Sylvia Menn

Pocket Interlinear New Testament

Pocket Interlinear New Testament

Jay P. Green, Sr., ***Editor***

BAKER BOOK HOUSE
Grand Rapids, Michigan 49506

Reprinted 1984 by
Baker Book House
with permission of copyright owner

ISBN: 0-8010-3777-8

Printed in the United States of America

PREFACE

"Every Scripture (is) God-breathed, and (is) profitable for teaching, for reproof, for correction, for instruction in righteousness; so that the man of God may be fitted out, having been fully furnished for every good work."

—2 Timothy 3:16

This Pocket Interlinear New Testament is presented to you and to all the Christian community with much exultation, tempered by fear and trembling and awe toward our almighty God and Savior, Jesus Christ.

It is hoped that you will discern that we have fully believed all the words of this holy Book, handling it with reverence, knowing that "man shall not live by bread alone, but by every word that proceeds out of the mouth of God" (Matt. 4:4), and that these words did not come "by the will of man, but men spoke from God, being borne along by (the) Holy Spirit" (2 Peter 1:21). It has also been written that each of the sons of men shall be judged by the words of this Book: "And if anyone hears My words, and does not believe, I do not judge him . . . the word which I spoke is that which will judge him in the last day" (John 12:47, 48). And the words of this Book being the ones that will judge every person having lived in all the ages, how important it must be that the very words of God, and no other, shall be contained in a portable book, to be distributed far and wide, in a form and in a commonly understood language easily and immediately taken into the heart and consciousness of all who have the privilege to read them. With these considerations in mind, and in holy fear inculcated by our God, we have sought to provide in *The Interlinear Hebrew-Greek-English Bible* all the original God-breathed Hebrew, Aramaic, and Greek words. And after much prayer and laborious study, we concluded that this could best be done by providing you with the two texts that alone have been uniquely preserved whole, and accepted in all generations, in all lands, by the vast majority of God's people as their "received texts". Other texts have been put forth from time to time, but none have been powerful enough to displace these two texts: the Masoretic Text of the Old Testament and the Received Text of the New.[1]

THE GREEK TEXT

The Greek text herein is purportedly that which directly underlies the King James Version, as reconstructed by F.H.A. Scrivener in 1894. It thus differs to a degree from all previously printed editions of the Received Text (e.g., there are over 250 differences—most of them quite minor—between this text and the Stephanus's "standard" textus receptus of 1550). The present text was typeset in England for the Trinitarian Bible Society by Stephen Austin and Sons, and it corresponds to *The New Testament in the Original Greek According to the Text Followed in the Authorized Version,* edited by Scrivener and originally published by Cambridge University Press in 1894 and 1902. The present Trinitarian Bible Society edition was first published in 1976.

Careful study, however, will show that this present text does not agree completely with the text used by the KJV translators (though it does agree virtually always). In places it has a dif-

---

1. For a defense of the superiority of the Received Text of the New Testament, see: Wilbur N. Pickering, *The Identity of the New Testament Text* (Nashville: Nelson, 1977); Zane C. Hodges, "Modern Textual Criticism and the Majority Text: A Response," *Journal of the Evangelical Theological Society* 21 (1978): 143–55.

ferent reading from that found in the KJV (e.g., Matt. 12:24, 27—Gk. "Beelzeboul, KJV "Beelzebub"; John 8:21—Gk. "sin," KJV "sins"; John 10:16—Gk. "one flock," KJV "one fold"; 1 Cor. 14:10—KJV "of these" omitted in Gk.; 1 Cor. 16:1—KJV "churches," Gk. "church," which has no manuscript support at all!) In other places the present text gives Greek words where the KJV translators indicate they had none by their use of italic type (e.g., the following words italicized in the KJV are actually given in the Greek of this TBS edition: Mark 8:14, *the disciples;* Mark 9:42, *these;* John 8:6, *as though he heard them not;* Acts 1:4, *them;* 1 John 3:16, *of God.* Some of these readings do have minority manuscript support, but it seems clear that these readings were not in the text chosen to underlie the KJV. Nevertheless, to all intents and purposes the TBS edition faithfully reproduces the KJV Greek text, as nearly as could be done at this date.

Although we admit that Erasmus added to this text a handful of readings from the Latin Vulgate, two or three without Greek manuscript authority (e.g., Acts 9:5, 6) and one from the Complutensian Bible (e.g., 1 John 5:7), we have not deleted these from the Greek text as supplied by the Trinitarian Bible Society—though we do not accept them as true Scripture.

THE ENGLISH TRANSLATIONS

There are two translations in this volume: the literal translation of the Greek words that is located directly under each Greek word, and *The King James II Version* on the side of the page. The latter provides a straightforward translation that makes it easy for the reader to see the proper word order in English and to assimilate the message given in God's words on that page. Both translations are word-for-word. We have rejected, and thus have studiously avoided, the conceptual-idea form of "translating" the Word of God. We hope these literal, word-for-word translations will demonstrate that such a translation can also be a readable and easily understood representation of God's Word.

INTERPRETATIONS

In the matter of interpretation—or as some would call it, bias—we do not hesitate to admit that many interpretative decisions must be made in any translation of the Bible. It has been our determination, backed by constant prayer, to let the text say what it says. And it is our hope and belief that we have not inserted a peculiar set of beliefs into the text by way of our translation. Nevertheless, by the very fact that a true translation must take into consideration the entire context of a word, phrase, sentence, or verse, interpretation must be present in making that translation—especially in those places where a Greek word, apart from the context, may be correctly translated by several different English words. It does make a difference, for instance, whether a person is "cured" or "saved." And conceivably there could be differences of opinion in the choice of an English word to express a Greek word in such cases. If a list of interpretative renditions were to be compiled, we would list these, at least, as present in this volume: (1) We have added punctuation, and of course the original manuscripts had none. (2) We also have used capitals and small letters, whereas the originals had only capitals. Especially we have attempted to aid the reader by capitalizing pronouns whenever the pronoun, or a name, is connected to a Person of the Godhead. Here there is undoubtedly room for differences of opinion. And in those places quoted from the Old Testament, the New Testament writers nearly always fix the deity of the persons quoted; therefore these are not so interpretative. But in another class of places, we have endeavored to capitalize, or not to capitalize, the pronouns according to whether or not the persons addressing Jesus acknowledged Him as God. Of course this is highly interpretative. (3) Wherever we have added a word or words to inform the reader of the sense, we have been careful in all those places to put the supplied words within parentheses. Therefore, any word within parentheses is not an expression of the actual Greek word.

PRESUPPOSITIONS

Being a willing slave of our God and Savior, Jesus Christ, and joyfully submitting to His higher thoughts, we gladly admit to a number of presuppositions: (1) We have acted upon the premise that "the Scriptures cannot be broken," meaning that not an iota or a point of them has been lost. With the firm conviction in our minds that each word was God-breathed, we dared not change a word, or supply a word, or change the word-order, so as to persuade the reader. If God used an ambiguous word, we tried to leave it that way, etc. (2) We have presupposed that Jesus Christ is not only our personal Savior and Lord, but that the Scriptures clearly reveal Him as equal with the Father and the Holy Spirit, one of the three Persons in the Godhead; (3) that He came to earth to give Himself a ransom for many; (4) that He both lived and died as a substitute for the sins of all those who shall come to a saving knowledge and belief in Him; (5) that He has risen to sit at the right of God the Father, ruling the world from there, interceding for and providentially guarding and guiding His own, until He destroys the earth by fire, coming to receive all of them at His right hand; and finally (6) that He will sit as supreme Judge of all men of all ages and will use the words of the Bible to judge the deeds of every person who will have inhabited the earth, casting all unbelievers into the Lake of Fire with the Devil.

DISTINCTIVE TRANSLATIONS

For easy apprehension and for continuity with the Old Testament, we have translated the Greek representing the names of Old Testament characters and places by the same English names that we have used in the Old Testament translation.

Due to our principle of translating each Greek word literally, a number of translations have emerged that are quite different from the usual.

The Greek word designating the mother of Jesus has always been translated "Mary," but the Greek word actually stands for "Mariam" (or"Miriam"); therefore we have so given it. Not that we think we can at this late date change her name in the mind of others from Mary to Mariam; we simply translated literally. It answers to the objection raised to there being two Marys in one family.

In translating the Greek words for "I am" in certain places, we have capitalized these words: viz., I AM (see John 8:59 and other places). It is our firm conviction that in those cases Jesus is identifying Himself as Jehovah (*Jehovah* properly translated meaning, I AM THAT I AM.) *Jesus* is of course the English name assigned to a word that means "Jehovah is salvation," and this same word in Greek would translate the Hebrew word for *Joshua.* Under the Greek we have translated literally, "to the ages," although we surely believe that the words are a clear idiomatic expression for "forever." In the marginal translation we have reversed this. Likewise we have translated "clean" heart, and also in other places where we firmly believe that "pure" could idiomatically be used. Another difference in this translation is that we have tried to translate in a way that would not be misleading as to sex. Many times other translators have put "any man" where "anyone" was literally correct. Male pronouns and male references abound in the Bible. We can see no good reason for supplying additional male references.

This is now the only interlinear New Testament in current, proper English; all others continue to use Elizabethan English. In the past we tried to defend the use of Elizabethan English in the Bible, but a four-year-old girl confounded us with two simple questions: (a) What means that? and (b) Why? Our studies soon revealed to us that the Bible was written in simple Hebrew and Greek, and that no special language was used when addressing God. The Bible was not intended to be encased in a stilted language of another age, whether it be Latin or Elizabethan English. As Tyndale said, every plowboy should be able to understand it. Otherwise we may as well leave it in the original languages.

Our constant aim in translation has been to represent the meaning of the Greek words in English as precisely and accurately as the English language will allow. This has included an attempt to display the meaning of compound words so that the parts of them are expressed. For example, in John 8:7 Jesus did not merely rise or stand up; He had bent down, and now He was bending back up. By these words we can visualize exactly what He was doing. We confess that this has been imperfectly accomplished, but in succeeding editions more of this type of accuracy can be achieved.

We have striven for consistency, having noted so much inconsistency in our seven previous translations and in the translations of others. And we believe that we have achieved more consistency in this translation than is present in others now available. Of course we were greatly aided by having others before us.

TRANSLATION PROBLEMS AND CHALLENGES

Just as there are difficult places to understand, so there are difficult places to translate. And sometimes the difficulty is not so much in assigning meanings to the Greek words as it is in punctuating them so as to catch the apostle's meaning. One example is 1 Corinthians 12:2.

As to other problems, we have made many decisions, some, if not all, of which may be challenged. We have in places left a Greek word untranslated, usually a particle or an article, where it was redundant or otherwise unsuitable to English transmission. Where the Greek order of words is difficult, we have not used superior figures, but have depended on the translation in the margin to give the English order. We have for the most part chosen to express each word of an idiomatic phrase where that would be more explanatory than the idiom. This is not consistently done, however. In some places where the present tense in Greek takes an English past for proper English, we have changed to a past tense. In a great many cases we have not done so, depending on the reader to realize that a difference in the two languages exists. This is also true of the aorist. In fact we believe that the New Testament writers themselves did not use the aorist in the strict (or restricted) way that Greek grammarians interpret it.

Due to space problems, we have not always been able to translate the participle where the English words *having been* are proper, but have many times merely used *being*. Also in other places where a Greek word is short and its English equivalent long, we have had to substitute (e.g., *by* instead of *through*). In the case of double-negative construction in the Greek, we have usually let it lie as it appears (rather than change one negative to a positive and thus make good English out of it). In some cases we have attempted to show the added strength of the negative, as intended in the Greek, by the use of punctuation.

There are of course many other problems encountered in rendering Greek into English. We respectfully refer the reader to other introductions to the Greek New Testament, especially to those in other interlinear New Testaments.

RESPONSIBILITY FOR THE TRANSLATION

The English translations in this volume, both the interlinear translation and the marginal *King James II Version*, have been improved and corrected by the suggestions of others who have reviewed the manuscript pages. The responsibility for the assignment of English equivalents belongs to me, however, since I was the sole judge of what would or would not be allowed in either translation. As for *The King James II Version*, this is the fourth edition of this very well received translation. Each edition has incorporated a host of helpful improvements submitted by men and women from all walks of life. In each edition an invitation for such suggestions has been issued. The results have been very gratifying indeed, proving that there are astute Bible students in all streams of English-reading Christians, both those who are disciplined scholars and those who can only question whether a certain translation could not be improved in a particular way.

Jay P. Green, Sr.
General Editor

ACKNOWLEDGMENTS

With thanksgiving, we acknowledge the immeasurable value of the work performed by our fellow-laborer, Rev. Maurice Robinson, who perused and offered suggestions on more than half these pages. We also are thankful to all the others who worked on various portions, giving many good suggestions for the improvement of the translations.

CONTENTS

THE GREEK ALPHABET

The Greek alphabet has twenty-four letters : —

Form.		Equivalent.	Name.		
Α	α	a		ἄλφα	*Alpha*
Β	β	b		βῆτα	*Beta*
Γ	γ	g		γάμμα	*Gamma*
Δ	δ	d		δέλτα	*Delta*
Ε	ϵ	e (*short*)	εἶ,	ἒ ψῑλόν	*Epsīlon*
Ζ	ζ	z		ζῆτα	*Zeta*
Η	η	e (*long*)		ἦτα	*Eta*
Θ	θ ϑ	th		θῆτα	*Theta*
Ι	ι	i		ἰῶτα	*Iota*
Κ	κ	k *or hard* c		κάππα	*Kappa*
Λ	λ	l		λά(μ)βδα	*Lambda*
Μ	μ	m		μῦ	*Mu*
Ν	ν	n		νῦ	*Nu*
Ξ	ξ	x	ξεῖ,	ξῖ	*Xi*
Ο	ο	o (*short*)	οὖ,	ὂ μῑκρόν	*Omīcron*
Π	π	p	πεῖ,	πῖ	*Pi*
Ρ	ρ	r		ῥῶ	*Rho*
Σ	σ ς	s		σίγμα	*Sigma*
Τ	τ	t		ταῦ	*Tau*
Υ	υ	(u) y	ὖ,	ὒ ψῑλόν	*Upsīlon*
Φ	φ	ph	φεῖ,	φῖ	*Phi*
Χ	χ	kh	χεῖ,	χῖ	*Chi*
Ψ	ψ	ps	ψεῖ,	ψῖ	*Psi*
Ω	ω	o (*long*)	ὦ,	ὦ μέγα	*Omĕga*

N. At the end of a word the form ς is used, elsewhere the form σ; thus, σύστασις.

ΕΥΑΓΓΕΛΙΟΝ
GOSPEL
ΤΟ ΚΑΤΑ ΜΑΤΘΑΙΟΝ
THE ACCORDING TO MATTHEW

KING JAMES II VERSION

THE GOSPEL ACCORDING TO MATTHEW

CHAPTER 1

1 The Book of the generation of Jesus Christ *the* son of David, *the* son of Abraham.

2 Abraham fathered Isaac, and Isaac fathered Jacob, and Jacob fathered Judah and his brothers. 3 And Judah fathered Pharez and Zarah out of Tamar, and Pharez fathered Hezron; and Hezron fathered Aram; 4 and Aram fathered Amminadab; and Amminadab fathered Nahshon; and Nahshon fathered Salmon; 5 and Salmon fathered Boaz out of Rahab; and Boaz fathered Obed out of Ruth; and Obed fathered Jesse; 6 and Jesse fathered David the king

7 And David the king fathered Solomon out of the *wife* of Uriah; 8 and Solomon fathered Rehoboam; and Rehoboam fathered Abijah; and Abijah fathered Asa; 8 and Asa fathered Jehoshaphat; and Jehoshaphat fathered Jehoram; and Jehoram fathered Uzziah; 9 and Uzziah fathered Jotham; and Jotham fathered Ahaz; and Ahaz fathered Hezekiah; 10 and Hezekiah fathered Manasseh; and Manasseh fathered Amon; and Amon fathered Josiah; 11 and Josiah fathered Jehoiachin and his brothers, at the carrying away of Babylon.

12 And after the carrying away of Babylon, Jehoiachin fathered Shealtiel; and Shealtiel fathered Zerubbabel; 13 and Zerubbabel fathered Abiud; and Abiud fathered Eliakim; and Eliakim fathered Azor; 14 and

CHAPTER 1

1 Βίβλος γενέσεως Ἰησοῦ Χριστοῦ, υἱοῦ Δαβίδ, υἱοῦ
(The) Book of generation of Jesus Christ, son of David, son
Ἀβραάμ.
of Abraham.
2 Ἀβραὰμ ἐγέννησε τὸν Ἰσαάκ· Ἰσαὰκ δὲ ἐγέννησε τὸν
Abraham fathered Isaac, Isaac and fathered
Ἰακώβ· Ἰακὼβ δὲ ἐγέννησε τὸν Ἰούδαν καὶ τοὺς ἀδελφοὺς
Jacob, Jacob and fathered Judah and the brothers
3 αὐτοῦ· Ἰούδας δὲ ἐγέννησε τὸν Φαρὲς καὶ τὸν Ζαρὰ ἐκ τῆς
of him. Judah And fathered Pharez and Zarah out of
Θάμαρ· Φαρὲς δὲ ἐγέννησε τὸν Ἐσρώμ· Ἐσρὼμ δὲ ἐγέννησε
Tamar; Pharez and fathered Hezron; Hezron and fathered
4 τὸν Ἀράμ· Ἀρὰμ δὲ ἐγέννησε τὸν Ἀμιναδάβ· Ἀμιναδὰβ
Aram; Aram and fathered Amminadab; Amminadab
δὲ ἐγέννησε τὸν Ναασσών· Ναασσὼν δὲ ἐγέννησε τὸν
and fathered Nahshon; Nahshon and fathered
5 Σαλμών· Σαλμὼν δὲ ἐγέννησε τὸν Βοόζ ἐκ τῆς Ῥαχάβ·
Salmon; Salmon and fathered Boaz out of Rahab;
Βοόζ δὲ ἐγέννησε τὸν Ὠβὴδ ἐκ τῆς Ῥούθ· Ὠβὴδ δὲ
Boaz and fathered Obed out of Ruth; Obed and
6 ἐγέννησε τὸν Ἰεσσαί· Ἰεσσαὶ δὲ ἐγέννησε τὸν Δαβὶδ τὸν
fathered Jesse; Jesse and fathered David the
βασιλέα.
king.
Δαβὶδ δὲ ὁ βασιλεὺς ἐγέννησε τὸν Σολομῶντα ἐκ τῆς
David And the king fathered Solomon out of the
7 τοῦ Οὐρίου· Σολομὼν δὲ ἐγέννησε τὸν Ῥοβοάμ· Ῥοβοὰμ
(wife) of Uriah; Solomon and fathered Rehoboam; Rehoboam
8 δὲ ἐγέννησε τὸν Ἀβιά· Ἀβιὰ δὲ ἐγέννησε τὸν Ἀσά· Ἀσὰ
and fathered Abijah; Abijah and fathered Asa; Asa
δὲ ἐγέννησε τὸν Ἰωσαφάτ· Ἰωσαφὰτ δὲ ἐγέννησε τὸν
and fathered Jehoshaphat; Jehoshaphat and fathered
9 Ἰωράμ· Ἰωρὰμ δὲ ἐγέννησε τὸν Ὀζίαν· Ὀζίας δὲ ἐγέννησε
Jehoram; Jehoram and fathered Uzziah; Uzziah and fathered
τὸν Ἰωάθαμ· Ἰωάθαμ δὲ ἐγέννησε τὸν Ἄχαζ· Ἄχαζ δὲ
Jotham; Jotham and fathered Ahaz; Ahaz and
10 ἐγέννησε τὸν Ἐζεκίαν· Ἐζεκίας δὲ ἐγέννησε τὸν Μανασσῆ·
fathered Hezekiah; Hezekiah and fathered Manasseh;
Μανασσῆς δὲ ἐγέννησε τὸν Ἀμών· Ἀμὼν δὲ ἐγέννησε τὸν
Manasseh and fathered Amon; Amon and fathered
11 Ἰωσίαν· Ἰωσίας δὲ ἐγέννησε τὸν Ἰεχονίαν καὶ τοὺς
Josiah; Josiah and fathered Jehoiachin and the
ἀδελφοὺς αὐτοῦ, ἐπὶ τῆς μετοικεσίας Βαβυλῶνος.
brothers of him, at the deportation of Babylon.
12 Μετὰ δὲ τὴν μετοικεσίαν Βαβυλῶνος, Ἰεχονίας ἐγέννησε
after And the deportation of Babylon, Jehoiachin fathered
τὸν Σαλαθιήλ· Σαλαθιὴλ δὲ ἐγέννησε τὸν Ζοροβάβελ·
Shealtiel; Shealtiel and fathered Zerubbabel;
13 Ζοροβάβελ δὲ ἐγέννησε τὸν Ἀβιούδ· Ἀβιοὺδ δὲ ἐγέννησε
Zerubbabel and fathered Abiud; Abiud and fathered
14 τὸν Ἐλιακείμ· Ἐλιακεὶμ δὲ ἐγέννησε τὸν Ἀζώρ· Ἀζὼρ δὲ
Eliakim; Eliakim and fathered Azor; Azor and

Azor fathered Sadoc; and Sadoc fathered Achim; and Achim fathered Eliud; [15] and Eliud fathered Eleazar; and Eleazar fathered Matthan; and Matthan fathered Jacob; [16] and Jacob fathered Joseph, the *betrothed* husband of Mary, of whom Jesus was born, who is called Christ.

[17] So all the generations from Abraham to David *were* fourteen generations; and from David to the carrying away to Babylon, fourteen generations, and from the carrying away into Babylon until Christ, fourteen generations.

[18] Now the birth of Jesus Christ was this way— for His mother Mary had been betrothed to Joseph— before they came together, she was discovered *to be* pregnant in womb by *the* Holy Spirit. [19] But her husband Joseph being just, and not willing to make her a public example, purposed to put her away secretly. [20] And *as* he *was* thinking about these things, behold, an angel of *the* Lord was seen by him in a dream, saying, Joseph, son of David, do not be afraid to take Mary *as* your wife. For that in her is fathered by *the* Holy Spirit. [21] And she will bear a son; and you shall call His name Jesus; for He shall save His people from their sins.

[22] Now all this happened so that might be fulfilled that spoken by the Lord through the prophet, saying, [23] "Behold! The virgin will conceive in *her* womb and will bear a son, and they will call His name Emmanuel, which translated is, God with us."

[24] And having been aroused from the sleep, Joseph did as the angel of *the* Lord commanded him, and took his wife; [25] and did not know her until she bore her son, the Firstborn. And he called His name Jesus.

ἐγέννησε τὸν Σαδώκ· Σαδὼκ δὲ ἐγέννησε τὸν Ἀχείμ· Ἀχεὶμ
fathered Sadoc; Sadoc and fathered Achim; Achim
15 δὲ ἐγέννησε τὸν Ἐλιούδ· Ἐλιοὺδ δὲ ἐγέννησε τὸν Ἐλεάζαρ·
and fathered Eliud; Eliud and fathered Eleazer;
Ἐλεάζαρ δὲ ἐγέννησε τὸν Ματθάν· Ματθὰν δὲ ἐγέννησε τὸν
Eleazer and fathered Matthan; Matthan and fathered
16 Ἰακώβ· Ἰακὼβ δὲ ἐγέννησε τὸν Ἰωσὴφ τὸν ἄνδρα Μαρίας,
Jacob; Jacob and fathered Joseph the husband of Mariam,
ἐξ ἧς ἐγεννήθη Ἰησοῦς ὁ λεγόμενος Χριστός.
out of who was born Jesus, He called Christ.
17 Πᾶσαι οὖν αἱ γενεαὶ ἀπὸ Ἀβραὰμ ἕως Δαβὶδ γενεαὶ
all Then the generations from Abraham until David, generations
δεκατέσσαρες· καὶ ἀπὸ Δαβὶδ ἕως τῆς μετοικεσίας Βαβυλῶνος
fourteen; and from David until the deportation to Babylon,
γενεαὶ δεκατέσσαρες· καὶ ἀπὸ τῆς μετοικεσίας Βαβυλῶνος
generations fourteen; and from the deportation to Babylon
ἕως τοῦ Χριστοῦ γενεαὶ δεκατέσσαρες.
until the Christ, generations fourteen.
18 Τοῦ δὲ Ἰησοῦ Χριστοῦ ἡ γέννησις οὕτως ἦν. μνηστευθεί-
Now of Jesus Christ the birth thus was: being betrothed
σης γὰρ τῆς μητρὸς αὐτοῦ Μαρίας τῷ Ἰωσήφ, πρὶν ἢ
for the mother of Him, Mariam, to Joseph, before
συνελθεῖν αὐτούς, εὑρέθη ἐν γαστρὶ ἔχουσα ἐκ Πνεύματος
joining of them, she was found in womb, pregnant by Spirit
19 Ἁγίου. Ἰωσὴφ δὲ ὁ ἀνὴρ αὐτῆς, δίκαιος ὤν, καὶ μὴ θέλων
Holy. Joseph And the husband of her, just being, and not willing
αὐτὴν παραδειγματίσαι, ἐβουλήθη λάθρα ἀπολῦσαι αὐτήν.
her to expose publicly, purposed secretly to put away her.
20 ταῦτα δὲ αὐτοῦ ἐνθυμηθέντος, ἰδού, ἄγγελος Κυρίου κατ'
these things And he meditating on, behold, an angel of (the) Lord by
ὄναρ ἐφάνη αὐτῷ, λέγων, Ἰωσήφ, υἱὸς Δαβίδ, μὴ φοβηθῇς
a dream was seen by him, saying, Joseph, son of David, not do fear
παραλαβεῖν Μαριὰμ τὴν γυναῖκά σου· τὸ γὰρ ἐν αὐτῇ
to take Mariam (as) the wife of you. that For in her
21 γεννηθὲν ἐκ Πνεύματός ἐστιν Ἁγίου. τέξεται δὲ υἱόν, καὶ
begotten by (the) Spirit is Holy. she will bear And a son, and
καλέσεις τὸ ὄνομα αὐτοῦ Ἰησοῦν· αὐτὸς γὰρ σώσει τὸν λαὸν
you shall call the name of Him Jesus. He For will save the people
22 αὐτοῦ ἀπὸ τῶν ἁμαρτιῶν αὐτῶν. τοῦτο δὲ ὅλον γέγονεν,
of Him from the sins of them. this Now all happened,
ἵνα πληρωθῇ τὸ ῥηθὲν ὑπὸ τοῦ Κυρίου διὰ τοῦ προφήτου,
that be fulfilled that spoken by the Lord through the prophet,
23 λέγοντος, Ἰδού, ἡ παρθένος ἐν γαστρὶ ἕξει καὶ τέξεται υἱόν,
saying, Behold, the virgin in womb will conceive and will bear a son.
καὶ καλέσουσι τὸ ὄνομα αὐτοῦ Ἐμμανουήλ, ὅ ἐστι μεθερμη-
and they will call the name of Him Emannuel, which is, translated,
24 νευόμενον, Μεθ' ἡμῶν ὁ Θεός. διεγερθεὶς δὲ ὁ Ἰωσὴφ ἀπὸ
with us God. being aroused And Joseph from
τοῦ ὕπνου ἐποίησεν ὡς προσέταξεν αὐτῷ ὁ ἄγγελος Κυρίου·
the sleep, he did as commanded him the angel of (the) Lord,
καὶ παρέλαβε τὴν γυναῖκα αὐτοῦ, καὶ οὐκ ἐγίνωσκεν αὐτὴν
and took (as) the wife of him, and not did know her
25 ἕως οὗ ἔτεκε τὸν υἱὸν αὐτῆς τὸν πρωτότοκον· καὶ ἐκάλεσε
until she bore the son of her, the firstborn. And he called
τὸ ὄνομα αὐτοῦ ἸΗΣΟΥΝ.
the name of Him, JESUS.

CHAPTER 2

1 Τοῦ δὲ Ἰησοῦ γεννηθέντος ἐν Βηθλεὲμ τῆς Ἰουδαίας, ἐν
And Jesus having been born in Bethlehem of Judea, in
ἡμέραις Ἡρῴδου τοῦ βασιλέως, ἰδού, μάγοι ἀπὸ ἀνατολῶν
(the) days of Herod the king, behold, Magi from (the) east
2 παρεγένοντο εἰς Ἱεροσόλυμα, λέγοντες, Ποῦ ἐστιν ὁ τεχθεὶς
arrived into Jerusalem, saying, where is he born
βασιλεὺς τῶν Ἰουδαίων; εἴδομεν γὰρ αὐτοῦ τὸν ἀστέρα ἐν
king of the Jews? we saw For of him the star in
3 τῇ ἀνατολῇ, καὶ ἤλθομεν προσκυνῆσαι αὐτῷ. ἀκούσας δὲ
the east, and came to worship him. hearing And
Ἡρῴδης ὁ βασιλεὺς ἐταράχθη, καὶ πᾶσα Ἱεροσόλυμα μετ'
Herod the king was troubled, and all Jerusalem with
4 αὐτοῦ. καὶ συναγαγὼν πάντας τοὺς ἀρχιερεῖς καὶ γραμ-
him. And gathering all the chief priests and scribes
ματεῖς τοῦ λαοῦ, ἐπυνθάνετο παρ' αὐτῶν ποῦ ὁ Χριστὸς
of the people, he inquired from them where the Christ
5 γεννᾶται. οἱ δὲ εἶπον αὐτῷ, Ἐν Βηθλεὲμ τῆς Ἰουδαίας·
was to be born. they And said to him, In Bethlehem of Judea.
6 οὕτω γὰρ γέγραπται διὰ τοῦ προφήτου, Καὶ σὺ Βηθλεέμ,
thus For it has been written by the prophet, And you, Bethlehem,
γῆ Ἰούδα, οὐδαμῶς ἐλαχίστη εἶ ἐν τοῖς ἡγεμόσιν Ἰούδα· ἐκ
land of Judah, not at all least are you among the governors of Judah. out of
σοῦ γὰρ ἐξελεύσεται ἡγούμενος, ὅστις ποιμανεῖ τὸν λαόν
of you For will come out a Governor who will shepherd the people
μου τὸν Ἰσραήλ. τότε Ἡρῴδης, λάθρα καλέσας τοὺς
of Me, (even) Israel. Then Herod, secretly calling the
μάγους, ἠκρίβωσε παρ' αὐτῶν τὸν χρόνον τοῦ φαινο-
Magi, asked exactly from them the time of the appearing
8 μένου ἀστέρος. καὶ πέμψας αὐτοὺς εἰς Βηθλεὲμ εἶπε, Πορευ-
star. And sending them to Bethlehem, he said, Having
θέντες ἀκριβῶς ἐξετάσατε περὶ τοῦ παιδίου· ἐπὰν δὲ εὕρητε,
gone, exactly inquire about the child. when And you find,
ἀπαγγείλατέ μοι, ὅπως κἀγὼ ἐλθὼν προσκυνήσω αὐτῷ.
report to me, so that I also coming may worship him.
9 οἱ δὲ ἀκούσαντες τοῦ βασιλέως ἐπορεύθησαν· καὶ ἰδού, ὁ
they And having heard the king departed. And, behold, the
ἀστήρ, ὃν εἶδον ἐν τῇ ἀνατολῇ, προῆγεν αὐτούς, ἕως ἐλθὼν
star which they saw in the east went before them until coming
10 ἔστη ἐπάνω οὗ ἦν τὸ παιδίον. ἰδόντες δὲ τὸν ἀστέρα,
it stood over where was the child. seeing And the star,
11 ἐχάρησαν χαρὰν μεγάλην σφόδρα. καὶ ἐλθόντες εἰς τὴν
they rejoiced a joy great, exceedingly. And coming into the
οἰκίαν, εἶδον τὸ παιδίον μετὰ Μαρίας τῆς μητρὸς αὐτοῦ,
house, they saw the child with Mariam the mother of Him.
καὶ πεσόντες προσεκύνησαν αὐτῷ, καὶ ἀνοίξαντες τοὺς
And falling down, they worshiped Him. And opening the
θησαυροὺς αὐτῶν προσήνεγκαν αὐτῷ δῶρα, χρυσὸν καὶ
treasures of them, they offered to Him gifts: gold and
12 λίβανον καὶ σμύρναν. καὶ χρηματισθέντες κατ' ὄναρ μὴ
frankincense and myrrh. And having been warned by a dream not
ἀνακάμψαι πρὸς Ἡρῴδην, δι' ἄλλης ὁδοῦ ἀνεχώρησαν εἰς
to return to Herod, by another way they departed into
τὴν χώραν αὐτῶν.
the country of them.

CHAPTER 2

1 Now when Jesus had been born in Bethlehem of Judea in *the* days of Herod the king, behold, wise men arrived from *the* east to Jerusalem, 2 saying, Where is He born king of the Jews? For we saw His star in the east and have come to worship Him. 3 But Herod the king having heard *this*, *he* was troubled, and all Jerusalem with him. 4 And having gathered all the chief priests and scribes of the people, he asked of them where the Christ was to be born.
5 And they said to him, In Bethlehem of Judea, for so it has been written by the prophet, 6 "And you, Bethlehem, land of Judah, in no way are the least among the governors of Judah, for out of you will come a Governor who will shepherd My people Israel."

7 Then secretly calling the wise men, Herod asked of them exactly the time of the star appearing. 8 And having sent them to Bethlehem, he said, Having gone, search carefully for the child. And when you find *him*, bring me word again so that having come, I may also worship him.
9 And having heard the king, they departed. And, behold! The star which they saw in the east went before them until it had come and stood over where the child was. 10 And seeing the star, they rejoiced exceedingly *with* a great joy. 11 And having come into the house, they saw the child with His mother Mary. And falling down, they worshiped Him. And having opened their treasures, they presented gifts to Him: gold and frankincense and myrrh. 12 And having been warned by a dream not to return to Herod, they went away into their own country by another way.

13 And they having departed, an angel of *the* Lord appeared to Joseph by a dream, saying, Rise up! Take the child and His mother with *you*, and flee into Egypt. And be there until I shall tell you. For Herod is about to look for the child in order to destroy Him.

14 And having risen up, he took along the child and his mother by night, and withdrew into Egypt. 15 And he was there until the end of Herod, that might be fulfilled that spoken by the Lord through the prophet, saying, "Out of Egypt I have called My Son."

16 Then having seen that he was fooled by the wise men, Herod was greatly enraged; and having sent, he killed all the boys in Bethlehem and in all its districts, from two years old and under—according to the time which he exactly asked from the wise men.

17 Then was fulfilled that spoken by Jeremiah the prophet, saying,

18 "A voice was heard in Ramah, wailing and bitter weeping, and great mourning, Rachel weeping for her children, and would not be comforted, because they were *not*."

19 But Herod having expired, behold, an angel of *the* Lord appears to Joseph by a dream in Egypt, 20 saying, Rising up, take along the child and His mother, and pass over into *the* land of Israel; for those seeking the soul of the child have expired.

21 And rising up, he took along the child and His mother and came into *the* land of Israel. 22 But hearing that Archelaus reigned over Judea in place of his father Herod, he feared to go there. And having been warned by a dream, he departed into the parts of Galilee. 23 And having come, he lived in a city called Nazareth; so as to fulfill that spoken by the prophet, "He shall be called a Nazarene."

13 Ἀναχωρησάντων δὲ αὐτῶν, ἰδού, ἄγγελος Κυρίου
having departed Now they, behold, an angel of (the) Lord
φαίνεται κατ' ὄναρ τῷ Ἰωσήφ, λέγων, Ἐγερθεὶς παράλαβε
appears by a dream to Joseph, saying, Rise up; take with (you
τὸ παιδίον καὶ τὴν μητέρα αὐτοῦ, καὶ φεῦγε εἰς Αἴγυπτον,
the child and the mother of Him, and flee into Egypt
καὶ ἴσθι ἐκεῖ ἕως ἂν εἴπω σοί· μέλλει γὰρ Ἡρῴδης ζητεῖν τὸ
and be there until I shall say to you. is about For Herod to seek the
14 παιδίον, τοῦ ἀπολέσαι αὐτό. ὁ δὲ ἐγερθεὶς παρέλαβε τὸ
child, to destroy Him. he And rising up took along the
παιδίον καὶ τὴν μητέρα αὐτοῦ νυκτός, καὶ ἀνεχώρησεν εἰς
child and the mother of Him by night, and departed into
15 Αἴγυπτον, καὶ ἦν ἐκεῖ ἕως τῆς τελευτῆς Ἡρῴδου· ἵνα
Egypt. And he was there until the end of Herod; that
πληρωθῇ τὸ ῥηθὲν ὑπὸ τοῦ Κυρίου διὰ τοῦ προφήτου,
be fulfilled that spoken by the Lord through the prophet,
16 λέγοντος, Ἐξ Αἰγύπτου ἐκάλεσα τὸν υἱόν μου. τότε
saying, Out of Egypt I have called the Son of Me. Then
Ἡρῴδης, ἰδὼν ὅτι ἐνεπαίχθη ὑπὸ τῶν μάγων, ἐθυμώθη
Herod, seeing that he was mocked by the Magi, was enraged,
λίαν, καὶ ἀποστείλας ἀνεῖλε πάντας τοὺς παῖδας τοὺς ἐν
greatly, and sending, he killed all the male-children in
Βηθλεὲμ καὶ ἐν πᾶσι τοῖς ὁρίοις αὐτῆς, ἀπὸ διετοῦς καὶ
Bethlehem and in all the districts of it, from two years and
κατωτέρω, κατὰ τὸν χρόνον ὃν ἠκρίβωσε παρὰ τῶν μάγων.
under, according to the time which he exactly asked from the Magi.
17 τότε ἐπληρώθη τὸ ῥηθὲν ὑπὸ Ἰερεμίου τοῦ προφήτου,
Then was fulfilled that spoken by Jeremiah the prophet,
18 λέγοντος, Φωνὴ ἐν Ῥαμᾶ ἠκούσθη, θρῆνος καὶ κλαυθμὸς
saying, A voice in Rama was heard, lamenting and weeping
καὶ ὀδυρμὸς πολύς, Ῥαχὴλ κλαίουσα τὰ τέκνα αὐτῆς, καὶ
and mourning much; Rachel weeping for the children of her, and
19 οὐκ ἤθελε παρακληθῆναι, ὅτι οὐκ εἰσί. τελευτήσαντος δὲ
not willing to be comforted, because not they were. having expired But
τοῦ Ἡρῴδου, ἰδού, ἄγγελος Κυρίου κατ' ὄναρ φαίνεται τῷ
Herod, behold, an angel of (the) Lord by a dream appears
20 Ἰωσὴφ ἐν Αἰγύπτῳ, λέγων, Ἐγερθεὶς παράλαβε τὸ παιδίον
to Joseph in Egypt, saying, Rising up, take along the child
καὶ τὴν μητέρα αὐτοῦ, καὶ πορεύου εἰς γῆν Ἰσραήλ· τεθνή-
and the mother of Him, and pass over into (the) land of Israel; have
21 κασι γὰρ οἱ ζητοῦντες τὴν ψυχὴν τοῦ παιδίου. ὁ δὲ ἐγερθεὶς
expired for those seeking the soul of the child. he And rising up
παρέλαβε τὸ παιδίον καὶ τὴν μητέρα αὐτοῦ, καὶ ἦλθεν εἰς
took along the child and the mother of Him, and came into
22 γῆν Ἰσραήλ. ἀκούσας δὲ ὅτι Ἀρχέλαος βασιλεύει ἐπὶ τῆς
(the) land of Israel. hearing But that Archelaus reigns over
Ἰουδαίας ἀντὶ Ἡρῴδου τοῦ πατρὸς αὐτοῦ, ἐφοβήθη ἐκεῖ
Judea in place of Herod the father of him, he feared there
ἀπελθεῖν· χρηματισθεὶς δὲ κατ' ὄναρ, ἀνεχώρησεν εἰς τὰ μέρη
to go. being warned And by a dream, he departed into the parts
23 τῆς Γαλιλαίας, καὶ ἐλθὼν κατῴκησεν εἰς πόλιν λεγομένην
of Galilee. And having come, he dwelt in a city called
Ναζαρέθ· ὅπως πληρωθῇ τὸ ῥηθὲν διὰ τῶν προφητῶν ὅτι
Nazareth; thus to fulfill that spoken through the prophet:
Ναζωραῖος κληθήσεται.
A Nazarene He shall be called.

CHAPTER 3

CHAPTER 3

[1]Now in those days John the Baptist comes preaching in the wilderness of Judea, [2]and saying, Repent! For the kingdom of Heaven has drawn near. [3]For this is he spoken of by Isaiah the prophet, saying, "The voice of *one* crying in the wilderness! Prepare the way of *the* Lord! Make His paths straight!"

[4]And John himself had his clothing from hairs of a camel, and a belt of leather about his loin. And his food was locusts and wild honey.

[5]Then Jerusalem and all Judea went out to him, and all the neighborhood of the Jordan; [6]and were baptized by him in the Jordan, confessing their sins. [7]But having seen many of the Pharisees and Sadducees coming to his baptism, he said to them, Offspring of vipers! Who warned you to flee from the wrath to come?

[8]Therefore, bring forth fruits worthy of repentance. [9]And do not think to say within yourselves, We have a father, Abraham. For I say to you that God is able to raise up children to Abraham from these stones. [10]But already the axe is even laid at the root of the trees; therefore, any tree not producing good fruit is cut down, and is thrown into fire. [11]I indeed baptize you in water to repentance; but He who *is* coming after me is stronger than me, whose sandals I am not fit to carry. He will baptize you in *the* Holy Spirit and fire; [12]whose fan *is* in His hand, and He will cleanse His floor, and will gather His wheat into the barn. But He will burn up the chaff with fire that cannot be put out.

[13]Then Jesus arrives from Galilee to the Jordan, to

1 Ἐν δὲ ταῖς ἡμέραις ἐκείναις παραγίνεται Ἰωάννης ὁ
in Now days those comes John the
βαπτιστής, κηρύσσων ἐν τῇ ἐρήμῳ τῆς Ἰουδαίας, καὶ λέγων,
Baptist proclaiming in the wilderness of Judea, and saying,
2 Μετανοεῖτε· ἤγγικε γὰρ ἡ βασιλεία τῶν οὐρανῶν. οὗτος
Repent! has come near For the kingdom of the heavens. this
γάρ ἐστιν ὁ ῥηθεὶς ὑπὸ Ἡσαΐου τοῦ προφήτου, λέγοντος,
3 For is he spoken of by Isaiah the prophet, saying,
Φωνὴ βοῶντος ἐν τῇ ἐρήμῳ, Ἑτοιμάσατε τὴν ὁδὸν Κυρίου·
A voice of (one) crying in the wilderness: Prepare the way of (the) Lord,
4 εὐθείας ποιεῖτε τὰς τρίβους αὐτοῦ. αὐτὸς δὲ ὁ Ἰωάννης εἶχε
straight make the paths of Him. he Now, John, had
τὸ ἔνδυμα αὐτοῦ ἀπὸ τριχῶν καμήλου, καὶ ζώνην δερ-
the clothing of him from hairs of a camel, and a belt of
ματίνην περὶ τὴν ὀσφὺν αὐτοῦ· ἡ δὲ τροφὴ αὐτοῦ ἦν
leather around the loin of him. the And food of him was
5 ἀκρίδες καὶ μέλι ἄγριον. τότε ἐξεπορεύετο πρὸς αὐτὸν
locusts and honey wild. Then went out to him
Ἱεροσόλυμα καὶ πᾶσα ἡ Ἰουδαία καὶ πᾶσα ἡ περίχωρος τοῦ
Jerusalem and all Judea, and all the neighborhood of the
6 Ἰορδάνου· καὶ ἐβαπτίζοντο ἐν τῷ Ἰορδάνῃ ὑπ' αὐτοῦ,
Jordan; and were baptized in the Jordan by him,
7 ἐξομολογούμενοι τὰς ἁμαρτίας αὐτῶν. Ἰδὼν δὲ πολλοὺς τῶν
confessing the sins of them. seeing And many of the
Φαρισαίων καὶ Σαδδουκαίων ἐρχομένους ἐπὶ τὸ βάπτισμα
Pharisees and Sadducees coming on the baptism
αὐτοῦ, εἶπεν αὐτοῖς, Γεννήματα ἐχιδνῶν, τίς ὑπέδειξεν ὑμῖν
of him, he said to them, Offspring of vipers! Who warned you
8 φυγεῖν ἀπὸ τῆς μελλούσης ὀργῆς; ποιήσατε οὖν καρποὺς
to flee from the coming wrath? Produce, then, fruits
9 ἀξίους τῆς μετανοίας· καὶ μὴ δόξητε λέγειν ἐν ἑαυτοῖς,
worthy of repentance; and not do think to say in yourselves,
Πατέρα ἔχομεν τὸν Ἀβραάμ· λέγω γὰρ ὑμῖν ὅτι δύναται ὁ
A father we have Abraham. I say For to you that is able
10 Θεὸς ἐκ τῶν λίθων τούτων ἐγεῖραι τέκνα τῷ Ἀβραάμ. ἤδη
God out of stones these to raise up children to Abraham. already
δὲ καὶ ἡ ἀξίνη πρὸς τὴν ῥίζαν τῶν δένδρων κεῖται· πᾶν οὖν
And even the axe at the root of the trees is laid. any Then
δένδρον μὴ ποιοῦν καρπὸν καλὸν ἐκκόπτεται καὶ εἰς πῦρ
tree not producing fruit good is cut off, and into fire
11 βάλλεται. ἐγὼ μὲν βαπτίζω ὑμᾶς ἐν ὕδατι εἰς μετάνοιαν· ὁ
is thrown. I indeed baptize you in water to repentance. He
δὲ ὀπίσω μου ἐρχόμενος ἰσχυρότερός μου ἐστίν, οὗ οὐκ εἰμὶ
But after me coming stronger than me is, of whom not I am
ἱκανὸς τὰ ὑποδήματα βαστάσαι· αὐτὸς ὑμᾶς βαπτίσει ἐν
worthy the sandals to bear. He you will baptize in
12 Πνεύματι Ἁγίῳ καὶ πυρί. οὗ τὸ πτύον ἐν τῇ χειρὶ αὐτοῦ,
(the) Spirit Holy and fire; of whom the fan (is) in the hand of Him.
καὶ διακαθαριεῖ τὴν ἅλωνα αὐτοῦ, καὶ συνάξει τὸν σῖτον
And He will cleanse the floor of Him, and will gather the wheat
αὐτοῦ εἰς τὴν ἀποθήκην, τὸ δὲ ἄχυρον κατακαύσει πυρὶ
of Him into the barn. the But chaff He will burn with fire
13 ἀσβέστῳ. Τότε παραγίνεται ὁ Ἰησοῦς ἀπὸ τῆς αλιλαίας
unquenchable. Then arrives Jesus from Galilee

John, to be baptized by him. 14 But John restrained Him, saying, I have need to be baptized by You, and do You come to me? 15 But answering, Jesus said to him, Allow *it* now, for it is becoming to us this way to fulfill all righteousness. Then he allowed Him. 16 And having been baptized, Jesus went up immediately from the water. And, behold! The heavens were opened to Him, and He saw the Spirit of God coming down as a dove, and coming upon Him. 17 And behold! A voice out of Heaven saying, This is My Son, the Beloved, in whom I have found delight.

CHAPTER 4

1 Then Jesus was led up into the wilderness by the Spirit, to be tempted by the Devil. 2 And having fasted forty days and forty nights, afterwards He hungered. 3 And coming to Him, the Tempter said, If You are *the* Son of God, speak that these stones may become loaves. 4 But answering, He said, It has been written, "Man shall not live by bread alone but by every word going out of *the* mouth of God."

5 Then the Devil takes Him to the holy city and sets Him on the edge of the Temple. 6 and says to Him, If You are *the* Son of God, throw Yourself down; for it has been written, "He shall give His angels charge concerning You, and they shall bear You on *their* hands, lest You strike Your foot against a stone." 7 Jesus said to him, Again it has been written, "You shall not tempt *the* Lord your God." 8 Again the Devil takes Him to a very high mountain, and shows to Him all the kingdoms of the world, and their glory. 9 And *he* says to Him, I will give all these things to You if falling down You will

ἐπὶ τὸν Ἰορδάνην πρὸς τὸν Ἰωάννην, τοῦ βαπτισθῆναι ὑπ’
at the Jordan to John, to be baptized by
αὐτοῦ. ὁ δὲ Ἰωάννης διεκώλυεν αὐτόν, λέγων, Ἐγὼ χρε-
14 him. But John restrained Him, saying, I need
ίαν ἔχω ὑπὸ σοῦ βαπτισθῆναι, καὶ σὺ ἔρχῃ πρός με; ἀποκ-
have by You to be baptized; and You come to me? an-
15 ριθεὶς δὲ ὁ Ἰησοῦς εἶπε πρὸς αὐτόν, Ἄφες ἄρτι· οὕτω γὰρ
swering But, Jesus said to him, Allow (it) now; thus for
πρέπον ἐστὶν ἡμῖν πληρῶσαι πᾶσαν δικαιοσύνην. τότε
fitting it is to us to fulfill all righteousness. Then
16 ἀφίησιν αὐτόν. καὶ βαπτισθεὶς ὁ Ἰησοῦς ἀνέβη εὐθὺς ἀπὸ τοῦ
he allows Him. And being baptized, Jesus went up at once from the
ὕδατος· καὶ ἰδού, ἀνεῴχθησαν αὐτῷ οἱ οὐρανοί, καὶ εἶδε τὸ
water. And, behold, were opened to Him the heavens; and He saw the
Πνεῦμα τοῦ Θεοῦ καταβαῖνον ὡσεὶ περιστερὰν καὶ ἐρχόμε-
Spirit of God descending as a dove, and coming
17 νον ἐπ’ αὐτόν. καὶ ἰδού, φωνὴ ἐκ τῶν οὐρανῶν, λέγουσα,
upon Him. And, behold, a voice out of the heavens, saying,
Οὗτός ἐστιν ὁ υἱός μου ὁ ἀγαπητός, ἐν ᾧ εὐδόκησα.
This is the Son of Me, the Beloved, in whom I have found delight.

CHAPTER 4

1 Τότε ὁ Ἰησοῦς ἀνήχθη εἰς τὴν ἔρημον ὑπὸ τοῦ Πνεύ-
Then Jesus was led up into the wilderness by the Spirit.
2 ματος, πειρασθῆναι ὑπὸ τοῦ διαβόλου. καὶ νηστεύσας
to be tested by the Devil. And having fasted
ἡμέρας τεσσαράκοντα καὶ νύκτας τεσσαράκοντα, ὕστερον
days forty and nights forty, afterward
3 ἐπείνασε. καὶ προσελθὼν αὐτῷ ὁ πειράζων εἶπεν, Εἰ υἱὸς
He hungered. And coming near Him, the Tempter said, If Son
4 εἶ τοῦ Θεοῦ, εἰπὲ ἵνα οἱ λίθοι οὗτοι ἄρτοι γένωνται. ὁ δὲ
You are of God, say that stones these loaves may become. He But
ἀποκριθεὶς εἶπε, Γέγραπται, Οὐκ ἐπ’ ἄρτῳ μόνῳ ζήσεται
answering said, It has been written: Not on bread alone shall live
ἄνθρωπος, ἀλλ’ ἐπὶ παντὶ ῥήματι ἐκπορευομένῳ διὰ στό-
man, but on every word proceeding through (the)
5 ματος Θεοῦ. τότε παραλαμβάνει αὐτὸν ὁ διάβολος εἰς τὴν
mouth of God. Then takes Him the Devil into the
ἁγίαν πόλιν, καὶ ἵστησιν αὐτὸν ἐπὶ τὸ πτερύγιον τοῦ ἱεροῦ,
holy city, and sets Him on the wing of the Temple,
6 καὶ λέγει αὐτῷ, Εἰ υἱὸς εἶ τοῦ Θεοῦ, βάλε σεαυτὸν κάτω·
and says to Him, If Son You are of God, Throw Yourself down;
γέγραπται γὰρ ὅτι Τοῖς ἀγγέλοις αὐτοῦ ἐντελεῖται περὶ
it has been written for: To the angels of Him He will give charge about
σοῦ, καὶ ἐπὶ χειρῶν ἀροῦσί σε, μήποτε προσκόψῃς πρὸς
You; and on hands they will bear You, lest You strike against
7 λίθον τὸν πόδα σου. ἔφη αὐτῷ ὁ Ἰησοῦς, Πάλιν γέγραπται,
a stone the foot of You. said to him Jesus, Again, it has been written,
8 Οὐκ ἐκπειράσεις Κύριον τὸν Θεόν σου. πάλιν παραλαμβάνει
Not you shall tempt (the) Lord God of you. Again takes
αὐτὸν ὁ διάβολος εἰς ὄρος ὑψηλὸν λίαν, καὶ δείκνυσιν αὐτῷ
Him the Devil to a mount high exceeding, and shows Him
9 πάσας τὰς βασιλείας τοῦ κόσμου καὶ τὴν δόξαν αὐτῶν, καὶ
all the kingdoms of the world, and the glory of them; and
λέγει αὐτῷ, Ταῦτα πάντα σοι δώσω, ἐὰν πεσὼν προσ-
says to Him, These things all to You I will give, if falling down You

worship me. [10]Then Jesus says to him, Go, Satan! For it has been written, "You shall worship *the* Lord God of you, and you shall serve Him only." [11]Then the Devil leaves Him. And behold! Angels came near and served Him.

[12]But Jesus having heard that John was delivered up, He withdrew into Galilee.

[13]And leaving Nazareth, coming He dwelt in Capernaum beside the sea, in *the* districts of Zebulun and Naphtali; [14]so that might be fulfilled that spoken by Isaiah the prophet, saying, [15]"Land of Zebulun and land of Naphtali, way of *the* sea, beyond the Jordan, Galilee of the nations: [16]The people sitting in darkness saw a great Light; and to those sitting in a region and shadow of death, Light sprang up to them.

[17]From that time Jesus began to preach and to say, Repent! For the kingdom of Heaven has drawn near.

[18]And walking beside the sea of Galilee, Jesus saw two brothers, Simon called Peter, and his brother Andrew, casting a net into the sea—for they were fishers. [19]And He said to them, Come after Me, and I will make you fishers of men. [20]And immediately they followed Him, leaving the nets.

[20]And going on from there, He saw two other brothers, James the *son* of Zebedee, and his brother John, in the boat with their father Zebedee, mending their nets. And He called them. [22]And at once leaving the boat and their father, they followed Him.

[23]And Jesus went around all Galilee teaching in their synagogues, and preaching the gospel of the Kingdom; and healing every disease

10 κυνήσης μοι. τότε λέγει αὐτῷ ὁ Ἰησοῦς, Ὕπαγε, Σατανᾶ
will worship me. Then says to him Jesus, Go, Satan
γέγραπται γάρ, Κύριον τὸν Θεόν σου προσκυνήσεις, καὶ
It has been written for: (The) Lord God of you you shall worship, and
11 αὐτῷ μόνῳ λατρεύσεις. τότε ἀφίησιν αὐτὸν ὁ διάβολος· καὶ
Him only you shall serve. Then leaves Him the Devil, and
12 ἰδού, ἄγγελοι προσῆλθον καὶ διηκόνουν αὐτῷ. Ἀκούσας δὲ
behold. angels came near and ministered to Him. having heard But
ὁ Ἰησοῦς ὅτι Ἰωάννης παρεδόθη, ἀνεχώρησεν εἰς τὴν
Jesus that John was delivered up, He withdrew into
13 Γαλιλαίαν· καὶ καταλιπὼν τὴν Ναζαρέθ ελθων κατῴκησεν
Galilee. And having left Nazareth, coming He dwelt
εἰς Καπερναοὺμ τὴν παραθαλασσίαν, ἐν ὁρίοις Ζαβουλὼν
in Capernaum beside the sea, in districts of Zebulun
14 καὶ Νεφθαλείμ· ἵνα πληρωθῇ τὸ ῥηθὲν διὰ Ἡσαΐου τοῦ προ-
and Naphtali; that may be fulfilled that spoken by Isaiah the
15 φήτου, λέγοντος, Γῆ Ζαβουλὼν καὶ γῆ Νεφθαλείμ, ὁδὸν
prophet, saying, Land of Zebulun and land of Naphtali, way
16 θαλάσσης, πέραν τοῦ Ἰορδάνου, Γαλιλαία τῶν ἐθνῶν, ὁ λαὸς
of (the) sea beyond the Jordan, Galilee of the nations; the people
ὁ καθήμενος ἐν σκότει εἶδε φῶς μέγα, καὶ τοῖς καθημένοις ἐν
sitting in darkness saw a light great, and to those sitting in
χώρᾳ καὶ σκιᾷ θανάτου, φῶς ἀνέτειλεν αυτοῖς.
a region and shadow of death, light sprang up to them.
17 Ἀπὸ τότε ἤρξατο ὁ Ἰησοῦς κηρύσσειν καὶ λέγειν,
From then began Jesus to proclaim and to say,
Μετανοεῖτε· ἤγγικε γὰρ ἡ βασιλεία τῶν οὐρανῶν.
Repent! has come near For the kingdom of the heavens.
18 Περιπατῶν δὲ ὁ Ἰησοῦς παρὰ τὴν θάλασσαν τῆς
walking And Jesus beside the sea
Γαλιλαίας εἶδε δύο ἀδελφούς, Σίμωνα τὸν λεγόμενον Πέτρον,
of Galilee, He saw two brothers, Simon called Peter,
καὶ Ἀνδρέαν τὸν ἀδελφὸν αὐτοῦ, βάλλοντας ἀμφίβληστρον
and Andrew the brother of him, casting a net
19 εἰς τὴν θάλασσαν· ἦσαν γὰρ ἁλιεῖς. καὶ λέγει αὐτοῖς, Δεῦτε
into the sea. they were For fishers. And He says to them, Come
20 ὀπίσω μου, καὶ ποιήσω ὑμᾶς ἁλιεῖς ἀνθρώπων. οἱ δὲ εὐθέως
after Me, and I will make you fishers of men. they And at once
21 ἀφέντες τὰ δίκτυα ἠκολούθησαν αὐτῷ. καὶ προβὰς ἐκεῖθεν,
forsaking the nets followed Him. And going on from there
εἶδεν ἄλλους δύο ἀδελφούς, Ἰάκωβον τὸν τοῦ Ζεβεδαίου καὶ
He saw other two brothers, James the (son) of Zebedee, and
Ἰωάννην τὸν ἀδελφὸν αὐτοῦ, ἐν τῷ πλοίῳ μετὰ Ζεβεδαίου
John the brother of him, in the boat with Zebedee
τοῦ πατρὸς αὐτῶν, καταρτίζοντας τὰ δίκτυα αὐτῶν·
the father of them, mending the nets of them.
22 καὶ ἐκάλεσεν αὐτούς. οἱ δὲ εὐθέως ἀφέντες τὸ πλοῖον καὶ τὸν
And He called them. they And at once forsaking the boat and the
πατέρα αὐτῶν ἠκολούθησαν αὐτῷ.
father of them followed Him.
23 Καὶ περιῆγεν ὅλην τὴν Γαλιλαίαν ὁ Ἰησοῦς, διδάσκων
And went about all Galilee Jesus, teaching
ἐν ταῖς συναγωγαῖς αὐτῶν, καὶ κηρύσσων τὸ εὐαγγέλιον
in the synagogues of them, and proclaiming the gospel
τῆς βασιλείας, καὶ θεραπεύων πᾶσαν νόσον καὶ πᾶσαν
of the kingdom, and healing every disease and every

[24]And the report of Him went out into all Syria. And they brought to Him all those having illness, suffering various diseases and torments; also *those* having been possessed by demons; and lunatics, and paralytics; and He healed them.

[25]And many crowds followed Him from Galilee and Decapolis, and Jerusalem, and Judea, and beyond the Jordan.

CHAPTER 5

[1]But seeing the crowds, He went up into the mountain, and having seated Himself, His disciples came to Him.

[2]And having opened His mouth, He taught them, saying,

[3]Blessed *are* the poor in spirit! For theirs is the kingdom of Heaven.

[4]Blessed *are* they who mourn! For they shall be comforted.

[5]Blessed *are* the meek! For they shall inherit the earth.

[6]Blessed *are* they who hunger and thirst after righteousness! For they shall be filled.

[7]Blessed *are* the merciful! For they shall obtain mercy.

[8]Blessed *are* the pure in heart! For they shall see God.

[9]Blessed *are* the peacemakers! For they shall be called sons of God.

[10]Blessed *are* they who have been persecuted for righteousness' sake! For theirs is the kingdom of Heaven.

[11]Blessed are you when they shall reproach you, and shall persecute *you,* and shall say every evil word against you, lying, on account of Me. [12]Rejoice and leap for joy, for your reward *is* great in Heaven; for in this way they persecuted the prophets who *were* before you.

[13]You are the salt of the earth; but if the salt becomes tasteless, with what shall it

24 μαλακίαν ἐν τῷ λαῷ. καὶ ἀπῆλθεν ἡ ἀκοὴ αὐτοῦ εἰς ὅλην
sicknesses among the people. And went the report of Him into all
τὴν Συρίαν· καὶ προσήνεγκαν αὐτῷ πάντας τοὺς κακῶς
Syria. And they brought to Him all those illness
ἔχοντας, ποικίλαις νόσοις καὶ βασάνοις συνεχομένους, καὶ
having, various diseases and torments suffering, and
δαιμονιζομένους, καὶ σεληνιαζομένους, καὶ παραλυτικούς·
demon-possessed, and lunatics, and paralytics.
25 καὶ ἐθεράπευσεν αὐτούς. καὶ ἠκολούθησαν αὐτῷ ὄχλοι
And He healed them. And followed Him crowds
πολλοὶ ἀπὸ τῆς Γαλιλαίας καὶ Δεκαπόλεως καὶ Ἱεροσολύμων
many from Galilee and Decapolis and Jerusalem
καὶ Ἰουδαίας καὶ πέραν τοῦ Ἰορδάνου.
and Judea, and beyond the Jordan.

CHAPTER 5

1 Ἰδὼν δὲ τοὺς ὄχλους ἀνέβη εἰς τὸ ὄρος καὶ καθίσαντος
seeing And the crowds, He went into the mount and sitting down
2 αὐτοῦ, προσῆλθον αὐτῷ οἱ μαθηταὶ αὐτοῦ· καὶ ἀνοίξας
Himself, came near to Him the disciples of Him. And opening
τὸ στομα αὐτοῦ, ἐδίδασκεν αὐτούς, λέγων,
the mouth of Him, He taught them, saying,
3 Μακάριοι οἱ πτωχοὶ τῷ πνεύματι· ὅτι αὐτῶν ἐστιν ἡ
Blessed (are) the poor in spirit, because of them is the
βασιλεία τῶν οὐρανῶν.
kingdom of the heavens.
4 Μακάριοι οἱ πενθοῦντες· ὅτι αὐτοὶ παρακληθήσονται.
Blessed (are) the (ones) mourning, because they shall be comforted.
5 Μακάριοι οἱ πρᾳεῖς· ὅτι αὐτοὶ κληρονομήσουσι τὴν γῆν.
Blessed (are) the meek, because they shall inherit the earth.
6 Μακάριοι οἱ πεινῶντες καὶ διψῶντες τὴν δικαιοσύνην·
Blessed (are) the (ones) hungering and thirsting (after) righteousness,
ὅτι αὐτοὶ χορτασθήσονται.
because they shall be filled.
7 Μακάριοι οἱ ἐλεήμονες· ὅτι αὐτοὶ ἐλεηθήσονται.
Blessed (are) the merciful, because they shall receive mercy.
8 Μακάριοι οἱ καθαροὶ τῇ καρδίᾳ· ὅτι αὐτοὶ τὸν Θεὸν
Blessed (are) the pure in heart, because they God
ὄψονται.
shall see.
9 Μακάριοι οἱ εἰρηνοποιοί· ὅτι αὐτοὶ υἱοὶ Θεοῦ κληθήσονται.
Blessed (are) the peacemakers, because they sons of God shall be called.
10 Μακάριοι οἱ δεδιωγμένοι ἕνεκεν δικαιοσύνης· ὅτι αὐτῶν
Blessed (are) those being persecuted because of righteousness, for of them
11 ἐστιν ἡ βασιλεία τῶν οὐρανῶν. Μακάριοί ἐστε, ὅταν ὀνειδί-
is the kingdom of the heavens. Blessed are you when they will
σωσιν ὑμᾶς καὶ διώξωσι, καὶ εἴπωσι πᾶν πονηρὸν ῥῆμα
reproach you and persecute, and shall say every evil word
12 καθ' ὑμῶν ψευδόμενοι, ἕνεκεν ἐμοῦ. χαίρετε καὶ ἀγαλλιᾶσθε,
against you, lying, for the sake of Me; rejoice and be glad,
ὅτι ὁ μισθὸς ὑμῶν πολὺς ἐν τοῖς οὐρανοῖς· οὕτω γὰρ ἐδίω-
because the reward of you (is) great in the heavens. thus For they per-
ξαν τοὺς προφήτας τοὺς πρὸ ὑμῶν.
secuted the prophets before you.
13 Ὑμεῖς ἐστε τὸ ἅλας τῆς γῆς· ἐὰν δὲ τὸ ἅλας μωρανθῇ, ἐν
You are the salt of the earth. if But the salt be tasteless, by

be salted? For it has strength for nothing any more, but to be thrown out, and to be trampled under by men.

[14]You are the light of the world, a city on a mountain cannot be hidden. [15]Nor do they light a lamp and put it under the grain measure, but on the lampstand; and it shines for all who *are* in the house. [16]So let your light shine before men, so that they may see your good works, and may glorify your Father in Heaven.

[17]Do not think that I came to abolish the Law or the Prophets; I did not come to do away, but to fulfill. [18]truly I say to you, Until the heavens and the earth pass away, in no way shall one iota or one tittle pass away from the law until all comes to pass. [19]Whoever then shall break one of these commandments, the least, and shall teach men so, he shall be called least in the kingdom of Heaven. But whoever does and teaches *them*, this one shall be called great in the kingdom of Heaven. [20]For I say to you, If your righteousness shall not exceed *that of* the scribes and Pharisees, you in no way shall go into the kingdom of Heaven.

[21]You have heard that it was said to the ancients: "Do not commit murder!" And, "Whoever commits murder shall be liable to the Judgment." [22]But I say to you, Everyone who is angry with his brother without a cause shall be liable to the Judgment. And whoever says, Fool! shall be liable *to be thrown* into the fire of Hell.

[23]Therefore, if you offer your gift on the altar, and remember there that your brother has something against you, [24]leave your gift there before the altar, and go. First, be reconciled to your brother, and then

τίνι ἁλισθήσεται ; εἰς οὐδὲν ἰσχύει ἔτι, εἰ μὴ βληθῆναι ἔξω
what shall it be salted? for nothing It is strong still, except to be thrown out,
14 καὶ καταπατεῖσθαι ὑπὸ τῶν ἀνθρώπων. ὑμεῖς ἐστε τὸ φῶς
and to be trampled under by men. You are the light
τοῦ κόσμου· οὐ δύναται πόλις κρυβῆναι ἐπάνω ὄρους
of the world; not is able a city to be hidden on a mount
15 κειμένη· οὐδὲ καίουσι λύχνον καὶ τιθέασιν αὐτὸν ὑπὸ τὸν
situated. Nor do they light a lamp and place it under the
μόδιον, ἀλλ' ἐπὶ τὴν λυχνίαν, καὶ λάμπει πᾶσι τοῖς ἐν τῇ
grain-measure, but on the lampstand, and it lightens all those in the
16 οἰκίᾳ. οὕτω λαμψάτω τὸ φῶς ὑμῶν ἔμπροσθεν τῶν ἀνθρώ-
house. Thus let shine the light of you before men,
πων, ὅπως ἴδωσιν ὑμῶν τὰ καλὰ ἔργα, καὶ δοξάσωσι τὸν
so that they may see of you the good works, and may glorify the
πατέρα ὑμῶν τὸν ἐν τοῖς οὐρανοῖς.
Father of you in the heavens.
17 Μὴ νομίσητε ὅτι ἦλθον καταλῦσαι τὸν νόμον ἢ τοὺς
Not do think that I came to annul the law or the
18 προφήτας· οὐκ ἦλθον καταλῦσαι ἀλλὰ πληρῶσαι. ἀμὴν
prophets. Not I came to annul, but to fulfill. truly
γὰρ λέγω ὑμῖν, ἕως ἂν παρέλθῃ ὁ οὐρανὸς καὶ ἡ γῆ, ἰῶτα
For I say to you, Until pass away the heavens and the earth, iota
ἓν ἢ μία κεραία οὐ μὴ παρέλθῃ ἀπὸ τοῦ νόμου, ἕως ἂν
one or one point in no way shall pass away from the law, until
19 πάντα γένηται. ὃς ἐὰν οὖν λύσῃ μίαν τῶν ἐντολῶν τούτων
all things occur. Whoever, then, relaxes one of commandments these
τῶν ἐλαχίστων, καὶ διδάξῃ οὕτω τοὺς ἀνθρώπους, ἐλά-
the least, and teaches so men, least
χιστος κληθήσεται ἐν τῇ βασιλείᾳ τῶν οὐρανῶν· ὃς δ' ἂν
he shall be called in the kingdom of the heavens. who But ever
ποιήσῃ καὶ διδάξῃ, οὗτος μέγας κληθήσεται ἐν τῇ βασιλείᾳ
does (them) and teaches, this one great shall be called in the kingdom
20 τῶν οὐρανῶν. λέγω γὰρ ὑμῖν ὅτι ἐὰν μὴ περισσεύσῃ ἡ
of the heavens. I say For to you that if not shall exceed the
δικαιοσύνη ὑμῶν πλεῖον τῶν γραμματέων καὶ Φαρισαίων,
righteousness of you more than the scribes and Pharisees,
οὐ μὴ εἰσέλθητε εἰς τὴν βασιλείαν τῶν οὐρανῶν.
in no way shall you go into the kingdom of the heavens.
21 Ἠκούσατε ὅτι ἐρρέθη τοῖς ἀρχαίοις, Οὐ φονεύσεις· ὃς
You heard that it was said to the ancients: Not do murder; who
22 δ' ἂν φονεύσῃ, ἔνοχος ἔσται τῇ κρίσει· ἐγὼ δὲ λέγω ὑμῖν
and ever murders, liable shall be to the Judgment. I But say to you
ὅτι πᾶς ὁ ὀργιζόμενος τῷ ἀδελφῷ αὐτοῦ εἰκῇ ἔνοχος ἔσται
that each who is angry with the brother of him without cause liable shall be
τῇ κρίσει· ὃς δ' ἂν εἴπῃ τῷ ἀδελφῷ αὐτοῦ, Ῥακά, ἔνοχος
to the Judgment. who And ever says to the brother of him, Raca, liable
ἔσται τῷ συνεδρίῳ· ὃς δ' ἂν εἴπῃ, Μωρέ, ἔνοχος ἔσται εἰς
shall be to the sanhedrin; who and ever says, Fool, liable shall be into
23 τὴν γέενναν τοῦ πυρός. ἐὰν οὖν προσφέρῃς τὸ δῶρόν σου
the Gehenna of fire. If, then, you offer the gift of you
ἐπὶ τὸ θυσιαστήριον, κἀκεῖ μνησθῇς ὅτι ὁ ἀδελφός σου ἔχει
on the altar, and there remember that the brother of you has
24 τι κατὰ σοῦ, ἄφες ἐκεῖ τὸ δῶρόν σου ἔμπροσθεν τοῦ θυσια-
something against you, leave there the gift of you before the altar,
στηρίου, καὶ ὕπαγε, πρῶτον διαλλάγηθι τῷ ἀδελφῷ σου,
and go; first be reconciled to the brother of you,

coming, offer your gift.

25 While you are in the way with him, be quickly well-intentioned toward your opponent, that the opponent not deliver you to the judge, and the judge deliver you to the officer, and you be thrown into prison. 26 Truly, I say to you, In no way shall you come out from there until you pay the last kodrantes.

27 You have heard that it was said to the ancients: Do not commit adultery. 28 But I say to you, Everyone looking at a woman to lust after her has already committed adultery with her in his heart.

29 But if your right eye offends you, take it out and throw *it* from you—for it is not profitable to you that one of your members should perish and not all your body be thrown into Hell. 30 And if your right hand cause you to offend, cut it off and throw *it* from you—for it is profitable to you that one of your members should perish, and not all your body be thrown into Hell.

31 It was also said, Whoever puts away his wife, let him give her a bill of divorce. 32 But I say to you, Whoever puts away his wife, apart from a matter of fornication, makes her commit adultery. And whoever shall marry the one put away commits adultery.

33 Again, you have heard that it was said to the ancients: You shall not swear falsely, but shall give your oaths to the Lord. 34 But I say to you, Do not swear *at* all, neither by Heaven, because it is God's throne; 35 nor by the earth, because it is the footstool of His feet; nor by Jerusalem, because it is *the* city of the great King. 36 Nor shall you swear by your head, because you are not able to make one hair white or black. 37 But let your word be Yes, yes; No, no. For whatever is more than these is from evil.

38 You have heard that it was said, Eye for eye, and tooth for tooth; 39 but I say to you, Do not resist evil;

25 καὶ τότε ἐλθὼν πρόσφερε τὸ δῶρόν σου. ἴσθι εὐνοῶν τῷ
and then coming offer the gift of you. Be well-minded with the
ἀντιδίκῳ σου ταχύ, ἕως ὅτου εἶ ἐν τῇ ὁδῷ μετ' αὐτοῦ,
opponent of you quickly, until that you are in the way with him,
μήποτέ σε παραδῷ ὁ ἀντίδικος τῷ κριτῇ, καὶ ὁ κριτής σε
lest you deliver the opponent to the judge, and the judge you
26 παραδῷ τῷ ὑπηρέτῃ, καὶ εἰς φυλακὴν βληθήσῃ. ἀμὴν λέγω
deliver to the officer, and into prison you be thrown. Truly, I say
σοι, οὐ μὴ ἐξέλθῃς ἐκεῖθεν, ἕως ἂν ἀποδῷς τὸν ἔσχατον
to you, in no way shall you exit from there until you pay the last
27 κοδράντην. Ἠκούσατε ὅτι ἐρρέθη τοῖς ἀρχαίοις, Οὐ μοιχεύ-
28 **kodrantes. You heard that it was said to the ancients, Not commit**
σεις· ἐγὼ δὲ λέγω ὑμῖν, ὅτι πᾶς ὁ βλέπων γυναῖκα πρὸς τὸ
adultery, I But I say to you that each one looking at a woman to
ἐπιθυμῆσαι αὐτῆς ἤδη ἐμοίχευσεν αὐτὴν ἐν τῇ καρδίᾳ αὐτοῦ.
lust after her already has committed adultery with her in the heart of him.
29 εἰ δὲ ὁ ὀφθαλμός σου ὁ δεξιὸς σκανδαλίζει σε, ἔξελε αὐτὸν
if But the eye of you right offends you, take out it
καὶ βάλε ἀπὸ σοῦ· συμφέρει γάρ σοι ἵνα ἀπόληται ἓν τῶν
and throw(it) from you. profitable For to you that should perish one of the
30 μελῶν σου, καὶ μὴ ὅλον τὸ σῶμά σου βληθῇ εἰς γέενναν. καὶ
parts of you, and not all the body of you be cast into Gehenna. And
εἰ ἡ δεξιά σου χεὶρ σκανδαλίζει σε, ἔκκοψον αὐτὴν καὶ βάλε
if the right of you hand causes to offend you, cut off it and throw
ἀπὸ σοῦ συμφέρειγαρ σοι ἵνα ἀπόληται ἓν τῶν μελῶν σου,
from you. profitable For you that should perish one of the parts of you,
31 καὶ μὴ ὅλον τὸ σῶμά σου βληθῇ εἰς γέενναν. ἐρρέθη δὲ ὅτι
and not all the body of you be cast into Gehenna. it was said And,
Ὃς ἂν ἀπολύσῃ τὴν γυναῖκα αὐτοῦ, δότω αὐτῇ ἀποσ-
Whoever puts away the wife of him, let him give her a bill
32 τάσιον· ἐγὼ δὲ λέγω ὑμῖν, ὅτι ὃς ἂν ἀπολύσῃ τὴν γυναῖκα
of divorce. I But say to you that whoever puts away the wife
αὐτοῦ, παρεκτὸς λόγου πορνείας, ποιεῖ αὐτὴν μοιχᾶσθαι·
of him, apart from a matter of fornication, makes her commit adultery;
καὶ ὃς ἐὰν ἀπολελυμένην γαμήσῃ μοιχᾶται.
and whoever the put away one shall marry commits adultery.
33 Πάλιν ἠκούσατε ὅτι ἐρρέθη τοῖς ἀρχαίοις, Οὐκ ἐπιορκή-
Again, you heard that it was said to the ancients, Not you shall per-
34 σεις, ἀποδώσεις δὲ τῷ Κυρίῳ τοὺς ὅρκους σου· ἐγὼ δὲ λέγω
jure, shall deliver but to the Lord the oaths of you. I But say
ὑμῖν μὴ ὀμόσαι ὅλως· μήτε ἐν τῷ οὐρανῷ, ὅτι θρόνος ἐστὶ
to you, Not do swear (at) all, neither by Heaven, because throne it is
35 τοῦ Θεοῦ· μήτε ἐν τῇ γῇ, ὅτι ὑποπόδιόν ἐστι τῶν ποδῶν
of God; neither by the earth, because footstool it is of the feet
αὐτοῦ· μήτε εἰς Ἱεροσόλυμα, ὅτι πόλις ἐστὶ τοῦ μεγάλου
of Him; neither to Jerusalem, because city it is of the great
36 βασιλέως· μήτε ἐν τῇ κεφαλῇ σου ὀμόσῃς, ὅτι οὐ δύνασαι
King; neither by the head of you swear, because not you are able
37 μίαν τρίχα λευκὴν ἢ μέλαιναν ποιῆσαι. ἔστω δὲ ὁ λόγος
one hair white or black to make. let be But the word
ὑμῶν, ναὶ ναί, οὒ οὔ· τὸ δὲ περισσὸν τούτων ἐκ τοῦ πονηροῦ
of you, Yes, yes, no, no. the And excess of these out of the evil one
38 ἐστιν. Ἠκούσατε ὅτι ἐρρέθη, Ὀφθαλμὸν ἀντὶ ὀφθαλμοῦ, καὶ
is. You heard that it was said, An eye instead of an eye, and
39 ὀδόντα ἀντὶ ὀδόντος· ἐγὼ δὲ λέγω ὑμῖν μὴ ἀντιστῆναι τῷ
a tooth instead of a tooth. I But say to you, Not do resist the

πονηρῷ· ἀλλ' ὅστις σε ῥαπίσει ἐπὶ τὴν δεξιάν σου σιαγόνα,
evil, but who you strikes on the right of you cheek
40 στρέψον αὐτῷ καὶ τὴν ἄλλην· καὶ τῷ θέλοντί σοι κριθῆναι
turn to him also the other; and he wishing you to sue,
41 καὶ τὸν χιτῶνά σου λαβεῖν, ἄφες αὐτῷ καὶ τὸ ἱμάτιον· καὶ
and the tunic of you to take, allow him also the coat. And
42 ὅστις σε ἀγγαρεύσει μίλιον ἕν, ὕπαγε μετ' αὐτοῦ δύο. τῷ
who you shall compel to go mile one, go with him two. He
αἰτοῦντί σε δίδου· καὶ τὸν θέλοντα ἀπὸ σοῦ δανείσασθαι μὴ
asking you to give, and he wishing from you to borrow, not
ἀποστραφῇς.
do turn away.
43 'Ηκούσατε ὅτι ἐρρέθη, 'Αγαπήσεις τὸν πλησίον σου, καὶ
You heard that it was said, You shall love the neighbor of you, and
44 μισήσεις τὸν ἐχθρόν σου· ἐγὼ δὲ λέγω ὑμῖν, ἀγαπᾶτε τοὺς
you shall hate the enemy of you. I But I say to you, Love the
ἐχθροὺς ὑμῶν, εὐλογεῖτε τοὺς καταρωμένους ὑμᾶς, καλῶς
enemies of you, bless those cursing you, well
ποιεῖτε τοὺς μισοῦντας ὑμᾶς, καὶ προσεύχεσθε ὑπὲρ τῶν
do to those hating you, and pray on behalf of those
45 ἐπηρεαζόντων ὑμᾶς, καὶ διωκόντων ὑμᾶς· ὅπως γένησθε
abusing you and persecuting you; so that you may be
υἱοὶ τοῦ πατρὸς ὑμῶν τοῦ ἐν οὐρανοῖς, ὅτι τὸν ἥλιον αὐτοῦ
sons of the Father of you in (the) heavens. Because the sun of Him
ἀνατέλλει ἐπὶ πονηροὺς καὶ ἀγαθούς, καὶ βρέχει ἐπὶ
He makes rise on (the) evil and (the) good, and sends rain on
46 δικαίους καὶ ἀδίκους. ἐὰν γὰρ ἀγαπήσητε τοὺς ἀγαπῶντας
(the) just and (the) unjust. if For you love those loving
ὑμᾶς, τίνα μισθὸν ἔχετε; οὐχὶ καὶ οἱ τελῶναι τὸ αὐτὸ
you, what reward have you? Not even do the tax-collectors the same
47 ποιοῦσι; καὶ ἐὰν ἀσπάσησθε τοὺς ἀδελφοὺς ὑμῶν μόνον,
practice? And if you greet the brothers of you only,
τί περισσὸν ποιεῖτε; οὐχὶ καὶ οἱ τελῶναι οὕτω ποιοῦσιν;
what exceptional do you? Not do even the tax-collectors so do?
48 ἔσεσθε οὖν ὑμεῖς τέλειοι, ὥσπερ ὁ πατὴρ ὑμῶν ὁ ἐν τοῖς
be then You perfect. even as the Father of you in the
οὐρανοῖς τέλειός ἐστι.
heavens perfect is.

CHAPTER 6

1 Προσέχετε τὴν ἐλεημοσύνην ὑμῶν μὴ ποιεῖν ἔμπροσθεν
Take care the merciful deeds of you not to do before
τῶν ἀνθρώπων, πρὸς τὸ θεαθῆναι αὐτοῖς· εἰ δὲ μήγε,
men, in order to be seen of them. if But not,
μισθὸν οὐκ ἔχετε παρὰ τῷ πατρὶ ὑμῶν τῷ ἐν τοῖς οὐρανοῖς.
reward not you have from the Father of you in the heavens
2 Ὅταν οὖν ποιῇς ἐλεημοσύνην, μὴ σαλπίσῃς ἔμπροσθέν
when Then you do merciful deeds, not do trumpet before
σου, ὥσπερ οἱ ὑποκριταὶ ποιοῦσιν ἐν ταῖς συναγωγαῖς καὶ
you, as the hypocrites do in the synagogues and
ἐν ταῖς ῥύμαις, ὅπως δοξασθῶσιν ὑπὸ τῶν ἀνθρώπων·
in the streets, so that they may be glorified by men.
3 ἀμὴν λέγω ὑμῖν, ἀπέχουσι τὸν μισθὸν αὐτῶν. σοῦ δὲ ποιοῦν-
Truly, I say to you, they have the reward of them. you But doing
τος ἐλεημοσύνην, μὴ γνώτω ἡ ἀριστερά σου τί ποιεῖ ἡ
merciful deeds, not do let know the left of you what does the

but whoever strikes you on the right cheek, turn the other to him also. [40]And to him desiring to sue you, and to take your tunic, allow him also *to have* the coat. [41]And whoever shall compel you to go one mile, go two with him. [42]He asking you to give, and he wishing to borrow from you, do not turn away.

[43]You have heard that it was said, You shall love your neighbor and hate your enemy. [44]But I say to you, Love your enemies, bless those cursing you; do well to those hating you, and pray for those abusing and persecuting you; [45]so that you may be sons of your Father in Heaven. Because He causes the sun to rise on *the* evil and *the* good, and sends rain on *the* just and unjust. [46]For if you love those loving you, what reward do you have? Do not the tax-collectors do the same? [47]And if you only greet your brothers, what exceptional *thing* do you do? Do not the tax-collectors do so? [48]Therefore, you be perfect, even as your Father in Heaven is perfect.

CHAPTER 6

[1]Be careful not to do your merciful deeds before men in order to be seen by them. Otherwise, you have no reward from your Father in Heaven. [2]Therefore, when you do merciful deeds, do not trumpet before you, as the hypocrites do in the synagogues and in the streets, so that they may be glorified by men. Truly I say to you, they have their reward. [3]But you doing merciful deeds, do not let your left

know what your right *hand* does, [4] so that your merciful deeds may be in secret. And your Father seeing in secret will Himself repay you in the open.

[5] And when you pray, you shall not be as the hypocrites, for they love to pray standing in the synagogues, and in the open streets, so that they may be seen of men. Truly I say to you, they have their reward. [6] But you, when you pray, enter into your room, and having shut your door, pray to your Father in secret. And your Father seeing in secret will repay you in the open. [7] But when you pray, do not babble vain words, as the heathen, for they think that they shall be heard in their much speaking. [8] Then do not be like them, for your Father knows what things you have need of before you ask Him. [9] Therefore, you *should* pray this way:

Our Father *who is* in Heaven, hallowed be Your name. [10] Let Your kingdom come; let Your will be done, on earth as it is in Heaven. [11] Give us today our daily bread, [12] and forgive us our debts as we also forgive our debtors. [13] And do not lead us into temptation, but deliver us from evil: for Yours is the kingdom, and the power, and the glory forever. Amen.

[14] For if you forgive men their offenses, your heavenly Father will also forgive your offenses. [15] But if you will not forgive men their offenses, neither will your Father forgive your offenses.

[16] And when you fast, do not be as the hypocrites, darkening the face, for they disfigure their faces so that

4 δεξιά σου, ὅπως ᾖ σου ἡ ἐλεημοσύνη ἐν τῷ κρυπτῷ· καὶ ὁ
right of you, so that of you the merciful deeds in secret, and the
πατήρ σου ὁ βλέπων ἐν τῷ κρυπτῷ αὐτὸς ἀποδώσει σοι ἐν
Father of you seeing in secret Him(self) will repay you in
τῷ φανερῷ.
the open

5 Καὶ ὅταν προσεύχῃ, οὐκ ἔσῃ ὥσπερ οἱ ὑποκριταί, ὅτι
And when you pray, not you shall be as the hypocrites, because
φιλοῦσιν ἐν ταῖς συναγωγαῖς καὶ ἐν ταῖς γωνίαις τῶν
they love in the synagogues and in the corners of the
πλατειῶν ἑστῶτες προσεύχεσθαι, ὅπως ἂν φανῶσι τοῖς
open streets standing to pray, so that may they appear
ἀνθρώποις· ἀμὴν λέγω ὑμῖν ὅτι ἀπέχουσι τὸν μισθὸν
to men. Truly, I say to you that they have the reward
6 αὐτῶν. σὺ δέ, ὅταν προσεύχῃ, εἴσελθε εἰς τὸ ταμιεῖόν σου,
of them. you But, when you pray, enter into the room of you
καὶ κλείσας τὴν θύραν σου, πρόσευξαι τῷ πατρί σου τῷ
and shutting the door of you, pray to the Father of you
ἐν τῷ κρυπτῷ· καὶ ὁ πατήρ σου ὁ βλέπων ἐν τῷ κρυπτῷ
in secret; and the Father of you seeing in secret
7 ἀποδώσει σοι ἐν τῷ φανερῷ. προσευχόμενοι δὲ μὴ βαττο-
will repay you in the open. when praying But, not do use
λογήσητε, ὥσπερ οἱ ἐθνικοί· δοκοῦσι γὰρ ὅτι ἐν τῇ πολυ-
vain repetition, as the nations; they think for that in much
8 λογίᾳ αὐτῶν εἰσακουσθήσονται. μὴ οὖν ὁμοιωθῆτε αὐτοῖς·
speaking of them they will be heard. not Then do be like them,
οἶδε γὰρ ὁ πατὴρ ὑμῶν ὧν χρείαν ἔχετε, πρὸ τοῦ ὑμᾶς
knows for the Father of you what things need you have before you
9 αἰτῆσαι αὐτόν. οὕτως οὖν προσεύχεσθε ὑμεῖς· Πάτερ ἡμῶν
ask Him. So then pray you, Father of us
10 ὁ ἐν τοῖς οὐρανοῖς, ἁγιασθήτω τὸ ὄνομά σου· ἐλθέτω ἡ
in the heavens, let be sanctified the name of You. Let come the
βασιλεία σου· γενηθήτω τὸ θέλημά σου, ὡς ἐν οὐρανῷ, καὶ
kingdom of You; let be done the will of You, as in Heaven, also
11 ἐπὶ τῆς γῆς· τὸν ἄρτον ἡμῶν τὸν ἐπιούσιον δὸς ἡμῖν
on the earth. The bread of us daily, give to us
12 σήμερον· καὶ ἄφες ἡμῖν τὰ ὀφειλήματα ἡμῶν, ὡς καὶ ἡμεῖς
today, and forgive us the debts of us, as also we
13 ἀφίεμεν τοῖς ὀφειλέταις ἡμῶν· καὶ μὴ εἰσενέγκῃς ἡμᾶς εἰς
forgive the debtors of us. And not lead us into
πειρασμόν, ἀλλὰ ῥῦσαι ἡμᾶς ἀπὸ τοῦ πονηροῦ. ὅτι σοῦ
temptation, but deliver us from evil; because of You
ἐστιν ἡ βασιλεία καὶ ἡ δύναμις καὶ ἡ δόξα εἰς τοὺς αἰῶνας.
is the kingdom, and the power, and the glory to the ages.
14 ἀμήν. ἐὰν γὰρ ἀφῆτε τοῖς ἀνθρώποις τὰ παραπτώματα
Amen. if For you forgive men the trespasses
15 αὐτῶν, ἀφήσει καὶ ὑμῖν ὁ πατὴρ ὑμῶν ὁ οὐράνιος· ἐὰν δὲ
of them, will forgive also you the Father of you heavenly. if But
μὴ ἀφῆτε τοῖς ἀνθρώποις τὰ παραπτώματα αὐτῶν, οὐδὲ ὁ
not you forgive men the trespasses of them, neither the
πατὴρ ὑμῶν ἀφήσει τὰ παραπτώματα ὑμῶν.
Father of you will forgive the trespasses of you.

16 Ὅταν δὲ νηστεύητε, μὴ γίνεσθε ὥσπερ οἱ ὑποκριταὶ
when And you fast, not do be as the hypocrites,
σκυθρωποί· ἀφανίζουσι γὰρ τὰ πρόσωπα αὐτῶν, ὅπως
darkening the face; they disfigure for the faces of them so as

they may appear to be fasting to men. Truly I say to you that they have their reward. [17]But you *in* fasting, anoint your head and wash your face. [18]so as not to appear to be fasting to men, but to your Father seeing in secret. And your Father seeing in secret will repay you in the open.

[19]Do not treasure up for you treasures on the earth, where moth and rust cause to vanish, and where thieves dig through and steal. [20]But treasure up for you treasures in Heaven, where neither moth nor rust cause to vanish, and where thieves do not dig through and steal. [21]For where your treasure is, there your heart will be also.

[22]The lamp of the body is the eye. If, then, your eye is sound, all your body is light. [23]But if your eye is evil, all your body is dark. If, then, the light in you is darkness, how great *is* the darkness!

[24]No one is able to serve two lords; for either he will hate the one, and he will love the other; or he will hold to the one, and he will despise the other. You are not able to serve God and wealth. [25]Because of this, I say to you, Do not be anxious for your soul, what you eat and what you drink; nor for your body, what you put on. Is not the soul more than the food, and the body than the clothing? [26]Look at the birds of the heaven, that they do not sow, nor do they reap, nor do *they* gather into barns; yet your heavenly Father feeds them. Do you not rather excel them?

[27]But who of you *by* being anxious is able to add one cubit onto his stature? [28]And why are you anxious about clothing? Consider the lilies of the field, how they grow. They do not labor nor

φανῶσι τοῖς ἀνθρώποις νηστεύοντες· ἀμὴν λέγω ὑμῖν ὅτι
they appear to men fasting. Truly, I say to you that

17 ἀπέχουσι τὸν μισθὸν αὐτῶν. σὺ δὲ νηστεύων ἄλειψαί σου
they have the reward of them. you but (in) fasting, anoint of you

18 τὴν κεφαλήν, καὶ τὸ πρόσωπόν σου νίψαι, ὅπως μὴ φανῇς
the head, and the face of you wash, so as not to appear

τοῖς ἀνθρώποις νηστεύων, ἀλλὰ τῷ πατρί σου τῷ ἐν τῷ
to men fasting, but to the Father of you in

κρυπτῷ· καὶ ὁ πατήρ σου ὁ βλέπων ἐν τῷ κρυπτῷ ἀποδώ-
secret; and the Father of you seeing in secret will repay

σει σοι ἐν τῷ φανερῷ.
you in the open.

19 Μὴ θησαυρίζετε ὑμῖν θησαυροὺς ἐπὶ τῆς γῆς, ὅπου σὴς
Not do treasure up for you treasures on the earth, where moth

καὶ βρῶσις ἀφανίζει, καὶ ὅπου κλέπται διορύσσουσι καὶ
and rust cause to vanish, and where thieves dig through and

20 κλέπτουσι· θησαυρίζετε δὲ ὑμῖν θησαυροὺς ἐν οὐρανῷ,
steal. treasure up But for you treasures in Heaven,

ὅπου οὔτε σὴς οὔτε βρῶσις ἀφανίζει, καὶ ὅπου κλέπται οὐ
where neither moth nor rust cause to vanish, and where thieves not

21 διορύσσουσιν οὐδὲ κλέπτουσιν. ὅπου γάρ ἐστιν ὁ θησαυρὸς
dig through nor steal. where For is the treasure

22 ὑμῶν, ἐκεῖ ἔσται καὶ ἡ καρδία ὑμῶν. ὁ λύχνος τοῦ σώματός
of you, there will be also the heart of you. The lamp of the body

ἐστιν ὁ ὀφθαλμός· ἐὰν οὖν ὁ ὀφθαλμός σου ἁπλοῦς ᾖ, ὅλον
is the eye. If, then, the eye of you sound be, all

23 τὸ σῶμά σου φωτεινὸν ἔσται· ἐὰν δὲ ὁ ὀφθαλμός σου πονη-
the body of you light is. if But the eye of you evil

ρὸς ᾖ, ὅλον τὸ σῶμά σου σκοτεινὸν ἔσται. εἰ οὖν τὸ φῶς τὸ
be, all the body of you dark is. If, then, the light

24 ἐν σοὶ σκότος ἐστί, τὸ σκότος πόσον; οὐδεὶς δύναται δυσὶ
in you darkness is, the darkness how great! No one is able two

κυρίοις δουλεύειν· ἢ γὰρ τὸν ἕνα μισήσει, καὶ τὸν ἕτερον
lords to serve. either For the one he will hate, and the other

ἀγαπήσει· ἢ ἑνὸς ἀνθέξεται, καὶ τοῦ ἑτέρου καταφρονήσει.
he will love, or one he will cleave to, and the other he will despise.

25 οὐ δύνασθε Θεῷ δουλεύειν καὶ μαμμωνᾷ. διὰ τοῦτο λέγω
not you are able God to serve and wealth. Because of this, I say

ὑμῖν, μὴ μεριμνᾶτε τῇ ψυχῇ ὑμῶν, τί φάγητε καὶ τί πίητε·
to you, not do be anxious for the soul of you, what you eat, and what drink;

μηδὲ τῷ σώματι ὑμῶν, τί ἐνδύσησθε. οὐχὶ ἡ ψυχὴ πλεῖόν
nor for the body of you, what you put on. not the soul more

26 ἐστι τῆς τροφῆς, καὶ τὸ σῶμα τοῦ ἐνδύματος; ἐμβλέψατε
Is than the food, and the body than the clothing? Look

εἰς τὰ πετεινὰ τοῦ οὐρανοῦ, ὅτι οὐ σπείρουσιν, οὐδὲ θερί-
at the birds of the heaven, that not they sow, nor do they

ζουσιν, οὐδὲ συνάγουσιν εἰς ἀποθήκας, καὶ ὁ πατὴρ ὑμῶν ὁ
reap, nor do gather into barns; yet the Father of you

οὐράνιος τρέφει αὐτά· οὐχ ὑμεῖς μᾶλλον διαφέρετε αὐτῶν;
heavenly feeds them. Not do you rather excel them?

27 τίς δὲ ἐξ ὑμῶν μεριμνῶν δύναται προσθεῖναι ἐπὶ τὴν
who But of you being anxious is able to add onto the

28 ἡλικίαν αὐτοῦ πῆχυν ἕνα; καὶ περὶ ἐνδύματος τί μεριμνᾶτε;
stature of him cubit one? And concerning clothing, why are you anxious?

καταμάθετε τὰ κρίνα τοῦ ἀγροῦ, πῶς αὐξάνει· οὐ κοπιᾷ,
Consider the lilies of the field, how they grow; not they labor,

do they spin; [29]but I say to you that not even Solomon in all his glory was clothed as one of these. [30]If God so enrobes the grass of the field —which is today, and is thrown into the oven tomorrow—*will He* not much rather you, *you* of little faith? [31]Then do not be anxious, saying, What may we eat? Or, what may we drink? Or, what may clothe us? [32]For all these things the heathen seek after. For your heavenly Father knows that you have need of all these things. [33]But seek first the kingdom of God and His righteousness, and all these things will be added to you. [34]Therefore, do not be anxious for tomorrow. For the morrow will be anxious of its own *things*. Sufficient to *each* day *is* its *own* badness.

CHAPTER 7

[1]Do not judge, that you may not be judged. [2]For with whatever judgment you judge, you will be judged; and with whatever measure you measure, it will be measured again to you. [3]But why do you look on the twig that *is* in the eye of your brother, but do not see the log in your eye? [4]Or how will you say to your brother, Allow me to cast out the twig from your eye; and behold, the log *is* in your eye! [5]Hypocrite, first cast the log out of your eye, and then you will see clearly to cast the twig out of the eye of your brother.

[6]Do not give that which *is* holy to the dogs, nor throw your pearls before the pigs, that they should not trample on them with their feet, and having turned they may charge you.

[7]Ask, and it will be given to you; seek, and you will find; knock, and it will be opened to you. [8]For each one that asks receives, and the *one* that seeks finds; and to the *one* knocking, it will be opened. [9]Or what man

29 οὐδὲ νήθει· λέγω δὲ ὑμῖν ὅτι οὐδὲ Σολομὼν ἐν πάσῃ τῇ
nor spin. I say But to you that not even Solomon in all the
30 δόξῃ αὐτοῦ περιεβάλετο ὡς ἓν τούτων. εἰ δὲ τὸν χόρτον τοῦ
glory of him was clothed as one of these. if But the grass of the
ἀγροῦ, σήμερον ὄντα, καὶ αὔριον εἰς κλίβανον βαλλόμενον,
field, today being, and tomorrow into a furnace being thrown,
ὁ Θεὸς οὕτως ἀμφιέννυσιν, οὐ πολλῷ μᾶλλον ὑμᾶς, ὀλιγό-
God thus enrobes; not much more (are) you, little-
31 πιστοι; μὴ οὖν μεριμνήσητε, λέγοντες, Τί φάγωμεν, ἢ τί
faiths? not Then be anxious, saying, What may we eat? Or, what
32 πίωμεν, ἢ τί περιβαλώμεθα; πάντα γὰρ ταῦτα τὰ ἔθνη
may we drink? Or, what may clothe us? all For these things the nations
ἐπιζητεῖ· οἶδε γὰρ ὁ πατὴρ ὑμῶν ὁ οὐράνιος ὅτι χρῄζετε
seek. knows For the Father of you heavenly that you need
33 τούτων ἁπάντων. ζητεῖτε δὲ πρῶτον τὴν βασιλείαν τοῦ
these of all. seek But first the kingdom
Θεοῦ καὶ τὴν δικαιοσύνην αὐτοῦ, καὶ ταῦτα πάντα προσ-
of God and the righteousness of Him, and these things all will be
34 τεθήσεται ὑμῖν. μὴ οὖν μεριμνήσητε εἰς τὴν αὔριον· ἡ γὰρ
added to you. not Then do be anxious for the morrow; the for
αὔριον μεριμνήσει τὰ ἑαυτῆς. ἀρκετὸν τῇ ἡμέρᾳ ἡ κακία
morrow will be anxious of itself. Sufficient to the day (is) the badness
αὐτῆς.
of it.

CHAPTER 7

1 Μὴ κρίνετε, ἵνα μὴ κριθῆτε· ἐν ᾧ γὰρ κρίματι κρίνετε,
2 Not do judge, that not you be judged. in what For judgment you judge,
κριθήσεσθε· καὶ ἐν ᾧ μέτρῳ μετρεῖτε, ἀντιμετρηθήσεται
you will be judged. And in what measure you measure, it will be measured
3 ὑμῖν. τί δὲ βλέπεις τὸ κάρφος τὸ ἐν τῷ ὀφθαλμῷ τοῦ ἀδελφοῦ
to you. why But do you see the twig in the eye of the brother
4 σου, τὴν δὲ ἐν τῷ σῷ ὀφθαλμῷ δοκὸν οὐ κατανοεῖς; ἢ πῶς
of you, the but in the of you eye log not you perceive? Or how
ἐρεῖς τῷ ἀδελφῷ σου, Ἄφες ἐκβάλω τὸ κάρφος ἀπὸ τοῦ
will you say to the brother of you, Permit (me) to take out the twig from the
ὀφθαλμοῦ σου· καὶ ἰδού, ἡ δοκὸς ἐν τῷ ὀφθαλμῷ σου;
the eye of you, and behold, the log (is) in the eye of you?
5 ὑποκριτά, ἔκβαλε πρῶτον τὴν δοκὸν ἐκ τοῦ ὀφθαλμοῦ σου,
Hypocrite! take out First the log out of the eye of you,
καὶ τότε διαβλέψεις ἐκβαλεῖν τὸ κάρφος ἐκ τοῦ ὀφθαλμοῦ
and then you will see clearly to take out the twig out of the eye
τοῦ ἀδελφοῦ σου.
of the brother of you.
6 Μὴ δῶτε τὸ ἅγιον τοῖς κυσί· μηδὲ βάλητε τοὺς μαργαρί-
Not do give the holy to the dogs, nor throw the pearls
τας ὑμῶν ἔμπροσθεν τῶν χοίρων, μήποτε καταπατήσωσιν
of you before the pigs, lest they trample
αὐτοὺς ἐν τοῖς ποσὶν αὐτῶν, καὶ στραφέντες ῥήξωσιν ὑμᾶς.
them with the feet of them, and turning they charge you.
7 Αἰτεῖτε, καὶ δοθήσεται ὑμῖν· ζητεῖτε, καὶ εὑρήσετε·
Ask, and it will be given to you; seek, and you will find;
8 κρούετε, καὶ ἀνοιγήσεται ὑμῖν. πᾶς γὰρ ὁ αἰτῶν λαμβάνει,
knock, and it will be opened to you. each For asking, receives;
9 καὶ ὁ ζητῶν εὑρίσκει, καὶ τῷ κρούοντι ἀνοιγήσεται. ἢ τίς
and he seeking, finds; and to the (one) knocking, it will be opened. Or who

of you is there who will give a stone if his son should ask a loaf of him? 10 And if he should ask a fish, will he give him a snake? 11 If, then, you, being evil, know to give good gifts to your children, how much more your Father who *is* in Heaven will give good things to those that ask Him?

12 Therefore, all things, whatever you desire that men should do to you, so also you should do to them; for this is the Law and the Prophets.

13 Go in through the narrow gate; for wide is the gate, and broad *is* the way that leads to death. And many are the ones who go through it. 14 For narrow is the gate, and constricted *is* the way that leads into life, and few are the ones who find it. 15 But beware of the false prophets who come to you in sheep's clothing, but inside they are plundering wolves. 16 From their fruits you shall know them. Do they gather grapes from thorns, or figs from thistles? 17 So every good tree produces good fruits; but the corrupt tree produces evil fruits. 18 A good tree cannot produce evil fruits, nor a corrupt tree produce good fruits. 19 Every tree not producing good fruits is cut out and is thrown into fire. 20 Surely you shall know them from their fruits.

21 Not everyone who says to Me, Lord, Lord, shall enter into the kingdom of Heaven, but the ones who do the will of My Father in Heaven. 22 Many will say to Me in that day, Lord, Lord, did we not prophesy in Your name, and in Your name cast out demons, and in Your name

ἐστιν ἐξ ὑμῶν ἄνθρωπος, ὃν ἐὰν αἰτήσῃ ὁ υἱὸς αὐτοῦ ἄρτον,
is of you a man, who if should ask the son of him a loaf,
10 μὴ λίθον ἐπιδώσει αὐτῷ; καὶ ἐὰν ἰχθὺν αἰτήσῃ, μὴ ὄφιν
a stone he will give him? And if a fish he should ask, a snake
11 ἐπιδώσει αὐτῷ; εἰ οὖν ὑμεῖς, πονηροὶ ὄντες, οἴδατε δόματα
he will give him? If, then, you, evil being, know gifts
ἀγαθὰ διδόναι τοῖς τέκνοις ὑμῶν, πόσῳ μᾶλλον ὁ πατὴρ
good to give to the children of you, how much more the Father
ὑμῶν ὁ ἐν τοῖς οὐρανοῖς δώσει ἀγαθὰ τοῖς αἰτοῦσιν αὐτόν;
of you in the heavens will give good things to those asking Him!
12 πάντα οὖν ὅσα ἂν θέλητε ἵνα ποιῶσιν ὑμῖν οἱ ἄνθρωποι,
all things Then, what ever you desire that may do to you men,
οὕτω καὶ ὑμεῖς ποιεῖτε αὐτοῖς· οὗτος γάρ ἐστιν ὁ νόμος καὶ
so also you do to them, this For is the Law and
οἱ προφῆται.
the Prophets.
13 Εἰσέλθετε διὰ τῆς στενῆς πύλης· ὅτι πλατεῖα ἡ πύλη, καὶ
Enter in through the narrow gate, because wide (is) the gate and
εὐρύχωρος ἡ ὁδὸς ἡ ἀπάγουσα εἰς τὴν ἀπώλειαν, καὶ πολλοί
broad (is) the way leading away into destruction; and many
14 εἰσιν οἱ εἰσερχόμενοι δι' αὐτῆς· ὅτι στενὴ ἡ πύλη, καὶ
are those entering in through it; because narrow the gate, and
τεθλιμμένη ἡ ὁδὸς ἡ ἀπάγουσα εἰς τὴν ζωήν, καὶ ὀλίγοι
constricted (is) the way leading away into Life; and few
εἰσὶν οἱ εὑρίσκοντες αὐτήν.
are those finding it.
15 Προσέχετε δὲ ἀπὸ τῶν ψευδοπροφητῶν, οἵτινες ἔρχονται
take care But from the false prophets, who come
πρὸς ὑμᾶς ἐν ἐνδύμασι προβάτων, ἔσωθεν δέ εἰσι λύκοι
to you in clothing of sheep; within but they are wolves
16 ἅρπαγες. ἀπὸ τῶν καρπῶν αὐτῶν ἐπιγνώσεσθε αὐτούς·
plundering. From the fruits of them, you shall know them.
μήτι συλλέγουσιν ἀπὸ ἀκανθῶν σταφυλήν, ἢ ἀπὸ τριβόλων
Neither do they gather from thorns grapes, or from thistles
17 σῦκα; οὕτω πᾶν δένδρον ἀγαθὸν καρποὺς καλοὺς ποιεῖ
figs? So every tree good fruits good produces.
18 τὸ δὲ σαπρὸν δένδρον καρποὺς πονηροὺς ποιεῖ. οὐ δύναται
the But corrupt tree fruits evil produces. Not is able
δένδρον ἀγαθὸν καρποὺς πονηροὺς ποιεῖν, οὐδὲ δένδρον
a tree good fruits evil to produce; nor a tree
19 σαπρὸν καρποὺς καλοὺς ποιεῖν. πᾶν δένδρον μὴ ποιοῦν
corrupt fruits good to produce. Every tree not producing
20 καρπὸν καλὸν ἐκκόπτεται καὶ εἰς πῦρ βάλλεται. ἄραγε ἀπὸ
fruits good is cut out, and into fire is thrown. Surely, from
21 τῶν καρπῶν αὐτῶν ἐπιγνώσεσθε αὐτούς. οὐ πᾶς ὁ λέγων
the fruits of them you will know them. Not everyone saying
μοι, Κύριε, Κύριε, εἰσελεύσεται εἰς τὴν βασιλείαν τῶν
to Me, Lord, Lord, will enter into the kingdom of the
οὐρανῶν· ἀλλ' ὁ ποιῶν τὸ θέλημα τοῦ πατρός μου τοῦ ἐν
heavens, but those doing the will of the Father of Me in
22 οὐρανοῖς. πολλοὶ ἐροῦσί μοι ἐν ἐκείνῃ τῇ ἡμέρᾳ, Κύριε, Κύριε,
(the) heavens. Many will say to Me in that **day, Lord, Lord,**
οὐ τῷ σῷ ὀνόματι προεφητεύσαμεν, καὶ τῷ σῷ ὀνόματι
not in Your name did we prophesy, and in Your name
δαιμόνια ἐξεβάλομεν, καὶ τῷ σῷ ὀνόματι δυνάμεις πολλὰς
demons cast out, and in Your name works of power many

do many mighty works? 23 And then I will declare to them, I never knew you; depart from Me, those working lawlessness!

24 Therefore, everyone who hears these words from Me, and does them, I will compare him to a wise man who built his house on the rock; 25 and the rains came down, and the waters came up, and the winds blew, and fell against that house; but it did not fall, for it had been founded on the rock. 26 And everyone who hears these words, and does not do them, *he* shall be compared to a foolish man who built his house on the sand; 27 and the rain came down, and the winds blew, and beat against that house; and it fell, and great was the fall of it.

28 And it happened, when Jesus had finished these sayings, the crowds were astonished at His teaching. 29 For He was teaching them as having authority, and not as the scribes.

CHAPTER 8

1 And He having come down from the mount, great crowds followed Him. 2 And behold, coming up, a leper worshiped Him, saying, Lord, If You will, You are able to cleanse me. 3 And stretching out His hand, Jesus touched him, saying, I will! Be cleansed! And instantly his leprosy was cleansed. 4 And Jesus said to him, See *that* you tell no one, but go, show yourself to the priest, and offer the gift which Moses commanded, for a testimony to them.

5 And Jesus having entered into Capernaum, a centurion came near Him, begging Him, 6 and saying,

23 ἐποιήσαμεν ; καὶ τότε ὁμολογήσω αὐτοῖς, ὅτι οὐδέποτε
we performed? And then I will declare to them, Never
ἔγνων ὑμᾶς· ἀποχωρεῖτε ἀπ' ἐμοῦ οἱ ἐργαζόμενοι τὴν
I knew you; depart from Me, those working
24 ἀνομίαν. πᾶς οὖν ὅστις ἀκούει μου τοὺς λόγους τούτους καὶ
lawlessness. Everyone then who hears from Me words these, and
ποιεῖ αὐτούς, ὁμοιώσω αὐτὸν ἀνδρὶ φρονίμῳ, ὅστις ᾠκοδό-
does them, I will compare him to a man prudent, who built
25 μησε τὴν οἰκίαν αὐτοῦ ἐπὶ τὴν πέτραν· καὶ κατέβη ἡ βροχὴ
the house of him on the rock. And came down the rain,
καὶ ἦλθον οἱ ποταμοὶ καὶ ἔπνευσαν οἱ ἄνεμοι, καὶ προσ-
and came up the rivers, and blew the winds, and fell
έπεσον τῇ οἰκίᾳ ἐκείνῃ, καὶ οὐκ ἔπεσε· τεθεμελίωτο γὰρ ἐπὶ
against house that; yet not it fell; it had been founded for on
26 τὴν πέτραν. καὶ πᾶς ὁ ἀκούων μου τοὺς λόγους τούτους
the rock. And everyone hearing of Me words these,
καὶ μὴ ποιῶν αὐτούς, ὁμοιωθήσεται ἀνδρὶ μωρῷ, ὅστις
and not doing them, will be compared to a man foolish, who
27 ᾠκοδόμησε τὴν οἰκίαν αὐτοῦ ἐπὶ τὴν ἄμμον· καὶ κατέβη ἡ
built the house of him on the sand; and came down the
βροχὴ καὶ ἦλθον οἱ ποταμοὶ καὶ ἔπνευσαν οἱ ἄνεμοι, καὶ
rain, and came up the rivers, and blew the winds, and
προσέκοψαν τῇ οἰκίᾳ ἐκείνῃ, καὶ ἔπεσε· καὶ ἦν ἡ πτῶσις
beat against house that; and it fell, and was the collapse
αὐτῆς μεγάλη.
of it great.
28 Καὶ ἐγένετο ὅτε συνετέλεσεν ὁ Ἰησοῦς τοὺς λόγους τού-
And happened, when had finished Jesus sayings these,
29 τους, ἐξεπλήσσοντο οἱ ὄχλοι ἐπὶ τῇ διδαχῇ αὐτοῦ· ἦν γὰρ
were astonished the crowds at the teaching of him. He was For
διδάσκων αὐτοὺς ὡς ἐξουσίαν ἔχων, καὶ οὐχ ὡς οἱ γραμ-
teaching them as authority having, and not as the
ματεῖς.
scribes.

CHAPTER 8

1 Καταβάντι δὲ αὐτῷ ἀπὸ τοῦ ὄρους, ἠκολούθησαν αὐτῷ
having come down And He from the mount, followed Him
2 ὄχλοι πολλοί καὶ ἰδού, λεπρὸς ἐλθὼν προσεκύνει αὐτῷ,
crowds great. And behold, a leper having come worshiped Him,
3 λέγων, Κύριε, ἐὰν θέλῃς, δύνασαί με καθαρίσαι. καὶ ἐκτείνας
saying, Lord, if You will, You are able me to cleanse. And stretching
τὴν χεῖρα, ἥψατο αὐτοῦ ὁ Ἰησοῦς, λέγων, Θέλω, καθαρί-
the hand, touched him Jesus, saying, I will, be
4 σθητι. καὶ εὐθέως ἐκαθαρίσθη αὐτοῦ ἡ λέπρα. καὶ λέγει
cleansed! And instantly was cleansed of Him the leprosy. And says
αὐτῷ ὁ Ἰησοῦς, Ὅρα μηδενὶ εἴπῃς· ἀλλ' ὕπαγε, σεαυτὸν
to him Jesus, See (that) no one you tell, but go, yourself
δεῖξον τῷ ἱερεῖ, καὶ προσένεγκε τὸ δῶρον ὃ προσέταξε
show to the priest, and offer the gift which ordered
Μωσῆς, εἰς μαρτύριον αὐτοῖς.
Moses, for a testimony to them.
5 Εἰσελθόντι δὲ τῷ Ἰησοῦ εἰς Καπερναούμ, προσῆλθεν
having entered And Jesus into Capernaum, came near
6 αὐτῷ ἑκατόνταρχος παρακαλῶν αὐτόν, καὶ λέγων, Κύριε,
to Him a centurion beseeching Him, and saying, Lord,

Lord, my child has been laid in the house, a paralytic, being grievously tormented. [7]And Jesus said to him, I will come and heal him. [8]And answering, the centurion said, Lord, I am not worthy that You should enter under my roof; but only speak a word, and my child will be healed. [9]For I am also a man under authority, having soldiers under myself. And I say to this one, Go; and he goes; and to another, Come; and he comes; and to my slave, Do this; and he does *it.*

[10]And hearing, Jesus marveled, and said to those following, Truly I say to you, Not even in Israel did I find such faith. [11]But I say to you that many will come from east and west, and will recline with Abraham and Isaac and Jacob in the kingdom of Heaven; [12]but the sons of the kingdom shall be cast out into the outer darkness; there shall be weeping and gnashing of the teeth. [13]And Jesus said to the centurion, Go, and as you have believed, so let it be to you. And his child was healed in that hour.

[14]And having come to the house of Peter, Jesus saw his mother-in-law laid out and in a fever. [15]And He touched her hand, and her fever left her. And she rose up and served them.

[16]And evening having come, they brought to Him many possessed by demons. And He cast out the spirits by a word, and He healed all who were ill; [17]so that it might be fulfilled that which was spoken by Isaiah the prophet, saying, "He took upon Himself our weaknesses, and bore *our* sicknesses."

[18]And seeing great crowds around Him, Jesus gave orders to go away to the other side. [19]And one, a scribe, coming near, said to Him, Teacher, I will follow You wherever you may go. [20]And Jesus said to him, The foxes have holes, and the

ὁ παῖς μου βέβληται ἐν τῇ οἰκίᾳ παραλυτικός, δεινῶς βασανι-
the child of me has been laid in the house a paralytic, grievously being
7 ζόμενος. καὶ λέγει αὐτῷ ὁ Ἰησοῦς, Ἐγὼ ἐλθὼν θεραπεύσω
tormented. And says to him Jesus, **I having come will heal**
8 αὐτόν. καὶ ἀποκριθεὶς ὁ ἑκατόνταρχος ἔφη, Κύριε, οὐκ εἰμὶ
him. And answering, the centurion said, Lord, not I am
ἱκανὸς ἵνα μου ὑπὸ τὴν στέγην εἰσέλθῃς· ἀλλὰ μόνον εἰπὲ
worthy that of me under the roof You may enter, but only say
9 λόγον, καὶ ἰαθήσεται ὁ παῖς μου. καὶ γὰρ ἐγὼ ἄνθρωπός
a word, and will be healed the child of me. also For I a man
εἰμι ὑπὸ ἐξουσίαν, ἔχων ὑπ' ἐμαυτὸν στρατιώτας· καὶ λέγω
am under authority, having under myself soldiers; and I say
τούτῳ, Πορεύθητι, καὶ πορεύεται· καὶ ἄλλῳ, Ἔρχου, καὶ
to this (one), Go And he goes. And to another, Come! And
ἔρχεται· καὶ τῷ δούλῳ μου, Ποίησον τοῦτο, καὶ ποιεῖ.
he comes. And to the slave of me, Do this! And he does.
10 ἀκούσας δὲ ὁ Ἰησοῦς ἐθαύμασε, καὶ εἶπε τοῖς ἀκολουθοῦσιν,
hearing And, Jesus marveled, and said to those following,
Ἀμὴν λέγω ὑμῖν, οὐδὲ ἐν τῷ Ἰσραὴλ τοσαύτην πίστιν
Truly, I say to you, Not even in Israel such faith
11 εὗρον. λέγω δὲ ὑμῖν, ὅτι πολλοὶ ἀπὸ ἀνατολῶν καὶ δυσμῶν
I found. I say And to you that many from east and vest
ἥξουσι, καὶ ἀνακλιθήσονται μετὰ Ἀβραὰμ καὶ Ἰσαὰκ καὶ
will come, and will recline with Abraham and Isaac and
12 Ἰακὼβ ἐν τῇ βασιλείᾳ τῶν οὐρανῶν· οἱ δὲ υἱοὶ ¯ - βασιλείας
Jacob in the kingdom of the heavens. the But sons of the kingdom
ἐκβληθήσονται εἰς τὸ σκότος τὸ ἐξώτερον· ἐκεῖ ἔσται ὁ
shall be cast out into the darkness outer; there shall be
13 κλαυθμὸς καὶ ὁ βρυγμὸς τῶν ὀδόντων. καὶ εἶπεν ὁ Ἰησοῦς
weeping and gnashing of the teeth. And said Jesus
τῷ ἑκατοντάρχῳ, Ὕπαγε, καὶ ὡς ἐπίστευσας γενηθήτω σοι.
to the centurion, Go! And as you believed, let it be to you.
καὶ ἰάθη ὁ παῖς αὐτοῦ ἐν τῇ ὥρᾳ ἐκείνῃ.
And was healed the child of him in hour that.
14 Καὶ ἐλθὼν ὁ Ἰησοῦς εἰς τὴν οἰκίαν Πέτρου, εἶδε τὴν
And having come, Jesus into the house of Peter, He saw the
15 πενθερὰν αὐτοῦ βεβλημένην καὶ πυρέσσουσαν, καὶ ἥψατο
mother-in-law of him having been laid and fever-stricken. And He touched
τῆς χειρὸς αὐτῆς, καὶ ἀφῆκεν αὐτὴν ὁ πυρετός· καὶ ἠγέρθη,
the hand of her, and left her the fever. And she arose
16 καὶ διηκόνει αὐτοῖς. ὀψίας δὲ γενομένης προσήνεγκαν αὐτῷ
and ministered to them. evening And having come, they brought to Him
δαιμονιζομένους πολλούς· καὶ ἐξέβαλε τὰ πνεύματα λόγῳ,
demon-possessed many. And He cast out the spirits by a word;
17 καὶ πάντας τοὺς κακῶς ἔχοντας ἐθεράπευσεν· ὅπως πληρωθῇ
and all those illness having, He healed; so as may be fulfilled
τὸ ῥηθὲν διὰ Ἡσαΐου τοῦ προφήτου, λέγοντος, Αὐτὸς τὰς
that spoken through Isaiah the prophet, saying, He the
ἀσθενείας ἡμῶν ἔλαβε, καὶ τὰς νόσους ἐβάστασεν.
weaknesses of us took, and the sicknesses He bore.
Ἰδὼν δὲ ὁ Ἰησοῦς πολλοὺς ὄχλους περὶ αὐτόν, ἐκέλευσεν
seeing And Jesus great crowds around Him, He ordered
18 ἀπελθεῖν εἰς τὸ πέραν. καὶ προσελθὼν εἷς γραμματεὺς εἶπεν
to go away to the other side. And coming near one scribe said
19 αὐτῷ, Διδάσκαλε, ἀκολουθήσω σοι ὅπου ἐὰν ἀπέρχῃ. καὶ
to Him, Teacher, I will follow you whereever you go. And
20 λέγει αὐτῷ ὁ Ἰησοῦς, Αἱ ἀλώπεκες φωλεοὺς ἔχουσι, καὶ τὰ
says to him Jesus, The foxes holes have, and the

birds of the heaven have nests, but the Son of man has nowhere He may lay *His* head. 21 And another of His disciples said to Him, Lord, allow me first to go and bury my father. 22 Jesus said to him, Follow Me, and leave the dead to bury their dead.

23 And He having entered into the boat, His disciples followed Him. 24 And, behold, a great storm rose up in the sea, so that the boat was covered by the waves; but He was sleeping. 25 And coming near, His disciples awakened Him, saying, Lord, save us! We are perishing. 26 And He said to them, Why are you afraid, *you* of little faith? Then rising up, He rebuked the winds and the sea. And there was a great calm. 27 And the men marveled, saying, What kind *of man* is this, that even the winds and the sea obey Him?

28 And when He had come to the other side, into the country of the Gergesenes, two demon-possessed ones met Him, coming out of the tombs, very violent, so that no one was able to pass through that way. 29 And, behold! They cried out, saying, What *is* to us and to You, Jesus, Son of God? Have You come here before time to torment us?

30 And there was far off from them a herd of many pigs feeding. 31 And the demons begged Him, saying, If You cast us out, allow us to go away into the herd of pigs. 32 And He said to them, Go! And coming out, these went away into the herd of pigs. and, behold, all the herd of pigs rushed down the cliff into the sea, and died in the waters.

33 But those who fed *them* fled, and going into the city, *they* told all the things of the

πετεινὰ τοῦ οὐρανοῦ κατασκηνώσεις· ὁ δὲ υἱὸς τοῦ ἀνθρώ-
birds of the heaven nests, the but Son of
21 που οὐκ ἔχει ποῦ τὴν κεφαλὴν κλίνῃ. ἕτερος δὲ τῶν μαθητῶν
man not has where the head He may lay. another And of the disciples
αὐτοῦ εἶπεν αὐτῷ, Κύριε, ἐπίτρεψόν μοι πρῶτον ἀπελθεῖν
of Him said to Him, Lord, allow me first to go away
22 καὶ θάψαι τὸν πατέρα μου. ὁ δὲ Ἰησοῦς εἶπεν αὐτῷ, Ἀκολού-
and to bury the father of me. And Jesus said to him, Follow
θει μοι, καὶ ἄφες τοὺς νεκροὺς θάψαι τοὺς ἑαυτῶν νεκρούς.
Me, and allow the dead to bury the of themselves dead.
23 Καὶ ἐμβάντι αὐτῷ εἰς τὸ πλοῖον, ἠκολούθησαν αὐτῷ οἱ
And having entered He into the boat, followed Him the
24 μαθηταὶ αὐτοῦ. καὶ ἰδού, σεισμὸς μέγας ἐγένετο ἐν τῇ θα-
disciples of Him. And behold, a shaking great occurred in the
λάσσῃ, ὥστε τὸ πλοῖον καλύπτεσθαι ὑπὸ τῶν κυμάτων·
sea, so that the boat was covered by the waves.
25 αὐτὸς δὲ ἐκάθευδε. καὶ προσελθόντες οἱ μαθηταὶ αὐτοῦ
He But was sleeping. And having come near, the disciples of Him
ἤγειραν αὐτόν, λέγοντες, Κύριε, σῶσον ἡμᾶς, ἀπολλύμεθα.
aroused Him, saying, Lord, save us; we are perishing.
καὶ λέγει αὐτοῖς, Τί δειλοί ἐστε, ὀλιγόπιστοι ; τότε ἐγερθεὶς
26 And He says to them, Why afraid are you, little-faiths? Then arising,
ἐπετίμησε τοῖς ἀνέμοις καὶ τῇ θαλάσσῃ, καὶ ἐγένετο γαλήνη
He rebuked the wind and the sea, and there was a calm
27 μεγάλη. οἱ δὲ ἄνθρωποι ἐθαύμασαν, λέγοντες, Ποταπός
great. the And men marveled, saying, Of what kind
ἐστιν οὗτος, ὅτι καὶ οἱ ἄνεμοι καὶ ἡ θάλασσα ὑπακούουσιν
is this, that even the winds and the sea obey
αὐτῷ ;
Him?

28 Καὶ ἐλθόντι αὐτῷ εἰς τὸ πέραν εἰς τὴν χώραν τῶν
And having come He to the other side, into the country of the
Γεργεσηνῶν, ὑπήντησαν αὐτῷ δύο δαιμονιζόμενοι ἐκ τῶν
Gergesenes, met Him two demon-possessed out of the
μνημείων ἐξερχόμενοι, χαλεποὶ λίαν, ὥστε μὴ ἰσχύειν τινὰ
tombs coming out, violent exceedingly, so as not was able any
29 παρελθεῖν διὰ τῆς ὁδοῦ ἐκείνης· καὶ ἰδού, ἔκραξαν λέγοντες,
to pass through way that. And behold, they cried out, saying,
Τί ἡμῖν καὶ σοί, Ἰησοῦ, υἱὲ τοῦ Θεοῦ ; ἦλθες ὧδε πρὸ καιροῦ
What to us and to You, Jesus, Son of God? Come You here before time
30 βασανίσαι ἡμᾶς ; ἦν δὲ μακρὰν ἀπ' αὐτῶν ἀγέλη χοίρων
to torment us? was And at a distance from them a herd of pigs
31 πολλῶν βοσκομένη. οἱ δὲ δαίμονες παρεκάλουν αὐτόν,
many feeding. the And demons begged Him,
λέγοντες, Εἰ ἐκβάλλεις ἡμᾶς, ἐπίτρεψον ἡμῖν ἀπελθεῖν εἰς τὴν
saying, If You expel us, allow us to go away into the
32 ἀγέλην τῶν χοίρων. καὶ εἶπεν αὐτοῖς, Ὑπάγετε. οἱ δὲ
herd. of the pigs. And He said to them, Go! those And
ἐξελθόντες ἀπῆλθον εἰς τὴν ἀγέλην τῶν χοίρων· καὶ ἰδού,
coming out went away into the herd of the pigs. And behold,
ὥρμησε πᾶσα ἡ ἀγέλη τῶν χοίρων κατὰ τοῦ κρημνοῦ εἰς
rushed all the herd of the pigs down the cliff into
33 τὴν θάλασσαν, καὶ ἀπέθανον ἐν τοῖς ὕδασιν. οἱ δὲ βόσκοντες
the sea, and died in the waters. those But feeding
ἔφυγον, καὶ ἀπελθόντες εἰς τὴν πόλιν ἀπήγγειλαν πάντα,
fled, and having gone into the city told all things,

demon-possessed ones. [34]And, behold, all the city went out to meet with Jesus. And seeing Him, they begged that He move away from their borders.

CHAPTER 9

[1]And entering into the boat, He passed over and came to *His* own city. [2]And, behold, they brought a paralytic on a cot to Him. And seeing their faith, Jesus said to the paralytic, Be comforted, child. Your sins have been forgiven you. [3]And, behold, some of the scribes said within themselves, This one blasphemes. [4]And seeing their thoughts, Jesus said, Why do you think evil in your hearts? [5]For what is easier, to say, *Your* sins have been forgiven you; or to say, Rise up and walk? [6]But that you may know that the Son of man has authority on earth to forgive sins, then He said to the paralytic, Rising up, lift up your cot and go to your house. [7]And rising up, he went away to his house. [8]And seeing, the crowds marveled, and *they* glorified God who gave such authority to men.

[9]And passing from there, Jesus saw a man named Matthew sitting at the tax office. And *He* said to him, Follow Me. And rising up, he followed Him.

[10]And it happened as He reclined in the house, Behold, many tax-collectors and sinners coming, *they* were reclining with Jesus and His disciples. [11]And seeing, the Pharisees said to His disciples, Why does your teacher eat with tax-collectors and sinners? [12]But Jesus hearing, He said to them, The ones who are strong have no need of a physician, but the ones who

34 καὶ τὰ τῶν δαιμονιζομένων. καὶ ἰδού, πᾶσα ἡ πόλις ἐξῆλ-
and the (things) of the demon-possessed. And behold, all the city went
θεν εἰς συνάντησιν τῷ Ἰησοῦ· καὶ ἰδόντες αὐτόν, παρεκά-
out to meet with Jesus; and seeing Him, they
λεσαν ὅπως μεταβῇ ἀπὸ τῶν ὁρίων αὐτῶν.
begged that He move from the borders of them.

CHAPTER 9

1 Καὶ ἐμβὰς εἰς τὸ πλοῖον διεπέρασε καὶ ἦλθεν εἰς τὴν ἰδίαν
And entering into the boat, He passed over and came into the own
2 πόλιν. καὶ ἰδού, προσέφερον αὐτῷ παραλυτικὸν ἐπὶ κλίνης
city. And behold, they brought to Him a paralytic on a cot
βεβλημένον· καὶ ἰδὼν ὁ Ἰησοῦς τὴν πίστιν αὐτῶν εἶπε τῷ
laid out. And seeing Jesus the faith of them, He said to the
παραλυτικῷ, Θάρσει, τέκνον· ἀφέωνταί σοι αἱ ἁμαρτίαι
paralytic, Be comforted, child; have been forgiven you the sins
3 σου. καὶ ἰδού, τινὲς τῶν γραμματέων εἶπον ἐν ἑαυτοῖς,
of you. And behold, some of the scribes said within themselves,
4 Οὗτος βλασφημεῖ. καὶ ἰδὼν ὁ Ἰησοῦς τὰς ἐνθυμήσεις αὐτῶν
This (one) blasphemes. And seeing Jesus the thoughts of them
εἶπεν, Ἱνατί ὑμεῖς ἐνθυμεῖσθε πονηρὰ ἐν ταῖς καρδίαις ὑμῶν;
He said, Why do you think evil in the hearts of you?
5 τί γάρ ἐστιν εὐκοπώτερον, εἰπεῖν, Ἀφέωνταί σοι αἱ
what For is easier, to say, Have been forgiven you the
6 ἁμαρτίαι· ἢ εἰπεῖν, Ἔγειραι καὶ περιπάτει; ἵνα δὲ εἰδῆτε,
sins; or to say, Rise up and walk? that But you may know
ὅτι ἐξουσίαν ἔχει ὁ υἱὸς τοῦ ἀνθρώπου ἐπὶ τῆς γῆς ἀφιέναι
that authority has the Son of man on the earth to forgive
ἁμαρτίας (τότε λέγει τῷ παραλυτικῷ), Ἐγερθεὶς ἆρόν σου
sins — then He says to the paralytic, Having risen, lift your
7 τὴν κλίνην, καὶ ὕπαγε εἰς τὸν οἶκόν σου. καὶ ἐγερθεὶς ἀπῆλ-
cot, and go to the house of you. And rising up, he went
8 θεν εἰς τὸν οἶκον αὐτοῦ. ἰδόντες δὲ οἱ ὄχλοι ἐθαύμασαν, καὶ
away to the house of him. having seen And the crowds marveled, and
ἐδόξασαν τὸν Θεόν, τὸν δόντα ἐξουσίαν τοιαύτην τοῖς
glorified God, the (One) giving authority such
ἀνθρώποις.
to men.

9 Καὶ παράγων ὁ Ἰησοῦς ἐκεῖθεν εἶδεν ἄνθρωπον καθήμενον
And passing by Jesus from there saw a man sitting
ἐπὶ τὸ τελώνιον, Ματθαῖον λεγόμενον, καὶ λέγει αὐτῷ,
at the tax-office, Matthew called; and says to him,
Ἀκολούθει μοι. καὶ ἀναστὰς ἠκολούθησεν αὐτῷ.
Follow me. And rising up, he followed Him.
10 Καὶ ἐγένετο αὐτοῦ ἀνακειμένου ἐν τῇ οἰκίᾳ, καὶ ἰδού,
And it happened, He reclining in the house, and behold,
πολλοὶ τελῶναι καὶ ἁμαρτωλοὶ ἐλθόντες συνανέκειντο τῷ
many tax-collectors and sinners having come were reclining
11 Ἰησοῦ καὶ τοῖς μαθηταῖς αὐτοῦ. καὶ ἰδόντες οἱ Φαρισαῖοι
with Jesus and the disciples of Him. And having seen, the Pharisees
εἶπον τοῖς μαθηταῖς αὐτοῦ, Διατί μετὰ τῶν τελωνῶν καὶ
said to the disciples of Him, Why with the tax-collectors and
12 ἁμαρτωλῶν ἐσθίει ὁ διδάσκαλος ὑμῶν; ὁ δὲ Ἰησοῦς ἀκούσας
sinners eats the teacher of you? But Jesus having heard,
εἶπεν αὐτοῖς, Οὐ χρείαν ἔχουσιν οἱ ἰσχύοντες ἰατροῦ, ἀλλ'
He said to them, Not need have those being strong of a healer, but

are sick. [13]But having gone, learn what this *is,* "I desire mercy, and not sacrifice." For I did not come to call the righteous to repentance, but sinners.

[14]Then the disciples of John came to Him, saying, Why do we and the Pharisees fast much, and Your disciples do not fast? [15]And Jesus said to them, Can the sons of the bridechamber mourn as long as the bridegroom is with them? But the days will come when the bridegroom will have been taken from them; and then they will fast. [16]But no one puts a piece of new cloth onto an old garment. For its filling up takes away from the garment, and a worse tear takes *its* place. [17]Nor do they put new wine into old skins; otherwise, the skins are burst, and the wine pours out, and the skins will be ruined. But they put new wine into new skins, and both are preserved together.

[18]As He spoke these things to them, behold, coming up a ruler bowed before Him, saying, My daughter has just now died; but coming lay Your hand on her, and she will live. [19]And rising up, Jesus and His disciples followed him.

[20]And, behold, a woman who had a flow of blood for twelve years came near, behind *Him, and* touched the hem of His robe. [21]For she said within herself, If only I shall touch His robe, I will be cured. [22]But turning and seeing her, Jesus said, Be comforted, daughter, your faith has saved you. And the woman was saved from that hour.

[23]And coming into the house of the ruler, and seeing the flute-players and the crowd causing a tumult,

[24]Jesus said to them, Go back, for the little girl has not died, but she sleeps. And they laughed at Him.

13 οἱ κακῶς ἔχοντες. πορευθέντες δὲ μάθετε τί ἐστιν, Ἔλεον
those illness having. having gone But, learn what it is: mercy
θέλω, καὶ οὐ θυσίαν· οὐ γὰρ ἦλθον καλέσαι δικαίους, ἀλλ'
I desire, and not sacrifice: not for I came to call righteous (ones) but
ἁμαρτωλοὺς εἰς μετάνοιαν.
sinners to repentance.
14 Τότε προσέρχονται αὐτῷ οἱ μαθηταὶ Ἰωάννου, λέγοντες,
Then came near to Him the disciples of John, saying,
Διατί ἡμεῖς καὶ οἱ Φαρισαῖοι νηστεύομεν πολλά, οἱ δὲ
Why we and the Pharisees do fast much, the but
15 μαθηταί σου οὐ νηστεύουσι; καὶ εἶπεν αὐτοῖς ὁ Ἰησοῦς, Μὴ
disciples of You not do fast? And said to them Jesus, not
δύνανται οἱ υἱοὶ τοῦ νυμφῶνος πενθεῖν, ἐφ' ὅσον μετ' αὐτῶν
Are able the sons of the bridechamber to mourn as long as with them
16 ἐστιν ὁ νυμφίος; ἐλεύσονται δὲ ἡμέραι ὅταν ἀπαρθῇ ἀπ'
is the bridegroom? will come But days when will have been taken from
αὐτῶν ὁ νυμφίος, καὶ τότε νηστεύσουσιν. οὐδεὶς δὲ ἐπιβάλ-
them the bridegroom, and then they will fast. no one But puts
λει ἐπίβλημα ῥάκους ἀγνάφου ἐπὶ ἱματίῳ παλαιῷ· αἴρει
a piece of cloth unfulled on a garment old; takes away
γὰρ τὸ πλήρωμα αὐτοῦ ἀπὸ τοῦ ἱματίου, καὶ χεῖρον
for the fullness of it from the garment, and a worse
17 σχίσμα γίνεται. οὐδὲ βάλλουσιν οἶνον νέον εἰς ἀσκοὺς
tear occurs. Neither do they put wine new into wineskins
παλαιούς· εἰ δὲ μήγε, ῥήγνυνται οἱ ἀσκοί, καὶ ὁ οἶνος
old; otherwise are burst the wineskins, and the wine
ἐκχεῖται, καὶ οἱ ἀσκοὶ ἀπολοῦνται· ἀλλὰ βάλλουσιν οἶνον
pours out, and the wineskins will be ruined; but they put wine
νέον εἰς ἀσκοὺς καινούς, καὶ ἀμφότερα συντηροῦνται.
new into wineskins fresh, and both are preserved together.
18 Ταῦτα αὐτοῦ λαλοῦντος αὐτοῖς, ἰδού, ἄρχων εἷς ἐλθὼν
(As) these things He is speaking to them, behold, a ruler one coming
προσεκύνει αὐτῷ, λέγων ὅτι Ἡ θυγάτηρ μου ἄρτι ἐτελεύ-
worshiped Him, saying, — The daughter of me just now has
τησεν· ἀλλὰ ἐλθὼν ἐπίθες τὴν χεῖρά σου ἐπ' αὐτήν, καὶ
died, but coming lay the hand of You on her, and
19 ζήσεται. καὶ ἐγερθεὶς ὁ Ἰησοῦς ἠκολούθησεν αὐτῷ καὶ οἱ
she will live. And rising up, — Jesus followed him, and the
20 μαθηταὶ αὐτοῦ. καὶ ἰδού, γυνὴ αἱμορροοῦσα δώδεκα ἔτη,
disciples of Him. And, behold, a woman having a flow of blood twelve years
προσελθοῦσα ὄπισθεν, ἥψατο τοῦ κρασπέδου τοῦ ἱματίου
coming near behind, touched the fringe of the garment
21 αὐτοῦ. ἔλεγε γὰρ ἐν ἑαυτῇ, Ἐὰν μόνον ἅψωμαι τοῦ ἱματίου
of Him. she said For within herself, If only I shall touch the garment
22 αὐτοῦ, σωθήσομαι. ὁ δὲ Ἰησοῦς ἐπιστραφεὶς καὶ ἰδὼν αὐτὴν
of Him, I shall be cured.— But Jesus having turned and seeing her
εἶπε, Θάρσει, θύγατερ· ἡ πίστις σου σέσωκέ σε. καὶ ἐσώθη
said, Be comforted, daughter; the faith of you has saved you. . And was saved
23 ἡ γυνὴ ἀπὸ τῆς ὥρας ἐκείνης. καὶ ἐλθὼν ὁ Ἰησοῦς εἰς τὴν
the woman from — hour that. And coming Jesus into the
οἰκίαν τοῦ ἄρχοντος, καὶ ἰδὼν τοὺς αὐλητὰς καὶ τὸν ὄχλον
house of the ruler, and seeing the flute-players and the crowd
24 θορυβούμενον, λέγει αὐτοῖς, Ἀναχωρεῖτε· οὐ γὰρ ἀπέθανε
causing a tumult, said to them, Go back not for has died
25 τὸ κοράσιον, ἀλλὰ καθεύδει. καὶ κατεγέλων αὐτοῦ. ὅτε δὲ
the girl, but she sleeps. And they laughed at Him. when But

25 But when the crowd had been put out, entering He took hold of her hand, and the little girl rose up. 26 And this report went out into all that land.

27 And Jesus passing on from there, two blind ones followed Him, crying and saying, Have pity on us, Son of David. 28 And coming into the house, the blind ones came near to Him. And Jesus said to them, Do you believe that I am able to do this? And they said to Him, Yes, Lord. 29 Then He touched their eyes, saying, According to your faith let it be to you. 30 And their eyes were opened. And Jesus strictly commanded them, saying, Let no one know. 31 But going out, they made Him known in all that land.

32 And as they were going out, behold, they brought to Him a dumb man possessed by a demon. 33 And the demon having been cast out, the dumb one spoke. And the crowds marveled, saying, Never was it seen this way in Israel. 34 But the Pharisees said, He casts out the demons by the ruler of the demons.

35 And Jesus went about all the cities and the villages teaching in their synagogues, and proclaiming the gospel of the kingdom, and healing every sickness and every weakness of body among the people. 36 And seeing the crowds, He was moved with pity for them, because they were tired and scattered, like sheep having no shepherd. 37 Then He said to His disciples, The harvest truly *is* great, but the workers few. 38 Pray then that the Lord may send out workers into His harvest.

ἐξεβλήθη ὁ ὄχλος, εἰσελθὼν ἐκράτησε τῆς χειρὸς αὐτῆς, καὶ
had been put out the crowd, entering He took hold of the hand of her, and
26 ἠγέρθη τὸ κοράσιον. καὶ ἐξῆλθεν ἡ φήμη αὕτη εἰς ὅλην τὴν
arose the girl. And went out the report this into all –
γῆν ἐκείνην.
land that.

27 Καὶ παράγοντι ἐκεῖθεν τῷ Ἰησοῦ, ἠκολούθησαν αὐτῷ δύο
And passing on from there – Jesus, followed Him two
τυφλοί, κράζοντες καὶ λέγοντες, Ἐλέησον ἡμᾶς, υἱὲ Δαβίδ.
blind ones, crying and saying, Have pity on us, Son of David.
28 ἐλθόντι δὲ εἰς τὴν οἰκίαν, προσῆλθον αὐτῷ οἱ τυφλοί, καὶ
coming And into the house, came near to Him the blind ones and
λέγει αὐτοῖς ὁ Ἰησοῦς, Πιστεύετε ὅτι δύναμαι τοῦτο ποιῆ-
said to them – Jesus, Do you believe that I am able this to do?
29 σαι; λέγουσιν αὐτῷ, Ναί, Κύριε. τότε ἥψατο τῶν ὀφθαλμῶν
They say to Him, Yes, Lord. Then He touched the eyes
30 αὐτῶν, λέγων, Κατὰ τὴν πίστιν ὑμῶν γενηθήτω ὑμῖν. καὶ
of them, saying, According to the faith of you let it be to you. And
ἀνεῴχθησαν αὐτῶν οἱ ὀφθαλμοί· καὶ ἐνεβριμήσατο αὐτοῖς ὁ
were opened their – eyes; and strictly ordered them –
31 Ἰησοῦς, λέγων, Ὁρᾶτε μηδεὶς γινωσκέτω. οἱ δὲ ἐξελθόντες
Jesus, saying, See, no one let know. they But going out
διεφήμισαν αὐτὸν ἐν ὅλῃ τῇ γῇ ἐκείνῃ.
declared Him in all – land that.

32 Αὐτῶν δὲ ἐξερχομένων, ἰδού, προσήνεγκαν αὐτῷ ἄνθρω-
(as) they And were going out, behold, they brought to Him a man
33 πον κωφὸν δαιμονιζόμενον. καὶ ἐκβληθέντος τοῦ δαιμονίου,
dumb demon-possessed. And having been cast out the demon,
ἐλάλησεν ὁ κωφός· καὶ ἐθαύμασαν οἱ ὄχλοι, λέγοντες,
spoke the dumb. And marveled the crowds, saying,
34 Οὐδέποτε ἐφάνη οὕτως ἐν τῷ Ἰσραήλ. οἱ δὲ Φαρισαῖοι
Never was it seen thus in Israel. the But Pharisees
ἔλεγον, Ἐν τῷ ἄρχοντι τῶν δαιμονίων ἐκβάλλει τὰ
said, By the prince of the demons He casts out the
δαιμόνια.
demons.

35 Καὶ περιῆγεν ὁ Ἰησοῦς τὰς πόλεις πάσας καὶ τὰς κώμας,
And went about – Jesus the cities all and the villages,
διδάσκων ἐν ταῖς συναγωγαῖς αὐτῶν, καὶ κηρύσσων τὸ
teaching in the synagogues of them, and proclaiming the
εὐαγγέλιον τῆς βασιλείας, καὶ θεραπεύων πᾶσαν νόσον καὶ
gospel of the kingdom, and healing every sickness and
36 πᾶσαν μαλακίαν ἐν τῷ λαῷ. Ἰδὼν δὲ τοὺς ὄχλους, ἐσπλαγ-
every weakness in the people. seeing And the crowds He was moved
χνίσθη περὶ αὐτῶν, ὅτι ἦσαν ἐκλελυμένοι καὶ ἐρριμμένοι
with pity for them, because they were tired and scattered
37 ὡσεὶ πρόβατα μὴ ἔχοντα ποιμένα. τότε λέγει τοῖς μαθηταῖς
as sheep not having a shepherd. Then He says to the disciples
αὐτοῦ, Ὁ μὲν θερισμὸς πολύς, οἱ δὲ ἐργάται ὀλίγοι·
of Him, the Indeed harvest (is) great, the but workmen few;
38 δεήθητε οὖν τοῦ Κυρίου τοῦ θερισμοῦ, ὅπως ἐκβάλῃ ἐργάτας
pray then the Lord of the harvest, that He may send workmen
εἰς τὸν θερισμὸν αὐτοῦ.
into the harvest of Him.

CHAPTER 10

1 And having called His twelve disciples, He gave them authority over unclean spirits, so as to throw them out, and to heal every disease and every weakness of body.

2 And the names of the twelve apostles are these: First, Simon who is called Peter, and his brother Andrew; James the *son* of Zebedee, and his brother John; 3 Philip, and Bartholomew; Thomas, and Matthew the tax-collector; James the *son* of Alpheus, and Lebbeus, whose last name *was* Thaddeus; 4 Simon the Canaanite, and Judas Iscariot, who also betrayed Him.

5 Jesus sent these twelve out, having charged them, saying: Do not go into the way of *the* nations, and do not go into a city of *the* Samaritans; 6 but rather go to the lost sheep of *the* house of Israel. 7 And going on, proclaim, saying, The kingdom of Heaven has drawn near. 8 Heal sick ones, cleanse lepers, raise dead ones, cast out demons. You have freely received, freely give. 9 Do not provide gold, nor silver, nor copper in your belt; 10 nor provision-bag for *the* road, nor two tunics, nor sandals, nor a staff. For the worker is worthy of his food.

11 And into whatever city or village you enter, ask who in it is worthy; and remain there until you go out. 12 But entering into the house, greet it; 13 and if the house truly is worthy, let your peace come upon it. But if it is not worthy, let your peace return to you. 14 And whoever will not receive you, nor will hear your words, having gone out of that house or city, shake off the dust from your feet. 15 Truly I say to you, It will be more bearable to the land of Sodom and Gomorrah in

CHAPTER 10

1 καὶ προσκαλεσάμενος τοὺς δώδεκα μαθητὰς αὐτοῦ, ἔδωκεν
And having called near the twelve disciples of Him, He gave
αὐτοῖς ἐξουσίαν πνευμάτων ἀκαθάρτων, ὥστε ἐκβάλλειν
to them authority over spirits unclean the so as to cast out
αὐτά, καὶ θεραπεύειν πᾶσαν νόσον καὶ πᾶσαν μαλακίαν.
them, and to heal every disease and every weakness.
2 Τῶν δὲ δώδεκα ἀποστόλων τὰ ὀνόματά ἐστι ταῦτα·
the And twelve apostles the names are these:
πρῶτος Σίμων ὁ λεγόμενος Πέτρος, καὶ Ἀνδρέας ὁ ἀδελφὸς
first Simon who is called Peter, and Andrew the brother
αὐτοῦ· Ἰάκωβος ὁ τοῦ Ζεβεδαίου, καὶ Ἰωάννης ὁ ἀδελφὸς
of him; James the (son of) Zebedee, and John the brother
3 αὐτοῦ· Φίλιππος, καὶ Βαρθολομαῖος· Θωμᾶς, καὶ Ματθαῖος
of him; Philip, and Bartholomew, Thomas, and Matthew
ὁ τελώνης· Ἰάκωβος ὁ τοῦ Ἀλφαίου, καὶ Λεββαῖος ὁ
the tax-collector; James the (son) of Alpheus, and Lebbeus who.
4 ἐπικληθεὶς Θαδδαῖος· Σίμων ὁ Κανανίτης, καὶ Ἰούδας
was surnamed Thaddeus; Simon the Canaanite, and Judas
5 Ἰσκαριώτης ὁ καὶ παραδοὺς αὐτόν. τούτους τοὺς δώδεκα
Iscariot who also betrayed Him. These — twelve
ἀπέστειλεν ὁ Ἰησοῦς, παραγγείλας αὐτοῖς, λέγων,
sent out — Jesus, having charged them, saying,
Εἰς ὁδὸν ἐθνῶν μὴ ἀπέλθητε, καὶ εἰς πόλιν Σαμαρειτῶν
Into the way of nations do not go, and into a city of (the) Samaritans
6 μὴ εἰσέλθητε· πορεύεσθε δὲ μᾶλλον πρὸς τὰ πρόβατα τὰ
not do enter, go but rather to the sheep, the
7 ἀπολωλότα οἴκου Ἰσραήλ. πορευόμενοι δὲ κηρύσσετε, λέγον-
lost of (the) house of Israel. going on. And proclaim, saying,
8 τες ὅτι Ἤγγικεν ἡ βασιλεία τῶν οὐρανῶν. ἀσθενοῦντας
— Has drawn near the kingdom of the heavens. Sick ones
θεραπεύετε, λεπροὺς καθαρίζετε, νεκροὺς ἐγείρετε, δαιμόνια
heal, lepers cleanse, dead ones raise, demons
9 ἐκβάλλετε. δωρεὰν ἐλάβετε, δωρεὰν δότε. μὴ κτήσησθε
cast out. Freely you received, freely give. Not provide
χρυσόν, μηδὲ ἄργυρον, μηδὲ χαλκὸν εἰς τὰς ζώνας ὑμῶν,
gold, nor silver, nor copper in the belts of you,
10 μὴ πήραν εἰς ὁδόν, μηδὲ δύο χιτῶνας, μηδὲ ὑποδήματα,
nor a bag for (the) way, nor two tunics, nor sandals,
μηδὲ ῥάβδους· ἄξιος γὰρ ὁ ἐργάτης τῆς τροφῆς αὐτοῦ ἐστιν.
nor staves, worthy for the worker of the food of him is.
11 εἰς ἣν δ' ἂν πόλιν ἢ κώμην εἰσέλθητε, ἐξετάσατε τίς ἐν αὐτῇ
into what And ever city village you enter, ask who in it
12 ἄξιός ἐστι· κἀκεῖ μείνατε, ἕως ἂν ἐξέλθητε. εἰσερχόμενοι δὲ
worthy is, and there remain until you go out. entering But
13 εἰς τὴν οἰκίαν, ἀσπάσασθε αὐτήν. καὶ ἐὰν μὲν ᾖ ἡ οἰκία ἀξία,
into the house, greet it; and if indeed be the house worthy,
ἐλθέτω ἡ εἰρήνη ὑμῶν ἐπ' αὐτήν· ἐὰν δὲ μὴ ᾖ ἀξία, ἡ εἰρήνη
let come the peace of you on it; if But not it is worthy, the peace
14 ὑμῶν πρὸς ὑμᾶς ἐπιστραφήτω. καὶ ὃς ἐὰν μὴ δέξηται ὑμᾶς
of you to you let return. And whoever not will receive you
μηδὲ ἀκούσῃ τοὺς λόγους ὑμῶν, ἐξερχόμενοι τῆς οἰκίας ἢ τῆς
nor will hear the words of you, going out (of) the house or —
πόλεως ἐκείνης, ἐκτινάξατε τὸν κονιορτὸν τῶν ποδῶν ὑμῶν.
city that shake off the dust of the feet of you.
15 ἀμὴν λέγω ὑμῖν, ἀνεκτότερον ἔσται γῇ Σοδόμων καὶ Γομόρ-
Truly I say to you, More bearable it will be to the land of Sodom and Gomor

Judgment Day than for that city.
16 Behold, I send you out as sheep in *the* midst of wolves. Therefore, be wise as serpents, and harmless as doves. 17 But beware of men. For they will betray you to sanhedrins, and they will flog you in their synagogues. 18 And also you will be brought before governors and kings for My sake, for a testimony to them and to the nations. 19 But when they deliver you up, do not be anxious how or what you should say, for it is given to you in that hour what you should say. 20 For you are not the *ones* speaking, but the Spirit of your Father who speaks in you. 21 But brother will betray brother to death, and *the* father *his* child. And children will rise up against parents and will put them to death. 22 And you will be hated by all on account of My name; but the *one* enduring to *the* end shall be saved. 23 But when they persecute you in this city, flee to another. For truly I say to you, In no way will you have finished the cities of Israel until the Son of man comes. 24 A disciples is not above the teacher, nor a slave above his lord. 25 *It is* enough for the disciple *to* become as his teacher, and the slave as his lord. If they call the Master of the house Beelzebub, how much more those of His household?
26 Therefore, you should not fear them, for nothing is covered which will not be uncovered, and hidden, which will not be made known. 27 What I say to you in the darkness, speak in the light. And what you hear in the ear, proclaim on the housetops. 28 And you should not fear the *ones* killing the body, but not being able to kill the soul. But rather fear Him being able to destroy both soul and body in Hell.
29 Are not two sparrows

ρων ἐν ἡμέρᾳ κρίσεως, ἢ τῇ πόλει ἐκείνῃ.
rah in (the) day of judgment than city that.
16 Ἰδού, ἐγὼ ἀποστέλλω ὑμᾶς ὡς πρόβατα ἐν μέσῳ λύκων·
Behold, I send out you as sheep in (the) midst of wolves;
γίνεσθε οὖν φρόνιμοι ὡς οἱ ὄφεις, καὶ ἀκέραιοι ὡς αἱ περιστε-
you be then wise as – serpents and harmless as – doves.
17 ραί. προσέχετε δὲ ἀπὸ τῶν ἀνθρώπων· παραδώσουσι γὰρ
beware And from – men; they will betray For
ὑμᾶς εἰς συνέδρια, καὶ ἐν ταῖς συναγωγαῖς αὐτῶν μαστιγώ-
you to sanhedrins and in the synagogues of them they will
18 σουσιν ὑμᾶς· καὶ ἐπὶ ἡγεμόνας δὲ καὶ βασιλεῖς ἀχθήσεσθε
scourge you; and before governors also and kings you will be brought
19 ἕνεκεν ἐμοῦ, εἰς μαρτύριον αὐτοῖς καὶ τοῖς ἔθνεσιν. ὅταν δὲ
for My sake, for a testimony to them and to the nations. when But
παραδιδῶσιν ὑμᾶς, μὴ μεριμνήσητε πῶς ἢ τί λαλήσητε·
they deliver up you, not be anxious how or what you may say;
20 δοθήσεται γὰρ ὑμῖν ἐν ἐκείνῃ τῇ ὥρᾳ τί λαλήσετε· οὐ γὰρ
it is given for to you in that – hour what you may say; not for
ὑμεῖς ἐστὲ οἱ λαλοῦντες, ἀλλὰ τὸ Πνεῦμα τοῦ πατρος υμων
you are the (ones) speaking, but the Spirit of the Father of you
21 τὸ λαλοῦν ἐν ὑμῖν. παραδώσει δὲ ἀδελφὸς ἀδελφὸν εἰς
which speaks in you. will deliver up But brother brother to
θάνατον, καὶ πατὴρ τέκνον· καὶ ἐπαναστήσονται τέκνα ἐπὶ
death, and Father (the) child; and will rise up children against
22 γονεῖς, καὶ θανατώσουσιν αὐτούς. καὶ ἔσεσθε μισούμενοι ὑπὸ
parents, and put to death them. And you will be hated by
πάντων διὰ τὸ ὄνομά μου· ὁ δὲ ὑπομείνας εἰς τέλος, οὗτος
all because of the name of Me. he But enduring to (the) end, this (one)
23 σωθήσεται. ὅταν δὲ διώκωσιν ὑμᾶς εν τῇ πόλει ταύτῃ,
shall be saved. when But they persecute you in city this,
φεύγετε εἰς τὴν ἄλλην· ἀμὴν γὰρ λέγω ὑμῖν, οὐ μὴ τελέσητε
flee to another; truly for I say to you, in no way will you finish
τὰς πόλεις τοῦ Ἰσραήλ, ἕως ἂν ἔλθῃ ὁ υἱὸς τοῦ ἀνθρώπου.
the cities of Israel, until may come the Son of man.
24 Οὐκ ἔστι μαθητὴς ὑπὲρ τὸν διδάσκαλον, οὐδὲ δοῦλος
Not is a disciple above the teacher, nor a slave
25 ὑπὲρ τὸν κύριον αὐτοῦ. ἀρκετὸν τῷ μαθητῇ ἵνα γένηται ὡς
above the Lord of him. (It is) enough for the disciple that he become as
ὁ διδάσκαλος αὐτοῦ, καὶ ὁ δοῦλος ὡς ὁ κύριος αὐτοῦ. εἰ τὸν
the teacher of him, and the slave as the the lord of him. If the
οἰκοδεσπότην Βεελζεβοὺβ ἐκάλεσαν, πόσῳ μᾶλλον τοὺς
master of the house Beelzebub they called, how much more those
26 οἰκιακοὺς αὐτοῦ ; μὴ οὖν φοβηθῆτε αὐτούς· οὐδὲν γάρ ἐστι
of his household? Not, then, you should fear them, nothing for is
κεκαλυμμένον ὃ οὐκ ἀποκαλυφθήσεται· καὶ κρυπτὸν ὃ οὐ
covered which will not be uncovered, and hidden which not
27 γνωσθήσεται. ὃ λέγω ὑμῖν ἐν τῇ σκοτίᾳ, εἴπατε ἐν τῷ φωτί·
will be made known. What I say to you in the dark, you say in the light;
28 καὶ ὃ εἰς τὸ οὖς ἀκούετε, κηρύξατε ἐπὶ τῶν δωμάτων. καὶ μὴ
and what in the ear you hear, proclaim on the housetops. And not
φοβηθῆτε ἀπὸ τῶν ἀποκτεινόντων τὸ σῶμα, τὴν δὲ ψυχὴν
you should fear – the (ones) killing the body, the but soul
μὴ δυναμένων ἀποκτεῖναι· φοβήθητε δὲ μᾶλλον τὸν δυνά-
not being able to kill; fear but rather the (one)
29 μενον καὶ ψυχὴν καὶ σῶμα ἀπολέσαι ἐν γεέννῃ. οὐχὶ δύο
being able both the soul and the body to destroy in Gehenna. Are not two

sold for an assarion? Yet not one of them shall fall to the ground without your Father. [30]But even the hairs of your head are all numbered. [31]For this reason you should not fear, you are better than many sparrows. [32]Therefore, everyone, whoever shall confess Me before men, I will also confess him before My Father in Heaven. [33]But whoever shall deny Me before men, I also will deny him before My Father in Heaven.

[34]Do not think that I came to bring peace on earth. I did not come to bring peace, but a sword. [35]I came to set a man against his father, and a daughter against her mother, and a daughter-in-law against her mother-in-law. [36]And a man's enemies *shall be* those of his *own* house. [37]He that loves father or mother above Me is not worthy of Me. And he that loves son or daughter above Me is not worthy of Me. [38]And he that does not take up his cross and follow after Me is not worthy of Me. [39]He that has found his life shall lose it. And he that has lost his life on account of Me shall find it. [40]He that receives you receives Me; and he receiving Me receives Him who sent Me. [41]He receiving a prophet in *the* name of a prophet will receive a prophet's reward; and he receiving a just *one* in the name of a just *one* will receive a just *one's* reward. [42]And whoever gives drink to one of these little ones, only a cup of cold *water,* in the name of a disciple, truly I say to you, In no way will he lose his reward.

CHAPTER 11

[1]And it happened, when Jesus had finished commanding His twelve disciples, He left there to teach

στρουθία ἀσσαρίου πωλεῖται ; καὶ ἓν ἐξ αὐτῶν οὐ πεσεῖται
sparrows for an assarion sold? And one of them not shall fall

30 ἐπὶ τὴν γῆν ἄνευ τοῦ πατρὸς ὑμῶν· ὑμῶν δὲ καὶ αἱ τρίχες τῆς
on the earth without the Father of you. of you But even the hairs of the

31 κεφαλῆς πᾶσαι ἠριθμημέναι εἰσί. μὴ οὖν φοβηθῆτε· πολλῶν
head all numbered are. not Then fear; many

32 στρουθίων διαφέρετε ὑμεῖς. πᾶς οὖν ὅστις ὁμολογήσει ἐν
sparrows excel you. Everyone then who shall confess —

ἐμοὶ ἔμπροσθεν τῶν ἀνθρώπων, ὁμολογήσω κἀγὼ ἐν αὐτῷ
Me before — men, will confess I also — him

33 ἔμπροσθεν τοῦ πατρός μου τοῦ ἐν οὐρανοῖς. ὅστις δ᾽ ἂν
before the Father of Me — in Heaven whoever and —

ἀρνήσηταί με ἔμπροσθεν τῶν ἀνθρώπων, ἀρνήσομαι αὐτὸν
denies Me before — men, will deny him

κἀγὼ ἔμπροσθεν τοῦ πατρός μου τοῦ ἐν οὐρανοῖς.
I also before the Father of Me who (is) in Heaven.

34 Μὴ νομίσητε ὅτι ἦλθον βαλεῖν εἰρήνην ἐπὶ τὴν γῆν· οὐκ
Not think that I came to cast peace on the earth; not

35 ἦλθον βαλεῖν εἰρήνην, ἀλλὰ μάχαιραν. ἦλθον γὰρ διχάσαι
I came to cast peace, but a sword. I came For to dissever

ἄνθρωπον κατὰ τοῦ πατρὸς αὐτοῦ, καὶ θυγατέρα κατὰ τῆς
a man with the father of him, and a daughter with the

36 μητρὸς αὐτῆς, καὶ νύμφην κατα τῆς πενθερᾶς αὐτῆς· καὶ
mother of her, and a bride with the mother-in-law of her, and

37 ἐχθροὶ τοῦ ἀνθρώπου οἱ οἰκιακοὶ αὐτοῦ. ὁ φιλῶν πατέρα ἢ
enemies of the man those of the house of him He loving father or

μητέρα ὑπὲρ ἐμέ, οὐκ ἔστι μου ἄξιος· καὶ ὁ φιλῶν υἱὸν ἢ
mother above Me not is of Me worthy; and he loving son or

38 θυγατέρα ὑπὲρ ἐμέ, οὐκ ἔστι μου ἄξιος· καὶ ὃς οὐ λαμβάνει
daughter above Me not is of Me worthy. And who not does take

τὸν σταυρὸν αὐτοῦ καὶ ἀκολουθεῖ ὀπίσω μου, οὐκ ἔστι μου
the cross of him and follow after Me not is of Me

39 ἄξιος. ὁ εὑρὼν τὴν ψυχὴν αὐτοῦ ἀπολέσει αὐτήν· καὶ ὁ
worthy. He finding the soul of him will lose it, and he

ἀπολέσας τὴν ψυχὴν αὐτοῦ ἕνεκεν ἐμοῦ εὑρήσει αὐτήν.
losing the soul of him for sake My will find it.

40 Ὁ δεχόμενος ὑμᾶς ἐμὲ δέχεται· καὶ ὁ ἐμὲ δεχόμενος δέχεται
He receiving you Me receives, and he Me receiving receives

41 τὸν ἀποστείλαντά με. ὁ δεχόμενος προφήτην εἰς ὄνομα
the (one) sending Me. He receiving a prophet in (the) name

προφήτου μισθὸν προφήτου λήψεται· καὶ ὁ δεχόμενος
of a prophet (the) reward of a prophet will receive; and he receiving

42 δίκαιον εἰς ὄνομα δικαίου μισθὸν δικαίου λήψεται. καὶ ὃς ἐὰν
(one) just in the name of a just (one), reward a just will receive. And whoever

ποτίσῃ ἕνα τῶν μικρῶν τούτων ποτήριον ψυχροῦ μόνον
gives drink to one little ones of these a cup of cold (water) only

εἰς ὄνομα μαθητοῦ, ἀμὴν λέγω ὑμῖν, οὐ μὴ ἀπολέσῃ τὸν
in (the) name of a disciple, truly I say to you, in no way will he lose the

μισθὸν αὐτοῦ.
reward of him.

CHAPTER 11

1 Καὶ ἐγένετο ὅτε ἐτέλεσεν ὁ Ἰησοῦς διατάσσων τοῖς
And it was, when finished — Jesus giving command to the

δώδεκα μαθηταῖς αὐτοῦ, μετέβη ἐκεῖθεν τοῦ διδάσκειν καὶ
disciples of Him, He moved from there — to teach and

and to proclaim in their cities.

[2]But hearing in the prison of the works of Christ, sending two of his disciples, [3]John said to Him, Are You the One coming, or are we to look for another? [4]And answering, Jesus said to them, Having returned, relate to John what you hear and see: [5]The blind receive sight, and the lame walk; lepers are cleansed, and the deaf hear; the dead are raised, and the poor are evangelized. [6]And blessed is he, whoever shall not be offended in Me.

[7]But as these were going, Jesus began to say to the crowds about John, What did you go out into the wilderness to see? A reed shaken with the wind? [8]But what did you go out to see? A man clothed in soft clothing? Behold, those who wear soft things are in the houses of kings. [9]But what did you go out to see? A prophet? yes, I say to you, and *one* more excellent than a prophet. [10]For this is *the one* about whom it has been written, "Behold, I send My messenger before Your face, who shall prepare Your way before You." [11]Truly I say to you, Not has arisen among *those* born of a woman a greater than John the Baptist. But the least in the kingdom of Heaven is greater than he is. [12]But from the days of John the Baptist until now, the kingdom of Heaven suffers violence, and the violent seize it. [13]For all the Prophets and the Law prophesied until John. [14]And if you are willing to receive, he is Elijah, the *one* about to come. [15]The *one* having ears to hear, let him hear.

[16]But to what shall I compare this generation? It is like little children sitting in *the* markets, and calling to their mates, [17]and saying, We piped to you, and you did not dance; we mourned to

κηρύσσειν ἐν ταῖς πόλεσιν αὐτῶν.
to proclaim in the cities of them.
2 Ὁ δὲ Ἰωάννης ἀκούσας ἐν τῷ δεσμωτηρίῳ τὰ ἔργα τοῦ
— But John having heard in the prison the works —
3 Χριστοῦ, πέμψας δύο τῶν μαθητῶν αὐτοῦ, εἶπεν αὐτῷ, Σὺ
of Christ, sending two of the disciples of him, said to Him, You
4 εἶ ὁ ἐρχόμενος, ἢ ἕτερον προσδοκῶμεν; καὶ ἀποκριθεὶς ὁ
are the coming (One), or another may we expect? And answering, —
Ἰησοῦς εἶπεν αὐτοῖς, Πορευθέντες ἀπαγγείλατε Ἰωάννῃ ἃ
Jesus said to them, Going relate to John what
5 ἀκούετε καὶ βλέπετε· τυφλοὶ ἀναβλέπουσι, καὶ χωλοὶ περι-
you hear and see: blind ones receive sight, and lame ones walk
πατοῦσι, λεπροὶ καθαρίζονται, καὶ κωφοὶ ἀκούουσι, νεκροὶ
about; lepers are cleansed, and deaf ones hear; dead ones
6 ἐγείρονται, καὶ πτωχοὶ εὐαγγελίζονται· καὶ μακάριός ἐστιν,
are raised, and poor ones are evangelized; and blessed he is,
7 ὃς ἐὰν μὴ σκανδαλισθῇ ἐν ἐμοί. τούτων δὲ πορευομένων,
whoever not shall be offended in Me. (as) these But were going,
ἤρξατο ὁ Ἰησοῦς λέγειν τοῖς ὄχλοις περὶ Ἰωάννου, Τί
began — Jesus to say to the crowds concerning John, What
ἐξήλθετε εἰς τὴν ἔρημον θεάσασθαι; κάλαμον ὑπὸ ἀνέμου
went you out to the wilderness to view? A reed by wind
8 σαλευόμενον; ἀλλὰ τί ἐξήλθετε ἰδεῖν; ἄνθρωπον ἐν μαλακοῖς
being shaken? But what went ye out to see? A man in soft
ἱματίοις ἠμφιεσμένον; ἰδού, οἱ τὰ μαλακὰ φοροῦντες ἐν τοῖς
garments clothed? Behold, those the soft wearing (are) in the
9 οἴκοις τῶν βασιλέων εἰσίν. ἀλλὰ τί ἐξήλθετε ἰδεῖν; προφήτην;
houses — of kings are. But what went you out to see? A prophet?
10 ναί, λέγω ὑμῖν, καὶ περισσότερον προφήτου. οὗτος γάρ
Yea, I say to you, and (one) more excellent than a prophet. this For
ἐστι περὶ οὗ γέγραπται, Ἰδού, ἐγὼ ἀποστέλλω τὸν
is (he) about whom it has been written, Behold, I send forth the
ἄγγελόν μου πρὸ προσώπου σου, ὃς κατασκευάσει τὴν
messenger of Me before your face, who shall prepare the
11 ὁδόν σου ἔμπροσθέν σου. ἀμὴν λέγω ὑμῖν, οὐκ ἐγήγερται ἐν
way of you before you. Truly I say to you not has arisen in
γεννητοῖς γυναικῶν μείζων Ἰωάννου τοῦ βαπτιστοῦ· ὁ δὲ
(those) born of a woman a greater (than) John the Baptist; the but
μικρότερος ἐν τῇ βασιλείᾳ τῶν οὐρανῶν μείζων αὐτοῦ ἐστιν.
lesser in the kingdom of the heavens greater (than) he is.
12 ἀπὸ δὲ τῶν ἡμερῶν Ἰωάννου τοῦ βαπτιστοῦ ἕως ἄρτι ἡ
from And the days of John the Baptist until now the
βασιλεία τῶν οὐρανῶν βιάζεται, καὶ βιασταὶ ἁρπάζουσιν
kingdom of the heavens suffers violence, and the violent seize
13 αὐτήν. πάντες γὰρ οἱ προφῆται καὶ ὁ νόμος ἕως Ἰωάννου
it. all For the prophets and the law until John
14 προεφήτευσαν· καὶ εἰ θέλετε δέξασθαι, αὐτός ἐστιν Ἠλίας ὁ
prophesied; and if you are willing to receive, he is Elijah, he
15 μέλλων ἔρχεσθαι. ὁ ἔχων ὦτα ἀκούειν ἀκουέτω. τίνι δὲ
16 **about to come. He having ears to hear, let him hear. to what But**
ὁμοιώσω τὴν γενεὰν ταύτην; ὁμοία ἐστὶ παιδαρίοις ἐν
shall I liken — generation this? like It is to little children in
ἀγοραῖς καθημένοις, καὶ προσφωνοῦσι τοῖς ἑταίροις αὐτῶν,
markets sitting, and calling to the mates of them,
17 καὶ λέγουσιν, Ηὐλήσαμεν ὑμῖν, καὶ οὐκ ὠρχήσασθε· ἐθρηνή-
and saying, We piped to you and not you did dance; we

you, and you did not wail. [18]For John came neither eating nor drinking, and they say, Behold, he has a demon. [19]The Son of man came eating and drinking, and they say, Behold, a gluttonous man and a winedrinker, and a friend of tax-collectors, and of sinners. And wisdom was justified by her children.

[20]Then He began to reproach the cities in which had occurred His most powerful *acts*, for they had not repented. [21]Woe to you, Chorazin! Woe to you, Bethsaida! For if the mighty works which have taken place in you had happened in Tyre and Sidon, they would have repented long ago in sackcloth and ashes. [22]But I say to you, it shall be more bearable for Tyre and Sidon in Judgment Day than for you. [23]And you, Capernaum, who have been exalted to the heaven, *you* will be thrown down to Hades. For if the powerful *acts* happening in you had taken place in Sodom, it still would *be* until today. [24]But I say to you, It will be more bearable for the land of Sodom in Judgment day than for you.

[25]Answering at that time, Jesus said, I praise You, Father, Lord of Heaven and of earth, because you hid these things from *the* sophisticated and cunning, and revealed them to babes. [26]Yes, Father, for so it was pleasing before You. [27]All things were yielded up to Me by My Father, and no one knows the Son except the Father, nor does anyone know the Father, except the Son, and to whomever the Son wills to reveal *Him*.

[28]Come to Me, all those laboring and being burdened, and I will give you rest. [29]Take My yoke upon you, and learn from Me, because I am meek and lowly in heart, and you will find rest to your souls. [30]For My yoke is easy, and My burden is light.

18 σαμεν ὑμῖν, καὶ οὐκ ἐκόψασθε. ἦλθε γὰρ Ἰωάννης μήτε ἐσθίων
mourned to you and not you did wail. came For John neither eating

19 μήτε πίνων, καὶ λέγουσι, Δαιμόνιον ἔχει. ἦλθεν ὁ υἱὸς τοῦ
nor drinking, and they say, A demon he has. Came the Son –

ἀνθρώπου ἐσθίων καὶ πίνων, καὶ λέγουσιν, Ἰδού, ἄνθρωπος
of man eating and drinking, and they say, Behold, a man

φάγος καὶ οἰνοπότης, τελωνῶν φίλος καὶ ἁμαρτωλῶν. καὶ
gluttonous, and a winedrinker, of tax-collectors a friend and of sinners. And

ἐδικαιώθη ἡ σοφία ἀπὸ τῶν τέκνων αὐτῆς.
was justified – wisdom by the children of her.

20 Τότε ἤρξατο ὀνειδίζειν τὰς πόλεις ἐν αἷς ἐγένοντο αἱ
Then He began to reproach the cities in which had occurred the

21 πλεῖσται δυνάμεις αὐτοῦ, ὅτι οὐ μετενόησαν. Οὐαί σοι,
most powerful (acts) of His; because not they repented. Woe to you,

Χοραζίν, οὐαί σοι, Βηθσαϊδά, ὅτι εἰ ἐν Τύρῳ καὶ Σιδῶνι
Chorazin; woe to you, Bethsaida! Because if in Tyre and Sidon

ἐγένοντο αἱ δυνάμεις αἱ γενόμεναι ἐν ὑμῖν, πάλαι ἂν ἐν σάκκῳ
occurred the powerful (acts) happening in you, long ago – in sackcloth

22 καὶ σποδῷ μετενόησαν. πλὴν λέγω ὑμῖν, Τύρῳ καὶ Σιδῶνι
and ashes they had repented. However, I say to you, For Tyre and for Sidon

23 ἀνεκτότερον ἔσται ἐν ἡμέρᾳ κρίσεως, ἢ ὑμῖν. καὶ σύ, Καπερ-
more tolerable it will be in (the) day of judgment than for you; and you, Ca-

ναούμ, ἡ ἕως τοῦ οὐρανοῦ ὑψωθεῖσα, ἕως ᾅδου καταβιβα-
pernaum, who to the heaven have been exalted, to Hades will be cast

σθήσῃ· ὅτι εἰ ἐν Σοδόμοις ἐγένοντο αἱ δυνάμεις αἱ γενόμεναι ἐν
down, because if in Sodom occurred the powerful (acts) happening in

24 σοί, ἔμειναν ἂν μέχρι τῆς σήμερον. πλὴν λέγω ὑμῖν, ὅτι γῇ
you, it would last until today. However, I tell you that for land

Σοδόμων ἀνεκτότερον ἔσται ἐν ἡμέρᾳ κρίσεως, ἢ σοί.
of Sodom more tolerable it will be in (the) day of judgment than for you.

25 Ἐν ἐκείνῳ τῷ καιρῷ ἀποκριθεὶς ὁ Ἰησοῦς εἶπεν, Ἐξομολο-
At that – time answering – Jesus said, I give praise

γοῦμαί σοι, πάτερ, Κύριε τοῦ οὐρανοῦ καὶ τῆς γῆς, ὅτι
to You, Father, Lord of the heaven and of the earth, for

ἀπέκρυψας ταῦτα ἀπὸ σοφῶν καὶ συνετῶν, καὶ ἀπεκάλυψας
You hid these things from sophisticated and cunning, and revealed

26 αὐτὰ νηπίοις. ναί ὁ πατήρ, ὅτι οὕτως ἐγένετο εὐδοκία
them to babes. Yea, – Father, because thus it was well-pleasing

27 ἔμπροσθέν σου. πάντα μοι παρεδόθη ὑπὸ τοῦ πατρός μου·
before You. All things to Me were yielded by the Father of Me;

καὶ οὐδεὶς ἐπιγινώσκει τὸν υἱόν, εἰ μὴ ὁ πατήρ· οὐδὲ τὸν
and no one knows the Son except the Father, nor the

πατέρα τις ἐπιγινώσκει, εἰ μὴ ὁ υἱός, καὶ ᾧ ἐὰν βούληται ὁ
Father anyone does know, except the Son, and to whomever wills the

28 υἱὸς ἀποκαλύψαι. δεῦτε πρός με πάντες οἱ κοπιῶντες καὶ
Son to reveal. Come to Me, all the (ones) laboring and

29 πεφορτισμένοι, κἀγὼ ἀναπαύσω ὑμᾶς. ἄρατε τὸν ζυγόν
being burdened, and I will give rest you. Take the yoke

μου ἐφ' ὑμᾶς καὶ μάθετε ἀπ' ἐμοῦ, ὅτι πρᾷός εἰμι καὶ ταπεινὸς
of Me on you and learn from Me, because meek I am and lowly

30 τῇ καρδίᾳ· καὶ εὑρήσετε ἀνάπαυσιν ταῖς ψυχαῖς ὑμῶν. ὁ
– in heart, and you will find rest to the souls of you; the

γὰρ ζυγός μου χρηστός, καὶ τὸ φορτίον μου ἐλαφρόν ἐστιν.
for yoke of Me pleasant and the burden of me light is.

CHAPTER 12

CHAPTER 12

1 At that time on the Sabbath, Jesus went through the grain fields. And His disciples were hungry, and began to pluck ears and to eat. 2 But seeing, the Pharisees said to Him, Behold, your disciples are doing what it is not lawful to do on the Sabbath. 3 But He said to them, Have you not read what David did, when he and those with him hungered? 4 How he entered into the house of God, and he ate the Showbread, which it was not lawful for him to eat, nor for those with him, but for the priests only? 5 Or have you not read in the Law that on the Sabbaths the priests in the Temple profane the Sabbath, and are not guilty? 6 But I say to you, One greater than the Temple is here. 7 But if you had known what *this* is, "I desire mercy, and not sacrifice," you would not have condemned those who are not guilty. 8 For the Son of man is also Lord of the Sabbath.

9 And moving from there, He came into their synagogue. 10 And, behold, a man having *a* withered hand was there. And they asked Him, saying, Is it lawful to heal on the sabbaths?—that they might accuse Him. 11 But He said to them, What man of you will be, who will have one sheep, and if this one fall into a pit on the sabbaths, will he not lay hold of it and raise *it* up? 12 How much more, then, does a man excel a sheep! So that it is lawful to do well on the sabbaths. 13 Then He said to the man, Stretch out your hand! And he stretched out. And it was restored sound as the other.

14 But they having left, the Pharisees took up a council against Him, how they might destroy Him. 15 But knowing, Jesus withdrew from there. And many crowds followed Him; and He healed them all, 16 and warned them that they not make Him manifest. 17 So that might be fulfilled that

1 Ἐν ἐκείνῳ τῷ καιρῷ ἐπορεύθη ὁ Ἰησοῦς τοῖς σάββασι διὰ
At that — time went — Jesus on the Sabbath through
τῶν σπορίμων· οἱ δὲ μαθηταὶ αὐτοῦ ἐπείνασαν, καὶ ἤρξαντο
the grainfields; the and disciples of Him hungered, and began
2 τίλλειν στάχυας καὶ ἐσθίειν. οἱ δὲ Φαρισαῖοι ἰδόντες εἶπον
to pluck ears and to eat. the But Pharisees seeing said
αὐτῷ, Ἰδού, οἱ μαθηταί σου ποιοῦσιν ὃ οὐκ ἔξεστι ποιεῖν
to Him, Behold, the disciples of You are doing what not it is lawful to do
3 ἐν σαββάτῳ. ὁ δὲ εἶπεν αὐτοῖς, Οὐκ ἀνέγνωτε τί ἐποίησε
on a Sabbath. He And said to them, Not did you read what did
4 Δαβίδ, ὅτε ἐπείνασεν αὐτὸς καὶ οἱ μετ' αὐτοῦ· πῶς εἰσῆλθεν
David, when he hungered Himself and those with him? How he went in
εἰς τὸν οἶκον τοῦ Θεοῦ, καὶ τοὺς ἄρτους τῆς προθέσεως
into the house — of God, and the loaves of the presentation
ἔφαγεν, οὓς οὐκ ἐξὸν ἦν αὐτῷ φαγεῖν, οὐδὲ τοῖς μετ' αὐτοῦ,
he ate, which not lawful it was for him to eat, nor for those with him,
5 εἰ μὴ τοῖς ἱερεῦσι μόνοις; ἢ οὐκ ἀνέγνωτε ἐν τῷ νόμῳ, ὅτι
except for the priests only? Or not did you read in the law that
τοῖς σάββασιν οἱ ἱερεῖς ἐν τῷ ἱερῷ τὸ σάββατον βεβηλοῦσι,
on the Sabbaths the priests in the Temple the Sabbath profane,
6 καὶ ἀναίτιοί εἰσι; λέγω δὲ ὑμῖν ὅτι τοῦ ἱεροῦ μείζων ἐστὶν
and guiltless are? I say But to you that the Temple a greater than is
7 ὧδε. εἰ δὲ ἐγνώκειτε τί ἐστιν, Ἔλεον θέλω καὶ οὐ θυσίαν,
here. if But you had known what it is, Mercy I desire, and not sacrifice,
8 οὐκ ἂν κατεδικάσατε τοὺς ἀναιτίους. κύριος γάρ ἐστι καὶ τοῦ
not would you have judged the guiltless. Lord For is also of the
σαββάτου ὁ υἱὸς τοῦ ἀνθρώπου.
Sabbath the Son — of man.
9 Καὶ μεταβὰς ἐκεῖθεν ἦλθεν εἰς τὴν συναγωγὴν αὐτῶν. καὶ
10 **And moving from there He came into the synagogue of them. And**
ἰδού, ἄνθρωπος ἦν τὴν χεῖρα ἔχων ξηράν· καὶ ἐπηρώτησαν
behold, a man was, the hand having withered, and they questioned
αὐτόν, λέγοντες, Εἰ ἔξεστι τοῖς σάββασι θεραπεύειν; ἵνα
Him, saying, If it is lawful on the Sabbaths to heal? That
11 κατηγορήσωσιν αὐτοῦ. ὁ δὲ εἶπεν αὐτοῖς, Τίς ἔσται ἐξ
they might accuse Him. He But said to them, What will be of
ὑμῶν ἄνθρωπος, ὃς ἕξει πρόβατον ἕν, καὶ ἐὰν ἐμπέσῃ τοῦτο
you a man who will have sheep one, and if fall (in) this
τοῖς σάββασιν εἰς βόθυνον, οὐχὶ κρατήσει αὐτὸ καὶ ἐγερεῖ;
on the Sabbaths into a pit, not will he lay hold of it and raise (it)?
12 πόσῳ οὖν διαφέρει ἄνθρωπος προβάτου. ὥστε ἔξεστι τοῖς
How much then surpasses a man a sheep! So that it is lawful on the
13 σάββασι καλῶς ποιεῖν. τότε λέγει τῷ ἀνθρώπῳ, Ἔκτεινον
Sabbaths well to do. Then He says to the man, Stretch out
τὴν χεῖρά σου. καὶ ἐξέτεινε, καὶ ἀποκατεστάθη ὑγιὴς ὡς ἡ
the hand of you, and he stretched and it was restored sound as the
14 ἄλλη. οἱ δὲ Φαρισαῖοι συμβούλιον ἔλαβον κατ' αὐτοῦ
other. the But Pharisees a council took against Him,
15 ἐξελθόντες, ὅπως αὐτὸν ἀπολέσωσιν. ὁ δὲ Ἰησοῦς γνοὺς
they having left, how Him they might destroy. But Jesus knowing
ἀνεχώρησεν ἐκεῖθεν· καὶ ἠκολούθησαν αὐτῷ ὄχλοι πολλοί,
withdrew from there. And followed Him crowds many,
16 καὶ ἐθεράπευσεν αὐτοὺς πάντας, καὶ ἐπετίμησεν αὐτοῖς,
and He healed them all, and warned them
17 ἵνα μὴ φανερὸν αὐτὸν ποιήσωσιν· ὅπως πληρωθῇ τὸ
that not manifest Him they should make; so that may be fulfilled that

spoken through the prophet, saying, [18]"Behold My child whom I chose, My Beloved, in whom My soul has found delight! I will put My Spirit on Him, and He shall declare judgment to the nations. [19]He shall not strive nor cry out, nor shall anyone hear His voice in the streets. [20]A bruised reed He will not break, and smoking flax He will not quench, until He bring forth judgment to victory. [21]And the nations will hope in His name." [22]Then one demon-possessed was brought to Him, blind and dumb. And He healed him, so that the blind and dumb could both speak and see. [23]And all the crowds were amazed, and said, Is this not the son of David? [24]But hearing, the Pharisees said, This one does not cast out demons except by Beelzebub, ruler of the demons. [25]But Jesus knowing their thoughts, He said to them, Every kingdom divided against itself is brought to ruin. And every city or house divided against itself will not stand. [26]And if Satan throws out Satan, he was divided against himself. How then will his kingdom stand? [27]And if I throw out the demons by Beelzebub, by whom do your sons throw them out? Because of this, they shall be your judges. [28]But if I cast out the demons by the Spirit of God, then the kingdom of God has come upon you. [29]Or how is anyone able to enter the house of the strong one and plunder his goods, unless he first tie up the strong one; and then he will plunder his house? [30]He who is not with Me is against Me; and he who does not gather with Me scatters. [31]Because of this, I say to you, Every sin and blasphemy shall be forgiven to men, but the blasphemy concerning the Spirit shall not be forgiven to men. [32]And whoever speaks a word against the Son of

18 ῥηθὲν διὰ Ἡσαΐου τοῦ προφήτου, λέγοντος, Ἰδού, ὁ παῖς
spoken through Isaiah the prophet, saying, Behold, the child
μου ὃν ᾑρέτισα· ὁ ἀγαπητός μου εἰς ὃν εὐδόκησεν ἡ ψυχή
of Me whom I chose, the beloved of Me in whom has delighted the soul
μου θήσω τὸ πνευμά μου ἐπ' αὐτὸν καὶ κρίσιν τοῖς ἔθνεσιν
of Me. I will put the Spirit of Me on Him, and judgment to the nations
19 ἀπαγγελεῖ. οὐκ ἐρίσει, οὐδὲ κραυγάσει· οὐδὲ ἀκούσει τις ἐν
He will declare. Not He will strive, nor cry out, nor will hear any in
20 ταῖς πλατείαις τὴν φωνὴν αὐτοῦ. κάλαμον συντετριμμένον
the streets the voice of Him. A reed bruised
οὐ κατεάξει, καὶ λῖνον τυφόμενον οὐ σβέσει· ἕως ἂν ἐκβάλῃ
not He will break, and flax smoking not He will quench, until He expel
21 εἰς νῖκος τὴν κρίσιν. καὶ ἐν τῷ ὀνόματι αὐτοῦ ἔθνη ἐλπιοῦσι.
to victory the judgment. And in the name of Him nations will hope.
22 Τότε προσηνέχθη αὐτῷ δαιμονιζόμενος, τυφλὸς· καὶ
Then was brought to Him a demon-possessed one blind and
κωφός· καὶ ἐθεράπευσεν αὐτόν, ὥστε τὸν τυφλὸν καὶ κωφὸν
dumb; and He healed him, so that the blind and dumb
23 καὶ λαλεῖν καὶ βλέπειν. καὶ ἐξίσταντο πάντες οἱ ὄχλοι καὶ
both could speak and see. And were amazed all the crowds, and
24 ἔλεγον, Μήτι οὗτός ἐστιν ὁ υἱὸς Δαβίδ; οἱ δὲ Φαρισαῖοι
said, Not this is the son of David? the But Pharisees
ἀκούσαντες εἶπον, Οὗτος οὐκ ἐκβάλλει τὰ δαιμόνια, εἰ μὴ
having heard said, This (one) not casts out the demons except
25 ἐν τῷ Βεελζεβοὺλ ἄρχοντι τῶν δαιμονίων. εἰδὼς δὲ ὁ
by — Beelzebub, ruler of the demons. knowing But
Ἰησοῦς τὰς ἐνθυμήσεις αὐτῶν εἶπεν αὐτοῖς, Πᾶσα βασιλεία
Jesus the thoughts of them, He said to them, Every kingdom
μερισθεῖσα καθ' ἑαυτῆς ἐρημοῦται· καὶ πᾶσα πόλις ἢ οἰκία
divided against itself is brought to ruin, and every city or house
26 μερισθεῖσα καθ' ἑαυτῆς οὐ σταθήσεται. καὶ εἰ ὁ Σατανᾶς τὸν
divided against itself not will stand, and if — Satan —
Σατανᾶν ἐκβάλλει, ἐφ' ἑαυτὸν ἐμερίσθη· πῶς οὖν σταθήσεται
Satan casts out, against himself he was divided. How then will stand
27 ἡ βασιλεία αὐτοῦ; καὶ εἰ ἐγὼ ἐν Βεελζεβοὺλ ἐκβάλλω τὰ
the kingdom of him? And if I by Beelzebub cast out the
δαιμόνια, οἱ υἱοὶ ὑμῶν ἐν τίνι ἐκβάλλουσι; διὰ τοῦτο αὐτοὶ
demons, the sons of you by whom do they cast out? Therefore they
28 ὑμῶν ἔσονται κριταί. εἰ δὲ ἐγὼ ἐν Πνεύματι Θεοῦ ἐκβάλλω
of you shall be judges. if But I by (the) Spirit of God cast out
29 τὰ δαιμόνια, ἄρα ἔφθασεν ἐφ' ὑμᾶς ἡ βασιλεία τοῦ Θεοῦ. ἢ
the demons, then has come upon you the kingdom — of God. Or
πῶς δύναταί τις εἰσελθεῖν εἰς τὴν οἰκίαν τοῦ ἰσχυροῦ καὶ τὰ
how can anyone enter into the house of the strong one and the
σκεύη αὐτοῦ διαρπάσαι, ἐὰν μὴ πρῶτον δήσῃ τὸν ἰσχυρόν;
vessels of him to plunder, if not first he binds the strong one?
30 καὶ τότε τὴν οἰκίαν αὐτοῦ διαρπάσει. ὁ μὴ ὢν μετ' ἐμοῦ,
And then the house of him he will plunder. He not being with Me
31 κατ' ἐμοῦ ἐστι, καὶ ὁ μὴ συνάγων μετ' ἐμοῦ, σκορπίζει. διὰ
against Me is; and he not gathering with Me scatters. Because
τοῦτο λέγω ὑμῖν, Πᾶσα ἁμαρτία καὶ βλασφημία ἀφεθήσεται
of this I say to you, Every sin and blasphemy shall be forgiven
τοῖς ἀνθρώποις· ἡ δὲ τοῦ Πνεύματος βλασφημία οὐκ ἀφεθή-
— to men; the but of the Spirit blasphemy not will be
32 σεται τοῖς ἀνθρώποις. καὶ ὃς ἂν εἴπῃ λόγον κατὰ τοῦ υἱοῦ
forgiven — to men. And whoever speaks a word against the Son

man, it shall be forgiven him. But whoever speaks against the Holy Spirit, it shall not be forgiven him, not in this age, nor in the coming *one*.

33 Either make the tree good, and its fruit good; or make the tree corrupt, and its fruit corrupt; for the tree is known by the fruit.

34 Offspring of vipers! How can you being evil speak good things? For out of the abundance of the heart the mouth speaks. 35 The good man out of the good treasure of the heart brings forth good things. And the evil man out of the evil treasure brings forth evil things. 36 But I say to you, that every idle word that men may speak, they shall give an account of it in Judgment Day. 37 For by your words you will be justified, and by your words you will be condemned.

38 Then some of the scribes and Pharisees answered, saying, Teacher, we desire to see a sign from you. 39 But answering He said to them, An evil and adulterous generation seeks a sign, and a sign shall not be given to it, except the sign of Jonah the prophet. 40 And even as Jonah was in the belly of the huge fish three days and three nights, so shall the Son of man be in the heart of the earth three days and three nights.

41 *The* men of Nineveh will stand up in the Judgment with this generation, and will condemn it. For they repented at the preaching of Jonah; and, behold, a Greater-than-Jonah *is* here. 42 The queen of *the* south will rise up in the Judgment with this generation, and will condemn it. For she came from the ends of the earth to hear the wisdom of Solomon; and, behold, a Greater-than-Solomon *is* here.

43 But when the unclean spirit goes from a man, he

τοῦ ἀνθρώπου, ἀφεθήσεται αὐτῷ· ὃς δ' ἂν εἴπῃ κατὰ τοῦ
— of man, it will be forgiven him; but whoever speaks against the
Πνεύματος τοῦ Ἁγίου, οὐκ ἀφεθήσεται αὐτῷ, οὔτε ἐν τούτῳ
Spirit the Holy, not it shall be forgiven him, neither in this
33 τῷ αἰῶνι οὔτε ἐν τῷ μέλλοντι. ἢ ποιήσατε τὸ δένδρον
— age nor in the coming (one). Either make the tree
καλόν, καὶ τὸν καρπὸν αὐτοῦ καλόν, ἢ ποιήσατε τὸ δένδρον
good and the fruit of it good, or make the tree
σαπρόν, καὶ τὸν καρπὸν αὐτοῦ σαπρόν· ἐκ γὰρ τοῦ καρποῦ
corrupt and the fruit of it corrupt; of for the fruit
34 τὸ δένδρον γινώσκεται. γεννήματα ἐχιδνῶν, πῶς δύνασθε
the tree is known. Offspring of vipers! How can you
ἀγαθὰ λαλεῖν, πονηροὶ ὄντες; ἐκ γὰρ τοῦ περισσεύματος
good things speak, evil being? out of For the abundance
35 τῆς καρδίας τὸ στόμα λαλεῖ. ὁ ἀγαθὸς ἄνθρωπος ἐκ τοῦ
of the heart the mouth speaks. The good man out of the
ἀγαθοῦ θησαυροῦ τῆς καρδίας ἐκβάλλει τὰ ἀγαθά· καὶ ὁ
good treasure of the heart puts forth the good things, and the
πονηρὸς ἄνθρωπος ἐκ τοῦ πονηροῦ θησαυροῦ ἐκβάλλει
evil man out of the evil treasure puts forth
36 πονηρά. λέγω δὲ ὑμῖν, ὅτι πᾶν ῥῆμα ἀργόν, ὃ ἐὰν λαλή-
evil things. I say But to you, that every word idle whatever may speak
σωσιν οἱ ἄνθρωποι, ἀποδώσουσι περὶ αὐτοῦ λόγον ἐν
— men, they will give concerning it account in
37 ἡμέρᾳ κρίσεως. ἐκ γὰρ τῶν λόγων σου δικαιωθήσῃ, καὶ ἐκ
(the) day of judgment, by For the words of you you will be justified, and by
τῶν λόγων σου καταδικασθήσῃ.
the words of you you will be condemned.
38 Τότε ἀπεκρίθησάν τινες τῶν γραμματέων καὶ Φαρισαίων,
Then answered some of the scribes and Pharisees,
39 λέγοντες, Διδάσκαλε, θέλομεν ἀπὸ σοῦ σημεῖον ἰδεῖν. ὁ δὲ
saying, Teacher, we wish from You a sign to see. He But
ἀποκριθεὶς εἶπεν αὐτοῖς, Γενεὰ πονηρὰ καὶ μοιχαλὶς σημεῖον
answering said to them, generation An evil and adulterous a sign
ἐπιζητεῖ· καὶ σημεῖον οὐ δοθήσεται αὐτῇ, εἰ μὴ τὸ σημεῖον
seeks, and a sign not shall be given to it except the sign
40 Ἰωνᾶ τοῦ προφήτου. ὥσπερ γὰρ ἦν Ἰωνᾶς ἐν τῇ κοιλίᾳ
of Jonah the prophet. even as For was Jonah in the belly
τοῦ κήτους τρεῖς ἡμέρας καὶ τρεῖς νύκτας, οὕτως ἔσται ὁ υἱὸς
of the huge fish three days and three nights, so will be the Son
τοῦ ἀνθρώπου ἐν τῇ καρδίᾳ τῆς γῆς τρεῖς ἡμέρας καὶ τρεῖς
— of man in the heart of the earth three days and three
41 νύκτας. ἄνδρες Νινευῖται ἀναστήσονται ἐν τῇ κρίσει μετὰ
nights. Men, Ninevites will stand up in the judgment with
τῆς γενεᾶς ταύτης καὶ κατακρινοῦσιν αὐτήν· ὅτι μετενόησαν
— generation this and will condemn it; because they repented
42 εἰς τὸ κήρυγμα Ἰωνᾶ· καὶ ἰδού, πλεῖον Ἰωνᾶ ὧδε. βασίλισσα
at the preaching of Jonah, and behold, a greater than Jonah (is) here. (The) queen
νότου ἐγερθήσεται ἐν τῇ κρίσει μετὰ τῆς γενεᾶς ταύτης καὶ
of (the) south will be raised in the judgment with — generation this and
κατακρινεῖ αὐτήν· ὅτι ἦλθεν ἐκ τῶν περάτων τῆς γῆς
will condemn it; because she came out of the limits of the earth
ἀκοῦσαι τὴν σοφίαν Σολομῶντος· καὶ ἰδού, πλεῖον Σολο-
to hear the wisdom of Solomon, and, behold, a greater than Solomon
43 μῶντος ὧδε. ὅταν δὲ τὸ ἀκάθαρτον πνεῦμα ἐξέλθῃ ἀπὸ τοῦ
(is) here. when Now the unclean spirit goes out from —

goes through dry places seeking rest, and does not find *it*. [44]Then he says, I will return to my house from which I came out. And coming, he finds *it* empty, swept and decorated. [45]Then he goes and takes with him seven other spirits more evil than himself. And entering, they dwell there. And the last things of that man become worse than the first. So it shall be also to this evil generation.

[46]But while He was yet speaking to the crowds, behold, *His* mother and brothers were standing outside, seeking to speak to Him. [47]Then one said to Him, Behold, Your mother and Your brothers are standing outside, seeking to speak to You. [48]But answering, He said to the *one* who spoke to Him, Who is My mother? And who are My brothers? [49]And stretching out His hand to His disciples, he said, Behold, My mother and My brothers. [50]For whoever shall do the will of My Father in Heaven, he is My brother and sister and mother.

[1]And going forth in that day from the house, Jesus sat down by the sea. [2]And great crowds were gathered to Him, so that entering into the boat, He sat down. And all the crowd stood on the shore. [3]And He spoke many things to them in parables, saying: Behold, the *one* sowing went out to sow. [4]And in his sowing, some indeed fell by the roadside; and the birds came and ate them. [5]And some fell on the stony places, where they did not have much earth. And immediately it sprang up because of not having deepness of earth; [6]and *the* sun rising, it was scorched; and because of not having root, it

ἀνθρώπου, διέρχεται δι' ἀνύδρων τόπων, ζητοῦν ἀνάπαυσιν,
a man, he goes through dry places seeking rest,
44 καὶ οὐχ εὑρίσκει. τότε λέγει, Ἐπιστρέψω εἰς τὸν οἶκόν μου
and not does find. Then he says, I will return to the house of me,
ὅθεν ἐξῆλθον· καὶ ἐλθὸν εὑρίσκει σχολάζοντα, σεσαρωμένον,
from where I came, and coming he finds (it) standing empty, swept
45 καὶ κεκοσμημένον. τότε πορεύεται καὶ παραλαμβάνει μεθ'
and decorated. Then he goes and takes along with
ἑαυτοῦ ἑπτὰ ἕτερα πνεύματα πονηρότερα ἑαυτοῦ, καὶ
him seven other spirits more evil (than) him, and
εἰσελθόντα κατοικεῖ ἐκεῖ· καὶ γίνεται τὰ ἔσχατα τοῦ ἀνθρώ-
entering dwells there; and becomes the last things – of man
που ἐκείνου χείρονα τῶν πρώτων. οὕτως ἔσται καὶ τῇ γενεᾷ
that worse than the first. Thus it will be also to gene-
ταύτῃ τῇ πονηρᾷ.
ration this – evil.
46 Ἔτι δὲ αὐτοῦ λαλοῦντος τοῖς ὄχλοις, ἰδού, ἡ μήτηρ καὶ
while But He is speaking to the crowds, behold, the mother and
οἱ ἀδελφοὶ αὐτοῦ εἱστήκεισαν ἔξω, ζητοῦντες αὐτῷ λαλῆσαι.
the brothers of Him stood outside, seeking to Him to speak.
47 εἶπε δέ τις αὐτῷ, Ἰδού, ἡ μήτηρ σου καὶ οἱ ἀδελφοί σου ἔξω
said And one to Him, Behold, the mother of You and the brothers of You out
48 ἑστήκασι, ζητοῦντές σοι λαλῆσαι. ὁ δὲ ἀποκριθεὶς εἶπε τῷ
are standing, seeking to You to speak. He And answering said to the
εἰπόντι αὐτῷ, Τίς ἐστιν ἡ μήτηρ μου; καὶ τίνες εἰσὶν οἱ
(one) saying to Him, Who is the mother of Me, and who are the
49 ἀδελφοί μου; καὶ ἐκτείνας τὴν χεῖρα αὐτοῦ ἐπὶ τοὺς
brothers of Me? And stretching out the hand of Him on the
μαθητὰς αὐτοῦ εἶπεν, Ἰδού, ἡ μήτηρ μου καὶ οἱ ἀδελφοί μου.
disciples of Him He said, Behold, the mother of Me and the brothers of Me.
50 ὅστις γὰρ ἂν ποιήσῃ τὸ θέλημα τοῦ πατρός μου τοῦ ἐν
who for ever does the will of the Father of Me
οὐρανοῖς, αὐτός μου ἀδελφὸς καὶ ἀδελφὴ καὶ μήτηρ ἐστίν.
heavens, he of Me brother and sister and mother is.

CHAPTER 13

1 Ἐν δὲ τῇ ἡμέρᾳ ἐκείνῃ ἐξελθὼν ὁ Ἰησοῦς ἀπὸ τῆς οἰκίας
in And – day that going forth – Jesus from the house
2 ἐκάθητο παρὰ τὴν θάλασσαν. καὶ συνήχθησαν πρὸς αὐτὸν
He sat down by the sea. And were assembled to Him
ὄχλοι πολλοί, ὥστε αὐτὸν εἰς τὸ πλοῖον ἐμβάντα καθῆσθαι·
crowds great, so that He into the boat having entered sat down,
3 καὶ πᾶς ὁ ὄχλος ἐπὶ τὸν αἰγιαλὸν εἱστήκει. καὶ ἐλάλησεν
and all the crowd on the shore stood. And He spoke
αὐτοῖς πολλὰ ἐν παραβολαῖς, λέγων, Ἰδού, ἐξῆλθεν ὁ
to them many things in parables, saying, Behold, went out the
4 σπείρων τοῦ σπείρειν. καὶ ἐν τῷ σπείρειν αὐτόν, ἃ μὲν ἔπεσε
(one) sowing – to sow, and in the sowing of him, some truly fell
παρὰ τὴν ὁδόν· καὶ ἦλθε τὰ πετεινὰ καὶ κατέφαγεν αὐτά.
by the wayside, and came the birds and ate them.
5 ἄλλα δὲ ἔπεσεν ἐπὶ τὰ πετρώδη, ὅπου οὐκ εἶχε γῆν πολλήν·
other and fell upon the rocky places, where not they had earth much
6 καὶ εὐθέως ἐξανέτειλε, διὰ τὸ μὴ ἔχειν βάθος γῆς· ἡλίου δὲ
and immediately it sprang up because not having depth of earth; sun and
ἀνατείλαντος ἐκαυματίσθη, καὶ διὰ τὸ μὴ ἔχειν ῥίζαν,
rising, it was scorched, and because of– not having root,

was dried up. 7 And some fell on the thorns; and the thorns grew up and choked them.

8 And some fell on the good ground, and yielded fruit—the one a hundred*fold*, and one sixty, and one thirty.

9 The *one* having ears to hear, let him hear.

10 And coming near the disciples said to Him, Why do You speak to them in parables? 11 And answering He said to them, Because it has been given to you to know the mysteries of the kingdom of Heaven, but it has not been given to them. 12 For whoever has, to him will be given; and he will have *an* overabundance. but whoever has not, even what he has will be taken away from him. 13 Because of this, I speak to them in parables, because seeing they do not see, and hearing they do not hear, nor do they understand. 14 And the prophecy of Isaiah is fulfilled on them, which says, "In hearing you will hear, and in no way know. And seeing you will see, and not at all perceive. 15 For the heart of this people has grown fat, and they heard sluggishly with the ears; and they closed their eyes that they not see with the eyes, and hear with the ears, and understand with the heart, and be converted, and I heal them." 16 But your eyes *are* blessed, because they see; and your ears, because they hear. 17 For truly I say to you, Many prophets and righteous ones desired to see what you see, and did not see; and to hear what you hear, and did not hear.

18 Therefore, hear the parable of the sower. 19 Everyone hearing the word of the kingdom, and not understanding, the evil one comes and catches away that which was sown in his heart. This is the *word* sown by the roadside. 20 And the *word* sown on the stony places is the *one* hearing the word, and immediately receiving it with joy; 21 but *he* has no root in himself, but is temporary; and

7 ἐξηράνθη. ἄλλα δὲ ἔπεσεν ἐπὶ τὰς ἀκάνθας, καὶ ἀνέβησαν αἱ
it was dried. And fell upon the thorns, and grew up the
8 ἄκανθαι καὶ ἀπέπνιξαν αὐτά. ἄλλα δὲ ἔπεσεν ἐπὶ τὴν γῆν
thorns and choked them. other And fell upon the earth
τὴν καλήν, καὶ ἐδίδου καρπόν, ὃ μὲν ἑκατόν, ὃ δὲ ἑξήκοντα,
– good, and yielded fruit, one in-deed a hundred, one and sixty
9 ὃ δὲ τριάκοντα. ὁ ἔχων ὦτα ἀκούειν ἀκουέτω.
one and thirty. The (one) having ears to hear, let him hear.
10 Καὶ προσελθόντες οἱ μαθηταὶ εἶπον αὐτῷ, Διατί ἐν
And having come, the disciples said to Him, Why in
11 παραβολαῖς λαλεῖς αὐτοῖς; ὁ δὲ ἀποκριθεὶς εἶπεν αὐτοῖς ὅτι
parables do You speak to them? He And answering said to them, Because
Ὑμῖν δέδοται γνῶναι τὰ μυστήρια τῆς βασιλείας τῶν
to you it has been given to know the mysteries of the kingdom of the
12 οὐρανῶν, ἐκείνοις δὲ οὐ δέδοται. ὅστις γὰρ ἔχει, δοθήσεται
heavens, to those but not it has been given. who for has, will be given
αὐτῷ καὶ περισσευθήσεται· ὅστις δὲ οὐκ ἔχει, καὶ ὃ ἔχει,
to him, and he will have abundance; who but not has, even what he has
13 ἀρθήσεται ἀπ᾽ αὐτοῦ. διὰ τοῦτο ἐν παραβολαῖς αὐτοῖς λαλῶ,
will be taken from him. Because of this, in parables to them I speak,
ὅτι βλέποντες οὐ βλέπουσι, καὶ ἀκούοντες οὐκ ἀκούουσιν,
because seeing not they see, and hearing not they hear.
14 οὐδὲ συνιοῦσι. καὶ ἀναπληροῦται ἐπ᾽ αὐτοῖς ἡ προφητεία
neither understand. And is fulfilled upon them the prophecy
Ἡσαΐου, ἡ λέγουσα, Ἀκοῇ ἀκούσετε καὶ οὐ μὴ συνῆτε· καὶ
of Isaiah, which says, In hearing you will hear and in no way know, and
15 βλέποντες βλέψετε, καὶ οὐ μὴ ἴδητε. ἐπαχύνθη γὰρ ἡ καρδία
seeing you will see and by no way perceive; has grown for the heart
τοῦ λαοῦ τούτου, καὶ τοῖς ὠσὶ βαρέως ἤκουσαν, καὶ τοὺς
– of people this and with the ears heavily they heard, and the
ὀφθαλμοὺς αὐτῶν ἐκάμμυσαν· μήποτε ἴδωσι τοῖς ὀφθαλμοῖς,
eyes of them they closed, lest they see with the eyes
καὶ τοῖς ὠσὶν ἀκούσωσι, καὶ τῇ καρδίᾳ συνῶσι, καὶ ἐπι-
and with the ears they hear, and with the heart understand, and be
16 στρέψωσι, καὶ ἰάσωμαι αὐτούς. ὑμῶν δὲ μακάριοι οἱ ὀφθαλ-
converted, and I heal them. of you But blessed (are) the eyes,
17 μοί, ὅτι βλέπουσι· καὶ τὰ ὦτα ὑμῶν, ὅτι ἀκούει. ἀμὴν γὰρ
because they see, and the ears of you, because they hear. truly For
λέγω ὑμῖν ὅτι πολλοὶ προφῆται καὶ δίκαιοι ἐπεθύμησαν
I say to you, that many prophets and righteous (ones) desired
ἰδεῖν ἃ βλέπετε, καὶ οὐκ εἶδον· καὶ ἀκοῦσαι ἃ ἀκούετε, καὶ
to see what you see, and not did see; and to hear what you hear, and
18 οὐκ ἤκουσαν. ὑμεῖς οὖν ἀκούσατε την παραβολὴν τοῦ
not did hear. You therefore hear the parable of the
19 σπείροντος. παντὸς ἀκούοντος τὸν λόγον τῆς βασιλείας καὶ
sower: Everyone hearing the word of the kingdom and
μὴ συνιέντος, ἔρχεται ὁ πονηρος, καὶ ἁρπάζει τὸ ἐσπαρ-
not understands, comes the evil one and catches away that which was
μένον ἐν τῇ καρδίᾳ αὐτοῦ· οὗτός ἐστιν ὁ παρὰ τὴν ὁδὸν
sown in the heart of him. This is the (word) by the wayside
20 σπαρείς. ὁ δὲ ἐπὶ τὰ πετρώδη σπαρείς, οὗτός ἐστιν ὁ τὸν
sown. the (word) and on the rocky places was sown, this is the (one) the
21 λόγον ἀκούων, καὶ εὐθὺς μετὰ χαρᾶς λαμβάνων αὐτόν· οὐκ
word hearing, and at once with joy receiving it; no
ἔχει δὲ ῥίζαν ἐν ἑαυτῷ, ἀλλὰ πρόσκαιρός ἐστι· γενομένης δὲ
has but root in himself, but temporary is; occurring but

tribulation or persecution having occurred because of the word, he is at once offended. [22]And the *word* sown into the thorns; this is the *one* hearing the word, and the anxiety of this age, and the deceit of riches choke the word, and it becomes unfruitful. [23]But the *word* sown in the good ground this is the *one* hearing the word and understanding *it*, who truly bears fruit and produces —one a hundred*fold*, and one sixty, and one thirty.

[24]He put another parable before them, saying, The kingdom of Heaven is compared to a man sowing good seed in his field. [25]But while the men slept, his enemy came and sowed darnel in *the* midst of the wheat, and went away. [26]And when the blade sprouted and produced fruit, then the darnel also appeared. [27]And coming near the slaves of the housemaster said to him, Sir, did you not sow good seed in your field? Then from where does it have the darnel? [28]And he said to them, A man, an enemy did this. And the slaves said to him, Then do you desire that going we should collect them? [29]But he said, No, lest collecting the darnel you should uproot the wheat with them. [30]Allow both to grow together until the harvest, and in the time of the harvest I will say to the reapers, First gather the darnel, and bind them into bundles in order to burn them. But bring the wheat together into my granary.

[31]He put another parable before them, saying, The kingdom of Heaven is like a grain of mustard, which a man took *and* sowed in his field; [32]which indeed is less than all the seeds, but when it is grown it is greater than the plants, and becomes a tree, so that the birds of the sky come and roost in its branches.

22 θλίψεως ἢ διωγμοῦ διὰ τὸν λόγον, εὐθὺς σκανδαλίζεται. ὁ
tribulation or persecution through the word, at once he is offended. he who
δὲ εἰς τὰς ἀκάνθας σπαρείς, οὗτός ἐστιν ὁ τὸν λόγον ἀκούων,
And in the thorns sown, this is the (one) the word hearing,
καὶ ἡ μέριμνα τοῦ αἰῶνος τούτου καὶ ἡ ἀπάτη τοῦ πλούτου
and the anxiety of the age this and the deceit of riches
23 συμπνίγει τὸν λόγον, καὶ ἄκαρπος γίνεται. ὁ δὲ ἐπὶ τὴν γῆν
choke the word, and unfruitful it becomes. he But on the earth
τὴν καλὴν σπαρείς, οὗτός ἐστιν ὁ τὸν λόγον ἀκούων καὶ
good was sown, this is the (one) the word hearing and
συνιών· ὃς δὴ καρποφορεῖ, καὶ ποιεῖ ὁ μὲν ἑκατόν, ὁ δὲ
understands; who indeed bears fruit and produces one truly a hundred, one and
ἑξήκοντα, ὁ δὲ τριάκοντα.
sixty, one and thirty.

24 Ἄλλην παραβολὴν παρέθηκεν αὐτοῖς, λέγων, Ὡμοιώθη
Another parable He put before them, saying, is likened
ἡ βασιλεία τῶν οὐρανῶν ἀνθρώπῳ σπείραντι καλὸν
the kingdom of the heavens to a man sowing good
25 σπέρμα ἐν τῷ ἀγρῷ αὐτοῦ· ἐν δὲ τῷ καθεύδειν τοὺς ἀνθρώ-
seed in the field of him: in but the sleeping of the men
πους, ἦλθεν αὐτοῦ ὁ ἐχθρὸς καὶ ἔσπειρε ζιζάνια ἀνὰ μέσον
came his enemy and sowed darnel amidst
26 τοῦ σίτου, καὶ ἀπῆλθεν. ὅτε δὲ ἐβλάστησεν ὁ χόρτος καὶ
the wheat, and went away. when And sprouted the blade, and
27 καρπὸν ἐποίησε, τότε ἐφάνη καὶ τὰ ζιζάνια. προσελθόντες
fruit produced, then appeared also the darnel. coming near
δὲ οἱ δοῦλοι τοῦ οἰκοδεσπότου εἶπον αὐτῷ, Κύριε, οὐχὶ
And the slaves of the master of the house said to him, Lord not
καλὸν σπέρμα ἔσπειρας ἐν τῷ σῷ ἀγρῷ; πόθεν οὖν ἔχει τὰ
good seed did you sow in the of you field? Whence then has it the
28 ζιζάνια; ὁ δὲ ἔφη αὐτοῖς, Ἐχθρὸς ἄνθρωπος τοῦτο ἐποίησεν.
darnel? he And said to them, An enemy, a man. this did.
οἱ δὲ δοῦλοι εἶπον αὐτῷ, Θέλεις οὖν ἀπελθόντες συλλέξωμεν
the And slaves said to him, Will you then having gone out we may collect
29 αὐτά; ὁ δὲ ἔφη, Οὔ· μήποτε, συλλέγοντες τὰ ζιζάνια,
them? he But said, No, lest collecting the darnel
30 ἐκριζώσητε ἅμα αὐτοῖς τὸν σῖτον. ἄφετε συναυξάνεσθαι
you may uproot with them the wheat. Allow to grow together
ἀμφότερα μέχρι τοῦ θερισμοῦ· καὶ ἐν τῷ καιρῷ τοῦ θερισμοῦ
both until the harvest; and in the time of the harvest
ἐρῶ τοῖς θερισταῖς, Συλλέξατε πρῶτον τὰ ζιζάνια, καὶ
I will say to the reapers, Collect first the darnel, and
δήσατε αὐτὰ εἰς δέσμας πρὸς τὸ κατακαῦσαι αὐτά· τὸν δὲ
bind them into bundles in order to burn them; the but
σῖτον συναγάγετε εἰς τὴν ἀποθήκην μου.
wheat bring together into the granary of me.

31 Ἄλλην παραβολὴν παρέθηκεν αὐτοῖς, λέγων, Ὁμοία
Another parable He presented to them, saying, Like
ἐστὶν ἡ βασιλεία τῶν οὐρανῶν κόκκῳ σινάπεως, ὃν λαβὼν
is the kingdom of the heavens to a grain of mustard, which taking
32 ἄνθρωπος ἔσπειρεν ἐν τῷ ἀγρῷ αὐτοῦ· ὃ μικρότερον μέν
a man sowed in the field of him, which lesser truly
ἐστι πάντων τῶν σπερμάτων· ὅταν δὲ αὐξηθῇ, μεῖζον τῶν
is than all the seeds, when but it is grown, greater than the
λαχάνων ἐστί, καὶ γίνεται δένδρον, ὥστε ἐλθεῖν τὰ πετεινὰ
plants is, and becomes a tree, so that come the birds

33 He spoke another parable to them: The kingdom of Heaven is like leaven, which taking a woman hid in three measures of meal, until the whole was leavened.

34 Jesus spoke of all these things in parables to the crowds; and He did not speak to them without a parable; 35 so that was fulfilled that spoken through the prophet, saying, "I will open My mouth in parables; I will say things hidden from *the* foundation of *the* world."

36 Then sending the crowds away, Jesus came into the house. And His disciples came to Him, saying, Explain to us the parable of the darnel of the field. 37 And answering He said to them, The *one* sowing the good seed is the Son of man. 38 And the field is the world; and the good seed, these are the sons of the kingdom; but the darnel are the sons of the evil. 39 And the enemy who sowed them is the Devil; and the harvest is the end of the age; and the angels are the reapers. 40 Therefore, as the darnel is gathered and is burned in the fire, so it will be in the end of this age. 41 The Son of man will send forth His angels, and they will gather out of His kingdom all the offenses, and those who practice lawlessness. 42 And they will throw them into the furnace of fire; there will be weeping and gnashing of the teeth. 43 Then the righteous will shine out like the sun in the kingdom of their Father. The *one* that has ears to hear, let him hear.

44 Again, the kingdom of Heaven is like treasure hidden in the field, which having found a man hid;

τοῦ οὐρανοῦ καὶ κατασκηνοῦν ἐν τοῖς κλάδοις αὐτοῦ.
of the heaven and roost in the branches of it.
33 Ἄλλην παραβολὴν ἐλάλησεν αὐτοῖς, Ὁμοία ἐστὶν ἡ
Another parable He spoke to them: Like is the
βασιλεία τῶν οὐρανῶν ζύμῃ, ἣν λαβοῦσα γυνὴ ἐνέκρυψεν
kingdom of the heavens to leaven, which taking a woman hid
εἰς ἀλεύρου σάτα τρία, ἕως οὗ ἐζυμώθη ὅλον.
in meal measures three, until was leavened the whole.
34 Ταῦτα πάντα ἐλάλησεν ὁ Ἰησοῦς ἐν παραβολαῖς τοῖς
These things all spoke — Jesus in parables to the
35 ὄχλοις, καὶ χωρὶς παραβολῆς οὐκ ἐλάλει αὐτοῖς· ὅπως
crowds, and without a parable not He spoke to them; so that
πληρωθῇ τὸ ῥηθὲν διὰ τοῦ προφήτου, λέγοντος, Ἀνοίξω
was fulfilled that spoken through the prophet, saying, I will open
ἐν παραβολαῖς τὸ στόμα μου, ἐρεύξομαι κεκρυμμένα ἀπὸ
in parables the mouth of Me; I will utter things hidden from
καταβολῆς κόσμου.
(the) foundation of (the) world.
36 Τότε ἀφεὶς τοὺς ὄχλους ἦλθεν εἰς τὴν οἰκίαν ὁ Ἰησοῦς· καὶ
Then sending away the crowds,came into the house — Jesus; and
προσῆλθον αὐτῷ οἱ μαθηταὶ αὐτοῦ, λέγοντες, Φράσον ἡμῖν
came to Him the disciples of Him, saying, Explain to us
37 τὴν παραβολὴν τῶν ζιζανίων τοῦ ἀγροῦ. ὁ δὲ ἀποκριθεὶς
the parable of the darnel of the field. He And answering
εἶπεν αὐτοῖς, Ὁ σπείρων τὸ καλὸν σπέρμα ἐστὶν ὁ υἱὸς τοῦ
said to them, The (one) sowing the good seed is the Son —
38 ἀνθρώπου· ὁ δὲ ἀγρός ἐστιν ὁ κόσμος· τὸ δὲ καλὸν σπέρμα,
of man; the and field is the world; the and good seed
οὗτοί εἰσιν οἱ υἱοὶ τῆς βασιλείας· τὰ δὲ ζιζάνιά εἰσιν οἱ υἱοὶ
these are the sons of the kingdom; the but darnel are the sons
39 τοῦ πονηροῦ· ὁ δὲ ἐχθρὸς ὁ σπείρας αὐτά ἐστιν ὁ διάβολος·
of the evil one; the and enemy who sowed them is the Devil;
ὁ δὲ θερισμὸς συντέλεια τοῦ αἰῶνός ἐστιν· οἱ δὲ θερισταὶ
the and harvest (the) completion of the age is, the and reapers
40 ἄγγελοί εἰσιν. ὥσπερ οὖν συλλέγεται τὰ ζιζάνια καὶ πυρὶ
angels are. As therefore is collected the darnel, and in fire
κατακαίεται, οὕτως ἔσται ἐν τῇ συντελείᾳ τοῦ αἰῶνος
is consumed, thus it shall be in the completion of the age
41 τούτου. ἀποστελεῖ ὁ υἱὸς τοῦ ἀνθρώπου τοὺς ἀγγέλους
this. Shall send out the Son — of man the angels
αὐτοῦ, καὶ συλλέξουσιν ἐκ τῆς βασιλείας αὐτοῦ πάντα τὰ
of Him, and they will collect out of the kingdom of Him all the
42 σκάνδαλα καὶ τοὺς ποιοῦντας τὴν ἀνομίαν, καὶ βαλοῦσιν
offenses and those who practice — lawlessness, and they will cast
αὐτοὺς εἰς τὴν κάμινον τοῦ πυρός· ἐκεῖ ἔσται ὁ κλαυθμὸς καὶ
them into the furnace of the fire: there shall be the weeping and
43 ὁ βρυγμὸς τῶν ὀδόντων. τότε οἱ δίκαιοι ἐκλάμψουσιν ὡς ὁ
the gnashing of the teeth. Then the righteous will shine forth as the
ἥλιος ἐν τῇ βασιλείᾳ τοῦ πατρὸς αὐτῶν. ὁ ἔχων ὦτα ἀκούειν
sun in the kingdom of the Father of them. He having ears to hear,
ἀκουέτω.
let him hear.

44 Πάλιν ὁμοία ἐστὶν ἡ βασιλεία τῶν οὐρανῶν θησαυρῷ
Again like is the kingdom of the heavens to treasure
κεκρυμμένῳ ἐν τῷ ἀγρῷ, ὃν εὑρὼν ἄνθρωπος ἔκρυψε· καὶ ἀπὸ
hid in the field, which having found a man hid, and from

and for the joy of it he goes and sells all things, as many as he has, and buys that field.

45 Again, the kingdom of Heaven is like a man, a merchant seeking excellent pearls; 46 who having found one very precious pearl, going away has sold all things, as many as he had, and bought it.

47 Again, the kingdom of Heaven is like a drag net thrown into the sea, and gathering together of every kind; 48 which when it was filled, drawing it up on the shore, and sitting down, *they* gathered the good into containers, and they threw out the bad. 49 So it will be in the end of the age: the angels will go out and will separate the wicked from *the* midst of the righteous; 50 and will throw them into the furnace of fire; there will be weeping and gnashing of the teeth.

51 Jesus said to them, Have you understood all these things? They said to Him, Yes, Lord. 52 And He said to them, Because of this every scribe schooled to the kingdom of Heaven is like a man, a master of a house, who puts forth out of his treasure new and old.

53 And it happened, when Jesus had finished these parables, He moved from there 54 And coming into His own country, He taught them in their synagogue, so that they were astonished, and said, Where did this one *get* this wisdom, and the mighty works? 55 Is this not the carpenter's son? *Is* not his mother called Mary, and his brothers, James, and Joseph, and Simon, and Judas? 56 And are not his sisters all with us? From where then did this one *get* all these things? 57 And they were offended in Him. But Jesus said to

τῆς χαρᾶς αὐτοῦ ὑπάγει, καὶ πάντα ὅσα ἔχει πωλεῖ, καὶ
the joy of it he goes, and all things what-ever he has, he sells, and
ἀγοράζει τὸν ἀγρὸν ἐκεῖνον.
buys — field that.
45 Πάλιν ὁμοία ἐστὶν ἡ βασιλεία τῶν οὐρανῶν ἀνθρώπῳ
Again like is the kingdom of the heavens to a man
46 ἐμπόρῳ ζητοῦντι καλοὺς μαργαρίτας· ὃς εὑρὼν ἕνα πολύ-
a merchant seeking excellent pearls; who finding one very
τιμον μαργαρίτην, ἀπελθὼν πέπρακε πάντα ὅσα εἶχε, καὶ
precious pearl, going away has sold all things that he has, and
ἠγόρασεν αὐτόν.
bought it.
47 Πάλιν ὁμοία ἐστὶν ἡ βασιλεία τῶν οὐρανῶν σαγήνῃ
Again like is the kingdom of the heavens to a net
βληθείσῃ εἰς τὴν θάλασσαν, καὶ ἐκ παντὸς γένους συναγα-
thrown into the sea, and of every kind gathering
48 γούσῃ· ἥν, ὅτε ἐπληρώθη, ἀναβιβάσαντες ἐπὶ τὸν αἰγιαλόν,
together; which when it was filled, drawing up onto the shore,
καὶ καθίσαντες, συνέλεξαν τὰ καλὰ εἰς ἀγγεῖα, τὰ δὲ σαπρὰ
and sitting down,(men)collected the good into vessels, the and corrupt
49 ἔξω ἔβαλον. οὕτως ἔσται ἐν τῃ συντελείᾳ τοῦ αἰῶνος· ἐξελεύ-
out they threw. Thus it will be in the completion of the age: will go
σονται οἱ ἄγγελοι, καὶ ἀφοριοῦσι τοὺς πονηροὺς ἐκ μέσου
out the angels, and will separate the evil from (the) midst
50 τῶν δικαίων, καὶ βαλοῦσιν αὐτοὺς εἰς τὴν κάμινον τοῦ πυρός·
of the righteous, and will throw them into the furnace of the fire;
ἐκεῖ ἔσται ὁ κλαυθμὸς καὶ ὁ βρυγμὸς τῶν ὀδόντων.
there will be the weeping and the gnashing of the teeth.
51 Λέγει αὐτοῖς ὁ Ἰησοῦς, Συνήκατε ταῦτα πάντα ; λέγουσιν
says to them — Jesus, Did you discern these things all? They say
52 αὐτῷ, Ναί, Κύριε. ὁ δὲ εἶπεν αὐτοῖς, Διὰ τοῦτο πᾶς γραμ-
to Him. Yes, Lord. He And said to them, Because of this every scribe
ματεὺς μαθητευθεὶς εἰς τὴν βασιλείαν τῶν οὐρανῶν ὅμοιός
discipled into the kingdom of the heavens like
ἐστιν ἀνθρώπῳ οἰκοδεσπότῃ, ὅστις ἐκβάλλει ἐκ τοῦ θησαυ-
is to a man, a master of a house, who puts forth out of the treasure
ροῦ αὐτοῦ καινὰ καὶ παλαιά.
of him new and old.
53 Καὶ ἐγένετο ὅτε ἐτέλεσεν ὁ Ἰησοῦς τὰς παραβολὰς ταύτας,
And it was, when had ended — Jesus — parables these,
54 μετῆρεν ἐκεῖθεν· καὶ ἐλθὼν εἰς τὴν πατρίδα αὐτοῦ ἐδίδασκεν
He moved from there;and coming into the country of Him, He taught
αὐτοὺς ἐν τῇ συναγωγῇ αὐτῶν, ὥστε ἐκπλήττεσθαι αὐτοὺς
them in the synagogue of them, so that were astounded they,
55 καὶ λέγειν, Πόθεν τούτῳ ἡ σοφία αὕτη καὶ αἱ δυνάμεις ; οὐχ
even to say, Whence to this one wisdom this, and the works of power? Not
οὗτός ἐστιν ὁ τοῦ τέκτονος υἱός ; οὐχὶ ἡ μήτηρ αὐτοῦ
this is the of the carpenter son? (Is) not the mother of him
λέγεται Μαριάμ, καὶ οἱ ἀδελφοὶ αὐτοῦ Ἰάκωβος καὶ Ἰωσῆς
called Mariam; and the brothers of him, James and Joseph
56 καὶ Σίμων καὶ Ἰούδας ; καὶ αἱ ἀδελφαὶ αὐτοῦ οὐχὶ πᾶσαι
and Simon and Judas? And the sisters of him not all
57 πρὸς ἡμᾶς εἰσί ; πόθεν οὖν τούτῳ ταῦτα πάντα ; καὶ
with us are? Whence then to this (one) these things all? And
ἐσκανδαλίζοντο ἐν αὐτῷ. ὁ δὲ Ἰησοῦς εἶπεν αὐτοῖς, Οὐκ
they were offended in Him. But Jesus said to them, Not

them. A prophet is not without honor, except in his own homeland, and in his own house. [58]And He did not do many mighty works there because of their unbelief.

CHAPTER 14

[1]At that time Herod the tetrarch heard the fame of Jesus. [2]And *he* said to his servants, This is John the Baptist. He has risen from the dead, and because of this mighty works are working in him. [3]For having seized John, Herod bound him and put *him* into prison, because of Herodias, the wife of his brother Philip. [4]For John said to him, It is not lawful for you to have her. [5]And desiring to kill him, he feared the multitude, because they held him as a prophet.

[6]But a birthday of Herod being celebrated, the daughter of Herodias danced in the midst, and pleased Herod. [7]So then he promised with an oath to give her whatever she should ask. [8]But she being urged on by her mother, she says, Give me here on a platter the head of John the Baptist. [9]And the king was grieved, because of the oaths, and those who had reclined with *him*, he ordered *it* to be given. [10]And sending, he beheaded John in the prison. [11]And his head was brought on a platter, and was given to the girl; and she brought *it* to her mother. [12]And having come, his disciples took the body and buried it; and coming, *they* reported to Jesus.

[13]And hearing, Jesus withdrew from there in a boat, into a desert place apart.

[14]And hearing, the crowds followed Him on foot from the cities. And going out, Jesus saw a great crowd, and was filled with pity toward them. And He

ἔστι προφήτης ἄτιμος, εἰ μὴ ἐν τῇ πατρίδι αὐτοῦ καὶ ἐν τῇ
is a prophet honorless, except in the homeland of him, and in the
58 οἰκίᾳ αὐτοῦ. καὶ οὐκ ἐποίησεν ἐκεῖ δυνάμεις πολλάς, διά
house of him. And not He did there power-works many, because
τὴν ἀπιστίαν αὐτῶν.
of the unbelief of them.

CHAPTER 14

1 Ἐν ἐκείνῳ τῷ καιρῷ ἤκουσεν Ἡρῴδης ὁ τετράρχης τὴν
At that time heard Herod the tetrarch the
2 ἀκοὴν Ἰησοῦ, καὶ εἶπε τοῖς παισὶν αὐτοῦ, Οὗτός ἐστιν
fame of Jesus, and said to the servants of him, **This is**
Ἰωάννης ὁ Βαπτιστής· αὐτὸς ἠγέρθη ἀπὸ τῶν νεκρῶν, καὶ
John the Baptist; he is risen from the dead, and
3 διὰ τοῦτο αἱ δυνάμεις ἐνεργοῦσιν ἐν αὐτῷ. ὁ γὰρ Ἡρῴδης
because of this the power works operate in him. For Herod
κρατήσας τὸν Ἰωάννην ἔδησεν αὐτὸν καὶ ἔθετο ἐν φυλακῇ,
having seized — John bound him and put in prison,
διὰ Ἡρωδιάδα τὴν γυναῖκα Φιλίππου τοῦ ἀδελφοῦ αὐτοῦ.
because of Herodias the wife of Philip, the brother of him.
4 ἔλεγε γὰρ αὐτῷ ὁ Ἰωάννης, Οὐκ ἔξεστί σοι ἔχειν αὐτήν.
said For to him — John, Not it is lawful for you to have her.
5 καὶ θέλων αὐτὸν ἀποκτεῖναι, ἐφοβήθη τὸν ὄχλον, ὅτι ὡς
And wishing him to kill, he feared the crowd, because as
6 προφήτην αὐτὸν εἶχον. γενεσίων δὲ ἀγομένων τοῦ Ἡρῴδου,
a prophet him they held. a birthday But being held — of Herod,
ὠρχήσατο ἡ θυγάτηρ τῆς Ἡρωδιάδος ἐν τῷ μέσῳ, καὶ
danced the daughter — of Herodias in the midst, and
7 ἤρεσε τῷ Ἡρῴδῃ. ὅθεν μεθ' ὅρκου ὡμολόγησεν αὐτῇ δοῦναι
pleased — Herod. Whence with an oath he acknowledged to her to give
8 ὃ ἐὰν αἰτήσηται. ἡ δέ, προβιβασθεῖσα ὑπὸ τῆς μητρὸς
whatever she might ask. she So being urged on by the mother
αὐτῆς, Δός μοι, φησίν, ὧδε ἐπὶ πίνακι τὴν κεφαλὴν Ἰωάννου
of her, Give me, she says, here on a platter the head of John
9 τοῦ Βαπτιστοῦ. καὶ ἐλυπήθη ὁ βασιλεύς, διὰ δὲ τοὺς ὅρκους
the Baptist. And was grieved the king, because of but the oaths
10 καὶ τοὺς συνανακειμένους ἐκέλευσε δοθῆναι· καὶ πέμψας
and those who reclined with (him), he ordered (it) be given. And sending
11 ἀπεκεφάλισε τὸν Ἰωάννην ἐν τῇ φυλακῇ. καὶ ἠνέχθη ἡ
he beheaded — John in the prison. And was brought the
κεφαλὴ αὐτοῦ ἐπὶ πίνακι, καὶ ἐδόθη τῷ κορασίῳ· καὶ ἤνεγκε
head of him on a platter, and was given to the girl, and she brought
12 τῇ μητρὶ αὐτῆς. καὶ προσελθόντες οἱ μαθηταὶ αὐτοῦ ἦραν
to the mother of her. And having come the disciples of him took
τὸ σῶμα, καὶ ἔθαψαν αὐτό καὶ ἐλθόντες ἀπήγγειλαν τῷ
the body, and buried it; and coming told —
Ἰησοῦ.
to Jesus.

13 Καὶ ἀκούσας ὁ Ἰησοῦς ἀνεχώρησεν ἐκεῖθεν ἐν πλοίῳ εἰς
And having heard Jesus withdrew from there in a boat into
ἔρημον τόπον κατ' ἰδίαν· καὶ ἀκούσαντες οἱ ὄχλοι ἠκολού-
a desert place privately. And having heard the crowds followed
14 θησαν αὐτῷ πεζῇ ἀπὸ τῶν πόλεων. καὶ ἐξελθὼν ὁ Ἰησοῦς
Him on foot from the cities. And going out, — Jesus
εἶδε πολὺν ὄχλον, καὶ ἐσπλαγχνίσθη ἐπ' αὐτούς, καὶ
saw great a crowd, and was filled with pity toward them, and

healed their infirm ones. [15]And evening coming, His disciples came to Him, saying, The place is desert, and the time is already gone. Dismiss the crowds, that going away into the villages they may buy food for themselves. [16]But Jesus said to them, They have no need to go away. You give them *food* to eat. [17]But they said to Him, We have nothing here except five loaves and two fish. [18]And He said, Bring them here to Me. [19]And commanding the crowds to recline on the grass, and taking the five loaves and two fish, looking up to Heaven, He blessed. And breaking, He gave the loaves to the disciples, and the disciples *gave* to the crowds. [20]And all ate, and were satisfied. And they took up the excess of the pieces, twelve handbaskets full. [21]And the ones eating were about five thousand men, besides women and children.

[22]And immediately Jesus made His disciples get into a boat, and to go before Him to the other side, until He should dismiss the crowds. [23]And having dismissed the crowds, He went up into the mountain alone to pray. And evening coming on, He was there alone. [24]But the boat was now in *the* middle of the sea, tossed by the waves, for the wind was contrary. [25]But in the fourth watch of the night, Jesus went out to them, walking on the sea. [26]And seeing Him walking on the sea, the disciples were troubled, saying, It is a ghost! and they cried out from the fear. [27]But immediately Jesus spoke to them, saying, Be comforted! I AM! Do not fear. [28]And answering Him, Peter said, Lord, if it is You, command me to come to You on the waters. [29]And He said, Come! And

15 ἐθεράπευσε τοὺς ἀρρώστους αὐτῶν. ὀψίας δὲ γενομένης,
He healed the infirm of them. evening And coming,
προσῆλθον αὐτῷ οἱ μαθηταὶ αὐτοῦ, λέγοντες, Ἔρημός
came near to Him the disciples of Him, saying, Desert
ἐστιν ὁ τόπος, καὶ ἡ ὥρα ἤδη παρῆλθεν· ἀπόλυσον τοὺς
is the place, and the hour already is gone by. Dismiss the
ὄχλους, ἵνα ἀπελθόντες εἰς τὰς κώμας ἀγοράσωσιν ἑαυτοῖς
crowds, that going away into the villages they may buy for themselves
16 βρώματα. ὁ δὲ Ἰησοῦς εἶπεν αὐτοῖς, Οὐ χρείαν ἔχουσιν
foods. – But Jesus said to them, Not need they have
17 ἀπελθεῖν· δότε αὐτοῖς ὑμεῖς φαγεῖν. οἱ δὲ λέγουσιν αὐτῷ,
to go away; give to them you to eat. they But say to Him,
Οὐκ ἔχομεν ὧδε εἰ μὴ πέντε ἄρτους καὶ δύο ἰχθύας. ὁ δὲ εἶπε,
Not we have here except five loaves and two fish. he And said,
19 Φέρετέ μοι αὐτοὺς ὧδε. καὶ κελεύσας τοὺς ὄχλους ἀνακλιθῆ-
Bear to Me them here. And commanding the crowds to recline
ναι ἐπὶ τοὺς χόρτους, καὶ λαβὼν τοὺς πέντε ἄρτους καὶ τοὺς
on the grass, and taking the five loaves and the
δύο ἰχθύας, ἀναβλέψας εἰς τὸν οὐρανόν, εὐλόγησε, καὶ
two fish, looking up to the Heaven, He blessed. and
κλάσας ἔδωκε τοῖς μαθηταῖς τοὺς ἄρτους, οἱ δὲ μαθηταὶ τοῖς
breaking He gave to the disciples the loaves, the and disciples to the
20 ὄχλοις. καὶ ἔφαγον πάντες, καὶ ἐχορτάσθησαν· καὶ ἦραν τὸ
crowds. And ate all and were satisfied; and they took the
21 περισσεῦον τῶν κλασμάτων, δώδεκα κοφίνους πλήρεις. οἱ
excess of the fragments, twelve handbaskets full. the (ones)
δὲ ἐσθίοντες ἦσαν ἄνδρες ὡσεὶ πεντακισχίλιοι, χωρὶς γυναι-
And eating were men about five thousand, apart from women
κῶν καὶ παιδίων.
and children.

22 Καὶ εὐθέως ἠνάγκασεν ὁ Ἰησοῦς τοὺς μαθητὰς αὐτοῦ
And instantly constrained Jesus the disciples of Him
ἐμβῆναι εἰς τὸ πλοῖον, καὶ προάγειν αὐτὸν εἰς τὸ πέραν,
to enter into the boat and to go before Him to the other side,
23 ἕως οὗ ἀπολύσῃ τοὺς ὄχλους. καὶ ἀπολύσας τοὺς ὄχλους,
until He should dismiss the crowds. And having dismissed the crowds,
ἀνέβη εἰς τὸ ὄρος κατ' ἰδίαν προσεύξασθαι· ὀψίας δὲ γενο-
He went into the mountain apart in order to pray: evening And com-
24 μένης, μόνος ἦν ἐκεῖ. τὸ δὲ πλοῖον ἤδη μέσον τῆς θαλάσσης
ing, alone He was there. the And boat now amidst the sea
ἦν, βασανιζόμενον ὑπὸ τῶν κυμάτων· ἦν γὰρ ἐναντίος ὁ
was, being tossed by the waves; was for contrary the
25 ἄνεμος. τεταρτῃ δὲ φυλακῇ τῆς νυκτὸς ἀπῆλθε πρὸς αὐτοὺς
wind. in fourth But watch of the night went toward them
26 ὁ Ἰησοῦς, περιπατῶν ἐπὶ τῆς θαλάσσης. καὶ ἰδόντες αὐτὸν
Jesus, walking on the sea. And seeing Him
οἱ μαθηταὶ ἐπὶ τὴν θάλασσαν περιπατοῦντα ἐταράχθησαν,
the disciples on the sea walking they were troubled,
λέγοντες ὅτι Φάντασμά ἐστι· καὶ ἀπὸ τοῦ φόβου ἔκραξαν.
saying, A phantom it is, and out of – fear they cried out.
27 εὐθέως δὲ ἐλάλησεν αὐτοῖς ὁ Ἰησοῦς, λέγων, Θαρσεῖτε· ἐγώ
at once But spoke to them – Jesus, saying, Be comforted, I
28 εἰμι· μὴ φοβεῖσθε. ἀποκριθεὶς δὲ αὐτῷ ὁ Πέτρος εἶπε, Κύριε,
AM! not Do fear. answering And Him – Peter said, Lord,
29 εἰ σὺ εἶ, κέλευσόν με πρός σε ἐλθεῖν ἐπὶ τὰ ὕδατα. ὁ δὲ εἶπεν,
if You are, command me to You to come on the waters. He And said,

descending from the boat, Peter walked on the waters to go to Jesus. [30] But seeing the strong wind, he was afraid, and beginning to sink, he cried out, saying, Lord, save me! [31] And immediately stretching out the hand, Jesus took hold of him, and said to him, Little-faith, why did you doubt? [32] And coming into the boat, the wind ceased. [33] And those in the boat came and worshiped Him, saying, Truly, You are the Son of God.

[34] And passing over, they came to the land of Gennesaret. [35] And recognizing Him, the men of that place sent to all that neighborhood, and brought to Him all those who had illness. [36] And *they* begged Him that they might touch the fringe of His robe. And as many as touched were made perfectly well.

CHAPTER 15

[1] Then the scribes and Pharisees came to Jesus from Jerusalem, saying, [2] Why do your disciples transgress the tradition of the elders? For they do not wash their hands when they eat bread. [3] But answering He said to them, Why do you also transgress the command of God on account of your tradition?

[4] For God commanded, saying, "Honor your father and mother," and, "He who speaks evil of father or mother, by death let him die." [5] But you say, Whoever says to the father or the mother, A gift, whatever you would gain from me; and in no way he honors his father or his mother. [6] And you annulled the command of God on account of your tradition. [7] Hypocrites! Well did Isaiah prophesy concerning you, saying, [8] "This people draws near

Ἐλθέ. καὶ καταβὰς ἀπὸ τοῦ πλοίου Πέτρος περιεπάτησεν
Come! And descending from the boat, — Peter walked
30 ἐπὶ τὰ ὕδατα, ἐλθεῖν πρὸς τὸν Ἰησοῦν. βλέπων δὲ τὸν
on the waters, to come toward — Jesus. seeing But the
ἄνεμον ἰσχυρὸν ἐφοβήθη· καὶ ἀρξάμενος καταποντίζεσθαι
wind strong, he was frightened, and beginning to sink
31 ἔκραξε, λέγων, Κύριε, σῶσόν με. εὐθέως δὲ ὁ Ἰησοῦς ἐκτείνας
he cried out, saying, Lord, save me! instantly And — Jesus extending
τὴν χεῖρα ἐπελάβετο αὐτοῦ, καὶ λέγει αὐτῷ, Ὀλιγόπιστε,
the hand took hold of him, and says to him, Little-faith,
32 εἰς τί ἐδίστασας; καὶ ἐμβάντων αὐτῶν εἰς τὸ πλοῖον,
why did you doubt? And going up they into the boat,
33 ἐκόπασεν ὁ ἄνεμος· οἱ δὲ ἐν τῷ πλοίῳ ἐλθόντες προσεκύνησαν
ceased the wind. the (ones) And in the boat coming worshiped
αὐτῷ, λέγοντες, Ἀληθῶς Θεοῦ υἱὸς εἶ.
Him, saying, Truly of God Son You are!
34 Καὶ διαπεράσαντες ἦλθον εἰς τὴν γῆν Γεννησαρέτ. καὶ
35 And passing over they came into the land of Gennessaret. And
ἐπιγνόντες αὐτὸν οἱ ἄνδρες τοῦ τόπου ἐκείνου ἀπέστειλαν
recognizing Him the men of place that sent
εἰς ὅλην τὴν περίχωρον ἐκείνην, καὶ προσήνεγκαν αὐτῷ
into all — neighborhood that, and brought to Him
πάντας τοὺς κακῶς ἔχοντας· καὶ παρεκάλουν αὐτόν, ἵνα
36 all those illness having, and begged Him that
μόνον ἅψωνται τοῦ κρασπέδου τοῦ ἱματίου αὐτοῦ· καὶ
only they might touch the fringe of the garment of Him. And
ὅσοι ἥψαντο διεσώθησαν.
as many as touched were made perfectly well.

CHAPTER 15

1 Τότε προσέρχονται τῷ Ἰησοῦ οἱ ἀπὸ Ἱεροσολύμων
Then approach — to Jesus the (ones) from Jerusalem,
2 γραμματεῖς καὶ Φαρισαῖοι, λέγοντες, Διατί οἱ μαθηταί σου
scribes and Pharisees, saying, Why the disciples of you
παραβαίνουσι τὴν παράδοσιν τῶν πρεσβυτέρων; οὐ γὰρ
transgress the tradition of the elders? not for
3 νίπτονται τὰς χεῖρας αὐτῶν, ὅταν ἄρτον ἐσθίωσιν. ὁ δὲ
they wash the hands of them, when bread they eat. He But
ἀποκριθεὶς εἶπεν αὐτοῖς, Διατί καὶ ὑμεῖς παραβαίνετε τὴν
answering said to them, Why also do you transgress the
4 ἐντολὴν τοῦ Θεοῦ διὰ τὴν παράδοσιν ὑμῶν; ὁ γὰρ Θεὸς
command — of God on account of the tradition of you? — For God
ἐνετείλατο, λέγων, Τίμα τὸν πατέρα σοῦ, καὶ τὴν μητέρα·
commanded, saying, Honor the father of you, and the mother;
καί, Ὁ κακολογῶν πατέρα ἢ μητέρα θανάτῳ τελευτάτω·
and, The (one) speaking evil of father or mother by death let him end.
5 ὑμεῖς δὲ λέγετε, Ὃς ἂν εἴπῃ τῷ πατρὶ ἢ τῇ μητρί, Δῶρον,
you But say, Whoever says to the father or the mother, A gift,
ὃ ἐὰν ἐξ ἐμοῦ ὠφεληθῇς, καὶ οὐ μὴ τιμήσῃ τὸν πατέρα
whatever by me you would gain, and in no way he honors the father
6 αὐτοῦ ἢ τὴν μητέρα αὐτοῦ· καὶ ἠκυρώσατε τὴν ἐντολὴν τοῦ
of him or the mother of him; and you annulled the command —
7 Θεοῦ διὰ τὴν παράδοσιν ὑμῶν. ὑποκριταί, καλῶς προεφή-
of God on account of tradition your. Hypocrites! Well proph-
8 τευσε περὶ ὑμῶν Ἡσαΐας, λέγων, Ἐγγίζει μοι ὁ λαὸς οὗτος
esied concerning you Isaiah, saying, Draws near to Me people this

to Me with their mouth, and with their lips honor Me; but their heart is far from Me. [9]But in vain they worship Me, teaching *the* ordinances of men *as* doctrines." [10]And calling near the crowd, He said to them, Hear and understand: [11]*It is* not that which enters into the mouth that defiles the man, but that which goes forth out of the mouth, this defiles the man.

[12]Then coming the disciples said to Him, You know that hearing the saying, the Pharisees were offended? [13]But answering He said, Every plant which My heavenly Father has not planted shall be rooted up. [14]Leave them alone. They are blind leaders of the blind; and if the blind lead, both will fall into a pit. [15]And answering Peter said to Him, Explain this parable to us. [16]But Jesus said, Are you also still without understanding? [17]Do you not yet perceive that everything entering into the mouth goes into the belly, and is thrown out into *the* wastebowl? [18]But the things which come out of the mouth come forth from the heart, and these defile the man. [19]For out of the heart comes forth evil thoughts, murders, adulteries, fornications, thefts, lies, blasphemies. [20]These things are the things defiling the man. But eating with unwashed hands does not defile the man.

[21]And going out from there, Jesus withdrew to the parts of Tyre and Sidon. [22]And, behold, a woman of Canaan coming forth cried out to Him, saying, have pity on me, Lord, Son of David! My daughter is vilely demon-possessed. [23]But He did not answer her a word. And coming near, His disciples asked Him, saying, Send her away, for she cries out after us? [24]But answering He said, I was not sent except

τῷ στόματι αὐτῶν, καὶ τοῖς χείλεσί με τιμᾷ· ἡ δὲ καρδία
with the mouth of them, and with the lips Me it honors; the but heart
9 αὐτῶν πόρρω ἀπέχει ἀπ' ἐμοῦ. μάτην δὲ σέβονταί με,
of them far is away from Me. in vain But they adore Me,
10 διδάσκοντες διδασκαλίας ἐντάλματα ἀνθρώπων. καὶ προσκα-
teaching (as) teachings ordinances of men. And calling
11 λεσάμενος τὸν ὄχλον, εἶπεν αὐτοῖς, Ἀκούετε καὶ συνίετε. οὐ
near the crowd, He said to them, Hear and understand, not
τὸ εἰσερχόμενον εἰς τὸ στόμα κοινοῖ τὸν ἄνθρωπον· ἀλλὰ τὸ
the (thing) entering into the mouth defiles the man. but the (thing)
ἐκπορευόμενον ἐκ τοῦ στόματος, τοῦτο κοινοῖ τὸν ἄνθρωπον.
coming forth from the mouth, this defiles the man.
12 τότε προσελθόντες οἱ μαθηταὶ αὐτοῦ εἶπον αὐτῷ, Οἶδας ὅτι
Then having come the disciples to Him, they said to Him, Do You know that
13 οἱ Φαρισαῖοι ἀκούσαντες τὸν λόγον ἐσκανδαλίσθησαν; ὁ
the Pharisees having heard the saying were offended? He
δὲ ἀποκριθεὶς εἶπε, Πᾶσα φυτεία, ἣν οὐκ ἐφύτευσεν ὁ πατήρ
But answering said, Every plant which not has planted the Father
14 μου ὁ οὐράνιος, ἐκριζωθήσεται. ἄφετε αὐτούς· ὁδηγοί εἰσι
of Me the heavenly shall be rooted up. Leave them; leaders they are
τυφλοὶ τυφλῶν· τυφλὸς δὲ τυφλὸν ἐὰν ὁδηγῇ, ἀμφότεροι εἰς
blind of blind; blind and blind if lead, both into
15 βόθυνον πεσοῦνται. ἀποκριθεὶς δὲ ὁ Πέτρος εἶπεν αὐτῷ,
a pit will fall. answering And — Peter said to Him,
16 Φράσον ἡμῖν τὴν παραβολὴν ταύτην. ὁ δὲ Ἰησοῦς εἶπεν,
Explain to us — parable this. — But Jesus said,
17 Ἀκμὴν καὶ ὑμεῖς ἀσύνετοί ἐστε; οὔπω νοεῖτε, ὅτι πᾶν τὸ
Yet also you unintelligent are? Not yet you perceive that everything
εἰσπορευόμενον εἰς τὸ στόμα εἰς τὴν κοιλίαν χωρεῖ, καὶ εἰς
entering into the mouth into the stomach goes, and into
18 ἀφεδρῶνα ἐκβάλλεται; τὰ δὲ ἐκπορευόμενα ἐκ τοῦ στόματος
(the) wastebowl is thrown out; the but (things) coming forth from the mouth
19 ἐκ τῆς καρδίας ἐξέρχεται, κἀκεῖνα κοινοῖ τὸν ἄνθρωπον. ἐκ
from the heart come forth, and those defile the man. from
γὰρ τῆς καρδίας ἐξέρχονται διαλογισμοὶ πονηροί, φόνοι,
For the heart come forth thoughts evil, murders,
μοιχεῖαι, πορνεῖαι, κλοπαί, ψευδομαρτυρίαι, βλασφημίαι·
adulteries, fornications, thefts, false witnessing, blasphemies;
20 ταῦτά ἐστι τὰ κοινοῦντα τὸν ἄνθρωπον· τὸ δὲ ἀνίπτοις
these things are the (ones) defiling the man; but with unwashed
χερσὶ φαγεῖν οὐ κοινοῖ τὸν ἄνθρωπον.
hands to eat not defiles the man.
21 Καὶ ἐξελθὼν ἐκεῖθεν ὁ Ἰησοῦς ἀνεχώρησεν εἰς τὰ μέρη
And going out from there — Jesus withdrew into the parts
22 Τύρου καὶ Σιδῶνος. καὶ ἰδού, γυνὴ Χαναναία ἀπὸ τῶν ὁρίων
of Tyre and Sidon. And behold, a woman Canaanite from — borders
ἐκείνων ἐξελθοῦσα ἐκραύγασεν αὐτῷ, λέγουσα, Ἐλέησόν
those coming forth cried out to Him, saying, Have pity on
23 με, Κύριε, υἱὲ Δαβίδ· ἡ θυγάτηρ μου κακῶς δαιμονίζεται. ὁ
me, Lord, Son of David; the daughter of me badly is demon-possessed. He
δὲ οὐκ ἀπεκρίθη αὐτῇ λόγον. καὶ προσελθόντες οἱ μαθηταὶ
But not answered her a word. And having come near the disciples
αὐτοῦ ἠρώτων αὐτόν, λέγοντες, Ἀπόλυσον αὐτήν, ὅτι
of Him asked Him, saying, Send away her, because
24 κράζει ὄπισθεν ἡμῶν. ὁ δὲ ἀποκριθεὶς εἶπεν, Οὐκ ἀπεστάλην
she cries out after us. He But answering said, not I was sent

to the lost sheep of *the* house of Israel. [25]But coming she worshiped Him, saying, Lord, help me! [26]But answering He said, It is not good to take the bread of the children and to throw *it* to the little dogs. [27]But she said, yes, Lord; for even the little dogs eat of the crumbs which fall from their masters' table. [28]Then answering Jesus said to her, O woman, your faith *is* great; let it be to you as you desire. And her daughter was healed from that hour.

[29]And moving from there, Jesus came beside the Sea of Galilee. And going up into the mountain, He sat there. [30]And great crowds came to Him, having with them *those* lame, blind, dumb, maimed, and many others. And they flung them down at the feet of Jesus. And He healed them; [31]so that the crowds marveled, seeing the dumb speaking, the maimed sound, the lame walking, and the blind seeing. And they glorified the God of Israel.

[32]But having called near His disciples, Jesus said, I am filled with pity on the crowd, because they already have remained with Me three days, and have nothing they may eat. And I do not desire to send them away fasting, that they may not faint in the way. [33]And His disciples said to Him, From where in a desert *will come* to us so many loaves as to satisfy so great a crowd? [34]And Jesus said to them, How many loaves do you have? And they said, Seven, and a few small fish. [35]And He commanded the crowds to recline on the ground. [36]And taking the seven loaves and the fish, giving thanks, He broke and gave to His disciples, and the disciples to the crowd. [37]And all ate, and were

25 εἰ μὴ εἰς τὰ πρόβατα τὰ ἀπολωλότα οἴκου Ἰσραήλ. ἡ δὲ
except to the sheep — lost of (the) house of Israel, she but
26 ἐλθοῦσα προσεκύνει αὐτῷ λέγουσα, Κύριε, βοήθει μοι. ὁ δὲ
coming worshiped Him, saying, Lord, help me! He But
ἀποκριθεὶς εἶπεν, Οὐκ ἔστι καλὸν λαβεῖν τὸν ἄρτον τῶν
answering said, not It is good to take the bread of the
27 τέκνων, καὶ βαλεῖν τοῖς κυναρίοις. ἡ δὲ εἶπε, Ναί, Κύριε· καὶ
children and to throw to the dogs. she And said, Yes, Lord, even
γὰρ τὰ κυνάρια ἐσθίει ἀπὸ τῶν ψιχίων τῶν πιπτόντων
For the dogs eat from the crumbs — falling
28 ἀπὸ τῆς τραπέζης τῶν κυρίων αὐτῶν. τότε ἀποκριθεὶς ὁ
from the table of the lords of them. Then answering —
Ἰησοῦς εἶπεν αὐτῇ, Ὦ γύναι, μεγάλη σου ἡ πίστις·
Jesus said to her, O woman, great (is) of you the faith;
γενηθήτω σοι ὡς θέλεις. καὶ ἰάθη ἡ θυγάτηρ αὐτῆς ἀπὸ τῆς
let it be to you as you will. And was healed the daughter of her from —
ὥρας ἐκείνης.
hour that.
29 Καὶ μεταβὰς ἐκεῖθεν ὁ Ἰησοῦς ἦλθε παρὰ τὴν θάλασσαν
And moving from there — Jesus came beside the Sea
30 τῆς Γαλιλαίας· καὶ ἀναβὰς εἰς τὸ ὄρος ἐκάθητο ἐκεῖ. καὶ
— of Galilee; and going up into the mountain He sat there. And
προσῆλθον αὐτῷ ὄχλοι πολλοί, ἔχοντες μεθ' ἑαυτῶν χωλούς,
came to Him crowds great, having with themselves (the) lame,
τυφλούς, κωφούς, κυλλούς, καὶ ἑτέρους πολλούς, καὶ ἔρριψαν
blind, dumb, maimed, and others many; and they flung
αὐτοὺς παρὰ τοὺς πόδας τοῦ Ἰησοῦ καὶ ἐθεράπευσεν αὐτούς·
them at the feet — of Jesus; and He healed them;
31 ὥστε τοὺς ὄχλους θαυμάσαι, βλέποντας κωφοὺς λαλοῦντας,
so that the crowds (had) to marvel, seeing dumb ones speaking,
κυλλοὺς ὑγιεῖς, χωλοὺς περιπατοῦντας, καὶ τυφλοὺς
maimed ones sound, lame ones walking, and blind ones
βλέποντας· καὶ ἐδόξασαν τὸν Θεὸν Ἰσραήλ.
seeing; and they glorified the God of Israel.
32 Ὁ δὲ Ἰησοῦς προσκαλεσάμενος τοὺς μαθητὰς αὐτοῦ εἶπε,
And Jesus having called near the disciples of Him said,
Σπλαγχνίζομαι ἐπὶ τὸν ὄχλον, ὅτι ἤδη ἡμέρας τρεῖς προσ-
I am filled with pity upon the crowd, because now days three they
μένουσί μοι, καὶ οὐκ ἔχουσι τί φάγωσι· καὶ ἀπολῦσαι
remain with Me, and not have anything they may eat; and to send away
33 αὐτοὺς νήστεις οὐ θέλω, μήποτε ἐκλυθῶσιν ἐν τῇ ὁδῷ. καὶ
them fasting not I desire, lest they be weary in the way. And
λέγουσιν αὐτῷ οἱ μαθηταὶ αὐτοῦ, Πόθεν ἡμῖν ἐν ἐρημίᾳ
say to Him the disciples of Him, From where to us in a desert
34 ἄρτοι τοσοῦτοι, ὥστε χορτάσαι ὄχλον τοσοῦτον; καὶ
loaves so many as to satisfy a crowd so great? And
λέγει αὐτοῖς ὁ Ἰησοῦς, Πόσους ἄρτους ἔχετε; οἱ δὲ εἶπον,
said to them — Jesus, How many loaves have you? they and said,
35 Ἑπτά, καὶ ὀλίγα ἰχθύδια. καὶ ἐκέλευσε τοῖς ὄχλοις ἀναπε-
Seven, and a few small fish, And He ordered the crowd to recline
36 σεῖν ἐπὶ τὴν γῆν· καὶ λαβὼν τοὺς ἑπτὰ ἄρτους καὶ τοὺς
on the ground; and taking the seven loaves and the
ἰχθύας, εὐχαριστήσας ἔκλασε, καὶ ἔδωκε τοῖς μαθηταῖς αὐτοῦ,
fish, giving thanks He broke, and gave to the disciples of Him,
37 οἱ δὲ μαθηταὶ τῷ ὄχλῳ. καὶ ἔφαγον πάντες καὶ ἐχορτά-
the and disciples to the crowd. And ate all, and were

satisfied. And they took up the excess pieces, seven lunch-baskets full. [38]And the ones eating were four thousand men, besides women and children. [39]And sending away the crowds, He went into the boat, and came to the borders of Magdala.

CHAPTER 16

[1]And having come, the Pharisees and Sadducees asked Him to show them a sign out of Heaven, tempting Him. [2]But answering He said to them, Evening coming on, you say, Clear sky; for the sky is red. [3]And at morning, Today a storm; for the sky is red, being overcast. Hypocrites! You indeed know how to discern the face of the sky, but you cannot the signs of the times. [4]An evil and adulterous generation seeks a sign, and a sign shall not be given to it, except the sign of Jonah the prophet. And leaving them, He went away.

[5]And His disciples coming to the other side, they forgot to take loaves. [6]And Jesus said to them, Watch! And beware of the leaven of the Pharisees and Sadducees. [7]And they reasoned among themselves, saying, Because we did not take loaves. [8]And knowing Jesus said to them, Why do you reason among yourselves because you took no loaves, little-faiths? [9]Do you not perceive nor recall the five loaves of the five thousand, and how many baskets you took up? [10]Nor the seven loaves of the four thousand, and how many lunch-baskets you took up? [11]How do you not perceive that *it was* not about loaves that I said to you to take heed from the leaven of the Pharisees and Sadducees? [12]Then they knew that He did not say to take heed from the leaven of bread, but from the teaching of the Pharisees and Sadducees.

σθησαν· καὶ ἦραν τὸ περισσεῦον τῶν κλασμάτων, ἑπτὰ
filled and they took up the excess of the fragments, seven
38 σπυρίδας πλήρεις. οἱ δὲ ἐσθίοντες ἦσαν τετρακισχίλιοι
lunch-baskets full. the And (ones) eating were four thousand
39 ἄνδρες, χωρὶς γυναικῶν καὶ παιδίων. καὶ ἀπολύσας τοὺς
men apart from women and children. And sending away the
ὄχλους ἐνέβη εἰς τὸ πλοῖον, καὶ ἦλθεν εἰς τὰ ὅρια Μαγδαλά.
crowds He went into the boat, and came into the borders of Magdala.

CHAPTER 16

1 Καὶ προσελθόντες οἱ Φαρισαῖοι καὶ Σαδδουκαῖοι πειρά-
And having come the Pharisees and Sadducees tempting
ζοντες ἐπηρώτησαν αὐτὸν σημεῖον ἐκ τοῦ οὐρανοῦ ἐπιδεῖξαι
asked Him a sign from — Heaven to show
2 αὐτοῖς. ὁ δὲ ἀποκριθεὶς εἶπεν αὐτοῖς, Ὀψίας γενομένης
them. He But answering said to them, Evening coming on
3 λέγετε, Εὐδία· πυρράζει γὰρ ὁ οὐρανός. καὶ πρωΐ, Σήμερον
you say, Clear sky; is red for the heaven. And at morning, Today
χειμών· πυρράζει γὰρ στυγνάζων ὁ οὐρανός. ὑποκριταί,
a storm; is red for being overcast the heaven. Hypocrites!
τὸ μὲν πρόσωπον τοῦ οὐρανοῦ γινώσκετε διακρίνειν, τὰ
the Indeed face of the heaven you know to discern, the
4 δὲ σημεῖα τῶν καιρῶν οὐ δύνασθε; γενεὰ πονηρὰ καὶ
but signs of the times not you are able. A generation evil and
μοιχαλὶς σημεῖον ἐπιζητεῖ· καὶ σημεῖον οὐ δοθήσεται αὐτῇ,
adulterous a sign seeks; and a sign not shall be given to it,
εἰ μὴ τὸ σημεῖον Ἰωνᾶ τοῦ προφήτου. καὶ καταλιπὼν
except the sign of Jonah the prophet. And forsaking
αὐτούς, ἀπῆλθε.
them He went away.

5 Καὶ ἐλθόντες οἱ μαθηταὶ αὐτοῦ εἰς τὸ πέραν ἐπελάθοντο
And coming the disciples of Him to the other side they forgot
6 ἄρτους λαβεῖν. ὁ δὲ Ἰησοῦς εἶπεν αὐτοῖς, Ὁρᾶτε καὶ προσ-
loaves to take. — And Jesus said to them, Beware and take
7 έχετε ἀπὸ τῆς ζύμης τῶν Φαρισαίων καὶ Σαδδουκαίων. οἱ
heed from the leaven of the Pharisees and the Sadducees. they
δὲ διελογίζοντο ἐν ἑαυτοῖς, λέγοντες ὅτι Ἄρτους οὐκ
But reasoned among themselves, saying, Because loaves not
8 ἐλάβομεν. γνοὺς δὲ ὁ Ἰησοῦς εἶπεν αὐτοῖς, Τί διαλογίζεσθε
we took. knowing And Jesus said to them, Why do you reason
9 ἐν ἑαυτοῖς, ὀλιγόπιστοι, ὅτι ἄρτους οὐκ ἐλάβετε; οὔπω
among yourselves, little-faiths, because loaves not you took? not
νοεῖτε, οὐδὲ μνημονεύετε τοὺς πέντε ἄρτους τῶν πεντακι-
you perceive nor remember the five loaves of the five
10 σχιλίων, καὶ πόσους κοφίνους ἐλάβετε; οὐδὲ τοὺς ἑπτὰ
thousand, and how many baskets you took? Neither the seven
ἄρτους τῶν τετρακισχιλίων, καὶ πόσας σπυρίδας ἐλάβετε;
loaves of the four thousand, and how many lunch-baskets you took?
11 πῶς οὐ νοεῖτε, ὅτι οὐ περὶ ἄρτου εἶπον ὑμῖν προσέχειν ἀπὸ
How not perceive that not about loaves I said to you to take heed from
12 τῆς ζύμης τῶν Φαρισαίων καὶ Σαδδουκαίων; τότε συνῆκαν
the leaven of the Pharisees and Sadducees. Then they knew
ὅτι οὐκ εἶπε προσέχειν ἀπὸ τῆς ζύμης τοῦ ἄρτου, ἀλλ' ἀπὸ
that not He said to take heed from the leaven of bread, but from
τῆς διδαχῆς τῶν Φαρισαίων καὶ Σαδδουκαίων.
the teaching of the Pharisees and Sadducees.

[13] And coming into the parts of Caesarea of Philip, Jesus questioned His disciples, saying, Whom do men say the Son of man is? [14] And they said, Some *say* John the Baptist; and others Elijah; and others Jeremiah, or one of the prophets. [15] He said to them, But you, whom do you say Me to be? [16] And answering, Simon Peter said, You are the Christ, the Son of the living God. [17] And answering Jesus said to him, Blessed are you, Simon, son of Jonah, for flesh and blood did not reveal *it* to you, but My Father in Heaven. [18] And I also say to you that you are Peter, and on this rock I will build My church, and *the* gates of Hades will not prevail against her. [19] And I will give to you the keys of the kingdom of Heaven. And whatever you bind on earth shall occur, having already been bound in Heaven. And whatever you may loose on the earth shall be, having been already loosed in Heaven. [20] Then He warned His disciples that they should not tell anyone that He is Jesus the Christ.

[21] From that time Jesus began to show to His disciples that it was necessary for Him to go away to Jerusalem, and to suffer many things from the elders and chief priests and scribes, and to be killed, and to be raised on the third day. [22] And having taken Him near, Peter began to rebuke Him, saying, *God be* gracious to You, Lord; this shall never be to You. [23] But turning He said to Peter, Go behind Me, Satan! You are an offense to Me, for your thoughts are not of the things of God, but the things of men.

[24] Then Jesus said to His disciples, If anyone desires to come after Me, let him deny himself, and let him bear his cross, and let him follow Me. [25] For whoever may desire to save his soul

13 Ἐλθὼν δὲ ὁ Ἰησοῦς εἰς τὰ μέρη Καισαρείας τῆς Φιλίππου
coming And — Jesus into the parts of Caesarea — of Philip
ἠρώτα τοὺς μαθητὰς αὐτοῦ, λέγων, Τίνα με λέγουσιν οἱ
He queried the disciples of Him, saying, Whom Me do say —
14 ἄνθρωποι εἶναι, τὸν υἱὸν τοῦ ἀνθρώπου ; οἱ δὲ εἶπον, Οἱ μὲν
men to be, the Son — of man? they And said, Some
Ἰωάννην τὸν Βαπτιστήν· ἄλλοι δὲ Ἠλίαν· ἕτεροι δὲ
John the Baptist; others and Elijah; others and
15 Ἰερεμίαν, ἢ ἕνα τῶν προφητῶν. λέγει αὐτοῖς, Ὑμεῖς δὲ τίνα
Jeremiah, or one of the prophets. He says to them, you But, whom
16 με λέγετε εἶναι ; ἀποκριθεὶς δὲ Σίμων Πέτρος εἶπε, Σὺ εἶ ὁ
Me do you say to be? answering And Simon Peter said, You are the
17 Χριστός, ὁ υἱὸς τοῦ Θεοῦ τοῦ ζῶντος. καὶ ἀποκριθεὶς ὁ
Christ, the Son — of God the living. And answering —
Ἰησοῦς εἶπεν αὐτῷ, Μακάριος εἶ, Σίμων Βὰρ Ἰωνᾶ, ὅτι σὰρξ
Jesus said to him, Blessed are you, Simon Bar-jonah because flesh
καὶ αἷμα οὐκ ἀπεκάλυψέ σοι, ἀλλ᾽ ὁ πατήρ μου ὁ ἐν τοῖς
and blood not did reveal to you, but the Father of Me — in the
18 οὐρανοῖς. κἀγὼ δέ σοι λέγω, ὅτι σὺ εἶ Πέτρος, καὶ ἐπὶ ταύτῃ
heavens. I also And to you say, — You are Peter, and on this
τῇ πέτρᾳ οἰκοδομήσω μου τὴν ἐκκλησίαν, καὶ πύλαι ᾅδου
— rock I will build of Me the church, and (the) gates of Hades
19 οὐ κατισχύσουσιν αὐτῆς. καὶ δώσω σοὶ τὰς κλεῖς τῆς
not will prevail against her. And I will give to you the keys of the
βασιλείας τῶν οὐρανῶν· καὶ ὃ ἐὰν δήσῃς ἐπὶ τῆς γῆς, ἔσται
kingdom of the heavens, and whatever you bind on the earth shall be
δεδεμένον ἐν τοῖς οὐρανοῖς· καὶ ὃ ἐὰν λύσῃς ἐπὶ τῆς γῆς,
having been bound in the heavens, and whatever you loose on the earth
20 ἔσται λελυμένον ἐν τοῖς οὐρανοῖς. τότε διεστείλατο τοῖς
shall be, having been loosed in the heavens. Then He warned the
μαθηταῖς αὐτοῦ ἵνα μηδενὶ εἴπωσιν ὅτι αὐτός ἐστιν Ἰησοῦς
disciples of Him that to no one they may tell that He is Jesus
ὁ Χριστός.
the Christ.

21 Ἀπὸ τότε ἤρξατο ὁ Ἰησοῦς δεικνύειν τοῖς μαθηταῖς
From then began — Jesus to show to the disciples
αὐτοῦ ὅτι δεῖ αὐτὸν ἀπελθεῖν εἰς Ἱεροσόλυμα, καὶ πολλὰ
of Him that it behoves Him to go away to Jerusalem, and many things
παθεῖν ἀπὸ τῶν πρεσβυτέρων καὶ ἀρχιερέων καὶ γραμ-
to suffer from the elders and chief priests and scribes,
ματέων, καὶ ἀποκτανθῆναι, καὶ τῇ τρίτῃ ἡμέρᾳ ἐγερθῆναι.
and to be killed, and on the third day to be raised.
22 καὶ προσλαβόμενος αὐτὸν ὁ Πέτρος ἤρξατο ἐπιτιμᾷν αὐτῷ
And taking near Him, — Peter began to rebuke Him,
23 λέγων, Ἵλεώς σοι, Κύριε· οὐ μὴ ἔσται σοι τοῦτο. ὁ δὲ στραφεὶς
saying, Gracious to You, Lord, in no way shall be to You this. He But turning
εἶπε τῷ Πέτρῳ, Ὕπαγε ὀπίσω μου, Σατανᾶ, σκάνδαλόν μου
said — to Peter, Go behind Me, Satan, an offense to Me
εἶ· ὅτι οὐ φρονεῖς τὰ τοῦ Θεοῦ, ἀλλὰ τὰ τῶν ἀνθρώπων.
you are, for not you think the things of God, but the things — of men.
24 τότε ὁ Ἰησοῦς εἶπε τοῖς μαθηταῖς αὐτοῦ, Εἴ τις θέλει ὀπίσω
Then — Jesus said to the disciples of Him, If anyone desires after
μου ἐλθεῖν, ἀπαρνησάσθω ἑαυτόν, καὶ ἀράτω τὸν σταυρὸν
Me to come, let him deny himself, and let him bear the cross
25 αὐτοῦ, καὶ ἀκολουθείτω μοι. ὃς γὰρ ἂν θέλῃ τὴν ψυχὴν
of him, and let him follow Me. whoever For may desire the soul

will lose it. But whoever may lose his soul for My sake will find it. [26]For what will a man be benefited if he should gain the whole world, but forfeits his soul? Or what will a man give *as* an exchange *for* his soul? [27]For the son of man is about to come in the glory of His Father, with His angels. And then He will give reward to each according to his works. [28]Truly I say to you, There are some standing here who in no way will taste of death until they see the Son of man coming in His kingdom.

CHAPTER 17

[1]And after six days, Jesus took Peter and James, and his brother John, and brought them up into a high mountain apart. [2]And He was transfigured before them, and His face shone like the sun, and His clothing became white as the light. [3]And, behold! Moses and Elijah appeared to them, talking with Him. [4]And answering Peter said to Jesus, Lord, it is good for us to be here. If You will, let us make three tabernacles here, one for You, one for Moses, and one for Elijah. [5]While he *was* yet speaking, behold, a bright cloud overshadowed them. And, behold, a voice out of the cloud saying, This is My beloved Son, in whom I have found delight; hear Him. [6]And hearing the disciples fell on their face and were greatly terrified. [7]And coming near, Jesus touched them and said, Rise up, and do not be terrified. [8]And lifting up their eyes, they did not see anyone except Jesus alone. [9]And as they were going down from the mountain,

αὐτοῦ σῶσαι ἀπολέσει αὐτήν· ὃς δ' ἂν ἀπολέσῃ τὴν ψυχὴν
of him to save he will lose it whoever and may lose the soul

26 αὐτοῦ ἕνεκεν ἐμοῦ εὑρήσει αὐτήν· τί γὰρ ὠφελεῖται ἄνθρω-
of him for the sake of Me,he will find it. what For will be benefited a

πος ἐὰν τὸν κόσμον ὅλον κερδήσῃ, τὴν δὲ ψυχὴν αὐτοῦ
man if the world whole he should gain, the but soul of him

27 ζημιωθῇ; ἢ τί δώσει ἄνθρωπος ἀντάλλαγμα τῆς ψυχῆς
forfeits? Or what will give a man (as) an exchange (for) the soul

αὐτοῦ; μέλλει γὰρ ὁ υἱὸς τοῦ ἀνθρώπου ἔρχεσθαι ἐν τῇ
of him? is about For the Son — of man to come in the

δόξῃ τοῦ πατρὸς αὐτοῦ μετὰ τῶν ἀγγέλων αὐτοῦ, καὶ
glory of the Father of Him with the angels of Him, and

28 τότε ἀποδώσει ἑκάστῳ κατὰ τὴν πρᾶξιν αὐτοῦ. ἀμὴν λέγω
then he will reward to each according to the works of him. Truly I say

ὑμῖν, εἰσί τινες τῶν ὧδε ἑστηκότων, οἵτινες ού μὴ γεύ-
to you, there are some — here standing who not at all will

σωνται θανάτου, ἕως ἂν ἴδωσι τὸν υἱὸν τοῦ ἀνθρώπου
taste of death until they see the Son — of man

ἐρχόμενον ἐν τῇ βασιλείᾳ αὐτοῦ.
coming in the kingdom of Him.

CHAPTER 17

1 Καὶ μεθ' ἡμέρας ἓξ παραλαμβάνει ὁ Ἰησοῦς τὸν Πέτρον καὶ
And after days six takes — Jesus — Peter and

Ἰάκωβον καὶ Ἰωάννην τὸν ἀδελφὸν αὐτοῦ, καὶ ἀναφέρει
James and John the brother of him, and leads up

2 αὐτοὺς εἰς ὄρος ὑψηλὸν κατ' ἰδίαν. καὶ μετεμορφώθη
them into mountain a high privately. And He was transfigured

ἔμπροσθεν αὐτῶν, καὶ ἔλαμψε τὸ πρόσωπον αὐτοῦ ὡς ὁ
before them, and shone the face of Him like the

3 ἥλιος, τὰ δὲ ἱμάτια αὐτοῦ ἐγένετο λευκὰ ὡς τὸ φῶς. καὶ ἰδού,
sun, the and garments of Him became white as the light, and behold,

ὤφθησαν αὐτοῖς Μωσῆς καὶ Ἠλίας, μετ' αὐτοῦ συλλαλοῦν-
appeared to them Moses and Elijah with Him talking to-

4 τες. ἀποκριθεὶς δὲ ὁ Πέτρος εἶπε τῷ Ἰησοῦ, Κύριε, καλόν
gether answering And — Peter said — to Jesus, Lord, good

ἐστιν ἡμᾶς ὧδε εἶναι· εἰ θέλεις, ποιήσωμεν ὧδε τρεῖς σκηνάς,
it is for us here to be. If You desire, let us make here three tents,

5 σοὶ μίαν, καὶ Μωσῇ μίαν, καὶ μίαν Ἠλίᾳ. ἔτι αὐτοῦ λαλοῦν-
for You one, and for Moses one, and one for Elijah. While he (was) speaking,

τος, ἰδού, νεφέλη φωτεινὴ ἐπεσκίασεν αὐτούς· καὶ ἰδού,
behold, a cloud radiant overshadowed them, and behold,

φωνὴ ἐκ τῆς νεφέλης, λέγουσα, Οὗτός ἐστιν ὁ υἱός μου
a voice out of the cloud, saying, This is the Son of Me,

6 ὁ ἀγαπητός, ἐν ᾧ εὐδόκησα· αὐτοῦ ἀκούετε. καὶ ἀκούσαντες
the beloved, in whom I delight; of Him hear. And hearing,

οἱ μαθηταὶ ἔπεσον ἐπὶ πρόσωπον αὐτῶν, καὶ ἐφοβήθησαν
the disciples fell on the face of them, and were terrified

7 σφόδρα. καὶ προσελθὼν ὁ Ἰησοῦς ἥψατο αὐτῶν καὶ εἶπεν,
greatly. And coming near,— Jesus touched them, and said,

8 Ἐγέρθητε καὶ μὴ φοβεῖσθε. ἐπάραντες δὲ τοὺς ὀφθαλμοὺς
Arise, and not fear. lifting up And the eyes

αὐτῶν, οὐδένα εἶδον, εἰ μὴ τὸν Ἰησοῦν μόνον.
of them, no one they saw except — Jesus alone.

9 Καὶ καταβαινόντων αὐτῶν ἀπὸ τοῦ ὄρους, ἐνετείλατο
And coming down they from the mountain, enjoined

Jesus charged them, saying, Tell the vision to no one until the Son of man is raised from the dead. [10]And His disciples asked Him, saying, Why then do the scribes say that Elijah must come first? [11]And answering Jesus said to them, Elijah indeed comes first, and shall restore all things. [12]But I say to you, Elijah has already come, and they did not know him, but did to him whatever they desired. So also the Son of man is about to suffer by them. [13]Then the disciples understood that He spoke to them about John the Baptist.

[14]And they having come to the crowd, a man came down to Him, kneeling down to Him, and saying, [15]Lord, pity my son. For he is moonstruck and suffers miserably. For he often falls into the fire, and often into the water. [16]And I brought him to Your disciples, and they were not able to heal him. [17]And answering Jesus said, O faithless and perverted generation! How long will I be with you? How long shall I bear with you? Bring him here to Me. [18]And Jesus rebuked it, and the demon went out from him; and the boy was healed from that hour.

[19]Then coming up to Jesus privately, the disciples said, Why were we not able to cast him out? [20]And Jesus said to them, Because of your unbelief. For truly I say to you, If you have faith as a grain of mustard, you shall say to this mountain, Move from here to there! And it will move. And nothing shall be impossible to you. [21]But this one does not go out except by prayer and fasting.

[22]And while they were staying in Galilee, Jesus said to them, The Son of man is about to be delivered into *the* hands of men.

αὐτοῖς ὁ Ἰησοῦς, λέγων, Μηδενὶ εἴπητε τὸ ὅραμα, ἕως οὗ ὁ
them — Jesus, saying, To no one tell the vision, until the

10 υἱὸς τοῦ ἀνθρώπου ἐκ νεκρῶν ἀναστῇ. καὶ ἐπηρώτησαν
Son — of man from the dead is raised. And questioned

αὐτὸν οἱ μαθηταὶ αὐτοῦ λέγοντες, Τί οὖν οἱ γραμματεῖς
Him the disciples of Him saying, Why then the scribes

11 λέγουσιν ὅτι Ἠλίαν δεῖ ἐλθεῖν πρῶτον; ὁ δὲ Ἰησοῦς ἀποκρι-
say that Elijah it behoves to come first? And Jesus, answering

θεὶς εἶπεν αὐτοῖς, Ἠλίας μὲν ἔρχεται πρῶτον, καὶ ἀποκατα-
said to them, Elijah indeed comes first and shall restore

12 στήσει πάντα· λέγω δὲ ὑμῖν ὅτι Ἠλίας ἤδη ἦλθε, καὶ οὐκ
all things; I tell but you that Elijah already is come, and not

ἐπέγνωσαν αὐτόν, ἀλλ' ἐποίησαν ἐν αὐτῷ ὅσα ἠθέλησαν·
they knew him, but did to him whatever they wished;

οὕτω καὶ ὁ υἱὸς τοῦ ἀνθρώπου μέλλει πάσχειν ὑπ' αὐτῶν.
thus also the Son — of man is about to suffer by them.

13 τότε συνῆκαν οἱ μαθηταὶ ὅτι περὶ Ἰωάννου τοῦ Βαπτιστοῦ
Then understood the disciples that concerning John the Baptist

εἶπεν αὐτοῖς.
He spoke to them.

14 Καὶ ἐλθόντων αὐτῶν πρὸς τὸν ὄχλον, προσῆλθεν αὐτῷ
And having come they toward the crowd, came near to Him

15 ἄνθρωπος γονυπετῶν αὐτῷ καὶ λέγων, Κύριε, ἐλέησόν μου
a man kneeling down to Him and saying, Lord, pity of me

τὸν υἱόν, ὅτι σεληνιάζεται καὶ κακῶς πάσχει· πολλάκις γὰρ
the son, because he is moonstruck and illness suffers; often for

16 πίπτει εἰς τὸ πῦρ, καὶ πολλάκις εἰς τὸ ὕδωρ. καὶ προσήνεγκα
he falls into the fire, and often into the water. And I brought

αὐτὸν τοῖς μαθηταῖς σου, καὶ οὐκ ἠδυνήθησαν αὐτὸν
him to the disciples of You, and not they were able him

17 θεραπεῦσαι. ἀποκριθεὶς δὲ ὁ Ἰησοῦς εἶπεν, Ὦ γενεὰ ἄπιστος
to heal. answering And — Jesus said, O generation faithless

καὶ διεστραμμένη, ἕως πότε ἔσομαι μεθ' ὑμῶν; ἕως πότε
and perverted, until when shall I be with you? Until when

18 ἀνέξομαι ὑμῶν; φέρετέ μοι αὐτὸν ὧδε. καὶ ἐπετίμησεν αὐτῷ
shall I endure you? Bring to Me him here. And rebuked it

ὁ Ἰησοῦς, καὶ ἐξῆλθεν ἀπ' αὐτοῦ τὸ δαιμόνιον, καὶ ἐθεραπεύ-
— Jesus, and came out from him the demon, and was healed

19 θη ὁ παῖς ἀπὸ τῆς ὥρας ἐκείνης. τότε προσελθόντες οἱ
the boy from — hour that. Then coming up the

μαθηταὶ τῷ Ἰησοῦ κατ' ἰδίαν εἶπον, Διατί ἡμεῖς οὐκ ἠδυνή-
disciples — to Jesus privately said, Why we not were

20 θημεν ἐκβαλεῖν αὐτό; ὁ δὲ Ἰησοῦς εἶπεν αὐτοῖς, Διὰ τὴν
able to cast out him? — And Jesus said to them, Through the

ἀπιστίαν ὑμῶν. ἀμὴν γὰρ λέγω ὑμῖν, ἐὰν ἔχητε πίστιν ὡς
unbelief of you. truly For I say to you, if you have faith as

κόκκον σινάπεως, ἐρεῖτε τῷ ὄρει τούτῳ, Μεταβηθι ἐντεῦθεν
a grain of mustard, you will say to mountain this, Move from here

21 ἐκεῖ, καὶ μεταβήσεται· καὶ οὐδὲν ἀδυνατήσει ὑμῖν. τοῦτο δὲ
to there and it will move, and nothing shall be impossible to you. this But

τὸ γένος οὐκ ἐκπορεύεται εἰ μὴ ἐν προσευχῇ καὶ νηστείᾳ.
kind not does go out except by prayer and fasting.

22 Ἀναστρεφομένων δὲ αὐτῶν ἐν τῇ Γαλιλαίᾳ, εἶπεν αὐτοῖς
while were remaining And they in Galilee, said to them

ὁ Ἰησοῦς, Μέλλει ὁ υἱὸς τοῦ ἀνθρώπου παραδίδοσθαι εἰς
— Jesus, is about the Son -- of man to be delivered into

23 And they will kill Him; and the third day He will be raised. And they grieved exceedingly.

24 And they coming into Capernaum, those receiving the didrachmas came to Peter and said, Does your Teacher pay the didrachmas? 25 He said, Yes. And when he entered into the house, Jesus anticipated him, saying, What do you think, Simon? From whom do the kings of the earth receive custom or tribute? From their sons, or from strangers? 26 Peter said to Him, From strangers. Jesus said to him, Then truly the sons are free. 27 But that we may not offend them, having gone to the sea, throw in a hook, and take the first fish coming up. And opening its mouth, you will find a stater. Taking that, give to them for you and Me.

CHAPTER 18

1 In that hour the disciples came to Jesus, saying, Who then is greater in the kingdom of Heaven? 2 And having called forward a little child, Jesus set him in their midst. 3 And *He* said, Truly I say to you, Unless you be converted, and become as the little children, in no way can you enter into the kingdom of Heaven.

4 Therefore, whoever will humble himself as this little child, this one is the greater in the kingdom of Heaven. 5 And whoever will receive one such little child in My name receives Me. 6 But whoever causes one of these little *ones* believing in Me to offend, it is better for him that a millstone turned by an ass should be hung on his neck, and he be sunk in the depth of the sea. 7 Woe to the world from *its* offenses! It is *a* necessity

23 χεῖρας ἀνθρώπων, καὶ ἀποκτενοῦσιν αὐτόν, καὶ τῇ τρίτῃ
(the) hands of men, and they will kill Him, and on the third

ἡμέρᾳ ἐγερθήσεται. καὶ ἐλυπήθησαν σφόδρα.
day He will be raised. And they grieved exceedingly.

24 Ἐλθόντων δὲ αὐτῶν εἰς Καπερναούμ, προσῆλθον οἱ τὰ
coming And they into Capernaum came up those the

δίδραχμα λαμβάνοντες τῷ Πέτρῳ καὶ εἶπον, Ὁ διδάσκαλος
didrachmas receiving — to Peter, and said, The teacher

25 ὑμῶν οὐ τελεῖ τὰ δίδραχμα; λέγει, Ναί. καὶ ὅτε εἰσῆλθεν εἰς
of you not pays the didrachma? He says, Yes. And when he entered into

τὴν οἰκίαν, προέφθασεν αὐτὸν ὁ Ἰησοῦς, λέγων, Τί σοι
the house, anticipated him — Jesus, saying, What you

δοκεῖ, Σίμων; οἱ βασιλεῖς τῆς γῆς ἀπὸ τίνων λαμβάνουσι
think, Simon? The kings of the earth, from whom do they receive

τέλη ἢ κῆνσον; ἀπὸ τῶν υἱῶν αὐτῶν, ἢ ἀπὸ τῶν
custom or poll-tax? From the sons of them, or from the

26 ἀλλοτρίων; λέγει αὐτῷ ὁ Πέτρος, Ἀπὸ τῶν ἀλλοτρίων.
strangers? says to Him — Peter, From the strangers.

27 ἔφη αὐτῷ ὁ Ἰησοῦς, Ἄραγε ἐλεύθεροί εἰσιν οἱ υἱοί. ἵνα δὲ μὴ
said to him — Jesus, Then indeed free are the sons. that But not

σκανδαλίσωμεν αὐτούς, πορευθεὶς εἰς τὴν θάλασσαν βάλε
we may offend them, having gone to the sea, throw

ἄγκιστρον, καὶ τὸν ἀναβάντα πρῶτον ἰχθὺν ἆρον· καὶ
a hook, and the coming up first fish take, and

ἀνοίξας τὸ στόμα αὐτοῦ, εὑρήσεις στατῆρα· ἐκεῖνον λαβὼν
opening the mouth of it, you will find a stater; that taking

δὸς αὐτοῖς ἀντὶ ἐμοῦ καὶ σοῦ.
give them for Me and you.

CHAPTER 18

1 Ἐν ἐκείνῃ τῇ ὥρᾳ προσῆλθον οἱ μαθηταὶ τῷ Ἰησοῦ,
In that — hour, came up the disciples — to Jesus,

λέγοντες Τίς ἄρα μείζων ἐστὶν ἐν τῇ βασιλείᾳ τῶν οὐρα-
saying, Who then greater is in the kingdom of the heavens?

2 νῶν; καὶ προσκαλεσάμενος ὁ Ἰησοῦς παιδίον ἔστησεν
And calling forward — Jesus a child, He set

3 αὐτὸ ἐν μέσῳ αὐτῶν, καὶ εἶπεν, Ἀμὴν λέγω ὑμῖν, ἐὰν μὴ
him in the midst of them, and said, Truly I say to you, except

στραφῆτε καὶ γένησθε ὡς τὰ παιδία, οὐ μὴ εἰσέλθητε εἰς τὴν
you convert and become as the children, cannot you enter into the

4 βασιλείαν τῶν οὐρανῶν. ὅστις οὖν ταπεινώσῃ ἑαυτὸν ὡς τὸ
kingdom of the heavens. Whoever then will humble himself as —

παιδίον τοῦτο, οὗτός ἐστιν ὁ μείζων ἐν τῇ βασιλείᾳ τῶν
child this, this (one) is the greater in the kingdom of the

5 οὐρανῶν. καὶ ὃς ἐὰν δέξηται παιδίον τοιοῦτον ἓν ἐπὶ τῷ
heavens. And whoever receives child such one on the

6 ὀνόματί μου, ἐμὲ δέχεται· ὃς δ' ἂν σκανδαλίσῃ ἕνα τῶν
name of Me, Me receives. who But ever causes to offend one of

μικρῶν τούτων τῶν πιστευόντων εἰς ἐμέ, συμφέρει αὐτῷ ἵνα
little (ones) these — believing in Me, it is gain for him that

κρεμασθῇ μύλος ὀνικὸς ἐπὶ τὸν τράχηλον αὐτοῦ, καὶ κατα-
be hung a millstone an ass's on the neck of him, and he be

7 ποντισθῇ ἐν τῷ πελάγει τῆς θαλάσσης. οὐαὶ τῷ κόσμῳ
sunk in the depth of the sea. Woe to the world

ἀπὸ τῶν σκανδάλων· ἀνάγκη γάρ ἐστιν ἐλθεῖν τὰ σκάνδαλα·
from — offenses; necessity for it is to come the offenses,

for the offenses to come, yet woe to that man through whom the offense comes! [8]And if your hand or your foot offends you, cut it off and throw *it* from you—it is good for you to enter into life maimed, than having two hands or two feet to be thrown into the everlasting fire. [9]And if your eye offends you, pluck it out and throw *it* from you—for it is good for you to enter into life one-eyed than having two eyes to be thrown into the Hell of fire. [10]See *that* you do not despise one of these little *ones*, for I tell you that their angels in Heaven continually look on the face of My Father in Heaven. [11]For the Son of man has come to save that which was lost. [12]What do you think? If there be to any man a hundred sheep, and one of them strays away, will he not leave the ninety-nine on the mountains; *and* going, he seek the straying *one*? [13]And if he happens to find it, truly I say to you that he rejoices over it more than over the ninety-nine not going astray. [14]So it is not *the* will before your Father in Heaven that one of these little *ones* should perish.

[15]But if your brother sins against you, go and reprove him between you and him alone. If he hears you, you have gained your brother. [16]But if he does not hear, take one or two more with you, so that on *the* mouth of two or three witnesses every word may stand. [17]But if he fails to hear them, tell *it* to the church. And if he also fails to hear the church, let him be to you as the heathen and the tax-collectors. [18]Truly say to you, Whatever you bind on the earth shall occur, having been bound in Heaven. And whatever you loose on the earth shall

πλὴν οὐαὶ τῷ ἀνθρωπῳ ἐκείνῳ, δι᾽ οὗ τὸ σκάνδαλον
yet woe to man that through whom the offense
8 ἔρχεται. εἰ δὲ ἡ χείρ σου ἢ ὁ πούς σου σκανδαλίζει σε,
comes! if And the hand of you or the foot of you offends you,
ἔκκοψον αὐτὰ καὶ βάλε ἀπὸ σοῦ· καλόν σοι ἐστὶν εἰσελθεῖν
cut off it and throw from you; good for you it is to enter
εἰς τὴν ζωὴν χωλὸν ἢ κυλλόν, ἢ δύο χεῖρας ἢ δύο πόδας
into — life lame or maimed than two hands or two feet
9 ἔχοντα βληθῆναι εἰς τὸ πῦρ τὸ αἰώνιον. καὶ εἰ ὁ ὀφθαλμός
having to be thrown into the fire — everlasting. And if the eye
σου σκανδαλίζει σε, ἔξελε αὐτὸν καὶ βάλε ἀπὸ σοῦ· καλόν
of you offends you, pluck out it and throw from you; good
σοι ἐστὶ μονόφθαλμον εἰς τὴν ζωὴν εἰσελθεῖν, ἢ δύο ὀφθαλ-
for you it is one-eyed into — life to enter, than two eyes
10 μοὺς ἔχοντα βληθῆναι εἰς τὴν γέενναν τοῦ πυρός. ὁρᾶτε μὴ
having to be thrown into Gehenna — of fire. See (that) not
καταφρονήσητε ἑνὸς τῶν μικρῶν τούτων, λέγω γὰρ ὑμῖν
you despise one of little (ones) these; I for you
ὅτι οἱ ἄγγελοι αὐτῶν ἐν οὐρανοῖς διὰ παντὸς βλέπουσι τὸ
that the angels of them in heavens always behold the
11 πρόσωπον τοῦ πατρός μου τοῦ ἐν οὐρανοῖς. ἦλθε γὰρ ὁ
face of the Father of Me — in heavens. is come For the
12 υἱὸς τοῦ ἀνθρώπου σῶσαι τὸ ἀπολωλός. τί ὑμῖν δοκεῖ ; ἐὰν
Son — of man to save that which was lost. What to you seems; if
γένηταί τινι ἀνθρώπῳ ἑκατὸν πρόβατα, καὶ πλανηθῇ ἓν ἐξ
there be to any man a hundred sheep, and strays one of
αὐτῶν· οὐχὶ ἀφεὶς τὰ ἐννενηκονταεννέα, ἐπὶ τὰ ὄρη πορευθεὶς
them, not will he leave the ninety-nine on the mounts, going
13 ζητεῖ τὸ πλανώμενον ; καὶ ἐὰν γένηται εὑρεῖν αὐτό, ἀμὴν
he seeks the straying (one)? And if he happens to find it, truly
λέγω ὑμῖν ὅτι χαίρει ἐπ᾽ αὐτῷ μᾶλλον, ἢ ἐπὶ τοῖς ἐννενη-
I say to you that he rejoices over it more than over the ninety-
14 κονταεννέα τοῖς μὴ πεπλανημένοις. οὕτως οὐκ ἔστι θέλημα
nine — not going astray. So not it is the will
ἔμπροσθεν τοῦ πατρὸς ὑμῶν τοῦ ἐν οὐρανοῖς, ἵνα ἀπόληται
before the Father of you — in Heaven that should perish
εἷς τῶν μικρῶν τούτων.
one of little (ones) these.
15 Ἐὰν δὲ ἁμαρτήσῃ εἰς σὲ ὁ ἀδελφός σου, ὕπαγε καὶ
if But sins against you the brother of you, go and
ἔλεγξον αὐτὸν μεταξὺ σοῦ καὶ αὐτοῦ μόνου. ἐάν σου
reprove him between you and him alone. If you
16 ἀκούσῃ, ἐκέρδησας τὸν ἀδελφόν σου· ἐὰν δὲ μὴ ἀκούσῃ,
he hear, you have gained the brother of you; if but not he hear,
παράλαβε μετὰ σοῦ ἔτι ἕνα ἢ δύο, ἵνα ἐπὶ στόματος δύο
take along with you besides one or two, that upon (the) mouth of two
17 μαρτύρων ἢ τριῶν σταθῇ πᾶν ῥῆμα. ἐὰν δὲ παρακούσῃ
witnesses or three may stand every word. if But he fails to hear
αὐτῶν, εἰπὲ τῇ ἐκκλησίᾳ· ἐὰν δὲ καὶ τῆς ἐκκλησίας
them, tell to the church; if and even the church
18 παρακούσῃ, ἔστω σοι ὥσπερ ὁ ἐθνικὸς καὶ ὁ τελώνης. ἀμὴν
he fails to hear, let him be to you as the nations and the tax-collector. Truly
λέγω ὑμῖν, ὅσα ἐὰν δήσητε ἐπὶ τῆς γῆς, ἔσται δεδεμένα ἐν
I say to you, whatever you bind on the earth shall occur, being bound in
τῷ οὐρανῷ· καὶ ὅσα ἐὰν λύσητε ἐπὶ τῆς γῆς, ἔσται λελυμένα
— Heaven; and whatever you loose on the earth shall occur, being loosed

occur, having been loosed in Heaven. [19] Again I say to you, If two of you agree on earth as to anything, whatever they shall ask, it shall be to them from My Father in Heaven. [20] For where two or three are gathered together in My name, there I am in their midst.

[21] Then coming up to Him, Peter said, Lord, how often shall my brother sin against me, and I forgive him? Until seven times? [22] Jesus said to him, I do not say to you, Until seven times, but, Until seventy times seven. [23] Because of this the kingdom of Heaven has been compared to a man, a king who decided to take account with his slaves. [24] And beginning to reckon, one debtor of ten thousand talents was brought near to him. [25] But he not having *any* to pay, the lord commanded him to be sold, also his wife and children, and all things, as much as he had, even to pay back. [26] Then falling down, the slave bowed the knee to him, saying, Lord, have patience with me, and I will pay all to you. [27] And being moved with pity, the lord of that slave released him, and forgave him the loan. [28] But going out, the slave found one of his fellow-slaves who owed him a hundred denarii. And seizing him, he choked *him,* saying, Pay me whatever you owe. [29] Then falling down at his feet, his fellow-slave begged him, saying, Have patience with me, and I will pay all to you. [30] But he would not, but going out he threw him into prison, until he pay back the *amount* owing. [31] But his fellow-slaves seeing the things happening, they were greatly grieved. And coming *they* reported all the things happening to their lord. [32] Then calling him near, his lord said to him, Wicked slave! I

19 ἐν τῷ οὐρανῷ. πάλιν λέγω ὑμῖν, ὅτι ἐὰν δύο ὑμῶν συμφωνή-
in — Heaven. Again, I say to you that if two of you may agree
σωσιν ἐπὶ τῆς γῆς περὶ παντὸς πράγματος οὗ ἐὰν αἰτή-
on the earth concerning every matter, whatever they
σωνται, γενήσεται αὐτοῖς παρὰ τοῦ πατρός μου τοῦ ἐν
may ask it shall occur to them from the Father of Me — in
20 οὐρανοῖς. οὗ γάρ εἰσι δύο ἢ τρεῖς συνηγμένοι εἰς τὸ ἐμὸν
heavens. where For are two or three gathered together in — my
ὄνομα, ἐκεῖ εἰμὶ ἐν μέσῳ αὐτῶν.
name, there I am in midst of them.
21 Τότε προσελθὼν αὐτῷ ὁ Πέτρος εἶπε, Κύριε, ποσάκις
Then coming up to Him — Peter said, Lord, how often
ἁμαρτήσει εἰς ἐμὲ ὁ ἀδελφός μου, καὶ ἀφήσω αὐτῷ; ἕως
shall sin against me the brother of me, and I forgive him? Until
22 ἑπτάκις; λέγει αὐτῷ ὁ Ἰησοῦς, Οὐ λέγω σοι ἕως ἑπτάκις,
seven times? Says to him — Jesus, not I say to you until seven times,
23 ἀλλ' ἕως ἑβδομηκοντάκις ἑπτά. διὰ τοῦτο ὡμοιώθη ἡ
but until seventy times seven. For this reason, was likened the
βασιλεία τῶν οὐρανῶν ἀνθρώπῳ βασιλεῖ, ὃς ἠθέλησε
kingdom of the heavens to a man, a king, who decided
24 συνᾶραι λόγον μετὰ τῶν δούλων αὐτοῦ. ἀρξαμένου δὲ
to take account with the slaves of him. beginning And
αὐτοῦ συναίρειν, προσηνέχθη αὐτῷ εἷς ὀφειλέτης μυρίων
him to reckon, was brought near to him one debtor of ten thousand
25 ταλάντων. μὴ ἔχοντος δὲ αὐτοῦ ἀποδοῦναι, ἐκέλευσεν αὐτὸν
talents. not having. And he to repay, commanded him
ὁ κύριος αὐτοῦ πραθῆναι, καὶ τὴν γυναῖκα αὐτοῦ καὶ τὰ
the lord of him to be sold, and the wife of him and the
26 τέκνα, καὶ πάντα ὅσα εἶχε, καὶ ἀποδοθῆναι. πεσὼν οὖν ὁ
children, and all as much as he had, and to pay back. Falling then the
δοῦλος προσεκύνει αὐτῷ, λέγων, Κύριε, μακροθύμησον ἐπ'
slave bowed the knee to him, saying, Lord, have patience over
27 ἐμοί, καὶ πάντα σοι ἀποδώσω. σπλαγχνισθεὶς δὲ ὁ κύριος
me, and all to you I will repay. filled with pity And, the lord
τοῦ δούλου ἐκείνου ἀπέλυσεν αὐτόν, καὶ τὸ δάνειον ἀφῆκεν
slave of that released him, and the loan forgave
28 αὐτῷ. ἐξελθὼν δὲ ὁ δοῦλος ἐκεῖνος εὗρεν ἕνα τῶν συνδούλων
him. going out But slave that found one of the fellow-slaves
αὐτοῦ, ὃς ὤφειλεν αὐτῷ ἑκατὸν δηνάρια, καὶ κρατήσας
of him, who owed him a hundred denarii, and seizing
29 αὐτὸν ἔπνιγε, λέγων, Ἀπόδος μοι ὅ τι ὀφείλεις. πεσὼν οὖν
him he throttled, saying, Pay back to me what ever you owed. Falling then
ὁ σύνδουλος αὐτοῦ εἰς τοὺς πόδας αὐτοῦ παρεκάλει αὐτόν,
the fellow-slave of him to the feet of him begged him,
λέγων, Μακροθύμησον ἐπ' ἐμοί, καὶ πάντα ἀποδώσω σοι.
saying, Have patience over me and all I will repay to you.
30 ὁ δὲ οὐκ ἤθελεν, ἀλλ' ἀπελθὼν ἔβαλεν αὐτὸν εἰς φυλακήν,
he But not willed (it), but going away threw him into prison
31 ἕως οὗ ἀποδῷ τὸ ὀφειλόμενον. ἰδόντες δὲ οἱ σύνδουλοι αὐτοῦ
until he pay back that owing. seeing And the fellow-slaves of him
τὰ γενόμενα ἐλυπήθησαν σφόδρα· καὶ ἐλθόντες διεσάφησαν
that occurring, they were grieved greatly, and coming reported
32 τῷ κυρίῳ αὐτῶν πάντα τὰ γενόμενα. τότε προσκαλεσά-
to the lord of them all the (things) occurring. Then calling near
μενος αὐτὸν ὁ κύριος αὐτοῦ λέγει αὐτῷ, Δοῦλε πονηρέ,
him, the lord of him says to him, slave Wicked,

forgave you all that debt, since you begged me. [33]Ought you not also to favor your fellow-slave, as I also favored you? [34]And being angry, his lord delivered him up to the tormentors until he pay back all that debt to him. [35]So also My heavenly Father will do to you unless each of you from your hearts forgive his brother their offenses.

CHAPTER 19

[1]And it happened when Jesus had finished these words, He moved from Galilee and came into the borders of Judah beyond the Jordan. [2]And great crowds followed Him; and He healed them there.

[3]And the Pharisees came near to Him, and saying to Him, Is it lawful for a man to put away his wife for every reason? [4]But answering He said to them, Have you not read that He who created them from the beginning made them male and female? [5]And He said, "For this reason a man shall leave father and mother, and shall be joined to his wife, and the two shall become one flesh. [6]So that they are no longer two, but one flesh. Therefore, what God has joined together, let not man separate." [7]They said to Him, Why then did Moses command to give a bill of divorce, and to put her away? [8]He said to them, In view of your hardheartedness Moses allowed you to put away your wives. But from the beginning it was not so. [9]And I say to you, Whoever shall put away his wife, if not for fornication, and shall marry another, *that one* commits adultery. And the *one* who marries her *who was* put away commits adultery.

[10]His disciples said to Him, If the case of the man

πᾶσαν τὴν ὀφειλὴν ἐκείνην ἀφῆκά σοι, ἐπεὶ παρεκάλεσάς με·
all — debt that I forgave you, since you begged me.

33 οὐκ ἔδει καὶ σὲ ἐλεῆσαι τὸν σύνδουλόν σου, ὡς καὶ ἐγώ σε
not must be even you to favor the fellow-slave of you, as also I you

34 ἠλέησα; καὶ ὀργισθεὶς ὁ κύριος αὐτοῦ παρέδωκεν αὐτὸν
had favored. And being angry, the lord of him delivered him

τοῖς βασανισταῖς, ἕως οὗ ἀποδῷ πᾶν τὸ ὀφειλόμενον αὐτῷ.
to the tormentors, until that he repay all that debt to him.

35 οὕτω καὶ ὁ πατήρ μου ὁ ἐπουράνιος ποιήσει ὑμῖν, ἐὰν μὴ
So also the Father of Me - heavenly will do to you, unless

ἀφῆτε ἕκαστος τῷ ἀδελφῷ αὐτοῦ ἀπὸ τῶν καρδιῶν ὑμῶν τὰ
you forgive each one the brother of him from the hearts of you the

παραπτώματα αὐτῶν.
offenses of them.

CHAPTER 19

1 Καὶ ἐγένετο ὅτε ἐτέλεσεν ὁ Ἰησοῦς τοὺς λόγους τούτους,
And it was, when ended — Jesus — words these,

μετῆρεν ἀπὸ τῆς Γαλιλαίας, καὶ ἦλθεν εἰς τὰ ὅρια τῆς
He moved from — Galilee and came into the borders —

2 Ἰουδαίας πέραν τοῦ Ἰορδάνου. καὶ ἠκολούθησαν αὐτῷ
of Judea, across the Jordan. And followed Him

ὄχλοι πολλοί, καὶ ἐθεράπευσεν αὐτοὺς ἐκεῖ.
crowds much, and He healed them there.

3 Καὶ προσῆλθον αὐτῷ οἱ Φαρισαῖοι πειράζοντες αὐτόν,
And approached him the Pharisees, tempting Him

καὶ λέγοντες αὐτῷ, Εἰ ἔξεστιν ἀνθρώπῳ ἀπολῦσαι τὴν
and saying to Him, If it is lawful for a man to put away the

4 γυναῖκα αὐτοῦ κατὰ πᾶσαν αἰτίαν; ὁ δὲ ἀποκριθεὶς εἶπεν
wife of him for every reason? He And answering said

αὐτοῖς, Οὐκ ἀνέγνωτε ὅτι ὁ ποιήσας ἀπ' ἀρχῆς ἄρσεν καὶ
to them, not Did you read that He making from beginning male and

5 θῆλυ ἐποίησεν αὐτούς, καὶ εἶπεν, Ἕνεκεν τούτου καταλείψει
female made them? And He said, For the sake of this shall leave

ἄνθρωπος τὸν πατέρα καὶ τὴν μητέρα, καὶ προσκολληθή-
a man — father and — mother, and shall be joined to

σεται τῇ γυναικὶ αὐτοῦ, καὶ ἔσονται οἱ δύο εἰς σάρκα μίαν;
the wife of him; and shall be the two for flesh one;

6 ὥστε οὐκέτι εἰσὶ δύο, ἀλλὰ σὰρξ μία· ὃ οὖν ὁ Θεὸς συνέζευξεν,
so that no longer are they two, but flesh one. What then God yoked together

7 ἄνθρωπος μὴ χωριζέτω. λέγουσιν αὐτῷ, Τί οὖν Μωσῆς
man do not let separate. They say to Him, Why then Moses

ἐνετείλατο δοῦναι βιβλίον ἀποστασίου, καὶ ἀπολῦσαι
did command to give a bill of divorce, and to put away

8 αὐτήν; λέγει αὐτοῖς ὅτι Μωσῆς πρὸς τὴν σκληροκαρδίαν
her? He says to them, — Moses in view of the obduracy

ὑμῶν ἐπέτρεψεν ὑμῖν ἀπολῦσαι τὰς γυναῖκας ὑμῶν· ἀπ'
of you allowed you to put away the wives of you. from

9 ἀρχῆς δὲ οὐ γέγονεν οὕτω. λέγω δὲ ὑμῖν ὅτι ὃς ἂν ἀπολύσῃ
the beginning but not it was so. I say And to you that whoever puts away

τὴν γυναικα αὐτοῦ, εἰ μὴ ἐπὶ πορνείᾳ, καὶ γαμήσῃ ἄλλην,
tne wife of him, if not for fornication, and shall marry another,

10 μοιχᾶται· καὶ ὁ ἀπολελυμένην γαμήσας μοιχᾶται. λέγουσιν
commits adultery and he her put away marrying commits adultery. Say

αὐτῷ οἱ μαθηταὶ αὐτοῦ, Εἰ οὕτως ἐστὶν ἡ αἰτία τοῦ
to Him the disciples of Him, If thus is the case of the

be so with his wife, it is not good to marry. [11] But He said to them, Not all receive this word, but *those* to whom it is given. [12] For there are eunuchs who were born thus from *their* mother's womb, and there are eunuchs who were made eunuchs by men; and there are eunuchs who made eunuchs *of* themselves for the sake of the kingdom of Heaven. He who is able to receive, let him receive *it*.

[13] Then little children were brought to Him, that He might lay hands on them and might pray. But the disciples rebuked them. [14] But Jesus said, Allow the little children and do not prevent them to come to Me; for of such is the kingdom of Heaven. [15] And laying hands on them, He went away from there.

[16] And, behold, one coming near said to Him, Good Teacher, what good thing shall I do that I may have eternal life? [17] And He said to him, Why do you call Me good? No one *is* good except One, God! But if you desire to enter into life, keep the commandments. [18] He said to Him, Which? And Jesus said, "You shall not commit murder; you shall not commit adultery; you shall not steal; you shall not bear false witness; [19] honor your father and your mother," and, "You shall love your neighbor as yourself." [20] The young man said to Him, All these things I have kept from my youth. What do I still lack? [21] Jesus said to him, If you desire to be perfect, go sell your property and give to *the* poor, and you will have treasure in Heaven; and come, follow Me. [22] But hearing the word, the young man went away sorrowful—for he had many possessions.

[23] And Jesus said to His disciples, Truly I say to you that a rich man will with great difficulty enter into the kingdom of Heaven. [24] And again I say to you, It is easier for a camel to pass through a

11 ἀνθρώπου μετὰ τῆς γυναικός, οὐ συμφέρει γαμῆσαι. ὁ δὲ εἶπεν
man with the wife, not it is gain to marry. He But said
αὐτοῖς, Οὐ πάντες χωροῦσι τὸν λόγον τοῦτον, ἀλλ' οἷς
to them, Not all make room for — word this. only to whom
12 δέδοται. εἰσὶ γὰρ εὐνοῦχοι, οἵτινες ἐκ κοιλίας μητρὸς
it is given, there are For eunuchs who from (the) womb of a mother
ἐγεννήθησαν οὕτω· καί εἰσιν εὐνοῦχοι, οἵτινες εὐνουχίσθησαν
were born so; and there are eunuchs who were made eunuchs
ὑπὸ τῶν ἀνθρώπων· καί εἰσιν εὐνοῦχοι, οἵτινες εὐνούχισαν
by — men; and there are eunuchs who made eunuchs
ἑαυτοὺς διὰ τὴν βασιλείαν τῶν οὐρανῶν. ὁ δυνάμενος
(of) themselves due to the kingdom of the heavens. The (one) able
χωρεῖν χωρείτω.
to receive, let him receive (it).
13 Τότε προσηνέχθη αὐτῷ παιδία, ἵνα τὰς χεῖρας ἐπιθῇ
Then were brought to Him children, that — hands He might lay
αὐτοῖς, καὶ προσεύξηται· οἱ δὲ μαθηταὶ ἐπετίμησαν αὐτοῖς.
on them and to pray; the but disciples rebuked them.
14 ὁ δὲ Ἰησοῦς εἶπεν, Ἄφετε τὰ παιδία, καὶ μὴ κωλύετε αὐτὰ
— But Jesus said, Permit the children, and not do prevent them
ἐλθεῖν πρός με· τῶν γὰρ τοιούτων ἐστὶν ἡ βασιλεία τῶν
to come to Me; — for of such is the kingdom of the
15 οὐρανῶν. καὶ ἐπιθεὶς αὐτοῖς τὰς χεῖρας, ἐπορεύθη ἐκεῖθεν.
heavens. And laying on them — hands, He went away from there.
16 Καὶ ἰδού, εἷς προσελθὼν εἶπεν αὐτῷ, Διδάσκαλε ἀγαθέ,
And behold! One coming near said to Him, teacher Good
17 τί ἀγαθὸν ποιήσω, ἵνα ἔχω ζωὴν αἰώνιον ; ὁ δὲ εἶπεν αὐτῷ,
what good shall I do that I may have life eternal? He And said to him,
Τί με λέγεις ἀγαθόν ; οὐδεὶς ἀγαθός, εἰ μὴ εἷς, ὁ Θεός. εἰ δὲ
Why Me you call good? No one (is) good except One — God. if But
18 θέλεις εἰσελθεῖν εἰς τὴν ζωήν, τήρησον τὰς ἐντολάς. λέγει
you desire to enter into — life, keep the commands. He says
αὐτῷ, Ποίας ; ὁ δὲ Ἰησοῦς εἶπε, Τὸ οὐ φονεύσεις· οὐ μοιχεύ-
to Him, Which? — And Jesus said, not You shall murder; not commit
19 σεις· οὐ κλέψεις· οὐ ψευδομαρτυρήσεις· τίμα τὸν πατέρα
adultery; not steal; not bear false witness; honor — father
σου καὶ τὴν μητέρα· καί, ἀγαπήσεις τὸν πλησίον σου ὡς
your and — mother; and, you shall love the neighbor of you as
20 σεαυτόν. λέγει αὐτῷ ὁ νεανίσκος, Πάντα ταῦτα ἐφυλαξάμην
yourself. says to Him The young man, All these things I have kept
21 ἐκ νεότητός μου· τί ἔτι ὑστερῶ ; ἔφη αὐτῷ ὁ Ἰησοῦς, Εἰ θέλεις
from my youth; What yet do I lack? said to him — Jesus, If you wish
τέλειος εἶναι, ὕπαγε, πώλησόν σου τὰ ὑπάρχοντα καὶ δὸς
perfect to be, go sell your — property and give
πτωχοῖς, καὶ ἕξεις θησαυρὸν ἐν οὐρανῷ· καὶ δεῦρο, ἀκολούθει
to (the) poor, and you will have treasure in Heaven; and come, follow
22 μοι. ἀκούσας δὲ ὁ νεανίσκος τὸν λόγον ἀπῆλθε λυπούμενος·
Me. hearing But the young man the word went away grieving,
ἦν γὰρ ἔχων κτήματα πολλά.
he was for having possessions many.
23 Ὁ δὲ Ἰησοῦς εἶπε τοῖς μαθηταῖς αὐτοῦ, Ἀμὴν λέγω ὑμῖν
— And Jesus said to the disciples of Him, Truly I say to you,
ὅτι δυσκόλως πλούσιος εἰσελεύσεται εἰς τὴν βασιλείαν τῶν
that with difficulty a rich man will enter into the kingdom of the
24 οὐρανῶν. πάλιν δὲ λέγω ὑμῖν, εὐκοπώτερόν ἐστι κάμηλον
heavens. again And I tell you, easier It is a camel

needle's eye than for a rich man to enter the kingdom of God. [25]And His disciples were exceedingly amazed when they heard this, saying, Who then can be saved? [26]But looking on *them,* Jesus said to them, With men this is impossible, but with God all things are possible.

[27]Then answering, Peter said to Him, Behold, we left all things and followed You. What then shall happen to us? [28]And Jesus said to them, Truly I say to you, You who have followed Me, in the regeneration, when the Son of man sits on the throne of glory, you also will sit on twelve thrones, judging the twelve tribes of Israel. [29]And everyone who left houses, or brothers, or sisters, or father, or mother, or wife, or children, or lands, for My name's sake shall receive a hundredfold, and shall inherit everlasting life. [30]But many first *ones* shall be last, and last *ones* first.

διὰ τρυπήματος ῥαφίδος διελθεῖν, ἢ πλούσιον εἰς τὴν βασι-
through (the) eye of a needle to pass, than a rich man into the king-
25 λείαν τοῦ Θεοῦ εἰσελθεῖν. ἀκούσαντες δὲ οἱ μαθηταὶ αὐτοῦ
dom – of God to enter. having heard And the disciples of Him
ἐξεπλήσσοντο σφόδρα, λέγοντες, Τίς ἄρα δύναται σωθῆναι ;
were astonished exceedingly, saying, Who then is able to be saved?
26 ἐμβλέψας δὲ ὁ Ἰησοῦς εἶπεν αὐτοῖς, Παρὰ ἀνθρώποις τοῦτο
looking But – Jesus said to them, With men this
27 ἀδύνατόν ἐστι, παρὰ δὲ Θεῷ πάντα δυνατά ἐστι. τότε
impossible is, with But God all things possible are. Then
ἀποκριθεὶς ὁ Πέτρος εἶπεν αὐτῷ, Ἰδού, ἡμεῖς ἀφήκαμεν
answering – Peter said to Him, Behold, we left
28 πάντα καὶ ἠκολουθήσαμέν σοι· τί ἄρα ἔσται ἡμῖν ; ὁ δὲ Ἰη-
all things and followed You. What then shall be to us? – And
σοῦς εἶπεν αὐτοῖς, Ἀμὴν λέγω ὑμῖν ὅτι ὑμεῖς οἱ ἀκολουθή-
Jesus said to them, Truly I tell you that you the (ones) having
σαντές μοι, ἐν τῇ παλιγγενεσίᾳ ὅταν καθίσῃ ὁ υἱὸς τοῦ
followed Me, in the regeneration, when sits the Son –
ἀνθρώπου ἐπὶ θρόνου δόξης αὐτοῦ, καθίσεσθε καὶ ὑμεῖς ἐπὶ
of man on (the) throne of glory of Him, You will sit even you on
δώδεκα θρόνους, κρίνοντες τὰς δώδεκα φυλὰς τοῦ Ἰσραήλ.
twelve thrones judging the twelve tribes – of Israel.
29 καὶ πᾶς ὃς ἀφῆκεν οἰκίας, ἢ ἀδελφούς, ἢ ἀδελφάς, ἢ πατέρα,
And everyone who left houses, or brothers, or sisters, or father,
ἢ μητέρα, ἢ γυναῖκα, ἢ τέκνα, ἢ ἀγρούς, ἕνεκεν τοῦ ὀνόματός
or mother, or wife, or children, or lands, for the sake of the name
μου, ἑκατονταπλασίονα λήψεται, καὶ ζωὴν αἰώνιον κλη-
of Me, a hundredfold shall receive, and life eternal shall
30 ρονομήσει. πολλοὶ δὲ ἔσονται πρῶτοι ἔσχατοι, καὶ ἔσχατοι
inherit. many But shall be first last, and last
πρῶτοι.
first.

CHAPTER 20

[1]For the kingdom of Heaven is like a man, a housemaster, who went out when *it was* early to hire workers into his vineyard. [2]And agreeing with the workers for a denarius *for* the day, he sent them into his vineyard. [3]And going out about the third hour, he saw others standing idle in the market. [4]And he said to them, You also go into the vineyard, and I will give you whatever is just. And they went. [5]Again, going out about *the* sixth and ninth hour, he did the same. [6]And going out about the eleventh hour, he found others standing idle, and said to them, Why do you stand here idle all day? [7]They said to him,

1 ὁμοία γάρ ἐστιν ἡ βασιλεία τῶν οὐρανῶν ἀνθρώπῳ
like For is the kingdom of the heavens to a man,
οἰκοδεσπότῃ, ὅστις ἐξῆλθεν ἅμα πρωῒ μισθώσασθαι ἐργάτας
a housemaster, who went out when early to hire workmen
2 εἰς τὸν ἀμπελῶνα αὐτοῦ. συμφωνήσας δὲ μετὰ τῶν ἐργατῶν
into the vineyard of him. agreeing And with the workmen
ἐκ δηναρίου τὴν ἡμέραν, ἀπέστειλεν αὐτοὺς εἰς τὸν ἀμπελῶνα
for a denarius the day, he sent them into the vineyard
3 αὐτοῦ. καὶ ἐξελθὼν περὶ τὴν τρίτην ὥραν, εἶδεν ἄλλους
of him. And going out about the third hour, he saw others
4 ἑστῶτας ἐν τῇ ἀγορᾷ ἀργούς· κἀκείνοις εἶπεν, Ὑπάγετε καὶ
standing in the market idle, and to them said, Go also
5 ὑμεῖς εἰς τὸν ἀμπελῶνα, καὶ ὃ ἐὰν ᾖ δίκαιον δώσω ὑμῖν. οἱ
you into the vineyard, and whatever is just I will give you, that
δὲ ἀπῆλθον. πάλιν ἐξελθὼν περὶ ἕκτην καὶ ἐννάτην ὥραν,
And went. Again going out about (the) sixth and ninth hour,
6 ἐποίησεν ὡσαύτως. περὶ δὲ τὴν ἑνδεκάτην ὥραν ἐξελθών,
he did likewise. about And the eleventh hour, going out
εὗρεν ἄλλους ἑστῶτας ἀργούς, καὶ λέγει αὐτοῖς, Τί ὧδε
he found others standing idle, and says to them, Why here
7 ἑστήκατε ὅλην τὴν ἡμέραν ἀργοί ; λέγουσιν αὐτῷ, Ὅτι
do you stand all the day idle? They say to him, Because

Because no one has hired us. He said to them, You also go into the vineyard, and you will receive whatever is just. [8]But evening coming, the lord of the vineyard said to his manager, Call the workers and pay them the wage, beginning from the last to the first. [9]And the ones coming the eleventh hour each received a denarius. [10]And coming, the first supposed that they would receive more. And they also each received a denarius. [11]And receiving *it*, they murmured against the housemaster, [12]saying, These last have performed one hour, and you have made them equal to us who have borne the burden and the heat of the day. [13]But answering he said to one of them, Friend, I am not unjust to you. Did you not agree to a denarius with me? [14]Take yours and go. But I desire to give to this last as also to you. [15]Or is it not lawful for me to do what I desire with my things? Or is your eye evil because I am good? [16]So the last shall be first, and the first last; for many are called, but few chosen.

[17]And going up to Jerusalem, Jesus took the twelve disciples aside in the way, and said to them, [18]Behold, we are going up to Jerusalem, and the Son of man will be betrayed to the chief priests and scribes. And they will condemn Him to death. [19]And they will deliver Him up to the heathen to mock, and to scourge, and to crucify. And the third day He will rise again.

[20]Then the mother of the sons of Zebedee came near to Him, along with her sons, bowing the knee and asking something from Him. [21]And He said to her, What do you desire? She said to Him, Say that these two sons of mine may sit one on Your right, and one on *Your* left *hand* in

οὐδεὶς ἡμᾶς ἐμισθώσατο. λέγει αὐτοῖς, Ὑπάγετε καὶ ὑμεῖς εἰς
no one us has hired. He says to them, Go also you into
8 τὸν ἀμπελῶνα, καὶ ὃ ἐὰν ᾖ δίκαιον λήψεσθε. ὀψίας δὲ γενο-
the vineyard, and whatever is just you will receive. eve But com-
μένης λέγει ὁ κύριος τοῦ ἀμπελῶνος τῷ ἐπιτρόπῳ αὐτοῦ,
ing, says the lord of the vineyard to the manager of him,
Κάλεσον τοὺς ἐργάτας, καὶ ἀπόδος αὐτοῖς τὸν μισθόν,
Call the workmen, and pay them the wage,
9 ἀρξάμενος ἀπὸ τῶν ἐσχάτων ἕως τῶν πρώτων. καὶ ἐλθόντες
beginning from the last ones until the first. And coming,
10 οἱ περὶ τὴν ἑνδεκάτην ὥραν ἔλαβον ἀνὰ δηνάριον. ἐλθόντες
those about the eleventh hour received each a denarius. coming
δὲ οἱ πρῶτοι ἐνόμισαν ὅτι πλείονα λήψονται· καὶ ἔλαβον καὶ
And the first supposed that more they will get; and they got also
11 αὐτοὶ ἀνὰ δηνάριον. λαβόντες δὲ ἐγόγγυζον κατὰ τοῦ
themselves each a denarius. receiving And they murmured against the
12 οἰκοδεσπότου, λέγοντες ὅτι Οὗτοι οἱ ἔσχατοι μίαν ὥραν
housemaster, saying, These — last one hour
ἐποίησαν, καὶ ἴσους ἡμῖν αὐτοὺς ἐποίησας, τοῖς βαστάσασι
performed and equal to us them you have made, who have borne
13 τὸ βάρος τῆς ἡμέρας καὶ τὸν καύσωνα. ὁ δὲ ἀποκριθεὶς
the burden of the day and the heat. he But answering
εἶπεν ἑνὶ αὐτῶν, Ἑταῖρε, οὐκ ἀδικῶ σε· οὐχὶ δηναρίου
said to one of them, Friend, not I am unjust to you; not of a denarius
14 συνεφώνησάς μοι; ἆρον τὸ σὸν καὶ ὕπαγε· θέλω δὲ τούτῳ
you agreed with me? Take — yours and go; I desire But to this
15 τῷ ἐσχάτῳ δοῦναι ὡς καὶ σοί. ἢ οὐκ ἔξεστί μοι ποιῆσαι ὃ
— last to give as also to you. Or not is it lawful for me to do what
θέλω ἐν τοῖς ἐμοῖς; εἰ ὁ ὀφθαλμός σου πονηρός ἐστιν, ὅτι
I desire in the things of me; or the eye of you evil is, because
16 ἐγὼ ἀγαθός εἰμι; οὕτως ἔσονται οἱ ἔσχατοι πρῶτοι, καὶ οἱ
I good am? So shall be the last first, and the
πρῶτοι ἔσχατοι· πολλοὶ γάρ εἰσι κλητοί, ὀλίγοι δὲ ἐκλεκτοί.
first last; many for are called, few but chosen.
17 Καὶ ἀναβαίνων ὁ Ἰησοῦς εἰς Ἱεροσόλυμα παρέλαβε τοὺς
And going up — Jesus to Jerusalem He took the
18 δώδεκα μαθητὰς κατ' ἰδίαν ἐν τῇ ὁδῷ, καὶ εἶπεν αὐτοῖς, Ἰδού,
twelve disciples privately, in the way and said to them, Behold,
ἀναβαίνομεν εἰς Ἱεροσόλυμα, καὶ ὁ υἱὸς τοῦ ἀνθρώπου
we are going up to Jerusalem, and the Son — of man
παραδοθήσεται τοῖς ἀρχιερεῦσι καὶ γραμματεῦσι· καὶ κατα-
will be delivered up to the chief priests and scribes. And they
19 κρινοῦσιν αὐτὸν θανάτῳ, καὶ παραδώσουσιν αὐτὸν τοῖς
will condemn Him to death. And they will deliver up Him to the
ἔθνεσιν εἰς τὸ ἐμπαῖξαι καὶ μαστιγῶσαι καὶ σταυρῶσαι·
nations to — mock and to scourge and to crucify.
καὶ τῇ τρίτῃ ἡμέρᾳ ἀναστήσεται.
And the third day He will rise again.
20 Τότε προσῆλθεν αὐτῷ ἡ μήτηρ τῶν υἱῶν Ζεβεδαίου μετὰ
Then came near to Him the mother of the sons of Zebedee with
τῶν υἱῶν αὐτῆς, προσκυνοῦσα καὶ αἰτοῦσά τι παρ' αὐτοῦ.
the sons of her, bowing the knee and asking something from Him.
21 ὁ δὲ εἶπεν αὐτῇ, Τί θέλεις; λέγει αὐτῷ, Εἰπὲ ἵνα καθίσωσιν
He And said to her, What desire you? She says to Him, Say that may sit
οὗτοι οἱ δύο υἱοί μου, εἷς ἐκ δεξιῶν σου, καὶ εἷς ἐξ εὐωνύμων,
these the two sons of me one on the right of You and one on the left

Your kingdom. 22 But answering Jesus said, You do not know what you ask. Are you able to drink the cup which I am about to drink, and to be baptized with the baptism with which I am to be baptized? They said to Him, We are able. 23 And He said to them, Indeed you shall drink My cup, and you shall be baptized with the baptism with which I am baptized; but to sit off My right and off My left *hand* is not Mine to give, but *to those* for whom it was prepared by My Father. 24 And hearing, the ten were indignant about the two brothers. 25 But having called them, Jesus said, You know that the rulers of the nations exercise lordship over them, and the great ones exercise authority over them. 26 But it will not be so among you. But whoever would become great among you, let him be your servant. 27 And whoever desires to be first among you, let him be your slave; 28 even as the Son of man did not come to be served, but to serve; and to give His life a ransom for many.

29 And as they were going out from Jericho, a great crowd followed Him. 30 And, behold, two blind ones sitting beside the way, having heard that Jesus was passing by, cried out, saying, Have pity on us, Lord, Son of David! 32 But the crowd rebuked them, that they be quiet. But they cried out the more, saying, Have pity on us, Lord, Son of David! 32 And stopping, Jesus called them, and said, What do you desire that I do to you? 33 They said to Him, Lord, that our eyes may be opened. 34 And moved with pity, Jesus touched their eyes. And instantly their eyes received sight, and they followed Him.

22 ἐν τῇ βασιλείᾳ σου. ἀποκριθεὶς δὲ ὁ Ἰησοῦς εἶπεν, Οὐκ
in the kingdom of You. answering But — Jesus said, not
οἴδατε τί αἰτεῖσθε. δύνασθε πιεῖν τὸ ποτήριον ὃ ἐγὼ μέλλω
You know what you ask. Can you drink the cup which I am about
πίνειν, καὶ τὸ βάπτισμα ὃ ἐγὼ βαπτίζομαι βαπτισθῆναι;
to drink, and the baptism which I am baptized to be baptized?
23 λέγουσιν αὐτῷ, Δυνάμεθα. καὶ λέγει αὐτοῖς, Τὸ μὲν
They say to Him, We can. And He says to them, the indeed
ποτήριόν μου πίεσθε, καὶ τὸ βάπτισμα ὃ ἐγὼ βαπτίζομαι
cup of Me you will drink, and the baptism which I am baptized
βαπτισθήσεσθε· τὸ δὲ καθίσαι ἐκ δεξιῶν μου καὶ ἐξ εὐωνύμων
you will be baptized (with), but to sit off the right of Me and off the left
μου, οὐκ ἔστιν ἐμὸν δοῦναι, ἀλλ' οἷς ἡτοίμασται ὑπὸ τοῦ
of Me, not is Mine to give, but for whom it was prepared by the
24 πατρός μου. καὶ ἀκούσαντες οἱ δέκα ἠγανάκτησαν περὶ τῶν
Father of Me. And having heard the ten were indignant about the
25 δύο ἀδελφῶν. ὁ δὲ Ἰησοῦς προσκαλεσάμενος αὐτοὺς εἶπεν,
two brothers. — But Jesus having called near them said,
Οἴδατε ὅτι οἱ ἄρχοντες τῶν ἐθνῶν κατακυριεύουσιν αὐτῶν,
You know that the rulers of the nations exercise lordship over them;
26 καὶ οἱ μεγάλοι κατεξουσιάζουσιν αὐτῶν. οὐχ οὕτως δὲ ἔσται
and the great ones exercise authority over them. not so But it will be
ἐν ὑμῖν· ἀλλ' ὃς ἐὰν θέλῃ ἐν ὑμῖν μέγας γενέσθαι ἔστω ὑμῶν
among you; but whoever would among you great become, let him be of you
27 διάκονος· καὶ ὃς ἐὰν θέλῃ ἐν ὑμῖν εἶναι πρῶτος ἔστω ὑμῶν
a servant. And whoever desires among you to be first, he shall be of you
28 δοῦλος· ὥσπερ ὁ υἱὸς τοῦ ἀνθρώπου οὐκ ἦλθε διακονηθῆναι,
a slave. even as the Son — of man not did come to be served,
ἀλλὰ διακονῆσαι, καὶ δοῦναι τὴν ψυχὴν αὐτοῦ λύτρον ἀντὶ
but to serve, and to give the life of Him a ransom for
πολλῶν.
many.

29 Καὶ ἐκπορευομένων αὐτῶν ἀπὸ Ἱεριχώ, ἠκολούθησεν
And going out they from Jericho, followed
30 αὐτῷ ὄχλος πολύς. καὶ ἰδού, δύο τυφλοὶ καθήμενοι παρὰ
Him a crowd great. And behold, two blind (ones) sitting beside
τὴν ὁδόν, ἀκούσαντες ὅτι Ἰησοῦς παράγει, ἔκραξαν,
the way, hearing that Jesus is passing by, cried out,
31 λέγοντες, Ἐλέησον ἡμᾶς, Κύριε, υἱὸς Δαβίδ. ὁ δὲ ὄχλος
saying, Have pity on us, Lord, Son of David. the But crowd
ἐπετίμησεν αὐτοῖς ἵνα σιωπήσωσιν. οἱ δὲ μεῖζον ἔκραζον,
rebuked them, that they be silent they But more cried out,
32 λέγοντες, Ἐλέησον ἡμᾶς, Κύριε, υἱὸς Δαβίδ. καὶ στὰς ὁ
saying, Have mercy on us, Lord, Son of David. And stopping —
Ἰησοῦς ἐφώνησεν αὐτούς, καὶ εἶπε, Τί θέλετε ποιήσω ὑμῖν;
Jesus called them, and said, What do you desire I do to you?
33 λέγουσιν αὐτῷ, Κύριε, ἵνα ἀνοιχθῶσιν ἡμῶν οἱ ὀφθαλμοί.
They say to Him, Lord, that may be opened of us the eyes.
34 σπλαγχνισθεὶς δὲ ὁ Ἰησοῦς ἥψατο τῶν ὀφθαλμῶν αὐτῶν·
moved with pity And — Jesus touched the eyes of them,
καὶ εὐθέως ἀνέβλεψαν αὐτῶν οἱ ὀφθαλμοί, καὶ ἠκολούθησαν
and instantly received sight of them the eyes, and they followed
αὐτῷ.
Him.

CHAPTER 21

[1] And when they drew near to Jerusalem and came to Bethphage, toward the Mount of Olives, then Jesus sent two disciples, [2] saying to them, Go into the village opposite you, and immediately you will find an ass tied, and a colt with her. Loosen *them and* lead *them* to Me. [3] And if anyone says anything to you, you shall say, The Lord has need of them. And he will send them at once. [4] But all this happened that might be fulfilled that which was spoken by the prophet, saying, [5] "Tell the daughter of Zion, Behold, your King comes to you, meek and mounted on an ass, even a colt, *the* son of an ass." [6] And going, and doing as Jesus had ordered them, the disciples brought the ass and the colt. And *they* put on them their garments; and He sat on them. [8] And most of *the* crowd spread their garments on the road. And others were cutting branches from the trees and were spreading them in the road. [9] And the crowd, the ones going before and the ones following, were crying out, saying, Hosanna to the Son of David! Blessed *is* He coming in *the* name of *the* Lord! Hosanna in the highest! [10] And as He entered into Jerusalem, all the city was shaken, saying, Who is this? [11] And the crowds said, This is Jesus, the Prophet, the *one* from Nazareth of Galilee.

[12] And Jesus entered into the temple of God, and threw out all those selling and buying in the temple. And He overthrew the tables of the moneychangers, and the seats of those selling the doves. [13] And He said to them, It has been written, "My house shall be called a house of prayer," but you have made it a den of robbers. [14] And blind and lame

CHAPTER 21

1 Καὶ ὅτε ἤγγισαν εἰς Ἱεροσόλυμα, καὶ ἦλθον εἰς Βηθφαγῆ
And when they drew near to Jerusalem, and came into Bethphage,
πρὸς τὸ ὄρος τῶν ἐλαιῶν, τότε ὁ Ἰησοῦς ἀπέστειλε δύο
towards the mount of the olives, then — Jesus sent two
2 μαθητάς, λέγων αὐτοῖς, Πορεύθητε εἰς τὴν κώμην τὴν ἀπέ-
disciples, telling them, You go into the village, that
ναντι ὑμῶν, καὶ εὐθέως εὑρήσετε ὄνον δεδεμένην, καὶ πῶλον
opposite you, and at once you will find an ass tied, and a colt
3 μετ' αὐτῆς· λύσαντες ἀγάγετέ μοι. καὶ ἐάν τις ὑμῖν εἴπῃ τι,
with her. Loosen (and) lead to Me. And if any to you says anything,
ἐρεῖτε ὅτι Ὁ Κύριος αὐτῶν χρείαν ἔχει· εὐθέως δὲ ἀποστελεῖ
you shall say, The Lord of them need has; at once and he will send
4 αὐτούς. τοῦτο δὲ ὅλον γέγονεν, ἵνα πληρωθῇ τὸ ῥηθὲν διὰ
them. this But all came to pass that may be fulfilled that spoken by
5 τοῦ προφήτου, λέγοντος, Εἴπατε τῇ θυγατρὶ Σιών, Ἰδού,
the prophet, saying, Tell the daughter of Zion, Behold,
ὁ βασιλεύς σου ἔρχεταί σοι, πραῢς καὶ ἐπιβεβηκὼς ἐπὶ ὄνον
the king of you comes to you, meek and mounted on an ass,
6 καὶ πῶλον υἱὸν ὑποζυγίου. πορευθέντες δὲ οἱ μαθηταί, καὶ
even a colt (the) son of an ass. having gone And the disciples, and
7 ποιήσαντες καθὼς προσέταξεν αὐτοῖς ὁ Ἰησοῦς, ἤγαγον
having done as ordered them — Jesus, they led
τὴν ὄνον καὶ τὸν πῶλον, καὶ ἐπέθηκαν ἐπάνω αὐτῶν τὰ
the ass and the colt, and put upon them the
8 ἱμάτια αὐτῶν, καὶ ἐπεκάθισαν ἐπάνω αὐτῶν. ὁ δὲ πλεῖστος
garments of them; and He sat on them. the And most of
ὄχλος ἔστρωσαν ἑαυτῶν τὰ ἱμάτια ἐν τῇ ὁδῷ· ἄλλοι δὲ
(the) crowd strewed of themselves the garments on the way. others And
ἔκοπτον κλάδους ἀπὸ τῶν δένδρων, καὶ ἐστρώννυον ἐν τῇ
were cutting branches from the trees and were spreading in the
9 ὁδῷ. οἱ δὲ ὄχλοι οἱ προάγοντες καὶ οἱ ἀκολουθοῦντες
way. the And crowds, the (ones) going before and the (ones) following,
ἔκραζον, λέγοντες, Ὡσαννὰ τῷ υἱῷ Δαβίδ· εὐλογημένος ὁ
were crying out, saying, Hosanna to the Son of David! Blessed (Is) He
ἐρχόμενος ἐν ὀνόματι Κυρίου· Ὡσαννὰ ἐν τοῖς ὑψίστοις.
coming in (the) name of the Lord; Hosanna in the highest!
10 καὶ εἰσελθόντος αὐτοῦ εἰς Ἱεροσόλυμα, ἐσείσθη πᾶσα ἡ
And entering He into Jerusalem, was shaken all the
11 πόλις, λέγουσα, Τίς ἐστιν οὗτος; οἱ δὲ ὄχλοι ἔλεγον,
city, saying, Who is this? the And crowds said,
Οὗτός ἐστιν Ἰησοῦς ὁ προφήτης, ὁ ἀπὸ Ναζαρὲθ τῆς
This is Jesus the prophet, the (one) from Nazareth —
Γαλιλαίας.
of Galilee.

12 Καὶ εἰσῆλθεν ὁ Ἰησοῦς εἰς τὸ ἱερὸν τοῦ Θεοῦ, καὶ ἐξέβαλε
And went in — Jesus into the Temple — of God, and threw out
πάντας τοὺς πωλοῦντας καὶ ἀγοράζοντας ἐν τῷ ἱερῷ, καὶ
all the (ones) selling and buying in the Temple. And
τὰς τραπέζας τῶν κολλυβιστῶν κατέστρεψε, καὶ τὰς
the tables of the moneychangers He overthrew, and the
13 καθέδρας τῶν πωλούντων τὰς περιστεράς. καὶ λέγει αὐτοῖς,
seats of the (ones) selling the doves. And He says to them,
Γέγραπται, Ὁ οἶκός μου οἶκος προσευχῆς κληθήσεται·
It has been written, The house of Me a house of prayer shall be called;
14 ὑμεῖς δὲ αὐτὸν ἐποιήσατε σπήλαιον λῃστῶν. καὶ προσῆλθον
you but it have made a den of robbers. And came near

ones came to Him in the Temple, and He healed them. [15]But the chief priests and the scribes, seeing the wonders which He did, and the children crying out in the Temple, and saying, Hosanna to the Son of David, they were incensed. [16]And *they* said to Him, Do you hear what these say? And Jesus said to them, Yes. Have you never read, "Out of *the* mouth of babes and sucklings You have perfected praise? [17]And leaving them, He went out of the city to Bethany, and spent the night there.

[18]And returning early to the city, He hungered. [19]And seeing one fig-tree by the road, He went up *to* it, and found nothing on it except leaves only. And He said to it, Let there be no more fruit from you forever. And the fig-tree immediately dried up. [20]And seeing, the disciples marveled, saying, How quickly the fig-tree is dried up! [21]And answering Jesus said to them, Truly I say to you, If you have faith and do not doubt, not only will you do the *miracle* of the fig-tree, but even if you should say to this mountain, Be taken up and thrown into the sea—it will be *so*. [22]And all things, whatever you may ask in prayer, believing, you shall receive.

[23]And He coming into the Temple, the chief priests and elders of the people came near to Him *as He was* teaching, saying, By what authority do you do these things? And who gave this authority? [24]And answering Jesus said to them, I also will ask you one thing, which if you tell Me, I also will tell you by what authority I do these things. [25]The baptism of John, from where was it? From Heaven, or from men? [26]And they reasoned by themselves, saying, If we should say, From Heaven, He will say to us, Then why did you not believe him? But if we should say, From men,

αὐτῷ τυφλοὶ καὶ χωλοὶ ἐν τῷ ἱερῷ· καὶ ἐθεράπευσεν αὐτούς.
to Him blind and lame in the Temple. and He healed them.
15 ἰδόντες δὲ οἱ ἀρχιερεῖς καὶ οἱ γραμματεῖς τὰ θαυμάσια ἃ
seeing But the chief priests and the scribes the wonders which
ἐποίησε, καὶ τοὺς παῖδας κράζοντας ἐν τῷ ἱερῷ, καὶ λέγον-
He did and the children crying out in the Temple, and saying,
16 τας, Ὡσαννὰ τῷ υἱῷ Δαβίδ, ἠγανάκτησαν, καὶ εἶπον αὐτῷ,
Hosanna to the Son of David, they were incensed, and said to Him,
Ἀκούεις τί οὗτοι λέγουσιν; ὁ δὲ Ἰησοῦς λέγει αὐτοῖς, Ναί·
Do you hear what these say? And Jesus says to them, Yes.
οὐδέποτε ἀνέγνωτε ὅτι Ἐκ στόματος νηπίων καὶ θηλα-
never Did you read, — Out of (the) mouth of babes and sucking
17 ζόντων κατηρτίσω αἶνον; καὶ καταλιπὼν αὐτοὺς ἐξῆλθεν
(ones) You have perfected praise? And leaving them He went
ἔξω τῆς πόλεως εἰς Βηθανίαν, καὶ ηὐλίσθη ἐκεῖ.
out of the city to Bethany, and lodged there.
18 Πρωΐας δὲ ἐπανάγων εἰς τὴν πόλιν, ἐπείνασε· καὶ ἰδὼν
19 early And returning to the city, He hungered. And seeing
συκῆν μίαν ἐπὶ τῆς ὁδοῦ, ἦλθεν ἐπ' αὐτήν, καὶ οὐδὲν εὗρεν
fig-tree one on the way, He went up (to) it, and nothing found
ἐν αὐτῇ εἰ μὴ φύλλα μόνον· καὶ λέγει αὐτῇ, Μηκέτι ἐκ σοῦ
in it, except leaves only, and He says to it, No longer of you
καρπὸς γένηται εἰς τὸν αἰῶνα. καὶ ἐξηράνθη παραχρῆμα ἡ
fruit may be to the age. And was dried up instantly the
20 συκῆ. καὶ ἰδόντες οἱ μαθηταὶ ἐθαύμασαν, λέγοντες, Πῶς
fig-tree. And seeing the disciples marveled, saying, How
21 παραχρῆμα ἐξηράνθη ἡ συκῆ; ἀποκριθεὶς δὲ ὁ Ἰησοῦς
instantly was withered the fig-tree! answering And — Jesus
εἶπεν αὐτοῖς, Ἀμὴν λέγω ὑμῖν, ἐὰν ἔχητε πίστιν, καὶ μὴ
said to them, Truly I say to you, If you have faith and not
διακριθῆτε, οὐ μόνον τὸ τῆς συκῆς ποιήσετε, ἀλλα κἂν τῷ
do doubt, not only that of the fig-tree you will do, but also if to
ὄρει τούτῳ εἴπητε, Ἄρθητι καὶ βλήθητι εἰς τὴν θάλασσαν,
mountain this you say, Be taken and thrown into the sea,
22 γενήσεται. καὶ πάντα ὅσα ἂν αἰτήσητε ἐν τῇ προσευχῇ,
it will be. And all things, whatever you ask in — prayer,
πιστεύοντες, λήψεσθε.
believing, you will receive.

23 Καὶ ἐλθόντι αὐτῷ εἰς τὸ ἱερόν, προσῆλθον αὐτῷ διδά-
And coming He into the Temple, approached to Him teach-
σκοντι οἱ ἀρχιερεῖς καὶ οἱ πρεσβύτεροι τοῦ λαοῦ, λέγοντες,
ing the chief priests and the elders of the people, saying
Ἐν ποίᾳ ἐξουσίᾳ ταῦτα ποιεῖς; καὶ τίς σοι ἔδωκε τὴν
By what authority these things do you? And who gave —
24 ἐξουσίαν ταύτην; ἀποκριθεὶς δὲ ὁ Ἰησοῦς εἶπεν αὐτοῖς,
authority this? answering And — Jesus said to them,
Ἐρωτήσω ὑμᾶς κἀγὼ λόγον ἕνα, ὃν ἐὰν εἴπητέ μοι, κἀγὼ
will question you I also word one, which if you tell Me, I also
25 ὑμιν ἐρῶ ἐν ποίᾳ ἐξουσίᾳ ταῦτα ποιῶ. τὸ βάπτισμα Ἰωάννου
you I will tell by what authority these I do: The baptism of John,
πόθεν ἦν; ἐξ οὐρανοῦ ἢ ἐξ ἀνθρώπων; οἱ δὲ διελογίζοντο
whence was it? From Heaven or from men? they And reasoned
παρ' ἑαυτοῖς, λέγοντες, Ἐὰν εἴπωμεν, ἐξ οὐρανοῦ, ἐρεῖ ἡμῖν,
by themselves, saying, If we say from Heaven, He will say to us
26 Διατί οὖν οὐκ ἐπιστεύσατε αὐτῷ; ἐὰν δὲ εἴπωμεν, ἐξ ἀνθρώ-
Why then not you did believe him? if But we say from men,

we fear the people. For all hold John to be a prophet. [27] And answering Jesus they said, We do not know. And He said to them, Neither do I tell you by what authority I do these things.

[28] But what do you think? A man had two children, and coming to the first he said, Child, go today; work in my vineyard. [29] And answering he said, I will not. But afterward, feeling sorry, he went. [30] And coming to the second, he said the same. And answering he said, I *go,* sir, but did not go. [31] Which of the two did the will of the father? They said to Him, The first. Jesus said to them, Truly I say to you, The tax-collectors and the harlots go before you into the kingdom of God. [32] For John came to you in *the* way of righteousness, and you did not believe him. But the tax-collectors and the harlots believed him. And seeing, you did not repent afterwards to believe him.

[33] Hear another parable: There was a certain man, a housemaster who planted a vineyard and placed a hedge around it, and dug a winepress in it, and built a tower. And *he* rented it to vinedressers, and left the country. [34] And when the season of the fruits came, he sent his slaves to the vinedressers to receive his fruits. [35] And the vinedressers taking his slaves, they beat this one, and they killed one; and they stoned another. [36] Again he sent other slaves, more than the first. And they did the same to them. [37] And at last he sent his son to them, saying, They will have respect for my son. [38] But seeing the son, the vinedressers said among themselves, This is the heir. Come,

πων, φοβούμεθα τὸν ὄχλον· πάντες γὰρ ἔχουσι τὸν Ἰωάννην
we fear the crowd. all For hold — John
27 ὡς προφήτην. καὶ ἀποκριθέντες τῷ Ἰησοῦ εἶπον, Οὐκ
as a prophet. And answering — Jesus they said, not
οἴδαμεν. ἔφη αὐτοῖς καὶ αὐτός, Οὐδὲ ἐγὼ λέγω ὑμῖν ἐν ποίᾳ
we do know. said to them And He, Neither I tell you by what
28 ἐξουσίᾳ ταῦτα ποιῶ. τί δὲ ὑμῖν δοκεῖ; ἄνθρωπος εἶχε
authority these things I do. what But to you seems it? A man had
τέκνα δύο, καὶ προσελθὼν τῷ πρώτῳ εἶπε, Τέκνον, ὕπαγε,
children two, and having come to the first he said, Child, go,
29 σήμερον ἐργάζου ἐν τῷ ἀμπελῶνί μου. ὁ δὲ ἀποκριθεὶς εἶπεν,
today work in the vineyard of me. he And answering said,
30 Οὐ θέλω· ὕστερον δὲ μεταμεληθείς, ἀπῆλθε. καὶ προσελθὼν
not I will. afterwards But feeling sorry he went. And having come
τῷ δευτέρῳ εἶπεν ὡσαύτως. ὁ δὲ ἀποκριθεὶς εἶπεν, Ἐγώ,
to the second, he said likewise. he And answering said, I (go),
31 κύριε· καὶ οὐκ ἀπῆλθε. τίς ἐκ τῶν δύο ἐποίησε τὸ θέλημα
lord, and not did leave. Who of the two did the will
τοῦ πατρός; λέγουσιν αὐτῷ, Ὁ πρῶτος. λέγει αὐτοῖς ὁ
of the father? They say to Him, The first. says to them —
Ἰησοῦς, Ἀμὴν λέγω ὑμῖν, ὅτι οἱ τελῶναι καὶ αἱ πόρναι
Jesus, Truly I say to you, that the tax-collectors and the harlots
32 προάγουσιν ὑμᾶς εἰς τὴν βασιλείαν τοῦ Θεοῦ. ἦλθε γὰρ
go before you into the kingdom — of God. came For
πρὸς ὑμᾶς Ἰωάννης ἐν ὁδῷ δικαιοσύνης, καὶ οὐκ ἐπιστεύ-
to you John in (the) way of righteousness, and not you did
σατε αὐτῷ· οἱ δὲ τελῶναι καὶ αἱ πόρναι ἐπίστευσαν αὐτῷ·
believe him; the but tax-collectors and the harlots believed him.
ὑμεῖς δὲ ἰδόντες οὐ μετεμελήθητε ὕστερον τοῦ πιστεῦσαι
you And seeing, not felt sorry afterwards — to believe
αὐτῷ.
him.

33 Ἄλλην παραβολὴν ἀκούσατε. ἄνθρωπός τις ἦν οἰκοδε-
Another parable hear: A man certain was a house-
σπότης, ὅστις ἐφύτευσεν ἀμπελῶνα, καὶ φραγμὸν αὐτῷ
master, who planted a vineyard, and a hedge it
περιέθηκε, καὶ ὤρυξεν ἐν αὐτῷ ληνόν, καὶ ᾠκοδόμησε πύργον,
put around, and dug in it a winepress, and built a tower,
34 καὶ ἐξέδοτο αὐτὸν γεωργοῖς, καὶ ἀπεδήμησεν. ὅτε δὲ
and rented it to vinedressers, and departed. when And
ἤγγισεν ὁ καιρὸς τῶν καρπῶν, ἀπέστειλε τοὺς δούλους
drew near the time of the fruits, he sent the slaves
αὐτοῦ πρὸς τοὺς γεωργούς, λαβεῖν τοὺς καρποὺς αὐτοῦ·
of him to the vinedressers, to receive the fruits of it.
35 καὶ λαβόντες οἱ γεωργοὶ τοὺς δούλους αὐτοῦ, ὃν μὲν ἔδειραν,
And taking the vinedressers the slaves of him, this one they beat,
36 ὃν δὲ ἀπέκτειναν, ὃν δὲ ἐλιθοβόλησαν. πάλιν ἀπέστειλεν
one and they killed; one and they stoned. Again he sent
ἄλλους δούλους πλείονας τῶν πρώτων· καὶ ἐποίησαν αὐτοῖς
other slaves, more (than) the first, and they did to them
37 ὡσαύτως. ὕστερον δὲ ἀπέστειλε πρὸς αὐτοὺς τὸν υἱὸν
likewise. later But he sent to them the son
38 αὐτοῦ, λέγων, Ἐντραπήσονται τὸν υἱόν μου. οἱ δὲ γεωργοὶ
of him, saying, They will respect the son of me. the But vinedressers
ἰδόντες τὸν υἱὸν εἶπον ἐν ἑαυτοῖς, Οὗτός ἐστιν ὁ κληρονόμος·
seeing the son said among themselves, This is the heir;

let us kill him, and get hold of his inheritance. [39]And taking him, they threw *him* out of the vineyard, and killed *him*. [40]Therefore, when the lord of the vineyard comes, what will he do to these vinedressers? [41]They said to Him, Bad men! He will miserably destroy them, and he will rent out the vineyard to other vinedressers who will give to him the fruits in their seasons. [42]Jesus said to them, Did you never read in the Scriptures, "*The* Stone which the builders rejected is the One that has become the head of the corner. This was from the Lord, and it is wonderful in our eyes"? [43]Because of this I say to you, The kingdom of God shall be taken from you, and it will be given to a nation bringing forth the fruits of it. [44]And he who falls on this Stone will be broken; but on whomever it falls, it will grind him to powder. [45]And hearing His parables, the chief priests and the Pharisees knew that He was speaking about them. [46]And seeking to lay hold of Him, they feared the crowds, because they held Him as a prophet.

δεῦτε, ἀποκτείνωμεν αὐτόν, καὶ κατάσχωμεν τὴν κληρονο-
come, let us kill him, and let us possess the inheritance
39 μίαν αὐτοῦ. καὶ λαβόντες αὐτὸν ἐξέβαλον ἔξω τοῦ ἀμπε-
of him. And taking him, they threw out the vine-
40 λῶνος καὶ ἀπέκτειναν. ὅταν οὖν ἔλθῃ ὁ κύριος τοῦ
yard and killed When therefore comes the lord of the
41 ἀμπελῶνος, τί ποιήσει τοῖς γεωργοῖς ἐκείνοις; λέγουσιν
vineyard, what will he do to vinedressers those? They say
αὐτῷ, Κακοὺς κακῶς ἀπολέσει αὐτούς, καὶ τὸν ἀμπελῶνα
to Him, Bad men, badly he will destroy them, and the vineyard
ἐκδόσεται ἄλλοις γεωργοῖς, οἵτινες ἀποδώσουσιν αὐτῷ
he will give out to other vinedressers, who will render to him
42 τοὺς καρποὺς ἐν τοῖς καιροῖς αὐτῶν. λέγει αὐτοῖς ὁ Ἰησοῦς,
the fruits in the seasons of them. says to them — Jesus,
Οὐδέποτε ἀνέγνωτε ἐν ταῖς γραφαῖς, Λίθον ὃν ἀπεδοκί-
never Did you read in the Scriptures: A stone which rejected
μασαν οἱ οἰκοδομοῦντες, οὗτος ἐγενήθη εἰς κεφαλὴν
the builders, this (one) became — head
γωνίας· παρὰ Κυρίου ἐγένετο αὕτη, καὶ ἔστι θαυμαστὴ ἐν
of corner; from (the) Lord happened this, and it is a wonder in
43 ὀφθαλμοῖς ἡμῶν; διὰ τοῦτο λέγω ὑμῖν ὅτι ἀρθήσεται ἀφ'
(the) eyes of us? Because of this I tell you, that will be taken from
ὑμῶν ἡ βασιλεία τοῦ Θεοῦ, καὶ δοθήσεται ἔθνει ποιοῦντι
you the kingdom — of God, and will be given to a nation producing
44 τοὺς καρποὺς ἐν τοῖς και ὁ πεσὼν ἐπὶ τὸν λίθον τοῦτον,
the fruits of it. And the (one) falling on — stone this
45 συνθλασθήσεται· ἐφ' ὃν δ' ἂν πέσῃ, λικμήσει αὐτόν. καὶ
will be broken up; upon whom but ever it fall, it will pulverize him. And
ἀκούσαντες οἱ ἀρχιερεῖς καὶ οἱ Φαρισαῖοι τὰς παραβολὰς
hearing the chief priests and the Pharisees the parables
46 αὐτοῦ ἔγνωσαν ὅτι περὶ αὐτῶν λέγει. καὶ ζητοῦντες αὐτὸν
of Him, they knew that about them He says; and seeking Him
κρατῆσαι, ἐφοβήθησαν τοὺς ὄχλους, ἐπειδὴ ὡς προφήτην
to seize, they feared the crowds, because as a prophet
αὐτὸν εἶχον.
Him they held.

CHAPTER 22

[1]And answering Jesus again spoke to them in parables, saying: [2]The kingdom of Heaven has been compared to a man, a king, who made a wedding feast for his son. [3]And *he* sent his slaves to call those who had been invited to the wedding feast but they would not come. [4]Again, he sent other slaves, saying, Tell the *ones* invited, Behold, I have prepared my supper, my oxen, and the fatlings are killed, and all things ready; come to the wedding feast. [5]But not caring they went away, one to his own field,

1 Καὶ ἀποκριθεὶς ὁ Ἰησοῦς πάλιν εἶπεν αὐτοῖς ἐν παρα-
And answering — Jesus again spoke to them in parables,
2 βολαῖς, λέγων, Ὡμοιώθη ἡ βασιλεία τῶν οὐρανῶν ἀνθρώπῳ
saying, Is likened the kingdom of the heavens to a man,
3 βασιλεῖ, ὅστις ἐποίησε γάμους τῷ υἱῷ αὐτοῦ· καὶ ἀπέστειλε
a king, who made a wedding feast to the son of him. And he sent
τοὺς δούλους αὐτοῦ καλέσαι τοὺς κεκλημένους εἰς τοὺς
the slaves of him to call the (ones) being called to the
4 γάμους, καὶ οὐκ ἤθελον ἐλθεῖν. πάλιν ἀπέστειλεν ἄλλους
wedding. And not they desired to come. Again he sent other
δούλους, λέγων, Εἴπατε τοῖς κεκλημένοις, Ἰδού, τὸ ἄριστόν
slaves, saying, Tell the (ones) called, Behold, the supper
μου ἡτοίμασα, οἱ ταῦροί μου καὶ τὰ σιτιστὰ τεθυμένα, καὶ
of me I have readied; the oxen of me and the fatted beasts are killed, and
5 πάντα ἕτοιμα· δεῦτε εἰς τοὺς γάμους. οἱ δὲ ἀμελήσαντες
all things ready. Come to the wedding feast they But not caring
ἀπῆλθον, ὁ μὲν εἰς τὸν ἴδιον ἀγρόν, ὁ δὲ εἰς τὴν ἐμπορίαν
went off, one to the own field, one and to the trading

and one to his trading. [6]And the rest, seizing his slaves, insulted and killed *them.* [7]And hearing, the king was angry. And sending his armies, *he* destroyed those murderers, and burned their city. [8]Then he said to his slaves, Indeed, the wedding feast is ready, but those having been called were not worthy. [9]Therefore, go onto the exits of the highways, and call to the wedding feast as many as you may find. [10]And going out into the highways, those slaves gathered all, as many as they found, both evil and good. And the wedding feast was filled with reclining guests. [11]And the king coming in to look over those reclining, he saw a man there who was not dressed *in* a wedding garment. [12]And he said to him, Friend, how did you get in here, not having a wedding garment? But he was silent. [13]Then the king said to the servants, Binding his feet and hands, take him away, and throw *him* out into the outer darkness. There shall be weeping and the gnashing of the teeth. [14]For many are called, but few chosen.

[15]Then going, the Pharisees took counsel so as they might trap Him in words. [16]And they sent to Him their disciples with the Herodians, saying, Teacher, we know that you are true, and teach the way of God in truth; and it does not concern you about anyone, for you do not look to *the* face of men. [17]Then tell us, what do you think? Is it lawful to give tribute to Caesar, or not?

[18]But knowing their wickedness, Jesus said, Why do you test Me, hypocrites? [19]Show Me the tribute coin. And they brought to Him a denarius. [20]And He said to them, Whose image and superscription is this?

[21]And they said to Him, Caesar's. Then He said to

6 αὐτοῦ· οἱ δὲ λοιποὶ κρατήσαντες τοὺς δούλους αὐτου
of him; the and rest seizing the slaves of him
7 ὕβρισαν καὶ ἀπέκτειναν. ἀκούσας δὲ ὁ βασιλεὺς ὠργίσθη,
insulted and killed. hearing And the king became angry,
καὶ πέμψας τὰ στρατεύματα αὐτοῦ ἀπώλεσε τοὺς φονεῖς
and sending the armies of him destroyed — murderers
8 ἐκείνους, καὶ τὴν πόλιν αὐτῶν ἐνέπρησε. τότε λέγει τοῖς
those, also the city of them burned. Then he says to the
δούλοις αὐτοῦ, Ὁ μὲν γάμος ἕτοιμός ἐστιν, οἱ δὲ κεκλημένοι
slaves of him, the Indeed wedding ready is, those but called
9 οὐκ ἦσαν ἄξιοι. πορεύεσθε οὖν ἐπὶ τὰς διεξόδους τῶν ὁδῶν,
not were worthy. You go therefore onto the exits of the ways,
10 καὶ ὅσους ἂν εὕρητε, καλέσατε εἰς τοὺς γάμους. καὶ ἐξελ-
and as many as you find call to the feast. And going
θόντες οἱ δοῦλοι ἐκεῖνοι εἰς τὰς ὁδοὺς συνήγαγον πάντας
forth slaves those into the ways gathered all
ὅσους εὗρον, πονηρούς τε καὶ ἀγαθούς· καὶ ἐπλήσθη ὁ
as many as they found; evil both and good; and was filled the
11 γάμος ἀνακειμένων. εἰσελθὼν δὲ ὁ βασιλεὺς θεάσασθαι τοὺς
wedding with recliners. coming in And the king to view those
ἀνακειμένους εἶδεν ἐκεῖ ἄνθρωπον οὐκ ἐνδεδυμένον ἔνδυμα
reclining he saw there a man not being dressed (in) a dress
12 γάμου· καὶ λέγει αὐτῷ, Ἑταῖρε, πῶς εἰσῆλθες ὧδε μὴ ἔχων
of wedding. And he to him, Friend, how did you enter here not having
13 ἔνδυμα γάμου; ὁ δὲ ἐφιμώθη. τότε εἶπεν ὁ βασιλεὺς τοῖς
a dress of wedding? he But was silent. Then said the king to the
διακόνοις, Δήσαντες αὐτοῦ πόδας καὶ χεῖρας, ἄρατε αὐτὸν
servants, Binding of him (the) feet and hands, take away him
καὶ ἐκβάλετε εἰς τὸ σκότος τὸ ἐξώτερον· ἐκεῖ ἔσται ὁ κλαυθμὸς
and throw out into the darkness outer, there shall be the weeping
14 καὶ ὁ βρυγμὸς τῶν ὀδόντων. πολλοὶ γάρ εἰσι κλητοί, ὀλίγοι
and the gnashing of the teeth. many For are called, few
δὲ ἐκλεκτοί.
but chosen.

15 Τότε πορευθέντες οἱ Φαρισαῖοι συμβούλιον ἔλαβον ὅπως
Then going the Pharisees counsel took so as
16 αὐτὸν παγιδεύσωσιν ἐν λόγῳ. καὶ ἀποστέλλουσιν αὐτῷ
Him they might trap in discourse. And they send forth to Him
τοὺς μαθητὰς αὐτῶν μετὰ τῶν Ἡρωδιανῶν, λέγοντες,
the disciples of them with the Herodians, saying,
Διδάσκαλε, οἴδαμεν ὅτι ἀληθὴς εἶ, καὶ τὴν ὁδὸν τοῦ Θεοῦ
Teacher, we know that truthful you are, and the way — of God
ἐν ἀληθείᾳ διδάσκεις, καὶ οὐ μέλει σοι περὶ οὐδενός, οὐ γὰρ
in truth you teach. and not it concerns you about no one; not for
17 βλέπεις εἰς πρόσωπον ἀνθρώπων. εἰπὲ οὖν ἡμῖν, τί σοι
you look to face of men. Tell therefore us, what you
18 δοκεῖ; ἔξεστι δοῦναι κῆνσον Καίσαρι, ἢ οὔ; γνοὺς δὲ ὁ
think: Is it lawful to give tribute to Caesar, or not? knowing But —
Ἰησοῦς τὴν πονηρίαν αὐτῶν εἶπε, Τί με πειράζετε, ὑπο-
Jesus the wickedness of them, said, Why Me you tempt, hypo-
19 κριταί; ἐπιδείξατέ μοι τὸ νόμισμα τοῦ κήνσου. οἱ δὲ προσ-
crites? Show Me the coin of the tribute. they And brought
20 ήνεγκαν αὐτῷ δηνάριον. καὶ λέγει αὐτοῖς, Τίνος ἡ εἰκὼν
to Him a denarius. And He says to them, Of whom — image
21 αὕτη καὶ ἡ ἐπιγραφή; λέγουσιν αὐτῷ, Καίσαρος. τότε λέγει
this and — superscription? They say to Him, Of Caesar. Then He says

them. Then give to Caesar the things of Caesar, and to God the things of God. [22] And hearing, they marveled. And leaving Him, they went away.

[23] On that day Sadducees came to Him, who say there is no resurrection. And they questioned Him, [24] saying, Teacher, Moses said, If anyone should die not having children, his brother shall marry his wife, and shall raise up seed to his brother. [25] And there were seven brothers with us, and having married, the first expired, and not having seed left his wife to his brother. [26] In the same way also the second, and the third, to the seven. [27] And last of all the woman died. [28] Therefore, in the resurrection, of which of the seven will she be wife? For all had her. [29] And answering Jesus said to them, You err, not knowing the Scriptures, nor the power of God. [30] For in the resurrection they neither marry nor are given in marriage, but they are as the angels of God in Heaven. [31] But concerning the resurrection of the dead, have you not read that which was spoken to you by God, saying, [32] "I am the God of Abraham, and the God of Isaac, and the God of Jacob"? God is not God of the dead, but of the living. [33] And hearing, the crowds were astonished at His teaching.

[34] But hearing that He had silenced the Sadducees, the Pharisees were gathered together. [35] And one of them, a lawyer, questioned *Him,* testing Him, and saying, [36] Teacher, which *is the* great commandment in the Law? [37] And Jesus said to him, You shall love *the* Lord your God with all your heart, and with all your soul, and with all your mind. [38] This is *the* first and great commandment.

[39] And *the* second *is* like it,

αὐτοῖς, Ἀπόδοτε οὖν τὰ Καίσαρος Καίσαρι· καὶ τὰ τοῦ
to them, Render then the things of Caesar to Caesar, and the things
22 Θεοῦ τῷ Θεῷ. καὶ ἀκούσαντες ἐθαύμασαν· καὶ ἀφέντες αὐτὸν
of God – to God. And hearing they marveled, and leaving Him
ἀπῆλθον.
they went away.

23 Ἐν ἐκείνῃ τῇ ἡμέρᾳ προσῆλθον αὐτῷ Σαδδουκαῖοι, οἱ
On that – day approaching to Him Sadducees, who
λέγοντες μὴ εἶναι ἀνάστασιν, καὶ ἐπηρώτησαν αὐτόν,
are saying not to be a resurrection. And they questioned Him,
24 λέγοντες, Διδάσκαλε, Μωσῆς εἶπεν, Ἐάν τις ἀποθάνῃ μὴ
saying, Teacher, Moses said, If any (man) die not
ἔχων τέκνα, ἐπιγαμβρεύσει ὁ ἀδελφὸς αὐτοῦ τὴν γυναῖκα
having children, shall take to wife the brother of him the wife
25 αὐτοῦ, καὶ ἀναστήσει σπέρμα τῷ ἀδελφῷ αὐτοῦ. ἦσαν δὲ
of him and shall raise up seed to the brother of him. were And
παρ' ἡμῖν ἑπτὰ ἀδελφοί· καὶ ὁ πρῶτος γαμήσας ἐτελεύτησε·
with us seven brothers; and the first having married ended (his life),
καὶ μὴ ἔχων σπέρμα, ἀφῆκε τὴν γυναῖκα αὐτοῦ τῷ ἀδελφῷ
and not having seed left the wife of him to the brother
26 αὐτοῦ. ὁμοίως καὶ ὁ δεύτερος, καὶ ὁ τρίτος, ἕως τῶν ἑπτά.
of him; likewise also the second, and the third, until the seven.
27 ὕστερον δὲ πάντων ἀπέθανε καὶ ἡ γυνή. ἐν τῇ οὖν ἀναστάσει,
28 **last And of all died also the woman. in the Then resurrection,**
τίνος τῶν ἑπτὰ ἔσται γυνή; πάντες γὰρ ἔσχον αὐτήν.
of which of the seven will she be wife? all For had her.
29 ἀποκριθεὶς δὲ ὁ Ἰησοῦς εἶπεν αὐτοῖς, Πλανᾶσθε, μὴ εἰδότες
answering And – Jesus said to them, You err, not knowing
30 τὰς γραφάς, μηδὲ τὴν δύναμιν τοῦ Θεοῦ. ἐν γὰρ τῇ ἀναστά-
the Scriptures, nor the power – of God. in For the resurrection
σει οὔτε γαμοῦσιν, οὔτε ἐκγαμίζονται, ἀλλ' ὡς ἄγγελοι τοῦ
neither they marry, nor are given in marriage; but as angels –
31 Θεοῦ ἐν οὐρανῷ εἰσι. περὶ δὲ τῆς ἀναστάσεως τῶν νεκρῶν,
of God. in Heaven they are. about But the resurrection of the dead,
32 οὐκ ἀνέγνωτε τὸ ῥηθὲν ὑμῖν ὑπὸ τοῦ Θεοῦ, λέγοντος, Ἐγώ
not have you read that spoken to you by – God, saying, I
εἰμι ὁ Θεὸς Ἀβραάμ, καὶ ὁ Θεὸς Ἰσαάκ, καὶ ὁ Θεὸς Ἰακώβ;
am the God of Abraham, and the God of Isaac, and the God of Jacob?
33 οὐκ ἔστιν ὁ Θεὸς Θεὸς νεκρῶν, ἀλλὰ ζώντων. καὶ ἀκού-
not is God God of the dead, but of (the) living. And having
σαντες οἱ ὄχλοι ἐξεπλήσσοντο ἐπὶ τῇ διδαχῇ αὐτοῦ.
heard, the crowds were astounded at the teaching of Him.
34 Οἱ δὲ Φαρισαῖοι, ἀκούσαντες ὅτι ἐφίμωσε τοὺς Σαδδου-
the But Pharisees hearing that He silenced the Sadducees,
35 καίους, συνήχθησαν ἐπὶ τὸ αὐτό. καὶ ἐπηρώτησεν εἷς ἐξ
were assembled together, and questioned one of
36 αὐτῶν νομικός, πειράζων αὐτόν, καὶ λέγων, Διδάσκαλε,
them, a lawyer, tempting Him; and saying, Teacher,
37 ποία ἐντολὴ μεγάλη ἐν τῷ νόμῳ; ὁ δὲ Ἰησοῦς εἶπεν αὐτῷ,
which command (is) great in the Law? And Jesus said to him,
Ἀγαπήσεις Κύριον τὸν Θεόν σου, ἐν ὅλῃ τῇ καρδίᾳ σου,
You shall love the Lord the God of you, with all the heart of you,
38 καὶ ἐν ὅλῃ τῇ ψυχῇ σου, καὶ ἐν ὅλῃ τῇ διανοίᾳ σου. αὕτη
and with all the soul of you, and with all the mind of you. This
39 ἐστὶ πρώτη καὶ μεγάλη ἐντολή. δευτέρα δὲ ὁμοία αὐτῇ,
is the first and great commandment; second and like to it,

You shall love your neighbor as yourself. [40]On these two commandments all the Law and the Prophets hang.

[41]But the Pharisees having been gathered, Jesus questioned them, [42]saying, What do you think about the Christ? Whose son is He? They say to Him, David's. [43]He said to them, Then how does David in Spirit call Him Lord, saying, [44]"The Lord said to my Lord, Sit on My right until I place your enemies as a footstool for Your feet"? [45]Therefore, if David calls Him Lord, how is He his son? [46]And no one was able to answer Him a word, nor did anyone dare from that day to question Him any more.

CHAPTER 23

[1]Then Jesus spoke to the crowd and to His disciples, [2]saying, The scribes and the Pharisees sat on Moses' seat. [3]Then all things, whatever they tell you to keep, keep and do. But do not do according to their works; for they say, and do not do.

[4]For they bind heavy and hard to bear burdens, and lay *them* on the shoulders of men; but they will not move them with their finger. [5]And they do all their works to be seen by men. And they make their phylacteries broad, and enlarge the borders of their robes. [6]And *they* love the first couch in the suppers, and the first seats in the synagogues, [7]and the greetings in the markets, and to be called by men, Rabbi, Rabbi. [8]But do not you be called Rabbi; for one is your leader, the Christ, and you are all brothers. [9]And do not call *anyone* father on earth, for one is your Father, the *One* in

40 Ἀγαπήσεις τὸν πλησίον σου ὡς σεαυτόν. ἐν ταύταις ταῖς
You shall love the neighbor of you as yourself. In these —
δυσὶν ἐντολαῖς ὅλος ὁ νόμος καὶ οἱ προφῆται κρέμανται.
two commandments all the Law and the prophets hang.
41 Συνηγμένων δὲ τῶν Φαρισαίων, ἐπηρώτησεν αὐτοὺς ὁ
having been assembled But the Pharisees, questioned them
42 Ἰησοῦς, λέγων, Τί ὑμῖν δοκεῖ περὶ τοῦ Χριστοῦ; τίνος υἱός
Jesus, saying, What to you seems about the Christ? Of whom son
43 ἐστι; λέγουσιν αὐτῷ, Τοῦ Δαβίδ. λέγει αὐτοῖς, Πῶς οὖν
is He? They say to Him, Of David. He says to them, How then
44 Δαβὶδ ἐν πνεύματι Κύριον αὐτὸν καλεῖ, λέγων, Εἶπεν ὁ
David by (the) Spirit Lord Him does call, saying, Said the
Κύριος τῷ Κυρίῳ μου, Κάθου ἐκ δεξιῶν μου, ἕως ἂν θῶ τοὺς
Lord to the Lord of me, Sit on the right of Me until I put the
45 ἐχθρούς σου ὑποπόδιον τῶν ποδῶν σου; εἰ οὖν Δαβὶδ
enemies of You (as) a footstool of the feet of You? If, then, David
46 καλεῖ αὐτὸν Κύριον, πῶς υἱὸς αὐτοῦ ἐστι; καὶ οὐδεὶς ἐδύνατο
calls Him Lord, how a son of him is He? And no one was able
αὐτῷ ἀποκριθῆναι λόγον· οὐδὲ ἐτόλμησέ τις ἀπ' ἐκείνης τῆς
Him to answer a word, nor dared anyone from that —
ἡμέρας ἐπερωτῆσαι αὐτὸν οὐκέτι.
day to question Him no longer.

CHAPTER 23

1 Τότε ὁ Ἰησοῦς ἐλάλησε τοῖς ὄχλοις καὶ τοῖς μαθηταῖς
Then — Jesus spoke to the crowd and to the disciples
2 αὐτοῦ, λέγων, Ἐπὶ τῆς Μωσέως καθέδρας ἐκάθισαν οἱ
of Him, saying, On the of Moses seat sat the
3 γραμματεῖς καὶ οἱ Φαρισαῖοι· πάντα οὖν ὅσα ἂν εἴπωσιν
scribes and the Pharisees. All things, then, whatever they tell
ὑμῖν τηρεῖν, τηρεῖτε καὶ ποιεῖτε· κατὰ δὲ τὰ ἔργα αὐτῶν μὴ
you to keep, keep and do. after But the works of them not
4 ποιεῖτε, λέγουσι γὰρ καὶ οὐ ποιοῦσι. δεσμεύουσι γὰρ φορτία
do you. they say For and not do. they bind For burdens
βαρέα καὶ δυσβάστακτα, καὶ ἐπιτιθέασιν ἐπὶ τοὺς ὤμους
heavy, and hard to bear, and lay (them) on the shoulders
τῶν ἀνθρώπων, τῷ δὲ δακτύλῳ αὐτῶν οὐ θέλουσι κινῆσαι
— of men; with the but finger of them not they wish to move
5 αὐτά. πάντα δὲ τὰ ἔργα αὐτῶν ποιοῦσι πρὸς τὸ θεαθῆναι
them. all But the works of them they do in order to be seen
τοῖς ἀνθρώποις· πλατύνουσι δὲ τὰ φυλακτήρια αὐτῶν, καὶ
— by men; they broaden And the phylacteries of them, and
6 μεγαλύνουσι τὰ κράσπεδα τῶν ἱματίων αὐτῶν· φιλοῦσί τε
enlarge the fringes of the garments of them; they love and
τὴν πρωτοκλισίαν ἐν τοῖς δείπνοις, καὶ τὰς πρωτοκαθεδρίας
the first couch in the suppers, and the first seats
7 ἐν ταῖς συναγωγαῖς, καὶ τοὺς ἀσπασμοὺς ἐν ταῖς ἀγοραῖς,
in the synagogues, and the greetings in the markets,
8 καὶ καλεῖσθαι ὑπὸ τῶν ἀνθρώπων, ῥαββί, ῥαββί· ὑμεῖς δὲ μὴ
and to be called by — men, Rabbi, Rabbi! you But not
κληθῆτε ῥαββί· εἷς γάρ ἐστιν ὑμῶν ὁ καθηγητής, ὁ Χριστός·
be called Rabbi; one for is of you the leader, the Christ,
9 πάντες δὲ ὑμεῖς ἀδελφοί ἐστε. καὶ πατέρα μὴ καλέσητε ὑμῶν
all and you brothers are. And Father not call of you
ἐπὶ τῆς γῆς· εἷς γάρ ἐστιν ὁ πατὴρ ὑμῶν, ὁ ἐν τοῖς οὐρανοῖς.
on the earth;one for is the Father of you, the (One) in the heavens

Heaven. 10 Nor be called leaders, for One is your Leader, the Christ. 11 But the greater of you shall be your servant. 12 And whoever will exalt himself shall be humbled. And whoever will humble himself shall be exalted.

13 But woe to you, scribes and Pharisees, hypocrites! For you shut up the kingdom of Heaven before men; for you do not enter, nor do you allow those entering to go in.

14 Woe to you, scribes and Pharisees, hypocrites! For you devour the houses of widows, and pray at length as a pretext. Because of this you will receive more abundant judgment.

15 Woe to you, scribes and Pharisees, hypocrites! For you go about the sea and the dry *land* to make one proselyte; and when he has become *so*, you make him twofold more a son of Hell than yourselves.

16 Woe to you, blind guides, who say, Whoever swears by the Temple, it is nothing; but whoever swears by the gold of the Temple is a debtor. 17 Fools and blind! For which is greater, the gold, or the Temple that sanctifies the gold? 18 And *you say*, Whoever swears by the altar, it is nothing; but whoever swears by the gift on it, *he is* a debtor. 19 Fools and blind! For which is greater, the gift, or the altar that sanctifies the gift? 20 Then the *one* swearing by the altar swears by it, and by all things on it. 21 And the *one* swearing by the Temple swears by it, and by the *One* dwelling in it. 22 And the *one* swearing by Heaven swears by the throne of God, and by the *One* sitting on it.

23 Woe to you, scribes and Pharisees, hypocrites! For you pay tithes of mint and dill and cummin, and you

10 μηδὲ κληθῆτε καθηγηταί· εἷς γάρ ὑμῶν ἐστιν ὁ καθηγητής,
Neither be called leaders; One for of you is the Leader,
11 ὁ Χριστός. ὁ δὲ μείζων ὑμῶν ἔσται ὑμῶν διάκονος. ὅστις δὲ
12 the Christ. the And greater of you shall be of you a servant, whoever And
ὑψώσει ἑαυτόν, ταπεινωθήσεται· καὶ ὅστις ταπεινώσει
will exalt himself shall be humbled, and whoever will humble
ἑαυτόν, ὑψωθήσεται.
himself shall be exalted.

13 Οὐαὶ δὲ ὑμῖν, γραμματεῖς καὶ Φαρισαῖοι, ὑποκριταί, ὅτι
woe But to you, scribes and Pharisees, hypocrites! Because
κλείετε τὴν βασιλείαν τῶν οὐρανῶν ἔμπροσθεν τῶν ἀνθρώ-
you shut the kingdom of the heavens before — men;
πων· ὑμεῖς γὰρ οὐκ εἰσέρχεσθε, οὐδὲ τοὺς εἰσερχομένους
you for not do enter, nor the (ones) entering
ἀφίετε εἰσελθεῖν.
do you allow to enter.

14 Οὐαὶ ὑμῖν, γραμματεῖς καὶ Φαρισαῖοι, ὑποκριταί, ὅτι
Woe to you, scribes and Pharisees, hypocrites! Because
κατεσθίετε τὰς οἰκίας τῶν χηρῶν, καὶ προφάσει μακρὰ
you devour the houses of the widows, and as a pretext (are) long
προσευχόμενοι· διὰ τοῦτο λήψεσθε περισσότερον κρίμα.
praying. Because of this you will receive more abundant judgment.

15 Οὐαὶ ὑμῖν, γραμματεῖς καὶ Φαρισαῖοι, ὑποκριταί, ὅτι
Woe to you, scribes and Pharisees, hypocrites! Because
περιάγετε τὴν θάλασσαν καὶ τὴν ξηρὰν ποιῆσαι ἕνα προσή-
you go about the sea and the dry (land) to make one prose-
λυτον, καὶ ὅταν γένηται, ποιεῖτε αὐτὸν υἱὸν γεέννης διπλό-
lyte, and when he becomes, you make him a son of Gehenna twofold
τερον ὑμῶν.
more than you.

16 Οὐαὶ ὑμῖν, ὁδηγοὶ τυφλοί, οἱ λέγοντες, Ὃς ἂν ὀμόσῃ ἐν
Woe to you, leaders blind, the (ones) saying, Whoever swears by
τῷ ναῷ, οὐδέν ἐστιν· ὃς δ᾽ ἂν ὀμόσῃ ἐν τῷ χρυσῷ τοῦ ναοῦ,
the Temple, nothing it is; who but ever swears by the gold of the Temple,
17 ὀφείλει. μωροὶ καὶ τυφλοί· τίς γὰρ μείζων ἐστίν, ὁ χρυσός, ἢ
is a debtor. Fools and blind! what For greater is, the gold or
18 ὁ ναὸς ὁ ἁγιάζων τὸν χρυσόν ; καί, Ὃς ἐὰν ὀμόσῃ ἐν τῷ
the Temple sanctifying the gold? And, whoever swears by the
θυσιαστηρίῳ, οὐδέν ἐστιν· ὃς δ᾽ ἂν ὀμόσῃ ἐν τῷ δώρῳ τῷ
altar, nothing it is; who but ever swears by the gift
19 ἐπάνω αὐτοῦ, ὀφείλει. μωροὶ καὶ τυφλοί· τί γὰρ μεῖζον,
upon it, is a debtor. Fools and blind! what For is greater
20 τὸ δῶρον, ἢ τὸ θυσιαστήριον τὸ ἁγιάζον τὸ δῶρον ; ὁ οὖν
the gift or the altar — sanctifying the gift? he Then
ὀμόσας ἐν τῷ θυσιαστηρίῳ ὀμνύει ἐν αὐτῷ καὶ ἐν πᾶσι τοῖς
swearing by the altar swears by it and by all the things
21 ἐπάνω αὐτοῦ· καὶ ὁ ὀμόσας ἐν τῷ ναῷ ὀμνύει ἐν αὐτῷ καὶ ἐν
upon it; and he swearing by the Temple swears by it and by
22 τῷ κατοικοῦντι αὐτόν· καὶ ὁ ὀμόσας ἐν τῷ οὐρανῷ ὀμνύει
the (One) inhabiting it. And the (one) swearing by Heaven swears
ἐν τῷ θρόνῳ τοῦ Θεοῦ καὶ ἐν τῷ καθημένῳ ἐπάνω αὐτοῦ.
by the throne — of God and by the (One) sitting upon it.

23 Οὐαὶ ὑμῖν, γραμματεῖς καὶ Φαρισαῖοι, ὑποκριταί, ὅτι
Woe to you, scribes and Pharisees, hypocrites! Because
ἀποδεκατοῦτε τὸ ἡδύοσμον καὶ τὸ ἄνηθον καὶ τὸ κύμινον,
you tithe the mint and the dill and the cummin,

have left aside the weightier *matters* of the Law: judgment, and mercy, and faith. It was right to do these, and not to have left those aside. [24]Blind guides, who strain out the gnat, but swallow the camel!

[25]Woe to you, scribes and Pharisees, hypocrites! For you cleanse the outside of the cup and of the dish, but within they are full of robbery and excess. [26]Blind Pharisee! First cleanse the inside of the cup and of the dish, that the outside of them may become clean also.

[27]Woe to you, scribes and Pharisees, hypocrites! For you are like whitened graves which outwardly indeed appear beautiful, but within are full of bones of *the* dead, and of all uncleanness. [28]So you also indeed outwardly appear righteous to men, but within are full of hypocrisy and lawlessness.

[29]Woe to you, scribes and Pharisees, hypocrites! For you build the tombs of the prophets, and adorn the tombs of the righteous. [30]And you say, If we had been in the days of our fathers, we would not have been partakers with them in the blood of the prophets. [31]So you witness to yourselves, that you are the sons of those who murdered the prophets. [32]And you fill up the measure of your fathers. [33]Serpents, offspring of vipers! How shall you escape the judgment of Hell? [34]Because of this, behold, I send to you prophets and wise ones and scribes. And *some* of them you will kill and crucify; and *some* of them you will flog in your synagogues, and will persecute from city to city; [35]so that should come on you all *the* righteous blood poured out on the earth, from the blood of righteous Abel to

καὶ ἀφήκατε τὰ βαρύτερα τοῦ νόμου, τὴν κρίσιν καὶ τὸν
and you have left the weightier matters of the law, – judgment and –
ἔλεον καὶ τὴν πίστιν· ταῦτα ἔδει ποιῆσαι, κἀκεῖνα μὴ ἀφιέναι.
mercy and – faith; these things one needs to do, and those not to leave.
24 ὁδηγοὶ τυφλοί, οἱ διϋλίζοντες τὸν κώνωπα, τὴν δὲ κάμηλον
leaders Blind, the (ones) straining out the gnat, the but camel
καταπίνοντες.
swallowing.

25 Οὐαὶ ὑμῖν, γραμματεῖς καὶ Φαρισαῖοι, ὑποκριταί, ὅτι
Woe to you, scribes and Pharisees, hypocrites! Because
καθαρίζετε τὸ ἔξωθεν τοῦ ποτηρίου καὶ τῆς παροψίδος,
you cleanse the outside of the cup and the dish,
26 ἔσωθεν δὲ γέμουσιν ἐξ ἁρπαγῆς καὶ ἀκρασίας. Φαρισαῖε τυφλέ,
within but they are full of robbery and excess. Pharisee Blind,
καθάρισον πρῶτον τὸ ἐντὸς τοῦ ποτηρίου καὶ τῆς παροψί-
cleanse first the inside of the cup and of the dish,
δος, ἵνα γένηται καὶ τὸ ἐκτὸς αὐτῶν καθαρόν.
that may become also the outside of them clean.
27 Οὐαὶ ὑμῖν, γραμματεῖς καὶ Φαρισαῖοι, ὑποκριταί, ὅτι
Woe to you, scribes and Pharisees, hypocrites! Because
παρομοιάζετε τάφοις κεκονιαμένοις, οἵτινες ἔξωθεν μὲν
you are like graves whitewashed, who outwardly indeed
φαίνονται ὡραῖοι, ἔσωθεν δὲ γέμουσιν ὀστέων νεκρῶν καὶ
appear beautiful, within but are full of bones of the dead and
28 πάσης ἀκαθαρσίας. οὕτω καὶ ὑμεῖς ἔξωθεν μὲν φαίνεσθε τοῖς
of all uncleanness. So also you outwardly indeed appear –
ἀνθρώποις δίκαιοι, ἔσωθεν δὲ μεστοί ἐστε ὑποκρίσεως καὶ
to men righteous, within but full are of hypocrisy and
ἀνομίας.
lawlessness.

29 Οὐαὶ ὑμῖν, γραμματεῖς καὶ Φαρισαῖοι, ὑποκριταί, ὅτι
Woe to you, scribes and Pharisees, hypocrites! Because
οἰκοδομεῖτε τοὺς τάφους τῶν προφητῶν, καὶ κοσμεῖτε τὰ
you build the graves of the prophets, and decorate the
30 μνημεῖα τῶν δικαίων, καὶ λέγετε, Εἰ ἦμεν ἐν ταῖς ἡμέραις
monuments of the righteous, and say, If we had been in the days
τῶν πατέρων ἡμῶν, οὐκ ἂν ἦμεν κοινωνοὶ αὐτῶν ἐν τῷ
of the fathers of us, not would we have been sharers of them in the
31 αἵματι τῶν προφητῶν. ὥστε μαρτυρεῖτε ἑαυτοῖς ὅτι υἱοί
blood of the prophets. So you witness to yourselves that sons
32 ἐστε τῶν φονευσάντων τοὺς προφήτας· καὶ ὑμεῖς πληρώσατε
you are of those murdering the prophets and you fill up
33 τὸ μέτρον τῶν πατέρων ὑμῶν. ὄφεις, γεννήματα ἐχιδνῶν,
the measure of the fathers of you. Serpents! Offspring of vipers!
34 πῶς φύγητε ἀπὸ τῆς κρίσεως τῆς γεέννης; διὰ τοῦτο, ἰδού,
How do you escape from the judgment – of Gehenna? Therefore, behold,
ἐγὼ ἀποστέλλω πρὸς ὑμᾶς προφήτας καὶ σοφοὺς καὶ γραμ-
I send to you prophets and wise ones and scribes;
ματεῖς· καὶ ἐξ αὐτῶν ἀποκτενεῖτε καὶ σταυρώσετε, καὶ ἐξ
and of them you will kill and crucify; and of
αὐτῶν μαστιγώσετε ἐν ταῖς συναγωγαῖς ὑμῶν καὶ διώξετε
them you will scourge in the synagogues of you, and persecute
35 ἀπὸ πόλεως εἰς πόλιν· ὅπως ἔλθῃ ἐφ' ὑμᾶς πᾶν αἷμα δίκαιον
from city to city; so comes upon you all blood righteous
ἐκχυνόμενον ἐπὶ τῆς γῆς, ἀπὸ τοῦ αἵματος Ἄβελ τοῦ
being poured out on the earth, from the blood of Abel the

the blood of Zechariah *the* son of Berechiah, whom you murdered between the Temple and the altar. [36] Truly I say to you, All these things will come on this generation.

[37] Jerusalem, Jerusalem, the *one* killing the prophets and stoning those who have been sent to her. How often I would have gathered your children together, in the way a bird gathers her chicks from under *her* wings! And you did not desire it. [38] Behold, your house is left to you desolate. [39] For I say to you, In no way shall you see Me from now on until you say, "Blessed is He who comes in *the* name of *the* Lord."

CHAPTER 24

[1] And going out, Jesus left the Temple. And His disciples came to point out to Him the buildings of the Temple. [2] But Jesus said to them, Do you not see all these things? Truly I say to you, There shall not be left here *one* stone on *a* stone which shall not be thrown down.

[3] And as He was sitting on the Mount of Olives, the disciples came to Him privately, saying, Tell us, when shall these things be? And, What is the sign of Your coming and of the end of the age? [4] And answering Jesus said to them, See that not any misleads you. [5] For many will come in My name, saying, I am the Christ. And they will mislead many. [6] But you will begin to hear of wars and rumors of wars. See, do not be disturbed. For all these things must take place, but the end is not yet. [7] For nation will be raised against nation, and kingdom against kingdom; and there will be famines and plagues and earthquakes against *many* places. [8] But all these *are* a beginning of throes. [9] Then they will deliver you up to affliction, and will kill you;

δικαίου, ἕως τοῦ αἵματος Ζαχαρίου υἱοῦ Βαραχίου, ὃν
righteous, to the blood of Zachariah (the) son of Barachiah, whom
36 ἐφονεύσατε μεταξὺ τοῦ ναοῦ καὶ τοῦ θυσιαστηρίου. ἀμὴν
you murdered between the Temple and the altar. Truly
λέγω ὑμῖν, ἥξει ταῦτα πάντα ἐπὶ τὴν γενεὰν ταύτην.
I say to you, will come all these things on — generation this.
37 Ἱερουσαλήμ, Ἱερουσαλήμ, ἡ ἀποκτείνουσα τοὺς προφή-
Jerusalem, Jerusalem, the (one) killing the prophets
τας καὶ λιθοβολοῦσα τοὺς ἀπεσταλμένους πρὸς αὐτήν,
and stoning the (ones) sent to her,
ποσάκις ἠθέλησα ἐπισυναγαγεῖν τὰ τέκνα σου, ὃν τρόπον
how often I desired to gather together the children of you, in the way
ἐπισυνάγει ὄρνις τὰ νοσσία ἑαυτῆς ὑπὸ τὰς πτέρυγας, καὶ
gathers together a bird the young of her under the wings, and
38 οὐκ ἠθελήσατε. ἰδού, ἀφίεται ὑμῖν ὁ οἶκος ὑμῶν ἔρημος.
not you desired. Behold, is left to you the house of you desolate;
39 λέγω γὰρ ὑμῖν, Οὐ μή με ἴδητε ἀπ' ἄρτι, ἕως ἂν εἴπητε,
I say For to you, Not at all Me shall you see from now until you say,
Εὐλογημένος ὁ ἐρχόμενος ἐν ὀνόματι Κυρίου.
Blessed the (one) coming in (the) name of (the) Lord.

CHAPTER 24

1 Καὶ ἐξελθὼν ὁ Ἰησοῦς ἐπορεύετο ἀπὸ τοῦ ἱεροῦ· καὶ
And going forth — Jesus went away from the Temple, and
προσῆλθον οἱ μαθηταὶ αὐτοῦ ἐπιδεῖξαι αὐτῷ τὰς οἰκοδομὰς
came up the disciples of Him to show Him the buildings
2 τοῦ ἱεροῦ. ὁ δὲ Ἰησοῦς εἶπεν αὐτοῖς, Οὐ βλέπετε πάντα
of the Temple. — And Jesus said to them, Not you see all
ταῦτα ; ἀμὴν λέγω ὑμῖν, οὐ μὴ ἀφεθῇ ὧδε λίθος ἐπὶ λίθον, ὃς
these? Truly I say to you, Not at all will be left here stone on stone which
οὐ μὴ καταλυθήσεται.
not at all shall be thrown down.
3 Καθημένου δὲ αὐτοῦ ἐπὶ τοῦ ὄρους τῶν ἐλαιῶν, προσῆλ-
sitting And He on the mount of the olives, came
θον αὐτῷ οἱ μαθηταὶ κατ' ἰδίαν, λέγοντες, Εἰπὲ ἡμῖν, πότε
up to Him the disciples privately, saying, Tell us, when
ταῦτα ἔσται ; καὶ τί τὸ σημεῖον τῆς σῆς παρουσίας, καὶ τῆς
these things will be; and what the sign — of Your presence, and of the
4 συντελείας τοῦ αἰῶνος ; καὶ ἀποκριθεὶς ὁ Ἰησοῦς εἶπεν αὐτοῖς,
termination of the age? And answering — Jesus said to them,
5 Βλέπετε, μή τις ὑμᾶς πλανήσῃ. πολλοὶ γὰρ ἐλεύσονται ἐπὶ
See, not any you misleads. many For will come on
τῷ ὀνόματί μου, λέγοντες, Ἐγώ εἰμι ὁ Χριστός· καὶ πολλοὺς
the name of Me, saying, I am the Christ, and many
6 πλανήσουσι. μελλήσετε δὲ ἀκούειν πολέμους καὶ ἀκοὰς
will cause to err. you will be about But to hear of wars and rumors
πολέμων· ὁρᾶτε, μὴ θροεῖσθε· δεῖ γὰρ πάντα γενέσθαι· ἀλλ'
of wars. See, do not be upset; it is right for all things to happen, but
7 οὔπω ἐστὶ τὸ τέλος. ἐγερθήσεται γὰρ ἔθνος ἐπὶ ἔθνος, καὶ
not yet is the end. will be raised For nation against nation, and
βασιλεία ἐπὶ βασιλείαν· καὶ ἔσονται λιμοὶ καὶ λοιμοὶ καὶ
kingdom against kingdom, and there will be famines and plagues and
8 σεισμοὶ κατὰ τόπους. πάντα δὲ ταῦτα ἀρχὴ ὠδίνων. τότε
9 **earthquakes against places all but these things beginning of throes. Then**
παραδώσουσιν ὑμᾶς εἰς θλῖψιν, καὶ ἀποκτενοῦσιν ὑμᾶς· καὶ
they will deliver up you to affliction, and will kill you, and

and you will be hated by all nations for My name's sake. [10]And then many will be offended, and they will deliver up one another, and will hate one another. [11]And many false prophets will arise, and will mislead many. [12]And because lawlessness shall have been multiplied, the love of many will grow cold. [13]But the *one* who endures to *the* end, that one will be saved. [14]And this gospel of the kingdom shall be preached in all the earth, for a testimony to all the nations; and then shall come the end.

[15]Therefore, when you see the abomination of desolation which was spoken of by Daniel the prophet, standing in *the* holy place—he who reads, let him understand—[16]then let those in Judea flee to the mountains; [17]the *one* on the housetop, let him not come down to take anything out of his house; [18]and the *one* in the field, let him not turn back to take his garment. [19]But woe to those that are with child and to those suckling in those days! [20]And pray that your flight will not be i winter, nor on a sabbath. [21]For there will be great affliction, such as has not happened from *the* beginning of *the* world until now; no, nor ever will be. [22]And except those days had been shortened, not any flesh would be saved—but on account of the elect, those days will be shortened. [23]Then if anyone says to you, Behold, here *is* the Christ; or, Here! Do not believe. [24]For false christs will rise up, and false prophets. And *they* will give great signs and wonders, so as to lead astray, if possible, even the elect. [25]Behold, I tell you beforehand. [26]Then if they say to you, Behold, He is in the wilderness; do not go out. Behold, *He is* in the inner rooms; do not believe. [27]For as the lightning comes forth from *the* east and shines as far as *the* west, so also will be the

ἔσεσθε μισούμενοι ὑπὸ πάντων τῶν ἐθνῶν διὰ τὸ ὄνομά μου.
you will be hated by all the nations for the name of Me.
10 καὶ τότε σκανδαλισθήσονται πολλοί, καὶ ἀλλήλους παραδώ-
And then will be offended many, and one another will
11 σουσι, καὶ μισήσουσιν ἀλλήλους. καὶ πολλοὶ ψευδοπρο-
deliver, and they will hate one another. And many false
12 φῆται ἐγερθήσονται, καὶ πλανήσουσι πολλούς. καὶ διὰ τὸ
prophets will be raised up, and will cause to err many; and because of
πληθυνθῆναι τὴν ἀνομίαν, ψυγήσεται ἡ ἀγάπη τῶν
shall have been multiplied lawlessness, will grow cold the love of the
13 πολλῶν· ὁ δὲ ὑπομείνας εἰς τέλος, οὗτος σωθήσεται. καὶ
14 **many. the (one) But enduring to (the) end, this one will be saved. And**
κηρυχθήσεται τοῦτο τὸ εὐαγγέλιον τῆς βασιλείας ἐν ὅλῃ
will be proclaimed this — gospel of the kingdom in all
τῇ οἰκουμένῃ εἰς μαρτύριον πᾶσι τοῖς ἔθνεσι· καὶ τότε ἥξει
the inhabited earth for a testimony to all the nations, and then will come
τὸ τέλος.
the end.
15 Ὅταν οὖν ἴδητε τὸ βδέλυγμα τῆς ἐρημώσεως, τὸ ῥηθὲν διὰ
When therefore you see the abomination of desolation — spoken via
Δανιὴλ τοῦ προφήτου, ἑστὼς ἐν τόπῳ ἁγίῳ (ὁ ἀναγινώ-
Daniel the prophet, standing in place holy [the one reading
16 σκων νοείτω), τότε οἱ ἐν τῇ Ἰουδαίᾳ φευγέτωσαν ἐπὶ τὰ
let him understand] then the(se) in Judea, let them flee upon the
17 ὄρη· ὁ ἐπὶ τοῦ δώματος μὴ καταβαινέτω ἆραί τι ἐκ τῆς
mounts, he on the housetop not let him descend to take things from the
18 οἰκίας αὐτοῦ· καὶ ὁ ἐν τῷ ἀγρῷ μὴ ἐπιστρεψάτω ὀπίσω
house of him; and the (one) in the field, not let him return behind
19 ἆραι τὰ ἱμάτια αὐτοῦ. οὐαὶ δὲ ταῖς ἐν γαστρὶ ἐχούσαις καὶ
to take the garment of him. Woe And to the(se) in womb having and
20 ταῖς θηλαζούσαις ἐν ἐκείναις ταῖς ἡμέραις. προσεύχεσθε δὲ
to those suckling in those — days. pray And
ἵνα μὴ γένηται ἡ φυγὴ ὑμῶν χειμῶνος, μηδὲ ἐν σαββάτῳ.
that not will occur the flight of you of winter, nor on a sabbath;
21 εσται γὰρ τότε θλίψις μεγάλη, οἵα οὐ γέγονεν ἀπ᾿ ἀρχῆς
will be for then affliction great, such as not has occurred from origin
22 κόσμου ἕως τοῦ νῦν, οὐδ᾿ οὐ μὴ γένηται. καὶ εἰ μὴ ἐκολοβώ-
of world until now; neither by no means occur. And except were cut
θησαν αἱ ἡμέραι ἐκεῖναι, οὐκ ἂν ἐσώθη πᾶσα σάρξ· διὰ δὲ
short — days those, not would be saved any flesh; because of the
23 τοὺς ἐκλεκτοὺς κολοβωθήσονται αἱ ἡμέραι ἐκεῖναι. τότε ἐάν
the elect will be cut short — days those. Then if
τις ὑμῖν εἴπῃ, Ἰδού, ὧδε ὁ Χριστός, ἢ ὧδε, μὴ πιστεύσητε.
anyone to you says, Behold, here the Christ; or, Here; not believe;
24 ἐγερθήσονται γὰρ ψευδόχριστοι καὶ ψευδοπροφῆται, καὶ
will arise for false Christs and false prophets, and
δώσουσι σημεῖα μεγάλα καὶ τέρατα, ὥστε πλανῆσαι, εἰ
they will give signs great and wonders, so as to cause to err, if
25 δυνατόν, καὶ τοὺς ἐκλεκτούς. ἰδού, προείρηκα ὑμῖν. ἐὰν οὖν
26 **possible, even the elect. Behold, I tell before to you. If then**
εἴπωσιν ὑμῖν, Ἰδού, ἐν τῇ ἐρήμῳ ἐστί, μὴ ἐξέλθητε· Ἰδού,
they say to you, Behold, in the desert He is, not go forth; Behold,
27 ἐν τοῖς ταμείοις, μὴ πιστεύσητε. ὥσπερ γὰρ ἡ ἀστραπὴ
in the private rooms, not believe. as For the lightning
ἐξέρχεται ἀπὸ ἀνατολῶν καὶ φαίνεται ἕως δυσμῶν, οὕτως
comes forth from (the) east and shines as far as (the) west, so

coming of the Son of man.
28 For wherever the dead
body may be, there the
eagles will be gathered.
29 And immediately after
the affliction of those days,
the sun will be darkened,
and the moon will not give
her light, and the stars will
fall from the heaven, and the
powers of the heavens will
be shaken. 30 And then the
sign of the Son of man will
appear in the heavens. And
then all the tribes of the land
will wail. And they will see
the Son of man coming on
the clouds of heaven with
power and much glory.
31 And He will send His
angels with a great sound of
a trumpet, and they will
gather His elect from the
four winds; from *the* ends of
the heavens to their ends.

32 But learn the parable of
the fig-tree: When its
branch has already become
tender, and it puts out
leaves, you know that the
summer *is* near; 33 so also
you when you see all these
things know that it is near, at
the doors. 34 Truly I say to
you, In no way will this
generation pass away until
all these things have occurred. 35 The heavens and the
earth will pass away, but My
words will never ever pass
away. 36 But as to that day
and that hour, no one knows,
neither the angels of Heaven,
but My Father only. 37 But as
the days of Noah, so will also
be the coming of the Son of
man. 38 For as they were in
the days before the flood:
eating, and drinking, marrying, and giving in marriage,
until *the* day *when* Noah
went into the ark—39 and
they did not know until the
flood came and took all
away—so also will be the
coming of the Son of man.
40 At that time two will be out

28 ἔσται καὶ ἡ παρουσία τοῦ υἱοῦ τοῦ ἀνθρώπου. ὅπου γὰρ
will be also the coming of the Son — of man. wherever For
ἐὰν ᾖ τὸ πτῶμα, ἐκεῖ συναχθήσονται οἱ ἀετοί.
if may be the carcase, there will be gathered the eagles.
29 Εὐθέως δὲ μετὰ τὴν θλίψιν τῶν ἡμερῶν ἐκείνων, ὁ ἥλιος
immediately And after the affliction — of days those, the sun
σκοτισθήσεται, καὶ ἡ σελήνη οὐ δώσει τὸ φέγγος αὐτῆς,
will be darkened, and the moon not will give the light of her,
καὶ οἱ ἀστέρες πεσοῦνται ἀπὸ τοῦ οὐρανοῦ, καὶ αἱ δυνάμεις
and the stars will fall from — heaven, and the powers
30 τῶν οὐρανῶν σαλευθήσονται. καὶ τότε φανήσεται τὸ
of the heavens will be shaken. And then will appear the
σημεῖον τοῦ υἱοῦ τοῦ ἀνθρώπου ἐν τῷ οὐρανῷ· καὶ τότε
sign of the Son — of man in the heaven; and then
κόψονται πᾶσαι αἱ φυλαὶ τῆς γῆς, καὶ ὄψονται τὸν υἱὸν τοῦ
will wail all the tribes of the land, and they will see the Son —
ἀνθρώπου ἐρχόμενον ἐπὶ τῶν νεφελῶν τοῦ οὐρανοῦ μετὰ
of man coming on the clouds of heaven with
31 δυνάμεως καὶ δόξης πολλῆς. καὶ ἀποστελεῖ τοὺς ἀγγέλους
power and glory much; and He will send the angels
αὐτοῦ μετὰ σάλπιγγος φωνῆς μεγάλης, καὶ ἐπισυνάξουσι
of Him with a trumpet sound great, and they will gather
τοὺς ἐκλεκτοὺς αὐτοῦ ἐκ τῶν τεσσάρων ἀνέμων, ἀπ' ἄκρων
the elect of Him out of the four winds from (the) ends
οὐρανῶν ἕως ἄκρων αὐτῶν.
of (the) heavens to (the) ends ot them.
32 Ἀπὸ δὲ τῆς συκῆς μάθετε τὴν παραβολήν· ὅταν ἤδη ὁ
from And the fig-tree learn the parable: When now the
κλάδος αὐτῆς γένηται ἁπαλός, καὶ τὰ φύλλα ἐκφύῃ, γινώ-
branch of it becomes tender, and the leaves it puts out, you
33 σκετε ὅτι ἐγγὺς τὸ θέρος· οὕτω καὶ ὑμεῖς, ὅταν ἴδητε πάντα
know that near (is) the summer: so also you when you see all
34 ταῦτα, γινώσκετε ὅτι ἐγγύς ἐστιν ἐπὶ θύραις. ἀμὴν λέγω
these things know that near it is on (the) doors. Truly I say
ὑμῖν, οὐ μὴ παρέλθῃ ἡ γενεὰ αὕτη, ἕως ἂν πάντα ταῦτα
to you, In no way passes away generation this until all these things
35 γένηται. ὁ οὐρανὸς καὶ ἡ γῆ παρελεύσονται, οἱ δὲ λόγοι
have occurred. The heavens and the earth will pass away, the but words
36 μου οὐ μὴ παρέλθωσι. περὶ δὲ τῆς ἡμέρας ἐκείνης καὶ τῆς
of Me in no way may pass away. about But — day that and the
ὥρας οὐδεὶς οἶδεν, οὐδὲ οἱ ἄγγελοι τῶν οὐρανῶν, εἰ μὴ ὁ
hour no one knows, neither the angels of the heavens, except the
37 πατήρ μου μόνος. ὥσπερ δὲ αἱ ἡμέραι τοῦ Νῶε, οὕτως
Father of Me only. as But the days — of Noah, so
38 ἔσται καὶ ἡ παρουσία τοῦ υἱοῦ τοῦ ἀνθρώπου. ὥσπερ γὰρ
will be also the coming of the Son — of man. as For
ἦσαν ἐν ταῖς ἡμέραις ταῖς πρὸ τοῦ κατακλυσμοῦ τρώγοντες
they were in the days before the flood, eating
καὶ πίνοντες, γαμοῦντες καὶ ἐκγαμίζοντες, ἄχρι ἧς ἡμέρας
and drinking, marrying and giving in marriage, until which day
39 εἰσῆλθε Νῶε εἰς τὴν κιβωτόν, καὶ οὐκ ἔγνωσαν, ἕως ἦλθεν
entered Noah into the ark, and not did know until came
ὁ κατακλυσμὸς καὶ ἦρεν ἅπαντας, οὕτως ἔσται καὶ ἡ παρου-
the flood and took all, so will be the coming
40 σία τοῦ υἱοῦ τοῦ ἀνθρώπου. τότε δύο ἔσονται ἐν τῷ ἀγρῷ·
of the Son — of man. Then two will be in the field,

in the field: the one is taken away, and the one is left; [41] two grinding at the mill, one is taken, and one is left. [42] Watch, then, for you do not know in what hour your Lord comes. [43] But know this, that if the housemaster had known in what watch the thief comes, he would have watched, and not have allowed his house to be broken into. [44] Because of this, you also be ready, for in that hour you think not, the Son of man comes. [45] Who then is the faithful and wise servant, whom his lord has set over his household, to give to them the food in season? [46] That servant whom his lord shall find so doing when he comes will be blessed. [47] Truly I say to you, He will set him over all his substance. [48] But if that evil servant should say in his heart, My lord delays to come, [49] and should begin to beat *his* fellow-slaves, and to eat and to drink with the drunkards, [50] the lord of that slave will come in a day in which he does not expect, and in an hour which he does not know, [51] and will cut him in two, and will appoint his portion with the hypocrites. There will be weeping and gnashing of the teeth.

41 ὁ εἷς παραλαμβάνεται, καὶ ὁ εἷς ἀφίεται. δύο ἀλήθουσαι ἐν
the one is taken away and the one is left. Two grinding in
42 τῷ μύλωνι· μία παραλαμβάνεται, καὶ μία ἀφίεται. γρηγο-
the mill, one is taken away and one is left. Watch
ρεῖτε οὖν, ὅτι οὐκ οἴδατε ποίᾳ ὥρᾳ ὁ Κύριος ὑμῶν ἔρχεται.
therefore that not you know on what hour the Lord of you is coming.
43 ἐκεῖνο δὲ γινώσκετε, ὅτι εἰ ᾔδει ὁ οἰκοδεσπότης ποίᾳ φυλακῇ
this And know, that if knew the housemaster in what watch
ὁ κλέπτης ἔρχεται, ἐγρηγόρησεν ἄν, καὶ οὐκ ἂν εἴασε διο-
the thief is coming, he would have watched and not might allow to be
44 ρυγῆναι τὴν οἰκίαν αὐτοῦ. διὰ τοῦτο καὶ ὑμεῖς γίνεσθε
dug through the house of him. Therefore also you be
ἕτοιμοι· ὅτι ᾗ ὥρᾳ οὐ δοκεῖτε, ὁ υἱὸς τοῦ ἀνθρώπου ἔρχεται.
ready, because that hour not you think the Son — of man comes.
45 τίς ἄρα ἐστὶν ὁ πιστὸς δοῦλος καὶ φρόνιμος, ὃν κατέστησεν ὁ
Who then is the faithful slave and prudent whom appointed the
κύριος αὐτοῦ ἐπὶ τῆς θεραπείας αὐτοῦ, τοῦ διδόναι αὐτοῖς
lord of him over the service of him — to give to them
46 τὴν τροφὴν ἐν καιρῷ; μακάριος ὁ δοῦλος ἐκεῖνος, ὃν ἐλθὼν
the food in season? Blessed (is) — slave that whom coming
47 ὁ κύριος αὐτοῦ εὑρήσει ποιοῦντα οὕτως. ἀμὴν λέγω ὑμῖν,
the lord of him will find doing so. Truly I say to you,
ὅτι ἐπὶ πᾶσι τοῖς ὑπάρχουσιν αὐτοῦ καταστήσει αὐτόν.
that over all the goods of him he will appoint him.
48 ἐὰν δὲ εἴπῃ ὁ κακὸς δοῦλος ἐκεῖνος ἐν τῇ καρδίᾳ αὐτοῦ,
if But says — wicked slave that in the heart of him,
49 Χρονίζει ὁ κύριός μου ἐλθεῖν, καὶ ἄρξηται τύπτειν τοὺς συν-
delays the lord of me to come, and should begin to beat the fellow-
50 δούλους, ἐσθίειν δὲ καὶ πίνειν μετὰ τῶν μεθυόντων, ἥξει ὁ
slaves, to eat and, and to drink with the (ones) drunk, comes the
κύριος τοῦ δούλου ἐκείνου ἐν ἡμέρᾳ ᾗ οὐ προσδοκᾷ, καὶ ἐν
lord of slave that on a day which not he expects, and in
51 ὥρᾳ ᾗ οὐ γινώσκει, καὶ διχοτομήσει αὐτόν, καὶ τὸ μέρος
an hour which not he knows, and will cut in two him, and the portion
αὐτοῦ μετὰ τῶν ὑποκριτῶν θήσει· ἐκεῖ ἔσται ὁ κλαυθμὸς καὶ
of him with the hypocrites will put; there will be the weeping and
ὁ βρυγμος τῶν ὀδόντων.
the gnashing of the teeth.

CHAPTER 25

[1] Then the kingdom of Heaven shall be compared to ten virgins who took their lamps and went out to meet the bridegroom. [2] And five of them were wise, and five foolish. [3] Those *being* foolish, having taken their lamps, did not take oil with them. [4] But the wise took oil in their vessels with their lamps. [5] But the bridegroom having delayed, all nodded and slept. [6] And *at* midnight a cry occurred: Behold, the

1 Τότε ὁμοιωθήσεται ἡ βασιλεία τῶν οὐρανῶν δέκα παρθέ-
Then shall be compared the kingdom of the heavens to ten virgins,
νοις, αἵτινες λαβοῦσαι τὰς λαμπάδας αὐτῶν ἐξῆλθον εἰς
who taking the lamps of them went out to
2 ἀπάντησιν τοῦ νυμφίου. πέντε δὲ ἦσαν ἐξ αὐτῶν φρόνιμοι,
a meeting of the bridegroom. five And were of them prudent
3 καὶ αἱ πέντε μωραί. αἵτινες μωραί, λαβοῦσαι τὰς λαμπάδας
and — five fools those (being) fools, having taken the lamps
4 ἑαυτῶν, οὐκ ἔλαβον μεθ᾽ ἑαυτῶν ἔλαιον· αἱ δὲ φρόνιμοι
of them, not did take with themselves oil; the but prudent
ἔλαβον ἔλαιον ἐν τοῖς ἀγγείοις αὐτῶν μετὰ τῶν λαμπάδων
took oil in the the vessels of them with the lamps
5 αὐτῶν. χρονίζοντος δὲ τοῦ νυμφίου, ἐνύσταξαν πᾶσαι καὶ
of them. delaying But the bridegroom, nodded all and
6 ἐκάθευδον. μέσης δὲ νυκτὸς κραυγὴ γέγονεν, Ἰδού, ὁ
slept. (at) mid- And night, a cry occurred: Behold, the

bridegroom is coming! Go out to meet him. Then all those virgins arose and prepared their lamps. [8]And the foolish said to the wise, Give us *some* of your oil, for our lamps are going out. [9]But the wise answered, saying, *No,* lest there not be enough for us and you. But rather go to those who sell, and buy for yourselves. [10]But as they went away to buy, the bridegroom came. And those ready went in with him to the wedding feast.

[11]And afterwards the other virgins also came, saying, Lord, Lord, open to us. [12]But answering he said, Truly I say to you, I do not know you. [13]Therefore, watch, for you do not know the day nor the hour in which the Son of man comes.

[14]For *it is* as if a man going abroad called *his* own slaves and delivered his goods to them. [15]And to one he gave five talents, and to another two, and to another one—to each according to his ability. And *he* went abroad at once. [16]And going, the *one* who received the five talents worked with them, and made another five talents. [17]In the same way, the *one* with the two also did; he also gained another two. [18]But the *one* who received the one *talent,* having gone away, dug in the earth and hid his lord's silver. [19]And after much time, the lord of those slaves came and took account with them. [20]And coming up, the *one* who received five talents brought another five talents near, saying, Lord, you delivered five talents to me. Behold, I gained another five talents above them. [21]And his lord said to him, Well *done,* good and faithful slave. You were faithful over a few things, I will set you over many. Enter into the joy of your lord.

7 νυμφίος ἔρχεται, ἐξέρχεσθε εἰς ἀπάντησιν αὐτοῦ. τότε
bridegroom comes! Go forth to a meeting of him. Then
ἠγέρθησαν πᾶσαι αἱ παρθένοι ἐκεῖναι, καὶ ἐκόσμησαν τὰς
arose all — virgins those, and prepared the
8 λαμπάδας αὐτῶν. αἱ δὲ μωραὶ ταῖς φρονίμοις εἶπον, Δότε
lamps of them. the And fools to the prudent said, Give
ἡμῖν ἐκ τοῦ ἐλαίου ὑμῶν, ὅτι αἱ λαμπάδες ἡμῶν σβέννυνται.
us the oil of you, for the lamps of us are going out.
9 ἀπεκρίθησαν δὲ αἱ φρόνιμοι, λέγουσαι, Μήποτε οὐκ
answered But the prudent, saying, (No,) lest not
ἀρκέσῃ ἡμῖν καὶ ὑμῖν· πορεύεσθε δὲ μᾶλλον πρὸς τοὺς
it suffices to us and to you. go But rather to the (ones)
10 πωλοῦντας καὶ ἀγοράσατε ἑαυταῖς. ἀπερχομένων δὲ αὐτῶν
selling and buy for yourselves. going away And they
ἀγοράσαι, ἦλθεν ὁ νυμφίος· καὶ αἱ ἕτοιμοι εἰσῆλθον μετ'
to buy, came the bridegroom and the ready (ones) went in with
11 αὐτοῦ εἰς τοὺς γάμους, καὶ ἐκλείσθη ἡ θύρα. ὕστερον δὲ
him to the wedding feast, and was shut the door. later And
ἔρχονται καὶ αἱ λοιπαὶ παρθένοι, λέγουσαι, Κύριε, κύριε,
come also the remaining virgins, saying, Lord, Lord,
12 ἄνοιξον ἡμῖν. ὁ δὲ ἀποκριθεὶς εἶπεν, Ἀμὴν λέγω ὑμῖν, οὐκ
open to us. he But answering said, Truly I say to you, not
13 οἶδα ὑμᾶς. γρηγορεῖτε οὖν, ὅτι οὐκ οἴδατε τὴν ἡμέραν οὐδὲ
I know you. Watch, therefore,for not you know the day nor
τὴν ὥραν, ἐν ᾗ ὁ υἱὸς τοῦ ἀνθρώπου ἔρχεται.
the hour in which the Son — of man comes.
14 Ὥσπερ γὰρ ἄνθρωπος ἀποδημῶν ἐκάλεσε τοὺς ἰδίους
(it is) as if For a man going abroad called the own
15 δούλους, καὶ παρέδωκεν αὐτοῖς τὰ ὑπάρχοντα αὐτοῦ· καὶ
slaves, and delivered to them the goods of him, and
ᾧ μὲν ἔδωκε πέντε τάλαντα, ᾧ δὲ δύο, ᾧ δὲ ἕν, ἑκάστῳ κατὰ
to one indeed he gave five talents; to one and two; to and one; to each one by
16 τὴν ἰδίαν δύναμιν· καὶ ἀπεδήμησεν εὐθέως. πορευθεὶς δὲ ὁ
the own ability, and went abroad Immediately. going And he
τὰ πέντε τάλαντα λαβὼν εἰργάσατο ἐν αὐτοῖς, καὶ ἐποίησεν
the five talents receiving worked with them and made
17 ἄλλα πέντε τάλαντα. ὡσαύτως καὶ ὁ τὰ δύο ἐκέρδησε καὶ
other five talents. Likewise, also the (one) the two ; gained also
18 αὐτὸς ἄλλα δύο. ὁ δὲ τὸ ἓν λαβὼν ἀπελθὼν ὤρυξεν ἐν τῇ
he other two. he But the one receiving , going away dug in the
19 γῇ, καὶ ἀπέκρυψε τὸ ἀργύριον τοῦ κυρίου αὐτοῦ. μετὰ δὲ
earth, and hid the silver of the lord of him. after And
χρόνον πολὺν ἔρχεται ὁ κύριος τῶν δούλων ἐκείνων, καὶ
time much comes the lord — of slaves those, and
20 συναίρει μετ' αὐτῶν λόγον. καὶ προσελθὼν ὁ τὰ πέντε
takes with them account. And coming up, the (one) the five
τάλαντα λαβὼν προσήνεγκεν ἄλλα πέντε τάλαντα, λέγων,
talents receiving brought near other five talents, saying,
Κύριε, πέντε τάλαντά μοι παρέδωκας· ἴδε, ἄλλα πέντε
Lord, five talents to me you delivered. Behold, other five
21 τάλαντα ἐκέρδησα ἐπ' αὐτοῖς. ἔφη δὲ αὐτῷ ὁ κύριος αὐτοῦ,
talents I gained over them. said And to him the lord of him,
Εὖ, δοῦλε ἀγαθὲ καὶ πιστέ, ἐπὶ ὀλίγα ἦς πιστός, ἐπὶ πολλῶν
Well, slave good and faithful, over a few you were faithful, over many
σε καταστήσω· εἴσελθε εἰς τὴν χαρὰν τοῦ κυρίου σου.
you I will set. Enter into the joy of the lord of you.

22 And the *one* who received two talents, coming up also said, Lord, you delivered two talents to me. Behold, I have gained two other talents above them. 23 His lord said to him, Well *done,* good and faithful slave. You were faithful over a few things; I will set you over many. Enter into the joy of your lord. 24 And the *one* who received the one talent also coming up, *he* said, Lord, I knew you, that you are a hard man, reaping where you did not sow, and gathering where you did not scatter. 25 And *I* fearing, having gone away, I hid your talent in the earth. Behold, you have yours. 26 And answering his lord said to him, Evil and slothful slave! You knew that I reaped where I did not sow, and gathered where I did not scatter. 27 Then you ought to have put my silver to the bankers; and coming I would have received my own with interest. 28 Therefore, take the talent from him, and give *it* to him who has the ten talents. 29 For to everyone who has, *more* will be given, and he will abound. But from him who does not have, even that which he has will be taken from him. 30 And throw the worthless slave out into the outer darkness. There will be weeping and gnashing of the teeth.

31 But when the Son of man comes in His glory, and all the holy angels with Him, then He will sit on the throne of His glory. 32 And before Him shall be gathered all the nations, and He will separate them from one another, as the shepherd separates the sheep from the goats. 33 And He will set the sheep on His right, but the goats off *the* left *hand.* 34 Then the King will say to those on His right, Come, the blessed of My Father. Inherit the kingdom prepared for you from *the* foundation of *the* world. 35 For I was hungry, and you

22 προσελθὼν δὲ καὶ ὁ τὰ δύο τάλαντα λαβὼν εἶπε, Κύριε,
coming up And also the (one) the two talents receiving said, Lord,
δύο τάλαντά μοι παρέδωκας· ἴδε, ἄλλα δύο τάλαντα
two talents to me you delivered. Behold, other two talents
23 ἐκέρδησα ἐπ' αὐτοῖς. ἔφη αὐτῷ ὁ κύριος αὐτοῦ, Εὖ, δοῦλε
I gained over them. said to him The lord of him, Well, slave
ἀγαθὲ καὶ πιστέ, ἐπὶ ὀλίγα ἦς πιστός, επὶ πολλῶν σε
good and faithful over a few you were faithful; over many you
24 καταστήσω· εἴσελθε εἰς τὴν χαρὰν τοῦ κυρίου σου. προσ-
I will set. Enter into the joy of the lord of you. coming
ελθὼν δὲ καὶ ὁ τὸ ἓν τάλαντον εἰληφὼς εἶπε, Κύριε, ἔγνων
up And also the (one) the one talent having received, said, Lord, I knew
σε ὅτι σκληρὸς εἶ ἄνθρωπος, θερίζων ὅπου οὐκ ἔσπειρας, καὶ
you, that hard you are a man, reaping where not you sowed, and
25 συνάγων ὅθεν οὐ διεσκόρπισας· καὶ φοβηθείς, ἀπελθὼν
gathering from where not you scattered; and fearing, going away,
ἔκρυψα τὸ τάλαντόν σου ἐν τῇ γῇ· ἴδε, ἔχεις τὸ σόν.
I hid the talent of you in the earth. Behold, you have yours.
26 ἀποκριθεὶς δὲ ὁ κύριος αὐτοῦ εἶπεν αὐτῷ, Πονηρὲ δοῦλε καὶ
answering And, the lord of him said to him, Evil slave and
ὀκνηρέ, ᾔδεις ὅτι θερίζω ὅπου οὐκ ἔσπειρα, καὶ συνάγω ὅθεν
slothful, you knew that I reap where not I sowed, and I gather where
27 οὐ διεσκόρπισα· ἔδει οὖν σε βαλεῖν τὸ ἀργύριόν μου τοῖς
not I scattered. It behoved then you to put the silver of me to the
τραπεζίταις, καὶ ἐλθὼν ἐγὼ ἐκομισάμην ἂν τὸ ἐμὸν σὺν
bankers, and coming I would have received again mine with
28 τόκῳ. ἄρατε οὖν ἀπ' αὐτοῦ τὸ τάλαντον, καὶ δότε τῷ
interest. Take, therefore, from him the talent, and give to him
29 ἔχοντι τὰ δέκα τάλαντα. τῷ γὰρ ἔχοντι παντὶ δοθήσεται,
having the ten talents. to him For having, each will be given
καὶ περισσευθήσεται· ἀπὸ δὲ τοῦ μὴ ἔχοντος, καὶ ὃ ἔχει,
and he will abound; from but the (one) not having even what he has
30 ἀρθήσεται ἀπ' αὐτοῦ. καὶ τὸν ἀχρεῖον δοῦλον ἐκβάλλετε
will be taken from him. And the worthless slave throw out
εἰς τὸ σκότος τὸ ἐξώτερον. ἐκεῖ ἔσται ὁ κλαυθμὸς καὶ ὁ
into the darkness – outer; there will be the weeping and the
βρυγμὸς τῶν ὀδόντων.
gnashing of the teeth.
31 Ὅταν δὲ ἔλθῃ ὁ υἱὸς τοῦ ἀνθρώπου ἐν τῇ δόξῃ αὐτοῦ,
when And comes the Son – of man in the glory of Him,
καὶ πάντες οἱ ἅγιοι ἄγγελοι μετ' αὐτοῦ, τότε καθίσει ἐπὶ
and all the holy angels with Him, then He will sit on
32 θρόνου δόξης αὐτοῦ, καὶ συναχθήσεται ἔμπροσθεν αὐτοῦ
a throne of glory of Him, and will be assembled before Him
πάντα τὰ ἔθνη, καὶ ἀφοριεῖ αὐτοὺς ἀπ' ἀλλήλων, ὥσπερ ὁ
all the nations, and He will part them from one another, as the
33 ποιμὴν ἀφορίζει τὰ πρόβατα ἀπὸ τῶν ἐρίφων· καὶ στήσει
shepherd parts the sheep from the goats, and will set
τὰ μὲν πρόβατα ἐκ δεξιῶν αὐτοῦ, τὰ δὲ ἐρίφια ἐξ εὐωνύμων.
the even sheep off right his, the but goats off (the) left.
34 τότε ἐρεῖ ὁ βασιλεὺς τοῖς ἐκ δεξιῶν αὐτοῦ, Δεῦτε, οἱ εὐλογη-
Then will say the King to those off His right, Come, the blessed
μένοι τοῦ πατρός μου, κληρονομήσατε τὴν ἡτοιμασμένην
of the Father of Me; inherit the prepared
35 ὑμῖν βασιλείαν ἀπὸ καταβολῆς κόσμου. ἐπείνασα γάρ, καὶ
for you kingdom from foundation of (the) world. I hungered For, and

ἐδώκατέ μοι φαγεῖν· ἐδίψησα, καὶ ἐποτίσατέ με· ξένος ἤμην,
you gave Me to eat; I thirsted, and you gave drink Me;an alien I was
36 καὶ συνηγάγετέ με· γυμνός, καὶ περιεβάλετέ με· ἠσθένησα,
and you took in Me; naked, and you clothed Me; I was sick,
καὶ ἐπεσκέψασθέ με· ἐν φυλακῇ ἤμην, καὶ ἤλθετε πρός με.
and you visited Me in prison I was, and you came to Me.
37 τότε ἀποκριθήσονται αὐτῷ οἱ δίκαιοι, λέγοντες, Κύριε,
Then will answer Him the righteous, saying, Lord,
πότε σὲ εἴδομεν πεινῶντα, καὶ ἐθρέψαμεν ; ἢ διψῶντα, καὶ
when You did we see hungering, and fed, or thirsting, and
38 ἐποτίσαμεν ; πότε δέ σε εἴδομεν ξένον, καὶ συνηγάγομεν ;
gave drink; when and You did we see an alien,,and gathered (You) in;
39 ἢ γυμνόν, καὶ περιεβάλομεν ; πότε δέ σε εἴδομεν ἀσθενῆ, ἢ ἐν
or naked, and clothed? when And You did we see sick, or in
40 φυλακῇ, καὶ ἤλθομεν πρός σε ; καὶ ἀποκριθεὶς ὁ βασιλεὺς ἐρεῖ
prison, and came to You? And answering the King will say
αὐτοῖς, Ἀμὴν λέγω ὑμῖν, ἐφ' ὅσον ἐποιήσατε ἑνὶ τούτων τῶν
to them, Truly I say to you, inasmuch as you did to one of these the
41 ἀδελφῶν μου τῶν ἐλαχίστων, ἐμοὶ ἐποιήσατε. τότε ἐρεῖ καὶ
brothers of Me the least, to Me you did. Then He says also
τοῖς ἐξ εὐωνύμων, Πορεύεσθε ἀπ' ἐμοῦ, οἱ κατηραμένοι, εἰς
to those off (the) left, Go from Me, those cursed into
τὸ πῦρ τὸ αἰώνιον, τὸ ἡτοιμασμένον τῷ διαβόλῳ καὶ τοῖς
the fire — everlasting — having been prepared for the Devil and the
42 ἀγγέλοις αὐτοῦ. ἐπείνασα γάρ, καὶ οὐκ ἐδώκατέ μοι φαγεῖν·
angels of him. I hungered For,and not you gave Me to eat;
43 ἐδίψησα, καὶ οὐκ ἐποτίσατέ με· ξένος ἤμην, καὶ οὐ συνηγά-
I thirsted, and not you gave drink to Me; an alien I was, and not you gathered
γετέ με· γυμνός, καὶ οὐ περιεβάλετέ με· ἀσθενής, καὶ ἐν
in Me; naked, and not you clothed Me; sick, and in
44 φυλακῇ, καὶ οὐκ ἐπεσκέψασθέ με. τότε ἀποκριθήσονται
prison, and not you visited Me. Then will answer
αὐτῷ καὶ αὐτοί, λέγοντες, Κύριε, πότε σὲ εἴδομεν πεινῶντα,
Him also they, saying, Lord, when You did we see hungering,
ἢ διψῶντα, ἢ ξένον, ἢ γυμνόν, ἢ ἀσθενῆ, ἢ ἐν φυλακῇ, καὶ
or thirsting, or an alien, or naked, or sick, or in prison, and
45 οὐ διηκονήσαμέν σοι ; τότε ἀποκριθήσεται αὐτοῖς, λέγων,
not did minister to You? Then He will answer them, saying,
Ἀμὴν λέγω ὑμῖν, ἐφ' ὅσον οὐκ ἐποιήσατε ἑνὶ τούτων τῶν
Truly I say to you; Inasmuch as not you did to one of these, the
46 ἐλαχίστων, οὐδὲ ἐμοὶ ἐποιήσατε. καὶ ἀπελεύσονται οὗτοι
least (ones), neither to Me you did. And will go away these
εἰς κόλασιν αἰώνιον· οἱ δὲ δίκαιοι εἰς ζωὴν αἰώνιον.
into punishment eternal, the but righteous into life eternal.

CHAPTER 26

1 Καὶ ἐγένετο ὅτε ἐτέλεσεν ὁ Ἰησοῦς πάντας τοὺς λόγους
And it was, when ended — Jesus all sayings
2 τούτους, εἶπε τοῖς μαθηταῖς αὐτοῦ, Οἴδατε ὅτι μετὰ δύο
these, He said to the disciples of Him, You know that after two
ἡμέρας τὸ πάσχα γίνεται, καὶ ὁ υἱὸς τοῦ ἀνθρώπου παραδί-
days the Passover comes, and the Son — of man is be-
3 δοται εἰς τὸ σταυρωθῆναι. τότε συνήχθησαν οἱ ἀρχιερεῖς
trayed to be crucified. Then were assembled the chief priests
καὶ οἱ γραμματεῖς καὶ οἱ πρεσβύτεροι τοῦ λαοῦ εἰς τὴν
and the scribes and the elders of the people to the

gave Me *food* to eat; I was thirsty, and you gave Me drink; I was a stranger, and you took Me in; 36 naked, and you clothed Me; I was sick, and you visited Me; I was in prison, and you came to Me. 37 Then the righteous will answer, saying, Lord, when did we see You hungry, and fed *You;* or thirsty, and gave *You* drink? 38 And when did we see You a stranger, and took *You* in; or naked, and clothed *You?* 39 And when did we see You sick, or in prison, and came to You? 40 And answering, the King will say to them, Truly I say to you, Inasmuch as you did *it* to one of these, the least of My brothers, you did *it* to Me. 41 Then He will also say to those on *His* left, Go away from Me, cursed ones, into the everlasting fire having been prepared for the Devil and his angels. 42 For I was hungry, and you gave Me nothing to eat; I was thirsty, and you gave me nothing to drink; 43 I was a stranger, and you did not take Me in; naked, and you did not clothe Me; sick, and in prison, and you did not visit Me. 44 Then they also will answer Him, saying, Lord, when did we see You hungry, or thirsty, or a stranger, or naked, or sick, or in prison, and did not minister to You? 45 Then He will answer them, saying, Truly I say to you, Inasmuch as you did not do *it* to one of these, the least, neither did you do *it* to Me. 46 And these shall go away into everlasting punishment, but the righteous into everlasting life.

CHAPTER 26

1 And it happened when Jesus finished all these sayings, He said to His disciples, 2 You know that the Passover is coming after two days, and the Son of man is betrayed to be crucified. 3 Then the chief priests and the scribes and the elders of the people were assembled

to the court of the high priest, the *one* named Caiaphas. [4]And *they* plotted together in order that they might seize Jesus by guile, and kill *Him.* [5]But they said, Not during the feast, that there be no uproar among the people.

[6]And Jesus being in Bethany in Simon the leper's house, [7]a woman came to Him having an alabaster vial of ointment, very precious. And *she* poured *it* on His head as He reclined. [8]But seeing this, His disciples were indignant, saying, For what *is* this waste? [9]For this ointment could have been sold for much, and have been given to *the* poor. [10]But knowing, Jesus said to them, Why do you cause trouble to the woman? For she worked a good work toward Me. [11]For you always have the poor with you, but do not always have Me. [12]For in putting this ointment on My body, she did *it* in order to bury Me. [13]Truly I say to you, Wherever this gospel is proclaimed in all the world, what she did will be spoken of as a memorial of her.

[14]Then one of the twelve, the *one* named Judas Iscariot, going to the chief priests [15]said, What will you give to me, and I will deliver Him up to you? And they weighed to him thirty silver pieces. [16]And from then he sought opportunity that he might betray Him.

[17]And on the first *day* of unleavened *bread* the disciples came to Jesus, saying to Him, Where do you desire we should prepare for You to eat the Passover? [18]And He said, Go into the city to a certain one and say to him, The Teacher says, My time is near; I will keep the Passover with My disciples with you. [19]And the disciples did as Jesus ordered them, and

4 αὐλὴν τοῦ ἀρχιερέως τοῦ λεγομένου Καϊάφα, καὶ συνεβου-
court of the high priest — named Caiaphas, and consulted
λεύσαντο ἵνα τὸν Ἰησοῦν κρατήσωσι δόλῳ καὶ ἀπο-
together that — Jesus they might seize by guile, and
5 κτείνωσιν. ἔλεγον δέ, Μὴ ἐν τῇ ἑορτῇ, ἵνα μὴ θόρυβος
kill (Him). they said But, Not at the feast, lest a turmoil
γένηται ἐν τῷ λαῷ.
occur among the people.

6 Τοῦ δὲ Ἰησοῦ γενομένου ἐν Βηθανίᾳ ἐν οἰκίᾳ Σίμωνος τοῦ
— And Jesus being in Bethany in (the) house of Simon the
7 λεπροῦ, προσῆλθεν αὐτῷ γυνὴ ἀλάβαστρον μύρου ἔχουσα
leper, came up to Him a woman an alabaster vial of ointment having
βαρυτίμου, καὶ κατέχεεν ἐπὶ τὴν κεφαλὴν αὐτοῦ ἀνακει-
very precious, and poured (it) on the head of Him reclining.
8 μένου. ἰδόντες δὲ οἱ μαθηταὶ αὐτοῦ ἠγανάκτησαν, λέγοντες,
seeing And the disciples of Him were indignant, saying,
9 Εἰς τί ἡ ἀπώλεια αὕτη; ἠδύνατο γὰρ τοῦτο τὸ μύρον
To what — waste this? could For this ointmen
10 πραθῆναι πολλοῦ, καὶ δοθῆναι πτωχοῖς. γνοὺς δὲ ὁ Ἰησοῦς
have been sold of much, and to be given to (the) poor? knowing And Jesus
εἶπεν αὐτοῖς, Τί κόπους παρέχετε τῇ γυναικί; ἔργον γὰρ
said to them, Why trouble do you cause to the woman? work For
11 καλὸν εἰργάσατο εἰς ἐμέ. πάντοτε γὰρ τοὺς πτωχοὺς ἔχετε
a good she worked toward Me, always for the poor you have
12 μεθ' ἑαυτῶν, ἐμὲ δὲ οὐ πάντοτε ἔχετε. βαλοῦσα γὰρ αὕτη
with yourselves, Me but not always you have. putting For she
τὸ μύρον τοῦτο ἐπὶ τοῦ σώματός μου, πρὸς τὸ ἐνταφιάσαι
ointment this on the body of Me, in order to bury
13 με ἐποίησεν. ἀμὴν λέγω ὑμῖν, ὅπου ἐὰν κηρυχθῇ τὸ εὐαγ-
Me she did (it). Truly I say to you, wherever is proclaimed gospel
γέλιον τοῦτο ἐν ὅλῳ τῷ κόσμῳ, λαληθήσεται καὶ ὃ ἐποίησεν
this in all the world, will be spoken also what did
αὕτη, εἰς μνημόσυνον αὐτῆς.
she for a memorial of her.

14 Τότε πορευθεὶς εἷς τῶν δώδεκα, ὁ λεγόμενος Ἰούδας
Then going one of the twelve, the (one) named Judas
15 Ἰσκαριώτης, πρὸς τοὺς ἀρχιερεῖς, εἶπε, Τί θέλετέ μοι δοῦναι,
Iscariot, to the chief priests, said, What will you me give,
κἀγὼ ὑμῖν παραδώσω αὐτόν; οἱ δὲ ἔστησαν αὐτῷ τριά-
and I to you will deliver up Him? they And weighed him thirty
16 κοντα ἀργύρια. καὶ ἀπὸ τότε ἐζήτει εὐκαιρίαν ἵνα αὐτὸν
silver pieces. And from then he sought opportunity that Him
παραδῷ.
he might deliver.

17 Τῇ δὲ πρώτῃ τῶν ἀζύμων προσῆλθον οἱ μαθηταὶ τῷ
on the And first unleavened came the disciples to
Ἰησοῦ, λέγοντες αὐτῷ, Ποῦ θέλεις ἑτοιμάσωμέν σοι φαγεῖν
Jesus, saying to Him, Where will You we may prepare for You to eat
18 τὸ πάσχα; ὁ δὲ εἶπεν, Ὑπάγετε εἰς τὴν πόλιν πρὸς τὸν
the Passover? He And said, Go into the city to such
δεῖνα, καὶ εἴπατε αὐτῷ, Ὁ διδάσκαλος λέγει, Ὁ καιρός μου
a one, and say to him, The Teacher says, The time of Me
ἐγγύς ἐστι· πρὸς σὲ ποιῶ τὸ πάσχα μετὰ τῶν μαθητῶν μου.
near is; toward you I make the Passover, with the disciples of Me.
19 καὶ ἐποίησαν οἱ μαθηταὶ ὡς συνέταξεν αὐτοῖς ὁ Ἰησοῦς, καὶ
And did the disciples as ordered them — Jesus, and

prepared the Passover.
[20] And evening coming,
He reclined with the Twelve.
[21] And as they were eating
He said, Truly I say to you
that one of you will betray
Me. [22] And grieving exceedingly, they began to say to
Him, each of them, Lord, Not
I am *the one*? [23] But answering He said, The *one* dipping
the hand with Me in the dish
will betray Me. [24] Indeed,
the Son of man goes, as it
has been written about Him.
But woe to that man by
whom the Son of man is
betrayed. It were good for
him if that man was never
born. [25] And answering
Judas, who was betraying
Him, said, Not I am *the one,*
Rabbi? He said to him, You
said *it*.
[26] And *as* they ate, Jesus
taking the bread, and blessing, broke and gave to the
disciples; and said, Take,
eat; this is My body. [27] And
taking the cup, and giving
thanks, He gave to them,
saying, Drink all of it. [28] For
this is My blood of the New
Covenant which concerning
many is poured out for
forgiveness of sins. [29] But I
say to you, I will not at all
drink of this fruit of the vine
after this, until that day
when I drink it new with you
in the kingdom of My Father.
[30] And having sung a
hymn, they went out to the
Mount of Olives. [31] Then
Jesus said to them, You all
will be offended in Me
during this night. For it has
been written, "I will smite
the Shepherd, and the
sheep of the flock will be
scattered." [32] But after My
resurrection I will go before
you into Galilee. [33] And
answering Peter said to
Him, Even if all will be
offended in You, I will never
be offended. [34] Jesus said
to him, Truly I say to you,
During this night, before *the*
cock crows, you will deny
Me three times. [35] Peter said

20 ἡτοίμασαν τὸ πάσχα. ὀψίας δὲ γενομένης ἀνέκειτο μετὰ τῶν
prepared the Passover. evening And coming, He reclined with the
21 δώδεκα. καὶ ἐσθιόντων αὐτῶν εἶπεν, Ἀμὴν λέγω ὑμῖν ὅτι
twelve. And eating they, He said, Truly I say to you that
22 εἷς ἐξ ὑμῶν παραδώσει με. καὶ λυπούμενοι σφόδρα ἤρξαντο
one from you will betray Me. And grieving exceedingly they began
23 λέγειν αὐτῷ ἕκαστος αὐτῶν, Μήτι ἐγώ εἰμι, Κύριε; ὁ δὲ
to say to Him, each of them, Not I am (he), Lord? He But
ἀποκριθεὶς εἶπεν, Ὁ ἐμβάψας μετ' ἐμοῦ ἐν τῷ τρυβλίῳ τὴν
answering said, The (one) dipping with Me in the dish the
24 χεῖρα, οὗτός με παραδώσει. ὁ μὲν υἱὸς τοῦ ἀνθρώπου ὑπάγει,
hand, Me will betray. the Indeed Son of man goes
καθὼς γέγραπται περὶ αὐτοῦ· οὐαὶ δὲ τῷ ἀνθρώπῳ ἐκείνῳ,
as it has been written about Him, woe but to man that
δι' οὗ ὁ υἱὸς τοῦ ἀνθρώπου παραδίδοται· καλὸν ἦν αὐτῷ εἰ
by whom the Son of man is betrayed; good were it for him if
25 οὐκ ἐγεννήθη ὁ ἄνθρωπος ἐκεῖνος. ἀποκριθεὶς δὲ Ἰούδας ὁ
not was born man that. answering And Judas who
παραδιδοὺς αὐτὸν εἶπε, Μήτι ἐγώ εἰμι, ῥαββί; λέγει αὐτῷ,
was betraying Him said, Not I am (he), Rabbi? He says to him,
26 Σὺ εἶπας. ἐσθιόντων δὲ αὐτῶν, λαβὼν ὁ Ἰησοῦς τὸν ἄρτον,
You said (it). eating And they, taking — Jesus the bread
καὶ εὐλογήσας, ἔκλασε καὶ ἐδίδου τοῖς μαθηταῖς, καὶ εἶπε,
and blessing, He broke and gave to the disciples, and said,
27 Λάβετε, φάγετε· τοῦτό ἐστι τὸ σῶμά μου. καὶ λαβὼν τὸ
Take, eat, this is the body of Me. And taking the
ποτήριον, καὶ εὐχαριστήσας, ἔδωκεν αὐτοῖς, λέγων, Πίετε
cup, and giving thanks, He gave to them, saying, Drink
28 ἐξ αὐτοῦ πάντες· τοῦτο γάρ ἐστι τὸ αἷμά μου, τὸ τῆς καινῆς
of it all; this for is the blood of Me — of the New
διαθήκης, τὸ περὶ πολλῶν ἐκχυνόμενον εἰς ἄφεσιν ἁμαρτιῶν.
Covenant, which concerning many is being poured out for forgiveness of sins.
29 λέγω δὲ ὑμῖν ὅτι οὐ μὴ πίω ἀπ' ἄρτι ἐκ τούτου τοῦ γεννή-
I say And to you that never will I drink from now of this fruit
ματος τῆς ἀμπέλου, ἕως τῆς ἡμέρας ἐκείνης ὅταν αὐτὸ πίνω
of the vine until — day that when it I drink
μεθ' ὑμῶν καινὸν ἐν τῇ βασιλείᾳ τοῦ πατρός μου.
with you new in the kingdom of the Father of Me.
30 Καὶ ὑμνήσαντες ἐξῆλθον εἰς τὸ ὄρος τῶν ἐλαιῶν.
And having sung a hymn they went into the mount of the olives.
31 Τότε λέγει αὐτοῖς ὁ Ἰησοῦς, Πάντες ὑμεῖς σκανδαλισθή-
Then says to them Jesus, All you will be offended
σεσθε ἐν ἐμοὶ ἐν τῇ νυκτὶ ταύτῃ· γέγραπται γάρ, Πατάξω
in Me during night this; it has been written for, I will strike
τὸν ποιμένα, καὶ διασκορπισθήσεται τὰ πρόβατα τῆς
the shepherd, and will be scattered the sheep of the
32 ποίμνης. μετὰ δὲ τὸ ἐγερθῆναί με, προάξω ὑμᾶς εἰς τὴν
flock; after but the rising (of) Me, I will go before you to —
33 Γαλιλαίαν. ἀποκριθεὶς δὲ ὁ Πέτρος εἶπεν αὐτῷ, Εἰ καὶ πάντες
Galilee. answering And Peter said to Him, If even all
σκανδαλισθήσονται ἐν σοί, ἐγὼ οὐδέποτε σκανδαλισθή-
be offended in You, I never will be offended.
34 σομαι. ἔφη αὐτῷ ὁ Ἰησοῦς, Ἀμὴν λέγω σοι ὅτι ἐν ταύτῃ τῇ
said to him Jesus, Truly I say to you that in this —
35 νυκτί, πρὶν ἀλέκτορα φωνῆσαι, τρὶς ἀπαρνήσῃ με. λέγει
night, before (the) cock crows, thrice you will deny Me. Says

to Him, Even if it were necessary for me to die with You, I will in no way deny You. And all the disciples said the same.

36 Then Jesus came with them to a place called Gethsemane. And He said to the disciples, Sit here until I going away shall pray there. 37 And taking along Peter and the two sons of Zebedee, He began to be sorrowful and deeply troubled. 38 Then He said to them, My soul is deeply grieved, even unto death. Stay here and watch with Me.

39 And going forward a little, He fell on His face praying and saying, My Father, if it is possible, let this cup pass from Me; yet, not as I will, but as You *will*. 40 And He came to the disciples and found them sleeping. And *He* said to Peter, So! Were you not able to watch one hour with Me? 41 Watch and pray that you do not enter into temptation. The spirit indeed *is* willing, but the flesh is weak. 42 Again, going away a second time, He prayed, saying, My Father, if this cup cannot pass away from Me without My drinking it, let Your will be done. 43 And coming He again found them sleeping, for their eyes were heavy.

44 And leaving them, going away again, He prayed a third time, saying the same thing. 45 Then He came to His disciples and said to them, Sleep on, and rest *for* what remains. Behold, the hour draws near, and the Son of man is betrayed into *the* hands of sinners. 46 Rise up, let us go. Behold, the *one* betraying Me draws near.

47 And as He was yet speaking, behold, Judas came, one of the Twelve. And with him *was* a numerous crowd with

αὐτῷ ὁ Πέτρος, Κἂν δέῃ με σὺν σοὶ ἀποθανεῖν, οὐ μή σε
to Him — Peter, Even if need I with You to die, in no way You
ἀπαρνήσομαι. ὁμοίως καὶ πάντες οἱ μαθηταὶ εἶπον.
I will deny. Likewise also all the disciples said.
36 Τότε ἔρχεται μετ' αὐτῶν ὁ Ἰησοῦς εἰς χωρίον λεγόμενον
Then comes with them — Jesus to a place called
Γεθσημανῆ, καὶ λέγει τοῖς μαθηταῖς, Καθίσατε αὐτοῦ, ἕως οὗ
Gethsemane, and says to the disciples, Sit on this until
37 ἀπελθὼν προσεύξωμαι ἐκεῖ. καὶ παραλαβὼν τὸν Πέτρον καὶ
going away I shall pray there. And taking along — Peter and
τοὺς δύο υἱοὺς Ζεβεδαίου, ἤρξατο λυπεῖσθαι καὶ ἀδημονεῖν.
the two sons of Zebedee, He began to grieve and be distressed.
38 τότε λέγει αὐτοῖς, Περίλυπός ἐστιν ἡ ψυχή μου ἕως θανάτου·
Then He says to them, deeply grieved is the soul of Me unto death;
39 μείνατε ὧδε καὶ γρηγορεῖτε μετ' ἐμοῦ. καὶ προελθὼν μικρόν,
remain here and watch with Me. And going forward a little,
ἔπεσεν ἐπὶ πρόσωπον αὐτοῦ προσευχόμενος καὶ λέγων,
He fell on (the) face of Him, praying and saying,
Πάτερ μου, εἰ δυνατόν ἐστι, παρελθέτω ἀπ' ἐμοῦ τὸ ποτή-
Father of Me, if possible it is, let pass from Me — cup
40 ριον τοῦτο· πλὴν οὐχ ὡς ἐγὼ θέλω, ἀλλ' ὡς σύ. καὶ ἔρχεται
this; yet not as I will, but as You. And He comes
πρὸς τοὺς μαθητάς, καὶ εὑρίσκει αὐτοὺς καθεύδοντας, καὶ
toward the disciples and finds them sleeping, and
λέγει τῷ Πέτρῳ, Οὕτως οὐκ ἰσχύσατε μίαν ὥραν γρηγορῆ-
says — to Peter, So, not were you able one hour to watch
41 σαι μετ' ἐμοῦ; γρηγορεῖτε καὶ προσεύχεσθε, ἵνα μὴ
with Me? Watch and pray, lest
εἰσέλθητε εἰς πειρασμόν· τὸ μὲν πνεῦμα πρόθυμον, ἡ δὲ
you enter into temptation; the indeed spirit (is) eager, the but
42 σὰρξ ἀσθενής. πάλιν ἐκ δευτέρου ἀπελθὼν προσηύξατο,
flesh (is) weak. Again, for a second (time) going away He prayed,
λέγων, Πάτερ μου, εἰ οὐ δύναται τοῦτο τὸ ποτήριον
saying, Father of Me, if not can this — cup
παρελθεῖν ἀπ' ἐμοῦ, ἐὰν μὴ αὐτὸ πίω, γενηθήτω τὸ θέλημά
pass away from Me unless it I drink, let be done the will
43 σου. καὶ ἐλθὼν εὑρίσκει αὐτοὺς πάλιν καθεύδοντας, ἦσαν
of You. And coming He finds them again sleeping, were
44 γὰρ αὐτῶν οἱ ὀφθαλμοὶ βεβαρημένοι. καὶ ἀφεὶς αὐτοὺς
for of them the eyes heavy. And leaving them
ἀπελθὼν πάλιν προσηύξατο ἐκ τρίτου, τὸν αὐτὸν λόγον
going away again, He prayed a third (time), the same word
45 εἰπών. τότε ἔρχεται πρὸς τοὺς μαθητὰς αὐτοῦ, καὶ λέγει
saying. Then He comes to the disciples of Him, and says
αὐτοῖς, Καθεύδετε τὸ λοιπὸν καὶ ἀναπαύεσθε· ἰδού, ἤγγικεν
to them, Sleep (for) what remains and rest; behold, draws near
ἡ ὥρα, καὶ ὁ υἱὸς τοῦ ἀνθρώπου παραδίδοται εἰς χεῖρας
the hour and the Son — of man is betrayed into hands
46 ἁμαρτωλῶν. ἐγείρεσθε, ἄγωμεν. ἰδού, ἤγγικεν ὁ παραδι-
of sinners. Rise, let us go, Behold, draws near the (one)
δούς με.
betraying Me.
47 Καὶ ἔτι αὐτοῦ λαλοῦντος, ἰδού, Ἰούδας εἷς τῶν δώδεκα
And while He was speaking, behold Judas, one of the twelve,
ἦλθε, καὶ μετ' αὐτοῦ ὄχλος πολὺς μετὰ μαχαιρῶν καὶ
came, and with him a crowd numerous with swords and

swords and clubs, from the chief priests and elders of the people. [48]And he who was betraying Him gave them a sign, saying, Whomever I may kiss, it is He. Seize Him. [49]And coming up at once to Jesus, he said, Greetings, Rabbi! And *he* ardently kissed Him. [50]But Jesus said to him, Friend, why are you here? Then coming up, they laid hands on Jesus and seized Him. [51]And, behold, one of those with Jesus, stretching out the hand, drew his sword and struck the slave of the high priest, *and* took off his ear. [52]Then Jesus said to him, Put your sword back into its place. For all who take *the* sword shall perish by a sword. [53]Or do you think that I am not able now to call on My Father, and He will place beside Me more than twelve legions of angels? [54]How then should the Scriptures be fulfilled, that it must happen this way?

[55]In that hour Jesus said to the crowds, Have you come out to take Me with swords and clubs, as against a robber? I sat daily with you, teaching in the Temple, and you did not lay hands on Me. [56]But all this is happening that the Scriptures of the prophets may be fulfilled.

Then all the disciples ran away, forsaking Him.

[57]And those who had seized Jesus led *Him* away to Caiaphas the high priest, where the scribes and the elders were assembled. [58]And Peter followed Him from a distance, even to the court of the high priest. And going inside, *he* sat with the under-officers to see the end. [59]And the chief priests and the elders and the whole Sanhedrin looked for false evidence against Jesus, so that they might put Him to death. [60]And none *were* found, even though *there were* many false witnesses coming forward, they did

48 ξύλων, ἀπὸ τῶν ἀρχιερέων καὶ πρεσβυτέρων τοῦ λαοῦ. ὁ
clubs, from the chief priests and elders of the people. he
δὲ παραδιδοὺς αὐτὸν ἔδωκεν αὐτοῖς σημεῖον, λέγων, Ὃν
And betraying Him gave to them a sign, saying, Whom-
49 ἂν φιλήσω, αὐτός ἐστι· κρατήσατε αὐτόν. καὶ εὐθέως
ever I may kiss, He it is; seize Him. And at once
προσελθὼν τῷ Ἰησοῦ εἶπε, Χαῖρε, ῥαββί· καὶ κατεφίλησεν
coming up — to Jesus he said, Hail, Rabbi, and ardently kissed
50 αὐτόν. ὁ δὲ Ἰησοῦς εἶπεν αὐτῷ, Ἑταῖρε, ἐφ' ᾧ πάρει ; τότε
Him. — But Jesus said to him, Friend, why are you here? Then
προσελθόντες ἐπέβαλον τὰς χεῖρας ἐπὶ τὸν Ἰησοῦν, καὶ
coming up, they laid on the hands, on — Jesus, and
51 ἐκράτησαν αὐτόν. καὶ ἰδού, εἷς τῶν μετὰ Ἰησοῦ, ἐκτείνας
seized Him. And behold, one of those with Jesus, stretching
τὴν χεῖρα, ἀπέσπασε τὴν μάχαιραν αὐτοῦ, καὶ πατάξας τὸν
the hand, drew the sword of him, and striking the
52 δοῦλον τοῦ ἀρχιερέως ἀφεῖλεν αὐτοῦ τὸ ὠτίον. τότε λέγει
slave of the high priest took off of him the ear. Then says
αὐτῷ ὁ Ἰησοῦς, Ἀπόστρεψόν σου τὴν μάχαιραν εἰς τὸν
to him — Jesus, Put back of you the sword to the
τόπον αὐτῆς· πάντες γὰρ οἱ λαβόντες μάχαιραν ἐν μαχαίρᾳ
place of it; all for those taking (the) sword by a sword
53 ἀπολοῦνται. ἢ δοκεῖς ὅτι οὐ δύναμαι ἄρτι παρακαλέσαι τὸν
shall perish. Or think you that not I can now call upon the
πατέρα μου, καὶ παραστήσει μοι πλείους ἢ δώδεκα λεγεῶνας
Father of Me, and He will place near Me more than twelve legions
54 ἀγγέλων ; πῶς οὖν πληρωθῶσιν αἱ γραφαί, ὅτι οὕτω δεῖ
of angels? How, then, should be fulfilled the Scriptures that so it must
55 γενέσθαι ; ἐν ἐκείνῃ τῇ ὥρᾳ εἶπεν ὁ Ἰησοῦς τοῖς ὄχλοις, Ὡς
be? In that — hour said — Jesus to the crowds, As
ἐπὶ λῃστὴν ἐξήλθετε μετὰ μαχαιρῶν καὶ ξύλων συλλαβεῖν
on a robber came you with swords and clubs together to take
με ; καθ' ἡμέραν πρὸς ὑμᾶς ἐκαθεζόμην διδάσκων ἐν τῷ ἱερῷ,
Me? Daily with you I sat teaching in the Temple,
56 καὶ οὐκ ἐκρατήσατέ με. τοῦτο δὲ ὅλον γέγονεν, ἵνα πληρωθῶ-
and not you seized Me. this But all has happened that may be ful-
σιν αἱ γραφαὶ τῶν προφητῶν. τότε οἱ μαθηταὶ πάντες
filled the Scriptures of the prophets. Then the disciples all
ἀφέντες αὐτὸν ἔφυγον.
leaving Him fled.
57 Οἱ δὲ κρατήσαντες τὸν Ἰησοῦν ἀπήγαγον πρὸς Καϊάφαν
the (ones) But seizing — Jesus led away to Caiaphas
τὸν ἀρχιερέα, ὅπου οἱ γραμματεῖς καὶ οἱ πρεσβύτεροι
the high priest, where the scribes and the elders
58 συνήχθησαν. ὁ δὲ Πέτρος ἠκολούθει αὐτῷ ἀπὸ μακρόθεν,
were assembled. — And Peter followed Him from afar
ἕως τῆς αὐλῆς τοῦ ἀρχιερέως, καὶ εἰσελθὼν ἔσω ἐκάθητο
up to the court of the high priest, and entering within sat
59 μετὰ τῶν ὑπηρετῶν, ἰδεῖν τὸ τέλος. οἱ δὲ ἀρχιερεῖς καὶ οἱ
with the under-officers to see the end. the And chief priests and the
πρεσβύτεροι καὶ τὸ συνέδριον ὅλον ἐζήτουν ψευδομαρτυ-
elders and the sanhedrin whole sought false testimony
60 ρίαν κατὰ τοῦ Ἰησοῦ, ὅπως αὐτὸν θανατώσωσι. καὶ οὐχ
against — Jesus so as Him they might execute.,but not
εὗρον· καὶ πολλῶν ψευδομαρτύρων προσελθόντων, οὐχ
did find,even many false witnesses coming forward not

not find *any.* But at last two false witnesses came up, [61] saying, This one said, I am able to destroy the Temple of God, and in three days to build it. [62] And standing up, the high priest said to Him, Do you answer nothing? What do these witness against you? [63] But Jesus was silent. And answering the high priest said to Him, I adjure you by the living God that you tell us if you are the Christ, the Son of God. [64] Jesus said to him, You said *it.* I tell you more. From this time you shall see the Son of man sitting at *the* right *hand* of power, and coming on the clouds of the heavens. [65] Then the high priest tore his garments, saying, He has blasphemed! Why do we have any more need of witnesses? Behold, now you have heard his blasphemy. [66] What do you think? And answering they said, He is deserving of death. [67] Then they spat in His face, and beat Him with the fist; and *some* slapped *Him,* [68] saying, Prophesy to us, Christ. Who is the *one* that struck you?

[69] And Peter sat outside in the court, and one girl came near to him, saying, And you were with Jesus the Galilean. [70] But he denied before all, saying, I do not know what you say. [71] And he going out into the porch, another saw him, and said to those there, And this one was with Jesus the Nazarene. [72] And again he denied with an oath, I do not know the man. [73] And after a little, coming near, those standing by said to Peter, Truly you also are of them, for even your speech makes you known. [74] Then he began to curse and to swear, I do not know the man. And immediately a cock crowed. [75] And Peter recalled the word of Jesus, saying to him, Before a cock crows, you will deny

εὗρον. ὕστερον δὲ προσελθόντες δύο ψευδομάρτυρες εἶπον,
did find. at last But coming up two false witnesses said,

61 Οὗτος ἔφη, Δύναμαι καταλῦσαι τὸν ναὸν τοῦ Θεοῦ, καὶ διὰ
This one said, I am able to destroy the temple – of God, and via

62 τριῶν ἡμερῶν οἰκοδομῆσαι αὐτόν. καὶ ἀναστὰς ὁ ἀρχιερεὺς
three days to build it. And standing up the high priest

εἶπεν αὐτῷ, Οὐδὲν ἀποκρίνῃ; τί οὗτοί σου καταμαρτυροῦ-
said to Him, Nothing do you reply of what these of you do witness

63 σιν; ὁ δὲ Ἰησοῦς ἐσιώπα. καὶ ἀποκριθεὶς ὁ ἀρχιερεὺς εἶπεν
against? But Jesus kept silent. And answering, the high priest said

αὐτῷ, Ἐξορκίζω σε κατὰ τοῦ Θεοῦ τοῦ ζῶντος, ἵνα ἡμῖν
to Him, I adjure you by God the living that us

εἴπῃς εἰ σὺ εἶ ὁ Χριστός, ὁ υἱὸς τοῦ Θεοῦ. λέγει αὐτῷ ὁ
you tell if you are the Christ, the Son of God! Says to him –

64 Ἰησοῦς, Σὺ εἶπας. πλὴν λέγω ὑμῖν, ἀπ' ἄρτι ὄψεσθε τὸν
Jesus, You said (it). Yet I tell you, from now you will see the

υἱὸν τοῦ ἀνθρώπου καθήμενον ἐκ δεξιῶν τῆς δυνάμεως καὶ
Son – of man sitting off (the) right (hand) of power and

65 ἐρχόμενον ἐπὶ τῶν νεφελῶν τοῦ οὐρανοῦ. τότε ὁ ἀρχιερεὺς
coming on the clouds – of Heaven. Then the high priest

διέρρηξε τὰ ἱμάτια αὐτοῦ, λέγων ὅτι Ἐβλασφήμησε· τί ἔτι
tore the garments of him, saying, – He blasphemed; Why yet

χρείαν ἔχομεν μαρτύρων; ἴδε, νῦν ἠκούσατε τὴν βλασφημίαν
need have we of witnesses? Behold, now, you heard the blasphemy.

66 αὐτοῦ. τί ὑμῖν δοκεῖ; οἱ δὲ ἀποκριθέντες εἶπον, Ἔνοχος
of him. What to you seems it? they And answering said, Liable

67 θανάτου ἐστί. τότε ἐνέπτυσαν εἰς τὸ πρόσωπον αὐτοῦ καὶ
of death he is. Then they spat in the face of Him, and

68 ἐκολάφισαν αὐτόν· οἱ δὲ ἐρράπισαν, λέγοντες, Προφή-
beat with the fist Him, they and slapped (Him), saying, Prophesy

τευσον ἡμῖν, Χριστέ, τίς ἐστιν ὁ παίσας σε;
to us, Christ, who is it, the (one) having struck you?

69 Ὁ δὲ Πέτρος ἔξω ἐκάθητο ἐν τῇ αὐλῇ· καὶ προσῆλθεν
– And Peter outside sat in the court; and came near

αὐτῷ μία παιδίσκη, λέγουσα, Καὶ σὺ ἦσθα μετὰ Ἰησοῦ τοῦ
to him one maid, saying, And you were with Jesus the

70 Γαλιλαίου. ὁ δὲ ἠρνήσατο ἔμπροσθεν πάντων, λέγων, Οὐκ
Galilean. he But denied before all, saying, not

71 οἶδα τί λέγεις. ἐξελθόντα δὲ αὐτὸν εἰς τὸν πυλῶνα, εἶδεν
I know what you say. going out And he into the porch, saw

αὐτὸν ἄλλη, καὶ λέγει τοῖς ἐκεῖ, Καὶ οὗτος ἦν μετὰ Ἰησοῦ
him another, and says to those there. And this one was with Jesus

72 τοῦ Ναζωραίου. καὶ πάλιν ἠρνήσατο μεθ' ὅρκου ὅτι Οὐκ
the Nazarene. And again he denied, with an oath, – not

73 οἶδα τὸν ἄνθρωπον. μετὰ μικρὸν δὲ προσελθόντες οἱ ἑστῶτες
I know the man. after a little And coming near those standing

εἶπον τῷ Πέτρῳ, Ἀληθῶς καὶ σὺ ἐξ αὐτῶν εἶ· καὶ γὰρ ἡ
said – to Peter, Truly also you of them are, even for the

74 λαλιά σου δῆλόν σε ποιεῖ. τότε ἤρξατο καταναθεματίζειν καὶ
speech of you manifest you makes. Then he began to curse and

ὀμνύειν ὅτι Οὐκ οἶδα τὸν ἄνθρωπον. καὶ εὐθέως ἀλέκτωρ
to swear, – not I know the man. And immediately a cock

75 ἐφώνησε. καὶ ἐμνήσθη ὁ Πέτρος τοῦ ῥήματος τοῦ Ἰησοῦ
crowed. And remembered – Peter the word – of Jesus,

εἰρηκότος αὐτῷ ὅτι Πρὶν ἀλέκτορα φωνῆσαι, τρὶς ἀπαρνήσῃ
having said to him, – Before a cock crows thrice you will deny

Me three times. And going out, he wept bitterly.

CHAPTER 27

[1]And *it* becoming early morning, all the chief priests and the elders of the people took counsel together against Jesus, so as to put Him to death. [2]And binding Him, they led *Him* away and delivered Him to Pontius Pilate the governor.

[3]Then Judas, the *one* betraying Him, seeing that He was condemned, sorrowing *he* returned the thirty pieces of silver to the chief priests and the elders, [4]saying, I sinned, betraying innocent blood. But they said, What *is it* to us? You see *to it*. [5]And tossing the silver pieces into the Temple, he left. And going away, *he* hanged himself. [6]And taking the pieces of silver, the chief priests said, It is not lawful to put them into the treasury, since it is *the* price of blood. [7]And taking counsel, they bought of them the potter's field, for burial for the strangers. [8]Therefore, that field was called Field of Blood until today. [9]Then was fulfilled that *which was* spoken by Jeremiah the prophet, saying, "And I took the thirty pieces of silver, the price of Him who was priced, on whom they of the sons of Israel set a price, [10]and gave them for the potter's field, as the Lord directed me."

[11]And Jesus stood before the governor. And the governor questioned Him, saying, Are you the king of the Jews? And Jesus said to him, You say *it*. [12]And when He was accused by the chief priests and the elders, He answered nothing. [13]Then Pilate said to Him, Do you not hear how many things they testify against you? [14]And He did not answer him, not even to one word, so that the governor greatly marveled.

[15]And at a feast the governor customarily released one prisoner to the crowd, whom they wished.

με. καὶ ἐξελθὼν ἔξω ἔκλαυσε πικρῶς.
Me. And going forth outside he wept bitterly.

CHAPTER 27

1 Πρωΐας δὲ γενομένης, συμβούλιον ἔλαβον πάντες οἱ
early morning And occurring, counsel together took all the
ἀρχιερεῖς καὶ οἱ πρεσβύτεροι τοῦ λαοῦ κατὰ τοῦ Ἰησοῦ,
chief priests and the elders of the people against — Jesus.
2 ὥστε θανατῶσαι αὐτόν· καὶ δήσαντες αὐτὸν ἀπήγαγον καὶ
so as to execute Him. And having bound Him, they led away and
παρέδωκαν αὐτὸν Ποντίῳ Πιλάτῳ τῷ ἡγεμόνι.
delivered Him to Pontius Pilate the governor.
3 Τότε ἰδὼν Ἰούδας ὁ παραδιδοὺς αὐτὸν ὅτι κατεκρίθη,
Then seeing Judas, the (one) betraying Him, that He was condemned,
μεταμεληθεὶς ἀπέστρεψε τὰ τριάκοντα ἀργύρια τοῖς ἀρχιε-
sorrowing returned the thirty pieces of silver to the chief
4 ρεῦσι καὶ τοῖς πρεσβυτέροις, λέγων, Ἥμαρτον παραδοὺς
priests and the elders, saying, I sinned, betraying
5 αἷμα ἀθῷον. οἱ δὲ εἶπον, Τί πρὸς ἡμᾶς; σὺ ὄψει. καὶ ῥίψας
blood innocent. they But said, What to us? You see (to it) And tossing
τὰ ἀργύρια εν τῷ ναῷ, ἀνεχωρησε· καὶ ἀπελθὼν ἀπήγξατο.
the silver pieces into the temple, he left, and going away hanged himself.
6 οἱ δὲ ἀρχιερεῖς λαβόντες τὰ ἀργύρια εἶπον, Οὐκ ἔξεστι
the But chief priests taking the silver pieces said, not It is lawful
βαλεῖν αὐτὰ εἰς τὸν κορβανᾶν, ἐπεὶ τιμὴ αἵματός ἐστι. συμ-
to put them into the treasury, since price of blood it is.
7 βούλιον δὲ λαβόντες ἠγόρασαν ἐξ αὐτῶν τὸν ἀγρὸν τοῦ
counsel And taking, they bought of them the field of the
8 κεραμέως, εἰς ταφὴν τοῖς ξένοις. διὸ ἐκλήθη ὁ ἀγρὸς ἐκεῖνος
potter for burial for the strangers. Thus was called field that,
9 ἀγρὸς αἵματος, ἕως τῆς σήμερον. τότε ἐπληρώθη τὸ ῥηθὲν
Field of Blood, until — today. Then was fulfilled that spoken
διὰ Ἱερεμίου τοῦ προφήτου, λέγοντος, Καὶ ἔλαβον τὰ
through Jeremiah the prophet, saying, And I took the
τριάκοντα ἀργύρια, τὴν τιμὴν τοῦ τετιμημένου, ὃν ἐτιμή-
thirty silver pieces, the price of the (one) priced, whom they
10 σαντο ἀπὸ υἱῶν Ἰσραήλ· καὶ ἔδωκαν αὐτὰ εἰς τὸν ἀγρὸν
priced from sons of Israel, and gave them for the field
τοῦ κεραμέως, καθὰ συνέταξέ μοι Κύριος.
of the potter, as directed me the Lord.
11 Ὁ δὲ Ἰησοῦς ἔστη ἔμπροσθεν τοῦ ἡγεμόνος· καὶ ἐπηρώ-
—And Jesus stood before the governor, and questioned
τησεν αὐτὸν ὁ ἡγεμών, λέγων, Σὺ εἶ ὁ βασιλεὺς τῶν
Him the governor, saying, You are the king of the
12 Ἰουδαίων; ὁ δὲ Ἰησοῦς ἔφη αὐτῷ, Σὺ λέγεις. καὶ ἐν τῷ
Jews? — And Jesus said to him, You say (it). And in the
κατηγορεῖσθαι αὐτὸν ὑπὸ τῶν ἀρχιερέων καὶ τῶν πρε-
accusing (of) Him by the chief priests and the
13 σβυτέρων, οὐδὲν ἀπεκρίνατο. τότε λέγει αὐτῷ ὁ Πιλάτος,
elders, nothing He answered. Then says to Him — Pilate,
14 Οὐκ ἀκούεις πόσα σοῦ καταμαρτυροῦσι; καὶ οὐκ ἀπεκρίθη
do not you hear what you they witness against? And not He answered
αὐτῷ πρὸς οὐδὲ ἓν ῥῆμα, ὥστε θαυμάζειν τὸν ἡγεμόνα λίαν.
him, to not even one word, so as to marvel the governor much
15 κατὰ δὲ ἑορτὴν εἰώθει ὁ ἡγεμὼν ἀπολύειν ἕνα τῷ ὄχλῳ
at And a feast used the governor to release one to the crowd

[16]And they had then a notable prisoner named Barabbas. [17]Then they having been assembled, Pilate said to them, Whom do you wish I may release to you, Barabbas, or Jesus called Christ? [18]For he knew they delivered Him up through envy. [19]But as he was sitting on the tribunal seat, his wife sent to him, saying, Let nothing *be* to you and that just one. For I have suffered many things today by a dream because of him. [20]But the chief priests and the elders persuaded the crowds, that they should ask *for* Barabbas, and to destroy Jesus. [21]And the governor said to them, Which do you wish from the two that I release to you? And they said, Barabbas. [22]Pilate said to them, What then should I do *to* Jesus called Christ? [23]They all say to him, Let him be crucified. But the governor said, For what wrong did he do? But they the more cried out, saying, Let him be crucified. [24]And seeing that nothing *is* gained, but rather an uproar occurs, taking water Pilate washed *his* hands before the crowd, saying, I am innocent of the blood of this righteous one; you will see. [25]And answering all the people said, His blood *be* on us and on our children. [26]Then he released Barabbas to them. But having flogged Jesus, he delivered *Him* up that He might be crucified.

[27]Then the soldiers of the governor, taking Jesus into the praetorium, gathered all the band against Him. [28]And having stripped Him, they put a scarlet cloak around Him. [29]And having plaited a crown of thorns and put it on His head, and a reed in His right *hand*, and bowing the knee before Him, they mocked at Him, saying, Hail, king of the Jews. [30]And having spit at Him, *they*

16 δέσμιον, ὃν ἤθελον. εἶχον δὲ τότε δέσμιον ἐπίσημον, λεγό-
prisoner, whom they wished. they had And then a prisoner notable called
17 μενον Βαραββᾶν. συνηγμένων οὖν αὐτῶν, εἶπεν αὐτοῖς ὁ
Barabbas. having assembled then they said to them –
Πιλάτος, Τίνα θέλετε ἀπολύσω ὑμῖν ; Βαραββᾶν, ἢ Ἰησοῦν
Pilate, Whom wish you I may release to you, Barabbas, or Jesus
18 τὸν λεγόμενον Χριστόν ; ᾔδει γὰρ ὅτι διὰ φθόνον παρέδωκαν
– called Christ? he knew For that through envy they delivered
19 αὐτόν. καθημένου δὲ αὐτοῦ ἐπὶ τοῦ βήματος, ἀπέστειλε
Him. sitting And he on the tribunal sent
πρὸς αὐτὸν ἡ γυνὴ αὐτοῦ, λέγουσα, Μηδέν σοι καὶ τῷ
to him the wife of him, saying, Nothing to you and to
δικαίῳ ἐκείνῳ· πολλὰ γὰρ ἔπαθον σήμερον κατ' ὄναρ δι'
just one that; many things for I suffered today by a dream via
20 αὐτόν. οἱ δὲ ἀρχιερεῖς καὶ οἱ πρεσβύτεροι ἔπεισαν τοὺς
him. the But chief priests and the elders persuaded the
ὄχλους ἵνα αἰτήσωνται τὸν Βαραββᾶν, τὸν δὲ Ἰησοῦν
crowds that they should ask – Barabbas, – and Jesus
21 ἀπολέσωσιν. ἀποκριθεὶς δὲ ὁ ἡγεμὼν εἶπεν αὐτοῖς, Τίνα
to destroy. answering And the governor said to them, Which
θέλετε ἀπὸ τῶν δύο ἀπολύσω ὑμῖν ; οἱ δὲ εἶπον, Βαραββᾶν.
wish you from the two I may release to you? they And said, Barabbas.
22 λέγει αὐτοῖς ὁ Πιλάτος, Τί οὖν ποιήσω Ἰησοῦν τὸν λεγό-
Says to them, – Pilate, What then may I do (to) Jesus – called
23 μενον Χριστόν ; λέγουσιν αὐτῷ πάντες, Σταυρωθήτω. ὁ
Christ? They say to him all, Let him be crucified. the
δὲ ἡγεμὼν ἔφη, Τί γὰρ κακὸν ἐποίησεν ; οἱ δὲ περισσῶς
But governor said, what For badness did he? they But more
24 ἔκραζον, λέγοντες, Σταυρωθήτω. ἰδὼν δὲ ὁ Πιλάτος ὅτι
cried out, saying, Let him be crucified. seeing And – Pilate that
οὐδὲν ὠφελεῖ, ἀλλὰ μᾶλλον θόρυβος γίνεται, λαβὼν ὕδωρ,
nothing is gained, but rather an uproar occurs, taking water
ἀπενίψατο τὰς χεῖρας ἀπέναντι τοῦ ὄχλου, λέγων, Ἀθῷός
he washed the hands before the crowd, saying, Innocent
25 εἰμι ἀπὸ τοῦ αἵματος τοῦ δικαίου τούτου· ὑμεῖς ὄψεσθε. καὶ
I am from the blood of righteous one this, you will see. And
ἀποκριθεὶς πᾶς ὁ λαὸς εἶπε, Τὸ αἷμα αὐτοῦ ἐφ' ἡμᾶς καὶ ἐπὶ
answering, all the people said, The blood of him on us and on
26 τὰ τέκνα ἡμῶν. τότε ἀπέλυσεν αὐτοῖς τὸν Βαραββᾶν· τὸν
the children of us. Then he released to them – Barabbas –
δὲ Ἰησοῦν φραγελλώσας παρέδωκεν ἵνα σταυρωθῇ.
But Jesus having whipped, he delivered that he might be crucified.
27 Τότε οἱ στρατιῶται τοῦ ἡγεμόνος, παραλαβόντες τὸν
Then the soldiers of the governor, having taken –
Ἰησοῦν εἰς τὸ πραιτώριον, συνήγαγον ἐπ' αὐτὸν ὅλην τὴν
Jesus into the praetorium, gathered against Him all the
28 σπεῖραν· καὶ ἐκδύσαντες αὐτόν, περιέθηκαν αὐτῷ χλαμύδα
cohort. And stripping Him, they put around Him a cloak
29 κοκκίνην. καὶ πλέξαντες στέφανον ἐξ ἀκανθῶν, ἐπέθηκαν
scarlet, and having plaited a crown of thorns, they placed
ἐπὶ τὴν κεφαλὴν αὐτοῦ, καὶ κάλαμον ἐπὶ τὴν δεξιὰν αὐτοῦ·
on the head of Him, and a reed upon the right of Him.
καὶ γονυπετήσαντες ἔμπροσθεν αὐτοῦ ἐνέπαιζον αὐτῷ,
And bowing the knee in front of Him they mocked at Him,
30 λέγοντες, Χαῖρε, ὁ βασιλεὺς τῶν Ἰουδαίων· καὶ ἐμπτύσαντες
saying, Hail, king of the Jews; and spitting

struck at His head. 31 And when they had mocked Him, they took the cloak off of Him, and they put His clothes on Him, and led Him away to crucify *Him.*

32 And going out, they found a man, a Cyrenean, Simon by name. This one they forced to bear His cross. 33 And coming to a place called Golgotha, which is called Place of a Skull, 34 they gave Him vinegar mingled with gall to drink. And having tasted, He would not drink. 35 And having crucified Him, they divided His garments, casting a lot—that might be fulfilled that spoken by the prophet, "They divided My garments *to* themselves, and they cast a lot for My clothing." 36 And sitting down they guarded Him there. 37 And they put up over His head His charge, *it* having been written: THIS IS JESUS THE KING OF THE JEWS. 38 Then two robbers were crucified with Him, one off *the* right, and one off *the* left *of Him.*

39 But those passing by blasphemed Him, shaking their heads, 40 and saying, *You* destroying the Temple, and building it in three days, if you are the Son of God, save yourself; come down from the cross. 41 And in the same way the chief priests, with the scribes and elders, mocking said, 42 He saved others; he is not able to save himself. If he is the king of Israel, let him come down now from the cross, and we will believe him. 43 He trusted on God. Let Him rescue him now, if He will *have* him. For he said, I am the Son of God. 44 And also the robbers crucified with Him reviled Him, *saying the* same.

45 And from *the* sixth hour there was darkness over all

εἰς αὐτόν, ἔλαβον τὸν κάλαμον, καὶ ἔτυπτον εἰς τὴν κεφαλὴν
at Him took the reed and struck at the head
31 αὐτοῦ. καὶ ὅτε ἐνέπαιξαν αὐτῷ, ἐξέδυσαν αὐτὸν τὴν
of Him. And when they mocked at Him, they stripped off Him the
χλαμύδα, καὶ ἐνέδυσαν αὐτὸν τὰ ἱμάτια αὐτοῦ, καὶ ἀπή-
cloak and put on Him the garments of Him, and led
γαγον αὐτὸν εἰς τὸ σταυρῶσαι.
away Him — — to crucify.
32 Ἐξερχόμενοι δὲ εὗρον ἄνθρωπον Κυρηναῖον, ὀνόματι
going forth And they found a man, a Cyrenian, by name
Σίμωνα· τοῦτον ἠγγάρευσαν ἵνα ἄρῃ τὸν σταυρὸν αὐτοῦ.
Simon. This one they compelled, that he bear the cross of Him.
33 καὶ ἐλθόντες εἰς τόπον λεγόμενον Γολγοθᾶ, ὅς ἐστι λεγόμενος
And coming to a place called Golgotha, which is saying,
34 κρανίου τόπος, ἔδωκαν αὐτῷ πιεῖν ὄξος μετὰ χολῆς μεμιγ-
Of a skull place, they gave Him to drink vinegar with gall mixed;
35 μένον· καὶ γευσάμενος οὐκ ἤθελε πιεῖν. σταυρώσαντες δὲ
and having tasted (it), not He would drink. having crucified And
αὐτόν, διεμερίσαντο τὰ ἱμάτια αὐτοῦ, βάλλοντες κλῆρον·
Him, they divided the garments of Him, casting a lot,
ἵνα πληρωθῇ τὸ ῥηθὲν ὑπὸ τοῦ προφήτου, Διεμερίσαντο τὰ
that may be fulfilled the spoken by the prophet, They divided the
ἱμάτιά μου ἑαυτοῖς, καὶ ἐπὶ τὸν ἱματισμόν μου ἔβαλον κλῆρον.
garments of Me themselves and on the clothing of Me they cast a lot.
36 καὶ καθήμενοι ἐτήρουν αὐτὸν ἐκεῖ. καὶ ἐπέθηκαν ἐπάνω τῆς
37 and sitting down they guarded Him there. And they placed above the
κεφαλῆς αὐτοῦ τὴν αἰτίαν αὐτοῦ γεγραμμένην, Οὗτός ἐστιν
the head of Him the charge of Him, having been written, THIS IS
38 Ἰησοῦς ὁ βασιλεὺς τῶν Ἰουδαίων. τότε σταυροῦνται σὺν
JESUS THE KING OF THE JEWS. Then are crucified with
39 αὐτῷ δύο λῃσταί, εἷς ἐκ δεξιῶν καὶ εἷς ἐξ εὐωνύμων. οἱ δὲ
Him two robbers, one off (the) right and one off (the) left. those And
παραπορευόμενοι ἐβλασφήμουν αὐτόν, κινοῦντες τὰς κεφα-
passing by blasphemed Him, shaking the heads
40 λὰς αὐτῶν, καὶ λέγοντες, Ὁ καταλύων τὸν ναὸν καὶ ἐν
of them, and saying, The (one) destroying the temple and in
τρισὶν ἡμέραις οἰκοδομῶν, σῶσον σεαυτόν· εἰ υἱὸς εἶ τοῦ
three days building (it), save yourself, if Son You are
41 Θεοῦ, κατάβηθι ἀπὸ τοῦ σταυροῦ. ὁμοίως δὲ καὶ οἱ
of God, come down from the cross. likewise And also the
ἀρχιερεῖς ἐμπαίζοντες μετὰ τῶν γραμματέων καὶ πρεσ-
chief priests mocking with the scribes and elders
42 βυτέρων ἔλεγον, Ἄλλους ἔσωσεν, ἑαυτὸν οὐ δύναται σῶσαι.
said, Others He saved, Himself not He is able to save.
εἰ βασιλεὺς Ἰσραήλ ἐστι, καταβάτω νῦν ἀπὸ τοῦ σταυροῦ,
if king of Israel He is, let Him descend now from the cross,
43 καὶ πιστεύσομεν αὐτῷ. πέποιθεν ἐπὶ τὸν Θεόν· ῥυσάσθω
and we will believe Him. He trusted on — God, let Him rescue
νῦν αὐτόν, εἰ θέλει αὐτόν. εἶπε γὰρ ὅτι Θεοῦ εἰμι υἱός. τὸ
now Him, if He desires Him. He said For, — of God I am Son. the
44 δ᾽ αὐτὸ καὶ οἱ λῃσταὶ οἱ συσταυρωθέντες αὐτῷ ὠνείδιζον
And same also the robbers — crucified together with Him reproached
αὐτῷ.
Him.

45 Ἀπὸ δὲ ἕκτης ὥρας σκότος ἐγένετο ἐπὶ πᾶσαν τὴν γῆν
from And sixth hour darkness occurred over all the land

the land until *the* ninth hour. 46 And about the ninth hour, Jesus cried out with a loud voice, saying, Eli, Eli, lama sabachthani—that is, My God, My God, why have Your forsaken Me? 47 And some of those standing there having heard, *they* said, This one calls Elijah. 48 And at once one of them running and taking a sponge, and filling *it* with vinegar, put *it* on a reed and gave drink to Him. 49 But the rest said, Let be; let us see if Elijah comes to save him.

50 And crying again with a great voice Jesus released *His* spirit. 51 And, behold, the veil of the Temple was torn into two from top to bottom. And the earth quaked, and the rocks were sheared! 52 And the tombs were opened, and many bodies of the saints who had fallen asleep arose. 53 And coming forth out of the tombs after His resurrection, *they* entered into the holy city and appeared to many.

54 But the centurion and those guarding Jesus with him, seeing the earthquake and the things taking place, *they* feared exceedingly, saying, Truly this One was Son of God.

55 And many women were there, watching from afar off, who followed Jesus from Galilee, ministering to Him; 56 among whom was Mary Magdalene, and Mary the mother of James and Joses, and the mother of the sons of Zebedee.

57 And evening having come, a rich man from Arimathea, Joseph by name, who also himself was discipled to Jesus; 58 this one coming to Pilate asked the body of Jesus. Then Pilate commanded the body to be given. 59 And taking the body, Joseph wrapped it in clean linen, 60 and laid it in his new tomb, which he had cut out in the rock. And having rolled a great stone

46 ἕως ὥρας ἐννάτης· περὶ δὲ τὴν ἐννάτην ὥραν ἀνεβόησεν ὁ
until hour (the) ninth. about And the ninth hour cried out —
Ἰησοῦς φωνῇ μεγάλῃ, λέγων, Ἠλί, Ἠλί, λαμὰ σαβαχθανί ;
Jesus a voice great, saying, Eli, Eli, lama sabachthani?
τοῦτ' ἔστι, Θεέ μου, Θεέ μου, ἱνατί με ἐγκατέλιπες ; τινὲς
this is, God of Me, God of Me, why Me did You forsake? some
47 δὲ τῶν ἐκεῖ ἑστώτων ἀκούσαντες ἔλεγον ὅτι Ἠλίαν φωνεῖ
And of those there standing hearing said, — Elijah calls
48 οὗτος. καὶ εὐθέως δραμὼν εἷς ἐξ αὐτῶν, καὶ λαβὼν σπόγγον,
this one. And at once running one of them and taking a sponge
49 πλήσας τε ὄξους, καὶ περιθεὶς καλάμῳ, ἐπότιζεν αὐτόν. οἱ δὲ
filling and with vinegar, and put on a reed, gave to drink Him. the But
λοιποὶ ἔλεγον, Ἄφες, ἴδωμεν εἰ ἔρχεται Ἠλίας σώσων αὐτόν.
rest said, Leave! Let us see if comes Elijah to save Him.
50 ὁ δὲ Ἰησοῦς πάλιν κράξας φωνῇ μεγάλῃ ἀφῆκε τὸ πνεῦμα.
—And Jesus again crying with a voice great released the spirit.
51 καὶ ἰδού, τὸ καταπέτασμα τοῦ ναοῦ ἐσχίσθη εἰς δύο ἀπὸ
And behold, the veil of the Temple was torn into two, from
ἄνωθεν ἕως κάτω· καὶ ἡ γῆ ἐσείσθη καὶ αἱ πέτραι ἐσχίσθη-
above until below and the earth was shaken,and the rocks were
52 σαν· καὶ τὰ μνημεῖα ἀνεῴχθησαν· καὶ πολλὰ σώματα τῶν
torn, and the tombs were opened, and many bodies of the
53 κεκοιμημένων ἁγίων ἠγέρθη· καὶ ἐξελθόντες ἐκ τῶν μνημείων
having fallen asleep saints were raised;and coming forth out of the tombs
μετὰ τὴν ἔγερσιν αὐτοῦ εἰσῆλθον εἰς τὴν ἁγίαν πόλιν, καὶ
after the rising of Him entered into the holy city and
54 ἐνεφανίσθησαν πολλοῖς. ὁ δὲ ἑκατόνταρχος καὶ οἱ μετ' αὐτοῦ
were manifested to many. the And centurion and those with him
τηροῦντες τὸν Ἰησοῦν, ἰδόντες τὸν σεισμὸν καὶ τὰ γενόμενα,
guarding — Jesus, seeing the earthquake and the happenings,
ἐφοβήθησαν σφόδρα, λέγοντες, Ἀληθῶς Θεοῦ υἱὸς ἦν
feared exceedingly, saying, Truly of God Son was
55 οὗτος. ἦσαν δὲ ἐκεῖ γυναῖκες πολλαὶ ἀπὸ μακρόθεν θεωροῦ-
this One. were And there women many from afar beholding
σαι, αἵτινες ἠκολούθησαν τῷ Ἰησοῦ ἀπὸ τῆς Γαλιλαίας,
who followed — Jesus from — Galilee,
56 διακονοῦσαι αὐτῷ· ἐν αἷς ἦν Μαρία ἡ Μαγδαληνή, καὶ
ministering to Him; among whom was Mary the Magdalene, and
Μαρία ἡ τοῦ Ἰακώβου καὶ Ἰωσῆ μήτηρ, καὶ ἡ μήτηρ τῶν
Mary the — of James and Joses mother, and the mother of the
υἱῶν Ζεβεδαίου.
sons of Zebedee.
57 Ὀψίας δὲ γενομένης, ἦλθεν ἄνθρωπος πλούσιος ἀπὸ
evening And having come, came a man rich from
Ἀριμαθαίας, τοὔνομα Ἰωσήφ, ὃς καὶ αὐτὸς ἐμαθήτευσε τῷ
Arimathea, by name Joseph, who also himself was discipled —
58 Ἰησοῦ· οὗτος προσελθὼν τῷ Πιλάτῳ, ᾐτήσατο τὸ σῶμα
to Jesus; this one coming up — to Pilate asked the body
τοῦ Ἰησοῦ. τότε ὁ Πιλάτος ἐκέλευσεν ἀποδοθῆναι τὸ σῶμα.
— of Jesus. Then — Pilate commanded to be given the body.
59 καὶ λαβὼν τὸ σῶμα ὁ Ἰωσὴφ ἐνετύλιξεν αὐτὸ σινδόνι
And taking the body, — Joseph wrapped it in linen
60 καθαρᾷ, καὶ ἔθηκεν αὐτὸ ἐν τῷ καινῷ αὐτοῦ μνημείῳ, ὃ
clean, and placed it in the new of him tomb, which
ἐλατόμησεν ἐν τῇ πέτρᾳ· καὶ προσκυλίσας λίθον μέγαν τῇ
he had hewed in the rock, and having rolled a stone great to the

to the door of the tomb, *he* departed. 61 And there was Mary Magdalene and the other Mary sitting across from the grave.

62 And on the morrow, which is after the Preparation, the chief priests and the Pharisees were gathered to Pilate, 63 saying, Sir, we have recalled that that deceiver said while living, After three days I will rise. 64 Therefore, command that the grave be secured until the third day, that his disciples may not come by night and steal him away, and may say to the people, He has risen from the dead. And the last deception will be worse than the first. 65 And Pilate said to them, You have a guard; go away; make *it as* secure as you know *how*. 66 And going they made the grave secure, sealing the stone, with the guard.

61 θύρα τοῦ μνημείου, ἀπῆλθεν. ἦν δὲ ἐκεῖ Μαρία ἡ Μαγδαληνή,
door of the tomb, he went away. was And there Mary the Magdalene,
καὶ ἡ ἄλλη Μαρία, καθήμεναι ἀπέναντι τοῦ τάφου.
and the other Mary, sitting opposite the grave.
62 Τῇ δὲ ἐπαύριον, ἥτις ἐστὶ μετὰ τὴν Παρασκευήν, συνή-
on the And morrow, which is after the Preparation, were
63 χθησαν οἱ ἀρχιερεῖς καὶ οἱ Φαρισαῖοι πρὸς Πιλάτον, λέγοντες,
assembled the chief priests and the Pharisees to Pilate, saying,
Κύριε, ἐμνήσθημεν ὅτι ἐκεῖνος ὁ πλάνος εἶπεν ἔτι ζῶν, Μετὰ
Sir, we have recalled that that — deceiver said yet living, After
64 τρεῖς ἡμέρας ἐγείρομαι. κέλευσον οὖν ἀσφαλισθῆναι τὸν
three days I arise. Command then to be made secure the
τάφον ἕως τῆς τρίτης ἡμέρας· μήποτε ἐλθόντες οἱ μαθηταὶ
grave until the third day, lest coming the disciples
αὐτοῦ νυκτὸς κλέψωσιν αὐτόν, καὶ εἴπωσι τῷ λαῷ, Ἠγέρ-
of him by night may steal him and may say to the people, He is
θη ἀπὸ τῶν νεκρῶν· καὶ ἔσται ἡ ἐσχάτη πλάνη χείρων τῆς
raised from the dead, and will be the last deceit worse than the
65 πρώτης. ἔφη δὲ αὐτοῖς ὁ Πιλάτος, Ἔχετε κουστωδίαν·
first. Said and to them — Pilate, You have a guard;
66 ὑπάγετε, ἀσφαλίσασθε ὡς οἴδατε. οἱ δὲ πορευθέντες ἠσφαλί-
go, make secure as you know. they And going made
σαντο τὸν τάφον, σφραγίσαντες τὸν λίθον, μετὰ τῆς
secure the grave, sealing the stone, with the
κουστωδίας.
guard.

CHAPTER 28

1 But late in the week, at the dawning into the first *day* of the week, Mary Magdalene and the other Mary came to see the grave.

2 And, behold, a great earthquake occurred! For an angel of *the* Lord coming down from Heaven, coming up, rolled away the stone from the door, and was sitting on it. 3 And his face was as lightning, and his clothing white as snow. 4 And those keeping guard were shaken from the fear of him, and they became as dead. 5 But answering the angel said to the women, You must not fear, for I know that you seek Jesus who has been crucified. 6 He is not here, for He was raised, as He said. Come, see the place where the Lord was lying. 7 And going quickly say to His disciples that He was raised from the dead. And, behold, He goes before you into Galilee. You will see Him there. See, I told you. 8 And going away quickly from the

1 Ὀψὲ δὲ σαββάτων, τῇ ἐπιφωσκούσῃ εἰς μίαν σαββάτων,
late in But the week, at the dawning into the first of (the) week,
ἦλθε Μαρία ἡ Μαγδαληνή, καὶ ἡ ἄλλη Μαρία, θεωρῆσαι
came Mary the Magdalene and the other Mary to view
2 τὸν τάφον. καὶ ἰδού, σεισμὸς ἐγένετο μέγας· ἄγγελος γὰρ
the grave. And, behold, an earthquake occurred great; an angel for
Κυρίου καταβὰς ἐξ οὐρανοῦ, προσελθὼν ἀπεκύλισε τὸν
of (the) Lord descending from Heaven, and coming up rolled away the
3 λίθον ἀπὸ τῆς θύρας, καὶ ἐκάθητο ἐπάνω αὐτοῦ. ἦν δὲ ἡ
stone from the door, and sitting on it. was And the
ἰδέα αὐτοῦ ὡς ἀστραπή, καὶ τὸ ἔνδυμα αὐτοῦ λευκὸν ὡσεὶ
look of him as lightning, and the dress of him white as
4 χιών. ἀπὸ δὲ τοῦ φόβου αὐτοῦ ἐσείσθησαν οἱ τηροῦντες
snow. from And the fear of him were shaken those guarding
5 καὶ ἐγένοντο ὡσεὶ νεκροί. ἀποκριθεὶς δὲ ὁ ἄγγελος εἶπε ταῖς
and they became as dead. answering And the angel said to the
γυναιξί, Μὴ φοβεῖσθε ὑμεῖς· οἶδα γὰρ ὅτι Ἰησοῦν τὸν
women, Do not fear you; I know for that Jesus the (One)
6 ἐσταυρωμένον ζητεῖτε. οὐκ ἔστιν ὧδε· ἠγέρθη γάρ, καθὼς
having been crucified you seek. not He is here; He was raised for, as
7 εἶπε. δεῦτε, ἴδετε τὸν τόπον ὅπου ἔκειτο ὁ Κύριος. καὶ ταχὺ
He said; come, see the place where lay the Lord. And quickly
πορευθεῖσαι εἴπατε τοῖς μαθηταῖς αὐτοῦ ὅτι Ἠγέρθη ἀπὸ
going tell to the disciples of Him that He was raised from
τῶν νεκρῶν· καὶ ἰδού, προάγει ὑμᾶς εἰς τὴν Γαλιλαίαν· ἐκεῖ
the dead, and, behold, He goes before you into — Galilee. There
8 αὐτὸν ὄψεσθε· ἰδού, εἶπον ὑμῖν. καὶ ἐξελθοῦσαι ταχὺ ἀπὸ
Him you will see. Behold, I told you. And going away quickly from

tomb, with fear and great joy, they ran to tell *it* to His disciples. 9 But as they were going to tell *it* to His disciples, behold, Jesus also met them, saying, Hail! And coming near they seized His feet, and worshiped Him. 10 Then Jesus said to them, Do not fear. Go tell My brothers that they may go into Galilee, and they will see Me there.

11 And as they were going, behold, some of the guard coming into the city reported to the chief priests all things that occurred. 12 And having been assembled with the elders, and taking counsel, they gave enough silver to the soldiers, 13 saying, Say that his disciples came *and* stole him by night, we being asleep. 14 And if this is heard by the governor, we will persuade him, and will make you free from anxiety. 15 And taking the silver, they did as they were taught. And this report is spread abroad among the Jews until today.

16 But the eleven disciples went into Galilee, to the Mount where Jesus appointed them. 17 And seeing Him, they worshiped Him. But they doubted. 18 And coming up Jesus talked with them, saying, All authority in Heaven and on earth was given to Me. 19 Therefore, go, disciple all nations, baptizing them into the name of the Father and of the Son and of the Holy Spirit; 20 teaching them to observe all things, whatever I commanded you. And, behold, I am with you all the days until the completion of the age. Amen.

τοῦ μνημείου μετὰ •φόβου καὶ χαρᾶς μεγάλης, ἔδραμον
the tomb, with fear and joy great, they ran

9 ἀπαγγεῖλαι τοῖς μαθηταῖς αὐτοῦ. ὡς δὲ ἐπορεύοντο ἀπαγ-
to announce to the disciples of Him. as But they were going to

γεῖλαι τοῖς μαθηταις αὐτοῦ, καὶ ἰδού, ὁ Ἰησοῦς ἀπήντησεν
tell (it) to the disciples of Him, also behold, — Jesus met

αὐταῖς, λέγων, Χαίρετε. αἱ δὲ προσελθοῦσαι ἐκράτησαν
them, saying, Hail! they And coming near seized

10 αὐτοῦ τοὺς πόδας, καὶ προσεκύνησαν αὐτῷ. τότε λέγει
of Him the feet, and worshiped Him. Then says

αὐταῖς ὁ Ἰησοῦς· Μὴ φοβεῖσθε· ὑπάγετε, ἀπαγγείλατε τοῖς
to them — Jesus, Do not fear. Go, announce to the

ἀδελφοῖς μου ἵνα ἀπέλθωσιν εἰς τὴν Γαλιλαίαν, κἀκεῖ με
brothers of Me that they may go into — Galilee, and there Me

ὄψονται.
they will see.

11 Πορευομένων δὲ αὐτῶν, ἰδού, τινὲς τῆς κουστωδίας
going And they, behold, some of the guard

ἐλθόντες εἰς τὴν πόλιν ἀπήγγειλαν τοῖς ἀρχιερεῦσιν ἅπαντα
coming into the city announced to the chief priests all things

12 τὰ γενόμενα. καὶ συναχθέντες μετὰ τῶν πρεσβυτέρων, συμ-
that occurred. And being assembled with the elders,

βούλιόν τε λαβόντες, ἀργύρια ἱκανὰ ἔδωκαν τοῖς στρατιώ-
counsel and taking, silver enough gave to the soldiers,

13 ταις, λέγοντες, Εἴπατε ὅτι Οἱ μαθηταὶ αὐτοῦ νυκτὸς
saying, Say, The disciples of Him by night

14 ἐλθόντες ἔκλεψαν αὐτὸν ἡμῶν κοιμωμένων. καὶ ἐὰν ἀκουσθῇ
coming stole Him, we being asleep. And if is heard

τοῦτο ἐπὶ τοῦ ἡγεμόνος, ἡμεῖς πείσομεν αὐτόν, καὶ ὑμᾶς
this before the governor, we will persuade him, and you

15 ἀμερίμνους ποιήσομεν. οἱ δὲ λαβόντες τὰ ἀργύρια ἐποίη-
free from anxiety we will make. they And taking the silver did

σαν ὡς ἐδιδάχθησαν. καὶ διεφημίσθη ὁ λόγος οὗτος παρὰ
as they were taught. And was spread — saying this by

Ἰουδαίοις μέχρι τῆς σήμερον.
Jews until — today.

16 Οἱ δὲ ἕνδεκα μαθηταὶ ἐπορεύθησαν εἰς τὴν Γαλιλαίαν, εἰς
the And eleven disciples went to — Galilee, to

17 τὸ ὄρος οὗ ἐτάξατο αὐτοῖς ὁ Ἰησοῦς. καὶ ἰδόντες αὐτὸν
the mount where appointed them — Jesus. And seeing Him,

18 προσεκύνησαν αὐτῷ· οἱ δὲ ἐδίστασαν. καὶ προσελθὼν ὁ
they worshiped Him, they but doubted. And coming up —

Ἰησοῦς ἐλάλησεν αὐτοῖς, λέγων, Ἐδόθη μοι πᾶσα ἐξουσία
Jesus talked with them, saying, was given Me All authority

19 ἐν οὐρανῷ καὶ ἐπὶ γῆς. πορευθέντες οὖν μαθητεύσατε πάντα
in Heaven and upon earth. Having gone, then, disciple all

τὰ ἔθνη, βαπτίζοντες αὐτοὺς εἰς τὸ ὄνομα τοῦ Πατρὸς καὶ
the nations, baptizing them into the name of the Father and

20 τοῦ Υἱοῦ καὶ τοῦ Ἁγίου Πνεύματος· διδάσκοντες αὐτοὺς
of the Son and of the Holy Spirit, teaching them

τηρεῖν πάντα ὅσα ἐνετειλάμην ὑμῖν· καὶ ἰδού, ἐγὼ μεθ'
to observe all things whatever I commanded you; and, behold, I with

ὑμῶν εἰμι πάσας τὰς ἡμέρας ἕως τῆς συντελείας τοῦ αἰῶνος.
you am all the days until the completion of the age.

Ἀμήν.
Amen.

KING JAMES II VERSION

THE

GOSPEL ACCORDING TO

MARK

CHAPTER 1

1 The beginning of the gospel of Jesus Christ, *the* Son of God, 2 as it has been written in the Prophets, "Behold, I send My messenger before Your face, who will prepare Your way before You; 3 *the* voice of one crying in the wilderness. Prepare the way of *the* Lord, make His paths straight."

4 John came baptizing in the wilderness, and proclaiming a baptism of repentance for forgiveness of sins. 5 And all the Judean country, and those of Jerusalem went out to him, and were all baptized by him in the Jordan River, confessing their sins. 6 And John was clothed in camel's hair, and a leather girdle about his loin; and eating locusts and wild honey. 7 And he proclaimed, saying, He who comes after me is mightier than me, of whom I am not fit to stoop down to loosen the thong of His sandals. 8 I indeed baptized you in water, but He will baptize you in *the* Holy Spirit.

9 And it happened in those days, Jesus came from Nazareth of Galilee, and was baptized by John in the Jordan. 10 And going up from the water immediately, He saw the heavens being torn, and the Spirit coming down as a dove upon Him.

ΕΥΑΓΓΕΛΙΟΝ
GOSPEL

ΤΟ ΚΑΤΑ ΜΑΡΚΟΝ
THE ACCORDING TO MARK

CHAPTER 1

1 Ἀρχὴ τοῦ εὐαγγελίου Ἰησοῦ Χριστοῦ, υἱοῦ τοῦ Θεοῦ·
(The) beginning of the gospel of Jesus Christ, Son – of God,

2 Ὡς γέγραπται ἐν τοῖς προφήταις, Ἰδού, ἐγὼ ἀποστέλλω
As it has been written in the prophets. Behold, I send

τὸν ἄγγελόν μου πρὸ προσώπου σου, ὃς κατασκευάσει τὴν
the messenger of Me before (the) face of you, who will prepare the

3 ὁδόν σου ἔμπροσθέν σου. φωνὴ βοῶντος ἐν τῇ ἐρήμῳ,
way of You before You. (The) voice of one crying in the wilderness.

Ἑτοιμάσατε τὴν ὁδὸν Κυρίου· εὐθείας ποιεῖτε τὰς τρίβους
Prepare the way of (the) Lord; straight make the paths

4 αὐτοῦ. ἐγένετο Ἰωάννης βαπτίζων ἐν τῇ ἐρήμῳ, καὶ κηρύσ-
of Him. came John baptizing in the desert, and proclaim-

5 σων βάπτισμα μετανοίας εἰς ἄφεσιν ἁμαρτιῶν. καὶ ἐξεπορεύ-
ing a baptism of repentance for forgiveness of sins. And went out

ετο πρὸς αὐτὸν πᾶσα ἡ Ἰουδαία χώρα, καὶ οἱ Ἱεροσολυμῖται,
to him all the Judean country, and the Jerusalemites,

καὶ ἐβαπτίζοντο πάντες ἐν τῷ Ἰορδάνῃ ποταμῷ ὑπ' αὐτοῦ,
and were baptised all in the Jordan River by him,

6 ἐξομολογούμενοι τὰς ἁμαρτίας αὐτῶν. ἦν δὲ Ἰωάννης
confessing the sins of them. was And John

ἐνδεδυμένος τρίχας καμήλου, καὶ ζώνην δερματίνην περὶ
clothed in hair of a camel, and a girdle leather about

τὴν ὀσφὺν αὐτοῦ, καὶ ἐσθίων ἀκρίδας καὶ μέλι ἄγριον.
the loin of him, and eating locusts and honey wild.

7 καὶ ἐκήρυσσε, λέγων, Ἔρχεται ὁ ἰσχυρότερός μου ὀπίσω
And he proclaimed, saying, Comes He stronger than me after

μου, οὗ οὐκ εἰμὶ ἱκανὸς κύψας λῦσαι τὸν ἱμάντα τῶν
me, of whom not **I am fit stooping down to loosen the thong of the**

8 ὑποδημάτων αὐτοῦ. ἐγὼ μὲν ἐβάπτισα ὑμᾶς ἐν ὕδατι· αὐτὸς
sandals of Him. I indeed baptized you in water. He

δὲ βαπτίσει ὑμᾶς ἐν Πνεύματι Ἁγίῳ.
but will baptize you **in (the) Spirit Holy.**

9 Καὶ ἐγένετο ἐν ἐκείναις ταῖς ἡμέραις, ἦλθεν Ἰησοῦς ἀπὸ
And it was in those – days, **came Jesus from**

Ναζαρὲθ τῆς Γαλιλαίας, καὶ ἐβαπτίσθη ὑπὸ Ἰωάννου εἰς τὸν
Nazareth of Galilee **and was baptized by John in the**

10 Ἰορδάνην. καὶ εὐθέως ἀναβαίνων ἀπὸ τοῦ ὕδατος, εἶδε
Jordan And immediately going up **from the water, he saw**

σχιζομένους τοὺς οὐρανούς, καὶ τὸ Πνεῦμα ὡσεὶ περιστερὰν
being torn the heavens, and **the Spirit as a dove**

[11] And there was a voice out of the heavens, You are My Son, the Beloved, in whom I take delight.

[12] And the Spirit at once drove Him out into the wilderness. [13] And He was there in the wilderness forty days, being tempted by Satan, and was with the wild beasts. And the angels ministered to Him.

[14] And after John was delivered up, Jesus came into Galilee, proclaiming the gospel of the kingdom of God, [15] and saying, The time has been fulfilled, and the kingdom of God draws near. Repent and believe in the gospel.

[16] And walking along beside the Sea of Galilee, He saw Simon and his brother Andrew casting a net in the sea; for they were fishers. [17] And Jesus said to them, Come after Me, and I will make you to become fishers of men. [18] And immediately they followed Him. [19] And going forward from there a little, He saw James the *son* of Zebedee, and his brother John. And they *were* in the boat mending the nets. [20] And He immediately called them. And leaving their father Zebedee in the boat with the hired servants, they went after Him.

[21] And they passed along into Capernaum. And He at once taught on the sabbaths, entering into the synagogue. [22] And they were astonished at His teaching, for He was teaching them as having authority, and not as the scribes. [23] And there was a man in their synagogue with an unclean spirit. And he cried out, [24] saying, What *is* to us and to You, Jesus, Nazarene? Have You come

11 καταβαῖνον ἐπ' αὐτόν· καὶ φωνὴ ἐγένετο ἐκ τῶν οὐρανῶν,
coming down upon Him. And a voice there was out of the heavens:
Σὺ εἶ ὁ υἱός μου ὁ ἀγαπητός, ἐν ᾧ εὐδόκησα.
You are the Son of Me the Beloved, in whom I take delight.
12 Καὶ εὐθὺς τὸ Πνεῦμα αὐτὸν ἐκβάλλει εἰς τὴν ἔρημον. καὶ
13 **And instantly the Spirit Him thrusts into the desert. And**
ἦν ἐκεῖ ἐν τῇ ἐρήμῳ ἡμέρας τεσσαράκοντα πειραζόμενος ὑπὸ
He was there in the desert days forty being tempted by
τοῦ Σατανᾶ, καὶ ἦν μετὰ τῶν θηρίων, καὶ οἱ ἄγγελοι διη-
— Satan, and was with the wild beasts, and the angels
κόνουν αὐτῷ.
ministered to Him.
14 Μετὰ δὲ τὸ παραδοθῆναι τὸν Ἰωάννην, ἦλθεν ὁ Ἰησοῦς
after And — was delivered up — John, came — Jesus
εἰς τὴν Γαλιλαίαν, κηρύσσων τὸ εὐαγγέλιον τῆς βασιλείας
into - Galilee, proclaiming the gospel of the kingdom
15 τοῦ Θεοῦ, καὶ λέγων ὅτι Πεπλήρωται ὁ καιρός, καὶ ἤγγικεν
— of God, and saying, — Has been fulfilled the time, and draw near
ἡ βασιλεία τοῦ Θεοῦ· μετανοεῖτε, καὶ πιστεύετε ἐν τῷ
the kingdom — of God; repent and believe in the
εὐαγγελίῳ.
gospel.
16 Περιπατῶν δὲ παρὰ τὴν θάλασσαν τῆς Γαλιλαίας εἶδε
walking along And beside the Sea — of Galilee, He saw
Σίμωνα καὶ Ἀνδρέαν τὸν ἀδελφὸν αὐτοῦ, βάλλοντας
Simon and Andrew the brother of him casting
17 ἀμφίβληστρον ἐν τῇ θαλάσσῃ· ἦσαν γὰρ ἁλιεῖς. καὶ εἶπεν
a small net in the sea; they were for fishers. And said
αὐτοῖς ὁ Ἰησοῦς, Δεῦτε ὀπίσω μου, καὶ ποιήσω ὑμᾶς
to them — Jesus, Come after Me, and I will make you
18 γενέσθαι ἁλιεῖς ἀνθρώπων. καὶ εὐθέως ἀφέντες τὰ δίκτυα
to become fishers of men. And at once leaving the nets
19 αὐτῶν, ἠκολούθησαν αὐτῷ. καὶ προβὰς ἐκεῖθεν ὀλίγον,
of them, they followed Him. And going forward from there a bit,
εἶδεν Ἰάκωβον τὸν τοῦ Ζεβεδαίου, καὶ Ἰωάννην τὸν
He saw James the (son) — of Zebedee and John the
ἀδελφὸν αὐτοῦ, καὶ αὐτοὺς ἐν τῷ πλοίῳ καταρτίζοντας τὰ
brother of him, and they in the boat mending the
20 δίκτυα. καὶ εὐθέως ἐκάλεσεν αὐτούς· καὶ ἀφέντες τὸν πατέρα
nets. And at once He called them. And leaving the father
αὐτῶν Ζεβεδαῖον ἐν τῷ πλοίῳ μετὰ τῶν μισθωτῶν ἀπῆλθον
of them, Zebedee, in the boat with the hired servants, they went
ὀπίσω αὐτοῦ.
after Him.
21 Καὶ εἰσπορεύονται εἰς Καπερναούμ· καὶ εὐθέως τοῖς
And they passed along into Capernaum, and at once on the
22 σάββασιν εἰσελθὼν εἰς τὴν συναγωγήν, ἐδίδασκε. καὶ
sabbaths entering into the synagogue. He taught. And
ἐξεπλήσσοντο ἐπὶ τῇ διδαχῇ αὐτοῦ· ἦν γὰρ διδάσκων
they were astounded at the teaching of Him, He was for teaching
23 αὐτοὺς ὡς ἐξουσίαν ἔχων, καὶ οὐχ ὡς οἱ γραμματεῖς. καὶ
them as authority having, and not as the scribes. And
ἦν ἐν τῇ συναγωγῇ αὐτῶν ἄνθρωπος ἐν πνεύματι ἀκαθάρτῳ,
was in the synagogue of them a man with a spirit unclean;
24 καὶ ἀνέκραξε, λέγων, Ἔα, τί ἡμῖν καὶ σοί, Ἰησοῦ Ναζαρηνέ;
and he cried out, saying, Ah! What to us and to You, Jesus, Nazarene?

to destroy us? I know You, who You are, the Holy One of God. [25]And Jesus rebuked him, saying, Be quiet, and come out of him. [26]And the unclean spirit convulsed him; and crying out with a loud voice, he came out of him. [27]And all were astonished, so as to discuss among themselves, saying, What is this? What new teaching *is* this, that He commands even the unclean spirits with authority, and they obey Him? [28]And His fame went out at once into all the Galilean neighborhood.

[29]And at once going out of the synagogue, they came into the house of Simon and Andrew, with James and John. [30]And the mother-in-law of Simon was laid out, stricken by fever. And they at once spoke to Him about her. [31]And coming near, He raised her up, holding her hand. And the fever left her instantly; and she served them.

[32]And evening coming, when the sun set, they brought to Him all those having illiness, and the demon-possessed ones. [33]And the whole city was gathered at the door. [34]And He healed many who had illness of various diseases. And he cast out many demons, and did not allow the demons to speak, because they knew Him.

[35]And rising up quite early in *the* night, He went out and went away into a desert place. And *He* was praying there. [36]And Simon and those with him searched for Him. [37]And finding Him, they said to Him, All are seeking You. [38]And He said to them, Let us go into the neighboring towns, that I may also proclaim there. For *it was* for this I came forth.

[39]And He was proclaiming in their synagogues in all Galilee, and casting out the

25 ἦλθες ἀπολέσαι ἡμᾶς ; οἶδά σε τίς εἶ, ὁ ἅγιος τοῦ Θεοῦ. καὶ
Came You to destroy us? I know You who You are, the Holy of God. And
ἐπετίμησεν αὐτῷ ὁ Ἰησοῦς, λέγων, Φιμώθητι, καὶ ἔξελθε
rebuked him — Jesus, saying, Be quiet, and come
26 ἐξ αὐτοῦ. καὶ σπαράξαν αὐτὸν τὸ πνεῦμα τὸ ἀκάθαρτον καὶ
out of him. And convulsing him the spirit — unclean, and
27 κράξαν φωνῇ μεγάλῃ, ἐξῆλθεν ἐξ αὐτοῦ. καὶ ἐθαμβήθησαν
crying out with a voice great, he came out of him. And were astounded
πάντες, ὥστε συζητεῖν πρὸς αὐτούς, λέγοντας, Τί ἐστι
all, so as to discuss to themselves, saying What is
τοῦτο ; τίς ἡ διδαχὴ ἡ καινὴ αὕτη, ὅτι κατ' ἐξουσίαν καὶ
this? What teaching new (is) this, that with authority even
τοῖς πνεύμασι τοῖς ἀκαθάρτοις ἐπιτάσσει, καὶ ὑπακούουσιν
the spirits — unclean he commands, and they obey
28 αὐτῷ ; ἐξῆλθε δὲ ἡ ἀκοὴ αὐτοῦ εὐθὺς εἰς ὅλην τὴν περίχωρον
Him. went out And the fame of Him at once in all the neighborhood
τῆς Γαλιλαίας.
— of Galilee.
29 Καὶ εὐθέως ἐκ τῆς συναγωγῆς ἐξελθόντες, ἦλθον εἰς τὴν
And at once out of the synagogue going forth, they came into the
οἰκίαν Σίμωνος καὶ Ἀνδρέου, μετὰ Ἰακώβου καὶ Ἰωάννου.
house of Simon and Andrew, with James and John.
30 ἡ δὲ πενθερὰ Σίμωνος κατέκειτο πυρέσσουσα, καὶ εὐθέως
the And mother-in-law of Simon was laid fever-stricken. And immediately
31 λέγουσιν αὐτῷ περὶ αὐτῆς· καὶ προσελθὼν ἤγειρεν αὐτήν,
they say to Him about her. And coming near He raised her,
κρατήσας τῆς χειρὸς αὐτῆς· καὶ ἀφῆκεν αὐτὴν ὁ πυρετὸς
holding the hand of her, and left her the fever.
εὐθέως, καὶ διηκόνει αὐτοῖς.
at once. And she served them.
32 Ὀψίας δὲ γενομένης, ὅτε ἔδυ ὁ ἥλιος, ἔφερον πρὸς αὐτὸν
evening And coming, when set the sun, they brought to Him
33 πάντας τοὺς κακῶς ἔχοντας καὶ τοὺς δαιμονιζομένους· καὶ
all the (ones) illness having, and the (ones) demon-possessed. And
34 ἡ πόλις ὅλη ἐπισυνηγμένη ἦν πρὸς τὴν θύραν. καὶ ἐθεράπευσε
the city whole gathered was at the door. And He healed
πολλοὺς κακῶς ἔχοντας ποικίλαις νόσοις, καὶ δαιμόνια
many illness having of various diseases, and demons
πολλὰ ἐξέβαλε, καὶ οὐκ ἤφιε λαλεῖν τὰ δαιμόνια, ὅτι ᾔδεισαν
many He cast out, and not allowed to speak the demons, because they knew
αὐτόν.
Him.
35 Καὶ πρωῒ ἔννυχον λίαν ἀναστὰς ἐξῆλθε, καὶ ἀπῆλθεν εἰς
And early in night quite rising up He went out, and went away to
36 ἔρημον τόπον, κἀκεῖ προσηύχετο. καὶ κατεδίωξαν αὐτὸν ὁ
a desert place, and there was praying. And searched for Him —
37 Σίμων καὶ οἱ μετ' αὐτοῦ· καὶ εὑρόντες αὐτὸν λέγουσιν αὐτῷ
Simon and those with him, and finding Him they say to Him,
38 ὅτι Πάντες ζητοῦσί σε. καὶ λέγει αὐτοῖς, Ἄγωμεν εἰς τὰς
— All are seeking You. And He says to them, Let us go into the
ἐχομένας κωμοπόλεις, ἵνα κἀκεῖ κηρύξω· εἰς τοῦτο γὰρ
neighboring towns, that there also I may proclaim. for this For
39 ἐξελήλυθα. καὶ ἦν κηρύσσων ἐν ταῖς συναγωγαῖς αὐτῶν εἰς
I came forth. And He was proclaiming in the synagogues of them in
ὅλην τὴν Γαλιλαίαν, καὶ τὰ δαιμόνια ἐκβάλλων.
all — Galilee, and the demons casting out

demons.

40 And a leper came to Him, falling on *his* knees to Him, and saying to Him, If You will, You are able to make me clean. 42 And being moved with pity, reaching out the hand, Jesus touched him, and said to him, I am willing. Be made clean! 42 And He having spoken, instantly the leprosy departed from him, and he was made clean. 43 And having strictly warned him, He at once put him out. 44 And He said to him, See, tell nothing to anyone, but go show yourself to the priest, and offer what Moses directed concerning your cleansing, for a testimony to them. 45 But going out he began to proclaim much, and to spread about the matter, so that He no longer was able to openly enter into a city. But He was outside in desert places. And they came to Him from every quarter.

CHAPTER 2

1 And again He entered into Capernaum after *some days.* And it was heard that He was in *a* house. 2 And at once many were gathered, so as none any longer had room, not even to the door. And He spoke the word to them. 3 And they came to Him carrying a paralytic, being borne by four. 4 And not being able to draw near to Him, due to the crowd, they unroofed the roof where He was. And digging through, they lowered the cot on which the paralytic was lying. 5 And seeing their faith, Jesus said to the paralytic, Child, your sins are forgiven to you. 6 But some of the scribes were sitting there, and reasoning in their hearts, 7 Why does this one speak blasphemies this way? Who is able to forgive sins, except One, God? 8 And instantly knowing in His spirit that they were thus reasoning within themselves, Jesus said to them, Why do

40 Καὶ ἔρχεται πρὸς αὐτὸν λεπρός, παρακαλῶν αὐτὸν καὶ
And comes to Him a leper. begging Him and
γονυπετῶν αὐτόν, καὶ λέγων αὐτῷ ὅτι Ἐὰν θέλῃς, δύνασαί
falling on knees to Him, and saying to Him, – If You will, You are able
41 με καθαρίσαι. ὁ δὲ Ἰησοῦς σπλαγχνισθείς, ἐκτείνας τὴν
me be made clean. – And Jesus being filled with pity, reaching out the
χεῖρα, ἥψατο αὐτοῦ, καὶ λέγει αὐτῷ, Θέλω, καθαρίσθητι.
hand, He touched him, and says to him, I am willing, be made clean.
42 καὶ εἰπόντος αὐτοῦ εὐθέως ἀπῆλθεν ἀπ' αὐτοῦ ἡ λέπρα,
And having spoken He instantly departed from him the leprosy,
43 καὶ ἐκαθαρίσθη. καὶ ἐμβριμησάμενος αὐτῷ, εὐθέως ἐξέβαλεν
and he was cleansed. And strictly warning him, immediately he put out
44 αὐτόν, καὶ λέγει αὐτῷ, Ὅρα, μηδενὶ μηδὲν εἴπῃς· ἀλλ'
him, and says to him, See, no one nothing tell, but
ὕπαγε, σεαυτὸν δεῖξον τῷ ἱερεῖ, καὶ προσένεγκε περὶ τοῦ
go yourself show to the priest and offer concerning the
καθαρισμοῦ σου ἃ προσέταξε Μωσῆς, εἰς μαρτύριον αὐτοῖς.
cleansing of you, what ordered Moses, for a testimony to them.
45 ὁ δὲ ἐξελθὼν ἤρξατο κηρύσσειν πολλὰ καὶ διαφημίζειν τὸν
he But going out began to proclaim much, and to spread about the
λογον; ὥστε μηκέτι αὐτὸν δύνασθαι φανερῶς εἰς πόλιν
matter, so as no longer He to be able openly into a city
εἰσελθεῖν, ἀλλ' ἔξω ἐν ἐρήμοις τόποις ἦν· καὶ ἤρχοντο πρὸς
to enter, but outside on desert places He was, and they came to
αὐτὸν πανταχόθεν.
Him from every quarter.

CHAPTER 2

Καὶ πάλιν εἰσῆλθεν εἰς Καπερναοὺμ δι' ἡμερῶν· καὶ
1 **And again He entered into Capernaum through days. And**
2 ἠκούσθη ὅτι εἰς οἶκόν ἐστι. καὶ εὐθέως συνήχθησαν πολλοί,
it was heard that in (a) house He is. And at once were assembled many,
ὥστε μηκέτι χωρεῖν μηδὲ τὰ προς τὴν θύραν· καὶ ἐλάλει
so as no longer to have room not even to the door, and He spoke
3 αὐτοις τὸν λόγον. καὶ ἔρχονται πρὸς αὐτόν, παραλυτικὸν
to them the word. And they come to Him a paralytic
4 φέροντες, αιρομενον ὑπὸ τεσσάρων. καὶ μὴ δυνάμενοι
carrying, being borne by four. And not being able
προσεγγίσαι αὐτῷ διὰ τὸν ὄχλον, ἀπεστέγασαν τὴν στέγην
to draw near to Him due to the crowd, they unroofed the roof
ὅπου ἦν, καὶ ἐξορύξαντες χαλῶσι τὸν κράββατον ἐφ' ᾧ ὁ
where He was, and digging through they lower the cot on which the
5 παραλυτικὸς κατέκειτο. ἰδὼν δὲ ὁ Ἰησοῦς τὴν πίστιν αὐτῶν
paralytic was lying. seeing And – Jesus the faith of them
λέγει τῷ παραλυτικῷ, Τέκνον, ἀφέωνταί σοι αἱ ἁμαρτίαι
He says to the paralytic, Child, are forgiven to you the sins
6 σου. ἦσαν δέ τινες τῶν γραμματέων ἐκεῖ καθήμενοι, καὶ
of you. were But some of the scribes there sitting, and
7 διαλογιζόμενοι ἐν ταῖς καρδίαις αὐτῶν, Τί οὗτος οὕτω
reasoning in the hearts of them, Why this one thus
λαλει βλασφημίας; τίς δύναται ἀφιέναι ἁμαρτίας εἰ μη εἷς,
speaks blasphemies? Who is able to forgive sins except one,
8 ὁ Θεός; καὶ ευθέως ἐπιγνους ὁ Ἰησοῦς τῷ πνεύματι αὐτοῦ
– God? And instantly knowing – Jesus in the spirit of Him
ὅτι οὕτως διαλογίζονται ἐν ἑαυτοῖς, εἰπεν αὐτοῖς, Τί ταῦτα
that so they reason among themselves, He says to them, Why these things

you reason these things in your hearts? [9]Which is easier? To say to the paralytic, *Your* sins are forgiven to you. Or to say, rise up and take your cot and walk? [10]But that you may know that the Son of man has authority to forgive sins on the earth, he said to the paralytic, [11]I say to you, Rise up and take up your cot, and go to your house. [12]And he at once rose up. And taking his cot, he went out before all; so that all were amazed and glorified God, saying, Never did we see *it* this way.

[13]And he went out by the sea again. And all the crowd came to Him. And He taught them. [14]And passing on, He saw Levi the *son* of Alpheus sitting at the tax-office. And *He* said to him, Follow Me. And rising up, he followed Him.

[15]And it happened as He reclined in his house, even many tax-collectors and sinners reclined with Jesus and His disciples, for they were many. And they followed Him. [16]And the scribes and Pharisees seeing Him eating with tax-collectors and sinners, *they* said to His disciples, Why *is it* that He eats and drinks with the tax-collectors and sinners? [17]And hearing, Jesus said to them, Those who are strong have no need of a physician, but those who have illness. I did not come to call the righteous to repentance, but sinners.

[18]And John's disciples, and those of the Pharisees, were fasting. And they came and said to Him, Why do John's disciples and those of the Pharisees fast, but your disciples do not fast? [19]And Jesus said to them, Can the sons of the bridechamber fast while the groom is with them? What

9 διαλογίζεσθε ἐν ταῖς καρδίαις ὑμῶν ; τί ἐστιν εὐκοπώτερον,
do you reason in the hearts of you? What is easier,
εἰπεῖν τῷ παραλυτικῷ, Ἀφέωνταί σοι αἱ ἁμαρτίαι, ἢ εἰπεῖν,
to say to the paralytic, are forgiven to you the sins, or to say,
10 Ἔγειραι, καὶ ἆρόν σου τὸν κράββατον, καὶ περιπάτει ; ἵνα
Rise and take up of you the cot and walk? that
δὲ εἰδῆτε ὅτι ἐξουσίαν ἔχει ὁ υἱὸς τοῦ ἀνθρώπου ἀφιέναι ἐπὶ
But you know that authority has the Son — of man to forgive on
11 τῆς γῆς ἁμαρτίας (λέγει τῷ παραλυτικῷ), Σοὶ λέγω,
the earth sins, He says to the paralytic, To you I say,
ἔγειραι, καὶ ἆρον τὸν κράββατόν σου, καὶ ὕπαγε εἰς τὸν
Rise, and take up the cot of you, and go to the
12 οἶκόν σου. καὶ ἠγέρθη εὐθέως, καὶ ἄρας τὸν κράββατον,
house of you. And he arose at once, and taking up the cot
ἐξῆλθεν ἐναντίον πάντων· ὥστε ἐξίστασθαι πάντας, καὶ
he went out before all, so as to be astounded all, and
δοξάζειν τὸν Θεόν, λέγοντας ὅτι Οὐδέποτε οὕτως εἴδομεν.
to glorify — God, saying, — Never thus we saw.
13 Καὶ ἐξῆλθε πάλιν παρὰ τὴν θάλασσαν· καὶ πᾶς ὁ ὄχλος
And He went out again by the sea. And all the crowd
14 ἤρχετο πρὸς αὐτόν, καὶ ἐδίδασκεν αὐτούς. καὶ παράγων
came to Him, and He taught them. And passing along
εἶδε Λευῒν τὸν τοῦ Ἀλφαίου καθήμενον ἐπὶ τὸ τελώνιον, καὶ
He saw Levi the (son) of Alpheus sitting at the tax-office, and
λέγει αὐτῷ, Ἀκολούθει μοι. καὶ ἀναστὰς ἠκολούθησεν
says to him, Follow Me. And rising up he followed
15 αὐτῷ. καὶ ἐγένετο ἐν τῷ κατακεῖσθαι αὐτὸν ἐν τῇ οἰκίᾳ
Him. And it was, while reclined He in the house
αὐτοῦ, καὶ πολλοὶ τελῶναι καὶ ἁμαρτωλοὶ συνανέκειντο τῷ
of him. and many tax-collectors and sinners reclined with —
Ἰησοῦ καὶ τοῖς μαθηταῖς αὐτοῦ· ἦσαν γὰρ πολλοί, καὶ
Jesus and the disciples of Him. they were For many, and
16 ἠκολούθησαν αὐτῷ. καὶ οἱ γραμματεῖς καὶ οἱ Φαρισαῖοι,
they followed Him. And the scribes and the Pharisees
ἰδόντες αὐτὸν ἐσθίοντα μετὰ τῶν τελωνῶν καὶ ἁμαρτωλῶν,
seeing Him eating with — tax-collectors and sinners,
ἔλεγον τοῖς μαθηταῖς αὐτοῦ, Τί ὅτι μετὰ τῶν τελωνῶν καὶ
said to the disciples of Him, Why that with the tax collectors and
17 ἁμαρτωλῶν ἐσθίει καὶ πίνει ; καὶ ἀκούσας ὁ Ἰησοῦς λέγει
sinners does He eat and drink? And hearing — Jesus says
αὐτοῖς, Οὐ χρείαν ἔχουσιν οἱ ἰσχύοντες ἰατροῦ, ἀλλ' οἱ
to them, Not need have those being strong of a physician, but those
κακῶς ἔχοντες. οὐκ ἦλθον καλέσαι δικαίους, ἀλλὰ ἁμαρ-
illness having. not I came to call righteous ones, but sin-
τωλοὺς εἰς μετάνοιαν.
ners to repentance.
18 Καὶ ἦσαν οἱ μαθηταὶ Ἰωάννου καὶ οἱ τῶν Φαρισαίων
And were the disciples of John and those of the Pharisees
νηστεύοντες· καὶ ἔρχονται καὶ λέγουσιν αὐτῷ, Διατί οἱ
fasting. And they come and say to Him, Why do the
μαθηταὶ Ἰωάννου καὶ οἱ τῶν Φαρισαίων νηστεύουσιν, οἱ
disciples of John and those of the Pharisees fast, —
19 δὲ σοὶ μαθηταὶ οὐ νηστεύουσι ; καὶ εἶπεν αὐτοῖς ὁ Ἰησοῦς,
but Your disciples not do fast? And said to them — Jesus,
Μὴ δύνανται οἱ υἱοὶ τοῦ νυμφῶνος, ἐν ᾧ ὁ νυμφίος μετ'
Not are able the sons of the bridechamber, while the groom with

time they have the groom with them, they cannot fast. [20]But the days will come when the groom will have been taken away from them, and then they will fast in those days. [21]And no one sews a patch of unmilled cloth on an old garment, else *it* takes away its fullness, the new *from* the old, and a worse tear occurs. [22]And no one puts new wine into old wineskins, else the new wine will burst the wineskins, and the wineskins will be destroyed. But new wine is put into fresh wineskins

[23]And it happened He went along through the grainfields in the sabbaths. And His disciples began to make way, plucking the heads *of grain.* [24]And the Pharisees said to Him, Behold, why do they do that which is not lawful on the sabbaths? [25]And He said to them, Did you never read what David did when he had need and hungered, and those with him, [26]how he entered the house of God in *the days of* Abiathar the high priest, and ate the Showbread, which it is not lawful to eat, except for the priests, and he even gave to those with him? [27]And He said to them, The sabbath came into being for man's sake, not man for the sabbath's sake. [28]So Then the Son of man is Lord of the sabbath also.

CHAPTER 3

And He again entered into the synagogue. And there was a man who had a withering *of* the hand. [2]And they watched Him, whether He will heal him on the sabbaths, that they might acuse Him. [3]And He said to the man who had a withering *of* the hand, Rise up into the middle. [4]And He said to them, *Is it* lawful to do good on the sabbaths, or to do

αὐτῶν ἐστι, νηστεύειν ; ὅσον χρόνον μεθ' ἑαυτῶν ἔχουσι τὸν
them is. to fast? What time with them they have the
20 νυμφίον, οὐ δύνανται νηστεύειν· ἐλεύσονται δὲ ἡμέραι ὅταν
bridegroom, not they are able to fast. will come But days when
ἀπαρθῇ ἀπ' αὐτῶν ὁ νυμφίος, καὶ τότε νηστεύσουσιν ἐν
will be taken away from them the bridegroom, and then they will fast in
21 ἐκείναις ταῖς ἡμέραις. καὶ οὐδεὶς ἐπίβλημα ῥάκους ἀγνάφου
those days. And no one a patch of cloth unfulled
ἐπιρράπτει ἐπὶ ἱματίῳ παλαιῷ· εἰ δὲ μή, αἴρει τὸ πλήρωμα
sews on a garment old; else takes away the fullness
αὐτοῦ τὸ καινὸν τοῦ παλαιοῦ, καὶ χεῖρον σχίσμα γίνεται.
of it the new (from) the old, and a worse tear occurs.
22 καὶ οὐδεὶς βάλλει οἶνον νέον εἰς ἀσκοὺς παλαιούς· εἰ δὲ μή,
And no one puts wine new into wineskins old; if But not,
ῥήσσει ὁ οἶνος ὁ νέος τοὺς ἀσκούς, καὶ ὁ οἶνος ἐκχεῖται καὶ οἱ
will burst the wine new the wineskins, and the wine pours out, and the
ἀσκοὶ ἀπολοῦνται· ἀλλὰ οἶνον νέον εἰς ἀσκοὺς καινοὺς
skins will be destroyed; but wine new into wineskins fresh
βλητέον.
is to be put.
23 Καὶ ἐγένετο παραπορεύεσθαι αὐτὸν ἐν τοῖς σάββασι διὰ
And it was, went along He in the sabbaths through
τῶν σπορίμων, καὶ ἤρξαντο οἱ μαθηταὶ αὐτοῦ ὁδὸν ποιεῖν
the grainfields, and began the disciples of Him (a) way to make
24 τίλλοντες τοὺς στάχυας. καὶ οἱ Φαρισαῖοι ἔλεγον αὐτῷ,
plucking the ears (of grain). And the Pharisees said to Him,
25 Ἴδε, τί ποιοῦσιν ἐν τοῖς σάββασιν ὃ οὐκ ἔξεστι ; καὶ αὐτὸς
Behold, why do they in the sabbaths what not is lawful? And He
ἔλεγεν αὐτοῖς, Οὐδέποτε ἀνέγνωτε τί ἐποίησε Δαβίδ, ὅτε
said to them, never Did you read what did David when
26 χρείαν ἔσχε καὶ ἐπείνασεν αὐτὸς καὶ οἱ μετ' αὐτοῦ ; πῶς
need he had, and hungered, he and the (ones) with him; how
εἰσῆλθεν εἰς τὸν οἶκον τοῦ Θεοῦ ἐπὶ Ἀβιάθαρ τοῦ ἀρχιερέως,
he entered into the house — of God on Abiathar the high priest,
καὶ τοὺς ἄρτους τῆς προθέσεως ἔφαγεν, οὓς οὐκ ἔξεστι
and the loaves of the presentation ate, which not is lawful
φαγεῖν εἰ μὴ τοῖς ἱερεῦσι, καὶ ἔδωκε καὶ τοῖς σὺν αὐτῷ οὖσι ;
to eat except the priests, and gave also to those with him; being?
27 καὶ ἔλεγεν αὐτοῖς, Τὸ σάββατον διὰ τὸν ἄνθρωπον ἐγένετο,
And He said to them, The sabbath for the sake of man came into being,
28 οὐχ ὁ ἄνθρωπος διὰ τὸ σάββατον· ὥστε Κύριός ἐστιν ὁ υἱὸς
not man for the sake of the sabbath; so then Lord is the Son
τοῦ ἀνθρώπου καὶ τοῦ σαββάτου.
— of man also of the sabbath.

CHAPTER 3

1 Καὶ εἰσῆλθε πάλιν εἰς τὴν συναγωγήν, καὶ ἦν ἐκεῖ ἄνθρω-
And He entered again into the synagogue, and was there a
2 πος ἐξηραμμένην ἔχων τὴν χεῖρα. καὶ παρετήρουν αὐτὸν εἰ
man a withering having (of) the hand. And they watched Him, if
τοῖς σάββασι θεραπεύσει αὐτόν, ἵνα κατηγορήσωσιν αὐτοῦ.
on the sabbaths He will heal him, that they might accuse Him.
3 καὶ λέγει τῷ ἀνθρώπῳ τῷ ἐξηραμμένην ἔχοντι τὴν χεῖρα,
And He says to the man — a withering having (of) the hand,
4 Ἔγειραι εἰς τὸ μέσον. καὶ λέγει αὐτοῖς, Ἔξεστι τοῖς σάββασιν
Rise into the midst. And he says to them, Lawful on the sabbaths

evil? To save a soul, or to kill? But they were silent. [5]And having looked around *on* them with anger, being greatly grieved with the hardness of their heart, He said to the man, Stretch out your hand! And he stretched out, and his hand was restored sound as the other. [6]And going out the Pharisees immediately took counsel with the Herodians against Him, how they might destroy Him.

[7]And Jesus withdrew to the sea with His disciples; and a great multitude from Galilee and from Judea followed Him; [8]also *some* from Jerusalem, and from Idumea, and beyond the Jordan; also those around Tyre and Sidon, a great multitude having heard how much He was doing came to Him. [9]And He spoke to His disciples that a small boat should stay near to Him because of the crowd, that they might not press upon Him. [10]For He healed many, so that they threw themselves on Him, that they might touch Him, as many as had plagues. [11]And when the unclean spirits saw Him, *they* fell down before Him, and cried out, saying, You are the Son of God! [12]And He very much warned them, so that they should not reveal Him.

[13]And He went up into the mountain, and He called near whom He desired. And they went to Him. [14]And He appointed twelve, that they might be with Him, and that He might send them to proclaim, [15]And to have authority to heal diseases and to cast out the demons.

[16]And He put on Simon *the* name Peter. [17]And He put on James *the* son of Zebedee, and John the brother of James, *the* name Boanerges, which is, Sons of Thunder. [18]Also *He appointed* Andrew, and Philip, and Bartholomew, and Matthew, and Thomas, and James the *son* of Alpheus, and Thaddeus, and

ἀγαθοποιῆσαι, ἢ κακοποιῆσαι; ψυχὴν σῶσαι, ἢ ἀπο-
to do good, or to do evil; a soul to save, or to
5 κτεῖναι; οἱ δὲ ἐσιώπων. καὶ περιβλεψάμενος αὐτοὺς μετ'
kill? they But were silent. And looking around (on) them with
ὀργῆς, συλλυπούμενος ἐπὶ τῇ πωρώσει τῆς καρδίας αὐτῶν,
anger, being greatly grieved on the hardness of the heart of them,
λέγει τῷ ἀνθρώπῳ, Ἔκτεινον τὴν χεῖρά σου. καὶ ἐξέτεινε,
He says to the man, Stretch out the hand of you. And he stretched,
6 καὶ ἀποκατεστάθη ἡ χεὶρ αὐτοῦ ὑγιὴς ὡς ἡ ἄλλη. καὶ
and was restored the hand of him sound as the other. And
ἐξελθόντες οἱ Φαρισαῖοι εὐθέως μετὰ τῶν Ἡρωδιανῶν
having gone out the Pharisees immediately with the Herodians
συμβούλιον ἐποίουν κατ' αὐτοῦ, ὅπως αὐτὸν ἀπολέσωσι.
counsel made against Him, how that Him they might destroy
7 Καὶ ὁ Ἰησοῦς ἀνεχώρησε μετὰ τῶν μαθητῶν αὐτοῦ πρὸς
And — Jesus withdrew with the disciples of Him to
τὴν θάλασσαν· καὶ πολὺ πλῆθος ἀπὸ τῆς Γαλιλαίας ἠκολού-
the sea; and a great multitude from — Galilee followed
8 θησαν αὐτῷ, καὶ ἀπὸ τῆς Ἰουδαίας, καὶ ἀπὸ Ἱεροσολύμων,
Him; and from — Judea, and from Jerusalem,
καὶ ἀπὸ τῆς Ἰδουμαίας, καὶ πέραν τοῦ Ἰορδάνου, καὶ οἱ
and from — Idumea, and beyond the Jordan, and those
περὶ Τύρον καὶ Σιδῶνα, πλῆθος πολύ, ἀκούσαντες ὅσα
around Tyre and Sidon; a multitude great, hearing what
9 ἐποίει, ἦλθον πρὸς αὐτόν. καὶ εἶπε τοῖς μαθηταῖς αὐτοῦ
He was doing came to Him. And He told the disciples of Him
ἵνα πλοιάριον προσκαρτερῇ αὐτῷ διὰ τὸν ὄχλον, ἵνα μὴ
that a small boat should stay near Him because of the crowd, lest
10 θλίβωσιν αὐτόν. πολλοὺς γὰρ ἐθεράπευσεν, ὥστε ἐπιπί-
they press on Him. many For He healed, so that (they) fell
11 πτειν αὐτῷ, ἵνα αὐτοῦ ἅψωνται, ὅσοι εἶχον μάστιγας. καὶ τὰ
upon Him, that Him they might touch, as many as had plagues; and the
πνεύματα τὰ ἀκάθαρτα, ὅταν αὐτὸν ἐθεώρει, προσέπιπτεν
spirits unclean wnen Him they saw fell before
12 αὐτῷ, καὶ ἔκραζε, λέγοντα ὅτι Σὺ εἶ ὁ υἱὸς τοῦ Θεοῦ. καὶ
Him and cried out, saying, — You are the Son — of God. And
πολλὰ ἐπετίμα αὐτοῖς ἵνα μὴ αὐτὸν φανερὸν ποιήσωσι.
much He warned them that not Him manifest they should make.
13 Καὶ ἀναβαίνει εἰς τὸ ὄρος, καὶ προσκαλεῖται οὓς ἤθελεν
And He goes up into the mountain, and called near whom wished
14 αὐτός· καὶ ἀπῆλθον πρὸς αὐτόν. καὶ ἐποίησε δώδεκα, ἵνα
He, and they went to Him. And He made twelve, that
15 ὦσι μετ' αὐτοῦ, καὶ ἵνα ἀποστέλλῃ αὐτοὺς κηρύσσειν καὶ
they might be with Him, and that He might send them to proclaim, and
ἔχειν ἐξουσίαν θεραπεύειν τὰς νόσους, καὶ ἐκβάλλειν τὰ
to have authority to heal the diseases, and to cast out the
16 δαιμόνια· καὶ ἐπέθηκε τῷ Σίμωνι ὄνομα Πέτρον· καὶ Ἰάκωβον
17 **demons. And He put upon Simon a name, Peter; and James**
τὸν τοῦ Ζεβεδαίου, καὶ Ἰωάννην τὸν ἀδελφὸν τοῦ Ἰακώβου·
the (son) of Zebedee, and John the brother of James,
καὶ ἐπέθηκεν αὐτοῖς ὀνόματα Βοανεργές, ὅ ἐστιν, Υἱοὶ
and He put upon them (the) names Boanerges, which is, Sons
18 βροντῆς· καὶ Ἀνδρέαν, καὶ Φίλιππον, καὶ Βαρθολομαῖον,
of Thunder; and Andrew and Philip; and Bartholomew
καὶ Ματθαῖον, καὶ Θωμᾶν, καὶ Ἰάκωβον τὸν τοῦ Ἀλφαίου,
and Matthew; and Thomas; and James the (son) of Alpheus,

Simon the Canaanite, [19]and Judas Iscariot, who also betrayed Him.

[20]And He came into a house. And again a crowd came together, so as they were not able to even eat bread. [21]And hearing, those with Him went out to take hold *of* Him; for they said, He is out of wits. [22]And the scribes coming down from Jerusalem said, He has Beelzebub, and He casts out demons by the ruler of the demons. [23]And calling them near, He spoke to them in parables, *saying*, How can Satan cast out Satan? [24]And if a kingdom is divided against itself, that kingdom cannot stand. [25]And if a house is divided against itself, that house is not able to stand. [26]And if Satan rises upon himself, and has been divided, he is not able to stand, but he has an end. [27]No one in any way is able to plunder the goods of the strong one, having entered into his house, unless he first ties up the strong one; and then he will plunder his house. [28]Truly I say to you, All the sins will be forgiven to the sons of men, and whatever blasphemies they have blasphemed. [29]But whoever blasphemes against the Holy Spirit has no forgiveness to eternity, but is liable to eternal judgment; because they said, He has an unclean spirit.

[31]Then His mother and brothers came. And standing outside, *they* sent to Him, calling Him. [32]And a crowd sat around Him. And they said to Him, Behold, Your mother and your brothers seek You outside. [33]And He answered them, saying, Who is My mother or My brothers? [34]And having looked around *on* those sitting around Him in a circle, He said, Behold, My mother and My brothers! [35]For whoever does the will

19 καὶ Θαδδαῖον, καὶ Σίμωνα τὸν Κανανίτην, καὶ Ἰούδαν
and Thaddeus, and Simon the Canaanite, and Judas
Ἰσκαριώτην, ὃς καὶ παρέδωκεν αὐτόν.
Iscariot, who also betrayed Him.
20 Καὶ ἔρχονται εἰς οἶκον· καὶ συνέρχεται πάλιν ὄχλος, ὥστε
And they come into a house; and comes together again a crowd so as
21 μὴ δύνασθαι αὐτοὺς μήτε ἄρτον φαγεῖν. καὶ ἀκούσαντες οἱ
not are able they not even bread to eat. And having heard those
παρ' αὐτοῦ ἐξῆλθον κρατῆσαι αὐτόν· ἔλεγον γὰρ ὅτι
with Him went forth to take hold (of) Him, they said for, —
22 Ἐξέστη. καὶ οἱ γραμματεῖς οἱ ἀπὸ Ἱεροσολύμων καταβάντες
He is insane. And the scribes — from Jerusalem coming down
ἔλεγον ὅτι Βεελζεβοὺλ ἔχει, καὶ ὅτι Ἐν τῷ ἄρχοντι τῶν
said, — Beelzebub He has, and, — By the ruler of the
23 δαιμονίων ἐκβάλλει τὰ δαιμόνια. καὶ προσκαλεσάμενος
demons he casts out the demons. And calling near
αὐτούς, ἐν παραβολαῖς ἔλεγεν αὐτοῖς, Πῶς δύναται Σατανᾶς
them, in parables He spoke to them, How is able Satan
24 Σατανᾶν ἐκβάλλειν; καὶ ἐὰν βασιλεία ἐφ' ἑαυτὴν μερισθῇ, οὐ
Satan to cast out? And if a kingdom against itself is divided, not
25 δύναται σταθῆναι ἡ βασιλεία ἐκείνη. καὶ ἐὰν οἰκία ἐφ'
is able to stand — kingdom that. And if a house against
26 ἑαυτὴν μερισθῇ, οὐ δύναται σταθῆναι ἡ οἰκία ἐκείνη. καὶ εἰ
itself is divided, not is able to stand — house that. And if
ὁ Σατανᾶς ἀνέστη ἐφ' ἑαυτὸν καὶ μεμέρισται, οὐ δύναται
— Satan rises upon himself and has been divided, **not he is able**
27 σταθῆναι, ἀλλὰ τέλος ἔχει. οὐ δύναται οὐδεὶς τὰ σκεύη τοῦ
to stand, but an end he has. not is able No one the goods of the
ἰσχυροῦ, εἰσελθὼν εἰς τὴν οἰκίαν αὐτοῦ, διαρπάσαι, ἐὰν μὴ
strong one having entered into the house of him, to plunder, unless
πρῶτον τὸν ἰσχυρὸν δήσῃ, καὶ τότε τὴν οἰκίαν αὐτοῦ διαρ-
first the strong one he bind, and then the house of him he will
28 πάσει. ἀμὴν λέγω ὑμῖν, ὅτι πάντα ἀφεθήσεται τὰ ἁμαρτή-
plunder. Truly I say to you, that all will be forgiven the sins
ματα τοῖς υἱοῖς τῶν ἀνθρώπων, καὶ βλασφημίαι ὅσας ἂν
of the sons — of men, and blasphemies whatever
29 βλασφημήσωσιν· ὃς δ' ἂν βλασφημήσῃ εἰς τὸ Πνεῦμα τὸ
they have blasphemed,who but ever blasphemes against the Spirit —
Ἅγιον, οὐκ ἔχει ἄφεσιν εἰς τὸν αἰῶνα, ἀλλ' ἔνοχός ἐστιν
Holy, not has forgiveness unto the age, but liable is
30 αἰωνίου κρίσεως. ὅτι ἔλεγον, Πνεῦμα ἀκάθαρτον ἔχει.
of an eternal judgment; for they said, A spirit unclean He has.
31 Ἔρχονται οὖν οἱ ἀδελφοὶ καὶ ἡ μήτηρ αὐτοῦ, καὶ ἔξω
come Then the brothers and the mother of Him, and outside
32 ἑστῶτες ἀπέστειλαν πρὸς αὐτόν, φωνοῦντες αὐτόν. καὶ
standing sent to Him, calling Him. And
ἐκάθητο ὄχλος περὶ αὐτόν· εἶπον δὲ αὐτῷ, Ἰδού, ἡ μήτηρ
sat a crowd around Him. they said And to Him, Behold the mother
33 σου καὶ οἱ ἀδελφοί σου ἔξω ζητοῦσί σε. καὶ ἀπεκρίθη αὐτοῖς
of you and the brothers of you outside seek You. And He answered them,
34 λέγων, Τίς ἐστιν ἡ μήτηρ μου ἢ οἱ ἀδελφοί μου; καὶ
saying, Who is the mother of Me or the brothers of Me? And
περιβλεψάμενος κύκλῳ τοὺς περὶ αὐτὸν καθημένους, λέγει,
looking around in a circle (at) those around Him sitting, He says
35 Ἴδε, ἡ μήτηρ μου καὶ οἱ ἀδελφοί μου. ὃς γὰρ ἂν ποιήσῃ τὸ
Behold, the mother of Me and the brothers of Me! who For ever does the

of God, this one is My brother, and My sister, and My mother.

CHAPTER 4

[1]And again He began to teach by the sea. And a large crowd was gathered to Him, so that He entered into the boat in order to sit in the sea. And all the crowd were on the land toward the sea. [2]And He taught them many things in parables, and said to them in His teaching: [3]Listen! Behold, the sower went out to sow. [4]And as he sowed, it happened that one indeed fell by the wayside; and the birds of the heaven ate it up. [5]And another fell on the rocky place where it did not have much earth. And it sprang up at once, due to not having deepness of earth. [6]And *the* sun rising, it was scorched. And through not having root, it was dried out.

[7]And another fell among the thorns, and the thorns grew up and choked it, and it did not yield fruit. [8]And another fell into the good ground, and yielded fruit, going up and increasing; and one bore thirty, and one sixty, and one a hundred-*fold*. [9]And He said to them, The *one* having ears to hear, let him hear.

[10]And when He was alone, those around Him, with the Twelve, asked Him *as to* the parable. [11]And He said to them, To you *it* has been given to know the mystery of the kingdom of God. But to these, those outside, all things *are* being *given* in parables, [12]that seeing they may see and not perceive; and hearing they may hear, and not understand, lest they should be converted, and sins be forgiven to them. [13]And He said to them, Do you not know this parable? And how will you know all parables? [14]The sower sows the word. [15]And these are those by the

θέλημα τοῦ Θεοῦ, οὗτος ἀδελφός μου καὶ ἀδελφή μου καὶ
will – of God, this one brother of Me and sister of Me and
μήτηρ ἐστί.
mother is.

CHAPTER 4

1 Καὶ πάλιν ἤρξατο διδάσκειν παρὰ τὴν θάλασσαν. καὶ
And again He began to teach by the sea. And
συνήχθη πρὸς αὐτὸν ὄχλος πολύς, ὥστε αὐτὸν ἐμβάντα εἰς
is assembled to Him a crowd large, so that He entering into
τὸ πλοῖον καθῆσθαι ἐν τῇ θαλάσσῃ· καὶ πᾶς ὁ ὄχλος πρὸς
the boat (had) to sit in the sea., and all the crowd toward
2 τὴν θάλασσαν ἐπὶ τῆς γῆς ἦν. καὶ ἐδίδασκεν αὐτοὺς ἐν
the sea on the land were. And He taught them in
παραβολαῖς πολλά, καὶ ἔλεγεν αὐτοῖς ἐν τῇ διδαχῇ αὐτοῦ,
parables many things, and said to them in the teaching of Him,
3 Ἀκούετε· ἰδού, ἐξῆλθεν ὁ σπείρων τοῦ σπεῖραι· καὶ ἐγένετο
4 **Hear! Behold, went out the (one) sowing to sow. And it was,**
ἐν τῷ σπείρειν, ὃ μὲν ἔπεσε παρὰ τὴν ὁδόν, καὶ ἦλθε τὰ
while sowing one indeed fell by the way, and came the
5 πετεινὰ τοῦ οὐρανοῦ καὶ κατέφαγεν αὐτό. ἄλλο δὲ ἔπεσεν
birds of the heaven and devoured it. other And fell
ἐπὶ τὸ πετρῶδες, ὅπου οὐκ εἶχε γῆν πολλήν· καὶ εὐθέως
on the rocky place where not it had earth much, and at once
6 ἐξανέτειλε, διὰ τὸ μὴ ἔχειν βάθος γῆς· ἡλίου δὲ ἀνατείλαντος
it sprang up, due to not having depth of earth; sun And arising,
7 ἐκαυματίσθη, καὶ διὰ τὸ μὴ ἔχειν ῥίζαν ἐξηράνθη. καὶ ἄλλο
it was scorched, and through not to have root it was dried up. And other
ἔπεσεν εἰς τὰς ἀκάνθας, καὶ ἀνέβησαν αἱ ἄκανθαι, καὶ συνέ-
fell into the thorns, and grew the thorns and choked
8 πνιξαν αὐτό, καὶ καρπὸν οὐκ ἔδωκε. καὶ ἄλλο ἔπεσεν εἰς τὴν
it, and fruit not it did give. And other fell into the
γῆν τὴν καλήν· καὶ ἐδίδου καρπὸν ἀναβαίνοντα καὶ
earth – good, and gave fruit going up and
αὐξάνοντα, καὶ ἔφερεν ἓν τριάκοντα, καὶ ἓν ἑξήκοντα, καὶ
increasing, and bore one thirty, and one sixty, and
9 ἓν ἑκατόν. καὶ ἔλεγεν αὐτοῖς, Ὁ ἔχων ὦτα ἀκούειν ἀκουέτω.
one a hundred. And He said to them, He having ears to hear, let him hear.
10 Ὅτε δὲ ἐγένετο καταμόνας, ἠρώτησαν αὐτὸν οἱ περὶ
when And He became alone, asked Him those around
11 αὐτὸν σὺν τοῖς δώδεκα τὴν παραβολήν. καὶ ἔλεγεν αὐτοῖς,
Him with the twelve the parable. And He said to them,
Ὑμῖν δέδοται γνῶναι τὸ μυστήριον τῆς βασιλείας τοῦ
To you has been given to know the mystery of the kingdom –
Θεοῦ· ἐκείνοις δὲ τοῖς ἔξω, ἐν παραβολαῖς τὰ πάντα γίνεται·
of God; to these but those outside in parables – all things became
12 ἵνα βλέποντες βλέπωσι, καὶ μὴ ἴδωσι· καὶ ἀκούοντες
that seeing they may see, and not perceive; and hearing
ἀκούωσι, καὶ μὴ συνιῶσι· μήποτε ἐπιστρέψωσι, καὶ
they may hear, and not understand, lest they should convert, and
13 ἀφεθῇ αὐτοῖς τὰ ἁμαρτήματα. καὶ λέγει αὐτοῖς, Οὐκ οἴδατε
be forgiven them the sins. And He says to them, not Know you
τὴν παραβολὴν ταύτην; καὶ πῶς πάσας τὰς παραβολὰς
– parable this? And how all the parables
14 γνώσεσθε; ὁ σπείρων τὸν λόγον σπείρει. οὗτοι δέ εἰσιν οἱ
15 **will you know? He sowing the word sows. these And are those**

wayside, where the word is sown. And when they hear, Satan comes at once and takes the word having been sown in their hearts. [16]And likewise, these are the ones being sown on the rocky places, who, when they hear the word, immediately receive it with joy, [17]yet they have no root in themselves, but are temporary. Then there being trouble or persecution through the word, they are immediately offended. [18]These are those being sown into the thorns, those hearing the word, [19]and the cares of this world, and the deceitfulness of riches, and the lusts about other things having entered in, *they* choke the word, and it becomes unfruitful. [20]And these are those being sown on the good ground, who hear and welcome the word, and bring forth fruit—one thirty, and one sixty, and one a hundred*fold*.

[21]And He said to them, Does the lamp come that it may be put under the grain measure, or under the bed? *Is it* not that it may be put on the lampstand? [22]For not anything is hidden but that it will be revealed; nor *anything* become covered but that it will come to light. [23]If anyone has ears to hear, let him hear.

[24]And He said to them, Be careful what you hear. With what measure you measure, it will be measured to you, and more will be given to you, the *ones* hearing. [25]For whoever may have, even that which he has will be taken from him.

[26]And He said, So is the kingdom of God, as if a man should cast seed on the earth, [27]and should sleep, and rise night and day, and the seed should sprout and lengthen of itself, as he does not know—[28]for of itself the earth bears fruit: first greenery, then an ear, then full grain in the ear. [29]And when the fruit yields, immediately he sends forth the sickle, for

παρὰ τὴν ὁδόν, ὅπου σπείρεται ὁ λόγος, καὶ ὅταν ἀκούσω-
by the way, where is sown the word; and when they hear,
σιν, εὐθέως ἔρχεται ὁ Σατανᾶς καὶ αἴρει τὸν λόγον τὸν
immediately comes — Satan and takes the word —
16 ἐσπαρμένον ἐν ταῖς καρδίαις αὐτῶν. καὶ οὗτοί εἰσιν ὁμοίως
having been sown in the hearts of them. And these are likewise
οἱ ἐπὶ τὰ πετρώδη σπειρόμενοι, οἵ, ὅταν ἀκούσωσι τὸν
these on the rocky places being sown, who when they hear the
17 λόγον, εὐθέως μετὰ χαρᾶς λαμβάνουσιν αὐτόν, καὶ οὐκ
word, immediately with joy they receive it, and not
ἔχουσι ῥίζαν ἐν ἑαυτοῖς, ἀλλὰ πρόσκαιροί εἰσιν· εἶτα γενο-
they have root in themselves, but temporary they are; then having
μένης θλίψεως ἢ διωγμοῦ διὰ τὸν λόγον, εὐθέως σκανδαλί-
become trouble or persecution through the word, immediately they are
18 ζονται. καὶ οὗτοί εἰσιν οἱ εἰς τὰς ἀκάνθας σπειρόμενοι, οἱ τὸν
offended. And these are those into the thorns being sown; those the
19 λόγον ἀκούοντες, καὶ αἱ μέριμναι τοῦ αἰῶνος τούτου, καὶ ἡ
word hearing, and the cares of — age this, and the
ἀπάτη τοῦ πλούτου, καὶ αἱ περὶ τὰ λοιπὰ ἐπιθυμίαι
deceitfulness — of riches, and the about the other things desires
εἰσπορευόμεναι συμπνίγουσι τὸν λόγον, καὶ ἄκαρπος
entering in choke the word, and unfruitful
20 γίνεται. καὶ οὗτοί εἰσιν οἱ ἐπὶ τὴν γῆν τὴν καλὴν σπαρέντες,
it becomes. And these are the (ones) on the earth — good being sown,
οἵτινες ἀκούουσι τὸν λόγον, καὶ παραδέχονται, καὶ καρ-
who hear the word, and welcome (it), and bring
ποφοροῦσιν, ἓν τριάκοντα, καὶ ἓν ἑξήκοντα, καὶ ἓν ἑκατόν.
forth fruit, one thirty, and one sixty, and one a hundred.
21 Καὶ ἔλεγεν αὐτοῖς, Μήτι ὁ λύχνος ἔρχεται ἵνα ὑπὸ τὸν
And He said to them, Not (is) the lamp come that under the
μόδιον τεθῇ ἢ ὑπὸ τὴν κλίνην; οὐχ ἵνα ἐπὶ τὴν λυχνίαν
bushel it be placed, or under the couch? (is it) not that on the lampstand
22 ἐπιτεθῇ; οὐ γάρ ἐστί τι κρυπτόν, ὃ ἐὰν μὴ φανερωθῇ· οὐδὲ
it be placed? not For is a thing hidden, which if not it may be revealed, nor
23 ἐγένετο ἀπόκρυφον, ἀλλ' ἵνα εἰς φανερὸν ἔλθῃ. εἴ τις ἔχει
became covered, but that to light it may come. If any have
24 ὦτα ἀκούειν ἀκουέτω. καὶ ἔλεγεν αὐτοῖς, Βλέπετε τί ἀκούετε.
ears to hear, let him hear. And He said to them, Be careful what you hear.
ἐν ᾧ μέτρῳ μετρεῖτε μετρηθήσεται ὑμῖν, καὶ προστεθήσεται
In what measure you measure it will be measured to you. And it will be added
25 ὑμῖν τοῖς ἀκούουσιν. ὃς γὰρ ἂν ἔχῃ, δοθήσεται αὐτῷ· καὶ
to you, the (ones) hearing. who For ever may have, it will be given to him; and
ὃς οὐκ ἔχει, καὶ ὃ ἔχει ἀρθήσεται ἀπ' αὐτοῦ.
who not has, even what he has will be taken from him.
26 Καὶ ἔλεγεν, Οὕτως ἐστὶν ἡ βασιλεία τοῦ Θεοῦ, ὡς ἐὰν
And He said, Thus is the kingdom — of God, as if
27 ἄνθρωπος βάλῃ τὸν σπόρον ἐπὶ τῆς γῆς, καὶ καθεύδῃ καὶ
a man should cast the seed on the earth, and should sleep and
ἐγείρηται νύκτα καὶ ἡμέραν, καὶ ὁ σπόρος βλαστάνῃ καὶ
rise night and day, and the seed should sprout and
28 μηκύνηται ὡς οὐκ οἶδεν αὐτός. αὐτομάτη γὰρ ἡ γῆ καρπο-
lengthen as not knows he of itself For the earth bears
φορεῖ, πρῶτον χόρτον, εἶτα στάχυν, εἶτα πλήρη σῖτον ἐν
fruit, first greenery, then an ear, then full grain in
29 τῷ στάχυϊ. ὅταν δὲ παραδῷ ὁ καρπός, εὐθέως ἀποστέλλει
the ear. when But yields the fruit, immediately he sends forth

the harvest has come. [30]And He said, To what shall we compare the kingdom of God? Or with what parable shall we compare it? [32]*It is* like a grain of mustard, which, when it is sown on the earth, it is less than all the seeds of those on the earth. [32]And when it is sown, *it* comes up, and becomes greater than all the plants, and produces great branches, so as to enable the birds of the heaven to roost under its shade.

[33]And with many such parables He spoke the word to them, even as they were able to hear. [34]But He did not speak to them without a parable. And He explained all things to His disciples privately.

[35]And evening having come, He said to them on that day, Let us pass over to the other side. [36]And dismissing the crowd, they took Him along, as He was in the boat. And other small boats also were with Him. [37]And a great windstorm occurred, and the waves beat into the boat, so that it was already filled. [38]And He was on the stern, sleeping on the headrest. And they awakened Him, and said to Him, Teacher, does it not matter to You that we are perishing? [39]And being awakened, He rebuked the wind, and said to the sea, Silence! Be still! And the wind ceased, and there was a great calm. [40]And He said to them, Why are you so fearful? How do you not have faith? [41]And they feared a great fear, and said to one another, who then is this, that even the wind and the sea obey Him?

CHAPTER 5

[1]And they came to the other side of the sea, to the country of the Gaderenes. [2]And He coming out from the boat, immediately out of the

τὸ δρέπανον, ὅτι παρέστηκεν ὁ θερισμός.
the sickle, because stands ready the harvest.
30 Καὶ ἔλεγε, Τίνι ὁμοιώσωμεν τὴν βασιλείαν τοῦ Θεοῦ;
And He said, How may we compare the kingdom — of God,
31 ἢ ἐν ποίᾳ παραβολῇ παραβάλωμεν αὐτήν; ὡς κόκκῳ
or by what parable may we compare it? As to a grain
σινάπεως, ὅς, ὅταν σπαρῇ ἐπὶ τῆς γῆς, μικρότερος πάντων
of mustard, which when it is sown on the earth, lesser than all
32 τῶν σπερμάτων ἐστὶ τῶν ἐπὶ τῆς γῆς· καὶ ὅταν σπαρῇ,
the seeds It is of those on the earth. And when it is sown,
ἀναβαίνει, καὶ γίνεται πάντων τῶν λαχάνων μείζων, καὶ
comes up, and becomes than all the plants greater, and
ποιεῖ κλάδους μεγάλους, ὥστε δύνασθαι ὑπὸ τὴν σκιὰν
makes branches great, so as to be able under the shade
αὐτοῦ τὰ πετεινὰ τοῦ οὐρανοῦ κατασκηνοῦν.
of it the birds of the heaven to roost.
33 Καὶ τοιαύταις παραβολαῖς πολλαῖς ἐλάλει αὐτοῖς τὸν
And such parables many He spoke to them the
34 λόγον, καθὼς ἠδύναντο ἀκούειν· χωρὶς δὲ παραβολῆς οὐκ
word, even as they were able to hear; without and a parable not
ἐλάλει αὐτοῖς· κατ᾽ ἰδίαν δὲ τοῖς μαθηταῖς αὐτοῦ ἐπέλυε
He spoke to them, privately but to the disciples of Him, He explained
πάντα.
all things.
35 Καὶ λέγει αὐτοῖς ἐν ἐκείνῃ τῇ ἡμέρᾳ, ὀψίας γενομένης,
And He says to them on that — day, evening having come,
36 Διέλθωμεν εἰς τὸ πέραν. καὶ ἀφέντες τὸν ὄχλον, παραλαμ-
Let us pass over to the other side. And dismissing the crowd, they take
βάνουσιν αὐτὸν ὡς ἦν ἐν τῷ πλοίῳ. καὶ ἄλλα δὲ πλοιάρια
along Him as He was in the boat. also other And small boats
37 ἦν μετ᾽ αὐτοῦ. καὶ γίνεται λαῖλαψ ἀνέμου μεγάλη· τὰ δὲ
were with Him. And occurs a storm of wind great the and
κύματα ἐπέβαλλεν εἰς τὸ πλοῖον, ὥστε αὐτὸ ἤδη γεμίζεσθαι.
waves beat into the boat, so as it already was filled.
38 καὶ ἦν αὐτὸς ἐπὶ τῇ πρύμνῃ ἐπὶ τὸ προσκεφάλαιον καθεύδων·
And was He on the stern, on the headrest sleeping.
καὶ διεγείρουσιν αὐτόν, καὶ λέγουσιν αὐτῷ, Διδάσκαλε, οὐ
And they awaken Him and say to Him, Teacher, not
39 μέλει σοι ὅτι ἀπολλύμεθα; καὶ διεγερθεὶς ἐπετίμησε τῷ
it matters to You that we are perishing? And being awakened He rebuked the
ἀνέμῳ, καὶ εἶπε τῇ θαλάσσῃ, Σιώπα, πεφίμωσο. καὶ ἐκόπα-
wind, and said to the sea, Silence! Be still! And cut off
40 σεν ὁ ἄνεμος, καὶ ἐγένετο γαλήνη μεγάλη. καὶ εἶπεν αὐτοῖς,
the wind, and there was a calm great. And He said to them,
41 Τί δειλοί ἐστε οὕτω; πῶς οὐκ ἔχετε πίστιν; καὶ ἐφοβήθησαν
Why fearful are you so? How not have you faith? And they feared
φόβον μέγαν, καὶ ἔλεγον πρὸς ἀλλήλους, Τίς ἄρα οὗτός
a fear great, and said to one another, Who then this One
ἐστιν, ὅτι καὶ ὁ ἄνεμος καὶ ἡ θάλασσα ὑπακούουσιν αὐτῷ,
is, that even the wind and the sea obey Him?

CHAPTER 5

1 Καὶ ἦλθον εἰς τὸ πέραν τῆς θαλάσσης, εἰς τὴν χώραν τῶν
And they came to the other side of the sea, into the country of the
2 Γαδαρηνῶν. καὶ ἐξελθόντι αὐτῷ ἐκ τοῦ πλοίου, εὐθέως
Gaderenes. And coming out He from the boat, immediately

tombs a man with an unclean spirit met Him. 3 who had *his* abode among the tombs, and no one was able to bind him, not even with a chain; 4 because he had often been bound with fetters and chains, and the chains had been torn by him, and the fetters had been shattered. And no one was able to subdue him. 5 And continually night and day in the mountains, and in the tombs, he was crying and cutting himself with stones. 6 And seeing Jesus from afar, he ran and bowed the knee to Him. 7 And crying with a loud voice, he said, What to me and to You, Jesus, Son of the most high God? I adjure You by God not *to* torment me. 8 For He was saying to him, Unclean spirit, come out of the man! 9 And He asked him, What *is* your name? And he answered, saying, My name *is* Legion, because we are many. 10 And he begged Him very much that He would not send them outside the country. 11 And a great herd of pigs were feeding there near the mountain. 12 And all the demons begged Him, saying, Send us into the pigs, that we may enter into them. 13 And Jesus immediately allowed them. And coming out, the unclean spirits entered into the pigs, and the herd rushed down the cliff into the sea—and they were about two thousand—and they were choked in the sea. 14 And those who fed the pigs fled, and *they* told *it* to the city, and to the fields. And they came out to see what it was that had been done. 15 And they came to Jesus, and stared at the one *who had been* demon-possessed, sitting and being clothed, and being in his senses, the one who had the legion. And they feared. 16 And those who had seen related how it happened to the demon-possessed one, and about the pigs.

17 And they began to beg

ἀπήντησεν αὐτῷ ἐκ τῶν μνημείων ἄνθρωπος ἐν πνεύματι
met Him out of the tombs a man in a spirit
3 ἀκαθάρτῳ, ὃς τὴν κατοίκησιν εἶχεν ἐν τοῖς μνημείοις· καὶ
unclean, who the dwelling had among the tombs, and
4 οὔτε ἀλύσεσιν οὐδεὶς ἠδύνατο αὐτὸν δῆσαι, διὰ τὸ αὐτὸν
not with a chain no one was able him to bind, because that he
πολλάκις πέδαις καὶ ἀλύσεσι δεδέσθαι, καὶ διεσπᾶσθαι ὑπ᾽
often with fetters and chains had been bound, and had been torn by
αὐτοῦ τὰς ἀλύσεις, καὶ τὰς πέδας συντετρίφθαι· καὶ οὐδεὶς
him the chains, and the fetters had been broken, and no one
5 αὐτὸν ἴσχυε δαμάσαι· καὶ διὰ παντός, νυκτὸς καὶ ἡμέρας,
him was able to subdue; and through all, night and day,
ἐν τοῖς ὄρεσι καὶ ἐν τοῖς μνήμασιν ἦν κράζων καὶ κατακόπτων
among the hills and in the tombs he was crying and cutting
6 ἑαυτὸν λίθοις. ἰδὼν δὲ τὸν Ἰησοῦν ἀπὸ μακρόθεν, ἔδραμε
himself with stones. seeing And Jesus from afar, he ran
7 καὶ προσεκύνησεν αὐτῷ, καὶ κράξας φωνῇ μεγάλῃ εἶπε. Τί
and bowed the knee to Him, and crying with a voice great said, What
ἐμοὶ καὶ σοί, Ἰησοῦ, υἱὲ τοῦ Θεοῦ τοῦ ὑψίστου; ὁρκίζω σε
to me and to You, Jesus, Son – of God the Most High? I adjure You
8 τὸν Θεόν, μή με βασανίσῃς. ἔλεγε γὰρ αὐτῷ, Ἔξελθε, τὸ
(by)God not me torment. He said For to him, Come out, the
9 πνεῦμα τὸ ἀκάθαρτον, ἐκ τοῦ ἀνθρώπου. καὶ ἐπηρώτα
spirit – unclean, out of the man! And He questioned
αὐτόν, Τί σοι ὄνομα; καὶ ἀπεκρίθη, λέγων, Λεγεὼν ὄνομά
him, What (is) to you name? And he answered, saying, Legion (the) name
10 μοι, ὅτι πολλοί ἐσμεν. καὶ παρεκάλει αὐτὸν πολλά, ἵνα μὴ
of me, for many we are. And he begged Him much, that not
11 αὐτοὺς ἀποστείλῃ ἔξω τῆς χώρας. ἦν δὲ ἐκεῖ πρὸς τὰ ὄρη
them He would send outside the country. was And there near the mount
12 ἀγέλη χοίρων μεγάλη βοσκομένη· καὶ παρεκάλεσαν αὐτὸν
herd of pigs a great feeding; and begged Him,
πάντες οἱ δαίμονες, λέγοντες, Πέμψον ἡμᾶς εἰς τοὺς χοίρους,
all the demons, saying, Send us into the pigs.
13 ἵνα εἰς αὐτοὺς εἰσέλθωμεν. καὶ ἐπέτρεψεν αὐτοῖς εὐθέως ὁ
that into them we may enter. And allowed them immediately–
Ἰησοῦς. καὶ ἐξελθόντα τὰ πνεύματα τὰ ἀκάθαρτα εἰσῆλθον
Jesus. And coming out, the spirits – unclean entered
εἰς τοὺς χοίρους· καὶ ὥρμησεν ἡ ἀγέλη κατὰ τοῦ κρημνοῦ
into the pigs, and rushed the herd down the precipice
εἰς τὴν θάλασσαν· ἦσαν δὲ ὡς δισχίλιοι· καὶ ἐπνίγοντο ἐν τῇ
into the sea, they were And about two thousand and were choked in the
14 θαλάσσῃ. οἱ δὲ βόσκοντες τοὺς χοίρους ἔφυγον, καὶ ἀνήγ-
sea. those And feeding the pigs fled, and told
γειλαν εἰς τὴν πόλιν καὶ εἰς τοὺς ἀγρούς. καὶ ἐξῆλθον ἰδεῖν
(it) to the city, and to the fields. And they came out to see
15 τί ἐστι τὸ γεγονός· καὶ ἔρχονται πρὸς τὸν Ἰησοῦν, καὶ
what is that having occurred, and they come to – Jesus, and
θεωροῦσι τὸν δαιμονιζόμενον καθήμενον καὶ ἱματισμένον
gaze upon the demon-possessed sitting and having been robed
καὶ σωφρονοῦντα, τὸν ἐσχηκότα τὸν λεγεῶνα· καὶ ἐφοβήθη-
and being in his senses, the one having had the legion, and they feared.
16 σαν. καὶ διηγήσαντο αὐτοῖς οἱ ἰδόντες πῶς ἐγένετο τῷ
And related to them the (ones) seeing how it occurred to the
17 δαιμονιζομένῳ, καὶ περὶ τῶν χοίρων. καὶ ἤρξαντο παρα-
demon possessed, one, and about the pigs. And they began to beg

Him to depart from their borders. [18]And He having entered into the boat, the *former* demoniac begged Him, that he be with Him. [19]But Jesus did not allow him, but said to him, Go to your house, to your own, and announce to them what the Lord has done to you, and favored you. [20]And he left and began to proclaim in Decapolis what Jesus did to him. And all marveled.

[21]And Jesus having crossed over in the boat again to the other side, a large crowd gathered upon Him; and He was by the sea. [22]And, behold, one of the rulers of the synagogue came Jairus by name; and seeing Him, *he* fell at His feet. [23]And he begged Him very much, saying, My daughter is at the last end. *I pray* that You will come *and* lay hands on her, that *she* may be cured, and live. [24]And He went with him. And a large crowd followed Him, and pressed on Him.

[25]And a certain woman being with a flow of blood twelve years, [26]and having suffered many things by many physicians, and having spent all things that she had, and having been in no way benefited, but rather having come to worse, [27]having come in the crowd behind *Him,* she touched His garment. [28]For she said, If I may but touch His garments, I will be cured. [29]And instantly the fountain of her blood was dried up, and she knew in *her* body that she was healed of the plague. [30]And knowing instantly within Himself that power had gone forth out of Him, turning in the crowd, Jesus said, Who touched My garments? [31]And His disciples said to Him, You see the crowd pressing on You, and do you say, Who touched Me? [32]And He looked around to see the *one* who had done this. [33]And being afraid, and

18 καλεῖν αὐτὸν ἀπελθεῖν ἀπὸ τῶν ὁρίων αὐτῶν. καὶ ἐμβάντος
Him to depart from the territory of them. And entering
αὐτοῦ εἰς τὸ πλοῖον, παρεκάλει αὐτὸν ὁ δαιμονισθείς, ἵνα ᾖ
He into the boat, begged Him · the demoniac, that he be
19 μετ᾽ αὐτοῦ. ὁ δὲ Ἰησοῦς οὐκ ἀφῆκεν αὐτόν, ἀλλὰ λέγει αὐτῷ,
with Him. – But Jesus not did allow him, but says to him
Ὕπαγε εἰς τὸν οἶκόν σου πρὸς τοὺς σούς, καὶ ἀνάγγειλον
Go to the house of you to those of you, and announce
20 αὐτοῖς ὅσα σοι ὁ Κύριος ἐποίησε, καὶ ἠλέησέ σε. καὶ ἀπῆλθε
to them how to you the Lord has done, and favored you. And he left
καὶ ἤρξατο κηρύσσειν ἐν τῇ Δεκαπόλει ὅσα ἐποίησεν αὐτῷ ὁ
and began to proclaim in – Decapolis how much did to him –
Ἰησοῦς· καὶ πάντες ἐθαύμαζον.
Jesus. And all marvelled.
21 Καὶ διαπεράσαντος τοῦ Ἰησοῦ ἐν τῷ πλοίῳ πάλιν εἰς τὸ
And crossing over – Jesus in the boat again to the
πέραν, συνήχθη ὄχλος πολὺς ἐπ᾽ αὐτόν, καὶ ἦν παρὰ τὴν
other side, was collected a crowd big upon Him, and He was by the
22 θάλασσαν. καὶ ἰδού, ἔρχεται εἷς τῶν ἀρχισυναγώγων,
sea. And behold, comes one of the synagogue chiefs,
ὀνόματι Ἰάειρος, καὶ ἰδὼν αὐτόν, πίπτει πρὸς τοὺς πόδας
by name Jairus, and seeing Him he falls at the feet
23 αὐτοῦ, καὶ παρεκάλει αὐτὸν πολλά, λέγων ὅτι Τὸ θυγάτριόν
of Him, and begs Him much, saying, – The daughter
μου ἐσχάτως ἔχει· ἵνα ἐλθὼν ἐπιθῇς αὐτῇ τὰς χεῖρας, ὅπως
of me is at the last end, that coming You may lay on her the hands,that (she)
24 σωθῇ καὶ ζήσεται. καὶ ἀπῆλθε μετ᾽ αὐτοῦ· καὶ ἠκολούθει
be cured and may live. And He went with him. And followed
αὐτῷ ὄχλος πολύς, καὶ συνέθλιβον αὐτόν.
Him a crowd great, and pressed upon Him.
25 Καὶ γυνή τις οὖσα ἐν ῥύσει αἵματος ἔτη δώδεκα, καὶ
26 And a woman certain being in a flow of blood years twelve, and
πολλὰ παθοῦσα ὑπὸ πολλῶν ἰατρῶν, καὶ δαπανήσασα τὰ
many things suffering by many physicians, and having spent that
παρ᾽ ἑαυτῆς πάντα, καὶ μηδὲν ὠφεληθεῖσα, ἀλλὰ μᾶλλον
by her all things, and nothing having been gained, but rather
27 εἰς τὸ χεῖρον ἐλθοῦσα, ἀκούσασα περὶ τοῦ Ἰησοῦ, ἐλθοῦσα
to the worse having come, hearing about – Jesus, coming
28 ἐν τῷ ὄχλῳ ὄπισθεν, ἥψατο τοῦ ἱματίου αὐτοῦ· ἔλεγε γὰρ
in the crowd behind she touched the garment of Him. she said For
29 ὅτι Κἂν τῶν ἱματίων αὐτοῦ ἅψωμαι, σωθήσομαι. καὶ
– If but the garments of Him I may touch, I will be cured. And
εὐθέως ἐξηράνθη ἡ πηγὴ τοῦ αἵματος αὐτῆς, καὶ ἔγνω τῷ
instantly was dried up the fountain of the blood of her, and she knew in
30 σώματι ὅτι ἴαται ἀπὸ τῆς μάστιγος. καὶ εὐθέως ὁ Ἰησοῦς
(her) body that she is healed of the plague And instantly – Jesus
ἐπιγνοὺς ἐν ἑαυτῷ τὴν ἐξ αὐτοῦ δύναμιν ἐξελθοῦσαν,
knowing within Himself that out of Him power had gone forth,
ἐπιστραφεὶς ἐν τῷ ὄχλῳ, ἔλεγε, Τίς μου ἥψατο τῶν ἱματίων;
turning in the crowd said, Who of Me touched the garments?
31 καὶ ἔλεγον αὐτῷ οἱ μαθηταὶ αὐτοῦ, Βλέπεις τὸν ὄχλον
And said to Him the disciples of Him, You see the crowd
32 συνθλίβοντά σε, καὶ λέγεις, Τίς μου ἥψατο; καὶ περιεβλέ-
pressing upon You, and You say, Who of Me touched? And He looked
33 πετο ἰδεῖν τὴν τοῦτο ποιήσασαν. ἡ δὲ γυνὴ φοβηθεῖσα καὶ
around to see the (one) this having done. the And woman fearing and

trembling, knowing what happened on her, the woman came and fell down before Him, and told Him all the truth. [34]And He said to her, Daughter, your faith has healed you. Go in peace, and be whole from your plague.

[35]As He was speaking, they came from the synagogue ruler, saying, Your daughter has died. Why do you still trouble the Teacher? [36]But hearing the word spoken, Jesus said to the synagogue ruler, Do not fear, only believe. [37]And He did not allow anyone to go with Him except Peter and James and John, the brother of James. [38]And they came into the synagogue ruler's house. And He saw a tumult, and weeping and much wailing. [39]And going in, He said to them, Why do you make a tumult and weep? The child has not died, but is sleeping. [40]And they laughed at Him. But putting all out, He takes along the father and the mother of the child, and those with Him, and passed on into where the child was lying. [41]And taking hold of the child's hand, He said to her, Talitha koumi; which is, being translated, Little girl, I say to you, Rise up! [42]And immediately the little girl rose up and walked. For she was twelve years *old*. And they were amazed with great amazement. [43]And He directed them that no one should know this. And *He* said to give her *something* to eat.

CHAPTER 6

[1]And He went out from there, and came to His native-place. And His disciples followed Him. [2]And a sabbath occurring, He began to teach in the synagogue. And hearing many were amazed, saying, From where did this one receive these things? And what *is*

τρέμουσα, εἰδυῖα ὃ γέγονεν ἐπ' αὐτῇ, ἦλθε καὶ προσέπεσεν
trembling, knowing what happened upon her, came and fell before
34 αὐτῷ, καὶ εἶπεν αὐτῷ πᾶσαν τὴν ἀλήθειαν. ὁ δὲ εἶπεν αὐτῇ,
Him, and told Him all the truth. He And said to her,
Θύγατερ, ἡ πίστις σου σέσωκέ σε· ὕπαγε εἰς εἰρήνην, καὶ
Daughter, the faith of you has healed you; go in peace, and
ἴσθι ὑγιὴς ἀπὸ τῆς μάστιγός σου.
be whole from the plague of you.
35 Ἔτι αὐτοῦ λαλοῦντος, ἔρχονται ἀπὸ τοῦ ἀρχισυναγώ-
While He was speaking, they come from the synagogue
γου, λέγοντες ὅτι Ἡ θυγάτηρ σου ἀπέθανε· τί ἔτι σκύλλεις
chief, saying, – The daughter of you has died: why still trouble
36 τὸν διδάσκαλον; ὁ δὲ Ἰησοῦς εὐθέως ἀκούσας τὸν λόγον
the Teacher? – But Jesus immediately, hearing the word
λαλούμενον λέγει τῷ ἀρχισυναγώγῳ, Μὴ φοβοῦ, μόνον
spoken, says to the synagogue chief, Do not fear; only
37 πίστευε. καὶ οὐκ ἀφῆκεν οὐδένα αὐτῷ συνακολουθῆσαι, εἰ
believe. And not He did allow no one Him to accompany, ex-
μὴ Πέτρον καὶ Ἰάκωβον καὶ Ἰωάννην τὸν ἀδελφὸν Ἰακώβου.
cept Peter and James and John the brother of James.
38 καὶ ἔρχεται εἰς τὸν οἶκον τοῦ ἀρχισυναγώγου, καὶ θεωρεῖ
And He comes into the house of the synagogue-chief, and He sees
39 θόρυβον, καὶ κλαίοντας καὶ ἀλαλάζοντας πολλά. καὶ
a tumult, and weeping and wailing much. And
εἰσελθὼν λέγει αὐτοῖς, Τί θορυβεῖσθε καὶ κλαίετε; τὸ
entering He says to them, Why do you make a tumult and weep? The
40 παιδίον οὐκ ἀπέθανεν, ἀλλὰ καθεύδει. καὶ κατεγέλων αὐτοῦ.
child not has died, but sleeps. And they laughed at Him.
ὁ δέ, ἐκβαλὼν ἅπαντας, παραλαμβάνει τὸν πατέρα τοῦ
He But having put out all takes along the father of the
παιδίου καὶ τὴν μητέρα καὶ τοὺς μετ' αὐτοῦ, καὶ εἰσπορεύε-
child and the mother and those with Him, and passes into
41 ται ὅπου ἦν τὸ παιδίον ἀνακείμενον. καὶ κρατήσας τῆς
where was the child lying. And taking hold of the
χειρὸς τοῦ παιδίου, λέγει αὐτῇ, Ταλιθά, κοῦμι· ὅ ἐστι
hand of the child, He says to her, Talitha koumi; which is,
42 μεθερμηνευόμενον, Τὸ κοράσιον, σοὶ λέγω, ἔγειραι. καὶ
being translated, – Little girl, to you I say, Arise! And
εὐθέως ἀνέστη τὸ κοράσιον καὶ περιεπάτει, ἦν γὰρ ἐτῶν
instantly rose up the little girl and walked. she was For of years
43 δώδεκα· καὶ ἐξέστησαν ἐκστάσει μεγάλῃ. καὶ διεστείλατο
twelve. And they were amazed with amazement great. And He ordered
αὐτοῖς πολλὰ ἵνα μηδεὶς γνῷ τοῦτο· καὶ εἶπε δοθῆναι
them much that no one should know this, and said to give
αὐτῇ φαγεῖν.
to her to eat.

CHAPTER 6

1 Καὶ ἐξῆλθεν ἐκεῖθεν, καὶ ἦλθεν εἰς τὴν πατρίδα αὐτοῦ·
And He went out from there, and comes to the native-place of Him,
2 καὶ ἀκολουθοῦσιν αὐτῷ οἱ μαθηταὶ αὐτοῦ. καὶ γενομένου
and follow Him the disciples of Him. And occurring
σαββάτου, ἤρξατο ἐν τῇ συναγωγῇ διδάσκειν· καὶ πολλοὶ
a sabbath, He began in the synagogue to teach, and many
ἀκούοντες ἐξεπλήσσοντο, λέγοντες, Πόθεν τούτῳ ταῦτα;
hearing were astonished, saying, From where to this one these things?

the wisdom given to him, that even such works of power come about through his hands? 3 Is this one not the carpenter, the son of Mary, and brother of James and Joseph and Judas and Simon? And are not his sisters here with us? And they were offended in Him. 4 And Jesus said to them, A prophet is not without honor, except in his native-place, and among the relatives, and in his *own* house. 5 And he could do no work of power there, except He healed on a few infirm ones, laying on *His* hands. 6 And He marveled because of their unbelief.

And He went around the villages in *a* circuit, teaching.

7 And He called the Twelve near, and began to send them out two by two. And *He* gave them authority *over* the unclean spirits, and charged them that they take nothing in *the* way, except only a staff—no bag, no bread, no copper in the belt; 9 but tying on sandals, and not putting on two tunics. 10 And He said to them, Wherever you enter into a house, remain there until you go out from there. 11 And as many as will not receive you, nor hear from you, having gone out from there shake off the dust under your feet for a testimony to them. Truly I say to you, it will be more tolerable for Sodom or Gomorrah in Judgment Day than for that city. 12 And going out they proclaimed that *men* should repent. 13 And they cast out many demons, and anointed with oil and healed many sick ones.

14 And Herod the king heard; for His name became publicly known. And he said, John the Baptist has been raised from the dead, and because of this the works of power operate in him.

καὶ τίς ἡ σοφία ἡ δοθεῖσα αὐτῷ, ὅτι καὶ δυνάμεις τοιαῦται
and what the wisdom given to Him that even works of power such
3 διὰ τῶν χειρῶν αὐτοῦ γίνονται; οὐχ οὗτός ἐστιν ὁ τέκτων,
through the hands of Him coming about? Not this one is the carpenter,
ὁ υἱὸς Μαρίας, ἀδελφὸς δὲ Ἰακώβου καὶ Ἰωσῆ καὶ Ἰούδα
the son of Mary, brother and of James and Joseph and Judas
καὶ Σίμωνος; καὶ οὐκ εἰσὶν αἱ ἀδελφαὶ αὐτοῦ ὧδε πρὸς ἡμᾶς;
and Simon? And not are the sisters of Him here with us?
4 καὶ ἐσκανδαλίζοντο ἐν αὐτῷ. ἔλεγε δὲ αὐτοῖς ὁ Ἰησοῦς ὅτι
And they were offended in Him. said And to them — Jesus, —
Οὐκ ἔστι προφήτης ἄτιμος, εἰ μὴ ἐν τῇ πατρίδι αὐτοῦ, καὶ
Not is a prophet unhonored, except in the native place of him, and
5 ἐν τοῖς συγγενέσι καὶ ἐν τῇ οἰκίᾳ αὐτοῦ. καὶ οὐκ ἠδύνατο
among the relatives and in the house of him. And not He could
ἐκεῖ οὐδεμίαν δύναμιν ποιῆσαι, εἰ μὴ ὀλίγοις ἀρρώστοις
there no work of power do, except on a few infirm ones
6 ἐπιθεὶς τὰς χεῖρας, ἐθεράπευσε. καὶ ἐθαύμαζε διὰ τὴν ἀπι-
laying on the hands He healed. And He marveled through the un-
στίαν αὐτῶν.
belief of them.

Καὶ περιῆγε τὰς κώμας κύκλῳ διδάσκων.
And He went around the villages in circuit teaching.

7 Καὶ προσκαλεῖται τοὺς δώδεκα, καὶ ἤρξατο αὐτοὺς
And He calls near the twelve, and began them
ἀποστέλλειν δύο δύο, καὶ ἐδίδου αὐτοῖς ἐξουσίαν τῶν
to send out two by two, and gave to them authority (over) the
8 πνευμάτων τῶν ἀκαθάρτων. καὶ παρήγγειλεν αὐτοῖς ἵνα
spirits — unclean, and charged them that
μηδὲν αἴρωσιν εἰς ὁδόν, εἰ μὴ ῥάβδον μόνον· μὴ πήραν, μὴ
nothing they take in (the) way, except a staff only, not a bag, nor
9 ἄρτον, μὴ εἰς τὴν ζώνην χαλκόν· ἀλλ' ὑποδεδεμένους
bread, nor in the belt copper; but having tied under
10 σανδάλια· καὶ μὴ ἐνδύσασθαι δύο χιτῶνας. καὶ ἔλεγεν
sandals, and not put on two tunics. And He said
αὐτοῖς, Ὅπου ἐὰν εἰσέλθητε εἰς οἰκίαν, ἐκεῖ μένετε ἕως ἂν
to them, Wherever you enter into a house, there remain until
11 ἐξέλθητε ἐκεῖθεν. καὶ ὅσοι ἂν μὴ δέξωνται ὑμᾶς, μηδὲ
you go out from there. And as many as not will receive you, nor
ἀκούσωσιν ὑμῶν, ἐκπορευόμενοι ἐκεῖθεν, ἐκτινάξατε τὸν
hear from you, going out from there shake off the
χοῦν τὸν ὑποκάτω τῶν ποδῶν ὑμῶν εἰς μαρτύριον αὐτοῖς.
dust — under the feet of you for a testimony to them.
ἀμὴν λέγω ὑμῖν, ἀνεκτότερον ἔσται Σοδόμοις ἢ Γομόρροις ἐν
Truly I say to you, more tolerable it will be for Sodom or Gomorrah in
12 ἡμέρᾳ κρίσεως, ἢ τῇ πόλει ἐκείνῃ. καὶ ἐξελθόντες ἐκήρυσσον
day of judgment, than for city that. And having gone out they preached
13 ἵνα μετανοήσωσι· καὶ δαιμόνια πολλὰ ἐξέβαλλον, καὶ
that (men) should repent And demons many they cast out; and
ἤλειφον ἐλαίῳ πολλοὺς ἀρρώστους καὶ ἐθεράπευον.
anointed with oil many sick ones, and healed.

14 Καὶ ἤκουσεν ὁ βασιλεὺς Ἡρώδης, φανερὸν γὰρ ἐγένετο τὸ
And heard the king, Herod, manifest for became the
ὄνομα αὐτοῦ, καὶ ἔλεγεν ὅτι Ἰωάννης ὁ βαπτίζων ἐκ νεκρῶν
name of Him. And he said, — John the Baptist from the dead
ἠγέρθη, καὶ διὰ τοῦτο ἐνεργοῦσιν αἱ δυνάμεις ἐν αὐτῷ.
has been raised, and therefore operate the works of power in him.

15 Others said, He is Elijah; and others said, He is a prophet, or one of the prophets. 16 But hearing, Herod said, This one is John, whom I beheaded. He has risen from the dead.

17 For having sent, Herod had seized John, and bound him in the prison, because of Herodias the wife of his brother Philip; because he had married her. 18 For John had said to Herod, It is not lawful for you to have the wife of your brother. 19 And Herodias held it against him, and desired to kill him, but was not able. 20 For Herod feared John, knowing him *to be* a holy and just man, and kept him safe. And hearing him, he did many things, and gladly heard from him.

21 And a suitable day having come, when Herod made a supper for his great ones, and the chiliarchs, and the first ones of Galilee. 22 And the daughter of Herodias entering, and dancing, she also pleased Herod and those reclining with *him*. The king said to the girl, Ask me whatever you wish, and I will give it to you. 23 And he swore to her, Whatever you ask me, I will give to you, up to half of my kingdom. 24 And going out, she said to her mother, What shall I ask? And she said, The head of John the Baptist. 25 And immediately going in with haste to the king, she asked, saying, I desire that you at once give to me the head of John the Baptist on a platter. 26 And becoming deeply grieved, the king did not wish to reject her, because of the oaths, and those reclining together. 27 And the king sending a guardsman at once, he ordered his head to be brought. 28 And going he beheaded him in

15 ἄλλοι ἔλεγον ὅτι Ἠλίας ἐστίν· ἄλλοι δὲ ἔλεγον ὅτι Προφήτης
Others said, Elijah He is, others and said, a prophet
16 ἐστίν, ἢ ὡς εἷς τῶν προφητῶν. ἀκούσας δὲ ὁ Ἡρώδης εἶπεν
He is or as one of the prophets. hearing But Herod said,
ὅτι Ὃν ἐγὼ ἀπεκεφάλισα Ἰωάννην, οὗτός ἐστιν· αὐτὸς
— whom I beheaded, John, this one he is. He
17 ἠγέρθη ἐκ νεκρῶν. αὐτὸς γὰρ ὁ Ἡρώδης ἀποστείλας
is risen from the dead. himself For — Herod sending
ἐκράτησε τὸν Ἰωάννην, καὶ ἔδησεν αὐτὸν ἐν τῇ φυλακῇ,
had seized — John, and bound him in the prison,
διὰ Ἡρωδιάδα τὴν γυναῖκα Φιλίππου τοῦ ἀδελφοῦ αὐτοῦ,
because of Herodias the wife of Philip, the brother of him;
18 ὅτι αὐτὴν ἐγάμησεν. ἔλεγε γὰρ ὁ Ἰωάννης τῷ Ἡρώδῃ
because her he had married, had said For — John — to Herod,
ὅτι Οὐκ ἔξεστί σοι ἔχειν τὴν γυναῖκα τοῦ ἀδελφοῦ σου.
— not it is lawful for you to have the wife of the brother of you.
19 ἡ δὲ Ἡρωδιὰς ἐνεῖχεν αὐτῷ, καὶ ἤθελεν αὐτὸν ἀποκτεῖναι·
— And Herodias held it against him, and wished him to kill,
20 καὶ οὐκ ἠδύνατο· ὁ γὰρ Ἡρώδης ἐφοβεῖτο τὸν Ἰωάννην,
and not was able; — for Herod feared John
εἰδὼς αὐτὸν ἄνδρα δίκαιον καὶ ἅγιον, καὶ συνετήρει αὐτόν·
knowing him a man just and holy, and kept safe him,
καὶ ἀκούσας αὐτοῦ, πολλὰ ἐποίει, καὶ ἡδέως αὐτοῦ ἤκουε.
and hearing him, many things he did, and gladly from him heard.
21 καὶ γενομένης ἡμέρας εὐκαίρου, ὅτε Ἡρώδης τοῖς γενεσίοις
And coming a day suitable when Herod on the birth-feast
αὐτοῦ δεῖπνον ἐποίει τοῖς μεγιστᾶσιν αὐτοῦ καὶ τοῖς
of him a supper made for the great ones of him, and the
22 χιλιάρχοις καὶ τοῖς πρώτοις τῆς Γαλιλαίας, καὶ εἰσελθούσης
chiliarchs, and the first ones — of Galilee. And entering
τῆς θυγατρὸς αὐτῆς τῆς Ἡρωδιάδος καὶ ὀρχησαμένης, καὶ
the daughter of her, — of Herodias, and dancing, and
ἀρεσάσης τῷ Ἡρώδῃ καὶ τοῖς συνανακειμένοις, εἶπεν ὁ
she pleased — Herod and those reclining with (him). said the
βασιλεὺς τῷ κορασίῳ, Αἴτησόν με ὃ ἐὰν θέλῃς, καὶ δώσω
king to the girl, Ask me whatever you wish, and I will give
23 σοί· καὶ ὤμοσεν αὐτῇ ὅτι Ὃ ἐάν με αἰτήσῃς, δώσω σοί,
to you. And he swore to her, — Whatever me you ask, I will give to you,
24 ἕως ἡμίσους τῆς βασιλείας μου. ἡ δὲ ἐξελθοῦσα εἶπε τῇ
up to half of the kingdom of me. she and going out said to the
μητρὶ αὐτῆς, Τί αἰτήσομαι; ἡ δὲ εἶπε, Τὴν κεφαλὴν
mother of her, What shall I ask? she And said, The head
25 Ἰωάννου τοῦ Βαπτιστοῦ. καὶ εἰσελθοῦσα εὐθέως μετὰ
of John the Baptist. And entering immediately with
σπουδῆς πρὸς τὸν βασιλέα, ᾐτήσατο, λέγουσα, Θέλω ἵνα
haste to the king, she asked, saying, I desire that
μοι δῷς ἐξαυτῆς ἐπὶ πίνακι τὴν κεφαλὴν Ἰωάννου τοῦ
to me you give at once on a dish the head of John the
26 Βαπτιστοῦ. καὶ περίλυπος γενόμενος ὁ βασιλεύς, διὰ τοὺς
Baptist. And deeply grieved becoming the king, because of the
ὅρκους καὶ τοὺς συνανακειμένους οὐκ ἠθέλησεν αὐτὴν ἀθε-
oaths, and those reclining together not did wish her to
27 τῆσαι. καὶ εὐθέως ἀποστείλας ὁ βασιλεὺς σπεκουλάτωρα
reject. And at once sending the king a guardsman
28 ἐπέταξεν ἐνεχθῆναι τὴν κεφαλὴν αὐτοῦ. ὁ δὲ ἀπελθὼν
he ordered to be brought the head of him. he And having gone

the prison, and brought his head on a platter, and gave it to the girl. And the girl gave it to her mother. [29]And hearing, his disciples went and took his corpse and placed it in a tomb.

[30]And the apostles gathered to Jesus. And *they* told Him all things, even what they did, and what they taught. [31]And He said to them, You come apart into a desert place, and rest a little. For those coming, and those going were many; and they did not even have opportunity to eat. [32]And they departed by boat into a desert place apart.

[33]And the crowds saw them going, and many recognized Him. And *they* ran together on foot there, from all the cities, and came before them, and came together to Him. [34]And going out Jesus saw a large crowd, and had pity on them, because they were as sheep having no shepherd. And He began to teach them many things. [35]And *it* now becoming a late hour, drawing near to Him, the disciples said, The place is desert, and *it is* now a late hour. [36]Send them away, that going away to the surrounding fields and villages they may buy bread for themselves. For they do not have what they may eat. [37]And answering He said to them, You give them *food* to eat. And they said to Him, Going, should we buy two hundred denarii of bread and give *it* to them to eat? [38]And He said to them, How many loaves do you have? Go and see. And knowing, they said, Five, and two fish. [39]And He ordered them all to recline, group *by* group, on the green grass. [40]And they sat group *by* group, by hundred and by fifty.

ἀπεκεφάλισεν αὐτὸν ἐν τῇ φυλακῇ, καὶ ἤνεγκε τὴν κεφαλὴν
beheaded him in the prison, and brought the head
αὐτοῦ ἐπὶ πίνακι, καὶ ἔδωκεν αὐτὴν τῷ κορασίῳ· καὶ τὸ
of him on a dish, and gave it to the girl; and the
29 κοράσιον ἔδωκεν αὐτὴν τῇ μητρὶ αὐτῆς. καὶ ἀκούσαντες
girl gave it to the mother of her. And having heard
οἱ μαθηταὶ αὐτοῦ ἦλθον, καὶ ἦραν τὸ πτῶμα αὐτοῦ, καὶ
the disciples of him went and took the corpse of him, and
ἔθηκαν αὐτὸ ἐν μνημείῳ.
placed it in a tomb.

30 Καὶ συνάγονται οἱ ἀπόστολοι πρὸς τὸν Ἰησοῦν, καὶ
And are assembled the apostles to — Jesus, and
ἀπήγγειλαν αὐτῷ πάντα, καὶ ὅσα ἐποίησαν καὶ ὅσα ἐδί-
told Him all things, even what they did and what they
31 δαξαν. καὶ εἶπεν αὐτοῖς, Δεῦτε ὑμεῖς αὐτοὶ κατ᾽ ἰδίαν εἰς
taught. And He said to them, Come yourselves privately to
ἔρημον τόπον, καὶ ἀναπαύεσθε ὀλίγον. ἦσαν γὰρ οἱ
a desert place, and rest a little. were For those
ἐρχόμενοι καὶ οἱ ὑπάγοντες πολλοί, καὶ οὐδὲ φαγεῖν ηὐκαί-
coming and the (ones) going many, and not even to eat they had
32 ρουν. καὶ ἀπῆλθον εἰς ἔρημον τόπον τῷ πλοίῳ κατ᾽ ἰδίαν.
opportunity. And they left into a desert place, by the boat, privately.
33 καὶ εἶδον αὐτοὺς ὑπάγοντας οἱ ὄχλοι, καὶ ἐπέγνωσαν αὐτὸν
And saw them going the crowds, and recognized Him
πολλοί, καὶ πεζῇ ἀπὸ πασῶν τῶν πόλεων συνέδραμον ἐκεῖ,
many, and on foot from all the cities ran together there,
34 καὶ προῆλθον αὐτούς, καὶ συνῆλθον πρὸς αὐτόν. καὶ
and came before them, and came together to Him. And
ἐξελθὼν εἶδεν ὁ Ἰησοῦς πολὺν ὄχλον, καὶ ἐσπλαγχνίσθη
going out saw — Jesus a much crowd, and had compassion
ἐπ᾽ αὐτοῖς, ὅτι ἦσαν ὡς πρόβατα μὴ ἔχοντα ποιμένα· καὶ
on them, because they were as sheep not having a shepherd. And
35 ἤρξατο διδάσκειν αὐτοὺς πολλά. καὶ ἤδη ὥρας πολλῆς
He began to teach them many things. And now an hour a much
γενομένης, προσελθόντες αὐτῷ οἱ μαθηταὶ αὐτοῦ λέγουσιν
occurring drawing near to Him the disciples of Him said,
36 ὅτι Ἔρημός ἐστιν ὁ τόπος, καὶ ἤδη ὥρα πολλή· ἀπόλυσον
— desert is The place, and now a hour much. Send away
αὐτούς, ἵνα ἀπελθόντες εἰς τοὺς κύκλῳ ἀγροὺς καὶ κώμας
them, that going away to the surrounding fields and villages
ἀγοράσωσιν ἑαυτοῖς ἄρτους. τί γὰρ φάγωσιν οὐκ ἔχουσιν.
they may buy for themselves bread, what For they may eat not they have.
37 ὁ δὲ ἀποκριθεὶς εἶπεν αὐτοῖς, Δότε αὐτοῖς ὑμεῖς φαγεῖν. καὶ
He But answering said to them, Give them you to eat. And
λέγουσιν αὐτῷ, Ἀπελθόντες ἀγοράσωμεν διακοσίων δηνα-
they say to Him, Having gone, should we buy two hundred de-
38 ρίων ἄρτους, καὶ δῶμεν αὐτοῖς φαγεῖν; ὁ δὲ λέγει αὐτοῖς,
narii of bread, and give them to eat? He And says to them,
Πόσους ἄρτους ἔχετε; ὑπάγετε καὶ ἴδετε. καὶ γνόντες
How many loaves do you have? Go and see. And knowing
39 λέγουσι, Πέντε, καὶ δύο ἰχθύας. καὶ ἐπέταξεν αὐτοῖς ἀνα-
they say, Five, and two fish. And He ordered them to
κλῖναι πάντας συμπόσια συμπόσια ἐπὶ τῷ χλωρῷ χόρτῳ.
recline all, companies (by) companies on the green grass.
40 καὶ ἀνέπεσον πρασιαὶ πρασιαί, ἀνὰ ἑκατὸν καὶ ἀνὰ πεντή-
And they sat group (by) group by hundred and by fifty.

[41]And taking the five loaves and the two fish, looking up to Heaven, He blessed, and broke the loaves, and gave to His disciples, that they might set before them. And He divided the two fish to all. [42]And all ate, and were satisfied. [43]And they took up twelve handbaskets full *of* fragments; also from the fish. [44]And those eating were about five thousand men.

[45]And at once He constrained His disciples to enter into the boat, and to go before to the other side, to Bethsaida, until He should dismiss the crowd. [46]And taking leave *of* them, He went away to the mountain to pray. [47]And *it* becoming evening, the boat was in *the* middle of the sea, and He alone on the land. [48]And He saw them being distressed in the rowing, for the wind was contrary to them. And *it was* about the fourth watch of the night *when* He came toward them, walking on the sea. And *He* willed to go by them. [49]But seeing Him walking on the sea, they thought *it* to be a ghost. And *they* cried out. [50]For all saw Him, and were troubled. And immediately He spoke to them and said to them, Have courage. I AM! Do not fear. [51]And He went up to them into the boat, and the wind was cut off. And they were amazed and marveled. [52]For they did not understand *the miracle* of the loaves; for their hearts were hardened.

[53]And crossing over, they came into the land of Gennesaret, and drew to shore. [54]And they coming out of the boat, at once knowing Him, [55]they ran around all that neighborhood. *And* they began to carry about those having illness on cots *to* where they heard that He is there. [56]And wherever He

41 κοντα. καὶ λαβὼν τοὺς πέντε ἄρτους καὶ τοὺς δύο ἰχθύας,
And taking the five loaves and the two fish,
ἀναβλέψας εἰς τὸν οὐρανόν, εὐλόγησε, καὶ κατέκλασε τοὺς
looking up to — Heaven, He blessed, and broke the
ἄρτους, καὶ ἐδίδου τοῖς μαθηταῖς αὐτοῦ ἵνα παραθῶσιν
loaves, and gave to the disciples of Him, that they may set before
42 αὐτοῖς· καὶ τοὺς δύο ἰχθύας ἐμέρισε πᾶσι. καὶ ἔφαγον πάντες,
them. And the two fish He divided to all. And ate all,
43 καὶ ἐχορτάσθησαν· καὶ ἦραν κλασμάτων δώδεκα κοφίνους
and were satisfied. And they took fragments, twelve handbaskets
44 πλήρεις, καὶ ἀπὸ τῶν ἰχθύων. καὶ ἦσαν οἱ φαγόντες τοὺς
full, and from the fish. And were the (ones) eating the
ἄρτους ὡσεὶ πεντακισχίλιοι ἄνδρες.
loaves about five thousand men.

45 Καὶ εὐθέως ἠνάγκασε τοὺς μαθητὰς αὐτοῦ ἐμβῆναι εἰς τὸ
And at once He constrained the disciples of Him to enter into the
πλοῖον, καὶ προάγειν εἰς τὸ πέραν πρὸς Βηθσαϊδά, ἕως
boat, and to go before to the other side, to Bethsaida, until
46 αὐτὸς ἀπολύσῃ τὸν ὄχλον. καὶ ἀποταξάμενος αὐτοῖς,
He should dismiss the crowd. And taking leave (of) them,
47 ἀπῆλθεν εἰς τὸ ὄρος προσεύξασθαι. καὶ ὀψίας γενομένης,
He went away to the mountain to pray. And evening occurring,
ἦν τὸ πλοῖον ἐν μέσῳ τῆς θαλάσσης, καὶ αὐτὸς μόνος ἐπὶ τῆς
was the boat in (the) midst of the sea, and He alone on the
48 γῆς. καὶ εἶδεν αὐτοὺς βασανιζομένους ἐν τῷ ἐλαύνειν, ἦν
land. And He saw them being distressed in the row(ing), was
γὰρ ὁ ἄνεμος ἐναντίος αὐτοῖς, καὶ περὶ τετάρτην φυλακὴν
for the wind contrary to them, and about (the) fourth watch
τῆς νυκτὸς ἔρχεται πρὸς αὐτούς, περιπατῶν ἐπὶ τῆς
of the night He comes toward them, walking on the
49 θαλάσσης· καὶ ἤθελε παρελθεῖν αὐτούς. οἱ δέ, ἰδόντες αὐτὸν
sea; and willed to go by them. they But, seeing Him
περιπατοῦντα ἐπὶ τῆς θαλάσσης, ἔδοξαν φάντασμα εἶναι,
walking on the sea, thought a ghost (it) to be,
50 καὶ ἀνέκραξαν· πάντες γὰρ αὐτὸν εἶδον, καὶ ἐταράχθησαν.
and cried out. all For Him saw, and were troubled.
καὶ εὐθέως ἐλάλησε μετ᾽ αὐτῶν, καὶ λέγει αὐτοῖς, Θαρσεῖτε·
And immediately He spoke with them, and says to them, Have courage,
51 ἐγώ εἰμι, μὴ φοβεῖσθε. καὶ ἀνέβη πρὸς αὐτοὺς εἰς τὸ πλοῖον,
I AM! Do not fear. And He went up to them into the boat,
καὶ ἐκόπασεν ὁ ἄνεμος· καὶ λίαν ἐκ περισσοῦ ἐν ἑαυτοῖς
and was cut the wind. And exceedingly beyond measure in themselves
52 ἐξίσταντο, καὶ ἐθαύμαζον. οὐ γὰρ συνῆκαν ἐπὶ τοῖς ἄρτοις·
they were amazed, and marveled. not For they understood by the loaves,
ἦν γὰρ ἡ καρδία αὐτῶν πεπωρωμένη.
was for the hearts of them hardened.

53 Καὶ διαπεράσαντες ἦλθον ἐπὶ τὴν γῆν Γεννησαρέτ, καὶ
And crossing over they came onto the land of Gennesaret, and
54 προσωρμίσθησαν. καὶ ἐξελθόντων αὐτῶν ἐκ τοῦ πλοίου,
drew to shore. And coming out they out of the boat,
55 εὐθέως ἐπιγνόντες αὐτόν, περιδραμόντες ὅλην τὴν περίχω-
at once knowing Him they ran around all — neighborhood
ρον ἐκείνην, ἤρξαντο ἐπὶ τοῖς κραββάτοις τοὺς κακῶς
that, they began on the cots those illness
56 ἔχοντας περιφέρειν, ὅπου ἤκουον ὅτι ἐκεῖ ἐστι. καὶ ὅπου ἂν
having to carry about, where they heard that there He is. And wherever

went into villages or cities or field, they laid the ailing *ones* in the markets, and begged Him that if even they may touch the fringe of His garment. And as many as touched Him were healed.

CHAPTER 7

[1]And the Pharisees were assembled to Him, also some of the scribes, coming from Jerusalem. [2]And seeing some of His disciples eating bread with unclean hands, that is unwashed *hands*, they found fault. [3]For the Pharisees and all the Jews do not eat unless they wash the hands with *the* fist, holding the tradition of the elders. [4]And *coming* from the market, they do not eat unless they wash themselves. And there are many other things which they received to hold: washings of cups, and of utensils, and of bronze vessels, and couches. [5]Then the Pharisees and scribes questioned Him: Why do your disciples not walk according to the tradition of the elders, but eat bread with unwashed hands? [6]And answering He said to them, Well did Isaiah prophesy concerning you, hypocrites; as it has been written, "This people honors Me with the lips, but their heart is far away from Me; [7]and in vain they worship Me, teaching *as* doctrines *the* commandments of men." [8]For forsaking the commandment of God, you hold the tradition of men: washings of utensils and cups, and many other such like things you do. [9]And He said to them, Do you do well to set aside the commandment of God so that you may keep your tradition? [10]For Moses said, "Honor your father and your mother," and, "The *one* speaking evil of father or mother, let him expire by death." [11]But you say, If a man says to *his*

εἰσεπορεύετο εἰς κώμας ἢ πόλεις ἢ ἀγρούς, ἐν ταῖς ἀγοραῖς
He entered into villages or cities or fields, in the markets
ἐτίθουν τοὺς ἀσθενοῦντας, καὶ παρεκάλουν αὐτὸν ἵνα κἂν
they laid the ailing (ones), and begged Him that if even
τοῦ κρασπέδου τοῦ ἱματίου αὐτοῦ ἅψωνται· καὶ ὅσοι ἂν
the fringe of the garment of Him they may touch; and as many as
ἥπτοντο αὐτοῦ ἐσῴζοντο.
touched Him were healed.

CHAPTER 7

1 Καὶ συνάγονται πρὸς αὐτὸν οἱ Φαρισαῖοι, καί τινες τῶν
And were assembled to Him the Pharisees, and some of the
2 γραμματέων, ἐλθόντες ἀπὸ Ἱεροσολύμων· καὶ ἰδόντες τινὰς
scribes, coming from Jerusalem. And seeing some
τῶν μαθητῶν αὐτοῦ κοιναῖς χερσί, τοῦτ᾽ ἔστιν ἀνίπτοις,
of the disciples of Him with unclean hands, that is unwashed,
3 ἐσθίοντας ἄρτους ἐμέμψαντο. οἱ γὰρ Φαρισαῖοι καὶ πάντες
eating bread, they found fault. the For Pharisees and all
οἱ Ἰουδαῖοι, ἐὰν μὴ πυγμῇ νίψωνται τὰς χεῖρας, οὐκ
the Jews unless with (the) fist they wash the hands, not
ἐσθίουσι, κρατοῦντες τὴν παράδοσιν τῶν πρεσβυτέρων·
do they eat, holding the tradition of the elders.
4 καὶ ἀπὸ ἀγορᾶς, ἐὰν μὴ βαπτίσωνται, οὐκ ἐσθίουσι· καὶ
And from market unless they wash themselves, not they eat, and
ἄλλα πολλά ἐστιν ἃ παρέλαβον κρατεῖν, βαπτισμοὺς
other things many there are which they received to hold, washings
5 ποτηρίων καὶ ξεστῶν καὶ χαλκίων καὶ κλινῶν. ἔπειτα
of cups and of utensils and of bronze vessels and couches. Then
ἐπερωτῶσιν αὐτὸν οἱ Φαρισαῖοι καὶ οἱ γραμματεῖς, Διατί οἱ
question Him the Pharisees and the scribes, Why the
μαθηταί σου οὐ περιπατοῦσι κατὰ τὴν παράδοσιν τῶν
disciples of you not walk according to the tradition of the
πρεσβυτέρων, ἀλλὰ ἀνίπτοις χερσὶν ἐσθίουσι τὸν ἄρτον;
elders, but with unwashed hands eat the bread?
6 ὁ δὲ ἀποκριθεὶς εἶπεν αὐτοῖς ὅτι Καλῶς προεφήτευσεν
He And answering said to them, – Well prophesied
Ἡσαΐας περὶ ὑμῶν τῶν ὑποκριτῶν, ὡς γέγραπται, Οὗτος ὁ
Isaiah concerning you, – hypocrites, as it has been written, This
λαὸς τοῖς χείλεσί με τιμᾷ, ἡ δὲ καρδία αὐτῶν πόρρω ἀπέχει
people with the lips Me honors, the but heart of them far is away
7 ἀπ᾽ ἐμοῦ. μάτην δὲ σέβονταί με, διδάσκοντες διδασκαλίας
from Me; in vain and they worship Me, teaching (as) teachings
8 ἐντάλματα ἀνθρώπων. ἀφέντες γὰρ τὴν ἐντολὴν τοῦ Θεοῦ,
commandments of men. forsaking For the commandment – of God,
κρατεῖτε τὴν παράδοσιν τῶν ἀνθρώπων, βαπτισμοὺς
you hold the tradition – of men washings
ξεστῶν καὶ ποτηρίων· καὶ ἄλλα παρόμοια τοιαῦτα πολλὰ
of utensils and cups and other like things such many
9 ποιεῖτε. καὶ ἔλεγεν αὐτοῖς, Καλῶς ἀθετεῖτε τὴν ἐντολὴν τοῦ
you do. And He said to them, Well do you set aside the commandment
10 Θεοῦ, ἵνα τὴν παράδοσιν ὑμῶν τηρήσητε. Μωσῆς γὰρ εἶπε,
of God, that the tradition of you you may keep. Moses For said,
Τίμα τὸν πατέρα σου καὶ τὴν μητέρα σου· καί, Ὁ κακολογῶν
Honor the father of you and the mother of you, and, He speaking evil
11 πατέρα ἢ μητέρα θανάτῳ τελευτάτω· ὑμεῖς δὲ λέγετε, Ἐὰν
of father or mother by death let him end. you But say, If

father or mother, Corban, which is, A gift—whatever you may profit by me. [12] And you no longer allow him to do anything for his father or his mother, [13] making the word of God of no effect by your tradition which you delivered. And many such like things you do.

[14] And calling all the crowd near, He said to them, All hear and understand Me. [15] There is nothing from outside the man which entering into him is able to defile *him.* But the things going out from him, those are the things defiling the man. [16] If anyone has an ear to hear, let him hear.

[17] And when He entered into a house from the crowd, His disciples questioned Him about the parable. [18] And He said to them, Are you also so undiscerning? Do you not perceive that everything that enters from the outside into the man is not able to defile him? [19] *This is* because it does not enter into his heart, but into the belly, and goes out into the wastebowl, purging all foods. [20] And He said, That passing out of the man, that defiles the man. [21] For from within, out of the heart of men, pass out the evil thoughts, adulteries, fornications, murders, [22] thefts, greedy desires, iniquities, deceit, lustful desires, a wicked eye, blasphemy, pride, foolishness—[23] all these evil things pass out from within and defile the man.

[24] And rising up from there, He went away into the borders of Tyre and Sidon. And entering into the house, He desired no one to know, but He could not be hidden. [25] For hearing about Him, a woman whose daughter had an unclean spirit came up *and* fell down at His feet.

[26] And the woman was a Greek, a Syro-phoenician by

εἴπῃ ἄνθρωπος τῷ πατρὶ ἢ τῇ μητρί, Κορβᾶν, ὅ ἐστι,
says a man to the father or to the mother, Corban—which is,
12 δῶρον, ὃ ἐὰν ἐξ ἐμοῦ ὠφεληθῇς· καὶ οὐκέτι ἀφίετε αὐτὸν
A gift — whatever by me you might profit;and no longer you allow him
13 οὐδὲν ποιῆσαι τῷ πατρὶ αὐτοῦ ἢ τῇ μητρὶ αὐτοῦ, ἀκυ-
nothing to do for the father of him or the mother of him, making
ροῦντες τὸν λόγον τοῦ Θεοῦ τῇ παραδόσει ὑμῶν ᾗ παρεδώ-
void the word — of God by the tradition of you which you
14 κατε· καὶ παρόμοια τοιαῦτα πολλὰ ποιεῖτε. καὶ προσκαλε-
delivered. And like things such many you do. And calling near
σάμενος πάντα τὸν ὄχλον, ἔλεγεν αὐτοῖς, Ἀκούετέ μου
(Him) all the crowd, He said to them, Hear Me
15 πάντες, καὶ συνίετε. οὐδέν ἐστιν ἔξωθεν τοῦ ἀνθρώπου
all, and understand. nothing There is from outside the man
εἰσπορευόμενον εἰς αὐτόν, ὃ δύναται αὐτὸν κοινῶσαι· ἀλλὰ
entering into him which is able him to profane; but
τὰ ἐκπορευόμενα ἀπ᾽ αὐτοῦ, ἐκεῖνά ἐστι τὰ κοινοῦντα τὸν
the things going out from him, those are the things profaning the
16 ἄνθρωπον. εἴ τις ἔχει ὦτα ἀκούειν ἀκουέτω. καὶ ὅτε εἰσῆλθεν
17 man. If anyone has ear to hear, let him hear. And when He entered
εἰς οἶκον ἀπὸ τοῦ ὄχλου, ἐπηρώτων αὐτὸν οἱ μαθηταὶ
into a house from the crowd, questioned Him the disciples
18 αὐτοῦ περὶ τῆς παραβολῆς. καὶ λέγει αὐτοῖς, Οὕτω καὶ
of Him about the parable. And He says to them, Thus also
ὑμεῖς ἀσύνετοί ἐστε; οὐ νοεῖτε ὅτι πᾶν τὸ ἔξωθεν εἰσπορευό-
you undiscerning are? Not perceive you that all that from outside enter-
19 μενον εἰς τὸν ἄνθρωπον οὐ δύναται αὐτὸν κοινῶσαι, ὅτι
ing into man not is able him to profane because
οὐκ εἰσπορεύεται αὐτοῦ εἰς τὴν καρδίαν, ἀλλ᾽ εἰς τὴν
not it does enter of him into the heart, but into the
κοιλίαν· καὶ εἰς τὸν ἀφεδρῶνα ἐκπορεύεται, καθαρίζον
belly, and into the waste-bowl goes out, purging
20 πάντα τὰ βρώματα. ἔλεγε δὲ ὅτι Τὸ ἐκ τοῦ ἀνθρώπου
all the foods? He said And — That out of the man
21 ἐκπορευόμενον, ἐκεῖνο κοινοῖ τὸν ἄνθρωπον. ἔσωθεν γάρ,
passing out that profanes the man. from within For,
ἐκ τῆς καρδίας τῶν ἀνθρώπων, οἱ διαλογισμοὶ οἱ κακοὶ
out of the heart — of men the thoughts — evil
22 ἐκπορεύονται, μοιχεῖαι, πορνεῖαι, φόνοι, κλοπαί, πλεονεξίαι,
pass out, adulteries, fornications, murders, thefts, greedy desires,
πονηρίαι, δόλος, ἀσέλγεια, ὀφθαλμὸς πονηρός, βλασφημία,
iniquities, deceit, lustful desires, an eye wicked, blasphemy,
23 ὑπερηφανία, ἀφροσύνη· πάντα ταῦτα τὰ πονηρὰ ἔσωθεν
pride, foolishness— all these — evil things from within
ἐκπορεύεται, καὶ κοινοῖ τὸν ἄνθρωπον.
pass out and profane the man.
24 Καὶ ἐκεῖθεν ἀναστὰς ἀπῆλθεν εἰς τὰ μεθόρια Τύρου καὶ
And from there rising up He went away into the borders of Tyre and
Σιδῶνος. καὶ εἰσελθὼν εἰς τὴν οἰκίαν, οὐδένα ἤθελε γνῶναι,
Sidon. And entering into the house, no one He desired to know,
25 καὶ οὐκ ἠδυνήθη λαθεῖν. ἀκούσασα γὰρ γυνὴ περὶ αὐτοῦ,
But not He could be hidden. hearing For a woman about Him,
ἧς εἶχε τὸ θυγάτριον αὐτῆς πνεῦμα ἀκάθαρτον, ἐλθοῦσα
of whom had the daughter of her a spirit unclean, coming
26 προσέπεσε πρὸς τοὺς πόδας αὐτοῦ· ἦν δὲ ἡ γυνὴ Ἑλληνίς,
fell down to the feet of Him;was and the woman a Greek,

race. And she asked that He would expel the demon from her daughter. [27]And Jesus said to her, First allow the children to be satisfied; for it is not good to take the children's bread and to throw *it* to the dogs. [28]But she answered and said to Him, Yes, Lord; for even the dogs under the table eat from the crumbs of the children. [29]And He said to her, Because of this word, go. The demon has gone out from your daughter.

[30]And going away to her house, she found the demon had gone out, and *her* daughter was laid on the couch.

[31]And again going out from the borders of Tyre and Sidon, He came to the sea of Galilee, in the midst of the borders of *the* Decapolis. [32]And they brought a deaf one to Him, hardly speaking. And they begged Him, that He put *His* hand on him. [33]And having taken him away, apart from the crowd, He put His fingers into his ears; and spitting, He touched his tongue; [34]and looking up into Heaven, He groaned, and said to him, Ephphatha! which is, Be opened! [35]And instantly his ears were opened, and the bond of his tongue was loosened, and he spoke correctly. [36]And He ordered them, that they should tell no one. But as much as He ordered them, much more abundantly they proclaimed. [37]And they were most exceedingly amazed, saying, He has done all things well. He makes even the deaf to hear, and the dumb to speak.

Συροφοίνισσα τῷ γένει· καὶ ἠρώτα αὐτὸν ἵνα τὸ δαιμόνιον
a Syrophoenician – by race. And she asked Him that the demon
27 ἐκβάλλῃ ἐκ τῆς θυγατρὸς αὐτῆς. ὁ δὲ Ἰησοῦς εἶπεν αὐτῇ,
He would expel from the daughter of her. – And Jesus said to her,
Ἄφες πρῶτον χορτασθῆναι τὰ τέκνα· οὐ γὰρ καλόν ἐστι
Allow first to be satisfied the children; not for good is
28 λαβεῖν τὸν ἄρτον τῶν τέκνων καὶ βαλεῖν τοις κυναρίοις. ἡ
to take the bread of the children and to throw to the dogs. she
δὲ ἀπεκρίθη καὶ λέγει αὐτῷ, Ναί, Κύριε· καὶ γὰρ τὰ κυνάρια
And answered and says to Him, Yes, Lord; even for the dogs
ὑποκάτω τῆς τραπέζης ἐσθίει ἀπὸ τῶν ψιχίων τῶν παιδίων.
under the table eat from the crumbs of the children.
29 καὶ εἶπεν αὐτῇ, Διὰ τοῦτον τὸν λόγον ὕπαγε· ἐξελήλυθε τὸ
And He said to her, Because of this – word, go; has gone out the
30 δαιμόνιον ἐκ τῆς θυγατρός σου. καὶ ἀπελθοῦσα εἰς τὸν οἶκον
demon – from the daughter of you. And going away to the house
αὐτῆς, εὗρε τὸ δαιμόνιον ἐξεληλυθός, καὶ τὴν θυγατέρα
of her, she found the demon had gone out, and the daughter
βεβλημένην ἐπὶ τῆς κλίνης.
was laid on the couch.

31 Καὶ πάλιν ἐξελθὼν ἐκ τῶν ὁρίων Τύρου καὶ Σιδῶνος, ἦλθε
And again going out from the borders of Tyre and Sidon, He came
πρὸς τὴν θάλασσαν τῆς Γαλιλαίας, ἀνὰ μέσον τῶν ὁρίων
to the sea – of Galilee in the midst of the borders
32 Δεκαπόλεως. καὶ φέρουσιν αὐτῷ κωφὸν μογιλάλον, καὶ
of (the) Decapolis. And they bring to Him a deaf one, hardly speaking, and
33 παρακαλοῦσιν αὐτὸν ἵνα ἐπιθῇ αὐτῷ τὴν χεῖρα. καὶ ἀπολα-
they begged Him that He put on him the hand. And taking
βόμενος αὐτὸν ἀπὸ τοῦ ὄχλου κατ' ἰδίαν, ἔβαλε τοὺς δα-
away him from the crowd, privately He put the
κτύλους αὐτοῦ εἰς τὰ ὦτα αὐτοῦ, καὶ πτύσας ἥψατο τῆς
fingers of Him into the ears of him, and spitting He touched the
34 γλώσσης αὐτοῦ, καὶ ἀναβλέψας εἰς τὸν οὐρανόν, ἐστέναξε,
tongue of him, and looking up into – Heaven, He groaned,
35 καὶ λέγει αὐτῷ, Ἐφφαθά, ὅ ἐστι, Διανοίχθητι. καὶ εὐθέως
and says to him, Ephphatha, which is, Be opened! And instantly
διηνοίχθησαν αὐτοῦ αἱ ἀκοαί· καὶ ἐλύθη ὁ δεσμὸς τῆς γλώσ-
were opened of him the hearing, and was loosened the bond of the tongue
36 σης αὐτοῦ, καὶ ἐλάλει ὀρθῶς. καὶ διεστείλατο αὐτοῖς ἵνα
of him, and He spoke correctly. And He ordered them that
μηδενὶ εἴπωσιν· ὅσον δὲ αὐτὸς αὐτοῖς διεστέλλετο, μᾶλλον
no one they should tell; as much as but He them ordered, much
37 περισσότερον ἐκήρυσσον. καὶ ὑπερπερισσῶς ἐξεπλήσσοντο,
more abundantly they proclaimed. And most exceedingly they were amazed,
λέγοντες, Καλῶς πάντα πεποίηκε· καὶ τοὺς κωφοὺς ποιεῖ
saying, Well all things He has done, even the deaf He makes
ἀκούειν, καὶ τοὺς ἀλάλους λαλεῖν.
to hear, and the dumb to speak.

CHAPTER 8

[1]The crowd being very great in those days, and not having anything they may eat, Jesus calling His disciples near, He said to them, [2]I have pity on the crowd,

1 Ἐν ἐκείναις ταῖς ἡμέραις, παμπόλλου ὄχλου ὄντος, καὶ
In those – days very great the crowd being, and
μὴ ἐχόντων τί φάγωσι, προσκαλεσάμενος ὁ Ἰησοῦς τοὺς
not having anything they may eat, calling near – Jesus the
2 μαθητὰς αὐτοῦ λέγει αὐτοῖς, Σπλαγχνίζομαι ἐπὶ τὸν ὄχλον·
disciples of Him, He says to them, I have pity on the crowd

because now three days they remain with Me, and they do not have what they may eat. [3]And if I send them away fasting to their house, they will faint in the way, for some of them come from afar. [4]And His disciples answered Him, From where will anyone here be able to satisfy these *with* bread on a desert? [5]And He asked them, How many loaves do you have. And they said, Seven. [6]And He ordered the crowd to recline on the ground. And taking the seven loaves, giving thanks, He broke and gave to His disciples, that they might serve. And they served the crowd. [7]And they had a few fish. And blessing, He said *for* these also to be served. [8]And they ate, and were satisfied. And *they* took up over and above seven lunch-baskets *of* fragments. [9]And those eating were about four thousand. And He sent them away. [10]And at once entering into the boat with His disciples, He came into the region of Dalmanutha.

[11]And the Pharisees went out and began to argue with Him, seeking from Him a sign from Heaven, tempting Him. [12]And groaning in His spirit, He said, Why does this generation seek a sign? Truly I say to you, *As* if this generation will be given a sign! [13]And leaving them, again entering into the boat, He went away to the other side.

[14]And the disciples forgot to take loaves. And they did not have *any* with them, except one loaf in the boat. [15]And He charged them, saying, See! Beware of the leaven of the Pharisees, and of the leaven of Herod. [16]And they reasoned with one another, saying, We have no loaves. [17]And knowing, Jesus said to them, Why do you reason because you have no loaves? Do you not yet perceive nor realize? Have you still hardened your

ὅτι ἤδη ἡμέρας τρεῖς προσμένουσί μοι, καὶ οὐκ ἔχουσι τί
because now days three they continue with Me, and not have what
3 φάγωσι· καὶ ἐὰν ἀπολύσω αὐτοὺς νήστεις εἰς οἶκον αὐτῶν,
they may eat; and if I send away them fasting to (the) house of them,
ἐκλυθήσονται ἐν τῇ ὁδῷ· τινὲς γὰρ αὐτῶν μακρόθεν ἥκασι.
they will faint in the way; some for of them from afar are come.
4 καὶ ἀπεκρίθησαν αὐτῷ οἱ μαθηταὶ αὐτοῦ, Πόθεν τούτους
And answered Him the disciples of Him, From where these
5 δυνήσεταί τις ὧδε χορτάσαι ἄρτων ἐπ' ἐρημίας; καὶ
will be able anyone here to satisfy (with) bread on a desert? And
ἐπηρώτα αὐτούς, Πόσους ἔχετε ἄρτους; οἱ δὲ εἶπον, Ἑπτά.
He asked them, How many have you loaves? they And said, Seven.
6 καὶ παρήγγειλε τῷ ὄχλῳ ἀναπεσεῖν ἐπὶ τῆς γῆς· καὶ λαβὼν
And He ordered the crowd to recline on the ground. And taking
τοὺς ἑπτὰ ἄρτους, εὐχαριστήσας ἔκλασε καὶ ἐδίδου τοῖς
the seven loaves, giving thanks, He broke and gave to the
μαθηταῖς αὐτοῦ, ἵνα παραθῶσι· καὶ παρέθηκαν τῷ ὄχλῳ.
disciples of Him, that they may serve. And they served the crowd
7 καὶ εἶχον ἰχθύδια ὀλίγα· καὶ εὐλογήσας εἶπε παραθεῖναι καὶ
And they had fish a few. And blessing He said to be served also
8 αὐτά. ἔφαγον δέ, καὶ ἐχορτάσθησαν· καὶ ἦραν περισσεύματα
these. they ate And, and were satisfied, and took up over and above
9 κλασμάτων ἑπτὰ σπυρίδας. ἦσαν δὲ οἱ φαγόντες ὡς
fragments, seven baskets. were And those eating about
10 τετρακισχίλιοι· καὶ ἀπέλυσεν αὐτούς. καὶ εὐθέως ἐμβὰς εἰς
four thousand. And He sent away them. And at once entering into
τὸ πλοῖον μετὰ τῶν μαθητῶν αὐτοῦ, ἦλθεν εἰς τὰ μέρη
the boat with the disciples of Him, He came into the region
Δαλμανουθά.
of Dalmanutha.

11 Καὶ ἐξῆλθον οἱ Φαρισαῖοι, καὶ ἤρξαντο συζητεῖν αὐτῷ,
And went out the Pharisees and began to argue with Him,
ζητοῦντες παρ' αὐτοῦ σημεῖον ἀπὸ τοῦ οὐρανοῦ, πειρά-
seeking from Him a sign from — Heaven, tempting
12 ζοντες αὐτόν. καὶ ἀναστενάξας τῷ πνεύματι αὐτοῦ λέγει,
Him. And groaning in the spirit of Him, He says,
Τί ἡ γενεὰ αὕτη σημεῖον ἐπιζητεῖ; ἀμὴν λέγω ὑμῖν, εἰ
Why — generation this a sign seeks? Truly, I say to you, (As) if
13 δοθήσεται τῇ γενεᾷ ταύτῃ σημεῖον. καὶ ἀφεὶς αὐτούς, ἐμβὰς
will be given — generation this a sign! And leaving them, entering
πάλιν εἰς τὸ πλοῖον, ἀπῆλθεν εἰς τὸ πέραν.
again into the boat, He went away to the other side.

14 Καὶ ἐπελάθοντο οἱ μαθηταὶ λαβεῖν ἄρτους, καὶ εἰ μὴ ἕνα
And forgot the disciples to take loaves, and except one
15 ἄρτον οὐκ εἶχον μεθ' ἑαυτῶν ἐν τῷ πλοίῳ. καὶ διεστέλλετο
loaf not they had with them in the boat. And He charged
αὐτοῖς, λέγων, Ὁρᾶτε, βλέπετε ἀπὸ τῆς ζύμης τῶν
them, saying, See, Look out! From the leaven of the
16 Φαρισαίων καὶ τῆς ζύμης Ἡρώδου. καὶ διελογίζοντο πρὸς
Pharisees, and of the leaven of Herod. And they reasoned with
17 ἀλλήλους, λέγοντες ὅτι Ἄρτους οὐκ ἔχομεν. καὶ γνοὺς ὁ
one another, saying, Loaves not we have. And knowing —
Ἰησοῦς λέγει αὐτοῖς, Τί διαλογίζεσθε ὅτι ἄρτους οὐκ ἔχετε;
Jesus says to them, Why do you reason because loaves not you have?
οὔπω νοεῖτε, οὐδὲ συνίετε; ἔτι πεπωρωμένην ἔχετε τὴν
not yet Do you perceive nor realize? yet hardened have you the

heart? [18]Having eyes, do you not see? And having ears, do you not hear? And do you not remember? [19]When I broke the five loaves to the five thousand, how many handbaskets full of fragments did you take up? They said to Him, Twelve. [20]And when the seven to the four thousand, how many lunch-baskets did you take up *with the* fillings of fragments? And they said, Seven. [21]And He said to them, How do you not understand?

[22]And He came to Bethsaida. And they carried a blind one to Him, and begged Him that He would touch him. [23]And laying hold of the hand of the blind one, He led him forth outside the village. And spitting into his eyes, laying *His* hands on him, He asked him if he saw anything. [24]And looking, he said, I see men as trees walking. [25]Then He again placed *His* hands on his eyes, and made him look up. And he was restored, and saw all clearly. [26]And He sent him to his house, saying, You may not go into the village, nor may tell anyone in the village.

[27]And Jesus and His disciples went out to the villages of Caesarea of Philip. And in the way He questioned His disciples, saying to them, Whom do men say Me to be? [28]And they answered, John the Baptist; and others *say* Elijah; but others, one of the prophets. [29]And He said to them, And you, whom do you say Me to be? And answering Peter said to Him, You are the Christ. [30]And He warned them that they may tell no one about Him. [31]And He began to teach them that it is necessary for the Son of man to suffer many things, and to be rejected of the elders and chief priests and

18 καρδίαν ὑμῶν; ὀφθαλμοὺς ἔχοντες οὐ βλέπετε; καὶ ὦτα
heart of you? eyes having, not do you see? And ears
19 ἔχοντες οὐκ ἀκούετε; καὶ οὐ μνημονεύετε; ὅτε τοὺς πέντε
having, not do you hear? And not do you remember when the five
ἄρτους ἔκλασα εἰς τοὺς πεντακισχιλίους, πόσους κοφίνους
loaves I broke to the five thousand, how many handbaskets
20 πλήρεις κλασμάτων ἤρατε; λέγουσιν αὐτῷ, Δώδεκα. Ὅτε
full of fragments you took? They say to Him, Twelve. when
δὲ τοὺς ἑπτὰ εἰς τοὺς τετρακισχιλίους, πόσων σπυρίδων
And the seven to the four thousand, of how many baskets
21 πληρώματα κλασμάτων ἤρατε; οἱ δὲ εἶπον, Ἑπτά. καὶ
(the) fillings of fragments you took? they And said, Seven. And
ἔλεγεν αὐτοῖς, Πῶς οὐ συνίετε;
He said to them, How not do you understand?
22 Καὶ ἔρχεται εἰς Βηθσαϊδά. καὶ φέρουσιν αὐτῷ τυφλόν,
And He comes to Bethsaida. And they bear to Him a blind one,
23 καὶ παρακαλοῦσιν αὐτὸν ἵνα αὐτοῦ ἅψηται. καὶ ἐπιλαβό-
and beg Him that him He would touch. And laying
μενος τῆς χειρὸς τοῦ τυφλοῦ, ἐξήγαγεν αὐτὸν ἔξω τῆς
hold of the hand of the blind one, He led forth him outside the
κώμης· καὶ πτύσας εἰς τὰ ὄμματα αὐτοῦ, ἐπιθεὶς τὰς χεῖρας
village. And having spit into the eyes of him, having laid the hands
24 αὐτῷ, ἐπηρώτα αὐτὸν εἴ τι βλέπει. καὶ ἀναβλέψας ἔλεγε,
on him, He asked him if anything he sees. And having looked he said,
25 Βλέπω τοὺς ἀνθρώπους ὡς δένδρα περιπατοῦντας. εἶτα
I see — men, as trees walking. Then
πάλιν ἐπέθηκε τὰς χεῖρας ἐπὶ τοὺς ὀφθαλμοὺς αὐτοῦ, καὶ
again He placed the hands upon the eyes of him, and
ἐποίησεν αὐτὸν ἀναβλέψαι. καὶ ἀποκατεστάθη, καὶ ἐνέβλεψε
made him look up. And he was restored, and saw
26 τηλαυγῶς ἅπαντας. καὶ ἀπέστειλεν αὐτὸν εἰς τὸν οἶκον
clearly all And He sent him to the house
αὐτοῦ, λέγων, Μηδὲ εἰς τὴν κώμην εἰσέλθῃς, μηδὲ εἴπῃς
of him, saying, Not into the village you may go in, nor may tell
τινὶ ἐν τῇ κώμῃ.
anyone in the village.
27 Καὶ ἐξῆλθεν ὁ Ἰησοῦς καὶ οἱ μαθηταὶ αὐτοῦ εἰς τὰς
And went out — Jesus and the disciples of Him to the
κώμας Καισαρείας τῆς Φιλίππου· καὶ ἐν τῇ ὁδῷ ἐπηρώτα
villages of Caesarea — of Philip. And in the way He questioned
τοὺς μαθητὰς αὐτοῦ, λέγων αὐτοῖς, Τίνα με λέγουσιν οἱ
the disciples of Him, saying to them, Whom Me say the
28 ἄνθρωποι εἶναι; οἱ δὲ ἀπεκρίθησαν, Ἰωάννην τὸν Βαπτι-
men to be? they And answered John the Baptist;
29 στήν· καὶ ἄλλοι Ἠλίαν, ἄλλοι δὲ ἕνα τῶν προφητῶν. καὶ
and others Elijah; others but, one of the prophets And
αὐτὸς λέγει αὐτοῖς, Ὑμεῖς δὲ τίνα με λέγετε εἶναι; ἀποκριθεὶς
He says to them. you And, whom Me say you to be? answering
30 δὲ ὁ Πέτρος λέγει αὐτῷ, Σὺ εἶ ὁ Χριστός. καὶ ἐπετίμησεν
And — Peter says to Him, You are the Christ! And He warned
31 αὐτοῖς, ἵνα μηδενὶ λέγωσι περὶ αὐτοῦ. καὶ ἤρξατο διδάσκειν
them, that no one they may tell about Him. And He began to teach
αὐτούς, ὅτι δεῖ τὸν υἱὸν τοῦ ἀνθρώπου πολλὰ παθεῖν, καὶ
them that it behoves the Son — of man many things to suffer, and
ἀποδοκιμασθῆναι ἀπὸ τῶν πρεσβυτέρων καὶ ἀρχιερέων καὶ
to be rejected of the elders and chief priests and

scribes, and to be killed, and after three days to rise again. [32]And He spoke the word openly. And taking Him aside, Peter began to rebuke Him. [33]But turning around and seeing His disciples, He rebuked Peter, saying, Go behind Me, Satan, because you do not mind the things of God, but the things of men.

[34]And calling near the crowd with His disciples, he said to them, Whoever desires to come after Me, let him deny himself and take his cross, and let him follow Me. [35]For whoever desires to save his soul, *he* shall lose it. But whoever shall lose his soul for My sake and the gospel, he shall save it. [36]For what shall it profit a man if he gain the whole world, yet damage his soul? [37]Or what shall a man give *as* an exchange *for* his soul? [38]For whoever may be ashamed of Me and My words in this adulterous and sinful generation, the Son of man will also be ashamed of him when He comes in the glory of His Father, along with the holy angels.

CHAPTER 9

[1]And He said to them, Truly I say to you, There are some standing here who in no way shall taste of death until they see the kingdom of God coming in power.

[2]And after six days Jesus takes along Peter and James and John, and carries them into a high mount apart alone. And He was transfigured before them. [3]And His garments became shining, very white like snow, such as a fuller on earth is not able to whiten. [4]And they saw Elijah with Moses, and they were speaking with

γραμματέων, καὶ ἀποκτανθῆναι, καὶ μετὰ τρεῖς ἡμέρας
scribes, and to be killed, and after three days
32 ἀναστῆναι· καὶ παρρησίᾳ τὸν λόγον ἐλάλει. καὶ προσλαβό-
to rise again. And openly the word He spoke. And taking aside
33 μενος αὐτὸν ὁ Πέτρος ἤρξατο ἐπιτιμᾷν αὐτῷ. ὁ δὲ ἐπιστρα-
Him, — Peter began to rebuke Him. He But turning
φείς, καὶ ἰδὼν τοὺς μαθητὰς αὐτοῦ, ἐπετίμησε τῷ Πέτρῳ,
around and seeing the disciples of Him rebuked — Peter,
λέγων, Ὕπαγε ὀπίσω μου, Σατανᾶ· ὅτι οὐ φρονεῖς τὰ τοῦ
saying, Get behind Me, Satan, because not you mind the things
34 Θεοῦ, ἀλλὰ τὰ τῶν ἀνθρώπων. καὶ προσκαλεσάμενος τὸν
of God, but the things of men. And calling near the
ὄχλον σὺν τοῖς μαθηταῖς αὐτοῦ, εἶπεν αὐτοῖς, Ὅστις θέλει
crowd with the disciples of Him, He said to them, Whoever desires
ὀπίσω μου ἐλθεῖν, ἀπαρνησάσθω ἑαυτόν, καὶ ἀράτω τὸν
after Me to come, let him deny himself and take the
35 σταυρὸν αὐτοῦ, καὶ ἀκολουθείτω μοι. ὃς γὰρ ἂν θέλῃ τὴν
cross of him, and let him follow Me. who For ever desires the
ψυχὴν αὐτοῦ σῶσαι, ἀπολέσει αὐτήν· ὃς δ' ἂν ἀπολέσῃ τὴν
soul of him to save, shall lose it: who but ever may lose the
ψυχὴν αὐτοῦ ἕνεκεν ἐμοῦ καὶ τοῦ εὐαγγελίου, οὗτος σώσει
soul of him for the sake of Me and the gospel, this one will save
36 αὐτήν. τί γὰρ ὠφελήσει ἄνθρωπον, ἐὰν κερδήσῃ τὸν
it. what For shall it profit a man if he gain the
37 κόσμον ὅλον, καὶ ζημιωθῇ τὴν ψυχὴν αὐτοῦ; ἢ τί δώσει
world whole, yet damage the soul of him. Or what shall give
38 ἄνθρωπος ἀντάλλαγμα τῆς ψυχῆς αὐτοῦ; ὃς γὰρ ἂν ἐπαι-
a man (as) an exchange (for) the soul of him? who For ever may be
σχυνθῇ με καὶ τοὺς ἐμοὺς λόγους ἐν τῇ γενεᾷ ταύτῃ τῇ
ashamed of Me and — My words in — generation this —
μοιχαλίδι καὶ ἁμαρτωλῷ, καὶ ὁ υἱὸς τοῦ ἀνθρώπου ἐπαι-
adulterous and sinful, also the Son — of man will be
σχυνθήσεται αὐτόν, ὅταν ἔλθῃ ἐν τῇ δόξῃ τοῦ πατρὸς
ashamed of him, when He comes in the glory of the Father
αὐτοῦ μετὰ τῶν ἀγγέλων τῶν ἁγίων.
of him, with the angels — holy.

CHAPTER 9

1 καὶ ἔλεγεν αὐτοῖς, Ἀμὴν λέγω ὑμῖν, ὅτι εἰσί τινες τῶν
And He said to them, Truly I say to you, that are some of those
ὧδε ἑστηκότων, οἵτινες οὐ μὴ γεύσωνται θανάτου, ἕως ἂν
here standing who in no way shall taste of death until
ἴδωσι τὴν βασιλείαν τοῦ Θεοῦ ἐληλυθυῖαν ἐν δυνάμει.
they see the kingdom — of God having come in power,
2 Καὶ μεθ' ἡμέρας ἓξ παραλαμβάνει ὁ Ἰησοῦς τὸν Πέτρον
And after days six takes along — Jesus — Peter
καὶ τὸν Ἰάκωβον καὶ τὸν Ἰωάννην, καὶ ἀναφέρει αὐτοὺς
and — James and — John, and carries them
εἰς ὄρος ὑψηλὸν κατ' ἰδίαν μόνους· καὶ μετεμορφώθη ἔμπρο-
into a mount high, privately, alone. And He was transfigured before
3 σθεν αὐτῶν· καὶ τὰ ἱμάτια αὐτοῦ ἐγένετο στίλβοντα, λευκὰ
them. And the garments of Him became shining, white
λίαν ὡς χιών, οἷα γναφεὺς ἐπὶ τῆς γῆς οὐ δύναται λευκᾶναι
very, as snow, such as a fuller on the earth not is able to whiten.
4 καὶ ὤφθη αὐτοῖς Ἠλίας σὺν Μωσεῖ, καὶ ἦσαν συλλαλοῦντε
And was seen by them Elijah with Moses, and they were speaking with

Jesus [5]And answering Peter said to Jesus, Rabbi, it is good *for* us to be here; and, Let us make three tabernacles, one for You, and one for Moses, and one for Elijah. [6]For he did not know what to say, for they were very fearful. [7]And a cloud was overshadowing them, and a voice came out of the cloud, saying, This is My Son, the Beloved; hear Him. [8]And suddenly, looking around, they no longer saw anyone, but Jesus alone with them. [9]And as they were coming down from the mount, He commanded them that they should tell no one what they saw, except when the Son of man should rise from *the* dead. [10]And they held the word to themselves, debating what *it* is to rise from *the* dead.

[11]And they asked Him, saying, Do *not* the scribes say that Elijah must come first? [12]And answering He said to them, Indeed Elijah coming first restores all things, and how it has been written of the Son of man that He suffer many things, and be despised. [13]But I say to you, Elijah also has come, and they did to him whatever they desired, even as it has been written of him.

[14]And coming to the disciples, He saw a great crowd around them, and scribes arguing with them. [15]And at once all the crowd seeing Him were greatly amazed. And running up, *they* greeted Him. [16]And He questioned the scribes, What are you arguing with them? [17]And one answered out of the crowd, saying, Teacher, I brought my son to You, having a dumb spirit. [18]and wherever it seizes him, it dashes him, and he foams and gnashes his teeth. And he wastes away. And I told Your disciples, that they might expel it. And they

5 τῷ Ἰησοῦ. καὶ ἀποκριθεὶς ὁ Πέτρος λέγει τῷ Ἰησοῦ, Ῥαββί,
— Jesus. And answering — Peter says — to Jesus, Rabbi,
καλόν ἐστιν ἡμᾶς ὧδε εἶναι· καὶ ποιήσωμεν σκηνὰς τρεῖς,
good it is us here to be, and let us make tents three,
6 σοὶ μίαν, καὶ Μωσεῖ μίαν, καὶ Ἠλίᾳ μίαν. οὐ γὰρ ᾔδει τί
for You one, and for Moses one , and for Elijah one. not For he knew who
7 λαλήσῃ· ἦσαν γὰρ ἔκφοβοι. καὶ ἐγένετο νεφέλη ἐπισκιάζουσα
to say, they were for very fearful. And was a cloud overshadowing
αὐτοῖς· καὶ ἦλθε φωνὴ ἐκ τῆς νεφέλης, λέγουσα, Οὗτός ἐστιν
them, and came a voice out of the cloud, saying, This is
8 ὁ υἱός μου ὁ ἀγαπητός· αὐτοῦ ἀκούετε. καὶ ἐξάπινα
the Son of Me, the Beloved; Him hear. And suddenly,
περιβλεψάμενοι, οὐκέτι οὐδένα εἶδον, ἀλλὰ τὸν Ἰησοῦν
looking around, no longer no one they saw, but — Jesus
μόνον μεθ' ἑαυτῶν.
alone with themselves.
9 Καταβαινόντων δὲ αὐτῶν ἀπὸ τοῦ ὄρους, διεστείλατο
as were descending And they from the mountain, He commanded
αὐτοῖς ἵνα μηδενὶ διηγήσωνται ἃ εἶδον, εἰ μὴ ὅταν ὁ υἱὸς
them that to no one they should tell what they saw, except when the Son
10 τοῦ ἀνθρώπου ἐκ νεκρῶν ἀναστῇ. καὶ τὸν λόγον ἐκράτησαν
— of man from (the) dead may rise. And the word they held
πρὸς ἑαυτούς, συζητοῦντες τί ἐστι τὸ ἐκ νεκρῶν ἀναστῆναι.
to themselves, debating what is (it) from (the) dead to rise.
11 καὶ ἐπηρώτων αὐτόν, λέγοντες ὅτι Λέγουσιν οἱ γραμματεῖς
And they asked Him, saying, Do (not) say the scribes
12 ὅτι Ἠλίαν δεῖ ἐλθεῖν πρῶτον ; ὁ δὲ ἀποκριθείς, εἶπεν αὐτοῖς,
that Elijah it behoves to come first? He And answering said to them,
Ἠλίας μὲν ἐλθὼν πρῶτον, ἀποκαθιστᾷ πάντα· καὶ πῶς
Elijah indeed having come first restores all things. And how
γέγραπται ἐπὶ τὸν υἱὸν τοῦ ἀνθρώπου, ἵνα πολλὰ πάθῃ
has it been written on the Son — of man, that many things He suffer
13 καὶ ἐξουδενωθῇ. ἀλλὰ λέγω ὑμῖν ὅτι καὶ Ἠλίας ἐλήλυθε,
and be despised. But I say to you, that also Elijah has come,
καὶ ἐποίησαν αὐτῷ ὅσα ἠθέλησαν, καθὼς γέγραπται ἐπ'
and they did to him whatever they desired, even as it has been written of
αὐτόν.
him.
14 Καὶ ἐλθὼν πρὸς τοὺς μαθητάς, εἶδεν ὄχλον πολὺν περὶ
And coming to the disciples, He saw a crowd great around
15 αὐτούς, καὶ γραμματεῖς συζητοῦντας αὐτοῖς. καὶ εὐθέως
them, and scribes arguing with them. And at once
πᾶς ὁ ὄχλος ἰδὼν αὐτὸν ἐξεθαμβήθη, καὶ προστρέχοντες
all the crowd seeing Him were greatly amazed, and running up
16 ἠσπάζοντο αὐτόν. καὶ ἐπηρώτησε τοὺς γραμματεῖς, Τί
greeted Him. And He questioned the scribes, What
17 συζητεῖτε πρὸς αὐτούς ; καὶ ἀποκριθεὶς εἷς ἐκ τοῦ ὄχλου
are you arguing with them? And answered, one out of the crowd,
εἶπε, Διδάσκαλε, ἤνεγκα τὸν υἱόν μου πρός σε, ἔχοντα
said, Teacher, I brought the son of me to You, having
18 πνεῦμα ἄλαλον. καὶ ὅπου ἂν αὐτὸν καταλάβῃ, ῥήσσει
a spirit dumb; and wherever him it seizes, it dashes
αὐτόν· καὶ ἀφρίζει, καὶ τρίζει τοὺς ὀδόντας αὐτοῦ, καὶ
him, and he foams, and gnashes the teeth of him and
ξηραίνεται· καὶ εἶπον τοῖς μαθηταῖς σου ἵνα αὐτὸ ἐκβάλωσι,
he wastes away. And I told the disciples of You that it they might expel,

were not able. [19]And answering them He said, O unbelieving generation! How long will I be with you? Bring him to Me. [20]And they brought him to Him. And seeing Him, the spirit immediately convulsed him. And falling on the ground, he wallowed, foaming. [21]And He questioned his father, How long a time is it while this has happened to him? And he said, From childhood. [22]And often it threw him both into fire and into water, that it might destroy him. But if You are able to do anything, help us, having pity on us. [23]And Jesus said to him, If you are able to believe, all things are possible to those believing. [24]And immediately crying out, the father of the child said with tears, Lord, I believe! Help my unbelief! [25]And seeing that a crowd is running together, Jesus rebuked the unclean spirit, saying, Dumb and deaf spirit, I command you, Come out from him, and you may no more go into him! [26]And crying out, and convulsing him very much, it came out. And he became as if dead, so as many to say that he died. [27]But taking hold of his hand, Jesus raised him up, and he stood up. [28]And He entering into a house, His disciples questioned Him privately, *Why* were we not able to cast it out? [29]And He said, This kind can go out by nothing except by prayer and fasting.

[30]And going forth from there, they passed by through Galilee. And He desired that no one know. [31]For He taught His disciples, and said to them, The Son of man is betrayed into *the* hands of men, and they will kill Him. And being killed, He will rise up the third day. [32]But they did not

19 καὶ οὐκ ἴσχυσαν. ὁ δὲ ἀποκριθεὶς αὐτῷ λέγει, Ὦ γενεὰ
and not they were able. He And answering him says, O generation
ἄπιστος, ἕως πότε πρὸς ὑμᾶς ἔσομαι; ἕως πότε ἀνέξομαι
unbelieving, until when with you will I be? Until when shall I endure
20 ὑμῶν; φέρετε αὐτὸν πρός με. καὶ ἤνεγκαν αὐτὸν πρὸς αὐτόν·
you? Bring him to Me. And they brought him to Him.
καὶ ἰδὼν αὐτόν, εὐθέως τὸ πνεῦμα ἐσπάραξεν αὐτόν· καὶ
And seeing Him, instantly the spirit convulsed him; and
21 πεσὼν ἐπὶ τῆς γῆς, ἐκυλίετο ἀφρίζων. καὶ ἐπηρώτησε τὸν
falling on the ground, he wallowed, foaming. And He questioned the
πατέρα αὐτοῦ, Πόσος χρόνος ἐστίν, ὡς τοῦτο γέγονεν αὐτῷ;
father of him, How long a time is it while this has happened to him?
22 ὁ δὲ εἶπε, Παιδιόθεν. καὶ πολλάκις αὐτὸν καὶ εἰς πῦρ ἔβαλε
he And said, From childhood. And often him both into fire it threw
καὶ εἰς ὕδατα, ἵνα ἀπολέσῃ αὐτόν· ἀλλ' εἴ τι δύνασαι,
and into water, that it might destroy him. But if anything You can do,
23 βοήθησον ἡμῖν, σπλαγχνισθεὶς ἐφ' ἡμᾶς. ὁ δὲ Ἰησοῦς εἶπεν
help us, having pity on us. — And Jesus said
αὐτῷ τό, Εἰ δύνασαι πιστεῦσαι, πάντα δυνατὰ τῷ
to him, — If you are able to believe, all things possible to the
24 πιστεύοντι. καὶ εὐθέως κράξας ὁ πατὴρ τοῦ παιδίου, μετὰ
believing. And immediately crying out the father of the child, with
δακρύων ἔλεγε, Πιστεύω, Κύριε, βοήθει μου τῇ ἀπιστίᾳ.
tears, said, I believe! Lord, help of me the unbelief!
25 Ἰδὼν δὲ ὁ Ἰησοῦς ὅτι ἐπισυντρέχει ὄχλος, ἐπετίμησε τῷ
seeing And — Jesus that is running together a crowd,, rebuked the
πνεύματι τῷ ἀκαθάρτῳ, λέγων αὐτῷ, Τὸ πνεῦμα τὸ ἄλαλον
spirit unclean, saying to it, — Spirit — dumb
καὶ κωφόν, ἐγώ σοι ἐπιτάσσω, ἔξελθε ἐξ αὐτοῦ, καὶ μηκέτι
and deaf, I you command, Come forth from him, and no more
26 εἰσέλθῃς εἰς αὐτόν. καὶ κράξαν, καὶ πολλὰ σπαράξαν αὐτόν,
may you go into him. And crying out, and much convulsing him,
ἐξῆλθε· καὶ ἐγένετο ὡσεὶ νεκρός, ὥστε πολλοὺς λέγειν ὅτι
it came out. And he became as if dead, so as many to say that
27 ἀπέθανεν. ὁ δὲ Ἰησοῦς κρατήσας αὐτὸν τῆς χειρός, ἤγειρεν
he died. — But Jesus having taken hold of him the hand raised
28 αὐτόν· καὶ ἀνέστη. καὶ εἰσελθόντα αὐτὸν εἰς οἶκον, οἱ
him, and he stood up. And entering He into a house, the
μαθηταὶ αὐτοῦ ἐπηρώτων αὐτὸν κατ' ἰδίαν ὅτι Ἡμεῖς οὐκ
disciples of Him questioned Him privately. (Why) we not
29 ἠδυνήθημεν ἐκβαλεῖν αὐτό; καὶ εἶπεν αὐτοῖς, Τοῦτο τὸ
were able to cast out it? And He said to them, This —
γένος ἐν οὐδενὶ δύναται ἐξελθεῖν, εἰ μὴ ἐν προσευχῇ καὶ
kind by nothing can go out, except by prayer and
νηστείᾳ.
fasting.

30 Καὶ ἐκεῖθεν ἐξελθόντες παρεπορεύοντο διὰ τῆς Γαλιλαίας·
And from there going forth, they passed by through — Galilee,
31 καὶ οὐκ ἤθελεν ἵνα τις γνῷ. ἐδίδασκε γὰρ τοὺς μαθητὰς
And not He desired that anyone know; He taught for the disciples
αὐτοῦ, καὶ ἔλεγεν αὐτοῖς ὅτι Ὁ υἱὸς τοῦ ἀνθρώπου παραδί-
of Him, and said to them, — The Son — of man is
δοται εἰς χεῖρας ἀνθρώπων, καὶ ἀποκτενοῦσιν αὐτόν· καὶ
betrayed into hands of men, and they will kill Him; and
32 ἀποκτανθείς, τῇ τρίτῃ ἡμέρᾳ ἀναστήσεται. οἱ δὲ ἠγνόουν
having been killed, the third day He will rise up. they But knew not

know the word, and feared to question Him. [33]And they came to Capernaum. And having come into the house, He questioned them, What were you disputing to yourselves in the way? [34]And they were silent, for they argued with one another in the way *as to* who was greater. [35]And sitting, He called the Twelve and said to them, If anyone desires to be first, he shall be last of all, and servant of all. [36]And taking a child, He set it in their midst, and having embraced it, He said to them, [37]Whoever receives one of such children on My name receives Me. And whoever receives Me not *only* receives Me, but the *One* having sent Me.

[38]And John answered Him, saying, Teacher, we saw someone casting out demons in Your name, who does not follow us. And we forbade him, because he does not follow us. [39]But Jesus said, Do not forbid him. For there is no one who shall do a work of power in My name, yet be able to quickly speak evil of Me. [40]For who is not against us is for us. [41]For whoever gives you a cup of cold water to drink in My name, because you are of Christ, truly I say to you, In no way he will lose his reward. [42]And whoever causes one of these little ones that believe in Me to offend, it is good for him if rather a millstone be laid about his neck, and he be thrown into the sea.

[43]And if your hand offend you, cut it off. For it is profitable for you to enter into life maimed, than having two hands to go away into Hell, into the fire that cannot be put out, [44]where their worm does not die, and the fire is not put out. [45]And if your foot causes you to offend, cut it off, for it is profitable

τὸ ῥῆμα, καὶ ἐφοβοῦντο αὐτὸν ἐπερωτῆσαι.

the word, and feared Him to question.

33 Καὶ ἦλθεν εἰς Καπερναούμ· καὶ ἐν τῇ οἰκίᾳ γενόμενος

And He came to Capernaum. And in the house having come;

ἐπηρώτα αὐτούς, Τί ἐν τῇ ὁδῷ πρὸς ἑαυτοὺς διελογίζεσθε ;

He questioned them, What in the way toward yourselves were you arguing?

34 οἱ δὲ ἐσιώπων· πρὸς ἀλλήλους γὰρ διελέχθησαν ἐν τῇ ὁδῷ,

they And were quiet with one another, for they argued in the way

35 τίς μείζων. καὶ καθίσας ἐφώνησε τοὺς δώδεκα, καὶ λέγει

who (was) greater. And sitting He called the twelve and says

αὐτοῖς, Εἴ τις θέλει πρῶτος εἶναι, ἔσται πάντων ἔσχατος,

to them, If anyone desires first to be, he shall be of all last,

36 καὶ πάντων διάκονος. καὶ λαβὼν παιδίον, ἔστησεν αὐτὸ

and of all servant. And having taken a child, He set it

ἐν μέσῳ αὐτῶν· καὶ ἐναγκαλισάμενος αὐτό, εἶπεν αὐτοῖς·

in (the) midst of them, and having embraced it, He said to them,

37 Ὃς ἐὰν ἓν τῶν τοιούτων παιδίων δέξηται ἐπὶ τῷ ὀνόματί

Whoever one — of such children receives on the name

μου, ἐμὲ δέχεται· καὶ ὃς ἐὰν ἐμὲ δέξηται, οὐκ ἐμὲ δέχεται,

of Me, Me receives; and whoever Me receives, not Me receives,

ἀλλὰ τὸν ἀποστείλαντά με.

but the (One) having sent Me.

38 Ἀπεκρίθη δὲ αὐτῷ ὁ Ἰωάννης, λέγων, Διδάσκαλε,

answered And Him — John, saying, Teacher,

εἴδομέν τινα ἐν τῷ ὀνόματί σου ἐκβάλλοντα δαιμόνια, ὃς

we saw someone in the name of You casting out demons, who

οὐκ ἀκολουθεῖ ἡμῖν· καὶ ἐκωλύσαμεν αὐτόν, ὅτι οὐκ

not does follow us; and we forbade him, because not

39 ἀκολουθεῖ ἡμῖν. ὁ δὲ Ἰησοῦς εἶπε, Μὴ κωλύετε αὐτόν·

he follows us. — But Jesus said, not Do forbid him;

οὐδεὶς γάρ ἐστιν ὃς ποιήσει δύναμιν ἐπὶ τῷ ὀνόματί μου,

no one for is who shall do a work of power on the name of Me,

40 καὶ δυνήσεται ταχὺ κακολογῆσαί με. ὃς γὰρ οὐκ ἔστι καθ'

yet be able quickly to speak evil of Me. who For not is against

41 ἡμῶν, ὑπὲρ ἡμῶν ἐστιν. ὃς γὰρ ἂν ποτίσῃ ὑμᾶς ποτήριον

us, for us is. who For ever gives drink you a cup

ὕδατος ἐν τῷ ὀνόματί μου, ὅτι Χριστοῦ ἐστέ, ἀμὴν λέγω

of water in the name of Me, because of Christ you are, truly I say

42 ὑμῖν, οὐ μὴ ἀπολέσῃ τὸν μισθὸν αὐτοῦ. καὶ ὃς ἂν σκαν-

to you, in no way he will lose the reward of him. And whoever causes to

δαλίσῃ ἕνα τῶν μικρῶν τούτων τῶν πιστευόντων εἰς ἐμέ,

offend one — little (ones) of these — believing in Me,

καλόν ἐστιν αὐτῷ μᾶλλον εἰ περίκειται λίθος μυλικὸς περὶ

good is it for him rather if be laid about of a stone of a mill around

43 τὸν τράχηλον αὐτοῦ, καὶ βέβληται εἰς τὴν θάλασσαν. καὶ

the neck of him, and he be thrown into the sea. And

ἐὰν σκανδαλίζῃ σε ἡ χείρ σου, ἀπόκοψον αὐτήν· καλόν σοι

if offend you the hand of you, cut off. it; well for you

ἐστὶ κυλλὸν εἰς τὴν ζωὴν εἰσελθεῖν, ἢ τὰς δύο χεῖρας ἔχοντα

is it maimed into — life to enter, than the two hands having

44 ἀπελθεῖν εἰς τὴν γέενναν, εἰς τὸ πῦρ τὸ ἄσβεστον. ὅπου ὁ

to go away into — Gehenna, into the fire — unquenchable, where the

45 σκώληξ αὐτῶν οὐ τελευτᾷ, καὶ τὸ πῦρ οὐ σβέννυται. καὶ

worm of them not has an end, and the fire not is quenched. And

ἐὰν ὁ πούς σου σκανδαλίζῃ σε, ἀπόκοψον αὐτόν· καλόν ἐστί

if the foot of you causes to offend you, cut off it; well is it

for you to enter into life lame, than having two feet to be thrown into Hell, into the fire that cannot be put out. [46]where their worm does not die, and the fire is not put out. [47]And if your eye offends you, cast it out. For it is profitable for you to enter into the kingdom of God one-eyed, than having two eyes to be thrown into the Hell of fire, [48]where their worm does not die, and the fire is not put out. [49]For everyone will be salted with fire, and every sacrifice will be salted with salt. [50]Salt *is* good, but if the salt becomes saltless, by what will you season? Have salt in yourselves, and be at peace with one another.

CHAPTER 10

[1]And rising up from there, He came into the borders of Judea by the other side of the Jordan. And again a crowd came together to Him, and as He usually did, He again taught them. [2]And coming near the Pharisees asked Him if it is lawful for a man to put away a wife, testing Him. [3]But answering He said to them, What did Moses command you? [4]And they said, Moses allowed to write a bill of divorce, and to put away. [5]And answering Jesus said to them, With respect to your hardheartedness he wrote this command to you. [6]But from the beginning of creation God made them male and female. [7]Because of this a man shall leave his father and mother, and shall be joined to his wife, [8]and the two shall be one flesh; so that they no longer are two, but one flesh. [9]Therefore, what God yoked together, let not man put apart. [10]And again in the house His disciples asked Him about the same. [11]And He said to them, Whoever

σοι εἰσελθεῖν εἰς τὴν ζωὴν χωλόν, ἢ τοὺς δύο πόδας ἔχοντα
you to enter into — life lame, than the two feet having
46 βληθῆναι εἰς τὴν γέενναν, εἰς τὸ πῦρ τὸ ἄσβεστον, ὅπου
to be thrown into — Gehenna into the fire unquenchable, where
47 ὁ σκώληξ αὐτῶν οὐ τελευτᾷ, καὶ τὸ πῦρ οὐ σβέννυται. καὶ
the worm of them not has an end, and the fire not is quenched. And
ἐὰν ὁ ὀφθαλμός σου σκανδαλίζῃ σε, ἔκβαλε αὐτόν· καλόν
if the eye of you offends you, cast out it; well
σοι ἐστὶ μονόφθαλμον εἰσελθεῖν εἰς τὴν βασιλείαν τοῦ Θεοῦ,
for you it is one-eyed to enter into the kingdom — of God,
ἢ δύο ὀφθαλμοὺς ἔχοντα βληθῆναι εἰς τὴν γέενναν τοῦ
than two eyes having to be thrown into the Gehenna —
48 πυρός, ὅπου ὁ σκώληξ αὐτῶν οὐ τελευτᾷ, καὶ τὸ πῦρ οὐ
of fire, where the worm of them not has an end, and the fire not
49 σβέννυται. πᾶς γὰρ πυρὶ ἁλισθήσεται, καὶ πᾶσα θυσία ἁλὶ
is quenched. everyone For with fire will be salted, and every sacrifice with salt
50 ἁλισθήσεται. καλὸν τὸ ἅλας· ἐὰν δὲ τὸ ἅλας ἄναλον γένηται,
will be salted. Good (is) the salt, if but the salt saltless becomes,
ἐν τίνι αὐτὸ ἀρτύσετε; ἔχετε ἐν ἑαυτοῖς ἅλας, καὶ εἰρηνεύετε
by what it will you season? Have in yourselves salt, and be at peace
ἐν ἀλλήλοις.
among one another.

CHAPTER 10

1 Κἀκεῖθεν ἀναστὰς ἔρχεται εἰς τὰ ὅρια τῆς Ἰουδαίας διὰ
And from there arising, He comes into the borders — of Judea by
τοῦ πέραν τοῦ Ἰορδάνου· καὶ συμπορεύονται πάλιν ὄχλοι
the other side of the Jordan. And came together again crowds
2 πρὸς αὐτόν· καί, ὡς εἰώθει, πάλιν ἐδίδασκεν αὐτούς. καὶ
with Him, and as He did usually, again He taught them. And
προσελθόντες οἱ Φαρισαῖοι ἐπηρώτησαν αὐτόν, Εἰ ἔξεστιν
coming up the Pharisees questioned Him Is it lawful
3 ἀνδρὶ γυναῖκα ἀπολῦσαι, πειράζοντες αὐτόν. ὁ δὲ ἀποκρι-
for a man a wife to dismiss, testing Him. He And answering
4 θεὶς εἶπεν αὐτοῖς, Τί ὑμῖν ἐνετείλατο Μωσῆς; οἱ δὲ εἶπον,
said to them, What you did command Moses? they And said,
Μωσῆς ἐπέτρεψε βιβλίον ἀποστασίου γράψαι, καὶ ἀπολῦ-
Moses allowed a roll of divorce to write, and to dismiss.
5 σαι. καὶ ἀποκριθεὶς ὁ Ἰησοῦς εἶπεν αὐτοῖς, Πρὸς τὴν
And answering, — Jesus said to them, For the
σκληροκαρδίαν ὑμῶν ἔγραψεν ὑμῖν τὴν ἐντολὴν ταύτην·
hardheartedness of you he wrote to you — commandment this.
6 ἀπὸ δὲ ἀρχῆς κτίσεως, ἄρσεν καὶ θῆλυ ἐποίησεν αὐτοὺς ὁ
from But beginning of creation male and female made them, —
7 Θεός. ἕνεκεν τούτου καταλείψει ἄνθρωπος τὸν πατέρα αὐτοῦ
God. On account of this shall leave a man the father of him
καὶ τὴν μητέρα· καὶ προσκολληθήσεται πρὸς τὴν γυναῖκα
and the mother, and shall be joined to the wife
8 αὐτοῦ, καὶ ἔσονται οἱ δύο εἰς σάρκα μίαν. ὥστε οὐκέτι εἰσὶ
of him, and shall become the two into flesh one ; so as no longer are they
9 δύο, ἀλλὰ μία σάρξ. ὃ οὖν ὁ Θεὸς συνέζευξεν, ἄνθρωπος μὴ
two, but one flesh. What then God yoked together, man not
10 χωριζέτω. καὶ ἐν τῇ οἰκίᾳ πάλιν οἱ μαθηταὶ αὐτοῦ περὶ τοῦ
let put apart. And in the house again the disciples of Him about the
11 αὐτοῦ ἐπηρώτησαν αὐτόν. καὶ λέγει αὐτοῖς, Ὃς ἐὰν ἀπο-
same questioned Him. And He says to them, Whoever may

puts away his wife, and shall marry another commits adultery with her. [12]And if a woman puts away her husband and marries another, she commits adultery.

[13]And they brought children to Him, that He might touch them. But the disciples rebuked those carrying *them.* [14]But seeing, Jesus was indignant. And He said to them, Allow the children to come to Me, and do not hinder them. For of such is the kingdom of God. [15]Truly I say to you, Whoever does not receive the kingdom of God as a child may in no way enter into it. [16]And having taken them in *His* arms, laying hands on them, He blessed them.

[17]And He having gone out into *the* highway, running up and kneeling down to Him, one questioned Him, Good Teacher, what shall I do that I may inherit eternal life? [18]But Jesus said to him, Why do you call Me good? No one *is* good except One, God. [19]You know the commandments: Do not commit adultery; do not commit murder, do not steal, do not bear false witness; do not defraud; honor your father and mother. [20]And answering he said to Him, Teacher, I observed all these from my youth. [21]And looking at him, Jesus loved him, and said to him, One *thing* is lacking to you. Go, sell what things you have, and give to the poor. And you will have treasure in Heaven. And come, follow Me, taking up the cross. [22]But being sad at the word, he went away grieving; for he had many possessions.

[23]And looking around Jesus said to His disciples, How hardly those having riches will enter into the kingdom of God! [24]And the disciples were astonished at His words. And answering

λύσῃ τὴν γυναῖκα αὐτοῦ καὶ γαμήσῃ ἄλλην, μοιχᾶται ἐπ'
dismiss the wife of him and marry another is in adultery with
12 αὐτήν· καὶ ἐὰν γυνὴ ἀπολύσῃ τὸν ἄνδρα αὐτῆς καὶ γαμηθῇ
her; and if a woman may dismiss husband her and marries
ἄλλῳ, μοιχᾶται.
another she commits adultery.

13 Καὶ προσέφερον αὐτῷ παιδία ἵνα ἅψηται αὐτῶν· οἱ δὲ
And they carried to Him children, that He might touch them. the But
14 μαθηταὶ ἐπετίμων τοῖς προσφέρουσιν. ἰδὼν δὲ ὁ Ἰησοῦς
disciples rebuked the (ones) carrying (them) seeing But — Jesus
ἠγανάκτησε, καὶ εἶπεν αὐτοῖς, Ἄφετε τὰ παιδία ἔρχεσθαι
was indignant, and He said to them, Allow the children to come
πρός με, καὶ μὴ κωλύετε αὐτά· τῶν γὰρ τοιούτων ἐστὶν ἡ
to Me; and not forbid them; of these for such is the
15 βασιλεία τοῦ Θεοῦ. ἀμὴν λέγω ὑμῖν, ὃς ἐὰν μὴ δέξηται τὴν
kingdom — of God. Truly I say to you, Whoever not receives the
βασιλείαν τοῦ Θεοῦ ὡς παιδίον, οὐ μὴ εἰσέλθῃ εἰς αὐτήν.
kingdom — of God as a child, in no way may enter into it.
16 καὶ ἐναγκαλισάμενος αὐτά, τιθεὶς τὰς χεῖρας ἐπ' αὐτά,
And having taken in arms them, having laid the hands on them,
ηὐλόγει αὐτά.
He blessed them .

17 Καὶ ἐκπορευομένου αὐτοῦ εἰς ὁδόν, προσδραμὼν εἷς καὶ
And going forth Him into (the) way, running up one and
γονυπετήσας αὐτὸν ἐπηρώτα αὐτόν, Διδάσκαλε ἀγαθέ, τί
kneeling down to Him questioned Him, teacher Good, What
18 ποιήσω ἵνα ζωὴν αἰώνιον κληρονομήσω; ὁ δὲ Ἰησοῦς
shall I do that life eternal I may inherit? — And Jesus
εἶπεν αὐτῷ, Τί με λέγεις ἀγαθόν; οὐδεὶς ἀγαθός, εἰ μὴ εἷς, ὁ
said to him, Why Me call you good? No one (is) good, except one, —
19 Θεός. τὰς ἐντολὰς οἶδας, Μὴ μοιχεύσῃς, μὴ φονεύσῃς, μὴ
God. The commandments you know: Do not adultery; do not murder; do not
κλέψῃς, μὴ ψευδομαρτυρήσῃς, μὴ ἀποστερήσῃς, τίμα τὸν
steal, do not bear false witness; do not defraud; honor the
20 πατέρα σου καὶ τὴν μητέρα. ὁ δὲ ἀποκριθεὶς εἶπεν αὐτῷ,
father of you and the mother. he And answering said to Him,
21 Διδάσκαλε, ταῦτα πάντα ἐφυλαξάμην ἐκ νεότητός μου. ὁ δὲ
Teacher, these All I observed from youth of me. But
Ἰησοῦς ἐμβλέψας αὐτῷ ἠγάπησεν αὐτόν, καὶ εἶπεν αὐτῷ,
Jesus, looking at him, loved him, and said to him,
Ἕν σοι ὑστερεῖ· ὕπαγε, ὅσα ἔχεις πώλησον, καὶ δὸς τοῖς
One to you is lacking; go, what things you have sell, and give to the
πτωχοῖς, καὶ ἕξεις θησαυρὸν ἐν οὐρανῷ· καὶ δεῦρο, ἀκολούθει
poor: and you will have treasure in Heaven; and come, follow
22 μοι, ἄρας τὸν σταυρόν. ὁ δὲ στυγνάσας ἐπὶ τῷ λόγῳ ἀπῆλθε
Me, taking up the cross. he But being sad at the word went away
λυπούμενος· ἦν γὰρ ἔχων κτήματα πολλά.
grieving; he was for having possessions many.
23 Καὶ περιβλεψάμενος ὁ Ἰησοῦς λέγει τοῖς μαθηταῖς αὐτοῦ,
And looking around, — Jesus says to the disciples of Him,
Πῶς δυσκόλως οἱ τὰ χρήματα ἔχοντες εἰς τὴν βασιλείαν τοῦ
How hardly the (ones) the riches having into the kingdom —
24 Θεοῦ εἰσελεύσονται. οἱ δὲ μαθηταὶ ἐθαμβοῦντο ἐπὶ τοῖς
of God will enter. the And disciples were amazed at the
λόγοις αὐτοῦ. ὁ δὲ Ἰησοῦς πάλιν ἀποκριθεὶς λέγει αὐτοῖς,
words of Him. — And Jesus again answering says to them,

again Jesus said to them, Children, how hard it is for those trusting on riches to enter into the kingdom of God! [25]It is easier *for* a camel to pass through the eye of the needle, than *for* a rich one to enter into the kingdom of God. [26]And they were exceedingly astonished, saying to themselves, And who is able to be saved? [27]But looking at them, Jesus said, From men *it is* impossible, but not from God— for all things are possible from God.

[28]And Peter began to say to Him, Behold, we left all and followed You. [29]But answering Jesus said, Truly I say to you, There is no one who forsook house, or brothers, or sisters, or father, or mother, or wife, or children, or land, for My sake and the gospel, [30]that will not receive a hundredfold now in this time; houses and brothers and sisters and mothers and children and lands, with persecutions. And in the coming age, eternal life. [31]But many first shall be last, and the last *shall be* first.

[32]And they were in the highway, going up to Jerusalem. And Jesus was going before them, and following they were astonished and afraid. And taking the Twelve again, He began to tell the things about to happen to Him: [33]Behold, we are going up to Jerusalem. And the Son of man will be betrayed to the chief priests and to the scribes. And they will condemn Him to death, and will deliver Him up to the heathen. [34]And they will mock Him, and will flog Him, and will spit at Him, and will kill Him. And on the third day He will rise again.

[35]And coming up to Him, James and John, the sons of

Τέκνα, πῶς δύσκολόν ἐστι τοὺς πεποιθότας ἐπὶ τοῖς
Children, how hard it is for those trusting on the
25 χρήμασιν εἰς τὴν βασιλείαν τοῦ Θεοῦ εἰσελθεῖν. εὐκοπώ-
riches into the kingdom — of God to enter! Easier
τερόν ἐστι κάμηλον διὰ τῆς τρυμαλιᾶς τῆς ῥαφίδος
it is (for) a camel through the eye of the needle
διελθεῖν, ἢ πλούσιον εἰς τὴν βασιλείαν τοῦ Θεοῦ εἰσελθεῖν.
to pass, than (for) a rich one into the kingdom — of God to enter.
26 οἱ δὲ περισσῶς ἐξεπλήσσοντο, λέγοντες πρὸς ἑαυτούς, Καὶ
they But exceedingly were astonished, saying to themselves, And
27 τίς δύναται σωθῆναι; ἐμβλέψας δὲ αὐτοῖς ὁ Ἰησοῦς λέγει,
who is able to be saved? looking at And them, — Jesus says,
Παρὰ ἀνθρώποις ἀδύνατον, ἀλλ' οὐ παρὰ τῷ Θεῷ· πάντα
From men (it is) impossible; but not from — God; all things
28 γὰρ δυνατά ἐστι παρὰ τῷ Θεῷ. καὶ ἤρξατο ὁ Πέτρος
for possible are from — God. And began — Peter
λέγειν αὐτῷ, Ἰδού, ἡμεῖς ἀφήκαμεν πάντα, καὶ ἠκολουθή-
to say to Him, Behold, we forsook all, and have followed
29 σαμέν σοι. ἀποκριθεὶς δὲ ὁ Ἰησοῦς εἶπεν, Ἀμὴν λέγω ὑμῖν,
You. answering But — Jesus said, Truly I say to you,
οὐδείς ἐστιν ὃς ἀφῆκεν οἰκίαν, ἢ ἀδελφούς, ἢ ἀδελφάς, ἢ
no one there is who forsook house, or brothers, or sisters, or
πατέρα, ἢ μητέρα, ἢ γυναῖκα, ἢ τέκνα, ἢ ἀγρούς, ἕνεκεν
father, or mother, or wife, or children, or fields for the sake
30 ἐμοῦ καὶ τοῦ εὐαγγελίου, ἐὰν μὴ λάβῃ ἑκατονταπλασίονα
of Me and the gospel, except he receives a hundredfold
νῦν ἐν τῷ καιρῷ τούτῳ, οἰκίας καὶ ἀδελφοὺς καὶ ἀδελφὰς
now in — time this, houses, and brothers, and sisters,
καὶ μητέρας καὶ τέκνα καὶ ἀγρούς, μετὰ διωγμῶν, καὶ ἐν τῷ
and mothers, and children, and fields, with persecutions; and in the
31 αἰῶνι τῷ ἐρχομένῳ ζωὴν αἰώνιον. πολλοὶ δὲ ἔσονται
age — coming, life eternal. many And will be
πρῶτοι ἔσχατοι, καὶ οἱ ἔσχατοι πρῶτοι.
first last; and the last, first.
32 Ἦσαν δὲ ἐν τῇ ὁδῷ ἀναβαίνοντες εἰς Ἱεροσόλυμα· καὶ
they were And in the way, going up to Jerusalem. And
ἦν προάγων αὐτοὺς ὁ Ἰησοῦς, καὶ ἐθαμβοῦντο, καὶ
was going before them — Jesus, and they were astonished and
ἀκολουθοῦντες ἐφοβοῦντο. καὶ παραλαβὼν πάλιν τοὺς
following were afraid And having taken again the
δώδεκα, ἤρξατο αὐτοῖς λέγειν τὰ μέλλοντα αὐτῷ συμβαίνειν
twelve, He began them to tell the things about to Him to happen,
33 ὅτι Ἰδού, ἀναβαίνομεν εἰς Ἱεροσόλυμα, καὶ ὁ υἱὸς τοῦ
— Behold, we are going up to Jerusalem, and the Son —
ἀνθρώπου παραδοθήσεται τοῖς ἀρχιερεῦσι καὶ τοῖς γραμ-
of man will be betrayed to the chief priests and to the
ματεῦσι, καὶ κατακρινοῦσιν αὐτὸν θανάτῳ, καὶ παραδώ-
scribes, and they will condemn Him to death, and will deliver
34 σουσιν αὐτὸν τοῖς ἔθνεσι, καὶ ἐμπαίξουσιν αὐτῷ, καὶ
up Him to the nations. And they will mock Him, and
μαστιγώσουσιν αὐτόν, καὶ ἐμπτύσουσιν αὐτῷ, καὶ ἀπο-
will scourge Him, and will spit at Him, and will
κτενοῦσιν αὐτόν· καὶ τῇ τρίτῃ ἡμέρᾳ ἀναστήσεται.
kill Him; and on the third day He will rise again.
35 Καὶ προσπορεύονται αὐτῷ Ἰάκωβος καὶ Ἰωάννης οἱ
And come up to Him James and John, the

Zebedee, said, Teacher, we desire that whatever we may ask You would do for us. [36]And He said to them, What do you desire for Me to do for you? [37]And they said to Him, Give us that we may sit one off *the* right of You, and one off *the* left of You, in Your glory. [38]But Jesus said to them, You do not know what you ask. Are you able to drink the cup which I drink, and to be baptized *with* the baptism I am baptized *with*? [39]And they said to Him, We are able. But Jesus said to them, Indeed you will drink the cup which I drink, and you will be baptized *with* the baptism *with* which I am baptized. [40]But to sit off My right and off My left is not Mine to give, but for whom it has been prepared.

[41]And hearing, the ten began to be indignant about James and John. [42]But calling them near, Jesus said to them, You know that those seeming to rule the nations lord it over them, and their great ones exercise authority over them. [43]But it is not so among you, but whoever desires to become great among you shall be your servant. [44]And whoever of you desires to become first, *he* shall be slave of all. [45]For even the Son of man did not come to be served, but to serve, and to give His soul *as* a ransom for many.

[46]And they came to Jericho. And He going out from Jericho, and His disciples, and a large crowd, a son of Timeus, Bartimeus the blind, was sitting beside the highway, begging. [47]And hearing that it was Jesus the Nazarene, he began to cry out and to say, Son of David, Jesus, have mercy on me! [48]And many warned him that he be quiet. But he much more cried out, Son of David, have mercy on me! [49]And standing still, Jesus said for him to be called. And they called the blind *one*, saying to him, Be

υἱοὶ Ζεβεδαίου, λέγοντες, Διδάσκαλε, θέλομεν ἵνα ὃ ἐὰν
sons of Zebedee, saying, Teacher, we desire that whatever

36 αἰτήσωμεν, ποιήσῃς ἡμῖν. ὁ δὲ εἶπεν αὐτοῖς, Τί θέλετε
we may ask You would do for us. He And said to them, What desire

37 ποιῆσαί με ὑμῖν; οἱ δὲ εἶπον αὐτῷ, Δὸς ἡμῖν, ἵνα εἷς ἐκ
to do Me for you? they And said to Him, Give us that one off

δεξιῶν σου καὶ εἷς ἐξ εὐωνύμων σου καθίσωμεν ἐν τῇ δόξῃ
(the) right of You and one off (the) left of You we may sit in the glory

38 σου. ὁ δὲ Ἰησοῦς εἶπεν αὐτοῖς, Οὐκ οἴδατε τί αἰτεῖσθε.
of You. And Jesus said to them, not You know what you ask.

δύνασθε πιεῖν τὸ ποτήριον ὃ ἐγὼ πίνω, καὶ τὸ βάπτισμα ὃ
Can you drink the cup which I drink, and the baptism which

39 ἐγὼ βαπτίζομαι βαπτισθῆναι; οἱ δὲ εἶπον αὐτῷ, Δυνάμεθα.
I am baptized to be baptized (with)? they And said to Him, We can.

ὁ δὲ Ἰησοῦς εἶπεν αὐτοῖς, Τὸ μὲν ποτήριον ὃ ἐγὼ πίνω
— And Jesus said to them, the Indeed cup which I drink

πίεσθε· καὶ τὸ βάπτισμα ὃ ἐγὼ βαπτίζομαι βαπτισθήσεσθε·
you will drink, and the baptism which I am baptized (with) you will be baptized;

40 τὸ δὲ καθίσαι ἐκ δεξιῶν μου καὶ ἐξ εὐωνύμων μου οὐκ ἔστιν
but to sit off (the) right of Me and off (the) left of Me not is

41 ἐμὸν δοῦναι, ἀλλ' οἷς ἡτοίμασται. καὶ ἀκούσαντες οἱ δέκα
Mine to give, but for whom it has been prepared. And hearing the ten

42 ἤρξαντο ἀγανακτεῖν περὶ Ἰακώβου καὶ Ἰωάννου. ὁ δὲ Ἰησοῦς
began to be indignant about James and John. — But Jesus

προσκαλεσάμενος αὐτοὺς λέγει αὐτοῖς, Οἴδατε ὅτι οἱ δοκοῦν-
having called near them says to them, You know that those seem-

τες ἄρχειν τῶν ἐθνῶν κατακυριεύουσιν αὐτῶν· καὶ οἱ μεγάλοι
ing to rule the nations lord it over them, and the great (ones)

43 αὐτῶν κατεξουσιάζουσιν αὐτῶν. οὐχ οὕτω δὲ ἔσται ἐν ὑμῖν·
of them exercise authority over them. not so But to be among you;

ἀλλ' ὃς ἐὰν θέλῃ γενέσθαι μέγας ἐν ὑμῖν, ἔσται διάκονος ὑμῶν·
but whoever desires to become great among you, shall be servant of you;

44 καὶ ὃς ἂν θέλῃ ὑμῶν γενέσθαι πρῶτος, ἔσται πάντων δοῦλος.
and whoever desires of you to become first, shall be of all slave.

45 καὶ γὰρ ὁ υἱὸς τοῦ ἀνθρώπου οὐκ ἦλθε διακονηθῆναι,
even For the Son — of man not did come to be served,

ἀλλὰ διακονῆσαι, καὶ δοῦναι τὴν ψυχὴν αὐτοῦ λύτρον ἀντὶ
but to serve and to give the soul of Him a ransom for

πολλῶν.
many.

46 Καὶ ἔρχονται εἰς Ἰεριχώ· καὶ ἐκπορευομένου αὐτοῦ ἀπὸ
And they come to Jericho. And going out He from

Ἰεριχώ, καὶ τῶν μαθητῶν αὐτοῦ, καὶ ὄχλου ἱκανοῦ, υἱὸς
Jericho, and the disciples of Him, and a crowd large, son

Τιμαίου Βαρτίμαιος ὁ τυφλὸς ἐκάθητο παρὰ τὴν ὁδὸν
of Timaeus Bartimaeus the blind sat by the way,

47 προσαιτῶν. καὶ ἀκούσας ὅτι Ἰησοῦς ὁ Ναζωραῖός ἐστιν,
begging. And having heard that Jesus the Nazarene it is,

ἤρξατο κράζειν καὶ λέγειν, Ὁ υἱὸς Δαβίδ, Ἰησοῦ, ἐλέησόν
he began to cry out and to say, — Son of David, Jesus, have mercy on

48 με. καὶ ἐπετίμων αὐτῷ πολλοί, ἵνα σιωπήσῃ· ὁ δὲ πολλῷ
me. And warned him many, that he be quiet. he But much

49 μᾶλλον ἔκραζεν, Υἱὲ Δαβίδ, ἐλέησόν με. καὶ στὰς ὁ Ἰησοῦς
more cried out, Son of David, have mercy on me! And standing Jesus

εἶπεν αὐτὸν φωνηθῆναι· καὶ φωνοῦσι τὸν τυφλόν, λέγοντες
said for him to be called. And they call the blind (one), saying

comforted, rise up. He calls you. [50]And throwing away his garment, rising up, he came to Jesus. [51]And answering Jesus said to him, What do you desire I should do to you? And the blind *one* said to Him, My Lord, that I may see again. [52]And Jesus said to him, Go, your faith has healed you. And instantly he saw again, and followed Jesus in the highway.

CHAPTER 11

[1]And when they drew near to Jerusalem, to Bethphage and Bethany, toward the Mount of Olives, He sent two of His disciples, [2]and said to them, Go into the village opposite you. And at once entering into it, you will find a colt tied, on which no one of men has sat. Untying it, bring *it*. [3]And if anyone says to you, Why do you do this? Say, The Lord has need of it. And he will at once send it here. [4]And they departed and found the colt tied at the door outside, by the crossway, and they untied it. [5]And some of those standing there said to them, What are you doing, untying the colt? [6]And they said to them as Jesus commanded. And they allowed them. [7]And they led the colt to Jesus. And they threw their garments on it, and He sat on it. [8]And many spread their garments on the highway, and others were cutting branches from the trees, and were spreading *them* on the highway. [9]And those going before, and those following after, were crying out, saying, Hosanna! Blessed *is* the *One* coming in *the* name of *the* Lord! [10]Blessed *is* the coming kingdom of our father David in *the* name of *the* Lord! Hosanna in the highest!

[11]And Jesus entered into Jerusalem, and into the

50 αὐτῷ, Θάρσει· ἔγειραι, φωνεῖ σε. ὁ δὲ ἀποβαλὼν τὸ ἱμάτιον
to him, Be comforted, arise, He calls you. he And casting away the garment
51 αὐτοῦ ἀναστὰς ἦλθε πρὸς τον Ἰησοῦν. καὶ ἀποκριθεὶς λέγει
of him, rising up, came to — Jesus. And answering says
αὐτῷ ὁ Ἰησοῦς, Τί θέλεις ποιήσω σοί; ὁ δὲ τυφλὸς εἶπεν
to him — Jesus, What desire you I do for you? the And blind one said
52 αὐτῷ, Ῥαββονί, ἵνα ἀναβλέψω. ὁ δὲ Ἰησοῦς εἶπεν αὐτῷ,
to Him, My Lord, that I may see again. And Jesus said to him,
Ὕπαγε· ἡ πίστις σου σέσωκέ σε. καὶ εὐθέως ἀνέβλεψε, καὶ
Go, the faith of you has healed you. And instantly he saw again, and
ἠκολούθει τῷ Ἰησοῦ ἐν τῇ ὁδῷ.
followed — Jesus in the way.

CHAPTER 11

1 Καὶ ὅτε ἐγγίζουσιν εἰς Ἱερουσαλήμ, εἰς Βηθφαγὴ καὶ
And when they draw near to Jerusalem, to Bethphage and
Βηθανίαν, πρὸς τὸ ὄρος τῶν ἐλαιῶν, ἀποστέλλει δύο τῶν
Bethany, towards the mount — of olives, He sends two of the
2 μαθητῶν αὐτοῦ, καὶ λέγει αὐτοῖς, Ὑπάγετε εἰς τὴν κώμην
disciples of Him and says to them, Go into the village
τὴν κατέναντι ὑμῶν· καὶ εὐθέως εἰσπορευόμενοι εἰς αὐτὴν
— opposite you, and at once entering into it
εὑρήσετε πῶλον δεδεμένον, ἐφ' ὃν οὐδεὶς ἀνθρώπων κεκάθικε·
you will find a colt having been tied, on which no one of men has sat.
3 λύσαντες αὐτὸν ἀγάγετε. καὶ ἐάν τις ὑμῖν εἴπῃ, Τί ποιεῖτε
Loosing it, lead. And if anyone to you says, Why do you do
τοῦτο; εἴπατε ὅτι Ὁ Κύριος αὐτοῦ χρείαν ἔχει· καὶ εὐθέως
this? Say, The Lord of it need has, and at once
4 αὐτὸν ἀποστελεῖ ὧδε. ἀπῆλθον δὲ καὶ εὗρον τὸν πῶλον
it he will send here. they departed And and found the colt
δεδεμένον πρὸς τὴν θύραν ἔξω ἐπὶ τοῦ ἀμφόδου, καὶ
having been tied to the door outside on the crossway, and
5 λύουσιν αὐτόν. καί τινες τῶν ἐκεῖ ἑστηκότων ἔλεγον αὐτοῖς,
they loosen it. And some of those there standing said to them,
6 Τί ποιεῖτε λύοντες τὸν πῶλον; οἱ δὲ εἶπον αὐτοῖς καθὼς
What do you do loosening the colt? they And said to them as
7 ἐνετείλατο ὁ Ἰησοῦς· καὶ ἀφῆκαν αὐτούς. καὶ ἤγαγον τὸν
commanded — Jesus, and they let go them. And they led the
πῶλον πρὸς τὸν Ἰησοῦν, καὶ ἐπέβαλον αὐτῷ τὰ ἱμάτια
colt to — Jesus; and they throw on it the garments
8 αὐτῶν, καὶ ἐκάθισεν ἐπ' αὐτῷ. πολλοὶ δὲ τὰ ἱμάτια αὐτῶν
of them and He sat on it. many And the garments of them
ἔστρωσαν εἰς τὴν ὁδόν· ἄλλοι δὲ στοιβάδας ἔκοπτον ἐκ
scattered into the way, others and branches were cutting from
9 τῶν δένδρων, καὶ ἐστρώννυον εἰς τὴν ὁδόν. καὶ οἱ προάγον-
the trees, and were scattering into the way. And those going be-
τες καὶ οἱ ἀκολουθοῦντες ἔκραζον, λέγοντες, Ὡσαννά·
fore, and those following, cried out, saying, Hosanna!
10 εὐλογημένος ὁ ἐρχόμενος ἐν ὀνόματι Κυρίου· εὐλογημένη
Blessed (be) the (One) coming in (the) name of (the) Lord! Blessed
ἡ ἐρχομένη βασιλεία ἐν ὀνόματι Κυρίου τοῦ πατρὸς ἡμῶν
the coming kingdom in (the) name of (the) Lord, of the father of us
Δαβίδ· Ὡσαννὰ ἐν τοῖς ὑψίστοις.
David! Hosanna in the highest!
11 Καὶ εἰσῆλθεν εἰς Ἱεροσόλυμα ὁ Ἰησοῦς, καὶ εἰς τὸ ἱερόν·
And entered into Jerusalem — Jesus, and into the Temple,

Temple. And having looked around at all things, the hour already being late, He went out to Bethany with the Twelve.

[12]And on the morrow, they going out from Bethany, He hungered. [13]And seeing a fig-tree having leaves afar off, He went *toward it,* if perhaps He would find anything on it. And coming on it, He found nothing except leaves, for it was not *the* time of figs. [14]And answering Jesus said to it, Let no one eat fruit of you any more forever. And His disciples heard.

[15]And they came to Jerusalem. And entering into the Temple, Jesus began to throw out those selling and buying in the Temple; also He overturned the tables of the moneychangers, and the seats of those selling the doves. [16]And *He* did not allow any to carry a vessel through the Temple. [17]And *He* taught, saying to them, Has it not been written, "My house shall be called a house of prayer for all the nations"? But you have made it a den of robbers. [18]And the scribes and the chief priests heard. And they sought how they might destroy Him; for they feared Him; because all the crowd was astonished at His teaching.

[19]And when evening came, He went outside the city. [20]And passing along early, they saw the fig-tree withered from *the* roots. [21]And remembering, Peter said to Him, Rabbi, behold, the fig-tree which You cursed has withered. [22]And answering Jesus said to them, Have faith *in* God. [23]For truly I say to you, Whoever says to this mountain, Be taken up and be thrown into the sea; and does not doubt in his heart, but believes that what he says will happen, it will be to him, whatever he says. [24]Therefore I say to you, All things, whatever you ask,

καὶ περιβλεψάμενος πάντα, ὀψίας ἤδη οὔσης τῆς ὥρας,
and looking around at all things, late already being the hour,
ἐξῆλθεν εἰς Βηθανίαν μετὰ τῶν δώδεκα.
He went out to Bethany with the twelve.
12 Καὶ τῇ ἐπαύριον ἐξελθόντων αὐτῶν ἀπὸ Βηθανίας,
And on the morrow having gone out they from Bethany,
13 ἐπείνασε. καὶ ἰδὼν συκῆν μακρόθεν, ἔχουσαν φύλλα, ἦλθεν
He hungered. And seeing a fig-tree afar off having leaves, He came
εἰ ἄρα εὑρήσει τι ἐν αὐτῇ· καὶ ἐλθὼν ἐπ' αὐτήν, οὐδὲν
if perhaps He will find any in it. And coming upon it, nothing
14 εὗρεν εἰ μὴ φύλλα· οὐ γὰρ ἦν καιρὸς σύκων. καὶ ἀποκριθεὶς
He found except leaves; not for it was time of figs. And answering
ὁ Ἰησοῦς εἶπεν αὐτῇ, Μηκέτι ἐκ σοῦ εἰς τὸν αἰῶνα μηδεὶς
— Jesus said to it, No more from you to the age no one
καρπὸν φάγοι. καὶ ἤκουον οἱ μαθηταὶ αὐτοῦ.
fruit may eat. And heard the disciples of Him.
15 Καὶ ἔρχονται εἰς Ἱεροσόλυμα· καὶ εἰσελθὼν ὁ Ἰησοῦς εἰς
And they come to Jerusalem. And entering Jesus into
τὸ ἱερὸν ἤρξατο ἐκβάλλειν τοὺς πωλοῦντας καὶ ἀγοράζοντας
the Temple, He began to cast out those selling, and buying
ἐν τῷ ἱερῷ· καὶ τὰς τραπέζας τῶν κολλυβιστῶν, καὶ τὰς
in the Temple, and the tables of the moneychangers, and the
16 καθέδρας τῶν πωλούντων τὰς περιστερὰς κατέστρεψε· καὶ
seats of those selling the doves He overturned, and
17 οὐκ ἤφιεν ἵνα τις διενέγκῃ σκεῦος διὰ τοῦ ἱεροῦ. καὶ ἐδίδασκε,
not did allow that any may carry a vessel through the Temple,and taught,
λέγων αὐτοῖς, Οὐ γέγραπται ὅτι Ὁ οἶκός μου οἶκος
saying to them, not Has it been written that the house of Me a house
προσευχῆς κληθήσεται πᾶσι τοῖς ἔθνεσιν ; ὑμεῖς δὲ ἐποιή-
of prayer shall be called for all the nations? you But have
18 σατε αὐτὸν σπήλαιον λῃστῶν. καὶ ἤκουσαν οἱ γραμματεῖς
made it a den of robbers. And heard the scribes
καὶ οἱ ἀρχιερεῖς, καὶ ἐζήτουν πῶς αὐτὸν ἀπολέσουσιν·
and the chief priests, and they sought how Him they might destroy;
ἐφοβοῦντο γὰρ αὐτόν, ὅτι πᾶς ὁ ὄχλος ἐξεπλήσσετο ἐπὶ
they feared for Him; because all the crowd was astounded at
τῇ διδαχῇ αὐτοῦ.
the teaching of Him.
19 Καὶ ὅτε ὀψὲ ἐγένετο, ἐξεπορεύετο ἔξω τῆς πόλεως.
And when evening came, He went forth out of the city.
20 Καὶ πρωῒ παραπορευόμενοι, εἶδον τὴν συκῆν ἐξηραμ-
And in the morning passing along they saw the fig-tree withered
21 μένην ἐκ ῥιζῶν. καὶ ἀναμνησθεὶς ὁ Πέτρος λέγει αὐτῷ,
from (the) roots. And remembering — Peter says to Him,
22 Ῥαββί, ἴδε, ἡ συκῆ ἣν κατηράσω ἐξήρανται. καὶ ἀποκριθεὶς
Rabbi, behold, the fig-tree which You cursed has withered. And answering
23 Ἰησοῦς λέγει αὐτοῖς, Ἔχετε πίστιν Θεοῦ. ἀμὴν γὰρ λέγω
Jesus says to them, Have faith (in) God. truly For I say
ὑμῖν ὅτι ὃς ἂν εἴπῃ τῷ ὄρει τούτῳ, Ἄρθητι, καὶ βλήθητι εἰς
to you that whoever says — mountain to this, Be taken, and be thrown into
τὴν θάλασσαν, καὶ μὴ διακριθῇ ἐν τῇ καρδίᾳ αὐτοῦ, ἀλλὰ
the sea, and not does doubt in the heart of him, but
24 πιστεύσῃ ὅτι ἃ λέγει γίνεται· ἔσται αὐτῷ ὃ ἐὰν εἴπῃ. διὰ
believes that what he says occurs, it will be to him, whatever he says. There-
τοῦτο λέγω ὑμῖν, Πάντα ὅσα ἂν προσευχόμενοι αἰτεῖσθε,
fore, I say to you, All things whatever praying you ask,

praying, believe that you will receive, and it will be to you. [25]And when you stand praying, if you have anything against anyone, forgive *it*, so that your Father in heaven may also forgive your sins. [26]But if you do not forgive, neither will your Father in Heaven forgive your sins.

[27]And they came again to Jerusalem. And as He was walking in the Temple, the chief priests and the scribes and the elders came to Him. [28]And they said to Him, By what authority do you do these things? And who gave this authority to you, that you do these things? [29]And answering Jesus said to them, I will also ask you one thing, and answer Me, and I will tell you by what authority I do these things:

[30]The baptism of John, was it from Heaven, or from men? Answer Me. [31]And they argued to themselves, saying, If we say, From Heaven, He will say, Why then did you not believe him? [32]But if we say, From men—they feared the people. For all held that John really was a prophet. [33]And answering they said to Jesus, We do not know. And answering Jesus said to them, Neither do I tell you by what authority I do these things.

CHAPTER 12

[1]And He began to speak to them in parables:

A man planted a vineyard, and set a fence around *it*, and dug a winevat, and built a tower. And *he* let it out to vinedressers, and left the country. [2]And at the season he sent a slave to the vinedressers, that he might receive from the vinedressers the fruit of the vineyard. [3]But taking him, they beat *him*, and sent *him* away empty. [4]And again he sent to them another

25 πιστεύετε ὅτι λαμβάνετε, καὶ ἔσται ὑμῖν. καὶ ὅταν στήκητε
believe that you receive, and it will be to you. And when you stand
προσευχόμενοι, ἀφίετε εἴ τι ἔχετε κατά τινος· ἵνα καὶ ὁ
praying, forgive if anything you have against any, that also the
πατὴρ ὑμῶν ὁ ἐν τοῖς οὐρανοῖς ἀφῇ ὑμῖν τὰ παραπτώματα
Father of you — in Heaven may forgive you the transgressions
26 ὑμῶν. εἰ δὲ ὑμεῖς οὐκ ἀφίετε, οὐδὲ ὁ πατὴρ ὑμῶν ὁ ἐν τοῖς
of you. if But you not do forgive, neither the Father of you — in the
οὐρανοῖς ἀφήσει τὰ παραπτώματα ὑμῶν.
heavens will forgive the transgressions of you.
27 Καὶ ἔρχονται πάλιν εἰς Ἱεροσόλυμα· καὶ ἐν τῷ ἱερῷ
And they come again to Jerusalem. And in the Temple
περιπατοῦντος αὐτοῦ, ἔρχονται πρὸς αὐτὸν οἱ ἀρχιερεῖς
walking Him, come to Him the chief priests
28 καὶ οἱ γραμματεῖς καὶ οἱ πρεσβύτεροι, καὶ λέγουσιν αὐτῷ,
and the scribes and the elders, and they say to Him,
Ἐν ποίᾳ ἐξουσίᾳ ταῦτα ποιεῖς; καὶ τίς σοι τὴν ἐξουσίαν
By what authority these things do You? And who You authority
29 ταύτην ἔδωκεν ἵνα ταῦτα ποιῇς; ὁ δὲ Ἰησοῦς ἀποκριθεὶς
this gave that these things You do? But Jesus answering
εἶπεν αὐτοῖς, Ἐπερωτήσω ὑμᾶς κἀγὼ ἕνα λόγον, καὶ
said to them, I will ask you, I also, one thing, and
ἀποκρίθητέ μοι, καὶ ἐρῶ ὑμῖν ἐν ποίᾳ ἐξουσίᾳ ταῦτα ποιῶ.
answer to Me, and I will tell you by what authority these things I do.
30 τὸ βάπτισμα Ἰωάννου. ἐξ οὐρανοῦ ἦν, ἢ ἐξ ἀνθρώπων;
The baptism of John, out of Heaven was it, or out of men?
31 ἀποκρίθητέ μοι. καὶ ἐλογίζοντο πρὸς ἑαυτούς, λέγοντες,
Answer Me. And they argued with themselves, saying,
Ἐὰν εἴπωμεν, Ἐξ οὐρανοῦ, ἐρεῖ, Διατί οὖν οὐκ ἐπιστεύσατε
if we say, Out of Heaven, He will say, Why then not did you believe
32 αὐτῷ ἀλλ' ἐὰν εἴπωμεν, Ἐξ ἀνθρώπων, ἐφοβοῦντο τὸν
him? But if we say, Out of men — they feared the
λαόν· ἅπαντες γὰρ εἶχον τὸν Ἰωάννην, ὅτι ὄντως προφήτης
people, all for held — John, that really a prophet
33 ἦν. καὶ ἀποκριθέντες λέγουσι τῷ Ἰησοῦ, Οὐκ οἴδαμεν. καὶ ὁ
he was. And answering they say — to Jesus, not We do know. And
Ἰησοῦς ἀποκριθεὶς λέγει αὐτοῖς, Οὐδὲ ἐγὼ λέγω ὑμῖν ἐν ποίᾳ
Jesus answering says to them, Neither I tell you by what
ἐξουσίᾳ ταῦτα ποιῶ.
authority these things I do.

CHAPTER 12

1 Καὶ ἤρξατο αὐτοῖς ἐν παραβολαῖς λέγειν, Ἀμπελῶνα
And He began to them in parables to speak, a vineyard
ἐφύτευσεν ἄνθρωπος, καὶ περιέθηκε φραγμόν, καὶ ὤρυξεν
planted A man, and put around (it) a fence, and dug
ὑπολήνιον, καὶ ᾠκοδόμησε πύργον, καὶ ἐξέδοτο αὐτὸν
a winevat and built a tower, and gave out it
2 γεωργοῖς, καὶ ἀπεδήμησε. καὶ ἀπέστειλε πρὸς τοὺς γεωργοὺς
to vinedressers, and went away. And he sent to the vinedressers
τῷ καιρῷ δοῦλον, ἵνα παρὰ τῶν γεωργῶν λάβῃ ἀπὸ τοῦ
at the time a slave, that from the vinedressers he receive from the
3 καρποῦ τοῦ ἀμπελῶνος. οἱ δὲ λαβόντες αὐτὸν ἔδειραν, καὶ
fruit of the vineyard. they But having taken him beat, and
4 ἀπέστειλαν κενόν. καὶ πάλιν ἀπέστειλε πρὸς αὐτοὺς ἄλλον
sent (him) away empty. And again he sent to them another

slave. And stoning that one, they struck *him* in the head, and sent *him* away, insulting him. [5]And again he sent another, and they killed him; also many others, indeed beating these, and killing these. [6]Yet having his own beloved son, then he sent him also to them last of all, saying, They will have respect for my son. [7]But these vinedressers said among themselves, This is the heir; come, let us kill him and the inheritance will be ours. [8]And taking *him,* they killed him, and threw *him* outside the vineyard. [9]Therefore, what will the lord of the vineyard do? He will come and will destroy the vinedressers, and will give the vineyard to others. [10]Have you not even read this Scripture, "*The* Stone which the builders rejected, this one became head of *the* corner; [11]this was from *the* Lord, and it is marvelous in our eyes"? [12]And they sought to seize Him, yet feared the crowd. For they knew that He spoke the parable against them. And leaving Him, they went away.

[13]And they sent some of the Pharisees and of the Herodians to Him, that they might catch Him in a word. [14]And coming they said to Him, Teacher, we know that you are true, and there is not a care to you about anyone, for you do not look to *the* face of men, but teach on the way of God *in* truth: Is it lawful to give tribute to Caesar, or not? [15]Should we give, or should we not give? But knowing their hypocrisy, He said to them, Why do you tempt Me? Bring Me a denarius, that I may see. [16]And they brought *one.* And He said to them, whose image and superscription *is* this? And they said to Him, Caesar's. [17]And answering Jesus said to them, Render the things of Caesar to Caesar, and the things of God to God. And

δοῦλον· κἀκεῖνον λιθοβολήσαντες ἐκεφαλαίωσαν, καὶ ἀπέ-
slave; that one having stoned they struck in the head, and sent
5 στειλαν ἠτιμωμένον. καὶ πάλιν ἄλλον ἀπέστειλε· κἀκεῖνον
(him) away, insulting him. And again another he sent, that one
ἀπέκτειναν· καὶ πολλοὺς ἄλλους, τοὺς μὲν δέροντες, τοὺς
they killed; and many others, these indeed beating, these
6 δὲ ἀποκτείνοντες. ἔτι οὖν ἕνα υἱὸν ἔχων ἀγαπητὸν αὐτοῦ,
and killing. Still, then, one son having beloved his own,
ἀπέστειλε καὶ αὐτὸν πρὸς αὐτοὺς ἔσχατον, λέγων ὅτι
he sent also him to them last, saying, —
7 Ἐντραπήσονται τὸν υἱόν μου. ἐκεῖνοι δὲ οἱ γεωργοὶ εἶπον
They will respect the son of me. those But — vinedressers said
πρὸς ἑαυτοὺς ὅτι Οὗτός ἐστιν ὁ κληρονόμος· δεῦτε, ἀπο-
to themselves, — This is the heir, come, let us
8 κτείνωμεν αὐτόν, καὶ ἡμῶν ἔσται ἡ κληρονομία. καὶ λαβόντες
kill him, and of us will be the inheritance. And taking
9 αὐτὸν ἀπέκτειναν, καὶ ἐξέβαλον ἔξω τοῦ ἀμπελῶνος. τί οὖν
him they killed, and cast (him) outside the vineyard. What then
ποιήσει ὁ κύριος τοῦ ἀμπελῶνος; ἐλεύσεται καὶ ἀπολέσει
will do the lord of the vineyard? He will come and will destroy
10 τοὺς γεωργούς, καὶ δώσει τὸν ἀμπελῶνα ἄλλοις. οὐδὲ τὴν
the vinedressers, and will give the vineyard to others. not even —
γραφὴν ταύτην ἀνέγνωτε, Λίθον ὃν ἀπεδοκίμασαν οἱ
scripture this Did you read? (The) Stone which rejected those
11 οἰκοδομοῦντες, οὗτος ἐγενήθη εἰς κεφαλὴν γωνίας· παρὰ
building, this one became for head of (the) corner; from
Κυρίου ἐγένετο αὕτη, καὶ ἔστι θαυμαστὴ ἐν ὀφθαλμοῖς
(the) Lord occurred this, and it is marvelous in eyes
12 ἡμῶν; καὶ ἐζήτουν αὐτὸν κρατῆσαι, καὶ ἐφοβήθησαν τὸν
of us? And they sought Him to seize, and feared the
ὄχλον· ἔγνωσαν γὰρ ὅτι πρὸς αὐτοὺς τὴν παραβολὴν
crowd; they knew for that to them the parable
εἶπε· καὶ ἀφέντες αὐτὸν ἀπῆλθον.
He told. And leaving Him, they went away.
13 Καὶ ἀποστέλλουσι πρὸς αὐτόν τινας τῶν Φαρισαίων καὶ
And they send to Him some of the Pharisees and
14 τῶν Ἡρωδιανῶν, ἵνα αὐτὸν ἀγρεύσωσι λόγῳ. οἱ δὲ
the Herodians, that Him they might catch in a word. they And
ἐλθόντες λέγουσιν αὐτῷ, Διδάσκαλε, οἴδαμεν ὅτι ἀληθὴς
having come say to Him, Teacher, we know that true
εἶ, καὶ οὐ μέλει σοι περὶ οὐδενός· οὐ γὰρ βλέπεις εἰς πρό-
you are, and not a care to you about no one; not for you look to (the)
σωπον ἀνθρώπων, ἀλλ' ἐπ' ἀληθείας τὴν ὁδὸν τοῦ Θεοῦ
face of men, but on truth the way — of God
15 διδάσκεις· ἔξεστι κῆνσον Καίσαρι δοῦναι ἢ οὔ; δῶμεν, ἢ
teach: Is it lawful tribute to Caesar to give, or not? Should we give or
μὴ δῶμεν; ὁ δὲ εἰδὼς αὐτῶν τὴν ὑπόκρισιν εἶπεν αὐτοῖς,
not should we give? He But knowing their hypocrisy said to them,
16 Τί με πειράζετε; φέρετέ μοι δηνάριον, ἵνα ἴδω. οἱ δὲ ἤνεγκαν.
Why Me tempt you? Bring Me a denarius, that I may see. they And brought.
καὶ λέγει αὐτοῖς, Τίνος ἡ εἰκὼν αὕτη καὶ ἡ ἐπιγραφή; οἱ
And He says to them, Whose (is) image this and — superscription? they
17 δὲ εἶπον αὐτῷ, Καίσαρος. καὶ ἀποκριθεὶς ὁ Ἰησοῦς εἶπεν
And said to Him, Caesar's. And answering, — Jesus said
αὐτοῖς, Ἀπόδοτε τὰ Καίσαρος Καίσαρι, καὶ τὰ τοῦ Θεοῦ
to them, Render the things of Caesar to Caesar, and the things of God

they marveled at Him.

18 And Sadducees came to Him, who say there is no resurrection. And they questioned Him, saying, 19 Teacher, Moses wrote for us that if a brother of anyone should die and leave behind a wife, and leave no children, that his brother should take his wife and raise up seed to his brother. 20 There were seven brothers. And the first took a wife, and dying, *he* left no seed. 21 And the second took her, and died, and neither did he leave seed; and the third likewise. 22 And the seven took her, and left no seed. Last of all, the woman also died. 23 Therefore, in the resurrection, when they rise again, of which of them will she be the wife? For the seven had her as wife. 24 And answering Jesus said to them, Do you not err because of this, not knowing the Scriptures, nor the power of God? 25 For when they rise again from *the* dead, neither they marry, nor are given in marriage, but are as angels in Heaven. 26 But concerning the dead, that they are raised, have you not read in the book of Moses, as God spoke to him at the Bush, saying, "I *am* the God of Abraham, and the God of Isaac, and the God of Jacob"? 27 He is not the God of *the* dead, but God of *the* living. Therefore, you greatly err.

28 And coming up one of the scribes, hearing them arguing, knowing that He answered them well, *he* questioned Him, Which is *the* first commandment of all? 29 And Jesus answered him, *The* first of all the commandments *is*: 'Hear, Israel. *The* Lord our God is one Lord, 30 and you shall love *the* Lord your God with all your heart, and with

τῷ Θεῷ. καὶ ἐθαύμασαν ἐπ' αὐτῷ.
– to God. And they marveled at Him.
18 Καὶ ἔρχονται Σαδδουκαῖοι πρὸς αὐτόν, οἵτινες λέγουσιν
And come Saddducees to Him, who say
ἀνάστασιν μὴ εἶναι· καὶ ἐπηρώτησαν αὐτόν, λέγοντες,
a resurrection not to be, and questioned Him, saying,
19 Διδάσκαλε, Μωσῆς ἔγραψεν ἡμῖν, ὅτι ἐάν τινος ἀδελφὸς
Teacher, Moses wrote to us that if of anyone a brother
ἀποθάνῃ, καὶ καταλίπῃ γυναῖκα, καὶ τέκνα μὴ ἀφῇ, ἵνα
should die and leave behind a wife, and children not leave, that
λάβῃ ὁ ἀδελφὸς αὐτοῦ τὴν γυναῖκα αὐτοῦ, καὶ ἐξαναστήσῃ
should take the brother of him the wife of him and should raise up
20 σπέρμα τῷ ἀδελφῷ αὐτοῦ· ἑπτὰ οὖν ἀδελφοὶ ἦσαν· καὶ ὁ
seed to the brother of him. Seven then brothers were; and the
πρῶτος ἔλαβε γυναῖκα, καὶ ἀποθνήσκων οὐκ ἀφῆκε σπέρμα·
first took a wife, and dying not did leave seed.
21 καὶ ὁ δεύτερος ἔλαβεν αὐτήν, καὶ ἀπέθανε, καὶ οὐδὲ αὐτὸς
And the second took her, and died, and neither he
22 ἀφῆκε σπέρμα· καὶ ὁ τρίτος ὡσαύτως. καὶ ἔλαβον αὐτὴν
left behind seed. And the third likewise. And took her
οἱ ἑπτά, καὶ οὐκ ἀφῆκαν σπέρμα. ἐσχάτη πάντων ἀπέθανε
the seven, and not did leave seed. Last of all died
23 καὶ ἡ γυνή. ἐν τῇ οὖν ἀναστάσει, ὅταν ἀναστῶσι, τίνος
also the wife. In the then resurrection, when they rise again, of which
αὐτῶν ἔσται γυνή; οἱ γὰρ ἑπτὰ ἔσχον αὐτὴν γυναῖκα.
of them will she be wife? the For seven had her (as) wife.
24 καὶ ἀποκριθεὶς ὁ Ἰησοῦς εἶπεν αὐτοῖς, Οὐ διὰ τοῦτο
And answering, – Jesus said to them, Not therefore
πλανᾶσθε, μὴ εἰδότες τὰς γραφάς, μηδὲ τὴν δύναμιν τοῦ
do you err, not knowing the Scriptures, nor the power –
25 Θεοῦ; ὅταν γὰρ ἐκ νεκρῶν ἀναστῶσιν, οὔτε γαμοῦσιν,
of God? when For from (the) dead they rise again, neither they marry,
οὔτε γαμίσκονται, ἀλλ' εἰσὶν ὡς ἄγγελοι οἱ ἐν τοῖς οὐρανοῖς.
nor are given in marriage, but are as angels – in the heavens.
26 περὶ δὲ τῶν νεκρῶν, ὅτι ἐγείρονται, οὐκ ἀνέγνωτε ἐν τῇ
about But the dead, that they are raised, not did you read in the
βίβλῳ Μωσέως, ἐπὶ τῆς βάτου, ὡς εἶπεν αὐτῷ ὁ Θεός, λέγων,
roll of Moses at the Bush, as spoke to him God, saying,
Ἐγὼ ὁ Θεὸς Ἀβραάμ, καὶ ὁ Θεὸς Ἰσαάκ, καὶ ὁ Θεὸς Ἰακώβ;
I (am) the God of Abraham, and the God of Isaac, and the God of Jacob?
27 οὐκ ἔστιν ὁ Θεὸς νεκρῶν, ἀλλὰ Θεὸς ζώντων· ὑμεῖς οὖν πολὺ
not He is the God of (the) dead, but God of (the) living You then much
πλανᾶσθε.
err.

28 Καὶ προσελθὼν εἷς τῶν γραμματέων, ἀκούσας αὐτῶν
And coming up one of the scribes, hearing them
συζητούντων, εἰδὼς ὅτι καλῶς αὐτοῖς ἀπεκρίθη, ἐπηρώ-
arguing, knowing that well to them He answered, asked
29 τησεν αὐτόν, Ποία ἐστὶ πρώτη πασῶν ἐντολή; ὁ δὲ
Him, What is (the) first of all commandments? – And
Ἰησοῦς ἀπεκρίθη αὐτῷ ὅτι Πρώτη πασῶν τῶν ἐντολῶν.
Jesus answered him, – The first of all the commandments (is)
30 Ἄκουε, Ἰσραήλ· Κύριος ὁ Θεὸς ἡμῶν, Κύριος εἷς ἐστί· καὶ
Hear, Israel, Lord the God of us Lord one is, and
ἀγαπήσεις Κύριον τὸν Θεόν σου ἐξ ὅλης τῆς καρδίας σου,
you shall love the Lord the God of you from all the heart of you,

all your soul and with all your mind, and with all your strength." This is the first commandment. [31]And *the* second *is* like this, You shall love your neighbor as yourself. There is not another commandment greater than these. [32]And the scribe said to Him, Right, Teacher. You have spoken according to truth, that God is one, and there is no other besides Him; [33]and to love Him with all the heart, and with all the understanding, and with all the soul, and with all the strength; and to love *one's* neighbor as oneself, is more than all the burnt offering and the sacrifices. [34]And seeing him, that he answered intelligently, Jesus said to him, You are not far from the kingdom of God. And no one dared to question Him any more.

[35]And answering Jesus said, teaching in the Temple, How do the scribes say that Christ is the son of David? [36]For David himself said by the Holy Spirit, "The Lord said to my Lord, Sit at My right hand until I place Your enemies as a footstool for Your feet." [37]Then David himself calls Him Lord. And from where is He his son? And the large crowd heard Him gladly.

[38]And He said to them in His teaching, Be careful of the scribes, those desiring to walk about in robes, and greetings in the markets, [39]and chief seats in the synagogues, and chief couches in the dinners, [40]those devouring the houses of widows, and for a pretense praying at length. These shall receive more abundant judgment.

[41]And sitting down opposite the treasury, Jesus watched how the crowd threw copper coins into the treasury. And many rich ones threw in much. [42]And

καὶ ἐξ ὅλης τῆς ψυχῆς σου, καὶ ἐξ ὅλης τῆς διανοίας σου,
and from all the soul of you, and from all the mind of you,
31 καὶ ἐξ ὅλης τῆς ἰσχύος σου. αὕτη πρώτη ἐντολή. καὶ δευτέρα
and from all the strength of you. This the first commandment; and second
ὁμοία αὕτη, Ἀγαπήσεις τὸν πλησίον σου ὡς σεαυτόν. μείζων
like this, You shall love the neighbor of you as yourself. Greater
32 τούτων ἄλλη ἐντολὴ οὐκ ἔστι. καὶ εἶπεν αὐτῷ ὁ γραμματεύς,
(than) these other command not is. And said to Him the scribe,
Καλῶς, διδάσκαλε, ἐπ' ἀληθείας εἶπας ὅτι εἷς ἐστι Θεός, καὶ
Well, Teacher, by truth you say that one is God, and
33 οὐκ ἔστιν ἄλλος πλὴν αὐτοῦ. καὶ τὸ ἀγαπᾷν αὐτὸν ἐξ
not there is another besides Him; and — to love Him out of
ὅλης τῆς καρδίας, καὶ ἐξ ὅλης τῆς συνέσεως, καὶ ἐξ ὅλης τῆς
all the heart, and out of all the understanding, and out of all the
ψυχῆς, καὶ ἐξ ὅλης τῆς ἰσχύος, καὶ τὸ ἀγαπᾷν τὸν πλησίον
soul, and from all the strength; and — to love the neighbor
ὡς ἑαυτόν, πλεῖόν ἐστι πάντων τῶν ὁλοκαυτωμάτων καὶ
as oneself, more is than all the burnt offerings and
34 τῶν θυσιῶν. καὶ ὁ Ἰησοῦς ἰδὼν αὐτὸν ὅτι νουνεχῶς
the sacrifices. And — Jesus seeing him, that intelligently
ἀπεκρίθη, εἶπεν αὐτῷ, Οὐ μακρὰν εἶ ἀπὸ τῆς βασιλείας τοῦ
he answered, said to him, Not far are you from the kingdom —
Θεοῦ. καὶ οὐδεὶς οὐκέτι ἐτόλμα αὐτὸν ἐπερωτῆσαι.
of God. And no one no more dared Him to question.
35 Καὶ ἀποκριθεὶς ὁ Ἰησοῦς ἔλεγε, διδάσκων ἐν τῷ ἱερῷ, Πῶς
And answering, — Jesus said, teaching in the Temple, How
λέγουσιν οἱ γραμματεῖς ὅτι ὁ Χριστὸς υἱός ἐστι Δαβίδ;
say the scribes that the Christ son is of David?
36 αὐτὸς γὰρ Δαβὶδ εἶπεν ἐν τῷ Πνεύματι τῷ Ἁγίῳ, Εἶπεν ὁ
himself For David said in the Spirit — Holy, Said the
Κύριος τῷ Κυρίῳ μου, Κάθου ἐκ δεξιῶν μου, ἕως ἂν θῶ τοὺς
Lord to the Lord of me, Sit off (the) right of Me until I put the
37 ἐχθρούς σου ὑποπόδιον τῶν ποδῶν σου. Αὐτὸς οὖν Δαβὶδ
enemies of You (as) a footstool for the feet of You. Himself, Then, David
λέγει αὐτὸν Κύριον· καὶ πόθεν υἱὸς αὐτοῦ ἐστι; καὶ ὁ πολὺς
says Him (to be) Lord, and from where son of him is He? And the large
ὄχλος ἤκουεν αὐτοῦ ἡδέως.
crowd heard Him gladly.
38 Καὶ ἔλεγεν αὐτοῖς ἐν τῇ διδαχῇ αὐτοῦ, Βλέπετε ἀπὸ τῶν
And He said to them in the teaching of Him, Be careful from the
γραμματέων, τῶν θελόντων ἐν στολαῖς περιπατεῖν, καὶ
scribes, the (ones) desiring in robes to walk about, and
39 ἀσπασμοὺς ἐν ταῖς ἀγοραῖς, καὶ πρωτοκαθεδρίας ἐν ταῖς
greetings in the markets, and chief seats in the
40 συναγωγαῖς, καὶ πρωτοκλισίας ἐν τοῖς δείπνοις· οἱ κατε-
synagogues, and chief couches in the dinners; the (ones)
σθίοντες τὰς οἰκίας τῶν χηρῶν, καὶ προφάσει μακρὰ
devouring the houses of the widows, and for a pretence lengthily
προσευχόμενοι· οὗτοι λήψονται περισσότερον κρίμα.
praying; these will receive more abundant judgment.
41 Καὶ καθίσας ὁ Ἰησοῦς κατέναντι τοῦ γαζοφυλακίου
And sitting — Jesus opposite the treasury,
ἐθεώρει πῶς ὁ ὄχλος βάλλει χαλκὸν εἰς τὸ γαζοφυλάκιον·
He watched how the crowd cast copper coins into the treasury.
42 καὶ πολλοὶ πλούσιοι ἔβαλλον πολλά. καὶ ἐλθοῦσα μία
And many rich ones cast in much; and coming one

coming one poor widow threw two lepta, which is a kodrantes. [43]And having called His disciples near, He said to them, Truly I say to you that this poor widow has thrown *in* more than all of those putting into the treasury. [44]For all threw *in* out of that abounding to them, but she out of her poverty threw *in* all, as much as she had, her whole livelihood.

CHAPTER 13

[1]And as He was going out of the Temple, one of His disciples said to Him, Teacher, see what stones and what buildings! [2]And answering Jesus said to him, Do you see these great buildings? Not one stone shall be left upon *a* stone which shall not be thrown down.

[3]And *as* He *was* sitting in the Mount of Olives opposite the Temple, Peter and James and John and Andrew questioned Him privately: [4]Tell us when these things shall be? And what *is* the sign when all these things are about to be done? [5]And answering Jesus began to say to them, Be careful that no one lead you astray. [6]For many will come in My name, saying I AM! And they will lead many astray. [7]But when you hear of wars and rumors of wars, do not be disturbed; for it must occur—but the end is not yet. [8]For nation will be raised against nation, and kingdom against kingdom. And there shall be earthquakes in many places; and there shall be famines and troubles. These things *are* the beginnings of anguishes.

[9]But you take heed to yourselves, for they will deliver you up to sanhedrins and to synagogues. You will be beaten, and you will be brought before governors and kings for My sake, for a testimony

43 χήρα πτωχὴ ἔβαλε λεπτὰ δύο, ὅ ἐστι κοδράντης. καὶ
widow poor cast lepta two, which is a quadrans. And
προσκαλεσάμενος τοὺς μαθητὰς αὐτοῦ, λέγει αὐτοῖς, Ἀμὴν
calling near the disciples of Him, He says to them, Truly
λέγω ὑμῖν ὅτι ἡ χήρα αὕτη ἡ πτωχὴ πλεῖον πάντων
I say to you that – widow, this – poor more than all
44 βέβληκε τῶν βαλόντων εἰς τὸ γαζοφυλάκιον· πάντες γὰρ
has cast the (ones) casting into the treasury; all for
ἐκ τοῦ περισσεύοντος αὐτοῖς ἔβαλον· αὕτη δὲ ἐκ τῆς
out of that abounding to them cast, she but out of the
ὑστερήσεως αὐτῆς πάντα ὅσα εἶχεν ἔβαλεν, ὅλον τὸν βίον
poverty of her all, as much as she had cast, all the living
αὐτῆς.
of her.

CHAPTER 13

1 Καὶ ἐκπορευομένου αὐτοῦ ἐκ τοῦ ἱεροῦ, λέγει αὐτῷ εἷς
And going forth He out of the Temple, says to Him one
τῶν μαθητῶν αὐτοῦ, Διδάσκαλε, ἴδε, ποταποὶ λίθοι καὶ
of the disciples of Him, Teacher, Behold, what kind of stones and
2 ποταπαὶ οἰκοδομαί. καὶ ὁ Ἰησοῦς ἀποκριθεὶς εἶπεν αὐτῷ,
what kind of buildings! And – Jesus answering said to him,
Βλέπεις ταύτας τὰς μεγάλας οἰκοδομάς; οὐ μὴ ἀφεθῇ λίθος
Do you see these – great buildings? In no way will be left stone
ἐπὶ λίθῳ, ὃς οὐ μὴ καταλυθῇ.
upon stone that not at all (will) be thrown down.
3 Καὶ καθημένου αὐτοῦ εἰς τὸ ὄρος τῶν ἐλαιῶν κατέναντι
And sitting He in the mount of the olives opposite
τοῦ ἱεροῦ, ἐπηρώτων αὐτὸν κατ' ἰδίαν Πέτρος καὶ Ἰάκωβος
the Temple, questioned Him privately Peter and James
4 καὶ Ἰωάννης καὶ Ἀνδρέας, Εἰπὲ ἡμῖν, πότε ταῦτα ἔσται;
and John and Andrew, Tell us, when these things will be?
καὶ τί τὸ σημεῖον ὅταν μέλλῃ πάντα ταῦτα συντελεῖσθαι;
And what the sign when are about all these things to be accomplished?
5 ὁ δὲ Ἰησοῦς ἀποκριθεὶς αὐτοῖς ἤρξατο λέγειν, Βλέπετε μή τις
And Jesus answering to them began to say, Be careful not any
6 ὑμᾶς πλανήσῃ. πολλοὶ γὰρ ἐλεύσονται ἐπὶ τῷ ὀνόματί μου,
you lead astray. many For will come on the name of Me,
7 λέγοντες ὅτι Ἐγώ εἰμι· καὶ πολλοὺς πλανήσουσιν. ὅταν δὲ
saying, – I AM! And many they will lead astray. when But
ἀκούσητε πολέμους καὶ ἀκοὰς πολέμων, μὴ θροεῖσθε· δεῖ
you hear (of) wars and rumors of wars, do not be alarmed. it must
8 γὰρ γενέσθαι· ἀλλ' οὔπω τὸ τέλος. ἐγερθήσεται γὰρ ἔθνος
For happen, but not yet the end. will be raised For nation
ἐπὶ ἔθνος, καὶ βασιλεία ἐπὶ βασιλείαν· καὶ ἔσονται σεισμοὶ
against nation, and kingdom against kingdom; and shall be earthquakes
κατὰ τόπους, καὶ ἔσονται λιμοὶ καὶ ταραχαί· ἀρχαὶ ὠδίνων
in many places; and shall be famines and troubles. Beginnings of travails
ταῦτα.
these things (are).
9 Βλέπετε δὲ ὑμεῖς ἑαυτούς· παραδώσουσι γὰρ ὑμᾶς εἰς
be careful But you yourselves; they will deliver for you to
συνέδρια, καὶ εἰς συναγωγὰς δαρήσεσθε, καὶ ἐπὶ ἡγεμόνων
sanhedrins, and to synagogues—you will be beaten; and before rulers
καὶ βασιλέων ἀχθήσεσθε ἕνεκεν ἐμοῦ, εἰς μαρτύριον αὐτοῖς.
and kings you will be led for the sake of Me, for a testimony to them.

to them. [10]And the gospel must first be proclaimed to all the nations. [11]But whenever they lead you away, delivering *you,* do not be anxious beforehand, what you should say or think. But whatever may be given to you in that hour, speak that. For you are not those speaking, but the Holy Spirit.

[12]And brother will deliver up brother to death, and a father the child. And children will rise up on parents, and will put them to death. [13]And you will be hated on account of My name. But the *one* enduring to the end this *one* will be saved.

[14]But when you see the abomination of desolation, the *one* spoken of by Daniel the prophet, standing where it ought not–he reading, let him understand—then let those in Judea flee into the mountains. [15]And he on the housetop, let him not go down into the house, nor go in to take anything out of his house. [16]And the *one* in the field, let him not return to the things behind, to take his garment. [17]But woe to those that are with child, and to those giving suck in those days! [18]And pray that your flight will not be in winter; [19]for there will be affliction *in* those days, such as has not been the like from *the* beginning of creation which God created until now, and never *will* be. [20]And if *the* Lord had not shortened the days, not any flesh would be saved; but because of the elect whom He chose, He has shortened the days. [21]And then if anyone says to you, Behold, here *is* the Christ! Or, Behold, there! You shall not believe. [22]For false christs and false prophets will be raised, and they will give signs and wonders in order to lead astray, if possible, the elect. [23]But you be careful. Behold, I have told you all things.

[24]But in those days, after that affliction, the sun will be

10 καὶ εἰς πάντα τὰ ἔθνη δεῖ πρῶτον κηρυχθῆναι τὸ εὐαγγέλιον
And to all the nations must first be proclaimed the gospel.
11 ὅταν δὲ ἀγάγωσιν ὑμᾶς παραδιδόντες, μὴ προμεριμνᾶτε τί
when And they lead away you, delivering (you), not be anxious before what
λαλήσητε, μηδὲ μελετᾶτε· ἀλλ' ὃ ἐὰν δοθῇ ὑμῖν ἐν ἐκείνῃ τῇ
you may say, nor meditate, but whatever is given you in that —
ὥρᾳ, τοῦτο λαλεῖτε· οὐ γάρ ἐστε ὑμεῖς οἱ λαλοῦντες, ἀλλὰ
hour, this speak; not for are you the (ones) speaking, but
12 τὸ Πνεῦμα τὸ Ἅγιον. παραδώσει δὲ ἀδελφὸς ἀδελφὸν εἰς
the Spirit — Holy. will deliver And a brother a brother to
θάνατον, καὶ πατὴρ τέκνον· καὶ ἐπαναστήσονται τέκνα ἐπὶ
to death, and a father a child; and will rise up children upon
13 γονεῖς, καὶ θανατώσουσιν αὐτούς· καὶ ἔσεσθε μισούμενοι
parents, and will put to death them; and you will be hated
ὑπὸ πάντων διὰ τὸ ὄνομά μου· ὁ δὲ ὑπομείνας εἰς τέλος,
by all on account of the name of Me. he But enduring to the end,
οὗτος σωθήσεται.
this (one) will be saved.
14 Ὅταν δὲ ἴδητε τὸ βδέλυγμα τῆς ἐρημώσεως, τὸ ῥηθὲν
when But you see the abomination — of desolation the (one) spoken
ὑπὸ Δανιὴλ τοῦ προφήτου, ἑστὼς ὅπου οὐ δεῖ (ὁ ἀναγινώ-
by Daniel the prophet, standing where not it ought, he reading
σκων νοείτω), τότε οἱ ἐν τῇ Ἰουδαίᾳ φευγέτωσαν εἰς τὰ
let him understand, then those in Judea, let them flee into the
15 ὄρη· ὁ δὲ ἐπὶ τοῦ δώματος μὴ καταβάτω εἰς τὴν οἰκίαν,
mounts. he And on the housetop, not let him descend into the house,
16 μηδὲ εἰσελθέτω ἆραί τι ἐκ τῆς οἰκίας αὐτοῦ· καὶ ὁ εἰς τὸν
nor enter to take anything out of the house of him; and he in the
ἀγρὸν ὢν μὴ ἐπιστρεψάτω εἰς τὰ ὀπίσω, ἆραι τὸ ἱμάτιον
field being, not let him return to the things behind to take the garment
17 αὐτοῦ. οὐαὶ δὲ ταῖς ἐν γαστρὶ ἐχούσαις καὶ ταῖς θηλαζού-
of him. woe But to those in womb holding, and to those giving
18 σαις ἐν ἐκείναις ταῖς ἡμέραις. προσεύχεσθε δὲ ἵνα μὴ γένηται
suck in those — days. pray But that not may occur
19 ἡ φυγὴ ὑμῶν χειμῶνος. ἔσονται γὰρ αἱ ἡμέραι ἐκεῖναι θλίψις,
the flight of you in winter, will be for — days those affliction
οἵα οὐ γέγονε τοιαύτη ἀπ' ἀρχῆς κτίσεως ἧς ἔκτισεν ὁ
such as not has been the like from beginning of creation which created —
20 Θεὸς ἕως τοῦ νῦν, καὶ ου μὴ γένηται. καὶ εἰ μὴ Κύριος
God until — now, and in no way may be. And unless (the) Lord
ἐκολόβωσε τὰς ἡμέρας, οὐκ ἂν ἐσώθη πᾶσα σάρξ· ἀλλὰ διὰ
had shortened the days, not would be saved any flesh; but because of
21 τοὺς ἐκλεκτούς, οὓς ἐξελέξατο, ἐκολόβωσε τὰς ἡμέρας. καὶ
the elect whom He elected, He shortened the days. And
τότε ἐάν τις ὑμῖν εἴπῃ, Ἰδού, ὧδε ὁ Χριστός, ἤ Ἰδού, ἐκεῖ, μὴ
then if anyone to you says, Behold, here the Christ, or behold, there, not
22 πιστεύσητε. ἐγερθήσονται γαρ ψευδόχριστοι καὶ ψευδο-
believe. will be raised For false Christs and false
προφῆται, καὶ δώσουσι σημεῖα καὶ τέρατα, πρὸς τὸ ἀπο-
prophets, and they will give signs and wonders in order to — lead
23 πλανᾶν, εἰ δυνατόν, καὶ τοὺς ἐκλεκτούς. ὑμεῖς δὲ βλέπετε·
astray, if possible, even the elect. you But be careful.
ἰδού, προείρηκα ὑμῖν πάντα.
Behold, I have told before you all things.
24 Ἀλλ' ἐν ἐκείναις ταῖς ἡμέραις, μετὰ τὴν θλίψιν ἐκείνην, ὁ
But in those — days, after — affliction that, the

darkened, and the moon will not give her light; [25]And the stars will be falling, and the powers in the heavens will be shaken. [26]And then they will see the Son of man coming in clouds with much power and glory. [27]And then He will send His angels, and they will gather His elect from the four winds, from *the* end of earth to *the* end of Heaven.

[28]And from the fig-tree learn the parable: When its branch becomes tender and puts out leaves, you know the summer is near. [29]So you also, when you see these things happening, know that it is near, at *the* doors. [30]Truly I say to you, Not at all will this generation pass away until all these things occur. [31]The heavens and the earth will pass away, but My word will not at all pass away. [32]But concerning that day and the hour, no one knows, not the angels, those in Heaven, nor the Son, but the Father. [33]Be careful; be wakeful, and pray. For you do not know when the time is. [34]As a man going abroad, leaving his house, and giving his slaves authority, and to each his work—and he commanded the doorkeeper, that he watch—[35]then you watch, for you do not know when the lord of the house is coming, *at* evening, or at midnight, or at cock-crowing, or early; [36]so that he may not come suddenly *and* find you sleeping. [37]And what I say to you, I say to all. Watch!

CHAPTER 14

[1]And it was the Passover, and the *Feast of* Unleavened Bread after two days. And the chief priests and the scribes were seeking how they might get hold of Him by guile, *and* they might kill Him. [2]But they said, Not during the feast, lest there

ἥλιος σκοτισθήσεται, καὶ ἡ σελήνη οὐ δώσει τὸ φέγγος
sun will be darkened, and the moon not will give the light
25 αὐτῆς, καὶ οἱ ἀστέρες τοῦ οὐρανοῦ ἔσονται ἐκπίπτοντες,
of her. And the stars of the heaven will be falling,
26 καὶ αἱ δυνάμεις αἱ ἐν τοῖς οὐρανοῖς σαλευθήσονται. καὶ τότε
and the powers — in the heavens will be shaken. And then
ὄψονται τὸν υἱὸν τοῦ ἀνθρώπου ἐρχόμενον ἐν νεφέλαις
they will see the Son — of man coming in clouds
27 μετὰ δυνάμεως πολλῆς καὶ δόξης. καὶ τότε ἀποστελεῖ τοὺς
with power much and glory. And then He will send the
ἀγγέλους αὐτοῦ, καὶ ἐπισυνάξει τοὺς ἐκλεκτοὺς αὐτοῦ ἐκ
angels of Him, and they will gather the elect of Him out of
τῶν τεσσάρων ἀνέμων, ἀπ' ἄκρου γῆς ἕως ἄκρου οὐρανοῦ.
the four winds, from (the) end of earth to (the) end of heaven.
28 Ἀπὸ δὲ τῆς συκῆς μάθετε τὴν παραβολήν· ὅταν αὐτῆς
from And the fig-tree learn the parable: when of it
ἤδη ὁ κλάδος ἁπαλὸς γένηται καὶ ἐκφύῃ τὰ φύλλα, γινώ-
now the branch tender becomes and puts out the leaves, you
29 σκετε ὅτι ἐγγὺς τὸ θέρος ἐστίν· οὕτω καὶ ὑμεῖς, ὅταν ταῦτα
know that near the summer is. So also you, when these things
30 ἴδητε γινόμενα, γινώσκετε ὅτι ἐγγύς ἐστιν ἐπὶ θύραις. ἀμὴν
you see happening, know that near is it, at (the) doors. Truly
λέγω ὑμῖν ὅτι οὐ μὴ παρέλθῃ ἡ γενεὰ αὕτη, μέχρις οὗ
I say to you that in no way will pass away generation this until
31 πάντα ταῦτα γένηται. ὁ οὐρανὸς καὶ ἡ γῆ παρελεύσονται·
all these things happen. The heaven and the earth will pass away,
32 οἱ δὲ λόγοι μου οὐ μὴ παρέλθωσι. περὶ δὲ τῆς ἡμέρας
the but words of Me in no way will pass away. concerning But day
ἐκείνης καὶ τῆς ὥρας οὐδεὶς οἶδεν, οὐδὲ οἱ ἄγγελοι οἱ ἐν
that and the hour no one knows, not the angels — in
33 οὐρανῷ, οὐδὲ ὁ υἱός, εἰ μὴ ὁ πατήρ. βλέπετε, ἀγρυπνεῖτε καὶ
Heaven, nor the Son, except the Father. Be careful, be wakeful, and
34 προσεύχεσθε· οὐκ οἴδατε γὰρ πότε ὁ καιρός ἐστιν. ὡς
pray. not you know For **when the time is. As**
ἄνθρωπος ἀπόδημος ἀφεὶς τὴν οἰκίαν αὐτοῦ, καὶ δοὺς τοῖς
a man going abroad, leaving the house of him, and giving to the
δούλοις αὐτοῦ τὴν ἐξουσίαν, καὶ ἑκάστῳ τὸ ἔργον αὐτοῦ,
slaves of him the authority, and to each the work of him,
35 καὶ τῷ θυρωρῷ ἐνετείλατο ἵνα γρηγορῇ. γρηγορεῖτε οὖν·
and the doorkeeper He ordered that he should watch. You watch, then,
οὐκ οἴδατε γὰρ πότε ὁ κύριος τῆς οἰκίας ἔρχεται, ὀψέ, ἢ
not you know for when the lord of the house comes, evening, or
36 μεσονυκτίου, ἢ ἀλεκτοροφωνίας, ἢ πρωΐ· μὴ ἐλθὼν ἐξαίφνης
at midnight, or at cock-crowing, or early; lest coming suddenly
37 εὕρῃ ὑμᾶς καθεύδοντας. ἃ δὲ ὑμῖν λέγω πᾶσι λέγω,
he find you sleeping. what And to you I say, to all I say,
Γρηγορεῖτε.
Watch!

CHAPTER 14

1 Ἦν δὲ τὸ πάσχα καὶ τὰ ἄζυμα μετὰ δύο ἡμέρας· καὶ
it was And the Passover and the unleavened bread bread after two days. And
ἐζήτουν οἱ ἀρχιερεῖς καὶ οἱ γραμματεῖς πῶς αὐτὸν ἐν δόλῳ
sought the chief priests and the scribes how Him by guile
2 κρατήσαντες ἀποκτείνωσιν· ἔλεγον δέ, Μὴ ἐν τῇ ἑορτῇ,
seizing they might kill. they said And, Not at the feast,

will be a tumult of the people.
3 And He being in Bethany in the house of Simon the leper, as He reclined, a woman having an alabaster vial of pure, costly ointment of nard, and breaking the alabaster vial, she poured *it* down His head. 4 And some were indignant to themselves, and saying, To what has this waste of the ointment occurred? For this could be sold *for* over three hundred denarii, and to be given to the poor. And they were incensed with her. 6 But Jesus said, Let her alone. Why do you cause her troubles? She worked a good work toward Me. 7 For you always have the poor with you, and when you wish, you can do well toward them. But you do not always have Me. 8 What this one held, she did. She took beforehand to anoint My body for the burial. 9 Truly I say to you, Wherever this gospel is proclaimed in all the world, what this *one* did will also be spoken of for a memorial of her.
10 And Judas Iscariot, one of the twelve, went away to the chief priests, that he might betray Him to them. 11 And hearing, they rejoiced and promised to give him silver. And he sought how he might opportunely betray Him.

12 And on the first day of the unleavened *bread*, when they killed the Passover, His disciples said to Him, Where do you desire *that* going we may prepare that You may eat the Passover? 13 And He sent two of His disciples, and said to them, Go into the city. And you will meet a man carrying a pitcher of water. Follow him. 14 And wherever he goes in, say to the housemaster, The Teacher says, Where is the guest room where I may eat the Passover with My disciples? 15 And he will show

μήποτε θόρυβος ἔσται τοῦ λαοῦ.
lest a tumult will be of the people.
3 Καὶ ὄντος αὐτοῦ ἐν Βηθανίᾳ, ἐν τῇ οἰκίᾳ Σίμωνος τοῦ
And being He in Bethany in the house of Simon the
λεπροῦ, κατακειμένου αὐτοῦ, ἦλθε γυνὴ ἔχουσα ἀλάβαστρον
leper, reclining He came a woman having an alabaster vial
μύρου νάρδου πιστικῆς πολυτελοῦς· καὶ συντρίψασα τὸ
of ointment of nard pure costly. And breaking the
4 ἀλάβαστρον, κατέχεεν αὐτοῦ κατὰ τῆς κεφαλῆς. ἦσαν δέ
alabaster vial she poured (it) of Him down the head. were And
τινες ἀγανακτοῦντες πρὸς ἑαυτούς, καὶ λέγοντες, Εἰς τί ἡ
some being indignant to themselves, and saying, To what –
5 ἀπώλεια αὕτη τοῦ μύρου γέγονεν; ἠδύνατο γὰρ τοῦτο
waste this of the ointment has occurred? could For this
πραθῆναι ἐπάνω τριακοσίων δηναρίων, καὶ δοθῆναι τοῖς
be sold (for) over three hundred denarii, and to be given to the
6 πτωχοῖς. καὶ ἐνεβριμῶντο αὐτῇ. ὁ δὲ Ἰησοῦς εἶπεν, Ἄφετε
poor. And they were incensed with her. But Jesus said, Let alone
αὐτήν· τί αὐτῇ κόπους παρέχετε; καλὸν ἔργον εἰργάσατο
her. Why to her troubles do you cause? a good work she worked
7 εἰς ἐμέ. πάντοτε γὰρ τοὺς πτωχοὺς ἔχετε μεθ' ἑαυτῶν, καὶ
to Me. always For the poor you have with yourselves, and
ὅταν θέλητε δύνασθε αὐτοὺς εὖ ποιῆσαι· ἐμὲ δὲ οὐ πάντοτε
when you wish you are able (to) them well to do, Me but not always
8 ἔχετε. ὃ εἶχεν αὕτη ἐποίησε· προέλαβε μυρίσαι μου τὸ
you have. What held this one, she did; she took beforehand to anoint of Me the
9 σῶμα εἰς τὸν ἐνταφιασμόν. ἀμὴν λέγω ὑμῖν, ὅπου ἂν
body for the burial. Truly I say to you, where ever
κηρυχθῇ τὸ εὐαγγέλιον τοῦτο εἰς ὅλον τὸν κόσμον, καὶ ὃ
is proclaimed gospel this in all the world, also what
ἐποίησεν αὕτη λαληθήσεται εἰς μνημόσυνον αὐτῆς.
did this (one) will be spoken for a memorial of her.
10 Καὶ ὁ Ἰούδας ὁ Ἰσκαριώτης, εἷς τῶν δώδεκα, ἀπῆλθε
And – Judas Iscariot, one of the twelve, went away
11 πρὸς τοὺς ἀρχιερεῖς, ἵνα παραδῷ αὐτὸν αὐτοῖς. οἱ δὲ ἀκού-
to the chief priests, that he might betray Him to them. they And
σαντες ἐχάρησαν, καὶ ἐπηγγείλαντο αὐτῷ ἀργύριον δοῦναι·
hearing rejoiced and promised him silver to give.
καὶ ἐζήτει πῶς εὐκαίρως αὐτὸν παραδῷ.
And he sought how opportunely Him he might betray.
12 Καὶ τῇ πρώτῃ ἡμέρᾳ τῶν ἀζύμων, ὅτε τὸ πάσχα ἔθυον,
And on the first day of the unleavened, when the Passover they killed,
λέγουσιν αὐτῷ οἱ μαθηταὶ αὐτοῦ, Ποῦ θέλεις ἀπελθόντες
say to Him the disciples of Him, Where do You wish going
13 ἑτοιμάσωμεν ἵνα φάγῃς τὸ πάσχα; καὶ ἀποστέλλει δύο τῶν
we may prepare that You eat the Passover? And He sends two of the
μαθητῶν αὐτοῦ, καὶ λέγει αὐτοῖς, Ὑπάγετε εἰς τὴν πόλιν,
disciples of Him, and says to them, Go into the city,
καὶ ἀπαντήσει ὑμῖν ἄνθρωπος κεράμιον ὕδατος βαστάζων·
and will meet you a man a pitcher of water carrying;
14 ἀκολουθήσατε αὐτῷ, καὶ ὅπου ἐὰν εἰσέλθῃ, εἴπατε τῷ
follow him. And where ever he enters, tell the
οἰκοδεσπότῃ ὅτι Ὁ διδάσκαλος λέγει, Ποῦ ἐστι τὸ κατά-
housemaster, – The Teacher says, Where is the guest-
15 λυμα, ὅπου τὸ πάσχα μετὰ τῶν μαθητῶν μου φάγω; καὶ
room where the Passover with the disciples of Me I may eat? And

you a large upper room, having been spread *and* made ready. Prepare for us there. [16]And His disciples went out and came into the city, and found *it* as He told them. And they prepared the Passover.

[17]And *it* becoming evening, He came with the Twelve. [18]And as they were reclining and eating, Jesus said, Truly I say to you, One of you will betray Me, the *one* eating with Me. [19]And they began to be grieved, and to say to Him one by one, Not at all I, *is it*? And another, Not at all I, *is it*? [20]But answering He said to them, *It is* one from the Twelve, the *one* dipping in the dish with Me. [21]Truly the Son of man goes as it has been written concerning Him, but woe to that man by whom the Son of man is betrayed! It were good for him if that man had never been born.

[22]And as they were eating, taking a loaf, Jesus broke and gave to them. And *He* said, Take, eat, this is My body. [23]And taking the cup, giving thanks, He gave to them. And they all drank out of it. [24]And He said to them, This is My blood, that of the New Covenant, which is poured out for many. [25]Truly I say to you, I will not at all drink of the fruit of the vine any more until that day when I drink it new in the kingdom of God.

[26]And singing a hymn, they went into the Mount of Olives.

[27]And Jesus said to them, All of you will be offended in Me in this night, because it has been written, "I will strike the Shepherd, and the sheep will be scattered." [28]But after My resurrection, I will go before you into Galilee. [29]But Peter said to Him, Even if all shall be

αὐτὸς ὑμῖν δείξει ἀνώγεον μέγα ἐστρωμένον ἕτοιμον· ἐκεῖ
he you will show an upper room large being spread, ready. There
16 ἑτοιμάσατε ἡμῖν. καὶ ἐξῆλθον οἱ μαθηταὶ αὐτοῦ, καὶ ἦλθον
you prepare for us. And went forth the disciples of Him, and came
εἰς τὴν πόλιν, καὶ εὗρον καθὼς εἶπεν αὐτοῖς, καὶ ἡτοίμασαν
into the city, and found as He told them, and they prepared
τὸ πάσχα.
the Passover.
17 Καὶ ὀψίας γενομένης ἔρχεται μετὰ τῶν δώδεκα. καὶ ἀνακει-
18 And evening occurring, He comes with the twelve. And reclining
μένων αὐτῶν καὶ ἐσθιόντων, εἶπεν ὁ Ἰησοῦς, Ἀμὴν λέγω
they, and eating, said — Jesus, Truly I say
19 ὑμῖν, ὅτι εἷς ἐξ ὑμῶν παραδώσει με, ὁ ἐσθίων μετ' ἐμοῦ. οἱ
to you that one from you will betray Me, the (one) eating with Me, they
δὲ ἤρξαντο λυπεῖσθαι, καὶ λέγειν αὐτῷ εἷς καθ' εἷς, Μή τι
And began to be grieved, and to say to Him one by one, Not at all
20 ἐγώ; καὶ ἄλλος, Μή τι ἐγώ; ὁ δὲ ἀποκριθεὶς εἶπεν αὐτοῖς,
I? And another, Not at all I? He And answering said to them,
Εἷς ἐκ τῶν δώδεκα, ὁ ἐμβαπτόμενος μετ' ἐμοῦ εἰς τὸ τρυβλίον.
One from the twelve, the (one) dipping in with Me in the dish.
21 ὁ μὲν υἱὸς τοῦ ἀνθρώπου ὑπάγει, καθὼς γέγραπται περὶ
the Indeed Son — of man is going as it has been written about
αὐτοῦ· οὐαὶ δὲ τῷ ἀνθρώπῳ ἐκείνῳ δι' οὗ ὁ υἱὸς τοῦ
Him. woe But to man that through whom the Son —
ἀνθρώπου παραδίδοται· καλὸν ἦν αὐτῷ εἰ οὐκ ἐγεννήθη ὁ
of man is betrayed; good were it for him if not was born
ἄνθρωπος ἐκεῖνος.
man that.
22 Καὶ ἐσθιόντων αὐτῶν, λαβὼν ὁ Ἰησοῦς ἄρτον εὐλογήσας
And eating they, taking Jesus a loaf, blessing,
ἔκλασε, καὶ ἔδωκεν αὐτοῖς, καὶ εἶπε, Λάβετε, φάγετε· τοῦτό
He broke and gave to them, and said, Take, eat, this
23 ἐστι τὸ σῶμά μου. καὶ λαβὼν τὸ ποτήριον εὐχαριστήσας
is the body of Me. And taking the cup, giving thanks,
24 ἔδωκεν αὐτοῖς· καὶ ἔπιον ἐξ αὐτοῦ πάντες. καὶ εἶπεν αὐτοῖς,
He gave to them, and drank from it all. And He said to them,
Τοῦτό ἐστι τὸ αἷμά μου, τὸ τῆς καινῆς διαθήκης, τὸ περὶ
This is the blood of Me, that of the New Covenant concerning
25 πολλῶν ἐκχυνόμενον. ἀμὴν λέγω ὑμῖν ὅτι οὐκέτι οὐ μὴ πίω
many being poured out. Truly I say to you that no more in no way I may drink
ἐκ τοῦ γεννήματος τῆς ἀμπέλου, ἕως τῆς ἡμέρας ἐκείνης ὅταν
of the offspring of the vine until — day that when
αὐτὸ πίνω καινὸν ἐν τῇ βασιλείᾳ τοῦ Θεοῦ.
it I drink new in the kingdom — of God.
26 Καὶ ὑμνήσαντες ἐξῆλθον εἰς τὸ ὄρος τῶν ἐλαιῶν.
And having sung a hymn they went into the mount of the olives.
27 Καὶ λέγει αὐτοῖς ὁ Ἰησοῦς ὅτι Πάντες σκανδαλισθήσεσθε
And says to them — Jesus, — All you will be offended
ἐν ἐμοὶ ἐν τῇ νυκτὶ ταύτῃ· ὅτι γέγραπται, Πατάξω τὸν
in Me in — night this, because it has been written: I will strike the
28 ποιμένα, καὶ διασκορπισθήσεται τὰ πρόβατα. ἀλλὰ μετὰ
Shepherd, and will be scattered the sheep. But after
29 τὸ ἐγερθῆναί με, προάξω ὑμᾶς εἰς τὴν Γαλιλαίαν. ὁ δὲ
the arising of Me, I will go before you into — Galilee. — And
Πέτρος ἔφη αὐτῷ, Καὶ εἰ πάντες σκανδαλισθήσονται, ἀλλ'
Peter said to Him, Even if all shall be offended, yet

offended, yet not I. 30 And Jesus said to him, Truly I say to you that today, in this night, before *the* cock crows twice, you will deny Me three times. 31 But he said more fervently, If it were needful for me to die with You, in no way will I deny You. And also all said the same.

32 And they came to a place of which the name *was* Gethsemane. And He said to His disciples, Sit here while I pray. 33 And He took along Peter and James and John with Him. And He began to be much amazed, and to be distressed. 34 And *He* said to them, My soul is deeply grieved, unto death. Remain here and watch. 35 And going forward a little, He fell on the ground, and prayed that if it were possible the hour might pass from Him. 36 And he said, Abba, Father, all things *are* possible to You; take this cup from Me. Yet not what I will, but what You *will.* 37 And He came and found them sleeping. And He said to Peter, Simon, do you sleep? Were you not strong enough to watch one hour? 38 Watch and pray, that you may not enter into temptation. The spirit truly *is* willing, but the flesh *is* weak. 39 And going away again, He prayed, saying the same thing. 40 And returning He found them sleeping again, for their eyes were heavy. And they did not know what to answer Him. 41 And He came a third time, and said to them, Sleep on now, and rest. It is enough. The hour has come. Behold, the Son of man is betrayed into the hands of sinners. 42 Rise up, let us go. Behold, the *one* betraying Me has drawn near.

43 And immediately, as He was yet speak-ing, Judas came up, being one of the Twelve. And with him *was* a great crowd with swords

30 οὐκ ἐγώ. καὶ λέγει αὐτῷ ὁ Ἰησοῦς, Ἀμὴν λέγω σοι, ὅτι
not I. And says to him — Jesus, Truly I say to you, —
σήμερον ἐν τῇ νυκτὶ ταύτῃ, πρὶν ἢ δὶς ἀλέκτορα φωνῆσαι,
Today, in — night this, before — twice (the) cock sounds,
31 τρὶς ἀπαρνήσῃ με. ὁ δὲ ἐκ περισσοῦ ἔλεγε μᾶλλον, Ἐάν με
thrice you will deny Me. he But exceedingly said more, If me
δέῃ συναποθανεῖν σοι, οὐ μή σε ἀπαρνήσομαι. ὡσαύτως
must die with You, in no way You will I deny. likewise
δὲ καὶ πάντες ἔλεγον.
And also all said.
32 Καὶ ἔρχονται εἰς χωρίον οὗ τὸ ὄνομα Γεθσημανῆ· καὶ
And they come to a place of which the name (was) Gethsemane. And
λέγει τοῖς μαθηταῖς αὐτοῦ, Καθίσατε ὧδε, ἕως προσεύξω-
He says to the disciples of Him, Sit here while I pray.
33 μαι. καὶ παραλαμβάνει τὸν Πέτρον καὶ τὸν Ἰάκωβον καὶ
And He takes along — Peter and — James and
Ἰωάννην μεθ' ἑαυτοῦ, καὶ ἤρξατο ἐκθαμβεῖσθαι καὶ ἀδη-
John with Him. And He began to be much amazed, and to be
34 μονεῖν. καὶ λέγει αὐτοῖς, Περίλυπός ἐστιν ἡ ψυχή μου ἕως
distressed, and says to them, Deeply grieved is the soul of Me unto
35 θανάτου· μείνατε ὧδε καὶ γρηγορεῖτε. καὶ προελθὼν μικρόν,
death. Remain here and watch. And going forward a little,
ἔπεσεν ἐπὶ τῆς γῆς, καὶ προσηύχετο ἵνα, εἰ δυνατόν ἐστι,
He fell on the ground, and prayed that if possible it is
36 παρέλθῃ ἀπ' αὐτοῦ ἡ ὥρα. καὶ ἔλεγεν, Ἀββᾶ, ὁ πατήρ,
might pass from Him the hour. And He said, Abba, — Father,
πάντα δυνατά σοι. παρένεγκε τὸ ποτήριον ἀπ' ἐμοῦ τοῦτο·
all things possible to You. Remove — cup from Me this;
37 ἀλλ' οὐ τί ἐγὼ θέλω, ἀλλὰ τί σύ. καὶ ἔρχεται καὶ εὑρίσκει
but not what I desire, but what You And He comes and finds
αὐτοὺς καθεύδοντας, καὶ λέγει τῷ Πέτρῳ, Σίμων, καθεύδεις;
them sleeping, and says — to Peter, Simon, do you sleep?
38 οὐκ ἴσχυσας μίαν ὥραν γρηγορῆσαι; γρηγορεῖτε καὶ
not were you strong one hour to watch? Watch and
προσεύχεσθε, ἵνα μὴ εἰσέλθητε εἰς πειρασμόν. τὸ μὲν πνεῦμα
pray, that not you enter into temptation; the indeed spirit
39 πρόθυμον, ἡ δὲ σὰρξ ἀσθενής. καὶ πάλιν ἀπελθὼν προσηύ-
(is) eager, the but flesh (is) weak. And again going away He prayed
40 ξατο, τὸν αὐτὸν λόγον εἰπών. καὶ ὑποστρέψας εὗρεν αὐτοὺς
the same word saying. And having returned He found them
πάλιν καθεύδοντας· ἦσαν γὰρ οἱ ὀφθαλμοὶ αὐτῶν βεβαρη-
again sleeping, were for the eyes of them heavy.
41 μένοι, καὶ οὐκ ᾔδεισαν τί αὐτῷ ἀποκριθῶσι. καὶ ἔρχεται τὸ
And not they knew what Him to answer. And He comes the
τρίτον, καὶ λέγει αὐτοῖς, Καθεύδετε τὸ λοιπὸν καὶ ἀναπαύε-
third, and says to them, Sleep now and rest;
σθε. ἀπέχει· ἦλθεν ἡ ὥρα· ἰδού, παραδίδοται ὁ υἱὸς τοῦ
it is enough; has come the hour; behold, is betrayed the Son —
42 ἀνθρώπου εἰς τὰς χεῖρας τῶν ἁμαρτωλῶν. ἐγείρεσθε, ἄγωμεν·
of man into the hands of the sinners. Arise, let us go;
ἰδού, ὁ παραδιδούς με ἤγγικε.
behold, the (one) betraying Me has drawn near.
43 Καὶ εὐθέως, ἔτι αὐτοῦ λαλοῦντος, παραγίνεται Ἰούδας,
And at once, yet He speaking, comes up Judas,
εἷς ὢν τῶν δώδεκα, καὶ μετ' αὐτοῦ ὄχλος πολὺς μετὰ μαχαι-
one being of the twelve, and with him a crowd large with swords

and staves, from the chief priests and the scribes and the elders. 44 And the *one* betraying Him had given them a sign, saying, Whomever I kiss, *it* is He; seize Him, and lead *Him* away safely. 45 And coming, at once coming near to Him, he said, Rabbi, Rabbi!. And he ardently kissed Him. 46 And they laid their hands on Him and seized Him. 47 But a certain one of those standing by, drawing *a* sword, struck the slave of the high priest, and took off his ear. 48 And answering Jesus said to them, Have you come out with swords and clubs to take Me, as against a robber? 49 I was with you daily teaching in the Temple, and you did not seize Me. But *it is* that the Scriptures may be fulfilled. 50 And leaving Him, all fled. 51 And one, a certain young man, was following Him, having thrown a linen cloth around *his* naked *body.* And the young men caught him. 52 But he, leaving behind the linen cloth, fled from them naked.

53 And they led Jesus away to the high priest. And they came together to him, all the chief priests and the elders and the scribes. 54 And Peter followed Him from a distance, to the inside of the hall of the chief priest. And he was sitting with the under-officers, also warming himself near the light. 55 And the chief priests and the whole sanhedrin sought testimony against Jesus, to put Him to death. And *they* did not find *any.* 56 For many bore false witness against Him, but their testimonies were not alike. 57 And standing up, some falsely testified against Him, saying, 58 We heard Him saying, I will destroy this Temple made with hands, and in three days I will build another not made with hands. 59 And

ρῶν καὶ ξύλων, παρὰ τῶν ἀρχιερέων καὶ τῶν γραμματέων
and clubs from the chief priests and the scribes
44 καὶ τῶν πρεσβυτέρων. δεδώκει δὲ ὁ παραδιδοὺς αὐτὸν
and the elders. had given And the (one) betraying Him
σύσσημον αὐτοῖς, λέγων, Ὃν ἂν φιλήσω, αὐτός ἐστι κρατή-
a signal them, saying, Whomever I kiss, He it is; seize
45 σατε αὐτόν, καὶ ἀπαγάγετε ἀσφαλῶς. καὶ ἐλθών, εὐθέως
Him, and lead away securely. And coming, at once
προσελθὼν αὐτῷ λέγει, Ῥαββί, ῥαββί· καὶ κατεφίλησεν
coming near to Him, he says, Rabbi, Rabbi; and fervently kissed
46 αὐτόν. οἱ δὲ ἐπέβαλον ἐπ' αὐτὸν τὰς χεῖρας αὐτῶν, καὶ
Him. they And laid on Him the hands of them and
47 ἐκράτησαν αὐτόν. εἷς δέ τις τῶν παρεστηκότων σπασά-
seized Him. one But certain of the (ones) standing by, drawing
μενος τὴν μάχαιραν ἔπαισε τὸν δοῦλον τοῦ ἀρχιερέως, καὶ
the sword struck the slave of the high priest, and
48 ἀφεῖλεν αὐτοῦ τὸ ὠτίον. καὶ ἀποκριθεὶς ὁ Ἰησοῦς εἶπεν
took off of him the ear. And answering — Jesus said
αὐτοῖς, Ὡς ἐπὶ λῃστὴν ἐξήλθετε μετὰ μαχαιρῶν καὶ ξύλων
to them, As against a robber come you out with swords and clubs
49 συλλαβεῖν με; καθ' ἡμέραν ἤμην πρὸς ὑμᾶς ἐν τῷ ἱερῷ
to take Me? Daily I was with you in the Temple
διδάσκων, καὶ οὐκ ἐκρατήσατέ με· ἀλλ' ἵνα πληρωθῶσιν αἱ
teaching, and not you did seize Me; but that may be fulfilled the
50 γραφαί. καὶ ἀφέντες αὐτὸν πάντες ἔφυγον.
Scriptures. And forsaking Him, all fled.
51 Καὶ εἷς τις νεανίσκος ἠκολούθει αὐτῷ, περιβεβλημένος
And one certain young man was following Him, having thrown about
52 σινδόνα ἐπὶ γυμνοῦ. καὶ κρατοῦσιν αὐτὸν οἱ νεανίσκοι· ὁ
a linen cloth upon (his) naked (body) And seized him the young men. he
δὲ καταλιπὼν τὴν σινδόνα γυμνὸς ἔφυγεν ἀπ' αὐτῶν.
But forsaking the linen cloth naked fled from them.
53 Καὶ ἀπήγαγον τὸν Ἰησοῦν πρὸς τὸν ἀρχιερέα· καὶ συνέρ-
And they led away — Jesus to the high priest, and come
χονται αὐτῷ πάντες οἱ ἀρχιερεῖς καὶ οἱ πρεσβύτεροι καὶ οἱ
together to him all the chief priests and the elders and the
54 γραμματεῖς. καὶ ὁ Πέτρος ἀπὸ μακρόθεν ἠκολούθησεν αὐτῷ
scribes. And — Peter from afar followed Him,
ἕως ἔσω εἰς τὴν αὐλὴν τοῦ ἀρχιερέως· καὶ ἦν συγκαθήμενος
until within, in the court of the high priest; and was sitting together
55 μετὰ τῶν ὑπηρετῶν, καὶ θερμαινόμενος πρὸς τὸ φῶς. οἱ δὲ
with the attendants, and warming himself toward the light. the And
ἀρχιερεῖς καὶ ὅλον τὸ συνέδριον ἐζήτουν κατὰ τοῦ Ἰησοῦ
chief priests and all the sanhedrin sought against — Jesus
μαρτυρίαν, εἰς τὸ θανατῶσαι αὐτόν· καὶ οὐχ εὕρισκον.
witness, for the putting to death Him, and not did find.
56 πολλοὶ γὰρ ἐψευδομαρτύρουν κατ' αὐτοῦ, καὶ ἴσαι αἱ
Many falsely testified against Him, and identical the
57 μαρτυρίαι οὐκ ἦσαν. καί τινες ἀναστάντες ἐψευδομαρτύρουν
testimonies not were. And some standing up falsely testified
58 κατ' αὐτοῦ, λέγοντες ὅτι Ἡμεῖς ἠκούσαμεν αὐτοῦ λέγοντος
against Him, saying, — We heard Him saying,
ὅτι Ἐγὼ καταλύσω τὸν ναὸν τοῦτον τὸν χειροποίητον, καὶ
— I will throw down Temple this — made with hands, and
59 διὰ τριῶν ἡμερῶν ἄλλον ἀχειροποίητον οἰκοδομήσω. καὶ
through three days another not made with hands I will build. And

neither in this was their testimony alike. 60 And standing up in the middle, the high priest questioned Jesus, saying, Do you not answer? Nothing? What do these testify against you? 61 But He was silent, and answered nothing. Again the high priest questioned Him, and said to Him, Are you the Christ, the son of the Blessed? 62 And Jesus said, I AM! And you will see the Son of man sitting at *the* right *hand* of power, and coming with the clouds of the heavens. 63 And tearing his garments, the high priest said, Why do we still have need of witnesses? 64 You heard the blasphemy. What appears to you? and they all condemned Him to be liable, *even* of death. 65 And some began to spit at Him, and to cover His face, and to beat Him with a fist, and to say to Him, Prophesy! And the under-officers struck Him with slaps.

66 And Peter being in the court below, one of the maids of the high priest came. 67 And seeing Peter warming himself, looking at him, *she* said, And you were with Jesus the Nazarene. 68 But he denied, saying, I do not know nor understand what you say. And he went out into the forecourt. And a cock crowed. 69 And seeing him again, the maid began to say to those standing by, This one is of them. 70 And again he denied. And after a little, those standing by again said to Peter, Truly you are from them, for you are both a Galilean and your speech agrees.

71 But he began to curse and to swear, I do not know this man whom you speak of. 72 And a second time a cock crowed. And Peter remembered the word Jesus said to him, Before a cock crows twice, you will deny Me three times. And thinking on *it*, he wept.

60 οὐδὲ οὕτως ἴση ἦν ἡ μαρτυρία αὐτῶν. καὶ ἀναστὰς ὁ ἀρχιε-
neither thus identical was the witness of them. And standing up the high

ρεὺς εἰς τὸ μέσον ἐπηρώτησε τὸν Ἰησοῦν, λέγων, Οὐκ ἀπο-
priest in the midst, he questioned — Jesus, saying, Do not you

61 κρίνῃ οὐδέν; τί οὗτοί σου καταμαρτυροῦσιν; ὁ δὲ ἐσιώπα,
answer nothing, what these you testify against? He But was silent,

καὶ οὐδὲν ἀπεκρίνατο. πάλιν ὁ ἀρχιερεὺς ἐπηρώτα αὐτόν, καὶ
and nothing answered. Again the high priest questioned Him, and

62 λέγει αὐτῷ, Σὺ εἶ ὁ Χριστός, ὁ υἱὸς τοῦ εὐλογητοῦ; ὁ δὲ
says to Him, You are the Christ, the Son of the Blessed (One)? — And

Ἰησοῦς εἶπεν, Ἐγώ εἰμι. καὶ ὄψεσθε τὸν υἱὸν τοῦ ἀνθρώπου
Jesus said, I AM! And you will see the Son — of man

καθήμενον ἐκ δεξιῶν τῆς δυνάμεως, καὶ ἐρχόμενον μετὰ τῶν
sitting off (the) right of the Power, and coming with the

63 νεφελῶν τοῦ οὐρανοῦ. ὁ δὲ ἀρχιερεὺς διαρρήξας τοὺς
clouds of Heaven. the And high priest, tearing the

χιτῶνας αὐτοῦ λέγει, Τί ἔτι χρείαν ἔχομεν μαρτύρων;
garments of him, says, Why still need do we have of witnesses?

64 ἠκούσατε τῆς βλασφημίας· τί ὑμῖν φαίνεται; οἱ δὲ πάντες
You heard the blasphemy. What to you appears it? they And all

65 κατέκριναν αὐτὸν εἶναι ἔνοχον θανάτου. καὶ ἤρξαντό τινες
condemned Him to be liable of death. And began some

ἐμπτύειν αὐτῷ, καὶ περικαλύπτειν τὸ πρόσωπον αὐτοῦ,
to spit at Him, and to cover the face of Him,

καὶ κολαφίζειν αὐτόν, καὶ λέγειν αὐτῷ, Προφήτευσον· καὶ
and to beat with a fist Him, and to say to Him, Prophesy! And

οἱ ὑπηρέται ῥαπίσμασιν αὐτὸν ἔβαλλον.
the attendants with slaps Him struck.

66 Καὶ ὄντος τοῦ Πέτρου ἐν τῇ αὐλῇ κάτω, ἔρχεται μία τῶν
And being — Peter in the court below, comes one of the

67 παιδισκῶν τοῦ ἀρχιερέως, καὶ ἰδοῦσα τὸν Πέτρον θερμαινό-
maids of the high priest, and seeing — Peter warming

μενον, ἐμβλέψασα αὐτῷ λέγει, Καὶ σὺ μετὰ τοῦ Ναζαρηνοῦ
himself, looking at him says, And you with the Nazarene

68 Ἰησοῦ ἦσθα. ὁ δὲ ἠρνήσατο, λέγων, Οὐκ οἶδα, οὐδὲ
Jesus were. he But denied, saying, not I know, nor

ἐπίσταμαι τί σὺ λέγεις. καὶ ἐξῆλθεν ἔξω εἰς τὸ προαύλιον·
understand what you say. And he went outside into the forecourt;

69 καὶ ἀλέκτωρ ἐφώνησε. καὶ ἡ παιδίσκη ἰδοῦσα αὐτὸν πάλιν
and a cock crowed. And the maid seeing him again

ἤρξατο λέγειν τοῖς παρεστηκόσιν ὅτι Οὗτος ἐξ αὐτῶν ἐστίν.
began to say to the (ones) standing by, This one of them is.

70 ὁ δὲ πάλιν ἠρνεῖτο. καὶ μετὰ μικρὸν πάλιν οἱ παρεστῶτες
he But again denied. And after a little again the (ones) standing by

ἔλεγον τῷ Πέτρῳ, Ἀληθῶς ἐξ αὐτῶν εἶ· καὶ γὰρ Γαλιλαῖος
said — to Peter, Truly of them you are; even for a Galilean

71 εἶ, καὶ ἡ λαλιά σου ὁμοιάζει. ὁ δὲ ἤρξατο ἀναθεματίζειν καὶ
you are, and the speech of you agrees. he And began to curse and

72 ὀμνύειν ὅτι Οὐκ οἶδα τὸν ἄνθρωπον τοῦτον ὃν λέγετε. καὶ
to swear, — not I know — man this whom you say. And

ἐκ δευτέρου ἀλέκτωρ ἐφώνησε. καὶ ἀνεμνήσθη ὁ Πέτρος τοῦ
for a second time a cock crowed. And remembered — Peter the

ῥήματος οὗ εἶπεν αὐτῷ ὁ Ἰησοῦς ὅτι Πρὶν ἀλέκτορα
word said to him — Jesus, — Before a cock

φωνῆσαι δίς, ἀπαρνήσῃ με τρίς. καὶ ἐπιβαλὼν ἔκλαιε.
crows twice, you will deny Me thrice. And thinking on (it) he wept.

CHAPTER 15

1 And immediately in the morning, the chief priests and scribes and all the sanhedrin forming a council, binding Jesus, *they* led *Him* away and delivered *Him* to Pilate. 2 And Pilate questioned Him, Are you the king of the Jews? And answering He said to him, You say *it*. 3 And the chief priests urgently accused Him of many things. But He answered nothing. 4 But Pilate again questioned Him, saying, Do you answer nothing? Behold, how many things they testify against you. 5 But Jesus answered nothing any more; so as *for* Pilate to marvel.

6 And at a feast he released to them one prisoner, whomever they asked. 7 And there was one called Barabbas, having been bound with the insurgents, who in the insurrection had committed murder. 8 And crying aloud, the crowd began to beg *him to do* as he always did to them. 9 But Pilate answered them, saying, Do you desire I should release to you the king of the Jews? 10 For he knew that the chief priests had delivered Him up through envy. 11 But the chief priests stirred up the crowd, that rather he should release Barabbas to them. 12 But answering again Pilate said to them, What then do you desire I do to *him* whom you call king of the Jews? 13 And again they cried out, Crucify him! 14 But Pilate said to them, For what evil did he do? But they much more cried out, Crucify him! 15 And deciding to do the easiest to the crowd, Pilate released Barabbas to them. And having flogged *Him, he* delivered up Jesus, that He might be crucified.

16 And the soldiers led Him away inside the court, which is *the* praetorium. And they called together all the cohort. 17 And they put

CHAPTER 15

1 Καὶ εὐθέως ἐπὶ τὸ πρωῒ συμβούλιον ποιήσαντες οἱ
And immediately on (morn) early, a council having made the
ἀρχιερεῖς μετὰ τῶν πρεσβυτέρων καὶ γραμματέων, καὶ ὅλον
chief priests with the elders and scribes, and all
τὸ συνέδριον, δήσαντες τὸν Ἰησοῦν ἀπήνεγκαν καὶ παρέδω-
the sanhedrin, having bound — Jesus led (Him) away and delivered
2 καν τῷ Πιλάτῳ. καὶ ἐπηρώτησεν αὐτὸν ὁ Πιλάτος, Σὺ εἶ ὁ
(Him) — to Pilate. And questioned Him — Pilate, You are the
βασιλεὺς τῶν Ἰουδαίων; ὁ δὲ ἀποκριθεὶς εἶπεν αὐτῷ, Σὺ
king of the Jews? He And answering said to him, You
3 λέγεις. καὶ κατηγόρουν αὐτοῦ οἱ ἀρχιερεῖς πολλά· αὐτὸς δὲ
say (it). And accused Him the chief priests many things, He but
4 οὐδὲν ἀπεκρίνατο. ὁ δὲ Πιλάτος πάλιν ἐπηρώτησεν αὐτόν,
nothing answered. — But Pilate again questioned Him,
λέγων, Οὐκ ἀποκρίνῃ οὐδέν; ἴδε, πόσα σου καταμαρτυ-
saying, not Do you answer nothing? Behold, how many things you they testify
5 ροῦσιν. ὁ δὲ Ἰησοῦς οὐκέτι οὐδὲν ἀπεκρίθη, ὥστε θαυμάζειν
against. — But Jesus no more nothing answered, so as to marvel
τὸν Πιλάτον.
Pilate.

6 Κατὰ δὲ ἑορτὴν ἀπέλυεν αὐτοῖς ἕνα δέσμιον, ὅνπερ
at And a feast he released to them one prisoner, whomever
7 ᾐτοῦντο. ἦν δὲ ὁ λεγόμενος Βαραββᾶς μετὰ τῶν συστασια-
they asked. was And one called Barabbas, with the insurgents
8 στῶν δεδεμένος, οἵτινες ἐν τῇ στάσει φόνον πεποιήκεισαν. καὶ
having been bound, who in the insurrection murder had committed. And
ἀναβοήσας ὁ ὄχλος ἤρξατο αἰτεῖσθαι καθὼς ἀεὶ ἐποίει αὐτοῖς.
crying aloud the crowd began to beg as always he did for them.
9 ὁ δὲ Πιλάτος ἀπεκρίθη αὐτοῖς, λέγων, Θέλετε ἀπολύσω ὑμῖν
—But Pilate answered them, saying, Desire you I may release to you
10 τὸν βασιλέα τῶν Ἰουδαίων; ἐγίνωσκε γὰρ ὅτι διὰ φθόνον
the king of the Jews? he knew For that for envy
11 παραδεδώκεισαν αὐτὸν οἱ ἀρχιερεῖς. οἱ δὲ ἀρχιερεῖς ἀνέσει-
had delivered over Him the chief priests. the But chief priests stirred
σαν τὸν ὄχλον, ἵνα μᾶλλον τὸν Βαραββᾶν ἀπολύσῃ αὐτοῖς.
up the crowd, that rather — Barabbas he should release to them.
12 ὁ δὲ Πιλάτος ἀποκριθεὶς πάλιν εἶπεν αὐτοῖς, Τί οὖν θέλετε
— But Pilate answering again said to them, What then wish you
13 ποιήσω ὃν λέγετε βασιλέα τῶν Ἰουδαίων; οἱ δὲ πάλιν
I do (with) whom you call king of the Jews? they And again
14 ἔκραξαν, Σταύρωσον αὐτόν. ὁ δὲ Πιλάτος ἔλεγεν αὐτοῖς, Τί
cried out, Crucify Him! — But Pilate said to them, what
γὰρ κακὸν ἐποίησεν; οἱ δὲ περισσοτέρως ἔκραξαν, Σταύ-
For evil did he do? they And much more cried out, Crucify
15 ρωσον αὐτόν. ὁ δὲ Πιλάτος βουλόμενος τῷ ὄχλῳ τὸ ἱκανὸν
Him! — But Pilate deciding the crowd the easiest
ποιῆσαι, ἀπέλυσεν αὐτοῖς τὸν Βαραββᾶν· καὶ παρέδωκε τὸν
to do, released to them Barabbas, and delivered up —
Ἰησοῦν, φραγελλώσας, ἵνα σταυρωθῇ.
Jesus, having whipped (Him) that He might be crucified.

16 Οἱ δὲ στρατιῶται ἀπήγαγον αὐτὸν ἔσω τῆς αὐλῆς, ὅ ἐστι
the And soldiers led away Him inside the court, which is
17 πραιτώριον, καὶ συγκαλοῦσιν ὅλην τὴν σπεῖραν. καὶ
praetorium, and they call together all the cohort. And

purple on Him, and they plaited and placed a crown of thorns on Him. [18]And they began to salute Him, Hail, King of the Jews! [19]And they struck His head with a reed, and spat at Him. And placing the knees, *they* bowed down to Him. [20]And when they had mocked Him, they took the purple off Him, and put His own garments on Him. and they led Him out, that they might crucify Him. [21]And they forced one passing by, Simon, a Cyrenian, coming from the field, the father of Alexander and Rufus, that he might carry His cross.

[22]And they brought Him to Golgotha Place, which translated is, Place of a Skull. [23]And they gave him wine having been spiced with myrrh to drink. But He did not take *it*. [24]And having crucified Him, they divided His garments, casting a lot on them, who *and* what *each* should take. [25]And it was *the* third hour, and they crucified Him. [26]And the superscription of His charge was written over *Him*, THE KING OF THE JEWS. [27]And they crucified two robbers with Him, one off *the* right, and one off *the* left of Him.

[28]And the Scripture was fulfilled which says, "And He was numbered with *the* lawless." [29]And those passing by blasphemed Him, shaking their heads, and saying, Aha! *You* razing the Temple, and in three days building *it*, [30]save yourself, and come down from the cross. [31]And also the chief priests and the scribes mocking to one another said the same, He saved others; he is not able to save himself. [32]The Christ, the King of Israel? Let him now come down from the cross, that we may see and believe. And the ones crucified with Him insulted Him.

[33]And *it* being *the* sixth hour, darkness came over all

ἐνδύουσιν αὐτὸν πορφύραν, καὶ περιτιθέασιν αὐτῷ πλέ-
they put on Him purple, and placed around Him having
18 ξαντες ἀκάνθινον στέφανον, καὶ ἤρξαντο ἀσπάζεσθαι αὐτόν,
plaited a thorny crown. And they began to salute Him,
19 Χαῖρε, βασιλεῦ τῶν Ἰουδαίων· καὶ ἔτυπτον αὐτοῦ τὴν
Hail, King of the Jews! And they struck of Him the
κεφαλὴν καλάμῳ, καὶ ἐνέπτυον αὐτῷ, καὶ τιθέντες τὰ γόνατα
head with a reed, and spit at Him; and placing the knees
20 προσεκύνουν αὐτῷ. καὶ ὅτε ἐνέπαιξαν αὐτῷ, ἐξέδυσαν
did homage to Him. And when they had mocked Him, they took off
αὐτὸν τὴν πορφύραν, καὶ ἐνέδυσαν αὐτὸν τὰ ἱμάτια τὰ ἴδια.
Him the purple, and put on Him the garments, his own.
21 Καὶ ἐξάγουσιν αὐτὸν ἵνα σταυρώσωσιν αὐτόν. καὶ
And they lead forth Him, that they might crucify Him. And
ἀγγαρεύουσι παράγοντά τινα Σίμωνα Κυρηναῖον, ἐρχόμενον
they compel passing by a certain Simon, a Cyrenian coming
ἀπ' ἀγροῦ, τὸν πατέρα Ἀλεξάνδρου καὶ Ῥούφου, ἵνα ἄρῃ
from a field, the father of Alexander and of Rufus, that he bear
22 τὸν σταυρὸν αὐτοῦ. καὶ φέρουσιν αὐτὸν ἐπὶ Γολγοθᾶ τόπον,
the cross of Him. And they bring Him to Golgotha place,
23 ὅ ἐστι μεθερμηνευόμενον, κρανίου τόπος καὶ ἐδίδουν αὐτῷ
which is, being translated, of a Skull Place. And they gave Him
24 πιεῖν ἐσμυρνισμένον οἶνον· ὁ δὲ οὐκ ἔλαβε. καὶ σταυρώσαντες
to drink spiced with myrrh wine, He but not did take. And having crucified
αὐτόν, διεμέριζον τὰ ἱμάτια αὐτοῦ, βάλλοντες κλῆρον ἐπ'
Him, they divided the garments of Him, casting a lot on
25 αὐτά, τίς τί ἄρῃ. ἦν δὲ ὥρα τρίτη, καὶ ἐσταύρωσαν αὐτόν.
them, who what may take. was And hour third, and they crucified Him.
26 καὶ ἦν ἡ ἐπιγραφὴ τῆς αἰτίας αὐτοῦ ἐπιγεγραμμένη, Ὁ
And was the superscription of the accusation of Him written over (Him), THE
27 βασιλεὺς τῶν Ἰουδαίων. καὶ σὺν αὐτῷ σταυροῦσι δύο
KING OF THE JEWS. And with Him they crucify two
28 λῃστάς, ἕνα ἐκ δεξιῶν καὶ ἕνα ἐξ εὐωνύμων αὐτοῦ. καὶ
robbers, one off (the) right, and one off (the) left of Him. And
ἐπληρώθη ἡ γραφὴ ἡ λέγουσα, Καὶ μετὰ ἀνόμων ἐλογίσθη.
was fulfilled the scripture which says, And with (the) lawless He was counted.
29 καὶ οἱ παραπορευόμενοι ἐβλασφήμουν αὐτόν, κινοῦντες τὰς
And those passing by blasphemed Him, shaking the
κεφαλὰς αὐτῶν, καὶ λέγοντες, Οὐά, ὁ καταλύων τὸν ναόν,
heads of them, and saying, Aha, the (one) razing the temple
30 καὶ ἐν τρισὶν ἡμέραις οἰκοδομῶν, σῶσον σεαυτόν. καὶ κατάβα
and in three days building, save yourself, and come down
31 ἀπὸ τοῦ σταυροῦ. ὁμοίως δὲ καὶ οἱ ἀρχιερεῖς ἐμπαίζοντες
from the cross. likewise And also the chief priests mocking
πρὸς ἀλλήλους μετὰ τῶν γραμματέων ἔλεγον, Ἄλλους
to one another, with the scribes, said, Others
32 ἔσωσεν, ἑαυτὸν οὐ δύναται σῶσαι. ὁ Χριστὸς ὁ βασιλεὺς
he saved, himself not he is able to save; the Christ, the king
τοῦ Ἰσραὴλ καταβάτω νῦν ἀπὸ τοῦ σταυροῦ, ἵνα ἴδωμεν
— of Israel, let Him descend now from the cross, that we may see
καὶ πιστεύσωμεν. καὶ οἱ συνεσταυρωμένοι αὐτῷ ὠνείδιζον
and believe. And the (ones) crucified with Him insulted
αὐτόν.
Him.
33 Γενομένης δὲ ὥρας ἕκτης, σκότος ἐγένετο ἐφ' ὅλην τὴν γῆν
occurring And hour sixth, darkness came over all the land

the land until *the* ninth hour. 34 And at the ninth hour Jesus cried with a loud voice, saying, Eloi, Eloi, lama sabachthani? which being translated is, My God, My God, why did You forsake Me? 35 And hearing, some of those standing by said, Behold, he calls Elijah. 36 And one running up, and filling a sponge with vinegar, and putting it on a reed, gave Him to drink. *But they* said, Leave *alone,* let us see if Elijah comes to take Him down.

37 And letting out a great cry, Jesus expired. 38 And the veil of the Temple was torn into two, from top to bottom. 39 And standing off across from Him, seeing that *He* had cried out so, *and* He expired, the centurion said, Truly, this Man was Son of God. 40 And women were watching from a distance, among whom also was Mary Magdalene; also Mary the mother of James the less, and of Joses, and Salome, 41 who also followed Him and ministered to Him when He was in Galilee; and many other *women* who came up to Jerusalem with Him.

42 And *it* becoming evening already, since it was *the* preparation, that is, *the* day before sabbath, 43 Joseph of Arimathea came, an honorable councillor, who himself was also waiting for the kingdom of God. *And* having boldness, he went in to Pilate and begged the body of Jesus. 44 And Pilate wondered if He were already dead. And calling the centurion near, he asked him if He died long ago. 45 And knowing from the centurion, he granted the body to Joseph. 46 And having bought a linen cloth, and having taken Him down, he wrapped *Him* in the linen, and laid Him in a tomb which was cut out of rock. And *he* rolled a stone to the mouth of the tomb. 47 And Mary Magdalene, and Mary

34 ἕως ὥρας ἐννάτης. καὶ τῇ ὥρᾳ τῇ ἐννάτῃ ἐβόησεν ὁ Ἰησοῦς
until hour ninth. And at the hour — ninth cried — Jesus
φωνῇ μεγάλῃ, λέγων, Ἐλωΐ, Ἐλωΐ, λαμμᾶ σαβαχθανί;
with a voice great, saying, Eloi, Eloi, Lama sabachthani?
ὅ ἐστι μεθερμηνευόμενον, Ὁ Θεός μου, ὁ Θεός μου, εἰς τί με
which is, being translated, The God of Me, the God of Me, why Me
35 ἐγκατέλιπες; καί τινες τῶν παρεστηκότων ἀκούσαντες
did You forsake? And some of the (ones) standing by having heard
36 ἔλεγον, Ἰδού, Ἠλίαν φωνεῖ. δραμὼν δὲ εἷς, καὶ γεμίσας
said, Behold, Elijah he calls. running And one, and having filled
σπόγγον ὄξους, περιθείς τε καλάμῳ, ἐπότιζεν αὐτόν, λέγων,
a sponge of vinegar, putting it and on a reed, gave to drink Him, saying,
37 Ἄφετε, ἴδωμεν εἰ ἔρχεται Ἠλίας καθελεῖν αὐτόν. ὁ δὲ
Leave, let us see if comes Elijah to take down Him. — But
38 Ἰησοῦς ἀφεὶς φωνὴν μεγάλην ἐξέπνευσε. καὶ τὸ καταπέτασμα
Jesus letting out a voice great expired. And the veil
39 τοῦ ναοῦ ἐσχίσθη εἰς δύο ἀπὸ ἄνωθεν ἕως κάτω. ἰδὼν δὲ ὁ
of the temple was torn into two, from top to bottom. seeing And the
κεντυρίων ὁ παρεστηκὼς ἐξ ἐναντίας αὐτοῦ ὅτι οὕτω
centurion — standing near off the opposite of Him, that thus
κράξας ἐξέπνευσεν, εἶπεν, Ἀληθῶς ὁ ἄνθρωπος οὗτος υἱὸς
having cried out He expired, said, Truly, — man this Son
40 ἦν Θεοῦ. ἦσαν δὲ καὶ γυναῖκες ἀπὸ μακρόθεν θεωροῦσαι,
was of God. were And also women from afar watching,
ἐν αἷς ἦν καὶ Μαρία ἡ Μαγδαληνή, καὶ Μαρία ἡ τοῦ
among whom was also Mary the Magdalene, and Mary the —
41 Ἰακώβου τοῦ μικροῦ καὶ Ἰωσῆ μήτηρ καὶ Σαλώμη, αἳ καί,
of James the less, and of Joses (the) mother and Salome, who also
ὅτε ἦν ἐν τῇ Γαλιλαίᾳ, ἠκολούθουν αὐτῷ, καὶ διηκόνουν
when He was in — Galilee had followed Him, and ministered
αὐτῷ, καὶ ἄλλαι πολλαὶ αἱ συναναβᾶσαι αὐτῷ εἰς
to Him, and other (women) many who came up with Him to
Ἱεροσόλυμα.
Jerusalem.

42 Καὶ ἤδη ὀψίας γενομένης, ἐπεὶ ἦν Παρασκευή, ὅ ἐστι
And now evening occurring, since it was (the) preparation which is
43 προσάββατον, ἦλθεν Ἰωσὴφ ὁ ἀπὸ Ἀριμαθαίας, εὐσχήμων
(the) day before sabbath, coming Joseph from Arimathea, an honorable
βουλευτής, ὃς καὶ αὐτὸς ἦν προσδεχόμενος τὴν βασιλείαν
councillor, who also (him)self was expecting the kingdom
τοῦ Θεοῦ· τολμήσας εἰσῆλθε πρὸς Πιλάτον, καὶ ᾐτήσατο
— of God, taking courage went in to Pilate, and asked
44 τὸ σῶμα τοῦ Ἰησοῦ. ὁ δὲ Πιλάτος ἐθαύμασεν εἰ ἤδη
the body — of Jesus. — And Pilate marveled if already
τέθνηκε· καὶ προσκαλεσάμενος τὸν κεντυρίωνα, ἐπηρώτησεν
He had died, and calling near the centurion, he questioned
45 αὐτὸν εἰ πάλαι ἀπέθανε. καὶ γνοὺς ἀπὸ τοῦ κεντυρίωνος,
him if long ago He died. And knowing from the centurion
46 ἐδωρήσατο τὸ σῶμα τῷ Ἰωσήφ. καὶ ἀγοράσας σινδόνα,
he granted the body to Joseph. And having bought a linen cloth
καὶ καθελὼν αὐτόν, ἐνείλησε τῇ σινδόνι, καὶ κατέθηκεν αὐτὸν
and having taken Him, he wrapped in the linen, and laid Him
ἐν μνημείῳ, ὃ ἦν λελατομημένον ἐκ πέτρας· καὶ προσεκύλισε
in a tomb, which was cut out of rock, and rolled
47 λίθον ἐπὶ τὴν θύραν τοῦ μνημείου. ἡ δὲ Μαρία ἡ Μαγδαληνὴ
a stone against the door of the tomb. —And Mary the Magdalene

of Joses, saw where He was laid.

CHAPTER 16

[1] And the sabbath passing, Mary Magdalene and Mary the *mother* of James and Salome, bought spices, so that coming they might anoint Him. [2] And very early on the first of the week, the sun having risen, they came upon the tomb. [3] And they said among themselves, Who will roll away the stone from the mouth of the tomb for us? [4] And looking up, they saw that the stone had been rolled back; for it was very large. [5] And entering into the tomb, they saw a young man sitting on the right, having been clothed *in* a white robe. And they were much amazed. [6] But He said to them, Do not be amazed. You seek Jesus the Nazarene, who has been crucified. He was raised. He is not here. See the place where they put Him? [7] But go, say to the disciples and to Peter, He goes before you into Galilee. You will see Him there, even as He told you. [8] And going out quickly, they fled from the tomb. And trembling and ecstasy took hold of them. And they told no one, not a thing, for they were afraid.

[9] And rising early on the first of the week, He first appeared to Mary Magdalene, from whom He had cast out seven demons. [10] That *one* had gone *and* reported to those who had been with Him, *who were* mourning and weeping. [11] And those hearing that He lives, and was seen by her, they did not believe.

[12] And after these things, He was revealed in a different form, going into the country. [13] And going those reported to the rest. Neither did they believe those.

[14] Afterward, as they reclined, He was revealed to

καὶ Μαρία Ἰωσῆ ἐθεώρουν ποῦ τίθεται.
and Mary of Joses beheld where He had been laid.

CHAPTER 16

1 Καὶ διαγενομένου τοῦ σαββάτου, Μαρία ἡ Μαγδαληνὴ
And passing the sabbath, Mary the Magdalene,
καὶ Μαρία ἡ τοῦ Ἰακώβου καὶ Σαλώμη ἠγόρασαν ἀρώματα,
and Mary the (mother) of James and Salome bought spices
2 ἵνα ἐλθοῦσαι ἀλείψωσιν αὐτόν. καὶ λίαν πρωῒ τῆς μιᾶς
that coming they might anoint Him. And very early on the first
σαββάτων ἔρχονται ἐπὶ τὸ μνημεῖον, ἀνατείλαντος τοῦ
of the week they come upon the tomb, having risen the
3 ἡλίου. καὶ ἔλεγον πρὸς ἑαυτάς, Τίς ἀποκυλίσει ἡμῖν τὸν
sun. And they said to themselves, Who will roll away for us the
4 λίθον ἐκ τῆς θύρας τοῦ μνημείου; καὶ ἀναβλέψασαι
stone from the door of the tomb? And looking up
θεωροῦσιν ὅτι ἀποκεκύλισται ὁ λίθος· ἦν γὰρ μέγας
they see that has been rolled back the stone. it was For great
5 σφόδρα. καὶ εἰσελθοῦσαι εἰς τὸ μνημεῖον, εἶδον νεανίσκον
exceedingly. And having entered into the tomb, they saw a young man
καθήμενον ἐν τοῖς δεξιοῖς, περιβεβλημένον στολὴν λευκήν·
sitting on the right, having been clothed (in) a robe white.
6 καὶ ἐξεθαμβήθησαν. ὁ δὲ λέγει αὐταῖς, Μὴ ἐκθαμβεῖσθε·
and they were much amazed. he But says to them, not Be much amazed;
Ἰησοῦν ζητεῖτε τὸν Ναζαρηνὸν τὸν ἐσταυρωμένον· ἠγέρθη,
Jesus you seek, the Nazarene; — having been crucified, He was raised
7 οὐκ ἔστιν ὧδε· ἴδε, ὁ τόπος ὅπου ἔθηκαν αὐτόν. ἀλλ'
not He is here; behold, the place where they put Him. But
ὑπάγετε, εἴπατε τοῖς μαθηταῖς αὐτοῦ καὶ τῷ Πέτρῳ ὅτι
go tell the disciples of Him, and — Peter, —
Προάγει ὑμᾶς εἰς τὴν Γαλιλαίαν· ἐκεῖ αὐτὸν ὄψεσθε, καθὼς
He goes before you into — Galilee; there Him you will see, even as
8 εἶπεν ὑμῖν. καὶ ἐξελθοῦσαι ταχὺ ἔφυγον ἀπὸ τοῦ μνημείου·
He told you. And going out quickly, they fled from the tomb.
εἶχε δὲ αὐτὰς τρόμος καὶ ἔκστασις· καὶ οὐδενὶ οὐδὲν εἶπον,
held And them trembling and ecstasy; and no one nothing they told;
ἐφοβοῦντο γάρ.
they were afraid for.

9 Ἀναστὰς δὲ πρωῒ πρώτῃ σαββάτου ἐφάνη πρῶτον
having risen And early on the first of the week, He appeared first
Μαρίᾳ τῇ Μαγδαληνῇ, ἀφ' ἧς ἐκβεβλήκει ἑπτὰ δαιμόνια.
to Mary the Magdalene, from whom He had cast seven demons.
10 ἐκείνη πορευθεῖσα ἀπήγγειλε τοῖς μετ' αὐτοῦ γενομένοις,
That (one) having gone reported to the (ones) with Him having been,
11 πενθοῦσι καὶ κλαίουσι. κἀκεῖνοι ἀκούσαντες ὅτι ζῇ καὶ
mourning and weeping. And those hearing that He lives and
ἐθεάθη ὑπ' αὐτῆς ἠπίστησαν.
was seen by her they disbelieved.

12 Μετὰ δὲ ταῦτα δυσὶν ἐξ αὐτῶν περιπατοῦσιν ἐφανερώθη
after And these things to two of them walking He was revealed
13 ἐν ἑτέρᾳ μορφῇ, πορευομένοις εἰς ἀγρόν. κἀκεῖνοι ἀπελθόντες
in a different form, going into the country. And those going
ἀπήγγειλαν τοῖς λοιποῖς· οὐδὲ ἐκείνοις ἐπίστευσαν.
reported to the rest; neither those they believed.

14 Ὕστερον ἀνακειμένοις αὐτοῖς τοῖς ἕνδεκα ἐφανερώθη, καὶ
Later as reclined they to the eleven He was revealed, and

the Eleven. And *He* reproached their unbelief and hardness of heart, because they did not believe those who had seen Him, having been raised. [15]And He said to them, Going into all the world, preach the gospel to all the creation. [16]The *one* believing and being baptized will be saved. And the *one* not believing will be condemned. [17]And these signs will follow those believing these things: they will cast out demons in My name; they will speak new languages;; [18]they will take up snakes; and if they drink anything deadly, it will in no way hurt them; they will lay hands on *the* sick, and they will be well.

[19]Then indeed, after speaking to them, the Lord was taken up into Heaven, and sat off *the* right of God. [20]And going out they preached everywhere, the Lord working with *them,* and confirming the word by the signs following. Amen.

ὠνείδισε τὴν·ἀπιστίαν αὐτῶν καὶ σκληροκαρδίαν, ὅτι τοῖς
reproached the unbelief of them and hardness of heart, because those
15 θεασαμένοις αὐτὸν ἐγηγερμένον οὐκ ἐπίστευσαν. καὶ εἶπεν
having seen Him, having been raised not they believed. And He said
αὐτοῖς, Πορευθέντες εἰς τὸν κόσμον ἅπαντα, κηρύξατε τὸ
to them, Going into the world all, preach the
16 εὐαγγέλιον πάσῃ τῇ κτίσει. ὁ πιστεύσας καὶ βαπτισθεὶς
gospel to all the creation. The (one) believing and being baptized
17 σωθήσεται· ὁ δὲ ἀπιστήσας κατακριθήσεται. σημεῖα δὲ τοῖς
will be saved; he but not believing will be condemned. signs And to those
πιστεύσασι ταῦτα παρακολουθήσει· ἐν τῷ ὀνόματί μου
believing these will follow, in the name of Me
18 δαιμόνια ἐκβαλοῦσι· γλώσσαις λαλήσουσι καιναῖς· ὄφεις
demons they will cast out; languages they shall speak new; snakes.
ἀροῦσι· κἂν θανάσιμόν τι πίωσιν, οὐ μὴ αὐτοὺς βλάψει· ἐπὶ
they will take;and if deadly anything they drink,not at all them it will hurt; on
ἀρρώστους χεῖρας ἐπιθήσουσι, καὶ καλῶς ἕξουσιν.
infirm ones hands they will place, and wellness they will have.
19 Ὁ μὲν οὖν Κύριος, μετὰ τὸ λαλῆσαι αὐτοῖς, ἀνελήφθη εἰς
The indeed then Lord, after the speaking to them, was taken up into
20 τὸν οὐρανόν, καὶ ἐκάθισεν ἐκ δεξιῶν τοῦ Θεοῦ. ἐκεῖνοι δὲ
— Heaven, and sat off (the) right of God. they But
ἐξελθόντες ἐκήρυξαν πανταχοῦ, τοῦ Κυρίου συνεργοῦντος,
having gone out preached everywhere, the Lord working with (them).
καὶ τὸν λόγον βεβαιοῦντος διὰ τῶν ἐπακολουθούντων
and the word confirming through the accompanying
σημείων. Ἀμήν.
signs. Amen.

KING JAMES II VERSION

THE GOSPEL ACCORDING TO LUKE

CHAPTER 1

1 Since many took in hand to draw up an account concerning the matters having been borne out among us, 2 as those from *the* beginning delivered to us, becoming eyewitnesses and ministers of the word, 3 it seemed good also to me, having traced out all things accurately from the first, to write in order to you, most excellent Theophilus, 4 that you may know the certainty concerning the words which you were taught.

5 In the days of Herod the king of Judea, there was a certain priest named Zacharias, of *the* daily course of Abijah. And his wife *was* of the daughters of Aaron, and her name *was* Elizabeth. 6 And they were both righteous before God, walking blameless in all the commandments and ordinances of the Lord. 7 And no child was *born* to them, because Elizabeth was barren. And both were advanced in their days.

8 And it happened in his serving as priest in the order of his course before God, 9 according to the custom of the priests, *Zacharias' lot* fell to burn incense, entering into the Temple of the Lord. 10 And all the multitude of the people was praying outside at the hour of incense. 11 And an angel of *the* Lord appeared to him, standing

ΕΥΑΓΓΕΛΙΟΝ
GOSPEL
ΤΟ ΚΑΤΑ ΛΟΥΚΑΝ
THE ACCORDING TO LUKE

CHAPTER 1

1 Ἐπειδήπερ πολλοὶ ἐπεχείρησαν ἀνατάξασθαι διήγησιν
Since many took in hand to draw up an account
2 περὶ τῶν πεπληροφορημένων ἐν ἡμῖν πραγμάτων, καθὼς
concerning the having been fully borne out among us matters. as
παρέδοσαν ἡμῖν οἱ ἀπ' ἀρχῆς αὐτόπται καὶ ὑπηρέται
delivered to us the (ones) from beginning, eyewitnesses and ministers
3 γενόμενοι τοῦ λόγου, ἔδοξε κἀμοί, παρηκολουθηκότι ἄνωθεν
becoming of the word, it seemed good also to me, following from the first
4 πᾶσιν ἀκριβῶς, καθεξῆς σοι γράψαι, κράτιστε Θεόφιλε, ἵνα
all things accurately, in order to you to write, most excellent Theophilus, that
ἐπιγνῷς περὶ ὧν κατηχήθης λόγων τὴν ἀσφάλειαν.
you may know about which you were taught (in) words the certainty.
5 Ἐγένετο ἐν ταῖς ἡμέραις Ἡρώδου τοῦ βασιλέως τῆς
There was in the days of Herod the king —
Ἰουδαίας ἱερεύς τις ὀνόματι Ζαχαρίας, ἐξ ἐφημερίας Ἀβιά·
of Judea a priest a certain by name Zacharias, of (the) daily course of Abia,
καὶ ἡ γυνὴ αὐτοῦ ἐκ τῶν θυγατέρων Ἀαρών, καὶ τὸ ὄνομα
and the wife of him of the daughters of Aaron, and the name
6 αὐτῆς Ἐλισάβετ. ἦσαν δὲ δίκαιοι ἀμφότεροι ἐνώπιον τοῦ
of her Elizabeth. they were And righteous both in (the) sight of —
Θεοῦ, πορευόμενοι ἐν πάσαις ταῖς ἐντολαῖς καὶ δικαιώμασι
God, walking in all the commandments and ordinances
7 τοῦ Κυρίου ἄμεμπτοι. καὶ οὐκ ἦν αὐτοῖς τέκνον, καθότι
of the Lord blameless. And not was to them a child, because
ἡ Ἐλισάβετ ἦν στεῖρα, καὶ ἀμφότεροι προβεβηκότες ἐν ταῖς
— Elizabeth was barren, and both advanced in the
ἡμέραις αὐτῶν ἦσαν.
days of them were.
8 Ἐγένετο δὲ ἐν τῷ ἱερατεύειν αὐτὸν ἐν τῇ τάξει τῆς ἐφη-
it was And, in the serving as priest of him in the order of the
9 μερίας αὐτοῦ ἔναντι τοῦ Θεοῦ, κατὰ τὸ ἔθος τῆς ἱερατείας,
course of him before — God, according to the custom of the priests,
10 ἔλαχε τοῦ θυμιάσαι εἰσελθὼν εἰς τὸν ναὸν τοῦ Κυρίου. καὶ
(his) lot to burn incense entering into the temple of the Lord. And
πᾶν τὸ πλῆθος τοῦ λαοῦ ἦν προσευχόμενον ἔξω τῇ ὥρᾳ
all the multitude of the people was praying outside at the hour
11 τοῦ θυμιάματος. ὤφθη δὲ αὐτῷ ἄγγελος Κυρίου, ἑστὼς ἐκ
— of incense. appeared And to him an angel of (the) Lord, standing on

on *the* right of the altar of incense. 12 And seeing, Zacharias was troubled, and fear fell on him. 13 But the angel said to him, Do not fear, Zacharias, because your prayer was heard, and your wife Elizabeth will bear a son to you; and you shall call his name John. 14 And he will be joy and exultation to you, and many will rejoice over his birth. 15 For he shall be great in the eyes of the Lord; and he shall not drink wine or strong drink. And he will be filled of *the* Holy Spirit, even from his mother's womb. 16 And many of the sons of Israel he wil turn to *the* Lord their God. 17 And he will go out before Him in *the* spirit and power of Elijah, to turn *the* hearts of fathers to *their* children, and disobedient ones to *the* wisdom of the just, to make ready a people having been prepared for *the* Lord. 18 And Zacharias said to the angel, By what shall I know this? For I am old, and my wife is advanced in her days.

19 And answering, the angel said to him, I am Gabriel, who stands before God, and I was sent to speak to you and to announce to you these glad tidings. 20 And behold, you shall be silent and not able to speak until the day in which these things take place, because you did not believe my words, which shall be fulfilled in their season.

21 And the people were expecting Zacharias, and they wondered at his delaying in the Temple. 22 But having come out, he was not able to speak to them, and they recognized that he had seen a vision in the Temple. And he was making signs to them, and continued dumb.

23 And it came to pass, when the days of his service were fulfilled, he departed to his house. 24 And after these days his wife Elizabeth conceived. And she

12 δεξιῶν τοῦ θυσιαστηρίου τοῦ θυμιάματος. καὶ ἐταράχθη
(the) right of the altar — of incense. And was troubled
Ζαχαρίας ἰδών, καὶ φόβος ἐπέπεσεν ἐπ' αὐτόν. εἶπε δὲ πρὸς
13 Zacharias seeing, and fear fell upon him. said But to
αὐτὸν ὁ ἄγγελος, Μὴ φοβοῦ, Ζαχαρία· διότι εἰσηκούσθη ἡ
him the angel, Do not fear, Zacharias because was heard the
δέησίς σου, καὶ ἡ γυνή σου Ἐλισάβετ γεννήσει υἱόν σοι, καὶ
request of you, and the wife of you, Elizabeth, will bear a son to you, and
14 καλέσεις τὸ ὄνομα αὐτοῦ Ἰωάννην. καὶ ἔσται χαρά σοι καὶ
you shall call the name of him John. And he shall be joy to you and
ἀγαλλίασις, καὶ πολλοὶ ἐπὶ τῇ γεννήσει αὐτοῦ χαρήσονται.
exultation and many over the birth of him will rejoice.
15 ἔσται γὰρ μέγας ἐνώπιον τοῦ Κυρίου, καὶ οἶνον καὶ σίκερα
he will be For great in the eyes of the Lord, and wine and strong drink
οὐ μὴ πίῃ, καὶ Πνεύματος Ἁγίου πλησθήσεται ἔτι ἐκ κοιλίας
not at all he may drink, and of (the) Spirit Holy he will be filled even from womb
16 μητρὸς αὐτοῦ. καὶ πολλοὺς τῶν υἱῶν Ἰσραὴλ ἐπιστρέψει
of mother of him. And many of the sons of Israel he will turn
17 ἐπὶ Κύριον τὸν Θεὸν αὐτῶν· καὶ αὐτὸς προελεύσεται
to (the) Lord the God of them; and he will go ahead
ἐνώπιον αὐτοῦ ἐν πνεύματι καὶ δυνάμει Ἠλίου, ἐπιστρέψαι
before Him in (the) spirit and power of Elijah, to turn
καρδίας πατέρων ἐπὶ τέκνα, καὶ ἀπειθεῖς ἐν φρονήσει
(the) hearts of fathers to children, and disobedient to (the) wisdom
18 δικαίων, ἑτοιμάσαι Κυρίῳ λαὸν κατεσκευασμένον. καὶ εἶπε
of (the) just, to prepare for (the) Lord a people having been prepared. And said
Ζαχαρίας πρὸς τὸν ἄγγελον, Κατὰ τί γνώσομαι τοῦτο;
Zacharias to the angel, By what shall I know this?
ἐγὼ γάρ εἰμι πρεσβύτης, καὶ ἡ γυνή μου προβεβηκυῖα ἐν
I For am old, and the wife of me is advanced in
19 ταῖς ἡμέραις αὐτῆς. καὶ ἀποκριθεὶς ὁ ἄγγελος εἶπεν αὐτῷ,
the days of her And answering the angel said to him,
Ἐγώ εἰμι Γαβριὴλ ὁ παρεστηκὼς ἐνώπιον τοῦ Θεοῦ· καὶ
I am Gabriel the (one) standing by before — God, and
ἀπεστάλην λαλῆσαι πρός σε, καὶ εὐαγγελίσασθαί σοι
I was sent to speak to you, and to give good news to you
20 ταῦτα. καὶ ἰδού, ἔσῃ σιωπῶν καὶ μὴ δυνάμενος λαλῆσαι,
of these. And behold, you will be silent and not able to speak
ἄχρι ἧς ἡμέρας γένηται ταῦτα, ἀνθ' ὧν οὐκ ἐπίστευσας
until which day occurs these things, because not you believed
τοῖς λόγοις μου, οἵτινες πληρωθήσονται εἰς τὸν καιρὸν
the words of me, which will be fulfilled in the time
21 αὐτῶν. καὶ ἦν ὁ λαὸς προσδοκῶν τὸν Ζαχαρίαν· καὶ
of them. And the people expecting — Zacharias, and
22 ἐθαύμαζον ἐν τῷ χρονίζειν αὐτὸν ἐν τῷ ναῷ. ἐξελθὼν δὲ οὐκ
they marveled in the delay of him in the temple coming out. And not
ἠδύνατο λαλῆσαι αὐτοῖς· καὶ ἐπέγνωσαν ὅτι ὀπτασίαν
he was able to speak to them, and they knew that a vision
ἑώρακεν ἐν τῷ ναῷ· καὶ αὐτὸς ἦν διανεύων αὐτοῖς, καὶ
he had seen in the Temple and he was signaling to them, and
23 διέμενε κωφός. καὶ ἐγένετο, ὡς ἐπλήσθησαν αἱ ἡμέραι τῆς
remained dumb. And it was, as were fulfilled the days of the
λειτουργίας αὐτοῦ, ἀπῆλθεν εἰς τὸν οἶκον αὐτοῦ.
service of him, he went away to the house of him.
24 Μετὰ δὲ ταύτας τὰς ἡμέρας συνέλαβεν Ἐλισάβετ ἡ γυνὴ
after And these — days, conceived Elizabeth the wife

hid herself five months, saying, 25 So has the Lord done to me in *the* days in which He looked on *me* to take away my reproach among men.

26 And in the sixth month, the angel Gabriel was sent by God to a city of Galilee named Nazareth, 27 to a virgin betrothed to a man whose name *was* Joseph, of *the* house of David; and the virgin's name *was* Mary. 28 And entering, the angel said to her, Hail, *O one* receiving grace! The Lord *is* with you. You *are* blessed among women!

29 And seeing *this*, she was disturbed at his word, and considered what kind of greeting this might be. 30 And the angel said to her, Do not fear, Mary, for you have found favor from God. 31 And behold! You will conceive in *your* womb and bear a Son; and you will call His name Jesus. 32 He will be great and will be called Son of *the* Most High. And the Lord God will give Him the throne of his father David. 33 And He will reign over the house of Jacob forever, and of His kingdom there will be no end.

34 But Mary said to the angel, How will this be since I do not know a man? 35 And answering, the angel said to her, *The* Holy Spirit will come on you, and *the* power of *the* Most High will overshadow you—for this reason that *One* being born of you will be called Son of God. 36 And behold, your kinswoman Elizabeth! She also conceived a son in her old age, and this is *the* sixth month to her who *was* called barren; 37 for nothing shall be impossible with God. 38 And Mary said, Behold, the slave of *the* Lord! May it be to me according to your word. And the angel departed from her.

39 And rising up in those days, Mary went into the hill-country with haste to a city of

αὐτοῦ, καὶ περιέκρυβεν ἑαυτὴν μῆνας πέντε, λέγουσα ὅτι
of him, and hid herself months five, saying,
25 οὕτω μοι πεποίηκεν ὁ Κύριος ἐν ἡμέραις αἷς ἐπεῖδεν ἀφελεῖν
Thus to me has done the Lord in days in which He saw to remove
τὸ ὄνειδός μου ἐν ἀνθρώποις.
the reproach of me among men.

26 Ἐν δὲ τῷ μηνὶ τῷ ἕκτῳ ἀπεστάλη ὁ ἄγγελος Γαβριὴλ
in And the month sixth was sent the angel Gabriel
ὑπὸ τοῦ Θεοῦ εἰς πόλιν τῆς Γαλιλαίας, ᾗ ὄνομα Ναζαρέθ,
by — God to a city — of Galilee, to which (the) name was Nazareth,
27 πρὸς παρθένον μεμνηστευμένην ἀνδρί, ᾧ ὄνομα Ἰωσήφ,
to a virgin having been betrothed to a man to whom (the) name (was) Joseph,
28 ἐξ οἴκου Δαβίδ· καὶ τὸ ὄνομα τῆς παρθένου Μαριάμ. καὶ
of house of David, and the name of the virgin (was) Mariam. And
εἰσελθὼν ὁ ἄγγελος πρὸς αὐτὴν εἶπε, Χαῖρε, κεχαριτωμένη·
entering the angel to her said, Hail,(one) receiving grace,
29 ὁ Κύριος μετὰ σου, εὐλογημένη σὺ ἐν γυναιξίν. ἡ δὲ ἰδοῦσα
the Lord (is) with you. Blessed (are) you among women. she And seeing
διεταράχθη ἐπὶ τῷ λόγῳ αὐτοῦ, καὶ διελογίζετο ποταπὸς
was disturbed at the word of him, and considered of what kind
30 εἴη ὁ ἀσπασμὸς οὗτος. καὶ εἶπεν ὁ ἄγγελος αὐτῇ, Μὴ φοβοῦ,
may be greeting this. And said the angel to her, Do not fear
31 Μαριάμ· εὗρες γὰρ χάριν παρὰ τῷ Θεῷ. καὶ ἰδού, συλλήψῃ
Mariam, you found for favor with — God. And, lo you will conceive
ἐν γαστρί, καὶ τέξῃ υἱόν, καὶ καλέσεις τὸ ὄνομα αὐτοῦ
in womb and bear a son, and you will call the name of Him
32 Ἰησοῦν. οὗτος ἔσται μέγας, καὶ υἱὸς ὑψίστου κληθήσεται·
Jesus. This One will be great. and Son of Most High will be called,
καὶ δώσει αὐτῷ Κύριος ὁ Θεὸς τὸν θρόνον Δαβὶδ τοῦ πατρὸς
and will give Him (the) Lord — God the throne of David the father
33 αὐτοῦ, καὶ βασιλεύσει ἐπὶ τὸν οἶκον Ἰακὼβ εἰς τοὺς αἰῶνας,
of Him; and He will reign over the house of Jacob to the ages,
34 καὶ τῆς βασιλείας αὐτοῦ οὐκ ἔσται τέλος. εἶπε δὲ Μαριὰμ πρὸς
and of the kingdom of Him not will be an end. said And Mariam to
35 τὸν ἄγγελον, Πῶς ἔσται τοῦτο, ἐπεὶ ἄνδρα οὐ γινώσκω ; καὶ
the angel, How will be this, since a man not I know? And
ἀποκριθεὶς ὁ ἄγγελος εἶπεν αὐτῇ, Πνεῦμα Ἅγιον ἐπελεύσεται
answering, the angel said to her, (The) Spirit Holy will come up
ἐπὶ σέ, καὶ δύναμις ὑψίστου ἐπισκιάσει σοι· διὸ καὶ τὸ γεννώ-
upon you, and power of Most High will overshadow you, so also that being
36 μενον ἐκ σοῦ ἅγιον κληθήσεται υἱὸς Θεοῦ. καὶ ἰδού, Ἐλισάβετ
born of you holy will be called Son of God. And, behold, Elizabeth
ἡ συγγενής σου, καὶ αὐτὴ συνειληφυῖα υἱὸν ἐν γήρᾳ αὐτῆς·
the relative of you, also she conceived a son in old age of her,
37 καὶ οὗτος μὴν ἕκτος ἐστὶν αὐτῇ τῇ καλουμένῃ στείρᾳ. ὅτι
and this month sixth is with her, the (one) called barren; because
38 οὐκ ἀδυνατήσει παρὰ τῷ Θεῷ πᾶν ῥῆμα. εἶπε δὲ Μαριάμ,
not will be impossible with — God every word. said And Mariam,
Ἰδού, ἡ δούλη Κυρίου· γένοιτό μοι κατὰ τὸ ῥῆμά σου. καὶ
Behold, the slave of (the) Lord; may it be to me as the word of you. And
ἀπῆλθεν ἀπ' αὐτῆς ὁ ἄγγελος.
went away from her the angel.

39 Ἀναστᾶσα δὲ Μαριὰμ ἐν ταῖς ἡμέραις ταύταις ἐπορεύθη
rising up And Mariam in days these, she went
εἰς τὴν ὀρεινὴν μετὰ σπουδῆς, εἰς πόλιν Ἰούδα, καὶ εἰσῆλθεν
to the hill-country with haste, to a city of Judah and entered

Judah. [40]And *she* entered into the house of Zacharias, and greeted Elizabeth. [41]And it happened, as Elizabeth heard Mary's greeting, the babe in her womb leaped, and Elizabeth was filled of *the* Holy Spirit. [42]And *she* cried out with a loud voice and said, Blessed *are* you among women, and blessed *is* the fruit of your womb. [43]And from where *is* this to me, that the mother of my Lord comes to me? [44]For behold, as the sound of your greeting came to my ears, the babe in my womb leaped in exultation. [45]And blessed is she believing, because there will be a completion to the things spoken to her from *the* Lord.

[46]And Mary said, My soul magnifies the Lord, [47]and my spirit exulted in God My Savior. [48]for He looked on the humiliation of His bondslave. For, behold, from now on all generations will count me blessed. [49]For the Mighty One did great things to me, and holy *is* His name. [50]And His mercy *is* to generations and generations to those fearing Him. [51]He worked power with His arm; He scattered proud ones in *the* thought of their heart. [52]He put down rulers from thrones, and exalted *the* lowly. [53]He filled *the* hungry with good things, and He sent *the* rich away empty. [54]He helped His servant Israel in order to remember mercy, [55]even as He spoke to our fathers, to Abraham, and to his seed forever.

[56]And Mary remained with her about three months, and returned to her house.

[57]And the time was fulfilled to Elizabeth *for* her to bear, and she bore a son. [58]And the neighbors and her relatives heard that *the* Lord magnified His mercy with

40 εἰς τὸν οἶκον Ζαχαρίου, καὶ ἠσπάσατο τὴν Ἐλισάβετ καὶ
into the house of Zacharias, and greeted – Elizabeth. And
41 ἐγένετο ὡς ἤκουσεν ἡ Ἐλισάβετ τὸν ἀσπασμὸν τῆς Μαρίας,
it was, as heard – Elizabeth the greeting – of Mariam,
ἐσκίρτησε τὸ βρέφος ἐν τῇ κοιλίᾳ αὐτῆς· καὶ ἐπλήσθη Πνεύ-
leaped the babe in the womb of her, and was filled of (the)
42 ματος Ἁγίου ἡ Ἐλισάβετ, καὶ ἀνεφώνησε φωνῇ μεγάλῃ
Spirit Holy – Elizabeth, and she called out with a voice great,
καὶ εἶπεν, Εὐλογημένη σὺ ἐν γυναιξί, καὶ εὐλογημένος ὁ
and said, Blessed (are) you among women, and blessed (is) the
43 καρπὸς τῆς κοιλίας σου. καὶ πόθεν μοι τοῦτο, ἵνα ἔλθῃ ἡ
fruit of the womb of you. And whence to me this, that comes the
44 μήτηρ τοῦ Κυρίου μου πρός με ; ἰδοὺ γάρ, ὡς ἐγένετο ἡ φωνὴ
mother of the Lord of me to me? behold For, as came the sound
τοῦ ἀσπασμοῦ σου εἰς τὰ ὦτά μου, ἐσκίρτησεν ἐν ἀγαλλιάσει
of the greeting of you to the ears of me, leaped in exultation
45 τὸ βρέφος ἐν τῇ κοιλίᾳ μου. καὶ μακαρία ἡ πιστεύσασα, ὅτι
the babe in the womb of me. And blessed the (one) believing, because
ἔσται τελείωσις τοῖς λελαλημένοις αὐτῇ παρὰ Κυρίου. καὶ
will be a completion to the things spoken to her from (the) Lord. And
46 εἶπε Μαριάμ, Μεγαλύνει ἡ ψυχή μου τὸν Κύριον, καὶ
said Mariam, magnifies The soul of me the Lord, and
47 ἠγαλλίασε τὸ πνεῦμά μου ἐπὶ τῷ Θεῷ τῷ σωτῆρί μου. ὅτι
exulted the spirit of me on – God the Savior of me; because
48 ἐπέβλεψεν ἐπὶ τὴν ταπείνωσιν τῆς δούλης αὐτοῦ. ἰδοὺ γάρ,
He looked upon the humiliation of the bondslave of Him. behold For,
ἀπὸ τοῦ νῦν μακαριοῦσί με πᾶσαι αἱ γενεαί. ὅτι ἐποίησέ μοι
from – now will count blessed me all the generations; for did to me
49 μεγαλεῖα ὁ δυνατός, καὶ ἅγιον τὸ ὄνομα αὐτοῦ. καὶ τὸ
great things the Mighty One. And holy the name of Him, and the
50 ἔλεος αὐτοῦ εἰς γενεὰς γενεῶν τοῖς φοβουμένοις αὐτόν.
mercy of Him to generations of generations to those fearing Him.
51 ἐποίησε κράτος ἐν βραχίονι αὐτοῦ· διεσκόρπισεν ὑπερη-
He did might(ily) with (the) arm of Him; He scattered proud
52 φάνους διανοίᾳ καρδίας αὐτῶν. καθεῖλε δυνάστας ἀπὸ
ones in (the) thought of the heart of them; He pulled down potentates from
53 θρόνων, καὶ ὕψωσε ταπεινούς. πεινῶντας ἐνέπλησεν
thrones, and exalted humble ones. hungering ones He filled
54 ἀγαθῶν, καὶ πλουτοῦντας ἐξαπέστειλε κενούς. ἀντελάβετο
of good things, and rich ones He sent away empty. He succored
55 Ἰσραὴλ παιδὸς αὐτου, μνησθῆναι ἐλέους (καθὼς ἐλάλησε
Israel (the) servant of Him, to remember mercy, even as He spoke
πρὸς τοὺς πατέρας ἡμῶν) τῷ Ἀβραὰμ καὶ τῷ σπέρματι
to the fathers of us, – to Abraham and to the seed
αὐτοῦ εἰς τὸν αἰῶνα.
of him to the age.

56 Ἔμεινε δὲ Μαριὰμ σὺν αὐτῇ ὡσεὶ μῆνας τρεῖς, καὶ ὑπέ-
remained And Mariam with her about months three, and
στρεψεν εἰς τὸν οἶκον αὐτῆς.
returned to the house of her.

57 Τῇ δὲ Ἐλισάβετ ἐπλήσθη ὁ χρόνος τοῦ τεκεῖν αὐτήν,
– And to Elizabeth was fulfilled the time – to bear her,
58 καὶ ἐγέννησεν υἱόν. καὶ ἤκουσαν οἱ περίοικοι καὶ οἱ συγ-
and she bore a son. And heard the neighbors and the
γενεῖς αὐτῆς ὅτι ἐμεγάλυνε Κύριος τὸ ἔλεος αὐτοῦ μετ'
relatives of her that magnified (the) Lord the mercy of Him with

her, and they rejoiced with her. 59 And it happened on the eighth day, they came to circumcise the child, and were calling it by his father's name, Zacharias. 60 And answering, his mother said, No, but he shall be called John. 61 And they said to her, No one is among your kindred who is called by this name. 62 And they signaled to his father *as to* what he might wish him to be called.

63 And asking for a writing tablet, he wrote, saying, John is his name. And all marveled. 64 And instantly his mouth was opened, and his tongue *loosed,* and he spoke, blessing God. 65 And fear came on all those who lived around them, and in all the hill-country of Judea these things were talked about. 66 And all who heard laid *them* up in their hearts, saying, What then will this child be? And the hand of *the* Lord was with him.

67 And his father Zacharias was filled of *the* Holy Spirit, and prophesied, saying, 68 Blessed be *the* Lord, the God of Israel, because He visited and worked redemption for His people. 69 And *He* raised up a Horn of salvation for us in the house of His servant David; 70 even as He spoke through the mouth of His holy prophets from the age *before:* 71 Salvation from our enemies, and from *the* hand of those hating us; 72 to execute mercy with our fathers, and to remember His holy covenant, 73 *the* oath which He swore to our father Abraham, 74 to give to us *that we* being delivered out of *the* hand of our enemies, should serve Him without fear, 75 in holiness and righteousness before Him all the days of our life. 76 And you, child, will be called Prophet of *the* Most

59 αὐτῆς, καὶ συνέχαιρον αὐτῇ. καὶ ἐγένετο ἐν τῇ ὀγδόῃ ἡμέρᾳ,
her, and they rejoiced with her. And it was, on the eighth day,
ἦλθον περιτεμεῖν τὸ παιδίον· καὶ ἐκάλουν αὐτὸ ἐπὶ τῷ
they came to circumcise the child, and were calling it by the
60 ὀνόματι τοῦ πατρὸς αὐτοῦ Ζαχαρίαν. καὶ ἀποκριθεῖσα ἡ
name of the father of him, Zacharias. And answering the
61 μήτηρ αὐτοῦ εἶπεν, Οὐχί, ἀλλὰ κληθήσεται Ἰωάννης. καὶ
mother of him said, Not so, but he shall be called John. And
εἶπον πρὸς αὐτὴν ὅτι Οὐδείς ἐστιν ἐν τῇ συγγενείᾳ σου
they said to her, — No one there is in the kindred of you
62 ὃς καλεῖται τῷ ὀνόματι τούτῳ. ἐνένευον δὲ τῷ πατρὶ αὐτοῦ,
who is called by name this. they signaled And to the father of him,
63 τὸ τί ἂν θέλοι καλεῖσθαι αὐτόν. καὶ αἰτήσας πινακίδιον
— what he may desire to be called him. And asking for a tablet,
64 ἔγραψε, λέγων, Ἰωάννης ἐστὶ τὸ ὄνομα αὐτοῦ· καὶ ἐθαύ-
he wrote, saying, John is the name of him. And mar-
μασαν πάντες. ἀνεῴχθη δὲ τὸ στόμα αὐτοῦ παραχρῆμα
veled all. was opened And the mouth of him instantly,
65 καὶ ἡ γλῶσσα αὐτοῦ, καὶ ἐλάλει εὐλογῶν τὸν Θεόν. καὶ
and the tongue of him, and he spoke blessing — God. And
ἐγένετο ἐπὶ πάντας φόβος τοὺς περιοικοῦντας αὐτούς· καὶ
came upon all fear the (ones) living around them, and
ἐν ὅλῃ τῇ ὀρεινῇ τῆς Ἰουδαίας διελαλεῖτο πάντα τὰ ῥήματα
in all the hill-country — of Judea were talked over all — facts
66 ταῦτα. καὶ ἔθεντο πάντες οἱ ἀκούσαντες ἐν τῇ καρδίᾳ αὐτῶν,
these And laid up all the (ones) hearing in the heart of them,
λέγοντες, Τί ἄρα τὸ παιδίον τοῦτο ἔσται; καὶ χεὶρ Κυρίου
saying, What then — child this will be? And (the) hand of Lord
ἦν μετ' αὐτοῦ.
was with him.
67 Καὶ Ζαχαρίας ὁ πατὴρ αὐτοῦ ἐπλήσθη Πνεύματος
And Zacharias the father of him was filled of (the) Spirit
68 Ἁγίου, καὶ προεφήτευσε, λέγων, Εὐλογητὸς Κύριος ὁ
Holy, and prophesied, saying, Blessed (be) (the) Lord the
Θεὸς τοῦ Ἰσραήλ, ὅτι ἐπεσκέψατο καὶ ἐποίησε λύτρωσιν
God — of Israel, because He visited and worked redemption
69 τῷ λαῷ αὐτοῦ, καὶ ἤγειρε κέρας σωτηρίας ἡμῖν ἐν τῷ οἴκῳ
for the people of Him, and raised a horn of salvation for us in the house
70 Δαβὶδ τοῦ παιδὸς αὐτοῦ (καθὼς ἐλάλησε διὰ στόματος τῶν
of David the servant of Him; even as He spoke through (the) mouth of the
71 ἁγίων τῶν ἀπ' αἰῶνος προφητῶν αὐτοῦ), σωτηρίαν ἐξ
holy — from (the) age prophets of Him. salvation out of
ἐχθρῶν ἡμῶν, καὶ ἐκ χειρὸς πάντων τῶν μισούντων ἡμᾶς·
(the) enemies of us, and out of hand of all the (ones) hating us,
72 ποιῆσαι ἔλεος μετὰ τῶν πατέρων ἡμῶν, καὶ μνησθῆναι
to execute mercy with the fathers of us, and to remember
73 διαθήκης ἁγίας αὐτοῦ, ὅρκον ὃν ὤμοσε πρὸς Ἀβραὰμ τὸν
(the) covenant holy of Him, (the) oath which He swore to Abraham the
74 πατέρα ἡμῶν, τοῦ δοῦναι ἡμῖν, ἀφόβως, ἐκ χειρὸς τῶν
father of us, — to give to us without fear out of (the) hand the
75 ἐχθρῶν ἡμῶν ῥυσθέντας, λατρεύειν αὐτῷ ἐν ὁσιότητι καὶ
enemies of us being delivered to serve Him in consecration and
δικαιοσύνῃ ἐνώπιον αὐτοῦ πάσας τὰς ἡμέρας τῆς ζωῆς
righteousness before Him all the days of the life
76 ἡμῶν. καὶ σύ, παιδίον, προφήτης ὑψίστου κληθήσῃ·
of us. And you, child, a prophet of (the) Most High will be called

High; for you will go before *the* face of *the* Lord to prepare His ways, [77] to give a knowledge of salvation to His people by forgiveness of their sins, [78] through *the* bowels of mercy of our God, in which *the* Dayspring from on high *will* visit us, [79] to appear to those sitting in darkness and in shadow of death, to direct our feet into *the* way of peace.
[80] And the child grew, and became strong in spirit. And *he* was in the desert until *the* days of his showing to Israel.

CHAPTER 2

[1] And it happened in those days, a decree went out from Caesar Augustus *for* all the habitable world to be registered. [2] This registration first occurred *under* the governing *by* Cyrenius. [3] And all went to be registered, each to his own city. [4] And Joseph also went from Galilee, out of *the* city of Nazareth of Judah, to a city of David which is called Bethlehem, because of his being of *the* house and family of David, [5] to be registered with Mary, she being betrothed to him *as* wife, *she* being pregnant. [6] And it happened *as* they were there, the days were fulfilled *for* her to bear. [7] And she bore her son, the Firstborn. And she wrapped Him, and laid Him in the manger—because there was no place for them in the inn.
[8] And shepherds were in the same country, living in the fields, and keeping guard over their flock *by* night. [9] And, behold, an angel of *the* Lord came on them. And *the* glory of *the* Lord shone around them. And they feared with a great fear. [10] And the angel said to them, do not fear. For, behold, I give good news to you, a great joy, which will be to all people, [11] because today a Savior who is Christ *the* Lord

προπορεύσῃ γὰρ πρὸ προσώπου Κυρίου ἑτοιμάσαι ὁδοὺς
you will go for before (the) face of (the) Lord to prepare (the) ways
77 αὐτοῦ· τοῦ δοῦναι γνῶσιν σωτηρίας τῷ λαῷ αὐτοῦ ἐν
of Him, – to give a knowledge of salvation to the people of Him by
78 ἀφέσει ἁμαρτιῶν αὐτῶν, διὰ σπλάγχνα ἐλέους Θεοῦ ἡμῶν,
forgiveness of sins of them, through (the) bowels of mercy of God of us,
79 ἐν οἷς ἐπεσκέψατο ἡμᾶς ἀνατολὴ ἐξ ὕψους, ἐπιφᾶναι τοῖς ἐν
in which (will) visit us (the) Dayspring from on high, to appear to those in
σκότει καὶ σκιᾷ θανάτου καθημένοις, τοῦ κατευθῦναι τοὺς
darkness and in shadow of death **sitting, – to direct the**
πόδας ἡμῶν εἰς ὁδὸν εἰρήνης.
feet of us into a way of peace.
80 Τὸ δὲ παιδίον ηὔξανε καὶ ἐκραταιοῦτο πνεύματι, καὶ ἦν ἐν
the And child grew and became strong in spirit, and was in
ταῖς ἐρήμοις ἕως ἡμέρας ἀναδείξεως αὐτοῦ πρὸς τὸν Ἰσραήλ.
the desert until (the) days of showing of him to – Israel.

CHAPTER 2

1 Ἐγένετο δὲ ἐν ταῖς ἡμέραις ἐκείναις, ἐξῆλθε δόγμα παρὰ
it was And, in – days those, went out a decree from
Καίσαρος Αὐγούστου, ἀπογράφεσθαι πᾶσαν τὴν οἰκου-
Caesar Augustus to be registered all the inhabited
2 μένην. αὕτη ἡ ἀπογραφὴ πρώτη ἐγένετο ἡγεμονεύοντος τῆς
earth. This registration first was (during the) governing of
3 Συρίας Κυρηνίου. καὶ ἐπορεύοντο πάντες ἀπογράφεσθαι,
Syria (by) Cyrenius. And went all to be registered,
4 ἕκαστος εἰς τὴν ἰδίαν πόλιν. ἀνέβη δὲ καὶ Ἰωσὴφ ἀπὸ τῆς
each one into (his) own city. went up And also Joseph from –
Γαλιλαίας, ἐκ πόλεως Ναζαρέθ, εἰς τὴν Ἰουδαίαν, εἰς πόλιν
Galilee out of (the) city Nazareth to – Judea, into (the) city
Δαβίδ, ἥτις καλεῖται Βηθλεέμ, διὰ τὸ εἶναι αὐτὸν ἐξ οἴκου καὶ
of David which is called Bethlehem, because of being him of (the) house and
5 πατριᾶς Δαβίδ, ἀπογράψασθαι σὺν Μαριὰμ τῇ μεμνηστευ-
family of David; to be registered with Mariam the (one) being be-
6 μένῃ αὐτῷ γυναικί, οὔσῃ ἐγκύῳ. ἐγένετο δὲ ἐν τῷ εἶναι
trothed to him (as) wife, **being pregnant. it was And, in being**
7 αὐτοὺς ἐκεῖ, ἐπλήσθησαν αἱ ἡμέραι τοῦ τεκεῖν αὐτήν. καὶ
they there, were fulfilled the days (for) the bearing (of) her; and
ἔτεκε τὸν υἱὸν αὐτῆς τὸν πρωτότοκον, καὶ ἐσπαργάνωσεν
she bore the son of her, the first-born, and she wrapped
αὐτόν, καὶ ἀνέκλινεν αὐτὸν ἐν τῇ φάτνῃ, διότι οὐκ ἦν αὐτοῖς
Him and laid Him in the manger, because not was for them
τόπος ἐν τῷ καταλύματι.
a place in the inn.
8 Καὶ ποιμένες ἦσαν ἐν τῇ χώρᾳ τῇ αὐτῇ ἀγραυλοῦντες καὶ
And shepherds were in the country same living in the fields and
φυλάσσοντες φυλακὰς τῆς νυκτὸς ἐπὶ τὴν ποίμνην αὐτῶν.
keeping guard of the night over the flock of them.
9 καὶ ἰδού, ἄγγελος Κυρίου ἐπέστη αὐτοῖς, καὶ δόξα Κυρίου
And behold, an angel of (the) Lord came on them, and (the) glory of Lord
10 περιέλαμψεν αὐτούς· καὶ ἐφοβήθησαν φόβον μέγαν. καὶ εἶπεν
shone around them, and they feared (with) a fear great. And said
αὐτοῖς ὁ ἄγγελος, Μὴ φοβεῖσθε· ἰδοὺ γάρ, εὐαγγελίζομαι
to them the angel, Do not fear, behold for, I give good news
11 ὑμῖν χαρὰν μεγάλην, ἥτις ἔσται παντὶ τῷ λαῷ· ὅτι ἐτέχθη
to you, a joy great, which will be to all the people, because was born

was born in *the* city of David. 12 And this *is* a sign to you: You will find a babe having been wrapped, lying in the manger. 13 And suddenly there was a multitude of *the* heavenly host, praising God and saying, 14 Glory to God in the highest, and peace on earth, good will among men.

15 And it happened as the angels departed from them into Heaven, even the men, the shepherds, said to one another, Indeed, let us go over to Bethlehem, and let us see this thing which has occurred, which the Lord made known to us. 16 And hurrying they came and sought out both Mary and Joseph, and the babe lying in the manger. 17 And seeing, they publicly told about the word spoken to them about this Child. 18 And all those hearing marveled about the things spoken to them by the shepherds. 19 And Mary kept all these sayings, meditating in her heart. 20 And the shepherds returned, glorifying and praising God for all things which they heard and saw, even as was spoken to them.

21 And when eight days were fulfilled to circumcise the child, His name was called Jesus, *the name* called by the angel before He was conceived in the womb.

22 And when the days of her purification according to the law of Moses, they took Him up to Jerusalem to present *Him* to the Lord, 23 as it has been written in *the* law of the Lord: "Every male opening a womb shall be called holy to the Lord:" 24 and to offer a sacrifice according to that said in the law of *the* Lord, a pair of turtledoves, or two nestlings of doves.

ὑμῖν σήμερον Σωτήρ, ὅς ἐστι Χριστὸς Κύριος, ἐν πόλει Δαβίδ.
to you today a Savior, who is Christ (the) Lord, into the city of David.
12 καὶ τοῦτο ὑμῖν τὸ σημεῖον· εὑρήσετε βρέφος ἐσπαργανω-
And this to you a sign, you will find a babe having been
13 μένον, κείμενον ἐν τῇ φάτνῃ. καὶ ἐξαίφνης ἐγένετο σὺν τῷ
wrapped, lying in manger. And suddenly there was with the
ἀγγέλῳ πλῆθος στρατιᾶς οὐρανίου, αἰνούντων τὸν Θεόν,
angel a multitude of (the) host heavenly, praising — God
14 καὶ λεγόντων, Δόξα ἐν ὑψίστοις Θεῷ, καὶ ἐπὶ γῆς εἰρήνη·
and saying, Glory in the highest to God, and on earth peace,
ἐν ἀνθρώποις εὐδοκία.
in men, good will.
15 Καὶ ἐγένετο, ὡς ἀπῆλθον ἀπ' αὐτῶν εἰς τὸν οὐρανὸν οἱ
And it was, as departed from them into — Heaven the
ἄγγελοι, καὶ οἱ ἄνθρωποι οἱ ποιμένες εἶπον πρὸς ἀλλήλους,
angels, even the men, the shepherds, said to one another,
Διέλθωμεν δὴ ἕως Βηθλεέμ, καὶ ἴδωμεν τὸ ῥῆμα τοῦτο τὸ
Let us go indeed unto Bethlehem, and let us see — thing this —
16 γεγονός, ὃ ὁ Κύριος ἐγνώρισεν ἡμῖν. καὶ ἦλθον σπεύσαντες,
having occurred, which the Lord made known to us. And they came, hurrying,
καὶ ἀνεῦρον τήν τε Μαριὰμ καὶ τὸν Ἰωσήφ, καὶ τὸ βρέφος
and sought out — both Mariam and — Joseph, and the babe
17 κείμενον ἐν τῇ φάτνῃ. ἰδόντες δὲ διεγνώρισαν περὶ τοῦ
lying in the manger. seeing And, they publicly told about the
ῥήματος τοῦ λαληθέντος αὐτοῖς περὶ τοῦ παιδίου τούτου.
saying spoken to them about — child this.
18 καὶ πάντες οἱ ἀκούσαντες ἐθαύμασαν περὶ τῶν λαληθέντων
And all those hearing marveled concerning the things spoken
19 ὑπὸ τῶν ποιμένων πρὸς αὐτούς. ἡ δὲ Μαριὰμ πάντα
by the shepherds to them. — And Mariam all
συνετήρει τὰ ῥήματα ταῦτα, συμβάλλουσα ἐν τῇ καρδίᾳ
kept — sayings these, meditating in the heart
20 αὐτῆς. καὶ ἐπέστρεψαν οἱ ποιμένες, δοξάζοντες καὶ αἰνοῦντες
of her. And returned the shepherds, glorifying and praising
τὸν Θεὸν ἐπὶ πᾶσιν οἷς ἤκουσαν καὶ εἶδον, καθὼς ἐλαλήθη
— God at all things which they heard and saw, even as was spoken
πρὸς αὐτούς.
to them.
21 Καὶ ὅτε ἐπλήσθησαν ἡμέραι ὀκτὼ τοῦ περιτεμεῖν τὸ
And when were fulfilled days eight — to circumcise the
παιδίον, καὶ ἐκλήθη τὸ ὄνομα αὐτοῦ Ἰησοῦς, τὸ κληθὲν ὑπὸ
child, and was called the name of Him Jesus, that called by
τοῦ ἀγγέλου πρὸ τοῦ συλληφθῆναι αὐτὸν ἐν τῇ κοιλίᾳ.
the angel before — was conceived Him in the womb.
22 Καὶ ὅτε ἐπλήσθησαν αἱ ἡμέραι τοῦ καθαρισμοῦ αὐτῆς
And when were fulfilled the days of the cleansing of her,
κατὰ τὸν νόμον Μωσέως, ἀνήγαγον αὐτὸν εἰς Ἱεροσόλυμα,
according to the law of Moses, they took up Him to Jerusalem
23 παραστῆσαι τῷ Κυρίῳ (καθὼς γέγραπται ἐν νόμῳ Κυρίου
to present to the Lord, as it has been written in (the) law of the Lord,
ὅτι Πᾶν ἄρσεν διανοῖγον μήτραν ἅγιον τῷ Κυρίῳ κληθήσε-
— Every male opening a womb holy to the Lord shall be
24 ται), καὶ τοῦ δοῦναι θυσίαν κατὰ τὸ εἰρημένον ἐν νόμῳ
called; and — to give a sacrifice according to that said in the Law
Κυρίου, Ζεῦγος τρυγόνων ἢ δύο νεοσσοὺς περιστερῶν. καὶ
of (the) Lord: a pair of turtledoves, or two nestlings of doves. And

25 And, behold, there was a man in Jerusalem whose name *was* Simeon. And this man *was* righteous and devout, eagerly expecting *the* Consolation of Israel. And *the* Holy Spirit was upon him. 26 And it happened to him, having been instructed by the Holy Spirit, *he was* not to see death before he would see the Christ of *the* Lord. 27 And by the Spirit he came into the Temple. And *as* the parents brought the child Jesus *for* them to do according to the custom of the law concerning Him, 28 even *Simeon* received Him into his arms. And *he* blessed God and said, 29 Now You will let Your slave go in peace, Master, according to Your word; 30 because my eyes saw Your Salvation, 31 which You prepared before *the* face of all the peoples, 32 a Light for revelation *to the* nations, and *the* Glory of Your people Israel.

33 And Joseph was marveling, and His mother, at the things being said concerning Him. 34 And Simeon blessed them, and said to His mother Mary, Behold, this One is set for *the* fall and rising up of many in Israel, and for a sign spoken against; 35 yea, a sword also will pierce your own soul, so that the thoughts of many hearts may be revealed.

36 And there was Anna, a prophetess, a daughter of Phanuel, of *the* tribe of Asher —she *was* advanced in many days, having lived seven years with a husband from her virginity, 37 and she *was* a widow eighty-four years—who did not depart from the Temple, serving with fastings and prayers. 38 And coming on at the very hour, she gave thanks to the Lord, and spoke concerning Him to all those in Jerusalem eagerly expecting redemption. 39 And when they had finished all things according to the law of *the* Lord, they

25 ἰδού, ἦν ἄνθρωπος ἐν Ἱερουσαλήμ, ᾧ ὄνομα Συμεών, καὶ ὁ
behold was a man in Jerusalem, to whom name Simeon. And —
ἄνθρωπος οὗτος δίκαιος καὶ εὐλαβής, προσδεχόμενος
man this (was) righteous and devout, expecting eagerly
παράκλησιν τοῦ Ἰσραήλ, καὶ Πνεῦμα Ἅγιον ἦν ἐπ' αὐτόν.
(the) consolation — of Israel; and (the) Spirit Holy was upon him.
26 καὶ ἦν αὐτῷ κεχρηματισμένον ὑπὸ τοῦ Πνεύματος τοῦ
And was to him, having been instructed by the Spirit —
Ἁγίου, μὴ ἰδεῖν θάνατον πρὶν ἢ ἴδῃ τὸν Χριστὸν Κυρίου.
Holy, not to see death before that he sees the Christ of (the) Lord.
27 καὶ ἦλθεν ἐν τῷ Πνεύματι εἰς τὸ ἱερόν· καὶ ἐν τῷ εἰσαγαγεῖν
And he came by the Spirit into the Temple; and in the bringing in
τοὺς γονεῖς τὸ παιδίον Ἰησοῦν, τοῦ ποιῆσαι αὐτοὺς κατὰ
the parents the child Jesus — to do them according
28 τὸ εἰθισμένον τοῦ νόμου περὶ αὐτοῦ, καὶ αὐτὸς ἐδέξατο αὐτὸ
to the custom of the law concerning Him; and he received Him
εἰς τὰς ἀγκάλας αὐτοῦ, καὶ εὐλόγησε τὸν Θεόν, καὶ εἶπε,
in the arms of him, and blessed — God and said,
29 Νῦν ἀπολύεις τὸν δοῦλόν σου, δέσποτα, κατὰ τὸ ῥῆμά σου,
Now let go the slave of You, Master, according to the word of You
30 ἐν εἰρήνῃ· ὅτι εἶδον οἱ ὀφθαλμοί μου τὸ σωτήριόν σου, ὃ
in peace; because saw the eyes of me the salvation of You which
31 ἡτοίμασας κατὰ πρόσωπον πάντων τῶν λαῶν· φῶς εἰς
You prepared before (the) face of all the peoples; a light for
32 ἀποκάλυψιν ἐθνῶν, καὶ δόξαν λαοῦ σου ισραηλ. καὶ ἦν
revelation (to the) nations, and a glory of people of You Israel. And was
33 Ἰωσὴφ καὶ ἡ μήτηρ αὐτοῦ θαυμάζοντες ἐπὶ τοῖς λαλου-
Joseph and the mother of Him marveling at the things being
34 μένοις περὶ αὐτοῦ. καὶ εὐλόγησεν αὐτοὺς Συμεών, καὶ εἶπε
said about Him. And blessed them Simeon, and said
πρὸς Μαριὰμ τὴν μητέρα αὐτοῦ, Ἰδού, οὗτος κεῖται εἰς
to Mariam the mother of Him, Behold, this (One) is set for
πτῶσιν καὶ ἀνάστασιν πολλῶν ἐν τῷ Ἰσραήλ, καὶ εἰς σημεῖον
fall and rising of many in — Israel, and for a sign
35 ἀντιλεγόμενον· καὶ σοῦ δὲ αὐτῆς τὴν ψυχὴν διελεύσεται
spoken against, and of you also of her soul will pierce
ῥομφαία· ὅπως ἂν ἀποκαλυφθῶσιν ἐκ πολλῶν καρδιῶν
a sword, so as — may be revealed of many hearts
36 διαλογισμοί. καὶ ἦν Ἄννα προφῆτις, θυγάτηρ Φανουήλ,
(the) thoughts. And was Anna a prophetess, a daughter of Phanuel,
ἐκ φυλῆς Ἀσήρ (αὕτη προβεβηκυῖα ἐν ἡμέραις πολλαῖς,
of (the) tribe of Asher; she advanced in days many,
ζήσασα ἔτη μετὰ ἀνδρὸς ἑπτὰ ἀπὸ τῆς παρθενίας αὐτῆς,
having lived years with a husband seven from the virginity of her,
37 καὶ αὕτη χήρα ὡς ἐτῶν ὀγδοηκοντατεσσάρων), ἣ οὐκ ἀφί-
and she a widow years eighty-four, who not
στατο ἀπὸ τοῦ ἱεροῦ, νηστείαις καὶ δεήσεσι λατρεύουσα
departed from the Temple, with fastings and petitionings serving
38 νύκτα καὶ ἡμέραν. καὶ αὕτη αὐτῇ τῇ ὥρᾳ ἐπιστᾶσα ἀνθω-
night and day And she at the very hour coming on, she
μολογεῖτο τῷ Κυρίῳ, καὶ ἐλάλει περὶ αὐτοῦ πᾶσι τοῖς
gave thanks to the Lord, and spoke concerning Him to all those
39 προσδεχομένοις λύτρωσιν ἐν Ἱερουσαλήμ. καὶ ὡς ἐτέλεσαν
expecting eagerly redemption in Jerusalem. And as they finished
ἅπαντα τὰ κατὰ τὸν νόμον Κυρίου, ὑπέστρεψαν εἰς τὴν
all things — according to the law of (the) Lord, they returned to —

returned to Galilee, to Nazareth their city.
40 And the child grew, and
became strong in spirit,
being filled with wisdom.
And the grace of God was
upon Him.
41 And His parents went
into Jerusalem year by year
at the Feast of the Passover.
42 And when He was twelve
years *old,* they going up to
Jerusalem according to the
custom of the Feast, 43 and
fulfilling the days, in their
returning, the boy Jesus
stayed in Jerusalem. And
Joseph and His mother did
not know. 44 But supposing
Him to be in the company,
they went a day on the way.
And they looked for Him
among the relatives and
friends. 45 And not finding
Him, they returned to Jerusalem, looking for Him.
46 And it happened after three
days they found Him in the
Temple, sitting in *the* midst
of the teachers, even hearing
them and questioning them.
47 And all those hearing Him
were amazed at His intelligence and His answers.
48 And seeing Him, they were
astounded. And His mother
said to Him, Child, why did
You do so to us? Behold, Your
father and I were looking for
You, greatly distressed.
49 And He said to them, Why
did You look for me? Did you
not know that I must be *busy*
in the *affairs* of My Father?
50 And they did not understand the word which He
spoke to them. 51 And He
went with them, and came to
Nazareth, and was being
subject to them. And His
mother carefully kept all
these sayings in her heart.
52 And Jesus progressed *in*
wisdom and stature and
favor before God and men.

CHAPTER 3

1 And in *the* fifteenth year
of the government of Tiberias Caesar, Pontius Pilate

Γαλιλαίαν, εἰς τὴν πόλιν αὐτῶν Ναζαρέθ.
Galilee, to the city of them, Nazareth.
40 Τὸ δὲ παιδίον ηὔξανε, καὶ ἐκραταιοῦτο πνεύματι, πληρού-
the And child grew, and became strong in spirit being
μενον σοφίας· καὶ χάρις Θεου ην επ αὐτό.
filled with wisdom, and the grace of God was upon Him.
41 Καὶ ἐπορεύοντο οἱ γονεῖς αὐτοῦ κατ' ἔτος εἰς Ἱερουσαλὴμ
And went the parents of Him year by year into Jerusalem
42 τῇ ἑορτῇ τοῦ πάσχα. καὶ ὅτε ἐγένετο ἐτῶν δώδεκα, ἀναβάν-
at the feast of the Passover. And when He was years twelve, going up
43 των αὐτῶν εἰς Ἱεροσόλυμα κατὰ τὸ ἔθος τῆς ἑορτῆς, καὶ
them to Jerusalem according to the custom of the feast, and
τελειωσάντων τὰς ἡμέρας, ἐν τῷ ὑποστρέφειν αὐτούς, ὑπέ-
fulfilling the days, in the returning of them,
μεινεν Ἰησοῦς ὁ παῖς ἐν Ἱερουσαλὴμ καὶ οὐκ ἔγνω Ἰωσὴφ
stayed Jesus the boy in Jerusalem; and not did know Joseph
44 καὶ ἡ μήτηρ αὐτοῦ· νομίσαντες δὲ αὐτὸν ἐν τῇ συνοδίᾳ εἶναι,
and the mother of Him. supposing But Him in the company to be,
ἦλθον ἡμέρας ὁδόν καὶ ἀνεζήτουν αὐτὸν ἐν τοῖς συγγενέσι
they went a day on the way, and looked for Him among the relatives
45 καὶ ἐν τοῖς γνωστοῖς· καὶ μὴ εὑρόντες αὐτόν, ὑπέστρεψαν εἰς
and among the friends, and not finding Him, they returned into
46 Ἱερουσαλήμ, ζητοῦντες αὐτόν. καὶ ἐγένετο, μεθ' ἡμέρας
Jerusalem seeking Him. And it was, after days
τρεῖς εὗρον αὐτὸν ἐν τῷ ἱερῷ, καθεζόμενον ἐν μέσῳ τῶν
three they found Him in the Temple, sitting in (the) midst of the
47 διδασκάλων, καὶ ἀκούοντα αὐτῶν, καὶ ἐπερωτῶντα αὐτούς.
teachers, even hearing them and questioning them
ἐξίσταντο δὲ πάντες οἱ ἀκούοντες αὐτοῦ ἐπὶ τῇ συνέσει καὶ
were amazed And all those hearing Him at the intelligence and
48 ταῖς ἀποκρίσεσιν αὐτοῦ. καὶ ἰδόντες αὐτὸν ἐξεπλάγησαν·
the answers of Him. And seeing Him, they were astounded
καὶ πρὸς αὐτὸν ἡ μήτηρ αὐτοῦ εἶπε, Τέκνον, τί ἐποίησας
and to Him the mother of Him said, Child, why did You do
ἡμῖν οὕτως; ἰδού, ὁ πατήρ σου κἀγὼ ὀδυνώμενοι ἐζητοῦμέν
to us thus? Behold, the father of You and I greatly distressed are seeking
49 σε. καὶ εἶπε πρὸς αὐτούς, Τί ὅτι ἐζητεῖτέ με; οὐκ ᾔδειτε ὅτι ἐν
You. And He said to them, Why that You sought Me? not know that in
50 τοῖς τοῦ πατρός μου δεῖ εἶναί με; καὶ αὐτοὶ οὐ συνῆκαν τὸ
the(affairs) of My Father must be Me? And they not understood the
51 ῥῆμα ὃ ἐλάλησεν αὐτοῖς. καὶ κατέβη μετ' αὐτῶν, καὶ ἦλθεν
word which He spoke to them. And He went with them, and came
εἰς Ναζαρέθ· καὶ ἦν ὑποτασσόμενος αὐτοῖς· καὶ ἡ μήτηρ
to Nazareth, and was being subject to them. And the mother
αὐτοῦ διετήρει πάντα τὰ ῥήματα ταῦτα ἐν τῇ καρδίᾳ
of Him carefully kept all sayings these in the heart
αὐτῆς.
of her.

52 Καὶ Ἰησοῦς προέκοπτε σοφίᾳ καὶ ἡλικίᾳ, καὶ χάριτι παρὰ
And Jesus progressed (in) wisdom and stature and favor before
Θεῷ καὶ ἀνθρώποις.
God and men.

CHAPTER 3

1 Ἐν ἔτει δὲ πεντεκαιδεκάτῳ τῆς ἡγεμονίας Τιβερίου
in (the) year And fifteenth of the government of Tiberias

governing Judea, and Herod ruling as tetrarch of Galilee; and his brother Philip ruling as tetrarch of Iturea and *the* Trachonitis country; and Lysanias ruling as tetrarch of Abilene, 2 upon *the* high priesthood of Annas and

Caiaphas, *the* word of God came on John the son of Zacharias in the desert. 3 And he came into the neighborhood of the Jordan, proclaiming a baptism of repentance for forgiveness of sins, 4 as it has been written in *the* book of *the* words of Isaiah the prophet, saying: "*The* voice of *one* crying in the wilderness, Prepare the way of *the* Lord, make His paths straight — 5 every valley shall be filled up, and every mountain and hill shall be made low; and the crooked *places* shall be made into straight; and the rough *places* into smooth ways; 6 and all flesh shall see the salvation of God."

7 Then he said to the crowds going out to be baptized by him, Offspring of vipers! Who warned you to flee from the coming wrath? 8 Therefore, bring forth fruits worthy of repentance, and do not begin to say within yourselves, We have Abraham *as* father. For I say to you that God is able to raise up children to Abraham out of these stones. 9 And also the axe is already laid to the root of the trees; therefore, every tree not producing good fruit is being cut down and being thrown into *the* fire. 10 And the crowd asked him, saying, What then shall we do? 11 And answering he said to them, The *one* that has two coats, let him give to him that has not. And the *one* that has foods, let him do the same.

12 And tax-collectors also came to be baptized. And they said to him, Teacher, what shall we do? 13 And he said to them, Do no more than that commanded to you.

Καίσαρος, ἡγεμονεύοντος Ποντίου Πιλάτου τῆς Ἰουδαίας,
Caesar, (in the) governing of Pontius Pilate of Judea
καὶ τετραρχοῦντος τῆς Γαλιλαίας Ἡρώδου, Φιλίππου δὲ
and ruling as tetrarch — of Galilee Herod, Philip and
τοῦ ἀδελφοῦ αὐτοῦ τετραρχοῦντος τῆς Ἰτουραίας καὶ
the brother of him ruling as tetrarch — of Iturea and
2 Τραχωνίτιδος χώρας, καὶ Λυσανίου τῆς Ἀβιληνῆς τετραρ-
of Trachonitis country, and Lysanias — of Abilene ruling as
χοῦντος, ἐπ' ἀρχιερέων Ἄννα καὶ Καϊάφα, ἐγένετο ῥῆμα
tetrarch, at high priesthood of Anna and Caiaphas **came a word**
Θεοῦ ἐπὶ Ἰωάννην τὸν τοῦ Ζαχαρίου υἱὸν ἐν τῇ ἐρήμῳ. καὶ
of God upon John the — of Zachariah son in the desert. And
3 ἦλθεν εἰς πᾶσαν τὴν περίχωρον τοῦ Ἰορδάνου, κηρύσσων
he came into all the neighborhood of the Jordan, proclaiming
4 βάπτισμα μετανοίας εἰς ἄφεσιν ἁμαρτιῶν· ὡς γέγραπται ἐν
a baptism of repentance for forgiveness of sins, as it has been written in
βίβλῳ λόγων Ἠσαΐου τοῦ προφήτου, λέγοντος, Φωνὴ
(the) roll of (the) words of Isaiah the prophet, saying, (The) voice
βοῶντος ἐν τῇ ἐρήμῳ, Ἑτοιμάσατε τὴν ὁδὸν Κυρίου· εὐθείας
of (one) crying in the wilderness, prepare the way of (the) Lord, straight
5 ποιεῖτε τὰς τρίβους αὐτοῦ. πᾶσα φάραγξ πληρωθήσεται,
make the paths of Him; every valley shall be filled up,
καὶ πᾶν ὄρος καὶ βουνὸς ταπεινωθήσεται· καὶ ἔσται τὰ
and every mountain and hill shall be laid low; and shall be the
6 σκολιὰ εἰς εὐθεῖαν, καὶ αἱ τραχεῖαι εἰς ὁδοὺς λείας· καὶ
crooked into straight, and the rough (places) into ways smooth; and
ὄψεται πᾶσα σὰρξ τὸ σωτήριον τοῦ Θεοῦ.
shall see all flesh the salvation — of God.
7 Ἔλεγεν οὖν τοῖς ἐκπορευομένοις ὄχλοις βαπτισθῆναι ὑπ'
He said therefore to the going out crowds to be baptized by
αὐτοῦ, Γεννήματα ἐχιδνῶν, τίς ὑπέδειξεν ὑμῖν φυγεῖν ἀπὸ
him, Offspring of vipers! Who warned you to flee from
8 τῆς μελλούσης ὀργῆς; ποιήσατε οὖν καρποὺς ἀξίους τῆς
the coming wrath? Produce therefore fruits worthy —
μετανοίας· καὶ μὴ ἄρξησθε λέγειν ἐν ἑαυτοῖς, Πατέρα ἔχομεν
of repentance; and not do begin to say among yourselves, Father we have
τὸν Ἀβραάμ· λέγω γὰρ ὑμῖν ὅτι δύναται ὁ Θεὸς ἐκ τῶν
Abraham, I say For to you that is able — God out of —
9 λίθων τούτων ἐγεῖραι τέκνα τῷ Ἀβραάμ. ἤδη δὲ καὶ ἡ ἀξίνη
stones these to raise up children to Abraham. now And even the axe
πρὸς τὴν ῥίζαν τῶν δένδρων κεῖται· πᾶν οὖν δένδρον μὴ
to the root of the trees is laid; every therefore tree not
ποιοῦν καρπὸν καλὸν ἐκκόπτεται καὶ εἰς πῦρ βάλλεται. καὶ
producing fruit good is being cut down and into fire being cast. And
10 ἐπηρώτων αὐτὸν οἱ ὄχλοι λέγοντες, Τί οὖν ποιήσομεν;
asked him the crowd, saying, What, then, may we do?
11 ἀποκριθεὶς δὲ λέγει αὐτοῖς, Ὁ ἔχων δύο χιτῶνας μεταδότω
answering And he says to them, He having two tunics, let him impart
τῷ μὴ ἔχοντι· καὶ ὁ ἔχων βρώματα ὁμοίως ποιείτω. ἦλθον
to (the one) not having; and (the one) having foods likewise let him do. came
12 δὲ καὶ τελῶναι βαπτισθῆναι, καὶ εἶπον πρὸς αὐτόν,
And also tax-collectors to be baptized, and said to him,
13 Διδάσκαλε, τί ποιήσομεν; ὁ δὲ εἶπε πρὸς αὐτούς, Μηδὲν
Teacher, what may we do? he And said to them, Nothing
πλέον παρὰ τὸ διατεταγμένον ὑμῖν πράσσετε. ἐπηρώ-
more besides that commanded to you keep doing. asked

[14] And also ones serving as soldiers asked him, saying, And we, what shall we do? And he said to them, Do not oppress anyone, nor accuse falsely; and be satisfied with your pay.

[15] But the people *were* expecting, and reasoning in their hearts about John, lest perhaps he is the Christ. [16] John answered all, saying, I indeed baptize you with water, but He stronger than me comes, of whom I am not fit to loosen the latchet of His sandals. He will baptize you in *the* Holy Spirit and fire; [17] whose sifting fan *is* in His hand; and He will fully purge His threshing-floor, and will gather the wheat into His barn—but He will burn the chaff with fire that cannot be put out.

[18] And then indeed exhorting many different things, he preached the gospel to the people. [19] But Herod the tetrarch, being reproved by him concerning his brother Philip's wife Herodias, and concerning all *the* evil things Herod did, [20] he also added this above all, he even shut up John in the prison.

[21] And it happened, in the baptizing *of* all the people, Jesus also being baptized, and praying, Heaven was opened, [22] and the Holy Spirit came down in a bodily form as a dove upon Him. And there was a voice out of Heaven, saying, You are My Son, the Beloved; I am delighted in You.

[23] And Jesus Himself was beginning to be about thirty years *old*, being, as was supposed, the son of Joseph, the *son* of Heli, [24] the *son* of Matthat, the *son* of Levi, the *son* of Melchi, the *son* of Janna, the *son* of Joseph, [25] the *son* of Mattathias, the *son* of Amos, the *son* of Nahum, the *son* of Esli, the *son* of Naggai, [26] the *son* of Maath, the *son* of Mattathias, the *son* of Semei, the *son* of Joseph, the *son* of Judah, [27] the *son* of Joannes, the *son* of Rhesa, the *son* of Zerubbabel, the *son* of Shealtiel, the *son* of Neri, [28] the *son* of

14 των δὲ αὐτὸν καὶ στρατευόμενοι, λέγοντες, Καὶ ἡμεῖς τί
— And him also ones serving as soldiers, saying, And we, what
ποιήσομεν; καὶ εἶπε πρὸς αὐτούς, Μηδένα διασείσητε,
may we do? And he said to them, No one oppress
μηδὲ συκοφαντήσητε· καὶ ἀρκεῖσθε τοῖς ὀψωνίοις ὑμῶν.
nor accuse falsely; and be satisfied with the pay of you.

15 Προσδοκῶντος δὲ τοῦ λαοῦ, καὶ διαλογιζομένων πάντων
expecting And the people, and reasoning all
ἐν ταῖς καρδίαις αὐτῶν περὶ τοῦ Ἰωάννου, μήποτε αὐτὸς
in the hearts of them about — John, lest perhaps he
16 εἴη ὁ Χριστός, ἀπεκρίνατο ὁ Ἰωάννης, ἅπασι λέγων, Ἐγὼ
is the Christ, answered — John to all, saying, I
μὲν ὕδατι βαπτίζω ὑμᾶς· ἔρχεται δὲ ὁ ἰσχυρότερός μου, οὗ
indeed with water baptize you; comes but (He) stronger than me, of whom
οὐκ εἰμὶ ἱκανὸς λῦσαι τὸν ἱμάντα τῶν ὑποδημάτων αὐτοῦ·
not I am fit to loose the latchet of the sandals of Him;
17 αὐτὸς ὑμᾶς βαπτίσει ἐν Πνεύματι Ἁγίῳ καὶ πυρί· οὗ τὸ
He you will baptize in (the) Spirit Holy and fire; of whom the
πτύον ἐν τῇ χειρὶ αυτοῦ, καὶ διακαθαριεῖ τὴν ἅλωνα αὐτοῦ,
fan (is) in the hand of Him, and He will fully purge the threshing-floor of Him,
καὶ συνάξει τὸν σῖτον εἰς τὴν ἀποθήκην αὐτοῦ, τὸ δὲ ἄχυρον
and will gather the wheat into the barn of Him; the but chaff
κατακαύσει πυρὶ ἀσβέστῳ.
He will burn up with fire unquenchable.

18 Πολλὰ μὲν οὖν καὶ ἕτερα παρακαλῶν εὐηγγελίζετο τὸν
Many things indeed then and different exhorting, he preached the gospel to the
19 λαόν· ὁ δὲ Ἡρώδης ὁ τετράρχης, ἐλεγχόμενος ὑπ' αὐτοῦ
people. — But Herod the tetrarch, being reproved by him
περὶ Ἡρωδιάδος τῆς γυναικὸς Φιλίππου τοῦ ἀδελφοῦ αὐτοῦ,
concerning Herodias the wife of Philip the brother of him,
καὶ περὶ πάντων ὧν ἐποίησε πονηρῶν ὁ Ἡρώδης, προσέ-
and concerning all things which did evil — Herod, he
20 θηκε καὶ τοῦτο ἐπὶ πᾶσι, καὶ κατέκλεισε τὸν Ἰωάννην ἐν τῇ
added also this above all, even he shut up — John in the
φυλακῇ.
prison.

21 Ἐγένετο δὲ ἐν τῷ βαπτισθῆναι ἅπαντα τὸν λαόν, καὶ
it was And in the baptizing (of) all the people, also
Ἰησοῦ βαπτισθέντος καὶ προσευχομένου, ἀνεῳχθῆναι τὸν
Jesus being baptized and praying, was opened the
22 οὐρανόν, καὶ καταβῆναι τὸ Πνεῦμα τὸ Ἅγιον σωματικῷ
heaven and came down the Spirit — Holy in a bodily
εἴδει ὡσεὶ περιστερὰν ἐπ' αὐτόν, καὶ φωνὴν ἐξ οὐρανοῦ
form as a dove upon Him, and a voice out of Heaven
γενέσθαι, λέγουσαν, Σὺ εἶ ὁ υἱός μου ὁ ἀγαπητός, ἐν σοὶ
occurred, saying, You are the Son of Me, the Beloved: in You
ηὐδόκησα.
I am delighted.

23 Καὶ αὐτὸς ἦν ὁ Ἰησοῦς ὡσεὶ ἐτῶν τριάκοντα ἀρχόμενος,
And Himself was — Jesus about years (old) thirty beginning,
24 ὢν (ὡς ἐνομίζετο) υἱὸς Ἰωσήφ, τοῦ Ἡλί, τοῦ Ματθάτ, τοῦ
being, as was supposed, son of Joseph. — of Heli — of Matthat. —
25 Λευΐ, τοῦ Μελχί, τοῦ Ἰαννά, τοῦ Ἰωσήφ, τοῦ Ματταθίου
of Levi, — of Melchi, of Janna, — of Joseph, — of Mattathias,
26 τοῦ Ἀμώς, τοῦ Ναούμ, τοῦ Ἐσλί, τοῦ Ναγγαί, τοῦ Μαάθ,
— of Amos, — of Nahum, — of Esli, — of Naggai, — of Maath,

Melchi, the *son* of Addi, the
son of Cosam, the *son* of
Elmodam, the *son* of Er, 29 the
son of Joseph, the *son* of
Eliezer, the *son* of Jorim, the
son of Matthat, the *son* of
Levi, 30 the *son* of Simeon,
the *son* of Judah, the *son* of
Joseph, the *son* of Jonan,
the *son* of Eliakim, 31 the *son*
of Melea, the *son* of Menam,
the *son* of Mattatha, the *son*
of Nathan, the *son* of David,
32 the *son* of Jesse, the *son* of
Obed, the *son* of Boaz, the
son of Salmon, the *son* of
Nahshon, 33 the *son* of
Amminadab, the *son* of Aram,
the *son* of Hezron, the *son* of
Pharez, the *son* of Judah,
34 the *son* of Jacob, the *son* of
Isaac, the *son* of Abraham, the
son of Terah, the *son* of Nahor,
35 the *son* of Serug, the *son* of
Reu, the *son* of Peleg, the *son*
of Eber, the *son* of Salah, 36 the
son of Cainan, the *son* of
Arphaxad, the *son* of Shem,
the *son* of Noah, the *son* of
Lamech, 37 the *son* of
Methuselah, the *son* of
Enoch, the *son* of Jared, the
son of Mahalalee, the *son* of
Cainan, 38 the *son* of Enos,
the *son* of Seth, the *son* of
Adam, the *son* of God.

CHAPTER 4

1 And full of *the* Holy
Spirit, Jesus returned from
the Jordan, and was led by
the Spirit into the wilderness 2 forty days, being
tempted by the Devil. And
He ate nothing in those
days, and they being ended,
He afterwards hungered.
3 And the Devil said to Him, If
You are Son of God, speak
to this stone that it become
a loaf. 4 And Jesus answered
to him, saying, It has been
written, "Man shall not live
by bread alone, but by every
word of God." 5 And lead-
ing Him up into a high mountain, the Devil showed Him
all the kingdoms of the
world in a moment of time.
6 And the Devil said to
Him, I will give all this
authority and their glory
to you, because it has
been delivered to me,
and I give it to whomever
I wish; 7 then if You

τοῦ Ματταθίου, τοῦ Σεμεΐ, τοῦ Ἰωσήφ, τοῦ Ἰούδα, τοῦ
— of Mattathias, — of Semei, — of Joseph, — of Judah, —
27 Ἰωαννᾶ, τοῦ Ῥησά, τοῦ Ζοροβάβελ, τοῦ Σαλαθιήλ, τοῦ
of Joannes, — of Rhesa, — of Zerubbabel, — of Salathiel, —
28 Νηρί, τοῦ Μελχί, τοῦ Ἀδδί, τοῦ Κωσάμ, τοῦ Ἐλμωδάμ,
of Neri, — of Melchi, — of Addi, — of Cosam, — of Elmodam,
29 τοῦ Ἤρ, τοῦ Ἰωσή, τοῦ Ἐλιέζερ, τοῦ Ἰωρείμ, τοῦ Ματθάτ,
of Er, of Joseph, — of Eliezer, — of Joreim, — of Matthai,
30 τοῦ Λευΐ, τοῦ Σιμεών, τοῦ Ἰούδα, τοῦ Ἰωσήφ, τοῦ Ἰωνάν,
— of Levi, — of Simeon, — of Judah, — of Joseph, — of Jonan,
31 τοῦ Ἐλιακείμ, τοῦ Μελεᾶ, τοῦ Μενάμ, τοῦ Ματταθά, τοῦ
— of Eliakim, — of Melea, — of Menam, — of Mattatha, —
32 Ναθάν, τοῦ Δαβίδ, τοῦ Ἰεσσαί, τοῦ Ὠβήδ, τοῦ Βοόζ, τοῦ
of Nathan, — of David, — of Jesse, — of Obed, — of Boaz, —
33 Σαλμών, τοῦ Ναασσών, τοῦ Ἀμιναδάβ, τοῦ Ἀράμ, τοῦ
of Salmon, — of Nahshon, — of Amminadab, — of Ram, —
34 Ἐσρώμ, τοῦ Φαρές, τοῦ Ἰούδα, τοῦ Ἰακώβ, τοῦ Ἰσαάκ,
of Hezron, — of Pharez, — of Judah, — of Jacob, — of Isaac,
35 τοῦ Ἀβραάμ, τοῦ Θάρα, τοῦ Ναχώρ, τοῦ Σαρούχ, τοῦ
— of Abraham, of Terah, — of Nahor, — of Serug, —
Ῥαγαῦ, τοῦ Φαλέκ, τοῦ Ἐβέρ, τοῦ Σαλά, τοῦ Καϊνάν, τοῦ
of Reu, — of Peleg, — of Eber, — of Salah, — of Cainan, —
36 Ἀρφαξάδ, τοῦ Σήμ, τοῦ Νῶε, τοῦ Λάμεχ, τοῦ Μαθουσάλα,
of Arphaxad, — of Shem, — of Noah, — of Lamech, — of Methuselah,
37 τοῦ Ἐνώχ, τοῦ Ἰαρέδ, τοῦ Μαλελεήλ, τοῦ Καϊνάν, τοῦ
— of Enoch, — of Jared, — of Mahalaleel, — of Cainan, —
38 Ἐνώς, τοῦ Σήθ, τοῦ Ἀδάμ, τοῦ Θεοῦ.
of Enos, — of Seth, — of Adam, — of God.

CHAPTER 4

1 Ἰησοῦς δὲ Πνεύματος Ἁγίου πλήρης ὑπέστρεψεν ἀπὸ τοῦ
Jesus And of (the) Spirit Holy full returned from the
2 Ἰορδάνου, καὶ ἤγετο ἐν τῷ Πνεύματι εἰς τὴν ἔρημον, ἡμέρας
Jordan, and was led by the Spirit into the wilderness, days
τεσσαράκοντα πειραζόμενος ὑπὸ τοῦ διαβόλου. καὶ οὐκ
forty being tempted by the Devil. And not
ἔφαγεν οὐδὲν ἐν ταῖς ἡμέραις ἐκείναις· καὶ συντελεσθεισῶν
He ate, nothing in — days those; and being ended
3 αὐτῶν, ὕστερον ἐπείνασε. καὶ εἶπεν αὐτῷ ὁ διάβολος, Εἰ
them, afterwards He hungered. And said to Him the Devil, If
υἱὸς εἶ τοῦ Θεοῦ, εἰπὲ τῷ λίθῳ τούτῳ ἵνα γένηται ἄρτος.
Son you are — of God say to stone this that it become a loaf.
4 καὶ ἀπεκρίθη Ἰησοῦς πρὸς αὐτόν, λέγων, Γέγραπται ὅτι
And made answer Jesus to him, saying, It has been written,
Οὐκ ἐπ' ἄρτῳ μόνῳ ζήσεται ὁ ἄνθρωπος, ἀλλ' ἐπὶ παντὶ
Not on bread only shall live — man, but on every
5 ῥήματι Θεοῦ. καὶ ἀναγαγὼν αὐτὸν ὁ διάβολος εἰς ὄρος
word of God. And leading up Him the Devil into a mount
ὑψηλὸν ἔδειξεν αὐτῷ πάσας τὰς βασιλείας τῆς οἰκουμένης
high, he showed Him all the kingdoms of the habitable world
6 ἐν στιγμῇ χρόνου. καὶ εἶπεν αὐτῷ ὁ διάβολος, Σοὶ δώσω τὴν
in a moment of time. And said to Him the Devil, To you I will give —
ἐξουσίαν ταύτην ἅπασαν καὶ τὴν δόξαν αὐτῶν· ὅτι ἐμοὶ
authority this all and the glory of them, because to me
παραδέδοται, καὶ ᾧ ἐὰν θέλω δίδωμι αὐτήν. σὺ οὖν ἐὰν
7 it has been delivered, and to whomever I wish I give it; you, then, if

worship before me, all will be Yours. [8]And answering to him, Jesus said, For it has been written, "You shall worship *the* Lord your God, and Him only you shall serve."

[9]And he led Him to Jerusalem, and stood Him on the pinnacle of the Temple, and said to him, If You are the Son of God, throw yourself down from here; [10]for it has been written, "He will command His angels about You, and to preserve You; [11]that on *their* hands they shall bear You, lest you strike Your foot against a stone." [12]And Jesus answering said to him, It has been said, "You shall not tempt *the* Lord your God." [13]And having finished every temptation, the Devil departed from Him until a time.

[14]And Jesus returned in the power of the Spirit to Galilee. And a rumor went out through all the neighborhood about Him. [15]And He taught in their synagogue, being glorified by all.

[16]And He came to Nazareth, where He was brought up. And He went in, as *was* His custom, on the day of the sabbaths, into the synagogue, and stood up to read. [17]And *the* book of Isaiah the prophet was handed to Him. And unrolling the book, He found the place where it was written, [18]"*The* Spirit of *the* Lord is upon Me; therefore He anointed Me to preach the gospel to *the* poor; He has sent Me to heal the brokenhearted, to preach deliverance to captives, and new sight to *the* blind; to send away crushed ones in deliverance; [19]to preach an acceptable year of *the* Lord." [20]And rolling up the book, returning *it* to the attendant, He sat down. and the eyes of all in the synagogue were fixed on Him. [21]And He began to say to

8 προσκυνήσῃς ἐνώπιόν μου, ἔσται σου πάντα. καὶ ἀποκρι-
you worship before me, will be of you all. And answering
θεὶς αὐτῷ εἶπεν ὁ Ἰησοῦς, Ὕπαγε ὀπίσω μου, Σατανᾶ·
to him said — Jesus, Get behind Me, Satan!
γέγραπται γάρ, Προσκυνήσεις Κύριον τὸν Θεόν σου, καὶ
it has been written For, You shall worship (the) Lord the God of you, and
9 αὐτῷ μόνῳ λατρεύσεις. καὶ ἤγαγεν αὐτὸν εἰς Ἱερουσαλήμ,
Him only you shall serve. And he led Him to Jerusalem,
καὶ ἔστησεν αὐτὸν ἐπὶ τὸ πτερύγιον τοῦ ἱεροῦ, καὶ εἶπεν
and stood Him on the pinnacle of the Temple, and said
αὐτῷ, Εἰ ὁ υἱὸς εἶ τοῦ Θεοῦ, βάλε σεαυτὸν ἐντεῦθεν κάτω·
to Him, If the Son you are — of God, throw yourself from here down;
10 γέγραπται γὰρ ὅτι Τοῖς ἀγγέλοις αὐτοῦ ἐντελεῖται περὶ
it has been written For, To the angels of Him He will command about
11 σοῦ, τοῦ διαφυλάξαι σε· καὶ ὅτι Ἐπὶ χειρῶν ἀροῦσί σε,
You — to preserve You and, In (their) hands they will bear You,
12 μήποτε προσκόψῃς πρὸς λίθον τὸν πόδα σου. καὶ ἀπο-
lest You strike against a stone the foot of You And answering
κριθεὶς εἶπεν αὐτῷ ὁ Ἰησοῦς ὅτι Εἴρηται, Οὐκ ἐκπειράσεις
said to him Jesus, — It has been said, not You shall tempt
13 Κύριον τὸν Θεόν σου. καὶ συντελέσας πάντα πειρασμὸν ὁ
(the) Lord the God of you. And having finished every temptation, the
διάβολος ἀπέστη ἀπ᾽ αὐτοῦ ἄχρι καιροῦ.
Devil departed from Him until a season.
14 Καὶ ὑπέστρεψεν ὁ Ἰησοῦς ἐν τῇ δυνάμει τοῦ Πνεύματος
And returned — Jesus in the power of the Spirit
εἰς τὴν Γαλιλαίαν· καὶ φήμη ἐξῆλθε καθ᾽ ὅλης τῆς περιχώρου
to — Galilee; and a rumor went out through all the neighborhood
15 περὶ αὐτοῦ. καὶ αὐτὸς ἐδίδασκεν ἐν ταῖς συναγωγαῖς
concerning Him. And He taught in the synagogues
αὐτῶν, δοξαζόμενος ὑπὸ πάντων.
of them, being glorified by all.
16 Καὶ ἦλθεν εἰς τὴν Ναζαρέθ, οὗ ἦν τεθραμμένος· καὶ
And He came to — Nazareth, where He was brought up and
εἰσῆλθε, κατὰ τὸ εἰωθὸς αὐτῷ, ἐν τῇ ἡμέρᾳ τῶν σαββάτων
He went in as (was) the custom to Him, on the day of the sabbaths,
17 εἰς τὴν συναγωγήν, καὶ ἀνέστη ἀναγνῶναι. καὶ ἐπεδόθη
into the synagogue, and stood up to read And was handed
αὐτῷ βιβλίον Ἠσαΐου τοῦ προφήτου. καὶ ἀναπτύξας τὸ
to Him a roll of Isaiah the prophet. And having unrolled the
18 βιβλίον, εὗρε τὸν τόπον οὗ ἦν γεγραμμένον, Πνεῦμα Κυρίου
roll, He found the place where it was written, (the) Spirit of (the) Lord
ἐπ᾽ ἐμέ, οὗ ἕνεκεν ἔχρισέ με εὐαγγελίζεσθαι πτωχοῖς· ἀπέ-
(is) on Me; therefore He anointed Me to preach the gospel to (the) poor; He
σταλκέ με ἰάσασθαι τοὺς συντετριμμένους τὴν καρδίαν·
has sent Me to heal the broken — (in) heart,
κηρύξαι αἰχμαλώτοις ἄφεσιν, καὶ τυφλοῖς ἀνάβλεψιν,
to preach to captives deliverance, and to (the) blind new sight,
19 ἀποστεῖλαι τεθραυσμένους ἐν ἀφέσει, κηρύξαι ἐνιαυτὸν
to send away crushed ones in deliverance, to preach a year
20 Κυρίου δεκτόν. καὶ πτύξας τὸ βιβλίον, ἀποδοὺς τῷ ὑπηρέτῃ,
(the) Lord acceptable. And closing the roll, returning (it) to the attendant,
ἐκάθισε· καὶ πάντων ἐν τῇ συναγωγῇ οἱ ὀφθαλμοὶ ἦσαν
He sat. And of all in the synagogue the eyes were
21 ἀτενίζοντες αὐτῷ. ἤρξατο δὲ λέγειν πρὸς αὐτοὺς ὅτι
fixed on Him. He began And to say to them, —

them, Today this Scripture has been fulfilled in your ears. 22 And all bore witness to Him, and marveled at the gracious words coming out of His mouth. And they said, Is this not the son of Joseph? 23 And He said to them, Surely you will speak this parable to Me, Physician, heal yourself. The things which we heard *were* happening in Capernaum, do also here in your native-place. 24 But He said, Truly I say to you that no prophet is acceptable in his native-place. 25 But truthfully I say to you, There were many widows in Israel in the days of Elijah, when the heaven was shut up over three years and six months, when a great famine came on all the land; 26 and *yet* Elijah was sent to none of them except to Zarephath of Sidon, to a widow woman. 27 And many lepers were in Israel during Elisha the prophet's *time*, and none of them was made clean except Naaman the Syrian.

28 And all were filled *with* anger, hearing these things in the synagogue. 29 And rising up, they threw Him outside the city, and led Him up to the brow of the hill on which their city was built, in order to throw Him down. 30 But He went away, passing through their midst.

31 And He went down to Capernaum, a city of Galilee. And He was teaching them in the sabbaths. 32 And they were astonished at His teaching, because His word was with authority. 33 And in the synagogue was a man who had a spirit of an unclean demon. And he cried out with a loud voice, 34 saying, Aha! What *is* to us and to You, Jesus, Nazarene? Did You come to destroy us? I know You. You are the Holy One of God. 35 And Jesus rebuked him, saying, Be silent, and come out of him! And throwing him into the

Σήμερον πεπλήρωται ἡ γραφὴ αὕτη ἐν τοῖς ὠσὶν ὑμῶν
Today has been fulfilled — scripture this in the ears of you.
22 καὶ πάντες ἐμαρτύρουν αὐτῷ, καὶ ἐθαύμαζον ἐπὶ τοῖς λόγοις
And all bore witness to Him and marveled at the words
τῆς χάριτος τοῖς ἐκπορευομένοις ἐκ τοῦ στόματος αὐτοῦ, καὶ
— of grace — proceeding from the mouth of Him. And
23 ἔλεγον, Οὐχ οὗτός ἐστιν ὁ υἱὸς Ἰωσήφ ; καὶ εἶπε πρὸς αὐτούς,
they said, Not this is the son of Joseph? And He said to them,
Πάντως ἐρεῖτέ μοι τὴν παραβολὴν ταύτην, Ἰατρέ, θεράπευσον σεαυτόν· ὅσα ἠκούσαμεν γενόμενα ἐν τῇ Καπερναουμ,
Surely you will say to Me — parable this, Physician, heal yourself! What things we heard happening in — Capernaum,
24 ποίησον καὶ ὧδε ἐν τῇ πατρίδι σου. εἶπε δέ, Ἀμὴν λέγω
do also here in the native-place of you. He said And, Truly, I say
ὑμῖν ὅτι οὐδεὶς προφήτης δεκτός ἐστιν ἐν τῇ πατρίδι αὐτοῦ.
to you that no prophet acceptable is in the native-place of him.
25 ἐπ' ἀληθείας δὲ λέγω ὑμῖν, πολλαὶ χῆραι ἦσαν ἐν ταῖς
on a truth But I say to you, Many widows were in the
ἡμέραις Ἠλίου ἐν τῷ Ἰσραήλ, ὅτε ἐκλείσθη ὁ οὐρανὸς ἐπὶ
days of Elijah in — Israel, when was shut up the heaven over
ἔτη τρία καὶ μῆνας ἕξ, ὡς ἐγένετο λιμὸς μέγας ἐπὶ πᾶσαν τὴν
years three and months six, when came a famine great upon all the
26 γῆν· καὶ πρὸς οὐδεμίαν αὐτῶν ἐπέμφθη Ἠλίας, εἰ μὴ εἰς
land; and to no one of them was sent Elijah except to
27 Σάρεπτα τῆς Σιδῶνος πρὸς γυναῖκα χήραν. καὶ πολλοὶ
Sarepta — of Sidon, to a woman, a widow. And many
λεπροὶ ἦσαν ἐπὶ Ἐλισσαίου τοῦ προφήτου ἐν τῷ Ἰσραήλ·
lepers were during Elisha the prophet in — Israel,
28 καὶ οὐδεὶς αὐτῶν ἐκαθαρίσθη, εἰ μὴ Νεεμὰν ὁ Σύρος. καὶ
and none of them was cleansed except Naaman the Syrian. And
ἐπλήσθησαν πάντες θυμοῦ ἐν τῇ συναγωγῇ, ἀκούοντες
were filled all (with) anger in the synagogue hearing
29 ταῦτα, καὶ ἀναστάντες ἐξέβαλον αὐτὸν ἔξω τῆς πόλεως, καὶ
these things, and rising up they threw Him outside the city. and
ἤγαγον αὐτὸν ἕως τῆς ὀφρύος τοῦ ὄρους ἐφ' οὗ ἡ πόλις
led Him up to the brow of the hill on which the city
30 αὐτῶν ᾠκοδόμητο, εἰς τὸ κατακρημνίσαι αὐτόν. αὐτὸς δὲ
of them was built, in order to — throw down Him. He But
διελθὼν διὰ μέσου αὐτῶν ἐπορεύετο.
passing through (the) midst of them went away.
31 Καὶ κατῆλθεν εἰς Καπερναοὺμ πόλιν τῆς Γαλιλαίας· καὶ
And He went down to Capernaum, a city — of Galilee. And
32 ἦν διδάσκων αὐτοὺς ἐν τοῖς σάββασι. καὶ ἐξεπλήσσοντο
He was teaching them in the sabbaths. And they were astounded
33 ἐπὶ τῇ διδαχῇ αὐτοῦ, ὅτι ἐν ἐξουσίᾳ ἦν ὁ λόγος αὐτοῦ. καὶ
at the teaching of Him, for with authority was the word of Him. And
ἐν τῇ συναγωγῇ ἦν ἄνθρωπος ἔχων πνεῦμα δαιμονίου
In the synagogue there was a man having a spirit of a demon
34 ἀκαθάρτου, καὶ ἀνέκραξε φωνῇ μεγάλῃ, λέγων, Ἔα, τί ἡμῖν
unclean, and cried out with a voice great, saying, Aha! What to us
καὶ σοί, Ἰησοῦ Ναζαρηνέ ; ἦλθες ἀπολέσαι ἡμᾶς ; οἶδά
and to You, Jesus, Nazarene? Did You come to destroy us? I know
35 σε τίς εἶ, ὁ ἅγιος τοῦ Θεοῦ. καὶ ἐπετίμησεν αὐτῷ ὁ Ἰησοῦς,
You, who you are, the holy of God. And rebuked him — Jesus,
λέγων, Φιμώθητι, καὶ ἔξελθε ἐξ αὐτοῦ. καὶ ῥίψαν αὐτὸν τὸ
saying, Be silent, and come out from him. And throwing him the

midst, the demon came out from him, not harming him. [36]And astonishment came on all. And they spoke with one another saying, What word *is* this, that He commands the unclean spirits with authority and power, and they come out? [37]And a report about Him went out into every place of the neighborhood.

[38]And rising up from the synagogue, He went into the house of Simon. And the mother-in-law of Simon was being seized with a great fever. and they asked Him concerning her. [39]And standing over her, He rebuked the fever, and it left her. And rising up instantly, she served them.

[40]And the sun sinking, all, as many as had sick ones with various diseases, brought them to Him. And laying hands on each one of them, He healed them. [41]And also demons came out from many, crying out and saying, You are the Christ, the Son of God! And rebuking *them,* He did not allow them to speak; for they knew Him to be the Christ.

[42]And day coming, going out He went into a desert place. And the crowds looked for Him, and came up to Him, and held Him fast, not to pass away from them. [43]But He said to them, It is right for Me to preach the gospel, the kingdom of God, to the other cities, because I was sent on this *mission.*

[44]And He was proclaiming in the synagogues of Galilee.

CHAPTER 5

[1]And it happened that the crowd was pressing on Him to hear the word of God. And He was standing by Lake Gennesaret. [2]And He saw two boats standing by the lake, but the fishermen had left them and were washing

δαιμόνιον εἰς τὸ μέσον ἐξῆλθεν ἀπ' αὐτοῦ, μηδὲν βλάψαν
demon in the midst came out from him, nothing injuring
36 αὐτόν. καὶ ἐγένετο θάμβος ἐπὶ πάντας, καὶ συνελάλουν πρὸς
him. And came astonishment on all, and they spoke with
ἀλλήλους, λέγοντες, Τίς ὁ λόγος οὗτος, ὅτι ἐν ἐξουσίᾳ καὶ
one another, saying, What (is) word this, that with authority and
δυνάμει ἐπιτάσσει τοῖς ἀκαθάρτοις πνεύμασι, καὶ ἐξέρχον-
power He commands the unclean spirits, and they come
37 ται ; καὶ ἐξεπορεύετο ἦχος περὶ αὐτοῦ εἰς πάντα τόπον τῆς
out? And went forth a rumor concerning Him into every place of the
περιχώρου.
neighborhood.
38 Ἀναστὰς δὲ ἐκ τῆς συναγωγῆς, εἰσῆλθεν εἰς τὴν οἰκίαν
rising up And from the synagogue, He went into the house
Σίμωνος· ἡ πενθερὰ δὲ τοῦ Σίμωνος ἦν συνεχομένη πυρετῷ
of Simon. the mother-in-law And of Simon was being seized with a fever
39 μεγάλῳ· καὶ ἠρώτησαν αὐτὸν περὶ αὐτῆς. καὶ ἐπιστὰς
great, and they ask Him concerning her. And standing
ἐπάνω αὐτῆς, ἐπετίμησε τῷ πυρετῷ, καὶ ἀφῆκεν αὐτήν·
over her, He rebuked the fever; and it left her.
παραχρῆμα δὲ ἀναστᾶσα διηκόνει αὐτοῖς.
at once And rising up she served them.
40 Δύνοντος δὲ τοῦ ἡλίου, πάντες ὅσοι εἶχον ἀσθενοῦντας
sinking And the sun, all, as many as had sick ones
νόσοις ποικίλαις ἤγαγον αὐτοὺς πρὸς αὐτόν· ὁ δὲ ἑνὶ
with various diseases, brought them to Him. He And one
ἑκάστῳ αὐτῶν τὰς χεῖρας ἐπιθεὶς ἐθεράπευσεν αὐτούς.
each of them the hands laying on healed them.
41 ἐξήρχετο δὲ καὶ δαιμόνια ἀπὸ πολλῶν, κράζοντα καὶ
came out And also demons from many, crying out and
λέγοντα ὅτι Σὺ εἶ ὁ Χριστὸς ὁ υἱὸς τοῦ Θεοῦ. καὶ ἐπιτιμῶν
saying, – You are the Christ, the Son – of God. And rebuking
οὐκ εἴα αὐτὰ λαλεῖν, ὅτι ᾔδεισαν τὸν Χριστὸν αὐτὸν εἶναι.
not He allowed them to speak, for they knew the Christ Him to be.
42 Γενομένης δὲ ἡμέρας, ἐξελθὼν ἐπορεύθη εἰς ἔρημον τόπον,
coming And day, going out He went to a desert place.
καὶ οἱ ὄχλοι ἐζήτουν αὐτόν, καὶ ἦλθον ἕως αὐτοῦ, καὶ
And the crowds looked for Him, and came up to Him, and
43 κατεῖχον αὐτὸν τοῦ μὴ πορεύεσθαι ἀπ' αὐτῶν. ὁ δὲ εἶπε
held fast Him, not to pass from them. He But said
πρὸς αὐτοὺς ὅτι Καὶ ταῖς ἑτέραις πόλεσιν εὐαγγελίσασθαί
to them, – Also to the other cities to preach the gospel
με δεῖ τὴν βασιλείαν τοῦ Θεοῦ· ὅτι εἰς τοῦτο ἀπέσταλμαι.
Me it behoves, the kingdom – of God, for on this I was sent.
44 Καὶ ἦν κηρύσσων ἐν ταῖς συναγωγαῖς τῆς Γαλιλαίας.
And He was proclaiming in the synagogues of Judea

CHAPTER 5

1 Ἐγένετο δὲ ἐν τῷ τὸν ὄχλον ἐπικεῖσθαι αὐτῷ τοῦ ἀκούειν
it was And in – the crowd pressing on Him – to hear
τὸν λόγον τοῦ Θεοῦ, καὶ αὐτὸς ἦν ἑστὼς παρὰ τὴν λίμνην
the word – of God, even He was standing by the lake
2 Γεννησαρέτ· καὶ εἶδε δύο πλοῖα ἑστῶτα παρὰ τὴν λίμνην·
Gennesaret. And He saw two boats standing by the lake;
οἱ δὲ ἁλιεῖς ἀποβάντες ἀπ' αὐτῶν ἀπέπλυναν τὰ δίκτυα
the but fishermen having gone from them were washing the nets

the nets. [3]And entering into one of the boats, which was Simon's, He asked him to put out a little from the land. And sitting down, he taught the crowd from the boat. [4]And as He quit speaking, He said to Simon, Put out into the deep, and let down your nets for a haul. [5]And answering said to Him, Master, laboring all through the night we took nothing. But at Your word I will let down the net. [6]And doing this, they netted a great multitude of fish; and their net was being torn. [7]And they signaled the partners, those in the other boat, to come *and* help them. And they came and filled both the boats, so that they were sinking. [8]And seeing, Simon Peter fell at the knees of Jesus, saying, Depart from me, for I am a sinful man, Lord. [9]For astonishment took hold of him, and all those with him, at the haul of fish which they took. [10]And in the same way also, James and John, *the* sons of Zebedee, who were partners with Simon. And Jesus said to Simon, Do not fear. From now on you will be taking men alive. [11]And bringing the boats down onto the land, forsaking all things, they followed Him.

[12]And it happened, in His being in one of the cities, even behold, a man full of leprosy. And seeing Jesus, falling on *his* face, he begged Him, saying, Lord, if You choose, You are able to cleanse me. [13]And stretching out the hand, He touched him, saying, I choose; be cleansed! And instantly the leprosy departed from him. [14]And He charged him to tell no one, but going away, show yourself to the priest, and offer for your cleansing, as Moses commanded, for a testimony

3 ἐμβὰς δὲ εἰς ἓν τῶν πλοίων, ὃ ἦν τοῦ Σίμωνος, ἠρώτησεν
entering And into one of the boats which was — Simon's, He asked

αὐτὸν ἀπὸ τῆς γῆς ἐπαναγαγεῖν ὀλίγον. καὶ καθίσας
him from the land to put out a little. And sitting

4 ἐδίδασκεν ἐκ τοῦ πλοίου τοὺς ὄχλους. ὡς δὲ ἐπαύσατο
He taught from the boat the crowd. as And He quit

λαλῶν, εἶπε πρὸς τὸν Σίμωνα, Ἐπανάγαγε εἰς τὸ βάθος,
speaking, He said to — Simon, Put out into the deep,

5 καὶ χαλάσατε τὰ δίκτυα ὑμῶν εἰς ἄγραν. καὶ ἀποκριθεὶς ὁ
and let down the nets of you for a haul. And answering

Σίμων εἶπεν αὐτῷ, Ἐπιστάτα, δι' ὅλης τῆς νυκτὸς κοπιά-
Simon said to Him, Master, through all the night

σαντες οὐδὲν ἐλάβομεν· ἐπὶ δὲ τῷ ῥήματί σου χαλάσω τὸ
laboring nothing we took, at but the word of You I will let down the

6 δίκτυον. καὶ τοῦτο ποιήσαντες, συνέκλεισαν ἰχθύων πλῆθος
net. And this doing, they enclosed of fish a multitude

7 πολύ· διερρήγνυτο δὲ τὸ δίκτυον αὐτῶν· καὶ κατένευσαν
much, was being torn and the nets of them. And they signaled

τοῖς μετόχοις τοῖς ἐν τῷ ἑτέρῳ πλοίῳ, τοῦ ἐλθόντας συλ-
the partners, those in the other boat, coming to

λαβέσθαι αὐτοῖς· καὶ ἦλθον καὶ ἔπλησαν ἀμφότερα τὰ
help them; and they came and filled both the

8 πλοῖα, ὥστε βυθίζεσθαι αὐτά. ἰδὼν δὲ Σίμων Πέτρος
boats, so as were sinking they. having seen And Simon Peter

προσέπεσε τοῖς γόνασι τοῦ Ἰησοῦ, λέγων, Ἔξελθε ἀπ' ἐμοῦ,
fell at the knees — of Jesus, saying, Depart from me,

9 ὅτι ἀνὴρ ἁμαρτωλός εἰμι, Κύριε. θάμβος γὰρ περιέσχεν
because a man sinful I am, Lord. astonishment For seized,

αὐτὸν καὶ πάντας τοὺς σὺν αὐτῷ, ἐπὶ τῇ ἄγρᾳ τῶν ἰχθύων
him and all the (ones) with him at the haul — of fish

10 ᾗ συνέλαβον· ὁμοίως δὲ καὶ Ἰάκωβον καὶ Ἰωάννην, υἱοὺς
which they took; likewise and both James and John, sons

Ζεβεδαίου, οἳ ἦσαν κοινωνοὶ τῷ Σίμωνι. καὶ εἶπε πρὸς τὸν
of Zebedee, who were sharers — with Simon. And said to —

Σίμωνα ὁ Ἰησοῦς, Μὴ φοβοῦ· ἀπὸ τοῦ νῦν ἀνθρώπους ἔσῃ
Simon — Jesus, Not do fear; from — now men you will be

11 ζωγρῶν. καὶ καταγαγόντες τὰ πλοῖα ἐπὶ τὴν γῆν, ἀφέντες
taking alive. And bringing down the boats onto the land, forsaking

ἅπαντα, ἠκολούθησαν αὐτῷ.
all things, they followed Him.

12 Καὶ ἐγένετο, ἐν τῷ εἶναι αὐτὸν ἐν μιᾷ τῶν πόλεων, καὶ
And it was, in the being of Him in one of the cities, and

ἰδού, ἀνὴρ πλήρης λέπρας· καὶ ἰδὼν τὸν Ἰησοῦν, πεσὼν
behold, a man full of leprosy; and seeing — Jesus, having fallen

ἐπὶ πρόσωπον, ἐδεήθη αὐτοῦ, λέγων, Κύριε, ἐὰν θέλῃς,
on (his) face, he begged Him, saying, Lord, if You choose

13 δύνασαί με καθαρίσαι. καὶ ἐκτείνας τὴν χεῖρα ἥψατο αὐτοῦ,
You are able Me to cleanse. And stretching the hand He touched him,

εἰπών, Θέλω, καθαρίσθητι. καὶ εὐθέως ἡ λέπρα ἀπῆλθεν ἀπ'
saying, I choose, be cleansed! And instantly the leprosy departed from

14 αὐτοῦ. καὶ αὐτὸς παρήγγειλεν αὐτῷ μηδενὶ εἰπεῖν· ἀλλὰ
him. And He charged him no one to tell, but

ἀπελθὼν δεῖξον σεαυτὸν τῷ ἱερεῖ, καὶ προσένεγκε περὶ τοῦ
going away show yourself to the priest, and offer concerning the

καθαρισμοῦ σου, καθὼς προσέταξε Μωσῆς, εἰς μαρτύριον
cleansing of you, as commanded Moses, for a testimony

to them.
[15]But the word about Him spread even more. And large crowds were coming to hear, and to be healed by Him from their infirmities. [16]But He was drawing back in the desert, and praying.
[17]And it happened on one of the days, even He was teaching. And Pharisees and teachers of *the* Law were sitting by, who were coming out of every village of Galilee and Judea, and Jerusalem. And *the* power of *the* Lord was there, for the curing of them. [18]And, behold, men carrying a man who was paralyzed on a cot. And they sought to bring him in, and to lay *him* before Him. [19]And not finding a way through *which* they might bring him in through the crowd, going up on the housetop, they let him down through the tiles with the cot, into the midst, in front of Jesus. [20]And seeing their faith, he said to him, Man, your sins have been forgiven you. [21]And the scribes and Pharisees began to reason, saying, Who is this who speaks blasphemies? Who is able to forgive sins, except God alone? [22]But knowing their thoughts, answering Jesus said to them, Why do you reason in your hearts? [23]Which is easier, to say, Your sins have been forgiven you; or to say, Rise up and walk? [24]But that you may know that the Son of man has authority on the earth to forgive sins, He said to the paralytic, I say to you, Rise up, and take your cot *and* go to your house. [25]And rising up at once before them, taking up *that* on which he was lying, he went to his house, glorifying God. [26]And amazement seized all, and they glorified God, and were filled *with* fear, saying, We saw wonderful things today.

15 αὐτοῖς. διήρχετο δὲ μᾶλλον ὁ λόγος περὶ αὐτοῦ· καὶ συν-
to them. spread But even more the word concerning Him, and were
ήρχοντο ὄχλοι πολλοὶ ἀκούειν, καὶ θεραπεύεσθαι ὑπ' αὐτοῦ
coming crowds great to hear, and to be healed by Him
16 ἀπὸ τῶν ἀσθενειῶν αὐτῶν. αὐτὸς δὲ ἦν ὑποχωρῶν ἐν ταῖς
from the infirmities of them. He But was withdrawing in the
ἐρήμοις καὶ προσευχόμενος.
desert and praying.
17 Καὶ ἐγένετο ἐν μιᾷ τῶν ἡμερῶν, καὶ αὐτὸς ἦν διδάσκων·
And it was, on one of the days, and He was teaching,
καὶ ἦσαν καθήμενοι Φαρισαῖοι καὶ νομοδιδάσκαλοι, οἳ ἦσαν
and were sitting Pharisees and teachers of law, who were
ἐληλυθότες ἐκ πάσης κώμης τῆς Γαλιλαίας καὶ Ἰουδαίας καὶ
coming out of every village – of Galilee and Judea and
Ἱερουσαλήμ· καὶ δύναμις Κυρίου ἦν εἰς τὸ ἰᾶσθαι αὐτούς.
Jerusalem. And power of (the) Lord was, to the curing (of) them.
18 καὶ ἰδού, ἄνδρες φέροντες ἐπὶ κλίνης ἄνθρωπον ὃς ἦν παρα-
And behold, men carrying on a cot a man who was
λελυμένος, καὶ ἐζήτουν αὐτὸν εἰσενεγκεῖν καὶ θεῖναι ἐνώπιον
paralyzed; and they sought him to bring in and to lay before
19 αὐτοῦ· καὶ μὴ εὑρόντες διὰ ποίας εἰσενέγκωσιν αὐτὸν διὰ
Him. And not finding by what way they may bring in him through
τὸν ὄχλον, ἀναβάντες ἐπὶ τὸ δῶμα, διὰ τῶν κεράμων
the crowd, going up on the housetop, through the tiles
καθῆκαν αὐτὸν σὺν τῷ κλινιδίῳ εἰς τὸ μέσον ἔμπροσθεν τοῦ
they let down him with the cot into the midst in front of –
20 Ἰησοῦ. καὶ ἰδὼν τὴν πίστιν αὐτῶν, εἶπεν αὐτῷ, Ἄνθρωπε,
Jesus. And seeing the faith of them, He said to him, Man,
21 ἀφέωνταί σοι αἱ ἁμαρτίαι σου. καὶ ἤρξαντο διαλογίζεσθαι
have been forgiven you the sins of you. And began to reason
οἱ γραμματεῖς καὶ οἱ Φαρισαῖοι, λέγοντες, Τίς ἐστιν οὗτος
the scribes and the Pharisees, saying, Who is this one
ὃς λαλεῖ βλασφημίας; τίς δύναται ἀφιέναι ἁμαρτίας, εἰ μὴ
who speaks blasphemies? Who is able to forgive sins, except
22 μόνος ὁ Θεός; ἐπιγνοὺς δὲ ὁ Ἰησοῦς τοὺς διαλογισμοὺς
only – God? knowing But – Jesus the reasonings
αὐτῶν ἀποκριθεὶς εἶπε πρὸς αὐτούς, Τί διαλογίζεσθε ἐν ταῖς
of them, answering said to them, Why do you reason in the
23 καρδίαις ὑμῶν; τί ἐστιν εὐκοπώτερον, εἰπεῖν, Ἀφέωνταί
hearts of you? What is easier, to say, Have been forgiven
σοι αἱ ἁμαρτίαι σου, ἢ εἰπεῖν, Ἔγειραι καὶ περιπάτει; ἵνα
you the sins of you, or to say, Rise up and walk? that
24 δὲ εἰδῆτε ὅτι ἐξουσίαν ἔχει ὁ υἱὸς τοῦ ἀνθρώπου ἐπὶ τῆς γῆς
But you may know authority has the Son – of man on the earth
ἀφιέναι ἁμαρτίας εἶπε τῷ παραλελυμένῳ Σοὶ λέγω,
to forgive sins, He said to the paralytic, To you I say,
ἔγειραι, καὶ ἄρας τὸ κλινίδιόν σου, πορεύου εἰς τὸν οἶκόν
Rise up, and taking the cot of you, go to the house
25 σου. καὶ παραχρῆμα ἀναστὰς ἐνώπιον αὐτῶν, ἄρας ἐφ' ᾧ
of you. And at once rising up before them taking on which
κατέκειτο, ἀπῆλθεν εἰς τὸν οἶκον αὐτοῦ, δοξάζων τὸν Θεόν.
he was lying, he went to the house of him, glorifying – God.
26 καὶ ἔκστασις ἔλαβεν ἅπαντας, καὶ ἐδόξαζον τὸν Θεόν, καὶ
And amazement seized all, and they glorified – God, and
ἐπλήσθησαν φόβου, λέγοντες ὅτι Εἴδομεν παράδοξα
were filled (with) fear, saying, – We saw wonderful things

[27]And after these things, He went out and saw a tax-collector named Levi, sitting at the tax office. And *He* said to him, Follow Me! [28]And leaving all, rising up he followed Him. [29]And Levi made a great feast for Him in his house. And there was a crowd of many tax-collectors reclining, and of others who were with them. [30]And their scribes and the Pharisees murmured at His disciples, saying, Why do you eat and drink with tax-collectors and sinners? [31]And answering Jesus said to them, Those who are sound have no need of a physician, but those who have sickness. [32]I did not come to call the righteous to repentance, but sinners.

[33]But they said to Him, Why do John's disciples fast often, and make prayers, and likewise those of the Pharisees, but those *close* to you eat and drink? [34]But He said to them, You are not able to make the sons of the bridechamber fast while the bridegroom is with them. [35]But days will come when the bridegroom is taken away from them, then in those days they will fast. [36]And He also told a parable to them: No one puts a piece of a new garment on an old garment; otherwise, both the new will tear, and the old does not match *the* piece from the new. [37]And no one puts new wine into old skins; otherwise, the new wine will burst the skins, and it will be poured out, and the skins will perish. [38]But new wine is to be put into new skins, and both are preserved together. [39]And no one drinking old *wine* immediately desires new; for he says, The old is better.

σήμερον.
today.

27 Καὶ μετὰ ταῦτα ἐξῆλθε, καὶ ἐθεάσατο τελώνην, ὀνόματι
And after these things He went, and saw a tax-collector, by name
Λευΐν, καθήμενον ἐπὶ τὸ τελώνιον, καὶ εἶπεν αὐτῷ, Ἀκολού-
Levi, sitting at the custom-house, and said to him, Follow
28 θει μοι. καὶ καταλιπὼν ἅπαντα, ἀναστὰς ἠκολούθησεν αὐτῷ.
Me! And having left all things, rising up he followed Him.
29 καὶ ἐποίησε δοχὴν μεγάλην ὁ Λευῒς αὐτῷ ἐν τῇ οἰκίᾳ αὐτοῦ·
And made a feast great — Levi for Him in the house of him;
καὶ ἦν ὄχλος τελωνῶν πολύς, καὶ ἄλλων οἳ ἦσαν μετ'
and was a crowd of tax-collectors, much, and of others who were with
30 αὐτῶν κατακείμενοι. καὶ ἐγόγγυζον οἱ γραμματεῖς αὐτῶν
them reclining And murmured the scribes of them
καὶ οἱ Φαρισαῖοι πρὸς τοὺς μαθητὰς αὐτοῦ, λέγοντες, Διατί
and the Pharisees at the disciples of Him, saying, Why
μετὰ τελωνῶν καὶ ἁμαρτωλῶν ἐσθίετε καὶ πίνετε; καὶ
with tax-collectors and sinners do you eat and drink? And
31 ἀποκριθεὶς ὁ Ἰησοῦς εἶπε πρὸς αὐτούς, Οὐ χρείαν ἔχουσιν
answering — Jesus said to them, Not need have
οἱ ὑγιαίνοντες ἰατροῦ, ἀλλ' οἱ κακῶς ἔχοντες. οὐκ ἐλήλυθα
32 **those being sound of a physician, but those illness having. not I have come**
καλέσαι δικαίους, ἀλλὰ ἁμαρτωλοὺς εἰς μετάνοιαν. οἱ δὲ
to call righteous ones, but sinners to repentance. they But
33 εἶπον πρὸς αὐτόν, Διατί οἱ μαθηταὶ Ἰωάννου νηστεύουσι
said to Him, Why the disciples of John fast
πυκνά, καὶ δεήσεις ποιοῦνται, ὁμοίως καὶ οἱ τῶν Φαρισαίων·
often, and prayers make, likewise also those of the Pharisees,
34 οἱ δὲ σοὶ ἐσθίουσι καὶ πίνουσιν; ὁ δὲ εἶπε πρὸς αὐτούς, Μὴ
those but to you eat and drink? He But said to them, Not
δύνασθε τοὺς υἱοὺς τοῦ νυμφῶνος, ἐν ᾧ ὁ νυμφίος μετ' αὐτῶν
are able the sons of the bride-chamber, while the groom with them
35 ἐστι, ποιῆσαι νηστεύειν: ἐλεύσονται δὲ ἡμέραι, καὶ ὅταν
is to make to fast, will come but days, and when
ἀπαρθῇ ἀπ' αὐτῶν ὁ νυμφίος, τότε νηστεύσουσιν ἐν
is taken away from them the bridegroom, then they will fast in
36 ἐκείναις ταῖς ἡμέραις. ἔλεγε δὲ καὶ παραβολὴν πρὸς αὐτοὺς
those — days. He told And also a parable to them,
ὅτι Οὐδεὶς ἐπίβλημα ἱματίου καινοῦ ἐπιβάλλει ἐπὶ ἱμάτιον
— No one a piece of a garment new puts on a garment
παλαιόν· εἰ δὲ μήγε, καὶ τὸ καινὸν σχίζει, καὶ τῷ παλαιῷ
old, otherwise, both the new will tear, and with the old
37 οὐ συμφωνεῖ ἐπίβλημα τὸ ἀπὸ τοῦ καινοῦ. καὶ οὐδεὶς βάλλει
not does agree (the) piece — from the new. And no one puts
οἶνον νέον εἰς ἀσκοὺς παλαιούς· εἰ δὲ μήγε, ῥήξει ὁ νέος οἶνος
wine new into wineskins old; otherwise, will burst the new wine
τοὺς ἀσκούς, καὶ αὐτὸς ἐκχυθήσεται, καὶ οἱ ἀσκοὶ ἀπολοῦν-
the wineskins, and it will be poured out, and the wineskins will
38 ται. ἀλλὰ οἶνον νέον εἰς ἀσκοὺς καινοὺς βλητέον, καὶ ἀμφό-
perish. But wine new into wineskins new is to be put, and both
τεροι συντηροῦνται. καὶ οὐδεὶς πιὼν παλαιὸν εὐθέως θέλει
are preserved together. And no one drinking old at once desires
νέον· λέγει γάρ, Ὁ παλαιὸς χρηστότερός ἐστιν.
new; he says for, The old better is.

CHAPTER 6

1 And it happened on the second chief sabbath, He passed along through the sown fields. And His disciples plucked the heads, and were eating, rubbing with the hands. 2 But some of the Pharisees said to them, Why do you do that which is not lawful to do on the sabbaths? 3 And answering Jesus said to them, Have you never read this, what David did when he and those being with him hungered? 4 *How* he went into the house of God, and he took the Showbread, and ate, and even gave to those with him–which it is not lawful to eat, except only the priests? 5 And He said to them, The Son of man is Lord of the sabbath also.

6 And it also happened on another sabbath, He going into the synagogue and teaching. And there was a man there, and his right hand was withered. 7 And the scribes and the Pharisees kept close by Him, *to see* if He would heal on the sabbath, so that they might find a charge against Him. 8 But He knew their reasonings. And *He* said to the man having the withered hand, Rise up, and stand in the middle! And rising up, he stood. 9 Then Jesus said to them, I will ask you one *thing,* Is it lawful to do good on the sabbaths, or to do ill; to save a soul, or to destroy *it?* 10 And having looked around at them all, He said to the man, Stretch out your hand! And he did so. And his hand was restored sound as the other. 11 But they were filled *with* madness, and talked to one another *as to* what they might do to Jesus.

12 And it happened in these days, He went out into the mountain to pray. And He was spending the night

CHAPTER 6

1 Ἐγένετο δὲ ἐν σαββάτῳ δευτεροπρώτῳ διαπορεύεσθαι
it was And on a sabbath, the second chief passed along
αὐτὸν διὰ τῶν σπορίμων· καὶ ἔτιλλον οἱ μαθηταὶ αὐτοῦ
He through the sown fields, and plucked the disciples of Him
2 τοὺς στάχυας, καὶ ἤσθιον, ψώχοντες ταῖς χερσί. τινὲς δὲ τῶν
the heads, and were eating, rubbing with the hands. some And of the
Φαρισαίων εἶπον αὐτοῖς, Τί ποιεῖτε ὃ οὐκ ἔξεστι ποιεῖν ἐν
Pharisees said to them, Why do you what not is lawful to do on
3 τοις σάββασι ; καὶ ἀποκριθεὶς πρὸς αὐτοὺς εἶπεν ὁ Ἰησοῦς,
the sabbaths? And answering to them said — Jesus,
Οὐδὲ τοῦτο ἀνέγνωτε, ὃ ἐποίησε Δαβίδ, ὁπότε ἐπείνασεν
Not this you read, what did David when he hungered,
4 αὐτὸς καὶ οἱ μετ᾽ αὐτοῦ ὄντες ; ὡς εἰσῆλθεν εἰς τὸν οἶκον τοῦ
he and those with him being? As he entered into the house —
Θεοῦ, καὶ τοὺς ἄρτους τῆς προθέσεως ἔλαβε, καὶ ἔφαγε, καὶ
of God, and the loaves of the presentation he took and ate, and
ἔδωκε καὶ τοῖς μετ᾽ αὐτοῦ, οὓς οὐκ ἔξεστι φαγεῖν εἰ μὴ μόνους
gave even to those with him, which not it is lawful to eat except only
5 τοὺς ἱερεῖς ; καὶ ἔλεγεν αὐτοῖς ὅτι Κύριός ἐστιν ὁ υἱὸς τοῦ
the priests? And He said to them, — Lord is The Son —
ἀνθρώπου καὶ τοῦ σαββάτου.
of man even of the sabbath.

6 Ἐγένετο δὲ καὶ ἐν ἑτέρῳ σαββάτῳ εἰσελθεῖν αὐτὸν εἰς τὴν
it was And also on another sabbath, entering He into the
συναγωγὴν καὶ διδάσκειν· καὶ ἦν ἐκεῖ ἄνθρωπος, καὶ ἡ χεὶρ
synagogue and teaching; and was there a man, and the hand
7 αὐτοῦ ἡ δεξιὰ ἦν ξηρά. παρετήρουν δὲ αὐτὸν οἱ γραμματεῖς
of him, the right, was withered. kept close by And Him the scribes
καὶ οἱ Φαρισαῖοι, εἰ ἐν τῷ σαββάτῳ θεραπεύσει· ἵνα εὕρωσι
and the Pharisees, if on the sabbath He will heal, that they might find
8 κατηγορίαν αὐτοῦ. αὐτὸς δὲ ᾔδει τοὺς διαλογισμοὺς αὐτῶν,
an accusation of Him. He But knew the reasonings of them,
καὶ εἶπε τῷ ἀνθρώπῳ τῷ ξηρὰν ἔχοντι τὴν χεῖρα, Ἔγειραι,
and said to the man — withered having the hand, Rise up
9 καὶ στῆθι εἰς τὸ μέσον. ὁ δὲ ἀναστὰς ἔστη. εἶπεν οὖν ὁ Ἰησοῦς
and stand in the middle! he And rising up stood. said Then — Jesus
πρὸς αὐτούς, Ἐπερωτήσω ὑμᾶς τί, Ἔξεστι τοῖς σάββασιν,
to them, I will ask you one: Is it lawful on the sabbaths
ἀγαθοποιῆσαι ἢ κακοποιῆσαι ; ψυχὴν σῶσαι η ἀπολέσαι ;
to do good, or to do ill? A soul to save, or to destroy?
10 καὶ περιβλεψάμενος πάντας αὐτούς, εἶπε τῷ ἀνθρώπῳ,
And looking around at all (of) them, He said to the man,
Ἔκτεινον τὴν χεῖρά σου. ὁ δὲ ἐποίησεν οὕτω. καὶ ἀποκατε-
Stretch out the hand of you. he And did so, and was
11 στάθη ἡ χειρ αὐτοῦ ὑγιὴς ὡς ἡ ἄλλη. αὐτοὶ δὲ ἐπλήσθησαν
restored the hand of him sound as the other. they But were filled
ἀνοίας· καὶ διελάλουν πρὸς ἀλλήλους, τί ἂν ποιήσειαν τῷ
(with) madness and talked to one another, what they might do —
Ἰησοῦ.
to Jesus.

12 Ἐγένετο δὲ ἐν ταῖς ἡμέραις ταύταις ἐξῆλθεν εἰς τὸ ὄρος
it was And in — days these, He went out into the mount
προσεύξασθαι· καὶ ἦν διανυκτερεύων ἐν τῇ προσευχῇ τοῦ
to pray, and He was spending the night in — prayer

in prayer to God. 13 And when it became day, he called His disciples. And *He* chose out twelve from them, whom He also named apostles: 14 Simon, whom He also named Peter, and his brother Andrew; James and John; Philip and Bartholomew; 15 Matthew and Thomas; James the *son* of Alpheus, and Simon, the *one* being called Zealot; 16 Judas *brother* of James, and Judas Iscariot, who also became *the* betrayer.

17 And coming down with them, he stood on a level place. And a crowd of His disciples, and a great multitude of the people from all Judea and Jerusalem, and *from* the coast country of Tyre and Sidon, *were there,* who came to hear Him, and to be healed from their diseases– 18 also those tormented by unclean spirits. And they were healed. 19 And all the crowd sought to touch Him, because power went out from Him and healed all.

20 And lifting up His eyes to His disciples, He said:

Blessed *are* the poor, for the kingdom of God is yours.

21 Blessed *are* those hungering now, for you will be filled.

Blessed *are* those weeping now, for you will laugh.

22 Blessed *are* you when men hate you, and when they cut you off, and will reproach *you,* and will cast out your name as evil, on account of the Son of man– 23 rejoice in that day, and leap for joy; for, behold, your reward *is* much in Heaven! For their fathers did according to these things to the prophets.

24 But woe to you, rich ones, for you have your comfort! 25 Woe to you, those having been filled, for you will hunger! Woe to you, those laughing now, for you will mourn and lament! 26 Woe to you when men speak well *of* you, for their

13 Θεοῦ. καὶ ὅτε ἐγένετο ἡμέρα, προσεφώνησε τοὺς μαθητὰς
of God. And when it became day, He called to the disciples
αὐτοῦ· καὶ ἐκλεξάμενος ἀπ' αὐτῶν δώδεκα, οὓς καὶ ἀποστό-
of Him, and elected from them twelve, whom also apostles
14 λους ὠνόμασε, Σίμωνα ὃν καὶ ὠνόμασε Πέτρον, καὶ Ἀνδρέαν
He named: Simon, whom also He named Peter; and Andrew
τὸν ἀδελφὸν αὐτοῦ, Ἰάκωβον καὶ Ἰωάννην, Φίλιππον καὶ
the brother of him; James and John; Philip and
15 Βαρθολομαῖον, Ματθαῖον καὶ Θωμᾶν, Ἰάκωβον τὸν τοῦ
Bartholomew; Matthew and Thomas; James the (son) –
16 Ἀλφαίου, καὶ Σίμωνα τὸν καλούμενον Ζηλωτήν, Ἰούδαν
of Alpheus; and Simon the (one) being called Zealot; Judas
Ἰακώβου, καὶ Ἰούδαν Ἰσκαριώτην, ὃς καὶ ἐγένετο προδό-
of James; and Judas Iscariot, who also became betrayer.
17 της, καὶ καταβὰς μετ' αὐτῶν, ἔστη ἐπὶ τόπου πεδινοῦ, καὶ
And coming down with them, He stood on a place level, and
ὄχλος μαθητῶν αὐτοῦ, καὶ πλῆθος πολὺ τοῦ λαοῦ ἀπὸ
crowd of disciples of Him, and a multitude much of the people from
πάσης τῆς Ἰουδαίας καὶ Ἱερουσαλήμ, καὶ τῆς παραλίου
all – Judea and Jerusalem, and the coast country
Τύρου καὶ Σιδῶνος, οἳ ἦλθον ἀκοῦσαι αὐτοῦ, καὶ ἰαθῆναι
of Tyre and Sidon, who came to hear Him, and to be healed
18 ἀπὸ τῶν νόσων αὐτῶν· καὶ οἱ ὀχλούμενοι ὑπὸ πνευμάτων
from the diseases of them, and those being tormented by spirits
19 ἀκαθάρτων, καὶ ἐθεραπεύοντο. καὶ πᾶς ὁ ὄχλος ἐζήτει
unclean, and they were healed. And all the crowd sought
ἅπτεσθαι αὐτοῦ· ὅτι δύναμις παρ' αὐτοῦ ἐξήρχετο καὶ ἰᾶτο
to touch Him, because power from Him went out and healed
πάντας.
all.
20 Καὶ αὐτὸς ἐπάρας τοὺς ὀφθαλμοὺς αὐτοῦ εἰς τοὺς μαθητὰς
And He lifting up the eyes of Him to the disciples
αὐτοῦ ἔλεγε, Μακάριοι οἱ πτωχοί, ὅτι ὑμετέρα ἐστὶν ἡ
of Him said, Blessed (are) the poor, because yours is the
21 βασιλεία τοῦ Θεοῦ. μακάριοι οἱ πεινῶντες νῦν, ὅτι χορτασθή-
kingdom of God. Blessed (are) those hungering now, for you will be
σεσθε. μακάριοι οἱ κλαίοντες νῦν, ὅτι γελάσετε. μακάριοί
filled. Blessed (are) those weeping now, because you will laugh. Blessed
22 ἐστε, ὅταν μισήσωσιν ὑμᾶς οἱ ἄνθρωποι, καὶ ὅταν ἀφο-
are you when hate you – men, and when they
ρίσωσιν ὑμᾶς, καὶ ὀνειδίσωσι, καὶ ἐκβάλωσι τὸ ὄνομα ὑμῶν
separate you, and will reproach, and will cast out the name of you
23 ὡς πονηρόν, ἕνεκα τοῦ υἱοῦ τοῦ ἀνθρώπου. χαίρετε ἐν
as evil, for the sake of the Son – of man. Rejoice in
ἐκείνῃ τῇ ἡμέρᾳ καὶ σκιρτήσατε· ἰδοὺ γάρ, ὁ μισθὸς ὑμῶν
that – day and leap for joy. behold For, the reward of you
πολὺς ἐν τῷ οὐρανῷ· κατὰ ταῦτα γὰρ ἐποίουν τοῖς προφή-
much in – Heaven! according to these For did to the prophets
24 ταις οἱ πατέρες αὐτῶν. πλὴν οὐαὶ ὑμῖν τοῖς πλουσίοις,
the fathers of them. But woe to you the rich ones,
25 ὅτι ἀπέχετε τὴν παράκλησιν ὑμῶν. οὐαὶ ὑμῖν, οἱ ἐμπεπλη-
because you have the comfort of you! Woe to you, those having
σμένοι, ὅτι πεινάσετε. οὐαὶ ὑμῖν, οἱ γελῶντες νῦν, ὅτι
been filled, for you will hunger. Woe to you,, **those laughing now because**
26 πενθήσετε καὶ κλαύσετε. οὐαὶ ὑμῖν, ὅταν καλῶς ὑμᾶς εἴπωσι
you will mourn and lament! Woe to you, when well (of) you speak

fathers did according to these things to the false prophets.

27 But I say to you, those hearing: Love your enemies; do good to those hating you; 28 bless those cursing you; and pray for those insulting you. 29 To those striking you on the cheek, turn the other also. And from those taking your garment, do not keep back the tunic also. 30 And to everyone asking you, give. And do not ask back from those taking your things. 31 And according as you desire that men should do to you, you also do the same to them. 32 And if you love those who love you, what thanks is there to you? For even sinners love those who love them. And if you do good to those who do good to you, what thanks is there to you? For even the sinners do the same. 34 And if you lend *to those* from whom you hope to receive, what thanks is there to you? For the sinners lend to sinners, so that they may receive the same.

35 But love your enemies, and do good, and lend, hoping for nothing *in return;* and your reward will be much; and you will be sons of the Most High, for He is kind to the unthankful and evil ones. 36 Therefore, be merciful, even as your Father also is merciful. 37 Judge not, and in no way be judged. Do not condemn, and in no way you will be condemned. Forgive, and you will be forgiven. 38 Give, and good measure will be given to you, pressed down and shaken together, and running over, they will give into your bosom. For the same measure which you measure, it will be measured back to you.

39 And He spoke a parable to them: A blind one is not

πάντες οἱ ἄνθρωποι· κατὰ ταῦτα γὰρ ἐποίουν τοῖς ψευδο-
all — men; according to these For did to the **false**
προφήταις οἱ πατέρες αὐτῶν.
prophets the fathers of them.

27 Ἀλλ' ὑμῖν λέγω τοῖς ἀκούουσιν, Ἀγαπᾶτε τοὺς ἐχθροὺς
But to you I say, those hearing, Love the enemies
28 ὑμῶν, καλῶς ποιεῖτε τοῖς μισοῦσιν ὑμᾶς, εὐλογεῖτε τοὺς
of you; well do to those hating you; bless those
καταρωμένους ὑμῖν, καὶ προσεύχεσθε ὑπὲρ τῶν ἐπηρεαζόν-
cursing you; and pray for those insulting
29 των ὑμᾶς. τῷ τύπτοντί σε ἐπὶ τὴν σιαγόνα, πάρεχε καὶ τὴν
you. To him striking you on the cheek, turn also the
ἄλλην· καὶ ἀπὸ τοῦ αἴροντός σου τὸ ἱμάτιον, καὶ τὸν
other, and from him taking of you the garment, also the
30 χιτῶνα μὴ κωλύσῃς. παντὶ δὲ τῷ αἰτοῦντί σε δίδου· καὶ
tunic not do keep back. To everyone And asking you, give; and
31 ἀπὸ τοῦ αἴροντος τὰ σά μὴ ἀπαίτει. καὶ καθὼς θέλετε ἵνα
from those taking your things, not do ask back. And as you desire that
ποιῶσιν ὑμῖν οἱ ἄνθρωποι, καὶ ὑμεῖς ποιεῖτε αὐτοῖς ὁμοίως.
may do to you men, also you do to them likewise.
32 καὶ εἰ ἀγαπᾶτε τοὺς ἀγαπῶντας ὑμᾶς, ποία ὑμῖν χάρις
And if you love those loving you, what to you thanks
ἐστί; καὶ γὰρ οἱ ἁμαρτωλοὶ τοὺς ἀγαπῶντας αὐτοὺς ἀγα-
is there? even For the sinners those loving them love.
33 πῶσι. καὶ ἐὰν ἀγαθοποιῆτε τοὺς ἀγαθοποιοῦντας ὑμᾶς,
And if you do good to those doing good to you,
ποία ὑμῖν χάρις ἐστί; καὶ γὰρ οἱ ἁμαρτωλοὶ τὸ αὐτὸ
what to you thanks is there? even For the sinners the same
34 ποιοῦσι. καὶ ἐὰν δανείζητε παρ' ὧν ἐλπίζητε ἀπολαβεῖν,
do. And if you lend from whom you hope to receive,
ποία ὑμῖν χάρις ἐστί; καὶ γὰρ οἱ ἁμαρτωλοὶ ἁμαρτωλοῖς
what to you thanks is there? even For the sinners to sinners
35 δανείζουσιν, ἵνα ἀπολάβωσι τὰ ἴσα. πλὴν ἀγαπᾶτε τοὺς
lend, that they may receive the same. But love the
ἐχθροὺς ὑμῶν, καὶ ἀγαθοποιεῖτε, καὶ δανείζετε, μηδὲν ἀπελ-
enemies of you, and do good and lend, nothing
πίζοντες· καὶ ἔσται ὁ μισθὸς ὑμῶν πολύς, καὶ ἔσεσθε υἱοὶ τοῦ
despairing, and will be the reward of you much; and you will be sons of the
ὑψίστου· ὅτι αὐτὸς χρηστός ἐστιν ἐπὶ τοὺς ἀχαρίστους καὶ
most High because He kind is to the unthankful and
36 πονηρούς. γίνεσθε οὖν οἰκτίρμονες, καθὼς καὶ ὁ πατὴρ
evil ones. Be then merciful, even as also the Father
37 ὑμῶν οἰκτίρμων ἐστί. μὴ κρίνετε, καὶ οὐ μὴ κριθῆτε. μὴ κατα-
of you merciful is. not Judge, and in no way be judged; do not
δικάζετε, καὶ οὐ μὴ καταδικασθῆτε· ἀπολύετε, καὶ ἀπολυθή-
condemn, and in no way you will be condemned; forgive, and you will be
38 σεσθε· δίδοτε, καὶ δοθήσεται ὑμῖν· μέτρον καλόν, πεπιε-
forgiven; give, and will be given to you measure good, pressed
σμένον καὶ σεσαλευμένον καὶ ὑπερεκχυνόμενον δώσουσιν εἰς
down and shaken together and running over shall they give into
τὸν κόλπον ὑμῶν. τῷ γὰρ αὐτῷ μέτρῳ ᾧ μετρεῖτε ἀντι-
the bosom of you. the For same measure which you mete, it will
μετρηθήσεται ὑμῖν.
be measured back to you.

39 Εἶπε δὲ παραβολὴν αὐτοῖς, Μήτι δύναται τυφλὸς τυφλὸν
He spoke And a parable to them, **Not is able a blind one** a blind one

able to guide a blind one. Will they not both fall into the ditch? [40]A disciple is not above his teacher, but everyone who has been perfected will be like his teacher. [41]But why do you look on the twig in your brother's eye, but do not consider the log in *your* own eye? [42]Or how can you say to your brother, Brother, let me pull out the twig in your eye, not yourself seeing the log in your eye? Hypocrite! First take the log out of your eye, and then you will see clearly to take out the twig in your brother's eye. [43]For there is not a good tree that produces bad fruit, nor a bad tree that produces good fruit. [44]For each tree is known by its own fruit. For they do not gather figs from thorns, nor do they gather grapes from a bramble bush. [45]The good man brings forth good out of the good treasure of his heart. And the evil man brings forth evil out of the evil treasure of his heart, for his mouth speaks out of the abundance of his heart.

[46]And why do you call Me Lord, Lord, and do not do what I say? [47]Everyone coming to Me and hearing My words, and doing them, I will show you to whom he is like: [48]He is like a man building a house, who dug and deepened, and laid a foundation on the rock; and a flood occurring, the stream burst against that house, and could not shake it, for it had been founded on the rock. [49]But he who heard and did not perform, *he* is like a man having built *his* house without a foundation, on which the stream burst, and it immediately fell; and the ruin of that house was great.

ὁδηγεῖν ; οὐχὶ ἀμφότεροι εἰς βόθυνον πεσοῦνται ; οὐκ ἔστι
guide. not Will they into the ditch fall in? Not is
40 μαθητὴς ὑπὲρ τὸν διδάσκαλον αὐτοῦ· κατηρτισμένος δὲ
a disciple above the teacher of him, having been perfected but
41 πᾶς ἔσται ὡς ὁ διδάσκαλος αὐτοῦ. τί δὲ βλέπεις τὸ κάρφος
everyone will be as the teacher of him. why And do you see the twig
τὸ ἐν τῷ ὀφθαλμῷ τοῦ ἀδελφοῦ σου, τὴν δὲ δοκὸν τὴν ἐν
— in the eye of the brother of you, the but log — in
42 τῷ ἰδίῳ ὀφθαλμῷ οὐ κατανοεῖς ; ἢ πῶς δύνασαι λέγειν τῷ
(your) own eye not you consider? Or how are you able to say to the
ἀδελφῷ σου, Ἀδελφέ, ἄφες ἐκβάλω τὸ κάρφος τὸ ἐν τῷ
brother of you, Brother, allow I may take out the twig — in the
ὀφθαλμῷ σου, αὐτὸς τὴν ἐν τῷ ὀφθαλμῷ σου δοκὸν οὐ
eye of you, yourself the in the eye of you log not
βλέπων ; ὑποκριτά, ἔκβαλε πρῶτον τὴν δοκὸν ἐκ τοῦ
seeing? Hypocrite, take out first the log out of the
ὀφθαλμοῦ σου, καὶ τότε διαβλέψεις ἐκβαλεῖν τὸ κάρφος τὸ
eye of you, and then you will see clearly to take out the twig
43 ἐν τῷ ὀφθαλμῷ τοῦ ἀδελφοῦ σου. οὐ γάρ ἐστι δένδρον
in the eye of the brother of you. not For is a tree
καλὸν ποιοῦν καρπὸν σαπρόν· οὐδὲ δένδρον σαπρὸν ποιοῦν
good producing fruit bad, nor tree a bad producing
44 καρπὸν καλόν. ἕκαστον γὰρ δένδρον ἐκ τοῦ ἰδίου καρποῦ
fruit good. each For tree out of the own fruit
γινώσκεται. οὐ γὰρ ἐξ ἀκανθῶν συλλέγουσι σῦκα, οὐδὲ ἐκ
is known. not For out of thorns do they gather figs, nor out of
45 βάτου τρυγῶσι σταφυλήν. ὁ ἀγαθὸς ἄνθρωπος ἐκ τοῦ
a bramble grapes do they gather. The good man out of the
ἀγαθοῦ θησαυροῦ τῆς καρδίας αὐτοῦ προφέρει τὸ ἀγαθόν
good treasure of the heart of him brings forth the good;
καὶ ὁ πονηρὸς ἄνθρωπος ἐκ τοῦ πονηροῦ θησαυροῦ τῆς
and the evil man out of the evil treasure of the
καρδίας αὐτοῦ προφέρει τὸ πονηρόν· ἐκ γὰρ τοῦ περισσεύ-
heart of him brings forth the evil; out of for the abundance
ματος τῆς καρδίας λαλεῖ τὸ στόμα αὐτοῦ.
of the heart speaks the mouth of him.

46 Τί δέ με καλεῖτε, Κύριε, Κύριε, καὶ οὐ ποιεῖτε ἃ λέγω ;
why And Me do you call, Lord, Lord, and not do what I say?
47 πᾶς ὁ ἐρχόμενος πρός με καὶ ἀκούων μου τῶν λόγων καὶ
Everyone coming to Me and hearing of Me the words, and
48 ποιῶν αὐτούς, ὑποδείξω ὑμῖν τίνι ἐστὶν ὅμοιος· ὅμοιός ἐστιν
doing them, I will show you to whom he is like. like He is
ἀνθρώπῳ οἰκοδομοῦντι οἰκίαν, ὃς ἔσκαψε καὶ ἐβάθυνε, καὶ
a man building a house, who dug and deepened, and
ἔθηκε θεμέλιον ἐπὶ τὴν πέτραν· πλημμύρας δὲ γενομένης,
laid a foundation on the rock; a flood and happening,
προσέρρηξεν ὁ ποταμὸς τῇ οἰκίᾳ ἐκείνῃ καὶ οὐκ ἴσχυσε
burst against the stream — house that, and not could
49 σαλεῦσαι αὐτήν· τεθεμελίωτο γὰρ ἐπὶ τὴν πέτραν. ὁ δὲ
shake it, it had been founded for on the rock. he But
ἀκούσας καὶ μὴ ποιήσας ὅμοιός ἐστιν ἀνθρώπῳ οἰκοδομή-
heard and not performed like is to a man having
σαντι οἰκίαν ἐπὶ τὴν γῆν χωρὶς θεμελίου· ᾗ προσέρρηξεν ὁ
built a house on the earth without a foundation, on which burst the
ποταμός, καὶ εὐθέως ἔπεσε, καὶ ἐγένετο τὸ ῥῆγμα τῆς
stream, and immediately it fell, and was the ruin —

CHAPTER 7

[1]And when He had completed all His words in the ears of the people, He went into Capernaum.

[2]And a certain slave of a centurion, *one* dear to him, having illness was about to expire. [3]And hearing about Jesus, he sent elders of the Jews to Him, asking Him that He might come *to* restore his slave. [4]And coming to Jesus, *they* earnestly begged Him, saying, He to whom You give this is worthy. [5]For he loves our nation, and he built the synagogue for us. [6]And Jesus went with them. But He being yet not far away from the house, the centurion sent friends to Him, saying to Him, Lord, do not trouble, for I am not worthy that You come under my roof. [7]For this reason I did not count myself worthy to come to You. But say a word, and let my servant be cured. [8]For I also am a man having been set under authority, having soldiers under myself. And I say to this one, Go! And he goes. And *to* another, Come! And he comes. And *to* my slave, Do this! And he does *it*. [9]And hearing these things, Jesus marveled at him. And turning to the crowd following Him, he said, I say to you, I did not find such faith in Israel. [10]And returning, those sent to the house found the sick slave well.

[11]And it happened on the next *day*, He went into a city being called Nain. And many of His disciples went with Him, also a great crowd. [12]And as He drew near to the gate of the city, even behold, *one* having died was being

οἰκίας ἐκείνης μέγα.
house of that great.

CHAPTER 7

1 Ἐπεὶ δὲ ἐπλήρωσε πάντα τὰ ῥήματα αὐτοῦ εἰς τὰς ἀκοὰς
when And He completed all the words of Him in the ears
τοῦ λαοῦ, εἰσῆλθεν εἰς Καπερναούμ.
of the people, He went into Capernaum.
2 Ἑκατοντάρχου δέ τινος δοῦλος κακῶς ἔχων ἤμελλε
of a centurion And a certain slave illness having was about
3 τελευτᾷν, ὃς ἦν αὐτῷ ἔντιμος. ἀκούσας δὲ περὶ τοῦ Ἰησοῦ,
to expire, who was to him dear. hearing And about — Jesus,
ἀπέστειλε πρὸς αὐτὸν πρεσβυτέρους τῶν Ἰουδαίων,
he sent to Him elders of the Jews
ἐρωτῶν αὐτόν, ὅπως ἐλθὼν διασώσῃ τὸν δοῦλον αὐτοῦ. οἱ
asking Him that coming He might restore the slave of him. they
4 δέ, παραγενομενοι πρὸς τὸν Ἰησοῦν, παρεκάλουν αὐτὸν
And coming to — Jesus begged Him
σπουδαιως, λέγοντες ὅτι ἄξιός ἐστιν ᾧ παρέξει τοῦτο·
earnestly, saying, — worthy He is for whom You give this.
5 ἀγαπᾷ γὰρ τὸ ἔθνος ἡμῶν, καὶ τὴν συναγωγὴν αὐτὸς
he loves For the nation of us, and the synagogue he
6 ᾠκοδόμησεν ἡμῖν. ὁ δὲ Ἰησοῦς ἐπορεύετο σὺν αὐτοῖς. ἤδη
built for us. — And Jesus went with them. yet
δὲ αὐτοῦ οὐ μακρὰν ἀπέχοντος ἀπὸ τῆς οἰκίας, ἔπεμψε πρὸς
And Him not far being away from the house, sent to
αὐτὸν ὁ ἑκατόνταρχος φίλους, λέγων αὐτῷ, Κύριε, μὴ
Him the centurion friends, saying to Him, Lord not
σκύλλου· οὐ γάρ εἰμι ἱκανὸς ἵνα ὑπὸ τὴν στέγην μου
do trouble. not For I am worthy that under the roof of me
7 εἰσέλθῃς· διὸ οὐδὲ ἐμαυτὸν ἠξίωσα πρός σε ἐλθεῖν· ἀλλὰ
You enter. Therefore not myself I counted worthy to You to come, but
8 εἰπὲ λογῳ, καὶ ἰαθήσεται ὁ παῖς μου. καὶ γὰρ ἐγὼ ἄνθρωπός
say in a word, and let be cured the servant of me. even For I a man
εἰμι ὑπὸ ἐξουσίαν τασσόμενος, ἔχων ὑπ' ἐμαυτὸν στρατιώ-
am under authority being set, having under myself soldiers,
τας, καὶ λέγω τούτῳ, Πορεύθητι, καὶ πορεύεται· καὶ ἄλλῳ,
and I tell this one, Go, and he goes; and another,
Ἔρχου, καὶ ἔρχεται· καὶ τῷ δούλῳ μου, Ποίησον τοῦτο, καὶ
Come, and he comes; and the slave of me, Do this, and
9 ποιεῖ. ἀκούσας δὲ ταῦτα ὁ Ἰησοῦς ἐθαύμασεν αὐτόν, καὶ
he does. hearing And these, — Jesus marveled at him, and
στραφεὶς τῷ ἀκολουθοῦντι αὐτῷ ὄχλῳ εἶπε, Λέγω ὑμῖν, οὐδὲ
turning to the following Him crowd said, I say to you, not
10 ἐν τῷ Ἰσραὴλ τοσαύτην πίστιν εὗρον. καὶ ὑποστρέψαντες οἱ
in — Israel such faith I found. And returning those
πεμφθέντες εἰς τὸν οἶκον εὗρον τὸν ἀσθενοῦντα δοῦλον
sent to the house found the sick slave
ὑγιαίνοντα.
well.

11 Καὶ ἐγενετο ἐν τῇ ἑξῆς, ἐπορεύετο εἰς πόλιν καλουμένην
And it was on the next (day), He went into a city being called
Ναῒν καὶ συνεπορεύοντο αὐτῷ οἱ μαθηταὶ αὐτοῦ ἱκανοί,
Nain, and went with Him the disciples of Him many,
12 καὶ ὄχλος πολύς. ὡς δὲ ἤγγισε τῇ πύλῃ τῆς πόλεως, και ἰδού,
and a crowd much. as And He drew near to the gate of the city, even behold,

borne, an only son born to his mother; and she was a widow. [13]And seeing her, the Lord felt pity for her, and said to her, Stop weeping. [14]And coming up, He touched the coffin; and those carrying *it* stood still. And He said, Young man, I say to you, arise! [15]And the dead one sat up and began to speak. And He gave him to his mother. [16]And fear took hold of all; and they glorified God, saying, A great prophet has risen up among us; and, God has visited His people. [17]And this word about Him went out in all Judea, and in all the neighborhood.

[18]And His disciples reported to John about all these things. [19]And having called near a certain two of his disciples, John sent to Jesus, saying, Are you the One coming? Or should we expect another? [20]And having come to Him, the men said, John the Baptist sent us to You, saying, Are You the One coming, or should we expect another? [21]And in the same hour He healed many from diseases and plagues and evil spirits. And He gave to many blind ones *ability* to see. [22]And answering Jesus said to them, , report to John what you saw and heard: Blind ones see again; lame ones walk about; lepers are being cleansed; deaf ones hear; dead ones are raised; poor ones are given the gospel. [23]And blessed is *he* who is not offended in Me.

[24]And John's messengers going away, He began to speak to the crowds about John. What did you go out to the wilderness to see? A reed being shaken by the

ἐξεκομίζετο τεθνηκώς, υἱὸς μονογενὴς τῇ μητρὶ αὐτοῦ, καὶ
was being borne, having died, son an only born to the mother of him; and
αὕτη ἦν χήρα· καὶ ὄχλος τῆς πόλεως ἱκανὸς ἦν σὺν αὐτῇ.
this was a widow. And a crowd of the city considerable was with her.
13 καὶ ἰδὼν αὐτὴν ὁ Κύριος ἐσπλαγχνίσθη ἐπ' αὐτῇ, καὶ εἶπεν
And seeing her the Lord felt pity over her, and said
14 αὐτῇ, Μὴ κλαῖε. καὶ προσελθὼν ἥψατο τῆς σοροῦ· οἱ δὲ
to her, Stop weeping. And coming up He touched the coffin, those and
βαστάζοντες ἔστησαν. καὶ εἶπε, Νεανίσκε, σοὶ λέγω,
bearing stood still. And He said, Young man, to you I say,
15 ἐγέρθητι. καὶ ἀνεκάθισεν ὁ νεκρός, καὶ ἤρξατο λαλεῖν. καὶ
Arise! And sat up the dead one, and began to speak; and
16 ἔδωκεν αὐτὸν τῇ μητρὶ αὐτοῦ. ἔλαβε δὲ φόβος ἅπαντας, καὶ
He gave him to the mother of him. took And fear all, and
ἐδόξαζον τὸν Θεόν, λέγοντες ὅτι Προφήτης μέγας ἐγήγερται
they glorified – God, saying, – A prophet great has risen up
17 ἐν ἡμῖν, καὶ ὅτι Ἐπεσκέψατο ὁ Θεὸς τὸν λαὸν αὐτοῦ. καὶ
among us, and, – has visited – God the people of Him. And
ἐξῆλθεν ὁ λόγος οὗτος ἐν ὅλῃ τῇ Ἰουδαίᾳ περὶ αὐτοῦ, καὶ
went out – word this in all – Judea concerning Him, and
ἐν πάσῃ τῇ περιχώρῳ.
in all the neighborhood.

18 Καὶ ἀπήγγειλαν Ἰωάννῃ οἱ μαθηταὶ αὐτοῦ περὶ πάντων
And reported to John the disciples of him about all
19 τούτων. καὶ προσκαλεσάμενος δύο τινὰς τῶν μαθητῶν
these things. And calling near two a certain of the disciples
αὐτοῦ ὁ Ἰωάννης ἔπεμψε πρὸς τὸν Ἰησοῦν, λέγων, Σὺ εἶ ὁ
of him, – John sent to – Jesus, saying, you Are the
20 ἐρχόμενος, ἢ ἄλλον προσδοκῶμεν; παραγενόμενοι δὲ πρὸς
coming One? Or another should we expect? coming And to
αὐτὸν οἱ ἄνδρες εἶπον, Ἰωάννης ὁ Βαπτιστὴς ἀπέσταλκεν
Him the men said, John the Baptist sent
ἡμᾶς πρός σε, λέγων, Σὺ εἶ ὁ ἐρχόμενος, ἢ ἄλλον προσδοκῶ-
us to You, saying, you Are the coming One, or another should we
21 μεν; ἐν αὐτῇ δὲ τῇ ὥρᾳ ἐθεράπευσε πολλοὺς ἀπὸ νόσων καὶ
expect? In the same And hour He healed many from diseases and
μαστίγων καὶ πνευμάτων πονηρῶν, καὶ τυφλοῖς πολλοῖς
plagues and spirits evil; and blind ones to many
22 ἐχαρίσατο τὸ βλέπειν. καὶ ἀποκριθεὶς ὁ Ἰησοῦς εἶπεν αὐτοῖς,
He gave to see. And answering – Jesus said to them,
Πορευθέντες ἀπαγγείλατε Ἰωάννῃ ἃ εἴδετε καὶ ἠκούσατε·
Going report to John what you saw and heard:
ὅτι τυφλοὶ ἀναβλέπουσι, χωλοὶ περιπατοῦσι, λεπροὶ
– Blind ones see again; lame ones walk about; lepers
καθαρίζονται, κωφοὶ ἀκούουσι, νεκροὶ ἐγείρονται, πτωχοὶ
are being cleansed; deaf ones hear; dead ones are raised; poor ones
23 εὐαγγελίζονται· καὶ μακάριός ἐστιν, ὃς ἐὰν μὴ σκανδαλισθῇ
are given the gospel; and blessed is whoever not is offended
ἐν ἐμοί.
in Me.

24 Ἀπελθόντων δὲ τῶν ἀγγέλων Ἰωάννου, ἤρξατο λέγειν
going away And the messengers of John, He began to say
πρὸς τοὺς ὄχλους περὶ Ἰωάννου, Τί ἐξεληλύθατε εἰς τὴν
to the crowds about John, What did you go out to the
ἔρημον θεάσασθαι; κάλαμον ὑπὸ ἀνέμου σαλευόμενον; ἀλλὰ
wilderness to see? A reed by wind being shaken? But

wind? 25 But what did you go out to see? A man dressed in soft clothing? Behold, thsoe in splendid clothing and being in luxury are in king's palaces. 26 But what did you go out to see? A prophet? Yes, I say to you, even more than a prophet. 27 This is he about whom it has been written: "Behold, I send My messenger before Your face, who will prepare Your way before You." 28 For I say to you, No one among *those* born of a woman is greater than he is.

29 And all the tax-collectors and the people hearing, *they* justified God, being baptized *with* the baptism of John. 30 But the Pharisees and the lawyers set aside God's counsel as to themselves, not having been baptized by John. 31 And the Lord said, Then to what shall I compare the men of this generation? And to what are they like? 32 They are like children sitting in a market and calling to one another, and saying, We piped to you, and you did not dance; we mourned to you, and you did not weep. 33 John the Baptist has come neither eating bread nor drinking wine, and you say, He has a demon. 34 The Son of man has come eating and drinking, and you say, Behold, a man, a glutton and a drunkard; a friend of tax-collectors and sinners.

35 But wisdom was justified from all her children.

36 And one of the Pharisees asked Him that He eat with him. And going into the Pharisee's house, He reclined. 37 And, behold, a woman who was a sinner in the city, knowing that He reclined in the Pharisee's house, taking an alabaster vial of ointment, 38 and standing at His feet, weeping behind *Him, she* began

25 τί ἐξεληλύθατε ἰδεῖν; ἄνθρωπον ἐν μαλακοῖς ἱματίοις
what did you go out to see? A man in soft clothing
ἠμφιεσμένον; ἰδού, οἱ ἐν ἱματισμῷ ἐνδόξῳ καὶ τρυφῇ
dressed? Behold, those in clothing splendid and in luxury
26 ὑπάρχοντες ἐν τοῖς βασιλείοις εἰσίν. ἀλλὰ τί ἐξεληλύθατε
being in — king's palaces are. But what did you go out
ἰδεῖν; προφήτην; ναί, λέγω ὑμῖν, καὶ περισσότερον προ-
to see? A prophet? Yes, I say to you, Even more than a
27 φήτου. οὗτός ἐστι περὶ οὗ γέγραπται, Ἰδού, ἐγὼ ἀπο-
prophet! This is he about whom it has been written, Behold, I
στέλλω τὸν ἄγγελόν μου πρὸ προσώπου σου, ὃς κατα-
send the messenger of Me before (the) face of You, who will
28 σκευάσει τὴν ὁδόν σου ἔμπροσθέν σου. λέγω γὰρ ὑμῖν, μείζων
prepare the way of You before You. I say For to you, greater
ἐν γεννητοῖς γυναικῶν προφήτης Ἰωάννου τοῦ Βαπτιστοῦ
among (those) born of women prophet than John the Baptist
οὐδείς ἐστιν· ὁ δὲ μικρότερος ἐν τῇ βασιλείᾳ τοῦ Θεοῦ
no one is. the But least (one) in the kingdom — of God
29 μείζων αὐτοῦ ἐστι. καὶ πᾶς ὁ λαὸς ἀκούσας καὶ οἱ τελῶναι
greater than he is. And all the people hearing, and the tax-collectors,
ἐδικαίωσαν τὸν Θεόν, βαπτισθέντες τὸ βάπτισμα Ἰωάννου·
justified — God, being baptized (with) the baptism of John.
30 οἱ δὲ Φαρισαῖοι καὶ οἱ νομικοὶ τὴν βουλὴν τοῦ Θεοῦ
the But Pharisees and the lawyers the counsel — of God
ἠθέτησαν εἰς ἑαυτούς, μὴ βαπτισθέντες ὑπ᾽ αὐτοῦ. εἶπε δὲ
set aside, for themselves not had been baptized by him. said And
31 ὁ Κύριος, Τίνι οὖν ὁμοιώσω τοὺς ἀνθρώπους τῆς γενεᾶς
the Lord, To what then shall I liken the men generation
32 ταύτης, καὶ τίνι εἰσὶν ὅμοιοι; ὅμοιοί εἰσι παιδίοις τοῖς ἐν
of this, and to what are they like? like They are children — in
ἀγορᾷ καθημένοις, καὶ προσφωνοῦσιν ἀλλήλοις, καὶ
a market sitting and calling to one another, and
λέγουσιν, Ηὐλήσαμεν ὑμῖν, καὶ οὐκ ὠρχήσασθε· ἐθρηνή-
saying, We piped to you, and not you danced; we
33 σαμεν ὑμῖν, καὶ οὐκ ἐκλαύσατε. ἐλήλυθε γὰρ Ἰωάννης ὁ
mourned to you, and not you wept. has come For John the
Βαπτιστὴς μήτε ἄρτον ἐσθίων μήτε οἶνον πίνων, καὶ λέγετε,
Baptist not bread eating, nor wine drinking, and you say,
34 Δαιμόνιον ἔχει. ἐλήλυθεν ὁ υἱὸς τοῦ ἀνθρώπου ἐσθίων καὶ
A demon he has. has come The Son — of man eating and
πίνων, καὶ λέγετε, Ἰδού, ἄνθρωπος φάγος καὶ οἰνοπότης,
drinking, and you say, Behold, a man, a glutton and a winebibber,
35 τελωνῶν φίλος καὶ ἁμαρτωλῶν. καὶ ἐδικαιώθη ἡ σοφία ἀπὸ
of tax-collectors friend and sinners. And was justified — wisdom from
τῶν τέκνων αὐτῆς πάντων.
the children of her all.
36 Ἠρώτα δέ τις αὐτὸν τῶν Φαρισαίων ἵνα φάγῃ μετ᾽
asked And a certain Him of the Pharisees, that He eat with
αὐτοῦ· καὶ εἰσελθὼν εἰς τὴν οἰκίαν τοῦ Φαρισαίου ἀνεκλίθη.
him. And going into the house of the Pharisee He reclined
37 καὶ ἰδού, γυνὴ ἐν τῇ πόλει, ἥτις ἦν ἁμαρτωλός, ἐπιγνοῦσα
And behold, a woman in the city who was a sinner, having known
ὅτι ἀνάκειται ἐν τῇ οἰκίᾳ τοῦ Φαρισαίου, κομίσασα ἀλά-
that He had reclined in the house of the Pharisee, having taken an
38 βαστρον μύρου, καὶ στᾶσα παρὰ τοὺς πόδας αὐτοῦ ὀπίσω
alabaster vial of ointment, and standing at the feet of Him behind

to wash His feet with tears.
And she was wiping with
the hairs of her head. And
she ardently kissed His feet,
and was anointing *them*
with the ointment. 39 But
the Pharisee who invited
Him spoke within himself,
saying, This one, if he were a
prophet, would have known
who and what the woman *is*
who touches him; for she is
a sinner. 40 And answering
Jesus said to the man,
Simon, I have a thing to say
to you. And he said, Teacher,
say *it*. 41 There were two
debtors to a certain creditor:
the one owed five hundred
denarii, and the other fifty.
42 But they not having *a thing*
to pay, he forgave both. Then
which of them do *you* say
will love him most? 43 And
answering, Simon said, I
suppose *the one* he forgave
the most. And He said to
him, You have judged rightly.
44 And turning to the woman,
He said to Simon, Do you see
this woman? I came into your
house. You did not give
water for My feet, but she
washed My feet with tears,
and wiped off with the hairs
of her head. 45 You gave
Me no kiss, but she from
when I entered did not stop
fervently kissing My feet.
46 You did not anoint My
head with oil, but she
anointed My feet with ointment. 47 For this reason I say
to you, her many sins are
forgiven, for she loved much.
But to whom little is forgiven, he loves little. 48 And
He said to her, Your sins are
forgiven. 49 And those
reclining began to say within themselves, Who is this
who even forgives sins?
50 But He said to the woman,
Your faith has saved you. Go
in peace.

CHAPTER 8

1 And it happened after-
wards, even He traveled in
every city and village,
preaching and announcing
the gospel of the kingdom of

κλαίουσα, ἤρξατο βρέχειν τοὺς πόδας αὐτοῦ τοῖς δάκρυσι,
weeping, began to wet the feet of Him with the tears,
καὶ ταῖς θριξὶ τῆς κεφαλῆς αὐτῆς ἐξέμασσε, καὶ κατεφίλει
and with the hairs of the head of her she was wiping, and kissing
39 τοὺς πόδας αὐτοῦ, καὶ ἤλειφε τῷ μύρῳ. ἰδὼν δὲ ὁ Φαρισαῖος
the feet of Him, and anointing with the ointment, seeing And the Pharisee
ὁ καλέσας αὐτὸν εἶπεν ἐν ἑαυτῷ λέγων, Οὗτος, εἰ ἦν
having invited Him, he spoke in himself, saying, This one, if he was
προφήτης, ἐγίνωσκεν ἂν τίς καὶ ποταπὴ ἡ γυνὴ ἥτις
a prophet would have known who and what the woman (is) who
40 ἅπτεται αὐτοῦ, ὅτι ἁμαρτωλός ἐστι. καὶ ἀποκριθεὶς ὁ
touches him, because a sinner she is. And answering —
Ἰησοῦς εἶπε πρὸς αὐτόν, Σίμων, ἔχω σοί τι εἰπεῖν. ὁ δέ φησι,
Jesus said to him, Simon, I have to you a thing to say. he And says,
41 Διδάσκαλε, εἰπέ. Δύο χρεωφειλέται ἦσαν δανειστῇ τινί·
Teacher, say. Two debtors were to a creditor certain.
42 ὁ εἷς ὤφειλε δηνάρια πεντακόσια, ὁ δὲ ἕτερος πεντήκοντα. μὴ
The one owed denarii five hundred, the and (the) other fifty. not
ἐχόντων δὲ αὐτῶν ἀποδοῦναι, ἀμφοτέροις ἐχαρίσατο. τίς
having And them (a thing) to repay, both he freely forgave. Who
43 οὖν αὐτῶν, εἰπέ, πλεῖον αὐτὸν ἀγαπήσει; ἀποκριθεὶς δὲ ὁ
then of them say (you) more him will love? answering And
Σίμων εἶπεν, Ὑπολαμβάνω ὅτι ᾧ τὸ πλεῖον ἐχαρίσατο. ὁ
Simon said, I suppose, —to whom the more he freely forgave. He
44 δὲ εἶπεν αὐτῷ, Ὀρθῶς ἔκρινας. καὶ στραφεὶς πρὸς τὴν
And said to him, Rightly you judged. And turning to the
γυναῖκα, τῷ Σίμωνι ἔφη, Βλέπεις ταύτην τὴν γυναῖκα;
woman, — to Simon He said, Do you see this — woman?
εἰσῆλθόν σου εἰς τὴν οἰκίαν, ὕδωρ ἐπὶ τοὺς πόδας μου οὐκ
I went of you into the house, water on the feet of Me not
ἔδωκας· αὕτη δὲ τοῖς δάκρυσιν ἔβρεξέ μου τοὺς πόδας, καὶ
you gave. she But with the tears wet of Me the feet, and
45 ταῖς θριξὶ τῆς κεφαλῆς αὐτῆς ἐξέμαξε. φίλημά μοι οὐκ ἔδωκας·
with the hairs — head of her wiped off. A kiss to Me not you gave,
αὕτη δέ, ἀφ' ἧς εἰσῆλθον, οὐ διέλιπε καταφιλοῦσά μου τοὺς
she but from (when) I entered not did stop fervently kissing of Me the
46 πόδας. ἐλαίῳ τὴν κεφαλήν μου οὐκ ἤλειψας· αὕτη δὲ μύρῳ
feet. With oil the head of Me not you anointed, she but with ointment
47 ἤλειψέ μου τοὺς πόδας. οὗ χάριν, λέγω σοι, ἀφέωνται αἱ
anointed of Me the feet. For this reason I say to you, are forgiven the
ἁμαρτίαι αὐτῆς αἱ πολλαί, ὅτι ἠγάπησε πολύ· ᾧ δὲ ὀλίγον
sins of her many, because she loved much, to whom but little
48 ἀφίεται, ὀλίγον ἀγαπᾷ. εἶπε δὲ αὐτῇ, Ἀφέωνταί σου αἱ
is forgiven, little he loves. He said And to her, are forgiven of you The
49 ἁμαρτίαι. καὶ ἤρξαντο οἱ συνανακείμενοι λέγειν ἐν ἑαυτοῖς,
sins. And began those reclining with (Him) to say in themselves,
50 Τίς οὗτός ἐστιν ὃς καὶ ἁμαρτίας ἀφίησιν; εἶπε δὲ πρὸς τὴν
Who this is, who even sins forgives? He said But to the
γυναῖκα, Ἡ πίστις σου σέσωκέ σε· πορεύου εἰς εἰρήνην.
woman, The faith of you has saved you; Go in peace.

CHAPTER 8

1 Καὶ ἐγένετο ἐν τῷ καθεξῆς, καὶ αὐτὸς διώδευε κατὰ πόλιν
And it was afterwards, and He traveled through every city
καὶ κώμην, κηρύσσων καὶ εὐαγγελιζόμενος τὴν βασιλείαν
and village, preaching and announcing the gospel of the kingdom

God. And the Twelve *were* with Him. 2 And certain women who had been healed from evil spirits and infirmities, Mary having been called Magdalene, from whom seven demons had gone out; and Joanna, wife of Chuza, Herod's steward; and Susanna; and many others, who were ministering to Him of their possessions.

4 And a great crowd coming together, and those in each city coming to Him, He spoke through a parable: 5 The sower went out to sow his seed. And as he sowed, some fell by the roadside, and was trampled, and the birds of the heaven ate it. 6 And other fell on the rock, and sprouting, it dried up, because of not having moisture. 7 And other fell in *the* midst of the thorns, and springing up with the thorns, *they* choked it. 8 And other fell on the good ground, and springing up it produced fruit a hundredfold. Saying these things, He cried out, The one having ears to hear, let him hear.

9 And His disciples questioned Him, saying, What might this parable be? 10 And He said, To you it has been given to know the mysteries of the kingdom of God, but to the rest in parables, that seeing they might not see, and hearing they might not understand. 11 And this is the parable: The seed is the word of God. 12 And those by the roadside are those who hear, then the Devil comes and takes away the word from their heart, lest believing they may be saved. 13 And those on the rock *are* those who, when they hear, receive the word with joy; and these have no root, those believing for a time, and in time of trial draw back. 14 And those falling in the thorns, these are

2 τοῦ Θεοῦ· καὶ οἱ δώδεκα σὺν αὐτῷ, καὶ γυναῖκές τινες αἳ
— of God, and the twelve with Him. also women certain who
ἦσαν τεθεραπευμέναι ἀπὸ πνευμάτων πονηρῶν καὶ
were healed from spirits evil and
ἀσθενειῶν, Μαρία ἡ καλουμένη Μαγδαληνή, ἀφ' ἧς δαιμόνια
infirmities Mary being called Magdalene, from whom demons
3 ἑπτὰ ἐξεληλύθει, καὶ Ἰωάννα γυνὴ Χουζᾶ ἐπιτρόπου Ἡρώ-
seven had gone out; and Joanna wife of Chuza, steward of
δου, καὶ Σουσάννα, καὶ ἕτεραι πολλαί, αἵτινες διηκόνουν
Herod; and Susanna; and others many; who ministered
αὐτῷ ἀπὸ τῶν ὑπαρχόντων αὐταῖς.
to them from the possessions of them.
4 Συνιόντος δὲ ὄχλου πολλοῦ, καὶ τῶν κατὰ πόλιν ἐπιπο-
coming together And crowd a much, and those in each city coming
ρευομένων πρὸς αὐτόν, εἶπε διὰ παραβολῆς, Ἐξῆλθεν ὁ
to Him, He said through a parable: Went out those
5 σπείρων τοῦ σπεῖραι τὸν σπόρον αὐτοῦ καὶ ἐν τῷ σπείρειν
sowing — to sow the seed of him. And in the sowing
αὐτόν, ὃ μὲν ἔπεσε παρὰ τὴν ὁδόν, καὶ κατεπατήθη, καὶ τὰ
of him, the one fell by the way, and was trampled; and the
6 πετεινὰ τοῦ οὐρανοῦ κατέφαγεν αὐτό. καὶ ἕτερον ἔπεσεν
birds of the heaven ate it. And other fell
ἐπὶ τὴν πέτραν, καὶ φυὲν ἐξηράνθη, διὰ τὸ μὴ ἔχειν ἰκμάδα.
on the rock, and growing it dried up, because of not having moisture.
7 καὶ ἕτερον ἔπεσεν ἐν μέσῳ τῶν ἀκανθων, καὶ συμφυεῖσαι αἱ
And other fell amidst the thorns, and growing up with the
8 ἄκανθαι ἀπέπνιξαν αὐτό. καὶ ἕτερον ἔπεσεν ἐπὶ τὴν
thorns choked it. And other fell on the
γῆν τὴν ἀγαθήν, καὶ φυὲν ἐποίησε καρπὸν εκατοντα-
earth — good. and growing it produced fruit a hundred-
πλασίονα. ταῦτα λέγων ἐφώνει, Ὁ ἔχων ὦτα ἀκούειν
fold. these things saying He called, Those having ears to hear,
ἀκουέτω.
let him hear.
9 Ἐπηρώτων δὲ αὐτὸν οἱ μαθηταὶ αὐτοῦ, λέγοντες, Τίς
questioned And Him the disciples of Him, saying, What
10 εἴη ἡ παραβολὴ αὕτη ; ὁ δὲ εἶπεν, Ὑμῖν δέδοται γνῶναι τὰ
might be parable this? He And said, To you it was given to know the
μυστήρια τῆς βασιλείας τοῦ Θεοῦ· τοῖς δὲ λοιποῖς ἐν
mysteries of the kingdom — of God, to the but rest in
παραβολαῖς, ἵνα βλέποντες μὴ βλέπωσι, καὶ ἀκούοντες μὴ
parables, that seeing not they might see, and hearing not
11 συνιῶσιν. ἔστι δὲ αὕτη ἡ παραβολή ὁ σπόρος ἐστὶν ὁ
they might know. is And this the parable: The seed is the
12 λόγος τοῦ Θεοῦ. οἱ δὲ παρὰ τὴν ὁδὸν εἰσὶν οἱ ἀκούοντες,
word — of God. the And (ones) by the way are those hearing;
εἶτα ἔρχεται ὁ διάβολος καὶ αἴρει τὸν λόγον ἀπὸ τῆς καρδίας
then comes the devil and takes the word from the heart
13 αὐτῶν, ἵνα μὴ πιστεύσαντες σωθῶσιν. οἱ δὲ ἐπὶ τῆς
of them, lest believing they may be saved. those And on the
πέτρας οἳ, ὅταν ἀκούσωσι, μετὰ χαρᾶς δέχονται τὸν λόγον,
rock who when they hear with joy receive the word,
καὶ οὗτοι ῥίζαν οὐκ ἔχουσιν, οἳ πρὸς καιρὸν πιστεύουσι,
and these root not do have, who for a time believe,
14 καὶ ἐν καιρῷ πειρασμοῦ ἀφίστανται. τὸ δὲ εἰς τὰς ἀκάνθας
and in time of trial draw back. that And in the thorns

those hearing, but under cares and riches and pleasures of life, having moving along, they are choked, and do not bear to maturity. [15]And those in the good ground, these are they who in a right and good heart having heard the word, they hold *it* and bear fruit in patience.

[16]And no one lighting a lamp covers it with a vessel, or puts *it* under a couch, but puts *it* on a lampstand, so that they who come in may see the light. [17]For nothing is hidden which will not be revealed, nor secret which will not be known, and come to *be* revealed. [18]Therefore, be careful how you hear. For whoever may have, more shall be given to him. And whoever may not have, even what he seems to have will be taken from him.

[19]And His brothers and mother came to Him, and were not able to get to Him because of the crowd. [20]And it was told Him, saying, Your mother and Your brothers are standing outside, wishing to see You. [21]And answering He said to them, My mother and My brothers are those hearing the word of God and doing it.

[22]And it happened on one of the days that He and His disciples entered into a boat. And He said to them, Let us go over to the other side of the lake. And they put out to sea. [23]And as they sailed, He fell asleep. And a windstorm came onto the lake, and they were flooded, and were in danger. [24]And coming up they awakened Him, saying, Master! Master! We are perishing. And being aroused, He rebuked the wind and the roughness of the water, and they ceased, and there was a calm. [25]And He said to them, Where is your faith? And fearing, they marveled, saying to one another, Who, then, is this One, that even the winds and

πεσόν, οὗτοί εἰσιν οἱ ἀκούσαντες, καὶ ὑπὸ μεριμνῶν καὶ
falling, these are those hearing, and under cares and
πλούτου καὶ ἡδονῶν τοῦ βίου πορευόμενοι συμπνίγονται,
riches and pleasures — of life moving along, they are choked
15 καὶ οὐ τελεσφοροῦσι. τὸ δὲ ἐν τῇ καλῇ γῇ, οὗτοί εἰσιν
and not do bear to maturity. that And in the good earth, these are
οἵτινες ἐν καρδίᾳ καλῇ καὶ ἀγαθῇ, ἀκούσαντες τὸν λόγον
(those) who in a heart right and good hearing the word,
κατέχουσι, καὶ καρποφοροῦσιν ἐν ὑπομονῇ.
they hold (it), and bear fruit in patience.
16 Οὐδεὶς δὲ λύχνον ἅψας καλύπτει αὐτὸν σκεύει, ἢ ὑποκάτω
no one But a lamp having lit covers it with a vessel, or underneath
κλίνης τίθησιν, ἀλλ' ἐπὶ λυχνίας ἐπιτίθησιν, ἵνα οἱ εἰσπορευό-
a couch puts (it),but on a lampstand puts (it), that those coming in
17 μενοι βλέπωσι τὸ φῶς. οὐ γάρ ἐστι κρυπτόν, ὃ οὐ φανερὸν
may see the light. not For is hidden which not revealed
γενήσεται· οὐδὲ ἀπόκρυφον, ὃ οὐ γνωσθήσεται καὶ εἰς
will be, nor secret which not will be known and to (be)
18 φανερὸν ἔλθῃ. βλέπετε οὖν πῶς ἀκούετε· ὃς γὰρ ἂν ἔχῃ,
revealed come. see Therefore how you hear; whoever for has,
δοθήσεται αὐτῷ· καὶ ὃς ἂν μὴ ἔχῃ, καὶ ὃ δοκεῖ ἔχειν ἀρθή-
it will be given to him, and who ever not has, even what he seems to have will
σεται ἀπ' αὐτοῦ.
be taken from him.
19 Παρεγένοντο δὲ πρὸς αὐτὸν ἡ μήτηρ καὶ οἱ ἀδελφοὶ
came And to Him the mother and the brothers
αὐτοῦ, καὶ οὐκ ἠδύναντο συντυχεῖν αὐτῷ διὰ τὸν ὄχλον.
of Him, and not were able to come up with Him through the crowd.
20 καὶ ἀπηγγέλη αὐτῷ, λεγόντων, Ἡ μήτηρ σου καὶ οἱ
And it was told to Him, saying, The mother of You and the
ἀδελφοί σου ἑστήκασιν ἔξω, ἰδεῖν σε θέλοντες. ὁ δὲ ἀποκριθεὶς
brothers of You are standing outside to see You desiring. He And answering
21 εἶπε πρὸς αὐτούς, Μήτηρ μου καὶ ἀδελφοί μου οὗτοί εἰσιν
said to them, Mother of Me and brothers of Me these are,
οἱ τὸν λόγον τοῦ Θεοῦ ἀκούοντες καὶ ποιοῦντες αὐτόν.
those the word — of God hearing and doing it.
22 Καὶ ἐγένετο ἐν μιᾷ τῶν ἡμερῶν, καὶ αὐτὸς ἐνέβη εἰς πλοῖον
And it was on one of the days, and He entered into a boat,
καὶ οἱ μαθηταὶ αὐτοῦ, καὶ εἶπε πρὸς αὐτούς, Διέλθωμεν εἰς
also the disciples of Him; and He said to them, Let us go over to
23 τὸ πέραν τῆς λίμνης· καὶ ἀνήχθησαν. πλεόντων δὲ αὐτῶν
the other side of the lake; and they put out to sea. sailing And them,
ἀφύπνωσε· καὶ κατέβη λαῖλαψ ἀνέμου εἰς τὴν λίμνην, καὶ
He fell asleep. And came down a storm of wind onto the lake, and
24 συνεπληροῦντο, καὶ ἐκινδύνευον. προσελθόντες δὲ διήγειραν
they were being filled, and were in danger. coming up And they awoke
αὐτόν, λέγοντες, Ἐπιστάτα, ἐπιστάτα, ἀπολλύμεθα. ὁ δὲ
Him, saying, Master! Master! We are perishing. He And
ἐγερθεὶς ἐπετίμησε τῷ ἀνέμῳ καὶ τῷ κλύδωνι τοῦ ὕδατος·
being aroused rebuked the wind and the roughness of the water,
25 καὶ ἐπαύσαντο, καὶ ἐγένετο γαλήνη. εἶπε δὲ αὐτοῖς, Ποῦ
and they ceased; and there was a calm. He said And to them, Where
ἐστιν ἡ πίστις ὑμῶν; φοβηθέντες δὲ ἐθαύμασαν, λέγοντες
is the faith of you? fearing And, they marveled, saying,
πρὸς ἀλλήλους, Τίς ἄρα οὗτός ἐστιν, ὅτι καὶ τοῖς ἀνέμοις
to one another, Who then this One is, that even the wind

the water obey Him?
[26]And they sailed down to the country of the Gaderenes, which is across from Galilee. [27]And He going out onto the land, a certain man out of the city, who had demons for a long time—and he put no garment on, and he did not stay in a house, but among the tombs. [28]And seeing Jesus, and crying out, he fell down before Him, and with a loud voice said, What to me and to You, Jesus, Son of God the Most High? I beg You, do not torment me. [29]For He charged the unclean spirit to come out of the man. For many times it had seized him, and he was bound with fetters and with chains, being guarded. And tearing apart the bonds, he was dirven by the demons into the deserts. [30]And Jesus asked him, saying, What is your name? And he said, Legion, because many demons entered into him.

[31]And he begged Him that He not order them to go away into the abyss. [32]And there was a herd of many pigs feeding there in the mount. And they begged Him that He would allow them to enter into those. And He allowed them. [33]And the demons coming out from the man entered into the pigs, and rushed down the cliff into the lake, and was choked. [34]And seeing the thing, those feeding *the pigs* fled, and leaving, *they* reported to the city and to the farms. [35]And they went out to see the thing happening, and came to Jesus. And *they* found the man from whom the demons had gone out, sitting clothed and of sound mind, at the feet of Jesus. And they were afraid. [36]And those seeing also related to them how the demon-possessed one was healed. [37]And all the multitude of

ἐπιτάσσει καὶ τῷ ὕδατι, καὶ ὑπακούουσιν αὐτῷ ;
He commands and the water, and they obey Him?
26 Καὶ κατέπλευσαν εἰς τὴν χώραν τῶν Γαδαρηνῶν, ἥτις
And they sailed down to the country of the Gadarenes, which
27 ἐστὶν ἀντιπέραν τῆς Γαλιλαίας. ἐξελθόντι δὲ αὐτῷ ἐπὶ τὴν
is opposite — Galilee. going out And Him onto the
γῆν, ὑπήντησεν αὐτῷ ἀνήρ τις ἐκ τῆς πόλεως, ὃς εἶχε δαι-
land, met Him a man certain out of the city, who had
μόνια ἐκ χρόνων ἱκανῶν, καὶ ἱμάτιον οὐκ ἐνεδιδύσκετο, καὶ
demons from a time long, and a garment not he put on, and
28 ἐν οἰκίᾳ οὐκ ἔμενεν, ἀλλ' ἐν τοῖς μνήμασιν. ἰδὼν δὲ τὸν
in a house not he stayed, but among the tombs. seeing And —
Ἰησοῦν, καὶ ἀνακράξας, προσέπεσεν αὐτῷ, καὶ φωνῇ μεγάλῃ
Jesus, and crying out, he fell down before Him, and with a voice great
εἶπε, Τί ἐμοὶ καὶ σοί, Ἰησοῦ, υἱὲ τοῦ Θεοῦ τοῦ ὑψίστου ;
said, What to me and to You, Jesus, Son — of God the Most High?
29 δέομαί σου, μή με βασανίσῃς. παρήγγειλε γὰρ τῷ πνεύματι
I beg You, not me do torment. He charged For the spirit
τῷ ἀκαθάρτῳ ἐξελθεῖν ἀπὸ τοῦ ἀνθρώπου· πολλοῖς γὰρ
— unclean to come out from the man. many For
χρόνοις συνηρπάκει αὐτόν, καὶ ἐδεσμεῖτο ἁλύσεσι καὶ πέδαις
times it had seized him, and he was bound with chains and fetters,
φυλασσόμενος, καὶ διαρρήσσων τὰ δεσμὰ ἠλαύνετο ὑπὸ τοῦ
being guarded, and tearing apart the bonds, he was driven by the
30 δαίμονος εἰς τὰς ἐρήμους. ἐπηρώτησε δὲ αὐτὸν ὁ Ἰησοῦς,
demons into the deserts. questioned And Him — Jesus,
λέγων, Τί σοι ἐστὶν ὄνομα ; ὁ δὲ εἶπε, Λεγεών· ὅτι δαιμόνια
saying, What to you is (the) name? he And said, Legion, because demons
31 πολλὰ εἰσῆλθεν εἰς αὐτόν. καὶ παρεκάλουν αὐτὸν ἵνα μὴ
many entered into him. And they begged Him that not
32 ἐπιτάξῃ αὐτοῖς εἰς τὴν ἄβυσσον ἀπελθεῖν. ἦν δὲ ἐκεῖ ἀγέλη
He order them into the abyss to go away. was And there a herd
χοίρων ἱκανῶν βοσκομένων ἐν τῷ ὄρει· καὶ παρεκάλουν
pigs of many feeding in the mountain; and they begged
αὐτὸν ἵνα ἐπιτρέψῃ αὐτοῖς εἰς ἐκείνους εἰσελθεῖν. καὶ ἐπέτρε-
Him that He would let them into those to enter. And He let
33 ψεν αὐτοῖς. ἐξελθόντα δὲ τὰ δαιμόνια ἀπὸ τοῦ ἀνθρώπου
them. coming out And the demons from the man
εἰσῆλθεν εἰς τοὺς χοίρους· καὶ ὥρμησεν ἡ ἀγέλη κατὰ τοῦ
entered into the pigs, and rushed the herd down the
34 κρημνοῦ εἰς τὴν λίμνην, καὶ ἀπεπνίγη. ἰδόντες δὲ οἱ
precipice into the lake, and was choked. seeing And those
βόσκοντες τὸ γεγενημένον ἔφυγον, καὶ ἀπελθόντες ἀπήγ-
feeding the thing happening, they fled and having left
35 γειλαν εἰς τὴν πόλιν καὶ εἰς τοὺς ἀγρούς. ἐξῆλθον δὲ ἰδεῖν
reported to the city and to the farms. they went And to see
τὸ γεγονός· καὶ ἦλθον πρὸς τὸν Ἰησοῦν, καὶ εὗρον καθή-
the thing happening and came to — Jesus, and found sitting
μενον τὸν ἄνθρωπον ἀφ' οὗ τὰ δαιμόνια ἐξεληλύθει, ἱματι-
the man from whom the demons had gone out, clothed
σμένον καὶ σωφρονοῦντα, παρὰ τοὺς πόδας τοῦ Ἰησοῦ· καὶ
and of sound mind, at the feet — of Jesus. And
36 ἐφοβήθησαν. ἀπήγγειλαν δὲ αὐτοῖς καὶ οἱ ἰδόντες πῶς ἐσώθη
they were afraid. related And to them also those seeing how was healed
37 ὁ δαιμονισθείς. καὶ ἠρώτησαν αὐτὸν ἅπαν τὸ πλῆθος τῆς
the demon-possessed. And asked Him all the multitude of the

the neighborhood of the Gadarenes were seized with a great fear and asked Him to depart from them. And entering into the boat, He returned. [38]And the man from whom the demons had gone out begged to be with Him. But Jesus sent him away, saying, [39]Go back to your house and tell what God did to you. And he went away proclaiming through all the city what things Jesus did to him.

[40]And it happened *as* Jesus returned, the crowd gladly received Him. [41]And, behold, a man named Jairus came, and this one was a synagogue ruler. And falling at the feet of Jesus, he begged Him to come into his house, [42]because an only daughter was born to him, about twelve years *old*, and she was dying. And in His going, the crowd pressed on Him. [43]And a woman being in a flow of blood from twelve years, who had spent *her* whole living to physicians, *and* could not be cured by anyone, [44]coming up behind, she touched the border of His garment. And instantly the flow of her blood stopped. [45]And Jesus said, Who *was* touching Me? And all having denied, Peter and those with Him said, Master, the crowds press and jostle You. And do You say, Who *was* touching Me? [46]But Jesus said, Someone touched Me; for I knew power had gone out from Me. [47]And seeing that she was not hidden, the woman came and kneeled down before Him, *and* told Him before all the people for what reason she touched Him, and how *she* was instantly cured. [248]And He said to her, Daughter, be comforted. Your faith has healed you. Go in peace.

περιχώρου τῶν Γαδαρηνῶν ἀπελθεῖν ἀπ' αὐτῶν, ὅτι φόβῳ
neighborhood of the Gadarenes to depart from them, for with a fear
μεγάλῳ συνείχοντο· αὐτὸς δὲ ἐμβὰς εἰς τὸ πλοῖον ὑπέ-
great they were seized; He and entering into the boat
38 στρεψεν. ἐδέετο δὲ αὐτοῦ ὁ ἀνὴρ ἀφ' οὗ ἐξεληλύθει τὰ
returned. begged And Him the man from whom had gone out the
δαιμόνια εἶναι σὺν αὐτῷ. ἀπέλυσε δὲ αὐτὸν ὁ Ἰησοῦς λέγων,
demons to be with Him; dismissed But him – Jesus, saying,
39 Ὑπόστρεφε εἰς τὸν οἶκόν σου, καὶ διηγοῦ ὅσα ἐποίησέ σοι
Go back to the house of you, and relate what did to you
ὁ Θεός. καὶ ἀπῆλθε, καθ' ὅλην τὴν πόλιν κηρύσσων ὅσα
– God. And he went away through all the city proclaiming what things
ἐποίησεν αὐτῷ ὁ Ἰησοῦς.
did to him – Jesus.
40 Ἐγένετο δὲ ἐν τῷ ὑποστρέψαι τὸν Ἰησοῦν, ἀπεδέξατο
it was And, in the returning – Jesus, gladly received
41 αὐτὸν ὁ ὄχλος· ἦσαν γὰρ πάντες προσδοκῶντες αὐτόν. καὶ
Him the crowd; they were for all expecting Him. And
ἰδού, ἦλθεν ἀνὴρ ᾧ ὄνομα Ἰάειρος, καὶ αὐτὸς ἄρχων τῆς
behold, came a man to whom name Jairus, and this one a ruler of the
συναγωγῆς ὑπῆρχε, καὶ πεσὼν παρὰ τοὺς πόδας τοῦ Ἰησοῦ
synagogue was. And falling at the feet – of Jesus,
42 παρεκάλει αὐτὸν εἰσελθεῖν εἰς τὸν οἶκον αὐτοῦ· ὅτι θυγάτηρ
he begged Him to come into the house of him, because daughter
μονογενὴς ἦν αὐτῷ ὡς ἐτῶν δώδεκα, καὶ αὕτη ἀπέθνη-
an only born was to him, about years twelve, and she was dying.
σκεν. ἐν δὲ τῷ ὑπάγειν αὐτὸν οἱ ὄχλοι συνέπνιγον αὐτόν.
in And the going (of) Him, the crowd pressed upon Him.
43 Καὶ γυνὴ οὖσα ἐν ῥύσει αἵματος ἀπὸ ἐτῶν δώδεκα, ἥτις
And a woman being in a flow of blood from years twelve, who
εἰς ἰατροὺς προσαναλώσασα ὅλον τὸν βίον οὐκ ἴσχυσεν
to physicians had spent whole – (her) living, not could
44 ὑπ' οὐδενὸς θεραπευθῆναι, προσελθοῦσα ὄπισθεν, ἥψατο
by no one be cured, having come up behind she touched
τοῦ κρασπέδου τοῦ ἱματίου αὐτοῦ· καὶ παραχρῆμα ἔστη
the border of the garment of Him, and immediately stopped
45 ἡ ῥύσις τοῦ αἵματος αὐτῆς. καὶ εἶπεν ὁ Ἰησοῦς, Τίς ὁ
the flow of the blood of her. And said – Jesus, Who
ἁψάμενός μου ; ἀρνουμένων δὲ πάντων, εἶπεν ὁ Πέτρος καὶ
(was) touching Me? denying And all, said – Peter and
οἱ μετ' αὐτοῦ, Ἐπιστάτα, οἱ ὄχλοι συνέχουσί σε, καὶ
those with Him, Master, the crowds press upon You and
46 ἀποθλίβουσι, καὶ λέγεις, Τίς ὁ ἁψάμενός μου ; ὁ δὲ Ἰησοῦς
jostle. And do You say, Who was touching Me? – But Jesus
εἶπεν, Ἥψατό μού τις· ἐγὼ γὰρ ἔγνων δύναμιν ἐξελθοῦσαν
said, touched Me Someone; I for knew power having gone forth
47 ἀπ' ἐμοῦ. ἰδοῦσα δὲ ἡ γυνὴ ὅτι οὐκ ἔλαθε, τρέμουσα ἦλθε,
from Me. seeing And the woman that not she was hid, trembling came
καὶ προσπεσοῦσα αὐτῷ, δι' ἣν αἰτίαν ἥψατο αὐτοῦ
and kneeled down before Him, for what cause she touched Him
ἀπήγγειλεν αὐτῷ ἐνώπιον παντὸς τοῦ λαοῦ, καὶ ὡς ἰάθη
she declared to Him before all the people, and how was cured
48 παραχρῆμα. ὁ δὲ εἶπεν αὐτῇ, Θάρσει, θύγατερ, ἡ πίστις
immediately. He And said to her, Be comforted, daughter, the faith
49 σου σέσωκέ σε· πορεύου εἰς εἰρήνην.
of you has healed you; go in peace.

49 As He was yet speaking, someone came from the synagogue ruler, saying to him, Your daughter has expired. Do not trouble the Teacher. 50 But hearing Jesus answered him, saying, Do not fear; only believe, and she will be healed. 51 And coming to the house, He did not allow anyone to enter except Peter and James and John, and the father and mother of the child. 52 And all were weeping and bewailing her. But He said, Stop weeping. She has not died, but is sleeping. 53 And they scoffed at Him, knowing that she died. 54 But putting all outside, and taking hold of her hand, He called out, saying, Child, rise up! 55 And her spirit returned, and she rose up immediately. And He ordered *something* to eat be given her. 56 And her parents were amazed. But He charged them to tell no one of that *which* happened.

CHAPTER 9

1 And having called together His twelve disciples, He gave them power and authority over all the demons, and to heal diseases. 2 And *He* sent them to proclaim the kingdom of God, and to heal those being sick. 3 And He said to them, Take nothing for the way, neither staffs, nor moneybags, nor bread, nor silver, nor each to have two tunics. 4 And into whatever house you enter, remain there, and go out from there. 5 And as many as may not receive you, going out from that city even shake off the dust from your feet, for a testimony against them. 6 And going out, they passed through the villages preaching the gospel, and healing everywhere.

7 And Herod the tetrarch heard all the things happen-

Ἔτι αὐτοῦ λαλοῦντος, ἔρχεταί τις παρὰ τοῦ ἀρχισυναγώ
Yet Him speaking, comes someone from the synagogue ruler
γου, λέγων αὐτῷ ὅτι Τέθνηκεν ἡ θυγάτηρ σου· μὴ σκύλλε
saying to Him, — has expired The daughter of you; not trouble
50 τὸν διδάσκαλον. ὁ δὲ Ἰησοῦς ἀκούσας ἀπεκρίθη αὐτῷ,
the Teacher. — But Jesus hearing answered him,
λέγων, Μὴ φοβοῦ· μόνον πίστευε, καὶ σωθήσεται. εἰσελθὼν
saying, Do not fear; only believe, and she will be healed. coming
51 δὲ εἰς τὴν οἰκίαν, οὐκ ἀφῆκεν εἰσελθεῖν οὐδένα, εἰ μὴ Πέτρον
And to the house, not He allowed to enter anyone except Peter
καὶ Ἰάκωβον καὶ Ἰωάννην, καὶ τὸν πατέρα τῆς παιδὸς καὶ
and James and John, and the father of the child, and
52 τὴν μητέρα. ἔκλαιον δὲ πάντες, καὶ ἐκόπτοντο αὐτήν. ὁ δὲ
the mother. were weeping And all and bewailing her. He But
53 εἶπε, Μὴ κλαίετε· οὐκ ἀπέθανεν, ἀλλὰ καθεύδει. καὶ κατε-
said, Stop weeping! not she died, but sleeps. And they
γέλων αὐτοῦ, εἰδότες ὅτι ἀπέθανεν. αὐτὸς δὲ ἐκβαλὼν ἔξω
ridiculed Him, knowing that she died. He But having put outside
54 πάντας, καὶ κρατήσας τῆς χειρὸς αὐτῆς, ἐφώνησε λέγων,
all, and having taken hold of the hand of her, He called, saying,
55 Ἡ παῖς ἐγείρου. καὶ ἐπέστρεψε τὸ πνεῦμα αὐτῆς. καὶ ἀνέστη
Child, arise! And returned the spirit of her, and she arose
56 παραχρῆμα· καὶ διέταξεν αὐτῇ δοθῆναι φαγεῖν. καὶ ἐξέστη-
immediately. And He ordered her to be given to eat. And were
σαν οἱ γονεῖς αὐτῆς· ὁ δὲ παρήγγειλεν αὐτοῖς μηδενὶ εἰπεῖν
amazed the parents of her. He But charged them to no one to tell
τὸ γεγονός.
the thing having happened.

CHAPTER 9

1 Συγκαλεσάμενος δὲ τοὺς δώδεκα μαθητὰς αὐτοῦ, ἔδωκεν
having called together And the twelve disciples of Him, He gave
αὐτοῖς δύναμιν καὶ ἐξουσίαν ἐπὶ πάντα τὰ δαιμόνια, καὶ
them power and authority over all the demons, and
2 νόσους θεραπεύειν. καὶ ἀπέστειλεν αὐτοὺς κηρύσσειν τὴν
diseases to heal. And He sent them to proclaim the
3 βασιλείαν τοῦ Θεοῦ, καὶ ἰᾶσθαι τοὺς ἀσθενοῦντας. καὶ εἶπε
kingdom — of God, and to cure those being sick. And He said
πρὸς αὐτούς, Μηδὲν αἴρετε εἰς τὴν ὁδόν· μήτε ῥάβδους,
to them, Nothing take for the way, neither staffs,
μήτε πήραν, μήτε ἄρτον, μήτε ἀργύριον, μήτε ἀνὰ δύο
nor moneybags, nor bread, nor silver, nor each two
4 χιτῶνας ἔχειν. καὶ εἰς ἣν ἂν οἰκίαν εἰσέλθητε, ἐκεῖ μένετε, καὶ
tunics to have. And into whatever house you go in, there remain, and
5 ἐκεῖθεν ἐξέρχεσθε. καὶ ὅσοι ἂν μὴ δέξωνται ὑμᾶς, ἐξερχό-
from there go out. And as many as not may receive you, going
μενοι ἀπὸ τῆς πόλεως ἐκείνης καὶ τὸν κονιορτὸν ἀπὸ τῶν
out from — city that even the dust from the
6 ποδῶν ὑμῶν ἀποτινάξατε εἰς μαρτύριον ἐπ' αὐτούς. ἐξερχό-
feet of you shake off, for a testimony against them. going
μενοι δὲ διήρχοντο κατὰ τὰς κώμας, εὐαγγελιζόμενοι καὶ
out And they passed through the villages preaching the gospel and
θεραπεύοντες πανταχοῦ.
healing everywhere.
7 Ἤκουσε δὲ Ἡρῴδης ὁ τετράρχης τὰ γινόμενα ὑπ' αὐτοῦ
heard And Herod the tetrarch the things happening by Him

ing by Him, and was puzzled, because of the saying by some that John had been raised from *the* dead; [8]and by some that Elijah had appeared; and others *said,* A prophet of the ancients rose again. [9]And Herod said, I

beheaded John, but who is this about whom I hear such things? And he sought to see Him.

[10]And returning the apostles told Him what things they did. And taking them, He went out privately to a desert place of a city called Bethsaida. [11]But knowing *it,* the crowds followed Him. And having received them, He spoke to them about the kingdom of God. And He cured those having need of healing. [12]But the day began to wane, and coming up the Twelve said to Him, Let the crowd go, that going to the surrounding villages and farms they may lodge, and find food supplies, because here we are in a desert place. [13]But He said to them, You give them to eat. But they said, There are not to us more than five loaves and two fish, unless going we buy foods for all this people. [14]For they were about five thousand men. But He said to His disciples, Make them recline in groups, by fifties. [15]And they did so, and made all recline. [16]And taking the five loaves and the two fish, looking up to Heaven, He blessed them, and broke, and gave to the disciples to set before the crowd. [17]And they ate and were all satisfied. And twelve handbaskets of fragments of that left over to them were taken up.

[18]And it happened *as* He was praying alone, the disciples were with Him. And He questioned them,

πάντα· καὶ διηπόρει, διὰ τὸ λέγεσθαι ὑπό τινων ὅτι
all, and was puzzled, because of the saying by some that
8 Ἰωάννης ἐγήγερται ἐκ νεκρῶν· ὑπό τινων δὲ ὅτι Ἠλίας
John has been raised from the dead, by some and that Elijah
ἐφάνη ἄλλων δὲ ὅτι Προφήτης εἷς τῶν ἀρχαίων ἀνέστη
had appeared; others and that a prophet of the ancients rose again.
9 καὶ εἶπεν ὁ Ἡρώδης, Ἰωάννην ἐγὼ ἀπεκεφάλισα· τίς δέ
And said — Herod, John I beheaded, who but
ἐστιν οὗτος, περὶ οὗ ἐγὼ ἀκούω τοιαῦτα; καὶ ἐζήτει ἰδεῖν
is this about whom I hear such things? And he tried to see
αὐτόν.
Him.
10 Καὶ ὑποστρέψαντες οἱ ἀπόστολοι διηγήσαντο αὐτῷ ὅσα
And having returned the apostles told Him what
ἐποίησαν. καὶ παραλαβὼν αὐτούς, ὑπεχώρησε κατ' ἰδίαν
they did. And taking them, He departed privately
11 εἰς τόπον ἔρημον πόλεως καλουμένης Βηθσαϊδά. οἱ δὲ ὄχλοι
to a place desert of a city called Bethsaida. the But crowds
γνόντες ἠκολούθησαν αὐτῷ· καὶ δεξάμενος αὐτούς, ἐλάλει
having known followed Him. And having received them, He spoke
αὐτοῖς περὶ τῆς βασιλείας τοῦ Θεοῦ, καὶ τοὺς χρείαν
to them about the kingdom — of God, and those need
12 ἔχοντας θεραπείας ἰᾶτο. ἡ δὲ ἡμέρα ἤρξατο κλίνειν· προσ-
having of healing He cured. the But day began to decline; coming
ελθόντες δὲ οἱ δώδεκα εἶπον αὐτῷ, Ἀπόλυσον τὸν ὄχλον,
up and the twelve said to Him, Let go the crowd,
ἵνα ἀπελθόντες εἰς τὰς κύκλῳ κώμας καὶ τοὺς ἀγροὺς κατα-
that going to the around villages and the farms they
λύσωσι, καὶ εὕρωσιν ἐπισιτισμόν· ὅτι ὧδε ἐν ἐρήμῳ τόπῳ
may lodge, and may find food supplies, because here in a desert place
13 ἐσμέν. εἶπε δὲ πρὸς αὐτούς, Δότε αὐτοῖς ὑμεῖς φαγεῖν. οἱ δὲ
we are. He said And to them, give them You to eat. they But
εἶπον, Οὐκ εἰσὶν ἡμῖν πλεῖον ἢ πέντε ἄρτοι καὶ δύο ἰχθύες,
said, Not is to us more than five loaves and two fish,
εἰ μήτι πορευθέντες ἡμεῖς ἀγοράσωμεν εἰς πάντα τὸν λαὸν
unless going we may buy for all people
14 τοῦτον βρώματα. ἦσαν γὰρ ὡσεὶ ἄνδρες πεντακισχίλιοι.
this foods. there were For about men five thousand.
εἶπε δὲ πρὸς τοὺς μαθητὰς αὐτοῦ, Κατακλίνατε αὐτοὺς
He said And to the disciples of Him, Cause to recline them
15 κλισίας ἀνὰ πεντήκοντα. καὶ ἐποίησαν οὕτω, καὶ ἀνέκλιναν
in groups by fifties. And they did so, and caused to recline
16 ἅπαντας. λαβὼν δὲ τοὺς πέντε ἄρτους καὶ τοὺς δύο ἰχθύας,
all. taking And the five loaves and the two fish,
ἀναβλέψας εἰς τὸν οὐρανόν, εὐλόγησεν αὐτούς, καὶ κατέ-
looking up to — Heaven, He blessed them, and broke
17 κλασε, καὶ ἐδίδου τοῖς μαθηταῖς παρατιθέναι τῷ ὄχλῳ. καὶ
and gave to the disciples to set before the crowd. And
ἔφαγον καὶ ἐχορτάσθησαν πάντες· καὶ ἤρθη τὸ περισσεῦσαν
they ate and were filled all; and were taken the excess
αὐτοῖς κλασμάτων, κόφινοι δώδεκα.
to them of fragments, baskets twelve.
18 Καὶ ἐγένετο ἐν τῷ εἶναι αὐτὸν προσευχόμενον καταμόνας,
And it was (as) was Him praying alone,
συνῆσαν αὐτῷ οἱ μαθηταί· καὶ ἐπηρώτησεν αὐτούς, λέγων,
were with Him the disciples, and He questioned them, saying,

saying, Whom do the crowds say Me to be? 19 And answering they said, John the Baptist, and others Elijah; and others that some prophet of the ancients has risen again. 20 And He said to them, But whom do you say Me to be? And answering Peter said, The Christ of God. 21 And strictly warning them, He ordered no one to tell this, 22 saying, The Son of man must suffer many things and be rejected by the elders and chief priests and scribes, and to be killed, and to be raised the third day. 23 And He said to all, If anyone desires to come after Me, let him deny himself and take up his cross daily. And let him follow Me. 24 For whoever desires to save his soul, he will lose it. But whoever loses his soul for My sake, this one will save it. 25 For what is a man profited *by* gaining the whole world, but destroying or suffering loss of himself? 26 For whoever is ashamed of Me and My words, the Son of man will be ashamed of that one when He comes in the glory of Him and of the Father, and of the holy angels. 27 But truly I say to you, There are some standing here who in no way will taste of death until they see the kingdom of God.

28 And about eight days after these sayings, it happened, taking Peter and John and James, He went into the mountain to pray. 29 And in His praying the appearance of His face became changed, and His clothing dazzling white. 30 And, behold, two men talked with Him, who were Moses and Elijah. 31 Appearing in glory, *they* spoke of His exodus, which He was about to accomplish in Jerusalem. 32 But Peter and those with him were

19 Τίνα με λέγουσιν οἱ ὄχλοι εἶναι; οἱ δὲ ἀποκριθέντες εἶπον,
Whom Me say the crowds to be? they And answering said,
Ἰωάννην τὸν Βαπτιστήν· ἄλλοι δὲ Ἠλίαν· ἄλλοι δέ, ὅτι
John the Baptist; others but Elijah; others and that
20 προφήτης τις τῶν ἀρχαίων ἀνέστη. εἶπε δὲ αὐτοῖς, Ὑμεῖς
prophet a certain of the ancients rose again. He said And to them, you
δὲ τίνα με λέγετε εἶναι; ἀποκριθεὶς δὲ ὁ Πέτρος εἶπε, Τὸν
And, whom Me say to be? answering And – Peter said, The
21 Χριστὸν τοῦ Θεοῦ. ὁ δὲ ἐπιτιμήσας αὐτοῖς παρήγγειλε
Christ – of God. He But warning them ordered
22 μηδενὶ εἰπεῖν τοῦτο, εἰπὼν ὅτι Δεῖ τὸν υἱὸν τοῦ ἀνθρώπου
no one to tell this, saying that it behoves the Son – of man
πολλὰ παθεῖν, καὶ ἀποδοκιμασθῆναι ἀπὸ τῶν πρεσβυτέ-
many things to suffer, and to be rejected from the elders
ρων καὶ ἀρχιερέων καὶ γραμματέων, καὶ ἀποκτανθῆναι,
and chief priests and scribes, and to be killed,
23 καὶ τῇ τρίτῃ ἡμέρᾳ ἐγερθῆναι. ἔλεγε δὲ πρὸς πάντας, Εἴ τις
and the third day to be raised. He said And to all, If anyone
θέλει ὀπίσω μου ἐλθεῖν, ἀπαρνησάσθω ἑαυτόν, καὶ ἀράτω
desires after Me to come, let him deny himself and take up
24 τὸν σταυρὸν αὐτοῦ καθ' ἡμέραν, καὶ ἀκολουθείτω μοι. ὃς
the cross of him daily. And let him follow Me who ever
γὰρ ἂν θέλῃ τὴν ψυχὴν αὐτοῦ σῶσαι, ἀπολέσει αὐτήν· ὃς
For desires the soul of him to save, he will lose it; whoever
δ' ἂν ἀπολέσῃ τὴν ψυχὴν αὐτοῦ ἕνεκεν ἐμοῦ, οὗτος σώσει
But loses the soul of him for My sake, this one will save
25 αὐτήν. τί γὰρ ὠφελεῖται ἄνθρωπος, κερδήσας τὸν κόσμον
it. what For is profited a man gaining the world
26 ὅλον, ἑαυτὸν δὲ ἀπολέσας ἢ ζημιωθείς; ὃς γὰρ ἂν ἐπαισχυνθῇ
whole, himself but destroying or suffering loss? whoever For is ashamed of
με καὶ τοὺς ἐμοὺς λόγους, τοῦτον ὁ υἱὸς τοῦ ἀνθρώπου
Me and – My words, this one the Son – of man
ἐπαισχυνθήσεται, ὅταν ἔλθῃ ἐν τῇ δόξῃ αὐτοῦ καὶ τοῦ
will be ashamed of when He comes in the glory of Him, and of the
27 πατρὸς καὶ τῶν ἁγίων ἀγγέλων. λέγω δὲ ὑμῖν ἀληθῶς,
Father, and of the holy angels. I say But to you truly,
εἰσί τινες τῶν ὧδε ἑστηκότων, οἳ οὐ μὴ γεύσονται θανάτου,
are some of those here standing who in no way shall taste of death
ἕως ἂν ἴδωσι τὴν βασιλείαν τοῦ Θεοῦ.
until they see the kingdom – of God.
28 Ἐγένετο δὲ μετὰ τοὺς λόγους τούτους ὡσεὶ ἡμέραι ὀκτώ,
it was And, after sayings these, about days eight,
καὶ παραλαβὼν τὸν Πέτρον καὶ Ἰωάννην καὶ Ἰάκωβον,
and taking – Peter and John and James,
29 ἀνέβη εἰς τὸ ὄρος προσεύξασθαι. καὶ ἐγένετο, ἐν τῷ
He went into the mountain to pray. And became in the
προσεύχεσθαι αὐτόν, τὸ εἶδος τοῦ προσώπου αὐτοῦ ἕτερον,
praying (of) Him the appearance of the face of Him different,
30 καὶ ὁ ἱματισμὸς αὐτοῦ λευκὸς ἐξαστράπτων. καὶ ἰδού,
and the clothing of Him white dazzling And, behold,
ἄνδρες δύο συνελάλουν αὐτῷ, οἵτινες ἦσαν Μωσῆς καὶ
men two talked with Him, who were Moses and
31 Ἠλίας, οἳ ὀφθέντες ἐν δόξῃ ἔλεγον τὴν ἔξοδον αὐτοῦ ἣν
Elijah, who appearing in glory spoke of the exodus of Him; which
32 ἔμελλε πληροῦν ἐν Ἱερουσαλήμ. ὁ δὲ Πέτρος καὶ οἱ σὺν αὐτῷ
He was about to finish in Jerusalem. – And Peter and those with him

pressed down with sleep. But awakening fully, they saw His glory, and the two men standing with Him. 33 And it happened in their parting from Him, Peter said to Jesus, Master, it is good *for* us to be here. And, Let us make three tabernacles, one for You, and one for Moses, and one for Elijah—not knowing what he said. 34 And he saying these things, a cloud came and overshadowed them. And they feared *as* those entered into the cloud. 35 And a voice came out of the cloud, saying, This is My Son, the Beloved; hear Him! 36 And *as* the voice occurred, Jesus was found alone. And they were quiet. And *they* did not tell anything which they had seen in those days.

37 And it happened on the next day, they coming down from the mountain, a huge crowd met Him. 38 And, behold, a man called aloud from the crowd, saying, Teacher, I beg You to look at my son, because he is my only-born. 39 And, behold, a spirit takes him, and *he* suddenly cries out. And *it* throws him into convulsions, with foaming. And *it* departs from him with pain, bruising him. 40 And I begged Your disciples, that they cast it out. And they were not able.

41 And answering Jesus said, O unbelieving and perverted generation, how long shall I be with you and endure you? Bring your son here. 42 But yet, *as* he *was* coming up, the demon tore him, and violently convulsed *him*. But Jesus rebuked the unclean spirit, and healed the child, and gave him back to his father. 43 And all were astonished at the majesty of God.

ἦσαν βεβαρημένοι ὕπνῳ· διαγρηγορήσαντες δὲ εἶδον τὴν
were pressed down with sleep. awakening fully But they saw the
δόξαν αὐτοῦ, καὶ τοὺς δύο ἄνδρας τοὺς συνεστῶτας αὐτῷ.
glory of Him, and the two men — standing with Him.
33 καὶ ἐγένετο, ἐν τῷ διαχωρίζεσθαι αὐτοὺς ἀπ' αὐτοῦ, εἶπεν
And it was, in the parting (of) them from Him, said
ὁ Πέτρος πρὸς τὸν Ἰησοῦν, Ἐπιστάτα, καλόν ἐστιν ἡμᾶς
— Peter to — Jesus, Master, good it is (for) us
ὧδε εἶναι· καὶ ποιήσωμεν σκηνὰς τρεῖς, μίαν σοί, καὶ
here to be, and let us make tents three, one for You, and
34 Μωσεῖ μίαν, καὶ μίαν Ἠλίᾳ· μὴ εἰδὼς ὃ λέγει. ταῦτα δὲ
Moses one, and one for Elijah, not knowing what he says. these And
αὐτοῦ λέγοντος, ἐγένετο νεφέλη καὶ ἐπεσκίασεν αὐτούς·
him saying, came a cloud and overshadowed them;
35 ἐφοβήθησαν δὲ ἐν τῷ ἐκείνους εἰσελθεῖν εἰς τὴν νεφέλην. καὶ
they feared and in the of those entering into the cloud. And
φωνὴ ἐγένετο ἐκ τῆς νεφέλης, λέγουσα, Οὗτός ἐστιν ὁ υἱός
a voice came out of the cloud, saying, This is the Son
36 μου ὁ ἀγαπητός· αὐτοῦ ἀκούετε. καὶ ἐν τῷ γενέσθαι τὴν
of Me, the Beloved; Him hear. And in the occurring of the
φωνήν, εὑρέθη ὁ Ἰησοῦς μόνος. καὶ αὐτοὶ ἐσίγησαν, καὶ
voice, was found — Jesus alone. And they were quiet; and
οὐδενὶ ἀπήγγειλαν ἐν ἐκείναις ταῖς ἡμέραις οὐδὲν ὧν
to no one reported in those — days, nothing which
ἑωράκασιν.
they had seen.
37 Ἐγένετο δὲ ἐν τῇ ἑξῆς ἡμέρᾳ, κατελθόντων αὐτῶν ἀπὸ
it was And on the next day, coming down them from
38 τοῦ ὄρους, συνήντησεν αὐτῷ ὄχλος πολύς. καὶ ἰδού, ἀνὴρ
the mountain, met Him a crowd much. And behold, a man
ἀπὸ τοῦ ὄχλου ἀνεβόησε, λέγων, Διδάσκαλε, δέομαί σου,
from the crowd called aloud, saying, Teacher, I beg You,
39 ἐπίβλεψον ἐπὶ τὸν υἱόν μου, ὅτι μονογενής ἐστί μοι· καὶ
to look at the son of me, because only born he is to me, and
ἰδού, πνεῦμα λαμβάνει αὐτόν, καὶ ἐξαίφνης κράζει, καὶ
behold, a spirit takes him, and suddenly cries out, and
σπαράσσει αὐτὸν μετὰ ἀφροῦ, καὶ μόγις ἀποχωρεῖ ἀπ'
convulses him with foam, and with pain departs from
40 αὐτοῦ, συντρῖβον αὐτόν. καὶ ἐδεήθην τῶν μαθητῶν σου
him, bruising him. And I begged the disciples of You
41 ἵνα ἐκβάλλωσιν αὐτό, καὶ οὐκ ἠδυνήθησαν. ἀποκριθεὶς δὲ
that they cast out it, and not they were able. answering And
ὁ Ἰησοῦς εἶπεν, Ὦ γενεὰ ἄπιστος καὶ διεστραμμένη, ἕως
— Jesus said, O generation unbelieving and having been perverted, until
πότε ἔσομαι πρὸς ὑμᾶς, καὶ ἀνέξομαι ὑμῶν; προσάγαγε
when shall I be with you, and endure you? Bring
42 ὧδε τὸν υἱόν σου. ἔτι δὲ προσερχομένου αὐτοῦ, ἔρρηξεν
here the son of you. yet But (as was) coming up him, tore
αὐτὸν τὸ δαιμόνιον καὶ συνεσπάραξεν· ἐπετίμησε δὲ ὁ
him the demon, and violently convulsed. rebuked But
Ἰησοῦς τῷ πνεύματι τῷ ἀκαθάρτῳ, καὶ ἰάσατο τὸν παῖδα,
Jesus the spirit — unclean, and healed the child,
43 καὶ ἀπέδωκεν αὐτὸν τῷ πατρὶ αὐτοῦ. ἐξεπλήσσοντο δὲ
and restored him to the father of him. were astounded And
πάντες ἐπὶ τῇ μεγαλειότητι τοῦ Θεοῦ.
all at the majesty — of God.

And *as* all were marveling at all things which He did, Jesus said to His disciples, 44 You lay into your ears these sayings. For the Son of man is about to be betrayed into *the* hands of men. 45 But they did not understand this saying, and it was veiled from them, that they not perceive it. And they feared to ask Him about this word.

46 But an argument came in among them, who might be *the greater of them.* 47 And seeing the argument of their heart, taking a child, Jesus stood it beside Himself, 48 and said to them, Whoever receives this child on My name receives Me. And whoever receives Me receives Him who sent Me. For the one being least among you all, this one is great.

49 And answering John said, Master, we saw someone casting out demons on Your name, and we forbade him, because he does not follow with us. 50 And Jesus said to him, Do not forbid; for whoever is not against us is for us.

51 And it happened in the fulfilling *of* the days of His taking up, even He set His face to go to Jerusalem. 52 And He sent messengers before His face. And going they went into a village of Samaritans, so as to make ready for Him. 53 And they did not receive Him, because His face was going toward Jerusalem. 54 And seeing, His disciples, James and John, said, Lord, do you desire *that* we tell fire to come down from Heaven, and to destroy them, even as Elijah did? 55 But turning

Πάντων δὲ θαυμαζόντων ἐπὶ πᾶσιν οἷς ἐποίησεν ὁ
all And marveling at all things which He did —
44 Ἰησοῦς, εἶπε πρὸς τοὺς μαθητὰς αὐτοῦ, Θέσθε ὑμεῖς εἰς τὰ
Jesus said to the disciples of Him, Lay you into the
ὦτα ὑμῶν τοὺς λόγους τούτους· ὁ γὰρ υἱὸς τοῦ ἀνθρώπου
ears of you — sayings these; the for Son — of man
45 μέλλει παραδίδοσθαι εἰς χεῖρας ἀνθρώπων. οἱ δὲ ἠγνόουν
is about to be betrayed into the hands of men. they But knew not
τὸ ῥῆμα τοῦτο, καὶ ἦν παρακεκαλυμμένον ἀπ᾽ αὐτῶν, ἵνα
— word this, and it was veiled from them, lest
μὴ αἴσθωνται αὐτό· καὶ ἐφοβοῦντο ἐρωτῆσαι αὐτὸν περὶ
they perceive it. And they feared to ask Him about
τοῦ ῥήματος τούτου.
word this.
46 Εἰσῆλθε δὲ διαλογισμὸς ἐν αὐτοῖς, τὸ τίς ἂν εἴη μείζων
came in But an argument among them, — who might be greater
47 αὐτῶν. ὁ δὲ Ἰησοῦς ἰδὼν τὸν διαλογισμὸν τῆς καρδίας
of them. — And Jesus having seen the argument of the heart
αὐτῶν, ἐπιλαβόμενος παιδίου, ἔστησεν αὐτὸ παρ᾽ ἑαυτῷ,
of them, taking a child stood it beside Himself,
48 καὶ εἶπεν αὐτοῖς, Ὃς ἐὰν δέξηται τοῦτο τὸ παιδίον ἐπὶ τῷ
and said to them, Whoever receives this — child upon the
ὀνόματί μου ἐμὲ δέχεται· καὶ ὃς ἐὰν ἐμὲ δέξηται δέχεται τὸν
name of Me, Me receives. And whoever Me receives receives the (One)
ἀποστείλαντά με· ὁ γὰρ μικρότερος ἐν πᾶσιν ὑμῖν ὑπάρχων
having sent Me. the For lesser among all you being,
οὗτος ἔσται μέγας.
this one is great.
49 Ἀποκριθεὶς δὲ ὁ Ἰωάννης εἶπεν, Ἐπιστάτα, εἴδομέν τινα
answering And — John said, Master, we saw someone
ἐπὶ τῷ ὀνόματί σου ἐκβάλλοντα τὰ δαιμόνια· καὶ ἐκωλύ-
on the name of You casting out — demons, and we pre-
50 σαμεν αὐτόν, ὅτι οὐκ ἀκολουθεῖ μεθ᾽ ἡμῶν. καὶ εἶπε πρὸς
vented him, because not he follows with us. And said to
αὐτὸν ὁ Ἰησοῦς, Μὴ κωλύετε· ὃς γὰρ οὐκ ἔστι καθ᾽ ἡμῶν
them — Jesus, Do not prevent; whoever for not is against us,
ὑπὲρ ἡμῶν ἐστιν.
for us is.
51 Ἐγένετο δὲ ἐν τῷ συμπληροῦσθαι τὰς ἡμέρας τῆς
it was And in the fulfilling (of) the days of the
ἀναλήψεως αὐτοῦ, καὶ αὐτὸς τὸ πρόσωπον αὐτοῦ ἐστήριξε
taking up of Him, even He the face of Him set
52 τοῦ πορεύεσθαι εἰς Ἱερουσαλήμ, καὶ ἀπέστειλεν ἀγγέλους
— to go to Jerusalem, and sent messengers
πρὸ προσώπου αὐτοῦ· καὶ πορευθέντες εἰσῆλθον εἰς κώμην
before the face of Him. And going they went into a village
53 Σαμαρειτῶν, ὥστε ἑτοιμάσαι αὐτῷ. καὶ οὐκ ἐδέξαντο αὐτόν,
of Samaritans, so as to prepare for Him. And not they received Him,
ὅτι τὸ πρόσωπον αὐτοῦ ἦν πορευόμενον εἰς Ἱερουσαλήμ.
because the face of Him was going to Jerusalem.
54 ἰδόντες δὲ οἱ μαθηταὶ αὐτοῦ Ἰάκωβος καὶ Ἰωάννης εἶπον,
seeing And the disciples of Him, James and John said,
Κύριε, θέλεις εἴπωμεν πῦρ καταβῆναι ἀπὸ τοῦ οὐρανοῦ, καὶ
Lord, desire You (that) we tell fire to come down from — Heaven and
55 ἀναλῶσαι αὐτούς, ὡς καὶ Ἠλίας ἐποίησε; στραφεὶς δὲ
to destroy them, as also Elijah did? turning But

He rebuked them, and said, You do not know of what spirit you are. [56]For the Son of man did not come to destroy men's lives, but to save. And they went to another village.

ἐπετίμησεν αὐτοῖς, καὶ εἶπεν, Οὐκ οἴδατε οἵου πνεύματός
He rebuked them, and said, Not you know of what spirit
56 ἐστε ὑμεῖς· ὁ γὰρ υἱὸς τοῦ ἀνθρώπου οὐκ ἦλθε ψυχὰς
are you. the For Son – of man not did come the lives
ἀνθρώπων ἀπολέσαι, ἀλλὰ σῶσαι. καὶ ἐπορεύθησαν εἰς
of men to destroy, but to save. And they went to
ἑτέραν κώμην.
another village.

[57]And it happened as they were going in the way, someone said to Him, I will follow You wherever You may go, Lord. [58]And Jesus said to him, The foxes have holes, and the birds of the heaven nests, but the Son of man has nowhere He may lay *His* head. [59]And He said to another, Follow Me. But he said, Lord, allow me to go first to bury my father. [60]But Jesus said to him, Leave the dead to bury their dead, but going out, you announce the kingdom of God. [61]And also another said, I will follow You, Lord, but first allow me to take leave of those in my house. [62]But Jesus said to him, No one putting his hand on the plow, and looking at the things behind, is fit for the kingdom of God.

57 Ἐγένετο δὲ πορευομένων αὐτῶν ἐν τῇ ὁδῷ, εἶπέ τις πρὸς
it was And, going them in the way, said one to
αὐτόν, Ἀκολουθήσω σοι ὅπου ἂν ἀπέρχῃ, Κύριε. καὶ εἶπεν
Him, I will follow You wherever You go, Lord. And said
58 αὐτῷ ὁ Ἰησοῦς, Αἱ ἀλώπεκες φωλεοὺς ἔχουσι, καὶ τὰ
to him – Jesus, The foxes holes have, and the
πετεινὰ τοῦ οὐρανοῦ κατασκηνώσεις· ὁ δὲ υἱὸς τοῦ ἀνθρώ-
birds of the heaven nests; the but Son – of man
59 που οὐκ ἔχει ποῦ τὴν κεφαλὴν κλίνῃ. εἶπε δὲ πρὸς ἕτερον,
not has where the head He may lay. He said And to another,
Ἀκολούθει μοι. ὁ δὲ εἶπε, Κύριε, ἐπίτρεψόν μοι ἀπελθόντι
Follow Me. he But said, Lord, allow me having gone
60 πρῶτον θάψαι τὸν πατέρα μου. εἶπε δὲ αὐτῷ ὁ Ἰησοῦς,
first to bury the father of me. said But to him – Jesus,
Ἄφες τοὺς νεκροὺς θάψαι τοὺς ἑαυτῶν νεκρούς· σὺ δὲ
Leave the dead to bury the of themselves dead; you but
61 ἀπελθὼν διάγγελλε τὴν βασιλείαν τοῦ Θεοῦ. εἶπε δὲ καὶ
going out announce the kingdom – of God. said And also
ἕτερος, Ἀκολουθήσω σοι, Κύριε· πρῶτον δὲ ἐπίτρεψόν μοι
another, I will follow You, Lord; first but allow me
62 ἀποτάξασθαι τοῖς εἰς τὸν οἶκόν μου. εἶπε δὲ πρὸς αὐτὸν ὁ
to take leave of those in the house of me. said But to him –
Ἰησοῦς, Οὐδείς, ἐπιβαλὼν τὴν χεῖρα αὐτοῦ ἐπ᾿ ἄροτρον,
Jesus, No one putting the hand of him on the plow
καὶ βλέπων εἰς τὰ ὀπίσω, εὔθετός ἐστιν εἰς τὴν βασιλείαν
and looking at the things behind fit is for the kingdom
τοῦ Θεοῦ.
- of God.

CHAPTER 10

[1]And after these things the Lord also appointed seventy others, and sent them two by two before His face into every city and where He was about to come. [2]Then He said to them, Indeed the harvest *is* much, but the laborers *are* few. Therefore, pray *to* the Lord of the harvest, that He send out workers into His harvest. [3]Go! Behold, I send you out as lambs in *the* midst of wolves. [4]Do not carry a purse, nor a moneybag, nor sandals; and greet no one by the way. [5]And into whatever house you may enter, first say, Peace to

1 Μετὰ δὲ ταῦτα ἀνέδειξεν ὁ Κύριος καὶ ἑτέρους ἑβδομή-
after And these things appointed the Lord and others seventy
κοντα, καὶ ἀπέστειλεν αὐτοὺς ἀνὰ δύο πρὸ προσώπου
and sent them two by two before (the) face
αὐτοῦ εἰς πᾶσαν πόλιν καὶ τόπον οὗ ἔμελλεν αὐτὸς ἔρχεσθαι.
of Him into every city and place where was about He to come.
2 ἔλεγεν οὖν πρὸς αὐτούς, Ὁ μὲν θερισμὸς πολύς, οἱ δὲ ἐργάται
He said Then to them, the Indeed harvest (is) much, the but workers
ὀλίγοι· δεήθητε οὖν τοῦ Κυρίου τοῦ θερισμοῦ, ὅπως ἐκβάλλῃ
few; pray therefore of the Lord of the harvest, that He send out
3 ἐργάτας εἰς τὸν θερισμὸν αὐτοῦ. ὑπάγετε· ἰδού, ἐγὼ ἀπο-
workers into the harvest of Him. Go! Behold, I send
4 στέλλω ὑμᾶς ὡς ἄρνας ἐν μέσῳ λύκων. μὴ βαστάζετε βαλάν-
out you as lambs in (the) midst of wolves. Do not carry a
τιον, μὴ πήραν, μηδὲ ὑποδήματα· καὶ μηδένα κατὰ τὴν
purse, nor a moneybag, nor sandals; and no one by the
5 ὁδὸν ἀσπάσησθε. εἰς ἣν δ᾿ ἂν οἰκίαν εἰσέρχησθε, πρῶτον
way greet. into whatever And house you may enter, first

this house. [6]And if a son of peace is truly there, your peace shall rest on it; but if not so, it shall return to you. [7]And remain in the same house, eating and drinking the things *shared* by them; for the laborer is worthy of his hire. Do not move from house to house.

[8]And into whatever city you enter, and they receive you, eat the things set before you. [9]And heal the sick in it, and say to them, The kingdom of God has drawn near to you. [10]But into whatever city you enter, and they do not receive you, having gone out into its streets, say, [11]Even the dust which clung to us out of your city we wipe off against you! Yet know this, that the kingdom of God has drawn near to you!

[12]And I say to you that it shall be more tolerable for Sodom in that day than for that city! [13]Woe to you, Chorazin! Woe to you, Bethsaida! For if the works of power which have been occurring in you had occurred in Tyre and Sidon, they long ago would have repented, sitting in sackcloth and ashes! [14]But it will be more tolerable for Tyre and Sidon in the Judgment than for you. [15]And you, Capernaum, were you not exalted to heaven? You will be thrust down to Hades!

[16]The one hearing you *also* hears Me, and the one rejecting you *also* rejects Me, and the one rejecting Me *also* rejects the *One* having sent Me.

[17]And the seventy returned with joy, saying, Lord, even the demons are subject to us through Your Name. [18]And He said to them, I saw Satan falling out of Heaven as lightning! [19]Behold, I have given you the authority to tread on snakes and scorpions, and on all the power of the Enemy, and nothing in any way shall hurt you. [20]But stop rejoicing in this, that the *evil* spirits submit to you. But rather

6 λέγετε, Εἰρήνη τῷ οἴκῳ τούτῳ. καὶ ἐὰν μὲν ᾖ ἐκεῖ ὁ υἱὸς
say, Peace — house to this. And if indeed is there — a son
εἰρήνης, ἐπαναπαύσεται ἐπ' αὐτὸν ἡ εἰρήνη ὑμῶν· εἰ δὲ
of peace, shall rest upon it the peace of you; if but
7 μήγε, ἐφ' ὑμᾶς ἀνακάμψει. ἐν αὐτῇ δὲ τῇ οἰκίᾳ μένετε, ἐσθίον-
not so, on you it shall return. In same And the house remain, eating
τες καὶ πίνοντες τὰ παρ' αὐτῶν· ἄξιος γὰρ ὁ ἐργάτης τοῦ
and drinking the things with them; worthy for the worker of the
8 μισθοῦ αὐτοῦ ἐστι. μὴ μεταβαίνετε ἐξ οἰκίας εἰς οἰκίαν. καὶ
pay of him is. Do not move from house to house. And
εἰς ἣν δ' ἂν πόλιν εἰσέρχησθε, καὶ δέχωνται ὑμᾶς, ἐσθίετε τὰ
into whatever city you enter, and they receive you, eat the things
9 παρατιθέμενα ὑμῖν, καὶ θεραπεύετε τοὺς ἐν αὐτῇ ἀσθενεῖς,
being set before you, and heal the in it sick,
καὶ λέγετε αὐτοῖς, Ἤγγικεν ἐφ' ὑμᾶς ἡ βασιλεία τοῦ Θεοῦ.
and say to them, has drawn near on you the kingdom — of God.
10 εἰς ἣν δ' ἂν πόλιν εἰσέρχησθε, καὶ μὴ δέχωνται ὑμᾶς, ἐξελ-
And into whatever city you enter, and not they receive you, going
11 θόντες εἰς τὰς πλατείας αὐτῆς εἴπατε, Καὶ τὸν κονιορτὸν τὸν
out into the streets of it say, Even the dust —
κολληθέντα ἡμῖν ἐκ τῆς πόλεως ὑμῶν ἀπομασσόμεθα ὑμῖν·
clinging to us out of the city of you we shake off to you
πλὴν τοῦτο γινώσκετε, ὅτι ἤγγικεν ἐφ' ὑμᾶς ἡ βασιλεία τοῦ
yet this know, that has drawn near on you the kingdom
12 Θεοῦ. λέγω δὲ ὑμῖν, ὅτι Σοδόμοις ἐν τῇ ἡμέρᾳ ἐκείνῃ ἀνε-
of God. I say And to you that for Sodom in — day that more
13 κτότερον ἔσται, ἢ τῇ πόλει ἐκείνῃ. οὐαί σοι, Χωραζίν, οὐαί
tolerable it will be than — city for that. Woe to you, Chorazin! Woe
σοι, Βηθσαϊδά· ὅτι εἰ ἐν Τύρῳ καὶ Σιδῶνι ἐγένοντο αἱ δυνά-
to you, Bethsaida! For if in Tyre and Sidon happened the works
μεις αἱ γενόμεναι ἐν ὑμῖν, πάλαι ἂν ἐν σάκκῳ καὶ σποδῷ
of power happening in you, long ago — in sackcloth and ashes
14 καθήμεναι μετενόησαν. πλὴν Τύρῳ καὶ Σιδῶνι ἀνεκτότερον
sitting they would have repented. But for Tyre and Sidon more tolerable
15 ἔσται ἐν τῇ κρίσει, ἢ ὑμῖν. καὶ σύ, Καπερναούμ, ἡ ἕως τοῦ
it will be in the Judgment than for you. And you, Capernaum, not to —
16 οὐρανοῦ ὑψωθεῖσα, ἕως ᾅδου καταβιβασθήσῃ. ὁ ἀκούων
Heaven were you lifted? To Hades you will come down. He hearing
ὑμῶν ἐμοῦ ἀκούει· καὶ ὁ ἀθετῶν ὑμᾶς ἐμὲ ἀθετεῖ· ὁ δὲ ἐμὲ
you Me hears, and he rejecting you Me rejects; he and Me
ἀθετῶν ἀθετεῖ τὸν ἀποστείλαντά με.
rejecting rejects the (One) having sent Me.
17 Ὑπέστρεψαν δὲ οἱ ἑβδομήκοντα μετὰ χαρᾶς, λέγοντες,
returned And the seventy with joy, saying,
Κύριε, καὶ τὰ δαιμόνια ὑποτάσσεται ἡμῖν ἐν τῷ ὀνόματί
Lord, even the demons submit to us in the name
18 σου. εἶπε δὲ αὐτοῖς, Ἐθεώρουν τὸν Σατανᾶν ὡς ἀστραπὴν
of You. He said But to them, I saw — Satan as lightning
19 ἐκ τοῦ οὐρανοῦ πεσόντα. ἰδού, δίδωμι ὑμῖν τὴν ἐξουσίαν
out of — Heaven fall. Behold, I give you the authority
τοῦ πατεῖν ἐπάνω ὄφεων καὶ σκορπίων, καὶ ἐπὶ πᾶσαν τὴν
— to tread on snakes and scorpions, and on all the
20 δύναμιν τοῦ ἐχθροῦ· καὶ οὐδὲν ὑμᾶς οὐ μὴ ἀδικήσει. πλὴν
power of the enemy, and nothing you in no way shall hurt. But
ἐν τούτῳ μὴ χαίρετε ὅτι τὰ πνεύματα ὑμῖν ὑποτάσσεται·
in this stop rejoicing that the spirits to you submit,

rejoice that your names are written in Heaven.

21 In the same hour Jesus rejoiced in the Spirit, and said, I praise You, Father, Lord of Heaven and of earth, that You hid these things from *the* sophisticated and cunning, and revealed them to babes; yes, Father, because so it was pleasing before You.

22 And having turned to the disciples alone, He said, 22 All things were delivered to Me by My Father, and no one knows who the Son is, except the Father; and who the Father is, except the Son, and whoever the son may desire to reveal *Him*. 23 And turning to the disciples private, He said, Blessed are the eyes seeing what you see. 24 For I say to you that many prophets and kings desired to see what you see, and did not see; and to hear what you hear, and did not hear.

25 And behold, a certain doctor of the Law stood up, tempting Him and saying, Teacher, what shall I do that I may inherit eternal life? 26 And He said to him, What has been written in the Law? How do you read *it*? 27 And answering he said, You shall love *the* Lord your God with all your heart, and with all your soul, and with all your strength, and with all your mind; and your neighbor as yourself. 28 And He said to him, You have answered rightly; do this, and you shall live.

29 But desiring to justify himself, he said to Jesus, And who is my neighbor? 30 And taking *it* up, Jesus said, A certain man was going down from Jerusalem to Jericho, and fell among robbers who both having stripped him and having inflicted wounds went away, having left *him*, being half-dead. 31 But by circumstance, a certain priest went down on that road, and

χαίρετε δὲ μᾶλλον ὅτι τὰ ὀνόματα ὑμῶν ἐγράφη ἐν τοῖς
rejoice but rather that the names of you are written in the
οὐρανοις.
heavens.

21 Ἐν αὐτῃ τῇ ὥρᾳ ἠγαλλιάσατο τῷ πνεύματι ὁ Ἰησοῦς
In same the hour exulted in the Spirit — Jesus
καὶ εἶπεν, Ἐξομολογοῦμαί σοι, πάτερ, Κύριε τοῦ οὐρανοῦ
and said, I praise You, Father, Lord — of Heaven
καὶ τῆς γῆς, ὅτι ἀπέκρυψας ταῦτα ἀπὸ σοφῶν καὶ συνετῶν,
and — of earth, for You hid these things from sophisticated and cunning
καὶ ἀπεκάλυψας αὐτὰ νηπίοις· ναί, ὁ πατήρ, ὅτι οὕτως
and revealed them to babes; yes, — Father, because thus
22 ἐγένετο εὐδοκία ἔμπροσθέν σου. πάντα παρεδόθη μοι ὑπὸ
it was well pleasing before You. All things were delivered to Me by
τοῦ πατρός μου· καὶ οὐδεὶς γινώσκει τίς ἐστιν ὁ υἱός, εἰ μὴ
the Father of Me, and no one knows who is the Son, except
ὁ πατήρ, καὶ τίς ἐστιν ὁ πατήρ, εἰ μὴ ὁ υἱός, καὶ ᾧ ἐὰν
the Father, and who is the Father, except the Son, and whoever
23 βούληται ὁ υἱὸς ἀποκαλύψαι. καὶ στραφεὶς πρὸς τοὺς
may desire the Son to reveal (Him). And having turned to the
μαθητὰς κατ᾽ ἰδίαν εἶπε, Μακάριοι οἱ ὀφθαλμοὶ οἱ βλέποντες
disciples, privately He said, Blessed the eyes — seeing
24 ἃ βλέπετε. λέγω γὰρ ὑμῖν, ὅτι πολλοὶ προφῆται καὶ
what you see. I say For to you that many prophets and
βασιλεῖς ἠθέλησαν ἰδεῖν ἃ ὑμεῖς βλέπετε, καὶ οὐκ εἶδον· καὶ
kings desired to see what you see, and not did see; and
ἀκοῦσαι ἃ ἀκούετε, καὶ οὐκ ἤκουσαν.
to hear what you hear, and not did hear.

25 Καὶ ἰδού, νομικός τις ἀνέστη, ἐκπειράζων αὐτόν, καὶ
And behold, lawyer a certain stood up, tempting Him, and
λέγων, Διδάσκαλε, τί ποιήσας ζωὴν αἰώνιον κληρονομήσω;
said, Teacher, what doing life eternal I may inherit?
26 ὁ δὲ εἶπε πρὸς αὐτόν, Ἐν τῷ νόμῳ τί γέγραπται; πῶς
He And said to him, In the law what is written? How
27 ἀναγινώσκεις; ὁ δὲ ἀποκριθεὶς εἶπεν, Ἀγαπήσεις Κύριον
do you read? he And answering said, You shall love (the) Lord
τὸν Θεόν σου, ἐξ ὅλης τῆς καρδίας σου, καὶ ἐξ ὅλης τῆς
the God of you from all the heart of you, and from all the
ψυχῆς σου, καὶ ἐξ ὅλης τῆς ἰσχύος σου, καὶ ἐξ ὅλης τῆς
soul of you, and from all the strength of you, and from all the
28 διανοίας σου· καὶ τὸν πλησίον σου ὡς σεαυτόν. εἶπε δὲ
mind of you; and the neighbor of you as yourself. He said And
29 αὐτῷ, Ὀρθῶς ἀπεκρίθης· τοῦτο ποίει, καὶ ζήσῃ. ὁ δὲ θέλων
to him, Rightly you answered; this do, and you will live. he But willing
δικαιοῦν ἑαυτὸν εἶπε πρὸς τὸν Ἰησοῦν, Καὶ τίς ἐστί μου
to justify himself said to — Jesus, And who is of me
30 πλησίον; ὑπολαβὼν δὲ ὁ Ἰησοῦς εἶπεν, Ἄνθρωπός τις
neighbor? Taking (it) up And, — Jesus said, man A certain
κατέβαινεν ἀπὸ Ἱερουσαλὴμ εἰς Ἱεριχώ καὶ λησταῖς
was going down from Jerusalem to Jericho, and robbers
περιέπεσεν, οἳ καὶ ἐκδύσαντες αὐτὸν καὶ πληγὰς ἐπιθέντες
fell in with, who both stripping him and blows laying on,
31 ἀπῆλθον, ἀφέντες ἡμιθανῆ τυγχάνοντα. κατὰ συγκυρίαν
went away, leaving (him) half dead being. by a coincidence
δὲ ἱερεύς τις κατέβαινεν ἐν τῇ ὁδῷ ἐκείνῃ· καὶ ἰδὼν αὐτὸν
And priest a certain was going in — way that and seeing him

having seen him, he passed by on the opposite side. [32]And in the same way a Levite, also being at the place, having come and seeing him, passed by opposite.

[33]But a certain traveling Samaritan came upon him, and seeing him, *he* was filled with pity. [34]And coming near, *he* bound up his wounds, pouring on oil and wine. And putting him on his own animal, *he* brought him to an inn, and cared for him. [35]And going forth on the morrow, having taken out two denarii, he gave *them* to the innkeeper, and said to him, Care for him, and whatever more you spend, I on my return will repay to you.

[36]Who, then, of these three seems to you to have become a neighbor to the one having fallen among the robbers? [37]And he said, The *one* having done the *deed of* mercy with him. Then Jesus said to him, Go, and you do likewise.

[38]And as they went on, it happened *that* He also entered into a certain village. And a certain woman, Martha by name, received Him into her house. [39]And she had a sister called Mary, who, even sitting alongside at the feet of Jesus, heard His word. [40]But Martha was distracted about much serving, and coming forward she said, Lord, do You not care that my sister has left me alone to serve? Then tell her that she should help me! [41]But answering, Jesus said to her, Martha, Martha, you are anxious and troubled about many things, [42]but there is need of *only* one; and Mary has chosen the good portion, which shall not be taken away from her.

CHAPTER 11

[1]And it happened as He was praying in a certain place, when He ceased, one of His disciples said to Him, Lord, teach us to pray, as John also taught his dis-

32 ἀντιπαρῆλθεν. ὁμοίως δὲ καὶ Λευΐτης γενόμενος κατὰ τὸν
passed opposite. likewise And also a Levite being at the
33 τόπον ἐλθὼν καὶ ἰδὼν ἀντιπαρῆλθε. Σαμαρείτης δέ τις
place, coming and seeing, passed opposite. Samaritan But a certain
ὁδεύων ἦλθε κατ' αὐτόν, καὶ ἰδὼν αὐτὸν ἐσπλαγχνίσθη,
traveling came upon him, and seeing him was filled with pity;
34 καὶ προσελθὼν κατέδησε τὰ τραύματα αὐτοῦ, ἐπιχέων
and coming up bound up the wounds of him, pouring
ἔλαιον καὶ οἶνον· ἐπιβιβάσας δὲ αὐτὸν ἐπὶ τὸ ἴδιον κτῆνος,
oil and wine, placing and him on the own beast
35 ἤγαγεν αὐτὸν εἰς πανδοχεῖον, καὶ ἐπεμελήθη αὐτοῦ. καὶ ἐπὶ
brought him to an inn, and cared for him. And on
τὴν αὔριον ἐξελθών, ἐκβαλὼν δύο δηνάρια ἔδωκε τῷ παν-
the morrow going out, taking out two denarii he gave to the inn-
δοχεῖ, καὶ εἶπεν αὐτῷ, Ἐπιμελήθητι αὐτοῦ· καὶ ὅ τι ἂν
keeper, and said to him, care for him, and whatever
προσδαπανήσῃς, ἐγὼ ἐν τῷ ἐπανέρχεσθαί με ἀποδώσω σοι.
you spend more, I in the returning (of) me will repay you.
36 τίς οὖν τούτων τῶν τριῶν δοκεῖ σοι πλησίον γεγονέναι
Who, then, of these — three seems it to you neighbor to have become
37 τοῦ ἐμπεσόντος εἰς τοὺς λῃστάς; ὁ δὲ εἶπεν, Ὁ ποιήσας τὸ
of those falling among the robbers? he And said, The (one) doing the
ἔλεος μετ' αὐτοῦ. εἶπεν οὖν αὐτῷ ὁ Ἰησοῦς, Πορεύου, καὶ
mercy with him. said Then to him — Jesus, Go, and
σὺ ποίει ὁμοίως.
you do likewise.
38 Ἐγένετο δὲ ἐν τῷ πορεύεσθαι αὐτούς, καὶ αὐτὸς εἰσῆλθεν
it occurred And in the going (of) them, also He entered
εἰς κώμην τινά· γυνὴ δέ τις ὀνόματι Μάρθα ὑπεδέξατο
into village a certain. woman And a certain by name Martha received
39 αὐτὸν εἰς τὸν οἶκον αὐτῆς. καὶ τῇδε ἦν ἀδελφὴ καλουμένη
Him into the house of her. And to this was a sister being called
Μαρία, ἣ καὶ παρακαθίσασα παρὰ τοὺς πόδας τοῦ Ἰησοῦ
Mary, who also sitting beside at the feet of Jesus
40 ἤκουε τὸν λόγον αὐτοῦ. ἡ δὲ Μάρθα περιεσπᾶτο περὶ
heard the word of Him. — But Martha was distracted about
πολλὴν διακονίαν· ἐπιστᾶσα δὲ εἶπε, Κύριε, οὐ μέλει σοι ὅτι
much serving; coming on And she said, Lord, not a care to You that
ἡ ἀδελφή μου μόνην με κατέλιπε διακονεῖν; εἰπὲ οὖν αὐτῇ
the sister of me alone me left to serve? tell Then her
41 ἵνα μοι συναντιλάβηται. ἀποκριθεὶς δὲ εἶπεν αὐτῇ ὁ Ἰησοῦς,
that me she should help. answering And said to her — Jesus,
Μάρθα, Μάρθα, μεριμνᾷς καὶ τυρβάζῃ περὶ πολλά· ἑνὸς
Martha, Martha, you are anxious and troubled about many things of one
42 δέ ἐστι χρεία· Μαρία δὲ τὴν ἀγαθὴν μερίδα ἐξελέξατο, ἥτις
but is need; Mary and the good part chose, which
οὐκ ἀφαιρεθήσεται ἀπ' αὐτῆς.
not shall be taken from her.

CHAPTER 11

1 Καὶ ἐγένετο ἐν τῷ εἶναι αὐτὸν ἐν τόπῳ τινὶ προσευχό-
And it was in the being (of) Him in place a certain praying,
μενον, ὡς ἐπαύσατο, εἶπέ τις τῶν μαθητῶν αὐτοῦ πρὸς
as He ceased, said a certain one of the disciples of Him to
αὐτόν, Κύριε, δίδαξον ἡμᾶς προσεύχεσθαι, καθὼς καὶ
Him, Lord, teach us to pray, even as also

ciples.[2] And He said to them, When you pray, say:

Our Father who *is* in Heaven, holy be Your name. May Your kingdom come; may Your will be done on earth as *it* also *is* in Heaven. [3]Give us our needed bread day by day; [4]and forgive us our sins, for we ourselves also forgive everyone indebted to us. And lead us not into temptation, but deliver us from evil.

[5]And He said to them, Who of you shall have a friend, and will come to him at midnight and say to him, Friend, lend me three loaves. [6]*For* a friend of mine arrived to me from a journey, and I do not have what I may set before him. [7]And he answering from within may say, Do not cause Me troubles. The door has already been shut, and my children are in bed with me. I cannot rise up to give to you. [8]I say to you, Even if he will not give to him, rising up because he is *a* friend, yet because of his shameless insisting, rising up he will give him as many as he needs.

[9]And I say to you, Ask, and it will be opened to you. [10]For everyone who asks receives. And those who seek find. And to the ones knocking, it will be opened. [11]And what father of you, *if* the son asks *for* bread, will he give him a stone? And if a fish, will he give him a snake instead of a fish? [12]And if he should ask an egg, will he give him a scorpion? [13]If, then, you being evil know to give good gifts to your children, how much more the Father out of Heaven will give *the* Holy Spirit to the ones asking Him.

[14]And he was casting out a demon, and it was dumb. And the demon going out, the dumb one spoke. And

2 Ἰωάννης ἐδίδαξε τοὺς μαθητὰς αὐτοῦ. εἶπε δὲ αὐτοῖς,
John taught the disciples of him. He said And to them,
Ὅταν προσεύχησθε, λέγετε, Πάτερ ἡμῶν ὁ ἐν τοῖς οὐρανοῖς
When you pray, say, Father Our, who in the heavens,
ἁγιασθήτω τὸ ὄνομά σου. ἐλθέτω ἡ βασιλεία σου. γενηθήτω
holy be the name of You; let come the kingdom of You. Let be done
3 τὸ θέλημά σου, ὡς ἐν οὐρανῷ, καὶ ἐπὶ τῆς γῆς. τὸν ἄρτον
the will of You, as in Heaven, also on the earth. The bread
4 ἡμῶν τὸν ἐπιούσιον δίδου ἡμῖν τὸ καθ' ἡμέραν. καὶ ἄφες
of us the needed give us — day by day. And forgive
ἡμῖν τὰς ἁμαρτίας ἡμῶν, καὶ γὰρ αὐτοὶ ἀφίεμεν παντὶ
us the sins of us, also for ourselves we forgive everyone
ὀφείλοντι ἡμῖν. καὶ μὴ εἰσενέγκῃς ἡμᾶς εἰς πειρασμόν, ἀλλὰ
indebted to us. And do not lead us into temptation, but
ῥῦσαι ἡμᾶς ἀπὸ τοῦ πονηροῦ.
deliver us from — evil.
5 Καὶ εἶπε πρὸς αὐτούς, Τίς ἐξ ὑμῶν ἕξει φίλον, καὶ πορεύ-
And He said to them, Who of you shall have a friend, and will
σεται πρὸς αὐτὸν μεσονυκτίου, καὶ εἴπῃ αὐτῷ, Φίλε,
come to him at midnight, and say to him, Friend,
6 χρῆσόν μοι τρεῖς ἄρτους, ἐπειδὴ φίλος μου παρεγένετο ἐξ
lend me three loaves, since a friend of me arrived off
7 ὁδοῦ πρός με, καὶ οὐκ ἔχω ὃ παραθήσω αὐτῷ· κἀκεῖνος
a journey to me, and not I have what I may set before him; and that one
ἔσωθεν ἀποκριθεὶς εἴπῃ, Μή μοι κόπους πάρεχε· ἤδη ἡ
within answering may say, Not me troubles cause; now the
θύρα κέκλεισται, καὶ τὰ παιδία μου μετ' ἐμοῦ εἰς τὴν κοίτην
door has been shut, and the children of me with me in the bed
8 εἰσίν· οὐ δύναμαι ἀναστὰς δοῦναί σοι. λέγω ὑμῖν, εἰ καὶ
are; not I am able rising up to give you. I say to you, if even
οὐ δώσει αὐτῷ ἀναστάς, διὰ τὸ εἶναι αὐτοῦ φίλον, διά γε
not he will give him, rising up on account of being of him friend, yet because of
τὴν ἀναίδειαν αὐτοῦ ἐγερθεὶς δώσει αὐτῷ ὅσων χρῄζει.
the importunity of him rising he will give him as many as he needs.
9 κἀγὼ ὑμῖν λέγω, Αἰτεῖτε, καὶ δοθήσεται ὑμῖν· ζητεῖτε, καὶ
And I to you say, Ask, and it will be given to you; seek, and
10 εὑρήσετε· κρούετε, καὶ ἀνοιγήσεται ὑμῖν. πᾶς γὰρ ὁ αἰτῶν
you will find; knock, and it will be opened to you. everyone For asking
λαμβάνει· καὶ ὁ ζητῶν εὑρίσκει· καὶ τῷ κρούοντι ἀνοιγή-
receives, and those seeking finds, and to those knocking, it will be
11 σεται. τίνα δὲ ὑμῶν τὸν πατέρα αἰτήσει ὁ υἱὸς ἄρτον, μὴ
opened. what And of you — father (of whom) asks the son bread,
λίθον ἐπιδώσει αὐτῷ; εἰ καὶ ἰχθύν, μὴ ἀντὶ ἰχθύος ὄφιν
a stone will he give him? if And a fish, instead of a fish, a snake
12 ἐπιδώσει αὐτῷ; ἢ καὶ ἐὰν αἰτήσῃ ᾠόν, μὴ ἐπιδώσει αὐτῷ
will he give him? Or also if he should ask an egg, will he give to him
13 σκορπίον; εἰ οὖν ὑμεῖς πονηροὶ ὑπάρχοντες οἴδατε ἀγαθὰ
a scorpion? If, then, you evil being know good
δόματα διδόναι τοῖς τέκνοις ὑμῶν, πόσῳ μᾶλλον ὁ πατὴρ
gifts to give to the children of you, how much more the Father
ὁ ἐξ οὐρανοῦ δώσει Πνεῦμα Ἅγιον τοῖς αἰτοῦσιν αὐτόν;
of Heaven will give (the) Spirit Holy to those asking Him.
14 Καὶ ἦν ἐκβάλλων δαιμόνιον, καὶ αὐτὸ ἦν κωφόν. ἐγένετο
And He was casting out a demon, and it was dumb. it was
δέ, τοῦ δαιμονίου ἐξελθόντος, ἐλάλησεν ὁ κωφός· καὶ
And, the demon going out, spoke the dumb one. And

the crowds marveled. 15 But some of them said, He casts out the demons by Beelzebub the chief of the demons. 16 And others tempting were seeking from Him a sign from Heaven. 17 But knowing their thoughts, He said to them, Every kingdom divided against itself is brought to ruin. And a house against a house falls. 18 And also if Satan is divided against himself, how shall his kingdom stand?—Because you say I cast out the demons by Beelzebub. 19 And if I cast out the demons by Beelzebub, by whom do your sons cast out? Because of this they shall be your judges. 20 But if I cast out the demons by *the* finger of God, then the kingdom of God has come upon you.

21 When the strong one being armed guards his dwelling, his goods are in peace. 22 But as soon as one stronger than he comes, *he* overcomes him; he takes away his armor on which he relied, and deals out his arms. 23 The *one* not being with Me is against Me. And the *one* not gathering with me scatters. 24 When the unclean spirit goes out from the man, he goes through dry places seeking rest. And not finding, *he* says, I will return to my house from where I came out. 25 And coming he finds *it* swept and decorated. 26 Then he goes and takes seven other spirits more wicked than himself; and entering he lives there. And the last things of that man becomes worse than the first.

27 And *as* He spoke these things, it happened that a certain woman lifted up *her* voice out of the crowd *and* said to Him, Blessed *is* the womb having borne You, and *the* breasts which You sucked. 28 And He said, No, rather, blessed *are* those hearing the word of God, and keeping it.

15 ἐθαύμασαν οἱ ὄχλοι. τινὲς δὲ ἐξ αὐτῶν εἶπον, Ἐν Βεελζεβοὺλ
marveled the crowds. some But of them said, By Beelzebub
16 ἄρχοντι τῶν δαιμονίων ἐκβάλλει τὰ δαιμόνια. ἕτεροι δὲ
the chief of the demons He casts out the demons. others And
17 πειράζοντες σημεῖον παρ' αὐτοῦ ἐζήτουν ἐξ οὐρανοῦ. αὐτὸς
tempting a sign from Him were seeking from Heaven. He
δὲ εἰδὼς αὐτῶν τὰ διανοήματα εἶπεν αὐτοῖς, Πᾶσα βασιλεία
But knowing of them the thoughts said to them, Every kingdom
ἐφ' ἑαυτὴν διαμερισθεῖσα ἐρημοῦται· καὶ οἶκος ἐπὶ οἶκον,
against itself divided is brought to ruin, and a house against a house
18 πίπτει. εἰ δὲ καὶ ὁ Σατανᾶς ἐφ' ἑαυτὸν διεμερίσθη, πῶς
falls. if And also — Satan against himself is divided, how
σταθήσεται ἡ βασιλεία αὐτοῦ; ὅτι λέγετε, ἐν Βεελζεβοὺλ
shall stand the kingdom of him? Because you say by Beelzebub
19 ἐκβάλλειν με τὰ δαιμόνια. εἰ δὲ ἐγὼ ἐν Βεελζεβοὺλ ἐκβάλλω
casting out I (am) the demons. if But I by Beelzebub cast out
τὰ δαιμόνια, οἱ υἱοὶ ὑμῶν ἐν τίνι ἐκβάλλουσι; διὰ τοῦτο
the demons, the sons of you, by what do they cast out? Therefore
20 κριταὶ ὑμῶν αὐτοὶ ἔσονται. εἰ δὲ ἐν δακτύλῳ Θεοῦ ἐκβάλλω
judges of you they shall be. **if But by (the) finger of God I cast out**
τὰ δαιμόνια, ἄρα ἔφθασεν ἐφ' ὑμᾶς ἡ βασιλεία τοῦ Θεοῦ.
the demons, then came upon you the kingdom — of God.
21 ὅταν ὁ ἰσχυρὸς καθωπλισμένος φυλάσσῃ τὴν ἑαυτοῦ αὐλήν,
When the strong one being armed guards the dwelling of him,
22 ἐν εἰρήνῃ ἐστὶ τὰ ὑπάρχοντα αὐτοῦ· ἐπὰν δὲ ὁ ἰσχυρότερος
in peace are the goods of him. when But one stronger
αὐτοῦ ἐπελθὼν νικήσῃ αὐτόν, τὴν πανοπλίαν αὐτοῦ αἴρει
(than) him coming overcomes him, the armor of him he takes,
23 ἐφ' ᾗ ἐπεποίθει, καὶ τὰ σκῦλα αὐτοῦ διαδίδωσιν. ὁ μὴ ὢν
on which he relied, and the arms of him distributes. Those not being
μετ' ἐμοῦ κατ' ἐμοῦ ἐστι· καὶ ὁ μὴ συνάγων μετ' ἐμοῦ σκορπί-
with Me, against Me is! And those not gathering with Me, scatters!
24 ζει. ὅταν τὸ ἀκάθαρτον πνεῦμα ἐξέλθῃ ἀπὸ τοῦ ἀνθρώπου,
When the unclean spirit goes out from the man,
διέρχεται δι' ἀνύδρων τόπων, ζητοῦν ἀνάπαυσιν· καὶ μὴ
he goes through dry places seeking rest, and not
εὑρίσκον λέγει, Ὑποστρέψω εἰς τὸν οἶκόν μου ὅθεν ἐξῆλθον.
finding says, I will return to the house of me from where I came.
25 καὶ ἐλθὸν εὑρίσκει σεσαρωμένον καὶ κεκοσμημένον. τότε
And coming he finds (it) having been swept and decorated. Then
26 πορεύεται καὶ παραλαμβάνει ἑπτὰ ἕτερα πνεύματα πονηρό-
he goes and takes seven other spirits more wicked
τερα ἑαυτοῦ, καὶ εἰσελθόντα κατοικεῖ ἐκεῖ· καὶ γίνεται τὰ
(than) himself, and entering he lives there; and becomes the
ἔσχατα τοῦ ἀνθρώπου ἐκείνου χείρονα τῶν πρώτων.
last things — man of that worse (than) the first.
27 Ἐγένετο δὲ ἐν τῷ λέγειν αὐτὸν ταῦτα, ἐπάρασά τις γυνὴ
it was And in the saying (of) Him these things, lifting a certain woman
φωνὴν ἐκ τοῦ ὄχλου εἶπεν αὐτῷ, Μακαρία ἡ κοιλία ἡ βαστά-
(her) voice out of the crowd said to Him, Blessed the womb having
28 σασά σε, καὶ μαστοὶ οὓς ἐθήλασας. αὐτὸς δὲ εἶπε, Μενοῦνγε
borne You, and (the) breasts which You sucked. He But said, No, rather
μακάριοι οἱ ἀκούοντες τὸν λόγον τοῦ Θεοῦ καὶ φυλάσσοντες
blessed those hearing the word of God and keeping
αὐτόν.
it.

[29]But the crowds pressing on *Him,* He began to say, This is an evil generation. It seeks a sign, and a sign will not be given to it, except the sign of Jonah the prophet. [30]For Jonah became a sign to the Ninevites; so also the Son of man will be to this generation. [31]*The* queen of *the* south will be raised in the Judgment with the men of this generation, and will condemn them, because she came from the ends of the earth to hear the wisdom of Solomon. And, behold, a Greater-than-Solomon *is* here. [32]Men, Ninevites will rise up in the Judgment with this generation, and will condemn it, because they repented at the preaching of Jonah. And, behold, a Greater-than-Jonah *is* here.

[33]But no one having lit a lamp places *it* in secret, nor under the grain-measure, but on the lampstand, that the ones entering may see the light. [34]The lamp of the body is the eye. Then when your eye is sound, also all your body is light. But when it is evil, also your body *is* dark. [35]Watch, then, that the light in you is not darkness. [36]If, then, your whole body *is* light, not having any part dark, all will be light, as when the lamp enlightens you with *its* shining.

[37]And *as He was* speaking, a certain Pharisee asked Him that He would dine with him. And going in, He reclined. [38]But watching, the Pharisee marveled that He did not first wash before the dinner. [39]But the Lord said to him, Now you Pharisees cleanse the outside of the cup and of the dish, but your inside is full of robbery and wickedness. [40]Fools! Did not He who made the outside also make the inside? [41]But give alms *of* the things which are within, and behold, all things *are* clean to you.

29 Τῶν δὲ ὄχλων ἐπαθροιζομένων ἤρξατο λέγειν, Ἡ γενεὰ
the And crowds pressing upon (Him), He began to say, generation
αὕτη πονηρά ἐστι· σημεῖον ἐπιζητεῖ, καὶ σημεῖον οὐ δοθή-
This an evil is. a sign It seeks, and a sign not will
30 σεται αὐτῇ, εἰ μὴ τὸ σημεῖον Ἰωνᾶ τοῦ προφήτου. καθὼς
be given to it, except the sign of Jonah the prophet. even as
γαρ ἐγένετο Ἰωνᾶς σημεῖον τοῖς Νινευΐταις οὕτως ἔσται
For became Jonah a sign to the Ninevites so will be
31 καὶ ὁ υἱὸς τοῦ ἀνθρώπου τῇ γενεᾷ ταύτῃ. βασίλισσα νότου
also the Son – of man – generation to this. (The) queen of south
ἐγερθήσεται ἐν τῇ κρίσει μετὰ τῶν ἀνδρῶν τῆς γενεᾶς ταύτης,
will be raised in the Judgment with the men – generation of this
καὶ κατακρινεῖ αὐτούς· ὅτι ἦλθεν ἐκ τῶν περάτων τῆς γῆς
and will condemn them; because she came from the ends of the earth
ἀκοῦσαι τὴν σοφίαν Σολομῶντος, καὶ ἰδού, πλεῖον Σολομῶν-
to hear the wisdom of Solomon, and behold, a greater than Solomon
32 τος ὧδε. ἄνδρες Νινευῒ ἀναστήσονται ἐν τῇ κρίσει μετὰ τῆς
(is) here. Men, Ninevites, will rise up in the Judgment with –
γενεᾶς ταύτης, καὶ κατακρινοῦσιν αὐτήν· ὅτι μετενόησαν
generation this, and will condemn it, because they repented
εἰς τὸ κήρυγμα Ἰωνᾶ, καὶ ἰδού, πλεῖον Ἰωνᾶ ὧδε.
at the preaching of Jonah; and behold, a greater than Jonah (is) here.

33 Οὐδεὶς δὲ λύχνον ἅψας εἰς κρυπτὸν τίθησιν, οὐδὲ ὑπὸ τὸν
No one But a lamp having lit in secret places (it), nor under the
μόδιον, ἀλλ' ἐπὶ τὴν λυχνίαν, ἵνα οἱ εἰσπορευόμενοι τὸ
grain-measure, but on the lampstand, that the (ones) entering the
34 φέγγος βλέπωσιν. ὁ λύχνος τοῦ σώματός ἐστιν ὁ ὀφθαλμός·
light may see. The lamp of the body is the eye.
ὅταν οὖν ὁ ὀφθαλμός σου ἁπλοῦς ᾖ, καὶ ὅλον τὸ σῶμά σου
When Then the eye of you single is, also all the body of you
φωτεινόν ἐστιν· ἐπὰν δὲ πονηρὸς ᾖ, καὶ τὸ σῶμά σου σκο-
bright is; when but evil it is, also the body of you (is)
35 τεινόν. σκόπει οὖν μὴ τὸ φῶς τὸ ἐν σοὶ σκότος ἐστίν. εἰ οὖν
dark. Watch, then, lest the light – in you darkness is. If, then,
36 τὸ σῶμά σου ὅλον φωτεινόν μὴ ἔχον τι μέρος σκοτεινόν
the body of you whole (is) bright, not having any part dark,
ἔσται φωτεινὸν ὅλον, ὡς ὅταν ὁ λύχνος τῇ ἀστραπῇ
will be bright all, as when the lamp with the shining
φωτίζῃ σε.
enlightens you.

37 Ἐν δὲ τῷ λαλῆσαι, ἠρώτα αὐτὸν Φαρισαῖός τις ὅπως
in And the speaking, asked Him Pharisee certain that
38 ἀριστήσῃ παρ' αὐτῷ· εἰσελθὼν δὲ ἀνέπεσεν. ὁ δὲ Φαρισαῖος
He would dine with him; entering and He reclined. the But Pharisee
ἰδὼν ἐθαύμασεν ὅτι οὐ πρῶτον ἐβαπτίσθη πρὸ τοῦ ἀρίστου.
seeing marveled, that not first He washed before the dinner.
39 εἶπε δὲ ὁ Κύριος πρὸς αὐτόν, Νῦν ὑμεῖς οἱ Φαρισαῖοι τὸ
said But the Lord to him, Now you – Pharisees the
ἔξωθεν τοῦ ποτηρίου καὶ τοῦ πίνακος καθαρίζετε, τὸ δὲ
outside of the cup and of the dish cleanse, the but
40 ἔσωθεν υμων γέμει ἁρπαγῆς καὶ πονηρίας. ἄφρονες, οὐχ
inside of you is full of robbery and evil. Fools! Did not
41 ὁ ποιήσας τὸ ἔξωθεν καὶ τὸ ἔσωθεν ἐποίησε; πλὴν τὰ
the (One) making the outside also the inside make; But (of) the things
ἐνόντα δότε ἐλεημοσύνην· καὶ ἰδού, πάντα καθαρὰ ὑμῖν
being within give alms, and behold, all things clean to you

[42] But woe to you, Pharisees, for you pay tithes of the mint, and the rue, and every plant, and pass by the judgment and the love of God. It was right to do these things, but not to leave aside those. [43] Woe to you, Pharisees! For you love the chief seat in the synagogues, and the greetings in the markets. [44] Woe to you, scribes and Pharisees! Hypocrites! For you are as the unseen tombs, and the men walking above do not know.

[45] And answering one of the lawyers said to Him, Teacher, saying these things You also insult us. [46] And He said, Woe to you lawyers also! For you load men *with* burdens heavy to bear, and you yourselves do not touch the burdens with one of your fingers. [47] Woe to you! For you build the tombs of the prophets, and your fathers killed them. [48] So you bear witness and consent to the works of your fathers; for they indeed killed them, and you build their tombs. [49] And because of this the wisdom of God said, "I will send prophets and apostles to them, and *some* of them they will kill and drive out, [50] in order that the blood of all the prophets poured out from *the* foundation of *the* world may be required from this generation, [51] from the blood of Abel to the blood of Zechariah, *who* perished between the altar and the House." Yea, I say to you, it will be required from this generation. [52] Woe to you, lawyers! For you took the key of knowledge, *but* you yourselves did not enter, and you kept out those entering

[53] And as He was saying these things to them, the

ἐστιν.
is.

42 Ἀλλ᾽ οὐαὶ ὑμῖν τοῖς Φαρισαίοις, ὅτι ἀποδεκατοῦτε τὸ
But woe to you — Pharisees, because you tithe the
ἡδύοσμον καὶ τὸ πήγανον καὶ πᾶν λάχανον, καὶ παρέρ-
mint and the rue and every plant, and pass
χεσθε τὴν κρίσιν καὶ τὴν ἀγάπην τοῦ Θεοῦ· ταῦτα ἔδει
by the judgment and the love — of God; these things must
43 ποιῆσαι, κἀκεῖνα μὴ ἀφιέναι. οὐαὶ ὑμῖν τοῖς Φαρισαίοις,
(you) do, and those not to leave aside. Woe to you — Pharisees,
ὅτι ἀγαπᾶτε τὴν πρωτοκαθεδρίαν ἐν ταῖς συναγωγαῖς,
because you love the chief seat in the synagogues,
44 καὶ τοὺς ἀσπασμοὺς ἐν ταῖς ἀγοραῖς. οὐαὶ ὑμῖν, γραμματεῖς
and the greetings in the markets! Woe to you, scribes
καὶ Φαρισαῖοι, ὑποκριταί, ὅτι ἐστὲ ὡς τὰ μνημεῖα τὰ ἄδηλα,
and Pharisees, hypocrites! For you are as the tombs — unseen,
καὶ οἱ ἄνθρωποι οἱ περιπατοῦντες ἐπάνω οὐκ οἴδασιν.
and the men — walking over not do know.
45 Ἀποκριθεὶς δέ τις τῶν νομικῶν λέγει αὐτῷ, Διδάσκαλε,
answering And one of the lawyers says to Him, Teacher,
46 ταῦτα λέγων καὶ ἡμᾶς ὑβρίζεις. ὁ δὲ εἶπε, Καὶ ὑμῖν τοῖς
these things saying also us You insult. He And said, Also to you
νομικοῖς οὐαί, ὅτι φορτίζετε τοὺς ἀνθρώπους φορτία
lawyers, woe! Because you burden — men (with) burdens
δυσβάστακτα, καὶ αὐτοὶ ἑνὶ τῶν δακτύλων ὑμῶν οὐ
difficult to carry, and yourselves with one of the fingers of you not
47 προσψαύετε τοῖς φορτίοις. οὐαὶ ὑμῖν, ὅτι οἰκοδομεῖτε τὰ
you touch the burdens. Woe to you, because you build the
μνημεῖα τῶν προφητῶν, οἱ δὲ πατέρες ὑμῶν ἀπέκτειναν
tombs of the prophets, the and fathers of you killed
48 αὐτούς. ἄρα μαρτυρεῖτε καὶ συνευδοκεῖτε τοῖς ἔργοις τῶν
them! Then you witness and consent to the works of the
πατέρων ὑμῶν· ὅτι αὐτοὶ μὲν ἀπέκτειναν αὐτούς, ὑμεῖς δὲ
fathers of you; for they indeed killed them, you but
49 οἰκοδομεῖτε αὐτῶν τὰ μνημεῖα. διὰ τοῦτο καὶ ἡ σοφία τοῦ
build of them the tombs. Because of this also the wisdom —
Θεοῦ εἶπεν, Ἀποστελῶ εἰς αὐτοὺς προφήτας καὶ ἀποστό-
of God said, I will send to them prophets and apostles,
50 λους, καὶ ἐξ αὐτῶν ἀποκτενοῦσι καὶ ἐκδιώξουσιν· ἵνα
and of them they will kill and drive out, that
ἐκζητηθῇ τὸ αἷμα πάντων τῶν προφητῶν τὸ ἐκχυνόμενον
may be required the blood of all the prophets — having been shed
51 ἀπὸ καταβολῆς κόσμου ἀπὸ τῆς γενεᾶς ταύτης, ἀπὸ τοῦ
from (the) foundation of world from — generation this, from the
αἵματος Ἄβελ ἕως τοῦ αἵματος Ζαχαρίου τοῦ ἀπολομένου
blood of Abel until the blood of Zechariah — (who) perished
μεταξὺ τοῦ θυσιαστηρίου καὶ τοῦ οἴκου· ναί, λέγω ὑμῖν,
between the altar and the house; yes, I say to you,
52 ἐκζητηθήσεται ἀπὸ τῆς γενεᾶς ταύτης. οὐαὶ ὑμῖν τοῖς
it will be required from — generation this. Woe to you, —
νομικοῖς, ὅτι ἤρατε τὴν κλεῖδα τῆς γνώσεως· αὐτοὶ οὐκ
lawyers! Because you took the key — of knowledge; yourselves not
εἰσήλθετε, καὶ τοὺς εἰσερχομένους ἐκωλύσατε.
you entered, and those entering you kept out.
53 Λέγοντος δὲ αὐτοῦ ταῦτα πρὸς αὐτούς, ἤρξαντο οἱ
as was saying And He these things to them, began the

scribes and Pharisees began to be terribly angry, and to draw Him out concerning many things, 54 lying in ambush for Him, and seeking to catch something out of His mouth, so that they might accuse Him.

CHAPTER 12

1 During which things thousands of the crowd *were* assembled, so as to trample on one another. He began first to say to His disciples, Take heed to yourselves from the leaven of the Pharisees, which is hypocrisy. 2 But nothing is completely concealed which will not be uncovered; and hidden, which will not be known. 3 Therefore, whatever you said in the darkness, it will be heard in the light. And what you spoke to the ear in the secret rooms, *it* will be proclaimed on the housetops. 4 But I say to you, My friends, stop being afraid of those killing the body, and after these things are not able to do anything more. 5 But I will warn you whom you should fear: fear those who after the killing have authority to cast into Hell. Yea, I say to you, Fear this One!

6 Are not five sparrows sold *for* two assaria? Yet not one of them has been forgotten before God. 7 But even the hairs of your head have all been numbered. Then stop being afraid. You substantially differ from many sparrows. 8 And I say to you, Everyone who confesses Me before men, the Son of man will also confess him befroe the angels of God. 9 But the *one* denying Me before men will be denied before the angels of God. 10 And everyone who says a word against the Son of man, it will be forgiven him. But those blaspheming the Holy Spirit will not be forgiven. 11 And when they

γραμματεῖς καὶ οἱ Φαρισαῖοι δεινῶς ἐνέχειν, καὶ ἀποστο-
scribes and the Pharisees terribly to be angry, and to draw
54 ματίζειν αὐτὸν περὶ πλειόνων, ἐνεδρεύοντες αὐτόν, καὶ
out Him concerning many things, lying in wait for Him, and
ζητοῦντες θηρεῦσαί τι ἐκ τοῦ στόματος αὐτοῦ ἵνα κατηγορή-
seeking to catch something from the mouth of Him, that they might
σωσιν αὐτοῦ.
accuse Him.

CHAPTER 12

1 Ἐν οἷς ἐπισυναχθεισῶν τῶν μυριάδων τοῦ ὄχλου, ὥστε
In which things being assembled the thousands of the crowd, so as
καταπατεῖν ἀλλήλους, ἤρξατο λέγειν πρὸς τοὺς μαθητὰς
to trample on one another, He began to say to the disciples
αὐτοῦ πρῶτον, Προσέχετε ἑαυτοῖς ἀπὸ τῆς ζύμης τῶν
of Him first, Beware to yourselves from the leaven of the
2 Φαρισαίων, ἥτις ἐστὶν ὑπόκρισις. οὐδὲν δὲ συγκεκαλυμ-
Pharisees, which is hypocrisy. nothing And being completely
μένον ἐστίν, ὃ οὐκ ἀποκαλυφθήσεται, καὶ κρυπτόν, ὃ οὐ
concealed is, which not will be uncovered; and hidden, which not
3 γνωσθήσεται. ἀνθ' ὧν ὅσα ἐν τῇ σκοτίᾳ εἴπατε, ἐν τῷ φωτὶ
will be known. Therefore, what in the darkness you said, in the light
ἀκουσθήσεται· καὶ ὃ πρὸς τὸ οὖς ἐλαλήσατε ἐν τοῖς ταμείοις,
it will be heard; and what to the ear you spoke in the secret rooms,
4 κηρυχθήσεται ἐπὶ τῶν δωμάτων. λέγω δὲ ὑμῖν τοῖς φίλοις
will be proclaimed on the housetops. I say But to you, the friends
μου, Μὴ φοβηθῆτε ἀπὸ τῶν ἀποκτεινόντων τὸ σῶμα, καὶ
of Me, Stop being afraid from those killing the body, and
5 μετὰ ταῦτα μὴ ἐχόντων περισσότερόν τι ποιῆσαι. ὑποδείξω
after these things not having anything more — to do. I will warn
δὲ ὑμῖν τίνα φοβηθῆτε· φοβήθητε τὸν μετὰ τὸ ἀποκτεῖναι
But you whom you may fear, fear him after the killing
ἐξουσίαν ἔχοντα ἐμβαλεῖν εἰς τὴν γέενναν· ναί, λέγω ὑμῖν,
authority having to throw into Gehenna. Yes, I say to you,
6 τοῦτον φοβήθητε. οὐχὶ πέντε στρουθία πωλεῖται ἀσσαρίων
this one fear! not five sparrows Are sold (for) assaria
δύο ; καὶ ἓν ἐξ αὐτῶν οὐκ ἔστιν ἐπιλελησμένον ἐνώπιον τοῦ
two? And one of them not is having been forgotten before —
7 Θεοῦ. ἀλλὰ καὶ αἱ τρίχες τῆς κεφαλῆς ὑμῶν πᾶσαι ἠρίθ-
God. But even the hairs of the head of you all have been
μηνται. μὴ οὖν φοβεῖσθε· πολλῶν στρουθίων διαφέρετε.
numbered. stop, Then, being afraid; from many sparrows you differ.
8 λέγω δὲ ὑμῖν, Πᾶς ὃς ἂν ὁμολογήσῃ ἐν ἐμοὶ ἔμπροσθεν τῶν
I say And to you, everyone who confesses — Me before —
ἀνθρώπων, καὶ ὁ υἱὸς τοῦ ἀνθρώπου ὁμολογήσει ἐν αὐτῷ
men, also the Son — of man will confess — him
9 ἔμπροσθεν τῶν ἀγγέλων τοῦ Θεοῦ· ὁ δὲ ἀρνησάμενός με
before the angels — of God. he And denying Me
ἐνώπιον τῶν ἀνθρώπων ἀπαρνηθήσεται ἐνώπιον τῶν
before — men will be denied before the
10 ἀγγέλων τοῦ Θεοῦ. καὶ πᾶς ὃς ἐρεῖ λόγον εἰς τὸν υἱὸν τοῦ
angels — of God. And everyone who says a word against the Son —
ἀνθρώπου, ἀφεθήσεται αὐτῷ· τῷ δὲ εἰς τὸ Ἅγιον Πνεῦμα
of man, it will be forgiven him; to him but against the Holy Spirit
11 βλασφημήσαντι οὐκ ἀφεθήσεται. ὅταν δὲ προσφέρωσιν ὑμᾶς
blaspheming not will be forgiven. when And they bring in you

bring you in before synagogues and rulers and authorities, do not be anxious how or what you should answer, or what you should say. 12 For the Holy Spirit will teach you in that same hour what you ought to say.

13 And one from the crowd said to Him, Teacher, tell my brother to divide the inheritance with me. 14 But He said to him, Man, who appointed Me a judge or a divider over you? 15 And He said to them, Beware, and keep back from covetousness. For one's life is not in the abundance of the things which are to him. 16 And He spoke a parable to them, saying, A certain rich man produced well *from* the land. 17 And he reasoned within himself, saying, What may I do, for I do not have where I may gather my fruits? 18 And he said, I will do this; I will tear down my barns, and I will build larger. And I will gather there all my produce and my goods. 19 And I will say to my soul, Soul, you have many goods laid *up* for many years; take rest, eat, drink, be merry. 20 But God said to him, Fool! This night they demand your soul from you; and to whom will it be, that which you prepared? 21 This *is* the *one* treasuring up for himself, and not being rich to God.

22 And He said to His disciples, Because of this I say to you, Do not be anxious as to your life, what you should eat, nor for the body, what you should put on. 23 The life is more than the food, and the body than the clothing. 24 Consider the ravens, for they do not sow, nor do they reap; to which there is no storehouse, nor barn. And God feeds them. How much rather you substantially differ from the birds! 25 And who of you *by* being anxious is able to add one cubit to his stature? 26 Then if you are not able to do even *the* least, why are you anxious about the other things?

ἐπὶ τὰς συναγωγὰς καὶ τὰς ἀρχὰς καὶ τὰς ἐξουσίας, μὴ
before – synagogues and – rulers and – authorities, do not
12 μεριμνᾶτε πῶς ἢ τί ἀπολογήσησθε, ἢ τί εἴπητε· τὸ γὰρ
be anxious how or what you may answer, or what you may say; the for
Ἅγιον Πνεῦμα διδάξει ὑμᾶς ἐν αὐτῇ τῇ ὥρᾳ, ἃ δεῖ εἰπεῖν.
Holy Spirit will teach you in same the hour what must you say.
13 Εἶπε δέ τις αὐτῷ ἐκ τοῦ ὄχλου, Διδάσκαλε, εἰπὲ τῷ ἀδελφῷ
said And one to Him from the crowd, Teacher, tell the brother
14 μου μερίσασθαι μετ' ἐμοῦ τὴν κληρονομίαν. ὁ δὲ εἶπεν αὐτῷ,
of me to divide with me the inheritance. He But said to him,
Ἄνθρωπε, τίς με κατέστησε δικαστὴν ἢ μεριστὴν ἐφ' ὑμᾶς;
Man, who Me appointed a judge or a divider over you?
15 εἶπε δὲ πρὸς αὐτούς, Ὁρᾶτε καὶ φυλάσσεσθε ἀπὸ τῆς πλεονε-
He said And to them, Beware, and keep back from covetous-
ξίας· ὅτι οὐκ ἐν τῷ περισσεύειν τινὶ ἡ ζωὴ αὐτοῦ ἐστὶν ἐκ
ness; for not in the abundance to anyone the life of him is out of
16 τῶν ὑπαρχόντων αὐτοῦ. εἶπε δὲ παραβολὴν πρὸς αὐτούς,
the things existing of him. He spoke And a parable to them,
17 λέγων, Ἀνθρώπου τινὸς πλουσίου εὐφόρησεν ἡ χώρα· καὶ
saying, A man certain rich produced well the land. And
διελογίζετο ἐν ἑαυτῷ λέγων, Τί ποιήσω, ὅτι οὐκ ἔχω ποῦ
he reasoned within himself, saying, What may I do, because not I have where
18 συνάξω τοὺς καρπούς μου; καὶ εἶπε, Τοῦτο ποιήσω· καθελῶ
I may gather the fruits of me? And he said, This I will do; I will raze
μου τὰς ἀποθήκας, καὶ μείζονας οἰκοδομήσω, καὶ συνάξω
of me the barns, and larger I will build; and I will gather
19 ἐκεῖ πάντα τὰ γενήματά μου καὶ τὰ ἀγαθά μου. καὶ ἐρῶ
there all the produce of me and the goods of me; and I will say
τῇ ψυχῇ μου, Ψυχή, ἔχεις πολλὰ ἀγαθὰ κείμενα εἰς ἔτη
to the soul of me, Soul you have many goods laid (up) for years
20 πολλά· ἀναπαύου, φάγε, πίε, εὐφραίνου. εἶπε δὲ αὐτῷ ὁ
many; take rest, eat, drink, be glad. said But to him –
Θεός, Ἄφρον, ταύτῃ τῇ νυκτὶ τὴν ψυχήν σου ἀπαιτοῦσιν
God, Fool! This – night the soul of you they demand
21 ἀπὸ σοῦ· ἃ δὲ ἡτοίμασας, τίνι ἔσται; οὕτως ὁ θησαυρίζων
from you; that and you prepared, to whom will it be? So the (one) treasuring
ἑαυτῷ, καὶ μὴ εἰς Θεὸν πλουτῶν.
for himself, and not to God, (they) being rich.
22 Εἶπε δὲ πρὸς τοὺς μαθητὰς αὐτοῦ, Διὰ τοῦτο ὑμῖν λέγω,
He said And to the disciples of Him, For this reason to you I say,
μὴ μεριμνᾶτε τῇ ψυχῇ ὑμῶν, τί φάγητε· μηδὲ τῷ σώματι,
Stop being anxious for the life of you, what you eat, nor for the body,
23 τί ἐνδύσησθε. ἡ ψυχὴ πλεῖόν ἐστι τῆς τροφῆς, καὶ τὸ σῶμα
what you put on. The life more is (than) the food, and the body
24 τοῦ ἐνδύματος. κατανοήσατε τοὺς κόρακας, ὅτι οὐ σπεί-
(than) the clothing. Consider the ravens, for not they
ρουσιν, οὐδὲ θερίζουσιν, οἷς οὐκ ἔστι ταμεῖον οὐδὲ ἀποθήκη,
sow, nor do they reap, to which not is storehouse nor barn
καὶ ὁ Θεὸς τρέφει αὐτούς· πόσῳ μᾶλλον ὑμεῖς διαφέρετε τῶν
and God feeds them; by how much rather you differ from the
25 πετεινῶν; τίς δὲ ἐξ ὑμῶν μεριμνῶν δύναται προσθεῖναι ἐπὶ
birds. who And of you being anxious is able to add on
26 τὴν ἡλικίαν αὐτοῦ πῆχυν ἕνα; εἰ οὖν οὔτε ἐλάχιστον
the stature of him cubit one? If, then, not (the) least
δύνασθε, τί περὶ τῶν λοιπῶν μεριμνᾶτε; κατανοήσατε τὰ
you are able, why about the other things are you anxious? Consider the

[27]Consider the lilies, how they grow. They do not labor, nor do they spin. But I say to you, Not even Solomon in all his glory was clothed like one of these. [28]But if God so clothes the grass, which today *is*, and tomorrow is thrown into the oven, how much rather you, *you* of little faith? [29]And you stop seeking what you eat, or what you drink. And stop being in anxiety. [30]For all the nations of the world seek after these things; and your Father knows that you need these. [31]But you seek the kingdom of God, and all these things will be added to you. [32]Stop fearing, little flock, for your Father was pleased to give you the kingdom. [33]Sell your possessions, and give alms. Make for yourselves purses that do not grow old, an unfailing treasure in Heaven, where a thief cannot come near, nor moth can corrupt. [34]For where your treasure is, there your heart will be also.

[35]Let your loins be girded, and the lamps burning; [36]and you *be* like men awaiting their lord when he returns from the wedding festivities, that coming and knocking, they immediately open to him. [37]Blessed *are* those slaves whom the lord when *he* comes will find watching. Truly I say to you, He will gird himself and will cause them to recline; and coming up, *he* will serve them. [38]And if he comes in the second watch, and in the third watch he comes and finds *it* so, blessed are those slaves. [39]But know this, that if the housemaster had known in what hour the thief is coming, he would have watched, and would not have allowed his house to be dug through. [40]And you, then, be ready. For in the hour you do not think the Son of man is coming.

27 κρίνα πῶς αὐξάνει· οὐ κοπιᾷ, οὐδὲ νήθει· λέγω δὲ ὑμῖν, οὐδὲ
lilies, how they grow; not they labor, nor spin, I say but to you, Not
Σολομὼν ἐν πάσῃ τῇ δόξῃ αὐτοῦ περιεβάλετο ὡς ἓν τούτων.
Solomon in all the glory of him was clothed as one of these.
28 εἰ δὲ τὸν χόρτον ἐν τῷ ἀγρῷ σήμερον ὄντα, καὶ αὔριον εἰς
if And the grass in the field, today (is) which, and tomorrow into
κλίβανον βαλλόμενον, ὁ Θεὸς οὕτως ἀμφιέννυσι. πόσῳ μᾶλλον
an oven is thrown, God so clothes, by how much rather
29 ὑμᾶς, ὀλιγόπιστοι ; καὶ ὑμεῖς μὴ ζητεῖτε τί φάγητε, ἢ τί
you, little-faiths? And you stop seeking what you eat, or what
30 πίητε· καὶ μὴ μετεωρίζεσθε. ταῦτα γὰρ πάντα τὰ ἔθνη τοῦ
you drink, and stop being in anxiety. these things For all the nations of the
κόσμου ἐπιζητεῖ· ὑμῶν δὲ ὁ πατὴρ οἶδεν ὅτι χρῄζετε τούτων.
world seek after; of you But the Father knows that you need these.
31 πλὴν ζητεῖτε τὴν βασιλείαν τοῦ Θεοῦ, καὶ ταῦτα πάντα
But you seek the kingdom — of God, and these things all
32 προστεθήσεται ὑμῖν. μὴ φοβοῦ, τὸ μικρὸν ποίμνιον· ὅτι
will be added to you. Stop fearing, — little flock; because
εὐδόκησεν ὁ πατὴρ ὑμῶν δοῦναι ὑμῖν τὴν βασιλείαν.
was pleased the Father of you to give you the kingdom.
33 πωλήσατε τὰ ὑπάρχοντα ὑμῶν καὶ δότε ἐλεημοσύνην.
Sell the possessions of you and give alms;
ποιήσατε ἑαυτοῖς βαλάντια μὴ παλαιούμενα, θησαυρὸν
make for yourselves purses not growing old, a treasure
ἀνέκλειπτον ἐν τοῖς οὐρανοῖς, ὅπου κλέπτης οὐκ ἐγγίζει οὐδὲ
unfailing in the heavens, where a thief not can approach, nor
34 σὴς διαφθείρει· ὅπου γάρ ἐστιν ὁ θησαυρὸς ὑμῶν, ἐκεῖ καὶ
moth can corrupt; where for is the treasure of you, there also
ἡ καρδία ὑμῶν ἔσται.
the heart of you will be.
35 Ἔστωσαν ὑμῶν αἱ ὀσφύες περιεζωσμέναι, καὶ οἱ λύχνοι
Let be of you the loins having been girded, and the lamps
36 καιόμενοι· καὶ ὑμεῖς ὅμοιοι ἀνθρώποις προσδεχομένοις τὸν
burning; and you like men awaiting the
κύριον ἑαυτῶν, πότε ἀναλύσει ἐκ τῶν γάμων, ἵνα, ἐλθόντος
lord of themselves, when he returns from the festivities, that, coming
37 καὶ κρούσαντος, εὐθέως ἀνοίξωσιν αὐτῷ. μακάριοι οἱ δοῦλοι
and knocking, at once they will open to him. Blessed — slaves
ἐκεῖνοι, οὓς ἐλθὼν ὁ κύριος εὑρήσει γρηγοροῦντας· ἀμὴν
those, whom coming the lord will find watching; truly
λέγω ὑμῖν ὅτι περιζώσεται καὶ ἀνακλινεῖ αὐτούς, καὶ παρ-
I say to you that he will gird himself and cause to recline them, and coming
38 ελθὼν διακονήσει αὐτοῖς. καὶ ἐὰν ἔλθῃ ἐν τῇ δευτέρᾳ φυλακῇ,
up to will serve them. And if he come in the second watch,
καὶ ἐν τῇ τρίτῃ φυλακῇ ἔλθῃ, καὶ εὕρῃ οὕτω μακάριοί εἰσιν
even in the third watch he come, and find (it) so, blessed are
39 οἱ δοῦλοι ἐκεῖνοι. τοῦτο δὲ γινώσκετε, ὅτι εἰ ᾔδει ὁ οἰκοδε-
— slaves those. this But know, that if had known the house
σπότης ποίᾳ ὥρᾳ ὁ κλέπτης ἔρχεται, ἐγρηγόρησεν ἄν, καὶ
master in what hour the thief is coming, he would have watched, and
40 οὐκ ἂν ἀφῆκε διορυγῆναι τὸν οἶκον αὐτοῦ. καὶ ὑμεῖς οὖν
not have allowed to be dug through the house of him. And you, then,
γίνεσθε ἕτοιμοι· ὅτι ᾗ ὥρᾳ οὐ δοκεῖτε ὁ υἱὸς τοῦ ἀνθρώπου
be prepared, for the hour not you think the Son — of man
ἔρχεται.
comes.

[41] And Peter said to Him, Lord, do you speak this parable to us, or also to all? [42] And the Lord said, Who then is the faithful and prudent steward, whom the lord will set over his house-servants, to give the portion of food in season? [43] Blessed *is* that slave whom the lord will find doing so *when he* comes. [44] Truly I say to you, he will appoint him over all his possessions. [45] But if that slave should say in his heart, My lord delays to come, and should begin to beat the men servants and the maid servants, and to eat and to drink and become drunk, [46] the lord of that slave will come in the day in which he does not expect, and in an hour which he does not know. And *he* will cut him apart, and will put his portion with the unbelievers. [47] But that slave knowing the will of his lord, and did not prepare, nor did according to his will, will be beaten with many *stripes*. [48] But he not knowing, and doing *things* worthy of stripes, will be beaten with few. And everyone given much, much will be demanded from him. And to whom much was deposited, more exceedingly they will ask him.

[49] I came to hurl fire into the earth, and what will I if it already was lit? [50] But I have a baptism to be immersed in, and now I am compressed until it is done! [51] Do you think that I came to give peace in the earth? No, I say to you, but rather division. [52] For from now on there will be five divided in one house, three against two, and two against three. [53] Father will be divided against son, and son against father; mother against daughter, and daughter against mother; mother-in-law against her daughter-in-law, and daughter-in-law against her mother-in-law.

[54] And He also said to the crowd, When you see the cloud rising up from *the* west, you immediately say, A storm is coming; and it

41 Εἶπε δὲ αὐτῷ ὁ Πέτρος, Κύριε, πρὸς ἡμᾶς τὴν παραβολὴν
said And to Him — Peter, Lord, to us — parable
42 ταύτην λέγεις, ἢ καὶ πρὸς πάντας ; εἶπε δὲ ὁ Κύριος, Τίς ἄρα
this do You say, or also to all? said And the Lord, Who then
ἐστὶν ὁ πιστὸς οἰκονόμος καὶ φρόνιμος, ὃν καταστήσει ὁ
is the faithful steward and prudent, whom will appoint the
κύριος ἐπὶ τῆς θεραπείας αὐτοῦ, τοῦ διδόναι ἐν καιρῷ τὸ
lord over the houseservants of him, — to give in season the
43 σιτομέτριον ; μακάριος ὁ δοῦλος ἐκεῖνος, ὃν ἐλθὼν ὁ κύριος
portion of food? Blessed — slave that, whom coming the lord
44 αὐτοῦ εὑρήσει ποιοῦντα οὕτως. ἀληθῶς λέγω ὑμῖν ὅτι ἐπὶ
of him will find doing so. Truly I say to you that over
45 πᾶσι τοῖς ὑπάρχουσιν αὐτοῦ καταστήσει αὐτόν. ἐὰν δὲ εἴπῃ
all the possessions of him he will appoint him. if But says
ὁ δοῦλος ἐκεῖνος ἐν τῇ καρδίᾳ αὐτοῦ, Χρονίζει ὁ κυριός μου
— slave that in the heart of him, Delays the lord of me
ἔρχεσθαι, καὶ ἄρξηται τύπτειν τοὺς παῖδας καὶ τὰς παιδί-
to come, and begins to beat the menservants and the maid
46 σκας, ἐσθίειν τε καὶ πίνειν καὶ μεθύσκεσθαι ἥξει ὁ κυριος τοῦ
servants. to eat both and to drink and to become drunk, will come the lord of
δούλου ἐκείνου ἐν ἡμέρᾳ ᾗ οὐ προσδοκᾷ, καὶ ἐν ὥρᾳ ᾗ οὐ
slave that in a day in which not he expects, and in an hour which not
γινώσκει· καὶ διχοτομήσει αὐτόν, καὶ τὸ μέρος αὐτοῦ μετὰ
he knows, and will cut apart him, and the portion of him with
47 τῶν ἀπίστων θήσει. ἐκεῖνος δὲ ὁ δοῦλος ὁ γνοὺς τὸ θέλημα
the unbelievers will place. that But — slave — having known the will
τοῦ κυρίου ἑαυτοῦ, καὶ μὴ ἑτοιμάσας μηδὲ ποιήσας πρὸς τὸ
of the Lord of him, and not did prepare nor did according to the
48 θέλημα αὐτοῦ, δαρήσεται πολλάς· ὁ δὲ μὴ γνούς, ποιήσας
will of Him, will be beaten with many. he But not knowing, doing
δὲ ἄξια πληγῶν, δαρήσεται ὀλίγας. παντὶ δὲ ᾧ ἐδόθη πολύ,
and worthy of stripes will be beaten with few. everyone And given much,
πολὺ ζητηθήσεται παρ' αὐτοῦ· καὶ ᾧ παρέθεντο πολύ,
much will be demanded from him; and to whom was deposited much,
περισσότερον αἰτήσουσιν αὐτόν.
more exceedingly they will ask him.
49 Πῦρ ἦλθον βαλεῖν εἰς τὴν γῆν, καὶ τί θέλω εἰ ἤδη ἀνήφθη ;
Fire I came to cast into the earth, and what will I if already it was lit?
50 βάπτισμα δὲ ἔχω βαπτισθῆναι, καὶ πῶς συνέχομαι ἕως οὗ
a baptism And I have to be baptized, and how I am compressed until
51 τελεσθῇ. δοκεῖτε ὅτι εἰρήνην παρεγενόμην δοῦναι ἐν τῇ γῇ ;
it is finished! Think that peace I came to give in the earth?
52 οὐχί, λέγω ὑμῖν, ἀλλ' ἢ διαμερισμόν. ἔσονται γὰρ ἀπὸ τοῦ
No, I say to you, but rather division. will be For from —
νῦν πέντε ἐν οἴκῳ ἑνὶ διαμεμερισμένοι, τρεῖς ἐπὶ δυσί, καὶ
now five in house one having been divided; three against two, and
53 δύο ἐπὶ τρισί. διαμερισθήσεται πατὴρ ἐφ' υἱῷ, καὶ υἱὸς ἐπὶ
two against three will be divided; father against son, and son against
πατρί· μήτηρ ἐπὶ θυγατρί, καὶ θυγάτηρ ἐπὶ μητρί πενθερὰ
father; mother against daughter, and daughter against mother; mother-in-law
ἐπὶ τὴν νύμφην αὐτῆς, καὶ νύμφη ἐπὶ τὴν πενθερὰν αὐτῆς.
against the daughter-in-law of her, and daughter-in-law against the mother-in-law of her.
54 Ἔλεγε δὲ καὶ τοῖς ὄχλοις, Ὅταν ἴδητε τὴν νεφέλην
He said And also to the crowds, When you see the cloud
ἀνατέλλουσαν ἀπὸ δυσμῶν, εὐθέως λέγετε Ὄμβρος ἔρχεται·
rising up from (the) west, at once you say, A storm is coming

happens so. 55 And when a south wind *is* blowing, you say, There will be heat; and it happens. 56 Hypocrites! You know to discern the face of the earth and of the heaven, but how *is it* you do not discern this time? 57 And why do you not judge what *is* right of yourselves? 58 For as you go with your adversary to a judge, give pains in the way to be set free from him, that he not drag you to the judge, and the judge deliver you to the officer, and the officer throw you into prison. 59 I say to you, In no way may you leave there until you pay even the last lepton.

CHAPTER 13

1 And some were present at the same time reporting to Him about the Galileans, whose blood Pilate mixed with their sacrifices. 2 And answering Jesus said to them, Do you think that these Galileans were sinners beyond all the Galileans, because they suffered such things? 3 No, I say to you; but if you do not repent, you will all perish in the same way. 4 Or those eighteen on whom the tower in Siloam fell, and killed them, do you think that these were sinners beyond all men who lived in Jerusalem? 5 No, I say to you; but if you do not repent, you will all perish in the same way.

6 And He spoke this parable:

A certain one had planted a fig-tree in his vineyard. And He came looking for fruit on it, and did not find *any*. 7 And he said to the vinedresser, Behold, three years I come looking for fruit on this fig-tree, and found none. Cut it down, and why does it waste the ground? 8 And the vinedresser said to him, Sir, leave it also this year, until I shall dig around

55 καὶ γίνεται οὕτω. καὶ ὅταν νότον πνέοντα, λέγετε ὅτι
and it happens so. And when a south wind blowing you say that

56 Καύσων ἔσται· καὶ γίνεται. ὑποκριταί, τὸ πρόσωπον τοῦ
heat will be, and it happens. Hypocrites! The face of the

οὐρανοῦ καὶ τῆς γῆς οἴδατε δοκιμάζειν· τὸν δὲ καιρὸν
heaven and the earth you know to discern, — but time

57 τοῦτον πῶς οὐ δοκιμάζετε; τί δὲ καὶ ἀφ' ἑαυτῶν οὐ κρίνετε
this how not do you discern? why And even from yourselves not do judge

58 τὸ δίκαιον; ὡς γὰρ ὑπάγεις μετὰ τοῦ ἀντιδίκου σου ἐπ'
the righteous? as For you go with the adversary of you to

ἄρχοντα, ἐν τῇ ὁδῷ δὸς ἐργασίαν ἀπηλλάχθαι ἀπ' αὐτοῦ·
a magistrate, in the way give pains to be freed from him,

μήποτε κατασύρῃ σε πρὸς τὸν κριτήν, καὶ ὁ κριτής σε
lest he drag you to the judge, and the judge you

παραδῷ τῷ πράκτορι, καὶ ὁ πράκτωρ σε βάλλῃ εἰς φυλακήν.
will deliver to the officer, and the officer you throw into prison.

59 λέγω σοι, οὐ μὴ ἐξέλθῃς ἐκεῖθεν, ἕως οὗ καὶ τὸ ἔσχατον
I say to you, in no way may you leave there until even the last

λεπτὸν ἀποδῷς.
lepton you pay.

CHAPTER 13

1 Παρῆσαν δέ τινες ἐν αὐτῷ τῷ καιρῷ ἀπαγγέλλοντες
were present And some at same the time reporting

αὐτῷ περὶ τῶν Γαλιλαίων, ὧν τὸ αἷμα Πιλάτος ἔμιξε μετὰ
to Him about the Galileans, of whom the blood Pilate mixed with

2 τῶν θυσιῶν αὐτῶν. καὶ ἀποκριθεὶς ὁ Ἰησοῦς εἶπεν αὐτοῖς,
the sacrifices of them. And answering — Jesus said to them,

Δοκεῖτε ὅτι οἱ Γαλιλαῖοι οὗτοι ἁμαρτωλοὶ παρὰ πάντας
Do you think that Galileans those sinners above all

3 τοὺς Γαλιλαίους ἐγένοντο, ὅτι τοιαῦτα πεπόνθασιν; οὐχί,
the Galileans were, because these things they have suffered? No,

λέγω ὑμῖν· ἀλλ' ἐὰν μὴ μετανοῆτε, πάντες ὡσαύτως
I say to you, but except you repent, all likewise

4 ἀπολεῖσθε. ἢ ἐκεῖνοι οἱ δέκα καὶ ὀκτώ, ἐφ' οὓς ἔπεσεν ὁ
you will perish. Or those — eighteen on whom fell the

πύργος ἐν τῷ Σιλωὰμ καὶ ἀπέκτεινεν αὐτούς, δοκεῖτε ὅτι
tower in — Siloam, and killed them, do you think that

οὗτοι ὀφειλέται ἐγένοντο παρὰ πάντας ἀνθρώπους τοὺς
they debtors were above all men, those

5 κατοικοῦντας ἐν Ἱερουσαλήμ; οὐχί, λέγω ὑμῖν· ἀλλ' ἐὰν
dwelling in Jerusalem? No, I say to you, but ex-

6 μὴ μετανοῆτε, πάντες ὁμοίως ἀπολεῖσθε. ἔλεγε δὲ ταύτην
cept you repent, all likewise you will perish. He told And this

τὴν παραβολήν· Συκῆν εἶχέ τις ἐν τῷ ἀμπελῶνι αὐτοῦ
— parable: A fig-tree had a certain in the vineyard of him

πεφυτευμένην· καὶ ἦλθε καρπὸν ζητῶν ἐν αὐτῇ, καὶ οὐχ
planted, and came fruit seeking in it, and not

7 εὗρεν. εἶπε δὲ πρὸς τὸν ἀμπελουργόν, Ἰδού, τρία ἔτη
he found. he said And to the vinedresser, Behold, three years

ἔρχομαι ζητῶν καρπὸν ἐν τῇ συκῇ ταύτῃ, καὶ οὐχ εὑρίσκω·
I come seeking fruit on — fig-tree this, and not do find;

8 ἔκκοψον αὐτήν· ἱνατί καὶ τὴν γῆν καταργεῖ; ὁ δὲ ἀποκριθεὶς
cut down it; why even the ground it spoils? he And answering

λέγει αὐτῷ, Κύριε, ἄφες αὐτὴν καὶ τοῦτο τὸ ἔτος, ἕως ὅτου
said to him, Lord, leave it also this — year, until

it and throw manure; 9 and *see* if it indeed makes fruit. But if not, in the future you may cut it down.

10 And He was teaching in one of the synagogues on the sabbaths. 11 And, behold, there was a woman having infirmity eighteen years, and was bent together, and was not able to be completely erect. 12 And seeing her, Jesus called *her* near, and said to her, Woman, you have been freed from your infirmity. 13 And He laid hands on her. And instantly she was made erect, and glorified God. 14 But answering the synagogue ruler, being angry that Jesus healed on the sabbath, said to the crowd, There are six days in which it is right to work. Therefore, coming in these, be healed, and not on the sabbath day. 15 Then the Lord answered him and said, Hypocrite! Each one of you on the sabbath, does he not untie his ox or ass from the manger, and leading *it* away give *it* drink? 16 And this one being a daughter of Abraham, whom Satan has bound, lo, eighteen years, ought *she* not to be loosened from this bond on the sabbath day? 17 And on His saying these things, all who were opposed to Him were ashamed. And all the crowd rejoiced over all the glorious things taking place by Him.

18 And He said, What is the kingdom of God like? And to what shall I compare it? 19 It is like a grain of mustard, which a man having taken threw into his garden. And it grew and became a great tree; and the birds of the heaven perched in its branches. 20 And again He said, To what shall I compare the kingdom of God? 21 It is like leaven, which taking a woman hid in three seahs of meal, until all was leavened.

22 And He went through by cities and villages teaching, and making progress toward

9 σκάψω περὶ αὐτήν, καὶ βάλω κοπρίαν· κἂν μὲν ποιήσῃ
I may dig around it, and throw manure; and if indeed it makes
καρπόν· εἰ δὲ μήγε, εἰς τὸ μέλλον ἐκκόψεις αὐτήν.
fruit; if but not, in the future you may cut down it.
10 Ἦν δὲ διδάσκων ἐν μιᾷ τῶν συναγωγῶν ἐν τοῖς σάββασι·
He was And teaching in one of the synagogues on the sabbaths.
11 καὶ ἰδού, γυνὴ ἦν πνεῦμα ἔχουσα ἀσθενείας ἔτη δέκα καὶ
And behold, a woman was a spirit having of infirmity years eighteen
ὀκτώ, καὶ ἦν συγκύπτουσα, καὶ μὴ δυναμένη ἀνακύψαι εἰς
and was bent together, and not was able to be erect com-
12 τὸ παντελές. ἰδὼν δὲ αὐτὴν ὁ Ἰησοῦς προσεφώνησε, καὶ
pletely. seeing And her, — Jesus called near and
13 ειπεν αὐτῇ, Γύναι, ἀπολέλυσαι της ἀσθενείας σοῦ. καὶ
said to her, Woman, you have been freed from the infirmity of you. And
ἐπεθηκεν αὐτῇ τὰς χεῖρας· και παραχρῆμα ἀνωρθώθη,
He laid on her the hands, and immediately she was made erect,
14 καὶ ἐδόξαζε τὸν Θεόν. ἀποκριθεὶς δὲ ὁ ἀρχισυνάγωγος,
and glorified — God. answering But the synagogue ruler,
ἀγανακτῶν ὅτι τῷ σαββάτῳ ἐθεράπευσεν ὁ Ἰησοῦς, ἔλεγε
being angry that on the sabbath healed — Jesus, said
τῷ ὄχλῳ, Ἓξ ἡμέραι εἰσὶν ἐν αἷς δεῖ ἐργάζεσθαι· ἐν ταύταις
to the crowd, Six days there are in which it is right to work; on these
οὖν ἐρχόμενοι θεραπεύεσθε, καὶ μὴ τῇ ἡμέρᾳ τοῦ σαββάτου.
then coming be healed, and not on the day of the sabbath.
15 ἀπεκρίθη οὖν αὐτῷ ὁ Κύριος, καὶ εἶπεν, Ὑποκριτά, ἕκαστος
answered Then him the Lord, and said, Hypocrites! Each one
ὑμῶν τῷ σαββάτῳ οὐ λύει τὸν βοῦν αὐτοῦ ἢ τὸν ὄνον ἀπὸ
of you on the sabbath, not loosen the ox of him or the ass from
16 τῆς φάτνης, καὶ ἀπαγαγὼν ποτίζει; ταύτην δέ, θυγατέρα
the manger, and leading away give drink? this one And, a daughter
Ἀβραὰμ οὖσαν, ἣν ἔδησεν ὁ Σατανᾶς, ἰδού, δέκα καὶ ὀκτὼ
of Abraham being, whom bound — Satan, behold, eighteen
ἔτη, οὐκ ἔδει λυθῆναι ἀπὸ τοῦ δεσμοῦ τούτου τῇ ἡμέρᾳ τοῦ
years, not was it right to free from — bond this on the day of the
17 σαββατου; καὶ ταυτα λέγοντος αὐτου, κατῃσχύνοντο
sabbath? And these things saying Him, were put to shame
πάντες οἱ ἀντικείμενοι αὐτῷ καὶ πᾶς ὁ ὄχλος ἔχαιρεν ἐπὶ
all those opposing Him, and all the crowd rejoiced over
πᾶσι τοῖς ἐνδόξοις τοῖς γινομένοις ὑπ' αὐτοῦ.
all the glorious things — happening by Him.
18 Ἔλεγε δέ, Τίνι ὁμοία ἐστὶν ἡ βασιλεία τοῦ Θεοῦ; καὶ τίνι
He said And, To what like is the kingdom — of God, and to what
19 ὁμοιώσω αυτην; ὁμοία ἐστὶ κόκκῳ σινάπεως, ὃν λαβὼν
may I compare it? like It is a grain of mustard, which taking
ἄνθρωπος ἔβαλεν εἰς κῆπον ἑαυτοῦ· καὶ ηὔξησε, καὶ ἐγένετο
a man threw into a garden of himself; and it grew, and became
εἰς δένδρον μεγα, καὶ τὰ πετεινὰ τοῦ οὐρανου κατεσκήνωσεν
into a tree great, and the birds of the heaven perched
20 ἐν τοῖς κλάδοις αὐτοῦ. καὶ πάλιν εἶπε, Τίνι ὁμοιώσω τὴν
in the branches of it. And again He said, To what may I compare the
21 βασιλείαν τοῦ Θεοῦ; ὁμοία ἐστὶ ζύμῃ, ἣν λαβοῦσα γυνὴ
kingdom — of God? like It is to leaven, which taking a woman
ἐνέκρυψεν εἰς ἀλεύρου σάτα τρία, ἕως οὗ ἐζυμώθη ὅλον.
hid in of meal measures three, until were leavened all.
22 Καὶ διεπορεύετο κατὰ πόλεις καὶ κώμας διδάσκων, καὶ
And He traveled throughout cities and villages teaching, and

Jerusalem. [23]And one said to Him, Lord, *are* the ones being saved few? But He said to them, [24]Labor to enter in through the narrow gate; for I say to you that many will seek to enter in, and will not have strength.

[25]From the time the Master of the house shall have risen up, and He shuts the door, and you begin to stand outside and to knock at the door, saying, Lord, Lord, open to us. And answering He will say to you, I do not know you. From where are you? [26]Then you will begin to say, We ate and drank in Your presence, and You taught in our streets.

[27]And He will say, I tell you, I do not know you, from where you are. Stand back from Me, all workers of unrighteousness. [28]There will be weeping and gnashing of the teeth when you see Abraham and Isaac and Jacob, and all the prophets, in the kingdom of God, but yourselves being thrust outside. [29]And they will come from east and west, and from north and south, and will recline in the kingdom of God. [30]And, behold, there are last ones who will be first, and there are first ones who will be last.

[31]In the same day certain Pharisees came saying to Him, Go out and go on from here, for Herod desires to kill you. [32]And He said to them, Going, say to that fox, Behold, today and tomorrow I cast out demons, and I complete cures, and the third *day* I am perfected. [33]But today and tomorrow, and on the following *day*, I must travel on. For it is not possible for a prophet to perish outside Jerusalem. [34]Jerusalem! Jerusalem! The *one* killing the prophets, and stoning those having been sent to her. How often I desired to gather your children in the way a hen *gathers* her brood under the wings; and you did not desire *it*. [35]Behold, your house is left to you desolate.

23 πορείαν ποιούμενος εἰς Ἱερουσαλήμ. εἶπε δέ τις αὐτῷ, Κύριε,
progress making toward Jerusalem. said And one to Him, Lord
24 εἰ ὀλίγοι οἱ σωζόμενοι ; ὁ δὲ εἶπε πρὸς αὐτούς, Ἀγωνίζεσθε
If few those being saved? He And said to them, Strive
εἰσελθεῖν διὰ τῆς στενῆς πύλης· ὅτι πολλοί, λέγω ὑμῖν,
to enter through the narrow gate, in that many, I say to you,
25 ζητήσουσιν εἰσελθεῖν, καὶ οὐκ ἰσχύσουσιν. ἀφ' οὗ ἂν ἐγερθῇ ὁ
will seek to enter in, and not will have strength. From when is risen the
οἰκοδεσπότης καὶ ἀποκλείσῃ τὴν θύραν, καὶ ἄρξησθε ἔξω
house-master, and he shuts the door, and you begin outside
ἑστάναι καὶ κρούειν τὴν θύραν, λέγοντες, Κύριε, Κύριε,
to stand and to knock the door, saying, Lord, Lord,
ἄνοιξον ἡμῖν· καὶ ἀποκριθεὶς ἐρεῖ ὑμῖν, Οὐκ οἶδα ὑμᾶς, πόθεν
open to us, and answering He say to you, not I know you, from where
26 ἐστέ· τότε ἄρξεσθε λέγειν, Ἐφάγομεν ἐνώπιόν σου καὶ
you are. Then you will begin to say, We ate before You and
27 ἐπίομεν, καὶ ἐν ταῖς πλατείαις ἡμῶν ἐδίδαξας. καὶ ἐρεῖ,
drank, and in the streets of us You taught. And He will say
Λέγω ὑμῖν, οὐκ οἶδα ὑμᾶς πόθεν ἐστέ· ἀπόστητε ἀπ' ἐμοῦ
I tell you, not I know you, from where you are. Stand back from Me,
28 πάντες οἱ ἐργάται τῆς ἀδικίας. ἐκεῖ ἔσται ὁ κλαυθμὸς καὶ ὁ
all the workers of unrighteousness. There will be the weeping and the
βρυγμὸς τῶν ὀδόντων, ὅταν ὄψησθε Ἀβραὰμ καὶ Ἰσαὰκ
gnashing of the teeth, when you see Abraham and Isaac
καὶ Ἰακὼβ καὶ πάντας τοὺς προφήτας ἐν τῇ βασιλείᾳ τοῦ
and Jacob and all the prophets in the kingdom —
29 Θεοῦ, ὑμᾶς δὲ ἐκβαλλομένους ἔξω. καὶ ἥξουσιν ἀπὸ ἀνατο-
of God, you and being thrust outside. And they will come from east
λῶν καὶ δυσμῶν, καὶ ἀπὸ βορρᾶ καὶ νότου, καὶ ἀνακλιθή-
and west, and from north and south, and will recline
30 σονται ἐν τῇ βασιλείᾳ τοῦ Θεοῦ. καὶ ἰδού, εἰσὶν ἔσχατοι οἳ
in the kingdom of God. And behold, are last ones who
ἔσονται πρῶτοι, καί εἰσὶ πρῶτοι οἳ ἔσονται ἔσχατοι.
will be first, and are first ones who will be last.
31 Ἐν αὐτῇ τῇ ἡμέρᾳ προσῆλθόν τινες Φαρισαῖοι, λέγοντες
In same the day came to (Him) certain Pharisees, saying
αὐτῷ, Ἔξελθε καὶ πορεύου ἐντεῦθεν, ὅτι Ἡρώδης θέλει σε
to Him, Go out and go on from here, because Herod desires you
32 ἀποκτεῖναι. καὶ εἶπεν αὐτοῖς, Πορευθέντες εἴπατε τῇ ἀλώπεκι
to kill. And He said to them, Going, say — fox
ταύτῃ, Ἰδού, ἐκβάλλω δαιμόνια καὶ ἰάσεις ἐπιτελῶ σήμερον
to that, Behold, I cast out demons and cures I finish today,
33 καὶ αὔριον, καὶ τῇ τρίτῃ τελειοῦμαι. πλὴν δεῖ με σήμερον
and tomorrow, and the third (day) I am perfected. But I must today
καὶ αὔριον καὶ τῇ ἐχομένῃ πορεύεσθαι· ὅτι οὐκ ἐνδέχεται
and tomorrow and on the following travel on, because not it is possible
34 προφήτην ἀπολέσθαι ἔξω Ἱερουσαλήμ. Ἱερουσαλήμ, Ἱερου-
a prophet to perish outside Jerusalem. Jerusalem! Jerus-
σαλήμ, ἡ ἀποκτείνουσα τοὺς προφήτας, καὶ λιθοβολοῦσα
alem! The (one) killing the prophets, and stoning
τοὺς ἀπεσταλμένους πρὸς αὐτήν, ποσάκις ἠθέλησα ἐπισυνά-
those having been sent to her. How often I desired to gather
ξαι τὰ τέκνα σου, ὃν τρόπον ὄρνις τὴν ἑαυτῆς νοσσιὰν ὑπὸ
the children of you in the way a bird (gathers) her brood under
35 τὰς πτέρυγας, καὶ οὐκ ἠθελήσατε. ἰδού, ἀφίεται ὑμῖν ὁ οἶκος
wings, and not you desired (it). Behold, is left to you the house

And truly I say to you, You shall not at all see Me until it come when you say, Blessed *is* the *One* coming in *the* name of *the* Lord.

CHAPTER 14

[1]And it happened in His going into a house of one of the leaders of the Pharisees on a sabbath to eat bread, and they were closely watching Him. [2]And, behold, a certain man was dropsical before Him. [3]And answering Jesus said to the lawyers and the Pharisees, saying, Is it lawful to heal on the sabbath? [4]And they were silent. And having taken *him,* He cured him, and let *him* go. [5]And answering to them He said, *If* an ox or an ass of yours should fall into a pit, will *you* not at once pull it up on the sabbath day? [6]And they could not reply to Him against these things.

[7]And He spoke a parable to those who were invited, noting how they were choosing out the chief seats, saying to them, [8]When you are invited by anyone to wedding feasts, do not recline at the chief seat, lest *one* more honorable than you be invited by him, [9]and coming he who invited you will say to you, Give this one place. And then you begin with shame to take the last place. [10]But when you are invited, going *in,* recline in the last place, so that when he inviting you comes, he will say to you, Friend, go up higher. then glory will be to you before those reclining with you. [11]For everyone exalting himself will be humbled; and the *one* humbling himself will be exalted.

[12]And He also said to him who had invited Him, When you make a dinner or supper, do not call your friends, nor your brothers, nor your relatives, nor rich neighbors, lest they also invite you in return, and it becomes a

ὑμῶν ἔρημος· ἀμὴν δὲ λέγω ὑμῖν ὅτι Οὐ μή με ἴδητε ἕως ἂν
of you desolate. truly And I say to you that in no way Me shall you see until
ἥξῃ, ὅτε εἴπητε, Εὐλογημένος ὁ ἐρχόμενος ἐν ὀνόματι Κυρίου.
it come when you say, Blessed the (One) coming in (the) name of (the) Lord.

CHAPTER 14

1 Καὶ ἐγένετο ἐν τῷ ἐλθεῖν αὐτὸν εἰς οἶκόν τινος τῶν
And it was in the going (of) Him into a house of one of the
ἀρχόντων τῶν Φαρισαιων σαββάτῳ φαγεῖν ἄρτον, καὶ
leaders of the Pharisees on a sabbath to eat bread, and
2 αὐτοὶ ἦσαν παρατηρούμενοι αὐτόν. καὶ ἰδού, ἄνθρωπός τις
they were carefully watching Him. And, behold, man a certain
3 ἦν ὑδρωπικὸς ἔμπροσθεν αὐτοῦ. καὶ ἀποκριθεὶς ὁ Ἰησοῦς
was dropsical before Him. And answering — Jesus
εἶπε πρὸς τοὺς νομικοὺς καὶ Φαρισαίους, λέγων, Εἰ ἔξεστι
said to the lawyers and Pharisees, saying, If it is lawful
4 τῷ σαββάτῳ θεραπεύειν ; οἱ δὲ ἡσύχασαν. καὶ ἐπιλαβόμενος
on the sabbath to heal, they and were silent. And taking (him),
5 ἰάσατο αὐτόν, καὶ ἀπέλυσε. καὶ ἀποκριθεὶς πρὸς αὐτοὺς
He cured him, and dismissed (him). And answering to them
εἶπε, Τίνος ὑμῶν ὄνος ἢ βοῦς εἰς φρέαρ ἐμπεσεῖται, καὶ οὐκ
He said, Of whom of you an ass or ox into a pit should fall, and not
6 εὐθέως ἀνασπάσει αὐτὸν ἐν τῇ ἡμέρᾳ τοῦ σαββάτου ; καὶ
at once he will pull up it on the day of the sabbath? And
οὐκ ἴσχυσαν ἀνταποκριθῆναι αὐτῷ πρὸς ταῦτα.
not they were able to reply to Him against these things.
7 Ἔλεγε δὲ πρὸς τοὺς κεκλημένους παραβολήν, ἐπέχων πῶς
He told And to those having been invited a parable noting how
8 τὰς πρωτοκλισιας ἐξελέγοντο, λέγων πρὸς αὐτούς, Ὅταν
the chief seats they were choosing, saying to them, When
κληθῇς ὑπό τινος εἰς γάμους, μὴ κατακλιθῇς εἰς τὴν πρωτοκλι-
you are invited by one to feasts, do not recline at the chief seat,
9 σίαν· μήποτε ἐντιμότερός σου ᾖ κεκλημένος ὑπ' αὐτοῦ, καὶ
lest (one) more honorable (than) you be invited by him, and
ἐλθὼν ὁ σὲ καὶ αὐτὸν καλέσας ἐρεῖ σοι, Δὸς τούτῳ τόπον· καὶ
coming he to you and him inviting will say to you, Give this one place. And
10 τότε ἄρξῃ μετ' αἰσχύνης τὸν ἔσχατον τόπον κατέχειν. ἀλλ'
then you begin with shame the last place to take. But
ὅταν κληθῇς, πορευθεὶς ἀνάπεσον εἰς τὸν ἔσχατον τόπον·
when you are invited, going recline in the last place,
ἵνα, ὅταν ἔλθῃ ὁ κεκληκώς σε, εἴπῃ σοι, Φίλε, προσανάβηθι
that when comes he inviting you, he say to you, Friend, go up
ἀνώτερον· τότε ἔσται σοι δόξα ἐνώπιον τῶν συνανακειμένων
higher. Then will be to you glory before those reclining with
11 σοι. ὅτι πᾶς ὁ ὑψῶν ἑαυτὸν ταπεινωθήσεται, καὶ ὁ ταπεινῶν
you. For everyone exalting himself will be humbled; and he humbling
ἑαυτὸν ὑψωθήσεται.
himself will be exalted.
12 Ἔλεγε δὲ καὶ τῷ κεκληκότι αὐτόν, Ὅταν ποιῇς ἄριστον ἢ
He said And also to those inviting Him, When you make a dinner or
δεῖπνον, μὴ φώνει τοὺς φίλους σου, μηδὲ τοὺς ἀδελφούς σου,
a supper, do not call the friends of you, nor the brothers of you,
μηδὲ τοὺς συγγενεῖς σου, μηδὲ γείτονας πλουσίους· μήποτε
nor the relatives of you, nor neighbors rich, lest
καὶ αὐτοί σε ἀντικαλέσωσι, καὶ γένηταί σοι ἀνταπόδομα.
also they you invite in return, and it becomes to you a repayment.

repayment to you. 13 But when you make a party, invite poor ones, maimed ones, lame ones, blind ones, 14 and you will be blessed, for they have nothing *with which* to repay you. For it will be repaid to you in the resurrection of the just. 15 And one of those reclining with *Him*, hearing these things, said to Him, Blessed *are* those eating bread in the kingdom of God. 16 But He said to him, A certain man made a great supper, and invited many. 17 And he sent his slave at the supper hour to say to those who had been invited, Come, for now it is all ready. 18 And they all with one *mind* began to beg off. The first said to him, I have bought a field, and I must also go out to see it; I beg you, have me excused. 19 And another said, I have bought five yoke of oxen, and I am going to try them out; I beg you, have me excused. 20 And another said, I have married a wife, and because of this I am not able to come. 21 And having come that slave reported these things to his lord. Then being angry, the housemaster said to his slave, Go out quickly into the streets and lanes of the city, and bring in here the poor and maimed and lame and blind. 22 And the slave said, Sir, it has been done as you ordered, and still there is room. 23 And the lord said to the slave, Go out into the highways and hedges, and compel *them* to come in, that my house may be filled. 24 For I say to you that not one of those men who had been invited shall taste of my supper.

25 And great crowds were going with Him. And turning He said to them, 26 If anyone comes to Me, and does not hate his father and mother, and wife, and

13 ἀλλ᾽ ὅταν ποιῇς δοχήν, κάλει πτωχούς, ἀναπήρους, χωλούς,
But when a party you make, invite poor ones, maimed ones, lame ones,
14 τυφλούς· καὶ μακάριος ἔσῃ, ὅτι οὐκ ἔχουσιν ἀνταποδοῦναί
blind ones, and blessed you will be, for not they have (with which) to repay
σοι· ἀνταποδοθήσεται γάρ σοι ἐν τῇ ἀναστάσει τῶν
you. it will be repaid For to you in the resurrection of the
δικαίων.
just.
15 Ἀκούσας δέ τις τῶν συνανακειμένων ταῦτα εἶπεν αὐτῷ,
hearing And one of those reclining with these things said to Him,
16 Μακάριος, ὃς φάγεται ἄρτον ἐν τῇ βασιλείᾳ τοῦ Θεοῦ. ὁ δὲ
Blessed those eating bread in the kingdom – of God. He But
εἶπεν αὐτῷ, Ἄνθρωπός τις ἐποίησε δεῖπνον μέγα, καὶ
said to him, man A certain made a supper great, and
17 ἐκάλεσε πολλούς· καὶ ἀπέστειλε τὸν δοῦλον αὐτοῦ τῇ ὥρᾳ
invited many, and sent the slave of him at the hour
τοῦ δείπνου εἰπεῖν τοῖς κεκλημένοις, Ἔρχεσθε, ὅτι ἤδη
of the supper to say to those having been invited, Come, because now
18 ἕτοιμά ἐστι πάντα. καὶ ἤρξαντο ἀπὸ μιᾶς παραιτεῖσθαι
ready it is all. And they began with one (mind) to beg off
πάντες. ὁ πρῶτος εἶπεν αὐτῷ, Ἀγρὸν ἠγόρασα, καὶ ἔχω
all. The first said to him, A field I have bought, and I have
ἀνάγκην ἐξελθεῖν καὶ ἰδεῖν αὐτόν· ἐρωτῶ σε, ἔχε με παρῃτη-
need to go out and to see it; I ask you, have me excused.
19 μένον. καὶ ἕτερος εἶπε, Ζεύγη βοῶν ἠγόρασα πέντε, καὶ
And another said, yoke of oxen I bought five, and
πορεύομαι δοκιμάσαι αὐτά· ἐρωτῶ σε, ἔχε με παρῃτημένον.
I am going to try out them; I ask you, have me excused.
20 καὶ ἕτερος εἶπε, Γυναῖκα ἔγημα, καὶ διὰ τοῦτο οὐ δύναμαι
And another said, a wife I married, and therefore not I am able
21 ἐλθεῖν. καὶ παραγενόμενος ὁ δοῦλος ἐκεῖνος ἀπήγγειλε τῷ
to come. And coming up slave that reported to the
κυρίῳ αὐτοῦ ταῦτα. τότε ὀργισθεὶς ὁ οἰκοδεσπότης εἶπε τῷ
lord of him these things. Then being angry the house-master said to the
δούλῳ αὐτοῦ, Ἔξελθε ταχέως εἰς τὰς πλατείας καὶ ῥύμας τῆς
slave of him, Go out quickly into the streets and lanes of the
πόλεως, καὶ τοὺς πτωχοὺς καὶ ἀναπήρους καὶ χωλοὺς καὶ
city, and the poor and maimed and lame and
22 τυφλοὺς εἰσάγαγε ὧδε. καὶ εἶπεν ὁ δοῦλος, Κύριε, γέγονεν ὡς
blind bring in here. And said the slave, Lord, has occurred as
23 ἐπέταξας, καὶ ἔτι τόπος ἐστί. καὶ εἶπεν ὁ κύριος πρὸς τὸν
you ordered, and yet room there is. And said the lord to the
δοῦλον, Ἔξελθε εἰς τὰς ὁδοὺς καὶ φραγμούς, καὶ ἀνάγκασον
slave, Go out into the ways and hedges, and compel (them)
24 εἰσελθεῖν, ἵνα γεμισθῇ ὁ οἶκός μου. λέγω γὰρ ὑμῖν ὅτι οὐδεὶς
to come in, that may be filled the house of me. I say For to you that not one
τῶν ἀνδρῶν ἐκείνων τῶν κεκλημένων γεύσεταί μου τοῦ
– men of those – having been invited shall taste of me the
δείπνου.
supper.
25 Συνεπορεύοντο δὲ αὐτῷ ὄχλοι πολλοί· καὶ στραφεὶς εἶπε
came together And to Him crowds many; and turning He said
26 πρὸς αὐτούς, Εἴ τις ἔρχεται πρός με, καὶ οὐ μισεῖ τὸν πατέρα
to them, If anyone comes to Me, and not hates the father
ἑαυτοῦ, καὶ τὴν μητέρα, καὶ τὴν γυναῖκα, καὶ τὰ τέκνα, καὶ
of him and the mother, and the wife, and the children, and

children, and brothers, and sisters, and even his own life, too, he is not able to be My disciple. [27]And whoever does not bear his cross and come after Me, he is not able to be My disciple. [28]For which of you desiring to build a tower does not first sit down *to* count the cost, whether he has *enough* to finish; [29]lest he may lay a foundation, and not have strength to finish, *and* all those seeing begin to mock him, saying, This man began to build, and did not have strength to finish? [31]Or what king going out to attack another king in war does not first sit down *to* take counsel whether he is able with ten thousand to meet those with twenty thousands coming on him? [32]But if not, he yet being far off, sending a delegation he asks the *terms* for peace. [33]So, then, everyone of you who does not abandon all his possessions is not able to be My disciple. [34]The salt *is* good, but if the salt becomes tasteless, with what will it be seasoned? [35]It is not fit for land nor for fertilizer. They throw it out. The *one* having ears to hear, let him hear.

CHAPTER 15

[1]And all the tax-collectors and sinners were drawing near to Him to hear Him. [2]And the Pharisees and the scribes murmured, saying, This one receives sinners, and eats with them. [3]And He spoke this parable, saying:

What man of you having a hundred sheep, and losing one of them, does not leave the ninety-nine in the desert, and goes after the lost until he finds it? [5]And finding *it*, *he* puts *it* on his shoulders, rejoicing. [6]And coming to

τοὺς ἀδελφούς, καὶ τὰς ἀδελφάς, ἔτι δὲ καὶ τὴν ἑαυτοῦ ψυχήν,
the brothers, , and the sisters, besides and even the of himself life,
27 οὐ δύναταί μου μαθητὴς εἶναι. καὶ ὅστις οὐ βαστάζει τὸν
not he is able of Me a disciple to be. And who not does bear the
σταυρὸν αὑτοῦ καὶ ἔρχεται ὀπίσω μου, οὐ δύναταί μου
cross of him and comes after Me, not he is able of Me
28 εἶναι μαθητής. τίς γὰρ ἐξ ὑμῶν, θέλων πύργον οἰκοδομῆσαι,
to be a disciple. who For of you desiring a tower to build,
οὐχὶ πρῶτον καθίσας ψηφίζει τὴν δαπάνην, εἰ ἔχει τὰ πρὸς
does not first sitting count the cost, if he has that to
29 ἀπαρτισμόν; ἵνα μήποτε, θέντος αὐτοῦ θεμέλιον καὶ μὴ
bring to completion; lest laying him a foundation, and not
ἰσχύοντος ἐκτελέσαι, πάντες οἱ θεωροῦντες ἄρξωνται ἐμπαί-
having strength to finish all, those seeing begin to mock
30 ζειν αὐτῷ, λέγοντες ὅτι Οὗτος ὁ ἄνθρωπος ἤρξατο οἰκοδο-
him, saying, — This man began to build,
31 μεῖν, καὶ οὐκ ἴσχυσεν ἐκτελέσαι. ἢ τίς βασιλεὺς πορευόμενος
and not had strength to finish. Or what king going
συμβαλεῖν ἑτέρῳ βασιλεῖ εἰς πόλεμον οὐχὶ καθίσας πρῶτον
to attack another king in war does not sitting first
βουλεύεται εἰ δυνατός ἐστιν ἐν δέκα χιλιάσιν ἀπαντῆσαι
take counsel whether able he is with ten thousands to meet
32 τῷ μετὰ εἴκοσι χιλιάδων ἐρχομένῳ ἐπ' αὐτόν; εἰ δὲ μήγε,
those with twenty thousands coming upon him? Otherwise,
ἔτι αὐτοῦ πόρρω ὄντος, πρεσβείαν ἀποστείλας ἐρωτᾷ τὰ
yet him afar being, a delegation sending he asks the
33 πρὸς εἰρήνην. οὕτως οὖν πᾶς ἐξ ὑμῶν ὃς οὐκ ἀποτάσσεται
for peace. So, then everyone of you who not does abandon
πᾶσι τοῖς ἑαυτοῦ ὑπάρχουσιν, οὐ δύναταί μου εἶναι
to all the of himself possessions not is able of Me to be
34 μαθητής. καλὸν τὸ ἅλας· ἐὰν δὲ τὸ ἅλας μωρανθῇ, ἐν τίνι
a disciple. Good (is) the salt; if but the salt becomes useless, with what
35 ἀρτυθήσεται; οὔτε εἰς γῆν οὔτε εἰς κοπρίαν εὔθετόν ἐστιν·
will it be seasoned? Not for soil nor for manure fit it is.
ἔξω βάλλουσιν αὐτό. ὁ ἔχων ὦτα ἀκούειν ἀκουέτω.
out They throw it. The (one) having ears to hear, let him hear.

CHAPTER 15

1 Ἦσαν δὲ ἐγγίζοντες αὐτῷ πάντες οἱ τελῶναι καὶ οἱ
were And drawing near to Him all the tax-collectors and the
2 ἁμαρτωλοί, ἀκούειν αὐτοῦ. καὶ διεγόγγυζον οἱ Φαρισαῖοι
sinners to hear Him. And murmured the Pharisees
καὶ οἱ γραμματεῖς λέγοντες ὅτι Οὗτος ἁμαρτωλοὺς προσδέ-
and the scribes, saying — This one sinners receives,
χεται, καὶ συνεσθίει αὐτοῖς.
and eats with them.
3 Εἶπε δὲ πρὸς αὐτοὺς τὴν παραβολὴν ταύτην, λέγων, Τίς
He spoke and to them — parable this, saying, What
4 ἄνθρωπος ἐξ ὑμῶν ἔχων ἑκατὸν πρόβατα, καὶ ἀπολέσας ἓν
man of you having a hundred sheep, and losing one
ἐξ αὐτῶν, οὐ καταλείπει τὰ ἐννενηκονταεννέα ἐν τῇ ἐρήμῳ,
of them, not does leave the ninety-nine in the desert
5 καὶ πορεύεται ἐπὶ τὸ ἀπολωλός, ἕως εὕρῃ αὐτό; καὶ εὑρὼν
and goes after the lost (one) until he finds it? And finding
6 ἐπιτίθησιν ἐπὶ τοὺς ὤμους ἑαυτοῦ χαίρων. καὶ ἐλθὼν εἰς τὸν
puts (it) on the shoulders of himself, rejoicing. And coming to the

the house, he calls together friends and neighbors, saying to them, Rejoice with me, for I have found my sheep that was lost. [7]And I say to you that the same joy is in Heaven over one sinner repenting, more than over ninety-nine just ones who have no need of repentance.

[8]Or what woman having ten drachmas, if she loses one drachma, does not light a lamp and sweep the house, and seek carefully until she finds *it*? [9]And finding, she calls together the friends and neighbors, saying, Rejoice with me, for I have found the drachma which I lost. [10]So I say to you, there is joy before the angels of God over one sinner repenting.

[11]And He said, A certain man had two sons. [12]And the younger of them said to *his* father, Father, give me the share of the property falling *to me*. And he divided the living to them. [13]And after not many days, gathering together all things, the younger son went way to a distant country. And there *he* wasted his property, living without restraint. [14]But he having spent all, a severe famine came throughout that country. And he began to be in need. [15]And going he was joined to one of the citizens of that country. And he sent him into the fields to feed his pigs. [16]And he was longing to fill his belly from the husks which the pigs ate. And no one gave to him. [17]But coming to himself, he said, How many servants of my father have plenty of loaves, but I am perishing with famine. [18]Rising up I will go to my father, and I will say to him, Father, I sinned against Heaven and before you. [19]And I am no longer worthy to be called your son. Make me as one of your hired servants.

οἶκον, συγκαλεῖ τοὺς φίλους καὶ τοὺς γείτονας, λέγων αὐτοῖς,
house, he calls together the friends and the neighbors, saying to them,
Συγχάρητέ μοι, ὅτι εὗρον τὸ πρόβατόν μου τὸ ἀπολωλός.
Rejoice with me, for I have found the sheep of me — having been lost.
7 λέγω ὑμῖν ὅτι οὕτω χαρὰ ἔσται ἐν τῷ οὐρανῷ ἐπὶ ἑνὶ ἁμαρ-
I say to you that thus joy is in — Heaven over one
τωλῷ μετανοοῦντι, ἢ ἐπὶ ἐννενηκονταεννέα δικαίοις, οἵτινες
sinner repenting, than over ninety-nine just ones who
οὐ χρείαν ἔχουσι μετανοίας.
no need have of repentance.
8 Ἢ τίς γυνὴ δραχμὰς ἔχουσα δέκα, ἐὰν ἀπολέσῃ δραχμὴν
Or what woman drachmas having ten, if she loses drachma
μίαν, οὐχὶ ἅπτει λύχνον, καὶ σαροῖ τὴν οἰκίαν, καὶ ζητεῖ
one, does not light a lamp and sweep the house, and seek
9 ἐπιμελῶς ἕως ὅτου εὕρῃ; καὶ εὑροῦσα συγκαλεῖται τὰς
carefully until she finds? And finding she calls together the
φίλας καὶ τὰς γείτονας, λέγουσα, Συγχάρητέ μοι, ὅτι εὗρον
friends and the neighbors, saying, Rejoice with me, for I have found
10 τὴν δραχμὴν ἣν ἀπώλεσα. οὕτω, λέγω ὑμῖν, χαρὰ γίνεται
the drachma which I lost. So, I say to you, joy there is
ἐνώπιον τῶν ἀγγέλων τοῦ Θεοῦ ἐπὶ ἑνὶ ἁμαρτωλῷ
before the angels — of God over one sinner
μετανοοῦντι.
11 **repenting.**
12 Εἶπε δέ, Ἄνθρωπός τις εἶχε δύο υἱούς· καὶ εἶπεν ὁ νεώτερος
He said And, man a certain had two sons. And said the younger
αὐτῶν τῷ πατρί, Πάτερ, δός μοι τὸ ἐπιβάλλον μέρος τῆς
of them to the father, Father, give me the falling (to me) share of the
13 οὐσίας. καὶ διεῖλεν αὐτοῖς τὸν βίον. καὶ μετ' οὐ πολλὰς
property. And he divided to them the living. And after not many
ἡμέρας συναγαγὼν ἅπαντα ὁ νεώτερος υἱὸς ἀπεδήμησεν εἰς
days, having gathered all things, the younger son went away to
χώραν μακράν, καὶ ἐκεῖ διεσκόρπισε τὴν οὐσίαν αὐτοῦ, ζῶν
a country distant, and there scattered the property of him, living
14 ἀσώτως. δαπανήσαντος δὲ αὐτοῦ πάντα, ἐγένετο λιμὸς
dissolutely. having spent But him all things, came famine
ἰσχυρὸς κατὰ τὴν χώραν ἐκείνην, καὶ αὐτὸς ἤρξατο ὑστερεῖ-
a severe throughout country that; and he began to be in
15 σθαι. καὶ πορευθεὶς ἐκολλήθη ἑνὶ τῶν πολιτῶν τῆς χώρας
need. And going he was joined to one of the citizens — country
ἐκείνης· καὶ ἔπεμψεν αὐτὸν εἰς τοὺς ἀγροὺς αὐτοῦ βόσκειν
of that, and he sent him into the fields of him to feed
16 χοίρους. καὶ ἐπεθύμει γεμίσαι τὴν κοιλίαν αὐτοῦ ἀπὸ τῶν
pigs. And he longed to fill the stomach of him from the
κερατίων ὧν ἤσθιον οἱ χοῖροι· καὶ οὐδεὶς ἐδίδου αὐτῷ. εἰς
husks which ate the pigs; and no one gave to him. to
17 ἑαυτὸν δὲ ἐλθὼν εἶπε, Πόσοι μίσθιοι τοῦ πατρός μου περισ-
himself But coming, he said, How many servants of the father of me
18 σεύουσιν ἄρτων, ἐγὼ δὲ λιμῷ ἀπόλλυμαι· ἀναστὰς πορεύ-
abound in loaves, I but with famine am perishing. Rising up I will
σομαι πρὸς τὸν πατέρα μου, καὶ ἐρῶ αὐτῷ, Πάτερ, ἥμαρτον
go to the father of me, and I will say to him, Father, I sinned
19 εἰς τὸν οὐρανὸν καὶ ἐνώπιόν σου· καὶ οὐκέτι εἰμὶ ἄξιος κληθῆ-
against Heaven, and before you; and no longer am I worthy to be
ναι υἱός σου· ποίησόν με ὡς ἕνα τῶν μισθίων σου. καὶ
called son of you. Make me as one of the servants of you. And

[20] And rising up he went to his father. But he yet being far away, his father saw him, and was moved with pity. And running, *he* fell on his neck and fervently kissed him. [21] And the son said to him, Father, I sinned against Heaven and before you. I am no longer worthy to be called your son. [22] But the father said to his slaves, Bring out the most excellent robe and clothe him. And give a ring for his hand, and sandals for the feet. [23] And bringing the fattened calf, kill *it*, and eating *it*, let us be merry. [24] For this son of mine was dead, and lived again; and was lost, and was found. And they began to be merry. [25] And his elder son was in a field. And as he drew near, coming to the house, he heard music and dances. [26] And calling one of the children to *him*, he inquired what this might be. [27] And he said to him, Your brother came, and your father killed the fattened calf, because he received him back healthy.

[28] But he was angry, and was not willing to go in. Then coming out his father begged him. [29] But answering he said to *his* father, Behold, so many years I served you, and never did I transgress a command of yours. Yet you never gave a goat to me, that I might be merry with my friends. [30] But when this son of yours came, having devoured your living with harlots, you killed the fattened calf for him. [31] But he said to him, Child, you are always with me, and all my things are yours. But it is right to make merry and to rejoice, because this brother of yours was dead, and has lived again; and being lost, also was found.

CHAPTER 16

[1] And He also said to His disciples, A certain man

20 ἀναστὰς ἦλθε πρὸς τὸν πατέρα ἑαυτοῦ. ἔτι δὲ αὐτοῦ μακρὰν
rising up he came to the father of himself. yet But him afar
ἀπέχοντος, εἶδεν αὐτὸν ὁ πατὴρ αὐτοῦ, καὶ ἐσπλαγχνίσθη,
being away, saw him the father of him, and was moved with pity;
καὶ δραμὼν ἐπέπεσεν ἐπὶ τὸν τράχηλον αὐτοῦ, καὶ κατε-
and running fell upon the neck of him, and fervently
21 φίλησεν αὐτόν. εἶπε δὲ αὐτῷ ὁ υἱός, Πάτερ, ἥμαρτον εἰς τὸν
kissed him. said And to him the son, Father, I sinned against —
οὐρανὸν καὶ ἐνώπιόν σου, καὶ οὐκέτι εἰμὶ ἄξιος κληθῆναι
Heaven and before you; and no longer am I worthy to be called
22 υἱός σου. εἶπε δὲ ὁ πατὴρ πρὸς τοὺς δούλους αὐτοῦ, Ἐξε-
son of you. said But the father to the slaves of him, Bring
νέγκατε τὴν στολὴν τὴν πρώτην καὶ ἐνδύσατε αὐτόν, καὶ
out robe the first, and clothe him, and
δότε δακτύλιον εἰς τὴν χεῖρα αὐτοῦ, καὶ ὑποδήματα εἰς τοὺς
give a ring to the hand of him, and sandals to the
23 πόδας· καὶ ἐνέγκαντες τὸν μόσχον τὸν σιτευτὸν θύσατε, καὶ
feet; and bringing the calf — fattened, kill, and
24 φαγόντες εὐφρανθῶμεν· ὅτι οὗτος ο υἱός μου νεκρὸς ἦν, καὶ
eating let us be merry; because this — son of me dead was, and
ἀνέζησε· καὶ ἀπολωλὼς ἦν, καὶ εὑρέθη. καὶ ἤρξαντο
lived again; and lost was, and was found. And they began
25 εὐφραίνεσθαι. ἦν δὲ ὁ υἱὸς αὐτοῦ ὁ πρεσβύτερος ἐν ἀγρῷ·
to be merry. was But the son of him — older in a field;
καὶ ὡς ἐρχόμενος ἤγγισε τῇ οἰκίᾳ, ἤκουσε συμφωνίας καὶ
and as coming he drew near to the house, he heard music and
26 χορῶν. καὶ προσκαλεσάμενος ἕνα τῶν παίδων, ἐπυνθάνετο
dances. And calling to (him) one of the children, he inquired
27 τί εἴη ταῦτα. ὁ δὲ εἶπεν αὐτῷ ὅτι Ὁ ἀδελφός σου ἥκει· καὶ
what may be this. he And said to him, — The brother of you came, and
ἔθυσεν ὁ πατήρ σου τὸν μόσχον τὸν σιτευτόν, ὅτι
killed the father of you the calf — fattened, because
28 ὑγιαίνοντα αὐτὸν ἀπέλαβεν. ὠργίσθη δέ, καὶ οὐκ ἤθελεν
being in health him he received back. he was angry But, and not desired
29 εἰσελθεῖν· ὁ οὖν πατὴρ αὐτοῦ ἐξελθὼν παρεκάλει αὐτόν. ὁ δὲ
to go in. the Then father of him coming out begged him. he But
ἀποκριθεὶς εἶπε τῷ πατρί, Ἰδού, τοσαῦτα ἔτη δουλεύω σοι,
answering said to the father, Behold, so many years I serve you,
καὶ οὐδέποτε ἐντολήν σου παρῆλθον, καὶ ἐμοὶ οὐδέποτε
and never a command of you I transgressed; and to me never
30 ἔδωκας ἔριφον, ἵνα μετὰ τῶν φίλων μου εὐφρανθῶ. ὅτε δὲ ὁ
you gave a goat that with the friends of me I might be merry. when But
υἱός σου οὗτος ὁ καταφαγών σου τὸν βίον μετὰ πορνῶν
son of you this, having devoured of you the living with harlots,
ἦλθεν, ἔθυσας αὐτῷ τὸν μόσχον τὸν σιτευτόν. ὁ δὲ εἶπεν
came, you killed for him the calf — fattened. he And said
31 αὐτῷ, Τέκνον, σὺ πάντοτε μετ᾽ ἐμοῦ εἶ, καὶ πάντα τὰ ἐμὰ σά
to him, Child, you always with me are, and all things(of) mine yours
32 ἐστιν. εὐφρανθῆναι δὲ καὶ χαρῆναι ἔδει· ὅτι ὁ ἀδελφός σου
are. to be merry And, and to rejoice must be, for the brother of you
οὗτος νεκρὸς ἦν, καὶ ἀνέζησε· καὶ ἀπολωλὼς ἦν, καὶ εὑρέθη.
this dead was, and lived again, and having been lost also was found.

CHAPTER 16

1 Ἔλεγε δὲ καὶ πρὸς τοὺς μαθητὰς αὐτοῦ, Ἄνθρωπός τις ἦν
He said And also to the disciples of Him, man A certain was

was rich, who had a steward. And this one was accused to him as wasting his possessions. [2] And calling him, he said to him, What *is* this I hear about you? Give the account of your stewardship; for you no longer can be steward. [3] And the steward said within himself, What shall I do, for my lord is taking away the stewardship from me. I am unable to dig, and I am ashamed to beg. [4] I know what I will do, that when I am removed *from* the stewardship, they will receive me into their houses. [5] And calling one each of the debtors of his lord to *him*, he said to the first, How much do you owe to my lord? [6] And he said, A hundred baths of oil. And he said to him, Take your statements, and sitting down quickly write fifty. [7] Then to another he said, And how much do you owe? And he said, A hundred cors of wheat. And he said to him, Take your statement and write eighty. [8] And the lord praised the unrighteous steward because he acted prudently. For the sons of this world are more prudent in their generation than *are* the sons of light. [9] And I say to you, Make friends to yourselves by the mammon of unrighteousness, so that when it fails, they may receive you into the eternal dwellings. [10] He that *is* faithful in *the* least is also faithful in much. And he that *is* unrighteous in *the* least also is unrighteous in much. [11] Then if you were not faithful in the unrighteous mammon, who will entrust the true to you? [12] And if you were not faithful in that of another, who will give your own to you? [13] No servant is able to serve two lords. For either he will hate the one, and he will love the other, or he will cling to one, and he will despise the other. You are not able to serve God and mammon.
[14] And being lovers of

πλούσιος, ὃς εἶχεν οἰκονόμον· καὶ οὗτος διεβλήθη αὐτῷ ὡς
rich, who had a steward, and this one was accused to him as
2 διασκορπίζων τὰ ὑπάρχοντα αὐτοῦ. καὶ φωνήσας αὐτὸν
wasting the possessions of him. And calling him,
εἶπεν αὐτῷ, Τί τοῦτο ἀκούω περὶ σοῦ; ἀπόδος τὸν λόγον
he said to him, What (is) this I hear about you? Render the account
3 τῆς οἰκονομίας σου· οὐ γὰρ δυνήσῃ ἔτι οἰκονομεῖν. εἶπε δὲ
of the stewardship of you; not for you can longer be steward. said And
ἐν ἑαυτῷ ὁ οἰκονόμος, Τί ποιήσω, ὅτι ὁ κύριός μου ἀφαι-
within himself the steward, What may I do, because the lord of me takes
ρεῖται τὴν οἰκονομίαν ἀπ' ἐμοῦ; σκάπτειν οὐκ ἰσχύω, ἐπαι-
away the stewardship from me? to dig not I am able; to
4 τεῖν αἰσχύνομαι. ἔγνων τί ποιήσω, ἵνα, ὅταν μετασταθῶ
beg I am ashamed. I know what I may do, that when I am removed (from)
5 τῆς οἰκονομίας, δέξωνταί με εἰς τοὺς οἴκους αὐτῶν. καὶ
(from) the stewardship, they receive me into the houses of them. And
προσκαλεσάμενος ἕνα ἕκαστον τῶν χρεωφειλετῶν τοῦ κυρίου
calling to (him) one each of the debtors of the lord
ἑαυτοῦ, ἔλεγε τῷ πρώτῳ, Πόσον ὀφείλεις τῷ κυρίῳ μου;
of himself, he said to the first, How much do you owe to the lord of me?
6 ὁ δὲ εἶπεν, Ἑκατὸν βάτους ἐλαίου. καὶ εἶπεν αὐτῷ, Δέξαι σου
he And said, A hundred baths of oil. And he said to him, Take of you
τὸ γράμμα, καὶ καθίσας ταχέως γράψον πεντήκοντα. ἔπειτα
the statements, and sitting quickly write fifty. Then
7 ἑτέρῳ εἶπε, Σὺ δὲ πόσον ὀφείλεις; ὁ δὲ εἶπεν, Ἑκατὸν κόρους
to another he said, you And how much owe you? he And said, A hundred cors
σίτου. καὶ λέγει αὐτῷ, Δέξαι σου τὸ γράμμα, καὶ γράψον
of wheat. And he said to him, Take of you the statement, and write
8 ὀγδοήκοντα. καὶ ἐπῄνεσεν ὁ κύριος τὸν οἰκονόμον τῆς ἀδικίας
eighty. And praised the lord the steward of unrighteousness
ὅτι φρονίμως ἐποίησεν· ὅτι οἱ υἱοὶ τοῦ αἰῶνος τουτου
because prudently he acted. For the sons — age of this
φρονιμώτεροι ὑπὲρ τοὺς υἱοὺς τοῦ φωτὸς εἰς τὴν γενεὰν
more prudent than the sons of the light in the generation
9 ἑαυτῶν εἰσί. κἀγὼ ὑμῖν λέγω, Ποιήσατε ἑαυτοῖς φίλους ἐκ
of themselves are. And I to you say, Make to yourselves friends by
τοῦ μαμωνᾶ τῆς ἀδικίας, ἵνα, ὅταν ἐκλίπητε, δέξωνται
the mammon of unrighteousness, that when it fails, they may receive
10 ὑμᾶς εἰς τὰς αἰωνίους σκηνας. ὁ πιστὸς ἐν ἐλαχίστῳ καὶ ἐν
you into the eternal dwellings. He faithful in least also in
πολλῷ πιστός ἐστι, καὶ ὁ ἐν ἐλαχίστῳ ἄδικος καὶ ἐν πολλῷ
much faithful is; and he in least (is) unrighteous also in much
11 ἄδικός ἐστιν. εἰ οὖν ἐν τῷ ἀδίκῳ μαμωνᾷ πιστοὶ οὐκ ἐγένεσθε,
unrighteous is. If, then, in the unrighteous mammon faithful not you were,
12 τὸ ἀληθινὸν τίς ὑμῖν πιστεύσει; καὶ εἰ ἐν τῷ ἀλλοτρίῳ
the true who to you will entrust? And if in that of another
13 πιστοὶ οὐκ ἐγένεσθε, τὸ ὑμέτερον τίς ὑμῖν δώσει; οὐδεὶς
faithful not you were, that being yours (is) who to you will give? No
οἰκέτης δύναται δυσὶ κυρίοις δουλεύειν· ἢ γὰρ τὸν ἕνα
houseslave is able two lords to serve; either for the one
μισήσει, καὶ τὸν ἕτερον ἀγαπήσει· ἢ ἑνὸς ἀνθέξεται, καὶ τοῦ
he will hate, and the other he will love, or one he will cling to, and the
ἑτέρου καταφρονήσει. οὐ δύνασθε Θεῷ δουλεύειν καὶ μαμωνᾷ.
other he will despise. not You are able God to serve and mammon.
Ἤκουον δὲ ταῦτα πάντα καὶ οἱ Φαρισαῖοι φιλάργυροι
heard And these things all also the Pharisees, moneylovers

money, the Pharisees also heard all these things, and they derided Him. [15] And He said to them, You are those justifying yourselves before men, but God knows your hearts. For the thing highly prized among men is a hateful thing before God. [16] The Law and the Prophets *were* until John; from then the kingdom of God was preached; and everyone is pressing into it. [17] But it is easier *for* the heaven and the earth to pass away, than for one tittle of the law to fail. [18] Everyone putting away his wife and marrying another commits adultery. And everyone marrying her having been put away from a husband commits adultery.

[19] And there was a certain rich man. And *he* customarily put on a purple robe and fine linen, being merry day by day, in luxury. [20] And there was a poor one; and *his* name was Lazarus, who had been laid at his porch, being plagued with sores. [21] And *he was* desiring to be filled from the crumbs that were falling from the table of the rich one. But having come, even the dogs licked his sores. [22] And it happened that the poor one died, and he was carried away by the angels into Abraham's bosom. And the rich one also died, and was buried. [23] And being in torments in Hell, lifting up his eyes, he sees Abraham from afar, and Lazarus in his bosoms. [24] And calling he said, Father Abraham, pity me, and send Lazarus, that he may dip the tip of his finger in water, and may cool my tongue; for I am suffering in this flame. [25] But Abraham said, Child, remember that you fully received your good things in your life, and Lazarus likewise the bad. But now he is comforted, but you are suffering. [26] And besides all these things, a great chasm has been fixed between us and you, so that

14 ὑπάρχοντες, καὶ ἐξεμυκτήριζον αὐτόν. καὶ εἶπεν αὐτοῖς,
15 being; and they derided Him. And He said to them,
Ὑμεῖς ἐστε οἱ δικαιοῦντες ἑαυτοὺς ἐνώπιον τῶν ἀνθρώπων
You are those justifying yourselves before — men,
ὁ δὲ Θεὸς γινώσκει τὰς καρδίας ὑμῶν· ὅτι τὸ ἐν ἀνθρώποις
—But God knows the hearts of you; for the thing among men
16 ὑψηλὸν βδέλυγμα ἐνώπιον τοῦ Θεοῦ ἐστιν. ὁ νόμος καὶ οἱ
highly prized an abomination before — God is. The Law and the
προφῆται ἕως Ἰωάννου· ἀπὸ τότε ἡ βασιλεία τοῦ Θεοῦ
Prophets (were) until John; from then the kingdom — of God
17 εὐαγγελίζεται, καὶ πᾶς εἰς αὐτὴν βιάζεται. εὐκοπώτερον δέ
is being preached; and everyone into it is pressing . easier But
ἐστι τὸν οὐρανὸν καὶ τὴν γῆν παρελθεῖν, ἢ τοῦ νόμου μίαν
it is the heaven and the earth to pass away, than of the law one
18 κεραίαν πεσεῖν. πᾶς ὁ ἀπολύων τὴν γυναῖκα αὐτοῦ καὶ
tittle to fall. Everyone putting away the wife of him and
γαμῶν ἑτέραν μοιχεύει· καὶ πᾶς ὁ ἀπολελυμένην ἀπὸ ἀνδρὸς
marrying another commits adultery and everyone having been put away her from a husband
γαμῶν μοιχεύει.
marrying, commits adultery.

19 Ἄνθρωπος δέ τις ἦν πλούσιος, καὶ ἐνεδιδύσκετο πορφύραν
man And a certain was rich, and customarily donned a purple robe
20 καὶ βύσσον, εὐφραινόμενος καθ' ἡμέραν λαμπρῶς. πτωχὸς
and fine linen, being merry day by day, in luxury poor one
δέ τις ἦν ὀνόματι Λάζαρος, ὃς ἐβέβλητο πρὸς τὸν πυλῶνα
And a was by name Lazarus who had been laid at the porch
21 αὐτοῦ ἡλκωμένος καὶ ἐπιθυμῶν χορτασθῆναι ἀπὸ τῶν
of him, being sore-plagued and desiring to be filled from the
ψιχίων τῶν πιπτόντων ἀπὸ τῆς τραπέζης τοῦ πλουσίου·
crumbs that were falling from the table of the rich one.
ἀλλὰ καὶ οἱ κύνες ἐρχόμενοι ἀπέλειχον τὰ ἕλκη αὐτοῦ.
But even the dogs coming licked the sores of him.
22 ἐγένετο δὲ ἀποθανεῖν τὸν πτωχόν, καὶ ἀπενεχθῆναι αὐτὸν
it was And, died the poor one, and was carried away him
ὑπὸ τῶν ἀγγέλων εἰς τὸν κόλπον τοῦ Ἀβραάμ· ἀπέθανε δὲ
by the angels into the bosom — of Abraham. died And
23 καὶ ὁ πλούσιος, καὶ ἐτάφη. καὶ ἐν τῷ ᾅδῃ ἐπάρας τοὺς
also the rich one, and was buried. And in — Hades lifting up the
ὀφθαλμοὺς αὐτοῦ, ὑπάρχων ἐν βασάνοις, ὁρᾷ τὸν Ἀβραὰμ
eyes of him, being in torments, he sees — Abraham
24 ἀπὸ μακρόθεν, καὶ Λάζαρον ἐν τοῖς κόλποις αὐτοῦ. καὶ αὐτὸς
from afar, and Lazarus in the bosoms of him. And he
φωνήσας εἶπε, Πάτερ Ἀβραάμ, ἐλέησόν με, καὶ πέμψον
calling said, Father Abraham, pity me, and send
Λάζαρον, ἵνα βάψῃ τὸ ἄκρον τοῦ δακτύλου αὐτοῦ ὕδατος,
Lazarus, that he may dip the tip of the finger of him of water
καὶ καταψύξῃ τὴν γλῶσσάν μου· ὅτι ὀδυνῶμαι ἐν τῇ
and may cool the tongue of me because I am suffering in —
25 φλογὶ ταύτῃ. εἶπε δὲ Ἀβραάμ, Τέκνον, μνήσθητι ὅτι ἀπέ-
flame this. said But Abraham, Child, remember that fully re-
λαβες σὺ τὰ ἀγαθά σου ἐν τῇ ζωῇ σου, καὶ Λάζαρος ὁμοίως
ceived you things good of you in the life of you, and Lazarus likewise
26 τὰ κακά· νῦν δὲ ὧδε παρακαλεῖται, σὺ δὲ ὀδυνᾶσαι. καὶ ἐπὶ
the bad. now But here he is comforted. you but are suffering. And besides
πᾶσι τούτοις, μεταξὺ ἡμῶν καὶ ὑμῶν χάσμα μέγα ἐστη-
all these things, between us and you a chasm great has

those desiring to pass from here to you are not able; nor may those from there pass over to us. [27] And he said, Then I beg you, father, that you send him to the house of my father, [28] for I have five brothers, so that he may testify to them, that they may not also come to this place of torment. [29] Abraham said to him, They have Moses and the Prophets, let them hear them. [30] But he said, No, Father Abraham, but if one from *the* dead should go to them, they will repent. [31] And he said to him, If they will not hear Moses and the Prophets, they will not be persuaded, not even if one from *the* dead should rise.

CHAPTER 17

[1] And He said to the disciples, It is impossible that offenses should not come, but woe *to him* through whom they come. [2] It is profitable for him if a millstone turned by an ass is put around his neck, and he be thrown into the sea, than that he should cause one of these little ones to offend. [3] Take heed to yourselves. And if your brother sins against you, rebuke him. And if he repents, forgive him. [4] And if seven times in a day he sins against you, and seven times in a day turns to you, saying, I repent; you shall forgive him.

[5] And the apostles said to the Lord, Add more faith to us. [6] But the Lord said, If you have faith as a grain of mustard, you may say to this sycamine tree, Be rooted up, and be planted in the sea!

And it would obey you. [7] But which of you having a slave plowing or feeding will say immediately *to him* who comes in out of the field, Come, recline? [8] But will *you* not say to him, Prepare something I may eat, and, Having girded yourself,

ρικται, ὅπως οἱ θέλοντες διαβῆναι ἐντεῦθεν πρὸς ὑμᾶς μὴ
been fixed so that those desiring to pass from here to you not
27 δύνωνται, μηδὲ οἱ ἐκεῖθεν πρὸς ἡμᾶς διαπερῶσιν. εἶπε δέ,
are able, nor those from there to us may cross over. he said And,
Ἐρωτῶ οὖν σε, πάτερ, ἵνα πέμψῃς αὐτὸν εἰς τὸν οἶκον τοῦ
I ask Then you, father, that you send him to the house of the
28 πατρός μου, ἔχω γὰρ πέντε ἀδελφούς, ὅπως διαμαρτύρηται
father of me; I have for five brothers; so that he may witness
αὐτοῖς, ἵνα μὴ καὶ αὐτοὶ ἔλθωσιν εἰς τὸν τόπον τοῦτον τῆς
to them, that not also they come to — place this —
29 βασάνου. λέγει αὐτῷ Ἀβραάμ, Ἔχουσι Μωσέα καὶ τοὺς
of torment. says to him Abraham, They have Moses and the
30 προφήτας· ἀκουσάτωσαν αὐτῶν. ὁ δὲ εἶπεν, Οὐχί, πάτερ
prophets, let them hear them. he But said, No, father
Ἀβραάμ· ἀλλ' ἐάν τις ἀπὸ νεκρῶν πορευθῇ πρὸς αὐτούς,
Abraham, but if one from (the) dead should go to them,
31 μετανοήσουσιν. εἶπε δὲ αὐτῷ, Εἰ Μωσέως καὶ τῶν προφη-
they will repent. he said And to him, If Moses and the prophets
τῶν οὐκ ἀκούουσιν, οὐδέ, ἐάν τις ἐκ νεκρῶν ἀναστῇ,
not they will hear, not even if one from (the) dead should rise
πεισθήσονται.
will they be persuaded.

CHAPTER 17

1 Εἶπε δὲ πρὸς τοὺς μαθητάς, Ἀνένδεκτόν ἐστι τοῦ μὴ
He said And to the disciples, Impossible it is — not
2 ἐλθεῖν τὰ σκάνδαλα· οὐαὶ δὲ δι' οὗ ἔρχεται. λυσιτελεῖ αὐτῷ
should come offenses, woe but through whom they come It profits him
εἰ μύλος ὀνικὸς περίκειται περὶ τὸν τράχηλον αὐτοῦ, καὶ
If a millstone of an ass is put around the neck of him, and
ἔρριπται εἰς τὴν θάλασσαν, ἢ ἵνα σκανδαλίσῃ ἕνα τῶν
he be cast into the sea, than that he should offend one —
3 μικρῶν τούτων. προσέχετε ἑαυτοῖς. ἐὰν δὲ ἁμάρτῃ εἰς σὲ ὁ
little ones of these. Take heed to yourselves. if And sins against you the
ἀδελφός σου, ἐπιτίμησον αὐτῷ· καὶ ἐὰν μετανοήσῃ, ἄφες
brother of you, rebuke him; and if he repents, forgive
4 αὐτῷ. καὶ ἐὰν ἑπτάκις τῆς ἡμέρας ἁμάρτῃ εἰς σέ, καὶ
him. And if seven times of the day he sins against you, and
ἑπτάκις τῆς ἡμέρας ἐπιστρέψῃ ἐπί σε, λέγων, Μετανοῶ,
seven times of the day turns to you, saying, I repent;
ἀφήσεις αὐτῷ.
you shall forgive him.
5 Καὶ εἶπον οἱ ἀπόστολοι τῷ Κυρίῳ, Πρόσθες ἡμῖν πίστιν.
And said the apostles to the Lord, Add to us faith.
6 εἶπε δὲ ὁ Κύριος, Εἰ εἴχετε πίστιν ὡς κόκκον σινάπεως,
said And the Lord, If you have faith as a grain of mustard,
ἐλέγετε ἂν τῇ συκαμίνῳ ταύτῃ, Ἐκριζώθητι, καὶ φυτεύθητι
you may say — sycamine to this, Be rooted up, and be planted
7 ἐν τῇ θαλάσσῃ· καὶ ὑπήκουσεν ἂν ὑμῖν. τίς δὲ ἐξ ὑμῶν δοῦλον
in the sea; even it would obey you. who But of you a slave
ἔχων ἀροτριῶντα ἢ ποιμαίνοντα, ὃς εἰσελθόντι ἐκ τοῦ
having plowing or shepherding, who (to him) come out of the
8 ἀγροῦ ἐρεῖ εὐθέως, Παρελθὼν ἀνάπεσαι· ἀλλ' οὐχὶ ἐρεῖ
field will say immediately, Having come, recline? But not will say
αὐτῷ, Ἑτοίμασον τί δειπνήσω, καὶ περιζωσάμενος διακόνει
to him, Prepare something I may eat; and having girded yourself serve

serve me until I eat and drink; and after these things you eat and drink? [9]Does he have thanks to that slave because he did the things commanded of him. I think not. [10]So also you, when you have all things commanded you, say, We are unprofitable slaves; what we ought to do, we have done.

[11]And it happened in His going to Jerusalem, He also passed through *the* middle of Samaria and Galilee. [12]And he having entered into a certain village, ten leprous men met Him, who stood afar off. [13]And they lifted up *their* voice, saying, Jesus, Master, pity us. [14]And seeing *them,* He said to them, Going, show yourselves to the priests. And it happened in their going, they were cleansed. [15]And one of them, seeing that he was cured, returned, glorifying God with a loud voice. [16]And *he* fell on *his* face at His feet, thanking Him. And he was a Samaritan. [17]And answering Jesus said, Were not the ten cleansed? But where *are* the nine? [18]Were there not found *any* returning to give glory to God except this stranger? [19]And He said to him, Rising up, go! Your faith has healed you.

[20]And being questioned by the Pharisees when the kingdom of God is coming, He answered them and said, The kingdom of God does not come with observation, [21]nor will they say, Behold, here; or behold, there! For behold the kingdom of God is within you.

[22]And He said to His disciples, Days will come when you will long to see one of the days of the Son of man, and will not see. [23]And they will say to you, Behold, here! Or, Behold, there! Do not go away, nor follow. [24]For as the lightning lights

μοι, ἕως φάγω καὶ πίω· καὶ μετὰ ταῦτα φάγεσαι καὶ πίεσαι
me until I eat and drink; and after these things eat and drink
9 σύ ; μὴ χάριν ἔχει τῷ δούλῳ ἐκείνῳ ὅτι ἐποίησε τὰ δια-
you. (Does) thanks he have slave to that because he did the things
10 ταχθέντα αὐτῷ ; οὐ δοκῶ. οὕτω καὶ ὑμεῖς, ὅταν ποιήσητε
commanded of him? not I think. So also you, when you have done
πάντα τὰ διαταχθέντα ὑμῖν, λέγετε ὅτι Δοῦλοι ἀχρεῖοί ἐσμεν·
all things commanded you, say, — Slaves unprofitable we are;
ὅτι ὃ ὠφείλομεν ποιῆσαι πεποιήκαμεν.
what we ought to do, we have done.
11 Καὶ ἐγένετο ἐν τῷ πορεύεσθαι αὐτὸν εἰς Ἱερουσαλήμ, καὶ
And it was, in the going of Him to Jerusalem, even
12 αὐτὸς διήρχετο διὰ μέσου Σαμαρείας καὶ Γαλιλαίας. καὶ
He passed through (the) midst of Samaria and Galilee. And
εἰσερχομένου αὐτοῦ εἴς τινα κώμην, ἀπήντησαν αὐτῷ δέκα
entering him into a certain village, met Him ten
13 λεπροὶ ἄνδρες, οἳ ἔστησαν πόρρωθεν· καὶ αὐτοὶ ἦραν φωνήν,
leprous men, who stood afar off, and they lifted voice,
14 λέγοντες, Ἰησοῦ, ἐπιστάτα, ἐλέησον ἡμᾶς. καὶ ἰδὼν εἶπεν
saying, Jesus, Master, pity us. And seeing He said
αὐτοῖς, Πορευθέντες ἐπιδείξατε ἑαυτοὺς τοῖς ἱερεῦσι. καὶ
to them, Going show yourselves to the priests. And
15 ἐγένετο ἐν τῷ ὑπάγειν αὐτούς, ἐκαθαρίσθησαν. εἷς δὲ ἐξ
it was. in the going (of) them, they were cleansed. one But of
αὐτῶν, ἰδὼν ὅτι ἰάθη, ὑπέστρεψε, μετὰ φωνῆς μεγάλης
them, seeing that he was cured, returned with a voice great
16 δοξάζων τὸν Θεόν· καὶ ἔπεσεν ἐπὶ πρόσωπον παρὰ τοὺς
glorifying — God, and fell upon (his) face at the
πόδας αὐτοῦ, εὐχαριστῶν αὐτῷ· καὶ αὐτὸς ἦν Σαμαρείτης.
feet of Him, thanking Him; and he was a Samaritan.
17 ἀποκριθεὶς δὲ ὁ Ἰησοῦς εἶπεν, Οὐχὶ οἱ δέκα ἐκαθαρίσθησαν ;
answering And — Jesus said, Not the ten were cleansed?
18 οἱ δὲ ἐννέα ποῦ ; οὐχ εὑρέθησαν ὑποστρέψαντες δοῦναι δόξαν
the But nine, where? not Were found returning to give glory
19 τῷ Θεῷ, εἰ μὴ ὁ ἀλλογενὴς οὗτος, καὶ εἶπεν αὐτῷ, Ἀναστὰς
to God, except stranger this? And He said to him, Rising up
πορεύου· ἡ πίστις σου σέσωκέ σε.
go! The faith of you has healed you.
20 Ἐπερωτηθεὶς δὲ ὑπὸ τῶν Φαρισαίων, πότε ἔρχεται ἡ
being questioned And by the Pharisees, when comes the
βασιλεία τοῦ Θεοῦ, ἀπεκρίθη αὐτοῖς καὶ εἶπεν, Οὐκ ἔρχεται
kingdom — of God, He answered them and said, does not come
21 ἡ βασιλεία τοῦ Θεοῦ μετὰ παρατηρήσεως· οὐδὲ ἐροῦσιν,
The kingdom — of God with observation, nor will they say,
Ἰδοὺ ὧδε, ἤ, Ἰδοὺ ἐκεῖ. ἰδοὺ γάρ, ἡ βασιλεία τοῦ Θεοῦ ἐντὸς
Behold, here; or behold, there. behold For, the kingdom — of God within
ὑμῶν ἐστιν.
you is.
22 Εἶπε δὲ πρὸς τοὺς μαθητάς, Ἐλεύσονται ἡμέραι ὅτε
He said And to the disciples, will come Days when
ἐπιθυμήσετε μίαν τῶν ἡμερῶν τοῦ υἱοῦ τοῦ ἀνθρώπου ἰδεῖν,
you will long one of the days of the Son — of man to see,
23 καὶ οὐκ ὄψεσθε. καὶ ἐροῦσιν ὑμῖν, Ἰδοὺ ὧδε, ἤ, Ἰδοὺ ἐκεῖ· μὴ
and not will see. And they will say to you, Behold here, or, behold, there; not
24 ἀπέλθητε, μηδὲ διώξητε. ὥσπερ γὰρ ἡ ἀστραπὴ ἡ ἀστρά-
do go away, nor follow. as For the lightning which lights up

up, flashing from the *one part* under heaven, and shines to the *other part* under heaven, so will the Son of man be in His day. [25]But first He must suffer many things, and to be rejected from this generation. [26]And as it was in the days of Noah, so also it will be in the days of the Son of man: [27]They were eating, drinking, marrying, giving in marriage, until *the* day Noah went into the ark. And the Flood came and destroyed all. [28]And likewise, as it was in the days of Lot: they were eating, drinking, buying, selling, planting, building; [29]but on *the* day Lot went out from Sodom, it rained fire and brimstone from Heaven, and destroyed all. [30]Even so it will be in the day the Son of man is revealed.

[31]In that day *he* who will be on the housetop, and his goods in the house, let him not come down to take them. And the *one* in the field likewise, let him not turn back to the things behind. [32]Remember Lot's wife. [33]Whoever seeks to save his soul will lose it. And whoever will lose it, he will preserve it. [34]I say to you, In that night there will be two on one bed; the one will be taken, and the other will be left. [35]Two will be grinding together; one will be taken, and the other will be left. [36]Two will be in the field; the one will be taken, and the other will be left. [37]And answering they said to Him, Where, Lord? And He said to them, Where the body *is*, there the eagles will be gathered.

CHAPTER 18

[1]And He also spoke a parable to them to *teach* it is always right to pray, and not to faint, [2]saying, A certain judge was in a city, not fearing God, and not respect-

πτουσα ἐκ τῆς ὑπ' οὐρανὸν εἰς τὴν ὑπ' οὐρανὸν λάμπει, οὕτως
flashing out of that under heaven to that under heaven shines, so
ἔσται καὶ ὁ υἱὸς τοῦ ἀνθρώπου ἐν τῇ ἡμέρᾳ αὐτοῦ. πρῶτον
will be also the Son — of man in the day of Him. first
25 δὲ δεῖ αὐτὸν πολλὰ παθεῖν καὶ ἀποδοκιμασθῆναι ἀπὸ τῆς
But must Him many things suffer, and to be rejected from —
26 γενεᾶς ταύτης. καὶ καθὼς ἐγένετο ἐν ταῖς ἡμέραις τοῦ Νῶε,
generation this. And as it was in the days — of Noah,
οὕτως ἔσται καὶ ἐν ταῖς ἡμέραις τοῦ υἱοῦ τοῦ ἀνθρώπου.
so it will be also in the days of the Son — of man.
27 ἤσθιον, ἔπινον, ἐγάμουν, ἐξεγαμίζοντο, ἄχρι ἧς ἡμέρας
They were eating, drinking, marrying, giving in marriage, until which day
εἰσῆλθε Νῶε εἰς τὴν κιβωτόν, καὶ ἦλθεν ὁ κατακλυσμός, καὶ
went in Noah into the ark. And came the Flood and
28 ἀπώλεσεν ἅπαντας. ὁμοίως καὶ ὡς ἐγένετο ἐν ταῖς ἡμέραις
destroyed all. Likewise also, as it was in the days
Λώτ· ἤσθιον, ἔπινον, ἠγόραζον, ἐπώλουν, ἐφύτευον,
of Lot, they were eating, drinking, buying, selling, planting,
29 ᾠκοδόμουν· ᾗ δὲ ἡμέρᾳ ἐξῆλθε Λὼτ ἀπὸ Σοδόμων, ἔβρεξε
building; on which but day went out Lot from Sodom, it rained
30 πῦρ καὶ θεῖον ἀπ' οὐρανοῦ, καὶ ἀπώλεσεν ἅπαντας· κατὰ
fire and brimstone from heaven and destroyed all. In this
ταῦτα ἔσται ᾗ ἡμέρᾳ ὁ υἱὸς τοῦ ἀνθρώπου ἀποκαλύπτεται
way it will be in the day the Son — of man is revealed.
31 ἐν ἐκείνῃ τῇ ἡμέρᾳ, ὃς ἔσται ἐπὶ τοῦ δώματος, καὶ τὰ
In that — day, who will be on the housetop, and the
σκεύη αὐτοῦ ἐν τῇ οἰκίᾳ, μὴ καταβάτω ἆραι αὐτά· καὶ ὁ
goods of him in the house, not let him descend to take them; and he
32 ἐν τῷ ἀγρῷ ὁμοίως μὴ ἐπιστρεψάτω εἰς τὰ ὀπίσω. μνη-
in the field likewise, not let him turn back to the things behind. Re-
33 μονεύετε τῆς γυναικὸς Λώτ. ὃς ἐὰν ζητήσῃ τὴν ψυχὴν
member the wife of Lot. Whoever seeks the soul
αὐτοῦ σῶσαι ἀπολέσει αὐτήν· καὶ ὃς ἐὰν ἀπολέσῃ αὐτὴν
of him to save, he will lose it; and whoever will lose it,
34 ζωογονήσει αὐτήν. λέγω ὑμῖν, ταύτῃ τῇ νυκτὶ ἔσονται δύο
will preserve it. I say to you, in this — night will be two
ἐπὶ κλίνης μιᾶς· ὁ εἷς παραληφθήσεται, καὶ ὁ ἕτερος ἀφεθή-
on bed one; the one will be taken, and the other will
35 σεται. δύο ἔσονται ἀλήθουσαι ἐπὶ τὸ αὐτό ἡ μία παρα-
be left. Two will be grinding together; the one will
36 ληφθήσεται, καὶ ἡ ἑτέρα ἀφεθήσεται. δύο ἔσονται ἐν τῷ
be taken, and the other will be left. Two will be in the
37 ἀγρῷ ὁ εἷς παραληφθήσεται, καὶ ὁ ἕτερος ἀφεθήσεται. καὶ
field; the one will be taken, and the other will be left. And
ἀποκριθέντες λέγουσιν αὐτῷ, Ποῦ, Κύριε; ὁ δὲ εἶπεν αὐτοῖς,
answering they say to Him, Where, Lord? He And said to them,
Ὅπου τὸ σῶμα, ἐκεῖ συναχθήσονται οἱ ἀετοί.
Where the body (is), there will be gathered the eagles.

CHAPTER 18

1 Ἔλεγε δὲ καὶ παραβολὴν αὐτοῖς πρὸς τὸ δεῖν πάντοτε
He told And also a parable to them to (teach) it is right always
2 προσεύχεσθαι, καὶ μὴ ἐκκακεῖν, λέγων, Κριτής τις ἦν ἔν τινι
to pray, and not to faint, saying, A judge certain was in a
πόλει, τὸν Θεὸν μὴ φοβούμενος, καὶ ἄνθρωπον μὴ ἐντρεπό-
city, God not fearing, and man not respecting.

ing man. 3 And a widow was in that city, and she came to him, saying, Avenge me of my adversary. 4 And he for a time would not. But after these things he said to himself, Even if I do not fear God, and do not respect man, 5 yet because this widow causes me trouble, I will avenge her, that coming in *the* end she may not subdue me. 6 And the Lord said, Hear what the unrighteous judge says; 7 and will God not at all carry out the avenging of His elect, those crying to Him day and night, and being patient over them? 8 I say to you that He will carry out the avenging of them speedily. But the Son of man coming then, will He find faith on the earth?

9 And He also spoke this parable to some *of* those relying on themselves, that they are righteous, and despising the rest:

10 Two men went up into the Temple to pray, the one a Pharisee, and the other a tax-collector. 11 The Pharisee was standing and praying these things to himself, God, I thank You that I am not as the rest of men, rapacious, unrighteous, adulterers, or even as this tax-collector. 12 I fast twice in the week, I tithe all things, as many as I get. 13 And standing at a distance, the tax-collector would not even lift up *his* eyes to Heaven, but smote on his breast, saying, God, be merciful to me, the sinner! 14 I say to you, This one went down to his house justified, rather than that one. For everyone exalting himself will be humbled. And the *one* humbling himself will be exalted.

15 And they brought infants to Him also, that He might touch them. But seeing, the disciples rebuked

3 μενος· χήρα δὲ ἦν ἐν τῇ πόλει ἐκείνῃ, καὶ ἤρχετο πρὸς αὐτόν
a widow And was in city that, and she came to him,

4 λέγουσα, Ἐκδίκησόν με ἀπὸ τοῦ ἀντιδίκου μου. καὶ οὐκ
saying, Avenge me from the adversary of me. And not

ἠθέλησεν ἐπὶ χρόνον· μετὰ δὲ ταῦτα εἶπεν ἐν ἑαυτῷ, Εἰ
he would for a time; after but these things he said in himself, If

καὶ τὸν Θεὸν οὐ φοβοῦμαι, καὶ ἄνθρωπον οὐκ ἐντρέπομαι·
even – God not I fear, and man not respect,

5 διά γε τὸ παρέχειν μοι κόπον τὴν χήραν ταύτην, ἐκδικήσω
yet because causes me trouble – widow this, I will avenge

6 αὐτήν, ἵνα μὴ εἰς τέλος ἐρχομένη ὑπωπιάζῃ με. εἶπε δὲ ὁ
her, lest in (the) end coming she subdue me. said And the

7 Κύριος, Ἀκούσατε τί ὁ κριτὴς τῆς ἀδικίας λέγει. ὁ δὲ Θεὸς
Lord, Hear what the judge of unrighteousness says; – and God

οὐ μὴ ποιήσει τὴν ἐκδίκησιν τῶν ἐκλεκτῶν αὐτοῦ τῶν
in no way will execute the avenging of the elect of Him, those

βοώντων πρὸς αὐτὸν ἡμέρας καὶ νυκτός, καὶ μακροθυμῶν
crying to Him day and night, and being patient

8 ἐπ᾽ αὐτοῖς; λέγω ὑμῖν ὅτι ποιήσει τὴν ἐκδίκησιν αὐτῶν ἐν
over them? I say to you that He will execute the avenging of them

τάχει. πλὴν ὁ υἱὸς τοῦ ἀνθρώπου ἐλθὼν ἆρα εὑρήσει τὴν
speedily But the Son – of man coming then, will He find –

πίστιν ἐπὶ τῆς γῆς;
faith on the earth?

9 Εἶπε δὲ καὶ πρός τινας τοὺς πεποιθότας ἐφ᾽ ἑαυτοῖς ὅτι
He said And also to some (of) those relying on themselves, that

εἰσὶ δίκαιοι, καὶ ἐξουθενοῦντας τοὺς λοιπούς, τὴν παρα-
they are righteous, also despising the rest;

10 βολὴν ταύτην· Ἄνθρωποι δύο ἀνέβησαν εἰς τὸ ἱερὸν
parable this, men Two went up to the Temple

11 προσεύξασθαι· ὁ εἷς Φαρισαῖος, καὶ ὁ ἕτερος τελώνης. ὁ
to pray, the one a Pharisee, and the other a tax-collector. The

Φαρισαῖος σταθεὶς πρὸς ἑαυτὸν ταῦτα προσηύχετο, Ὁ
Pharisee standing, to himself these things praying,

Θεός, εὐχαριστῶ σοι ὅτι οὐκ εἰμὶ ὥσπερ οἱ λοιποὶ τῶν
God, I thank You that not I am as the rest –

ἀνθρώπων, ἅρπαγες, ἄδικοι, μοιχοί, ἢ καὶ ὡς οὗτος ὁ
of men, rapacious, unrighteous, adulterers, or even as this

12 τελώνης. νηστεύω δὶς τοῦ σαββάτου, ἀποδεκατῶ πάντα
tax-collector. I fast twice (in) the week; I tithe all things,

13 ὅσα κτῶμαι. καὶ ὁ τελώνης μακρόθεν ἑστὼς οὐκ ἤθελεν οὐδὲ
as many as I get. And the tax-collector afar off standing not would not even

τοὺς ὀφθαλμοὺς εἰς τὸν οὐρανὸν ἐπᾶραι, ἀλλ᾽ ἔτυπτεν εἰς τὸ
the eyes to – Heaven lift up, but smote on the

στῆθος αὐτοῦ, λέγων, Ὁ Θεός, ἱλάσθητί μοι τῷ ἁμαρτωλῷ.
breast of him, saying, God, be merciful to me the sinner.

14 λέγω ὑμῖν, κατέβη οὗτος δεδικαιωμένος εἰς τὸν οἶκον αὐτοῦ
I say to you, went down this one having been justified to the house of him

ἢ ἐκεῖνος· ὅτι πᾶς ὁ ὑψῶν ἑαυτὸν ταπεινωθήσεται, ὁ δὲ τα-
than that one, for everyone exalting himself will be humbled; he And

πεινῶν ἑαυτὸν ὑψωθήσεται.
humbling himself will be exalted.

15 Προσέφερον δὲ αὐτῷ καὶ τὰ βρέφη, ἵνα αὐτῶν ἅπτηται·
they brought And to Him also the babes, that them He might touch;

ἰδόντες δὲ οἱ μαθηταὶ ἐπετίμησαν αὐτοῖς. ὁ δὲ Ἰησοῦς
seeing but, the disciples rebuked them. – But Jesus

them. [16]But Jesus called them near, saying, Allow the children to come to Me, and do not prevent them. For of such is the kingdom of God. [17]Truly I say to you, Whoever does not receive the kingdom of God like a child, not at all will enter into it.

[18]And a certain ruler asked Him, saying, Good Teacher, what may I do to inherit eternal life? [19]But Jesus said to him, Why do you say I *am* good? No one *is* good, except One: God. [20]You know the commandments: Do not commit adultery, do not murder, do not steal, do not bear false witness, honor your father and your mother. [21]And he said, I have kept all these things from my youth. [22]And hearing these things, Jesus said to him, Yet one thing is lacking to you: sell all, as much as you have, and give to *the* poor, and you will have treasure in Heaven. And come, follow Me. [23]But hearing these things, he became exceedingly grieved, for he was exceedingly rich. [24]And seeing him having become exceedingly grieved, Jesus said, How hardly those having riches shall enter into the kingdom of God! [25]For it is easier *for* a camel to go in through a needle's eye than *for* a rich one to enter into the kingdom of God. [26]And those hearing said, And who is able to be saved? [27]But He said, The things impossible with men are possible with God. [28]And Peter said, Behold, we left all and followed You. [29]And he said to them, Truly I say to you, There is no one who has left house, or parents, or brothers, or wife, or children, for the sake of the kingdom of God, [30]who shall not receive many times more in this time, and in the age that is coming everlasting life.

[31]And taking the Twelve, He said to them, Behold, we are going up to Jerusalem, and all things will be fulfilled

16 προσκαλεσάμενος αὐτὰ εἶπεν, Ἄφετε τὰ παιδία ἔρχεσθαι
called near them, saying, Allow the children to come
πρός με, καὶ μὴ κωλύετε αὐτά· τῶν γὰρ τοιούτων ἐστὶν ἡ
to Me, and not do prevent them, – for of such is the
17 βασιλεία τοῦ Θεοῦ. ἀμὴν λέγω ὑμῖν, ὃς ἐὰν μὴ δέξηται τὴν
kingdom – of God. Truly I say to you, whoever not receives the
βασιλείαν τοῦ Θεοῦ ὡς παιδίον, οὐ μὴ εἰσέλθῃ εἰς αὐτήν.
kingdom – of God as a child, in no way enters into it.
18 Καὶ ἐπηρώτησέ τις αὐτὸν ἄρχων, λέγων, Διδάσκαλε
And questioned a certain Him ruler, saying, Teacher
19 ἀγαθέ, τί ποιήσας ζωὴν αἰώνιον κληρονομήσω; εἶπε δὲ
good, what doing life eternal I may inherit? said And
αὐτῷ ὁ Ἰησοῦς, Τί με λέγεις ἀγαθόν; οὐδεὶς ἀγαθός, εἰ μὴ
to him – Jesus, Why Me you say (is) good? No one (is) good, except
20 εἷς, ὁ Θεός. τὰς ἐντολὰς οἶδας, Μὴ μοιχεύσῃς, μὴ φονεύσῃς,
One, God. The commands you know, Not do adultery, not kill,
μὴ κλέψῃς, μὴ ψευδομαρτυρήσῃς, τίμα τὸν πατέρα σου καὶ
not steal, not bear false witness, honor the father of you and
21 τὴν μητέρα σου. ὁ δὲ εἶπε, Ταῦτα πάντα ἐφυλαξάμην ἐκ
the mother of you. he And said, these things All I have kept from
22 νεότητός μου. ἀκούσας δὲ ταῦτα ὁ Ἰησοῦς εἶπεν αὐτῷ, Ἔτι
youth my. hearing But these things, Jesus said to him, Yet
ἕν σοι λείπει· πάντα ὅσα ἔχεις πώλησον, καὶ διάδος πτωχοῖς,
one to you is lacking: all, as much as you have, sell, and distribute to (the) poor,
καὶ ἕξεις θησαυρὸν ἐν οὐρανῷ· καὶ δεῦρο, ἀκολούθει μοι. ὁ δὲ
and you will have treasure in Heaven; and come, follow Me. he But
23 ἀκούσας ταῦτα περίλυπος ἐγένετο· ἦν γὰρ πλούσιος σφόδρα.
hearing these things very grieved became, he was for rich exceedingly.
24 Ἰδὼν δὲ αὐτὸν ὁ Ἰησοῦς περίλυπον γενόμενον εἶπε, Πῶς
seeing And him, Jesus very grieved having become said, How
δυσκόλως οἱ τὰ χρήματα ἔχοντες εἰσελεύσονται εἰς τὴν
hardly those – riches having shall enter into the
25 βασιλείαν τοῦ Θεοῦ. εὐκοπώτερον γάρ ἐστι κάμηλον διὰ
kingdom – of God. easier For it is (for) a camel through
τρυμαλιᾶς ῥαφίδος εἰσελθεῖν, ἢ πλούσιον εἰς τὴν βασιλείαν
(the) eye of a needle to go in, than a rich one into the kingdom
26 τοῦ Θεοῦ εἰσελθεῖν. εἶπον δὲ οἱ ἀκούσαντες, Καὶ τίς δύναται
– of God to enter. said And those hearing, And who is able
27 σωθῆναι; ὁ δὲ εἶπε, Τὰ ἀδύνατα παρὰ ἀνθρώποις δυνατά
to be saved? He And said, The things impossible with men possible
28 ἐστι παρὰ τῷ Θεῷ. εἶπε δὲ ὁ Πέτρος, Ἰδού, ἡμεῖς ἀφή-
is with – God. said And – Peter, Behold, we
29 καμεν πάντα, καὶ ἠκολουθήσαμέν σοι. ὁ δὲ εἶπεν αὐτοῖς,
left all and followed You. He And said to them,
Ἀμὴν λέγω ὑμῖν ὅτι οὐδείς ἐστιν ὃς ἀφῆκεν οἰκίαν, ἢ
Truly I say to you that no one there is who has left house, or
γονεῖς, ἢ ἀδελφούς, ἢ γυναῖκα, ἢ τέκνα, ἕνεκεν τῆς βασιλείας
parents, or brothers, or wife, or children for the sake of the kingdom
30 τοῦ Θεοῦ, ὃς οὐ μὴ ἀπολάβῃ πολλαπλασίονα ἐν τῷ καιρῷ
of God, who – not shall receive many times more in – time
τούτῳ, καὶ ἐν τῷ αἰῶνι τῷ ἐρχομένῳ ζωὴν αἰώνιον.
this and in the age coming life everlasting.
31 Παραλαβὼν δὲ τοὺς δώδεκα, εἶπε πρὸς αὐτούς, Ἰδού,
taking And the twelve, He said to them, Behold,
ἀναβαίνομεν εἰς Ἱεροσόλυμα, καὶ τελεσθήσεται πάντα τὰ
we are going up to Jerusalem, and will be completed all things –

which have been written through the prophets to the Son of man. [32]For He will be delivered up to the heathen, and will be mocked, and will be insulted, and will be spat upon. [33]And flogging *Him*, they will kill Him. And on the third day He will rise again. [34]And they did not understand these things, nothing. And this saying had been hidden from them, and they did not know the things being said.

[35]And it happened *as* He drew near to Jericho, a certain blind one sat by the highway begging. [36]And a crowd having passed through, he asked what this might be. [37]And they told him that Jesus the Nazarene is passing by. [38]And he cried out, saying, Jesus, son of David, pity me! [39]And those going before rebuked him, that he be quiet. But he much more cried out, Son of David, pity me! [40]And standing still, Jesus commanded him to be brought to Him. And he drawing near, He asked him, [41]saying, What do you desire I do to you? And he said, Lord, that I may see again. [42]And Jesus said to him, See again! Your faith has healed you. [43]And instantly he saw again. And *he* followed Him, glorifying God. And seeing, all the people gave praise to God.

CHAPTER 19

[1]And going in, He passed through Jericho. [2]And, behold, a man called by name Zaccheus. And he was a chief tax-collector, and he was rich. [3]And he was seeking to see Jesus, who He is. And he was not able, because of the crowd, and he was little in stature. [4]And running ahead, he went up onto a sycamore-tree, so that he might see Him; for He was going to pass that way. [5]And as He came to the place, looking up Jesus saw him, and said to him,

γεγραμμένα διὰ τῶν προφητῶν τῷ υἱῷ τοῦ ἀνθρώπου.
having been written via the prophets to the Son — of man.
τούτῳ, καὶ ἐν τῷ αἰῶνι τῷ ἐρχομένῳ ζωὴν αἰώνιον.
this, and in the age — coming life eternal.
32 παραδοθήσεται γὰρ τοῖς ἔθνεσι, καὶ ἐμπαιχθήσεται, καὶ
He will be delivered for to the nations, and will be mocked, and
33 ὑβρισθήσεται, καὶ ἐμπτυσθήσεται, καὶ μαστιγώσαντες
will be insulted, and will be spat upon. And having scourged
ἀποκτενοῦσιν αὐτόν· καὶ τῇ ἡμέρᾳ τῇ τρίτῃ ἀναστήσεται.
they will kill Him; and on the day — third He will rise again.
34 καὶ αὐτοὶ οὐδὲν τούτων συνῆκαν, καὶ ἦν τὸ ῥῆμα τοῦτο
And they none of these things understood, and was — saying this
κεκρυμμένον ἀπ' αὐτῶν, καὶ οὐκ ἐγίνωσκον τα λεγόμενα.
having been hidden from them; and not they knew the things being said.
35 Ἐγένετο δὲ ἐν τῷ ἐγγίζειν αὐτὸν εἰς Ἱεριχώ, τυφλός τις
it was And in the drawing near (of) Him to Jericho, blind one a certain
36 ἐκάθητο παρὰ τὴν ὁδὸν προσαιτῶν· ἀκούσας δὲ ὄχλου
sat by the way begging. hearing And a crowd
37 διαπορευομένου, ἐπυνθάνετο τί εἴη τοῦτο. ἀπήγγειλαν δὲ
passing through, he asked what might be this. they reported And
38 αὐτῷ ὅτι Ἰησοῦς ὁ Ναζωραῖος παρέρχεται. καὶ ἐβόησε,
to him that Jesus the Nazarene is passing by. And he cried,
39 λέγων, Ἰησοῦ, υἱὲ Δαβίδ, ἐλέησόν με. καὶ οἱ προάγοντες
saying, Jesus, son of David, pity me. And those going before
ἐπετίμων αὐτῷ ἵνα σιωπήσῃ· αὐτὸς δὲ πολλῷ μᾶλλον
rebuked him, that he be quiet. he But by much more
40 ἔκραζεν, Υἱὲ Δαβίδ, ἐλέησόν με. σταθεὶς δὲ ὁ Ἰησοῦς ἐκέλευσεν
cried out, Son of David, pity me. standing And — Jesus commanded
αὐτὸν ἀχθῆναι πρὸς αὐτόν· ἐγγίσαντος δὲ αὐτοῦ ἐπηρώ-
41 **him to be brought to Him. drawing near And him, He asked**
τησεν αὐτόν, λέγων, Τί σοι θέλεις ποιήσω; ὁ δὲ εἶπε, Κύριε,
him, saying, What to you wish you I do? he And said, Lord,
42 ἵνα ἀναβλέψω. καὶ ὁ Ἰησοῦς εἶπεν αὐτῷ, Ἀνάβλεψον· ἡ
that I may see again. And Jesus said to him, See again! The
43 πίστις σου σέσωκέ σε. καὶ παραχρῆμα ἀνέβλεψε, καὶ
faith of you has healed you. And at once he saw again, and
ἠκολούθει αὐτῷ, δοξάζων τὸν Θεόν· καὶ πᾶς ὁ λαὸς ἰδὼν
followed Him, glorifying — God. And all the people seeing
ἔδωκεν αἶνον τῷ Θεῷ.
gave praise — to God.

CHAPTER 19

1 Καὶ εἰσελθὼν διήρχετο τὴν Ἱεριχώ. καὶ ἰδού, ἀνὴρ
2 **And having entered He traversed — Jericho. And behold, a man**
ὀνόματι καλούμενος Ζακχαῖος, καὶ αὐτὸς ἦν ἀρχιτελώνης,
by name being called Zaccheus; and he was a chief tax-collector.
3 καὶ οὗτος ἦν πλούσιος. καὶ ἐζήτει ἰδεῖν τὸν Ἰησοῦν τίς ἐστι,
and he was rich. And he sought to see — Jesus, who He is,
καὶ οὐκ ἠδύνατο ἀπὸ τοῦ ὄχλου, ὅτι τῇ ἡλικίᾳ μικρὸς ἦν.
And not he was able from the crowd, because — in stature little he was.
καὶ προδραμὼν ἔμπροσθεν ἀνέβη ἐπὶ συκομωραίαν ἵνα ἴδῃ
4 **And having run ahead before, he went up onto a sycamore-tree,** that he see
5 αὐτόν· ὅτι δι' ἐκείνης ἤμελλε διέρχεσθαι. καὶ ὡς ἦλθεν ἐπὶ
Him, because via that (way) He was going to pass. And as He came on
τὸν τόπον, ἀναβλέψας ὁ Ἰησοῦς εἶδεν αὐτόν, καὶ εἶπε πρὸς
the place, looking up — Jesus saw him, and said to

Zaccheus, hurry, come down, for today I must stay in your house. 6 And hastening he came down and welcomed Him, rejoicing. 7 And seeing, all murmured, saying, He has gone in to stay with a sinful man. 8 But standing, Zaccheus said to the Lord, Behold, Lord, half of my possessions I give to the poor. And if I accused anyone falsely, I restore *it* fourfold. 9 And Jesus said to him, Today salvation has come to this house; for he also is a son of Abraham. 10 For the Son of man came to seek and to save that which has been lost.

11 But as they were hearing these things, He spoke, adding a parable, because He was near to Jerusalem, and they thought that the kingdom of God was immediately to be revealed: 12 Therefore, He said: A certain well-born man went to a distant country to receive a kingdom for himself, and to return. 13 And calling ten of his slaves, He gave to them ten minas, and said to them, Trade until I come. 14 But his citizens hated him, and sent a delegation after him, saying, We do not desire this one to reign over us. 15 And it happened *as* he returned, having received the kingdom, he even said *for* those slaves to be called, to whom he gave the silver, that he might know what each had gained by trading. 16 And the first came, saying, Lord, your mina has gained ten minas. 17 And he said to him, Well done, good slave! Because you were faithful in a least thing, have authority over ten cities. 18 And the second came, saying, Lord, your mina has made five minas. 19 And he said to this one also, And you be over five cities. 20 And another came, saying, Lord, behold, your mina which I had kept

αὐτόν, Ζακχαῖε, σπεύσας κατάβηθι· σήμερον γὰρ ἐν τῷ
him, Zaccheus, making haste, come down; today for in the

6 οἴκῳ σου δεῖ με μεῖναι. καὶ σπεύσας κατέβη, καὶ ὑπεδέξατο
house of you must Me to stay. And hastening he came down, and welcomed

7 αὐτὸν χαίρων. καὶ ἰδόντες ἅπαντες διεγόγγυζον, λέγοντες
Him, rejoicing. And seeing all murmured, saying,

8 ὅτι Παρὰ ἁμαρτωλῷ ἀνδρὶ εἰσῆλθε καταλῦσαι. σταθεὶς δὲ
— With a sinful man He went in to lodge. standing And

Ζακχαῖος εἶπε πρὸς τὸν Κύριον, Ἰδού, τὰ ἡμίση τῶν
Zaccheus said to the Lord, Behold, the half of the

ὑπαρχόντων μου, Κύριε, δίδωμι τοῖς πτωχοῖς· καὶ εἴ τινός
possessions of me, Lord, I give to the poor; and if anyone

9 τι ἐσυκοφάντησα, ἀποδίδωμι τετραπλοῦν. εἶπε δὲ πρὸς
anything I accused falsely, I restore fourfold said And to

αὐτὸν ὁ Ἰησοῦς ὅτι Σήμερον σωτηρία τῷ οἴκῳ τούτῳ ἐγέ-
him — Jesus, — Today salvation — house to this is

10 νετο, καθότι καὶ αὐτὸς υἱὸς Ἀβραάμ ἐστιν. ἦλθε γὰρ ὁ υἱὸς
come, because even he a son of Abraham is. came For the Son

τοῦ ἀνθρώπου ζητῆσαι καὶ σῶσαι τὸ ἀπολωλός.
— of man to seek and to save the thing having been lost.

11 Ἀκουόντων δὲ αὐτῶν ταῦτα, προσθεὶς εἶπε παραβολήν,
hearing And them these things, adding He told a parable,

διὰ τὸ ἐγγὺς αὐτὸν εἶναι Ἱερουσαλήμ, καὶ δοκεῖν αὐτοὺς ὅτι
because near He was to Jerusalem, and thought they that

12 παραχρῆμα μέλλει ἡ βασιλεία τοῦ Θεοῦ ἀναφαίνεσθαι.
immediately was about the kingdom — of God to be revealed.

13 εἶπεν οὖν, Ἄνθρωπός τις εὐγενὴς ἐπορεύθη εἰς χώραν μακράν,
He said, then, man a certain well-born went to a country distant

λαβεῖν ἑαυτῷ βασιλείαν, καὶ ὑποστρέψαι. καλέσας δὲ δέκα
to receive for himself a kingdom, and to return. having called And ten

14 δούλους ἑαυτοῦ, ἔδωκεν αὐτοῖς δέκα μνᾶς, καὶ εἶπε πρὸς
slaves of himself, He gave to them ten minas, and said to

αὐτούς, Πραγματεύσασθε ἕως ἔρχομαι. οἱ δὲ πολῖται
them, Trade until I come. the But citizens

αὐτοῦ ἐμίσουν αὐτόν, καὶ ἀπέστειλαν πρεσβείαν ὀπίσω
of him hated him, and sent a delegation after

αὐτοῦ, λέγοντες, Οὐ θέλομεν τοῦτον βασιλεῦσαι ἐφ' ἡμᾶς.
him, saying, not We desire this one to reign over us.

15 καὶ ἐγένετο ἐν τῷ ἐπανελθεῖν αὐτὸν λαβόντα τὴν βασιλείαν,
And it was, in the returning (of) him, having received the kingdom,

καὶ εἶπε φωνηθῆναι αὐτῷ τοὺς δούλους τούτους, οἷς ἔδωκε
even he said to be called to him — slaves those to whom he gave

16 τὸ ἀργύριον, ἵνα γνῷ τίς τί διεπραγματεύσατο. παρε-
the silver, that he know what each had gained by trading. came

γένετο δὲ ὁ πρῶτος, λέγων, Κύριε, ἡ μνᾶ σου προσειργάσατο
And the first, saying, Lord, the mina of you has gained

17 δέκα μνᾶς. καὶ εἶπεν αὐτῷ, Εὖ, ἀγαθὲ δοῦλε· ὅτι ἐν ἐλαχίστῳ
ten minas. And he said to him, Well, good slave, for in a least thing

18 πιστὸς ἐγένου, ἴσθι ἐξουσίαν ἔχων ἐπάνω δέκα πόλεων. καὶ
faithful you were; be authority having over ten cities. And

ἦλθεν ὁ δεύτερος, λέγων, Κύριε, ἡ μνᾶ σου ἐποίησε πέντε
came the second, saying, Lord, the mina of you has made five

19 μνᾶς. εἶπε δὲ καὶ τούτῳ, Καὶ σὺ γίνου ἐπάνω πέντε πόλεων.
minas. he said And also to this, **And you be over five cities.**

20 καὶ ἕτερος ἦλθε, λέγων, Κύριε, ἰδού, ἡ μνᾶ σου, ἣν εἶχον
And another came, saying, Lord, Behold, the mina of you which I had

in a napkin. [21] For I feared you, because you are an exacting man, taking what you did not lay down, and reaping what you did not sow. [22] But he said to him, I will judge you out of your own mouth, wicked slave. You knew that I am an exacting man, taking what I did not lay down, and reaping what I did not sow. [23] And why did you not give my silver on the *bank* table? And coming I might have required it with interest. [24] And to those standing by he said, Take the mina from him, and give it to him who has ten minas. [25] And they said to him, Lord, he has ten minas. [26] For I say to you, that to everyone who has, it will be given. And from the *one* who does not have, even what he has will be taken from him. [27] But these enemies of mine, those not desiring me to reign over them, bring here and execute *them* before me. [28] And saying these things, He went in front, going up to Jerusalem.

[29] And it happened as He drew near to Bethphage and Bethany toward the Mount called Of Olives, He sent two of His disciples, [30] saying, Go into the village opposite *you*, in which having entered you will find a colt being tied, on which no one of men ever yet sat. Untying it, bring *it*. [31] And if anyone asks, Why do you untie *it*? You shall say to them, The Lord has need of it. [32] And going, those having been sent found as He told them. [33] And *as* they were untying the colt, its owners said to them, Why do you untie the colt? [34] And they said, The Lord has need of it. [35] And they led it to Jesus. And throwing their garments on the colt, they put Jesus on *it*. [36] And as He went, they were spreading their garments in the highway. [37] And

21 ἀποκειμένην ἐν σουδαρίῳ· ἐφοβούμην γάρ σε, ὅτι ἄνθρωπος
reserved in a napkin; I feared for you, for a man
αὐστηρὸς εἶ· αἴρεις ὃ οὐκ ἔθηκας, καὶ θερίζεις ὃ οὐκ ἔσπειρας.
exacting you are, taking what not you lay, and reaping what not you sowed.
22 λέγει δὲ αὐτῷ, Ἐκ τοῦ στόματός σου κρινῶ σε, πονηρὲ δοῦλε.
he says And to him, From the mouth of you I will judge you, wicked slave.
ᾔδεις ὅτι ἐγὼ ἄνθρωπος αὐστηρός εἰμι, αἴρων ὃ οὐκ ἔθηκα,
You knew that I an exacting man am, taking what not I laid,
23 καὶ θερίζων ὃ οὐκ ἔσπειρα· καὶ διατί οὐκ ἔδωκας τὸ ἀργύριόν
and reaping what not I sowed. And why not did you give the silver
μου ἐπὶ τὴν τράπεζαν, καὶ ἐγὼ ἐλθὼν σὺν τόκῳ ἂν ἔπραξα
of me on the (bank) table? And I coming, with interest may have exacted
24 αὐτό; καὶ τοῖς παρεστῶσιν εἶπεν, Ἄρατε ἀπ' αὐτοῦ τὴν
it. And to those standing by he said, Take from him the
25 μνᾶν, καὶ δότε τῷ τὰς δέκα μνᾶς ἔχοντι. καὶ εἶπον αὐτῷ,
mina, and give to the (one) ten minas having. And they said to him,
26 Κύριε, ἔχει δέκα μνᾶς. λέγω γὰρ ὑμῖν, ὅτι παντὶ τῷ ἔχοντι
Lord, he has ten minas. I say For to you, that to everyone having,
δοθήσεται· ἀπὸ δὲ τοῦ μὴ ἔχοντος, καὶ ὃ ἔχει ἀρθήσεται
it will be given, from and the (one) not having, even what he has will be taken
27 ἀπ' αὐτοῦ. πλὴν τοὺς ἐχθρούς μου ἐκείνους, τοὺς μὴ θελή-
from him. But — enemies of me these, those not
σαντάς με βασιλεῦσαι ἐπ' αὐτούς, ἀγάγετε ὧδε, καὶ
desiring me to reign over them, bring here, and
κατασφάξατε ἔμπροσθέν μου.
execute before me.
28 Καὶ εἰπὼν ταῦτα, ἐπορεύετο ἔμπροσθεν, ἀναβαίνων εἰς
And having said these things, He went in front, going up to
Ἱεροσόλυμα.
Jerusalem.
29 Καὶ ἐγένετο ὡς ἤγγισεν εἰς Βηθφαγὴ καὶ Βηθανίαν πρὸς
And it was, as He drew near to Bethphage and Bethany toward
τὸ ὄρος τὸ καλούμενον ἐλαιῶν, ἀπέστειλε δύο τῶν μαθητῶν
the mount — being called of olives, He sent two of the disciples
30 αὐτοῦ, εἰπών, Ὑπάγετε εἰς τὴν κατέναντι κώμην· ἐν ᾗ
of Him, saying, Go into the opposite village, in which
εἰσπορευόμενοι εὑρήσετε πῶλον δεδεμένον, ἐφ' ὃν οὐδεὶς
entering you will find a colt having been tied, on which no one
πώποτε ἀνθρώπων ἐκάθισε· λύσαντες αὐτὸν ἀγάγετε. καὶ
ever yet of men sat. Having untied it, bring (it) And
31 ἐάν τις ὑμᾶς ἐρωτᾷ, Διατί λύετε; οὕτως ἐρεῖτε αὐτῷ ὅτι
if anyone you asks, Why do you untie, thus you shall say to them,—
32 Ὁ Κύριος αὐτοῦ χρείαν ἔχει. ἀπελθόντες δὲ οἱ ἀπεσταλ-
The Lord of it need has. having gone And, those having been
33 μένοι εὗρον καθὼς εἶπεν αὐτοῖς. λυόντων δὲ αὐτῶν τὸν
sent found as He told them. untying And them the
πῶλον, εἶπον οἱ κύριοι αὐτοῦ πρὸς αὐτούς, Τί λύετε τὸν
colt, said the owners of it to them, Why do you untie the
34 πῶλον; οἱ δὲ εἶπον, Ὁ Κύριος αὐτοῦ χρείαν ἔχει. καὶ
colt? they And said, The Lord of it need has. And
35 ἤγαγον αὐτὸν πρὸς τὸν Ἰησοῦν· καὶ ἐπιρρίψαντες ἑαυτῶν
they led it to — Jesus, and throwing of themselves
τὰ ἱμάτια ἐπὶ τὸν πῶλον ἐπεβίβασαν τὸν Ἰησοῦν. πορευο-
the garments on the colt, they put on (it) — Jesus. going
36 μένου δὲ αὐτοῦ, ὑπεστρώννυον τὰ ἱμάτια αὐτῶν ἐν τῇ ὁδῷ.
And Him, they spread out the garments of them in the way.

as He was drawing near, already to the descent of the Mount of Olives, all the multitude of the disciples began rejoicing, to praise God with a loud voice concerning all *the* mighty works that they saw, [38] saying, Blessed *is* the One coming in the name of the Lord, the King. Peace in Heaven, and glory in *the* highest!

[39] And some of the Pharisees from the crowd said to Him, Teacher, rebuke your disciples. [40] And answering He said to them, I say to you, If these should be silent, the stones will cry out.

[41] And as He drew near, seeing the city, He wept over it, [42] saying, If you had known, even you, even at least in this day of yours, the things for your peace! But now they are hidden from your eyes. [43] For the days will come on you, and your enemies will raise up a rampart to you, and will surround you, and will keep you in on every side; [44] and will tear you down, and your children in you, and not will leave a stone on a stone, because you did not know the time of your visitation.

[45] And entering into the Temple, He began to throw out those selling and buying in it, [46] saying to them, It has been written, "My house is a house of prayer," but you made it a den of robbers. [47] And He was teaching day by day in the Temple. But the chief priests and the scribes and the chief of the people sought to kill Him. [48] And *they* did not find what they might do; for all the people hung on Him, listening.

CHAPTER 20

[1] And it happened on one of those days, *as* He was teaching the people and preaching the gospel in the Temple, the chief priests and the scribes and the

37 ἐγγίζοντος δὲ αὐτοῦ ἤδη πρὸς τῇ καταβάσει τοῦ ὄρους τῶν
drawing near And Him now to the descent of the mount of the
ἐλαιῶν, ἤρξαντο ἅπαν τὸ πλῆθος τῶν μαθητῶν χαίροντες
olives, began all the multitude of the disciples rejoicing
αἰνεῖν τὸν Θεὸν φωνῇ μεγάλῃ περὶ πασῶν ὧν εἶδον δυνά-
to praise — God with a voice great about all which they saw, works
38 μεων, λέγοντες,
of power, saying,

Εὐλογημένος ὁ ἐρχόμενος βασιλεὺς ἐν ὀνόματι Κυρίου·
Blessed the coming One, the king, in the name of the Lord;
εἰρήνη ἐν οὐρανῷ, καὶ δόξα ἐν ὑψίστοις.
peace in Heaven, and glory in highest places.

39 Καί τινες τῶν Φαρισαίων ἀπὸ τοῦ ὄχλου εἶπον πρὸς
And some of the Pharisees from the crowd said to
40 αὐτόν, Διδάσκαλε, ἐπιτίμησον τοῖς μαθηταῖς σου. καὶ ἀπο-
Him, Teacher, rebuke the disciples of you. And
κριθεὶς εἶπεν αὐτοῖς, Λέγω ὑμῖν ὅτι, ἐὰν οὗτοι σιωπήσωσιν,
answering He said to them, I say to you, — if these shall be silent,
οἱ λίθοι κεκράξονται.
the stones will cry out.

41 Καὶ ὡς ἤγγισεν, ἰδὼν τὴν πόλιν, ἔκλαυσεν ἐπ' αὐτῇ,
And as He drew near, seeing the city, He wept over it,
42 λέγων ὅτι Εἰ ἔγνως καὶ σύ, καί γε ἐν τῇ ἡμέρᾳ σου ταύτῃ,
saying, — If you knew, even you, even at least in day of you this,
43 τὰ πρὸς εἰρήνην σου· νῦν δὲ ἐκρύβη ἀπὸ ὀφθαλμῶν σου. ὅτι
the things for peace of you, now but were hid from the eyes of you. For
ἥξουσιν ἡμέραι ἐπὶ σέ, καὶ περιβαλοῦσιν οἱ ἐχθροί σου
will come days on you, and will raise up the enemies of you
χάρακά σοι, καὶ περικυκλώσουσί σε, καὶ συνέξουσί σε πάντο-
a rampart to you, and will surround you, and will keep in you on all
44 θεν, καὶ ἐδαφιοῦσί σε καὶ τὰ τέκνα σου ἐν σοί, καὶ οὐκ
sides, and raze you, and the children of you in you, and not
ἀφήσουσιν ἐν σοὶ λίθον ἐπὶ λίθῳ· ἀνθ' ὧν οὐκ ἔγνως τὸν
will leave in you stone upon stone because not you knew the
καιρὸν τῆς ἐπισκοπῆς σου.
time of the visitation of you.

45 Καὶ εἰσελθὼν εἰς τὸ ἱερόν, ἤρξατο ἐκβάλλειν τοὺς πωλοῦν-
And entering into the Temple, He began to throw out the(ones) selling
46 τας ἐν αὐτῷ καὶ ἀγοράζοντας, λέγων αὐτοῖς, Γέγραπται,
in it, and buying, saying to them, It has been written
Ὁ οἶκός μου οἶκος προσευχῆς ἐστίν· ὑμεῖς δὲ αὐτὸν ἐποιήσατε
The house of Me a house of prayer is; you but it made
47 σπήλαιον λῃστῶν. καὶ ἦν διδάσκων τὸ καθ' ἡμέραν ἐν τῷ
a den of robbers. And He was teaching day by day in the
ἱερῷ· οἱ δὲ ἀρχιερεῖς καὶ οἱ γραμματεῖς ἐζήτουν αὐτὸν
Temple. the But chief priests and the scribes sought Him
48 ἀπολέσαι, καὶ οἱ πρῶτοι τοῦ λαοῦ· καὶ οὐχ εὕρισκον τὸ τί
to destroy, and the chief men of the people; and not did find — what
ποιήσωσιν, ὁ λαὸς γὰρ ἅπας ἐξεκρέματο αὐτοῦ ἀκούων.
they might do; the people for all hung upon Him, hearing.

CHAPTER 20

1 Καὶ ἐγένετο ἐν μιᾷ τῶν ἡμερῶν ἐκείνων, διδάσκοντος αὐτοῦ
And it was, on one of — days those, teaching Him
τὸν λαὸν ἐν τῷ ἱερῷ καὶ εὐαγγελιζομένου, ἐπέστησαν οἱ
the people in the Temple, and preaching the gospel; came upon the

elders came up, 2 and spoke to Him, saying, Tell us by what authority you do these things, or who is it who gave to you this authority? 3 And answering He said to them, I will ask you one thing, and tell me, 4 The baptism of John, was it from Heaven, or from men? 5 And they reasoned with themselves, saying, If we say, From Heaven, he will say, Why, then, did you not believe him? 6 But if we say, From men, all the people will stone us, being convinced that John was a prophet. 7 And they answered, they did not know from where. 8 And Jesus said to them, Neither do I tell you by what authority I do these things.

9 And He began to speak this parable to the people: A certain man planted a vineyard, and let it out to vinedressers. And *he* left the country for long periods *of time*. 10 And in season he sent a slave to the vine dressers, that they might give him the fruit of the vineyard. But the vinedressers sent him away empty, beating *him*. 11 And he again sent another slave. But they also sent that one away empty, beating and insulting *him*. 12 And he again sent a third. But they also threw out this one, wounding *him*. 13 And the lord of the vineyard said, What shall I do? I will send my beloved son. Perhaps seeing this one, they will respect *him*. 14 And seeing him, the vinedressers reasoned with themselves, saying, this is the heir. Come, let us kill him, so that the inheritance may become ours. 15 And throwing him out of the vineyard, they killed *him*. Therefore, what will the lord of the vineyard do to them? 16 He will come and will destroy these vinedressers, and will give the vineyard to others.

2 ἀρχιερεῖς καὶ οἱ γραμματεῖς σὺν τοῖς πρεσβυτέροις, καὶ εἶπον
chief priests and the scribes with the elders, and spoke,
πρὸς αὐτόν, λέγοντες, Εἰπὲ ἡμῖν, ἐν ποίᾳ ἐξουσίᾳ ταῦτα
to Him, saying, Tell us, by what authority these things
ποιεῖς, ἢ τίς ἐστιν ὁ δούς σοι τὴν ἐξουσίαν ταύτην ; ἀπο-
you do, or who is the (one) giving you authority this?
3 κριθεὶς δὲ εἶπε πρὸς αὐτούς, Ἐρωτήσω ὑμᾶς κἀγὼ ἕνα
answering And He said to them, will ask you I also one
4 λόγον, καὶ εἴπατέ μοι· Τὸ βάπτισμα Ἰωάννου ἐξ οὐρανοῦ
word, and you tell Me: The baptism of John, from Heaven
5 ἦν, ἢ ἐξ ἀνθρώπων ; οἱ δὲ συνελογίσαντο πρὸς ἑαυτούς,
was it, or from men? they And debated with themselves
λέγοντες ὅτι Ἐὰν εἴπωμεν, Ἐξ οὐρανοῦ, ἐρεῖ, Διατί οὖν οὐκ
saying, — If we say, From Heaven, he will say, Why, then, not
6 ἐπιστεύσατε αὐτῷ ; ἐὰν δὲ εἴπωμεν, Ἐξ ἀνθρώπων, πᾶς ὁ
you believed him? if And we say From men, all the
λαὸς καταλιθάσει ἡμᾶς· πεπεισμένος γάρ ἐστιν Ἰωάννην
people will stone us, having been convinced for John
7 προφήτην εἶναι. καὶ ἀπεκρίθησαν μὴ εἰδέναι πόθεν. καὶ ὁ
a prophet was. And they answered not they knew from where. And
8 Ἰησοῦς εἶπεν αὐτοῖς, Οὐδὲ ἐγὼ λέγω ὑμῖν ἐν ποίᾳ ἐξουσίᾳ
Jesus said to them, Neither do I tell you by what authority
ταῦτα ποιῶ.
these things I do.

9 Ἤρξατο δὲ πρὸς τὸν λαὸν λέγειν τὴν παραβολὴν ταύτην·
He began And to the people to tell — parable this:
Ἄνθρωπός τις ἐφύτευσεν ἀμπελῶνα, καὶ ἐξέδοτο αὐτὸν
A man certain planted a vineyard, and let out it
10 γεωργοῖς, καὶ ἀπεδήμησε χρόνους ἱκανούς· καὶ ἐν καιρῷ
to vinedressers, and went away periods for considerable. And in time
ἀπέστειλε πρὸς τοὺς γεωργοὺς δοῦλον, ἵνα ἀπὸ τοῦ καρποῦ
he sent to the vinedressers a slave, that from the fruit
τοῦ ἀμπελῶνος δῶσιν αὐτῷ· οἱ δὲ γεωργοὶ δείραντες αὐτὸν
of the vineyard they will give him. the But vinedressers sent away him,
11 ἐξαπέστειλαν κενόν. καὶ προσέθετο πέμψαι ἕτερον δοῦλον·
beating (him) empty. And he added to send another slave
οἱ δὲ κἀκεῖνον δείραντες καὶ ἀτιμάσαντες ἐξαπέστειλαν κενόν.
they but that one also, beating and insulting (him), sent away empty.
12 καὶ προσέθετο πέμψαι τρίτον· οἱ δὲ καὶ τοῦτον τραυματί-
And he added to send a third. they But also this one, wounding
13 σαντες ἐξέβαλον. εἶπε δὲ ὁ κύριος τοῦ ἀμπελῶνος, Τί ποιήσω ;
(him) threw out. said And the lord of the vineyard, What shall I do?
πέμψω τὸν υἱόν μου τὸν ἀγαπητόν· ἴσως τοῦτον ἰδόντες
I will send the son of me, the beloved; perhaps this one having seen
14 ἐντραπήσονται. ἰδόντες δὲ αὐτὸν οἱ γεωργοὶ διελογίζοντο
they will respect. seeing And him, the vinedressers reasoned
πρὸς ἑαυτούς, λέγοντες, Οὗτός ἐστιν ὁ κληρονόμος· δεῦτε,
with themselves, saying, This is the heir; come,
15 ἀποκτείνωμεν αὐτόν, ἵνα ἡμῶν γένηται ἡ κληρονομία. καὶ
let us kill him, that of us may become the inheritance. And
ἐκβαλόντες αὐτὸν ἔξω τοῦ ἀμπελῶνος, ἀπέκτειναν. τί οὖν
throwing out him out of the vineyard, they killed. What, then,
16 ποιήσει αὐτοῖς ὁ κύριος τοῦ ἀμπελῶνος ; ἐλεύσεται καὶ
will do to them the lord of the vineyard? He will come and
ἀπολέσει τοὺς γεωργοὺς τούτους, καὶ δώσει τὸν ἀμπελῶνα
will destroy vinedressers these, and will give the vineyard

And hearing *this*, they said, Let it not be! 17 And looking at them He said, What, then, is this having been written, "*The* stone that those building rejected, this one became to be for *the* Head of *the* corner? 18 Everyone falling on that Stone will be broken in pieces; but on whomever it falls, it will crush him.

19 And the chief priests and the scribes sought to lay hands on Him in the same hour. And *they* feared the people, for they knew that He told this parable against them.

20 And watching carefully, they sent spies, pretending themselves to be righteous, in order that they might seize upon a word of His, so as to deliver Him to the power and to the authority of the governor. 21 And they questioned Him, saying, Teacher, we know that you say and teach rightly, and do not receive *the* face *of anyone*, but you teach the way of God with truth. 22 Is it lawful to give tribute to Caesar, or not? 23 But perceiving their slyness, He said to them, Why do you tempt Me? 24 Show Me a denarius. Whose image and superscription does it have? And answering they said, Caesar's. 25 And He said to them, Then give the things of Caesar to Caesar, and the things of God to God. 26 And they were not able to lay hold of His speech before the people. And marveling at His answer, they were silent.

27 And some of the Sadducees coming up, those speaking against a resurrection, they questioned Him, 28 saying, Teacher, Moses wrote to us, If anyone's brother dies having a wife, and this one should die childless, that his brother should take the wife and raise up seed to his brother. 29 Then there were seven brothers. And having taken a wife, the first died childless. 30 And the second took the

ἄλλοις. ἀκούσαντες δὲ εἶπον, Μὴ γένοιτο. ὁ δὲ ἐμβλέψας
to others. hearing And, they said, Not let it be! He And looking at
17 αὐτοῖς εἶπε, Τί οὖν ἐστι τὸ γεγραμμένον τοῦτο, Λίθον ὃν
them said, What, then, is having been written this: (The) stone that
ἀπεδοκίμασαν οἱ οἰκοδομοῦντες, οὗτος ἐγενήθη εἰς κεφαλὴν
rejected those building, this one came to be for (the) head
18 γωνίας; πᾶς ὁ πεσὼν ἐπ' ἐκεῖνον τὸν λίθον συνθλασθή-
of (the) corner? Everyone falling on that — stone will be broken in
σεται ἐφ' ὃν δ' ἂν πέσῃ, λικμήσει αὐτόν.
pieces; on whomever but it falls, it will crush him.
19 Καὶ ἐζήτησαν οἱ ἀρχιερεῖς καὶ οἱ γραμματεῖς ἐπιβαλεῖν
And sought the chief priests and the scribes to lay
ἐπ' αὐτὸν τὰς χεῖρας ἐν αὐτῇ τῇ ὥρᾳ, καὶ ἐφοβήθησαν τὸν
on Him the hands in same the hour; and feared the
20 λαόν· ἔγνωσαν γὰρ ὅτι πρὸς αὐτοὺς τὴν παραβολὴν ταύτην
people; they knew for that at them — parable this
εἶπε. καὶ παρατηρήσαντες ἀπέστειλαν ἐγκαθέτους ὑπο-
He told. And watching carefully they sent spies,
κρινομένους ἑαυτοὺς δικαίους εἶναι, ἵνα ἐπιλάβωνται αὐτοῦ
pretending themselves righteous to be; that they might seize of Him
λόγου, εἰς τὸ παραδοῦναι αὐτὸν τῇ ἀρχῇ καὶ τῇ ἐξουσίᾳ
a word, in order to deliver Him to the power and to the authority
21 τοῦ ἡγεμόνος. καὶ ἐπηρώτησαν αὐτόν, λέγοντες, Διδάσκαλε,
of the governor And they questioned Him, saying, Teacher,
οἴδαμεν ὅτι ὀρθῶς λέγεις καὶ διδάσκεις, καὶ οὐ λαμβάνεις
we know that rightly you speak, and teach, and not do receive
πρόσωπον, ἀλλ' ἐπ' ἀληθείας τὴν ὁδὸν τοῦ Θεοῦ διδάσκεις.
a face, but upon truth the way — of God you teach.
22 ἔξεστιν ἡμῖν Καίσαρι φόρον δοῦναι, ἢ οὔ; κατανοήσας δὲ
23 **Is it lawful for us to Caesar tribute to give, or not? perceiving And**
αὐτῶν τὴν πανουργίαν, εἶπε πρὸς αὐτούς, Τί με πειράζετε;
of them the slyness, He said to them, Why Me do you tempt;
24 ἐπιδείξατέ μοι δηνάριον· τίνος ἔχει εἰκόνα καὶ ἐπιγραφήν;
show Me a denarius; of whom has it an image and superscription?
25 ἀποκριθέντες δὲ εἶπον, Καίσαρος. ὁ δὲ εἶπεν αὐτοῖς, Ἀπόδοτε
answering And they said, Of Caesar. He And said to them, Render
τοίνυν τὰ Καίσαρος Καίσαρι, καὶ τὰ τοῦ Θεοῦ τῷ Θεῷ.
then the things of Caesar to Caesar, and the things — of God — to God.
26 καὶ οὐκ ἴσχυσαν ἐπιλαβέσθαι αὐτοῦ ῥήματος ἐναντίον τοῦ
And not they were able to lay hold of Him (the) speech before the
λαοῦ· καὶ θαυμάσαντες ἐπὶ τῇ ἀποκρίσει αὐτοῦ, ἐσίγησαν.
people and marveling at the answer of Him, they were silent.
27 Προσελθόντες δέ τινες τῶν Σαδδουκαίων, οἱ ἀντιλέγοντες
coming up And some of the Sadducees, those speaking against
28 ἀνάστασιν μὴ εἶναι, ἐπηρώτησαν αὐτόν, λέγοντες, Διδά-
a resurrection not to be. They questioned Him, saying, Teacher,
σκαλε, Μωσῆς ἔγραψεν ἡμῖν, ἐάν τινος ἀδελφὸς ἀποθάνῃ
Moses wrote to us, If of anyone a brother dies
ἔχων γυναῖκα, καὶ οὗτος ἄτεκνος ἀποθάνῃ, ἵνα λάβῃ ὁ
having a wife, and this one childless should die, that should take the
ἀδελφὸς αὐτοῦ τὴν γυναῖκα, καὶ ἐξαναστήσῃ σπέρμα τῷ
brother of him the wife, and raise up seed to the
29 ἀδελφῷ αὐτοῦ. ἑπτὰ οὖν ἀδελφοὶ ἦσαν· καὶ ὁ πρῶτος
brother of him. seven Then brothers there were, and the first
30 λαβὼν γυναῖκα ἀπέθανεν ἄτεκνος· καὶ ἔλαβεν ὁ δεύτερος
having taken a wife died childless; and took the second

woman, and this one died childless. [31] And the third took her, and likewise also the seven died and did not leave children. [32] And last of all the woman also died. [33] Therefore, in the resurrection, of which of them does she become wife? For the seven had her *as* wife. [34] And answering Jesus said to them, The sons of this world marry and are given in marriage. [35] But those counted worthy to obtain that world, and the resurrection from *the* dead, neither marry nor are given in marriage. [36] For they are not able to die *any* more; they are equal to angels, and are sons of God, being sons of the resurrection. [37] But that the dead are raised, even Moses pointed out at the Bush, when he calls *the* Lord the God of Abraham, and the God of Isaac, and the God of Jacob— [38] but He is not God of *the* dead, but of *the* living; for all live to Him. [39] And anwering some of the scribes said, Teacher, you have spoken well. [40] And they did not dare to question Him any more, nothing.

[41] And He said to them, How do you say the Christ is David's son? [42] Even David himself said in *the* book of Psalms, "The Lord said to my Lord, Sit at My right *hand* [43] until I place Your enemies *as* a footstool of Your feet." [44] David then calls Him Lord, and how is He his son?

[45] And *as* all the people were listening, He said to His disciples, [46] Beware of the scribes, those desiring to walk about in robes, and liking greetings in the markets, and chief seats in the synagogues, and chief couches in the suppers; [47] who devour the houses of the widows, and under pretense pray long. These will receive a more severe

τὴν γυναῖκα, καὶ οὗτος ἀπέθανεν ἄτεκνος. καὶ ὁ τρίτος
the wife, and this one died childless. And the third
31 ἔλαβεν αὐτήν. ὡσαύτως δὲ καὶ οἱ ἑπτά· καὶ οὐ κατέλιπον
took her, likewise and also the seven even not did leave
32 τέκνα, καὶ ἀπέθανον. ὕστερον πάντων ἀπέθανε καὶ ἡ γυνή.
children, and died. Lastly of all died also the woman.
33 ἐν τῇ οὖν ἀναστάσει, τίνος αὐτῶν γίνεται γυνή; οἱ γὰρ
in the Then resurrection, of which of them becomes she wife; the for
34 ἑπτὰ ἔσχον αὐτὴν γυναῖκα. καὶ ἀποκριθεὶς εἶπεν αὐτοῖς ὁ
seven had her (for)wife? And answering, said to them
Ἰησοῦς, Οἱ υἱοὶ τοῦ αἰῶνος τούτου γαμοῦσι καὶ ἐκγαμί-
Jesus, The sons — age of this marry and are given
35 σκονται· οἱ δὲ καταξιωθέντες τοῦ αἰῶνος ἐκείνου τυχεῖν καὶ
marriage, those but counted worthy — age of that to obtain, and
τῆς ἀναστάσεως τῆς ἐκ νεκρῶν οὔτε γαμοῦσιν οὔτε ἐκγαμί-
the resurrection from among (the) dead neither marry nor are given
36 σκονται· οὔτε γὰρ ἀποθανεῖν ἔτι δύνανται· ἰσάγγελοι γάρ
in marriage, not even for to die (any) more they are able, equal to angels for
εἰσι, καὶ υἱοί εἰσι τοῦ Θεοῦ, τῆς ἀναστάσεως υἱοὶ ὄντες. ὅτι
they are: and sons are — of God, of the resurrection sons being. that
37 δὲ ἐγείρονται οἱ νεκροί, καὶ Μωσῆς ἐμήνυσεν ἐπὶ τῆς βάτου,
But are raised the dead, even Moses pointed out at the Bush,
ὡς λέγει Κύριον τὸν Θεὸν Ἀβραὰμ καὶ τὸν Θεὸν Ἰσαὰκ καὶ
as he calls (the) Lord the God of Abraham and the God of Isaac and
38 τὸν Θεὸν Ἰακώβ. Θεὸς δὲ οὐκ ἔστι νεκρῶν, ἀλλὰ ζώντων·
the God of Jacob. God But not He is of dead ones, but of living ones
39 πάντες γὰρ αὐτῷ ζῶσιν. ἀποκριθέντες δέ τινες τῶν γραμ-
all for to Him live. answering And some of the
40 ματέων εἶπον, Διδάσκαλε, καλῶς εἶπας. Οὐκέτι δὲ ἐτόλμων
scribes said, Teacher, Well you say. no more And they dared
ἐπερωτᾷν αὐτὸν οὐδέν.
to question Him, nothing.

41 Εἶπε δὲ πρὸς αὐτούς, Πῶς λέγουσι τὸν Χριστὸν υἱὸν
He said And to them, How do they say the Christ son
42 Δαβὶδ εἶναι; καὶ αὐτὸς Δαβὶδ λέγει ἐν βίβλῳ ψαλμῶν,
of David is? Even himself David says in (the) roll of Psalms:
43 Εἶπεν ὁ Κύριος τῷ Κυρίῳ μου, Κάθου ἐκ δεξιῶν μου, ἕως ἂν
Said the Lord to the Lord of me, Sit at (the) right of Me until
44 θῶ τοὺς ἐχθρούς σου ὑποπόδιον τῶν ποδῶν σου. Δαβὶδ
I put the enemies of You a footstool of the foot of You. David
οὖν Κύριον αὐτὸν καλεῖ, καὶ πῶς υἱὸς αὐτοῦ ἐστιν;
then Lord Him calls. And how son of him is He?

45 Ἀκούοντος δὲ παντὸς τοῦ λαοῦ, εἶπε τοῖς μαθηταῖς αὐτοῦ,
hearing And all the people, He said to the disciples of Him,
46 Προσέχετε ἀπὸ τῶν γραμματέων τῶν θελόντων περιπατεῖν
Beware of the scribes, those desiring to walk about
ἐν στολαῖς, καὶ φιλούντων ἀσπασμοὺς ἐν ταῖς ἀγοραῖς, καὶ
in robes, and liking greetings in the markets, and
πρωτοκαθεδρίας ἐν ταῖς συναγωγαῖς, καὶ πρωτοκλισίας ἐν
chief seats in the synagogues, and chief couches in
47 τοῖς δείπνοις· οἳ κατεσθίουσι τὰς οἰκίας τῶν χηρῶν, καὶ
the suppers; those devouring the houses of the widows, and
προφάσει μακρὰ προσεύχονται. οὗτοι λήψονται περισσό-
under pretence long pray. These will receive a more

judgment.

CHAPTER 21

[1]And looking up He saw the rich ones putting their gifts into the treasury. [2]And He also saw a certain poor widow putting two lepta there. [3]And He said, Truly I say to you, This poor widow put *in* more than all; [4]for all these out of their abundance put in the gifts to God, but she out of her poverty put in all the living which she had.

[5]And as some were speaking about the Temple, that it had been adorned with beautiful stones and gifts, He said, [6]*As to* these things that you see, days will come in which a stone will not be left on a stone, which will not be thrown down.

[7]And they asked him, saying, Teacher, then when will these things be? And what *will be* the sign when these things are about to happen? [8]And He said, Watch that you not be led astray. For many will come on My name, saying, I AM! and, The time has come. Do not go after them. [9]And when you hear of wars and disturbances, do not be afraid. For these things must first occur, but the end *is* not at once. [10]Then He said to them, Nation will be lifted up against nation, and kingdom against kingdom; [11]also there will be great earthquakes from place to place, and famines, and plagues. And also there will be great signs from Heaven. [12]But before all these things they all will lay their hands on you, and will persecute *you*, delivering *you* into the synagogues and prisons, being led away before kings and governors on account of My name. [13]But it will return to you for a testimony. [14]Therefore, put into your hearts not to premeditate to make a defense. [15]For I will give you a mouth and

τερον κρίμα.
severe judgment.

CHAPTER 21

1 Ἀναβλέψας δὲ εἶδε τοὺς βάλλοντας τὰ δῶρα αὐτῶν εἰς
looking up And He saw those putting the gifts of them into
2 τὸ γαζοφυλάκιον πλουσίους· εἶδε δὲ καί τινα χήραν
the treasury rich ones. He saw And also a certain widow
3 πενιχρὰν βάλλουσαν ἐκεῖ δύο λεπτά, καὶ εἶπεν, Ἀληθῶς
poor putting there two lepta; and He said, Truly
λέγω ὑμῖν, ὅτι ἡ χήρα ἡ πτωχὴ αὕτη πλεῖον πάντων ἔβαλεν·
I say to you, widow poor This more (than) all cast.
4 ἅπαντες γὰρ οὗτοι ἐκ τοῦ περισσεύοντος αὐτοῖς ἔβαλον εἰς
all For these out of the abundance to them cast into
τὰ δῶρα τοῦ Θεοῦ, αὕτη δὲ ἐκ τοῦ ὑστερήματος αὐτῆς
the gifts — to God, she but out of the want of her
ἅπαντα τὸν βίον ὃν εἶχεν ἔβαλε.
all the living which she had put.

5 Καί τινων λεγόντων περὶ τοῦ ἱεροῦ, ὅτι λίθοις καλοῖς
And some speaking about the Temple, that with stones beautiful
6 καὶ ἀναθήμασι κεκόσμηται, εἶπε, Ταῦτα ἃ θεωρεῖτε, ἐλεύ-
and gifts it has been decorated, He said, These things that you see, will
σονται ἡμέραι ἐν αἷς οὐκ ἀφεθήσεται λίθος ἐπὶ λίθῳ, ὃς ου
come days in which not will be left stone on stone which not
7 καταλυθήσεται. ἐπηρώτησαν δὲ αὐτόν, λέγοντες, Διδά-
will be thrown down. they questioned And Him, saying, Teacher
σκαλε, πότε οὖν ταῦτα ἔσται : καὶ τί τὸ σημεῖον, ὅταν μέλλῃ
when, then, these things will be? And what the sign when are about
8 ταῦτα γίνεσθαι ; ὁ δὲ εἶπε, Βλέπετε μὴ πλανηθῆτε· πολλοὶ
these things to occur? He And said, Watch, lest you be led astray; many
γὰρ ἐλεύσονται ἐπὶ τῷ ὀνόματί μου, λέγοντες ὅτι Ἐγώ εἰμι·
for will come on the name of Me, saying, — I AM;
9 καί, Ὁ καιρὸς ἤγγικε. μὴ οὖν πορευθῆτε ὀπίσω αὐτῶν. ὅταν
and, The time has come. not Therefore go after them. when
δὲ ἀκούσητε πολέμους καὶ ἀκαταστασίας, μὴ πτοηθῆτε·
And you hear of wars and disturbances, Do not be afraid.
δεῖ γὰρ ταῦτα γενέσθαι πρῶτον, ἀλλ' οὐκ εὐθέως τὸ τέλος.
must For these things occur first, but not at once the end.
10 Τότε ἔλεγεν αὐτοῖς, Ἐγερθήσεται ἔθνος ἐπὶ ἔθνος, καὶ
Then He said to them, will be raised Nation against nation, and
11 βασιλεία ἐπὶ βασιλείαν· σεισμοί τε μεγαλοι κατὰ τόπους
kingdom against kingdom, earthquakes and great from place to place;
καὶ λιμοὶ καὶ λοιμοὶ ἔσονται, φόβητρά τε καὶ σημεῖα ἀπ'
and famines and plagues there will be; terrors and, also signs from
12 οὐρανοῦ μεγάλα ἔσται. πρὸ δὲ τούτων ἁπάντων ἐπι-
Heaven great will be. before But these things all they
βαλοῦσιν ἐφ' ὑμᾶς τὰς χεῖρας αὐτῶν, καὶ διώξουσι, παραδι-
will lay on you the hands of them, and will persecute, delivering
δόντες εἰς συναγωγὰς καὶ φυλακάς, ἀγομένους ἐπὶ βασιλεῖς
into the synagogues and prisons, being led away before kings
13 καὶ ἡγεμόνας, ἕνεκεν τοῦ ὀνόματός μου. ἀποβήσεται δὲ
and governors, on account of the name of Me. It will return But
14 ὑμῖν εἰς μαρτύριον. θέσθε οὖν εἰς τὰς καρδίας ὑμῶν μὴ
to you for a testimony. put Therefore into the hearts of you not
15 προμελετᾷν ἀπολογηθῆναι· ἐγὼ γὰρ δώσω ὑμῖν στόμα καὶ
to premeditate to make a defense. I For will give you a mouth and

wisdom, which those having been set against you will not be able to withstand or contradict. [16]But you will be betrayed also by parents, and brothers, and relatives, and friends. And they will put you to death. [17]And you will be hated by all because of My name. [18]And a hair of your head shall in no way perish. [19]By your patience, you will gain your souls.

[20]But when you see Jerusalem being encircled by armies, then know that its destruction has come near. [21]Then let those in Judea flee into the mountains; and those in its midst, let them go out. And those in the open spaces, let them not go into her. [22]For these are days of vengeance *when* all things that have been written are to be fulfilled. [23]But woe to the pregnant women, and those suckling in those days; for great distress will be on the earth, and wrath on this people. [24]And they will fall by *the* mouth of *the* sword, and will be led captive to all the nations. And Jerusalem will be trodden down by nations, until *the* time of *the* nations are fulfilled. [25]And there will be signs in sun and moon and stars. And on the earth *will be* anxiety of nations with bewilderment, roaring of sea and of surf, [26]men fainting at heart from fear and expecting of the things which have come on the earth. For the powers of the heavens will be shaken. [27]And then they will see the Son of man coming in a cloud with power and much glory. [28]But when these things begin to happen, stand up and lift up your heads, because your redemption draws near.

[29]And He spoke a parable to them: Watch the fig-tree and all the trees; [30]now when they sprout leaves, seeing *it* you will know that now the summer is near. [31]So also when you see

σοφίαν, ᾗ οὐ δυνήσονται ἀντειπεῖν οὐδὲ ἀντιστῆναι πάντες
wisdom, which not will be able to withstand nor contradict all

16 οἱ ἀντικείμενοι ὑμῖν. παραδοθήσεσθε δὲ καὶ ὑπὸ γονέων
those opposing you. you will be betrayed And also by parents

καὶ ἀδελφῶν καὶ συγγενῶν καὶ φίλων, καὶ θανατώσουσιν
and brothers and relatives and friends, and they will execute

17 ἐξ ὑμῶν. καὶ ἔσεσθε μισούμενοι ὑπὸ πάντων διὰ τὸ ὄνομά
of you. And you will be hated by all because of the name

18 μου. καὶ θρὶξ ἐκ τῆς κεφαλῆς ὑμῶν οὐ μη ἀπόληται. ἐν τῇ
of Me. And a hair of the head of you in no way shall perish in the

19 ὑπομονῇ ὑμῶν κτήσασθε τὰς ψυχὰς ὑμῶν.
patience of you, you will gain the souls of you.

20 Ὅταν δὲ ἴδητε κυκλουμένην ὑπὸ στρατοπέδων τὴν
when And you see being encircled by armies —

Ἱερουσαλήμ, τότε γνῶτε ὅτι ἤγγικεν ἡ ἐρήμωσις αὐτῆς
Jerusalem, then know that has come the ruin of it.

21 τότε οἱ ἐν τῇ Ἰουδαίᾳ φευγέτωσαν εἰς τὰ ὄρη καὶ οἱ ἐν
Then those in — Judea, let them flee into the mounts, and those in

μέσῳ αὐτῆς ἐκχωρείτωσαν· καὶ οἱ ἐν ταῖς χώραις μὴ εἰσερχέ-
midst of it, let them go out, and those in the open spaces not let them

22 σθωσαν εἰς αὐτήν. ὅτι ἡμέραι ἐκδικήσεως αὗταί εἰσι, τοῦ
enter into it. For days of vengeance these are, —

23 πληρωθῆναι πάντα τὰ γεγραμμένα. οὐαὶ δὲ ταῖς ἐν γαστρὶ
to be fulfilled all the things having been written woe But to the pregnant

ἐχούσαις καὶ ταῖς θηλαζούσαις ἐν ἐκείναις ταῖς ἡμέραις·
women, and those giving suck in those — days;

ἔσται γὰρ ἀνάγκη μεγάλη ἐπὶ τῆς γῆς, καὶ ὀργὴ ἐν τῷ λαῷ
will be for distress great on the earth, and wrath on people

24 τούτῳ. καὶ πεσοῦνται στόματι μαχαίρας, καὶ αἰχμαλω-
this. And they will fall by (the) mouth of (the) sword, and will be led

τισθήσονται εἰς πάντα τὰ ἔθνη· καὶ Ἱερουσαλὴμ ἔσται
captive to all the nations. And Jerusalem will be

25 πατουμένη ὑπὸ ἐθνῶν, ἄχρι πληρωθῶσι καιροὶ ἐθνῶν. καὶ
trodden down by nations; until are fulfilled (the) times of nations. And

ἔσται σημεῖα ἐν ἡλίῳ καὶ σελήνῃ καὶ ἄστροις, καὶ ἐπὶ τῆς
will be signs in sun and moon and stars. And on the

γῆς συνοχὴ ἐθνῶν ἐν ἀπορίᾳ, ἠχούσης θαλάσσης καὶ σάλου,
earth, anxiety of nations in perplexity of sound, of sea, and of surf,

26 ἀποψυχόντων ἀνθρώπων ἀπὸ φόβου καὶ προσδοκίας τῶν
fainting men from fear and expectation of the

ἐπερχομένων τῇ οἰκουμένῃ· αἱ γὰρ δυνάμεις τῶν οὐρανῶν
things coming on the habitable earth; the for powers of the heavens

27 σαλευθήσονται. καὶ τότε ὄψονται τὸν υἱὸν τοῦ ἀνθρώπου
will be shaken. And then they will see the Son — of man

28 ἐρχόμενον ἐν νεφέλῃ μετὰ δυνάμεως καὶ δόξης πολλῆς. ἀρχο-
coming in a cloud with power and glory much. begin-

μένων δὲ τούτων γίνεσθαι, ἀνακύψατε καὶ ἐπάρατε τὰς
ning And these things to happen, stand erect and lift up the

κεφαλὰς ὑμῶν· διότι ἐγγίζει ἡ ἀπολύτρωσις ὑμῶν.
heads of you, because draws near the redemption of you.

29 Καὶ εἶπε παραβολὴν αὐτοῖς, Ἴδετε τὴν συκῆν καὶ πάντα
And He told a parable to them: You see the fig-tree and all

30 τὰ δένδρα· ὅταν προβάλωσιν ἤδη, βλέποντες ἀφ' ἑαυτῶν
the trees; when they sprout leaves now, seeing from yourselves

31 γινώσκετε ὅτι ἤδη ἐγγὺς τὸ θέρος ἐστίν. οὕτω καὶ ὑμεῖς,
you know that now near the summer is. So also you,

these things happening, you know that the kingdom of God is near. [32]Truly I say to you, In no way will this generation pass away until all *these* things occur. [33]The heaven and the earth will pass away, but My words in no way will pass away.

[34]But take heed to yourselves, that your hearts not be loaded down with headaches, and drinking, and anxieties of life, and that day come suddenly upon you [35]as a snare, for it will come in on all those sitting on *the* face of all the earth. [36]Then be watchful at every time, begging that you be counted worthy to escape all these things which are about to happen, and to stand before the Son of man.

[37]And *in* the days He was teaching in the Temple. And *in* the nights going out, He lodged in the Mount of Olives. [38]And all the people came early to Him in the Temple, to hear Him.

CHAPTER 22

[1]And the Feast of Unleavened Bread, being called Passover, drew near. [2]And the chief priests and the scribes sought how to destroy Him, for they feared the people.

[3]And Satan entered into Judas, the *one* having been called Iscariot, being of the number of the Twelve. [4]And going, he talked with the chief priests and the captains *as to* how he might betray Him. [5]And they exulted, and they agreed to give him silver. [6]And he fully consented, and sought opportunity to betray Him to them, away from *the* crowd.

[7]And the day of the unleavened came, on which the Passover must be killed. [8]And He sent Peter and John, saying, Going, prepare for us the Passover, that we may eat. [9]And they said to Him, Where do You desire that we prepare? [10]And He said to them, Behold, you going into the

ὅταν ἴδητε ταῦτα γινόμενα, γινώσκετε ὅτι ἐγγύς ἐστιν ἡ
when you see these things occurring, know that near is the
32 βασιλεία τοῦ Θεοῦ. ἀμὴν λέγω ὑμῖν ὅτι οὐ μὴ παρέλθῃ ἡ
kingdom — of God. Truly I say to you that in no way will pass away
33 γενεὰ αὕτη, ἕως ἂν πάντα γένηται. ὁ οὐρανὸς καὶ ἡ γῆ
generation this until all things occur. The heaven and the earth
παρελεύσονται, οἱ δὲ λόγοι μου οὐ μὴ παρέλθωσι.
will pass away, the but words of Me in no way will pass away.
34 Προσέχετε δὲ ἑαυτοῖς, μήποτε βαρυνθῶσιν ὑμῶν αἱ
take heed And to yourselves, lest be loaded down of you the
καρδίαι ἐν κραιπάλῃ καὶ μέθῃ καὶ μερίμναις βιωτικαῖς. καὶ
hearts in headaches and drinking and anxieties of life. And
35 αἰφνίδιος ἐφ᾽ ὑμᾶς ἐπιστῇ ἡ ἡμέρα ἐκείνη· ὡς παγὶς γὰρ
come on you suddenly — day that; as a snare for
ἐπελεύσεται ἐπὶ πάντας τοὺς καθημένους ἐπὶ πρόσωπον
it will come in on all those sitting on (the) face
36 πάσης τῆς γῆς. ἀγρυπνεῖτε οὖν ἐν παντὶ καιρῷ δεόμενοι, ἵνα
of all the earth. you be watchful Then at every time, begging that
καταξιωθῆτε ἐκφυγεῖν ταῦτα πάντα τὰ μέλλοντα γίνεσθαι,
you be counted worthy to escape these all things being about to occur,
καὶ σταθῆναι ἔμπροσθεν τοῦ υἱοῦ τοῦ ἀνθρώπου.
and to stand before the Son — of man.
37 Ἦν δὲ τὰς ἡμέρας ἐν τῷ ἱερῷ διδάσκων· τὰς δὲ νύκτας
He was And (in) the days in the Temple teaching, (in) the and nights
38 ἐξερχόμενος ηὐλίζετο εἰς τὸ ὄρος τὸ καλούμενον ἐλαιῶν. καὶ
going out He lodged in the mountain being called of olives. And
πᾶς ὁ λαὸς ὤρθριζε πρὸς αὐτὸν ἐν τῷ ἱερῷ ἀκούειν αὐτοῦ.
all the people came early to Him in the Temple to hear Him.

CHAPTER 22

1 Ἤγγιζε δὲ ἡ ἑορτὴ τῶν ἀζύμων, ἡ λεγομένη πάσχα.
drew near And the feast of the unleavened (bread), being called Passover.
2 καὶ ἐζήτουν οἱ ἀρχιερεῖς καὶ οἱ γραμματεῖς τὸ πῶς ἀνέλωσιν
And sought the chief priests and the scribes — how to destroy
αὐτόν· ἐφοβοῦντο γὰρ τὸν λαόν.
Him, they feared for the people.
3 Εἰσῆλθε δὲ ὁ Σατανᾶς εἰς Ἰούδαν τον ἐπικαλούμενον
entered And — Satan into Judas the (one) being called
4 Ἰσκαριώτην, ὄντα ἐκ τοῦ ἀριθμοῦ τῶν δώδεκα. καὶ ἀπελθὼν
Iscariot, being of the number of the twelve. And going,
συνελάλησε τοῖς ἀρχιερεῦσι καὶ τοις στρατηγοῖς τὸ πῶς
he talked with the chief priests and the captains (as to) how
5 αὐτὸν παραδῷ αὐτοῖς. καὶ ἐχάρησαν, καὶ συνέθεντο αὐτῷ
he might betray Him. And they exulted, and they agreed him
6 ἀργύριον δοῦναι. καὶ ἐξωμολόγησε, καὶ ἐζήτει εὐκαιρίαν
silver to give. And he fully consented, and sought opportunity
τοῦ παραδοῦναι αὐτὸν αὐτοῖς ἄτερ ὄχλου.
— to betray Him to them away from (the) crowd.
7 Ἦλθε δὲ ἡ ἡμέρα τῶν ἀζύμων, ἐν ᾗ ἔδει θύεσθαι τὸ πασχα.
came And the day of the unleavened, on which must be killed the passover.
8 καὶ ἀπέστειλε Πέτρον καὶ Ἰωάννην, εἰπών, Πορευθέντες
And He sent Peter and John, saying, Going,
9 ἑτοιμάσατε ἡμῖν τὸ πάσχα, ἵνα φάγωμεν. οἱ δὲ εἶπον αὐτῷ,
prepare for us the passover, that we may eat. they And said to Him,
10 Ποῦ θέλεις ἑτοιμάσωμεν ; ὁ δὲ εἶπεν αὐτοῖς, Ἰδού, εἰσελθόντων
Where You desire we prepare? He And told them, Behold, going in

city, you will meet a man carrying a pitcher of water. Follow him into the house where he goes in. 11 And you will say to the house-master, The Teacher says to you, Where is the guest-room where I may eat the Passover with My disciples? 12 And he will show you a large upper room having been spread; prepare there. 13 And going they found as He had told them, and they prepared the Passover.

14 And when the hour came, He reclined, and the twelve apostles with Him. 15 And He said to them, With desire I desired to eat this Passover with you before My suffering. 16 For I say to you that I will never in any way eat of it until it is fulfilled in the kingdom of God. 17 And having taken a cup, giving thanks, He said, Take this and divide *it* among yourselves. 18 For I say to you that in no way will I drink from the fruit of the vine until the kingdom of God has come. 19 And taking a loaf, giving thanks, He broke and gave to them, saying, This is My body being given for you. Do this for My remembrance. 20 In the same way the cup also, after having supped, saying, This cup *is* the new covenant in My blood, which is being poured out for you. 21 But, behold, the hand of My betrayer on the table with Me! 22 And, indeed, the Son of man goes according as was determined, but woe to that man by whom He is betrayed! 23 And they began to examine themselves who then it may be of them, the *one* being about to do this.

24 And there was also a dispute among them, who of them seems to be greater. 25 And He said to them, The kings of the nations lord it over them, and the authorities over them are called

ὑμῶν εἰς τὴν πόλιν, συναντήσει ὑμῖν ἄνθρωπος κεράμιον
you into the city, will meet you a man a pitcher
ὕδατος βαστάζων· ἀκολουθήσατε αὐτῷ εἰς τὴν οἰκίαν οὗ
of water carrying. Follow him into the house where e
11 εἰσπορεύεται. καὶ ἐρεῖτε τῷ οἰκοδεσπότῃ τῆς οἰκίας, Λέγει
he goes in. And you will say to the house-master of the house, Says
σοι ὁ διδάσκαλος, Ποῦ ἐστι τὸ κατάλυμα, ὅπου τὸ πάσχα
to you the Teacher, Where is the guest room where the passover
12 μετὰ τῶν μαθητῶν μου φάγω; κἀκεῖνος ὑμῖν δείξει ἀνώγεον
with the disciples of Me I may eat? And that one you will show an upper room
13 μέγα ἐστρωμένον· ἐκεῖ ἑτοιμάσατε. ἀπελθόντες δὲ εὗρον
large having been spread; there prepare. going And they found
καθὼς εἴρηκεν αὐτοῖς· καὶ ἡτοίμασαν τὸ πάσχα.
as He had told them, and they prepared the passover.
14 Καὶ ὅτε ἐγένετο ἡ ὥρα, ἀνέπεσε, καὶ οἱ δώδεκα ἀπόστολοι
And when came the hour, He reclined, and the twelve apostles
15 σὺν αὐτῷ. καὶ εἶπε πρὸς αὐτούς, Ἐπιθυμίᾳ ἐπεθύμησα τοῦτο
with Him. And He said to them, With desire I desired this
16 τὸ πάσχα φαγεῖν μεθ' ὑμῶν πρὸ τοῦ με παθεῖν· λέγω γὰρ
— passover to eat with you, before the Me to suffer. I say For
ὑμῖν ὅτι οὐκέτι οὐ μὴ φάγω ἐξ αὐτοῦ, ἕως ὅτου πληρωθῇ ἐν
to you that never in any way I eat of it, until when it is fulfilled in
17 τῇ βασιλείᾳ τοῦ Θεοῦ. καὶ δεξάμενος ποτήριον, εὐχαριστή-
the kingdom — of God. And taking a cup, having given thanks,
18 σας εἶπε, Λάβετε τοῦτο, καὶ διαμερίσατε ἑαυτοῖς· λέγω γὰρ
He said, Take this, and divide among yourselves. I say For
ὑμῖν ὅτι οὐ μὴ πίω ἀπὸ τοῦ γεννήματος τῆς ἀμπέλου, ἕως
to you that in no way I drink from the produce of the vine until
19 ὅτου ἡ βασιλεία τοῦ Θεοῦ ἔλθῃ. καὶ λαβὼν ἄρτον, εὐχαριστή-
when the kingdom — of God comes. And taking a loaf, having given
σας ἔκλασε, καὶ ἔδωκεν αὐτοῖς, λέγων, Τοῦτό ἐστι τὸ σῶμά
thanks, He broke, and gave to them, saying, This is the body
μου, τὸ ὑπὲρ ὑμῶν διδόμενον· τοῦτο ποιεῖτε εἰς τὴν ἐμὴν
of Me, — for you being given; this do for — My
20 ἀνάμνησιν. ὡσαύτως καὶ τὸ ποτήριον μετὰ τὸ δειπνῆσαι,
remembrance. in like manner And the cup after having supped,
λέγων, Τοῦτο τὸ ποτήριον ἡ καινὴ διαθήκη ἐν τῷ αἵματί
saying, This — cup (is) the new covenant in the blood
21 μου, τὸ ὑπὲρ ὑμῶν ἐκχυνόμενον. πλὴν ἰδού, ἡ χεὶρ τοῦ
of Me, — for you being poured out. But, behold, the hand of the
22 παραδιδόντος με μετ' ἐμοῦ ἐπὶ τῆς τραπέζης. καὶ ὁ μὲν υἱὸς
betrayer of Me with Me on the table. And, indeed, the Son
τοῦ ἀνθρώπου πορεύεται κατὰ τὸ ὡρισμένον· πλὴν οὐαὶ τῷ
— of man goes, according as was determined, but woe —
23 ἀνθρώπῳ ἐκείνῳ δι' οὗ παραδίδοται. καὶ αὐτοὶ ἤρξαντο
man to that through whom He is betrayed! And they began
συζητεῖν πρὸς ἑαυτοὺς τὸ τίς ἄρα εἴη ἐξ αὐτῶν ὁ τοῦτο
to argue with themselves — who then it may be of them, he this
μέλλων πράσσειν.
being about to do.
24 Ἐγένετο δὲ καὶ φιλονεικία ἐν αὐτοῖς τὸ τίς αὐτῶν δοκεῖ
there was And also a dispute among them, — who of them seems
25 εἶναι μείζων. ὁ δὲ εἶπεν αὐτοῖς, Οἱ βασιλεῖς τῶν ἐθνῶν
to be greater. He And said to them, The kings of the nations
κυριεύουσιν αὐτῶν, καὶ οἱ ἐξουσιάζοντες αὐτῶν εὐεργέται
lord it over them, and the authorities over them benefactors

benefactors. [26]But you *be* not so, but the greater among you, let him be as the lesser, and the *one* governing as the *one* serving. [27]For who *is* greater, the *one* serving, or the *one* reclining? *Is it* not the *one* reclining? But I am in your midst as *One* serving. [28]But you are those having continued with Me in My trials. [29]And I appoint a kingdom to you, as My Father appointed to Me, [30]that you may eat and drink at My table in My kingdom. And you will sit on thrones judging the twelve tribes of Israel.

[31]And the Lord said, Simon, Simon, behold, Satan asked for you, to sift *you* as wheat, [32]but I prayed concerning you that your faith might not fail. And when you have turned back, confirm your brothers. [33]And he said to Him, Lord, I am ready to go both to prison and to death with You. [34]And He said, I say to you, Peter, a cock will not crow today before you will deny knowing Me three times.

[35]And He said to them, When I sent you without a purse, or a wallet, or sandals, did you lack anything? And they said, Nothing. [36]Then He said to them, But now the *one* having a purse, let him take *it*, likewise also a wallet. And the *one* not having, let him sell his garment and let him buy a sword. [37]For I say to you that this that has been written must yet be fulfilled in Me, "And He was numbered with *the* lawless," for the things concerning Me also have an end. [38]And they said, Lord, behold, here *are* two swords. And He said to them, it is enough.

[39]And going out, according to *His* custom, He went to the Mount of Olives; and His disciples also followed Him. [40]And having come on the place, He said to them, Pray you *will* not enter

26 καλοῦνται. ὑμεῖς δὲ οὐχ οὕτως· ἀλλ' ὁ μείζων ἐν ὑμῖν
are called. you But not so, but the greater among you
γενέσθω ὡς ὁ νεώτερος· καὶ ὁ ἡγούμενος ὡς ὁ διακονῶν. τίς
let him be as the lesser, and he governing as he serving. who
27 γὰρ μείζων, ὁ ἀνακείμενος ἢ ὁ διακονῶν; οὐχὶ ὁ ἀνακεί-
For (is)greater, he reclining or he serving? (Is it) not he reclining?
28 μενος; ἐγὼ δέ εἰμι ἐν μέσῳ ὑμῶν ὡς ὁ διακονῶν. ὑμεῖς δέ
I But am in (the) midst of you as (one) serving. you But
ἐστε οἱ διαμεμενηκότες μετ' ἐμοῦ ἐν τοῖς πειρασμοῖς μου·
are those having continued with Me in the temptations of Me;
29 κἀγὼ διατίθεμαι ὑμῖν, καθὼς διέθετό μοι ὁ πατήρ μου,
and I appoint to you, as appointed to Me the Father of Me
30 βασιλείαν, ἵνα ἐσθίητε καὶ πίνητε ἐπὶ τῆς τραπέζης μου
a kingdom, that you may eat and drink at the table of Me
ἐν τῇ βασιλείᾳ μου, καὶ καθίσησθε ἐπὶ θρόνων, κρίνοντες
in the kingdom of Me; and you will sit on thrones judging
31 τὰς δώδεκα φυλὰς τοῦ Ἰσραήλ. εἶπε δὲ ὁ Κύριος, Σίμων,
the twelve tribes — Of Israel. said And the Lord, Simon,
Σίμων, ἰδού, ὁ Σατανᾶς ἐξῃτήσατο ὑμᾶς, τοῦ σινιάσαι ὡς
Simon, behold, — Satan asked for you — to sift (you) as
32 τὸν σῖτον· ἐγὼ δὲ ἐδεήθην περὶ σοῦ, ἵνα μὴ ἐκλείπῃ ἡ πίστις
the wheat; I but entreated about you, that not might fail the faith
σου· καὶ σύ ποτε ἐπιστρέψας στήριξον τοὺς ἀδελφούς σου.
of you; and you when having turned confirm the brothers of you.
33 ὁ δὲ εἶπεν αὐτῷ, Κύριε, μετὰ σοῦ ἕτοιμός εἰμι καὶ εἰς φυλακὴν
he And said to him, Lord, with You prepared I am both to prison
34 καὶ εἰς θάνατον πορεύεσθαι. ὁ δὲ εἶπε, Λέγω σοι, Πέτρε, οὐ
and to death to go. He But said, I say to you, Peter, not
μὴ φωνήσει σήμερον ἀλέκτωρ, πρὶν ἢ τρὶς ἀπαρνήσῃ μὴ
will sound today a cock before thrice you will deny –
εἰδέναι με.
knowing Me.
35 Καὶ εἶπεν αὐτοῖς, Ὅτε ἀπέστειλα ὑμᾶς ἄτερ βαλαντίου καὶ
And He said to them, When I sent you without a purse and
πήρας καὶ ὑποδημάτων, μή τινος ὑστερήσατε; οἱ δὲ εἶπον,
a wallet and sandals, not anything you lacked? they And said,
36 Οὐδενός. εἶπεν οὖν αὐτοῖς, Ἀλλὰ νῦν ὁ ἔχων βαλάντιον
Nothing. He said Then to them, But now he having a purse,
ἀράτω, ὁμοίως καὶ πήραν· καὶ ὁ μὴ ἔχων, πωλησάτω τὸ
let him take; likewise also a wallet; and he not having, let him sell the
37 ἱμάτιον αὐτοῦ, καὶ ἀγορασάτω μάχαιραν. λέγω γὰρ ὑμῖν
garment of him and let him buy a sword. I say For to you
ὅτι ἔτι τοῦτο τὸ γεγραμμένον δεῖ τελεσθῆναι ἐν ἐμοί, τὸ Καὶ
that yet this that has been written must be completed in Me: — And
μετὰ ἀνόμων ἐλογίσθη· καὶ γὰρ τὰ περὶ ἐμοῦ τέλος ἔχει. οἱ
with (the) lawless He was counted; also for that about Me an end has. they
38 δὲ εἶπον, Κύριε, ἰδού, μάχαιραι ὧδε δύο. ὁ δὲ εἶπεν αὐτοῖς,
And said, Lord, behold, swords here (are) two. He And said to them,
Ἱκανόν ἐστι.
Enough it is.
39 Καὶ ἐξελθὼν ἐπορεύθη κατὰ τὸ ἔθος εἰς τὸ ὄρος τῶν
And going forth He went according to the custom to the mount of the
ἐλαιῶν· ἠκολούθησαν δὲ αὐτῷ καὶ οἱ μαθηταὶ αὐτοῦ. γενό-
olives; followed and Him also the disciples of Him.
40 μενος δὲ ἐπὶ τοῦ τόπου, εἶπεν αὐτοῖς, Προσεύχεσθε μὴ εἰσελ-
coming And on the place, He said to them, Pray you (will) not enter

into temptation. [41]And He was withdrawn from them, about a stone's throw. And falling on *His* knees, He prayed, [42]saying, Father, if You will, take away this cup from Me; but let not My will be done, but Your *will.* [43]And an angel from Heaven appeared to Him, strengthening Him. [44]And being in an agony, He prayed more intently. And His sweat became as drops of blood falling down onto the earth. [45]And rising up from the prayer, coming to His disciples, He found them sleeping from grief. [46]And He said to them, Why do you sleep? Rising up, pray, that you do not enter into temptation. [47]And *as* He was yet speaking, behold, a crowd! And the *one* called Judas, one of the Twelve, came in front of them and drew near to Jesus to kiss Him. [48]But Jesus said to him, Judas, do you betray the Son of man with a kiss? [49]And those around Him seeing that about to occur, *they* said to Him, Lord, shall we strike with a sword? [50]And a certain one of them struck the high priest's slave, and cut off his right ear. [51]And answering Jesus said, Allow *it* until this. And having touched his ear, He healed him. [52]And Jesus said to those coming upon Him, chief priests, and captains of the Temple, and elders, Have you come out with swords and clubs as against a robber? [53]When I was with you day by day in the Temple, you did not stretch out your hand on Me. But this is your hour, and the authority of the darkness.

[54]And laying hold of Him, they led Him away and brought *Him* into the high priest's house. And Peter followed at a distance. [55]And lighting a fire in *the* midst of the court, and they sitting down, Peter sat in

41 θεῖν εἰς πειρασμόν. καὶ αὐτὸς ἀπεσπάσθη ἀπ' αὐτῶν ὡσεὶ
into temptation. And He was withdrawn from them, about
42 λίθου βολήν, καὶ θεὶς τὰ γόνατα προσηύχετο, λέγων, Πάτερ,
a stone's throw. And placing the knees, He prayed, saying, Father,
εἰ βούλει, παρένεγκε τὸ ποτήριον τοῦτο ἀπ' ἐμοῦ· πλὴν μὴ
if You will, take away – cup this from Me; but not
43 τὸ θέλημά μου, ἀλλὰ τὸ σὸν γενέσθω. ὤφθη δὲ αὐτῷ ἄγγελος
the will of Me, but – of You let be. **appeared And to Him an angel**
44 ἀπ' οὐρανοῦ ἐνισχύων αὐτόν. καὶ γενόμενος ἐν ἀγωνίᾳ,
from Heaven strengthening Him. And becoming in an agony,
ἐκτενέστερον προσηύχετο. ἐγένετο δὲ ὁ ἱδρὼς αὐτοῦ ὡσεὶ
more instantly He prayed. became And the sweat of Him as
45 θρόμβοι αἵματος καταβαίνοντες ἐπὶ τὴν γῆν. καὶ ἀναστὰς
drops of blood falling down onto the earth. And rising up
ἀπὸ τῆς προσευχῆς, ἐλθὼν πρὸς τοὺς μαθητάς αὐτοῦ,
from the prayer, coming to the disciples of Him,
46 εὗρεν αὐτοὺς κοιμωμένους ἀπὸ τῆς λύπης, καὶ εἶπεν αὐτοῖς,
He found them sleeping from the grief, and said to them,
Τί καθεύδετε; ἀναστάντες προσεύχεσθε, ἵνα μὴ εἰσέλθητε
Why do you sleep? Having arisen, pray, lest you enter
εἰς πειρασμόν.
into temptation.
47 Ἔτι δὲ αὐτοῦ λαλοῦντος, ἰδού, ὄχλος, καὶ ὁ λεγόμενος
yet And Him speaking, behold, a crowd. And the (one) called
Ἰούδας, εἷς τῶν δώδεκα, προήρχετο αὐτῶν. καὶ ἤγγισε τῷ
Judas, one of the twelve, came before them, and drew near to
48 Ἰησοῦ φιλῆσαι αὐτόν. ὁ δὲ Ἰησοῦς εἶπεν αὐτῷ, Ἰούδα,
Jesus in order to kiss Him. – But Jesus said to him, Judas,
49 φιλήματι τὸν υἱὸν τοῦ ἀνθρώπου παραδίδως; ἰδόντες δὲ οἱ
with a kiss the Son – of man do you betray? seeing And those
περὶ αὐτὸν τὸ ἐσόμενον εἶπον αὐτῷ, Κύριε, εἰ πατάξομεν ἐν
around him that about to occur said to Him, Lord, if we shall strike with
50 μαχαίρᾳ; καὶ ἐπάταξεν εἷς τις ἐξ αὐτῶν τὸν δοῦλον τοῦ
a sword? And struck a certain one of them of the slave of the
51 ἀρχιερέως, καὶ ἀφεῖλεν αὐτοῦ τὸ οὖς τὸ δεξιόν. ἀποκριθεὶς
high priest, and cut off of him the ear, the right. answering
δὲ ὁ Ἰησοῦς εἶπεν, Ἐᾶτε ἕως τούτου. καὶ ἁψάμενος τοῦ
And Jesus said, Allow (it) until this. And touching the
52 ὠτίου αὐτοῦ, ἰάσατο αὐτόν. εἶπε δὲ ὁ Ἰησοῦς πρὸς τοὺς
ear of him, He cured him. said And – Jesus to those
παραγενομένους ἐπ' αὐτὸν ἀρχιερεῖς καὶ στρατηγοὺς τοῦ
coming upon Him, chief priests, and captains of the
ἱεροῦ καὶ πρεσβυτέρους, Ὡς ἐπὶ λῃστὴν ἐξεληλύθατε μετὰ
Temple, and elders: As against a robber did you come out with
53 μαχαιρῶν καὶ ξύλων: καθ' ἡμέραν ὄντος μου μεθ' ὑμῶν
swords and clubs? Day by day being Me with you
ἐν τῷ ἱερῷ, οὐκ ἐξετείνατε τὰς χεῖρας ἐπ' ἐμέ. ἀλλ' αὕτη
in the Temple, not you stretched the hand on Me. But this
ὑμῶν ἐστιν ἡ ὥρα, καὶ ἡ ἐξουσία τοῦ σκότους.
your is – hour, and the authority of the darkness.
54 Συλλαβόντες δὲ αὐτὸν ἤγαγον, καὶ εἰσήγαγον αὐτὸν
having seized And Him, they led away, and brought Him
εἰς τὸν οἶκον τοῦ ἀρχιερέως. ὁ δὲ Πέτρος ἠκολούθει μακρόθεν.
into the house of the high priest.–And Peter followed afar off.
55 ἁψάντων δὲ πῦρ ἐν μέσῳ τῆς αὐλῆς, καὶ συγκαθισάντων
lighting And a fire in (the) midst of the court, and sitting down

their midst. 56 And a
certain maidservant *was*
sitting near the light. And
looking intently at him, *she*
said, And this one was with
him. 57 But he denied Him,
saying, Woman, I do not
know Him. 58 And after a
while another seeing him
said, And you are of them.
But Peter said, Man, I am
not. 59 And about an hour
intervening, a certain other
one boldly charged, saying,
Truly this one also was with
him, for he also is a Galilean.
60 And Peter said, Man I do
not know what you say. And
immediately, while he yet
spoke, the cock crowed.
61 And turning, the Lord
looked at Peter. And Peter
remembered the word of the
Lord, how he told him,
Before a cock would crow,
you will deny Me three
times. 62 And going outside
Peter wept bitterly.

63 And the men who were
holding Jesus mocked Him,
beating *Him*. 64 And blind-
folding Him, *they were*
striking His face and questioning Him, saying,
Prophesy, who is the *one*
stinging you? 65 And many
other things they said to
Him, blaspheming.

66 And when day came,
the body of elders of the
people, the chief priests and
scribes, were gathered. And
they led Him away into their
sanhedrin, saying, 67 If you
are the Christ, tell us. And
He said to them, If I tell you,
you will in no way believe.
68 And also if I ask, in no way
will you answer Me, or let
Me go. 69 From now on the
Son of man will be sitting at
the right *hand* of the power
of God. 70 And they all said,
Then are you the Son of
God? And He said, You say
it, because I AM! 71 And
they said, Why do we yet
have need of witness? For
we ourselves heard *it* from
His mouth.

56 αὐτῶν, ἐκάθητο ὁ Πέτρος ἐν μέσῳ αὐτῶν. ἰδοῦσα δὲ αὐτὸν
they, sat — Peter in (the) midst of them. seeing And him
παιδίσκη τις καθήμενον πρὸς τὸ φῶς, καὶ ἀτενίσασα αὐτῷ,
maidservant a certain sitting near the light, and looking intently at him,
57 εἶπε, Καὶ οὗτος σὺν αὐτῷ ἦν. ὁ δὲ ἠρνήσατο αὐτόν, λέγων,
said, And this one with him was. he But denied Him, saying,
58 Γύναι, οὐκ οἶδα αὐτόν. καὶ μετὰ βραχὺ ἕτερος ἰδὼν αὐτὸν
Woman, not I know Him. And after a while another seeing him
ἔφη, Καὶ σὺ ἐξ αὐτῶν εἶ. ὁ δὲ Πέτρος εἶπεν, Ἄνθρωπε, οὐκ
said, And you of them are. — But Peter said, Man, not
59 εἰμί. καὶ διαστάσης ὡσεὶ ὥρας μιᾶς, ἄλλος τις διϊσχυρίζετο,
I am. And intervening about hour one, other a certain boldly charged,
λέγων, Ἐπ᾽ ἀληθείας καὶ οὗτος μετ᾽ αὐτοῦ ἦν· καὶ γὰρ
saying, In truth also this one with him was, also for
60 Γαλιλαῖός ἐστιν. εἶπε δὲ ὁ Πέτρος, Ἄνθρωπε, οὐκ οἶδα ὃ
a Galilean he is. said And — Peter, Man, not I know what
λέγεις. καὶ παραχρῆμα, ἔτι λαλοῦντος αὐτοῦ, ἐφώνησεν ὁ
you say. And immediately, yet speaking him, sounded the
61 ἀλέκτωρ. καὶ στραφεὶς ὁ Κύριος ἐνέβλεψε τῷ Πέτρῳ. καὶ
cock. And turning the Lord looked at — Peter. And
ὑπεμνήσθη ὁ Πέτρος τοῦ λόγου τοῦ Κυρίου, ὡς εἶπεν αὐτῷ
remembered — Peter the word of the Lord, as He told him
62 ὅτι Πρὶν ἀλέκτορα φωνῆσαι, ἀπαρνήσῃ με τρίς. καὶ ἐξελθὼν
Before a cock would sound, you will deny Me thrice. And going
ἔξω ὁ Πέτρος ἔκλαυσε πικρῶς.
outside Peter wept bitterly.

63 Καὶ οἱ ἄνδρες οἱ συνέχοντες τὸν Ἰησοῦν ἐνέπαιζον αὐτῷ,
And the men — having in charge — Jesus mocked Him,
64 δέροντες. καὶ περικαλύψαντες αὐτόν, ἔτυπτον αὐτοῦ τὸ
beating (Him) And having blindfolded Him, striking of Him the
πρόσωπον, καὶ ἐπηρώτων αὐτόν, λέγοντες, Προφήτευσον·
face, and questioned Him, saying, Prophesy,
65 τίς ἐστιν ὁ παίσας σε; καὶ ἕτερα πολλὰ βλασφημοῦντες
who is the (one) stinging you? And other things many, blaspheming,
ἔλεγον εἰς αὐτόν.
they said to Him.

66 Καὶ ὡς ἐγένετο ἡμέρα, συνήχθη τὸ πρεσβυτέριον τοῦ
And when came day, was assembled the body of elders of the
λαοῦ, ἀρχιερεῖς τε καὶ γραμματεῖς, καὶ ἀνήγαγον αὐτὸν εἰς
people, chief priests and scribes, and led away Him to
67 τὸ συνέδριον ἑαυτῶν, λέγοντες, Εἰ σὺ εἶ ὁ Χριστός, εἰπὲ
the sanhedrin of themselves, saying, If you are the Christ, tell
ἡμῖν. εἶπε δὲ αὐτοῖς, Ἐὰν ὑμῖν εἴπω, οὐ μὴ πιστεύσητε·
us. He said And to them, If you I tell, in no way will you believe.
68 ἐὰν δὲ καὶ ἐρωτήσω, οὐ μὴ ἀποκριθῆτέ μοι, ἢ ἀπολύσητε.
if And also I ask, in no way you will answer Me, or let Me go.
69 ἀπὸ τοῦ νῦν ἔσται ὁ υἱὸς τοῦ ἀνθρώπου καθήμενος ἐκ
From now on will be the Son — of man sitting at
70 δεξιῶν τῆς δυνάμεως τοῦ Θεοῦ. εἶπον δὲ πάντες, Σὺ οὖν εἶ ὁ
the right of the power — of God. they said And all, You, then, are the
υἱὸς τοῦ Θεοῦ; ὁ δὲ πρὸς αὐτοὺς ἔφη, Ὑμεῖς λέγετε ὅτι ἐγώ
Son — of God? He And to them said, You say (it), because I
71 εἰμι. οἱ δὲ εἶπον, Τί ἔτι χρείαν ἔχομεν μαρτυρίας; αὐτοὶ γὰρ
am. they And said, Why yet have we need of witness? ourselves For
ἠκούσαμεν ἀπὸ τοῦ στόματος αὐτοῦ.
we heard from the mouth of Him.

CHAPTER 23

CHAPTER 23

[1]And rising up all the multitude of them led Him before Pilate. [2]And they began to accuse Him, saying, We found this one perverting the nation, and forbidding to give tribute to Caesar, saying himself to be a king, Christ. [3]And Pilate questioned Him, saying, Are you the king of the Jews? And answering him He said, You say *it.* [4]And Pilate said to the chief priests and the crowd, I find nothing blameable in this man. [5]And they insisted, saying, He stirs up the people, teaching throughout all Judea, beginning from Galilee to here. [6]And hearing Galilee, Pilate asked if the man is a Galilean. [7]And knowing that He is from Herod's jurisdiction, he sent Him up to Herod, he also being in Jerusalem these days.

1 Καὶ ἀναστὰν ἅπαν τὸ πλῆθος αὐτῶν, ἤγαγεν αὐτὸν ἐπὶ
And rising up all the multitude of them led Him before
2 τὸν Πιλάτον. ἤρξαντο δὲ κατηγορεῖν αὐτοῦ, λέγοντες,
– Pilate. they began And to accuse Him, saying,
Τοῦτον εὕρομεν διαστρέφοντα τὸ ἔθνος, καὶ κωλύοντα Καί-
This one we found perverting the nation, and forbidding to
σαρι φόρους διδόναι, λέγοντα ἑαυτὸν Χριστὸν βασιλέα εἶναι.
Caesar tribute to give, saying himself Christ a king to be.
3 ὁ δὲ Πιλάτος ἐπηρώτησεν αὐτόν, λέγων, Σὺ εἶ ὁ βασιλεὺς
—And Pilate questioned Him, saying, you Are the king
4 τῶν Ἰουδαίων; ὁ δὲ ἀποκριθεὶς αὐτῷ ἔφη, Σὺ λέγεις. ὁ δὲ
of the Jews? He And answering him said, You say (it). —And
Πιλάτος εἶπε πρὸς τοὺς ἀρχιερεῖς καὶ τοὺς ὄχλους, Οὐδὲν
Pilate said to the chief priests and the crowds Nothing
5 εὑρίσκω αἴτιον ἐν τῷ ἀνθρώπῳ τούτῳ. οἱ δὲ ἐπίσχυον,
I find blameable in — man this. they But insisted,
λέγοντες ὅτι Ἀνασείει τὸν λαόν, διδάσκων καθ' ὅλης τῆς
saying, — He stirs up the people, teaching throughout all —
6 Ἰουδαίας, ἀρξάμενος ἀπὸ τῆς Γαλιλαίας ἕως ὧδε. Πιλάτος δὲ
Judea, beginning from — Galilee to here. Pilate And
ἀκούσας Γαλιλαίαν ἐπηρώτησεν εἰ ὁ ἄνθρωπος Γαλιλαῖός
hearing Galilee, (he) asked if the man a Galilean
7 ἐστι. καὶ ἐπιγνοὺς ὅτι ἐκ τῆς ἐξουσίας Ἡρώδου ἐστίν, ἀνέ-
is. And having known that from the jurisdiction of Herod He is, he
πεμψεν αὐτὸν πρὸς Ἡρώδην, ὄντα καὶ αὐτὸν ἐν Ἱεροσολύ-
sent up Him to Herod, being also him in Jerusalem
μοις ἐν ταύταις ταῖς ἡμέραις.
in these — days.

[8]And seeing Jesus, Herod greatly rejoiced; for he was wishing to see Him *for* a long *time,* because of hearing many things about Him. [9]And he questioned Him in many words. But He answered him nothing. [10]And the chief priests and the scribes stood fiercely accusing Him.

8 Ὁ δὲ Ἡρώδης ἰδὼν τὸν Ἰησοῦν ἐχάρη λίαν· ἦν γὰρ
— And Herod seeing — Jesus rejoiced greatly; he was for
θέλων ἐξ ἱκανοῦ ἰδεῖν αὐτόν, διὰ τὸ ἀκούειν πολλὰ περὶ
wishing of a long (time) to see Him, because of hearing many things about
αὐτοῦ· καὶ ἤλπιζέ τι σημεῖον ἰδεῖν ὑπ' αὐτοῦ γινομενον.
Him. And he hoped some sign to see by Him brought about.
9 ἐπηρώτα δὲ αὐτὸν ἐν λόγοις ἱκανοῖς· αὐτὸς δὲ οὐδὲν ἀπεκρί-
questioned And Him in words many. He But nothing
10 νατο αὐτῷ. εἱστήκεισαν δὲ οἱ ἀρχιερεῖς καὶ οἱ γραμματεῖς,
answered him. stood And the chief priests and the scribes
εὐτόνως κατηγοροῦντες αὐτοῦ. ἐξουθενήσας δὲ αὐτὸν ὁ
vehemently accusing Him. having humiliated And Him, —

[11]And Herod having humiliated Him with his guardsmen, and mocking Him *by* putting luxurious clothing around *Him, he* sent Him back to Pilate. [12]And on that same day both Pilate and Herod became friends with each other, for before they were at enmity *between* themselves.
[13]And having called together the chief priests and the rulers and the people, [14]Pilate said to them, You brought this man to me as perverting the people.

11 Ἡρώδης σὺν τοῖς στρατεύμασιν αὐτοῦ, καὶ ἐμπαίξας,
Herod with the soldiery of him, and mocking
περιβαλὼν αὐτὸν ἐσθῆτα λαμπράν, ἀνέπεμψεν αὐτὸν τῷ
putting around Him clothing luxurious, sent back Him —
12 Πιλάτῳ. ἐγένοντο δὲ φίλοι ὅ τε Πιλάτος καὶ ὁ Ἡρώδης ἐν
to Pilate. became And friends — both Pilate and — Herod on
αὐτῇ τῇ ἡμέρᾳ μετ' ἀλλήλων· προϋπῆρχον γὰρ ἐν ἔχθρᾳ
same the day with each other; they before for in enmity
ὄντες πρὸς ἑαυτούς.
being with themselves.
13 Πιλάτος δὲ συγκαλεσάμενος τοὺς ἀρχιερεῖς καὶ τοὺς ἄρχον-
Pilate And calling together the chief priests and the leaders
14 τας καὶ τὸν λαόν, εἶπε πρὸς αὐτούς, Προσηνέγκατέ μοι τὸν
and the people, said to them, You brought to me —
ἄνθρωπον τοῦτον, ὡς ἀποστρέφοντα τὸν λαόν· καὶ ἰδού,
man this, as perverting the people, and behold,

And, behold, examining him before you I found nothing blameable in this man *regarding that* which you charge against him. [15] But neither did Herod; for I sent you up to him, and, behold, nothing worthy of death is done by him. [16] Therefore, chastising him, I will release *him.* [17] And he had to release to them one at *the* Feast. [18] And they all together shouted, saying, Take this one, and release Barabbas to us; [19] who was thrown into prison due to some revolt and murder occurring in the city. [20] Then Pilate again called out, desiring to release Jesus. [21] But they shouted, saying, Crucify! Crucify him! [22] And a third *time* he said to them, For what evil did this one do? I found no cause of death in him. Therefore, chastising him, I will release *him.* [23] But with loud voices they insisted, asking for Him to be crucified. And their voices and of the chief priests prevailed. [24] And Pilate adjudged their request to be done. [25] And he released to them *the one* thrown into prison due to revolt and murder, whom they asked. But he delivered Jesus to their will.

[26] And as they led Him away, having laid hold on a certain Simon, a Cyrenian, coming from a field, they put the cross on him, to bear *it* behind Jesus.

[27] And a great multitude of people were following Him, and of women who also were bewailing and lamenting Him. [28] And turning to them, Jesus said, Daughters of Jerusalem, do not weep over Me, but weep over yourselves and over your children. [29] For, behold, days will come in which they will say, Blessed *are* the barren, and the wombs which did not bear, and breasts that did not suckle. [30] Then they will begin to say to the mountains, Fall on us! And to the hills, Cover us!

ἐγὼ ἐνώπιον ὑμῶν ἀνακρίνας οὐδὲν εὗρον ἐν τῷ ἀνθρώπῳ
I before you examining nothing found in — man

15 τούτῳ αἴτιον ὧν κατηγορεῖτε κατ' αὐτοῦ· ἀλλ' οὐδὲ
this blameable of which you bring charge against him. But neither

Ἡρώδης· ἀνέπεμψα γὰρ ὑμᾶς πρὸς αὐτόν, καὶ ἰδού, οὐδὲν
Herod; I sent up for you to him, and, behold, nothing

16 ἄξιον θανάτου ἐστὶ πεπραγμένον αὐτῷ. παιδεύσας οὖν
worthy of death is done by him. Having chastised, then,

17 αὐτὸν ἀπολύσω. ἀνάγκην δὲ εἶχεν ἀπολύειν αὐτοῖς κατὰ
him I will release. need And he had to release to them at

18 ἑορτὴν ἕνα. ἀνέκραξαν δὲ παμπληθεί, λέγοντες, Αἶρε τοῦτον,
(the) feast one. they shouted And, all enmass, saying, Take this one,

ἀπόλυσον δὲ ἡμῖν τὸν Βαραββᾶν· ὅστις ἦν διὰ στάσιν τινὰ
release and to us — Barabbas; who was due to revolt some

19 γενομένην ἐν τῇ πόλει καὶ φόνον βεβλημένος εἰς φυλακήν.
occurring in the city, and murder, thrown into prison.

20 πάλιν οὖν ὁ Πιλάτος προσεφώνησε, θέλων ἀπολῦσαι τὸν
again Then — Pilate called (to them), desiring to release —

21 Ἰησοῦν. οἱ δὲ ἐπεφώνουν, λέγοντες, Σταύρωσον, σταύρωσον
Jesus. they But shouted, saying, Crucify! Crucify

22 αὐτόν. ὁ δὲ τρίτον εἶπε πρὸς αὐτούς, Τί γὰρ κακὸν ἐποίησεν
him! he But a third said to them, what For evil did

οὗτος; οὐδὲν αἴτιον θανάτου εὗρον ἐν αὐτῷ· παιδεύσας οὖν
this one? nothing cause of death I found in him; having chastised, then,

23 αὐτὸν ἀπολύσω. οἱ δὲ ἐπέκειντο φωναῖς μεγάλαις, αἰτού-
him I will release. they But insisted voices with great, asking

μενοι αὐτὸν σταυρωθῆναι· καὶ κατίσχυον αἱ φωναὶ αὐτῶν
for Him to be crucified. And prevailed the voices of them

24 καὶ τῶν ἀρχιερέων. ὁ δὲ Πιλάτος ἐπέκρινε γενέσθαι τὸ αἴτημα
and of the chief priests. And Pilate adjudged to be done the request

25 αὐτῶν. ἀπέλυσε δὲ αὐτοῖς τὸν διὰ στάσιν καὶ φόνον βεβλη-
of them. he released And to them(him) due to revolt and murder had been

μένον εἰς τὴν φυλακήν, ὃν ᾐτοῦντο· τὸν δὲ Ἰησοῦν παρέδωκε
thrown into the prison, whom they asked; — but Jesus he delivered

τῷ θελήματι αὐτῶν.
to the will of them.

26 Καὶ ὡς ἀπήγαγον αὐτόν, ἐπιλαβόμενοι Σίμωνός τινος
And as they led away Him, having laid hold on Simon a certain

Κυρηναίου τοῦ ἐρχομένου ἀπ' ἀγροῦ, ἐπέθηκαν αὐτῷ τὸν
a Cyrenian — coming from a field, they put on him the

σταυρόν, φέρειν ὄπισθεν τοῦ Ἰησοῦ.
cross, to bear (it) behind — Jesus.

27 Ἠκολούθει δὲ αὐτῷ πολὺ πλῆθος τοῦ λαοῦ, καὶ γυναικῶν
were following And Him a much multitude of the people, and of women

28 αἳ καὶ ἐκόπτοντο καὶ ἐθρήνουν αὐτόν. στραφεὶς δὲ πρὸς
who also were bewailing and lamenting Him. turning And to

αὐτὰς ὁ Ἰησοῦς εἶπε, Θυγατέρες Ἱερουσαλήμ, μὴ κλαίετε
them — Jesus said, Daughters of Jerusalem, not do weep

29 ἐπ' ἐμέ, πλὴν ἐφ' ἑαυτὰς κλαίετε καὶ ἐπὶ τὰ τέκνα ὑμῶν. ὅτι
over Me, but over yourselves weep, and over the children of you. For,

ἰδού, ἔρχονται ἡμέραι ἐν αἷς ἐροῦσι, Μακάριαι αἱ στεῖραι,
behold, will come days in which they will say, Blessed the barren,

καὶ κοιλίαι αἳ οὐκ ἐγέννησαν, καὶ μαστοὶ οἳ οὐκ ἐθήλασαν.
and the wombs which not did bear, and breasts that not did give suck.

30 τότε ἄρξονται λέγειν τοῖς ὄρεσι, Πέσετε ἐφ' ἡμᾶς· καὶ τοῖς
Then they will begin to say to the mountains, Fall on us! And to the

For if they do these things in the green tree, what may take place in the dry?

32 And two others, two criminals, were led with Him to be put to death.

33 And when they came upon the place being called Skull, they crucified Him and the criminals there, one on *the* right, and one on *the* left.

34 And Jesus said, Father, forgive them, for they do not know what they are doing. And dividing His garments, they cast a lot. 35 And the people stood watching. And the rulers also *were* with them, scoffing, saying, He saved others, let him save himself, if this one is the Christ, the elect of God. 36 And coming near the soldiers also mocked Him, and offering vinegar to Him, 37 and saying, If you are the king of the Jews, save yourself. 38 And also a superscription was written over Him, in Greek and Latin and Hebrew letters: THIS IS THE KING OF THE JEWS.

39 And one of the hanged criminals blasphemed Him, saying, If you are the Christ, save yourself and us. 40 But answering the other rebuked him, saying, Do you not fear God, for *you* are in the same judgment? 41 And we indeed justly, for we receive things worthy of what we did; but this One did nothing wrong. 42 And he said to Jesus, Lord, remember me when You come in Your kingdom. 43 And Jesus said to him, Truly I say to you, Today you will be with Me in Paradise.

44 And it was about *the* sixth hour, and darkness came over all the land until *the* ninth hour. 45 And the sun was darkened; and the veil of the Temple was torn in the middle. 46 And crying with a loud voice, Jesus

31 βουνοις, Καλύψατε ἡμᾶς. ὅτι εἰ ἐν τῷ ὑγρῷ ξύλῳ ταῦτα
hills, Cover us, because If in the sappy tree these things
ποιοῦσιν, ἐν τῷ ξηρῷ τί γένηται ;
they do, in the dry what may occur?
32 Ἤγοντο δὲ καὶ ἕτεροι δύο κακοῦργοι σὺν αὐτῷ ἀναι-
were led And also others, two criminals, with Him to be
ρεθῆναι.
executed.
33 Καὶ ὅτε ἀπῆλθον ἐπὶ τὸν τόπον τὸν καλούμενον Κρανίον,
And when they came upon the place — being called Skull,
ἐκεῖ ἐσταύρωσαν αὐτόν, καὶ τοὺς κακούργους, ὃν μὲν ἐκ
there they crucified Him, and the criminals, one on
34 δεξιῶν, ὃν δὲ ἐξ ἀριστερῶν. ὁ δὲ Ἰησοῦς ἔλεγε, Πάτερ, ἄφες
(the) right, and one on (the) left. — And Jesus said, Father, forgive
αὐτοῖς· οὐ γὰρ οἴδασι τί ποιοῦσι. διαμεριζόμενοι δὲ τὰ
them, not for they know what they are doing. dividing And the
35 ἱμάτια αὐτοῦ, ἔβαλον κλῆρον. καὶ εἱστήκει ὁ λαὸς θεωρῶν.
garments of Him, they cast a lot. And stood the people watching.
ἐξεμυκτήριζον δὲ καὶ οἱ ἄρχοντες σὺν αὐτοῖς, λέγοντες,
scoffed And also the rulers with them, saying,
Ἄλλους ἔσωσε, σωσάτω ἑαυτόν, εἰ οὗτός ἐστιν ὁ Χριστός, ὁ
Others he saved, let him save himself, if this one is the Christ, the
36 τοῦ Θεοῦ ἐκλεκτός. ἐνέπαιζον δὲ αὐτῷ καὶ οἱ στρατιῶται,
of God elect. mocked And Him also the soldiers,
37 προσερχόμενοι καὶ ὄξος προσφέροντες αὐτῷ, καὶ λέγοντες,
coming near and vinegar offering to Him, and saying,
38 Εἰ σὺ εἶ ὁ βασιλεὺς τῶν Ἰουδαίων, σῶσον σεαυτόν. ἦν δὲ καὶ
If you are the king of the Jews, save yourself. was And also
ἐπιγραφὴ γεγραμμένη ἐπ' αὐτῷ γράμμασιν Ἑλληνικοῖς καὶ
an epigraph written over Him in letters Greek and
Ῥωμαϊκοῖς καὶ Ἑβραϊκοῖς, Οὗτός ἐστιν ὁ βασιλεὺς τῶν
Latin and Hebrew, THIS IS THE KING OF THE
Ἰουδαίων.
JEWS.
39 Εἷς δὲ τῶν κρεμασθέντων κακούργων ἐβλασφήμει αὐτόν,
one And of the hanged criminals blasphemed Him,
λέγων, Εἰ σὺ εἶ ὁ Χριστός, σῶσον σεαυτὸν καὶ ἡμᾶς. ἀπο-
saying, If you are the Christ, save yourself and us.
40 κριθεὶς δὲ ὁ ἕτερος ἐπετίμα αὐτῷ, λέγων, Οὐδὲ φοβῇ σὺ τὸν
answering But the other rebuked him, saying, Do not fear you —
41 Θεόν, ὅτι ἐν τῷ αὐτῷ κρίματι εἶ ; καὶ ἡμεῖς μὲν δικαίως, ἄξια
God, because in the same judgment are? And we indeed justly, things worthy
γὰρ ὧν ἐπράξαμεν ἀπολαμβάνομεν· οὗτος δὲ οὐδὲν ἄτοπον
for of what we did we receive. this One But nothing amiss
42 ἔπραξε. καὶ ἔλεγε τῷ Ἰησοῦ, Μνήσθητί μου, Κύριε, ὅταν
did. And he said — to Jesus, Remember me, Lord, when
43 ἔλθῃς ἐν τῇ βασιλείᾳ σου. καὶ εἶπεν αὐτῷ ὁ Ἰησοῦς, Ἀμὴν
You come in the kingdom of You. And said to him Jesus, Truly
λέγω σοι, σήμερον μετ' ἐμοῦ ἔσῃ ἐν τῷ παραδείσῳ.
I say to you, Today with Me you will be in Paradise.
44 Ἦν δὲ ὡσεὶ ὥρα ἕκτη, καὶ σκότος ἐγένετο ἐφ' ὅλην τὴν
it was And about hour sixth, and darkness came over all the
45 γῆν ἕως ὥρας ἐννάτης. καὶ ἐσκοτίσθη ὁ ἥλιος, καὶ ἐσχίσθη τὸ
land, until hour ninth, and was darkened the sun, and was torn the
46 καταπέτασμα τοῦ ναοῦ μέσον. καὶ φωνήσας φωνῇ μεγάλῃ ὁ
veil of the temple in two. And crying with a voice great

said, Father, Into Your hands I commit My spirit. And saying this, He breathed out the Spirit.

[47]And seeing the thing happening, the centurion glorified God, saying, This Man was righteous. [48]And all the crowd arriving together at this sight, watching the things happening, beating their breasts, returned. [49]And all those known to Him stood at a distance, and *the* women, those accompanying Him from Galilee, *were* seeing these things.

[50]And, behold, a man named Joseph, being a councillor, a good and righteous man; [51]this one was not assenting to their counsel and deed—*he was* from Arimathea, a city of the Jews, and who himself also was eagerly expecting the kingdom of God—[52]coming near to Pilate, this one asked the body of Jesus. [53]And taking it down, he wrapped it in linen, and placed it in a quarried tomb, where no one was ever yet laid. [54]And it was Preparation Day, and a sabbath was coming on. [55]And also women *were* following, who were accompanying Him out of Galilee, *who* watched the tomb, and how His body was placed. [56]And returning, *they* prepared spices and ointment.

And they remained quiet *on* the sabbath, according to the commandment.

CHAPTER 24

[1]But the first of the week, while still very early, they came on the tomb, carrying spices which they prepared; and some *were* with them. [2]And they found the stone having been rolled away from the tomb. [3]And going in, they did not find the body of the Lord Jesus. [4]And it happened, *as* they *were* perplexed about this, even behold, two men stood by them, in shining clothing.

Ἰησοῦς εἶπε, Πάτερ, εἰς χεῖράς σου παραθήσομαι τὸ πνεῦμά
47 **Jesus said Father, into the hands of You I commit the spirit**
μου· καὶ ταῦτα εἰπὼν ἐξέπνευσεν. Ἰδὼν δὲ ὁ ἑκατόνταρχος
of Me. And this saying, He breathed out the Spirit seeing And, the centurion
τὸ γενόμενον ἐδόξασε τὸν Θεόν, λέγων, Ὄντως ὁ ἄνθρωπος
48 **the thing happening glorified — God, saying, Truly — man**
οὗτος δίκαιος ἦν. καὶ πάντες οἱ συμπαραγενόμενοι ὄχλοι
this righteous was. And all the arriving together crowd
ἐπὶ τὴν θεωρίαν ταύτην, θεωροῦντες τὰ γενόμενα, τύπτοντες
49 **at — sight this, watching the things occurring, beating**
ἑαυτῶν τὰ στήθη ὑπέστρεφον. εἱστήκεισαν δὲ πάντες οἱ
of themselves the breasts, returned. stood And all those
γνωστοὶ αὐτοῦ μακρόθεν, καὶ γυναῖκες αἱ συνακολουθήσασαι
known to Him afar off, and women, those accompanying
αὐτῷ ἀπὸ τῆς Γαλιλαίας, ὁρῶσαι ταῦτα.
50 **Him from — Galilee, seeing these things.**
Καὶ ἰδού, ἀνὴρ ὀνόματι Ἰωσήφ, βουλευτὴς ὑπάρχων
And behold, a man by name Joseph, a councillor being,
ἀνὴρ ἀγαθὸς καὶ δίκαιος (οὗτος οὐκ ἦν συγκατατεθειμένος
51 **a man good and righteous; this one not was agreeing with**
τῇ βουλῇ καὶ τῇ πράξει αὐτῶν), ἀπὸ Ἀριμαθαίας πόλεως
the counsel and the action of them; from Arimathea a city
τῶν Ἰουδαίων, ὃς καὶ προσεδέχετο καὶ αὐτὸς τὴν βασιλείαν
52 **of the Jews, who and was eagerly expecting also himself kingdom**
τοῦ Θεοῦ· οὗτος προσελθὼν τῷ Πιλάτῳ ᾐτήσατο τὸ σῶμα
53 **— of God; this one coming near — to Pilate asked the body**
τοῦ Ἰησοῦ. καὶ καθελὼν αὐτὸ ἐνετύλιξεν αὐτὸ σινδόνι, καὶ
— of Jesus. And taking down it, he wrapped it in linen, and
ἔθηκεν αὐτὸ ἐν μνήματι λαξευτῷ, οὗ οὐκ ἦν οὐδέπω οὐδεὶς
54 **placed it in a tomb hewn, where not was no one not yet**
κείμενος. καὶ ἡμέρα ἦν Παρασκευή, καὶ σάββατον ἐπέφωσκε.
55 **laid. And day it was of preparation, and a sabbath was coming on.**
κατακολουθήσασαι δὲ καὶ γυναῖκες, αἵτινες ἦσαν συνεληλυ-
following And also women, who were accompanying
θυῖαι αὐτῷ ἐκ τῆς Γαλιλαίας, ἐθεάσαντο τὸ μνημεῖον, καὶ ὡς
56 **Him out of Galilee, watched the tomb, and how**
ἐτέθη τὸ σῶμα αὐτοῦ. ὑποστρέψασαι δὲ ἡτοίμασαν ἀρώ-
was placed the body of Him. returning And prepared
ματα καὶ μύρα.
spices and ointment.

CHAPTER 24

1 Καὶ τὸ μὲν σάββατον ἡσύχασαν κατὰ τὴν ἐντολήν. τῇ δὲ
And (on) the sabbath they rested according to the command. the But
μιᾷ τῶν σαββάτων, ὄρθρου βαθέος, ἦλθον ἐπὶ τὸ μνῆμα,
one of the week, while still very early, they came on the tomb,
2 φέρουσαι ἃ ἡτοίμασαν ἀρώματα, καί τινες σὺν αὐταῖς. εὗρον
carrying which they prepared spices, and some with them. they found
3 δὲ τὸν λίθον ἀποκεκυλισμένον ἀπὸ τοῦ μνημείου. καὶ
And the stone having been rolled away from the tomb. And
4 εἰσελθοῦσαι οὐχ εὗρον τὸ σῶμα τοῦ Κυρίου Ἰησοῦ. καὶ
going in not they found the body of the Lord Jesus. And
ἐγένετο ἐν τῷ διαπορεῖσθαι αὐτὰς περὶ τούτου, καὶ ἰδού,
it was in the perplexing (of) them about this; and behold,
δύο ἄνδρες ἐπέστησαν αὐταῖς ἐν ἐσθήσεσιν ἀστραπτούσαις·
two men stood by them in clothing shining.

5 And they becoming terrified, and bowing *their* faces to the earth, they said to them, Why do you seek the living with the dead? 6 He is not here, but was raised. Remember how He spoke to you, yet being in Galilee, 7 saying, The Son of man must be delivered into *the* hands of sinful men, and to be crucified, and the third day to rise again. 8 And they remembered His words. 9 And returning from the tomb, they reported all these things to the Eleven, and to all the rest. 10 And they were Mary Magdalene, and Joanna, and Mary *mother* of James, and the rest with them, who told these things to the apostles. 11 And their words seemed like foolishness to them, and they did not believe them. 12 But rising up, Peter ran to the tomb, and stooping down he saw the linen lying alone. And *he* went away wondering to himself *at what* had happened.

13 And, behold, two of them were going on the same day to a village being sixty furlongs distant from Jerusalem, which *was* named Emmaus. 14 And they talked to each other about all these things taking place. 15 And it happened *as* they talked and reasoned that coming near Jesus Himself traveled with them. 16 But their eyes were held *so as* not to recognize Him. 17 And He said to them, What words *are* these which you exchange with each other *while* walking, and are sad of face? 18 And answering, one of them whose name *was* Cleopas, said to Him, *Are* you only a stranger in Jerusalem, and do not know the things happening in it in these days? 19 And He said to them, What things? And they said to Him, The things concerning Jesus the Nazarene, who was a man, a prophet mighty in

5 ἐμφόβων δὲ γενομένων αὐτῶν, καὶ κλινουσῶν το πρόσωπον
terrified And becoming them, and bending the faces
εἰς τὴν γῆν, εἶπον πρὸς αὐτάς, Τί ζητεῖτε τὸν ζῶντα μετὰ
to the earth, they said to them, Why seek you the Living One with
6 τῶν νεκρῶν; οὐκ ἔστιν ὧδε, ἀλλ' ἠγέρθη· μνήσθητε ὡς
the dead ones? not He is here, but was raised. Remember how
7 ἐλάλησεν ὑμῖν, ἔτι ὢν ἐν τῇ Γαλιλαίᾳ, λέγων ὅτι δεῖ τὸν υἱὸν
He spoke to you, yet being in — Galilee, saying, that must the Son
τοῦ ἀνθρώπου παραδοθῆναι εἰς χεῖρας ἀνθρώπων ἁμαρτω-
— of man be delivered into (the) hands men of sinful,
λῶν, καὶ σταυρωθῆναι, καὶ τῇ τρίτῃ ἡμέρᾳ ἀναστῆναι.
and to be crucified, and the third day to rise again.
8 καὶ ἐμνήσθησαν τῶν ῥημάτων αὐτοῦ, καὶ ὑποστρέψασαι
And they remembered the words of Him, and returning
9 ἀπὸ τοῦ μνημείου, ἀπήγγειλαν ταῦτα πάντα τοῖς ἕνδεκα
from the tomb reported these things all to the eleven,
10 καὶ πᾶσι τοῖς λοιποῖς. ἦσαν δὲ ἡ Μαγδαληνὴ Μαρία καὶ
and to all the rest. they were And the Magdalene Mary, and
Ἰωάννα καὶ Μαρία Ἰακώβου, καὶ αἱ λοιπαὶ σὺν αὐταῖς, αἳ
Joanna, and Mary of James, and the rest with them, who
11 ἔλεγον πρὸς τοὺς ἀποστόλους ταῦτα. καὶ ἐφάνησαν ἐνώπιον
told to the apostles these things. And seemed before
αὐτῶν ὡσεὶ λῆρος τὰ ῥήματα αὐτῶν, καὶ ἠπίστουν αὐταῖς.
them as folly the words of them, and they disbelieved them.
12 ὁ δὲ Πέτρος ἀναστὰς ἔδραμεν ἐπὶ τὸ μνημεῖον, καὶ παρα-
And Peter having arisen ran to the tomb, and stooping
κύψας βλέπει τὰ ὀθόνια κείμενα μόνα· καὶ ἀπῆλθε πρὸς
down he sees the linen lying alone, and went away to
ἑαυτὸν θαυμάζων τὸ γεγονός.
himself wondering (at what) had happened.
13 Καὶ ἰδού, δύο ἐξ αὐτῶν ἦσαν πορευόμενοι ἐν αὐτῇ τῇ
And behold, two of them were going on same the
ἡμέρᾳ εἰς κώμην ἀπέχουσαν σταδίους ἑξήκοντα ἀπὸ
day to a village being distant furlongs sixty from
14 Ἰερουσαλήμ, ᾗ ὄνομα Ἐμμαούς. καὶ αὐτοὶ ὡμίλουν πρὸς
Jerusalem, to which name Emmaus; and they talked to
15 ἀλλήλους περὶ πάντων τῶν συμβεβηκότων τούτων. καὶ
each other about all having happened these things. And
ἐγένετο ἐν τῷ ὁμιλεῖν αὐτοὺς καὶ συζητεῖν, καὶ αὐτὸς ὁ
it was, in the talking (of) them and discussing, even Himself,
16 Ἰησοῦς ἐγγίσας συνεπορεύετο αὐτοῖς. οἱ δὲ ὀφθαλμοὶ αὐτῶν
Jesus, coming near traveled with them. the And eyes of them
17 ἐκρατοῦντο τοῦ μὴ ἐπιγνῶναι αὐτόν. εἶπε δὲ πρὸς αὐτούς,
were held — not to recognize Him. He said And to them,
Τίνες οἱ λόγοι οὗτοι οὓς ἀντιβάλλετε πρὸς ἀλλήλους
What — words these which you exchange with each other
18 περιπατοῦντες, καί ἐστε σκυθρωποί; ἀποκριθεὶς δὲ ὁ εἷς, ᾧ
(while) walking, and are downcast? answering And one, whose
ὄνομα Κλεόπας, εἶπε πρὸς αὐτόν, Σὺ μόνος παροικεῖς ἐν
name (was) Cleopas, said to Him, (Are) you only a stranger in
Ἰερουσαλήμ, καὶ οὐκ ἔγνως τὰ γενόμενα ἐν αὐτῇ ἐν ταῖς
Jerusalem, and not know the things occurring in it in —
19 ἡμέραις ταύταις; καὶ εἶπεν αὐτοῖς, Ποῖα; οἱ δὲ εἶπον αὐτῷ,
days these? And He said to them, What? they And said to Him,
Τὰ περὶ Ἰησοῦ τοῦ Ναζωραίου, ὃς ἐγένετο ἀνὴρ προφήτης
The things about Jesus the Nazarene, who was a man, a prophet

deed and word before God and all the people; 20 and how the chief priests delivered Him up to judgment of death, and crucified Him. 21 But we were hoping that He is the *One* going to redeem Israel. But with all these things, this third day comes today since these things happened. 22 And also certain women from among us astonished us, having been early at the tomb, 23 and not finding His body, *they* came saying to also have seen a vision of angels, who say He is alive. 24 And some of those with us went to the tomb, and found *it* so, even as the women also said; but they did not see Him. 25 And He said to them, O fools, and slow of heart to believe on all things which the prophets spoke! 26 Was it not necessary for the Christ to suffer these things, and to enter into His glory? 27 And beginning from Moses, and from all the prophets, He explained to them all the Scriptures, the things about Himself. 28 And they drew near to the village where they were going, and He seemed to be going further. 29 And they constrained Him, sayiing, Stay with us, for it is toward evening, and the day has declined. And He went in to stay with them. 30 And it happened *as* He reclined with them, taking the loaf, He blessed; and breaking He gave to them. 31 And their eyes were opened, and they knew Him. And He became invisible from them. 32 And they said to one another, Was not our heart burning in us as He spoke to us in the highway, and as He opened up to us the Scriptures? 33 And rising up in the same hour, they went back to Jerusalem, and *they* found the Eleven and those with

δυνατὸς ἐν ἔργῳ καὶ λόγῳ ἐναντίον τοῦ Θεοῦ καὶ παντὸς
powerful in work and word before — God and all
20 τοῦ λαοῦ· ὅπως τε παρέδωκαν αὐτὸν οἱ ἀρχιερεῖς καὶ οἱ
the people, how both delivered Him the chief priests and the
ἄρχοντες ἡμῶν εἰς κρίμα θανάτου, καὶ ἐσταύρωσαν αὐτόν.
rulers of us to (the) judgment of death, and crucified Him.
21 ἡμεῖς δὲ ἠλπίζομεν ὅτι αὐτός ἐστιν ὁ μέλλων λυτροῦσθαι τὸν
we But were hoping that He is the (One) going to redeem —
Ἰσραήλ. ἀλλά γε σὺν πᾶσι τούτοις τρίτην ταύτην ἡμέραν
Israel. But with all these things third this day
22 ἄγει σήμερον ἀφ' οὗ ταῦτα ἐγένετο. ἀλλὰ καὶ γυναῖκές τινες
comes today since these things occurred. But also women some
ἐξ ἡμῶν ἐξέστησαν ἡμᾶς, γενόμεναι ὄρθριαι ἐπὶ τὸ μνημεῖον·
of us astounded us, being early at the tomb,
23 καὶ μὴ εὑροῦσαι τὸ σῶμα αὐτοῦ, ἦλθον λέγουσαι καὶ ὀπτα-
and not finding the body of Him, came saying also a vision
24 σίαν ἀγγέλων ἑωρακέναι, οἳ λέγουσιν αὐτὸν ζῆν. καὶ ἀπ-
of angels to have seen, who say Him to live. And
ῆλθόν τινες τῶν σὺν ἡμῖν ἐπὶ τὸ μνημεῖον, καὶ εὗρον οὕτω
went some of those with us to the tomb, and found so
25 καθὼς καὶ αἱ γυναῖκες εἶπον· αὐτὸν δὲ οὐκ εἶδον. καὶ αὐτὸς
as also the women said; Him but not they saw. And He
εἶπε πρὸς αὐτούς, Ὦ ἀνόητοι καὶ βραδεῖς τῇ καρδίᾳ τοῦ
said to them, O fools and slow — in heart —
26 πιστεύειν ἐπὶ πᾶσιν οἷς ἐλάλησαν οἱ προφῆται· οὐχὶ ταῦτα
to believe on all things which spoke the prophets! Not these things
ἔδει παθεῖν τὸν Χριστόν, καὶ εἰσελθεῖν εἰς τὴν δόξαν αὐτοῦ;
must suffer the Christ, and to enter into the glory of Him?
27 καὶ ἀρξάμενος ἀπὸ Μωσέως καὶ ἀπὸ πάντων τῶν προφητῶν,
And beginning from Moses and from all the prophets,
διηρμήνευεν αὐτοῖς ἐν πάσαις ταῖς γραφαῖς τὰ περὶ ἑαυτοῦ.
He interpreted to them in all the Scriptures that about Himself.
28 καὶ ἤγγισαν εἰς τὴν κώμην οὗ ἐπορεύοντο· καὶ αὐτὸς
And they drew near to the village where they were going, and He
29 προσεποιεῖτο πορρωτέρω πορεύεσθαι. καὶ παρεβιάσαντο
appeared further to be going. And they constrained
αὐτόν, λέγοντες, Μεῖνον μεθ' ἡμῶν, ὅτι πρὸς ἑσπέραν ἐστί,
Him, saying, Stay with us, because toward evening it is,
30 καὶ κέκλικεν ἡ ἡμέρα. καὶ εἰσῆλθε τοῦ μεῖναι σὺν αὐτοῖς. καὶ
and has declined the day. And He went in — to stay with them. And
ἐγένετο ἐν τῷ κατακλιθῆναι αὐτὸν μετ' αὐτῶν, λαβὼν τὸν
it was, in the reclining (of) Him with them, taking the
31 ἄρτον εὐλόγησε, καὶ κλάσας ἐπεδίδου αὐτοῖς. αὐτῶν δὲ
loaf He blessed, and having broken He gave to them. of them And
διηνοίχθησαν οἱ ὀφθαλμοί, καὶ ἐπέγνωσαν αὐτόν· καὶ
was opened the eyes, and they remembered Him. And
32 αὐτὸς ἄφαντος ἐγένετο ἀπ' αὐτῶν. καὶ εἶπον πρὸς ἀλλή-
He invisible became from them. And they said to each
λους, Οὐχὶ ἡ καρδία ἡμῶν καιομένη ἦν ἐν ἡμῖν, ὡς ἐλάλει
other, Not the heart of us burning was in us as He spoke
33 ἡμῖν ἐν τῇ ὁδῷ, καὶ ὡς διήνοιγεν ἡμῖν τὰς γραφάς; καὶ
to us in the way, and as He opened up to us the Scriptures? And
ἀναστάντες αὐτῇ τῇ ὥρᾳ ὑπέστρεψαν εἰς Ἱερουσαλήμ, καὶ
rising up same in the hour they returned to Jerusalem, and
εὗρον συνηθροισμένους τοὺς ἕνδεκα καὶ τοὺς σὺν αὐτοῖς,
found, having been gathered, the eleven and those with them,

them, having been gathered,
34 saying, The Lord really was
raised, and appeared to
Simon. 35 And they related
the things in the highway,
and how He was known to
them in the breaking of the
loaf.
36 And as they were telling
these things, Jesus Himself
stood in their midst, and said
to them, Peace to you! 37 But
being terrified and filled with
fear, they thought they saw a
spirit. 38 And He said to
them, Why are you troubled?
And why do reasonings
come up in your hearts. 39 See
My hands and My feet, that I
am He? Feel Me and see,
because a spirit does not
have flesh and bones, as you
see Me having. 40 And
saying this, He showed
them *His* hands and feet.
41 But yet they not believing
from the joy, and marveling,
He said to them, Have you
any food here? 42 And they
handed a broiled part of a
fish to Him, and from a
honeycomb. 43 And taking
these before them, He ate.
44 And He said to them,
These *are* the words which I
spoke to you, yet being with
you, that must be fulfilled, all
the things having been
written in the Law of Moses,
and the Prophets, and the
Psalms, concerning Me.
45 Then He opened up their
mind to understand the Scriptures. 46 And He said to them,
So it has been written, and so
it was necessary that the
Christ should suffer, and to
rise from *the* dead the third
day; 47 and repentance and
forgiveness of sins should be
preached on His name to all
the nations, beginning at
Jerusalem. 48 And you are
witnesses of these things.
49 And, behold, I send forth
the promise of My Father on
you. But you sit in the city of
Jerusalem until you are
clothed with power from on
high.
50 And He led them out as
far as to Bethany. And lifting

34 λέγοντας ὅτι Ἠγέρθη ὁ Κύριος ὄντως, καὶ ὤφθη Σίμωνι. καὶ
35 **saying, — was raised the Lord really, and appeared to Simon. And**
αὐτοὶ ἐξηγοῦντο τὰ ἐν τῇ ὁδῷ, καὶ ὡς ἐγνώσθη αὐτοῖς ἐν
they related the things in the way, and how He was known to them in
τῇ κλάσει τοῦ ἄρτου.
the breaking of the loaf.

36 Ταῦτα δὲ αὐτῶν λαλούντων, αὐτὸς ὁ Ἰησοῦς ἔστη ἐν
these things And them saying, Himself, — Jesus, stood in
37 μέσῳ αὐτῶν, καὶ λέγει αὐτοῖς, Εἰρήνη ὑμῖν. πτοηθέντες δὲ
(the) midst of them, and says to them, Peace to you. terrified But
38 καὶ ἔμφοβοι γενόμενοι ἐδόκουν πνεῦμα θεωρεῖν. καὶ εἶπεν
and filled with fear being, they thought a spirit they beheld. And He said
αὐτοῖς, Τί τεταραγμένοι ἐστέ; καὶ διατί διαλογισμοὶ
to them, Why troubled are you? And why do reasonings
39 ἀναβαίνουσιν ἐν ταῖς καρδίαις ὑμῶν; ἴδετε τὰς χεῖράς μου
come up in the hearts of you? See the hands of Me
καὶ τοὺς πόδας μου, ὅτι αὐτὸς ἐγώ εἰμι· ψηλαφήσατέ με καὶ
and the feet of Me, that He I am. Feel Me and
ἴδετε, ὅτι πνεῦμα σάρκα καὶ ὀστέα οὐκ ἔχει, καθὼς ἐμὲ
see, because a spirit flesh and bones not has, as Me
40 θεωρεῖτε ἔχοντα. καὶ τοῦτο εἰπὼν ἐπέδειξεν αὐτοῖς τὰς
you behold having. And this having said, He showed to them the
41 χεῖρας καὶ τοὺς πόδας. ἔτι δὲ ἀπιστούντων αὐτῶν ἀπὸ τῆς
hands and the feet. yet And disbelieving them, from the
χαρᾶς καὶ θαυμαζόντων, εἶπεν αὐτοῖς, Ἔχετέ τι βρώσιμον
joy and marveling, He said to them, Have you any food
42 ἐνθάδε; οἱ δὲ ἐπέδωκαν αὐτῷ ἰχθύος ὀπτοῦ μέρος, καὶ ἀπὸ
here? they And handed to Him of a fish broiled part, and from
43 μελισσίου κηρίου. καὶ λαβὼν ἐνώπιον αὐτῶν ἔφαγεν.
a honey-comb. And taking before them, He ate.

44 Εἶπε δὲ αὐτοῖς, Οὗτοι οἱ λόγοι, οὓς ἐλάλησα πρὸς ὑμᾶς
He said And to them, These — words which I spoke to you,
ἔτι ὢν σὺν ὑμῖν, ὅτι δεῖ πληρωθῆναι πάντα τὰ γεγραμμένα
yet being with you, that must be fulfilled all the things being written
ἐν τῷ νόμῳ Μωσέως καὶ προφήταις καὶ ψαλμοῖς περὶ ἐμοῦ.
in the law of Moses and (the) prophets and Psalms, about Me.
45 τότε διήνοιξεν αὐτῶν τὸν νοῦν, τοῦ συνιέναι τὰς γραφάς·
Then He opened up of them the mind — to understand the Scriptures;
46 καὶ εἶπεν αὐτοῖς ὅτι Οὕτω γέγραπται, καὶ οὕτως ἔδει παθεῖν
and said to them, — Thus it is written, and thus must suffer
τὸν Χριστόν, καὶ ἀναστῆναι ἐκ νεκρῶν τῇ τρίτῃ ἡμέρᾳ, καὶ
the Christ, and to rise from (the) dead the third day, and
47 κηρυχθῆναι ἐπὶ τῷ ὀνόματι αὐτοῦ μετάνοιαν καὶ ἄφεσιν
to be preached on the name of Him repentance and forgiveness
ἁμαρτιῶν εἰς πάντα τὰ ἔθνη, ἀρξάμενον ἀπὸ Ἱερουσαλήμ.
of sins to all the nations, beginning from Jerusalem.
48 ὑμεῖς δέ ἐστε μάρτυρες τούτων. καὶ ἰδού, ἐγὼ ἀποστέλλω
49 **You And are witnesses of these things. And behold, I send forth**
τὴν ἐπαγγελίαν τοῦ πατρός μου ἐφ᾽ ὑμᾶς· ὑμεῖς δὲ καθίσατε
the promise of the Father of Me on you. you But sit
ἐν τῇ πόλει Ἱερουσαλήμ, ἕως οὗ ἐνδύσησθε δύναμιν ἐξ
in the city of Jerusalem until you are clothed with power **from**
ὕψους.
on high.

50 Ἐξήγαγε δὲ αὐτοὺς ἔξω ἕως εἰς Βηθανίαν καὶ ἐπάρας τὰς
He led And them out until to Bethany, and lifting up the

up His hands, He blessed them. [51] And it happened *as* He blessed them, He withdrew from them, and was carried into Heaven. [52] And worshiping Him, they returned to Jerusalem with great joy, and were continually in the Temple, praising and blessing God. Amen.

51 χεῖρας αὐτοῦ εὐλόγησεν αὐτούς. καὶ ἐγένετο ἐν τῷ εὐλογεῖν
hands of Him, He blessed them. And it was, in the blessing
αὐτὸν αὐτούς, διέστη ἀπ' αὐτῶν, καὶ ἀνεφέρετο εἰς τὸ
(of) Him them, He withdrew from them, and was carried into —
52 ουρανόν. καὶ αὐτοὶ προσκυνήσαντες αὐτόν, ὑπέστρεψαν
Heaven. And they having worshiped Him returned
53 εἰς Ἱερουσαλὴμ μετὰ χαρᾶς μεγάλης· καὶ ἦσαν διὰ παντὸς
to Jerusalem with joy great, and were continually
ἐν τῷ ἱερῷ, αἰνοῦντες καὶ εὐλογοῦντες τὸν Θεόν. Ἀμήν.
in the Temple, praising and blessing — God. Amen.

KING JAMES II VERSION

THE GOSPEL ACCORDING TO JOHN

CHAPTER 1

1 In *the* beginning was the Word, and the Word was with God, and the Word was God. 2 He was in the beginning with God. 3 All things came into being through Him, and without Him not even one *thing* came into being. 4 In Him was life, and the life was the light of men. 5 and the light shines in the darkness, and the darkness did not overtake it.

6 There was a man sent from God, his name *was* John. 7 He came for a witness, that he might witness concerning the Light, that all might believe through Him. 8 He was not that Light, but that he might witness concerning the Light. 9 He was the true Light; He enlightens every man coming into the world. 10 He was in the world, and the world came into being through Him. Yet the world did not know Him. 11 He came into *His* own, and *His* own did not receive Him. 12 But as many as received Him, to them He gave authority to become children of God, to the ones believing into His name; 13 who were born not of bloods, nor of *the* will of *the* flesh, nor of *the* will of man, but were born of God.

14 And the Word became flesh, and tabernacled among us. And we beheld His glory, glory as of an only-begotten from *the* Father, full of grace and of truth. 15 John witnesses concerning Him, and has cried out, saying, This One was *He* of whom I said, He coming after me has been before me, for He was preceding me. 16 And out of His

ΕΥΑΓΓΕΛΙΟΝ
GOSPEL
ΤΟ ΚΑΤΑ ΙΩΑΝΝΗΝ
THE ACCORDING TO JOHN

CHAPTER 1

1 Ἐν ἀρχῇ ἦν ὁ λόγος, καὶ ὁ λόγος ἦν πρὸς τὸν Θεόν, καὶ
In (the) beginning was the Word, and the Word was with — God, and
2 Θεὸς ἦν ὁ λόγος. οὗτος ἦν ἐν ἀρχῇ πρὸς τὸν Θεόν. πάντα
3 **God was the Word. This One was in beginning with — God. All things**
δι' αὐτοῦ ἐγένετο, καὶ χωρὶς αὐτοῦ ἐγένετο οὐδὲ ἓν ὃ γέγονεν.
through Him came into being, and without Him came into being not even one (thing) that came into being.
4 ἐν αὐτῷ ζωὴ ἦν, καὶ ἡ ζωὴ ἦν τὸ φῶς τῶν ἀνθρώπων, καὶ
5 **In Him life was, and the life was the light — of men, and**
τὸ φῶς ἐν τῇ σκοτίᾳ φαίνει, καὶ ἡ σκοτία αὐτὸ οὐ κατέλαβεν.
the light in the darkness shines, and the darkness it not did overtake.
6 ἐγένετο ἄνθρωπος ἀπεσταλμένος παρὰ Θεοῦ, ὄνομα αὐτῷ
There was a man having been sent from God, (the) name to him,
7 Ἰωάννης. οὗτος ἦλθεν εἰς μαρτυρίαν, ἵνα μαρτυρήσῃ περὶ
John; this one came for a witness, that he might witness about
8 τοῦ φωτός, ἵνα πάντες πιστεύσωσι δι' αὐτοῦ. οὐκ ἦν ἐκεῖνος
the light, that all might believe through Him. not He was that
9 τὸ φῶς, ἀλλ' ἵνα μαρτυρήσῃ περὶ τοῦ φωτός. ἦν τὸ φῶς τὸ
— light, but that he might witness about the light. He was the light —
ἀληθινόν, ὃ φωτίζει πάντα ἄνθρωπον ἐρχόμενον εἰς τὸν
true, which enlightens every man coming into the
10 κόσμον. ἐν τῷ κόσμῳ ἦν, καὶ ὁ κόσμος δι' αὐτοῦ ἐγένετο, καὶ
world. In the world He was, and the world through Him became, and
11 ὁ κόσμος αὐτὸν οὐκ ἔγνω. εἰς τὰ ἴδια ἦλθε, καὶ οἱ ἴδιοι αὐτὸν
the world Him did not know. Into (His) own He came, and (His) own Him
12 οὐ παρέλαβον. ὅσοι δὲ ἔλαβον αὐτόν, ἔδωκεν αὐτοῖς ἐξουσίαν
not did receive. as many as But received Him, He gave to them authority
τέκνα Θεοῦ γενέσθαι, τοῖς πιστεύουσιν εἰς τὸ ὄνομα αὐτοῦ·
children of God to become, to those believing into the name of Him,
13 οἳ οὐκ ἐξ αἱμάτων, οὐδὲ ἐκ θελήματος σαρκός, οὐδὲ ἐκ θελή-
who not of bloods, nor of (the) will of (the) flesh, nor of (the)
14 ματος ἀνδρός, ἀλλ' ἐκ Θεοῦ ἐγεννήθησαν. καὶ ὁ λόγος σὰρξ
will of man, but of God were born. And the Word flesh
ἐγένετο, καὶ ἐσκήνωσεν ἐν ἡμῖν (καὶ ἐθεασάμεθα τὴν δόξαν
became, and tabernacled among us, and we beheld the glory
αὐτοῦ, δόξαν ὡς μονογενοῦς παρὰ πατρός), πλήρης χάριτος
of Him, glory as of an only-begotten from (the) Father, full of grace
15 καὶ ἀληθείας. Ἰωάννης μαρτυρεῖ περὶ αὐτοῦ, καὶ κέκραγε
and of truth. John witnesses concerning Him, and has cried out
λέγων, Οὗτος ἦν ὃν εἶπον, Ὁ ὀπίσω μου ἐρχόμενος ἔμπρο-
saying, This One was of whom I said, He after me coming before
16 σθέν μου γέγονεν· ὅτι πρῶτός μου ἦν. καὶ ἐκ τοῦ πληρώματος
me has become, for preceding me He was. And out of the fullness

fullness we all received, and grace on top of grace, for the Law came through Moses, *but* grace and truth came through Jesus Christ. [18] No one has seen God at any time; the only-begotten Son, who is in the bosom of the Father, He reveals *Him*.

[19] And this is the witness of John, when the Jews sent priests and Levites that they might ask him, Who are you? [20] And he acknowledged and did not deny, and acknowledged, I am not the Christ. [21] And they asked him, What, then? Are you Elijah? And he said, I am not. Are you the Prophet? And he answered, No. [22] Then they said to him, Who are you, that we may give an answer to those who sent us? What do you say about yourself? [23] He said, "*I am* a voice crying in the wilderness: Make straight the way of the Lord," as Isaiah the prophet said. [24] And those who had been sent were of the Pharisees. [25] And they asked him and said to him, Why then do you baptize, if you are not the Christ, nor Elijah, nor the Prophet? [26] John answered them, saying, I baptize in water, but *One* stands in your midst whom you do not know. [27] He it is who comes after me, who has been before me, of whom I am not worthy that I should untie the latchet of His sandal. [28] These things took place in Bethabara beyond the Jordan, where John was baptizing.

[29] On the morrow, John sees Jesus coming toward him, and said, Behold, the Lamb of God, who takes away the sin of the world! [30] This is He about whom I said, After me comes a Man who has been before me, for He was preceding me. [31] And I did not know Him, but that He be revealed to Israel. For this reason I came baptizing in

17 αὐτοῦ ἡμεῖς πάντες ἐλάβομεν, καὶ χάριν ἀντὶ χάριτος. ὅτι ὁ
of Him we all received, and grace on top of grace, because the
νόμος διὰ Μωσέως ἐδόθη, ἡ χάρις καὶ ἡ ἀλήθεια διὰ Ἰησοῦ
Law through Moses was given, grace and truth through Jesus
18 Χριστοῦ ἐγένετο. Θεὸν οὐδεὶς ἑώρακε πώποτε· ὁ μονογενὴς
Christ came into being. God no one has seen, at any time; the only-begotten
υἱός, ὁ ὢν εἰς τὸν κόλπον τοῦ πατρός, ἐκεῖνος ἐξηγήσατο.
Son, who is in the bosom of the Father, that One explains (Him).
19 Καὶ αὕτη ἐστὶν ἡ μαρτυρία τοῦ Ἰωάννου, ὅτε ἀπέστειλαν
And this is the witness — of John, when sent
οἱ Ἰουδαῖοι ἐξ Ἱεροσολύμων ἱερεῖς καὶ Λευΐτας ἵνα ἐρωτή-
the Jews from Jerusalem priests and Levites, that they might
20 σωσιν αὐτόν, Σὺ τίς εἶ; καὶ ὡμολόγησε, καὶ οὐκ ἠρνήσατο·
ask him, you Who are? And he acknowledged and not denied,
21 καὶ ὡμολόγησεν ὅτι Οὐκ εἰμὶ ἐγὼ ὁ Χριστός. καὶ ἠρώτησαν
and he acknowledged, not am I the Christ. And they asked
αὐτόν, Τί οὖν; Ἠλίας εἶ σύ; καὶ λέγει, Οὐκ εἰμί. Ὁ προφή-
him, What, then? Elijah you? And he says, not I am. The prophet
22 της εἶ σύ; καὶ ἀπεκρίθη, Οὔ. εἶπον οὖν αὐτῷ, Τίς εἶ; ἵνα
are you? And he answered, No. They said then to him, Who are you, that
ἀπόκρισιν δῶμεν τοῖς πέμψασιν ἡμᾶς. τί λέγεις περὶ
an answer we may give to those sending us. What do you say about
23 σεαυτοῦ; ἔφη, Ἐγὼ φωνὴ βοῶντος ἐν τῇ ἐρήμῳ, Εὐθύνατε
yourself? He said, I (am) a voice crying in the wilderness, Make straight
24 τὴν ὁδὸν Κυρίου. καθὼς εἶπεν Ἠσαΐας ὁ προφήτης. καὶ οἱ
the way of (the) Lord, as said Isaiah the prophet. And those
25 ἀπεσταλμένοι ἦσαν ἐκ τῶν Φαρισαίων. καὶ ἠρώτησαν
having been sent were of the Pharisees. And they asked
αὐτόν, καὶ εἶπον αὐτῷ, Τί οὖν βαπτίζεις, εἰ σὺ οὐκ εἶ ὁ
him, and said to him, Why then do you baptize, if you not are the
26 Χριστός, οὔτε Ἠλίας, οὔτε ὁ προφήτης; ἀπεκρίθη αὐτοῖς ὁ
Christ, nor Elijah, nor the prophet? Answered them —
Ἰωάννης λέγων, Ἐγὼ βαπτίζω ἐν ὕδατι· μέσος δὲ ὑμῶν
John, saying, I baptize in water; amidst but you
27 ἕστηκεν ὃν ὑμεῖς οὐκ οἴδατε. αὐτός ἐστιν ὁ ὀπίσω μου
stands (One) whom you not do know. This One it is who after me
ἐρχόμενος, ὃς ἔμπροσθέν μου γέγονεν· οὗ ἐγὼ οὐκ εἰμὶ ἄξιος
coming, who before me has become, of whom I not am worthy
28 ἵνα λύσω αὐτοῦ τὸν ἱμάντα τοῦ ὑποδήματος. ταῦτα ἐν
that I should untie of Him the latchet of the sandal. These things in
Βηθαβαρᾷ ἐγένετο πέραν τοῦ Ἰορδάνου, ὅπου ἦν Ἰωάννης
Bethabara occurred beyond the Jordan, where was John
βαπτίζων.
baptizing.

29 Τῇ ἐπαύριον βλέπει ὁ Ἰωάννης τὸν Ἰησοῦν ἐρχόμενον
On the morrow sees — John — Jesus coming
πρὸς αὐτόν, καὶ λέγει, Ἴδε ὁ ἀμνὸς τοῦ Θεοῦ, ὁ αἴρων τὴν
toward him, and says, Behold, the Lamb — of God, taking the
30 ἁμαρτίαν τοῦ κόσμου. οὗτός ἐστι περὶ οὗ ἐγὼ εἶπον,
sin of the world. This is He about whom I said,
Ὀπίσω μου ἔρχεται ἀνὴρ ὃς ἔμπροσθέν μου γέγονεν, ὅτι
After me comes a Man who before me has become, for
31 πρῶτός μου ἦν. κἀγὼ οὐκ ᾔδειν αὐτόν· ἀλλ' ἵνα φανερωθῇ
preceding me He was. And I not did know Him, but that He be revealed
τῷ Ἰσραήλ, διὰ τοῦτο ἦλθον ἐγὼ ἐν τῷ ὕδατι βαπτίζων.
— to Israel, therefore came I in the water baptizing.

water. [32]And John witnessed, saying, I have seen the Spirit coming down as a dove out of Heaven, and He abode on Him. [33]And I did not know Him, but He who sent me to baptize in water, that One said to me, on whomever you see the Spirit coming down and abiding on Him, this is He who baptizes in *the* Holy Spirit. [34]And I have seen, and have witnessed that this One is the Son of God.

[35]Again on the morrow, John and two from his disciples stood. [36]And looking at Jesus walking, he said, Behold, the Lamb of God! [37]And the two disciples heard him speaking, and followed Jesus. [38]But seeing them following, Jesus said to them, What do you seek? And they said to Him, Rabbi—which being translated is called Teacher—where are You staying? [39]He said to them, Come and see. They went and saw where He lodged, and remained with Him that day. And *the* hour was about *the* tenth. [40]Andrew the brother of Simon Peter was one of the two who heard this from John, and followed Him. [41]This one first found *his* own brother Simon, and told him, We have found the Messiah, which being translated is the Christ. [42]And he led him to Jesus. And looking at him, Jesus said, You are Simon the son of Jonah; you shall be called Cephas—which translated is Peter.

[43]And on the morrow Jesus desired to go out into Galilee. And He found Philip, and said to him, Follow me! [44]And Philip was from Bethsaida, of the city of Andrew and Peter. [45]Philip found Nathanael, and said to him, We have found *the One* whom Moses wrote about in the Law and the Prophets,

32 καὶ ἐμαρτύρησεν Ἰωάννης λέγων ὅτι Τεθέαμαι τὸ Πνεῦμα
And witnessed John saying, I have beheld the Spirit
καταβαῖνον ὡσεὶ περιστερὰν ἐξ οὐρανοῦ, καὶ ἔμεινεν ἐπ᾽
coming down as a dove out of Heaven, and He abode on
33 αὐτόν. κἀγὼ οὐκ ᾔδειν αὐτόν· ἀλλ᾽ ὁ πέμψας με βαπτίζειν
Him. And I did not know Him, but the (One) sending me to baptize
ἐν ὕδατι, ἐκεῖνός μοι εἶπεν, Ἐφ᾽ ὃν ἂν ἴδῃς τὸ Πνεῦμα κατα-
in water, that One to me said, On whomever you see the Spirit coming
βαῖνον καὶ μένον ἐπ᾽ αὐτόν, οὗτός ἐστιν ὁ βαπτίζων ἐν
down and abiding on Him, this is the (One) baptizing in
34 Πνεύματι Ἁγίῳ. κἀγὼ ἑώρακα, καὶ μεμαρτύρηκα ὅτι οὗτός
(the) Spirit Holy. And I have seen, and have witnessed, that this One
ἐστιν ὁ υἱὸς τοῦ Θεοῦ.
is the Son – of God.

35 Τῇ ἐπαύριον πάλιν εἱστήκει ὁ Ἰωάννης, καὶ ἐκ τῶν
On the morrow again stood – John, and out of the
36 μαθητῶν αὐτοῦ δύο· καὶ ἐμβλέψας τῷ Ἰησοῦ περιπατοῦντι,
disciples of him two; and looking at – Jesus walking,
37 λέγει, Ἴδε ὁ ἀμνὸς τοῦ Θεοῦ. καὶ ἤκουσαν αὐτοῦ οἱ δύο
he says, Behold, the Lamb – of God. And heard him the two
38 μαθηταὶ λαλοῦντος, καὶ ἠκολούθησαν τῷ Ἰησοῦ. στραφεὶς
disciples speaking, and they followed – Jesus. turning
δὲ ὁ Ἰησοῦς καὶ θεασάμενος αὐτοὺς ἀκολουθοῦντας, λέγει
And – Jesus, and beholding them following, He says
αὐτοῖς, Τί ζητεῖτε; οἱ δὲ εἶπον αὐτῷ, Ῥαββί (ὃ λέγεται
to them, What do you seek? they And said to Him, Rabbi, which is called,
39 ἑρμηνευόμενον, Διδάσκαλε), ποῦ μένεις; λέγει αὐτοῖς, Ἔρχε-
being translated, Teacher, where do you stay? He says to them, Come
σθε καὶ ἴδετε. ἦλθον καὶ εἶδον ποῦ μένει· καὶ παρ᾽ αὐτῷ
and see. They went and saw where He stayed, and with Him
40 ἔμειναν τὴν ἡμέραν ἐκείνην· ὥρα δὲ ἦν ὡς δεκάτη. ἦν
abode. – day that; (the) hour and was about (the) tenth. was
Ἀνδρέας ὁ ἀδελφὸς Σίμωνος Πέτρου εἷς ἐκ τῶν δύο τῶν
Andrew the brother of Simon Peter, one of the two –
ἀκουσάντων παρὰ Ἰωάννου καὶ ἀκολουθησάντων αὐτῷ.
hearing from John, and following Him.
41 εὑρίσκει οὗτος πρῶτος τὸν ἀδελφὸν τὸν ἴδιον Σίμωνα, καὶ
finds This one first brother (his) own Simon, and
λέγει αὐτῷ, Εὑρήκαμεν τὸν Μεσσίαν (ὅ ἐστι μεθερμηνευό-
tells him, We have found the Messiah – which is, being translated
42 μενον, ὁ Χριστός). καὶ ἤγαγεν αὐτὸν πρὸς τὸν Ἰησοῦν.
the Christ – and he led him to – Jesus.
ἐμβλέψας δὲ αὐτῷ ὁ Ἰησοῦς εἶπε, Σὺ εἶ Σίμων ὁ υἱὸς Ἰωνᾶ·
looking at And him – Jesus said, You are Simon the son of Jonah;
σὺ κληθήσῃ Κηφᾶς (ὃ ἑρμηνεύεται Πέτρος).
you shall be called Cephas—which translated is Peter.

43 Τῇ ἐπαύριον ἠθέλησεν ὁ Ἰησοῦς ἐξελθεῖν εἰς τὴν Γαλιλαίαν,
On the morrow decided – Jesus to go out into – Galilee.
44 καὶ εὑρίσκει Φίλιππον, καὶ λέγει αὐτῷ, Ἀκολούθει μοι. ἦν δὲ
And He finds Philip, and says to him, Follow me. was And
ὁ Φίλιππος ἀπὸ Βηθσαϊδά, ἐκ τῆς πόλεως Ἀνδρέου καὶ
– Philip from Bethsaida, of the city of Andrew and
45 Πέτρου. εὑρίσκει Φίλιππος τὸν Ναθαναήλ, καὶ λέγει αὐτῷ,
Peter. finds Philip Nathanael, and says to him,
Ὃν ἔγραψε Μωσῆς ἐν τῷ νόμῳ καὶ οἱ προφῆται εὑρήκαμεν,
(He) whom wrote Moses in the Law and the Prophets, we have found

Jesus the son of Joseph from Nazareth. [46]And Nathanael said to him, Can any good thing be out of Nazareth? Philip said to him, Come and see.

[47]Jesus saw Nathanael coming toward Him, and said concerning him, Behold, truly an Israelite in whom is no guile! [48]Nathanael said to Him, From where do You know me? Jesus answered and said to him, Before Philip called, you being under the fig-tree, I saw you. [49]Nathanael answered and said to Him, Rabbi, You are the Son of God; You are the King of Israel. [50]Jesus answered and said to him, Because I said to you I saw you under the fig-tree, do you believe? You will see greater things than these. [51]And He said to him, Truly, truly, I say to you, From now on you will see Heaven opened, and the angels of God ascending and descending on the Son of man.

CHAPTER 2

[1]And on the third day a marriage took place in Cana of Galilee, and the mother of Jesus was there. [2]And Jesus and His disciples were also invited to the marriage. [3]And being short of wine, the mother of Jesus said to Him, They have no wine. [4]Jesus said to her, What is that to Me and to you, woman? My hour has not yet come. [5]His mother said to the servants, Whatever He says to you, do. [6]And there were six stone waterpots standing, according to the purification of the Jews, each containing two or three measures. [7]Jesus said to them, Fill the waterpots with water. And they filled them to *the* top. [8]And He said to them, Now draw out and carry to the master of the feast. And they carried *it*. [9]But when the master of the feast tasted the water that had become wine, and did not know from where it was— but the servants draw-

46 Ἰησοῦν τὸν υἱὸν τοῦ Ἰωσὴφ τὸν ἀπὸ Ναζαρέθ. καὶ εἶπεν
Jesus the son — of Joseph — from Nazareth. And said
αὐτῷ Ναθαναήλ, Ἐκ Ναζαρὲθ δύναταί τι ἀγαθὸν εἶναι;
to him Nathanael, Out of Nazareth can anything good be?
47 λέγει αὐτῷ Φίλιππος, Ἔρχου καὶ ἴδε. εἶδεν ὁ Ἰησοῦς τὸν
Says to him Philip, Come and see. saw — Jesus —
Ναθαναὴλ ἐρχόμενον πρὸς αὐτόν, καὶ λέγει περὶ αὐτοῦ, Ἴδε
Nathanael coming toward Him, and says about him, Behold,
48 ἀληθῶς Ἰσραηλίτης, ἐν ᾧ δόλος οὐκ ἔστι. λέγει αὐτῷ
truly an Israelite, in whom guile not is. says to Him
Ναθαναήλ, Πόθεν με γινώσκεις; ἀπεκρίθη ὁ Ἰησοῦς καὶ
Nathanael, From where me do You know? Answered — Jesus and
εἶπεν αὐτῷ, Πρὸ τοῦ σε Φίλιππον φωνῆσαι, ὄντα ὑπὸ τὴν
said to him, Before — you Philip called, being under the
49 συκῆν, εἶδόν σε. ἀπεκρίθη Ναθαναὴλ καὶ λέγει αὐτῷ, Ῥαββί,
fig-tree, I saw you. answered Nathanael and says to Him, Rabbi,
50 σὺ εἶ ὁ υἱὸς τοῦ Θεοῦ, σὺ εἶ ὁ βασιλεὺς τοῦ Ἰσραήλ. ἀπεκρίθη
You are the Son — of God; You are the king — of Israel. answered
Ἰησοῦς καὶ εἶπεν αὐτῷ, Ὅτι εἶπόν σοι, εἶδόν σε ὑποκάτω
Jesus and said to him, Because I told you I saw you underneath
51 τῆς συκῆς, πιστεύεις; μείζω τούτων ὄψει. καὶ λέγει αὐτῷ,
the fig-tree, you believe? Greater than these you will see; and He says to him,
Ἀμὴν ἀμὴν λέγω ὑμῖν, ἀπ' ἄρτι ὄψεσθε τὸν οὐρανὸν ἀνεῳ-
Truly, truly I say to you, from now on you will see the heaven opened
γότα, καὶ τοὺς ἀγγέλους τοῦ Θεοῦ ἀναβαίνοντας καὶ κατα-
and the angels — of God ascending and
βαίνοντας ἐπὶ τὸν υἱὸν τοῦ ἀνθρώπου.
descending on the Son — of man.

CHAPTER 2

1 Καὶ τῇ ἡμέρᾳ τῇ τρίτῃ γάμος ἐγένετο ἐν Κανᾶ τῆς
And on the day — third a wedding there was in Cana —
2 Γαλιλαίας, καὶ ἦν ἡ μήτηρ τοῦ Ἰησοῦ ἐκεῖ· ἐκλήθη δὲ καὶ ὁ
of Galilee, and was the mother — of Jesus there. was invited And also
3 Ἰησοῦς καὶ οἱ μαθηταὶ αὐτοῦ εἰς τὸν γάμον. καὶ ὑστερή-
Jesus and the disciples of Him to the wedding. And being
σαντος οἴνου, λέγει ἡ μήτηρ τοῦ Ἰησοῦ πρὸς αὐτόν, Οἶνον
short of wine, says the mother — of Jesus to Him, wine
4 οὐκ ἔχουσι. λέγει αὐτῇ ὁ Ἰησοῦς, Τί ἐμοὶ καὶ σοί, γύναι;
not They have. says to her — Jesus, What to Me and to you, woman?
5 οὔπω ἥκει ἡ ὥρα μου. λέγει ἡ μήτηρ αὐτοῦ τοῖς διακόνοις,
Not yet is come the hour of Me. Says the mother of Him to the servants,
6 Ὅ τι ἂν λέγῃ ὑμῖν, ποιήσατε. ἦσαν δὲ ἐκεῖ ὑδρίαι λίθιναι
Whatever He says to you, do. were And there waterpots stone
ἓξ κείμεναι κατὰ τὸν καθαρισμὸν τῶν Ἰουδαίων, χωροῦσαι
six standing according to the purification of the Jews, containing
7 ἀνὰ μετρητὰς δύο ἢ τρεῖς. λέγει αὐτοῖς ὁ Ἰησοῦς, Γεμίσατε
each measures two or three. says to them Jesus, Fill
8 τὰς ὑδρίας ὕδατος. καὶ ἐγέμισαν αὐτὰς ἕως ἄνω. καὶ λέγει
the waterpots of water. And they filled them up to (the) top. And He says
αὐτοῖς, Ἀντλήσατε νῦν, καὶ φέρετε τῷ ἀρχιτρικλίνῳ. καὶ
to them Draw out now, and carry to the master of the feast. And
9 ἤνεγκαν. ὡς δὲ ἐγεύσατο ὁ ἀρχιτρίκλινος τὸ ὕδωρ οἶνον
they carried. as But tasted the master of the feast the water wine
γεγενημένον, καὶ οὐκ ᾔδει πόθεν ἐστίν (οἱ δὲ διάκονοι
having become, and not knew from where it is—the but servants

ing the water knew—the master of the feast called the bridegroom, 10 and said to him, Every man first sets on the good wine; and when they have drunk freely, then the worse. You have kept the good wine until now. 11 This beginning of the miracles Jesus did in Cana of Galilee. And *it* revealed His glory, and His disciples believed in Him.

12 After this He went down to Capernaum, He and His mother and His brothers and His disciples. And He remained there not many days.

13 And the Passover of the Jews was near. And Jesus went up to Jerusalem. 14 And He found those selling oxen and sheep and doves in the Temple, and the money-changers sitting. 15 And making a whip out of ropes, He threw all out of the Temple, both the sheep, and the oxen, and the money-changers, pouring out the money and overturning the tables. 16 And to the ones selling the doves, He said, Take these things from here! Do not make My Father's house a house of merchandise. 17 And His disciples remembered that it was written, "The zeal of Your house has consumed Me."

18 Then the Jews answered and said to Him, What sign do you show to us, since you do these things? 19 Jesus said to them, Destroy this Temple, and in three days I will raise it up. 20 Then the Jews said, This Temple was forty-six years being built, and do you raise it up in three days? 21 But He spoke about the Temple of His body. 22 Then when He was raised from *the* dead, His disciples recalled that He said this to them. And they believed the Scripture, and the word which Jesus spoke.

ᾔδεισαν οἱ ἠντληκότες τὸ ὕδωρ), φωνεῖ τὸν νυμφίον ὁ
knew, those having drawn the water — calls the bridegroom the
10 ἀρχιτρίκλινος, καὶ λέγει αὐτῷ, Πᾶς ἄνθρωπος πρῶτον τὸν
master of the feast, and says to him, Every man first the
καλὸν οἶνον τίθησι, καὶ ὅταν μεθυσθῶσι, τότε τὸν ἐλάσσω·
good wine sets on, and when they have drunk, then the worse;
11 σὺ τετήρηκας τὸν καλὸν οἶνον ἕως ἄρτι. ταύτην ἐποίησε
you have kept the good wine until now. This did
τὴν ἀρχὴν τῶν σημείων ὁ Ἰησοῦς ἐν Κανᾷ τῆς Γαλιλαίας,
the beginning of the signs — Jesus in Cana — of Galilee.
καὶ ἐφανέρωσε τὴν δόξαν αὐτοῦ· καὶ ἐπίστευσαν εἰς αὐτὸν οἱ
And (it) revealed the glory of Him, and believed in Him the
μαθηταὶ αὐτοῦ.
disciples of Him.

12 Μετὰ τοῦτο κατέβη εἰς Καπερναούμ, αὐτὸς καὶ ἡ μήτηρ
After this went down to Capernaum He, and the mother
αὐτοῦ, καὶ οἱ ἀδελφοὶ αὐτοῦ, καὶ οἱ μαθηταὶ αὐτοῦ· καὶ ἐκεῖ
of Him, and the brothers of Him, and the disciples of Him, and there
ἔμειναν οὐ πολλὰς ἡμέρας.
He abode not many days.

13 Καὶ ἐγγὺς ἦν τὸ πάσχα τῶν Ἰουδαίων, καὶ ἀνέβη εἰς
And near was the Passover of the Jews. And went up to
14 Ἱεροσόλυμα ὁ Ἰησοῦς. καὶ εὗρεν ἐν τῷ ἱερῷ τοὺς πωλοῦντας
Jerusalem — Jesus. And He found in the Temple those selling
βόας καὶ πρόβατα καὶ περιστεράς, καὶ τοὺς κερματιστὰς
oxen and sheep and doves, and the money merchants
15 καθημένους. καὶ ποιήσας φραγέλλιον ἐκ σχοινίων πάντας
sitting. And having made a whip out of ropes, all
ἐξέβαλεν ἐκ τοῦ ἱεροῦ, τά τε πρόβατα καὶ τοὺς βόας· καὶ τῶν
He threw out of the Temple, the both sheep and the oxen and the
κολλυβιστῶν ἐξέχεε τὸ κέρμα, καὶ τὰς τραπέζας ἀνέστρεψε·
moneychangers, pouring out the money, and the tables overturning.
16 καὶ τοῖς τὰς περιστερὰς πωλοῦσιν εἶπεν, Ἄρατε ταῦτα
And to those doves selling He said, Take these things
ἐντεῦθεν· μὴ ποιεῖτε τὸν οἶκον τοῦ πατρός μου οἶκον
from here! Do not make the house of the Father of Me a house
17 ἐμπορίου. ἐμνήσθησαν δὲ οἱ μαθηταὶ αὐτοῦ ὅτι γεγραμ-
of merchandise. remembered And the disciples of Him that having been
18 μένον ἐστίν, Ὁ ζῆλος τοῦ οἴκου σου κατέφαγέ με. ἀπεκρίθη-
written is: The zeal of the house of You has devoured Me. answered
σαν οὖν οἱ Ἰουδαῖοι καὶ εἶπον αὐτῷ, Τί σημεῖον δεικνύεις
Then the Jews and said to Him, What sign do You show
19 ἡμῖν, ὅτι ταῦτα ποιεῖς; ἀπεκρίθη ὁ Ἰησοῦς καὶ εἶπεν αὐτοῖς,
to us, since these things You do? answered — Jesus and said to them,
Λύσατε τὸν ναὸν τοῦτον, καὶ ἐν τρισὶν ἡμέραις ἐγερῶ αὐτόν.
Destroy — temple this, and in three days I will raise it.
20 εἶπον οὖν οἱ Ἰουδαῖοι, Τεσσαράκοντα καὶ ἓξ ἔτεσιν ᾠκο-
said Then the Jews, Forty and six years is being
δομήθη ὁ ναὸς οὗτος, καὶ σὺ ἐν τρισὶν ἡμέραις ἐγερεῖς αὐτόν;
built Temple this, and you in three days will raise it?
21 ἐκεῖνος δὲ ἔλεγε περὶ τοῦ ναοῦ τοῦ σώματος αὐτοῦ. ὅτε
22 **that One But spoke about the temple of the body of Him. When**
οὖν ἠγέρθη ἐκ νεκρῶν, ἐμνήσθησαν οἱ μαθηταὶ αὐτοῦ ὅτι
then He was raised from (the) dead, recalled the disciples of Him that
τοῦτο ἔλεγεν αὐτοῖς· καὶ ἐπίστευσαν τῇ γραφῇ, καὶ τῷ λόγῳ
this He said to them; and they believed the Scripture and the word

23 And as He was in Jerusalem, at the Passover, at the Feast, many believed into His name, seeing the miracles which He did. 24 But Jesus Himself did not commit Himself to them, because He knew all; 25 and because He had no need that anyone should witness concerning man; for He knew what was in man.

ᾧ εἶπεν ὁ Ἰησοῦς.
which said — Jesus.
23 Ὡς δὲ ἦν ἐν Ἱεροσολύμοις ἐν τῷ πάσχα, ἐν τῇ ἑορτῇ,
as And He was in Jerusalem, at the Passover, at the feast,
πολλοὶ ἐπίστευσαν εἰς τὸ ὄνομα αὐτοῦ, θεωροῦντες αὐτοῦ τὰ
many believed in the name of Him, beholding of Him the
24 σημεῖα ἃ ἐποίει. αὐτὸς δὲ ὁ Ἰησοῦς οὐκ ἐπίστευεν ἑαυτὸν
signs which He did. Himself But, — Jesus not did commit Himself
25 αὐτοῖς, διὰ τὸ αὐτὸν γινώσκειν πάντας, καὶ ὅτι οὐ χρείαν
to them, because (of) Him knowing all, and because no need
εἶχεν ἵνα τις μαρτυρήσῃ περὶ τοῦ ἀνθρώπου· αὐτὸς γὰρ
He had that any should witness concerning man He for
ἐγίνωσκε τί ἦν ἐν τῷ ἀνθρώπῳ.
knew what was in — man.

CHAPTER 3

CHAPTER 3

1 But there was a man from the Pharisees, Nicodemus his name, a ruler of the Jews. 2 This one came to Jesus by night, and said to Him, Rabbi, we know that You have come *as* a teacher from God. For no one is able to do these miracles which You do, except God be with Him. 3 Jesus answered and said to him, Truly, truly, I say to you, If one does not receive birth from above, he is not able to see the kingdom of God. 4 Nicodemus said to Him, How is a man able to be born, being old? He is not able to enter into his mother's womb a second *time* and be born? 5 Jesus answered, Truly, truly, I say to you, If one does not receive birth out of water and Spirit, he is not able to enter into the kingdom of God. 6 That receiving birth from the flesh is flesh; and that receiving birth from the Spirit is spirit. 7 Do not wonder because I told you, You must receive birth from above. 8 The Spirit breathes where He desires, and you hear His voice; but you do not know from where He comes, and where He goes—so is everyone who has received birth from the Spirit. 9 Nicodemus answered and said to Him, How can these things come about? 10 Jesus answered and said to him, You are the teacher of Israel, and you do

1 Ἦν δὲ ἄνθρωπος ἐκ τῶν Φαρισαίων, Νικόδημος ὄνομα
was And a man out of the Pharisees. Nicodemus (the) name
2 αὐτῷ, ἄρχων τῶν Ἰουδαίων· οὗτος ἦλθε πρὸς τὸν Ἰησοῦν
to him, a ruler of the Jews. This one came to — Jesus
νυκτός, καὶ εἶπεν αὐτῷ, Ῥαββί, οἴδαμεν ὅτι ἀπὸ Θεοῦ ἐλή-
by night, and said to Him, Rabbi, we know that from God You
λυθας διδάσκαλος· οὐδεὶς γὰρ ταῦτα τὰ σημεῖα δύναται
have come a teacher; no one for these — signs is able
3 ποιεῖν ἃ σὺ ποιεῖς, ἐὰν μὴ ᾖ ὁ Θεὸς μετ' αὐτοῦ. ἀπεκρίθη ὁ
to do which You do, except be God with Him. answered —
Ἰησοῦς καὶ εἶπεν αὐτῷ. Ἀμὴν ἀμὴν λέγω σοι, ἐὰν μή τις
Jesus and said to him, Truly, truly, I say to you, Except one
γεννηθῇ ἄνωθεν, οὐ δύναται ἰδεῖν τὴν βασιλείαν τοῦ Θεοῦ.
receive birth from above, not he is able to see the kingdom — of God.
4 λέγει πρὸς αὐτὸν ὁ Νικόδημος, Πῶς δύναται ἄνθρωπος
says to Him — Nicodemus, How is able a man
γεννηθῆναι γέρων ὤν; μὴ δύναται εἰς τὴν κοιλίαν τῆς
to be born, old being? Not he is able into the womb of the
5 μητρὸς αὐτοῦ δεύτερον εἰσελθεῖν καὶ γεννηθῆναι; ἀπεκρίθη
mother of him a second (time) to enter and be born? answered
ὁ Ἰησοῦς, Ἀμὴν ἀμὴν λέγω σοι, ἐὰν μή τις γεννηθῇ ἐξ
Jesus, Truly, truly, I say to you, Except one receive birth of
ὕδατος καὶ Πνεύματος, οὐ δύναται εἰσελθεῖν εἰς τὴν βασιλείαν
water and Spirit, not he is able to enter into the kingdom
6 τοῦ Θεοῦ. τὸ γεγεννημένον ἐκ τῆς σαρκὸς σάρξ ἐστι· καὶ τὸ
of God. That receiving birth from the flesh, flesh is; and that
7 γεγεννημένον ἐκ τοῦ πνεύματος πνεῦμά ἐστι. μὴ θαυμάσῃς
receiving birth from the Spirit, spirit is. Do not wonder
8 ὅτι εἶπόν σοι, Δεῖ ὑμᾶς γεννηθῆναι ἄνωθεν. τὸ πνεῦμα ὅπου
because I told you, must You receive birth from above. The Spirit where
θέλει πνεῖ, καὶ τὴν φωνὴν αὐτοῦ ἀκούεις, ἀλλ' οὐκ οἶδας
He desires breathes, and the voice of Him you hear, but not you know
πόθεν ἔρχεται καὶ ποῦ ὑπάγει· οὕτως ἐστὶ πᾶς ὁ γεγεννη-
from where He comes and where He goes; so is everyone having received
9 μένος ἐκ τοῦ πνεύματος. ἀπεκρίθη Νικόδημος καὶ εἶπεν αὐτῷ,
birth from the Spirit. answered Nicodemus and said to Him,
10 Πῶς δύναται ταῦτα γενέσθαι; ἀπεκρίθη ὁ Ἰησοῦς καὶ εἶπεν
How can these things come about? answered — Jesus and said
αὐτῷ, Σὺ εἶ ὁ διδάσκαλος τοῦ Ἰσραήλ, καὶ ταῦτα οὐ
to him, You are the teacher — of Israel, and these things not

not know these things? [11] Truly, truly, I say to you, That which we know we speak, and that which we have seen, we testify. And you do not receive our testimony. [12] If I tell you earthly things, and you do not believe; how will you believe if I tell you heavenly things? [13] And no one has gone up into Heaven, except He having come down out of Heaven, the Son of Man who is in Heaven. [14] And even as Moses lifted up the serpent in the wilderness, so must the Son of man be lifted up, [15] that everyone believing into Him should not perish, but have everlasting life.

[16] For God so loved the world that He gave His only-begotten Son, that everyone believing into Him should not perish, but have everlasting life. [17] For God did not send His Son into the world that He might judge the world, but that the world might be saved through Him. [18] The *one* believing into Him is not judged; but the *one* not believing has already been judged; for he has not believed into the name of the only-begotten Son of God. [19] And this is the judgment, that the Light has come into the world, and men loved the darkness more than the Light; for their works were evil. [20] For everyone practicing wickedness hates the Light, and does not come to the Light, that his works may not be exposed. [21] But the *one* doing the truth comes to the Light, that his works may be revealed, that they have been worked in God.

[22] After these things Jesus and His disciples came into the land of Judea. And *He* continued there with them, and baptized. [23] And John was also baptizing in Aenon, near Salim, for many waters were there; and they came and were being baptized.

[24] For John had not yet been thrown into prison.

11 γινώσκεις ; ἀμὴν ἀμὴν λέγω σοι ὅτι ὃ οἴδαμεν λαλοῦμεν, καὶ
you do know? Truly, truly, I say to you, —what we know we speak. and
ὃ ἑωράκαμεν μαρτυροῦμεν· καὶ τὴν μαρτυρίαν ἡμῶν οὐ
what we have seen we witness, and the witness of us not
12 λαμβάνετε. εἰ τὰ ἐπίγεια εἶπον ὑμῖν καὶ οὐ πιστεύετε, πῶς,
you receive. If earthly things I told you and not you believe, how,
13 ἐὰν εἴπω ὑμῖν τὰ ἐπουράνια, πιστεύσετε ; καὶ οὐδεὶς ἀναβέ-
if I tell you the heavenly things, will you believe? And no one has gone
βηκεν εἰς τὸν οὐρανόν, εἰ μὴ ὁ ἐκ τοῦ οὐρανοῦ καταβάς, ὁ
up into — Heaven except He out of — Heaven having come down, the
14 υἱὸς τοῦ ἀνθρώπου ὁ ὢν ἐν τῷ οὐρανῷ. καὶ καθὼς Μωσῆς
Son — of man, who is in — Heaven. And as Moses
ὕψωσε τὸν ὄφιν ἐν τῇ ἐρήμῳ, οὕτως ὑψωθῆναι δεῖ τὸν υἱὸν
lifted up the serpent in the wilderness, so to be lifted up must the Son
15 τοῦ ἀνθρώπου· ἵνα πᾶς ὁ πιστεύων εἰς αὐτὸν μὴ ἀπόληται,
— of man, that everyone believing in Him not may perish,
ἀλλ' ἔχῃ ζωὴν αἰώνιον.
but have life everlasting.
16 Οὕτω γὰρ ἠγάπησεν ὁ Θεὸς τὸν κόσμον, ὥστε τὸν υἱὸν
so For loved God the world, so as the Son
αὐτοῦ τὸν μονογενῆ ἔδωκεν, ἵνα πᾶς ὁ πιστεύων εἰς αὐτὸν
of Him, the only-begotten, He gave, that everyone believing into Him
17 μὴ ἀπόληται, ἀλλ' ἔχῃ ζωὴν αἰώνιον. οὐ γὰρ ἀπέστειλεν ὁ
not may perish, but have life everlasting. not For sent
Θεὸς τὸν υἱὸν αὐτοῦ εἰς τὸν κόσμον ἵνα κρίνῃ τὸν κόσμον,
God the Son of Him into the world that He judge the world,
18 ἀλλ' ἵνα σωθῇ ὁ κόσμος δι' αὐτοῦ. ὁ πιστεύων εἰς αὐτὸν οὐ
but that may be saved the world via Him. The (one) believing in Him not
κρίνεται· ὁ δὲ μὴ πιστεύων ἤδη κέκριται, ὅτι μὴ πεπί-
is judged; the (one) but not believing already has been judged, for not he has
19 στευκεν εἰς τὸ ὄνομα τοῦ μονογενοῦς υἱοῦ τοῦ Θεοῦ. αὕτη δέ
believed into the name of the only-begotten Son — of God. this And
ἐστιν ἡ κρίσις, ὅτι τὸ φῶς ἐλήλυθεν εἰς τὸν κόσμον, καὶ
is the judgment, that the light has come into the world, and
ἠγάπησαν οἱ ἄνθρωποι μᾶλλον τὸ σκότος ἢ τὸ φῶς· ἦν
loved — men more the darkness than the light; were
20 γὰρ πονηρὰ αὐτῶν τὰ ἔργα. πᾶς γὰρ ὁ φαῦλα πράσσων
for evil of them the works. everyone For wickedness practicing
μισεῖ τὸ φῶς, καὶ οὐκ ἔρχεται πρὸς τὸ φῶς, ἵνα μὴ ἐλεγχθῇ
hates the light, and not does come to the light, that not be reproved
21 τὰ ἔργα αὐτοῦ. ὁ δὲ ποιῶν τὴν ἀλήθειαν ἔρχεται πρὸς τὸ
the works of him. the (one) But doing the truth comes to the
φῶς, ἵνα φανερωθῇ αὐτοῦ τὰ ἔργα, ὅτι ἐν Θεῷ ἐστιν
light, that may be revealed of him the works, that in God they are
εἰργασμένα.
having been worked.
22 Μετὰ ταῦτα ἦλθεν ὁ Ἰησοῦς καὶ οἱ μαθηταὶ αὐτοῦ εἰς
After these things came — Jesus and the disciples of Him into
τὴν Ἰουδαίαν γῆν· καὶ ἐκεῖ διέτριβε μετ' αὐτῶν καὶ ἐβάπτι-
the Judean land, and there continued with them and baptized.
23 ζεν. ἦν δὲ καὶ Ἰωάννης βαπτίζων ἐν Αἰνὼν ἐγγὺς τοῦ Σαλείμ,
was And also John baptizing in Aenon near — Salem,
ὅτι ὕδατα πολλὰ ἦν ἐκεῖ· καὶ παρεγίνοντο καὶ ἐβαπτίζοντο.
for waters many were there; and they came and were being baptized.
24 οὔπω γὰρ ἦν βεβλημένος εἰς τὴν φυλακὴν ὁ Ἰωάννης.
not yet For was having been cast into the prison — John.

25 Then a questioning arose from John's disciples with *the* Jews concerning purifying. 26 And they came to John and said to him, Teacher, *He* who was with you beyond the Jordan, to whom you have witnessed, behold, this one baptizes, and all are coming to Him. 27 John answered and said, A man is able to receive nothing unless it has been given to him from Heaven. 28 You yourselves witness to me, that I said, I am not the Christ, but that having been sent I am going before that One. 29 The *one* having the bride is *the* bridegroom. But the friend of the bridegroom, standing and hearing him, rejoices with joy because of the bridegroom's voice. Then this my joy has been fulfilled. 30 That One must increase, but I *must* decrease.

31 The *One* coming from above is above all. The *one* being of the earth is of the earth, and speaks of the earth. The *One* coming out of Heaven is above all. 32 And what He has seen and heard, this He testifies; and no one receives His testimony. 33 The *one* receiving His testimony has sealed that God is true; 34 for *the One* whom God sent speaks the words of God; for God does not give the Spirit by measure. 35 The Father loves the Son, and has given all things into His hand. 36 The *one* believing into His name has everlasting life; but the *one* refusing to believe the Son will not see life, but the wrath of God remains on him.

CHAPTER 4

1 Then when the Lord knew that the Pharisees heard that Jesus made more disciples and baptized *more* than John — 2 though indeed Jesus Himself was not baptizing, but His disciples— 3 He left Judea and went away into Galilee again. 4 And it was necessary for Him to pass through Samaria. 5 And He

25 ἐγένετο οὖν ζήτησις ἐκ τῶν μαθητῶν Ἰωάννου μετὰ
was Therefore a questioning of the disciples of John with
26 Ἰουδαίων περὶ καθαρισμοῦ. καὶ ἦλθον πρὸς τὸν Ἰωάννην
Jews concerning purifying. And they came to — John
καὶ εἶπον αὐτῷ, Ῥαββί, ὃς ἦν μετὰ σοῦ πέραν τοῦ Ἰορδάνου,
and said to him, Rabbi, (He)who was with you beyond the Jordan,
ᾧ σὺ μεμαρτύρηκας, ἴδε οὗτος βαπτίζει, καὶ πάντες ἔρχονται
to whom you have witnessed, behold, this one baptizes, and all are coming
27 πρὸς αὐτόν. ἀπεκρίθη Ἰωάννης καὶ εἶπεν, Οὐ δύναται
to Him. answered John and said, not is able
ἄνθρωπος λαμβάνειν οὐδέν, ἐὰν μὴ ᾖ δεδομένον αὐτῷ ἐκ τοῦ
A man to receive nothing unless it is having been given to him from
28 οὐρανοῦ. αὐτοὶ ὑμεῖς μοι μαρτυρεῖτε ὅτι εἶπον, Οὐκ εἰμὶ
Heaven. (your)selves You to me witness that I said, not am
ἐγὼ ὁ Χριστός, ἀλλ' ὅτι ἀπεσταλμένος εἰμὶ ἔμπροσθεν
I the Christ, but that having been sent I am preceding
29 ἐκείνου. ὁ ἔχων τὴν νύμφην νυμφίος ἐστίν· ὁ δὲ φίλος τοῦ
that One. He having the bride (the) bridegroom is, the but friend of the
νυμφίου, ὁ ἑστηκὼς καὶ ἀκούων αὐτοῦ, χαρᾷ χαίρει διὰ τὴν
bridegroom, standing and hearing him, with joy rejoices for the
φωνὴν τοῦ νυμφίου· αὕτη οὖν ἡ χαρὰ ἡ ἐμὴ πεπλήρωται.
voice of the bridegroom. this Then the joy of me has been fulfilled.
30 ἐκεῖνον δεῖ αὐξάνειν, ἐμὲ δὲ ἐλαττοῦσθαι.
That One must increase, me but to decrease.
31 Ὁ ἄνωθεν ἐρχόμενος ἐπάνω πάντων ἐστίν. ὁ ὢν ἐκ τῆς
The One from above coming above all is, the (one) being of the
γῆς, ἐκ τῆς γῆς ἐστι, καὶ ἐκ τῆς γῆς λαλεῖ· ὁ ἐκ τοῦ οὐρανοῦ
earth of the earth is, and of the earth speaks. He from Heaven
32 ἐρχόμενος ἐπάνω πάντων ἐστί. καὶ ὃ ἑώρακε καὶ ἤκουσε,
coming above all is. And what He has seen and heard,
τοῦτο μαρτυρεῖ· καὶ τὴν μαρτυρίαν αὐτοῦ οὐδεὶς λαμβάνει.
this He witnesses, and the witness of Him no one receives.
33 ὁ λαβὼν αὐτοῦ τὴν μαρτυρίαν ἐσφράγισεν ὅτι ὁ Θεὸς ἀληθής
He receiving of Him the witness has sealed that — God true.
34 ἐστιν. ὃν γὰρ ἀπέστειλεν ὁ Θεός, τὰ ῥήματα τοῦ Θεοῦ λαλεῖ·
is.(He) whom For sent — God, the words — of God speaks;
35 οὐ γὰρ ἐκ μέτρου δίδωσιν ὁ Θεὸς τὸ Πνεῦμα. ὁ πατὴρ ἀγαπᾷ
not for by measure gives — God the Spirit. The Father loves
36 τὸν υἱόν, καὶ πάντα δέδωκεν ἐν τῇ χειρὶ αὐτοῦ. ὁ πιστεύων
the Son, and all things has given into the hand of Him. he believing
εἰς τὸν υἱὸν ἔχει ζωὴν αἰώνιον· ὁ δὲ ἀπειθῶν τῷ υἱῷ οὐκ
into the Son has life everlasting; the (one) but disobeying the Son not
ὄψεται ζωήν, ἀλλ' ἡ ὀργὴ τοῦ Θεοῦ μένει ἐπ' αὐτόν.
will see life, but the wrath — of God remains on him.

CHAPTER 4

1 Ὡς οὖν ἔγνω ὁ Κύριος ὅτι ἤκουσαν οἱ Φαρισαῖοι ὅτι
As therefore knew the Lord that heard the Pharisees that
Ἰησοῦς πλείονας μαθητὰς ποιεῖ καὶ βαπτίζει ἢ Ἰωάννης
Jesus more disciples makes and baptizes than John,
2 (καίτοιγε Ἰησοῦς αὐτὸς οὐκ ἐβάπτιζεν, ἀλλ' οἱ μαθηταὶ
though Jesus Himself not baptized but the disciples
3 αὐτοῦ), ἀφῆκε τὴν Ἰουδαίαν, καὶ ἀπῆλθε πάλιν εἰς τὴν
of Him; He left — Judea and went away again into —
4 Γαλιλαίαν. ἔδει δὲ αὐτὸν διέρχεσθαι διὰ τῆς Σαμαρείας. ἔρχε-
5 **Galilee. it behoved And Him to pass through — Samaria. He**

came to a city of Samaria called Sychar, near the piece of land Jacob gave to his son Joseph. [6]And Jacob's fountain was there. Then having been wearied by the journey, Jesus sat thus on the fountain. *The* hour was about *the* sixth.

[7]A woman came out of Samaria to draw water. Jesus said to her, Give Me to drink. [8]For His disciples had gone away into the city that they might buy provisions. [9]Then the woman said to Him, How do you, being a Jew, ask to drink from me, *I* being a Samaritan woman? For Jews do not associate with Samaritans. [10]Jesus answered and said to her, If you knew the gift of God, and who is the *One* saying to you, Give Me to drink, you would have asked Him, and He would give you living water. [11]The woman said to Him, Sir, you have no vessel, and the well is deep. From where then do you have living water? [12]Are you greater than our father Jacob who gave us the well, and he and his sons and his livestock drank out of it?

[13]Jesus answered and said to her, Everyone drinking of this water will thirst again; but the water which I give to him will never ever thirst forever, but the water which I will give to him will become a fountain of water in him, springing up into everlasting life. [15]The woman said to Him, Sir, give me this water, that I may not thirst, nor come here to draw. [16]Jesus said to her, Go, call your husband, and come here. [17]And the woman answered and said, I have no husband. Jesus said to her, Well did you say, I have no husband. [18]For you have had five husbands, and now *he* whom you have is not your husband. You have spoken this truly. [19]The woman said to Him, Sir, I perceive that you are a prophet. [20]Our

ται οὖν εἰς πόλιν τῆς Σαμαρείας λεγομένην Συχάρ, πλησίον
comes then to a city — of Samaria called Sychar, near
6 τοῦ χωρίου ὃ ἔδωκεν Ἰακὼβ Ἰωσὴφ τῷ υἱῷ αὐτοῦ· ἦν δὲ
the piece of land that gave Jacob to Joseph the son of him. was And
ἐκεῖ πηγὴ τοῦ Ἰακώβ. ὁ οὖν Ἰησοῦς κεκοπιακὼς ἐκ τῆς
there a fountain — of Jacob. Therefore, Jesus having wearied from the
ὁδοιπορίας ἐκαθέζετο οὕτως ἐπὶ τῇ πηγῇ. ὥρα ἦν ὡσεὶ
journey sat thus on the fountain; hour was about
7 ἕκτη. ἔρχεται γυνὴ ἐκ τῆς Σαμαρείας ἀντλῆσαι ὕδωρ· λέγει
sixth. Comes a woman of — Samaria to draw water. says
8 αὐτῇ ὁ Ἰησοῦς, Δός μοι πιεῖν. οἱ γὰρ μαθηταὶ αὐτοῦ ἀπελη-
to her Jesus, Give Me to drink. the For disciples of Him had gone
9 λύθεισαν εἰς τὴν πόλιν, ἵνα τροφὰς ἀγοράσωσι. λέγει οὖν
away into the city, that foods they might buy. says Then
αὐτῷ ἡ γυνὴ ἡ Σαμαρεῖτις, Πῶς σὺ Ἰουδαῖος ὢν παρ᾽ ἐμοῦ
to Him the woman Samaritan, How do you, a Jew being, from me
πιεῖν αἰτεῖς, οὔσης γυναικὸς Σαμαρείτιδος; (οὐ γὰρ συγ-
to drink ask , (I) being woman a Samaritan? not For
10 χρῶνται Ἰουδαῖοι Σαμαρείταις.) ἀπεκρίθη Ἰησοῦς καὶ εἶπεν
associate Jews with Samaritans. answered Jesus and said
αὐτῇ, Εἰ ᾔδεις τὴν δωρεὰν τοῦ Θεοῦ, καὶ τίς ἐστιν ὁ λέγων
to her, If you knew the gift — of God, and who is the (one) saying
σοι, Δός μοι πιεῖν, σὺ ἂν ᾔτησας αὐτόν, καὶ ἔδωκεν ἄν σοι
to you, Give me to drink, you would have asked Him, and He would give you
11 ὕδωρ ζῶν. λέγει αὐτῷ ἡ γυνή, Κύριε, οὔτε ἄντλημα ἔχεις, καὶ
water living. says to Him The woman, Lord, no vessel you have, and
12 τὸ φρέαρ ἐστὶ βαθύ· πόθεν οὖν ἔχεις τὸ ὕδωρ τὸ ζῶν; μὴ σὺ
the well is deep; from where then have you water living? not You
μείζων εἶ τοῦ πατρὸς ἡμῶν Ἰακώβ, ὃς ἔδωκεν ἡμῖν το φρέαρ,
greater are (than) the father of us, Jacob, who gave us the well,
καὶ αὐτὸς ἐξ αὐτοῦ ἔπιε, καὶ οἱ υἱοὶ αὐτοῦ, καὶ τὰ θρέμματα
and he it drank, and the sons of him, and the livestock
13 αὐτοῦ; ἀπεκρίθη ὁ Ἰησοῦς καὶ εἶπεν αὐτῇ, Πᾶς ὁ πίνων ἐκ
of him? answered — Jesus and said to her, Everyone drinking of
14 τοῦ ὕδατος τούτου, διψήσει πάλιν· ὃς δ᾽ ἂν πίῃ ἐκ τοῦ
— water this will thirst again; who but ever drinks of the
ὕδατος οὗ ἐγὼ δώσω αὐτῷ, οὐ μὴ διψήσῃ εἰς τὸν αἰῶνα·
water which I will give him, in no way will thirst unto the age,
ἀλλὰ τὸ ὕδωρ ὃ δώσω αὐτῷ γενήσεται ἐν αὐτῷ πηγὴ
but the water which I will give him will become in him a fountain
15 ὕδατος ἁλλομένου εἰς ζωὴν αἰώνιον. λέγει πρὸς αὐτὸν ἡ
of water springing to life everlasting. says to Him The
γυνή, Κύριε, δός μοι τοῦτο τὸ ὕδωρ, ἵνα μὴ διψῶ, μηδὲ
woman, Lord, give me this — water, that not I thirst, nor
16 ἔρχωμαι ἐνθάδε ἀντλεῖν. λέγει αὐτῇ ὁ Ἰησοῦς, Ὕπαγε,
come here to draw. says to her — Jesus, Go,
17 φώνησον τὸν ἄνδρα σοῦ, καὶ ἐλθὲ ἐνθάδε. ἀπεκρίθη ἡ γυνὴ
call the husband of you, and come here. answered The woman
καὶ εἶπεν, Οὐκ ἔχω ἄνδρα. λέγει αὐτῇ ὁ Ἰησοῦς, Καλῶς εἶπας
and said, not I have a husband. says to her — Jesus, well You say,
18 ὅτι Ἄνδρα οὐκ ἔχω· πέντε γὰρ ἄνδρας ἔσχες, καὶ νῦν ὃν
— A husband not I have; five for husbands you had. and now whom
19 ἔχεις οὐκ ἔστι σου ἀνήρ· τοῦτο ἀληθὲς εἴρηκας. λέγει αὐτῷ
you have not is your husband; this truly you have said. says to Him
20 ἡ γυνή, Κύριε, θεωρῶ ὅτι προφήτης εἶ σύ. οἱ πατέρες ἡμῶν
The woman, Lord, I perceive that a prophet are you. The fathers of us

fathers worshiped in this mountain, and you say that in Jerusalem is the place where it is necessary to worship. 21 Jesus said to her, Woman, believe Me that an hour is coming when you will worship the Father neither in this mountain nor in Jerusalem. 22 You worship what you do not know, for salvation is of the Jews. 23 But an hour is coming, and now is, when the true worshipers will worship the Father in spirit and in truth. For the Father also seeks such *ones* that worship Him. 24 God *is* a spirit, and the ones worshiping Him must worship in spirit and truth. 25 The woman said to Him, I know that Messiah is coming, the *One* called Christ. When that One comes, He will announce to us all things. 26 Jesus said to her, I AM, the *One* speaking to you.

27 And on this His disciples came and marveled that He was speaking with a woman. However, no one said, What do you seek? Or, Why do You speak with her?
28 Then the woman left her waterpot and went away into the city, and said to the men, 29 Come, see a Man who told me all things, whatever I did. Is this One not the Christ? 30 Therefore, they went out of the city and came to Him.
31 But in the meantime the disciples asked Him, saying, Rabbi eat. 32 But He said to them, I have food to eat which you do not know. 33 Then the disciples said to one another, No one brought Him *food* to eat? 34 Jesus said to them, My food is that I should do the the will of *Him* who sent Me, and that I may finish His work. 35 You should not say, It is yet four months and the harvest comes. Behold, I

ἐν τούτῳ τῷ ὄρει προσεκύνησαν· καὶ ὑμεῖς λέγετε ὅτι ἐν
in this — mountain worshiped, and you say that in
21 Ἱεροσολύμοις ἐστὶν ὁ τόπος ὅπου δεῖ προσκυνεῖν. λέγει
Jerusalem is the place where it is right to worship. says
αὐτῇ ὁ Ἰησοῦς, Γύναι, πίστευσόν μοι, ὅτι ἔρχεται ὥρα,
to her — Jesus, Woman, believe me, that comes an hour
ὅτε οὔτε ἐν τῷ ὄρει τούτῳ οὔτε ἐν Ἱεροσολύμοις προσκυνή-
when neither in — mountain this, nor in Jerusalem, will you worship
22 σετε τῷ πατρί. ὑμεῖς προσκυνεῖτε ὃ οὐκ οἴδατε· ἡμεῖς
the Father You worship what not you know, we
προσκυνοῦμεν ὃ οἴδαμεν· ὅτι ἡ σωτηρία ἐκ τῶν Ἰουδαίων
worship what we know, since salvation of the Jews
23 ἐστίν. ἀλλ' ἔρχεται ὥρα καὶ νῦν ἐστιν, ὅτε οἱ ἀληθινοὶ
is. But is coming an hour, and now is, when the true
προσκυνηταὶ προσκυνήσουσι τῷ πατρὶ ἐν πνεύματι καὶ
worshipers will worship the Father in spirit and
ἀληθείᾳ· καὶ γὰρ ὁ πατὴρ τοιούτους ζητεῖ τοὺς προσ-
truth; also for the Father such seeks, those
24 κυνοῦντας αὐτόν. Πνεῦμα ὁ Θεός· καὶ τοὺς προσκυνοῦντας
worshiping Him. A spirit — God (is) and those worshiping
25 αὐτόν, ἐν πνεύματι καὶ ἀληθείᾳ δεῖ προσκυνεῖν. λέγει αὐτῷ
Him in spirit and truth need to worship. says to Him
ἡ γυνή, Οἶδα ὅτι Μεσσίας ἔρχεται (ὁ λεγόμενος Χριστός)·
The woman, I know that Messiah is coming, the (One) called Christ;
26 ὅταν ἔλθῃ ἐκεῖνος, ἀναγγελεῖ ἡμῖν πάντα. λέγει αὐτῇ ὁ
when comes that One, He will announce to us all things. says to her —
Ἰησοῦς, Ἐγώ εἰμι, ὁ λαλῶν σοι.
Jesus, I AM, He speaking to you.
27 Καὶ ἐπὶ τούτῳ ἦλθον οἱ μαθηταὶ αὐτοῦ, καὶ ἐθαύμασαν
And on this came the disciples of Him, and marveled
ὅτι μετὰ γυναικὸς ἐλάλει· οὐδεὶς μέντοι εἶπε, Τί ζητεῖς;
that with a woman He was speaking; no one, though, said, What seek you?
28 ἤ, Τί λαλεῖς μετ' αὐτῆς; ἀφῆκεν οὖν τὴν ὑδρίαν αὐτῆς ἡ
or, Why speak You with her? left, then, the waterpot of her The
γυνή, καὶ ἀπῆλθεν εἰς τὴν πόλιν, καὶ λέγει τοῖς ἀνθρώποις,
woman, and went away into the city, and says to the men,
29 Δεῦτε, ἴδετε ἄνθρωπον, ὃς εἶπέ μοι πάντα ὅσα ἐποίησα· μήτι
Come! See a man who told me all things whatever I did. Not
30 οὗτός ἐστιν ὁ Χριστός; ἐξῆλθον οὖν ἐκ τῆς πόλεως, καὶ
this One Is the Christ? They went out, then, from the city, and
31 ἤρχοντο πρὸς αὐτόν. ἐν δὲ τῷ μεταξὺ ἠρώτων αὐτὸν οἱ
came to Him. In And the meantime asked Him the
32 μαθηταί, λέγοντες, Ῥαββί, φάγε. ὁ δὲ εἶπεν αὐτοῖς, Ἐγὼ
disciples, saying, Rabbi, eat. He But said to them, I
33 βρῶσιν ἔχω φαγεῖν ἣν ὑμεῖς οὐκ οἴδατε. ἔλεγον οὖν οἱ
food have to eat which you not do know. said Therefore the
μαθηταὶ πρὸς ἀλλήλους, Μήτις ἤνεγκεν αὐτῷ φαγεῖν;
disciples to one another, No one brought Him to eat?
34 λέγει αὐτοῖς ὁ Ἰησοῦς, Ἐμὸν βρῶμά ἐστιν, ἵνα ποιῶ τὸ θέλημα
says to them Jesus, My food is that I may do the will
35 τοῦ πέμψαντός με, καὶ τελειώσω αὐτοῦ τὸ ἔργον. οὐχ ὑμεῖς
of (Him) having sent Me, and I may finish of Him the work. Not you
λέγετε ὅτι Ἔτι τετράμηνόν ἐστι, καὶ ὁ θερισμὸς ἔρχεται;
say, Yet four months it is, and the harvest comes.
ἰδού, λέγω ὑμῖν, Ἐπάρατε τοὺς ὀφθαλμοὺς ὑμῶν, καὶ
Behold, I say to you, Lift up the eyes of you, and

say to you, Lift up your eyes and behold the fields, for they are already white to harvest. 36 And the *one* reaping receives reward, and gathers fruit to everlasting life, so that both the *one* sowing and the *one* reaping may rejoice together. 37 For in this the word is true, that another *is* the *one* sowing, and another the *one* reaping. 38 I sent you to reap what you have not labored over. Others have labored, and you have entered into their labor.

39 And many of the Samaritans out of that city believed into Him, because of the word of the woman testifying, He told me all things, whatever I did. 40 Then as the Samaritans came to Him, they asked Him to remain with them. And He remained there two days. 41 And many more believed because of His word. 42 And they said to the woman, We no longer believe because of your saying; for we ourselves have heard, and we know that this One is truly the Savior of the world, the Christ.

43 But after the two days, He went out from there, and went away into Galilee. 44 For Jesus Himself testified that a prophet has no honor in *his* own native-place. 45 Therefore, when He came into Galilee, the Galileans received Him, seeing all things which He did in Jerusalem at the Feast. For they also went to the Feast.

46 Then Jesus came again to Cana of Galilee, where He made the water *into* wine. And there was a certain nobleman whose son was sick in Capernaum. 47 Hearing that Jesus is coming from Judea into Galilee, this one went out to Him, and asked Him that He would come and heal his son; for he was about to die. 48 Then Jesus said to him, Unless you see signs and wonders, you will not at all

θεάσασθε τὰς χώρας, ὅτι λευκαί εἰσι πρὸς θερισμὸν ἤδη.
behold the fields, because white they are to harvest already.
36 καὶ ὁ θερίζων μισθὸν λαμβάνει, καὶ συνάγει καρπὸν εἰς ζωὴν
And he reaping reward receives, and gathers fruit to life
αἰώνιον· ἵνα καὶ ὁ σπείρων ὁμοῦ χαίρῃ καὶ ὁ θερίζων.
eternal, that also he sowing together may rejoice and he reaping.
37 ἐν γὰρ τούτῳ ὁ λόγος ἐστὶν ἀληθινός, ὅτι ἄλλος ἐστὶν ὁ
in For this the word is true, that another is the (one)
38 σπείρων, καὶ ἄλλος ὁ θερίζων. ἐγὼ ἀπέστειλα ὑμᾶς θερίζειν
sowing, and another the (one) reaping. I sent you to reap
ὃ οὐχ ὑμεῖς κεκοπιάκατε· ἄλλοι κεκοπιάκασι, καὶ ὑμεῖς εἰς τὸν
what not you have labored over. Others have labored, and you into the
κόπον αὐτῶν εἰσεληλύθατε.
labor of them have entered.
39 Ἐκ δὲ τῆς πόλεως ἐκείνης πολλοὶ ἐπίστευσαν εἰς αὐτὸν
out of And the city that many believed in Him
τῶν Σαμαρειτῶν διὰ τὸν λόγον τῆς γυναικὸς μαρτυρούσης
of the Samaritans because of the word of the woman testifying,
40 ὅτι Εἶπέ μοι πάντα ὅσα ἐποίησα. ὡς οὖν ἦλθον πρὸς αὐτὸν
— He told me all things whatever I did. As therefore came to Him
οἱ Σαμαρεῖται, ἠρώτων αὐτὸν μεῖναι παρ' αὐτοῖς· καὶ ἔμεινεν
the Samaritans, they asked Him to stay with them; and He stayed
41 ἐκεῖ δύο ἡμέρας. καὶ πολλῷ πλείους ἐπίστευσαν διὰ τὸν
there two days. And more many believed through the
42 λόγον αὐτοῦ, τῇ τε γυναικὶ ἔλεγον ὅτι Οὐκέτι διὰ τὴν σὴν
word of Him. to the And woman they said, No longer because of your
λαλιὰν πιστεύομεν· αὐτοὶ γὰρ ἀκηκόαμεν, καὶ οἴδαμεν ὅτι
speaking we believe; (our)selves for we have heard, and we know that
οὗτός ἐστιν ἀληθῶς ὁ Σωτὴρ τοῦ κόσμου, ὁ Χριστός.
this One is truly the Savior of the world, the Christ.
43 Μετα δὲ τὰς δύο ἡμερας ἐξῆλθεν ἐκεῖθεν, καὶ ἀπῆλθεν εἰς
after And the two days, He went out from there, and went into
44 τὴν Γαλιλαίαν. αὐτὸς γὰρ ὁ Ἰησοῦς ἐμαρτύρησεν ὅτι προφή-
— Galilee. (Him)self For, — Jesus testified that a prophet
45 της ἐν τῇ ἰδίᾳ πατρίδι τιμὴν οὐκ ἔχει. ὅτε οὖν ἦλθεν εἰς τὴν
in the own native-place honor not has. When, then, He came into —
Γαλιλαίαν, ἐδέξαντο αὐτὸν οἱ Γαλιλαῖοι, πάντα ἑωρακότες
Galilee, received Him the Galileans, all things having seen
ἃ ἐποίησεν ἐν Ἱεροσολύμοις ἐν τῇ ἑορτῇ· καὶ αὐτοὶ γὰρ ἦλθον
which He did in Jerusalem at the feast. also they For went
εἰς τὴν ἑορτήν.
to the feast.
46 Ἦλθεν οὖν ὁ Ἰησοῦς πάλιν εἰς τὴν Κανᾶ τῆς Γαλιλαίας,
came then — Jesus again to — Cana — of Galilee,
ὅπου ἐποίησε τὸ ὕδωρ οἶνον. καὶ ἦν τις βασιλικός, οὗ ὁ υἱὸς
where He made the water wine. And was one noble of whom the son
47 ἠσθένει ἐν Καπερναούμ. οὗτος ἀκούσας ὅτι Ἰησοῦς ἥκει ἐκ
was ill in Capernaum. This one hearing that Jesus comes from
τῆς Ἰουδαίας εἰς τὴν Γαλιλαίαν, ἀπῆλθε πρὸς αὐτόν, καὶ
— Judea into — Galilee, went out to Him, and
ἠρώτα αὐτὸν ἵνα καταβῇ καὶ ἰάσηται αὐτοῦ τὸν υἱόν·
asked Him, that He would come and would cure of him the son;
48 ἤμελλε γὰρ ἀποθνῄσκειν. εἶπεν οὖν ὁ Ἰησοῦς πρὸς αὐτόν,
he was For about to die. said Then — Jesus to him,
49 Ἐὰν μὴ σημεῖα καὶ τέρατα ἴδητε, οὐ μὴ πιστεύσητε. λέγει
Except signs and wonders you see, in no way you believe. says
will

believe. 49 The nobleman said to Him, Sir, come down before my child dies. 50 Jesus said to him, Go! Your son lives. and the man believed the word which Jesus said to him, and went away. 51 But already, as he was going down, his slaves met him and reported, saying, Your child lives. 52 He then asked from them the hour in which he had gotten better. And they said to him, Yesterday, *at the* seventh hour, the fever left him. 53 Then the father knew that *it was* at that hour in which Jesus said to him, Your son lives. And he himself, and his whole household, believed. 54 Again, this second miracle Jesus did, coming from Judea into Galilee.

πρὸς αὐτὸν ὁ βασιλικός, Κύριε, κατάβηθι πρὶν ἀποθανεῖν
to Him The noble Lord, come down before dies
50 τὸ παιδίον μου. λέγει αὐτῷ ὁ Ἰησοῦς, Πορεύου· ὁ υἱός σου
the child of me. says to him — Jesus, Go, the son of you
ζῇ. καὶ ἐπίστευσεν ὁ ἄνθρωπος τῷ λόγῳ ᾧ εἶπεν αὐτῷ
lives. And believed the man the word which said to him
51 Ἰησοῦς, καὶ ἐπορεύετο. ἤδη δὲ αὐτοῦ καταβαίνοντος, οἱ
Jesus, and went away. already And (as) he (was) going down the
δοῦλοι αὐτοῦ ἀπήντησαν αὐτῷ, καὶ ἀπήγγειλαν λέγοντες
slaves of him met him, and reported, saying,
52 ὅτι Ὁ παῖς σου ζῇ. ἐπύθετο οὖν παρ' αὐτῶν τὴν ὥραν ἐν
— The child of you lives. He asked then from them the hour in
ᾗ κομψότερον ἔσχε. καὶ εἶπον αὐτῷ ὅτι Χθὲς ὥραν ἑβδόμην
which better he had. And they said to him, Yesterday (at) hour seventh
53 ἀφῆκεν αὐτὸν ὁ πυρετός. ἔγνω οὖν ὁ πατὴρ ὅτι ἐν ἐκείνῃ τῇ
left him the fever. Knew, then, the father that in that —
ὥρᾳ, ἐν ᾗ εἶπεν αὐτῷ ὁ Ἰησοῦς ὅτι Ὁ υἱός σου ζῇ· καὶ
hour in which said to him — Jesus, — The son of you lives. And
54 ἐπίστευσεν αὐτὸς καὶ ἡ οἰκία αὐτοῦ ὅλη. τοῦτο πάλιν
he believed, himself and the house of him whole. This again,
δεύτερον σημεῖον ἐποίησεν ὁ Ἰησοῦς, ἐλθὼν ἐκ τῆς Ἰουδαίας
a second sign, did — Jesus, having come from Judea
εἰς τὴν Γαλιλαίαν.
into — Galilee.

CHAPTER 5

CHAPTER 5

1 After these things there was a feast of the Jews, and Jesus went up to Jerusalem.

2 And at Jerusalem is a pool at the Sheep Gate which *is* called in Hebrew, Bethesda, having five porches. 3 In these was a great multitude of the infirm lying: blind ones, lame ones, withered ones; awaiting the stirring of the water. 4 For an angel from time to time descended in the pool, and agitated the water. Then the *one* first entering after the agitation of the water became well, whatever disease he was held by.

5 But a certain man was there, being in infirmity thirty-eight years. 6 Seeing him lying, and knowing that he had already *spent* much time, Jesus said to him, Do you desire to become well? 7 The infirm one answered Him, Lord, I do not have a man, that when the water is agitated he may throw me into the pool; but while I am coming,

1 Μετὰ ταῦτα ἦν ἑορτὴ τῶν Ἰουδαίων, καὶ ἀνέβη ὁ
After these things was a feast of the Jews, and went up —
Ἰησοῦς εἰς Ἱεροσόλυμα.
Jesus to Jerusalem.
2 Ἔστι δὲ ἐν τοῖς Ἱεροσολύμοις ἐπὶ τῇ προβατικῇ κολυμ-
is And in — Jerusalem at the Sheep Gate a pool,
βήθρα, ἡ ἐπιλεγομένη Ἑβραϊστὶ Βηθεσδά, πέντε στοὰς
which (is) called in Hebrew Bethesda, five porches
3 ἔχουσα. ἐν ταύταις κατέκειτο πλῆθος πολὺ τῶν ἀσθενούν-
having. In these was lying a multitude great of the infirm,
των, τυφλῶν, χωλῶν, ξηρῶν, ἐκδεχομένων τὴν τοῦ ὕδατος
blind ones, lame ones, withered ones, awaiting the of the water
4 κίνησιν. ἄγγελος γὰρ κατὰ καιρὸν κατέβαινεν ἐν τῇ
stirring. an angel For at a time descended in the
κολυμβήθρᾳ, καὶ ἐτάρασσε τὸ ὕδωρ· ὁ οὖν πρῶτος ἐμβὰς
pool, and agitated the water. he Then first entering
μετὰ τὴν ταραχὴν τοῦ ὕδατος, ὑγιὴς ἐγίνετο, ᾧ δήποτε
after the agitation of the water, whole became, to what ever
5 κατείχετο νοσήματι. ἦν δέ τις ἄνθρωπος ἐκεῖ τριάκοντα καὶ
he was held by disease. was But a certain man there thirty and
6 ὀκτὼ ἔτη ἔχων ἐν τῇ ἀσθενείᾳ. τοῦτον ἰδὼν ὁ Ἰησοῦς
eight years being in — infirmity. this one, seeing — Jesus,
κατακείμενον, καὶ γνοὺς ὅτι πολὺν ἤδη χρόνον ἔχει, λέγει
lying (there) and knowing that much already time he has (spent), says
7 αὐτῷ, Θέλεις ὑγιὴς γενέσθαι; ἀπεκρίθη αὐτῷ ὁ ἀσθενῶν,
to him, Desire you whole to become? answered Him The sick one,
Κύριε, ἄνθρωπον οὐκ ἔχω ἵνα, ὅταν ταραχθῇ τὸ ὕδωρ,
Lord, a man not I have, that when is agitated the water
βάλλῃ με εἰς τὴν κολυμβήθραν· ἐν ᾧ δὲ ἔρχομαι ἐγώ, ἄλλος
he cast me into the pool; while but am coming I, another

another goes down before me. [8]Jesus said to him, Rise up, Take up your cot and walk! [9]And instantly the man became well, and took up his cot and walked. And it was a sabbath that day. [10]Therefore, the Jews said to the *one* having been healed, It is a sabbath. It is not lawful for you to lift up the cot. [11]He answered them, The *One* making me well, that One said to me, Lift up your cot and walk. [12]Then they asked him, Who is the man who told you, Lift up your cot and walk? [13]But he did not know the *One* who cured him, for a crowd being in that place, Jesus had withdrawn. [14]After these things Jesus found him in the Temple, and said to him, Behold, you have become well; sin no more, that a worse thing not happen to you. [15]The man went away and told the Jews that Jesus is the *One* making him well. [16]And because of this, the Jews persecuted Jesus, and lusted to kill Him, because He did these things on a sabbath. [17]But Jesus answered them, My Father works until now, and I work. [18]Because of this, therefore, the Jews the more lusted to kill Him, for not only did He break the sabbath, but also called God His own Father, making Himself equal to God.

[19]Then Jesus answered and said to them, Truly, truly, I say to you, The Son is not able to do anything from Himself, except what He may see the Father doing. For whatever that One does, these things also the Son does the same way. [20]For the Father loves the Son, and shows to Him all things which He does. And He will show Him greater works than these in order that you may marvel. [21]For even as the Father raises the dead, and gives life, so also the Son gives life to whomever He

8 πρὸ ἐμοῦ καταβαίνει. λέγει αὐτῷ ὁ Ἰησοῦς, Ἔγειραι, ἆρον
before me goes down. says to him Jesus, Rise, Take up
9 τὸν κράββατόν σου, καὶ περιπάτει. καὶ εὐθέως ἐγένετο ὑγιὴς
the mattress of you, and walk! And instantly became whole
ὁ ἄνθρωπος, καὶ ἦρε τὸν κράββατον αὐτοῦ καὶ περιεπάτει.
the man, and took up the mattress of him and walked.
10 Ἦν δὲ σάββατον ἐν ἐκείνῃ τῇ ἡμέρᾳ. ἔλεγον οὖν οἱ
it was And a sabbath on that — day. said Therefore the
Ἰουδαῖοι τῷ τεθεραπευμένῳ, Σάββατόν ἐστιν· οὐκ ἔξεστί
Jews to the (one) having been healed, A sabbath it is; not it is lawful
11 σοι ἆραι τὸν κράββατον. ἀπεκρίθη αὐτοῖς, Ὁ ποιήσας με
for you to lift the mattress. He answered them, The (One) making me
ὑγιῆ, ἐκεῖνός μοι εἶπεν, Ἆρον τὸν κράββατόν σου καὶ
whole, that One to me said, Lift up the mattress of you, and
12 περιπάτει. ἠρώτησαν οὖν αὐτόν, Τίς ἐστιν ὁ ἄνθρωπος ὁ
walk. they asked Therefore him, Who is the man who
13 εἰπών σοι, Ἆρον τὸν κράββατόν σου καὶ περιπάτει; ὁ δὲ
told you, Lift up the mattress of you and walk? he But
ἰαθεὶς οὐκ ᾔδει τίς ἐστιν· ὁ γὰρ Ἰησοῦς ἐξένευσεν, ὄχλου
cured not did know who it is. — For Jesus had withdrawn, a crowd
14 ὄντος ἐν τῷ τόπῳ. μετὰ ταῦτα εὑρίσκει αὐτὸν ὁ Ἰησοῦς
being in the place. After these things finds him — Jesus
ἐν τῷ ἱερῷ, καὶ εἶπεν αὐτῷ, Ἴδε ὑγιὴς γέγονας· μηκέτι
in the Temple, and said to him, Behold, whole you have become; no more
15 ἁμάρτανε, ἵνα μὴ χεῖρόν τί σοι γένηται. ἀπῆλθεν ὁ ἄνθρω-
sin, lest a worse thing to you occur. went away The man
πος, καὶ ἀνήγγειλε τοῖς Ἰουδαίοις ὅτι Ἰησοῦς ἐστιν ὁ ποιή-
and told the Jews that Jesus is He
16 σας αὐτὸν ὑγιῆ. καὶ διὰ τοῦτο ἐδίωκον τὸν Ἰησοῦν οἱ
making him whole. And therefore persecuted — Jesus the
Ἰουδαῖοι, καὶ ἐζήτουν αὐτὸν ἀποκτεῖναι, ὅτι ταῦτα ἐποίει
Jews, and sought Him to kill, because these things He did
17 ἐν σαββάτῳ. ὁ δὲ Ἰησοῦς ἀπεκρίνατο αὐτοῖς, Ὁ πατήρ μου
on a sabbath. — But Jesus answered to them, The Father of Me
18 ἕως ἄρτι ἐργάζεται, κἀγὼ ἐργάζομαι. διὰ τοῦτο οὖν μᾶλλον
until now works, and I work. Because of this, then, the more
ἐζήτουν αὐτὸν οἱ Ἰουδαῖοι ἀποκτεῖναι, ὅτι οὐ μόνον ἔλυε τὸ
sought him the Jews to kill, because not only He broke the
σάββατον, ἀλλὰ καὶ πατέρα ἴδιον ἔλεγε τὸν Θεόν, ἴσον
sabbath, but also Father His own called — God, equal
ἑαυτὸν ποιῶν τῷ Θεῷ.
Himself making — to God.
19 Ἀπεκρίνατο οὖν ὁ Ἰησοῦς καὶ εἶπεν αὐτοῖς, Ἀμὴν ἀμὴν
answered Therefore Jesus and said to them, Truly, truly
λέγω ὑμῖν, οὐ δύναται ὁ υἱὸς ποιεῖν ἀφ' ἑαυτοῦ οὐδέν, ἐὰν
I say to you, not is able the Son to do from Himself nothing, un-
μή τι βλέπῃ τὸν πατέρα ποιοῦντα· ἃ γὰρ ἂν ἐκεῖνος ποιῇ,
less what He may see the Father doing; what For ever that One does,
20 ταῦτα καὶ ὁ υἱὸς ὁμοίως ποιεῖ. ὁ γὰρ πατὴρ φιλεῖ τὸν υἱόν,
these things also the Son likewise does. the For Father loves the Son,
καὶ πάντα δείκνυσιν αὐτῷ ἃ αὐτὸς ποιεῖ καὶ μείζονα τούτων
and all things shows to Him which He does; and greater (than) these
21 δείξει αὐτῷ ἔργα, ἵνα ὑμεῖς θαυμάζητε. ὥσπερ γὰρ ὁ πατὴρ
He will show Him works, that you may marvel. even as For the Father
ἐγείρει τοὺς νεκροὺς καὶ ζωοποιεῖ, οὕτω καὶ ὁ υἱὸς οὓς θέλει
raises up the dead and makes alive so also the Son whom He wills

wills. [22] For the Father judges no one, but has given all judgment to the Son, [23] so that all may honor the Son, even as they honor the Father. The *one* not honoring the Son does not honor the Father who has sent Him. [24] Truly, truly, I say to you, The *one* who hears My word, and believes the *One* who has sent Me, has everlasting life, and does not come into judgment, but has passed out of death into life. [25] Truly, truly, I say to you that an hour is coming, and now is, when the dead will hear the voice of the Son of God, and the ones hearing will live. [26] For even as the Father has life in Himself, so He gave also to the Son to have life in Himself. [27] And He gave authority to Him to also execute judgment, for He is *the* Son of man. [28] Do not marvel at this, for an hour is coming in which all those in the tombs will hear His voice. [29] And *they* will come out, the ones having done good into a resurrection of life; and the ones having practiced evil into a resurrection of judgment.

[30] I am not able to do anything from Myself; just as I hear, I judge; and My judgment is just. For I do not seek My will, but the will of Him sending Me, *the* Father. [31] If I witness concerning Myself, My witness is not true; [32] it is Another that witnesses concerning Me, and I know that the witness which He witnesses concerning Me is true. [33] You have sent to John, and he has testified to the truth. [34] But I do not receive witness from man, but I say these things that you may be saved. [35] That one was the burning and shining lamp, and you were willing to rejoice in his light for an hour. [36] But I have the greater witness than John's, for the works which the Father has given Me, that I

22 ζωοποιεῖ. οὐδὲ γὰρ ὁ πατὴρ κρίνει οὐδένα, ἀλλὰ τὴν κρίσιν
He makes alive. not For the Father judges no one, but — judgment
23 πᾶσαν δέδωκε τῷ υἱῷ· ἵνα πάντες τιμῶσι τὸν υἱόν, καθὼς
all He has given to the Son, that all may honor the Son, even as
τιμῶσι τὸν πατέρα ὁ μὴ τιμῶν τὸν υἱόν, οὐ τιμᾷ τὸν
they honor the Father. He not honoring the Son not does honor the
24 πατέρα τὸν πέμψαντα αὐτόν. ἀμὴν ἀμὴν λέγω ὑμῖν ὅτι ὁ
Father, the (One) having sent Him. Truly, truly I say to you, The (one)
τὸν λόγον μου ἀκούων, καὶ πιστεύων τῷ πέμψαντί με, ἔχει
the word of Me hearing, and believing the (One) having sent Me, has
ζωὴν αἰώνιον· καὶ εἰς κρίσιν οὐκ ἔρχεται, ἀλλὰ μεταβέβηκεν
life everlasting and into judgment not comes, but has passed
25 ἐκ τοῦ θανάτου εἰς τὴν ζωήν. ἀμὴν ἀμὴν λέγω ὑμῖν ὅτι
out of — death into — life. Truly, truly, I say to you, —
ἔρχεται ὥρα καὶ νῦν ἐστιν, ὅτε οἱ νεκροὶ ἀκούσονται τῆς
comes An hour, and now is, when the dead will hear from the
φωνῆς τοῦ υἱοῦ τοῦ Θεοῦ, καὶ οἱ ἀκούσαντες ζήσονται.
voice of the Son — of God, and those hearing will live.
26 ὥσπερ γὰρ ὁ πατὴρ ἔχει ζωὴν ἐν ἑαυτῷ, οὕτως ἔδωκε καὶ
even as For the Father has life in Himself, so He gave also
27 τῷ υἱῷ ζωὴν ἔχειν ἐν ἑαυτῷ· καὶ ἐξουσίαν ἔδωκεν αὐτῷ καὶ
to the Son life to have in Himself. And authority He gave to Him, also
28 κρίσιν ποιεῖν, ὅτι υἱὸς ἀνθρώπου ἐστί. μὴ θαυμάζετε τοῦτο·
judgment to do, because (the) Son of man He is. not Marvel (at) this,
ὅτι ἔρχεται ὥρα, ἐν ᾗ πάντες οἱ ἐν τοῖς μνημείοις ἀκούσονται
for comes an hour in which all those in the tombs will hear
29 τῆς φωνῆς αὐτοῦ, καὶ ἐκπορεύσονται, οἱ τὰ ἀγαθὰ ποιή-
the voice of Him, and will come out; those the good having
σαντες, εἰς ἀνάστασιν ζωῆς· οἱ δὲ τὰ φαῦλα πράξαντες, εἰς
done; into a resurrection of life; those and the evil having practiced into
ἀνάστασιν κρίσεως.
a resurrection of judgment.
30 Οὐ δύναμαι ἐγὼ ποιεῖν ἀπ᾽ ἐμαυτοῦ οὐδέν· καθὼς ἀκούω,
not am able I to do from Myself nothing; just as I hear,
κρίνω· καὶ ἡ κρίσις ἡ ἐμὴ δικαία ἐστίν· ὅτι οὐ ζητῶ τὸ
I judge; and judgment — My just is, because not I seek —
θέλημα τὸ ἐμόν, ἀλλὰ τὸ θέλημα τοῦ πέμψαντός με πατρός.
will — My, but the will of the (One) sending Me, (the) Father.
31 ἐὰν ἐγὼ μαρτυρῶ περὶ ἐμαυτοῦ, ἡ μαρτυρία μου οὐκ ἔστιν
If I witness concerning Myself, the witness of Me not is
32 ἀληθής. ἄλλος ἐστὶν ὁ μαρτυρῶν περὶ ἐμοῦ, καὶ οἶδα ὅτι
true; another there is that witnesses concerning Me, and I know that
33 ἀληθής ἐστιν ἡ μαρτυρία ἣν μαρτυρεῖ περὶ ἐμοῦ. ὑμεῖς
true is the witness which He witnesses concerning Me. You
ἀπεστάλκατε πρὸς Ἰωάννην, καὶ μεμαρτύρηκε τῇ ἀληθείᾳ.
have sent to John, and he has witnessed to the truth;
34 ἐγὼ δὲ οὐ παρὰ ἀνθρώπου τὴν μαρτυρίαν λαμβάνω, ἀλλὰ
I but not from man the witness receive, but
35 ταῦτα λέγω ἵνα ὑμεῖς σωθῆτε. ἐκεῖνος ἦν ὁ λύχνος ὁ καιό-
these things I say that you may be saved. That one was the lamp —
μενος καὶ φαίνων, ὑμεῖς δὲ ἠθελήσατε ἀγαλλιασθῆναι πρὸς
burning and shining; you and were willing to exult for
36 ὥραν ἐν τῷ φωτὶ αὐτοῦ. ἐγὼ δὲ ἔχω τὴν μαρτυρίαν μείζω
an hour in the light of him. I But have the witness greater
τοῦ Ἰωάννου· τὰ γὰρ ἔργα ἃ ἔδωκέ μοι ὁ πατὴρ ἵνα
than of John; the for works which has given Me the Father that

should finish them, the works which I do themselves witness concerning Me, that the Father has sent Me. [37]And the Father who sent Me has Himself borne witness concerning Me. You have neither heard His voice at any time, nor have you seen His form. [38]And you do not have His word abiding in you, for you do not believe the One whom He sent. [39]You search the Scriptures, for you think in them you have everlasting life. And they are the ones witnessing concerning Me. [40]And you are not willing to come to Me that you may have life. [41]I do not receive glory from men; [42]but I have known you, that you do not have the love of God in yourselves. [43]I have come in the name of My Father, and you do not receive Me. If another comes in *his* own name, you will receive that one. [44]How are you able to believe, *you who* receive glory from one another, and the glory which *is* from the only God you do not seek? [45]Do not think that I will accuse you to the Father; there is *one* accusing you, Moses, in whom you have hoped. [46]For if you were believing Moses, you would then believe Me; for that one wrote concerning Me. [47]But if you do not believe his writings, how will you believe My words?

CHAPTER 6

[1]After these things Jesus went away over the Sea of Galilee, the Tiberian *Sea*. [2]And a great crowd followed Him, for they saw His miracles which He did on the sick ones. [3]And Jesus went up into the mountain, and sat with His disciples. [4]And the Passover was near, the feast of the Jews.
[5]Then Jesus lifting up *His* eyes and seeing that a great

τελειώσω αὐτά, αὐτὰ τὰ ἔργα ἃ ἐγὼ ποιῶ, μαρτυρεῖ περὶ
I may finish them, themselves the works that I do witness about
37 ἐμοῦ ὅτι ὁ πατήρ με ἀπέσταλκε. καὶ ὁ πέμψας με πατήρ,
Me, that the Father Me has sent. And He having sent Me (the) Father,
αὐτὸς μεμαρτύρηκε περὶ ἐμοῦ. οὔτε φωνὴν αὐτοῦ ἀκηκόατε
He has witnessed concerning Me. Neither the voice of Him have you heard
38 πώποτε, οὔτε εἶδος αὐτοῦ ἑωράκατε. καὶ τὸν λόγον αὐτοῦ
at any time, nor form His have you seen. And the word of Him
οὐκ ἔχετε μένοντα ἐν ὑμῖν, ὅτι ὃν ἀπέστειλεν ἐκεῖνος, τούτῳ
not you have abiding in you, for whom sent that One, this One
39 ὑμεῖς οὐ πιστεύετε. ἐρευνᾶτε τὰς γραφάς, ὅτι ὑμεῖς δοκεῖτε
you do not believe. You search the Scriptures, because you think
ἐν αὐταῖς ζωὴν αἰώνιον ἔχειν, καὶ ἐκεῖναί εἰσιν αἱ μαρτυ-
in them life everlasting you have, and those are the (ones)
40 ροῦσαι περὶ ἐμοῦ· καὶ οὐ θέλετε ἐλθεῖν πρός με, ἵνα ζωὴν
witnessing about Me. And not you desire to come to Me, that life
41 ἔχητε. δόξαν παρὰ ἀνθρώπων οὐ λαμβάνω· ἀλλ' ἔγνωκα
42 you may have. glory from men not I receive, but I have known
ὑμᾶς, ὅτι τὴν ἀγάπην τοῦ Θεοῦ οὐκ ἔχετε ἐν ἑαυτοῖς.
you, that the love — of God not you have in yourselves.
43 ἐγὼ ἐλήλυθα ἐν τῷ ὀνόματι τοῦ πατρός μου, καὶ οὐ
I have come in the name of the Father of Me, and not
λαμβάνετέ με· ἐὰν ἄλλος ἔλθῃ ἐν τῷ ὀνόματι τῷ ἰδίῳ, ἐκεῖνον
you receive Me; if another comes in — name the own, that one
44 λήψεσθε. πῶς δύνασθε ὑμεῖς πιστεῦσαι, δόξαν παρὰ ἀλλή-
you will receive. How can you believe, glory from one
λων λαμβάνοντες, καὶ τὴν δόξαν τὴν παρὰ τοῦ μόνου Θεοῦ
another receiving, and the glory — from the only God
45 οὐ ζητεῖτε; μὴ δοκεῖτε ὅτι ἐγὼ κατηγορήσω ὑμῶν πρὸς τὸν
not you seek? Do not think that I will accuse you to the
πατέρα· ἔστιν ὁ κατηγορῶν ὑμῶν, Μωσῆς, εἰς ὃν ὑμεῖς
Father; there is the (one) accusing you, Moses, in whom you
46 ἠλπίκατε. εἰ γὰρ ἐπιστεύετε Μωσῇ, ἐπιστεύετε ἂν ἐμοί·
have hoped. if For you were believing Moses, you were believing then Me;
47 περὶ γὰρ ἐμοῦ ἐκεῖνος ἔγραψεν. εἰ δὲ τοῖς ἐκείνου γράμμασιν
about for Me that one wrote. if But the of that one writings
οὐ πιστεύετε, πῶς τοῖς ἐμοῖς ῥήμασι πιστεύσετε;
not you believe, how — My words will you believe?

CHAPTER 6

1 Μετὰ ταῦτα ἀπῆλθεν ὁ Ἰησοῦς πέραν τῆς θαλάσσης τῆς
After these things went away Jesus across the sea —
2 Γαλιλαίας, τῆς Τιβεριάδος. καὶ ἠκολούθει αὐτῷ ὄχλος πολύς,
of Galilee, — of Tiberias. And followed Him a crowd great
ὅτι ἑώρων αὐτοῦ τὰ σημεῖα ἃ ἐποίει ἐπὶ τῶν ἀσθενούντων.
for they saw of Him the signs which He did on the sick ones.
3 ἀνῆλθε δὲ εἰς τὸ ὄρος ὁ Ἰησοῦς, καὶ ἐκεῖ ἐκάθητο μετὰ τῶν
went up And to the mountain Jesus, and there sat with the
4 μαθητῶν αὐτοῦ. ἦν δὲ ἐγγὺς τὸ πάσχα, ἡ ἑορτὴ τῶν
disciples of Him. was And near the Passover, the feast of the
5 Ἰουδαίων. ἐπάρας οὖν ὁ Ἰησοῦς τοὺς ὀφθαλμούς, καὶ
Jews. lifting up Then Jesus the eyes, and
θεασάμενος ὅτι πολὺς ὄχλος ἔρχεται πρὸς αὐτόν, λέγει πρὸς
beholding that a great crowd is coming to Him, He says to
τὸν Φίλιππον, Πόθεν ἀγοράσομεν ἄρτους, ἵνα φάγωσιν
Philip, From where may we buy loaves that may eat

crowd is coming to Him, He said to Philip, From where may we buy loaves that these may eat? 6 But He said this to test him, for He knew what He was about to do. 7 Philip answered Him, Loaves for two hundred denarii are not enough for them, that each of them may receive a little. 8 One of His disciples said to Him, Andrew the brother of Simon Peter, 9 A little boy is here who has five barley loaves and two fish; but what are these for so many? 10 And Jesus said, Make the men to recline. And much grass was in the place, therefore the men reclined, the number about five thousand. 11 And Jesus took the loaves, and giving thanks distributed to the disciples, and the disciples to those reclining. And in the same way the fish, as much as they desired. 12 And when they were filled, He said to His disciples, Gather up the fragments left over, that not anything be lost. 13 Then they gathered and filled twelve handbaskets with fragments of the five barley loaves which were left over to those who had eaten. 14 Then seeing what miracle Jesus did, the men said, This is truly the Prophet, the *one* coming into the world. 15 Then knowing that they were about to come and seize Him, that they might make Him king, Jesus withdrew again to the mountain, alone *by* Himself.

16 And when it became evening, His disciples went down on the sea. 17 And entering into the boat, they were going across the sea to Capernaum. And darkness had already occurred, and Jesus had not come to them. 18 And the sea was aroused by a great wind blowing. 19 Then having rowed about twenty-five or thirty furlongs, they saw Jesus walking on the sea. And *He* having come near the boat, they were afraid. 20 But He said to them, I AM! Do not fear.

6 οὗτοι; τοῦτο δὲ ἔλεγε πειράζων αὐτόν· αὐτὸς γὰρ ᾔδει τί
these? this And He said testing him; He for knew what
7 ἔμελλε ποιεῖν. ἀπεκρίθη αὐτῷ Φίλιππος, Διακοσίων
He was going to do. answered Him Philip, Of two hundred
δηναρίων ἄρτοι οὐκ ἀρκοῦσιν αὐτοῖς, ἵνα ἕκαστος αὐτῶν
denarii loaves not for them, that each of them
8 βραχύ τι λάβῃ. λέγει αὐτῷ εἷς ἐκ τῶν μαθητῶν αὐτοῦ,
a little may receive, says to Him one of the disciples of Him,
9 Ἀνδρέας ὁ ἀδελφὸς Σίμωνος Πέτρου, Ἔστι παιδάριον ἓν
Andrew the brother of Simon Peter, There is little boy one
ὧδε, ὃ ἔχει πέντε ἄρτους κριθίνους καὶ δύο ὀψάρια· ἀλλὰ
here, who has five loaves (of) barley, and two fish; but
10 ταῦτα τί ἐστιν εἰς τοσούτους; εἶπε δὲ ὁ Ἰησοῦς, Ποιήσατε
these what are to so many? said And— Jesus, Make
τοὺς ἀνθρώπους ἀναπεσεῖν. ἦν δὲ χόρτος πολὺς ἐν τῷ τόπῳ.
the men to recline. was And grass much in the place.
ἀνέπεσον οὖν οἱ ἄνδρες τὸν ἀριθμὸν ὡσεὶ πεντακισχίλιοι.
Reclined, therefore, the men, the number about five thousand.
11 ἔλαβε δὲ τοὺς ἄρτους ὁ Ἰησοῦς, καὶ εὐχαριστήσας διέδωκε
took And the loaves — Jesus, and having given thanks dealt out
τοῖς μαθηταῖς, οἱ δὲ μαθηταὶ τοῖς ἀνακειμένοις· ὁμοίως καὶ ἐκ
to the disciples, the and disciples to those reclining; likewise and of
12 τῶν ὀψαρίων ὅσον ἤθελον. ὡς δὲ ἐνεπλήσθησαν, λέγει τοῖς
the fish, as much as they desired. as and they were filled, He says to the
μαθηταῖς αὐτοῦ, Συναγάγετε τὰ περισσεύσαντα κλάσματα,
disciples of Him, Gather together the left over fragments,
13 ἵνα μή τι ἀπόληται. συνήγαγον οὖν, καὶ ἐγέμισαν δώδεκα
that not anything be lost. they gathered Then, and filled twelve
κοφίνους κλασμάτων ἐκ τῶν πέντε ἄρτων τῶν κριθίνων, ἃ
baskets with fragments of the five loaves — (of) barley which
14 ἐπερίσσευσε τοῖς βεβρωκόσιν. οἱ οὖν ἄνθρωποι ἰδόντες ὃ
were left over to those having eaten. the Therefore men seeing what
ἐποίησε σημεῖον ὁ Ἰησοῦς, ἔλεγον ὅτι Οὗτός ἐστιν ἀληθῶς ὁ
did sign — Jesus, said, — This is truly the
15 προφήτης ὁ ἐρχόμενος εἰς τὸν κόσμον. Ἰησοῦς οὖν γνοὺς
prophet, the (one) coming into the world. Jesus Then, knowing
ὅτι μέλλουσιν ἔρχεσθαι καὶ ἁρπάζειν αὐτόν, ἵνα ποιήσωσιν
that they are about to come and seize Him, that they may make
αὐτὸν βασιλέα, ἀνεχώρησε πάλιν εἰς τὸ ὄρος αὐτὸς μόνος.
Him king, withdrew again into the mountain, Himself alone
16 Ὡς δὲ ὀψία ἐγένετο, κατέβησαν οἱ μαθηταὶ αὐτοῦ ἐπὶ τὴν
when And evening it was, went down the disciples of Him on the
17 θάλασσαν, καὶ ἐμβάντες εἰς τὸ πλοῖον, ἤρχοντο πέραν τῆς
sea. And having entered into the boat, they were going across the
θαλάσσης εἰς Καπερναούμ. καὶ σκοτία ἤδη ἐγεγόνει, καὶ οὐκ
sea to Capernaum. And darkness already occurred, and not
18 ἐληλύθει πρὸς αὐτοὺς ὁ Ἰησοῦς. ἥ τε θάλασσα ἀνέμου μεγά-
had come to them — Jesus. And the sea by a wind great
19 λου πνέοντος διηγείρετο. ἐληλακότες οὖν ὡς σταδίους εἰκοσι-
blowing was aroused. having rowed Then about furlongs twenty-
πέντε ἢ τριάκοντα, θεωροῦσι τὸν Ἰησοῦν περιπατοῦντα ἐπὶ
five, or thirty, they behold — Jesus walking on
τῆς θαλάσσης, καὶ ἐγγὺς τοῦ πλοίου γινόμενον· καὶ ἐφοβήθη-
the sea, and near the boat becoming; and they feared.
20 σαν. ὁ δὲ λέγει αὐτοῖς, Ἐγώ εἰμι· μὴ φοβεῖσθε. ἤθελον οὖν
21 He But says to them, I AM! Do not fear. they desired Then

[21]Then they desired to take Him into the boat. And the boat was instantly at the land to which they were going.

[22]On the morrow the crowd standing on the other side of the sea had seen that no other little boat was there, except one, that one into which His disciples entered, and that Jesus did not go with His disciples into the small boat, but that the disciples went away alone. [23]But other small boats came from Tiberias near the place where they ate the bread, the Lord having given thanks.

[24]Therefore, when the crowd saw that Jesus was not there, nor His disciples, they themselves also entered into the boats and came to Capernaum seeking Jesus. [25]And finding Him across the sea, they said to Him, Rabbi, when did you come here? [26]Jesus answered them and said, Truly, truly, I say to you, you seek Me not because you saw miracles, but because you ate of the loaves and were satisfied. [27]Do not labor *for* the food which perishes, but for the food which endures to everlasting life, which the Son of man will give to you; for God the Father sealed this One. [28]Then they said to Him, What may we do that we may work the works of God? [29]Jesus answered and said to them, This is the work of God, that you believe into *Him* whom that One sent. [30]Then they said to Him, Then what miracle do you do, that we may see and may believe you? What do you work? [31]Our fathers ate the manna in the wilderness, as it is written, "He gave them bread out of Heaven to eat." [32]Then Jesus said to them, Truly, truly, I say to you, Moses has not given you the bread out of Heaven, but My Father gives you the true bread out of

λαβεῖν αὐτὸν εἰς τὸ πλοῖον· καὶ εὐθέως τὸ πλοῖον ἐγένετο
to take Him into the boat; and instantly the boat became
ἐπὶ τῆς γῆς εἰς ἣν ὑπῆγον.
at the land to which they were going.
22 Τῇ ἐπαύριον ὁ ὄχλος ὁ ἑστηκὼς πέραν τῆς θαλάσσης,
On the morrow the crowd — standing across the sea
ἰδὼν ὅτι πλοιάριον ἄλλο οὐκ ἦν ἐκεῖ εἰ μὴ ἓν ἐκεῖνο εἰς ὃ
had seen that little boat another not was there, except one, that into which
ἐνέβησαν οἱ μαθηταὶ αὐτοῦ, καὶ ὅτι οὐ συνεισῆλθε τοῖς
entered the disciples of Him; and that not went with the
μαθηταῖς αὐτοῦ ὁ Ἰησοῦς εἰς τὸ πλοιάριον, ἀλλὰ μόνοι οἱ
disciples of Him — Jesus into the but alone the
23 μαθηταὶ αὐτοῦ ἀπῆλθον, (ἄλλα δὲ ἦλθε πλοιάρια ἐκ
disciples of Him went away. other But came little boats from
Τιβεριάδος ἐγγὺς τοῦ τόπου ὅπου ἔφαγον τὸν ἄρτον,
Tiberias near the place where they ate the loaves,
24 εὐχαριστήσαντος τοῦ Κυρίου)· ὅτε οὖν εἶδεν ὁ ὄχλος ὅτι
having given thanks the Lord. when Therefore saw the crowd that
Ἰησοῦς οὐκ ἔστιν ἐκεῖ οὐδὲ οἱ μαθηταὶ αὐτοῦ, ἐνέβησαν καὶ
Jesus not is there, nor the disciples of Him, they entered also
αὐτοὶ εἰς τὰ πλοῖα, καὶ ἦλθον εἰς Καπερναούμ, ζητοῦντες τὸν
themselves into the boats, and came to Capernaum seeking —
25 Ἰησοῦν. καὶ εὑρόντες αὐτὸν πέραν τῆς θαλάσσης, εἶπον
Jesus. And having found Him across the sea, they said
26 αὐτῷ, Ῥαββί, πότε ὧδε γέγονας; ἀπεκρίθη αὐτοῖς ὁ
to Him, Rabbi, when here did you come? answered them —
Ἰησοῦς καὶ εἶπεν, Ἀμὴν ἀμὴν λέγω ὑμῖν, ζητεῖτέ με, οὐχ ὅτι
Jesus and said, Truly, truly, I say to you, You seek Me, not because
εἴδετε σημεῖα, ἀλλ' ὅτι ἐφάγετε ἐκ τῶν ἄρτων καὶ ἐχορτά-
you saw signs, but because you ate of the loaves and were
27 σθητε. ἐργάζεσθε μὴ τὴν βρῶσιν τὴν ἀπολλυμένην, ἀλλὰ
satisfied. Work not (for) the food — perishing, but
τὴν βρῶσιν τὴν μένουσαν εἰς ζωὴν αἰώνιον, ἣν ὁ υἱὸς τοῦ
the food — enduring to life everlasting, which the Son —
ἀνθρώπου ὑμῖν δώσει· τοῦτον γὰρ ὁ πατὴρ ἐσφράγισεν,
of man to you will give; this One for the Father sealed,
28 ὁ Θεός. εἶπον οὖν πρὸς αὐτόν, Τί ποιῶμεν, ἵνα ἐργαζώμεθα
— God. they said Then to Him, What may we do that we may work
29 τὰ ἔργα τοῦ Θεοῦ; ἀπεκρίθη ὁ Ἰησοῦς καὶ εἶπεν αὐτοῖς,
the works — of God? answered — Jesus and said to them,
Τοῦτό ἐστι τὸ ἔργον τοῦ Θεοῦ, ἵνα πιστεύσητε εἰς ὃν
This is the work — of God, that you believe into whom
30 ἀπέστειλεν ἐκεῖνος. εἶπον οὖν αὐτῷ, Τί οὖν ποιεῖς σὺ
sent that One. They said, then, to Him, What then do You
31 σημεῖον, ἵνα ἴδωμεν καὶ πιστεύσωμέν σοι; τί ἐργάζῃ; οἱ
(as) a sign, that we may see and may believe You? What do You work? The
πατέρες ἡμῶν τὸ μάννα ἔφαγον ἐν τῇ ἐρήμῳ, καθώς ἐστι
fathers of us the manna ate in the wilderness, as it is
γεγραμμένον, Ἄρτον ἐκ τοῦ οὐρανοῦ ἔδωκεν αὐτοῖς φαγεῖν.
having been written, Bread out of — Heaven He gave to them to eat.
32 εἶπεν οὖν αὐτοῖς ὁ Ἰησοῦς, Ἀμὴν ἀμὴν λέγω ὑμῖν, Οὐ
said therefore to them — Jesus, Truly, truly, I say to you, not
Μωσῆς δέδωκεν ὑμῖν τὸν ἄρτον ἐκ τοῦ οὐρανοῦ· ἀλλ' ὁ
Moses has given you the bread out of — Heaven, but the
πατήρ μου δίδωσιν ὑμῖν τὸν ἄρτον ἐκ τοῦ οὐρανοῦ τὸν
Father of Me gives to you the bread out of — Heaven —

Heaven. [33]For the bread of God is the *One* coming down out of Heaven and giving life to the world. [34]Then they said to Him, Lord, always give us this bread. [35]Jesus said to them, I am the Bread of life; the *one* coming to Me will not at all hunger, and the *one* believing into Me will never ever thirst.

[36]But I said to you that you also have seen Me and did not believe. [37]All that My Father gives to Me shall come to Me, and the *one* coming to Me I will in no way cast out. [38]For I have not come down out of Heaven that I should do My will, but the will of Him who sent Me. [39]And this is the will of the Father who sent Me, that *of* all that He has given Me, I should not lose *any* of it, but should raise it up at the last day. [40]And this is the will of the *One* who sent Me, that everyone seeing the Son and believing into Him should have everlasting life; and I will raise him up at the last day.

[41]Then the Jews murmured concerning Him, because He said, I am the Bread coming down out of Heaven. [42]And *they* said, Is this not Jesus the son of Joseph, of whom we know the father and the mother? How does this one now say, I have come down out of Heaven? [43]Then Jesus answered and said to them, Do not murmur with one another. [44]No one is able to come to Me unless the Father who sent Me draws him; and I will raise him up in the last day. [45]It has been written in the Prophets, "They shall all be taught of God." So then everyone who hears and learns from the Father comes to Me; [46]not that anyone has seen the Father, except the *One* being from God, He has seen the Father. [47]Truly, truly, I say to you, the *one* believing into Me has everlasting life. [48]I am the Bread of life. [49]Your

33 ἀληθινόν. ὁ γὰρ ἄρτος τοῦ Θεοῦ ἐστιν ὁ καταβαίνων ἐκ τοῦ
true. the For bread — of God is the (One) coming down out of
34 οὐρανοῦ καὶ ζωὴν διδοὺς τῷ κόσμῳ. εἶπον οὖν πρὸς αὐτόν,
Heaven and life giving to the world. They said, then, to Him,
35 Κύριε, πάντοτε δὸς ἡμῖν τὸν ἄρτον τοῦτον. εἶπε δὲ αὐτοῖς
Lord, always give us — bread this. said And to them
ὁ Ἰησοῦς, Ἐγώ εἰμι ὁ ἄρτος τῆς ζωῆς· ὁ ἐρχόμενος πρός με
— Jesus, I am the bread — of life, the (one) coming to Me
οὐ μὴ πεινάσῃ· καὶ ὁ πιστεύων εἰς ἐμὲ οὐ μὴ διψήσῃ
not at all will hunger, and the (one) believing in Me in no way will thirst,
36 πώποτε. ἀλλ' εἶπον ὑμῖν ὅτι καὶ ἑωράκατέ με, καὶ οὐ
ever! But I told you that both you have seen Me, and not
37 πιστεύετε. πᾶν ὃ δίδωσί μοι ὁ πατὴρ πρὸς ἐμὲ ἥξει· καὶ τὸν
believe. All that gives to Me the Father to Me will come, and he
38 ἐρχόμενον πρός με οὐ μὴ ἐκβάλω ἔξω. ὅτι καταβέβηκα ἐκ
coming to Me in no way I will cast out. For I have descended from
τοῦ οὐρανοῦ, οὐχ ἵνα ποιῶ τὸ θέλημα τὸ ἐμόν, ἀλλὰ τὸ
— Heaven not that I may do will — My, but the
39 θέλημα τοῦ πέμψαντός με. τοῦτο δέ ἐστι τὸ θέλημα τοῦ
will of the (One) sending Me. this And is the will of the
πέμψαντός με πατρός, ἵνα πᾶν ὃ δέδωκέ μοι, μὴ ἀπολέσω
having sent Me Father, that all which He has given Me, not I shall lose
40 ἐξ αὐτοῦ, ἀλλὰ ἀναστήσω αὐτὸ ἐν τῇ ἐσχάτῃ ἡμέρᾳ. τοῦτο
of it, but shall raise up it in the last day. this
δέ ἐστι τὸ θέλημα τοῦ πέμψαντός με, ἵνα πᾶς ὁ θεωρῶν τὸν
And is the will of the (One) sending Me, that everyone seeing the
υἱὸν καὶ πιστεύων εἰς αὐτόν, ἔχῃ ζωὴν αἰώνιον, καὶ ἀνα-
Son and believing in Him should have life everlasting; and will
στήσω αὐτὸν ἐγὼ τῇ ἐσχάτῃ ἡμέρᾳ.
raise up him I at the last day.
41 Ἐγόγγυζον οὖν οἱ Ἰουδαῖοι περὶ αὐτοῦ, ὅτι εἶπεν, Ἐγώ
murmured Therefore the Jews concerning Him, because He said, I
42 εἰμι ὁ ἄρτος ὁ καταβὰς ἐκ τοῦ οὐρανοῦ. καὶ ἔλεγον, Οὐχ
am the bread — coming down out of Heaven. And they said, not
οὗτός ἐστιν Ἰησοῦς ὁ υἱὸς Ἰωσήφ, οὗ ἡμεῖς οἴδαμεν τὸν
this Is Jesus the son of Joseph, of whom we know the
πατέρα καὶ τὴν μητέρα; πῶς οὖν λέγει οὗτος ὅτι Ἐκ τοῦ
father and the mother? How now says this one — Out of —
43 οὐρανοῦ καταβέβηκα; ἀπεκρίθη οὖν ὁ Ἰησοῦς καὶ εἶπεν αὐτοῖς,
Heaven I have come down? answered Then Jesus and said to them,
44 Μὴ γογγύζετε μετ' ἀλλήλων. οὐδεὶς δύναται ἐλθεῖν πρός με,
Do not murmur with one another. No one is able to come to Me
ἐὰν μὴ ὁ πατὴρ ὁ πέμψας με ἑλκύσῃ αὐτόν, καὶ ἐγὼ ἀναστή-
unless the Father who sent Me draws him, and I will raise
45 σω αὐτὸν τῇ ἐσχάτῃ ἡμέρᾳ. ἔστι γεγραμμένον ἐν τοῖς προφή-
up him in the last day. It is having been written in the prophets,
ταις, Καὶ ἔσονται πάντες διδακτοὶ τοῦ Θεοῦ. πᾶς οὖν ὁ
And they shall be all taught — of God; everyone, then,
46 ἀκούσας παρὰ τοῦ πατρὸς καὶ μαθών, ἔρχεται πρός με. οὐχ
hearing from the Father and learning, comes to Me. Not
ὅτι τὸν πατέρα τις ἑώρακεν, εἰ μὴ ὁ ὢν παρὰ τοῦ Θεοῦ,
that the Father anyone has seen, except the (One) being from God,
47 οὗτος ἑώρακε τὸν πατέρα. ἀμὴν ἀμὴν λέγω ὑμῖν, ὁ πιστεύων
this One has seen the Father. Truly, truly, I say to you, he believing
48 εἰς ἐμέ, ἔχει ζωὴν αἰώνιον. ἐγώ εἰμι ὁ ἄρτος τῆς ζωῆς. οἱ
49 in Me has life everlasting. I am the bread — of life. The

fathers ate the manna in the wilderness, and died. [50]This is the Bread coming down out of Heaven, that anyone may eat of it and not die. [51]I am the Living Bread that came down from Heaven. If anyone eats of this Bread, he will live forever. And indeed the bread which I will give is My flesh, which I will give for the life of the world.

[52]Then the Jews argued with one another, saying, How can this one give us *his* flesh to eat? [53]Then Jesus said to them, Truly, truly, I say to you, Except you eat the flesh of the Son of man, and drink His blood, you do not have life in yourselves. [54]The *one* partaking of My flesh and drinking of My blood has everlasting life, and I will raise him up at the last day. [55]For My flesh is truly food, and My blood is truly drink. [56]The *one* partaking of My flesh and drinking of My blood abides in Me, and I in him. [57]Even as the living Father sent Me, and I live through the Father, also the *one* partaking Me, even that one will live through Me. [58]This is the Bread which came down out of Heaven, not as your fathers ate the manna, and died; the *one* partaking of this Bread will live forever. [59]He said these things teaching in a synagogue in Capernaum.

[60]Then many of His disciples having heard, *they* said, This word is hard; who is able to hear it? [61]But knowing in Himself that His disciples were murmuring about this, Jesus said to them, Does this offend you? [62]Then *what* if you see the Son of man going up where He was at first? [63]It is the Spirit that gives life. The flesh does not profit— nothing! The words which I speak are spirit and are life.

πατέρες ὑμῶν ἔφαγον τὸ μάννα ἐν τῇ ἐρήμῳ, καὶ ἀπέθανον.
fathers of you ate the manna in the wilderness, and died.
50 οὗτός ἐστιν ὁ ἄρτος ὁ ἐκ τοῦ οὐρανοῦ καταβαίνων, ἵνα τις
This is the bread out of — Heaven coming down, that anyone
51 ἐξ αὐτοῦ φάγῃ καὶ μὴ ἀποθάνῃ. ἐγώ εἰμι ὁ ἄρτος ὁ ζῶν, ὁ ἐκ
of it may eat and not die. I am the bread — living that from
τοῦ οὐρανοῦ καταβάς· ἐάν τις φάγῃ ἐκ τούτου τοῦ ἄρτου,
— Heaven came down; if anyone eats of this — bread,
ζήσεται εἰς τὸν αἰῶνα. καὶ ὁ ἄρτος δὲ ὃν ἐγὼ δώσω, ἡ σάρξ
he will live to the age. indeed the bread And which I will give, the flesh
μου ἐστίν, ἣν ἐγὼ δώσω ὑπὲρ τῆς τοῦ κόσμου ζωῆς.
of Me is, which I will give for the of the world life.
52 Ἐμάχοντο οὖν πρὸς ἀλλήλους οἱ Ἰουδαῖοι λέγοντες, Πῶς
Argued therefore with one another the Jews, saying How
53 δύναται οὗτος ἡμῖν δοῦναι τὴν σάρκα φαγεῖν; εἶπεν οὖν
can this one us give the flesh to eat? said Then
αὐτοῖς ὁ Ἰησοῦς, Ἀμὴν ἀμὴν λέγω ὑμῖν, ἐὰν μὴ φάγητε τὴν
to them — Jesus, Truly, truly, I say to you, Except you eat the
σάρκα τοῦ υἱοῦ τοῦ ἀνθρώπου καὶ πίητε αὐτοῦ τὸ αἷμα,
flesh of the Son — of man and drink of Him the blood,
54 οὐκ ἔχετε ζωὴν ἐν ἑαυτοῖς. ὁ τρώγων μου τὴν σάρκα καὶ
not you do have life in yourselves. He partaking of Me the flesh and
πίνων μου τὸ αἷμα, ἔχει ζωὴν αἰώνιον, καὶ ἐγὼ ἀναστήσω
drinking of Me the blood has life everlasting, and I will raise up
55 αὐτὸν τῇ ἐσχάτῃ ἡμέρᾳ. ἡ γὰρ σάρξ μου ἀληθῶς ἐστι
him at the last day the For flesh of Me truly is
56 βρῶσις, καὶ τὸ αἷμά μου ἀληθῶς ἐστι πόσις. ὁ τρώγων μου
food, and the blood of Me truly is drink. He partaking of Me
τὴν σάρκα καὶ πίνων μου τὸ αἷμα, ἐν ἐμοὶ μένει, κἀγὼ ἐν
the flesh and drinking of Me the blood in Me abides, and I in
57 αὐτῷ. καθὼς ἀπέστειλέ με ὁ ζῶν πατήρ, κἀγὼ ζῶ διὰ τὸν
him. Even as sent Me the living Father, and I live via the
58 πατέρα· καὶ ὁ τρώγων με, κἀκεῖνος ζήσεται δι' ἐμέ. οὗτός
Father, also he partaking Me, even that one will live via Me. This
ἐστιν ὁ ἄρτος ὁ ἐκ τοῦ οὐρανοῦ καταβάς· οὐ καθὼς ἔφαγον
is the bread which out of Heaven came down, not as ate
οἱ πατέρες ὑμῶν τὸ μάννα, καὶ ἀπέθανον· ὁ τρώγων τοῦτον
the fathers of you the manna, and died; he partaking this
59 τὸν ἄρτον, ζήσεται εἰς τὸν αἰῶνα. ταῦτα εἶπεν ἐν συναγωγῇ
— bread will live to the age. These things He said in a synagogue
διδάσκων ἐν Καπερναούμ.
teaching in Capernaum.
60 Πολλοὶ οὖν ἀκούσαντες ἐκ τῶν μαθητῶν αὐτοῦ εἶπον,
many Therefore hearing of the disciples of Him said,
Σκληρός ἐστιν οὗτος ὁ λόγος· τίς δύναται αὐτοῦ ἀκούειν;
Hard is this — word; who is able it to hear?
61 εἰδὼς δὲ ὁ Ἰησοῦς ἐν ἑαυτῷ ὅτι γογγύζουσι περὶ τούτου
knowing But Jesus in Himself that are murmuring about this
οἱ μαθηταὶ αὐτοῦ, εἶπεν αὐτοῖς, Τοῦτο ὑμᾶς σκανδαλίζει;
the disciples of Him, He said to them, Does this you offend?
62 ἐὰν οὖν θεωρῆτε τὸν υἱὸν τοῦ ἀνθρώπου ἀναβαίνοντα ὅπου
If then you behold the Son — of man going up where
63 ἦν τὸ πρότερον; τὸ πνεῦμά ἐστι τὸ ζωοποιοῦν, ἡ σὰρξ οὐκ
He was at first? The Spirit it is (that) makes alive; the flesh not
ὠφελεῖ οὐδέν· τὰ ῥήματα ἃ ἐγὼ λαλῶ ὑμῖν, πνεῦμά ἐστι
profits nothing; the words which I speak to you spirit is

[64] But there are some of you who are not believing. For Jesus knew from *the* beginning who they were who did not believe, and who was the *one* betraying Him. [65] And He said, For this reason I have told you that no one is able to come to Me except it is given to him from My Father.

[66] From this *time* many of His disciples went away into the things behind, and no longer walked with Him. [67] Therefore, Jesus said to the Twelve, Do you also wish to go? [68] Then Simon Peter answered Him, Lord, to whom shall we go? You have *the* words of eternal life. [69] And we have believed and have known that You are the Christ, the Son of the living God. [70] Jesus answered them, Did I not choose you, the Twelve? Yet one *of* you is a devil! [71] But He spoke *of* Judas Iscariot, Simon's *son*, for this one was about to betray Him, being one of the Twelve.

CHAPTER 7

[1] And after these things Jesus was walking in Galilee; for He did not desire to walk in Judea, because the Jews were lusting to kill Him. [2] And the Jewish Feast of the Tabernacles was near. [3] Therefore, His brothers said to Him, Move away from here and go to Judea, so that your disciples will also see your works which you do— [4] for no one does anything in secret, and himself seeks to be in public. If you do these things, reveal yourself to the world. [5] For His brothers did not believe into Him. [6] Then Jesus said to them, My time is not yet here, but your time is always ready. [7] The world cannot

64 καὶ ζωή ἐστιν. ἀλλ' εἰσὶν ἐξ ὑμῶν τινες οἳ οὐ πιστεύουσιν.
and life is. But are of you some who not are believing
ᾔδει γὰρ ἐξ ἀρχῆς ὁ Ἰησοῦς, τίνες εἰσὶν οἱ μὴ πιστεύοντες,
knew For from beginning Jesus who are those not believing,
65 καὶ τίς ἐστιν ὁ παραδώσων αὐτόν. καὶ ἔλεγε, Διὰ τοῦτο
and who is the (one) betraying Him. And He said, Therefore
εἴρηκα ὑμῖν, ὅτι οὐδεὶς δύναται ἐλθεῖν πρός με, ἐὰν μὴ ᾖ
I have told you, that no one is able to come to Me unless it is
δεδομένον αὐτῷ ἐκ τοῦ πατρός μου.
given to him from the Father of Me.
66 Ἐκ τούτου πολλοὶ ἀπῆλθον τῶν μαθητῶν αὐτοῦ εἰς
From this many went away of the disciples of Him into
67 τὰ ὀπίσω, καὶ οὐκέτι μετ' αὐτοῦ περιεπάτουν. εἶπεν οὖν ὁ
the things behind, and no longer with Him walked. said Therefore
68 Ἰησοῦς τοῖς δώδεκα, Μὴ καὶ ὑμεῖς θέλετε ὑπάγειν; ἀπεκρίθη
Jesus to the twelve, Not also you wish to go? answered
οὖν αὐτῷ Σίμων Πέτρος, Κύριε, πρὸς τίνα ἀπελευσόμεθα;
Then Him Simon Peter, Lord, to whom shall we go?
69 ῥήματα ζωῆς αἰωνίου ἔχεις. καὶ ἡμεῖς πεπιστεύκαμεν καὶ
words of life eternal You have. And we have believed and
ἐγνώκαμεν ὅτι σὺ εἶ ὁ Χριστὸς ὁ υἱὸς τοῦ Θεοῦ τοῦ ζῶντος.
have known that You are the Christ, the Son — of God the living.
70 ἀπεκρίθη αὐτοῖς ὁ Ἰησοῦς, Οὐκ ἐγὼ ὑμᾶς τοὺς δώδεκα
answered them — Jesus, Did not I you the twelve
71 ἐξελεξάμην, καὶ ἐξ ὑμῶν εἷς διάβολός ἐστιν; ἔλεγε δὲ τὸν
choose? And (of) you one a devil is. He spoke And —
Ἰούδαν Σίμωνος Ἰσκαριώτην· οὗτος γὰρ ἤμελλεν αὐτὸν
Judas of Simon Iscariot; this one for was about Him
παραδιδόναι, εἷς ὢν ἐκ τῶν δώδεκα.
to betray, one being of the twelve.

CHAPTER 7

1 Καὶ περιεπάτει ὁ Ἰησοῦς μετὰ ταῦτα ἐν τῇ Γαλιλαίᾳ· οὐ
And was walking — Jesus after these things in — Galilee; not
γὰρ ἤθελεν ἐν τῇ Ἰουδαίᾳ περιπατεῖν, ὅτι ἐζήτουν αὐτὸν
For He desired in — Judea to walk, because were seeking Him
2 οἱ Ἰουδαῖοι ἀποκτεῖναι. ἦν δὲ ἐγγὺς ἡ ἑορτὴ τῶν Ἰουδαίων
the Jews to kill. was And near the feast of the Jews,
3 ἡ σκηνοπηγία. εἶπον οὖν πρὸς αὐτὸν οἱ ἀδελφοὶ αὐτοῦ,
The Tabernacles. said Therefore to Him the brothers of Him,
Μετάβηθι ἐντεῦθεν, καὶ ὕπαγε εἰς τὴν Ἰουδαίαν, ἵνα καὶ οἱ
Depart from here, and go to — Judea, that also the
4 μαθηταί σου θεωρήσωσι τὰ ἔργα σου ἃ ποιεῖς. οὐδεὶς γὰρ
disciples of you will behold the works of you which you do. no one For
ἐν κρυπτῷ τι ποιεῖ, καὶ ζητεῖ αὐτὸς ἐν παρρησίᾳ εἶναι. εἰ
in secret anything does, and seeks himself in public to be. If
5 ταῦτα ποιεῖς, φανέρωσον σεαυτὸν τῷ κόσμῳ. οὐδὲ γὰρ οἱ
these things you do, reveal yourself to the world. not even For the
6 ἀδελφοὶ αὐτοῦ ἐπίστευον εἰς αὐτόν. λέγει οὖν αὐτοῖς ὁ
brothers of Him believed in Him. says Then to them —
Ἰησοῦς, Ὁ καιρὸς ὁ ἐμὸς οὔπω πάρεστιν, ὁ δὲ καιρὸς ὁ
Jesus, The time — of Me not yet is present, but time —
7 ὑμέτερος πάντοτέ ἐστιν ἕτοιμος. οὐ δύναται ὁ κόσμος
your always is ready. not is able The world
μισεῖν ὑμᾶς· ἐμὲ δὲ μισεῖ, ὅτι ἐγὼ μαρτυρῶ περὶ αὐτοῦ, ὅτι
to hate you; Me but it hates, because I witness about it, that

hate you; but it hates Me because I witness about it, that its works are evil. [8]You go up to this feast. I am not yet going up to the feast, for My time has not yet been fulfilled. [9]And saying these things to them, He remained in Galilee.

[10]But when His brothers went up, then He also went up to the feast–not openly, but as in secret. [11]Then the Jews sought Him in the feast, and said, Where is He? [12]And there was much murmuring about Him in the crowds. Some said, he is good; but others said, No, but he deceives the crowd. [13]However, no one publicly spoke about Him, because of the fear of the Jews.

[14]But the feast now being half over, Jesus went up into the Temple and was teaching. [15]And the Jews marveled, saying, How does this one know letters, not being taught? [16]Jesus answered them and said, My teaching is not Mine, but of the *One* who sent Me. [17]If anyone desires to do His will, he will know concerning the teaching, whether it is of God, or I speak from Myself. [18]The *one* speaking from himself seeks *his* own glory. But the *one* seeking the glory of the *One* who sent Him, this One is true, and unrighteousness is not in Him. [19]Has not Moses given you the Law, and not one of you does the Law? Why do you lust to kill Me? [20]The crowd answered and said, You have a demon. Who lusts to kill you? [21]Jesus answered and said to them, I did one work, and you all marvel. [22]Because of this Moses has given you circumcision; not that it is of Moses, but of the fathers. And on a sabbath you circumcise a man. [23]If a man receives circumcision on a sabbath, so that the Law of Moses is not broken, are you angry with Me because I made a

8 τὰ ἔργα αὐτοῦ πονηρά ἐστιν. ὑμεῖς ἀνάβητε εἰς τὴν ἑορτὴν
the works of it evil are. You go up to feast
ταύτην· ἐγὼ οὔπω ἀναβαίνω εἰς τὴν ἑορτὴν ταύτην, ὅτι ὁ
this; I not yet am going to – feast this, because
9 καιρὸς ὁ ἐμὸς οὔπω πεπλήρωται. ταῦτα δὲ εἰπὼν αὐτοῖς,
time My not yet has been fulfilled. these things And saying to them,
ἔμεινεν ἐν τῇ Γαλιλαίᾳ.
He stayed in – Galilee.
10 Ὡς δὲ ἀνέβησαν οἱ ἀδελφοὶ αὐτοῦ, τότε καὶ αὐτὸς ἀνέβη
when But went up the brothers of Him, then also He went up
11 εἰς τὴν ἑορτήν, οὐ φανερῶς, ἀλλ' ὡς ἐν κρυπτῷ. οἱ οὖν
to the feast, not openly, but as in secret. the Then
Ἰουδαῖοι ἐζήτουν αὐτὸν ἐν τῇ ἑορτῇ, καὶ ἔλεγον, Ποῦ ἐστιν
the Jews sought Him in the feast, and said, Where is
12 ἐκεῖνος; καὶ γογγυσμὸς πολὺς περὶ αὐτοῦ ἦν ἐν τοῖς ὄχλοις
that one? And murmuring much about Him was in the crowds;
οἱ μὲν ἔλεγον ὅτι Ἀγαθός ἐστιν· ἄλλοι δὲ ἔλεγον, Οὔ, ἀλλὰ
some said, – A good one He is; others but said, No, but
13 πλανᾷ τὸν ὄχλον. οὐδεὶς μέντοι παρρησίᾳ ἐλάλει περὶ αὐτοῦ
he deceives the crowd. No one however publicly spoke about Him,
διὰ τὸν φόβον τῶν Ἰουδαίων.
because of the fear of the Jews.
14 Ἤδη δὲ τῆς ἑορτῆς μεσούσης, ἀνέβη ὁ Ἰησοῦς εἰς τὸ ἱερόν,
now But the feast being in middle went up Jesus to the Temple
15 καὶ ἐδίδασκε. καὶ ἐθαύμαζον οἱ Ἰουδαῖοι λέγοντες, Πῶς οὗτος
and taught. And marveled the Jews, saying, How this one
16 γράμματα οἶδε, μὴ μεμαθηκώς; ἀπεκρίθη αὐτοῖς ὁ Ἰησοῦς
letters knows, not being taught? answered them – Jesus
καὶ εἶπεν, Ἡ ἐμὴ διδαχὴ οὐκ ἔστιν ἐμή, ἀλλὰ τοῦ πέμψαντός
and said, My teaching not is Mine, but of the (One) sending
17 με. ἐάν τις θέλῃ τὸ θέλημα αὐτοῦ ποιεῖν, γνώσεται περὶ τῆς
Me. If anyone desires the will of Him to do, he will know concerning the
διδαχῆς, πότερον ἐκ τοῦ Θεοῦ ἐστιν, ἢ ἐγὼ ἀπ' ἐμαυτοῦ
teaching, whether of – God it is, or I from Myself
18 λαλῶ. ὁ ἀφ' ἑαυτοῦ λαλῶν, τὴν δόξαν τὴν ἰδίαν ζητεῖ· ὁ δὲ
speak. The (one) from himself speaking the glory – own seeks; he But
ζητῶν τὴν δόξαν τοῦ πέμψαντος αὐτόν, οὗτος ἀληθής ἐστι,
seeking the glory of the (One) sending Him, this one true is,
19 καὶ ἀδικία ἐν αὐτῷ οὐκ ἔστιν. οὐ Μωσῆς δέδωκεν ὑμῖν τὸν
and unrighteousness in him not is. Did not Moses give you the
νόμον, καὶ οὐδεὶς ἐξ ὑμῶν ποιεῖ τὸν νόμον; τί με ζητεῖτε
law, and no one of you does the law. Why Me seek you
20 ἀποκτεῖναι; ἀπεκρίθη ὁ ὄχλος καὶ εἶπε, Δαιμόνιον ἔχεις· τίς
to kill? answered the crowd and said, A demon you have, Who
21 σε ζητεῖ ἀποκτεῖναι; ἀπεκρίθη ὁ Ἰησοῦς καὶ εἶπεν αὐτοῖς,
you seeks to kill? answered – Jesus and said to them,
22 Ἓν ἔργον ἐποίησα, καὶ πάντες θαυμάζετε. διὰ τοῦτο Μωσῆς
One work I did, and all you marvel. Because of this Moses
δέδωκεν ὑμῖν τὴν περιτομήν (οὐχ ὅτι ἐκ τοῦ Μωσέως ἐστίν,
has given you – circumcision; not that of – Moses it is,
ἀλλ' ἐκ τῶν πατέρων)· καὶ ἐν σαββάτῳ περιτέμνετε
but of the fathers; and on a sabbath you circumcise
23 ἄνθρωπον. εἰ περιτομὴν λαμβάνει ἄνθρωπος ἐν σαββάτῳ,
a man. If circumcision receives a man on a sabbath,
ἵνα μὴ λυθῇ ὁ νόμος Μωσέως, ἐμοὶ χολᾶτε ὅτι ὅλον ἄνθρω-
that not is broken the law of Moses, with Me are you angry that a whole man

man entirely sound on a sabbath? 24 Do not judge according to sight, but judge righteous judgment.

25 Then some of the Jerusalemites said, Is this not the one they are seeking to kill? 26 And, behold, He speaks publicly, and they say nothing to him. Perhaps the rulers truly knew that this is indeed the Christ? 27 But we know this one, from where he is. But when the Christ comes, no one knows from where He is.

28 Then Jesus cried out in the Temple, and saying, You both know Me, and you know from where I am. And I have not come from Myself, but He sending Me is true, whom you do not know. 29 But I know Him, because I am from Him; and He sent Me. 30 Then they lusted to seize Him; yet no one laid *a* hand on Him, because His hour had not yet come. 31 But many of the crowd believed into Him, and said, The Christ, when He comes, will He do more miracles than these which this One did?

32 The Pharisees heard the crowd murmuring these things about Him, and the Pharisees and the scribes sent officers that they might seize Him. 33 Therefore, Jesus said to them, Yet a little while I am with you, and I go to Him who sent Me.

34 You will seek Me, and will not find *Me*, and where I am you are not able to come. 35 Then the Jews said amongst themselves, Where is this one about to go that we will not find him? Is he about to go to the Dispersion of the Greeks, and to teach the Greeks? 36 What is this word which he said, You will seek Me and will not find *Me*, and where I am, you are not able to come?

37 And in the last day of the great feast, Jesus stood and

24 που ὑγιῆ ἐποίησα ἐν σαββάτῳ ; μὴ κρίνετε κατ' ὄψιν, ἀλλὰ
healthy I made on a sabbath? Do not judge by sight, but
τὴν δικαίαν κρίσιν κρίνατε.
— righteous judgment judge.
25 Ἔλεγον οὖν τινες ἐκ τῶν Ἱεροσολυμιτῶν, Οὐχ οὗτός ἐστιν
said Therefore some of the Jerusalemites not this one Is it
26 ὃν ζητοῦσιν ἀποκτεῖναι ; καὶ ἴδε παρρησίᾳ λαλεῖ, καὶ οὐδὲν
whom they are seeking to kill? And behold, publicly He speaks, and nothing
αὐτῷ λέγουσι. μήποτε ἀληθῶς ἔγνωσαν οἱ ἄρχοντες ὅτι
to Him they say. Perhaps truly knew the rulers that
27 οὗτός ἐστιν ἀληθῶς ὁ Χριστός ; ἀλλὰ τοῦτον οἴδαμεν πόθεν
this is indeed the Christ? But this one we know from where
ἐστίν· ὁ δὲ Χριστὸς ὅταν ἔρχηται, οὐδεὶς γινώσκει πόθεν
he is; the but Christ when comes, no one knows from where
28 ἐστίν. ἔκραξεν οὖν ἐν τῷ ἱερῷ διδάσκων ὁ Ἰησοῦς καὶ λέγων,
He is. cried out Then in the Temple teaching — Jesus, and saying,
Κἀμὲ οἴδατε, καὶ οἴδατε πόθεν εἰμί· καὶ ἀπ' ἐμαυτοῦ οὐκ
And Me you know, and you know from where I am; and from Myself not
ἐλήλυθα, ἀλλ' ἔστιν ἀληθινὸς ὁ πέμψας με, ὃν ὑμεῖς οὐκ
I have come, but He is true, the (One) sending Me, whom you not
29 οἴδατε. ἐγὼ δὲ οἶδα αὐτόν, ὅτι παρ' αὐτοῦ εἰμι, κἀκεῖνός με
do know. I But know Him, because from Him I am, and that One Me
30 ἀπέστειλεν. ἐζήτουν οὖν αὐτὸν πιάσαι. καὶ οὐδεὶς ἐπέβαλεν
sent. they sought Then Him to seize; and no one laid
ἐπ' αὐτὸν τὴν χεῖρα, ὅτι οὔπω ἐληλύθει ἡ ὥρα αὐτοῦ.
on Him the hand, because not yet had come the hour of Him.
31 πολλοὶ δὲ ἐκ τοῦ ὄχλου ἐπίστευσαν εἰς αὐτόν, καὶ ἔλεγον
many But of the crowd believed in Him, and said,
ὅτι Ὁ Χριστὸς ὅταν ἔλθῃ, μήτι πλείονα σημεῖα τούτων
— The Christ, when He comes, not greater signs than these
32 ποιήσει ὧν οὗτος ἐποίησεν ; ἤκουσαν οἱ Φαρισαῖοι τοῦ
will He do which this One did? Heard the Pharisees the
ὄχλου γογγύζοντος περὶ αὐτοῦ ταῦτα· καὶ ἀπέστειλαν οἱ
crowd murmuring concerning Him these things and sent the
Φαρισαῖοι καὶ οἱ ἀρχιερεῖς ὑπηρέτας ἵνα πιάσωσιν αὐτόν.
Pharisees and the chief priests officers, that they might seize Him.
33 εἶπεν οὖν αὐτοῖς ὁ Ἰησοῦς, Ἔτι μικρὸν χρόνον μεθ' ὑμῶν
said Therefore to them Jesus, Yet a little time with you
34 εἰμι, καὶ ὑπάγω πρὸς τὸν πέμψαντά με. ζητήσετέ με, καὶ
I am, and I go to the (One) sending Me. You will seek Me, and
οὐχ εὑρήσετε· καὶ ὅπου εἰμὶ ἐγώ, ὑμεῖς οὐ δύνασθε ἐλθεῖν.
not will find, and where am I, you not are able to come.
35 εἶπον οὖν οἱ Ἰουδαῖοι πρὸς ἑαυτούς, Ποῦ οὗτος μέλλει
said Then the Jews to themselves, Where this one is about
πορεύεσθαι ὅτι ἡμεῖς οὐχ εὑρήσομεν αὐτόν ; μὴ εἰς τὴν
to go that we not will find Him? not to the
διασπορὰν τῶν Ἑλλήνων μέλλει πορεύεσθαι, καὶ διδάσκειν
Dispersion of the Greeks is he about to go, and to teach
36 τοὺς Ἕλληνας ; τίς ἐστιν οὗτος ὁ λόγος ὃν εἶπε, Ζητήσετέ
the Greeks? What is this — word which He said: You will see
με, καὶ οὐχ εὑρήσετε· καὶ ὅπου εἰμὶ ἐγώ, ὑμεῖς οὐ δύνασθε
Me, and not you will find, and where am I, you not are able
ἐλθεῖν ;
to come?
37 Ἐν δὲ τῇ ἐσχάτῃ ἡμέρᾳ τῇ μεγάλῃ τῆς ἑορτῆς εἱστήκει
in And the last day, the great, of the feast stood

cried out, saying, If anyone thirsts, let him come to Me and drink. 38 The *one* believing into Me, as the Scripture said, "Out of his belly will flow rivers of living water." 39 But He said this concerning the Spirit, whom the ones believing into Him were about to receive; for *the* Holy Spirit was not yet *given*, because Jesus was not yet glorified.

40 Then hearing the word, many of the crowd said, This is truly the Prophet. 41 Others said, This is the Christ. But others said, No! For does the Christ come out of Galilee? 42 Has not the Scripture said that the Christ comes from the seed of David, and from Bethlehem, the village where David was? 43 Therefore, a division occurred in the crowd because of Him. 44 And some of them desired to seize Him, but no one laid hands on Him.

45 Then the officers came to the chief priests and Pharisees, and they said to them, Why did you not bring him? 46 The officers answered, Never did a man so speak as does this man. 47 Then the Pharisees answered them, Have you not also been deceived? 48 Has any from the rulers believed into him, or from the Pharisees? 49 But not knowing the Law this crowd is cursed. 50 Nicodemus said to them—the *one* coming *by* night to Him, being one of themselves— Our Law does not judge the man unless it hear from him first, and know what he does? 52 They answered and said to him, Are you also from Galilee? Search the Scripture and see that a prophet has not been raised out of Galilee.

And they each one went to his house.

CHAPTER 8

1 But Jesus went to the

ὁ Ἰησοῦς καὶ ἔκραξε, λέγων, Ἐάν τις διψᾷ, ἐρχέσθω πρός
— Jesus and cried out, saying, If anyone thirst, let him come to

38 με καὶ πινέτω. ὁ πιστεύων εἰς ἐμέ, καθὼς εἶπεν ἡ γραφή,
Me and drink. He believing into Me, as said the Writing,

ποταμοὶ ἐκ τῆς κοιλίας αὐτοῦ ῥεύσουσιν ὕδατος ζῶντος.
rivers out of the belly of him will flow water of living.

39 τοῦτο δὲ εἶπε περὶ τοῦ Πνεύματος οὗ ἔμελλον λαμβάνειν οἱ
this But He said about the Spirit whom were about to receive those

πιστεύοντες εἰς αὐτόν· οὔπω γὰρ ἦν Πνεῦμα Ἅγιον, ὅτι
believing in Him; not yet for was (the) Spirit Holy, because,

40 ὁ Ἰησοῦς οὐδέπω ἐδοξάσθη. πολλοὶ οὖν ἐκ τοῦ ὄχλου
— Jesus not yet was glorified. Many therefore of the crowd

ἀκούσαντες τὸν λόγον ἔλεγον, Οὗτός ἐστιν ἀληθῶς ὁ προφή-
hearing the word said, This is truly the prophet.

41 της. ἄλλοι ἔλεγον, Οὗτός ἐστιν ὁ Χριστός. ἄλλοι δὲ ἔλεγον,
Others said, This is the Christ. others But said, (No!)

42 Μὴ γὰρ ἐκ τῆς Γαλιλαίας ὁ Χριστὸς ἔρχεται; οὐχὶ ἡ γραφὴ
not For out of — Galilee the Christ comes? Has not the Scripture

εἶπεν ὅτι ἐκ τοῦ σπέρματος Δαβίδ, καὶ ἀπὸ Βηθλεέμ, τῆς
said that out of the seed of David, and from Bethlehem, the

43 κώμης ὅπου ἦν Δαβίδ, ὁ Χριστὸς ἔρχεται; σχίσμα οὖν ἐν
village where was David, the Christ comes? a division Then in

44 τῷ ὄχλῳ ἐγένετο δι' αὐτόν. τινὲς δὲ ἤθελον ἐξ αὐτῶν
the crowd occurred, because of Him. some And desired of them

πιάσαι αὐτόν, ἀλλ' οὐδεὶς ἐπέβαλεν ἐπ' αὐτὸν τὰς χεῖρας.
to seize Him, but no one laid on Him the hands.

45 Ἦλθον οὖν οἱ ὑπηρέται πρὸς τοὺς ἀρχιερεῖς καὶ Φαρι-
came Then the officers to the chief priests and

σαίους· καὶ εἶπον αὐτοῖς ἐκεῖνοι, Διατί οὐκ ἠγάγετε αὐτόν;
Pharisees, and said to them those, Why not did you bring him?

46 ἀπεκρίθησαν οἱ ὑπηρέται, Οὐδέποτε οὕτως ἐλάλησεν
answered The officers, Never so spoke

47 ἄνθρωπος, ὡς οὗτος ὁ ἄνθρωπος. ἀπεκρίθησαν οὖν αὐτοῖς
a man as this man. answered Then them

48 οἱ Φαρισαῖοι, Μὴ καὶ ὑμεῖς πεπλάνησθε; μή τις ἐκ τῶν
the Pharisees, Not also you have been deceived? Not any from the

49 ἀρχόντων ἐπίστευσεν εἰς αὐτόν, ἢ ἐκ τῶν Φαρισαίων; ἀλλ'
rulers have believed into him, or from the Pharisees? But

ὁ ὄχλος οὗτος ὁ μὴ γινώσκων τὸν νόμον ἐπικατάρατοί εἰσι.
crowd this not knowing the Law cursed upon are

50 λέγει Νικόδημος πρὸς αὐτούς (ὁ ἐλθὼν νυκτὸς πρὸς αὐτόν,
says Nicodemus to them —he having come (by) night to Him,

51 εἷς ὢν ἐξ αὐτῶν), Μὴ ὁ νόμος ἡμῶν κρίνει τὸν ἄνθρωπον,
one being of themselves—Not the Law of us does judge the man

ἐὰν μὴ ἀκούσῃ παρ' αὐτοῦ πρότερον καὶ γνῷ τί ποιεῖ;
unless it hear from him first and know what he does

52 ἀπεκρίθησαν καὶ εἶπον αὐτῷ, Μὴ καὶ σὺ ἐκ τῆς Γαλιλαίας εἶ;
They answered and said to him, Not also you of — Galilee are?

53 ἐρεύνησον καὶ ἴδε ὅτι προφήτης ἐκ τῆς Γαλιλαίας οὐκ
Search (the Scripture) and see that a prophet out of — Galilee not

ἐγήγερται. Καὶ ἐπορεύθη ἕκαστος εἰς τὸν οἶκον αὐτοῦ·
has been raised. And they went each one to the house of him.

CHAPTER 8

1 Ἰησοῦς δὲ ἐπορεύθη εἰς τὸ
Jesus And went to the

Mount of Olives. 2 And at dawn He came again into the Temple, and all the people came to Him. And sitting down, He taught them. 3 And the scribes and the Pharisees brought to Him a woman having been taken in adultery. And standing her in *the* middle, 4 they said to Him, Teacher, this woman was taken in the very act, committing adultery. 5 And in the Law Moses gave us command that such should be stoned. You, then, what do you say? 6 But they said this to tempt Him, that they may have *reason* to accuse Him. But bending down, Jesus wrote with the finger in the earth, not appearing *to hear*. 7 But as they continued questioning Him, bending back up, He said to them, He that *is* without sin, let him cast the first stone at her. 8 And bending down again, He wrote in the earth. 9 But hearing, and being convicted by the conscience, they went out one by one, beginning from the older ones, until the last. And Jesus was left alone, and the woman standing in *the* middle. 10 And Jesus bending back up, and having seen no one but the woman, He said to her, Woman, where are those who accused you? Did no one give judgment against you? 11 And she said, No one, Lord. And Jesus said to her,, Neither do I give judgment. Go, and sin no more.

12 Then Jesus again spoke to them, saying, I am the Light of the world; the *one* following Me will in no way walk in the darkness, but will have the light of life. 13 Then the Pharisees said to Him, You witnessed concerning yourself; your witness is not true. 14 Jesus answered and said to them, Even if I witness concerning Myself, My witness is true, for I know from where I came, and where I go. But you

2 ὄρος τῶν ἐλαιῶν. ὄρθρου δὲ πάλιν παρε-
mount of the olives. at dawn And again He
γένετο εἰς τὸ ἱερόν, καὶ πᾶς ὁ λαὸς ἤρχετο πρὸς αὐτόν· καὶ
arrived in the Temple, and all the people came to Him, and
3 καθίσας ἐδίδασκεν αὐτούς. ἄγουσι δὲ οἱ γραμματεῖς καὶ οἱ
sitting He taught them. lead And the scribes and the
Φαρισαῖοι πρὸς αὐτὸν γυναῖκα ἐν μοιχείᾳ κατειλημμένην,
Pharisees to Him a woman in adultery having been taken,
4 καὶ στήσαντες αὐτὴν ἐν μέσῳ, λέγουσιν αὐτῷ, Διδάσκαλε,
and standing her in (the) midst they say to Him, Teacher,
5 αὕτη ἡ γυνὴ κατειλήφθη ἐπαυτοφώρῳ μοιχευομένη. ἐν δὲ τῷ
this woman has been taken in the very act committing adultery. in And the
νόμῳ Μωσῆς ἡμῖν ἐνετείλατο τὰς τοιαύτας λιθοβολεῖσθαι·
Law Moses to us commanded such (women) to be stoned
6 σὺ οὖν τί λέγεις; τοῦτο δὲ ἔλεγον πειράζοντες αὐτόν, ἵνα
you, then, what say you? this But they said tempting Him, that
ἔχωσι κατηγορεῖν αὐτοῦ. ὁ δὲ Ἰησοῦς κάτω κύψας, τῷ
they may have to accuse Him. — But Jesus down stooping with the
7 δακτύλῳ ἔγραφεν εἰς τὴν γῆν, μὴ προσποιούμενος. ὡς δὲ
finger wrote in the earth, not appearing (to hear). as And
ἐπέμενον ἐρωτῶντες αὐτόν, ἀνακύψας εἶπε πρὸς αὐτούς,
they continued questioning Him. bending back up, He said to them,
Ὁ ἀναμάρτητος ὑμῶν, πρῶτος τὸν λίθον ἐπ' αὐτῇ βαλέτω.
The (one) sinless of you, first the stone on her let him cast.
8 9 καὶ πάλιν κάτω κύψας ἔγραφεν εἰς τὴν γῆν. οἱ δέ, ἀκούσαν-
And again down stooping He wrote in the earth. they But, having
τες, καὶ ὑπὸ τῆς συνειδήσεως ἐλεγχόμενοι, ἐξήρχοντο εἷς καθ'
heard, and by the conscience being convicted, went out one by
εἷς, ἀρξάμενοι ἀπὸ τῶν πρεσβυτέρων ἕως τῶν ἐσχάτων· καὶ
one, beginning from the older ones, until the last. And
κατελείφθη μόνος ὁ Ἰησοῦς, καὶ ἡ γυνὴ ἐν μέσῳ ἑστῶσα.
was left alone — Jesus, and the woman in (the) midst standing.
10 ἀνακύψας δὲ ὁ Ἰησοῦς, καὶ μηδένα θεασάμενος πλὴν τῆς
bending back up And Jesus, and no one observing but the
γυναικός, εἶπεν αὐτῇ Ἡ γυνή, ποῦ εἰσιν ἐκεῖνοι οἱ κατήγοροί
woman, He said to her, Woman, where are those, the accusers
11 σου; οὐδείς σε κατέκρινεν; ἡ δὲ εἶπεν, Οὐδείς, Κύριε. εἶπε δὲ
of you? No one you judged? she And said, No one, Lord. said And
αὐτῇ ὁ Ἰησοῦς, Οὐδὲ ἐγώ σε κατακρίνω· πορεύου καὶ μηκέτι
to her Jesus, Neither I you do judge; go, and no more
ἁμάρτανε.
sin.
12 Πάλιν οὖν ὁ Ἰησοῦς αὐτοῖς ἐλάλησε λέγων, Ἐγώ εἰμι τὸ
Again, then, Jesus to them spoke, saying, I am the
φῶς τοῦ κόσμου· ὁ ἀκολουθῶν ἐμοὶ οὐ μὴ περιπατήσει ἐν τῇ
light of the world; the (one) following Me in no way will walk in the
13 σκοτίᾳ, ἀλλ' ἕξει τὸ φῶς τῆς ζωῆς. εἶπον οὖν αὐτῷ οἱ
darkness, but will have the light of life. said Then to Him the
Φαρισαῖοι, Σὺ περὶ σεαυτοῦ μαρτυρεῖς· ἡ μαρτυρία σου οὐκ
Pharisees, You about yourself witnessed. The witness of you not
14 ἔστιν ἀληθής. ἀπεκρίθη Ἰησοῦς καὶ εἶπεν αὐτοῖς, Κἂν
is true. answered Jesus and said to them, Even if
ἐγὼ μαρτυρῶ περὶ ἐμαυτοῦ, ἀληθής ἐστιν ἡ μαρτυρία μου·
I witness about Myself, true is the witness of Me,
ὅτι οἶδα πόθεν ἦλθον, καὶ ποῦ ὑπάγω· ὑμεῖς δὲ οὐκ οἴδατε
because I know from where I came, and where I go; you but not do know

do not know from where I come, and where I go. [15]You judge according to the flesh. I judge no one. [16]But even if I judge, My judgment is true because I am not alone, but I and *the* Father who sent Me. [17]And in your Law it has been written that the witness of two men is true. [18]I am the *one* witnessing concerning Myself, and He who sent Me, *the* Father witnesses concerning Me. [19]Then they said to Him, Where is your father? Jesus answered, You neither know Me, nor My Father. If you had known Me, then you also would have known My Father. [20]Jesus spoke these words in the treasury, teaching in the Temple, for His hour had not yet come.

[21]Then Jesus said to them again, I go, and you will seek Me. And you will die in your sin. Where I go, you are not able to come. [22]Then the Jews said, Will he kill himself, because he says, Where I go, you are not able to come? [23]And He said to them, You are from below; I am from above. You are from this world; I am not from this world. [24]Therefore, I said to you that you will die in your sins. For if you do not believe that I AM, you will die in your sins. [25]Then they said to Him, Who are you? And Jesus said to them, Altogether what I also say to you. [26]I have many things to say and to judge, but the *One* sending Me is true, and what I heard from Him, these things I say to the world. [27]They did not know that He spoke to them *of* the Father.

[28]Then Jesus said to them, When you lift up the Son of man, then you will know that I AM; and from Myself I do nothing, but (as) My Father taught Me, these things I

15 πόθεν ἔρχομαι, καὶ ποῦ ὑπάγω. ὑμεῖς κατὰ τὴν σάρκα
from where I come, or where I go. You according to the flesh
16 κρίνετε· ἐγὼ οὐ κρίνω οὐδένα. καὶ ἐὰν κρίνω δὲ ἐγώ, ἡ
judge. I do not judge no one. even if judge But I,
κρίσις ἡ ἐμὴ ἀληθής ἐστιν· ὅτι μόνος οὐκ εἰμί, ἀλλ' ἐγὼ καὶ
judgment My true is, because alone not I am, but I and
17 ὁ πέμψας με πατήρ. καὶ ἐν τῷ νόμῳ δὲ τῷ ὑμετέρῳ γέγρα-
He sending Me, (the) Father. Also in Law and your it has been
18 πται ὅτι δύο ἀνθρώπων ἡ μαρτυρία ἀληθής ἐστιν. ἐγώ εἰμι
written that of two men the witness true is. I am
ὁ μαρτυρῶν περὶ ἐμαυτοῦ, καὶ μαρτυρεῖ περὶ ἐμοῦ ὁ πέμψας
the (one) witnessing about Myself, and witnesses about Me He sending,
19 με πατήρ. ἔλεγον οὖν αὐτῷ, Ποῦ ἐστιν ὁ πατήρ σου
Me, (the) Father. they said Then to Him, Where is the father of you?
ἀπεκρίθη ὁ Ἰησοῦς, Οὔτε ἐμὲ οἴδατε, οὔτε τὸν πατέρα μου·
answered Jesus, Neither Me you know, nor the Father of Me;
20 εἰ ἐμὲ ᾔδειτε, καὶ τὸν πατέρα μου ᾔδειτε ἄν. ταῦτα τὰ
if Me you had known the Father of Me you had known then. These —
ῥήματα ἐλάλησεν ὁ Ἰησοῦς ἐν τῷ γαζοφυλακίῳ, διδάσκων
words spoke Jesus in the treasury, teaching
ἐν τῷ ἱερῷ· καὶ οὐδεὶς ἐπίασεν αὐτόν, ὅτι οὔπω ἐληλύθει ἡ
in the Temple. And no one seized Him, because not yet had come the
ὥρα αὐτοῦ.
hour of Him.

21 Εἶπεν οὖν πάλιν αὐτοῖς ὁ Ἰησοῦς, Ἐγὼ ὑπάγω, καὶ
said therefore again to them — Jesus, I go, and
ζητήσετέ με, καὶ ἐν τῇ ἁμαρτίᾳ ὑμῶν ἀποθανεῖσθε· ὅπου
you will seek Me; and in the sin of you you will die. Where
22 ἐγὼ ὑπάγω, ὑμεῖς οὐ δύνασθε ἐλθεῖν. ἔλεγον οὖν οἱ Ἰουδαῖοι,
I go, you not are able to come. said Then the Jews,
Μήτι ἀποκτενεῖ ἑαυτόν, ὅτι λέγει, Ὅπου ἐγὼ ὑπάγω,
Not will he kill himself, because he says, Where I go,
23 ὑμεῖς οὐ δύνασθε ἐλθεῖν; καὶ εἶπεν αὐτοῖς, Ὑμεῖς ἐκ τῶν κάτω
you not are able to come? And He said to them, You from below
ἐστέ, ἐγὼ ἐκ τῶν ἄνω εἰμί· ὑμεῖς ἐκ τοῦ κόσμου τούτου ἐστέ,
are; I from above am. You from world this are;
24 ἐγὼ οὐκ εἰμὶ ἐκ τοῦ κόσμου τούτου. εἶπον οὖν ὑμῖν ὅτι
I not am from — world this. I said therefore to you that
ἀποθανεῖσθε ἐν ταῖς ἁμαρτίαις ὑμῶν· ἐὰν γὰρ μὴ πιστεύσητε
you will die in the sins of you; if for not you believe
25 ὅτι ἐγώ εἰμι, ἀποθανεῖσθε ἐν ταῖς ἁμαρτίαις ὑμῶν. ἔλεγον
that I AM, you will die in the sins of you. They said
οὖν αὐτῷ, Σὺ τίς εἶ; καὶ εἶπεν αὐτοῖς ὁ Ἰησοῦς, Τὴν ἀρχὴν
then to Him, you Who are? And said to them — Jesus, Altogether
26 ὅ τι καὶ λαλῶ ὑμῖν. πολλὰ ἔχω περὶ ὑμῶν λαλεῖν καὶ
what even I say to you. Many things I have about you to say and
κρίνειν· ἀλλ' ὁ πέμψας με ἀληθής ἐστι, κἀγὼ ἃ ἤκουσα παρ'
to judge, but the (One) sending Me true is, and I what I heard from
27 αὐτοῦ, ταῦτα λέγω εἰς τὸν κόσμον. οὐκ ἔγνωσαν ὅτι τὸν
Him, these things I say to the world. not They knew that (of) the
28 πατέρα αὐτοῖς ἔλεγεν. εἶπεν οὖν αὐτοῖς ὁ Ἰησοῦς, Ὅταν
Father to them He spoke. said therefore to them Jesus, When
ὑψώσητε τὸν υἱὸν τοῦ ἀνθρώπου, τότε γνώσεσθε ὅτι ἐγώ
you lift up the Son — of man, then you will know that I
εἰμι, καὶ ἀπ' ἐμαυτοῦ ποιῶ οὐδέν, ἀλλὰ καθὼς ἐδίδαξέ με ὁ
AM; and from Myself I do nothing, but as taught Me the

speak. [29]And the *One* who sent Me is with Me. The Father did not leave Me alone, for I do the things pleasing to Him. [30]*As* He spoke these things, many believed into Him.

[31]Then Jesus said to the Jews who had believed in Him, If you continue in My word, you are truly My disciples. [32]And you will know the truth, and the truth will set you free. [33]They answered Him, We are Abraham's seed, and we have been in slavery to no one, never! How do you say, You will become free? [34]Jesus answered them, Truly, truly, I say to you, Everyone practicing sin is a slave of sin. [35]But the slave does not remain in the house forever; the son remains forever. [36]Therefore, if the Son sets you free, you are free indeed.

[37]I know that you are Abraham's seed, but you seek to kill Me because My word has no place in you. [38]I speak what I have seen with My Father. And you therefore do what you have seen with your father. [39]They answered and said to Him, Abraham is our father. Jesus said to them, If you were children of Abraham, you would do the works of Abraham. [40]But now you seek to kill Me, a man who has spoken the truth to you, which I heard alongside *of* God. Abraham did not do this.

[41]You do the works of your father. They said to Him, We were not born of fornication; we have one father, God. [42]Then Jesus said to them, If God were your Father you would love Me, for I went forth and have come from God. For I have not come from Myself, but that One sent Me. [43]Why do you not understand My speech? *It is* because you are not able to hear My word.

29 πατήρ μου, ταῦτα λαλῶ. καὶ ὁ πέμψας με μετ' ἐμοῦ ἐστιν·
Father of Me, these things I say. And the (One) sending Me with Me is.
οὐκ ἀφῆκέ με μόνον ὁ πατήρ, ὅτι ἐγὼ τὰ ἀρεστὰ αὐτῷ ποιῶ
Not left Me alone the Father, for I the things pleasing to Him do
30 πάντοτε. ταῦτα αὐτοῦ λαλοῦντος πολλοὶ ἐπίστευσαν εἰς
always. These things He saying, many believed in
αὐτόν.
Him.

31 Ἔλεγεν οὖν ὁ Ἰησοῦς πρὸς τοὺς πεπιστευκότας αὐτῷ
said Therefore Jesus to the having believed in Him
Ἰουδαίους, Ἐὰν ὑμεῖς μείνητε ἐν τῷ λόγῳ τῷ ἐμῷ, ἀληθῶς
Jews, If you continue in the word – My, truly
32 μαθηταί μου ἐστέ· καὶ γνώσεσθε τὴν ἀλήθειαν, καὶ ἡ ἀλήθεια
disciples of Me you are; and you will know the truth, and the truth
33 ἐλευθερώσει ὑμᾶς. ἀπεκρίθησαν αὐτῷ, Σπέρμα Ἀβραάμ
will set free you. They answered to Him, seed of Abraham
ἐσμεν, καὶ οὐδενὶ δεδουλεύκαμεν πώποτε· πῶς σὺ λέγεις ὅτι
We are, and to no one have we been enslaved, never. How do you say, –
34 Ἐλεύθεροι γενήσεσθε; ἀπεκρίθη αὐτοῖς ὁ Ἰησοῦς, Ἀμὴν
free You will become? answered them – Jesus, Truly,
ἀμὴν λέγω ὑμῖν, ὅτι πᾶς ὁ ποιῶν τὴν ἁμαρτίαν δοῦλός ἐστι
truly, I say to you, that everyone doing – sin a slave is
35 τῆς ἁμαρτίας. ὁ δὲ δοῦλος οὐ μένει ἐν τῇ οἰκίᾳ εἰς τὸν αἰῶνα·
– of sin. the But slave not remains in the house to the age;
36 ὁ υἱὸς μένει εἰς τὸν αἰῶνα. ἐὰν οὖν ὁ υἱὸς ὑμᾶς ἐλευθερώσῃ,
the son remains to the age. If, then, the Son you sets free,
37 ὄντως ἐλεύθεροι ἔσεσθε. οἶδα ὅτι σπέρμα Ἀβραάμ ἐστε·
really free you are. I know that the seed of Abraham you are
ἀλλὰ ζητεῖτέ με ἀποκτεῖναι, ὅτι ὁ λόγος ὁ ἐμὸς οὐ χωρεῖ ἐν
but you seek Me to kill, because word – My not has place in
38 ὑμῖν. ἐγὼ ὃ ἑώρακα παρὰ τῷ πατρί μου, λαλῶ· καὶ ὑμεῖς οὖν
you. I what I have seen with the Father of Me, I speak; and you, then,
39 ὃ ἑωράκατε παρὰ τῷ πατρὶ ὑμῶν, ποιεῖτε. ἀπεκρίθησαν καὶ
what you have seen with the father of you, you do. They answered and
εἶπον αὐτῷ, Ὁ πατὴρ ἡμῶν Ἀβραάμ ἐστι. λέγει αὐτοῖς ὁ
said to Him, The father of us Abraham is. says to them –
Ἰησοῦς, Εἰ τέκνα τοῦ Ἀβραὰμ ἦτε, τὰ ἔργα τοῦ Ἀβραὰμ
Jesus, If children – of Abraham you were, the works – of Abraham
40 ἐποιεῖτε ἄν. νῦν δὲ ζητεῖτέ με ἀποκτεῖναι, ἄνθρωπον ὃς τὴν
you would do. now And you seek Me to kill, a man who the
ἀλήθειαν ὑμῖν λελάληκα, ἣν ἤκουσα παρὰ τοῦ Θεοῦ· τοῦτο
truth to you has spoken, which I heard beside – God; this
41 Ἀβραὰμ οὐκ ἐποίησεν. ὑμεῖς ποιεῖτε τὰ ἔργα τοῦ πατρὸς
Abraham not did do. You do the works of the father
ὑμῶν. εἶπον οὖν αὐτῷ, Ἡμεῖς ἐκ πορνείας οὐ γεγεννήμεθα·
of you. They said, then, to Him, We of fornication not were born;
42 ἕνα πατέρα ἔχομεν, τὸν Θεόν. εἶπεν αὐτοῖς ὁ Ἰησοῦς, Εἰ ὁ
one father we have, – God. said to them – Jesus, If –
Θεὸς πατὴρ ὑμῶν ἦν, ἠγαπᾶτε ἂν ἐμέ· ἐγὼ γὰρ ἐκ τοῦ Θεοῦ
God Father of you was, you would love Me; I for from – God
ἐξῆλθον καὶ ἥκω· οὐδὲ γὰρ ἀπ' ἐμαυτοῦ ἐλήλυθα, ἀλλ'
went forth, and have come; not for from Myself I have come, but
43 ἐκεῖνός με ἀπέστειλε. διατί τὴν λαλιὰν τὴν ἐμὴν οὐ γινώ-
that One Me sent. Why – speech – My not you
44 σκετε; ὅτι οὐ δύνασθε ἀκούειν τὸν λόγον τὸν ἐμόν. ὑμεῖς
know? Because not you are able to hear – word – My. You

44 You are of the Devil *as* father, and the lusts of your father you desire to do. That one was a murderer from *the* beginning, and he has not stood in the truth because there is no truth in him. When he speaks *a* lie, he speaks from *his* own, because he is a liar, and the father of it. 45 And because I speak the truth, you do not believe Me. 46 Who of you reproves Me concerning sin? But if I speak truth, why do you not believe Me? 47 The *one* who is of God hears the words of God; for this reason you do not hear, because you are not of God. 48 Then the Jews answered and said to Him, Do we not say well that you are a Samaritan, and have a demon? 49 Jesus answered, I do not have a demon, but I honor My Father, and you dishonor Me. 50 But I do not seek My glory; there is One who seeks and judges. 51 Truly, truly, I say to you, If anyone keeps My word, he will never ever see death.

52 Then the Jews said to Him, Now we know that you have a demon. Abraham died, and the prophets, and you say, If anyone keeps My word, he will never ever taste of death. 53 Are you greater than our father Abraham who died? And the prophets died! Whom do you make yourself?

54 Jesus answered, If I glorify Myself, My glory is nothing; it is My Father who glorifies Me, whom you say is your God. 55 And you have not known Him; but I know Him, and if I say that I do not know Him, I shall be like you, a liar. But I know Him, and I keep His word. 56 Your father Abraham leaped for joy that he should see My day, and he saw, and rejoiced. 57 Then the Jews said to Him, You do not yet have fifty years, and have you

ἐκ πατρὸς τοῦ διαβόλου ἐστέ, καὶ τὰς ἐπιθυμίας τοῦ πατρὸς
from (your) father the Devil are; and the lusts of the father

ὑμῶν θέλετε ποιεῖν. ἐκεῖνος ἀνθρωποκτόνος ἦν ἀπ᾽ ἀρχῆς,
of you you desire to do. That one a murderer was from (the) first,

καὶ ἐν τῇ ἀληθείᾳ οὐχ ἕστηκεν, ὅτι οὐκ ἔστιν ἀλήθεια ἐν αὐτῷ.
and in the truth not has stood, because not is truth in him.

ὅταν λαλῇ τὸ ψεῦδος, ἐκ τῶν ἰδίων λαλεῖ· ὅτι ψεύστης ἐστὶ
When he speaks the lie, out of the own he speaks, for a liar he is,

45 καὶ ὁ πατὴρ αὐτοῦ. ἐγὼ δὲ ὅτι τὴν ἀλήθειαν λέγω, οὐ πι-
and the father of it. I But because the truth I say, not you

46 στεύετέ μοι. τίς ἐξ ὑμῶν ἐλέγχει με περὶ ἁμαρτίας ; εἰ δὲ ἀλή-
believe Me. Who of you reproves Me concerning sin? if And

47 θειαν λέγω, διατί ὑμεῖς οὐ πιστεύετέ μοι ; ὁ ὢν ἐκ τοῦ Θεοῦ
truth I say, why you do not believe Me? He being of — God

τὰ ῥήματα τοῦ Θεοῦ ἀκούει· διὰ τοῦτο ὑμεῖς οὐκ ἀκούετε,
the words — of God hears; therefore you do not hear,

48 ὅτι ἐκ τοῦ Θεοῦ οὐκ ἐστέ. ἀπεκρίθησαν οὖν οἱ Ἰουδαῖοι καὶ
since from God not you are. answered, then, The Jews and

εἶπον αὐτῷ, Οὐ καλῶς λέγομεν ἡμεῖς ὅτι Σαμαρείτης εἶ σύ,
said to Him, Not well say we that a Samaritan are you,

49 καὶ δαιμόνιον ἔχεις ; ἀπεκρίθη Ἰησοῦς, Ἐγὼ δαιμόνιον οὐκ
and a demon you have? answered Jesus, I a demon not

ἔχω, ἀλλὰ τιμῶ τὸν πατέρα μου, καὶ ὑμεῖς ἀτιμάζετέ με.
have, but I honor the Father of Me, and you dishonor Me.

50 ἐγὼ δὲ οὐ ζητῶ τὴν δόξαν μου· ἔστιν ὁ ζητῶν καὶ κρίνων.
I But not do seek the glory of Me; One is seeking and judging.

51 ἀμὴν ἀμὴν λέγω ὑμῖν, ἐάν τις τὸν λόγον τὸν ἐμὸν τηρήσῃ,
Truly, truly, I say to you, if anyone — word — My keeps,

52 θάνατον οὐ μὴ θεωρήσῃ εἰς τὸν αἰῶνα. εἶπον οὖν αὐτῷ
death in no way will he behold for ever. said, then, to Him

οἱ Ἰουδαῖοι, Νῦν ἐγνώκαμεν ὅτι δαιμόνιον ἔχεις. Ἀβραὰμ
The Jews, Now we have known that a demon you have. Abraham

ἀπέθανε καὶ οἱ προφῆται, καὶ σὺ λέγεις, Ἐάν τις τὸν λόγον
died, and the prophets, and you say, If anyone the word

53 μου τηρήσῃ, οὐ μὴ γεύσεται θανάτου εἰς τὸν αἰῶνα. μὴ σὺ
of Me keeps, in no way will he taste of death to the age. Not you

μείζων εἶ τοῦ πατρὸς ἡμῶν Ἀβραάμ, ὅστις ἀπέθανε ; καὶ
greater are than the father of us, Abraham, who died? Also

54 οἱ προφῆται ἀπέθανον· τίνα σεαυτὸν σὺ ποιεῖς ; ἀπεκρίθη
the prophets died. Whom Yourself you do make? answered

Ἰησοῦς, Ἐὰν ἐγὼ δοξάζω ἐμαυτόν, ἡ δόξα μου οὐδέν ἐστιν·
Jesus, If I glorify Myself, the glory of Me nothing is;

ἔστιν ὁ πατήρ μου ὁ δοξάζων με, ὃν ὑμεῖς λέγετε ὅτι Θεὸς
it is the Father of Me glorifying Me, whom you say that God

55 ὑμῶν ἐστι, καὶ οὐκ ἐγνώκατε αὐτόν· ἐγὼ δὲ οἶδα αὐτόν,
of you is. And not you have known Him; I but know Him,

καὶ ἐὰν εἴπω ὅτι οὐκ οἶδα αὐτόν, ἔσομαι ὅμοιος ὑμῶν,
and if I say that not I know Him, I shall be like you,

ψεύστης· ἀλλ᾽ οἶδα αὐτόν, καὶ τὸν λόγον αὐτοῦ τηρῶ.
a liar. But I know Him, and the word of Him I keep.

56 Ἀβραὰμ ὁ πατὴρ ὑμῶν ἠγαλλιάσατο ἵνα ἴδῃ τὴν ἡμέραν
Abraham the father of you leaped for joy that he may see day

57 τὴν ἐμήν, καὶ εἶδε καὶ ἐχάρη. εἶπον οὖν οἱ Ἰουδαῖοι πρὸς
— My, and he saw and rejoiced. said Then the Jews to

αὐτόν, Πεντήκοντα ἔτη οὔπω ἔχεις, καὶ Ἀβραὰμ ἑώρακας ;
Him, Fifty years not yet you have, and Abraham you have seen?

seen Abraham? 58 Jesus said to them, Truly, truly, I say to you, Before Abraham came into being, I AM. 59 Therefore, they took up stones that they might throw *them* on Him. But Jesus was hidden, and went forth out of the Temple, going through *the* midst of them, and so passed by.

CHAPTER 9

1 And passing by, He saw a man blind from birth. 2 And His disciples asked Him, saying, Teacher, who sinned, this one, or his parents, that he was born blind? 3 Jesus answered, Neither this one nor his parents, but that the works of God might be revealed in him. 4 It is necessary for Me to work the works of Him who sent Me while it is day. Night comes when no one is able to work. 5 While I am in the world, I am *the* Light of the world. 6 Saying these things, He spat on the ground and made clay out of the spittle, and anointed clay on the blind one's eyes.

7 And He said to him, Go, wash in the pool of Siloam, which translated is Sent. Then he went, and washed, and came seeing. 8 Then the neighbors and those who formerly saw him, that he was blind, said, Is this one not the *one* who had sat and begged? 9 It is he; and others, He is like him. That one said, I am *he*. 10 Then they said to him, How were your eyes opened? 11 He answered and said, A man called Jesus made clay and anointed my eyes, and told me, Go to the pool of Siloam, and wash. And going in, and washing, I received sight. 12 Then they said to him, Where is that one? He said, I do not know.

13 They brought him to the Pharisees, the *one* once

58 εἶπεν αὐτοῖς ὁ Ἰησοῦς, Ἀμὴν ἀμὴν λέγω ὑμῖν, πρὶν Ἀβραὰμ
said to them — Jesus, Truly, truly I say to you, before Abraham
59 γενέσθαι, ἐγώ εἰμι. ἦραν οὖν λίθους ἵνα βάλωσιν ἐπ' αὐτόν·
came into being, I AM. they took Then stones that they might cast on Him;
Ἰησοῦς δὲ ἐκρύβη, καὶ ἐξῆλθεν ἐκ τοῦ ἱεροῦ, διελθὼν διὰ
Jesus but was hidden, and went forth out of the Temple, going through
μέσου αὐτῶν· καὶ παρῆγεν οὕτως.
(the) midst of them, and passed by thus.

CHAPTER 9

1 Καὶ παράγων εἶδεν ἄνθρωπον τυφλὸν ἐκ γενετῆς. καὶ
And passing by, He saw a man blind from birth. And
2 ἠρώτησαν αὐτὸν οἱ μαθηταὶ αὐτοῦ λέγοντες, Ῥαββί, τίς
asked Him the disciples of Him, saying, Rabbi, who
ἥμαρτεν, οὗτος ἢ οἱ γονεῖς αὐτοῦ, ἵνα τυφλὸς γεννηθῇ;
sinned, this one, or the parents of him, that blind he was born?
3 ἀπεκρίθη ὁ Ἰησοῦς, Οὔτε οὗτος ἥμαρτεν οὔτε οἱ γονεῖς
answered — Jesus, Neither this one sinned, nor the parents
αὐτοῦ· ἀλλ' ἵνα φανερωθῇ τὰ ἔργα τοῦ Θεοῦ ἐν αὐτῷ.
of him, but that might be revealed the works — of God in him.
4 ἐμὲ δεῖ ἐργάζεσθαι τὰ ἔργα τοῦ πέμψαντός με ἕως ἡμέρα
Me it behoves to work the works of the (One) sending Me while day
5 ἐστίν· ἔρχεται νύξ, ὅτε οὐδεὶς δύναται ἐργάζεσθαι. ὅταν ἐν
it is. comes Night, when no one is able to work. When in
6 τῷ κόσμῳ ὦ, φῶς εἰμι τοῦ κόσμου. ταῦτα εἰπών, ἔπτυσε
the world I am, (the) light I am of the world. These things saying, He spat
χαμαί, καὶ ἐποίησε πηλὸν ἐκ τοῦ πτύσματος, καὶ ἐπέχρισε
on earth and made clay out of the spittle, and anointed
7 τὸν πηλὸν ἐπὶ τοὺς ὀφθαλμοὺς τοῦ τυφλοῦ, καὶ εἶπεν αὐτῷ,
the clay on the eyes of the blind one, and said to him,
Ὕπαγε νίψαι εἰς τὴν κολυμβήθραν τοῦ Σιλωάμ (ὃ ἑρμη-
Go, wash in the pool — of Siloam; which is
νεύεται, ἀπεσταλμένος). ἀπῆλθεν οὖν καὶ ἐνίψατο, καὶ ἦλθε
translated, having been sent. He went then, and washed, and came
8 βλέπων. οἱ οὖν γείτονες καὶ οἱ θεωροῦντες αὐτὸν τὸ πρό-
seeing. the Then neighbors and those beholding him formerly,
τερον ὅτι τυφλὸς ἦν, ἔλεγον, Οὐχ οὗτός ἐστιν ὁ καθή-
that blind he was, said, Not this one is the (one)
9 μενος καὶ προσαιτῶν; ἄλλοι ἔλεγον ὅτι Οὗτός ἐστιν· ἄλλοι
sitting and begging? Others said, — This is he; others
δὲ ὅτι Ὅμοιος αὐτῷ ἐστιν. ἐκεῖνος ἔλεγεν ὅτι Ἐγώ εἰμι.
and like him he is. That one said, I am.
10 ἔλεγον οὖν αὐτῷ, Πῶς ἀνεῴχθησάν σου οἱ ὀφθαλμοί;
they said Then to him, How were opened of you the eyes?
11 ἀπεκρίθη ἐκεῖνος καὶ εἶπεν, Ἄνθρωπος λεγόμενος Ἰησοῦς
answered That one and said, (The) man being called Jesus
πηλὸν ἐποίησε, καὶ ἐπέχρισέ μου τοὺς ὀφθαλμούς, καὶ εἶπέ
clay made and anointed of me the eyes, and told
μοι, Ὕπαγε εἰς τὴν κολυμβήθραν τοῦ Σιλωάμ, καὶ νίψαι.
me, Go to the pool — of Siloam, and wash.
12 ἀπελθὼν δὲ καὶ νιψάμενος, ἀνέβλεψα. εἶπον οὖν αὐτῷ, Ποῦ
going And, and washing, I received sight. They said then to him, Where
ἐστιν ἐκεῖνος; λέγει, Οὐκ οἶδα.
is that one? He says, Not I do know.
13 Ἄγουσιν αὐτὸν πρὸς τοὺς Φαρισαίους, τόν ποτε τυφλόν.
They lead him to the Pharisees, the (one) once blind.

blind. [14]And it was a sabbath when Jesus made the clay and opened his eyes. [15]Then also the Pharisees again asked him how he received sight. And he said to them, He put clay on my eyes, and I washed, and I see. [16]Then some of the Pharisees said, This man is not from God, because He does not keep the sabbath. Others said, How can a man, a sinner, do such miracles? And there was a division among them. [17]They said to the blind one again, What do you say about him, because he opened your eyes? And he said, He is a prophet. [18]Then the Jews did not believe concerning him, that he was blind and received sight, until they called the parents of him having received sight. [19]And they asked them, saying, Is this your son, whom you say that he was born blind? [21]Then how does he now see? [20]His parents answered them and said, We know that this is our son, and that he was born blind. [21]But how he now sees, we do not know; or who opened his eyes, we do not know. He is of age, ask him. He will speak about himself. [22]His parents said these things because they feared the Jews; for the Jews had already agreed that if anyone should confess Him *as* Christ, he would be expelled from the synagogue. [23]Because of this his parents said, He is of age, ask him. [24]Then they called the man who was blind a second time, and said to him, Give glory to God. We know that this man is a sinner. [25]Then he answered and said, Whether he is a sinner, I do not know. One *thing* I do know, that being blind, now I see. [26]And they said to him again, What did he do to you? How did he

14 ἦν δὲ σάββατον ὅτε τὸν πηλὸν ἐποίησεν ὁ Ἰησοῦς, καὶ
it was And a sabbath when the clay made — Jesus, and
15 ἀνέῳξεν αὐτοῦ τοὺς ὀφθαλμούς. πάλιν οὖν ἠρώτων αὐτὸν
opened of him the eyes. Again, therefore, asked him
καὶ οἱ Φαρισαῖοι, πῶς ἀνέβλεψεν. ὁ δὲ εἶπεν αὐτοῖς, Πηλὸν
also the Pharisees how he received sight. he And said to them, Clay
ἐπέθηκεν ἐπὶ τοὺς ὀφθαλμούς μου, καὶ ἐνιψάμην, καὶ
He put on the eyes of me, and I washed, and
16 βλέπω. ἔλεγον οὖν ἐκ τῶν Φαρισαίων τινές, Οὗτος ὁ ἄνθρω-
I see. said Then of the Pharisees some, This man
πος οὐκ ἔστι παρὰ τοῦ Θεοῦ, ὅτι τὸ σάββατον οὐ τηρεῖ.
not is from — God, because the sabbath not He keeps.
ἄλλοι ἔλεγον, Πῶς δύναται ἄνθρωπος ἁμαρτωλὸς τοιαῦτα
Others said, How is able a man, a sinner, such
17 σημεῖα ποιεῖν; καὶ σχίσμα ἦν ἐν αὐτοῖς. λέγουσι τῷ τυφλῷ
signs do? And a division was among them. They say to the blind one
πάλιν, Σὺ τί λέγεις περὶ αὐτοῦ, ὅτι ἤνοιξέ σου τοὺς ὀφθαλ-
again, you What say concerning him, because he opened of you the eyes?
18 μούς; ὁ δὲ εἶπεν ὅτι Προφήτης ἐστίν. οὐκ ἐπίστευσαν οὖν οἱ
he And said, — A prophet He is. Not did believe, therefore, the
Ἰουδαῖοι περὶ αὐτοῦ, ὅτι τυφλὸς ἦν καὶ ἀνέβλεψεν, ἕως
Jews concerning him, that blind he was and received sight until
19 ὅτου ἐφώνησαν τοὺς γονεῖς αὐτοῦ τοῦ ἀναβλέψαντος, καὶ
when they called the parents of him — having received sight; and
ἠρώτησαν αὐτοὺς λέγοντες, Οὗτός ἐστιν ὁ υἱὸς ὑμῶν, ὃν
they asked them, saying, this Is the son of you, whom
ὑμεῖς λέγετε ὅτι τυφλὸς ἐγεννήθη; πῶς οὖν ἄρτι βλέπει;
you say that blind he was born? How, then, just now he sees?
20 ἀπεκρίθησαν αὐτοῖς οἱ γονεῖς αὐτοῦ καὶ εἶπον, Οἴδαμεν ὅτι
answered them The parents of him and said, We know that
21 οὗτός ἐστιν ὁ υἱὸς ἡμῶν, καὶ ὅτι τυφλὸς ἐγεννήθη· πῶς δὲ νῦν
this is the son of us, and that blind he was born. how But now
βλέπει, οὐκ οἴδαμεν· ἢ τίς ἤνοιξεν αὐτοῦ τοὺς ὀφθαλμούς,
he sees, not we know, or who opened of him the eyes
ἡμεῖς οὐκ οἴδαμεν· αὐτὸς ἡλικίαν ἔχει· αὐτὸν ἐρωτήσατε,
we not know. He age has, him ask.
22 αὐτὸς περὶ αὐτοῦ λαλήσει. ταῦτα εἶπον οἱ γονεῖς αὐτοῦ, ὅτι
He concerning himself will speak. These things said the parents of him, for
ἐφοβοῦντο τοὺς Ἰουδαίους· ἤδη γὰρ συνετέθειντο οἱ
they feared the Jews; already for had agreed the
Ἰουδαῖοι, ἵνα ἐάν τις αὐτὸν ὁμολογήσῃ Χριστόν, ἀποσυνά-
Jews that if anyone Him should confess (as) Christ, from synagogue
23 γωγος γένηται. διὰ τοῦτο οἱ γονεῖς αὐτοῦ εἶπον ὅτι
expelled he would be. Because of this the parents of him said, —
24 Ἡλικίαν ἔχει, αὐτὸν ἐρωτήσατε. ἐφώνησαν οὖν ἐκ δευτέρου
age He has, him ask. They called therefore a second time
τὸν ἄνθρωπον ὃς ἦν τυφλός, καὶ εἶπον αὐτῷ, Δὸς δόξαν τῷ
the man who was blind, and said to him, Give glory to
Θεῷ· ἡμεῖς οἴδαμεν ὅτι ὁ ἄνθρωπος οὗτος ἁμαρτωλός ἐστιν.
God; we know that man this a sinner is.
25 ἀπεκρίθη οὖν ἐκεῖνος καὶ εἶπεν, Εἰ ἁμαρτωλός ἐστιν, οὐκ
answered Then that one and said, If a sinner He is, not
26 οἶδα· ἓν οἶδα, ὅτι τυφλὸς ὤν, ἄρτι βλέπω. εἶπον δὲ αὐτῷ
I know; one I know, that blind being, just now I see. they said And to him
πάλιν, Τί ἐποίησέ σοι; πῶς ἤνοιξέ σου τοὺς ὀφθαλμούς;
again, What did he to you? How opened he of you the eyes?

open your eyes? [27] He answered them, I told you already, and you did not hear. Why do you wish to hear again? Do you also desire to become disciples of Him? [28] Then they reviled him and said, You are a disciple of that one, but we are disciples of Moses. [29] We know that God has spoken by Moses, but this one, we do not know from where he is. [30] The man answered and said to them, For there is a marvel in this, that you do not know from where He is, and He opened my eyes. [31] But we know that God does not hear sinful ones, but if anyone is God-fearing, and does His will, He hears that one. [32] Never was it ever heard that anyone opened the eyes of one having been born blind. [33] If this One was not from God, He could not do anything. [34] They answered and said to him, You were born wholly in sins, and do you teach us? And they threw him outside.

[35] Jesus heard that they threw him outside, and finding him, He said to him, Do you believe into the Son of God? [36] And he answered and said, Who is He, Lord, that I may believe into Him? [37] And Jesus said to him, You have both seen Him, and He speaking with you is that One. [38] And he said, I believe, Lord! And he worshiped Him. [39] And Jesus said, I came into this world for judgment, that the ones who see may become blind. [40] And those of the Pharisees who were with Him heard, and said to Him, Are we also blind? [41] Jesus said to them, If you were blind, you would have no sin. But now you say, We see, therefore, your sin remains.

CHAPTER 10

[1] Truly, truly, I say to you, the *one* not entering through

27 ἀπεκρίθη αὐτοῖς, Εἶπον ὑμῖν ἤδη, καὶ οὐκ ἠκούσατε. τί πάλιν
He answered them, I told you already, and not you heard. Why again
θέλετε ἀκούειν ; μὴ καὶ ὑμεῖς θέλετε αὐτοῦ μαθηταὶ γενέσθαι ;
do you wish to hear? Not also you wish of Him disciples to become?
28 ἐλοιδόρησαν οὖν αὐτόν, καὶ εἶπον, Σὺ εἶ μαθητὴς ἐκείνου·
they reviled Then him and said, You are a disciple of that one,
29 ἡμεῖς δὲ τοῦ Μωσέως ἐσμὲν μαθηταί. ἡμεῖς οἴδαμεν ὅτι Μωσῇ
we but — of Moses are disciples. We know that by Moses
λελάληκεν ὁ Θεός· τοῦτον δὲ οὐκ οἴδαμεν πόθεν ἐστίν.
has spoken God, this one but not we know from where he is.
30 ἀπεκρίθη ὁ ἄνθρωπος καὶ εἶπεν αὐτοῖς, Ἐν γὰρ τούτῳ
answered The man and said to them, in For this
θαυμαστόν ἐστιν, ὅτι ὑμεῖς οὐκ οἴδατε πόθεν ἐστί, καὶ
a marvel is, that you do not know from where He is, and
31 ἀνέῳξέ μου τοὺς ὀφθαλμούς. οἴδαμεν δὲ ὅτι ἁμαρτωλῶν ὁ
He opened of me the eyes. we know And that sinful ones
Θεὸς οὐκ ἀκούει· ἀλλ' ἐάν τις θεοσεβὴς ᾖ, καὶ τὸ θέλημα
God not hears, but if anyone God-fearing is, and the will
32 αὐτοῦ ποιῇ, τούτου ἀκούει. ἐκ τοῦ αἰῶνος οὐκ ἠκούσθη
of Him does, this one He hears. From the age not it was heard
33 ὅτι ἤνοιξέ τις ὀφθαλμοὺς τυφλοῦ γεγεννημένου. εἰ μὴ ἦν
that opened anyone eyes of one blind having been born. If not was
34 οὗτος παρὰ Θεοῦ, οὐκ ἠδύνατο ποιεῖν οὐδέν. ἀπεκρίθησαν
this One from God, not He could do nothing. They answered
καὶ εἶπον αὐτῷ, Ἐν ἁμαρτίαις σὺ ἐγεννήθης ὅλος, καὶ σὺ
and said to him, In sins you were born wholly, and you
διδάσκεις ἡμᾶς ; καὶ ἐξέβαλον αὐτὸν ἔξω.
teach us? And they threw him outside.
35 Ἤκουσεν ὁ Ἰησοῦς ὅτι ἐξέβαλον αὐτὸν ἔξω· καὶ εὑρὼν
heard Jesus that they threw him outside, and finding
36 αὐτόν, εἶπεν αὐτῷ, Σὺ πιστεύεις εἰς τὸν υἱὸν τοῦ Θεοῦ ; ἀπε-
him. He said to him, You do believe in the Son — of God?
κρίθη ἐκεῖνος καὶ εἶπε, Τίς ἐστι, Κύριε, ἵνα πιστεύσω εἰς
answered That one and said, Who is He, Lord, that I may believe in
37 αὐτόν ; εἶπε δὲ αὐτῷ ὁ Ἰησοῦς, Καὶ ἑώρακας αὐτόν, καὶ ὁ
Him? said And to him — Jesus, Even you have seen him, and He
38 λαλῶν μετὰ σοῦ ἐκεῖνός ἐστιν. ὁ δὲ ἔφη, Πιστεύω, Κύριε·
speaking with you that One is. he And said, I believe, Lord;
39 καὶ προσεκύνησεν αὐτῷ. καὶ εἶπεν ὁ Ἰησοῦς, Εἰς κρίμα ἐγὼ
and he worshiped Him. And said — Jesus, For judgment I
εἰς τὸν κόσμον τοῦτον ἦλθον, ἵνα οἱ μὴ βλέποντες βλέπω-
to — world this came, that the (ones) not seeing may see,
40 σι, καὶ οἱ βλέποντες τυφλοὶ γένωνται. καὶ ἤκουσαν ἐκ τῶν
and those seeing blind may become. And heard of the
Φαρισαίων ταῦτα οἱ ὄντες μετ' αὐτοῦ, καὶ εἶπον αὐτῷ, Μὴ
Pharisees these things those being with Him, and said to Him, Not
41 καὶ ἡμεῖς τυφλοί ἐσμεν ; εἶπεν αὐτοῖς ὁ Ἰησοῦς, Εἰ τυφλοὶ
also we blind are? said to them Jesus, If blind
ἦτε, οὐκ ἂν εἴχετε ἁμαρτίαν· νῦν δὲ λέγετε ὅτι Βλέπομεν·
you were, not you would have sin; now but you say, — We see;
ἡ οὖν ἁμαρτία ὑμῶν μένει.
the then sin of you remains.

CHAPTER 10

1 Ἀμὴν ἀμὴν λέγω ὑμῖν, ὁ μὴ εἰσερχόμενος διὰ τῆς θύρας
Truly, truly I say to you, he not entering through the door

the door into the sheepfold, but going up by another way, that one is a thief and a robber. 2 But the *one* entering through the door is the shepherd of the sheep. 3 The doorkeeper opens to him, and the sheep hear his voice, and he calls *his* own sheep by name, and leads them out. 4 And when he puts forth *his* own sheep, he goes in front of them, and the sheep follow because they know his voice. 5 But they never follow a stranger, but will flee from him, because they do not know the voice of the strangers. 6 Jesus spoke this allegory to them, but they did not know what it was which He spoke to them.

7 Then Jesus again said to them, Truly, truly, I say to you that I am the door of the sheep. 8 All who came before Me are thieves and robbers; but the sheep did not hear them. 9 I am the door. If anyone enters through Me, he will be saved, and will go in, and will go out, and will find pasture. 10 The thief does not come except that he may steal, and kill, and destroy. I came that they may have life, and may have *it* abundantly. 11 I am the Good Shepherd! The Good Shepherd lays down His life for the sheep. 12 But the hireling, not even being a shepherd, who does not own the sheep, sees the wolf coming and forsakes the sheep, and flees. And the wolf seizes them, and scatters the sheep. 13 But the hireling flees because he is a hireling, and there is not a care to him concerning the sheep. 14 I am the Good Shepherd, and I know those that *are* Mine; and I am known by the *ones that are* Mine. 15 Even as the Father knows Me, I also know the Father, and I lay down My soul for the sheep. 16 And I have other sheep which are not of this fold. I

εἰς τὴν αὐλὴν τῶν προβάτων, ἀλλὰ ἀναβαίνων ἀλλαχόθεν,
into the fold of the sheep, but going up by another way,

2 ἐκεῖνος κλέπτης ἐστὶ καὶ λῃστής. ὁ δὲ εἰσερχόμενος διὰ τῆς
that one a thief is and a robber. he But entering through the

3 θύρας ποιμήν ἐστι τῶν προβάτων. τούτῳ ὁ θυρωρὸς
door shepherd is of the sheep. To this one the doorkeeper

ἀνοίγει, καὶ τὰ πρόβατα τῆς φωνῆς αὐτοῦ ἀκούει, καὶ τὰ
opens, and the sheep the voice of him hears, and the

4 ἴδια πρόβατα καλεῖ κατ' ὄνομα, καὶ ἐξάγει αὐτά. καὶ ὅταν
own sheep he calls by name, and leads out them. And when

τὰ ἴδια πρόβατα ἐκβάλῃ, ἔμπροσθεν αὐτῶν πορεύεται· καὶ
the own sheep he passes, in front of them he passes, and

τὰ πρόβατα αὐτῷ ἀκολουθεῖ, ὅτι οἴδασι τὴν φωνὴν αὐτοῦ.
the sheep to him follow, because they know the voice of him.

5 ἀλλοτρίῳ δὲ οὐ μὴ ἀκολουθήσωσιν, ἀλλὰ φεύξονται ἀπ'
a stranger But in no way should they follow. but will flee from

6 αὐτοῦ· ὅτι οὐκ οἴδασι τῶν ἀλλοτρίων τὴν φωνήν. ταύτην
him, because not they know of the strangers the voice. This

τὴν παροιμίαν εἶπεν αὐτοῖς ὁ Ἰησοῦς· ἐκεῖνοι δὲ οὐκ ἔγνωσαν
— allegory said to them — Jesus, those but not knew

τίνα ἦν ἃ ἐλάλει αὐτοῖς.
what it was which He spoke to them.

7 Εἶπεν οὖν πάλιν αὐτοῖς ὁ Ἰησοῦς, Ἀμὴν ἀμὴν λέγω ὑμῖν
said Therefore again to them — Jesus, Truly, truly, I say to you

8 ὅτι Ἐγώ εἰμι ἡ θύρα τῶν προβάτων. πάντες ὅσοι πρὸ ἐμοῦ
that I am the door of the sheep. All who before Me

ἦλθον κλέπται εἰσὶ καὶ λῃσταί· ἀλλ' οὐκ ἤκουσαν αὐτῶν τὰ
came thieves are and robbers; but did not hear them the

9 πρόβατα. ἐγώ εἰμι ἡ θύρα· δι' ἐμοῦ ἐάν τις εἰσέλθῃ, σωθή-
sheep. I am the door; through Me If anyone enter he will

σεται, καὶ εἰσελεύσεται καὶ ἐξελεύσεται, καὶ νομὴν εὑρήσει.
be saved, and will go in and will go out, and pasture will find.

10 ὁ κλέπτης οὐκ ἔρχεται εἰ μὴ ἵνα κλέψῃ καὶ θύσῃ καὶ ἀπολέσῃ·
The thief not comes except that he may steal and slay and destroy;

11 ἐγὼ ἦλθον ἵνα ζωὴν ἔχωσι, καὶ περισσὸν ἔχωσιν. ἐγώ εἰμι
I came that life they may have, and abundantly may have. I am

ὁ ποιμὴν ὁ καλός· ὁ ποιμὴν ὁ καλὸς τὴν ψυχὴν αὐτοῦ
the Shepherd — Good. The Shepherd — Good the soul of Him

12 τίθησιν ὑπὲρ τῶν προβάτων. ὁ μισθωτὸς δέ, καὶ οὐκ ὢν
lays down for the sheep. the hireling And, even not being

ποιμήν, οὗ οὐκ εἰσὶ τὰ πρόβατα ἴδια, θεωρεῖ τὸν λύκον
a shepherd, whose not are the sheep (his) own, beholds the wolf

ἐρχόμενον, καὶ ἀφίησι τὰ πρόβατα, καὶ φεύγει· καὶ ὁ λύκος
coming, and forsakes the sheep, and flees, and the wolf

13 ἁρπάζει αὐτά, καὶ σκορπίζει τὰ πρόβατα. ὁ δὲ μισθωτὸς
seizes them and scatters the sheep. the Now hireling

φεύγει, ὅτι μισθωτός ἐστι, καὶ οὐ μέλει αὐτῷ περὶ τῶν
flees because a hireling he is, and not is care to him about the

14 προβάτων. ἐγώ εἰμι ὁ ποιμὴν ὁ καλός, καὶ γινώσκω τὰ ἐμά,
sheep. I am the Shepherd Good, and I know — Mine,

15 καὶ γινώσκομαι ὑπὸ τῶν ἐμῶν. καθὼς γινώσκει με ὁ πατήρ,
and am known by — Mine. As knows Me the Father,

κἀγὼ γινώσκω τὸν πατέρα· καὶ τὴν ψυχήν μου τίθημι ὑπὲρ
I also know the Father; and the soul of Me I lay down for

16 τῶν προβάτων. καὶ ἄλλα πρόβατα ἔχω, ἃ οὐκ ἔστιν ἐκ τῆς
the sheep. And other sheep I have, which not are of —

must also lead those, and they will hear My voice; and there will be one flock, one Shepherd. [17]For this reason My Father loves Me, because I lay down My soul, that I may take it again. [18]No one takes it from Me, but I lay it down from Myself. I have authority to lay it down, and I have authority to take it again. I received this commandment from My Father.

[19]Then a division again occurred among the Jews, because of these words. [20]And many of them said, He has a demon and is insane. Why do you hear him? [21]Others said, These are not words of one having been possessed by a demon. A demon is not able to open *the* eyes of blind ones.

[22]And *the Feast* of Dedication took place in Jerusalem, and it was winter. [23]And Jesus was walking in the Temple, in Solomon's Porch. [24]Then the Jews encircled Him, and said to Him, How long do you lift up our soul? If you are the Christ, tell us publicly. [25]Jesus answered them, I told you, and you did not believe. The works which I do in the name of My Father, these bear witness about Me. [26]But you do not believe, for you are not of My sheep, as I said to you. [27]My sheep hear My voice, and I know them, and they follow Me. [28]And I give eternal life to them, and they shall never ever perish; and not anyone shall pluck them out of My hand. [29]My Father who has given *them* to Me is greater than all, and no one is able to pluck out of My Father's hand. [30]I and the Father are one! [31]Then the Jews again took up stones, that they might stone Him. [32]Jesus answered them, I showed you many good

αὐλῆς ταύτης· κἀκεῖνά με δεῖ ἀγαγεῖν, καὶ τῆς φωνῆ- μου
fold this; those also Me it is right to lead, and of the voice of Me

17 ἀκούσουσι· καὶ γενήσεται μία ποίμνη, εἷς ποιμήν. διὰ τοῦτο
they will hear, and will become one flock, one Shepherd. Therefore

ὁ πατήρ με ἀγαπᾷ, ὅτι ἐγὼ τίθημι τὴν ψυχήν μου, ἵνα
the Father Me loves, because I lay down the soul of Me. that

18 πάλιν λάβω αὐτήν οὐδεὶς αἴρει αὐτὴν ἀπ' ἐμοῦ, ἀλλ' ἐγὼ
again I may take it. No one takes up it from Me, but I

τίθημι αὐτὴν ἀπ' ἐμαυτοῦ. ἐξουσιαν ἐχω θεῖναι αὐτήν, καὶ
lay down it from Myself. authority I have to lay down it, and

ἐξουσίαν ἔχω πάλιν λαβεῖν αὐτήν· ταύτην τὴν ἐντολὴν
authority I have again to take it. This — commandment

ἔλαβον παρὰ τοῦ πατρός μου.
I received from the Father of Me.

19 Σχίσμα οὖν πάλιν ἐγένετο ἐν τοῖς Ἰουδαίοις διὰ τοὺς
a division Therefore again occurred among the Jews, because of —

20 λόγους τούτους. ἔλεγον δὲ πολλοὶ ἐξ αὐτῶν, Δαιμόνιον ἔχει
words these. said And many of them, A demon he has,

21 καὶ μαίνεται· τί αὐτοῦ ἀκούετε ; ἄλλοι ἔλεγον, Ταῦτα τὰ
and is insane. Why him do you hear? Others said, These —

ῥήματα οὐκ ἔστι δαιμονιζομένου· μὴ δαιμόνιον δύναται
words not are of one demon-possessed; not a demon is able

τυφλῶν ὀφθαλμοὺς ἀνοίγειν ;
of blind ones eyes to open?

22 Ἐγένετο δὲ τὰ ἐγκαίνια· ἐν τοῖς Ἱεροσολύμοις, καὶ
occurred And the Dedication in — Jerusalem; and

23 χειμὼν ἦν· καὶ περιεπάτει ὁ Ἰησοῦς ἐν τῷ ἱερῷ ἐν τῇ στοᾷ
winter it was. And walked — Jesus in the Temple in the porch

24 τοῦ Σολομῶντος. ἐκύκλωσαν οὖν αὐτὸν οἱ Ἰουδαῖοι, καὶ
— of Solomon. encircled Then Him the Jews, and

ἔλεγον αὐτῷ, Ἕως πότε τὴν ψυχὴν ἡμῶν αἴρεις ; εἰ σὺ εἶ ὁ
said to Him, Until when the soul of us you lift up? If you are the

25 Χριστός, εἰπὲ ἡμῖν παρρησίᾳ. ἀπεκρίθη αὐτοῖς ὁ Ἰησοῦς,
Christ, tell us publicly. answered them — Jesus,

Εἶπον ὑμῖν, καὶ οὐ πιστεύετε· τὰ ἔργα ἃ ἐγὼ ποιῶ ἐν τῷ
I said to you, and not you believe; the works which I do in the

26 ὀνόματι τοῦ πατρός μου, ταῦτα μαρτυρεῖ περὶ ἐμοῦ· ἀλλ'
name of the Father of Me, these witness concerning Me; but

ὑμεῖς οὐ πιστεύετε· οὐ γάρ ἐστε ἐκ τῶν προβάτων τῶν ἐμῶν,
you not do believe not for you are of the sheep — of Me.

27 καθὼς εἶπον ὑμῖν. τὰ πρόβατα τὰ ἐμὰ τῆς φωνῆς μου ἀκούει,
As I said to you, — sheep — My of the voice of Me hear,

28 κἀγὼ γινώσκω αὐτά, καὶ ἀκολουθοῦσί μοι· κἀγὼ ζωὴν
and I know them, and they follow Me; and I life

αἰώνιον δίδωμι αὐτοῖς· καὶ οὐ μὴ ἀπόλωνται εἰς τὸν αἰῶνα,
eternal give to them; and in no way shall they perish for ever,.

29 καὶ οὐχ ἁρπάσει τις αὐτὰ ἐκ τῆς χειρός μου. ὁ πατήρ μου
and not shall pluck anyone them out of the hand of Me. The Father of Me

ὃς δέδωκέ μοι, μείζων πάντων ἐστί· καὶ οὐδεὶς δύναται
who has given to Me, greater than all is, and no one is able

30 ἁρπάζειν ἐκ τῆς χειρὸς τοῦ πατρός μου. ἐγὼ καὶ ὁ πατὴρ
to pluck out of the hand of the Father of Me. I and the Father

31 ἕν ἐσμεν. ἐβάστασαν οὖν πάλιν λίθους οἱ Ἰουδαῖοι ἵνα
one are. took up Therefore again stones the Jews, that

32 λιθάσωσιν αὐτόν. ἀπεκρίθη αὐτοῖς ὁ Ἰησοῦς, Πολλὰ καλὰ
they might stone Him. answered them — Jesus, Many good

works from My Father. For which work of them do you stone Me? 33 The Jews answered Him, say-ing, We do not stone you concerning a good work, but concerning blasphemy, and because you, being a man, make yourself God. 34 Jesus answered them, Is it not writ-ten in your Law, "I said, you are gods"? 35 If He called those gods with whom the word of God was—and Scripture cannot be broken—36 do you say *of Him* whom the Father sanctified and sent into the world, You blaspheme, be-cause I said, I am Son of God? 37 If I do not do the works of My Father, do not believe Me. 38 But if I do, even if you do not believe Me, believe the works, that you may perceive and may believe that the Father *is* in Me, and I in Him. 39 Then they again sought to seize Him. And He went forth out of their hand. 40 And He went away again across the Jordan to the place where John was at first baptizing, and remained there. 41 And many came to Him and said, John indeed did no miracle, but all things that John said concerning this One were true. 42 And many believed into Him there.

CHAPTER 11

1 And there was a certain sick one, Lazarus from Bethany, of the village of Mary and her sister Martha. 2 And it was Mary who anointed the Lord with oint-ment, and wiped His feet with her hair, whose brother Lazarus was sick. 3 There-fore, the sisters sent to Him, saying, Lord, behold, *the one* whom You love is sick. 4 And hearing, Jesus said, This is not sickness to death, but for the glory of God, that the Son of God be glorified by it. 5 And Jesus loved Martha, and her sister, and Lazarus. 6 Therefore, when

ἔργα ἔδειξα ὑμῖν ἐκ τοῦ πατρός μου· διὰ ποῖον αὐτῶν ἔργον
works I showed you from the Father of Me; for which of them work
33 λιθάζετέ με ; ἀπεκρίθησαν αὐτῷ οἱ Ἰουδαῖοι λέγοντες, Περὶ
do you stone Me? answered Him the Jews, saying, Concerning
καλοῦ ἔργου οὐ λιθάζομέν σε, ἀλλὰ περὶ βλασφημίας, καὶ
a good work not we stone you, but concerning blasphemy, and
34 ὅτι σὺ ἄνθρωπος ὢν ποιεῖς σεαυτὸν Θεόν. ἀπεκρίθη αὐτοῖς
because you a man being make yourself God. answered them
ὁ Ἰησοῦς, Οὐκ ἔστι γεγραμμένον ἐν τῷ νόμῳ ὑμῶν, Ἐγὼ
— Jesus, not Is it having been written in the Law of you, I
35 εἶπα, θεοί ἐστε ; εἰ ἐκείνους εἶπε θεούς, πρὸς οὓς ὁ λόγος τοῦ
said, gods you are. If those He called gods, with whom the word —
36 Θεοῦ ἐγένετο (καὶ οὐ δύναται λυθῆναι ἡ γραφή), ὃν ὁ
of God was — and not can be broken the Scripture — whom the
πατὴρ ἡγίασε καὶ ἀπέστειλεν εἰς τὸν κόσμον, ὑμεῖς λέγετε
Father sanctified and sent into the world, you say,
37 ὅτι Βλασφημεῖς, ὅτι εἶπον, Υἱὸς τοῦ Θεοῦ εἰμι ; εἰ οὐ ποιῶ
— You blaspheme! Because I said, Son — of God I am? If not I do
38 τὰ ἔργα τοῦ πατρός μου, μὴ πιστεύετέ μοι· εἰ δὲ ποιῶ, κἂν
the works of the Father of Me, not do believe Me. if But I do, even if
ἐμοὶ μὴ πιστεύητε, τοῖς ἔργοις πιστεύσατε· ἵνα γνῶτε καὶ
Me not you believe, the works believe, that you may know and
39 πιστεύσητε ὅτι ἐν ἐμοὶ ὁ πατήρ, κἀγὼ ἐν αὐτῷ. ἐζήτουν
may believe that in Me the Father (is), and I in Him. they sought
οὖν πάλιν αὐτὸν πιάσαι· καὶ ἐξῆλθεν ἐκ τῆς χειρὸς αὐτῶν.
then again Him to seize. And He went out of the hand of them.
40 Καὶ ἀπῆλθε πάλιν πέραν τοῦ Ἰορδάνου εἰς τὸν τόπον
And He went away again across the Jordan to the place
41 ὅπου ἦν Ἰωάννης τὸ πρῶτον βαπτίζων· καὶ ἔμεινεν ἐκεῖ. καὶ
where was John at first baptizing, and remained there. And
πολλοὶ ἦλθον πρὸς αὐτόν, καὶ ἔλεγον ὅτι Ἰωάννης μὲν
many came to Him, and said, — John indeed
σημεῖον ἐποίησεν οὐδέν· πάντα δὲ ὅσα εἶπεν Ἰωάννης περὶ
sign did none, all things but whatever said John concerning
42 τούτου, ἀληθῆ ἦν. καὶ ἐπίστευσαν πολλοὶ ἐκεῖ εἰς αὐτόν.
this One true were. And believed many there in Him.

CHAPTER 11

1 Ἦν δέ τις ἀσθενῶν Λάζαρος ἀπὸ Βηθανίας, ἐκ τῆς κώμης
was And a certain sick one, Lazarus from Bethany, of the village
2 Μαρίας καὶ Μάρθας τῆς ἀδελφῆς αὐτῆς. ἦν δὲ Μαρία ἡ
of Mary and Martha the sister of her. was And Mary the (one)
ἀλείψασα τὸν Κύριον μύρῳ, καὶ ἐκμάξασα τοὺς πόδας αὐτοῦ
rubbing the Lord with ointment, and wiping off the feet of Him
3 ταῖς θριξὶν αὐτῆς, ἧς ὁ ἀδελφὸς Λάζαρος ἠσθένει. ἀπέστειλαν
with the hairs of her, of whom the brother Lazarus was sick. sent
οὖν αἱ ἀδελφαὶ πρὸς αὐτὸν λέγουσαι, Κύριε, ἴδε ὃν φιλεῖς
Then the sisters to Him, saying, Lord, behold, whom You love
4 ἀσθενεῖ. ἀκούσας δὲ ὁ Ἰησοῦς εἶπεν, Αὕτη ἡ ἀσθένεια οὐκ ἔστι
is sick. hearing And,— Jesus said, This — sickness not is
πρὸς θάνατον, ἀλλ᾽ ὑπὲρ τῆς δόξης τοῦ Θεοῦ, ἵνα δοξασθῇ ὁ
to death, but for the glory — of God, that be glorified the
5 υἱὸς τοῦ Θεοῦ δι᾽ αὐτῆς. ἠγάπα δὲ ὁ Ἰησοῦς τὴν Μάρθαν καὶ
Son — of God by it. loved Now — Jesus — Martha and
6 τὴν ἀδελφὴν αὐτῆς καὶ τὸν Λάζαρον. ὡς οὖν ἤκουσεν ὅτι
the sister of her and — Lazarus. As, then, He heard that

He heard that he is sick, then, indeed, He remained in the place where He was two days. 7 Then after this he said to the disciples, Let us go to Judea again. 8 The disciples said to Him, Rabbi, just now the Jews were seeking to stone You, and do you go there again? 9 Jesus answered, Are there not twelve hours in the day? If anyone walks in the day, he does not stumble because he sees the light of the world. 10 but if anyone walks in the night, he stumbles because the light is not in him. 11 He said these things. And after this He said to them, Our friend Lazarus has fallen asleep, but I am going that I may awaken him. 12 Then His disciples said, Lord, if he has fallen asleep, he will recover. 13 But Jesus had spoken about his death, but they thought that he spoke of the sleep of slumber. 14 Then Jesus said to them plainly, Lazarus has died. 15 And I rejoice on your account, in order that you may believe, for I was not there. But let us go to him. 16 Then Thomas called Didymus said to the fellow-disciples, Let us go, even we, that we may die with Him. 17 Then coming, Jesus found him already being held in the tomb four days. 19 And Bethany was near Jerusalem, *about* fifteen furlongs off. 19 And many of the Jews had come to those around Martha and Mary, that they might console them concerning their brother. 20 Therefore, when Martha heard that Jesus is coming, she met Him; but Mary was sitting in the house. 21 Then Martha said to Jesus, Lord, if You had been here, my brother would not be dead. 22 But even now I know that whatever You may ask God, God will give You. 23 Jesus said to her, Your brother will

7 ἀσθενεῖ, τότε μὲν ἔμεινεν ἐν ᾧ ἦν τόπῳ δύο ἡμέρας. ἔπειτα
he is sick, then, indeed, He abode in which was He place two days. Then
μετὰ τοῦτο λέγει τοῖς μαθηταῖς, Ἄγωμεν εἰς τὴν Ἰουδαίαν
after this He says to the disciples, Let us go to — Judea
8 πάλιν. λέγουσιν αὐτῷ οἱ μαθηταί, Ῥαββί, νῦν ἐζήτουν σε
again. Say to Him the disciples, Rabbi, now were seeking You
9 λιθάσαι οἱ Ἰουδαῖοι, καὶ πάλιν ὑπάγεις ἐκεῖ; ἀπεκρίθη ὁ
to stone the Jews, and again do You go there? answered —
Ἰησοῦς, Οὐχὶ δώδεκά εἰσιν ὧραι τῆς ἡμέρας; ἐάν τις περι-
Jesus, Not twelve are there hours of the day? If anyone walks
πατῇ ἐν τῇ ἡμέρᾳ, οὐ προσκόπτει, ὅτι τὸ φῶς τοῦ κόσμου
in the day, not he stumbles, because the light — world
10 τούτου βλέπει. ἐὰν δέ τις περιπατῇ ἐν τῇ νυκτί, προσκόπτει,
this he sees. if But anyone walk in the night, he stumbles,
11 ὅτι τὸ φῶς οὐκ ἔστιν ἐν αὐτῷ. ταῦτα εἶπε, καὶ μετὰ τοῦτο
because the light not is in him. These things He said, and after this
λέγει αὐτοῖς, Λάζαρος ὁ φίλος ἡμῶν κεκοίμηται· ἀλλὰ
He says to them, Lazarus the friend of us has fallen asleep; but
12 πορεύομαι ἵνα ἐξυπνίσω αὐτόν. εἶπον οὖν οἱ μαθηταὶ αὐτοῦ,
I am going that I may awaken him. said Then the disciples of Him,
13 Κύριε, εἰ κεκοίμηται, σωθήσεται. εἰρήκει δὲ ὁ Ἰησοῦς περὶ τοῦ
Lord, if he has slept, he will recover. had spoken And Jesus about the
θανάτου αὐτοῦ· ἐκεῖνοι δὲ ἔδοξαν ὅτι περὶ τῆς κοιμήσεως τοῦ
death of him, those but thought that about the sleep —
14 ὕπνου λέγει. τότε οὖν εἶπεν αὐτοῖς ὁ Ἰησοῦς παρρησίᾳ,
of slumber He says. Then therefore told them — Jesus openly,
15 Λάζαρος ἀπέθανε. καὶ χαίρω δι' ὑμᾶς, ἵνα πιστεύσητε, ὅτι
Lazarus has died. And I rejoice because of you, that you may believe, that
16 οὐκ ἤμην ἐκεῖ· ἀλλ' ἄγωμεν πρὸς αὐτόν. εἶπεν οὖν Θωμᾶς, ὁ
not I was there. But let us go to him. said Then Thomas —
λεγόμενος Δίδυμος, τοῖς συμμαθηταῖς, Ἄγωμεν καὶ ἡμεῖς, ἵνα
being called Twin, to the fellow-disciples, Let us go, even we, that
ἀποθάνωμεν μετ' αὐτοῦ.
we may die with Him.
17 Ἐλθὼν οὖν ὁ Ἰησοῦς εὗρεν αὐτὸν τέσσαρας ἡμέρας ἤδη
coming Then — Jesus found him four days already
18 ἔχοντα ἐν τῷ μνημείῳ. ἦν δὲ ἡ Βηθανία ἐγγὺς τῶν Ἱεροσολύ-
being held in the tomb. was And Bethany near — Jerusalem,
19 μων, ὡς ἀπὸ σταδίων δεκαπέντε· καὶ πολλοὶ ἐκ τῶν
as from stadia fifteen. And many of the
Ἰουδαίων ἐληλύθεισαν πρὸς τὰς περὶ Μάρθαν καὶ Μαρίαν,
Jews had come to those around Martha and Mary,
20 ἵνα παραμυθήσωνται αὐτὰς περὶ τοῦ ἀδελφοῦ αὐτῶν. ἡ
that they might console them concerning the brother of them.
οὖν Μάρθα, ὡς ἤκουσεν ὅτι ὁ Ἰησοῦς ἔρχεται, ὑπήντησεν
Therefore Martha, when she heard that Jesus is coming, met
21 αὐτῷ· Μαρία δὲ ἐν τῷ οἴκῳ ἐκαθέζετο. εἶπεν οὖν ἡ Μάρθα
Him; Mary but in the house was sitting. said Then Martha
πρὸς τὸν Ἰησοῦν, Κύριε, εἰ ἦς ὧδε, ὁ ἀδελφός μου οὐκ ἂν
to — Jesus, Lord, if You were here, the brother of me not would
22 ἐτεθνήκει. ἀλλὰ καὶ νῦν οἶδα ὅτι ὅσα ἂν αἰτήσῃ τὸν Θεόν,
be dead. But also now I know that whatever You may ask, God
23 δώσει σοι ὁ Θεός. λέγει αὐτῇ ὁ Ἰησοῦς, Ἀναστήσεται ὁ
will give You God. says to her — Jesus, will rise again The
24 ἀδελφός σου. λέγει αὐτῷ Μάρθα, Οἶδα ὅτι ἀναστήσεται ἐν
brother of you. says to Him Martha, I know that he will rise again in

rise again in the resurrection in the last day. [25]Jesus said to her, I am the Resurrection and the Life; the *one* believing into Me, though he die, he shall live. [26]And everyone living and believing into Me shall never ever die. Do you believe this? [27]She said to Him, yes, Lord, I have believed that You are the Christ the Son of God who comes into the world.

[28]And saying these things, she went away and called her sister Mary secretly, saying, The Teacher is here and calls you. [29]That one, when she heard, rose up quickly and came to Him. [30]And Jesus had not yet come into the village, but was in the place where Martha met Him. [31]Then the Jews who were with her in the house, and consoling her, seeing that Mary quickly rose up and went out, *they* followed her, saying, She is going to the tomb so that she may weep there. [32]Then when she came where Jesus was, seeing Him, she fell at His feet, saying to Him, Lord, if You were here, my brother would not have died. [33]Then when He saw her weeping, and the Jews coming down with her weeping, Jesus groaned in the spirit and troubled Himself. [34]And *He* said, Where have you put him? They said to him, Lord, come and see. [35]Jesus wept. [36]Then the Jews said, See how He loved him! [37]But some of them said, Was this One, the *one* opening the eyes of the blind, not able to have caused that this one should not have died? [38]Then groaning again within Himself, Jesus came to the tomb. And it was a cave, and a stone lying on it. [39]Jesus said, Take away the stone. Martha, the sister of him that died, said, Lord, he already smells, for it is *the* fourth *day*. [40]Jesus said to her, Did I not say to you that if

25 τῇ ἀναστασει ἐν τῇ ἐσχάτῃ ἡμέρᾳ. εἶπεν αὐτῇ ὁ Ἰησοῦς,
the resurrection in the last Day. said to her — Jesus,
Ἐγώ εἰμι ἡ ἀνάστασις καὶ ἡ ζωή· ὁ πιστεύων εἰς ἐμέ, κἂν
I am the resurrection and the life; the (one) believing in Me, though
26 ἀποθάνῃ, ζήσεται· καὶ πᾶς ὁ ζῶν καὶ πιστεύων εἰς ἐμέ, οὐ
he die, he shall live; and everyone living and believing in Me, in no
27 μὴ ἀποθάνῃ εἰς τὸν αἰῶνα. πιστεύεις τοῦτο; λέγει αὐτῷ,
way shall die to the age. Do you believe this? She says to Him,
Ναί, Κύριε· ἐγὼ πεπίστευκα, ὅτι σὺ εἶ ὁ Χριστός, ὁ υἱὸς τοῦ
Yes, Lord, I have believed that You are the Christ, the Son —
28 Θεοῦ, ὁ εἰς τὸν κόσμον ἐρχόμενος. καὶ ταῦτα εἰποῦσα
of God, who into the world comes. And these things having said,
ἀπῆλθε, καὶ ἐφώνησε Μαρίαν τὴν ἀδελφὴν αὐτῆς λάθρα,
she went away, and called Mary the sister of her secretly,
29 εἰποῦσα, Ὁ διδάσκαλος πάρεστι καὶ φωνεῖ σε. ἐκείνη ὡς
saying, The Teacher is here and calls you. That one as
30 ἤκουσεν, ἐγείρεται ταχὺ καὶ ἔρχεται πρὸς αὐτόν. (οὔπω
she heard rises up quickly and comes to Him. not yet
δὲ ἐληλύθει ὁ Ἰησοῦς εἰς τὴν κώμην, ἀλλ' ἦν ἐν τῷ τόπῳ
And had come — Jesus into the village, but was in the place
31 ὅπου ὑπήντησεν αὐτῷ ἡ Μάρθα.) οἱ οὖν Ἰουδαῖοι οἱ ὄντες
where met Him Martha. the Then Jews, those being
μετ' αὐτῆς ἐν τῇ οἰκίᾳ καὶ παραμυθούμενοι αὐτήν, ἰδόντες
with her in the house and consoling her, seeing
τὴν Μαρίαν ὅτι ταχέως ἀνέστη καὶ ἐξῆλθεν, ἠκολούθησαν
— Mary that quickly she rose up and went out, followed
αὐτῇ, λέγοντες ὅτι ὑπάγει εἰς τὸ μνημεῖον, ἵνα κλαύσῃ ἐκεῖ.
her, saying that she goes to the tomb, that she may weep there
32 ἡ οὖν Μαρία, ὡς ἦλθεν ὅπου ἦν ὁ Ἰησοῦς, ἰδοῦσα αὐτον,
Then Mary, when she came where was — Jesus, seeing Him,
ἔπεσεν εἰς τοὺς πόδας αὐτοῦ, λέγουσα αὐτῷ, Κύριε, εἰ ἦς
fell at the feet of Him, saying to Him, Lord, if You were
33 ὧδε, οὐκ ἂν ἀπέθανέ μου ὁ ἀδελφός. Ἰησοῦς οὖν ὡς εἶδεν
here, not would have died of me the brother. Jesus Then, as He saw
αὐτὴν κλαίουσαν, καὶ τοὺς συνελθόντας αὐτῇ Ἰουδαίους
her weeping, and the coming down with her Jews
κλαίοντας, ἐνεβριμήσατο τῷ πνεύματι, καὶ ἐτάραξεν ἑαυτόν,
weeping, groaned in the spirit, and troubled Himself,
34 καὶ εἶπε, Ποῦ τεθείκατε αὐτόν; λέγουσιν αὐτῷ, Κύριε, ἔρχου
and said, Where have you put him? They say to Him, Lord, come
35 καὶ ἴδε. ἐδάκρυσεν ὁ Ἰησοῦς. ἔλεγον οὖν οἱ Ἰουδαῖοι, Ἴδε
36 **and see. shed tears — Jesus. said Therefore the Jews, See**
37 πῶς ἐφίλει αὐτόν. τινὲς δὲ ἐξ αὐτῶν εἶπον, Οὐκ ἠδύνατο
how He loved him. some And of them said, Not was able
οὗτος, ὁ ἀνοίξας τοὺς ὀφθαλμοὺς τοῦ τυφλοῦ, ποιῆσαι ἵνα
this One, He opening the eyes of the blind, to have caused that
38 καὶ οὗτος μὴ ἀποθάνῃ; Ἰησοῦς οὖν πάλιν ἐμβριμώμενος
also this one not should die. Jesus Then again groaning
ἐν ἑαυτῷ ἔρχεται εἰς τὸ μνημεῖον. ἦν δὲ σπήλαιον, καὶ λίθος
in Himself comes to the tomb. it was And a cave, and a stone
39 ἐπέκειτο ἐπ' αὐτῷ. λέγει ὁ Ἰησοῦς, Ἄρατε τὸν λίθον. λέγει
was lying on it. says — Jesus, Lift the stone. says
αὐτῷ ἡ ἀδελφὴ τοῦ τεθνηκότος Μάρθα, Κύριε, ἤδη ὄζει·
to Him the sister of the (one) having died, Martha, Lord, already he smells,
40 τεταρταῖος γάρ ἐστι. λέγει αὐτῇ ὁ Ἰησοῦς, Οὐκ εἶπόν σοι,
(the) fourth (day) for it is. says to her — Jesus, Did not I say to you,

you would believe you will see the glory of God? 41 Then they took away the stone where the dead one was laid. And Jesus lifted *His* eyes upward and said, Father, I thank You that You heard Me. 42 And I know that you always hear Me; but because of the crowd who stand around I said *it*, that they might believe that You sent Me. 43 And saying these things, He cried out with a loud voice, Lazarus! Here! Outside! 44 And the *one* who had died came out, having the feet and the hands bound with sheets, and his face being bound with a cloth. Jesus said to them, Untie him, and let *him* go.

45 Therefore, many of the Jews, those coming to Mary, and having seen what Jesus did, believed into Him. 46 But some of them went away to the Pharisees, and told them what Jesus had done.

47 Then the chief priests and the Pharisees assembled a sanhedrin, and said, What are we doing, for this man does many miracles? 48 If we let him alone this way, all will believe into him, and the Romans will come and will take away from us both the place and the nation. 49 But a certain one of them, Caiaphas, being high priest of that year, said to them, You know nothing, 50 nor consider that it is to our benefit that one man die for the people, and not all the nation to perish. 51 But he did not say this from himself, but being high priest that year he prophesied that Jesus was about to die on behalf of the nation, 52 and not only on behalf of the nation, but that He also might gather into one the children of God who had been scattered. 53 Then from that day they took counsel that they might kill Him.

41 ὅτι ἐὰν πιστεύσῃς, ὄψει τὴν δόξαν τοῦ Θεοῦ ; ἦραν οὖν τὸν
that if you believe you will see the glory — of God? they lifted Then the
λίθον, οὗ ἦν ὁ τεθνηκὼς κείμενος. ὁ δὲ Ἰησοῦς ἦρε τοὺς
stone, where was the dead one laid. And Jesus lifted the
ὀφθαλμοὺς ἄνω, καὶ εἶπε, Πάτερ, εὐχαριστῶ σοι ὅτι ἤκουσάς
eyes upward, and said, Father, I thank You that You heard
42 μου. ἐγὼ δὲ ᾔδειν ὅτι πάντοτέ μου ἀκούεις· ἀλλὰ διὰ τὸν
Me. I And knew that always Me You hear. But because of the
ὄχλον τὸν περιεστῶτα εἶπον, ἵνα πιστεύσωσιν ὅτι σύ με
crowd — standing around I said, that they might believe that You Me
43 ἀπέστειλας. καὶ ταῦτα εἰπών, φωνῇ μεγάλῃ ἐκραύγασε,
did send. And these things saying, with a voice great He cried out,
44 Λάζαρε, δεῦρο ἔξω. καὶ ἐξῆλθεν ὁ τεθνηκώς, δεδεμένος τοὺς
Lazarus, Here! Outside! And came out the (one) having died, being bound the
πόδας καὶ τὰς χεῖρας κειρίαις, καὶ ἡ ὄψις αὐτοῦ σουδαρίῳ
feet and the hands with sheets, and the face of him with a cloth
περιεδέδετο. λέγει αὐτοῖς ὁ Ἰησοῦς, Λύσατε αὐτόν, καὶ ἄφετε
being bound. says to them — Jesus, Loosen him, and allow (him)
ὑπάγειν.
to depart.

45 Πολλοὶ οὖν ἐκ τῶν Ἰουδαίων, οἱ ἐλθόντες πρὸς τὴν Μαρίαν
Many therefore of the Jews, those coming to — Mary
καὶ θεασάμενοι ἃ ἐποίησεν ὁ Ἰησοῦς, ἐπίστευσαν εἰς αὐτόν.
and having beheld what did Jesus, believed in Him.
46 τινὲς δὲ ἐξ αὐτῶν ἀπῆλθον πρὸς τοὺς Φαρισαίους, καὶ εἶπον
some But of them went away to the Pharisees and told
αὐτοῖς ἃ ἐποίησεν ὁ Ἰησοῦς.
them what had done — Jesus.

47 Συνήγαγον οὖν οἱ ἀρχιερεῖς καὶ οἱ Φαρισαῖοι συνέδριον,
assembled Then the chief priests and the Pharisees a sanhedrin,
καὶ ἔλεγον, Τί ποιοῦμεν ; ὅτι οὗτος ὁ ἄνθρωπος πολλὰ
and said, What are we doing, because this man many
48 σημεῖα ποιεῖ. ἐὰν ἀφῶμεν αὐτὸν οὕτω, πάντες πιστεύσουσιν
signs does? If we leave him thus, all will believe
εἰς αὐτόν· καὶ ἐλεύσονται οἱ Ῥωμαῖοι καὶ ἀροῦσιν ἡμῶν καὶ
in him, and will come the Romans and will take of us both
49 τὸν τόπον καὶ τὸ ἔθνος. εἷς δέ τις ἐξ αὐτῶν Καϊάφας, ἀρχιερεὺς
the place and the nation. one But man of them, Caiaphas, high priest
ὢν τοῦ ἐνιαυτοῦ ἐκείνου, εἶπεν αὐτοῖς, Ὑμεῖς οὐκ οἴδατε
being of year that, said to them, You do not know
50 οὐδέν, οὐδὲ διαλογίζεσθε ὅτι συμφέρει ἡμῖν ἵνα εἷς ἄνθρωπος
nothing, nor consider that it is profitable for us that one man
ἀποθάνῃ ὑπὲρ τοῦ λαοῦ, καὶ μὴ ὅλον τὸ ἔθνος ἀπόληται.
die for the people, and not all the nation to perish.
51 τοῦτο δὲ ἀφ' ἑαυτοῦ οὐκ εἶπεν, ἀλλὰ ἀρχιερεὺς ὢν τοῦ ἐνιαυ-
this But from himself not he said, but high priest being year
τοῦ ἐκείνου, προεφήτευσεν ὅτι ἔμελλεν ὁ Ἰησοῦς ἀποθνή-
— that, he prophesied that was about — Jesus to die
52 σκειν ὑπὲρ τοῦ ἔθνους, καὶ οὐχ ὑπὲρ τοῦ ἔθνους μόνον, ἀλλ'
on behalf of the nation, and not on behalf of the nation only, but
ἵνα καὶ τὰ τέκνα τοῦ Θεοῦ τὰ διεσκορπισμένα συναγάγῃ
that also the children — of God — having been scattered He might gather
53 εἰς ἕν. ἀπ' ἐκείνης οὖν τῆς ἡμέρας συνεβουλεύσαντο ἵνα
into one. from that Therefore — day, they took counsel that
ἀποκτείνωσιν αὐτόν.
they might kill Him.

54 Therefore, Jesus no longer walked publicly among the Jews, but went away from there into the country near the desert, to a city being called Ephraim, and stayed there with His disciples.

55 And the Passover of the Jews was near. And many went up to Jerusalem out of the country before the Passover, that they might purify themselves. 56 Then they sought Jesus, and said with one another, standing in the temple, What does it seem to you? That He does not at all come to the Feast? 57 And all the chief priests and the Pharisees had given commands that if anyone knew where He is, he should inform so that they might seize Him.

CHAPTER 12

1 Then six days before the Passover, Jesus came to Bethany, where Lazarus was, who had died, whom He raised from *the* dead. 2 Then they made Him a supper there, and Martha served. But Lazarus was one of those reclining with Him. 3 Then taking a pound of ointment of pure, costly spikenard, Mary anointed the feet of Jesus, and wiped off with her hairs. And the house was filled with the odor of the ointment. 4 Then Simon's son, Judas Iscariot, one of His disciples, who was about to betray Him, said, 5 Why was this ointment not sold *for* three hundred denarii, and given to *the* poor? 6 But he said this not that he was caring for the poor, but that he was a thief, and held the moneybag, and carried away the things being put *in*. 7 Then Jesus said, Allow her, for she has kept it for the day of My burial. 8 For you always have the poor with you, but you do not always have Me.

9 Then a great crowd of the Jews learned that He

54 Ἰησοῦς οὖν οὐκέτι παρρησίᾳ περιεπάτει ἐν τοῖς Ἰουδαίοις,
Jesus Therefore no longer publicly walked among the Jews
ἀλλὰ ἀπῆλθεν ἐκεῖθεν εἰς τὴν χώραν ἐγγὺς τῆς ἐρήμου, εἰς
but went away from there into the country near the desert, to
Ἐφραῒμ λεγομένην πόλιν, κἀκεῖ διέτριβε μετὰ τῶν μαθητῶν
Ephraim being called a city, and there stayed with the disciples
55 αὐτοῦ. ἦν δὲ ἐγγὺς τὸ πάσχα τῶν Ἰουδαίων· καὶ ἀνέβησαν
of Him. was And near the Passover of the Jews, and went up
πολλοὶ εἰς Ἱεροσόλυμα ἐκ τῆς χώρας πρὸ τοῦ πάσχα, ἵνα
many to Jerusalem out of the country before the Passover, that
56 ἁγνίσωσιν ἑαυτούς. ἐζήτουν οὖν τὸν Ἰησοῦν, καὶ ἔλεγον μετ'
they might purify themselves. they sought Then Jesus, and said with
ἀλλήλων ἐν τῷ ἱερῷ ἑστηκότες, Τί δοκεῖ ὑμῖν; ὅτι οὐ μὴ
one another in the Temple standing, What seems it to you? That not at all
57 ἔλθῃ εἰς τὴν ἑορτήν; δεδώκεισαν δὲ καὶ οἱ ἀρχιερεῖς καὶ οἱ
He comes to the feast? had given And also the chief priests and the
Φαρισαῖοι ἐντολήν, ἵνα ἐάν τις γνῷ ποῦ ἐστι, μηνύσῃ, ὅπως
Pharisees commands that if anyone knew where He is, he should inform so
πιάσωσιν αὐτόν.
they might seize Him.

CHAPTER 12

1 Ὁ οὖν Ἰησοῦς πρὸ ἓξ ἡμερῶν τοῦ πάσχα ἦλθεν εἰς
Therefore Jesus before six days the Passover came to
Βηθανίαν, ὅπου ἦν Λάζαρος ὁ τεθνηκώς, ὃν ἤγειρεν ἐκ νε-
Bethany, where was Lazarus, who had died, whom He raised out of
2 κρῶν. ἐποίησαν οὖν αὐτῷ δεῖπνον ἐκεῖ, καὶ ἡ Μάρθα διηκόνει·
(the) dead. they made Then for Him a supper there, and Martha served,
3 ὁ δὲ Λάζαρος εἷς ἦν τῶν συνανακειμένων αὐτῷ. ἡ οὖν Μαρία
but Lazarus one was of those reclining with Him. Then Mary
λαβοῦσα λίτραν μύρου νάρδου πιστικῆς πολυτίμου,
taking a pound of ointment of spikenard pure costly
ἤλειψε τοὺς πόδας τοῦ Ἰησοῦ, καὶ ἐξέμαξε ταῖς θριξὶν αὐτῆς
rubbed the feet — of Jesus, and wiped off with the hairs of her
τοὺς πόδας αὐτοῦ· ἡ δὲ οἰκία ἐπληρώθη ἐκ τῆς ὀσμῆς τοῦ
the feet of Him. the And house was filled of the odor of the
4 μύρου. λέγει οὖν εἷς ἐκ τῶν μαθητῶν αὐτοῦ, Ἰούδας Σίμωνος
ointment. says Then one of the disciples of Him, Judas of Simon
5 Ἰσκαριώτης, ὁ μέλλων αὐτὸν παραδιδόναι, Διατί τοῦτο τὸ
Iscariot, the (one) being about Him to betray, Why this —
μύρον οὐκ ἐπράθη τριακοσίων δηναρίων, καὶ ἐδόθη πτω-
ointment not was sold (for) three hundred denarii, and given to (the)
6 χοῖς; εἶπε δὲ τοῦτο, οὐχ ὅτι περὶ τῶν πτωχῶν ἔμελεν αὐτῷ,
poor? he said But this, not because about the poor was a care to him,
ἀλλ' ὅτι κλέπτης ἦν, καὶ τὸ γλωσσόκομον εἶχε, καὶ τὰ
but that a thief he was, and the moneybag held and that
7 βαλλόμενα ἐβάσταζεν. εἶπεν οὖν ὁ Ἰησοῦς, Ἄφες αὐτήν·
being put (in) carried away. said Therefore Jesus, Allow her;
8 εἰς τὴν ἡμέραν τοῦ ἐνταφιασμοῦ μου τετήρηκεν αὐτό. τοὺς
for the day of the burial of Me she has kept it. the
πτωχοὺς γὰρ πάντοτε ἔχετε μεθ' ἑαυτῶν, ἐμὲ δὲ οὐ πάντοτε
poor For always you have with yourselves, Me but not always
ἔχετε.
you have.

9 Ἔγνω οὖν ὄχλος πολὺς ἐκ τῶν Ἰουδαίων ὅτι ἐκεῖ ἐστι
knew Then crowd the much of the Jews that there He is,

was there. And they came not because of Jesus alone, but that they also might see Lazarus whom He raised from *the* dead. [10]But the chief priests took counsel that they also might put Lazarus to death, [11]because many of the Jews went away and believed into Jesus.

[12]On the morrow, coming to the Feast, hearing that Jesus is coming to Jerusalem, a great crowd [13]took palm branches and went out to a meeting with Him, and were crying out, Hosanna! Blessed *is* He coming in *the* name of *the* Lord, the King of Israel! [14]And having found an ass colt, Jesus sat on it, even as it had been written, [15]"Do not fear, daughter of Zion. Behold, your king comes sitting on the foal of an ass." [16]But His disciples did not know at the first, but when Jesus was glorified, then they recalled that these things had been written on Him; and they did these things to Him. [17]Then the crowd which was with Him when He called Lazarus out of the tomb, and raising him from *the* dead, witnessed. [18]Because of this also the crowds met Him, because it heard *of* this miracle He had done. [19]Then the Pharisees said among themselves, Observe that you gain nothing. Behold, the world has gone after Him.

[20]And there were some Greeks among those coming up, that they might worship at the Feast. [21]Then these came to Philip, the *one* from Bethsaida of Galilee, and asked him, saying, Sir, we desire to see Jesus. [22]Philip came and told Andrew, and again Andrew and Philip told Jesus. [23]But Jesus answered them, saying, The hour has come that the Son of man should be glorified. [24]Truly, truly, I say to you, Unless the grain of wheat that falls into the earth dies,

καὶ ἦλθον οὐ διὰ τὸν Ἰησοῦν μόνον, ἀλλ᾽ ἵνα καὶ τὸν
and they came not because of Jesus alone, but that also —
10 Λάζαρον ἴδωσιν, ὃν ἤγειρεν ἐκ νεκρῶν. ἐβουλεύσαντο δὲ οἱ
Lazarus they might see, whom He raised from dead. took counsel But the
11 ἀρχιερεῖς ἵνα καὶ τὸν Λάζαρον ἀποκτείνωσιν· ὅτι πολλοὶ δι᾽
chief priests that also — Lazarus they might kill, because many through
αὐτὸν ὑπῆγον τῶν Ἰουδαίων, καὶ ἐπίστευον εἰς τὸν Ἰησοῦν.
him departed of the Jews, and believed in — Jesus.
12 Τῇ ἐπαύριον ὄχλος πολὺς ὁ ἐλθὼν εἰς τὴν ἑορτήν, ἀκού-
On the morrow a crowd much coming to the feast,
13 σαντες ὅτι ἔρχεται ὁ Ἰησοῦς εἰς Ἱεροσόλυμα, ἔλαβον τὰ
hearing that is coming — Jesus to Jerusalem, took the
βαΐα τῶν φοινίκων, καὶ ἐξῆλθον εἰς ὑπάντησιν αὐτῷ, καὶ
branches of the palm-trees and went out to a meeting with Him, and
ἔκραζον, Ὡσαννά· εὐλογημένος ὁ ἐρχόμενος ἐν ὀνόματι
cried out, Hosanna! Blessed (is) He coming in (the) name
14 Κυρίου, ὁ βασιλεὺς τοῦ Ἰσραήλ. εὑρὼν δὲ ὁ Ἰησοῦς ὀνάριον,
of (the) Lord, the king + of Israel. finding And Jesus an ass colt,
15 ἐκάθισεν ἐπ᾽ αὐτό, καθώς ἐστι γεγραμμένον, Μὴ φοβοῦ,
He sat upon it, even as it is having been written, Do not fear,
θύγατερ Σιών· ἰδού, ὁ βασιλεύς σου ἔρχεται, καθήμενος ἐπὶ
daughter of Zion. Behold, the King of you comes, sitting on
16 πῶλον ὄνου. ταῦτα δὲ οὐκ ἔγνωσαν οἱ μαθηταὶ αὐτοῦ τὸ
the foal of an ass. these things But not knew the disciples of Him at the
πρῶτον· ἀλλ᾽ ὅτε ἐδοξάσθη ὁ Ἰησοῦς, τότε ἐμνήσθησαν ὅτι
first, but when was glorified Jesus, then they remembered that
ταῦτα ἦν ἐπ᾽ αὐτῷ γεγραμμένα, καὶ ταῦτα ἐποίησαν αὐτῷ.
these things were on Him having been written, and these they did to Him.
17 ἐμαρτύρει οὖν ὁ ὄχλος ὁ ὢν μετ᾽ αὐτοῦ ὅτε τὸν Λάζαρον
witnessed Therefore the crowd which was with Him when — Lazarus
18 ἐφώνησεν ἐκ τοῦ μνημείου, καὶ ἤγειρεν αὐτὸν ἐκ νεκρῶν. διὰ
He called out of the tomb, and raised him out of (the) dead. There-
τοῦτο καὶ ὑπήντησεν αὐτῷ ὁ ὄχλος, ὅτι ἤκουσε τοῦτο
fore also met with Him the crowd, because it heard this
19 αὐτὸν πεποιηκέναι τὸ σημεῖον. οἱ οὖν Φαρισαῖοι εἶπον πρὸς
(which) He had done sign. the Then Pharisees said to
ἑαυτούς, Θεωρεῖτε ὅτι οὐκ ὠφελεῖτε οὐδέν· ἴδε ὁ κόσμος
themselves, Observe, that not you profit nothing. Behold, the world
ὀπίσω αὐτοῦ ἀπῆλθεν.
after Him has gone
20 Ἦσαν δέ τινες Ἕλληνες ἐκ τῶν ἀναβαινόντων ἵνα προσ-
were And some Greeks of those going up that they
21 κυνήσωσιν ἐν τῇ ἑορτῇ· οὗτοι οὖν προσῆλθον Φιλίππῳ
might worship at the feast. these Then came toward Philip
τῷ ἀπὸ Βηθσαϊδὰ τῆς Γαλιλαίας, καὶ ἠρώτων αὐτὸν
the (one) from Bethsaida — of Galilee, and asked him
22 λέγοντες, Κύριε, θέλομεν τὸν Ἰησοῦν ἰδεῖν. ἔρχεται Φίλιππος
saying, Sir, we desire Jesus to see. Comes Philip
καὶ λέγει τῷ Ἀνδρέᾳ· καὶ πάλιν Ἀνδρέας καὶ Φίλιππος
and tells — Andrew, and again Andrew and Philip
23 λέγουσι τῷ Ἰησοῦ. ὁ δὲ Ἰησοῦς ἀπεκρίνατο αὐτοῖς λέγων,
tell — Jesus. And Jesus answers them, saying,
24 Ἐλήλυθεν ἡ ὥρα ἵνα δοξασθῇ ὁ υἱὸς τοῦ ἀνθρώπου. ἀμὴν
has come The hour that should be glorified the Son — of man. Truly,
ἀμὴν λέγω ὑμῖν, ἐὰν μὴ ὁ κόκκος τοῦ σίτου πεσὼν εἰς τὴν
truly, I say to you, Unless the grain — of wheat falling into the

it remains alone. But if it dies, it bears much fruit. [25]The *one* who loves his soul loses it; and he who hates his soul in this world will keep it to everlasting life. [26]If anyone serves Me, let him follow Me; and where I am, there My servant will also be. And if anyone serves Me, the Father will honor him.

[27]And My soul is troubled, and what may I say? Father, save Me out of this hour. but on this account I came to this hour. [28]Father, glorify Your name. Then a voice came out of the heaven, I both glorified *it*, and I will again glorify *it*. [29]Then standing and hearing, the crowd said that thunder occurred. Others said, An angel has spoken to Him. [30]Jesus answered and said, this voice has not occurred because of Me, but because of you. [31]Now is *the* judgment of this world; not the ruler of this world shall be cast out. [32]And I, if I be lifted up from the earth, I will draw all to Myself. [33]But He said this, signifying by what kind *of* death He was about to die. [34]The crowd answered Him, We heard out of the Law that the Christ lives forever. And how do you say that the Son of man must be lifted up? Who is this Son of man? [35]Then Jesus said to them, Yet a little while the Light is with you. Walk while you have the Light, that darkness not overtake you. And the *one* walking in the darkness does not know where he is going. [36]While you have the Light, believe into the Light, that you may become sons of Light.

Jesus spoke these things, and going away was hidden from them.

[37]But *though* He had done so many miracles before them, they did not believe into Him, [38]so that the word of Isaiah the prophet might be fulfilled, which he said, "Lord, who has believed our report? And the

γῆν ἀποθάνῃ, αὐτὸς μόνος μένει· ἐὰν δὲ ἀποθάνῃ, πολὺν
earth dies, it alone remains; if but it die much
25 καρπὸν φέρει. ὁ φιλῶν τὴν ψυχὴν αὐτοῦ ἀπολέσει αὐτήν·
fruit it bears. He loving the soul of him loses it;
καὶ ὁ μισῶν τὴν ψυχὴν αὐτοῦ ἐν τῷ κόσμῳ τούτῳ εἰς ζωὴν
and he hating the soul of him in world this, to life
26 αἰώνιον φυλάξει αὐτήν. ἐὰν ἐμοὶ διακονῇ τις, ἐμοὶ ἀκολου-
eternal will keep it. If Me serves anyone, Me let him
θείτω· καὶ ὅπου εἰμὶ ἐγώ, ἐκεῖ καὶ ὁ διάκονος ὁ ἐμὸς ἔσται·
follow; and where am I, there also servant My will be.
27 καὶ ἐάν τις ἐμοὶ διακονῇ, τιμήσει αὐτὸν ὁ πατήρ. νῦν ἡ ψυχή
And if anyone Me serves, will honor him the Father. Now the soul
μου τετάρακται· καὶ τί εἴπω ; πάτερ, σῶσόν με ἐκ τῆς ὥρας
of Me is agitated, and what may I say? Father, save Me out of hour
28 ταύτης. ἀλλὰ διὰ τοῦτο ἦλθον εἰς τὴν ὥραν ταύτην. πάτερ,
this. But on account of this I came to hour this. Father,
δόξασόν σου τὸ ὄνομα. ἦλθεν οὖν φωνὴ ἐκ τοῦ οὐρανοῦ,
glorify of You the name. came Then a voice out of Heaven:
29 Καὶ ἐδόξασα, καὶ πάλιν δοξάσω. ὁ οὖν ὄχλος ὁ ἑστὼς καὶ
Both I glorified and again I will glorify. the Then crowd standing and
ἀκούσας ἔλεγε βροντὴν γεγονέναι· ἄλλοι ἔλεγον, Ἄγγελος
hearing said thunder to have occurred. Others said, An angel
30 αὐτῷ λελάληκεν. ἀπεκρίθη ὁ Ἰησοῦς καὶ εἶπεν, Οὐ δι' ἐμὲ
to Him has spoken, answered — Jesus and said, Not via Me
31 αὕτη ἡ φωνὴ γέγονεν, ἀλλὰ δι' ὑμᾶς. νῦν κρίσις ἐστὶ τοῦ
this voice occurred, but because of you. Now judgment is —
κόσμου τούτου· νῦν ὁ ἄρχων τοῦ κόσμου τούτου ἐκβληθή-
of world this; now the ruler of world this shall be
32 σεται ἔξω. κἀγὼ ἐὰν ὑψωθῶ ἐκ τῆς γῆς, πάντας ἑλκύσω
thrown out. And I if I be lifted up from the earth, all I will draw
33 πρὸς ἐμαυτόν. τοῦτο δὲ ἔλεγε, σημαίνων ποίῳ θανάτῳ
to Myself. this And He said, signifying by what kind (of) death
34 ἤμελλεν ἀποθνήσκειν. ἀπεκρίθη αὐτῷ ὁ ὄχλος, Ἡμεῖς ἠκού-
He was about to die. answered Him The crowd, We heard
σαμεν ἐκ τοῦ νόμου ὅτι ὁ Χριστὸς μένει εἰς τὸν αἰῶνα· καὶ πῶς
out of the law that the Christ abides to the age; and how
σὺ λέγεις ὅτι Δεῖ ὑψωθῆναι τὸν υἱὸν τοῦ ἀνθρώπου ; τίς
do you say that it behoves to be lifted up the Son — of man? Who
35 ἐστιν οὗτος ὁ υἱὸς τοῦ ἀνθρώπου ; εἶπεν οὖν αὐτοῖς ὁ Ἰησοῦς,
is this Son — of man? said Then to them Jesus,
Ἔτι μικρὸν χρόνον τὸ φῶς μεθ' ὑμῶν ἐστι. περιπατεῖτε ἕως
Yet a little time the light with you is. Walk while
τὸ φῶς ἔχετε, ἵνα μὴ σκοτία ὑμᾶς καταλάβῃ· καὶ ὁ περιπα-
the light you have, lest darkness you overtake; and the (one) walk-
36 τῶν ἐν τῇ σκοτίᾳ οὐκ οἶδε ποῦ ὑπάγει. ἕως τὸ φῶς ἔχετε,
ing in the darkness not knows where he is going. While the light you have,
πιστεύετε εἰς τὸ φῶς, ἵνα υἱοὶ φωτὸς γένησθε.
believe in the light, that sons of light you may become.

Ταῦτα ἐλάλησεν ὁ Ἰησοῦς, καὶ ἀπελθὼν ἐκρύβη ἀπ'
These things spoke — Jesus, and going away was hidden from
37 αὐτῶν. τοσαῦτα δὲ αὐτοῦ σημεῖα πεποιηκότος ἔμπροσθεν
them. so many But He signs having done before
38 αὐτῶν, οὐκ ἐπίστευον εἰς αὐτόν· ἵνα ὁ λόγος Ἠσαΐου τοῦ
them, not they believed in Him that the word of Isaiah the
προφήτου πληρωθῇ, ὃν εἶπε, Κύριε, τίς ἐπίστευσε τῇ ἀκοῇ
prophet might be fulfilled which he said, Lord, who has believed the report

arm of the Lord, to whom was it revealed?" 39 Because of this they could not believe, because Isaiah said again, 40 "He has blinded their eyes and has hardened their heart, that they might not see with the eyes, and understand with the heart, and be converted, and I should heal them." 41 Isaiah said these things when he saw His glory, and spoke about Him. 42 Still, even among the rulers, many did not believe into Him. But because of the Pharisees, they were not confessing, so that they not be put out of the synagogue. 43 For they loved the glory of men more than the glory of God.

44 But Jesus cried out and said, The *one* believing into Me does not believe into Me, but into the *One* sending Me. 45 And the *one* seeing Me sees the *One* who sent Me. 46 I have come *as* a Light to the world, that everyone who believes into Me may not remain in the darkness. 47 And if anyone hears My words, and does not believe, I do not judge him; for I did not come that I might judge the world, but that I might save the world. 48 The *one* who rejects Me and not receiving My words has that judging him: the word which I spoke, that will judge him in the last Day. 49 For I did not speak from Myself, but He who sent Me, *the* Father, He has given Me command, what I should say, and what I should speak. 50 And I know that His command is everlasting life. Therefore, what things I speak, as the Father has said to Me, so I speak.

CHAPTER 13

1 And before the feast of the Passover, Jesus knowing that His hour had come that He should move from this world to the Father, loving *His* own in the world, He loved them to *the* end. 2 And supper taking place, the

39 ἡμῶν ; καὶ ὁ βραχίων Κυρίου τίνι ἀπεκαλύφθη ; διὰ τοῦτο
of us? And the arm of (the) Lord, to whom was it revealed? Therefore
40 οὐκ ἠδύναντο πιστεύειν, ὅτι πάλιν εἶπεν Ἠσαΐας, Τετύ-
not they could believe, because again said Isaiah, He has
φλωκεν αὐτῶν τοὺς ὀφθαλμούς, καὶ πεπώρωκεν αὐτῶν τὴν
blinded of them the eyes, and hardened of them the
41 καρδίαν· ἵνα μὴ ἴδωσι τοῖς ὀφθαλμοῖς, καὶ νοήσωσι τῇ
heart, lest they might see with the eyes, and understand with the
καρδίᾳ, καὶ ἐπιστραφῶσι, καὶ ἰάσωμαι αὐτούς. ταῦτα εἶπεν
heart, and be converted, and I should heal them. These things said
Ἠσαΐας, ὅτε εἶδε τὴν δόξαν αὐτοῦ, καὶ ἐλάλησε περὶ αὐτοῦ.
Isaiah when he saw the glory of Him, and spoke about Him.
42 ὅμως μέντοι καὶ ἐκ τῶν ἀρχόντων πολλοὶ ἐπίστευσαν εἰς
Still, however, even of the rulers many believed in
αὐτόν· ἀλλὰ διὰ τοὺς Φαρισαίους οὐχ ὡμολόγουν, ἵνα μὴ
Him, but because of the Pharisees not were confessing lest
43 ἀποσυνάγωγοι γένωνται. ἠγάπησαν γὰρ τὴν δόξαν τῶν
put out of the synagogue they be. they loved For the glory —
ἀνθρώπων μᾶλλον ἤπερ τὴν δόξαν τοῦ Θεοῦ.
of men more than the glory — of God.
44 Ἰησοῦς δὲ ἔκραξε καὶ εἶπεν, Ὁ πιστεύων εἰς ἐμέ, οὐ
Jesus But cried out and said, The (one) believing in Me, not
45 πιστεύει εἰς ἐμέ, ἀλλ᾽ εἰς τὸν πέμψαντά με· καὶ ὁ θεωρῶν
believes in Me, but in the (One) sending Me; and he seeing
46 ἐμέ, θεωρεῖ τὸν πέμψαντά με. ἐγὼ φῶς εἰς τὸν κόσμον
Me sees the (One) sending Me. I a light to the world
ἐλήλυθα, ἵνα πᾶς ὁ πιστεύων εἰς ἐμέ, ἐν τῇ σκοτίᾳ μὴ μείνῃ.
have come, that everyone believing in Me in the darkness not may abide.
47 καὶ ἐάν τις μου ἀκούσῃ τῶν ῥημάτων καὶ μὴ πιστεύσῃ,
And if anyone of Me hears the words, and not believes,
ἐγὼ οὐ κρίνω αὐτόν· οὐ γὰρ ἦλθον ἵνα κρίνω τὸν κόσμον,
I do not judge him; not for I came that I might judge the world,
48 ἀλλ᾽ ἵνα σώσω τὸν κόσμον. ὁ ἀθετῶν ἐμὲ καὶ μὴ λαμβάνων
but that I might save the world. The (one) rejecting Me and not receiving
τὰ ῥήματά μου, ἔχει τὸν κρίνοντα αὐτόν· ὁ λόγος ὃν
the words of Me has that judging him: the word which
49 ἐλάλησα, ἐκεῖνος κρινεῖ αὐτὸν ἐν τῇ ἐσχάτῃ ἡμέρᾳ. ὅτι ἐγὼ
I spoke, that will judge him in the last Day. Because I
ἐξ ἐμαυτοῦ οὐκ ἐλάλησα· ἀλλ᾽ ὁ πέμψας με πατήρ, αὐτός μοι
from Myself not spoke, but He sending Me, (the) Father, He Me
50 ἐντολὴν ἔδωκε, τί εἴπω καὶ τί λαλήσω. καὶ οἶδα ὅτι ἡ
command has given, what I may say and what I may speak. And I know that the
ἐντολὴ αὐτοῦ ζωὴ αἰώνιός ἐστιν· ἃ οὖν λαλῶ ἐγώ, καθὼς
command of Him life eternal is. What things then speak I, as
εἴρηκέ μοι ὁ πατήρ, οὕτω λαλῶ.
has said to Me the Father, so I speak.

CHAPTER 13

1 Πρὸ δὲ τῆς ἑορτῆς τοῦ πάσχα, εἰδὼς ὁ Ἰησοῦς ὅτι
before And the feast of the Passover, knowing Jesus that
ἐλήλυθεν αὐτοῦ ἡ ὥρα ἵνα μεταβῇ ἐκ τοῦ κόσμου τούτου
had come of Him the hour that He should move from world this,
πρὸς τὸν πατέρα, ἀγαπήσας τοὺς ἰδίους τοὺς ἐν τῷ κόσμῳ,
to the Father, loving the own — in the world,
2 εἰς τέλος ἠγάπησεν αὐτούς. καὶ δείπνου γενομένου, τοῦ
to (the) end He loved them. And supper having occurred the

Devil having already put into the heart of Simon's son Judas Iscariot that he should betray Him, [3]Jesus knowing that His Father has given all things into *His* hands, and that He came out from God, and goes to God, [4]He rose up from the supper, and laid aside *His* garments. And taking a towel, He girded Himself. [5]Then He put water into the basin and began to wash the feet of the disciples, and to wipe off with the towel with which He was girded. [6]He then came to Simon Peter. And that one said to Him, Lord, do You wash my feet? [7]Jesus answered and said to him, What I am doing, you do not yet know. But you will know after these things. [8]Peter said to Him, You may in no way wash my feet forever. Jesus answered him, Unless I wash you, you have no part with Me. [9]Simon Peter said to Him, Lord, not my feet only but also the hands and the head. [10]Jesus said to him, The *one* having been bathed has no need *other* than to wash the feet, but is wholly clean. And you are clean, but not all. [11]For He knew the *one* betraying Him. For this reason He said, You are not all clean.

[12]Then when He had washed their feet, and had taken His garments, reclining again, He said to them, Do you know what I have done to you? [13]You call Me the Teacher, and, The Lord. And you say well, for I am. [14]If then I washed your feet, the Lord and the Teacher, you also ought to wash the feet of one another. [15]For I gave you an example, that as I did to you, you also should do. [16]Truly, truly, I say to you, A slave is not greater than his lord, or a messenger greater than the *one* sending him. [17]If you know these things, blessed are you if you do them. [18]I do not speak concerning all of you; I know whom I chose out; but that the Scripture might be

διαβόλου ἤδη βεβληκότος εἰς τὴν καρδίαν Ἰούδα Σίμωνος
Devil already having put into the heart of Judas of Simon
3 Ἰσκαριώτου ἵνα αὐτὸν παραδῷ, εἰδὼς ὁ Ἰησοῦς ὅτι πάντα
Iscariot, that Him he should betray, knowing Jesus that all things
δέδωκεν αὐτῷ ὁ πατὴρ εἰς τὰς χεῖρας, καὶ ὅτι ἀπὸ Θεοῦ
has given Him the Father into the hands, and that from God
4 ἐξῆλθε καὶ πρὸς τὸν Θεὸν ὑπάγει, ἐγείρεται ἐκ τοῦ δείπνου,
He came, and to — God departs, He rises from the supper
καὶ τίθησι τὰ ἱμάτια, καὶ λαβὼν λέντιον διέζωσεν ἑαυτόν.
and lays aside the garments, and taking a towel He girded Himself.
5 εἶτα βάλλει ὕδωρ εἰς τὸν νιπτῆρα, καὶ ἤρξατο νίπτειν τοὺς
Then He puts water into the basin, and began to wash the
πόδας τῶν μαθητῶν, καὶ ἐκμάσσειν τῷ λεντίῳ ᾧ ἦν διεζω-
feet of the disciples, and to wipe off with the towel with which He
6 σμένος. ἔρχεται οὖν πρὸς Σίμωνα Πέτρον· καὶ λέγει αὐτῷ
was girded. He comes then to Simon Peter; and said to Him
7 ἐκεῖνος, Κύριε, σύ μου νίπτεις τοὺς πόδας; ἀπεκρίθη Ἰησοῦς
that one, Lord, Do You of me wash the feet? answered Jesus
καὶ εἶπεν αὐτῷ, Ὃ ἐγὼ ποιῶ, σὺ οὐκ οἶδας ἄρτι, γνώσῃ
and said to him, What I am doing, you not know yet, you will know
8 δὲ μετὰ ταῦτα. λέγει αὐτῷ Πέτρος, Οὐ μὴ νίψῃς τοὺς πόδας
but after these things. says to Him Peter, In no way may You wash the feet
μου εἰς τὸν αἰῶνα. ἀπεκρίθη αὐτῷ ὁ Ἰησοῦς, Ἐὰν μὴ νίψω
of me to the age. answered to him — Jesus, Unless I wash
9 σε, οὐκ ἔχεις μέρος μετ' ἐμοῦ. λέγει αὐτῷ Σίμων Πέτρος,
you, not you have part with Me. says to Him Simon Peter,
Κύριε, μὴ τοὺς πόδας μου μόνον, ἀλλὰ καὶ τὰς χεῖρας καὶ
Lord, not the feet of Me only, but also the hands and
10 τὴν κεφαλήν. λέγει αὐτῷ ὁ Ἰησοῦς, Ὁ λελουμένος οὐ χρείαν
the head. says to him Jesus, He having bathed no need
ἔχει ἢ τοὺς πόδας νίψασθαι, ἀλλ' ἔστι καθαρὸς ὅλος· καὶ
has than the feet to wash, but is clean wholly; and
11 ὑμεῖς καθαροί ἐστε, ἀλλ' οὐχὶ πάντες. ᾔδει γὰρ τὸν παραδι-
you clean are, but not all. He knew For the (one) betray-
δόντα αὐτόν· διὰ τοῦτο εἶπεν, Οὐχὶ πάντες καθαροί ἐστε.
ing Him; for this reason He said, Not all clean you are.
12 Ὅτε οὖν ἔνιψε τοὺς πόδας αὐτῶν, καὶ ἔλαβε τὰ ἱμάτια
When, therefore, He washed the feet of them, and took the garments
αὐτοῦ, ἀναπεσὼν πάλιν, εἶπεν αὐτοῖς, Γινώσκετε τί πεποίη-
of Him. Reclining again, He said to them, Do you know what I have
13 κα ὑμῖν; ὑμεῖς φωνεῖτέ με, Ὁ διδάσκαλος, καὶ Ὁ κύριος· καὶ
done to you? You call Me, The Teacher, and, The Lord; and
14 καλῶς λέγετε, εἰμὶ γάρ. εἰ οὖν ἐγὼ ἔνιψα ὑμῶν τοὺς πόδας,
well you say; I am for. If, then, I washed of you the feet,
ὁ κύριος καὶ ὁ διδάσκαλος, καὶ ὑμεῖς ὀφείλετε ἀλλήλων
the Lord and the Teacher; also you ought of one another
15 νίπτειν τοὺς πόδας. ὑπόδειγμα γὰρ ἔδωκα ὑμῖν, ἵνα καθὼς
to wash the feet. an example For I gave you, that as
16 ἐγὼ ἐποίησα ὑμῖν, καὶ ὑμεῖς ποιῆτε. ἀμὴν ἀμὴν λέγω ὑμῖν,
I did to you, also you should do. Truly, truly, I say to you,
Οὐκ ἔστι δοῦλος μείζων τοῦ κυρίου αὐτοῦ, οὐδὲ ἀπόστολος
not is A slave greater than the lord of him, nor a messenger
17 μείζων τοῦ πέμψαντος αὐτόν. εἰ ταῦτα οἴδατε, μακάριοί
greater than the (one) sending him. If these things you know, blessed
18 ἐστε ἐὰν ποιῆτε αὐτά. οὐ περὶ πάντων ὑμῶν λέγω· ἐγὼ
are you if you do them. Not concerning all of you I speak; I

fulfilled, "The *one* eating the bread with Me lifted up his heel against Me." 19 From this time I tell you, before *it* happens, that when it happens you may believe that I AM. 20 Truly, truly, I say to you, The *one* who receives whomever I may send receives Me; and the *one* who receives Me receives the *One* who sent Me.

21 Having said these things, Jesus was troubled in spirit, and testified and said, Indeed I tell you truly that one of you will betray Me. 22 Then the disciples looked upon one another, doubting of whom He spoke. 23 But there was one of His disciples reclining at the bosom of Jesus, whom Jesus loved. 24 Therefore Simon Peter signaled to him to ask whom it might be of whom He spoke. 25 And he having leaned upon the breast of Jesus said to Him, Lord, who is it? 26 Jesus answered, It is he to whom I, having dipped the morsel, shall give *it*. And having dipped in the morsel, He gave *it* to Judas Iscariot, *son* of Simon. 27 And after the morsel, then Satan entered into him. Then Jesus said to him, What you do, do quickly. 28 But no one of those reclining knew for what He spoke to him; 29 for some thought, since Judas held the purse, that Jesus was saying to him, Buy what things we have need *of* for the feast; or that he should give something to the poor. 30 Therefore, having received the morsel, he immediately went out; and it was night.

31 When therefore he had gone out, Jesus said, Now the Son of Man has been glorified, and God has been glorified in Him. 32 If God has been glorified in Him, God also shall glorify Him in Himself, and immediately shall glorify Him. 33 Little children, yet a little while I am with you. You will seek Me; and, as I said to the Jews that, where I go, you

οἶδα οὓς ἐξελεξάμην· ἀλλ' ἵνα ἡ γραφὴ πληρωθῇ, Ὁ τρώγων
know whom I chose out, but that the Scripture be fulfilled: The (one) eating
19 μετ' ἐμοῦ τὸν ἄρτον ἐπῆρεν ἐπ' ἐμὲ τὴν πτέρναν αὐτοῦ. ἀπ'
with Me the bread lifted up against Me the heel of him. From
ἄρτι λέγω ὑμῖν πρὸ τοῦ γενέσθαι, ἵνα, ὅταν γένηται,
now I tell you, before the happening, that when it happens
20 πιστεύσητε ὅτι ἐγώ εἰμι. ἀμὴν ἀμὴν λέγω ὑμῖν, Ὁ λαμβάνων
you may believe that I AM. Truly, truly, I say to you, he receiving
ἐάν τινα πέμψω, ἐμὲ λαμβάνει· ὁ δὲ ἐμὲ λαμβάνων, λαμβάνει
whomever I may send, Me receives, he and Me receiving, receives
τὸν πέμψαντά με.
the (one) sending Me.

21 Ταῦτα εἰπὼν ὁ Ἰησοῦς ἐταράχθη τῷ πνεύματι, καὶ
These things saying — Jesus was agitated in the spirit, and
ἐμαρτύρησε καὶ εἶπεν, Ἀμὴν ἀμὴν λέγω ὑμῖν ὅτι εἷς ἐξ ὑμῶν
witnessed and said, Truly, truly, I say to you that one of you
22 παραδώσει με. ἔβλεπον οὖν εἰς ἀλλήλους οἱ μαθηταί,
will betray Me. looked Then at one another the disciples,
23 ἀπορούμενοι περὶ τίνος λέγει. ἦν δὲ ἀνακείμενος εἷς τῶν
being perplexed about whom He speaks. was And reclining one of the
μαθητῶν αὐτοῦ ἐν τῷ κόλπῳ τοῦ Ἰησοῦ, ὃν ἠγάπα ὁ
disciples of Him on the bosom — of Jesus, whom loved —
24 Ἰησοῦς· νεύει οὖν τούτῳ Σίμων Πέτρος πυθέσθαι τίς ἂν εἴη
Jesus; nods then to this one Simon Peter to ask who it might be
25 περὶ οὗ λέγει. ἐπιπεσὼν δὲ ἐκεῖνος ἐπὶ τὸ στῆθος τοῦ Ἰησοῦ,
about whom He speaks. leaning And that one on the breast — of Jesus,
26 λέγει αὐτῷ, Κύριε, τίς ἐστιν; ἀποκρίνεται ὁ Ἰησοῦς,
he said to Him, Lord, who is it? answers — Jesus,
Ἐκεῖνός ἐστιν ᾧ ἐγὼ βάψας τὸ ψωμίον ἐπιδώσω. καὶ ἐμβά-
That one it is to whom I having dipped the morsel shall give it. And dipping
27 ψας τὸ ψωμίον, δίδωσιν Ἰούδᾳ Σίμωνος Ἰσκαριώτῃ. καὶ
the morsel, He gave to Judas of Simon Iscariot. And
μετὰ τὸ ψωμίον, τότε εἰσῆλθεν εἰς ἐκεῖνον ὁ Σατανᾶς. λέγει
after the morsel, then entered into that one Satan. says
28 οὖν αὐτῷ ὁ Ἰησοῦς, Ὃ ποιεῖς, ποίησον τάχιον. τοῦτο δὲ
Then to him Jesus, What you do, do quickly. this But
29 οὐδεὶς ἔγνω τῶν ἀνακειμένων πρὸς τί εἶπεν αὐτῷ. τινὲς γὰρ
no one knew of those reclining for what He spoke to him. some For
ἐδόκουν, ἐπεὶ τὸ γλωσσόκομον εἶχεν ὁ Ἰούδας, ὅτι λέγει
thought, since the money-bag held — Judas, that tells
αὐτῷ ὁ Ἰησοῦς, Ἀγόρασον ὧν χρείαν ἔχομεν εἰς τὴν
him Jesus, Buy of what things need we have for the
30 ἑορτήν· ἢ τοῖς πτωχοῖς ἵνα τι δῷ. λαβὼν οὖν τὸ ψωμίον
feast; or, to the poor that a thing he give. Receiving, then, the morsel
ἐκεῖνος, εὐθέως ἐξῆλθεν· ἦν δὲ νύξ.
that one, at once went out. it was And night.

31 Ὅτε οὖν ἐξῆλθε, λέγει ὁ Ἰησοῦς, Νῦν ἐδοξάσθη ὁ υἱὸς τοῦ
when Then he went, says Jesus, Now was glorified the Son —
32 ἀνθρώπου, καὶ ὁ Θεὸς ἐδοξάσθη ἐν αὐτῷ. εἰ ὁ Θεὸς ἐδοξάσθη
of man, and God was glorified in Him; if God was glorified
ἐν αὐτῷ, καὶ ὁ Θεὸς δοξάσει αὐτὸν ἐν ἑαυτῷ, καὶ εὐθὺς
in Him, both God will glorify Him in Himself, and at once
33 δοξάσει αὐτόν. τεκνία, ἔτι μικρὸν μεθ' ὑμῶν εἰμι. ζητήσετέ
will glorify Him. Children, yet a little with you I am. You will seek
με, καὶ καθὼς εἶπον τοῖς Ἰουδαίοις ὅτι Ὅπου ὑπάγω ἐγώ,
Me, and as I said to the Jews, — Where go I,

are not able to come; I also say to you now. [34]I give a new commandment to you, that you should love one another, according as I loved you, you should also love one another. [35]By this all shall know that you are My disciples, if you have love among one another. [36]Simon Peter said to Him, Lord, where do You go? Jesus answered him, Where I go you are not able to follow now, but afterwards you shall follow Me. [37]Peter said to Him, Lord, why am I not able to follow You now? I will lay down my life for you! [38]Jesus answered him, Will you lay down your life for Me? Indeed, I tell you truly, in no way shall *the* cock crow until that you shall deny Me three times.

CHAPTER 14

[1]Do not let your heart be troubled; you believe in God, believe also in Me. [2]In My father's house are many dwelling places. If it were not so, I would have told you. I am going to prepare a place for you! [3]And if I go and prepare a place for you, I am coming again, and will receive you to Myself, that where I am you may be also. [4]And where I go you know, and the way you know.

[5]Thomas said to Him, Lord, we do not know where You go, and how can we know the way? [6]Jesus said to him, I am the Way, and the Truth, and the Life. No one comes to the Father but by Me. [7]If you had known Me, you would have known My Father also; and from now on you do know Him, and have seen Him. [8]And Philip said to Him, Lord, show us the Father, and it suffices us. [9]Jesus said to him, Am I so long a time with you, and you have not known Me, Philip? He that has seen Me has seen the Father! And how do

34 ὑμεῖς οὐ δύνασθε ἐλθεῖν, καὶ ὑμῖν λέγω ἄρτι. ἐντολὴν
you not are able to come, also to you I say now. A command
καινὴν δίδωμι ὑμῖν, ἵνα ἀγαπᾶτε ἀλλήλους· καθὼς ἠγά-
A new I give you, that you love one another as I
35 πησα ὑμᾶς, ἵνα καὶ ὑμεῖς ἀγαπᾶτε ἀλλήλους. ἐν τούτῳ γνώ-
loved you that also you should love one another. By this will
σονται πάντες ὅτι ἐμοὶ μαθηταί ἐστε, ἐὰν ἀγάπην ἔχητε ἐν
know all that to Me disciples you are, if love you have among
ἀλλήλοις.
one another.
36 Λέγει αὐτῷ Σίμων Πέτρος, Κύριε, ποῦ ὑπάγεις ; ἀπεκρίθη
says to Him Simon Peter, Lord, where do You go? answered
αὐτῷ ὁ Ἰησοῦς, Ὅπου ὑπάγω, οὐ δύνασαί μοι νῦν ἀκο-
him Jesus, Where I go, not you are able Me now to
37 λουθῆσαι, ὕστερον δὲ ἀκολουθήσεις μοι. λέγει αὐτῷ ὁ
follow, later but you will follow Me. says to Him
Πέτρος, Κύριε, διατί οὐ δύναμαί σοι ἀκολουθῆσαι ἄρτι ;
Peter, Lord, why not am I able You to follow now?
38 τὴν ψυχήν μου ὑπὲρ σοῦ θήσω. ἀπεκρίθη αὐτῷ ὁ Ἰησοῦς,
The soul of me for You I will lay down. answers him — Jesus,
Τὴν ψυχήν σου ὑπὲρ ἐμοῦ θήσεις ; ἀμὴν ἀμὴν λέγω σοι, οὐ
The soul of you for Me you will lay down? Truly, truly I say to you, in
μὴ ἀλέκτωρ φωνήσει ἕως οὗ ἀπαρνήσῃ με τρίς.
no way a cock will crow until you deny Me three times.

CHAPTER 14

1 Μὴ ταρασσέσθω ὑμῶν ἡ καρδία· πιστεύετε εἰς τὸν Θεόν,
Not let be agitated of you the heart; believe in God,
2 καὶ εἰς ἐμὲ πιστεύετε. ἐν τῇ οἰκίᾳ τοῦ πατρός μου μοναὶ
and in Me believe. In the house of the Father of Me dwellings
πολλαί εἰσιν· εἰ δὲ μή, εἶπον ἂν ὑμῖν· πορεύομαι ἑτοιμάσαι
many are. Otherwise, I would have told you. I go to prepare
3 τόπον ὑμῖν. καὶ ἐὰν πορευθῶ καὶ ἑτοιμάσω ὑμῖν τόπον,
a place for you, and if I go and prepare for you a place,
πάλιν ἔρχομαι καὶ παραλήψομαι ὑμᾶς πρὸς ἐμαυτόν· ἵνα
again I am coming and will receive you to Myself, that
4 ὅπου εἰμὶ ἐγώ, καὶ ὑμεῖς ἦτε. καὶ ὅπου ἐγὼ ὑπάγω οἴδατε,
where am I, also you may be. And where I go you know,
5 καὶ τὴν ὁδὸν οἴδατε. λέγει αὐτῷ Θωμᾶς, Κύριε, οὐκ οἴδαμεν
and the way you know. says to Him Thomas, Lord, not we know
6 ποῦ ὑπάγεις· καὶ πῶς δυνάμεθα τὴν ὁδὸν εἰδέναι ; λέγει
where You go, and how are we able the way to know? says
αὐτῷ ὁ Ἰησοῦς, Ἐγώ εἰμι ἡ ὁδὸς καὶ ἡ ἀλήθεια καὶ ἡ ζωή·
to him — Jesus, I am the way and the truth and the life;
7 οὐδεὶς ἔρχεται πρὸς τὸν πατέρα, εἰ μὴ δι' ἐμοῦ. εἰ ἐγνώκειτέ
no one comes to the Father except through Me. If you had known
με, καὶ τὸν πατέρα μου ἐγνώκειτε ἄν· καὶ ἀπ' ἄρτι γινώ-
Me, also the Father of Me you would have known, and from now you
8 σκετε αὐτόν, καὶ ἑωράκατε αὐτόν. λέγει αὐτῷ Φίλιππος,
know Him, and have seen Him. says to Him Philip,
9 Κύριε, δεῖξον ἡμῖν τὸν πατέρα, καὶ ἀρκεῖ ἡμῖν. λέγει αὐτῷ
Lord, show us the Father, and it suffices us. says to him
ὁ Ἰησοῦς, Τοσοῦτον χρόνον μεθ' ὑμῶν εἰμι, καὶ οὐκ ἔγνωκάς
— Jesus, so long a time with you Am I, and not you know
με, Φίλιππε ; ὁ ἑωρακὼς ἐμέ, ἑώρακε τὸν πατέρα· καὶ πῶς σὺ
Me, Philip? The (one) seeing Me has seen the Father; and how do you

you say, Show us the Father? [10]Do you not believe that I *am* in the Father and the Father is in Me? The words which I speak to you I do not speak from Myself, but the Father who abides in Me, He does the works.

[11]Believe Me that I *am* in the Father, and the Father *is* in Me; but if not, believe Me because of the works themselves. [12]Indeed, I tell you truly, He that believes in Me, the works which I do he shall also do, and greater than these he shall do, because I go to My Father. [13]And whatever you may ask in My Name, this I will do, that the Father may be glorified in the Son. [14]If you ask anything in My Name, I will do *it*. [15]If you love Me, keep My commandments.

[16]And I will petition the Father, and He will give you another Comforter, that He may remain with you forever: [17]the Spirit of Truth, whom the world cannot receive because it does not see Him nor know Him. But you know Him, for He abides with you, and shall be in you.

[18]I will not leave you orphans; I am coming to you. [19]Yet a little *while* and the world no longer sees Me, but you see Me. Because I live, you also shall live. [20]In that day you shall know that I *am* in My Father, and you *are* in Me, and I *am* in you. [21]He that has My commandments and keeps them, he it is that loves Me; and he that loves Me shall be loved by My Father, and I shall love him and shall reveal Myself to him.

[22]Judas said to him (not the Iscariot), Lord, what has happened that You are about to reveal Yourself to us and not to the world? [23]Jesus answered and said to him, If anyone loves Me, he will keep My word, and My Father shall love him. And we shall come to him and shall make a dwelling-place with him. [24]He who does not love Me does not keep My words—and the

10 λέγεις, Δεῖξον ἡμῖν τὸν πατέρα ; οὐ πιστεύεις ὅτι ἐγὼ ἐν τῷ
say, Show us the Father? Not do you believe that I in the
πατρί, καὶ ὁ πατὴρ ἐν ἐμοί ἐστι ; τὰ ῥήματα ἃ ἐγὼ λαλῶ
Father (am), and the Father in Me is? The words which I speak
ὑμῖν, ἀπ' ἐμαυτοῦ οὐ λαλῶ· ὁ δὲ πατὴρ ὁ ἐν ἐμοὶ μένων,
to you, from Myself not I speak, the but Father who in Me abides;
11 αὐτὸς ποιεῖ τὰ ἔργα. πιστεύετέ μοι ὅτι ἐγὼ ἐν τῷ πατρί,
He does the works. Believe Me, that I (am) in the Father,
καὶ ὁ πατὴρ ἐν ἐμοί· εἰ δὲ μή, διὰ τὰ ἔργα αὐτὰ πιστεύετέ
and the Father in Me (is). if And not, for the works themselves believe
12 μοι. ἀμὴν ἀμὴν λέγω ὑμῖν, ὁ πιστεύων εἰς ἐμέ, τὰ ἔργα ἃ ἐγὼ
Me. Truly, truly, I say to you, the (one) believing in Me, the works that I
ποιῶ κἀκεῖνος ποιήσει, καὶ μείζονα τούτων ποιήσει· ὅτι
do, also that one will do, and greater (than) these he will do, because
13 ἐγὼ πρὸς τὸν πατέρα μου πορεύομαι. καὶ ὅ τι ἂν αἰτήσητε
I to the Father of Me go. And whatever you may ask
ἐν τῷ ὀνόματί μου, τοῦτο ποιήσω, ἵνα δοξασθῇ ὁ πατὴρ ἐν
in the name of Me, this I will do, that may be glorified the Father in
14 τῷ υἱῷ. ἐάν τι αἰτήσητε ἐν τῷ ὀνόματί μου, ἐγὼ ποιήσω.
the Son. If anything you ask in the name of Me, I will do
15 ἐὰν ἀγαπᾶτέ με, τὰς ἐντολὰς τὰς ἐμὰς τηρήσατε. καὶ ἐγὼ
16 **If you love Me, commandments — My you will keep. And I**
ἐρωτήσω τὸν πατέρα, καὶ ἄλλον παράκλητον δώσει ὑμῖν,
will petition the Father, and another Paraclete He will give you,
17 ἵνα μένῃ μεθ' ὑμῶν εἰς τὸν αἰῶνα, τὸ πνεῦμα τῆς ἀληθείας, ὃ
that He abide with you for ever, the Spirit — of Truth, whom
ὁ κόσμος οὐ δύναται λαβεῖν, ὅτι οὐ θεωρεῖ αὐτό, οὐδὲ γινώ-
the world not is able to receive, because not it sees Him, nor knows.
σκει αὐτό· ὑμεῖς δὲ γινώσκετε αὐτό, ὅτι παρ' ὑμῖν μένει, καὶ
Him. you But know Him, because with you He abides, and
18 ἐν ὑμῖν ἔσται. οὐκ ἀφήσω ὑμᾶς ὀρφανούς· ἔρχομαι πρὸς
in you will be. Not I will leave you orphans; I am coming to
19 ὑμᾶς. ἔτι μικρὸν καὶ ὁ κόσμος με οὐκέτι θεωρεῖ, ὑμεῖς δὲ θεω-
you. Yet a little and the world Me no longer beholds. you But behold
20 ρεῖτέ με· ὅτι ἐγὼ ζῶ, καὶ ὑμεῖς ζήσεσθε. ἐν ἐκείνῃ τῇ ἡμέρᾳ
Me, because I live, also you will live. In that — day
γνώσεσθε ὑμεῖς ὅτι ἐγὼ ἐν τῷ πατρί μου, καὶ ὑμεῖς ἐν ἐμοί,
will know you that I (am) in the Father of Me, and you in Me,
21 κἀγὼ ἐν ὑμῖν. ὁ ἔχων τὰς ἐντολάς μου καὶ τηρῶν αὐτάς,
and I in you. He having the commandments of Me and keeping them,
ἐκεῖνός ἐστιν ὁ ἀγαπῶν με· ὁ δὲ ἀγαπῶν με, ἀγαπηθήσεται
that one is the (one) loving Me; he And loving Me will be loved
ὑπὸ τοῦ πατρός μου· καὶ ἐγὼ ἀγαπήσω αὐτόν, καὶ ἐμφανίσω
by the Father of Me, and I will love him, and will reveal
22 αὐτῷ ἐμαυτόν. λέγει αὐτῷ Ἰούδας, οὐχ ὁ Ἰσκαριώτης,
to him Myself. says to him Judas, not the Iscariot.
Κύριε, τί γέγονεν ὅτι ἡμῖν μέλλεις ἐμφανίζειν σεαυτόν, καὶ
Lord, what has occurred that to us you are about to reveal Yourself, and
23 οὐχὶ τῷ κόσμῳ ; ἀπεκρίθη ὁ Ἰησοῦς καὶ εἶπεν αὐτῷ, Ἐάν
not at all to the world? answered Jesus and said to him, If
τις ἀγαπᾷ με, τὸν λόγον μου τηρήσει, καὶ ὁ πατήρ μου
anyone loves Me, the word of Me he will keep, and the Father of Me
ἀγαπήσει αὐτόν, καὶ πρὸς αὐτὸν ἐλευσόμεθα, καὶ μονὴν
will love him, and to him we will come, and an abode
24 παρ' αὐτῷ ποιήσομεν. ὁ μὴ ἀγαπῶν με, τοὺς λόγους μου
with him we will make. The (one) not loving Me, the words of Me

word which you hear is not Mine but of the Father who sent Me!

[25] I have spoken these things to you, abiding with you; [26] but the Comforter, the Holy Spirit, whom the Father shall send in My name, He shall teach you all things, and shall remind you of all things that I said to you. [27] I leave peace to you; My peace I give to you. Not as the world gives do I give to you. Let not your heart be troubled, nor let it be timid. [28] You heard that I said to you, I am going away and I am coming *again* to you. If you loved Me, you would have rejoiced that I said, I am going to the Father, for My Father is greater than I. [29] And now I have told you before it occurs, that when it shall occur you may believe.

[30] I shall no longer speak many things with you, for the ruler of this world is coming, and he has nothing in Me. [31] But that the world may know that I love the Father, even as the Father commanded Me, so I do. Rise up, let us go from here.

CHAPTER 15

[1] I am the True Vine, and My Father is the Vinedresser. [2] Every branch in Me not bearing fruit, He takes away; and every *branch* bearing fruit, He prunes so that it may bear more fruit. [3] You are already pruned because of the word which I have spoken to you. [4] Remain in Me, and I in you. As the branch is not able to bear fruit of itself, unless it remain in the vine, so neither *can* you unless you remain in Me. [5] I am the Vine; you *are* the branches. He that remains in Me, and I in him, this one bears much fruit, for apart from Me you are not able to do anything. [6] Unless one remains in Me, he is cast out as the branch, and is dried up; and they gather and

οὐ τηρεῖ· καὶ ὁ λόγος ὃν ἀκούετε οὐκ ἔστιν ἐμός, ἀλλὰ τοῦ
not keeps; and the word which you hear not is Mine, but of Him
πέμψαντός με πατρός.
having sent Me (the) Father.
25 Ταῦτα λελάληκα ὑμῖν παρ' ὑμῖν μένων. ὁ δὲ παράκλητος,
26 **These things I have spoken to you with you abiding. the But Paraclete,**
τὸ Πνεῦμα τὸ Ἅγιον, ὃ πέμψει ὁ πατὴρ ἐν τῷ ὀνόματί μου,
the Spirit — Holy which will send the Father in the name of Me,
ἐκεῖνος ὑμᾶς διδάξει πάντα, καὶ ὑπομνήσει ὑμᾶς πάντα ἃ
that One you will teach all things, and remind you (of) all which
27 εἶπον ὑμῖν. εἰρήνην ἀφίημι ὑμῖν, εἰρήνην τὴν ἐμὴν δίδωμι
I told you. Peace I leave to you; peace — My I give
ὑμῖν· οὐ καθὼς ὁ κόσμος δίδωσιν, ἐγὼ δίδωμι ὑμῖν. μὴ
you; not as the world gives I give you. Not
28 ταρασσέσθω ὑμῶν ἡ καρδία, μηδὲ δειλιάτω. ἠκούσατε ὅτι
let be agitated of you the heart, not let it be fearful. You heard that
ἐγὼ εἶπον ὑμῖν, Ὑπάγω καὶ ἔρχομαι πρὸς ὑμᾶς. εἰ ἠγαπᾶτέ
I told you: I go, and come to you. If you loved
με, ἐχάρητε ἂν ὅτι εἶπον, Πορεύομαι πρὸς τὸν πατέρα·
Me, you would have rejoiced that I said, I am going to the Father,
29 ὅτι ὁ πατήρ μου μείζων μού ἐστι. καὶ νῦν εἴρηκα ὑμῖν πρὶν
for the Father of Me greater than Me is. And now I have told you before
30 γενέσθαι· ἵνα, ὅταν γένηται, πιστεύσητε. οὐκέτι πολλὰ
(it) happens, that when it happens you may believe. No longer many things
λαλήσω μεθ' ὑμῶν· ἔρχεται γὰρ ὁ τοῦ κόσμου τούτου
I will speak with you, is coming for the of world this
31 ἄρχων, καὶ ἐν ἐμοὶ οὐκ ἔχει οὐδέν· ἀλλ' ἵνα γνῷ ὁ κόσμος
ruler, and in Me not He has nothing. But that may know the world
ὅτι ἀγαπῶ τὸν πατέρα, καὶ καθὼς ἐνετείλατό μοι ὁ πατήρ,
that I love the Father, and as commanded Me the Father,
οὕτω ποιῶ. ἐγείρεσθε, ἄγωμεν ἐντεῦθεν.
so I do. Rise, let us go from here.

CHAPTER 15

1 Ἐγώ εἰμι ἡ ἄμπελος ἡ ἀληθινή, καὶ ὁ πατήρ μου ὁ
I am the vine — true, and the Father of Me the
2 γεωργός ἐστι. πᾶν κλῆμα ἐν ἐμοὶ μὴ φέρον καρπόν, αἴρει
Vinedresser is. Every branch in Me not bearing fruit, He takes
αὐτό· καὶ πᾶν τὸ καρπὸν φέρον, καθαίρει αὐτό, ἵνα πλείονα
it. And each the fruit bearing, He prunes it so that more
3 καρπὸν φέρῃ. ἤδη ὑμεῖς καθαροί ἐστε διὰ τὸν λόγον ὃν
fruit it may bear. Now you pruned are because of the word which
4 λελάληκα ὑμῖν. μείνατε ἐν ἐμοί, κἀγὼ ἐν ὑμῖν. καθὼς τὸ
I have spoken to you. Remain in Me, and I in you. As the
κλῆμα οὐ δύναται καρπὸν φέρειν ἀφ' ἑαυτοῦ, ἐὰν μὴ μείνῃ
branch not is able fruit to bear from itself unless it remain
5 ἐν τῇ ἀμπέλῳ, οὕτως οὐδὲ ὑμεῖς, ἐὰν μὴ ἐν ἐμοὶ μείνητε. ἐγώ
in the vine, so neither you unless in Me you remain. I
εἰμι ἡ ἄμπελος, ὑμεῖς τὰ κλήματα. ὁ μένων ἐν ἐμοί, κἀγὼ ἐν
am the vine, you (are) the branches. He remaining in Me, and I in
αὐτῷ, οὗτος φέρει καρπὸν πολύν· ὅτι χωρὶς ἐμοῦ οὐ δύνασθε
him, this one bears fruit much, because apart from Me not you can
6 ποιεῖν οὐδέν. ἐὰν μή τις μείνῃ ἐν ἐμοί, ἐβλήθη ἔξω ὡς τὸ
do nothing. Unless anyone remains in Me, he is cast out as the
κλῆμα, καὶ ἐξηράνθη, καὶ συνάγουσιν αὐτὰ καὶ εἰς πῦρ
branch, and is withered and they gather them and into a fire

throw them into a fire, and they are burned. [7]If you remain in Me, and My words remain in you, whatever you desire you shall ask, and it shall happen to you. [8]In this My Father is glorified, that you should bear much fruit; and you will be My disciples. [9]As the Father loved Me, I also loved you; continue in My love. [10]If you keep My commandments, you will continue in My love; as I have kept My Father's commandments and continue in His love. [11]I have spoken these things to you that My joy may abide in you, and your joy may be full. [12]This is My commandment, that you love one another as I loved you. [13]Greater love than this has no one, that anyone should lay down his soul for his friends— [14]you are My friends if you do whatever I command you. [15]I no longer call you slaves, for the slave does not know what his lord does. But I called you friends, because all things which I heard from My Father I made known to you. [16]You have not chosen Me, but I chose you out and planted you, that you should go and should bear fruit, and your fruit remain; that whatever you should ask the Father in My name, He may give you. [17]These things I command you, that you love one another. [18]If the world hates you, you know that it has hated Me before *it has hated* you. [19]If you were of the world, the world would love its own. But because you are not of the world, but I chose you out of the world, for this reason the world hates you. [20]Remember the word which I said to you, A slave is not greater than his lord. If they persecuted Me, they also will persecute you. If they kept My word, they also will keep yours. [21]But all these things they will do to you on account of My name, because they do not know the *One* who sent Me.

7 βάλλουσι, καὶ καίεται. ἐὰν μείνητε ἐν ἐμοί, καὶ τὰ ῥήματά
they throw, and they are burned. If you remain in Me, and the words
μου ἐν ὑμῖν μείνῃ, ὃ ἐὰν θέλητε αἰτήσεσθε, καὶ γενήσεται
of Me in you remain, whatever you desire you will ask, and it shall happen
8 ὑμῖν. ἐν τούτῳ ἐδοξάσθη ὁ πατήρ μου, ἵνα καρπὸν πολὺν
to you. In this is glorified the Father of Me, that fruit much
9 φέρητε· καὶ γενήσεσθε ἐμοὶ μαθηταί. καθὼς ἠγάπησέ με ὁ
you shall bear. and you will be to Me disciples. As loved Me the
πατηρ, κἀγὼ ἠγάπησα ὑμᾶς· μείνατε ἐν τῇ ἀγάπῃ τῇ ἐμῇ
Father, I also loved you; remain in love — My.
10 ἐὰν τὰς ἐντολάς μου τηρήσητε, μενεῖτε ἐν τῇ ἀγάπῃ μου·
If the commandments of Me you keep, you will remain in the love of Me.
καθὼς ἐγὼ τὰς ἐντολὰς τοῦ πατρός μου τετήρηκα, καὶ μένω
as I the command of the Father of Me have kept, and remain
11 αὐτοῦ ἐν τῇ ἀγάπῃ. ταῦτα λελάληκα ὑμῖν, ἵνα ἡ χαρὰ ἡ
of Him in the love. These things I have spoken to you that joy
12 ἐμὴ ἐν ὑμῖν μείνῃ, καὶ ἡ χαρὰ ὑμῶν πληρωθῇ. αὕτη ἐστὶν ἡ
of Me in you remain, and the joy of you may be filled. This is the
ἐντολὴ ἡ ἐμή, ἵνα ἀγαπᾶτε ἀλλήλους, καθὼς ἠγάπησα
commandment My, that you love one another even as I loved
13 ὑμᾶς. μείζονα ταύτης ἀγάπην οὐδεὶς ἔχει, ἵνα τις την ψυχὴν
you. Greater than this love no one has, that anyone the soul
14 αὐτοῦ θῇ ὑπὲρ τῶν φίλων αὐτοῦ. ὑμεῖς φίλοι μου ἐστέ, ἐὰν
of him lay down for the friends of him. You friends of Me are, if
15 ποιῆτε ὅσα ἐγὼ ἐντέλλομαι ὑμῖν. οὐκέτι ὑμᾶς λέγω δούλους,
you do whatever I command you. No longer you I call slaves,
ὅτι ὁ δοῦλος οὐκ οἶδε τί ποιεῖ αὐτοῦ ὁ κύριος· ὑμᾶς δὲ εἴρηκα
for the slave not knows what does of him the lord; you but I called
φίλους, ὅτι πάντα ἃ ἤκουσα παρὰ τοῦ πατρός μου ἐγνώ-
friends because all things which I heard from the Father of Me I made
16 ρισα ὑμῖν. οὐχ ὑμεῖς με ἐξελέξασθε, ἀλλ' ἐγὼ ἐξελεξάμην ὑμᾶς,
known to you. not You Me have chosen, but I chose out you,
καὶ ἔθηκα ὑμᾶς, ἵνα ὑμεῖς ὑπάγητε καὶ καρπὸν φέρητε, καὶ ὁ
and planted you, that you should go and fruit should bear, and the
καρπὸς ὑμῶν μένῃ· ἵνα ὅ τι ἂν αἰτήσητε τὸν πατέρα ἐν τῷ
fruit of you remain, that whatever you may ask the Father in the
17 ὀνόματί μου, δῷ ὑμῖν. ταῦτα ἐντέλλομαι ὑμῖν, ἵνα
name of Me, He may give you. These things I command you, that
18 ἀγαπᾶτε ἀλλήλους. εἰ ὁ κόσμος ὑμᾶς μισεῖ, γινώσκετε ὅτι
you love one another. If the world you hates you know that
19 ἐμὲ πρῶτον ὑμῶν μεμίσηκεν. εἰ ἐκ τοῦ κόσμου ἦτε, ὁ κόσμος
Me before you it has hated. If of the world you were, the world
ἂν τὸ ἴδιον ἐφίλει· ὅτι δὲ ἐκ τοῦ κόσμου οὐκ ἐστέ, ἀλλ' ἐγὼ
would the own have loved; that but of the world not you are, but I
ἐξελεξάμην ὑμᾶς ἐκ τοῦ κόσμου, διὰ τοῦτο μισεῖ ὑμᾶς ὁ
chose out you out of the world, therefore hates you the
20 κόσμος. μνημονεύετε τοῦ λόγου οὗ ἐγὼ εἶπον ὑμῖν, Οὐκ ἔστι
world. Remember the word which I said to you: Not is
δοῦλος μείζων τοῦ κυρίου αὐτοῦ. εἰ ἐμὲ ἐδίωξαν, καὶ ὑμᾶς
a slave greater than the lord of him. If Me they persecuted, also you
διώξουσιν· εἰ τὸν λόγον μου ἐτήρησαν, καὶ τὸν ὑμέτερον
they will persecute; if the word of Me they kept, also — yours
21 τηρήσουσιν. ἀλλὰ ταῦτα πάντα ποιήσουσιν ὑμῖν διὰ τὸ
they will keep. But these things all they will do to you because of
22 ὄνομά μου, ὅτι οὐκ οἴδασι τὸν πέμψαντά με. εἰ μὴ ἦλθον καὶ
name My, for not they know the (One) sending Me. Unless I came and

[22] If I did not come and speak to them, they had no sin. But now they do not have excuse as to their sin. [23] The *one* hating Me also hates My Father. [24] If I did not do the works among them which no other did, they had no sin. But now they both have seen and have also hated Me and My Father. [25] But that may be fulfilled the word that has been written in their Law, "they hated Me without a cause." [26] And when the Comforter comes, whom I will send to you from the Father, the Spirit of truth who proceeds from the Father, that One will witness concerning Me. [27] And you also witness, because from *the* beginning you were with Me.

CHAPTER 16

[1] I have spoken these things to you so that you may not be offended. [2] They will put you out of *the* synagogue, but an hour is coming that everyone killing you will think to bear a service before God. [3] And they will do these things to you because they do not know the Father nor Me. [4] But I have spoken these things to you so that when the hour comes you may recall them, that I told you these things. But I did not say these things to you from *the* beginning because I was with you. [5] But now I am going to Him who sent Me. And not one of you asks Me, Where are you going? [6] But because I have said these things to you, grief has filled your heart. [7] But I tell you the truth, it is advantageous for you that I should go; for if I do not go away, the Comforter will not come to you. But if I go, I will send Him to you. [8] And when that One comes, *He* will convict the world concerning sin, and concerning righteousness, and concerning judgment. [9] Concerning sin, because they do not believe into Me; [10] and concerning righteousness because I am going to the Father, and you no longer see Me; [11] and concerning

ἐλάλησα αὐτοῖς, ἁμαρτίαν οὐκ εἶχον· νῦν δὲ πρόφασιν οὐκ
spoke to them sin not they had; now but an excuse not
23 ἔχουσι περὶ τῆς ἁμαρτίας αὐτῶν. ὁ ἐμὲ μισῶν, καὶ τὸν
they have concerning the sin of them. The (one) Me hating also the
24 πατέρα μου μισεῖ. εἰ τὰ ἔργα μὴ ἐποίησα ἐν αὐτοῖς ἃ οὐδεὶς
Father of Me hates. If the works not I did among them which none
ἄλλος πεποίηκεν, ἁμαρτίαν οὐκ εἶχον· νῦν δὲ καὶ ἑωράκασι
other did, sin not they had; now but both they have seen
25 καὶ μεμισήκασι καὶ ἐμὲ καὶ τὸν πατέρα μου. ἀλλ' ἵνα πλη-
and have hated both Me and the Father of Me. But that may be
ρωθῇ ὁ λόγος ὁ γεγραμμένος ἐν τῷ νόμῳ αὐτῶν ὅτι Ἐμίση-
fulfilled the word that has been written in the law of them, — They
σάν με δωρεάν.
hated Me freely.

26 Ὅταν δὲ ἔλθῃ ὁ παράκλητος, ὃν ἐγὼ πέμψω ὑμῖν παρὰ
when And comes the Paraclete whom I will send to you from
τοῦ πατρός, τὸ πνεῦμα τῆς ἀληθείας, ὃ παρὰ τοῦ πατρὸς
the Father, the Spirit — of truth who from the Father
27 ἐκπορεύεται, ἐκεῖνος μαρτυρήσει περὶ ἐμοῦ· καὶ ὑμεῖς δὲ
proceeds, that One will witness concerning Me; also you and
μαρτυρεῖτε, ὅτι ἀπ' ἀρχῆς μετ' ἐμοῦ ἐστε.
witness, because from (the) beginning with Me you are.

CHAPTER 16

1 Ταῦτα λελάληκα ὑμῖν, ἵνα μὴ σκανδαλισθῆτε. ἀπο-
2 **These things I have spoken to you that not you be offended. Put from**
συναγώγους ποιήσουσιν ὑμᾶς· ἀλλ' ἔρχεται ὥρα, ἵνα πᾶς
(the) synagogue they will make you, but comes an hour that everyone
3 ὁ ἀποκτείνας ὑμᾶς δόξῃ λατρείαν προσφέρειν τῷ Θεῷ. καὶ
killing you will think a service to bear before — God. And
ταῦτα ποιήσουσιν ὑμῖν, ὅτι οὐκ ἔγνωσαν τὸν πατέρα οὐδὲ
these things they will do to you because not they knew the Father nor
4 ἐμέ. ἀλλὰ ταῦτα λελάληκα ὑμῖν, ἵνα ὅταν ἔλθῃ ἡ ὥρα,
Me. But these things I have spoken to you that when comes the hour
μνημονεύητε αὐτῶν, ὅτι ἐγὼ εἶπον ὑμῖν. ταῦτα δὲ ὑμῖν ἐξ
you may recall them, that I told to you these things And to you from
5 ἀρχῆς οὐκ εἶπον, ὅτι μεθ' ὑμῶν ἤμην. νῦν δὲ ὑπάγω πρὸς
(the) first not I said, because with you I was. now But I am going to
τὸν πέμψαντά με, καὶ οὐδεὶς ἐξ ὑμῶν ἐρωτᾷ με, Ποῦ ὑπάγεις ;
the (One) sending Me, and not one of you asks Me, Where are you going?
6 ἀλλ' ὅτι ταῦτα λελάληκα ὑμῖν, ἡ λύπη πεπλήρωκεν ὑμῶν
But because these things I have said to you, grief has filled of you
7 τὴν καρδίαν. ἀλλ' ἐγὼ τὴν ἀλήθειαν λέγω ὑμῖν· συμφέρει
the heart. But I the truth tell you, it is profitable
ὑμῖν ἵνα ἐγὼ ἀπέλθω· ἐὰν γὰρ μὴ ἀπέλθω, ὁ παράκλητος
for you that I should go. if For not I go away, the Paraclete
οὐκ ἐλεύσεται πρὸς ὑμᾶς· ἐὰν δὲ πορευθῶ, πέμψω αὐτὸν
not will come to you; if but I go, I will send Him
8 πρὸς ὑμᾶς. καὶ ἐλθὼν ἐκεῖνος ἐλέγξει τὸν κόσμον περὶ ἁμαρ-
to you. And coming that One will convict the world concerning sin,
9 τίας καὶ περὶ δικαιοσύνης καὶ περὶ κρίσεως· περὶ ἁμαρτίας
and concerning righteousness and concerning judgment; concerning sin
10 μέν, ὅτι οὐ πιστεύουσιν εἰς ἐμέ· περὶ δικαιοσύνης δέ, ὅτι
because not they believe in Me; concerning righteousness and because
11 πρὸς τὸν πατέρα μου ὑπάγω, καὶ οὐκέτι θεωρεῖτέ με· περὶ
to the Father of Me I am going; and no longer you behold Me; concerning

judgment because the ruler of this world has been judged. 12 Yet I have many things to tell you, but you are not able to bear now. 13 But when the Spirit of truth comes, He will guide you into all truth; for He will not speak from Himself, but whatever He hears, He will speak; and He will announce the coming things to you. 14 He will glorify Me, for He will receive from Mine and will announce to you. 15 All things which the Father has are Mine. For this reason I said that He receives from Mine, and will announce to you. 16 A little and you do not see Me. And again a little *while,* and you will see Me, because I go away to the Father.

17 Then they said, What is this that He says, The little *while?* We do not know what He says. 19 Then Jesus knew that they desired to ask Him, and said to them, Do you seek *answers* with one another concerning this, because I said, A little *while,* and you do not see Me; and again a little *while,* and you will see Me? 20 Truly, truly, I say to you that you will weep and will lament. But the world will rejoice. And you will be grieved, but your grief will become joy. 21 The woman has grief when she bears, because her hour came, but when she brings forth the child, she no longer remembers the distress, because of the joy that a man was born into the world. 22 And you, then, truly have grief now; but I will see you again, and your heart will rejoice; and no one takes your joy from you. 23 And in that day you will ask Me nothing. Truly, truly, I say to you, Whatever you shall ask the Father in My name, He will give you. 24 Until now you asked nothing in My name: ask, and you will receive, so that your joy may be full.

12 δὲ κρίσεως, ὅτι ὁ ἄρχων τοῦ κόσμου τούτου κέκριται. ἔτι
and judgment, because the ruler of world this has been judged. Yet
πολλὰ ἔχω λέγειν ὑμῖν, ἀλλ' οὐ δύνασθε βαστάζειν ἄρτι.
many things I have to tell you, but not you are able to bear now;
13 ὅταν δὲ ἔλθῃ ἐκεῖνος, τὸ πνεῦμα τῆς ἀληθείας, ὁδηγήσει
when but comes that One, the Spirit — of truth, He will guide
ὑμᾶς εἰς πᾶσαν τὴν ἀλήθειαν· οὐ γὰρ λαλήσει ἀφ' ἑαυτοῦ,
you into all the truth; not for will He speak from Himself,
ἀλλ' ὅσα ἂν ἀκούσῃ λαλήσει, καὶ τὰ ἐρχόμενα ἀναγγελεῖ
but what ever He hears He will speak, and the coming things He will announce
14 ὑμῖν. ἐκεῖνος ἐμὲ δοξάσει, ὅτι ἐκ τοῦ ἐμοῦ λήψεται, καὶ
to you. That One Me will glorify because from Mine He will receive and
15 ἀναγγελεῖ ὑμῖν. πάντα ὅσα ἔχει ὁ πατὴρ ἐμά ἐστι· διὰ
will announce to you. All things which has the Father, Mine is; for this
τοῦτο εἶπον, ὅτι ἐκ τοῦ ἐμοῦ λήψεται, καὶ ἀναγγελεῖ ὑμιν.
reason I said that from Mine He receives, and will announce to you.
16 μικρὸν καὶ οὐ θεωρεῖτέ με, καὶ πάλιν μικρὸν καὶ ὄψεσθέ με,
A little and not you behold Me, and again a little and you will see Me.
17 ὅτι ἐγὼ ὑπάγω πρὸς τὸν πατέρα. εἶπον οὖν ἐκ τῶν
because I go to the Father. said Therefore of the
μαθητῶν αὐτοῦ πρὸς ἀλλήλους, Τί ἐστι τοῦτο ὃ λέγει ἡμῖν,
disciples of Him to one another, What is this which He tells us:
Μικρὸν καὶ οὐ θεωρεῖτέ με, καὶ πάλιν μικρὸν καὶ ὄψεσθέ με ;
A little and not you behold Me, and again a little and you will see Me?
18 καὶ ὅτι Ἐγὼ ὑπάγω πρὸς τὸν πατέρα ; ἔλεγον οὖν, Τοῦτο
Also, Because I go to the Father? they said Therefore, this
19 τί ἐστιν ὃ λέγει, τὸ μικρόν ; οὐκ οἴδαμεν τί λαλεῖ. ἔγνω οὖν
What is that He says, The little? do not We know what He says. knew Then
ὁ Ἰησοῦς ὅτι ἤθελον αὐτὸν ἐρωτᾷν, καὶ εἶπεν αὐτοῖς, Περὶ
Jesus that they desired Him to question, and said to them, Concerning
τούτου ζητεῖτε μετ' ἀλλήλων, ὅτι εἶπον, Μικρὸν καὶ οὐ
this do you seek with one another, because I said, A little and not
20 θεωρεῖτέ με, καὶ πάλιν μικρὸν καὶ ὄψεσθέ με ; ἀμὴν ἀμὴν
you behold Me, and again a little and you will see Me? Truly, truly,
λέγω ὑμῖν ὅτι κλαύσετε καὶ θρηνήσετε ὑμεῖς, ὁ δὲ κόσμος
I say to you that will weep and will lament you, the and world
χαρήσεται· ὑμεῖς δὲ λυπηθήσεσθε, ἀλλ' ἡ λύπη ὑμῶν εἰς
will rejoice you And will be grieved, but the grief of you into
21 χαρὰν γενήσεται. ἡ γυνὴ ὅταν τίκτῃ λύπην ἔχει, ὅτι ἦλθεν
joy will become. The woman when she bears grief has, because came
ἡ ὥρα αὐτῆς· ὅταν δὲ γεννήσῃ τὸ παιδίον, οὐκέτι μνημονεύει
the hour of her; when but she brings forth the child, no longer she remembers
τῆς θλίψεως, διὰ τὴν χαρὰν ὅτι ἐγεννήθη ἄνθρωπος εἰς
the distress, because of the joy that was born a man into
22 τὸν κόσμον. καὶ ὑμεῖς οὖν λύπην μὲν νῦν ἔχετε· πάλιν δὲ
the world. And you, therefore, grief indeed now have; again but
ὄψομαι ὑμᾶς, καὶ χαρήσεται ὑμῶν ἡ καρδία, καὶ τὴν χαρὰν
will see you, and will rejoice of you the heart, and the joy
23 ὑμῶν οὐδεὶς αἴρει ἀφ' ὑμῶν. καὶ ἐν ἐκείνῃ τῇ ἡμέρᾳ ἐμὲ οὐκ
of you no one takes from you. And in that — day Me not
ἐρωτήσετε οὐδέν. ἀμὴν ἀμὴν λέγω ὑμῖν ὅτι ὅσα ἂν αἰτή-
you will question nothing. Truly, truly, I say to you that whatever you
24 σητε τὸν πατέρα ἐν τῷ ὀνοματί μου, δώσει ὑμῖν. ἕως ἄρτι
ask the Father in the name of Me, He will give you. Until now
οὐκ ᾐτήσατε οὐδὲν ἐν τῷ ὀνόματί μου· αἰτεῖτε, καὶ λήψεσθε,
not you asked nothing in the name of Me; ask, and you will receive

[25]I have spoken these things to you in allegories. And hour comes when I will no longer speak to you in allegories, but I will reveal the Father plainly to you. [26]In that day you will ask in My name, and I do not tell you that I will petition the Father about you; [27]for the Father Himself loves you, because you have loved Me, and have believed that I came out from God. [28]I came out from the Father, and have come into the world; I leave the world again and go to the Father. [29]His disciples said to Him, Behold, now You speak plainly and You say no allegory. [30]Now we know that You know all things, and do not need for You to question anyone. By this we believe that You came out from God. [31]Jesus answered them, Do you believe now? [32]Behold, an hour is coming, and now has come, that you are scattered, each one to *his* own things, and you will leave Me alone. Yet I am not alone, because the Father is with Me. [33]I have spoken these things to you that you may have peace in Me. You have pain in the world; but be encouraged; I have overcome the world.

CHAPTER 17

[1]Jesus said these things, and lifted up His eyes to Heaven, and said, Father, the hour has come. Glorify Your son, that Your Son may also glorify You. [2]As You gave to Him authority over all flesh, so that all which You gave to Him, He may give to them everlasting life. [3]And this is everlasting life, that they may know You, the only true God, and Jesus Christ, whom You have sent. [4]I have glorified You on the earth. I finished the work that You have given Me to do. [5]And now Father, glorify Me with Yourself, with the glory which I had

ἵνα ἡ χαρὰ ὑμῶν ᾖ πεπληρωμένη.
that the joy of you may be filled.
25 Ταῦτα ἐν παροιμίαις λελάληκα ὑμῖν· ἔρχεται ὥρα ὅτε
These things in allegories I have spoken to you; comes an hour when
οὐκέτι ἐν παροιμίαις λαλήσω ὑμῖν, ἀλλὰ παρρησίᾳ περὶ τοῦ
no longer in allegories I will speak to you, but plainly concerning the
26 πατρὸς ἀναγγελῶ ὑμῖν. ἐν ἐκείνῃ τῇ ἡμέρᾳ ἐν τῷ ὀνόματί μου
Father I will declare to you. In that — day in the name of Me
αἰτήσεσθε· καὶ οὐ λέγω ὑμῖν ὅτι ἐγὼ ἐρωτήσω τὸν πατέρα
you will ask, and not I tell you that I will petition the Father
27 περὶ ὑμῶν· αὐτὸς γὰρ ὁ πατὴρ φιλεῖ ὑμᾶς, ὅτι ὑμεῖς ἐμὲ
concerning you; Himself for the Father loves you, because you Me
πεφιλήκατε, καὶ πεπιστεύκατε ὅτι ἐγὼ παρὰ τοῦ Θεοῦ
have loved, and have believed that I from — God
28 ἐξῆλθον. ἐξῆλθον παρὰ τοῦ πατρός, καὶ ἐλήλυθα εἰς τὸν
came forth. I came forth from the Father, and have come into the
κόσμον· πάλιν ἀφίημι τὸν κόσμον, καὶ πορεύομαι πρὸς τὸν
world; again I leave the world, and go to the
29 πατέρα. λέγουσιν αὐτῷ οἱ μαθηταὶ αὐτοῦ, Ἴδε, νῦν παρ-
Father. say to Him The disciples of Him, Behold, now
30 ρησίᾳ λαλεῖς, καὶ παροιμίαν οὐδεμίαν λέγεις. νῦν οἴδαμεν
plainly You speak, and allegory not one You say. Now we know
ὅτι οἶδας πάντα, καὶ οὐ χρείαν ἔχεις ἵνα τίς σε ἐρωτᾷ· ἐν
that You know all things, and no need have that anyone You query; by
31 τούτῳ πιστεύομεν ὅτι ἀπὸ Θεοῦ ἐξῆλθες. ἀπεκρίθη αὐτοῖς ὁ
this we believe that from God You came. answered them —
32 Ἰησοῦς, Ἄρτι πιστεύετε; ἰδού, ἔρχεται ὥρα καὶ νῦν ἐλή-
Jesus, Now do you believe? Behold, comes an hour and now has
λυθεν, ἵνα σκορπισθῆτε ἕκαστος εἰς τὰ ἴδια, καὶ ἐμὲ μόνον
come, that you are scattered, each one to the own things and Me alone
33 ἀφῆτε· καὶ οὐκ εἰμὶ μόνος, ὅτι ὁ πατὴρ μετ' ἐμοῦ ἐστι. ταῦτα
you leave; and not I am alone, because the Father with Me is. These things
λελάληκα ὑμῖν, ἵνα ἐν ἐμοὶ εἰρήνην ἔχητε. ἐν τῷ κόσμῳ
I have spoken to you, that in Me peace you may have. In the world
θλῖψιν ἕξετε· ἀλλὰ θαρσεῖτε, ἐγὼ νενίκηκα τὸν κόσμον.
distress you have, but be encouraged, I have overcome the world.

CHAPTER 17

1 Ταῦτα ἐλάλησεν ὁ Ἰησοῦς, καὶ ἐπῆρε τοὺς ὀφθαλμοὺς
These things spoke — Jesus, and lifting up the eyes
αὐτοῦ εἰς τὸν οὐρανόν, καὶ εἶπε, Πάτερ, ἐλήλυθεν ἡ ὥρα·
of Him to — Heaven, and said, Father, has come the hour
2 δόξασόν σου τὸν υἱόν, ἵνα καὶ ὁ υἱός σου δοξάσῃ σε· καθὼς
glorify of You the Son, that also the Son of You may glorify You. As
ἔδωκας αὐτῷ ἐξουσίαν πάσης σαρκός, ἵνα πᾶν ὃ δέδωκας
You gave Him authority of all flesh, that all which You gave
3 αὐτῷ, δώσῃ αὐτοῖς ζωὴν αἰώνιον. αὕτη δέ ἐστιν ἡ αἰώνιος
to Him, He may give to them life everlasting. this And is everlasting
ζωή, ἵνα γινώσκωσί σε τὸν μόνον ἀληθινὸν Θεόν, καὶ ὃν
life, that they may know You the only true God, and whom
4 ἀπέστειλας Ἰησοῦν Χριστόν. ἐγώ σε ἐδόξασα ἐπὶ τῆς γῆς·
You sent. Jesus Christ. I You glorified on the earth,
5 τὸ ἔργον ἐτελείωσα ὃ δέδωκάς μοι ἵνα ποιήσω. καὶ νῦν
the work finishing which You gave to Me that I should do. And now
δόξασόν με σύ, πάτερ, παρὰ σεαυτῷ τῇ δόξῃ ᾗ εἶχον πρὸ
glorify Me You, Father, with Yourself with the glory that I had before

with You before the existence of the world. [6] I revealed Your name to the men whom You gave to Me out of the world. They were Yours, and You have given them to Me; and they have kept Your word. [7] Now they have known that all things, whatever You gave to Me, are from You. [8] For the words which You have given Me, I have given to them. And they received, and truly knew that I came out from You; and they believed that You sent Me. [9] I pray for them; I do not pray for the world, but for those whom You have given to Me; for they are Yours. [10] And all My things are Yours, and Yours are Mine; and I have been glorified in them. [11] And I no longer am in the world, yet these are in the world; and I come to You. Holy Father, keep them in Your name; those whom You gave to Me, that *they* may be one as We *are*.

[12] While I was with them in the world, I kept them in Your name; I guarded those whom You gave to Me, and not one of them was lost, except the son of perdition, that the Scripture might be fulfilled. [13] And now I come to You, and I speak these things in the world that they may have My joy fulfilled in them. [14] I have given them Your word, and the world hated them because they are not of the world, as I am not of the world. [15] I do not pray for You to take them out of the world, but for You to keep them from evil. [16] They are not of the world, even as I am not of the world. [17] Sanctify them by Your truth —Your word is truth. [18] As You sent Me into the world, I also sent them into the world; [19] and I sanctify Myself for them, that they may also be sanctified in truth. [20] And I do not pray about these only, but also about those who will believe in Me through their words; [21] that all may be one, as You *are* in Me, Father, and I in

6 τοῦ τὸν κόσμον εἶναι παρὰ σοί. ἐφανέρωσά σου τὸ ὄνομα
the of the world being with You. I revealed of You the name

τοῖς ἀνθρώποις οὓς δέδωκάς μοι ἐκ τοῦ κόσμου· σοὶ ἦσαν,
to the men whom You gave to Me out of the world. To You they were

καὶ ἐμοὶ αὐτοὺς δέδωκας· καὶ τὸν λόγον σου τετηρήκασι.
and to Me them You gave; and the word of You they have kept.

7 νῦν ἔγνωκαν ὅτι πάντα ὅσα δέδωκάς μοι, παρὰ σοῦ ἐστιν·
Now they have known that all whatever You gave to Me from You is;

8 ὅτι τὰ ῥήματα ἃ δέδωκάς μοι, δέδωκα αὐτοῖς· καὶ αὐτοὶ
because the words which You gave to Me I have given to them, and they

ἔλαβον, καὶ ἔγνωσαν ἀληθῶς ὅτι παρὰ σοῦ ἐξῆλθον, καὶ
received, and knew truly that from beside You I came forth; and

9 ἐπίστευσαν ὅτι σύ με ἀπέστειλας. ἐγὼ περὶ αὐτῶν ἐρωτῶ·
they believed that You Me sent. I concerning them petition;

οὐ περὶ τοῦ κόσμου ἐρωτῶ, ἀλλὰ περὶ ὧν δέδωκάς μοι, ὅτι
not about the world I petition, but concerning whom You gave Me, for

10 σοί εἰσι· καὶ τὰ ἐμὰ πάντα σά ἐστι, καὶ τὰ σὰ ἐμά· καὶ
to You they are, and things My all Yours are, and Your things Mine; and

11 δεδόξασμαι ἐν αὐτοῖς. καὶ οὐκέτι εἰμὶ εν τῷ κόσμῳ, καὶ
I have been glorified in them. And no longer am I in the world, and

οὗτοι ἐν τῷ κόσμῳ εἰσί, καὶ ἐγὼ πρός σε ἔρχομαι. πάτερ
these in the world are, and I to You come. Father

ἅγιε, τήρησον αὐτοὺς ἐν τῷ ὀνόματί σου, οὓς δέδωκάς μοι,
Holy, keep them in the name of You, whom You gave to Me

12 ἵνα ὦσιν ἕν, καθὼς ἡμεῖς. ὅτε ἤμην μετ᾽ αὐτῶν ἐν τῷ κόσμῳ,
that may be one, as we. When I was with them in the world,

ἐγὼ ἐτήρουν αὐτοὺς ἐν τῷ ὀνόματί σου· οὓς δέδωκάς μοι
I was keeping them in the name of You; whom You gave to Me

ἐφύλαξα, καὶ οὐδεὶς ἐξ αὐτῶν ἀπώλετο, εἰ μὴ ὁ υἱὸς τῆς
I guarded, and not one of them perished, except the son —

13 ἀπωλείας, ἵνα ἡ γραφὴ πληρωθῇ. νῦν δὲ πρός σε ἔρχομαι,
of perdition, that the Scripture might be fulfilled. now And to You I come,

καὶ ταῦτα λαλῶ ἐν τῷ κόσμῳ, ἵνα ἔχωσι τὴν χαρὰν τὴν
and these things I speak in the world, that they have joy —

14 ἐμὴν πεπληρωμένην ἐν αὐτοῖς. ἐγὼ δέδωκα αὐτοῖς τὸν
My having been fulfilled in them. I have given them the

λόγον σου, καὶ ὁ κόσμος ἐμίσησεν αὐτούς, ὅτι οὐκ εἰσὶν ἐκ
word of You, and the world hated them because not they are of

15 τοῦ κόσμου, καθὼς ἐγὼ οὐκ εἰμὶ ἐκ τοῦ κόσμου. οὐκ ἐρωτῶ
the world, even as I not am of the world. not I petition

ἵνα ἄρῃς αὐτοὺς ἐκ τοῦ κόσμου, ἀλλ᾽ ἵνα τηρήσῃς αὐτοὺς
that You take them out of the world, but that You keep them

16 ἐκ τοῦ πονηροῦ. ἐκ τοῦ κόσμου οὐκ εἰσί, καθὼς ἐγὼ ἐκ τοῦ
from — evil. Of the world not they are, even as I of the

17 κόσμου οὐκ εἰμί. ἁγίασον αὐτοὺς ἐν τῇ ἀληθείᾳ σου· ὁ
world not am. Sanctify them in the truth of You; —

18 λόγος ὁ σὸς ἀλήθειά ἐστι. καθὼς ἐμὲ ἀπέστειλας εἰς τὸν
word — Your truth is. Even as Me You sent into the

19 κόσμον, κἀγὼ ἀπέστειλα αὐτοὺς εἰς τὸν κόσμον. καὶ ὑπὲρ
world, I also sent them into the world. And for

αὐτῶν ἐγὼ ἁγιάζω ἐμαυτόν, ἵνα καὶ αὐτοὶ ὦσιν ἡγιασμένοι
them I sanctify Myself, that also they may be sanctified

20 ἐν ἀληθείᾳ. οὐ περὶ τούτων δὲ ἐρωτῶ μόνον, ἀλλὰ καὶ περὶ
in truth. not concerning these And I petition only, but also concerning

21 τῶν πιστευσόντων διὰ τοῦ λόγου αὐτῶν εἰς ἐμέ· ἵνα πάντες
those who shall believe through the word of them into Me; that all

You, that they also may be one in Us, that the world may believe that You sent Me. [22]And I have given them the glory which You have given Me, that they may be one, as We are one, [23]I in them, and You in Me, that they may be perfected in one, and that the world may know that You sent Me and loved them, even as You loved Me. [24]Father, I desire that *those* whom You have given Me, that where I am, they may also be with Me, that they may behold My glory which You gave Me, because You loved Me before *the* foundation of *the* world. [25]Righteous Father, truly the world did not know You, but I knew You, and these have known that You sent Me. [26]And I made Your name known to them, and will make *it* known, that the love *with* which You loved Me may be in them, and I in them.

CHAPTER 18

[1]Having said these things, Jesus went out with His disciples across the winter-stream Kidron, where there was a garden into which He and His disciples entered. [2]And Judas, the *one* betraying Him, also knew the place, because Jesus many times assembled there with His disciples. [3]Therefore, having received a cohort and assistants from among the chief priests and the Pharisees, Judas comes there with torches and lamps and weapons. [4]Jesus then, knowing all the things coming upon Him, said to them, Whom do you seek? [5]They answered Him, Jesus the Nazarene. Jesus said to them, I AM! And Judas, the *one* betraying Him, also stood with them. [6]When therefore He said to them, I AM, they departed into the rear and fell to *the* ground. [7]Then again He asked, Whom do you seek? And they said, Jesus the Nazarene. [8]Jesus answered, I

ἐν ὦσι· καθὼς σύ, πάτερ, ἐν ἐμοί, κἀγὼ ἐν σοί, ἵνα καὶ αὐτοὶ
one may be, as You, Father, in Me, and I in You, that also they
ἐν ἡμῖν ἓν ὦσιν· ἵνα ὁ κόσμος πιστεύσῃ ὅτι σύ με ἀπέστειλας.
in Us one may be, that the world may believe that You Me sent.
22 καὶ ἐγὼ τὴν δόξαν ἣν δέδωκάς μοι, δέδωκα αὐτοῖς, ἵνα
And I the glory which You have given Me have given to them, that
23 ὦσιν ἕν, καθὼς ἡμεῖς ἕν ἐσμεν. ἐγὼ ἐν αὐτοῖς, καὶ σὺ ἐν ἐμοί,
they may be one, as We one are; I in them, and You in Me,
ἵνα ὦσι τετελειωμένοι εἰς ἕν, καὶ ἵνα γινώσκῃ ὁ κόσμος ὅτι
that they may be perfected into one, and that may know the world that
σύ με ἀπέστειλας, καὶ ἠγάπησας αὐτούς, καθὼς ἐμὲ ἠγάπη-
You Me sent and loved them even as Me You
24 σας. πάτερ, οὓς δέδωκάς μοι, θέλω ἵνα ὅπου εἰμὶ ἐγώ,
loved. Father, whom You have given to Me, I desire that where am I,
κἀκεῖνοι ὦσι μετ᾽ ἐμοῦ· ἵνα θεωρῶσι τὴν δόξαν τὴν ἐμήν,
those also may be with Me, that they may behold glory — My,
ἣν ἔδωκάς μοι, ὅτι ἠγάπησάς με πρὸ καταβολῆς κόσμου.
which You gave Me because You loved Me before foundation of (the) world.
25 πάτερ δίκαιε, καὶ ὁ κόσμος σε οὐκ ἔγνω, ἐγὼ δέ σε ἔγνων,
Father Righteous, indeed the world You not knew, I but You knew,
26 καὶ οὗτοι ἔγνωσαν ὅτι σύ με ἀπέστειλας· καὶ ἐγνώρισα
and these knew that You Me sent; and I made known
αὐτοῖς τὸ ὄνομά σου, καὶ γνωρίσω· ἵνα ἡ ἀγάπη, ἣν
to them the name of You, and will make known; that the love (with) which
ἠγάπησάς με, ἐν αὐτοῖς ᾖ, κἀγὼ ἐν αὐτοῖς.
You loved Me in them may be, and I in them.

CHAPTER 18

1 Ταῦτα εἰπὼν ὁ Ἰησοῦς ἐξῆλθε σὺν τοῖς μαθηταῖς αὐτοῦ
These things having said Jesus went forth with the disciples of Him
πέραν τοῦ χειμάρρου τῶν Κέδρων, ὅπου ἦν κῆπος, εἰς ὃν
across the torrent — of Kidron, where was a garden, into which
2 εἰσῆλθεν αὐτὸς καὶ οἱ μαθηταὶ αὐτοῦ. ᾔδει δὲ καὶ Ἰούδας, ὁ
entered He and the disciples of Him. knew And also Judas, he
παραδιδοὺς αὐτόν, τὸν τόπον· ὅτι πολλάκις συνήχθη ὁ
betraying Him, the place, because many times assembled
3 Ἰησοῦς ἐκεῖ μετὰ τῶν μαθητῶν αὐτοῦ. ὁ οὖν Ἰούδας, λαβὼν
Jesus there with the disciples of Him. Therefore Judas, receiving
τὴν σπεῖραν, καὶ ἐκ τῶν ἀρχιερέων καὶ Φαρισαίων ὑπηρέτας,
the band, and from the chief priests and the Pharisees officers,
4 ἔρχεται ἐκεῖ μετὰ φανῶν καὶ λαμπάδων καὶ ὅπλων. Ἰησοῦς
comes there with torches and lamps and weapons. Jesus
οὖν, εἰδὼς πάντα τὰ ἐρχόμενα ἐπ᾽ αὐτόν, ἐξελθὼν εἶπεν
Then, knowing all the things coming on Him, going forth said
5 αὐτοῖς, Τίνα ζητεῖτε; ἀπεκρίθησαν αὐτῷ, Ἰησοῦν τὸν
to them, Whom do you seek? They answered Him, Jesus the
Ναζωραῖον. λέγει αὐτοῖς ὁ Ἰησοῦς, Ἐγώ εἰμι. εἱστήκει δὲ
Nazarene. tells them — Jesus, I AM. stood And
6 καὶ Ἰούδας ὁ παραδιδοὺς αὐτὸν μετ᾽ αὐτῶν. ὡς οὖν εἶπεν
also Judas, the (one) betraying Him, with them. when Then He told
αὐτοῖς ὅτι Ἐγώ εἰμι, ἀπῆλθον εἰς τὰ ὀπίσω, καὶ ἔπεσον
them, — I AM, they went away into the rear, and fell
7 χαμαί. πάλιν οὖν αὐτοὺς ἐπηρώτησε, Τίνα ζητεῖτε; οἱ δὲ
to earth. Again, then, He inquired, Whom do you seek? they And
8 εἶπον, Ἰησοῦν τὸν Ναζωραῖον. ἀπεκρίθη ὁ Ἰησοῦς, Εἶπον
said, Jesus the Nazarene. answered — Jesus, I told

told you that I AM; if therefore, you seek Me, allow these to depart— 9 that the word might be fulfilled which said, "*Of* those whom You have given to Me, I lost not one of them."

10 Then Simon Peter, having a sword, drew it and struck the slave of the High Priest, and cut off his right ear. And the slave's name was Malchus. 11 Then Jesus said to Peter, Put your sword into the sheath: the cup which the Father has given Me, shall I in no way drink it?

12 Then the cohort and the chiliarch and the court-officers of the Jews together seized Jesus and bound Him. 13 And they led Him away first to Annas, for he was *the* father-in-law of Caiaphas, who was *the* High Priest of that year. 14 And it was Caiaphas who *had* given counsel to the Jews that it was advantageous *for* one man to perish for the people.

15 Now Simon Peter and another disciple followed Jesus, and that disciple was known to the High Priest, and entered together with Jesus into the court of the High Priest, 16 but Peter stood at the door outside. The other disciple who was known to the High Priest therefore went out and spoke to The doorkeeper, and brought Peter in. 17 Then the maidservant, the doorkeeper, said to Peter, Are you not also of the disciples of this man? He said, I am not. 18 Now the slaves and the court-officers were standing, and warming themselves, having made a fire of coals, for it was cold; and Peter was standing with them and warming himself.

19 Then the High Priest questioned Jesus about His disciples and about His teaching. 20 Jesus answered him, I openly spoke to the world; I continually taught in the synagogue and in the Temple where the Jews

ὑμῖν ὅτι ἐγώ εἰμι· εἰ οὖν ἐμὲ ζητεῖτε, ἄφετε τούτους ὑπάγειν·
you that I AM. If, then, Me you seek, allow these to go;
9 ἵνα πληρωθῇ ὁ λόγος ὃν εἶπεν ὅτι Οὓς δέδωκάς μοι, οὐκ
that might be fulfilled the word which said, — Whom You gave to Me, not
10 ἀπώλεσα ἐξ αὐτῶν οὐδένα. Σίμων οὖν Πέτρος ἔχων μάχαιραν
I lost (any) of them, no one. Simon Then Peter having a sword,
εἵλκυσεν αὐτήν, καὶ ἔπαισε τὸν τοῦ ἀρχιερέως δοῦλον, καὶ
drew it, and struck the of the high priest slave, and
ἀπέκοψεν αὐτοῦ τὸ ὠτίον τὸ δεξιόν. ἦν δὲ ὄνομα τῷ δούλῳ
cut off of him the ear — right. was And a name to the slave,
11 Μάλχος. εἶπεν οὖν ὁ Ἰησοῦς τῷ Πέτρῳ, Βάλε τὴν μάχαιράν
Malchus. said Then — Jesus to Peter, Put the sword
σου εἰς τὴν θήκην· τὸ ποτήριον ὃ δέδωκέ μοι ὁ πατήρ, οὐ μὴ
of you into the sheath; the cup which has given Me the Father, in no way
πίω αὐτό;
shall I drink it?

12 Ἡ οὖν σπεῖρα καὶ ὁ χιλίαρχος καὶ οἱ ὑπηρέται τῶν Ἰου-
the Then band and the chiliarch and the officers of the
13 δαίων συνέλαβον τὸν Ἰησοῦν, καὶ ἔδησαν αὐτόν, καὶ ἀπή-
Jews together seized Jesus, and bound Him, and led
γαγον αὐτὸν πρὸς Ἄνναν πρῶτον· ἦν γὰρ πενθερὸς τοῦ
away Him to Annas first, he was for father-in-law —
14 Καϊάφα, ὃς ἦν ἀρχιερεὺς τοῦ ἐνιαυτοῦ ἐκείνου. ἦν δὲ Καϊάφας
of Caiaphas, who was high priest — of year that. was And Caiaphas
ὁ συμβουλεύσας τοῖς Ἰουδαίοις, ὅτι συμφέρει ἕνα ἄνθρωπον
the (one) having advised the Jews that it is profitable for one man
ἀπολέσθαι ὑπὲρ τοῦ λαοῦ.
to perish for the people.

15 Ἠκολούθει δὲ τῷ Ἰησοῦ Σίμων Πέτρος, καὶ ἄλλος μαθητής.
followed And — Jesus Simon Peter and another disciple.
ὁ δὲ μαθητὴς ἐκεῖνος ἦν γνωστὸς τῷ ἀρχιερεῖ, καὶ συνεισῆλθε
And disciple that was known to the high priest, and went in with
16 τῷ Ἰησοῦ εἰς τὴν αὐλὴν τοῦ ἀρχιερέως· ὁ δὲ Πέτρος εἱστήκει
Jesus into the court of the high priest; —but Peter stood
πρὸς τῇ θύρᾳ ἔξω. ἐξῆλθεν οὖν ὁ μαθητὴς ὁ ἄλλος ὃς ἦν
at the door outside. went out Then the disciple — other who was
γνωστὸς τῷ ἀρχιερεῖ, καὶ εἶπε τῇ θυρωρῷ, καὶ εἰσήγαγε τὸν
known to the high priest, and spoke to the portress, and brought in —
17 Πέτρον. λέγει οὖν ἡ παιδίσκη ἡ θυρωρὸς τῷ Πέτρῳ, Μὴ καὶ
Peter. says Then the maidservant, the portress, — to Peter, Not also
σὺ ἐκ τῶν μαθητῶν εἶ τοῦ ἀνθρώπου τούτου; λέγει ἐκεῖνος,
you of the disciples are — of man this? says That one
18 Οὐκ εἰμί. εἱστήκεισαν δὲ οἱ δοῦλοι καὶ οἱ ὑπηρέται ἀνθρακιὰν
Not I am. were standing And the slaves and the officers, a fire of coals
πεποιηκότες, ὅτι ψύχος ἦν, καὶ ἐθερμαίνοντο· ἦν δὲ μετ᾽
having made, because cold it was, and were warming; was and with
αὐτῶν ὁ Πέτρος ἑστὼς καὶ θερμαινόμενος.
them — Peter standing and warming himself.

19 Ὁ οὖν ἀρχιερεὺς ἠρώτησε τὸν Ἰησοῦν περὶ τῶν μαθητῶν
the Then high priest questioned — Jesus concerning the disciples
20 αὐτοῦ, καὶ περὶ τῆς διδαχῆς αὐτοῦ. ἀπεκρίθη αὐτῷ ὁ
of Him, and concerning the teaching of Him. answered him —
Ἰησοῦς, Ἐγὼ παρρησίᾳ ἐλάλησα τῷ κόσμῳ· ἐγὼ πάντοτε
Jesus, I publicly spoke to the world; I always
ἐδίδαξα ἐν τῇ συναγωγῇ καὶ ἐν τῷ ἱερῷ, ὅπου πάντοτε οἱ
taught in the synagogue and in the Temple, where always the

continually come together, and I spoke nothing in secret. 21 Why do you question Me? Ask those who have heard what I spoke to them: behold, these know what I said! 22 But *on* His having said these things, one of the court-officers standing by gave Jesus a blow with the palm, saying, Do you answer the High Priest this way? 23 Jesus answered him, If I spoke evil, bear witness concerning the evil; but if well, why do you strike Me? 24 Then Annas sent Him out, having been bound, to Caiaphas the High Priest.

25 Now Simon Peter was standing and warming himself. They therefore said to him, Are you not also of His disciples? He denied and said, I am not. 26 One of the slaves of the High Priest, being a relative *of him* of whom Peter cut off the ear, said, Did I not see you in the garden with Him? 27 Again therefore Peter denied, and immediately a cock crowed.

28 Then they led Jesus from Caiaphas into the Praetorium, and it was early. And they did not enter into the Praetorium, that they might not be defiled, but that they might eat the Passover. 29 Therefore, Pilate went out to them and said, What accusation do you bring against this man? 30 They answered and said to him, If this one were not an evildoer, then we would not have delivered him to you. 31 Then Pilate said to them, You take him and judge him according to your *own* Law. Then the Jews said to him, It is not lawful for us to put anyone to death— 32 that the word of Jesus which He said might be fulfilled, signifying by what kind *of* death He was about to die.

33 Then Pilate again went in to the praetorium and called Jesus, and said to Him, Are you the king of the Jews? 34 Jesus answered him, Do you say this from yourself, or

21 Ἰουδαῖοι συνέρχονται, καὶ ἐν κρυπτῷ ἐλάλησα οὐδέν. τί με
Jews come together, and in secret I spoke nothing. Why Me
ἐπερωτᾷς; ἐπερώτησον τοὺς ἀκηκοότας, τί ἐλάλησα αὐτοῖς·
do you question? Question those having heard what I spoke to them.
22 ἴδε, οὗτοι οἴδασιν ἃ εἶπον ἐγώ. ταῦτα δὲ αὐτοῦ εἰπόντος,
Behold, these know what said I. these things And He saying,
εἷς τῶν ὑπηρετῶν παρεστηκὼς ἔδωκε ῥάπισμα τῷ Ἰησοῦ,
one of the officers standing by gave a blow — to Jesus,
23 εἰπών, Οὕτως ἀποκρίνῃ τῷ ἀρχιερεῖ; ἀπεκρίθη αὐτῷ ὁ
saying, Thus answer you the high priest? answered to him. —
Ἰησοῦς, Εἰ κακῶς ἐλάλησα, μαρτύρησον περὶ τοῦ κακοῦ·
Jesus, If evilly I spoke, bear witness concerning the evil;
24 εἰ δὲ καλῶς, τί με δέρεις; ἀπέστειλεν οὖν αὐτὸν ὁ Ἄννας
if but well, why Me do you beat? Sent therefore Him — Annas
δεδεμένον πρὸς Καϊάφαν τὸν ἀρχιερέα.
being bound to Caiaphas the high priest.
25 Ἦν δὲ Σίμων Πέτρος ἑστὼς καὶ θερμαινόμενος· εἶπον οὖν
was And Simon Peter standing and warming himself. they said Then
αὐτῷ, Μὴ καὶ σὺ ἐκ τῶν μαθητῶν αὐτοῦ εἶ; ἠρνήσατο
to him, Not also you of the disciples of him are? denied
26 ἐκεῖνος, καὶ εἶπεν, Οὐκ εἰμί. λέγει εἷς ἐκ τῶν δούλων τοῦ
That one, and said, not I am. says One of the slaves of the
ἀρχιερέως, συγγενὴς ὢν οὗ ἀπέκοψε Πέτρος τὸ ὠτίον,
high priest, a relative being of whom cut off Peter the ear,
27 Οὐκ ἐγώ σε εἶδον ἐν τῷ κήπῳ μετ' αὐτοῦ; πάλιν οὖν
Not I you did see in the garden with Him? again Then
ἠρνήσατο ὁ Πέτρος, καὶ εὐθέως ἀλέκτωρ ἐφώνησεν.
denied — Peter, and at once a cock sounded.
28 Ἄγουσιν οὖν τὸν Ἰησοῦν ἀπὸ τοῦ Καϊάφα εἰς τὸ πραιτώ-
they lead Then — Jesus from — Caiaphas to the praetorium;
ριον· ἦν δὲ πρωΐα, καὶ αὐτοὶ οὐκ εἰσῆλθον εἰς τὸ πραιτώ-
it was and early; and they did not enter into the praetorium,
29 ριον, ἵνα μὴ μιανθῶσιν, ἀλλ' ἵνα φάγωσι τὸ πάσχα. ἐξῆλθεν
lest they be defiled, but that they may eat the Passover. went out
οὖν ὁ Πιλάτος πρὸς αὐτούς, καὶ εἶπε, Τίνα κατηγορίαν
Therefore Pilate to them, and said, What accusation
30 φέρετε κατὰ τοῦ ἀνθρώπου τούτου; ἀπεκρίθησαν καὶ εἶπον
bring you against man this? They answered and said
αὐτῷ, Εἰ μὴ ἦν οὗτος κακοποιός, οὐκ ἄν σοι παρεδώκαμεν
to him, Unless was this one an evildoer, not then to you we had delivered
31 αὐτόν. εἶπεν οὖν αὐτοῖς ὁ Πιλάτος, Λάβετε αὐτὸν ὑμεῖς, καὶ
him. said Then to them Pilate, take him You, and
κατὰ τὸν νόμον ὑμῶν κρίνατε αὐτόν. εἶπον οὖν αὐτῷ οἱ
according to the law of you judge him. said Then to him the
32 Ἰουδαῖοι, Ἡμῖν οὐκ ἔξεστιν ἀποκτεῖναι οὐδένα· ἵνα ὁ λόγος
Jews, for us Not it is lawful to put to death no one; that the word
τοῦ Ἰησοῦ πληρωθῇ, ὃν εἶπε, σημαίνων ποίῳ θανάτῳ
— of Jesus might be fulfilled, which He said, signifying by what kind (of) death
ἤμελλεν ἀποθνήσκειν.
He was about to die.
33 Εἰσῆλθεν οὖν εἰς τὸ πραιτώριον πάλιν ὁ Πιλάτος, καὶ
entered Then into the praetorium again Pilate, and
ἐφώνησε τὸν Ἰησοῦν, καὶ εἶπεν αὐτῷ, Σὺ εἶ ὁ βασιλεὺς τῶν
called — Jesus, and said to Him, you Are the king of the
34 Ἰουδαίων; ἀπεκρίθη αὐτῷ ὁ Ἰησοῦς, Ἀφ' ἑαυτοῦ σὺ τοῦτο
Jews? answered him — Jesus, From yourself you this

did others tell you about Me? [35] Pilate answered, Am I a Jew? Your nation and the chief priests delivered you up to me. What did you do? [36] Jesus answered, My kingdom is not of this world. If My kingdom were of this world, My servants would fight, that I might not be delivered up to the Jews. But now My kingdom is not from here. [37] Then Pilate said to Him, Then are you a king? Jesus answered, You say that I am a king, for I have been born for this, and for this I have come into the world, that I might witness to the truth. Everyone that is of the truth hears My voice. [38] Pilate said to Him, What is truth?

And having said this, he again went out to the Jews and said to them, I do not find one crime in him. [39] But there is a custom to you, that I should release one to you at the Passover. Therefore, you decide: Should I release the king of the Jews to you? [40] Then all cried out again, saying, Not this one, but Barabbas! But Barabbas was a robber.

35 λέγεις, ἢ ἄλλοι σοι εἶπον περὶ ἐμοῦ ; ἀπεκρίθη ὁ Πιλάτος,
say, or others you told about Me? answered Pilate,
Μήτι ἐγὼ Ἰουδαῖός εἰμι ; τὸ ἔθνος τὸ σὸν καὶ οἱ ἀρχιερεῖς
Not I a Jew am? nation Your and the chief priests
36 παρέδωκάν σε ἐμοί· τί ἐποίησας ; ἀπεκρίθη ὁ Ἰησοῦς, Ἡ
delivered up You to me; what did you do? answered — Jesus,
βασιλεία ἡ ἐμὴ οὐκ ἔστιν ἐκ τοῦ κόσμου τούτου· εἰ ἐκ τοῦ
kingdom My not is of world this; If of
κόσμου τούτου ἦν ἡ βασιλεία ἡ ἐμή, οἱ ὑπηρέται ἂν οἱ ἐμοὶ
world this was kingdom My, servants would My
ἠγωνίζοντο, ἵνα μὴ παραδοθῶ τοῖς Ἰουδαίοις· νῦν δὲ ἡ
have fought, that not I should be delivered to the Jews. now But
37 βασιλεία ἡ ἐμὴ οὐκ ἔστιν ἐντεῦθεν. εἶπεν οὖν αὐτῷ ὁ Πιλάτος,
kingdom My not is from here. said Then to Him Pilate,
Οὐκοῦν βασιλεὺς εἶ σύ ; ἀπεκρίθη ὁ Ἰησοῦς, Σὺ λέγεις ὅτι
Really not a king are you? answered — Jesus, You say that
βασιλεύς εἰμι ἐγώ. ἐγὼ εἰς τοῦτο γεγέννημαι, καὶ εἰς τοῦτο
a king am I I for this have been born, and for this
ἐλήλυθα εἰς τὸν κόσμον, ἵνα μαρτυρήσω τῇ ἀληθείᾳ. πᾶς ὁ
I have come into the world, that I might witness to the truth, everyone
38 ὢν ἐκ τῆς ἀληθείας ἀκούει μου τῆς φωνῆς. λέγει αὐτῷ ὁ
being of the truth hears of Me the voice. says to Him
Πιλάτος, Τί ἐστιν ἀλήθεια ;
Pilate, What is truth?
Καὶ τοῦτο εἰπών, πάλιν ἐξῆλθε πρὸς τοὺς Ἰουδαίους, καὶ
And this having said, again he went out to the Jews, and
39 λέγει αὐτοῖς, Ἐγὼ οὐδεμίαν αἰτίαν εὑρίσκω ἐν αὐτῷ. ἔστι
tells them, I not one crime find in him. is
δὲ συνήθεια ὑμῖν, ἵνα ἕνα ὑμῖν ἀπολύσω ἐν τῷ πάσχα·
But a custom to you, that one to you I should release at the Passover;
βούλεσθε οὖν ὑμῖν ἀπολύσω τὸν βασιλέα τῶν Ἰουδαίων ;
decide you, then, to you I should release the king of the Jews?
40 ἐκραύγασαν οὖν πάλιν πάντες, λέγοντες, Μὴ τοῦτον, ἀλλὰ
cried out Then again all, saying, Not this one, but
τὸν Βαραββᾶν· ἦν δὲ ὁ Βαραββᾶς λῃστής.
— Barabbas. was But Barabbas a robber.

CHAPTER 19

[1] So Pilate then took Jesus and flogged *Him*. [2] And having plaited a wreath out of thorns, the soldiers put *it* on His head. And *they* threw a purple robe around Him, [3] and said, Hail, king of the Jews! And they gave Him blows with the palm. [4] Then Pilate went outside again and said to them, Behold, I bring him out to you that you may know that I do not find even one crime in him! [5] Then Jesus came outside, wearing the thorny wreath and the purple mantle. And he said to them, Behold, the man! [6] When, therefore, the chief priests

CHAPTER 19

1 Τότε οὖν ἔλαβεν ὁ Πιλάτος τὸν Ἰησοῦν, καὶ ἐμαστίγωσε.
Then, therefore, took Pilate — Jesus and scourged (Him).
2 καὶ οἱ στρατιῶται πλέξαντες στέφανον ἐξ ἀκανθῶν ἐπέθηκαν
And the soldiers having plaited a wreath out of thorns put (it) on
αὐτοῦ τῇ κεφαλῇ, καὶ ἱμάτιον πορφυροῦν περιέβαλον αὐτόν,
of Him the head, and a garment purple threw around Him;
3 καὶ ἔλεγον, Χαῖρε, ὁ βασιλεὺς τῶν Ἰουδαίων· καὶ ἐδίδουν
and said, Hail, king of the Jews; and they gave
4 αὐτῷ ῥαπίσματα. ἐξῆλθεν οὖν πάλιν ἔξω ὁ Πιλάτος, καὶ
Him slaps. went out Then again outside Pilate and
λέγει αὐτοῖς, Ἴδε, ἄγω ὑμῖν αὐτὸν ἔξω, ἵνα γνῶτε ὅτι ἐν
said to them, Behold, I bring to you him out, that you may know that in
5 αὐτῷ οὐδεμίαν αἰτίαν εὑρίσκω. ἐξῆλθεν οὖν ὁ Ἰησοῦς ἔξω,
him not one crime I find. came out Then Jesus outside,
φορῶν τὸν ἀκάνθινον στέφανον καὶ τὸ πορφυροῦν ἱμάτιον.
bearing the thorny wreath and the purple garment.
6 καὶ λέγει αὐτοῖς, Ἴδε, ὁ ἄνθρωπος. ὅτε οὖν εἶδον αὐτὸν οἱ
And he says to them, Behold, the man! when Then saw Him the

and the under-officers saw Him, they cried out, saying, Crucify! Crucify! Pilate said to them, You take him and crucify *him*, for I do not find *one* crime in him! 7 The Jews answered him, We have a Law, and according to our Law he ought to die, because he made himself Son of God! 8 When therefore Pilate heard this word, he was more afraid, 9 and entered into the Praetorium again, and said to Jesus, Where are you from? But Jesus did not give him an answer. 10 So Pilate said to Him, Do you not speak to me? Do you not know that I have authority to crucify you, and I have authority to release you? 11 Jesus answered, You would have no authority against Me if it were not given to you from above. Because of this the *one* delivering Me to you has a greater sin. 12 From this *time* Pilate sought to release Him. But the Jews cried out, saying, If you release this one, you are not a friend of Caesar. Everyone making himself a king speaks against Caesar. 13 Then hearing this word, Pilate led Jesus out. And *he* sat down on the judgment seat, at a place called Pavement, but in Hebrew, Gabbatha. 14 And it was *the* preparation of the Passover, and about *the* sixth hour. And he said to the Jews, Behold, your king! 15 But they cried out, Away, Away! Crucify him! Pilate said to them, Shall I crucify your king? The chief priests answered, We have no king except Caesar. 16 There-fore, then, he delivered Him up to them, that He might be crucified.

And they took Jesus and led *Him* away.

17 And He went out bearing His cross, to *the* place called Of a Skull, which is called in Hebrew, Golgotha; 18 where

ἀρχιερεῖς καὶ οἱ ὑπηρέται, ἐκραύγασαν λέγοντες, Σταύρω-
chief priests and the officers, they cried out saying Crucify!
σον, σταύρωσον. λέγει αὐτοῖς ὁ Πιλάτος, Λάβετε αὐτὸν
Crucify! says to them Pilate, Take Him
ὑμεῖς καὶ σταυρώσατε· ἐγὼ γὰρ οὐχ εὑρίσκω ἐν αὐτῷ αἰτίαν.
you, and crucify, I for not do find in him a crime.
7 ἀπεκρίθησαν αὐτῷ οἱ Ἰουδαῖοι, Ἡμεῖς νόμον ἔχομεν, καὶ
answered him The Jews, We a law have, and
κατὰ τὸν νόμον ἡμῶν ὀφείλει ἀποθανεῖν, ὅτι ἑαυτὸν υἱὸν τοῦ
according to the law of us he ought to die, because himself Son —
8 Θεοῦ ἐποίησεν. ὅτε οὖν ἤκουσεν ὁ Πιλάτος τοῦτον τὸν
of God he has made when Then heard Pilate this —
9 λόγον, μᾶλλον ἐφοβήθη, καὶ εἰσῆλθεν εἰς τὸ πραιτώριον
word, more he was afraid, and entered into the praetorium
πάλιν, καὶ λέγει τῷ Ἰησοῦ, Πόθεν εἶ σύ; ὁ δὲ Ἰησοῦς ἀπό-
again and says — to Jesus, From where are You? But Jesus an
10 κρισιν οὐκ ἔδωκεν αὐτῷ. λέγει οὖν αὐτῷ ὁ Πιλάτος, Ἐμοὶ
answer did not give him. says Then to Him Pilate, To me
οὐ λαλεῖς; οὐκ οἶδας ὅτι ἐξουσίαν ἔχω σταυρῶσαί σε, καὶ
not you speak? not you know that authority I have to crucify you, and
11 ἐξουσίαν ἔχω ἀπολῦσαί σε; ἀπεκρίθη ὁ Ἰησοῦς, Οὐκ εἶχες
authority I have to release you? answered Jesus, not You had
ἐξουσίαν οὐδεμίαν κατ' ἐμοῦ, εἰ μὴ ἦν σοι δεδομένον ἄνωθεν·
authority, not any against Me, if not it was to you being given from above;
12 διὰ τοῦτο ὁ παραδιδούς μέ σοι μείζονα ἁμαρτίαν ἔχει. ἐκ
therefore the (one) delivering Me to you a greater sin has. From
τούτου ἐζήτει ὁ Πιλάτος ἀπολῦσαι αὐτόν. οἱ δὲ Ἰουδαῖοι
this sought Pilate to release Him. the but Jews
ἔκραζον λέγοντες, Ἐὰν τοῦτον ἀπολύσῃς, οὐκ εἶ φίλος τοῦ
cried out saying, If this one you release not you are friend —
Καίσαρος· πᾶς ὁ βασιλέα αὐτὸν ποιῶν, ἀντιλέγει τῷ
of Caesar; everyone a king himself making speaks against
13 Καίσαρι. ὁ οὖν Πιλάτος ἀκούσας τοῦτον τὸν λόγον ἤγαγεν
Caesar. Therefore Pilate hearing this word led
ἔξω τὸν Ἰησοῦν, καὶ ἐκάθισεν ἐπὶ τοῦ βήματος, εἰς τόπον
out — Jesus, and sat down on the judgment seat at a place
14 λεγόμενον Λιθόστρωτον, Ἑβραϊστὶ δὲ Γαββαθᾶ· ἦν δὲ
called (The) Pavement, in Hebrew but, Gabbatha. it was And
Παρασκευὴ τοῦ πάσχα, ὥρα δὲ ὡσεὶ ἕκτη· καὶ λέγει τοῖς
preparation of the Passover, hour and about (the) sixth, and he says to the
15 Ἰουδαίοις, Ἴδε, ὁ βασιλεὺς ὑμῶν. οἱ δὲ ἐκραύγασαν, Ἆρον,
Jews, Behold, the king of you. they But cried out, Away,
ἆρον, σταύρωσον αὐτόν. λέγει αὐτοῖς ὁ Πιλάτος, Τὸν
away, crucify him! says to them Pilate, The
βασιλέα ὑμῶν σταυρώσω; ἀπεκρίθησαν οἱ ἀρχιερεῖς, Οὐκ
king of you shall I crucify? answered The chief priests, not
16 ἔχομεν βασιλέα εἰ μὴ Καίσαρα. τότε οὖν παρέδωκεν αὐτὸν
We have a king except Caesar. Then, therefore, he delivered up Him
αὐτοῖς, ἵνα σταυρωθῇ.
to them, that He might be crucified.

17 Παρέλαβον δὲ τὸν Ἰησοῦν καὶ ἀπήγαγον· καὶ βαστάζων
they took And Jesus and led away, and bearing
τὸν σταυρὸν αὐτοῦ ἐξῆλθεν εἰς τὸν λεγόμενον Κρανίου
the cross of Him, He went out to that called Of a skull,
18 τόπον, ὃς λέγεται Ἑβραϊστὶ Γολγοθᾶ· ὅπου αὐτὸν ἐσταύ-
(the) place, which is called in Hebrew, Golgotha; where Him they

they crucified Him, and two others with Him, on this side and on that side, and Jesus in the middle. 19 And Pilate also wrote a title and put *it* on the cross. And having been written, it was: JESUS THE NAZARENE—THE KING OF THE JEWS. 20 Therefore, many of the Jews read this title, because the place where Jesus was crucified was near the city. And it was written in Hebrew, in Greek, in Latin. 21 Then the chief priests of the Jews said to Pilate, Do not write, The king of the Jews; but that that one said, I am King of the Jews. 22 Pilate answered, What I have written, I have written.

23 Then when they crucified Jesus, the soldiers took His garments and made four parts, a part to each soldier, also the robe, and the robe was seamless, woven from the top throughout. 24 Then they said to one another, Let us not tear it, but let us cast lots about it, whose it will be —that the Scripture might be fulfilled which said, "They divided My garments among them, and they threw a lot *for* My garment." Therefore the soldiers did these things.

25 And His mother, and His mother's sister Mary, the *wife* of Clopas, and Mary Magdalene stood by the cross of Jesus. 26 Then seeing *His* mother, and the disciple whom he loved standing by, Jesus said to His mother, Woman, behold your son! 27 Then He said to the disciple, Behold, your mother! And from that hour the disciple took her into *his* own home.

28 After this, knowing that all things have now been finished, that the Scripture be fulfilled, Jesus said, I thirst. 29 Then a vessel full of vinegar was set. And filling a sponge *with* vinegar, and putting hyssop around *it*, they

ρωσαν, καὶ μετ' αὐτοῦ ἄλλους δύο, ἐντεῦθεν καὶ ἐντεῦθεν,
crucified, and with him others two, on this side and on that side,
19 μέσον δὲ τὸν Ἰησοῦν. ἔγραψε δὲ καὶ τίτλον ὁ Πιλάτος,
in center and Jesus. wrote And also a title Pilate,
καὶ ἔθηκεν ἐπὶ τοῦ σταυροῦ· ἦν δὲ γεγραμμένον, Ἰησοῦς ὁ
and put (it) on the cross; it was and having been written, JESUS THE
20 Ναζωραῖος ὁ βασιλεὺς τῶν Ἰουδαίων. τοῦτον οὖν τὸν
NAZARENE, THE KING OF THE JEWS. This, therefore —
τίτλον πολλοὶ ἀνέγνωσαν τῶν Ἰουδαίων, ὅτι ἐγγὺς ἦν
title many read of the Jews, because near was
τῆς πόλεως ὁ τόπος ὅπου ἐσταυρώθη ὁ Ἰησοῦς· καὶ ἦν
the city the place where was crucified Jesus; and it was
21 γεγραμμένον Ἑβραϊστί, Ἑλληνιστί, Ῥωμαϊστί. ἔλεγον
having been written in Hebrew, in Greek, in Latin. said
οὖν τῷ Πιλάτῳ οἱ ἀρχιερεῖς τῶν Ἰουδαίων, Μὴ γράφε,
Therefore to Pilate the chief priests of the Jews, Not do write,
Ὁ βασιλεὺς τῶν Ἰουδαίων· ἀλλ' ὅτι ἐκεῖνος εἶπε, Βασιλεύς
The king of the Jews; but that that one said, king
22 εἰμι τῶν Ἰουδαίων. ἀπεκρίθη ὁ Πιλάτος, Ὃ γέγραφα,
I am of the Jews. answered Pilate, What I have written,
γέγραφα.
I have written.

23 Οἱ οὖν στρατιῶται, ὅτε ἐσταύρωσαν τὸν Ἰησοῦν, ἔλαβον
the Then soldiers, when they crucified — Jesus, took
τὰ ἱμάτια αὐτοῦ, καὶ ἐποίησαν τέσσαρα μέρη, ἑκάστῳ
the garments of Him, and made four parts, to each
στρατιώτῃ μέρος, καὶ τὸν χιτῶνα· ἦν δὲ ὁ χιτὼν ἄρραφος,
soldier a part: also the tunic. was And the tunic seamless,
24 ἐκ τῶν ἄνωθεν ὑφαντὸς δι' ὅλου. εἶπον οὖν πρὸς ἀλλήλους,
from the top woven throughout. They said, then, to one another,
Μὴ σχίσωμεν αὐτόν, ἀλλὰ λάχωμεν περὶ αὐτοῦ, τίνος
Not let us tear it, but let us cast lots about it, whose
ἔσται· ἵνα ἡ γραφὴ πληρωθῇ ἡ λέγουσα, Διεμερίσαντο τὰ
it will be; that the Scripture be fulfilled which said, They divided the
ἱμάτιά μου ἑαυτοῖς, καὶ ἐπὶ τὸν ἱματισμόν μου ἔβαλον κλῆρον.
the garments of Me to themselves on the garment of Me cast a lot.
25 οἱ μὲν οὖν στρατιῶται ταῦτα ἐποίησαν. εἱστήκεισαν δὲ
the Therefore soldiers these things did. there stood But
παρὰ τῷ σταυρῷ τοῦ Ἰησοῦ ἡ μήτηρ αὐτοῦ, καὶ ἡ ἀδελφὴ
by the cross — of Jesus the mother of Him, and the sister
τῆς μητρὸς αὐτοῦ, Μαρία ἡ τοῦ Κλωπᾶ, καὶ Μαρία ἡ
of the mother of Him, Mary the (wife) of Cleopas, and Mary the
26 Μαγδαληνή. Ἰησοῦς οὖν ἰδὼν τὴν μητέρα, καὶ τὸν μαθητὴν
Magdalene. Jesus Therefore seeing the mother, and the disciple
παρεστῶτα ὃν ἠγάπα, λέγει τῇ μητρὶ αὐτοῦ, Γύναι, ἰδοὺ ὁ
standing by, whom He loved, says to the mother of Him, Woman, behold the
27 υἱός σου. εἶτα λέγει τῷ μαθητῇ, Ἰδοὺ ἡ μήτηρ σου. καὶ ἀπ'
son of you. Then He says to the disciple. Behold, the mother of you. And from
ἐκείνης τῆς ὥρας ἔλαβεν αὐτὴν ὁ μαθητὴς εἰς τὰ ἴδια.
that — hour took her the disciple into the own (home).

28 Μετὰ τοῦτο εἰδὼς ὁ Ἰησοῦς ὅτι πάντα ἤδη τετέλεσται,
After this knowing Jesus that all things already have been finished,
29 ἵνα τελειωθῇ ἡ γραφή, λέγει, Διψῶ. σκεῦος οὖν ἔκειτο ὄξους
that be completed the Scripture, says, I thirst. a vessel Then was set, of vinegar
μεστόν· οἱ δέ, πλήσαντες σπόγγον ὄξους, καὶ ὑσσώπῳ
full; they and, having filled a sponge (with) vinegar, and hyssop

[30]Then when Jesus took the vinegar, He said, It has been finished! And bowing *His* head, *He* delivered up *His* spirit.

[31]Then the Jews asked Pilate that their legs might be broken, and they be taken away, so that the bodies might not remain on the cross on the sabbath—since it was *the* Preparation. [32]Then the soldiers came and broke the legs of the first, and of the other crucified with Him. [33]But on coming *to* Jesus, when they saw He already was dead, they did not break His legs. [34]But one of the soldiers pierced His side *with* a spear, and at once blood and water came out. [35]And the *one* seeing has borne witness, and his witness is true; and that One knows that he speaks truly, that you may believe. [36]For these things happened that the Scripture might be fulfilled, "Not a bone of Him shall be broken." [37]And again, a different Scripture says, "They shall look at *Him* whom they have pierced.

[38]And after these things, Joseph from Arimathea—being a disciple of Jesus, but concealed because of fear of the Jews—asked Pilate that he might take the body of Jesus. And Pilate gave permission. Then he came and took the body of Jesus. [39]And Nicodemus also came, the *one* coming at first to Jesus by night, bearing a mixture of myrrh and aloes, about a hundred Roman pounds. [40]Then they took the body of Jesus and bound it in linens, with the spices, as is usual with the Jews *in* burying. [41]And there was a garden in the place where He was crucified, and a new tomb in the garden, in which no one yet ever was put. [42]There, then, because of the Preparation of

30 περιθέντες, προσήνεγκαν αὐτοῦ τῷ στόματι. ὅτε οὖν ἔλαβε
putting around, they brought to of Him the mouth, when Then took
τὸ ὄξος ὁ Ἰησοῦς, εἶπε, Τετέλεσται· καὶ κλίνας τὴν κεφαλήν,
the vinegar Jesus, He said, It has been completed, and bowing the head
παρέδωκε τὸ πνεῦμα.
delivered up the spirit.

31 Οἱ οὖν Ἰουδαῖοι, ἐπεὶ Παρασκευὴ ἦν, ἵνα μὴ μείνῃ ἐπὶ τοῦ
the Therefore Jews, since preparation it was, that not may remain on the
σταυροῦ τὰ σώματα ἐν τῷ σαββάτῳ (ἦν γὰρ μεγάλη ἡ
cross the bodies on the sabbath, was for great the
ἡμέρα ἐκείνου τοῦ σαββάτου), ἠρώτησαν τὸν Πιλάτον ἵνα
day of that — sabbath; they asked Pilate that
32 κατεαγῶσιν αὐτῶν τὰ σκέλη, καὶ ἀρθῶσιν. ἦλθον οὖν οἱ
might be broken of them the legs, and they be taken. came Then the
στρατιῶται, καὶ τοῦ μὲν πρώτου κατέαξαν τὰ σκέλη καὶ τοῦ
soldiers, and of the first broke the legs, and of the
33 ἄλλου τοῦ συσταυρωθέντος αὐτῷ· ἐπὶ δὲ τὸν Ἰησοῦν ἐλ-
other — crucified with Him; upon but — Jesus
θόντες, ὡς εἶδον αὐτὸν ἤδη τεθνηκότα, οὐ κατέαξαν αὐτοῦ
coming, when they saw He already was dead, not they broke of Him
34 τὰ σκέλη· ἀλλ' εἷς τῶν στρατιωτῶν λόγχῃ αὐτοῦ τὴν πλευ-
the legs, but one of the soldiers a lance of him the side
35 ρὰν ἔνυξε, καὶ εὐθὺς ἐξῆλθεν αἷμα καὶ ὕδωρ. καὶ ὁ ἑωρακὼς
pierced, and at once came out blood and water. And the (one) seeing
μεμαρτύρηκε, καὶ ἀληθινὴ αὐτοῦ ἐστιν ἡ μαρτυρία, κἀκεῖνος
has witnessed, and true of him is the witness, and that one
36 οἶδεν ὅτι ἀληθῆ λέγει, ἵνα ὑμεῖς πιστεύσητε. ἐγένετο γὰρ
knows that true he speaks, that you may believe. happened For
ταῦτα ἵνα ἡ γραφὴ πληρωθῇ, Ὀστοῦν οὐ συντριβήσεται
these things that the Scripture be fulfilled: A bone not shall be splintered
37 αὐτοῦ. καὶ πάλιν ἑτέρα γραφὴ λέγει, Ὄψονται εἰς ὃν
of Him. And again a different Scripture says, They shall look at whom
ἐξεκέντησαν.
they have pierced.

38 Μετὰ δὲ ταῦτα ἠρώτησε τὸν Πιλάτον ὁ Ἰωσὴφ ὁ ἀπὸ
after And these things asked Pilate Joseph from
Ἀριμαθαίας, ὢν μαθητὴς τοῦ Ἰησοῦ, κεκρυμμένος δὲ διὰ
Arimathea, being a disciple — of Jesus, concealed but through
τὸν φόβον τῶν Ἰουδαίων, ἵνα ἄρῃ τὸ σῶμα τοῦ Ἰησοῦ· καὶ
the fear of the Jews, that he take the body — of Jesus. And
ἐπέτρεψεν ὁ Πιλάτος. ἦλθεν οὖν καὶ ἦρε τὸ σῶμα τοῦ Ἰησοῦ.
allowed (it) Pilate. He came, then, and took the body — of Jesus.
39 ἦλθε δὲ καὶ Νικόδημος, ὁ ἐλθὼν πρὸς τὸν Ἰησοῦν νυκτὸς τὸ
came And also Nicodemus, the (one) coming to — Jesus (by) night at
πρῶτον, φέρων μίγμα σμύρνης καὶ ἀλόης ὡσεὶ λίτρας ἑκατόν.
first, bearing a mixture of myrrh and aloes, about litrae a hundred.
40 ἔλαβον οὖν τὸ σῶμα τοῦ Ἰησοῦ, καὶ ἔδησαν αὐτὸ ὀθονίοις
they took Then the body — of Jesus, and bound it in linens
μετὰ τῶν ἀρωμάτων, καθὼς ἔθος ἐστὶ τοῖς Ἰουδαίοις
with the spices, as custom is with the Jews
41 ἐνταφιάζειν. ἦν δὲ ἐν τῷ τόπῳ ὅπου ἐσταυρώθη κῆπος, καὶ
to bury. was And in the place where He was crucified a garden and
42 ἐν τῷ κήπῳ μνημεῖον καινόν, ἐν ᾧ οὐδέπω οὐδεὶς ἐτέθη. ἐκεῖ
in the garden a tomb new, in which never yet no one was put. There,
οὖν διὰ τὴν Παρασκευὴν τῶν Ἰουδαίων, ὅτι ἐγγὺς ἦν τὸ
then, because of the preparation of the Jews, because near was the

the Jews, because the tomb was near, they put Jesus.

CHAPTER 20

[1]But on the first of the week Mary Magdalene came early to the tomb, darkness yet being *on it.* And *she* saw the stone had been removed from the tomb. [2]Then she ran and came to Simon Peter, and to the other disciples whom Jesus loved, and said to them, They took away the Lord out of the tomb, and we do not know where they laid Him. [3]Then Peter and the other disciple went out and came to the tomb. [4]And the two ran together, and the other disciple ran in front more quickly than Peter, and came first to the tomb. [5]And stooping down, he saw the linens lying; however, he did not go in. [6]Then Simon Peter came following him, and entered into the tomb, and saw the linens lying. [7]And the gravecloth which was on His head *was* not lying with the linens, but was wrapped up in one place by itself. [8]Therefore, then the other disciple also entered, having come first to the tomb. And he saw and believed. [9]For they did not yet know the Scripture, that it was necessary for Him to rise from *the* dead. [10]Then the disciples went away again to themselves.

[11]But Mary stood outside at the tomb, weeping. Then as she wept, she stooped down into the tomb. [12]And *she* saw two angels in white, sitting one at the head, and one at the feet, where the body of Jesus lay. [13]And they said to her, Woman, why do you weep? She said to them, Because they took away my Lord, and I do not know where they put Him. [14]And saying these things, she turned backward, and saw Jesus standing, and did not know that it was Jesus. [15]Jesus said to her, Woman, why do you

μνημεῖον, ἔθηκαν τὸν Ἰησοῦν.
tomb, they put — Jesus.

CHAPTER 20

1 Τῇ δὲ μιᾷ τῶν σαββάτων Μαρία ἡ Μαγδαληνὴ ἔρχεται
on the And first of the sabbaths, Mary the Magdalene comes
πρωΐ, σκοτίας ἔτι οὔσης, εἰς τὸ μνημεῖον, καὶ βλέπει τὸν
early, darkness yet being to the tomb, and sees the
2 λίθον ἠρμένον ἐκ τοῦ μνημείου. τρέχει οὖν καὶ ἔρχεται πρὸς
stone being removed from the tomb. she runs Then and comes to
Σίμωνα Πέτρον καὶ πρὸς τὸν ἄλλον μαθητὴν ὃν ἐφίλει ὁ
Simon Peter, and to the other disciple whom loved
Ἰησοῦς, καὶ λέγει αὐτοῖς, Ἦραν τὸν Κύριον ἐκ τοῦ μνημείου,
Jesus; and says to them, They took the Lord out of the tomb,
3 καὶ οὐκ οἴδαμεν ποῦ ἔθηκαν αὐτόν. ἐξῆλθεν οὖν ὁ Πέτρος καὶ
and not we know where they put Him. went out Then Peter and
4 ὁ ἄλλος μαθητής, καὶ ἤρχοντο εἰς τὸ μνημεῖον. ἔτρεχον δὲ οἱ
the other disciple, and came to the tomb. ran And the
δύο ὁμοῦ· καὶ ὁ ἄλλος μαθητὴς προέδραμε τάχιον τοῦ
two together; and the other disciple ran in front, more quickly than
5 Πέτρου, καὶ ἦλθε πρῶτος εἰς τὸ μνημεῖον, καὶ παρακύψας
Peter, and came first to the tomb, and stooping
6 βλέπει κείμενα τὰ ὀθόνια, οὐ μέντοι εἰσῆλθεν. ἔρχεται οὖν
sees lying the linens; not, however, he went in. Comes, therefore,
Σίμων Πέτρος ἀκολουθῶν αὐτῷ, καὶ εἰσῆλθεν εἰς τὸ μνημεῖον,
Simon Peter following him, and entered into the tomb.
7 καὶ θεωρεῖ τὰ ὀθόνια κείμενα, καὶ τὸ σουδάριον ὃ ἦν ἐπὶ τῆς
And he beholds the linens lying, and the cloth which was on the
κεφαλῆς αὐτοῦ, οὐ μετὰ τῶν ὀθονίων κείμενον, ἀλλὰ χωρὶς
head of Him, not with the linens lying, but apart
8 ἐντετυλιγμένον εἰς ἕνα τόπον. τότε οὖν εἰσῆλθε καὶ ὁ ἄλλος
being wrapped up into one place. Then, therefore entered also the other
μαθητὴς ὁ ἐλθὼν πρῶτος εἰς τὸ μνημεῖον, καὶ εἶδε, καὶ
disciple having come first to the tomb, and he saw, and
9 ἐπίστευσεν· οὐδέπω γὰρ ᾔδεισαν τὴν γραφήν, ὅτι δεῖ
believed. not yet For they knew the Scripture, that it behoves
10 αὐτὸν ἐκ νεκρῶν ἀναστῆναι. ἀπῆλθον οὖν πάλιν πρὸς
Him from (the) dead to rise. went away Then again to
ἑαυτοὺς οἱ μαθηταί.
themselves the disciples.

11 Μαρία δὲ εἱστήκει πρὸς τὸ μνημεῖον κλαίουσα ἔξω· ὡς
Mary And stood at the tomb weeping outside. As
12 οὖν ἔκλαιε, παρέκυψεν εἰς τὸ μνημεῖον, καὶ θεωρεῖ δύο
then she wept, she stooped into the tomb, and beholds two
ἀγγέλους ἐν λευκοῖς καθεζομένους, ἕνα πρὸς τῇ κεφαλῇ, καὶ
angels in white sitting, one at the head, and
13 ἕνα πρὸς τοῖς ποσίν, ὅπου ἔκειτο τὸ σῶμα τοῦ Ἰησοῦ. καὶ
one at the feet, where had lain the body — of Jesus. And
λέγουσιν αὐτῇ ἐκεῖνοι, Γύναι, τί κλαίεις; λέγει αὐτοῖς, Ὅτι
say to her those, Woman, why do you weep? She says to them, For
14 ἦραν τὸν Κύριόν μου, καὶ οὐκ οἶδα ποῦ ἔθηκαν αὐτόν. καὶ
they removed the Lord of me, and not I know where they put Him. And
ταῦτα εἰποῦσα ἐστράφη εἰς τὰ ὀπίσω, καὶ θεωρεῖ τὸν
these things Saying, she turned into the rear, and beholds —
15 Ἰησοῦν ἑστῶτα, καὶ οὐκ ᾔδει ὅτι ὁ Ἰησοῦς ἐστι. λέγει αὐτῇ
Jesus standing, and not knows that Jesus it is. says to her

weep? Whom do you seek? Thinking that it was the gardener, she said to Him, Sir, if you carried Him away, tell me where you put Him, and I will take Him away. [16] Jesus said to her, Mary! Turning around, she said to Him, Rabboni!—that is to say, Teacher. [17] Jesus said to her, Do not touch Me, for I have not yet ascended to My Father, and your Father, and My God, and your God. [18] Mary Magdalene came bringing word to the disciples that she had seen the Lord, and that He told her these things.

[19] Then it being evening on that day, the first of the week, and the doors having been locked where the disciples were assembled, because of fear of the Jews, Jesus came and stood in the midst, and said to them, Peace to you. [20] And saying this, He showed them His hands and side. Then seeing the Lord, the disciples rejoiced. [21] Then Jesus said to them, Peace to you. As the Father has sent Me, I also send you. [22] And saying this, He breathed on *them,* and said to them, Receive *the* Holy Spirit. [23] Of whomever you forgive the sins, they are forgiven to them. Of whomever you may retain, they are retained. [24] But Thomas, one of the Twelve, the *one* called Twin, was not with them when Jesus came. [25] Then the other disciples said to him, We have seen the Lord. But he said to them, Unless I see the mark of the nails in His hands, and thrust my finger into the mark of the nails, and thrust my hand into His side, in no way will I believe.
[26] And after eight days His disciples were inside again,

ὁ Ἰησοῦς, Γύναι, τί κλαίεις; τίνα ζητεῖς; ἐκείνη, δοκοῦσα
Jesus, Woman, why do you weep? Whom seek you? That one, thinking
ὅτι ὁ κηπουρός ἐστι, λέγει αὐτῷ, Κύριε, εἰ σὺ ἐβάστασας
that the gardener it is, says to Him, Sir, if you carried away
16 αὐτόν, εἰπέ μοι ποῦ αὐτὸν ἔθηκας, κἀγὼ αὐτὸν ἀρῶ. λέγει
Him, tell me where Him you put, and I Him will take. says
αὐτῇ ὁ Ἰησοῦς, Μαρία. στραφεῖσα ἐκείνη λέγει αὐτῷ,
to her Jesus, Mary! turning That one says to Him
17 Ῥαββουνί· ὃ λέγεται, Διδάσκαλε. λέγει αὐτῇ ὁ Ἰησοῦς, Μή
Rabboni, that is to say, Teacher. says to her Jesus, Do not
μου ἅπτου, οὔπω γὰρ ἀναβέβηκα πρὸς τὸν πατέρα μου·
Me touch, not yet for I have ascended to the Father of Me.
πορεύου δὲ πρὸς τοὺς ἀδελφούς μου, καὶ εἰπὲ αὐτοῖς,
go But to the brothers of Me, and say to them,
Ἀναβαίνω πρὸς τὸν πατέρα μου καὶ πατέρα ὑμῶν, καὶ
I ascend to the Father of Me and the Father of you, and
18 Θεόν μου καὶ Θεὸν ὑμῶν. ἔρχεται Μαρία ἡ Μαγδαληνὴ
the God of Me and the God of you. comes Mary the Magdalene
ἀπαγγέλλουσα τοῖς μαθηταῖς ὅτι ἑώρακε τὸν Κύριον, καὶ
bringing word to the disciples, that she has seen the Lord, and
ταῦτα εἶπεν αὐτῇ.
these things He told her.

19 Οὔσης οὖν ὀψίας, τῇ ἡμέρᾳ ἐκείνῃ τῇ μιᾷ τῶν σαββάτων,
it being Then evening — day on that, the first of the sabbaths,
καὶ τῶν θυρῶν κεκλεισμένων ὅπου ἦσαν οἱ μαθηταὶ συνηγ-
and the doors having been locked where were the disciples gathered
μένοι, διὰ τὸν φόβον τῶν Ἰουδαίων, ἦλθεν ὁ Ἰησοῦς καὶ
together, because of the fear of the Jews, came Jesus and
20 ἔστη εἰς τὸ μέσον, καὶ λέγει αὐτοῖς, Εἰρήνη ὑμῖν. καὶ τοῦτο
stood in the midst, and says to them, Peace to you. And this
εἰπὼν ἔδειξεν αὐτοῖς τὰς χεῖρας καὶ τὴν πλευρὰν αὐτοῦ.
saying He showed them the hands and the side of Him.
21 ἐχάρησαν οὖν οἱ μαθηταὶ ἰδόντες τὸν Κύριον. εἶπεν οὖν
Rejoiced, therefore, the disciples seeing the Lord. said Then
αὐτοῖς ὁ Ἰησοῦς πάλιν, Εἰρήνη ὑμῖν· καθὼς ἀπέσταλκέ με ὁ
to them Jesus again, Peace to you. As has sent Me the
22 πατήρ, κἀγὼ πέμπω ὑμᾶς. καὶ τοῦτο εἰπὼν ἐνεφύσησε καὶ
Father, I also send you. And this having said, He breathed on, and
23 λέγει αὐτοῖς, Λάβετε Πνεῦμα Ἅγιον. ἄν τινων ἀφῆτε τὰς
said to them, Receive (the) Spirit Holy. Ever of whom you forgive the
ἁμαρτίας, ἀφίενται αὐτοῖς· ἄν τινων κρατῆτε, κεκράτηνται.
sins, they are forgiven to them; ever of whom you retain, they are retained.
24 Θωμᾶς δέ, εἷς ἐκ τῶν δώδεκα, ὁ λεγόμενος Δίδυμος, οὐκ ἦν
Thomas But, one of the twelve, the (one) called Twin, not was
25 μετ' αὐτῶν ὅτε ἦλθεν ὁ Ἰησοῦς. ἔλεγον οὖν αὐτῷ οἱ ἄλλοι
with them when came Jesus. said Then to him the other
μαθηταί, Ἑωράκαμεν τὸν Κύριον. ὁ δὲ εἶπεν αὐτοῖς, Ἐὰν μὴ
disciples, We have seen the Lord. he But said to them, Unless
ἴδω ἐν ταῖς χερσὶν αὐτοῦ τὸν τύπον τῶν ἥλων, καὶ βάλω
I see in the hands of Him the mark of the nails, and thrust
τὸν δάκτυλόν μου εἰς τὸν τύπον τῶν ἥλων, καὶ βάλω τὴν
the finger of me into the mark of the nails, and thrust the
χεῖρά μου εἰς τὴν πλευρὰν αὐτοῦ, οὐ μὴ πιστεύσω.
hand of me into the side of Him, in no way will I believe.
26 Καὶ μεθ' ἡμέρας ὀκτὼ πάλιν ἦσαν ἔσω οἱ μαθηταὶ αὐτοῦ,
And after days eight, again were inside the disciples of Him.

and Thomas was with them. The door having been locked, Jesus came and stood in the midst, and said, Peace to you. [27]Then He said to Thomas, Bring your finger here and see My hands; and bring your hand and thrust into My side, and be not unbelieving, but believing. [28]And Thomas answered and said to Him, My Lord and my God! [29]Jesus said to him, Because you have seen Me, Thomas, you have believed. Blessed *are* the ones not seeing, and believing.

[30]Then truly Jesus did many other miracles in the presence of His disciples, which are not written in this book. [31]But these have been written that you may believe that Jesus is the Christ, the Son of God; and that believing you may have life in His name.

CHAPTER 21

[1]After these things Jesus revealed Himself again to the disciples at the sea of Tiberias. And He revealed *Himself* this way: [2]Simon Peter, and Thomas, being called Twin, and Nathanael from Cana of Galilee, and the *sons* of Zebedee, and two others of His disciples were together. [3]Simon Peter said to them, I am going out to fish. They said to him, We also are coming with you. They went and entered into the boat at once. And in that night they caught nothing. [4]And *it* now becoming early morning, Jesus stood on the shore. However, the disciples did not know that it was Jesus. [5]Then Jesus said to them, Children, Do you not have anything to eat? They answered Him, No. [6]And He said to them, Cast the net into the right side of the boat, and you will find. Then they cast, and they no longer had *the* strength to draw, from the multitude of the fish. [7]Then

καὶ Θωμᾶς μετ' αὐτῶν. ἔρχεται ὁ Ἰησοῦς, τῶν θυρῶν
and Thomas with them. comes — Jesus, the doors
κεκλεισμένων, καὶ ἔστη εἰς τὸ μέσον καὶ εἶπεν, Εἰρήνη ὑμῖν.
having been locked, and stood in the midst, and said, Peace to you.
27 εἶτα λέγει τῷ Θωμᾷ, Φέρε τὸν δάκτυλόν σου ὧδε, καὶ ἴδε τὰς
Then He says — to Thomas, Bring the finger of you here, and see the
χεῖράς μου· καὶ φέρε τὴν χεῖρά σου, καὶ βάλε εἰς τὴν πλευ-
hands of Me, and bring the hand of you, and thrust into the side
28 ράν μου· καὶ μὴ γίνου ἄπιστος, ἀλλὰ πιστός. καὶ ἀπεκρίθη
of Me, and not become unbelieving, but believing. And answered
29 ὁ Θωμᾶς, καὶ εἶπεν αὐτῷ, Ὁ Κύριός μου καὶ ὁ Θεός μου. λέγει
Thomas, and said to Him, The Lord of me and the God of me. says
αὐτῷ ὁ Ἰησοῦς, Ὅτι ἑώρακάς με, Θωμᾶ, πεπίστευκας·
to him Jesus, Because you have seen Me, Thomas, you have believed.
μακάριοι οἱ μὴ ἰδόντες, καὶ πιστεύσαντες.
Blessed those not seeing, and believing.
30 Πολλὰ μὲν οὖν καὶ ἄλλα σημεῖα ἐποίησεν ὁ Ἰησοῦς ἐνώ-
Many, therefore, and other signs did Jesus in (the)
πιον τῶν μαθητῶν αὐτοῦ, ἃ οὐκ ἔστι γεγραμμένα ἐν τῷ
sight of the disciples of Him, which not is written in
31 βιβλίῳ τούτῳ. ταῦτα δὲ γέγραπται, ἵνα πιστεύσητε ὅτι ὁ
roll this. these things But have been written that you believe that
Ἰησοῦς ἐστιν ὁ Χριστὸς ὁ υἱὸς τοῦ Θεοῦ, καὶ ἵνα πιστεύοντες
Jesus is the Christ the Son — of God, and that believing
ζωὴν ἔχητε ἐν τῷ ὀνόματι αὐτοῦ.
life you may have in the name of Him.

CHAPTER 21

1 Μετὰ ταῦτα ἐφανέρωσεν ἑαυτὸν πάλιν ὁ Ἰησοῦς τοῖς
After these things revealed Himself again Jesus to the
μαθηταῖς ἐπὶ τῆς θαλάσσης τῆς Τιβεριάδος· ἐφανέρωσε δὲ
disciples on the sea — of Tiberias: He revealed and
2 οὕτως. ἦσαν ὁμοῦ Σίμων Πέτρος, καὶ Θωμᾶς ὁ λεγόμενος
thus: Were together Simon Peter, and Thomas being called
Δίδυμος, καὶ Ναθαναὴλ ὁ ἀπὸ Κανᾶ τῆς Γαλιλαίας, καὶ οἱ
Twin, and Nathanael from Cana, of Galilee, and those
τοῦ Ζεβεδαίου, καὶ ἄλλοι ἐκ τῶν μαθητῶν αὐτοῦ δύο.
— of Zebedee, and others of the disciples of Him two.
3 λέγει αὐτοῖς Σίμων Πέτρος, Ὑπάγω ἁλιεύειν. λέγουσιν
says to them Simon Peter, I am going out to fish. They say
αὐτῷ, Ἐρχόμεθα καὶ ἡμεῖς σὺν σοί. ἐξῆλθον καὶ ἀνέβησαν
to him, are coming also We with you. They went and entered
εἰς τὸ πλοῖον εὐθύς, καὶ ἐν ἐκείνῃ τῇ νυκτὶ ἐπίασαν οὐδέν.
into the boat at once. And in that — night, they caught nothing.
4 πρωΐας δὲ ἤδη γενομένης ἔστη ὁ Ἰησοῦς εἰς τὸν αἰγιαλόν·
early morn But now (it) becoming, stood Jesus in the shore;
5 οὐ μέντοι ᾔδεισαν οἱ μαθηταὶ ὅτι Ἰησοῦς ἐστι. λέγει οὖν
not, however, knew the disciples that Jesus it is. says Then
αὐτοῖς ὁ Ἰησοῦς, Παιδία, μή τι προσφάγιον ἔχετε; ἀπεκρί-
to them Jesus, Children, not anything for eating have you? They
6 θησαν αὐτῷ, Οὔ. ὁ δὲ εἶπεν αὐτοῖς, Βάλετε εἰς τὰ δεξιὰ
answered Him, No. He And said to them, Cast into the right
μέρη τοῦ πλοίου τὸ δίκτυον, καὶ εὑρήσετε. ἔβαλον οὖν, καὶ
parts of the boat the net, and you will find. They cast, then, and
οὐκέτι αὐτὸ ἑλκύσαι ἴσχυσαν ἀπὸ τοῦ πλήθους τῶν ἰχθύων.
no longer it to draw had they might from the multitude of the fish.

the disciple whom Jesus loved said to Peter, It is the Lord. Then hearing that it is the Lord, Simon Peter girded on *his* coat—for he was naked—and threw himself into the sea. [8]And the other disciples came in the little boat; for they were not far from the land, only about two hundred cubits, dragging the net of the fish. [9]Then when they went up on the land, they saw a coal fire lying, and a fish lying on *it*, and bread. [10]Jesus said to them, Bring from the little fish which you caught now. [11]Simon Peter went up and dragged the net onto the land, full of big fish, a hundred and fifty-three. And *though* being so many, the net was not torn. [12]Jesus said to them, Come, break fast. And no one of the disciples dared to ask Him, Who are You, knowing that it is the Lord. [13]Then Jesus came and took the bread, and gave to them; and in the same way the little fish. [14]This now *is* the three times Jesus was revealed to His disciples, *He* being raised from *the* dead.

[15]Then when they broke fast, Jesus said to Simon Peter, Simon *son* of Jonah, do you love Me more than these? He said to Him, Yes, Lord; You know that I love you. He said to him, Feed My lambs! [16]Again He says to him, secondly, Simon *son* of Jonah, do you love Me? He says to Him, Yes, Lord; You know that I love You. He said to him, Shepherd My sheep! [17]Thirdly, He said to him, Simon *son* of Jonah, do you love Me? Peter was grieved that He said to him *a* third *time*, Do you love Me? And he said to Him, Lord, You perceive all things; You know that I love You! Jesus said to him, Feed My sheep!

[18]Truly, truly, I say to you, When you were younger, you girded yourself, and you walked where you desired. But when you grow old, you will stretch out your hands,

7 λέγει οὖν ὁ μαθητὴς ἐκεῖνος ὃν ἠγάπα ὁ Ἰησοῦς τῷ Πέτρῳ,
says Then disciple that whom loved Jesus — to Peter,
Ὁ Κύριός ἐστι. Σίμων οὖν Πέτρος, ἀκούσας ὅτι ὁ Κύριός
The Lord it is. Simon Then Peter, hearing that the Lord
ἐστι, τὸν ἐπενδύτην διεζώσατο (ἦν γὰρ γυμνός), καὶ
it is, the coat (having) girded on. he was For naked, and
8 ἔβαλεν ἑαυτὸν εἰς τὴν θάλασσαν. οἱ δὲ ἄλλοι μαθηταὶ τῷ
threw himself into the sea. the And other disciples in the
πλοιαρίῳ ἦλθον (οὐ γὰρ ἦσαν μακρὰν ἀπὸ τῆς γῆς, ἀλλ'
little boat came, not for they were far from the land, but
ὡς ἀπὸ πηχῶν διακοσίων), σύροντες τὸ δίκτυον τῶν
about from cubits two hundred, dragging the net of the
9 ἰχθύων. ὡς οὖν ἀπέβησαν εἰς τὴν γῆν, βλέπουσιν ἀνθρακιὰν
fish. when Then they went up on the land, they saw a coal fire
10 κειμένην καὶ ὀψάριον ἐπικείμενον, καὶ ἄρτον. λέγει αὐτοῖς
lying, and a fish lying on, and bread. says to them
ὁ Ἰησοῦς, Ἐνέγκατε ἀπὸ τῶν ὀψαρίων ὧν ἐπιάσατε νῦν.
Jesus, Bring from the little fish which you caught now.
11 ἀνέβη Σίμων Πέτρος, καὶ εἵλκυσε τὸ δίκτυον ἐπὶ τῆς γῆς,
went up Simon Peter, and dragged the net onto the land,
μεστὸν ἰχθύων μεγάλων ἑκατὸν πεντηκοντατριῶν· καὶ
full fish of great a hundred fifty three. And
12 τοσούτων ὄντων, οὐκ ἐσχίσθη τὸ δίκτυον. λέγει αὐτοῖς ὁ
so many being not was torn the net. says to them
Ἰησοῦς, Δεῦτε ἀριστήσατε. οὐδεὶς δὲ ἐτόλμα τῶν μαθητῶν
Jesus, Come, break fast. no one And dared of the disciples
ἐξετάσαι αὐτόν, Σὺ τίς εἶ; εἰδότες ὅτι ὁ Κύριός ἐστιν.
to question Him, You Who are, knowing that the Lord it is.
13 ἔρχεται οὖν ὁ Ἰησοῦς, καὶ λαμβάνει τὸν ἄρτον, καὶ δίδωσιν
comes Then Jesus and takes the bread, and gives
14 αὐτοῖς, καὶ τὸ ὀψάριον ὁμοίως. τοῦτο ἤδη τρίτον ἐφανερώθη
to them, and the little fish likewise. This already thrice was revealed
ὁ Ἰησοῦς τοῖς μαθηταῖς αὐτοῦ, ἐγερθεὶς ἐκ νεκρῶν.
Jesus to the disciples of Him, having been raised from (the) dead.
15 Ὅτε οὖν ἠρίστησαν, λέγει τῷ Σίμωνι Πέτρῳ ὁ Ἰησοῦς,
when Then they breakfasted, says to Simon Peter Jesus,
Σίμων Ἰωνᾶ, ἀγαπᾷς με πλεῖον τούτων; λέγει αὐτῷ, Ναὶ
Simon of Jonah, do you love Me more (than) these? He says to Him, Yes,
Κύριε· σὺ οἶδας ὅτι φιλῶ σε. λέγει αὐτῷ, Βόσκε τὰ ἀρνία μου.
Lord, You know that I love You. He says to him, Feed the lambs of Me.
16 λέγει αὐτῷ πάλιν δεύτερον, Σίμων Ἰωνᾶ, ἀγαπᾷς με; λέγει
He says to him again secondly, Simon of Jonah, do you love Me? He says
αὐτῷ, Ναὶ Κύριε· σὺ οἶδας ὅτι φιλῶ σε. λέγει αὐτῷ, Ποίμαινε
to Him, Yes, Lord, You know that I love You. He says to him, Shepherd
17 τὰ πρόβατά μου. λέγει αὐτῷ τὸ τρίτον, Σίμων Ἰωνᾶ, φιλεῖς
the sheep of Me. He says to him thirdly, Simon of Jonah do you love
με; ἐλυπήθη ὁ Πέτρος ὅτι εἶπεν αὐτῷ τὸ τρίτον, φιλεῖς με;
Me? was grieved Peter that He said to him thirdly, Do you love Me?
καὶ εἶπεν αὐτῷ, Κύριε, σὺ πάντα οἶδας· σὺ γινώσκεις ὅτι
And he said to Him, Lord You all things perceive, You know that
18 φιλῶ σε. λέγει αὐτῷ ὁ Ἰησοῦς, Βόσκε τὰ πρόβατά μου. ἀμὴν
I love You. says to him Jesus, Feed the little sheep of Me. Truly,
ἀμὴν λέγω σοι, ὅτε ἦς νεώτερος, ἐζώννυες σεαυτόν, καὶ
truly, I say to you, when you were younger, you girded yourself, and
περιεπάτεις ὅπου ἤθελες· ὅταν δὲ γηράσῃς, ἐκτενεῖς τὰς
you walked where you desired, when but you grow old you will stretch the

and another will gird you, and will carry *you* where you do not desire. [19]But He said this signifying by what death he would glorify God. And having said this, He told him, Follow Me. [20]But turning, Peter saw the disciple whom Jesus loved following *them*, who also leaned on His breast at the Supper, and said, Lord, who is the *one* betraying You? [21]Seeing him, Peter said to Jesus, Lord, and what *of* this one? [22]Jesus said to him, If I desire him to remain until I come, what *is that* to you? You follow Me. [23]Therefore, the word went out to the brothers that that disciple does not die. Yet Jesus did not say to him that he does not die, but, If I desire him to remain until I come, what *is that* to you?

[24]This is the disciple witnessing concerning these other things, writing these things, and we know that his witness is true.

[25]And there are also many things, whatever Jesus did, which if they were written singly, I suppose the world itself *could* not contain the books having been written. Amen.

χεῖράς σου, καὶ ἄλλος σε ζώσει, καὶ οἴσει ὅπου οὐ θέλεις.
hands of you, and another you will gird, and will carry where not you want
19 τοῦτο δὲ εἶπε, σημαίνων ποίῳ θανάτῳ δοξάσει τὸν Θεόν.
this And He said, signifying by what death he will glorify — God.
20 καὶ τοῦτο εἰπὼν λέγει αὐτῷ, Ἀκολούθει μοι. ἐπιστραφεὶς δὲ
And this saying, He tells him, Follow Me. turning And
ὁ Πέτρος βλέπει τὸν μαθητὴν ὃν ἠγάπα ὁ Ἰησοῦς ἀκολου-
Peter sees the disciple whom loved Jesus, following,
θοῦντα, ὃς καὶ ἀνέπεσεν ἐν τῷ δείπνῳ ἐπὶ τὸ στῆθος αὐτοῦ
who also leaned at the supper on the breast of Him
21 καὶ εἶπε, Κύριε, τίς ἐστιν ὁ παραδιδούς σε; τοῦτον ἰδὼν ὁ
and said, Lord, who is the (one) betraying You? This one seeing —
22 Πέτρος λέγει τῷ Ἰησοῦ, Κύριε, οὗτος δὲ τί; λέγει αὐτῷ ὁ
Peter says — to Jesus, Lord, this one and what? says to him —
Ἰησοῦς, Ἐὰν αὐτὸν θέλω μένειν ἕως ἔρχομαι, τί πρός σε;
Jesus, If him I desire to remain until I come, what to you?
23 σὺ ἀκολούθει μοι. ἐξῆλθεν οὖν ὁ λόγος οὗτος εἰς τοὺς ἀδελ-
You follow Me. went out Therefore word this to the brothers,
φούς, ὅτι ὁ μαθητὴς ἐκεῖνος οὐκ ἀποθνήσκει· καὶ οὐκ εἶπεν
that disciple that not does die; and not said
αὐτῷ ὁ Ἰησοῦς, ὅτι οὐκ ἀποθνήσκει· ἀλλ', Ἐὰν αὐτὸν θέλω
to him — Jesus that not he does die; but, If him I desire
μένειν ἕως ἔρχομαι, τί πρός σε;
to remain until I come, what to you?
24 Οὗτός ἐστιν ὁ μαθητὴς ὁ μαρτυρῶν περὶ τούτων, καὶ
This is the disciple witnessing concerning other things
γράψας ταῦτα· καὶ οἴδαμεν ὅτι ἀληθής ἐστιν ἡ μαρτυρία
writing these things, and we know that true is the witness
αὐτοῦ.
of him.
25 Ἔστι δὲ καὶ ἄλλα πολλὰ ὅσα ἐποίησεν ὁ Ἰησοῦς, ἅτινα
are And also the things many, whatever did — Jesus, which
ἐὰν γράφηται καθ' ἕν, οὐδὲ αὐτὸν οἶμαι τὸν κόσμον χωρῆσαι
if they were written singly, not itself I suppose the world to contain
τὰ γραφόμενα βιβλία. Ἀμήν.
those being written rolls. Amen.

KING JAMES II VERSION

THE ACTS OF THE APOSTLES

CHAPTER 1

[1]Indeed, O Theophilus, I made the first report as to all things which Jesus began both to do and to teach, [2]until the day He was taken up, having given directions to the apostles through *the* Holy Spirit; [3]to whom also He presented Himself living after His suffering, by many infallible proofs being seen by them through forty days, and speaking the things concerning the kingdom of God. [4]And being gathered together, He charged them not to leave Jerusalem, but to await the promise of the Father, "which you heard of Me. [5]For John indeed baptized in water, but you will be baptized in *the* Holy Spirit not many days after."

[6]Then, indeed, coming together they questioned Him, saying, Lord, Do You restore the kingdom to Israel at this time? [7]And He said to them, It is not yours to know times or seasons, which the Father placed in His own authority; [8]but you will receive power, the Holy Spirit coming upon you, and you will be witnesses of Me both in Jerusalem, and in Judea, and Samaria, and to *the* end of the earth. [9]And saying these things, *as* they looked on, He was taken up; and a cloud received Him from their eyes. [10]And as they were looking intently into the heaven, He having gone, even

ΠΡΑΞΕΙΣ ΤΩΝ ΑΠΟΣΤΟΛΩΝ

ACTS OF THE APOSTLES

CHAPTER 1

1 Τὸν μὲν πρῶτον λόγον ἐποιησάμην περὶ πάντων, ὦ
The — first account I made concerning all things, O
2 Θεόφιλε, ὧν ἤρξατο ὁ Ἰησοῦς ποιεῖν τε καὶ διδάσκειν, ἄχρι
Theophilus, which began — Jesus to do both and to teach, until
ἧς ἡμέρας, ἐντειλάμενος τοῖς ἀποστόλοις διὰ Πνεύματος
which day, having given directions to the apostles through (the) Spirit
3 Ἁγίου οὓς ἐξελέξατο, ἀνελήφθη· οἷς καὶ παρέστησεν ἑαυτὸν
Holy whom He chose, He was taken up; to whom also He showed Himself
ζῶντα μετὰ τὸ παθεῖν αὐτὸν ἐν πολλοῖς τεκμηρίοις, δι'
living after the suffering (of) Him by many infallible proofs through
ἡμερῶν τεσσαράκοντα ὀπτανόμενος αὐτοῖς, καὶ λέγων τὰ
days forty being seen by them, and saying the things
4 περὶ τῆς βασιλείας τοῦ Θεοῦ. καὶ συναλιζόμενος μετ' αὐτῶν
about the kingdom — of God. And meeting with them
παρήγγειλεν αὐτοῖς ἀπὸ Ἱεροσολύμων μὴ χωρίζεσθαι,
He charged them from Jerusalem not to depart,
ἀλλὰ περιμένειν τὴν ἐπαγγελίαν τοῦ πατρός, ἣν ἠκούσατέ
but to await the promise of the Father, which you heard
5 μου· ὅτι Ἰωάννης μὲν ἐβάπτισεν ὕδατι, ὑμεῖς δὲ βαπτισθή-
of Me, because John indeed baptized in water, you but will be
σεσθε ἐν Πνεύματι Ἁγίῳ οὐ μετὰ πολλὰς ταύτας ἡμέρας.
baptized in (the) Spirit Holy not after many these days.
6 Οἱ μὲν οὖν συνελθόντες ἐπηρώτων αὐτὸν λέγοντες, Κύριε,
those So then coming together questioned Him, saying, Lord,
εἰ ἐν τῷ χρόνῳ τούτῳ ἀποκαθιστάνεις τὴν βασιλείαν τῷ
if at — time this restore You the kingdom —
7 Ἰσραήλ; εἶπε δὲ πρὸς αὐτούς, Οὐχ ὑμῶν ἐστι γνῶναι
to Israel? He said And to them, Not of you it is to know
χρόνους ἢ καιροὺς οὓς ὁ πατὴρ ἔθετο ἐν τῇ ἰδίᾳ ἐξουσίᾳ.
times or seasons which the Father placed in the own authority.
8 ἀλλὰ λήψεσθε δύναμιν, ἐπελθόντος τοῦ Ἁγίου Πνεύματος
But you will receive power, coming the Holy Spirit
ἐφ' ὑμᾶς· καὶ ἔσεσθέ μοι μάρτυρες ἔν τε Ἱερουσαλήμ, καὶ ἐν
upon you, and you will be of Me witnesses in both Jerusalem, and in
πάσῃ τῇ Ἰουδαίᾳ καὶ Σαμαρείᾳ, καὶ ἕως ἐσχάτου τῆς γῆς.
all — Judea, and Samaria, and unto (the) end of the earth.
9 καὶ ταῦτα εἰπών, βλεπόντων αὐτῶν ἐπήρθη, καὶ νεφέλη
And these things saying, looking them, He was taken up, and a cloud
10 ὑπέλαβεν αὐτὸν ἀπὸ τῶν ὀφθαλμῶν αὐτῶν. καὶ ὡς ἀτενί-
received Him from the eyes of them. And as gazing
ζοντες ἦσαν εἰς τὸν οὐρανόν, πορευομένου αὐτοῦ, καὶ ἰδοὺ
they were to Heaven, going Him, and behold,

behold, two men in white clothing stood by them, [11]who also said, Men, Galileans, why do you stand looking up to the heaven? This Jesus, the *One* being taken from you into Heaven, will come in the way you saw Him going into Heaven.

[12]Then they returned to Jerusalem from *the* mount being called Of Olive Grove, which is near Jerusalem, a sabbath's *journey* away. [13]And when they went in, they went up to the upper room where they were waiting: both Peter and James, and John and Andrew, Philip and Thomas, Bartholomew and Matthew, James *the son* of Alpheus and Simon the Zealot, and Judas *the brother* of James. [14]These all were continuing steadfastly in prayer and in supplication with one mind, with *the* women, and *with* Mary the mother of Jesus, and with His brothers.

[15]And in these days, Peter standing up in *the* middle of the disciples said—and *the* number of names together *being* about a hundred and twenty—[16]Men, brothers, it was necessary *for* this Scripture to be fulfilled which the Holy Spirit spoke before by David's mouth concerning Judas, the *one* having become guide to those seizing Jesus; [17]for he was numbered with us, and obtained a portion of this ministry. [18]Indeed, then, this one bought a field out of the reward of unrighteousness, and having become headlong, he burst in *the* middle, and poured out all his bowels. [19]And it became known to all those living in Jerusalem, so as to be called in their own dialect, Akeldama; that is, Field of Blood. [20]For it has been written in *the* book of Psalms, "Let his estate become forsaken, and he not be living in it" and, "let another take his office."

11 ἄνδρες δύο παρειστήκεισαν αὐτοῖς ἐν ἐσθῆτι λευκῇ, οἳ καὶ
men two stood by them in clothing white, who also
εἶπον, Ἄνδρες Γαλιλαῖοι, τί ἑστήκατε ἐμβλέποντες εἰς τὸν
said, Men, Galileans, why do you stand looking to —
οὐρανόν; οὗτος ὁ Ἰησοῦς, ὁ ἀναληφθεὶς ἀφ' ὑμῶν εἰς τὸν
Heaven? This — Jesus, the (one) being taken from you to —
οὐρανόν, οὕτως ἐλεύσεται ὃν τρόπον ἐθεάσασθε αὐτὸν
Heaven, thus will come in the way you beheld Him
πορευόμενον εἰς τὸν οὐρανόν.
going into — Heaven.
12 Τοτε ὑπέστρεψαν εἰς Ἱερουσαλὴμ ἀπὸ ὄρους τοῦ καλου-
Then they returned to Jerusalem from (the) mount being
μένου Ἐλαιῶνος, ὅ ἐστιν ἐγγὺς Ἱερουσαλήμ, σαββάτου
called Of olive grove, which is near Jerusalem, a sabbath's
13 ἔχον ὁδόν. καὶ ὅτε εἰσῆλθον, ἀνέβησαν εἰς τὸ ὑπερῷον οὗ
having a way. And when they entered, they went up to the upper room where
ἦσαν καταμένοντες, ὅ τε Πέτρος καὶ Ἰάκωβος καὶ Ἰωάννης καὶ
they were waiting, both Peter and James and John and
Ἀνδρέας, Φίλιππος καὶ Θωμᾶς, Βαρθολομαῖος καὶ Ματθαῖος,
Andrew, Philip and Thomas, Bartholomew and Matthew,
Ἰάκωβος Ἀλφαίου καὶ Σίμων ὁ Ζηλωτής, καὶ Ἰούδας Ἰακώ-
James of Alpheus and Simon the Zealot, and Judas of
14 βου. οὗτοι πάντες ἦσαν προσκαρτεροῦντες ὁμοθυμαδὸν τῇ
James. These all were continuing steadfastly with one mind —
προσευχῇ καὶ τῇ δεήσει, σὺν γυναιξὶ καὶ Μαρίᾳ τῇ μητρὶ τοῦ
in prayer and in supplication, with (the) women, and Mary the mother —
Ἰησοῦ, καὶ σὺν τοῖς ἀδελφοῖς αὐτοῦ.
of Jesus, and with the brothers of Him.
15 Και ἐν ταῖς ἡμέραις ταύταις ἀναστὰς Πέτρος ἐν μέσῳ τῶν
And in days these standing up Peter in (the) midst of the
μαθητῶν εἶπεν (ἦν τε ὄχλος ὀνομάτων ἐπὶ τὸ αὐτὸ ὡς ἑκατὸν
disciples said; was and the crowd of names together about a hundred
16 εἴκοσιν), Ἄνδρες ἀδελφοί, ἔδει πληρωθῆναι τὴν γραφὴν
twenty; Men, brothers, it behoved to be fulfilled — Scripture
ταύτην, ἣν προεῖπε τὸ Πνεῦμα τὸ Ἅγιον διὰ στόματος
this, which spoke the Spirit — Holy through (the) mouth
Δαβὶδ περὶ Ἰούδα, τοῦ γενομένου ὁδηγοῦ τοῖς συλλαβοῦσι
David concerning Judas, the (one) being guide to the (ones) taking
17 τὸν Ἰησοῦν. ὅτι κατηριθμημένος ἦν σὺν ἡμῖν, καὶ ἔλαχε τὸν
— Jesus; because being numbered he was with us, and obtained the
18 κλῆρον τῆς διακονίας ταύτης. (οὗτος μὲν οὖν ἐκτήσατο
portion — of ministry this; this one therefore bought
χωρίον ἐκ τοῦ μισθοῦ τῆς ἀδικίας, καὶ πρηνὴς γενόμενος
a field out of the reward — of unrighteousnes, and headlong becoming
19 ἐλάκησε μέσος, καὶ ἐξεχύθη πάντα τὰ σπλάγχνα αὐτοῦ. καὶ
he burst in (the) middle, and poured out all the bowels of him. And
γνωστὸν ἐγένετο πᾶσι τοις κατοικοῦσιν Ἱερουσαλήμ, ὥστε
known it became to all those inhabiting Jerusalem, so as
κληθῆναι τὸ χωρίον ἐκεῖνο τῇ ἰδίᾳ διαλέκτῳ αὐτῶν Ἀκελ-
to be called — field that in the own dialect of them Akel-
20 δαμά, τοῦτ' ἔστι, χωρίον αἵματος.) γέγραπται γὰρ ἐν βίβλῳ
dama, that is, Field of Blood. it has been written For in (the) roll
Ψαλμῶν, Γενηθήτω ἡ ἔπαυλις αὐτοῦ ἔρημος, καὶ μὴ ἔστω ὁ
of Psalms, Let become the estate of him forsaken, and not be he
21 κατοικῶν ἐν αὐτῇ· καί, Τὴν ἐπισκοπὴν αὐτοῦ λάβοι ἕτερος.
dwelling in it; and, The office of him let take another.

[21] Therefore, it is right that one of these men being with us all the time in which the Lord Jesus came in and went out among us, [22] beginning from the baptism of John until the day when He was taken from us, one of these to become a witness of His resurrection with us. [23] And they set out two: Joseph, he being called Barsabas, who was surnamed Justus; and Matthias. [24] And having prayed, they said, You, Lord, knower of all hearts, show which one from these two You chose [25] to take the share of this ministry and apostleship, from which Judas fell, to go to *his* own place. [26] And they gave their lots. And the lot fell on Matthias; and he was numbered with the eleven apostles.

CHAPTER 2

[1] And in the fulfilling of the Day of Pentecost, they were all with one mind in the same place. [2] And suddenly a sound came out of the heaven, as being borne along by a violent wind! And it filled all the house where they were sitting. [3] And tongues as of fire appeared to them, being distributed; and it sat on each one of them. [4] And they were all filled of *the* Holy Spirit, and began to speak in other languages, as the Spirit gave *ability* to them to speak.
[5] And Jews were living in Jerusalem, devout men from every nation of those under the heaven. [6] But this sound occurring, the multitude came together and were confounded, because they each heard them speaking in his own dialect. [7] And all were amazed and marveled, saying to one another, Behold, are all these, those speaking, Galileans? [8] And how do we hear each in our own dialect in which we

δεῖ οὖν τῶν συνελθόντων ἡμῖν ἀνδρῶν ἐν παντὶ χρόνῳ ἐν ᾧ
must Then of the accompanying us men in all (the) time in which
εἰσῆλθε καὶ ἐξῆλθεν ἐφ' ἡμᾶς ὁ Κύριος Ἰησοῦς, ἀρξάμενος ἀπὸ
went in and went out among us the Lord Jesus, beginning from
22 τοῦ βαπτίσματος Ἰωάννου, ἕως τῆς ἡμέρας ἧς ἀνελήφθη ἀφ'
the baptism of John until the day when He was taken from
ἡμῶν, μάρτυρα τῆς ἀναστάσεως αὐτοῦ γενέσθαι σὺν ἡμῖν
us, a witness of the resurrection of Him to become with us
23 ἕνα τούτων. καὶ ἔστησαν δύο, Ἰωσὴφ τὸν καλούμενον
one of these. And they set two, Joseph the (one) being called
24 Βαρσαβᾶν, ὃς ἐπεκλήθη Ἰοῦστος, καὶ Ματθίαν. καὶ προσ-
Barsabas, who was surnamed Justus, and Matthias. And
ευξάμενοι εἶπον, Σὺ Κύριε καρδιογνῶστα πάντων, ἀνά-
praying they said, You, Lord, Heart-knower of all, show
25 δειξον ἐκ τούτων τῶν δύο ὃν ἕνα ἐξελέξω, λαβεῖν τὸν κλῆρον
out of these — two which one You chose to take the part
τῆς διακονίας ταύτης καὶ ἀποστολῆς, ἐξ ἧς παρέβη Ἰούδας,
of ministry this and apostleship, from which fell Judas,
26 πορευθῆναι εἰς τὸν τόπον τὸν ἴδιον. καὶ ἔδωκαν κλήρους
to go to the place — own. And they gave lots
αὐτῶν, καὶ ἔπεσεν ὁ κλῆρος ἐπὶ Ματθίαν, καὶ συγκατεψη-
for them, and fell the lot on Matthias; and he was counted
φίσθη μετὰ τῶν ἕνδεκα ἀποστόλων.
with the eleven apostles.

CHAPTER 2

1 Καὶ ἐν τῷ συμπληροῦσθαι τὴν ἡμέραν τῆς Πεντηκοστῆς,
And in the fulfilling of the Day — of Pentecost,
2 ἦσαν ἅπαντες ὁμοθυμαδὸν ἐπὶ τὸ αὐτό. καὶ ἐγένετο ἄφνω
they were all with one mind in the same place. And was suddenly
ἐκ τοῦ οὐρανοῦ ἦχος ὥσπερ φερομένης πνοῆς βιαίας, καὶ
out of Heaven a sound as being borne of a wind violent, and
3 ἐπλήρωσεν ὅλον τὸν οἶκον οὗ ἦσαν καθήμενοι. καὶ ὤφθησαν
it filled all the house where they were sitting. And appeared
αὐτοῖς διαμεριζόμεναι γλῶσσαι ὡσεὶ πυρός, ἐκάθισέ τε ἐφ'
to them being distributed tongues as of fire, it sat and on
4 ἕνα ἕκαστον αὐτῶν. καὶ ἐπλήσθησαν ἅπαντες Πνεύματος
one each of them. And they were filled all of (the) Spirit
Ἁγίου, καὶ ἤρξαντο λαλεῖν ἑτέραις γλώσσαις, καθὼς τὸ
Holy, and began to speak in other languages, as the
Πνεῦμα ἐδίδου αὐτοῖς ἀποφθέγγεσθαι.
Spirit gave to them to speak.
5 Ἦσαν δὲ ἐν Ἱερουσαλὴμ κατοικοῦντες Ἰουδαῖοι, ἄνδρες
were And in Jerusalem living Jews, men
6 εὐλαβεῖς, ἀπὸ παντὸς ἔθνους τῶν ὑπὸ τὸν οὐρανόν. γενο-
devout from every nation of those under — Heaven. happen-
μένης δὲ τῆς φωνῆς ταύτης, συνῆλθε τὸ πλῆθος καὶ συνεχύθη,
ing And — sound this, came together the multitude and were confounded
ὅτι ἤκουον εἷς ἕκαστος τῇ ἰδίᾳ διαλέκτω λαλούντων αὐτῶν.
because they heard each in the own dialect speaking them.
7 ἐξίσταντο δὲ πάντες καὶ ἐθαύμαζον, λέγοντες πρὸς ἀλλή-
were amazed And all and marveled, saying to one
λους, Οὐκ ἰδοὺ πάντες οὗτοί εἰσιν οἱ λαλοῦντες Γαλιλαῖοι;
another, not, Behold, all these are those speaking Galileans?
8 καὶ πῶς ἡμεῖς ἀκούομεν ἕκαστος τῇ ἰδίᾳ διαλέκτῳ ἡμῶν ἐν
And how we hear each in the own dialect of us in

were born. 9 Parthians, and Medes, and Elamites, and those living in Mesopotamia, both Judea and Cappadocia, Pontus and Asia, 10 both Phrygia and Pamphylia, Egypt, and the regions of Libya over against Cyrene, and the temporarily residing Romans, both Jews and proselytes, 11 Cretans and Arabians, we hear them speaking the great things of God in our own languages? 12 And all were amazed and puzzled, saying to one another, What would this wish to be? 13 But ridiculng, others said, They are full of sweet wine.

14 But standing up with the Eleven, Peter lifted up his voice and spoke out to them, Men, Jews, and all you living in Jerusalem, let this be known to you, and listen to my words: 15 For these are not drunk, as you imagine, for it is *the* third hour of the day. 16 But this is that which has been spoken by the prophet Joel, 17 "And it shall be in the last days, God says, I will pour from My Spirit on all flesh, and your sons and your daughters shall prophesy; and your young men shall see visions; and your old men shall dream dreams; 18 and also I will pour out My Spirit on My slaves and slave-girls in those days, and they shall prophesy. 19 And I will give wonders in the heaven above, and miracles on the earth below, blood and fire and vapor of smoke. 20 The sun will be turned into darkness, and the moon into blood, before the coming of the great and notable day of the Lord. 21 And it shall be that everyone who shall call on the name of *the* Lord will be saved."
22 Men, Israelites, hear

9 ᾗ ἐγεννήθημεν; Πάρθοι καὶ Μῆδοι καὶ Ἐλαμῖται, καὶ οἱ
which we were born, Parthians and Medes and Elamites, and those
κατοικοῦντες τὴν Μεσοποταμίαν, Ἰουδαίαν τε καὶ Καπ-
inhabiting — Mesopotamia, Judea both and Cappa-
10 παδοκίαν, Πόντον καὶ τὴν Ἀσίαν, Φρυγίαν τε καὶ Παμφυ-
docia, Pontus and — Asia, Phrygia both and Pam-
λίαν, Αἴγυπτον καὶ τὰ μέρη τῆς Λιβύης τῆς κατὰ Κυρήνην,
phylia, Egypt and the regions — of Libya — over against Cyrene,
καὶ οἱ ἐπιδημοῦντες Ῥωμαῖοι, Ἰουδαῖοί τε καὶ προσήλυτοι,
and the temporarily residing Romans, Jews both and proselytes,
11 Κρῆτες καὶ Ἄραβες, ἀκούομεν λαλούντων αὐτῶν ταῖς
Cretans and Arabians, we hear speaking them in
ἡμετέραις γλώσσαις τὰ μεγαλεῖα τοῦ Θεοῦ. ἐξίσταντο δὲ
our languages the great deeds — of God. were amazed And
12 πάντες καὶ διηπόρουν, ἄλλος πρὸς ἄλλον λέγοντες, Τί ἂν
all and were puzzled, other to other saying, What would
13 θέλοι τοῦτο εἶναι; ἕτεροι δὲ χλευάζοντες ἔλεγον ὅτι λεύκους
you wish this to be? others But mocking said, — Of sweet wine
μεμεστωμένοι εἰσί.
full they are.
14 Σταθεὶς δὲ Πέτρος σὺν τοῖς ἕνδεκα, ἐπῆρε τὴν φωνὴν αὐ-
standing But Peter with the eleven lifted up the voice of
τοῦ, καὶ ἀπεφθέγξατο αὐτοῖς, Ἄνδρες Ἰουδαῖοι, καὶ οἱ κατ-
him and spoke out to them, Men, Jews, and those
οικοῦντες Ἱερουσαλὴμ ἅπαντες, τοῦτο ὑμῖν γνωστὸν ἔστω,
inhabiting Jerusalem all, this to you known let be,
15 καὶ ἐνωτίσασθε τὰ ῥήματά μου. οὐ γάρ, ὡς ὑμεῖς ὑπολαμ-
and give ear to the words of me. not For, as you imagine,
βάνετε, οὗτοι μεθύουσιν· ἔστι γὰρ ὥρα τρίτη της ἡμέρας·
these are drunk, it is for hour third of the day;
16 ἀλλὰ τοῦτό ἐστι τὸ εἰρημένον διὰ τοῦ προφήτου Ἰωήλ,
but this is the thing being spoken through the prophet Joel:
17 Καὶ ἔσται ἐν ταῖς ἐσχάταις ἡμέραις, λέγει ὁ Θεός, ἐκχεῶ ἀπὸ
And it shall be in the last days, says — God, I will pour from
τοῦ πνεύματός μου ἐπὶ πᾶσαν σάρκα· καὶ προφητεύσουσιν
the Spirit of Me on all flesh, and will prophesy
οἱ υἱοὶ ὑμῶν καὶ αἱ θυγατέρες ὑμῶν. καὶ οἱ νεανίσκοι ὑμῶν
the sons of you, and the daughters of you, and the young men of you
ὁράσεις ὄψονται, καὶ οἱ πρεσβύτεροι ὑμῶν ἐνύπνια ἐνυπνια-
visions will see, and the old men of you dreams will
18 σθήσονται· καί γε ἐπὶ τοὺς δούλους μου καὶ ἐπὶ τὰς δούλας
dream, and — on the male slaves of Me, and on the female slave
μου ἐν ταῖς ἡμέραις ἐκείναις ἐκχεῶ ἀπὸ τοῦ πνεύματός μου, καὶ
of Me, in — days those I will pour from the Spirit of Me, and
19 προφητεύσουσι. καὶ δώσω τέρατα ἐν τῷ οὐρανῷ ἄνω, καὶ
they will prophesy. And I will give wonders in the heaven above, and
σημεῖα ἐπὶ τῆς γῆς κάτω, αἷμα καὶ πῦρ καὶ ἀτμίδα καπνοῦ·
signs on the earth below, blood and fire and vapor of smoke.
20 ὁ ἥλιος μεταστραφήσεται εἰς σκότος, καὶ ἡ σελήνη εἰς
The sun will be turned into darkness and the moon into
αἷμα, πρὶν ἢ ἐλθεῖν τὴν ἡμέραν Κυρίου τὴν μεγάλην καὶ
blood, before comes the day of (the) Lord the great and
21 ἐπιφανῆ· καὶ ἔσται, πᾶς ὃς ἂν ἐπικαλέσηται τὸ ὄνομα Κυρίου
notable. And it will be everyone whoever calls on the name of (the) Lord
22 σωθήσεται. ἄνδρες Ἰσραηλῖται, ἀκούσατε τοὺς λόγους
will be saved. Men, Israelites, hear — words

these words, Jesus the Nazarene, a man from God, having been approved among you by mighty works and wonders and miracles, which God did in your midst, as you yourselves also know, [23]this One given to you by the before-determined counsel and foreknowledge of God, *you* having taken *Him* by lawless hands, having crucified *Him*, you put *Him* to death. [24]*But* God raised *Him* up, loosing the throes of death, because it was not possible for Him to be held by it. [25]For David said as to Him, "I always foresaw the Lord before Me, because He is at My right *hand*, that I not be moved. [26]For this reason My heart rejoiced, and My tongue was glad; and My flesh also will dwell on hope, [27]because You will not leave My soul in Hades, nor will You give Your Holy One to see corruption. [28]You revealed to Me paths of life; You will fill Me with joy with Your face."

[29]Men, brothers, it is permitted to say to you with plainness as to the patriarch David, that he both died and was buried, and his tomb is among us until this day. [30]Being a prophet, then, and knowing that God swore with an oath to him that of *the* fruit of his loin, as concerning flesh, to raise the Christ to sit on his throne; [31]foreseeing, he spoke about the resurrection of the Christ, that His soul was not left in Hades, nor did His flesh see corruption. [32]This Jesus God raised up, of which we all are witnesses. [33]Therefore, being exalted to the right of God, and receiving the promise of the Holy Spirit from the Father, He poured out this which you now see and hear. [34]For David did not ascend into Heaven, but he says, "The Lord said to my Lord, Sit at My right [35]until I place Your enemies as a

τούτους· Ἰησοῦν τὸν Ναζωραῖον, ἄνδρα ἀπὸ τοῦ Θεοῦ
these: Jesus the Nazarene, a man from – God
ἀποδεδειγμένον εἰς ὑμᾶς δυνάμεσι καὶ τέρασι καὶ σημείοις,
having been approved among you by powerful deeds and wonders and signs,
οἷς ἐποίησε δι' αὐτοῦ ὁ Θεὸς εν μεσῳ υμῶν, καθὼς καὶ αὐτοὶ
which did through Him God amidst you, as also yourselves
23 οἴδατε, τοῦτον τῇ ὡρισμένῃ βουλῇ καὶ προγνώσει τοῦ Θεοῦ
you know, this One by the before determined counsel and foreknowledge – of God
ἔκδοτον λαβόντες, διὰ χειρῶν ἀνόμων προσπήξαντες
given up having taken by hands lawless, having crucified,
24 ἀνείλετε· ὃν ὁ Θεὸς ἀνέστησε, λύσας τὰς ὠδῖνας τοῦ θανάτου,
you killed, whom God raised up, having loosed the throes – of death,
25 καθότι οὐκ ἦν δυνατὸν κρατεῖσθαι αὐτὸν ὑπ' αὐτοῦ. Δαβὶδ
because not it was possible to be held Him by it. David
γὰρ λέγει εἰς αὐτόν, Προωρώμην τὸν Κύριον ἐνώπιόν μου
For says (as) to Him, I foresaw the Lord before Me
26 διὰ παντός· ὅτι ἐκ δεξιῶν μου ἐστίν, ἵνα μὴ σαλευθῶ· διὰ
always, because on (the) right Me He is, that not I be moved. There-
τοῦτο εὐφράνθη ἡ καρδία μου, καὶ ἠγαλλιάσατο ἡ γλῶσσά
fore was glad the heart of Me and exulted the tongue
27 μου· ἔτι δὲ καὶ ἡ σάρξ μου κατασκηνώσει ἐπ' ἐλπίδι· ὅτι οὐκ
of Me; yet And also the flesh of Me will dwell on hope, because not
ἐγκαταλείψεις τὴν ψυχήν μου εἰς ᾅδου, οὐδὲ δώσεις τὸν
You will leave the soul of Me in Hades, nor will You give the
28 ὅσιόν σου ἰδεῖν διαφθοράν. ἐγνώρισάς μοι ὁδοὺς ζωῆς·
Holy One of You to see corruption. You revealed to Me paths of life.
29 πληρώσεις με εὐφροσύνης μετὰ τοῦ προσώπου σου. ἄνδρες
You will fill Me with joy with the face of You. Men,
ἀδελφοί, ἐξὸν εἰπεῖν μετὰ παρρησίας πρὸς ὑμᾶς περὶ τοῦ
brothers, it is permitted to say with plainness to you concerning the
πατριάρχου Δαβίδ, ὅτι καὶ ἐτελεύτησε καὶ ἐτάφη, καὶ τὸ
patriarch David, that both he died and was buried, and the
30 μνῆμα αὐτοῦ ἔστιν ἐν ἡμῖν ἄχρι τῆς ἡμέρας ταύτης. προφή-
tomb of him is among us until – day this. a prophet
της οὖν ὑπάρχων, καὶ εἰδὼς ὅτι ὅρκῳ ὤμοσεν αὐτῷ ὁ Θεός,
Then being, and knowing that with an oath sworn to him God
ἐκ καρποῦ τῆς ὀσφύος αὐτοῦ τὸ κατὰ σάρκα ἀναστήσειν
of (the) fruit of the loin of him as concerning flesh to raise up
31 τὸν Χριστόν, καθίσαι ἐπὶ τοῦ θρόνου αὐτοῦ, προϊδὼν
the Christ, to sit on the throne of him, foreseeing
ἐλάλησε περὶ τῆς ἀναστάσεως τοῦ Χριστοῦ, ὅτι οὐ κατελείφθη
he spoke concerning the resurrection of the Christ, that not was left
ἡ ψυχὴ αὐτοῦ εἰς ᾅδου, οὐδὲ ἡ σὰρξ αὐτοῦ εἶδε διαφθοράν.
the soul of Him in Hades, nor the flesh of Him saw corruption.
32 τοῦτον τὸν Ἰησοῦν ἀνέστησεν ὁ Θεός, οὗ πάντες ἡμεῖς ἐσμεν
This – Jesus raised up God, of which all we are
33 μάρτυρες. τῇ δεξιᾷ οὖν τοῦ Θεοῦ ὑψωθείς, τήν τε ἐπαγγελίαν
witnesses; to the right, therefore, of God being exalted, the and promise
τοῦ Ἁγίου Πνεύματος λαβὼν παρὰ τοῦ πατρός, ἐξέχεε
of the Holy Spirit receiving from the Father, He poured
34 τοῦτο ὃ νῦν ὑμεῖς βλέπετε καὶ ἀκούετε. οὐ γὰρ Δαβὶδ ἀνέβη
this which now you see and hear. not For David ascended
εἰς τοὺς οὐρανούς, λέγει δὲ αὐτός, Εἶπεν ὁ Κύριος τῷ Κυρίῳ
to the heavens, says but he, said The Lord to the Lord
35 μου, Κάθου ἐκ δεξιῶν μου, ἕως ἂν θῶ τοὺς ἐχθρούς σου
of me, Sit at (the) right of Me until I place the enemies of You

footstool for Your feet."
36 Then assuredly, let all *the* house of Israel acknowledge that God made Him both Lord and Christ, this same Jesus whom you crucified.
37 And hearing they were stabbed in the heart, and said to Peter and the other apostles, What shall we do, men, brothers?
38 And Peter said to them, Repent and be baptized, each of you in the name of Jesus Christ unto forgiveness of sins. And you will receive the gift of the Holy Spirit. 39 For the promise is to you and to your children, and to all those afar off, as many as *the* Lord our God shall call. 40 And with many other words he earnestly testified and exhorted, saying, Be saved from this perverse generation. 41 Then those who gladly welcomed his words were baptized. And about three thousand souls were added that day. 42 And they were continuing steadfastly in the teaching of the apostles, and in fellowship, and in the breaking of bread, and in prayers.

43 And fear came on every soul, and many wonders and miracles took place through the apostles. 44 And all the believers were together, and had all things common. 45 And they sold possessions and goods, and distributed them to all, according as anyone had need. 46 And continuing steadfastly with one mind day by day in the Temple, and breaking bread from house to house, they shared food in gladness and simplicity of heart, 47 praising God, and having favor with all the people. And the Lord added to the church those being saved from day to day.

36 ὑποπόδιον τῶν ποδῶν σου. ἀσφαλῶς οὖν γινωσκέτω πᾶς
a footstool to the feet of You. Assuredly, therefore, let know all
οἶκος Ἰσραήλ, ὅτι καὶ Κύριον καὶ Χριστὸν αὐτὸν ὁ Θεὸς
the house of Israel that both Lord and Christ Him God
ἐποίησε, τοῦτον τὸν Ἰησοῦν ὃν ὑμεῖς ἐσταυρώσατε.
made, this — Jesus whom you crucified.
37 Ἀκούσαντες δὲ κατενύγησαν τῇ καρδίᾳ, εἶπόν τε πρὸς
having heard And, they were stabbed in the heart, said and to
τὸν Πέτρον καὶ τοὺς λοιποὺς ἀποστόλους, Τί ποιήσομεν,
— Peter, and the remaining apostles, What may we do,
38 ἄνδρες ἀδελφοί ; Πέτρος δὲ ἔφη πρὸς αὐτούς, Μετανοήσατε,
men, brothers? Peter And said to them, Repent
καὶ βαπτισθήτω ἕκαστος ὑμῶν ἐπὶ τῷ ὀνόματι Ἰησοῦ
and be baptized each of you on the name of Jesus
Χριστοῦ εἰς ἄφεσιν ἁμαρτιῶν, καὶ λήψεσθε τὴν δωρεὰν
Christ to forgiveness of sins, and you will receive the gift
39 τοῦ Ἁγίου Πνεύματος. ὑμῖν γάρ ἐστιν ἡ ἐπαγγελία, καὶ
of the Holy Spirit. to you For is the promise, and
τοῖς τέκνοις ὑμῶν, καὶ πᾶσι τοῖς εἰς μακράν, ὅσους ἂν προσ-
to the children of you, even to all those at a distance, as many as may
40 καλέσηται Κύριος ὁ Θεὸς ἡμῶν. ἑτέροις τε λόγοις πλείοσι
call (the) Lord, the God of us. with other And words many
διεμαρτύρετο καὶ παρεκάλει λέγων, Σώθητε ἀπὸ τῆς γενεᾶς
he earnestly testified and exhorted, saying, Be saved from — generation
41 τῆς σκολιᾶς ταύτης. οἱ μὲν οὖν ἀσμένως ἀποδεξάμενοι τὸν
— perverse this. Those, then, gladly welcoming the
λόγον αὐτοῦ ἐβαπτίσθησαν· καὶ προσετέθησαν τῇ ἡμέρᾳ
word of him were baptized, and there were added — day
42 ἐκείνῃ ψυχαὶ ὡσεὶ τρισχίλιαι. ἦσαν δὲ προσκαρτεροῦντες
that souls, about three thousand. they were And steadfastly continuing
τῇ διδαχῇ τῶν ἀποστόλων καὶ τῇ κοινωνίᾳ, καὶ τῇ κλάσει
in the teaching of the apostles, and in the fellowship, and in the breaking
τοῦ ἄρτου καὶ ταῖς προσευχαῖς.
of the bread, and in the prayers.
43 Ἐγένετο δὲ πάσῃ ψυχῇ φόβος, πολλά τε τέρατα καὶ
came And to every soul fear; many and wonders and
44 σημεῖα διὰ τῶν ἀποστόλων ἐγίνετο. πάντες δὲ οἱ πιστεύ-
signs through the apostles occurred. all And the believing
45 οντες ἦσαν ἐπὶ τὸ αὐτό, καὶ εἶχον ἅπαντα κοινά, καὶ τὰ
ones were together, and had all things common, and the
κτήματα καὶ τὰς ὑπάρξεις ἐπίπρασκον, καὶ διεμέριζον αὐτὰ
goods and the possessions they sold and distributed them
46 πᾶσι, καθότι ἄν τις χρείαν εἶχε. καθ' ἡμέραν τε προσκαρτε-
to all, according as anyone need had. from day to day And continuing
ροῦντες ὁμοθυμαδὸν ἐν τῷ ἱερῷ, κλῶντές τε κατ' οἶκον
steadfastly with one mind in the Temple breaking and from house to house
ἄρτον, μετελάμβανον τροφῆς ἐν ἀγαλλιάσει καὶ ἀφελότητι
bread, they shared food in gladness and simplicity
47 καρδίας, αἰνοῦντες τὸν Θεόν, καὶ ἔχοντες χάριν πρὸς ὅλον
of heart, praising — God, and having favor with all
τὸν λαόν. ὁ δὲ Κύριος προσετίθει τοὺς σωζομένους καθ'
the people. the And Lord added those being saved from
ἡμέραν τῇ ἐκκλησίᾳ.
day to the church.

CHAPTER 3

CHAPTER 3

[1]And Peter and John were going up on the same *day* into the Temple at the hour of prayer, the ninth. [2]And a certain man, being lame from his mother's womb, was being carried, whom they put at the door of the Temple being called Beautiful from day to day, to ask alms from those going into the Temple; [3]who, seeing Peter and John being about to go into the Temple, asked alms. [4]And Peter, with John, looking intently toward him, he said, Look to us! [5]And he paid heed to them, expecting to receive something from them. [6]But Peter said, There is no silver and gold to me, but what I have, this I give to you: In the name of Jesus Christ the Nazarean, rise up and walk! [7]And taking him by the right hand, he raised *him* up. And immediately his feet and ankle-bones were made firm. [8]And leaping up, he stood and walked, and went in with them into the Temple, walking and leaping, and praising God. [10]And they recognized him, that it was the *one* who was sitting at the Beautiful Gate of the Temple for alms. And they were filled with amazement and ecstasy at the thing that happened to him.

[11]And the lame one *who was* healed holding to Peter and John, all the people ran together to them on the porch called Solomon's, greatly amazed. [12]And seeing, Peter answered to the people, Men, Israelites, why do you marvel at this one? Or why do you stare at us, as *if* by our own power or godliness *we* have made him to walk? [13]The God of Abraham and Isaac and Jacob, the God of our fathers, glorified His Child

1 Ἐπὶ τὸ αὐτὸ δὲ Πέτρος καὶ Ἰωάννης ἀνέβαινον εἰς τὸ
on the same (day) And Peter and John were going into the
2 ἱερὸν ἐπὶ τὴν ὥραν τῆς προσευχῆς τὴν ἐννάτην. καί τις
Temple at the hour — of prayer, the ninth, and a certain
ἀνὴρ χωλὸς ἐκ κοιλίας μητρὸς αὐτοῦ ὑπάρχων ἐβαστάζετο·
man lame from womb mother's his being, was being carried
ὃν ἐτίθουν καθ' ἡμέραν πρὸς τὴν θύραν τοῦ ἱεροῦ τὴν
whom they put from day to day at the door of the Temple —
λεγομένην Ὡραίαν, τοῦ αἰτεῖν ἐλεημοσύνην παρὰ τῶν
being called Beautiful, — to ask alms from those
3 εἰσπορευομένων εἰς τὸ ἱερόν. ὃς ἰδὼν Πέτρον καὶ Ἰωάννην
going into the Temple, who seeing Peter and John
μέλλοντας εἰσιέναι εἰς τὸ ἱερόν, ἠρώτα ἐλεημοσύνην. ἀτενίσας
being about to go into the Temple, asked alms. gazing intently
4 δὲ Πέτρος εἰς αὐτὸν σὺν τῷ Ἰωάννῃ, εἶπε, Βλέψον εἰς ἡμᾶς. ὁ
And Peter at him, with — John, he said, Look to us! he
5 δὲ ἐπεῖχεν αὐτοῖς, προσδοκῶν τι παρ' αὐτῶν λαβεῖν. εἶπε δὲ
And paid heed to them, expecting something from them to receive. said And
6 Πέτρος, Ἀργύριον καὶ χρυσίον οὐχ ὑπάρχει μοι· ὃ δὲ ἔχω,
Peter, Silver and gold not is to me, what but I have,
τοῦτό σοι δίδωμι. ἐν τῷ ὀνόματι Ἰησοῦ Χριστοῦ τοῦ Ναζω-
this to you I give, in the name of Jesus Christ the Naza-
7 ραίου, ἔγειραι καὶ περιπάτει. καὶ πιάσας αὐτὸν τῆς δεξιᾶς
rean, rise up and walk! And taking him by the right
χειρὸς ἤγειρε· παραχρῆμα δὲ ἐστερεώθησαν αὐτοῦ αἱ βάσεις
hand, he raised up immediately and were made firm of him the feet
8 καὶ τὰ σφυρά. καὶ ἐξαλλόμενος ἔστη καὶ περιεπάτει, καὶ
and the ankle-bones. And leaping up he stood, and walked, and
εἰσῆλθε σὺν αὐτοῖς εἰς τὸ ἱερόν, περιπατῶν καὶ ἁλλόμενος
went in with them into the Temple, walking and leaping
9 καὶ αἰνῶν τὸν Θεόν. καὶ εἶδεν αὐτὸν πᾶς ὁ λαὸς περιπα-
and praising — God. And saw him all the people walking
10 τοῦντα καὶ αἰνοῦντα τὸν Θεόν· ἐπεγίνωσκόν τε αὐτὸν ὅτι
and praising — God; they recognized and him, that
οὗτος ἦν ὁ πρὸς τὴν ἐλεημοσύνην καθήμενος ἐπὶ τῇ Ὡραίᾳ
this was he for — alms sitting at the Beautiful
πύλῃ τοῦ ἱεροῦ· καὶ ἐπλήσθησαν θάμβους καὶ ἐκστάσεως
Gate of the Temple. And they were filled of amazement and ecstasy
ἐπὶ τῷ συμβεβηκότι αὐτῷ.
at the thing having happened to him.

11 Κρατοῦντος δὲ τοῦ ἰαθέντος χωλοῦ τὸν Πέτρον καὶ
holding And the healed lame (one) Peter and
Ἰωάννην, συνέδραμε πρὸς αὐτοὺς πᾶς ὁ λαὸς ἐπὶ τῇ στοᾷ
John, ran together to them all the people on the porch
12 τῇ καλουμένῃ Σολομῶντος, ἔκθαμβοι. ἰδὼν δὲ Πέτρος ἀπε-
— called Solomon's, greatly amazed. seeing And Peter
κρίνατο πρὸς τὸν λαόν, Ἄνδρες Ἰσραηλῖται, τί θαυμάζετε
answered to the people, Men, Israelites, Why do you marvel
ἐπὶ τούτῳ, ἢ ἡμῖν τί ἀτενίζετε, ὡς ἰδίᾳ δυνάμει ἢ εὐσεβείᾳ
at this one, or at us why do you gaze, as by own power or piety
13 πεποιηκόσι τοῦ περιπατεῖν αὐτόν; ὁ Θεὸς Ἀβραὰμ καὶ
having made — to walk him? The God of Abraham and
Ἰσαὰκ καὶ Ἰακώβ, ὁ Θεὸς τῶν πατέρων ἡμῶν, ἐδόξασε τὸν
of Isaac and of Jacob, the God of the fathers of us, glorified the

Jesus, whom you delivered up, and denied Him in the presence of Pilate, that one having decided to set *Him* free. 14 But you denied the holy and righteous *One*, and requested a man, a murderer, to be granted to you. 15 And the Author of Life you killed, whom God raised up from *the* dead, of which we are witnesses. 16 And on the faith of His Name, this one whom you behold and know, His Name made firm; and the faith which *came* through Him gave to him this complete soundness before you all. 17 And now, brothers, I know that you acted according to ignorance, as also *did* your rulers. 18 But what things God before announced through *the* mouth of all His prophets *that* the Christ should suffer, He fulfilled in this manner. 19 Repent, therefore, and convert, for the blotting out of your sins, so that times of refreshing may come from *the* face of the Lord, 20 and *that* He may send forth the *One* before proclaimed to you, Jesus Christ, 21 whom Heaven needs to receive until *the* times of restoration of all things, of which God spoke through *the* mouth of all His holy prophets from *the* age *past*. 22 For Moses indeed said to the fathers, "*The* Lord your God will raise up to you a Prophet from among your brothers, *One* like me; you shall hear Him according to all things, whatever He may speak to you. 23 And it shall be *that of* every soul, whoever will not hear that Prophet shall be utterly destroyed from among the people." 24 And also all the prophets, from Samuel and those following after, as many as spoke, also before announced these days.

25 You are *the* sons of the prophets, and of the covenant which God appointed to our fathers, saying to Abraham, "Even in your Seed all the families of the earth shall be blessed."

παῖδα αὐτοῦ Ἰησοῦν· ὃν ὑμεῖς παρεδώκατε, καὶ ἠρνήσασθε
servant of Him, Jesus, whom you delivered up, and denied
αὐτὸν κατὰ πρόσωπον Πιλάτου, κρίναντος ἐκείνου ἀπο-
Him in the presence of Pilate, having decided that one to re-
14 λύειν. ὑμεῖς δὲ τὸν ἅγιον καὶ δίκαιον ἠρνήσασθε, καὶ ᾐτή-
lease (Him), you but the holy and righteous One denied, and
15 σασθε ἄνδρα φονέα χαρισθῆναι ὑμῖν, τὸν δὲ ἀρχηγὸν τῆς
asked a man, a murderer, to be granted to you, the and Author —
ζωῆς ἀπεκτείνατε· ὃν ὁ Θεὸς ἤγειρεν ἐκ νεκρῶν, οὗ ἡμεῖς
of life you killed, whom God raised from (the) dead, of which we
16 μάρτυρές ἐσμεν. καὶ ἐπὶ τῇ πίστει τοῦ ὀνόματος αὐτοῦ,
witnesses are. And on the faith of the name of Him,
τοῦτον ὃν θεωρεῖτε καὶ οἴδατε ἐστερέωσε τὸ ὄνομα αὐτοῦ·
this one whom you behold and know made firm by the name of Him,
καὶ ἡ πίστις ἡ δι' αὐτοῦ ἔδωκεν αὐτῷ τὴν ὁλοκληρίαν
and the faith which through Him gave to him complete soundness
17 ταύτην ἀπέναντι πάντων ὑμῶν. καὶ νῦν, ἀδελφοί, οἶδα ὅτι
this before all of you. And now, brothers, I know that
18 κατὰ ἄγνοιαν ἐπράξατε, ὥσπερ καὶ οἱ ἄρχοντες ὑμῶν. ὁ δὲ
by way of ignorance you acted, as also the rulers of you, But
Θεὸς ἃ προκατήγγειλε διὰ στόματος πάντων τῶν προ-
God that He before announced through (the) mouth of all the
φητῶν αὐτοῦ, παθεῖν τὸν Χριστόν, ἐπλήρωσεν οὕτω.
prophets of Him, to suffer the Christ, He fulfilled thus.
19 μετανοήσατε οὖν καὶ ἐπιστρέψατε, εἰς τὸ ἐξαλειφθῆναι ὑμῶν
Repent, therefore, and be converted, for the blotting out of you
τὰς ἁμαρτίας, ὅπως ἂν ἔλθωσι καιροὶ ἀναψύξεως ἀπὸ προσ-
the sins, so as when may come times of refreshing from (the)
20 ώπου τοῦ Κυρίου, καὶ ἀποστείλῃ τὸν προκεκηρυγμένον
presence of the Lord, and He may send the (One) before proclaimed
21 ὑμῖν Ἰησοῦν Χριστόν· ὃν δεῖ οὐρανὸν μὲν δέξασθαι ἄχρι
to you, Jesus Christ, whom it is right Heaven to receive until
χρόνων ἀποκαταστάσεως πάντων, ὧν ἐλάλησεν ὁ Θεὸς
(the) times of restitution of all things, which spoke God
διὰ στόματος πάντων ἁγίων αὐτοῦ προφητῶν ἀπ' αἰῶνος.
through (the) mouth of all holy of Him prophets from (the) age.
22 Μωσῆς μὲν γὰρ πρὸς τοὺς πατέρας εἶπεν ὅτι Προφήτην
Moses indeed For to the fathers said, — A prophet
ὑμῖν ἀναστήσει Κύριος ὁ Θεὸς ὑμῶν ἐκ τῶν ἀδελφῶν ὑμῶν
for you will raise up (the) Lord God of you from the brothers of you
ὡς ἐμέ· αὐτοῦ ἀκούσεσθε κατὰ πάντα ὅσα ἂν λαλήσῃ πρὸς
like me; Him you shall hear according to all, whatever He may speak to
23 ὑμᾶς. ἔσται δέ, πᾶσα ψυχή, ἥτις ἂν μὴ ἀκούσῃ τοῦ προφή-
you. it shall be And, every soul, whoever may not hear — prophet
24 του ἐκείνου, ἐξολοθρευθήσεται ἐκ τοῦ λαοῦ. καὶ πάντες δὲ
that, will be utterly destroyed from the people. also all And
οἱ προφῆται ἀπὸ Σαμουὴλ καὶ τῶν καθεξῆς, ὅσοι ἐλάλησαν,
the prophets from Samuel, and those in order, as many as spoke,
25 καὶ προκατήγγειλαν τὰς ἡμέρας ταύτας. ὑμεῖς ἐστε υἱοὶ τῶν
also before announced — days these. You are sons of the
προφητῶν, καὶ τῆς διαθήκης ἧς διέθετο ὁ Θεὸς πρὸς τοὺς
prophets, and of the covenant which appointed God to the
πατέρας ἡμῶν, λέγων πρὸς Ἀβραάμ, Καὶ τῷ σπέρματί σου
fathers of us, saying to Abraham, And in the seed of you
26 ἐνευλογηθήσονται πᾶσαι αἱ πατριαὶ τῆς γῆς. ὑμῖν πρῶτον
shall be blessed all the families of the earth. To you first

Jesus, God sent Him first to you, blessing you in turning away each one from your evil deeds.

CHAPTER 4

And *as* they were speaking to the people, the priests and the commander of the Temple *guard* and the Sadducees stood near them, [2]being distressed because they taught the people and announced in Jesus the resurrection from *the* dead. [3]And they laid hands *on* them, and put *them* into custody until the morrow; for it was already evening. [4]But many of those having heard the word believed, and the number of the men became about five thousand.

[5]And it happened on the morrow *that* the rulers and elders and scribes assembled together in Jerusalem; [6]also Annas the High Priest, and Caiaphas, and John, and Alexander, and as many as were of the high-priestly family. [7]And having stood them in the midst, they were inquiring, By what sort of power, or by what sort of Name, did you do this? [8]Then Peter, having been filled from *the* Holy Spirit, said to them, Rulers of the people, and elders of Israel: [9]if we are being examined today upon a good work for an infirm man, *regarding* by what this one has been healed, [10]let it be known to you all and to all the people of Israel that by the Name of Jesus Christ the Nazarean, whom you crucified, whom God raised up from *the* dead— in this *Name* this one stands near before you whole! [11]This *One* is the Stone counted worthless by you the builders, which has become *placed* into *the* Head of *the* corner. [12]and there is salvation in no other One, for neither is there any other name under Heaven

ὁ Θεός, ἀναστήσας τὸν παῖδα αὐτοῦ Ἰησοῦν, ἀπέστειλεν
God having raised up the Child of Him, Jesus, sent
αὐτὸν εὐλογοῦντα ὑμᾶς, ἐν τῷ ἀποστρέφειν ἕκαστον ἀπὸ
Him, blessing you in the turning away (of) each one from
τῶν πονηριῶν ὑμῶν.
the evilnesses of you.

CHAPTER 4

1 Λαλούντων δὲ αὐτῶν πρὸς τὸν λαόν, ἐπέστησαν αὐτοῖς
speaking And they to the people, came upon them
οἱ ἱερεῖς καὶ ὁ στρατηγὸς τοῦ ἱεροῦ καὶ οἱ Σαδδουκαῖοι,
the priests and the commander of the Temple and the Sadducees,
2 διαπονούμενοι διὰ τὸ διδάσκειν αὐτοὺς τὸν λαόν, καὶ
being distressed because of the teaching (of) them the people, even
καταγγέλλειν ἐν τῷ Ἰησοῦ τὴν ἀνάστασιν τὴν ἐκ νεκρῶν.
to announce by – Jesus the resurrection – from (the) dead
3 καὶ ἐπέβαλον αὐτοῖς τὰς χεῖρας, καὶ ἔθεντο εἰς τήρησιν εἰς
And (they) laid on them the hands, and put into custody unto
4 τὴν αὔριον· ἦν γὰρ ἑσπέρα ἤδη. πολλοὶ δὲ τῶν ἀκουσάντων
the morrow; it was for evening now. many And of those hearing
τὸν λόγον ἐπίστευσαν· και ἐγενήθη ὁ ἀριθμὸς τῶν ἀνδρῶν
the word believed, and became the number of the men
ὡσεὶ χιλιάδες πέντε.
about thousands five.

5 Ἐγένετο δὲ ἐπὶ τὴν αὔριον συναχθῆναι αὐτῶν τοὺς
it was And, on the morrow to be assembled of them the
ἄρχοντας καὶ πρεσβυτέρους καὶ γραμματεῖς εἰς Ἱερουσαλήμ,
rulers and elders and scribes to Jerusalem,
6 καὶ Ἄνναν τὸν ἀρχιερέα, καὶ Καϊάφαν, καὶ Ἰωάννην, καὶ
and Annas the high priest, and Caiaphas, and John, and
7 Ἀλέξανδρον, καὶ ὅσοι ἦσαν ἐκ γένους ἀρχιερατικοῦ. καὶ
Alexander, and as many as were of (the) family high priestly. And
στήσαντες αὐτοὺς ἐν τῷ μέσῳ ἐπυνθάνοντο, Ἐν ποίᾳ
having stood them in the midst inquired, By what
8 δυνάμει ἢ ἐν ποίῳ ὀνόματι ἐποιήσατε τοῦτο ὑμεῖς ; τότε
power or in what name did do this you? Then
Πέτρος πλησθεὶς Πνεύματος Ἁγίου εἶπε πρὸς αὐτούς,
Peter filled of (the) Spirit Holy said to them,
9 Ἄρχοντες τοῦ λαοῦ καὶ πρεσβύτεροι τοῦ Ἰσραήλ, εἰ ἡμεῖς
Rulers of the people and elders of Israel, if we
σήμερον ἀνακρινόμεθα ἐπὶ εὐεργεσίᾳ ἀνθρώπου ἀσθενοῦς,
today are being examined on a good work of a man infirm
10 ἐν τίνι οὗτος σέσωσται· γνωστὸν ἔστω πᾶσιν ὑμῖν καὶ
by what this one has been healed, known let it be to all of you and
παντὶ τῷ λαῷ Ἰσραήλ, ὅτι ἐν τῷ ὀνόματι Ἰησοῦ Χριστοῦ
to all the people of Israel, that in the name of Jesus Christ
τοῦ Ναζωραίου, ὃν ὑμεῖς ἐσταυρώσατε, ὃν ὁ Θεὸς ἤγειρεν
the Nazarean, whom you crucified, whom God raised
ἐκ νεκρῶν, ἐν τούτῳ οὗτος παρέστηκεν ἐνώπιον ὑμῶν ὑγιής.
from (the) dead, in this, this one stands before you whole.
11 οὗτός ἐστιν ὁ λίθος ὁ ἐξουθενηθεὶς ὑφ' ὑμῶν τῶν οἰκοδο-
This is the Stone counted worthless by you the builders,
μούντων, ὁ γενόμενος εἰς κεφαλὴν γωνίας. καὶ οὐκ ἔστιν ἐν
which has become to (be the) head of (the) corner. And not is in
12 ἄλλῳ οὐδενὶ ἡ σωτηρία· οὔτε γὰρ ὄνομά ἐστιν ἕτερον ὑπὸ τὸν
other none the salvation, neither for name is another under –

having been given among men by which we must be saved.

[13]But seeing the boldness of Peter and John, and having perceived that they are untaught and uneducated men, they marveled. And they recognized them, that they were with Jesus. [14]But seeing the man standing with them, the *one* having been healed, they had nothing to say against *him*. [15]But commanding them to go outside the sanhedrin, they conferred with one another, [16]saying, What may we do to these men? For that a notable miracle has indeed occurred through them *is* plain to all those living in Jerusalem; and we are not able to deny *it*. [17]But that it may not spread abroad further to the people, let us threaten them with a threat, *that* they no longer speak on this name to any men.

[18]And calling them, they ordered them not to speak at all, nor to teach on the name of Jesus. [19]But answering to them, Peter and John said, Whether it is right before God to listen to you rather than God, you judge. [20]For we are not able to not speak what we saw and heard. [21]But having threatened again, they let them go, finding nothing *as to* how they might punish them, on account of the people, because all glorified God on the thing happening. [22]For the man on whom this miracle of healing had occurred was more than forty.

[23]And being let go, they came to their own and reported to them what the chief priests and elders said. [24]And hearing, *they* with one passion lifted voice to God and said, Master, You *are* the God who made the heaven and the earth and the sea, and all things in them, [25]who through *the* mouth of Your servant David said, "Why did the nations rage,

οὐρανὸν τὸ δεδομένον ἐν ἀνθρώποις, ἐν ᾧ δεῖ σωθῆναι ἡμᾶς.
Heaven —having been given among men by which must be saved us.
13 Θεωροῦντες δὲ τὴν τοῦ Πέτρου παρρησίαν καὶ Ἰωάννου,
beholding And the — of Peter boldness and of John,
καὶ καταλαβόμενοι ὅτι ἄνθρωποι ἀγράμματοί εἰσι καὶ
and having perceived that men unlettered they are, and
ἰδιῶται, ἐθαύμαζον, ἐπεγίνωσκόν τε αὐτοὺς ὅτι σὺν τῷ
private, they marveled, recognized and them that with —
14 Ἰησοῦ ἦσαν. τὸν δὲ ἄνθρωπον βλέποντες σὺν αὐτοῖς ἑστῶτα
Jesus they were. the And man seeing with them standing,
15 τὸν τεθεραπευμένον, οὐδὲν εἶχον ἀντειπεῖν. κελεύσαντες δὲ
the (one) having been healed, nothing they had to gainsay. commanding And
αὐτοὺς ἔξω τοῦ συνεδρίου ἀπελθεῖν, συνέβαλον πρὸς ἀλλή-
them outside the sanhedrin to go, they conferred with one
16 λους, λέγοντες, Τί ποιήσομεν τοῖς ἀνθρώποις τούτοις; ὅτι
another, saying, What may we do to men these; that
μὲν γὰρ γνωστὸν σημεῖον γέγονε δι' αὐτῶν, πᾶσι τοῖς κατοι-
indeed for a notable sign has occurred through them, to all those inhabit-
κοῦσιν Ἱερουσαλὴμ φανερόν, καὶ οὐ δυνάμεθα ἀρνήσασθαι.
ing Jerusalem (is) manifest, and not we are able to deny;
17 ἀλλ' ἵνα μὴ ἐπὶ πλεῖον διανεμηθῇ εἰς τὸν λαόν, ἀπειλῇ
but lest — more it be spread abroad to the people, let us with a threat
ἀπειλησώμεθα αὐτοῖς μηκέτι λαλεῖν ἐπὶ τῷ ὀνόματι τούτῳ
threaten them no longer to speak on name this
18 μηδενὶ ἀνθρώπων. καὶ καλέσαντες αὐτούς, παρήγγειλαν
to no one of men. And calling them, they ordered
αὐτοῖς τὸ καθόλου μὴ φθέγγεσθαι μηδὲ διδάσκειν ἐπὶ τῷ
them — at all not to speak nor to teach on the
19 ὀνόματι τοῦ Ἰησοῦ. ὁ δὲ Πέτρος καὶ Ἰωάννης ἀποκριθέντες
name — of Jesus. But Peter and John answering
πρὸς αὐτοὺς εἶπον, Εἰ δίκαιόν ἐστιν ἐνώπιον τοῦ Θεοῦ ὑμῶν
to them said, If right it is before — God you
20 ἀκούειν μᾶλλον ἢ τοῦ Θεοῦ, κρίνατε. οὐ δυνάμεθα γὰρ ἡμεῖς,
to hear rather than — God, you judge. not are able For we
21 ἃ εἴδομεν καὶ ἠκούσαμεν, μὴ λαλεῖν. οἱ δὲ προσαπειλησά-
what we saw and heard not to speak. they But having threatened
μενοι ἀπέλυσαν αὐτούς, μηδὲν εὑρίσκοντες τὸ πῶς κολάσων-
again released them, nothing finding — how they might
ται αὐτούς, διὰ τὸν λαόν, ὅτι πάντες ἐδόξαζον τὸν Θεὸν ἐπὶ
punish them, due to the people, because all glorified — God on
22 τῷ γεγονότι. ἐτῶν γὰρ ἦν πλειόνων τεσσαράκοντα ὁ ἄν-
the thing occurring. of years For was more (than) forty the
θρωπος ἐφ' ὃν ἐγεγόνει τὸ σημεῖον τοῦτο τῆς ἰάσεως.
man on whom had happened sign this — of healing.
23 Ἀπολυθέντες δὲ ἦλθον πρὸς τοὺς ἰδίους, καὶ ἀπήγγειλαν
being released And they came to the own, and reported
ὅσα πρὸς αὐτοὺς οἱ ἀρχιερεῖς καὶ οἱ πρεσβύτεροι εἶπον. οἱ
what to them the chief priests and the elders said. they
24 δὲ ἀκούσαντες ὁμοθυμαδὸν ἦραν φωνὴν πρὸς τὸν Θεόν, καὶ
And having heard, with one passion lifted voice to — God, and
εἶπον, Δέσποτα, σὺ ὁ Θεὸς ὁ ποιήσας τὸν οὐρανὸν καὶ τὴν
said, Master, You the God who made the heaven and the
γῆν καὶ τὴν θάλασσαν καὶ πάντα τὰ ἐν αὐτοῖς· ὁ διὰ στό-
earth and the sea and all things in them, who through (the)
25 ματος Δαβὶδ τοῦ παιδός σου εἰπών, Ἱνατί ἐφρύαξαν ἔθνη,
mouth of David the child of You said, ' Why did rage the nations,

and *the* peoples devised foolish things? [26]The kings of the earth stood up, and the rulers were assembled on the same *day* against the Lord, yea, against His Christ."

[27]For truly both Herod and Pontius Pilate, with the nations and *the* peoples of Israel were gathered together against Your holy child Jesus, whom You anointed, [28]to do whatever Your hand and counsel before-determined to be done. [29]And now, Lord, look upon their threatenings, and give to Your slave to speak Your word with all boldness, [30]in the extending of Your hand for healing and miracles and wonders to happen through the name of Your holy child Jesus. [31]And they having prayed, the place in which they were gathered was shaken, and they were all filled with *the* Holy Spirit, and spoke the word of God with boldness.

[32]And of the multitude of those who believed, the heart and the soul were one. And no one said any of the possessions to be his own, but all things were common to them. [33]And with great power the apostles gave testimony of the resurrection of the Lord Jesus, and great grace was upon them all. [34]For neither was anyone needy among them, for as many as were owners of lands or houses, selling *them*, they bore the value of the *things* being sold, [35]and laid them at the feet of the apostles. And it was distributed to each according as any had need.

[36]And Joses, the *one* surnamed Barnabas by the apostles, which being translated is Son of Consolation, a Levite, a Cypriot by race, [37]a field being his, selling *it*, he bore the proceeds and placed *them* at the feet of the apostles.

26 καὶ λαοὶ ἐμελέτησαν κενά ; παρέστησαν οἱ βασιλεῖς τῆς γῆς,
and peoples devised vain things? stood up The kings of the earth,
καὶ οἱ ἄρχοντες συνήχθησαν ἐπὶ τὸ αὐτὸ κατὰ τοῦ Κυρίου,
and the rulers were assembled on the same (day) against the Lord,
27 καὶ κατὰ τοῦ Χριστοῦ αὐτοῦ· συνήχθησαν γὰρ ἐπ' ἀληθείας
and against the Christ of Him; were assembled for on a truth
ἐπὶ τὸν ἅγιον παῖδά σου Ἰησοῦν, ὃν ἔχρισας, Ἡρώδης τε
against the holy child of You, Jesus, whom You anointed, Herod both
καὶ Πόντιος Πιλάτος, σὺν ἔθνεσι καὶ λαοῖς Ἰσραήλ, ποιῆσαι
and Pontius Pilate, with nations and peoples of Israel, to do
28 ὅσα ἡ χείρ σου καὶ ἡ βουλή σου προώρισε γενέσθαι. καὶ
whatever the hand of You and the counsel of You predetermined to occur. And
29 τὰ νῦν, Κύριε, ἔπιδε ἐπὶ τὰς ἀπειλὰς αὐτῶν, καὶ δὸς τοῖς
— now, Lord, look upon the threatenings of them, and give to the
δούλοις σου μετὰ παρρησίας πάσης λαλεῖν τὸν λόγον σου,
slaves of You with boldness all to speak the word of You,
30 ἐν τῷ τὴν χεῖρά σου ἐκτείνειν σε εἰς ἴασιν, καὶ σημεῖα καὶ
by the hand of You stretching You for healing, and signs and
τέρατα γίνεσθαι διὰ τοῦ ὀνόματος τοῦ ἁγίου παιδός σου
wonders to happen through the name of the holy child of You,
31 Ἰησοῦ. καὶ δεηθέντων αὐτῶν ἐσαλεύθη ὁ τόπος ἐν ᾧ ἦσαν
Jesus. And having petitioned they, was shaken the place in which they were
συνηγμένοι, καὶ ἐπλήσθησαν ἅπαντες Πνεύματος Ἁγίου,
assembled, and they were filled all with (the) Spirit Holy,
καὶ ἐλάλουν τὸν λόγον τοῦ Θεοῦ μετὰ παρρησίας.
and spoke the word — of God with boldness.
32 Τοῦ δὲ πλήθους τῶν πιστευσάντων ἦν ἡ καρδία καὶ ἡ
of the And multitude of those believing were the heart and the
ψυχὴ μία· καὶ οὐδ' εἷς τι τῶν ὑπαρχόντων αὐτῷ ἔλεγεν
soul one, and not one anything of the possessions to him he said
33 ἴδιον εἶναι, ἀλλ' ἦν αὐτοῖς ἅπαντα κοινά. καὶ μεγάλῃ
own to be, but were to them all things common. And with great
δυνάμει ἀπεδίδουν τὸ μαρτύριον οἱ ἀπόστολοι τῆς ἀναστά-
power gave the testimony the apostles of the resurrection
σεως τοῦ Κυρίου Ἰησοῦ, χάρις τε μεγάλη ἦν ἐπὶ πάντας
of the Lord Jesus, grace and great was upon all
34 αὐτούς. οὐδὲ γὰρ ἐνδεής τις ὑπῆρχεν ἐν αὐτοῖς· ὅσοι γὰρ
(of) them. neither For needy anyone was among them, as many as for
κτήτορες χωρίων ἢ οἰκιῶν ὑπῆρχον, πωλοῦντες ἔφερον τὰς
owners of lands or houses were, having sold bore the
35 τιμὰς τῶν πιπρασκομένων, καὶ ἐτίθουν παρὰ τοὺς πόδας
values of those being sold, and placed at the feet
τῶν ἀποστόλων· διεδίδοτο δὲ ἑκάστῳ καθότι ἄν τις χρείαν
of the apostles; it was distributed and to each according as any need
εἶχεν.
had.
36 Ἰωσῆς δέ, ὁ ἐπικληθεὶς Βαρνάβας ὑπὸ τῶν ἀποστόλων
Joses And, he surnamed Barnabas by the apostles,
(ὅ ἐστι, μεθερμηνευόμενον, υἱὸς παρακλήσεως), Λευΐτης,
which is, being translated, Son of Consolation, a Levite,
37 Κύπριος τῷ γένει, ὑπάρχοντος αὐτῷ ἀγροῦ, πωλήσας
a Cypriot — by race, being to him a field, having sold
ἤνεγκε τὸ χρῆμα, καὶ ἔθηκε παρὰ τοὺς πόδας τῶν ἀποστόλων.
bore the proceeds and placed at the feet of the apostles.

CHAPTER 5

CHAPTER 5

[1]But a certain man named Ananias, with his wife Sapphira, sold a property, [2]and kept back from the price, his wife also aware of *it*, and bringing a certain part, *he* put *it* at the feet of the apostles. [3]But Peter said, Ananias, why did Satan fill your heart *for* you to lie to the Holy Spirit, and to keep back from the price of the land? [4]Remaining, did it not remain yours? And being sold, was it *not* in your authority? Why *is it* that this action was put in your heart? You did not lie to men, but to God!

[5]And hearing these words, Ananias fell down *and* expired. And great fear came on all those hearing these things. [6]And the younger ones wrapped him, and carrying out, *they* buried *him*.

[7]And about three hours afterwards, his wife also entered, not knowing that happening. [8]And Peter answered her, Tell me if you gave over the land *for* so much? And she said, Yes, *for* so much. [9]And Peter said to her, Why *was it* that it was agreed with you to tempt the Spirit of *the* Lord? Behold, the feet of those burying your husband at the door! Yea, they will carry you out. [10]And she immediately fell at his feet, and expired. And entering, the younger ones found her dead; and carrying *her* out, *they* buried her beside her husband. [11]And great fear came on all the church, and on all those hearing these things.

[12]And many miracles and wonders among the people took place through the hands of the apostles. And they were all with one passion in Solomon's Porch. [13]And of the rest, no one

1 Ἀνὴρ δέ τις Ἀνανίας ὀνόματι, σὺν Σαπφείρῃ τῇ γυναικὶ
man And a certain, Ananias by name, with Sapphira the wife
2 αὐτοῦ, ἐπώλησε κτῆμα, καὶ ἐνοσφίσατο ἀπὸ τῆς τιμῆς,
of him, sold a property, and secretly kept back from the price,
συνειδυίας καὶ τῆς γυναικὸς αὐτοῦ, καὶ ἐνέγκας μέρος τι
aware of (it) also the wife of him, and bringing a part certain
3 παρὰ τοὺς πόδας τῶν ἀποστόλων ἔθηκεν. εἶπε δὲ Πέτρος,
to the feet of the apostles placed (it). said But Peter,
Ἀνανία, διατί ἐπλήρωσεν ὁ Σατανᾶς τὴν καρδίαν σου,
Ananias, why filled — Satan the heart of you,
ψεύσασθαί σε τὸ Πνεῦμα τὸ Ἅγιον, καὶ νοσφίσασθαι ἀπὸ
to lie to you the Spirit Holy, and to secretly keep back from
4 τῆς τιμῆς τοῦ χωρίου; οὐχὶ μένον σοὶ ἔμενε, καὶ πραθὲν ἐν
the price of the land? not Remaining to you remain, and sold in
τῇ σῇ ἐξουσίᾳ ὑπῆρχε; τί ὅτι ἔθου ἐν τῇ καρδίᾳ σου τὸ
— your authority it was? What (is it) that was put in the heart of you —
πρᾶγμα τοῦτο; οὐκ ἐψεύσω ἀνθρώποις, ἀλλὰ τῷ Θεῷ.
action this? not You lied to men, but — to God.
5 ἀκούων δὲ Ἀνανίας τοὺς λόγους τούτους, πεσὼν ἐξέψυξε·
hearing And Ananias words these, falling expired.
καὶ ἐγένετο φόβος μέγας ἐπὶ πάντας τοὺς ἀκούοντας ταῦτα.
And came fear great on all those hearing these things.
6 ἀναστάντες δὲ οἱ νεώτεροι συνέστειλαν αὐτόν, καὶ ἐξενέγ-
rising up And the younger ones, they wrapped him, and carrying
καντες ἔθαψαν.
out, buried (him).
7 Ἐγένετο δὲ ὡς ὡρῶν τριῶν διάστημα, καὶ ἡ γυνὴ αὐτοῦ
it was And about hours three afterwards, also the wife of him
8 μὴ εἰδυῖα τὸ γεγονὸς εἰσῆλθεν. ἀπεκρίθη δὲ αὐτῇ ὁ Πέτρος,
not knowing the happening, entered. answered And her — Peter,
Εἰπέ μοι, εἰ τοσούτου τὸ χωρίον ἀπέδοσθε. ἡ δὲ εἶπε, Ναί,
Tell me, if of so much the land you gave over? she And said, Yes,
9 τοσούτου. ὁ δὲ Πέτρος εἶπε πρὸς αὐτήν, Τί ὅτι συνεφωνήθη
of so much. And Peter said to her, What (was it) that it was agreed
ὑμῖν πειράσαι τὸ Πνεῦμα Κυρίου; ἰδού, οἱ πόδες τῶν θαψάν-
with you to tempt the Spirit of (the) Lord? Behold, the feet of those burying
10 των τὸν ἄνδρα σου ἐπὶ τῇ θύρᾳ, καὶ ἐξοίσουσί σε. ἔπεσε δὲ
the husband of you at the door, and they will carry you. she fell And
παραχρῆμα παρὰ τοὺς πόδας αὐτοῦ, καὶ ἐξέψυξεν· εἰσελ-
immediately at the feet of him, and expired. entering
θόντες δὲ οἱ νεανίσκοι εὗρον αὐτὴν νεκράν, καὶ ἐξενέγκαντες
And, the young men found her dead, and carrying out
11 ἔθαψαν πρὸς τὸν ἄνδρα αὐτῆς. καὶ ἐγένετο φόβος μέγας
buried her near the husband of her. And came fear great
ἐφ' ὅλην τὴν ἐκκλησίαν, καὶ ἐπὶ πάντας τους ἀκούοντας
on all the church, and on all those hearing
ταῦτα.
these things.
12 Διὰ δὲ τῶν χειρῶν τῶν ἀποστόλων ἐγίνετο σημεῖα καὶ
through And the hands of the apostles happened signs and
τέρατα ἐν τῷ λαῷ πολλά· καὶ ἦσαν ὁμοθυμαδὸν ἅπαντες
wonders among the people many; and were with one passion all
13 ἐν τῇ στοᾷ Σολομῶντος. τῶν δὲ λοιπῶν οὐδεὶς ἐτόλμα
in the porch of Solomon. of the And rest, no one dared

dared to be joined to them, but the people greatly magnified them
14 And more believing ones were added to *the* Lord, multitudes of both men and of women; 15 so as to carry out the sick in the streets, and to place *them* on cots and mattresses, that *at the* coming *of* Peter, if even *his* shadow might overshadow some of them.
16 And also the multitude came together *from* the cities around Jerusalem, bringing sick ones and those being tormented by unclean spirits; who were all healed.
17 And rising up, the high priest and all those with him, which is *the* sect of the Sadducees, were filled with zeal, 18 and laid their hands on the apostles, and put them in public custody.
19 But an angel of *the* Lord opened the doors of the prison during the night, and leading them out, *he* said, 20 Go! And standing in the Temple, speak to the people all the words of this Life.
21 And hearing, they went into the Temple about dawn, and taught. But having come near, the officers did not find them in the prison. And returning, they reported,

23 saying, Indeed we found the jail having been shut with all security, and the guards outside standing before the doors. But opening *it*, we found no one inside. 24 And when they heard these words, both the priest and the Temple commander and the chief priests were in doubt concerning them, what this might be. 25 But having come, one reported to them, saying, Behold, the men whom you put in the prison are in the Temple, standing

κολλᾶσθαι αὐτοῖς, ἀλλ' ἐμεγάλυνεν αὐτοὺς ὁ λαός· μᾶλλον
to be joined to them, but magnified them the people; more
14 δὲ προσετίθεντο πιστεύοντες τῷ Κυρίῳ, πλήθη ἀνδρῶν τε
and were added believing ones to (the) Lord, multitudes of men both
15 καὶ γυναικῶν· ὥστε κατὰ τὰς πλατείας ἐκφέρειν τοὺς
and of women; so as in the streets to carry out the
ἀσθενεῖς, καὶ τιθέναι ἐπὶ κλινῶν καὶ κραββάτων, ἵνα ἐρχο-
sick, and to place on cots and mattresses, that coming
μένου Πέτρου κἂν ἡ σκιὰ ἐπισκιάσῃ τινὶ αὐτῶν. συνήρχετο
Peter, if even the shadow overshadow some of them. assembled
16 δὲ καὶ τὸ πλῆθος τῶν πέριξ πόλεων εἰς Ἱερουσαλήμ,
And also the multitude of the round about cities to Jerusalem,
φέροντες ἀσθενεῖς καὶ ὀχλουμένους ὑπὸ πνευμάτων ἀκαθάρ-
carrying sick (ones) and those being tormented by spirits unclean,
των, οἵτινες ἐθεραπεύοντο ἅπαντες.
who were healed all.
17 Ἀναστὰς δὲ ὁ ἀρχιερεὺς καὶ πάντες οἱ σὺν αὐτῷ (ἡ οὖσα
rising up And the high priest and all those with him, which is
αἵρεσις τῶν Σαδδουκαίων), ἐπλήσθησαν ζήλου, καὶ ἐπέ-
(the) sect of the Sadducees, were filled of jealousy and
18 βαλον τὰς χεῖρας αὐτῶν ἐπὶ τοὺς ἀποστόλους, καὶ ἔθεντο
laid on the hands of them on the apostles, and put
19 αὐτοὺς ἐν τηρήσει δημοσίᾳ. ἄγγελος δὲ Κυρίου διὰ τῆς νυκτὸς
them in custody publicly. an angel But of (the) Lord by night
ἤνοιξε τὰς θύρας τῆς φυλακῆς, ἐξαγαγών τε αὐτοὺς εἶπε,
opened the doors of the prison, leading out and them said,
20 Πορεύεσθε, καὶ σταθέντες λαλεῖτε ἐν τῷ ἱερῷ τῷ λαῷ πάντα
Go, and standing speak in the Temple to the people all
21 τὰ ῥήματα τῆς ζωῆς ταύτης. ἀκούσαντες δὲ εἰσῆλθον ὑπὸ
the words of life this. having heard And, they entered about
τὸν ὄρθρον εἰς τὸ ἱερόν, καὶ ἐδίδασκον. παραγενόμενος δὲ ὁ
the dawn into the Temple, and taught. having come near And the
ἀρχιερεὺς καὶ οἱ σὺν αὐτῷ, συνεκάλεσαν τὸ συνέδριον καὶ
high priest and those with him, he called together the sanhedrin and
πᾶσαν τὴν γερουσίαν τῶν υἱῶν Ἰσραήλ, καὶ ἀπέστειλαν εἰς
all the elderhood of the sons of Israel. And they sent to
22 τὸ δεσμωτήριον, ἀχθῆναι αὐτούς. οἱ δὲ ὑπηρέται παρα-
the jail to be brought them. the But officers having
γενόμενοι οὐχ εὗρον αὐτοὺς ἐν τῇ φυλακῇ· ἀναστρέψαντες
come near not did find them in the prison; having returned
23 δὲ ἀπήγγειλαν, λέγοντες ὅτι Τὸ μὲν δεσμωτήριον εὕρομεν
and they reported, saying, — the Indeed jail we found
κεκλεισμένον ἐν πάσῃ ἀσφαλείᾳ, καὶ τοὺς φύλακας ἔξω
having been shut in all security, and the guards outside
ἑστῶτας πρὸ τῶν θυρῶν· ἀνοίξαντες δέ, ἔσω οὐδένα εὕρο-
standing at the doors, having opened but, inside no one we
24 μεν. ὡς δὲ ἤκουσαν τοὺς λόγους τούτους ὅ τε ἱερεὺς καὶ ὁ
found as And heard words these the both priest and the
στρατηγὸς τοῦ ἱεροῦ καὶ οἱ ἀρχιερεῖς, διηπόρουν περὶ
commander of the Temple and the chief priests, they were in doubt concerning
25 αὐτῶν, τί ἂν γένοιτο τοῦτο. παραγενόμενος δέ τις ἀπήγ-
them, what might become this. having come And one reported
γειλεν αὐτοῖς λέγων ὅτι Ἰδού, οἱ ἄνδρες οὓς ἔθεσθε ἐν τῇ
to them, saying, — Behold, the men whom you put in the
φυλακῇ εἰσὶν ἐν τῷ ἱερῷ ἑστῶτες καὶ διδάσκοντες τὸν λαόν.
prison are in the Temple standing and teaching the people.

and teaching the people. 26 Then the commander going with the officers, *they* brought them, not with force, for they feared the people, that they might not be stoned.

27 And bringing them, they stood in the sanhedrin. And the high priest asked them, 28 saying, Did we not command you by a command *that* you not teach in this Name? And, behold, you have filled Jerusalem with your teaching, and intend to bring on us the blood of this man. 29 But answering Peter and the apostles said, It is right to obey God rather than man. 30 The God of our fathers raised up Jesus, whom you seized, hanging *Him* on a tree. 31 This One God *has* exalted *as* a Ruler and Savior to His right *hand,* to give to Israel repentance and forgiveness of sins. 32 And we are His witnesses of these things, and also the Holy Spirit, whom God gave to those obeying Him.

33 But those hearing were cut, and *they* took counsel to do away with them. 34 But one standing up in the sanhedrin, a Pharisee named Gamaliel, a teacher of the Law honored by all the people, commanded the apostles to be put outside a little while. 35 And he said to them, Men, Israelites, take heed to yourselves what you intend to do on these men. 36 For before these days Theudas rose up, claiming himself to be somebody, to whom was joined a number of men, about four hundred; who was done away, and all, as many as obeyed him, were dispersed and came to nothing.

37 After this, Judas the Galilean rose up in the days of the Registration. And *he* drew much people after him. Yet that one perished, and all were scattered, as many as obeyed him. 38 And now I say to you, draw away from

26 τότε ἀπελθὼν ὁ στρατηγὸς σὺν τοῖς ὑπηρέταις ἤγαγεν
Then going the commander with the officers brought
αὐτους, οὐ μετὰ βίας, ἐφοβοῦντο γὰρ τὸν λαόν, ἵνα μὴ
them, not with force, they feared for the people, lest
27 λιθασθῶσιν. ἀγαγόντες δὲ αὐτοὺς ἔστησαν ἐν τῷ συνεδρίῳ.
they be stoned. bringing And them, they stood in the sanhedrin.
28 καὶ ἐπηρώτησεν αὐτοὺς ὁ ἀρχιερεύς, λέγων, Οὐ παραγ-
And questioned them the high priest, saying, Not by a
γελίᾳ παρηγγείλαμεν ὑμῖν μὴ διδάσκειν ἐπὶ τῷ ὀνόματι
charge did we charge to you not to teach on — name
τούτῳ; καὶ ἰδοὺ πεπληρώκατε τὴν Ἱερουσαλὴμ τῆς δι-
this? And, behold, you have filled — Jerusalem of the
δαχῆς ὑμῶν, καὶ βούλεσθε ἐπαγαγεῖν ἐφ' ἡμᾶς τὸ αἷμα τοῦ
teaching of you, and purpose to bring on us the blood —
29 ἀνθρώπου τούτου. ἀποκριθεὶς δὲ ὁ Πέτρος καὶ οἱ ἀπόστολοι
of man this. answering But — Peter and the apostles
30 εἶπον, Πειθαρχεῖν δεῖ Θεῷ μᾶλλον ἢ ἀνθρώποις. ὁ Θεὸς τῶν
said, to obey It is right God rather than men. The God of the
πατέρων ἡμῶν ἤγειρεν Ἰησοῦν, ὃν ὑμεῖς διεχειρίσασθε,
fathers of us raised Jesus, whom you laid hands upon,
31 κρεμάσαντες ἐπὶ ξύλου. τοῦτον ὁ Θεὸς ἀρχηγὸν καὶ σωτῆρα
hanging (Him) on a tree. This One God (as) Ruler and Savior
ὕψωσε τῇ δεξιᾷ αὐτοῦ, δοῦναι μετάνοιαν τῷ Ἰσραὴλ καὶ
exalted to the right (hand) of Him, to give repentance — to Israel and
32 ἄφεσιν ἁμαρτιῶν. καὶ ἡμεῖς ἐσμεν αὐτοῦ μάρτυρες τῶν
forgiveness of sins. And we are of Him witnesses —
ῥημάτων τούτων, καὶ τὸ Πνεῦμα δὲ τὸ Ἅγιον, ὃ ἔδωκεν ὁ
of words these, also the Spirit and — Holy which gave
Θεὸς τοῖς πειθαρχοῦσιν αὐτῷ.
God to those obeying Him.
33 Οἱ δὲ ἀκούσαντες διεπρίοντο, καὶ ἐβουλεύοντο ἀνελεῖν
those And hearing were cut, and took counsel to take away
34 αὐτούς. ἀναστὰς δέ τις ἐν τῷ συνεδρίῳ Φαρισαῖος, ὀνό-
them. standing up But one in the sanhedrin, a Pharisee by
ματι Γαμαλιήλ, νομοδιδάσκαλος, τίμιος παντὶ τῷ λαῷ,
name Gamaliel, a teacher of the Law, honored by all the people,
35 ἐκέλευσεν ἔξω βραχύ τι τοὺς ἀποστόλους ποιῆσαι. εἶπέ τε
commanded outside a little while the apostles to put. he said And
πρὸς αὐτούς, Ἄνδρες Ἰσραηλῖται, προσέχετε ἑαυτοῖς ἐπὶ
to them, Men, Israelites, take heed to yourselves on
36 τοῖς ἀνθρώποις τούτοις, τί μέλλετε πράσσειν. πρὸ γὰρ
— men these, what you intend to do. before For
τούτων τῶν ἡμερῶν ἀνέστη Θευδᾶς, λέγων εἶναί τινα
these — days stood up Theudas, saying to be someone
ἑαυτόν, ᾧ προσεκολλήθη ἀριθμὸς ἀνδρῶν ὡσεὶ τετρακοσίων·
himself, to whom were joined a number of men, about four hundred,
ὃς ἀνῃρέθη, καὶ πάντες ὅσοι ἐπείθοντο αὐτῷ διελύθησαν καὶ
who was taken away, and all as many as obeyed him were dispersed and
37 ἐγένοντο εἰς οὐδέν. μετὰ τοῦτον ἀνέστη Ἰούδας ὁ Γαλιλαῖος
came to nothing. After this stood up Judas the Galilean
ἐν ταῖς ἡμέραις τῆς ἀπογραφῆς, καὶ ἀπέστησε λαὸν ἱκανὸν
in the days of the registration, and drew away people much
ὀπίσω αὐτοῦ· κἀκεῖνος ἀπώλετο, καὶ πάντες ὅσοι ἐπείθοντο
after him; and that one perished, and all as many as obeyed
38 αὐτῷ διεσκορπίσθησαν. καὶ τὰ νῦν λέγω ὑμῖν, ἀπόστητε
him were scattered. And — now I say to you, draw away

these men, and permit them; because if this counsel is of men, or this work, it will be destroyed. [39]But if it is from God, you will not be able to destroy it, lest you be found even fighters against God. [40]And they obeyed him. And having called the apostles, beating *them,* they commanded not to speak on the name of Jesus, and let them go. [41]Then they indeed departed from *the* presence of the sanhedrin, rejoicing that they were deemed worthy to be dishonored on behalf of His name. [42]And every day they did not cease teaching and preaching the gospel *of* Jesus the Christ in the Temple.

CHAPTER 6

[1]But in those days, the disciples having multiplied, a murmuring of the Hellenists toward the Hebrews occurred, because their widows were being overlooked in the daily serving. [2]And the Twelve, having called near the multitude of the disciples, said, It is not pleasing us, having left the word of God, to serve tables! [3]Therefore, brothers, be looking for men among you receiving testimony—seven *men,* full of *the* Holy Spirit and wisdom, whom we shall appoint over this need. [4]But we shall continue steadfast in prayer and the service of the word!

[5]And the saying *was* pleasing before all the multitude. And they chose out Stephen, a man full of faith and *the* Holy Spirit, and Philip, and Prochorus, and Nicanor, and Timon, and Parmenas, and Nicolas, a proselyte from Antioch— [6]*each of* whom they made stand before the apostles. And having prayed, they placed *their* hands on them.

[7]And the word of God was increasing, and the number of the disciples in Jerusalem was multiplying exceedingly— even a great

ἀπὸ τῶν ἀνθρώπων τούτων, καὶ ἐάσατε αὐτούς· ὅτι ἐὰν ᾖ
from — men these, and allow them; because if be
ἐξ ἀνθρώπων ἡ βουλὴ αὕτη ἢ τὸ ἔργον τοῦτο, καταλυθή-
of men counsel this, or — work this, it will be
39 σεται· εἰ δὲ ἐκ Θεοῦ ἐστιν, οὐ δύνασθε καταλῦσαι αὐτό,
destroyed. if But of God it is, not you will be able to destroy it,
40 μήποτε καὶ θεομάχοι εὑρεθῆτε. ἐπείσθησαν δὲ αὐτῷ· καὶ
lest even God-fighters you be found. they obeyed And him, and
προσκαλεσάμενοι τοὺς ἀποστόλους, δείραντες παρήγγειλαν
having called the apostles, beating (them) they charged
μὴ λαλεῖν ἐπὶ τῷ ὀνόματι τοῦ Ἰησοῦ, καὶ ἀπέλυσαν αὐτούς.
not to speak on the name — of Jesus, and released them.
41 οἱ μὲν οὖν ἐπορεύοντο χαίροντες ἀπὸ προσώπου τοῦ συνε-
They indeed then departed rejoicing from (the) presence of the san-
δρίου, ὅτι ὑπὲρ τοῦ ὀνόματος αὐτοῦ κατηξιώθησαν ἀτιμασθῆ-
hedrin, that for the name of Him they were deemed worthy to be
42 ναι. πᾶσάν τε ἡμέραν, ἐν τῷ ἱερῷ καὶ κατ' οἶκον, οὐκ ἐπαύ-
dishonored every And day, in the Temple and house to house, not they
οντο διδάσκοντες καὶ εὐαγγελιζόμενοι Ἰησοῦν τὸν Χριστόν.
ceased teaching and preaching the gospel— Jesus the Christ.

CHAPTER 6

1 Ἐν δὲ ταῖς ἡμέραις ταύταις, πληθυνόντων τῶν μαθητῶν,
in And — days these, multiplying the disciples,
ἐγένετο γογγυσμὸς τῶν Ἑλληνιστῶν πρὸς τοὺς Ἑβραίους,
there was a murmuring of the Hellenists against the Hebrews,
ὅτι παρεθεωροῦντο ἐν τῇ διακονίᾳ τῇ καθημερινῇ αἱ χῆραι
because were overlooked in the service near daily the widows
2 αὐτῶν. προσκαλεσάμενοι δὲ οἱ δώδεκα τὸ πλῆθος τῶν
of them. having called near And the twelve the multitude of the
μαθητῶν, εἶπον, Οὐκ ἀρεστόν ἐστιν ἡμᾶς, καταλείψαντας
disciples, they said, not pleasing It is to us leaving
3 τὸν λόγον τοῦ Θεοῦ, διακονεῖν τραπέζαις. ἐπισκέψασθε οὖν,
the word — of God to serve tables. Look out, therefore,
ἀδελφοί, ἄνδρας ἐξ ὑμῶν μαρτυρουμένους ἑπτά, πλήρεις
brothers, men from you being witnessed to, seven, full
Πνεύματος Ἁγίου καὶ σοφίας, οὓς καταστήσομεν ἐπὶ τῆς
of (the) Spirit Holy, and of wisdom, whom we will appoint over —
4 χρείας ταύτης. ἡμεῖς δὲ τῇ προσευχῇ καὶ τῇ διακονίᾳ τοῦ
duty this. we But to prayer and the service of the
5 λόγου προσκαρτερήσομεν. καὶ ἤρεσεν ὁ λόγος ἐνώπιον
word will continue steadfast And was pleasing the word before
παντὸς τοῦ πλήθους· καὶ ἐξελέξαντο Στέφανον, ἄνδρα πλήρη
all the multitude, and they chose Stephen, a man full
πίστεως καὶ Πνεύματος Ἁγίου, καὶ Φίλιππον, καὶ Πρόχο-
of faith and (the) Spirit Holy, and Philip, and Prochorus,
ρον, καὶ Νικάνορα, καὶ Τίμωνα, καὶ Παρμενᾶν, καὶ Νικόλαον
and Nicanor, and Timon, and Parmenas, and Nicolas
6 προσήλυτον Ἀντιοχέα, οὓς ἔστησαν ἐνώπιον τῶν ἀποστό-
a proselyte of Antioch; whom they set before the apostles;
λων· καὶ προσευξάμενοι ἐπέθηκαν αὐτοῖς τὰς χεῖρας.
and having prayed they placed on them the hands.
7 Καὶ ὁ λόγος τοῦ Θεοῦ ηὔξανε, καὶ ἐπληθύνετο ὁ ἀριθμὸς
And the word — of God increased, and was multipled the number
τῶν μαθητῶν ἐν Ἱερουσαλὴμ σφόδρα, πολύς τε ὄχλος τῶν
of the disciples in Jerusalem exceedingly; a much and crowd of the

crowd of the priests were hearkening to the faith! [8]And Stephen, full of faith and power, was doing wonders and great signs among the people. [9]But some of those of the synagogue, called Libertines, rose up, also *some* Cyrenians and Alexandrians, and *some* of those from Cilicia and Asia Minor, disputing with Stephen. [10]And they had no strength to stand against the wisdom and the Spirit by which he was speaking. [11]Then they induced *some* men *to be* saying, We have heard him speaking blasphemous words against Moses and God! [12]And they stirred up together the people and the elders and the scribes; and having stood near, they together seized him, and led *him* into the Sanhedrin. [13]And they stood up false witnesses, *who were* saying, This man does not cease speaking blasphemous words against this holy place and the Law; [14]for we have heard him saying that this Jesus the Nazarene will destroy this place, and will change the customs which Moses delivered over to us. [15]And having looked intently at him, all those seating themselves in the Sanhedrin saw his face as if *it were the* face of an angel.

CHAPTER 7

[1]And the High Priest said, *Tell me* if, then, you thus hold these things? [2]And he said, Men, brothers, and fathers, listen! The God of glory was seen by our father Abraham, being in Mesopotamia before he lived in Haran; [3]and said to him, Go out from your land and from your kindred, and come into a land which I will show to you. [4]Then going out from *the* land of Chaldea, he lived in Haran. And after his father died, *God* moved him from there into this land in which you now live. [5]And He did not give to him an

ἱερέων ὑπήκουον τῇ πίστει.
priests obeved the faith.

8 Στέφανος δὲ πλήρης πίστεως καὶ δυνάμεως ἐποίει τέρατα
Stephen And full of faith and power did wonders

9 καὶ σημεῖα μεγάλα ἐν τῷ λαῷ. ἀνέστησαν δέ τινες τῶν ἐκ
and signs great among the people. rose up But some of those of

τῆς συναγωγῆς τῆς λεγομένης Λιβερτίνων, καὶ Κυρηναίων,
the synagogue – called of (the) Libertines, and of Cyrenians

καὶ Ἀλεξανδρέων, καὶ τῶν ἀπὸ Κιλικίας καὶ Ἀσίας, συζη-
and of Alexandrians, and of those from Cilicia and Asia,

10 τοῦντες τῷ Στεφάνῳ. καὶ οὐκ ἴσχυον ἀντιστῆναι τῇ σοφίᾳ
disputing – with Stephen. And not were able to stand against the wisdom

11 καὶ τῷ πνεύματι ᾧ ἐλάλει. τότε ὑπέβαλον ἄνδρας λέγοντας
and the spirit by which he spoke. Then they suborned men, saying,

ὅτι Ἀκηκόαμεν αὐτοῦ λαλοῦντος ῥήματα βλάσφημα εἰς
– We have heard from him speaking words blasphemous against

12 Μωσῆν καὶ τὸν Θεόν. συνεκίνησάν τε τὸν λαὸν καὶ τοὺς
Moses and – God. they stirred up And the people and the

πρεσβυτέρους καὶ τοὺς γραμματεῖς, καὶ ἐπιστάντες συν-
elders and the scribes, and coming on they

13 ήρπασαν αὐτόν, καὶ ἤγαγον εἰς τὸ συνέδριον, ἔστησάν τε
seized him and led to the sanhedrin they stood And

μάρτυρας ψευδεῖς λέγοντας, Ὁ ἄνθρωπος οὗτος οὐ παύεται
witnesses false, saying, man This not ceases

ῥήματα βλάσφημα λαλῶν κατὰ τοῦ τόπου τοῦ ἁγίου
words blasphemous speaking against – place – holy

14 τούτου καὶ τοῦ νόμου· ἀκηκόαμεν γὰρ αὐτοῦ λέγοντος ὅτι
this, and the Law; we have heard for from him, saying

Ἰησοῦς ὁ Ναζωραῖος οὗτος καταλύσει τὸν τόπον τοῦτον,
Jesus the Nazarene, this One, will destroy – place this,

15 καὶ ἀλλάξει τὰ ἔθη ἃ παρέδωκεν ἡμῖν Μωϋσῆς. καὶ ἀτενί-
and will change the customs which delivered to us Moses. And looking

σαντες εἰς αὐτὸν ἅπαντες οἱ καθεζόμενοι ἐν τῷ συνεδρίῳ,
intently at him, all those sitting in the sanhedrin

εἶδον τὸ πρόσωπον αὐτοῦ ὡσεὶ πρόσωπον ἀγγέλου.
saw the face of him as if a face of an angel.

CHAPTER 7

1 Εἶπε δὲ ὁ ἀρχιερεύς, Εἰ ἄρα ταῦτα οὕτως ἔχει; ὁ δὲ ἔφη,
said And the high priest, If, then, these things thus hold? he And said,

2 Ἄνδρες ἀδελφοὶ καὶ πατέρες, ἀκούσατε. ὁ Θεὸς τῆς δόξης
Men, brothers and fathers, hear: The God – of glory

ὤφθη τῷ πατρὶ ἡμῶν Ἀβραὰμ ὄντι ἐν τῇ Μεσοποταμίᾳ,
appeared to the father of us, Abraham, being in – Mesopotamia

3 πρὶν ἢ κατοικῆσαι αὐτὸν ἐν Χαρράν, καὶ εἶπε πρὸς αὐτόν,
before even dwelt him in Haran; and said to him,

Ἔξελθε ἐκ τῆς γῆς σου καὶ ἐκ τῆς συγγενείας σου, καὶ δεῦρο
Go out of the land of you and from the kindred of you, and come

4 εἰς γῆν ἣν ἄν σοι δείξω. τότε ἐξελθὼν ἐκ γῆς Χαλδαίων
into a land which to you I will show. Then going out (of) the land of Chaldea,

κατῴκησεν ἐν Χαρράν· κἀκεῖθεν, μετὰ τὸ ἀποθανεῖν τὸν
he dwelt in Haran. And from there after the dying of the

πατέρα αὐτοῦ, μετῴκισεν αὐτὸν εἰς τὴν γῆν ταύτην εἰς ἣν
father of him, (God) moved him into – land this, in which

5 ὑμεῖς νῦν κατοικεῖτε· καὶ οὐκ ἔδωκεν αὐτῷ κληρονομίαν ἐν
you now dwell. And not He gave to him an inheritance in

inheritance in it not even a footbreadth. And *He* promised to give it to him for a possession, and to his seed after him, there being no child to him. [6]And God spoke thus, that his seed would be a sojourner in another land, and they would enslave it and oppress *it* four hundred years. [7]And God said, I will judge the nation to which you will be in bondage; and, After these things they will come out and will serve Me in this place. [8]And He gave to him a covenant of circumcision; and so he fathered Isaac, and circumcised him on the eighth day. And Isaac *fathered* Jacob, and Jacob the twelve patriarchs. [9]And being jealous of Joseph, the patriarchs sold *him* into Egypt. [10]And God was with him, and plucked him out from all his afflictions, and gave him favor and wisdom over against Pharaoh *the* king of Egypt. And he appointed him governor over Egypt and all his household. [11]But a famine came over all the land of Egypt and Canaan, and great affliction. And our fathers did not find food. [12]But hearing grain was in Egypt, Jacob sent our fathers out first. [13]And at the second *time,* Joseph was made known to his brothers, and Joseph's race became known to Pharaoh.

[14]And sending, Joseph called his father and all his kindred, seventy-five souls in *all.* [15]And Jacob went down into Egypt, and expired, he and our fathers. [16]And they were moved into Shechem, and were put in the tomb which Abraham bought *for* a price of silver from the sons of Hamor of Shechem. [17]But as the time of the promise drew near, which God swore to Abraham, the people increased and multiplied in Egypt.

αὐτῇ, οὐδὲ βῆμα ποδός· καὶ ἐπηγγείλατο αὐτῷ δοῦναι εἰς
it, nor space of a foot, and promised him to give for
κατάσχεσιν αὐτήν, καὶ τῷ σπέρματι αὐτοῦ μετ' αὐτόν, οὐκ
a possession it, and to the seed of him after him, not
6 ὄντος αὐτῷ τέκνου. ἐλάλησε δὲ οὕτως ὁ Θεός, ὅτι ἔσται τὸ
being to him a child. spoke And thus — God, that will be the
σπέρμα αὐτοῦ πάροικον ἐν γῇ ἀλλοτρίᾳ, καὶ δουλώσουσιν
seed of him a sojourner in a land another, and they will enslave
7 αὐτὸ καὶ κακώσουσιν, ἔτη τετρακόσια. καὶ τὸ ἔθνος, ᾧ ἐὰν
it, and will oppress years four hundred. And the nation to whom may
δουλεύσωσι, κρινῶ ἐγώ, εἶπεν ὁ Θεός· καὶ μετὰ ταῦτα
they serve, will judge I; said God and, After these things
8 ἐξελεύσονται, καὶ λατρεύσουσί μοι ἐν τῷ τόπῳ τούτῳ. καὶ
they will come out, and will do service to Me in — place this. And
ἔδωκεν αὐτῷ διαθήκην περιτομῆς· καὶ οὕτως ἐγέννησε τὸν
He gave to him a covenant of circumcision; and thus he fathered —
Ἰσαάκ, καὶ περιέτεμεν αὐτὸν τῇ ἡμέρᾳ τῇ ὀγδόῃ· καὶ ὁ
Isaac, and circumcised him on the day — eighth. And
Ἰσαὰκ τὸν Ἰακώβ, καὶ ὁ Ἰακὼβ τοὺς δώδεκα πατριάρχας.
Isaac (fathered) Jacob, and Jacob the twelve patriarchs.
9 καὶ οἱ πατριάρχαι ζηλώσαντες τὸν Ἰωσὴφ ἀπέδοντο εἰς
And the patriarchs being jealous — Joseph gave over into
10 Αἴγυπτον· καὶ ἦν ὁ Θεὸς μετ' αὐτοῦ. καὶ ἐξείλετο αὐτὸν ἐκ
Egypt; and was — God with him, and plucked out him from
πασῶν τῶν θλίψεων αὐτοῦ, καὶ ἔδωκεν αὐτῷ χάριν καὶ
all the afflictions of him; and gave him favor and
σοφίαν ἐναντίον Φαραὼ βασιλέως Αἰγύπτου, καὶ κατέστησεν
wisdom over against Pharaoh king of Egypt, and he appointed
αὐτὸν ἡγούμενον ἐπ' Αἴγυπτον καὶ ὅλον τὸν οἶκον αὐτοῦ.
him governor over Egypt and all the house of him.
11 ἦλθε δὲ λιμὸς ἐφ' ὅλην τὴν γῆν Αἰγύπτου καὶ Χαναάν, καὶ
came But a famine over all the land of Egypt and Canaan, and
θλίψις μεγάλη καὶ οὐχ εὕρισκον χορτάσματα οἱ πατέρες
affliction great; and did not did find sustenance the fathers
12 ἡμῶν. ἀκούσας δὲ Ἰακὼβ ὄντα σῖτα ἐν Αἰγύπτῳ, ἐξαπέστειλε
of us. having heard But Jacob being grain in Egypt, he sent forth
13 τοὺς πατέρας ἡμῶν πρῶτον. καὶ ἐν τῷ δευτέρῳ ἀνεγνωρίσθη
the fathers of us first. And in the second was made known
Ἰωσὴφ τοῖς ἀδελφοῖς αὐτοῦ, καὶ φανερὸν ἐγένετο τῷ Φαραὼ
Joseph to the brothers of him, and manifest became — to Pharaoh
14 τὸ γένος τοῦ Ἰωσήφ. ἀποστείλας δὲ Ἰωσὴφ μετεκαλέσατο
the race — of Joseph. sending And Joseph, called
τὸν πατέρα αὐτοῦ Ἰακώβ, καὶ πᾶσαν τὴν συγγένειαν αὐτοῦ,
the father of him, Jacob, and all the kindred of him,
15 ἐν ψυχαῖς ἑβδομήκοντα πέντε. κατέβη δὲ Ἰακὼβ εἰς Αἴγυ-
in souls, seventy five. went down And Jacob into Egypt,
πτον, καὶ ἐτελεύτησεν αὐτὸς καὶ οἱ πατέρες ἡμῶν· καὶ μετετέ-
and expired he and the fathers of us, and they were
16 θησαν εἰς Συχέμ, καὶ ἐτέθησαν ἐν τῷ μνήματι ὃ ὠνήσατο
moved into Shechem, and were placed in the tomb which bought
Ἀβραὰμ τιμῆς ἀργυρίου παρὰ τῶν υἱῶν Ἐμὸρ τοῦ Συχέμ.
Abraham (for) a price of silver from the sons of Hamor — of Shechem.
17 καθὼς δὲ ἤγγιζεν ὁ χρόνος τῆς ἐπαγγελίας ἧς ὤμοσεν ὁ Θεὸς
as And drew near the time of the promise which swore — God
τῷ Ἀβραάμ, ηὔξησεν ὁ λαὸς καὶ ἐπληθύνθη ἐν Αἰγύπτῳ,
— to Abraham, grew the people, and were multiplied in Egypt,

18 until another king rose up, who did not know Joseph. 19 Dealing slyly with our race, this one oppressed our fathers, causing their infants *to be* exposed *so as* not to be kept alive.

20 In which time Moses was born, and was beautiful to God; who was reared three months in his father's house. 21 And he being cast out, Pharaoh's daughter took him up and reared him for a son to her. 22 And Moses was instructed in all *the* wisdom of Egyptians; and was powerful in words and in works. 23 And when a period of forty years was fulfilled to him, it arose in his heart to look upon his brothers, the sons of Israel.

24 And seeing one being wronged, he defended *him*, and he avenged the *one* getting the worse, striking the Egyptian. 25 And he thought his brothers *would* understand that God would give them deliverance by his hand. But they did not understand. 26 And on the following day he appeared to them *while* fighting. And *he* urged them to peace, saying, Men, you are brothers. Why do you wrong one another? 27 But the *one* wronging the neighbor thrust him away, saying, Who appointed you a ruler and a judge over us? 28 Do you not want to do away with me *in the* way you did away with the Egyptian yesterday? 29 And Moses fled at this word. And he became a resident in Midian land, where he fathered two sons.

30 And forty years being fulfilled to him, *the* Angel of *the* Lord appeared to him in the desert of Mount Sinai, in a flame of fire *in* a bush. 31 And seeing, Moses marveled at the sight. And he coming up to look, a voice of *the* Lord came to him: 32 I *am* the God of your fathers, the God of Abraham, and the God of Isaac, and the God of Jacob. But becoming trembly, Moses did not dare to look. 33 And the Lord

18 ἄχρις οὗ ἀνέστη βασιλεὺς ἕτερος, ὃς οὐκ ᾔδει τὸν Ἰωσήφ.
until rose up king another, who not knew — Joseph.
19 οὗτος κατασοφισάμενος τὸ γένος ἡμῶν, ἐκάκωσε τοὺς πατέ-
This one dealing slyly with the race of us oppressed the fathers
ρας ἡμῶν, τοῦ ποιεῖν ἔκθετα τὰ βρέφη αὐτῶν, εἰς τὸ μὴ
of us — to make exposed the babes of them unto — not
20 ζωογονεῖσθαι. ἐν ᾧ καιρῷ ἐγεννήθη Μωσῆς, καὶ ἦν ἀστεῖος
being preserved alive. At which time was born Moses, and he was beautiful
τῷ Θεῷ· ὃς ἀνετράφη μῆνας τρεῖς ἐν τῷ οἴκῳ τοῦ πατρὸς
— to God, who was reared months three in the house of the father
21 αὐτοῦ. ἐκτεθέντα δὲ αὐτόν, ἀνείλετο αὐτὸν ἡ θυγάτηρ
of him. being exposed And he, took up him the daughter
22 Φαραώ, καὶ ἀνεθρέψατο αὐτὸν ἑαυτῇ εἰς υἱόν. καὶ ἐπαιδεύθη
of Pharaoh, and reared him to herself for a son. And was instructed
Μωσῆς πάσῃ σοφίᾳ Αἰγυπτίων· ἦν δὲ δυνατὸς ἐν λόγοις καὶ
Moses in all (the) wisdom of Egyptians, was and powerful in words and
23 ἐν ἔργοις. ὡς δὲ ἐπληροῦτο αὐτῷ τεσσαρακονταετὴς χρόνος,
in works. as But was fulfilled to him of forty years a time,
ἀνέβη ἐπὶ τὴν καρδίαν αὐτοῦ ἐπισκέψασθαι τοὺς ἀδελφοὺς
it arose on the heart of him to look upon the brothers
24 αὐτοῦ τοὺς υἱοὺς Ἰσραήλ. καὶ ἰδών τινα ἀδικούμενον, ἠμύ-
of him, the sons of Israel. And seeing one being wronged, he de-
νατο καὶ ἐποίησεν ἐκδίκησιν τῷ καταπονουμένῳ, πατάξας
fended, and he did vengeance for the (one) getting the worse, striking
25 τὸν Αἰγύπτιον· ἐνόμιζε δὲ συνιέναι τοὺς ἀδελφοὺς αὐτοῦ ὅτι
the Egyptian. he thought And to understand the brothers of him that
ὁ Θεὸς διὰ χειρὸς αὐτοῦ δίδωσιν αὐτοῖς σωτηρίαν· οἱ δὲ οὐ
— God through hand of him would give to them deliverance; they but not
26 συνῆκαν. τῇ δὲ ἐπιούσῃ ἡμέρᾳ ὤφθη αὐτοῖς μαχομένοις, καὶ
understood. the But following day he appeared to them fighting, and
συνήλασεν αὐτοὺς εἰς εἰρήνην, εἰπών, Ἄνδρες, ἀδελφοί ἐστε
urged them to peace, saying, Men, brothers are
27 ὑμεῖς· ἱνατί ἀδικεῖτε ἀλλήλους; ὁ δὲ ἀδικῶν τὸν πλησίον
you, why do you wrong one another? he But wronging the neighbor
ἀπώσατο αὐτόν, εἰπών, Τίς σε κατέστησεν ἄρχοντα καὶ
thrust away him, saying, Who you appointed a ruler and
28 δικαστὴν ἐφ' ἡμᾶς; μὴ ἀνελεῖν με σὺ θέλεις, ὃν τρόπον ἀνεῖλες
a judge over us? Do not to take away me you desire, (in) what way you took away
29 χθὲς τὸν Αἰγύπτιον; ἔφυγε δὲ Μωσῆς ἐν τῷ λόγῳ τούτῳ,
yesterday the Egyptian? fled And Moses at — word this.
καὶ ἐγένετο πάροικος ἐν γῇ Μαδιάμ, οὗ ἐγέννησεν υἱοὺς δύο.
And he became a sojourner in land Midian, where he fathered sons two.
30 καὶ πληρωθέντων ἐτῶν τεσσαράκοντα, ὤφθη αὐτῷ ἐν τῇ
And being fulfilled years forty, appeared to him in the
ἐρήμῳ τοῦ ὄρους Σινᾶ ἄγγελος Κυρίου ἐν φλογὶ πυρὸς
desert of the Mount Sinai, (the) angel of (the) Lord in a flame of fire
31 βάτου. ὁ δὲ Μωσῆς ἰδὼν ἐθαύμασε τὸ ὅραμα· προσερχο-
of a bush. And Moses seeing marveled at the sight coming
μένου δὲ αὐτοῦ κατανοῆσαι, ἐγένετο φωνὴ Κυρίου πρὸς
up And he to look, came a voice of (the) Lord to
32 αὐτόν, Ἐγὼ ὁ Θεὸς των πατέρων σου, ὁ Θεὸς Ἀβραὰμ καὶ
him. I (am) the God of the fathers of you, the God of Abraham and
ὁ Θεὸς Ἰσαὰκ καὶ ὁ Θεὸς Ἰακώβ. ἔντρομος δὲ γενόμενος
the God of Isaac and the God of Jacob (am). trembling But becoming
33 Μωσῆς οὐκ ἐτόλμα κατανοῆσαι. εἶπε δὲ αὐτῷ ὁ Κύριος,
Moses not did dare to observe, said And to him the Lord,

said to him, "Untie the sandal from your feet, for the place where you stand is holy ground." [34] "I surely saw the affliction of My people in Egypt, and I have heard their groan; and I came down to pluck them out. And now, come, I will send you to Egypt."

[35] This Moses, whom they denied, saying, Who appointed you a ruler and a judge, this one God has sent *as* ruler and redeemer by *the* hand of *the* Angel who appeared to him in the Bush. [36] This one led them out, having worked wonders and miracles in *the* land of Egypt, and in *the* Red Sea, and forty years in the wilderness. [37] This is the Moses who said to the sons of Israel, "*The* Lord your God will raise up a Prophet to you from your brothers, *One* like me. You shall hear Him." [38] This is the *one* who was in the congregation in the wilderness with the Angel who spoke to him in Mount Sinai, and *with* our fathers, who received living words to give to us; [39] to whom our fathers did not desire to be subject, but thrust *him* away, and turned their hearts back to Egypt, [40] saying, "Make for us gods which will go before us; for this Moses who led us out of *the* land of Egypt, we do not know what has happened to him." [41] And they made a calf in those days, and led a sacrifice up to the idol, and made merry in the works of their hands. [42] But God turned and gave them over to serve the host of the heaven; as it has been written in *the* book of the Prophets: "Did you bring slain beasts and sacrifices to Me forty years in the wilderness, O house of Israel? [43] And you took up the the tent of Moloch, and the star of your god Remphan, the figures which you made in order to worship them? And I

Λῦσον τὸ ὑπόδημα τῶν ποδῶν σου· ὁ γὰρ τόπος ἐν ᾧ
Loosen the sandal of the feet of you, the for place on which
34 ἕστηκας γῆ ἁγία ἐστίν. ἰδὼν εἶδον τὴν κάκωσιν τοῦ λαοῦ
you stand ground holy is. Seeing I saw the oppression of the people
μου τοῦ ἐν Αἰγύπτῳ, καὶ τοῦ στεναγμοῦ αὐτῶν ἤκουσα·
of Me – in Egypt, and the groan of them I heard,
καὶ κατέβην ἐξελέσθαι αὐτούς· καὶ νῦν δεῦρο, ἀποστελῶ σε
and I came down to rescue them; and now come, I will send you
35 εἰς Αἴγυπτον. τοῦτον τὸν Μωϋσῆν ὃν ἠρνήσαντο εἰπόντες,
to Egypt. This – Moses whom they denied, saying,
Τίς σε κατέστησεν ἄρχοντα καὶ δικαστήν; τοῦτον ὁ Θεὸς
Who you appointed a ruler and a judge? This one – God
ἄρχοντα καὶ λυτρωτὴν ἀπέστειλεν ἐν χειρὶ ἀγγέλου τοῦ
a ruler and a deliverer has sent by (the) hand of (the) Angel
36 ὀφθέντος αὐτῷ ἐν τῇ βάτῳ. οὗτος ἐξήγαγεν αὐτούς,
appearing to him in the Bush. This one led out them,
ποιήσας τέρατα καὶ σημεῖα ἐν γῇ Αἰγύπτου καὶ ἐν Ἐρυθρᾷ
doing wonders and signs in (the) land of Egypt, and in (the) Red
37 θαλάσσῃ, καὶ ἐν τῇ ἐρήμῳ ἔτη τεσσαράκοντα. οὗτός ἐστιν
Sea, and in the desert years forty. This is
ὁ Μωϋσῆς ὁ εἰπὼν τοῖς υἱοῖς Ἰσραήλ, Προφήτην ὑμῖν
the Moses – saying to the sons of Israel, A prophet for you
ἀναστήσει Κύριος ὁ Θεὸς ὑμῶν ἐκ τῶν ἀδελφῶν ὑμῶν ὡς ἐμέ·
will raise up (the) Lord God of you from the brothers of you, like me.
38 αὐτοῦ ἀκούσεσθε. οὗτός ἐστιν ὁ γενόμενος ἐν τῇ ἐκκλησίᾳ
Him you shall hear. This is the (one) having been in the assembly
ἐν τῇ ἐρήμῳ μετὰ τοῦ ἀγγέλου τοῦ λαλοῦντος αὐτῷ ἐν τῷ
in the desert with the Angel – speaking to him in the
ὄρει Σινᾶ καὶ τῶν πατέρων ἡμῶν· ὃς ἐδέξατο λόγια ζῶντα
Mount Sinai, and (with) the fathers of us, who received words living
39 δοῦναι ἡμῖν· ᾧ οὐκ ἠθέλησαν ὑπήκοοι γενέσθαι οἱ πατέρες
to give to us, to whom not desired subject to be the fathers
ἡμῶν, ἀλλ' ἀπώσαντο, καὶ ἐστράφησαν ταῖς καρδίαις αὐτῶν
of us, but thrust away, and turned away the hearts of them
40 εἰς Αἴγυπτον, εἰπόντες τῷ Ἀαρών, Ποίησον ἡμῖν θεοὺς οἳ
to Egypt, saying – to Aaron, Make for us gods which
προπορεύσονται ἡμῶν· ὁ γὰρ Μωσῆς οὗτος, ὃς ἐξήγαγεν
will go before us; – for Moses this, who led
41 ἡμᾶς ἐκ γῆς Αἰγύπτου, οὐκ οἴδαμεν τί γέγονεν αὐτῷ. καὶ
us out of (the) land of Egypt, not we know what has occurred to him. And
ἐμοσχοποίησαν ἐν ταῖς ἡμέραις ἐκείναις, καὶ ἀνήγαγον
they made a calf in – days those, and led up
θυσίαν τῷ εἰδώλῳ, καὶ εὐφραίνοντο ἐν τοῖς ἔργοις τῶν
a sacrifice to the idol, and made merry in the works of the
42 χειρῶν αὐτῶν. ἔστρεψε δὲ ὁ Θεός, καὶ παρέδωκεν αὐτοὺς
hands of them. turned And – God, and gave over them
λατρεύειν τῇ στρατιᾷ τοῦ οὐρανοῦ· καθὼς γέγραπται ἐν
to worship the host – of heaven, as it has been written in
βίβλῳ τῶν προφητῶν, Μὴ σφάγια καὶ θυσίας προσηνέγ-
(the) roll of the prophets, Not victims and sacrifices you brought
κατέ μοι ἔτη τεσσαράκοντα ἐν τῇ ἐρήμῳ, οἶκος Ἰσραήλ;
near to Me years forty in the desert, house of Israel;
43 καὶ ἀνελάβετε τὴν σκηνὴν τοῦ Μολόχ, καὶ τὸ ἄστρον τοῦ
and you took up the tent – of Moloch, and the star of the
θεοῦ ὑμῶν Ῥεμφάν, τοὺς τύπους οὓς ἐποιήσατε προσκυνεῖν
god of you, Remphan, the models which you made to worship

will remove you beyond
Babylon." 44 The tabernacle
of the testimony was among
our fathers in the wilderness,
as He who spoke to Moses
commanded to make it
according to the pattern
which he had seen; 45 which
also *was* brought in *by* our
fathers with Joshua, in the
taking of possession of the
nations *which they* had
inherited; whom God drove
out from the face of our
fathers, until the days of
David; 46 who found favor
before God, and asked to
find a tabernacle for the God
of Jacob; 47 but Solomon
built Him a house. 48 But
the Most High does not
dwell in temples made by
hand; as the prophet says,
49 "Heaven *is* My throne, and
the earth a footstool of My
feet; what house will you
build Me, says *the* Lord; or
what the place of My rest?
50 Did not My hands make all
these things?"
51 *O* stiffnecked and
uncircumcised in heart and
in the ears! You always fell
against the Holy Spirit. As
your fathers did, so you also
did. 52 Which of the
prophets did your fathers not
persecute? And they killed
those who before an-
nounced the coming of the
Just One, of whom you now
have become betrayers and
murderers; 53 who received
the Law by the disposition of
angels, and did not keep *it*.
54 And hearing these
things, they were cut to their
hearts, and gnashed the
teeth on him. 55 But being
full of *the* Holy Spirit, looking
intently into Heaven, he saw
the glory of God, and Jesus
standing at *the* right of God.
56 And *he* said, Behold, I see
the heavens having been
opened, and the Son of man
standing at the right of God!
57 And crying out with a loud
voice, they held their ears,
and rushed on him with one
passion. 58 And throwing *him*
outside the city, they stoned

44 αὐτοῖς· καὶ μετοικιῶ ὑμᾶς ἐπέκεινα Βαβυλῶνος. ἡ σκηνὴ τοῦ
them, and I will remove you beyond Babylon. The tent —
μαρτυρίου ἦν τοῖς πατράσιν ἡμῶν ἐν τῇ ἐρήμῳ, καθὼς
of witness was to the fathers of us in the desert, as
διετάξατο ὁ λαλῶν τῷ Μωσῇ, ποιῆσαι αὐτὴν κατὰ τὸν
commanded the (One) speaking to Moses, to make it according to the
45 τύπον ὃν ἑωράκει. ἣν καὶ εἰσήγαγον διαδεξάμενοι οἱ πατέρες
pattern which he had seen, which also was led, having inherited the fathers
ἡμῶν μετὰ Ἰησοῦ ἐν τῇ κατασχέσει τῶν ἐθνῶν, ὧν ἐξῶσεν ὁ
of us with Joshua in the taking of possession of the nations, whom put out
Θεὸς ἀπὸ προσώπου τῶν πατέρων ἡμῶν, ἕως τῶν ἡμερῶν
God from the face of the fathers of us, until the days
46 Δαβίδ· ὃς εὗρε χάριν ἐνώπιον τοῦ Θεοῦ, καὶ ᾐτήσατο εὑρεῖν
of David, who found favor before — God, and asked to find
47 σκήνωμα τῷ Θεῷ Ἰακώβ. Σολομῶν δὲ ᾠκοδόμησεν αὐτῷ
a tent for the God of Jacob. Solomon But built for Him
48 οἶκον. ἀλλ' οὐχ ὁ ὕψιστος ἐν χειροποιήτοις ναοῖς κατοικεῖ,
a house. But not the Most High in made by hand temples dwells;
49 καθὼς ὁ προφήτης λέγει, Ὁ οὐρανός μοι θρόνος, ἡ δὲ γῆ
as the prophet says, The Heaven to Me a throne, the and earth
ὑποπόδιον τῶν ποδῶν μου· ποῖον οἶκον οἰκοδομήσετέ μοι ;
a footstool of the feet of Me; what sort of house will you build for Me,
50 λέγει Κύριος· ἢ τίς τόπος τῆς καταπαύσεώς μου ; οὐχὶ ἡ
says (the) Lord, or what place of the resting of Me? Did not the
χείρ μου ἐποίησε ταῦτα πάντα ;
hand of Me make these things all?
51 Σκληροτράχηλοι καὶ ἀπερίτμητοι τῇ καρδίᾳ καὶ τοῖς ὠσίν,
Stiffnecked and uncircumcised in the heart and in the ears,
ὑμεῖς ἀεὶ τῷ Πνεύματι τῷ Ἁγίῳ ἀντιπίπτετε· ὡς οἱ πατέρες
you always the Spirit — Holy fell against, as the fathers
52 ὑμῶν, καὶ ὑμεῖς. τίνα τῶν προφητῶν οὐκ ἐδίωξαν οἱ πατέρες
of you, also you. Which of the prophets not persecuted the fathers
ὑμῶν ; καὶ ἀπέκτειναν τοὺς προκαταγγείλαντας περὶ τῆς
of you? And they killed those before announcing concerning the
ἐλεύσεως τοῦ δικαίου, οὗ νῦν ὑμεῖς προδόται καὶ φονεῖς
coming of the Just One, of whom now you betrayers and murderers
53 γεγένησθε· οἵτινες ἐλάβετε τὸν νόμον εἰς διαταγὰς ἀγγέλων,
have become, who received the Law by disposition of angels,
καὶ οὐκ ἐφυλάξατε.
and not kept (it).
54 Ἀκούοντες δὲ ταῦτα, διεπρίοντο ταῖς καρδίαις αὐτῶν, καὶ
hearing And these things, they were cut to the hearts of them, and
55 ἔβρυχον τοὺς ὀδόντας ἐπ' αὐτόν. ὑπάρχων δὲ πλήρης
gnashed the teeth at him. being But full
Πνεύματος Ἁγίου, ἀτενίσας εἰς τὸν οὐρανόν, εἶδε δόξαν Θεοῦ,
of (the) Spirit Holy looking intently into Heaven, he saw (the) glory of God,
56 καὶ Ἰησοῦν ἑστῶτα ἐκ δεξιῶν τοῦ Θεοῦ, καὶ εἶπεν, Ἰδού,
and Jesus standing at (the) right — of God, and said, Behold,
θεωρῶ τοὺς οὐρανοὺς ἀνεῳγμένους, καὶ τὸν υἱὸν τοῦ ἀνθρώ-
I see the heavens having been opened and the Son — of
57 που ἐκ δεξιῶν ἑστῶτα τοῦ Θεοῦ. κράξαντες δὲ φωνῇ μεγάλῃ,
man at (the) right standing — of God. crying out And with a voice great,
συνέσχον τὰ ὦτα αὐτῶν, καὶ ὥρμησαν ὁμοθυμαδὸν ἐπ'
they held the ears of them, and rushed with one passion on
58 αὐτόν· καὶ ἐκβαλόντες ἔξω τῆς πόλεως, ἐλιθοβόλουν· καὶ οἱ
him, and throwing outside the city, they stoned (him). And the

him. And the witnesses put off their garments at the feet of a young man called Saul. [59]And they stoned Stephen, invoking and saying, Lord Jesus, receive my spirit. [60]And placing the knees, he cried out with a loud voice, Lord, do not make this sin stand to them. And saying this, he fell asleep.

CHAPTER 8

[1]And Saul was consenting to the doing away of him. And in that day a great persecution took place on the church which *was* in Jerusalem; and all were scattered throughout the regions of Judea and Samaria, except the apostles. [2]And devout men together carried Stephen, and made a great lamentation over him. [3]But Saul ravaged the church, entering house by house, dragging both men and women, he delivered *them* to prison.

[4]Then, indeed, the ones who had been scattered passed through, preaching the gospel, the word. [5]And going down to a city of Samaria, Philip proclaimed Christ to them. [6]And with one passion the crowds heeded that being said by Philip, when they heard and saw the miracles which he did. [7]For out of those having unclean spirits, *they* came out, crying with a loud voice. And many who had been paralyzed and lame were healed. [8]And great joy was in that city. [9]But a certain man named Simon had long been conjuring in the city, and amazing the nation of Samaria, claiming himself to be some great one. [10]All were paying attention to *him,* from small to great, saying, This one is the power of God, which *is* great. [11]And they were paying attention to him, because for a long time *he*

μάρτυρες ἀπέθεντο τὰ ἱμάτια αὐτῶν παρὰ τοὺς πόδας
witnesses put off the garments of them at the feet
59 νεανίου καλουμένου Σαύλου. καὶ ἐλιθοβόλουν τὸν Στέφανον,
of a young man called Saul. And they stoned – Stephen
ἐπικαλούμενον καὶ λέγοντα, Κύριε Ἰησοῦ, δέξαι τὸ πνεῦμά
invoking (God) and saying, Lord Jesus, receive the spirit
60 μου. θεὶς δὲ τὰ γόνατα, ἔκραξε φωνῇ μεγάλῃ, Κύριε, μὴ
of me. placing And the knees, he cried with a voice great, Lord, Not
στήσῃς αὐτοῖς τὴν ἁμαρτίαν ταύτην. καὶ τοῦτο εἰπὼν
make stand to them sin this. And this having said
ἐκοιμήθη
he fell asleep.

CHAPTER 8

1 Σαῦλος δὲ ἦν συνευδοκῶν τῇ ἀναιρέσει αὐτοῦ.
Saul And was consenting to the doing away of him.
Ἐγένετο δὲ ἐν ἐκείνῃ τῇ ἡμέρᾳ διωγμὸς μέγας ἐπὶ τὴν
it was And in that day a persecution great on the
ἐκκλησίαν τὴν ἐν Ἱεροσολύμοις· πάντες τε διεσπάρησαν
church – in Jerusalem, all and were scattered
κατὰ τὰς χώρας τῆς Ἰουδαίας καὶ Σαμαρείας, πλὴν τῶν
through the countries of Judea and Samaria, except the
2 ἀποστόλων. συνεκόμισαν δὲ τὸν Στέφανον ἄνδρες εὐλαβεῖς,
apostles. together carried And Stephen men devout,
3 καὶ ἐποιήσαντο κοπετὸν μέγαν ἐπ᾽ αὐτῷ. Σαῦλος δὲ
and made a lamentation great over him. Saul And
ἐλυμαίνετο τὴν ἐκκλησίαν, κατὰ τοὺς οἴκους εἰσπορευό-
ravaged the church, house by house having gone
μενος, σύρων τε ἄνδρας καὶ γυναῖκας παρεδίδου εἰς φυλακήν.
in, dragging both men and women, he delivered to prison.
4 Οἱ μὲν οὖν διασπαρέντες διῆλθον, εὐαγγελιζόμενοι τὸν
Those, therefore, being scattered passed through preaching the
5 λόγον. Φίλιππος δὲ κατελθὼν εἰς πόλιν τῆς Σαμαρείας,
word. Philip And going down to a city of Samaria
6 ἐκήρυσσεν αὐτοῖς τὸν Χριστόν. προσεῖχόν τε οἱ ὄχλοι τοῖς
proclaimed to them the Christ heeded And the crowds that
λεγομένοις ὑπὸ τοῦ Φιλίππου ὁμοθυμαδόν, ἐν τῷ ἀκούειν
being said by – Philip, with one passion in the hearing
7 αὐτοὺς καὶ βλέπειν τὰ σημεῖα ἃ ἐποίει. πολλῶν γὰρ τῶν
(of) them and seeing the signs which he was doing. many For of the
ἐχόντων πνεύματα ἀκάθαρτα, βοῶντα μεγάλῃ φωνῇ
(ones) having spirits unclean, crying with a great voice
ἐξήρχετο· πολλοὶ δὲ παραλελυμένοι καὶ χωλοὶ ἐθεραπεύθη-
came out many and having been paralyzed and lame were healed.
8 σαν. καὶ ἐγένετο χαρὰ μεγάλη ἐν τῇ πόλει ἐκείνῃ.
And there was joy great in city that.
9 Ἀνὴρ δέ τις ὀνόματι Σίμων προϋπῆρχεν ἐν τῇ πόλει
a man And certain by name Simon had long been in the city
μαγεύων καὶ ἐξιστῶν τὸ ἔθνος τῆς Σαμαρείας, λέγων εἶναί
conjuring and amazing the nation of Samaria, saying to be
10 τινα ἑαυτὸν μέγαν· ᾧ προσεῖχον πάντες ἀπὸ μικροῦ ἕως
someone himself great, to whom took heed all, from small to
μεγάλου, λέγοντες, Οὗτός ἐστιν ἡ δύναμις τοῦ Θεοῦ ἡ
great, saying, This one is the power of God
11 μεγάλη. προσεῖχον δὲ αὐτῷ, διὰ τὸ ἱκανῷ χρόνῳ ταῖς
great. they were heeding And him, because for a long time with the

had amazed them *with his* conjuring. [12]But when they believed Philip preaching the gospel, the things concerning the kingdom of God, and the name of Jesus Christ, they were baptized, both men and women. [13]And Simon himself also believed, and being baptized was continuing steadfastly with Philip. And seeing miracles and mighty works happening, he was amazed.

[14]And the apostles in Jerusalem hearing that Samaria had received the word of God, they sent Peter and John to them, [15]who going down prayed concerning them, so that they might receive *the* Holy Spirit. [16]For He had not yet fallen on any of them, but they were only baptized into the name of the Lord Jesus. [17]Then they laid hands on them, and they received *the* Holy Spirit.

[18]But Simon seeing that the Spirit is given through the laying on of the hands of the apostles, he offered them money, [19]saying, Give to me this authority, that on whomever I may lay on the hands, he may receive *the* Holy Spirit. [20]But Peter said to him, May your silver be with you into perdition, because you thought to get the gift of God through money. [21]There is neither part nor lot to you in this matter, for your heart is not upright in the sight of God. [22]Therefore, repent of this wickedness of yours, and petition God if perhaps the thought of your heart may be forgiven to you; [23]for I see you to be in *the* gall of bitterness and a bundle of unrighteousness. [24]And answering Simon said, You petition to the Lord for me, so that nothing of which you have spoken come on me.

[25]Then having earnestly testified, and having spoken

12 μαγείαις ἐξεστακέναι αὐτούς. ὅτε δὲ ἐπίστευσαν τῷ Φιλίππῳ
conjuring (he) had amazed them. when But they believed — Philip
εὐαγγελιζομένῳ τὰ περὶ τῆς βασιλείας τοῦ Θεοῦ καὶ τοῦ
preaching the gospel, the things about the kingdom — of God, and the
ὀνόματος τοῦ Ἰησοῦ Χριστοῦ, ἐβαπτίζοντο ἄνδρες τε καὶ
name of Jesus Christ, they were baptized, men both and
13 γυναῖκες. ὁ δὲ Σίμων καὶ αὐτὸς ἐπίστευσε, καὶ βαπτισθεὶς
women. But Simon also himself believed, and being baptized
ἦν προσκαρτερῶν τῷ Φιλίππῳ· θεωρῶν τε δυνάμεις καὶ
was steadfastly continuing to Philip, beholding and works of power and
σημεῖα γινόμενα, ἐξίστατο.
signs happening, he was amazed.

14 Ἀκούσαντες δὲ οἱ ἐν Ἱεροσολύμοις ἀπόστολοι ὅτι
hearing And the in Jerusalem apostles that
δέδεκται ἡ Σαμάρεια τὸν λόγον τοῦ Θεοῦ, ἀπέστειλαν πρὸς
has received Samaria the word — of God, they sent to
15 αὐτοὺς τὸν Πέτρον καὶ Ἰωάννην· οἵτινες καταβάντες
them — Peter and John, who going down
προσηύξαντο περὶ αὐτῶν, ὅπως λάβωσι Πνεῦμα Ἅγιον·
prayed concerning them, so as they might receive (the) Spirit Holy
16 οὔπω γὰρ ἦν ἐπ' οὐδενὶ αὐτῶν ἐπιπεπτωκός, μόνον δὲ
not yet for He was on no one of them having fallen only but
βεβαπτισμένοι ὑπῆρχον εἰς τὸ ὄνομα τοῦ Κυρίου Ἰησοῦ.
having been baptized they were in the name the Lord Jesus.
17 τότε ἐπετίθουν τὰς χεῖρας ἐπ' αὐτούς, καὶ ἐλάμβανον
Then they laid on the hands on them, and they received
18 Πνεῦμα Ἅγιον. θεασάμενος δὲ ὁ Σίμων ὅτι διὰ τῆς ἐπιθέ-
(the) Spirit Holy. beholding And Simon that through the laying
σεως τῶν χειρῶν τῶν ἀποστόλων δίδοται τὸ Πνεῦμα τὸ
on of the hands of the apostles is given the Spirit —
19 Ἅγιον, προσήνεγκεν αὐτοῖς χρήματα, λέγων, Δότε κἀμοὶ
Holy, he offered them money, saying, Give also to me
τὴν ἐξουσίαν ταύτην, ἵνα ᾧ ἐὰν ἐπιθῶ τὰς χεῖρας, λαμβάνῃ
— authority this, that to whom may I lay on the hands, he may receive
20 Πνεῦμα Ἅγιον. Πέτρος δὲ εἶπε πρὸς αὐτόν, Τὸ ἀργύριόν σου
(the) Spirit Holy. Peter But said to him, The silver of you
σὺν σοὶ εἴη εἰς ἀπώλειαν, ὅτι τὴν δωρεὰν τοῦ Θεοῦ ἐνόμισας
with you be into perdition, because the gift — of God you thought
21 διὰ χρημάτων κτᾶσθαι. οὐκ ἔστι σοι μερὶς οὐδὲ κλῆρος ἐν
through money to get. not There is to you part nor lot in
τῷ λόγῳ τούτῳ. ἡ γὰρ καρδία σου οὐκ ἔστιν εὐθεῖα ἐνώπιον
— matter this. the For heart of you not is right before
22 τοῦ Θεοῦ. μετανόησον οὖν ἀπὸ τῆς κακίας σου ταύτης, καὶ
— God. Repent, therefore, from — wickedness of you this, and
δεήθητι τοῦ Θεοῦ, εἰ ἄρα ἀφεθήσεταί σοι ἡ ἐπίνοια τῆς
petition — God if perhaps will be forgiven you the thought of the
23 καρδίας σου. εἰς γὰρ χολὴν πικρίας καὶ σύνδεσμον ἀδικίας
heart of you. in For (the) gall of bitterness and a bundle of unrighteousness
24 ὁρῶ σε ὄντα. ἀποκριθεὶς δὲ ὁ Σίμων εἶπε, Δεήθητε ὑμεῖς ὑπὲρ
I see you being. answering And Simon said, Petition you for
ἐμοῦ πρὸς τὸν Κύριον, ὅπως μηδὲν ἐπέλθῃ ἐπ' ἐμὲ ὧν εἰρή-
me to the Lord, so as not one may come on me of what you
κατε.
have spoken.

25 Οἱ μὲν οὖν διαμαρτυράμενοι καὶ λαλήσαντες τὸν λόγον
They, therefore, having earnestly testified and having spoken the word

the word, and having preached the gospel to many villages of the Samaritans, they returned to Jerusalem.

[26] But an angel of *the* Lord spoke to Philip, saying, Rise up and go along south on the highway going down from Jerusalem to Gaza; this is desert. [27] And rising up, he went. And, behold, an Ethiopian man, a eunuch, one in power *with* Candace the queen of *the* Ethiopians, who was over all her treasure, who had come to Jerusalem to worship. [28] And *he* was returning. And sitting on his chariot, he read the prophet Isaiah.

[29] And the Spirit said to Philip, Come up and join yourself to this chariot. [30] And running near, Philip heard him reading the prophet Isaiah, and said, Then do you know what you are reading? [31] But he said, How should I be able, unless someone shall guide me? And he called Philip near, to come up and sit with him. [32] And *the* content of the Scripture which he was reading was this: "He was led as a sheep to slaughter, and as a lamb dumb before His shearer, so He does not open His mouth. [33] In His humiliation, His judgment was taken away; and who will recount His generation? For His life is taken away from the earth."

[34] And answering, the eunuch said to Philip, I beg you, about whom does the prophet say this? About himself, or about some other? [35] And opening his mouth, and beginning from this Scripture, Philip preached to him the gospel *of* Jesus. [36] And as they passed along the highway, they came on some water. And the eunuch said, Behold, water! What hinders me from being baptized? [37] And Philip said, If you believe out of all the heart, it is lawful. And answering, he said, I

τοῦ Κυρίου, ὑπέστρεψαν εἰς Ἱερουσαλήμ, πολλάς τε κώμας
of the Lord, returned to Jerusalem, many and villages
τῶν Σαμαρειτῶν εὐηγγελίσαντο.
of the Samaritans having preached the gospel.
26 Ἄγγελος δὲ Κυρίου ἐλάλησε προς Φίλιππον, λέγων,
an angel And of (the) Lord spoke to Philip, saying,
Ἀνάστηθι καὶ πορεύου κατὰ μεσημβρίαν ἐπὶ τὴν ὁδὸν τὴν
Rise up and go along south, on the highway –
καταβαίνουσαν ἀπὸ Ἱερουσαλὴμ εἰς Γάζαν· αὕτη ἐστὶν
going down from Jerusalem to Gaza; this is
27 ἔρημος. καὶ ἀναστὰς ἐπορεύθη· καὶ ἰδού, ἀνὴρ Αἰθίοψ εὐνοῦ-
desert. And rising up he went. And, behold, a man Ethiopian, a eunuch,
χος δυνάστης Κανδάκης τῆς βασιλίσσης Αἰθιόπων, ὃς ἦν ἐπὶ
a power of Candace the queen of Ethiopians, who was over
πάσης τῆς γάζης αὐτῆς, ὃς ἐληλυθει προσκυνήσων εἰς
all the treasure of her, who had come to worship to
28 Ἱερουσαλήμ, ἦν τε ὑποστρέφων καὶ καθήμενος ἐπὶ τοῦ
Jerusalem, was and returning and sitting on the
ἅρματος αὐτοῦ, ἀνεγίνωσκε τὸν προφήτην Ἠσαΐαν. εἶπε
chariot of him, he read the prophet Isaiah. said
29 δὲ τὸ Πνεῦμα τῷ Φιλίππῳ, Πρόσελθε καὶ κολλήθητι τῷ
And the Spirit – to Philip, Go near and join yourself to –
30 ἅρματι τούτῳ. προσδραμὼν δὲ ὁ Φίλιππος ἤκουσεν αὐτοῦ
chariot this. running near And, Philip heard from him
ἀναγινώσκοντος τὸν προφήτην Ἠσαΐαν, καὶ εἶπεν, Ἆρά
reading the prophet Isaiah, and said, Indeed,
31 γε γινώσκεις ἃ ἀναγινώσκεις ; ὁ δὲ εἶπε, Πῶς γὰρ ἂν δυναί-
do you know what you are reading? he And said, how For should I be
μην, ἐὰν μή τις ὁδηγήσῃ με ; παρεκάλεσέ τε τὸν Φίλιππον
able, unless someone shall guide me? he called near And – Philip
32 ἀναβάντα καθίσαι σὺν αὐτῷ. ἡ δὲ περιοχὴ τῆς γραφῆς ἣν
coming up to sit with him. the And (the) content of the Scripture which
ἀνεγίνωσκεν ἦν αὕτη, Ὡς πρόβατον ἐπὶ σφαγὴν ἤχθη, καὶ
he was reading was this: As a sheep to slaughter He was led, and
ὡς ἀμνὸς ἐναντίον τοῦ κείροντος αὐτὸν ἄφωνος, οὕτως οὐκ
as a lamb before he shearing it (is) voiceless, so not
33 ἀνοίγει τὸ στόμα αὐτοῦ. ἐν τῇ ταπεινώσει αὐτοῦ ἡ κρίσις
He opens the mouth of Him. In the humiliation of Him, the judgment
αὐτοῦ ἤρθη, τὴν δὲ γενεὰν αὐτοῦ τίς διηγήσεται ; ὅτι
of Him was taken; the but generation of Him who will recount? Because
34 αἴρεται ἀπὸ τῆς γῆς ἡ ζωὴ αὐτοῦ. ἀποκριθεὶς δὲ ὁ εὐνοῦχος
is taken from the earth the life of Him. answering And the eunuch
τῷ Φιλίππῳ εἶπε, Δέομαί σου, περὶ τίνος ὁ προφήτης λέγει
to Philip said, I ask you, about whom the prophet says
35 τοῦτο ; περὶ ἑαυτοῦ, ἢ περὶ ἑτέρου τινός ; ἀνοίξας δὲ ὁ
this? (Is it) about himself, or about other someone? opening And
Φίλιππος τὸ στόμα αὐτοῦ, καὶ ἀρξάμενος ἀπὸ τῆς γραφῆς
Philip the mouth of him, and beginning from Scripture
36 ταύτης, εὐηγγελίσατο αὐτῷ τὸν Ἰησοῦν. ὡς δὲ ἐπορεύοντο
this, preached the gospel to him, Jesus. as And they were going
κατὰ τὴν ὁδόν, ἦλθον ἐπί τι ὕδωρ· καί φησιν ὁ εὐνοῦχος,
along the highway, they came on some water, and says the eunuch,
37 Ἰδού, ὕδωρ· τί κωλύει με βαπτισθῆναι ; εἶπε δὲ ὁ Φίλιππος,
Behold, water! What prevents me to be baptized? said And Philip,
Εἰ πιστεύεις ἐξ ὅλης τῆς καρδίας, ἔξεστιν. ἀποκριθεὶς δὲ εἶπε,
If you believe from all the heart, it is lawful. answering And he said,

believe Jesus Christ to be the
Son of God.
38 And he commanded the
chariot to stand still. And
both went down into the
water, both Philip and the
eunuch; and he baptized
him. 39 But when they
came up out of the water,
the Spirit of *the* Lord caught
Philip away, and the eunuch
did not see him any more;
for he went his way rejoicing.
40 And Philip was found at
Azotus, and passing through
he preached the gospel *to* all
the cities, until he came to
Caesarea.

CHAPTER 9

1 But still breathing threats
and murder toward the disciples of the Lord, coming to
the high priest, 2 Saul
asked from him letters to
Damascus, to the syna-
gogues, so that if he found
any being of the Way, both
men and women, having
bound them he might bring
them to Jerusalem. 3 But in
going, it happened *as* he
drew near to Damascus,
even suddenly a light from
Heaven shone around him.
4 And falling on the earth, he
heard a voice saying to him,
Saul, Saul, why do you
persecute Me? 5 And he
said, Who are you, Sir? And
the Lord said, I am Jesus
whom you persecute. *It is*
hard for you to kick against
the prods. 6 Both trembling
and being astonished, he
said, Lord, what do you
desire me to do? And the
Lord *said* to him, Rise up and
go into the city, and it will be
told you what you must do.
7 But the men who were
traveling with him had been
standing speechless, hearing, indeed, the voice, but
seeing no one. 8 And Saul
was lifted up from the
ground, his eyes having
been opened, *but* he saw no
one. But leading him by the
hand, they brought *him* to
Damascus. 9 And he was
three days not seeing, and
did not eat or drink. 10 And
there was a certain disciple
in Damascus named Ananias.

38 Πιστεύω τὸν υἱὸν τοῦ Θεοῦ εἶναι τὸν Ἰησοῦν Χριστόν. καὶ
I believe the Son – of God to be – Jesus Christ. And
ἐκέλευσε στῆναι τὸ ἅρμα· καὶ κατέβησαν ἀμφότεροι εἰς τὸ
he ordered to stand the chariot, and went down both into the
ὕδωρ, ὅ τε Φίλιππος καὶ ὁ εὐνοῦχος· καὶ ἐβάπτισεν αὐτόν.
water, – both Philip and the eunuch, and he baptized him.
39 ὅτε δὲ ἀνέβησαν ἐκ τοῦ ὕδατος, Πνεῦμα Κυρίου ἥρπασε τὸν
when And they came up out of the water (the) Spirit of (the) Lord caught away
Φίλιππον· καὶ οὐκ εἶδεν αὐτὸν οὐκέτι ὁ εὐνοῦχος, ἐπορεύετο
Philip, and not did see him any more the eunuch, he went
40 γὰρ τὴν ὁδὸν αὐτοῦ χαίρων. Φίλιππος δὲ εὑρέθη εἰς Ἄζωτον·
for the way of him rejoicing. Philip And was found at Azotus,
καὶ διερχόμενος εὐηγγελίζετο τὰς πόλεις πάσας, ἕως τοῦ
and passing through he preached the gospel to the cities all, until the
ἐλθεῖν αὐτὸν εἰς Καισάρειαν.
coming (of) him to Caesarea.

CHAPTER 9

1 Ὁ δὲ Σαῦλος ἔτι ἐμπνέων ἀπειλῆς καὶ φόνου εἰς τοὺς
– But Saul still breathing in threats and murder toward the
2 μαθητὰς τοῦ Κυρίου, προσελθὼν τῷ ἀρχιερεῖ, ᾐτήσατο
disciples of the Lord, having come to the high priest, asked
παρ' αὐτοῦ ἐπιστολὰς εἰς Δαμασκὸν πρὸς τὰς συναγωγάς,
from him letters to Damascus, to the synagogues,
ὅπως ἐάν τινας εὕρῃ τῆς ὁδοῦ ὄντας ἄνδρας τε καὶ γυναῖκας,
so that if any he found of the way being, men both and women.
3 δεδεμένους ἀγάγῃ εἰς Ἱερουσαλήμ. ἐν δὲ τῷ πορεύεσθαι,
binding (them) he may bring to Jerusalem. in And the going
ἐγένετο αὐτὸν ἐγγίζειν τῇ Δαμασκῷ· καὶ ἐξαίφνης περι-
happened he drew near – to Damascus, and suddenly shone
4 ήστραψεν αὐτὸν φῶς ἀπὸ τοῦ οὐρανοῦ· καὶ πεσὼν ἐπὶ τὴν
around him a light from – Heaven; and falling on the
γῆν, ἤκουσε φωνὴν λέγουσαν αὐτῷ, Σαούλ, Σαούλ, τί με
earth, he heard a voice saying to him, Saul, Saul! Why Me
5 διώκεις; εἶπε δέ, Τίς εἶ, Κύριε; ὁ δὲ Κύριος εἶπεν, Ἐγώ εἰμι
you persecute? he said And, Who are you, Sir? And the Lord said, I am
Ἰησοῦς ὃν σὺ διώκεις· σκληρόν σοι πρὸς κέντρα λακτίζειν.
Jesus, whom you persecute; (It is) hard for you against prods to kick.
6 τρέμων τε καὶ θαμβῶν εἶπε, Κύριε, τί με θέλεις ποιῆσαι; καὶ
trembling both And astonished he said, Lord, what me desire You to do? And
ὁ Κύριος πρὸς αὐτόν, Ἀνάστηθι καὶ εἴσελθε εἰς τὴν πόλιν,
the Lord (said) to him, Rise up and go into the city,
7 καὶ λαληθήσεταί σοι τί σε δεῖ ποιεῖν. οἱ δὲ ἄνδρες οἱ συν-
and it shall be told you what you must do. the And men –
οδεύοντες αὐτῷ εἱστήκεισαν ἐννεοί, ἀκούοντες μὲν τῆς φω-
traveling with him had been standing speechless, hearing indeed the sound,
8 νῆς, μηδένα δὲ θεωροῦντες. ἠγέρθη δὲ ὁ Σαῦλος ἀπὸ τῆς
no one but beholding. was lifted And Saul from the
γῆς· ἀνεῳγμένων δὲ τῶν ὀφθαλμῶν αὐτοῦ, οὐδένα ἔβλεπε,
earth, having been opened the eyes of him, no one he saw.
χειραγωγοῦντες δὲ αὐτὸν εἰσήγαγον εἰς Δαμασκόν. καὶ ἦν
leading by the hand And him, they brought to Damascus. And he was
9 ἡμέρας τρεῖς μὴ βλέπων, καὶ οὐκ ἔφαγεν οὐδὲ ἔπιεν.
days three not seeing, and did not eat nor drink.
10 Ἦν δέ τις μαθητὴς ἐν Δαμασκῷ ὀνόματι Ἀνανίας, καὶ
was And a certain disciple in Damascus by name Ananias, and

And the Lord said to him in a vision, Ananias. And he said, Behold me, Lord. 11 And the Lord *said* to him, Rising up, pass along on the street being called Straight, and seek a Tarsian named Saul in *the* house of Judas. For, behold, he is praying. 12 And he has seen in a vision a man named Ananias coming and putting a hand on him, so that he may see again. 13 And Ananias answered, Lord, I have heard from many about this man, how many bad things he did to Your saints in Jerusalem. 14 And here he has authority from the chief priests to bind all who call on Your name. 15 And the Lord said to him, Go, for this one is a chosen vessel to Me, to bear My name before nations and kings and *the* sons of Israel; 61 for I will show him how much he must suffer for My name.

17 And Ananias went away and entered into the house. And putting hands on him, *he* said, Brother Saul, the Lord Jesus has sent me, the *One* who appeared to you in the highway *on* which you came, that you may see again, and be filled with *the* Holy Spirit. 18 And instantly scales as it were fell from his eyes, and he saw again. And rising up, *he* was baptized. 19 And taking food, *he* was strengthened. And Saul was with the disciples in Damascus some days.

20 And he at once proclaimed Christ in the synagogues, that this One is the Son of God. 21 And all those hearing were amazed, and said, Is this not the *one* destroying the ones invoking this Name in Jerusalem, and he had come here for this, that binding them he may lead *them* before the chief priests? 22 But Saul was more filled with power, and confounded the Jews living in Damascus, proving

εἶπε πρὸς αὐτὸν ὁ Κύριος ἐν ὁράματι, Ἀνανία. ὁ δὲ εἶπεν,
said to him the Lord in a vision, Ananias. he And said,
11 Ἰδοὺ ἐγώ, Κύριε. ὁ δὲ Κύριος πρὸς αὐτόν, Ἀναστὰς
Behold, I, Lord. the And Lord to him, Rising up
πορεύθητι ἐπὶ τὴν ῥύμην τὴν καλουμένην Εὐθεῖαν, καὶ ζητη-
pass along on the street — being called Straight, and seek
σον ἐν οἰκίᾳ Ἰούδα Σαῦλον ὀνόματι, Ταρσέα· ἰδοὺ γὰρ
in (the) house of Judas Saul by name a Tarsian; behold for
12 προσεύχεται, καὶ εἶδεν ἐν ὁράματι ἄνδρα ὀνόματι Ἀνανίαν
he is praying, and has seen in a vision a man by name Ananias
εἰσελθόντα καὶ ἐπιθέντα αὐτῷ χεῖρα, ὅπως ἀναβλέψῃ.
coming in and putting on him a hand so as he may see again.
13 ἀπεκρίθη δὲ ὁ Ἀνανίας, Κύριε, ἀκήκοα ἀπὸ πολλῶν περὶ
answered And — Ananias, Lord, I have heard from many about
τοῦ ἀνδρὸς τούτου, ὅσα κακὰ ἐποίησε τοῖς ἁγίοις σου ἐν
— man this, how many bad things he did to the saints of You in
14 Ἱερουσαλήμ· καὶ ὧδε ἔχει ἐξουσίαν παρὰ τῶν ἀρχιερέων,
Jerusalem; and here he has authority from the chief priests
15 δῆσαι πάντας τοὺς ἐπικαλουμένους τὸ ὄνομά σου. εἶπε δὲ
to bind all the (ones) invoking the name of You. said But
πρὸς αὐτὸν ὁ Κύριος, Πορεύου, ὅτι σκεῦος ἐκλογῆς μοι ἐστὶν
to him the Lord, Go because a vessel of election to Me is
οὗτος, τοῦ βαστάσαι τὸ ὄνομά μου ἐνώπιον ἐθνῶν καὶ
this one, — to bear the name of Me before nations and
16 βασιλέων, υἱῶν τε Ἰσραήλ· ἐγὼ γὰρ ὑποδείξω αὐτῷ ὅσα
kings, sons and of Israel; I for will show him how many
17 δεῖ αὐτὸν ὑπὲρ τοῦ ὀνόματός μου παθεῖν. ἀπῆλθε δὲ
must he on behalf of the name of Me suffer. went away And
Ἀνανίας καὶ εἰσῆλθεν εἰς τὴν οἰκίαν, καὶ ἐπιθεὶς ἐπ' αὐτὸν τὰς
Ananias and entered into the house, and putting on him the
χεῖρας εἶπε, Σαοὺλ ἀδελφέ, ὁ Κύριος ἀπέσταλκέ με, Ἰησοῦς
hands said, Saul Brother, the Lord has sent me, Jesus
ὁ ὀφθείς σοι ἐν τῇ ὁδῷ ᾗ ἤρχου, ὅπως ἀναβλέψῃς καὶ πλη-
He appearing to you in the way which you came, so as you may see and be
18 σθῇς Πνεύματος Ἁγίου. καὶ εὐθέως ἀπέπεσον ἀπὸ τῶν
filled of (the) Spirit Holy. And at once fell away from the
ὀφθαλμῶν αὐτοῦ ὡσεὶ λεπίδες, ἀνέβλεψέ τε παραχρῆμα,
eyes of him as if scales, he saw again and, instantly
19 καὶ ἀναστὰς ἐβαπτίσθη, καὶ λαβὼν τροφὴν ἐνίσχυσεν.
and rising up was baptized; and taking food was strengthened.
Ἐγένετο δὲ ὁ Σαῦλος μετὰ τῶν ἐν Δαμασκῷ μαθητῶν
was And — Saul with the in Damascus disciples
20 ἡμέρας τινάς. καὶ εὐθέως ἐν ταῖς συναγωγαῖς ἐκήρυσσε τὸν
days some, and at once in the synagogues he proclaimed the
21 Χριστόν, ὅτι οὗτός ἐστιν ὁ υἱὸς τοῦ Θεοῦ. ἐξίσταντο δὲ
Christ, that this One is the Son — of God. were amazed And
πάντες οἱ ἀκούοντες καὶ ἔλεγον, Οὐχ οὗτός ἐστιν ὁ πορθήσας
all those hearing, and said, not this one Is the (one) destroying
ἐν Ἱερουσαλὴμ τοὺς ἐπικαλουμένους τὸ ὄνομα τοῦτο, καὶ
in Jerusalem those invoking — name this, and
ὧδε εἰς τοῦτο ἐληλύθει ἵνα δεδεμένους αὐτοὺς ἀγάγῃ ἐπὶ
here for this he had come, that binding them he may lead before
22 τοὺς ἀρχιερεῖς; Σαῦλος δὲ μᾶλλον ἐνεδυναμοῦτο, καὶ συνέ-
the chief priests? Saul And more was filled with power and con-
χυνε τοὺς Ἰουδαίους τοὺς κατοικοῦντας ἐν Δαμασκῷ,
founded the Jews living in Damascus,

that this One is the Christ.
23 And when many days were fulfilled, the Jews plotted together to do away with him. 24 But their plot was known to Saul. And they carefully watched the gates both by day and by night, so that they might do away with him. 25 But taking him by night, the disciples let him down through the wall, lowering *him* in a basket.
26 And arriving in Jerusalem, he tried to be joined to the disciples; yet all feared him, not believing that he was a disciple. 27 But taking hold of him, Barnabas led him to the apostles. And *he* told them how he saw the Lord in the highway, and that He spoke to him; and how he spoke boldly in Damascus in the name of Jesus. 29 And he spoke and disputed with the Hellenists, but they seized him in order to do away with him. 30 But knowing *this*, the brothers brought him down to Caesarea, and sent him out to Tarsus. 31 Then, indeed, the churches throughout all Judea, and Galilee, and Samaria, had peace, being built up and going on in the fear of the Lord. And *they* were increased in the comfort of the Holy Spirit.

32 And it happened, passing through all, Peter came down to the saints living in Lydda also. 33 And he found that a certain man named Aeneas *was* there, lying on a mattress eight years, who was paralyzed. 34 And Peter said to him, Aeneas, Jesus the Christ heals you; rise up and spread for yourself! And he instantly rose up. 35 And all those living in Lydda and the Sharon *Plain* saw him, who

συμβιβάζων ὅτι οὗτός ἐστιν ὁ Χριστός.
proving that this One is the Christ.
23 Ὡς δὲ ἐπληροῦντο ἡμέραι ἱκαναί, συνεβουλεύσαντο οἱ
when And were fulfilled days many, plotted together the
24 Ἰουδαῖοι ἀνελεῖν αὐτόν· ἐγνώσθη δὲ τῷ Σαύλῳ ἡ ἐπιβουλὴ
Jews to do away (with) him, was known but to Saul the plot
αὐτῶν. παρετήρουν τε τὰς πύλας ἡμέρας τε καὶ νυκτός,
of them. they carefully watched And the gates by day both and by night,
25 ὅπως αὐτὸν ἀνέλωσι· λαβόντες δὲ αὐτὸν οἱ μαθηταὶ νυκτός,
so as him they may do away; taking but him the disciples by night
καθῆκαν διὰ τοῦ τείχους, χαλάσαντες ἐν σπυρίδι.
let down through the wall, lowering (him) in a basket.
26 Παραγενόμενος δὲ ὁ Σαῦλος εἰς Ἱερουσαλήμ, ἐπειρᾶτο
arriving And — Saul in Jerusalem, he tried
κολλᾶσθαι τοῖς μαθηταῖς· καὶ πάντες ἐφοβοῦντο αὐτόν, μὴ
to be joined to the disciples; and all feared him, not
27 πιστεύοντες ὅτι ἐστὶ μαθητής. Βαρνάβας δὲ ἐπιλαβόμενος
believing that he is a disciple. Barnabas But taking hold of
αὐτὸν ἤγαγε πρὸς τοὺς ἀποστόλους, καὶ διηγήσατο αὐτοῖς
him led to the apostles, and told them
πῶς ἐν τῇ ὁδῷ εἶδε τὸν Κύριον, καὶ ὅτι ἐλάλησεν αὐτῷ,
how in the way he saw the Lord, and that He spoke to him,
καὶ πῶς ἐν Δαμασκῷ ἐπαρρησιάσατο ἐν τῷ ὀνόματι τοῦ
and how in Damascus he spoke boldly in the name —
28 Ἰησοῦ. καὶ ἦν μετ' αὐτῶν εἰσπορευόμενος καὶ ἐκπορευό-
of Jesus. And he was with them going in and going
μενος ἐν Ἱερουσαλήμ, καὶ παρρησιαζόμενος ἐν τῷ ὀνόματι
out in Jerusalem, and speaking boldly in the name
29 τοῦ Κυρίου Ἰησοῦ, ἐλάλει τε καὶ συνεζήτει πρὸς τοὺς
of the Lord Jesus. he spoke And and discussed with the
30 Ἑλληνιστάς· οἱ δὲ ἐπεχείρουν αὐτὸν ἀνελεῖν. ἐπιγνόντες δὲ
Hellenists; they and took in hand him to do away. knowing But
οἱ ἀδελφοὶ κατήγαγον αὐτὸν εἰς Καισάρειαν, καὶ ἐξαπέ-
the brothers led down him to Caesarea, and sent
31 στειλαν αὐτὸν εἰς Ταρσόν. αἱ μὲν οὖν ἐκκλησίαι καθ'
forth him to Tarsus. the Therefore churches throughout
ὅλης τῆς Ἰουδαίας καὶ Γαλιλαίας καὶ Σαμαρείας εἶχον εἰρήνην
all — Judea and Galilee and Samaria had peace,
οἰκοδομούμεναι, καὶ πορευόμεναι τῷ φόβῳ τοῦ Κυρίου καὶ
being built up, and going on in the fear of the Lord, and
τῇ παρακλήσει τοῦ Ἁγίου Πνεύματος ἐπληθύνοντο.
in the comfort of the Holy Spirit were multiplied.
32 Ἐγένετο δὲ Πέτρον διερχόμενον διὰ πάντων κατελθεῖν καὶ
it was And, Peter passing through all came down also
33 πρὸς τοὺς ἁγίους τοὺς κατοικοῦντας Λύδδαν. εὗρε δὲ ἐκεῖ
to the saints — inhabiting Lydda. he found And there
ἄνθρωπόν τινα Αἰνέαν ὀνόματι, ἐξ ἐτῶν ὀκτὼ κατακείμενον
a man certain, Aeneas by name, of years eight lying
34 ἐπὶ κραββάτῳ, ὃς ἦν παραλελυμένος. καὶ εἶπεν αὐτῷ ὁ
on a mattress, who was paralyzed. And said to him —
Πέτρος, Αἰνέα, ἰᾶταί σε Ἰησοῦς ὁ Χριστός· ἀνάστηθι καὶ
Peter, Aeneas, heals you Jesus the Christ; rise up and
στρῶσον σεαυτῷ. καὶ εὐθέως ἀνέστη. καὶ εἶδον αὐτὸν
spread for yourself. And instantly he rose up. And saw him
35 πάντες οἱ κατοικοῦντες Λύδδαν καὶ τὸν Σάρωνα, οἵτινες
all those inhabiting Lydda and the Sharon (plain), who

then turned to the Lord.

[36]And in Joppa was a certain disciple named Tabitha, which translated is called Gazelle. She was full of good works and of alms which she did. [37]And it happened in those days, becoming ill she died. And having washed her, they put *her* in an upper room. [38]And Lydda being near to Joppa, the disciples hearing that Peter is in it, they sent two men to him, begging *him* not to delay to come to them.

[39]And rising up, Peter went with them. *And he* having arrived, they led *him* up to the upper room, and all the widows stood by him, weeping and showing tunics and garments which Dorcas made being with them. [40]And putting all out, placing the knees, Peter prayed. And turning to the body, he said, Tabitha, Arise! And she opened her eyes, and seeing Peter, she sat up. [41]And giving her a hand, he raised her up. And calling the saints and the widows, he presented her living. [42]And it became known throughout all Joppa, and many believed on the Lord. [43]And it was many days *that* he remained in Joppa, with a certain Simon, a tanner.

CHAPTER 10

[1]But a certain man named Cornelius was in Caesarea, a centurion of a cohort being called Italian; [2]*one* devout and fearing God, with all his household, both doing many alms to the people, and praying continually to God. [3]About *the* ninth hour of the day, he saw in a vision an angel coming to him, and saying to him, Cornelius! [4]And he was staring at him, and becoming

ἐπέστρεψαν ἐπὶ τὸν Κύριον.
turned to the Lord.
36 Ἐν Ἰόππῃ δέ τις ἦν μαθήτρια ὀνόματι Ταβιθά, ἣ διερμη-
in Joppa And a certain was disciple, by name Tabitha, which being
νευομένη λέγεται Δορκάς· αὕτη ἦν πλήρης ἀγαθῶν ἔργων καὶ
translated is called Gazelle. She was full of good works and
37 ἐλεημοσυνῶν ὧν ἐποίει. ἐγένετο δὲ ἐν ταῖς ἡμέραις ἐκείναις
of alms which she did. it was And, in — days those,
ἀσθενήσασαν αὐτὴν ἀποθανεῖν· λούσαντες δὲ αὐτὴν ἔθηκαν
having ailed, she died. having washed And, her they put
38 ἐν ὑπερῴῳ. ἐγγὺς δὲ οὔσης Λύδδης τῇ Ἰόππῃ, οἱ μαθηταὶ
in an upper room. near And being Lydda — to Joppa, the disciples
ἀκούσαντες ὅτι Πέτρος ἐστὶν ἐν αὐτῇ, ἀπέστειλαν δύο
having heard that Peter is in it, they sent two
ἄνδρας πρὸς αὐτόν, παρακαλοῦντες μὴ ὀκνῆσαι διελθεῖν
men to him, begging (him) not to delay to come
39 ἕως αὐτῶν. ἀναστὰς δὲ Πέτρος συνῆλθεν αὐτοῖς· ὃν παρα-
to them. rising And Peter went with them; whom arriving
γενόμενον ἀνήγαγον εἰς τὸ ὑπερῷον, καὶ παρέστησαν αὐτῷ
they led up to the upper room, and stood by him
πᾶσαι αἱ χῆραι κλαίουσαι καὶ ἐπιδεικνύμεναι χιτῶνας καὶ
all the widows weeping and showing tunics and
ἱμάτια ὅσα ἐποίει μετ᾽ αὐτῶν οὖσα ἡ Δορκάς. ἐκβαλὼν δὲ
garments such as made with them being — Dorcas. thrusting And
40 ἔξω πάντας ὁ Πέτρος θεὶς τὰ γόνατα προσηύξατο· καὶ
out all, Peter placing the knees prayed; and
ἐπιστρέψας πρὸς τὸ σῶμα, εἶπε, Ταβιθά, ἀνάστηθι. ἡ δὲ
turning to the body, he said, Tabitha, Arise. she And
ἤνοιξε τοὺς ὀφθαλμοὺς αὐτῆς· καὶ ἰδοῦσα τὸν Πέτρον,
opened the eyes of her and seeing — Peter,
41 ἀνεκάθισε. δοὺς δὲ αὐτῇ χεῖρα, ἀνέστησεν αὐτήν· φωνήσας δὲ
she sat up. giving And her a hand, he raised up her; calling and
τοὺς ἁγίους καὶ τὰς χήρας, παρέστησεν αὐτὴν ζῶσαν. γνω-
the saints and the widows, he presented her living.
42 στὸν δὲ ἐγένετο καθ᾽ ὅλης τῆς Ἰόππης, καὶ πολλοὶ ἐπί-
known And it became through all — Joppa, and many
43 στευσαν ἐπὶ τὸν Κύριον. ἐγένετο δὲ ἡμέρας ἱκανὰς μεῖνι
believed on the Lord. it was And days sufficient remained
αὐτὸν ἐν Ἰόππῃ παρά τινι Σίμωνι βυρσεῖ.
he in Joppa with one Simon, a tanner.

CHAPTER 10

1 Ἀνὴρ δέ τις ἦν ἐν Καισαρείᾳ ὀνόματι Κορνήλιος, ἑκατοντ-
a man And certain was in Caesarea, by name Cornelius, a centurion
2 άρχης ἐκ σπείρης τῆς καλουμένης Ἰταλικῆς, εὐσεβὴς καὶ
of a cohort — being called Italian; devout and
φοβούμενος τὸν Θεὸν σὺν παντὶ τῷ οἴκῳ αὐτοῦ, ποιῶν τε
fearing — God with all the house of him, doing both
ἐλεημοσύνας πολλὰς τῷ λαῷ, καὶ δεόμενος τοῦ Θεοῦ διὰ
alms many to the people, and petitioning — God con-
3 παντός. εἶδεν ἐν ὁράματι φανερῶς, ὡσεὶ ὥραν ἐννάτην τῆς
tinually. He saw in a vision plainly, about hour ninth of the
ἡμέρας, ἄγγελον τοῦ Θεοῦ εἰσελθόντα πρὸς αὐτόν, καὶ
day, an angel — of God coming in to him, and
4 εἰπόντα αὐτῷ, Κορνήλιε. ὁ δὲ ἀτενίσας αὐτῷ καὶ ἔμφοβος
saying to him, Cornelius! he And was gazing at him and terrified

terrified he said, What is it, Sir? And he said to him, Your prayers and your alms have gone up for a memorial before God. [5]And now send men to Joppa, and call for Simon who is surnamed Peter. [6]This one is lodged with one Simon, a tanner whose house is by *the* sea. He will tell you what you must do. [7]And when the angel speaking to Cornelius went away, calling two of his servants, and a devout soldier of those continually waiting on him, [8]and having explained all things them, he sent them to Joppa.

[9]And on the morrow, these passing along on *the* road, and drawing near to the city, Peter went up on the roof to pray, about *the* sixth hour. [10]And he became hungry, and wished to taste *food*. But *as* they *were* preparing, an ecstasy fell on him. [11]And he saw the heaven being opened, and a certain vessel like a great sheet coming down, being bound by four corners, and let down onto the earth; [12]in which were all the four-footed animals of the earth, and the wild beasts, and the creeping things, and the birds of the heaven. [13]And a voice came to him, Rise up, Peter, slay and eat. [14]But Peter said, Not at all, Lord, because I never did eat anything common or unclean. [15]And again a voice *came* to him a second *time*, What things God made clean, you do not make common. [16]And this happened three *times*, and the vessel was taken up into the heaven again.

[17]And as Peter was doubting within himself what the vision which he saw might be, even behold, the men who were sent from Cornelius stood on the porch, having asked out the house of Simon. [18]And calling out, they inquired if Simon being

γενόμενος εἶπε, Τί ἐστι, Κύριε; εἶπε δὲ αὐτῷ, Αἱ προσευχαί
becoming he said, What is it, Sir? he said And to him, The prayers
σου καὶ αἱ ἐλεημοσύναι σου ἀνέβησαν εἰς μνημόσυνον
of you and the alms of you went up for a memorial
5 ἐνώπιον τοῦ Θεοῦ. καὶ νῦν πέμψον εἰς Ἰόππην ἄνδρας, καὶ
before — God. And now send to Joppa men, and
6 μετάπεμψαι Σίμωνα ὃς ἐπικαλεῖται Πέτρος· οὗτος ξενίζεται
call for Simon who is surnamed Peter; this one is lodged
παρά τινι Σίμωνι βυρσεῖ, ᾧ ἐστιν οἰκία παρὰ θάλασσαν·
with one Simon, a tanner, to whom is a house by (the) sea
7 οὗτος λαλήσει σοι τί σε δεῖ ποιεῖν. ὡς δὲ ἀπῆλθεν ὁ ἄγγελος
this one will tell you what you must do. as And went away the angel
ὁ λαλῶν τῷ Κορνηλίῳ, φωνήσας δύο τῶν οἰκετῶν αὐτοῦ,
— speaking — to Cornelius, having called two of the servants of him,
καὶ στρατιώτην εὐσεβῆ τῶν προσκαρτερούντων αὐτῷ, καὶ
and a soldier devout of those continually waiting on him, and
8 ἐξηγησάμενος αὐτοῖς ἅπαντα, ἀπέστειλεν αὐτοὺς εἰς τὴν
having explained to them all things, he sent forth them to —
Ἰόππην.
Joppa.
9 Τῇ δὲ ἐπαύριον, ὁδοιπορούντων ἐκείνων καὶ τῇ πόλει
on the And morrow, passing along (the) road these, and to the city
ἐγγιζόντων, ἀνέβη Πέτρος ἐπὶ τὸ δῶμα προσεύξασθαι, περὶ
drawing near, went up Peter on the roof to pray, about
10 ὥραν ἕκτην· ἐγένετο δὲ πρόσπεινος, καὶ ἤθελε γεύσασθαι·
hour sixth. he became And hungry, and desired to taste;
παρασκευαζόντων δὲ ἐκείνων, ἐπέπεσεν ἐπ' αὐτὸν ἔκστασις,
preparing and they fell on him an ecstasy,
11 καὶ θεωρεῖ τὸν οὐρανὸν ἀνεῳγμένον, καὶ καταβαῖνον ἐπ'
And he beholds the heaven being opened, and coming down on
αὐτὸν σκεῦός τι ὡς ὀθόνην μεγάλην, τέσσαρσιν ἀρχαῖς
him a vessel certain like a sheet great, by four corners
12 δεδεμένον, καὶ καθιέμενον ἐπὶ τῆς γῆς· ἐν ᾧ ὑπῆρχε πάντα
being bound, and let down onto the earth; in which were all
τὰ τετράποδα τῆς γῆς καὶ τὰ θηρία καὶ τὰ ἑρπετὰ καὶ τὰ
the quadrupeds of the earth, and the beasts, and the reptiles, and the
13 πετεινὰ τοῦ οὐρανοῦ. καὶ ἐγένετο φωνὴ πρὸς αὐτόν,
birds of the heaven. And came a voice to him,
14 Ἀναστάς, Πέτρε, θῦσον καὶ φάγε. ὁ δὲ Πέτρος εἶπε,
Rise up, Peter, slay and eat. — But Peter said,
Μηδαμῶς, Κύριε· ὅτι οὐδέποτε ἔφαγον πᾶν κοινὸν ἢ ἀκάθαρ-
Not at all, Lord, because never did I eat anything common or un
15 τον. καὶ φωνὴ πάλιν ἐκ δευτέρου πρὸς αὐτόν, Ἃ ὁ Θεὸς
clean. And a voice again from a second (time) to him, what things God
16 ἐκαθάρισε, σὺ μὴ κοίνου. τοῦτο δὲ ἐγένετο ἐπὶ τρίς καὶ
cleansed you not make common. this And happened on three, and
πάλιν ἀνελήφθη τὸ σκεῦος εἰς τὸν οὐρανόν.
again was taken up the vessel into the heaven.
17 Ὡς δὲ ἐν ἑαυτῷ διηπόρει ὁ Πέτρος τί ἂν εἴη τὸ ὅραμα ὃ
as And in himself was doubting Peter, what might be the vision which
εἶδε, καὶ ἰδού, οἱ ἄνδρες οἱ ἀπεσταλμένοι ἀπὸ τοῦ Κορνηλίου,
he saw, and behold, the men having been sent from Cornelius
διερωτήσαντες τὴν οἰκίαν Σίμωνος, ἐπέστησαν ἐπὶ τὸν
having asked out the house of Simon stood at the
18 πυλῶνα, καὶ φωνήσαντες ἐπυνθάνοντο εἰ Σίμων, ὁ ἐπικαλού-
porch. And calling they inquired if Simon, being

surnamed Peter is lodged *here.* [19]And as Peter pondered concerning the vision, the Spirit said to him, Three men are seeking you. [20]But rising up, go down and go with them, not having discriminated, because I have sent them. [21]And going down to the men, the ones sent from Cornelius to him, Peter said, Behold, I am *the one* you seek. What *is* the cause for which you are here? [22]And they said, Cornelius, a centurion, a just man and *one* fearing God, and being testified to by all the nation of the Jews, was divinely warned by a holy angel to call you to his house, and to hear words from you. [23]Then calling them in, he lodged *them.*

And on the morrow Peter went out with them. And some of the brothers from Joppa went out with them, accompanying him. [24]And on the morrow they entered Caesarea. And Cornelius was expecting them, having called together his relatives and *his* intimate friends. [25]And as Peter was coming in, meeting him, Cornelius fell at *his* feet *and* worshiped. [26]But Peter lifted him up, saying, Stand up! I myself am also a man. [27]And talking with him, he went in and found many having come together. [28]And he said to them, You know how unlawful it is for a man, a Jew, to unite himself or to come near to one of another race. Yet God showed to me not to call a man common or unclean.

[29]Therefore, I also came without complaint, having been sent for. Then for what reason did you send for me? [30]And Cornelius said, From *the* fourth day until this hour I have been fasting, and the ninth hour *I* was praying in my house. And, behold, a

19 μενος Πέτρος, ἐνθάδε ξενίζεται. τοῦ δὲ Πέτρου ἐνθυμουμένου
surnamed Peter, here is lodged. — And Peter pondering
περὶ τοῦ ὁράματος, εἶπεν αὐτῷ τὸ Πνεῦμα, Ἰδού, ἄνδρες
about the vision, said to him the Spirit Behold, men
20 τρεῖς ζητοῦσί σε. ἀλλὰ ἀναστὰς κατάβηθι, καὶ πορεύου σὺν
three are seeking you. But rising up, go down, and go with
αὐτοῖς, μηδὲν διακρινόμενος· διότι ἐγὼ ἀπέσταλκα αὐτούς.
them nothing discriminating, because I have sent them.
21 καταβὰς δὲ Πέτρος πρὸς τοὺς ἄνδρας τοὺς ἀπεσταλμένους ἀπὸ
going down And Peter to the men, those sent from
τοῦ Κορνηλίου πρὸς αὐτόν, εἶπεν, Ἰδού, ἐγώ εἰμι ὃν ζητεῖτε·
— Cornelius to him, said, Behold, I am whom you seek;
22 τίς ἡ αἰτία δι' ἣν πάρεστε; οἱ δὲ εἶπον, Κορνήλιος ἑκατοντάρ-
what (is) the cause for which you are here? they And said, Cornelius, a centurion
χης, ἀνὴρ δίκαιος καὶ φοβούμενος τὸν Θεόν, μαρτυρούμενός
a man just and fearing — God, being testified to
τε ὑπὸ ὅλου τοῦ ἔθνους τῶν Ἰουδαίων, ἐχρηματίσθη ὑπὸ
and by all of the nation of the Jews, was warned by
ἀγγέλου ἁγίου μεταπέμψασθαί σε εἰς τὸν οἶκον αὐτοῦ, καὶ
an angel holy to call you to the house of him, and
23 ἀκοῦσαι ῥήματα παρὰ σοῦ. εἰσκαλεσάμενος οὖν αὐτοὺς
to hear words from you. Calling in, therefore, them,
ἐξένισε.
he lodged.

Τῇ δὲ ἐπαύριον ὁ Πέτρος ἐξῆλθε σὺν αὐτοῖς, καί τινες τῶν
on the And morrow, Peter went out with them, and some of the
24 ἀδελφῶν τῶν ἀπὸ τῆς Ἰόππης συνῆλθον αὐτῷ. καὶ τῇ
brothers — from — Joppa accompanied him. And on the
ἐπαύριον εἰσῆλθον εἰς τὴν Καισάρειαν. ὁ δὲ Κορνήλιος ἦν
morrow they entered into — Caesarea. And Cornelius was
προσδοκῶν αὐτούς, συγκαλεσάμενος τοὺς συγγενεῖς αὐτοῦ
awaiting them, having called together the relatives of him
25 καὶ τοὺς ἀναγκαίους φίλους. ὡς δὲ ἐγένετο εἰσελθεῖν τὸν
and the intimate friends. when And was entering —
Πέτρον, συναντήσας αὐτῷ ὁ Κορνήλιος, πεσὼν ἐπὶ τοὺς
Peter, meeting him — Cornelius, falling at the
26 πόδας, προσεκύνησεν. ὁ δὲ Πέτρος αὐτὸν ἤγειρε λέγων,
feet worshiped. — But Peter him raised, saying,
27 Ἀνάστηθι· κἀγὼ αὐτὸς ἄνθρωπός εἰμι. καὶ συνομιλῶν αὐτῷ
Stand up; also I (my)self a man am. And talking with him
εἰσῆλθε, καὶ εὑρίσκει συνεληλυθότας πολλούς, ἔφη τε πρὸς
he entered, and finds having come together many, said and to
28 αὐτούς, Ὑμεῖς ἐπίστασθε ὡς ἀθέμιτόν ἐστιν ἀνδρὶ Ἰουδαίῳ
them, You understand how unlawful it is for a man, a Jew,
κολλᾶσθαι ἢ προσέρχεσθαι ἀλλοφύλῳ· καὶ ἐμοὶ ὁ Θεὸς
to unite with or to approach one of another race; and to me — God
ἔδειξε μηδένα κοινὸν ἢ ἀκάθαρτον λέγειν ἄνθρωπον· διὸ καὶ
showed not one common or unclean to call a man. Because of this, also
29 ἀναντιρρήτως ἦλθον μεταπεμφθείς. πυνθάνομαι οὖν, τίνι
without complaint I came, being sent for. I ask, therefore, for what
30 λόγῳ μετεπέμψασθέ με. καὶ ὁ Κορνήλιος ἔφη, Ἀπὸ τετάρτης
reason you sent for me. And Cornelius said, From fourth
ἡμέρας μέχρι ταύτης τῆς ὥρας ἤμην νηστεύων, καὶ τὴν
day until this — hour, I have been fasting, and the
ἐννάτην ὥραν προσευχόμενος ἐν τῷ οἴκῳ μου· καὶ ἰδού,
ninth hour was praying in the house of me, and behold,

man stood before me in bright clothing. [31]And *he* said, Cornelius, your prayer was heard, and your alms remembered before God. [32]Therefore, send to Joppa and call for Simon who is surnamed Peter; this one is lodged in *the* house of Simon, a tanner, by *the* sea. Having come, *he* will speak to you. [33]Then at once I sent to you; and you did well *to* come. Now, then, we are all present before God to hear all the things having been commanded you by God.

[34]And opening *his* mouth, Peter said, Truly I see that God is not a receiver of faces, [35]but in every nation the *one* fearing Him and working righteousness is acceptable to Him. [36]The word which He sent to the sons of Israel, preaching the gospel of peace through Jesus Christ. He is lord of all. [37]You know the things that happened throughout all Judea, beginning from Galilee after the baptism which John proclaimed: [38]Jesus from Nazareth, how God anointed Him with *the* Holy Spirit and with power, who went through doing good, and healing all those having been oppressed by the Devil, because God was with Him. [39]And we are witnesses of all things which He did, both in the country of the Jews, and in Jerusalem—they did away with *Him,* hanging *Him* on a tree— [40]God raised up this One the third day, and granted Him to become visible; [41]not to all the people, but to witnesses, the ones having been before hand-picked by God, to us who ate and drank with Him after His rising again from *the* dead. [42]And He commanded us to proclaim to the people, and to solemnly witness that it is He who has been marked out by God *to be* Judge of *the* living and *the* dead.

31 ἀνὴρ ἔστη ἐνώπιόν μου ἐν ἐσθῆτι λαμπρᾷ, καί φησι,
a man stood before me in clothing bright, and says,
Κορνήλιε, εἰσηκούσθη σου ἡ προσευχή, καὶ αἱ ἐλεημοσύναι
Cornelius, was listened (to) of you the prayer, and the alms
32 σου ἐμνήσθησαν ἐνώπιον τοῦ Θεοῦ. πέμψον οὖν εἰς Ἰόππην,
of you were remembered before – God. send Therefore to Joppa,
καὶ μετακάλεσαι Σίμωνα ὃς ἐπικαλεῖται Πέτρος· οὗτος ξενί-
and call for Simon who is surnamed Peter; this one is
ζεται ἐν οἰκίᾳ Σίμωνος βυρσέως παρὰ θάλασσαν· ὃς παρα-
lodged in (the) house of Simon, a tanner, by (the) sea, who having
33 γενόμενος λαλήσει σοι. Ἐξαυτῆς οὖν ἔπεμψα πρός σε· σύ τε
come will speak to you. At once, then, I sent to you; you and
καλῶς ἐποίησας παραγενόμενος. νῦν οὖν πάντες ἡμεῖς ἐνώ-
well did having come. Now, then, all we
πιον τοῦ Θεοῦ πάρεσμεν ἀκοῦσαι πάντα τὰ προστεταγμένα
before – God are present to hear all the things being commanded
34 σοι ὑπὸ τοῦ Θεοῦ. ἀνοίξας δὲ Πέτρος τὸ στόμα εἶπεν,
you by – God. opening And Peter the mouth said,
Ἐπ᾽ ἀληθείας καταλαμβάνομαι ὅτι οὐκ ἔστι προσωπολή-
On truth, I perceive that not is a receiver of
35 πτης ὁ Θεός· ἀλλ᾽ ἐν παντὶ ἔθνει ὁ φοβούμενος αὐτὸν καὶ
faces God, but in every nation he fearing Him and
36 ἐργαζόμενος δικαιοσύνην, δεκτὸς αὐτῷ ἐστι. τὸν λόγον ὃν
working righteousness acceptable to Him is. The word which
ἀπέστειλε τοῖς υἱοῖς Ἰσραήλ, εὐαγγελιζόμενος εἰρήνην διὰ
He sent to the sons of Israel, preaching the gospel peace through
37 Ἰησοῦ Χριστοῦ (οὗτός ἐστι πάντων Κύριος)—ὑμεῖς οἴδατε,
Jesus Christ; this One is of all Lord. You know
τὸ γενόμενον ῥῆμα καθ᾽ ὅλης τῆς Ἰουδαίας, ἀρξάμενον ἀπὸ
that happened the thing through all – of Judea, beginning from
τῆς Γαλιλαίας, μετὰ τὸ βάπτισμα ὃ ἐκήρυξεν Ἰωάννης·
– Galilee after the baptism which proclaimed John;
38 Ἰησοῦν τὸν ἀπὸ Ναζαρέθ, ὡς ἔχρισεν αὐτὸν ὁ Θεὸς Πνεύ-
Jesus the (One) from Nazareth, how anointed Him God with (the)
ματι Ἁγίῳ καὶ δυνάμει, ὃς διῆλθεν εὐεργετῶν καὶ ἰώμενος
Spirit Holy, and with power, who went about doing good and healing
πάντας τοὺς καταδυναστευομένους ὑπὸ τοῦ διαβόλου, ὅτι
all those having been oppressed by the Devil, because
39 ὁ Θεὸς ἦν μετ᾽ αὐτοῦ. καὶ ἡμεῖς ἐσμεν μάρτυρες πάντων ὧν
God was with Him. And we are witnesses of all things which
ἐποίησεν ἔν τε τῇ χώρᾳ τῶν Ἰουδαίων καὶ ἐν Ἱερουσαλήμ·
He did, in both the country of the Jews and in Jerusalem;
40 ὃν ἀνεῖλον κρεμάσαντες ἐπὶ ξύλου. τοῦτον ὁ Θεὸς ἤγειρε τῇ
whom they did away (with) hanging on a tree. This One God raised the
41 τρίτῃ ἡμέρᾳ, καὶ ἔδωκεν αὐτὸν ἐμφανῆ γενέσθαι, οὐ παντὶ
third day, and gave Him visible to become, not to all
τῷ λαῷ, ἀλλὰ μάρτυσι τοῖς προκεχειροτονημένοις ὑπὸ
the people, but to witnesses, those having been before hand-picked by
τοῦ Θεοῦ, ἡμιν, οἵτινες συνεφάγομεν καὶ συνεπίομεν αὐτῷ
– God, to us, who ate with and drank with Him
42 μετὰ τὸ ἀναστῆναι αὐτὸν ἐκ νεκρῶν. καὶ παρήγγειλεν
after the rising again (of) Him out of (the) dead. And He commanded
ἡμῖν κηρύξαι τῷ λαῷ, καὶ διαμαρτύρασθαι ὅτι αὐτός
us to proclaim to the people, and to solemnly witness that He
43 ἐστιν ὁ ὡρισμένος ὑπὸ τοῦ Θεοῦ κριτὴς ζώντων καὶ νεκρῶν.
it is who has been marked out by – God (as) judge of living and of dead.

[43]To this One all the prophets witness, *that* through His name everyone believing into Him *will* receive forgiveness of sins. [44]*As* Peter was yet speaking these words, the Holy Spirit fell on all those hearing the word. [45]And the faithful of *the* circumcision were amazed, as many as came with Peter, because the gift of the Holy Spirit was also poured out on the nations. [46]For they heard them speaking in languages, and magnifying God. Then Peter answered, [47]Can anyone forbid the water that these not be baptized, who the Holy Spirit received, even as we also? [48]And he commanded them to be baptized in the name of the Lord. Then they asked him to remain some days.

CHAPTER 11

[1]And the apostles and the brothers who were throughout Judea heard that the nations received the word of God. [2]And when Peter went up to Jerusalem, those of the circumcision contended with him, [3]saying, You went in to uncircumcised men, and ate with them. [4]But beginning, Peter set out to them in order, saying, [5]I was being in *the* city of Joppa, praying. And in an ecstasy, I saw a vision: a vessel *was* coming down, like a huge sheet, being let down by four corners out of the heaven; and it came as far as me. [6]Looking intently on *this,* I observed. And I saw the four-footed animals of the earth, and the wild beasts, and the creeping things, and the birds of the heaven. [7]And I heard a voice saying to me, Peter, rise up, slay and eat. [8]But I said, Not at all, Lord, because never *has* anything common or unclean entered into my mouth. [9]But a voice answered me the

τούτῳ πάντες οἱ προφῆται μαρτυροῦσιν, ἄφεσιν ἁμαρτιῶν
To this One all the prophets witness, forgiveness of sins
λαβεῖν διὰ τοῦ ὀνόματος αὐτοῦ πάντα τὸν πιστεύοντα
to receive through the name of Him everyone – believing
εἰς αὐτόν.
in Him.
44 Ἔτι λαλοῦντος τοῦ Πέτρου τὰ ῥήματα ταῦτα, ἐπέπεσε τὸ
(As) yet speaking – Peter – words these, fell the
Πνεῦμα τὸ Ἅγιον ἐπὶ πάντας τοὺς ἀκούοντας τὸν λόγον.
Spirit – Holy on all those hearing the word.
45 καὶ ἐξέστησαν οἱ ἐκ περιτομῆς πιστοί, ὅσοι συνῆλθον τῷ
And were amazed those of circumcision faithful, as many as came with –
Πέτρῳ, ὅτι καὶ ἐπὶ τὰ ἔθνη ἡ δωρεὰ τοῦ Ἁγίου Πνεύματος
Peter, because also on the nations the gift of the Holy Spirit
46 ἐκκέχυται. ἤκουον γὰρ αὐτῶν λαλούντων γλώσσαις, καὶ
was poured out. they heard For them speaking in languages, and
μεγαλυνόντων τὸν Θεόν. τότε ἀπεκρίθη ὁ Πέτρος, Μήτι
magnifying – God. Then answered – Peter, Not
47 τὸ ὕδωρ κωλῦσαι δύναταί τις, τοῦ μὴ βαπτισθῆναι τούτους,
the water forbid can anyone, – not to be baptized these,
οἵτινες τὸ Πνεῦμα τὸ Ἅγιον ἔλαβον καθὼς καὶ ἡμεῖς; προσ-
who the Spirit – Holy received even as also we? he com-
48 έταξέ τε αὐτοὺς βαπτισθῆναι ἐν τῷ ὀνόματι τοῦ Κυρίου.
manded. And them to be baptized in the name of the Lord.
τότε ἠρώτησαν αὐτὸν ἐπιμεῖναι ἡμέρας τινάς.
Then they asked him to remain days some.

CHAPTER 11

1 Ἤκουσαν δὲ οἱ ἀπόστολοι καὶ οἱ ἀδελφοὶ οἱ ὄντες κατὰ
heard And the apostles and the brothers – being throughout
τὴν Ἰουδαίαν ὅτι καὶ τὰ ἔθνη ἐδέξαντο τὸν λόγον τοῦ Θεοῦ.
– Judea that also the nations received the word – of God.
2 καὶ ὅτε ἀνέβη Πέτρος εἰς Ἱεροσόλυμα, διεκρίνοντο πρὸς αὐτὸν
And when went Peter to Jerusalem, disputed with him
3 οἱ ἐκ περιτομῆς, λέγοντες ὅτι Πρὸς ἄνδρας ἀκροβυστίαν
those of circumcision, saying, – To men uncircumcision
4 ἔχοντας εἰσῆλθες, καὶ συνέφαγες αὐτοῖς. ἀρξάμενος δὲ ὁ
having you went in, and you ate with them. beginning And,
5 Πέτρος ἐξετίθετο αὐτοῖς καθεξῆς λέγων, Ἐγὼ ἤμην ἐν πόλει
Peter explained to them in order, saying, I was being in (the) city
Ἰόππῃ προσευχόμενος, καὶ εἶδον ἐν ἐκστάσει ὅραμα, κατα-
of Joppa praying, and I saw in an ecstasy a vision, coming
βαῖνον σκεῦός τι, ὡς ὀθόνην μεγάλην τέσσαρσιν ἀρχαῖς
down a vessel certain, as a sheet great by four corners
6 καθιεμένην ἐκ τοῦ οὐρανοῦ, καὶ ἦλθεν ἄχρις ἐμοῦ· εἰς ἣν
being let down out of the heaven, and it came to me; into which
ἀτενίσας κατενόουν, καὶ εἶδον τὰ τετράποδα τῆς γῆς καὶ
gazing I perceived, and I saw the quadrupeds of the earth, and
7 τὰ θηρία καὶ τὰ ἑρπετὰ καὶ τὰ πετεινὰ τοῦ οὐρανοῦ. ἤκουσα
the beasts, and the reptiles, and the birds of the heaven. I heard
δὲ φωνῆς λεγούσης μοι, Ἀναστάς, Πέτρε, θῦσον καὶ φάγε.
And a voice saying to me, Rise up, Peter; slay and eat.
8 εἶπον δέ, Μηδαμῶς, Κύριε· ὅτι πᾶν κοινὸν ἢ ἀκάθαρτον
I said And, Not at all, Lord, because anything common or unclean
9 οὐδέποτε εἰσῆλθεν εἰς τὸ στόμα μου. ἀπεκρίθη δέ μοι φωνὴ
never entered into the mouth of me. answered And me a voice

second *time* out of the heaven. What God has cleansed, you do not make common. [10]And this took place three *times;* and all things were again pulled up into the heaven again. [11]And, behold, three men stood at the house in which I was, having been sent from Caesarea to me. [12]And the Spirit said to me to go with them, not discriminating. And these six brothers also went with me, and we went into the man's house. [13]And he told us how he saw an angel in his house, standing and saying to him, Send men to Joppa, and send for Simon who is surnamed Peter, [14]who will speak words to you by which you and all your household will be saved. [15]And in my beginning to speak, the Holy Spirit fell on them, even as also on us in *the* beginning. [16]And I recalled the word of *the* Lord, how He said, John indeed baptized with water, but you shall be baptized in *the* Holy Spirit. [17]Then if God gave the same gift to them as also to us, having believed on the Lord Jesus Christ, and I, who was I *to be* able to prevent God? [18]And hearing these things, they kept silent, and glorified God, saying, Then truly God has granted repentance unto life to the nations also.

[19]Then, indeed, they who were scattered by the oppression taking place over Stephen passed through to Phoenicia and Cyprus and Antioch, speaking the word to no one except only to Jews. [20]But some men from them, Cypriots and Cyrenians, who had come to Antioch, spoke to the Hellenists, preaching the gospel of the Lord Jesus. [21]And *the* hand of *the* Lord was with them, and a great number believing, *they* turned to the Lord. [22]And the word was heard in the ears of the

ἐκ δευτέρου ἐκ τοῦ οὐρανοῦ, Ἃ ὁ Θεὸς ἐκαθάρισε, σὺ μὴ
a second (time) out of — Heaven, What God has cleansed, you not
10 κοίνου. τοῦτο δὲ ἐγένετο ἐπὶ τρίς, καὶ πάλιν ἀνεσπάσθη
make common. this And happened on three, and again were pulled up
11 ἅπαντα εἰς τὸν οὐρανόν. καὶ ἰδού, ἐξαυτῆς τρεῖς ἄνδρες
all things into — Heaven. And, behold, at once three men
ἐπέστησαν ἐπὶ τὴν οἰκίαν ἐν ᾗ ἤμην, ἀπεσταλμένοι ἀπὸ
stood at the house in which I was, having been sent from
12 Καισαρείας πρός με. εἶπε δέ μοι τὸ Πνεῦμα συνελθεῖν αὐτοῖς,
Caesarea to me. said And to me the Spirit to go with them,
μηδὲν διακρινόμενον. ἦλθον δὲ σὺν ἐμοὶ καὶ οἱ ἓξ ἀδελφοὶ
nothing discriminating. came And with me also — six brothers
οὗτοι, καὶ εἰσήλθομεν εἰς τὸν οἶκον τοῦ ἀνδρός· ἀπήγγειλέ
these, and we entered into the house of the man. he reported
13 τε ἡμῖν πῶς εἶδε τὸν ἄγγελον ἐν τῷ οἴκῳ αὐτοῦ σταθέντα,
And to us how he saw the angel in the house of him standing,
καὶ εἰπόντα αὐτῷ, Ἀπόστειλον εἰς Ἰόππην ἄνδρας, καὶ
and saying to him, Send forth to Joppa men, and
14 μετάπεμψαι Σίμωνα, τὸν ἐπικαλούμενον Πέτρον, ὃς λαλήσει
send for Simon, the (one) surnamed Peter, who will speak
ῥήματα πρός σε, ἐν οἷς σωθήσῃ σὺ καὶ πᾶς ὁ οἶκός σου.
words to you, by which will be saved you and all the house of you.
15 ἐν δὲ τῷ ἄρξασθαί με λαλεῖν, ἐπέπεσε τὸ Πνεῦμα τὸ Ἅγιον
in And beginning me to speak, fell the Spirit — Holy
16 ἐπ' αὐτούς, ὥσπερ καὶ ἐφ' ἡμᾶς ἐν ἀρχῇ. ἐμνήσθην δὲ τοῦ
on them, as also on us at first. I remembered And the
ῥήματος Κυρίου, ὡς ἔλεγεν, Ἰωάννης μεν ἐβάπτισεν ὕδατι,
word of (the) Lord, how He said, John indeed baptized with water,
17 ὑμεῖς δὲ βαπτισθήσεσθε ἐν Πνεύματι Ἁγίῳ. εἰ οὖν τὴν ἴσην
you but will be baptized in (the) Spirit Holy. If, then, the same
δωρεὰν ἔδωκεν αὐτοῖς ὁ Θεὸς ὡς καὶ ἡμῖν, πιστεύσασιν ἐπὶ
gift gave them God, as also to us, having believed on
τὸν Κύριον Ἰησοῦν Χριστόν, ἐγὼ δὲ τίς ἤμην δυνατὸς
the Lord Jesus Christ I, and who was able
18 κωλῦσαι τὸν Θεόν; ἀκούσαντες δὲ ταῦτα ἡσύχασαν, καὶ
to prevent God? hearing And these things, they kept silent, and
ἐδόξαζον τὸν Θεόν, λέγοντες, Ἄραγε καὶ τοῖς ἔθνεσιν ὁ Θεὸς
glorified God, saying, Then also to the nations God
τὴν μετάνοιαν ἔδωκεν εἰς ζωήν.
— repentance has given unto life.

19 Οἱ μὲν οὖν διασπαρέντες ἀπὸ τῆς θλίψεως τῆς γενομένης
they indeed Then who were scattered from the affliction — occurring
ἐπὶ Στεφάνῳ διῆλθον ἕως Φοινίκης καὶ Κύπρου καὶ
over Stephen passed through to Phoenicia and Cyprus and
Ἀντιοχείας, μηδενὶ λαλοῦντες τὸν λόγον εἰ μὴ μόνον
Antioch, to no one speaking the word except only
20 Ἰουδαίοις. ἦσαν δέ τινες ἐξ αὐτῶν ἄνδρες Κύπριοι καὶ Κυρη-
to Jews. were But some of them men, Cypriots and Cyren-
ναῖοι, οἵτινες εἰσελθόντες εἰς Ἀντιόχειαν, ἐλάλουν πρὸς τοὺς
ians, who coming to Antioch spoke to the
21 Ἑλληνιστάς, εὐαγγελιζόμενοι τὸν Κύριον Ἰησοῦν. καὶ ἦν
Hellenists, preaching the gospel of the Lord Jesus. And was
χεὶρ Κυρίου μετ' αὐτῶν· πολύς τε ἀριθμὸς πιστεύσας ἐπέ-
hand (the) Lord's with them, a much and number, believing
22 στρεψεν ἐπὶ τὸν Κύριον. ἠκούσθη δὲ ὁ λόγος εἰς τὰ ὦτα τῆς
turned upon the Lord. was heard And the word into the ears of the

church in Jerusalem con-
cerning them. And they sent
out Barnabas to go through
as far as Antioch; 23 who
having come, and seeing
the grace of God, rejoiced.
And *he* exhorted all with
purpose of heart to abide
near the Lord. 24 For he
was a good man, and full of
the Holy Spirit, and of faith.
And a considerable crowd
was added to the Lord.
25 And Barnabas went out to
Tarsus to seek Saul. 26 And
finding him, he brought him
to Antioch. And it happened
that *many* of them were
gathered to them in the
church a whole year. And
they taught a considerable
crowd. And the disciples
were first called Christians
at Antioch.
27 And in these days
prophets came down from
Jerusalem to Antioch. 28 And
one of them named Agabus
rising up, *he* signified
through the Spirit that a
great famine was about to
be over all the habitable
earth—which also happen-
ed on Claudius Caesar's *time*.
29 And according as any was
prospered, each of the
disciples determined to send
to those living in Judea to
minister *to them*; 30 which
they also did, sending to the
elders through *the* hand of
Barnabas and Saul.

CHAPTER 12

1 And at that time Herod
the king threw on the hands
to oppress some of the
church. 2 And he did away
with James the brother of
John, with a sword. 3 And
seeing that it was pleasing to
the Jews, he added also to
seize Peter–and they were
days of unleavened *bread*–
4 also capturing *him*, he put
him into prison, delivering to
four sets of four soldiers to
guard him; intending to bring
him up to the people after the
Passover. 5 Then Peter was
indeed kept in the prison; but

ἐκκλησίας τῆς ἐν Ἱεροσολύμοις περὶ αὐτῶν· καὶ ἐξαπέστειλαν
church — in Jerusalem about them; and they sent forth
23 Βαρνάβαν διελθεῖν ἕως Ἀντιοχείας· ὃς παραγενόμενος καὶ
Barnabas to go through to Antioch; who having come and
ἰδὼν τὴν χάριν τοῦ Θεοῦ ἐχάρη, καὶ παρεκάλει πάντας τῇ
seeing the grace of God rejoiced, and exhorted all —
24 προθέσει τῆς καρδίας προσμένειν τῷ Κυρίῳ· ὅτι ἦν ἀνὴρ
with purpose — of heart to remain near the Lord; for he was a man
ἀγαθὸς καὶ πλήρης Πνεύματος Ἁγίου καὶ πίστεως· καὶ
good, and full of (the) Spirit Holy and of faith. And
25 προσετέθη ὄχλος ἱκανὸς τῷ Κυρίῳ. ἐξῆλθε δὲ εἰς Ταρσὸν ὁ
was added a crowd considerable to the Lord. went And to Tarsus
26 Βαρνάβας ἀναζητῆσαι Σαῦλον, καὶ εὑρὼν αὐτὸν ἤγαγεν
Barnabas to seek Saul, and finding him he led
αὐτὸν εἰς Ἀντιόχειαν. ἐγένετο δὲ αὐτοὺς ἐνιαυτὸν ὅλον
him to Antioch. it was And, to them a year whole
συναχθῆναι ἐν τῇ ἐκκλησίᾳ καὶ διδάξαι ὄχλον ἱκανόν, χρη-
were assembled in the church, and taught a crowd considerable,
ματίσαι τε πρῶτον ἐν Ἀντιοχείᾳ τοὺς μαθητὰς Χριστιανούς.
were called and (at) first Antioch the disciples Christians.
27 Ἐν ταύταις δὲ ταῖς ἡμέραις κατῆλθον ἀπὸ Ἱεροσολύμων
in these And — days came down from Jerusalem
28 προφῆται εἰς Ἀντιόχειαν. ἀναστὰς δὲ εἷς ἐξ αὐτῶν ὀνόματι
prophets to Antioch. having risen And one of them by name
Ἄγαβος, ἐσήμανε διὰ τοῦ Πνεύματος λιμὸν μέγαν μέλλειν
Agabus signified through the Spirit a famine great to be about
ἔσεσθαι ἐφ' ὅλην τὴν οἰκουμένην· ὅστις καὶ ἐγένετο ἐπὶ
to be over all the inhabited earth; which also happened on
29 Κλαυδίου Καίσαρος. τῶν δὲ μαθητῶν καθὼς ηὐπορεῖτό τις,
(the time) of Claudius Caesar. the And disciples, as was prospered any,
ὥρισαν ἕκαστος αὐτῶν εἰς διακονίαν πέμψαι τοῖς κατοι-
determined each of them for ministration to send to those
30 κοῦσιν ἐν τῇ Ἰουδαίᾳ ἀδελφοῖς· ὃ καὶ ἐποίησαν, ἀποστεί-
living in — Judea brothers; which also they did, sending
λαντες πρὸς τοὺς πρεσβυτέρους διὰ χειρὸς Βαρνάβα καὶ
to the elders through (the) hand of Barnabas and
Σαύλου.
of Saul.

CHAPTER 12

1 Κατ' ἐκεῖνον δὲ τὸν καιρὸν ἐπέβαλεν Ἡρώδης ὁ βασιλεὺς
at that And — time threw on Herod the king
2 τὰς χεῖρας κακῶσαί τινας τῶν ἀπὸ τῆς ἐκκλησίας. ἀνεῖλε δὲ
the hands to oppress some of those from the church. he did away And
3 Ἰάκωβον τὸν ἀδελφὸν Ἰωάννου μαχαίρᾳ. καὶ ἰδὼν ὅτι ἀρε-
James the brother of John with a sword. And seeing that
στόν ἐστι τοῖς Ἰουδαίοις, προσέθετο συλλαβεῖν καὶ Πέτρον·
pleasing is to the Jews, he added to seize also Peter;
4 ἦσαν δὲ ἡμέραι τῶν ἀζύμων· ὃν καὶ πιάσας ἔθετο εἰς φυλακήν,
were and days — of unleaven whom also capturing, he put in prison,
παραδοὺς τέσσαρσι τετραδίοις στρατιωτῶν φυλάσσειν
delivering to four quaternions of soldiers to guard
αὐτόν, βουλόμενος μετὰ τὸ πάσχα ἀναγαγεῖν αὐτὸν τῷ
him; intending after the Passover to lead up him to the
5 λαῷ. ὁ μὲν οὖν Πέτρος ἐτηρεῖτο ἐν τῇ φυλακῇ· προσευχὴ
people. Therefore Peter was kept in the prison; prayer

fervent prayer was made by the church to God on his behalf. [6]But when Herod was about to bring him out, in that night Peter was sleeping between two soldiers, bound with two chains, also guards were keeping the prison before the door. [7]And, behold, an angel of *the* Lord stood by, and a light shone in the building. And striking Peter's side, he raised him up, saying, Rise up in haste! And the chains fell off from his hands. [8]And the angel said to him, Gird yourself, and put on your sandals. And he did so. And he said to him, Throw around your garment, and follow me. [9]And going out, he followed him, and did not know that this happening through the angel was real; but he thought he saw a vision. [10]And going through a first and a second guard, they came on the iron gate carrying *one* into the city, which opened to them of itself. And going out, they went on one street; and instantly the angel withdrew from him. [11]And having come , Peter said within himself, Now I know truly that *the* Lord sent out His angel and plucked me out of Herod's hand, and *out* of all the expectation of the people of the Jews. [12]And considering, he came to the house of Mary the mother of John, the *one* being surnamed Mark, where many were gathered together, and praying. [13]And Peter having knocked *at* the door of the porch, a servant-girl named Rhoda came near to listen. [14]And recognizing Peter's voice, from joy she did not open the porch, but running in she reported Peter *was* standing before the porch. [15]But they said to her, You are raving. But she insisted it was so. And they said, It is his angel. [16]But Peter

δὲ ἦν ἐκτενὴς γινομένη ὑπὸ τῆς ἐκκλησίας πρὸς τὸν Θεὸν
But was earnestly being made by the church to — God

6 ὑπὲρ αὐτοῦ. ὅτε δὲ ἔμελλεν αὐτὸν προάγειν ὁ Ἡρώδης, τῇ
about him. when And was about him to lead forth — Herod, —

νυκτὶ ἐκείνῃ ἦν ὁ Πέτρος κοιμώμενος μεταξὺ δύο στρατιω-
in night that was Peter sleeping between two soldiers,

τῶν, δεδεμένος ἁλύσεσι δυσί· φύλακές τε πρὸ τῆς θύρας
having been bound with chains two; guards and before the door

7 ἐτήρουν τὴν φυλακήν. καὶ ἰδού, ἄγγελος Κυρίου ἐπέστη, καὶ
were keeping the prison. And behold, an angel of (the) Lord stood by, and

φῶς ἔλαμψεν ἐν τῷ οἰκήματι· πατάξας δὲ τὴν πλευρὰν τοῦ
a light shone in the building; striking and the side —

Πέτρου, ἤγειρεν αὐτὸν λέγων, Ἀνάστα ἐν τάχει. καὶ ἐξέπεσον
of Peter, he raised him, saying, Rise up in haste. And fell off

8 αὐτοῦ αἱ ἁλύσεις ἐκ τῶν χειρῶν. εἶπέ τε ὁ ἄγγελος πρὸς
of him the chains from the hands. said And the angel to

αὐτόν, Περίζωσαι καὶ ὑπόδησαι τὰ σανδάλιά σου. ἐποίησε
him, Gird yourself, and put on the sandals of you. he did

δὲ οὕτω. καὶ λέγει αὐτῷ, Περιβαλοῦ τὸ ἱμάτιόν σου, καὶ
And so. And he says to him, Throw around the garment of you, and

9 ἀκολούθει μοι. καὶ ἐξελθὼν ἠκολούθει αὐτῷ· καὶ οὐκ ᾔδει ὅτι
follow me. And going out he followed him, and not knew that

ἀληθές ἐστι τὸ γινόμενον διὰ τοῦ ἀγγέλου, ἐδόκει δὲ ὅραμα
true was that happening through the angel; he thought but a vision

10 βλέπειν. διελθόντες δὲ πρώτην φυλακὴν καὶ δευτέραν, ἦλθον
to see. going through And (the) first guard and (the) second, they came

ἐπὶ τὴν πύλην τὴν σιδηρᾶν, τὴν φέρουσαν εἰς τὴν πόλιν,
on the gate — iron — carrying (one) to the city,

ἥτις αὐτομάτη ἠνοίχθη αὐτοῖς· καὶ ἐξελθόντες προῆλθον
which of itself was opened to them; and going out they went on

11 ῥύμην μίαν, καὶ εὐθέως ἀπέστη ὁ ἄγγελος ἀπ' αὐτοῦ. καὶ ὁ
street one; and instantly withdrew the angel from him. And

Πέτρος, γενόμενος ἐν ἑαυτῷ, εἶπε, Νῦν οἶδα ἀληθῶς ὅτι
Peter having come within himself said, Now I know truly that

ἐξαπέστειλε Κύριος τὸν ἄγγελον αὐτοῦ, καὶ ἐξείλετό με ἐκ
sent out (the) Lord the angel of Him, and plucked me out of

χειρὸς Ἡρώδου καὶ πάσης τῆς προσδοκίας τοῦ λαοῦ τῶν
hand Herod's, and of all the expectation of the people of the

12 Ἰουδαίων. συνιδών τε ἦλθεν ἐπὶ τὴν οἰκίαν Μαρίας τῆς
Jews. considering And he came to the house of Mary the

μητρὸς Ἰωάννου τοῦ ἐπικαλουμένου Μάρκου, οὗ ἦσαν
mother of John, — surnamed Mark, where were

13 ἱκανοὶ συνηθροισμένοι καὶ προσευχόμενοι. κρούσαντος δὲ
many gathered together and praying. knocking And

τοῦ Πέτρου τὴν θύραν τοῦ πυλῶνος, προσῆλθε παιδίσκη
— Peter (at) the door of the porch, came near a maidservant

14 ὑπακοῦσαι, ὀνόματι Ῥόδη. καὶ ἐπιγνοῦσα τὴν φωνὴν τοῦ
to listen, by name, Rhoda. And recognizing the voice —

Πέτρου, ἀπὸ τῆς χαρᾶς οὐκ ἤνοιξε τὸν πυλῶνα, εἰσδραμοῦσα
of Peter, from — joy not she opened the porch, running

15 δὲ ἀπήγγειλεν ἑστάναι τὸν Πέτρον πρὸ τοῦ πυλῶνος. οἱ δὲ
but reported to stand — Peter before the porch. they But

πρὸς αὐτὴν εἶπον, Μαίνῃ. ἡ δὲ διϊσχυρίζετο οὕτως ἔχειν.
to her said, You are raving. she But insisted so (it) to hold.

16 οἱ δ' ἔλεγον, Ὁ ἄγγελος αὐτοῦ ἐστιν. ὁ δὲ Πέτρος ἐπέμενε
they And said, The angel of him it is. But Peter continued

continued knocking. And opening, they saw him, and were amazed. 17 And signaling to them with the hand to be silent, he told them how the Lord led him out of the prison. And he said, Report these things to James and the brothers. And going out, he went to another place. 18 And day having come, there was not a little disturbance among the soldiers, *saying*, What, then, became of Peter? 19 And searching for him, and not finding, examining the guards, Herod commanded *them* to be led away. And going down from Judea to Caesarea, *he* stayed.

20 And Herod was in bitter hostility with *the* Tyrians and Sidonians. But they with one passion came to him. And persuading Blastus, the *one* over the king's bedroom, they begged peace—because their country was fed from the royal *bounty*. 21 And on a set day, having been clothed in a regal garment, and sitting on the tribunal, Herod made a speech to them. 22 And the mass *of people* cried out, *The* voice of a god, and not of a man! 23 And instantly an angel of *the* Lord struck him, because he did not give the glory to God. And being eaten by worms, his soul went out.

24 But the word of God grew and increased.

25 And Barnabas and Saul returned from Jerusalem, having fulfilled the service, and having taken John with *them*, the *one* surnamed Mark.

CHAPTER 13

1 And in Antioch some among the existing church *were* prophets and teachers: both Barnabas and Simeon, he being called Niger, and Lucius the Cyrenian; and Manaen *the* foster-brother of Herod the tetrarch; and Saul. 2 And *while* they *were* doing service to the Lord, and fasting, the Holy

κρούων· ἀνοίξαντες δὲ εἶδον αὐτόν, καὶ ἐξέστησαν. κατα-
knocking; having opened and they saw him, and were amazed.

17 σείσας δὲ αὐτοῖς τῇ χειρὶ σιγᾶν, διηγήσατο αὐτοῖς πῶς ὁ
signaling And to them with the hand to be silent, he told them how the

Κύριος αὐτὸν ἐξήγαγεν ἐκ τῆς φυλακῆς. εἶπε δέ, Ἀπαγγεί-
Lord him led out from the prison. he said And, Report

λατε Ἰακώβῳ καὶ τοῖς ἀδελφοῖς ταῦτα. καὶ ἐξελθὼν ἐπορεύθη
to James and the brothers these things. And going out, he went

18 εἰς ἕτερον τόπον. γενομένης δὲ ἡμέρας, ἦν τάραχος οὐκ
to another place. becoming And day, there was disturbance not

ὀλίγος ἐν τοῖς στρατιώταις, τί ἄρα ὁ Πέτρος ἐγένετο.
a little among the soldiers: what then (of) Peter became?

19 Ἡρώδης δὲ ἐπιζητήσας αὐτὸν καὶ μὴ εὑρών, ἀνακρίνας
Herod And searching for him, and not finding, examining

τοὺς φύλακας, ἐκέλευσεν ἀπαχθῆναι. καὶ κατελθὼν ἀπὸ τῆς
the guards, commanded to be led away; and going down from —

Ἰουδαίας εἰς τὴν Καισάρειαν διέτριβεν.
Judea to — Caesarea stayed.

20 Ἦν δὲ ὁ Ἡρώδης θυμομαχῶν Τυρίοις καὶ Σιδωνίοις·
was And Herod in bitter hostility with Tyrians and Sidonians;

ὁμοθυμαδὸν δὲ παρῆσαν πρὸς αὐτόν, καὶ πείσαντες Βλάστον
with one mind and they came to him, and persuading Blastus,

τὸν ἐπὶ τοῦ κοιτῶνος τοῦ βασιλέως, ᾐτοῦντο εἰρήνην, διὰ τὸ
the (one) over the bedroom of the king, they asked peace, because the

21 τρέφεσθαι αὐτῶν τὴν χώραν ἀπὸ τῆς βασιλικῆς. τακτῇ δὲ
feeding of them the country from the royal (bounty). on a set And

ἡμέρᾳ ὁ Ἡρώδης ἐνδυσάμενος ἐσθῆτα βασιλικήν, καὶ καθίσας
day, Herod being clothed in a garment regal, and sitting

22 ἐπὶ τοῦ βήματος, ἐδημηγόρει πρὸς αὐτούς· ὁ δὲ δῆμος
on the tribunal, made a speech to them. the And mass

23 ἐπεφώνει, Θεοῦ φωνὴ καὶ οὐκ ἀνθρώπου. παραχρῆμα δὲ
cried out, of a god A voice, and not of a man! immediately And

ἐπάταξεν αὐτὸν ἄγγελος Κυρίου, ἀνθ᾽ ὧν οὐκ ἔδωκε τὴν
struck him an angel of (the) Lord, because not he gave the

δόξαν τῷ Θεῷ· καὶ γενόμενος σκωληκόβρωτος, ἐξέψυξεν.
glory — to God. And becoming eaten by worms, his soul went out.

24 Ὁ δὲ λόγος τοῦ Θεοῦ ηὔξανε καὶ ἐπληθύνετο.
the But word — of God grew and increased.

25 Βαρνάβας δὲ καὶ Σαῦλος ὑπέστρεψαν ἐξ Ἱερουσαλήμ,
Barnabas And and Saul returned out of Jerusalem

πληρώσαντες τὴν διακονίαν, συμπαραλαβόντες καὶ Ἰωάννην
having fulfilled the service, having taken with (them) and John,

τὸν ἐπικληθέντα Μάρκον.
— being surnamed Mark.

CHAPTER 13

1 Ἦσαν δέ τινες ἐν Ἀντιοχείᾳ κατὰ τὴν οὖσαν ἐκκλησίαν
were And some in Antioch among the existing church

προφῆται καὶ διδάσκαλοι, ὅ τε Βαρνάβας καὶ Συμεὼν ὁ
prophets and teachers. Both Barnabas and Simeon, he

καλούμενος Νίγερ, καὶ Λούκιος ὁ Κυρηναῖος, Μαναήν τε
being called Niger, and Lucius the Cyrenian, Manaen and

2 Ἡρώδου τοῦ τετράρχου σύντροφος, καὶ Σαῦλος. λειτουρ-
of Herod the tetrarch foster-brother, and Saul. (while) doing service

γούντων δὲ αὐτῶν τῷ Κυρίῳ καὶ νηστευόντων, εἶπε τὸ
And they to the Lord, and fasting, said the

Spirit said, So, then, separate both Barnabas and Saul to Me, for the work to which I have called them.
[3]Then, having fasted and prayed, and placing hands on them, they let *them* go.

[4]Then these indeed sent out by the Holy Spirit went down to Seleucia, and from there sailed away to Cyprus. [5]And having been in Salamis, they announced the word of God in the synagogues of the Jews. And they also had John *as* a helper. [6]And passing through the island as far as Paphos, they found a certain conjurer, a false prophet, a Jew whose name *was* Barjesus. [7]*He* was with the proconsul, Sergius Paulus, an intelligent man. This one having called Barnabas and Saul to *him*, *he* sought to hear the word of God. [8]But Elymas, the conjurer—for so his name was translated—withstood them, seeking to turn the proconsul away from the faith. [9]But Saul, who *is* also Paul, being filled with *the* Holy Spirit, and looking intently on him, [10]*he* said, O son of the Devil, full of all guile and of all cunning, enemy of all righteousness, will you not stop perverting the right ways of *the* Lord? [11]And now, behold, *the* hand of the Lord *is* on you, and you will be blind, not seeing the sun until a time. And instantly a mist and darkness fell on him; and going about he sought *some to* lead *him* by the hand. [12]Then seeing the thing happening, the proconsul believed, having been astounded at the teaching of the Lord.
[13]And putting out from Paphos *with* those around *him*, Paul came to Perga of Pamphylia. And separating from them, John returned to Jerusalem. [14]But going through from Perga, they came to Antioch-Pisidia, and

Πνεῦμα τὸ Ἅγιον, Ἀφορίσατε δή μοι τόν τε Βαρνάβαν καὶ
Spirit — Holy, separate So then to me — both Barnabas and
3 τὸν Σαῦλον εἰς τὸ ἔργον ὃ προσκέκλημαι αὐτούς. τότε νηστεύ-
Saul for the work to which I have called them. Then having
σαντες καὶ προσευξάμενοι καὶ ἐπιθέντες τὰς χεῖρας αὐτοῖς,
fasted and having prayed, and placing on the hands to them,
ἀπέλυσαν.
they let (them) go.
4 Οὗτοι μὲν οὖν, ἐκπεμφθέντες ὑπὸ τοῦ Πνεύματος τοῦ
These indeed therefore sent out by the Spirit —
Ἁγίου, κατῆλθον εἰς τὴν Σελεύκειαν, ἐκεῖθέν τε ἀπέπλευσαν
Holy went down to — Seleucia, from there sailed away
5 εἰς τὴν Κύπρον. καὶ γενόμενοι ἐν Σαλαμῖνι, κατήγγελλον τὸν
to — Cyprus. And being in Salamis, they announced the
λόγον τοῦ Θεοῦ ἐν ταῖς συναγωγαῖς τῶν Ἰουδαίων· εἶχον δὲ
word — of God in the synagogues of the Jews. they had And
5 καὶ Ἰωάννην ὑπηρέτην. διελθόντες δὲ τὴν νῆσον ἄχρι
also John (as) assistant. passing through And the island as far as
Πάφου, εὗρόν τινα μάγον ψευδοπροφήτην Ἰουδαῖον, ᾧ
Paphos, they found a certain conjurer, a false prophet, a Jew, whose
7 ὄνομα Βαριησοῦς, ὃς ἦν σὺν τῷ ἀνθυπάτῳ Σεργίῳ Παύλῳ,
name (was) Barjesus, who was with the Proconsul, Sergius Paulus,
ἀνδρὶ συνετῷ. οὗτος προσκαλεσάμενος Βαρνάβαν καὶ
a man intelligent. This one calling to (him) Barnabas and
Σαῦλον ἐπεζήτησεν ἀκοῦσαι τὸν λόγον τοῦ Θεοῦ. ἀνθίστατο
Saul sought to hear the word — of God. withstood
8 δὲ αὐτοῖς Ἐλύμας, ὁ μάγος (οὕτω γὰρ μεθερμηνεύεται τὸ
But them Elymas, the conjurer, so for was translated the
ὄνομα αὐτοῦ), ζητῶν διαστρέψαι τὸν ἀνθύπατον ἀπὸ τῆς
name of him — seeking to turn away the Proconsul from the
9 πίστεως. Σαῦλος δέ, ὁ καὶ Παῦλος, πλησθεὶς Πνεύματος
faith. Saul But, who also (is) Paul, being filled with (the) Spirit
10 Ἁγίου, καὶ ἀτενίσας εἰς αὐτὸν εἶπεν, Ὦ πλήρης παντὸς
Holy, and looking intently on him said, O full of all
δόλου καὶ πάσης ῥᾳδιουργίας, υἱὲ διαβόλου, ἐχθρὲ πάσης
deceit, and of all cunning, son of (the) Devil, enemy of all
δικαιοσύνης, οὐ παύσῃ διαστρέφων τὰς ὁδοὺς Κυρίου τὰς
righteousness, not will you cease turning away the ways of (the) Lord —
11 εὐθείας; καὶ νῦν ἰδού, χεὶρ τοῦ Κυρίου ἐπὶ σέ, καὶ ἔσῃ τυφλός,
right? And now behold, hand the Lord's on you, and you will be blind,
μὴ βλέπων τὸν ἥλιον ἄχρι καιροῦ. παραχρῆμα δὲ ἐπέπεσεν
not seeing the sun until a time. instantly And fell
ἐπ' αὐτὸν ἀχλὺς καὶ σκότος, καὶ περιάγων ἐζήτει χειραγω-
on him a mist and darkness, and going about he sought leaders by
12 γούς. τότε ἰδὼν ὁ ἀνθύπατος τὸ γεγονὸς ἐπίστευσεν,
the hand. Then seeing the Proconsul the thing having occurred believed,
ἐκπλησσόμενος ἐπὶ τῇ διδαχῇ τοῦ Κυρίου.
being astounded at the teaching of the Lord.
13 Ἀναχθέντες δὲ ἀπὸ τῆς Πάφου οἱ περὶ τὸν Παῦλον ἦλθον
having put out And from — Paphos those around — Paul came
εἰς Πέργην τῆς Παμφυλίας. Ἰωάννης δὲ ἀποχωρήσας ἀπ'
to Perga — of Pamphylia. John And having separated from
14 αὐτῶν ὑπέστρεψεν εἰς Ἱεροσόλυμα. αὐτοὶ δὲ διελθόντες ἀπὸ
them returned to Jerusalem. they And going through from
τῆς Πέργης, παρεγένοντο εἰς Ἀντιόχειαν τῆς Πισιδίας, καὶ
— Perga arrived in Antioch the Pisidian. And

going into the synagogue on the day of the sabbaths, they sat down. [15]And after the reading of the Law, and of the Prophets, the synagogue rulers sent to them, saying, Men, brothers, if there is a word of exhortation to the people, speak.

[16]And rising up, and signaling with his hand, Paul said:

Men, Israelites, and those fearing God, listen. [17]The God of this people Israel chose out our fathers, and exalted the people in *their* stay in *the* land *of* Egypt. And with a high arm, He led them out of it. [18]And as forty years time *passed*, He endured them in the wilderness. [19]And *He* pulled down seven nations in Canaan land *and* gave their land to them as an inheritance.

[20]And after these things, as four hundred and fifty years *passed*, He gave judges until Samuel the prophet. [21]And then they asked for a king. And God gave Saul the son of Kish to them, a man of *the* tribe of Benjamin, *for* forty years. [22]And removing him, He raised up to them David for a king, to whom He also said, witnessing, "I found David the *son* of Jesse *to be* a man according to My *own* heart, who will do all My will." [23]Of the seed of this one, according to promise, God raised up to Israel a Savior, Jesus; [24]John having before proclaimed a baptism of repentance to all the people of Israel before *the* face of His entrance. [25]And as John fulfilled his course, he said, Whom do you suppose me to be? I am not *He*, but, behold, He comes after me, of whom I am not worthy to loosen the sandal of *His* feet. [26]Men, brothers, sons of *the* race of Abraham, and the ones among you fearing God, to you the word of this salvation was sent. [27]For those dwelling in Jerusalem, and

εἰσελθόντες εἰς τὴν συναγωγὴν τῇ ἡμέρᾳ τῶν σαββάτων,
going into the synagogue on the day of the sabbaths
15 ἐκάθισαν. μετὰ δὲ τὴν ἀνάγνωσιν τοῦ νόμου καὶ τῶν
sat down. after And the reading of the Law and of the
προφητῶν, ἀπέστειλαν οἱ ἀρχισυνάγωγοι πρὸς αὐτούς,
Prophets, sent forth the synagogue rulers to them,
λέγοντες, Ἄνδρες ἀδελφοί, εἰ ἔστι λόγος ἐν ὑμῖν παρακλή-
saying, Men, brothers, if is a word among you of exhort-
16 σεως πρὸς τὸν λαόν, λέγετε. ἀναστὰς δὲ Παῦλος, καὶ
ation to the people, say (it). rising up And Paul, and
κατασείσας τῇ χειρί, εἶπεν,
signaling with the hand, he said,
Ἄνδρες Ἰσραηλῖται, καὶ οἱ φοβούμενοι τὸν Θεόν, ἀκού-
Men, Israelites, and those fearing — God,
17 σατε. ὁ Θεὸς τοῦ λαοῦ τούτου Ἰσραὴλ ἐξελέξατο τοὺς
hear: The God — of people this Israel chose out the
πατέρας ἡμῶν, καὶ τὸν λαὸν ὕψωσεν ἐν τῇ παροικίᾳ ἐν γῇ
fathers of us, and the people exalted in the sojourn in land
Αἰγύπτῳ, καὶ μετὰ βραχίονος ὑψηλοῦ ἐξήγαγεν αὐτοὺς ἐξ
(of) Egypt, and with an arm high He led out them out of
18 αὐτῆς. καὶ ὡς τεσσαρακονταετῆ χρόνον ἐτροποφόρησεν
it. And as (passed) forty years time, He endured
19 αὐτοὺς ἐν τῇ ἐρήμῳ. καὶ καθελὼν ἔθνη ἑπτὰ ἐν γῇ Χαναάν,
them in the desert. And pulled down nations seven in land Canaan,
20 κατεκληροδότησεν αὐτοῖς τὴν γῆν αὐτῶν. καὶ μετὰ ταῦτα,
gave as an inheritance to them the land of them. And after these things,
ὡς ἔτεσι τετρακοσίοις καὶ πεντήκοντα, ἔδωκε κριτὰς ἕως
as years four hundred and fifty, He gave judges until
21 Σαμουὴλ τοῦ προφήτου. κἀκεῖθεν ᾐτήσαντο βασιλέα, καὶ
Samuel the prophet. And from there they asked a king, and
ἔδωκεν αὐτοῖς ὁ Θεὸς τὸν Σαοὺλ υἱὸν Κίς, ἄνδρα ἐκ φυλῆς
gave them God — Saul son of Kish, a man of tribe
22 Βενιαμίν, ἔτη τεσσαράκοντα. καὶ μεταστήσας αὐτόν, ἤγειρεν
of Benjamin, years forty. And removing him, He raised
αὐτοῖς τὸν Δαβὶδ εἰς βασιλέα, ᾧ καὶ εἶπε μαρτυρήσας, Εὗρον
to them — David for a king, to whom also He said, witnessing, I found
Δαβὶδ τὸν τοῦ Ἰεσσαί, ἄνδρα κατὰ τὴν καρδίαν μου, ὃς
David the (son) of Jesse a man according to the heart of Me, who
23 ποιήσει πάντα τὰ θελήματά μου. τούτου ὁ Θεὸς ἀπὸ τοῦ
will do all the desires of Me. Of this one God from the
σπέρματος κατ' ἐπαγγελίαν ἤγειρε τῷ Ἰσραὴλ σωτῆρα
seed according to promise raised — to Israel a Savior,
24 Ἰησοῦν, προκηρύξαντος Ἰωάννου πρὸ προσώπου τῆς
Jesus. Previously proclaiming John, before (the) face of the
εἰσόδου αὐτοῦ βάπτισμα μετανοίας παντὶ τῷ λαῷ Ἰσραήλ.
coming of Him a baptism of repentance to all the people of Israel.
25 ὡς δὲ ἐπλήρου ὁ Ἰωάννης τὸν δρόμον, ἔλεγε, Τίνα με
as And fulfilled — John the course, he said, Whom me
ὑπονοεῖτε εἶναι ; οὐκ εἰμὶ ἐγώ. ἀλλ' ἰδού, ἔρχεται μετ' ἐμέ,
do you suppose to be? not am I (He). but behold, He comes after me,
26 οὗ οὐκ εἰμὶ ἄξιος τὸ ὑπόδημα τῶν ποδῶν λῦσαι. ἄνδρες
of whom not I am worthy the sandal of (His) feet to loosen. Men,
ἀδελφοί, υἱοὶ γένους Ἀβραάμ, καὶ οἱ ἐν ὑμῖν φοβούμενοι τὸν
brothers, sons of (the) race of Abraham, and those in you fearing —
27 Θεόν, ὑμῖν ὁ λόγος τῆς σωτηρίας ταύτης ἀπεστάλη. οἱ γὰρ
God. to you the word of salvation this was sent forth. those For

their rulers, not having known this One, and having read the voices of the prophets throughout every sabbath, judging *Him*, they fulfilled *the Scriptures*. [28]And finding not one cause of death, they asked Pilate to do away with Him. [29]And when they finished all the things having been written concerning Him, taking *Him* down from the tree, they laid *Him* in a tomb. [30]But God raised Him from *the* dead; [31]who appeared for many days to those coming up with Him from Galilee to Jerusalem, who are witnesses of Him to the people. [32]And we preach the gospel *to* you, the promise made to the fathers, that this God has fulfilled to us, their children, raising up Jesus; [33]as also it has been written in the second Psalm, "You are My Son; today I have begotten You." [34]And that He raised Him from *the* dead, no more being about to return to corruption, so He has said, "I will give You the holy things of faithful David." [35]So He also said in another, "You will not give Your Holy One to see corruption." [36]For having served *his* own generation by the counsel of God, David truly fell asleep, and was added to his fathers, and saw corruption. [37]But *He* whom God raised up, He did not see corruption. [38]Then let it be known to you, men, brothers, that through this One forgiveness of sin is announced to you. [39]And everyone believing in this One is justified from all things which you could not be justified by the Law of Moses. [40]Then watch *that* the thing spoken in the prophets may not come on you: [41]"Behold, *you* despisers, and marvel, and perish, because I work a work in your days, a work which you would in no way believe if anyone declares *it* to you." [42]But the Jews having gone out of the synagogue, the

κατοικοῦντες ἐν Ἱερουσαλὴμ καὶ οἱ ἄρχοντες αὐτῶν, τοῦτον
dwelling in Jerusalem and the rulers of them, this One
ἀγνοήσαντες, καὶ τὰς φωνὰς τῶν προφητῶν τὰς κατὰ πᾶν
not knowing, and the voices of the prophets throughout every
28 σάββατον ἀναγινωσκομένας, κρίναντες ἐπλήρωσαν. καὶ
sabbath being read, having judged (Him), they fulfilled And
μηδεμίαν αἰτίαν θανάτου εὑρόντες, ᾐτήσαντο Πιλάτον
not one cause of death having found, they asked Pilate
29 ἀναιρεθῆναι αὐτόν. ὡς δὲ ἐτέλεσαν ἅπαντα τὰ περὶ αὐτοῦ
do away (with) Him. when And they finished all the things about Him
γεγραμμένα, καθελόντες ἀπὸ τοῦ ξύλου, ἔθηκαν εἰς μνημεῖον.
having been written, taking down from the tree, they laid in a tomb.
30 ὁ δὲ Θεὸς ἤγειρεν αὐτὸν ἐκ νεκρῶν· ὃς ὤφθη ἐπὶ ἡμέρας
31 But God raised Him from (the) dead; who appeared for days
πλείους τοῖς συναναβᾶσιν αὐτῷ ἀπὸ τῆς Γαλιλαίας εἰς
many to those coming up with Him from — Galilee to
32 Ἱερουσαλήμ, οἵτινές εἰσι μάρτυρες αὐτοῦ πρὸς τὸν λαόν. καὶ
Jerusalem, who are witnesses of Him to the people. And
ἡμεῖς ὑμᾶς εὐαγγελιζόμεθα τὴν πρὸς τοὺς πατέρας ἐπαγ-
we (to) you preach the gospel, the to the fathers promise
γελίαν γενομένην, ὅτι ταύτην ὁ Θεὸς ἐκπεπλήρωκε τοῖς
having come, that this (promise) God has fulfilled to the
33 τέκνοις αὐτῶν ἡμῖν, ἀναστήσας Ἰησοῦν· ὡς καὶ ἐν τῷ ψαλμῷ
children of them to us, raising up Jesus, as also in the Psalm
τῷ δευτέρῳ γέγραπται, Υἱός μου εἶ σύ, ἐγὼ σήμερον
second, it has been written: Son of Me are You, I today
34 γεγέννηκά σε. ὅτι δὲ ἀνέστησεν αὐτὸν ἐκ νεκρῶν, μηκέτι
have begotten You. that And He raised up Him from (the) dead, no more
μέλλοντα ὑποστρέφειν εἰς διαφθοράν, οὕτως εἴρηκεν ὅτι
being about to return to corruption, thus He has said, —
35 Δώσω ὑμῖν τὰ ὅσια Δαβὶδ τὰ πιστά. διὸ καὶ ἐν ἑτέρῳ λέγει,
I will give You the holy things of David faithful. Thus also in another He says,
36 Οὐ δώσεις τὸν ὅσιόν σου ἰδεῖν διαφθοράν. Δαβὶδ μὲν γὰρ
Not You will give the holy one of You to see corruption. David indeed For
ἰδίᾳ γενεᾷ ὑπηρετήσας τῇ τοῦ Θεοῦ βουλῇ ἐκοιμήθη, καὶ
own generation having served by the — of God counsel fell asleep, and
37 προσετέθη πρὸς τοὺς πατέρας αὐτοῦ, καὶ εἶδε διαφθοράν· ὃν
was added to the fathers of him, and saw corruption. whom
38 δὲ ὁ Θεὸς ἤγειρεν, οὐκ εἶδε διαφθοράν. γνωστὸν οὖν ἔστω
But God raised up, not He saw corruption. Known, therefore, let it be
ὑμῖν, ἄνδρες ἀδελφοί, ὅτι διὰ τούτου ὑμῖν ἄφεσις ἁμαρτιῶν
to you, men, brothers, that through this One to you forgiveness of sins
39 καταγγέλλεται· καὶ ἀπὸ πάντων ὧν οὐκ ἠδυνήθητε ἐν τῷ
is announced, and from all things which not you could by the
νόμῳ Μωσέως δικαιωθῆναι, ἐν τούτῳ πᾶς ὁ πιστεύων
law of Moses be justified, in this One everyone — believing
40 δικαιοῦται. βλέπετε οὖν μὴ ἐπέλθῃ ἐφ' ὑμᾶς τὸ εἰρημένον ἐν
is justified. Look, then, (that) not come on you the thing spoken in
41 τοῖς προφήταις, Ἴδετε, οἱ καταφρονηταί, καὶ θαυμάσατε,
the prophets; See, the despisers, and marvel
καὶ ἀφανίσθητε· ὅτι ἔργον ἐγὼ ἐργάζομαι ἐν ταῖς ἡμέραις
and vanish, because a work I work in the days
ὑμῶν, ἔργον ᾧ οὐ μὴ πιστεύσητε, ἐάν τις ἐκδιηγῆται ὑμῖν.
of you; a work which in no way you believe if anyone declare (it) to you.
42 Ἐξιόντων δὲ ἐκ τῆς συναγωγῆς τῶν Ἰουδαίων, παρεκά-
going out And of the synagogue, the Jews begged

Gentiles begged that these words be spoken to them on the next sabbath. [43] And the synagogue being broken up, many of the Jews and of the devout proselytes followed Paul and Barnabas; who speaking to them persuaded them to continue in the grace of God.

[44] And the sabbath coming, almost all the city was gathered to hear the word of God. [45] And the Jews seeing the crowds, they were filled with jealousy, and contradicted the things being spoken by Paul, contradicting and blaspheming. [46] But speaking boldly, Paul and Barnabas said, It was necessary the word of God to be spoken first to you; but since you indeed thrust it away, and judge yourselves not worthy of eternal life, behold, we turn to the Gentiles. [47] For so the Lord has commanded us, "I have set You for a Light of nations, that You be for salvation to *the* end of the earth."

[48] And hearing, the Gentiles rejoiced, and glorified the word of the Lord. And as many as had been appointed to eternal life believed. [49] And the word of the Lord was carried through all the country. [50] But the Jews excited the devout and honorable women, and the chief ones of the city, and raised up a persecution against Paul and Barnabas, and threw them out from their borders. [51] But they shaking the dust of their feet off on them, they came into Iconium. [52] And the disciples were filled with joy and *the* Holy Spirit.

CHAPTER 14

[1] And it happened in Iconium, they went in together into the synagogue of the Jews, and spoke so as for a huge multitude of both Jews and Greeks to believe. [2] But

λουν τὰ ἔθνη εἰς τὸ μεταξὺ σάββατον λαληθῆναι αὐτοῖς
the Gentiles on the next sabbath to be spoken to them

43 τὰ ῥήματα ταῦτα. λυθείσης δὲ τῆς συναγωγῆς, ἠκολούθησαν
words these. being broken And the synagogue, followed

πολλοὶ τῶν Ἰουδαίων καὶ τῶν σεβομένων προσηλύτων τῷ
many of the Jews and of the devout proselytes —

Παύλῳ καὶ τῷ Βαρνάβᾳ· οἵτινες προσλαλοῦντες αὐτοῖς,
Paul and — Barnabas, who speaking to them

ἔπειθον αὐτοὺς ἐπιμένειν τῇ χάριτι τοῦ Θεοῦ.
persuaded them to continue in the grace of God.

44 Τῷ δὲ ἐρχομένῳ σαββάτῳ σχεδὸν πᾶσα ἡ πόλις συνήχθη
in the And coming sabbath almost all the city was gathered

45 ἀκοῦσαι τὸν λόγον τοῦ Θεοῦ. ἰδόντες δὲ οἱ Ἰουδαῖοι τοὺς
to hear the word — of God. seeing And the Jews the

ὄχλους ἐπλήσθησαν ζήλου, καὶ ἀντέλεγον τοῖς ὑπὸ τοῦ
crowds, they were filled of jealousy, and contradicted the things by —

Παύλου λεγομένοις, ἀντιλέγοντες καὶ βλασφημοῦντες
Paul, being spoken, contradicting and blaspheming.

46 παρρησιασάμενοι δὲ ὁ Παῦλος καὶ ὁ Βαρνάβας εἶπον, Ὑμῖν
speaking boldly But — Paul and — Barnabas said, To you

ἦν ἀναγκαῖον πρῶτον λαληθῆναι τὸν λόγον τοῦ Θεοῦ.
it was necessary firstly to be spoken the word — of God.

ἐπειδὴ δὲ ἀπωθεῖσθε αὐτόν, καὶ οὐκ ἀξίους κρίνετε ἑαυτοὺς
since indeed But you put away it, and not worthy judge yourselves

47 τῆς αἰωνίου ζωῆς, ἰδοὺ στρεφόμεθα εἰς τὰ ἔθνη. οὕτω γὰρ
of the eternal life, behold, we turn to the nations. so For

ἐντέταλται ἡμῖν ὁ Κύριος, Τέθεικά σε εἰς φῶς ἐθνῶν, τοῦ
has commanded us the Lord: I have set You for a light of nations —

48 εἶναί σε εἰς σωτηρίαν ἕως ἐσχάτου τῆς γῆς. ἀκούοντα δὲ τὰ
to be You for salvation to (the) end of the earth. hearing And the

ἔθνη ἔχαιρον, καὶ ἐδόξαζον τὸν λόγον τοῦ Κυρίου, καὶ
nations rejoiced, and glorified the word of the Lord. And

49 ἐπίστευσαν ὅσοι ἦσαν τεταγμένοι εἰς ζωὴν αἰώνιον. διεφέ-
believed as many as were appointed to life eternal. was

50 ρετο δὲ ὁ λόγος του Κυρίου δι' ὅλης τῆς χώρας. οἱ δὲ
carried And the word of the Lord through all the country. the But

Ἰουδαῖοι παρώτρυναν τὰς σεβομένας γυναῖκας καὶ τὰς
Jews urged on the devout women and —

εὐσχήμονας καὶ τοὺς πρώτους τῆς πόλεως, καὶ ἐπήγειραν
honorable and the chief ones of the city; and raised up

διωγμὸν ἐπὶ τὸν Παῦλον καὶ τὸν Βαρνάβαν, καὶ ἐξέβαλον
persecution against — Paul and — Barnabas, and threw out

51 αὐτοὺς ἀπὸ τῶν ὁρίων αὐτῶν. οἱ δὲ ἐκτιναξάμενοι τὸν
them from the borders of them. they And shaking off the

κονιορτὸν τῶν ποδῶν αὐτῶν ἐπ' αὐτούς, ἦλθον εἰς Ἰκόνιον.
dust of the feet of them on them, they came into Iconium.

52 οἱ δὲ μαθηταὶ ἐπληροῦντο χαρᾶς καὶ Πνεύματος Ἁγίου.
the And disciples were filled from joy, and from (the) Spirit Holy.

CHAPTER 14

1 Ἐγένετο δὲ ἐν Ἰκονίῳ, κατὰ τὸ αὐτὸ εἰσελθεῖν αὐτοὺς εἰς
it happened And in Iconium together entered them into

τὴν συναγωγὴν τῶν Ἰουδαίων, καὶ λαλῆσαι οὕτως ὥστε
the synagogue of the Jews, and to speak so as

πιστεῦσαι Ἰουδαίων τε καὶ Ἑλλήνων πολὺ πλῆθος. οἱ δὲ
to believe of Jews both and of Greeks, a much multitude. the But

the unbelieving Jews raised up and made malignant the souls of the Gentiles against the brothers. 3 Then, indeed, they stayed a considerable time, speaking boldly on the Lord, witnessing to the word of His grace, and giving miracles and wonders to occur through their hands. 4 And the multitude of the city was divided; and some were with the Jews, but others with the apostles. 5 And when a rush of the Gentiles occurred, and both the Jews and their rulers *came* to insult and to stone them; 6 perceiving *this,* they fled to the cities of Lycaonia, Lystra and Derbe, and the surrounding country. 7 And they were preaching the gospel there.

8 And a certain man was sitting in Lystra, powerless in the feet, being lame from his mother's womb, who had never walked. 9 This one heard Paul speaking, who looking intently at him, and seeing that he had faith to be cured, 10 *he* said with a loud voice, Stand upright on your feet! And he leaped up and walked about. 11 And seeing what Paul did, the crowd lifted up their voice in Lycaonian, saying, The gods have come down to us, becoming like men. 12 And they called Barnabas, Zeus; and Paul, Hermes, because he was the leader in speaking. 13 And the priest of Zeus being before their city, carrying bulls and garlands, *he* wished to sacrifice along with the crowds. 14 But Paul and Barnabas, the apostles, hearing, they tore their garments *and* sprang into the crowd, crying out, 15 and saying, Men, why do you do these things? We also are men of like feelings to you, to turn from these vanities to the living God, who made the Heaven and the earth and the sea, and all things in them; 16 who in the past generations

2 ἀπειθοῦντες Ἰουδαῖοι ἐπήγειραν καὶ ἐκάκωσαν τὰς ψυχὰς
disobeying Jews raised up and embittered the souls

3 τῶν ἐθνῶν κατὰ τῶν ἀδελφῶν. ἱκανὸν μὲν οὖν χρόνον
of the Gentiles against the brothers. A considerable therefore time

διέτριψαν παρρησιαζόμενοι ἐπὶ τῷ Κυρίῳ τῷ μαρτυροῦντι
they stayed speaking boldly on the Lord witnessing

τῷ λόγῳ τῆς χάριτος αὐτοῦ, καὶ διδόντι σημεῖα καὶ τέρατα
to the word of the grace of Him, and giving signs and wonders

4 γίνεσθαι διὰ τῶν χειρῶν αὐτῶν. ἐσχίσθη δὲ τὸ πλῆθος τῆς
to happen through the hands of them. was divided But the multitude of the

πόλεως· καὶ οἱ μὲν ἦσαν σὺν τοῖς Ἰουδαίοις, οἱ δὲ σὺν τοῖς
city, and some were with the Jews, others but with the

5 ἀποστόλοις. ὡς δὲ ἐγένετο ὁρμὴ τῶν ἐθνῶν τε καὶ Ἰουδαίων
apostles. when And occurred a rush of the Gentitles, even and Jews,

σὺν τοῖς ἄρχουσιν αὐτῶν, ὑβρίσαι καὶ λιθοβολῆσαι αὐτούς,
with the rulers of them, to insult and to stone them;

6 συνιδόντες κατέφυγον εἰς τὰς πόλεις τῆς Λυκαονίας, Λύστραν
perceiving they fled to the cities — of Lycaonia, Lystra,

7 καὶ Δέρβην, καὶ τὴν περίχωρον· κἀκεῖ ἦσαν εὐαγγελιζόμενοι.
and Derbe, and the surrounding country; and there they were evangelizing.

8 Καί τις ἀνὴρ ἐν Λύστροις ἀδύνατος τοῖς ποσὶν ἐκάθητο,
And a certain man in Lystra powerless in the feet was sitting

χωλὸς ἐκ κοιλίας μητρὸς αὐτοῦ ὑπάρχων, ὃς οὐδέποτε
lame from (the) womb of (the) mother of him being, who never

9 περιεπεπατήκει. οὗτος ἤκουε τοῦ Παύλου λαλοῦντος· ὃς
had walked. This one heard — Paul speaking, who

10 ἀτενίσας αὐτῷ, καὶ ἰδὼν ὅτι πίστιν ἔχει τοῦ σωθῆναι, εἶπε
looking at him and seeing that faith he has — to be cured, said

μεγάλῃ τῇ φωνῇ, Ἀνάστηθι ἐπὶ τοὺς πόδας σου ὀρθός. καὶ
with a great voice, Stand up on the feet of you erect. And

11 ἥλλετο καὶ περιεπάτει. οἱ δὲ ὄχλοι, ἰδόντες ὃ ἐποίησεν ὁ
he leaped and walked about. the And crowds seeing what did

Παῦλος, ἐπῆραν τὴν φωνὴν αὐτῶν Λυκαονιστὶ λέγοντες, Οἱ
Paul lifted up the voice of them in Lycaonian, saying, The

12 θεοὶ ὁμοιωθέντες ἀνθρώποις κατέβησαν πρὸς ἡμᾶς. ἐκάλουν
gods having become like men have come down to us. they called

τε τὸν μὲν Βαρνάβαν, Δία· τὸν δὲ Παῦλον, Ἑρμῆν, ἐπειδὴ
And — Barnabas, Zeus; — and Paul, Hermes; since

13 αὐτὸς ἦν ὁ ἡγούμενος τοῦ λόγου. ὁ δὲ ἱερεὺς τοῦ Διὸς τοῦ
he was the leader of the speaking. the But priest — of Zeus —

ὄντος πρὸ τῆς πόλεως αὐτῶν, ταύρους καὶ στέμματα ἐπὶ τοὺς
being before the city of them, bulls and garlands to the

14 πυλῶνας ἐνέγκας, σὺν τοῖς ὄχλοις ἤθελε θύειν. ἀκούσαντες δὲ
gates carrying, with the crowds wished to sacrifice. hearing And

οἱ ἀπόστολοι Βαρνάβας καὶ Παῦλος, διαρρήξαντες τὰ ἱμάτια
the apostles Barnabas and Paul, having torn the garments

αὐτῶν, εἰσεπήδησαν εἰς τὸν ὄχλον, κράζοντες καὶ λέγοντες,
of them, sprang into the crowd, crying out and saying,

15 Ἄνδρες, τί ταῦτα ποιεῖτε; καὶ ἡμεῖς ὁμοιοπαθεῖς ἐσμεν ὑμῖν
Men, why these things do you? Also we of like feelings are to you

ἄνθρωποι, εὐαγγελιζόμενοι ὑμᾶς ἀπὸ τούτων τῶν ματαίων
men, preaching the gospel to you from these — vanities

ἐπιστρέφειν ἐπὶ τὸν Θεὸν τὸν ζῶντα, ὃς ἐποίησε τὸν οὐρανὸν
to turn to the God living; who made the heaven

16 καὶ τὴν γῆν καὶ τὴν θάλασσαν καὶ πάντα τὰ ἐν αὐτοῖς· ὃς ἐν
and the earth and the sea, and all things in them; who in

allowed all the nations to go in their *own* ways, [17]though indeed He did not leave Himself without witness, doing good, giving rain and fruitful seasons to us from Heaven, filling our hearts with food and gladness. [18]And saying these things, they hardly stopped the crowds, *that they* not sacrifice to them.

[19]But Jews came there from Antioch and Iconium, and persuading the crowds, and stoning Paul, they dragged *him* outside the city, supposing him to have died.

[20]But the disciples surrounding him, arising he entered into the city. And on the morrow he went away with Barnabas to Derbe. [21]And having preached the gospel to that city, and having made many disciples, they returned to Lystra and Iconium and Antioch, [22]confirming the souls of the disciples, exhorting to continue in the faith, and that through many afflictions we must enter into the kingdom of God. [23]And having hand-picked elders for them in every church, having prayed with fastings, they committed them to the Lord into whom they had believed.

[24]And passing through Pisidia, they came to Pamphylia. [25]And speaking the word in Perga, they came down to Attalia, [26]and from there they sailed to Antioch, from where they had been committed to the grace of God for the work which they fulfilled.

[27]And having arrived, and gathering the church, they reported what things God did with them, and that He opened a door of faith to the nations. [28]And they stayed there not a little time with the disciples.

CHAPTER 15

[1]And some, having come down from Judea, taught

ταῖς παρῳχημέναις γενεαῖς εἴασε πάντα τὰ ἔθνη πορεύεσθαι
the having passed by generations allowed all the nations to go
17 ταῖς ὁδοῖς αὐτῶν. καίτοιγε οὐκ ἀμάρτυρον ἑαυτὸν ἀφῆκεν
the ways of them. And yet not without witness Himself left,
ἀγαθοποιῶν, οὐρανόθεν ἡμῖν ὑετοὺς διδοὺς καὶ καιροὺς
doing good, from heaven to us rain giving and seasons
καρποφόρους, ἐμπιπλῶν τροφῆς καὶ εὐφροσύνης τὰς καρδίας
fruit-bearing filling of food and of gladness the hearts
18 ἡμῶν. καὶ ταῦτα λέγοντες, μόλις κατέπαυσαν τοὺς ὄχλους
of us. And these things saying, hardly they stopped the crowds
τοῦ μὴ θύειν αὐτοῖς.
— not to sacrifice to them.
19 Ἐπῆλθον δὲ ἀπὸ Ἀντιοχείας καὶ Ἰκονίου Ἰουδαῖοι, καὶ
came over And from Antioch and Iconium Jews, and
πείσαντες τοὺς ὄχλους, καὶ λιθάσαντες τὸν Παῦλον, ἔσυρον
persuading the crowds, and stoning — Paul, they dragged
ἔξω τῆς πόλεως, νομίσαντες αὐτὸν τεθνάναι. κυκλωσάντων
outside the city, supposing him to have died. having surrounded
20 δὲ αὐτὸν τῶν μαθητῶν, ἀναστὰς εἰσῆλθεν εἰς τὴν πόλιν· καὶ
But him the disciples, rising up he entered into the city. And
21 τῇ ἐπαύριον ἐξῆλθε σὺν τῷ Βαρνάβᾳ εἰς Δέρβην. εὐαγγελι-
on the morrow he went with — Barnabas to Derbe. preaching
σάμενοί τε τὴν πόλιν ἐκείνην, καὶ μαθητεύσαντες ἱκανούς,
the gospel And — city to that, and having made disciples many,
ὑπέστρεψαν εἰς τὴν Λύστραν καὶ Ἰκόνιον καὶ Ἀντιόχειαν,
they returned to — Lystra and Iconium and Antioch,
22 ἐπιστηρίζοντες τὰς ψυχὰς τῶν μαθητῶν, παρακαλοῦντες
confirming the souls of the disciples, exhorting
ἐμμένειν τῇ πίστει, καὶ ὅτι διὰ πολλῶν θλίψεων δεῖ ἡμᾶς
to continue in the faith, and that through many afflictions must we
23 εἰσελθεῖν εἰς τὴν βασιλείαν τοῦ Θεοῦ. χειροτονήσαντες δὲ
enter into the kingdom — of God. having hand-picked And
αὐτοῖς πρεσβυτέρους κατ' ἐκκλησίαν, προσευξάμενοι μετὰ
for them elders in (every) church praying with
νηστειῶν, παρέθεντο αὐτοὺς τῷ Κυρίῳ εἰς ὃν πεπιστεύ-
fastings, they committed them to the Lord in whom they had
24 κεισαν. καὶ διελθόντες τὴν Πισιδίαν ἦλθον εἰς Παμφυλίαν.
believed. And passing through — Pisidia, they came to Pamphylia
25 καὶ λαλήσαντες ἐν Πέργῃ τὸν λόγον, κατέβησαν εἰς Ἀττά-
And speaking in Perga the word, they came down to Attalia,
26 λειαν· κἀκεῖθεν ἀπέπλευσαν εἰς Ἀντιόχειαν, ὅθεν ἦσαν
and from there sailed away to Antioch, from where they had
παραδεδομένοι τῇ χάριτι τοῦ Θεοῦ εἰς τὸ ἔργον ὃ ἐπλή-
been committed to the grace of God for the work which they
27 ρωσαν. παραγενομενοι δὲ καὶ συναγαγόντες τὴν ἐκκλησίαν,
fulfilled having arrived And, and gathering the church,
ἀνήγγειλαν ὅσα ἐποίησεν ὁ Θεὸς μετ' αὐτῶν, καὶ ὅτι ἤνοιξε
they reported what things did God with them, and that He opened
28 τοῖς ἔθνεσι θύραν πίστεως. διέτριβον δὲ ἐκεῖ χρόνον οὐκ
to the nations a door of faith. they continued And there a time not
ὀλίγον σὺν τοῖς μαθηταῖς.
little with the disciples.

CHAPTER 15

1 Καί τινες κατελθόντες ἀπὸ τῆς Ἰουδαίας, ἐδίδασκον τοὺς
And some going down from — Judea taught the

the brothers, If you are not circumcised *according* to the custom of Moses, you cannot be saved. [2]Therefore, dissension and not a little disputation having occurred with them by Paul and Barnabas, they appointed Paul and Barnabas and some others of them to go up into Jerusalem to the apostles and elders concerning this question. [3]Indeed, therefore, they, having been sent forward by the church, passed through Phoenecia and Samaria, fully narrating the conversion of the Gentiles. And they were producing great joy *among* all the brothers.

[4]And having arrived in Jerusalem, they were welcomed by the church and the apostles and the elders. And they reported what things God had done with them. [5]But some of those *who* had believed from the sect of the Pharisees rose up, saying, It is necessary to circumcise them, and to command *them* to keep the Law of Moses.

[6]And the apostles and the elders were assembled to see about this matter. [7]And much disputation having occurred, Peter having risen said to them: Men, brothers, you recognize that from ancient days, God chose among us *that* through my mouth the nations *should* hear the word of the Gospel, and *should* believe. [8]And the heart-knowing God testified to them, giving them the Holy Spirit, even as also to us. [9]And He made distinction in nothing between both us and them, having purified their hearts by faith.

[10]Therefore, why do you now test God, *by* putting a yoke on the neck of the disciples which neither our fathers nor we had strength to bear? [11]But through the grace of *the* Lord Jesus Christ, we believe *in order* to be saved according to which

ἀδελφοὺς ὅτι Ἐὰν μὴ περιτέμνησθε τῷ ἔθει Μωϋσέως, οὐ
brothers If not are circumcised by the custom of Moses, not
2 δύνασθε σωθῆναι. γενομένης οὖν στάσεως καὶ συζητήσεως
you can be saved. occurring Then discord and discussion
οὐκ ὀλίγης τῷ Παύλῳ καὶ τῷ Βαρνάβᾳ πρὸς αὐτούς, ἔταξαν
not a little – by Paul and – Barnabas with them, they chose
ἀναβαίνειν Παῦλον καὶ Βαρνάβαν καί τινας ἄλλους ἐξ
to go up Paul and Barnabas and some others of
αὐτῶν πρὸς τοὺς ἀποστόλους καὶ πρεσβυτέρους εἰς Ἱερου-
them to the apostles and elders to
3 σαλὴμ περὶ τοῦ ζητήματος τούτου. οἱ μὲν οὖν, προπεμ-
Jerusalem about – question this. they Therefore being set
φθέντες ὑπὸ τῆς ἐκκλησίας, διήρχοντο τὴν Φοινίκην καὶ
forward by the church, passed through – Phoenicia and
Σαμάρειαν, ἐκδιηγούμενοι τὴν ἐπιστροφὴν τῶν ἐθνῶν· καὶ
Samaria, telling about the conversion of the Gentiles and
4 ἐποίουν χαρὰν μεγάλην πᾶσι τοῖς ἀδελφοῖς. παραγενό-
they caused joy great to all the brothers. having arrived
μενοι δὲ εἰς Ἱερουσαλήμ, ἀπεδέχθησαν ὑπὸ τῆς ἐκκλησίας
And to Jerusalem, they were welcomed by the church,
καὶ τῶν ἀποστόλων καὶ τῶν πρεσβυτέρων, ἀνήγγειλάν τε
and the apostles and the elders, reported and
5 ὅσα ὁ Θεὸς ἐποίησε μετ' αὐτῶν. ἐξανέστησαν δέ τινες τῶν
what things God did with them. rise forth But some of those
ἀπὸ τῆς αἱρέσεως τῶν Φαρισαίων πεπιστευκότες, λέγοντες
from the sect of the Pharisees having believed, saying,
ὅτι Δεῖ περιτέμνειν αὐτούς, παραγγέλλειν τε τηρεῖν τὸν
–It is right to circumcise them, to command and to keep the
νόμον Μωϋσέως.
law of Moses.

6 Συνήχθησαν δὲ οἱ ἀπόστολοι καὶ οἱ πρεσβύτεροι ἰδεῖν
were assembled And the apostles and the elders to see
7 περὶ τοῦ λόγου τούτου. πολλῆς δὲ συζητήσεως γενομένης,
about – matter this. much And discussion having occurred,
ἀναστὰς Πέτρος εἶπε πρὸς αὐτούς,
rising up Peter said to them,
Ἄνδρες ἀδελφοί, ὑμεῖς ἐπίστασθε ὅτι ἀφ' ἡμερῶν ἀρχαίων
Men, brothers, you understand that from days ancient
ὁ Θεὸς ἐν ἡμῖν ἐξελέξατο, διὰ τοῦ στόματός μου ἀκοῦσαι
God among us chose through the mouth of me to hear
8 τὰ ἔθνη τὸν λόγον τοῦ εὐαγγελίου, καὶ πιστεῦσαι. καὶ ὁ
the nations the word of the gospel, and to believe. And the
καρδιογνώστης Θεὸς ἐμαρτύρησεν αὐτοῖς, δοὺς αὐτοῖς τὸ
heart-knowing God witnessed to them, giving them the
9 Πνεῦμα τὸ Ἅγιον, καθὼς καὶ ἡμῖν· καὶ οὐδὲν διέκρινε μεταξὺ
Spirit – Holy, as also to us, and nothing distinguished between
ἡμῶν τε καὶ αὐτῶν, τῇ πίστει καθαρίσας τὰς καρδίας αὐτῶν.
us both and them, by faith having cleansed the hearts of them.
10 νῦν οὖν τί πειράζετε τὸν Θεόν, ἐπιθεῖναι ζυγὸν ἐπὶ τὸν
Now, then, why do you tempt – God, to put a yoke on the
τράχηλον τῶν μαθητῶν, ὃν οὔτε οἱ πατέρες ἡμῶν οὔτε ἡμεῖς
neck of the disciples, which neither the fathers of us nor we
11 ἰσχύσαμεν βαστάσαι; ἀλλὰ διὰ τῆς χάριτος Κυρίου Ἰησοῦ
were able to bear? But through the grace of (the) Lord Jesus
Χριστοῦ πιστεύομεν σωθῆναι, καθ' ὃν τρόπον κἀκεῖνοι.
Christ we believe to be saved by which means (as) even they.

manner they also *believed*.
[12]And all the multitude kept silent, and were hearing Barnabas and Paul recounting what things God did through them among the Gentiles, *even* the signs and wonders. [13]And after they were silent, James responded, saying, Men, brothers, hear me: [14]Simon has recounted *how* even as *at* first God oversaw to take a people out from *among the* Gentiles for His Name. [15]And with this agree the words of the prophets, as it has been written, [16]"After these things I will return and will build again the tabernacle of David *which* had fallen, and I will rebuild its things, and I will set it up, [17]so as the rest of men may seek the Lord, even all the nations on whom My name has been called, says the Lord, who is doing these things." [18]All His words are known to God from eternity. [19]For this reason I judge not to trouble those from the Gentiles turning to God; [20]but to write to them to hold back from the pollutions of idols, and *from* fornication, and that strangled, and blood. [21]For Moses from ancient generations has those proclaiming him, being read in the synagogues on every sabbath.

[22]Then it seemed *good* to the apostles and the elders, with all the church, to send chosen men from them to Antioch with Paul and Barnabas: Judas being called Barsabas, and Silas, leading men among the brothers, [23]writing by their hand these things: The apostles and the elders and the brothers, to those throughout Antioch, and Syria, and Cilicia, brothers from *the* Gentiles: Greeting. [24]Since we heard that some of us having gone out have troubled you with

12 Ἐσίγησε δὲ πᾶν τὸ πλῆθος, καὶ ἤκουον Βαρνάβα καὶ
was silent And all the multitude, and heard Barnabas and

Παύλου ἐξηγουμένων ὅσα ἐποίησεν ὁ Θεὸς σημεῖα καὶ
Paul recounting what did — God signs and

13 τέρατα ἐν τοῖς ἔθνεσι δι' αὐτῶν. μετὰ δὲ τὸ σιγῆσαι αὐτούς,
wonders among the nations through them. after And the silence of them,

ἀπεκρίθη Ἰάκωβος λέγων,
answered James, saying,

14 Ἄνδρες ἀδελφοί, ἀκούσατέ μου· Συμεὼν ἐξηγήσατο καθὼς
Men, brothers, hear me. Simeon recounted even as

πρῶτον ὁ Θεὸς ἐπεσκέψατο λαβεῖν ἐξ ἐθνῶν λαὸν ἐπὶ τῷ
first God oversaw to take out of nations a people for the

15 ὀνόματι αὐτοῦ. καὶ τούτῳ συμφωνοῦσιν οἱ λόγοι τῶν προ-
name of Him. And to this agree together the words of the

16 φητῶν, καθὼς γέγραπται, Μετὰ ταῦτα ἀναστρέψω, καὶ
prophets, as it has been written, After these things I will return, and

ἀνοικοδομήσω τὴν σκηνὴν Δαβὶδ τὴν πεπτωκυῖαν· καὶ τὰ
I will rebuild the tent of David — having fallen, and that

κατεσκαμμένα αὐτῆς ἀνοικοδομήσω, καὶ ἀνορθώσω αὐτήν·
being demolished of it I will rebuild, and I will set up it,

17 ὅπως ἂν ἐκζητήσωσιν οἱ κατάλοιποι τῶν ἀνθρώπων τὸν
so as — may seek the rest — of men the

Κύριον, καὶ πάντα τὰ ἔθνη, ἐφ' οὓς ἐπικέκληται τὸ ὄνομά μου
Lord, even all the nations on whom has been invoked the name of Me

18 ἐπ' αὐτούς, λέγει Κύριος ὁ ποιῶν ταῦτα πάντα. γνωστὰ
upon them, says (the) Lord who is doing these things all. known

19 ἀπ' αἰῶνός ἐστι τῷ Θεῷ πάντα τὰ ἔργα αὐτοῦ. διὸ ἐγὼ
from eternity are to God All · the works of Him Because of this, I

κρίνω μὴ παρενοχλεῖν τοῖς ἀπὸ τῶν ἐθνῶν ἐπιστρέφουσιν
judge not to trouble those from the nations turning

20 ἐπὶ τὸν Θεόν· ἀλλὰ ἐπιστεῖλαι αὐτοῖς τοῦ ἀπέχεσθαι ἀπὸ
to God, but to write to them — to hold back from

τῶν ἀλισγημάτων τῶν εἰδώλων καὶ τῆς πορνείας καὶ τοῦ
pollutions of the idols, and — fornication, and the

21 πνικτοῦ καὶ τοῦ αἵματος. Μωσῆς γὰρ ἐκ γενεῶν ἀρχαίων
strangled, and — blood. Moses For from generations ancient

κατὰ πόλιν τοὺς κηρύσσοντας αὐτὸν ἔχει, ἐν ταῖς συναγω-
in every city those proclaiming him he has, in the synagogues

γαῖς κατὰ πᾶν σάββατον ἀναγινωσκόμενος.
on every sabbath being read.

22 Τότε ἔδοξε τοῖς ἀποστόλοις καὶ τοῖς πρεσβυτέροις σὺν
Then it seemed to the apostles and the elders, with

ὅλῃ τῇ ἐκκλησίᾳ, ἐκλεξαμένους ἄνδρας ἐξ αὐτῶν πέμψαι εἰς
all the church, chosen men of them to send to

Ἀντιόχειαν σὺν τῷ Παύλῳ καὶ Βαρνάβᾳ, Ἰούδαν τὸν
Antioch with — Paul and Barnabas, Judas —

ἐπικαλούμενον Βαρσαβᾶν, καὶ Σίλαν, ἄνδρας ἡγουμένους ἐν
surnamed Barsabas, and Silas, men leading among

23 τοῖς ἀδελφοῖς, γράψαντες διὰ χειρὸς αὐτῶν τάδε, Οἱ ἀπό-
the brothers, writing through (the) hand of them these things: The

στολοι καὶ οἱ πρεσβύτεροι καὶ οἱ ἀδελφοὶ τοῖς κατὰ τὴν
apostles and the elders and the brothers to those throughout

Ἀντιόχειαν καὶ Συρίαν καὶ Κιλικίαν ἀδελφοῖς τοῖς ἐξ ἐθνῶν,
Antioch and Syria and Cilicia, brothers from (the) Gentiles,

24 χαίρειν· ἐπειδὴ ἠκούσαμεν ὅτι τινὲς ἐξ ἡμῶν ἐξελθόντες ἐτά-
Greeting. Since we heard that some of us having gone out

words, unsettling your souls, saying, Be circumcised and keep the Law; to whom we gave no command; [25]it seemed *good* to us, having become of one mind, to send chosen men to you along with our beloved Barnabas and Paul, [26]men who have given up their souls on behalf of the name of our Lord, Jesus Christ. [27]We have sent, therefore, Judas and Silas, they also through word announcing the same things. [28]For it seemed *good* to the Holy Spirit and to us to put not one greater burden on you than these necessary things: [29]To hold back from idol sacrifices, and blood, and that strangled, and *from* fornication; from which continually keeping yourselves, you will do well. Be prospered.

[30]Then they indeed being let go, they went to Antioch. And gathering the multitude, *they* delivered the letter. [31]And reading *it*, they rejoiced at the comfort. [32]And Judas and Silas, themselves also being prophets, exhorted the brothers through much speech, and confirmed *them*. [33]And continuing for a time, they were let go with peace from the brothers to the apostles. [34]But it seemed *good* to Silas to remain. [35]And Paul and Barnabas stayed in Antioch, teaching and preaching the gospel, the word of the Lord, with many others also.

[36]And after some days Paul said to Barnabas, Indeed, having turned back, let us look after our brothers throughout every city in which we announced the word of the Lord; how they are holding *it*. [37]But Barnabas purposed to take with *them John, the one* being called Mark. [38]But Paul thought *it* well not to take that one with *them, he* having withdrawn from them

ραξαν ὑμᾶς λόγοις, ἀνασκευάζοντες τὰς ψυχὰς ὑμῶν,
troubled you with words, unsettling the souls of you,
λέγοντες περιτέμνεσθαι καὶ τηρεῖν τὸν νόμον, οἷς οὐ διεστει-
saying, Be circumcised and keep the Law; to whom not we gave
25 λάμεθα· ἔδοξεν ἡμῖν γενομένοις ὁμοθυμαδόν, ἐκλεξαμένους
command; it seemed to us becoming of one passion chosen
ἄνδρας πέμψαι πρὸς ὑμᾶς, σὺν τοῖς ἀγαπητοῖς ἡμῶν
men to send to you, with the beloved of us
26 Βαρνάβᾳ καὶ Παύλῳ, ἀνθρώποις παραδεδωκόσι τὰς ψυχὰς
Barnabas and Paul, men having given up the souls
αὐτῶν ὑπὲρ τοῦ ὀνόματος τοῦ Κυρίου ἡμῶν Ἰησοῦ Χρι-
of them on behalf of the name of the Lord of us, Jesus Christ.
27 στοῦ. ἀπεστάλκαμεν οὖν Ἰούδαν καὶ Σίλαν, καὶ αὐτοὺς διὰ
We have sent, therefore, Judas and Silas, and they through
28 λόγου ἀπαγγέλλοντας τὰ αὐτά. ἔδοξε γὰρ τῷ Ἁγίῳ
word announcing, the same things. it seemed For to the Holy
Πνεύματι, καὶ ἡμῖν, μηδὲν πλέον ἐπιτίθεσθαι ὑμῖν βάρος,
Spirit and to us not one greater to put on you burden
29 πλὴν τῶν ἐπάναγκες τούτων, ἀπέχεσθαι εἰδωλοθύτων καὶ
than — necessary things these: to abstain from idol sacrifices, and
αἵματος καὶ πνικτοῦ καὶ πορνείας· ἐξ ὧν διατηροῦντες
blood, and that strangled, and fornication; from which continually keeping
ἑαυτούς, εὖ πράξετε. ἔρρωσθε.
yourselves well you will do. Be prospered.

30 Οἱ μὲν οὖν ἀπολυθέντες ἦλθον εἰς Ἀντιόχειαν· καὶ συν-
They, therefore, being let go, they went to Antioch; and having
31 αγαγόντες τὸ πλῆθος, ἐπέδωκαν τὴν ἐπιστολήν. ἀναγνόντες
gathered the multitude, delivered the letter. having read
32 δέ, ἐχάρησαν ἐπὶ τῇ παρακλήσει. Ἰούδας δὲ καὶ Σίλας, καὶ
And they rejoiced at the comfort. Judas And and Silas, also
αὐτοὶ προφῆται ὄντες, διὰ λόγου πολλοῦ παρεκάλεσαν
themselves prophets being, through speech much exhorted
33 τοὺς ἀδελφούς, καὶ ἐπεστήριξαν. ποιήσαντες δὲ χρόνον,
the brothers, and confirmed. having continued And a time,
ἀπελύθησαν μετ᾽ εἰρήνης ἀπὸ τῶν ἀδελφῶν πρὸς τοὺς
they were let go with peace from the brothers to the
34 ἀποστόλους. ἔδοξε δὲ τῷ Σίλᾳ ἐπιμεῖναι αὐτοῦ. Παῦλος δὲ
35 apostles. it seemed (good) But to Silas to remain (there). Paul And
καὶ Βαρνάβας διέτριβον ἐν Ἀντιοχείᾳ, διδάσκοντες καὶ
and Barnabas stayed in Antioch, teaching and
εὐαγγελιζόμενοι, μετὰ καὶ ἑτέρων πολλῶν, τὸν λόγον τοῦ
preaching the gospel, with also others many the word of the
Κυρίου.
Lord.

36 Μετὰ δέ τινας ἡμέρας εἶπε Παῦλος πρὸς Βαρνάβαν,
after And some days said Paul to Barnabas,
Ἐπιστρέψαντες δὴ ἐπισκεψώμεθα τοὺς ἀδελφοὺς ἡμῶν
Having turned back indeed let us look after the brothers of us
κατὰ πᾶσαν πόλιν, ἐν αἷς κατηγγείλαμεν τὸν λόγον τοῦ
throughout every city in which we announced the word of the
37 Κυρίου, πῶς ἔχουσι. Βαρνάβας δὲ ἐβουλεύσατο συμπαραλα-
Lord, how they are holding. Barnabas And purposed to take with
38 βεῖν τὸν Ἰωάννην, τὸν καλούμενον Μάρκον. Παῦλος δὲ
(them) — John, — being called Mark. Paul But
ἠξίου, τὸν ἀποστάντα ἀπ᾽ αὐτῶν ἀπὸ Παμφυλίας, καὶ μὴ
thought fit (he) having withdrawn from them from Pamphilia, and not

from Pamphylia, and not going with them to the work. 39 Then there was sharp feeling, so as to separate them from each other. And taking Mark, Barnabas sailed away to Cyprus. 40 But having chosen Silas, Paul went out, being commended to the grace of God by the brothers, 41 and passed through Syria and Cilicia, making the churches strong.

CHAPTER 16

1 And he arrived in Derbe and Lystra. And behold, a certain disciple named Timothy was there, *the* son of a certain believing Jewish woman—but *his* father *was* a Greek— 2 *This one* was being testified of by the brothers in Lystra and Iconium. 3 Paul desired this one to go forth with him, and having taken *him* he circumcised him, because of the Jews *who* were in those places—for they all knew his father, that he continued being a Greek — 4 And as they passed through the cities, they were delivering over to them *the need* to keep the decrees having been determined by the apostles and the elders who *were* in Jerusalem. 5 Indeed, therefore, the churches were being made strong in the faith, and were becoming more abundant in number by *every* day.

6 And having come through the Phrygian and the Galatian region—having been forbidden by the Holy Spirit to speak the word in Asia— 7 having come to Mysia, they were attempting to go to Bithynia; and the Spirit did not allow them. 8 And having passed by Mysia, they came down into Troas. 9 And a vision was seen by Paul during the night: a certain man of Macedonia had stood, entreating him and saying, Having crossed over into Macedonia, help us! 10 And *as soon* as he saw the vision, we immediately sought to go forth into Macedonia, concluding that the Lord had called us near to announce the gospel *to* them.

συνελθόντα αὐτοῖς εἰς τὸ ἔργον, μὴ συμπαραλαβεῖν τοῦτον.
going with them to the work, not to take with (them) that one.
39 ἐγένετο οὖν παροξυσμός, ὥστε ἀποχωρισθῆναι αὐτοὺς ἀπ'
there was Then sharp feeling, so as to separate them from
ἀλλήλων, τόν τε Βαρνάβαν παραλαβόντα τὸν Μάρκον
each other; — and Barnabas taking — Mark
40 ἐκπλεῦσαι εἰς Κύπρον· Παῦλος δὲ ἐπιλεξάμενος Σίλαν ἐξῆλθε,
to sail way to Cyprus. Paul But having chosen Silas went out,
41 παραδοθεὶς τῇ χάριτι τοῦ Θεοῦ ὑπὸ τῶν ἀδελφῶν. διήρχετο
being commended to the grace of God by the brothers. went through
δὲ τὴν Συρίαν καὶ Κιλικίαν, ἐπιστηρίζων τὰς ἐκκλησίας.
And — Syria and Cilicia, making strong the churches.

CHAPTER 16

1 Κατήντησε δὲ εἰς Δέρβην καὶ Λύστραν· καὶ ἰδού, μαθητής
he came down And to Derbe and Lystra. And behold, a disciple
τις ἦν ἐκεῖ, ὀνόματι Τιμόθεος, υἱὸς γυναικός τινος Ἰουδαίας
certain was there by name Timothy, son of a woman certain Jewish
2 πιστῆς, πατρὸς δὲ Ἕλληνος· ὃς ἐμαρτυρεῖτο ὑπὸ τῶν ἐν
faithful, father but (was) a Greek; who was witnessed to by the in
3 Λύστροις καὶ Ἰκονίῳ ἀδελφῶν. τοῦτον ἠθέλησεν ὁ Παῦλος
Lystra and Iconium brothers. This one desired — Paul
σὺν αὐτῷ ἐξελθεῖν, καὶ λαβὼν περιέτεμεν αὐτόν, διὰ τοὺς
with him to go forth, and taking circumcised him because of the
Ἰουδαίους τοὺς ὄντας ἐν τοῖς τόποις ἐκείνοις· ᾔδεισαν γὰρ
Jews — being in — places those; they knew for
4 ἅπαντες τὸν πατέρα αὐτοῦ, ὅτι Ἕλλην ὑπῆρχεν. ὡς δὲ
all the father of him, that a Greek he was. as And
διεπορεύοντο τὰς πόλεις, παρεδίδουν αὐτοῖς φυλάσσειν τὰ
they went through the cities, they delivered to them to keep the
δόγματα τὰ κεκριμένα ὑπὸ τῶν ἀποστόλων καὶ τῶν πρεσ-
decrees — being decided by the apostles and the
5 βυτέρων τῶν ἐν Ἱερουσαλήμ. αἱ μὲν οὖν ἐκκλησίαι ἐστερεοῦν-
elders — in Jerusalem. the Therefore churches were made
το τῇ πίστει, καὶ ἐπερίσσευον τῷ ἀριθμῷ καθ' ἡμέραν.
strong in the faith, and increased — in number day by day.
6 Διελθόντες δὲ τὴν Φρυγίαν καὶ τὴν Γαλατικὴν χώραν,
having passed through And the Phrygia and the Galatian country,
κωλυθέντες ὑπὸ τοῦ Ἁγίου Πνεύματος λαλῆσαι τὸν λόγον
being prevented by the Holy Spirit to speak the word
7 ἐν τῇ Ἀσίᾳ, ἐλθόντες κατὰ τὴν Μυσίαν ἐπείραζον κατὰ τὴν
in — Asia, coming against — Mysia, they attempted along
Βιθυνίαν πορεύεσθαι· καὶ οὐκ εἴασεν αὐτοὺς τὸ Πνεῦμα·
Bithynia to go, and not allowed them the Spirit.
8 παρελθόντες δὲ τὴν Μυσίαν κατέβησαν εἰς Τρωάδα. καὶ
passing by And — Mysia they came down to Troas. And
9 ὅραμα διὰ τῆς νυκτὸς ὤφθη τῷ Παύλῳ· ἀνήρ τις ἦν Μακεδὼν
a vision during the night appeared — to Paul, a man certain was of Macedonia
ἑστώς, παρακαλῶν αὐτὸν καὶ λέγων, Διαβὰς εἰς Μακεδονίαν,
standing, begging him and saying, Passing over to Macedonia,
10 βοήθησον ἡμῖν. ὡς δὲ τὸ ὅραμα εἶδεν, εὐθέως ἐζητήσαμεν
help us. when And the vision he saw, at once we sought
ἐξελθεῖν εἰς τὴν Μακεδονίαν, συμβιβάζοντες ὅτι προσκέκλη-
to go forth to — Macedonia, concluding that has called
ται ἡμᾶς ὁ Κύριος εὐαγγελίσασθαι αὐτούς.
us the Lord to preach the gospel to them.

[11] Then having set sail from Troas, we came with a straight course into Samothrace, and on the morrow into Neapolis; [12] and from there into Philippi, which is a chief *city* of *that* part of Macedonia, a colony. And we continued spending time in this city some days. [13] And on the day of the sabbaths, we went outside the city beside a river, where it was customary *for* prayer to be *made*. And having sat down, we were speaking to the women who came together *there*. [14] And a certain woman named Lydia, a seller of purple of *the* city of Thyatira, *one* reverencing God, was listening, whose heart the Lord opened thoroughly to pay attention to the things being spoken by Paul. [15] And as she and her household were baptized, she entreated *Paul*, saying, If you have judged me to be believing in the Lord, having entered into my house, remain *a while*. And she strongly urged us.

[16] And it happened, *as* we went into *the place* of prayer, a certain maidservant having a Pythonic spirit *came* to meet us, whose divining brought much gain to her lords. [17] Having followed after Paul and us, she cried out, saying, These men are slaves of the Most High God, who are announcing to us a way of salvation! [18] And she continually did this over many days. But having become distressed, and having turned to the *demonic* spirit, Paul said, I command you in the Name of Jesus Christ to come out from her! And it came out in that *same* hour.

[19] And seeing that the hope of their gain went out, having seized Paul and Silas, her lords dragged *them* to the market before the rulers. [20] And bringing them near to the governor, *they* said, These men are very much troubling our city, being Jews,

11 Ἀναχθέντες οὖν ἀπὸ τῆς Τρῳάδος, εὐθυδρομήσαμεν εἰς
setting sail Then from — Troas, we ran a straight course to
12 Σαμοθρᾴκην, τῇ τε ἐπιούσῃ εἰς Νεάπολιν, ἐκεῖθέν τε εἰς
Samothrace, on the and next day to Neapolis, from there and to
Φιλίππους, ἥτις ἐστὶ πρώτη τῆς μερίδος τῆς Μακεδονίας
Philippi, which is (the) first of the part — of Macedonia
πόλις, κολωνία· ἦμεν δὲ ἐν ταύτῃ τῇ πόλει διατρίβοντες
city, a colony. we were And in this — city staying
13 ἡμέρας τινάς. τῇ τε ἡμέρᾳ τῶν σαββάτων ἐξήλθομεν ἔξω τῆς
days some. on the And day of the sabbaths, we went out outside the
πόλεως παρὰ ποταμόν, οὗ ἐνομίζετο προσευχὴ εἶναι, καὶ
city by a river, where was customary prayer to be; and
14 καθίσαντες ἐλαλοῦμεν ταῖς συνελθούσαις γυναιξί. καί τις
sitting down we spoke to the who came together women. And a certain
γυνὴ ὀνόματι Λυδία, πορφυρόπωλις πόλεως Θυατείρων,
woman, by name Lydia, a seller of purple, of (the) city of Thyatira,
σεβομένη τὸν Θεόν, ἤκουεν· ἧς ὁ Κύριος διήνοιξε τὴν καρδίαν,
revering — God, heard, of whom the Lord opened the heart
15 προσέχειν τοῖς λαλουμένοις ὑπὸ τοῦ Παύλου. ὡς δὲ ἐβαπτί-
to attend to the things spoken by — Paul. when And she was
σθη, καὶ ὁ οἶκος αὐτῆς, παρεκάλεσε λέγουσα, Εἰ κεκρίκατέ
baptized, and the house of her, she beseeched, saying, If you have judged
με πιστὴν τῷ Κυρίῳ εἶναι, εἰσελθόντες εἰς τὸν οἶκόν μου,
me believing in the Lord to be, entering into the house of me,
μείνατε. καὶ παρεβιάσατο ἡμᾶς.
remain. And she urged us.

16 Ἐγένετο δὲ πορευομένων ἡμῶν εἰς προσευχήν, παιδίσκην
it was And, going us into (a place of) prayer, a girl
τινὰ ἔχουσαν πνεῦμα Πύθωνος ἀπαντῆσαι ἡμῖν, ἥτις
certain having a spirit of Python met us, who
ἐργασίαν πολλὴν παρεῖχε τοῖς κυρίοις αὐτῆς, μαντευομένη.
gain much brought to the lords of her divining.
17 αὕτη κατακολουθήσασα τῷ Παύλῳ καὶ ἡμῖν, ἔκραζε λέγουσα,
She following after — Paul and us, cried out saying,
Οὗτοι οἱ ἄνθρωποι δοῦλοι τοῦ Θεοῦ τοῦ ὑψίστου εἰσίν,
These — men slaves of the God — most high are,
18 οἵτινες καταγγέλλουσιν ἡμῖν ὁδὸν σωτηρίας. τοῦτο δὲ
who announce to us a way of salvation. this And
ἐποίει ἐπὶ πολλὰς ἡμέρας. διαπονηθεὶς δὲ ὁ Παῦλος, καὶ
she did over many days. becoming distressed But Paul, and
ἐπιστρέψας, τῷ πνεύματι εἶπε, Παραγγέλλω σοι ἐν τῷ
turning to the spirit said, I command you in the
ὀνόματι Ἰησοῦ Χριστοῦ, ἐξελθεῖν ἀπ' αὐτῆς. καὶ ἐξῆλθεν
name of Jesus Christ to come out from her. And it came out
αὐτῇ τῇ ὥρᾳ.
in that hour.

19 Ἰδόντες δὲ οἱ κύριοι αὐτῆς ὅτι ἐξῆλθεν ἡ ἐλπὶς τῆς
seeing And the lords of her that went out the hope of the
ἐργασίας αὐτῶν, ἐπιλαβόμενοι τὸν Παῦλον καὶ τὸν Σίλαν,
gain of them, having seized — Paul and — Silas,
20 εἵλκυσαν εἰς τὴν ἀγορὰν ἐπὶ τοὺς ἄρχοντας, καὶ προσ-
dragged to the market before the rulers, and having
αγαγόντες αὐτοὺς τοῖς στρατηγοῖς εἶπον, Οὗτοι οἱ ἄνθρω-
led near them to the governor said, These — men
21 ποι ἐκταράσσουσιν ἡμῶν τὴν πόλιν, Ἰουδαῖοι ὑπάρχοντες,
are very much troubling of us the city, Jews being,

[21]and announce customs which it is not lawful for us to receive, nor to do, being Romans.[22]And the crowd rose against them, and tearing off their clothes, the governors commanded to flog *them*. [23]And laying on them many stripes, they threw *them* into prison, charging the jailer to keep them securely; [24]who, receiving them, threw them into the inner prison, and locked their feet in the stocks.

[26]And having prayed, toward midnight Paul and Silas praised God in a hymn. And the prisoners listened to them. [26]And suddenly there was a great earthquake, so that the foundations of the jail were shaken. And immediately all the doors were opened, and all the bonds were loosened. [27]And the jailer being awakened, and seeing the doors of the prison being open, having drawn a sword, was about to do away with himself, supposing the prisoners to have escaped. [28]But Paul called out with a loud voice, saying, Do no harm *to* yourself! For we are all here. [29]And asking for lights, he rushed in. And becoming trembly, he fell before Paul and Silas. [30]And leading them outside, *he* said, Sirs, what must I do that I may be saved? [31]And they said, Believe on the Lord Jesus Christ, and you will be saved, you and your household. [32]And they spoke the word of the Lord to him, and to all those in his household. [33]And taking them in that hour of the night, he washed from *their* stripes. And he and those of his were baptized at once. [34]And bringing them up to the house, he set a table before *them*, and exulted with all his household, believing God.
[35]And day having come,

καὶ καταγγέλλουσιν ἔθη ἃ οὐκ ἔξεστιν ἡμῖν παραδέχεσθαι
and they announce customs which not it is lawful for us to receive,
22 οὐδὲ ποιεῖν, Ῥωμαίοις οὖσι. καὶ συνεπέστη ὁ ὄχλος κατ'
nor to do, Romans being. And rose together the crowd against
αὐτῶν, καὶ οἱ στρατηγοὶ περιρρήξαντες αὐτῶν τὰ ἱμάτια
them, and the governors tearing off of them the clothes
23 ἐκέλευον ῥαβδίζειν. πολλάς τε ἐπιθέντες αὐτοῖς πληγὰς
commanded to flog; many and laying on them stripes
ἔβαλον εἰς φυλακήν, παραγγείλαντες τῷ δεσμοφύλακι
threw into prison, charging the jailer
24 ἀσφαλῶς τηρεῖν αὐτούς· ὅς, παραγγελίαν τοιαύτην εἰληφώς,
securely to keep them; who a charge such having received,
ἔβαλεν αὐτοὺς εἰς τὴν ἐσωτέραν φυλακήν, καὶ τοὺς πόδας
threw them into the inner prison, and the feet
25 αὐτῶν ἠσφαλίσατο εἰς τὸ ξύλον. κατὰ δε τὸ μεσονύκτιον
of them secured in the stocks. about And — midnight,
Παῦλος καὶ Σίλας προσευχόμενοι ὕμνουν τὸν Θεόν, ἐπη-
Paul and Silas praying praised in a hymn — God,
26 κροῶντο δὲ αὐτῶν οἱ δέσμιοι· ἄφνω δὲ σεισμὸς ἐγένετο
listened and to them the prisoners. suddenly And an earthquake was
μέγας, ὥστε σαλευθῆναι τὰ θεμέλια τοῦ δεσμωτηρίου·
great, so as to be shaken the foundations of the jail.
ἀνεῴχθησάν τε παραχρῆμα αἱ θύραι πᾶσαι, καὶ πάντων
were opened And immediately the doors all, and of all
27 τὰ δεσμὰ ἀνέθη. ἔξυπνος δὲ γενόμενος ὁ δεσμοφύλαξ, καὶ
the bonds were loosened. awake And becoming the jailer, and
ἰδὼν ἀνεῳγμένας τὰς θύρας τῆς φυλακῆς, σπασάμενος
seeing having been opened the doors of the prison, having drawn
μάχαιραν, ἔμελλεν ἑαυτὸν ἀναιρεῖν, νομίζων ἐκπεφευγέναι
a sword, was about himself to do away, supposing to have escaped
28 τοὺς δεσμίους. ἐφώνησε δὲ φωνῇ μεγάλῃ ὁ Παῦλος λέγων,
the prisoners. called But with a voice great — Paul, saying,
Μηδὲν πράξῃς σεαυτῷ κακόν· ἅπαντες γάρ ἐσμεν ἐνθάδε.
nothing Do (to) yourself harm, all for we are here.
29 αἰτήσας δὲ φῶτα εἰσεπήδησε, καὶ ἔντρομος γενόμενος
asking And lights, he rushed in, and trembling becoming
30 προσέπεσε τῷ Παύλῳ καὶ τῷ Σίλᾳ, καὶ προαγαγὼν αὐτοὺς
he fell before — Paul and — Silas, and having led them
31 ἔξω ἔφη, Κύριοι, τί με δεῖ ποιεῖν ἵνα σωθῶ; οἱ δὲ εἶπον,
outside said, Sirs, what me must do that I may be saved? they And said,
Πίστευσον ἐπὶ τὸν Κύριον Ἰησοῦν Χριστόν, καὶ σωθήσῃ
Believe on the Lord Jesus Christ, and you will be saved,
32 σὺ καὶ ὁ οἶκός σου. καὶ ἐλάλησαν αὐτῷ τὸν λόγον τοῦ
you and the house of you. And they spoke to him the word of the
33 Κυρίου, καὶ πᾶσι τοῖς ἐν τῇ οἰκίᾳ αὐτοῦ. καὶ παραλαβὼν
Lord, and all those in the house of him. And taking
αὐτοὺς ἐν ἐκείνῃ τῇ ὥρᾳ τῆς νυκτὸς ἔλουσεν ἀπὸ τῶν πλη-
them in that — hour of the night, he washed from the stripes,
γῶν, καὶ ἐβαπτίσθη αὐτὸς καὶ οἱ αὐτοῦ πάντες παραχρῆμα.
and was baptized he and those of him all at once,
34 ἀναγαγών τε αὐτοὺς εἰς τὸν οἶκον αὐτοῦ παρέθηκε τράπε-
bringing up and them to the house, he set before (them) a table,
ζαν, καὶ ἠγαλλιάσατο πανοικὶ πεπιστευκὼς τῷ Θεῷ.
and exulted with all the house, having believed — God.
35 Ἡμέρας δὲ γενομένης, ἀπέστειλαν οἱ στρατηγοὶ τοὺς
day And coming, sent the governors the

the governors sent the floggers, saying, Let those men go. 36 And the jailer announced these words to Paul, The governors have sent that you be let go. Now, then, going out, proceed in peace. 37 But Paul said to them, Having beaten us publicly, being Romans *and* uncondemned men, they threw *us* into prison. And now do they throw us out secretly? No, indeed! But coming themselves, let them bring us out. 38 And the floggers reported these words to the governors. And hearing that they were Romans, they were afraid. 39 And coming, *they* begged them. And bringing *them* out, *they* asked *them* to go out of the city. 40 And going out from the prison, they went into the *house of* Lydia. And seeing the brothers, they exhorted them, and went out.

CHAPTER 17

1 And traveling through Amphipolis and Apollonia, they came to Thessalonica, where a synagogue of the Jews was. 2 And according to Paul's custom, he went in to them and reasoned with them from the Scriptures on three sabbaths, 3 opening and setting forth that the Christ must have suffered, and to have risen from *the* dead, and that this is the Christ, Jesus, whom I announce to you. 4 And some of them were persuaded, and joined themselves to Paul and Silas, both a great multitude of the worshiping Greeks, and not a few of the leading women. 5 But the disobeying Jews becoming jealous, and having taken aside some wicked men of the market-loafers, and gathering a crowd, set the city into turmoil. And coming on the house of Jason, they sought to bring them on to the mob. 6 But not finding them, they dragged Jason

ῥαβδούχους λέγοντες, Ἀπόλυσον τοὺς ἀνθρώπους ἐκείνους.
floggers, saying, Let go — men those.
36 ἀπήγγειλε δὲ ὁ δεσμοφύλαξ τοὺς λόγους τούτους πρὸς
announced And the jailer — words these to
τὸν Παῦλον ὅτι Ἀπεστάλκασιν οἱ στρατηγοί, ἵνα ἀπο-
— Paul, — have sent The governors, that you
37 λυθῆτε· νῦν οὖν ἐξελθόντες πορεύεσθε ἐν εἰρήνῃ. ὁ δὲ Παῦλος
be let go. Now, then, going out proceed in peace. But Paul
ἔφη πρὸς αὐτούς, Δείραντες ἡμᾶς δημοσίᾳ, ἀκατακρίτους,
said to them, Having beaten us publicly, uncondemned
ἀνθρώπους Ῥωμαίους ὑπάρχοντας, ἔβαλον εἰς φυλακήν, καὶ
men, Romans being, they threw into prison; and
νῦν λάθρα ἡμᾶς ἐκβάλλουσιν ; οὐ γάρ· ἀλλὰ ἐλθόντες αὐτοὶ
now secretly us they throw out? No indeed, but coming themselves
38 ἡμᾶς ἐξαγαγέτωσαν. ἀνήγγειλαν δὲ τοῖς στρατηγοῖς οἱ
us let them bring out. reported And to the governors the
ῥαβδοῦχοι τὰ ῥήματα ταῦτα· καὶ ἐφοβήθησαν ἀκούσαντες
floggers — words these. And they were afraid, hearing
39 ὅτι Ῥωμαῖοί εἰσι, καὶ ἐλθόντες παρεκάλεσαν αὐτούς, καὶ
that Romans they are; and coming begged them, and
40 ἐξαγαγόντες ἠρώτων ἐξελθεῖν τῆς πόλεως. ἐξελθόντες δὲ ἐκ
bringing out asked to go out of the city. going out And from
τῆς φυλακῆς εἰσῆλθον εἰς τὴν Λυδίαν· καὶ ἰδόντες τοὺς ἀδελ-
the prison, entered into the (house of) Lydia, and seeing the brothers,
φούς, παρεκάλεσαν αὐτούς, καὶ ἐξῆλθον.
they exhorted them, and went forth.

CHAPTER 17

1 Διοδεύσαντες δὲ τὴν Ἀμφίπολιν καὶ Ἀπολλωνίαν, ἦλθον
traveling through And — Amphipolis and Apollonia, they came
εἰς Θεσσαλονίκην, ὅπου ἦν ἡ συναγωγὴ τῶν Ἰουδαίων·
to Thessalonica, where was a synagogue of the Jews.
2 κατὰ δὲ τὸ εἰωθὸς τῷ Παύλῳ εἰσῆλθε πρὸς αὐτούς, καὶ ἐπὶ
as And the custom with Paul, he entered to them, and on
3 σάββατα τρία διελέγετο αὐτοῖς ἀπὸ τῶν γραφῶν, διανοίγων
sabbaths three reasoned with them from the Scriptures, opening
καὶ παρατιθέμενος, ὅτι τὸν Χριστὸν ἔδει παθεῖν καὶ ἀναστῆ-
and setting forth that the Christ must have suffered and to have
ναι ἐκ νεκρῶν, καὶ ὅτι οὗτός ἐστιν ὁ Χριστὸς Ἰησοῦς, ὃν ἐγὼ
risen from (the) dead, and that this is the Christ, Jesus, whom I
4 καταγγέλλω ὑμῖν. καί τινες ἐξ αὐτῶν ἐπείσθησαν, καὶ
announce to you. And some of them were persuaded, and
προσεκληρώθησαν τῷ Παύλῳ καὶ τῷ Σίλᾳ, τῶν τε σεβο-
joined themselves — to Paul and — Silas, of the both worship-
μένων Ἑλλήνων πολὺ πλῆθος, γυναικῶν τε τῶν πρώτων
ing Greeks a great multitude, of women and the chief,
5 οὐκ ὀλίγαι. ζηλώσαντες δὲ οἱ ἀπειθοῦντες Ἰουδαῖοι, καὶ
not a few. becoming jealous But the disobeying Jews, and
προσλαβόμενοι τῶν ἀγοραίων τινὰς ἄνδρας πονηρούς, καὶ
taking aside of the market-loafers some, men wicked, and
ὀχλοποιήσαντες, ἐθορύβουν τὴν πόλιν· ἐπιστάντες τε τῇ
gathering a crowd, set into turmoil the city, coming on and the
6 οἰκίᾳ Ἰάσονος, ἐζήτουν αὐτοὺς ἀγαγεῖν εἰς τὸν δῆμον. μὴ
house of Jason sought them to bring on to the mob; not
εὑρόντες δὲ αὐτούς, ἔσυρον τὸν Ἰάσονα καί τινας ἀδελφοὺς
finding but them, they dragged — Jason and some brothers

and some brothers before the city judges, crying, Those who have turned the world upside down have come here, too; [7]whom Jason has received. And these all act contrary to the decrees of Caesar, saying there is another king, Jesus. [8]And hearing these things, they troubled the crowd and the city judges. [9]And taking security from Jason and the rest, they let them go.

[10]But the brothers at once sent both Paul and Silas to Berea during the night; who having arrived went into the synagogue of the Jews. [11]And these were more noble than those in Thessalonica; *for they* received the word with all readiness, daily examining the Scriptures if these things *are* so. [12]Then many from among them truly believed, and not a few of the honorable Grecian women and men. [13]But when the Jews from Thessalonica knew that the word of God was also announced in Berea by Paul, they came there also, shaking up the crowd. [14]And immediately, then, the brothers sent away Paul, to go as toward the sea. But both Silas and Timothy remained there. [15]But those conducting Paul brought him as far as Athens. And receiving a command to Silas and Timothy, that they come to him quickly, they departed.

[16]But awaiting them in Athens, Paul's spirit was pained within him, seeing the city full of images. [17]Then, indeed, he addressed the Jews in the synagogue, and those worshiping; also in the market every day, to those happening to be *there*. [18]And some of the

ἐπὶ τοὺς πολιτάρχας, βοῶντες ὅτι Οἱ τὴν οἰκουμένην
to the the city judges, crying, — Those the habitable world
7 ἀναστατώσαντες, οὗτοι καὶ ἐνθάδε πάρεισιν, οὓς ὑποδέδε-
having turned upside down, these also here have come, whom has received
κται Ἰάσων· καὶ οὗτοι πάντες ἀπέναντι τῶν δογμάτων
Jason; and these all contrary to the decrees
Καίσαρος πράττουσι, βασιλέα λέγοντες ἕτερον εἶναι, Ἰησοῦν.
of Caesar act, king saying another to be, Jesus.
8 ἐτάραξαν δὲ τὸν ὄχλον καὶ τοὺς πολιτάρχας ἀκούοντας
they troubled And the crowd and the city judges hearing
9 ταῦτα. καὶ λαβόντες τὸ ἱκανὸν παρὰ τοῦ Ἰάσονος καὶ τῶν
these things. And taking the security from — Jason and the
λοιπῶν, ἀπέλυσαν αὐτούς.
rest, they let go them.
10 Οἱ δὲ ἀδελφοὶ εὐθέως διὰ τῆς νυκτὸς ἐξέπεμψαν τόν τε
the But brothers at once during the night sent — both
Παῦλον καὶ τὸν Σίλαν εἰς Βέροιαν· οἵτινες παραγενόμενοι
Paul and — Silas to Berea, who having arrived
11 εἰς τὴν συναγωγὴν τῶν Ἰουδαίων ἀπῄεσαν. οὗτοι δὲ ἦσαν
into the synagogue of the Jews went. these And were
εὐγενέστεροι τῶν ἐν Θεσσαλονίκῃ, οἵτινες ἐδέξαντο τὸν
more noble (than) those in Thessalonica, who received the
λόγον μετὰ πάσης προθυμίας, τὸ καθ' ἡμέραν ἀνακρίνοντες
word with all readiness, daily examining
12 τὰς γραφάς, εἰ ἔχοι ταῦτα οὕτως. πολλοὶ μὲν οὖν ἐξ αὐτῶν
the Scriptures, if have these things so. Many, therefore of them
ἐπίστευσαν, καὶ τῶν Ἑλληνίδων γυναικῶν τῶν εὐσχη-
believed and of the Greek women — honorable
13 μόνων καὶ ἀνδρῶν οὐκ ὀλίγοι. ὡς δὲ ἔγνωσαν οἱ ἀπὸ τῆς
and men not a few. when But knew the from —
Θεσσαλονίκης Ἰουδαῖοι ὅτι καὶ ἐν τῇ Βεροίᾳ κατηγγέλη
Thessalonica Jews that also in — Berea was announced
ὑπὸ τοῦ Παύλου ὁ λόγος τοῦ Θεοῦ, ἦλθον κἀκεῖ σαλεύοντες
by Paul the word of God, they came there also shaking
14 τοὺς ὄχλους. εὐθέως δὲ τότε τὸν Παῦλον ἐξαπέστειλαν οἱ
the crowd. at once And, then, — Paul sent away the
ἀδελφοὶ πορεύεσθαι ὡς ἐπὶ τὴν θάλασσαν· ὑπέμενον δὲ ὅ
brothers to go as to the sea. remained But —
15 τε Σίλας καὶ ὁ Τιμόθεος ἐκεῖ. οἱ δὲ καθιστῶντες τὸν Παῦλον,
both Silas and — Timothy there. those And conducting — Paul
ἤγαγον αὐτὸν ἕως Ἀθηνῶν· καὶ λαβόντες ἐντολὴν πρὸς
brought him as far as Athens; and having received a command to
τὸν Σίλαν καὶ Τιμόθεον, ἵνα ὡς τάχιστα ἔλθωσι πρὸς αὐτόν,
— Silas and Timothy, that as quickly they come to him,
ἐξῄεσαν.
they departed.

16 Ἐν δὲ ταῖς Ἀθήναις ἐκδεχομένου αὐτοὺς τοῦ Παύλου,
in And — Athens awaiting them — Paul
παρωξύνετο τὸ πνεῦμα αὐτοῦ ἐν αὐτῷ, θεωροῦντι κατεί-
was pained the spirit of him in him, beholding full of
17 δωλον οὖσαν τὴν πόλιν. διελέγετο μὲν οὖν ἐν τῇ συναγωγῇ
images being the city. He addressed, therefore, in the synagogue
τοῖς Ἰουδαίοις καὶ τοῖς σεβομένοις, καὶ ἐν τῇ ἀγορᾷ κατὰ
the Jews and those worshiping; also in the market —
18 πᾶσαν ἡμέραν πρὸς τοὺς παρατυγχάνοντας. τινὲς δὲ τῶν
every day to those happening to be (there). some And of the

Epicureans and of the Stoics, philosophers, fell in with him. And some said, What may this chatterer wish to say? And these *others*, He seems to be an announcer of foreign demons–because he announced Jesus and the resurrection to them. 19 And taking hold of him, they led *him* to the Areopagus, saying, Are we able to know what this new teaching being spoken by you *is*? 20 For you bring startling things to our ears. We are minded, then, to know what these things wish to be. 21 And all Athenians and the strangers living *there* have leisure for nothing else than to say and to hear something newer.

22 And standing in *the* middle of the Areopagus, Paul said, Men, Athenians, I see how you in everything *are* fearful of gods; 23 for passing through and looking up at the objects of your worship, I also found an altar on which had been written, TO AN UNKNOWN GOD. Not knowing, then, whom you worship, I make Him known to you.

24 The God who made the world and all things in it, this One being Lord of Heaven and of earth does not dwell in handmade temples, 25 nor is served by hands of men, *as* having need of anything, *for* He gives life and breath to all. 26 And He made every nation of men of one blood, to live on all the face of the earth, ordaining fore-appointed seasons and boundaries of their dwelling, 27 to seek the Lord, if perhaps they might feel after Him and might find Him, though indeed not being far from each one of us. 28 For in Him we live and move and are; as also some of the poets among you have said, For we are also His offspring. 29 Therefore, being offspring of God, we ought not to suppose that the Godhead is like gold or silver or stone, engraved by art and the ought not to think that the Godhead is like gold or

Ἐπικουρείων καὶ τῶν Στωϊκῶν φιλοσόφων συνέβαλλον αὐτῷ.
Epicureans and of the Stoics, philosophers, fell in with him.
καί τινες ἔλεγον, Τί ἂν θέλοι ὁ σπερμολόγος οὗτος λέγειν;
And some said, What may desire — chatterer this to say?
οἱ δέ, Ξένων δαιμονίων δοκεῖ καταγγελεὺς εἶναι· ὅτι τὸν
these And, Of foreign demons he seems an announcer to be; because —
19 Ἰησοῦν καὶ τὴν ἀνάστασιν αὐτοῖς εὐηγγελίζετο. ἐπιλα-
Jesus and the resurrection to them he announced. taking
βόμενοί τε αὐτοῦ, ἐπὶ τὸν Ἄρειον πάγον ἤγαγον λέγοντες,
hold And of him, to the Areopagus they led (him), saying,
Δυνάμεθα γνῶναι, τίς ἡ καινὴ αὕτη ἡ ὑπὸ σοῦ λαλουμένη
Are we able to know what — new this — by you being spoken
20 διδαχή; ξενίζοντα γάρ τινα εἰσφέρεις εἰς τὰς ἀκοὰς ἡμῶν·
teaching (is)? startling things For some you bring to the ears of us;
21 βουλόμεθα οὖν γνῶναι, τί ἂν θέλοι ταῦτα εἶναι. (Ἀθηναῖοι
we are minded, then, to know what wishes these things to be. Athenians
δὲ πάντες καὶ οἱ ἐπιδημοῦντες ξένοι εἰς οὐδὲν ἕτερον εὐκαί-
And all and the living strangers for nothing different have
ρουν, ἢ λέγειν τι καὶ ἀκούειν καινότερον.)
leisure either to say something, and to hear newer (things).
22 Σταθεὶς δὲ ὁ Παῦλος ἐν μέσῳ τοῦ Ἀρείου πάγου ἔφη,
standing And — Paul in (the) midst of the Areopagus said,
Ἄνδρες Ἀθηναῖοι, κατὰ πάντα ὡς δεισιδαιμονεστέρους ὑμᾶς
Men, Athenians, in everything how very fearful of gods you
23 θεωρῶ. διερχόμενος γὰρ καὶ ἀναθεωρων τὰ σεβάσματα
I behold. passing through For and looking up at the objects of worship
ὑμῶν, εὗρον καὶ βωμὸν ἐν ᾧ ἐπεγέγραπτο, Ἀγνώστῳ Θεῷ.
of you, I found also an altar in which had been written, To an Unknown God.
ὃν οὖν ἀγνοοῦντες εὐσεβεῖτε, τοῦτον ἐγὼ καταγγέλλω ὑμῖν.
Whom, then, not knowing you reverence, this One I announce to you.
24 ὁ Θεὸς ὁ ποιήσας τὸν κόσμον καὶ πάντα τὰ ἐν αὐτῷ, οὗτος,
The God, He having made the world and all things in it, this One
οὐρανοῦ καὶ γῆς κύριος ὑπάρχων, οὐκ ἐν χειροποιήτοις
of Heaven and of earth Lord being, not in handmade
25 ναοῖς κατοικεῖ, οὐδὲ ὑπὸ χειρῶν ἀνθρώπων θεραπεύεται,
temples dwells, nor by hands of men is served
προσδεόμενός τινος, αὐτὸς διδοὺς πᾶσι ζωὴν καὶ πνοὴν καὶ
having need of anything. He is giving to all life and breath, and
26 τὰ πάντα· ἐποίησέ τε ἐξ ἑνὸς αἵματος πᾶν ἔθνος ἀνθρώπων,
all things. He made And of one blood every nation of men,
κατοικεῖν ἐπὶ πᾶν τὸ πρόσωπον τῆς γῆς, ὁρίσας προτεταγ-
to live on all the face of the earth, ordaining fore-appointed
27 μένους καιροὺς καὶ τὰς ὁροθεσίας τῆς κατοικίας αὐτῶν· ζητεῖν
seasons and the boundaries of the dwelling of them, to seek
τὸν Κύριον, εἰ ἄραγε ψηλαφήσειαν αὐτὸν καὶ εὕροιεν, καί-
the Lord, if perhaps they might feel after Him and might find,
τοιγε οὐ μακρὰν ἀπὸ ἑνὸς ἑκάστου ἡμῶν ὑπάρχοντα. ἐν
though not far from one each of us being. in
28 αὐτῷ γὰρ ζῶμεν καὶ κινούμεθα καί ἐσμεν· ὡς καί τινες τῶν
Him For we live and move and are, as indeed some of the
29 καθ' ὑμᾶς ποιητῶν εἰρήκασι, Τοῦ γὰρ καὶ γένος ἐσμέν. γένος
among you poets have said: of Him For also offspring we are. offspring
οὖν ὑπάρχοντες τοῦ Θεοῦ, οὐκ ὀφείλομεν νομίζειν χρυσῷ ἢ
Then being — of God, not we ought to suppose to gold, or
ἀργύρῳ ἢ λίθῳ, χαράγματι τέχνης καὶ ἐνθυμήσεως ἀνθρώ-
to silver, or to stone, to an engraving of art and of imagination of man,

imagination of man. [30]Truly, then, God overlooking the times of ignorance now strictly charges all men everywhere to repent, [31]because He set a day in which He is going to judge the world in righteousness, by a Man whom He appointed, having given proof to all *by* raising Him from *the* dead. [32]And hearing *of* a resurrection of *the* dead, some indeed ridiculed, and said, We will hear you again concerning this. [33]And so Paul went out from their midst. [34]But some men believed, joining themselves to him, among whom also *were* Dionysius the Areopagite and a woman named Damaris, and others with them.

CHAPTER 18

[1]And after these things, departing from Athens, Paul came to Corinth. [2]And finding a certain Jew named Aquila, of Pontus by race, having recently come from Italy *with* his wife Priscilla—because Claudius had ordered all the Jews to leave Rome—he came to them. [3]And because *he* was of the same trade, he lived and worked with them; for they were tentmakers by trade. [4]And he reasoned in the synagogue on every sabbath, persuading both Jews and Greeks. [5]And when both Silas and Timothy came down from Macedonia, Paul was pressed by the Spirit, earnestly testifying to the Jews *that* Jesus *is* the Christ. [6]But they having resisted, and blaspheming, having shaken *his* garments, he said to them, Your blood *be* on your head. I *am* pure *from it*; from now on I will go to the Gentiles. [7]And moving from there, he went into *the* house of one named Justus, *one* worshiping God, whose

30 που, τὸ θεῖον εἶναι ὅμοιον. τοὺς μὲν οὖν χρόνους τῆς ἀγνοίας
the Godhead is like. the indeed Then times – of ignorance
ὑπεριδὼν ὁ Θεός, τὰ νῦν παραγγέλλει τοῖς ἀνθρώποις πᾶσι
overlooking, God now declares to men all
31 πανταχοῦ μετανοεῖν· διότι ἔστησεν ἡμέραν, ἐν ᾗ μέλλει
everywhere to repent, because He set a day in which He is going
κρίνειν τὴν οἰκουμένην ἐν δικαιοσύνῃ, ἐν ἀνδρὶ ᾧ ὥρισε,
to judge the habitable world in righteousness, by a Man whom He appointed
πίστιν παρασχὼν πᾶσιν, ἀναστήσας αὐτὸν ἐκ νεκρῶν.
proof having given to all, having raised Him from (the) dead.
32 Ἀκούσαντες δὲ ἀνάστασιν νεκρῶν, οἱ μὲν ἐχλεύαζον· οἱ
hearing (of) And a resurrection of (the) dead, some indeed ridiculed;
33 δὲ εἶπον, Ἀκουσόμεθά σου πάλιν περὶ τούτου. καὶ οὕτως ὁ
but said, We will hear you again concerning this. And thus
34 Παῦλος ἐξῆλθεν ἐκ μέσου αὐτῶν. τινὲς δὲ ἄνδρες κολληθέντες
Paul went out from (the) midst of them. some But men adhering
αὐτῷ, ἐπίστευσαν· ἐν οἷς καὶ Διονύσιος ὁ Ἀρεοπαγίτης, καὶ
to him believed, among whom both Dionysius the Areopagite, and
γυνὴ ὀνόματι Δάμαρις, καὶ ἕτεροι σὺν αὐτοῖς.
a woman by name Damaris, and others with them.

CHAPTER 18

1 Μετὰ δὲ ταῦτα χωρισθεὶς ὁ Παῦλος ἐκ τῶν Ἀθηνῶν ἦλθεν
after And these things departing Paul from – Athens came
2 εἰς Κόρινθον. καὶ εὑρών τινα Ἰουδαῖον ὀνόματι Ἀκύλαν,
to Corinth. And finding a certain Jew by name Aquila,
Ποντικὸν τῷ γένει, προσφάτως ἐληλυθότα ἀπὸ τῆς Ἰταλίας,
of Pontus – by race, recently having come from – Italy,
καὶ Πρίσκιλλαν γυναῖκα αὐτοῦ, διὰ τὸ διατεταχέναι Κλαύ-
and Priscilla the wife of him, because had ordered Claud-
διον χωρίζεσθαι πάντας τοὺς Ἰουδαίους ἐκ τῆς Ῥώμης,
ius to depart all the Jews from – Rome,
3 προσῆλθεν αὐτοῖς· καὶ διὰ τὸ ὁμότεχνον εἶναι, ἔμενε παρ'
he came to them. and because the same trade being, he abode with
αὐτοῖς καὶ εἰργάζετο· ἦσαν γὰρ σκηνοποιοὶ τὴν τέχνην.
them and worked; they were for tentmakers – by trade.
4 διελέγετο δὲ ἐν τῇ συναγωγῇ κατὰ πᾶν σάββατον, ἔπειθέ τε
he reasoned And in the synagogue on every sabbath, persuading both
Ἰουδαίους καὶ Ἕλληνας.
Jews and Greeks.
5 Ὡς δὲ κατῆλθον ἀπὸ τῆς Μακεδονίας ὅ τε Σίλας καὶ ὁ
when And came down from – Macedonia – both Silas and –
Τιμόθεος, συνείχετο τῷ πνεύματι ὁ Παῦλος, διαμαρτυρό-
Timothy, was pressed by the Spirit – Paul, earnestly testifying
μενος τοῖς Ἰουδαίοις τὸν Χριστὸν Ἰησοῦν. ἀντιτασσο-
to the Jews (that) Christ Jesus (is). having re-
6 μένων δὲ αὐτῶν καὶ βλασφημούντων, ἐκτιναξάμενος τὰ
sisted But they, and blaspheming, he having shaken the
ἱμάτια, εἶπε πρὸς αὐτούς, Τὸ αἷμα ὑμῶν ἐπὶ τὴν κεφαλὴν
garments said to them, The blood of you on the head
ὑμῶν· καθαρὸς ἐγώ· ἀπὸ τοῦ νῦν εἰς τὰ ἔθνη πορεύσομαι.
of you (is); clean I from – now to the nations I will go
7 καὶ μεταβὰς ἐκεῖθεν ἦλθεν εἰς οἰκίαν τινὸς ὀνόματι Ἰούστου,
And moving from there he went into house of one by name Justus,
σεβομένου τὸν Θεόν, οὗ ἡ οἰκία ἦν συνομοροῦσα τῇ
(one) worshiping God, of whom the house was being next door to the

house was next door to the synagogue. [8]And Crispus, the synagogue ruler, believed the Lord along with all his household. And hearing, many of the Corinthians believed and were baptized. [9]And the Lord said to Paul through a vision in *the* night, Do not fear, but speak, and do not keep silence; [10]because I am with you, and no one shall set on you to oppress you; because there is much people to Me in this city. [11]And he remained a year and six months teaching the word of God among them.

[12]But Gallio *being* proconsul of Achaia, the Jews rushed against Paul with one passion, and led him to the tribunal, [13]saying, This one persuades men to worship God contrary to the Law. [14]But Paul being about to open *his* mouth, Gallio said to the Jews, If, indeed, then, it was some wrong or wicked criminality, O Jews, according to reason I would endure you. [15]But if it is a question about a word, and names, and the law according to you, you will see to *it* yourselves; for I do not wish to be a judge of these things. [16]And he drove them from the tribunal. [17]And all the Greeks having seized Sosthenes the ruler of the synagogue, they beat *him* before the tribunal. And not one of these things mattered to Gallio.

[18]And having remained many days more, having taken leave of the brothers, Paul sailed to Syria—and Priscilla and Aquila *were* with him—having shaved *his* head in Cenchrea, for he had a vow. [19]And he came to Ephesus, and he left them there. But going into the synagogue, he reasoned with the Jews. [20]And they asking *him* to remain a longer time with them, he did not agree; [21]but took leave of them, saying, I must

8 συναγωγῇ. Κρίσπος δὲ ὁ ἀρχισυνάγωγος ἐπίστευσε τῷ
synagogue. Crispus And the synagogue ruler believed the
Κυρίῳ σὺν ὅλῳ τῷ οἴκῳ αὐτοῦ· καὶ πολλοὶ τῶν Κορινθίων
Lord with all the house of him, and many of the Corinthians
9 ἀκούοντες ἐπίστευον καὶ ἐβαπτίζοντο. εἶπε δὲ ὁ Κύριος δι'
hearing believed and were baptized. said And the Lord through
ὁράματος ἐν νυκτὶ τῷ Παύλῳ, Μὴ φοβοῦ, ἀλλὰ λάλει καὶ
a vision in (the) night — to Paul, Do not fear, but speak and
10 μὴ σιωπήσῃς· διότι ἐγώ εἰμι μετὰ σοῦ, καὶ οὐδεὶς ἐπιθή-
do not keep silence, because I am with you, and no one shall
σεταί σοι τοῦ κακῶσαί σε· διότι λαός ἐστί μοι πολὺς ἐν τῇ
set on you — to oppress you; because people is to me much in —
11 πόλει ταύτῃ. ἐκάθισέ τε ἐνιαυτὸν καὶ μῆνας ἕξ, διδάσκων
city this. he sat And a year and months six teaching
ἐν αὐτοῖς τὸν λόγον τοῦ Θεοῦ.
among them the word — of God.
12 Γαλλίωνος δὲ ἀνθυπατεύοντος τῆς Ἀχαΐας, κατεπέστησαν
Gallio (being) And proconsul — of Achaia, rushed against
ὁμοθυμαδὸν οἱ Ἰουδαῖοι τῷ Παύλῳ, καὶ ἤγαγον αὐτὸν
with one mind the Jews — Paul, and led him
13 ἐπὶ τὸ βῆμα, λέγοντες ὅτι Παρὰ τὸν νόμον οὗτος ἀναπείθει
to the tribunal, saying, Contrary to the law, this one persuades
14 τοὺς ἀνθρώπους σέβεσθαι τὸν Θεόν. μέλλοντος δὲ τοῦ
— men to worship — God. being about And —
Παύλου ἀνοίγειν τὸ στόμα, εἶπεν ὁ Γαλλίων πρὸς τοὺς
Paul to open the mouth, said — Gallio to the
Ἰουδαίους, Εἰ μὲν οὖν ἦν ἀδίκημά τι ἢ ῥᾳδιούργημα
Jews, If indeed, then, it was wrong some or criminality
πονηρόν, ὦ Ἰουδαῖοι, κατὰ λόγον ἂν ἠνεσχόμην ὑμῶν·
wicked, O Jews, according to reason I would endure you;
15 εἰ δὲ ζήτημά ἐστι περὶ λόγου καὶ ὀνομάτων καὶ νόμου τοῦ
if but a question it is about a word and names and law the
καθ' ὑμᾶς, ὄψεσθε αὐτοί· κριτὴς γὰρ ἐγὼ τούτων οὐ βού-
according to you, you will see to (it) (your)selves; a judge for I of these things not
16 λομαι εἶναι. καὶ ἀπήλασεν αὐτοὺς ἀπὸ τοῦ βήματος.
intend to be. And he drove them from the tribunal.
17 ἐπιλαβόμενοι δὲ πάντες οἱ Ἕλληνες Σωσθένην τὸν ἀρχι-
seizing But all the Greeks Sosthenes the ruler
συνάγωγον ἔτυπτον ἔμπροσθεν τοῦ βήματος. καὶ οὐδὲν
of the synagogue, they struck (him) before the tribunal; and not one
τούτων τῷ Γαλλίωνι ἔμελεν.
of these things to Gallio mattered.
18 Ὁ δὲ Παῦλος ἔτι προσμείνας ἡμέρας ἱκανάς, τοῖς ἀδελφοῖς
And Paul yet having remained days many, to the brothers
ἀποταξάμενος, ἐξέπλει εἰς τὴν Συρίαν, καὶ σὺν αὐτῷ
taking leave, he sailed to — Syria, and with him
Πρίσκιλλα καὶ Ἀκύλας, κειράμενος τὴν κεφαλὴν ἐν Κεγχρεαῖς·
Priscilla and Aquila, having shorn the head in Cenchrea;
19 εἶχε γὰρ εὐχήν. κατήντησε δὲ εἰς Ἔφεσον, κἀκείνους κατέ-
he had for a vow. he came down And to Ephesus, and those he
λιπεν αὐτοῦ· αὐτὸς δὲ εἰσελθὼν εἰς τὴν συναγωγὴν διε-
left there. he But entering into the synagogue reasoned
20 λέχθη τοῖς Ἰουδαίοις. ἐρωτώντων δὲ αὐτῶν ἐπὶ πλείονα
with the Jews. asking And they over a longer
21 χρόνον μεῖναι παρ' αὐτοῖς, οὐκ ἐπένευσεν· ἀλλ' ἀπετάξατο
time to remain with them, not he did agree, but took leave

by all means keep the coming feast at Jerusalem; but I will come again to you, God willing. And he sailed from Ephesus. [22] And having landed at Caesarea, going up and greeting the church, he went down to Antioch. [23] And having spent some time, he went out, passing through the Galatian and Phrygian country in order, making the disciples strong.

[24] But a certain Jew named Apollos, an Alexandrian by birth, an eloquent man, came to Ephesus, being powerful in the Scriptures. [25] This one was taught in the way of the Lord by mouth; and *being* fervent in spirit, he spoke and taught accurately the things about the Lord, having understood only the baptism of John. [26] And he began to speak boldly in the synagogue. And Priscilla and Aquila heard him. And *they* took him and more accurately expounded the way of God to him. [27] And he having intended to go through into Achaia, being encouraged the brothers wrote to the disciples to welcome him; who, having arrived much helped those who were believing through grace. [28] For he powerfully confuted the Jews publicly, proving through the Scriptures Jesus to be the Christ.

CHAPTER 19

[1] And it happened, in the *time* Apollos was in Corinth, Paul *was* passing through the higher parts to come to Ephesus. And finding some disciples, [2] he said to them, Believing, did you receive *the* Holy Spirit? And they said to him, We did not even hear whether *the* Holy Spirit is. [3] And he said to them, Then to what were you baptized? And they said, To the baptism of John.

αὐτοῖς εἰπών, Δεῖ με πάντως τὴν ἑορτὴν τὴν ἐρχομένην ποιῆ-
of them saying, It behoves me by all means the feast — coming to
σαι εἰς Ἱεροσόλυμα· πάλιν δὲ ἀνακάμψω πρὸς ὑμᾶς, τοῦ Θεοῦ
keep at Jerusalem, again but I will come to you, — God
22 θέλοντος. καὶ ἀνήχθη ἀπὸ τῆς Ἐφέσου. καὶ κατελθὼν εἰς
willing. And he sailed from — Ephesus. And landing at
Καισάρειαν, ἀναβὰς καὶ ἀσπασάμενος τὴν ἐκκλησίαν,
Caesarea, having gone up and having greeted the church,
23 κατέβη εἰς Ἀντιόχειαν. καὶ ποιήσας χρόνον τινὰ ἐξῆλθε,
he went down to Antioch. And having spent time some he went out,
διερχόμενος καθεξῆς τὴν Γαλατικὴν χώραν καὶ Φρυγίαν,
passing through in order the Galatian country and Phrygian
ἐπιστηρίζων πάντας τοὺς μαθητάς.
strengthening all the disciples.
24 Ἰουδαῖος δέ τις Ἀπολλὼς ὀνόματι, Ἀλεξανδρεὺς τῷ
a Jew And certain, Apollos by name, an Alexandrian —
γένει, ἀνὴρ λόγιος, κατήντησεν εἰς Ἔφεσον, δυνατὸς ὢν ἐν
by race, a man eloquent, came to Ephesus, powerful being in
25 ταῖς γραφαῖς. οὗτος ἦν κατηχημένος τὴν ὁδὸν τοῦ Κυρίου,
the Scriptures. This one was orally taught in the way of the Lord,
καὶ ζέων τῷ πνεύματι ἐλάλει καὶ ἐδίδασκεν ἀκριβῶς τὰ περὶ
and fervent — in spirit he spoke and taught accurately the things about
τοῦ Κυρίου, ἐπιστάμενος μόνον τὸ βάπτισμα Ἰωάννου·
the Lord, understanding only the baptism of John.
26 οὗτός τε ἤρξατο παρρησιάζεσθαι ἐν τῇ συναγωγῇ. ἀκού-
this one And began to speak boldly in the synagogue. hearing
σαντες δὲ αὐτοῦ Ἀκύλας καὶ Πρίσκιλλα, προσελάβοντο
And him, Aquila and Priscilla took
αὐτόν, καὶ ἀκριβέστερον αὐτῷ ἐξέθεντο τὴν τοῦ Θεοῦ ὁδόν.
him and more accurately to him expounded the of God way.
27 βουλομένου δὲ αὐτοῦ διελθεῖν εἰς τὴν Ἀχαΐαν, προτρεψά-
intending And him to go through into Achaia, being encour-
μενοι οἱ ἀδελφοὶ ἔγραψαν τοῖς μαθηταῖς ἀποδέξασθαι αὐτόν·
aged the brothers wrote to the disciples to welcome him;
ὃς παραγενόμενος συνεβάλετο πολὺ τοῖς πεπιστευκόσι διὰ
who having arrived helped much those having believed through
28 τῆς χάριτος· εὐτόνως γὰρ τοῖς Ἰουδαίοις διακατηλέγχετο
— grace; vehemently for the Jews he confuted
δημοσίᾳ, ἐπιδεικνὺς διὰ τῶν γραφῶν εἶναι τὸν Χριστὸν
publicly, proving through the Scriptures to be the Christ
Ἰησοῦν.
Jesus.

CHAPTER 19

1 Ἐγένετο δέ, ἐν τῷ τὸν Ἀπολλὼ εἶναι ἐν Κορίνθῳ, Παῦλον
it was And, in the (time) Apollos was in Corinth, Paul
διελθόντα τὰ ἀνωτερικὰ μέρη ἐλθεῖν εἰς Ἔφεσον· καὶ εὑρών
passing through the higher parts came to Ephesus, and finding
2 τινας μαθητὰς εἶπε πρὸς αὐτούς, Εἰ Πνεῦμα Ἅγιον ἐλάβετε
some disciples, said to them, If (the) Spirit Holy you received
πιστεύσαντες; οἱ δὲ εἶπον πρὸς αὐτόν, Ἀλλ' οὐδὲ εἰ Πνεῦμα
believing? they And said to him, But not even if (the) Spirit
3 Ἅγιόν ἐστιν, ἠκούσαμεν. εἶπέ τε πρὸς αὐτούς, Εἰς τί οὖν
Holy is we heard. he said And to them, To what, then,
ἐβαπτίσθητε; οἱ δὲ εἶπον, Εἰς τὸ Ἰωάννου βάπτισμα; εἶπε
were you baptized? they And said, To the of John baptism. said

[4] And Paul said, John indeed baptized *with* a baptism of repentance, saying to the people that they should believe into the *One* coming after him; that is, into the Christ, Jesus. [5] And hearing, they were baptized into the name of the Lord Jesus. [6] And Paul laying hands on them, the Holy Spirit came on them; and they spoke in languages and prophesied. [7] And all the men were about twelve.

[8] And going into the synagogue, he spoke boldly over three months, having reasoned with *them*, and persuading concerning the things of the kingdom of God. [9] But when some were hardened, and did not obey, speaking evil of the Way before the multitude, departing from them He separated the disciples, conversing day by day in the school of a certain Tyrannus. [10] And this happened over two years, so as all those living in Asia heard the word of the Lord Jesus, both Jews and Greeks. [11] And God did works of power through Paul's hands, not common *works;* [12] *but* so as even handkerchiefs or aprons from his skin to be brought, and the diseases to be released from them; and the evil spirits to go out from them.

[13] But certain from the strolling Jews, exorcists, undertook to name the name of the Lord Jesus over those having evil spirits, saying, We exorcise you *by* Jesus whom Paul preaches. [14] And there were seven sons of Sceva, a Jewish priest, doing this.

[15] But the evil spirit said, I know Jesus, and I comprehend Paul, but who are you? [16] And the man in whom was the evil spirit leaped on them; and overcoming them, he

4 δὲ Παῦλος, Ἰωάννης μὲν ἐβάπτισε βάπτισμα μετανοίας, τῷ
And Paul, John indeed baptized a baptism of repentance to the
λαῷ λέγων εἰς τὸν ἐρχόμενον μετ᾽ αὐτὸν ἵνα πιστεύσωσι,
people saying into the (One) coming after him that they should believe,
5 τοῦτ᾽ ἔστιν, εἰς τὸν Χριστὸν Ἰησοῦν. ἀκούσαντες δὲ ἐβαπτί-
this is, in the Christ, Jesus. hearing And they were
6 σθησαν εἰς τὸ ὄνομα τοῦ Κυρίου Ἰησοῦ. καὶ ἐπιθέντος
baptized into the name of the Lord Jesus. And laying on
αὐτοῖς τοῦ Παύλου τὰς χεῖρας, ἦλθε τὸ Πνεῦμα τὸ Ἅγιον
them — Paul the hands, came the Spirit — Holy
7 ἐπ᾽ αὐτούς, ἐλάλουν τε γλώσσαις καὶ προεφήτευον. ἦσαν
on them, they spoke and in languages and prophesied. were
δὲ οἱ πάντες ἄνδρες ὡσεὶ δεκαδύο.
And the all men about twelve.
8 Εἰσελθὼν δὲ εἰς τὴν συναγωγὴν ἐπαρρησιάζετο, ἐπὶ
entering And into the synagogue, he spoke boldly over
μῆνας τρεῖς διαλεγόμενος καὶ πείθων τὰ περὶ τῆς βασιλείας
months three conversing with and persuading the things concerning the kingdom
9 τοῦ Θεοῦ. ὡς δέ τινες ἐσκληρύνοντο καὶ ἠπείθουν, κακολο-
of God. as But some were hardened and disobeyed, speaking
γοῦντες τὴν ὁδὸν ἐνώπιον τοῦ πλήθους, ἀποστὰς ἀπ᾽
evil of the Way before the multitude, having departed from
αὐτῶν ἀφώρισε τοὺς μαθητάς, καθ᾽ ἡμέραν διαλεγόμενος
them, he separated the disciples, day by day conversing
10 ἐν τῇ σχολῇ Τυράννου τινός. τοῦτο δὲ ἐγένετο ἐπὶ ἔτη δύο,
in the school of Tyrannus a certain. this And happened over years two,
ὥστε πάντας τοὺς κατοικοῦντας τὴν Ἀσίαν ἀκοῦσαι τὸν
so as all those inhabiting — Asia heard the
λόγον τοῦ Κυρίου Ἰησοῦ, Ἰουδαίους τε καὶ Ἕλληνας.
word of the Lord Jesus, Jews both and Greeks.
11 δυνάμεις τε οὐ τὰς τυχούσας ἐποίει ὁ Θεὸς διὰ τῶν χειρῶν
works of power And not the common did God through the hands
12 Παύλου, ὥστε καὶ ἐπὶ τοὺς ἀσθενοῦντας ἐπιφέρεσθαι ἀπὸ
of Paul, so as even onto those sick to be brought from
τοῦ χρωτὸς αὐτοῦ σουδάρια ἢ σιμικίνθια, καὶ ἀπαλλάσσε-
the skin of him handkerchiefs or aprons, and to be released
σθαι ἀπ᾽ αὐτῶν τὰς νόσους, τά τε πνεύματα τὰ πονηρὰ
from them the diseases, the and spirits — evil
13 ἐξέρχεσθαι ἀπ᾽ αὐτῶν. ἐπεχείρησαν δέ τινες ἀπὸ τῶν περιερ-
to go out from them. undertook But some from the strolling
χομένων Ἰουδαίων ἐξορκιστῶν ὀνομάζειν ἐπὶ τοὺς ἔχοντας
Jews, exorcists, to name over those having
τὰ πνεύματα τὰ πονηρὰ τὸ ὄνομα τοῦ Κυρίου Ἰησοῦ,
the spirits — evil the name of the Lord Jesus,
λέγοντες, Ὁρκίζομεν ὑμᾶς τὸν Ἰησοῦν ὃν ὁ Παῦλος κηρύσ-
saying, we exorcise you (by) Jesus whom Paul proclaims.
14 σει. ἦσαν δέ τινες υἱοὶ Σκευᾶ Ἰουδαίου ἀρχιερέως ἑπτὰ οἱ
were And of one sons, of Sceva, a Jewish chief priest, seven —
15 τοῦτο ποιοῦντες. ἀποκριθὲν δὲ τὸ πνεῦμα τὸ πονηρὸν
this doing. answering And the spirit — evil
εἶπε, Τὸν Ἰησοῦν γινώσκω, καὶ τὸν Παῦλον ἐπίσταμαι·
said, — Jesus I know, and — Paul I comprehend,
16 ὑμεῖς δὲ τίνες ἐστέ; καὶ ἐφαλλόμενος ἐπ᾽ αὐτοὺς ὁ ἄνθρωπος
you but, who are? And leaping on them the man
ἐν ᾧ ἦν τὸ πνεῦμα τὸ πονηρόν, καὶ κατακυριεύσας αὐτῶν,
in whom was the spirit — evil, and overmastering them,

ἴσχυσε κατ' αὐτῶν, ὥστε γυμνοὺς καὶ τετραυματισμένους
was strong against them, so as naked and having been wounded
17 ἐκφυγεῖν ἐκ τοῦ οἴκου ἐκείνου. τοῦτο δὲ ἐγένετο γνωστὸν
to escape out of — house that. this And became known
πᾶσιν Ἰουδαίοις τε καὶ Ἕλλησι τοῖς κατοικοῦσι τὴν Ἔφεσον,
to all, Jews both and Greeks, those inhabiting — Ephesus;
καὶ ἐπέπεσε φόβος ἐπὶ πάντας αὐτούς, καὶ ἐμεγαλύνετο τὸ
and fell on fear on all them, and was magnified the
18 ὄνομα τοῦ Κυρίου Ἰησοῦ. πολλοί τε τῶν πεπιστευκότων
name of the Lord Jesus. many And of those having believed
ἤρχοντο, ἐξομολογούμενοι, καὶ ἀναγγέλλοντες τὰς πράξεις
came confessing and telling the doings
19 αὐτῶν. ἱκανοὶ δὲ τῶν τὰ περίεργα πραξάντων συνενέγκαντες
of them. many And of those the curious arts practicing, bringing together
τὰς βίβλους κατέκαιον ἐνώπιον πάντων· καὶ συνεψήφισαν
the rolls, burned (them) before all, and they counted
20 τὰς τιμὰς αὐτῶν, καὶ εὗρον ἀργυρίου μυριάδας πέντε. οὕτω
the prices of them, and found of silver thousand five. Thus
κατὰ κράτος ὁ λόγος τοῦ Κυρίου ηὔξανε καὶ ἴσχυεν.
with might, the word of the Lord increased and was strong.

21 Ὡς δὲ ἐπληρώθη ταῦτα, ἔθετο ὁ Παῦλος ἐν τῷ πνεύματι,
when And were fulfilled these things, purposed Paul in the Spirit
διελθὼν τὴν Μακεδονίαν καὶ Ἀχαΐαν, πορεύεσθαι εἰς
passing through Macedonia and Achaia to go to
Ἱερουσαλήμ, εἰπὼν ὅτι Μετὰ τὸ γενέσθαι με ἐκεῖ, δεῖ με καὶ
Jerusalem, saying, — After becoming me there, must me also
22 Ῥώμην ἰδεῖν. ἀποστείλας δὲ εἰς τὴν Μακεδονίαν δύο τῶν
Rome see. sending And into — Macedonia two of those
διακονούντων αὐτῷ, Τιμόθεον καὶ Ἔραστον, αὐτὸς ἐπέσχε
ministering to him, Timothy and Erastus, he delayed
χρόνον εἰς τὴν Ἀσίαν.
a time in — Asia.

23 Ἐγένετο δὲ κατὰ τὸν καιρὸν ἐκεῖνον τάραχος οὐκ ὀλίγος
there was And about — time that disturbance not a little
24 περὶ τῆς ὁδοῦ. Δημήτριος γάρ τις ὀνόματι, ἀργυροκόπος,
about the Way. Demetrius For one by name, a silversmith,
ποιῶν ναοὺς ἀργυροῦς Ἀρτέμιδος, παρείχετο τοῖς τεχνίταις
making shrines silver of Artemis provided the craftsmen
25 ἐργασίαν οὐκ ὀλίγην· οὓς συναθροίσας, καὶ τοὺς περὶ τὰ
trade not a little; whom assembling also the about
τοιαῦτα ἐργάτας, εἶπεν, Ἄνδρες, ἐπίστασθε ὅτι ἐκ ταύτης
such things workmen, he said, Men, you understand that from this
26 τῆς ἐργασίας ἡ εὐπορία ἡμῶν ἐστι. καὶ θεωρεῖτε καὶ ἀκούετε
— trade the gain to us is. And you behold and hear
ὅτι οὐ μόνον Ἐφέσου, ἀλλὰ σχεδὸν πάσης τῆς Ἀσίας, ὁ
that not only Ephesus, but almost all — of Asia —
Παῦλος οὗτος πείσας μετέστησεν ἱκανὸν ὄχλον, λέγων ὅτι
Paul this persuading perverted a huge crowd, saying that
27 οὐκ εἰσὶ θεοὶ οἱ διὰ χειρῶν γινόμενοι. οὐ μόνον δὲ τοῦτο
not are gods those through hands being made. not only And this,
κινδυνεύει ἡμῖν τὸ μέρος εἰς ἀπελεγμὸν ἐλθεῖν, ἀλλὰ καὶ τὸ
is in danger to us the share into disrepute to come, but also the
τῆς μεγάλης θεᾶς Ἀρτέμιδος ἱερὸν εἰς οὐδὲν λογισθῆναι,
of the great goddess Artemis temple for nothing will be counted,
μέλλειν τε καὶ καθαιρεῖσθαι τὴν μεγαλειότητα αὐτῆς, ἣν ὅλη
is going and also to be diminished the greatness of her, whom all

was strong against them, so that they fled out of the house naked and wounded. [17]And this became known to all, both Jews and Greeks, those living in Ephesus. And fear fell on them all, and the name of the Lord Jesus was magnified. [18]And many of those who had believed came confessing, and declaring their deeds. [19]And many of the ones practicing the curious arts, bringing together the books, burned *them* before all. And they counted the prices of them, and found *it to be* five thousand of silver. [20]So with might the word of the Lord increased and was strong.

[21]And when these things were fulfilled, passing through Macedonia and Achaia, Paul purposed to go to Jerusalem, saying, After I have come there, I must also see Rome. [22]And sending into Macedonia two who ministered to him, Timothy and Erastus, he delayed a time in Asia.

[23]And about that time there was a disturbance about the Way. [24]For a certain silversmith named Demetrius *was* making silver shrines of Diana, providing no little trade *for* the craftsmen. [25]And assembling the workmen about such things, he said, Men, you understand that from this trade is our wealth. [26]And you see and hear that not only Ephesus, but almost all of Asia Paul has perverted, persuading a huge crowd, saying that those being made by hands are not gods. [27]And not only is this dangerous to us, *lest our* part come to *be in* contempt, but also the temple of the great goddess Diana will be counted nothing, and her majesty is also about to be destroyed, whom all Asia and

the world worships. 28 And hearing, and having become full of anger, they cried out, saying, Great *is* Diana of *the* Ephesians! 29 And all the city was filled with confusion. And they rushed with one passion into the theater, keeping a firm grip on Gaius and Aristarchus, Macedonians, traveling companions of Paul. 30 And Paul intending to go in to the mob, the disciples did not allow him. 31 And also some of the Asiarchs, being his friends, sending to him begged *him* not to give himself into the theater. 32 Then others indeed cried out a different thing, for the assembly was confused; and the majority did not know on what account they came together.

33 But they dragged Alexander forward out of the crowd, the Jews pushing him in front. And waving *his* hand, Alexander desired to defend himself to the mob. 34 But knowing that he is a Jew, one voice was for all, as *they were* crying out over two hours, Great *is* Diana of *the* Ephesians! 35 And the town clerk quieting the crowd, he said, Men, Ephesians, for what man is there who does not know the city of the Ephesians to be temple-keepers of the great goddess Diana, and of That Fallen from the Sky. 36 Then these things being undeniable, it is necessary for you having been calmed to be *so*, and to do nothing rash. 37 For you brought these men, neither temple-robbers nor blaspheming your goddess. 38 If then, indeed, Demetrius and those craftsmen with him have a matter against anyone, courts are being *held*, and there are proconsuls. Let them accuse one another. 39 But if you seek concerning other things, it will be settled in a lawful assembly. 40 For we are in danger to be accused of revolt concerning today, there being no cause about which we will be able to give

28 ἡ Ἀσία καὶ ἡ οἰκουμένη σέβεται. ἀκούσαντες δὲ καὶ γενό-
Asia and the habitable world worships. hearing And, and
μενοι πλήρεις θυμοῦ, ἔκραζον λέγοντες, Μεγάλη ἡ Ἄρτεμις
becoming full of anger, they cried out saying, Great (is) Artemis
29 Ἐφεσίων. καὶ ἐπλήσθη ἡ πόλις ὅλη συγχύσεως· ὥρμησάν τε
of (the) Ephesians! And was filled the city all of confusion, they rushed and
ὁμοθυμαδὸν εἰς τὸ θέατρον, συναρπάσαντες Γάϊον καὶ
with one mind to the theatre, keeping a firm grip on Gaius and
30 Ἀρίσταρχον Μακεδόνας, συνεκδήμους τοῦ Παύλου. τοῦ δὲ
Aristarchus, Macedonians, traveling companions of Paul. —And
Παύλου βουλομένου εἰσελθεῖν εἰς τὸν δῆμον, οὐκ εἴων αὐτὸν
Paul intending to enter into the mob, not allowed him
31 οἱ μαθηταί. τινὲς δὲ καὶ τῶν Ἀσιαρχῶν, ὄντες αὐτῷ φίλοι,
the disciples. some And also of the Asiarchs, being of him friends,
πέμψαντες πρὸς αὐτόν, παρεκάλουν μὴ δοῦναι ἑαυτὸν εἰς
sending to him, begged not to give himself into
32 τὸ θέατρον. ἄλλοι μὲν οὖν ἄλλο τι ἔκραζον· ἦν γὰρ ἡ
the theatre. Others indeed, then, other some cried out, was for the
ἐκκλησία συγκεχυμένη, καὶ οἱ πλείους οὐκ ᾔδεισαν τίνος
assembly confounded, and the majority not did know of what
33 ἕνεκεν συνεληλύθεισαν. ἐκ δὲ τοῦ ὄχλου προεβίβασαν Ἀλέ-
on account they came together out of But the crowd, they dragged forward
ξανδρον, προβαλλόντων αὐτὸν τῶν Ἰουδαίων. ὁ δὲ Ἀλέξαν-
Alexander, thrusting forward him the Jews. And Alexander
δρος, κατασείσας τὴν χεῖρα, ἤθελεν ἀπολογεῖσθαι τῷ δήμῳ.
waving the hand desired to defend himself to the mob.
34 ἐπιγνόντων δὲ ὅτι Ἰουδαῖός ἐστι, φωνὴ ἐγένετο μία ἐκ
knowing. But that a Jew he is, voice there was one from
πάντων ὡς ἐπὶ ὥρας δύο κραζόντων, Μεγάλη ἡ Ἄρτεμις
all, as over hours two crying out, Great (is) Artemis
35 Ἐφεσίων. καταστείλας δὲ ὁ γραμματεὺς τὸν ὄχλον φησίν,
of (the) Ephesians! quieting And the town clerk the crowd, he says,
Ἄνδρες Ἐφέσιοι, τίς γάρ ἐστιν ἄνθρωπος ὃς οὐ γινώσκει
Men, Ephesians, what for is there man who not does know
τὴν Ἐφεσίων πόλιν νεωκόρον οὖσαν τῆς μεγάλης θεᾶς
the of (the) Ephesians city temple-keeper being of the great goddess
36 Ἀρτέμιδος καὶ τοῦ Διοπετοῦς; ἀναντιρρήτων οὖν ὄντων
Artemis, and of that fallen from the sky? undeniable Then being
τούτων, δέον ἐστὶν ὑμᾶς κατεσταλμένους ὑπάρχειν, καὶ
these things, necessary it is you having been quietened to be (so), and
37 μηδὲν προπετὲς πράττειν. ἠγάγετε γὰρ τοὺς ἄνδρας
nothing rash to do. you brought For — men
τούτους, οὔτε ἱεροσύλους οὔτε βλασφημοῦντας τὴν θεὰν
these, neither temple-robbers nor blaspheming the goddess
38 ὑμῶν. εἰ μὲν οὖν Δημήτριος καὶ οἱ σὺν αὐτῷ τεχνῖται πρός
of you. If indeed, then, Demetrius and those with him craftsmen against
τινα λόγον ἔχουσιν, ἀγοραῖοι ἄγονται, καὶ ἀνθύπατοί
anyone a matter have, courts are being (held), and proconsuls
39 εἰσιν· ἐγκαλείτωσαν ἀλλήλοις. εἰ δέ τι περὶ ἑτέρων ἐπιζητεῖτε,
are; let them accuse one another. if But any about other things you seek,
40 ἐν τῇ ἐννόμῳ ἐκκλησίᾳ ἐπιλυθήσεται. καὶ γὰρ κινδυνεύομεν
in the lawful assembly it will be settled. also For we are in danger
ἐγκαλεῖσθαι στάσεως περὶ τῆς σήμερον, μηδενὸς αἰτίου
to be accused of insurrection concerning today; nothing cause
ὑπάρχοντος περὶ οὗ δυνησόμεθα ἀποδοῦναι λόγον τῆς
there being concerning which we shall be able to give account —

account of this crowding together. [41]And saying these things, he dismissed the assembly.

CHAPTER 20

[1]And after the ceasing of the tumult, having called the disciples, and having greeted *them,* Paul went away to go into Macedonia. [2]And passing through those parts, and exhorting them with much speech, he came into Greece. [3]And spending three months there, a plot by the Jews being *against* him, being about to sail into Syria, he was of a mind to return through Macedonia. [4]And Sopater, a Berean; and Aristarchus and Secundus of the Thessalonians; and Gaius of Derbe; and Timothy; and Tychicus and Trophimus of Asia accompanied him as far as Asia. [5]Going forward, these awaited us in Troas. [6]But we sailed along after the days of unleavened *bread* from Philippi, and came to them at Troas *in* five days, where we stayed seven days.

[7]And on the first of the week, the disciples having been assembled to break bread, being about to depart on the morrow, Paul reasoned to them. And he continued his speech until midnight. [8]And many lamps were in the upper room where they were assembled. [9]And a certain young man named Eutychus was sitting on the window sill, being overborne by deep sleep. Paul reasoning for a longer time, being overborne by the sleep, he fell from the third floor down, and was taken up dead. [10]But going down Paul fell on him, and embracing *him, he* said, Do not be terrified; for his soul is in him. [11]And going up, and breaking bread, and tasting, and conversing over a long *time,* until daybreak, he went out thus. [12]And they brought the boy alive, and were comforted not a

41 συστροφῆς ταύτης. καὶ ταῦτα εἰπών, ἀπέλυσε τὴν ἐκκλησίαν.
crowding together of this. And these saying, he dismissed the assembly.

CHAPTER 20

1 Μετὰ δὲ τὸ παύσασθαι τὸν θόρυβον, προσκαλεσάμενος
after And the ceasing of the tumult, having called
ὁ Παῦλος τοὺς μαθητάς, καὶ ἀσπασάμενος, ἐξῆλθε πορευθῆναι
Paul the disciples, and greeting, went away to go
2 εἰς τὴν Μακεδονίαν. διελθὼν δὲ τὰ μέρη ἐκεῖνα, καὶ παρα-
to — Macedonia. passing through And parts those, and having
καλέσας αὐτοὺς λόγῳ πολλῷ, ἦλθεν εἰς τὴν Ἑλλάδα. ποιή-
exhorted them with speech much, he came into — Greece spending
3 σας τε μῆνας τρεῖς, γενομένης αὐτῷ ἐπιβουλῆς ὑπὸ τῶν
And months three, there being (against) him a plot by the
Ἰουδαίων μέλλοντι ἀνάγεσθαι εἰς τὴν Συρίαν, ἐγένετο
Jews, being about to set sail to — Syria, he was
4 γνώμη τοῦ ὑποστρέφειν διὰ Μακεδονίας. συνείπετο δὲ
of a mind — to return through Macedonia. accompanied And
αὐτῷ ἄχρι τῆς Ἀσίας Σώπατρος Βεροιαῖος· Θεσσαλονι-
him as far as — Asia Sopater, a Berean, of Thessalonians
κέων δέ, Ἀρίσταρχος καὶ Σεκοῦνδος, καὶ Γάϊος Δερβαῖος,
and, Aristarchus and Secundus; and Gaius of Derbe,
5 καὶ Τιμόθεος· Ἀσιανοὶ δέ, Τυχικὸς καὶ Τρόφιμος. οὗτοι
and Timothy, of Asia and, Tychicus and Trophimus. These
6 προελθόντες ἔμενον ἡμᾶς ἐν Τρῳάδι. ἡμεῖς δὲ ἐξεπλεύσαμεν
going forward awaited us in Troas. we And sailed away
μετὰ τὰς ἡμέρας τῶν ἀζύμων ἀπὸ Φιλίππων, καὶ ἤλθομεν
after the days — of unleavened from Philippi, and came
πρὸς αὐτοὺς εἰς τὴν Τρῳάδα ἄχρις ἡμερῶν πέντε, οὗ
to them in — Troas until days five, where
διετρίψαμεν ἡμέρας ἑπτά.
we stayed days seven.
7 Ἐν δὲ τῇ μιᾷ τῶν σαββάτων, συνηγμένων τῶν μαθητῶν
on And the one of the sabbaths, having been assembled the disciples
τοῦ κλάσαι ἄρτον, ὁ Παῦλος διελέγετο αὐτοῖς, μέλλων
— to break bread, Paul reasoned to them, being about to
ἐξιέναι τῇ ἐπαύριον, παρέτεινέ τε τὸν λόγον μέχρι μεσονυ-
depart on the morrow; he continued and the discourse until midnight.
8 κτίου. ἦσαν δὲ λαμπάδες ἱκαναὶ ἐν τῷ ὑπερῴῳ οὗ ἦσαν
there were And lamps many in the upper room where they were
9 συνηγμένοι. καθήμενος δέ τις νεανίας ὀνόματι Εὔτυχος ἐπὶ
assembled. sitting And a certain young man by name Eutuchus on
τῆς θυρίδος, καταφερόμενος ὕπνῳ βαθεῖ, διαλεγομένου τοῦ
the window sill, being overborne by sleep deep, reasoning —
Παύλου ἐπὶ πλεῖον, κατενεχθεὶς ἀπὸ τοῦ ὕπνου ἔπεσεν ἀπὸ
Paul for a longer time, being overborne by the sleep, he fell from
10 τοῦ τριστέγου κάτω, καὶ ἤρθη νεκρός. καταβὰς δὲ ὁ Παῦλος
the third floor down, and was taken up dead. going down But Paul
ἐπέπεσεν αὐτῷ, καὶ συμπεριλαβὼν εἶπε, Μὴ θορυβεῖσθε
fell on him, and having embraced said, Do not be terrified;
11 ἡ γὰρ ψυχὴ αὐτοῦ ἐν αὐτῷ ἐστιν. ἀναβὰς δὲ καὶ κλάσας
the for soul of him in him is. going up And, and breaking
ἄρτον καὶ γευσάμενος, ἐφ' ἱκανόν τε ὁμιλήσας ἄχρις αὐγῆς,
bread, and tasting, over a long (time) and conversing until dawn,
12 οὕτως ἐξῆλθεν. ἤγαγον δὲ τὸν παῖδα ζῶντα, καὶ παρεκλήθη-
thus he went out. they brought and the boy living, and were comforted

little.

[13]But going before onto the ship, we set sail for Assos, being about to take Paul in there; for it was *thus it* had been arranged, he being about to go on foot. [14]And when he met us in Assos, taking him up we came to Mitylene. [15]And sailing away from there, on the next *day* we arrived off Chios, and on the next we crossed to Samos. And remaining at Trogyllium, the next *day* we came to Miletus. [16]For Paul had decided to sail by Ephesus, so as it might not happen to him to spend time in Asia; for he hastened if it were possible for him to be in Jerusalem *on* the day of Pentecost.

[17]And sending to Ephesus from Miletus, he called for the elders of the church. [18]And when they came to him, he said to them:

You understand, from the first day *on* which I set foot in Asia, how I was with you all the time, [19]serving the Lord with all humility, and many tears and trials happening to me by the plots of the Jews; [20]as I kept nothing back of what is profitable, *so as* not to tell you; and to teach you publicly, and from house to house, [21]earnestly testifying both to Jews and to Greeks repentance toward God and faith toward our Lord Jesus Christ. [22]And now, behold, I being bound by the Spirit go to Jerusalem, not knowing the things going to meet me in it, [23]but that the Holy Spirit testifies city by city saying that bonds and afflictions await me. [24]But I do not think anything, nor do I hold my soul precious to myself, so that I might finish my course with joy, and the

σαν οὐ μετρίως.
not moderately.

13 Ἡμεῖς δέ, προελθόντες ἐπὶ τὸ πλοῖον, ἀνήχθημεν εἰς τὴν
we And, going before onto the ship, set sail for —
Ἄσσον, ἐκεῖθεν μέλλοντες ἀναλαμβάνειν τὸν Παῦλον· οὕτω
Assos, from there intending to take up — Paul; so
14 γὰρ ἦν διατεταγμένος, μέλλων αὐτὸς πεζεύειν. ὡς δὲ συνέ-
For it was having been arranged, intending he to go afoot. when And he
βαλεν ἡμῖν εἰς τὴν Ἄσσον, ἀναλαβόντες αὐτὸν ἤλθομεν εἰς
met with us in — Assos, taking up him we came to
15 Μιτυλήνην. κἀκεῖθεν ἀποπλεύσαντες, τῇ ἐπιούσῃ κατηντή-
Mitylene; and from there sailing away, on the next we
σαμεν ἀντικρὺ Χίου· τῇ δὲ ἑτέρᾳ παρεβάλομεν εἰς Σάμον· καὶ
arrived off Chios, on the and other we crossed to Samos, and
μείναντες ἐν Τρωγυλλίῳ, τῇ ἐχομένῃ ἤλθομεν εἰς Μίλητον.
having remained at Trogyllium, the next (day) we came to Miletus.
16 ἔκρινε γὰρ ὁ Παῦλος παραπλεῦσαι τὴν Ἔφεσον, ὅπως μὴ
had decided For Paul to sail past — Ephesus, so as not
γένηται αὐτῷ χρονοτριβῆσαι ἐν τῇ Ἀσίᾳ· ἔσπευδε γάρ, εἰ
be to him to spend time in — Asia; he hastened for, if
δυνατὸν ἦν αὐτῷ, τὴν ἡμέραν τῆς Πεντηκοστῆς γενέσθαι
possible it was for him the day — of Pentecost to be
17 εἰς Ἱεροσόλυμα. Ἀπὸ δὲ τῆς Μιλήτου πέμψας εἰς Ἔφεσον
in Jerusalem. from And — Miletus sending to Ephesus
18 μετεκαλέσατο τοὺς πρεσβυτέρους τῆς ἐκκλησίας. ὡς δὲ παρε
he called for the elders of the church. when And they
γένοντο πρὸς αὐτόν, εἶπεν αὐτοῖς,
came to him, he said to them,
Ὑμεῖς ἐπίστασθε, ἀπὸ πρώτης ἡμέρας ἀφ' ἧς ἐπέβην εἰς
You understand from (the) first day from which I set foot in
τὴν Ἀσίαν, πῶς μεθ' ὑμῶν τὸν πάντα χρόνον ἐγενόμην,
— Asia, how with you the all time I was,
19 δουλεύων τῷ Κυρίῳ μετὰ πάσης ταπεινοφροσύνης καὶ
serving the Lord with all humility and
πολλῶν δακρύων καὶ πειρασμῶν τῶν συμβάντων μοι ἐν
many tears and trials — happening to me by
20 ταῖς ἐπιβουλαῖς τῶν Ἰουδαίων· ὡς οὐδὲν ὑπεστειλάμην τῶν
the plots of the Jews, as nothing I kept back of the
συμφερόντων, τοῦ μὴ ἀναγγεῖλαι ὑμῖν καὶ διδάξαι ὑμᾶς
profitable (things), — not to tell you, and to teach you
21 δημοσίᾳ καὶ κατ' οἴκους, διαμαρτυρόμενος Ἰουδαίοις τε καὶ
publicly, and from house to house, earnestly testifying to Jews and also
Ἕλλησι τὴν εἰς τὸν Θεὸν μετάνοιαν, καὶ πίστιν τὴν εἰς τὸν
to Greeks — toward — God repentance, and faith — toward the
22 Κύριον ἡμῶν Ἰησοῦν Χριστόν. καὶ νῦν ἰδού, ἐγὼ δεδεμένος
Lord of us, Jesus Christ. And now behold, I being bound
τῷ πνεύματι πορεύομαι εἰς Ἱερουσαλήμ, τὰ ἐν αὐτῇ συναντή-
by the Spirit am going to Jerusalem, the things in it going
23 σοντά μοι μὴ εἰδώς, πλὴν ὅτι τὸ Πνεῦμα τὸ Ἅγιον κατὰ
to meet me not knowing, but that the Spirit — Holy city
πόλιν διαμαρτύρεται λέγον ὅτι δεσμά με καὶ θλίψεις μένουσιν.
by city testifies saying that bonds me and afflictions await.
24 ἀλλ' οὐδενὸς λόγον ποιοῦμαι, οὐδὲ ἔχω τὴν ψυχήν μου
But of nothing account I make, nor hold the soul of me
τιμίαν ἐμαυτῷ, ὡς τελειῶσαι τὸν δρόμον μου μετὰ χαρᾶς,
precious to myself, so as I may finish the course of me with joy,

ministry which I received from the Lord Jesus Christ, to fully testify the gospel of the grace of God. 25 And now, behold, I know that you all will see my face no more, among whom I went about proclaiming the kingdom of God. 26 Therefore, I testify to you on this day that I am clean from the blood of all. 27 For I did not keep back from declaring to you all the counsel of God. 28 Therefore, take heed to yourselves and to all the flock, in which the Holy Spirit placed you overseers to shepherd the church of God which He purchased through *His* own blood. 29 For I know this, that after my departure grievous wolves will come in among you, not sparing the flock; 30 and from among your own selves will rise up men speaking perverted things, in order to draw away the disciples after themselves.

31 Therefore, watch, remembering that I did not cease admonishing each one with tears three years, night and day. 32 And now I commend you to God, brothers, and to the word of His grace, which is able to build up and to give you inheritance among all those having been sanctified. 33 I have desired *the* silver, or gold, or clothing of no one. 34 But you yourselves know that these hands ministered to my needs, and to those who were with me. 35 I showed you all things, that working in this way we ought to help those being weak, and to remember the words of the Lord Jesus, that He said, It is more blessed to give than to receive. 36 And saying these things, placing his knees, he prayed with them all. 37 And there was much weeping of all, and falling on the neck of Paul, they ardently kissed him.

καὶ τὴν διακονίαν ἣν ἔλαβον παρὰ τοῦ Κυρίου Ἰησοῦ,
and the ministry which I received from the Lord Jesus,
25 διαμαρτύρασθαι τὸ εὐαγγέλιον τῆς χάριτος τοῦ Θεοῦ. καὶ
to fully testify the gospel of the grace — of God. And
νῦν ἰδού, ἐγὼ οἶδα ὅτι οὐκέτι ὄψεσθε τὸ πρόσωπόν μου
now behold, I know that no more will see the face of me
ὑμεῖς πάντες, ἐν οἷς διῆλθον κηρύσσων τὴν βασιλείαν τοῦ
you all, among whom I went about proclaiming the kingdom —
26 Θεοῦ. διὸ μαρτύρομαι ὑμῖν ἐν τῇ σήμερον ἡμέρᾳ, ὅτι καθαρὸς
of God. Therefore I testify to you on — this day that clean
27 ἐγὼ ἀπὸ τοῦ αἵματος πάντων. οὐ γὰρ ὑπεστειλάμην τοῦ
I am from the blood of all; not for I kept back —
μὴ ἀναγγεῖλαι ὑμῖν πᾶσαν τὴν βουλὴν τοῦ Θεοῦ. προσ-
not to declare to you all the counsel — of God. take
28 έχετε οὖν ἑαυτοῖς καὶ παντὶ τῷ ποιμνίῳ, ἐν ᾧ ὑμᾶς τὸ
heed, therefore, to yourselves and to all the flock, in which you the
Πνεῦμα τὸ Ἅγιον ἔθετο ἐπισκόπους, ποιμαίνειν τὴν ἐκκλη-
Spirit — Holy placed overseers, to shepherd the church
σίαν τοῦ Θεοῦ, ἣν περιεποιήσατο διὰ τοῦ ἰδίου αἵματος.
— of God, which He purchased through the own blood.
29 ἐγὼ γὰρ οἶδα τοῦτο, ὅτι εἰσελεύσονται μετὰ τὴν ἄφιξίν
I For know this, that will come in after the departure
30 μου λύκοι βαρεῖς εἰς ὑμᾶς, μὴ φειδόμενοι τοῦ ποιμνίου· καὶ
of me wolves grievous into you, not sparing the flock, and
ἐξ ὑμῶν αὐτῶν ἀναστήσονται ἄνδρες λαλοῦντες διεστραμ-
out of you yourselves will rise up men speaking perverted
31 μένα, τοῦ ἀποσπᾶν τοὺς μαθητὰς ὀπίσω αὐτῶν. διὸ
things, — to draw away the disciples after themselves. Therefore
γρηγορεῖτε, μνημονεύοντες ὅτι τριετίαν νύκτα καὶ ἡμέραν
watch, remembering that three years night and day
32 οὐκ ἐπαυσάμην μετὰ δακρύων νουθετῶν ἕνα ἕκαστον. καὶ
not I ceased with tears admonishing one each. And
τὰ νῦν παρατίθεμαι ὑμᾶς, ἀδελφοί, τῷ Θεῷ καὶ τῷ λόγῳ
— now I commend you, brothers, — to God and to the word
τῆς χάριτος αὐτοῦ, τῷ δυναμένῳ ἐποικοδομῆσαι, καὶ
— of grace of Him, — being able to build up and
33 δοῦναι ὑμῖν κληρονομίαν ἐν τοῖς ἡγιασμένοις πᾶσιν. ἀργυ-
to give you inheritance among those having been sanctified all. Silver
34 ρίου ἢ χρυσίου ἢ ἱματισμοῦ οὐδενὸς ἐπεθύμησα. αὐτοὶ δὲ
or gold or clothing of no one I desired. yourselves But
γινώσκετε ὅτι ταῖς χρείαις μου καὶ τοῖς οὖσι μετ' ἐμοῦ
know that to the needs of me and those being with me
35 ὑπηρέτησαν αἱ χεῖρες αὗται. πάντα ὑπέδειξα ὑμῖν, ὅτι
ministered hands these. All things I showed to you, that
οὕτω κοπιῶντας δεῖ ἀντιλαμβάνεσθαι τῶν ἀσθενούντων,
thus working it behoves to help those infirm (ones),
μνημονεύειν τε τῶν λόγων τοῦ Κυρίου Ἰησοῦ, ὅτι αὐτὸς
to remember and the words of the Lord Jesus, that He
εἶπε, Μακάριόν ἐστι διδόναι μᾶλλον ἢ λαμβάνειν.
said, Blessed it is to give rather than to receive.
36 Καὶ ταῦτα εἰπών, θεὶς τὰ γόνατα αὐτοῦ, σὺν πᾶσιν
And these things having said, placing the knees of him, with all
37 αὐτοῖς προσηύξατο. ἱκανὸς δὲ ἐγένετο κλαυθμὸς πάντων·
them he prayed. much And was weeping of all,
καὶ ἐπιπεσόντες ἐπὶ τὸν τράχηλον τοῦ Παύλου κατεφίλουν
and falling on the neck — of Paul they ardently kissed

[38] Most of all *they were* grieving for the word which he had said, that they no more were going to see his face. And they went with him to the ship.

CHAPTER 21

[1] And when it was *time* to sail, we having been torn away from them, running direct we came to Coos; and on the next *day* to Rhodes, and from there to Patara. [2] And finding a ship crossing over to Phoenice, going on board we set sail. [3] And sighting Cyprus, and leaving it on the left, we sailed to Syria, and came down to Tyre; for the ship was unloading the cargo there. [4] And finding disciples, we remained there seven days; who told Paul through the Spirit not to go up to Jerusalem. [5] But when it was *time for* us to complete the days, going out we traveled, with all *the* women and children going with us as far as outside the city. And placing the knees on the shore, *we* prayed. [6] And giving parting greetings to one another, we boarded the ship; and those went back to their own.

[7] And completing the voyage from Tyre, we arrived at Ptolemais. And having greeted the brothers, we remained one day with them. [8] And on the morrow, those around *him* going out, Paul came to Caesarea. And going into the house of Philip the evangelist, *he* being of the Seven, we stayed with him. [9] And there were four virgin daughters to this one, who prophesied. [10] And we remaining more days, a certain prophet named Agabus came down. [11] And coming to us, and taking Paul's girdle, and binding his hands and feet, he said, The

38 αὐτόν, ὀδυνώμενοι μάλιστα ἐπὶ τῷ λόγῳ ᾧ εἰρήκει, ὅτι
him, grieving most over the word which he said, that
οὐκέτι μέλλουσι τὸ πρόσωπον αὐτοῦ θεωρεῖν. προέπεμπον
no more they are the face of him to behold. they escorted
δὲ αὐτὸν εἰς τὸ πλοῖον.
And him to the ship.

CHAPTER 21

1 Ὡς δὲ ἐγένετο ἀναχθῆναι ἡμᾶς ἀποσπασθέντας ἀπ'
when And it was (time) to sail, we having been withdrawn from
αὐτῶν, εὐθυδρομήσαντες ἤλθομεν εἰς τὴν Κῶν, τῇ δὲ ἑξῆς
them, having run direct, we came to — Coos; on the and next
2 εἰς τὴν Ῥόδον, κἀκεῖθεν εἰς Πάταρα· καὶ εὑρόντες πλοῖον
to — Rhodes, and from there to Patara; and having found a ship
διαπερῶν εἰς Φοινίκην, ἐπιβάντες ἀνήχθημεν. ἀναφάναντες
crossing over to Phoenice, entering we set sail. having sighted
3 δὲ τὴν Κύπρον, καὶ καταλιπόντες αὐτὴν εὐώνυμον, ἐπλέομεν
And — Cyprus, and leaving it on the left, we sailed
εἰς Συρίαν, καὶ κατήχθημεν εἰς Τύρον· ἐκεῖσε γὰρ ἦν τὸ
to Syria, and came down to Tyre; there for was the
4 πλοῖον ἀποφορτιζόμενον τὸν γόμον. καὶ ἀνευρόντες
ship unloading the cargo. And having found
μαθητάς, ἐπεμείναμεν αὐτοῦ ἡμέρας ἑπτά· οἵτινες τῷ Παύλῳ
disciples, we remained there days seven; who — Paul
ἔλεγον διὰ τοῦ Πνεύματος, μὴ ἀναβαίνειν εἰς Ἱερουσαλήμ.
told through the Spirit not to go up to Jerusalem.
5 ὅτε δὲ ἐγένετο ἡμᾶς ἐξαρτίσαι τὰς ἡμέρας, ἐξελθόντες ἐπο-
when But it was (time) us to complete the days, having gone out we
ρευόμεθα, προπεμπόντων ἡμᾶς πάντων σὺν γυναιξὶ καὶ
traveled, accompanying us all with women and
τέκνοις ἕως ἔξω τῆς πόλεως· καὶ θέντες τὰ γόνατα ἐπὶ τὸν
children as far as outside the city; and placing the knees on the
6 αἰγιαλὸν προσηυξάμεθα. καὶ ἀσπασάμενοι ἀλλήλους, ἐπέ-
shore, praying, And giving parting greetings to one another, we
βημεν εἰς τὸ πλοῖον, ἐκεῖνοι δὲ ὑπέστρεψαν εἰς τὰ ἴδια.
went up into the ship, those and returned to the own.
7 Ἡμεῖς δέ, τὸν πλοῦν διανύσαντες ἀπὸ Τύρου, κατηντή-
we And, the voyage completing from Tyre, arrived
σαμεν εἰς Πτολεμαΐδα, καὶ ἀσπασάμενοι τοὺς ἀδελφοὺς
at Ptolemais; and greeting the brothers,
8 ἐμείναμεν ἡμέραν μίαν παρ' αὐτοῖς. τῇ δὲ ἐπαύριον ἐξελθόντες
we remained day one with them. on the And morrow going out
οἱ περὶ τὸν Παῦλον ἦλθομεν εἰς Καισάρειαν· καὶ εἰσελθόντες
those around (him), Paul came to Caesarea, and having gone
εἰς τὸν οἶκον Φιλίππου τοῦ εὐαγγελιστοῦ, τοῦ ὄντος ἐκ τῶν
to the house of Philip the evangelist, — being of the
9 ἑπτά, ἐμείναμεν παρ' αὐτῷ. τούτῳ δὲ ἦσαν θυγατέρες
seven, we stayed with him. to this one And were daughters
10 παρθένοι τέσσαρες προφητεύουσαι. ἐπιμενόντων δὲ ἡμῶν
virgin four prophesying. remaining And we
ἡμέρας πλείους, κατῆλθέ τις ἀπὸ τῆς Ἰουδαίας προφήτης
days more, came down a certain from — Judea prophet,
11 ὀνόματι Ἄγαβος. καὶ ἐλθὼν πρὸς ἡμᾶς, καὶ ἄρας τὴν ζώνην
by name Agabus, and coming to us, and taking the girdle
τοῦ Παύλου, δήσας τε αὐτοῦ τὰς χεῖρας καὶ τοὺς πόδας εἶπε,
— of Paul, binding and of himself the hands and the feet, he said,

Holy Spirit says these *things:* The Jews will bind the man whose girdle this is, in Jerusalem, and will deliver *him* up into *the* hands of *the* Gentiles. [12] And when we heard these things, both we and those of *the* place begged him not to go up to Jerusalem. [13] But Paul answered, What are you doing, weeping and breaking my heart? For I not only am ready to be bound, but also to die at Jerusalem for the name of the Lord Jesus. [14] And he not being persuaded, we were silent, saying, The will of the Lord be *done.*

[15] And after these days, having made ready, we went up to Jerusalem. [16] And also *some* of the disciples from Caesarea went with us, bringing Mnason, a certain Cypriot, an ancient disciple, with whom we might lodge. [17] And we being in Jerusalem, the brothers joyfully received us. [18] And on the next *day,* Paul went in with us to James. And all the elders came. [19] And having greeted them, he related one by one what things God had worked among the Gentiles through his ministry. [20] And hearing, they glorified the Lord, and said to him, You see brother how many myriads there are of Jews that have believed, and all are zealous ones of the Law. [21] And they were informed about you, that you teach falling away from Moses, telling all the Jews throughout the nations not to circumcise their children, nor to walk in the customs. [22] What then is it? At all events, a multitude must come together, for they will hear that you have come. [23] Then, do this, what we say to you: four men are with us, having a vow on themselves; [24] taking

Τάδε λέγει τὸ Πνεῦμα τὸ Ἅγιον, Τὸν ἄνδρα οὗ ἐστιν ἡ ζώνη
These says the Spirit – Holy, The man of whom is girdle
αὕτη, οὕτω δήσουσιν ἐν Ἱερουσαλὴμ οἱ Ἰουδαῖοι, καὶ
this, thus will bind in Jerusalem the Jews, and
12 παραδώσουσιν εἰς χεῖρας ἐθνῶν. ὡς δὲ ἠκούσαμεν ταῦτα,
will deliver into (the) hands of nations. when And we heard these things,
παρεκαλοῦμεν ἡμεῖς τε καὶ οἱ ἐντόπιοι, τοῦ μὴ ἀναβαίνειν
begged we both and the residents – not to go up
13 αὐτὸν εἰς Ἱερουσαλήμ. ἀπεκρίθη δὲ ὁ Παῦλος, Τί ποιεῖτε
him to Jerusalem. answered And Paul, What are you doing,
κλαίοντες καὶ συνθρύπτοντές μου τὴν καρδίαν ; ἐγὼ γὰρ οὐ
weeping and crushing of me the heart? ! For not
μόνον δεθῆναι, ἀλλὰ καὶ ἀποθανεῖν εἰς Ἱερουσαλὴμ ἑτοίμως
only to be bound, but also to die in Jerusalem readiness
14 ἔχω ὑπὲρ τοῦ ὀνόματος τοῦ Κυρίου Ἰησοῦ. μὴ πειθομένου
I have for the name of the Lord Jesus. not being persuaded
δὲ αὐτοῦ, ἡσυχάσαμεν εἰπόντες, Τὸ θέλημα τοῦ Κυρίου
And him, we kept silence, having said, Of the will of the Lord
γενέσθω.
let be (done).

15 Μετὰ δὲ τὰς ἡμέρας ταύτας ἀποσκευασάμενοι ἀνεβαίνομεν
after And – days these having made ready, we went up
16 εἰς Ἱερουσαλήμ. συνῆλθον δὲ καὶ τῶν μαθητῶν ἀπὸ Καισα-
to Jerusalem. went And also of the disciples from Caesarea
ρείας σὺν ἡμῖν, ἄγοντες παρ' ᾧ ξενισθῶμεν, Μνάσωνί τινι
with us, bringing (one) with whom we may lodge, Mnason a certain
Κυπρίῳ, ἀρχαίῳ μαθητῇ.
Cypriot, an ancient disciple.
17 Γενομένων δὲ ἡμῶν εἰς Ἱεροσόλυμα, ἀσμένως ἐδέξαντο
being And us in Jerusalem, joyfully received
ἡμᾶς οἱ ἀδελφοί. τῇ δὲ ἐπιούσῃ εἰσῄει ὁ Παῦλος σὺν ἡμῖν πρὸς
us the brothers. on the And next went in Paul with us to
18 Ἰάκωβον, πάντες τε παρεγένοντο οἱ πρεσβύτεροι. καὶ
James, all and came the elders. And
19 ἀσπασάμενος αὐτούς, ἐξηγεῖτο καθ' ἓν ἕκαστον ὧν ἐποίησεν
having greeted them, he related one by one of which did
20 ὁ Θεὸς ἐν τοῖς ἔθνεσι διὰ τῆς διακονίας αὐτοῦ. οἱ δὲ ἀκού-
God among the nations through the ministry of him. they And
σαντες ἐδόξαζον τὸν Κύριον· εἰπόν τε αὐτῷ, Θεωρεῖς, ἀδελφέ,
hearing glorified the Lord, said and to him, You see, brother
πόσαι μυριάδες εἰσὶν Ἰουδαίων τῶν πεπιστευκότων· καὶ
how many myriads there are of Jews having believed, and
21 πάντες ζηλωταὶ τοῦ νόμου ὑπάρχουσι· κατηχήθησαν δὲ
all zealous ones of the law are; they were informed and
περὶ σοῦ, ὅτι ἀποστασίαν διδάσκεις ἀπὸ Μωσέως τοὺς
about you, that falling away you teach from Moses
κατὰ τὰ ἔθνη πάντας Ἰουδαίους, λέγων μὴ περιτέμνειν
throughout the nations all Jews, telling not to circumcise
22 αὐτοὺς τὰ τέκνα, μηδὲ τοῖς ἔθεσι περιπατεῖν. τί οὖν ἐστι ;
them the children, nor in the customs to walk. What, then, is it?
πάντως δεῖ πλῆθος συνελθεῖν· ἀκούσονται γὰρ ὅτι ἐλή-
At all events must a multitude come together, will hear for that you
23 λυθας. τοῦτο οὖν ποίησον ὅ σοι λέγομεν· εἰσὶν ἡμῖν ἄνδρες
have come. This, then, do what you we tell. There are to us men
24 τέσσαρες εὐχὴν ἔχοντες ἐφ' ἑαυτῶν· τούτους παραλαβὼν
four having a vow upon themselves; these taking

these, be purified with them, and be at expense for them, that they may shave the head. And all shall know that what they have been told about you is nothing, but you yourself walk orderly, keeping the Law. 25 And as to the believing Gentiles, we joined in writing, judging them to observe no such thing, except to keep themselves from both idol sacrifice, and the blood, and a thing strangled, and *from* fornication. 26 then taking the men on the next day, being purified with them, Paul went into the Temple, declaring the fulfillment of the days of the purification, until the offering should be offered for each one of them.

27 But when the seven days were about to be completed, having seen him in the Temple, the Jews from Asia stirred up all the crowd, and laid hands on him, 28 crying out, Men, Israelites, help! This is the man who teaches everywhere against the Law and this place. And even more, he also brought Greeks into the Temple, and has defiled this holy place. 29 For they had before seen Trophimus the Ephesian in the city with him, whom they supposed that Paul brought into the Temple. 30 And the whole city was moved, and there was a running together of people. And having laid hold of Paul, they drew him outside of the Temple, and at once the doors were shut. 31 But *as* they *were* seeking to kill him, a report came up to the chiliarch of the cohort that all Jerusalem is in a tumult. 32 *He* at once ran down to them, taking soldiers and centurions. And seeing the chiliarch and the soldiers, they stopped beating Paul. 33 Then going near, the chiliarch laid hold of him,

ἁγνίσθητι σὺν αὐτοῖς, καὶ δαπάνησον ἐπ' αὐτοῖς, ἵνα
be purified with them, and be at expense on them, that
ξυρήσωνται τὴν κεφαλήν, καὶ γνῶσι πάντες ὅτι ὧν κατή-
they may shave the head, and may know all that of which they
χηνται περὶ σοῦ οὐδέν ἐστιν, ἀλλὰ στοιχεῖς καὶ αὐτὸς τὸν
have been told about you nothing is, but you walk also yourself the
25 νόμον φυλάσσων. περὶ δὲ τῶν πεπιστευκότων ἐθνῶν ἡμεῖς
Law keeping. concerning And the believing nations, we
ἐπεστείλαμεν, κρίναντες μηδὲν τοιοῦτον τηρεῖν αὐτούς, εἰ
joined in writing, judging no such thing to observe them, ex-
μὴ φυλάσσεσθαι αὐτοὺς τό τε εἰδωλόθυτον καὶ τὸ αἷμα καὶ
cept to keep from themselves the both idol sacrifice and the blood and
26 πνικτὸν καὶ πορνείαν. τότε ὁ Παῦλος παραλαβὼν τοὺς
a thing strangled and fornication, Then Paul taking the
ἄνδρας, τῇ ἐχομένῃ ἡμέρᾳ σὺν αὐτοῖς ἁγνισθεὶς εἰσῄει εἰς
men, on the next day with them having been purified went into
τὸ ἱερόν, διαγγέλλων τὴν ἐκπλήρωσιν τῶν ἡμερῶν τοῦ
the Temple, declaring the fulfillment of the days of the
ἁγνισμοῦ, ἕως οὗ προσηνέχθη ὑπὲρ ἑνὸς ἑκάστου αὐτῶν
purification, until should be offered for one each of them
ἡ προσφορά.
the offering.
27 Ὡς δὲ ἔμελλον αἱ ἑπτὰ ἡμέραι συντελεῖσθαι, οἱ ἀπὸ τῆς
as But about to be the seven days completed, the from —
Ἀσίας Ἰουδαῖοι, θεασάμενοι αὐτὸν ἐν τῷ ἱερῷ, συνέχεον
Asia Jews, having seen him in the Temple, stirred up
πάντα τὸν ὄχλον, καὶ ἐπέβαλον τὰς χεῖρας ἐπ' αὐτόν,
all the crowd, and laid the hands on him,
28 κράζοντες, Ἄνδρες Ἰσραηλῖται, βοηθεῖτε. οὗτός ἐστιν ὁ
crying out, Men, Israelites, help! This is the
ἄνθρωπος ὁ κατὰ τοῦ λαοῦ καὶ τοῦ νόμου καὶ τοῦ τόπου
man who against the people and the Law and — place
τούτου πάντας πανταχοῦ διδάσκων· ἔτι τε καὶ Ἕλληνας
this all everywhere teaching. further And also Greeks
εἰσήγαγεν εἰς τὸ ἱερόν, καὶ κεκοίνωκε τὸν ἅγιον τόπον
brought in to the Temple, and has defiled — holy place
29 τοῦτον. ἦσαν γὰρ προεωρακότες Τρόφιμον τὸν Ἐφέσιον ἐν
this. they were For previously seen Trophimus the Ephesian in
τῇ πόλει σὺν αὐτῷ, ὃν ἐνόμιζον ὅτι εἰς τὸ ἱερὸν εἰσήγαγεν
the city with him, whom they supposed that into the Temple brought in
30 ὁ Παῦλος. ἐκινήθη τε ἡ πόλις ὅλη, καὶ ἐγένετο συνδρομὴ τοῦ
Paul, was moved And the city whole, and there was running together the
λαοῦ· καὶ ἐπιλαβόμενοι τοῦ Παύλου εἷλκον αὐτὸν ἔξω τοῦ
people, and having seized — Paul, they drew him outside of the
31 ἱεροῦ· καὶ εὐθέως ἐκλείσθησαν αἱ θύραι. ζητούντων δὲ αὐτὸν
Temple, and at once were shut the doors. they seeking And him
ἀποκτεῖναι, ἀνέβη φάσις τῷ χιλιάρχῳ τῆς σπείρης, ὅτι
to kill, came up a report to the chiliarch of the cohort, that
32 ὅλη συγκέχυται Ἱερουσαλήμ· ὃς ἐξαυτῆς παραλαβὼν
all is in a tumult Jerusalem; who at once having taken
στρατιώτας καὶ ἑκατοντάρχους, κατέδραμεν ἐπ' αὐτούς·
soldiers and centurions ran down on them;
οἱ δέ, ἰδόντες τὸν χιλίαρχον καὶ τοὺς στρατιώτας, ἐπαύσαντο
they and seeing the chiliarch and the soldiers ceased
33 τύπτοντες τὸν Παῦλον. τότε ἐγγίσας ὁ χιλίαρχος ἐπελάβετο
beating — Paul. Then going near the chiliarch laid hold

and commanded *him* to be bound with two chains. And *he* asked who he might be, and what he is doing. [34]But others cried something else in the crowd, and not being able to know the certainty because of the uproar, he commanded him brought into the fortress.

[35]But when he came on the stairs, it happened he was borne by the soldiers because of the violence of the crowd. [36]For the multitude of the people followed, crying out, Take him away!

[37]But being about to be brought into the fortress, Paul said to the chiliarch, Is it lawful for me to say a thing to you? And he said, Do you know *to speak* in Greek? [38]Then are you not the Egyptian who before these days caused a riot, and led four thousand men of the assassins out into the desert? [39]But Paul said, I am indeed a Jew of Tarsus, of Cilicia, a citizen *of* no mean city. And I beg you, allow me to speak to the people. [40]And he allowing him, standing on the stairs Paul signaled with *his* hand to the people. And much silence taking place, he spoke in the Hebrew dialect, saying,

CHAPTER 22

[1]Men, brothers and fathers, hear my defense now to you. [2]And hearing that he spoke in the Hebrew dialect to them, they showed more quietness. And he said:

[3]I am indeed a man, a Jew born in Tarsus of Cilicia, but having been brought up in this city at the feet of Gamaliel, having been trained according to the exactness of the ancestral law, being a zealous one of God, even as you all are today. [4] persecuted this Way as far as

αὐτοῦ, καὶ ἐκέλευσε δεθῆναι ἁλύσεσι δυσί· καὶ ἐπυνθάνετο τίς
of him. and commanded to be bound with chains two, and asked who
34 ἂν εἴη, καὶ τί ἐστι πεποιηκώς. ἄλλοι δὲ ἄλλο τι ἐβόων ἐν τῷ
he may be, and what he is doing. others And else something cried in the
ὄχλῳ· μὴ δυνάμενος δὲ γνῶναι τὸ ἀσφαλὲς διὰ τὸν θόρυβον,
crowd, not being able and to know the certain thing for the uproar,
35 ἐκέλευσεν ἄγεσθαι αὐτὸν εἰς τὴν παρεμβολήν. ὅτε δὲ ἐγένετο
he commanded to bring him into the fortress. when But he came
ἐπὶ τοὺς ἀναβαθμούς, συνέβη βαστάζεσθαι αὐτὸν ὑπὸ τῶν
on the steps, it happened to be carried him by the
36 στρατιωτῶν διὰ τὴν βίαν τοῦ ὄχλου. ἠκολούθει γὰρ τὸ
soldiers because of the violence of the crowd. followed For the
πλῆθος τοῦ λαοῦ κρᾶζον, Αἶρε αὐτόν.
multitude of the people crying out, Take away him.
37 Μέλλων τε εἰσάγεσθαι εἰς τὴν παρεμβολὴν ο Παῦλος λεγει
being about And to be brought into the fortress, Paul said
τῷ χιλιάρχῳ, Εἰ ἔξεστί μοι εἰπεῖν τι πρός σε; ὁ δὲ ἔφη,
to the chiliarch, If it is lawful for me to say a thing to you? he And said,
38 Ἑλληνιστὶ γινώσκεις; οὐκ ἄρα σὺ εἶ ὁ Αἰγύπτιος ὁ πρὸ
in Greek do you know? Not, then, you are the Egyptian, he before
τούτων τῶν ἡμερῶν ἀναστατώσας καὶ ἐξαγαγὼν εἰς τὴν
these — days caused a riot and leading out into the
39 ἔρημον τοὺς τετρακισχιλίους ἄνδρας τῶν σικαρίων; εἶπε δὲ ὁ
desert the four thousand men of the assassins? said And
Παῦλος, Ἐγὼ ἄνθρωπος μέν εἰμι Ἰουδαῖος, Ταρσεὺς τῆς
Paul, I a man indeed am, a Jew, a Tarsian —
Κιλικίας, οὐκ ἀσήμου πόλεως πολίτης· δέομαι δέ σου, ἐπί-
of Cilicia, not of a mean city a citizen. I beg And of you,
40 τρεψόν μοι λαλῆσαι πρὸς τὸν λαόν. ἐπιτρέψαντος δὲ αὐτοῦ,
allow me to speak to the people. he having allowed And him,
ὁ Παῦλος ἑστὼς ἐπὶ τῶν ἀναβαθμῶν κατέσεισε τῇ χειρὶ τῷ
Paul standing on the steps signaled with the hand to the
λαῷ· πολλῆς δὲ σιγῆς γενομένης, προσεφώνησε τῇ Ἑβραΐδι
people; much and silence occurring, he spoke in the Hebrew
διαλέκτῳ λέγων,
dialect, saying,

CHAPTER 22

1 Ἄνδρες ἀδελφοὶ καὶ πατέρες, ἀκούσατέ μου τῆς πρὸς
Men, brothers and fathers, hear of me the to
ὑμᾶς νῦν ἀπολογίας.
you now defense.
2 Ἀκούσαντες δὲ ὅτι τῇ Ἑβραΐδι διαλέκτῳ προσεφώνει
hearing And that in the Hebrew dialect he spoke
αὐτοῖς, μᾶλλον παρέσχον ἡσυχίαν. καί φησιν,
to them, more they showed quietness. And he says,
3 Ἐγὼ μέν εἰμι ἀνὴρ Ἰουδαῖος, γεγεννημένος ἐν Ταρσῷ τῆς
I indeed am a man, a Jew, having been born in Tarsus —
Κιλικίας, ἀνατεθραμμένος δὲ ἐν τῇ πόλει ταύτῃ παρὰ τοὺς
of Cilicia, having been brought up and in — city this at the
πόδας Γαμαλιήλ, πεπαιδευμένος κατὰ ἀκρίβειαν τοῦ πα-
feet of Gamaliel; having been trained according to exactness of the
τρῴου νόμου, ζηλωτὴς ὑπάρχων τοῦ Θεοῦ, καθὼς πάντες
ancestral Law, a zealous one being — of God, even as all
4 ὑμεῖς ἐστε σήμερον· ὃς ταύτην τὴν ὁδὸν ἐδίωξα ἄχρι θανάτου,
you are today; who this — Way persecuted as far as to death,

death, binding and delivering up both men and women to prisons; 5 as also the high priest and all the elderhood witnesses to me. And having received letters from *them*, I traveled into Damascus to indeed lead those being bound there to Jerusalem, in order that they might be punished. 6 And it happened to me, traveling and drawing near to Damascus: suddenly, about midday, a great light out of the heaven shone around me. 7 And I fell to the ground, and heard a voice saying to me, Saul, Saul, why do you persecute Me? 8 And I answered, Who are you, Sir? And He said to me, I am Jesus the Nazarene whom you persecute. 9 But those being with me indeed saw the light, and were alarmed, but did not hear His voice speaking to me. 10 And I said, What shall I do, Lord? And the Lord said to me, Rising up, go into Damascus, and there you will be told about all things which has been appointed to you to do. 11 And as I did not see, from the glory of that light, being led by the hand by those being with me, I went into Damascus.

12 And a certain Ananias, a devout man according to the Law, testified *to* by all the Jews living *there*, 13 coming to me and standing by, *he* said to me, Brother Saul look up. And in the same hour I looked up on him. 14 And he said, The God of our fathers appointed you to know His will, and to see the Just One, and to hear a voice out of His mouth; 15 for you shall be a witness for Him to all men, of what you have seen and heard. 16 And now what do you intend? Rising up, be baptized, and wash away your sins, calling on the name of the Lord. 17 And it happened to me, returning to Jerusalem and praying in the Temple:

δεσμεύων καὶ παραδιδοὺς εἰς φυλακὰς ἄνδρας τε καὶ γυναῖκας.
binding and delivering to prisons men both and women.
5 ὡς καὶ ὁ ἀρχιερεὺς μαρτυρεῖ μοι, καὶ πᾶν τὸ πρεσβυτέριον·
as Even the high priest witnesses to me, and all the elderhood;
παρ' ὧν καὶ ἐπιστολὰς δεξάμενος πρὸς τοὺς ἀδελφούς, εἰς
from whom also letters having received to the brothers in
Δαμασκὸν ἐπορευόμην, ἄξων καὶ τοὺς ἐκεῖσε ὄντας δεδεμένους
Damascus, I traveled leading also those there being bound
6 εἰς Ἱερουσαλήμ, ἵνα τιμωρηθῶσιν. ἐγένετο δέ μοι πορευο-
to Jerusalem, that they might be punished. it was And to me traveling
μένῳ καὶ ἐγγίζοντι τῇ Δαμασκῷ, περὶ μεσημβρίαν, ἐξαίφνης
and drawing near to Damascus, about midday suddenly
7 ἐκ τοῦ οὐρανοῦ περιαστράψαι φῶς ἱκανὸν περὶ ἐμέ. ἔπεσόν
out of the heaven shone light a great about me. I fell
τε εἰς τὸ ἔδαφος, καὶ ἤκουσα φωνῆς λεγούσης μοι, Σαούλ,
And to the ground, and heard a voice saying to me, Saul,
8 Σαούλ, τί με διώκεις ; ἐγὼ δὲ ἀπεκρίθην, Τίς εἶ, Κύριε ; εἶπέ
Saul, why Me you persecute? I And answered, Who are you, Sir? He said
τε πρός με, Ἐγώ εἰμι Ἰησοῦς ὁ Ναζωραῖος ὃν σὺ διώκεις.
And to me, I am Jesus the Nazarene, whom you persecute.
9 οἱ δὲ σὺν ἐμοὶ ὄντες τὸ μὲν φῶς ἐθεάσαντο, καὶ ἔμφοβοι
those And with me being, the indeed light beheld, and alarmed
ἐγένοντο· τὴν δὲ φωνὴν οὐκ ἤκουσαν τοῦ λαλοῦντός μοι.
were, the but voice not they heard of Him speaking to me.
10 εἶπον δέ, Τί ποιήσω, Κύριε ; ὁ δὲ Κύριος εἶπε πρός με,
I said And, What may I do, Lord? the And Lord said to me,
Ἀναστὰς πορεύου εἰς Δαμασκόν· κἀκεῖ σοι λαληθήσεται
Rising up, go into Damascus, and there to you it will be told
11 περὶ πάντων ὧν τέτακταί σοι ποιῆσαι. ὡς δὲ οὐκ ἐνέβλεπον
about all things which is appointed to you to do. as And not I saw
ἀπὸ τῆς δόξης τοῦ φωτὸς ἐκείνου, χειραγωγούμενος ὑπὸ
from the glory light of that, being led by the hand by
12 τῶν συνόντων μοι, ἦλθον εἰς Δαμασκόν. Ἀνανίας δέ τις,
the (ones) being with me, I went into Damascus. Ananias And a certain,
ἀνὴρ εὐσεβὴς κατὰ τὸν νόμον, μαρτυρούμενος ὑπὸ πάντων
a man devout according to the Law, testified (to) by all
13 τῶν κατοικούντων Ἰουδαίων, ἐλθὼν πρός με καὶ ἐπιστὰς
the living (there) Jews, coming to me and standing by
εἶπέ μοι, Σαοὺλ ἀδελφέ, ἀνάβλεψον. κἀγὼ αὐτῇ τῇ ὥρᾳ
said to me, Saul, brother, look up. And I in that hour
14 ἀνέβλεψα εἰς αὐτόν. ὁ δὲ εἶπεν, Ὁ Θεὸς τῶν πατέρων ἡμῶν
looked up at him. he And said, The God of the fathers of us
προεχειρίσατό σε γνῶναι τὸ θέλημα αὐτοῦ, καὶ ἰδεῖν τὸν
before appointed you to know the will of Him, and to see the
15 δίκαιον, καὶ ἀκοῦσαι φωνὴν ἐκ τοῦ στόματος αὐτοῦ. ὅτι ἔσῃ
Just One, and to hear a voice out of the mouth of Him, for you will be
μάρτυς αὐτῷ πρὸς πάντας ἀνθρώπους ὧν ἑώρακας καὶ
a witness to Him to all men of which you have seen and
16 ἤκουσας. καὶ νῦν τί μέλλεις ; ἀναστὰς βάπτισαι καὶ ἀπό-
heard. And now what intend you? Rising up, be baptized and wash
λουσαι τὰς ἁμαρτίας σου, ἐπικαλεσάμενος τὸ ὄνομα τοῦ
away the sins of you, calling on the name of the
17 Κυρίου. ἐγένετο δέ μοι ὑποστρέψαντι εἰς Ἱερουσαλήμ, καὶ
Lord. it was And to me, having returned to Jerusalem, and
προσευχομένου μου ἐν τῷ ἱερῷ, γενέσθαι με ἐν ἐκστάσει, καὶ
praying me in the Temple, becoming me in an ecstasy, and

became in an ecstasy, [18]and I saw Him saying to me, Hurry and go out quickly from Jerusalem, because they will not receive your testimony concerning Me. [19]And I said, Lord, they understand that I was imprisoning and beating the ones believing on You throughout the synagogues. [20]And when the blood of Your witness Stephen was poured out, I myself also was standing by and consenting to his execution, and holding the garments of those killing him. [21]And He said to me, Go, for I will send you to the nations afar off.

[22]And they heard him until this word, and lifted up their voice, saying, Take such a one from the earth, for it is not fitting that he should live! [23]And they shouting, and tearing the garments, and throwing dust into the air, [24]the chiliarch ordered to bring him into the fortress, saying for him to be examined with scourges, that he may know for what cause they cried out so against him.

[25]But as they stretched him with the thongs, Paul said to the centurion standing by, Is it lawful for you to flog a man, even a Roman not found guilty? [26]And hearing, coming near the centurion reported to the chiliarch, saying, Watch what you are about to do, for this man is a Roman. [27]And coming up, the chiliarch said to him, Tell me, are you a Roman? And he said, yes. [28]And the chiliarch answered, I bought this citizenship with a great sum. And Paul said, I also was born *free.* [29]Then at once those being about to examine him stood away from him. And the chiliarch also feared, fully knowing that he was a Roman, and that he had bound him. [30]And on the morrow, desiring to know the certainty *as to* why he was

18 ἰδεῖν αὐτὸν λέγοντά μοι, Σπεῦσον καὶ ἔξελθε ἐν τάχει ἐξ
saw Him saying to me, Hurry and go out quickly from
Ἱερουσαλήμ· διότι οὐ παραδέξονταί σου τὴν μαρτυρίαν
Jerusalem, because not they will receive of you the testimony
19 περὶ ἐμοῦ. κἀγὼ εἶπον, Κύριε, αὐτοὶ ἐπίστανται ὅτι ἐγὼ
concerning Me. And I said, Lord, they understand that I
ἤμην φυλακίζων καὶ δέρων κατὰ τὰς συναγωγὰς τοὺς
was imprisoning and beating throughout the synagogues those
20 πιστεύοντας ἐπὶ σέ· καὶ ὅτε ἐξεχεῖτο τὸ αἷμα Στεφάνου τοῦ
believing on You; and when was poured out the blood of Stephen the
μάρτυρός σου, καὶ αὐτὸς ἤμην ἐφεστὼς καὶ συνευδοκῶν τῇ
witness of You, also myself I was standing by and consenting to the
ἀναιρέσει αὐτοῦ, καὶ φυλάσσων τὰ ἱμάτια τῶν ἀναιρούντων
execution of him, and keeping the garments of those killing
21 αὐτόν. καὶ εἶπε πρός με, Πορεύου, ὅτι ἐγὼ εἰς ἔθνη μακρὰν
him And He said to me, Go, because I to the nations afar off
ἐξαποστελῶ σε.
will send you.

22 Ἤκουον δὲ αὐτοῦ ἄχρι τούτου τοῦ λόγου, καὶ ἐπῆραν
they heard And him as far as to this — word, and lifted up
τὴν φωνὴν αὐτῶν λέγοντες, Αἶρε ἀπὸ τῆς γῆς τὸν τοιοῦτον·
the voice of them saying, Take from the earth — such a one;
23 οὐ γὰρ καθῆκον αὐτὸν ζῆν. κραυγαζόντων δὲ αὐτῶν, καὶ
not for it is fitting he should live. shouting And them, and
ῥιπτούντων τὰ ἱμάτια, καὶ κονιορτὸν βαλλόντων εἰς τὸν
tearing the garments, and dust throwing into the
24 ἀέρα, ἐκέλευσεν αὐτὸν ὁ χιλίαρχος ἄγεσθαι εἰς τὴν παρεμβο-
air, commanded him the chiliarch to bring into the fortress,
λήν, εἰπὼν μάστιξιν ἀνετάζεσθαι αὐτόν, ἵνα ἐπιγνῷ δι' ἣν
saying with scourges to be examined him, that he may know for what
25 αἰτίαν οὕτως ἐπεφώνουν αὐτῷ. ὡς δὲ προέτειναν αὐτὸν τοῖς
crime thus they cried against him. as But they stretched him with the
ἱμᾶσιν, εἶπε πρὸς τὸν ἑστῶτα ἑκατόνταρχον ὁ Παῦλος, Εἰ
thongs, said to the standing by centurion — Paul, If
ἄνθρωπον Ῥωμαῖον καὶ ἀκατάκριτον ἔξεστιν ὑμῖν μαστίζειν;
a man, a Roman, and (one) not found guilty it is lawful for you to whip?
26 ἀκούσας δὲ ὁ ἑκατόνταρχος, προσελθὼν ἀπήγγειλε τῷ
hearing And the centurion coming near reported to the
χιλιάρχῳ λέγων, Ὅρα τί μέλλεις ποιεῖν· ὁ γὰρ ἄνθρωπος
chiliarch, saying, See what you are about to do, for man
27 οὗτος Ῥωμαῖός ἐστι. προσελθὼν δὲ ὁ χιλίαρχος εἶπεν αὐτῷ,
this a Roman is. having come up And the chiliarch, he said to him,
28 Λέγε μοι, εἰ σὺ Ῥωμαῖος εἶ; ὁ δὲ ἔφη, Ναί. ἀπεκρίθη τε ὁ
Tell me if you a Roman are he And said, Yes. answered And the
χιλίαρχος, Ἐγὼ πολλοῦ κεφαλαίου τὴν πολιτείαν ταύτην
chiliarch, I of a much sum — citizenship this
ἐκτησάμην. ὁ δὲ Παῦλος ἔφη, Ἐγὼ δὲ καὶ γεγέννημαι.
bought. And Paul said, I But even have been born.
29 εὐθέως οὖν ἀπέστησαν ἀπ' αὐτοῦ οἱ μέλλοντες αὐτὸν ἀνε-
At once, then, stood away from him those being about him to
τάζειν. καὶ ὁ χιλίαρχος δὲ ἐφοβήθη, ἐπιγνοὺς ὅτι Ῥωμαῖός
examine. also the chiliarch And feared, fully knowing that a Roman
ἐστι, καὶ ὅτι ἦν αὐτὸν δεδεκώς.
he is, and that he was him having bound.

30 Τῇ δὲ ἐπαύριον βουλόμενος γνῶναι τὸ ἀσφαλές, τὸ τί
on the And morrow, being minded to know the certain thing — why

accused by the Jews, he freed him from the bonds. And *he* commanded the chief priests and all their sanhedrin to come. And bringing Paul down, *he* set *him* among them.

CHAPTER 23

[1] And looking on the sanhedrin, Paul said, Men, brothers, I in all good conscience have conducted myself toward God to this day. [2] But Ananias the high priest ordered those standing by him to strike his mouth. [3] Then Paul said to him, God is going to strike you, whitened wall! And do you sit judging me according to the Law, and contrary to the Law command me to be struck? [4] And those standing by said, Do you revile the high priest of God? [5] And Paul said, I did not know that he is high priest; for it has been written, "You shall not speak evil of a ruler of your people." [6] But knowing that the one part consisted of Sadducees, and the other of Pharisees, Paul cried out in the sanhedrin, Men, brothers, I am a Pharisee, a son of Pharisees; I am being judged concerning hope and resurrection of *the* dead! [7] And he having spoken this, there was a discord of the Pharisees and the Sadducees; and the multitude was divided. [8] For the Sadducees indeed say there is no resurrection, nor angel, nor spirit. But Pharisees confess both. [9] And there was a great cry. And the scribes of the part of the Pharisees rising up, they were contending, saying, We find nothing evil in this man. And, If a spirit spoke to him, or an angel, let us not fight against God. [10] And discord having arisen, fearing lest Paul should be torn by them, the chiliarch commanded the soldiery to go down to take him out of their midst,

κατηγορεῖται παρὰ τῶν Ἰουδαίων, ἔλυσεν αὐτὸν ἀπὸ τῶν
he was accused by the Jews, he freed him from the
δεσμῶν, καὶ ἐκέλευσεν ἐλθεῖν τοὺς ἀρχιερεῖς καὶ ὅλον τὸ
bonds, and commanded to come the chief priests and all the
συνέδριον αὐτῶν, καὶ καταγαγὼν τὸν Παῦλον ἔστησεν εἰς
sanhedrin of them; and having brought down Paul set (him) among
αὐτούς.
them.

CHAPTER 23

1 Ἀτενίσας δὲ ὁ Παῦλος τῷ συνεδρίῳ εἶπεν, Ἄνδρες ἀδελφοί,
having looked And Paul on the sanhedrin, he said, Men, brothers,
ἐγὼ πάσῃ συνειδήσει ἀγαθῇ πεπολίτευμαι τῷ Θεῷ ἄχρι
I in all conscience good have lived — to God until
2 ταύτης τῆς ἡμέρας. ὁ δὲ ἀρχιερεὺς Ἀνανίας ἐπέταξε τοῖς
this — day. the But high priest, Ananias, ordered those
3 παρεστῶσιν αὐτῷ τύπτειν αὐτοῦ τὸ στόμα. τότε ὁ Παῦλος
standing by him to strike of him the mouth. Then Paul
πρὸς αὐτὸν εἶπε, Τύπτειν σε μέλλει ὁ Θεός, τοῖχε κεκονιαμένε·
to him said, to strike you is about God, wall whitened!
καὶ σὺ κάθῃ κρίνων με κατὰ τὸν νόμον, καὶ παρανομῶν
And you sit judging me according to the Law, and contrary to law
4 κελεύεις με τύπτεσθαι; οἱ δὲ παρεστῶτες εἶπον, Τὸν ἀρχιερέα
command me to be struck? those And standing by said, The high priest
5 τοῦ Θεοῦ λοιδορεῖς; ἔφη τε ὁ Παῦλος, Οὐκ ᾔδειν, ἀδελφοί,
— of God do you revile? said And Paul, Not I knew, brothers,
ὅτι ἐστὶν ἀρχιερεύς· γέγραπται γάρ, Ἄρχοντα τοῦ λαοῦ σου
that he is high priest; it has been written for, A ruler of the people of you
6 οὐκ ἐρεῖς κακῶς. γνοὺς δὲ ὁ Παῦλος ὅτι τὸ ἓν μέρος ἐστὶ
not speak of evilly. knowing And Paul that the one part is
Σαδδουκαίων, τὸ δὲ ἕτερον Φαρισαίων, ἔκραξεν ἐν τῷ
of Sadducees, the and other of Pharisees, cried out in the
συνεδρίῳ, Ἄνδρες ἀδελφοί, ἐγὼ Φαρισαῖός εἰμι, υἱὸς Φαρι-
sanhedrin, Men, brothers, I a Pharisee am, a son of Phari-
σαίου· περὶ ἐλπίδος καὶ ἀναστάσεως νεκρῶν ἐγὼ κρίνομαι.
sees; concerning hope and resurrection of (the) dead I am being judged.
7 τοῦτο δὲ αὐτοῦ λαλήσαντος, ἐγένετο στάσις τῶν Φαρισαίων
this And him having spoken, there was a discord of the Pharisees
8 καὶ τῶν Σαδδουκαίων, καὶ ἐσχίσθη τὸ πλῆθος. Σαδδουκαῖοι
and the Sadducees, and was divided the multitude. Sadducees
μὲν γὰρ λέγουσι μὴ εἶναι ἀνάστασιν, μηδὲ ἄγγελον, μήτε
indeed For say not to be a resurrection, neither angel nor
9 πνεῦμα· Φαρισαῖοι δὲ ὁμολογοῦσι τὰ ἀμφότερα. ἐγένετο δὲ
spirit. Pharisees But confess — both. there was And
κραυγὴ μεγάλη· καὶ ἀναστάντες οἱ γραμματεῖς τοῦ μέρους
a cry great, and having risen up the scribes of the part
τῶν Φαρισαίων διεμάχοντο λέγοντες, Οὐδὲν κακὸν εὑρί-
the Pharisees, they were contending, saying, Nothing evil we
σκομεν ἐν τῷ ἀνθρώπῳ τούτῳ· εἰ δὲ πνεῦμα ἐλάλησεν αὐτῷ
find in — man this; if and a spirit spoke to him
10 ἢ ἄγγελος, μὴ θεομαχῶμεν. πολλῆς δὲ γενομένης στάσεως,
or an angel, not let us fight against God. much And arising discord,
εὐλαβηθεὶς ὁ χιλίαρχος μὴ διασπασθῇ ὁ Παῦλος ὑπ' αὐτῶν,
fearing the chiliarch lest should be torn Paul by them,
ἐκέλευσε τὸ στράτευμα καταβὰν ἁρπάσαι αὐτὸν ἐκ μέσου
commanded the soldiery going down to seize him out of (the) midst

and to bring *him* into the fortress. [11] And coming to him in the following night the Lord said, Be cheered, Paul, for as you fully testified the things concerning Me in Jerusalem, so you must also testify at Rome. [12] And day having come about, some of the Jews making a conspiracy cursed themselves, saying neither to eat nor to drink until they should kill Paul. [13] And those making this plot were more than forty; [14] who coming near to the chief priests and to the elders said, With a curse we have cursed ourselves to taste of nothing until we may kill Paul. [15] Now, then, you with the sanhedrin inform the chiliarch, so as tomorrow he may bring him down to you, as intending to more accurately find out about him. And before the drawing near of him, we are ready to kill him. [16] But the son of Paul's sister hearing, having come near and entering into the fortress, reported to Paul. [17] And calling one of the centurions, Paul said, Bring this young man to the chiliarch, for he has something to report to him. [18] Then indeed taking him, he brought *him* to the chiliarch, and said, Paul the prisoner having called me near asked me to bring this young man to you. [19] And laying hold of his hand, and drawing aside privately, the chiliarch asked, What is *it* that you have to report to me? [20] And he said, The Jews agreed to ask you that tomorrow you bring down Paul into the sanhedrin, as being about to inquire more accurately concerning him.

[21] Therefore, you be not persuaded by them, for more than forty men of them lie in wait for him.

αὐτῶν, ἄγειν τε εἰς τὴν παρεμβολήν.
of them, to bring and into the fortress.
11 Τῇ δὲ ἐπιούσῃ νυκτὶ ἐπιστὰς αὐτῷ ὁ Κύριος εἶπε, Θάρσει
in the And following night coming on to him the Lord said, Be cheered,
Παῦλε· ὡς γὰρ διεμαρτύρω τὰ περὶ ἐμοῦ εἰς Ἱερουσαλήμ,
Paul; as for you fully testified the things about Me in Jerusalem,
οὕτω σε δεῖ καὶ εἰς Ῥώμην μαρτυρῆσαι.
so you must also in Rome testify.
12 Γενομένης δὲ ἡμέρας, ποιήσαντές τινες τῶν Ἰουδαίων
becoming And day, making some of the Jews
συστροφήν, ἀνεθεμάτισαν ἑαυτούς, λέγοντες μήτε φαγεῖν
a conspiracy, cursed themselves, saying neither to eat
13 μήτε πιεῖν ἕως οὗ ἀποκτείνωσι τὸν Παῦλον. ἦσαν δὲ πλείους
nor to drink until they should kill — Paul. were And more (than)
τεσσαράκοντα οἱ ταύτην τὴν συνωμοσίαν πεποιηκότες·
forty those this — plot making;
14 οἵτινες προσελθόντες τοῖς ἀρχιερεῦσι καὶ τοῖς πρεσβυτέροις
who having come near to the chief priests and to the elders
εἶπον, Ἀναθέματι ἀνεθεματίσαμεν ἑαυτούς, μηδενὸς γεύσα-
said, With a curse we cursed ourselves of nothing to taste
15 σθαι ἕως οὗ ἀποκτείνωμεν τὸν Παῦλον. νῦν οὖν ὑμεῖς ἐμφανί-
until we may kill — Paul. Now, then, you inform
σατε τῷ χιλιάρχῳ σὺν τῷ συνεδρίῳ, ὅπως αὔριον αὐτὸν
the chiliarch with the sanhedrin, so as tomorrow him
καταγάγῃ πρὸς ὑμᾶς, ὡς μέλλοντας διαγινώσκειν ἀκριβέ-
he bring down to you as intending to ascertain more
στερον τὰ περὶ αὐτοῦ· ἡμεῖς δέ, πρὸ τοῦ ἐγγίσαι αὐτόν,
accurately that about him; we and before the drawing near of him
16 ἕτοιμοί ἐσμεν τοῦ ἀνελεῖν αὐτόν. ἀκούσας δὲ ὁ υἱὸς τῆς
ready are — to kill him. hearing And the son of the
ἀδελφῆς Παύλου τὴν ἐνέδραν, παραγενόμενος καὶ εἰσελθὼν
sister of Paul of the ambush, having come near and entering
εἰς τὴν παρεμβολήν, ἀπήγγειλε τῷ Παύλῳ. προσκαλεσά-
into the fortress reported — to Paul. calling to (him)
17 μενος δὲ ὁ Παῦλος ἕνα τῶν ἑκατοντάρχων ἔφη, Τὸν νεανίαν
And Paul one of the centurions said, — youth
τοῦτον ἀπάγαγε πρὸς τὸν χιλίαρχον· ἔχει γάρ τι ἀπαγγεῖ-
This bring up to the chiliarch, he has for something to
18 λαι αὐτῷ. ὁ μὲν οὖν παραλαβὼν αὐτὸν ἤγαγε πρὸς τὸν
report to him. he Then taking him brought to the
χιλίαρχον, καί φησιν, Ὁ δέσμιος Παῦλος προσκαλεσάμενός
chiliarch, and says, The prisoner Paul calling near
με ἠρώτησε τοῦτον τὸν νεανίαν ἀγαγεῖν πρός σε, ἔχοντά τι
me asked this — youth to bring to you, having a thing
19 λαλῆσαί σοι. ἐπιλαβόμενος δὲ τῆς χειρὸς αὐτοῦ ὁ χιλίαρχος,
to tell you. laying hold And of the hand of him the chiliarch
καὶ ἀναχωρήσας κατ' ἰδίαν ἐπυνθάνετο, Τί ἐστιν ὃ ἔχεις
and having withdrawn privately asked, What is (it) which you have
20 ἀπαγγεῖλαί μοι; εἶπε δὲ ὅτι Οἱ Ἰουδαῖοι συνέθεντο τοῦ
to report to me? he said And, — The Jews agreed —
ἐρωτῆσαί σε, ὅπως αὔριον εἰς τὸ συνέδριον καταγάγῃς τὸν
to ask you so as tomorrow to the sanhedrin you bring down —
Παῦλον, ὡς μέλλοντές τι ἀκριβέστερον πυνθάνεσθαι περὶ
Paul, as intending something more accurately to inquire concerning
21 αὐτοῦ. σὺ οὖν μὴ πεισθῇς αὐτοῖς· ἐνεδρεύουσι γὰρ αὐτὸν
him. You, then, not be persuaded by them; lie in wait for for him

who put themselves under a curse neither to eat nor to drink until they kill him. And now they are ready, awaiting the promise from you. 22 Then the chiliarch sent the young man away, charging *him* to tell no one that you reported these things to me.

23 And having called near a certain two of the centurions, he said, Get two hundred soldiers ready, so that they may go to Caesarea, and seventy horsemen, and two hundred spearmen, for the third hour of the night; 24 and animals to stand by, so that setting Paul on, they may bring *him* to Felix the governor. 25 *For he* was writing a letter, having this form:

26 Claudius Lysias to the most excellent governor, Felix, greeting. 27 This man being seized by the Jews, and being about to be killed by them, coming on with the soldiers I rescued him, learning that he was a Roman. 28 And being minded to know the charge for which they were accusing him, I brought him down to their sanhedrin; 29 whom I found to be accused concerning questions of their law, and nothing worthy of death or having bonds. 30 And it being revealed to me that a plot against the man was about to be *executed* by the Jews, I at once sent to you, also commanding the accusers to say the things against him before you. Farewell.

31 Then indeed taking up Paul according to the thing appointed to them, the soldiers brought *him* through the night to Antipatris. 32 And on the morrow, allowing the horsemen to go with him, they returned to the fortress. 33 Entering into Caesarea, and giving the letter to the governor, *they* also presented Paul to him. 34 And read-

ἐξ αὐτῶν ἄνδρες πλείους τεσσαράκοντα, οἵτινες ἀνεθεμάτισαν
of them men more (than) forty, who cursed
ἑαυτοὺς μήτε φαγεῖν μήτε πιεῖν ἕως οὗ ἀνέλωσιν αὐτόν· καὶ
themselves neither to eat nor drink until they kill him, and
νῦν ἕτοιμοί εἰσι προσδεχόμενοι τὴν ἀπὸ σοῦ ἐπαγγελίαν. ὁ
now ready they are, awaiting the from you promise. the
22 μὲν οὖν χιλίαρχος ἀπέλυσε τὸν νεανίαν, παραγγείλας μηδενὶ
Then chiliarch dismissed the youth, charging (him) no one
23 ἐκλαλῆσαι ὅτι ταῦτα ἐνεφάνισας πρός με. καὶ προσκαλεσά-
to tell that these things you reported to me. And calling near
μενος δύο τινὰς τῶν ἑκατοντάρχων εἶπεν, Ἑτοιμάσατε
two a certain of the centurions he said, Prepare
στρατιώτας διακοσίους ὅπως πορευθῶσιν ἕως Καισαρείας,
soldiers two hundred, so as they may go to Caesarea,
καὶ ἱππεῖς ἑβδομήκοντα, καὶ δεξιολάβους διακοσίους, ἀπὸ
and horsemen seventy, and spearmen two hundred, from
24 τρίτης ὥρας τῆς νυκτός· κτήνη τε παραστῆσαι, ἵνα ἐπιβιβά-
third hour of the night; beasts and to stand by, that having
σαντες τὸν Παῦλον διασώσωσι πρὸς Φήλικα τὸν ἡγεμόνα·
set on — Paul they may bring to Felix the governor;
25 γράψας ἐπιστολὴν περιέχουσαν τὸν τύπον τοῦτον·
writing a letter, having — form this:
26 Κλαύδιος Λυσίας τῷ κρατίστῳ ἡγεμόνι Φήλικι χαίρειν.
Claudius Lysias to the most excellent governor, Felix, greeting.
27 τὸν ἄνδρα τοῦτον συλληφθέντα ὑπὸ τῶν Ἰουδαίων, καὶ
— man This having been seized by the Jews, and
μέλλοντα ἀναιρεῖσθαι ὑπ' αὐτῶν, ἐπιστὰς σὺν τῷ στρατεύ-
being about to be killed by them, coming on with the soldiers
28 ματι ἐξειλόμην αὐτόν, μαθὼν ὅτι Ῥωμαῖός ἐστι. βουλόμενος
I rescued him, having learned that a Roman he is. being minded
δὲ γνῶναι τὴν αἰτίαν δι' ἣν ἐνεκάλουν αὐτῷ, κατήγαγον
And to know the charge for which they were accusing him, I brought down
29 αὐτὸν εἰς τὸ συνέδριον αὐτῶν· ὃν εὗρον ἐγκαλούμενον περὶ
him to the sanhedrin of them; whom I found being accused concerning
ζητημάτων τοῦ νόμου αὐτῶν, μηδὲν δὲ ἄξιον θανάτου ἢ
questions of the law of them, nothing and worthy of death, or
30 δεσμῶν ἔγκλημα ἔχοντα. μηνυθείσης δέ μοι ἐπιβουλῆς εἰς τὸν
of bonds charge having. being revealed And to me a plot against the
ἄνδρα μέλλειν ἔσεσθαι ὑπὸ τῶν Ἰουδαίων, ἐξαυτῆς ἔπεμψα
man being about to be by the Jews, at once I sent
πρός σε, παραγγείλας καὶ τοῖς κατηγόροις λέγειν τὰ πρὸς
to you, commanding also the accusers to say — to
αὐτὸν ἐπὶ σοῦ. ἔρρωσο.
him before you. Farewell.
31 Οἱ μὲν οὖν στρατιῶται, κατὰ τὸ διατεταγμένον αὐτοῖς,
the Therefore soldiers, according to the thing appointed to them,
ἀναλαβόντες τὸν Παῦλον, ἤγαγον διὰ τῆς νυκτὸς εἰς τὴν
taking up — Paul, brought through the night to —
32 Ἀντιπατρίδα. τῇ δὲ ἐπαύριον ἐάσαντες τοὺς ἱππεῖς πορεύ-
Antipatris; on the and morrow, allowing the horsemen to go
33 εσθαι σὺν αὐτῷ, ὑπέστρεψαν εἰς τὴν παρεμβολήν· οἵτινες
with him, they returned to the fortress; who
εἰσελθόντες εἰς τὴν Καισάρειαν, καὶ ἀναδόντες τὴν ἐπιστολὴν
having entered into — Caesarea, and giving over the letter
34 τῷ ἡγεμόνι, παρέστησαν καὶ τὸν Παῦλον αὐτῷ. ἀναγνοὺς
to the governor, presented also — Paul to him. having read

ing *it*, the governor asked from what province he is. And having learned that *he was* from Cilicia, [35] he said, I will hear you fully when your accusers arrive. And *he* commanded him to be kept in the praetorium of Herod.

δὲ ὁ ἡγεμών, καὶ ἐπερωτήσας ἐκ ποίας ἐπαρχίας ἐστί, καὶ
And the governor, and asking of what province he is, and
35 πυθόμενος ὅτι ἀπὸ Κιλικίας, Διακούσομαί σου, ἔφη, ὅταν καὶ
learning that from Cilicia, I will hear you, he said, when also
οἱ κατήγοροί σου παραγένωνται. ἐκέλευσέ τε αὐτὸν ἐν τῷ
the accusers of you arrive; commanding and him in the
πραιτωρίῳ τοῦ Ἡρῴδου φυλάσσεσθαι.
praetorium — of Herod to be kept.

CHAPTER 24

[1] And after five days the high priest came down with the elders, and a certain orator, Tertullus, who made a statement to the governor against Paul. [2] And Tertullus being called, he began to accuse, saying [3] Obtaining much peace through you, and excellent achievements having come to this nation due to your forethought, in everything and everywhere we accept with all thankfulness, most excellent Felix. [4] But that I not hinder you more, I beseech you to hear us briefly in your fairness. [5] For finding this man pestilent, and moving insurrection among all the Jews throughout the world, and a ringleader of the Nazarene sect; [6] who also attempted to profane the Temple; whom we also seized and wished to judge according to our law; [7] but Lysias the chiliarch coming up with much force took him away out of our hands, commanding his accusers to come to you; [8] from whom you will be able yourself, having examined as to all these things of which we accuse him, to know. [9] And the Jews also joined in, saying these things to be so.

1 Μετὰ δὲ πέντε ἡμέρας κατέβη ο ἀρχιερεὺς Ἀνανίας μετὰ
after And five days came down the high priest, Ananias, with
τῶν πρεσβυτέρων καὶ ῥήτορος Τερτύλλου τινός, οἵτινες
the elders and an orator, Tertullus one, who
2 ἐνεφάνισαν τῷ ἡγεμόνι κατὰ τοῦ Παύλου. κληθέντος δὲ
informed the governor against — Paul. being called And
αὐτοῦ, ἤρξατο κατηγορεῖν ὁ Τέρτυλλος λέγων,
him, began to accuse Tertullas, saying,
3 Πολλῆς εἰρήνης τυγχάνοντες διὰ σοῦ, καὶ κατορθωμάτων
Much peace obtaining through you, and excellent measures
γινομένων τῷ ἔθνει τούτῳ διὰ τῆς σῆς προνοίας, πάντῃ τε
having come to nation this through your forethought, in everything both
καὶ πανταχοῦ ἀποδεχόμεθα, κράτιστε Φῆλιξ, μετὰ πάσης
and everywhere we welcome, most excellent Felix, with all
4 εὐχαριστίας. ἵνα δὲ μὴ ἐπὶ πλεῖόν σε ἐγκόπτω, παρακαλῶ
thankfulness. that But not more you I hinder, I beseech
5 ἀκοῦσαί σε ἡμῶν συντόμως τῇ σῇ ἐπιεικείᾳ. εὑρόντες γὰρ
to hear you us briefly — in your forbearance. finding For
τὸν ἄνδρα τοῦτον λοιμόν, καὶ κινοῦντα στάσιν πᾶσι τοῖς
— man this pestilent and moving insurrection among all the
Ἰουδαίοις τοῖς κατὰ τὴν οἰκουμένην, πρωτοστάτην τε τῆς
Jews throughout the habitable world, a ringleader and of the
6 τῶν Ναζωραίων αἱρέσεως· ὃς καὶ τὸ ἱερὸν ἐπείρασε βεβηλῶ-
— Nazarene sect, who also the Temple attempted to profane,
σαι· ὃν καὶ ἐκρατήσαμεν καὶ κατὰ τὸν ἡμέτερον νόμον ἠθελή-
whom also we seized, and according to our law wished
7 σαμεν κρίνειν. παρελθὼν δὲ Λυσίας ὁ χιλίαρχος μετὰ πολλῆς
to judge. coming up But Lysias the chiliarch with much
βίας ἐκ τῶν χειρῶν ἡμῶν ἀπήγαγε, κελεύσας τοὺς κατηγό-
force out of the hands of us took away, commanding the accusers
8 ρους αὐτοῦ ἔρχεσθαι ἐπὶ σέ· παρ' οὗ δυνήσῃ, αὐτὸς ἀνα-
of him to come to you; from whom you can yourself, having
κρίνας, περὶ πάντων τούτων ἐπιγνῶναι ὧν ἡμεῖς κατηγο-
examined about all these things, know fully of which we accuse
9 ροῦμεν αὐτοῦ. συνέθεντο δὲ καὶ οἱ Ἰουδαῖοι, φάσκοντες
him. joined in And also the Jews, alleging
ταῦτα οὕτως ἔχειν.
these things so to be.

[10] But the governor signaling to him to speak, Paul answered:

Understanding you as being *a* judge to this nation many years, I cheerfully defend myself *as to* the things concerning myself.

10 Ἀπεκρίθη δὲ ὁ Παῦλος, νεύσαντος αὐτῷ τοῦ ἡγεμόνος
answered And Paul, having signaled to him the governor
λέγειν,
to speak,
Ἐκ πολλῶν ἐτῶν ὄντα σε κριτὴν τῷ ἔθνει τούτῳ ἐπιστά-
Of many years being you a judge nation to this under-
μενος, εὐθυμότερον τὰ περὶ ἐμαυτοῦ ἀπολογοῦμαι, δυνα-
standing, cheerfully (as to) that about myself I defend myself, being

11 You being able to know that not more than twelve days are to me since I went worshiping in Jerusalem; 12 and neither did they find me reasoning with anyone in the Temple, or making a gathering of a crowd; neither in the synagogues, nor throughout the city; 13 nor are they able to prove that of which they now accuse me. 14 But I confess this to you, that according to the Way, which they say *is* a sect, so I worship the ancestral God, believing all things according to that having been written *in* the Law and the Prophets, 15 having a hope toward God, which these themselves admit, *of* a resurrection being about to be of *the* dead, both of just and unjust ones. 16 And in this I exercise myself to have always a blameless conscience toward God and men. 17 And after many years I arrived doing alms and offerings to my nation, 18 Among which they found me purified in the Temple, not with a crowd, nor with tumult, *but by* some Jews from Asia, 19 who ought to be present before you and to accuse, if they have anything against me. 20 Or these themselves say if they found anything unjust in me, I standing before the sanhedrin, 21 than concerning this one voice which I cried out standing among them, that I am being judged today before you concerning a resurrection of *the* dead.

22 And hearing these things, Felix put them off, knowing more accurately about the Way, saying, When Lysias the chiliarch comes down, I will examine the things as to you. 23 And having ordered the centurion to keep Paul, and to have ease, and not to forbid anyone of his own to minister or to come to him.

24 And after some days, Felix having arrived with his wife Drusilla, who was a Jewess, he sent for Paul.

11 μένου σου γνῶναι ὅτι οὐ πλείους εἰσί μοι ἡμέραι ἢ δεκαδύο,
able you to know that not more are to me days twelve,
12 ἀφ' ἧς ἀνέβην προσκυνήσων ἐν Ἱερουσαλήμ· καὶ οὔτε ἐν τῷ
from which I went worshiping in Jerusalem and neither in the
ἱερῷ εὗρόν με πρός τινα διαλεγόμενον ἢ ἐπισύστασιν
Temple they found me with anyone reasoning, or a gathering
ποιοῦντα ὄχλου, οὔτε ἐν ταῖς συναγωγαῖς, οὔτε κατα τὴν
making of a crowd, neither in the synagogues, nor throughout the
13 πόλιν. οὔτε παραστῆσαι δύνανται περὶ ὧν νῦν κατηγοροῦσί
city, nor to prove they are able about which now they accuse
14 μου. ὁμολογῶ δὲ τοῦτό σοι, ὅτι κατὰ τὴν ὁδὸν ἣν λέγουσιν
me. I confess But this to you, that according to the Way which they say
αἵρεσιν, οὕτω λατρεύω τῷ πατρῴῳ Θεῷ, πιστεύων πᾶσι
a sect (is), thus I worship the ancestral God, believing all
τοῖς κατὰ τὸν νόμον καὶ τοῖς προφήταις γεγραμμένοις·
the things as to the Law and the Prophets having been written;
15 ἐλπίδα ἔχων εἰς τὸν Θεόν, ἣν καὶ αὐτοὶ οὗτοι προσδέχονται,
hope having toward God, which also themselves these admit,
ἀνάστασιν μέλλειν ἔσεσθαι νεκρῶν, δικαίων τε καὶ ἀδίκων.
a resurrection being about to be of (the) dead, of just both and unjust.
16 ἐν τούτῳ δὲ αὐτὸς ἀσκῶ, ἀπρόσκοπον συνείδησιν ἔχειν πρὸς
by this And myself I exercise a blameless conscience to have toward
17 τὸν Θεὸν καὶ τοὺς ἀνθρώπους διὰ παντός. δι' ἐτῶν δὲ
— God and — men always. after years And
πλειόνων παρεγενόμην ἐλεημοσύνας ποιήσων εἰς τὸ ἔθνος
many I arrived alms doing to the nation
18 μου καὶ προσφοράς· ἐν οἷς εὗρόν με ἡγνισμένον ἐν τῷ ἱερῷ,
of me and offerings, among which they found me purified in the Temple,
οὐ μετὰ ὄχλου οὐδὲ μετὰ θορύβου, τινὲς ἀπὸ τῆς Ἀσίας
not with a crowd, nor with tumult; some from — Asia
19 Ἰουδαῖοι· οὓς ἔδει ἐπὶ σοῦ παρεῖναι καὶ κατηγορεῖν εἴ τι
Jews, whom it is right before you to be present and to accuse if a thing
20 ἔχοιεν πρός με. ἢ αὐτοὶ οὗτοι εἰπάτωσαν, εἴ τι εὗρον ἐν ἐμοὶ
they have against me. Or them these let say if anything they found in me
21 ἀδίκημα, στάντος μου ἐπὶ τοῦ συνεδρίου, ἢ περὶ μιᾶς ταύτης
unjust, standing me before the sanhedrin, than about one this
φωνῆς, ἧς ἔκραξα ἑστὼς ἐν αὐτοῖς, ὅτι Περὶ ἀναστάσεως
voice which I cried out standing among them, that concerning a resurrection
νεκρῶν ἐγὼ κρίνομαι σήμερον ὑφ' ὑμῶν.
of (the) dead I am being judged today before you.
22 Ἀκούσας δὲ ταῦτα ὁ Φῆλιξ ἀνεβάλετο αὐτούς, ἀκριβέ-
having heard And these things Felix put off them, more
στερον εἰδὼς τὰ περὶ τῆς ὁδοῦ, εἰπών, Ὅταν Λυσίας ὁ χιλί-
accurately knowing about the Way, saying, When Lysias the chili-
23 αρχος καταβῇ, διαγνώσομαι τὰ καθ' ὑμᾶς· διαταξάμενός τε
arch comes down I will examine the things as to you; having ordered and
τῷ ἑκατοντάρχῃ τηρεῖσθαι τὸν Παῦλον, ἔχειν τε ἄνεσιν, καὶ
the centurion to keep — Paul, to have and ease, and
μηδένα κωλύειν τῶν ἰδίων αὐτοῦ ὑπηρετεῖν ἢ προσέρχεσθαι
no one to forbid of the own him to minister or to come
αὐτῷ.
to him.
24 Μετὰ δὲ ἡμέρας τινάς, παραγενόμενος ὁ Φῆλιξ σὺν
after And days some, having arrived Felix with
Δρουσίλλῃ τῇ γυναικὶ αὐτοῦ οὔσῃ Ἰουδαίᾳ, μετεπέμψατο
Drusilla the wife of him, being a Jewess, he sent for

And *he* heard him concerning the faith in Christ. [25] And he having reasoned concerning righteousness and self-control, and the Judgment that is about to be, becoming afraid Felix answered, For the present, go; but taking time later, I will call for you; [26] and with it all also hoping that silver would be given to him by Paul, that he might free him. Therefore, *he* also more frequently sent for him *and* conversed with him. [27] But two years being completed, Felix welcomed a successor, Porcius Festus. And wishing to show a favor to the Jews, Felix left Paul bound.

CHAPTER 25

[1] Then entering the province, Festus went up to Jerusalem from Caesarea. [2] And the high priest and the chief of the Jews made a statement before him against Paul, and they begged him, [3] asking a favor against him, so as he might send for him to Jerusalem, making a plot to kill him on the way. [4] Then indeed Festus answered that Paul should be kept at Caesarea, he himself even being about to go shortly. [5] Then he said, those having power among you may go down with *me*. If there is a thing amiss in this man, let them accuse him.

[6] And remaining among them more than ten days, going down to Caesarea, on the next day sitting on the tribunal, he ordered Paul to be brought. [7] And he having arrived, the Jews coming down from Jerusalem stood around, also bringing many weighty charges against Paul, which they were not able to prove. [8] Defending himself, *Paul* said, Neither against the Law of the Jews, nor against the Temple, nor against Caesar have I sinned

τὸν Παῦλον, καὶ ἤκουσεν αὐτοῦ περὶ τῆς εἰς Χριστὸν πί-
Paul, and heard him concerning the in Christ
25 στεως. διαλεγομένου δὲ αὐτοῦ περὶ δικαιοσύνης καὶ ἐγκρατείας
faith. reasoning And him concerning righteousness and self-control
καὶ τοῦ κρίματος τοῦ μέλλοντος ἔσεσθαι, ἔμφοβος γενόμενος
and the judgment — being about to be, afraid becoming
ὁ Φῆλιξ ἀπεκρίθη, Τὸ νῦν ἔχον πορεύου· καιρὸν δὲ μεταλα-
Felix answered, For the present go, time but taking
26 βὼν μετακαλέσομαί σε· ἅμα δὲ καὶ ἐλπίζων ὅτι χρήματα
later I will send for you; withal but also hoping that silver
δοθήσεται αὐτῷ ὑπὸ τοῦ Παύλου, ὅπως λύσῃ αὐτόν· διὸ
will be given him by — Paul; that he might free him. So
καὶ πυκνότερον αὐτὸν μεταπεμπόμενος ὡμίλει αὐτῷ.
also more frequently him sending for, he conversed with him.
27 διετίας δὲ πληρωθείσης, ἔλαβε διάδοχον ὁ Φῆλιξ Πόρκιον
two years And being completed, received a successor Felix, Porcius
Φῆστον· θέλων τε χάριτας καταθέσθαι τοῖς Ἰουδαίοις ὁ Φῆλιξ
Festus; wishing and a favor to show to the Jews, Felix
κατέλιπε τὸν Παῦλον δεδεμένον.
left Paul bound.

CHAPTER 25

1 Φῆστος οὖν ἐπιβὰς τῇ ἐπαρχίᾳ, μετὰ τρεῖς ἡμέρας ἀνέβη
Festus, therefore, entering the province after three days went up
2 εἰς Ἱεροσόλυμα ἀπὸ Καισαρείας. ἐνεφάνισαν δὲ αὐτῷ ὁ
to Jerusalem from Caesarea. made a statement And to him the
ἀρχιερεὺς καὶ οἱ πρῶτοι τῶν Ἰουδαίων κατὰ τοῦ Παύλου,
chief priest and the chief of the Jews against — Paul.
3 καὶ παρεκάλουν αὐτόν, αἰτούμενοι χάριν κατ' αὐτοῦ, ὅπως
And they besought him, asking a favor against him, so as
μεταπέμψηται αὐτὸν εἰς Ἱερουσαλήμ, ἐνέδραν ποιοῦντες
he might send for him to Jerusalem, a plot making
4 ἀνελεῖν αὐτὸν κατὰ τὴν ὁδόν. ὁ μὲν οὖν Φῆστος ἀπεκρίθη,
to kill him by the way. Therefore Festus answered
τηρεῖσθαι τὸν Παῦλον ἐν Καισαρείᾳ, ἑαυτὸν δὲ μέλλειν ἐν
to be kept — Paul in Caesarea, himself and being about to
5 τάχει ἐκπορεύεσθαι. οἱ οὖν δυνατοὶ ἐν ὑμῖν, φησί, συγκατα-
quickly go forth. the Then able ones among you, he says, going down
βάντες, εἴ τι ἐστὶν ἄτοπον ἐν τῷ ἀνδρὶ τούτῳ, κατηγορεί-
with (me), if a thing is amiss in — man this, let them
τωσαν αὐτοῦ.
accuse him.

6 Διατρίψας δὲ ἐν αὐτοῖς ἡμέρας πλείους ἢ δέκα, καταβὰς
having stayed And among them days more than ten, going down
εἰς Καισάρειαν, τῇ ἐπαύριον καθίσας ἐπὶ τοῦ βήματος ἐκέ-
to Caesarea, on the morrow sitting on the tribunal he
7 λευσε τὸν Παῦλον ἀχθῆναι. παραγενομένου δὲ αὐτοῦ,
ordered — Paul to be brought. arriving And him,
περιέστησαν οἱ ἀπὸ Ἱεροσολύμων καταβεβηκότες Ἰουδαῖοι,
stood around the from Jerusalem having come down Jews,
πολλὰ καὶ βαρέα αἰτιάματα φέροντες κατὰ τοῦ Παύλου, ἃ
many and weighty charges bringing against — Paul, which
8 οὐκ ἴσχυον ἀποδεῖξαι, ἀπολογουμένου αὐτοῦ ὅτι Οὔτε εἰς
not they were able to prove. Defending himself, he said, — Neither against
τὸν νόμον τῶν Ἰουδαίων, οὔτε εἰς τὸ ἱερόν, οὔτε εἰς Καίσαρά
the law of the Jews, nor against the Temple, nor against Caesar

in anything. [9]But desiring to show a favor to the Jews, answering Paul, Festus said, Do you desire to go up to Jerusalem to be judged before me there about these things? [10]But Paul said, I am standing before the tribunal of Caesar where I ought to be judged. I did nothing to the Jews, as also you very well know. [11]For if I indeed do wrong and have done anything worthy of death, I do not refuse to die. But if there is nothing of which they accuse me, no one can give me up to them. I appeal to Caesar. [12]Then conferring with the sanhedrin, Festus answered, You have appealed to Caesar, you shall go before Caesar.

[13]And certain days having passed, king Agrippa and Bernice arrived at Caesarea, greeting Festus. [14]And when they stayed there more days, Festus set out to the king the things as to Paul, saying, A certain man has been left by Felix, [15]about whom, on my being in Jerusalem, the chief priests and the elders of the Jews made a statement, asking judgment against him; [16]to whom I answered, It is not a custom with Romans to give up any man to destruction before the *one* being accused may have the accusers face to face, and may receive place of defense concerning the accusation. [17]Then they coming together here, making no delay, sitting on the tribunal on the next *day*, I commanded the man to be brought; [18]about whom, standing up, the accusers brought no charge of which I suspected, [19]but they had certain questions about *their* own demon-worship, and about a certain Jesus dying, whom Paul claimed to live.

[20]And being puzzled as to this inquiry, I said, Did he

9 τι ἥμαρτον. ὁ Φῆστος δὲ τοῖς Ἰουδαίοις θέλων χάριν
anything I sinned. Festus But the Jews wishing a favor
καταθέσθαι, ἀποκριθεὶς τῷ Παύλῳ εἶπε, Θέλεις εἰς Ἱεροσό-
to show, answering — Paul said, Desire you to Jerusalem
10 λυμα ἀναβάς, ἐκεῖ περὶ τούτων κρίνεσθαι ἐπ' ἐμοῦ; εἶπε δὲ
to go up, there about these things to be judged before me? said And
ὁ Παῦλος, Ἐπὶ τοῦ βήματος Καίσαρος ἑστώς εἰμι, οὗ με δεῖ
Paul, Before the tribunal of Caesar standing I am; where me must
κρίνεσθαι· Ἰουδαίους οὐδὲν ἠδίκησα, ὡς καὶ σὺ κάλλιον
be judged. Jews nothing I have wronged, as indeed you very well
11 ἐπιγινώσκεις. εἰ μὲν γὰρ ἀδικῶ καὶ ἄξιον θανάτου πέπραχά
know. if indeed For I do wrong and worthy of death I have done
τι, οὐ παραιτοῦμαι τὸ ἀποθανεῖν· εἰ δὲ οὐδέν ἐστιν ὧν οὗτοι
a thing, not I refuse — to die; if but not one is of which these
κατηγοροῦσί μου, οὐδείς με δύναται αὐτοῖς χαρίσασθαι.
accuse me, no one me is able to them to grant.
12 Καίσαρα ἐπικαλοῦμαι. τότε ὁ Φῆστος συλλαλήσας μετὰ τοῦ
Caesar I appeal to. Then Festus having conferred with the
συμβουλίου ἀπεκρίθη, Καίσαρα ἐπικέκλησαι; ἐπὶ Καίσαρα
sanhedrin answered, Caesar you have appealed to, before Caesar
πορεύσῃ.
you shall go.
13 Ἡμερῶν δὲ διαγενομένων τινῶν, Ἀγρίππας ὁ βασιλεὺς
days And passing some, Agrippa the king
καὶ Βερνίκη κατήντησαν εἰς Καισάρειαν, ἀσπασόμενοι τὸν
and Bernice arrived at Caesarea, greeting
14 Φῆστον. ὡς δὲ πλείους ἡμέρας διέτριβον ἐκεῖ, ὁ Φῆστος τῷ
Festus. as And more days they stayed there, Festus to the
βασιλεῖ ἀνέθετο τὰ κατὰ τὸν Παῦλον, λέγων, Ἀνήρ τίς ἐστι
king set out the things as to — Paul, saying, a man certain is
15 καταλελειμμένος ὑπὸ Φήλικος δέσμιος, περὶ οὗ, γενομένου
having been left by Felix a prisoner, about whom, being
μου εἰς Ἱεροσόλυμα, ἐνεφάνισαν οἱ ἀρχιερεῖς καὶ οἱ πρεσ-
me in Jerusalem, made a statement the chief priests and the
16 βύτεροι τῶν Ἰουδαίων, αἰτούμενοι κατ' αὐτοῦ δίκην. πρὸς
elders of the Jews, asking against him sentence; to
οὓς ἀπεκρίθην, ὅτι οὐκ ἔστιν ἔθος Ῥωμαίοις χαρίζεσθαί τινα
whom I answered that not it is a custom with Romans to grant any
ἄνθρωπον εἰς ἀπώλειαν, πρὶν ἢ ὁ κατηγορούμενος κατὰ
man to destruction before the (one) being accused face
πρόσωπον ἔχοι τοὺς κατηγόρους, τόπον τε ἀπολογίας
to face should have the accusers, place and of defense
17 λάβοι περὶ τοῦ ἐγκλήματος. συνελθόντων οὖν αὐτῶν ἐνθάδε,
receive concerning the charge. Coming together, then, they to here,
ἀναβολὴν μηδεμίαν ποιησάμενος, τῇ ἑξῆς καθίσας ἐπὶ τοῦ
delay no making, on the next sitting on the
18 βήματος, ἐκέλευσα ἀχθῆναι τὸν ἄνδρα· περὶ οὗ σταθέντες οἱ
tribunal, I commanded to be brought the man; about whom standing the
κατήγοροι οὐδεμίαν αἰτίαν ἐπέφερον ὧν ὑπενόουν ἐγώ,
accusers no charge brought of which suspected I,
19 ζητήματα δέ τινα περὶ τῆς ἰδίας δεισιδαιμονίας εἶχον πρὸς
questions but certain about the own demon-worship they had with
αὐτόν, καὶ περί τινος Ἰησοῦ τεθνηκότος, ὃν ἔφασκεν ὁ Παῦλος
him, and about a certain Jesus having died, whom claimed Paul
20 ζῆν. ἀπορούμενος δὲ ἐγὼ εἰς τὴν περὶ τούτου ζήτησιν,
to live. being puzzled And I as to the concerning this inquiry.

desire to go to Jerusalem, and to be judged there concerning these things? [21] But Paul having appealed for himself to be kept to the examination of Augustus, I commanded him to be held until I might send him to Caesar. [22] And Agrippa said to Festus, I also was myself minded to hear the man. And he said, Tomorrow you shall hear him.

[23] Then on the next day, Agrippa and Bernice coming with much pomp and entering into the auditorium, with both the chiliarchs and the chief men, being of the city, also Festus commanding, Paul was led out. [24] And Festus said, King Agrippa, and all those men present with us, you see this one about whom all the multitude of the Jews pleaded with me both here and in Jerusalem, crying out that he ought to live no longer. [25] But I having perceived nothing he had done worthy of death, also this one himself having appealed to Augustus, I decided to send him; [26] concerning whom I have nothing certain to write to *my* lord. Therefore, I brought him before you, and most of all before you, king Agrippa, so as the examination taking place, I may have somewhat to write to *my* lord. [27] for it seems unreasonable to me to send a prisoner, and not to signify the charges against him.

CHAPTER 26

[1] And Agrippa said to Paul, It is allowed for you yourself to speak. Then Paul made a defense, stretching out the hand:

[2] Concerning all of which I am accused by Jews, King Agrippa, I count myself happy being about to make defense before you today, [3] you being most of all expert knowing of all the customs

ἔλεγον, εἰ βούλοιτο πορεύεσθαι εἰς Ἱερουσαλήμ, κἀκεῖ κρίνε-
said if he desired to go to Jerusalem and there to be
21 σθαι περὶ τούτων. τοῦ δὲ Παύλου ἐπικαλεσαμένου τηρηθῆναι
judged about these things. But Paul having appealed to be kept
αὐτὸν εἰς τὴν τοῦ Σεβαστοῦ διάγνωσιν, ἐκέλευσα τηρεῖσθαι
him to the — of Augustus examination, I commanded to be kept
22 αὐτόν, ἕως οὗ πέμψω αὐτὸν πρὸς Καίσαρα. Ἀγρίππας δὲ
him until I may send him to Caesar. Agrippa And
πρὸς τὸν Φῆστον ἔφη, Ἐβουλόμην καὶ αὐτὸς τοῦ ἀνθρώπου
to — Festus said, I was minded also myself the man
ἀκοῦσαι. ὁ δέ, Αὔριον, φησίν, ἀκούσῃ αὐτοῦ.
to hear. he And, Tomorrow, said, you will hear him.
23 Τῇ οὖν ἐπαύριον, ἐλθόντος τοῦ Ἀγρίππα καὶ τῆς Βερνίκης
on the Then morrow coming — Agrippa and — Bernice
μετὰ πολλῆς φαντασίας, καὶ εἰσελθόντων εἰς τὸ ἀκροατήριον,
with much pomp, and entering into the auditorium,
σύν τε τοῖς χιλιάρχοις καὶ ἀνδράσι τοῖς κατ᾽ ἐξοχὴν οὖσι τῆς
with both the chiliarchs and men the chief being of the
24 πόλεως, καὶ κελεύσαντος τοῦ Φήστου, ἤχθη ὁ Παῦλος. καί
city, and having commanded Festus, was brought Paul. And
φησιν ὁ Φῆστος, Ἀγρίππα βασιλεῦ, καὶ πάντες οἱ συμπαρόν-
says Festus, Agrippa King, and all those present with
τες ἡμῖν ἄνδρες, θεωρεῖτε τοῦτον περὶ οὗ πᾶν τὸ πλῆθος τῶν
us, Men, you behold this one about whom all the multitude of the
Ἰουδαίων ἐνέτυχόν μοι ἔν τε Ἱεροσολύμοις καὶ ἐνθάδε, ἐπι-
Jews petitioned me in both Jerusalem and here,
25 βοῶντες μὴ δεῖν ζῆν αὐτὸν μηκέτι. ἐγὼ δὲ καταλαβόμενος
crying not ought to live him no longer. I And having perceived
μηδὲν ἄξιον θανάτου αὐτὸν πεπραχέναι, καὶ αὐτοῦ δὲ τούτου
nothing worthy of death he had done, also himself but this one
26 ἐπικαλεσαμένου τὸν Σεβαστόν, ἔκρινα πέμπειν αὐτόν. περὶ
appealing to — Augustus, I decided to send him. Concerning
οὗ ἀσφαλές τι γράψαι τῷ κυρίῳ οὐκ ἔχω. διὸ προήγαγον
whom certain anything to write to the lord not I have. So I brought forth
αὐτὸν ἐφ᾽ ὑμῶν, καὶ μάλιστα ἐπὶ σοῦ, βασιλεῦ Ἀγρίππα,
him before you, and most before you, king Agrippa,
27 ὅπως τῆς ἀνακρίσεως γενομένης σχῶ τι γράψαι. ἄλογον
so as the examination being, I may have what to write. unreasonable
γάρ μοι δοκεῖ, πέμποντα δέσμιον, μὴ καὶ τὰς κατ᾽ αὐτοῦ
For to me it seems sending a prisoner, not also the against him
αἰτίας σημᾶναι.
charges to signify.

CHAPTER 26

1 Ἀγρίππας δὲ πρὸς τὸν Παῦλον ἔφη, Ἐπιτρέπεταί σοι
Agrippa And to — Paul said, It is allowed for you
ὑπὲρ σεαυτοῦ λέγειν. τότε ὁ Παῦλος ἀπελογεῖτο, ἐκτείνας
for yourself to speak. Then Paul made a defense, stretching
τὴν χεῖρα,
the hand,
2 Περὶ πάντων ὧν ἐγκαλοῦμαι ὑπὸ Ἰουδαίων, βασιλεῦ
Concerning all things of which I am accused by Jews, king
Ἀγρίππα, ἥγημαι ἐμαυτὸν μακάριον μέλλων ἀπολογεῖσθαι
Agrippa, I count myself happy being about to make defense
3 ἐπὶ σοῦ σήμερον· μάλιστα γνώστην ὄντα σὲ εἰδὼς πάντων
before you today, most of all an expert being you knowing of all

and questions also among the Jews. Therefore, I beg you to patiently hear me. [4]Truly, then, all the Jews know my way of life from youth, which from *the* beginning was among my nation in Jerusalem; [5]who before knew me from the first, if they wish to testify, that according to the most exact sect of our religion, I lived a Pharisee. [6]And now for *the* hope of the promise made by God to the fathers, I stand being judged; [7]to which our twelve tribes hope to arrive, worshiping in earnestness night and day; concerning which hope I am accused by the Jews, king Agrippa. [8]Why is it judged unbelievable by you if God raises *the* dead? [9]Indeed, I then thought within myself that I ought to do many things contrary to the name of Jesus the Nazarene.

[10]Which I also did in Jerusalem; and I shut up many of the saints in prisons, having received authority from the chief priests; and they being put to death, I cast a vote. [11]And often punishing them through all the synagogues, I compelled them to blaspheme. And *being* exceedingly furious against them, I even persecuted even unto the outside cities. [12]In which also traveling to Damascus with authority and decision power from the chief priests, [13]at midday along the highway, *O* king, I and those with me saw a light shining around me, above the brightness of the sun. [14]And all of us falling to the ground, I heard a voice speaking to me, and saying in the Hebrew dialect, Saul, Saul why do you persecute Me? *It is* hard for you to kick against the prods. [15]And I said, Who are you, Sir? And He said, I am Jesus whom you persecute; [16]but rise up and stand on your feet, for *it*

τῶν κατὰ Ἰουδαίους ἐθῶν τε καὶ ζητημάτων· διὸ δέομαί σου,
the among Jews customs both and questions; therefore I beg you,
4 μακροθύμως ἀκοῦσαί μου. τὴν μὲν οὖν βίωσίν μου τὴν ἐκ
patiently to hear me. the Indeed then way of life of me from
νεότητος, τὴν ἀπ' ἀρχῆς γενομένην ἐν τῷ ἔθνει μου ἐν
youth — from the beginning having been in the nation of me in
5 Ἱεροσολύμοις, ἴσασι πάντες οἱ Ἰουδαῖοι, προγινώσκοντές
Jerusalem, know all the Jews, before knowing
με ἄνωθεν, ἐὰν θέλωσι μαρτυρεῖν, ὅτι κατὰ τὴν ἀκριβεστά-
me from the first, if they will to testify, that according to the most exact
6 την αἵρεσιν τῆς ἡμετέρας θρησκείας ἔζησα Φαρισαῖος. καὶ
sect — of our religion I lived a Pharisee. And
νῦν ἐπ' ἐλπίδι τῆς πρὸς τοὺς πατέρας ἐπαγγελιας γενομένης
now on hope of the to the fathers promise having been
7 ὑπὸ τοῦ Θεοῦ ἕστηκα κρινόμενος, εἰς ἣν τὸ δωδεκάφυλον
by — God, I stand being judged, to which the twelve tribes
ἡμῶν ἐν ἐκτενείᾳ νύκτα καὶ ἡμέραν λατρεῦον ἐλπίζει καταν-
of us in earnestness night and day worshiping hopes to
τῆσαι· περὶ ἧς ἐλπίδος ἐγκαλοῦμαι, βασιλεῦ Ἀγρίππα, ὑπὸ
arrive; concerning which hope I am accused, king Agrippa, by
8 τῶν Ἰουδαίων. τί ἄπιστον κρίνεται παρ' ὑμῖν, εἰ ὁ Θεὸς
the Jews. Why unbelievable is it judged by you if God
9 νεκροὺς ἐγείρει ; ἐγὼ μὲν οὖν ἔδοξα ἐμαυτῷ πρὸς τὸ ὄνομα
(the) dead raises? I indeed then thought to myself to the name
10 Ἰησοῦ τοῦ Ναζωραίου δεῖν πολλὰ ἐναντία πρᾶξαι· ὃ καὶ
of Jesus the Nazarene ought many things contrary to do; which also
ἐποίησα ἐν Ἱεροσολύμοις, καὶ πολλοὺς τῶν ἁγίων ἐγὼ
I did in Jerusalem, and many of the saints I
φυλακαῖς κατέκλεισα, τὴν παρὰ τῶν ἀρχιερέων ἐξουσίαν
in prisons shut up, the from the chief priests authority
11 λαβών, ἀναιρουμένων τε αὐτῶν κατήνεγκα ψῆφον. καὶ κατὰ
receiving, being killed and them, I cast a vote. And through
πάσας τὰς συναγωγὰς πολλάκις τιμωρῶν αὐτούς, ἠνάγ-
all the synagogues often punishing them, I
καζον βλασφημεῖν· περισσῶς τε ἐμμαινόμενος αὐτοῖς,
compelled to blaspheme, exceedingly and furious against them,
12 ἐδίωκον ἕως καὶ εἰς τὰς ἔξω πόλεις. ἐν οἷς καὶ πορευόμενος
I persecuted until even to the outside cities. In which also traveling
εἰς τὴν Δαμασκὸν μετ' ἐξουσίας καὶ ἐπιτροπῆς τῆς παρὰ τῶν
to — Damascus with authority and decision power — from the
13 ἀρχιερέων, ἡμέρας μέσης, κατὰ τὴν ὁδὸν εἶδον, βασιλεῦ,
chief priests, at day mid- along the way I saw, king,
οὐρανόθεν ὑπὲρ τὴν λαμπρότητα τοῦ ἡλίου, περιλάμψαν
from Heaven above the brightness of the sun shining around
14 με φῶς καὶ τοὺς σὺν ἐμοὶ πορευομένους. πάντων δὲ κατα-
me a light, also those with me traveling. all And having
πεσόντων ἡμῶν εἰς τὴν γῆν, ἤκουσα φωνὴν λαλοῦσαν πρός
fallen down us to the earth, I heard a voice speaking to
με καὶ λέγουσαν τῇ Ἑβραΐδι διαλέκτῳ, Σαούλ, Σαούλ, τί
me, and saying in the Hebrew dialect, Saul Saul, why
15 με διώκεις ; σκληρόν σοι πρὸς κέντρα λακτίζειν. ἐγὼ δὲ
Me persecute you? (It is) hard for you to kick against the prods. I And
εἶπον, Τίς εἶ, Κύριε ; ὁ δὲ εἶπεν, Ἐγώ εἰμι Ἰησοῦς ὃν σὺ
said, Who are you, Sir? He And said, I am Jesus whom you
16 διώκεις. ἀλλὰ ἀνάστηθι, καὶ στῆθι ἐπὶ τοὺς πόδας σου· εἰς
persecute. But rise up, and stand on the feet of you. for

is for this reason I appear to you, to appoint you a servant and a witness both of what you saw, and in what I shall appear to you, [17]having delivered you from the people and the nations, to whom I now send you, [18]to open their eyes, so that *they* may turn from darkness to light, and *from* the authority of Satan to God; in order that they may receive forgiveness of sins, and an inheritance among those being sanctified by faith in Me. [19]Upon this, king Agrippa, I was not disobedient to the heavenly vision; [20]but to those first in Damascus, and Jerusalem, and to all the country of Judea, and to the nations, making known *the command* to repent and to turn to God, doing works worthy of repentance. [21]Because of these things, having seized *me* in the Temple, the Jews tried to kill *me*. [22]Then obtaining help from God, I stand until this day, witnessing both to small and to great, saying nothing else than what the prophets and Moses also said was going to happen: [23]*that* Christ *was* to suffer, *that* by a resurrection of *the* dead He was first going to proclaim light to the people and to the nations.

[24]And he defending himself *with* these things, Festus said with a *loud* voice, Paul, You rave! Your many letters turned *you* to madness. [25]But he said, Not to madness, most excellent Festus, but I speak words of truth and sanity. [26]For the king understands about these things, to whom I speak. For I am persuaded not any of these things are hidden *from* him, nothing. For *the* doing of this is not in a corner. [27]Do you believe the prophets, king Agrippa? I know that you believe. [28]And Agrippa said to Paul, Do you persuade me to become a Christian in *but* a little?

τοῦτο γὰρ ὤφθην σοι, προχειρίσασθαί σε ὑπηρέτην καὶ
this For I appeared to you, to appoint you a servant and
17 μάρτυρα ὧν τε εἶδες ὧν τε ὀφθήσομαί σοι, ἐξαιρούμενός σε
a witness of what both you saw, of what and I will appear to you, delivering you
ἐκ τοῦ λαοῦ καὶ τῶν ἐθνῶν, εἰς οὓς νῦν σε ἀποστέλλω,
from the people and the nations, to whom now you I send,
18 ἀνοῖξαι ὀφθαλμοὺς αὐτῶν, καὶ ἐπιστρέψαι ἀπὸ σκότους
to open the eyes of them, and to turn from darkness
εἰς φῶς καὶ τῆς ἐξουσίας τοῦ Σατανᾶ ἐπὶ τὸν Θεόν, τοῦ
to light, and the authority — of Satan to — God, —
λαβεῖν αὐτοὺς ἄφεσιν ἁμαρτιῶν, καὶ κλῆρον ἐν τοῖς ἡγια-
to receive them forgiveness of sins, and a lot among those being
19 σμένοις πίστει τῇ εἰς ἐμέ. ὅθεν, βασιλεῦ Ἀγρίππα, οὐκ
sanctified by faith — in Me. Upon this, king Agrippa, not
20 ἐγενόμην ἀπειθὴς τῇ οὐρανίῳ ὀπτασίᾳ· ἀλλὰ τοῖς ἐν
I was disobedient to the heavenly vision, but to those in
Δαμασκῷ πρῶτον καὶ Ἱεροσολύμοις, εἰς πᾶσάν τε τὴν
Damascus firstly, and (in) Jerusalem, to all and the
χώραν τῆς Ἰουδαίας, καὶ τοῖς ἔθνεσιν, ἀπήγγελλον μετανοεῖν,
country — of Judea, and to the nations. I announced to repent
καὶ ἐπιστρέφειν ἐπὶ τὸν Θεόν, ἄξια τῆς μετανοίας ἔργα
and to turn to — God, worthy of the repentance works
21 πράσσοντας. ἕνεκα τούτων με οἱ Ἰουδαῖοι συλλαβόμενοι ἐν
doing. Because of these things me the Jews having seized in
22 τῷ ἱερῷ ἐπειρῶντο διαχειρίσασθαι. ἐπικουρίας οὖν τυχὼν
the Temple tried to kill (me). Help, then, obtaining
τῆς παρὰ τοῦ Θεοῦ, ἄχρι τῆς ἡμέρας ταύτης ἕστηκα
— from — God until — day this, I stand
μαρτυρούμενος μικρῷ τε καὶ μεγάλῳ, οὐδὲν ἐκτὸς λέγων ὧν
witnessing to small and also to great, nothing else than saying what
23 τε οἱ προφῆται ἐλάλησαν μελλόντων γίνεσθαι καὶ Μωσῆς, εἰ
both the prophets said being about to happen, and Moses, if
παθητὸς ὁ Χριστός, εἰ πρῶτος ἐξ ἀναστάσεως νεκρῶν φῶς
to suffer the Christ, if first by a resurrection of (the) dead, a light
μέλλει καταγγέλλειν τῷ λαῷ καὶ τοῖς ἔθνεσι.
He is going to announce to the people and to the nations.
24 Ταῦτα δὲ αὐτοῦ ἀπολογουμένου, ὁ Φῆστος μεγάλῃ τῇ
these things And him defending himself, Festus great with the
φωνῇ ἔφη, Μαίνῃ Παῦλε· τὰ πολλά σε γράμματα εἰς μανίαν
voice says, You rave, Paul; the many of you letters to madness
25 περιτρέπει. ὁ δέ, Οὐ μαίνομαι, φησί, κράτιστε Φῆστε, ἀλλ'
turn (you). But, Not to madness, he says, most excellent Festus, but
ἀληθείας καὶ σωφροσύνης ῥήματα ἀποφθέγγομαι. ἐπίσταται
of truth and sanity words I speak. understands
26 γὰρ περὶ τούτων ὁ βασιλεύς, πρὸς ὃν καὶ παρρησιαζόμενος
For about these things the king, to whom even being bold of speech
λαλῶ· λανθάνειν γὰρ αὐτόν τι τούτων οὐ πείθομαι οὐδέν·
I speak, to be hidden for (from) him any of these not, I am persuaded nothing.
27 οὐ γάρ ἐστιν ἐν γωνίᾳ πεπραγμένον τοῦτο. πιστεύεις,
not For is in a corner (the) doing of this. Do you believe,
28 βασιλεῦ Ἀγρίππα, τοῖς προφήταις ; οἶδα ὅτι πιστεύεις. ὁ δὲ
king Agrippa, the prophets? I know that you believe. And
Ἀγρίππας πρὸς τὸν Παῦλον ἔφη, Ἐν ὀλίγῳ με πείθεις
Agrippa to — Paul said, In a little me you persuade
Χριστιανὸν γενέσθαι. ὁ δὲ Παῦλος εἶπεν, Εὐξαίμην ἂν τῷ
a Christian to become? And Paul said, I would pray

29 And Paul said, I would pray to God, both in a little and in much, not only you, but also these hearing me today to become as I also am, except for these bonds. 30 And saying these things, the king and the governor and Bernice rose up, and those who sat with them. 31 And withdrawing, they spoke to one another saying, This man does nothing worthy of death or of bonds. 32 And Agrippa said to Festus, This man was able to have been let go, if he had not appealed to Caesar.

29 Θεῷ, καὶ ἐν ὀλίγῳ καὶ ἐν πολλῷ οὐ μόνον σε, ἀλλὰ καὶ
God, both in a little and in much, not only you, but also
πάντας τοὺς ἀκούοντάς μου σήμερον, γενέσθαι τοιούτους
all those hearing me today, to become such
ὁποῖος κἀγώ εἰμι, παρεκτὸς τῶν δεσμῶν τούτων.
as also I am, except — bonds these.
30 Καὶ ταῦτα εἰπόντος αὐτοῦ, ἀνέστη ὁ βασιλεὺς καὶ ὁ
And these things having said he, rose up the king and the
ἡγεμών, ἥ τε Βερνίκη, καὶ οἱ συγκαθήμενοι αὐτοῖς· καὶ
governor, and Bernice, and those sitting with them; and
31 ἀναχωρήσαντες ἐλάλουν πρὸς ἀλλήλους, λέγοντες ὅτι
having left spoke to one another, saying, —
Οὐδὲν θανάτου ἄξιον ἢ δεσμῶν πράσσει ὁ ἄνθρωπος οὗτος.
Nothing of death worthy or bonds does man this.
32 Ἀγρίππας δὲ τῷ Φήστῳ ἔφη, Ἀπολελύσθαι ἐδύνατο ὁ
Agrippa And to Festus said, to have been released was able
ἄνθρωπος οὗτος, εἰ μὴ ἐπεκέκλητο Καίσαρα.
man this, if not he had appealed to Caesar.

CHAPTER 27

1 And when it was decided that we should sail to Italy, they delivered up both Paul and certain other prisoners to a centurion named Julius, of a cohort of Augustus. 2 And boarding a ship of Adramyttium which was about to sail alongside Asian places, we set sail; Aristarchus a Macedonian of Thessalonica being with us. 3 And on the next *day* we landed at Sidon. And treating Paul kindly, Julius allowed *him* to go to *his* friends to receive care. 4 And setting sail from there, we sailed close to Cyprus, because of the winds being contrary.

5 And sailing over the sea against Cilicia and Pamphylia, we came to Myra of Lycia.

6 And the centurion finding there an Alexandrian ship sailing to Italy, he put us on it.

7 And in many days, sailing slowly and with difficulty, having come against Cnidus, the wind not allowing us, we sailed close to Crete against Salmone. 8 And coasting along it with difficulty, we came to a certain place named Fair Havens, near to which was a city, Lasea.

1 Ὡς δὲ ἐκρίθη τοῦ ἀποπλεῖν ἡμᾶς εἰς τὴν Ἰταλίαν, παρεδί-
when And it was decided to sail us to — Italy, they de-
δουν τόν τε Παῦλον καί τινας ἑτέρους δεσμώτας ἑκατοντ-
livered — both Paul and some other prisoners to a cen-
2 άρχῃ, ὀνόματι Ἰουλίῳ, σπείρης Σεβαστῆς. ἐπιβάντες δὲ
turion, by name Julius, of a cohort Augustan. embarking And
πλοίῳ Ἀδραμυττηνῷ, μέλλοντες πλεῖν τοὺς κατὰ τὴν Ἀσίαν
a ship of Adramyttium, being about to sail to the alongside Asia
τόπους, ἀνήχθημεν, ὄντος σὺν ἡμῖν Ἀριστάρχου Μακεδόνος
places, we set sail, being with us Aristarchus, a Macedonian
3 Θεσσαλονικέως. τῇ τε ἑτέρᾳ κατήχθημεν εἰς Σιδῶνα· φιλαν-
of Thessalonica. on the And next we were landed at Sidon, kindly
θρώπως τε ὁ Ἰούλιος τῷ Παύλῳ χρησάμενος ἐπέτρεψε πρὸς
And Julius Paul treating allowed to
4 τοὺς φίλους πορευθέντα ἐπιμελείας τυχεῖν. κἀκεῖθεν ἀναχθέν-
the friends going care to receive. And from there putting
τες ὑπεπλεύσαμεν τὴν Κύπρον, διὰ τὸ τοὺς ἀνέμους εἶναι
to sea, we sailed close to Cyprus, because of the winds being
5 ἐναντίους. τό τε πέλαγος τὸ κατὰ τὴν Κιλικίαν καὶ Παμφυ-
contrary the And sea — against — Cilicia and Pam-
6 λίαν διαπλεύσαντες, κατήλθομεν εἰς Μύρα τῆς Λυκίας. κἀκεῖ
phylia sailing over we came down to Myra — of Lycia. And there
εὑρὼν ὁ ἑκατόνταρχος πλοῖον Ἀλεξανδρῖνον πλέον εἰς τὴν
having found the centurion ship an Alexandrian sailing to —
7 Ἰταλίαν, ἐνεβίβασεν ἡμᾶς εἰς αὐτό. ἐν ἱκαναῖς δὲ ἡμέραις
Italy, he placed us in it. in many And days
βραδυπλοοῦντες, καὶ μόλις γενόμενοι κατὰ τὴν Κνίδον, μὴ
sailing slowly, and hardly coming against — Cnidus, not
προσεῶντος ἡμᾶς τοῦ ἀνέμου, ὑπεπλεύσαμεν τὴν Κρήτην
allowing us the wind, we sailed close to — Crete
8 κατὰ Σαλμώνην· μόλις τε παραλεγόμενοι αὐτὴν ἤλθομεν
against Salmone, hardly and sailing along it we came
εἰς τόπον τινὰ καλούμενον Καλοὺς Λιμένας, ᾧ ἐγγὺς ἦν
to a place certain being called Fair Haven, to which near was
πόλις Λασαία.
a city, Lasea

9 And much time having passed, and the voyage already being dangerous, because the Fast already had gone by, Paul warned them, 10 saying, Men, I see that the voyage is about to be with injury, and not only much loss of the cargo and of the ship, but also of our souls.
11 But the centurion was rather persuaded by the helmsman and the shipmaster, than by the things spoken by Paul. 12 And the port not being fit for wintering, the most gave counsel to set sail from there, if somehow they may be able to pass the winter, arriving at Phoenice, a port of Crete looking toward *the* southwest and northwest.
13 And a south wind blowing gently, thinking to have gained the purpose, lifting *anchor* they sailed along close by Crete. 14 And not much after, a stormy wind called Euroclydon beat down *on* it. 15 And the ship being seized, and not being able to beat against the wind, giving way we were borne along.
16 But running under an islet being called Clauda, we were hardly able to get mastery of the boat; 17 which taking, they used helps, undergirding the ship. And fearing lest they fall into Syrtis, lowering the tackle, so they were borne along.
18 But we being exceedingly storm-tossed, they made a casting on the next *day*.
19 And on the third *day* they threw out the ship's tackle with their hands. 20 And neither sun nor stars appearing for many days, and no small tempest pressing hard, now all hope of our being saved was taken away. 21 And there being much fasting, then standing up in their midst, Paul said, Truly, O men, being obedient to me *you* ought not to have set sail from Crete, and to have come by this injury and loss. 22 And

9 Ἱκανοῦ δὲ χρόνου διαγενομένου, καὶ ὄντος ἤδη ἐπισφα-
much And time having passed, and being now dangerous
λοῦς τοῦ πλοός, διὰ τὸ καὶ τὴν νηστείαν ἤδη παρεληλυ-
the voyage, because also the Fast now to have gone
10 θέναι, παρῄνει ὁ Παῦλος λέγων αὐτοῖς, Ἄνδρες, θεωρῶ ὅτι
by, advised Paul saying to them, Men, I see that
μετὰ ὕβρεως καὶ πολλῆς ζημίας, οὐ μόνον τοῦ φόρτου καὶ
with injury and much loss, not only of the cargo and
τοῦ πλοίου ἀλλὰ καὶ τῶν ψυχῶν ἡμῶν, μέλλειν ἔσεσθαι τὸν
of the ship, but also the souls of us, to be about to be the
11 πλοῦν. ὁ δὲ ἑκατόνταρχος τῷ κυβερνήτῃ καὶ τῷ ναυκλήρῳ
voyage. the But centurion by the steersman and the shipmaster
ἐπείθετο μᾶλλον ἢ τοῖς ὑπὸ τοῦ Παύλου λεγομένοις.
was persuaded, rather than the things by Paul said.
12 ἀνευθέτου δὲ τοῦ λιμένος ὑπάρχοντος πρὸς παραχειμασίαν,
not fit And the port being for wintering,
οἱ πλείους ἔθεντο βουλὴν ἀναχθῆναι κἀκεῖθεν, εἴπως δύ-
the most gave counsel to set sail from there, if somehow they
ναιντο καταντήσαντες εἰς Φοίνικα παραχειμάσαι, λιμένα τῆς
may be able having arrived at Phoenice to pass the winter, a port
13 Κρήτης βλέποντα κατὰ λίβα καὶ κατὰ χῶρον. ὑποπνεύ-
of Crete looking toward southwest and toward northwest. blowing
σαντος δὲ νότου, δόξαντες τῆς προθέσεως κεκρατηκέναι,
gently And a south wind, thinking the purpose to have gained,
14 ἄραντες ἆσσον παρελέγοντο τὴν Κρήτην. μετ' οὐ πολὺ δὲ
raising (anchor) close they sailed by — Crete. after not much And
ἔβαλε κατ' αὐτῆς ἄνεμος τυφωνικός, ὁ καλούμενος Εὐροκλύ-
beat down it wind a stormy, being called Euroclydon,
15 δων· συναρπασθέντος δὲ τοῦ πλοίου, καὶ μὴ δυναμένου
being seized and the ship, and not being able
16 ἀντοφθαλμεῖν τῷ ἀνέμῳ, ἐπιδόντες ἐφερόμεθα. νησίον δέ τι
to beat against the wind, giving way we were borne. islet But an
ὑποδραμόντες καλούμενον Κλαύδην μόλις ἰσχύσαμεν περι-
running under, being called Clauda, hardly we were able
17 κρατεῖς γενέσθαι τῆς σκάφης· ἣν ἄραντες, βοηθείαις ἐχρῶντο,
mastery to get of the boat, which taking helps they used,
ὑποζωννύντες τὸ πλοῖον· φοβούμενοί τε μὴ εἰς τὴν σύρτιν
undergirding the ship; fearing and lest into — Syrtis
18 ἐκπέσωσι, χαλάσαντες τὸ σκεῦος, οὕτως ἐφέροντο. σφοδρῶς
they fall, lowering the tackle, thus they were borne. exceedingly
19 δὲ χειμαζομένων ἡμῶν, τῇ ἑξῆς ἐκβολὴν ἐποιοῦντο· καὶ τῇ
But being tempest-tossed we, on the next a casting out they made, and on the
τρίτῃ αὐτόχειρες τὴν σκευὴν τοῦ πλοίου ἐρρίψαμεν. μήτε
third with their hands the tackle of the ship they threw. neither
20 δὲ ἡλίου μήτε ἄστρων ἐπιφαινόντων ἐπὶ πλείονας ἡμέρας,
And sun nor stars appearing over many days,
χειμῶνός τε οὐκ ὀλίγου ἐπικειμένου, λοιπὸν περιῃρεῖτο πᾶσα
tempest and no small pressing hard, now was taken away all
21 ἐλπὶς τοῦ σώζεσθαι ἡμᾶς. πολλῆς δὲ ἀσιτίας ὑπαρχούσης,
hope — to be saved us. much And fasting being,
τότε σταθεὶς ὁ Παῦλος ἐν μέσῳ αὐτῶν εἶπεν, Ἔδει μέν, ὦ
then standing Paul in (the) midst of them said, (You) ought, O
ἄνδρες, πειθαρχήσαντάς μοι μὴ ἀνάγεσθαι ἀπὸ τῆς Κρήτης,
men, having been obedient to me not to have set sail from — Crete,
22 κερδῆσαί τε τὴν ὕβριν ταύτην καὶ τὴν ζημίαν. καὶ τὰ νῦν
to come by and — injury this and — loss. And — now

now I exhort you to be cheered, for there will be no casting away of soul from among you, only of the ship. 23 For tonight an angel of God stood by me, whose I am, and whom I serve, 24 saying, Do not fear, Paul. You must stand before Caesar. And, behold, God has granted to you all those sailing with you. 25 Therefore, be cheered, men, for I believe God, that it will be so, according to the way it was spoken to me. 26 But we must fall on a certain island.

27 And when the fourteenth night came, we being carried about in the Adriatic *Sea*, toward the middle of the night the sailors supposed *us to* come near some country. 28 And sounding, they found twenty fathoms; and moving, also sounding again, they found fifteen fathoms. 29 And fearing lest they should fall on rock places, and casting anchors out of *the* stern, they wished day to come.

30 But the sailors seeking to flee out of the ship, and lowering the boat into the sea, pretending to be about to cast out anchors from *the* prow, 31 Paul said to the centurion, and to the soldiers, Unless these remain in the ship, you cannot be saved. 32 Then the soldiers cut away the ropes of the boat, and let it fall.

33 And until day was about to come, Paul begged all to partake of food, saying, Today *is the* fourteenth day you continued waiting without food, not having taken anything. 34 Therefore, I beg you to take of food; for not a hair of your head shall perish. 35 And saying these things, and taking bread, he gave thanks to God before all; and breaking he began to eat.

36 And all having become cheered, they took food.

παραινῶ ὑμᾶς εὐθυμεῖν· ἀποβολὴ γὰρ ψυχῆς οὐδεμία ἔσται
I advise you to be cheered, casting away for of soul no will be
23 ἐξ ὑμῶν, πλὴν τοῦ πλοίου. παρέστη γάρ μοι τῇ νυκτὶ ταύτῃ
of you, but of the ship. stood by For me – night this
24 ἄγγελος τοῦ Θεοῦ, οὗ εἰμι, ᾧ καὶ λατρεύω, λέγων, Μὴ
an angel – of God, whose I am, whom also I serve, saying, Do not
φοβοῦ, Παῦλε· Καίσαρί σε δεῖ παραστῆναι· καὶ ἰδού, κεχάρι-
fear, Paul, Caesar you must stand before, and behold, has given
25 σταί σοι ὁ Θεὸς πάντας τοὺς πλέοντας μετὰ σοῦ. διὸ εὐθυμεῖτε
you God all those sailing with you. So be cheered,
ἄνδρες· πιστεύω γὰρ τῷ Θεῷ ὅτι οὕτως ἔσται καθ' ὃν
men, I believe for – God, that so it will be in the way
26 τρόπον λελάληταί μοι. εἰς νῆσον δέ τινα δεῖ ἡμᾶς ἐκπεσεῖν.
of which it was spoken to me. Onto island But an must we fall off.
27 Ὡς δὲ τεσσαρεσκαιδεκάτη νὺξ ἐγένετο, διαφερομένων
when And (the) fourteenth night came, being carried about
ἡμῶν ἐν τῷ Ἀδρίᾳ, κατὰ μέσον τῆς νυκτὸς ὑπενόουν οἱ
us in the Adriatic, toward the middle of the night supposed the
28 ναῦται προσάγειν τινὰ αὐτοῖς χώραν· καὶ βολίσαντες εὗρον
sailors to approach some to them country. And sounding they found
ὀργυιὰς εἴκοσι· βραχὺ δὲ διαστήσαντες, καὶ πάλιν βολί-
fathoms twenty, a little and having moved also again sounding,
29 σαντες, εὗρον ὀργυιὰς δεκαπέντε· φοβούμενοί τε μήπως εἰς
they found fathoms fifteen; fearing and lest on
τραχεῖς τόπους ἐκπέσωμεν, ἐκ πρύμνης ῥίψαντες ἀγκύρας
rough places they may fall off, our of (the) stern throwing anchors
30 τέσσαρας, ηὔχοντο ἡμέραν γενέσθαι. τῶν δὲ ναυτῶν ζητούν-
four, they wished day to come. the And sailors seeking
των φυγεῖν ἐκ τοῦ πλοίου, καὶ χαλασάντων τὴν σκάφην εἰς
to flee out of the ship, and lowering the boat into
τὴν θάλασσαν, προφάσει ὡς ἐκ πρώρας μελλόντων ἀγκύρας
the sea, pretending as out of (the) prow being about anchors
31 ἐκτείνειν, εἶπεν ὁ Παῦλος τῷ ἑκατοντάρχῃ καὶ τοῖς στρατιώ-
to cast out, said Paul to the centurion and to the soldiers
ταις, Ἐὰν μὴ οὗτοι μείνωσιν ἐν τῷ πλοίῳ, ὑμεῖς σωθῆναι οὐ
If not these remain in the ship, you to be saved not
32 δύνασθε. τότε οἱ στρατιῶται ἀπέκοψαν τὰ σχοινία τῆς
are able. Then the soldiers cut away the ropes of the
33 σκάφης, καὶ εἴασαν αὐτὴν ἐκπεσεῖν. ἄχρι δὲ οὗ ἔμελλεν ἡμέρα
boat, and let it fall off. until And was about day
γίνεσθαι, παρεκάλει ὁ Παῦλος ἅπαντας μεταλαβεῖν τροφῆς,
to come, begged Paul all to partake of food,
λέγων, Τεσσαρεσκαιδεκάτην σήμερον ἡμέραν προσδοκῶντες
saying, (The) fourteenth today (is) day waiting
34 ἄσιτοι διατελεῖτε, μηδὲν προσλαβόμενοι. διὸ παρακαλῶ
without food you continued, nothing having taken. Therefore I beg
ὑμᾶς προσλαβεῖν τροφῆς· τοῦτο γὰρ πρὸς τῆς ὑμετέρας
you to take of food; this for to – your
σωτηρίας ὑπάρχει· οὐδενὸς γὰρ ὑμῶν θρὶξ ἐκ τῆς κεφαλῆς
deliverance is; of no one for of you a hair from the head
35 πεσεῖται. εἰπὼν δὲ ταῦτα, καὶ λαβὼν ἄρτον, εὐχαρίστησε
shall perish. saying And these things, and taking bread, he gave thanks
36 τῷ Θεῷ ἐνώπιον πάντων· καὶ κλάσας ἤρξατο ἐσθίειν. εὔθυμοι
– to God before all, and breaking began to eat. cheered
δὲ γενόμενοι πάντες καὶ αὐτοὶ προσελάβοντο τροφῆς. ἦμεν
And becoming all, also they took food. we were

[37] And in the ship all the souls *were* two hundred seventy-six. [38] And being filled *with* food, they lightened the ship, throwing the wheat out into the sea.

[39] And when day came, they did not recognize the land, but they noted a certain bay having a shore, into which they purposed, if they were able, to drive the ship. [40] And casting off the anchors, they left *them* in the sea, at the same time loosening the bands of the rudders, and raising the foresail to the breeze, they held to the shore. [41] And coming on a place between two seas, they drove the vessel. And indeed the prow stuck firmly, but the stern was broken by the violence of the waves. [42] And the mind of the soldiers was that they should kill the prisoners, lest any swimming out should escape. [43] But the centurion being minded to save Paul prevented them *of their* purpose, and commanded those able to swim, first casting *themselves* overboard, to go out on the land. [44] And the rest, some indeed on boards, and others on some of the things from the ship. And so it happened that all *were* saved on the land.

CHAPTER 28

And being saved, then they knew that the island is called Melita. [2] And the foreigners *were* showing not the common kindness to us, for having kindled a fire because of the rain coming on, and because of the cold, they welcomed us all. [3] And Paul gathering a bunch of sticks, and putting *them* on the fire, a snake coming out from the heat fastened on his hand. [4] And when the foreigners saw the beast hanging from his hand, they said to one another, By all means this man is a murderer, whom being saved out of the sea,

37 δὲ ἐν τῷ πλοίῳ αἱ πᾶσαι ψυχαί, διακόσιαι ἑβδομηκονταέξ.
And in the ship the all souls, two hundred seventy-six.
38 κορεσθέντες δὲ τροφῆς ἐκούφιζον τὸ πλοῖον, ἐκβαλλόμενοι
having been filled And of food, they lightened the ship, throwing out
39 τὸν σῖτον εἰς τὴν θάλασσαν. ὅτε δὲ ἡμέρα ἐγένετο, τὴν γῆν
the wheat into the sea. when And day came, the land
οὐκ ἐπεγίνωσκον· κόλπον δέ τινα κατενόουν ἔχοντα αἰγια-
not did recognize, a bay but certain they noted having a shore,
40 λόν, εἰς ὃν ἐβουλεύσαντο, εἰ δύναιντο, ἐξῶσαι τὸ πλοῖον. καὶ
into which they purposed, if they could, to drive the ship. And
τὰς ἀγκύρας περιελόντες εἴων εἰς τὴν θάλασσαν, ἅμα ἀνέντες
the anchors having cast off they left in the sea, at the same time freeing
τὰς ζευκτηρίας τῶν πηδαλίων· καὶ ἐπάραντες τὸν ἀρτέμονα
the bands of the rudders, and raising the foresail
41 τῇ πνεούσῃ κατεῖχον εἰς τὸν αἰγιαλόν. περιπεσόντες δὲ εἰς
to the breeze, they held to the shore. coming upon And —
τόπον διθάλασσον ἐπώκειλαν τὴν ναῦν· καὶ ἡ μὲν πρῶρα
a place between two seas, they drove the vessel, and the prow
ἐρείσασα ἔμεινεν ἀσάλευτος, ἡ δὲ πρύμνα ἐλύετο ὑπὸ τῆς
having stuck remained immovable, the but stern was broken by the
42 βίας τῶν κυμάτων. τῶν δὲ στρατιωτῶν βουλὴ ἐγένετο ἵνα
violence of the waves. of the And soldiers (the) mind was that
τοὺς δεσμώτας ἀποκτείνωσι, μήτις ἐκκολυμβήσας διαφύγοι.
the prisoners they should kill, lest any swimming out should escape.
43 ὁ δὲ ἑκατόνταρχος, βουλόμενος διασῶσαι τὸν Παῦλον,
the But centurion being minded to save — Paul,
ἐκώλυσεν αὐτοὺς τοῦ βουλήματος, ἐκέλευσέ τε τοὺς δυνα-
prevented them the purpose, commanded and those being
μένους κολυμβᾷν ἀπορρίψαντας πρώτους ἐπὶ τὴν γῆν
able to swim, throwing overboard first, onto the land
44 ἐξιέναι· καὶ τοὺς λοιπούς, οὓς μὲν ἐπὶ σανίσιν, οὓς δὲ ἐπί
to go out. And the rest, some indeed on planks, others and on
τινων τῶν ἀπὸ τοῦ πλοίου. καὶ οὕτως ἐγένετο πάντας
some of the things from the ship. And so it was, all
διασωθῆναι ἐπὶ τὴν γῆν.
to be saved on the land.

CHAPTER 28

1 Καὶ διασωθέντες, τότε ἐπέγνωσαν ὅτι Μελίτη ἡ νῆσος
And having been saved, then they knew that Melita the island
2 καλεῖται. οἱ δὲ βάρβαροι παρεῖχον οὐ τὴν τυχοῦσαν
is called. the And foreigners showed not the common
φιλανθρωπίαν ἡμῖν· ἀνάψαντες γὰρ πυράν, προσελάβοντο
kindness us; having kindled for a fire, they welcomed
πάντας ἡμᾶς, διὰ τὸν ὑετὸν τὸν ἐφεστῶτα, καὶ διὰ τὸ ψῦχος.
all us, because of the rain — coming on, and due to the cold.
3 συστρέψαντος δὲ τοῦ Παύλου φρυγάνων πλῆθος, καὶ
having gathered And — Paul of sticks a bunch, and
ἐπιθέντος ἐπὶ τὴν πυράν, ἔχιδνα ἐκ τῆς θέρμης ἐξελθοῦσα
putting on the fire, a snake from the heat coming out
4 καθῆψε τῆς χειρὸς αὐτοῦ. ὡς δὲ εἶδον οἱ βάρβαροι κρεμά-
fastened on the hand of him. when And saw the foreigners hanging
μενον τὸ θηρίον ἐκ τῆς χειρὸς αὐτοῦ, ἔλεγον πρὸς ἀλλήλους,
the beast from the hand of him, they said to one another,
Πάντως φονεύς ἐστιν ὁ ἄνθρωπος οὗτος, ὃν διασωθέντα ἐκ
By all means a murderer is man this, whom being saved out of

Justice did not permit to live. [5]Then he indeed shaking the beast off into the fire, *he* suffered no harm. [6]But they expected him to be about to become inflamed, or to suddenly fall down dead. but over much *time*, they expecting and seeing nothing amiss happening to him, changing their minds, they said him to be a god.

[7]And in the *parts* about that place were lands to the chief of the island, Publius by name. Welcoming us, *he* housed us in a friendly way. [8]And it happened the father of Publius was lying down, suffering from fevers and dysentery; to whom Paul went in. And praying, laying on his hands, *Paul* cured him. [9]Then, this taking place, the rest who *were* having infirmities in the island also came, and *they* were healed. [10]*They* also honored us with many honors. And on *our* setting sail, they laid on *us* the things for *our* need.

[11]And after three months we sailed in a ship which had wintered in the island, an Alexandrian with an ensign, *The* Twin Brothers. [12]And landing at Syracuse, we remained three days. [13]Going around from there, we arrived at Rhegium. And after one day, a south wind having come on, on the second we came to Puteoli; [14]where finding brothers, we were begged by them to remain seven days. And so we went toward Rome. [15]And the brothers from there hearing about us, *they* came out to meet us, as far as *the* marketplace of Appius, and Three Taverns; whom Paul seeing, thanking God, he took courage.

[16]And when we went into Rome, the centurion delivered the prisoners to the camp commander. But Paul was allowed to remain by himself, with the soldier guarding him.

5 τῆς θαλάσσης ἡ Δίκη ζῆν οὐκ εἴασεν. ὁ μὲν οὖν, ἀποτινάξας
the sea — justice to live not allowed. He then, shaking off
6 τὸ θηρίον εἰς τὸ πῦρ, ἔπαθεν οὐδὲν κακόν. οἱ δὲ προσεδόκων
the beast into the fire, suffered no harm. they But expected
αὐτὸν μέλλειν πίμπρασθαι ἢ καταπίπτειν ἄφνω νεκρόν· ἐπὶ
him to be about to swell, or to fall down suddenly dead. over
πολὺ δὲ αὐτῶν προσδοκώντων, καὶ θεωρούντων μηδὲν
much But they expecting, and beholding nothing
ἄτοπον εἰς αὐτὸν γινόμενον, μεταβαλλόμενοι ἔλεγον θεὸν
amiss to him happening, changing their minds they said a god
αὐτὸν εἶναι.
him to be.
7 Ἐν δὲ τοῖς περὶ τὸν τόπον ἐκεῖνον ὑπῆρχε χωρία τῷ
in And the (parts) about place that, were lands to the
πρώτῳ τῆς νήσου, ὀνόματι Ποπλίῳ, ὃς ἀναδεξάμενος ἡμᾶς
chief of the island, by name Publius, who welcoming us
8 τρεῖς ἡμέρας φιλοφρόνως ἐξένισεν. ἐγένετο δὲ τὸν πατέρα τοῦ
three days in a friendly way lodged (us). it was And, the father —
Ποπλίου πυρετοῖς καὶ δυσεντερίᾳ συνεχόμενον κατακεῖσθαι·
of Publius fevers and dysentery suffering from was lying down,
πρὸς ὃν ὁ Παῦλος εἰσελθών, καὶ προσευξάμενος, ἐπιθεὶς τὰς
to whom Paul having entered and praying, laying on the
9 χεῖρας αὐτῷ, ἰάσατο αὐτόν. τούτου οὖν γενομένου, καὶ οἱ
hands him, cured him. this Then happening, also the
λοιποὶ οἱ ἔχοντες ἀσθενείας ἐν τῇ νήσῳ προσήρχοντο καὶ
rest of those having infirmities in the island came up and
10 ἐθεραπεύοντο· οἳ καὶ πολλαῖς τιμαῖς ἐτίμησαν ἡμᾶς, καὶ
were healed; who also with many honors honored us, and
ἀναγομένοις ἐπέθεντο τὰ πρὸς τὴν χρείαν.
on our sailing laid on the things for the needs (of us).
11 Μετὰ δὲ τρεῖς μῆνας ἀνήχθημεν ἐν πλοίῳ παρακεχει-
after And three months we sailed in a ship having
μακότι ἐν τῇ νήσῳ, Ἀλεξανδρίνῳ, παρασήμῳ Διοσκούροις.
wintered in the island, an Alexandrian, with an ensign, Twin Brothers.
12 καὶ καταχθέντες εἰς Συρακούσας ἐπεμείναμεν ἡμέρας τρεῖς·
And having been landed at Syracuse, we remained days three,
13 ὅθεν περιελθόντες κατηντήσαμεν εἰς Ῥήγιον, καὶ μετὰ μίαν
from where tacking we arrived at Rhegium. And after one
ἡμέραν ἐπιγενομένου νότου, δευτεραῖοι ἤλθομεν εἰς Ποτιό-
day, coming on a south wind, on the second we came to Puteoli,
14 λους· οὗ εὑρόντες ἀδελφούς, παρεκλήθημεν ἐπ' αὐτοῖς
where having found brothers, we were besought by them
ἐπιμεῖναι ἡμέρας ἑπτά· καὶ οὕτως εἰς τὴν Ῥώμην ἤλθομεν.
to remain days seven; and thus to — Rome we went.
15 κἀκεῖθεν οἱ ἀδελφοὶ ἀκούσαντες τὰ περὶ ἡμῶν, ἐξῆλθον εἰς
And from there the brothers having heard about us came out to
ἀπάντησιν ἡμῖν ἄχρις Ἀππίου Φόρου καὶ Τριῶν Ταβερνῶν·
meet us as far as Appius Forum and Three Taverns,
οὓς ἰδὼν ὁ Παῦλος, εὐχαριστήσας τῷ Θεῷ, ἔλαβε θάρσος.
whom seeing Paul, thanking — God, he took courage.
16 Ὅτε δὲ ἤλθομεν εἰς Ῥώμην, ὁ ἑκατόνταρχος παρέδωκε
when And we went into Rome, the centurion delivered
τοὺς δεσμίους τῷ στρατοπεδάρχῃ· τῷ δὲ Παύλῳ ἐπετράπη
the prisoners to the camp commander; but Paul was allowed
μένειν καθ' ἑαυτόν, σὺν τῷ φυλάσσοντι αὐτὸν στρατιώτῃ.
to remain by himself, with the guarding him soldier.

[17]And after three days, it happened that Paul called together those being chief of the Jews. And they coming together, he said to them, Men, brothers, I did nothing contrary to the people, or to the ancestral customs. I was delivered a prisoner from Jerusalem into the hands of the Romans; [18]who examining me were of a mind to let me go, because no cause of death was in me. [19]But the Jews speaking against *it*, I was compelled to appeal to Caesar, not as having anything to accuse my nation. [20]On account of this, then, I called for you, to see and to speak to *you*. For I have this chain around *me* for the sake of the hope of Israel. [21]And they said to him, We neither received letters concerning you from the Jews, nor having arrived has any one of the brothers reported or spoken anything evil concerning you.

17 Ἐγένετο δὲ μετὰ ἡμέρας τρεῖς συγκαλέσασθαι τὸν Παῦλον
it was And, after days three called together — Paul
τοὺς ὄντας τῶν Ἰουδαίων πρώτους· συνελθόντων δὲ αὐτῶν,
those being of the Jews chief. coming together And them,
ἔλεγε πρὸς αὐτούς, Ἄνδρες ἀδελφοί, ἐγὼ οὐδὲν ἐναντίον
he said to them, Men, brothers, I nothing contrary
ποιήσας τῷ λαῷ ἢ τοῖς ἔθεσι τοῖς πατρῴοις, δέσμιος ἐξ
did to the people or to the customs ancestral, a prisoner from
Ἱεροσολύμων παρεδόθην εἰς τὰς χεῖρας τῶν Ῥωμαίων·
Jerusalem I was delivered to the hands of the Romans,
18 οἵτινες ἀνακρίναντές με ἐβούλοντο ἀπολῦσαι, διὰ τὸ μηδε-
who having examined me were minded to let me go, because no
19 μίαν αἰτίαν θανάτου ὑπάρχειν ἐν ἐμοί. ἀντιλεγόντων δὲ τῶν
cause of death to be in me. speaking against But the
Ἰουδαίων, ἠναγκάσθην ἐπικαλέσασθαι Καίσαρα, οὐχ ὡς
Jews, I was compelled to appeal to Caesar; not as
20 τοῦ ἔθνους μου ἔχων τι κατηγορῆσαι. διὰ ταύτην οὖν τὴν
the nation of me having anything to accuse. Because of this, then,
αἰτίαν παρεκάλεσα ὑμᾶς ἰδεῖν καὶ προσλαλῆσαι· ἕνεκεν γὰρ
cause I called fo you to see and to speak to; for the sake of for
τῆς ἐλπίδος τοῦ Ἰσραὴλ τὴν ἅλυσιν ταύτην περίκειμαι.
the hope — of Israel, — chain this I have around (me).
21 οἱ δὲ πρὸς αὐτὸν εἶπον, Ἡμεῖς οὔτε γράμματα περὶ σοῦ
they And to him said, We neither letters about you
ἐδεξάμεθα ἀπὸ τῆς Ἰουδαίας, οὔτε παραγενόμενός τις τῶν
received from the Jews, nor arriving anyone of the
ἀδελφῶν ἀπήγγειλεν ἢ ἐλάλησέ τι περὶ σοῦ πονηρόν.
brothers told or spoke anything about you evil.

[22]But we think *it* fitting to hear from you *as to* what you think, for truly as concerning this sect, it is known to us that it is spoken against everywhere.

22 ἀξιοῦμεν δὲ παρὰ σοῦ ἀκοῦσαι ἃ φρονεῖς· περὶ μὲν γὰρ τῆς
we think fit But from you to hear what you think about indeed for
αἱρέσεως ταύτης γνωστόν ἐστιν ἡμῖν ὅτι πανταχοῦ ἀντιλέ-
sect this known is us, that everywhere it is
γεται.
spoken against.

[23]And having appointed him a day, more came to him in the lodging, to whom he expounded, earnestly testifying the kingdom of God, and persuading them the things concerning Jesus, both from the law of Moses and the Prophets, from morning until evening. [24]And some indeed were persuaded by that being said; others disbelieved. [25]And disagreeing with one another, they were let go, Paul saying one word: Well did the Holy Spirit speak through the prophet Isaiah to our fathers, [26]saying, "Go to this people and say, You will surely hear, and not at all understand; and you will surely see, and not at all perceive.; [27]for the heart of this people was fattened,

23 Ταξάμενοι δὲ αὐτῷ ἡμέραν, ἧκον πρὸς αὐτὸν εἰς τὴν
appointing And him a day, came to him in the
ξενίαν πλείονες· οἷς ἐξετίθετο διαμαρτυρόμενος τὴν βασι-
lodging more, to whom he set forth earnestly testifying the king-
λείαν τοῦ Θεοῦ, πείθων τε αὐτοὺς τὰ περὶ τοῦ Ἰησοῦ, ἀπό
dom — of God, persuading and them concerning — Jesus, from
τε τοῦ νόμου Μωσέως καὶ τῶν προφητῶν, ἀπὸ πρωῒ ἕως
and the law of Moses and the Prophets, from morning until
24 ἑσπέρας. καὶ οἱ μὲν ἐπείθοντο τοῖς λεγομένοις, οἱ δὲ ἠπίστουν.
evening. And some were persuaded by that being said, others disbelieved.
25 ἀσύμφωνοι δὲ ὄντες πρὸς ἀλλήλους ἀπελύοντο, εἰπόντος
being disagreed And being with one another, they were let go, having said
τοῦ Παύλου ῥῆμα ἕν, ὅτι Καλῶς τὸ Πνεῦμα τὸ Ἅγιον
— Paul word one, — Well the Spirit — Holy
ἐλάλησε διὰ Ἡσαΐου τοῦ προφήτου πρὸς τοὺς πατέρας
spoke through Isaiah the prophet to the fathers
26 ἡμῶν, λέγον, Πορεύθητι πρὸς τὸν λαὸν τοῦτον καὶ εἰπέ,
of us, saying, Go to — people this and say:
Ἀκοῇ ἀκούσετε, καὶ οὐ μὴ συνῆτε· καὶ βλέποντες βλέψετε,
In hearing you will hear, and not at all understand, and seeing you will see,
27 καὶ οὐ μὴ ἴδητε· ἐπαχύνθη γὰρ ἡ καρδία τοῦ λαοῦ τούτου,
and not at all perceive, was fattened for the heart — people of this,

and they have heard with the ears heavily; and they closed their eyes lest at any time they see with *their* eyes and hear with *their* ears, and understand with *their* heart, and be converted, and I should heal them." [28] Therefore, let it be known to you that the salvation of God was sent to the nations; and they will hear. [29] And he saying these things, the Jews went away, having much discussion among themselves.

[30] And Paul remained two whole years in *his* own rented place, and *he* welcomed all those coming in to him, [31] proclaiming the kingdom of God, and teaching the things concerning the Lord Jesus Christ, with all freedom, *and* without hindrance.

καὶ τοῖς ὠσὶ βαρέως ἤκουσαν, καὶ τοὺς ὀφθαλμοὺς αὐτῶν
and with the ears heavily they heard, and the eyes of them
ἐκάμμυσαν· μήποτε ἴδωσι τοῖς ὀφθαλμοῖς, καὶ τοῖς ὠσὶν
they closed, lest at any time they see with the eyes, and with the ears
ἀκούσωσι, καὶ τῇ καρδίᾳ συνῶσι, καὶ ἐπιστρέψωσι, καὶ
hear, and with the heart understand, and be converted, and
28 ἰάσωμαι αὐτούς. γνωστὸν οὖν ἔστω ὑμῖν, ὅτι τοῖς ἔθνεσιν
I should heal them. Known, therefore, be it to you, that to the nations
ἀπεστάλη τὸ σωτήριον τοῦ Θεοῦ, αὐτοὶ καὶ ἀκούσονται.
was sent the salvation — of God, they and will hear.
29 καὶ ταῦτα αὐτοῦ εἰπόντος, ἀπῆλθον οἱ Ἰουδαῖοι, πολλὴν
And these things he having said, went away the Jews much
ἔχοντες ἐν ἑαυτοῖς συζήτησιν.
having among themselves discussion.
30 Ἔμεινε δὲ ὁ Παῦλος διετίαν ὅλην ἐν ἰδίῳ μισθώματι, καὶ
remained And Paul two years a whole in (his) own rented place, and
ἀπεδέχετο πάντας τοὺς εἰσπορευομένους πρὸς αὐτόν,
welcomed all those coming in to him,
31 κηρύσσων τὴν βασιλείαν τοῦ Θεοῦ, καὶ διδάσκων τὰ περὶ
proclaiming the kingdom — of God, and teaching the things about
τοῦ Κυρίου Ἰησοῦ Χριστοῦ, μετὰ πάσης παρρησίας,
the Lord Jesus Christ, with all freedom,
ἀκωλύτως.
without hindrance.

ΠΑΥΛΟΥ ΤΟΥ ΑΠΟΣΤΟΛΟΥ
PAUL THE APOSTLE

Η ΠΡΟΣ
TO (THE)

ΡΩΜΑΙΟΥΣ ΕΠΙΣΤΟΛΗ
ROMANS EPISTLE

KING JAMES II VERSION

THE EPISTLE TO THE ROMANS

CHAPTER 1

1 Paul, a slave of Jesus Christ, a called apostle, separated to the gospel of God, 2 which He before promised through His prophets in holy Scriptures, 3 concerning His Son who came of the seed of David according to flesh, 4 who was marked out Son of God in power, according to the Spirit of holiness, by resurrection of *the* dead, Jesus Christ our Lord; 5 by whom we received grace and apostleship to obedience of faith among all the nations, for His name's sake, 6 among whom are you also, the called-out ones of Jesus Christ; 7 to all those who are in Rome, beloved of God, called-out saints, grace and peace to you from God our Father and *the* Lord Jesus Christ.

8 First, I thank my God through Jesus Christ for you all, that your faith is spoken of in all the world. 9 for God is my witness, whom I serve in my spirit in the gospel of His Son, how without ceasing I make mention of you 10 always in my prayers, beseeching if by any means now at length I shall be blessed by the will of God to come to you. 11 For I long to see you, that I may impart some spiritual gift to you, for the establishing of you 12 that is, to be comforted together among you, through the faith in one another, both yours and mine. 13 But I do

CHAPTER 1

1 Παῦλος, δοῦλος Ἰησοῦ Χριστοῦ, κλητὸς ἀπόστολος,
Paul, a slave of Jesus Christ, called (to be) an apostle,
2 ἀφωρισμένος εἰς εὐαγγέλιον Θεοῦ, ὃ προεπηγγείλατο διὰ
being separated to (the) gospel of God, which He promised before through
3 τῶν προφητῶν αὐτοῦ ἐν γραφαῖς ἁγίαις, περὶ τοῦ υἱοῦ
the prophets of Him in Scriptures holy, concerning the Son
αὐτοῦ, τοῦ γενομένου ἐκ σπέρματος Δαβὶδ κατὰ σάρκα,
of Him, — come of the seed of David according to flesh,
4 τοῦ ὁρισθέντος υἱοῦ Θεοῦ ἐν δυνάμει, κατὰ πνεῦμα ἁγιω-
— marked out Son of God in power according to (the) Spirit of
σύνης, ἐξ ἀναστάσεως νεκρῶν, Ἰησοῦ Χριστοῦ τοῦ Κυρίου
holiness, by resurrection of (the) dead, Jesus Christ the Lord
5 ἡμῶν, δι' οὗ ἐλάβομεν χάριν καὶ ἀποστολὴν εἰς ὑπακοὴν
of us, through whom we received grace and apostleship to obedience
6 πίστεως ἐν πᾶσι τοῖς ἔθνεσιν, ὑπὲρ τοῦ ὀνόματος αὐτοῦ, ἐν
of faith among all the nations, for the sake of the name of Him, among
7 οἷς ἐστὲ καὶ ὑμεῖς, κλητοὶ Ἰησοῦ Χριστοῦ· πᾶσι τοῖς οὖσιν
whom are also you called out ones of Jesus Christ. To all those being
ἐν Ῥώμῃ ἀγαπητοῖς Θεοῦ, κλητοῖς ἁγίοις· χάρις ὑμῖν καὶ
in Rome beloved of God, called out saints, grace to you and
εἰρήνη ἀπὸ Θεοῦ πατρὸς ἡμῶν καὶ Κυρίου Ἰησοῦ Χριστοῦ.
peace from God (the) Father of us, and (the) Lord Jesus Christ.
8 Πρῶτον μὲν εὐχαριστῶ τῷ Θεῷ μου διὰ Ἰησοῦ Χριστοῦ
Firstly, truly I thank the God of me through Jesus Christ
ὑπὲρ πάντων ὑμῶν, ὅτι ἡ πίστις ὑμῶν καταγγέλλεται ἐν
for all of you, that the faith of you is spoken of in
9 ὅλῳ τῷ κόσμῳ. μάρτυς γάρ μού ἐστιν ὁ Θεός, ᾧ λατρεύω
all the world. the witness For of me is God, whom I serve
ἐν τῷ πνεύματί μου ἐν τῷ εὐαγγελίῳ τοῦ υἱοῦ αὐτοῦ, ὡς
in the spirit of me in the gospel of the Son of Him, how
10 ἀδιαλείπτως μνείαν ὑμῶν ποιοῦμαι, πάντοτε ἐπὶ τῶν
without ceasing mention of you I make always on the
προσευχῶν μου δεόμενος, εἴπως ἤδη ποτὲ εὐοδωθήσομαι ἐν
prayers of me beseeching, if at all now at length I shall be blessed by
11 τῷ θελήματι τοῦ Θεοῦ ἐλθεῖν πρὸς ὑμᾶς. ἐπιποθῶ γὰρ ἰδεῖν
the will — of God to come to you. I long For to see
ὑμᾶς, ἵνα τι μεταδῶ χάρισμα ὑμῖν πνευματικόν, εἰς τὸ
you, that some I may impart gift to you spiritual, for the
12 στηριχθῆναι ὑμᾶς. τοῦτο δέ ἐστι, συμπαρακληθῆναι ἐν ὑμῖν
establishing of you. this And is to be comforted together among you
13 διὰ τῆς ἐν ἀλλήλοις πίστεως ὑμῶν τε καὶ ἐμοῦ. οὐ θέλω δὲ
through the in one another faith of you both and of me. not I wish But

not wish you to be ignorant, brothers, that many times I purposed to come to you, and was kept back until the present, that I might have some fruit among you also, even as among the other nations. [14]I am a debtor both to Greeks and to foreigners, both to wise, and to foolish, [15]so as far as in me *lies*, I am eager to preach the gospel to you in Rome also. [16]for I am not ashamed of the gospel of Christ, for it is power of God to salvation to everyone believing, both to Jew first, and to Greek; [17]for in it the righteousness of God is revealed from faith to faith; even as it has been written, "But the just shall live by faith."

[18]For God's wrath is revealed from Heaven on all ungodliness and unrighteousness of men, holding the truth in unrighteousness, [19]because the thing known of God is clearly known within them, for God revealed *it* to them— [20]for the unseen things of Him from the creation of the world are clearly seen, being understood by the things made, both His eternal power and Godhead, for them to be without excuse. [21]Because knowing God, they did not glorify Him as God, nor were thankful; but became vain in their reasonings, and their foolish heart was darkened. [22]Professing to be wise, they became foolish, [23]and changed the glory of the incorruptible God into a likeness of an image of corruptible man, and of birds, and four-footed animals, and creeping things. [24]Therefore God also gave them up to uncleanness in the lusts of their hearts, their bodies to be dishonored among themselves; [25]who changed the truth of God into the lie, and worshiped and served the created thing more than the Creator, who is blessed forever. Amen.

ὑμᾶς ἀγνοεῖν, ἀδελφοί, ὅτι πολλάκις προεθέμην ἐλθεῖν πρὸς
you to be ignorant, brothers, that often I purposed to come to
ὑμᾶς (καὶ ἐκωλύθην ἄχρι τοῦ δεῦρο), ἵνα καρπόν τινα σχῶ
you, and was hindered until the present, that fruit some I have
14 καὶ ἐν ὑμῖν, καθὼς καὶ ἐν τοῖς λοιποῖς ἔθνεσιν. Ἕλλησί τε καὶ
also among you, even as also in the remaining nations. to Greeks Both and
15 βαρβάροις, σοφοῖς τε καὶ ἀνοήτοις ὀφειλέτης εἰμί· οὕτω τὸ
to foreigners, to wise both and foolish, a debtor I am; so as
κατ' ἐμὲ πρόθυμον καὶ ὑμῖν τοῖς ἐν Ῥώμῃ εὐαγγελίσασθαι.
far as in me (lies) I am eager also to you in Rome to preach the gospel.
16 οὐ γὰρ ἐπαισχύνομαι τὸ εὐαγγέλιον τοῦ Χριστοῦ· δύναμις
not For I am ashamed of the gospel — of Christ, power
γὰρ Θεοῦ ἐστιν εἰς σωτηρίαν παντὶ τῷ πιστεύοντι, Ἰουδαίῳ
for of God it is to salvation to everyone believing, to Jew
17 τε πρῶτον καὶ Ἕλληνι. δικαιοσύνη γὰρ Θεοῦ ἐν αὐτῷ
both firstly, and to Greek. a righteousness For of God in it
ἀποκαλύπτεται ἐκ πίστεως εἰς πίστιν, καθὼς γέγραπται,
is revealed from faith to faith, even as it has been written,
Ὁ δὲ δίκαιος ἐκ πίστεως ζήσεται.
the But just by faith shall live.
18 Ἀποκαλύπτεται γὰρ ὀργὴ Θεοῦ ἀπ' οὐρανοῦ ἐπὶ πᾶσαν
is revealed For (the) wrath of God from Heaven on all
ἀσέβειαν καὶ ἀδικίαν ἀνθρώπων τῶν τὴν ἀλήθειαν ἐν ἀδικίᾳ
ungodliness and unrighteousness of men — the truth in unrighteousness
19 κατεχόντων· διότι τὸ γνωστὸν τοῦ Θεοῦ φανερόν ἐστιν ἐν
holding; because the thing known — of God clearly known is in
20 αὐτοῖς· ὁ γὰρ Θεὸς αὐτοῖς ἐφανέρωσε. τὰ γὰρ ἀόρατα αὐτοῦ
them, for God to them revealed (it). the For unseen things of Him
ἀπὸ κτίσεως κόσμου τοῖς ποιήμασι νοούμενα καθορᾶται.
from (the) creation of (the) world by the things made being understood are clearly seen,
ἥ τε ἀΐδιος αὐτοῦ δύναμις καὶ θειότης, εἰς τὸ εἶναι αὐτοὺς
the both eternal of Him power and Godhead; for to be them
21 ἀναπολογήτους· διότι γνόντες τὸν Θεόν, οὐχ ὡς Θεὸν
without excuse. Because having known — God, not as God
ἐδόξασαν ἢ εὐχαρίστησαν, ἀλλ' ἐματαιώθησαν ἐν τοῖς
they glorified, nor were thankful; but became vain in the
διαλογισμοῖς αὐτῶν, καὶ ἐσκοτίσθη ἡ ἀσύνετος αὐτῶν
reasonings of them, and was darkened the undiscerning of them
22 καρδία. φάσκοντες εἶναι σοφοὶ ἐμωράνθησαν, καὶ ἤλλαξαν
heart. Professing to be wise, they became foolish, and changed
23 τὴν δόξαν τοῦ ἀφθάρτου Θεοῦ ἐν ὁμοιώματι εἰκόνος φθαρτοῦ
the glory of the incorruptible God into a likeness of an image of corruptible
ἀνθρώπου καὶ πετεινῶν καὶ τετραπόδων καὶ ἑρπετῶν.
man, and birds, and four-footed animals, and reptiles.
24 Διὸ καὶ παρέδωκεν αὐτοὺς ὁ Θεὸς ἐν ταῖς ἐπιθυμίαις τῶν
Therefore also gave up them God in the lusts of the
καρδιῶν αὐτῶν εἰς ἀκαθαρσίαν τοῦ ἀτιμάζεσθαι τὰ σώματα
hearts of them to uncleanness, — to be dishonored the bodies
25 αὐτῶν ἐν ἑαυτοῖς· οἵτινες μετήλλαξαν τὴν ἀλήθειαν τοῦ
of them among themselves; who changed the truth —
Θεοῦ ἐν τῷ ψεύδει, καὶ ἐσεβάσθησαν καὶ ἐλάτρευσαν τῇ
of God into the lie, and worshiped and served the
κτίσει παρὰ τὸν κτίσαντα, ὅς ἐστιν εὐλογητὸς εἰς τοὺς
creature rather than the Creator, who is blessed to the
αἰῶνας. ἀμήν.
ages. Amen.

[26]Because of this, God gave them up to dishonorable passions, for even their females changed the natural use to that contrary to nature. [27]And likewise, the males also forsaking the natural use of the female burned in their lust toward one another, males with males working out shamefulness, and receiving back the reward which was fitting for their error.

[28]And even as they did not think fit to have God in *their* knowledge, God gave them up to a reprobate mind, to do the things not right, [29]having been filled with all unrighteousness, fornication, iniquity, covetousness, malice; *being* full of envy, murder, quarrels, deceit, evil habits; *becoming* whisperers, [30]slanderers, God-haters, insolent, proud, braggarts, devisers of evil things, disobedient to parents, [31]without discernment, perfidious, without natural affection, unforgiving, unmerciful–[32]who knowing the righteous order of God, that those practicing such things are worthy of death, not only do them, but also applaud those practicing *them*.

CHAPTER 2

[1]Therefore, O man, you are without excuse,. everyone who judges, for in that in which you judge the other, you condemn yourself; for you who judge do the same things. [2]But we know that the judgment of God is according to truth on those that practice such things. [3]And, O man, the *one* judging those that practice such things, and practice them *yourself*, do you think you will escape the judgment of God? [4]Or do you despise the riches of His kindness, and the forbearance and the long-suffering, not knowing that the kindness of God leads you to repentance? [5]But according to your hardness and your impenitent heart, do you treasure up to yourself wrath

26 Διὰ τοῦτο παρέδωκεν αὐτοὺς ὁ Θεὸς εἰς πάθη ἀτιμίας·
Therefore gave up them God to passions of dishonor;
αἵ τε γὰρ θήλειαι αὐτῶν μετήλλαξαν τὴν φυσικὴν χρῆσιν
the even for females of them changed the natural use
27 εἰς τὴν παρὰ φύσιν· ὁμοίως τε καὶ οἱ ἄρσενες, ἀφέντες τὴν
to the (use) against nature; likewise and also the males having forsaken the
φυσικὴν χρῆσιν τῆς θηλείας, ἐξεκαύθησαν ἐν τῇ ὀρέξει αὐτῶν
natural use of the female, burned in the lust of them
εἰς ἀλλήλους, ἄρσενες ἐν ἄρσεσι τὴν ἀσχημοσύνην κατερ-
toward one another, males among males the shamefulness working
γαζόμενοι, καὶ τὴν ἀντιμισθίαν ἣν ἔδει τῆς πλάνης αὐτῶν
out, and the reward which behoved the straying of them,
ἐν ἑαυτοῖς ἀπολαμβάνοντες.
in themselves receiving back.

28 Καὶ καθὼς οὐκ ἐδοκίμασαν τὸν Θεὸν ἔχειν ἐν ἐπιγνώσει,
And even as not they thought fit – God to have in knowledge,
παρέδωκεν αὐτοὺς ὁ Θεὸς εἰς ἀδόκιμον νοῦν, ποιεῖν τὰ μὴ
gave up them God to a reprobate mind, to do the things not
29 καθήκοντα, πεπληρωμένους πάσῃ ἀδικίᾳ, πορνείᾳ, πονηρίᾳ,
right, having been filled with all unrighteousness, fornication, iniquity,
πλεονεξίᾳ, κακίᾳ· μεστοὺς φθόνου, φόνου, ἔριδος, δόλου,
covetousness, malice, full of envy, murder, quarrels, deceit,
30 κακοηθείας· ψιθυριστάς, καταλάλους, θεοστυγεῖς, ὑβριστάς,
evil habits, whisperers, slanderers, God-haters, insolent,
ὑπερηφάνους, ἀλαζόνας, ἐφευρετὰς κακῶν. γονεῦσιν ἀπει-
proud, braggarts; devisers of evil things, to parents diso-
31 θεῖς, ἀσυνέτους, ἀσυνθέτους, ἀστόργους, ἀσπόνδους, ἀνελεή-
bedient, undiscerning, perfidious. without affection, implacable, unmerci-
32 μονας· οἵτινες τὸ δικαίωμα τοῦ Θεοῦ ἐπιγνόντες, ὅτι οἱ τὰ
ful; who the righteous order of God having known, that those
τοιαῦτα πράσσοντες ἄξιοι θανάτου εἰσίν, οὐ μόνον αὐτὰ
such things practicing worthy of death are, not only them
ποιοῦσιν, ἀλλὰ καὶ συνευδοκοῦσι τοῖς πράσσουσι.
do, but also consent to those practicing (them).

CHAPTER 2

1 Διὸ ἀναπολόγητος εἶ, ὦ ἄνθρωπε πᾶς ὁ κρίνων· ἐν ᾧ γὰρ
Therefore without excuse are you, O man, everyone judging; in what for
κρίνεις τὸν ἕτερον, σεαυτὸν κατακρίνεις, τὰ γὰρ αὐτὰ πράσ-
you judge the other, yourself you condemn; the for same things you
2 σεις ὁ κρίνων. οἴδαμεν δὲ ὅτι τὸ κρίμα τοῦ Θεοῦ ἐστι κατὰ
practice those judging. we know But that the judgment of God is according to
3 ἀλήθειαν ἐπὶ τοὺς τὰ τοιαῦτα πράσσοντας. λογίζῃ δὲ τοῦτο,
truth on those that such things practice. do you think And this,
ὦ ἄνθρωπε ὁ κρίνων τοὺς τὰ τοιαῦτα πράσσοντας καὶ ποιῶν
O man, he judging those such things practicing and doing
4 αὐτά, ὅτι σὺ ἐκφεύξῃ τὸ κρίμα τοῦ Θεοῦ; ἢ τοῦ πλούτου
them, that you will escape the judgment – of God? Or the riches
τῆς χρηστότητος αὐτοῦ καὶ τῆς ἀνοχῆς καὶ τῆς μακροθυμίας
of the kindness of Him, and the forbearance and the longsuffering
καταφρονεῖς, ἀγνοῶν ὅτι τὸ χρηστὸν τοῦ Θεοῦ εἰς μετάνοιάν
do you despise, not knowing that the kindness – of God to repentance
5 σε ἄγει; κατὰ δὲ τὴν σκληρότητά σου καὶ ἀμετανόητον
you leads? according to But the hardness of you and the impenitent
καρδίαν θησαυρίζεις σεαυτῷ ὀργὴν ἐν ἡμέρᾳ ὀργῆς καὶ
heart, do you treasure for yourself wrath in a day of wrath, and

in a day of wrath, and revelation of a righteous judgment of God, [6]who will give to each according to his works; [7]everlasting life indeed to those who with patience *in* good work *are* seeking glory and honor and incorruptibility; [8]but to those even disobeying the truth out of self-interest, and obeying unrighteousness *will be* anger and wrath, [9]trouble and pain on every soul of man that works out evil, both of Jew first, and of Greek. [10]But glory and honor and peace *will be* to everyone that works out good, to *the* Jew first, and to *the* Greek. [11]For there is no respect of persons with God. [12]For as many as sinned without Law will also perish without Law. And as many as sinned within Law will be judged through Law. [13]For not the hearers of the Law are just with God, but the doers of the Law shall be justified. [14]For when nations not having Law do by nature the things of the Law, they are a law to themselves; [15]who show the work of the law written in their hearts, their conscience witnessing with *them*; and the thoughts between one another accusing or excusing, [16]in a day when God shall judge the hidden things of men, according to my gospel, through Jesus Christ.

[17]Behold, you are called a Jew, and rest in the Law, and boast in God, [18]and know the will, and approve the things excelling, being instructed out of the Law; [19]and persuading yourself to be a guide of blind ones, a light to those in darkness, [20]an instructor of foolish ones, a teacher of infants, having the form of knowledge and of the truth in the Law—[21]then the *one* teaching another, do you teach yourself? The *one* preaching not to steal, do you steal? [22]The *one* saying not to commit adultery, do you commit adultery? The *one* detesting the idols, do

6 ἀποκαλύψεως δικαιοκρισίας τοῦ Θεοῦ, ὃς ἀποδώσει ἑκάστῳ
revelation of a righteous judgment of God, who will give to each one
7 κατὰ τὰ ἔργα αὐτοῦ· τοῖς μὲν καθ' ὑπομονὴν ἔργου ἀγαθοῦ
according to the works of him to those by patience work good,
δόξαν καὶ τιμὴν καὶ ἀφθαρσίαν ζητοῦσι, ζωὴν αἰώνιον· τοῖς
glory and honor and incorruptibility seeking, life everlasting. to those
8 δὲ ἐξ ἐριθείας, καὶ ἀπειθοῦσι μὲν τῇ ἀληθείᾳ, πειθομένοις δὲ
But out of self-interest even disobeying indeed the truth, obeying but
9 τῇ ἀδικίᾳ, θυμος καὶ ὀργή, θλίψις καὶ στενοχωρία, ἐπὶ
unrighteousness, anger and wrath, trouble and pain on
πᾶσαν ψυχὴν ἀνθρώπου τοῦ κατεργαζομένου τὸ κακόν,
every soul of man — working out the evil,
10 Ἰουδαίου τε πρῶτον καὶ Ἕλληνος· δόξα δὲ καὶ τιμὴ καὶ
of Jew both firstly, and of Greek. glory But and honor and
εἰρήνη παντὶ τῷ ἐργαζομένῳ τὸ ἀγαθόν, Ἰουδαίῳ τε πρῶτον
peace to everyone working out the good, to Jew both firstly,
11 καὶ Ἕλληνι· οὐ γάρ ἐστι προσωποληψία παρὰ τῷ Θεῷ.
and to Greek. not For is respect of persons with — God.
12 ὅσοι γὰρ ἀνόμως ἥμαρτον, ἀνόμως καὶ ἀπολοῦνται· καὶ
as many as For without law sinned, without law also will perish; and
13 ὅσοι ἐν νόμῳ ἥμαρτον, διὰ νόμου κριθήσονται· οὐ γὰρ οἱ
as many as in law sinned, through law will be judged; not for the
ἀκροαταὶ τοῦ νόμου δίκαιοι παρὰ τῷ Θεῷ, ἀλλ' οἱ ποιηταὶ
hearers of the law are just with — God, but the doers
14 τοῦ νόμου δικαιωθήσονται. ὅταν γὰρ ἔθνη τὰ μὴ νόμον
of the law shall be justified. when For nations — not law
ἔχοντα φύσει τὰ τοῦ νόμου ποιῇ, οὗτοι, νόμον μὴ ἔχοντες,
having by nature the things of the law do, these law not having
15 ἑαυτοῖς εἰσι νόμος· οἵτινες ἐνδείκνυνται τὸ ἔργον τοῦ νόμου
to themselves are a law; who show the work of the law
γραπτὸν ἐν ταῖς καρδίαις αὐτῶν, συμμαρτυρούσης αὐτῶν
written in the hearts of them, witnessing with of them
τῆς συνειδήσεως, καὶ μεταξὺ ἀλλήλων τῶν λογισμῶν
the conscience, and between one another the thoughts
16 κατηγορούντων ἢ καὶ ἀπολογουμένων, ἐν ἡμέρᾳ ὅτε κρινεῖ
accusing or even excusing, in a day when judges
ὁ Θεὸς τὰ κρυπτὰ τῶν ἀνθρώπων, κατὰ τὸ εὐαγγέλιόν μου
God the hidden things of men according to the gospel of me
διὰ Ἰησοῦ Χριστοῦ.
through Jesus Christ.
17 Ἴδε σὺ Ἰουδαῖος ἐπονομάζῃ, καὶ ἐπαναπαύῃ τῷ νόμῳ,
Behold, you a Jew are named, and rest in the law,
18 καὶ καυχᾶσαι ἐν Θεῷ, καὶ γινώσκεις τὸ θέλημα, καὶ δοκι-
and boast in God, and know the will, and approve
19 μάζεις τὰ διαφέροντα, κατηχούμενος ἐκ τοῦ νόμου, πέποιθάς
the things excelling, being instructed out of the law, having persuaded
τε σεαυτὸν ὁδηγὸν εἶναι τυφλῶν, φῶς τῶν ἐν σκότει, παι-
and yourself a guide to be of blind ones, a light to those in darkness, an
20 δευτὴν ἀφρόνων, διδάσκαλον νηπίων, ἔχοντα τὴν μόρφωσιν
instructor of foolish ones, a teacher of infants, having the form
21 τῆς γνώσεως καὶ τῆς ἀληθείας ἐν τῷ νόμῳ· ὁ οὖν διδάσκων
of knowledge and of the truth in the law; the one then, teaching
ἕτερον, σεαυτὸν οὐ διδάσκεις; ὁ κηρύσσων μὴ κλέπτειν,
another, yourself not do you teach? the one proclaiming not to steal,
22 κλέπτεις; ὁ λέγων μὴ μοιχεύειν, μοιχεύεις; ὁ βδελυσσόμενος
do you steal? the one saying not to commit adultery, do you commit adultery? the one detesting

you rob temples? 23 *You* who boasts in Law, do you dishonor God through transgression of the Law? 24 For the name of God is blasphemed among the nations because of you, even as it has been written: 25 "For indeed circumcision profits if you practice *the* Law, but if you are a transgressor of Law, your circumcision becomes uncircumcision. 26 If, then, the uncircumcision keeps the demands of the Law, *will* not his uncircumcision be counted for circumcision? 27 And will *not* the uncircumcision by nature *by* keeping the Law judge you, the *one who* through letter and circumcision *becomes* transgressor of Law? 28 For he is not a Jew that *is one* outwardly, nor *is* circumcision that outwardly in flesh; 29 but he *is* a Jew that *is one* inwardly, and circumcision *is* of heart, in spirit, not in letter, of whom the praise *is* not from men, but from God.

CHAPTER 3

1 What then *is* the superiority of the Jew? Or what the profit of circumcision? 2 Much every way. For first, indeed, that they were entrusted with the oracles of God. 3 For what if some did not believe? Will their unbelief destroy the faith of God? 4 Let it not be! But let God be true, and every man a liar; even as it has been written, "That You should be justified in Your words, and will overcome in Your being judged."

5 But if our unrighteousness commends God's righteousness, what shall we say? *Is* God unrighteous who lays on wrath? I speak according to man. 6 Let it not be! Otherwise, how will God judge the world? 7 for if in my lie the truth of God abounded to His glory, why am I yet judged as a sinner? 8 And not, as we are wrongly accused, and as some report us to say, Let us do bad things so that good things may come. *The* judgment of whom is just

23 τὰ εἴδωλα, ἱεροσυλεῖς; ὃς ἐν νόμῳ καυχᾶσαι διὰ τῆς
the idols, do you rob temples? Who in law boasts, through
24 παραβάσεως τοῦ νόμου τὸν Θεὸν ἀτιμάζεις; τὸ γὰρ ὄνομα
transgression of the law — God do you dishonor? the For name
τοῦ Θεοῦ δι᾽ ὑμᾶς βλασφημεῖται ἐν τοῖς ἔθνεσι, καθὼς
— of God through you is blasphemed among the nations; even as
25 γέγραπται. περιτομὴ μὲν γὰρ ὠφελεῖ, ἐὰν νόμον πράσσῃς·
it has been written. circumcision For profits, if law you practice;
ἐὰν δὲ παραβάτης νόμου ᾖς, ἡ περιτομή σου ἀκροβυστία
if but a transgressor of law you are, the circumcision of you uncircumcision
26 γέγονεν. ἐὰν οὖν ἡ ἀκροβυστία τὰ δικαιώματα τοῦ νόμου
becomes. If, then, the uncircumcision the ordinances of the law
φυλάσσῃ, οὐχὶ ἡ ἀκροβυστία αὐτοῦ εἰς περιτομὴν λογισθή-
keeps, (will) not the uncircumcision of him for circumcision be counted?
27 σεται; καὶ κρινεῖ ἡ ἐκ φύσεως ἀκροβυστία, τὸν νόμον
And will judge the by nature uncircumcision the law
τελοῦσα, σὲ τὸν διὰ γράμματος καὶ περιτομῆς παραβάτην
keeping you the through letter and circumcision transgressor
28 νόμου; οὐ γὰρ ὁ ἐν τῷ φανερῷ Ἰουδαῖός ἐστιν, οὐδὲ ἡ ἐν τῷ
of law? not For the (one) apparent a Jew is, nor (is) the
29 φανερῷ ἐν σαρκὶ περιτομή· ἀλλ᾽ ὁ ἐν τῷ κρυπτῷ Ἰουδαῖος,
apparent in flesh circumcision, but the (one) in private Jew (is),
καὶ περιτομὴ καρδίας ἐν πνεύματι, οὐ γράμματι· οὗ ὁ
and circumcision (is) of heart, in spirit, not in letter; of whom the
ἔπαινος οὐκ ἐξ ἀνθρώπων, ἀλλ᾽ ἐκ τοῦ Θεοῦ.
praise (is) not from men, but from — God.

CHAPTER 3

1 Τί οὖν τὸ περισσὸν τοῦ Ἰουδαίου, ἢ τίς ἡ ὠφέλεια τῆς
What, then, the superiority of the Jew, or what the profit —
2 περιτομῆς; πολὺ κατὰ πάντα τρόπον· πρῶτον μὲν γὰρ ὅτι
of circumcision? Much by every way. firstly, indeed, For, that
3 ἐπιστεύθησαν τὰ λόγια τοῦ Θεοῦ. τί γὰρ εἰ ἠπίστησάν
they were entrusted with the oracles of God. what For? If disbelieved
τινες· μὴ ἡ ἀπιστία αὐτῶν τὴν πίστιν τοῦ Θεοῦ καταργή-
some, Not the unbelief of them the faith of God destroy?
4 σει; μὴ γένοιτο· γινέσθω δὲ ὁ Θεὸς ἀληθής, πᾶς δὲ ἄνθρωπος
Not let it be! let be But God true, every and man
ψεύστης, καθὼς γέγραπται, Ὅπως ἂν δικαιωθῇς ἐν τοῖς
a liar, even as it has been written, So as you may be justified in the
5 λόγοις σου, καὶ νικήσῃς ἐν τῷ κρίνεσθαί σε. εἰ δὲ ἡ ἀδικία
sayings of you, and will overcome in the being judged you. if But the unrighteousness
ἡμῶν Θεοῦ δικαιοσύνην συνίστησι, τί ἐροῦμεν; μὴ ἄδικος
of us of God a righteousness commends, what shall we say? unrighteous
6 ὁ Θεὸς ὁ ἐπιφέρων τὴν ὀργήν (κατὰ ἄνθρωπον λέγω); μὴ
(Is) God inflicting — wrath? —according to man I say — not
7 γένοιτο· ἐπεὶ πῶς κρινεῖ ὁ Θεὸς τὸν κόσμον; εἰ γὰρ ἡ
let it be! Otherwise how will judge God the world? if For the
ἀλήθεια τοῦ Θεοῦ ἐν τῷ ἐμῷ ψεύσματι ἐπερίσσευσεν εἰς τὴν
truth of God by my lie abounded to the
8 δόξαν αὐτοῦ, τί ἔτι κἀγὼ ὡς ἁμαρτωλὸς κρίνομαι; καὶ μή
glory of Him, why yet I also as a sinner am judged? And not
(καθὼς βλασφημούμεθα, καὶ καθώς φασί τινες ἡμᾶς λέγειν
— as we are wrongly accused, and as report some us to say—
ὅτι), Ποιήσωμεν τὰ κακὰ ἵνα ἔλθῃ τὰ ἀγαθά; ὧν τὸ κρίμα
Let us do bad things that may come good things. Of whom judgment

[9]What, then? Do we excel?
Not at all! For we have before
charged both Jews and
Greeks all *with* being under
sin; [10]according as it has been
written, "There is none
righteous, no, not one!
[11]There is none that understands, there is not one that
seeks after God. [12]All turned
away; *they* became worthless
together; not *one* is doing
kindness, not so much as
one! [13]Their throat *is* an
opened grave; they used
deceit with their tongues; *the*
poison of asps *is* under their
lips; [14]whose mouth is full
of cursing and bitterness.
[15]Their feet *are* swift to shed
blood; [16]ruin and misery
are in their way; [17]and they
do not know a way of peace;
[18]there is no fear of God
before their eyes."
[19]Now we know that
whatever the law says, it
speaks to those within the
law, so that every mouth may
be stopped, and all the world
be under judgment to God.
[20]Because by works of law
no flesh will be justified before Him—for through law *is*
full knowledge of sin.
[21]But now a righteousness
of God has been revealed
apart from Law, being witnessed by the Law and the
Prophets, [22]even the
righteousness of God through
the faith of Jesus Christ
toward all and upon all those
believing; for there is no
difference, [23]for all sinned
and come short of the glory of
God, [24]being justified as a
free gift by His grace through
the redemption in Christ
Jesus; [25]whom God set
forth *as* a propitiation through
faith in His blood, for a showing forth of His righteousness
through the passing by of the
sins that had taken place
before, in the forbearance of
God— [26]for *the* showing
forth of His righteousness in
the present time, for His
being just and justifying him
that *is* of *the* faith of Jesus.
[27]Then where *is* the boasting? It was excluded. Through
what law? Of works? No, but

ἔνδικόν ἐστι.
just is.

9 Τί οὖν; προεχόμεθα; οὐ πάντως· προῃτιασάμεθα γὰρ
What, then? Do we excel? Not at all! we before charged For

10 Ἰουδαίους τε καὶ Ἕλληνας πάντας ὑφ' ἁμαρτίαν εἶναι, καθὼς
Jews both and Greeks all under sin to be, even as

11 γέγραπται ὅτι Οὐκ ἔστι δίκαιος οὐδὲ εἷς· οὐκ ἔστιν ὁ συνιῶν,
has been written, Not a righteous, not one; not is (one) understanding

12 οὐκ ἔστιν ὁ ἐκζητῶν τὸν Θεόν· πάντες ἐξέκλιναν, ἅμα ἠχρειώ-
not is (one) seeking — God; all turned away, together became

θησαν· οὐκ ἔστι ποιῶν χρηστότητα, οὐκ ἔστιν ἕως ἑνός·
worthless, not is (one) doing kindness, not is so much as one.

13 τάφος ἀνεῳγμένος ὁ λάρυγξ αὐτῶν, ταῖς γλώσσαις αὐτῶν
A grave opened (is) the throat of them, with the tongues of them

14 ἐδολιοῦσαν· ἰὸς ἀσπίδων ὑπὸ τὰ χείλη αὐτῶν· ὧν τὸ στόμα
they used deceit, poison of asps under the lips of them; of whom the mouth

15 ἀρᾶς καὶ πικρίας γέμει· ὀξεῖς οἱ πόδες αὐτῶν ἐκχέαι αἷμα·
of cursing and bitterness is full; swift the feet of them to shed blood;

16 σύντριμμα καὶ ταλαιπωρία ἐν ταῖς ὁδοῖς αὐτῶν, καὶ ὁδὸν
ruin and misery in the way of them: and a way

17 εἰρήνης οὐκ ἔγνωσαν· οὐκ ἔστι φόβος Θεοῦ ἀπέναντι τῶν
of peace not they knew. Not is fear of God before the

18 ὀφθαλμῶν αὐτῶν.
eyes of them.

19 Οἴδαμεν δὲ ὅτι ὅσα ὁ νόμος λέγει, τοῖς ἐν τῷ νόμῳ λαλεῖ,
we know But that what the law says to those in the law it speaks,

ἵνα πᾶν στόμα φραγῇ, καὶ ὑπόδικος γένηται πᾶς ὁ κόσμος
that every mouth be stopped, and under judgment may become all the world

20 τῷ Θεῷ· διότι ἐξ ἔργων νόμου οὐ δικαιωθήσεται πᾶσα σὰρξ
to God; because by works of law not will be justified all flesh

21 ἐνώπιον αὐτοῦ· διὰ γὰρ νόμου ἐπίγνωσις ἁμαρτίας. νυνὶ δὲ
before Him; through for law (is) full knowledge of sin. now But

22 χωρὶς νόμου δικαιοσύνη Θεοῦ πεφανέρωται, μαρτυρουμένη
without law a righteousness of God has been revealed being witnessed

ὑπὸ τοῦ νόμου καὶ τῶν προφητῶν· δικαιοσύνη δὲ Θεοῦ διὰ
by the Law and the Prophets, a righteousness and of God via

πίστεως Ἰησοῦ Χριστοῦ εἰς πάντας καὶ ἐπὶ πάντας τοὺς
faith of Jesus Christ to all and upon all those

23 πιστεύοντας· οὐ γάρ ἐστι διαστολή· πάντες γὰρ ἥμαρτον
believing; not for there is a difference; all for sinned

24 καὶ ὑστεροῦνται τῆς δόξης τοῦ Θεοῦ, δικαιούμενοι δωρεὰν
and come short of the glory — of God, being justified freely

τῇ αὐτοῦ χάριτι διὰ τῆς ἀπολυτρώσεως τῆς ἐν Χριστῷ
by the of Him grace through the redemption — in Christ

25 Ἰησοῦ· ὃν προέθετο ὁ Θεὸς ἱλαστήριον, διὰ τῆς πίστεως,
Jesus; whom set forth God a propitiation through — faith,

ἐν τῷ αὐτοῦ αἵματι, εἰς ἔνδειξιν τῆς δικαιοσύνης αὐτοῦ, διὰ
by the of Him blood, for a display of the righteousness of Him, through

τὴν πάρεσιν τῶν προγεγονότων ἁμαρτημάτων, ἐν τῇ ἀνοχῇ
the passing by of the that before had occurred sins, in the forbearance

26 τοῦ Θεοῦ· πρὸς ἔνδειξιν τῆς δικαιοσύνης αὐτοῦ ἐν τῷ νῦν
— of God for the display of the righteousness of Him in the present

καιρῷ, εἰς τὸ εἶναι αὐτὸν δίκαιον καὶ δικαιοῦντα τὸν ἐκ
time, for the being (of) Him just and justifying the (one) of

27 πίστεως Ἰησοῦ. ποῦ οὖν ἡ καύχησις; ἐξεκλείσθη. διὰ ποίου
faith of Jesus. Where, then, the boasting? It was excluded. Through what

through a law of faith. [28]Then we conclude a man to be justified without works of Law. [29]Or *is He* the God of Jews only, and not also of *the* nations? [30]Yes, also of nations, since *it is* one God who will justify circumcision by faith, and uncircumcision through faith. [31]Then do we make the Law of no effect through faith? Let it not be! But we establish Law.

CHAPTER 4

[1]What then shall we say our father Abraham to have found according to flesh? [2]For if Abraham was justified by works, he has a boast—but not with God. [3]For what says the Scripture? "And Abraham believed God, and it was counted to him for righteousness." [4]Now *to one* working, the reward is not counted according to grace, but according to debt. [5]But to the *one* not working, but believing on Him justifying the ungodly, his faith is counted for righteousness. [6]Even as also David says of the blessedness of the man to whom God counts righteousness apart from works: [7]"Blessed *are those* whose lawlessnesses are forgiven, and whose sins are covered; [8]blessed *the* man to whom *the* Lord will in no way charge sin."

[9]*Is* this blessedness then on the circumcision, or also on the uncircumcision? For we say the faith was counted to Abraham for righteousness. [10]How then was it counted? Being in circumcusion, or in uncircumcision? Not in circumcision, but in uncircumcision! [11]And he received a sign of circumcision *as* a seal of the righteousness of faith *while* in uncircumcision, for him to be a father of those believing through uncircumcision, for righteousness to be counted to them also; [12]and a father of circumcision to those not of circumcision only, but also to those walking by the steps of the uncircumcision faith of

28 νόμου ; τῶν ἔργων ; οὐχί, ἀλλὰ διὰ νόμου πίστεως. λογιζό-
law? Of works? No, but through a law of faith. we con-
μεθα οὖν πίστει δικαιοῦσθαι ἄνθρωπον, χωρὶς ἔργων νόμου.
clude Then by faith to be justified a man without works of law.
29 ἢ Ἰουδαίων ὁ Θεὸς μόνον ; οὐχὶ δὲ καὶ ἐθνῶν ; ναὶ καὶ
Or of Jews (is He) the God only, not and also of nations? Yes, also
30 ἐθνῶν· ἐπείπερ εἷς ὁ Θεός, ὃς δικαιώσει περιτομὴν ἐκ πί-
of nations, since (it is) one God who will justify circumcision by
31 στεως, καὶ ἀκροβυστίαν διὰ τῆς πίστεως. νόμον οὖν καταρ-
faith, and uncircumcision through the faith. law Then do we
γοῦμεν διὰ τῆς πίστεως ; μὴ γένοιτο· ἀλλὰ νόμον ἱστῶμεν.
destroy though the faith? Not let it be! But law we establish.

CHAPTER 4

1 Τί οὖν ἐροῦμεν Ἀβραὰμ τὸν πατέρα ἡμῶν εὑρηκέναι κατὰ
What then shall we say Abraham the father of us to have found according
2 σάρκα ; εἰ γὰρ Ἀβραὰμ ἐξ ἔργων ἐδικαιώθη, ἔχει καύχημα,
to flesh? if For Abraham by works was justified, he has a boast;
3 ἀλλ' οὐ πρὸς τὸν Θεόν. τί γὰρ ἡ γραφὴ λέγει ; Ἐπίστευσε
but not with — God. what For the Scripture says? believed
δὲ Ἀβραὰμ τῷ Θεῷ, καὶ ἐλογίσθη αὐτῷ εἰς δικαιοσύνην. τῷ
And Abraham God, and it was counted to him for righteousness. to the
4 δὲ ἐργαζομένῳ ὁ μισθὸς οὐ λογίζεται κατὰ χάριν, ἀλλὰ
Now (one) working the reward not is counted according to grace, but
5 κατὰ τὸ ὀφείλημα. τῷ δὲ μὴ ἐργαζομένῳ, πιστεύοντι δὲ ἐπὶ
according to debt. to the But not working (one), believing but on
τὸν δικαιοῦντα τὸν ἀσεβῆ, λογίζεται ἡ πίστις αὐτοῦ εἰς
the (One) justifying the ungodly, is counted the faith of him for
6 δικαιοσύνην. καθάπερ καὶ Δαβὶδ λέγει τὸν μακαρισμὸν τοῦ
righteousness, even as also David says of the blessedness of the
ἀνθρώπου, ᾧ ὁ Θεὸς λογίζεται δικαιοσύνην χωρὶς ἔργων,
man to whom God counts righteousness without works,
7 Μακάριοι ὧν ἀφέθησαν αἱ ἀνομίαι, καὶ ὧν ἐπεκαλύφθησαν
Blessed of whom are forgiven the lawlessnesses, and of whom are covered
8 αἱ ἁμαρτίαι. μακάριος ἀνὴρ ᾧ οὐ μὴ λογίσηται Κύριος
the sins; Blessed (the) man to whom in no way will charge (the) Lord
9 ἁμαρτίαν. ὁ μακαρισμὸς οὖν οὗτος ἐπὶ τὴν περιτομήν, ἢ καὶ
sin. (Is) blessedness then this on the circumcision, or also
ἐπὶ τὴν ἀκροβυστίαν ; λέγομεν γὰρ ὅτι Ἐλογίσθη τῷ
on the uncircumcision? we say For, — was counted
10 Ἀβραὰμ ἡ πίστις εἰς δικαιοσύνην. πῶς οὖν ἐλογίσθη ; ἐν
to Abraham The faith for righteousness. How, then, was it counted? In
περιτομῇ ὄντι, ἢ ἐν ἀκροβυστίᾳ ; οὐκ ἐν περιτομῇ, ἀλλ' ἐν
circumcision being, or in uncircumcision? Not in circumcision, but in
11 ἀκροβυστίᾳ· καὶ σημεῖον ἔλαβε περιτομῆς, σφραγῖδα τῆς
uncircumcision; and a sign he received of circumcision, a seal of the
δικαιοσύνης τῆς πίστεως τῆς ἐν τῇ ἀκροβυστίᾳ εἰς τὸ
righteousness of the faith (while) in — uncircumcision, for the
εἶναι αὐτὸν πατέρα πάντων τῶν πιστευόντων δι' ἀκροβυ-
being (of) him a father of all the believing ones through uncir-
στίας, εἰς τὸ λογισθῆναι καὶ αὐτοῖς τὴν δικαιοσύνην· καὶ
cumcision, for to be counted also to them — righteousness, and
12 πατέρα περιτομῆς τοῖς οὐκ ἐκ περιτομῆς μόνον, ἀλλὰ καὶ
a father of circumcision to those not of circumcision only, but also
τοῖς στοιχοῦσι τοῖς ἴχνεσι τῆς ἐν τῇ ἀκροβυστίᾳ πίστεως
to those walking in the steps of the in — uncircumcision faith

our father Abraham.

[13]For the promise *was* not through law to Abraham, or to his seed, *for* him to be the heir of the world, but through a righteousness of faith. [14]For if the heirs *are* of Law, faith has been made of no effect, and the promise has been destroyed. [15]For the Law works out wrath; for where no law is, neither *is* transgression. [16]On account of this, *it is* of faith, that *it be* according to grace, for the promise to be made sure to all the seed—not to that of the Law only, but also to that of *the* faith of Abraham, who is father of us all—[17]according as it has been written, "I have made you a father of many nations;"—before God, whom he believed, who gives life to the dead, and calling the things that are not as being. [18]*He* against hope believed in hope, for him to become father of many nations, according to what has been said, "So shall your seed be."

[19]And he did not consider his body to have died, not weakening in faith—being about a hundred years *old; nor* yet the death of Sarah's womb — [20]but did not stagger by unbelief at the promise of God, but was empowered by faith, giving glory to God, [21]and being fully persuaded that what He has promised, He is also able to do. [22]Therefore, it was also counted to him for righteousness. [23]But it was not written for him only, that it was counted to him, [24]but also on account of us, to whom it is about to be counted, to the ones believing on Him who has raised our Lord Jesus from *the* dead; [25]who was delivered for our offenses, and was raised for our justification.

13 τοῦ πατρὸς ἡμῶν Ἀβραάμ. οὐ γὰρ διὰ νόμου ἡ ἐπαγγελία
of the father of us, Abraham. not For through law the promise
τῷ Ἀβραὰμ η τῷ σπέρματι αὐτοῦ, τὸ κληρονόμον αὐτὸν
to Abraham, or to the seed of him, the heir him
14 εἶναι τοῦ κόσμου, ἀλλὰ διὰ δικαιοσύνης πίστεως. εἰ γὰρ οἱ
to be of the world, but through a righteousness of faith. if For the
ἐκ νόμου κληρονόμοι, κεκένωται ἡ πίστις, καὶ κατήργηται ἡ
of law (are) heirs, has been voided faith, and been destroyed **the**
15 ἐπαγγελία· ὁ γὰρ νόμος ὀργὴν κατεργάζεται· οὐ γὰρ οὐκ
promise. the For law wrath works out, where for not
16 ἔστι νόμος, οὐδὲ παράβασις. διὰ τοῦτο ἐκ πίστεως, ἵνα κατὰ
is law, neither (is) transgression. Therefore (it is) of faith, that according
χάριν, εἰς τὸ εἶναι βεβαίαν τὴν ἐπαγγελίαν παντὶ τῷ
grace, for the being made sure the promise to all the
σπέρματι, οὐ τῷ ἐκ τοῦ νόμου μόνον, ἀλλὰ καὶ τῷ ἐκ
seed, not to the (seed) of the law only, but also to (that) of
πίστεως Ἀβραάμ, ὅς ἐστι πατὴρ πάντων ἡμῶν (καθὼς
(the) faith of Abraham who is father of all us — even as
17 γέγραπται ὅτι Πατέρα πολλῶν ἐθνῶν τέθεικά σε) κατέναντι
it has been written, A father of many nations I have appointed you — before
οὗ ἐπίστευσε Θεοῦ, τοῦ ζωοποιοῦντος τοὺς νεκρούς, καὶ
whom he believed God, the (one) making live the dead, and
18 καλοῦντος τὰ μὴ ὄντα ὡς ὄντα. ὃς παρ' ἐλπίδα ἐπ' ἐλπίδι
calling the things not being as being; who beyond hope on hope
ἐπίστευσεν, εἰς τὸ γενέσθαι αὐτὸν πατέρα πολλῶν ἐθνῶν,
believed, for the becoming (of) him a father of many nations,
19 κατὰ τὸ εἰρημένον, Οὕτως ἔσται τὸ σπέρμα σου. καὶ μὴ
according to what was said, So shall be the seed of you. And not
ἀσθενήσας τῇ πίστει, οὐ κατενόησε τὸ ἑαυτοῦ σῶμα ἤδη
weakening — in faith, not he considered the of himself body already
νενεκρωμένον (ἑκατονταέτης που ὑπάρχων), καὶ τὴν νέ-
to have died, a hundred years about being, and the
20 κρωσιν τῆς μήτρας Σάρρας· εἰς δὲ τὴν ἐπαγγελίαν τοῦ Θεοῦ
death of the womb of Sarah; at but the promise of God
οὐ διεκρίθη τῇ ἀπιστίᾳ, ἀλλ' ἐνεδυναμώθη τῇ πίστει, δοὺς
not hesitated — by unbelief, but was empowered — by faith, giving
21 δόξαν τῷ Θεῷ, καὶ πληροφορηθεὶς ὅτι ὃ ἐπήγγελται,
glory — to God, and being fully persuaded that what He has promised
22 δυνατός ἐστι καὶ ποιῆσαι. διὸ καὶ ἐλογίσθη αὐτῷ εἰς δικαιο-
able He is also to do. Therefore also it was counted to him for right-
23 σύνην. οὐκ ἐγράφη δὲ δι' αὐτὸν μόνον, ὅτι ἐλογίσθη αὐτῷ·
eousness. not it was written But for him only that it was counted to him
24 ἀλλὰ καὶ δι' ἡμᾶς, οἷς μέλλει λογίζεσθαι, τοῖς πιστεύουσιν
but also for us, to whom it is going to be counted, to those believing
25 ἐπὶ τὸν ἐγείραντα Ἰησοῦν τὸν Κύριον ἡμῶν ἐκ νεκρῶν, ὃς
on the (One) having raised Jesus the Lord of us out of (the) dead, who
παρεδόθη διὰ τὰ παραπτώματα ἡμῶν, καὶ ἠγέρθη διὰ τὴν
was delivered for the offenses of us, and was raised for the
δικαίωσιν ἡμῶν.
justification of us.

CHAPTER 5

1 Δικαιωθέντες οὖν ἐκ πίστεως, εἰρήνην ἔχομεν πρὸς τὸν
having been justified Then by faith, peace we have with —
2 Θεὸν διὰ τοῦ Κυρίου ἡμῶν Ἰησοῦ Χριστοῦ, δι' οὗ καὶ τὴν
God through the Lord of us, Jesus Christ, through whom also the

CHAPTER 5

[1]Then being justified by faith, we have peace with God through our Lord Jesus Christ; [2]through whom also

we have had access by faith into this grace in which we stand, and *we* glory on the hope of the glory of God. [3]And not only so, but we also glory in afflictions, knowing that affliction works out patience, [4]and patience *works out* proven character, and proven character, hope. [5]And the hope does not put *us* to shame, because the love of God has been poured out in our hearts through *the* Holy Spirit given to us; [6]for we yet being without strength, in due time Christ died for the ungodly. [7]For one will with difficulty die for a just one—for perhaps one even dares to die for the sake of the good one—[8]but God commends His love to us in that we yet being sinners, Christ died for us. [9]Much more, then, being justified now by His blood, we shall be saved from wrath through Him. [10]For if being enemies, we were reconciled to God through the death of His Son, much more being reconciled we shall be saved by His life. [11]And not only *so*, but also glorying in God through our Lord Jesus Christ, through whom we now received the reconciliation.

[12]Because of this, even as sin entered the world through one man, and death through sin, so also death passed to all men, inasmuch as all sinned; [13]for sin was in *the* world until Law, but sin is not charged *where* there is no law; [14]but death reigned from Adam until Moses, even on those who had not sinned in the likeness of Adam's transgression, who is a type of the coming *One*. [15]But the free gift *shall* not *be* also like the offense. for if by the offense of the one the many died, much more the grace of God, and

προσαγωγὴν ἐσχήκαμεν τῇ πίστει εἰς τὴν χάριν ταύτην ἐν
access we have had — by faith into — grace this in
ᾗ ἑστήκαμεν, καὶ καυχώμεθα ἐπ' ἐλπίδι τῆς δόξης τοῦ Θεοῦ.
which we stand, and boast on the hope of the glory — of God.
3 οὐ μόνον δέ, ἀλλὰ καὶ καυχώμεθα ἐν ταῖς θλίψεσιν, εἰδότες
not only And (so), but also we boast in — troubles, knowing
4 ὅτι ἡ θλίψις ὑπομονὴν κατεργάζεται, ἡ δὲ ὑπομονὴ δοκιμήν,
that trouble patience works out, and patience proof,
5 ἡ δὲ δοκιμὴ ἐλπίδα· ἡ δὲ ἐλπὶς οὐ καταισχύνει, ὅτι ἡ ἀγάπη
and proof hope, and hope not does put to shame, for the love
τοῦ Θεοῦ ἐκκέχυται ἐν ταῖς καρδίαις ἡμῶν διὰ Πνεύματος
of God has been poured out in the hearts of us through (the) Spirit
6 Ἁγίου τοῦ δοθέντος ἡμῖν. ἔτι γὰρ Χριστός, ὄντων ἡμῶν
Holy — given to us. yet For Christ — being us
7 ἀσθενῶν, κατὰ καιρὸν ὑπὲρ ἀσεβῶν ἀπέθανε. μόλις γὰρ ὑπὲρ
weak — according to time for ungodly ones died. hardly For for
δικαίου τις ἀποθανεῖται· ὑπὲρ γὰρ τοῦ ἀγαθοῦ τάχα τις
a just one anyone will die; on behalf of for the good one perhaps one
8 καὶ τολμᾷ ἀποθανεῖν. συνίστησι δὲ τὴν ἑαυτοῦ ἀγάπην εἰς
even dares to die; commends but the of Himself love to
ἡμᾶς ὁ Θεός, ὅτι ἔτι ἁμαρτωλῶν ὄντων ἡμῶν Χριστος ὑπὲρ
us God, that yet sinners being us, Christ for
9 ἡμῶν ἀπέθανε. πολλῷ οὖν μᾶλλον, δικαιωθέντες νῦν ἐν τῷ
us died. much Then more having been justified now by the
10 αἵματι αὐτοῦ, σωθησόμεθα δι' αὐτοῦ ἀπὸ τῆς ὀργῆς. εἰ
blood of Him, we shall be saved through Him from the wrath. if
γὰρ ἐχθροὶ ὄντες κατηλλάγημεν τῷ Θεῷ διὰ τοῦ θανάτου
For enemies being we were reconciled — to God through the death
τοῦ υἱοῦ αὐτοῦ, πολλῷ μᾶλλον καταλλαγέντες σωθησό-
of the Son of Him, by much more having been reconciled we shall be
11 μεθα ἐν τῇ ζωῇ αὐτοῦ· οὐ μόνον δέ, ἀλλὰ καὶ καυχώμενοι ἐν
saved by the life of Him; not only (so) And, but also boasting in
τῷ Θεῷ διὰ τοῦ Κυρίου ἡμῶν Ἰησοῦ Χριστοῦ, δι' οὗ νῦν τὴν
— God through the Lord of us, Jesus Christ, through whom now the
καταλλαγὴν ἐλάβομεν.
reconciliation we received.
12 Διὰ τοῦτο, ὥσπερ δι' ἑνὸς ἀνθρώπου ἡ ἁμαρτία εἰς τὸν
Therefore as through one man sin into the
κόσμον εἰσῆλθε, καὶ διὰ τῆς ἁμαρτίας ὁ θάνατος, καὶ οὕτως
world entered, and through sin death, also so
13 εἰς πάντας ἀνθρώπους ὁ θάνατος διῆλθεν, ἐφ' ᾧ πάντες
to all men death passed, inasmuch as all
ἥμαρτον· ἄχρι γὰρ νόμου ἁμαρτία ἦν ἐν κόσμῳ· ἁμαρτία
sinned —until for law sin was in (the) world, sin
14 δὲ οὐκ ἐλλογεῖται, μὴ ὄντος νόμου. ἀλλ' ἐβασίλευσεν ὁ
but not is charged there not being law; but reigned
θάνατος ἀπὸ Ἀδὰμ μέχρι Μωσέως καὶ ἐπὶ τοὺς μὴ ἁμαρτή-
death from Adam until Moses even over those not sinning
σαντας ἐπὶ τῷ ὁμοιώματι τῆς παραβάσεως Ἀδάμ, ὅς ἐστι
on the likeness of the transgression of Adam, who is
15 τύπος τοῦ μέλλοντος. ἀλλ' οὐχ ὡς τὸ παράπτωμα, οὕτω
a type of the (One) coming. But not as the offense, so
καὶ τὸ χάρισμα. εἰ γὰρ τῷ τοῦ ἑνὸς παραπτώματι οἱ
also the free gift; if for by the of the one offense the
πολλοὶ ἀπέθανον, πολλῷ μᾶλλον ἡ χάρις του Θεοῦ καὶ ἡ
many died, much more the grace — of God and the

the gift in grace, which *is* of
the one Man, Jesus Christ, did
abound to the many. 16 And
the gift *shall* not *be* as by one
having sinned; for indeed the
judgment *was* of one to
condemnation; but the free
gift *is* of many offenses to
justification. 17 For if by the
offense of the one death
reigned by the one, much
more those who are receiving
the abundance of grace and
the gift of righteousness shall
rule in life by the One, Jesus
Christ. 18 So, then, as through
one offense *it was* toward all
men to condemnation, so
also by one accomplished
righteousness toward all men
to justification of life. 19 For
as through the one man's
disobedience the many were
constituted sinners, so also
by the obedience of the One
the many shall be constituted
righteous. 20 But Law came
in beside, that the offense
might abound. But where sin
abounded, grace much more
abounded, 21 that as sin
ruled in death, so also grace
might rule through righteousness
to everlasting life,
through Jesus Christ our Lord.

δωρεὰ ἐν χάριτι τῇ τοῦ ἑνὸς ἀνθρώπου Ἰησοῦ Χριστοῦ εἰς
gift in grace — of the one Man, Jesus Christ, to
16 τοὺς πολλοὺς ἐπερίσσευσε. καὶ οὐχ ὡς δι' ἑνὸς ἁμαρτή-
the many abounded. And not as through one sinning
σαντος, τὸ δώρημα· τὸ μὲν γὰρ κρίμα ἐξ ἑνὸς εἰς κατάκριμα,
of life, (be) the gift; the indeed for judgment of one to condemnation,
17 τὸ δὲ χάρισμα ἐκ πολλῶν παραπτωμάτων εἰς δικαίωμα. εἰ
the But free gift (is) of many offenses to justification. if
γὰρ τῷ τοῦ ἑνὸς παραπτώματι ὁ θάνατος ἐβασίλευσε διὰ
For by the of the one offense death reigned through
τοῦ ἑνός, πολλῷ μᾶλλον οἱ τὴν περισσείαν τῆς χάριτος καὶ
the one, much more those the abundance of the grace and
τῆς δωρεᾶς τῆς δικαιοσύνης λαμβάνοντες ἐν ζωῇ βασιλεύ-
of the gift of righteousness receiving in life will
18 σουσι διὰ τοῦ ἑνὸς Ἰησοῦ Χριστοῦ. ἄρα οὖν ὡς δι' ἑνὸς
reign through the One, Jesus Christ. So then, as through one
παραπτώματος εἰς πάντας ἀνθρώπους εἰς κατάκριμα, οὕτω
offense to all men to condemnation, so
καὶ δι' ἑνὸς δικαιώματος εἰς πάντας ἀνθρώπους εἰς δικαίωσιν
also through one righteous act to all men to justification
19 ζωῆς. ὥσπερ γὰρ διὰ τῆς παρακοῆς τοῦ ἑνὸς ἀνθρώπου
of life. as For through the disobedience of the one man
ἁμαρτωλοὶ κατεστάθησαν οἱ πολλοί, οὕτω καὶ διὰ τῆς
sinners were constituted the many, so also through the
ὑπακοῆς τοῦ ἑνὸς δίκαιοι κατασταθήσονται οἱ πολλοί.
obedience of the One righteous will be constituted the many.
20 νόμος δὲ παρεισῆλθεν, ἵνα πλεονάσῃ τὸ παράπτωμα· οὗ
Law But came in beside, that might abound the offense; where
δὲ ἐπλεόνασεν ἡ ἁμαρτία, ὑπερεπερίσσευσεν ἡ χάρις· ἵνα
but abounded the sin, more abounded grace, that
21 ὥσπερ ἐβασίλευσεν ἡ ἁμαρτία ἐν τῷ θανάτῳ, οὕτω καὶ ἡ
as reigned sin in death, so also
χάρις βασιλεύσῃ διὰ δικαιοσύνης εἰς ζωὴν αἰώνιον, διὰ
grace might reign through righteousness to life everlasting through
Ἰησοῦ Χριστοῦ τοῦ Κυρίου ἡμῶν.
Jesus Christ the Lord of us.

CHAPTER 6

CHAPTER 6

1 What then shall we say?
Shall we continue in sin that
grace may abound? 2 Let it
not be! We who died to sin,
how shall we still live in it?
3 Or are you ignorant that all
who were baptized into
Christ Jesus were baptized
into His death? 4 Therefore,
we were buried with Him
through baptism into death,
that as Christ was raised up
from *the* dead by the glory of
the Father, so also we should
walk in newness of life. 5 For
if we have been joined
together in the likeness of
His death, so also shall we be

1 Τί οὖν ἐροῦμεν; ἐπιμενοῦμεν τῇ ἁμαρτίᾳ, ἵνα ἡ χάρις
What, then, shall we say? Shall we continue in sin, that grace
2 πλεονάσῃ; μὴ γένοιτο. οἵτινες ἀπεθάνομεν τῇ ἁμαρτίᾳ,
may abound? Not let it be! who We died to sin,
3 πῶς ἔτι ζήσομεν ἐν αὐτῇ; ἢ ἀγνοεῖτε ὅτι ὅσοι ἐβαπτίσθημεν
how still shall we live in it? Or are you ignorant that all who were baptized
εἰς Χριστὸν Ἰησοῦν, εἰς τὸν θάνατον αὐτοῦ ἐβαπτίσθημεν;
into Christ Jesus, into the death of Him were baptized?
4 συνετάφημεν οὖν αὐτῷ διὰ τοῦ βαπτίσματος εἰς τὸν
we were buried with Then Him through — baptism into
θάνατον· ἵνα ὥσπερ ἠγέρθη Χριστὸς ἐκ νεκρῶν διὰ τῆς
death, that as was raised Christ from (the) dead through the
δόξης τοῦ πατρός, οὕτω καὶ ἡμεῖς ἐν καινότητι ζωῆς περι-
glory of the Father, so also we in newness of life might
5 πατήσωμεν. εἰ γὰρ σύμφυτοι γεγόναμεν τῷ ὁμοιώματι τοῦ
walk. if For united with we have become in the likeness of the
θανάτου αὐτοῦ, ἀλλὰ καὶ τῆς ἀναστάσεως ἐσόμεθα· τοῦτο
death of Him, but also of the resurrection we shall be. this

in the resurrection; 6 knowing this, that our old man was crucified with *Him*, that the body of sin might be annulled, so that we no longer serve sin. 7 For the *one* that died has been justified from sin. 8 But if we died with Christ, we believe that we also shall live with Him, 9 knowing that Christ being raised from *the* dead dies no more; death no longer lords it over Him. 10 For in that He died, He died to sin once for all; but in that He lives, He lives to God. 11 So also you count yourselves to be truly dead to sin, but alive to God, in Christ Jesus our Lord.

12 Therefore, do not let sin rule in your mortal body, to obey it in its lusts. 13 Do not yield your members *as* instruments of unrighteousness to sin; but yield yourselves to God as living from *the* dead, and your members instruments of righteousness to God. 14 For your sin shall not lord it over you, for you are not under law, but under grace.

15 What then? Shall we sin because we are not under law, but under grace? Let it not be! 16 Do you not know that to whom you yield yourselves for obedience, you are slaves to whom you obey, whether of sin to death, or obedience to righteousness? 17 But thanks to God that you were slaves of sin, but you obeyed from *the* heart the form of teaching to which you were delivered. 18 And having been set free from sin, you were enslaved to righteousness. 19 I speak as a man on account of the weakness of your flesh. For as you yielded your members *as* slaves to uncleanness and to lawless act unto lawless act, so now yield your members *as* slaves to righteousness unto sanctification. 20 For when you were slaves of sin, you were free as to righteousness. 21 Therefore, what fruit did you

6 γινώσκοντες, ὅτι ὁ παλαιὸς ἡμῶν ἄνθρωπος συνεσταυρώθη,
Knowing, that the old of us man was crucified with,
ἵνα καταργηθῇ τὸ σῶμα τῆς ἁμαρτίας, τοῦ μηκέτι δουλεύειν
that might be annulled the body of sin, no longer to serve
7 ἡμᾶς τῇ ἁμαρτίᾳ· ὁ γὰρ ἀποθανὼν δεδικαίωται ἀπὸ τῆς
us sin; the (one) for having died has been justified from
8 ἁμαρτίας. εἰ δὲ ἀπεθάνομεν σὺν Χριστῷ, πιστεύομεν ὅτι καὶ
sin. if But we died with Christ, we believe that also
9 συζήσομεν αὐτῷ· εἰδότες ὅτι Χριστὸς ἐγερθεὶς ἐκ νεκρῶν
we shall live with Him, knowing that Christ having been raised from dead
10 οὐκέτι ἀποθνήσκει· θάνατος αὐτοῦ οὐκέτι κυριεύει. ὃ γὰρ
no more dies; death Him no more lords it over. that For
ἀπέθανε, τῇ ἁμαρτίᾳ ἀπέθανεν ἐφάπαξ· ὃ δὲ ζῇ, ζῇ τῷ Θεῷ.
He died, to sin He died once for all in that but he lives, he lives to God,
11 οὕτω καὶ ὑμεῖς λογίζεσθε ἑαυτοὺς νεκροὺς μὲν εἶναι τῇ
So also you count yourselves dead indeed to be —
ἁμαρτίᾳ, ζῶντας δὲ τῷ Θεῷ ἐν Χριστῷ Ἰησοῦ τῷ Κυρίῳ
to sin, living but to God in Christ Jesus the Lord
ἡμῶν.
of us.

12 Μὴ οὖν βασιλευέτω ἡ ἁμαρτία ἐν τῷ θνητῷ ὑμῶν σώματι,
Do not, therefore, let reign sin in the mortal of you body,
13 εἰς τὸ ὑπακούειν αὐτῇ ἐν ταῖς ἐπιθυμίαις αὐτοῦ· μηδὲ παρι-
to obey it in the lusts of it, neither
στάνετε τὰ μέλη ὑμῶν ὅπλα ἀδικίας τῇ ἁμαρτίᾳ· ἀλλὰ
yield the members of you weapons of unrighteousness to sin, but
παραστήσατε ἑαυτοὺς τῷ Θεῷ ὡς ἐκ νεκρῶν ζῶντας, καὶ τὰ
yield yourselves to God as from (the) dead living, and the
14 μέλη ὑμῶν ὅπλα δικαιοσύνης τῷ Θεῷ. ἁμαρτία γὰρ ὑμῶν οὐ
members of you weapons of righteousness to God; sin for of you not
κυριεύσει· οὐ γάρ ἐστε ὑπὸ νόμον, ἀλλ' ὑπὸ χάριν.
shall lord it over. not for you are under law, but under grace.
15 Τί οὖν; ἁμαρτήσομεν, ὅτι οὐκ ἐσμὲν ὑπὸ νόμον, ἀλλ' ὑπὸ
What then? Shall we sin because not we are under law, but under
16 χάριν; μὴ γένοιτο. οὐκ οἴδατε ὅτι ᾧ παριστάνετε ἑαυτοὺς
grace? Not let it be! not Know you that to whom you yield yourselves
δούλους εἰς ὑπακοήν, δοῦλοί ἐστε ᾧ ὑπακούετε, ἤτοι ἁμαρ-
slaves for obedience, slaves you are whom you obey, whether of
17 τίας εἰς θάνατον, ἢ ὑπακοῆς εἰς δικαιοσύνην; χάρις δὲ τῷ
sin unto death, or obedience unto righteousness? thanks But
Θεῷ, ὅτι ἦτε δοῦλοι τῆς ἁμαρτίας, ὑπηκούσατε δὲ ἐκ καρδίας
to God that you were slaves of sin, you obeyed and from the heart
18 εἰς ὃν παρεδόθητε τύπον διδαχῆς· ἐλευθερωθέντες δὲ ἀπὸ
to which you were delivered a form of teaching; having been freed And from
19 τῆς ἁμαρτίας, ἐδουλώθητε τῇ δικαιοσύνῃ. ἀνθρώπινον λέγω
sin, you were enslaved to righteousness. As a man I speak
διὰ τὴν ἀσθένειαν τῆς σαρκὸς ὑμῶν· ὥσπερ γὰρ παρεστή-
because of the weakness of the flesh of you. as For you yielded
σατε τὰ μέλη ὑμῶν δοῦλα τῇ ἀκαθαρσίᾳ καὶ τῇ ἀνομίᾳ εἰς
the members of you slaves — to uncleanness and to iniquity unto
τὴν ἀνομίαν, οὕτω νῦν παραστήσατε τὰ μέλη ὑμῶν δοῦλα
iniquity, so now yield the members of you slaves
20 τῇ δικαιοσύνῃ εἰς ἁγιασμόν. ὅτε γὰρ δοῦλοι ἦτε τῆς
to righteousness unto sanctification. when For slaves you were
21 ἁμαρτίας, ἐλεύθεροι ἦτε τῇ δικαιοσύνῃ. τίνα οὖν καρπὸν
of sin, free you were to righteousness. what Therefore fruit

have then in the *things* over which you now are ashamed? For the end of those things *is* death. [22]But now being set free from sin, and being enslaved to God, you have your fruit unto sanctification, and the end everlasting life. [23]For the wages of sin *is* death; but the free gift of God *is* everlasting life in Christ Jesus our Lord.

CHAPTER 7

[1]Or are you ignorant, brothers—for I speak to those knowing law—that the law rules over the man for as long a time as he may live? [2]For the married woman was bound by law to the living husband; but if the husband dies, she is set free from the law of the husband. [3]So, then, *if* the husband *is* living, she will be called an adulteress if she becomes another man's. But if the husband dies, she is free from the law, *so as for* her not to be an adulteress *by* becoming another man's *wife*. [4]So that, my brothers, you also were made dead to the law through the body of Christ, *for* you to become Another's, to *One* raised from *the* dead, so that we may bear fruit to God. [5]For when we were in the flesh, the passions of sin worked in our members through the law for the bearing of fruit unto death. [6]But now we have been set free from the law, having died *to that* in which we were held, so that we serve in newness of spirit, and not *in* oldness of letter.

[7]What, then, shall we say? *Is* the law sin? Let it not be! But I did not know sin except through law; for also I did not know lust except the law said, You shall not lust. [8]But sin taking occasion through the commandment worked every lust in me; for apart from law, sin was dead. [9]And I was

εἴχετε τότε ἐφ' οἷς νῦν ἐπαισχύνεσθε; τὸ γὰρ τέλος ἐκείνων
had you then? Over which now you are ashamed; the for end of those
22 θάνατος. νυνὶ δὲ ἐλευθερωθέντες ἀπὸ τῆς ἁμαρτίας, δουλω-
(is) death. now But having been freed from sin, having been
θέντες δὲ τῷ Θεῷ, ἔχετε τὸν καρπὸν ὑμῶν εἰς ἁγιασμόν, τὸ
enslaved and to God, you have the fruit of you to sanctification, the
23 δὲ τέλος ζωὴν αἰώνιον. τὰ γὰρ ὀψώνια τῆς ἁμαρτίας
and end life everlasting. the For wages of sin
θάνατος, τὸ δὲ χάρισμα τοῦ Θεοῦ ζωὴ αἰώνιος ἐν Χριστῷ
(is) death, the and gift of God life everlasting in Christ
Ἰησοῦ τῷ Κυρίῳ ἡμῶν.
Jesus the Lord of us.

CHAPTER 7

1 Ἢ ἀγνοεῖτε, ἀδελφοί (γινώσκουσι γὰρ νόμον λαλῶ),
Or are you ignorant, brothers — to those knowing for law I speak —
ὅτι ὁ νόμος κυριεύει τοῦ ἀνθρώπου ἐφ' ὅσον χρόνον ζῇ; ἡ
that the law lords it over the man over such time (as) He lives. the
2 γὰρ ὕπανδρος γυνὴ τῷ ζῶντι ἀνδρὶ δέδεται νόμῳ· ἐὰν δὲ
For married woman to the living husband was bound by law; if but
ἀποθάνῃ ὁ ἀνήρ, κατήργηται ἀπὸ τοῦ νόμου τοῦ ἀνδρός.
dies the husband, she is freed from the law of the husband.
3 ἄρα οὖν ζῶντος τοῦ ἀνδρὸς μοιχαλὶς χρηματίσει, ἐὰν
Therefore living the husband, an adulteress she will be called, if
γένηται ἀνδρὶ ἑτέρῳ· ἐὰν δὲ ἀποθάνῃ ὁ ἀνήρ, ἐλευθέρα
she becomes man to another. if But dies the husband, free
ἐστὶν ἀπὸ τοῦ νόμου, τοῦ μὴ εἶναι αὐτὴν μοιχαλίδα, γενομέ-
she is from the law, not being her an adulteress becoming
4 νην ἀνδρὶ ἑτέρῳ. ὥστε, ἀδελφοί μου, καὶ ὑμεῖς ἐθανατώθητε
(wife) man to another. So, brothers of me, also you were made dead
τῷ νόμῳ διὰ τοῦ σώματος τοῦ Χριστοῦ, εἰς τὸ γενέσθαι
to the law through the body — of Christ, to become
ὑμᾶς ἑτέρῳ, τῷ ἐκ νεκρῶν ἐγερθέντι, ἵνα καρποφορήσωμεν
you to Another, to (One) from dead raised, that we may bear fruit
5 τῷ Θεῷ. ὅτε γὰρ ἦμεν ἐν τῇ σαρκί, τὰ παθήματα τῶν
to God. when For we were in the flesh, the passions
ἁμαρτιῶν τὰ διὰ τοῦ νόμου ἐνηργεῖτο ἐν τοῖς μέλεσιν
of sin through the law working in the members
6 ἡμῶν εἰς τὸ καρποφορῆσαι τῷ θανάτῳ. νυνὶ δὲ κατηργήθη-
of us for the bearing of fruit to death. now But we were freed
μεν ἀπὸ τοῦ νόμου, ἀποθανόντος ἐν ᾧ κατειχόμεθα, ὥστε
from the law, having died (to that) in which we were held, so as
δουλεύειν ἡμᾶς ἐν καινότητι πνεύματος, καὶ οὐ παλαιότητι
to serve us in newness of spirit and not (in) oldness
γράμματος.
of letter.

7 Τί οὖν ἐροῦμεν; ὁ νόμος ἁμαρτία; μὴ γένοιτο· ἀλλὰ τὴν
What then shall we say? (is) the law sin? Not let it be! But
ἁμαρτίαν οὐκ ἔγνων, εἰ μὴ διὰ νόμου· τήν τε γὰρ ἐπιθυμίαν
sin not I knew, except through law also For lust
8 οὐκ ᾔδειν, εἰ μὴ ὁ νόμος ἔλεγεν, Οὐκ ἐπιθυμήσεις· ἀφορμὴν
not I knew, except the law said, not You shall lust. occasion
δὲ λαβοῦσα ἡ ἁμαρτία διὰ τῆς ἐντολῆς κατειργάσατο ἐν
But taking sin through the commandment worked in
ἐμοὶ πᾶσαν ἐπιθυμίαν· χωρὶς γὰρ νόμου ἁμαρτία νεκρά.
me every lust; without for law sin (is) dead.

alive apart from law once, but the commandment came, and sin came alive, and I died. [10]And the commandment which *was* to life, this was found *to be* death to me; [11]for sin taking occasion through the commandment deceived me, and through it killed *me*.

[12]So indeed the law *is* holy, and the commandment holy and just and good. [13]Then that which *is* good, has it become death to me? Let it not be! But sin, that it might appear *to be* sin, having worked out death through the good to me, in order that sin might become excessively sinful through the commandment. [14]For we know that the law is spiritual, and I am fleshly, having been sold under sin. [15]For what I work out, I do not know. For what I do not will, this I do. But what I hate, this I do. [16]But if I do what I do not will, I agree with the law, that *it is* good. [17]But now I no longer work it out, but the sin dwelling in me. [18]For I know that in me, that is in my flesh, dwells no good. For to will is present to me, but to work out the good I do not find. [19]For what good I desire, I do not. But the evil I do not desire, this I do. [20]But if I do what I do not desire, *it is* no longer I working it out, but sin dwelling in me. [21]I find then the law, *when* I desire to do the right, that evil is present with me. [22]For I delight in the law of God according to the inward man; [23]but I see another law in my members warring against the law of my mind, and taking me captive by the law of sin being in my members. [24]O wretched man *that* I *am*! Who shall deliver me from the body of this death? [25]I thank God through Jesus Christ our Lord. So then I myself with the mind truly

9 ἐγὼ δὲ ἔζων χωρὶς νόμου ποτέ· ἐλθούσης δὲ τῆς ἐντολῆς,
I And was living without law then, coming but the commandment,
10 ἡ ἁμαρτία ἀνέζησεν, ἐγὼ δὲ ἀπέθανον· καὶ εὑρέθη μοι ἡ
sin revived, I and died, and was found to me the
11 ἐντολὴ ἡ εἰς ζωήν, αὕτη εἰς θάνατον· ἡ γὰρ ἁμαρτία
command- ment for life, this to death (was). For sin
ἀφορμὴν λαβοῦσα διὰ τῆς ἐντολῆς ἐξηπάτησέ με, καὶ δι'
occasion taking through the commandment deceived me, and through
12 αὐτῆς ἀπέκτεινεν. ὥστε ὁ μὲν νόμος ἅγιος, καὶ ἡ ἐντολὴ
it killed (me). So the indeed law (is) holy, and the command- ment
13 ἁγία καὶ δικαία καὶ ἀγαθή. τὸ οὖν ἀγαθὸν ἐμοὶ γέγονε
holy and just and good. the Then good to me (has it) become
θάνατος; μὴ γένοιτο. ἀλλὰ ἡ ἁμαρτία, ἵνα φανῇ ἁμαρτία,
death? | Not let it be! But sin, that it appear sin,
διὰ τοῦ ἀγαθοῦ μοι κατεργαζομένη θάνατον,—ἵνα γένηται
through the good to me working out death, that may become
καθ' ὑπερβολὴν ἁμαρτωλὸς ἡ ἁμαρτία διὰ τῆς ἐντολῆς.
excessively sinful sin through the commandment.
14 οἴδαμεν γὰρ ὅτι ὁ νόμος πνευματικός ἐστιν· ἐγὼ δὲ σαρκικός
we know For that the law spiritual is; I but fleshly
15 εἰμι, πεπραμένος ὑπὸ τὴν ἁμαρτίαν. ὃ γὰρ κατεργάζομαι,
am, having been sold under sin. what For I work,
οὐ γινώσκω· οὐ γὰρ ὃ θέλω, τοῦτο πράσσω· ἀλλ' ὃ μισῶ,
not I know; not for what I desire, this I practice; but what I hate,
16 τοῦτο ποιῶ. εἰ δὲ ὃ οὐ θέλω, τοῦτο ποιῶ, σύμφημι τῷ
this I do. if But what not I desire, this I do, I agree with the
17 νόμῳ ὅτι καλός. νυνὶ δὲ οὐκέτι ἐγὼ κατεργάζομαι αὐτό,
law that (it is) good. now But no longer I work out it,
18 ἀλλ' ἡ οἰκοῦσα ἐν ἐμοὶ ἁμαρτία. οἶδα γὰρ ὅτι οὐκ οἰκεῖ ἐν
but the indwelling in me sin. I know For that not dwells in
ἐμοί, τοῦτ' ἔστιν ἐν τῇ σαρκί μου, ἀγαθόν· τὸ γὰρ θέλειν
me this is in the flesh of me — the good; for to desire
παράκειταί μοι, τὸ δὲ κατεργάζεσθαι τὸ καλὸν οὐχ εὑρίσκω.
is present to me, but to work out the good not I find.
19 οὐ γὰρ ὃ θέλω, ποιῶ ἀγαθόν· ἀλλ' ὃ οὐ θέλω κακόν, τοῦτο
not For what I desire I do good, but what not I desire, evil this
20 πράσσω. εἰ δὲ ὃ οὐ θέλω ἐγώ, τοῦτο ποιῶ, οὐκέτι ἐγὼ κατερ-
I practice. if But what not desire I, this I do, no longer I work
21 γάζομαι αὐτό, ἀλλ' ἡ οἰκοῦσα ἐν ἐμοὶ ἁμαρτία. εὑρίσκω ἄρα
out it, but the dwelling in me sin. I find, then,
τὸν νόμον τῷ θέλοντι ἐμοὶ ποιεῖν τὸ καλόν, ὅτι ἐμοὶ τὸ κακὸν
the law, the (one) desiring me to do the good, that to me the evil
22 παράκειται. συνήδομαι γὰρ τῷ νόμῳ τοῦ Θεοῦ κατὰ τὸν
is present. I delight For in the law of God according to the
23 ἔσω ἄνθρωπον· βλέπω δὲ ἕτερον νόμον ἐν τοῖς μέλεσί μου
inner man. I see But another law in the members of me
ἀντιστρατευόμενον τῷ νόμῳ τοῦ νοός μου, καὶ αἰχμαλωτί-
warring against the law of the mind of me, and taking captive
ζοντά με τῷ νόμῳ τῆς ἁμαρτίας τῷ ὄντι ἐν τοῖς μέλεσί μου.
me by the law of sin, the (one) being in the members of me.
24 ταλαίπωρος ἐγὼ ἄνθρωπος· τίς με ῥύσεται ἐκ τοῦ σώματος
Wretched I man! Who me will deliver from the body
25 τοῦ θανάτου τούτου; εὐχαριστῶ τῷ Θεῷ διὰ Ἰησοῦ Χρι-
death of this? I thank God through Jesus Christ
στοῦ τοῦ Κυρίου ἡμῶν. ἄρα οὖν αὐτὸς ἐγὼ τῷ μὲν νοῒ δουλεύω
the Lord of us. So then myself, I with the mind serve

serve *the* law of God, and the flesh *the* law of sin.

CHAPTER 8

[1] *There is* now no condemnation to those in Christ Jesus, who do not walk according to flesh, but according to Spirit. [2] For the law of the Spirit of life in Christ Jesus set me free from the law of sin and of death. [3] For the law *being* powerless, in that it was weak through the flesh, God sending His own Son in *the* likeness of sinful flesh, and concerning sin, condemned sin in the flesh. [4] So that the righteous demand of the law might be fulfilled in us, those not walking according to flesh, but according to Spirit. [5] For the ones that are according to flesh mind the things of the flesh. And they according to Spirit *mind* the things of the Spirit. [6] For the mind of the flesh *is* death; but the mind of the Spirit *is* life and peace; [7] because the mind of the flesh *is* enmity towards God; for it is not subject to the law of God, for neither can *it be*. [8] And those being in the flesh are not able to please God. [9] But you are not in flesh, but in Spirit, since *the* Spirit of God dwells in you. But if anyone has not *the* Spirit of Christ, this one is not His. [10] But if Christ *is* in you, the body indeed is dead because of sin, but the Spirit *is* life because of righteousness. [11] But if the Spirit of the *One* having raised Jesus from *the* dead dwells in you, the *One* having raised the Christ from *the* dead will also make your mortal bodies live through the indwelling of His Spirit in you.

[12] So, then, brothers, we are debtors, not to the flesh, to live according to flesh; [13] for if you live according to flesh, you are going to die. But if by *the* Spirit you put to death the practices of the body, you will live. [14] For as many as are led by *the* Spirit of God, these are sons of God.

νόμῳ Θεοῦ, τῇ δὲ σαρκὶ νόμῳ ἁμαρτίας.
(the) law of God, the and flesh (the) law of sin.

CHAPTER 8

1 Οὐδὲν ἄρα νῦν κατάκριμα τοῖς ἐν Χριστῷ Ἰησοῦ, μὴ κατὰ
no Therefore now condemnation to those in Christ Jesus, not according to
2 σάρκα περιπατοῦσιν, ἀλλὰ κατὰ πνεῦμα. ὁ γὰρ νόμος του
flesh walking, but according to Spirit. the For law of the
πνεύματος τῆς ζωῆς ἐν Χριστῷ Ἰησοῦ ἠλευθέρωσέ με ἀπὸ
Spirit of life in Christ Jesus set free me from
3 τοῦ νόμου τῆς ἁμαρτίας καὶ τοῦ θανάτου. τὸ γὰρ ἀδύνατον
the law of sin and of death. the For powerless
τοῦ νόμου, ἐν ᾧ ἠσθένει διὰ τῆς σαρκός, ὁ Θεὸς τὸν ἑαυτοῦ
law, in which it was weak via the flesh, God the of Himself
υἱὸν πέμψας ἐν ὁμοιώματι σαρκὸς ἁμαρτίας καὶ περὶ ἁμαρ-
Son sending in likeness of flesh of sin, and concerning sin
4 τίας κατέκρινε τὴν ἁμαρτίαν ἐν τῇ σαρκί· ἵνα τὸ δικαίωμα
condemned sin in the flesh, that demand
τοῦ νόμου πληρωθῇ ἐν ἡμῖν. τοῖς μὴ κατὰ σάρκα περιπατοῦ-
of the law may be fulfilled in us, those not by flesh walking,
5 σιν, ἀλλὰ κατὰ πνεῦμα. οἱ γὰρ κατὰ σάρκα ὄντες τὰ τῆς
but according to Spirit. those For according to flesh being the things
σαρκὸς φρονοῦσιν· οἱ δὲ κατὰ πνεῦμα τὰ τοῦ πνεύματος. τὸ
of flesh mind; those but by Spirit the things of the Spirit. the
6 γὰρ φρόνημα τῆς σαρκὸς θάνατος· τὸ δὲ φρόνημα τοῦ πνεύ-
For mind of the flesh (is) death; the but mind of the Spirit
7 ματος ζωὴ καὶ εἰρήνη· διότι τὸ φρόνημα τῆς σαρκὸς ἔχθρα
(is) life and peace. Therefore the mind of the flesh (is) enmity
εἰς Θεόν, τῷ γὰρ νόμῳ τοῦ Θεοῦ οὐχ ὑποτάσσεται, οὐδὲ
against God, to the for law of God not it is subject, neither
8 γὰρ δύναται· οἱ δὲ ἐν σαρκὶ ὄντες Θεῷ ἀρέσαι οὐ δύνανται.
for can (be); those and in flesh being God to please not are able
9 ὑμεῖς δὲ οὐκ ἐστὲ ἐν σαρκί, ἀλλ' ἐν πνεύματι. εἴπερ Πνεῦμα
you But not are in flesh, but in Spirit, since (the) Spirit
Θεοῦ οἰκεῖ ἐν ὑμῖν. εἰ δέ τις Πνεῦμα Χριστοῦ οὐκ ἔχει, οὗτος
of God dwells in you. if But anyone (the) Spirit of Christ not has, this one
10 οὐκ ἔστιν αὐτοῦ. εἰ δὲ Χριστὸς ἐν ὑμῖν, τὸ μὲν σῶμα νεκρὸν
not is of Him. if But Christ (is) in you, the indeed body (is) dead
11 δι' ἁμαρτίαν, τὸ δὲ πνεῦμα ζωὴ διὰ δικαιοσύνην. εἰ δὲ τὸ
because of sin, the but Spirit (is) life because of righteousness. if But the
Πνεῦμα τοῦ ἐγείραντος Ἰησοῦν ἐκ νεκρῶν οἰκεῖ ἐν ὑμῖν, ὁ
Spirit of the (One) having raised Jesus from (the) dead dwells in you, the (One)
ἐγείρας τὸν Χριστὸν ἐκ νεκρῶν ζωοποιήσει καὶ τὰ θνητὰ
having raised the Christ from (the) dead will make live also the mortal
σώματα ὑμῶν, διὰ τοῦ ἐνοικοῦντος αὐτοῦ Πνεύματος ἐν
bodies of you, through the indwelling of Him Spirit in
ὑμῖν.
you.

12 Ἄρα οὖν, ἀδελφοί, ὀφειλέται ἐσμέν, οὐ τῇ σαρκί, τοῦ κατὰ
So then, brothers, debtors we are, not to the flesh — according to
13 σάρκα ζῆν· εἰ γὰρ κατὰ σάρκα ζῆτε, μέλλετε ἀποθνήσκειν·
flesh to live. if For according to flesh you live, you are going to die;
εἰ δὲ πνεύματι τὰς πράξεις τοῦ σώματος θανατοῦτε, ζήσεσθε.
if but by (the) Spirit the practices of the body you put to death, you will live.
14 ὅσοι γὰρ Πνεύματι Θεοῦ ἄγονται, οὗτοί εἰσιν υἱοὶ Θεοῦ.
as many as For by Spirit of God are led, these are sons of God.

[15]For you did not receive a spirit of slavery again to fear, but you received a Spirit of adoption by which we cry, Abba! Father! [16]The Spirit Himself witnesses with our spirit that we are children of God. [17]And if children, also heirs; truly heirs of God, and joint-heirs of Christ; if indeed we suffer together, that we may also be glorified together.

[18]For I calculate that the sufferings of the present time *are* not worthy *to compare* to the coming glory to be revealed in us. [19]For the earnest expectation of the creation eagerly awaits the revelation of the sons of God. [20]For the creation was not willingly subjected to vanity, but through Him subjecting *it*, on hope; [21]that also the creation will be freed from the slavery of corruption to the freedom of the glory of the children of God. [22]For we know that all the creation groans together and travails together until now. [23]And not only *so*, but even we ourselves also groan within ourselves having eagerly expected adoption, the redemption of our body; [24]for we were saved by hope; but hope being seen is not hope; for what anyone sees, why does he also hope? [25]But if we hope for what we do not see, through patience we wait eagerly.

[26]And likewise the Spirit also joins in to help our weaknesses. For we do not know what we should pray *for* as we ought, but the Spirit Himself pleads our case for us with groanings that cannot be uttered. [27]But the *One* searching the hearts knows what *is the* mind of the Spirit, because He intercedes for the saints according to God. [28]But we know that all things work together for good to those who love God, to those who are called according to purpose; [29]because whom He foreknew, He also predestinated *to be* conformed to the image of His Son, for Him to

15 οὐ γὰρ ἐλάβετε πνεῦμα δουλείας πάλιν εἰς φόβον, ἀλλ'
not For you received a spirit of slavery again to fear, but
ἐλάβετε πνεῦμα υἱοθεσίας, ἐν ᾧ κράζομεν, Ἀββᾶ, ὁ πατήρ.
you received a Spirit of adoption, by which we cry. Abba, Father!
16 αὐτὸ τὸ Πνεῦμα συμμαρτυρεῖ τῷ πνεύματι ἡμῶν, ὅτι ἐσμὲν
itself The Spirit bears witness with the spirit of us, that we are
17 τέκνα Θεοῦ· εἰ δὲ τέκνα, καὶ κληρονόμοι· κληρονόμοι μὲν
children of God. if And children, also heirs; heirs truly
Θεοῦ, συγκληρονόμοι δὲ Χριστοῦ· εἴπερ συμπάσχομεν, ἵνα
of God, joint-heirs and of Christ; if indeed we suffer together, that
καὶ συνδοξασθῶμεν.
also we may be glorified together.
18 Λογίζομαι γὰρ ὅτι οὐκ ἄξια τὰ παθήματα τοῦ νῦν καιροῦ
I calculate For that not worthy the sufferings of the present time
19 πρὸς τὴν μέλλουσαν δόξαν ἀποκαλυφθῆναι εἰς ἡμᾶς. ἡ γὰρ
to the coming glory to be revealed in us. the For
ἀποκαραδοκία τῆς κτίσεως τὴν ἀποκάλυψιν τῶν υἱῶν τοῦ
earnest expectation of the creation the revelation of the sons
20 Θεοῦ ἀπεκδέχεται. τῇ γὰρ ματαιότητι ἡ κτίσις ὑπετάγη,
of God is eagerly expecting. For to vanity the creation was subjected,
21 οὐχ ἑκοῦσα, ἀλλὰ διὰ τὸν ὑποτάξαντα, ἐπ' ἐλπίδι· ὅτι καὶ
not willingly, but through Him subjecting, on hope, that also
αὐτὴ ἡ κτίσις ἐλευθερωθήσεται ἀπὸ τῆς δουλείας τῆς
itself the creation will be freed from the slavery —
φθορᾶς εἰς τὴν ἐλευθερίαν τῆς δόξης τῶν τέκνων τοῦ Θεοῦ.
of corruption to the freedom of the glory of the children — of God.
22 οἴδαμεν γὰρ ὅτι πᾶσα ἡ κτίσις συστενάζει καὶ συνωδίνει
we know For that all the creation groans together and travails
23 ἄχρι τοῦ νῦν. οὐ μόνον δέ, ἀλλὰ καὶ αὐτοὶ τὴν ἀπαρχὴν
until now. not only And (so) but also ourselves the firstfruit
τοῦ Πνεύματος ἔχοντες, καὶ ἡμεῖς αὐτοὶ ἐν ἑαυτοῖς στενά-
of the Spirit having, also we ourselves in ourselves groan,
ζομεν, υἱοθεσίαν ἀπεκδεχόμενοι, τὴν ἀπολύτρωσιν τοῦ
adoption eagerly expecting, the redemption of the
24 σώματος ἡμῶν. τῇ γὰρ ἐλπίδι ἐσώθημεν· ἐλπὶς δὲ βλεπομένη
body of us. For by hope we were saved, hope but being seen
25 οὐκ ἔστιν ἐλπίς· ὃ γὰρ βλέπει τις, τί καὶ ἐλπίζει; εἰ δὲ ὃ οὐ
not is hope; what for sees anyone, why also he hopes? if But what not
βλέπομεν ἐλπίζομεν, δι' ὑπομονῆς ἀπεκδεχόμεθα.
we see we hope (for). through patience we eagerly expect.
26 Ὡσαύτως δὲ καὶ τὸ Πνεῦμα συναντιλαμβάνεται ταῖς
likewise And also the Spirit joins in to help the
ἀσθενείαις ἡμῶν· τὸ γὰρ τί προσευξώμεθα καθὸ δεῖ, οὐκ
weaknesses of us, — for what we may pray (for) as we ought, not
οἴδαμεν, ἀλλ' αὐτὸ τὸ πνεῦμα ὑπερεντυγχάνει ὑπὲρ ἡμῶν
we know, but itself the Spirit pleads our case for us
27 στεναγμοῖς ἀλαλήτοις· ὁ δὲ ἐρευνῶν τὰς καρδίας οἶδε τί τὸ
with groanings unutterable. He But searching the hearts knows what (is)
φρόνημα τοῦ Πνεύματος, ὅτι κατὰ Θεὸν ἐντυγχάνει ὑπὲρ
(the) mind of the Spirit, because according to God He intercedes for
28 ἁγίων. οἴδαμεν δὲ ὅτι τοῖς ἀγαπῶσι τὸν Θεὸν πάντα
saints. we know And that to the (ones) loving God, all things
29 συνεργεῖ εἰς ἀγαθόν, τοῖς κατὰ πρόθεσιν κλητοῖς οὖσιν. ὅτι
work together for good, to those according to purpose called being. Because
οὓς προέγνω, καὶ προώρισε συμμόρφους τῆς εἰκόνος τοῦ υἱοῦ
whom He foreknew also He predestinated conformed to the image of the Son

be *the* firstborn among many brothers. [30]But whom He predestinated, these He also called; and whom He called, these He also justified; but whom He justified, these He also glorified.

[31]What then shall we say to these things? If God *be* for us, who against us? [32]Truly *He* who did not spare His own Son, but gave Him up for us all, how will He not freely give us all things with Him? [33]Who will bring any charge against the God's elect? God *is* the *One* justifying! [34]Who *is he* condemning? *It is* Christ who has died, but rather also *is* raised, who also is at *the* right *hand* of God; who also intercedes for us. [35]Who shall separate us from the love of Christ? *Shall* tribulation, or distress, or persecution, or famine, or nakedness, or danger, or sword? [36]Even as it has been written, "For Your sake we are killed all the day *long*; we are counted as sheep of slaughter." [37]But in all these things we more than conquer through Him who has loved us. [38]For I am persuaded that neither death, nor life, nor angels, nor rulers, nor powers, nor things present, nor things to come, [39]nor height, nor depth, nor any other creature will be able to separate us from the love of God in Christ Jesus, our Lord.

CHAPTER 9

[1]I tell *the* truth in Christ, I do not lie, my conscience bearing witness with me in *the* Holy Spirit, [2]that my grief is great, and *a* never-ceasing pain *is* in my heart, [3]for I myself was wishing to be a curse from Christ on behalf of my brothers, my kinsmen according to flesh; [4]who are Israelites; whose *are* the adoption and the glory, and the covenants, and the Law-giving, and the service, and the promises; [5]whose *are* the fathers; and of whom *is* the Christ according to flesh, He being God over all, blessed

αὐτοῦ, εἰς τὸ εἶναι αὐτὸν πρωτότοκον ἐν πολλοῖς ἀδελφοῖς·
of Him, for to be Him firstborn among many brothers;
30 οὓς δὲ προώρισε, τούτους καὶ ἐκάλεσε· καὶ οὓς ἐκάλεσε, τού-
whom but He predestinated, these also He called, and whom He called,
τους καὶ ἐδικαίωσεν· οὓς δὲ ἐδικαίωσε, τούτους καὶ ἐδόξασε.
these also He justified; whom but He justified, these also He glorified.
31 Τί οὖν ἐροῦμεν πρὸς ταῦτα; εἰ ὁ Θεὸς ὑπὲρ ἡμῶν, τίς
What then shall we say to these things? If God (be) for us, who
32 καθ' ἡμῶν; ὅς γε τοῦ ἰδίου υἱοῦ οὐκ ἐφείσατο, ἀλλ' ὑπὲρ
against us? (He) who truly the own Son not spared, but for
ἡμῶν πάντων παρέδωκεν αὐτόν, πῶς οὐχὶ καὶ σὺν αὐτῷ
us all gave up Him, how not also with Him
33 τὰ πάντα ἡμῖν χαρίσεται; τίς ἐγκαλέσει κατὰ ἐκλεκτῶν
all things to us will He freely give? Who will bring charge against the elect
34 Θεοῦ; Θεὸς ὁ δικαιῶν· τίς ὁ κατακρίνων; Χριστὸς ὁ ἀπο-
of God? God (is) the (One) justifying. Who condemning? Christ (is) He having
θανών, μᾶλλον δὲ καὶ ἐγερθείς, ὃς καὶ ἔστιν ἐν δεξιᾷ τοῦ Θεοῦ,
died, rather but also raised, who also is at (the) right (hand) of God,
35 ὃς καὶ ἐντυγχάνει ὑπὲρ ἡμῶν. τίς ἡμᾶς χωρίσει ἀπὸ τῆς
who also intercedes for us. Who us shall separate from the
ἀγάπης τοῦ Χριστοῦ; θλίψις, ἢ στενοχωρία, ἢ διωγμός, ἢ
love of Christ? (Shall) tribulation, or distress, or persecuting, or
36 λιμός, ἢ γυμνότης, ἢ κίνδυνος, ἢ μάχαιρα; καθὼς γέγραπται
famine, or nakedness, or danger, or sword? Even as it has been written,
ὅτι Ἕνεκά σου θανατούμεθα ὅλην τὴν ἡμέραν· ἐλογίσθημεν
— For the sake of You we are killed all the day; we are counted
37 ὡς πρόβατα σφαγῆς. ἀλλ' ἐν τούτοις πᾶσιν ὑπερνικῶμεν διὰ
as sheep of slaughter. But in these things all we overconquer through
38 τοῦ ἀγαπήσαντος ἡμᾶς. πέπεισμαι γαρ ὅτι οὔτε θάνατος
the (One) having loved us. I have been persuaded For that not death
οὔτε ζωὴ οὔτε ἄγγελοι οὔτε ἀρχαὶ οὔτε δυνάμεις οὔτε
nor life nor angels nor rulers nor powers nor
39 ἐνεστῶτα οὔτε μέλλοντα οὔτε ὕψωμα οὔτε βάθος οὔτε τις
things present nor things coming nor height nor depth nor any
κτίσις ἑτέρα δυνήσεται ἡμᾶς χωρίσαι ἀπὸ τῆς ἀγάπης τοῦ
creature other will be able us to separate from the love —
Θεοῦ τῆς ἐν Χριστῷ Ἰησοῦ τῷ Κυρίῳ ἡμῶν.
of God in Christ Jesus the Lord of us.

CHAPTER 9

1 Ἀλήθειαν λέγω ἐν Χριστῷ, οὐ ψεύδομαι, συμμαρτυρούσης
(the) truth I tell in Christ, not I lie, bearing witness with
2 μοι τῆς συνειδήσεώς μου ἐν Πνεύματι Ἁγίῳ, ὅτι λύπη μοι
me the conscience of me in (the) Spirit Holy, that grief to me
3 ἐστὶ μεγάλη, καὶ ἀδιάλειπτος ὀδύνη τῇ καρδίᾳ μου. ηὐχόμην
is great and never ceasing pain in the heart of me. was wishing
γὰρ αὐτὸς ἐγὼ ἀνάθεμα εἶναι ἀπὸ τοῦ Χριστοῦ ὑπὲρ τῶν
For myself I a curse to be from — Christ on behalf of the
4 ἀδελφῶν μου, τῶν συγγενῶν μου κατὰ σάρκα· οἵτινές εἰσιν
brothers of me, the kinsmen of me according to flesh; who are
Ἰσραηλῖται, ὧν ἡ υἱοθεσία καὶ ἡ δόξα καὶ αἱ διαθῆκαι καὶ ἡ
Israelites, of whom the adoption and the glory, and the covenants and the
5 νομοθεσία καὶ ἡ λατρεία καὶ αἱ ἐπαγγελίαι, ὧν οἱ πατέρες,
law-giving, and the service and the promises; of whom the fathers,
καὶ ἐξ ὧν ὁ Χριστὸς τὸ κατὰ σάρκα, ὁ ὢν ἐπὶ πάντων, Θεὸς
and from whom the Christ according to flesh, He being over all, God

forever. Amen. [6]Not, however, that God's word has failed. For not all those of Israel *are* Israel; [7]nor because they are Abraham's seed *are* all children, but "In Isaac a Seed shall be called to you." [8]That is: Not the children of flesh *are* children of God, but the children of the promise *are* counted for a seed. [9]For the word of promise is this, "According to this time I will come, and a son will be to Sarah." [10]And not only *so*, but also Rebecca conceiving of one, our father Isaac; [11]for *the children* not yet being born, nor having done any good or evil, that the purpose of God according to election might stand, not of works, but of the *One* calling, [12]it was said to her, "The greater shall serve the lesser;" [13]even as it has been written, "I loved Jacob, and I hated Esau."

[14]What then shall we say? *Is there* not unrighteousness with God? Let it not be! [15]For He said to Moses, "I will have mercy on whomever I have mercy, and I will pity whomever I will pity." [16]So, then, *it is* not of the *one* willing, nor of the *one* running, but of the *One* showing mercy, of God. [17]For the Scripture says to Pharaoh, "For this very thing I raised you up, so that I might show forth My power in you, and so that My name might be publicized in all the earth." [18]So, then, to whom He desires, He shows mercy. And whom He desires, He hardens. [19]You will then say to me, why does He yet find fault? For who has resisted His will? [20]Yes, rather, O man, who are you answering against God? Shall the thing formed say to the *One* forming *it*, Why did You make me like this? [21]Or does not the potter have authority over the clay, out of the one lump to make one vessel to honor, and one to dishonor? [22]But if God, desiring to show forth wrath, and to make His power known, endured in much long-suffering vessels of wrath having been fitted out

6 εὐλογητὸς εἰς τοὺς αἰῶνας. ἀμήν. οὐχ οἷον δὲ ὅτι ἐκπέπτωκεν
blessed to the ages. Amen. Not, however, that has failed
ὁ λόγος τοῦ Θεοῦ. οὐ γὰρ πάντες οἱ ἐξ Ἰσραήλ, οὗτοι
the word — of God. not For all those of Israel, these
7 Ἰσραήλ· οὐδ' ὅτι εἰσὶ σπέρμα Ἀβραάμ, πάντες τέκνα· ἀλλ'
(are of) Israel; nor because they are seed of Abraham (are they) all children, but
8 Ἐν Ἰσαὰκ κληθήσεταί σοι σπέρμα. τοῦτ' ἔστιν, οὐ τὰ
In Isaac will be called to you seed. This is, not the
τέκνα τῆς σαρκός, ταῦτα τέκνα τοῦ Θεοῦ· ἀλλὰ τὰ τέκνα τῆς
children of the flesh these children — of God, but the children of the
9 ἐπαγγελίας λογίζεται εἰς σπέρμα. ἐπαγγελίας γὰρ ὁ λόγος
promise (is) counted for a seed. of promise For the word
οὗτος, Κατὰ τὸν καιρὸν τοῦτον ἐλεύσομαι, καὶ ἔσται τῇ
this (is): According to time this I will come, and will be —
10 Σάρρᾳ υἱός. οὐ μόνον δέ, ἀλλὰ καὶ Ῥεβέκκα ἐξ ἑνὸς κοίτην
to Sarah a son. not only (so) And, but also Rebecca from one con-
11 ἔχουσα, Ἰσαὰκ τοῦ πατρὸς ἡμῶν—μήπω γὰρ γεννηθέντων,
ceiving, Isaac the father of us; not yet for being born,
μηδὲ πραξάντων τι ἀγαθὸν ἢ κακόν, ἵνα ἡ κατ' ἐκλογὴν τοῦ
nor practicing anything good or evil, that the according to election
Θεοῦ πρόθεσις μένῃ, οὐκ ἐξ ἔργων, ἀλλ' ἐκ τοῦ καλοῦντος,
of God purpose might stand, not of works, but of the (One) calling,
12 ἐρρήθη αὐτῇ ὅτι Ὁ μείζων δουλεύσει τῷ ἐλάσσονι. καθὼς
13 **it was said to her — The greater shall serve the lesser; even as**
γέγραπται, Τὸν Ἰακὼβ ἠγάπησα, τὸν δὲ Ἠσαῦ ἐμίσησα.
it has been written: Jacob I loved, — and Esau I hated.
14 Τί οὖν ἐροῦμεν; μὴ ἀδικία παρὰ τῷ Θεῷ; μὴ γένοιτο.
What then shall we say? Not unrightesousness with God? Not let it be!
15 τῷ γὰρ Μωσῇ λέγει, Ἐλεήσω ὃν ἂν ἐλεῶ, καὶ οἰκτειρήσω
— For to Moses He says: I will have mercy whomever I have mercy and I will pity
16 ὃν ἂν οἰκτείρω. ἄρα οὖν οὐ τοῦ θέλοντος, οὐδὲ τοῦ τρέ-
whomever I pity. So therefore not of the (one) willing, nor of the (one)
17 χοντος, ἀλλὰ τοῦ ἐλεοῦντος Θεοῦ. λέγει γὰρ ἡ γραφὴ τῷ
running, but of the (One) showing mercy, God says For the Scripture —
Φαραὼ ὅτι Εἰς αὐτὸ τοῦτο ἐξήγειρά σε, ὅπως ἐνδείξωμαι
to Pharaoh, — For this very thing I raised up you, so as I may show forth
ἐν σοὶ τὴν δύναμίν μου, καὶ ὅπως διαγγελῇ τὸ ὄνομά μου
in you the power of me, and so as might be publicized the name of Me
18 ἐν πάσῃ τῇ γῇ. ἄρα οὖν ὃν θέλει ἐλεεῖ· ὃν δὲ θέλει σκληρύνει.
in all the earth. So, then, to whom He wills He has mercy whom and He wills, He hardens.
19 Ἐρεῖς οὖν μοι, Τί ἔτι μέμφεται; τῷ γὰρ βουλήματι αὐτοῦ
You will say then to me, Why yet finds He fault? the For counsel of Him
20 τίς ἀνθέστηκε; μενοῦνγε, ὦ ἄνθρωπε, σὺ τίς εἶ ὁ ἀνταπο-
who resisted? Yes, rather, O man, you who are the (one)
κρινόμενος τῷ Θεῷ; μὴ ἐρεῖ τὸ πλάσμα τῷ πλάσαντι, Τί με
answering against God; not will say, that formed to the Former: Why me
21 ἐποίησας οὕτως; ἢ οὐκ ἔχει ἐξουσίαν ὁ κεραμεὺς τοῦ πηλοῦ,
made You this way? Or not has authority the potter of the clay,
ἐκ τοῦ αὐτοῦ φυράματος ποιῆσαι ὃ μὲν εἰς τιμὴν σκεῦος, ὃ
out of the same lump to make one to honor vessel,
22 δὲ εἰς ἀτιμίαν; εἰ δὲ θέλων ὁ Θεὸς ἐνδείξασθαι τὴν ὀργήν,
and one to dishonor? if But desiring God to show forth wrath,
καὶ γνωρίσαι τὸ δυνατὸν αὐτοῦ, ἤνεγκεν ἐν πολλῇ μα-
and to make known the power of Him, endured in much long-
κροθυμίᾳ σκεύη ὀργῆς κατηρτισμένα εἰς ἀπώλειαν· καὶ ἵνα
suffering vessels of wrath having been fitted for destruction; and that

for destruction; [23]and that He make known the riches of His glory on vessels of mercy which He before prepared for glory, [24]whom He also called, not only us, of Jews, but also out of nations. [25]As also He says in Hosea, "I will call those not a people, My people! And those not beloved, Beloved! [26]And it shall be, in the place where it was said to them, You are not My people—there they will be called, Sons of the living God." [27]But Isaiah cries on behalf of Israel, "If the number of the sons of Israel be as the sand of the sea, the remnant will be saved. [28]For *He is* bringing *the* matter to an end, and cutting short in righteousness, because *the* Lord will do a thing cut short on the earth." [29]And as Isaiah has said before, "Except *the* Lord of hosts left a seed to us, we would have become as Sodom, and we would have become as Gomorrah."

[30]What then shall we say? That *the* nations not following after righteousness have taken on righteousness, but a righteousness of faith; [31]but Israel following after a law of righteousness did not arrive at a law of righteousness? [32]Why? Because *it was* not of faith, but as of works of Law. For they stumbled at the Stone-of-stumbling, as it has been written, "Behold, I place in Zion a Stone-of-stumbling, and a Rock-of-offense; and everyone believing on Him will not be put to shame."

CHAPTER 10

[1]Brothers, truly my heart's pleasure and request to God on behalf of Israel is for *it* to be saved. [2]For I testify to them that they have zeal to God, but not according to knowledge. [3]For being ignorant of the righteousness of God, and seeking to establish their own righteousness, they did not submit to the righteousness of God. [4]For Christ is the end of law for righteousness

23 γνωρίσῃ τὸν πλοῦτον τῆς δόξης αὐτοῦ ἐπὶ σκεύη ἐλέους,
He make known the riches of the glory of Him on vessels of mercy,
24 ἃ προητοίμασεν εἰς δόξαν, οὓς καὶ ἐκάλεσεν ἡμᾶς οὐ μόνον
which He before prepared for glory, whom also He called, us not only
25 ἐξ Ἰουδαίων, ἀλλὰ καὶ ἐξ ἐθνῶν ; ὡς καὶ ἐν τῷ Ὡσηὲ λέγει,
of Jews, but also of nations. As also in Hosea He says:
Καλέσω τὸν οὐ λαόν μου λαόν μου· καὶ τὴν οὐκ ἠγαπη-
I will call the not people of Me a people of Me, and the not beloved
26 μένην ἠγαπημένην. καὶ ἔσται, ἐν τῷ τόπῳ οὗ ἐρρήθη αὐτοῖς,
ones, Beloved; and it shall be, in the place where it was said to them,
Οὐ λαός μου ὑμεῖς, ἐκεῖ κληθήσονται υἱοὶ Θεοῦ ζῶντος.
not a people of Me you, there they will be called sons God of a living.
27 Ἠσαΐας δὲ κράζει ὑπὲρ τοῦ Ἰσραήλ, Ἐὰν ᾖ ὁ ἀριθμὸς τῶν
Isaiah But cries on behalf of — Israel, If be the number of the
υἱῶν Ἰσραὴλ ὡς ἡ ἄμμος τῆς θαλάσσης, τὸ κατάλειμμα
sons of Israel as the sand of the sea, the remnant
28 σωθήσεται· λόγον γὰρ συντελῶν καὶ συντέμνων ἐν δικαιο-
will be saved; the matter for bringing to an end and cutting short in righteous-
σύνῃ· ὅτι λόγον συντετμημένον ποιήσει Κύριος ἐπὶ τῆς
ness, because a matter cut short will do (the) Lord on the
29 γῆς. καὶ καθὼς προείρηκεν Ἠσαΐας, Εἰ μὴ Κύριος Σαβαὼθ
earth. And as has said before, Isaiah: Except (the) Lord of hosts
ἐγκατέλιπεν ἡμῖν σπέρμα, ὡς Σόδομα ἂν ἐγενήθημεν, καὶ ὡς
left to us a seed, as Sodom we would have become, and as
Γόμορρα ἂν ὡμοιώθημεν.
Gomorrah we would have become.
30 Τί οὖν ἐροῦμεν ; ὅτι ἔθνη, τὰ μὴ διώκοντα δικαιοσύνην,
What then shall we say? That nations not following after righteousness
κατέλαβε δικαιοσύνην, δικαιοσύνην δὲ τὴν ἐκ πίστεως· Ἰσ-
have taken on righteousness, a righteousness but of faith;
31 ραὴλ δέ, διώκων νόμον δικαιοσύνης, εἰς νόμον δικαιοσύνης
Israel but following after a law of righteousness at a law of righteousness
32 οὐκ ἔφθασε. διατί ; ὅτι οὐκ ἐκ πίστεως, ἀλλ᾽ ὡς ἐξ ἔργων
not did arrive? Why? Because not of faith, but as of works
νόμου. προσέκοψαν γὰρ τῷ λίθῳ τοῦ προσκόμματος, καθὼς
of law. they stumbled For at the Stone of stumbling, even as
γέγραπται, Ἰδοὺ τίθημι ἐν Σιὼν λίθον προσκόμματος καὶ
it has been written: Behold, I place in Zion a Stone-of stumbling, and
πέτραν σκανδάλου· καὶ πᾶς ὁ πιστεύων ἐπ᾽ αὐτῷ οὐ καται-
a Rock-of-offense, and everyone believing on Him not will be
σχυνθήσεται.
put to shame.

CHAPTER 10

1 Ἀδελφοί, ἡ μὲν εὐδοκία τῆς ἐμῆς καρδίας καὶ ἡ δέησις ἡ
Brothers, the indeed pleasure of My heart and the request
2 πρὸς τὸν Θεὸν ὑπὲρ τοῦ Ἰσραήλ ἐστιν εἰς σωτηρίαν. μαρ-
to God on behalf of Israel is for to be saved. I
τυρῶ γὰρ αὐτοῖς ὅτι ζῆλον Θεοῦ ἔχουσιν, ἀλλ᾽ οὐ κατ᾽
testify For to them that zeal to God they have, but not according to
3 ἐπίγνωσιν. ἀγνοοῦντες γὰρ τὴν τοῦ Θεοῦ δικαιοσύνην, καὶ
knowledge. being ignorant For the — of God righteousness, and
τὴν ἰδίαν δικαιοσύνην ζητοῦντες στῆσαι, τῇ δικαιοσύνῃ τοῦ
the own righteousness seeking to establish, to the righteousness —
4 Θεοῦ οὐχ ὑπετάγησαν. τέλος γὰρ νόμου Χριστὸς εἰς δικαιο-
of God not they submitted. the end For of law Christ (is) for righteous-

to every one that believes. [5]For Moses writes *of* the righteousness *which is* of the law: "The man doing these things shall live by them." [6]But the righteousness of faith says this: "Do not say in your heart, Who will go up into Heaven?"—that is, to bring down Christ; or, [7]"Who will go down into the abyss?"—that is, to bring Christ up from *the* dead. [8]But what does it say? "The word is near you, in your mouth and in your heart" —that is, the word of faith which we proclaim. [9]Because if you confess *the* Lord Jesus with your mouth, and believe in your heart that God raised Him from *the* dead, you will be saved. [10]For with *the* heart *one* believes unto righteousness, and with *the* mouth *one* confesses unto salvation. [11]For the Scripture says, "Everyone believing on Him will not be put to shame." [12]For there is no difference both of Jew and of Greek, for the same Lord of all is rich toward all the ones calling on Him. [13]For everyone, whoever may call on the name of *the* Lord, will be saved. [14]How then may they call on *One* in whom they have not believed? And how may they believe *One* of whom they have not heard? And how may they hear without preaching? [15]And how may they preach if they are not sent? Even as it has been written, "How beautiful the feet of those preaching the gospel of peace, of those preaching the gospel of good things." [16]But not all obeyed the gospel, for Isaiah says, "Lord, who has believed our report?" [17]Then faith *is* of hearing, and hearing through God's word. [18]But I say, Did they not hear? Yes, rather, into all the earth their voice went out, and to the ends of the world their words. [19]But I say, Did not Israel know? First, Moses says, "I will provoke you to jealousy by a nation; by an unwise nation I will anger

5 σύνην παντὶ τῷ πιστεύοντι. Μωσῆς γὰρ γράφει τὴν δι-
ness to everyone believing. Moses For writes: The
καιοσύνην τὴν ἐκ τοῦ νόμου, ὅτι ὁ ποιήσας αὐτὰ ἄνθρωπος
righteousness of law, the doing of these things man
6 ζήσεται ἐν αὐτοῖς. ἡ δὲ ἐκ πίστεως δικαιοσύνη οὕτω λέγει,
shall live by them. the But of faith righteousness thus says:
Μὴ εἴπῃς ἐν τῇ καρδίᾳ σου, Τίς ἀναβήσεται εἰς τὸν οὐρανόν ;
not Say in the heart of you, Who will go up into Heaven?
7 (τοῦτ' ἔστι Χριστὸν καταγαγεῖν·) ἤ, Τίς καταβήσεται εἰς
– this is, Christ to bring down – or, Who will go down into
τὴν ἄβυσσον ; (τοῦτ' ἔστι Χριστὸν ἐκ νεκρῶν ἀναγαγεῖν.)
the abyss – this is, Christ from (the) dead to bring up –
8 ἀλλὰ τί λέγει ; Ἐγγύς σου τὸ ῥῆμά ἐστιν, ἐν τῷ στόματί
but what says it? near you The word is, in the mouth
σου καὶ ἐν τῇ καρδίᾳ σου· τοῦτ' ἔστι τὸ ῥῆμα τῆς πίστεως
of you and in the heart of you; this is the word of faith
9 ὃ κηρύσσομεν· ὅτι ἐὰν ὁμολογήσῃς ἐν τῷ στόματί σου
which we proclaim. Because if you confess with the mouth of you
Κύριον Ἰησοῦν, καὶ πιστεύσῃς ἐν τῇ καρδίᾳ σου ὅτι ὁ Θεὸς
(the) Lord Jesus, and believe in the heart of you that God
10 αὐτὸν ἤγειρεν ἐκ νεκρῶν, σωθήσῃ· καρδίᾳ γὰρ πιστεύεται
Him raised from (the) dead, you will be saved. with heart For (one) believes
11 εἰς δικαιοσύνην, στόματι δὲ ὁμολογεῖται εἰς σωτηρίαν. λέγει
to righteousness, with mouth and (one) confesses to salvation. says
γὰρ ἡ γραφή, Πᾶς ὁ πιστεύων ἐπ' αὐτῷ οὐ καταισχυνθή-
For the Scripture: Everyone believing on Him not will be put to
12 σεται. οὐ γάρ ἐστι διαστολὴ Ἰουδαίου τε καὶ Ἕλληνος· ὁ
shame. not For is difference of Jew both and of Greek, the
γὰρ αὐτὸς Κύριος πάντων, πλουτῶν εἰς πάντας τοὺς ἐπι-
for same Lord of all is rich to all those
13 καλουμένους αὐτόν. πᾶς γὰρ ὃς ἂν ἐπικαλέσηται τὸ ὄνομα
calling on Him. everyone For whoever calls on the name
14 Κυρίου σωθήσεται. πῶς οὖν ἐπικαλέσονται εἰς ὃν οὐκ ἐπί-
of (the) Lord will be saved. How then may they call on (One) in whom not
στευσαν ; πῶς δὲ πιστεύσουσιν οὗ οὐκ ἤκουσαν ; πῶς δὲ
they believed? how And may they believe of whom not they heard? how And
15 ἀκούσουσι χωρὶς κηρύσσοντος ; πῶς δὲ κηρύξουσιν ἐὰν μὴ
may they hear without preaching? how And may they preach if not
ἀποσταλῶσι ; καθὼς γέγραπται, Ὡς ὡραῖοι οἱ πόδες τῶν
they are sent? Even as it has been written: How beautiful the feet of those
εὐαγγελιζομένων εἰρήνην, τῶν εὐαγγελιζομένων τὰ ἀγαθά.
preaching the gospel of peace, of those preaching the gospel of good things.
16 Ἀλλ' οὐ πάντες ὑπήκουσαν τῷ εὐαγγελίῳ. Ἡσαΐας γὰρ
But not all obeyed the gospel. Isaiah For
17 λέγει, Κύριε, τίς ἐπίστευσε τῇ ἀκοῇ ἡμῶν ; ἄρα ἡ πίστις ἐξ
says, Lord, who has believed the report of us? Then faith (is) of
18 ἀκοῆς, ἡ δὲ ἀκοὴ διὰ ῥήματος Θεοῦ. ἀλλὰ λέγω, Μὴ οὐκ
hearing, the and hearing through a word of God. But I say, Did not
ἤκουσαν ; μενοῦνγε· εἰς πᾶσαν τὴν γῆν ἐξῆλθεν ὁ φθόγγος
they hear? Yes, rather, to all the earth went out the utterance
αὐτῶν, καὶ εἰς τὰ πέρατα τῆς οἰκουμένης τὰ ῥήματα αὐτῶν.
of them, and to the ends of the habitable world the words of them.
19 ἀλλὰ λέγω, Μὴ οὐκ ἔγνω Ἰσραήλ ; πρῶτος Μωσῆς λέγει,
But I say, Did not know Israel? First, Moses says,
Ἐγὼ παραζηλώσω ὑμᾶς ἐπ' οὐκ ἔθνει, ἐπὶ ἔθνει ἀσυνέτῳ
I will provoke to jealousy you by not a nation, by a nation unwise

you." [20]But Isaiah *is* very bold and says, "I was found by those not seeking Me; I became known to those not inquiring after Me." [21]But to Israel He says, "All the day I stretched out My hands to a disobeying and contradicting people."

CHAPTER 11

[1]I say, then, Did not God thrust away His people? Let it not be! For I am an Israelite, out of Abraham's seed, of *the* tribe of Benjamin. [2]God did not thrust away His people whom He foreknew. Or do you not know what the Scripture said to Elijah, how he pleaded with God against Israel, saying, [3]"Lord, they killed Your prophets, and they dug down Your altars; and only I am left, and they seek my soul." [4]But what does the Divine answer say, "I reserved to Myself seven thousand men who did not bow a knee to Baal." [5]So then, also in the present time a remnant according to election of grace has come into being. [6]But if by grace, no longer *is* it of works; else grace no longer becomes grace. But if of works, it is no longer grace; else work is no longer work. [7]What then? What Israel seeks, this he did not obtain, but the election obtained *it*, and the rest were hardened; [8]even as it has been written, "God gave to them a spirit of slumber, eyes not seeing and ears not hearing" until this day. [9]And David said, "Let their table become for a snare and a trap, and for a stumbling-block, and a recompense to them; [10]let their eyes be darkened, not to see, and their back always bowing."

[11]I say, then, Did not they stumble that they fall? Let it not be! But by their slipping away *came* salvation to the nations, to provoke them to

20 παροργιῶ ὑμᾶς. Ἠσαΐας δὲ ἀποτολμᾷ καὶ λέγει, Εὑρέθην
I will anger you. Isaiah But very bold and says, I was found
τοῖς ἐμὲ μὴ ζητοῦσιν, ἐμφανὴς ἐγενόμην τοῖς ἐμὲ μὴ ἐπερω-
by those Me not seeking, revealed I became to those Me not inquiring
21 τῶσι. πρὸς δὲ τὸν Ἰσραὴλ λέγει, Ὅλην τὴν ἡμέραν ἐξεπέ-
after. to But — Israel He says, All the day I stretched
τασα τὰς χεῖράς μου πρὸς λαὸν ἀπειθοῦντα καὶ ἀντιλέγοντα.
out the hands of Me to a people disobeying and contradicting.

1 Λέγω οὖν, Μὴ ἀπώσατο ὁ Θεὸς τὸν λαὸν αὐτοῦ; μὴ
I say, then, Did not put away God the people of Him? Not
γένοιτο. καὶ γὰρ ἐγὼ Ἰσραηλίτης εἰμί, ἐκ σπέρματος
let it be! even For I an Israelite am, out of (the) seed
2 Ἀβραάμ, φυλῆς Βενϊαμίν. οὐκ ἀπώσατο ὁ Θεὸς τὸν λαὸν
of Abraham, of tribe of Benjamin. not did thrust away God the people
αὐτοῦ ὃν προέγνω. ἢ οὐκ οἴδατε ἐν Ἠλίᾳ τί λέγει ἡ γραφή;
of Him whom He fore-knew. Or not you know in Elijah what says the Scripture,
3 ὡς ἐντυγχάνει τῷ Θεῷ κατὰ τοῦ Ἰσραήλ, λέγων, Κύριε,
how he pleads with God against — Israel, saying: Lord,
τοὺς προφήτας σου ἀπέκτειναν, καὶ τὰ θυσιαστήριά σου
the prophets of You they killed, and the altars of You
κατέσκαψαν· κἀγὼ ὑπελείφθην μόνος, καὶ ζητοῦσι τὴν
they dug down, and I am left alone, and they seek the
4 ψυχήν μου. ἀλλὰ τί λέγει αὐτῷ ὁ χρηματισμός; Κατέλιπον
soul of me. But what says to him the divine answer? I reserved
ἐμαυτῷ ἑπτακισχιλίους ἄνδρας, οἵτινες οὐκ ἔκαμψαν γόνυ
to Myself seven thousand men who not bowed (the) knee
5 τῇ Βάαλ. οὕτως οὖν καὶ ἐν τῷ νῦν καιρῷ λεῖμμα κατ'
to Baal. So, then, also in the present time a remnant according to
6 ἐκλογὴν χάριτος γέγονεν. εἰ δὲ χάριτι, οὐκέτι ἐξ ἔργων·
election of grace has become. if And by grace, no longer of works;
ἐπεὶ ἡ χάρις οὐκέτι γίνεται χάρις. εἰ δὲ ἐξ ἔργων, οὐκέτι ἐστὶ
else grace no longer becomes grace. if But of works, no longer is it
7 χάρις· ἐπεὶ τὸ ἔργον οὐκέτι ἐστὶν ἔργον. τί οὖν; ὃ ἐπιζητεῖ
grace, else work no longer is work. What then? What seeks for
Ἰσραήλ, τούτου οὐκ ἐπέτυχεν, ἡ δὲ ἐκλογὴ ἐπέτυχεν, οἱ δὲ
Israel, this not he obtained; the but election obtained (it), the and
8 λοιποὶ ἐπωρώθησαν· καθὼς γέγραπται. Ἔδωκεν αὐτοῖς ὁ
rest were hardened; as it has been written: gave to them
Θεὸς πνεῦμα κατανύξεως, ὀφθαλμοὺς τοῦ μὴ βλέπειν, καὶ
God a spirit of slumber, eyes not seeing, and
9 ὦτα τοῦ μὴ ἀκούειν, ἕως τῆς σήμερον ἡμέρας. καὶ Δαβὶδ
ears not hearing; until the present day. And David
λέγει, Γενηθήτω ἡ τράπεζα αὐτῶν εἰς παγίδα, καὶ εἰς θήραν,
says: Let become the table of them for a snare, and for a trap,
10 καὶ εἰς σκάνδαλον, καὶ εἰς ἀνταπόδομα αὐτοῖς· σκοτισθή-
and for a stumbling-block, and for a recompense to them; let be darkened
τωσαν οἱ ὀφθαλμοὶ αὐτῶν τοῦ μὴ βλέπειν καὶ τὸν νῶτον
the eyes of them not to see, and the back
11 αὐτῶν διὰ παντὸς σύγκαμψον. λέγω οὖν, μὴ ἔπταισαν ἵνα
of them always bowing. I say, then, Did not they stumble that
πέσωσι; μὴ γένοιτο· ἀλλὰ τῷ αὐτῶν παραπτώματι ἡ
they fall? Not let it be! But by the of them slipping away (came)
σωτηρία τοῖς ἔθνεσιν, εἰς τὸ παραζηλῶσαι αὐτούς. εἰ δὲ τὸ
salvation to the nations, to provoke to jealousy them. if But the

jealousy. 12 But if their slipping away *is the* riches of *the* world, and their default *the* riches of *the* nations, how much more their fullness? 13 For I speak to you, the nations, since I am an apostle of *the* nations; I glorify my ministry, 14 if somehow I may provoke to jealousy my flesh, and may save some of them. 15 For if their casting away *is the* reconciliation of *the* world, what the reception, except life from *the* dead? 16 Now if the firstfruit *is* holy, also the lump. And if the root, also the branches. 17 But if some of the branches were broken off, and you being a wild olive were grafted in among them, and became a sharer of the root and the fatness of the olive-tree, 18 do not boast against the branches. But if you do boast, *it is* not you *that* bears the root, but the root bears you. 19 You will then say, The branches were broken off that I might be grafted in. 20 Well! For unbelief they were broken off. And you stand by faith. Do not *be* highminded, but fear. 21 For if God did not spare the natural branches, lest perhaps He will not spare you either. 22 Behold, then, *the* kindness and severity of God. On those having fallen, severity. But on you, kindness—if you continue in the kindness. Otherwise, you will also be cut off. 23 And those also, if they do not continue in unbelief, will be grafted in. For God is able to again graft them in. 24 For if you were cut out of the natural wild olive tree, and were against nature grafted into a good olive tree—how much more these *being* according to nature will be grafted into *their* own olive tree.

25 For I do not want you to be ignorant of this mystery, brothers—so that you may not be wise within yourselves—that hardness *in* part has happened to Israel, until the fullness of the nations comes in; 26 and so all Israel will be saved, even as it has been

12 παράπτωμα αὐτῶν πλοῦτος κόσμου, καὶ τὸ ἥττημα αὐτῶν
slipping away of them (is the) riches of (the) world, and the default of them
πλοῦτος ἐθνῶν, πόσῳ μᾶλλον τὸ πλήρωμα αὐτῶν;
(the) riches of (the) nations, how much more the fullness of them!
13 Ὑμῖν γὰρ λέγω τοῖς ἔθνεσιν. ἐφ' ὅσον μέν εἰμι ἐγὼ ἐθνῶν
to you For I speak, the nations, since indeed am I of nations
14 ἀπόστολος, τὴν διακονίαν μου δοξάζω· εἴ πως παραζηλώσω
an apostle, the ministry of me I glorify, if somehow I may provoke to jealousy
15 μου τὴν σάρκα, καὶ σώσω τινὰς ἐξ αὐτῶν. εἰ γὰρ ἡ ἀπο-
of me the flesh and may save some of them. if For the casting
βολὴ αὐτῶν καταλλαγὴ κόσμου, τίς ἡ πρόσληψις, εἰ μὴ
away of them (the) reconciliation of world, what the reception, except
16 ζωὴ ἐκ νεκρῶν; εἰ δὲ ἡ ἀπαρχὴ ἁγία, καὶ τὸ φύραμα· καὶ εἰ
life from (the) dead? if Now the firstfruit (is) holy, also the lump; and if
17 ἡ ῥίζα ἁγία, καὶ οἱ κλάδοι. εἰ δέ τινες τῶν κλάδων ἐξεκλάσθη-
the root, also the branches. if But some of the branches were broken
σαν, σὺ δὲ ἀγριέλαιος ὢν ἐνεκεντρίσθης ἐν αὐτοῖς, καὶ
off, you and, a wild olive being were grafted in among them, and
συγκοινωνὸς τῆς ῥίζης καὶ τῆς πιότητος τῆς ἐλαίας ἐγένου,
a partaker of the root and of the fatness of the olive-tree became,
18 μὴ κατακαυχῶ τῶν κλάδων· εἰ δὲ κατακαυχᾶσαι, οὐ σὺ τὴν
do not boast against the branches; if but you boast, not you the
19 ῥίζαν βαστάζεις, ἀλλ' ἡ ῥίζα σέ. ἐρεῖς οὖν, Ἐξεκλάσθησαν οἱ
root bears, but the root you. You will say then, were broken off
20 κλάδοι, ἵνα ἐγὼ ἐγκεντρισθῶ. καλῶς· τῇ ἀπιστίᾳ ἐξεκλά-
Branches, that I might be grafted in. Well, — for unbelief they were
σθησαν, σὺ δὲ τῇ πίστει ἕστηκας. μὴ ὑψηλοφρόνει, ἀλλὰ
broken off, you and by faith stand. not high minded (Be), but
21 φοβοῦ· εἰ γὰρ ὁ Θεὸς τῶν κατὰ φύσιν κλάδων οὐκ ἐφείσατο,
fear; if for God the according to nature branches not spared,
22 μήπως οὐδέ σου φείσηται. ἴδε οὖν χρηστότητα καὶ ἀποτο-
lest neither you He will spare. Behold, then, (the) kindness and severity
μίαν Θεοῦ· ἐπὶ μὲν τοὺς πεσόντας, ἀποτομίαν· ἐπὶ δέ σε,
of God on indeed those having fallen, severity; on but you,
χρηστότητα, ἐὰν ἐπιμείνῃς τῇ χρηστότητι· ἐπεὶ καὶ σὺ
kindness. if you continue in the kindness, otherwise also you
23 ἐκκοπήσῃ. καὶ ἐκεῖνοι δέ, ἐὰν μὴ ἐπιμείνωσι τῇ ἀπιστίᾳ,
will be cut off also those And, if not they continue in unbelief,
ἐγκεντρισθήσονται· δυνατὸς γάρ ἐστιν ὁ Θεὸς πάλιν ἐγκεν-
will be grafted in; able for is God again to graft
24 τρίσαι αὐτούς. εἰ γὰρ σὺ ἐκ τῆς κατὰ φύσιν ἐξεκόπης ἀγρι-
in them. if For you out of the natural were cut out wild
ελαίου, καὶ παρὰ φύσιν ἐνεκεντρίσθης εἰς καλλιέλαιον, πόσῳ
olive, and against nature were grafted in into a good olive, how much
μᾶλλον οὗτοι, οἱ κατὰ φύσιν, ἐγκεντρισθήσονται τῇ ἰδίᾳ
more these, those according to nature, will be grafted in the own
ἐλαίᾳ,
olive-tree?

25 Οὐ γὰρ θέλω ὑμᾶς ἀγνοεῖν, ἀδελφοί, τὸ μυστήριον τοῦτο,
not For I wish you to be ignorant, brothers, (of) mystery this
ἵνα μὴ ἦτε παρ' ἑαυτοῖς φρόνιμοι, ὅτι πώρωσις ἀπὸ μέρους
that not you be in yourselves wise, that hardness from (in) part
τῷ Ἰσραὴλ γέγονεν, ἄχρις οὗ τὸ πλήρωμα τῶν ἐθνῶν εἰσ-
to Israel has happened, until the fullness of the nations comes
26 έλθῃ· καὶ οὕτω πᾶς Ἰσραὴλ σωθήσεται· καθὼς γέγραπται,
in, and so all Israel will be saved, even as it has been written:

written, "The Deliverer will come out of Zion, and He will turn away ungodliness from Jacob. [27]And this *is* My covenant with them, when I take away their sins." [28]Indeed, as regards the gospel, enemies for you; but as regards the election, beloved for the sake of the fathers. [29]For the free gifts and the calling of God *are* without repentance. [30]For as you also then disobeyed God, but now have obtained mercy by the disobedience of these; [31]so also these now *have* disobeyed by your mercy, so that they also may obtain mercy. [32]For God shut up all in disobedience, that He may show mercy to all.

[33]O *the* depth of *the* riches and of *the* wisdom and *the* knowledge of God! How unsearchable *are* His judgments, and His ways past finding out! [34]For who has known the mind of *the* Lord? Or who became His counselor? [35]Or who first gave to Him, and it will be repaid to him? [36]Because of Him, and through Him, and to Him *are* all things. To Him be the glory forever! Amen.

CHAPTER 12

[1]Therefore, brothers, I call on you through the mercies of God to present your bodies a living sacrifice, holy, pleasing to God, *which is* your reasonable service. [2]And be not conformed to this age, but be transformed by the renewing of your mind, in order to prove by you what *is* the good and pleasing and perfect will of God. [3]For I say through the grace which is given to me, to everyone being among you, not to have high thoughts beyond what is right to think. But set your mind so as to think to be right-minded, even as God divided a measure of faith to each. [4]For even as we have many members in one body, but all members do not have the same function; [5]so we

Ἥξει ἐκ Σιὼν ὁ ῥυόμενος, καὶ ἀποστρέψει ἀσεβείας ἀπὸ
Will come out of Zion the Deliverer and He will turn away ungodliness from
27 Ἰακώβ· καὶ αὕτη αὐτοῖς ἡ παρ' ἐμοῦ διαθήκη, ὅταν ἀφέλω-
Jacob. And this (is) with them the from Me covenant, when I take away
28 μαι τὰς ἁμαρτίας αὐτῶν. κατὰ μὲν τὸ εὐαγγέλιον, ἐχθροὶ δι'
the sins of them as regards Indeed the gospel, enemies for
ὑμᾶς· κατὰ δὲ τὴν ἐκλογήν, ἀγαπητοὶ διὰ τοὺς πατέρας.
you; as regards but the election, beloved for the sake of the fathers.
29 ἀμεταμέλητα γὰρ τὰ χαρίσματα καὶ ἡ κλῆσις τοῦ Θεοῦ.
without repentance For the free gifts and the calling — of God.
30 ὥσπερ γὰρ καὶ ὑμεῖς ποτὲ ἠπειθήσατε τῷ Θεῷ, νῦν δὲ
as For also you then disobeyed God, now but
31 ἠλεήθητε τῇ τούτων ἀπειθείᾳ· οὕτω καὶ οὗτοι νῦν ἠπείθη-
you obtained mercy by the of these disobedience, so also these now disobeyed
32 σαν, τῷ ὑμετέρῳ ἐλέει ἵνα καὶ αὐτοὶ ἐλεηθῶσι. συνέκλεισε
by your mercy that also they may obtain mercy. shut up
γὰρ ὁ Θεὸς τοὺς πάντας εἰς ἀπείθειαν, ἵνα τοὺς πάντας
For God — all in disobedience, that — to all
ἐλεήσῃ.
He may show mercy.
33 Ὦ βάθος πλούτου καὶ σοφίας καὶ γνώσεως Θεοῦ. ὡς
O (the) depth of (the) riches and of (the) wisdom and (the) knowledge of God; how
ἀνεξερεύνητα τὰ κρίματα αὐτοῦ, καὶ ἀνεξιχνίαστοι αἱ ὁδοὶ
unsearchable the judgments of Him, and past finding out the ways
34 αὐτοῦ. τίς γὰρ ἔγνω νοῦν Κυρίου; ἢ τίς σύμβουλος αὐτοῦ
of Him! who For has known the mind of (the) Lord? or who His counselor
35 ἐγένετο; ἢ τίς προέδωκεν αὐτῷ, καὶ ἀνταποδοθήσεται
became? or who first gave to Him, and it will be repaid
36 αὐτῷ; ὅτι ἐξ αὐτοῦ καὶ δι' αὐτοῦ καὶ εἰς αὐτὸν τὰ πάντα·
to him? Because of Him, and through Him, and to Him (are) all things;
αὐτῷ ἡ δόξα εἰς τοὺς αἰῶνας. ἀμήν.
to Him be the glory to the ages! Amen.

CHAPTER 12

1 Παρακαλῶ οὖν ὑμᾶς, ἀδελφοί, διὰ τῶν οἰκτιρμῶν τοῦ
I beseech Therefore you, brothers, through the compassion
Θεοῦ, παραστῆσαι τὰ σώματα ὑμῶν θυσίαν ζῶσαν, ἁγίαν,
of God, to present the body of you sacrifice a living, holy,
2 εὐάρεστον τῷ Θεῷ, τὴν λογικὴν λατρείαν ὑμῶν. καὶ μὴ
well-pleasing to God, the reasonable service of you. And not
συσχηματίζεσθε τῷ αἰῶνι τούτῳ, ἀλλὰ μεταμορφοῦσθε τῇ
be conformed to age this, but be transformed by the
ἀνακαινώσει τοῦ νοὸς ὑμῶν, εἰς τὸ δοκιμάζειν ὑμᾶς τί τὸ
renewing of the mind of you, to prove you what the
θέλημα τοῦ Θεοῦ τὸ ἀγαθὸν καὶ εὐάρεστον καὶ τέλειον.
will of God, the good and well-pleasing and perfect.
3 Λέγω γάρ, διὰ τῆς χάριτος τῆς δοθείσης μοι, παντὶ τῷ
I say For, through the grace — given to me to everyone
ὄντι ἐν ὑμῖν, μὴ ὑπερφρονεῖν παρ' ὃ δεῖ φρονεῖν, ἀλλὰ
being among you, not to have high thoughts beyond what is right to think, but
φρονεῖν εἰς τὸ σωφρονεῖν, ἑκάστῳ ὡς ὁ Θεὸς ἐμέρισε μέτρον
to think to be sober-minded, to each as God divided a measure
4 πίστεως. καθάπερ γὰρ ἐν ἑνὶ σώματι μέλη πολλὰ ἔχομεν, τὰ
of faith. as For in one body members many we have, the
5 δὲ μέλη πάντα οὐ τὴν αὐτὴν ἔχει πρᾶξιν· οὕτως οἱ πολλοὶ
but members all not the same have function, so the many

the many are one body in Christ, and each one members of one another. [6]But having different gifts according to the grace given to us, whether prophecy, according to the proportion of faith; [7]or ministry, in the ministry; or the *one* teaching, in the teaching; [8]or the *one* exhorting, in the encouragement; the *one* sharing, in simplicity; the *one* taking the lead, in diligence; the *one* showing mercy, in cheerfulness.

[9]*Let* love *be* without dissimulation, shrinking from evil, cleaving to good; [10]in brotherly love to one another loving fervently, having gone before one another in honor. [11]As to diligence, not slothful; warm in spirit, serving the Lord; [12]in hope, rejoicing; in affliction, enduring; in prayer, steadfastly continuing; [13]imparting to the needs of the saints; pursuing hospitality.

[14]Bless those who persecute you; bless, and do not curse. [15]Rejoice with rejoicing ones, and weep with weeping ones; [16]minding the same thing toward one another, not minding high things, but yielding to the lowly. do not become wise within yourselves. [17]Repay no one evil for evil; providing right things before all men. [18]If possible, as far as *is* in you, seeking peace with all men; [19]not avenging yourselves, beloved, but giving place to wrath—for it has been written, "Vengeance is Mine, I will repay, says *the* Lord." [20]Therefore, if your enemy hungers, feed him; if he thirsts, give him drink; for doing this you will heap coals of fire on his head. [21]Do not be overcome by evil, but overcome the evil with good.

CHAPTER 13

[1]Let every soul be subject to higher authorities, for there is no authority except from God; but the authorities

ἓν σῶμά ἐσμεν ἐν Χριστῷ, ὁ δὲ καθ' εἷς ἀλλήλων μέλη.
one body we are in Christ, and each one of one another members
6 ἔχοντες δὲ χαρίσματα κατὰ τὴν χάριν τὴν δοθεῖσαν ἡμῖν
having And gifts according to the grace given to us
διάφορα, εἴτε προφητείαν, κατὰ τὴν ἀναλογίαν τῆς πίστεως·
differing, whether prophecy, according to the proportion of faith;
7 εἴτε διακονίαν, ἐν τῇ διακονίᾳ· εἴτε ὁ διδάσκων, ἐν τῇ
or ministry, in the ministry; or the (one) teaching, in the
8 διδασκαλίᾳ· εἴτε ὁ παρακαλῶν, ἐν τῇ παρακλήσει· ὁ μεταδι-
teaching; or the (one) exhorting, in the exhortation; the (one) sharing,
δούς, ἐν ἁπλότητι· ὁ προϊστάμενος, ἐν σπουδῇ· ὁ ἐλεῶν ἐν
in simplicity; the (one) taking the lead in diligence, he showing mercy, in
9 ἱλαρότητι. ἡ ἀγάπη ἀνυπόκριτος. ἀποστυγοῦντες τὸ
cheerfulness. (let) Love (be) without dissimulation; shrinking from
10 πονηρόν, κολλώμενοι τῷ ἀγαθῷ. τῇ φιλαδελφίᾳ εἰς ἀλλή-
evil, cleaving to the good; in brotherly love to one
λους φιλόστοργοι· τῇ τιμῇ ἀλλήλους προηγούμενοι· τῇ
another loving fervently, in honor one another preferring;
11 σπουδῇ μὴ ὀκνηροί· τῷ πνεύματι ζέοντες· τῷ Κυρίῳ δου-
in diligence, not slothful; in spirit burning, the Lord
12 λεύοντες· τῇ ἐλπίδι χαίροντες· τῇ θλίψει ὑπομένοντες· τῇ
serving; in hope, rejoicing; in trouble, enduring;
13 προσευχῇ προσκαρτεροῦντες· ταῖς χρείαις τῶν ἁγίων
in prayer, steadfastly continuing, to the needs of the saints
14 κοινωνοῦντες· τὴν φιλοξενίαν διώκοντες. εὐλογεῖτε τοὺς
imparting, hospitality pursuing. Bless those
15 διώκοντας ὑμᾶς· εὐλογεῖτε, καὶ μὴ καταρᾶσθε. χαίρειν μετὰ
persecuting you; bless, and do not curse. Rejoice with
16 χαιρόντων, καὶ κλαίειν μετὰ κλαιόντων. τὸ αὐτὸ εἰς ἀλλή-
rejoicing ones; and weep with weeping ones. The same toward one
λους φρονοῦντες. μὴ τὰ ὑψηλὰ φρονοῦντες, ἀλλὰ τοῖς
another minding; not the things high minding, but to the
ταπεινοῖς συναπαγόμενοι. μὴ γίνεσθε φρόνιμοι παρ' ἑαυτοῖς.
humble yield, do not become wise with yourselves.
17 μηδενὶ κακὸν ἀντὶ κακοῦ ἀποδιδόντες. προνοούμενοι καλὰ
To no one evil for evil returning; providing for right things
18 ἐνώπιον πάντων ἀνθρώπων. εἰ δυνατόν, τὸ ἐξ ὑμῶν, μετὰ
before all men; if possible, as far as in you, with
19 πάντων ἀνθρώπων εἰρηνεύοντες. μὴ ἑαυτοὺς ἐκδικοῦντες,
all men seeking peace; not yourselves avenging,
ἀγαπητοί, ἀλλὰ δότε τόπον τῇ ὀργῇ· γέγραπται γάρ,
beloved, but give place to wrath, it has been written for,
20 Ἐμοὶ ἐκδίκησις, ἐγὼ ἀνταποδώσω, λέγει Κύριος. ἐὰν οὖν πεινᾷ
To Me (is) vengeance, I will repay, says (the) Lord. if Then hungers
ὁ ἐχθρός σου, ψώμιζε αὐτόν· ἐὰν διψᾷ, πότιζε αὐτόν· τοῦτο
the enemy of you, feed him; if he thirsts, give drink to him; this
γὰρ ποιῶν, ἄνθρακας πυρὸς σωρεύσεις ἐπὶ τὴν κεφαλὴν αὐτοῦ.
for doing, coals of fire you will heap on the head of him.
21 μὴ νικῶ ὑπὸ τοῦ κακοῦ, ἀλλὰ νίκα ἐν τῷ ἀγαθῷ τὸ κακόν.
Not be conquered by evil, but conquer with good the evil.

CHAPTER 13

1 Πᾶσα ψυχὴ ἐξουσίαις ὑπερεχούσαις ὑποτασσέσθω· οὐ
Every soul to authorities higher be subject to. no
γάρ ἐστιν ἐξουσία εἰ μὴ ἀπὸ Θεοῦ, αἱ δὲ οὖσαι ἐξουσίαι ὑπὸ
For there is authority except from God, the but existing authorities by

that exist have been ordained by God. 2 So that the *one* resisting authority has opposed the ordinance of God; and the ones opposing will receive judgment to themselves. 3 For the rulers are not a terror to good works, but to the bad. And do you desire not to be afraid of the authority? Do the good, and you will have praise from it; 4 for it is a servant of God to you for good. But if you practice evil, be afraid; for he does not bear the sword in vain; for he is a servant of God, an avenger for wrath to the *one* practicing evil. 5 Because of this, *it is* necessary to be subject, not only on account of wrath, but also on account of conscience. 6 For on this account you also pay taxes; for they are ministers of God, always giving attention to this very thing. 7 Then give to all *their* dues: to the *one due* tax, the tax; to the *one due* tribute, the tribute; to the *one due* honor, the honor. 8 Owe no one anything, except to love one another. For the *one* loving the other has fulfilled the law. 9 For, "Do not commit adultery; do not murder; do not steal; do not bear false witness; do not lust," and if *there is* any other commandment, it is summed up in this word: "You shall love your neighbor as yourself." 10 Love does not work evil to the neighbor. Then love *is* the fulfillment of law.

11 Also this, knowing the time, that *it is* the hour for you to be aroused from sleep, for now our salvation is nearer than when we believed. 12 The night is far gone, and the day has drawn near; therefore, let us cast off the works of darkness, and let us put on the weapons of the light. 13 Let us walk becomingly, as in *the* day; not in carousings and drinking; not in co-habitation and lustful acts; not in fighting and envy. 14 But put on the Lord Jesus Christ and do not take

2 τοῦ Θεοῦ τεταγμέναι εἰσίν. ὥστε ὁ ἀντιτασσόμενος τῇ
— God having been ordained are. So the (one) resisting the
ἐξουσίᾳ, τῇ τοῦ Θεοῦ διαταγῇ ἀνθέστηκεν· οἱ δὲ ἀνθεστη-
authority the of God ordinance has opposed; those and having
3 κότες ἑαυτοῖς κρίμα λήψονται. οἱ γὰρ ἄρχοντες οὐκ εἰσὶ
opposed, to themselves judgment will receive. the For rulers not are
φόβος τῶν ἀγαθῶν ἔργων, ἀλλὰ τῶν κακῶν. θέλεις δὲ μὴ
a terror to good works, but to the bad. wish you And not
φοβεῖσθαι τὴν ἐξουσίαν ; τὸ ἀγαθὸν ποίει, καὶ ἕξεις ἔπαινον
to fear the authority? the good Do, and you will have praise
4 ἐξ αὐτῆς· Θεοῦ γὰρ διάκονός ἐστί σοι εἰς τὸ ἀγαθόν. ἐὰν δὲ
from it; of God For a servant he is to you for the good. if But
τὸ κακὸν ποιῇς, φοβοῦ· οὐ γὰρ εἰκῇ τὴν μάχαιραν φορεῖ·
the evil you do, fear; not for in vain the sword he bears;
Θεοῦ γὰρ διάκονός ἐστιν, ἔκδικος εἰς ὀργὴν τῷ τὸ κακὸν
of God for a servant he is, an avenger for wrath to the (one) evil
5 πράσσοντι. διὸ ἀνάγκη ὑποτάσσεσθαι, οὐ μόνον διὰ τὴν
practicing. Therefore it is necessary to be subject, not only because of
ὀργήν, ἀλλὰ καὶ διὰ τὴν συνείδησιν. διὰ τοῦτο γὰρ καὶ
wrath, but also because of conscience. on account of this For also
6 φόρους τελεῖτε· λειτουργοὶ γὰρ Θεοῦ εἰσιν, εἰς αὐτὸ τοῦτο
taxes you pay; ministers for of God they are, for this very thing
7 προσκαρτεροῦντες. ἀπόδοτε οὖν πᾶσι τὰς ὀφειλάς· τῷ τὸν
always giving attention. give Then to all the dues: to the (one) the
φόρον τὸν φόρον· τῷ τὸ τέλος τὸ τέλος· τῷ τὸν φόβον τὸν
tax (due) the tax; to the (one) the tribute the tribute, fear (due) the
φόβον· τῷ τὴν τιμὴν τὴν τιμήν.
fear; honor (due) the honor.
8 Μηδενὶ μηδὲν ὀφείλετε, εἰ μὴ τὸ ἀγαπᾷν ἀλλήλους· ὁ γὰρ
To no one nothing owe, except to love one another; he for
9 ἀγαπῶν τὸν ἕτερον, νόμον πεπλήρωκε. τὸ γάρ, Οὐ μοιχεύ-
loving the other, the law has fulfilled. — For: Do not commit
σεις, οὐ φονεύσεις, οὐ κλέψεις, οὐ ψευδομαρτυρήσεις, οὐκ
adultery; not do murder; not do steal; Do not bear false witness; not
ἐπιθυμήσεις, καὶ εἴ τις ἑτέρα ἐντολή, ἐν τούτῳ τῷ λόγῳ
lust; and if any other commandment, in this word
ἀνακεφαλαιοῦται, ἐν τῷ, Ἀγαπήσεις τὸν πλησίον σου ὡς
it is summed up: You shall love the neighbor of you as
10 ἑαυτόν. ἡ ἀγάπη τῷ πλησίον κακὸν οὐκ ἐργάζεται·
yourself. Love to the neighbor evil does not work;
πλήρωμα οὖν νόμου ἡ ἀγάπη.
fulfillment then of law (is) love.
11 Καὶ τοῦτο, εἰδότες τὸν καιρόν, ὅτι ὥρα ἡμᾶς ἤδη ἐξ ὕπνου
And this, knowing the time, that an hour (is for you) now out of sleep
ἐγερθῆναι· νῦν γὰρ ἐγγύτερον ἡμῶν ἡ σωτηρία ἢ ὅτε ἐπι-
to be raised; now for nearer of us the salvation than when we
12 στεύσαμεν. ἡ νὺξ προέκοψεν, ἡ δὲ ἡμέρα ἤγγικεν· ἀποθώμεθα
believed. The night (is) far gone, the and day has drawn near. Let us cast off
οὖν τὰ ἔργα τοῦ σκότους, καὶ ἐνδυσώμεθα τὰ ὅπλα τοῦ
then the works of the darkness, and let us put on the weapons of the
13 φωτός. ὡς ἐν ἡμέρᾳ, εὐσχημόνως περιπατήσωμεν, μὴ κώμοις
light. As in (the) day, becomingly let us walk, not in carousings
14 καὶ μέθαις, μὴ κοίταις καὶ ἀσελγείαις, μὴ ἔριδι καὶ ζήλῳ. ἀλλ
and drinking, not in cohabitation and lustful acts, not in fighting and envy. But
ἐνδύσασθε τὸν Κύριον Ἰησοῦν Χριστόν, καὶ τῆς σαρκὸς
put on the Lord Jesus Christ, and of the flesh

thought for the lusts of the flesh.

CHAPTER 14

[1]And receive the *one* who is weak in the faith, not to judgments of *your* thoughts. [2]One believes to eat all things; but being weak, *another* one eats vegetables. [3]The *one* eating do not despise the *one* not eating. And the *one* not eating, do not judge the *one* eating—for God received him. [4]Who are you judging another's servant? To his own master he stands or falls. But he will stand, for God is able to make him stand. [5]One indeed judges a day above *another* day; and *another* one judges every day *alike*. Let each one be fully assured in his own mind. [6]The *one* minding the days, he minds *it* to *the* Lord. The *one* eating, he eats to *the* Lord; for he gives thanks to God. And the *one* not eating, he does not eat to *the* Lord, and gives thanks to God. [7]For no one of us lives to himself; and no one dies to himself. [8]For both if we live, we live to *the* Lord; and if we die, we die to *the* Lord. Then both if we live, and if we die, we are the Lord's. [9]For this Christ both died and rose and lived again, that He might be Lord over both *the* dead and the living. [10]But why do you judge your brother? Or why do you also despise your brother? For all shall stand before the judgment seat of Christ. [11]For it has been written, "I live, says the Lord, that every knee will bow to Me, and every tongue confess to God." [12]So then each one of us will give account concerning himself to God. [13]Then let us no longer judge one another, but rather judge this, not to put a stumblingblock or an offense toward a brother. [14]I know and am persuaded in *the* Lord Jesus that nothing itself *is*

πρόνοιαν μὴ ποιεῖσθε, εἰς ἐπιθυμίας.
forethought do not make for (its) lusts.

CHAPTER 14

1 Τὸν δὲ ἀσθενοῦντα τῇ πίστει προσλαμβάνεσθε, μὴ εἰς
the (one) And being weak in the faith receive, not to
2 διακρίσεις διαλογισμῶν. ὃς μὲν πιστεύει φαγεῖν πάντα, ὁ
judgments of thoughts. One indeed believes to eat all things, one
3 δὲ ἀσθενῶν λάχανα ἐσθίει. ὁ ἐσθίων τὸν μὴ ἐσθίοντα μὴ
but being weak vegetables eats. The (one) eating the (one) not eating do not
ἐξουθενείτω, καὶ ὁ μὴ ἐσθίων τὸν ἐσθίοντα μὴ κρινέτω· ὁ
despise; and the (one) not eating the (one) eating do not judge. —
4 Θεὸς γὰρ αὐτὸν προσελάβετο. σὺ τίς εἶ ὁ κρίνων ἀλλότριον
God For him received. You who are judging of another
οἰκέτην; τῷ ἰδίῳ κυρίῳ στήκει ἢ πίπτει. σταθήσεται δέ·
a servant, to the own lord he stands or falls he will stand but,
5 δυνατὸς γάρ ἐστιν ὁ Θεὸς στῆσαι αὐτόν. ὃς μὲν κρίνει
able for is God to stand him. One indeed judges
ἡμέραν παρ' ἡμέραν, ὃς δὲ κρίνει πᾶσαν ἡμέραν. ἕκαστος
a day above a day; one and judges every day (alike). Each
6 ἐν τῷ ἰδίῳ νοῒ πληροφορείσθω. ὁ φρονῶν τὴν ἡμέραν,
in the own mind let him be fully assured. He minding the day,
Κυρίῳ φρονεῖ· καὶ ὁ μὴ φρονῶν τὴν ἡμέραν, Κυρίῳ οὐ
to (the) Lord he minds; and he not minding the day, to (the) Lord not
φρονεῖ. ὁ ἐσθίων Κυρίῳ ἐσθίει, εὐχαριστεῖ γὰρ τῷ Θεῷ· καὶ
he minds. He eating, to (the) Lord he eats; he gives thanks for to God; and
ὁ μὴ ἐσθίων Κυρίῳ οὐκ ἐσθίει, καὶ εὐχαριστεῖ τῷ Θεῷ.
he not eating, to (the) Lord not he eats; and gives thanks to God.
7 οὐδεὶς γὰρ ἡμῶν ἑαυτῷ ζῇ, καὶ οὐδεὶς ἑαυτῷ ἀποθνήσκει.
no one For of us to himself lives, and no one to himself dies.
8 ἐάν τε γὰρ ζῶμεν, τῷ Κυρίῳ ζῶμεν· ἐάν τε ἀποθνήσκωμεν,
if both For we live, to (the) Lord we live; if and we die,
τῷ Κυρίῳ ἀποθνήσκομεν· ἐάν τε οὖν ζῶμεν, ἐάν τε ἀποθνή-
to (the) Lord we die. if And therefore we live, if and we
9 σκωμεν, τοῦ Κυρίου ἐσμέν. εἰς τοῦτο γὰρ Χριστὸς καὶ
die, of the Lord we are. for this For Christ also
ἀπέθανε καὶ ἀνέστη καὶ ἀνέζησεν, ἵνα καὶ νεκρῶν καὶ
died and rose and lived again, that both of dead and
10 ζώντων κυριεύσῃ. σὺ δὲ τί κρίνεις τὸν ἀδελφόν σου; ἢ καὶ
of living He might be Lord. you And why judge the brother of you? Or also
σὺ τί ἐξουθενεῖς τὸν ἀδελφόν σου; πάντες γὰρ παραστη-
you why despise the brother of you? all For shall stand
11 σόμεθα τῷ βήματι τοῦ Χριστοῦ. γέγραπται γάρ, Ζῶ ἐγώ,
before the judgment seat of Christ. it has been written For, live I,
λέγει Κύριος· ὅτι ἐμοὶ κάμψει πᾶν γόνυ, καὶ πᾶσα γλῶσσα
says (the) Lord, that to Me will bow every knee, and every tongue
12 ἐξομολογήσεται τῷ Θεῷ. ἄρα οὖν ἕκαστος ἡμῶν περὶ
will confess to God. So then, each one of us concerning
ἑαυτοῦ λόγον δώσει τῷ Θεῷ.
himself account will give to God.
13 Μηκέτι οὖν ἀλλήλους κρίνωμεν· ἀλλὰ τοῦτο κρίνατε
No longer, then, one another let us judge; but this judge
μᾶλλον, τὸ μὴ τιθέναι πρόσκομμα τῷ ἀδελφῷ ἢ σκάνδαλον.
rather, not to put a stumbling-block to the brother or an offense.
14 οἶδα καὶ πέπεισμαι ἐν Κυρίῳ Ἰησοῦ, ὅτι οὐδὲν κοινὸν δι'
I know and am persuaded in (the) Lord Jesus, that nothing (is) common
by

ἑαυτοῦ· εἰ μὴ τῷ λογιζομένῳ τι κοινὸν εἶναι, ἐκείνῳ κοινόν.
itself, except to the (one) counting anything common to be, to that one (it is) common.
15 εἰ δὲ διὰ βρῶμα ὁ ἀδελφός σου λυπεῖται, οὐκέτι κατὰ ἀγάπην
if And for (your) food the brother of you is grieved, no longer according to love
περιπατεῖς. μὴ τῷ βρώματί σου ἐκεῖνον ἀπόλλυε, ὑπὲρ οὗ
do you walk. Not by the food of you that one destroy, for whom
16 Χριστὸς ἀπέθανε. μὴ βλασφημείσθω οὖν ὑμῶν τὸ ἀγαθόν·
Christ died, let not be evil spoken of Then of you the good.
17 οὐ γάρ ἐστιν ἡ βασιλεία τοῦ Θεοῦ βρῶσις καὶ πόσις, ἀλλὰ
not For is the kingdom Of God eating and drinking, but
18 δικαιοσύνη καὶ εἰρήνη καὶ χαρὰ ἐν Πνεύματι Ἁγίῳ. ὁ γὰρ
righteousness and peace and joy in (the) Spirit Holy. the For
ἐν τούτοις δουλεύων τῷ Χριστῷ εὐάρεστος τῷ Θεῷ, καὶ
in these serving Christ (is) well-pleasing to God, and
19 δόκιμος τοῖς ἀνθρώποις. ἄρα οὖν τὰ τῆς εἰρήνης διώκωμεν,
approved by men. So then the things of peace let us pursue,
20 καὶ τὰ τῆς οἰκοδομῆς τῆς εἰς ἀλλήλους. μὴ ἕνεκεν βρώματος
and the things for building up for one another. Do not because of food
κατάλυε τὸ ἔργον τοῦ Θεοῦ. πάντα μὲν καθαρά, ἀλλὰ κακὸν
undo the work of God. All things truly (are) clean, but bad
21 τῷ ἀνθρώπῳ τῷ διὰ προσκόμματος ἐσθίοντι. καλὸν τὸ μὴ
to the man through a stumbling-block eating. (It is) good not
φαγεῖν κρέα, μηδὲ πιεῖν οἶνον, μηδὲ ἐν ᾧ ὁ ἀδελφός σου
to eat flesh, nor to drink wine, nor (any) by which the brother of you
22 προσκόπτει ἢ σκανδαλίζεται ἢ ἀσθενεῖ. σὺ πίστιν ἔχεις;
stumbles, or be offended, or be weak. Do you faith have?
κατὰ σαυτὸν ἔχε ἐνώπιον τοῦ Θεοῦ. μακάριος ὁ μὴ κρίνων
By yourself have (it) before God. Blessed the (one) not judging
23 ἑαυτὸν ἐν ᾧ δοκιμάζει. ὁ δὲ διακρινόμενος, ἐὰν φάγῃ, κατα-
himself in what he approves; he but doubting, if he eats, has been
κέκριται, ὅτι οὐκ ἐκ πίστεως· πᾶν δὲ ὃ οὐκ ἐκ πίστεως,
condemned, because not of faith; all and not of faith
ἁμαρτία ἐστίν.
sin is.

CHAPTER 15

1 Ὀφείλομεν δὲ ἡμεῖς οἱ δυνατοὶ τὰ ἀσθενήματα τῶν ἀδυνά-
ought And we the strong the weaknesses of the not
2 των βαστάζειν, καὶ μὴ ἑαυτοῖς ἀρέσκειν. ἕκαστος γὰρ
strong to bear, and not ourselves please. let each one For
ἡμῶν τῷ πλησίον ἀρεσκέτω εἰς τὸ ἀγαθὸν πρὸς οἰκοδομήν.
of us the neighbor to please for good, to building up.
3 καὶ γὰρ ὁ Χριστὸς οὐχ ἑαυτῷ ἤρεσεν, ἀλλά, καθὼς
even For Christ not Himself pleased, but even as
γέγραπται, Οἱ ὀνειδισμοὶ τῶν ὀνειδιζόντων σε ἐπέπεσον
it has been written: The reproaches of those reproaching You fell
4 ἐπ' ἐμέ. ὅσα γὰρ προεγράφη, εἰς τὴν ἡμετέραν διδασκαλίαν
on Me. whatever For were written before. for our teaching
προεγράφη, ἵνα διὰ τῆς ὑπομονῆς καὶ τῆς παρακλήσεως
were written before. that through patience and encouragement
5 τῶν γραφῶν τὴν ἐλπίδα ἔχωμεν. ὁ δὲ Θεὸς τῆς ὑπομονῆς
of the Scriptures hope we might have. the And God of patience
καὶ τῆς παρακλήσεως δῴη ὑμῖν τὸ αὐτὸ φρονεῖν ἐν ἀλλήλοις
and of encouragement give to you the same, to mind among one another
κατὰ Χριστὸν Ἰησοῦν· ἵνα ὁμοθυμαδὸν ἐν ἑνὶ στόματι
according to Christ Jesus, that with one accord, with one mouth

---

common. [15]But if your brother is grieved because of *your* food, you no longer walk according to love. Do not destroy that one for whom Christ died by your food. [16]Then do not let your good be spoken evil of. [17]For the kingdom of God is not eating and drinking, but righteousness and peace and joy in *the* Holy Spirit. [18]For the *one* serving Christ in these things *is* well-pleasing to God, and approved by men. [19]So then let us pursue the things of peace, and the things for building up one another. [20]Do not undo the work of God because of food. Truly, all things *are* clean, but *it is* bad to the man who eats through a stumblingblock. [21]*It is* good not to eat flesh, nor to drink wine, nor *anything* by which your brother stumbles, or is offended, or is weak. [22]Do you have faith? Have *it* to yourself before God. Blessed *is* the *one* not condemning himself in what he approves. [23]But the *one* doubting, if he eats, *he* has been condemned, because it is not of faith—and whatever *is* not of faith is sin.

CHAPTER 15

[1]But we who *are* strong ought to bear the weaknesses of those not strong, and not to please ourselves. [2]For let everyone of us please his neighbor for good, to building up. [3]For also Christ did not please Himself, but even as it has been written, "The curses of those cursing You fell on Me." [4]For whatever things were written before were written for our instruction, that through patience and encouragement of the Scriptures we might have hope. [5]And may the God of patience and encouragement give you to mind the same thing among one another according to Christ Jesus, [6]that with one accord

and with one mouth you may glorify *the* God and Father of our Lord Jesus Christ. 7 Therefore, receive one another as Christ also received us, to *the* glory of God. 8 And I say, Jesus has become a minister of circumcision for *the* truth of God, to confirm the promises of the fathers, 9 and for the nations to glorify God for mercy, even as it has been written, "Because of this I will confess to You in the nations, and I will give praise to Your name." 10 And again He says, "Rejoice, nations, with His people." 11 And again, "Praise the Lord, all the nations, and praise Him all the peoples."
12 And again Isaiah says, "The Root of Jesse shall be, and He rising up to rule the nations; on Him nations will hope." 13 And may the God of hope fill you with all joy and peace in believing, for you to abound in hope, in power of *the* Holy Spirit.
14 But, my brothers, I myself am persuaded concerning you, that you yourselves are also full of goodness, being filled with all knowledge, being able to warn one another. 15 But I wrote to you more boldly, brothers, as reminding you in part, because of the grace given to me by God, 16 for me to be a minister of Jesus Christ to the nations, sacredly ministering the gospel of God, that the offering of the nations might be acceptable *and* sanctified by *the* Holy Spirit. 17 Therefore, I have boasting in Christ Jesus *as to* the things pertaining to God. 18 For I will not dare to speak of anything which Christ did not work out through me for *the* obedience of the nations in word and work, 4 19 in power of miracles and wonders, in power of *the* Spirit of God, so as *for* me to have fulfilled the gospel of Christ from Jerusalem and in a circle as far as Illyricum. 20 And so eagerly striving to

δοξάζητε τὸν Θεὸν καὶ πατέρα τοῦ Κυρίου ἡμῶν Ἰησοῦ
you may glorify God and Father of the Lord of us Jesus
7 Χριστοῦ. διὸ προσλαμβάνεσθε ἀλλήλους. καθὼς καὶ ὁ Χρι-
Christ. Therefore receive one another, even as also Christ
8 στὸς προσελάβετο ἡμᾶς, εἰς δόξαν Θεοῦ. λέγω δέ, Ἰησοῦν
received us, to (the) glory of God. I say And, Jesus
Χριστὸν διάκονον γεγενῆσθαι περιτομῆς ὑπὲρ ἀληθείας
Christ a minister has become of circumcision for (the) truth
Θεοῦ, εἰς τὸ βεβαιῶσαι τὰς ἐπαγγελίας τῶν πατέρων· τὰ
of God, to confirm the promises of the fathers, the
9 δὲ ἔθνη ὑπὲρ ἐλέους δοξάσαι τὸν Θεόν, καθὼς γέγραπται.
and nations for mercy to glorify God, even as it has been written,
Διὰ τοῦτο ἐξομολογήσομαί σοι ἐν ἔθνεσι, καὶ τῷ ὀνόματί σου
Therefore I will confess to You among nations, and to Your name
10 ψαλῶ. καὶ πάλιν λέγει, Εὐφράνθητε, ἔθνη, μετὰ τοῦ λαοῦ
I will praise. And again he says, Rejoice, nations, with the people
11 αὐτοῦ. καὶ πάλιν, Αἰνεῖτε τὸν Κύριον πάντα τὰ ἔθνη, καὶ
of Him. And again, Praise the Lord all the nations, and
12 ἐπαινέσατε αὐτὸν πάντες οἱ λαοί. καὶ πάλιν Ἠσαΐας λέγει,
praise Him all the peoples And again, Isaiah says,
Ἔσται ἡ ῥίζα τοῦ Ἰεσσαί, καὶ ὁ ἀνιστάμενος ἄρχειν ἐθνῶν·
Shall be the Root of Jesse, and the (One) rising up to rule the nations;
13 ἐπ' αὐτῷ ἔθνη ἐλπιοῦσιν. ὁ δὲ Θεὸς τῆς ἐλπίδος πληρώσαι
on Him nations will hope. the And God of hope fill
ὑμᾶς πάσης χαρᾶς καὶ εἰρήνης ἐν τῷ πιστεύειν, εἰς τὸ περισ-
you of all joy and peace in believing, for to
σεύειν ὑμᾶς ἐν τῇ ἐλπίδι, ἐν δυνάμει Πνεύματος Ἁγίου.
abound you in hope, in power of (the) Spirit Holy.
14 Πέπεισμαι δέ, ἀδελφοί μου, καὶ αὐτὸς ἐγὼ περὶ ὑμῶν, ὅτι
I am persuaded But, brothers of me, even myself, I, concerning you, that
καὶ αὐτοὶ μεστοί ἐστε ἀγαθωσύνης, πεπληρωμένοι πάσης
also yourselves full you are of goodness, having been filled of all
15 γνώσεως, δυνάμενοι καὶ ἀλλήλους νουθετεῖν. τολμηρότερον
knowledge, being able also one another to warn. more boldly
δὲ ἔγραψα ὑμῖν, ἀδελφοί, ἀπὸ μέρους, ὡς ἐπαναμιμνήσκων
And I wrote to you, brothers, in part as reminding
16 ὑμᾶς, διὰ τὴν χάριν τὴν δοθεῖσάν μοι ὑπὸ τοῦ Θεοῦ, εἰς τὸ
you, because of the grace given to me by God, for
εἶναί με λειτουργὸν Ἰησοῦ Χριστοῦ εἰς τὰ ἔθνη, ἱερουρ-
to be me a minister of Jesus Christ to the nations, sacredly
γοῦντα τὸ εὐαγγέλιον τοῦ Θεοῦ, ἵνα γένηται ἡ προσφορὰ
ministering the gospel of God, that may be the offering
17 τῶν ἐθνῶν εὐπρόσδεκτος, ἡγιασμένη ἐν Πνεύματι Ἁγίῳ. ἔχω
of the nations acceptable, sanctified by (the) Spirit Holy. I have
18 οὖν καύχησιν ἐν Χριστῷ Ἰησοῦ τὰ πρὸς Θεόν. οὐ γὰρ
therefore boasting in Christ Jesus the things with God. not for
τολμήσω λαλεῖν τι ὧν οὐ κατειργάσατο Χριστὸς δι' ἐμοῦ,
I will dare to speak anything of which not did work out Christ through me,
19 εἰς ὑπακοὴν ἐθνῶν λόγῳ καὶ ἔργῳ, ἐν δυνάμει σημείων καὶ
for obedience of (the) nations in word and work, in power of signs and
τεράτων, ἐν δυνάμει Πνεύματος Θεοῦ· ὥστε με ἀπὸ Ἱερου-
wonders, in power of (the) Spirit of God, so as me from Jerus-
σαλὴμ καὶ κύκλῳ μέχρι τοῦ Ἰλλυρικοῦ πεπληρωκέναι τὸ
alem and around to — Illyricum to have fulfilled the
20 εὐαγγέλιον τοῦ Χριστοῦ· οὕτω δὲ φιλοτιμούμενον εὐαγγελί-
gospel of Christ. so And eagerly striving to preach the

preach the gospel where Christ was named, so that I should not build on another's foundation; [21]but even as it has been written, "They shall see, to whom nothing was announced concerning Him; and the ones that have not heard shall understand."

[22]Therefore, I also was much hindered from coming to you, [23]but now having no more place in these regions, and having a longing to come to you for many years, [24]whenever I may go into Spain, I will come to you; for I hope *in* traveling through to see you, and to be set forward there by you, if first I may be filled of you in part. [25]But now I am going to Jerusalem, doing service to the saints. [26]For Macedonia and Achaia thought it good to make certain gifts to the poor of the saints in Jerusalem. [27]For they thought it good, also being debtors of them; for if the nations shared in their spiritual things, they ought also to minister to them in the fleshly things. [28]Then completing and having sealed this fruit to them, I will go through you into Spain. [29]And I know that I will come to you in the fullness of *the* blessing of the gospel of Christ *when* I come. [30]But I exhort you, brothers, by our Lord Jesus Christ, and by the love of the Spirit, to strive together with me in *your* prayers to God on my behalf,

[31]that I be delivered from those disobeying in Judea, and that my ministry to Jerusalem may be acceptable to the saints; [32]that *I may* come to you through *the* will of God, and that I may be refreshed with you. [33]And the God of peace *be* with all of you. Amen.

ζεσθαι, οὐχ ὅπου ὠνομάσθη Χριστός, ἵνα μὴ ἐπ' ἀλλότριον
gospel, not where was named Christ, that not on another's
21 θεμέλιον οἰκοδομῶ· ἀλλά, καθὼς γέγραπται, Οἷς οὐκ
foundation I should build, but, even as it has been written: To whom not
ἀνηγγέλη περὶ αὐτοῦ, ὄψονται· καὶ οἳ οὐκ ἀκηκόασι,
it was announced about Him, they shall see; and those not having heard,
συνήσουσι.
they shall understand.
22 Διὸ καὶ ἐνεκοπτόμην τὰ πολλὰ τοῦ ἐλθεῖν πρὸς ὑμᾶς·
Therefore also I was hindered much to come to you;
23 νυνὶ δὲ μηκέτι τόπον ἔχων ἐν τοῖς κλίμασι τούτοις, ἐπιποθίαν
now but no longer place having in — regions these, a desire
24 δὲ ἔχων τοῦ ἐλθεῖν πρὸς ὑμᾶς ἀπὸ πολλῶν ἐτῶν, ὡς ἐὰν
and having to come to you from many years, whenever
πορεύωμαι εἰς τὴν Σπανίαν, ἐλεύσομαι πρὸς ὑμᾶς· ἐλπίζω
I may go into Spain, I will come to you; I hope
γὰρ διαπορευόμενος θεάσασθαι ὑμᾶς, καὶ ὑφ' ὑμῶν προ-
for traveling through to behold you, and by you to be
πεμφθῆναι ἐκεῖ, ἐὰν ὑμῶν πρῶτον ἀπὸ μέρους ἐμπλησθῶ.
set forward there. if of you firstly in part I may be filled.
25 νυνὶ δὲ πορεύομαι εἰς Ἱερουσαλήμ, διακονῶν τοῖς ἁγίοις.
now And I am going to Jerusalem ministering to the saints.
26 εὐδόκησαν γὰρ Μακεδονία καὶ Ἀχαΐα κοινωνίαν τινὰ
thought it good For Macedonia and Achaia gifts certain
ποιήσασθαι εἰς τοὺς πτωχοὺς τῶν ἁγίων τῶν ἐν Ἱερου-
to make to the poor of the saints — in Jeru-
27 σαλήμ. εὐδόκησαν γάρ, καὶ ὀφειλέται αὐτῶν εἰσιν. εἰ γὰρ
salem. they thought it good For, and debtors of them are. if For
τοῖς πνευματικοῖς αὐτῶν ἐκοινώνησαν τὰ ἔθνη, ὀφείλουσι
in the spiritual things of them shared the nations, they ought
28 καὶ ἐν τοῖς σαρκικοῖς λειτουργῆσαι αὐτοῖς. τοῦτο οὖν
also in the fleshly things to minister to them. this Then
ἐπιτελέσας, καὶ σφραγισάμενος αὐτοῖς τὸν καρπὸν τοῦτον,
having finished, and having sealed to them fruit this,
29 ἀπελεύσομαι δι' ὑμῶν εἰς τὴν Σπανίαν. οἶδα δὲ ὅτι ἐρχό-
I will go away through you to Spain. I know And that coming
μενος πρὸς ὑμᾶς ἐν πληρώματι εὐλογίας τοῦ εὐαγγελίου τοῦ
to you in the fullness of (the) blessing of the gospel
Χριστοῦ ἐλεύσομαι.
of Christ I will come.
30 Παρακαλῶ δὲ ὑμᾶς, ἀδελφοί, διὰ τοῦ Κυρίου ἡμῶν Ἰησοῦ
I exhort And you, brothers, by the Lord of us, Jesus
Χριστοῦ, καὶ διὰ τῆς ἀγάπης τοῦ Πνεύματος, συναγωνί-
Christ, and by the love of the Spirit, to strive
σασθαί μοι ἐν ταῖς προσευχαῖς ὑπὲρ ἐμοῦ πρὸς τὸν Θεόν·
together with me in the prayers on behalf of me to — God,
31 ἵνα ῥυσθῶ ἀπὸ τῶν ἀπειθούντων ἐν τῇ Ἰουδαίᾳ, καὶ ἵνα ἡ
that I be delivered from those disobeying in — Judea, and that the
διακονία μου ἡ εἰς Ἱερουσαλὴμ εὐπρόσδεκτος γένηται τοῖς
ministry of me which (is) to Jerusalem acceptable may be to the
32 ἁγίοις· ἵνα ἐν χαρᾷ ἔλθω πρὸς ὑμᾶς διὰ θελήματος Θεοῦ, καὶ
saints, that in joy coming to you through (the) will of God, and
33 συναναπαύσωμαι ὑμῖν. ὁ δὲ Θεὸς τῆς εἰρήνης μετα πάντωκ
I may be refreshed with you. the And God of peace with all
ὑμῶν. ἀμήν.
of you. Amen.

CHAPTER 16

[1]But I commend our sister Phoebe to you, being a servant of the church in Cenchrea; [2]that you may receive her in *the* Lord, *as is* worthy of the saints, and may assist her in whatever she may need of you. For she also became a helper of many, and of myself.

[3]Greet Priscilla and Aquila, my fellow-workers in Christ Jesus, [4]who laid down their neck for my soul; to whom I not only give thanks, but also all the churches of the nations. [5]And greet the church at their house, and my beloved Epenetus, who is a firstfruit of Achaia for Christ.

[6]Greet Mary, who did much labor for us. [7]Greet Andronicus and Junias, my kinsmen and fellow-prisoners, noted among the apostles, who also were in Christ before me. [8]Greet Amplias my beloved in the Lord. [9]Greet Urbanus, our helper in Christ, and my beloved Stachys. [10]Greet Apelles, the approved in Christ, *and* those of Aristobulus. [11]Greet Herodion, my kinsman. Greet those of Narcissus, those being in *the* Lord. [12]Greet Tryphena and Tryphosa, those laboring in *the* Lord. Greet Persis the beloved, who *has* labored *in* many things in *the* Lord. [13]Greet Rufus, the chosen in *the* Lord, and his mother and mine. [14]Greet Asyncritus, Phlegon, Hermas, Petrobas, Hermes, and the brothers with them. [15]Greet Philogus and Julias, Nereus and his sister, and Olympas, and all the saints with him.

CHAPTER 16

1 Συνίστημι δὲ ὑμῖν Φοίβην τὴν ἀδελφὴν ἡμῶν, οὖσαν
I commend And to you Phoebe the sister of us, being
διάκονον τῆς ἐκκλησίας τῆς ἐν Κεγχρεαῖς· ἵνα αὐτὴν προσδέ-
a servant of the church in Cenchrea, that her you may
2 ξησθε ἐν Κυρίῳ ἀξίως τῶν ἁγίων, καὶ παραστῆτε αὐτῇ ἐν ᾧ
receive in (the) Lord worthily of the saints, and may assist her in what-
ἂν ὑμῶν χρῄζῃ πράγματι· καὶ γὰρ αὕτη προστάτις πολλῶν
ever of you she may have need. also For she a helper of many
ἐγενήθη, καὶ αὐτοῦ ἐμοῦ.
became, and of myself.
3 Ἀσπάσασθε Πρίσκιλλαν καὶ Ἀκύλαν τοὺς συνεργούς μου
Greet Priscilla and Aquilla the fellow-workers of me
4 ἐν Χριστῷ Ἰησοῦ, οἵτινες ὑπὲρ τῆς ψυχῆς μου τὸν ἑαυτῶν
In Christ Jesus, who for the soul of me the of themselves
τράχηλον ὑπέθηκαν, οἷς οὐκ ἐγὼ μόνος εὐχαριστῶ, ἀλλὰ
neck they laid down; to whom not I only give thanks, but
καὶ πᾶσαι αἱ ἐκκλησίαι τῶν ἐθνῶν· καὶ τὴν κατ' οἶκον αὐτῶν
also all the churches of the nations; and the in house of them
5 ἐκκλησίαν. ἀσπάσασθε Ἐπαίνετον τὸν ἀγαπητόν μου, ὅς
church. Greet Epenetus the beloved of me, who
ἐστιν ἀπαρχὴ τῆς Ἀχαΐας εἰς Χριστόν. ἀσπάσασθε Μαριάμ,
is firstfruit of Achaia for Christ. Greet Mariam,
6 ἥτις πολλὰ εκοπίασεν εἰς ἡμᾶς. ἀσπάσασθε Ἀνδρόνικον καὶ
who many things labored for you. Greet Andronicus and
7 Ἰουνιαν τοὺς συγγενεῖς μου καὶ συναιχμαλώτους μου,
Junias the Kinsmen of me and fellow-prisoners of me,
οἵτινές εἰσιν ἐπίσημοι ἐν τοῖς ἀποστόλοις, οἳ καὶ πρὸ ἐμοῦ
who are notable among the apostles, who and before me
8 γεγόνασιν ἐν Χριστῷ. ἀσπάσασθε Ἀμπλίαν τὸν ἀγαπητόν
have been in Christ. Greet Amplias the beloved
9 μου ἐν Κυρίῳ. ἀσπάσασθε Οὐρβανὸν τὸν συνεργὸν ἡμῶν ἐν
of me in (the) Lord. Greet Urbanus the fellow-worker of us in
10 Χριστῷ, καὶ Στάχυν τὸν ἀγαπητόν μου. ἀσπάσασθε Ἀπελ-
Christ, and Stachys the beloved of me. Greet Apelles
λῆν τὸν δοκιμον ἐν Χριστῷ. ἀσπάσασθε τοὺς ἐκ τῶν Ἀριστο-
the approved in Christ. Greet those of Aristo-
11 βούλου. ἀσπάσασθε Ἡροδίωνα τὸν συγγενῆ μου. ἀσπά-
bulus. Greet Herodian the kinsman of me. Greet
12 σασθε τοὺς ἐκ τῶν Ναρκίσσου, τοὺς ὄντας ἐν Κυρίῳ. ἀσπά-
those of Narcissus, those being in (the) Lord. Greet
σασθε Τρύφαιναν καὶ Τρυφῶσαν τὰς κοπιώσας ἐν Κυρίῳ.
Tryphena and Tryphosa, those laboring in (the) Lord
ἀσπάσασθε Περσίδα τὴν ἀγαπητήν, ἥτις πολλὰ ἐκοπίασεν
Greet Persis the beloved, who many things labored
13 ἐν Κυρίῳ. ἀσπάσασθε Ῥοῦφον τὸν ἐκλεκτὸν ἐν Κυρίῳ, καὶ τὴν
in (the) Lord. Greet Rufus the chosen in (the) Lord, and the
μητέρα αὐτοῦ καὶ ἐμοῦ. ἀσπάσασθε Ἀσύγκριτον, Φλέγοντα,
mother of him and of me. Greet Asyncritus, Phlegon,
14 Ἑρμᾶν, Πατρόβαν, Ἑρμῆν, καὶ τοὺς σὺν αὐτοῖς ἀδελφούς.
Hermas, Patrobas, Hermes, and the with them brothers.
15 ἀσπάσασθε Φιλόλογον καὶ Ἰουλίαν, Νηρέα καὶ τὴν ἀδελφὴν
Greet Philologus and Julias, Nereus and the sister
αὐτοῦ, καὶ Ὀλυμπᾶν, καὶ τοὺς σὺν αὐτοῖς πάντας ἁγίους.
of him, and Olympas, and the with him all saints.

[16]Greet one another with a holy kiss. The churches of Christ greet you.

[17]And I exhort you, brothers, to watch those making the divisions and causes of stumbling contrary to the teaching which you learned; and turn away from them. [18]For such ones do not serve our Lord Jesus Christ, but their own belly; and by smooth speaking and flattering *they* deceive the hearts of those without guile. [19]For your obedience reached to all; therefore, I rejoice over you. But I desire you to be truly wise *as* to good, but simple toward evil. [20]And the God of peace shall bruise Satan under your feet shortly.

The grace of our Lord Jesus Christ be with you.

[21]Timothy my fellow-worker, and Lucius, and Jason, and Sosipater my kinsman, greet you. [22]I, Tertius, the *one* writing the epistle, greet you in *the* Lord. [23]Gaius, the host of all the church and me, greets you. Erastus, the steward of the city, and Quartus the brother, greet you. [24]The grace of our Lord Jesus Christ be with you all. Amen.

[25]Now to Him *who is* able to establish you according to my gospel, and the preaching of Jesus Christ, according to the revelation of *the* mystery during eternal times, [26]but now has been made plain, and by prophetic Scriptures, according to the commandment of the eternal God, made known for obedience of faith to all the nations; [27]the only wise God through Jesus Christ, to whom *be* the glory forever. Amen.

16 ἀσπάσασθε ἀλλήλους ἐν φιλήματι ἁγίῳ. ἀσπάζονται ὑμᾶς
Greet one another with a kiss holy. greet you
αἱ ἐκκλησίαι τοῦ Χριστοῦ.
the churches of Christ.
17 Παρακαλῶ δὲ ὑμᾶς, ἀδελφοί, σκοπεῖν τοὺς τὰς διχοστα-
I exhort And you, brothers, to watch those the divisions
σίας καὶ τὰ σκάνδαλα, παρὰ τὴν διδαχὴν ἣν ὑμεῖς ἐμάθετε,
and the offenses, against the teaching which you learned,
18 ποιοῦντας· καὶ ἐκκλίνατε ἀπ' αὐτῶν. οἱ γὰρ τοιοῦτοι τῷ
making, and turn away from them. For such ones the
Κυρίῳ ἡμῶν Ἰησοῦ Χριστῷ οὐ δουλεύουσιν, ἀλλὰ τῇ
Lord of us, Jesus Christ, not do serve; but the
ἑαυτῶν κοιλίᾳ· καὶ διὰ τῆς χρηστολογίας καὶ εὐλογίας
of themselves belly; and through smooth speech and flattering
19 ἐξαπατῶσι τὰς καρδίας τῶν ἀκάκων. ἡ γὰρ ὑμῶν ὑπακοὴ
deceive the hearts of the guileless. the For of you obedience
εις πάντας ἀφίκετο. χαίρω οὖν τὸ ἐφ' ὑμῖν· θέλω δὲ ὑμᾶς
to all reached. I rejoice Therefore over you; I desire and you
σοφοὺς μὲν εἶναι εἰς τὸ ἀγαθόν, ἀκεραίους δὲ εἴς τὸ κακόν.
wise truly to be to the good; simple but toward the evil.
20 ὁ δὲ Θεὸς τῆς εἰρήνης συντρίψει τὸν Σατανᾶν ὑπὸ τοὺς
the And God of peace will crush Satan under the
πόδας ὑμῶν ἐν τάχει.
feet of you shortly.
Ἡ χάρις τοῦ Κυρίου ἡμῶν Ἰησοῦ Χριστοῦ μεθ' ὑμῶν.
The grace of the Lord of us, Jesus Christ, (be) with you.
ἀμήν.
Amen.
21 Ἀσπάζονται ὑμᾶς Τιμόθεος ὁ συνεργός μου, καὶ Λούκιος
greets you Timothy the fellow-worker of me, and Lucius
καὶ Ἰάσων καὶ Σωσίπατρος οἱ συγγενεῖς μου. ἀσπάζομαι
and Jason, and Sosipater the kinsman of me. greet
22 ὑμᾶς ἐγω Τέρτιος, ὁ γράψας τὴν ἐπιστολήν, ἐν Κυρίῳ.
you I, Tertius, the (one) writing the epistle, in (the) Lord.
23 ἀσπάζεται ὑμᾶς Γάϊος ὁ ξένος μου καὶ τῆς ἐκκλησίας ὅλης.
greets you Gaius the host of me, and the church of all.
ασπάζεται ὑμᾶς Ἔραστος ὁ οἰκονόμος τῆς πόλεως, καὶ
greets you Erastus the treasurer of the city, and
Κουαρτος ὁ ἀδελφός.
Quartus the brother.
24 Ἡ χάρις τοῦ Κυρίου ἡμῶν Ἰησοῦ Χριστοῦ μετὰ πάντων
The grace of the Lord of us, Jesus Christ, with all
25 ὑμῶν. ἀμήν. Τῷ δὲ δυναμένῳ ὑμᾶς στηρίξαι κατὰ τὸ
you. Amen. to the (One) And able you to establish according to
εὐαγγέλιόν μου καὶ τὸ κήρυγμα Ἰησοῦ Χριστοῦ, κατὰ
the gospel of me, and the proclamation of Jesus Christ, according
ἀποκάλυψιν μυστηριου χρονοις αἰωνίοις σεσιγημένου,
to the revelation of (the) mystery in times eternal having been kept silent,
26 φανερωθέντος δὲ νῦν, διά τε γραφῶν προφητικῶν, κατ'
revealed but now, through and writings prophetic, according
ἐπιταγὴν τοῦ αἰωνίου Θεοῦ, εἰς ὑπακοὴν πίστεως εἰς
to the command of the eternal God for obedience of faith to
27 παντα τὰ ἔθνη γνωρισθέντος, μόνῳ σοφῷ Θεῷ, διὰ
all the nations made known, only wise to God through
Ἰησοῦ Χριστοῦ, ᾧ ἡ δόξα εἰς τοὺς αἰῶνας. ἀμήν.
Jesus Christ, to whom (be) glory to the ages. Amen.

KING JAMES II VERSION

THE FIRST EPISTLE TO THE CORINTHIANS

CHAPTER 1

1 Paul, a called apostle of Jesus Christ, by *the* will of God, and Sosthenes the brother, 2 to the church of God which is in Corinth, those having been sanctified in Christ Jesus, called-out saints, with all those calling on the name of our Lord Jesus Christ in every place, both theirs and ours: 3 Grace to you, and peace, from God our Father and the Lord Jesus Christ.

4 I give thanks to my God always concerning you *for* the grace of God given to you in Christ Jesus, 5 that in everything you were enriched in Him, in all discourse and all knowledge, 6 even as the testimony of Christ was confirmed in you, 7 so that you *are* not lacking in any gift, awaiting the revelation of our Lord Jesus Christ, 8 who also will confirm you until *the* end, blameless in the day of our Lord Jesus Christ. 9 God *is* faithful, through whom you were called into *the* fellowship of His Son, Jesus Christ our Lord.

10 Now I exhort you, brothers, through the name of our Lord Jesus Christ that you all say the same thing, and there not be divisions among you; but you be united in the same mind and in the same judgment. 11 For, my brothers,

ΠΑΥΛΟΥ ΤΟΥ ΑΠΟΣΤΟΛΟΥ
PAUL THE APOSTLE

Η ΠΡΟΣ
THE TO

ΚΟΡΙΝΘΙΟΥΣ
(THE) CORINTHIANS

ΕΠΙΣΤΟΛΗ ΠΡΩΤΗ
EPISTLE FIRST

CHAPTER 1

1 Παῦλος κλητὸς ἀπόστολος Ἰησοῦ Χριστοῦ διὰ θελήματος
Paul a called apostle of Jesus Christ through (the) will
2 Θεοῦ, καὶ Σωσθένης ὁ ἀδελφός, τῇ ἐκκλησίᾳ τοῦ Θεοῦ τῇ
of God, and Sosthenes the brother, to the church of God
οὔσῃ ἐν Κορίνθῳ, ἡγιασμένοις ἐν Χριστῷ Ἰησοῦ, κλητοῖς
existing in Corinth, those having been sanctified in Christ Jesus called out
ἁγίοις, σὺν πᾶσι τοῖς ἐπικαλουμένοις τὸ ὄνομα τοῦ Κυρίου
saints, with all those calling on the name of the Lord
ἡμῶν Ἰησοῦ Χριστοῦ ἐν παντὶ τόπῳ, αὐτῶν τε καὶ ἡμῶν·
of us, Jesus Christ, in every place, of them both and of us;
3 χάρις ὑμῖν καὶ εἰρήνη ἀπὸ Θεοῦ πατρὸς ἡμῶν καὶ Κυρίου
grace to you, and peace, from God (the) Father of us and (the) Lord
Ἰησοῦ Χριστοῦ.
Jesus Christ.
4 Εὐχαριστῶ τῷ Θεῷ μου πάντοτε περὶ ὑμῶν, ἐπὶ τῇ
I give thanks to the God of me always concerning you, on the
5 χάριτι τοῦ Θεοῦ τῇ δοθείσῃ ὑμῖν ἐν Χριστῷ Ἰησοῦ· ὅτι ἐν
grace of God given to you in Christ Jesus, that in
παντὶ ἐπλουτίσθητε ἐν αὐτῷ, ἐν παντὶ λόγῳ καὶ πάσῃ
everything you were enriched in Him, in all discourse and all
6 γνώσει, καθὼς τὸ μαρτύριον τοῦ Χριστοῦ ἐβεβαιώθη ἐν
knowledge, even as the testimony of Christ was confirmed in
7 ὑμῖν· ὥστε ὑμᾶς μὴ ὑστερεῖσθαι ἐν μηδενὶ χαρίσματι, ἀπεκ-
you, so as you not to be lacking in no gift,
δεχομένους τὴν ἀποκάλυψιν τοῦ Κυρίου ἡμῶν Ἰησοῦ
awaiting the revelation of the Lord of us, Jesus
8 Χριστοῦ, ὃς καὶ βεβαιώσει ὑμᾶς ἕως τέλους, ἀνεγκλήτους ἐν
Christ, who also will confirm you until (the) end, blameless in
9 τῇ ἡμέρᾳ τοῦ Κυρίου ἡμῶν Ἰησοῦ Χριστοῦ. πιστὸς ὁ Θεός,
the day of the Lord of us, Jesus Christ. Faithful (is) God,
δι' οὗ ἐκλήθητε εἰς κοινωνίαν τοῦ υἱοῦ αὐτοῦ Ἰησοῦ Χριστοῦ
through whom you were called into fellowship of the Son of Him, Jesus Christ
τοῦ Κυρίου ἡμῶν.
the Lord of us.

10 Παρακαλῶ δὲ ὑμᾶς, ἀδελφοί, διὰ τοῦ ὀνόματος τοῦ
I exhort Now you, brothers, through the name of the
Κυρίου ἡμῶν Ἰησοῦ Χριστοῦ, ἵνα τὸ αὐτὸ λέγητε πάντες,
Lord of us, Jesus Christ, that the same thing you say all,
καὶ μὴ ᾖ ἐν ὑμῖν σχίσματα, ἦτε δὲ κατηρτισμένοι ἐν τῷ αὐτῷ
and not be among you divisions, you be but united in the same
11 νοῒ καὶ ἐν τῇ αὐτῇ γνώμῃ. ἐδηλώθη γάρ μοι περὶ ὑμῶν,
mind and in the same judgment. it was shown For to me about you.

concerning you it was shown to me by those of Chloe that there are strifes among you. [12] But I say this, that each of you says, I am of Paul, and I of Apollos, and I of Cephas, and I of Christ. [13] Has Christ been divided? Was Paul crucified for you? Or were you baptized into the name of Paul? [14] I give thanks to God that I did not baptize one of you, except Crispus and Gaius, [15] that not anyone should say that you were baptized in my name. [16] And I also baptized the household of Stephanas. For the rest, I do not know if I baptized any other. [17] For Christ did not send me to baptize, but to preach the gospel; not in wisdom of words, lest the cross of Christ be nullified.

[18] For the word of the cross is foolishness to those being lost; but to us being saved, *it is the* power of God. [19] For it has been written, "I will destroy the wisdom of the wise, and I will set aside the understanding of those perceiving." [20] Where *is the* wise? Where *the* scribe? Where *the* lawyer of this world? Did God not make the wisdom of this world foolish? [21] For since in the wisdom of God the world *by* wisdom did not know God, God was pleased to save the ones believing through the foolishness of preaching. [22] And since Jews ask for a sign, and Greeks seek wisdom, [23] but we preach Christ crucified— truly an offense to Jews, and foolishness to Greeks, [24] but to the called-out ones, both to Jews and to Greeks, Christ *is* the power of God and *the* wisdom of God; [25] because the foolish thing of God is wiser *than* men; and the weak thing of God is stronger *than* men.

[26] For you see your calling, brothers, that *there are* not many wise according to flesh, nor many powerful, not many wellborn. [27] But God chose the foolish things of the world

12 ἀδελφοί μου, ὑπὸ τῶν Χλόης, ὅτι ἔριδες ἐν ὑμῖν εἰσι. λέγω
brothers of me, by those of Chloe, that strifes among you are. I say
δὲ τοῦτο, ὅτι ἕκαστος ὑμῶν λέγει, Ἐγὼ μέν εἰμι Παύλου,
And this, that each of you says, I indeed am of Paul,
13 Ἐγὼ δὲ Ἀπολλώ, Ἐγὼ δὲ Κηφᾶ, Ἐγὼ δὲ Χριστοῦ. μεμέ-
I and of Apollos, I and of Cephas, I and of Christ Has
ρισται ὁ Χριστός; μὴ Παῦλος ἐσταυρώθη ὑπὲρ ὑμῶν, ἢ εἰς
been divided Christ? Not Paul was crucified for you? Or in
14 τὸ ὄνομα Παύλου ἐβαπτίσθητε; εὐχαριστῶ τῷ Θεῷ ὅτι
the name of Paul were you baptized? I give thanks to God that
15 οὐδένα ὑμῶν ἐβάπτισα, εἰ μὴ Κρισπον καὶ Γάϊον· ἵνα μή τις
not one of you I baptized, except Crispus and Gaius; lest anyone
16 εἴπῃ ὅτι εἰς τὸ ἐμὸν ὄνομα ἐβάπτισα. ἐβάπτισα δὲ καὶ τὸν Στε-
should say that in my name you were baptized. I baptized And also the of
17 φανᾶ οἶκον· λοιπὸν οὐκ οἶδα εἴ τινα ἄλλον ἐβάπτισα. οὐ γὰρ
Stephanas house. For the rest not I know if any other I baptized. not For
ἀπέστειλέ με Χριστος βαπτίζειν, ἀλλ' εὐαγγελίζεσθαι οὐκ
sent me Christ to baptize, but to preach the gospel, not
ἐν σοφίᾳ λόγου, ἵνα μὴ κενωθῇ ὁ σταυρὸς τοῦ Χριστοῦ.
in wisdom of words, lest be nullified the cross of Christ.
18 Ὁ λόγος γὰρ ὁ τοῦ σταυροῦ τοῖς μὲν ἀπολλυμένοις
the word For of the cross to those truly perishing
μωρία ἐστί, τοῖς δὲ σωζομένοις ἡμῖν δύναμις Θεοῦ ἐστι.
foolishness is; to those and being saved to us (the) power of God is.
19 γέγραπται γάρ, Ἀπολῶ τὴν σοφίαν τῶν σοφῶν, καὶ τὴν
it has been written For, I will destroy the wisdom of the wise, and the
20 σύνεσιν τῶν συνετῶν ἀθετήσω. ποῦ σοφός; ποῦ γραμ-
understanding of the perceiving I will set aside. Where (the) wise? Where (the)
ματεύς; ποῦ συζητητὴς τοῦ αἰῶνος τούτου; οὐχὶ ἐμώ-
scribe? Where (the) disputer age of this? Did not make
21 ρανεν ὁ Θεὸς τὴν σοφίαν τοῦ κόσμου τούτου; ἐπειδὴ γὰρ
foolish God the wisdom of world this? since For,
ἐν τῇ σοφίᾳ τοῦ Θεοῦ οὐκ ἔγνω ὁ κόσμος διὰ τῆς σοφίας τὸν
in the wisdom of God, not knew the world through the wisdom —
Θεόν, εὐδόκησεν ὁ Θεὸς διὰ τῆς μωρίας τοῦ κηρύγματος
God., was pleased God through the foolishness of preaching
22 σῶσαι τοὺς πιστεύοντας. ἐπειδὴ καὶ Ἰουδαῖοι σημεῖον
to save those believing. since And Jews ask
23 αἰτοῦσι, καὶ Ἕλληνες σοφίαν ζητοῦσιν· ἡμεῖς δὲ κηρύσσομεν
a sign and Greeks wisdom seek, we but preach
Χριστὸν ἐσταυρωμένον, Ἰουδαίοις μὲν σκάνδαλον, Ἕλλησι
Christ having been crucified: to Jews indeed an offense; to Greeks
24 δὲ μωρίαν· αὐτοῖς δὲ τοῖς κλητοῖς, Ἰουδαίοις τε καὶ Ἕλλησι,
and foolishness; to them but the called ones, to Jews both and to Greeks,
25 Χριστὸν Θεοῦ δύναμιν καὶ Θεοῦ σοφίαν. ὅτι τὸ μωρὸν τοῦ
Christ of God (the) power and of God (the) wisdom. For the foolish thing
Θεοῦ σοφώτερον τῶν ἀνθρώπων ἐστί, καὶ τὸ ἀσθενὲς τοῦ
of God wiser (than) men is; and the weak thing
Θεοῦ ἰσχυρότερον τῶν ἀνθρώπων ἐστί.
of God stronger (than) men is.
26 Βλέπετε γὰρ τὴν κλῆσιν ὑμῶν, ἀδελφοί, ὅτι οὐ πολλοὶ
you see For the calling of you, brothers, that not many
σοφοὶ κατὰ σάρκα, οὐ πολλοὶ δυνατοί, οὐ πολλοὶ εὐγενεῖς·
wise ones as to flesh, not many powerful, not many well born;
27 ἀλλὰ τὰ μωρὰ τοῦ κόσμου ἐξελέξατο ὁ Θεός, ἵνα τοὺς
but the foolish things of the world chose God, that the

that the wise might be put to shame, and God chose the weak things of the world so that He might put to shame the strong things. [28] And God chose the low-born of the world, and the despised, and the things that are not, so that He might bring to nothing the things that are; [29] so that no flesh might glory in His presence. [30] But of Him, you are in Christ Jesus, who was made to us wisdom from God, both righteousness and sanctification and redemption, [31] so that even as it has been written, "He that glories, let him glory in *the* Lord."

CHAPTER 2

[1] And when I came to you, brothers, I did not come with excellency of word or wisdom, declaring to you the testimony of God. [2] For I decided not to know anything among you except Jesus Christ, and Him having been crucified. [3] And I was with you in weakness, and in fear, and in much trembling. [4] And my word and my preaching *was* not in moving words of human wisdom, but in proof of *the* Spirit and of power, [5] that your faith might not be in *the* wisdom of men, but in *the* power of God.

[6] But we speak wisdom among the perfect; but not the wisdom of this age, nor of the rulers of this age, those being brought to nothing. [7] But we speak *the* wisdom of God in a mystery having been hidden, which God predetermined before the ages for our glory, [8] which none of the rulers of this age has known; for if they had known, they would not have crucified the Lord of glory, [9] but according as it has been written, "Eye has not seen and ear has not heard," nor has it risen up into the heart of man, "the things which God has prepared for those that love Him." [10] But God revealed *them* to us by His Spirit, for the Spirit searches all things, even the depths of God. [11] For who

28 σοφοὺς καταισχύνῃ· καὶ τὰ ἀσθενῆ τοῦ κόσμου ἐξελέξατο ὁ
wise might be shamed; and the weak things of the world chose
Θεός, ἵνα καταισχύνῃ τὰ ἰσχυρά· καὶ τὰ ἀγενῆ τοῦ κόσμου
God, that He might shame the strong things; and the base things of the world
καὶ τὰ ἐξουθενημένα ἐξελέξατο ὁ Θεός, καὶ τὰ μὴ ὄντα, ἵνα
and the things despised chose God, and the things not being, that
29 τὰ ὄντα καταργήσῃ· ὅπως μὴ καυχήσηται πᾶσα σὰρξ
the things being He nullify; so as not might boast all flesh
30 ἐνώπιον αὐτοῦ. ἐξ αὐτοῦ δὲ ὑμεῖς ἐστε ἐν Χριστῷ Ἰησοῦ,
before Him. of Him And you are in Christ Jesus,
ὃς ἐγενήθη ἡμῖν σοφία ἀπὸ Θεοῦ, δικαιοσύνη τε καὶ
who became to us wisdom from God, righteousness both and
31 ἁγιασμός, καὶ ἀπολύτρωσις· ἵνα, καθὼς γέγραπται, Ὁ
sanctification and redemption, that even as has been written: Those
καυχώμενος, ἐν Κυρίῳ καυχάσθω.
boasting, in (the) Lord let him boast

CHAPTER 2

1 Κἀγὼ ἐλθὼν πρὸς ὑμᾶς, ἀδελφοί, ἦλθον οὐ καθ' ὑπεροχὴν
And I coming to you, brothers, came not according to excellence
λόγου ἢ σοφίας καταγγέλλων ὑμῖν τὸ μαρτύριον τοῦ Θεοῦ.
of word or wisdom, announcing to you the testimony of God.
2 οὐ γὰρ ἔκρινα τοῦ εἰδέναι τι ἐν ὑμῖν, εἰ μὴ Ἰησοῦν Χριστόν,
not For I decided to know anything among you, except Jesus Christ,
3 καὶ τοῦτον ἐσταυρωμένον. καὶ ἐγὼ ἐν ἀσθενείᾳ καὶ ἐν φόβῳ
and this (One) having been crucified. And I in weakness and in fear
4 καὶ ἐν τρόμῳ πολλῷ ἐγενόμην πρὸς ὑμᾶς. καὶ ὁ λόγος μου
and in trembling much was with you. And the word of me
καὶ τὸ κήρυγμά μου οὐκ ἐν πειθοῖς ἀνθρωπίνης σοφίας
and the preaching of me not in persuasive of human wisdom
5 λόγοις, ἀλλ' ἐν ἀποδείξει πνεύματος καὶ δυνάμεως· ἵνα ἡ
words but in proof of (the) Spirit and of power; that the
πίστις ὑμῶν μὴ ᾖ ἐν σοφίᾳ ἀνθρώπων, ἀλλ' ἐν δυνάμει Θεοῦ.
faith of you not be in wisdom of men, but in power of God.
6 Σοφίαν δὲ λαλοῦμεν ἐν τοῖς τελείοις· σοφίαν δὲ οὐ τοῦ
wisdom But we speak among the perfect; the wisdom but not—
αἰῶνος τούτου, οὐδὲ τῶν ἀρχόντων τοῦ αἰῶνος τούτου,
age of this, neither of the rulers — age of this.
7 τῶν καταργουμένων· ἀλλὰ λαλοῦμεν σοφίαν Θεοῦ ἐν μυστη-
those being brought to nothing; but we speak a wisdom of God in mystery,
ρίῳ, τὴν ἀποκεκρυμμένην, ἣν προώρισεν ὁ Θεὸς πρὸ τῶν
— having been hidden, which predetermined God before the
8 αἰώνων εἰς δόξαν ἡμῶν· ἣν οὐδεὶς τῶν ἀρχόντων τοῦ αἰῶνος
ages for glory of us; which not one of the rulers — age
τούτου ἔγνωκεν· εἰ γὰρ ἔγνωσαν, οὐκ ἂν τὸν Κύριον τῆς
of this has known; if for they knew, not the Lord —
9 δόξης ἐσταύρωσαν· ἀλλὰ καθὼς γέγραπται, Ἃ ὀφθαλμὸς
of glory they had crucified. But even as it has been written: Things that eye
οὐκ εἶδε, καὶ οὖς οὐκ ἤκουσε, καὶ ἐπὶ καρδίαν ἀνθρώπου οὐκ
did not see, and ear not did hear, and on the heart of man not
10 ἀνέβη, ἃ ἡτοίμασεν ὁ Θεὸς τοῖς ἀγαπῶσιν αὐτόν. ἡμῖν δὲ ὁ
came up, how prepared God those loving Him. to us But
Θεὸς ἀπεκάλυψε διὰ τοῦ πνεύματος αὐτοῦ· τὸ γὰρ πνεῦμα
God revealed through the Spirit of Him, the for Spirit
11 πάντα ἐρευνᾷ, καὶ τὰ βάθη τοῦ Θεοῦ. τίς γὰρ οἶδεν ἀνθρώ-
all things searches, even the deep things of God. who For knows of men

among men knows the things of a man, except the spirit of a man within him? So also no one has known the things of God except the Spirit of God. [12] But we have not received the spirit of the world, but the Spirit from God, that we may know the things freely given to us by God; [13] which things we also speak, not in words taught in human wisdom, but in *words* taught of *the* Holy Spirit, comparing spiritual things with spiritual *things*. [14] But a natural man does not receive the things of *the* Spirit of God, for they are foolishness to him, and he is not able to know *them*, because they are spiritually discerned. [15] But the spiritual one discerns all things, but he is discerned by no one. [16] For who knew *the* mind of *the* Lord? Who will teach Him? But we have *the* mind of Christ.

CHAPTER 3

[1] And, brothers, I was not able to speak to you as to spiritual ones, but as to fleshly, as to babes in Christ. [2] I gave you milk to drink, and not food, for you were not then able; but neither now are you yet able. [3] For you are yet fleshly. For where among you *is* jealousy, and strife, and divisions, are you not fleshly and walk according to man? [4] For when one may say, I am of Paul, and another, I of Apollos, are you not fleshly? [5] Who then is Paul? And who Apollos? But ministers through whom you believed, and to each as the Lord gave. [6] I planted, Apollos watered, but God made to grow. [7] So as neither he planting is anything, nor he watering, but God making to grow. [8] So he planting and he watering are one, and each one will receive *his* own reward according to *his* own labor. [9] For we are fellow-workers, a field of God, *and* you are a building of God.

[10] According to God's grace

πων τὰ τοῦ ἀνθρώπου, εἰ μὴ τὸ πνεῦμα τοῦ ἀνθρώπου τὸ ἐν
the things of a man, except the spirit of a man in
αὐτῷ; οὕτω καὶ τὰ τοῦ Θεοῦ οὐδεὶς οἶδεν, εἰ μὴ τὸ Πνεῦμα
him? So also the things of God no one has known except the Spirit
12 τοῦ Θεοῦ. ἡμεῖς δὲ οὐ τὸ πνεῦμα τοῦ κόσμου ἐλάβομεν, ἀλλὰ
of God. we And not the spirit of the world received, but
τὸ πνεῦμα τὸ ἐκ τοῦ Θεοῦ, ἵνα εἰδῶμεν τὰ ὑπὸ τοῦ Θεοῦ
the Spirit from God, that we may know the things by God
13 χαρισθέντα ἡμῖν. ἃ καὶ λαλοῦμεν, οὐκ ἐν διδακτοῖς ἀνθρω-
freely given to us; which things also we speak, not in taught of
πίνης σοφίας λόγοις, ἀλλ' ἐν διδακτοῖς Πνεύματος Ἁγίου,
human wisdom words, but in (words) taught of (the) Spirit Holy,
14 πνευματικοῖς πνευματικὰ συγκρίνοντες. ψυχικὸς δὲ ἄνθρω-
with spiritual things spiritual things comparing. a natural But man
πος οὐ δέχεται τὰ τοῦ Πνεύματος τοῦ Θεοῦ· μωρία γὰρ
not receives the things of (the) Spirit of God; foolishness for
αὐτῷ ἐστι, καὶ οὐ δύναται γνῶναι, ὅτι πνευματικῶς ἀνακρί-
to him they are; and not he is able to know, because spiritually they are dis-
15 νεται. ὁ δὲ πνευματικὸς ἀνακρίνει μὲν πάντα, αὐτὸς δὲ ὑπ'
cerned. the But spiritual one discerns indeed all things, he but by
16 οὐδενὸς ἀνακρίνεται. τίς γὰρ ἔγνω νοῦν Κυρίου, ὃς συμβιβά-
no one is discerned. who For knew (the) mind of Lord, who will teach
σει αὐτόν; ἡμεῖς δὲ νοῦν Χριστοῦ ἔχομεν.
Him? we But (the) mind of Christ have.

CHAPTER 3

1 Καὶ ἐγώ, ἀδελφοί, οὐκ ἠδυνήθην λαλῆσαι ὑμῖν ὡς πνευ-
And I, brothers, not was able to speak to you as spiritual
2 ματικοῖς, ἀλλ' ὡς σαρκικοῖς, ὡς νηπίοις ἐν Χριστῷ. γάλα
ones, but as to fleshly, as to infants in Christ. milk
ὑμᾶς ἐπότισα, καὶ οὐ βρῶμα· οὔπω γὰρ ἠδύνασθε, ἀλλ'
you I gave to drink, and not food, not then for you were able, but
3 οὔτε ἔτι νῦν δύνασθε· ἔτι γὰρ σαρκικοί ἐστε· ὅπου γὰρ ἐν
neither yet now are you able; still for fleshly you are. where For among
ὑμῖν ζῆλος καὶ ἔρις καὶ διχοστασίαι, οὐχὶ σαρκικοί ἐστε,
you (is) jealousy and strife and divisions, not fleshly are you,
4 καὶ κατὰ ἄνθρωπον περιπατεῖτε; ὅταν γὰρ λέγῃ τις, Ἐγὼ
and according to man walk? when For may say one, I
μέν εἰμι Παύλου, ἕτερος δέ, Ἐγὼ Ἀπολλώ, οὐχὶ σαρκικοί
truly am of Paul, another and, I of Apollos, not fleshly
5 ἐστε; τίς οὖν ἐστι Παῦλος, τίς δὲ Ἀπολλὼς ἀλλ' ἢ διάκονοι
are you? What then is Paul; what and Apollos? But ministers
6 δι' ὧν ἐπιστεύσατε, καὶ ἑκάστῳ ὡς ὁ Κύριος ἔδωκεν; ἐγὼ
through whom you believed, and to each as the Lord gave. I
7 ἐφύτευσα, Ἀπολλὼς ἐπότισεν, ἀλλ' ὁ Θεὸς ηὔξανεν. ὥστε
planted, Apollos watered, but God made to grow. So as
οὔτε ὁ φυτεύων ἐστί τι, οὔτε ὁ ποτίζων, ἀλλ' ὁ αὐξάνων
neither he planting is anything, nor he watering, but He making grow,
8 Θεός. ὁ φυτεύων δὲ καὶ ὁ ποτίζων ἕν εἰσιν· ἕκαστος δὲ τὸν
God. he planting So and he watering one are, each one and the
9 ἴδιον μισθὸν λήψεται κατὰ τὸν ἴδιον κόπον. Θεοῦ γάρ ἐσμεν
own reward will receive according to the own labor. of God For we are
συνεργοί· Θεοῦ γεώργιον, Θεοῦ οἰκοδομή ἐστε.
fellow-workers; Of God, a field; of God a building you are.
10 Κατὰ τὴν χάριν τοῦ Θεοῦ τὴν δοθεῖσάν μοι, ὡς σοφὸς
According to the grace of God given to me, as a wise

given to me, as a wise master-builder, I laid a foundation; but another builds on *it*. But let each one be careful how he builds. [11] For no one is able to lay *any* other foundation beside the *One* having been laid, who is Jesus Christ. [12] And if anyone builds on this foundation gold, silver, precious stones, wood, grass, straw, [13] the work of each will be revealed; for the Day will make *it* known, because it is revealed in fire; and the fire will prove the work of each, what sort it is. [14] If the work of anyone which he built remains, he will receive a reward. [15] If the work of anyone shall be consumed, he shall suffer loss; but he will be saved, but so as through fire.

[16] Do you not know that you are a temple of God, and the Spirit of God dwells in you? [17] If anyone corrupts the temple of God, God will bring that one to corruption; for the temple of God is holy, which you are. [18] Let no one deceive himself; if anyone thinks to be wise among you in this age, let him become foolish, that he may become wise. [19] For the wisdom of this world is foolishness with God; for it has been written, "He takes the wise in their own craftiness." [20] And again, "*The* Lord knows the reasonings of the wise, that they are worthless." [21] So let no one glory in men; for all things are yours, [22] whether Paul, or Apollos, or Cephas, or *the* world, or life, or death, or things present, or things to come—all are yours, [23] and you are Christ's, and Christ *is* God's.

CHAPTER 4

[1] Let a man think of us as ministers of Christ, and stewards of *the* mysteries of God. [2] And the rest, it is sought among stewards that one be found faithful. [3] But to me it is a small thing that I

ἀρχιτέκτων θεμέλιον τέθεικα, ἄλλος δὲ ἐποικοδομεῖ. ἕκαστος
master builder a foundation I laid, another but builds on (it). each one
11 δὲ βλεπέτω πῶς ἐποικοδομεῖ. θεμέλιον γὰρ ἄλλον οὐδεὶς
But let him look how he builds on(it). foundation For other no one
δύναται θεῖναι παρὰ τὸν κείμενον, ὅς ἐστιν Ἰησοῦς ὁ
is able to lay beside the (One) being laid, who is Jesus the
12 Χριστός. εἰ δέ τις ἐποικοδομεῖ ἐπὶ τὸν θεμέλιον τοῦτον
Christ. if And anyone builds on foundation this
χρυσόν, ἄργυρον, λίθους τιμίους, ξύλα, χόρτον, καλάμην,
gold, silver, stones precious, woods, hay, stubble,
13 ἑκάστου τὸ ἔργον φανερὸν γενήσεται· ἡ γὰρ ἡμέρα δηλώσει,
of each one the work manifest will be; the for day will declare,
ὅτι ἐν πυρὶ ἀποκαλύπτεται· καὶ ἑκάστου τὸ ἔργον ὁποῖόν
for by fire it is revealed, and of each one the work of what sort
14 ἐστι τὸ πῦρ δοκιμάσει. εἴ τινος τὸ ἔργον μένει ὃ ἐπῳκοδό-
it is, the fire it will prove. If of someone the work remains, which he built
15 μησε, μισθὸν λήψεται. εἴ τινος τὸ ἔργον κατακαήσεται,
on, a reward he will receive. If anyone the work will be consumed,
ζημιωθήσεται· αὐτὸς δὲ σωθήσεται, οὕτω δὲ ὡς διὰ πυρός.
he will suffer loss, he but will be saved, so but as through fire.
16 Οὐκ οἴδατε ὅτι ναὸς Θεοῦ ἐστε, καὶ τὸ Πνεῦμα τοῦ Θεοῦ
Do not you know that a temple of God you are, and the Spirit of God
17 οἰκεῖ ἐν ὑμῖν; εἴ τις τὸν ναὸν τοῦ Θεοῦ φθείρει. φθερεῖ
dwells in you? If anyone the temple of God corrupts, will corrupt
τοῦτον ὁ Θεός· ὁ γὰρ ναὸς τοῦ Θεοῦ ἅγιός ἐστιν, οἵτινές
this one God. the For temple of God holy is, who
ἐστε ὑμεῖς.
are you.
18 Μηδεὶς ἑαυτὸν ἐξαπατάτω· εἴ τις δοκεῖ σοφὸς εἶναι ἐν
No one himself let deceive; if anyone thinks wise to be among
ὑμῖν ἐν τῷ αἰῶνι τούτῳ, μωρὸς γενέσθω, ἵνα γένηται σοφός.
you in age this, foolish let him become, that he become wise.
19 ἡ γὰρ σοφία τοῦ κόσμου τούτου μωρία παρὰ τῷ Θεῷ ἐστι.
the For wisdom world of this foolishness with God is.
γέγραπται γάρ, Ὁ δρασσόμενος τοὺς σοφοὺς ἐν τῇ πανουρ-
it has been written For: He (is) taking the wise in the craftiness
20 γίᾳ αὐτῶν. καὶ πάλιν, Κύριος γινώσκει τοὺς διαλογισμοὺς
of them. And again: (The) Lord knows the reasonings
21 τῶν σοφῶν, ὅτι εἰσὶ μάταιοι. ὥστε μηδεὶς καυχάσθω ἐν
of the wise, that they are vain. So as no one let boast in
22 ἀνθρώποις· πάντα γὰρ ὑμῶν ἐστιν, εἴτε Παῦλος, εἴτε
men; all things for of you is, whether Paul, or
Ἀπολλώς, εἴτε Κηφᾶς, εἴτε κόσμος, εἴτε ζωή, εἴτε θάνατος
Apollos, or Cephas, or (the) world, or life, or death,
23 εἴτε ἐνεστῶτα, εἴτε μέλλοντα· πάντα ὑμῶν ἐστιν, ὑμεῖς δὲ
or things present, or things coming, all things of you are, you and
Χριστοῦ, Χριστὸς δὲ Θεοῦ.
of Christ, Christ and of God.

CHAPTER 4

1 Οὕτως ἡμᾶς λογιζέσθω ἄνθρωπος, ὡς ὑπηρέτας Χριστοῦ
So us let count a man as ministers of Christ,
2 καὶ οἰκονόμους μυστηρίων Θεοῦ. ὃ δὲ λοιπόν, ζητεῖται ἐν
and stewards of (the) mysteries of God. the And rest, it is sought among
3 τοῖς οἰκονόμοις, ἵνα πιστός τις εὑρεθῇ. ἐμοὶ δὲ εἰς ἐλάχιστόν
— stewards, that faithful anyone be found. to me And for a little thing

should be judged by you, or by a man's day. But neither do I judge myself. [4]For I know nothing of myself, but I have not been justified by this, but He judging me is *the* Lord. [5]Then do not judge anything before time, until the Lord comes, who will both shed light on the hidden things of darkness, and will reveal the counsels of the hearts. And then praise will be to each one from God.

[6]And, brothers, I transferred these things to myself and Apollos because of you, that in us you may learn not to think above what has been written, that you not *be* puffed up one over the other. [7]For who makes you to differ? And what do you have that you did not receive? And if you received *it*, why do you boast as *if you* did not receive? [8]You are already satisfied; you already became rich; you reigned without us—and oh that you really did reign, so that we also might reign with you! [9]For I think that God set us out last, the apostles, as appointed to death, because we became a spectacle to the world, even to angels and to men. [10]We *are* fools for the sake of Christ, but you *are* wise in Christ. We *are* weak, but you *are* strong. You *are* honored, but we not honored. [11]Until the present hour we also hunger and thirst, and are naked, and are buffeted, and wander homeless, [12]and labor, working with our own hands. Being cursed, we bless; persecuted, we bear; [13]defamed, we entreat—we have become as filth of the world, dirt wiped off by all until now. [14]I do not write these things shaming you, but warning you as my beloved children. [15]for if you should have myriads of teachers in Christ, yet not many fathers; for I fathered you in Christ Jesus through the gospel. [16]Then I urge you, be imitators

ἐστιν ἵνα ὑφ' ὑμῶν ἀνακριθῶ, ἢ ὑπὸ ἀνθρωπίνης ἡμέρας·
it is that by you I am judged, or by a man's day;
4 ἀλλ' οὐδὲ ἐμαυτὸν ἀνακρίνω. οὐδὲν γὰρ ἐμαυτῷ σύνοιδα,
but not myself I judge; nothing for against myself I know,
ἀλλ' οὐκ ἐν τούτῳ δεδικαίωμαι· ὁ δὲ ἀνακρίνων με Κύριός
but not by this have I been justified; He but judging me Lord
5 ἐστιν. ὥστε μὴ πρὸ καιροῦ τι κρίνετε, ἕως ἂν ἔλθῃ ὁ Κύριος,
is. So as not before time anything judge, until comes the Lord,
ὃς καὶ φωτίσει τὰ κρυπτὰ τοῦ σκότους, καὶ φανερώσει τὰς
who both will shed light on the hidden things of darkness, and will reveal the
βουλὰς τῶν καρδιῶν· καὶ τότε ὁ ἔπαινος γενήσεται ἑκάστῳ
counsels of the hearts; and then the praise will be to each one
ἀπὸ τοῦ Θεοῦ.
from God.
6 Ταῦτα δέ, ἀδελφοί, μετεσχημάτισα εἰς ἐμαυτὸν καὶ
these things And, brothers, I transferred to myself and
Ἀπολλὼ δι' ὑμᾶς, ἵνα ἐν ἡμῖν μάθητε τὸ μὴ ὑπὲρ ὃ γέγρα-
Apollos because of you, that in us you may learn not above what has been
πται φρονεῖν, ἵνα μὴ εἷς ὑπὲρ τοῦ ἑνὸς φυσιοῦσθε κατὰ τοῦ
written to think, that not one over one you are puffed up against the
7 ἑτέρου. τίς γάρ σε διακρίνει ; τί δὲ ἔχεις ὃ οὐκ ἔλαβες ; εἰ δὲ
other. who For you makes differ? what And have you not you received? if
8 καὶ ἔλαβες, τί καυχᾶσαι ὡς μὴ λαβών ; ἤδη κεκορεσμένοι
And you received, why boast you as not receiving? Already being sated
ἐστέ, ἤδη ἐπλουτήσατε, χωρὶς ἡμῶν ἐβασιλεύσατε· καὶ
you are; already you became rich; without us you reigned, and
ὄφελόν γε ἐβασιλεύσατε, ἵνα καὶ ἡμεῖς ὑμῖν συμβασιλεύσω-
oh that really you did reign, that also we you might reign with.
9 μεν. δοκῶ γὰρ ὅτι ὁ Θεὸς ἡμᾶς τοὺς ἀποστόλους ἐσχάτους
I think For that God us, the apostles, last
ἀπέδειξεν ὡς ἐπιθανατίους· ὅτι θέατρον ἐγενήθημεν τῷ
set out, as appointed to death, because a spectacle we became to the
10 κόσμῳ, καὶ ἀγγέλοις, καὶ ἀνθρώποις. ἡμεῖς μωροὶ διὰ
world, and to angels and to men. We (are) fools because of
Χριστόν, ὑμεῖς δὲ φρόνιμοι ἐν Χριστῷ· ἡμεῖς ἀσθενεῖς, ὑμεῖς
Christ, you but prudent in Christ; we (are) weak, you
11 δὲ ἰσχυροί ὑμεῖς ἔνδοξοι, ἡμεῖς δὲ ἄτιμοι. ἄχρι τῆς ἄρτι
but strong; you (are) honored, we but unhonored. Until the present
ὥρας καὶ πεινῶμεν, καὶ διψῶμεν, καὶ γυμνητεύομεν, καὶ
hour both we hunger, and thirst, and are naked, and
12 κολαφιζόμεθα, και ἀστατοῦμεν, και κοπιῶμεν ἐργαζομενοι
are buffeted, and wander homeless, and labor, working
ταις ἰδίαις χερσί· λοιδορούμενοι εὐλογοῦμεν· διωκόμενοι
with the own hands. Cursed, we bless; persecuted
13 ἀνεχόμεθα· βλασφημούμενοι παρακαλοῦμεν· ὡς περικαθάρ-
we bear; evilly spoken to, we beg; as filth
ματα τοῦ κόσμου ἐγενήθημεν, πάντων περίψημα ἕως ἄρτι.
of the world, we are become; of all dirt wiped off until now.
Οὐκ ἐντρέπων ὑμᾶς γράφω ταῦτα, ἀλλ' ὡς τέκνα μου
not shaming you I write these things, but as children of me
15 ἀγαπητὰ νουθετῶ. ἐὰν γὰρ μυρίους παιδαγωγοὺς ἔχητε ἐν
beloved warning. if For myriads teachers you have in
Χριστῷ, ἀλλ' οὐ πολλοὺς πατέρας· ἐν γὰρ Χριστῷ Ἰησοῦ
Christ, yet not many fathers; in for Christ Jesus
16 διὰ τοῦ εὐαγγελίου· ἐγὼ ὑμᾶς ἐγέννησα. παρακαλῶ οὖν
through the gospel I you fathered. I urge then,

of me. [17]Because of this I sent Timothy to you, who is my beloved child, and faithful in *the* Lord, who will remind you *of* my ways in Christ, even as I teach in every church. [18]As to my not coming to you now, some were puffed up. [19]But if the Lord wills, I will come to you shortly. And I will not know the word of those who have been puffed up, but the power. [20]For the kingdom of God *is* not in word, but in power. [21]What do you desire? *Shall* I come to you with a rod, or in love and a spirit of meekness?

17 ὑμᾶς, μιμηταί μου γίνεσθε. διὰ τοῦτο ἔπεμψα ὑμῖν Τιμόθεον,
you, imitators of me become. Because of this I sent to you Timothy,
ὅς ἐστι τέκνον μου ἀγαπητὸν καὶ πιστὸν ἐν Κυρίῳ, ὃς ὑμᾶς
who is a child of me, beloved and faithful in (the) Lord, who you
ἀναμνήσει τὰς ὁδούς μου τὰς ἐν Χριστῷ, καθὼς πανταχοῦ
will remind (of) the ways of me in Christ, as everywhere
18 ἐν πάσῃ ἐκκλησίᾳ διδάσκω. ὡς μὴ ἐρχομένου δέ μου πρὸς
in every church I teach. When not coming now me to
19 ὑμᾶς ἐφυσιώθησάν τινες. ἐλεύσομαι δὲ ταχέως πρὸς ὑμᾶς,
you were puffed up some. I will come But shortly to you,
ἐὰν ὁ Κύριος θελήσῃ, καὶ γνώσομαι οὐ τὸν λόγον τῶν
if the Lord wills, and I will know not the word of those
20 πεφυσιωμένων, ἀλλὰ τὴν δύναμιν. οὐ γὰρ ἐν λόγῳ ἡ
having been puffed up, but the power. not For in word the
21 βασιλεία τοῦ Θεοῦ, ἀλλ' ἐν δυνάμει. τί θέλετε ; ἐν ῥάβδῳ
kingdom of God, but in power. What desire you? With a rod
ἔλθω πρὸς ὑμᾶς, ἢ ἐν ἀγάπῃ πνεύματί τε πρᾳότητος ;
I come to you, or in love, a spirit and of meekness?

CHAPTER 5

CHAPTER 5

[1]Everywhere *it* is heard that fornication *is* among you, and such fornication which *is* not named among the heathen, so as one to have *his* father's wife. [2]And you are puffed up, and have not rather mourned, that he that did this deed might be taken from your midst. [3]For as being absent in body, but being present in spirit, I have already judged the *one* who has worked out this thing, as *if I were* present. [4]In the name of our Lord Jesus Christ—you being gathered together with my spirit, with the power of our Lord Jesus Christ— [5]to deliver such a one to Satan for destruction of the flesh, that the spirit may be saved in the day of the Lord Jesus. [6]Your boast *is* not good. Do you not know that a little leaven leavens all the lump? [7]Therefore, purge out the old leaven so that you may be a new lump, even as you are unleavened. For also Christ our Passover was sacrificed for us. [8]So let us keep *the* feast, not with old leaven, nor with leaven of malice and of evil but with unleavened *bread* of sincerity and truth.

1 Ὅλως ἀκούεται ἐν ὑμῖν πορνεία, καὶ τοιαύτη πορνεία,
Everywhere (it) is heard among you fornication, and such fornication
ἥτις οὐδὲ ἐν τοῖς ἔθνεσιν ὀνομάζεται, ὥστε γυναῖκά τινα
which (is) not among the nations named, so as (the) wife one
2 τοῦ πατρὸς ἔχειν. καὶ ὑμεῖς πεφυσιωμένοι ἐστέ, καὶ οὐχὶ
of the father to have. And you having been puffed up are, and not
μᾶλλον ἐπενθήσατε, ἵνα ἐξαρθῇ ἐκ μέσου ὑμῶν ὁ τὸ ἔργον
rather mourned, that might be taken from your midst he deed
3 τοῦτο ποιήσας. ἐγὼ μὲν γὰρ ὡς ἀπὼν τῷ σώματι παρὼν
this did. I indeed For as being absent in the body, but present
δὲ τῷ πνεύματι, ἤδη κέκρικα ὡς παρών, τὸν οὕτω τοῦτο
in the spirit, already have judged as being present he thus this thing
4 κατεργασάμενον, ἐν τῷ ὀνόματι τοῦ Κυρίου ἡμῶν Ἰησοῦ
having worked out. In the name of the Lord of us, Jesus
Χριστοῦ, συναχθέντων ὑμῶν καὶ τοῦ ἐμοῦ πνεύματος, σὺν
Christ, being gathered together you and the of me spirit, with
5 τῇ δυνάμει τοῦ Κυρίου ἡμῶν Ἰησοῦ Χριστοῦ, παραδοῦναι
the power of the Lord of us, Jesus Christ, to deliver
τὸν τοιοῦτον τῷ Σατανᾷ εἰς ὄλεθρον τῆς σαρκός, ἵνα τὸ
such a one to Satan for destruction of the flesh, that the
6 πνεῦμα σωθῇ ἐν τῇ ἡμέρᾳ τοῦ Κυρίου Ἰησοῦ. οὐ καλὸν τὸ
spirit may be saved in the day of the Lord Jesus. Not good (is) the
καύχημα ὑμῶν. οὐκ οἴδατε ὅτι μικρὰ ζύμη ὅλον τὸ φύραμα
boast of you. Do not you know that a little leaven all the lump
7 ζυμοῖ ; ἐκκαθάρατε οὖν τὴν παλαιὰν ζύμην, ἵνα ἦτε νέον
leavens? purge out Then the old leaven, that you be a new
φύραμα, καθώς ἐστε ἄζυμοι. καὶ γὰρ τὸ πάσχα ἡμῶν ὑπὲρ
lump, as you are unleavened. also For the Passover of us for
8 ἡμῶν ἐθύθη Χριστός· ὥστε ἑορτάζωμεν, μὴ ἐν ζύμῃ παλαιᾷ,
us was sacrificed, Christ, so as let us keep feast, not with leaven old,
μηδὲ ἐν ζύμῃ κακίας καὶ πονηρίας, ἀλλ' ἐν ἀζύμοις εἰλι-
not with leaven of malice and of evil: but with unleavened of
κρινείας καὶ ἀληθείας.
sincerity and truth.

[9]I wrote to you in the letter

9 Ἔγραψα ὑμῖν ἐν τῇ ἐπιστολῇ μὴ συναναμίγνυσθαι
I wrote to you in the epistle not to associate intimately

not to associate with fornicators; [10] and not altogether with this world's fornicators, or with the covetous, or with plunderers, or with idolaters, since then you must go out of the world. [11] But now I wrote to you not to intimately associate if anyone is called a brother *and is* either a fornicator, or an idolater, or a reviler, or a drunkard, or a plunderer, with such a one not to eat. [12] For what *is it* to me to also judge the ones outside? Do you not judge those inside? [13] But God will judge those outside. And you shall put out the evil one from you.

CHAPTER 6

[1] Does anyone of you having a matter against another dare to be judged before the unjust, and not before the saints? [2] Do you not know that the saints will judge the world? And if the world is judged by you, are you unworthy of small judgments? [3] Or do you not know that we shall judge angels, not to speak of this life? [4] If, then, you truly have judgments of this life, those being least esteemed in the church, you sit these. [5] For I speak shame to you. So, is there not a wise one among you, not even one who will be able to judge his brother in your midst? [6] But brother is judged with brother, and this before unbelievers! [7] Indeed, then, a failure is already with you all, that you have lawsuits with yourselves. Why not instead be deprived? Why not instead be wronged? [8] But you do wrong, and defraud; and these things *to* brothers! [9] Or do you not know that unjust ones will not inherit *the* kingdom of God? Do not be led astray, neither fornicators, nor idolaters, nor adulterers, no abusers, nor homosexuals, [10] nor thieves, nor covetous ones, nor drunkards, nor revilers, nor plunderers shall inherit *the* kingdom of God. [11] And some were these things, but you were washed; but you were sanctified; but you were justified in the name of the

10 πόρνοις· καὶ οὐ πάντως τοῖς πόρνοις τοῦ κόσμου τούτου,
with fornicators, and not altogether with the fornicators world of this,
ἢ τοῖς πλεονέκταις, ἢ ἅρπαξιν, ἢ εἰδωλολάτραις· ἐπεὶ
or with the covetous, or with plunderers, or with idolaters, since
11 ὀφείλετε ἄρα ἐκ τοῦ κόσμου ἐξελθεῖν. νυνὶ δὲ ἔγραψα ὑμῖν
you ought then out of the world to go out. now But I wrote to you
μὴ συναναμίγνυσθαι, ἐάν τις ἀδελφὸς ὀνομαζόμενος ᾖ
not to associate intimately if anyone a brother is called (is) either
πόρνος, ἢ πλεονέκτης, ἢ εἰδωλολάτρης, ἢ λοίδορος, ἢ
a fornicator, or a covetous, or an idolater, or a reviler, or
12 μέθυσος, ἢ ἅρπαξ· τῷ τοιούτῳ μηδὲ συνεσθίειν. τί γάρ μοι
drunkard, or a plunderer, with such a one not to eat. what For to me
13 καὶ τοὺς ἔξω κρίνειν ; οὐχὶ τοὺς ἔσω ὑμεῖς κρίνετε ; τοὺς δὲ
also those outside to judge? Do not those inside you judge? those But
ἔξω ὁ Θεὸς κρίνει. καὶ ἐξαρεῖτε τὸν πονηρὸν ἐξ ὑμῶν αὐτῶν
outside God will judge. And you shall put out the evil one from yourselves.

CHAPTER 6

1 Τολμᾷ τις ὑμῶν, πρᾶγμα ἔχων πρὸς τὸν ἕτερον, κρίνεσθαι
Dares anyone of you a matter having against another to be judged
2 ἐπὶ τῶν ἀδίκων, καὶ οὐχὶ ἐπὶ τῶν ἁγίων ; οὐκ οἴδατε ὅτι οἱ
before the unjust, and not before the saints? Do not you know that the
ἅγιοι τὸν κόσμον κρινοῦσι ; καὶ εἰ ἐν ὑμῖν κρίνεται ὁ κόσμος,
saints the world will judge? And if by you is judged the world,
3 ἀνάξιοί ἐστε κριτηρίων ἐλαχίστων ; οὐκ οἴδατε ὅτι ἀγγέ-
unworthy are you judgments of small? Do not you know that angels
4 λους κρινοῦμεν ; μήτι γε βιωτικά ; βιωτικὰ μὲν οὖν κριτήρια
we will judge, not to speak of this life? Of this life truly then judgments
ἐὰν ἔχητε, τοὺς ἐξουθενημένους ἐν τῇ ἐκκλησίᾳ, τούτους
if you have, those being least esteemed in the church, these
5 καθίζετε. πρὸς ἐντροπὴν ὑμῖν λέγω. οὕτως οὐκ ἔστιν ἐν
sit you. For shame to you I say. Thus, not is among
ὑμῖν σοφὸς οὐδὲ εἷς, ὃς δυνήσεται διακρῖναι ἀνὰ μέσον τοῦ
you a wise one, not one who will be able to discern in your midst the
6 ἀδελφοῦ αὐτοῦ, ἀλλὰ ἀδελφὸς μετὰ ἀδελφοῦ κρίνεται, καὶ
brother of him? But brother with brother is judged, and
7 τοῦτο ἐπὶ ἀπίστων ; ἤδη μὲν οὖν ὅλως ἥττημα ἐν ὑμῖν ἐστιν,
this before unbelievers. Already indeed, then all a failure with you is,
ὅτι κρίματα ἔχετε μεθ' ἑαυτῶν. διατί οὐχὶ μᾶλλον ἀδικεῖσθε ;
that lawsuits you have with yourselves. Why not instead be wronged?
8 διατί οὐχὶ μᾶλλον ἀποστερεῖσθε ; ἀλλὰ ὑμεῖς ἀδικεῖτε καὶ
Why not instead be despoiled? But you do wrong and
9 ἀποστερεῖτε, καὶ ταῦτα ἀδελφούς. ἢ οὐκ οἴδατε ὅτι ἄδικοι
despoil, and these things (to) brothers. Or not you know that unjust ones
βασιλείαν Θεοῦ οὐ κληρονομήσουσι ; μὴ πλανᾶσθε· οὔτε
(the) kingdom of God not will inherit? Be not led astray; not
πόρνοι, οὔτε εἰδωλολάτραι, οὔτε μοιχοί, οὔτε μαλακοί, οὔτε
fornicators, nor idolaters, nor adulterers, nor abusers, nor
10 ἀρσενοκοῖται, οὔτε κλέπται, οὔτε πλεονέκται, οὔτε μέθυσοι,
homosexuals, nor thieves, nor covetous ones, nor drunkards,
οὐ λοίδοροι, οὐχ ἅρπαγες, βασιλείαν Θεοῦ οὐ κληρονομή-
not revilers, not plunderers (the) kingdom of God not shall
11 σουσι. καὶ ταῦτά τινες ἦτε· ἀλλὰ ἀπελούσασθε, ἀλλὰ
inherit. And these things some were. But you were washed; but
ἡγιάσθητε, ἀλλ' ἐδικαιώθητε ἐν τῷ ὀνόματι τοῦ Κυρίου
you were sanctified; but you were justified in the name of the Lord

Lord Jesus, and in the Spirit of our God.

[12] All things are lawful to me, but not all things profit. All things are lawful to me, but I will not be ruled by anyone. [13] Foods for the belly, and the belly for foods; but God will destroy both this and these. But the body *is* not for fornication, but for the Lord. [14] And God also raised up the Lord, and will raise us up through His power. [15] Do you not know that your bodies are members of Christ? Then taking the members of Christ, shall I make *them* members of a harlot? Let it not be! [16] Or do you not know that he being joined to a harlot is one body? For He says, "The two *shall be* into one flesh." [17] But he being joined to the Lord is one spirit. [18] Flee fornication. Every sin which a man may do is outside the body, but he doing fornication sins against *his* own body. [19] Or do you not know that your body is a temple of *the* Holy Spirit in you, which you have from God, and you are not of yourselves? [20] You were bought with a price; then glorify God in your body, and in your spirit, which are of God.

CHAPTER 7

[1] But concerning what you wrote to me, *it is* good for a man not to touch a woman; [2] but because of fornication, let each have his *own* wife, and let each have *her* own husband. [3] Let the husband give due kindness to the wife; and likewise the wife also to the husband. [4] The wife does not have authority of *her* own body, but the husband. And likewise also the husband does not have authority *over his* own body, but the wife. [5] Do not deprive one another, unless by agreement for a time, that you may be free for fasting and prayer. And come together again on the same *place*, that Satan may not

Ἰησοῦ, καὶ ἐν τῷ Πνεύματι τοῦ Θεοῦ ἡμῶν.
Jesus, and in the Spirit God of us.
12 Πάντα μοι ἔξεστιν, ἀλλ' οὐ πάντα συμφέρει· πάντα μοι
All things to me are lawful, but not all things contribute. All things to me
ἔξεστιν, ἀλλ' οὐκ ἐγὼ ἐξουσιασθήσομαι ὑπό τινος. τὰ
are lawful, but not I will be ruled by anyone. –
13 βρώματα τῇ κοιλίᾳ, καὶ ἡ κοιλία τοῖς βρώμασιν· ὁ δὲ Θεὸς
Foods for the belly, and the belly – for foods; but God
καὶ ταύτην καὶ ταῦτα καταργήσει. τὸ δὲ σῶμα οὐ τῇ
both this and these will destroy. the But body not(is)
14 πορνείᾳ, ἀλλὰ τῷ Κυρίῳ, καὶ ὁ Κύριος τῷ σώματι· ὁ δὲ
for fornication, but for the Lord, and the Lord for the body. And
Θεὸς καὶ τὸν Κύριον ἤγειρε, καὶ ἡμᾶς ἐξεγερεῖ διὰ της
God also the Lord raised, and us will raise up through the
15 δυνάμεως αὐτοῦ. οὐκ οἴδατε ὅτι τὰ σώματα ὑμῶν μέλη
power of Him. Do not you know that the bodies of you members
Χριστοῦ ἐστιν; ἄρας οὖν τὰ μέλη τοῦ Χριστοῦ ποιήσω
of Christ are? having taken Then the members of Christ, Shall I make
16 πόρνης μέλη; μὴ γένοιτο. ἢ οὐκ οἴδατε ὅτι ὁ κολλώμενος τῇ
of a harlot members? Not let it be! Or not you know that he being joined
πόρνῃ ἓν σῶμά ἐστιν; Ἔσονται γάρ, φησίν, οἱ δύο εἰς σάρκα
to a harlot one body is? will be For, He says, the two into flesh
17 μίαν. ὁ δὲ κολλώμενος τῷ Κυρίῳ ἓν πνεῦμά ἐστι. φεύγετε τὴν
18 one. he But being joined to the Lord one spirit is. Flee –
πορνείαν. πᾶν ἁμάρτημα ὃ ἐὰν ποιήσῃ ἄνθρωπος ἐκτὸς τοῦ
fornication. Every sin which if may do a man outside the
σώματός ἐστιν· ὁ δὲ πορνεύων εἰς τὸ ἴδιον σῶμα ἁμαρτάνει.
body is, he but doing fornication against the own body sins.
19 ἢ οὐκ οἴδατε ὅτι τὸ σῶμα ὑμῶν ναὸς τοῦ ἐν ὑμῖν Ἁγίου
Or not you know that the body of you a temple of the in you Holy
Πνεύματός ἐστιν, οὗ ἔχετε ἀπὸ Θεοῦ; καὶ οὐκ ἐστὲ ἑαυτῶν,
Spirit is, which you have from God; and not are you of yourselves?
20 ἠγοράσθητε γὰρ τιμῆς· δοξάσατε δὴ τὸν Θεὸν ἐν τῷ σώματι
you were bought For of a price; glorify then God in the body
ὑμῶν, καὶ ἐν τῷ πνεύματι ὑμῶν, ἅτινά ἐστι τοῦ Θεοῦ.
of you, and in the spirit of you, which are of God.

CHAPTER 7

1 Περὶ δὲ ὧν ἐγράψατέ μοι, καλὸν ἀνθρώπῳ γυναικὸς μὴ
concerning But what you wrote to me, (it is) good for a man a woman not
2 ἅπτεσθαι. διὰ δὲ τὰς πορνείας ἕκαστος τὴν ἑαυτοῦ γυναῖκα
to touch; because of but the fornications each one the of himself wife
3 ἐχέτω, καὶ ἑκάστη τὸν ἴδιον ἄνδρα ἐχέτω. τῇ γυναικὶ ὁ ἀνὴρ
have; and each one the own husband have. To the wife the husband
τὴν ὀφειλομένην εὔνοιαν ἀποδιδότω· ὁμοίως δὲ καὶ ἡ γυνὴ
due kindness let pay; likewise and also the wife
4 τῷ ἀνδρί. ἡ γυνὴ τοῦ ἰδίου σώματος οὐκ ἐξουσιάζει, ἀλλ'
to the husband. The wife of the own body not has authority, but
ὁ ἀνήρ· ὁμοίως δὲ καὶ ὁ ἀνὴρ τοῦ ἰδίου σώματος οὐκ ἐξου-
the husband; likewise and also the husband the own body not has
5 σιάζει, ἀλλ' ἡ γυνή. μὴ ἀποστερεῖτε ἀλλήλους, εἰ μή τι ἂν
authority, but the wife. Do not deprive one another, unless
ἐκ συμφώνου πρὸς καιρόν, ἵνα σχολάζητε τῇ νηστείᾳ καὶ
by agreement for a time, that you may be free for fasting and
τῇ προσευχῇ, καὶ πάλιν ἐπὶ τὸ αὐτὸ συνέρχησθε, ἵνα μὴ
for prayer; and again on the same (place) come together, that not

tempt you through your incontinence. 6 But I say this by permission, not by command. 7 But I desire all men also to be as myself. But each has his own gift from God, one this way, and one that way. 8 But I say to the unmarried men, and to the widows, it is good for them if they also remain as I. 9 But if they do not have self-control, let them marry; for it is better to marry than to be inflamed. 10 But I command the ones being married—not I, but the Lord—a woman not to be separated from *her* husband; 11 but if she indeed is separated, remain unmarried; or be reconciled to the husband; and a husband not to leave *his* wife. 12 But to the rest I say, not the Lord, if any brother has an unbelieving wife, and she consents to live with him, let him not leave her. 13 And a woman who has an unbelieving husband, and he consents to live with her, let her not leave him. 14 For the unbelieving husband has been sanctified by the wife; and the unbelieving wife has been sanctified by the husband; else, then, your children are unclean; but now they are holy. 15 But if the unbelieving one separates, let *them* be separated; the brother or the sister is not in bondage in such matters; but God has called us in peace. 16 For what do you know, wife, whether you will save the husband; or what do you know, husband, whether you will save the wife? 17 Only as God has divided to each, each as the Lord has called, so let him walk. So I command in the churches.

18 *Was* anyone called having been circumcised? Do not be uncircumcised. Was anyone called in uncircumcision? Do not be circumcised. 19 Circumcision is nothing, and uncircumcision is nothing; but the keeping of God's commands. 20 Each one in the calling in which he was called, in this remain. 21 Were you called *as* a slave? It does not matter to you. But if you are able to

6 πειράζῃ ὑμᾶς ὁ Σατανᾶς διὰ τὴν ἀκρασίαν ὑμῶν. τοῦτο δὲ
may tempt you Satan through the incontinence of you. this And
7 λέγω κατὰ συγγνώμην, οὐ κατ' ἐπιταγήν. θέλω γὰρ
I say by permission, not by command. I desire For
πάντας ἀνθρώπους εἶναι ὡς καὶ ἐμαυτόν· ἀλλ' ἕκαστος ἴδιον
all men to be as also myself; but each one (his) own
χάρισμα ἔχει ἐκ Θεοῦ, ὃς μὲν οὕτως, ὃς δὲ οὕτως.
gift has from God, one thus, one and thus.
8 Λέγω δὲ τοῖς ἀγάμοις καὶ ταῖς χήραις, καλὸν αὐτοῖς
I say And to the bachelors and to the widows, good for them
9 ἐστιν ἐὰν μείνωσιν ὡς κἀγώ. εἰ δὲ οὐκ ἐγκρατεύονται,
it is if they remain as I also. if But not have self-control,
γαμησάτωσαν· κρεῖσσον γάρ ἐστι γαμῆσαι ἢ πυροῦσθαι.
let them marry; better for it is to marry than to be inflamed.
10 τοῖς δὲ γεγαμηκόσι παραγγέλλω, οὐκ ἐγώ, ἀλλ' ὁ Κύριος,
to those But having married I enjoin, not I, but the Lord,
11 γυναῖκα ἀπὸ ἀνδρὸς μὴ χωρισθῆναι (ἐὰν δὲ καὶ χωρισθῇ,
a woman from (her) husband not to be separated — if but indeed she is separated
μενέτω ἄγαμος, ἢ τῷ ἀνδρὶ καταλλαγήτω)· καὶ ἄνδρα
remain unmarried, or to the husband be reconciled — and a husband
12 γυναῖκα μὴ ἀφιέναι. τοῖς δὲ λοιποῖς ἐγὼ λέγω, οὐχ ὁ
(his) wife not to leave. to the And rest I say, not the
Κύριος· εἴ τις ἀδελφὸς γυναῖκα ἔχει ἄπιστον, καὶ αὐτὴ
Lord: If any brother a wife has unbelieving, and she
13 συνευδοκεῖ οἰκεῖν μετ' αὐτοῦ, μὴ ἀφιέτω αὐτήν. καὶ γυνὴ
consents to live with him, not let him leave her. And a woman
ἥτις ἔχει ἄνδρα ἄπιστον, καὶ αὐτὸς συνευδοκεῖ οἰκεῖν μετ'
who has a husband unbelieving, and he consents to live with
14 αὐτῆς, μὴ ἀφιέτω αὐτόν. ἡγίασται γὰρ ὁ ἀνὴρ ὁ ἄπιστος
her, not let her leave him. has been sanctified For the husband unbelieving
ἐν τῇ γυναικί, καὶ ἡγίασται ἡ γυνὴ ἡ ἄπιστος ἐν τῷ ἀνδρί·
by the wife; and has been sanctified the wife unbelieving by the husband;
ἐπεὶ ἄρα τὰ τέκνα ὑμῶν ἀκάθαρτά ἐστι, νῦν δὲ ἅγιά ἐστιν.
else then the children of you unclean is; now but holy they are.
15 εἰ δὲ ὁ ἄπιστος χωρίζεται, χωριζέσθω. οὐ δεδούλωται ὁ
if But the unbelieving separates, let be separated; not is in bondage the
ἀδελφὸς ἢ ἡ ἀδελφὴ ἐν τοῖς τοιούτοις· ἐν δὲ εἰρήνῃ κέκληκεν
brother or the sister in such matters; in but peace has called
16 ἡμᾶς ὁ Θεός. τί γὰρ οἶδας, γύναι, εἰ τὸν ἄνδρα σώσεις ; ἢ τί
us God. what For know you, wife, if the husband you will save; what
17 οἶδας, ἄνερ, εἰ τὴν γυναῖκα σώσεις ; εἰ μὴ ἑκάστῳ ὡς ἐμέρισεν
know you, husband, if the wife you will save? Only to each as has divided
ὁ Θεός, ἕκαστον ὡς κέκληκεν ὁ Κύριος, οὕτω περιπατείτω.
God, each as has called the Lord, so let him walk.
18 καὶ οὕτως ἐν ταῖς ἐκκλησίαις πάσαις διατάσσομαι. περι-
And so in the churches all I command. Having
τετμημένος τις ἐκλήθη ; μὴ ἐπισπάσθω. ἐν ἀκροβυστίᾳ τις
been circumcised any was called not be uncircumcised; uncircumcision any
ἐκλήθη ; μὴ περιτεμνέσθω. ἡ περιτομὴ οὐδέν ἐστι, καὶ ἡ
was called, not be circumcised. Circumcision nothing is, and
19 ἀκροβυστία οὐδέν ἐστιν, ἀλλὰ τήρησις ἐντολῶν Θεοῦ.
uncircumcision nothing is, but the keeping of the commands of God.
20 ἕκαστος ἐν τῇ κλήσει ᾗ ἐκλήθη, ἐν ταύτῃ μενέτω. δοῦλος
Each one in the calling in which he was called, in this remain. a slave
21 ἐκλήθης ; μή σοι μελέτω· ἀλλ' εἰ καὶ δύνασαι ἐλεύθερος
Were you called? Not to you it matters. But if also you are able free

be free, rather use *it*. [22]For the *one* called a slave in *the* Lord is a freed man of *the* Lord. And likewise, the *one* called a free man is a slave of Christ. [23]You were redeemed with a price; do not become slaves of men. [24]Each in whatever *state* called, brothers, in this remain with God.

[25]But about virgins, I have no command of *the* Lord. But I give judgment, as having received mercy by *the* Lord to be faithful. [26]Then I think this to be good, because of the present necessity: that *it is* good for a man to be thus; [27]Have you been bound to a wife? Do not seek to be released. Have you been released from a wife? Do not seek a wife. [28]But if you also marry, you do not sin; and if the virgin marries, she does not sin. But such will have trouble in the flesh. But I am sparing you. [29]But I say this, brothers, that the time has been cut short. For the rest is that even the *ones* having wives should be as not having; [30]and those weeping as not weeping; and those rejoicing as not rejoicing; and those buying as not possessing; [31]and those using this world as not abusing *it*; for the mode of this world is passing away.

[32]But I desire you to be without care. The unmarried one cares for the things of *the* Lord, how to please the Lord; [33]but the *one* marrying cares for the things of the world, how to please the wife. [34]The wife and the virgin *are* different. The unmarried cares for the things of *the* Lord, that she be holy in both body and spirit. But the married cares for the things of the world, how to please the husband. [35]And I say this for your advantage, not that I put a snare *before* you; but for the fitting thing, and waiting on the Lord without distraction.

[36]But if anyone thinks *it* behaving indecently toward his virginity—if he *is* beyond *his* prime, and so it ought to be—let him do what he desires; he does not sin; let

22 γενέσθαι, μᾶλλον χρῆσαι. ὁ γὰρ ἐν Κυρίῳ κληθεὶς δοῦλος,
to become, rather use (it). the (one) For in (the) Lord called a slave
ἀπελεύθερος Κυρίου ἐστίν· ὁμοίως καὶ ὁ ἐλεύθερος κληθείς,
a freed man of (the) Lord is. likewise And the (one) a free man called
23 δοῦλός ἐστι Χριστοῦ. τιμῆς ἠγοράσθητε· μὴ γίνεσθε δοῦλοι
a slave is of Christ. Of a price you were bought; not become slaves
24 ἀνθρώπων. ἕκαστος ἐν ᾧ ἐκλήθη, ἀδελφοί, ἐν τούτῳ μενέτω
of men. Each one in what (state) called, brothers, in this remain
παρὰ τῷ Θεῷ.
with God.

25 Περὶ δὲ τῶν παρθένων ἐπιταγὴν Κυρίου οὐκ ἔχω· γνώμην
about And the virgins a command of (the) Lord not I have, judgment
26 δὲ δίδωμι ὡς ἠλεημένος ὑπὸ Κυρίου πιστὸς εἶναι. νομίζω οὖν
but I give as having had mercy by (the) Lord faithful to be. I think, then,
τοῦτο καλὸν ὑπάρχειν διὰ τὴν ἐνεστῶσαν ἀνάγκην, ὅτι
this good to be because of the present necessity; that (is)
27 καλὸν ἀνθρώπῳ τὸ οὕτως εἶναι. δέδεσαι γυναικί; μὴ ζήτει
good for a men — so to be. Have you been bound to a woman? Not seek
28 λύσιν. λέλυσαι ἀπὸ γυναικός; μὴ ζήτει γυναῖκα. ἐὰν δὲ καὶ
to be loosed. Have you been loosed from a woman? Not seek a woman. if But indeed
γήμῃς, οὐχ ἥμαρτες· καὶ ἐὰν γήμῃ ἡ παρθενος, οὐχ ἥμαρτε.
you marry, not you sin. And if marries the virgin, not she sinned.
θλίψιν δὲ τῇ σαρκὶ ἕξουσιν οἱ τοιοῦτοι· ἐγὼ δὲ ὑμῶν φείδομαι.
trouble But in the flesh will have such. I But you am sparing.
29 τοῦτο δέ φημι, ἀδελφοί, ὅτι ὁ καιρὸς συνεσταλμένος· τὸ
this But I say, brothers, that the time has been shortened; for
λοιπόν ἐστιν ἵνα καὶ οἱ ἔχοντες γυναῖκας ὡς μὴ ἔχοντες ὦσι·
the rest is, that even those having wives, as not having be;
30 καὶ οἱ κλαίοντες, ὡς μὴ κλαίοντες· καὶ οἱ χαίροντες, ὡς μὴ
and those weeping, as not weeping; and those rejoicing, as not
31 χαίροντες· καὶ οἱ ἀγοράζοντες, ὡς μὴ κατέχοντες· καὶ οἱ
rejoicing; and those buying, as not possessing; and those
χρώμενοι τῷ κόσμῳ τούτῳ, ὡς μὴ καταγρώμενοι· παράγει
using world this, as not abusing (it); is passing away
32 γὰρ τὸ σχῆμα τοῦ κόσμου τούτου. θέλω δὲ ὑμᾶς ἀμερίμνους
for the mode world of this. I desire But you without care
33 εἶναι. ὁ ἄγαμος μεριμνᾷ τὰ τοῦ Κυρίου, πῶς ἀρέσει τῷ
to be. The unmarried one cares for the things of (the) Lord, how to please the
Κυρίῳ· ὁ δὲ γαμήσας μεριμνᾷ τὰ τοῦ κόσμου, πῶς ἀρέσει
Lord; he but having married cares for the things of the world, how to please
34 τῇ γυναικί. μεμέρισται ἡ γυνὴ καὶ ἡ παρθένος. ἡ ἄγαμος
the wife, Different (are) the wife and the virgin. The unmarried
μεριμνᾷ τὰ τοῦ Κυρίου, ἵνα ᾖ ἁγία καὶ σώματι καὶ πνεύματι·
cares for the things of (the) Lord, that she be holy both in body and in spirit;
ἡ δὲ γαμήσασα μεριμνᾷ τὰ τοῦ κόσμου, πῶς ἀρέσει τῷ
the but married cares for the things of (the) world, how to please the
35 ἀνδρί. τοῦτο δὲ πρὸς τὸ ὑμῶν αὐτῶν συμφέρον λέγω· οὐχ
husband. this And for the of yourselves advantage I say, not
ἵνα βρόχον ὑμῖν ἐπιβάλω, ἀλλὰ πρὸς τὸ εὔσχημον καὶ
that a snare (before) you I put; but for the thing fitting and
36 εὐπρόσεδρον τῷ Κυρίῳ ἀπερισπάστως. εἰ δέ τις ἀσχημονεῖν
waiting on the Lord without distraction. If But any to behave indecently
ἐπὶ τὴν παρθένον αὐτοῦ νομίζει, ἐὰν ᾖ ὑπέρακμος, καὶ οὕτως
toward the virginity of him thinks — if he is beyond (his) prime, and so
ὀφείλει γίνεσθαι, ὃ θέλει ποιείτω· οὐχ ἁμαρτάνει· γαμείτω-
(it) ought to be, what he desires let him do; not he sins; let them

them marry. [37]But *he* who stands firm in heart, not having necessity, but has authority as to *his* own will, and has judged this in his heart, to keep his virginity; he does well. [38]So that he that gives in marriage does well; and he that does not give in marriage does better. [39]A wife is bound by law for as long a time as her husband lives; but if her husband sleeps, she is free to be married to whomever she desires, only in *the* Lord. [40]But she is happier if she remains so, according to my judgment. And I think I also have *the* Spirit of God.

CHAPTER 8

[1]But concerning the sacrifices to idols, we know that we have all knowledge. Knowledge puffs up, but love builds up. [2]But if anyone thinks to know anything, he still has known nothing as he ought to know. [3]But if anyone loves God, he has been known by Him. [4]Then concerning the eating of things sacrificed to idols, we know that an idol *is* nothing in *the* world, and that *there is* no other God except one. [5]For even if *some* are called gods, either in Heaven or on the earth; even as there are many gods, and many lords; [6]but to us *is* one God, the Father, of whom *are* all things, and we for Him; and one Lord, Jesus Christ, through whom *are* all things, and we by Him. [7]But the knowledge *is* not in all; but some being aware of the idol eat as an idolatrous sacrifice until now; and their conscience being weak is defiled. [8]But food will not commend us to God. For neither if we eat do we excel, nor if we do not eat are we behind. [9]But be careful lest this authority of yours become a cause of stumbling to the weak ones. [10]For if anyone sees you, he having knowledge, sitting in an idol-temple, will not the weak one's conscience be lifted up

37 σαν. ὃς δὲ ἕστηκεν ἑδραῖος ἐν τῇ καρδίᾳ, μὴ ἔχων ἀνάγκην,
marry. (he) who but stands firm in the heart, not having necessity,
ἐξουσίαν δὲ ἔχει περὶ τοῦ ἰδίου θελήματος, καὶ τοῦτο
authority but has concerning the own will, and this
κέκρικεν ἐν τῇ καρδίᾳ αὐτοῦ, τοῦ τηρεῖν τὴν ἑαυτοῦ
has judged in the heart of him, to keep the of himself
38 παρθένον, καλῶς ποιεῖ. ὥστε καὶ ὁ ἐκγαμίζων καλῶς ποιεῖ·
virginity, well he does. So as both he giving in marriage well does,
39 ὁ δὲ μὴ ἐκγαμίζων κρεῖσσον ποιεῖ. γυνὴ δέδεται νόμῳ ἐφ'
he and not giving in marriage better does. A wife has been bound by law for
ὅσον χρόνον ζῇ ὁ ἀνὴρ αὐτῆς· ἐὰν δὲ κοιμηθῇ ὁ ἀνὴρ αὐτῆς,
as long a time as lives her husband; if but sleeps the husband of her,
ἐλευθέρα ἐστὶν ᾧ θέλει γαμηθῆναι, μόνον ἐν Κυρίῳ. μακα-
free she is to whom she desires to be married, only in (the) Lord.
40 ριωτέρα δέ ἐστιν ἐὰν οὕτω μείνῃ, κατὰ τὴν ἐμὴν γνώμην·
happier But she is if so she remains, according to my judgment;
δοκῶ δὲ κἀγὼ Πνεῦμα Θεοῦ ἔχειν.
I think and I also (the) Spirit of God have.

CHAPTER 8

1 Περὶ δὲ τῶν εἰδωλοθύτων, οἴδαμεν ὅτι πάντες γνῶσιν
concerning And the idolatrous sacrifices, we know that all knowledge
2 ἔχομεν. ἡ γνῶσις φυσιοῖ, ἡ δὲ ἀγάπη οἰκοδομεῖ. εἰ δέ τις
we have. Knowledge puffs up, but love builds up. if But any
δοκεῖ εἰδέναι τι, οὐδέπω οὐδὲν ἔγνωκε καθὼς δεῖ γνῶναι·
thinks to know anything, nothing yet he has known as ought he to know.
3 εἰ δέ τις ἀγαπᾷ τὸν Θεόν, οὗτος ἔγνωσται ὑπ' αὐτοῦ.
if But anyone loves God, this one has been known by Him.
4 περὶ τῆς βρώσεως οὖν τῶν εἰδωλοθύτων, οἴδαμεν ὅτι οὐδὲν
about the eating Then of the idolatrous sacrifices, we know that (is) not
εἴδωλον ἐν κόσμῳ, καὶ ὅτι οὐδεὶς Θεὸς ἕτερος εἰ μὴ εἷς.
an idol in (the) world, and that (there is) no God other except one.
5 καὶ γὰρ εἴπερ εἰσὶ λεγόμενοι θεοί, εἴτε ἐν οὐρανῷ, εἴτε ἐπὶ
even For if there are (that) called gods, either in Heaven, or upon
6 τῆς γῆς· ὥσπερ εἰσὶ θεοὶ πολλοί, καὶ κύριοι πολλοί· ἀλλ'
the earth; even as there are gods many, and lords many, but
ἡμῖν εἷς Θεὸς ὁ πατήρ, ἐξ οὗ τὰ πάντα, καὶ ἡμεῖς εἰς αὐτόν·
to us one God the Father, of whom all things, and we for Him,
καὶ εἷς Κύριος Ἰησοῦς Χριστός, δι' οὗ τὰ πάντα, καὶ ἡμεῖς
and one Lord Jesus Christ, through whom all things, and we
7 δι' αὐτοῦ. ἀλλ' οὐκ ἐν πᾶσιν ἡ γνῶσις· τινὲς δὲ τῇ συνειδήσει
by Him. But not in all (is) the knowledge; some and conscious
τοῦ εἰδώλου ἕως ἄρτι ὡς εἰδωλόθυτον ἐσθίουσι, καὶ ἡ
of the idol until now as an idolatrous sacrifice eat, and the
8 συνείδησις αὐτῶν ἀσθενὴς οὖσα μολύνεται. βρῶμα δὲ ἡμᾶς
conscience of them weak being is defiled. food But us
οὐ παρίστησι τῷ Θεῷ· οὔτε γὰρ ἐὰν φάγωμεν περισσεύο-
not will commend to God, neither for if we eat do we excel,
9 μεν, οὔτε ἐὰν μὴ φάγωμεν ὑστερούμεθα. βλέπετε δὲ μήπως
nor if not we eat are we behind. watch But lest
ἡ ἐξουσία ὑμῶν αὕτη πρόσκομμα γένηται τοῖς ἀσθενοῦσιν.
the authority of you this a stumbling-block becomes to the weak ones.
10 ἐὰν γάρ τις ἴδῃ σε τὸν ἔχοντα γνῶσιν ἐν εἰδωλείῳ κατακεί-
if For anyone sees you, the (one) having knowledge in an idol temple
μενον, οὐχὶ ἡ συνείδησις αὐτοῦ ἀσθενοῦς ὄντος οἰκοδομηθή-
sitting, not the conscience of him, weak being, be built up

so as to eat things sacrificed to idols? 11 And on your knowledge the weak brother will fall, for whom Christ died. 12 And sinning in this way against *your* brothers, and wounding their conscience, being weak, you sin against Christ. 13 Therefore, if food offends my brother, I will not at all eat flesh forever, so that I do not offend my brother.

CHAPTER 9

1 Am I not an apostle? Am I not free? Have I not seen our Lord Jesus Christ? Are you not my work in *the* Lord? 2 If I am not an apostle to others, yet I am indeed to you; for you are the seal of my apostleship in *the* Lord. 3 My defense to those examining me is this: 4 Have we not authority to eat and to drink? 5 Have we not authority to lead about a sister, a wife, as the rest of the apostles also, and Cephas, and the Lord's brothers *do*? 6 Or *is it* only Barnabas and I *who* have no authority to quit work? 7 Who serves as a soldier at *his* own wages at any time? Who plants a vineyard, and does not eat of its fruit? Or who shepherds a flock, and does not eat of the milk of the flock? 8 Do I speak these things according to man, or does not the Law say these things? 9 For it has been written in the Law of Moses, "You shall not muzzle an ox treading out grain." Is it *that* it matters to God *as to* oxen? 10 Or does He say *it* altogether because of us? Because of us it is written, so that the *one* plowing ought to plow *in* hope; and the *one* threshing *in* hope to partake of hope.

11 If we have sowed spiritual things to you, *is it* a great thing if we shall reap of your fleshly things? 12 If others have a share of the authority *over* you, *should* not rather we? But we did not use this authority, but we endured all things, so that we might not give a hindrance to the

11 σεται εἰς τὸ τὰ εἰδωλόθυτα ἐσθίειν; καὶ ἀπολεῖται ὁ ἀσθε-
— — the idolatrous sacrifices to eat? And is destroyed the weak
νῶν ἀδελφὸς ἐπὶ τῇ σῇ γνώσει, δι' ὃν Χριστὸς ἀπέθανεν;
brother by the of you knowledge, for whom Christ died.
12 οὕτω δὲ ἁμαρτάνοντες εἰς τοὺς ἀδελφούς, καὶ τύπτοντες
so And sinning against the brothers, and wounding
αὐτῶν τὴν συνείδησιν ἀσθενοῦσαν, εἰς Χριστὸν ἁμαρτάνετε.
of them the conscience being weak, against Christ you sin.
13 διόπερ εἰ βρῶμα σκανδαλίζει τὸν ἀδελφόν μου, οὐ μὴ φάγω
Therefore, if food offends the brother of you, in no way I eat
κρέα εἰς τὸν αἰῶνα, ἵνα μὴ τὸν ἀδελφόν μου σκανδαλίσω.
flesh to the age, that not the brother of me I offend.

CHAPTER 9

1 Οὐκ εἰμὶ ἀπόστολος; οὐκ εἰμὶ ἐλεύθερος; οὐχὶ Ἰησοῦν
not Am I an apostle? not Am I free? (Have) not Jesus
Χριστὸν τὸν Κύριον ἡμῶν ἑώρακα; οὐ τὸ ἔργον μου ὑμεῖς
Christ the Lord of us I have seen? not the work of me you
2 ἐστε ἐν Κυρίῳ; εἰ ἄλλοις οὐκ εἰμὶ ἀπόστολος, ἀλλά γε ὑμῖν
Are in (the) Lord? If to others not I am an apostle, yet indeed to you
εἰμι· ἡ γὰρ σφραγὶς τῆς ἐμῆς ἀποστολῆς ὑμεῖς ἐστε ἐν Κυρίῳ.
I am; the for seal of my apostleship you are in (the) Lord.
3 ἡ ἐμὴ ἀπολογία τοῖς ἐμὲ ἀνακρίνουσιν αὕτη ἐστί. μὴ οὐκ
My defense to those me examining this is. not
4 ἔχομεν ἐξουσίαν φαγεῖν καὶ πιεῖν; μὴ οὐκ ἔχομεν ἐξουσίαν
5 Have we authority to eat and to drink? not Have we authority
ἀδελφὴν γυναῖκα περιάγειν, ὡς καὶ οἱ λοιποὶ ἀπόστολοι,
a sister, a wife, to lead about, as also the rest of (the) apostles,
6 καὶ οἱ ἀδελφοὶ τοῦ Κυρίου, καὶ Κηφᾶς; ἢ μόνος ἐγὼ καὶ
and the brothers of the Lord, and Cephas? Or only I and
7 Βαρνάβας οὐκ ἔχομεν ἐξουσίαν τοῦ μὴ ἐργάζεσθαι; τίς
Barnabas not we have authority not to work? Who
στρατεύεται ἰδίοις ὀψωνίοις ποτέ; τίς φυτεύει ἀμπελῶνα,
soldiers at (his) own wages at any time? Who plants a vineyard
καὶ ἐκ τοῦ καρποῦ αὐτοῦ οὐκ ἐσθίει; ἢ τίς ποιμαίνει ποίμνην,
and from the fruit of it not eats? Or who shepherds a flock,
8 καὶ ἐκ τοῦ γάλακτος τῆς ποίμνης οὐκ ἐσθίει; μὴ κατὰ ἄνθρω-
and of the milk of the flock not eats? Not according to
9 πον ταῦτα λαλῶ; ἢ οὐχὶ καὶ ὁ νόμος ταῦτα λέγει; ἐν γὰρ
man these things I speak, or not also the law these things says? in For
10 τῷ Μωσέως νόμῳ γέγραπται, Οὐ φιμώσεις βοῦν ἀλοῶντα.
the of Moses law it has been written: not You shall muzzle an ox threshing
μὴ τῶν βοῶν μέλει τῷ Θεῷ; ἢ δι' ἡμᾶς πάντως λέγει; δι'
Not of oxen matters it to God, or because of us altogether He says? For
ἡμᾶς γὰρ ἐγράφη, ὅτι ἐπ' ἐλπίδι ὀφείλει ὁ ἀροτριῶν
us, for it was written; because on hope ought the (one) plowing
ἀροτριᾷν, καὶ ὁ ἀλοῶν τῆς ἐλπίδος αὐτοῦ μετέχειν ἐπ' ἐλπίδι.
to plow; and the (one) threshing of his hope to partake on hope.
11 εἰ ἡμεῖς ὑμῖν τὰ πνευματικὰ ἐσπείραμεν, μέγα εἰ ἡμεῖς ὑμῶν
If we to you spiritual things sowed, (is it) a great thing if we of you
12 τὰ σαρκικὰ θερίσομεν; εἰ ἄλλοι τῆς ἐξουσίας ὑμῶν μετέ-
fleshly things shall reap? If others of the authority of you have a
χουσιν, οὐ μᾶλλον ἡμεῖς; ἀλλ' οὐκ ἐχρησάμεθα τῇ ἐξουσίᾳ
share, not rather we? But not we used authority
ταύτῃ· ἀλλὰ πάντα στέγομεν, ἵνα μὴ ἐγκοπήν τινα δῶμεν
this, but all things we endured, that not an obstacle anyone we give

gospel of Christ. 13 Do you not know that those having labored eat of the holy things of the Temple? Those attending *on* the altar partake with the altar. 14 So also the Lord ordained those preaching the gospel to live from the gospel. 15 But I have not used one of these. And I do not write these things that it be so with me. For *it is* good to me rather to die than that anyone nullify my glorying. 16 For if I preach the gospel, no glory is to me; for necessity is laid on me, and it is woe to me if I do not preach the gospel. 17 For if I do this willingly, I have a reward; but if unwillingly, I am entrusted with a stewardship. 18 What then is my reward? That preaching the gospel I may make the gospel of Christ free, so as not to fully use my authority in the gospel. 19 For being free of all, I enslaved myself to all, that I might gain the more. 20 And I became as a Jew to the Jews, that I might gain Jews; to those under Law as under Law, that I might gain those under Law; 21 to those without Law as without Law—not being without law of God, but under *the* law of Christ—that I might gain *those* without Law. 22 I became to the weak as weak, that I might gain the weak. To all I have become all things, that in any case I might save some. 23 And I do this for the gospel, that I might become a fellow-partaker of it.

24 Do you not know that those running in a stadium indeed all run, but one receives the prize? So run that you may obtain. 25 But everyone striving *in* all things controls himself. Then those truly that they may receive a corruptible crown, but we an incorruptible. 26 So I run accordingly, as not uncertainly; so I fight, as not beating air; 27 but I buffet my body and lead *it* captive, lest

13 τῷ εὐαγγελίῳ τοῦ Χριστοῦ. οὐκ οἴδατε ὅτι οἱ τὰ ἱερὰ
to the gospel of Christ Do not you know that those holy things
ἐργαζόμενοι ἐκ τοῦ ἱεροῦ ἐσθίουσιν, οἱ τῷ θυσιαστηρίῳ
laboring (about) of the temple eat, those the altar
14 προσεδρεύοντες τῷ θυσιαστηρίῳ συμμερίζονται; οὕτω καὶ
attending (on), the altar partake with. So also
ὁ Κύριος διέταξε τοῖς τὸ εὐαγγέλιον καταγγέλλουσιν ἐκ τοῦ
the Lord ordained those of the gospel announcing, of the
15 εὐαγγελίου ζῇν. ἐγὼ δὲ οὐδενὶ ἐχρησάμην τούτων· οὐκ
gospel to live. I But not one have used of these. not
ἔγραψα δὲ ταῦτα ἵνα οὕτω γένηται ἐν ἐμοί· καλὸν γάρ μοι
I write And these things that so it should be with me; good For to me
μᾶλλον ἀποθανεῖν ἢ τὸ καύχημά μου ἵνα τις κενώσῃ. ἐὰν
rather to die, than the glorying of me that anyone void. if
16 γὰρ εὐαγγελίζωμαι, οὐκ ἔστι μοι καύχημα· ἀνάγκη γάρ
For I preach the gospel, not there is to me glory; necessity for
μοι ἐπίκειται· οὐαὶ δέ μοι ἐστίν, ἐὰν μὴ εὐαγγελίζωμαι. εἰ
me is laid on; woe and to me is, if not I preach the gospel. if
17 γὰρ ἑκὼν τοῦτο πράσσω, μισθὸν ἔχω· εἰ δὲ ἄκων, οἰκονομίαν
For willingly this I do, a reward I have; if but unwillingly, a stewardship
18 πεπίστευμαι. τίς οὖν μοί ἐστιν ὁ μισθός; ἵνα εὐαγγελιζό-
I am entrusted with. What then of me is the reward? That preaching the
μενος ἀδάπανον θήσω τὸ εὐαγγέλιον τοῦ Χριστοῦ, εἰς τὸ μὴ
gospel without charge I place the gospel of Christ, so as not
19 καταχρήσασθαι τῇ ἐξουσίᾳ μου ἐν τῷ εὐαγγελίῳ. ἐλεύ-
to use to the full the authority of me in the gospel. free
θερος γὰρ ὢν ἐκ πάντων, πᾶσιν ἐμαυτὸν ἐδούλωσα, ἵνα
For being of all, to all myself I enslaved, that
20 τοὺς πλείονας κερδήσω. καὶ ἐγενόμην τοῖς Ἰουδαίοις ὡς
the more I might gain. And I became to the Jews as
Ἰουδαῖος, ἵνα Ἰουδαίους κερδήσω· τοῖς ὑπὸ νόμον ὡς ὑπὸ
a Jew, that Jews I might gain; to those under law as under
21 νόμον, ἵνα τοὺς ὑπὸ νόμον κερδήσω· τοῖς ἀνόμοις ὡς ἄνομος,
law, that those under law I might gain; to those without law as without law
μὴ ὢν ἄνομος Θεῷ ἀλλ' ἔννομος Χριστῷ, ἵνα κερδήσω ἀνό-
not being without law of God, but under law of Christ, that I might gain with-
22 μους. ἐγενόμην τοῖς ἀσθενέσιν ὡς ἀσθενής, ἵνα τοὺς ἀσθενεῖς
out law. I became to the weak as weak, that the weak
κερδήσω. τοῖς πᾶσι γέγονα τὰ πάντα, ἵνα πάντως τινὰς
I might gain. To all I have become all things, that in any case some
23 σώσω. τοῦτο δὲ ποιῶ διὰ τὸ εὐαγγέλιον, ἵνα συγκοινωνὸς
I might save. this And I do for the gospel, that a fellow-partaker
24 αὐτοῦ γένωμαι. οὐκ οἴδατε ὅτι οἱ ἐν σταδίῳ τρέχοντες πάν-
of it I might become. Not know you that those in a stadium running all
τες μὲν τρέχουσιν, εἷς δὲ λαμβάνει τὸ βραβεῖον; οὕτω
indeed run, one but receives the prize? So
25 τρέχετε, ἵνα καταλάβητε. πᾶς δὲ ὁ ἀγωνιζόμενος πάντα
run that you may obtain. everyone And striving (in) all things
ἐγκρατεύεται· ἐκεῖνοι μὲν οὖν ἵνα φθαρτὸν στέφανον λάβω-
controls himself; those truly, then, that a corruptible crown they may
26 σιν, ἡμεῖς δὲ ἄφθαρτον. ἐγὼ τοίνυν οὕτω τρέχω, ὡς οὐκ
receive, we but an incorruptible. I accordingly so run, as not
27 ἀδήλως· οὕτω πυκτεύω, ὡς οὐκ ἀέρα δέρων· ἀλλ' ὑπωπιάζω
uncertainly; so I fight, as not air beating; but I buffet
μου τὸ σῶμα καὶ δουλαγωγῶ, μήπως, ἄλλοις κηρύξας,
of me the body and lead (it) captive, lest to others proclaiming,

proclaiming to others I myself might be rejected.

CHAPTER 10

[1]And I do not want you to be ignorant, brothers, that our fathers were all under the cloud, and all passed through the Sea. [2]And all were baptized to Moses in the cloud, and in the Sea; [3]and all ate the same spiritual food. [4]And all drank the same spiritual drink; for they drank of the spiritual rock following—and that Rock was Christ. [5]Yet God was not pleased with most of them; for they were scattered in the desert. [6]But these things became examples for us, so that we may not be lusters after evil, even as those indeed lusted. [7]Neither be idolaters, even as some of them, as it has been written, "The people sat down to eat and drink, and stood up to play." [8]Nor should we commit fornication, as some of them fornicated, and twenty-three thousand fell in one day. [9]Neither overtempt Christ, as some of them tempted, and perished by serpents. [10]Neither should you murmur, as also some of them murmured, and perished by the destroyer. [1]And all these things happened to those *as* examples, and *it* was written for our warning, on whom the ends of the ages have come. [12]So that he that thinks to stand, let him be careful that he not fall.

[13]No temptation has taken you except *what is* human; but God is faithful, who will not allow you to be tempted above what you are able. But with the temptation, *He* will also make the way out, so that you may be able to bear *it*.

[14]Therefore, my beloved, flee from idolatry. [15]I speak as to prudent ones; you judge what I say. [16]The cup of blessing that we bless, is it not a partaking of the blood

αὐτὸς ἀδόκιμος γένωμαι.
myself rejected I may become.

CHAPTER 10

1 Οὐ θέλω δὲ ὑμᾶς ἀγνοεῖν, ἀδελφοί, ὅτι οἱ πατέρες ἡμῶν
not I desire And you to be ignorant, brothers, that the fathers of us
πάντες ὑπὸ τὴν νεφέλην ἦσαν, καὶ πάντες διὰ τῆς θαλάσσης
all under the cloud were, and all through the sea
2 διῆλθον, καὶ πάντες εἰς τὸν Μωσῆν ἐβαπτίσαντο ἐν τῇ νεφέλῃ
passed and all to Moses were baptized in the cloud
3 καὶ ἐν τῇ θαλάσσῃ, καὶ πάντες τὸ αὐτὸ βρῶμα πνευματικὸν
and in the sea, and all the same food spiritual
4 ἔφαγον, καὶ πάντες τὸ αὐτὸ πόμα πνευματικὸν ἔπιον·
ate, and all the same drink spiritual drank;
ἔπινον γὰρ ἐκ πνευματικῆς ἀκολουθούσης πέτρας· ἡ δὲ
they drank for of a spiritual following rock, the and
5 πέτρα ἦν ὁ Χριστός. ἀλλ' οὐκ ἐν τοῖς πλείοσιν αὐτῶν
Rock was Christ. But not in the most of them
εὐδόκησεν ὁ Θεός· κατεστρώθησαν γὰρ ἐν τῇ ἐρήμῳ. ταῦτα
was well-pleased God; they were scattered for in the desert. these things
6 δὲ τύποι ἡμῶν ἐγενήθησαν, εἰς τὸ μὴ εἶναι ἡμᾶς ἐπιθυμητὰς
And examples of us were, for not to be us lusters after
7 κακῶν, καθὼς κἀκεῖνοι ἐπεθύμησαν. μηδὲ εἰδωλολάτραι
evil, even as those indeed lusted. Neither idolaters
γίνεσθε, καθώς τινες αὐτῶν· ὡς γέγραπται, Ἐκάθισεν ὁ λαὸς
be, even as some of them, as it has been written: Sat the people
8 φαγεῖν καὶ πιεῖν, καὶ ἀνέστησαν παίζειν. μηδὲ πορνεύωμεν,
to eat and drink, and stood up to play. Neither do fornication,
καθώς τινες αὐτῶν ἐπόρνευσαν, καὶ ἔπεσον ἐν μιᾷ ἡμέρᾳ
even as some of them fornicated, and fell in one day
9 εἰκοσιτρεῖς χιλιάδες. μηδὲ ἐκπειράζωμεν τὸν Χριστόν, καθὼς
twenty-three thousands. Neither overtempt the Christ, even as
καί τινες αὐτῶν ἐπείρασαν, καὶ ὑπὸ τῶν ὄφεων ἀπώλοντο.
also some of them tempted, and by serpents were destroyed.
10 μηδὲ γογγύζετε, καθὼς καί τινες αὐτῶν ἐγόγγυσαν, καὶ
Neither murmur even as also some of them murmured, and
11 ἀπώλοντο ὑπὸ τοῦ ὀλοθρευτοῦ. ταῦτα δὲ πάντα τύποι
were destroyed by the destroyer. these things And all (as) examples
συνέβαινον ἐκείνοις· ἐγράφη δὲ πρὸς νουθεσίαν ἡμῶν, εἰς
happened to those, was written and for warning of us,, to
12 οὓς τὰ τέλη τῶν αἰώνων κατήντησεν. ὥστε ὁ δοκῶν
whom the ends of the ages has arrived. So as the (one) thinking
13 ἑστάναι, βλεπέτω μὴ πέσῃ. πειρασμὸς ὑμᾶς οὐκ εἴληφεν εἰ
to stand, let watch lest he falls. Temptation you not has taken ex-
μὴ ἀνθρώπινος· πιστὸς δὲ ὁ Θεός, ὃς οὐκ ἐάσει ὑμᾶς πει-
cept (what is) human; faithful but (is) God, who not will allow you to be
ρασθῆναι ὑπὲρ ὃ δύνασθε, ἀλλὰ ποιήσει σὺν τῷ πειρασμῷ
tempted beyond what you are able; but will make with the temptation
καὶ τὴν ἔκβασιν, τοῦ δύνασθαι ὑμᾶς ὑπενεγκεῖν.
also the way out, to be able you to bear (it).
14 Διόπερ, ἀγαπητοί μου, φεύγετε ἀπὸ τῆς εἰδωλολατρείας.
Therefore, beloved of me, flee from idolatry.
15 ὡς φρονίμοις λέγω, κρίνατε ὑμεῖς ὅ φημι. τὸ ποτήριον τῆς
As to prudent ones I say, judge you what I say. The cup
16 εὐλογίας ὃ εὐλογοῦμεν, οὐχὶ κοινωνία τοῦ αἵματος τοῦ
of blessing which we bless, not a partaking of the blood

of Christ? The bread which we break, is it not a partaking of the body of Christ? [17]Because we, the many, are one bread, one body, for we all partake of the one bread. [18]Look at Israel according to flesh; are not those eating the sacrifices partakers of the altar? [19]What then do I say, that an idol is anything, or that an idolatrous sacrifice is anything? [20]But the things the nations sacrifice, *they* sacrifice to demons, not to God. But I do not want you to become sharers of demons; [21]you cannot drink *the* cup of the Lord and a cup of demons; you cannot partake of the table of *the* Lord, and a table of demons. [22]Or do we provoke the Lord to jealousy? Are we stronger than He?

[23]All things are lawful to me, but not all things profit. All things are lawful to me, but not all things build up. [24]Let no one seek the things of himself, but each on that of the other. [25]Eat everything being sold in a meat market, examining nothing because of conscience, [26]for "the earth *is* the Lord's, and the fullness of it." [27]And if any of the unbelievers invite you, and you desire to go, eat everything set before you, examining nothing because of conscience. [28]but if anyone tells you, This is slain in sacrifice; do not eat, because of that one pointing *it* out, and the conscience; for "the earth *is* the Lord's, and the fullness of it." [29]But I say conscience, not that of himself, but that of the other. For why is my freedom judged by another's conscience? [30]But if I partake by grace, why am I evil spoken of because of what I give thanks *for*? [31]Then whether you eat or drink, or whatever you do, do all things to the glory of God. [32]Be without offense both to Jews and Greeks, and to the church of God. [33]Even as I also please *in* all things, not seeking my own advantage, but that of the many, that

Χριστοῦ ἐστί; τὸν ἄρτον ὃν κλῶμεν, οὐχὶ κοινωνία τοῦ
of Christ is? The bread which we break not a partaking of the
17 σώματος τοῦ Χριστοῦ ἐστίν; ὅτι εἷς ἄρτος, ἓν σῶμα, οἱ
body of Christ is it? Because one bread, one body the
πολλοί ἐσμεν· οἱ γὰρ πάντες ἐκ τοῦ ἑνὸς ἄρτου μετέχομεν.
many we are; for all of the one bread we partake.
18 βλέπετε τὸν Ἰσραὴλ κατὰ σάρκα· οὐχὶ οἱ ἐσθίοντες τὰς
See Israel according to flesh; not those eating the
19 θυσίας κοινωνοὶ τοῦ θυσιαστηρίου εἰσί; τί οὖν φημι; ὅτι
sacrifices sharers of the altar are? What then do I say, that
20 εἴδωλόν τί ἐστιν; ἢ ὅτι εἰδωλόθυτόν τί ἐστιν; ἀλλ' ὅτι ἃ
an idol anything is? Or that an idolatrous sacrifice anything is? But what things
θύει τὰ ἔθνη, δαιμονίοις θύει, καὶ οὐ Θεῷ· οὐ θέλω δὲ ὑμᾶς
sacrifice the nations, to demons sacrifice, and not to God. not I want But you
21 κοινωνοὺς τῶν δαιμονίων γίνεσθαι. οὐ δύνασθε ποτήριον
sharers of demons to become. not You are able a cup
Κυρίου πίνειν καὶ ποτήριον δαιμονίων· οὐ δύνασθε τραπέζης
of (the) Lord to drink and a cup of demons; not you are able of a table
22 Κυρίου μετέχειν καὶ τραπέζης δαιμονίων. ἢ παραζηλοῦμεν
of (the) Lord to partake and a table of demons. Or do we make jealous
τὸν Κύριον; μὴ ἰσχυρότεροι αὐτοῦ ἐσμέν;
the Lord? Not stronger (than) He we are?

Πάντα μοι ἔξεστιν, ἀλλ' οὐ πάντα συμφέρει. πάντα μοι
23 All things to me are lawful, but not all things contribute. All things to me
ἔξεστιν, ἀλλ' οὐ πάντα οἰκοδομεῖ. μηδεὶς τὸ ἑαυτοῦ ζητείτω,
24 are lawful, but not all things build up. No one the thing of himself seeks,
ἀλλὰ τὸ τοῦ ἑτέρου ἕκαστος. πᾶν τὸ ἐν μακέλλῳ πωλού-
25 but that of the other each one. Everything in a meat market being
μενον ἐσθίετε, μηδὲν ἀνακρίνοντες διὰ τὴν συνείδησιν· τοῦ
26 sold eat, nothing examining because of conscience; of the
27 γὰρ Κυρίου ἡ γῆ καὶ τὸ πλήρωμα αὐτῆς. εἰ δέ τις καλεῖ ὑμᾶς
for Lord the earth and the fullness of it. if And anyone invites you
τῶν ἀπίστων, καὶ θέλετε πορεύεσθαι, πᾶν τὸ παρατιθέ-
of the unbelievers, and you desire to go, everything set before
μενον ὑμῖν ἐσθίετε, μηδὲν ἀνακρίνοντες διὰ τὴν συνείδησιν.
you eat, nothing examining because of conscience.
ἐὰν δέ τις ὑμῖν εἴπῃ, Τοῦτο εἰδωλόθυτόν ἐστι, μὴ ἐσθίετε, δι'
28 if But anyone you tells, This slain in sacrifice is, do not eat, because
ἐκεῖνον τὸν μηνύσαντα καὶ τὴν συνείδησιν· τοῦ γὰρ Κυρίου
that one pointing out, and conscience; the for (is the) Lord's
29 ἡ γῆ καὶ τὸ πλήρωμα αὐτῆς. συνείδησιν δὲ λέγω, οὐχὶ τὴν
the earth and the fullness of it. conscience But I say, not (that)
ἑαυτοῦ, ἀλλὰ τὴν τοῦ ἑτέρου· ἱνατί γὰρ ἡ ἐλευθερία μου
of himself, but the (one) of the other. why For the freedom of me
κρίνεται ὑπὸ ἄλλης συνειδήσεως; εἰ δὲ ἐγὼ χάριτι μετέχω, τί
30 is judged by another's conscience? if And I by grace partake, why
βλασφημοῦμαι ὑπὲρ οὗ ἐγὼ εὐχαριστῶ; εἴτε οὖν ἐσθίετε,
31 am I evil spoken of because of what I give thanks (for)? Whether then you eat
εἴτε πίνετε, εἴτε τι ποιεῖτε, πάντα εἰς δόξαν Θεοῦ ποιεῖτε.
or drink, or what you do, all things to the glory of God do.
32 ἀπρόσκοποι γίνεσθε καὶ Ἰουδαίοις καὶ Ἕλλησι καὶ τῇ
without offense Be both to Jews and to Greeks and to the
33 ἐκκλησίᾳ τοῦ Θεοῦ· καθὼς κἀγὼ πάντα πᾶσιν ἀρέσκω, μὴ
church of God, as I also (in) all things all please, not
ζητῶν τὸ ἐμαυτοῦ συμφέρον, ἀλλὰ τὸ τῶν πολλῶν, ἵνα
seeking the of myself advantage, but of the many, that

they may be saved.

CHAPTER 11

[1] Be imitators of me, as I also of Christ.

[2] But I praise you, brothers, that in all things you have remembered me; and even as I delivered to you, you hold fast the traditions. [3] But I want you to know that Christ is the Head of every man, and the man *is* the head of a woman, and God *is the* head of Christ. [4] Every man praying or prophesying, having *anything* down over *his* head shames his Head. [5] And every woman praying or prophesying with the head uncovered shames her head; for it is the same *as* being shaved. [6] For if a woman is not covered, let her also be shorn. But if *it is* shameful for a woman to be shorn, or to be shaved, let her be covered. [7] For truly man ought not to have the head covered, being *the* image and glory of God. But woman is *the* glory of man— [8] for man is not of the woman, but woman of man; [9] for also man was not created for the sake of the woman, but woman for the sake of the man; [10] because of this, the woman ought to have authority on the head, because of the angels— [11] however, man *is* not apart from woman, nor woman apart from man, in *the* Lord. [12] For as the woman *is* out of the man, so also the man through the woman; but all things from God. [13] You judge among yourselves: is it fitting *for* a woman to pray to God uncovered? [14] Or does not nature herself teach you that if a man indeed wears long hair, it is a dishonor to him? [15] But if a woman wears hair long, it is a glory to her, because the long hair has been given to her instead of a veil. [16] But if anyone thinks to be contentious, we do not have such a custom, nor the churches of God.

σωθῶσι.
they may be saved.

CHAPTER 11

1 μιμηταί μου γίνεσθε, καθὼς κἀγὼ Χριστοῦ.
imitators of me Be, as also I of Christ.
2 Ἐπαινῶ δὲ ὑμᾶς, ἀδελφοί, ὅτι πάντα μου μέμνησθε, καὶ
I praise But you, brothers, because all things of me you recalled, and
καθὼς παρέδωκα ὑμῖν τὰς παραδόσεις κατέχετε. θέλω δὲ
3 **as I delivered to you, the traditions you hold fast. I wish But**
ὑμᾶς εἰδέναι, ὅτι παντὸς ἀνδρὸς ἡ κεφαλὴ ὁ Χριστός ἐστι·
you to know, that of every man the head Christ is;
4 κεφαλὴ δὲ γυναικός, ὁ ἀνήρ· κεφαλὴ δὲ Χριστοῦ, ὁ Θεός. πᾶς
head and of a woman, the man; (the) head and of Christ, God. Every
ἀνὴρ προσευχόμενος ἢ προφητεύων, κατὰ κεφαλῆς ἔχων,
man praying or prophesying down over (his) head having,
5 καταισχύνει τὴν κεφαλὴν αὐτοῦ. πᾶσα δὲ γυνὴ προσευχο-
shames the Head of him. every But woman praying
μένη ἢ προφητεύουσα ἀκατακαλύπτῳ τῇ κεφαλῇ, καται-
or prophesying uncovered with the head, shames
σχύνει τὴν κεφαλὴν ἑαυτῆς· ἓν γάρ ἐστι καὶ τὸ αὐτὸ τῇ ἐξυρη-
the head of herself, one for it is and the same with the being
6 μένῃ. εἰ γὰρ οὐ κατακαλύπτεται γυνή, καὶ κειράσθω· εἰ δὲ
shaved. if For not is covered a woman, also let her be shorn. if But
αἰσχρὸν γυναικὶ τὸ κείρασθαι ἢ ξυρᾶσθαι, κατακαλυ-
shameful for a woman to be shorn or to be shaved, let her be
7 πτέσθω. ἀνὴρ μὲν γὰρ οὐκ ὀφείλει κατακαλύπτεσθαι τὴν
covered. a man indeed For not ought to be covered the
κεφαλήν, εἰκὼν καὶ δόξα Θεοῦ ὑπάρχων· γυνὴ δὲ δόξα
head, (the) image and glory of God being. the woman But glory
8 ἀνδρός ἐστιν. οὐ γάρ ἐστιν ἀνὴρ ἐκ γυναικός, ἀλλὰ γυνὴ
of a man is. not For is man of woman, but woman
9 ἐξ ἀνδρός· καὶ γὰρ οὐκ ἐκτίσθη ἀνὴρ διὰ τὴν γυναῖκα, ἀλλὰ
of man; also for not was created man because of the woman, but
10 γυνὴ διὰ τὸν ἄνδρα· διὰ τοῦτο ὀφείλει ἡ γυνὴ ἐξουσίαν
woman because of the man. Therefore ought the woman authority
11 ἔχειν ἐπὶ τῆς κεφαλῆς διὰ τοὺς ἀγγέλους. πλὴν οὔτε ἀνὴρ
to have on the head because of the angels. But neither man
12 χωρὶς γυναικός, οὔτε γυνὴ χωρὶς ἀνδρός, ἐν Κυρίῳ. ὥσπερ
without woman, nor woman without man, in (the) Lord. as
γὰρ ἡ γυνὴ ἐκ τοῦ ἀνδρός, οὕτω καὶ ὁ ἀνὴρ διὰ τῆς
For the woman of the man, so also the man through the
13 γυναικός, τὰ δὲ πάντα ἐκ τοῦ Θεοῦ. ἐν ὑμῖν αὐτοῖς κρίνατε·
woman, but all things of God. Among you yourselves judge:
πρέπον ἐστὶ γυναῖκα ἀκατακάλυπτον τῷ Θεῷ προσεύχε-
fitting Is it (for) a woman uncovered to God to pray?
14 σθαι; ἢ οὐδὲ αὐτὴ ἡ φύσις διδάσκει ὑμᾶς, ὅτι ἀνὴρ μὲν ἐὰν
Does not herself nature teaches you that a man indeed if
15 κομᾷ, ἀτιμία αὐτῷ ἐστί; γυνὴ δὲ ἐὰν κομᾷ, δόξα αὐτῇ
wears long hair, a dishonor to him it is; a woman but if wears hair long, a glory to her
16 ἐστίν. ὅτι ἡ κόμη ἀντὶ περιβολαίου δέδοται αὐτῇ. εἰ δέ τις
it is? Because the long hair instead of a veil has been given to her. But anyone
δοκεῖ φιλόνεικος εἶναι, ἡμεῖς τοιαύτην συνήθειαν οὐκ ἔχομεν,
thinks contentious to be, we such a custom do not have,
οὐδὲ αἱ ἐκκλησίαι τοῦ Θεοῦ.
neither the churches of God.

[17]But enjoining this, I do not praise *you*, because you come together not for the better, but for the worse. [18]Indeed, first, I hear divisions to be among you *when* you come together in the church. And I believe some part. [19]For there must also be heresies among you, so that the approved ones may become revealed among you. [20]Then you coming together into one place, it is not to eat *the* Lord's supper. [21]For each one takes his own supper first in the eating; and one is hungry, and another drunken. [22]For do you not have houses to eat and to drink? Or do you despise the church of God, and shame those who have not? What do I say to you? Shall I praise you for this? I do not praise.

[23]For I received from the Lord what I also delivered to you, that the Lord Jesus in the night in which He was betrayed took bread; [24]and giving thanks He broke and said, Take, eat; this is My body which *is* broken on behalf of you; this do in remembrance of Me. [25]In the same way the cup also, after supping, saying, This cup is the New Covenant in My blood; as often as you drink do this in remembrance of Me. [26]For as often as you may eat this bread, and drink this cup, you solemnly proclaim the death of the Lord, until He shall come. [27]So that whoever should eat this bread, or drink the cup of the Lord, unworthily, *that one* will be guilty of the body and of the blood of the Lord. [28]But let a man examine himself, and so let him eat, and let him drink of the cup; [29]for he eating and drinking unworthily eats and drinks judgment to himself, not discerning the body of the Lord. [30]For this reason many among you *are* weak and feeble, and many sleep. [31]for if we discerned ourselves,

17 Τοῦτο δὲ παραγγέλλων οὐκ ἐπαινῶ, ὅτι οὐκ εἰς τὸ
this But enjoining, not I praise (you), because not for the
18 ρεῖττον ἀλλ' εἰς τὸ ἧττον συνέρχεσθε. πρῶτον μὲν γὰρ
better, but for the worse you come together. firstly indeed For
συνερχομένων ὑμῶν ἐν τῇ ἐκκλησίᾳ, ἀκούω σχίσματα ἐν
coming together you, in the church, I hear divisions among
19 ὑμῖν ὑπάρχειν, καὶ μέρος τι πιστεύω. δεῖ γὰρ καὶ αἱρέσεις ἐν
you to be, and part some I believe. must For also heresies among
20 ὑμῖν εἶναι, ἵνα οἱ δόκιμοι φανεροὶ γένωνται ἐν ὑμῖν. συνερχο-
you be, that the approved ones revealed may become among you. Coming
μένων οὖν ὑμῶν ἐπὶ τὸ αὐτό, οὐκ ἔστι Κυριακὸν δεῖπνον
together, then, you together, not it is of the Lord a supper
21 φαγεῖν. ἕκαστος γὰρ τὸ ἴδιον δεῖπνον προλαμβάνει ἐν τῷ
to eat. each one For the own supper takes before
22 φαγεῖν, καὶ ὃς μὲν πεινᾷ, ὃς δὲ μεθύει. μὴ γὰρ οἰκίας οὐκ
to eat; and one hungers, another drunken. not For houses not
ἔχετε εἰς τὸ ἐσθίειν καὶ πίνειν; ἢ τῆς ἐκκλησίας τοῦ Θεοῦ κατα-
you have to eat and to drink? Or the church of God do you
φρονεῖτε, καὶ καταισχύνετε τοὺς μὴ ἔχοντας; τί ὑμῖν εἴπω;
despise, and shame those not having? What to you do I say?
23 ἐπαινέσω ὑμᾶς ἐν τούτῳ; οὐκ ἐπαινῶ. ἐγὼ γὰρ παρέλαβον
Shall I praise you in this? not I praise. I For I received
ἀπὸ τοῦ Κυρίου, ὃ καὶ παρέδωκα ὑμῖν, ὅτι ὁ Κύριος
from the Lord what also I delivered to you, that the Lord
24 Ἰησοῦς ἐν τῇ νυκτὶ ᾗ παρεδίδοτο ἔλαβεν ἄρτον, καὶ
Jesus in the night in which He was betrayed took bread, and
εὐχαριστήσας ἔκλασε, καὶ εἶπε, Λάβετε, φάγετε, τοῦτό μού
having given thanks broke and said, Take, eat, this of Me
ἐστι τὸ σῶμα τὸ ὑπὲρ ὑμῶν κλώμενον· τοῦτο ποιεῖτε εἰς
is the body on behalf of you broken; this do for
25 τὴν ἐμὴν ἀνάμνησιν. ὡσαύτως καὶ τὸ ποτήριον, μετὰ τὸ
my remembrance. In the same way And the cup, after the
δειπνῆσαι, λέγων, Τοῦτο τὸ ποτήριον ἡ καινὴ διαθήκη
supping, saying, This cup the new covenant
ἐστὶν ἐν τῷ ἐμῷ αἵματι· τοῦτο ποιεῖτε, ὁσάκις ἂν πίνητε,
is in My blood; this do, as often as you drink,
26 εἰς τὴν ἐμὴν ἀνάμνησιν. ὁσάκις γὰρ ἂν ἐσθίητε τὸν ἄρτον
for My remembrance. as often For (as) you may eat bread
τοῦτον, καὶ τὸ ποτήριον τοῦτο πίνητε, τὸν θάνατον τοῦ
this, and cup this drink. the death of the
27 Κυρίου καταγγέλλετε ἄχρις οὗ ἂν ἔλθῃ. ὥστε ὃς ἂν ἐσθίῃ
Lord you declare, until He may come. So as whoever may eat
τὸν ἄρτον τοῦτον ἢ πίνῃ τὸ ποτήριον τοῦ Κυρίου ἀναξίως,
the bread this, or drinks the cup of the Lord unworthily
28 ἔνοχος ἔσται τοῦ σώματος καὶ αἵματος τοῦ Κυρίου. δοκι-
guilty will be of the body and of the blood of the Lord. let
μαζέτω δὲ ἄνθρωπος ἑαυτόν, καὶ οὕτως ἐκ τοῦ ἄρτου
prove But a man himself, and so of the bread
29 ἐσθιέτω, καὶ ἐκ τοῦ ποτηρίου πινέτω. ὁ γὰρ ἐσθίων καὶ πίνων
let him eat, and of the cup let him drink. he For eating and drinking
ἀναξίως, κρίμα ἑαυτῷ ἐσθίει καὶ πίνει, μὴ διακρίνων τὸ
unworthily judgment to himself eats and drinks, not discerning the
30 σῶμα τοῦ Κυρίου. διὰ τοῦτο ἐν ὑμῖν πολλοὶ ἀσθενεῖς καὶ
body of the Lord. Therefore among you (are) many weak and
31 ἄρρωστοι, καὶ κοιμῶνται ἱκανοί. εἰ γὰρ ἑαυτοὺς διεκρίνομεν,
feeble, and sleep many. if For ourselves we discerned,

32 οὐκ ἂν ἐκρινόμεθα. κρινόμενοι δέ, ὑπὸ Κυρίου παιδευόμεθα,
not we would be judged. being judged But by (the) Lord, we are chastened,
33 ἵνα μὴ σὺν τῷ κόσμῳ κατακριθῶμεν. ὥστε, ἀδελφοί μου,
lest with the world we are condemned. So as, brothers of me,
34 συνερχόμενοι εἰς τὸ φαγεῖν, ἀλλήλους ἐκδέχεσθε. εἰ δέ τις
coming together to eat, one another await. if And anyone
πεινᾷ, ἐν οἴκῳ ἐσθιέτω· ἵνα μὴ εἰς κρίμα συνέρχησθε. τὰ δὲ
hungers, at home let him eat, lest to judgment you come together. the And
λοιπά, ὡς ἂν ἔλθω, διατάξομαι.
rest, whenever I come, I will set in order.

CHAPTER 12

1 Περὶ δὲ τῶν πνευματικῶν, ἀδελφοί, οὐ θέλω ὑμᾶς ἀγνοεῖν.
about And the spiritual matters, brothers, not I wish you to be ignorant.
2 οἴδατε ὅτι ἔθνη ἦτε πρὸς τὰ εἴδωλα τὰ ἄφωνα, ὡς ἂν
You know that nations you were to the idols dumb,
3 ἤγεσθε, ἀπαγόμενοι. διὸ γνωρίζω ὑμῖν, ὅτι οὐδεὶς ἐν Πνεύ-
you were led, being led away. Therefore I make known to you that no one by
ματι Θεοῦ λαλῶν λέγει ἀνάθεμα Ἰησοῦν· καὶ οὐδεὶς δύναται
(the) Spirit of God speaking says, A curse (is) Jesus; and no one is able
εἰπεῖν Κύριον Ἰησοῦν, εἰ μὴ ἐν Πνεύματι Ἁγίῳ.
to say, Lord Jesus, except by (the) Spirit Holy.
4 Διαιρέσεις δὲ χαρισμάτων εἰσί, τὸ δὲ αὐτὸ Πνεῦμα. καὶ
differences But of gifts there are, the but same Spirit. And
5 διαιρέσεις διακονιων εἰσί, καὶ ὁ αὐτὸς Κύριος. καὶ διαιρέσεις
6 differences of ministries there are, yet the same Lord. And differences
ἐνεργημάτων εἰσίν, ὁ δὲ αὐτός ἐστι Θεός, ὁ ἐνεργῶν τὰ
of workings there are, the and same is God working
7 πάντα ἐν πᾶσιν. ἑκάστῳ δὲ δίδοται ἡ φανέρωσις τοῦ
all things in all. to each one But is given the showing forth of the
Πνεύματος πρὸς τὸ συμφέρον. ᾧ μὲν γὰρ διὰ τοῦ Πνεύματος
Spirit to the advantage. to one For through the Spirit
8 δίδοται λόγος σοφίας, ἄλλῳ δὲ λόγος γνώσεως, κατὰ τὸ αὐτὸ
is given a word of wisdom; to another and a word of knowledge per the same
9 Πνεῦμα· ἑτέρῳ δὲ πίστις, ἐν τῷ αὐτῷ Πνεύματι· ἄλλῳ δὲ
Spirit; to another and faith, by the same Spirit; to another and
10 χαρίσματα ἰαμάτων, ἐν τῷ αὐτῷ Πνεύματι· ἄλλῳ δὲ ἐνεργή-
gifts of healing, by the same Spirit, to another and workings
ματα δυνάμεων, ἄλλῳ δὲ προφητεία, ἄλλῳ δὲ διακρίσεις
of powers; to another and prophecy; to another and discerning
πνευμάτων, ἑτέρῳ δὲ γένη γλωσσῶν, ἄλλῳ δὲ ἑρμηνεία
of spirits; to another and kinds of languages; to another and interpretation
11 γλωσσῶν· πάντα δὲ ταῦτα ἐνεργεῖ τὸ ἓν καὶ τὸ αὐτὸ Πνεῦμα,
of languages; all and these things works the one and the same Spirit,
διαιροῦν ἰδίᾳ ἑκάστῳ καθὼς βούλεται.
distributing separately to each as He purposes.
12 Καθάπερ γὰρ τὸ σῶμα ἕν ἐστι, καὶ μέλη ἔχει πολλά,
as For the body one is, and members has many,
πάντα δὲ τὰ μέλη τοῦ σώματος τοῦ ἑνός, πολλὰ ὄντα, ἕν
all but the members of the body one, many being, one
13 ἐστι σῶμα· οὕτω καὶ ὁ Χριστός. καὶ γὰρ ἐν ἑνὶ Πνεύματι
is body; so also the Christ. also For by one Spirit
ἡμεῖς πάντες εἰς ἓν σῶμα ἐβαπτίσθημεν, εἴτε Ἰουδαῖοι εἴτε
we all into one body were baptized, whether Jews or
Ἕλληνες, εἴτε δοῦλοι εἴτε ἐλεύθεροι· καὶ πάντες εἰς ἓν Πνεῦμα
Greeks, whether slaves or free, and all into one Spirit

we would not be judged. [32] But being judged, we are corrected by *the* Lord, that we not be condemned with the world. [33] So that, my brothers, coming together to eat, wait for one another. [34] But if anyone is hungry, let him eat at home, that you may not come together for judgment; and the other things I will set in order whenever I come.

CHAPTER 12

[1] But as to spiritual things, brothers, I do not wish you to be ignorant. [2] You know that being led away you Gentiles were led to dumb idols. [3] Therefore, I make known to you that no one speaking by *the* Spirit of God says, Jesus is a curse. And no one is able to say Jesus *is* Lord, except by *the* Holy Spirit. [4] But there are differences of gifts, but the same Spirit; [5] and there are differences of ministries, yet the same Lord. [6] And there are differences of workings, but the same God is working all things in all. [7] But to each one is given the showing forth of the Spirit to *our* profit. [8] For through the Spirit is given to one a word of wisdom; and to another a word of knowledge, according to the same Spirit; [9] and to another, faith by the same Spirit; and to another, gifts of healing by the same Spirit; [10] and to another, workings of powers; and to another, prophecy; and to another, discerning of spirits; and to another, kinds of languages; and to another, interpretation of languages. [11] But the one and the same Spirit works all these things, distributing separately to each as He wills.

[12] Even as the body is one, and has many members, but all the members of the body, being many, *are* one body; so also *is* Christ. [13] For also we all were baptized by one Spirit into one body, whether

Jews or Greeks, whether slaves or free, even all were given to drink into one Spirit. 14 For also the body is not one member, but many. 15 If the foot says, Because I am not a hand, I am not of the body; on account of this, is it not of the body? 17 If all the body *was* an eye, where *would be* the hearing? If all hearing, where the smelling? 18 But now God set the members, each one of them, in the body, even as He desired. 19 But if all was one member, where *would* the body *be*? 20 But now, indeed, many *are* the members, but one body. 21 And the eye is not able to say to the hand, I have no need of you; or again the head to the feet, I have no need of you. 22 But much rather the members of the body seeming to be weaker are necessary. 23 And those of the body we think to be less honorable, to these we put more abundant honor around *them*. And our unpresentable *members* have more abundant propriety. 24 But our presentable one have no need. But God tempered the body together, giving more abundant honor to the the *member* having need, 25 that there not be division in the body, but that the members might have the same care for one another. 26 And if one member suffers, all the members suffer with *it*. If one member is glorified, all the members rejoice with *it*.

27 And you are a body of Christ, and members in part. 28 And God placed some in the church: firstly apostles; secondly, prophets; thirdly, teachers; then works of power; then gifts of healing, helps, governings, kinds of languages. 29 *Are* all apostles? All prophets? All teachers? All workers of power? 30 Do all have gifts of healing? Do all speak languages? Do all interpret? 31 But zealously strive after the better gifts. And yet I

14 ἐποτίσθημεν. καὶ γὰρ τὸ σῶμα οὐκ ἔστιν ἓν μέλος, ἀλλὰ
we were given to drink. also For the body not is one member, but

15 πολλά. ἐὰν εἴπῃ ὁ πούς, Ὅτι οὐκ εἰμὶ χείρ, οὐκ εἰμὶ ἐκ τοῦ
many. If says the foot: Because not I am a hand, not I am of the

16 σώματος· οὐ παρὰ τοῦτο οὐκ ἔστιν ἐκ τοῦ σώματος; καὶ
body; on account of this not is it of the body? And

ἐὰν εἴπῃ τὸ οὖς, Ὅτι οὐκ εἰμὶ ὀφθαλμός, οὐκ εἰμὶ ἐκ τοῦ
if says the ear: Because not I am an eye, not I am of the

17 σώματος· οὐ παρὰ τοῦτο οὐκ ἔστιν ἐκ τοῦ σώματος; εἰ
body; on account of this, not is it of the body; If

ὅλον τὸ σῶμα ὀφθαλμός, ποῦ ἡ ἀκοή; εἰ ὅλον ἀκοή, ποῦ
all the body (was) an eye, where the hearing? If all hearing, where

18 ἡ ὄσφρησις; νυνὶ δὲ ὁ Θεὸς ἔθετο τὰ μέλη ἓν ἕκαστον αὐτῶν
the smelling. now But God set the members, one each of them

19 ἐν τῷ σώματι, καθὼς ἠθέλησεν. εἰ δὲ ἦν τὰ πάντα ἓν μέλος,
in the body, as He desired. if And was all one member,

20 ποῦ τὸ σῶμα; νῦν δὲ πολλὰ μὲν μέλη, ἓν δὲ σῶμα. οὐ
where the body? now But many indeed members, one but body. not

21 δύναται δὲ ὀφθαλμὸς εἰπεῖν τῇ χειρί, Χρείαν σου οὐκ ἔχω·
can And the eye say to the hand, need of you not I have;

22 ἢ πάλιν ἡ κεφαλὴ τοῖς ποσί, Χρείαν ὑμῶν οὐκ ἔχω. ἀλλὰ
or again the head to the feet, need of you not I have. But

πολλῷ μᾶλλον τὰ δοκοῦντα μέλη τοῦ σώματος ἀσθενέ-
by much more the seeming members of the body weaker

23 στερα ὑπάρχειν, ἀναγκαῖά ἐστι· καὶ ἃ δοκοῦμεν ἀτιμότερα
to be, necessary is; and those which we think less honorable

εἶναι τοῦ σώματος, τούτοις τιμὴν περισσοτέραν περιτίθεμεν·
to be of the body, to these honor more abundant we put around;

καὶ τὰ ἀσχήμονα ἡμῶν εὐσχημοσύνην περισσοτέραν ἔχει·
and the unpresentable of us propriety more abundant has;

24 τὰ δὲ εὐσχήμονα ἡμῶν οὐ χρείαν ἔχει· ἀλλ' ὁ Θεὸς συνε-
the but presentable (members) of us not need has. But God tempered

κέρασε τὸ σῶμα, τῷ ὑστεροῦντι περισσοτέραν δοὺς τιμήν,
together the body, to the (member) lacking, more abundant giving honor,

25 ἵνα μὴ ᾖ σχίσμα ἐν τῷ σώματι, ἀλλὰ τὸ αὐτὸ ὑπὲρ ἀλλήλων
lest be division in the body; but the same on behalf of one another

26 μεριμνῶσι τὰ μέλη. καὶ εἴτε πάσχει ἓν μέλος, συμπάσχει
should care the members. And whether suffers one member, suffers with (it)

πάντα τὰ μέλη· εἴτε δοξάζεται ἓν μέλος, συγχαίρει πάντα
all the members; or is glorified one member, rejoices with (it) all

27 τὰ μέλη. ὑμεῖς δέ ἐστε σῶμα Χριστοῦ, καὶ μέλη ἐκ μέρους.
the members. you And are a body of Christ, and members in part.

28 καὶ οὓς μὲν ἔθετο ὁ Θεὸς ἐν τῇ ἐκκλησίᾳ πρῶτον ἀποστόλους,
And some placed God in the church firstly apostles;

δεύτερον προφήτας, τρίτον διδασκάλους, ἔπειτα δυνάμεις,
secondly prophets; thirdly, teachers; then works of power;

εἶτα χαρίσματα ἰαμάτων, ἀντιλήψεις, κυβερνήσεις, γένη
then gifts of healing; helps; governings; kinds

29 γλωσσῶν. μὴ πάντες ἀπόστολοι; μὴ πάντες προφῆται;
of languages. Not all (are) apostles? Not all (are) prophets?

30 μὴ πάντες διδάσκαλοι; μὴ πάντες δυνάμεις; μὴ πάντες
Not all (are) teachers? Not all workers of power? Not all

χαρίσματα ἔχουσιν ἰαμάτων; μὴ πάντες γλώσσαις λαλοῦσι;
gifts have of healings? Not all languages speak?

31 μὴ πάντες διερμηνεύουσι; ζηλοῦτε δὲ τὰ χαρίσματα τὰ
Not all interpret? zealously strive after But the gifts

show you a way according to excellence:

CHAPTER 13

[1]If I speak with the tongues of men and of angels, but I do not have love, I have become *as* sounding brass or a clanging cymbal. [2]And if I have prophecies, and know all mysteries and all knowledge, and if I have all faith so as to move mountains, but do not have love, I am nothing. [3]And if I give out all my goods, and if I deliver my body that I be burned, but I do not have love, I am not profited anything. [4]Love has patience, is kind; love is not envious; love is not vain, is not puffed up; [5]does not behave indecently; does not pursue its own things; is not easily provoked; thinks no evil; [6]does not rejoice in unrighteousness, but rejoices in the truth; [7]quietly covers all things; believes all things; hopes all things; endures all things; [8]love never fails. But if *there are* prophecies, they will be abolished; if tongues, they shall cease; if knowledge, it will be abolished. [9]For we know in part, and we prophesy in part; [10]but when the perfect thing comes, then that *which is* in part will be caused to cease. [11]When I was an infant, I spoke as an infant, I thought as an infant, I reasoned as an infant. But when I became a man, I did away with the things of the infant. [12]For now we see through a mirror in dimness, but then face to face. Now I know in part, but then I will fully know even as I also was fully known. [13]And now faith, hope, and love, these three things remain; but the greatest of these *is* love.

CHAPTER 14

[1]Pursue love, and seek eagerly the spiritual things, but rather that you may prophesy. [2]For the *one* speaking in a tongue does not speak to men, but to God;

κρείττονα. καὶ ἔτι καθ' ὑπερβολὴν ὁδὸν ὑμῖν δείκνυμι.
better. And yet according to excellence a way to you I show.

CHAPTER 13

1 Ἐὰν ταῖς γλώσσαις τῶν ἀνθρώπων λαλῶ καὶ τῶν
If in the languages of men I speak, even
ἀγγέλων, ἀγάπην δὲ μὴ ἔχω, γέγονα χαλκὸς ἠχῶν ἢ
of angels, love and not I have, I have become brass sounding, or
2 κύμβαλον ἀλαλάζον. καὶ ἐὰν ἔχω προφητείαν, καὶ εἰδῶ τὰ
a cymbal clanging. And if I have prophecies, and know
μυστήρια πάντα καὶ πᾶσαν τὴν γνῶσιν, καὶ ἐὰν ἔχω πᾶσαν
mysteries all, and all knowledge, and if I have all
τὴν πίστιν, ὥστε ὄρη μεθιστάνειν, ἀγάπην δὲ μὴ ἔχω, οὐδέν
faith, so as mountains to move, love but not have, nothing
3 εἰμι. καὶ ἐὰν ψωμίσω πάντα τὰ ὑπάρχοντά μου, καὶ ἐὰν
I am. And if I distribute all the goods of me, and if
παραδῶ τὸ σῶμά μου ἵνα καυθήσωμαι, ἀγάπην δὲ μὴ ἔχω,
I deliver the body of me that I be burned, love but not I have,
4 οὐδὲν ὠφελοῦμαι. ἡ ἀγάπη μακροθυμεῖ, χρηστεύεται· ἡ
nothing I am profited. Love suffers long, is kind;
ἀγάπη οὐ ζηλοῖ· ἡ ἀγάπη οὐ περπερεύεται, οὐ φυσιοῦται,
love not is envious; love not vaunts itself, not is puffed up,
5 οὐκ ἀσχημονεῖ, οὐ ζητεῖ τὰ ἑαυτῆς, οὐ παροξύνεται, οὐ
not behaves indecently, not seeks things of itself, not is provoked, not
6 λογίζεται τὸ κακόν, οὐ χαίρει ἐπὶ τῇ ἀδικίᾳ, συγχαίρει δὲ τῇ
thinks evil, not rejoices over the wrong, rejoices with but the
7 ἀληθείᾳ, πάντα στέγει, πάντα πιστεύει, πάντα ἐλπίζει,
truth; all things covers quietly, all things believes, all things hopes,
8 πάντα ὑπομένει. ἡ ἀγάπη οὐδέποτε ἐκπίπτει· εἴτε δὲ προφη-
all things endures. Love never fails; whether but prophecies,
τεῖαι, καταργηθήσονται· εἴτε γλῶσσαι, παύσονται· εἴτε
they will be abolished; if languages, they shall cease; if
9 γνῶσις, καταργηθήσεται. ἐκ μέρους γὰρ γινώσκομεν, καὶ ἐκ
knowledge, it shall be abolished. in part For we know, and in
10 μέρους προφητεύομεν· ὅταν δὲ ἔλθῃ τὸ τέλειον, τότε τὸ ἐκ
part we prophesy; when but comes the perfect thing, then that in
11 μέρους καταργηθήσεται. ὅτε ἤμην νήπιος, ὡς νήπιος
part will be abolished. When I was an infant, as an infant
ἐλάλουν, ὡς νήπιος ἐφρόνουν, ὡς νήπιος ἐλογιζόμην· ὅτε δὲ
I spoke, as an infant I thought, as an infant I reasoned; when but
12 γέγονα ἀνήρ, κατήργηκα τὰ τοῦ νηπίου. βλέπομεν γὰρ
I became a man, I did away with the things of the infant. we see For
ἄρτι δι' ἐσόπτρου ἐν αἰνίγματι, τότε δὲ πρόσωπον πρὸς
yet through a mirror in obscureness, then but face to
πρόσωπον· ἄρτι γινώσκω ἐκ μέρους, τότε δὲ ἐπιγνώσομαι
face; yet I know in part, then but I will fully know
13 καθὼς καὶ ἐπεγνώσθην. νυνὶ δὲ μένει πίστις, ἐλπίς, ἀγάπη,
even as also I was fully known. now But remains faith, hope, love,
τὰ τρία ταῦτα· μείζων δὲ τούτων ἡ ἀγάπη.
three these things; (the) greater and of these (is) love.

CHAPTER 14

1 Διώκετε τὴν ἀγάπην· ζηλοῦτε δὲ τὰ πνευματικά, μᾶλλον
Pursue love, seek eagerly and the spiritual things; rather
2 δὲ ἵνα προφητεύητε. ὁ γὰρ λαλῶν γλώσσῃ οὐκ ἀνθρώποις
and that you may prophesy he for speaking in a tongue not to men

for no one hears, but in spirit he speaks mysteries. 3 But the *one* prophesying to men speaks *for* building up, and encouragement, and comfort. 4 The *one* speaking in a tongue builds himself up; but he prophesying builds up a church. 5 And I wish all of you to speak in languages, but rather that you may prophesy—for greater is the *one* prophesying than the *one* speaking in tongues, unless he interpret that the church may receive building up. 6 But now, brothers, if I come to you speaking in tongues, what will I profit you, except I speak to you either in revelation, or in knowledge, or in prophecy, or in teaching? 7 Yet lifeless things giving a sound, whether pipe or harp, if they do not give a distinction in the sound, how will it be known what *is* being piped or harped? 8 For also if a trumpet gives an uncertain sound, who will get himself ready for war?

9 So also you, if you do not give a clear word through the language, how will it be known what *is* being said? For you will be speaking into air. 10 So it may be many kinds of sounds are in *the* world, and not one is without *distinct* sound. 11 If, then, I do not know the power of the sound, I will be a foreigner to him speaking, and he speaking in me a foreigner. 12 So also you, since you are zealots of spiritual things, seek to build up the church that you may abound. 13 So then, the *one* speaking in a language, let him pray that he may interpret. 14 For if I pray in a tongue, my spirit prays, but my mind is unfruitful. 15 What then is it? I will pray with the spirit, and I will also pray with the mind; I will sing with the spirit, and I will also sing with the mind. 16 Else, if you bless in the spirit, the *one* occupying the place of the unlearned, how will he say the amen at your giving of thanks, since he does not know what you say? 17 For you truly give thanks well, but the other is not built up. 18 I

3 λαλεῖ, ἀλλὰ τῷ Θεῷ· οὐδεὶς γὰρ ἀκούει, πνεύματι δὲ λαλεῖ
speaks, but to God; no one for hears, in spirit but he speaks
μυστήρια. ὁ δὲ προφητεύων ἀνθρώποις λαλεῖ οἰκοδομὴν καὶ
mysteries. the (one) but prophesying to men speaks (for) building up and
4 παράκλησιν καὶ παραμυθίαν ὁ λαλῶν γλώσσῃ ἑαυτὸν οἰκο-
encouragement and comfort. The (one) speaking in a tongue himself builds
5 δομεῖ, ὁ δὲ προφητεύων ἐκκλησίαν οἰκοδομεῖ. θέλω δὲ πάντας
up, the (one) but prophesying a church builds up. I desire And all
ὑμᾶς λαλεῖν γλώσσαις, μᾶλλον δὲ ἵνα προφητεύητε· μείζων
you to speak in languages, rather but that you may prophesy; greater
γὰρ ὁ προφητεύων ἢ ὁ λαλῶν γλώσσαις, ἐκτὸς εἰ μὴ διερμη-
for the (one) prophesying than he speaking in tongues, unless he interpret,
6 νεύῃ, ἵνα ἡ ἐκκλησία οἰκοδομὴν λάβῃ. νυνὶ δέ, ἀδελφοί, ἐὰν
that the church building up may receive. now But, brothers, if
ἔλθω πρὸς ὑμᾶς γλώσσαις λαλῶν, τί ὑμᾶς ὠφελήσω, ἐὰν μὴ
I come to you in languages speaking, what you will I profit, except
ὑμῖν λαλήσω ἢ ἐν ἀποκαλύψει, ἢ ἐν γνώσει, ἢ ἐν προφητείᾳ,
to you I speak either in revelation, or in knowledge, or in prophecy,
7 ἢ ἐν διδαχῇ; ὅμως τὰ ἄψυχα φωνὴν διδόντα, εἴτε αὐλός,
or in teaching? Yet lifeless things a sound giving, whether pipe
εἴτε κιθάρα, ἐὰν διαστολὴν τοῖς φθόγγοις μὴ δῷ, πῶς
or harp, if a distinction in the sound not they give, how
8 γνωσθήσεται τὸ αὐλούμενον ἢ τὸ κιθαριζόμενον; καὶ γὰρ
will it be known the thing being piped or the thing being harped? indeed For
ἐὰν ἄδηλον φωνὴν σάλπιγξ δῷ, τίς παρασκευάσεται εἰς
if an uncertain sound a trumpet gives, who will get himself ready for
9 πόλεμον; οὕτω καὶ ὑμεῖς διὰ τῆς γλώσσης ἐὰν μὴ εὔσημον
war? So also you through the language if not a clear
λόγον δῶτε, πῶς γνωσθήσεται τὸ λαλούμενον; ἔσεσθε γὰρ
word give, how will it be known the thing being said? you For
10 εἰς ἀέρα λαλοῦντες. τοσαῦτα, εἰ τύχοι, γένη φωνῶν ἐστὶν
into air will be speaking. So many it may be kinds of sounds are
11 ἐν κόσμῳ καὶ οὐδὲν ἄφωνον. ἐὰν οὖν μὴ εἰδῶ τὴν δύναμιν
in (the) world, and not one is voiceless. If, then, not I know the power
τῆς φωνῆς, ἔσομαι τῷ λαλοῦντι βάρβαρος, καὶ ὁ λαλῶν ἐν
of the sound, I will be to the (one) speaking a foreigner, and he speaking in
12 ἐμοὶ βάρβαρος. οὕτω καὶ ὑμεῖς, ἐπεὶ ζηλωταί ἐστε πνευ-
me a foreigner. So also you, since zealots you are of
μάτων, πρὸς τὴν οἰκοδομὴν τῆς ἐκκλησίας ζητεῖτε ἵνα περισ-
spiritual things, to the building up of the church seek, that you may
13 σεύητε. διόπερ ὁ λαλῶν γλώσσῃ προσευχέσθω ἵνα διερμη-
abound. Therefore, he speaking in a language let him pray that he may
14 νεύῃ. ἐὰν γὰρ προσεύχωμαι γλώσσῃ, τὸ πνεῦμά μου
interpret. if For I pray in a tongue, the spirit of me
15 προσεύχεται, ὁ δὲ νοῦς μου ἄκαρπός ἐστι. τί οὖν ἐστί;
prays, the but mind of me unfruitful is. What then is it?
προσεύξομαι τῷ πνεύματι, προσεύξομαι δὲ καὶ τῷ νοΐ· ψαλῶ
I will pray with the spirit, I will pray and also with the mind; I sing
16 τῷ πνεύματι, ψαλῶ δὲ καὶ τῷ νοΐ. ἐπεὶ ἐὰν εὐλογήσῃς τῷ
with the spirit, I sing and also with the mind. Else if you bless in the
πνεύματι, ὁ ἀναπληρῶν τὸν τόπον τοῦ ἰδιώτου πῶς ἐρεῖ
spirit, the (one) occupying the place of the unlearned, how will he say
τὸ ἀμὴν ἐπὶ τῇ σῇ εὐχαριστίᾳ, ἐπειδὴ τί λέγεις οὐκ οἶδε;
the amen at your giving thanks? Since what you say not he knows;
17 σὺ μὲν γὰρ καλῶς εὐχαριστεῖς, ἀλλ' ὁ ἕτερος οὐκ οἰκοδο-
you indeed for well give thanks, but the other not is built up

thank my God *that* I speak more languages than all of you. [19]But in a church I desire to speak five words with my mind, that I may also instruct others, than myriads of words in a foreign language.

[20]Do not be children in your minds, but in malice be like infants, and in your minds be mature. [21]It has been written in the Law, "By other tongues and by other lips I will speak to this people, and even so they will not hear Me, says *the* Lord." [22]So that tongues are not a sign to those believing, but to those not believing. But prophecy is not to those not believing, but to those believing. [23]Therefore, if the whole church comes together, and all speak in languages, and uninstructed ones or unbelievers come in, will they not say that you rave? [24]But if all prophesy, and some unbeliever or one not instructed comes in, he is convicted by all, he is judged by all. [25]And so the secrets of his heart become revealed; and so, falling on *his* face, he will worship God, declaring that God is truly among you.

[26]Then what is it, brothers? When you come together, each one of you has a psalm; he has a teaching; he has a language; he has a revelation; he has an interpretation. Let all things be for building up. [27]If one speaks in a language, *let it be* by two or three *at* the most; and in turn, also let one interpret. [28]And if there is no interpreter, let him be silent in church; and let him speak to himself and to God. [29]And *if there are* two or three prophets, let them speak, and let the others discern. [30]But if a revelation *occurs* to another sitting by, let the first be silent. [31]For you can all prophesy one by one, that all may learn, and all may be encouraged. [32]And the spirits of prophets *are*

18 μεῖται. εὐχαριστῶ τῷ Θεῷ μου, πάντων ὑμῶν μᾶλλον
I thank the God of me, all of you more than
19 γλώσσαις λαλῶν· ἀλλ' ἐν ἐκκλησίᾳ θέλω πέντε λόγους διὰ
in languages I speak, but in a church I desire five words with
τοῦ νοός μου λαλῆσαι, ἵνα καὶ ἄλλους κατηχήσω, ἢ μυρίους
the mind of me to speak, that also others I may instruct, than myriads
λόγους ἐν γλώσσῃ.
of words in a foreign language.

20 Ἀδελφοί, μὴ παιδία γίνεσθε ταῖς φρεσίν· ἀλλὰ τῇ κακίᾳ
Brothers, not children be in the minds, but in malice
21 νηπιάζετε, ταῖς δὲ φρεσὶ τέλειοι γίνεσθε. ἐν τῷ νόμῳ
be like infants in the and minds mature be. In the law
γέγραπται ὅτι Ἐν ἑτερογλώσσοις καὶ ἐν χείλεσιν ἑτέροις
it has been written: In other tongues and in lips other
λαλήσω τῷ λαῷ τούτῳ, καὶ οὐδ' οὕτως εἰσακούσονταί μου,
I will speak to people this, and not so will they hear Me,
22 λέγει Κύριος. ὥστε αἱ γλῶσσαι εἰς σημεῖόν εἰσιν, οὐ τοῖς
says (the) Lord. So as tongues for a sign are, not to those
πιστεύουσιν, ἀλλὰ τοῖς ἀπίστοις· ἡ δὲ προφητεία, οὐ τοῖς
believing, but to those not believing; and prophecy (is) not to the
23 ἀπίστοις, ἀλλὰ τοῖς πιστεύουσιν. ἐὰν οὖν συνέλθῃ ἡ
unbelievers, but to those believing. If, therefore, comes the
ἐκκλησία ὅλη ἐπὶ τὸ αὐτό, καὶ πάντες γλώσσαις λαλῶσιν,
church whole together, and all in languages speak,
εἰσέλθωσι δὲ ἰδιῶται ἢ ἄπιστοι, οὐκ ἐροῦσιν ὅτι μαίνεσθε;
come in and uninstructed or unbelievers, not will they say that you rave?
24 ἐὰν δὲ πάντες προφητεύωσιν, εἰσέλθῃ δέ τις ἄπιστος ἢ
if But all prophesy, comes in and some unbeliever or
ἰδιώτης, ἐλέγχεται ὑπὸ πάντων, ἀνακρίνεται ὑπὸ πάντων,
uninstructed, he is convicted by all, he is judged by all;
25 καὶ οὕτω τὰ κρυπτὰ τῆς καρδίας αὐτοῦ φανερὰ γίνεται· καὶ
and so the secrets of the heart of him revealed become, and
οὕτω πεσὼν ἐπὶ πρόσωπον προσκυνήσει τῷ Θεῷ ἀπαγ-
so falling on (his) face, he will worship God, declaring
γέλλων ὅτι ὁ Θεὸς ὄντως ἐν ὑμῖν ἐστι.
that God truly among you is.

26 Τί οὖν ἐστίν, ἀδελφοί; ὅταν συνέρχησθε, ἕκαστος ὑμῶν
What then is it, brothers? When you come together, each one of you
ψαλμὸν ἔχει, διδαχὴν ἔχει, γλῶσσαν ἔχει, ἀποκάλυψιν ἔχει,
a psalm has, a teaching he has, a language he has, a revelation he has,
27 ἑρμηνείαν ἔχει. πάντα πρὸς οἰκοδομὴν γενέσθω. εἴτε
an interpretation he has. all things for building up let be. If
γλώσσῃ τις λαλεῖ, κατὰ δύο ἢ τὸ πλεῖστον τρεῖς, καὶ ἀνὰ
in a language one speaks, by two or the most three, and in
28 μέρος, καὶ εἷς διερμηνευέτω· ἐὰν δὲ μὴ ᾖ διερμηνευτής, σιγάτω
turn, and one let interpret; if but not (is) an interpreter, be silent
29 ἐν ἐκκλησίᾳ· ἑαυτῷ δὲ λαλείτω καὶ τῷ Θεῷ. προφῆται δὲ
in church, to himself and let him speak, and to God. prophets And
30 δύο ἢ τρεῖς λαλείτωσαν, καὶ οἱ ἄλλοι διακρινέτωσαν. ἐὰν δὲ
two or three let them speak, and the others let discern; if and
31 ἄλλῳ ἀποκαλυφθῇ καθημένῳ, ὁ πρῶτος σιγάτω. δύνασθε
to another is revealed sitting the first let be silent. you can
γὰρ καθ' ἕνα πάντες προφητεύειν, ἵνα πάντες μανθάνωσι,
For one by one all prophesy, that all may learn
32 καὶ πάντες παρακαλῶνται· καὶ πνεύματα προφητῶν προφή-
and all may be encouraged. And the spirits of prophets to prophets

subject to prophets. 33 For God is not *God* of confusion, but of peace, as in all the churches of the saints.

34 Let your women be silent in the churches, for it is not allowed to them to speak, but to be in subjection, as also the law says. 35 But if they desire to learn anything, let them question their husbands at home; for it is a shame for a woman to speak in a church. 36 Or did the word of God go out from you? Or did it reach only to you?

37 If anyone thinks to be a prophet, or a spiritual one, let him recognize what I write to you, that they are a command of the Lord. 38 But if any be ignorant, let him be ignorant. 39 So as, brothers, seek eagerly to prophesy, and do not forbid to speak in languages. 40 And let all things be done decently and in order.

CHAPTER 15

1 But, brothers, I reveal to you the gospel which I preached to you, which you also received, in which you also stand, 2 by which you also are being saved, if you hold fast the word which I preached to you; unless you believed in vain. 3 For I delivered to you in the first place what I also received, that Christ died for our sins, according to the Scriptures; 4 and that He was buried; and that He was raised the third day, according to the Scriptures; 5 and that He appeared to Peter, then to the Twelve. 6 Then He appeared to over five hundred brothers at once, of whom the most remain until now; but some also fell asleep. 7 Then He was seen by James; then by all the apostles; 8 and last of all, even as if to *one* born out of time, He was also seen by me. 9 for I am the least of the apostles, who am not sufficient to be called an apostle, because I persecuted the church of God. 10 But

33 ταις ὑποτάσσεται. οὐ γάρ ἐστιν ἀκαταστασίας ὁ Θεός, ἀλλ'
(are) subject. not For is of confusion God, but
εἰρήνης, ὡς ἐν πάσαις ταῖς ἐκκλησίαις τῶν ἁγίων.
of peace, as in all the churches of the saints.
34 Αἱ γυναῖκες ὑμῶν ἐν ταῖς ἐκκλησίαις σιγάτωσαν· οὐ γὰρ
Let the women of you in the churches be silent, not for
ἐπιτέτραπται αὐταῖς λαλεῖν, ἀλλ' ὑποτάσσεσθαι, καθὼς καὶ
it is allowed to them to speak, but let them be subject, as also
35 ὁ νόμος λέγει. εἰ δέ τι μαθεῖν θέλουσιν, ἐν οἴκῳ τοὺς ἰδίους
the law says. if But anything to learn they desire, at home the own
ἄνδρας ἐπερωτάτωσαν· αἰσχρὸν γάρ ἐστι γυναιξὶν ἐν
husbands let them question; a shame for it is for women in
36 ἐκκλησίᾳ λαλεῖν. ἢ ἀφ' ὑμῶν ὁ λόγος τοῦ Θεοῦ ἐξῆλθεν ; ἢ
a church to speak. Or from you the word of God went out, or
εἰς ὑμᾶς μόνους κατήντησεν
to you only did it reach?
37 Εἴ τις δοκεῖ προφήτης εἶναι ἢ πνευματικός, ἐπιγινωσκέτω
If anyone thinks a prophet to be, or a spiritual one, let him recognize
38 ἃ γράφω ὑμῖν, ὅτι τοῦ Κυρίου εἰσὶν ἐντολαί. εἰ δέ τις ἀγνοεῖ,
what I write to you, that of the Lord they are a command. if But any be ignorant,
ἀγνοείτω.
let him be ignorant.
39 Ὥστε, ἀδελφοί, ζηλοῦτε τὸ προφητεύειν, καὶ τὸ λαλεῖν
So as, brothers, seek eagerly to prophesy, and to speak
40 γλώσσαις μὴ κωλύετε. πάντα εὐσχημόνως καὶ κατὰ τάξιν
in languages not do forbid; all things decently and according to order
γινέσθω.
let be done.

CHAPTER 15

1 Γνωρίζω δὲ ὑμῖν, ἀδελφοί, τὸ εὐαγγέλιον ὃ εὐηγγελισάμην
I make known And to you, brothers, the gospel which I preached
2 ὑμῖν, ὃ καὶ παρελάβετε, ἐν ᾧ καὶ ἑστήκατε, δι οὗ καὶ σώζεσθε·
to you, which also you received, in which also you stand, by which also you are saved,
τίνι λόγῳ εὐηγγελισάμην ὑμῖν, εἰ κατέχετε, ἐκτὸς εἰ μὴ εἰκῇ
to what word I preached to you if you hold fast, unless in vain
3 ἐπιστεύσατε. παρέδωκα γὰρ ὑμῖν ἐν πρώτοις, ὃ καὶ παρέ-
you believed. I delivered For to you among the first what also I
λαβον, ὅτι Χριστὸς ἀπέθανεν ὑπὲρ τῶν ἁμαρτιῶν ἡμῶν
received, that Christ died for the sins of us
4 κατὰ τὰς γραφάς· καὶ ὅτι ἐτάφη· καὶ ὅτι ἐγήγερται τῇ τρίτῃ
according to the Scriptures, and that He was buried, and has been raised the third
5 ἡμέρα κατὰ τὰς γραφάς· καὶ ὅτι ὤφθη Κηφᾷ, εἶτα τοῖς δώδεκα·
day according to the Scriptures, and he was seen by Cephas, then by the twelve;
6 ἔπειτα ὤφθη ἐπάνω πεντακοσίοις ἀδελφοῖς ἐφάπαξ, ἐξ ὧν οἱ
afterward He was seen over by five hundreds brothers at one time, of whom the
7 πλείους μένουσιν ἕως ἄρτι τινὲς δὲ καὶ ἐκοιμήθησαν· ἔπειτα
most remain until now, some but also fell asleep. Afterward
8 ὤφθη Ἰακώβῳ, εἶτα τοῖς ἀποστόλοις πᾶσιν· ἔσχατον δὲ
He was seen by James, then by the apostles all; lastly and
9 πάντων, ὡσπερεὶ τῷ ἐκτρώματι, ὤφθη κἀμοί. ἐγὼ γάρ
of all, even as if to the untimely birth, He was seen by me also. I For
10 εἰμι ὁ ἐλάχιστος τῶν ἀποστόλων, ὃς οὐκ εἰμὶ ἱκανὸς καλεῖσθαι
am the least of the apostles, who not am sufficient to be called
ἀπόστολος, διότι ἐδίωξα τὴν ἐκκλησίαν τοῦ Θεοῦ. χάριτι δὲ
an apostle, because I persecuted the church of God. by grace But

by the grace of God I am what I am, and His grace which *was* toward me has not been without fruit, but I labored more abundantly than all of them—yet not I, but the grace of God with me. 11 Therefore, whether they or I, so we preach, and so you believed.

12 But if Christ is proclaimed, that He was raised from *the* dead, how do some among you say that there is not a resurrection of *the* dead? 13 But if there is not a resurrection, neither has Christ been raised. 14 But if Christ has not been raised, then our proclamation is worthless, and our faith is also worthless. 15 And also we are found *to be* false witnesses of God, because we witnessed as to God that He raised Christ, whom He did not raise, then, if *the* dead are not raised. 16 For if *the* dead are not raised, Christ has not been raised. 17 But if Christ has not been raised, your faith *is* foolish; you are still in your sins. 18 And then those that fell asleep in Christ were lost. 19 if we only have hope in Christ in this life, we are of all men most miserable.

20 But now Christ has been raised from *the* dead; He became the firstfruit of those having fallen asleep. 21 For since death *is* through man, also through a Man *is* a resurrection of *the* dead; 22 for as all die in Adam, so also all will be made alive in Christ. 23 But each in *his* own order: Christ, the firstfruit; afterward those of Christ at His coming. 24 Then *is* the end—when He delivers the kingdom to God, even the Father, when He abolishes all rule, and all authority and power—25 for it is right for Him to reign until He puts all the enemies under His feet; 26 *the* last enemy made to cease is death. 27 For He subjected

Θεοῦ εἰμὶ ὅ εἰμι, καὶ ἡ χάρις αὐτοῦ ἡ εἰς ἐμὲ οὐ κενὴ ἐγενήθη,
of God I am what I am, and His grace to me not empty was,

ἀλλὰ περισσότερον αὐτῶν πάντων ἐκοπίασα· οὐκ ἐγὼ δέ,
but more abundantly (than) them all I labored, not I yet,

11 ἀλλ' ἡ χάρις τοῦ Θεοῦ ἡ σὺν ἐμοί. εἴτε οὖν ἐγώ, εἴτε ἐκεῖνοι
but the grace of God with me.Whether, then, I or those,

οὕτω κηρύσσομεν, καὶ οὕτως ἐπιστεύσατε.
so we proclaim, and so you believed.

12 Εἰ δὲ Χριστὸς κηρύσσεται ὅτι ἐκ νεκρῶν ἐγήγερται, πῶς
If But Christ is proclaimed that from (the) dead He was raised. how

13 λέγουσί τινες ἐν ὑμῖν ὅτι ἀνάστασις νεκρῶν οὐκ ἔστιν ; εἰ δὲ
say some among you that a resurrection of dead not is? if But

ἀνάστασις νεκρῶν οὐκ ἔστιν, οὐδὲ Χριστὸς ἐγήγερται·
a resurrection of dead not is, neither Christ has been raised;

14 εἰ δὲ Χριστὸς οὐκ ἐγήγερται, κενὸν ἄρα τὸ κήρυγμα
if and Christ not has been raised, worthless then the proclamation

15 ἡμῶν, κενὴ δὲ καὶ ἡ πίστις ὑμῶν. εὑρισκόμεθα δὲ καὶ ψευδο-
of us, worthless and also the faith of us. we are found And also false

μάρτυρες τοῦ Θεοῦ, ὅτι ἐμαρτυρήσαμεν κατὰ τοῦ Θεοῦ ὅτι
witnesses of God, because we witnessed as to God that

16 ἤγειρε τὸν Χριστόν, ὃν οὐκ ἤγειρεν, εἴπερ ἄρα νεκροὶ οὐκ
He raised Christ, whom not He raised if then dead ones not

ἐγείρονται. εἰ γὰρ νεκροὶ οὐκ ἐγείρονται, οὐδὲ Χριστὸς
are raised. if For dead ones not are raised, neither Christ

17 ἐγήγερται· εἰ δὲ Χριστὸς οὐκ ἐγήγερται, ματαία ἡ πίστις
has been raised; if but Christ not has been raised, foolish the faith

18 ὑμῶν· ἔτι ἐστὲ ἐν ταῖς ἁμαρτίαις ὑμῶν. ἄρα καὶ οἱ κοιμη-
of you; still you are in the sins of you. Then also those having

19 θέντες ἐν Χριστῷ ἀπώλοντο. εἰ ἐν τῇ ζωῇ ταύτῃ ἠλπικότες
slept in Christ were lost If in life this having hoped

ἐσμὲν ἐν Χριστῷ μόνον, ἐλεεινότεροι πάντων ἀνθρώπων
we are in Christ only, more miserable of all men

ἐσμέν.
we are.

20 Νυνὶ δὲ Χριστὸς ἐγήγερται ἐκ νεκρῶν, ἀπαρχὴ τῶν
now But Christ has been raised from (the) dead,firstfruit of those

21 κεκοιμημένων ἐγένετο. ἐπειδὴ γὰρ δι' ἀνθρώπου ὁ θάνατος,
having fallen asleep He became. since For through man (is) death,

22 καὶ δι' ἀνθρώπου ἀνάστασις νεκρῶν. ὥσπερ γὰρ ἐν τῷ
and through a Man a resurrection of (the) dead. as For in

Ἀδὰμ πάντες ἀποθνήσκουσιν, οὕτω καὶ ἐν τῷ Χριστῷ
Adam all die, so also in Christ

23 πάντες ζωοποιηθήσονται. ἕκαστος δὲ ἐν τῷ ἰδίῳ τάγματι·
all will be made alive. each But in the own order:

ἀπαρχὴ Χριστός, ἔπειτα οἱ Χριστοῦ ἐν τῇ παρουσίᾳ αὐτοῦ.
the firstfruit Christ, afterward those of Christ in the coming of Him.

24 εἶτα τὸ τέλος, ὅταν παραδῷ τὴν βασιλείαν τῷ Θεῷ καὶ
Then the end — when He delivers the kingdom to God, even

πατρί, ὅταν καταργήσῃ πᾶσαν ἀρχὴν καὶ πᾶσαν ἐξουσίαν
the Father; when He abolishes all rule and all authority

25 καὶ δύναμιν. δεῖ γὰρ αὐτὸν βασιλεύειν, ἄχρις οὗ ἂν θῇ
and power — it is right For Him to reign until He puts

26 πάντας τοὺς ἐχθροὺς ὑπὸ τοὺς πόδας αὐτοῦ. ἔσχατος
all the enemies under the feet of Him — (the) last

27 ἐχθρὸς καταργεῖται ὁ θάνατος. Πάντα γὰρ ὑπέταξεν ὑπὸ
enemy is abolished, death — all things for He subjected under

all things under His feet; but when He says that all things have been subjected, *it is* plain that *it* excepts Him who has subjected all things to Him. 28 But when all things are subjected to Him, then the Son Himself will be subjected to the *One* who has subjected all things to Him, that God may be all things in all.

29 Otherwise, what will they do, those being baptized on behalf of the dead? If *the* dead are not at all raised, why indeed are they baptized on behalf of the dead? 30 Why are we also in danger every hour? 31 Day by day I die, by your boasting, which I have in Christ Jesus our Lord. 32 If according to man I fought with beasts in Ephesus, what the profit to me if *the* dead are not raised? —"Let us eat and drink, for tomorrow we die." 33 Do not be led astray; bad companionships ruin good habits. 34 Be righteously awake, and do not sin; for some have ignorance of God. I speak to your shame.

35 But someone will say, How are the dead raised? And with what body do they come? 36 Foolish one! What you sow is not made alive unless it dies. 37 And what you sow, you do not sow the body that *is* going to be, but a bare grain—it may be of wheat, or of some of the rest— 38 and God gives it a body according as He willed, and to each of the seeds its own body. 39 Not every flesh *is* the same flesh, but one flesh of men, and another flesh of beasts, and another of fish, and another of birds. 40 And *there are* heavenly bodies, and earthly bodies. But the glory of the heavenly *is* truly different, and that of the earthly different; 41 one glory of *the* sun, and another of *the* moon, and another glory of *the* stars, for star differs from star in glory. 42 So also the resurrection of the dead. It is sown in corruption; it is raised in

τοὺς πόδας αὐτοῦ. ὅταν δὲ εἴπῃ ὅτι Πάντα ὑποτέτακται,
the feet of Him. when But He says that all things have been subjected,
28 δῆλον ὅτι ἐκτὸς τοῦ ὑποτάξαντος αὐτῷ τὰ πάντα. ὅταν δὲ
(it is) plain that excepted the (One) having subjected to Him all things. when But
ὑποταγῇ αὐτῷ τὰ πάντα, τότε καὶ αὐτὸς ὁ υἱὸς ὑποταγή-
is subjected to Him all things, then also Himself, the Son, will be sub-
σεται τῷ ὑποτάξαντι αὐτῷ τὰ πάντα, ἵνα ᾖ ὁ Θεὸς τὰ
jected to the (One) having subjected to Him all things, that may be God
πάντα ἐν πᾶσιν.
all things in all.
29 Ἐπεὶ τί ποιήσουσιν οἱ βαπτιζόμενοι ὑπὲρ τῶν νεκρῶν ;
Otherwise what will they do, those being baptized on behalf of the dead?
εἰ ὅλως νεκροὶ οὐκ ἐγείρονται, τί καὶ βαπτίζονται ὑπὲρ τῶν
If not at all dead ones not are raised, why indeed are they baptized for the
30 νεκρῶν ; τί καὶ ἡμεῖς κινδυνεύομεν πᾶσαν ὥραν ; καθ' ἡμέραν
31 **dead; why also we are in danger every hour? Day by day**
ἀποθνήσκω, νὴ τὴν ὑμετέραν καύχησιν, ἣν ἔχω ἐν Χριστῷ
I die, by your boasting, which I have in Christ
32 Ἰησοῦ τῷ Κυρίῳ ἡμῶν. εἰ κατὰ ἄνθρωπον ἐθηριομάχησα
Jesus the Lord of us. If according to man I fought with beasts
ἐν Ἐφέσῳ, τί μοι τὸ ὄφελος, εἰ νεκροὶ οὐκ ἐγείρονται ;
in Ephesus, what to me the profit? If dead ones not are raised,
33 φάγωμεν καὶ πίωμεν, αὔριον γὰρ ἀποθνήσκομεν. μὴ πλανᾶ-
let us eat and drink, tomorrow for we die. not Be led
34 σθε· Φθείρουσιν ἤθη χρήσθ' ὁμιλίαι κακαί. ἐκνήψατε δικαίως,
astray, will corrupt habits good companionships bad. Be aroused righteously,
καὶ μὴ ἁμαρτάνετε· ἀγνωσίαν γὰρ Θεοῦ τινὲς ἔχουσι· πρὸς
and not sin; ignorance for of God some have; for
ἐντροπὴν ὑμῖν λέγω.
shame to you I speak.
35 Ἀλλ' ἐρεῖ τις, Πῶς ἐγείρονται οἱ νεκροί ; ποίῳ δὲ σώματι
But will say someone, How are raised the dead? with what And body
36 ἔρχονται ; ἄφρον, σὺ ὃ σπείρεις, οὐ ζωοποιεῖται, ἐὰν μὴ
do they come? Foolish one, you what sow, not is made alive unless
37 ἀποθάνῃ· καὶ ὃ σπείρεις, οὐ τὸ σῶμα τὸ γενησόμενον σπεί-
it dies; and what you sow, not the body going to become you
ρεις, ἀλλὰ γυμνὸν κόκκον, εἰ τύχοι, σίτου ἤ τινος τῶν
sow, but a naked grain it may be of wheat or some of the
38 λοιπῶν· ὁ δὲ Θεὸς αὐτῷ δίδωσι σῶμα καθὼς ἠθέλησε, καὶ
rest; but God to it gives a body as He desired, and
39 ἑκάστῳ τῶν σπερμάτων τὸ ἴδιον σῶμα. οὐ πᾶσα σὰρξ ἡ
to each of the seeds the own body. (is) not All flesh the
αὐτὴ σάρξ· ἀλλὰ ἄλλη μὲν σὰρξ ἀνθρώπων, ἄλλη δὲ σὰρξ
same flesh, but other indeed flesh of men, other and flesh
40 κτηνῶν, ἄλλη δὲ ἰχθύων, ἄλλη δὲ πτηνῶν. καὶ σώματα
of animals, other and of fish, other and of birds. And (are) bodies
ἐπουράνια, καὶ σώματα ἐπίγεια· ἀλλ' ἑτέρα μὲν ἡ τῶν ἐπου-
heavenly, and bodies earthly, but other (is) truly the of the
41 ρανίων δόξα, ἑτέρα δὲ ἡ τῶν ἐπιγείων. ἄλλη δόξα ἡλίου, καὶ
heavenly glory, other and that of the earthly; other glory of the sun, and
ἄλλη δόξα σελήνης, καὶ ἄλλη δόξα ἀστέρων· ἀστὴρ γὰρ
other glory of the moon, and other glory of (the) stars; star for
42 ἀστέρος διαφέρει ἐν δόξῃ οὕτω. καὶ ἡ ἀνάστασις τῶν
from star differs in glory. So also the resurrection of the
νεκρῶν. σπείρεται ἐν φθορᾷ, ἐγείρεται ἐν ἀφθαρσίᾳ· σπεί-
dead. It is sown in corruption; it is raised in incorruption; it is

incorruption. 43 It is sown in dishonor, it is raised in glory. It is sown in weakness, it is raised in power. 44 It is sown a natural body, it is raised a spiritual body; there is a spiritual body, and there is a natural body. 45 So also it has been written, "The first man, Adam, became a living soul," the last Adam *became* a life-giving Spirit. 46 But not the spiritual first, but the natural; afterward the spiritual. 47 The first man *was* out of earth, earthy. The second Man *was* the Lord out of Heaven. 48 Such the earth, such also the earthy. And such the heavenly Man, such also the heavenly ones. 49 And as we bore the image of the earthy *man*, we shall also bear the image of the heavenly *Man*. 50 And I say this, brothers, that flesh and blood is not able to inherit *the* kingdom of God, nor does corruption inherit incorruption. 51 Behold, I speak a mystery to you: we shall not all fall asleep, but we all shall be changed. 52 In a moment, in a glance of an eye, at the last trumpet; for a trumpet will sound, and the dead will be raised incorruptible, and we shall all be changed. 53 For this corruptible must put on incorruption, and this mortal must put on immortality. 54 But when this corruptible shall put on incorruption, and this mortal shall put on immortality, then will take place the word that has been written, "Death was swallowed up in victory. 55 O death, where *is your* sting? Hades, where *is your* victory?" 56 Now the sting of death *is* sin, and the power of sin *is* the law; 57 but thanks *be* to God who gives us the victory through our Lord Jesus Christ! 58 So that, my beloved brothers, *you* be firm, unmoveable, abounding in the work of the Lord always, knowing that your labor is not without fruit in *the* Lord.

43 ρεται ἐν ἀτιμίᾳ, ἐγείρεται ἐν δόξῃ· σπείρεται ἐν ἀσθενείᾳ,
sown in dishonor; it is raised in glory; it is sown in weakness;

44 ἐγείρεται ἐν δυνάμει· σπείρεται σῶμα ψυχικόν, ἐγείρεται
it is raised in power; it is sown a body natural; it is raised

σῶμα πνευματικόν. ἔστι σῶμα ψυχικόν, καὶ ἔστι σῶμα
body spiritual. There is a body natural, and there is a body

45 πνευματικόν. οὕτω καὶ γέγραπται, Ἐγένετο ὁ πρῶτος
spiritual. So also it has been written: became The first

ἄνθρωπος Ἀδὰμ εἰς ψυχὴν ζῶσαν. ὁ ἔσχατος Ἀδὰμ εἰς
man Adam soul a living; the last Adam

46 πνεῦμα ζωοποιοῦν. ἀλλ’ οὐ πρῶτον τὸ πνευματικόν, ἀλλὰ
Spirit a life-giving. But not firstly the spiritual (body), but

47 τὸ ψυχικόν, ἔπειτα τὸ πνευματικόν. ὁ πρῶτος ἄνθρωπος ἐκ
the natural; afterward the spiritual. The first man (was) out of

γῆς, χοϊκός· ὁ δεύτερος ἄνθρωπος, ὁ Κύριος ἐξ οὐρανοῦ.
earth, earthy; the second Man the Lord out of Heaven.

48 οἷος ὁ χοϊκός, τοιοῦτοι καὶ οἱ χοϊκοί· καὶ οἷος ὁ ἐπουράνιος,
Such the earth, such also the earthy ones; and such the heavenly Man,

49 τοιοῦτοι καὶ οἱ ἐπουράνιοι· καὶ καθὼς ἐφορέσαμεν τὴν εἰκόνα
such also the heavenly ones. And as we bore the image

τοῦ χοϊκοῦ, φορέσομεν καὶ τὴν εἰκόνα τοῦ ἐπουρανίου.
of the earthy man, we shall bear also the image of the heavenly Man.

50 Τοῦτο δέ φημι, ἀδελφοί, ὅτι σὰρξ καὶ αἷμα βασιλείαν
this And I say, brothers, that flesh and blood (the) kingdom

Θεοῦ κληρονομῆσαι οὐ δύνανται, οὐδὲ ἡ φθορὰ τὴν ἀφθαρ-
of God inherit not is able to, nor corruption incorrup-

51 σίαν κληρονομεῖ. ἰδού, μυστήριον ὑμῖν λέγω· Πάντες μὲν οὐ
tion inherit. Behold, a mystery to you I tell: all indeed not

52 κοιμηθησόμεθα, πάντες δὲ ἀλλαγησόμεθα, ἐν ἀτόμῳ, ἐν ῥιπῇ
we shall fall asleep, all but we shall be changed, in a moment, in a glance

ὀφθαλμοῦ, ἐν τῇ ἐσχάτῃ σάλπιγγι· σαλπίσει γάρ, καὶ οἱ
of an eye, at the last trumpet; will trumpet for, and the

νεκροὶ ἐγερθήσονται ἄφθαρτοι, καὶ ἡμεῖς ἀλλαγησόμεθα.
dead will be raised incorruptible and we shall be changed.

53 δεῖ γὰρ τὸ φθαρτὸν τοῦτο ἐνδύσασθαι ἀφθαρσίαν, καὶ τὸ
must For corruptible this put on incorruption, and

54 θνητὸν τοῦτο ἐνδύσασθαι ἀθανασίαν. ὅταν δὲ τὸ φθαρτὸν
mortal this put on immortality. when And corruptible

τοῦτο ἐνδύσηται ἀφθαρσίαν καὶ τὸ θνητὸν τοῦτο ἐνδύσηται
this shall put on incorruption, and mortal this put on

ἀθανασίαν, τότε γενήσεται ὁ λόγος ὁ γεγραμμένος, Κατε-
immortality, then will occur the word having been written: was

55 πόθη ὁ θάνατος εἰς νῖκος. Ποῦ σου, θάνατε, τὸ κέντρον ; ποῦ
swallowed Death in victory. Where of you, death the sting; where

56 σου, ᾅδη, τὸ νῖκος ; τὸ δὲ κέντρον τοῦ θανάτου ἡ ἁμαρτία· ἡ
of you Hades the victory? the And sting of death (is) sin,

57 δὲ δύναμις τῆς ἁμαρτίας ὁ νόμος· τῷ δὲ Θεῷ χάρις τῷ
and the power of sin (is) the law; but to God thanks, He

διδόντι ἡμῖν τὸ νῖκος διὰ τοῦ Κυρίου ἡμῶν Ἰησοῦ Χριστοῦ.
giving to us the victory through the Lord of us, Jesus Christ.

58 ὥστε, ἀδελφοί μου ἀγαπητοί, ἑδραῖοι γίνεσθε, ἀμετακίνητοι,
So as, brothers of me, beloved, firm be, unmoveable,

περισσεύοντες ἐν τῷ ἔργῳ τοῦ Κυρίου πάντοτε, εἰδότες ὅτι
abounding in the work of the Lord always, knowing that

ὁ κόπος ὑμῶν οὐκ ἔστι κενὸς ἐν Κυρίῳ.
the labor of you not is fruitless in (the) Lord.

CHAPTER 16

CHAPTER 16

[1]And about the collection for the saints, as I charged the churches of Galatia, so also you do. [2]On the first of a week, let each of you put by himself, storing up whatever he is prospered, that there not be then collections when I come. [3]And when I arrive, whomever you approve, through these epistles, I will send to carry your grace to Jerusalem. [4]And if it is suitable for me to go also, they shall go with me. [5]But I will come to you when I have gone through Macedonia. [6]For I am going through Macedonia, and it may be I shall stay with you, or even spend the winter, that you may set me forward wherever I go. [7]For I do not want to see you now in passing, but I hope to stay a while with you, if the Lord permits. [8]But I will remain in Ephesus until Pentecost. [9]for a door has been opened to me, wonderful and mighty; and many *are* opposing.

[10]But if Timothy comes, see that he is with you without fear; for he works the work of *the* Lord, even as I. [11]Then let no one despise him; but send him on in peace, that he may come to me. For I am waiting for him, with the brothers. [12]And about Apollos the brother, I much urged him that he come to you with the brothers, and it *was* not altogether *his* will that he come now. But he will come when he has opportunity.

[13]Watch! Stand fast in the faith! Be men! Be strong! [14]Let all your things be done in love.

[15]But I entreat you, brothers: you know the house of Stephanas, that it is Achaia's firstfruit, and they appointed themselves for service to the saints; [16]that also you be subject to such ones, and to everyone working and laboring with *me*. [17]But I rejoice at the

1 Περὶ δὲ τῆς λογίας τῆς εἰς τοὺς ἁγίους, ὥσπερ διέταξα ταῖς
about And the collection for the saints, as I charged the
2 ἐκκλησίαις τῆς Γαλατίας, οὕτω καὶ ὑμεῖς ποιήσατε. κατὰ
churches of Galatia, so also you do. Every
μίαν σαββάτων ἕκαστος ὑμῶν παρ' ἑαυτῷ τιθέτω, θησαυ-
one of a week each of you by himself let him put, storing
ρίζων ὅ τι ἂν εὐοδῶται, ἵνα μή, ὅταν ἔλθω, τότε λογίαι
up whatever he is prospered, that not when I come then collections
3 γίνωνται. ὅταν δὲ παραγένωμαι, οὓς ἐὰν δοκιμάσητε δι'
there be. when But I arrive, whomever you approve, through
ἐπιστολῶν, τούτους πέμψω ἀπενεγκεῖν τὴν χάριν ὑμῶν εἰς
epistles these I will send to carry the grace of you to
4 Ἱερουσαλήμ· ἐὰν δὲ ᾖ ἄξιον τοῦ κἀμὲ πορεύεσθαι, σὺν ἐμοὶ
Jerusalem. if But it is suitable me also to go, with me
5 πορεύσονται. ἐλεύσομαι δὲ πρὸς ὑμᾶς, ὅταν Μακεδονίαν
they shall go. I will come And to you when Macadonia
6 διέλθω· Μακεδονίαν γὰρ διέρχομαι· πρὸς ὑμᾶς δὲ τυχὸν
I go through. Macedonia For I am going through , with you and possibly
παραμενῶ, ἢ καὶ παραχειμάσω, ἵνα ὑμεῖς με προπέμψητε οὗ
I will stay, or even spend the winter, that you me may set forward
7 ἐὰν πορεύωμαι. οὐ θέλω γὰρ ὑμᾶς ἄρτι ἐν παρόδῳ ἰδεῖν·
wherever I may go. not I desire For you yet in passage to see;
ἐλπίζω δὲ χρόνον τινὰ ἐπιμεῖναι πρὸς ὑμᾶς, ἐὰν ὁ Κύριος
I am hoping and time some to remain with you, if the Lord
8 ἐπιτρέπῃ. ἐπιμενῶ δὲ ἐν Ἐφέσῳ ἕως τῆς Πεντηκοστῆς· θύρα
permits. I will remain But in Ephesus until Pentecost, a door
9 γάρ μοι ἀνέῳγε μεγάλη καὶ ἐνεργής, καὶ ἀντικείμενοι πολλοί.
for to me opened great and effective, and (are) opposing many.
10 Ἐὰν δὲ ἔλθῃ Τιμόθεος, βλέπετε ἵνα ἀφόβως γένηται πρὸς
if But comes Timothy, see that without fear he is with
11 ὑμᾶς· τὸ γὰρ ἔργον Κυρίου ἐργάζεται ὡς καὶ ἐγώ. μή τις
you, the for work of (the) Lord he works, as also I. Let not any
οὖν αὐτὸν ἐξουθενήσῃ· προπέμψατε δὲ αὐτὸν ἐν εἰρήνῃ, ἵνα
then him despise, set forward but him in peace, that
12 ἔλθῃ πρός με· ἐκδέχομαι γὰρ αὐτὸν μετὰ τῶν ἀδελφῶν. περὶ
he come to me; I am awaiting for him with the brothers. about
δὲ Ἀπολλὼ τοῦ ἀδελφοῦ, πολλὰ παρεκάλεσα αὐτὸν ἵνα
And Apollos the brother, much I besought him that
ἔλθῃ πρὸς ὑμᾶς μετὰ τῶν ἀδελφῶν· καὶ πάντως οὐκ ἦν
he come to you with the brothers, and altogether not it was
θέλημα ἵνα νῦν ἔλθῃ, ἐλεύσεται δὲ ὅταν εὐκαιρήσῃ
(his) will that now he come; he will come but when he has opportunity.
13 Γρηγορεῖτε, στήκετε ἐν τῇ πίστει, ἀνδρίζεσθε, κραταιοῦ-
Watch! Stand in the faith! Be men! Be strong!
14 σθε. πάντα ὑμῶν ἐν ἀγάπῃ γινέσθω.
All things of you in love let it be.
15 Παρακαλῶ δὲ ὑμᾶς, ἀδελφοί (οἴδατε τὴν οἰκίαν Στεφανᾶ,
I beseech And you, brothers, you know the house of Stephanas,
ὅτι ἐστὶν ἀπαρχὴ τῆς Ἀχαΐας, καὶ εἰς διακονίαν τοῖς ἁγίοις
that it is firstfruit of Achaia, and to ministry to the saints
16 ἔταξαν ἑαυτούς), ἵνα καὶ ὑμεῖς ὑποτάσσησθε τοῖς τοιούτοις,
they appointed themselves, that also you may submit to such ones,
17 καὶ παντὶ τῷ συνεργοῦντι καὶ κοπιῶντι. χαίρω δὲ ἐπὶ τῇ
and to everyone working with (me) and laboring. I rejoice And at the

presence of Stephanas, and of Fortunatus, and of Achaicus, because these supplied your lack. [18]For they refreshed my spirit and yours. Therefore, recognize such ones.

[19]The churches of Asia greet you. Aquila and Priscilla much greet you in *the* Lord, with the church in their house. [20]All the brothers greet you. Greet one another with a holy kiss.

[21]The greeting with my hand, Paul. [22]If anyone does not love the Lord Jesus Christ, let him be a curse; the Lord comes.

[23]The grace of the Lord Jesus Christ *be* with you. [24]My love *be* with all of you in Christ Jesus. Amen.

παρουσίᾳ Στεφανᾶ καὶ Φουρτουνάτου καὶ Ἀχαϊκοῦ ὅτι τὸ
presence of Stephanas, and of Fortunatus, and of Achaicus, that
18 ὑμῶν ὑστέρημα οὗτοι ἀνεπλήρωσαν. ἀνέπαυσαν γὰρ τὸ ἐμὸν
your lack these supplied; they refreshed for my
πνεῦμα καὶ τὸ ὑμῶν· ἐπιγινώσκετε οὖν τοὺς τοιούτους.
spirit and of you. Recognize, therefore, such ones.
19 Ἀσπάζονται ὑμᾶς αἱ ἐκκλησίαι τῆς Ἀσίας· ἀσπάζονται
Greet you the churches of Asia Greets
ὑμᾶς ἐν Κυρίῳ πολλὰ Ἀκύλας καὶ Πρίσκιλλα, σὺν τῇ κατ'
you in (the) Lord much Aquila and Priscilla, with the in
20 οἶκον αὐτῶν ἐκκλησίᾳ. ἀσπάζονται ὑμᾶς οἱ ἀδελφοὶ πάντες.
(the) house of them church. Greet you the brothers all.
ἀσπάσασθε ἀλλήλους ἐν φιλήματι ἁγίῳ.
Greet one another with kiss a holy.
21 Ὁ ἀσπασμὸς τῇ ἐμῇ χειρὶ Παύλου. εἴ τις οὐ φιλεῖ τὸν
22 **The greeting with my hand, Paul. If anyone not love the**
23 Κύριον Ἰησοῦν Χριστόν, ἤτω ἀνάθεμα. Μαρὰν ἀθά. ἡ χάρις
Lord Jesus Christ, let him be a curse. The Lord comes. The grace
24 τοῦ Κυρίου Ἰησοῦ Χριστοῦ μεθ' ὑμῶν. ἡ ἀγάπη μου μετὰ
of the Lord Jesus Christ (be) with you. The love of me (be) with
πάντων ὑμῶν ἐν Χριστῷ Ἰησοῦ. ἀμήν.
all of you in Christ Jesus. Amen.

ΠΑΥΛΟΥ ΤΟΥ ΑΠΟΣΤΟΛΟΥ
PAUL THE APOSTLE

Η ΠΡΟΣ
THE TO

ΚΟΡΙΝΘΙΟΥΣ
(THE) CORINTHIANS

ΕΠΙΣΤΟΛΗ ΔΕΥΤΕΡΑ
EPISTLE SECOND

2 CORINTHIANS

CHAPTER 1

KING JAMES II VERSION

THE SECOND EPISTLE TO THE CORINTHIANS

CHAPTER 1

[1] Paul, an apostle of Jesus Christ, through *the* will of God, and Timothy the brother, to the church of God being in Corinth, with all the saints being in all Achaia, [2] Grace and peace from God our Father and *the* Lord Jesus Christ.

[3] Blessed *be* the God and Father of our Lord Jesus Christ, the Father of compassions and God of all comfort, [4] the *One* comforting us on all our affliction, for us to be able to comfort those in every affliction, through the comfort by which we ourselves are comforted by God. [5] Because the sufferings of Christ abound in us, so also our comfort abounds through Christ. [6] But if we are afflicted, *it is* for your comfort and salvation, being worked out in *the* endurance of the same sufferings which we also suffer. If we are comforted, *it is* for your comfort and salvation; [7] and our hope for you *is* certain, knowing that even as you are sharers of the sufferings, so also of the comfort.

[8] For, brothers, we do not want you to be ignorant as to our affliction having happened to us in Asia, that we were excessively pressed down beyond *our* power, so as for us even to despair *of life*. [9] But we ourselves have the

1 Παῦλος ἀπόστολος Ἰησοῦ Χριστοῦ διὰ θελήματος Θεοῦ,
Paul an apostle of Jesus Christ through (the) will of God,
καὶ Τιμόθεος ὁ ἀδελφός, τῇ ἐκκλησίᾳ τοῦ Θεοῦ τῇ οὔσῃ ἐν
and Timothy the brother to the church of God being in
Κορίνθῳ, σὺν τοῖς ἁγίοις πᾶσι τοῖς οὖσιν ἐν ὅλῃ τῇ Ἀχαΐᾳ·
Corinth, with the saints all being in all Achaia;
2 χάρις ὑμῖν καὶ εἰρήνη ἀπὸ Θεοῦ πατρὸς ἡμῶν καὶ Κυρίου
Grace to you and peace from God (the) Father of us and (the) Lord
Ἰησοῦ Χριστοῦ.
Jesus Christ.
3 Εὐλογητὸς ὁ Θεὸς καὶ πατὴρ τοῦ Κυρίου ἡμῶν Ἰησοῦ
Blessed (be) the God and Father of the Lord of us Jesus
Χριστοῦ, ὁ πατὴρ τῶν οἰκτιρμῶν καὶ Θεὸς πάσης παρα-
Christ, the Father of compassions and the God of all com-
4 κλήσεως, ὁ παρακαλῶν ἡμᾶς ἐπὶ πάσῃ τῇ θλίψει ἡμῶν,
fort, the (One) comforting us on all the trouble of us,
εἰς τὸ δύνασθαι ἡμᾶς παρακαλεῖν τοὺς ἐν πάσῃ θλίψει, διὰ
for to be able us to comfort those in every trouble, through
τῆς παρακλήσεως ἧς παρακαλούμεθα αὐτοὶ ὑπὸ τοῦ Θεοῦ.
the comfort of which we are comforted ourselves by God.
5 ὅτι καθὼς περισσεύει τὰ παθήματα τοῦ Χριστοῦ εἰς ἡμᾶς,
Because as abounds the sufferings of Christ in us,
6 οὕτω διὰ Χριστοῦ περισσεύει καὶ ἡ παράκλησις ἡμῶν. εἴτε
so through Christ abounds also the comfort of us. whether
δὲ θλιβόμεθα, ὑπὲρ τῆς ὑμῶν παρακλήσεως καὶ σωτηρίας,
And we are troubled for the of you comfort and salvation,
τῆς ἐνεργουμένης ἐν ὑπομονῇ τῶν αὐτῶν παθημάτων ὧν
being worked out in (the) endurance of the same sufferings which
καὶ ἡμεῖς πάσχομεν· εἴτε παρακαλούμεθα, ὑπὲρ τῆς ὑμῶν
also we suffer, whether we are comforted, (it is) for your
7 παρακλήσεως καὶ σωτηρίας· καὶ ἡ ἐλπὶς ἡμῶν βεβαία ὑπὲρ
comfort and salvation; and the hope of us (is) certain for
ὑμῶν· εἰδότες ὅτι ὥσπερ κοινωνοί ἐστε τῶν παθημάτων,
you, knowing that as sharers you are of the sufferings,
8 οὕτω καὶ τῆς παρακλήσεως. οὐ γὰρ θέλομεν ὑμᾶς ἀγνοεῖν,
so also of the comfort. not For we desire you to be ignorant,
ἀδελφοί, ὑπὲρ τῆς θλίψεως ἡμῶν τῆς γενομένης ἡμῖν ἐν τῇ
brothers, as to the trouble of us having been to us in
Ἀσίᾳ, ὅτι καθ' ὑπερβολὴν ἐβαρήθημεν ὑπὲρ δύναμιν, ὥστε
Asia, that excessively we were burdened beyond power, so as
9 ἐξαπορηθῆναι ἡμᾶς καὶ τοῦ ζῆν. ἀλλὰ αὐτοὶ ἐν ἑαυτοῖς τὸ
to despair (of life) us, even to live. But (our)selves in ourselves the

sentence of death in ourselves, that we should not trust on ourselves, but on God, the *One* raising the dead; [10]who delivered us from so great a death, and does deliver, in whom we have hope that He will still deliver *us,* [11]you also laboring together for us in prayer, that the gracious gift by many may be *the cause of* thanksgiving through many for us.

[12]For our glorying is this, the testimony of our conscience, that we had our conduct in the world in simplicity and sincerity of God, not in fleshly wisdom, but in the grace of God, and more abundantly toward you. [13]For we do not write other things to you than what you read, or even recognize; and I hope that you will recognize even to *the* end, [14]even as you also in part recognized us, that we are your glorying, even as also you *are* ours in the day of the Lord Jesus.

[15]And in this confidence, I purposed to come to you before now, that you might have a second benefit, [16]and to go through you into Macedonia, and again from Macedonia to come to you; and to be set forward by you to Judea. [17]Then purposing this, did I indeed use lightness? Or what I purposed, did I purpose according to flesh, that may be with me yes, yes, and no, no? [18]But God *is* faithful, that our word to you did not become Yes and No. [19]for Jesus Christ the Son of God, the *One* proclaimed among you by us, through me and Silvanus and Timothy, was not Yes and No, but has been Yes in Him. [20]For as many promises as *are* of God, in Him *they are* Yes, and in Him *are* Amen, for glory to God through us. [21]But He confirming us and anointing us with you in Christ *is* God. [22]And He having sealed us, and giving the earnest of the Spirit in our hearts.

ἀπόκριμα τοῦ θανάτου ἐσχήκαμεν, ἵνα μὴ πεποιθότες ὦμεν
sentence of death we have, that not should trust we
10 ἐφ' ἑαυτοῖς, ἀλλ' ἐπὶ τῷ Θεῷ τῷ ἐγείροντι τοὺς νεκρούς· ὃς
on ourselves, but on God, the (One) raising the dead: who
ἐκ τηλικούτου θανάτου ἐρρύσατο ἡμᾶς καὶ ῥύεται, εἰς ὃν
out of so great a death delivered us and does deliver, in whom
11 ἠλπίκαμεν ὅτι καὶ ἔτι ῥύσεται· συνυπουργούντων καὶ ὑμῶν
we have hope that even yet He will deliver, laboring together also you
ὑπὲρ ἡμῶν τῇ δεήσει, ἵνα ἐκ πολλῶν προσώπων τὸ εἰς ἡμᾶς
for us in prayer, that by many persons the for us
χάρισμα διὰ πολλῶν εὐχαριστηθῇ ὑπὲρ ἡμῶν.
gift through many thanks may be given for us.
12 Ἡ γὰρ καύχησις ἡμῶν αὕτη ἐστί, τὸ μαρτύριον τῆς
the For boasting of us this is, the testimony of the
συνειδήσεως ἡμῶν, ὅτι ἐν ἁπλότητι καὶ εἰλικρινείᾳ Θεοῦ,
conscience of us, that in simplicity and sincerity of God,
οὐκ ἐν σοφίᾳ σαρκικῇ, ἀλλ' ἐν χάριτι Θεοῦ, ἀνεστράφημεν
not in wisdom fleshly, but in the grace of God we behaved
13 ἐν τῷ κόσμῳ, περισσοτέρως δὲ πρὸς ὑμᾶς. οὐ γὰρ ἄλλα
in the world, more abundantly and toward you. not For other things
γράφομεν ὑμῖν, ἀλλ' ἢ ἃ ἀναγινώσκετε ἢ καὶ ἐπιγινώσκετε
we write to you, other than what you read, or even perceive,
14 ἐλπίζω δὲ ὅτι καὶ ἕως τέλους ἐπιγνώσεσθε· καθὼς καὶ ἐπέ-
I hope and that also until the end you will perceive, as also you
γνωτε ἡμᾶς ἀπὸ μέρους, ὅτι καύχημα ὑμῶν ἐσμέν, καθάπερ
perceived us from (in) part, because boasting of you we are, even as
καὶ ὑμεῖς ἡμῶν, ἐν τῇ ἡμέρᾳ τοῦ Κυρίου Ἰησοῦ.
also you of us, in the day of the Lord Jesus.
15 Καὶ ταύτῃ τῇ πεποιθήσει ἐβουλόμην πρὸς ὑμᾶς ἐλθεῖν
And in this confidence I purposed to you to come
16 πρότερον, ἵνα δευτέραν χάριν ἔχητε· καὶ δι' ὑμῶν διελθεῖν εἰς
previously, that a second benefit you have, and through you to go through to
Μακεδονίαν, καὶ πάλιν ἀπὸ Μακεδονίας ἐλθεῖν πρὸς ὑμᾶς,
Macedonia, and again from Macedonia to come to you,
17 καὶ ὑφ' ὑμῶν προπεμφθῆναι εἰς τὴν Ἰουδαίαν. τοῦτο οὖν
and by you to be set forward to Judea. This, then,
βουλευόμενος, μή τι ἄρα τῇ ἐλαφρίᾳ ἐχρησάμην; ἢ ἃ βου-
purposing, not indeed lightness I used? Or what I
λεύομαι, κατὰ σάρκα βουλεύομαι, ἵνα ᾖ παρ' ἐμοὶ τὸ ναὶ ναὶ
purposed, according to flesh do I purpose, that may be with me the Yes, Yes,
18 καὶ τὸ οὒ οὔ; πιστὸς δὲ ὁ Θεός, ὅτι ὁ λόγος ἡμῶν ὁ πρὸς
and the No, No? faithful But (is) God, that the word of us to
19 ὑμᾶς οὐκ ἐγένετο ναὶ καὶ οὔ. ὁ γὰρ τοῦ Θεοῦ υἱὸς Ἰησοῦς
you not became Yes, and No. For the of God Son, Jesus
Χριστὸς ὁ ἐν ὑμῖν δι' ἡμῶν κηρυχθείς, δι' ἐμοῦ καὶ Σιλουανοῦ
Christ, the (One) among you by us proclaimed, through me and Silvanus
καὶ Τιμοθέου, οὐκ ἐγένετο ναὶ καὶ οὔ, ἀλλὰ ναὶ ἐν αὐτῷ
and Timothy, not became Yes, and No, but Yes in Him
20 γέγονεν. ὅσαι γὰρ ἐπαγγελίαι Θεοῦ, ἐν αὐτῷ τὸ ναί, καὶ ἐν
has been. as many as For (are) promises of God, in Him the Yes, and in
21 αὐτῷ τὸ ἀμήν, τῷ Θεῷ πρὸς δόξαν δι' ἡμῶν. ὁ δὲ βεβαιῶν
Him the Amen, to God unto glory through us. He But confirming
22 ἡμᾶς σὺν ὑμῖν εἰς Χριστόν, καὶ χρίσας ἡμᾶς, Θεός· ὁ καὶ
us with you in Christ, and anointing us (is) God, He and
σφραγισάμενος ἡμᾶς, καὶ δοὺς τὸν ἀρραβῶνα τοῦ Πνεύ-
having sealed us and having given the earnest of the Spirit

[23]And I call God *as* witness to my soul that I came no more to Corinth to spare you. [24]Not that we rule over your faith, but we are fellow-workers of your joy. For you stand by faith.

CHAPTER 2

[1]But I decided this within myself, not to come to you again in grief. [2]For if I grieved you, who yet will be making me glad, if not the *one* being grieved by me? [3]And I wrote this same thing to you, lest coming I might have grief from *those* of whom I ought to rejoice; trusting in you all that my joy is *the joy of* all of you. [4]For out of much affliction and agony of heart I wrote to you, through many tears, not that you be grieved, but that you know the love which I have more abundantly toward you.

[5]But if anyone has grieved, he has not grieved me, but in part, that I not overbear all of you. [6]This censure by the majority *is* enough for such a one. [7]So that on the contrary, you should rather forgive and comfort such a one, that *he* not be swallowed up *by* the overflowing grief. [8]So I beseech you to confirm *your* love to him. [9]For to this end I also wrote, that I might know the proof of you, if you are obedient in everything. [10]But to whom you forgive anything, I also. For also if I have forgiven anything, I have forgiven it for you, in Christ's person; [11]so that we should not be overreached by Satan, for we are not ignorant of his devices.

[12]And coming to Troas for the gospel of Christ, and a door having been opened to me in *the* Lord, [13]I had no ease in my spirit at my not finding my brother Titus; but I

ματος ἐν ταῖς καρδίαις ἡμῶν.
in the hearts of us.
23 Ἐγὼ δὲ μάρτυρα τὸν Θεὸν ἐπικαλοῦμαι ἐπὶ τὴν ἐμὴν
I And (as) witness God call on my
24 ψυχήν, ὅτι φειδόμενος ὑμῶν οὐκέτι ἦλθον εἰς Κόρινθον. οὐχ
soul, that sparing you no more I came to Corinth. Not
ὅτι κυριεύομεν ὑμῶν τῆς πίστεως, ἀλλὰ συνεργοί ἐσμεν τῆς
that we rule over of you the faith, but fellow-workers we are of the
χαρᾶς ὑμῶν· τῇ γὰρ πίστει ἑστήκατε.
joy of you; for by faith you stand.

CHAPTER 2

1 ἔκρινα δὲ ἐμαυτῷ τοῦτο, τὸ μὴ πάλιν ἐλθεῖν ἐν λύπῃ
I decided And in myself this, not again to come in grief
2 πρὸς ὑμᾶς. εἰ γὰρ ἐγὼ λυπῶ ὑμᾶς, καὶ τίς ἐστιν ὁ
to you. if For I grieve you, even who is it
3 εὐφραίνων με, εἰ μὴ ὁ λυπούμενος ἐξ ἐμοῦ; καὶ ἔγραψα
making glad me, if not the (one) being grieved by me? And I wrote
ὑμῖν τοῦτο αὐτό, ἵνα μὴ ἐλθὼν λύπην ἔχω ἀφ' ὧν ἔδει
to you this same thing, that not coming grief I should have from whom it behoved
4 με χαίρειν, πεποιθὼς ἐπὶ πάντας ὑμᾶς, ὅτι ἡ ἐμὴ χαρὰ
me to rejoice, trusting in all of you, that my joy
πάντων ὑμῶν ἐστιν. ἐκ γὰρ πολλῆς θλίψεως καὶ συνοχῆς
all of you is. out of For much trouble and anxiety
καρδίας ἔγραψα ὑμῖν διὰ πολλῶν δακρύων, οὐχ ἵνα
of heart I wrote to you through many tears, not that
λυπηθῆτε, ἀλλὰ τὴν ἀγάπην ἵνα γνῶτε ἣν ἔχω περισ
you be grieved, but the love that you know which I have more
σοτέρως εἰς ὑμᾶς.
abundantly to you.
5 Εἰ δέ τις λελύπηκεν, οὐκ ἐμὲ λελύπηκεν, ἀλλ' ἀπὸ μέρους
if But anyone has grieved, not me he has grieved, but from part,
6 ἵνα μὴ ἐπιβαρῶ πάντας ὑμᾶς. ἱκανὸν τῷ τοιούτῳ ἡ ἐπιτιμία
lest I overbear all of you. Enough for such a one censure
7 αὕτη ἡ ὑπὸ τῶν πλειόνων· ὥστε τοὐναντίον μᾶλλον ὑμᾶς
this by the majority, so as on the contrary rather you
χαρίσασθαι καὶ παρακαλέσαι, μή πως τῇ περισσοτέρᾳ
to forgive and to comfort, lest (by) the more abundant
8 λύπῃ καταποθῇ ὁ τοιοῦτος. διὸ παρακαλῶ ὑμᾶς κυρῶσαι
grief be swallowed such a one. Therefore I beseech you to confirm
9 εἰς αὐτὸν ἀγάπην. εἰς τοῦτο γὰρ καὶ ἔγραψα, ἵνα γνῶ τὴν
to him (your) love. to this For also I wrote, that I might know
10 δοκιμὴν ὑμῶν, εἰ εἰς πάντα ὑπήκοοί ἐστε. ᾧ δέ τι χαρίζεσθε,
proof of you, if in all things obedient you are. to whom But anything you forgive
καὶ ἐγώ· καὶ γὰρ ἐγὼ εἴ τι κεχάρισμαι, ᾧ κεχάρισμαι, δι'
also I; indeed for I if anything I have forgiven of whom I have forgiven, for
11 ὑμᾶς ἐν προσώπῳ Χριστοῦ, ἵνα μὴ πλεονεκτηθῶμεν ὑπὸ
you (it is) in (the) person of Christ, that not we be overreached by
τοῦ Σατανᾶ· οὐ γὰρ αὐτοῦ τὰ νοήματα ἀγνοοῦμεν.
Satan, not for of him the devices we are ignorant.
12 Ἐλθὼν δὲ εἰς τὴν Τρῳάδα εἰς τὸ εὐαγγέλιον τοῦ Χριστοῦ
having come And to Troas in the gospel of Christ,
13 καὶ θύρας μοι ἀνεῳγμένης ἐν Κυρίῳ, οὐκ ἔσχηκα ἄνεσιν τῷ
and a door to me having been opened in (the) Lord, not I had rest to the
πνεύματί μου, τῷ μὴ εὑρεῖν με Τίτον τὸν ἀδελφόν μου· ἀλλὰ
spirit of me, in the not finding me Titus the brother of me, but

14 ἀποταξάμενος αὐτοῖς ἐξῆλθον εἰς Μακεδονίαν. τῷ δὲ Θεῷ
saying farewell to them I went out to Macedonia. But to God
χάρις τῷ πάντοτε θριαμβεύοντι ἡμᾶς ἐν τῷ Χριστῷ, καὶ τὴν
thanks, He always leading in triumph us in Christ, and the
ὀσμὴν τῆς γνώσεως αὐτοῦ φανεροῦντι δι' ἡμῶν ἐν παντὶ
odor of the knowledge of Him revealing through us in every
15 τόπῳ. ὅτι Χριστοῦ εὐωδία ἐσμὲν τῷ Θεῷ ἐν τοῖς σωζομένοις
place; because of Christ a sweet smell we are to God in those being saved
16 καὶ ἐν τοῖς ἀπολλυμένοις· οἷς μὲν ὀσμὴ θανάτου εἰς θάνατον,
and in those being lost; to the one, an odor of death unto death;
17 οἷς δὲ ὀσμὴ ζωῆς εἰς ζωήν. καὶ πρὸς ταῦτα τίς ἱκανός; οὐ
the others and an odor of life unto life. And for these things who is enough? not
γὰρ ἐσμεν ὡς οἱ πολλοί, καπηλεύοντες τὸν λόγον τοῦ Θεοῦ·
For we are as the many, hawking the word of God,
ἀλλ' ὡς ἐξ εἰλικρινείας, ἀλλ' ὡς ἐκ Θεοῦ, κατενώπιον τοῦ
but as of sincerity, but as of God, in the sight of
Θεοῦ, ἐν Χριστῷ λαλοῦμεν.
God, in Christ we speak.

CHAPTER 3

1 Ἀρχόμεθα πάλιν ἑαυτοὺς συνιστάνειν; ἢ μὴ χρῄζομεν,
Do we begin again ourselves to commend? Or not need we
ὥς τινες, συστατικῶν ἐπιστολῶν πρὸς ὑμᾶς, ἢ ἐξ ὑμῶν
as some commendatory epistles to you, or from you
2 συστατικῶν; ἡ ἐπιστολὴ ἡμῶν ὑμεῖς ἐστε, ἐγγεγραμμένη
commendatory (ones)? The epistle of us you are, having been inscribed
ἐν ταῖς καρδίαις ἡμῶν, γινωσκομένη καὶ ἀναγινωσκομένη
in the hearts of us, being known and being read
3 ὑπὸ πάντων ἀνθρώπων· φανερούμενοι ὅτι ἐστὲ ἐπιστολὴ
by all men, being manifested that you are an epistle
Χριστοῦ διακονηθεῖσα ὑφ' ἡμῶν, ἐγγεγραμμένη οὐ μέλανι,
of Christ ministered by us, having been inscribed not by ink,
ἀλλὰ Πνεύματι Θεοῦ ζῶντος, οὐκ ἐν πλαξὶ λιθίναις, ἀλλ' ἐν
but by (the) Spirit of God a living, not in tables of stone, but in
4 πλαξὶ καρδίας σαρκίναις. πεποίθησιν δὲ τοιαύτην ἔχομεν
tablets (of the) heart fleshly. confidence And such we have
5 διὰ τοῦ Χριστοῦ πρὸς τὸν Θεόν· οὐχ ὅτι ἱκανοί ἐσμεν ἀφ'
through Christ toward God. Not that sufficient we are of
ἑαυτῶν λογίσασθαί τι ὡς ἐξ ἑαυτῶν, ἀλλ' ἡ ἱκανότης ἡμῶν
ourselves to reason out anything as out of ourselves, but the sufficiency of us
6 ἐκ τοῦ Θεοῦ· ὃς καὶ ἱκάνωσεν ἡμᾶς διακόνους καινῆς
(is) of God, who also made sufficient us (as) ministers of a new
διαθήκης, οὐ γράμματος, ἀλλὰ πνεύματος· τὸ γὰρ γράμμα
covenant, not of letter, but of spirit; the for letter
7 ἀποκτείνει, τὸ δὲ πνεῦμα ζωοποιεῖ. εἰ δὲ ἡ διακονία τοῦ
kills, the but Spirit makes alive. if And the ministry
θανάτου ἐν γράμμασιν, ἐντετυπωμένη ἐν λίθοις, ἐγενήθη ἐν
of death in letters having been engraved in stone was in
δόξῃ, ὥστε μὴ δύνασθαι ἀτενίσαι τοὺς υἱοὺς Ἰσραὴλ εἰς τὸ
glory, so as not to be able to gaze the sons of Israel into the
πρόσωπον Μωσέως διὰ τὴν δόξαν τοῦ προσώπου αὐτοῦ,
face of Moses because of the glory of the face of him,
8 τὴν καταργουμένην· πῶς οὐχὶ μᾶλλον ἡ διακονία τοῦ πνεύ-
being done away, how not rather the ministry of the Spirit
9 ματος ἔσται ἐν δόξῃ; εἰ γὰρ ἡ διακονία τῆς κατακρίσεως
will be in glory? if For the ministry of condemnation

went out to Macedonia. 14 But thanks *be* to God, He always leading us in triumph in Christ, and *the One* revealing through us the odor of the knowledge of Him in every place. 15 For we are a sweet smell to God because of Christ in those being saved, and in those being lost— 16 to the one, an odor of death unto death; and to the others an odor of life unto life. And who is sufficient for these things? 17 For we are not as the many, hawking the word of God; but as of sincerity, but as of God. We speak in Christ, in the sight of God.

CHAPTER 3

1 Do we begin again to commend ourselves? Or do we, as some, need commendatory letters to you, or commendatory *ones* from you? 2 You are our letter, having been inscribed in our hearts, being known and read by all men, 3 *it* having been made plain that you are Christ's letter, served by us; not having been inscribed by ink, but by *the* Spirit of *the* living God; not on tablets of stone, but in fleshly tablets *of the* heart. 4 And we have such confidence through Christ toward God; 5 not that we are sufficient of ourselves to reason out anything as out of ourselves, but our sufficiency *is* of God, 6 who also made us able ministers of a new covenant; not of letter, but of Spirit. For the letter kills, but the Spirit makes alive. 7 But the ministry of death having been engraved in letters in stone was with glory, so as the sons of Israel *were* not able to gaze into the face of Moses because of the glory of his face; which was to cease. 8 How much rather the ministry of the Spirit will be in glory! 9 For if the ministry of condemnation

was glory, much rather the ministry of righteousness abounds in glory. 10 For even that which has been made glorious has not been made glorious in this respect, because of the surpassing glory. 11 For if the thing done away *was* through glory, much rather the thing remaining in glory.

12 Therefore, having such hope, we use much boldness. 13 And not as Moses *who* put a veil over his face, for the sons of Israel not to gaze at the end of the *thing* being done away. 14 But their thoughts were hardened; for until the present the same veil remains on the reading of the Old Covenant, not being revealed that it is being done away in Christ. 15 But until today, when Moses is being read, a veil lies on their heart. 16 But whenever it turns to *the* Lord, the veil is taken away. 17 And the Lord is the Spirit; and where the Spirit of *the* Lord *is*, there *is* freedom. 18 But we all with *our* face having been unveiled, having beheld the glory of *the* Lord in a mirror, are being changed *into* the same image from glory to glory, as from *the* Lord Spirit.

CHAPTER 4

1 Therefore, having this ministry, even as we obtained mercy, we do not faint. 2 But we have renounced the hidden things of shame, not walking in craftiness, nor falsifying the word of God, but *by* the revelation of the truth commending ourselves to every conscience of men before God. 3 But also if our gospel is being hidden, it has been hidden in those being lost; 4 in whom the god of this age has blinded the thoughts of the unbelieving, so that the brightness of the gospel of the glory of Christ,

δόξα, πολλῷ μᾶλλον περισσεύει ἡ διακονία τῆς δικαιοσύνης
(was) glory, much rather abounds the ministry of righteousness
10 ἐν δόξῃ. καὶ γὰρ οὐδὲ δεδόξασται τὸ δεδοξασμένον ἐν τούτῳ
in glory. indeed For not has been glorified the thing glorified in this
11 τῷ μέρει, ἕνεκεν τῆς ὑπερβαλλούσης δόξης. εἰ γὰρ τὸ κατ-
respect, because of the excelling glory. if For the thing
αργούμενον, διὰ δόξης, πολλῷ μᾶλλον τὸ μένον, ἐν δόξῃ.
being done away (was) via glory, much rather the thing remaining in glory.
12 Ἔχοντες οὖν τοιαύτην ἐλπίδα, πολλῇ παρρησίᾳ χρώ-
having Therefore such hope, much boldness we
13 μεθα· καὶ οὐ καθάπερ Μωσῆς ἐτίθει κάλυμμα ἐπὶ τὸ πρόσω-
use, and not as Moses put a veil over the face
πον ἑαυτοῦ, πρὸς τὸ μὴ ἀτενίσαι τοὺς υἱοὺς Ἰσραὴλ εἰς τὸ
of himself, for not to gaze the sons of Israel at the
14 τέλος τοῦ καταργουμένου· ἀλλ' ἐπωρώθη τὰ νοήματα
end of the (thing) being done away. But were hardened the thoughts
αὐτῶν· ἄχρι γὰρ τῆς σήμερον τὸ αὐτὸ κάλυμμα ἐπὶ τῇ
of them. until For the present the same veil on the
ἀναγνώσει τῆς παλαιᾶς διαθήκης μένει μὴ ἀνακαλυπτόμενον,
reading of the Old Covenant remains, not being unveiled
15 ὅ τι ἐν Χριστῷ καταργεῖται. ἀλλ' ἕως σήμερον, ἡνίκα
that in Christ it is being done away. But until today, when
ἀναγινώσκεται Μωσῆς, κάλυμμα ἐπὶ τὴν καρδίαν αὐτῶν
is being read Moses, a veil on the heart of them
16 κεῖται. ἡνίκα δ' ἂν ἐπιστρέψῃ πρὸς Κύριον, περιαιρεῖται τὸ
lies; whenever But it turns to (the) Lord, is taken away the
17 κάλυμμα. ὁ δὲ Κύριος τὸ Πνεῦμά ἐστιν· οὗ δὲ τὸ Πνεῦμα
veil. the And Lord the Spirit is, where and the Spirit
18 Κυρίου, ἐκεῖ ἐλευθερία. ἡμεῖς δὲ πάντες, ἀνακεκαλυμμένῳ
of (the) Lord (is), there freedom (is). we But all, having been unveiled
προσώπῳ τὴν δόξαν Κυρίου κατοπτριζόμενοι, τὴν αὐτὴν
with face the glory of (the) Lord beholding in a mirror, the same
εἰκόνα μεταμορφούμεθα ἀπὸ δόξης εἰς δόξαν, καθάπερ ἀπὸ
image are being changed (into), from glory to glory, even as from
Κυρίου Πνεύματος.
(the) Lord Spirit.

CHAPTER 4

1 Διὰ τοῦτο ἔχοντες τὴν διακονίαν ταύτην, καθὼς ἠλεήθη-
Therefore, having ministry this, even as we obtained
2 μεν, οὐκ ἐκκακοῦμεν· ἀλλ' ἀπειπάμεθα τὰ κρυπτὰ τῆς
mercy, not we faint; but we have renounced the hidden things
αἰσχύνης, μὴ περιπατοῦντες ἐν πανουργίᾳ μηδὲ δολοῦντες
of shame, not walking in craftiness, nor adulterating
τὸν λόγον τοῦ Θεοῦ, ἀλλὰ τῇ φανερώσει τῆς ἀληθείας
the word of God, but the revelation of the truth
συνιστῶντες ἑαυτοὺς πρὸς πᾶσαν συνείδησιν ἀνθρώπων
commending ourselves to every conscience of men
3 ἐνώπιον τοῦ Θεοῦ. εἰ δὲ καὶ ἔστι κεκαλυμμένον τὸ εὐαγγέλιον
before God. if But indeed is being hidden the gospel
4 ἡμῶν, ἐν τοῖς ἀπολλυμένοις ἐστὶ κεκαλυμμένον· ἐν οἷς ὁ Θεὸς
of us, in those being lost it is hidden, in whom the god
τοῦ αἰῶνος τούτου ἐτύφλωσε τὰ νοήματα τῶν ἀπίστων,
age of this has blinded the thoughts of the unbelieving,
εἰς τὸ μὴ αὐγάσαι αὐτοῖς τὸν φωτισμὸν τοῦ εὐαγγελίου
— — not to dawn on them the brightness of the gospel

who is the image of God, should not dawn on them. [5]For we do not proclaim ourselves, but Christ Jesus *as* Lord, and ourselves your slaves for the sake of Jesus. [6]Because *it is* God who said, "Out of darkness Light shall shine," who shone in our hearts to *give the* brightness of the knowledge of the glory of God in *the* face of Jesus Christ.

[7]But we have this treasure in earthen vessels, so that the excellence of the power may be of God, and not from us; [8]in every *way* being pressed down, but not hemmed in; in doubt, but not utterly at a loss; [9]being persecuted, but not forsaken; being thrown down, but not destroyed; [10]always bearing about the dying of the Lord Jesus in the body, that also the life of Jesus may be revealed in our body. [11]For we who live are always being delivered up on account of Jesus, that also the life of Jesus may be revealed in our mortal flesh; [12]so that death indeed works in us, and life in you. [13]But having the same spirit of faith, according to what has been written, "I believed, therefore I spoke," we also believe, therefore we also speak; [14]knowing that He who raised up the Lord Jesus will also raise us up through Jesus, and will present *us* with you. [15]For all things *are* for your sake, that the superabounding grace may be made to abound through the thanksgiving of the greater number, to the glory of God.

[16]Therefore, we do not faint, but if indeed our outward man is being decayed, yet the inward *man* is being renewed day by day. [17]For the lightness of our present affliction works out for us a far more excellent weight of glory; [18]we not considering the things seen, but the things not being seen; for the things seen *are*

τῆς δόξης τοῦ Χριστοῦ, ὅς ἐστιν εἰκὼν τοῦ Θεοῦ. οὐ γὰρ
of the glory of Christ, who is (the) image of God. not For
5 ἑαυτοὺς κηρύσσομεν, ἀλλὰ Χριστὸν Ἰησοῦν Κύριον·
ourselves we proclaim, but Christ Jesus (as) Lord,
6 ἑαυτοὺς δὲ δούλους ὑμῶν διὰ Ἰησοῦν. ὅτι ὁ Θεὸς ὁ εἰπὼν ἐκ
ourselves and slaves of you for the sake of Jesus. Because God saying: Out of
σκότους φῶς λάμψαι, ὃς ἔλαμψεν ἐν ταῖς καρδίαις ἡμῶν,
darkness light shall shine, Who shone in the hearts of us
πρὸς φωτισμὸν τῆς γνώσεως τῆς δόξης τοῦ Θεοῦ ἐν
to (give the) brightness of the knowledge of the glory of God in
προσώπῳ Ἰησοῦ Χριστοῦ.
(the) face of Jesus Christ.

7 Ἔχομεν δὲ τὸν θησαυρὸν τοῦτον ἐν ὀστρακίνοις σκεύεσιν,
we have And treasure this in earthen vessels,
ἵνα ἡ ὑπερβολὴ τῆς δυνάμεως ᾖ τοῦ Θεοῦ, καὶ μὴ ἐξ ἡμῶν·
that the excellence of the power may be of God, and not of us;
8 ἐν παντὶ θλιβόμενοι, ἀλλ' οὐ στενοχωρούμενοι· ἀπορού-
in every (way) being troubled, but not hemmed in; being per-
9 μενοι, ἀλλ' οὐκ ἐξαπορούμενοι· διωκόμενοι, ἀλλ' οὐκ ἐγκατα-
plexed, but not utterly at a loss; being persecuted, but not forsaken,
10 λειπόμενοι· καταβαλλόμενοι, ἀλλ' οὐκ ἀπολλύμενοι· πάν-
being thrown down, but not destroyed; always
τοτε τὴν νέκρωσιν τοῦ Κυρίου Ἰησοῦ ἐν τῷ σώματι περιφέ-
the dying of the Lord Jesus in the body bearing
ροντες, ἵνα καὶ ἡ ζωὴ τοῦ Ἰησοῦ ἐν τῷ σώματι ἡμῶν
about, that also the life of Jesus in the body of us
11 φανερωθῇ. ἀεὶ γὰρ ἡμεῖς οἱ ζῶντες εἰς θάνατον παραδιδό-
may be revealed. always For we the (ones) living to death are being deliv-
μεθα διὰ Ἰησοῦν, ἵνα καὶ ἡ ζωὴ τοῦ Ἰησοῦ φανερωθῇ ἐν τῇ
ered on account Jesus, that also the life of Jesus may be revealed in the
12 θνητῇ σαρκὶ ἡμῶν. ὥστε ὁ μὲν θάνατος ἐν ἡμῖν ἐνεργεῖται,
mortal flesh of us. So as indeed death in us works,
13 ἡ δὲ ζωὴ ἐν ὑμῖν. ἔχοντες δὲ τὸ αὐτὸ πνεῦμα τῆς πίστεως,
and life in you. having But the same spirit of faith,
κατὰ τὸ γεγραμμένον, Ἐπίστευσα, διὸ ἐλάλησα, καὶ ἡμεῖς
according to that having been written: I believed, so I spoke; both we
14 πιστεύομεν, διὸ καὶ λαλοῦμεν· εἰδότες ὅτι ὁ ἐγείρας τὸν
believe, therefore and we speak, knowing that He having raised the
Κύριον Ἰησοῦν καὶ ἡμᾶς διὰ Ἰησοῦ ἐγερεῖ, καὶ παραστήσει
Lord Jesus also us with Jesus will raise, and will present (us)
15 σὺν ὑμῖν. τὰ γὰρ πάντα δι' ὑμᾶς, ἵνα ἡ χάρις πλεονάσασα
with you. For all things for your sake, that grace may superabound
διὰ τῶν πλειόνων τὴν εὐχαριστίαν περισσεύσῃ εἰς τὴν
through the greater number the thanksgiving may make abound to the
δόξαν τοῦ Θεοῦ.
glory of God.

16 Διὸ οὐκ ἐκκακοῦμεν· ἀλλ' εἰ καὶ ὁ ἔξω ἡμῶν ἄνθρωπος
Therefore not we faint, but if indeed the outward of us man
διαφθείρεται, ἀλλ' ὁ ἔσωθεν ἀνακαινοῦται ἡμέρᾳ καὶ ἡμέρᾳ.
is being decayed yet the inward (man) is being renewed day by day
17 τὸ γὰρ παραυτίκα ἐλαφρὸν τῆς θλίψεως ἡμῶν καθ' ὑπερ-
the For present lightness of the affliction of us — surpassing
βολὴν εἰς ὑπερβολὴν αἰώνιον βάρος δόξης κατεργάζεται
(moment) by surpassing (moment) an eternal weight of glory work out
18 ἡμῖν, μὴ σκοπούντων ἡμῶν τὰ βλεπόμενα, ἀλλὰ τὰ μὴ
for us, not considering us the things being seen, but the things not

not lasting, but the things not
seen *are* everlasting.

CHAPTER 5

1 For we know that if our
earthly house of *this* tabernacle is taken down, we have
a building from God, a house
not made with hands, eternal
in Heaven. 2 For indeed in
this we groan, greatly
desiring to put on our dwelling place out of Heaven; 3 if
indeed *in* being clothed, we
shall not be found naked;
4 For indeed being in the
tabernacle, we groan, having
been weighted down, inas-
much as we do not wish to
be unclothed, but to be
clothed, so that the mortal
may be swallowed up by the
life. 5 And He having
worked in us for this same
thing *is* God, who also *is*
giving us the earnest of the
Spirit. 6 Then always being
fully assured, and knowing
that being at home in the
body we are away from
home from the Lord— 7 for
we walk by faith, not by
sight— 8 we are fully
assured and are pleased
rather to go away from home
out of the body, and to come
home to the Lord. 9 Therefore, we also are striving to
be well-pleasing to Him,
whether at home, or being
away from home. 10 For we
all must apear before the
judgment-seat of Christ, so
that each one may receive
the things *done* in the body,
according to what we did,
whether good or bad.
11 Then knowing the fear
of the Lord, we persuade
men, and we have been
manifest to God, and I also
hope to have been manifest
in your conscience. 12 For
we do not again commend
ourselves to you, but are
giving you occasion of glorying on our behalf, that you
may have *it* toward those
boasting in appearance, and
not in heart. 13 For if we
are insane, *it is* to God; or *if*
we are in our senses, *it is* for
you. 14 For the love of
Christ constrains us, having

βλεπόμενα· τὰ γὰρ βλεπόμενα πρόσκαιρα· τὰ δὲ μὴ βλεπό-
being seen, the things For being seen (are) temporary, the things but not
μενα αἰώνια.
being seen (are) everlasting.

CHAPTER 5

1 Οἴδαμεν γὰρ ὅτι ἐὰν ἡ ἐπίγειος ἡμῶν οἰκία τοῦ σκήνους
we know For that if the earthly of us house of the tabernacle
καταλυθῇ, οἰκοδομὴν ἐκ Θεοῦ ἔχομεν, οἰκίαν ἀχειροποίητον,
is destroyed, a building of God we have, a house not made by hands,
2 αἰώνιον ἐν τοῖς οὐρανοῖς. καὶ γὰρ ἐν τούτῳ στενάζομεν, τὸ
eternal in the heavens. indeed For in this we groan, the
οἰκητήριον ἡμῶν τὸ ἐξ οὐρανοῦ ἐπενδύσασθαι ἐπιποθοῦντες·
dwelling place of us out of Heaven to put on greatly desiring,
3 εἴ γε καὶ ἐνδυσάμενοι οὐ γυμνοὶ εὑρεθησόμεθα. καὶ γὰρ οἱ
4 if indeed being clothed, not naked we shall be found. indeed For
ὄντες ἐν τῷ σκήνει στενάζομεν βαρούμενοι· ἐφ' ᾧ οὐ θέλομεν
being in the tabernacle, we groan, being burdened, inasmuch as not we wish
ἐκδύσασθαι, ἀλλ' ἐπενδύσασθαι, ἵνα καταποθῇ τὸ θνητὸν
to be unclothed, but to be clothed, that may be swallowed the mortal
5 ὑπὸ τῆς ζωῆς. ὁ δὲ κατεργασάμενος ἡμᾶς εἰς αὐτὸ τοῦτο
by the life. He Now having worked in us for this same thing
Θεός, ὁ καὶ δοὺς ἡμῖν τὸν ἀρραβῶνα τοῦ Πνεύματος.
(is) God, He also giving us the earnest of the Spirit.
6 θαρροῦντες οὖν πάντοτε, καὶ εἰδότες ὅτι ἐνδημοῦντες ἐν τῷ
being assured Therefore always, and knowing that being at home in the
7 σώματι ἐκδημοῦμεν ἀπὸ τοῦ Κυρίου (διὰ πίστεως γὰρ
body we are away from home from the Lord through faith For
8 περιπατοῦμεν, οὐ διὰ εἴδους), θαρροῦμεν δέ, καὶ εὐδοκοῦμεν
we walk, not through sight — we are assured, then, and think it good
μᾶλλον ἐκδημῆσαι ἐκ τοῦ σώματος, καὶ ἐνδημῆσαι πρὸς τὸν
rather to go away from home out of the body, and to come home to the
9 Κύριον. διὸ καὶ φιλοτιμούμεθα, εἴτε ἐνδημοῦντες, εἴτε ἐκδη-
Lord. Therefore also we are striving, whether being at home, or being away
10 μοῦντες, εὐάρεστοι αὐτῷ εἶναι. τοὺς γὰρ πάντας ἡμᾶς
from home, well-pleasing to Him to be. — For all us
φανερωθῆναι δεῖ ἔμπροσθεν τοῦ βήματος τοῦ Χριστοῦ, ἵνα
to be revealed it behoves before the judgment-seat of Christ, that
κομίσηται ἕκαστος τὰ διὰ τοῦ σώματος, πρὸς ἃ ἔπραξεν,
may receive each one the things through the body, according to what we did,
εἴτε ἀγαθόν, εἴτε κακόν.
whether good or bad.
11 Εἰδότες οὖν τὸν φόβον τοῦ Κυρίου ἀνθρώπους πείθομεν,
Knowing, then, the fear of the Lord, men we persuade,
Θεῷ δὲ πεφανερώμεθα· ἐλπίζω δὲ καὶ ἐν ταῖς συνειδήσεσιν
to God and we have been manifest; I hope and also in the conscience
12 ὑμῶν πεφανερῶσθαι. οὐ γὰρ πάλιν ἑαυτοὺς συνιστάνομεν
of you to have been manifest, not For again ourselves we commend
ὑμῖν, ἀλλὰ ἀφορμὴν διδόντες ὑμῖν καυχήματος ὑπὲρ ἡμῶν,
to you, but an occasion giving to you of boasting on behalf of us,
ἵνα ἔχητε πρὸς τοὺς ἐν προσώπῳ καυχωμένους, καὶ οὐ
that you may have (it) toward those in appearance boasting, and not
13 καρδίᾳ. εἴτε γὰρ ἐξέστημεν, Θεῷ· εἴτε σωφρονοῦμεν, ὑμῖν.
in heart. whether For we are insane, (it is) to God; or we are in our senses, for you.
14 ἡ γὰρ ἀγάπη τοῦ Χριστοῦ συνέχει ἡμᾶς, κρίναντας τοῦτο,
the For love of Christ constrains us, having judged this

judged this, that if One died for all, then all died; [15]and He died for all, that the living ones may live no more to themselves, but to the *One* having died for them, and having been raised. [16]So as we now know no one according to flesh, but even if we have known Christ according to flesh, but now we no more know. [17]So that if anyone *is* in Christ, *that one* is a new creation; the old things have passed away; behold, all things have become new! [18]And all things *are* of God, who reconciled us to Himself through Jesus Christ, and giving to us the ministry of reconciliation; [19]whereas God was in Christ reconciling *the* world to Himself, not charging their trespasses to them, and putting the word of reconciliation in us.

[20]Therefore, on behalf of Christ, we are ambassadors, as God exhorting through us, we beseech on behalf of Christ, Be reconciled to God. [21]For He made Him who knew no sin *to be* sin for us, that we might become *the* righteousness of God in Him.

CHAPTER 6

[1]But working together, we also call on you not to receive the grace of God in vain. [2]For He says, "In an acceptable time I heard you, and in a day of salvation I helped you;" behold, now *is* the day of salvation! [3]*Let us* not give a cause of stumbling in anything, that the ministry may not be blamed, [4]but in everything setting ourselves out as God's servants in much patience, in troubles, in emergencies, in difficulties, [5]in stripes, in imprisonments, in riots, in labors, in watchings, in fastings, [6]in pureness, in knowledge, in longsuffering, in kindness, in the Holy Spirit in true love, [7]in *the* word of truth, in *the* power of God, through the

ὅτι εἰ εἷς ὑπὲρ πάντων ἀπέθανεν, ἄρα οἱ πάντες ἀπέθανον·
that if One for all died, then the all died;
15 καὶ ὑπὲρ πάντων ἀπέθανεν, ἵνα οἱ ζῶντες μηκέτι ἑαυτοῖς
and for all He died, that those living no more to themselves
16 ζῶσιν, ἀλλὰ τῷ ὑπὲρ αὐτῶν ἀποθανόντι καὶ ἐγερθέντι. ὥστε
may live, but to the (One) for them having died, and having been raised So as
ἡμεῖς ἀπὸ τοῦ νῦν οὐδένα οἴδαμεν κατὰ σάρκα· εἰ δὲ καὶ
we from now no one know according to flesh; if but even
ἐγνώκαμεν κατὰ σάρκα Χριστόν, ἀλλὰ νῦν οὐκέτι γινώ-
we have known according to flesh Christ, but now no more we know
17 σκομεν. ὥστε εἴ τις ἐν Χριστῷ, καινὴ κτίσις· τὰ ἀρχαῖα
(Him). So as if anyone (is) in Christ, (he is) a new creation; the old things
18 παρῆλθεν, ἰδοὺ γέγονε καινὰ τὰ πάντα. τὰ δὲ πάντα ἐκ τοῦ
passed away behold, have become new all things. the things and all (are) out of
Θεοῦ, τοῦ καταλλάξαντος ἡμᾶς ἑαυτῷ διὰ Ἰησοῦ Χριστοῦ,
God, the (One) having reconciled us to Himself through Jesus Christ,
19 καὶ δόντος ἡμῖν τὴν διακονίαν τῆς καταλλαγῆς· ὡς ὅτι Θεὸς
and having given to us the ministry of reconciliation, as that God
ἦν ἐν Χριστῷ κόσμον καταλλάσσων ἑαυτῷ, μὴ λογιζό-
was in Christ (the) world reconciling to Himself, not charging
μενος αὐτοῖς τὰ παραπτώματα αὐτῶν, καὶ θέμενος ἐν ἡμῖν
to them the trespasses of them, and putting in us
τὸν λόγον τῆς καταλλαγῆς.
the word of reconciliation.
20 Ὑπὲρ Χριστοῦ οὖν πρεσβεύομεν, ὡς τοῦ Θεοῦ παρακαλ-
On behalf of Christ, therefore, we are ambassadors as God exhorting
οῦντος δι' ἡμῶν· δεόμεθα ὑπὲρ Χριστοῦ, καταλλάγητε τῷ
through us; we beseech on behalf of Christ, be reconciled
21 Θεῷ. τὸν γὰρ μὴ γνόντα ἁμαρτίαν, ὑπὲρ ἡμῶν ἁμαρτίαν
to God. the (One) For not knowing sin on behalf of us sin
ἐποίησεν, ἵνα ἡμεῖς γινώμεθα δικαιοσύνη Θεοῦ ἐν αὐτῷ.
He made. so that we might become (the) righteousness of God in Him.

CHAPTER 6

1 συνεργοῦντες δὲ καὶ παρακαλοῦμεν μὴ εἰς κενὸν τὴν χάριν
working together And also we exhort not to in vain the grace
2 τοῦ Θεοῦ δέξασθαι ὑμᾶς (λέγει γάρ, Καιρῷ δεκτῷ ἐπήκουσά
of God to receive you – He says For, In a time acceptable I heard
σου, καὶ ἐν ἡμέρᾳ σωτηρίας ἐβοήθησά σοι· ἰδού, νῦν καιρὸς
you, and in a day of salvation I helped you – behold, now a time
3 εὐπρόσδεκτος, ἰδού, νῦν ἡμέρα σωτηρίας) μηδεμίαν ἐν
acceptable; behold, now a day of salvation – no in
4 μηδενὶ διδόντες προσκοπήν, ἵνα μὴ μωμηθῇ ἡ διακονία· ἀλλ'
nothing giving cause of stumbling, that not be blamed the ministry, but
ἐν παντὶ συνιστῶντες ἑαυτοὺς ὡς Θεοῦ διάκονοι, ἐν ὑπομονῇ
in everything commending ourselves as of God ministers, in patience
5 πολλῇ, ἐν θλίψεσιν, ἐν ἀνάγκαις, ἐν στενοχωρίαις, ἐν πλη-
much, in troubles, in emergencies, in difficulties, in stripes,
γαῖς, ἐν φυλακαῖς, ἐν ἀκαταστασίαις, ἐν κόποις, ἐν ἀγρυ-
in imprisonments, in riots, in labors, in watchings,
6 πνίαις, ἐν νηστείαις, ἐν ἁγνότητι, ἐν γνώσει, ἐν μα-
in fastings, in pureness, in knowledge, in
κροθυμίᾳ, ἐν χρηστότητι, ἐν Πνεύματι Ἁγίῳ, ἐν ἀγάπῃ
long-suffering, in kindness, in spirit a holy, in love
7 ἀνυποκρίτῳ, ἐν λόγῳ ἀληθείας, ἐν δυνάμει Θεοῦ, διὰ τῶν
unfeigned, in a word of truth, in (the) power of God, through the

weapons of righteousness on the right *hand* and on the left, [8]through glory and dishonor, through evil report and good report—as deceivers, and yet true; [9]as unknown, and yet well-known; as dying, and yet, look, we live!; as flogged, and yet not put to death; [10]as sorrowful, but yet always rejoicing; as poor, but yet enriching many; as having nothing, yet possessing all things.

[11]Our mouth is opened to you, Corinthians, our heart has been made larger. [12]You are not restrained in us, but you are restrained in your *own* bowels. [13]But for the same reward—I speak as to children—you also be made larger.

[14]Do not be unequally yoked *with* unbelievers. For what partnership does righteousness *have* with lawlessness? And what fellowship does light *have* with darkness? [15]And what agreement does Christ *have* with Belial? Or what part does a believer *have* with an unbeliever? [16]And what agreement does a temple of God *have* with idols? For you are a temple of *the* living God, even as God said, "I will dwell in them, and walk among *them*; and I will be their God, and they shall be My people." [17]Therefore, come out from among them, and be separated, says *the* Lord, and do not touch *the* unclean thing; and I will receive you. [18]And I will be a Father to you, and you will be sons and daughters to Me, says *the* Almighty.

CHAPTER 7

[1]Then having these promises, beloved, let us cleanse ourselves from all defilements of flesh and of spirit, perfecting holiness in *the* fear of God. [2]Make room for us. We wronged no one; we plundered no one; we overreached no one. [3]I do not speak to condemnation,

8 ὅπλων τῆς δικαιοσύνης τῶν δεξιῶν καὶ ἀριστερῶν, διὰ
weapons of righteousness on the right and of left; through
δόξης καὶ ἀτιμίας, διὰ δυσφημίας καὶ εὐφημίας· ὡς πλάνοι,
glory and dishonor; through evil report and good report, as deceivers
9 καὶ ἀληθεῖς· ὡς ἀγνοούμενοι, καὶ ἐπιγινωσκόμενοι· ὡς
and(yet) true; as unknown, and (yet) well-known; as
ἀποθνήσκοντες, καὶ ἰδού, ζῶμεν· ὡς παιδευόμενοι, καὶ μὴ
dying, and behold, we live; as flogged, and not
10 θανατούμενοι· ὡς λυπούμενοι, ἀεὶ δὲ χαίροντες· ὡς πτωχοί,
put to death; as grieved, always and rejoicing; as poor,
πολλοὺς δὲ πλουτίζοντες· ὡς μηδὲν ἔχοντες, καὶ πάντα
many but enriching; as nothing having, and all things
κατέχοντες.
possessing.

11 Τὸ στόμα ἡμῶν ἀνέῳγε πρὸς ὑμᾶς, Κορίνθιοι, ἡ καρδια
The mouth of us is opened to you, Corinthians, the heart
12 ἡμῶν πεπλάτυνται. οὐ στενοχωρεῖσθε ἐν ἡμῖν, στενοχω-
of us has been made larger. not You are restrained in us, you are
13 ρεῖσθε δὲ ἐν τοῖς σπλάγχνοις ὑμῶν. τὴν δὲ αὐτὴν ἀντιμισθίαν
restrained but in the bowels of you. for the But same reward
(ὡς τέκνοις λέγω), πλατύνθητε καὶ ὑμεῖς.
—as to children I speak — be enlarged also you.

14 Μὴ γίνεσθε ἑτεροζυγοῦντες ἀπίστοις· τίς γὰρ μετοχὴ
Do not become unequally yoked (with) unbelievers, what for partnership
δικαιοσύνῃ καὶ ἀνομίᾳ ; τίς δὲ κοινωνία φωτὶ πρὸς σκότος ;
(have) righteousness and lawlessness? what And fellowship light with darkness?
15 τίς δὲ συμφώνησις Χριστῷ πρὸς Βελίαλ ; ἢ τίς μερὶς πιστῷ
what And agreement (has) Christ with Belial? Or what part a believer
16 μετὰ ἀπίστου : τίς δὲ συγκατάθεσις ναῷ Θεοῦ μετὰ εἰδώλων ;
with an unbeliever? what And union the temple of God with idols?
ὑμεῖς γὰρ ναὸς Θεοῦ ἐστε ζῶντος, καθὼς εἶπεν ὁ Θεός ὅτι
you For a temple of God are of a living, even as said God: —
Ἐνοικήσω ἐν αὐτοῖς, καὶ ἐμπεριπατήσω· καὶ ἔσομαι αὐτῶν
I will dwell among them, and I will walk among (them) and I will be of them
17 Θεός, καὶ αὐτοὶ ἔσονταί μοι λαός. διὸ Ἐξέλθετε ἐκ μέσου
God, and they shall be of me a people. Therefore come out from amidst
αὐτῶν καὶ ἀφορίσθητε, λέγει Κύριος, καὶ ἀκαθάρτου μὴ
them, and be separated, says (the) Lord, and an unclean thing not
18 ἅπτεσθε· κἀγὼ εἰσδέξομαι ὑμᾶς, καὶ ἔσομαι ὑμῖν εἰς πατέρα,
touch, and I will receive you, and I will be to you for a Father,
καὶ ὑμεῖς ἔσεσθέ μοι εἰς υἱοὺς καὶ θυγατέρας, λέγει Κύριος
and you will be to Me for sons and daughters, says (the) Lord
παντοκράτωρ.
Almighty.

CHAPTER 7

1 ταύτας οὖν ἔχοντες τὰς ἐπαγγελίας, ἀγαπη-
these Then having promises, beloved,
τοί, καθαρίσωμεν ἑαυτοὺς ἀπὸ παντὸς μολυσμοῦ σαρκὸς
let us cleanse ourselves from all defilements of flesh
καὶ πνεύματος, ἐπιτελοῦντες ἁγιωσύνην ἐν φόβῳ Θεοῦ.
and of spirit, perfecting holiness in (the) fear of God.
2 Χωρήσατε ἡμᾶς· οὐδένα ἠδικήσαμεν, οὐδένα ἐφθείραμεν,
Make room for us; no one we wronged, no one we spoiled,
3 οὐδένα ἐπλεονεκτήσαμεν. οὐ πρὸς κατάκρισιν λέγω· προεί-
no one we overreached. Not for condemnation I speak, I have

for I have said before that you are in our hearts, for *us* to die together, and to live together. [4]My boldness toward you *is* great. My boasting on your behalf *is* much. I have been filled with comfort; I overflow with joy on all our trouble.

[5]For, indeed, we coming into Macedonia, our flesh had no rest, but being troubled in every way, *with* fightings *on the* outside, and fears *on the* inside. [6]But He who comforts the lowly comforted us by the presence of Titus. [7]And not only by his coming, but also by the comfort with which he was comforted over you, telling us your longing, your mourning, your zeal for me; so as for me to rejoice more. [8]For even if I grieved you in the letter, I do not regret; if indeed I did regret; for I see that the letter grieved you for an hour. [9]Now I rejoice, not that you were grieved, but that you were grieved to repentance. For you were grieved according to God, that you might suffer loss in nothing by us. [10]For the grief according to God works repentance to salvation, not to be regretted. But the grief of the world works out death. [11]For behold this same thing, you being grieved according to God, how much it worked out earnestness in you; but *also* defense; but *also* indignation; but *also* fear; but *also* desire; but *also* zeal; but *also* vengeance! In everything you commended yourselves to be clear in the matter. [12]Then even if I wrote to you, *it was* not for the sake of him who had done wrong, nor for the sake of him who had been wronged, but for the sake of revealing our earnestness on your behalf, for you before God. [13]For this reason we have been comforted in your comfort, and we rejoice the rather more abundantly over the joy of Titus, because his spirit has been refreshed by all of

ρηκα γάρ, ὅτι ἐν ταῖς καρδίαις ἡμῶν ἐστὲ εἰς τὸ σύναποθα-
before said for, that in the hearts of us you are for to die with (you)
4 νεῖν καὶ συζῆν. πολλή μοι παρρησία πρὸς ὑμᾶς, πολλή μοι
and to live with (you) Great (is) my boldness toward you, Much to me
καύχησις ὑπὲρ ὑμῶν· πεπλήρωμαι τῇ παρακλήσει, ὑπερ-
boasting on behalf of you. I have been filled with comfort, I
περισσεύομαι τῇ χαρᾷ ἐπὶ πάσῃ τῇ θλίψει ἡμῶν.
overflow with joy on all the trouble of us.
5 Καὶ γὰρ ἐλθόντων ἡμῶν εἰς Μακεδονίαν οὐδεμίαν ἔσχηκεν
indeed For coming us into Macedonia no has had
ἄνεσιν ἡ σὰρξ ἡμῶν, ἀλλ' ἐν παντὶ θλιβόμενοι· ἔξωθεν μάχαι,
rest the flesh of us, but in every way being troubled; without fightings,
6 ἔσωθεν φόβοι. ἀλλ' ὁ παρακαλῶν τοὺς ταπεινοὺς παρε-
within fears. But the (One) comforting the lowly
7 κάλεσεν ἡμᾶς, ὁ Θεός, ἐν τῇ παρουσίᾳ Τίτου· οὐ μόνον δὲ ἐν
comforted us, God, by the presence of Titus; not only and by
τῇ παρουσίᾳ αὐτοῦ, ἀλλὰ καὶ ἐν τῇ παρακλήσει ᾗ παρεκλήθη
the presence of him, but also by the comfort with which he was comforted
ἐφ' ὑμῖν, ἀναγγέλλων ἡμῖν τὴν ὑμῶν ἐπιπόθησιν, τὸν ὑμῶν
over you, telling us your longing, your
ὀδυρμόν, τὸν ὑμῶν ζῆλον ὑπὲρ ἐμοῦ, ὥστε με μᾶλλον
mourning, your zeal for me, so as for me more
8 χαρῆναι. ὅτι εἰ καὶ ἐλύπησα ὑμᾶς ἐν τῇ ἐπιστολῇ, οὐ μετα-
to rejoice. Because if even I grieved you by the epistle, not I
μέλομαι, εἰ καὶ μετεμελόμην· βλέπω γὰρ ὅτι ἡ ἐπιστολὴ
regret; if indeed I regretted, I see for that epistle
9 ἐκείνη, εἰ καὶ πρὸς ὥραν, ἐλύπησεν ὑμᾶς. νῦν χαίρω, οὐχ
that if indeed for an hour it grieved you, now I rejoice, not
ὅτι ἐλυπήθητε, ἀλλ' ὅτι ἐλυπήθητε εἰς μετάνοιαν· ἐλυπήθητε
that you were grieved, but that you were grieved to repentance; you grieved
10 γὰρ κατὰ Θεόν, ἵνα ἐν μηδενὶ ζημιωθῆτε ἐξ ἡμῶν. ἡ γὰρ
for according to God, that in nothing you might suffer loss by us. the For
κατὰ Θεὸν λύπη μετάνοιαν εἰς σωτηρίαν ἀμεταμέλητον
according to God grief repentance to salvation unregrettable
κατεργάζεται· ἡ δὲ τοῦ κόσμου λύπη θάνατον κατεργά-
works: the but of the world grief death works
11 ζεται. ἰδοὺ γάρ, αὐτὸ τοῦτο, τὸ κατὰ Θεὸν λυπηθῆναι ὑμᾶς,
out. behold For, this same thing, according to God to be grieved you,
πόσην κατειργάσατο ὑμῖν σπουδήν, ἀλλὰ ἀπολογίαν,
how much it worked out in you earnestness, but defense,
ἀλλὰ ἀγανάκτησιν, ἀλλὰ φόβον, ἀλλὰ ἐπιπόθησιν, ἀλλὰ
but indignation, but fear, but eager desire, but
ζῆλον, ἀλλ' ἐκδίκησιν. ἐν παντὶ συνεστήσατε ἑαυτοὺς ἁγνοὺς
zeal, but vengeance! In everything you commended yourselves clear
12 εἶναι ἐν τῷ πράγματι. ἄρα εἰ καὶ ἔγραψα ὑμῖν, οὐχ εἵνεκεν
to be in the affair. Then if even I wrote to you (it was) not for
τοῦ ἀδικήσαντος, οὐδὲ εἵνεκεν τοῦ ἀδικηθέντος, ἀλλ' εἵνεκεν
the (one) having done wrong, nor for the (one) having been wronged, but for
τοῦ φανερωθῆναι τὴν σπουδὴν ἡμῶν τὴν ὑπὲρ ὑμῶν πρὸς
to be revealed the earnestness of us on behalf of you toward
13 ὑμᾶς ἐνώπιον τοῦ Θεοῦ. διὰ τοῦτο παρακεκλήμεθα ἐπὶ τῇ
you before God. For this reason we have been comforted as to the
παρακλήσει ὑμῶν· περισσοτέρως δὲ μᾶλλον ἐχάρημεν ἐπὶ τῇ
comfort of you, abundantly and more we rejoice over the
χαρᾷ Τίτου, ὅτι ἀναπέπαυται τὸ πνεῦμα αὐτοῦ ἀπὸ πάντων
joy of Titus, because has been rested the spirit of him from all

you. [14]Because if I have boasted anything to him about you, I was not ashamed. But as we spoke all things in truth to you, so also our boasting as to Titus became truth. [15]And his tender feelings are abundant toward you, remembering the obedience of all of you, as you received him with fear and trembling. [16]Therefore, I rejoice, that in everything I am fully assured in you.

CHAPTER 8

[1]But we make known to you the grace of God, brothers, which has been given among the churches of Macedonia, [2]that in much testing of trouble, the overflowing of their joy, and the depth of their poverty, abounded to the riches of their generosity. [3]For I testify *that* according to *their* ability, and beyond *their* ability, *they* willingly *gave,* [4]with much entreating, begging us *that they might* receive of us the grace and the fellowship of the ministry to the saints. [5]And not as we hoped, but they first gave themselves to the Lord, and to us, through *the* will of God, [6]for us to call on Titus, that even as he began before, so also he might complete this grace to you also. [7]But even as you abound in every-thing—in faith, and in word, and in knowledge, and in all earnestness, and in your love in us—that you also should abound in this grace. [8]I do not speak according to command, but through the earnestness of others, and testing the trueness of your love.

[9]For you know the grace of our Lord Jesus Christ, that being rich, He became poor for your sake, so that you might be made rich by the poverty of that One. [10]And I give judgment in this, for this is profitable for you, who began before not only to do, but also to be willing from last year. [11]But now also finish the doing *of it,* so that

14 ὑμῶν. ὅτι εἴ τι αὐτῷ ὑπὲρ ὑμῶν κεκαύχημαι, οὐ κατησχύν-
you, because if anything to him for you I have boasted, not I was ashamed
θην· ἀλλ' ὡς πάντα ἐν ἀληθείᾳ ἐλαλήσαμεν ὑμῖν, οὕτω καὶ ἡ
but as all things in truth we spoke to you, so also the
15 καύχησις ἡμῶν, ἡ ἐπὶ Τίτου, ἀλήθεια ἐγενήθη. καὶ τὰ σπλάγ-
boasting of us as to Titus truth became, and the bowels
χνα αὐτοῦ περισσοτέρως εἰς ὑμᾶς ἐστίν, ἀναμιμνησκομένου
of him abundantly toward you are, remembering
τὴν πάντων ὑμῶν ὑπακοήν, ὡς μετὰ φόβου καὶ τρόμου
the of all of you obedience, as with fear and trembling
16 ἐδέξασθε αὐτόν. χαίρω οὖν ὅτι ἐν παντὶ θαρρῶ ἐν ὑμῖν.
you received him. I rejoice Then that in everything I am assured in you.

CHAPTER 8

1 Γνωρίζομεν δὲ ὑμῖν, ἀδελφοί, τὴν χάριν τοῦ Θεοῦ τὴν
we make known But to you, brothers, the grace of God
2 δεδομένην ἐν ταῖς ἐκκλησίαις τῆς Μακεδονίας· ὅτι ἐν πολλῇ
being given among the churches of Macedonia, that in much
δοκιμῇ θλίψεως ἡ περισσεία τῆς χαρᾶς αὐτῶν καὶ ἡ κατὰ
testing of trouble the overflowing of the joy of them, and the
βάθους πτωχεία αὐτῶν ἐπερίσσευσεν εἰς τὸν πλοῦτον τῆς
depth poverty of them abounded to the riches of the
3 ἁπλότητος αὐτῶν. ὅτι κατὰ δύναμιν, μαρτυρῶ, καὶ ὑπὲρ
liberality of them. Because according to ability, I witness, and beyond
4 δύναμιν αὐθαίρετοι, μετὰ πολλῆς παρακλήσεως δεόμενοι
(their) ability voluntarily with much beseeching begging
ἡμῶν, τὴν χάριν καὶ τὴν κοινωνίαν τῆς διακονίας τῆς εἰς
us the grace and the fellowship of the ministry to
5 τοὺς ἁγίους δέξασθαι ἡμᾶς· καὶ οὐ καθὼς ἠλπίσαμεν, ἀλλ'
the saints to receive of us, and not as we hoped, but
ἑαυτοὺς ἔδωκαν πρῶτον τῷ Κυρίῳ, καὶ ἡμῖν διὰ θελήματος
themselves gave firstly to the Lord, and to us, through the will
6 Θεοῦ. εἰς τὸ παρακαλέσαι ἡμᾶς Τίτον, ἵνα καθὼς προενήρ-
of God. For to call us on Titus, that as he began
ξατο, οὕτω καὶ ἐπιτελέσῃ εἰς ὑμᾶς καὶ τὴν χάριν ταύτην.
before, so also he should complete to you also grace this.
7 ἀλλ' ὥσπερ ἐν παντὶ περισσεύετε, πίστει, καὶ λόγῳ, καὶ
But as in everything you abound, in faith, and in word, and
γνώσει, καὶ πάσῃ σπουδῇ, καὶ τῇ ἐξ ὑμῶν ἐν ἡμῖν ἀγάπῃ,
in knowledge, and all earnestness, and the of you in us love.
8 ἵνα καὶ ἐν ταύτῃ τῇ χάριτι περισσεύητε. οὐ κατ' ἐπιταγὴν
that also in this grace you may abound. Not by command
λέγω, ἀλλὰ διὰ τῆς ἑτέρων σπουδῆς καὶ τὸ τῆς ὑμετέρας
I say, but through the of others earnestness also the of your
9 ἀγάπης γνήσιον δοκιμάζων. γινώσκετε γὰρ τὴν χάριν τοῦ
love trueness testing; you know for the grace of the
Κυρίου ἡμῶν Ἰησοῦ Χριστοῦ, ὅτι δι' ὑμᾶς ἐπτώχευσε,
Lord of us, Jesus Christ that because of you He became poor,
10 πλούσιος ὤν, ἵνα ὑμεῖς τῇ ἐκείνου πτωχείᾳ πλουτήσητε. καὶ
rich being, that you by the of that One poverty might become rich. And
γνώμην ἐν τούτῳ δίδωμι· τοῦτο γὰρ ὑμῖν συμφέρει, οἵτινες
a judgment in this I give, this for to you is profitable, who
οὐ μόνον τὸ ποιῆσαι ἀλλὰ καὶ τὸ θέλειν προενήρξασθε ἀπὸ
not only the to do but also the to will you before began from
11 πέρυσι. νυνὶ δὲ καὶ τὸ ποιῆσαι ἐπιτελέσατε, ὅπως, καθάπερ
last year. now But also the doing (of it) finish, so as, as

even as *there was* the eagerness *in* the willing, so also the finishing, *giving* out of what *you* have. [12] For if the eagerness is present, it is acceptable according to *what* one has, not according to *what* one does not have. [13] For *it is* not that others *have* ease, but you trouble; [14] but by equality in the present time: your abundance for their need, so that their abundance may also be for your need, so that there may be equality; [15] even as it has been written, He *taking* much, he had nothing left over, and he *taking* little did not have less."

[16] But thanks *be* to God, who gives the same earnestness for you in the heart of Titus. For truly he received the entreating; but being more earnest, he went out to you of his own accord. [18] But we sent with him the brother whose praise *is* in the gospel throughout all the churches; [19] and not only *so*, but also he having been chosen by the churches *as* our traveling companion with this gift being ministered by us to the glory of the Lord Himself, and your eagerness; [20] avoiding this, lest anyone should blame us in this bounty being ministered by us; [21] providing right things not only before the Lord, but also before men. [22] And we sent with them our brother whom we often proved in many things to be earnest, and now much more earnest by the great assurance which *I have* toward you. [23] If *any asks* as to Titus, *he is* my partner, and a fellow-worker for you; or *about* our brothers, *they are* messengers of the churches, *the* glory of Christ. [24] Therefore, show them a proof of your love and of our boastings toward you, even in the sight of the churches.

CHAPTER 9

[1] For indeed concerning the ministry to the saints, it is

ἡ προθυμία τοῦ θέλειν, οὕτω καὶ τὸ ἐπιτελέσαι ἐκ τοῦ ἔχειν.
the eagerness of the willing, so also the finishing out of (what) you have.
12 εἰ γὰρ ἡ προθυμία πρόκειται, καθὸ ἐὰν ἔχῃ τις, εὐπρόσδε-
if For the eagerness is present, according to what one has, it is acceptable,
13 κτος, οὐ καθὸ οὐκ ἔχει. οὐ γὰρ ἵνα ἄλλοις ἄνεσις, ὑμῖν δὲ
not according to (what) one not has. not For that to others ease, you but
14 θλίψις· ἀλλ' ἐξ ἰσότητος, ἐν τῷ νῦν καιρῷ τὸ ὑμῶν περίσ-
trouble, but by equality, in the present time the of you abun-
σευμα εἰς τὸ ἐκείνων ὑστέρημα, ἵνα καὶ τὸ ἐκείνων περίσσευμα
dance for the of those lack, that also the of those abundance
γένηται εἰς τὸ ὑμῶν ὑστέρημα· ὅπως γένηται ἰσότης,
may be for the of you lack, so as may be equality,
15 καθὼς γέγραπται, Ὁ τὸ πολύ, οὐκ ἐπλεόνασε· καὶ ὁ τὸ
even as it has been written: He (taking) much, not he had over, and he (taking)
ὀλίγον, οὐκ ἠλαττόνησε.
little, not had less.
16 Χάρις δὲ τῷ Θεῷ τῷ διδόντι τὴν αὐτὴν σπουδὴν ὑπὲρ
thanks But to God giving the same earnestness for
17 ὑμῶν ἐν τῇ καρδίᾳ Τίτου. ὅτι τὴν μὲν παράκλησιν ἐδέξατο,
you in the heart of Titus, because the indeed beseeching he received,
σπουδαιότερος δὲ ὑπάρχων, αὐθαίρετος ἐξῆλθε πρὸς ὑμᾶς.
more earnest and being, of his own accord he went out to you.
18 συνεπέμψαμεν δὲ μετ' αὐτοῦ τὸν ἀδελφόν, οὗ ὁ ἔπαινος ἐν τῷ
we sent And with him the brother, of whom the praise is in the
19 εὐαγγελίῳ διὰ πασῶν τῶν ἐκκλησιῶν· οὐ μόνον δέ, ἀλλὰ
gospel throughout all the churches, not only and, but
καὶ χειροτονηθεὶς ὑπὸ τῶν ἐκκλησιῶν συνέκδημος ἡμῶν
also having been chosen by the churches a traveling companion to us
σὺν τῇ χάριτι ταύτῃ τῇ διακονουμένῃ ὑφ' ἡμῶν πρὸς τὴν
with gift this being ministered by us to the
20 αὐτοῦ τοῦ Κυρίου δόξαν, καὶ προθυμίαν ὑμῶν· στελλόμενοι
Himself of the Lord glory, and (the) eagerness of you; avoiding
τοῦτο, μή τις ἡμᾶς μωμήσηται ἐν τῇ ἁδρότητι ταύτῃ τῇ
this, lest anyone us should blame in bounty this
21 διακονουμένῃ ὑφ' ἡμῶν· προνοούμενοι καλὰ οὐ μόνον
being ministered by us; providing right things not only
22 ἐνώπιον Κυρίου ἀλλὰ καὶ ἐνώπιον ἀνθρώπων. συνεπέμψα-
before (the) Lord, but also before men. we sent with
μεν δὲ αὐτοῖς τὸν ἀδελφὸν ἡμῶν, ὃν ἐδοκιμάσαμεν ἐν πολλοῖς
And them the brother of us, whom we proved in many things
πολλάκις σπουδαῖον ὄντα, νυνὶ δὲ πολὺ σπουδαιότερον,
many times earnest being, now and much more earnest,
23 πεποιθήσει πολλῇ τῇ εἰς ὑμᾶς. εἴτε ὑπὲρ Τίτου, κοινωνὸς
in assurance much toward you. Whether as to Titus, partner
ἐμὸς καὶ εἰς ὑμᾶς συνεργός· εἴτε ἀδελφοὶ ἡμῶν, ἀπόστολοι
my and for you fellow-worker, or brothers of us, apostles
24 ἐκκλησιῶν, δόξα Χριστοῦ. τὴν οὖν ἔνδειξιν τῆς ἀγάπης
of churches, (the) glory of Christ. the Therefore proof of the love
ὑμῶν, καὶ ἡμῶν καυχήσεως ὑπὲρ ὑμῶν, εἰς αὐτοὺς ἐνδείξασθε
of you and of us the boasting as to you to them showing forth
καὶ εἰς πρόσωπον τῶν ἐκκλησιῶν.
and in the presence of the churches.

CHAPTER 9

1 Περὶ μὲν γὰρ τῆς διακονίας τῆς εἰς τοὺς ἁγίους περισσόν
concerning indeed For the ministry to the saints, superfluous

unnecessary for me to write to you. [2]For I know your eagerness, *of* which I boast to Macedonia on your behalf, that Achaia has made ready from last year; and your zeal arouses the greater number. [3]But I sent the brothers that our boasting which *is* on your behalf should not be in vain in this respect, that as I said, you were ready; [4]lest if Macedonians come with me, and find you not ready, that we—we do not say you—should be ashamed in this assurance of . boasting. [5]Therefore, I thought *it* necessary to exhort the brothers, that they go forward to you, and arrange beforehand your promised blessing; this to be ready, thus as a blessing, and not as greediness.

[6]And this: the *one* sowing sparingly will also reap sparingly; and the *one* sowing on *hope of* blessing will also reap on blessing. [7]Each one as he purposes in his heart, not of grief or of necessity, for God loves a cheerful giver. [8]And God is able to make all grace to abound toward you, that in everything, always having all self-sufficiency, you may abound to every good work; [9]even as it has been written, "He scattered; he gave to the poor; his righteousness abides forever." [10]Now He that supplies seed to the sower, and bread for eating, may He supply and multiply your seed, and increase the fruits of your righteousness, [11]in everything *you* being enriched to all generosity, which works out thanksgiving to God through us. [12]Because the ministry of this service is not only making up the things lacking of the saints, but also multiplying through many thanksgivings to God, [13]through the proof of this service, *they* glorifying

2 μοί ἐστι τὸ γράφειν ὑμῖν· οἶδα γὰρ τὴν προθυμίαν ὑμῶν, ἣν
to me it is to write you; I know for the eagerness of you, which
ὑπὲρ ὑμῶν καυχῶμαι Μακεδόσιν, ὅτι Ἀχαΐα παρεσκεύασται
as to you I boast to Macedonia, that Achaia has made ready
ἀπὸ πέρυσι· καὶ ὁ ἐξ ὑμῶν ζῆλος ἠρέθισε τοὺς πλείονας.
from last year, and the of you zeal arouses the greater number.
3 ἔπεμψα δὲ τοὺς ἀδελφούς, ἵνα μὴ τὸ καύχημα ἡμῶν τὸ ὑπὲρ
I sent And the brothers, lest the boast of us as to
ὑμῶν κενωθῇ ἐν τῷ μέρει τούτῳ· ἵνα, καθὼς ἔλεγον, παρε-
you should be in vain in respect this, that, as I said, having
4 σκευασμένοι ἦτε· μή πως, ἐὰν ἔλθωσι σὺν ἐμοὶ Μακεδόνες καὶ
been ready you were, lest if come with me Macedonians and
εὕρωσιν ὑμᾶς ἀπαρασκευάστους, καταισχυνθῶμεν ἡμεῖς (ἵνα
find you not ready should be ashamed we — that
μὴ λέγωμεν ὑμεῖς) ἐν τῇ ὑποστάσει ταύτῃ τῆς καυχήσεως.
not we say you — in assurance this of boasting.
5 ἀναγκαῖον οὖν ἡγησάμην παρακαλέσαι τοὺς ἀδελφούς, ἵνα
necessary Therefore I thought (it) to exhort the brothers, that
προέλθωσιν εἰς ὑμᾶς, καὶ προκαταρτίσωσι τὴν προκατηγ-
they go forward to you, and arrange beforehand the having been
γελμένην εὐλογίαν ὑμῶν, ταύτην ἑτοίμην εἶναι, οὕτως ὡς
promised blessing of you, this ready to be, thus as
εὐλογίαν, καὶ μὴ ὥσπερ πλεονεξίαν.
a blessing, and not as greediness.

6 Τοῦτο δέ, ὁ σπείρων φειδομένως, φειδομένως καὶ θερίσει·
this And: he sowing sparingly, sparingly also will reap;
καὶ ὁ σπείρων ἐπ' εὐλογίαις, ἐπ' εὐλογίαις καὶ θερίσει.
and he sowing on (hope of) blessing on blessing also will reap.
7 ἕκαστος καθὼς προαιρεῖται τῇ καρδίᾳ· μὴ ἐκ λύπης ἢ ἐξ
Each one as he purposes in the heart, not of grief or of
8 ἀνάγκης· ἱλαρὸν γὰρ δότην ἀγαπᾷ ὁ Θεός. δυνατὸς δὲ ὁ
necessity; a cheerful for giver loves God. is able And
Θεὸς πᾶσαν χάριν περισσεῦσαι εἰς ὑμᾶς, ἵνα ἐν παντὶ
God all grace to make abound toward you, that in everything
πάντοτε πᾶσαν αὐτάρκειαν ἔχοντες περισσεύητε εἰς πᾶν
always all self-sufficiency having you may abound to every
9 ἔργον ἀγαθόν· καθὼς γέγραπται, Ἐσκόρπισεν, ἔδωκε τοῖς
work good; even as it has been written: He scattered; he gave to the
10 πένησιν· ἡ δικαιοσύνη αὐτοῦ μένει εἰς τὸν αἰῶνα. ὁ δὲ
poor; the righteousness of him remains to the age. He Now
ἐπιχορηγῶν σπέρμα τῷ σπείροντι, καὶ ἄρτον εἰς βρῶσιν
that supplies seed to the sower, and bread for eating,
χορηγήσαι, καὶ πληθύναι τὸν σπόρον ὑμῶν, καὶ αὐξήσαι
may He supply and multiply the seed of you, and increase
11 τὰ γεννήματα τῆς δικαιοσύνης ὑμῶν· ἐν παντὶ πλουτιζό-
the fruits of the righteousness of you in everything being en-
μενοι εἰς πᾶσαν ἁπλότητα, ἥτις κατεργάζεται δι' ἡμῶν
riched to all liberality, which works out through us
12 εὐχαριστίαν τῷ Θεῷ. ὅτι ἡ διακονία τῆς λειτουργίας ταύτης
thanksgiving to God. Because the ministry service of this
οὐ μόνον ἐστὶ προσαναπληροῦσα τὰ ὑστερήματα τῶν
not only is making up the things lacking of the
ἁγίων, ἀλλὰ καὶ περισσεύουσα διὰ πολλῶν εὐχαριστιῶν
saints, but also abounding through many thanksgivings
13 τῷ Θεῷ· διὰ τῆς δοκιμῆς τῆς διακονίας ταύτης δοξάζοντες
to God, through the proof ministry of this glorifying

God by your freely expressed obedience to the gospel of Christ, and *the* generosity of the fellowship toward them and toward all; [14]and *in* their prayer for you, a longing after you, because of the overflowing grace of God on you. [15]But thanks *be* to God for His unspeakable gift.

CHAPTER 10

[1]And I myself, Paul, call on you through the meekness and gentleness of Christ—I, who indeed to look upon am lowly among you, but being absent am bold toward you; [2]but I ask, not being present, that I may not be bold with the confidence which I think to be daring against some, those having thought *of* us as walking according to flesh; [3]for walking about in flesh, we do not war according to flesh; [4]for the weapons of our warfare *are* not fleshly, but powerful to God in order to pull down strongholds; [5]pulling down imaginations and every high thing lifting *itself* up against the knowledge of God, and bringing into captivity every thought into the obedience of Christ; [6]and having readiness to avenge all disobedience, whenever your obedience is fulfilled. [7]Do you look at things according to appearance? If anyone has persuaded himself to be of Christ, let him think this again as to himself, that as he *is* of Christ, so also we *are* of Christ. [8]For even if I also somewhat more fully should boast about our authority—which the Lord gave us for building up, and not for pulling you down—I will not be put to shame; [9]so that I may not seem to frighten you by letters—[10]because, he says, the letters *are* weighty and strong, but the bodily presence *is* weak, and *his* speech being despised—[11]let such a one think this, that such as we are in word

τὸν Θεὸν ἐπὶ τῇ ὑποταγῇ τῆς ὁμολογίας ὑμῶν εἰς τὸ
God on the submission by the confession of you to the
εὐαγγέλιον τοῦ Χριστοῦ, καὶ ἁπλότητι τῆς κοινωνίας εἰς
gospel of Christ, and (the) liberality of the fellowship toward
14 αὐτοὺς καὶ εἰς πάντας· καὶ αὐτῶν δεήσει ὑπὲρ ὑμῶν
them and toward all; and them with petition for you
ἐπιποθούντων ὑμᾶς διὰ τὴν ὑπερβάλλουσαν χάριν τοῦ
longing after you on account of the surpassing grace
15 Θεοῦ ἐφ' ὑμῖν. χάρις δὲ τῷ Θεῷ ἐπὶ τῇ ἀνεκδιηγήτῳ αὐτοῦ
of God upon you. thanks But to God for the unspeakable of Him
δωρεᾷ.
gift.

CHAPTER 10

1 Αὐτὸς δὲ ἐγὼ Παῦλος παρακαλῶ ὑμᾶς διὰ τῆς πρᾳότητος
myself And I, Paul, exhort you through the meekness
καὶ ἐπιεικείας τοῦ Χριστοῦ, ὃς κατὰ πρόσωπον μὲν ταπεινὸς
and forbearance of Christ, who according to face indeed humble
2 ἐν ὑμῖν, ἀπὼν δὲ θαρρῶ εἰς ὑμᾶς· δέομαι δέ, τὸ μὴ παρὼν
among you being absent, but am bold toward you; I ask but, not being present,
θαρρῆσαι τῇ πεποιθήσει ᾗ λογίζομαι τολμῆσαι ἐπί τινας
to be bold in the confidence which I think to be daring toward some,
τοὺς λογιζομένους ἡμᾶς ὡς κατὰ σάρκα περιπατοῦντας.
those thinking us as according to flesh walking.
3 ἐν σαρκὶ γὰρ περιπατοῦντες, οὐ κατὰ σάρκα στρατευόμεθα
in flesh For walking, not according to flesh we war;
4 (τὰ γὰρ ὅπλα τῆς στρατείας ἡμῶν οὐ σαρκικά, ἀλλὰ
the for weapons of the warfare of us (are) not fleshly, but
5 δυνατὰ τῷ Θεῷ πρὸς καθαίρεσιν ὀχυρωμάτων), λογισμοὺς
powerful to God in order to demolish strongholds, imaginations
καθαιροῦντες καὶ πᾶν ὕψωμα ἐπαιρόμενον κατὰ τῆς γνώσεως
demolishing, and every high thing lifting up (itself) against the knowledge
τοῦ Θεοῦ, καὶ αἰχμαλωτίζοντες πᾶν νόημα εἰς τὴν ὑπακοὴν
of God, and bringing into captivity every thought into the obedience
6 τοῦ Χριστοῦ, καὶ ἐν ἑτοίμῳ ἔχοντες ἐκδικῆσαι πᾶσαν
of Christ, and readiness having to avenge all
7 παρακοήν, ὅταν πληρωθῇ ὑμῶν ἡ ὑπακοή. τὰ κατὰ
disobedience, whenever is fulfilled of you the obedience. The things as to
πρόσωπον βλέπετε; εἴ τις πέποιθεν ἑαυτῷ Χριστοῦ εἶναι,
face you look (at)? If anyone has persuaded himself of Christ to be,
τοῦτο λογιζέσθω πάλιν ἀφ' ἑαυτοῦ, ὅτι καθὼς αὐτὸς
this let him think again as to himself, that as he (is)
8 Χριστοῦ, οὕτω καὶ ἡμεῖς Χριστοῦ. ἐάν τε γὰρ καὶ περισσό-
of Christ, so also we of Christ. if even For also more abun-
τερόν τι καυχήσωμαι περὶ τῆς ἐξουσίας ἡμῶν (ἧς ἔδωκεν ὁ
dantly somewhat I should more fully boast about the authority of us; which gave the
Κύριος ἡμῖν εἰς οἰκοδομήν, καὶ οὐκ εἰς καθαίρεσιν ὑμῶν),
Lord to us for building up, and not for pulling down of you;
9 οὐκ αἰσχυνθήσομαι· ἵνα μὴ δόξω ὡς ἂν ἐκφοβεῖν ὑμᾶς διὰ
not I will be put to shame, that not I seem as though to scare you through
10 τῶν ἐπιστολῶν. ὅτι Αἱ μὲν ἐπιστολαί, φησί, βαρεῖαι καὶ
the epistles. Because the truly epistles, he says, (are) weighty and
ἰσχυραί· ἡ δὲ παρουσία τοῦ σώματος ἀσθενής, καὶ ὁ λόγος
strong, the but presence of the body (is) weak, and the speech
11 ἐξουθενημένος. τοῦτο λογιζέσθω ὁ τοιοῦτος, ὅτι οἷοί ἐσμεν
being despised. this Let think such a one, that such as we are

through letters, being absent, such *we are* also being present in deed. [12] For we dare not rank or compare ourselves with some of those commending themselves—but they measuring themselves among themselves, and comparing themselves to themselves, *are* not perceptive. [13] But we will not boast beyond measure, but according to measure of the rule which the God of measure distributed to us, to reach even to you. [14] For we do not overstretch ourselves as *if not* reaching to you; for we also came to you in the gospel of Christ; [15] not boasting beyond measure in the labors of others, having hope that the growing faith among you will be made larger according to our rule, to overflowing, [16] in order to preach the gospel to that beyond you, not to boast in another's rule in things ready. [17] But the *one* boasting, let him boast in *the* Lord. [18] For not the *one* commending himself is the one approved, but *the one* whom the Lord commends.

CHAPTER 11

[1] I would that you were bearing with me a little in foolishness; but, indeed, bear with me. [2] For I am jealous *over* you with a jealousy of God. For I have promised you to one Man, to present *you* a pure virgin to Christ. [3] But I fear lest by any means as the serpent deceived Eve in his craftiness, so your thoughts should be corrupted from the purity which *is due* to Christ. [4] For if, indeed, the *one* coming preaches another Jesus, whom we have not preached, or *if* you receive another spirit which you have not received, or another gospel which you never accepted, you might well endure. [5] For I judge *myself* to have come behind the highest apostles *in* nothing. [6] But even if *I am* unskilled in speech, yet not in knowledge. But in every way *I* have been clearly revealed to you in all things. [7] Or did I commit sin, humbling myself that you might be

τῷ λόγῳ δι' ἐπιστολῶν ἀπόντες, τοιοῦτοι καὶ παρόντες
in word through epistles being absent, such also being present
12 τῷ ἔργῳ. οὐ γὰρ τολμῶμεν ἐγκρῖναι ἢ συγκρῖναι ἑαυτούς
in work. not For we dare to rank with or compare ourselves
τισι τῶν ἑαυτοὺς συνιστανόντων· ἀλλὰ αὐτοὶ ἐν ἑαυτοῖς
with some of those themselves commending—but they among themselves
ἑαυτοὺς μετροῦντες, καὶ συγκρίνοντες ἑαυτοὺς ἑαυτοῖς, οὐ
themselves measuring, and comparing themselves to themselves, not
13 συνιοῦσιν. ἡμεῖς δὲ οὐχὶ εἰς τὰ ἄμετρα καυχησόμεθα, ἀλλὰ
(are) perceptive. we But not beyond measure will boast, but
κατὰ τὸ μέτρον τοῦ κανόνος οὗ ἐμέρισεν ἡμῖν ὁ Θεός, μέτρου
according to measure of the rule which divided to us the God of measure,
14 ἐφικέσθαι ἄχρι καὶ ὑμῶν. οὐ γὰρ ὡς μὴ ἐφικνούμενοι εἰς ὑμᾶς
to reach as far as even you. not For as not reaching to you
ὑπερεκτείνομεν ἑαυτούς· ἄχρι γὰρ καὶ ὑμῶν ἐφθάσαμεν ἐν τῷ
do we overstretch ourselves until for even to you we came in the
15 εὐαγγελίῳ τοῦ Χριστοῦ· οὐκ εἰς τὰ ἄμετρα καυχώμενοι, ἐν
gospel of Christ, not beyond measure boasting in
ἀλλοτρίοις κόποις, ἐλπίδα δὲ ἔχοντες, αὐξανομένης τῆς
of others the labors, hope but having growing the
πίστεως ὑμῶν, ἐν ὑμῖν μεγαλυνθῆναι κατὰ τὸν κανόνα ἡμῶν
faith of you among you to be magnified according to the rule of us
16 εἰς περισσείαν, εἰς τὰ ὑπερέκεινα ὑμῶν εὐαγγελίσασθαι, οὐκ
to overflowing, in order to (in) that beyond you to preach the gospel, not
17 ἐν ἀλλοτρίῳ κανόνι εἰς τὰ ἕτοιμα καυχήσασθαι. ὁ δὲ καυχώ-
in of another (the) rule in things ready to boast those But boasting,
18 μενος, ἐν Κυρίῳ καυχάσθω. οὐ γὰρ ὁ ἑαυτὸν συνιστῶν,
in (the) Lord let him boast. not For the (one) himself commending,
ἐκεῖνός ἐστι δόκιμος, ἀλλ' ὃν ὁ Κύριος συνίστησιν.
that one is approved, but whom the Lord commends.

CHAPTER 11

1 Ὄφελον ἀνείχεσθέ μου μικρὸν τῇ ἀφροσύνῃ· ἀλλὰ καὶ
I would that you endured me a little of foolishness, but, indeed,
2 ἀνέχεσθέ μου. ζηλῶ γὰρ ὑμᾶς Θεοῦ ζήλῳ· ἡρμοσάμην γὰρ
bear with me. I am jealous For (of) you of God, with a jealousy I joined for
ὑμᾶς ἑνὶ ἀνδρὶ παρθένον ἁγνὴν παραστῆσαι τῷ Χριστῷ.
you to one husband a virgin pure to present to Christ.
3 φοβοῦμαι δὲ μή πως ὡς ὁ ὄφις Εὔαν ἐξηπάτησεν ἐν τῇ πανουρ-
I fear And lest somehow as the serpent Eve deceived in the craftiness
γίᾳ αὐτοῦ, οὕτω φθαρῇ τὰ νοήματα ὑμῶν ἀπὸ τῆς ἁπλό-
of him so should be spoiled the thoughts of you from the simplic-
4 τητος τῆς εἰς τὸν Χριστόν. εἰ μὲν γὰρ ὁ ἐρχόμενος ἄλλον
ity (due) to Christ. if indeed For he coming another
Ἰησοῦν κηρύσσει ὃν οὐκ ἐκηρύξαμεν, ἢ πνεῦμα ἕτερον λαμ-
Jesus proclaims, whom not we have proclaimed, or spirit another you
βάνετε ὃ οὐκ ἐλάβετε, ἢ εὐαγγέλιον ἕτερον ὃ οὐκ ἐδέξασθε,
receive which not you received, or gospel another which not you accepted,
5 καλῶς ἠνείχεσθε. λογίζομαι γὰρ μηδὲν ὑστερηκέναι τῶν
(these) well you endure. I judge For nothing to have come behind the
6 ὑπὲρ λίαν ἀποστόλων. εἰ δὲ καὶ ἰδιώτης τῷ λόγῳ, ἀλλ' οὐ
highest apostles. if But indeed unskilled in speech, yet not
7 τῇ γνώσει· ἀλλ' ἐν παντὶ φανερωθέντες ἐν πᾶσιν εἰς ὑμᾶς. ἢ
in knowledge, but in every way having been revealed in all things to you. Or
ἁμαρτίαν ἐποίησα ἐμαυτὸν ταπεινῶν ἵνα ὑμεῖς ὑψωθῆτε,
sin did I commit myself humbling that you might be exalted,

exalted, because I preached the gospel of God to you without charge? 8 I stripped other churches, receiving wages in order to serve you. 9 And being present with you, and lacking, I was not a burden to anyone. The brothers coming from Macedonia made up for my lack. And in every way I kept myself without burden *to you*, and I will keep *myself*. 10 The truth of Christ is in me, that this boasting shall not be silenced in me in the regions of Achaia. 11 Why? Because I do not love you? God knows. 12 But what I do, I also will do, that I may cut off the opportunity of those desiring an opportunity, so that in that which they boast, they be found also as we. 13 For such ones *are* false apostles, deceitful workers transforming themselves into apostles of Christ. 14 Did not even Satan marvelously transform himself into an angel of light? 15 *It is* not a great thing, then, if also his ministers transform themselves as ministers of righteousness; whose end will be according to their works.

16 Again I say, let not anyone think me to be foolish. But if not, even if as foolish, receive me, that I also may boast a little. 17 What I speak, I speak not according to *the* Lord, but as in foolishness, in this boldness of boasting. 18 Since many boast according to the flesh, I also will boast. 19 For you gladly endure fools, being wise. 20 For you endure if anyone enslaves you, if anyone devours, if anyone receives, if anyone exalts *self*, if anyone beats you in the face. 21 I speak according to dishonor, as *if* we have been weak. But in whatever anyone dares—I say *it* in foolishness—I also dare. 22 Are they Hebrews? I also. Are they Israelites? I also. Are they Abraham's seed? I also. 23 Are they ministers of Christ—I speak as beside myself—I beyond *them* in labors more

ὅτι δωρεὰν τὸ τοῦ Θεοῦ εὐαγγέλιον εὐηγγελισάμην ὑμῖν;
because freely the of God gospel I preached to you?
8 ἄλλας ἐκκλησίας ἐσύλησα, λαβὼν ὀψώνιον πρὸς τὴν ὑμῶν
Other churches I stripped, having received wages for the of you
9 διακονίαν· καὶ παρὼν πρὸς ὑμᾶς καὶ ὑστερηθείς, οὐ κατενάρ-
ministry, and being present with you and lacking, not I was a
κησα οὐδενός· τὸ γὰρ ὑστέρημά μου προσανεπλήρωσαν
burden of no one; the for lack of me made up
οἱ ἀδελφοί, ἐλθόντες ἀπὸ Μακεδονίας· καὶ ἐν παντὶ ἀβαρῆ
the brothers coming from Macedonia; and in every way without burden
10 ὑμῖν ἐμαυτὸν ἐτήρησα καὶ τηρήσω. ἔστιν ἀλήθεια Χριστοῦ
to you, myself I kept and I will keep. is (The) truth of Christ
ἐν ἐμοί, ὅτι ἡ καύχησις αὕτη οὐ φραγήσεται εἰς ἐμὲ ἐν τοῖς
in me, that boasting this not shall be silenced in me in the
11 κλίμασι τῆς Ἀχαΐας. διατί; ὅτι οὐκ ἀγαπῶ ὑμᾶς; ὁ Θεὸς
regions of Achaia. Why? Because not I love you? God
12 οἶδεν. ὃ δὲ ποιῶ, καὶ ποιήσω, ἵνα ἐκκόψω τὴν ἀφορμὴν τῶν
knows. what But I do, also I will do, that I may cut off the opportunity of those
θελόντων ἀφορμήν, ἵνα ἐν ᾧ καυχῶνται, εὑρεθῶσι καθὼς
desiring an opportunity, that in that which they boast, they be found as
13 καὶ ἡμεῖς. οἱ γὰρ τοιοῦτοι ψευδαπόστολοι, ἐργάται δόλιοι,
also we (are). For such (are) false apostles, workers deceitful,
14 μετασχηματιζόμενοι εἰς ἀποστόλους Χριστοῦ. καὶ οὐ
transforming themselves into apostles of Christ. And not
θαυμαστόν· αὐτὸς γὰρ ὁ Σατανᾶς μετασχηματίζεται εἰς
marvelously himself For Satan transform himself into
15 ἄγγελον φωτός. οὐ μέγα οὖν εἰ καὶ οἱ διάκονοι αὐτοῦ
an angel of light? (It is) not a great thing, then, if also the ministers of him
μετασχηματίζονται ὡς διάκονοι δικαιοσύνης, ὧν τὸ τέλος
transform themselves as ministers of righteousness; of whom the end
ἔσται κατὰ τὰ ἔργα αὐτῶν.
will be according to the works of them.
16 Πάλιν λέγω, μή τίς με δόξῃ ἄφρονα εἶναι· εἰ δὲ μή γε, κἂν
Again I say, not anyone me think foolish to be; if but not, even if
17 ὡς ἄφρονα δέξασθέ με, ἵνα μικρόν τι κἀγὼ καυχήσωμαι. ὃ
as foolish receive me, that a little I also may boast. What
λαλῶ, οὐ λαλῶ κατὰ Κύριον, ἀλλ᾽ ὡς ἐν ἀφροσύνῃ, ἐν ταύτῃ
I speak, not I speak according to (the) Lord, but as in foolishness, in this
18 τῇ ὑποστάσει τῆς καυχήσεως. ἐπεὶ πολλοὶ καυχῶνται κατὰ
boldness of boasting. Since many boast according to
19 τὴν σάρκα, κἀγὼ καυχήσομαι. ἡδέως γὰρ ἀνέχεσθε τῶν
the flesh, I also will boast. gladly For you endure
20 ἀφρόνων, φρόνιμοι ὄντες. ἀνέχεσθε γάρ, εἴ τις ὑμᾶς κατα-
fools, wise being. you endure For, if anyone you
δουλοῖ, εἴ τις κατεσθίει, εἴ τις λαμβάνει, εἴ τις ἐπαίρεται, εἴ
enslaves, if anyone devours, if anyone receives (you), if anyone lifts (himself) if
21 τις ὑμᾶς εἰς πρόσωπον δέρει. κατὰ ἀτιμίαν λέγω, ὡς ὅτι
anyone you in the face beats. According to dishonor I say, as that
ἡμεῖς ἠσθενήσαμεν· ἐν ᾧ δ᾽ ἄν τις τολμᾷ (ἐν ἀφροσύνῃ
we have been weak; in what but ever anyone dares — in foolishness
22 λέγω), τολμῶ κἀγώ. Ἑβραῖοί εἰσι; κἀγώ· Ἰσραηλῖταί
I say (it) — dare I also. Hebrews Are they? I also! Israelites
23 εἰσι; κἀγώ· σπέρμα Ἀβραάμ εἰσι; κἀγώ· διάκονοι Χριστοῦ
are they? I also! Seed of Abraham are they? I also! Ministers of Christ
εἰσι; (παραφρονῶν λαλῶ) ὑπὲρ ἐγώ· ἐν κόποις περισσοτέ-
are they? As beside myself I speak - beyond (them) I in labors more abun-

abundantly, in stripes beyond measure; in prisons, much more; in deaths, many times. [24]Five times I received forty *stripes* minus one from the Jews. [25]I was flogged three times; I was stoned once; I was shipwrecked three times; I have spent a night and a day in the deep. [26]*I have been* in travels often, in dangers of rivers; in dangers of robbers; in dangers from *my* race; in dangers from *the* nations; in dangers in *the* city; in dangers in *the* desert; in dangers on *the* sea; in dangers among false brothers; [27]in hardship and toil; often in watchings; in hunger and thirst; often in fastings, in cold and nakedness. [28]Besides the things outside conspiring against me day by day, the care of all the churches. [29]Who is weak, and I am not weak? Who is offended, and I do not burn?

[30]If it is right to boast *in* the things of my weakness, I will boast. [31]The God and Father of our Lord Jesus Christ knows, He who is blessed forever, that I do not lie. [32]In Damascus, the governor of Aretas the king guarded the city of *the* Damascenes, desiring to seize me. [33]And I was let down through the wall in a basket, and escaped their hands.

CHAPTER 12

[1]Indeed, to boast *is* not profitable to me; for I will come to visions and revelations of *the* Lord. [2]I know a man in Christ fourteen years ago—whether in the body, I do not know; or out of the body, I do not know; God knows—such a one *was* caught up to *the* third Heaven. And I know such a man—whether in the body, or out of the body, I do not know; God knows— [4]that he was caught into Paradise and heard unspeakable words, which it is not allowed a man to speak. [5]On behalf of such

ρως, ἐν πληγαῖς ὑπερβαλλόντως, ἐν φυλακαῖς περισσοτέρως,
dantly, in stripes surpassing measure, in prisons more abundantly,
24 ἐν θανάτοις πολλάκις. ὑπὸ Ἰουδαίων πεντάκις τεσσαρά-
in deaths many times. By Jews five times forty
25 κοντα παρὰ μίαν ἔλαβον. τρὶς ἐρραβδίσθην, ἅπαξ ἐλιθάσθην,
(stripes) less one I received; thrice I was flogged; once I was stoned;
τρὶς ἐναυάγησα, νυχθήμερον ἐν τῷ βυθῷ πεποίηκα·
thrice I was shipwrecked; a night and a day in the deep I have done;
26 ὁδοιπορίαις πολλάκις, κινδύνοις ποταμῶν, κινδύνοις λη-
in travels many times; in dangers of rivers, in dangers of
στῶν, κινδύνοις ἐκ γένους, κινδύνοις ἐξ ἐθνῶν, κινδύνοις ἐν
robbers, in dangers from (my) race, in dangers from nations; in dangers in
πόλει, κινδύνοις ἐν ἐρημίᾳ, κινδύνοις ἐν θαλάσσῃ, κινδύνοις
a city; in dangers in a desert; in dangers in (the) sea; in dangers
27 ἐν ψευδαδέλφοις· ἐν κόπῳ καὶ μόχθῳ, ἐν ἀγρυπνίαις
among false brothers; in labor and hardship; in watchings
πολλάκις, ἐν λιμῷ καὶ δίψει, ἐν νηστείαις πολλάκις, ἐν ψύχει
many times; in hunger and thirst; in fastings many times; in cold
28 καὶ γυμνότητι. χωρὶς τῶν παρεκτός, ἡ ἐπισύστασίς μου
and nakedness; apart from the things outside, the conspiring against me
29 ἡ καθ' ἡμέραν, ἡ μέριμνα πασῶν τῶν ἐκκλησιῶν. τίς
day by day; the care of all the churches. Who
ἀσθενεῖ, καὶ οὐκ ἀσθενῶ ; τίς σκανδαλίζεται, καὶ οὐκ ἐγὼ
is weak, and not I am weak? Who is offended, and not I
30 πυροῦμαι ; εἰ καυχᾶσθαι δεῖ, τὰ τῆς ἀσθενείας μου καυχήσο-
burn? If to boast it is right, the things of my weakness I will
31 μαι. ὁ Θεὸς καὶ πατὴρ τοῦ Κυρίου ἡμῶν Ἰησοῦ Χριστοῦ
boast. The God and Father of the Lord of us Jesus Christ,
32 οἶδεν, ὁ ὢν εὐλογητὸς εἰς τοὺς αἰῶνας, ὅτι οὐ ψεύδομαι. ἐν
knows, He being blessed to the ages, that not I am lying. In
Δαμασκῷ ὁ ἐθνάρχης Ἀρέτα τοῦ βασιλέως ἐφρούρει τὴν
Damascus the governor of Aretas the king guarded the
33 Δαμασκηνῶν πόλιν, πιάσαι με θέλων· καὶ διὰ θυρίδος ἐν
of (the) Damascenes city, to seize me desiring, and through a window in
σαργάνῃ ἐχαλάσθην διὰ τοῦ τείχους, καὶ ἐξέφυγον τὰς
a basket I was lowered through the wall and escaped the
χεῖρας αὐτοῦ.
hands of them.

CHAPTER 12

1 Καυχᾶσθαι δὴ οὐ συμφέρει μοι· ἐλεύσομαι γὰρ εἰς ὀπτα-
To boast indeed not (is) profitable to me, I will come for to visions
2 σίας καὶ ἀποκαλύψεις Κυρίου. οἶδα ἄνθρωπον ἐν Χριστῷ
and revelations of (the) Lord. I know a man in Christ
πρὸ ἐτῶν δεκατεσσάρων (εἴτε ἐν σώματι, οὐκ οἶδα· εἴτε ἐκτὸς
before years fourteen —whether in (the) body, not I know; or outside
τοῦ σώματος, οὐκ οἶδα· ο Θεὸς οἶδεν), ἁρπαγέντα τὸν τοιοῦ-
the body, not I know; God knows — caught up such
3 τον ἕως τρίτου οὐρανοῦ. καὶ οἶδα τον τοιοῦτον ἄνθρωπον
a one to third Heaven. And I know such a man
(εἴτε ἐν σώματι, εἴτε ἐκτὸς τοῦ σώματος, οὐκ οἶδα· ὁ Θεὸς
—whether in (the) body, or outside the body, not I know; God
4 οἶδεν), ὅτι ἡρπάγη εἰς τὸν παράδεισον, καὶ ἤκουσεν ἄρρητα
knows— that he was caught into Paradise and heard unspeakable
5 ῥήματα. ἃ οὐκ ἐξὸν ἀνθρώπῳ λαλῆσαι. ὑπὲρ τοῦ τοιούτου
words, which not it is allowed a man to speak. On behalf of such a one

a one I will boast. But I will not boast on my behalf, except in my weaknesses. [6] For if I desire to boast, I shall not be foolish; for I speak the truth. but I spare, lest anyone reckons me *to be* beyond what he sees me, or hears of me; [7] and by the surpassing revelations, that I not be made haughty, a thorn in the flesh was given to me, a messenger of Satan, that he might buffet me, that I not be made haughty. [8] As to this, I entreated the Lord three times, that it depart from me. [9] And He said to me, My grace is sufficient for you; for My power is perfected in weaknesses. Therefore, I will rather gladly boast in my weaknesses, that the power of Christ may overshadow me. [10] Therefore, I am pleased in weaknesses, in insults, in dire needs, in persecutions, in distresses, for the sake of Christ. For when I may be weak, then I am powerful.

[11] Boasting, I have become foolish. You compelled me. For I ought to be commended by you, for I lacked nothing of the highest apostles, even though I am nothing. [12] Truly the signs of the apostles were worked out among you in all patience, in miracles, and in wonders, and by works of power. [13] For what is it in which you were less than the rest of the churches, except that I myself did not burden you? Forgive me this wrong.

[14] Behold, I am ready to come to you a third *time*. And I will not burden you, for I do not seek your things, but you. For the children ought not to lay up treasure for the parents, but the parents for the children. [15] But I will most gladly spend and be spent for your souls, even if loving you more and more, I am loved *the* less. [16] But let it be *so*, I did not burden you, but being crafty, I caught you with bait. [17] By any whom I have sent to you, did I

καυχήσομαι· ὑπὲρ δὲ ἐμαυτοῦ οὐ καυχήσομαι, εἰ μὴ ἐν ταῖς
I will boast; on behalf of but myself not I will boast, except in the
6 ἀσθενείαις μου· ἐὰν γὰρ θελήσω καυχήσασθαι, οὐκ ἔσομαι
weaknesses of me, if For I should desire to boast, not I shall be
ἄφρων· ἀλήθειαν γὰρ ἐρῶ· φείδομαι δέ, μή τις εἰς ἐμὲ λογίση-
foolish, truth for I will speak; I spare but, lest anyone to me reckons
7 ται ὑπὲρ ὃ βλέπει με, ἢ ἀκούει τι ἐξ ἐμοῦ. καὶ τῇ ὑπερβολῇ
beyond what he sees me, or hears of me, and by the surpassing
τῶν ἀποκαλύψεων ἵνα μὴ ὑπεραίρωμαι, ἐδόθη μοι σκόλοψ
revelations, that not I be made haughty, was given to me a thorn
τῇ σαρκί, ἄγγελος Σατᾶν ἵνα με κολαφίζῃ, ἵνα μὴ ὑπεραί-
in the flesh, a messenger of Satan, that me he might buffet, lest I be made
8 ρωμαι. ὑπὲρ τούτου τρὶς τὸν Κύριον παρεκάλεσα, ἵνα ἀποστῇ
haughty. As to this thrice the Lord I besought, that it depart
9 ἀπ' ἐμοῦ. καὶ εἴρηκέ μοι, Ἀρκεῖ σοι ἡ χάρις μου· ἡ γὰρ
from me. And He said to me, Enough for you (is) the grace of Me; the for
δύναμίς μου ἐν ἀσθενείᾳ τελειοῦται. ἥδιστα οὖν μᾶλλον
power of Me in weaknesses is perfected. gladly Therefore rather
καυχήσομαι ἐν ταῖς ἀσθενείαις μου, ἵνα ἐπισκηνώσῃ ἐπ' ἐμὲ
I will boast in the weaknesses of me, that may overshadow me
10 ἡ δύναμις τοῦ Χριστοῦ. διὸ εὐδοκῶ ἐν ἀσθενείαις, ἐν ὕβρεσιν,
the power of Christ. Therefore I am pleased in weaknesses, in insults,
ἐν ἀνάγκαις, ἐν διωγμοῖς, ἐν στενοχωρίαις, ὑπὲρ Χριστοῦ·
in dire needs, in persecutions, in distresses, for the sake of Christ.
ὅταν γὰρ ἀσθενῶ, τότε δυνατός εἰμι.
when For I may be weak, then powerful I am.
11 Γέγονα ἄφρων καυχώμενος· ὑμεῖς με ἠναγκάσατε· ἐγὼ
I have become foolish boasting; you me compelled. I
γὰρ ὤφειλον ὑφ' ὑμῶν συνίστασθαι· οὐδὲν γὰρ ὑστέρησα
For ought by you to be commended. nothing For I lacked
12 τῶν ὑπὲρ λίαν ἀποστόλων, εἰ καὶ οὐδέν εἰμι. τὰ μὲν σημεῖα
of the highest apostles, if even nothing I am. the Indeed signs
τοῦ ἀποστόλου κατειργάσθη ἐν ὑμῖν ἐν πάσῃ ὑπομονῇ, ἐν
of the apostles were worked out among you in all patience, by
13 σημείοις καὶ τέρασι καὶ δυνάμεσι. τί γάρ ἐστιν ὃ ἡττήθητε
signs and wonders, and by works of power. what For is it which you were less
ὑπὲρ τὰς λοιπὰς ἐκκλησίας, εἰ μὴ ὅτι αὐτὸς ἐγὼ οὐ κατε-
than the rest of the churches, except that myself I not
νάρκησα ὑμῶν; χαρίσασθέ μοι τὴν ἀδικίαν ταύτην.
burdened you? Forgive me wrong this.
14 Ἰδού, τρίτον ἑτοίμως ἔχω ἐλθεῖν πρὸς ὑμᾶς, καὶ οὐ
Behold, a third (time) I am ready to come to you, and not
καταναρκήσω ὑμῶν· ου γὰρ ζητῶ τὰ ὑμῶν, ἀλλ' ὑμᾶς· οὐ
I will burden you; not for I seek the things of you, but you. not
γὰρ ὀφείλει τὰ τέκνα τοῖς γονεῦσι θησαυρίζειν, ἀλλ' οἱ
For ought the children for the parents to lay up treasure, but the
15 γονεῖς τοῖς τέκνοις. ἐγὼ δὲ ἥδιστα δαπανήσω καὶ ἐκδα-
parents for the children. I But most gladly will spend and be
πανηθήσομαι ὑπὲρ τῶν ψυχῶν ὑμῶν, εἰ καὶ περισσοτέρως
spent out on behalf of the souls of you; if even more abundantly
16 ὑμᾶς ἀγαπῶν, ἧττον ἀγαπῶμαι. ἔστω δέ, ἐγὼ οὐ κατε-
you I love, (the) less I am loved. let it be But, I not
βάρησα ὑμᾶς· ἀλλ' ὑπάρχων πανοῦργος, δόλῳ ὑμᾶς
burdened you; but being crafty, with guile you
17 ἔλαβον. μή τινα ὧν ἀπέσταλκα πρὸς ὑμᾶς, δι' αὐτοῦ
I took. Not anyone whom I have sent to you, through him

overreach you by him? [18] I begged Titus, and sent the brother with *him.* Did Titus overreach you? Did we not walk in the same spirit? Did *we* not *walk* in the same steps?

[19] Again, do you think we are defending to you? We speak before God in Christ, but in all things for your building up, beloved. [20] For I fear lest somehow coming I not find you as I wish, and I be found by you such as you do not wish; lest somehow *there be* strifes, envyings, anger, rivalries, evil-speakings, whisperings, proud thoughts, disturbances; [21] lest *in* my coming again my God may humble me with you, and I shall mourn many of those previously sinning, and not repenting over the uncleanness, and fornication, and lustfulness which they have practiced.

CHAPTER 13

[1] I am coming to you this third *time.* In *the* mouth of two or of three witnesses every matter shall be established. [2] I have said before, and I say beforehand, as being present the second *time* and being absent now, I write to those previously sinning, and all the rest, that if I come again, I will not spare. [3] Since you seek a proof of Christ speaking in me; who is not weak toward you, but is powerful in you— [4] for even if He was crucified in weakness, yet He lives by *the* power of God —for indeed we are weak in Him, but we shall live with Him by the power of God toward you— [5] examine yourselves, whether you are in the faith; prove your own selves. Or do you not recognize that Jesus Christ is in you, unless you are reprobates? [6] And I hope you will know that we are not reprobates. [7] But I pray to God *for* you not to do evil, none. *And* not that we may appear approved, but that you may do the good; but we *deemed* to be reprobates.

[8] For we have no power

18 ἐπλεονέκτησα ὑμᾶς; παρεκάλεσα Τίτον, καὶ συναπέστειλα
did I overreach you? I besought Titus, and sent with (him)
τὸν ἀδελφόν· μή τι ἐπλεονέκτησεν ὑμᾶς Τίτος; οὐ τῷ αὐτῷ
the brother, not overreached you Titus? Did not in the same
Πνεύματι περιεπατήσαμεν; οὐ τοῖς αὐτοῖς ἴχνεσι;
spirit we walk? Did not in the same steps (we walk)?
19 Πάλιν δοκεῖτε ὅτι ὑμῖν ἀπολογούμεθα; κατενώπιον τοῦ
Again, do you think that to you we are defending? Before
Θεοῦ ἐν Χριστῷ λαλοῦμεν· τὰ δὲ πάντα, ἀγαπητοί, ὑπὲρ
God in Christ we speak; but in all things, beloved, on behalf of
20 τῆς ὑμῶν οἰκοδομῆς. φοβοῦμαι γάρ, μή πως ἐλθὼν οὐχ
the of you building up. I fear For lest somehow coming not
οἵους θέλω εὕρω ὑμᾶς, κἀγὼ εὑρεθῶ ὑμῖν οἷον οὐ θέλετε· μή
such as I wish I find you, and I am found by you such as not you wish,
πως ἔρεις, ζῆλοι, θυμοί, ἐριθεῖαι, καταλαλιαί, ψιθυρισμοί,
somehow (be) strifes, envyings, anger, rivalries, evil speakings, whisperings,
21 φυσιώσεις, ἀκαταστασίαι· μὴ πάλιν ἐλθόντα με ταπεινώσῃ
proud thoughts, disturbances; lest again coming me may humble
ὁ Θεός μου πρὸς ὑμᾶς, καὶ πενθήσω πολλοὺς τῶν προη-
the God of me with you, and I shall mourn many of those having
μαρτηκότων, καὶ μὴ μετανοησάντων ἐπὶ τῇ ἀκαθαρσίᾳ καὶ
previously sinned, and not repenting over the uncleanness and
πορνείᾳ καὶ ἀσελγείᾳ ᾗ ἔπραξαν.
fornication and lustfulness which they have practiced.

CHAPTER 13

1 Τρίτον τοῦτο ἔρχομαι πρὸς ὑμᾶς. ἐπὶ στόματος δύο
(The) third (time) this (is) I am coming to you. At (the) mouth of two
2 μαρτύρων καὶ τριῶν σταθήσεται πᾶν ῥῆμα. προείρηκα καὶ
witnesses and of three shall be established every matter. I said before, and
προλέγω, ὡς παρὼν τὸ δεύτερον, καὶ ἀπὼν νῦν γράφω
I say beforehand, as being present the second, and being absent now, I write
τοῖς προημαρτηκόσι καὶ τοῖς λοιποῖς πᾶσιν, ὅτι ἐὰν ἔλθω
to those having previously sinned, and the rest all, that if I come
3 εἰς τὸ πάλιν, οὐ φείσομαι· ἐπεὶ δοκιμὴν ζητεῖτε τοῦ ἐν ἐμοὶ
— — again, not I will spare, since a proof you seek in me
λαλοῦντος Χριστοῦ, ὃς εἰς ὑμᾶς οὐκ ἀσθενεῖ, ἀλλὰ δυνατεῖ
speaking of Christ, who toward you not is weak, but is powerful
4 ἐν ὑμῖν· καὶ γὰρ εἰ ἐσταυρώθη ἐξ ἀσθενείας, ἀλλὰ ζῇ ἐκ
in you. even For if He was crucified out of weakness, but He lives by
δυνάμεως Θεοῦ. καὶ γὰρ καὶ ἡμεῖς ἀσθενοῦμεν ἐν αὐτῷ, ἀλλὰ
(the) power of God. indeed For even we are weak in Him, but
5 ζησόμεθα σὺν αὐτῷ ἐκ δυνάμεως Θεοῦ εἰς ὑμᾶς. ἑαυτοὺς
we shall live with Him by (the) power of God toward you. Yourselves
πειράζετε εἰ ἐστὲ ἐν τῇ πίστει, ἑαυτοὺς δοκιμάζετε. ἢ οὐκ
examine, if you are in the faith, yourselves test; or do not
ἐπιγινώσκετε ἑαυτούς, ὅτι Ἰησοῦς Χριστὸς ἐν ὑμῖν ἐστίν;
you perceive yourselves that Jesus Christ in you is.
6 εἰ μή τι ἀδόκιμοί ἐστε. ἐλπίζω δὲ ὅτι γνώσεσθε ὅτι ἡμεῖς οὐκ
unless reprobates you are. I hope And that you will know that we not
7 ἐσμὲν ἀδόκιμοι. εὔχομαι δὲ πρὸς τὸν Θεόν, μὴ ποιῆσαι ὑμᾶς
are reprobates. I pray And to God not to do you
κακὸν μηδέν, οὐχ ἵνα ἡμεῖς δόκιμοι φανῶμεν, ἀλλ' ἵνα ὑμεῖς
evil, none; not that we approved may appear, but that you
8 τὸ καλὸν ποιῆτε, ἡμεῖς δὲ ὡς ἀδόκιμοι ὦμεν. οὐ γὰρ δυνά-
the good may do; we and (deemed) reprobates to be. not For we can

against the truth, but for the truth. 9 For we rejoice when we are weak, and you are powerful. But we pray for this also, your perfection. 10 Because of this, I write these things while absent, that being present I may not deal sharply *with you* according to the authority which the Lord gave me for building up, and not for pulling down.

11 Finally, brothers, rejoice. Perfect yourselves, encourage yourselves; mind the same thing; be at peace; and the God of love and of peace will be with you.

12 Greet one another with a holy kiss.

13 All the saints greet you.

14 The grace of the Lord Jesus Christ, and the love of God, and the fellowship of the Holy Spirit *be* with you all. Amen.

9 μεθά τι κατὰ τῆς ἀληθείας, ἀλλ' ὑπὲρ τῆς ἀληθείας. χαίρομεν
anything against the truth, but for the truth. we rejoice
γὰρ ὅταν ἡμεῖς ἀσθενῶμεν, ὑμεῖς δὲ δυνατοὶ ἦτε· τοῦτο δὲ
For when we are weak, you and powerful are; this also
10 καὶ εὐχόμεθα, τὴν ὑμῶν κατάρτισιν. διὰ τοῦτο ταῦτα ἀπὼν
and we pray, the of you perfection. Therefore these things being absent
γράφω, ἵνα παρὼν μὴ ἀποτόμως χρήσωμαι, κατὰ τὴν
I write, that being present not sharply I may deal according to the
ἐξουσίαν ἣν ἔδωκέ μοι ὁ Κύριος εἰς οἰκοδομήν, καὶ οὐκ εἰς
authority which gave me the Lord for building up and not for
καθαίρεσιν.
pulling down.
11 Λοιπόν, ἀδελφοί, χαίρετε· καταρτίζεσθε, παρακαλεῖσθε,
For the rest, brothers, rejoice; perfect yourselves, encourage yourselves
τὸ αὐτὸ φρονεῖτε, εἰρηνεύετε· καὶ ὁ Θεὸς τῆς ἀγάπης καὶ
the same thing mind, be at peace, and the God of love and
12 εἰρήνης ἔσται μεθ' ὑμῶν. ἀσπάσασθε ἀλλήλους ἐν ἁγίῳ
of peace will be with you. Greet one another with a holy
φιλήματι.
kiss.
13 Ἀσπάζονται ὑμᾶς οἱ ἅγιοι πάντες.
Greet you the saints all.
14 Ἡ χάρις τοῦ Κυρίου Ἰησοῦ Χριστοῦ, καὶ ἡ ἀγάπη τοῦ
The grace of the Lord Jesus Christ, and the love
Θεοῦ, καὶ ἡ κοινωνία τοῦ Ἁγίου Πνεύματος μετὰ πάντων
of God, and the fellowship of the Holy Spirit (be) with all
ὑμῶν. ἀμήν.
you. Amen.

ΠΑΥΛΟΥ
PAUL
Η ΠΡΟΣ
THE TO
ΓΑΛΑΤΑΣ ΕΠΙΣΤΟΛΗ
(THE) GALATIANS EPISTLE

KING JAMES II VERSION

THE EPISTLE TO *THE* GALATIANS

CHAPTER 1

[1] Paul, an apostle, not from men, nor through man, but through Jesus Christ and God *the* Father, the *One* raising Him from *the* dead; [2] and all the brothers with me, to the churches of Galatia. [3] Grace to you, and peace, from God *the* Father and our Lord Jesus Christ, [4] who gave Himself for our sins, so that He might deliver us out of the present evil age, according to the will of our God and Father, [5] to whom *be* the glory forever and ever. Amen.

[6] I wonder that you so quickly are being transferred from Him having called you by *the* grace of Christ to another gospel, [7] which is not another; only some there are troubling you and desiring to pervert the gospel of Christ. [8] But even if we, or an angel from Heaven, should preach a gospel to you beside what we preached to you, let him be accursed. [9] As we have said before, and now I say again, if anyone preaches a gospel to you beside what you received, let him be accursed.

[10] For do I now persuade men, or God? Or do I seek to please men? For if I yet pleased men, I would not have been a slave of Christ.

[11] And, brothers, I make known to you the gospel which was preached by me, that it is not according to man. [12] for I did not receive

CHAPTER 1

1 Παῦλος ἀπόστολος (οὐκ ἀπ' ἀνθρώπων, οὐδὲ δι'
Paul an apostle not from men, nor through
ἀνθρώπου, ἀλλὰ διὰ Ἰησοῦ Χριστοῦ, καὶ Θεοῦ πατρὸς
man, but through Jesus Christ, and God (the) Father
2 τοῦ ἐγείραντος αὐτὸν ἐκ νεκρῶν), καὶ οἱ σὺν ἐμοὶ πάντες
He having raised Him from (the) dead; and those with me all
3 ἀδελφοί, ταῖς ἐκκλησίαις τῆς Γαλατίας· χάρις ὑμῖν καὶ εἰρήνη
brothers, to the churches of Galatia, Grace to you and peace
4 ἀπὸ Θεοῦ πατρός, καὶ Κυρίου ἡμῶν Ἰησοῦ Χριστοῦ, τοῦ
from God (the) Father, and (the) Lord of us, Jesus Christ, the (One)
δόντος ἑαυτὸν ὑπὲρ τῶν ἁμαρτιῶν ἡμῶν, ὅπως ἐξέληται
having given Himself for the sins of us, so as He might deliver
ἡμᾶς ἐκ τοῦ ἐνεστῶτος αἰῶνος πονηροῦ, κατὰ τὸ θέλημα
us out of the present age of evil, according to the will
5 τοῦ Θεοῦ καὶ πατρὸς ἡμῶν· ᾧ ἡ δόξα εἰς τοὺς αἰῶνας τῶν
of the God and Father of us, whose (is) the glory to the ages of the
αἰώνων. ἀμήν.
ages. Amen.

6 Θαυμάζω ὅτι οὕτω ταχέως μετατίθεσθε ἀπὸ τοῦ καλέ-
I wonder that so quickly are being transferred from the (One) hav-
7 σαντος ὑμᾶς ἐν χάριτι Χριστοῦ εἰς ἕτερον εὐαγγέλιον· ὃ
ing called you by (the) grace of Christ to another gospel, which
οὐκ ἔστιν ἄλλο, εἰ μή τινές εἰσιν οἱ ταράσσοντες ὑμᾶς καὶ
not is another, only some there are troubling you and
8 θέλοντες μεταστρέψαι τὸ εὐαγγέλιον τοῦ Χριστοῦ. ἀλλὰ
desiring to pervert the gospel of Christ. But
καὶ ἐὰν ἡμεῖς ἢ ἄγγελος ἐξ οὐρανοῦ εὐαγγελίζηται ὑμῖν παρ'
even if we or an angel out of Heaven preach a gospel to you beside
9 ὃ εὐηγγελισάμεθα ὑμῖν, ἀνάθεμα ἔστω. ὡς προειρήκαμεν,
what we preached to you, accursed let him be. As we have said before,
καὶ ἄρτι πάλιν λέγω, εἴ τις ὑμᾶς εὐαγγελίζεται παρ' ὃ
and now again I say, if anyone you preaches a gospel beside what
10 παρελάβετε, ἀνάθεμα ἔστω. ἄρτι γὰρ ἀνθρώπους πείθω
you received, accursed let him be. now For men do I persuade,
ἢ τὸν Θεόν; ἢ ζητῶ ἀνθρώποις ἀρέσκειν; εἰ γὰρ ἔτι ἀνθρώ-
or God? Or do I seek men to please? if For yet men
ποις ἤρεσκον, Χριστοῦ δοῦλος οὐκ ἂν ἤμην.
I pleased, of Christ a slave not would I have been.

11 Γνωρίζω δὲ ὑμῖν, ἀδελφοί, τὸ εὐαγγέλιον τὸ εὐαγγελισθὲν
I make known And to you, brothers, the gospel preached
12 ὑπ' ἐμοῦ, ὅτι οὐκ ἔστι κατὰ ἄνθρωπον. οὐδὲ γὰρ ἐγὼ παρὰ
by me, that not it is according to man. not For I from

it from man, nor was I taught *it* but by a revelation of Jesus Christ. 13 For you heard my way of life when *I was* in Judaism, that with surpassing *zeal* I persecuted the church of God, and ravaged it. 14 And *I* progressed in Judaism beyond many contemporaries in my race, being much more a zealot of the ancestral traditions. 15 But when God was pleased, He having separated me from my mother's womb, and having called through His grace, 16 to reveal His Son in me, that I might preach Him among the nations; immediately I did not confer with flesh and blood, 17 nor did I go up to Jerusalem to those apostles before me; but I went away into Arabia, and returned again to Damascus.
18 Then after three years I went up to Jerusalem to learn from Peter, and remained with him fifteen days. 19 But I saw *no* other of the apostles, except James the brother of the Lord. 20 And what I write to you, behold, before God I do not lie. 21 Then I went into the regions of Syria and of Cilicia; 22 but I was not known by face to the churches of Judea in Christ. 23 But only they were hearing that the *one* who then was persecuting us now preaches the faith which he then ravaged; 24 and they glorified God in me.

CHAPTER 2

1 Then through fourteen years I again went up to Jerusalem with Barnabas, also taking Titus with *me*. 2 And I went up according to revelation. And I put before them the gospel which I proclaim in the nations, but privately to the *ones* seeming *to be* pillars, lest I run, or I ran, into vanity. 3 But not even Titus, the *one* with me,

ἀνθρώπου παρέλαβον αὐτό, οὔτε ἐδιδάχθην, ἀλλὰ δι'
man received it, nor was I taught (by man), but by
13 ἀποκαλύψεως Ἰησοῦ Χριστοῦ. ἠκούσατε γὰρ τὴν ἐμὴν
a revelation of Jesus Christ. you heard For my
ἀναστροφήν ποτε ἐν τῷ Ἰουδαϊσμῷ, ὅτι καθ' ὑπερβολὴν
way of life when in the Judaism, that with surpassing (zeal)
14 ἐδίωκον τὴν ἐκκλησίαν τοῦ Θεοῦ, καὶ ἐπόρθουν αὐτήν· καὶ
I persecuted the church of God, and ravaged it, and
προέκοπτον ἐν τῷ Ἰουδαϊσμῷ ὑπὲρ πολλοὺς συνηλικιώτας
progressed in Judaism beyond many contemporaries
ἐν τῷ γένει μου, περισσοτέρως ζηλωτὴς ὑπάρχων τῶν
in the race of me, much more a zealot being of the
15 πατρικῶν μου παραδόσεων. ὅτε δὲ εὐδόκησεν ὁ Θεός, ὁ
ancestral of me traditions. when But was pleased God, He
ἀφορίσας με ἐκ κοιλίας μητρός μου καὶ καλέσας διὰ τῆς
having separated me from my mother's womb, and having called through the
16 χάριτος αὐτοῦ, ἀποκαλύψαι τὸν υἱὸν αὐτοῦ ἐν ἐμοί, ἵνα
grace of Him to reveal the Son of Him in me, that
εὐαγγελίζωμαι αὐτὸν ἐν τοῖς ἔθνεσιν, εὐθέως οὐ προσανε-
I might preach Him among the nations, immediately not I conferred
17 θέμην σαρκὶ καὶ αἵματι· οὐδὲ ἀνῆλθον εἰς Ἱεροσόλυμα πρὸς
with flesh and blood, neither did I go up to Jerusalem to
τοὺς πρὸ ἐμοῦ ἀποστόλους, ἀλλ' ἀπῆλθον εἰς Ἀραβίαν, καὶ
the before me apostles, but I went away into Arabia, and
πάλιν ὑπέστρεψα εἰς Δαμασκόν.
again returned to Damascus.
18 Ἔπειτα μετὰ ἔτη τρία ἀνῆλθον εἰς Ἱεροσόλυμα ἱστορῆσαι
Then after years three I went up to Jerusalem to learn from
19 Πέτρον, καὶ ἐπέμεινα πρὸς αὐτὸν ἡμέρας δεκαπέντε. ἕτερον
Peter, and remained with him days fifteen, other
δὲ τῶν ἀποστόλων οὐκ εἶδον, εἰ μὴ Ἰάκωβον τὸν ἀδελφὸν
but of the apostles not I saw, except James the brother
20 τοῦ Κυρίου. ἃ δὲ γράφω ὑμῖν, ἰδοὺ ἐνώπιον τοῦ Θεοῦ, ὅτι
of the Lord. what And I write to you, behold before God, that
21 οὐ ψεύδομαι. ἔπειτα ἦλθον εἰς τὰ κλίματα τῆς Συρίας καὶ τῆς
not I lie. Then I went into the regions of Syria and
22 Κιλικίας. ἤμην δὲ ἀγνοούμενος τῷ προσώπῳ ταῖς ἐκκλησίαις
of Cilicia. I was And unknown by face to the churches
23 τῆς Ἰουδαίας ταῖς ἐν Χριστῷ· μόνον δὲ ἀκούοντες ἦσαν ὅτι
of Judea in Christ. only But hearing they were that
Ὁ διώκων ἡμᾶς ποτέ, νῦν εὐαγγελίζεται τὴν πίστιν ἥν ποτε
the (one) persecuting us then, now preaches the faith which then
24 ἐπόρθει. καὶ ἐδόξαζον ἐν ἐμοὶ τὸν Θεόν.
he ravaged and they glorified in me God.

CHAPTER 2

1 Ἔπειτα διὰ δεκατεσσάρων ἐτῶν πάλιν ἀνέβην εἰς Ἱεροσό-
Then through fourteen years again I went up to Jerusa-
2 λυμα μετὰ Βαρνάβα, συμπαραλαβὼν καὶ Τίτον. ἀνέβην δὲ
lem with Barnabas, taking with (me) also Titus. I went up And
κατὰ ἀποκάλυψιν, καὶ ἀνεθέμην αὐτοῖς τὸ εὐαγγέλιον ὃ
according to a revelation, and I put before them the gospel which
κηρύσσω ἐν τοῖς ἔθνεσι, κατ' ἰδίαν δὲ τοῖς δοκοῦσι, μή πως εἰς
I proclaim in the nations, privately but to those seeming, lest into
3 κενὸν τρέχω ἢ ἔδραμον. ἀλλ' οὐδὲ Τίτος ὁ σὺν ἐμοί, Ἕλλην
vanity I run or I ran. But not even Titus, he with me, a Greek

A Greek, was compelled to be circumcised. [4]But because of those false brothers stealing in, who stole in to spy on our freedom which we have in Christ Jesus, they desiring to enslave us; [5]to whom not even for an hour we yielded in subjection, that the truth of the gospel might continue with you. [6]But from those seeming to be something—what kind they were then does not matter to me; God does not accept the face of man—for those seeming *important* conferred nothing to me. [7]But on the contrary, seeing that I have been entrusted *with* the gospel of the uncircumcision, even as Peter to the circumcision— [8]for He working in Peter to an apostleship of the circumcision also worked in me to the nations—[9]and knowing the grace given to me, James and Cephas and John, those seeming to be pillars, gave right *hands* of fellowship to Barnabas and to me, that we *go* to the nations, but they to the circumcision; [10]only that we might remember the poor, which same thing I was eager to do.

[11]But when Peter came to Antioch, I opposed *him* to his face, because he was to be blamed. [12]For before some came from James, he ate with the Gentiles. But when they came, he drew back and separated himself, being afraid of those of the circumcision. [13]And the rest of the Jews also dissembled with him, so as even Barnabas was led away with their dissembling. [14]But when I saw that they did not walk uprightly with the truth of the gospel, I said to Peter before all, If you being a Jew live *as* a Gentile, and not *as the* Jews, why do you compel the Gentiles to judaize? [15]We Jews by nature, and not sinners of *the* Gentiles —[16]knowing that a man is not justified by works of law, except through faith *in* Jesus Christ—we also

4 ὤν, ἠναγκάσθη περιτμηθῆναι· διὰ δὲ τοὺς παρεισάκτους
being, was compelled to be circumcised; because of but those stealing
ψευδαδέλφους, οἵτινες παρεισῆλθον κατασκοπῆσαι τὴν
false brothers, who stole in to spy on the
ἐλευθερίαν ἡμῶν ἣν ἔχομεν ἐν Χριστῷ Ἰησοῦ, ἵνα ἡμᾶς
freedom of us which we have in Christ Jesus, that us
5 καταδουλώσωνται· οἷς οὐδὲ πρὸς ὥραν εἴξαμεν τῇ ὑποταγῇ,
they desire to enslave; to whom not for an hour yielded we in subjection
6 ἵνα ἡ ἀλήθεια τοῦ εὐαγγελίου διαμείνῃ πρὸς ὑμᾶς. ἀπὸ δὲ
that the truth of the gospel might continue with you. from But
τῶν δοκούντων εἶναί τι (ὁποῖοί ποτε ἦσαν οὐδέν μοι
those seeming to be something —of what kind then they were not to me
διαφέρει· πρόσωπον Θεὸς ἀνθρώπου οὐ λαμβάνει)—ἐμοὶ
matters; the face God of man does not accept – to me
7 γὰρ οἱ δοκοῦντες οὐδὲν προσανέθεντο· ἀλλὰ τοὐναντίον,
for those seeming nothing conferred but on the contrary
ἰδόντες ὅτι πεπίστευμαι τὸ εὐαγγέλιον τῆς ἀκροβυστίας,
seeing that I have been entrusted (with) the gospel of the uncircumcision,
8 καθὼς Πέτρος τῆς περιτομῆς (ὁ γὰρ ἐνεργήσας Πέτρῳ εἰς
even as Peter to the circumcision —the (One) for working in Peter to
ἀποστολὴν τῆς περιτομῆς, ἐνήργησε καὶ ἐμοὶ εἰς τὰ ἔθνη),
an apostleship of the circumcision, worked also in me to the nations—
9 καὶ γνόντες τὴν χάριν τὴν δοθεῖσάν μοι, Ἰάκωβος καὶ
and knowing the grace given to me, James and
Κηφᾶς καὶ Ἰωάννης, οἱ δοκοῦντες στύλοι εἶναι, δεξιὰς
Cephas and John, those seeming pillars to be, right (hands)
ἔδωκαν ἐμοὶ καὶ Βαρνάβᾳ κοινωνίας, ἵνα ἡμεῖς εἰς τὰ ἔθνη,
gave to me and to Barnabas of fellowship, that we to the nations,
10 αὐτοὶ δὲ εἰς τὴν περιτομήν· μόνον τῶν πτωχῶν ἵνα μνημο-
they but to the circumcision; only the poor that we might
νεύωμεν, ὃ καὶ ἐσπούδασα αὐτὸ τοῦτο ποιῆσαι.
remember, which indeed I was eager this same thing to do.
11 Ὅτε δὲ ἦλθε Πέτρος εἰς Ἀντιόχειαν, κατὰ πρόσωπον
when But came Peter to Antioch, against face
12 αὐτῷ ἀντέστην, ὅτι κατεγνωσμένος ἦν. πρὸ τοῦ γὰρ ἐλθεῖν
to him I opposed, because to be condemned he was. before the for coming
τινὰς ἀπὸ Ἰακώβου, μετὰ τῶν ἐθνῶν συνήσθιεν· ὅτε δὲ
of some from James, with the nations he ate; when but
ἦλθον, ὑπέστελλε καὶ ἀφώριζεν ἑαυτόν, φοβούμενος τοὺς ἐκ
they came, he drew back and separated himself, being afraid of those of
13 περιτομῆς. καὶ συνυπεκρίθησαν αὐτῷ καὶ οἱ λοιποὶ Ἰουδαῖοι,
the circumcision. And dissembled with him also the rest of the Jews,
14 ὥστε καὶ Βαρνάβας συναπήχθη αὐτῶν τῇ ὑποκρίσει. ἀλλ᾽
so as even Barnabas was led away with of them the dissembling. But
ὅτε εἶδον ὅτι οὐκ ὀρθοποδοῦσι πρὸς τὴν ἀλήθειαν τοῦ
when I saw that not they walked uprightly with the truth of the
εὐαγγελίου, εἶπον τῷ Πέτρῳ ἔμπροσθεν πάντων, Εἰ σύ,
gospel, I said to Peter, in front of all, If you
Ἰουδαῖος ὑπάρχων, ἐθνικῶς ζῇς καὶ οὐκ Ἰουδαϊκῶς, τί τὰ
a Jew being, a Gentile live, and not (as the) Jews why the
15 ἔθνη ἀναγκάζεις Ἰουδαΐζειν; ἡμεῖς φύσει Ἰουδαῖοι, καὶ οὐκ
Gentiles you compel to judaize? We by nature Jews, and not
16 ἐξ ἐθνῶν ἁμαρτωλοί, εἰδότες ὅτι οὐ δικαιοῦται ἄνθρωπος
of (the) Gentiles sinners, knowing that not is justified a man
ἐξ ἔργων νόμου, ἐὰν μὴ διὰ πίστεως Ἰησοῦ Χριστοῦ, καὶ
by works of law, except through faith (in) Jesus Christ, even

believed in Christ Jesus, that we may be justified by faith *in* Christ, and not by works of law, because all flesh will not be justified by works of law. 17 But if seeking to be justified in Christ, we also were found *to be* sinners, *is* Christ then a minister of sin? Let it not be! 18 For if I build again these things which I destroyed, I confirm myself *as* a transgressor. 19 For I through the Law died to Law, that I might live to God. 20 I have been crucified with Christ; and I live, *yet* no longer I, but Christ lives in me. And that *life* I now live, I live by faith toward the Son of God, the *One* loving me and giving Himself over on my behalf. 21 I do not set aside the grace of God; for if righteousness is through law, then Christ died without cause.

CHAPTER 3

1 O foolish Galatians! Who bewitched you not to obey the truth, to whom before *your* eyes Jesus Christ was written among you crucified? 2 This only I desire to learn from you: Did you receive the Spirit by works of Law, or by hearing of faith? 3 Are you so foolish? Having begun in *the* Spirit, do you now perfect *yourself* in *the* flesh? 4 Did you suffer so much vainly? If indeed *it* also *was* vainly? 5 Then He supplying the Spirit to you, and working mighty works in you, *is it* by works of Law, or by hearing of faith? 6 Even as Abraham believed God, and it was counted to him for righteousness. 7 Know, then, that those of faith, these are sons of Abraham. 8 And the Scripture foreseeing that God would justify the nations by faith, preached the gospel before to Abraham: "All the nations will be blessed in you." 9 So that those of faith are blessed with the faithful Abraham. 10 For as many as are out of works of law, *these* are under a curse. For it has been written, "Cursed *is* everyone who

ἡμεῖς εἰς Χριστὸν Ἰησοῦν ἐπιστεύσαμεν, ἵνα δικαιωθῶμεν ἐκ
we in Christ Jesus believed that we may be justified by
πίστεως Χριστοῦ, καὶ οὐκ ἐξ ἔργων νόμου· διότι οὐ δικαιωθή-
faith (in) Christ, and not of works of law, because not will be just-
17 σεται ἐξ ἔργων νόμου πᾶσα σάρξ. εἰ δέ, ζητοῦντες δικαιωθῆ-
ified by works of law all flesh. if But seeking to be justified
ναι ἐν Χριστῷ, εὑρέθημεν καὶ αὐτοὶ ἁμαρτωλοί, ἄρα
in Christ we were found also ourselves sinners, then
18 Χριστὸς ἁμαρτίας διάκονος; μὴ γένοιτο. εἰ γὰρ ἃ κατέλυσα,
(is) Christ of sin a minister? Let it not be! if For what I destroyed,
19 ταῦτα πάλιν οἰκοδομῶ, παραβάτην ἐμαυτὸν συνίστημι. ἐγὼ
these things again I build, a transgressor myself I establish. I
20 γὰρ διὰ νόμου νόμῳ ἀπέθανον, ἵνα Θεῷ ζήσω. Χριστῷ
For through law to law died, that to God I might live. With Christ
συνεσταύρωμαι· ζῶ δέ, οὐκέτι ἐγώ, ζῇ δὲ ἐν ἐμοὶ Χριστός·
I have been crucified: I live and, no longer I, lives but in me Christ;
ὃ δὲ νῦν ζῶ ἐν σαρκί, ἐν πίστει ζῶ τῇ τοῦ υἱοῦ τοῦ Θεοῦ, τοῦ
what and now I live in flesh, by faith I live to the Son of God,
21 ἀγαπήσαντός με καὶ παραδόντος ἑαυτὸν ὑπὲρ ἐμοῦ. οὐκ
loving me and giving over Himself on behalf of me. not
ἀθετῶ τὴν χάριν τοῦ Θεοῦ· εἰ γὰρ διὰ νόμου δικαιοσύνη,
I set aside the grace of God; if for through law righteousness,
ἄρα Χριστὸς δωρεὰν ἀπέθανεν.
then Christ without cause died.

CHAPTER 3

1 Ὦ ἀνόητοι Γαλάται, τίς ὑμᾶς ἐβάσκανε τῇ ἀληθείᾳ μὴ
O foolish Galatians, who you bewitched the truth not
πείθεσθαι, οἷς κατ' ὀφθαλμοὺς Ἰησοῦς Χριστὸς προεγράφη
to obey, to whom before the eyes Jesus Christ was written afore
2 ἐν ὑμῖν ἐσταυρωμένος; τοῦτο μόνον θέλω μαθεῖν ἀφ' ὑμῶν,
among you crucified? This only I desire to learn from you,
ἐξ ἔργων νόμου τὸ Πνεῦμα ἐλάβετε, ἢ ἐξ ἀκοῆς πίστεως;
by works of law the Spirit did you receive, or by hearing of faith?
3 οὕτως ἀνόητοί ἐστε; ἐναρξάμενοι Πνεύματι, νῦν σαρκὶ
so foolish Are you? Having begun in (the) Spirit, now in (the) flesh
4 ἐπιτελεῖσθε; τοσαῦτα ἐπάθετε εἰκῇ; εἴ γε καὶ εἰκῇ. ὁ οὖν
5 do you finish? So much suffered you vainly? If indeed even vainly? He then
ἐπιχορηγῶν ὑμῖν τὸ Πνεῦμα καὶ ἐνεργῶν δυνάμεις ἐν ὑμῖν,
supplying to you the Spirit and working works of power in you,
6 ἐξ ἔργων νόμου, ἢ ἐξ ἀκοῆς πίστεως; καθὼς Ἀβραὰμ ἐπί-
by works of law, or by hearing of faith? As Abraham
7 στευσε τῷ Θεῷ, καὶ ἐλογίσθη αὐτῷ εἰς δικαιοσύνην. γινώ-
believed God, and it was counted to him for righteousness. Know
σκετε ἄρα ὅτι οἱ ἐκ πίστεως, οὗτοί εἰσιν υἱοὶ Ἀβραάμ.
then that those of faith, these are sons of Abraham.
8 προϊδοῦσα δὲ ἡ γραφὴ ὅτι ἐκ πίστεως δικαιοῖ τὰ ἔθνη ὁ
foreseeing And the Scripture that by faith would justify the nations
Θεός, προευηγγελίσατο τῷ Ἀβραὰμ ὅτι Εὐλογηθήσονται
God, preached the gospel before to Abraham that will be blessed
9 ἐν σοὶ πάντα τὰ ἔθνη. ὥστε οἱ ἐκ πίστεως εὐλογοῦνται σὺν
in you all the nations. So as those of faith are blessed with
10 τῷ πιστῷ Ἀβραάμ. ὅσοι γὰρ ἐξ ἔργων νόμου εἰσίν, ὑπὸ
the faithful Abraham. as many as For out of works of law are, under
κατάραν εἰσί· γέγραπται γάρ, Ἐπικατάρατος πᾶς ὃς οὐκ
a curse are; it has been written for: Cursed (is) everyone who not

does not continue in all the things having been written in the book of the Law, to do them. 11 And that no one is justified by Law before God *is* clear, because, "The just shall live by faith." 12 But the Law is not of faith, but, "The man doing these things shall live in them." 13 Christ redeemed us from the curse of the law, having become a curse for us; for it has been written, "Cursed *is* everyone having been hung on a tree;" 14 that the blessing of Abraham might be to the nations in Christ Jesus, that we might receive the promise of the Spirit through faith.

15 Brothers, I speak according to man, a covenant having been ratified, even *among* mankind, no one sets aside or adds to *it.* 16 but the promises were spoken to Abraham and to his Seed—it does not say, And to seeds, as of many; but as of one, "And to your Seed," which is Christ— 17 And I say this, A covenant having been ratified before to Christ by God, *the* Law coming into being four hundred and thirty years after does not annul the promise, so as to abolish *it.* 18 For if the inheritance *is* of Law, *it is* no more of promise; but God has given *it* to Abraham through promise. 19 Why, then, the Law? It was added because of transgressions, until the Seed should come *to those* to whom it had been promised, being ordained through angels in a mediator's hand. 20 But the Mediator is not of one, but God is one.

21 Then *is* the Law against the promises? Let it not be! For if a law had been given which had been able to make alive, indeed righteousness would have been out of law. 22 But the Scripture locked up all under sin, that the promise by faith of Jesus Christ might be given to the ones believing. 23 But before faith came, we were guarded under law, having been locked up to the faith about to be revealed.

ἐμμένει ἐν πᾶσι τοῖς γεγραμμένοις ἐν τῷ βιβλίῳ τοῦ νόμου,
continues in all the things having been written in the roll of the law
11 τοῦ ποιῆσαι αὐτά. ὅτι δὲ ἐν νόμῳ οὐδεὶς δικαιοῦται παρὰ
to do them. that And by law no one is justified before
12 τῷ Θεῷ, δῆλον· ὅτι Ὁ δίκαιος ἐκ πίστεως ζήσεται· ὁ δὲ
God (is) clear, because the just one by faith will live; the and
νόμος οὐκ ἔστιν ἐκ πίστεως, ἀλλ' Ὁ ποιήσας αὐτὰ ἄνθρωπος
law not is of faith, but: The doing these things man
13 ζήσεται ἐν αὐτοῖς. Χριστὸς ἡμᾶς ἐξηγόρασεν ἐκ τῆς κατάρας
shall live in them. Christ us redeemed out of the curse
τοῦ νόμου, γενόμενος ὑπὲρ ἡμῶν κατάρα· γέγραπται γάρ,
of the law, having become for us a curse; it has been written for:
14 Ἐπικατάρατος πᾶς ὁ κρεμάμενος ἐπὶ ξύλου· ἵνα εἰς τὰ ἔθνη
Cursed (is) everyone who hangs on a tree; that to the nations
ἡ εὐλογία τοῦ Ἀβραὰμ γένηται ἐν Χριστῷ Ἰησοῦ, ἵνα τὴν
the blessing of Abraham might be in Christ Jesus, that the
ἐπαγγελίαν τοῦ Πνεύματος λάβωμεν διὰ τῆς πίστεως.
promise of the Spirit we might receive through faith.
15 Ἀδελφοί, κατὰ ἄνθρωπον λέγω· ὅμως ἀνθρώπου κεκυρω-
Brothers, according to man I say, even of man having been
16 μένην διαθήκην οὐδεὶς ἀθετεῖ ἢ ἐπιδιατάσσεται. τῷ δὲ
ratified a covenant, no one sets aside or adds to (it). And
Ἀβραὰμ ἐρρήθησαν αἱ ἐπαγγελίαι, καὶ τῷ σπέρματι αὐτοῦ.
to Abraham were said the promises, and to the Seed of him.
οὐ λέγει, Καὶ τοῖς σπέρμασιν, ὡς ἐπὶ πολλῶν, ἀλλ' ὡς ἐφ'
Not it says, And to thc seeds, as upon many, but as of
17 ἑνός, Καὶ τῷ σπέρματί σου, ὅς ἐστι Χριστός. τοῦτο δὲ λέγω,
One: And to the Seed of you, who is Christ. this And I say,
διαθήκην προκεκυρωμένην ὑπὸ τοῦ Θεοῦ εἰς Χριστὸν ὁ μετὰ
A covenant having been ratified before by God to Christ, the after
ἔτη τετρακόσια καὶ τριάκοντα γεγονὼς νόμος οὐκ ἀκυροῖ, εἰς
years four hundred and thirty coming into being Law not annuls, so
18 τὸ καταργῆσαι τὴν ἐπαγγελίαν. εἰ γὰρ ἐκ νόμου ἡ κληρονο-
as to abolish the promise. if For of law the inheritance
μία, οὐκέτι ἐξ ἐπαγγελίας· τῷ δὲ Ἀβραὰμ δι' ἐπαγγελίας
(is), no more (is it) of promise; but to Abraham through promise
19 κεχάρισται ὁ Θεός. τί οὖν ὁ νόμος ; τῶν παραβάσεων χάριν
has given (it) God. Why, then, the law? the transgressions because of
προσετέθη, ἄχρις οὗ ἔλθῃ τὸ σπέρμα ᾧ ἐπήγγελται, διατα-
It was added, until should come the Seed to whom it had been promised, being
20 γεὶς δι' ἀγγέλων ἐν χειρὶ μεσίτου. ὁ δὲ μεσίτης ἑνὸς οὐκ
ordained through angels in hand a mediator's. the But mediator of one not
21 ἔστιν, ὁ δὲ Θεὸς εἷς ἐστίν. ὁ οὖν νόμος κατὰ τῶν ἐπαγγελιῶν
is, but God one is. the Then law against the promises
τοῦ Θεοῦ; μὴ γένοιτο. εἰ γὰρ ἐδόθη νόμος ὁ δυνάμενος
God (is)? Let it not be! if For had been given a law which was able
22 ζωοποιῆσαι, ὄντως ἂν ἐκ νόμου ἦν ἡ δικαιοσύνη. ἀλλὰ
to make alive, indeed would out of (that) law have been the righteousness. But
συνέκλεισεν ἡ γραφὴ τὰ πάντα ὑπὸ ἁμαρτίαν, ἵνα ἡ
locked up the Scripture all under sin, that the
ἐπαγγελία ἐκ πίστεως Ἰησοῦ Χριστοῦ δοθῇ τοῖς πιστεύουσι.
promise by faith of Jesus Christ might be given to those believing.
23 Πρὸ τοῦ δὲ ἐλθεῖν τὴν πίστιν, ὑπὸ νόμον ἐφρουρούμεθα,
before the But coming faith, under law we were guarded,
συγκεκλεισμένοι εἰς τὴν μέλλουσαν πίστιν ἀποκαλυφθῆναι.
having been locked up to the being about faith to be revealed.

[24]So that the Law has become a trainer of us *until* Christ, that we might be justified by faith. [25]But faith coming, we are no longer under a trainer, [26]for you are sons of God through faith in Christ Jesus. [27]For as many as were baptized into Christ, you put on Christ. [28]There cannot be Jew nor Greek; there is no slave nor freeman; there is no male and female; for you are all one in Christ Jesus. [29]And if you *are* of Christ, then you are a seed of Abraham, even heirs according to promise.

24 ὥστε ὁ νόμος παιδαγωγὸς ἡμῶν γέγονεν εἰς Χριστόν, ἵνα
So as the law a trainer of us has become (until) Christ, that
25 ἐκ πίστεως δικαιωθῶμεν. ἐλθούσης δὲ τῆς πίστεως, οὐκέτι
by faith we might be justified. having come But faith, no more
26 ὑπὸ παιδαγωγόν ἐσμεν. πάντες γὰρ υἱοὶ Θεοῦ ἐστὲ διὰ τῆς
under a trainer we are. all For sons of God you are through
27 πίστεως ἐν Χριστῷ Ἰησοῦ. ὅσοι γὰρ εἰς Χριστὸν ἐβαπτί-
faith in Christ Jesus. as many as For into Christ were
28 σθητε, Χριστὸν ἐνεδύσασθε. οὐκ ἔνι Ἰουδαῖος οὐδὲ Ἕλλην,
baptized, Christ you put on. not There is Jew nor Greek,
οὐκ ἔνι δοῦλος οὐδὲ ἐλεύθερος, οὐκ ἔνι ἄρσεν καὶ θῆλυ· πάντες
not is slave nor freeman; not is male and female; all
29 γὰρ ὑμεῖς εἷς ἐστὲ ἐν Χριστῷ Ἰησοῦ. εἰ δὲ ὑμεῖς Χριστοῦ, ἄρα
for you one are in Christ Jesus. if And you (are) of Christ, then
τοῦ Ἀβραὰμ σπέρμα ἐστέ, καὶ κατ' ἐπαγγελίαν κληρονό-
of Abraham a seed you are, even according to promise heirs.
μοι.

CHAPTER 4

CHAPTER 4

[1]But say, for as long a time as the heir is an infant, he being lord of all does not differ *from* a slave, but is under guardians and housemasters until the *term* set before by the father. [3]So we also, when we were infants, we were under the elements of the world, being enslaved. [4]But when the fullness of the time came, God sent forth His Son, having come out of a woman, having come under Law, [5]that He might redeem the ones under law, that we might receive the adoption of sons. [6]And because you are sons, God sent forth the Spirit of His Son into your hearts, crying, Abba! Father! [7]So that you no more are a slave, but a son; and if a son, also an heir of God through Christ.

[8]But then, indeed, not knowing God, you served as slaves *to* the ones not by nature being gods. [9]But now, knowing God, but rather being known by God, how do you turn again to the weak and poor elements, *to* which you again desire to slave anew? [10]You observe days, and months, and seasons, and years. [11]I fear *for* you, lest somehow I have labored among you in vain.

1 Λέγω δέ, ἐφ' ὅσον χρόνον ὁ κληρονόμος νήπιός ἐστιν,
I say But, over so long a time the heir an infant is,
2 οὐδὲν διαφέρει δούλου, κύριος πάντων ὤν· ἀλλὰ ὑπὸ
nothing he differs (from) a slave, lord of all being, but under
ἐπιτρόπους ἐστὶ καὶ οἰκονόμους, ἄχρι τῆς προθεσμίας τοῦ
guardians is, and housemasters, until the (term) set before by the
3 πατρός. οὕτω καὶ ἡμεῖς, ὅτε ἦμεν νήπιοι, ὑπὸ τὰ στοιχεῖα
father. So also we, when we were infants, under the elements
4 τοῦ κόσμου ἦμεν δεδουλωμένοι· ὅτε δὲ ἦλθε τὸ πλήρωμα
of the world we were, being enslaved; when but came the fullness
τοῦ χρόνου, ἐξαπέστειλεν ὁ Θεὸς τὸν υἱὸν αὐτοῦ, γενό-
of the time, sent forth God the Son of Him, becoming
5 μενον ἐκ γυναικός, γενόμενον ὑπὸ νόμον, ἵνα τοὺς ὑπὸ
of a woman, becoming under law, that those under
6 νόμον ἐξαγοράσῃ, ἵνα τὴν υἱοθεσίαν ἀπολάβωμεν. ὅτι δέ
law He might redeem, that the adoption of sons we may receive. because And
ἐστε υἱοί, ἐξαπέστειλεν ὁ Θεὸς τὸ Πνεῦμα τοῦ υἱοῦ αὐτοῦ
you are sons, sent forth God the Spirit of the Son of Him
7 εἰς τὰς καρδίας ὑμῶν, κρᾶζον, Ἀββᾶ, ὁ πατήρ. ὥστε οὐκέτι
into the hearts of you, crying, Abba, Father! So as no more
εἶ δοῦλος, ἀλλ' υἱός· εἰ δὲ υἱός, καὶ κληρονόμος Θεοῦ διὰ
are you a slave, but a son; if and a son, also an heir of God by
Χριστοῦ.
Christ.
8 Ἀλλὰ τότε μέν, οὐκ εἰδότες Θεόν, ἐδουλεύσατε τοῖς μὴ
But then indeed not knowing God, you served as slaves those not
9 φύσει οὖσι θεοῖς· νῦν δέ, γνόντες Θεόν, μᾶλλον δὲ γνωσθέντες
by nature being gods; now but knowing God, rather but being known
ὑπὸ Θεοῦ, πῶς ἐπιστρέφετε πάλιν ἐπὶ τὰ ἀσθενῆ καὶ
by God, how do you turn again upon the weak and
10 πτωχὰ στοιχεῖα, οἷς πάλιν ἄνωθεν δουλεύειν θέλετε; ἡμέρας
poor elements, which again anew to slave for you desire? days
11 παρατηρεῖσθε, καὶ μῆνας, καὶ καιρούς, καὶ ἐνιαυτούς. φοβοῦ-
You observe, and months, and seasons, and years. I fear
μαι ὑμᾶς, μή πως εἰκῇ κεκοπίακα εἰς ὑμᾶς.
(for) you, lest some how in vain I have labored among you.

[12]Brothers, I beg of you, be as I *am*, because I *am* as you. You wronged me *in* nothing. [13]But you know that because of weakness of the flesh, I preached the gospel to you before; [14]and you did not despise my temptation in my flesh, nor spurn *it*, but you received me as an angel of God, as Christ Jesus. [15]What then was your blessedness? For I testify to you that if you were able, *you* would have plucked out your eyes and given to me. [16]So then did I become your enemy speaking truth to you? [17]They are zealous for you, but they desire to shut you out, that you be zealous *to* them. [18]But *it is* good to always be zealous in a good thing, and not only in my being present with you. [19]My children, *for* whom I again travail until Christ should be formed in you, [20]even now I desired to be present with, and to change my voice; for I am in doubt *as to* you.

[21]Tell me, those desiring to be under Law, do you hear the Law? [22]For it has been written: Abraham had two sons, one out of the slave-woman, and one out of the free woman. [23]But, indeed, he of the slave-woman has been born according to flesh; and he of the free woman through the promise; [24]which things are being allegorized; for these are two covenants, one, indeed, from Mount Sinai bringing forth to slavery—which is Hagar, [25]for Hagar is Mount Sinai in Arabia, and corresponds to the present Jerusalem, and she is in slavery with her children— [26]But the Jerusalem *from* above is free, who is the mother of us all; [27]for it has been written, "Be glad, barren *one* not bearing; break forth and shout, the *one* travailing, for more *are* the children of the desolate rather than she having the husband." [28]But, brothers, we are children of promise according to Isaac. [29]But then even as he born according to flesh persecuted the

12 Γίνεσθε ὡς ἐγώ, ὅτι κἀγὼ ὡς ὑμεῖς, ἀδελφοί, δέομαι ὑμῶν.
Be as I because I also as you, brothers, I beg of you.
13 οὐδέν με ἠδικήσατε· οἴδατε δὲ ὅτι δι' ἀσθένειαν τῆς σαρκὸς
Nothing me you wronged; you know and that because of weakness of the flesh
14 εὐηγγελισάμην ὑμῖν τὸ πρότερον. καὶ τὸν πειρασμόν μου
I preached the gospel to you before, and the temptation of me
τὸν ἐν τῇ σαρκί μου οὐκ ἐξουθενήσατε οὐδὲ ἐξεπτύσατε,
in the flesh of me not you despised, not disdained,
ἀλλ' ὡς ἄγγελον Θεοῦ ἐδέξασθέ με, ὡς Χριστὸν Ἰησοῦν.
but as an angel of God you received me, as Christ Jesus.
15 τίς οὖν ἦν ὁ μακαρισμὸς ὑμῶν; μαρτυρῶ γὰρ ὑμῖν ὅτι, εἰ
What then was the blessedness of you? I witness for to you that, if
δυνατόν, τοὺς ὀφθαλμοὺς ὑμῶν ἐξορύξαντες ἂν ἐδώκατέ μοι.
you could, the eyes of you plucking out would have given me.
16 ὥστε ἐχθρὸς ὑμῶν γέγονα ἀληθεύων ὑμῖν; ζηλοῦσιν ὑμᾶς
17 **So then an enemy of you became I speaking truth to you? They are zealous for you,**
οὐ καλῶς, ἀλλὰ ἐκκλεῖσαι ὑμᾶς θέλουσιν, ἵνα αὐτοὺς ζηλοῦτε.
not well, but to shut out you they desire, that(to) them you be zealous:
18 καλὸν δὲ τὸ ζηλοῦσθαι ἐν καλῷ πάντοτε, καὶ μὴ μόνον ἐν
(it is) good but to be zealous in a good thing always, and not only in
19 τῷ παρεῖναί με πρὸς ὑμᾶς. τεκνία μου, οὓς πάλιν ὠδίνω,
being present me with you. Children of me, (for) whom again I travail,
20 ἄχρις οὗ μορφωθῇ Χριστὸς ἐν ὑμῖν, ἤθελον δὲ παρεῖναι πρὸς
until should be formed Christ in you, I desired and to be present with
ὑμᾶς ἄρτι, καὶ ἀλλάξαι τὴν φωνήν μου, ὅτι ἀποροῦμαι ἐν
you now, and to change the voice of me because I am in doubt in
ὑμῖν.
you.

21 Λέγετέ μοι, οἱ ὑπὸ νόμον θέλοντες εἶναι, τὸν νόμον οὐκ
Tell me, those under law desiring to be, the law do not
22 ἀκούετε; γέγραπται γάρ, ὅτι Ἀβραὰμ δύο υἱοὺς ἔσχεν· ἕνα
you hear? it has been written For: — Abraham two sons had, one
23 ἐκ τῆς παιδίσκης, καὶ ἕνα ἐκ τῆς ἐλευθέρας. ἀλλ' ὁ μὲν ἐκ τῆς
of the slave-woman, and one of the free woman. But he indeed of the
παιδίσκης κατὰ σάρκα γεγέννηται, ὁ δὲ ἐκ τῆς ἐλευθέρας διὰ
slave-woman according to flesh has been born; he and of the free woman via
24 τῆς ἐπαγγελίας. ἅτινά ἐστιν ἀλληγορούμενα· αὗται γάρ
the promise. Which things is being allegorized; these for
εἰσιν αἱ δύο διαθῆκαι· μία μὲν ἀπὸ ὄρους Σινᾶ, εἰς δουλείαν
are two covenants: one indeed from Mount Sinai, to slavery
25 γεννῶσα, ἥτις ἐστὶν Ἄγαρ. τὸ γὰρ Ἄγαρ Σινᾶ ὄρος ἐστὶν ἐν
bringing forth, which is Hagar. the For Hagar Sinai Mount is in
τῇ Ἀραβίᾳ, συστοιχεῖ δὲ τῇ νῦν Ἱερουσαλήμ, δουλεύει δὲ
Arabia, corresponds and to the now Jerusalem, she slaves and
26 μετὰ τῶν τέκνων αὐτῆς. ἡ δὲ ἄνω Ἱερουσαλὴμ ἐλευθέρα ἐστίν,
with the children of her. the But above Jerusalem free is,
27 ἥτις ἐστὶ μήτηρ πάντων ἡμῶν. γέγραπται γάρ, Εὐφράνθητι
who is mother of all of us; it has been written for: Be glad
στεῖρα ἡ οὐ τίκτουσα· ῥῆξον καὶ βόησον ἡ οὐκ ὠδίνουσα·
barren (one) not bearing, break forth and shout, the (one) not travailing;
ὅτι πολλὰ τὰ τέκνα τῆς ἐρήμου μᾶλλον ἢ τῆς ἐχούσης τὸν
because more (are) the children of the desolate rather than she having the
28 ἄνδρα. ἡμεῖς δέ, ἀδελφοί, κατα Ἰσαάκ, ἐπαγγελίας τέκνα
husband. we But, brothers, according to Isaac, of promise children
29 ἐσμέν. ἀλλ' ὥσπερ τότε ὁ κατὰ σάρκα γεννηθεὶς ἐδίωκε τὸν
we are. But even as then he according to flesh born persecuted the (one)

one according to Spirit, so also now. [30] But what says the Scripture? "Cast out the slave-woman and her son, for in no way shall the son of the slave-woman inherit with the son of the free. [31] Then, brothers, we are not children of a slave-woman, but of the free woman.

CHAPTER 5

[1] Then stand firm in the freedom with which Christ made us free, and do not again be held with a yoke of slavery.

[2] Behold, I, Paul, say to you that if you are circumcised, Christ will profit you nothing. [3] And I testify again to every man being circumcised, that he is a debtor to do all the law. [4] You who are justified by law are deprived of all effect from Christ—you fell from grace. [5] For we through *the* Spirit eagerly wait for *the* hope of righteousness out of faith. [6] For in Christ Jesus neither circumcision nor uncircumcision has any strength, but faith working through love. [7] You were running well; who held you back *that* you do not obey the truth? [8] The persuasion *is* not from Him calling you. [9] A little leaven leavens all the lump. [10] I trust as to you in *the* Lord that you will think nothing else, but that the *one* troubling you shall bear the judgment, whoever he may be. [11] But I, brothers, if I proclaim circumcision, why am I still persecuted? Then the offense of the Cross has passed away. [12] I would that the ones causing you to doubt will cut themselves off.

[13] For, brothers, you were called to freedom. Only do not *use* the freedom for gain to the flesh. But serve one another as slaves by love. [14] For the whole law is fulfilled in one word, "You shall love your neighbor as yourself." [15] But if you bite and devour one another, be careful that you are not consumed.

30 κατὰ Πνεῦμα, οὕτω καὶ νῦν. ἀλλὰ τί λέγει ἡ γραφή ; "Ἔκβαλε
according to Spirit, so also now. But what says the Scripture? Cast out
τὴν παιδίσκην καὶ τὸν υἱὸν αὐτῆς, οὐ γὰρ μὴ κληρονομήσῃ
the slave-woman and the son of her, in no For way shall inherit
31 ὁ υἱὸς τῆς παιδίσκης μετὰ τοῦ υἱοῦ τῆς ἐλευθέρας. ἄρα, ἀδελ-
the son of the slave-woman with the Son of the free. Then, brothers,
φοί, οὐκ ἐσμὲν παιδίσκης τέκνα, ἀλλὰ τῆς ἐλευθέρας.
not we are of a slave-woman children, but of the free woman.

CHAPTER 5

1 τῇ ἐλευθερίᾳ οὖν ᾗ Χριστὸς ἡμᾶς ἠλευθέρωσε, στήκετε, καὶ
In the freedom, then, with which Christ us made free, stand firm, and
μὴ πάλιν ζυγῷ δουλείας ἐνέχεσθε.
not again with a yoke of slavery be held.
2 Ἴδε, ἐγὼ Παῦλος λέγω ὑμῖν, ὅτι ἐὰν περιτέμνησθε, Χριστὸς
Behold, I, Paul, tell you, that if you are circumcised, Christ
3 ὑμᾶς οὐδὲν ὠφελήσει. μαρτύρομαι δὲ πάλιν παντὶ ἀνθρώπῳ
you nothing will profit. I testify And again to every man
περιτεμνομένῳ, ὅτι ὀφειλέτης ἐστὶν ὅλον τὸν νόμον ποιῆσαι.
being circumcised, that a debtor he is all the law to do.
4 κατηργήθητε ἀπὸ τοῦ Χριστοῦ, οἵτινες ἐν νόμῳ δικαιοῦσθε·
You were passed away from Christ, whoever by law are justified,
5 τῆς χάριτος ἐξεπέσατε. ἡμεῖς γὰρ Πνεύματι ἐκ πίστεως
grace you fell from. we For by (the) Spirit from faith
6 ἐλπίδα δικαιοσύνης ἀπεκδεχόμεθα. ἐν γὰρ Χριστῷ Ἰησοῦ
(the) hope of righteousness eagerly wait. in For Christ Jesus
οὔτε περιτομή τι ἰσχύει, οὔτε ἀκροβυστία, ἀλλὰ πίστις δι'
neither circumcision any strength has nor uncircumcision, but faith through
7 ἀγάπης ἐνεργουμένη. ἐτρέχετε καλῶς· τίς ὑμᾶς ἀνέκοψε τῇ
love working. You were running well, who you held back the
8 ἀληθείᾳ μὴ πείθεσθαι ; ἡ πεισμονὴ οὐκ ἐκ τοῦ καλοῦντος
truth not you obey? the persuasion (is) not from Him calling
9 ὑμᾶς. μικρὰ ζύμη ὅλον τὸ φύραμα ζυμοῖ. ἐγὼ πέποιθα εἰς
10 **you. A little leaven all the lump leavens. I trust as to**
ὑμᾶς ἐν Κυρίῳ, ὅτι οὐδὲν ἄλλο φρονήσετε· ὁ δὲ ταράσσων
you in (the) Lord, that nothing other you will think; the (one) but troubling
11 ὑμᾶς βαστάσει τὸ κρίμα, ὅστις ἂν ᾖ. ἐγὼ δέ, ἀδελφοί, εἰ
you shall bear the judgment, whoever he may be. I But, brothers, if
περιτομὴν ἔτι κηρύσσω, τί ἔτι διώκομαι ; ἄρα κατήργηται
circumcision still proclaim, why yet am I persecuted? Then has passed away
12 τὸ σκάνδαλον τοῦ σταυροῦ. ὄφελον καὶ ἀποκόψονται οἱ
the offense of the cross. Would that also will cut themselves off those
ἀναστατοῦντες ὑμᾶς.
causing to doubt you.
13 Ὑμεῖς γὰρ ἐπ' ἐλευθερίᾳ ἐκλήθητε, ἀδελφοί· μόνον μὴ τὴν
you For for freedom were called, brothers, only not the
ἐλευθερίαν εἰς ἀφορμὴν τῇ σαρκί, ἀλλὰ διὰ τῆς ἀγάπης
freedom for gain to the flesh, but through love
14 δουλεύετε ἀλλήλοις. ὁ γὰρ πᾶς νόμος ἐν ἑνὶ λόγῳ πληροῦται,
serve as slaves to one another. the For whole law in one word is fulfilled
15 ἐν τῷ, Ἀγαπήσεις τὸν πλησίον σου ὡς ἑαυτόν. εἰ δὲ
in the (word): You shall love the neighbor of you as yourself. if But
ἀλλήλους δάκνετε καὶ κατεσθίετε, βλέπετε μὴ ὑπὸ ἀλλήλων
one another you bite and devour, see lest by one another
ἀναλωθῆτε.
you are consumed.

16 But I say, Walk in *the* Spirit, and you will not fullfill *the* lust of *the* flesh. 17 For the flesh lusts against the Spirit, and the Spirit against the flesh; and these are contrary to one another, lest whatever you may will, these things you do. 18 But if you are led by *the* Spirit, you are not under Law. 19 Now the works of the flesh are clearly revealed: adultery, fornication, uncleanness, lustfulness, 20 idolatry, sorcery, hatreds, fightings, jealousies, angers, rivalries, divisions, heresies, 21 envyings, murders, drunkennesses, wild parties, and things like these; *of* which I tell you beforehand, as I also said before, that those practicing such things will not inherit *the* kingdom of God.

22 But the fruit of the Spirit is: love, joy, peace, longsuffering, kindness, goodness, faith, 23 meekness, self-control—against such things there is not a law. 24 But the ones belonging to Christ crucified the flesh with *its* passions and lusts.

25 If we live in *the* Spirit, let us also walk in *the* Spirit. 26 Let us not become glory-seeking, provoking one another, envying one another.

CHAPTER 6

1 Brothers, if a man is taken in some fault, you, the spiritual ones, restore such a one in the spirit of meekness, considering yourself, that you not also be tempted. 2 Bear one another's burdens, and so you will fulfill the law of Christ. 3 For if anyone thinks to be something, he deceives himself, being nothing. 4 But let each one prove his work, and then he alone will have a boast, and not as to another. 5 For each one will bear *his* own load.

6 But let him share, the *one* being taught in the word,

16 Λέγω·δέ, Πνεύματι περιπατεῖτε. καὶ ἐπιθυμίαν σαρκὸς οὐ
I say And, in (the) Spirit walk, and (the) lust of (the) flesh not
17 μὴ τελέσητε. ἡ γὰρ σὰρξ ἐπιθυμεῖ κατὰ τοῦ Πνεύματος, τὸ
at all you will fulfill. the For flesh lusts against the Spirit, the
δὲ Πνεῦμα κατὰ τῆς σαρκός· ταῦτα δὲ ἀντίκειται ἀλλήλοις,
and (the) Spirit against the flesh, these and are contrary to one another.
18 ἵνα μὴ ἃ ἂν θέλητε, ταῦτα ποιῆτε. εἰ δὲ Πνεύματι ἄγεσθε,
lest whatever you may will, these you do. if But by (the) Spirit you are led,
19 οὐκ ἐστὲ ὑπὸ νόμον. φανερὰ δέ ἐστι τὰ ἔργα τῆς σαρκός,
not you are under law. clearly revealed Now are the works of the flesh,
20 ἅτινά ἐστι μοιχεία, πορνεία, ἀκαθαρσία, ἀσέλγεια, εἰδω-
which are: adultery, fornication, uncleanness, lustfulness, idol-
λολατρεία, φαρμακεία, ἔχθραι, ἔρεις, ζῆλοι, θυμοί, ἐριθεῖαι,
service, sorcery, enmities, fightings, jealousies, angers, rivalries,
21 διχοστασίαι, αἱρέσεις, φθόνοι, φόνοι, μέθαι, κῶμοι, καὶ τὰ
divisions, heresies, envyings, murders,drunkennesses, revellings, and
ὅμοια τούτοις· ἃ προλέγω ὑμῖν, καθὼς καὶ προεῖπον, ὅτι
like things to these, which I tell before you, as also I said previously, that
οἱ τὰ τοιαῦτα πράσσοντες βασιλείαν Θεοῦ οὐ κληρονομή-
those such things practicing (the) kingdom of God not will inherit.
22 σουσιν. ὁ δὲ καρπὸς τοῦ Πνεύματός ἐστιν ἀγάπη, χαρά,
the But fruit of the Spirit is: love, joy,
23 εἰρήνη, μακροθυμία, χρηστότης, ἀγαθωσύνη, πίστις, πρᾳό-
peace, longsuffering, kindness, goodness, faith meek-
24 της, ἐγκράτεια· κατὰ τῶν τοιούτων οὐκ ἔστι νόμος. οἱ δὲ τοῦ
ness, self-control; against such things not is a law. those And
Χριστοῦ, τὴν σάρκα ἐσταύρωσαν σὺν τοῖς παθήμασι καὶ
of Christ the flesh crucified with the passions and
ταῖς ἐπιθυμίαις.
the lusts
25 Εἰ ζῶμεν Πνεύματι, Πνεύματι καὶ στοιχῶμεν. μὴ γινώ-
26 **If we live in (the) Spirit, in (the) Spirit also let us walk. not Let us be-**
μεθα κενόδοξοι, ἀλλήλους προκαλούμενοι, ἀλλήλοις φθονοῦν-
come vainglorious, one another provoking one another envying.
τες.

CHAPTER 6

1 Ἀδελφοί, ἐὰν καὶ προληφθῇ ἄνθρωπος ἔν τινι παραπτώ-
Brothers, if indeed is overtaken a man in some fault,
ματι, ὑμεῖς οἱ πνευματικοὶ καταρτίζετε τὸν τοιοῦτον ἐν
you the spiritual ones restore such a one in
πνεύματι πρᾳότητος, σκοπῶν σεαυτὸν μὴ καὶ σὺ πειρασθῇς.
the spirit of meekness, considering yourself, lest also you be tempted
2 ἀλλήλων τὰ βάρη βαστάζετε, καὶ οὕτως ἀναπληρωσατε τὸν
Of one another the burdens bear, and so you will fulfill the
3 νόμον τοῦ Χριστοῦ. εἰ γὰρ δοκεῖ τις εἶναί τι, μηδὲν ὤν,
law of Christ. if For thinks anyone to be something, nothing being,
4 ἑαυτὸν φρεναπατᾷ. τὸ δὲ ἔργον ἑαυτοῦ δοκιμαζέτω ἕκαστος,
himself he deceives. the But work of himself let prove each one,
καὶ τότε εἰς ἑαυτὸν μόνον τὸ καύχημα ἕξει, καὶ οὐκ εἰς τὸν
and then in himself alone the boast he will have, and not in the
5 ἕτερον. ἕκαστος γὰρ τὸ ἴδιον φορτίον βαστάσει.
other one. each one For the own load will bear.
6 Κοινωνείτω δὲ ὁ κατηχούμενος τὸν λόγον τῷ κατηχοῦντι
let him share And, he being taught in the word, with the (one) teaching

with the *one* teaching in all good things. [7]Do not be deceived. God is not mocked. For whatever a man may sow, that he also will reap. [8]For the *one* sowing to his flesh will reap corruption of the flesh. But the *one* sowing to the Spirit will reap everlasting life from the Spirit. [9]But we should not lose heart in doing good, for in due time we shall reap, if *we* do ot faint. [10]So, then, as we have time, let us work good toward all, and especially toward the household of the faith.

[11]See in what large letters I write to you with my hand. [12]As many as desire to look well in *the* flesh, these compel you to be circumcised; only that they may not be persecuted for the cross of Christ. [13]For they themselves having been circumcised do not even keep *the* Law; but they desire you to be circumcised so that they may boast in your flesh. [14]But may it never be for me to boast, except in the cross of the Lord Jesus Christ, through whom the world has been crucified to me, and I to the world. [15]For in Christ Jesus neither circumcision *has* any strength, nor uncircumcision; but a new creation. [16]And as many as shall walk by this rule, peace and mercy *be* on them, and on the Israel of God.

[17]For the rest, let no one give troubles to me, for I bear in my body the brands of the Lord Jesus.

[18]The grace of our Lord Jesus Christ *be* with your spirit, brothers. Amen.

7 ἐν πᾶσιν ἀγαθοῖς. μὴ πλανᾶσθε, Θεὸς οὐ μυκτηρίζεται· ὃ γὰρ
in all good things. not Be led astray, God not is mocked; what For
8 ἐὰν σπείρῃ ἄνθρωπος, τοῦτο καὶ θερίσει. ὅτι ὁ σπείρων εἰς
ever may sow a man, this also he will reap.; because he sowing to
τὴν σάρκα ἑαυτοῦ, ἐκ τῆς σαρκὸς θερίσει φθοράν· ὁ δὲ σπεί-
the flesh of himself, of the flesh will reap corruption; he but
ρων εἰς τὸ Πνεῦμα, ἐκ τοῦ Πνεύματος θερίσει ζωὴν αἰώνιον.
sowing to the Spirit, of the Spirit will reap life everlasting.
9 τὸ δὲ καλὸν ποιοῦντες μὴ ἐκκακῶμεν· καιρῷ γὰρ ἰδίῳ θερίσο-
the And good doing, not let us weaken. in time For in its own we shall
10 μεν, μὴ ἐκλυόμενοι. ἄρα οὖν ὡς καιρὸν ἔχομεν, ἐργαζώμεθα
reap, not (we) are) fainting Then therefore as time we have, let us work
τὸ ἀγαθὸν πρὸς πάντας, μάλιστα δὲ πρὸς τοὺς οἰκείους τῆς
the good to all, most of all and to the household of the
πίστεως.
faith.
11 Ἴδετε πηλίκοις ὑμῖν γράμμασιν ἔγραψα τῇ ἐμῇ χειρί. ὅσοι
12 See in how large to you letters I write with my hand. As many as
θέλουσιν εὐπροσωπῆσαι ἐν σαρκί, οὗτοι ἀναγκάζουσιν
desire to look well in (the) flesh, these compel
ὑμᾶς περιτέμνεσθαι, μόνον ἵνα μὴ τῷ σταυρῷ τοῦ Χριστοῦ
you to be circumcised, only that not for the cross of Christ
13 διώκωνται. οὐδὲ γὰρ οἱ περιτεμνόμενοι αὐτοὶ νόμον φυλάσ-
they are persecuted; not even For those having been circumcised themselves law keep.
σουσιν· ἀλλὰ θέλουσιν ὑμᾶς περιτέμνεσθαι, ἵνα ἐν τῇ ὑμετέρᾳ
but they desire you to be circumcised that in your
14 σαρκὶ καυχήσωνται. ἐμοὶ δὲ μὴ γένοιτο καυχᾶσθαι εἰ μὴ ἐν
flesh they may boast. to me But not it may be to boast, except in
τῷ σταυρῷ τοῦ Κυρίου ἡμῶν Ἰησοῦ Χριστοῦ· δι' οὗ ἐμοὶ
the cross of (the) Lord of us, Jesus Christ, through whom to me
15 κόσμος ἐσταύρωται, κἀγὼ τῷ κόσμῳ. ἐν γὰρ Χριστῷ Ἰησοῦ
(the) world has been crucified, and I to the world. in For Christ Jesus
οὔτε περιτομή τι ἰσχύει, οὔτε ἀκροβυστία, ἀλλὰ καινὴ
neither circumcision any strength (has), nor uncircumcision, but a new
16 κτίσις. καὶ ὅσοι τῷ κανόνι τούτῳ στοιχήσουσιν, εἰρήνη ἐπ'
creation. And as many as by rule this shall walk, peace on
αὐτούς, καὶ ἔλεος, καὶ ἐπὶ τὸν Ἰσραὴλ τοῦ Θεοῦ.
them, and mercy, and on the Israel of God.
17 Τοῦ λοιποῦ, κόπους μοι μηδεὶς παρεχέτω· ἐγὼ γὰρ τὰ
For the rest, troubles to me no one let cause; I for the
στίγματα τοῦ Κυρίου Ἰησοῦ ἐν τῷ σώματί μου βαστάζω.
brands of the Lord Jesus in the body of me bear.
18 Ἡ χάρις τοῦ Κυρίου ἡμῶν Ἰησοῦ Χριστοῦ μετὰ τοῦ
The grace of the Lord of us, Jesus Christ, (be) with the
πνεύματος ὑμῶν, ἀδελφοί. ἀμήν.
spirit of you, brothers. Amen.

ΠΑΥΛΟΥ ΤΟΥ ΑΠΟΣΤΟΛΟΥ
PAUL THE APOSTLE
Η ΠΡΟΣ
THE TO
ΕΦΕΣΙΟΥΣ ΕΠΙΣΤΟΛΗ
EPHESIANS EPISTLE

KING JAMES II VERSION

THE EPISTLE TO *THE* EPHESIANS

CHAPTER 1

[1] Paul, *an* apostle of Jesus Christ through *the* will of God, to the saints being in Ephesus, and faithful in Christ Jesus: [2] Grace to you and peace from God our Father and the Lord Jesus Christ.

[3] Blessed *is* the God and Father of our Lord Jesus Christ, who blessed us with every spiritual blessing in the heavenlies with Christ; [4] according as He chose us in Him before *the* foundation of *the* world, for us to be holy and without blemish before Him in love; [5] predestinating us to adoption through Jesus Christ to Himself, according to the good pleasure of His will, [6] to *the* praise of *the* glory of His grace, in which He favored us in the Beloved, [7] in whom we have redemption through His blood, the forgiveness of sins, according to the riches of His grace; [8] which He caused to abound toward us in all wisdom and understanding, [9] making known to us the mystery of His will, according to the good pleasure which He purposed in Himself, [10] for the administration of the fullness of time; to head up all things in Christ, both the things in Heaven, and the things on earth, in Him, [11] in whom we also have been chosen to an inheritance, being predestinated according to *the* purpose of the *One* working all things according to the counsel of His *own*

CHAPTER 1

1 Παῦλος, ἀπόστολος Ἰησοῦ Χριστοῦ διὰ θελήματος Θεοῦ,
Paul, an apostle of Jesus Christ through (the) will of God,
τοῖς ἁγίοις τοῖς οὖσιν ἐν Ἐφέσῳ καὶ πιστοῖς ἐν Χριστῷ
to the saints being in Ephesus and faithful in Christ
2 Ἰησοῦ· χάρις ὑμῖν καὶ εἰρήνη ἀπὸ Θεοῦ πατρὸς ἡμῶν καὶ
Jesus: Grace to you and peace from God the Father of us, and
Κυρίου Ἰησοῦ Χριστοῦ.
(the) Lord Jesus Christ.
3 Εὐλογητὸς ὁ Θεὸς καὶ πατὴρ τοῦ Κυρίου ἡμῶν Ἰησοῦ
Blessed (is) the God and Father of the Lord of us, Jesus
Χριστοῦ, ὁ εὐλογήσας ἡμᾶς ἐν πάσῃ εὐλογίᾳ πνευματικῇ
Christ, who blessed us with every blessing spiritual
4 ἐν τοῖς ἐπουρανίοις ἐν Χριστῷ· καθὼς ἐξελέξατο ἡμᾶς ἐν
in the heavenlies in Christ; according as He chose us in
αὐτῷ πρὸ καταβολῆς κόσμου, εἶναι ἡμᾶς ἁγίους καὶ
Him before (the) foundation of (the) world, to be us holy and
5 ἀμώμους κατενώπιον αὐτοῦ ἐν ἀγάπῃ, προορίσας ἡμᾶς εἰς
unblemished before Him, in love predestinating us to
υἱοθεσίαν διὰ Ἰησοῦ Χριστοῦ εἰς αὐτόν, κατὰ τὴν εὐδοκίαν
adoption through Jesus Christ to Himself, according to the good pleasure
6 τοῦ θελήματος αὐτοῦ, εἰς ἔπαινον δόξης τῆς χάριτος αὐτοῦ,
of the will of Him, to (the) praise of (the) glory of the grace of Him,
7 ἐν ᾗ ἐχαρίτωσεν ἡμᾶς ἐν τῷ ἠγαπημένῳ· ἐν ᾧ ἔχομεν τὴν
with which He favored us in the (One) having been loved; in whom we have the
ἀπολύτρωσιν διὰ τοῦ αἵματος αὐτοῦ, τὴν ἄφεσιν τῶν
redemption through the blood of Him, the forgiveness
παραπτωμάτων, κατὰ τὸν πλοῦτον τῆς χάριτος αὐτοῦ,
of trespasses, according to the riches of the grace of Him,
8 ἧς ἐπερίσσευσεν εἰς ἡμᾶς ἐν πάσῃ σοφίᾳ καὶ φρονήσει,
which he caused to abound to us in all wisdom and intelligence,
9 γνωρίσας ἡμῖν τὸ μυστήριον τοῦ θελήματος αὐτοῦ, κατὰ
making known to us the mystery of the will of Him, according to
10 τὴν εὐδοκίαν αὐτοῦ, ἣν προέθετο ἐν αὐτῷ εἰς οἰκονομίαν τοῦ
the good pleasure of Him, which He purposed in Himself for a stewardship of the
πληρώματος τῶν καιρῶν, ἀνακεφαλαιώσασθαι τὰ πάντα
fullness of the times, to head up all things
ἐν τῷ Χριστῷ, τά τε ἐν τοῖς οὐρανοῖς καὶ τὰ ἐπὶ τῆς γῆς·
in Christ, the things both in the heavens and the things on the earth
11 ἐν αὐτῷ, ἐν ᾧ καὶ ἐκληρώθημεν, προορισθέντες κατὰ
in Him, in whom also we have been chosen to an inheritance being predestinated according to
πρόθεσιν τοῦ τὰ πάντα ἐνεργοῦντος κατὰ τὴν βουλὴν τοῦ
(the) purpose of the (One) all things working according to the counsel of the

will, [12] for us to be to *the* praise of His glory, the ones first trusting in Christ; [13] in whom also you hearing the word of truth, the gospel of your salvation, in whom also believing you were sealed with the Holy Spirit of promise, [14] who is an earnest of our inheritance, to *the* redemption of the purchased possession, to *the* praise of His glory.

[15] Because of this, hearing of your faith in the Lord Jesus, and love toward all the saints, I also [16] do not cease giving thanks on your behalf, making mention of you in my prayers, [17] that the God of our Lord Jesus Christ, the Father of glory, may give to you a spirit of wisdom and revelation in *the* knowledge of Him, [18] the eyes of your mind having been enlightened for you to know what is the hope of His calling, and what the riches of the glory of His inheritance in the saints, [19] and what is the surpassing greatness of His power toward us, the ones believing according to the working of His mighty strength [20] which He worked in Christ *in* raising Him from *the* dead—yea, *He* seated *Him* at His right *hand* in the heavenlies, [21] far above all principality, and authority, and power, and lordship, and every name being named, not only in this age, but also in the coming *age;* [22] and He put all things under His feet, and gave Him *to be* Head over all things to the church, [23] which is His body, the fullness of Him filling all things in all—

CHAPTER 2

[1] and *He worked in* you who were once dead in trespass-
es and sins, [2] in which you d

12 θελήματος αὐτοῦ, εἰς τὸ εἶναι ἡμᾶς εἰς ἔπαινον τῆς δόξης
will of Him, for to be us to (the) praise of the glory
13 αὐτοῦ, τοὺς προηλπικότας ἐν τῷ Χριστῷ· ἐν ᾧ καὶ ὑμεῖς,
of Him, those having previously trusted in Christ; in whom also you,
ἀκούσαντες τὸν λόγον τῆς ἀληθείας, τὸ εὐαγγέλιον τῆς
hearing the word of truth, the gospel of the
σωτηρίας ὑμῶν,—ἐν ᾧ καὶ πιστεύσαντες ἐσφραγίσθητε τῷ
salvation of you, in whom also believing you were sealed with the
14 Πνεύματι τῆς ἐπαγγελίας τῷ Ἁγίῳ, ὅς ἐστιν ἀρραβὼν τῆς
Spirit of promise the Holy, who is an earnest of the
κληρονομίας ἡμῶν, εἰς ἀπολύτρωσιν τῆς περιποιήσεως, εἰς
inheritance of us, until (the) redemption of the possession, to
ἔπαινον τῆς δόξης αὐτοῦ.
(the) praise of the glory of Him.
15 Διὰ τοῦτο κἀγώ, ἀκούσας τὴν καθ' ὑμᾶς πίστιν ἐν τῷ
Therefore I also, hearing the among you faith in the
Κυρίῳ Ἰησοῦ καὶ τὴν ἀγάπην τὴν εἰς πάντας τοὺς ἁγίους,
Lord Jesus and the love to all the saints,
16 οὐ παύομαι εὐχαριστῶν ὑπὲρ ὑμῶν, μνείαν ὑμῶν ποιού-
not do cease giving thanks on behalf of you, mention of you making
17 μενος ἐπὶ τῶν προσευχῶν μου· ἵνα ὁ Θεὸς τοῦ Κυρίου ἡμῶν
on the prayers of me, that the God of the Lord of us,
Ἰησοῦ Χριστοῦ, ὁ πατὴρ τῆς δόξης, δώῃ ὑμῖν πνεῦμα
Jesus Christ, the Father of glory, may give to you a spirit
18 σοφίας καὶ ἀποκαλύψεως, ἐν ἐπιγνώσει αὐτοῦ· πεφωτι-
of wisdom and revelation in (the) knowledge of Him, having been
σμένους τοὺς ὀφθαλμοὺς τῆς διανοίας ὑμῶν, εἰς τὸ εἰδέναι
enlightened the eyes of the mind of you, for to know
ὑμᾶς τίς ἐστιν ἡ ἐλπὶς τῆς κλήσεως αὐτοῦ, καὶ τίς ὁ πλοῦτος
you what is the hope of the calling of Him, and what the riches
19 τῆς δόξης τῆς κληρονομίας αὐτοῦ ἐν τοῖς ἁγίοις, καὶ τί τὸ
of the glory of the inheritance of Him in the saints; and what the
ὑπερβάλλον μέγεθος τῆς δυνάμεως αὐτοῦ εἰς ἡμᾶς τοὺς
surpassing greatness of the power of Him toward us, those
πιστεύοντας, κατὰ τὴν ἐνέργειαν τοῦ κράτους τῆς ἰσχύος
believing according to the working of the might of the strength
20 αὐτοῦ ἣν ἐνήργησεν ἐν τῷ Χριστῷ, ἐγείρας αὐτὸν ἐκ νεκρῶν,
of Him, which He worked in Christ raising Him from (the) dead;
21 καὶ ἐκάθισεν ἐν δεξιᾷ αὐτοῦ ἐν τοῖς ἐπουρανίοις, ὑπεράνω
and He seated (Him) at the right of Him in the heavenlies far above
πάσης ἀρχῆς καὶ ἐξουσίας καὶ δυνάμεως καὶ κυριότητος,
all rule and authority and power and lordship,
καὶ παντὸς ὀνόματος ὀνομαζομένου οὐ μόνον ἐν τῷ αἰῶνι
and every name being named not only in age
22 τούτῳ, ἀλλὰ καὶ ἐν τῷ μέλλοντι· καὶ πάντα ὑπέταξεν ὑπὸ
this, but also in the coming (age), and all things subjected under
τοὺς πόδας αὐτοῦ, καὶ αὐτὸν ἔδωκε κεφαλὴν ὑπὲρ πάντα τῇ
the feet of Him, and Him gave (to be) Head over all things to the
23 ἐκκλησίᾳ, ἥτις ἐστὶ τὸ σῶμα αὐτοῦ, τὸ πλήρωμα τοῦ πάντα
church, which is the body of Him, the fullness of the (One) all things
ἐν πᾶσι πληρουμένου.
with all things filling.

CHAPTER 2

1 Καὶ ὑμᾶς ὄντας νεκροὺς τοῖς παραπτώμασι καὶ ταῖς
And you being dead in the trespasses and in the

then walked according to the course of this world, according to the ruler of the authority of the air, the spirit now working in the sons of disobedience; [3]among whom we also conducted ourselves in times past in the lusts of our flesh, doing the things willed of the flesh and of the minds, and were by nature the children of wrath, even as the rest. [4]But God, being rich in mercy, because of His great love *with* which He loved us, [5]even we being dead in sins, *He* made us alive together with Christ—by grace you are being saved—[6]and raised *us* up together, and seated *us* together in the heavenlies in Christ Jesus, [7]that He might show in the coming ages the exceeding great riches of His grace in kindness toward us in Christ Jesus. [8]For by grace you are saved, through faith, and this not of yourselves; *it is* the gift of God; [9]not of works, that not anyone should boast; [10]for we are *His* workmanship, created in Christ Jesus unto good works, which God before prepared that we should walk in them.

[11]Therefore, remember that you, the nations, *were* then in *the* flesh, those having been called Uncircumcision by those having been called Circumcision in *the* flesh made by hand, [12]that at that time you were without Christ, alienated from the commonwealth of Israel, and strangers of the covenants of promise, having no hope, and without God in the world. [13]But now in Christ Jesus you who then were afar off became near by the blood of Christ. [14]For He is our peace, He making *us* both one, and breaking down the middle wall of partition, [15]annulling in His flesh the enmity, the Law of

2 ἁμαρτίαις, ἐν αἷς ποτὲ περιεπατήσατε κατὰ τὸν αἰῶνα τοῦ
sins, in which then you walked according to the age
κόσμου τούτου, κατὰ τὸν ἄρχοντα τῆς ἐξουσίας τοῦ ἀέρος,
world of this, according to the ruler of the authority of the air,
τοῦ πνεύματος τοῦ νῦν ἐνεργοῦντος ἐν τοῖς υἱοῖς τῆς ἀπει-
the spirit now working in the sons of dis-
3 θείας· ἐν οἷς καὶ ἡμεῖς παντες ἀνεστράφημέν ποτε ἐν ταῖς
obedience, among whom also we all conducted ourselves then in the
ἐπιθυμίαις τῆς σαρκὸς ἡμῶν, ποιοῦντες τὰ θελήματα τῆς
lusts of the flesh of us, doing the things willed of the
σαρκὸς καὶ τῶν διανοιῶν, καὶ ἥμεν τέκνα φύσει ὀργῆς, ὡς
flesh and of the understandings, and were children by nature of wrath, as
4 καὶ οἱ λοιποί·—ὁ δὲ Θεός, πλούσιος ὢν ἐν ἐλέει, διὰ τὴν
also the rest — but God rich being in mercy, because of the
5 πολλὴν ἀγάπην αὐτοῦ ἣν ἠγάπησεν ημᾶς, καὶ ὄντας ἡμᾶς
much love of Him (with) which He loved us, even being us
νεκροὺς τοῖς παραπτώμασι συνεζωοποίησε τῷ Χριστῷ
dead in trespasses (He) made us alive with Christ;
6 (χάριτί ἐστε σεσωσμένοι), καὶ συνήγειρε, καὶ συνεκάθισεν
by grace you are being saved; and raised (us) with, and seated (us) with
7 ἐν τοῖς ἐπουρανίοις ἐν Χριστῷ Ἰησοῦ· ἵνα ἐνδείξηται ἐν τοῖς
in the heavenlies in Christ Jesus, that He might show in the
αἰῶσι τοῖς ἐπερχομένοις τὸ ὑπερβάλλοντα πλοῦτον τῆς
ages coming on the surpassing riches of the
χάριτος αὐτοῦ ἐν χρηστότητι ἐφ' ἡμᾶς ἐν Χριστῷ Ἰησοῦ·
grace of Him in kindness toward us in Christ Jesus.
8 τῇ γὰρ χάριτι ἐστε σεσωσμένοι διὰ τῆς πίστεως, καὶ τοῦτο
For by grace you are saved, through faith, and this
9 οὐκ ἐξ ὑμῶν· Θεοῦ τὸ δῶρον· οὐκ ἐξ ἔργων, ἵνα μή τις
not of you, of God (is) the gift; not of works, lest anyone
10 καυχήσηται αὐτοῦ γάρ εσμεν ποίημα, κτισθέντες ἐν Χριστῷ
should boast. of Him For we are (His) doing, created in Christ
Ἰησοῦ ἐπὶ ἔργοις ἀγαθοῖς, οις προητοίμασεν ὁ Θεος, ἵνα
Jesus unto works good, which before prepared God that
ἐν αὐτοῖς περιπατήσωμεν.
in them we should walk

11 Διὸ μνημονεύετε, ὅτι ὑμεῖς ποτὲ τὰ ἔθνη ἐν σαρκί, οἱ
Therefore remember that you then the nations in (the) flesh, those
λεγόμενοι ἀκροβυστία ὑπὸ τῆς λεγομένης περιτομῆς ἐν
being called uncircumcision by those being called circumcision in
12 σαρκὶ χειροποιήτου, ὅτι ἦτε ἐν τῷ καιρῷ ἐκείνῳ χωρὶς
(the) flesh made by hand, that you were at time that without
Χριστοῦ, ἀπηλλοτριωμένοι τῆς πολιτείας τοῦ Ἰσραήλ, καὶ
Christ, having been alienated from the commonwealth of Israel, and
ξένοι τῶν διαθηκῶν τῆς ἐπαγγελίας, ἐλπίδα μὴ ἔχοντες,
strangers of the covenants of promise, hope not having,
13 καὶ ἄθεοι ἐν τῷ κόσμῳ. νυνὶ δὲ ἐν Χριστῷ Ἰησοῦ ὑμεῖς οἱ
and godless in the world. now But in Christ Jesus you, those
ποτὲ ὄντες μακρὰν ἐγγὺς ἐγενήθητε ἐν τῷ αἵματι τοῦ
then being afar off, near became by the blood
14 Χριστοῦ. αὐτὸς γάρ ἐστιν ἡ εἰρήνη ἡμῶν, ὁ ποιήσας τὰ
of Christ. He For is the peace of us, the (One) making
15 ἀμφότερα ἕν, καὶ τὸ μεσότοιχον τοῦ φραγμοῦ λύσας, τὴν
both one, and the middle wall of partition having broken, the
ἔχθραν ἐν τῇ σαρκὶ αὐτοῦ, τὸν νόμον τῶν ἐντολῶν ἐν
enmity in the flesh of Him, the law of the commandments in

the commandments in decrees, that He might in Himself create the two into one new man, making peace; 16 and might reconcile both in one body to God through the cross, slaying the enmity in Himself. 17 And coming, *He* preached peace to you, the ones afar off, and to the ones near. 18 For through Him we both have access by one Spirit to the Father. 19 So, then, you are no longer strangers and tenants, but *you are* fellow-citizens of the saints and *of the* household of God, 20 being built up on the foundation of the apostles and prophets, Jesus Christ Himself being *the* cornerstone; 21 in whom all the building fitted together grows into a holy temple in *the* Lord; 22 also in whom you are being built together into a dwelling-place of God in *the* Spirit.

CHAPTER 3

1 For this reason I, Paul, the prisoner of Christ Jesus on behalf of you, the nations, 2 if, indeed, you heard of the stewardship of the grace of God given to me for you, 3 that by revelation He revealed to me the mystery, as I wrote before in brief, 4 by the reading of which you are able to realize my understandinging in the mystery of Christ; 5 which was not made known to the sons of men in other generations, as it now has been revealed to His holy apostles and prophets in *the* Spirit, 6 *for* the nations to be joint-heirs, and of the same body and sharers of His promise in Christ, through the gospel; 7 of which I was made a minister, according to the gift of the grace of God given to me, according to the working of His power.
8 This grace was given to me, the least of all the saints, to preach the gospel of the

δόγμασι, καταργήσας· ἵνα τοὺς δύο κτίσῃ ἐν ἑαυτῷ εἰς ἕνα
decrees, having abolished, that the two He create in Himself into one
16 καινὸν ἄνθρωπον, ποιῶν εἰρήνην, καὶ ἀποκαταλλάξῃ τοὺς
new man, making peace, and might reconcile
ἀμφοτέρους ἐν ἑνὶ σώματι τῷ Θεῷ διὰ τοῦ σταυροῦ,
both in one body to God through the cross
17 ἀποκτείνας τὴν ἔχθραν ἐν αὐτῷ· καὶ ἐλθὼν εὐηγγελίσατο
slaying the enmity in Himself, and coming preached
18 εἰρήνην ὑμῖν τοῖς μακρὰν καὶ τοῖς ἐγγύς· ὅτι δι' αὐτοῦ
peace to you, those afar off, and to the (ones) near, for through Him
ἔχομεν τὴν προσαγωγὴν οἱ ἀμφότεροι ἐν ἑνὶ Πνεύματι πρὸς
we have access both by one Spirit unto
19 τὸν πατέρα. ἄρα οὖν οὐκέτι ἐστὲ ξένοι καὶ πάροικοι, ἀλλὰ
the Father. Then therefore no more are you strangers and sojourners, but
20 συμπολῖται τῶν ἁγίων καὶ οἰκεῖοι τοῦ Θεοῦ, ἐποικοδομη-
fellow-citizens of the saints and (of the) household of God, having been
θέντες ἐπὶ τῷ θεμελίῳ τῶν ἀποστόλων καὶ προφητῶν, ὄντος
built on the foundation of the apostles and prophets, being
21 ἀκρογωνιαίου αὐτοῦ Ἰησοῦ Χριστοῦ, ἐν ᾧ πᾶσα ἡ οἰκοδομὴ
(the) cornerstone (Him)self Jesus Christ, in whom all the building
22 συναρμολογουμένη αὔξει εἰς ναὸν ἅγιον ἐν Κυρίῳ, ἐν ᾧ καὶ
fitted together grows into a temple holy in (the) Lord, in whom also
ὑμεῖς συνοικοδομεῖσθε εἰς κατοικητήριον τοῦ Θεοῦ ἐν
you are being built together into a dwelling-place of God in
Πνεύματι.
(the) Spirit.

CHAPTER 3

1 Τούτου χάριν ἐγὼ Παῦλος ὁ δέσμιος τοῦ Χριστοῦ Ἰησοῦ
of this By reason I, Paul, the prisoner of Christ Jesus
2 ὑπὲρ ὑμῶν τῶν ἐθνῶν,—εἴγε ἠκούσατε τὴν οἰκονομίαν τῆς
on behalf of you the nations — if indeed you heard the stewardship of the
3 χάριτος τοῦ Θεοῦ τῆς δοθείσης μοι εἰς ὑμᾶς, ὅτι κατὰ
grace of God given to me for you, that by way of
ἀποκάλυψιν ἐγνώρισέ μοι τὸ μυστήριον, καθὼς προέγραψα
revelation was made known to me the mystery, as I wrote before
4 ἐν ὀλίγῳ, πρὸς ὃ δύνασθε ἀναγινώσκοντες νοῆσαι τὴν
in brief, as to which you are able reading to realize the
5 σύνεσίν μου ἐν τῷ μυστηρίῳ τοῦ Χριστοῦ· ὃ ἐν ἑτέραις
understanding of me in the mystery of Christ, which in other
γενεαῖς οὐκ ἐγνωρίσθη τοῖς υἱοῖς τῶν ἀνθρώπων, ὡς νῦν
generations not was made known to the sons of men as now
ἀπεκαλύφθη τοῖς ἁγίοις ἀποστόλοις αὐτοῦ καὶ προφήταις
it was revealed to the holy apostles of Him and prophets
6 ἐν Πνεύματι· εἶναι τὰ ἔθνη συγκληρονόμα καὶ σύσσωμα καὶ
in (the) Spirit to be the nations joint-heirs and a joint-body and
συμμέτοχα τῆς ἐπαγγελίας αὐτοῦ ἐν τῷ Χριστῷ, διὰ τοῦ
joint-sharers of the promise of Him in Christ, through the
7 εὐαγγελίου, οὗ ἐγενόμην διάκονος κατὰ τὴν δωρεὰν τῆς
gospel, of which I became a minister according to the gift of the
χάριτος τοῦ Θεοῦ, τὴν δοθεῖσάν μοι κατὰ τὴν ἐνέργειαν τῆς
grace of God, given to me according to the working of the
8 δυνάμεως αὐτοῦ. ἐμοὶ τῷ ἐλαχιστοτέρῳ πάντων τῶν
power of Him. To me, the least of all the
ἁγίων ἐδόθη ἡ χάρις αὕτη, ἐν τοῖς ἔθνεσιν εὐαγγελίσασθαι
saints, was given grace this, in the nations to preach

unsearchable riches of Christ among the nations, [9]and to bring to light what *is* the fellowship of the mystery having been hidden from eternity in God, the *One* creating all things through Jesus Christ, [10]so that now to the rulers and to the authorities in the heavenlies might be made known through the church the manifold wisdom of God, [11]according to the eternal purpose which He accomplished in Christ Jesus our Lord, [12]in whom we have boldness and access in confidence through His faith. [13]Therefore, I beg *you* not to faint at my troubles on your behalf, which is your glory.

[14]For this reason I bow my knees to the Father of our Lord Jesus Christ, [15]of whom every family in Heaven and on earth is named, [16]that He may give you according to the riches of His glory by *His* power to become mighty in the inward man through His Spirit, [17]that through faith Christ may dwell in your hearts, having been rooted and founded in love, [18]that you may be given strength to grasp, with all the saints, what *is* the breadth and length and depth and height, [19]and to know the love of Christ which surpasses knowledge, that you may be filled with all the fullness of God. [20]Now to Him being able to do exceedingly above all that we ask or think, according to the power working in us, [21]to Him *be* the glory in the church in Christ Jesus, to all the generations of the age forever. Amen.

9 τὸν ἀνεξιχνίαστον πλοῦτον τοῦ Χριστοῦ, καὶ φωτίσαι
the unsearchable riches of Christ, and to bring to light
πάντας τίς ἡ κοινωνία τοῦ μυστηρίου τοῦ ἀποκεκρυμμένου
all, what (is) the fellowship of the mystery having been hidden
ἀπὸ τῶν αἰώνων ἐν τῷ Θεῷ τῷ τὰ πάντα κτίσαντι διὰ
from the ages in God, the (One) all things having created via
10 Ἰησοῦ Χριστοῦ, ἵνα γνωρισθῇ νῦν ταῖς ἀρχαῖς καὶ ταῖς
Jesus Christ, that might be made known now to the rulers and to the
ἐξουσίαις ἐν τοῖς ἐπουρανίοις διὰ τῆς ἐκκλησίας ἡ πολυποί-
authorities in the heavenlies through the church the manifold
11 κιλος σοφία τοῦ Θεοῦ, κατὰ πρόθεσιν τῶν αἰώνων ἣν ἐποίη-
wisdom of God, according to the purpose of the ages which He
12 σεν ἐν Χριστῷ Ἰησοῦ τῷ Κυρίῳ ἡμῶν· ἐν ᾧ ἔχομεν τὴν
made in Christ Jesus the Lord of us, in whom we have
παρρησίαν καὶ τὴν προσαγωγὴν ἐν πεποιθήσει διὰ τῆς
boldness and access in confidence through the
13 πίστεως αὐτοῦ. διὸ αἰτοῦμαι μὴ ἐκκακεῖν ἐν ταῖς θλίψεσί μου
faith of Him. Therefore I ask (you) not to faint among the troubles of me
ὑπὲρ ὑμῶν, ἥτις ἐστὶ δόξα ὑμῶν.
on your behalf, which is glory of you.
14 Τούτου χάριν κάμπτω τὰ γόνατά μου πρὸς τὸν πατέρα
of this By reason I bow the knees of me to the Father
15 τοῦ Κυρίου ἡμῶν Ἰησοῦ Χριστοῦ, ἐξ οὗ πᾶσα πατριὰ ἐν οὐ-
of the Lord of us, Jesus Christ, of whom every family in
16 ρανοῖς καὶ ἐπὶ γῆς ὀνομάζεται, ἵνα δῴη ὑμῖν, κατὰ τὸν πλοῦ-
Heaven and on earth is named, that He may give you per the riches
τον τῆς δόξης αὐτοῦ, δυνάμει κραταιωθῆναι διὰ τοῦ Πνεύ-
of the glory of Him by power to become mighty through the
17 ματος αὐτοῦ εἰς τὸν ἔσω ἄνθρωπον, κατοικῆσαι τὸν Χριστὸν
Spirit of Him in the inward man, to dwell Christ
διὰ τῆς πίστεως ἐν ταῖς καρδίαις ὑμῶν· ἐν ἀγάπῃ ἐρριζω-
through faith in the hearts of you, in love having been
18 μένοι καὶ τεθεμελιωμένοι ἵνα ἐξισχύσητε καταλαβέσθαι σὺν
rooted and having been founded, that you be strengthened to grasp with
πᾶσι τοῖς ἁγίοις, τί τὸ πλάτος καὶ μῆκος καὶ βάθος καὶ ὕψος,
all the saints, what (is) the breadth and length and depth and height,
19 γνῶναί τε τὴν ὑπερβάλλουσαν τῆς γνώσεως ἀγάπην τοῦ
to know and the surpassing knowledge love
Χριστοῦ, ἵνα πληρωθῆτε εἰς πᾶν τὸ πλήρωμα τοῦ Θεοῦ.
of Christ, that you may be filled to all the fullness of God.
20 Τῷ δὲ δυναμένῳ ὑπὲρ πάντα ποιῆσαι ὑπὲρ ἐκ περισσοῦ
the (One) Now being able beyond all things to do exceedingly above
ὧν αἰτούμεθα ἢ νοοῦμεν, κατὰ τὴν δύναμιν τὴν ἐνεργου-
what we ask or think, according to the power working
21 μένην ἐν ἡμῖν, αὐτῷ ἡ δόξα ἐν τῇ ἐκκλησίᾳ ἐν Χριστῷ Ἰησοῦ
in us, to Him (be) the glory in the church in Christ Jesus
εἰς πάσας τὰς γενεὰς τοῦ αἰῶνος τῶν αἰώνων. ἀμήν.
to all the generations of the age of the ages. Amen.

CHAPTER 4

[1]Therefore, I exhort you, I the prisoner in *the* Lord, to walk worthily of the calling in which you were called, [2]with all humility and meekness, with long-suffering, bearing

1 Παρακαλῶ οὖν ὑμᾶς ἐγώ, ὁ δέσμιος ἐν Κυρίῳ, ἀξίως
exhort therefore you I, the prisoner in (the) Lord, worthily
2 περιπατῆσαι τῆς κλήσεως ἧς ἐκλήθητε, μετὰ πάσης ταπει-
to walk of the calling of which you were called, with all
νοφροσύνης καὶ πρᾳότητος, μετὰ μακροθυμίας, ἀνεχό-
humility, and meekness, with long-suffering, bearing

with one another in love; [3]being eager to keep the unity of the Spirit in the bond of peace. [4]*There is* one body and one Spirit, even as you also were called in one hope of your calling; [5]one Lord, one faith, one baptism, [6]one God and Father of all, He above all and through all and in you all. [7]But to each one of us was given grace according to the measure of the gift of Christ. [8]Therefore, He says, "Having gone up on high, He led captivity captive, and gave gifts to men." [9]But that He went up, what is it except that He also first came down into the lower parts of the earth? [10]He that came down is the same who also went up above all the heavens, that He might fill all things. [11]And He gave some *to be* apostles; some, prophets; some, evangelists; some, pastors, and teachers; [12]with a view to the perfecting of the saints, for the work of the ministry, for the building up of the body of Christ; [13]until we all may come to the unity of the faith and of the knowledge of the Son of God, to a full-grown man, to *the* measure of *the* stature of the fullness of Christ, [14]so that we may no longer be infants, having been blown and carried to and fro by every wind of doctrine, in the underhandedness of men, in craftiness with a view to the trickery of error, [15]but speaking the truth in love, we may grow up into Him in all things, who is the Head, the Christ; [16]from whom all the body having been fitted and compacted together through every assisting bond, according to *the* working of each part in *its* measure, producing the growth of the body to the building up of itself in love.

[17]Therefore, I say this, and testify in *the* Lord, that you no longer walk even as also

3 μενοι ἀλλήλων ἐν ἀγάπῃ, σπουδάζοντες τηρεῖν τὴν ἑνότητα
with one another in love, being eager to keep the unity
4 τοῦ Πνεύματος ἐν τῷ συνδέσμῳ τῆς εἰρήνης. ἓν σῶμα καὶ
of the Spirit in the bond of peace. One body and
ἓν Πνεῦμα, καθὼς καὶ ἐκλήθητε ἐν μιᾷ ἐλπίδι τῆς κλήσεως
one Spirit (is), as also you were called in one hope of the calling
5/6 ὑμῶν· εἷς Κύριος, μία πίστις, ἓν βάπτισμα, εἷς Θεὸς καὶ
of you, one Lord, one faith, one baptism, one God and
πατὴρ πάντων, ὁ ἐπὶ πάντων, καὶ διὰ πάντων, καὶ ἐν
Father of all, the (One) above all, and through all, and in
7 πᾶσιν ὑμῖν. ἑνὶ δὲ ἑκάστῳ ἡμῶν ἐδόθη ἡ χάρις κατὰ τὸ
all you. to one But each of us was given grace according to the
8 μέτρον τῆς δωρεᾶς τοῦ Χριστοῦ. διὸ λέγει, Ἀναβὰς εἰς
measure of the gift of Christ. Therefore He says, Having gone up on
ὕψος ᾐχμαλώτευσεν αἰχμαλωσίαν, καὶ ἔδωκε δόματα τοῖς
high, He led captive captivity, and gave gifts
9 ἀνθρώποις. (τὸ δέ, Ἀνέβη, τί ἐστιν εἰ μὴ ὅτι καὶ κατέβη
to men — the Now: He went up; what is it except that also He came down
10 πρῶτον εἰς τὰ κατώτερα μέρη τῆς γῆς; ὁ καταβάς, αὐτός
first into the lower parts of the earth? The (One) coming down
ἐστι καὶ ὁ ἀναβὰς ὑπεράνω πάντων τῶν οὐρανῶν, ἵνα
is also the (One) going up far above all the heavens, that
11 πληρώσῃ τὰ πάντα.) καὶ αὐτὸς ἔδωκε τοὺς μὲν ἀποστό-
He might fill all things — and He gave some apostles,
λους, τοὺς δὲ προφήτας, τοὺς δὲ εὐαγγελιστάς, τοὺς δὲ
some prophets, some evangelists, some
12 ποιμένας καὶ διδασκάλους, πρὸς τὸν καταρτισμὸν τῶν
pastors, and teachers, for the perfecting of the
ἁγίων, εἰς ἔργον διακονίας, εἰς οἰκοδομὴν τοῦ σώματος τοῦ
saints; for (the) work of ministry, to building of the body
13 Χριστοῦ· μέχρι καταντήσωμεν οἱ πάντες εἰς τὴν ἑνότητα
of Christ, until we may come all to the unity
τῆς πίστεως καὶ τῆς ἐπιγνώσεως τοῦ υἱοῦ τοῦ Θεοῦ, εἰς
of the faith and of the knowledge of the Son of God to
ἄνδρα τέλειον, εἰς μέτρον ἡλικίας τοῦ πληρώματος τοῦ
a man full-grown, to (the) measure of (the) stature of the fullness
14 Χριστοῦ· ἵνα μηκέτι ὦμεν νήπιοι, κλυδωνιζόμενοι καὶ
of Christ, that no longer we may be infants, being blown and
περιφερόμενοι παντὶ ἀνέμῳ τῆς διδασκαλίας, ἐν τῇ κυβείᾳ
being carried about by every wind of doctrine, in the sleight
τῶν ἀνθρώπων, ἐν πανουργίᾳ, πρὸς τὴν μεθοδείαν τῆς
of men, in craftiness to the trickery
15 πλάνης· ἀληθεύοντες δὲ ἐν ἀγάπῃ αὐξήσωμεν εἰς αὐτὸν τὰ
of error; speaking truth but in love, we may grow into Him in all
16 πάντα, ὅς ἐστιν ἡ κεφαλή, ὁ Χριστός, ἐξ οὗ πᾶν τὸ σῶμα
respects, who is the Head, Christ, of whom all the body
συναρμολογούμενον καὶ συμβιβαζόμενον διὰ πάσης ἁφῆς
being fitted together and being brought together through every band
τῆς ἐπιχορηγίας, κατ' ἐνέργειαν ἐν μέτρῳ ἑνὸς ἑκάστου
of assistance, according to (the) working in measure of one each
μέρους, τὴν αὔξησιν τοῦ σώματος ποιεῖται εἰς οἰκοδομὴν
part, the growth of the body producing, to the building up
ἑαυτοῦ ἐν ἀγάπῃ.
of itself in love.

17 Τοῦτο οὖν λέγω καὶ μαρτύρομαι ἐν Κυρίῳ, μηκέτι ὑμᾶς
this Therefore I say, and testify in (the) Lord, no longer you

the rest *of the* nations walk, in *the* vanity of their mind, 18 having been darkened in the understanding, being alienated *from* the life of God through the ignorance which is in them because of the hardness of their heart, 19 who having cast off all feeling gave themselves up to lust, for *the* working of all uncleanness with greediness. 20 But you have not so learned Christ, 21 if truly you heard Him, and were taught in Him, as *the* truth is in Jesus; 22 for you have put off the old man, as regards the former behavior, having been corrupted according to the deceitful lusts; 23 and to be renewed in the spirit of your mind; 24 and to have put on the new man *which* according to God was created in righteousness and true holiness. 25 Therefore, putting off the false, speak truth each with his neighbor, because we are members of one another. 26 Be angry, but do not sin; do not let the sun go down on your wrath, 27 nor give place to the Devil. 28 The *one* stealing, let him steal no more, but rather let him labor, working what *is* good with the hands, that he may have *something* to give to the *one* that has need. 29 Let not every filthy word go out of your mouth, but if anything, *for* good to building up in respect of need, that it may give grace to the ones hearing. 30 And do not grieve the Holy Spirit of God, by whom you were sealed to *the* day of redemption. 31 Let all bitterness, and anger, and wrath, and tumult, and evil speaking be put away from you, along with all evil things. 32 And be kind to one another, tenderhearted, having forgiven one another, even as also God forgave you in Christ.

περιπατεῖν, καθὼς καὶ τὰ λοιπὰ ἔθνη περιπατεῖ ἐν ματαιό-
walk even as also the rest (of the) nations walk, in vanity
18 τητι τοῦ νοὸς αὐτῶν, ἐσκοτισμένοι τῇ διανοίᾳ, ὄντες
of the mind of them, having been darkened in the intellect, being
ἀπηλλοτριωμένοι τῆς ζωῆς τοῦ Θεοῦ διὰ τὴν ἄγνοιαν τὴν
alienated (from) the life of God through the ignorance
οὖσαν ἐν αὐτοῖς, διὰ τὴν πώρωσιν τῆς καρδίας αὐτῶν·
being in them, on account of the hardness of the heart of them,
19 οἵτινες ἀπηλγηκότες ἑαυτοὺς παρέδωκαν τῇ ἀσελγείᾳ, εἰς
who having cast off all feeling themselves gave up to lust, to
20 ἐργασίαν ἀκαθαρσίας πάσης ἐν πλεονεξίᾳ. ὑμεῖς δὲ οὐχ
(the) working of uncleanness all with greediness. you But not
21 οὕτως ἐμάθετε τὸν Χριστόν, εἴγε αὐτὸν ἠκούσατε καὶ ἐν
so learned Christ, if indeed Him you heard and by
αὐτῷ ἐδιδάχθητε, καθώς ἐστιν ἀλήθεια ἐν τῷ Ἰησοῦ·
Him were taught, even as is (the) truth in Jesus,
22 ἀποθέσθαι ὑμᾶς, κατὰ τὴν προτέραν ἀναστροφήν, τὸν
to put off you, as regards the former behavior, of the
παλαιὸν ἄνθρωπον, τὸν φθειρόμενον κατὰ τὰς ἐπιθυμίας
old man, being corrupted according to the lusts
23 τῆς ἀπάτης· ἀνανεοῦσθαι δὲ τῷ πνεύματι τοῦ νοὸς ὑμῶν,
of deceit, to be renewed and in the spirit of the mind of you,
24 καὶ ἐνδύσασθαι τὸν καινὸν ἄνθρωπον, τὸν κατὰ Θεὸν κτι-
and to put on the new man according to God
σθέντα ἐν δικαιοσύνῃ καὶ ὁσιότητι τῆς ἀληθείας.
created in righteousness and holiness of truth.
25 Διὸ ἀποθέμενοι τὸ ψεῦδος λαλεῖτε ἀλήθειαν ἕκαστος μετὰ
Therefore putting off the false, speak truth each with
26 τοῦ πλησίον αὐτοῦ· ὅτι ἐσμὲν ἀλλήλων μέλη. ὀργίζεσθε καὶ
the neighbor of him, because we are one another's members. Be angry and
μὴ ἁμαρτάνετε· ὁ ἥλιος μὴ ἐπιδυέτω ἐπὶ τῷ παροργισμῷ
do not sin, the sun not let set on the provocation
27/ ὑμῶν· μήτε δίδοτε τόπον τῷ διαβόλῳ. ὁ κλέπτων μηκέτι
28 **of you; nor give place to the Devil. The (one) stealing, no more**
κλεπτέτω· μᾶλλον δὲ κοπιάτω, ἐργαζόμενος τὸ ἀγαθὸν ταῖς
let him steal, rather but let him labor, working the good with the
29 χερσίν, ἵνα ἔχῃ μεταδιδόναι τῷ χρείαν ἔχοντι. πᾶς λόγος
hands, that he may have to give to the (one) need having. Every word
σαπρὸς ἐκ τοῦ στόματος ὑμῶν μὴ ἐκπορευέσθω, ἀλλ' εἴ τις
corrupt out of the mouth of you not let go, but if any
ἀγαθὸς πρὸς οἰκοδομὴν τῆς χρείας, ἵνα δῷ χάριν τοῖς ἀκού-
(is) good to building up the need, that it may give grace to those
30 ουσι. καὶ μὴ λυπεῖτε τὸ Πνεῦμα τὸ Ἅγιον τοῦ Θεοῦ, ἐν ᾧ
hearing. And do not grieve the Spirit Holy of God, by whom
31 ἐσφραγίσθητε εἰς ἡμέραν ἀπολυτρώσεως. πᾶσα πικρία καὶ
you were sealed for a day of redemption. All bitterness and
θυμὸς καὶ ὀργὴ καὶ κραυγὴ καὶ βλασφημία ἀρθήτω ἀφ' ὑμῶν,
anger and wrath and tumult and evil speaking put away from you,
32 σὺν πάσῃ κακίᾳ· γίνεσθε δὲ εἰς ἀλλήλους χρηστοί, εὔσπλαγ-
with all evil things. be And to one another kind, tender-
χνοι, χαριζόμενοι ἑαυτοῖς, καθὼς καὶ ὁ Θεὸς ἐν Χριστῷ ἐχαρί-
hearted, forgiving yourselves, as also God in Christ
σατο ὑμῖν.
forgave you.

CHAPTER 5

[1]Then be imitators of God, as beloved children, [2]and walk in love, even as Christ also loved us, and gave Himself for us, an offering and a sacrifice to God for an odor of a sweet smell.

[3]But let not be named among you fornication, and all uncleanness, or greediness, as is fitting for saints; [4]also filthiness, and foolish talking, or joking—these things are not becoming—but rather thanksgiving. [5]For be knowing this, that every fornicator, or unclean one, or covetous *one,* who is an idolater, has no inheritance in the kingdom of Christ and of God. [6]Let no one deceive you with empty words, for through these the wrath of God comes on the sons of disobedience. [7]Then do not be partners with them; [8]for you then were darkness, but now light in *the* Lord—walk as children of light. [9]For the fruit of the Spirit *is* in all goodness and righteousness and truth, [10]proving what is well-pleasing to the Lord. [11]And have no fellowship with the unfruitful works of darkness, but rather even reprove *them.* [12]For it is shameful even to speak of the things being done by them in secret. [13]But all things being exposed by the light are clearly revealed, for everything having been revealed *is* light. [14]Therefore, He says, "Arise, sleeping one, and stand up from the dead ones, and Christ will shine on you."

[15]Then watch how carefully you walk, not as unwise, but as wise ones, [16]redeeming the time, because the days are evil. [17]For this reason, do not be foolish, but understanding what the will of the Lord *is.* [18]And do not be drunk with wine, in which is debauchery, but be filled by *the* Spirit, [19]speaking to yourselves in psalms and hymns and spiritual songs,

CHAPTER 5

1 Γίνεσθε οὖν μιμηταὶ τοῦ Θεοῦ, ὡς τέκνα ἀγαπητά καὶ
be. Then imitators of God, as children beloved, and
2 περιπατεῖτε ἐν ἀγάπῃ, καθὼς καὶ ὁ Χριστὸς ἠγάπησεν ἡμᾶς,
walk in love, even as also Christ loved us
καὶ παρέδωκεν ἑαυτὸν ὑπὲρ ἡμῶν προσφορὰν καὶ θυσίαν
and gave up Himself for us an offering and a sacrifice
3 τῷ Θεῷ εἰς ὀσμὴν εὐωδίας. πορνεία δὲ καὶ πᾶσα ἀκαθαρσία
to God for an odor of sweet smell. fornication But and all uncleanness
ἢ πλεονεξία μηδὲ ὀνομαζέσθω ἐν ὑμῖν, καθὼς πρέπει ἁγίοις·
or greediness not let it be named among you, as is fitting for saints,
4 καὶ αἰσχρότης, καὶ μωρολογία ἢ εὐτραπελία, τὰ οὐκ ἀνή-
and filthiness, and foolish talking or joking, the things not be-
5 κοντα· ἀλλὰ μᾶλλον εὐχαριστία. τοῦτο γάρ ἐστε γινώ-
coming, but rather thanksgiving. this For be
σκοντες, ὅτι πᾶς πόρνος, ἢ ἀκάθαρτος, ἢ πλεονέκτης, ὅς ἐστιν
knowing, that every fornicator; or unclean one; or greedy, who is
εἰδωλολάτρης, οὐκ ἔχει κληρονομίαν ἐν τῇ βασιλείᾳ τοῦ
an idolater; not has inheritance in the kingdom
6 Χριστοῦ καὶ Θεοῦ. μηδεὶς ὑμᾶς ἀπατάτω κενοῖς λόγοις·
of Christ and of God. Let no one you deceive with empty words;
διὰ ταῦτα γὰρ ἔρχεται ἡ ὀργὴ τοῦ Θεοῦ ἐπὶ τοὺς υἱοὺς
through these for comes the wrath of God on the sons
7/8 τῆς ἀπειθείας. μὴ οὖν γίνεσθε συμμέτοχοι αὐτῶν· ἦτε γάρ
of disobedience. not Then be partners with them; you were for
ποτε σκότος, νῦν δὲ φῶς ἐν Κυρίῳ· ὡς τέκνα φωτὸς περι-
then darkness, now and light in (the) Lord, as children of light walk,
9 πατεῖτε (ὁ γὰρ καρπὸς τοῦ Πνεύματος ἐν πάσῃ ἀγαθωσύνῃ
—the for fruit of the Spirit (is) in all goodness
10 καὶ δικαιοσύνῃ καὶ ἀληθείᾳ), δοκιμάζοντες τί ἐστιν εὐάρε-
and righteousness and truth — proving what is well-
11 στον τῷ Κυρίῳ· καὶ μὴ συγκοινωνεῖτε τοῖς ἔργοις τοῖς
pleasing to the Lord; and do not have fellowship with the works
12 ἀκάρποις τοῦ σκότους, μᾶλλον δὲ καὶ ἐλέγχετε· τὰ γὰρ
unfruitful of darkness, rather but even reprove; the for
13 κρυφῇ γινόμενα ὑπ' αὐτῶν αἰσχρόν ἐστι καὶ λέγειν. τὰ δὲ
hidden things being done by them shameful it is even to speak; but
πάντα ἐλεγχόμενα ὑπὸ τοῦ φωτὸς φανεροῦται· πᾶν γὰρ
all things being reproved by the light is revealed; everything for
14 τὸ φανερούμενον φῶς ἐστί. διὸ λέγει, Ἔγειραι ὁ καθεύδων
being revealed light is. Therefore He says: Arise sleeping one
καὶ ἀνάστα ἐκ τῶν νεκρῶν, καὶ ἐπιφαύσει σοι ὁ Χριστός.
and stand up from the dead ones, and will shine on you Christ.
15 Βλέπετε οὖν πῶς ἀκριβῶς περιπατεῖτε, μὴ ὡς ἄσοφοι,
See, therefore, how carefully you walk, not as unwise,
16 ἀλλ' ὡς σοφοί, ἐξαγοραζόμενοι τὸν καιρόν, ὅτι αἱ ἡμέραι
but as wise ones, redeeming the time, because the days
17 πονηραί εἰσι. διὰ τοῦτο μὴ γίνεσθε ἄφρονες, ἀλλὰ συνιέντες
evil are. Because of this, do not be foolish, but understanding
18 τί τὸ θέλημα τοῦ Κυρίου. καὶ μὴ μεθύσκεσθε οἴνῳ, ἐν ᾧ
what the will of the Lord (Is). And do not be drunk with wine, in which
19 ἐστὶν ἀσωτία, ἀλλὰ πληροῦσθε ἐν Πνεύματι, λαλοῦντες
is debauchery, but be filled by (the) Spirit, speaking
ἑαυτοῖς ψαλμοῖς καὶ ὕμνοις καὶ ᾠδαῖς πνευματικαῖς, ᾄδοντες
to yourselves in psalms and hymns and songs spiritual, singing

singing and praising in your heart to the Lord, 20 giving thanks at all times for all things in the name of our Lord Jesus Christ, even to God *the* Father, 21 having been subject to one another in *the* fear of God.

22 Wives, subject yourselves to *your* own husbands, as to the Lord; 23 because a husband is head of the wife, as also Christ *is* Head of the church, and He is Savior of the body. 24 But even as the church is subject to Christ, so also the wives to their own husbands in everything.

25 Husbands, love your wives, even as Christ also loved the church and gave Himself up on its behalf, 26 that He might sanctify it, cleansing *it* by the washing of the water in *the* word, 27 that He might present it to Himself *as* the glorious church, not having spot or wrinkle, or any such things; but that it be holy and without blemish. 28 So, husbands ought to love their wives as their *own* bodies—he loving his wife loves himself— 29 for then no one hated his *own* flesh, but nourishes and cherishes it, even as also the Lord the church. 30 For we are members of His body, of His flesh, and of His bones. 31 "For this a man shall leave his father and mother, and shall be joined to his wife; and the two shall be one flesh." 32 The mystery is great, but I speak as to Christ and as to the church. 33 However, you also, everyone, let each love his wife as himself, and the wife, that she fears the husband.

CHAPTER 6

1 Children, obey your parents in *the* Lord, for this is

20 καὶ ψάλλοντες ἐν τῇ καρδίᾳ ὑμῶν τῷ Κυρίῳ, εὐχαριστοῦντες
and psalming in the heart of you to the Lord, giving thanks
πάντοτε ὑπὲρ πάντων ἐν ὀνόματι τοῦ Κυρίου ἡμῶν Ἰησοῦ
always for all things in the name of the Lord of us, Jesus
21 Χριστοῦ τῷ Θεῷ καὶ πατρί, ὑποτασσόμενοι ἀλλήλοις ἐν
Christ, to God, even (the) Father, being subject to one another in
φόβῳ Θεοῦ.
(the) fear of God.
22 Αἱ γυναῖκες, τοῖς ἰδίοις ἀνδράσιν ὑποτάσσεσθε, ὡς τῷ
The wives to the own husbands subject yourselves, as to the
23 Κυρίῳ. ὅτι ὁ ἀνήρ ἐστι κεφαλὴ τῆς γυναικός, ὡς καὶ ὁ
Lord, because a man is head of the woman, as also the
Χριστὸς κεφαλὴ τῆς ἐκκλησίας, καὶ αὐτός ἐστι σωτὴρ τοῦ
Christ (is) Head of the church, and He is Savior of the
24 σώματος. ἀλλ' ὥσπερ ἡ ἐκκλησία ὑποτάσσεται τῷ Χριστῷ,
body. But as the church is subject to Christ,
25 οὕτω καὶ αἱ γυναῖκες τοῖς ἰδίοις ἀνδράσιν ἐν παντί. οἱ
so also the wives to the own husbands in everything. The
ἄνδρες, ἀγαπᾶτε τὰς γυναῖκας ἑαυτῶν, καθὼς καὶ ὁ Χριστὸς
husbands, love the wives (of) yourselves, even as also Christ
ἠγάπησε τὴν ἐκκλησίαν, καὶ ἑαυτὸν παρέδωκεν ὑπὲρ αὐτῆς·
loved the church, and Himself gave up on behalf of it,
26 ἵνα αὐτὴν ἁγιάσῃ, καθαρίσας τῷ λουτρῷ τοῦ ὕδατος ἐν
that it He might sanctify, cleansing by the washing of the water by
27 ῥήματι, ἵνα παραστήσῃ αὐτὴν ἑαυτῷ ἔνδοξον τὴν ἐκκλη-
(the) word, that might present it to Himself glorious the church,
σίαν, μὴ ἔχουσαν σπῖλον ἢ ῥυτίδα ἤ τι τῶν τοιούτων, ἀλλ'
not having spot or wrinkle or any of the such things, but
28 ἵνα ᾖ ἁγία καὶ ἄμωμος. οὕτως ὀφείλουσιν οἱ ἄνδρες ἀγαπᾷν
that it be holy and unblemished. So ought the husbands to love
τὰς ἑαυτῶν γυναῖκας ὡς τὰ ἑαυτῶν σώματα. ὁ ἀγαπῶν τὴν
the of themselves wives as the of themselves bodies. The (one) loving the
29 ἑαυτοῦ γυναῖκα ἑαυτὸν ἀγαπᾷ· οὐδεὶς γάρ ποτε τὴν ἑαυτοῦ
of himself wife himself loves; no one for then the of himself
σάρκα ἐμίσησεν, ἀλλ' ἐκτρέφει καὶ θάλπει αὐτήν, καθὼς καὶ
flesh hated, but nourishes and cherishes it, even as also
30 ὁ Κύριος τὴν ἐκκλησίαν· ὅτι μέλη ἐσμὲν τοῦ σώματος αὐτοῦ,
the Lord the church, because members we are of the body of Him,
31 ἐκ τῆς σαρκὸς αὐτοῦ καὶ ἐκ τῶν ὀστέων αὐτοῦ. Ἀντὶ τοῦ-
of the flesh of Him and of the bones of Him. For this
του καταλείψει ἄνθρωπος τὸν πατέρα αὐτοῦ καὶ τὴν
shall leave a man the father of him and the
μητέρα, καὶ προσκολληθήσεται πρὸς τὴν γυναῖκα αὐτοῦ,
mother and shall cleave to the wife of him,
32 καὶ ἔσονται οἱ δύο εἰς σάρκα μίαν. τὸ μυστήριον τοῦτο μέγα
and shall be the two for flesh one. mystery This great
33 ἐστίν· ἐγὼ δὲ λέγω εἰς Χριστόν, καὶ εἰς τὴν ἐκκλησίαν. πλὴν
is, I but say as to Christ and as to the church. But
καὶ ὑμεῖς οἱ καθ' ἕνα, ἕκαστος τὴν ἑαυτοῦ γυναῖκα οὕτως
also you one by one, each the of himself wife, so
ἀγαπάτω ὡς ἑαυτόν· ἡ δὲ γυνὴ ἵνα φοβῆται τὸν ἄνδρα.
let him love as himself, the and wife that she fears the husband.

CHAPTER 6

1 Τὰ τέκνα, ὑπακούετε τοῖς γονεῦσιν ὑμῶν ἐν Κυρίῳ· τοῦτο
The children: obey the parents of you in (the) Lord, this

right. [2]Honor your father and mother, which is *the* first commandment with a promise, [3]that it may be well with you, and you may be long-lived on the earth. [4]And fathers, do not provoke your children, but bring them up in *the* discipline and admonition of *the* Lord.

[5]Slaves, obey *your* lords according to flesh, with fear and trembling, in singleness of your heart, as to Christ; [6]not with eye-service as men-pleasers, but as slaves of Christ doing the will of God from *the* soul, [7]serving as slaves with good will to the Lord, and not *as to* men; [8]each one knowing that whatever good thing he has done, this he shall receive from the Lord, whether a slave, or a freeman. [9]And lords, do the same things toward them, forbearing the threatening, knowing that the Lord of both of you is in Heaven, and there is no respect of persons with Him. [10]For the rest, my brothers, be made powerful in *the* Lord, and in the might of His strength. [11]Put on all the armor of God, for you to be able to stand against the wiles of the Devil; [12]because we are not wrestling against flesh and blood, but against the rulers, against the authorities, against the rulers of this world, of the darkness of this age, against the spiritual *powers* of evil in the heavenlies. [13]Because of this, take up all of the armor of God, that you may be able to resist in the evil day, and having worked out all things, to stand. [14]Therefore, stand firm, having girded your loins about with truth, and having put on the breastplate of righteousness, [15]and having shod the feet with *the* preparation of the gospel of peace; [16]above all, taking up the shield of faith, with which

2 γάρ ἐστι δίκαιον. Τιμα τὸν πατέρα σου καὶ τὴν μητέρα
for is right. Honor the father of you and the mother
3 (ἥτις ἐστὶν ἐντολὴ πρώτη ἐν ἐπαγγελίᾳ), ἵνα εὖ σοι
—which is commandment (the) first with a promise — that well with you
4 γένηται, καὶ ἔσῃ μακροχρόνιος ἐπὶ τῆς γῆς. καὶ οἱ πατέρες,
I may be, and you may be long-lived on the earth. And the fathers:
μὴ παροργίζετε τὰ τέκνα ὑμῶν, ἀλλ᾽ ἐκτρέφετε αὐτὰ ἐν
do not provoke the children of you, but nurture them in
παιδείᾳ καὶ νουθεσίᾳ Κυρίου.
(the) discipline and admonition of (the) Lord.
5 Οἱ δοῦλοι, ὑπακούετε τοῖς κυρίοις κατὰ σάρκα μετὰ φόβου
The slaves: obey the lords according to flesh with fear
καὶ τρόμου, ἐν ἁπλότητι τῆς καρδίας ὑμῶν, ὡς τῷ Χριστῷ·
and trembling, in singleness of the heart of you, as to Christ
6 μὴ κατ᾽ ὀφθαλμοδουλείαν ὡς ἀνθρωπάρεσκοι, ἀλλ᾽ ὡς δοῦλοι
not by way of eye-service as men-pleasers, but as slaves
7 τοῦ Χριστοῦ, ποιοῦντες το θέλημα τοῦ Θεοῦ ἐκ ψυχῆς, μετ᾽
of Christ doing the will of God from (the) soul, with
εὐνοίας δουλεύοντες ὡς τῷ Κυρίῳ καὶ οὐκ ἀνθρώποις·
goodwill serving as slaves as to the Lord and not (as to) men,
8 εἰδότες ὅτι ὃ ἐάν τι ἕκαστος ποιήσῃ ἀγαθόν, τοῦτο κομιεῖται
knowing that whatever each one he does good thing, this he will get
9 παρὰ τοῦ Κυρίου, εἴτε δοῦλος, εἴτε ἐλεύθερος. καὶ οἱ κύριοι,
from the Lord, whether a slave, or a freeman. And the lords:
τὰ αὐτὰ ποιεῖτε πρὸς αὐτούς, ἀνιέντες τὴν ἀπειλήν· εἰδότες
The same things do toward them, forbearing the threatening, knowing
ὅτι καὶ ὑμῶν αὐτῶν ὁ Κύριός ἐστιν ἐν οὐρανοῖς, καὶ προσω-
that also of you of them the Lord is in Heaven, and respect
ποληψία οὐκ ἔστι παρ᾽ αὐτῷ.
of persons not is with Him.
10 Τὸ λοιπόν, ἀδελφοί μου, ἐνδυναμοῦσθε ἐν Κυρίῳ, καὶ ἐν
For the rest, brothers of me, be empowered in (the) Lord, and in
11 τῷ κράτει τῆς ἰσχύος αὐτοῦ. ἐνδύσασθε τὴν πανοπλίαν τοῦ
the might of the strength of Him. Put on the whole armor
Θεοῦ, πρὸς τὸ δύνασθαι ὑμᾶς στῆναι πρὸς τὰς μεθοδείας τοῦ
of God, for to be able you to stand against the wiles of the
12 διαβόλου. ὅτι οὐκ ἔστιν ἡμῖν ἡ πάλη πρὸς αἷμα καὶ σάρκα,
Devil. Because not is to us wrestling against blood and flesh,
ἀλλὰ πρὸς τὰς ἀρχάς, πρὸς τὰς ἐξουσίας, πρὸς τοὺς κο-
but against the rulers, against the authorities, against the
σμοκράτορας τοῦ σκότους τοῦ αἰῶνος τούτου, πρὸς τὰ
world's rulers of the darkness age of this, against the
13 πνευματικὰ τῆς πονηρίας ἐν τοῖς ἐπουρανίοις. διὰ τοῦτο
spiritual (powers) of evil in the heavenlies. Because of this
ἀναλάβετε τὴν πανοπλίαν τοῦ Θεοῦ, ἵνα δυνηθῆτε ἀντιστῆ-
take up the whole armor of God, that you be able to resist
ναι ἐν τῇ ἡμέρᾳ τῇ πονηρᾷ, καὶ ἅπαντα κατεργασάμενοι
in the day evil, and all things having worked out
14 στῆναι. στῆτε οὖν περιζωσάμενοι τὴν ὀσφὺν ὑμῶν ἐν
to stand. Stand, therefore, having girded about the loins of you with
15 ἀληθείᾳ, καὶ ἐνδυσάμενοι τὸν θώρακα τῆς δικαιοσύνης, καὶ
truth, and putting on the breastplace of righteousness, and
ὑποδησάμενοι τοὺς πόδας ἐν ἑτοιμασίᾳ τοῦ εὐαγγελίου τῆς
having shod the feet with (the) preparation of the gospel
16 εἰρήνης· ἐπὶ πᾶσιν ἀναλαβόντες τὸν θυρεὸν τῆς πίστεως,
of peace; above all, having taken up the shield of faith,

you will be able to quench all the darts of the evil one, the things having been made fiery. [17] Also, take the helmet of salvation, and the sword of the Spirit, which is the word of God; [18] through all prayer and petition, praying at every time in *the* Spirit, and watching to this same thing with all perseverance and petition concerning all the saints. [19] *Pray* also for me, that to me may be given speech in *the* opening of my mouth with boldness to make known the mystery of the gospel, [20] for which I am an ambassador in a chain, that in it I may speak boldly as it is right for me to speak.

[21] But that you also may know the things about me, what I am doing, Tychichus the beloved brother and fellow-servant will make known all things to you, [22] whom I sent to you for this same thing, that you might know the things about us, and *he* may comfort your hearts.

[23] Peace and love to the brothers, with faith from God *the* Father and *the* Lord Jesus Christ. [24] Grace *be* with all those that love our Lord Jesus Christ in incorruptibility.

ἐν ᾧ δυνήσεσθε πάντα τὰ βέλη τοῦ πονηροῦ τὰ πεπυρωμένα
by which you will be able all the darts of the evil one having been made fiery

17 σβέσαι. καὶ τὴν περικεφαλαίαν τοῦ σωτηρίου δέξασθε, καὶ
to quench. And the helmet of salvation take, and

18 τὴν μάχαιραν τοῦ Πνεύματος, ὅ ἐστι ῥῆμα Θεοῦ· διὰ πάσης
the sword of the Spirit, which is (the) word of God via all

προσευχῆς καὶ δεήσεως προσευχόμενοι ἐν παντὶ καιρῷ ἐν
prayer and petition, praying at every time in

Πνεύματι, καὶ εἰς αὐτὸ τοῦτο ἀγρυπνοῦντες ἐν πάσῃ
(the) Spirit, and to same thing this watching in all

19 προσκαρτερήσει καὶ δεήσει περὶ πάντων τῶν ἁγίων, καὶ
perseverance and petition concerning all the saints, and

ὑπὲρ ἐμοῦ, ἵνα μοι δοθείη λόγος ἐν ἀνοίξει τοῦ στόματός
for me, that to me may be given speech in opening of the mouth

μου ἐν παρρησίᾳ, γνωρίσαι τὸ μυστήριον τοῦ εὐαγγελίου,
of me in boldness, to make known the mystery of the gospel,

20 ὑπὲρ οὗ πρεσβεύω ἐν ἁλύσει, ἵνα ἐν αὐτῷ παρρησιάσωμαι,
for which I am an ambassador in a chain, that in it I may speak boldly

ὡς δεῖ με λαλῆσαι.
as it behoves me to speak.

21 Ἵνα δὲ εἰδῆτε καὶ ὑμεῖς τὰ κατ' ἐμέ, τί πράσσω, πάντα
that Now may know also you the things about me, what I am doing, all things

ὑμῖν γνωρίσει Τυχικὸς ὁ ἀγαπητὸς ἀδελφὸς καὶ πιστὸς
to you will make known Tychicus the beloved brother and faithful

22 διάκονος ἐν Κυρίῳ· ὃν ἔπεμψα πρὸς ὑμᾶς εἰς αὐτὸ τοῦτο,
minister in (the) Lord whom I sent to you for this same thing,

ἵνα γνῶτε τὰ περὶ ἡμῶν, καὶ παρακαλέσῃ τὰς καρδίας
that you may know the things about us, and may comfort the hearts

ὑμῶν.
of you.

23 Εἰρήνη τοῖς ἀδελφοῖς καὶ ἀγάπη μετὰ πίστεως ἀπὸ Θεοῦ
Peace to the brothers and love with faith from God

24 πατρὸς καὶ Κυρίου Ἰησοῦ Χριστοῦ. ἡ χάρις μετὰ πάντων
(the) Father and (the) Lord Jesus Christ. Grace (be) with all

τῶν ἀγαπώντων τὸν Κύριον ἡμῶν Ἰησοῦν Χριστὸν ἐν
those loving the Lord of us, Jesus Christ in

ἀφθαρσίᾳ.
incorruptibility.

ΠΑΥΛΟΥ ΤΟΥ ΑΠΟΣΤΟΛΟΥ
PAUL THE APOSTLE

Η ΠΡΟΣ
THE TO (THE)

ΦΙΛΙΠΠΗΣΙΟΥΣ ΕΠΙΣΤΟΛΗ
PHILIPPIANS EPISTLE

KING JAMES II VERSION

THE EPISTLE TO *THE* PHILIPPIANS

CHAPTER 1

1 Paul, and Timothy, slaves of Jesus Christ, to all saints in Christ Jesus who are in Philippi, with the overseers and ministers: 2 Grace to you and peace from God our Father and *the* Lord Jesus Christ.

3 I thank my God on all the remembrance of you, 4 always in my every prayer on your behalf making *my* prayer with joy 5 over your fellowship in the gospel, from *the* first day until now, 6 being persuaded of this very thing, that the *One* having begun a good work in you will finish *it* until *the* day of Jesus Christ; 7 as it is righteous for me to think this of you all, because you have me in *your* heart, both in my bonds and in the defense and confirmation of the gospel, you are all sharers of the grace with me. 8 For God is my witness how I long after you all in *the* bowels of Jesus Christ. 9 And I pray that your love may yet abound more and more in full knowledge and all perception, 10 for you *to* approve of the things that differ, that you may be pure and without blame for *the* day of Christ, 11 being filled *with the* fruits of righteousness through Jesus Christ, to *the* glory and praise of God. 12 But I want you to know, brothers, that the things concerning me have more fully come to *the* advancement of the gospel,

CHAPTER 1

1 Παῦλος καὶ Τιμόθεος, δοῦλοι Ἰησοῦ Χριστοῦ, πᾶσι τοῖς
Paul and Timothy, slaves of Jesus Christ, to all the
ἁγίοις ἐν Χριστῷ Ἰησοῦ τοῖς οὖσιν ἐν Φιλίπποις, σὺν ἐπι-
saints in Christ Jesus being in Philippi with
2 σκόποις καὶ διακόνοις· χάρις ὑμῖν καὶ εἰρήνη ἀπὸ Θεοῦ
overseers and ministers: Grace to you and peace from God
πατρὸς ἡμῶν καὶ Κυρίου Ἰησοῦ Χριστοῦ.
(the) Father of us and (the) Lord Jesus Christ.
3 Εὐχαριστῶ τῷ Θεῷ μου ἐπὶ πάσῃ τῇ μνείᾳ ὑμῶν, πάντοτε
4 I thank the God of me at all the remembrance of you, always
ἐν πάσῃ δεήσει μου ὑπὲρ πάντων ὑμῶν μετὰ χαρᾶς τὴν
in every petition of me on behalf of all you with joy the
5 δέησιν ποιούμενος, ἐπὶ τῇ κοινωνίᾳ ὑμῶν εἰς τὸ εὐαγγέλιον,
petition making, over the fellowship of you in the gospel
6 ἀπὸ πρώτης ἡμέρας ἄχρι τοῦ νῦν· πεποιθὼς αὐτὸ τοῦτο,
from (the) first day until now, being persuaded very this thing,
ὅτι ὁ ἐναρξάμενος ἐν ὑμῖν ἔργον ἀγαθὸν ἐπιτελέσει ἄχρις
that the (One) having begun in you a work good will finish (it) until
7 ἡμέρας Ἰησοῦ Χριστοῦ· καθώς ἐστι δίκαιον ἐμοὶ τοῦτο
(the) day of Jesus Christ, as it is righteous for me this
φρονεῖν ὑπὲρ πάντων ὑμῶν, διὰ τὸ ἔχειν με ἐν τῇ καρδίᾳ
to think of all you, because of having me in the heart
ὑμᾶς, ἔν τε τοῖς δεσμοῖς μου καὶ τῇ ἀπολογίᾳ καὶ βεβαιώσει
you, in both the bonds of me and in the defense and confirmation
τοῦ εὐαγγελίου, συγκοινωνούς μου τῆς χάριτος πάντας
of the gospel, sharers with me of the grace all
8 ὑμᾶς ὄντας. μάρτυς γάρ μού ἐστιν ὁ Θεός, ὡς ἐπιποθῶ
you being. witness For of me is God, how I long after
9 πάντας ὑμᾶς ἐν σπλάγχνοις Ἰησοῦ Χριστοῦ. καὶ τοῦτο
all you in (the) bowels of Jesus Christ. And this
προσεύχομαι, ἵνα ἡ ἀγάπη ὑμῶν ἔτι μᾶλλον καὶ μᾶλλον
I pray, that the love of you yet more and more
10 περισσεύῃ ἐν ἐπιγνώσει καὶ πάσῃ αἰσθήσει, εἰς τὸ δοκιμάζειν
may abound in full knowledge and all perception, for the approving
ὑμᾶς τὰ διαφέροντα, ἵνα ἦτε εἰλικρινεῖς καὶ ἀπρόσκοποι εἰς
of you the things differing, that you be sincere and without blame for
11 ἡμέραν Χριστοῦ, πεπληρωμένοι καρπῶν δικαιοσύνης τῶν
(the) day of Christ, having been filled (with) fruits of righteousness
διὰ Ἰησοῦ Χριστοῦ, εἰς δόξαν καὶ ἔπαινον Θεοῦ.
through Jesus Christ, to (the) glory and praise of God.
12 Γινώσκειν δὲ ὑμᾶς βούλομαι, ἀδελφοί, ὅτι τὰ κατ' ἐμὲ
to know And you I want, brothers, that the things about me
13 μᾶλλον εἰς προκοπὴν τοῦ εὐαγγελίου ἐλήλυθεν· ὥστε τοὺς
rather to (the) advance of the gospel has come, so as the

[13]so that in all the praetorium, and to all the rest, my bonds have become clearly revealed *to be* in Christ; [14]and the most of the brothers in *the* Lord, being confident in my bonds, more exceedingly dare to fearlessly speak the word. [15]Some, indeed, even proclaim Christ because of envy and strife; but some also because of good will. [16]These, indeed, announce Christ out of party spirit, not sincerely, thinking to add affliction to my bonds. [17]But these *others* out of love, knowing that I am set tor defense of the gospel. [18]For what? Yet in every way, whether in pretense or in truth, Christ is announced; and I rejoice in this; I will also yet rejoice. [19]For I know that this will result in salvation to me through your petition, and *the* supply of the Spirit of Jesus Christ, [20]according to my earnest expectation and hope, that in nothing I shall be ashamed, but as always in all boldness even now Christ will be magnified in my body, whether through life or through death.

[21]For me to live *is* Christ, and to die is gain. [22]But if I live in *the* flesh, this *is* to me fruit of *my* labor, and what I shall choose, I do not know. [23]For I am pressed together by the two: having a desire to depart and be with Christ, *which is* far better—[24]but to remain in the flesh *is* more necessary on account of you. [25]And being persuaded of this, I know that I will remain and will continue with you all for your advancement and joy of faith; [26]so that your glorying may abound in Christ Jesus in me, through my presence with you again. [27]Only behave yourself worthily of the gospel of Christ, so that whether coming and seeing you, or being absent, I hear the things concerning you, that you stand fast in one spirit and one soul, striving together in the faith of the gospel, [28]and not being

δεσμούς μου φανερούς ἐν Χριστῷ γενέσθαι ἐν ὅλῳ τῷ πραι-
bonds of me clearly revealed in Christ become in all the prae-
14 τωρίῳ καὶ τοῖς λοιποῖς πᾶσι, καὶ τοὺς πλείονας τῶν ἀδελφῶν
torium, and to the rest all, and the most of the brothers
ἐν Κυρίῳ, πεποιθότας τοῖς δεσμοῖς μου, περισσοτέρως
in (the) Lord being confident in the bonds of me, more exceedingly
15 τολμᾷν ἀφόβως τὸν λόγον λαλεῖν. τινὲς μὲν καὶ διὰ φθόνον
to dare fearlessly the word to speak. Some indeed even for envy
καὶ ἔριν, τινὲς δὲ καὶ δι' εὐδοκίαν τὸν Χριστὸν κηρύσσουσιν·
and strife, some but also for goodwill Christ proclaim;
16 οἱ μὲν ἐξ ἐριθείας τὸν Χριστὸν καταγγέλλουσιν, οὐχ ἁγνῶς,
These indeed of rivalry Christ announce, not sincerely,
17 οἰόμενοι θλίψιν ἐπιφέρειν τοῖς δεσμοῖς μου· οἱ δὲ ἐξ ἀγάπης,
thinking trouble to add to the bonds of me. But these out of love,
18 εἰδότες ὅτι εἰς ἀπολογίαν τοῦ εὐαγγελίου κεῖμαι. τί γάρ;
knowing that for defense of the gospel I am set. what For?
πλὴν παντὶ τρόπῳ, εἴτε προφάσει εἴτε ἀληθείᾳ, Χριστὸς
Yet in every way, whether in pretense or in truth, Christ
καταγγέλλεται· καὶ ἐν τούτῳ χαίρω, ἀλλὰ καὶ χαρήσομαι.
is announced, and in this I rejoice; yet also I will rejoice.
19 οἶδα γὰρ ὅτι τοῦτό μοι ἀποβήσεται εἰς σωτηρίαν διὰ τῆς
I know For that this to me will result in salvation through the
ὑμῶν δεήσεως, καὶ ἐπιχορηγίας τοῦ Πνεύματος Ἰησοῦ
of you petition, and supply of the Spirit of Jesus
20 Χριστοῦ, κατὰ τὴν ἀποκαραδοκίαν καὶ ἐλπίδα μου, ὅτι ἐν
Christ, according to the earnest expectation and hope of me, that in
οὐδενὶ αἰσχυνθήσομαι, ἀλλ' ἐν πάσῃ παρρησίᾳ, ὡς πάν-
nothing I shall be ashamed, but in all boldness, as always,
τοτε, καὶ νῦν μεγαλυνθήσεται Χριστὸς ἐν τῷ σώματί μου,
and now will be magnified Christ in the body of me,
21 εἴτε διὰ ζωῆς εἴτε διὰ θανάτου. ἐμοὶ γὰρ τὸ ζῆν, Χριστός·
whether via life or via death. to me For to live (is) Christ,
22 καὶ τὸ ἀποθανεῖν, κέρδος. εἰ δὲ τὸ ζῆν ἐν σαρκί, τοῦτό μοι
and to die is gain. if But to live in (the) flesh, this to me
23 καρπὸς ἔργου· καὶ τί αἱρήσομαι οὐ γνωρίζω. συνέχομαι
(is) fruit of (my) work, and what I shall choose not I perceive. I am constrained
γὰρ ἐκ τῶν δύο, τὴν ἐπιθυμίαν ἔχων εἰς τὸ ἀναλῦσαι καὶ σὺν
For by the two, the desire having to depart and with
24 Χριστῷ εἶναι, πολλῷ μᾶλλον κρεῖσσον· τὸ δὲ ἐπιμένειν ἐν
Christ be, much rather better; but to remain in
25 τῇ σαρκὶ ἀναγκαιότερον δι' ὑμᾶς. καὶ τοῦτο πεποιθὼς
the flesh (is) more necessary on account of you. And this being assured
οἶδα ὅτι μενῶ, καὶ συμπαραμενῶ πᾶσιν ὑμῖν εἰς τὴν ὑμῶν
I know that I will remain, and will continue with all you for the of you
26 προκοπὴν καὶ χαρὰν τῆς πίστεως, ἵνα τὸ καύχημα ὑμῶν
advancement and joy of the faith, that the boast of you
περισσεύῃ ἐν Χριστῷ Ἰησοῦ ἐν ἐμοί, διὰ τῆς ἐμῆς παρου-
may abound in Christ Jesus in me, through my presence
27 σίας πάλιν πρὸς ὑμᾶς. μόνον ἀξίως τοῦ εὐαγγελίου τοῦ
again with you. Only worthily of the gospel
Χριστοῦ πολιτεύεσθε, ἵνα εἴτε ἐλθὼν καὶ ἰδὼν ὑμᾶς, εἴτε
of Christ conduct yourself, that whether coming and seeing you, or
ἀπών, ἀκούσω τὰ περὶ ὑμῶν, ὅτι στήκετε ἐν ἑνὶ πνεύματι,
being absent, I hear the things about you, that you stand in one spirit,
28 μιᾷ ψυχῇ συναθλοῦντες τῇ πίστει τοῦ εὐαγγελίου, καὶ μὴ
with one soul striving together in the faith of the gospel, and not

terrified in anything by those who oppose, which to them truly is a proof of destruction, but to you of salvation, and this from God: [29]because it was granted to you on behalf of Christ not only to believe in Him, but also to suffer on His behalf, [30]having the same struggle which you saw in me, and now hear *to be* in me.

CHAPTER 2

[1]Then if *there is* any comfort in Christ, if any fellowship of *the* Spirit, if any tendernesses and compassions, [2]fulfill my joy, that you think the same, having the same love, one in soul, minding the one thing, [3]*doing* nothing according to party-spirit or self-glory, but in humility esteeming one another to surpass themselves; [4]each not looking at their own things, but each also *at the* things of others. [5]For let this mind be in you which also *was* in Christ Jesus, [6]who subsisting in the form of God thought *it* not robbery to be equal with God, [7]but emptied Himself, taking *the* form of a slave, having become in *the* likeness of men, [8]and being found in fashion as a man, He humbled Himself, having become obedient until death, even *the* death of a cross. [9]Therefore, God highly exalted Him and gave Him a name above every name, [10]that at the name of Jesus every knee should bow, of *those* of Heaven, and *those* of earth, and *those* under *the* earth; [11]and every tongue should confess that Jesus Christ *is* Lord, to *the* glory of God *the* Father.

[12]So, then, my beloved, even as you always obeyed, not as in my presence only, but now much rather in my absence, work out your salvation with fear and trembling, [13]for it is God who is working in you both to

πτυρόμενοι ἐν μηδενὶ ὑπὸ τῶν ἀντικειμένων· ἥτις αὐτοῖς
being terrified in nothing by those opposing, which to them
μέν ἐστιν ἔνδειξις ἀπωλείας, ὑμῖν δὲ σωτηρίας, καὶ τοῦτο
indeed is a proof of destruction, to you but of salvation, and this
29 ἀπὸ Θεοῦ· ὅτι ὑμῖν ἐχαρίσθη τὸ ὑπὲρ Χριστοῦ, οὐ μόνον τὸ
from God, because to you it was granted for Christ, not only
30 εἰς αὐτὸν πιστεύειν, ἀλλὰ καὶ τὸ ὑπὲρ αὐτοῦ πάσχειν· τὸν
in Him to believe, but also on behalf of Him to suffer, the
αὐτὸν ἀγῶνα ἔχοντες οἷον εἴδετε ἐν ἐμοί, καὶ νῦν ἀκούετε ἐν
same struggle having which you saw in me, and now hear in
ἐμοί.
me.

CHAPTER 2

1 Εἴ τις οὖν παράκλησις ἐν Χριστῷ, εἴ τι παραμύθιον
If (is) any Then comfort in Christ, if any consolation
ἀγάπης, εἴ τις κοινωνία Πνεύματος, εἴ τινα σπλάγχνα καὶ
of love, if any fellowship of (the) Spirit, if any compassions and
2 οἰκτιρμοί, πληρώσατέ μου τὴν χαράν, ἵνα τὸ αὐτὸ φρονῆτε,
pities, fulfill of me the joy, that the same you think,
τὴν αὐτὴν ἀγάπην ἔχοντες, σύμψυχοι, τὸ ἓν φρονοῦντες·
the same love having, one in soul, the one thing minding,
3 μηδὲν κατὰ ἐρίθειαν ἢ κενοδοξίαν, ἀλλὰ τῇ ταπεινοφροσύνῃ
nothing according to rivalry or self-glory, but in humility
4 ἀλλήλους ἡγούμενοι ὑπερέχοντας ἑαυτῶν· μὴ τὰ ἑαυτῶν
one another esteeming surpassing themselves; not their own things
5 ἕκαστος σκοπεῖτε, ἀλλὰ καὶ τὰ ἑτέρων ἕκαστος. τοῦτο γὰρ
each looking at, but also other's things each. this For
6 φρονείσθω ἐν ὑμῖν ὃ καὶ ἐν Χριστῷ Ἰησοῦ· ὃς ἐν μορφῇ Θεοῦ
think among you, which also (was) in Christ Jesus, who in (the) form of God
7 ὑπάρχων, οὐχ ἁρπαγμὸν ἡγήσατο τὸ εἶναι ἴσα Θεῷ, ἀλλ᾽
subsisting, not robbery thought (it) to be equal with God, but
ἑαυτὸν ἐκένωσε, μορφὴν δούλου λαβών, ἐν ὁμοιώματι ἀνθρώ-
Himself emptied, (the) form of a slave taking, in likeness of men
8 πων γενόμενος· καὶ σχήματι εὑρεθεὶς ὡς ἄνθρωπος, ἐταπείνω-
becoming; and in fashion being found as a man, He humbled
σεν ἑαυτόν, γενόμενος ὑπήκοος μέχρι θανάτου, θανάτου δὲ
Himself, becoming obedient until death, (the) death even
9 σταυροῦ. διὸ καὶ ὁ Θεὸς αὐτὸν ὑπερύψωσε, καὶ ἐχαρίσατο
of a cross. Therefore also God Him highly exalted, and gave
10 αὐτῷ ὄνομα τὸ ὑπὲρ πᾶν ὄνομα· ἵνα ἐν τῷ ὀνόματι Ἰησοῦ
to Him a name above every name, that in the name of Jesus
πᾶν γόνυ κάμψῃ ἐπουρανίων καὶ ἐπιγείων καὶ καταχθονίων,
every knee should bow, of heavenly and of earthly, and those under earth,
11 καὶ πᾶσα γλῶσσα ἐξομολογήσηται ὅτι Κύριος Ἰησοῦς
and every tongue should confess that Lord Jesus
Χριστός, εἰς δόξαν Θεοῦ πατρός.
Christ (is), to (the) glory of God (the) Father.
12 Ὥστε, ἀγαπητοί μου, καθὼς πάντοτε ὑπηκούσατε, μὴ ὡς
So as, beloved of me, as always you obeyed, not as
ἐν τῇ παρουσίᾳ μου μόνον, ἀλλὰ νῦν πολλῷ μᾶλλον ἐν τῇ
in the presence of me only, but now by more rather in the
ἀπουσίᾳ μου, μετὰ φόβου καὶ τρόμου τὴν ἑαυτῶν σωτηρίαν
absence of me, with fear and trembling the of yourselves salvation
13 κατεργάζεσθε· ὁ Θεὸς γάρ ἐστιν ὁ ἐνεργῶν ἐν ὑμῖν καὶ τὸ
work out; God for is the (One) working in you both

will and to work for the sake of *His* good pleasure. [14] Do all things without murmurings and disputings, [15] that you may be blameless and harmless, children of God, without fault in the midst of a crooked generation, even having been perverted— among whom you shine as luminaries in *the* world, [16] holding up a word of life, for a boast to me in *the* day of Christ, that I ran not in vain, nor labored in vain. [17] But if indeed I am poured out on the sacrifice and service of your faith, I rejoice; and I rejoice with you all. [18] And you also rejoice *in* the same, and rejoice with me.

[19] But I hope in the Lord Jesus to send Timothy to you soon, that I may also be of good cheer, knowing the things about you. [20] For I have no one likeminded, who genuinely will care for the things about you. [21] For all seek their own things, not the things of Christ Jesus. [22] But you know the proof of him, that as a child to a father, he served with me for the gospel. [23] Therefore, I hope to send this one at once, whenever I shall see the things about me. [24] But I trust in *the* Lord that I myself also will come soon. [25] But I thought it needful to send to you Epaphroditus, my brother and fellow-worker, and my fellow-soldier, and your messenger and minister of my need; [26] since he was longing for you all, and has been troubled because you heard that he was sick. [27] For indeed he was sick, coming near to death; but God had mercy on him, but also me, lest I should have grief on grief. [28] Therefore, I sent him eagerly, that seeing him again you may rejoice, and I may be less grieved. [29] Then receive him in *the* Lord with all joy, and hold such in honor, [30] that through the work of Christ he drew near to death, exposing *his* soul, that he may fill up your lack of

14 θέλειν καὶ τὸ ἐνεργεῖν ὑπὲρ τῆς εὐδοκίας. πάντα ποιεῖτε
to will and to work on behalf of (His) good pleasure. All things do
15 χωρὶς γογγυσμῶν καὶ διαλογισμῶν, ἵνα γένησθε ἄμεμπτοι
without murmurings and disputings, that you may be blameless
καὶ ἀκέραιοι, τέκνα Θεοῦ ἀμώμητα ἐν μέσῳ γενεᾶς σκολιᾶς
and harmless, children of God faultless amidst a generation crooked
καὶ διεστραμμένης, ἐν οἷς φαίνεσθε ὡς φωστῆρες ἐν κόσμῳ,
and having been perverted, among whom you shine as luminaries in (the) world,
16 λόγον ζωῆς ἐπέχοντες, εἰς καύχημα ἐμοὶ εἰς ἡμέραν Χριστοῦ,
a word of life holding up, for a boast to me in (the) day of Christ,
17 ὅτι οὐκ εἰς κενὸν ἔδραμον, οὐδὲ εἰς κενὸν ἐκοπίασα. ἀλλ' εἰ
that not in vain I ran, nor in vain labored. But if
καὶ σπένδομαι ἐπὶ τῇ θυσίᾳ καὶ λειτουργίᾳ τῆς πίστεως
indeed I am poured out on the sacrifice and service of the faith
18 ὑμῶν, χαίρω καὶ συγχαίρω πᾶσιν ὑμῖν· τὸ δ' αὐτὸ καὶ ὑμεῖς
of you, I rejoice, and I rejoice with all you; the and same also you
χαίρετε καὶ συγχαίρετέ μοι.
rejoice, and rejoice with me.
19 Ἐλπίζω δὲ ἐν Κυρίῳ Ἰησοῦ, Τιμόθεον ταχέως πέμψαι
I hope But in (the) Lord Jesus Timothy shortly to send
20 ὑμῖν, ἵνα κἀγὼ εὐψυχῶ, γνοὺς τὰ περὶ ὑμῶν. οὐδένα γὰρ ἔχω
to you, that I also may be of good cheer. knowing the things about you. no one For I have
21 ἰσόψυχον, ὅστις γνησίως τὰ περὶ ὑμῶν μεριμνήσει. οἱ πάντες
likeminded, who genuinely the things about you will care for all
22 γὰρ τὰ ἑαυτῶν ζητοῦσιν, οὐ τὰ τοῦ Χριστοῦ Ἰησοῦ. τὴν δὲ
For the things of themselves seek, not the things of Christ Jesus. the But
δοκιμὴν αὐτοῦ γινώσκετε, ὅτι ὡς πατρὶ τέκνον, σὺν ἐμοὶ
proof of him you know, that as to a father a child, with me
23 ἐδούλευσεν εἰς τὸ εὐαγγέλιον. τοῦτον μὲν οὖν ἐλπίζω πέμψαι,
he served for the gospel. This one, therefore, I hope to send,
24 ὡς ἂν ἀπίδω τὰ περὶ ἐμέ, ἐξαυτῆς· πέποιθα δὲ ἐν Κυρίῳ, ὅτι
whenever I shall see the things about me at once; I trust but in (the) Lord that
25 καὶ αὐτὸς ταχέως ἐλεύσομαι. ἀναγκαῖον δὲ ἡγησάμην
also myself shortly I will come. necessary But I thought (it)
Ἐπαφρόδιτον τὸν ἀδελφὸν καὶ συνεργὸν καὶ συστρατιώτην
Epaphroditus the brother and fellow-worker and fellow-soldier
μου, ὑμῶν δὲ ἀπόστολον, καὶ λειτουργὸν τῆς χρείας μου,
of me, of you and, apostle and minister of the need of me,
26 πέμψαι πρὸς ὑμᾶς· ἐπειδὴ ἐπιποθῶν ἦν πάντας ὑμᾶς, καὶ
to send to you since longing after he was all you, and
27 ἀδημονῶν, διότι ἠκούσατε ὅτι ἠσθένησε· καὶ γὰρ ἠσθένησε
being troubled, because you heard that he was sick. indeed For he was sick,
παραπλήσιον θανάτῳ· ἀλλ' ὁ Θεὸς αὐτὸν ἠλέησεν, οὐκ αὐτὸν
coming near to death, but God him had mercy on, not on him
28 δὲ μόνον, ἀλλὰ καὶ ἐμέ, ἵνα μὴ λύπην ἐπὶ λύπῃ σχῶ. σπου-
and only, but also me, lest grief on grief I should have. More
δαιοτέρως οὖν ἔπεμψα αὐτόν, ἵνα, ἰδόντες αὐτὸν πάλιν,
eagerly, therefore, I sent him, that seeing him again
29 χαρῆτε, κἀγὼ ἀλυπότερος ὦ. προσδέχεσθε οὖν αὐτὸν ἐν
you may rejoice, and I less grieved may be. receive Therefore him in
Κυρίῳ μετὰ πάσης χαρᾶς, καὶ τοὺς τοιούτους ἐντίμους ἔχετε·
(the) Lord with all joy, and such ones honored hold,
30 ὅτι διὰ τὸ ἔργον τοῦ Χριστοῦ μέχρι θανάτου ἤγγισε,
that through the work of Christ as far as death he drew near,
παραβουλευσάμενος τῇ ψυχῇ, ἵνα ἀναπληρώσῃ τὸ ὑμῶν
exposing the soul, that he might fill up the of you

service toward me.

CHAPTER 3

[1]For the rest, my brothers, rejoice in *the* Lord. To write the same things to you *is* not truly tiresome to me, but safe for you. [2]Look out *for* the dogs; look out *for* the evil workers; look out *for* the concision *party*. [3]For we are the circumcision who worship by the Spirit of God, and glorying in Christ Jesus, and do not trust in flesh. [4]Though I also might have trust in flesh—if any other thinks to trust in flesh, I more—[5]in circumcision, *the* eighth day; of *the* race of Israel, *the* tribe of Benjamin; a Hebrew of the Hebrews, according to Law, a Pharisee; [6]according to zeal, persecuting the church; according to righteousness in Law, being blameless. [7]But what things were gain to me, these I have counted loss because of Christ. [8]But, nay, rather I also count all things to be loss because of the excellency of the knowledge of Christ Jesus, my Lord, for whose sake I have suffered the loss of all things, and count *them* to be trash, that I might gain Christ, [9]and be found in Him; not having my own righteousness of Law, but through *the* faith of Christ *having* the righteousness of God *based* on faith, [10]to know Him and the power of His resurrection, and the fellowship of His sufferings, having been conformed to His death; [11]if somehow I may attain to the resurrection from the dead. [12]Not that I already received, or already have been perfected, but I press on, if I also may lay hold, inasmuch as I also was laid hold of by Christ Jesus. [13]Brothers, I do not count myself to have laid hold, but one *thing I do*, forgetting the things behind, and reaching out to those things before, [14]I press on after the mark, for the prize of the high calling of God in Christ Jesus. [15]Then as many as *are* perfect, let us be of this mind; and if you

ὑστέρημα τῆς πρός με λειτουργίας.
lack toward me of service.

CHAPTER 3

1 Τὸ λοιπόν, ἀδελφοί μου, χαίρετε ἐν Κυρίῳ. τὰ αὐτὰ
For the rest, brothers of me, rejoice in (the) Lord. The same things
2 γράφειν ὑμῖν, ἐμοὶ μὲν οὐκ ὀκνηρόν, ὑμῖν δὲ ἀσφαλές. βλέπετε
to write to you for me indeed not is tiresome, for you but safe. Look (to)
τοὺς κύνας, βλέπετε τοὺς κακοὺς ἐργάτας, βλέπετε τὴν
the dogs, Look (to) the evil workers, look (to) the
3 κατατομήν· ἡμεῖς γάρ ἐσμεν ἡ περιτομή, οἱ πνεύματι Θεῷ
concision. we For are the circumcision, those by Spirit of God
λατρεύοντες, καὶ καυχώμενοι ἐν Χριστῷ Ἰησοῦ, καὶ οὐκ ἐν
worshiping, and boasting in Christ Jesus, and not in
4 σαρκὶ πεποιθότες· καίπερ ἐγὼ ἔχων πεποίθησιν καὶ ἐν σαρκί·
(the) flesh trusting; even though I having trust also in (the) flesh
5 εἴ τις δοκεῖ ἄλλος πεποιθέναι ἐν σαρκί, ἐγὼ μᾶλλον· περιτομῇ
—if any thinks other to trust in (the) flesh, I more: in circumcision
ὀκταήμερος, ἐκ γένους Ἰσραήλ, φυλῆς Βενιαμίν, Ἑβραῖος ἐξ
(the) eighth day; of (the) race of Israel; (the) tribe of Benjamin; a Hebrew of
6 Ἑβραίων, κατὰ νόμον Φαρισαῖος, κατα ζῆλον διώκων τὴν
Hebrews; according to law, a Pharisee; according to zeal, persecuting the
ἐκκλησίαν, κατὰ δικαιοσύνην τὴν ἐν νόμῳ γενόμενος ἄμεμ-
church; according to righteousness in (the) law, being blame-
7 πτος. ἀλλ ἅτινα ἦν μοι κέρδη, ταῦτα ἥγημαι διὰ τὸν Χριστὸν
less. But what things were to me gain, these I have counted because of Christ
8 ζημίαν. ἀλλὰ μενοῦνγε καὶ ἡγοῦμαι πάντα ζημίαν εἶναι διὰ
loss. But nay, rather also I count all things loss to be because of
τὸ ὑπερέχον τῆς γνώσεως Χριστοῦ Ἰησοῦ τοῦ Κυρίου μου·
the excellency of the knowledge of Christ Jesus the Lord of me,
δι' ὃν τὰ πάντα ἐζημιώθην, καὶ ἡγοῦμαι σκύβαλα εἶναι, ἵνα
for whose sake all things I suffered loss, and count refuse to be, that
9 Χριστὸν κερδήσω, καὶ εὑρεθῶ ἐν αὐτῷ, μὴ ἔχων ἐμὴν δικαιο-
Christ I might gain, and be found in Him, not having my right-
σύνην τὴν ἐκ νόμου, ἀλλὰ τὴν διὰ πίστεως Χριστοῦ, τὴν ἐκ
eousness of law, But through faith of Christ, the of
10 Θεοῦ δικαιοσύνην ἐπὶ τῇ πίστει· τοῦ γνῶναι αὐτόν, καὶ
God righteousness (based) on faith, to know Him and
τὴν δύναμιν τῆς ἀναστάσεως αὐτοῦ, καὶ τὴν κοινωνίαν τῶν
the power of the resurrection of Him, and the fellowship of the
11 παθημάτων αὐτοῦ, συμμορφούμενος τῷ θανάτῳ αὐτοῦ, εἴ
sufferings of Him, being conformed to the death of Him; if
12 πως καταντήσω εἰς τὴν ἐξανάστασιν τῶν νεκρῶν. οὐχ ὅτι
somehow I may attain to the resurrection out of the dead. Not that
ἤδη ἔλαβον, ἢ ἤδη τετελείωμαι· διώκω δέ, εἰ καὶ καταλάβω
already I received, or already been perfected, I follow but, if also I may lay hold,
13 ἐφ' ᾧ καὶ κατελήφθην ὑπὸ τοῦ Χριστοῦ Ἰησοῦ. ἀδελφοί,
inasmuch as also I was laid hold of by Christ Jesus. Brothers,
ἐγὼ ἐμαυτὸν οὐ λογίζομαι κατειληφέναι· ἓν δέ, τὰ μὲν ὀπίσω
I myself not reckon to have laid hold, one but, the things behind
14 ἐπιλανθανόμενος, τοῖς δὲ ἔμπροσθεν ἐπεκτεινόμενος, κατὰ
forgetting, the things and before stretching forward to, after
σκοπὸν διώκω ἐπὶ τὸ βραβεῖον τῆς ἄνω κλήσεως τοῦ Θεοῦ
a mark I pursue, for the prize of the high calling of God
15 ἐν Χριστῷ Ἰησοῦ. ὅσοι οὖν τέλειοι, τοῦτο φρονῶμεν· καὶ εἴ
in Christ Jesus. as many as Then (are) perfect, this let us think; and if

think anything differently, God will also reveal this to you.

[16]Yet *as* to where we have reached, *let us* walk to the same rule, *being* of the same mind. [17]Be fellow-imitators of me, brothers, and consider those walking this way, even as you have us *for* a pattern. [18]For many walk *as* the enemies of the cross of Christ —of whom I often told you, and now even weeping I say *it*—[19]whose end *is* destruction, whose god *is* the belly, and *who* glory in their shame, those who mind earthly things. [20]For our citizenship is in Heaven, from where we also wait for a Savior, *the* Lord Jesus Christ, [21]who will transform our body of humiliation, for it to be conformed to His body of glory, according to the working of His mighty power, even to put all things under Himself.

CHAPTER 4

[1]So that, my brothers, ones loved and longed for, my joy and crown, so stand firm in *the* Lord, beloved ones.

[2]I entreat Euodia, and I entreat Syntyche, to mind the same thing in *the* Lord. [3]And I also ask you, true yoke-fellow, help those who struggled along with me and with Clement, and the rest, fellow-workers with me, whose names *are* in *the* Book of Life.

[4]Rejoice in *the* Lord always. Again I say, Rejoice! [5]Let your reasonableness be known to all men. The Lord *is* near. [6]Do not be anxious about anything, but in everything by prayer and by petition, with thanksgivings, let your requests be made known to God; [7]and the peace of God which surpasses all understanding will keep your hearts and your minds in Christ Jesus. [8]For the rest, brothers, whatever is true, whatever honorable,

16 τι ἑτέρως φρονεῖτε, καὶ τοῦτο ὁ Θεὸς ὑμῖν ἀποκαλύψει· πλὴν
anything other you think, even this God to you will reveal. Yet
εἰς ὃ ἐφθάσαμεν, τῷ αὐτῷ στοιχεῖν κανόνι, τὸ αὐτὸ φρονεῖν.
to what we arrived, by the same to walk rule, of the same mind.
17 Συμμιμηταί μου γίνεσθε, ἀδελφοί, καὶ σκοπεῖτε τοὺς οὕτω
fellow-imitators of me Be, brothers, and mark those thus
18 περιπατοῦντας, καθὼς ἔχετε τύπον ἡμᾶς. πολλοὶ γὰρ περι-
walking, as you have an example us. many For
πατοῦσιν, οὓς πολλάκις ἔλεγον ὑμῖν, νῦν δὲ καὶ κλαίων λέγω,
walk —of whom often I told you, now and also weeping I say —
19 τοὺς ἐχθροὺς τοῦ σταυροῦ τοῦ Χριστοῦ· ὧν τὸ τέλος ἀπώ-
(as) the enemies of the cross of Christ, of whom the end (is) destruc-
λεια, ὧν ὁ θεὸς ἡ κοιλία, καὶ ἡ δόξα ἐν τῇ αἰσχύνῃ αὐτῶν, οἱ
tion, of whom the god the belly (is) and glory in the shame of them, those
20 τὰ ἐπίγεια φρονοῦντες. ἡμῶν γὰρ τὸ πολίτευμα ἐν οὐρανοῖς
the earthly things thinking. of us For the citizenship in Heaven
ὑπάρχει, ἐξ οὗ καὶ Σωτῆρα ἀπεκδεχόμεθα, Κύριον Ἰησοῦν
is, from where also a Savior we wait for, (the) Lord Jesus
21 Χριστόν· ὃς μετασχηματίσει τὸ σῶμα τῆς ταπεινώσεως
Christ, who will change the body of the humiliation
ἡμῶν, εἰς τὸ γενέσθαι αὐτὸ σύμμορφον τῷ σώματι τῆς δόξης
of us for to be it conformed to the body of the glory
αὐτοῦ, κατὰ τὴν ἐνέργειαν τοῦ δύνασθαι αὐτὸν καὶ ὑποτάξαι
of Him, according to the working of the ability (of) Him, even to subject
ἑαυτῷ τὰ πάντα.
to Himself all things.

CHAPTER 4

1 Ὥστε, ἀδελφοί μου ἀγαπητοὶ καὶ ἐπιπόθητοι, χαρὰ καὶ
So as, brothers of me, beloved and longed for, joy and
στέφανός μου, οὕτω στήκετε ἐν Κυρίῳ, ἀγαπητοί.
crown of me, so stand in (the) Lord, beloved.
2 Εὐοδίαν παρακαλῶ, καὶ Συντύχην παρακαλῶ, τὸ αὐτὸ
Euodia I beseech, and Syntyche I beseech, the same thing
3 φρονεῖν ἐν Κυρίῳ. καὶ ἐρωτῶ καί σε, σύζυγε γνήσιε, συλλαμ-
to think in (the) Lord. And I ask also you, yoke-fellow true, help
βάνου αὐταῖς, αἵτινες ἐν τῷ εὐαγγελίῳ συνήθλησάν μοι,
them, who in the gospel struggled with me,
μετὰ καὶ Κλήμεντος, καὶ τῶν λοιπῶν συνεργῶν μου, ὧν τὰ
with and Clement, and the rest, fellow-workers with me of whom the
ὀνόματα ἐν βίβλῳ ζωῆς.
names (are) in (the) Scroll of Life.
4 Χαίρετε ἐν Κυρίῳ πάντοτε· πάλιν ἐρῶ, χαίρετε. τὸ ἐπιεικὲς
5 Rejoice in (the) Lord always; again I will say, Rejoice. The mildness
6 ὑμῶν γνωσθήτω πᾶσιν ἀνθρώποις. ὁ Κύριος ἐγγύς. μηδὲν
of you let it be known to all men. The Lord (is) near. Nothing
μεριμνᾶτε, ἀλλ' ἐν παντὶ τῇ προσευχῇ καὶ τῇ δεήσει μετὰ
be anxious about, but in everything, by prayer and by petition with
εὐχαριστίας τὰ αἰτήματα ὑμῶν γνωριζέσθω πρὸς τὸν Θεόν.
thanksgivings, the requests of you let be made known to God.
καὶ ἡ εἰρήνη τοῦ Θεοῦ, ἡ ὑπερέχουσα πάντα νοῦν, φρουρήσει
And the peace of God which surpasses all understanding will keep
τὰς καρδίας ὑμῶν καὶ τὰ νοήματα ὑμῶν ἐν Χριστῷ Ἰησοῦ.
the hearts of you and the minds of you in Christ Jesus.
8 Τὸ λοιπόν, ἀδελφοί, ὅσα ἐστὶν ἀληθῆ, ὅσα σεμνά, ὅσα
For the rest, brothers, whatever is true, whatever honorable, whatever

whatever *is* right, whatever pure, whatever lovely, whatever of good report; if *of* any virtue, and if *of* any praise, think on these things. 9 And what things you learned and received and heard and saw in me, practice these things; and the God of peace will be with you.

10 But I rejoiced in *the* Lord greatly that now at last you revived *your* thinking of me— although you indeed did think, but lacked opportunity. 11 Not that I speak as to great need; for I have learned to be content in whatever state I am. 12 But I know to be humbled, and I know to abound; in everything, and in all things, I am taught both to be filled, and to hunger, both to abound, and to lack. 13 I can do all things through Christ, the *One* giving me power. 14 Yet you did well in sharing my troubles. 15 And you know, too, *O* Philipians, that in *the* beginning of the gospel, when I went out from Macedonia, not one church shared with me in *the* matter of giving and receiving, except you only. 16 Because truly in Thessalonica you sent to my need, both once and twice. 17 Not that I seek a gift, but I seek the fruit multiplying to your account. 18 But I have all things, and more than enough; I have been filled, receiving from Epaphroditus the things from you, an odor of sweet smell, an acceptable sacrifice, well-pleasing to God.

19 And my God will fill your every need according to His riches in glory, in Christ Jesus.

20 Now may glory be to our God and Father forever and ever. Amen.

21 Greet every saint in Christ Jesus. The brothers with me greet you. 22 All the saints greet you, most of all those of Caesar's house.

23 The grace of our Lord Jesus Christ be with all of you. Amen.

δίκαια, ὅσα ἁγνά, ὅσα προσφιλῆ, ὅσα εὔφημα, εἴ τις ἀρετὴ
just, whatever pure, whatever loveable, whatever of good report, if any virtue
9 καὶ εἴ τις ἔπαινος, ταῦτα λογίζεσθε. ἃ καὶ ἐμάθετε καὶ παρε-
and if any praise, these things consider. What things you learned and re-
λάβετε καὶ ἠκούσατε καὶ εἴδετε ἐν ἐμοί, ταῦτα πράσσετε· καὶ
ceived, and heard and saw, in me, these things practice; and
ὁ Θεὸς τῆς εἰρήνης ἔσται μεθ' ὑμῶν.
the God of peace will be with you.
10 Ἐχάρην δὲ ἐν Κυρίῳ μεγάλως, ὅτι ἤδη ποτὲ ἀνεθάλετε τὸ
I rejoiced Now in (the) Lord greatly, that now at last you revived
11 ὑπὲρ ἐμοῦ φρονεῖν· ἐφ' ᾧ καὶ ἐφρονεῖτε, ἠκαιρεῖσθε δέ. οὐχ
of me thinking, as to which indeed you thought, lacked opportunity. but Not
ὅτι καθ' ὑστέρησιν λέγω· ἐγὼ γὰρ ἔμαθον, ἐν οἷς εἰμί,
that by way of lack I say; I for learned in what state I am,
12 αὐτάρκης εἶναι. οἶδα καὶ ταπεινοῦσθαι, οἶδα καὶ περισ-
self-sufficient to be. I know both to be humbled, I know and to
σεύειν· ἐν παντὶ και ἐν πᾶσι μεμύημαι καὶ χορτάζεσθαι καὶ
abound; in everything and in all things I am taught both to be filled and
13 πεινᾷν, καὶ περισσεύειν καὶ ὑστερεῖσθαι. πάντα ἰσχύω ἐν
to hunger, both to abound and to lack. All things I can do in
14 τῷ ἐνδυναμοῦντί με Χριστῷ. πλὴν καλῶς ἐποιήσατε
the (One) empowering me, Christ. Yet well you did
15 συγκοινωνήσαντές μου τῇ θλίψει. οἴδατε δὲ καὶ ὑμεῖς,
sharing in of me the troubles. know And also you,
Φιλιππήσιοι, ὅτι ἐν ἀρχῇ τοῦ εὐαγγελίου, ὅτε ἐξῆλθον
Philippians, that in (the) beginning of the gospel, when I went out
ἀπὸ Μακεδονίας, οὐδεμία μοι ἐκκλησία ἐκοινώνησεν εἰς
from Macedonia, not one me church shared with in
16 λόγον δόσεως καὶ λήψεως, εἰ μὴ ὑμεῖς μόνοι· ὅτι καὶ ἐν
(the) matter of giving and receiving, except you only, because truly in
Θεσσαλονίκῃ καὶ ἅπαξ καὶ δὶς εἰς τὴν χρείαν μοι ἐπέμψατε.
Thessalonica both once and twice to the need of me you sent.
17 οὐχ ὅτι ἐπιζητῶ τὸ δόμα, ἀλλ' ἐπιζητῶ τὸν καρπὸν τὸν
Not that I seek the gift, but I seek the fruit
18 πλεονάζοντα εἰς λόγον ὑμῶν. ἀπέχω δὲ πάντα καὶ περισ-
multiplying to (the) account of you. I have But all things and abound;
σεύω· πεπλήρωμαι, δεξάμενος παρὰ Ἐπαφροδίτου τὰ παρ'
I have been filled, receiving from Epaphroditus the things from
ὑμῶν, ὀσμὴν εὐωδίας, θυσίαν δεκτήν, εὐάρεστον τῷ Θεῷ.
you, an odor of sweet smell, a sacrifice acceptable, well-pleasing to God.
19 ὁ δὲ Θεός μου πληρώσει πᾶσαν χρείαν ὑμῶν κατὰ τὸν
the And God of me will fill every need of you according to the
20 πλοῦτον αὐτοῦ ἐν δόξῃ, ἐν Χριστῷ Ἰησοῦ. τῷ δὲ Θεῷ καὶ
riches of Him in glory, in Christ Jesus. to the Now God and
πατρὶ ἡμῶν ἡ δόξα εἰς τοὺς αἰῶνας τῶν αἰώνων. ἀμήν.
Father of us (be) the glory to the ages of the ages. Amen.
21 Ἀσπάσασθε πάντα ἅγιον ἐν Χριστῷ Ἰησοῦ. ἀσπά-
Greet every saint in Christ Jesus. Greet
22 ζονται ὑμᾶς οἱ σὺν ἐμοὶ ἀδελφοί. ἀσπάζονται ὑμᾶς πάντες
you the with me brothers. Greet you all
οἱ ἅγιοι, μάλιστα δὲ οἱ ἐκ τῆς Καίσαρος οἰκίας.
the saints, most of all but those of the of Caesar house.
23 Ἡ χάρις τοῦ Κυρίου ἡμῶν Ἰησοῦ Χριστοῦ μετὰ πάντων
The grace of the Lord of us, Jesus Christ (be) with all
ὑμῶν. ἀμήν.
of you. Amen.

ΠΑΥΛΟΥ ΤΟΥ ΑΠΟΣΤΟΛΟΥ
PAUL THE APOSTLE

Η ΠΡΟΣ
THE TO

ΚΟΛΟΣΣΑΕΙΣ ΕΠΙΣΤΟΛΗ
(THE) COLOSSIANS EPISTLE

KING JAMES II VERSION

THE EPISTLE TO THE COLOSSIANS

CHAPTER 1

1 Paul, *an* apostle of Jesus Christ through the will of God, and Timothy the brother, 2 to the saints and faithful brothers in Christ in Colossee: Grace and peace to you from God our Father and *the* Lord Jesus Christ. 3 We give thanks to God and *the* Father of our Lord Jesus Christ, praying continually about you, 4 hearing of your faith in Christ Jesus, and the love which *you have* toward all the saints, 5 through the hope being laid up for you in Heaven; which you heard before in the word of the truth of the gospel, 6 coming to you, as also in all the world, and is bearing fruit, even also among you, from the day in which you heard and knew the grace of God in truth; 7 even as you also learned from Epaphras our beloved fellow-slave, who is a faithful minister of Christ for you, 8 he also showing to us your love in *the* Spirit.

9 For this cause also, from the day in which we heard, we do not cease praying for you and asking that you may be filled *with* the knowledge of His will in all wisdom and spiritual understanding, 10 *for* you to walk worthily of the Lord to all pleasing, bearing fruit in every good work, and growing into the full knowledge of God; 11 being empowered with all

COLOSSIANS

CHAPTER 1

1 Παῦλος ἀπόστολος Ἰησοῦ Χριστοῦ διὰ θελήματος Θεοῦ,
Paul an apostle of Jesus Christ through (the) will of God,
2 καὶ Τιμόθεος ὁ ἀδελφός, τοῖς ἐν Κολοσσαῖς ἁγίοις καὶ πιστοῖς
and Timothy the brother, to the in Colosse saints and faithful
ἀδελφοῖς ἐν Χριστῷ· χάρις ὑμῖν καὶ εἰρήνη ἀπὸ Θεοῦ πατρὸς
brothers in Christ: Grace to you and peace from God (the) Father
ἡμῶν καὶ Κυρίου Ἰησοῦ Χριστοῦ.
of us and (the) Lord Jesus Christ.
3 Εὐχαριστοῦμεν τῷ Θεῷ καὶ πατρὶ τοῦ Κυρίου ἡμῶν
We give thanks to God and Father of the Lord of us,
4 Ἰησοῦ Χριστοῦ, πάντοτε περὶ ὑμῶν προσευχόμενοι, ἀκού-
Jesus Christ, always concerning you praying, having
σαντες τὴν πίστιν ὑμῶν ἐν Χριστῷ Ἰησοῦ, καὶ τὴν ἀγάπην
heard the faith of you in Christ Jesus, and the love
5 τὴν εἰς πάντας τοὺς ἁγίους, διὰ τὴν ἐλπίδα τὴν ἀποκειμένην
of all the saints, through the hope being laid up
ὑμῖν ἐν τοῖς οὐρανοῖς, ἣν προηκούσατε ἐν τῷ λόγῳ τῆς
for you in the heavens, which you heard before in the word of the
6 ἀληθείας τοῦ εὐαγγελίου, τοῦ παρόντος εἰς ὑμᾶς, καθὼς καὶ
truth of the gospel, coming to you, as also
ἐν παντὶ τῷ κόσμῳ, καὶ ἔστι καρποφορούμενον, καθὼς καὶ
in all the world, and it is bearing fruit, even also
ἐν ὑμῖν, ἀφ' ἧς ἡμέρας ἠκούσατε καὶ ἐπέγνωτε τὴν χάριν τοῦ
among you, from which day you heard and fully knew the grace
7 Θεοῦ ἐν ἀληθείᾳ· καθὼς καὶ ἐμάθετε ἀπὸ Ἐπαφρᾶ τοῦ
of God in truth, as also you learned from Epaphras the
ἀγαπητοῦ συνδούλου ἡμῶν, ὅς ἐστι πιστὸς ὑπὲρ ὑμῶν
beloved fellow-slave of us, who is a faithful for you
8 διάκονος τοῦ Χριστοῦ, ὁ καὶ δηλώσας ἡμῖν τὴν ὑμῶν ἀγάπην
minister of Christ, he also having shown to us the of you love
ἐν Πνεύματι.
in (the) Spirit.
9 Διὰ τοῦτο καὶ ἡμεῖς, ἀφ' ἧς ἡμέρας ἠκούσαμεν, οὐ παυό-
Therefore also we, from which day we heard, do not cease
μεθα ὑπὲρ ὑμῶν προσευχόμενοι, καὶ αἰτούμενοι ἵνα πλη-
on behalf of you praying and asking that you
ρωθῆτε τὴν ἐπίγνωσιν τοῦ θελήματος αὐτοῦ ἐν πάσῃ σοφίᾳ
may be filled (with) the knowledge of the will of Him in all wisdom
10 καὶ συνέσει πνευματικῇ, περιπατῆσαι ὑμᾶς ἀξίως τοῦ Κυρίου
and understanding spiritual, to walk you worthily of the Lord
εἰς πᾶσαν ἀρέσκειαν, ἐν παντὶ ἔργῳ ἀγαθῷ καρποφοροῦντες
to all pleasing, in every work good bearing fruit
11 καὶ αὐξανόμενοι εἰς τὴν ἐπίγνωσιν τοῦ Θεοῦ· ἐν πάσῃ δυνάμει
and growing into the full knowledge of God, with all power

power according to the might of His glory, to all patience and long-suffering with joy; [12]giving thanks to the Father, who has made us fit for a share of the inheritance of the saints in light, [13]who delivered us out of the power of darkness, and translated *us* into the kingdom of the Son of His love; [14]in whom we have redemption through His blood, the forgiveness of sins; [15]who is *the* image of the invisible God, *the* Firstborn of all creation—[16]for all things were created in Him, the things in the heavens, and the things on the earth; the visible and the invisible; whether thrones, or lordships, or rulers, or authorities, all things have been created through Him and for Him.

[17]And He is before all things, and all things consist in Him. [18]And He is the Head of the body, the church; who is *the* Beginning, *the* Firstborn from *the* dead, that He be pre-eminent in all things; [19]because all the fullness was pleased to dwell in Him, [20]and through Him making peace by the blood of His cross, to reconcile all things to Himself through Him, whether the things on the earth, or the things in the heavens. [21]And you then were once alienated and enemies in *your* mind by evil works. But now He reconciled [22]in the body of His flesh, through death, to present you holy and without blame, and without charge before Him, [23]if you continue in the faith grounded and settled, and not being moved away from the hope of the gospel which you heard proclaimed in all the creation under Heaven, of which I, Paul, became a minister.

[24]Now *I* rejoice in my sufferings on your behalf,

δυναμούμενοι, κατὰ τὸ κράτος τῆς δόξης αὐτοῦ, εἰς πᾶσαν
being empowered, according to the might of the glory of Him, to all
12 ὑπομονὴν καὶ μακροθυμίαν μετὰ χαρᾶς· εὐχαριστοῦντες τῷ
patience and long-suffering, with joy, giving thanks to the
πατρὶ τῷ ἱκανώσαντι ἡμᾶς εἰς τὴν μερίδα τοῦ κλήρου τῶν
Father having made fit us for the share of the lot of the
13 ἁγίων ἐν τῷ φωτί, ὃς ἐρρύσατο ἡμᾶς ἐκ τῆς ἐξουσίας τοῦ
saints in light, who delivered us out of the authority
σκότους, καὶ μετέστησεν εἰς τὴν βασιλείαν τοῦ υἱοῦ τῆς
of darkness, and translated (us) into the kingdom of the Son of the
14 ἀγάπης αὐτοῦ, ἐν ᾧ ἔχομεν τὴν ἀπολύτρωσιν διὰ τοῦ
love of Him, in whom we have redemption through the
15 αἵματος αὐτοῦ, τὴν ἄφεσιν τῶν ἁμαρτιῶν· ὅς ἐστιν εἰκὼν
blood of Him, the forgiveness of sins; who is (the) image
16 τοῦ Θεοῦ τοῦ ἀοράτου, πρωτότοκος πάσης κτίσεως· ὅτι
of God the invisible, (the) firstborn of all creation, because
ἐν αὐτῷ ἐκτίσθη τὰ πάντα, τὰ ἐν τοῖς οὐρανοῖς καὶ τὰ ἐπὶ
in Him were created all things, the things in the heavens, and the things on
τῆς γῆς, τὰ ὁρατὰ καὶ τὰ ἀόρατα, εἴτε θρόνοι, εἴτε κυριό-
the earth, the visible and the invisible, whether thrones, or lordships
τητες, εἴτε ἀρχαί, εἴτε ἐξουσίαι· τὰ πάντα δι' αὐτοῦ καὶ εἰς
or rulers, or authorities; all things through Him and for
17 αὐτὸν ἔκτισται· καὶ αὐτός ἐστι πρὸ πάντων, καὶ τὰ πάντα
Him have been created, and He is before all things, and all things
18 ἐν αὐτῷ συνέστηκε. καὶ αὐτός ἐστιν ἡ κεφαλὴ τοῦ σώματος,
in Him consisted; and He is the Head of the body,
τῆς ἐκκλησίας· ὅς ἐστιν ἀρχή, πρωτότοκος ἐκ τῶν νεκρῶν,
the church, who is (the) beginning, firstborn from the dead,
19 ἵνα γένηται ἐν πᾶσιν αὐτὸς πρωτεύων· ὅτι ἐν αὐτῷ εὐδόκησε
that may be in all things He pre-eminent, because in Him was pleased
20 πᾶν τὸ πλήρωμα κατοικῆσαι, καὶ δι' αὐτοῦ ἀποκαταλλάξαι
all the fullness to dwell, and through Him to reconcile
τὰ πάντα εἰς αὐτόν, εἰρηνοποιήσας διὰ τοῦ αἵματος τοῦ
all things to Himself, making peace through the blood of the
σταυροῦ αὐτοῦ, δι' αὐτοῦ, εἴτε τὰ ἐπὶ τῆς γῆς, εἴτε τὰ ἐν
cross of Him, through Him, whether the things on the earth, or those in
21 τοῖς οὐρανοῖς. Καὶ ὑμᾶς ποτὲ ὄντας ἀπηλλοτριωμένους καὶ
the heavens. And you, then, being alienated and
ἐχθροὺς τῇ διανοίᾳ ἐν τοῖς ἔργοις τοῖς πονηροῖς, νυνὶ δὲ
enemies in the mind by (your) works evil. now But
22 ἀποκατήλλαξεν ἐν τῷ σώματι τῆς σαρκὸς αὐτοῦ διὰ τοῦ
He reconciled in the body of the flesh of Him through the
θανάτου, παραστῆσαι ὑμᾶς ἁγίους καὶ ἀμώμους καὶ
death (of Him), to present you holy and blameless and
23 ἀνεγκλήτους κατενώπιον αὐτοῦ· εἴγε ἐπιμένετε τῇ πίστει
without charge before Him, if indeed you continue in the faith
τεθεμελιωμένοι καὶ ἑδραῖοι, καὶ μὴ μετακινούμενοι ἀπὸ τῆς
having been founded and steadfast, and not being moved away from the
ἐλπίδος τοῦ εὐαγγελίου οὗ ἠκούσατε, τοῦ κηρυχθέντος ἐν
hope of the gospel which you heard proclaimed in
πάσῃ τῇ κτίσει τῇ ὑπὸ τὸν οὐρανόν, οὗ ἐγενόμην ἐγὼ
all the creation under Heaven, of which became I,
Παῦλος διάκονος.
Paul, a minister.

24 Ὃς νῦν χαίρω ἐν τοῖς παθήμασί μου ὑπὲρ ὑμῶν, καὶ
Who now rejoice in the sufferings of me on behalf of you, and

and I fill up in my flesh the things lacking of the afflictions of Christ, on behalf of His body, which is the church; 25 of which I became a minister, according to the administration of God given to me to fulfill the word of God, 26 the mystery having been hidden from the ages, and from the generations, but now was revealed to His saints; 27 to whom God desired to make known what *are* the riches of the glory of this mystery among the nations, which is Christ in you, the hope of glory; 28 whom we announce, warning every man and teaching every man in all wisdom, that we may present every man full-grown in Christ Jesus. 29 For which I labor, working according to the working of Him who works in me in power.

CHAPTER 2

1 For I want you to know how great a struggle I have concerning you, and those in Laodicea, and as many as have not seen my face in *the* flesh; 2 that their hearts may be comforted, being joined together in love, and to all riches of the full assurance of the understanding, to *the* full knowledge of the mystery of God, even of *the* Father and of Christ, 3 in whom are hidden all the treasures of wisdom and of knowledge. 4 And I say this, that no one may beguile you with persuasive words. 5 For though I am indeed absent in the flesh, yet I am with you in spirit, rejoicing and seeing your order, and the firmness of your faith in Christ. 6 Therefore, as you received Christ Jesus the Lord, walk in Him, 7 having been rooted and built up in Him, and having been confirmed in the faith, even as you were taught, abound-

ἀνταναπληρῶ τὰ ὑστερήματα τῶν θλίψεων τοῦ Χριστοῦ
fill up the things lacking of the afflictions of Christ
ἐν τῇ σαρκί μου ὑπὲρ τοῦ σώματος αὐτοῦ, ὅ ἐστιν ἡ
in the flesh of me on behalf of the body of Him, which is the
25 ἐκκλησία· ἧς ἐγενόμην ἐγὼ διάκονος, κατὰ τὴν οἰκονομίαν
church, of which became I a minister as regards the stewardship
τοῦ Θεοῦ τὴν δοθεῖσάν μοι εἰς ὑμᾶς, πληρῶσαι τὸν λόγον
of God given to me for you, to fulfill the word
26 τοῦ Θεοῦ, τὸ μυστήριον τὸ ἀποκεκρυμμένον ἀπὸ τῶν
of God, the mystery having been hidden from the
αἰώνων καὶ ἀπὸ τῶν γενεῶν· νυνὶ δὲ ἐφανερώθη τοῖς ἁγίοις
ages and from the generations, now but was revealed to the saints
27 αὐτοῦ, οἷς ἠθέλησεν ὁ Θεὸς γνωρίσαι τίς ὁ πλοῦτος τῆς
of Him, to whom desired God to make known what (are) the riches of the
δόξης τοῦ μυστηρίου τούτου ἐν τοῖς ἔθνεσιν, ὅς ἐστι Χριστὸς
glory mystery of this among the nations, who is Christ
28 ἐν ὑμῖν, ἡ ἐλπὶς τῆς δόξης· ὃν ἡμεῖς καταγγέλλομεν, νου-
in you, the hope of the glory, whom we announce,
θετοῦντες πάντα ἄνθρωπον, καὶ διδάσκοντες πάντα ἄνθρω-
warning every man, and teaching every man
πον ἐν πάσῃ σοφίᾳ, ἵνα παραστήσωμεν πάντα ἄνθρωπον
in all wisdom that we may present every man
29 τέλειον ἐν Χριστῷ Ἰησοῦ· εἰς ὃ καὶ κοπιῶ, ἀγωνιζόμενος
full-grown in Christ Jesus, for which also I labor, struggling
κατὰ τὴν ἐνέργειαν αὐτοῦ, τὴν ἐνεργουμένην ἐν ἐμοὶ ἐν
according to the working of Him, the (One) working in me in
δυνάμει.
power.

CHAPTER 2

1 Θέλω γὰρ ὑμᾶς εἰδέναι ἡλίκον ἀγῶνα ἔχω περὶ ὑμῶν καὶ
I want For you to know how great a struggle I have as to you and
τῶν ἐν Λαοδικείᾳ, καὶ ὅσοι οὐχ ἑωράκασι τὸ πρόσωπόν μου
those in Laodicea, and as many as not have seen the face of me
2 ἐν σαρκί, ἵνα παρακληθῶσιν αἱ καρδίαι αὐτῶν, συμβιβασθέν-
in (the) flesh, that may be comforted the hearts of them, being joined to-
των ἐν ἀγάπῃ, καὶ εἰς πάντα πλοῦτον τῆς πληροφορίας τῆς
gether in love, and for all riches of the full assurance of the
συνέσεως, εἰς ἐπίγνωσιν τοῦ μυστηρίου τοῦ Θεοῦ καὶ πατρὸς
understanding, for full knowledge of the mystery of God, and of Father,
3 καὶ τοῦ Χριστοῦ, ἐν ᾧ εἰσὶ πάντες οἱ θησαυροὶ τῆς σοφίας
and of Christ, in whom are all the treasures of wisdom
4 καὶ τῆς γνώσεως ἀπόκρυφοι. τοῦτο δὲ λέγω, ἵνα μή τις ὑμᾶς
and knowledge hidden. this And I say, that not anyone you
5 παραλογίζηται ἐν πιθανολογίᾳ. εἰ γὰρ καὶ τῇ σαρκὶ ἄπειμι,
beguile by persuasive words. if For indeed in the flesh I am absent,
ἀλλὰ τῷ πνεύματι σὺν ὑμῖν εἰμί, χαίρων καὶ βλέπων ὑμῶν
yet in the spirit with you I am, rejoicing and seeing of you
τὴν τάξιν, καὶ τὸ στερέωμα τῆς εἰς Χριστὸν πίστεως ὑμῶν.
the order, and the firmness of the in Christ faith of you.
6 Ὡς οὖν παρελάβετε τὸν Χριστὸν Ἰησοῦν τὸν Κύριον, ἐν
As, therefore, you received Christ Jesus the Lord, in
7 αὐτῷ περιπατεῖτε, ἐρριζωμένοι καὶ ἐποικοδομούμενοι ἐν
Him walk, having been rooted and having been built up in
αὐτῷ, καὶ βεβαιούμενοι ἐν τῇ πίστει, καθὼς ἐδιδάχθητε,
Him, and being confirmed in the faith, as you were taught,

ing in it with thanksgiving.
[8]Watch, that there not be one robbing you through philosophy and empty deceit, according to the tradition of men, according to the elements of the world, and not according to Christ. [9]For in Him dwells all the fullness of the Godhead bodily; [10]and having been filled, you are in Him; who is the Head of all rule and authority, [11]in whom also you were circumcised with a circumcision not made by hand, in the putting off of the body of the sins of the flesh, by the circumcision of Christ; [12]being buried with Him in baptism, in whom also you were raised through the faith of the working of God, raising Him from the dead. [13]And you, being dead in the offenses and the circumcision of your flesh, He made alive together with Him, having forgiven us all the offenses; [14]blotting out the handwriting in the ordinances against us, which were contrary to us, even *He* has taken it out of the midst, nailing it to the cross; [15]having stripped the rulers and the authorities, He made a show of them in public, triumphing *over* them in it.

[16]Then do not let anything judge you in eating or in drinking, or in respect of a feast, or the new moon, or of sabbaths, [17]which are a shadow of coming things; but the body *is* of Christ. [18]Let no one judge you unworthy, willing in humility and worship of the angels, pushing into things which he has not seen, *being* puffed up by the mind of his flesh without a cause, [19]and not holding fast the Head, from whom all the body having been supplied *with* the joints and bands, and having been joined together, will grow with the growth *which comes* from God.

[20]If, then, you died with Christ from the elements of the world, why are you under *its* decrees, as living in *the* world? [21]Do not handle; do

περισσεύοντες ἐν αὐτῇ ἐν εὐχαριστίᾳ.
abounding in it in thanksgiving.
8 Βλέπετε μή τις ὑμᾶς ἔσται ὁ συλαγωγῶν διὰ τῆς φιλοσο-
Watch, lest anyone you shall be robbing through philoso-
φίας καὶ κενῆς ἀπάτης, κατὰ τὴν παράδοσιν τῶν ἀνθρώπων,
phy and vain deceit, according to the tradition of men,
9 κατὰ τὰ στοιχεῖα τοῦ κόσμου, καὶ οὐ κατὰ Χριστόν· ὅτι ἐν
according to the elements of the world, and not according to Christ; for in
αὐτῷ κατοικεῖ πᾶν τὸ πλήρωμα τῆς θεότητος σωματικῶς,
Him dwells all the fullness of the Godhead bodily,
10 καί ἐστε ἐν αὐτῷ πεπληρωμένοι, ὅς ἐστιν ἡ κεφαλὴ πασης
and you are in Him having been filled, who is the Head of all
11 ἀρχῆς καὶ ἐξουσίας· ἐν ᾧ καὶ περιετμήθητε περιτομῇ ἀχει-
rule and authority, in whom also you were circumcised with a circumcision not
ροποιήτῳ, ἐν τῇ ἀπεκδύσει του σώματος τῶν ἁμαρτιῶν
made by hand, by the putting off of the body of the sins
12 τῆς σαρκός, ἐν τῇ περιτομῇ τοῦ Χριστοῦ, συνταφέντες αὐτῷ
of the flesh, by the circumcision of Christ, co-buried with Him
ἐν τῷ βαπτίσματι, ἐν ᾧ καὶ συνηγέρθητε διὰ τῆς πίστεως τῆς
in the baptism, in whom also you were raised through the faith of the
ἐνεργείας τοῦ Θεοῦ, τοῦ ἐγείραντος αὐτὸν ἐκ τῶν νεκρῶν.
working of God, raising Him from the dead;
13 καὶ ὑμᾶς, νεκροὺς ὄντας εν τοῖς παραπτώμασι καὶ τῇ ἀκρο-
and you dead being in the offenses and the uncir-
βυστίᾳ τῆς σαρκὸς ὑμῶν, συνεζωοποίησε σὺν αὐτῷ, χαρισά-
cumcision of the flesh of you, He made alive you with Him, having for-
14 μενος ὑμῖν πάντα τὰ παραπτώματα, ἐξαλείψας τὸ καθ' ἡμῶν
given you all the offenses; blotting out the against us
χειρόγραφον τοῖς δόγμασιν, ὃ ἦν ὑπεναντίον ἡμῖν· καὶ αὐτὸ
handwriting in ordinances which were contrary to us, and it
15 ἦρκεν ἐκ τοῦ μέσου, προσηλώσας αὐτὸ τῷ σταυρῷ· ἀπεκδυ-
has taken out of the midst, nailing it to the cross; having
σάμενος τὰς ἀρχὰς καὶ τὰς ἐξουσίας, ἐδειγμάτισεν ἐν παρ-
stripped the rulers and the authorities, He displayed (them) in
ρησίᾳ, θριαμβεύσας αὐτοὺς ἐν αὐτῷ.
public, triumphing (over) them in it.

16 Μὴ οὖν τις ὑμᾶς κρινέτω ἐν βρώσει ἢ ἐν πόσει, ἢ ἐν μέρει
Not, therefore, anyone you let judge in eating or in drinking, or in respect
17 ἑορτῆς ἢ νουμηνίας ἢ σαββάτων· ἅ ἐστι σκιὰ τῶν μελλόν-
of a feast, or of a new moon, or of sabbaths, which is a shadow of things
18 των, τὸ δὲ σῶμα τοῦ Χριστοῦ. μηδεὶς ὑμᾶς καταβραβευέτω
coming, the but body (is) of Christ. No one you let give judgment
θέλων ἐν ταπεινοφροσύνῃ καὶ θρησκείᾳ τῶν ἀγγέλων, ἃ
wishing in humility and worship of the angels, things which
μὴ ἑώρακεν ἐμβατεύων, εἰκῆ φυσιούμενος ὑπὸ τοῦ νοὸς
not he has seen pushing into, without a cause puffed up by the mind
19 τῆς σαρκὸς αὐτοῦ, καὶ οὐ κρατῶν τὴν κεφαλήν, ἐξ οὗ πᾶν
of the flesh of him, and not holding the Head, from whom all
τὸ σῶμα, διὰ τῶν ἁφῶν καὶ συνδέσμων ἐπιχορηγούμενον
the body, through the joints and bands having been supplied
καὶ συμβιβαζόμενον, αὔξει τὴν αὔξησιν τοῦ Θεοῦ.
and having been joined together will grow with the growth of God.
20 Εἰ οὖν ἀπεθάνετε σὺν τῷ Χριστῷ ἀπὸ τῶν· στοιχείων
If, then, you died with Christ from the elements
21 τοῦ κόσμου, τί, ὡς ζῶντες ἐν κόσμῳ, δογματίζεσθε, Μὴ
of the world, why as living in (the) world, are you under decrees: Not

not taste; do not touch— [22]which things are all to rot away in the using, according to the injunctions and teachings of men. [23]Which things indeed have a reputation of wisdom in will-worship and humility, and unsparing *abuse* of *the* body, not in any honor for satisfaction of the flesh.

CHAPTER 3

[1]If, then, you were raised with Christ, seek the things above, where Christ is sitting at *the* right of God; [2]mind the things above, not the things on the earth, [3]for you died, and your life has been hidden with Christ in God. [4]Whenever Christ our life is revealed, then also you will be revealed in glory with Him.

[5]Therefore, put to death your members on the earth: fornication, uncleanness, passion, evil lust, and covetousness, which is idolatry; [6]on account of which things the wrath of God is coming on the sons of disobedience; [7]among whom you also walked at one time, when you were living in these. [8]But now also put off all *these* things: wrath, anger, malice, evil speaking, shameful words out of your mouth. [9]Do not lie to one another, having put off the old man with his practices, and having put on the new, having been renewed in full knowledge according to *the* image of the *One* creating him; [11]where there is no Greek and Jew, circumcision and uncircumcision, foreigner, Scythian, slave *or* freeman —but Christ *is* all things in all.

[12]Then put on as the elect of God, holy and beloved, tender feelings of compassions, kindness, humility, meekness, long-suffering, [13]bearing with one another, and forgiving each other, if any has a complaint against anyone; even as Christ forgave you, so you also *do*.

22 ἄψῃ, μηδὲ γεύσῃ, μηδὲ θίγῃς (ἅ ἐστι πάντα εἰς φθορὰν τῇ
touch, nor taste, nor handle· which things are all for corruption in the
ἀποχρήσει), κατὰ τὰ ἐντάλματα καὶ διδασκαλίας τῶν
using — according to the injunctions and teachings
23 ἀνθρώπων; ἅτινά ἐστι λόγον μὲν ἔχοντα σοφίας ἐν ἐθε-
of men? Which things is a repute indeed having of wisdom in self-
λοθρησκείᾳ καὶ ταπεινοφροσύνῃ καὶ ἀφειδίᾳ σώματος, οὐκ
imposed worship and humility and unsparing (abuse) of (the) body, not
ἐν τιμῇ τινὶ πρὸς πλησμονὴν τῆς σαρκός.
in honor any for satisfaction of the flesh.

CHAPTER 3

1 Εἰ οὖν συνηγέρθητε τῷ Χριστῷ, τὰ ἄνω ζητεῖτε, οὗ ὁ
If, then, you were raised with Christ, the things above seek, where
2 Χριστός ἐστιν ἐν δεξιᾷ τοῦ Θεοῦ καθήμενος. τὰ ἄνω φρονεῖτε,
Christ is at (the) right of God sitting; the things above mind,
3 μὴ τὰ ἐπὶ τῆς γῆς. ἀπεθάνετε γάρ, καὶ ἡ ζωὴ ὑμῶν κέκρυ-
not the things on the earth. you died For, and the life of you has been
4 πται σὺν τῷ Χριστῷ ἐν τῷ Θεῷ. ὅταν ὁ Χριστὸς φανερωθῇ,
hidden with Christ in God. Whenever Christ is revealed,
ἡ ζωὴ ἡμῶν, τότε καὶ ὑμεῖς σὺν αὐτῷ φανερωθήσεσθε ἐν
the life of us, then also you with Him will be revealed in
δόξῃ.
glory.

5 Νεκρώσατε οὖν τὰ μέλη ὑμῶν τὰ ἐπὶ τῆς γῆς, πορνείαν,
put to death Therefore the members of you on the earth, fornication,
ἀκαθαρσίαν, πάθος, ἐπιθυμίαν κακήν, καὶ τὴν πλεονεξίαν,
uncleanness, passion, lust evil, and covetousness,
6 ἥτις ἐστὶν εἰδωλολατρεία, δι' ἃ ἔρχεται ἡ ὀργὴ τοῦ Θεοῦ
which is idolatry; for which things is coming the wrath of God
7 ἐπὶ τοὺς υἱοὺς τῆς ἀπειθείας· ἐν οἷς καὶ ὑμεῖς περιεπατήσατέ
on the sons of disobedience, among whom also you . walked
8 ποτε, ὅτε ἐζῆτε ἐν αὐτοῖς. νυνὶ δὲ ἀπόθεσθε καὶ ὑμεῖς τὰ
then, when you were living in these. now But, put off also you
πάντα, ὀργήν, θυμόν, κακίαν, βλασφημίαν, αἰσχρολογίαν
all things: wrath, anger, malice, evil speaking, shameful words
9 ἐκ τοῦ στόματος ὑμῶν· μὴ ψεύδεσθε εἰς ἀλλήλους, ἀπεκδυσά-
out of the mouth of you. Do not lie to one another, having put
μενοι τὸν παλαιὸν ἄνθρωπον σὺν ταῖς πράξεσιν αὐτοῦ,
off the old man with the practices of him,
10 καὶ ἐνδυσάμενοι τὸν νέον, τὸν ἀνακαινούμενον εἰς ἐπίγνωσιν
and having put on the new (man) being renewed in full knowledge
11 κατ' εἰκόνα τοῦ κτίσαντος αὐτόν· ὅπου οὐκ ἔνι Ἕλλην καὶ
according to (the) image of Him creating him, where not there is Greek and
Ἰουδαῖος, περιτομὴ καὶ ἀκροβυστία, βάρβαρος, Σκύθης,
Jew, circumcision and uncircumcision, foreigner, Scythian,
δοῦλος, ἐλεύθερος· ἀλλὰ τὰ πάντα καὶ ἐν πᾶσι Χριστός.
slave, freeman, but all things and in all Christ (is).
12 Ἐνδύσασθε οὖν. ὡς ἐκλεκτοὶ τοῦ Θεοῦ, ἅγιοι καὶ
put on Therefore, as elect ones of God, holy and
ἠγαπημένοι, σπλάγχνα οἰκτιρμῶν, χρηστότητα, ταπεινο-
having been loved, bowels of compassions, kindness, humility,
13 φροσύνην, πρᾳότητα, μακροθυμίαν· ἀνεχόμενοι ἀλλήλων,
meekness, long-suffering, forbearing one another,
καὶ χαριζόμενοι ἑαυτοῖς, ἐάν τις πρός τινα ἔχῃ μομφήν· καθὼς
and forgiving yourselves, if anyone against any has a complaint; as

14 And above all these, *add* love, which is *the* bond of perfectness. 15 And let the peace of God rule in your hearts, to which you also were called in one body, and be thankful. 16 Let the word of Christ live in you richly, in all wisdom, teaching and exhorting yourselves in psalms and hymns and spiritual songs, singing with grace in your hearts to the Lord. 17 And everything, whatever you do in word or in work, *do* all things in the name of *the* Lord Jesus, giving thanks to God and *the* Father through Him.

18 Wives, be subject to *your* own husbands, as is becoming in *the* Lord. 19 Husbands, love the wives, and do not be bitter against them. 20 Children, obey the parents in all things; for this is well-pleasing to the Lord. 21 Fathers, do not provoke your children, that they may not be disheartened. 22 Slaves, obey the lords according to flesh in all respects, not with eye-service as men-pleasers, but in singleness of heart, fearing God. 23 And whatever you may do, work from the soul, as to the Lord, and not to men, 24 knowing that from *the* Lord you shall receive the reward of the inheritance. For you serve *the* Lord Christ. 25 But the *one* doing wrong will receive what he did wrong, and there is no respect of persons.

CHAPTER 4

1 Lords, give that which *is* just and that which *is* equal to the slaves, knowing that you have a Lord in Heaven.

2 Steadfastly continue in prayer, watching in it with thanksgiving, 3 praying together about us also, that

14 καὶ ὁ Χριστὸς ἐχαρίσατο ὑμῖν, οὕτω καὶ ὑμεῖς· ἐπὶ πᾶσι δὲ
indeed Christ forgave you, so also you; above all and
τούτοις τὴν ἀγάπην, ἥτις ἐστὶ σύνδεσμος τῆς τελειότητος.
these things love, which is (the) bond of perfectness.
15 καὶ ἡ εἰρήνη τοῦ Θεοῦ βραβευέτω ἐν ταῖς καρδίαις ὑμῶν,
And the peace of God let rule in the hearts of you,
16 εἰς ἣν καὶ ἐκλήθητε ἐν ἑνὶ σώματι· καὶ εὐχάριστοι γίνεσθε. ὁ
to which indeed you were called in one body, and thankful be. The
λόγος τοῦ Χριστοῦ ἐνοικείτω ἐν ὑμῖν πλουσίως ἐν πάσῃ
word of Christ let dwell in you richly, in all
σοφίᾳ· διδάσκοντες καὶ νουθετοῦντες ἑαυτούς, ψαλμοῖς, καὶ
wisdom teaching and exhorting yourselves, in psalms and
17 ὕμνοις, καὶ ᾠδαῖς πνευματικαῖς, ἐν χάριτι ᾄδοντες ἐν τῇ
hymns and songs spiritual, with grace singing in the
καρδίᾳ ὑμῶν τῷ Κυρίῳ. καὶ πᾶν ὅ τι ἂν ποιῆτε, ἐν λόγῳ ἢ
hearts of you to the Lord. And everything, whatever you do in word or
ἐν ἔργῳ, πάντα ἐν ὀνόματι Κυρίου Ἰησοῦ, εὐχαριστοῦντες
in work, all things (do) in the name of (the) Lord Jesus, giving thanks
τῷ Θεῷ καὶ πατρὶ δι' αὐτοῦ.
to God and (the) Father through Him.
18 Αἱ γυναῖκες, ὑποτάσσεσθε τοῖς ἰδίοις ἀνδράσιν, ὡς ἀνῆκεν
The wives: be subject to the own husbands, as is befitting
19 ἐν Κυρίῳ. οἱ ἄνδρες, ἀγαπᾶτε τὰς γυναῖκας, καὶ μὴ πικραί-
in (the) Lord. The husbands: love the wives, and not be
20 νεσθε πρὸς αὐτάς. τὰ τέκνα, ὑπακούετε τοῖς γονεῦσι κατὰ
bitter toward them. The children: obey the parents all in
21 πάντα· τοῦτο γάρ ἐστιν εὐάρεστον τῷ Κυρίῳ. οἱ πατέρες,
all, this for is well-pleasing to the Lord. The fathers:
22 μὴ ἐρεθίζετε τὰ τέκνα ὑμῶν, ἵνα μὴ ἀθυμῶσιν. οἱ δοῦλοι,
do not provoke the children of you, that not they be disheartened. The slaves:
ὑπακούετε κατὰ πάντα τοῖς κατὰ σάρκα κυρίοις, μὴ ἐν
obey all in all those according to flesh lords, not with
ὀφθαλμοδουλείαις ὡς ἀνθρωπάρεσκοι, ἀλλ' ἐν ἁπλότητι
eye-services as men-pleasers, but in singleness
23 καρδίας, φοβούμενοι τὸν Θεόν· καὶ πᾶν ὅ τι ἐὰν ποιῆτε, ἐκ
of heart, fearing God. And everything whatever you do, from
24 ψυχῆς ἐργάζεσθε, ὡς τῷ Κυρίῳ καὶ οὐκ ἀνθρώποις· εἰδότες
the soul work as to the Lord and not to men, knowing
ὅτι ἀπὸ Κυρίου ἀπολήψεσθε τὴν ἀνταπόδοσιν τῆς κληρονο-
that from (the) Lord you will receive the reward of the inheritance.
25 μίας· τῷ γὰρ Κυρίῳ Χριστῷ δουλεύετε. ὁ δὲ ἀδικῶν
the For Lord Christ you serve; the (one) and doing wrong
κομιεῖται ὃ ἠδίκησε· καὶ οὐκ ἔστι προσωποληψία.
will receive what he did wrong. and not is (any) respect of persons.

CHAPTER 4

1 οἱ κύριοι, τὸ δίκαιον καὶ τὴν
The lords: the just thing and the
ἰσότητα τοῖς δούλοις παρέχεσθε, εἰδότες ὅτι καὶ ὑμεῖς ἔχετε
equality to the slaves supply, knowing that also you have
Κύριον ἐν οὐρανοῖς.
a Lord in Heaven.
2 Τῇ προσευχῇ προσκαρτερεῖτε, γρηγοροῦντες ἐν αὐτῇ ἐν
In the prayer steadfastly continue, watching in it with
3 εὐχαριστίᾳ· προσευχόμενοι ἅμα καὶ περὶ ἡμῶν, ἵνα ὁ Θεὸς
thanksgiving, praying together also about us, that God

God may open to us a door of the word, to speak the mystery of Christ, on account of which I also have been bound, [4]that I may make it clear, as I ought to speak. [5]Walk in wisdom toward the ones outside, redeeming the time. [6]Let your word *be* always with grace, seasoned with salt, to know how you ought to answer each one.

[7]Tychichus the beloved brother and faithful minister, and fellow-slave in *the* Lord, will make known to you the things about me, [8]whom I sent to you for this very thing, that he know the things about you, and that he might comfort your hearts; [9]with Onesimus the faithful and beloved brother, who is of you. They will make known to you all the things here.

[10]Aristarchus, my fellow-prisoner, greets you; also Mark the cousin of Barnabas, about whom you received orders—if he comes to you, receive him—[11]and Jesus, the *one* being called Justus, those being of the circumcision, these only fellow-workers for the kingdom of God, who became a comfort to me. [12]Epaphras greets you, he of you, a slave of Christ, always striving for you in prayers, that you may stand full-grown and complete in every will of God. [13]For I bear witness to him, that he has much zeal on your behalf, and those in Laodicea, and those in Hierapolis. [14]Luke the beloved physician greets you, also Demas. [15]Greet the brothers in Laodicea, and Nymphas, and the church in his house.

[16]And when this letter is read before you, cause that it be read also in the Laodicean church; and the *one* of Laodicea, that you also read. [17]And say to Archippus, Look to the ministry which you received in *the* Lord, that you may fulfill it.

ἀνοίξῃ ἡμῖν θύραν τοῦ λόγου, λαλῆσαι τὸ μυστήριον τοῦ
may open to us a door of the word, to speak the mystery
4 Χριστοῦ, δι' ὃ καὶ δέδεμαι ἵνα φανερώσω αὐτό, ὡς δεῖ με
of Christ, for which also I have been bound, that I may reveal it as it behoves me
5 λαλῆσαι. ἐν σοφίᾳ περιπατεῖτε πρὸς τοὺς ἔξω, τὸν καιρὸν
to speak: In wisdom walk toward those outside, the time
6 ἐξαγοραζόμενοι. ὁ λόγος ὑμῶν πάντοτε ἐν χάριτι, ἅλατι
redeeming. The speech of you (let be) always with grace, with salt
ἠρτυμένος, εἰδέναι πῶς δεῖ ὑμᾶς ἑνὶ ἑκάστῳ ἀποκρίνεσθαι.
being seasoned, to know how it behoves you one each to answer.
7 Τὰ κατ' ἐμὲ πάντα γνωρίσει ὑμῖν Τυχικός, ὁ ἀγαπητὸς
The things about me all will make known to you Tychicus the beloved
8 ἀδελφὸς καὶ πιστὸς διάκονος καὶ σύνδουλος ἐν Κυρίῳ ὃν
brother and faithful minister, and fellow-slave in (the) Lord, whom
ἔπεμψα πρὸς ὑμᾶς εἰς αὐτὸ τοῦτο, ἵνα γνῷ τὰ περὶ ὑμῶν καὶ
I sent to you for this same thing, that he know the things about us, and
9 παρακαλέσῃ τὰς καρδίας ὑμῶν· σὺν Ὀνησίμῳ τῷ πιστῷ
he might comfort the hearts of you, with Onesimus the faithful
καὶ ἀγαπητῷ ἀδελφῷ, ὅς ἐστιν ἐξ ὑμῶν. πάντα ὑμῖν
and beloved brother, who is of you; all to you
γνωριοῦσι τὰ ὧδε.
they will make known the things here.
10 Ἀσπάζεται ὑμᾶς Ἀρίσταρχος ὁ συναιχμάλωτός μου,
Greets you Aristarchus the fellow-captive of me,
καὶ Μάρκος ὁ ἀνεψιὸς Βαρνάβα (περὶ οὗ ἐλάβετε ἐντολάς·
and Mark the cousin of Barnabas about whom you received orders;
11 ἐὰν ἔλθῃ πρὸς ὑμᾶς, δέξασθε αὐτόν), καὶ Ἰησοῦς ὁ λεγό-
if he comes to you, receive him — and Jesus, the (one)
μενος Ἰοῦστος, οἱ ὄντες ἐκ περιτομῆς· οὗτοι μόνοι συνεργοὶ
named Justus, those being of the circumcision, these only fellow-workers
εἰς τὴν βασιλείαν τοῦ Θεοῦ, οἵτινες ἐγενήθησάν μοι
for the kingdom of God, who became to me
12 παρηγορία. ἀσπάζεται ὑμᾶς Ἐπαφρᾶς ὁ ἐξ ὑμῶν, δοῦλος
a comfort. Greets you Epaphras the (one) of you, a slave
Χριστοῦ, πάντοτε ἀγωνιζόμενος ὑπὲρ ὑμῶν ἐν ταῖς προσ-
of Christ, always struggling on behalf of you in the
ευχαῖς, ἵνα στῆτε τέλειοι καὶ πεπληρωμένοι ἐν παντὶ
prayers, that you may stand full-grown and being complete in all
13 θελήματι τοῦ Θεοῦ. μαρτυρῶ γὰρ αὐτῷ ὅτι ἔχει ζῆλον
(the) will of God. I bear witness For to him that he has zeal
πολὺν ὑπὲρ ὑμῶν καὶ τῶν ἐν Λαοδικείᾳ καὶ τῶν ἐν Ἱεραπό-
much on behalf of you, and those in Laodicea, and those in Hierapolis.
14 λει. ἀσπάζεται ὑμᾶς Λουκᾶς ὁ ἰατρὸς ὁ ἀγαπητός, καὶ
Greets you Luke the physician beloved, and
15 Δημᾶς. ἀσπάσασθε τοὺς ἐν Λαοδικείᾳ ἀδελφούς, καὶ Νυμφᾶν,
Demas. Greet the in Laodicea brothers, and Nymphas
16 καὶ τὴν κατ' οἶκον αὐτοῦ ἐκκλησίαν. καὶ ὅταν ἀναγνωσθῇ
and the at (the) house of him church. And whenever is read
παρ' ὑμῖν ἡ ἐπιστολή, ποιήσατε ἵνα καὶ ἐν τῇ Λαοδικέων
before you the epistle, cause that also in the Laodicean
ἐκκλησίᾳ ἀναγνωσθῇ, καὶ τὴν ἐκ Λαοδικείας ἵνα καὶ ὑμεῖς
church it is read, and the (one) of Laodicea, that also you
17 ἀναγνῶτε. καὶ εἴπατε Ἀρχίππῳ, Βλέπε τὴν διακονίαν ἣν
read. And tell Archippus: Look (to) the ministry which
παρέλαβες ἐν Κυρίῳ, ἵνα αὐτὴν πληροῖς.
you received in (the) Lord, that it you may fulfill.

[18]The greeting of Paul by my own hand. Remember my bonds. Grace *be* with you. Amen.

18 Ὁ ἀσπασμὸς τῇ ἐμῇ χειρὶ Παύλου. μνημονεύετέ μου τῶν
The greeting by my hand, of Paul. Remember of me the
δεσμῶν. ἡ χάρις μεθ' ὑμῶν. ἀμήν.
bonds. Grace (be) with you. Amen.

ΠΑΥΛΟΥ ΤΟΥ ΑΠΟΣΤΟΛΟΥ
PAUL THE APOSTLE
Η ΠΡΟΣ
TO THE
ΘΕΣΣΑΛΟΝΙΚΕΙΣ
THESSALONIANS
ΕΠΙΣΤΟΛΗ ΠΡΩΤΗ
EPISTLE FIRST
THESSALONIANS
CHAPTER 1

KING JAMES II VERSION

THE FIRST EPISTLE TO *THE* THESSALONIANS

CHAPTER 1

1 Paul and Silvanus and Timothy to the church of Thessalonians in God *the* Father and *the* Lord Jesus Christ: Grace and peace to you from God our Father and *the* Lord Jesus Christ.

2 We give thanks to God always concerning you all, making mention of you at our prayers, 3 remembering without ceasing your work of faith and labor of love, and the patience of hope of our Lord Jesus Christ, before our God and Father; 4 knowing, brothers, beloved by God, your election. 5 For our gospel did not come to you in word only, but also in power, and in *the* Holy Spirit, and in much assurance, even as you know what we were among you for your sake. 6 And you became imitators of us and of the Lord, welcoming the word in much affliction with joy of *the* Holy Spirit, 7 so that you became examples to all those believing in Macedonia and Achaia. 8 For the word of the Lord sounded out from you, not only in Macedonia and Achaia, but also in every place your faith toward God has gone out, so that there is no need for us to have to say anything. 9 for they themselves announce concerning us, what kind of entrance we have to you, and

1 Παῦλος καὶ Σιλουανὸς καὶ Τιμόθεος, τῇ ἐκκλησίᾳ Θεσ-
Paul and Silvanus and Timothy to the church of
σαλονικέων ἐν Θεῷ πατρί, καὶ Κυρίῳ Ἰησοῦ Χριστῷ· χάρις
Thessalonians in God (the) Father, and (the) Lord Jesus Christ: Grace
ὑμῖν καὶ εἰρήνη ἀπὸ Θεοῦ πατρὸς ἡμῶν καὶ Κυρίου Ἰησοῦ
to you and peace from God (the) Father of us and (the) Lord Jesus
Χριστοῦ.
Christ.
2 Εὐχαριστοῦμεν τῷ Θεῷ πάντοτε περὶ πάντων ὑμῶν,
We give thanks to God always concerning all you,
3 μνείαν ὑμῶν ποιούμενοι ἐπὶ τῶν προσευχῶν ἡμῶν, ἀδια-
mention of you making on the prayers of us, un-
λείπτως μνημονεύοντες ὑμῶν τοῦ ἔργου τῆς πίστεως, καὶ
ceasingly remembering of you the work of faith, and
τοῦ κόπου τῆς ἀγάπης, καὶ τῆς ὑπομονῆς τῆς ἐλπίδος τοῦ
the labor of love, and the patience of hope of the
Κυρίου ἡμῶν Ἰησοῦ Χριστοῦ, ἔμπροσθεν τοῦ Θεοῦ καὶ
Lord of us, Jesus Christ, before the God and
4 πατρὸς ἡμῶν· εἰδότες, ἀδελφοὶ ἠγαπημένοι, ὑπὸ Θεοῦ τὴν
Father of us, knowing, brothers, having been loved by God the
5 ἐκλογὴν ὑμῶν· ὅτι τὸ εὐαγγέλιον ἡμῶν οὐκ ἐγενήθη εἰς ὑμᾶς
election of you; because the gospel of us not came to you
ἐν λόγῳ μόνον, ἀλλὰ καὶ ἐν δυνάμει, καὶ ἐν Πνεύματι Ἁγίῳ,
in word only, but also in power, and in (the) Spirit Holy,
καὶ ἐν πληροφορίᾳ πολλῇ, καθὼς οἴδατε οἷοι ἐγενήθημεν ἐν
and in assurance much, as you know what sort we were among
6 ὑμῖν δι' ὑμᾶς. καὶ ὑμεῖς μιμηταὶ ἡμῶν ἐγενήθητε καὶ τοῦ
you because of you. And you imitators of us became and of the
Κυρίου, δεξάμενοι τὸν λόγον ἐν θλίψει πολλῇ μετὰ χαρᾶς
Lord, welcoming the word in affliction much with joy
7 Πνεύματος Ἁγίου, ὥστε γενέσθαι ὑμᾶς τύπους πᾶσι τοῖς
of (the) Spirit Holy, so as to become you patterns to all those
8 πιστεύουσιν ἐν τῇ Μακεδονίᾳ καὶ τῇ Ἀχαΐα. ἀφ' ὑμῶν γὰρ
believing in Macedonia and Achaia. from you For
ἐξήχηται ὁ λόγος τοῦ Κυρίου οὐ μόνον ἐν τῇ Μακεδονίᾳ
sounded the word of the Lord not only in Macedonia
καὶ Ἀχαΐᾳ, ἀλλὰ καὶ ἐν παντὶ τόπῳ ἡ πίστις ὑμῶν ἡ πρὸς
and Achaia, but also in every place the faith of you toward
τὸν Θεὸν ἐξελήλυθεν, ὥστε μὴ χρείαν ἡμᾶς ἔχειν λαλεῖν τι.
God has gone out, so as not need for us to have to speak anything;
9 αὐτοὶ γὰρ περὶ ἡμῶν ἀπαγγέλλουσιν ὁποίαν εἴσοδον ἔσχο-
themselves for about us announce what kind of entrance we

how you had turned to God from the idols, to serve *the* true and living God, [10]and to eagerly await His Son from Heaven, whom He raised from *the* dead, Jesus, the *One* delivering us from the wrath to come.

CHAPTER 2

[1]For brothers, you yourselves know our coming in to you, that it has not been without fruit. [2]But also suffering before and being insulted in Philippi, as you know, we were bold in our God to speak the gospel of God to you in much agony. [3]For our exhortation *was* not of error, nor of uncleanness, nor in guile; [4]but even as we have been approved by God to be entrusted *with* the gospel, so we speak; not as pleasing men, but God, who tests our hearts. [5]For neither were we then *found* with words of flattery, even as you know, nor with pretense of covetousness—God is witness—[6]nor seeking glory from men; neither from you, nor from others, having been able to be *so* with heaviness as apostles of Christ. [7]But we were gentle in your midst, even as a nurse should warmly cherish her children.

[8]Longing over you in this way, we were pleased to impart to you not only the gospel of God, but also our own souls, because you have become beloved to us. [9]For you remember, brothers, our labor and toil, for we proclaimed the gospel of God to you night and day, working in order not to put a burden on anyone of you. [10]You and God *are* witnesses how holily and righteously and blamelessly we were to you, those believing; [11]even as you know how *I was to* each one of you, as a father *to* his children, exhorting and

μεν πρὸς ὑμᾶς, καὶ πῶς ἐπεστρέψατε πρὸς τὸν Θεὸν ἀπὸ τῶν
have to you, and how you had turned to God from the
10 εἰδώλων, δουλεύειν Θεῷ ζῶντι καὶ ἀληθινῷ καὶ ἀναμένειν
idols, to serve God living and true, and to await
τὸν υἱὸν αὐτοῦ ἐκ τῶν οὐρανῶν, ὃν ἤγειρεν ἐκ νεκρῶν,
the Son of Him from the heavens, whom He raised from (the) dead,
Ἰησοῦν, τὸν ῥυόμενον ἡμᾶς ἀπὸ τῆς ὀργῆς τῆς ἐρχομένης.
Jesus, He delivering us from the wrath coming.

CHAPTER 2

1 Αὐτοὶ γὰρ οἴδατε, ἀδελφοί, τὴν εἴσοδον ἡμῶν τὴν πρὸς
yourselves For, you know, brothers the entrance of us to
2 ὑμᾶς, ὅτι οὐ κενὴ γέγονεν· ἀλλὰ καὶ προπαθόντες καὶ
you, that not in vain it has been, but also having suffered before and
ὑβρισθέντες, καθὼς οἴδατε, ἐν Φιλίπποις, ἐπαρρησιασάμεθα
having been insulted, as you know, in Philippi we were bold
ἐν τῷ Θεῷ ἡμῶν λαλῆσαι πρὸς ὑμᾶς τὸ εὐαγγέλιον τοῦ
in the God of us to speak to you the gospel
3 Θεοῦ ἐν πολλῷ ἀγῶνι. ἡ γὰρ παράκλησις ἡμῶν οὐκ ἐκ
of God ,in much struggle. the For exhortation of us not of
4 πλάνης, οὐδὲ ἐξ ἀκαθαρσίας, οὔτε ἐν δόλῳ· ἀλλὰ καθὼς
error, nor of uncleanness. nor in guile, but as
δεδοκιμάσμεθα ὑπὸ τοῦ Θεοῦ πιστευθῆναι τὸ εὐαγγέλιον,
we have been approved by God to be entrusted (with) the gospel,
οὕτω λαλοῦμεν, οὐχ ὡς ἀνθρώποις ἀρέσκοντες, ἀλλὰ τῷ Θεῷ
so we speak, not as men pleasing, but God
5 τῷ δοκιμάζοντι τὰς καρδίας ἡμῶν. οὔτε γάρ ποτε ἐν λόγῳ
the (one) testing the hearts of us. neither For then in words
κολακείας ἐγενήθημεν, καθὼς οἴδατε, οὔτε ἐν προφάσει
of flattery were we, as you know, not with pretext
6 πλεονεξίας· Θεὸς μάρτυς· οὔτε ζητοῦντες ἐξ ἀνθρώπων
of covetousness—God (is) witness— nor seeking from men
δόξαν, οὔτε ἀφ' ὑμῶν οὔτε ἀπ' ἄλλων, δυνάμενοι ἐν βάρει
glory, neither from you, nor from others, being able with heaviness
7 εἶναι, ὡς Χριστοῦ ἀπόστολοι, ἀλλ' ἐγενήθημεν ἤπιοι ἐν
to be, as of Christ apostles; but we were gentle in
8 μέσῳ ὑμῶν, ὡς ἂν τροφὸς θάλπῃ τὰ ἑαυτῆς τέκνα· οὕτως,
(the) midst of you, as if a nurse should cherish the of herself children, so
ἱμειρόμενοι ὑμῶν, εὐδοκοῦμεν μεταδοῦναι ὑμῖν οὐ μόνον τὸ
longing for you, we were well-pleased to impart to you not only the
εὐαγγέλιον τοῦ Θεοῦ, ἀλλὰ καὶ τας ἑαυτῶν ψυχάς, διότι
gospel of God, but also the of ourselves souls, because
9 ἀγαπητοὶ ἡμῖν γεγένησθε. μνημονεύετε γάρ, ἀδελφοί, τὸν
beloved to us you have become. you remember For, brothers, the
κόπον ἡμῶν καὶ τὸν μόχθον· νυκτὸς γὰρ καὶ ἡμέρας ἐργαζό-
labor of us and the toil, night for and day working
μενοι, πρὸς τὸ μὴ ἐπιβαρῆσαί τινα ὑμῶν, ἐκηρύξαμεν εἰς
in order to not put a burden on anyone of you, we proclaimed to
10 ὑμᾶς τὸ εὐαγγέλιον τοῦ Θεοῦ. ὑμεῖς μάρτυρες καὶ ὁ Θεός,
you the gospel of God. You (are) witnesses, and God,
ὡς ὁσίως καὶ δικαίως καὶ ἀμέμπτως ὑμῖν τοῖς πιστεύουσιν
how holily and righteously and blamelessly to you, those believing,
11 ἐγενήθημεν· καθάπερ οἴδατε ὡς ἕνα ἕκαστον ὑμῶν, ὡς πατὴρ
we were, even as you know how one each of you, as a father
τέκνα ἑαυτοῦ, παρακαλοῦντες ὑμᾶς καὶ παραμυθούμενοι καὶ
children of himself, exhorting you and consoling, and

consoling you, [12] testifying for you to walk worthily of God, He calling you to His kingdom and glory.

[13] And because of this we give thanks to God without ceasing, that having received *the* word of hearing from us, you welcomed *it as* of God, not *as* a word of men, but as it is, truly *the* word of God, which also works in you, the *ones* believing. [14] For, brothers, you became imitators of the churches of God being in Judea in Christ Jesus, because you also suffered these things by *your* own fellow-countrymen, as they also by the Jews, [15] who both killed the Lord Jesus and *their* own prophets, also driving us out, and not pleasing God, and *being* contrary to all men; [16] forbidding us to speak to the nations in order that they be saved, to fill up their sins always. But the wrath has come on them to *the* uttermost.

[17] But, brothers, we being taken away from you for an hour's time, in presence, not in heart, we were much more eager with much desire to see your face. [18] Therefore, we desired to come to you, truly I, Paul, both once and twice; but Satan hindered us.

[19] For what *is* our hope or joy, or crown of glorying? *Are* you not even *to be* before our Lord Jesus at His coming? [20] For you are our glory and joy.

CHAPTER 3

[1] So no longer enduring, we were pleased to be left in Athens alone, [2] and sent our brother and minister of God, Timothy, and our fellow-worker in the gospel of Christ, in order to establish you and to encourage you

12 μαρτυρούμενοι, εἰς τὸ περιπατῆσαι ὑμᾶς ἀξίως τοῦ Θεοῦ
testifying for to have walked you worthily of God,
τοῦ καλοῦντος ὑμᾶς εἰς τὴν ἑαυτοῦ βασιλείαν καὶ δόξαν.
the (One) calling you to the of Himself kingdom and glory.
13 Διὰ τοῦτο καὶ ἡμεῖς εὐχαριστοῦμεν τῷ Θεῷ ἀδιαλείπτως,
therefore And we give thanks to God without ceasing,
ὅτι παραλαβόντες λόγον ἀκοῆς παρ' ἡμῶν τοῦ Θεοῦ,
that having received (the) word of hearing from us of God,
ἐδέξασθε οὐ λόγον ἀνθρώπων, ἀλλὰ καθώς ἐστιν ἀληθῶς,
you welcomed, not (as) a word of men, but as it is truly,
λόγον Θεοῦ, ὃς καὶ ἐνεργεῖται ἐν ὑμῖν τοῖς πιστεύουσιν.
a word of God, which also works in you, those believing.
14 ὑμεῖς γὰρ μιμηταὶ ἐγενήθητε, ἀδελφοί, τῶν ἐκκλησιῶν τοῦ
you For imitators became, brothers, of the churches
Θεοῦ τῶν οὐσῶν ἐν τῇ Ἰουδαίᾳ ἐν Χριστῷ Ἰησοῦ· ὅτι ταυτὰ
of God being in Judea in Christ Jesus, because these things
ἐπάθετε καὶ ὑμεῖς ὑπὸ τῶν ἰδίων συμφυλετῶν, καθὼς και
suffered also you by the own fellow-countrymen, as also
15 αὐτοί ὑπὸ τῶν Ἰουδαίων, τῶν καὶ τὸν Κύριον ἀποκτεινάν-
they by the Jews, those both the Lord killing,
των Ἰησοῦν καὶ τοὺς ἰδίους προφήτας, καὶ ἡμᾶς ἐκδιωξάν-
Jesus, and the own prophets, and us driving out
των, καὶ Θεῷ μὴ ἀρεσκόντων, καὶ πᾶσιν ἀνθρώποις
and God not pleasing, and to all men
16 ἐναντίων, κωλυόντων ἡμᾶς τοῖς ἔθνεσι λαλῆσαι ἵνα σωθῶσιν,
contrary, hindering us to the nations to speak, that they be saved,
εἰς τὸ ἀναπληρῶσαι αὐτῶν τὰς ἁμαρτίας πάντοτε· ἔφθασε
to fill up of them the sins always. has come
δὲ ἐπ' αὐτοὺς ἡ ὀργὴ εἰς τέλος.
But on them the wrath to (the) end.
17 Ἡμεῖς δέ, ἀδελφοί, ἀπορφανισθέντες ἀφ' ὑμῶν πρὸς καιρὸν
we But, brothers being taken away from you for time
ὥρας, προσώπῳ οὐ καρδίᾳ, περισσοτέρως ἐσπουδάσαμεν
of an hour, in face, not in heart, more abundantly were eager
18 τὸ πρόσωπον ὑμῶν ἰδεῖν ἐν πολλῇ ἐπιθυμίᾳ· διὸ ἠθελήσαμεν
the face of you to see with much desire. Therefore we desired
ἐλθεῖν πρὸς ὑμᾶς, ἐγὼ μὲν Παῦλος καὶ ἅπαξ καὶ δίς, καὶ ἐνέ-
to come to you, I indeed Paul, both once and twice, and
19 κοψεν ἡμᾶς ὁ Σατανᾶς. τίς γὰρ ἡμῶν ἐλπὶς ἢ χαρὰ ἢ στέ-
hindered us Satan. what For of us hope or joy or
φανος καυχήσεως; ἢ οὐχὶ καὶ ὑμεῖς, ἔμπροσθεν τοῦ Κυρίου
crown of boasting? Not even you before the Lord
20 ἡμῶν Ἰησοῦ Χριστοῦ ἐν τῇ αὐτοῦ παρουσίᾳ; ὑμεῖς γάρ
of us, Jesus Christ at the of Him coming? you For
ἐστε ἡ δόξα ἡμῶν καὶ ἡ χαρά.
you are the glory of us and the joy.

CHAPTER 3

1 Διὸ μηκέτι στέγοντες, εὐδοκήσαμεν καταλειφθῆναι ἐν
So no longer enduring, we were pleased to be left in
2 Ἀθήναις μόνοι, καὶ ἐπέμψαμεν Τιμόθεον τὸν ἀδελφὸν ἡμῶν
Athens alone, and sent Timothy the brother of us
καὶ διάκονον τοῦ Θεοῦ καὶ συνεργὸν ἡμῶν ἐν τῷ εὐαγγελίῳ
and minister of God, and fellow-worker of us in the gospel
τοῦ Χριστοῦ, εἰς τὸ στηρίξαι ὑμᾶς καὶ παρακαλέσαι ὑμᾶς περὶ
of Christ, to establish you and to encourage you about

concerning your faith, [3]that no one be drawn aside by these afflictions. For you yourselves know that we are appointed to this. [4]For even when we were with you, we told before that we are about to be afflicted, as it also happened, even you know. [5]Because of this, no longer enduring, I also sent to know your faith, that the tempting *one* not somehow tempt you, and our labor should become to no avail. [6]But now Timothy coming to us from you, and announcing good news to us *of* your love and faith, and that you have good remembrance of us always, longing to see us, even as also we *long to see* you, [7]because of this we were comforted as to you, brothers, on *knowing* all our affliction and distress through your faith, [8]for we now live, if you should stand fast in *the* Lord. [9]For what thanks are we able to return to God as to you, as to all the joy *with* which we rejoice on account of you before our God, [10]night and day praying to see your face, and to complete the things lacking in your faith?

[11]But may our God and Father Himself, and our Lord Jesus Christ, direct our way to you. [12]And may the Lord make you to increase and to abound in love toward one another and toward all, even as we also toward you, [13]in order to establish your hearts blameless in holiness before our God and Father at the coming of our Lord Jesus Christ with all His saints.

CHAPTER 4

[1]For the rest, then, brothers, we beg you and we exhort in *the* Lord Jesus, even as you received from us

3 τῆς πίστεως ὑμῶν, τῷ μηδένα σαίνεσθαι ἐν ταῖς θλίψεσι
the faith of you no one to be drawn aside by afflictions
4 ταύταις· αὐτοὶ γὰρ οἴδατε ὅτι εἰς τοῦτο κείμεθα. καὶ γὰρ
these. yourselves For you know that to this we are appointed. even For
ὅτε πρὸς ὑμᾶς ἦμεν, προελέγομεν ὑμῖν ὅτι μέλλομεν θλί-
when with you we were, we said before to you that we are about to be
5 βεσθαι, καθὼς καὶ ἐγένετο καὶ οἴδατε. διὰ τοῦτο κἀγώ,
afflicted, as also it happened, and you know. Therefore I also
μηκέτι στέγων, ἔπεμψα εἰς τὸ γνῶναι τὴν πίστιν ὑμῶν, μή
no longer enduring sent to know the faith of you, lest
πως ἐπείρασεν ὑμᾶς ὁ πειράζων, καὶ εἰς κενὸν γένηται ὁ
somehow tempted you the tempting (one), and in vain became the
6 κόπος ἡμῶν. ἄρτι δὲ ἐλθόντος Τιμοθέου πρὸς ἡμᾶς ἀφ'
labor of us. now But coming Timothy to us from
ὑμῶν, καὶ εὐαγγελισαμένου ἡμῖν τὴν πίστιν καὶ τὴν ἀγάπην
you, and announcing good news to us (of) the faith and the love
ὑμῶν, καὶ ὅτι ἔχετε μνείαν ἡμῶν ἀγαθὴν πάντοτε, ἐπιπο-
of you, and that you have remembrance of us good always, longing
7 θοῦντες ἡμᾶς ἰδεῖν, καθάπερ καὶ ἡμεῖς ὑμᾶς· διὰ τοῦτο
us to see, even as also we you, for this reason
παρεκλήθημεν, ἀδελφοί, ἐφ' ὑμῖν ἐπὶ πάσῃ τῇ θλίψει καὶ
we were comforted, brothers, over you on all the affliction and
8 ἀνάγκῃ ἡμῶν διὰ τῆς ὑμῶν πίστεως· ὅτι νῦν ζῶμεν, ἐὰν
distress of us through the of you faith, because now we live if
9 ὑμεῖς στήκητε ἐν Κυρίῳ. τίνα γὰρ εὐχαριστίαν δυνάμεθα τῷ
you stand in (the) Lord. what For thanks are we able
Θεῷ ἀνταποδοῦναι περὶ ὑμῶν, ἐπὶ πάσῃ τῇ χαρᾷ ᾗ χαί-
to God to return concerning you, over all the joy (with) which
10 ρομεν δι' ὑμᾶς ἔμπροσθεν τοῦ Θεοῦ ἡμῶν, νυκτὸς καὶ ἡμέρας
we rejoice by you before the God of us, night and day
ὑπὲρ ἐκ περισσοῦ δεόμενοι εἰς τὸ ἰδεῖν ὑμῶν τὸ πρόσωπον,
superabundantly petitioning for to see of you the face,
καὶ καταρτίσαι τὰ ὑστερήματα τῆς πίστεως ὑμῶν;
and to complete the things lacking in the faith of you?
11 Αὐτὸς δὲ ὁ Θεὸς καὶ πατὴρ ἡμῶν, καὶ ὁ Κύριος ἡμῶν
Himself And, the God and Father of us, and the Lord of us,
12 Ἰησοῦς Χριστός, κατευθύναι τὴν ὁδὸν ἡμῶν πρὸς ὑμᾶς· ὑμᾶς
Jesus Christ, may He direct the way of us to you, you
δὲ ὁ Κύριος πλεονάσαι καὶ περισσεύσαι τῇ ἀγάπῃ εἰς ἀλλή-
and the Lord make to abound and to exceed in love toward one
13 λους καὶ εἰς πάντας, καθάπερ καὶ ἡμεῖς εἰς ὑμᾶς, εἰς τὸ
another and toward all, even as also we toward you, to
στηρίξαι ὑμῶν τὰς καρδίας ἀμέμπτους ἐν ἁγιωσύνῃ,
establish of you the hearts blameless in holiness,
ἔμπροσθεν τοῦ Θεοῦ καὶ πατρὸς ἡμῶν, ἐν τῇ παρουσίᾳ τοῦ
before the God and Father of us, in the presence of the
Κυρίου ἡμῶν Ἰησοῦ Χριστοῦ μετὰ πάντων τῶν ἁγίων
Lord of us, Jesus Christ, with all the saints
αὐτοῦ.
of Him.

CHAPTER 4

1 Τὸ λοιπὸν οὖν, ἀδελφοί, ἐρωτῶμεν ὑμᾶς καὶ παρακαλοῦ-
For the rest, then, brothers, we beseech you and we exhort
μεν ἐν Κυρίῳ Ἰησοῦ καθὼς παρελάβετε παρ' ἡμῶν τὸ πῶς
in (the) Lord Jesus, even as you received from us how

how you ought to walk and to please God, that you abound more. 2 For you know what injunctions we gave you through the Lord Jesus. 3 For this is God's will, your sanctification, *for* you to abstain from fornication, 4 each one of you to know to possess his vessel in purity and honor, 5 not in passion of lust, even as also the nations not knowing God *do*, 6 not to go beyond and to overreach in the matter of his brother, because *the* avenger concerning all these *is* the Lord, even as we told you before, and solemnly testified. 7 For God did not call us to uncleanness, but in purity. 8 Therefore, the *one* that despises does not despise man, but God, even He giving His Holy Spirit to us.

9 Now as to brotherly love, you have no need *for me* to write to you, for you yourselves are taught by God to love one another. 10 For you also do it to the brothers in all Macedonia; but, brothers, we exhort you to abound more. 11 And try earnestly to be quiet, and to do *your* own things, and to work with your own hands, as we enjoined you, 12 that you may walk becomingly toward those outside, and that you may have need of nothing.

13 But I do not want you to be ignorant, brothers, concerning those who sleep, that you not grieve, as the rest also, not having hope. 14 For if we believe that Jesus died and rose again, even so God will also bring with Him all those who have fallen asleep through Jesus. 15 For we say this to you in *the* word of *the* Lord, that we the living who remain to the coming of the Lord not at all will go before those who have fallen asleep; 16 because the Lord Himself shall come down from Heaven with a commanding shout by an archangel's voice, and with God's

δεῖ ὑμᾶς περιπατεῖν καὶ ἀρέσκειν Θεῷ, ἵνα περισσεύητε
it behoves you to walk and to please God, that you abound
2 μᾶλλον. οἴδατε γὰρ τίνας παραγγελίας ἐδώκαμεν ὑμῖν διὰ
more. you know For what injunctions we gave you through
3 τοῦ Κυρίου Ἰησοῦ. τοῦτο γάρ ἐστι θέλημα τοῦ Θεοῦ, ὁ
the Lord Jesus. this For is (the) will of God, the
4 ἁγιασμὸς ὑμῶν, ἀπέχεσθαι ὑμᾶς ἀπὸ τῆς πορνείας· εἰδέναι
sanctification of you, to abstain you from fornication, to know
ἕκαστον ὑμῶν τὸ ἑαυτοῦ σκεῦος κτᾶσθαι ἐν ἁγιασμῷ καὶ τιμῇ,
each one of you the of himself vessel to possess in purity and honor,
5 μὴ ἐν πάθει ἐπιθυμίας, καθάπερ καὶ τὰ ἔθνη τὰ μὴ εἰδότα τὸν
not in passion of lust, even as also the nations not knowing
6 Θεόν· τὸ μὴ ὑπερβαίνειν καὶ πλεονεκτεῖν ἐν τῷ πράγματι
God, not to go beyond and to overreach in the matter
τὸν ἀδελφὸν αὐτοῦ· διότι ἔκδικος ὁ Κύριος περὶ πάντων
the brother of him, because (the) avenger the Lord (is) concerning all
τούτων, καθὼς καὶ προείπαμεν ὑμῖν καὶ διεμαρτυράμεθα.
these, as indeed we before told you and solemnly witnessed.
7 οὐ γὰρ ἐκάλεσεν ἡμᾶς ὁ Θεὸς ἐπὶ ἀκαθαρσίᾳ, ἀλλ' ἐν
not For called us God to uncleanness, but in
8 ἁγιασμῷ. τοιγαροῦν ὁ ἀθετῶν οὐκ ἄνθρωπον ἀθετεῖ, ἀλλὰ
purity. Therefore those despising not man despises, but
τον Θεὸν τὸν καὶ δόντα τὸ Πνεῦμα αὐτοῦ τὸ Ἅγιον εἰς ἡμᾶς.
God, the (One) also giving the Spirit of him the Holy to you.
9 Περὶ δὲ τῆς φιλαδελφίας οὐ χρείαν ἔχετε γράφειν ὑμῖν·
concerning And brotherly love, no need you have to write to you,
αὐτοὶ γὰρ ὑμεῖς θεοδίδακτοί ἐστε εἰς τὸ ἀγαπᾷν ἀλλήλους·
yourselves for you taught by God are to love one another;
10 καὶ γὰρ ποιεῖτε αὐτὸ εἰς πάντας τοὺς ἀδελφοὺς τοὺς ἐν ὅλῃ
indeed for you do it toward all the brothers in all
τῇ Μακεδονίᾳ. παρακαλοῦμεν δὲ ὑμᾶς, ἀδελφοί, περισσεύειν
Macedonia. we exhort But you, brothers, to abound
11 μᾶλλον, καὶ φιλοτιμεῖσθαι ἡσυχάζειν, καὶ πράσσειν τὰ ἴδια,
more, and to try earnestly to be quiet, and to practice the own,
καὶ ἐργάζεσθαι ταῖς ἰδίαις χερσὶν ὑμῶν, καθὼς ὑμῖν παρηγ-
and to work with the own hands of you, as you we
12 γείλαμεν· ἵνα περιπατῆτε εὐσχημόνως πρὸς τοὺς ἔξω, καὶ
enjoined, that you may walk becomingly toward those outside, and
μηδενὸς χρείαν ἔχητε.
of nothing need you may have.
13 Οὐ θέλω δὲ ὑμᾶς ἀγνοεῖν, ἀδελφοί, περὶ τῶν κεκοιμη-
not I do desire And you to be ignorant, brothers, about those sleeping,
μένων, ἵνα μὴ λυπῆσθε, καθὼς καὶ οἱ λοιποὶ οἱ μὴ ἔχοντες
lest you grieve as also the rest not having
14 ἐλπίδα. εἰ γὰρ πιστεύομεν ὅτι Ἰησοῦς ἀπέθανε καὶ ἀνέστη,
hope. if For we believe that Jesus died and rose again,
οὕτω καὶ ὁ Θεὸς τοὺς κοιμηθέντας διὰ τοῦ Ἰησοῦ ἄξει σὺν
so also God those having slept through Jesus will bring with
15 αὐτῷ. τοῦτο γὰρ ὑμῖν λέγομεν ἐν λόγῳ Κυρίου, ὅτι ἡμεῖς οἱ
Him. this For to you we say by a word of (the) Lord, that we the
ζῶντες οἱ περιλειπόμενοι εἰς τὴν παρουσίαν τοῦ Κυρίου, οὐ
living remaining to the coming of the Lord, not
16 μὴ φθάσωμεν τοὺς κοιμηθέντας. ὅτι αὐτὸς ὁ Κύριος ἐν κελεύ-
at all may go before those having slept; because Himself the Lord with a word
σματι, ἐν φωνῇ ἀρχαγγέλου, καὶ ἐν σάλπιγγι Θεοῦ καταβή-
of command by a voice of an archangel, and with a trumpet of God, will

trumpet. And the dead in Christ will rise again first. [17] then we who remain alive will be caught up in *the* clouds to a meeting with the Lord in *the* air. And so we will always be with *the* Lord. [18] So, then, comfort each other with these words.

CHAPTER 5

[1] But as to the times and the seasons, brothers, you have no need for you to be written *to*, [2] for you yourselves know accurately the day of *the* Lord comes as a thief in the night. [3] For when they say, Peace and safety! Then suddenly destruction comes upon them, like travail to the pregnant woman, and they shall not at all escape. [4] But you, brothers, are not in darkness, that the Day should overtake you as a thief. [5] You are all sons of light and sons of day; we are not of night, nor of darkness.

[6] So, then, we should not sleep as the rest also *do*, but we should watch and be calm. [7] For the *ones* who sleep sleep by night, and the *ones* having been drunk are drunk by night; [8] but we being of day should be calm, having put on *the* breastplate of faith and love, and *the* hope of salvation *as* a helmet; [9] because God has not appointed us to wrath, but for obtaining salvation through our Lord Jesus Christ, [10] He dying on our behalf, so that whether we watch or we sleep, we may live together with Him. [11] Therefore, comfort one another, and build up one another, as you indeed do.

[12] But, brothers, we beg you to know those laboring among you, and taking the lead of you in *the* Lord, and warning you; [13] even esteem them most exceedingly in love because of their work. Be at peace among yourselves.

[14] And we exhort you,

σεται ἀπ' οὐρανοῦ, καὶ οἱ νεκροὶ ἐν Χριστῷ ἀναστήσονται
descend from Heaven, and the dead in Christ will rise again
17 πρῶτον· ἔπειτα ἡμεῖς οἱ ζῶντες, οἱ περιλειπόμενοι, ἅμα σὺν
firstly, then we the living· remaining together with
αὐτοῖς ἁρπαγησόμεθα ἐν νεφέλαις εἰς ἀπάντησιν τοῦ Κυρίου
them will be caught up in clouds to a meeting of the Lord
18 εἰς ἀέρα· καὶ οὕτω πάντοτε σὺν Κυρίῳ ἐσόμεθα. ὥστε παρα-
in (the) air, and so always with (the) Lord we will be. So then
καλεῖτε ἀλλήλους ἐν τοῖς λόγοις τούτοις.
comfort one another with words these.

CHAPTER 5

1 Περὶ δὲ τῶν χρόνων καὶ τῶν καιρῶν, ἀδελφοί, οὐ χρείαν
concerning And the times and the seasons, brothers, not need
2 ἔχετε ὑμῖν γράφεσθαι. αὐτοὶ γὰρ ἀκριβῶς οἴδατε ὅτι ἡ ἡμέρα
have you to be written, yourselves for accurately you know that (the) day
3 Κυρίου ὡς κλέπτης ἐν νυκτὶ οὕτως ἔρχεται· ὅταν γὰρ
of (the) Lord as a thief at night so it comes. when For
λέγωσιν, Εἰρήνη καὶ ἀσφάλεια, τότε αἰφνίδιος αὐτοῖς
they say, Peace and safety! Then sudden them
ἐφίσταται ὄλεθρος, ὥσπερ ἡ ὠδὶν τῇ ἐν γαστρὶ ἐχούσῃ, καὶ
comes on destruction, as the travail to the pregnant woman, and
4 οὐ μὴ ἐκφύγωσιν. ὑμεῖς δέ, ἀδελφοί, οὐκ ἐστὲ ἐν σκότει, ἵνα
not at all may they escape. you But, brothers, not are in darkness, that
5 ἡ ἡμέρα ὑμᾶς ὡς κλέπτης καταλάβῃ· πάντες ὑμεῖς υἱοὶ φωτός
the day you as a thief should overtake; all you sons of light
6 ἐστε καὶ υἱοὶ ἡμέρας· οὐκ ἐσμὲν νυκτὸς οὐδὲ σκότους· ἄρα οὖν
are, and sons of day. not We are of night, nor of darkness; therefore
μὴ καθεύδωμεν ὡς καὶ οἱ λοιποί, ἀλλὰ γρηγορῶμεν καὶ
not let us sleep as also the rest, but let us watch and
7 νήφωμεν. οἱ γὰρ καθεύδοντες νυκτὸς καθεύδουσι· καὶ οἱ
be sober. those For sleeping, by night sleep, and those
8 μεθυσκόμενοι νυκτὸς μεθύουσιν. ἡμεῖς δέ, ἡμέρας ὄντες, νήφω-
being drunk by night are drunk; we but, of day being, let us be
μεν, ἐνδυσάμενοι θώρακα πίστεως καὶ ἀγάπης, καὶ περικεφα-
sober, putting on a breastplate of faith and of love, and a helmet
9 λαίαν, ἐλπίδα σωτηρίας. ὅτι οὐκ ἔθετο ἡμᾶς ὁ Θεὸς εἰς
of hope of salvation; because not appointed us God to
ὀργήν, ἀλλ' εἰς περιποίησιν σωτηρίας διὰ τοῦ Κυρίου ἡμῶν
wrath, but for obtainment of salvation through the Lord of us,
10 Ἰησοῦ Χριστοῦ, τοῦ ἀποθανόντος ὑπὲρ ἡμῶν, ἵνα, εἴτε
Jesus Christ, the (One) having died on behalf of us, that whether
11 γρηγορῶμεν εἴτε καθεύδωμεν, ἅμα σὺν αὐτῷ ζήσωμεν. διὸ
we watch or we sleep, together with Him we may live. So
παρακαλεῖτε ἀλλήλους, καὶ οἰκοδομεῖτε εἷς τὸν ἕνα, καθὼς
comfort one another, and build up one the other, as
καὶ ποιεῖτε.
indeed you do.

12 Ἐρωτῶμεν δὲ ὑμᾶς, ἀδελφοί, εἰδέναι τοὺς κοπιῶντας ἐν
we ask And you, brothers, to know those laboring among
ὑμῖν, καὶ προϊσταμένους ὑμῶν ἐν Κυρίῳ, καὶ νουθετοῦντας
you, and taking the lead of you in (the) Lord, and warning
13 ὑμᾶς, καὶ ἡγεῖσθαι αὐτοὺς ὑπὲρ ἐκ περισσοῦ ἐν ἀγάπῃ διὰ
you, and esteem them most exceedingly in love because of
14 τὸ ἔργον αὐτῶν. εἰρηνεύετε ἐν ἑαυτοῖς. παρακαλοῦμεν δέ
the work of them. Be at peace among yourselves. we exhort And

brothers, to warn the unruly ones, comfort the faint-hearted, sustain the weak, be patient towards all. [15]See *that* no one renders evil for evil, but always pursue the good, both towards one another and toward all.

[16]Rejoice evermore. [17]Pray without ceasing. [18]In everything give thanks, for this *is the* will of God in Christ Jesus, toward you. [19]Do not quench the Spirit. [20]Do not despise prophecies. [21]Test all things, hold fast to the good. [22]Keep back from every form of evil.

[23]And may the God of peace Himself fully sanctify you, and may your whole spirit and soul and body be kept blameless at the coming of our Lord Jesus Christ. [24]*He* who calls you *is* faithful, who also will perform *it*.

[25]Brothers, pray concerning us.

[26]Greet all the brothers with a holy kiss. [27]I charge you by the Lord that this letter be read to all the holy brothers.

[28]The grace of our Lord Jesus Christ *be* with you. Amen.

ὑμᾶς, ἀδελφοί, νουθετεῖτε τοὺς ἀτάκτους, παραμυθεῖσθε τοὺς
you, brothers, warn the insubordinate, comfort the
ὀλιγοψύχους, ἀντέχεσθε τῶν ἀσθενῶν, μακροθυμεῖτε πρὸς
faint-hearted, care for those being weak, be long-suffering toward
15 πάντας. ὁρᾶτε μή τις κακὸν ἀντὶ κακοῦ τινὶ ἀποδῷ· ἀλλὰ
all. See (that) not anyone evil for evil to anyone returns, but
πάντοτε τὸ ἀγαθὸν διώκετε καὶ εἰς ἀλλήλους καὶ εἰς πάντας.
always the good follow even toward one another and toward all.
16 πάντοτε χαίρετε· ἀδιαλείπτως προσεύχεσθε· ἐν παντὶ
17 always Rejoice. without ceasing Pray. In everything
18 εὐχαριστεῖτε· τοῦτο γὰρ θέλημα Θεοῦ ἐν Χριστῷ Ἰησοῦ εἰς
give thanks, this for (is) (the) will of God in Christ Jesus as to
19 ὑμᾶς. τὸ Πνεῦμα μὴ σβέννυτε· προφητείας μὴ ἐξουθενεῖτε·
20 you. The Spirit not do quench. Prophecies not despise.
21 πάντα δοκιμάζετε· τὸ καλὸν κατέχετε· ἀπὸ παντὸς εἴδους
22 All things test, the good hold fast. From every form
πονηροῦ ἀπέχεσθε.
of evil keep back.

23 Αὐτὸς δὲ ὁ Θεὸς τῆς εἰρήνης ἁγιάσαι ὑμᾶς ὁλοτελεῖς· καὶ
Himself And, the God of peace, may He sanctify you fully, and
ὁλόκληρον ὑμῶν τὸ πνεῦμα καὶ ἡ ψυχὴ καὶ τὸ σῶμα
whole of you the spirit, and the soul, and the body,
ἀμέμπτως ἐν τῇ παρουσίᾳ τοῦ Κυρίου ἡμῶν Ἰησοῦ Χριστοῦ
blamelessly at the coming of the Lord of us, Jesus Christ
24 τηρηθείη. πιστὸς ὁ καλῶν ὑμᾶς, ὃς καὶ ποιήσει.
may be kept. Faithful (is) He calling you, who also will do (it).

25 Ἀδελφοί, προσεύχεσθε περὶ ἡμῶν.
Brothers, pray concerning us.

26 Ἀσπάσασθε τοὺς ἀδελφοὺς πάντας ἐν φιλήματι ἁγίῳ.
Greet the brothers all with kiss a holy.
27 ὁρκίζω ὑμᾶς τὸν Κύριον, ἀναγνωσθῆναι τὴν ἐπιστολὴν
I charge you by the Lord to be read the epistle
πᾶσι τοῖς ἁγίοις ἀδελφοῖς.
to all the holy brothers.

28 Ἡ χάρις τοῦ Κυρίου ἡμῶν Ἰησοῦ Χριστοῦ μεθ' ὑμῶν.
The grace of the Lord of us, Jesus Christ, (be) with you.
ἀμήν.
Amen.

KING JAMES II VERSION

THE SECOND EPISTLE TO *THE* THESSALONIANS

CHAPTER 1

1 Paul and Silvanus and Timothy to the church of Thessalonians in God our Father and *the* Lord Jesus Christ: 2 Grace to you and peace from God our Father and *the* Lord Jesus Christ.

3 We are bound to give thanks to God always concerning you, even as it is right, because your faith grows exceedingly, and the love of each one of you all multiplies toward one another; 4 so as for us to boast ourselves in you in the churches of God for your patience and faith in all your persecutions, and the afflictions which you endure, 5 a clear token of the just judgment of God, for you to be counted worthy of the kingdom of God, for which you indeed suffer; 6 since *it is* a just thing with God to repay affliction to the ones afflicting you; 7 and to you, those being afflicted, rest with us at the revelation of the Lord Jesus from Heaven with angels of His power, 8 in flaming fire giving full vengeance to those not knowing God, and to those not obeying the gospel of our Lord Jesus Christ; 9 who will pay *the* penalty: everlasting destruction from *the* face of the Lord, and from the glory of His strength, 10 when He comes to be glorified in His saints, and to be admired in all those who believe in that Day, because our testimony

ΠΑΥΛΟΥ ΤΟΥ ΑΠΟΣΤΟΛΟΥ
PAUL THE APOSTLE

Η ΠΡΟΣ
THE TO

ΘΕΣΣΑΛΟΝΙΚΕΙΣ
(THE) THESSALONIANS

ΕΠΙΣΤΟΛΗ ΔΕΥΤΕΡΑ
EPISTLE SECOND

CHAPTER 1

1 Παῦλος καὶ Σιλουανὸς καὶ Τιμόθεος τῇ ἐκκλησίᾳ Θεσσα-
Paul and Silvanus and Timothy to the church of Thess-
λονικέων ἐν Θεῷ πατρὶ ἡμῶν καὶ Κυρίῳ Ἰησοῦ Χριστῷ·
alonians in God (the) Father of us and (the) Lord Jesus Christ :
2 χάρις ὑμῖν καὶ εἰρήνη ἀπὸ Θεοῦ πατρὸς ἡμῶν καὶ Κυρίου
Grace to you and peace from God (the) Father of us and (the) Lord
Ἰησοῦ Χριστοῦ.
Jesus Christ.
3 Εὐχαριστεῖν ὀφείλομεν τῷ Θεῷ πάντοτε περὶ ὑμῶν,
to give thanks We ought to God always concerning you,
ἀδελφοί, καθὼς ἄξιόν ἐστιν, ὅτι ὑπεραυξάνει ἡ πίστις ὑμῶν,
brothers, even as right it is; because grows exceedingly the faith of you,
καὶ πλεονάζει ἡ ἀγάπη ἑνὸς ἑκάστου πάντων ὑμῶν εἰς ἀλλή-
and multiplies the love one of each all of you to one
4 λους· ὥστε ἡμᾶς αὐτοὺς ἐν ὑμῖν καυχᾶσθαι ἐν ταῖς ἐκκλησίαις
another, so as us ourselves in you to boast among the churches
τοῦ Θεοῦ ὑπὲρ τῆς ὑπομονῆς ὑμῶν καὶ πίστεως ἐν πᾶσι
of God for the patience of you and faith in all
5 τοῖς διωγμοῖς ὑμῶν καὶ ταῖς θλίψεσιν αἷς ἀνέχεσθε· ἔνδειγμα
the persecutions of you and the afflictions which you endure, a clear token
τῆς δικαίας κρίσεως τοῦ Θεοῦ, εἰς τὸ καταξιωθῆναι ὑμᾶς τῆς
of the just judgment of God for to be counted worthy you of the
6 βασιλείας τοῦ Θεοῦ, ὑπὲρ ἧς καὶ πάσχετε· εἴπερ δίκαιον παρὰ
kingdom of God, for which indeed you suffer, since a just thing with
7 Θεῷ ἀνταποδοῦναι τοῖς θλίβουσιν ὑμᾶς θλίψιν, καὶ ὑμῖν τοῖς
God to repay to those afflicting you affliction, and to you those
θλιβομένοις ἄνεσιν μεθ' ἡμῶν, ἐν τῇ ἀποκαλύψει τοῦ Κυρίου
being afflicted rest with us, at the revelation of the Lord
8 Ἰησοῦ ἀπ' οὐρανοῦ μετ' ἀγγέλων δυνάμεως αὐτοῦ, ἐν πυρὶ
Jesus from Heaven with angels of power of Him, in fire
φλογός, διδόντος ἐκδίκησιν τοῖς μὴ εἰδόσι Θεόν, καὶ τοῖς
of flame, giving full vengeance to those not knowing God, and to those
μὴ ὑπακούουσι τῷ εὐαγγελίῳ τοῦ Κυρίου ἡμῶν Ἰησοῦ
not obeying the gospel of the Lord of us, Jesus
9 Χριστοῦ· οἵτινες δίκην τίσουσιν, ὄλεθρον αἰώνιον ἀπὸ προσ-
Christ, who (the) penalty will pay, destruction eternal from (the)
ώπου τοῦ Κυρίου καὶ ἀπὸ τῆς δόξης τῆς ἰσχύος αὐτοῦ,
face of the Lord and from the glory of the strength of Him,
10 ὅταν ἔλθῃ ἐνδοξασθῆναι ἐν τοῖς ἁγίοις αὐτοῦ, καὶ θαυμασθῆ-
when He comes to be glorified in the saints of Him, and to be admired
ναι ἐν πᾶσι τοῖς πιστεύουσιν (ὅτι ἐπιστεύθη τὸ μαρτύριον
in all those having believed, because was believed the testimony

to you was believed. [11]For which we also always pray concerning you, that our God may count you worthy of the calling, and may fulfill every good pleasure of goodness, and work of faith in power, [12]so that the name of our Lord may be glorified in you, and you in Him, according to the grace of our God and of *the* Lord Jesus Christ.

CHAPTER 2

[1]And we beg you, brothers, by the coming of our Lord Jesus Christ, and of our gathering together to Him, [2]for you not to be quickly shaken *in* mind, nor to be troubled; neither through a spirit, nor through speech, nor through letter, as through us, as if the day of Christ has come. [3]Do not let anyone deceive you in any way, because *that Day will not come* unless first comes the falling away, and the man of sin is revealed, the son of perdition, [4]the *one* opposing and exalting himself over everything being called God, or object of worship, so as *for* him to sit in the temple of God as God, showing himself that he is a god. [5]Do you not remember that I told you these things, *I* yet being with you? [6]And now you know the thing holding back, for him to be revealed in his time. [7]For the mystery of lawlessness already works, only he holding back now, until it comes out of *the* midst; [8]and then the Lawless One will be revealed, whom the Lord will consume by the spirit of His mouth; and *He* will bring to nothing by the brightness of His coming; [9]*His* coming is according to the working of Satan in all power and miracles and lying wonders, [10]and in all deceit of unrighteousness in those being lost, because they did not receive the love of the truth in order for them to be saved. [11]And because of this, God will send to them a

11 ἡμῶν ἐφ' ὑμᾶς) ἐν τῇ ἡμέρᾳ ἐκείνῃ. εἰς ὃ καὶ προσευχόμεθ
of us to you in day that. For which indeed we pray
πάντοτε περι ὑμῶν, ἵνα ὑμᾶς ἀξιώσῃ τῆς κλήσεως ὁ Θεὸς
always concerning you, that you may count worthy of the calling the God
ἡμῶν, καὶ πληρώσῃ πᾶσαν εὐδοκίαν ἀγαθωσύνης καὶ ἔργον
of us, and may fulfill every good pleasure of goodness and work
12 πίστεως ἐν δυνάμει· ὅπως ἐνδοξασθῇ τὸ ὄνομα τοῦ Κυρίου
of faith in power, so as may be glorified the name of the Lord
ἡμῶν Ἰησοῦ Χριστοῦ ἐν ὑμῖν, καὶ ὑμεῖς ἐν αὐτῷ, κατὰ τὴν
of us. Jesus Christ in you, and you in Him, according to the
χάριν τοῦ Θεοῦ ἡμῶν καὶ Κυρίου Ἰησοῦ Χριστοῦ.
grace of the God of us and (the) Lord Jesus Christ.

CHAPTER 2

1 Ἐρωτῶμεν δὲ ὑμᾶς, ἀδελφοί, ὑπὲρ τῆς παρουσίας τοῦ
we ask And you, brothers, by the presence of the
Κυρίου ἡμῶν Ἰησοῦ Χριστοῦ, καὶ ἡμῶν ἐπισυναγωγῆς ἐπ'
Lord of us, Jesus Christ, and of us gathering together to
2 αὐτόν, εἰς τὸ μὴ ταχέως σαλευθῆναι ὑμᾶς ἀπὸ τοῦ νοός,
Him, for not quickly to be shaken you from the mind,
μήτε θροεῖσθαι, μήτε διὰ πνεύματος, μήτε διὰ λόγου, μήτε
nor to be troubled, neither through a spirit, nor through speech, nor
δι' ἐπιστολῆς ὡς δι' ἡμῶν, ὡς ὅτι ἐνέστηκεν ἡ ἡμέρα τοῦ
through epistle, as through us, as that is come the day of the
3 Χριστοῦ· μή τις ὑμᾶς ἐξαπατήσῃ κατὰ μηδένα τρόπον· ὅτι
Christ. Let not anyone you deceive, by no way, because
ἐὰν μὴ ἔλθῃ ἡ ἀποστασία πρῶτον, καὶ ἀποκαλυφθῇ ὁ ἄνθρω-
unless comes the falling away first, and is revealed the man
4 πος τῆς ἁμαρτίας, ὁ υἱὸς τῆς ἀπωλείας, ὁ ἀντικείμενος καὶ
of sin, the son of perdition, he opposing and
ὑπεραιρόμενος ἐπὶ πᾶν τὸ λεγόμενον Θεὸν η σέβασμα, ὥστε
exalting himself over everything being called God, or object of worship, so
αὐτὸν εἰς τὸν ναὸν τοῦ Θεοῦ ὡς Θεὸν καθίσαι, ἀποδεικνύντα
him in the temple of God as God to sit, showing
5 ἑαυτὸν ὅτι ἐστὶ Θεός. οὐ μνημονεύετε ὅτι ἔτι ὢν πρὸς ὑμᾶς
himself that he is a God. Do not you remember that yet being with you,
6 ταῦτα ἔλεγον ὑμῖν; καὶ νῦν τὸ κατέχον οἴδατε, εἰς το ἀπο-
these things I told you? And now the thing restraining you know, for to be
7 καλυφθῆναι αὐτὸν ἐν τῷ ἑαυτοῦ καιρῷ. τὸ γὰρ μυστήριον
revealed him in the of him time. the For mystery
ἤδη ἐνεργεῖται τῆς ἀνομίας· μόνον ὁ κατέχων ἄρτι, ἕως ἐκ
already works of lawlessness, only he restraining now, until out of
8 μέσου γένηται. καὶ τότε ἀποκαλυφθήσεται ὁ ἄνομος, ὃν ὁ
(the) midst it comes. And then will be revealed the lawless one, whom the
Κύριος ἀναλώσει τῷ πνεύματι τοῦ στόματος αὐτοῦ, καὶ
Lord will consume by the spirit of the mouth of Him, and
9 καταργήσει τῇ ἐπιφανείᾳ τῆς παρουσίας αὐτοῦ· οὗ ἐστὶν
bring to nothing by the brightness of the coming of Him; of whom is
ἡ παρουσία κατ' ἐνέργειαν τοῦ Σατανᾶ ἐν πάσῃ δυνάμει καὶ
the coming according to the working of Satan in all power and
10 σημείοις καὶ τέρασι ψεύδους, καὶ ἐν πάσῃ ἀπάτῃ τῆς ἀδικίας
signs and wonders of a lie, and with all deceit of unrighteousness
ἐν τοῖς ἀπολλυμένοις, ἀνθ' ὧν τὴν ἀγάπην τῆς ἀληθείας
in those being lost; because the love of the truth
11 οὐκ ἐδέξαντο εἰς τὸ σωθῆναι αὐτούς. καὶ διὰ τοῦτο πέμψει
not they received for to be saved them. And because of this will send

working of error, for them to believe the lie. [12]that all may be judged, those not believing the truth, but who have delighted in unrighteousness.

[13]But we ought to thank God always concerning you, brothers, beloved by *the* Lord, because God chose you from the beginning to salvation in sanctification of *the* Spirit and belief of *the* truth, [14]to which He called you through our gospel, to obtain *the* glory of our Lord Jesus Christ. [15]So, then, brothers, stand firm and strongly hold the teachings you were taught, whether by word or by our letter. [16]But may our Lord Himself, Jesus Christ, and our God and Father, He who loves and gives us everlasting encouragement and good hope by grace, [17]encourage your hearts, and may He establish you in every good word and work.

CHAPTER 3

[1]For the rest, brothers, pray concerning us, that the word of the Lord may run and be glorified, even as also with you, [2]and that we may be delivered from perverse and evil men—for faith *is* not in all. [3]But the Lord is faithful, who will establish and will guard you from the evil one. [4]But we trust in *the* Lord as to you, that whatever things we enjoin you, you both do and will do. [5]And the Lord direct your hearts into the love of God and into the patience of Christ.

[6]And we enjoin you, brothers, in the name of our Lord Jesus Christ, to draw yourselves back from every brother walking *in an* unruly *way*, and not according to the teaching which you received from us. [7]For you yourselves know how it is right to act like us, because

αὐτοῖς ὁ Θεὸς ἐνέργειαν πλάνης, εἰς τὸ πιστεῦσαι αὐτοὺς
to them God a working of error for to believe them

12 τῷ ψεύδει· ἵνα κριθῶσι πάντες οἱ μὴ πιστεύσαντες τῇ
the lie, that may be judged all those not having believed the

ἀληθείᾳ, ἀλλ' εὐδοκήσαντες ἐν τῇ ἀδικίᾳ.
truth, but having had pleasure in unrighteousness.

13 Ἡμεῖς δὲ ὀφείλομεν εὐχαριστεῖν τῷ Θεῷ πάντοτε περὶ
we But ought to thank God always concerning

ὑμῶν, ἀδελφοὶ ἠγαπημένοι ὑπὸ Κυρίου, ὅτι εἵλετο ὑμᾶς
you, brothers, having been loved by (the) Lord, because chose you

ὁ Θεὸς ἀπ' ἀρχῆς εἰς σωτηρίαν ἐν ἁγιασμῷ Πνεύματος καὶ
God from (the) beginning to salvation in sanctification of (the) Spirit and

14 πίστει ἀληθείας· εἰς ὃ ἐκάλεσεν ὑμᾶς διὰ τοῦ εὐαγγελίου
belief of (the) truth, to which He called you through the gospel

ἡμῶν, εἰς περιποίησιν δόξης τοῦ Κυρίου ἡμῶν Ἰησοῦ
of us, to obtainment of (the) glory of the Lord of us, Jesus

15 Χριστοῦ. ἄρα οὖν, ἀδελφοί, στήκετε, καὶ κρατεῖτε τὰς παρα-
Christ. So then, brothers, stand, and hold the tra-

δόσεις ἃς ἐδιδάχθητε, εἴτε διὰ λόγου εἴτε δι' ἐπιστολῆς ἡμῶν.
ditions which you were taught either by word or by an epistle of us.

16 Αὐτὸς δὲ ὁ Κύριος ἡμῶν Ἰησοῦς Χριστός, καὶ ὁ Θεὸς καὶ
Himself And the Lord of us, Jesus Christ, and the God and

πατὴρ ἡμῶν ὁ ἀγαπήσας ἡμᾶς καὶ δοὺς παράκλησιν αἰωνίαν
Father of us, the (One) loving us and giving comfort eternal

17 καὶ ἐλπίδα ἀγαθὴν ἐν χάριτι, παρακαλέσαι ὑμῶν τὰς
and a hope good by grace, may He comfort of you the

καρδίας καὶ στηρίξαι ὑμᾶς ἐν παντὶ λόγῳ καὶ ἔργῳ ἀγαθῷ.
hearts and establish you in every word and work good.

CHAPTER 3

1 Τὸ λοιπόν, προσεύχεσθε, ἀδελφοί, περὶ ἡμῶν, ἵνα ὁ λόγος
For the rest, pray, brothers, about us, that the word

2 τοῦ Κυρίου τρέχῃ καὶ δοξάζηται, καθὼς καὶ πρὸς ὑμᾶς, καὶ
of the Lord may run and be glorified, as indeed with you, and

ἵνα ῥυσθῶμεν ἀπὸ τῶν ἀτόπων καὶ πονηρῶν ἀνθρώπων·
that we be delivered from perverse and evil men;

3 οὐ γὰρ πάντων ἡ πίστις. πιστὸς δέ ἐστιν ὁ Κύριος, ὃς
(is) not For of all the faith. faithful But is the Lord, who

4 στηρίξει ὑμᾶς καὶ φυλάξει ἀπὸ τοῦ πονηροῦ. πεποίθαμεν
will establish you and will guard from the evil one. we are persuaded

δὲ ἐν Κυρίῳ ἐφ' ὑμᾶς, ὅτι ἃ παραγγέλλομεν ὑμῖν καὶ
And in (the) Lord as to you, that what things we enjoin you both

5 ποιεῖτε καὶ ποιήσετε. ὁ δὲ Κύριος κατευθύναι ὑμῶν τὰς
you do and will do. the And Lord direct of you the

καρδίας εἰς τὴν ἀγάπην τοῦ Θεοῦ, καὶ εἰς τὴν ὑπομονὴν τοῦ
hearts into the love of God, and into the patience

Χριστοῦ.
of Christ.

6 Παραγγέλλομεν δὲ ὑμῖν, ἀδελφοί, ἐν ὀνόματι τοῦ Κυρίου
we enjoin And you, brothers, in the name of the Lord

ἡμῶν Ἰησοῦ Χριστοῦ, στέλλεσθαι ὑμᾶς ἀπὸ παντὸς ἀδελφοῦ
of us, Jesus Christ, to draw back you from every brother

ἀτάκτως περιπατοῦντος, καὶ μὴ κατὰ τὴν παράδοσιν ἣν
insubordinately walking, and not according to the tradition which

7 παρέλαβε παρ' ἡμῶν. αὐτοὶ γὰρ οἴδατε πῶς δεῖ μιμεῖσθαι
you received from us. yourselves For, you know how it is right to imitate

we were not disorderly among you; [8]nor did we eat bread from anyone *as* a gift; but by labor and toil working night and day in order not to burden anyone of you. [9]Not that we do not have authority, but that we give ourselves an example to you, for *you* to act like us. [10]For even when we were with you, we enjoined you: If anyone does not desire to work, let him not eat. [11]For we hear some are walking in an unruly way among you, not working at all, but being busybodies. [12]And we enjoin such and exhort through our Lord Jesus Christ that they may eat their own bread, working with quietness. [13]And you, brothers, do not lose heart *in* well-doing. [14]But if anyone does not obey our word through the letter, mark that one, and do not associate with him, that he be shamed; [15]but do not count *him* an enemy, but warn *him* as a brother.

[16]And may the Lord of peace continually give to you in every way. The Lord *be* with all of you.

[17]The greeting of Paul by my hand is *the* sign in every letter; so I write. [18]The grace of our Lord Jesus Christ *be* with you all. Amen.

8 ἡμᾶς· ὅτι οὐκ ἠτακτήσαμεν ἐν ὑμῖν, οὐδὲ δωρεὰν ἄρτον
us, because not we were disorderly among you, nor (as) a gift bread
ἐφάγομεν παρά τινος, ἀλλ᾽ ἐν κόπῳ καὶ μόχθῳ, νύκτα καὶ
ate from anyone, but by labor and toil night and
ἡμέραν ἐργαζόμενοι, πρὸς τὸ μὴ ἐπιβαρῆσαί τινα ὑμῶν·
day working for not to burden anyone of you;
9 οὐχ ὅτι οὐκ ἔχομεν ἐξουσίαν, ἀλλ᾽ ἵνα ἑαυτοὺς τύπον δῶμεν
not that not we have authority, but that ourselves an example we give
10 ὑμῖν εἰς τὸ μιμεῖσθαι ἡμᾶς. καὶ γὰρ ὅτε ἦμεν πρὸς ὑμᾶς, τοῦτο
to you for to imitate us, even For when we were with you, this
παρηγγέλλομεν ὑμῖν ὅτι Εἴ τις οὐ θέλει ἐργάζεσθαι, μηδὲ
we enjoined you, — If anyone not desires to work, not
11 ἐσθιέτω. ἀκούομεν γάρ τινας περιπατοῦντας ἐν ὑμῖν
let him eat. we hear (of) For some walking among you
12 ἀτάκτως, μηδὲν ἐργαζομένους, ἀλλὰ περιεργαζομένους. τοῖς
disorderly, nothing working, but working all about,
δὲ τοιούτοις παραγγέλλομεν, καὶ παρακαλοῦμεν διὰ τοῦ
and such we enjoin and exhort through the
Κυρίου ἡμῶν Ἰησοῦ Χριστοῦ, ἵνα μετὰ ἡσυχίας ἐργαζόμενοι
Lord of us, Jesus Christ, that with quietness working
13 τὸν ἑαυτῶν ἄρτον ἐσθίωσιν. ὑμεῖς δέ, ἀδελφοί, μὴ ἐκκακήσητε
the of themselves bread they may eat. you And, brothers, do not lose heart
14 καλοποιοῦντες. εἰ δέ τις οὐχ ὑπακούει τῷ λόγῳ ἡμῶν διὰ τῆς
(in) welldoing. if And any not obeys the word of us via the
ἐπιστολῆς, τοῦτον σημειοῦσθε, καὶ μὴ συναναμίγνυσθε αὐτῷ,
epistle, this one mark, and do not associate with him,
15 ἵνα ἐντραπῇ· καὶ μὴ ὡς ἐχθρὸν ἡγεῖσθε, ἀλλὰ νουθετεῖτε ὡς
that he be shamed; and not as an enemy esteem (him), but warn as
ἀδελφόν.
a brother.

16 Αὐτὸς δὲ ὁ Κύριος τῆς εἰρήνης δῴη ὑμῖν τὴν εἰρήνην διὰ
Himself And, the Lord of peace give to you the peace con-
παντὸς ἐν παντὶ τρόπῳ. ὁ Κύριος μετὰ πάντων ὑμῶν.
tinually in every way. The Lord (be) with all you.

17 Ὁ ἀσπασμὸς τῇ ἐμῇ χειρὶ Παύλου, ὅ ἐστι σημεῖον ἐν πάσῃ
The greeting by my hand, of Paul, which is a sign in every
18 ἐπιστολῇ· οὕτω γράφω. ἡ χάρις τοῦ Κυρίου ἡμῶν Ἰησοῦ
epistle; thus I write. The grace of the Lord of us, Jesus
Χριστοῦ μετὰ πάντων ὑμῶν. ἀμήν.
Christ (be) with all you. Amen.

ΠΑΥΛΟΥ ΤΟΥ ΑΠΟΣΤΟΛΟΥ
PAUL THE APOSTLE

Η ΠΡΟΣ
THE TO

ΤΙΜΟΘΕΟΝ
TIMOTHY

ΕΠΙΣΤΟΛΗ ΠΡΩΤΗ
EPISTLE FIRST

KING JAMES II VERSION

THE FIRST EPISTLE TO TIMOTHY

CHAPTER 1

1 Paul, an apostle of Jesus Christ according to a command of God our Savior, even *the* Lord Jesus Christ, our Hope, 2 to Timothy, a true child in *the* faith: Grace, mercy, peace from God our Father and our Lord Jesus Christ.

3 Even as I begged you to remain *in* Ephesus —*I* going to Macedonia—that you might charge some not to teach other *doctrines* 4 nor to give heed to fables and to endless genealogies — which provide doubts rather than a stewardship of God in faith— 5 but the end of the commandment is love out of a pure heart and a good conscience, and faith not pretended; 6 from which having missed the mark some turned aside to empty talking, 7 wishing to be teachers of Law, neither understanding what they say, nor about that which they strongly affirm. 8 And we know that the law *is* good, if anyone uses it lawfully, 9 knowing this, that law is not laid down for a righteous one but for lawless and unruly ones, for ungodly and sinful ones, for unholy and profane ones, for slayers of fathers and slayers of mothers, for murderers, 10 for fornicators, for homosexuals, for slave-traders, for liars, for perjurers, and if any other thing opposes sound teaching, 11 according to the gospel of the glory of the blessed God *with* which I was entrusted.

CHAPTER 1

1 Παῦλος ἀπόστολος Ἰησοῦ Χριστοῦ κατ' ἐπιταγὴν Θεοῦ
Paul an apostle of Jesus Christ according to a command of God
σωτῆρος ἡμῶν, καὶ Κυρίου Ἰησοῦ Χριστοῦ τῆς ἐλπίδος
the Savior of us, even (the) Lord Jesus Christ the hope
2 ἡμῶν, Τιμοθέῳ γνησίῳ τέκνῳ ἐν πίστει· χάρις, ἔλεος, εἰρήνη
of us, to Timothy, a true child in (the) faith: Grace, mercy, peace
ἀπὸ Θεοῦ πατρὸς ἡμῶν καὶ Ἰησοῦ Χριστοῦ τοῦ Κυρίου
from God (the) Father of us, and Jesus Christ the Lord
ἡμῶν.
of us.

3 Καθὼς παρεκάλεσά σε προσμεῖναι ἐν Ἐφέσῳ, πορευό-
As I besought you to remain in Ephesus, (I) going
μενος εἰς Μακεδονίαν, ἵνα παραγγείλῃς τισὶ μὴ ἑτεροδιδα-
into Macedonia, that you might enjoin certain ones not to teach
4 σκαλεῖν, μηδὲ προσέχειν μύθοις καὶ γενεαλογίαις ἀπεράντοις,
other (doctrines), nor to attend to tales and to genealogies endless,
αἵτινες ζητήσεις παρέχουσι μᾶλλον ἢ οἰκοδομίαν Θεοῦ τὴν
which doubts provide rather than a stewardship of God
5 ἐν πίστει—.τὸ δὲ τέλος τῆς παραγγελίας ἐστὶν ἀγάπη ἐκ
in faith. the Now end of the commandment is love out of
καθαρᾶς καρδίας καὶ συνειδήσεως ἀγαθῆς καὶ πίστεως
a clean heart and a conscience good and faith
6 ἀνυποκρίτου· ὧν τινὲς ἀστοχήσαντες ἐξετράπησαν εἰς
unpretended, which some missing the mark turned aside to
7 ματαιολογίαν, θέλοντες εἶναι νομοδιδάσκαλοι, μὴ νοοῦντες
empty talking, wishing to be teachers of law, not understanding
8 μήτε ἃ λέγουσι, μήτε περὶ τίνων διαβεβαιοῦνται. οἴδαμεν
either what they say, or about what things they strongly affirm we know
9 δὲ ὅτι καλὸς ὁ νόμος, ἐάν τις αὐτῷ νομίμως χρῆται, εἰδὼς
And that (is) good the law, if anyone it lawfully uses, knowing
τοῦτο, ὅτι δικαίῳ νόμος οὐ κεῖται, ἀνόμοις δὲ καὶ ἀνυπο-
this, that for a just one law not is laid down, for lawless but and for in-
τάκτοις, ἀσεβέσι καὶ ἁμαρτωλοῖς, ἀνοσίοις καὶ βεβήλοις,
subordinate, for ungodly and sinful ones, for unholy and profane ones,
10 πατραλῴαις καὶ μητραλῴαις, ἀνδροφόνοις, πόρνοις, ἀρσενο-
for father-slayers and mother-slayers, for men-slayers, for fornicators, for
κοίταις, ἀνδραποδισταῖς, ψεύσταις, ἐπιόρκοις, καὶ εἴ τι
homosexuals, for slave-traders, for liars, for perjurers, and if any
11 ἕτερον τῇ ὑγιαινούσῃ διδασκαλίᾳ ἀντίκειται, κατὰ τὸ
other thing the sound teaching opposes, according to the
εὐαγγέλιον τῆς δόξης τοῦ μακαρίου Θεοῦ, ὃ ἐπιστεύθην
gospel of the glory of the blessed God, which was entrusted (with)

[12] And I have thanks to Him empowering me, our Lord Jesus Christ, because He counted me faithful, putting *me* into the ministry, [13] the *one* who before was a blasphemer, and a persecutor, and insolent; but I obtained mercy, because being ignorant I did *it* in unbelief. [14] But the grace of our Lord abounded exceedingly with faith and love in Christ Jesus. [15] Faithful *is* the word, and worthy of all acceptance, that Christ Jesus came into the world to save sinners, of whom I am chief. [16] But for this reason I obtained mercy, that in me first Jesus Christ might show forth all longsuffering, for an example to those being about to believe on Him to everlasting life. [17] Now to the King eternal, invisible, incorruptible, *the* only wise God, *be* honor and glory forever and ever. Amen.

[18] This charge I commit to you, *my* child Timothy, according to the prophecies going before as to you, that you might war a good warfare by them, [19] having faith and a good conscience, which some having thrust away made shipwreck concerning the faith; [20] of whom are Hymeneus and Alexander, whom I delivered to Satan, that they may be taught not to blaspheme.

CHAPTER 2

[1] First of all, then, I exhort *that* petitions, prayers, intercessions, thanksgivings be made on behalf of all men; [2] for kings and all those being in high position, that we may lead a tranquil and quiet existence in all godliness and reverence. [3] For this *is* good and acceptable before our deliverer, God, [4] who desires all men to be delivered, and to come to a full knowledge of the truth. [5] For God *is*

ἐγώ.
I
12 Καὶ χάριν ἔχω τῷ ἐνδυναμώσαντί με Χριστῷ Ἰησοῦ τῷ
And thanks I have to the (One) empowering me, Christ Jesus the
Κυρίῳ ἡμῶν, ὅτι πιστόν με ἡγήσατο, θέμενος εἰς διακονίαν,
Lord of us, because faithful me He counted, putting (me) into ministry,
13 τὸν πρότερον ὄντα βλάσφημον καὶ διώκτην καὶ ὑβριστήν·
the (one) before being a blasphemer and a persecutor and insolent;
14 ἀλλ' ἠλεήθην, ὅτι ἀγνοῶν ἐποίησα ἐν ἀπιστίᾳ· ὑπερ-
but I obtained mercy, because being ignorant I did (it) in unbelief, super-
επλεόνασε δὲ ἡ χάρις τοῦ Κυρίου ἡμῶν μετὰ πίστεως καὶ
abounded the grace of the Lord, of us with faith and
15 ἀγάπης τῆς ἐν Χριστῷ Ἰησοῦ. πιστὸς ὁ λόγος καὶ πάσης
love in Christ Jesus. Faithful (is) the word and of all
ἀποδοχῆς ἄξιος, ὅτι Χριστὸς Ἰησοῦς ἦλθεν εἰς τὸν κόσμον
acceptance worthy, that Christ Jesus came into the world
16 ἁμαρτωλοὺς σῶσαι, ὧν πρῶτός εἰμι ἐγώ· ἀλλὰ διὰ τοῦτο
sinners to save, of whom chief am I; but because of this
ἠλεήθην, ἵνα ἐν ἐμοὶ πρώτῳ ἐνδείξηται Ἰησοῦς Χριστὸς τὴν
I obtained mercy, that in me first might show forth Jesus Christ
πᾶσαν μακροθυμίαν, πρὸς ὑποτύπωσιν τῶν μελλόντων
all long-suffering, for a pattern to those being about
17 πιστεύειν ἐπ' αὐτῷ εἰς ζωὴν αἰώνιον. τῷ δὲ βασιλεῖ τῶν
to believe on Him for life everlasting. to the Now King of the
αἰώνων, ἀφθάρτῳ, ἀοράτῳ, μόνῳ σοφῷ Θεῷ, τιμὴ καὶ δόξα
ages, invisible, incorruptible, (the) only wise God, (be) honor and glory
εἰς τοὺς αἰῶνας τῶν αἰώνων. ἀμήν.
to the ages of the ages. Amen.
18 Ταύτην τὴν παραγγελίαν παρατίθεμαί σοι, τέκνον
This charge I commit to you, child,
Τιμόθεε, κατὰ τὰς προαγούσας ἐπί σε προφητείας, ἵνα
Timothy, according to the going before as to you prophecies that
19 στρατεύῃ ἐν αὐταῖς τὴν καλὴν στρατείαν, ἔχων πίστιν καὶ
you might war by them the good warfare, having faith and
ἀγαθὴν συνείδησιν, ἥν τινες ἀπωσάμενοι περὶ τὴν πίστιν
a good conscience, which some having thrust away concerning the faith
20 ἐναυάγησαν· ὧν ἐστιν Ὑμέναιος καὶ Ἀλέξανδρος, οὓς
made shipwreck; of whom is Hymeneus and Alexander, whom
παρέδωκα τῷ Σατανᾷ, ἵνα παιδευθῶσι μὴ βλασφημεῖν.
I delivered to Satan, that they may be taught not to blaspheme.

CHAPTER 2

1 Παρακαλῶ οὖν πρῶτον πάντων ποιεῖσθαι δεήσεις, προσ-
I exhort Therefore firstly of all to be made petitions, prayers,
ευχάς, ἐντεύξεις, εὐχαριστίας, ὑπὲρ πάντων ἀνθρώπων·
intercessions, thanksgivings on behalf of all men;
2 ὑπὲρ βασιλέων καὶ πάντων τῶν ἐν ὑπεροχῇ ὄντων, ἵνα
for kings and all those in high position being, that
ἤρεμον καὶ ἡσύχιον βίον διάγωμεν ἐν πάσῃ εὐσεβείᾳ καὶ
a tranquil and quiet existence we may lead in all godliness and
3 σεμνότητι. τοῦτο γὰρ καλὸν καὶ ἀπόδεκτον ἐνώπιον τοῦ
reverence. this (is) For good and acceptable before the
4 σωτῆρος ἡμῶν Θεοῦ, ὃς πάντας ἀνθρώπους θέλει σωθῆναι
deliverer of us, God, who all men desires to be delivered
5 καὶ εἰς ἐπίγνωσιν ἀληθείας ἐλθεῖν. εἷς γὰρ Θεός, εἷς καὶ
and to a full knowledge of truth to come. one For God (is), one also

one, also *there is* one Mediator of God and of men, *the* Man Christ Jesus, [6]the *One* having given Himself a ransom on behalf of all, the testimony *to be given* in its own times; [7]to which I was appointed a herald and apostle —I speak the truth in Christ and do not lie—a teacher of *the* nations, in faith and truth.

[8]Therefore, I desire the men to pray in every place, lifting up holy hands without wrath and doubting. [9]Likewise also the women to adorn themselves in decent clothing, with modesty and sensibleness, not with plaiting, or gold, or pearls, or expensive garments, [10]but what becomes women professing fear of God through good works. [11]Let a woman learn in silence, in all subjection. [12]But I do not allow a woman to teach, nor to exercise authority *over* a man, but to be in silence. [13]For Adam was formed first, then Eve. [14]And Adam was not deceived, but the woman being deceived has come to be in transgression; [15]but she will be delivered through the bearing of children, if they remain in faith and love and holiness, with sensibleness.

CHAPTER 3

[1]Faithful *is* the word: If anyone reaches out to overseership, he desires a good work. [2]Then the overseer must be blameless, husband of one wife, temperate, sensible, modest, hospitable, apt at teaching; [3]not a drinker, not a contentious one, not greedy of ill gain—but gentle, not quarrelsome, not loving money; [4]ruling his own house well, having children in subjection with all reverence—[5]but if anyone does not know to rule *his* own house, how will he care for a church of God?—[6]not a novice, lest being puffed up he may fall into *the* judgment of the Devil. [7]But he must also have a good witness from those outside, that he not fall into reproach, and

μεσίτης Θεοῦ καὶ ἀνθρώπων, ἄνθρωπος Χριστὸς Ἰησοῦς,
Mediator of God and of men, (the) man Christ Jesus,
6 ὁ δοὺς ἑαυτὸν ἀντίλυτρον ὑπὲρ πάντων, τὸ μαρτύριον
He having given Himself a ransom on behalf of all, the testimony
7 καιροῖς ἰδίοις, εἰς ὃ ἐτέθην ἐγὼ κήρυξ καὶ ἀπόστολος (ἀλή-
in its own times; to which was appointed I a herald and apostle — truth
θειαν λέγω ἐν Χριστῷ, οὐ ψεύδομαι), διδάσκαλος ἐθνῶν ἐν
I say in Christ, do not I lie — a teacher of nations in
πίστει καὶ ἀληθείᾳ.
faith and truth.
8 Βούλομαι οὖν προσεύχεσθαι τοὺς ἄνδρας ἐν παντὶ τόπῳ,
I desire Therefore to pray the men in every place,
ἐπαίροντας ὁσίους χεῖρας, χωρὶς ὀργῆς καὶ διαλογισμοῦ.
lifting up holy hands, without wrath and doubting.
9 ὡσαύτως καὶ τὰς γυναῖκας ἐν καταστολῇ κοσμίῳ, μετὰ αἰδοῦς
Likewise also the women in clothing decent, with modesty
καὶ σωφροσύνης, κοσμεῖν ἑαυτάς, μὴ ἐν πλέγμασιν, ἢ χρυσῷ,
and sensibleness to adorn themselves, not with plaiting, or gold,
10 ἢ μαργαρίταις, ἢ ἱματισμῷ πολυτελεῖ, ἀλλ' (ὃ πρέπει
or pearls, or garments expensive, but what becomes
γυναιξὶν ἐπαγγελλομέναις θεοσέβειαν) δι' ἔργων ἀγαθῶν.
women professing fear of God, by means of works good.
11 γυνὴ ἐν ἡσυχίᾳ μανθανέτω ἐν πάσῃ ὑποταγῇ. γυναικὶ δὲ
A woman in silence let learn in all subjection. a woman But
12 διδάσκειν οὐκ ἐπιτρέπω, οὐδὲ αὐθεντεῖν ἀνδρός, ἀλλ' εἶναι
to teach not I allow, nor to exercise authority of a man, but to be
13 ἐν ἡσυχίᾳ. Ἀδὰμ γὰρ πρῶτος ἐπλάσθη, εἶτα Εὔα· καὶ
in silence. Adam For first was formed, then Eve. And
14 Ἀδὰμ οὐκ ἠπατήθη, ἡ δὲ γυνὴ ἀπατηθεῖσα ἐν παραβάσει
Adam not was deceived, the but woman being deceived in transgression
15 γέγονε· σωθήσεται δὲ διὰ τῆς τεκνογονίας, ἐὰν μείνωσιν ἐν
has become; she will be saved but through the childbearing, if they remain in
πίστει καὶ ἀγάπῃ καὶ ἁγιασμῷ μετὰ σωφροσυνης.
faith and love and holiness with sensibleness.

CHAPTER 3

1 Πιστὸς ὁ λόγος· Εἴ τις ἐπισκοπῆς ὀρέγεται, καλοῦ ἔργου
Faithful (is) the word: If anyone overseership aspires to, a good work
2 ἐπιθυμεῖ. δεῖ οὖν τὸν ἐπίσκοπον ἀνεπίληπτον εἶναι, μιᾶς
he desires. It behoves, then, the overseer without reproach to be, of one
γυναικὸς ἄνδρα, νηφάλιον, σώφρονα, κόσμιον, φιλόξενον,
wife husband, temperate, sensible, modest, hospitable,
3 διδακτικόν· μὴ πάροινον, μὴ πλήκτην, μὴ αἰσχροκερδῆ,
apt at teaching, not a drinker, not a striker, not greedy of ill gain,
4 ἀλλ' ἐπιεικῆ, ἄμαχον, ἀφιλάργυρον· τοῦ ἰδίου οἴκου καλῶς
but gentle, not quarrelsome, not avaricious, the own house well
προϊστάμενον, τέκνα ἔχοντα ἐν ὑποταγῇ μετὰ πάσης
ruling, children having in subjection with all
5 σεμνότητος (εἰ δέ τις τοῦ ἰδίου οἴκου προστῆναι οὐκ οἶδε,
reverence — if but anyone the own house to rule not knows,
6 πῶς ἐκκλησίας Θεοῦ ἐπιμελήσεται ;)· μὴ νεόφυτον, ἵνα μὴ
how a church of God will he care for? — not a novice, lest
7 τυφωθεὶς εἰς κρίμα ἐμπέσῃ τοῦ διαβόλου. δεῖ δὲ αὐτὸν καὶ
being puffed up into judgment he fall of the Devil. it behoves And him also
μαρτυρίαν καλὴν ἔχειν ἀπὸ τῶν ἔξωθεν, ἵνα μὴ εἰς ὀνειδισμὸν
a witness good to have from those outside, lest into reproach

into a snare of the Devil. [8]Likewise, deacons *to be* reverent, not double-tongued, not addicted to much wine, not greedy of ill gain, [9]having the mystery of the faith with a pure conscience. [10]And also let these be tested first, then let them serve, being blameless. [11]Likewise, *their* wives *to be* reverent, not slanderers, temperate, faithful in all things. [12]Let deacons be husbands of one wife, ruling *their* own households and children well. [13]For those having served well gain a good grade for themselves, and much boldness in faith, those in Christ Jesus.

[14]I write these things to you, hoping to come to you shortly. [15]But if I delay, that you may know how to behave in the house of God, which is *the* church of the living God, *the* pillar and foundation of the truth. [16]And confessedly, great is the mystery of godliness: God was manifested in flesh, was justified in Spirit, was seen by angels, was proclaimed among nations, was believed on in *the* world, was taken up in glory.

CHAPTER 4

[1]But the Spirit expressly says that in the latter times some will depart from the faith, cleaving to deceiving spirits and teachings of demons, [2]in hypocrisy of liars, being seared in *their* own conscience, [3]forbidding to marry, *saying* to abstain from foods, which God created for partaking with thanksgiving by the believers, and *those* knowing the truth. [4]Because every creature of God *is* good and nothing to be thrust away, but having been received with thanksgiving; [5]for through God's word and prayerful intercourse it is sanctified. [6]Having suggested these things to the brothers, you will be a

8 ἐμπέσῃ καὶ παγίδα τοῦ διαβόλου. διακόνους ὡσαύτως
he fall, and (into) a snare of the Devil. deacons Likewise
σεμνούς, μὴ διλόγους, μὴ οἴνῳ πολλῷ προσέχοντας, μὴ
reverent (to be), not double-tongued, not wine to much addicted, not
9 αἰσχροκερδεῖς, ἔχοντας τὸ μυστήριον τῆς πίστεως ἐν καθαρᾷ
greedy of ill gain, having the mystery of the faith with a clean
10 συνειδήσει. καὶ οὗτοι δὲ δοκιμαζέσθωσαν πρῶτον, εἶτα
conscience. also these And let be tested first, then
11 διακονείτωσαν, ἀνέγκλητοι ὄντες. γυναῖκας ὡσαύτως
let them minister, without reproach being. wives Likewise
12 σεμνάς, μὴ διαβόλους, νηφαλίους, πιστὰς ἐν πᾶσι. διάκονοι
reverent (to be), not slanderers, temperate, faithful in all things. deacons
ἔστωσαν μιᾶς γυναικὸς ἄνδρες, τέκνων καλῶς προϊστάμενοι
Let be of one wife husbands children well ruling
13 καὶ τῶν ἰδίων οἴκων. οἱ γὰρ καλῶς διακονήσαντες βαθμὸν
and the own households. those For well having ministered a grade
ἑαυτοῖς καλὸν περιποιοῦνται, καὶ πολλὴν παρρησίαν ἐν
for themselves good gain, and much boldness in
πίστει τῇ ἐν Χριστῷ Ἰησοῦ.
faith, those in Christ Jesus.
14 Ταῦτά σοι γράφω, ἐλπίζων ἐλθεῖν πρός σε τάχιον· ἐὰν δὲ
These things to you I write, hoping to come to you shortly; if but
15 βραδύνω, ἵνα εἰδῇς πῶς δεῖ ἐν οἴκῳ Θεοῦ ἀναστρέφεσθαι,
I delay, that you may know how must in (the) house of God to behave,
ἥτις ἐστὶν ἐκκλησία Θεοῦ ζῶντος, στύλος καὶ ἑδραίωμα τῆς
which is (the) church of God (the) living, pillar and foundation of the
16 ἀληθείας. καὶ ὁμολογουμένως μέγα ἐστὶ τὸ τῆς εὐσεβείας
truth. And confessedly, great is the of godliness
μυστήριον· Θεὸς ἐφανερώθη ἐν σαρκί, ἐδικαιώθη ἐν πνεύματι,
mystery, God was manifested in flesh, was justified in spirit,
ὤφθη ἀγγέλοις, ἐκηρύχθη ἐν ἔθνεσιν, ἐπιστεύθη ἐν κόσμῳ,
was seen by angels, was proclaimed among nations, was believed in (the) world,
ἀνελήφθη ἐν δόξῃ.
was taken up in glory.

CHAPTER 4

1 Τὸ δὲ Πνεῦμα ῥητῶς λέγει, ὅτι ἐν ὑστέροις καιροῖς ἀποστή-
the But Spirit in words says that in latter times will
σονταί τινες τῆς πίστεως, προσέχοντες πνεύμασι πλάνοις
depart from some the faith, adhering to spirits deceiving
2 καὶ διδασκαλίαις δαιμονίων, ἐν ὑποκρίσει ψευδολόγων,
and teachings of demons, in hypocrisy of liars,
3 κεκαυτηριασμένων τὴν ἰδίαν συνείδησιν, κωλυόντων γαμεῖν,
having been seared on the own conscience, forbidding to marry,
ἀπέχεσθαι βρωμάτων, ἃ ὁ Θεὸς ἔκτισεν εἰς μετάληψιν μετὰ
(saying) to abstain from foods which God created for partaking with
4 εὐχαριστίας τοῖς πιστοῖς καὶ ἐπεγνωκόσι τὴν ἀλήθειαν. ὅτι
thanksgiving by the believers and (those) knowing the truth. Because
πᾶν κτίσμα Θεοῦ καλόν, καὶ οὐδὲν ἀπόβλητον, μετὰ εὐχαρι-
every creature of God (is) good, and nothing to be put away, with thanks-
5 στίας λαμβανόμενον· ἁγιάζεται γὰρ διὰ λόγου Θεοῦ καὶ
giving having been received; it is sanctified for through a word of God and
ἐντεύξεως.
prayerful intercourse.
6 Ταῦτα ὑποτιθέμενος τοῖς ἀδελφοῖς καλὸς ἔσῃ διάκονος
These things having suggested to the brothers, good you will be minister

minister of Jesus Christ, having been nourished by the words of faith, and by the good teaching which you have followed. [7]But refuse the profane and old-womanish tales. And exercise yourself to godliness. [8]For bodily exercise is profitable for a little, but godliness is profitable to all things, having promise of the present life, and of that coming. [9]Faithful *is* the word, and worthy of all acceptance; [10]for to this we labor and *are* reproached, because we hope on *the* living God, who is deliverer of all men, especially of believers. [11]Enjoin and teach these things.

[12]Let no one despise your youth, but become an example of the believers in word, in conduct, in love, in spirit, in faith, in purity. [13]Until I come, attend to reading, to exhortation, to teaching. [14]Do not be neglectful of the gift in you, which was given to you through prophecy, with laying on of the hands of the elderhood. [15]Meditate on these things; be in these things in order that your progress may be plain to all. [16]Hold on to yourself and to the teaching; continue in them; for doing this, you will both deliver yourself and those hearing you.

CHAPTER 5

[1]Do not sharply rebuke an elder, but exhort as a father, *and* younger ones as brothers; [2]elder women as mothers; younger women as sisters in all purity. [3]Honor widows, the *ones* really being widows; [4]but if any widow has children or grandchildren, let them learn first to be godly to their own house, and to make a return payment to *their* forebears; for this is good and pleasing before God. [5]But she really being a widow, even having been left alone, has set *her* hope on God, and continues in petitions and prayers night and day. [6]But she who lives in self-pleasure has died *while* living. [7]And enjoin

Ἰησοῦ Χριστοῦ, ἐντρεφόμενος τοῖς λόγοις τῆς πίστεως, καὶ
of Jesus Christ, being nourished by the words of the faith, and
7 τῆς καλῆς διδασκαλίας ᾗ παρηκολούθηκας. τοὺς δὲ βεβήλους
by the good teaching which you have followed. the But profane
καὶ γραώδεις μύθους παραιτοῦ. γύμναζε δὲ σεαυτὸν πρὸς
and old-womanish tales refuse. exercise And yourself to
8 εὐσέβειαν· ἡ γὰρ σωματικὴ γυμνασία πρὸς ὀλίγον ἐστὶν
godliness. For bodily exercise for a little is
ὠφέλιμος· ἡ δὲ εὐσέβεια πρὸς πάντα ὠφέλιμός ἐστιν, ἐπαγ-
profitable, but godliness to all things profitable is,
9 γελίαν ἔχουσα ζωῆς τῆς νῦν καὶ τῆς μελλούσης. πιστὸς ὁ
promise having life of the now and of the coming. Faithful (is) the
10 λόγος καὶ πάσης ἀποδοχῆς ἄξιος. εἰς τοῦτο γὰρ καὶ κοπιῶ-
word and of all acceptance worthy. to this For also we labor
μεν καὶ ὀνειδιζόμεθα, ὅτι ἠλπίκαμεν ἐπὶ Θεῷ ζῶντι, ὅς ἐστι
and (are) reproached because we have set hope on God (the) living, who is
11 σωτὴρ πάντων ἀνθρώπων, μάλιστα πιστῶν. παράγγελλε
deliverer of all men, especially of believers. Enjoin
12 ταῦτα καὶ δίδασκε. μηδείς σου τῆς νεότητος καταφρονείτω,
these things and teach. no one of you the youth Let despise,
ἀλλὰ τύπος γίνου τῶν πιστῶν ἐν λόγῳ, ἐν ἀναστροφῇ, ἐν
but an example become of the believers in word, in conduct, in
13 ἀγάπῃ, ἐν πνεύματι, ἐν πίστει, ἐν ἁγνείᾳ. ἕως ἔρχομαι,
love, in spirit, in faith, in purity. Until I come,
14 πρόσεχε τῇ ἀναγνώσει, τῇ παρακλήσει, τῇ διδασκαλίᾳ. μὴ
attend to the reading, to the exhortation, to the teaching. Do not
ἀμέλει τοῦ ἐν σοὶ χαρίσματος, ὃ ἐδόθη σοι διὰ προφητείας
be neglectful of the in you gift, which was given you via prophecy
15 μετὰ ἐπιθέσεως τῶν χειρῶν τοῦ πρεσβυτερίου. ταῦτα μελέτα,
with laying on of the hands of the elderhood. these things Give care to
16 ἐν τούτοις ἴσθι, ἵνα σου ἡ προκοπὴ φανερὰ ᾖ ἐν πᾶσιν. ἔπεχε
in these things be, that of you the progress plain may be to all. Hold on
σεαυτῷ καὶ τῇ διδασκαλίᾳ. ἐπίμενε αὐτοῖς· τοῦτο γὰρ ποιῶν
to yourself and to the teaching; continue in them; this for doing
καὶ σεαυτὸν σώσεις καὶ τοὺς ἀκούοντάς σου.
both yourself you will deliver, and those hearing you.

CHAPTER 5

1 Πρεσβυτέρῳ μὴ ἐπιπλήξῃς, ἀλλὰ παρακάλει ὡς πατέρα·
an older man Do not rebuke, but exhort as a father;
2 νεωτέρους, ὡς ἀδελφούς· πρεσβυτέρας, ὡς μητέρας· νεωτέρας,
younger ones as brothers; older women as mothers; younger women
3 ὡς ἀδελφάς, ἐν πάσῃ ἁγνείᾳ. χήρας τίμα τὰς ὄντως χήρας.
as sisters, in all purity. widows Honor, those being really widows.
4 εἰ δέ τις χήρα τέκνα ἢ ἔκγονα ἔχει, μανθανέτωσαν πρῶτον
if But any widow children or grandchildren has, let them learn firstly
τὸν ἴδιον οἶκον εὐσεβεῖν, καὶ ἀμοιβὰς ἀποδιδόναι τοῖς προγό-
the own house to be godly to, and repayments return to the fore-
νοις· τοῦτο γάρ ἐστι καλὸν καὶ ἀπόδεκτον ἐνώπιον τοῦ Θεοῦ.
bears; this for is good and acceptable before God.
5 ἡ δὲ ὄντως χήρα καὶ μεμονωμένη ἤλπικεν ἐπὶ τὸν Θεόν,
the But being really widow even having been left has set hope on God,
καὶ προσμένει ταῖς δεήσεσι καὶ ταῖς προσευχαῖς νυκτὸς καὶ
and continues in the petitions and the prayers night and
6 ἡμέρας. ἡ δὲ σπαταλῶσα, ζῶσα τέθνηκε. καὶ ταῦτα παράγ-
7 day. the But (one) living in self-pleasure (while) living has died. And these things enjoin

these things that they may be blameless. [8]But if anyone does not provide for *his* own, and especially *his* family, he has denied the faith, and is worse than an unbeliever. [9]Let a widow be enrolled having become not less than sixty years, wife of one man, [10]being witnessed by good works; if she brought up children; if she hosted strangers; if she washed the feet of the saints; if she relieved afflicted ones; if she followed after every good work. [11]But refuse younger widows; for whenever they grow lustful against Christ, they desire to marry, [12]having guilt because they set aside the first faith; [13]and with it all, they also learn *to be* idle, but also gossips and busybodies, speaking the things not proper. [14]Therefore, I desire *the* young women to marry, to bear children, to rule the house, giving no occasion to the adversary on account of reproach. [15]For some already have turned aside behind Satan. [16]If any believing man or believing woman has widows, let them relieve *them*, and do not burden the church, that it may relieve those being really widows.

[17]Let the elders who take the lead well be counted worthy of double honor, especially those laboring in word and teaching. [18]For the Scripture says, "You shall not muzzle an ox treading out *grain*," and, "The laborer *is* worthy of his pay." [19]Do not receive an accusation against an elder unless on *the testimony of* two or three witnesses. [20]The ones sinning before all, rebuke; that the rest also may have fear. [21]I solemnly witness before God and *the* Lord Jesus Christ, and the elect angels, that you should guard these things without prejudice, doing nothing by way of partiality.

[22]Lay hands quickly on no one, nor share in *the* sins of others. Keep yourself pure. [23]No longer drink water, but

8 γελλε, ἵνα ἀνεπίληπτοι ὦσιν. εἰ δέ τις τῶν ἰδίων καὶ
that without reproach they may be. if But anyone the own, and
μάλιστα τῶν οἰκείων οὐ προνοεῖ, τὴν πίστιν ἤρνηται, καὶ
especially the family, not provides for, the faith he has denied, and
9 ἔστιν ἀπίστου χείρων. χήρα καταλεγέσθω μὴ ἔλαττον ἐτῶν
is an unbeliever worse than. A widow let be enrolled not less (than) years
10 ἑξήκοντα, γεγονυῖα ἑνὸς ἀνδρὸς γυνή, ἐν ἔργοις καλοῖς
sixty having become, of one man wife, by works good
μαρτυρουμένη, εἰ ἐτεκνοτρόφησεν, εἰ ἐξενοδόχησεν, εἰ ἁγίων
being witnessed, if she brought up children, if she hosted strangers, if of saints
πόδας ἔνιψεν, εἰ θλιβομένοις ἐπήρκεσεν, εἰ παντὶ ἔργῳ
feet she washed, if afflicted ones she relieved, if every work
11 ἀγαθῷ ἐπηκολούθησε. νεωτέρας δὲ χήρας παραιτοῦ· ὅταν
good she followed after. younger But widows refuse; whenever
γὰρ καταστρηνιάσωσι τοῦ Χριστοῦ, γαμεῖν θέλουσιν,
for they grow lustful against Christ, to marry they desire,
12 ἔχουσαι κρίμα, ὅτι τὴν πρώτην πίστιν ἠθέτησαν. ἅμα δὲ
having (a) judgment, because the first faith they set aside; withal and
13 καὶ ἀργαὶ μανθάνουσι, περιερχόμεναι τὰς οἰκίας, οὐ μόνον
also idle they learn (to be), going around the houses, not only
δὲ ἀργαί, ἀλλὰ καὶ φλύαροι καὶ περίεργοι, λαλοῦσαι τὰ
and idle, but also gossips and busybodies, speaking the things
14 μὴ δέοντα. βούλομαι οὖν νεωτέρας γαμεῖν, τεκνογονεῖν,
not proper. I will, therefore, younger women to marry, to bear children,
οἰκοδεσποτεῖν, μηδεμίαν ἀφορμὴν διδόναι τῷ ἀντικειμένῳ
to rule the house, no occasion to give to the (one) opposing
15 λοιδορίας χάριν. ἤδη γάρ τινες ἐξετράπησαν ὀπίσω τοῦ
reproach on account of. already For some turned aside behind
16 Σατανᾶ. εἴ τις πιστὸς ἢ πιστὴ ἔχει χήρας, ἐπαρκείτω αὐταῖς,
Satan. If any believing man or believing woman has widows, relieve them,
καὶ μὴ βαρείσθω ἡ ἐκκλησία, ἵνα ταῖς ὄντως χήραις ἐπαρ-
and not burden the church, that those being really widows it may
κέσῃ.
relieve.

17 Οἱ καλῶς προεστῶτες πρεσβύτεροι διπλῆς τιμῆς ἀξιού-
The well ruling elders of double honor count
σθωσαν, μάλιστα οἱ κοπιῶντες ἐν λόγῳ καὶ διδασκαλίᾳ.
worthy, expecially those laboring in word and teaching.
18 λέγει γὰρ ἡ γραφή, Βοῦν ἀλοῶντα οὐ φιμώσεις. καί, Ἄξιος
says For the Scripture: An ox threshing not you shall muzzle, and, Worthy
19 ὁ ἐργάτης τοῦ μισθοῦ αὐτοῦ. κατὰ πρεσβυτέρου κατη-
the workman of the pay of him. Against an elder
γορίαν μὴ παραδέχου, ἐκτὸς εἰ μὴ ἐπὶ δύο ἢ τριῶν μαρτύ-
accusation not receive, unless on two or three wit-
20 ρων. τοὺς ἁμαρτάνοντας ἐνώπιον πάντων ἔλεγχε, ἵνα καὶ
nesses. Those sinning before all, reprove; that also
21 οἱ λοιποὶ φόβον ἔχωσι. διαμαρτύρομαι ἐνώπιον τοῦ Θεοῦ
the rest fear may have. I solemnly witness before God
καὶ Κυρίου Ἰησοῦ Χριστοῦ καὶ τῶν ἐκλεκτῶν ἀγγέλων, ἵνα
and (the) Lord Jesus Christ, and the elect angels, that
ταῦτα φυλάξῃς χωρὶς προκρίματος, μηδὲν ποιῶν κατὰ
these things you guard without prejudice, nothing doing by way of
22 πρόσκλισιν. χεῖρας ταχέως μηδενὶ ἐπιτίθει, μηδὲ κοινώνει
partiality. hands quickly no one Lay on, nor share in
23 ἁμαρτίαις ἀλλοτρίαις· σεαυτὸν ἁγνὸν τήρει. μηκέτι ὑδροπό-
sins of others; yourself pure keep. No longer drink

use a little wine on account of your stomach and your frequent infirmities. [24]The sins of some men are plain before, going before to judgment; and *of* some, they also follow after. [25]Likewise, also the good works are plain beforehand, and those otherwise cannot be hidden.

CHAPTER 6

[1]Let as many as *are* slaves under a yoke count their masters worthy of all honor, that the name and teaching of God may not be blasphemed. [2]And those having believing masters, let them not despise *them* because they are brothers, but rather let them serve because they are believing and beloved ones, those receiving of the good service in return. Teach and exhort these things.

[3]If anyone teaches differently, and does not consent to sound words, those of our Lord Jesus Christ, and the teaching according to godliness, [4]he has been puffed up, understanding nothing, but *is* sick concerning doubts and arguments, out of which comes envy, strife, evil-speakings, evil suspicions, [5]meddling, of men whose mind has been corrupted and deprived of the truth, supposing gain to be godliness. Withdraw from such *persons.* [6]But godliness with contentment is great gain. [7]For we did not bring anything into the world, *and it is* plain that neither can we carry anything out. [8]But having food and clothing, we will be satisfied with these. [9]But those having purposed to be rich fall into temptation and a snare, and many foolish and hurtful lusts which plunge men into death and destruction. [10]For the love of money is a root of all evils, which some having lusted after were seduced from the faith, and *they* themselves pierced through

τει, ἀλλ' οἴνῳ ὀλίγῳ χρῶ, διὰ τὸν στόμαχόν σου καὶ τὰς
water, but wine a little use, because of the stomach of you and the
24 πυκνάς σου ἀσθενείας. τινῶν ἀνθρώπων αἱ ἁμαρτίαι
frequent of you weaknesses. of some men The sins
προδηλοί εἰσι, προάγουσαι εἰς κρίσιν· τισὶ δὲ καὶ ἐπακο-
plain before are, going before to judgment; some but indeed they
25 λουθοῦσιν. ὡσαύτως καὶ τὰ καλὰ ἔργα πρόδηλά ἐστι· καὶ
follow on; likewise also the good works plain before are, and
τὰ ἄλλως ἔχοντα κρυβῆναι οὐ δύναται.
those otherwise (being) be hidden not can.

CHAPTER 6

1 Ὅσοι εἰσὶν ὑπὸ ζυγὸν δοῦλοι, τοὺς ἰδίους δεσπότας πάσης
As many as are under a yoke, slaves, the own masters of all
τιμῆς ἀξίους ἡγείσθωσαν, ἵνα μὴ τὸ ὄνομα τοῦ Θεοῦ καὶ ἡ
honor worthy esteem, that not the name of God and the
2 διδασκαλία βλασφημῆται. οἱ δὲ πιστοὺς ἔχοντες δεσπότας
teaching be blasphemed, those And believing having masters,
μὴ καταφρονείτωσαν, ὅτι ἀδελφοί εἰσιν· ἀλλὰ μᾶλλον δου-
not let them despise because brothers they are, but rather let them
λευέτωσαν, οτι πιστοί εἰσι καὶ ἀγαπητοὶ οἱ τῆς εὐεργεσίας
serve as slaves, because believing are and beloved those of the good service
ἀντιλαμβανόμενοι. ταῦτα δίδασκε καὶ παρακάλει.
receiving in return. these things Teach and exhort.

3 Εἴ τις ἑτεροδιδασκαλεῖ, καὶ μὴ προσέρχεται ὑγιαίνουσι
If anyone teaches differently, and not consents to sound
λόγοις, τοῖς τοῦ Κυρίου ἡμῶν Ἰησοῦ Χριστοῦ, καὶ τῇ κατ'
words, those of the Lord of us, Jesus Christ, and to the according to
4 εὐσέβειαν διδασκαλίᾳ, τετύφωται, μηδὲν ἐπιστάμενος, ἀλλὰ
godliness teaching, he has been puffed up, nothing understanding, but
νοσῶν περὶ ζητήσεις καὶ λογομαχίας, ἐξ ὧν γίνεται φθόνος,
is sick concerning doubts and arguments, out of which comes envy,
5 ἔρις, βλασφημίαι, ὑπόνοιαι πονηραί, παραδιατριβαὶ διε-
strife, evil-speakings, suspicions evil, wearing disputes, having
φθαρμένων ἀνθρώπων τὸν νοῦν, καὶ ἀπεστερημένων τῆς
been corrupted of men the mind, and deprived of the
ἀληθείας, νομιζόντων πορισμὸν εἶναι τὴν εὐσέβειαν. ἀφί-
truth, supposing gain to be godliness; with-
6 στασο ἀπὸ τῶν τοιούτων. ἔστι δὲ πορισμὸς μέγας ἡ εὐσέβεια
draw from such. is But gain great godliness
7 μετὰ αὐταρκείας· οὐδὲν γὰρ εἰσηνέγκαμεν εἰς τὸν κόσμον,
with contentment; nothing for we have brought into the world,
8 δῆλον ὅτι οὐδὲ ἐξενεγκεῖν τι δυνάμεθα· ἔχοντες δὲ διατροφὰς
(it is) plain that neither carry out anything can we; having but foods
9 καὶ σκεπάσματα τούτοις ἀρκεσθησόμεθα. οἱ δὲ βουλόμενοι
and clothings, with these things we will be satisfied. those but resolving
πλουτεῖν ἐμπίπτουσιν εἰς πειρασμὸν καὶ παγίδα καὶ ἐπιθυ-
to be rich fall into temptation and a snare, and lusts
μίας πολλὰς ἀνοήτους καὶ βλαβεράς, αἵτινες βυθίζουσι τοὺς
many foolish and hurtful, which cause to sink
10 ἀνθρώπους εἰς ὄλεθρον καὶ ἀπώλειαν. ῥίζα γὰρ πάντων τῶν
men into ruin and destruction. a root For of all
κακῶν ἐστὶν ἡ φιλαργυρία· ἧς τινὲς ὀρεγόμενοι ἀπεπλανήθη-
evils is the love of money, of which some lusting after were seduced
σαν ἀπὸ τῆς πίστεως, καὶ ἑαυτους περιέπειραν ὀδύναις
from the faith, and themselves pierced around pains

by many pains.

11 But you, O man of God, flee these things, and pursue righteousness, godliness, faith, love, patience, meekness. 12 Fight the good fight of faith. Lay hold on eternal life, to which you were also called, and confessed the good confession before many witnesses. 13 I charge you before God, He making all things alive, and Christ Jesus, He witnessing the good confession *to* Pilate, 14 that you keep the commandment spotless, blameless, until the appearing of our Lord Jesus Christ; 15 who in His own time will reveal the blessed and only Potentate, the King of kings and Lord of lords; 16 the only *One* having immortality, living in light that cannot be approached; whom no one of men saw, nor can see; to whom be honor and everlasting might. Amen.

17 Charge the rich in the present age not to be highminded, nor to have hope in *the* uncertainty of riches, but in the living God, He offering to us richly all things for enjoyment; 18 to do good, to be rich in good works, to be ready to share, generous, 19 treasuring up for themselves a good foundation for the coming *age*, that they may lay hold on everlasting life.

20 O Timothy, guard the deposit, having turned away from the profane, empty babblings and opposing theories of the falsely named knowledge, which some having asserted have missed the mark concerning the faith.

Grace *be* with you. Amen.

πολλαῖς.
by many.

11 Σὺ δέ, ὦ ἄνθρωπε τοῦ Θεοῦ, ταῦτα φεῦγε· δίωκε δὲ δικαιο-
you But, O man of God, these things flee, pursue and after
σύνην, εὐσέβειαν, πίστιν, ἀγάπην, ὑπομονήν, πρᾳότητα.
righteousness, godliness, faith, love, patience, meekness.
12 ἀγωνίζου τὸν καλὸν ἀγῶνα τῆς πίστεως, ἐπιλαβοῦ τῆς
Fight the good fight of faith. Lay hold on
αἰωνίου ζωῆς, εἰς ἣν καὶ ἐκλήθης, καὶ ὡμολόγησας τὴν καλὴν
everlasting life, to which also you were called, and confessed the good
13 ὁμολογίαν ἐνώπιον πολλῶν μαρτύρων. παραγγέλλω σοι
confession before many witnesses. I enjoin you
ἐνώπιον τοῦ Θεοῦ τοῦ ζωοποιοῦντος τὰ πάντα, καὶ Χριστοῦ
before God, the (One) making alive all things, and Christ
Ἰησοῦ τοῦ μαρτυρήσαντος ἐπὶ Ποντίου Πιλάτου τὴν καλὴν
Jesus, the (One) having witnessed on Pontius Pilate the good
14 ὁμολογίαν, τηρῆσαί σε τὴν ἐντολὴν ἄσπιλον, ἀνεπίληπτον,
confession, to keep you the commandment unspotted, irreproachable,
15 μέχρι τῆς ἐπιφανείας τοῦ Κυρίου ἡμῶν Ἰησοῦ Χριστοῦ, ἣν
until the appearing of the Lord of us, Jesus Christ, which
καιροῖς ἰδίοις δείξει ὁ μακάριος καὶ μόνος δυνάστης, ὁ Βασι-
in its own time will reveal the blessed and only Potentate, the King
16 λεὺς τῶν βασιλευόντων, καὶ Κύριος τῶν κυριευόντων, ὁ
of kings, and Lord of lords, the
μόνος ἔχων ἀθανασίαν, φῶς οἰκῶν ἀπρόσιτον, ὃν εἶδεν οὐδεὶς
only (One) having immortality, light living in unapproachable, whom saw no one
ἀνθρώπων, οὐδὲ ἰδεῖν δύναται· ᾧ τιμὴ καὶ κράτος αἰώνιον.
of men, nor see can; to whom honor and might everlasting.
ἀμήν.
Amen.

17 Τοῖς πλουσίοις ἐν τῷ νῦν αἰῶνι παράγγελλε, μὴ ὑψη-
The rich in the present age enjoin not to be
λοφρονεῖν, μηδὲ ἠλπικέναι ἐπὶ πλούτου ἀδηλότητι, ἀλλ' ἐν
highminded, nor to set hope on of riches (the) uncertainty, but on
τῷ Θεῷ τῷ ζῶντι, τῷ παρέχοντι ἡμῖν πλουσίως πάντα
God the living, the (One) offering to us richly all things
18 εἰς ἀπόλαυσιν· ἀγαθοεργεῖν, πλουτεῖν ἐν ἔργοις καλοῖς,
for enjoyment, to work good, to be rich in works good,
19 εὐμεταδότους εἶναι, κοινωνικούς, ἀποθησαυρίζοντας ἑαυτοῖς
ready to impart to be, generous, treasuring away for themselves
θεμέλιον καλὸν εἰς τὸ μέλλον, ἵνα ἐπιλάβωνται τῆς αἰωνίου
foundation a good for the coming (age), that they lay hold on everlasting
ζωῆς.
life.

20 Ὦ Τιμόθεε, τὴν παρακαταθήκην φύλαξον, ἐκτρεπόμενος
O Timothy, the deposit guard, having turned from
τὰς βεβήλους κενοφωνίας καὶ ἀντιθέσεις τῆς ψευδωνύμου
the profane, empty babblings and opposing theories of the falsely named
21 γνώσεως· ἥν τινες ἐπαγγελλόμενοι περὶ τὴν πίστιν
knowledge, which some asserting concerning the faith
ἠστόχησαν.
have missed the mark.

Ἡ χάρις μετὰ σοῦ. ἀμήν.
Grace (be) with you. Amen.

ΠΑΥΛΟΥ ΤΟΥ ΑΠΟΣΤΟΛΟΥ
PAUL THE APOSTLE

Η ΠΡΟΣ
THE TO

ΤΙΜΟΘΕΟΝ
TIMOTHY

ΕΠΙΣΤΟΛΗ ΔΕΥΤΕΡΑ
EPISTLE SECOND

KING JAMES II VERSION

THE SECOND EPISTLE TO TIMOTHY

CHAPTER 1

[1] Paul *an* apostle of Jesus Christ by *the* will of God, according to the promise of life which *is* in Christ Jesus, [2] to *my* beloved child Timothy: Grace, mercy, peace from God *the* Father and Christ Jesus our Lord.

[3] I have thanks to God, whom I worship from *my* forebears in a pure conscience, how unceasingly I have remembrance concerning you in my petitions night and day, [4] longing to see you, being reminded of your tears, that I may be filled with joy; [5] taking recollection of the unpretended faith which first dwelt in your grandmother Lois, and *in* your mother Eunice; and I am assured that *it is* also in you. [6] For which cause I remind you to fan the flame of the gift of God, which is in you through the laying on of my hands. [7] For God did not give a spirit of fearfulness to us, but of power, and of love, and of self-control. [8] Then do not be ashamed of the testimony of our Lord, nor *of* me, His prisoner. But suffer hardship with the gospel, according to the power of God, [9] He having saved us and having called us with a holy calling, not according to our works, but according to *His* own purpose and grace given to us in Christ Jesus before eternal times, [10] but now revealed by the appearance of our Savior, Jesus Christ, making death of no

CHAPTER 1

1 Παῦλος, ἀπόστολος Ἰησοῦ Χριστοῦ διὰ θελήματος Θεοῦ,
Paul an apostle of Jesus Christ through (the) will of God,
2 κατ' ἐπαγγελίαν ζωῆς τῆς ἐν Χριστῷ Ἰησοῦ, Τιμοθέῳ
by way of a promise of life in Christ Jesus, to Timothy
ἀγαπητῷ τέκνῳ· χάρις, ἔλεος, εἰρήνη ἀπὸ Θεοῦ πατρὸς καὶ
beloved child, Grace, hope, peace from God (the) Father and
Χριστοῦ Ἰησοῦ τοῦ Κυρίου ἡμῶν.
Christ Jesus the Lord of us.
3 Χάριν ἔχω τῷ Θεῷ, ᾧ λατρεύω ἀπὸ προγόνων ἐν καθαρᾷ
Thanks I have to God, whom I worship from (my) forebears in a clean
συνειδήσει, ὡς ἀδιάλειπτον ἔχω τὴν περὶ σοῦ μνείαν ἐν ταῖς
conscience, as without ceasing I have the concerning you remembrance in the
4 δεήσεσί μου νυκτὸς καὶ ἡμέρας, ἐπιποθῶν σε ἰδεῖν, μεμνημένος
petitions of me night and day, longing you to see, being reminded
5 σου τῶν δακρύων, ἵνα χαρᾶς πληρωθῶ, ὑπόμνησιν λαμ-
of you the tears, that with joy I may be filled, recollection taking
βάνων τῆς ἐν σοὶ ἀνυποκρίτου πίστεως, ἥτις ἐνῴκησε
of the in you unpretended faith, which indwelt
πρῶτον ἐν τῇ μάμμῃ σου Λωΐδι καὶ τῇ μητρί σου Εὐνίκῃ,
firstly in your grandmother Lois, and (in) the mother of you Eunice,
6 πέπεισμαι δὲ ὅτι καὶ ἐν σοί. δι' ἣν αἰτίαν ἀναμιμνήσκω σε
I am assured and that also in you (is) For which cause I remind you
ἀναζωπυρεῖν τὸ χάρισμα τοῦ Θεοῦ, ὅ ἐστιν ἐν σοὶ διὰ τῆς
to fan the flame of the gift of God, which is in you through the
7 ἐπιθέσεως τῶν χειρῶν μου. οὐ γὰρ ἔδωκεν ἡμῖν ὁ Θεὸς
laying on of the hands of me. not For gave to us God
πνεῦμα δειλίας, ἀλλὰ δυνάμεως καὶ ἀγάπης καὶ σωφρονι-
a spirit of cowardice, but of power and of love and of self-
8 σμοῦ. μὴ οὖν ἐπαισχυνθῇς τὸ μαρτύριον τοῦ Κυρίου ἡμῶν,
control. not Therefore be ashamed of the testimony of the Lord of us,
μηδὲ ἐμὲ τὸν δέσμιον αὐτοῦ· ἀλλὰ συγκακοπάθησον τῷ
nor (of) me, the prisoner of Him, but suffer hardship with the
9 εὐαγγελίῳ κατὰ δύναμιν Θεοῦ, τοῦ σώσαντος ἡμᾶς καὶ
gospel according to (the) power of God, the (One) having saved us and
καλέσαντος κλήσει ἁγίᾳ, οὐ κατὰ τὰ ἔργα ἡμῶν, ἀλλὰ κατ'
having called calling with a holy, not according to the works of us, but by
ἰδίαν πρόθεσιν καὶ χάριν τὴν δοθεῖσαν ἡμῖν ἐν Χριστῷ Ἰησοῦ
(His) own purpose and grace given to us in Christ Jesus
10 πρὸ χρόνων αἰωνίων, φανερωθεῖσαν δὲ νῦν διὰ τῆς ἐπι-
before times eternal; revealed but now through the
φανείας τοῦ σωτῆρος ἡμῶν Ἰησοῦ Χριστοῦ, καταργήσαντος
appearance of the Savior of us, Jesus Christ, making of no effect

effect *and* bringing life and incorruption to light through the gospel. 11 for which I was appointed a herald and apostle, and a teacher of nations. 12 For which cause I also suffer these things; but I am not ashamed, for I know whom I have believed, and I am persuaded that He is able to guard my deposit until that Day. 13 Hold a pattern of sound words which you heard from me, in faith and love in Christ Jesus. 14 Guard the good deposit *given* through *the* Holy Spirit indwelling in us.

15 You know this, that all those in Asia turned away from me, of whom is Phygellus and Hermogenes. 16 May the Lord give mercy to the house of Onesiphorus, because he often refreshed me, and he was not ashamed *of* my chain; 17 but having come to Rome, he more diligently sought and found me. 18 May the Lord give to him to find mercy from *the* Lord in that Day. And what things he served in Ephesus, you know very well.

CHAPTER 2

1 Therefore, my child, you be empowered by grace in Christ Jesus. 2 And what things you heard from me through many witnesses, commit these things to faithful men, such as will be competent to also teach others. 3 Therefore, you suffer hardship as a good soldier of Jesus Christ. 4 No one serving as a soldier tangles with the affairs of this life, so that he might please the *one* enlisting *him*. 5 And also if anyone competes, he is not crowned unless he competes lawfully. 6 *It is* right *that* the laboring farmer partake first of the fruits. 7 Consider what I say, for the Lord will give you understanding in all things. 8 Remember Jesus Christ having been raised from *the* dead, of the seed of David, according to my gospel, 9 in

μὲν τὸν θάνατον, φωτίσαντος δὲ ζωὴν καὶ ἀφθαρσίαν διὰ τοῦ
death, bringing to light and life and incorruption through the
11 εὐαγγελίου, εἰς ὃ ἐτέθην ἐγὼ κήρυξ καὶ ἀπόστολος καὶ
gospel, for which was appointed I a herald and apostle and
12 διδάσκαλος ἐθνῶν δι' ἣν αἰτίαν καὶ ταῦτα πάσχω, ἀλλ' οὐκ
a teacher of nations; for which cause also these things I suffer, but not
ἐπαισχύνομαι οἶδα γὰρ ᾧ πεπίστευκα, καὶ πέπεισμαι ὅτι
I am ashamed, I know for whom I have believed, and I am persuaded that
δυνατός ἐστι τὴν παραθήκην μου φυλάξαι εἰς ἐκείνην τὴν
able He is the deposit of me to guard unto that
13 ἡμέραν. ὑποτύπωσιν ἔχε ὑγιαινόντων λόγων ὧν παρ ἐμοῦ
Day. a pattern Have of sound words which from me
14 ἤκουσας, ἐν πίστει καὶ ἀγάπῃ τῇ ἐν Χριστῷ Ἰησοῦ. τὴν
you heard, in faith and love in Christ Jesus. The
καλὴν παρακαταθήκην φύλαξον διὰ Πνεύματος Ἁγίου τοῦ
good deposit guard through (the) Spirit Holy
ἐνοικοῦντος ἐν ἡμῖν.
indwelling in us.

15 Οἶδας τοῦτο, ὅτι ἀπεστράφησάν με πάντες οἱ ἐν τῇ Ἀσίᾳ,
You know this, that turned away from me all those in Asia,
16 ὧν ἐστὶ Φύγελλος καὶ Ἑρμογένης. δῴη ἔλεος ὁ Κύριος τῷ
of whom is Phygellus and Hermogenes. May give mercy the Lord to the
Ὀνησιφόρου οἴκῳ· ὅτι πολλάκις με ἀνέψυξε, καὶ τὴν ἅλυσίν
of Onesiphorus house because often me he refreshed, and the chain
17 μου οὐκ ἐπῃσχύνθη, ἀλλὰ γενόμενος ἐν Ῥώμῃ, σπουδαιό-
of me not he was ashamed (of); but coming to Rome, more diligently
18 τερον ἐζήτησέ με καὶ εὗρε (δῴη αὐτῷ ὁ Κύριος εὑρεῖν ἔλεος
he sought me and found —may give to him the Lord to find mercy
παρὰ Κυρίου ἐν ἐκείνῃ τῇ ἡμέρᾳ)· καὶ ὅσα ἐν Ἐφέσῳ
from (the) Lord in that Day — and what things in Ephesus
διηκόνησε, βέλτιον σὺ γινώσκεις.
he served, very well you know.

CHAPTER 2

1 Σὺ οὖν, τέκνον μου, ἐνδυναμοῦ ἐν τῇ χάριτι τῇ ἐν Χριστῷ
You, therefore, child of me, be empowered by grace in Christ
2 Ἰησοῦ. καὶ ἃ ἤκουσας παρ' ἐμοῦ διὰ πολλῶν μαρτύρων,
Jesus. And what things you heard from me through many witnesses,
ταῦτα παράθου πιστοῖς ἀνθρώποις, οἵτινες ἱκανοὶ ἔσονται
these things commit to faithful men, who competent will be
3 καὶ ἑτέρους διδάξαι. σὺ οὖν κακοπάθησον ὡς καλὸς στρατιώ-
also others to teach. You, then, suffer hardship as a good soldier
4 της Ἰησοῦ Χριστοῦ. οὐδεὶς στρατευόμενος ἐμπλέκεται ταῖς
of Jesus Christ. No one serving as a soldier tangles with the
τοῦ βίου πραγματείαις, ἵνα τῷ στρατολογήσαντι ἀρέσῃ.
of life affairs, that the (One) having enlisted (him) he please.
5 ἐὰν δὲ καὶ ἀθλῇ τις, οὐ στεφανοῦται ἐὰν μὴ νομίμως ἀθλήσῃ.
if And also competes any, not he is crowned unless lawfully he competes.
6 τὸν κοπιῶντα γεωργὸν δεῖ πρῶτον τῶν καρπῶν μετα-
The laboring farmer it behoves firstly of the fruits to
7 λαμβάνειν. νόει ἃ λέγω· δῴη γάρ σοι ὁ Κύριος σύνεσιν ἐν
partake. Consider what I say, will give for you the Lord understanding in
8 πᾶσι. μνημόνευε Ἰησοῦν Χριστὸν ἐγηγερμένον ἐκ νεκρῶν,
all. Remember Jesus Christ having been raised from (the) dead,
9 ἐκ σπέρματος Δαβίδ, κατὰ τὸ εὐαγγέλιόν μου· ἐν ᾧ κακο-
of (the) seed of David, according to the gospel of me; in which I

which I suffer ill as an evildoer, unto bonds; but the word of God has not been bound. 10 Because of this, I endure all things on account of the elect, that they also may obtain salvation in Christ Jesus, with everlasting glory. 11 Faithful *is* the word: for if we died with *Him,* we also shall live with *Him.* If we deny *Him,* that One will deny us. 13 If we are unfaithful, that One remains faithful; He is not able to deny Himself.

14 Remind *them of* these things, solemnly testifying before the Lord not to dispute about words for nothing useful, to *the* throwing down *of* those hearing. 15 Earnestly *study* to show yourself approved to God, a workman unashamed, rightly dividing the word of truth. 16 But shun profane, empty babblings, for they will go on to more ungodliness, 17 and their word will have growth like gangrene—of whom is Hymeneus and Philetus; 18 who missed the mark concerning the truth, saying the resurrection already has come, and overturn the faith of some.

19 Nevertheless, the foundation of God stands firm, having this seal, "*The* Lord knew those being His;" and, "Let everyone naming the name of Christ depart from unrighteousness." 20 But in a great house not only is there vessels of gold and silver, but also of wood and of earth; and some to honor, and some to dishonor. 21 Therefore, if anyone purifies himself from these, he will be a vessel to honor, having been sanctified and made useful to the Master, having been prepared to every good work. 22 But flee youthful lusts, and pursue righteousness, faith, love, peace, with the *ones* calling on the Lord out of a pure heart. 23 But refuse the foolish and undisciplined questionings, knowing that they generate quarrels. 24 But a slave of *the* Lord ought not to

παθῶ μέχρι δεσμῶν, ὡς κακοῦργος· ἀλλ᾽ ὁ λόγος τοῦ Θεοῦ
suffer ill unto bonds as an evildoer; but the word of God
10 οὐ δέδεται. διὰ τοῦτο πάντα ὑπομένω διὰ τοὺς ἐκλεκτούς,
not has been bound Therefore all things I endure on account of the elect
ἵνα καὶ αὐτοὶ σωτηρίας τύχωσι τῆς ἐν Χριστῷ Ἰησοῦ, μετὰ
that also they salvation may obtain in Christ Jesus, with
11 δόξης αἰωνίου. πιστὸς ὁ λόγος· Εἰ γὰρ συναπεθάνομεν, καὶ
glory everlasting. Faithful (is) the word; if for we died with (Him), also
12 συζήσομεν· εἰ ὑπομένομεν, καὶ συμβασιλεύσομεν· εἰ ἀρνού-
we shall live with (Him); if we endure, also we shall reign with (Him); if we de-
13 μεθα, κἀκεῖνος ἀρνήσεται ἡμᾶς· εἰ ἀπιστοῦμεν, ἐκεῖνος πιστὸς
ny (Him), that One will deny us; if we are unfaithful, that One faithful
μένει· ἀρνήσασθαι ἑαυτὸν οὐ δύναται.
remains; to deny Himself not He is able.
14 Ταῦτα ὑπομίμνησκε, διαμαρτυρόμενος ἐνώπιον τοῦ
These things remind (them), solemnly testifying before the
Κυρίου μὴ λογομαχεῖν εἰς οὐδὲν χρήσιμον, ἐπὶ καταστροφῇ
Lord not to dispute about words for nothing useful, to throwing down
15 τῶν ἀκουόντων. σπούδασον σεαυτὸν δόκιμον παραστῆσαι
those hearing. Earnestly (study) yourself approved to show
τῷ Θεῷ, ἐργάτην ἀνεπαίσχυντον, ὀρθοτομοῦντα τὸν λόγον
to God a workman unashamed, rightly dividing the word
16 τῆς ἀληθείας. τὰς δὲ βεβήλους κενοφωνίας περιΐστασο· ἐπὶ
of truth. the But profane, empty babblings shun; to
17 πλεῖον γὰρ προκόψουσιν ἀσεβείας, καὶ ὁ λόγος αὐτῶν ὡς
more for they will advance ungodliness, and the word of them as
18 γάγγραινα νομὴν ἕξει· ὧν ἐστὶν Ὑμέναιος καὶ Φιλητός· οἵτινες
gangrene feeding will have; of whom is Hymeneus and Philetus, who
περὶ τὴν ἀλήθειαν ἠστόχησαν, λέγοντες τὴν ἀνάστασιν
concerning the truth missed the mark, saying the resurrection
19 ἤδη γεγονέναι, καὶ ἀνατρέπουσι τήν τινων πίστιν. ὁ μέντοι
already to have come, and overturn the of some faith. the However,
στερεὸς θεμέλιος τοῦ Θεοῦ ἕστηκεν, ἔχων τὴν σφραγῖδα
firm foundation of God stands, having seal
ταύτην, Ἔγνω Κύριος τοὺς ὄντας αὐτοῦ, καί, Ἀποστήτω
this, knew (the) Lord those being His, and, Let depart
20 ἀπὸ ἀδικίας πᾶς ὁ ὀνομάζων τὸ ὄνομα Χριστοῦ. ἐν μεγάλῃ
from iniquity everyone naming the name of Christ. in a great
δὲ οἰκίᾳ οὐκ ἔστι μόνον σκεύη χρυσᾶ καὶ ἀργυρᾶ, ἀλλὰ καὶ
Now house, not is there only vessels golden and silver, but also
ξύλινα καὶ ὀστράκινα, καὶ ἃ μὲν εἰς τιμήν, ἃ δὲ εἰς ἀτιμίαν.
wooden and earthen; and some to honor, and some to dishonor
21 ἐὰν οὖν τις ἐκκαθάρῃ ἑαυτὸν ἀπὸ τούτων, ἔσται σκεῦος εἰς
If, therefore anyone cleanses himself from these, he will be a vessel to
τιμήν, ἡγιασμένον, καὶ εὔχρηστον τῷ δεσπότῃ, εἰς πᾶν
honor, having been sanctified, and useful to the master, to every
22 ἔργον ἀγαθὸν ἡτοιμασμένον. τὰς δὲ νεωτερικὰς ἐπιθυμίας
work good having been prepared. the And youthful lusts
φεῦγε· δίωκε δὲ δικαιοσύνην, πίστιν, ἀγάπην, εἰρήνην, μετὰ
flee, pursue but righteousness, faith, love, peace, with
23 τῶν ἐπικαλουμένων τὸν Κύριον ἐκ καθαρᾶς καρδίας. τὰς δὲ
those calling on the Lord out of a clean heart. But
μωρὰς καὶ ἀπαιδεύτους ζητήσεις παραιτοῦ, εἰδὼς ὅτι
foolish and uninstructed questionings refuse, knowing that
24 γεννῶσι μάχας. δοῦλον δὲ Κυρίου οὐ δεῖ μάχεσθαι, ἀλλ᾽
they generate quarrels; a slave and of (the) Lord not it behoves to quarrel, but

quarrel, but to be gentle towards all, apt to teach, forbearing, [25] in meekness teaching those who oppose, *if* perhaps God may give them repentance for a full knowledge of *the* truth, [26] and they may awake out of the snare of the Devil, having been taken captive by him, so as to do the will of that one.

CHAPTER 3

[1] But know this, that in *the* last days grievous times will be at hand. [2] For men will be lovers of themselves, lovers of money, braggarts, arrogant, blasphemers, disobedient to parents, unthankful, unholy, [3] without natural feeling, unyielding, slanderers, without self-control, savage, haters of good, [4] betrayers, reckless, puffed up, lovers of pleasure rather than lovers of God, [5] having a form of godliness, but denying the power of it—even turn away from these. [6] For of these are those creeping into houses and leading silly women captive, *the ones* having been heaped with sins, being led away by various lusts, [7] always learning, but never being able to come to a full knowledge of *the* truth. [8] But in the way Jannes and Jambres withstood Moses, so also these withstand the truth, men having been corrupted *in* mind, found worthless as to the faith. [9] But they will not go further, for their foolishness will be plain to all, as also that of those became.

[10] But you have closely followed my teaching, the conduct, the purpose, the faith, the long-suffering, the love, the patient endurance, [11] the persecutions, the sufferings, such as happened to me in Antioch, in Iconium, in Lystra; what persecutions I bore. And the Lord delivered me out of all. [12] And, indeed, all desiring to live godly in Christ Jesus will be persecuted. [13] But evil men and

25 ἤπιον εἶναι πρὸς πάντας, διδακτικόν, ἀνεξίκακον, ἐν πρᾳό-
gentle to be toward all, apt to teach, forbearing, in meek-
τητι παιδεύοντα τοὺς ἀντιδιατιθεμένους· μήποτε δῷ αὐτοῖς
ness teaching those opposing, (if) perhaps may give them
26 ὁ Θεὸς μετάνοιαν εἰς ἐπίγνωσιν ἀληθείας, καὶ ἀνανήψωσιν
God repentance for a full knowledge of truth, and they regain senses
ἐκ τῆς τοῦ διαβόλου παγίδος, ἐζωγρημένοι ὑπ' αὐτοῦ εἰς τὸ
out of the devil snare, having been captured by him to (do) the
ἐκείνου θέλημα.
of that one will.

CHAPTER 3

1 Τοῦτο δὲ γίνωσκε, ὅτι ἐν ἐσχάταις ἡμέραις ἐνστήσονται
this And know, that in (the) last days will be at hand
2 καιροὶ χαλεποί. ἔσονται γὰρ οἱ ἄνθρωποι φίλαυτοι, φιλ-
times grievous. will be For men self-lovers, money-
άργυροι, ἀλαζόνες, ὑπερήφανοι, βλάσφημοι, γονεῦσιν ἀπει-
lovers, braggarts, arrogant, blasphemers, to parents diso-
3 θεῖς, ἀχάριστοι, ἀνόσιοι, ἄστοργοι, ἄσπονδοι, διάβολοι,
bedient, unthankful, unholy, without natural feeling, implacable, slanderers,
4 ἀκρατεῖς, ἀνήμεροι, ἀφιλάγαθοι, προδόται, προπετεῖς, τετυ-
without self-control, savage, haters of good, betrayers, reckless, puffed
5 φωμένοι, φιλήδονοι μᾶλλον ἢ φιλόθεοι, ἔχοντες μόρφωσιν
up, pleasure-lovers rather than God-lovers, having a form
εὐσεβείας, τὴν δὲ δύναμιν αὐτῆς ἠρνημένοι· καὶ τούτους
of godliness, the but power of it having denied—even these
6 ἀποτρέπου. ἐκ τούτων γάρ εἰσιν οἱ ἐνδύνοντες εἰς τὰς οἰκίας,
turn away from. of these For are those creeping into houses,
καὶ αἰχμαλωτεύοντες τὰ γυναικάρια σεσωρευμένα ἁμαρ-
and leading captive silly women having been heaped with
7 τίαις, ἀγόμενα ἐπιθυμίαις ποικίλαις, πάντοτε μανθάνοντα,
sins, being led lusts by various, always learning
8 καὶ μηδέποτε εἰς ἐπίγνωσιν ἀληθείας ἐλθεῖν δυνάμενα. ὃν
and never to a full knowledge of truth to come being able. by
τρόπον δὲ Ἰαννῆς καὶ Ἰαμβρῆς ἀντέστησαν Μωϋσεῖ, οὕτω
what way And Jannes and Jambres opposed Moses, so
καὶ οὗτοι ἀνθίστανται τῇ ἀληθείᾳ, ἄνθρωποι κατεφθαρ-
also these oppose the truth, men having been
9 μένοι τὸν νοῦν, ἀδόκιμοι περὶ τὴν πίστιν. ἀλλ' οὐ προκό-
corrupted the mind, reprobate concerning the faith. But not they will
ψουσιν ἐπὶ πλεῖον· ἡ γὰρ ἄνοια αὐτῶν ἔκδηλος ἔσται πᾶσιν,
advance to more; the for folly of them plain will be to all,
10 ὡς καὶ ἡ ἐκείνων ἐγένετο. σὺ δὲ παρηκολούθηκάς μου τῇ
as also the (folly) of those became. you But have closely followed of me the
διδασκαλίᾳ, τῇ ἀγωγῇ, τῇ προθέσει, τῇ πίστει, τῇ μα-
teaching, the conduct, the purpose, the faith, the long-
11 κροθυμίᾳ, τῇ ἀγάπῃ, τῇ ὑπομονῇ, τοῖς διωγμοῖς, τοῖς παθή-
suffering, the love, the patience, the persecutions, the sufferings
μασιν, οἷά μοι ἐγένετο ἐν Ἀντιοχείᾳ, ἐν Ἰκονίῳ, ἐν Λύστροις,
which to me happened in Antioch, in Iconium, in Lystra;
οἵους διωγμοὺς ὑπήνεγκα· καὶ ἐκ πάντων με ἐρρύσατο ὁ
what persecutions I bore; yet out of all me delivered the
12 Κύριος. καὶ πάντες δὲ οἱ θέλοντες εὐσεβῶς ζῆν ἐν Χριστῷ
Lord. indeed all And those desiring godly to live in Christ
13 Ἰησοῦ διωχθήσονται. πονηροὶ δὲ ἄνθρωποι καὶ γόητες
Jesus will be persecuted. evil But men and pretenders

pretenders will go forward to worse, leading astray, and being led astray. [14] But you keep on in what you learned and were assured of, knowing from whom you learned, [15] and that from a babe you know the Holy Scriptures, those being able to make you wise to salvation through belief in Christ Jesus. [16] Every Scripture *is* God-breathed and profitable for teaching, for reproof, for correction, for instruction in righteousness; [17] so that the man of God may be perfect, fully furnished for every good work.

CHAPTER 4

[1] Then I solemnly witness before God and the Lord Jesus Christ, He being about to judge living and dead according to His appearance and His kingdom, [2] preach the word; be urgent in season, out of season; convict, warn, encourage with all long-suffering and teaching. [3] For a time will be when they will not endure sound doctrine, but according to their own lusts, having itching ears, they will heap up to themselves teachers tickling the ear, [4] and *they* will turn away the ear from the truth, and will be turned aside to myths. [5] But you be clear-minded in all; suffer hardship, do *the* work of an evangelist; fully carry out your ministry. [6] For I am already being poured out, and the time of my release is here. [7] I have fought the good fight. I have finished the course. I have kept the faith. [8] For the rest, the crown of righteousness is laid up for me, which the Lord, the righteous Judge, will give to me in that Day—and not only to me, but also to all the ones loving His appearance. [9] Make haste to come to me shortly; [10] for Demas deserted me, loving the present age; and *he* went to Thessalonica. Cres-

προκόψουσιν ἐπὶ τὸ χεῖρον, πλανῶντες καὶ πλανώμενοι.
will go forward to worse, deceiving and being deceived.
14 σὺ δὲ μένε ἐν οἷς ἔμαθες καὶ ἐπιστώθης, εἰδὼς παρὰ τίνος
you But continue in what you learned and were assured of, knowing from whom
15 ἔμαθες, καὶ ὅτι ἀπὸ βρέφους τὰ ἱερὰ γράμματα οἶδας, τὰ
you learned, and that from a babe the holy scriptures you know, those
δυνάμενά σε σοφίσαι εἰς σωτηρίαν διὰ πίστεως τῆς εν
being able you to make wise to salvation through belief in
16 Χριστῷ Ἰησοῦ. πᾶσα γραφὴ θεόπνευστος καὶ ὠφέλιμος
Christ Jesus. Every Scripture (is) God-breathed and profitable
πρὸς διδασκαλίαν, πρὸς ἔλεγχον, πρὸς ἐπανόρθωσιν, πρὸς
for teaching, for reproof, for correction, for
17 παιδείαν τὴν ἐν δικαιοσύνῃ· ἵνα ἄρτιος ᾖ ὁ τοῦ Θεοῦ
instruction in righteousness, that fitted may be the of God
ἄνθρωπος, πρὸς πᾶν ἔργον ἀγαθὸν ἐξηρτισμένος.
man, for every work good having been furnished.

CHAPTER 4

1 Διαμαρτύρομαι οὖν ἐγὼ ἐνώπιον τοῦ Θεοῦ, καὶ τοῦ
solemnly witness Then I before God, and the
Κυρίου Ἰησοῦ Χριστοῦ, τοῦ μέλλοντος κρίνειν ζῶντας καὶ
Lord Jesus Christ, the (One) being about to judge living ones and
νεκροὺς κατὰ τὴν ἐπιφάνειαν αὐτοῦ καὶ τὴν βασιλείαν
dead, according to the appearance of Him and the kingdom
2 αὐτοῦ, κήρυξον τὸν λόγον, ἐπίστηθι εὐκαίρως, ἀκαίρως,
of Him, proclaim the word, be urgent in season, out of season,
ἔλεγξον, ἐπιτίμησον, παρακάλεσον, ἐν πάσῃ μακροθυμίᾳ
reprove, warn, encourage with all long-suffering
3 καὶ διδαχῇ. ἔσται γὰρ καιρὸς ὅτε τῆς ὑγιαινούσης διδα-
and teaching. there will For a time when the sound
σκαλίας οὐκ ἀνέξονται, ἀλλὰ κατὰ τὰς ἐπιθυμίας τὰς ἰδίας
doctrine not they will bear, but according to the lusts the own
ἑαυτοῖς ἐπισωρεύσουσι διδασκάλους, κνηθόμενοι τὴν ἀκοήν·
to themselves they will heap up teachers tickling the ear,
4 καὶ ἀπὸ μὲν τῆς ἀληθείας τὴν ἀκοὴν ἀποστρέψουσιν, ἐπὶ
and from indeed the truth the ear will turn away, to
5 δὲ τοὺς μύθους ἐκτραπήσονται. σὺ δὲ νῆφε ἐν πᾶσι, κακοπά-
and myths will be turned. you But be sober in all, suffer
θησον, ἔργον ποίησον εὐαγγελιστοῦ, τὴν διακονίαν σου
evil, (the) work do of an evangelist, the ministry of you
6 πληροφόρησον. ἐγὼ γὰρ ἤδη σπένδομαι, καὶ ὁ καιρὸς τῆς
fulfill. I For already am being poured out, and the time of the
7 ἐμῆς ἀναλύσεως ἐφέστηκε. τὸν ἀγῶνα τὸν καλὸν ἠγώνισμαι,
of me departure has arrived. The fight good I have fought,
8 τὸν δρόμον τετέλεκα, τὴν πίστιν τετήρηκα· λοιπόν, ἀπό-
the course I have finished, the faith I have kept; for the rest, is laid
κειταί μοι ὁ τῆς δικαιοσύνης στέφανος, ὃν ἀποδώσει μοι ὁ
up for me the of righteousness crown, which will give to me the
Κύριος ἐν ἐκείνῃ τῇ ἡμέρᾳ, ὁ δίκαιος κριτής· οὐ μόνον δὲ
Lord in that Day, the righteous Judge; not only and
ἐμοί, ἀλλὰ καὶ πασι τοῖς ἠγαπηκόσι τὴν ἐπιφάνειαν αὐτοῦ.
to me; but also all those having loved the appearance of Him.
9 Σπούδασον ἐλθεῖν πρός με ταχέως· Δημᾶς γάρ με ἐγκατέ-
10 Make haste to come to me shortly. Demas For me deserted,
λιπεν, ἀγαπήσας τὸν νῦν αἰῶνα, καὶ ἐπορεύθη εἰς Θεσ-
loving the present age, and went to Thessa-

cens *went* to Galatia, Titus to Dalmatia. [11]Only Luke is with me. Taking Mark, bring *him* with you, for he is useful to me for ministry. [12]But I sent Tychicus to Ephesus. [13]Bring the cloak which I left in Troas with Carpus, and the books, especially the parchments, when *you* come. [14]Alexander the coppersmith showed many evil things to me. The Lord will give to him according to his works. [15]You also guard against *him*, for he greatly resisted our words.

[16]In my first defense, no one was beside me, but all deserted me. May it not be reckoned to them. [17]But the Lord stood with me and gave me power, that through me the preaching might be fulfilled, and all the nations might hear. And I was delivered out of *the* mouth of the lion. [18]And the Lord will deliver me from every wicked work, and will save *me* for His heavenly kingdom; to whom *be* the glory forever and ever. Amen.

[19]Greet Priscilla and Aquila, and the house of Onesiphorus. [20]Erastus remained in Corinth, but I left Trophimus sick in Miletus.

[21]Try to come before winter. Eubulus greets you, and Pudens, and Linus, and Claudia, and all the brothers.

[22]The Lord Jesus Christ *be* with your spirit. Grace *be* with you. Amen.

σαλονίκην· Κρήσκης εἰς Γαλατίαν, Τίτος εἰς Δαλματίαν.
Ionica, Crescens to Galatia; Titus to Dalmatia.
11 Λουκᾶς ἐστὶ μόνος μετ' ἐμοῦ. Μάρκον ἀναλαβὼν ἄγε μετὰ
Luke is only with me. Mark having taken, bring with
12 σεαυτοῦ· ἔστι γάρ μοι εὔχρηστος εἰς διακονίαν. Τυχικὸν δὲ
yourself, he is for to me useful for ministry. Tychichus But
13 ἀπέστειλα εἰς Ἔφεσον. τὸν φελόνην ὃν ἀπέλιπον ἐν Τρῳάδι
I sent to Ephesus. The cloak which I left in Troas
παρὰ Κάρπῳ, ἐρχόμενος φέρε, καὶ τὰ βιβλία, μάλιστα τὰς
with Carpus, coming bring, and the scrolls, especially the
14 μεμβράνας. Ἀλέξανδρος ὁ χαλκεὺς πολλά μοι κακὰ ἐνεδεί-
parchments. Alexander the coppersmith much to me evils showed;
15 ξατο· ἀποδῴη αὐτῷ ὁ Κύριος κατὰ τὰ ἔργα αὐτοῦ· ὃν καὶ
will give to him the Lord according to the works of him; whom also
σὺ φυλάσσου, λίαν γὰρ ἀνθέστηκε τοῖς ἡμετέροις λόγοις.
you guard (against), greatly for he opposed our words.
16 ἐν τῇ πρώτῃ μου ἀπολογίᾳ οὐδείς μοι συμπαρεγένετο, ἀλλὰ
At the first of me defense no one me was beside, but
17 πάντες με ἐγκατέλιπον· μὴ αὐτοῖς λογισθείη. ὁ δὲ Κύριός
all me deserted. May it not to them be reckoned. the But Lord
μοι παρέστη, καὶ ἐνεδυνάμωσέ με, ἵνα δι' ἐμοῦ τὸ κήρυγμα
me stood with, and empowered me, that through me the preaching
πληροφορηθῇ, καὶ ἀκούσῃ πάντα τὰ ἔθνη· καὶ ἐρρύσθην ἐκ
might be fulfilled, and might hear all the nations. And I was delivered out of
18 στόματος λέοντος. καὶ ῥύσεταί με ὁ Κύριος ἀπὸ παντος εργου
(the) mouth of (the) lion. And will deliver me The Lord from every work
πονηροῦ. καὶ σώσει εἰς τὴν βασιλείαν αὐτοῦ τὴν ἐπουράνιον·
wicked, and will save for the kingdom of Him heavenly;
ᾧ ἡ δόξα εἰς τοὺς αἰῶνας τῶν αἰώνων. ἀμήν.
to whom (be) the glory to the ages of the ages. Amen.
19 Ἄσπασαι Πρίσκαν καὶ Ἀκύλαν, καὶ τὸν Ὀνησιφόρου
Greet Priscilla and Aquila, and the of Onesiphorus
20 οἶκον. Ἔραστος ἔμεινεν ἐν Κορίνθῳ· Τρόφιμον δὲ ἀπέλιπον
house. Erastus remained in Corinth, Trophimus But I left
21 ἐν Μιλήτῳ ἀσθενοῦντα. σπούδασον πρὸ χειμῶνος ἐλθεῖν.
in Miletus sick. Make haste before winter to come.
ἀσπάζεταί σε Εὔβουλος, καὶ Πούδης, καὶ Λῖνος, καὶ Κλαυδία,
Greets you Eubulus and Pudens and Linus and Claudia,
καὶ οἱ ἀδελφοὶ πάντες.
and the brothers all.
22 Ὁ Κύριος Ἰησοῦς Χριστὸς μετὰ τοῦ πνεύματός σου. ἡ
The Lord Jesus Christ (be) with the spirit of you.
χάρις μεθ' ὑμῶν. ἀμήν.
Grace (be) with you. Amen.

KING JAMES II VERSION

THE EPISTLE TO TITUS

CHAPTER 1

1 Paul, a slave and an apostle of Jesus Christ according to *the* faith of *the* elect of God and full knowledge of *the* truth according to godliness, 2 on hope of eternal life which the God that does not lie promised before *the* eternal times, 3 but revealed in its own times in a proclamation of His word, with which I was entrusted by *the* command of our Savior God: 4 to Titus, a true child according to *our* common faith. Grace, mercy, peace from God *the* Father and *the* Lord Jesus Christ our Savior.

5 For this cause I left you in Crete, that you might set in order the things lacking, and to appoint elders in every city, as I ordered you: 6 If anyone is blameless, husband of one wife, having believing children, not in accusation of loose behavior, or unruly. 7 For the overseer must be blameless, as a steward of God, not self-pleasing, not full of passion, not given to wine, not a quarreler, not greedy of ill gain; 8 but hospitable, a lover of good, discreet, just, holy, temperate, 9 clinging to the faithful word according to the teaching, that he may be able both to encourage with sound teaching, and to convict the *ones* speaking against.

10 For there are indeed many unruly men, empty talkers and mind-deluders, especially those of *the* circumcision, 11 whose mouth you must stop, who overturn whole houses, teaching things which *they*

ΠΑΥΛΟΥ
PAUL
Η ΠΡΟΣ
THE TO
ΤΙΤΟΝ ΕΠΙΣΤΟΛΗ
TITUS EPISTLE

CHAPTER 1

1 Παῦλος, δοῦλος Θεοῦ, ἀπόστολος δὲ Ἰησοῦ Χριστοῦ, κατὰ
Paul, a slave of God, an apostle and of Jesus Christ, according to
πίστιν ἐκλεκτῶν Θεοῦ καὶ ἐπίγνωσιν ἀληθείας τῆς κατ
(the) faith of (the) elect of God and full knowledge of (the) truth according to
2 εὐσέβειαν, ἐπ' ἐλπίδι ζωῆς αἰωνίου, ἣν ἐπηγγείλατο ὁ
godliness, on hope life of eternal which promised the
3 ἀψευδὴς Θεὸς πρὸ χρόνων αἰωνίων, ἐφανέρωσε δὲ καιροῖς
not lying God before times eternal, revealed but times
ἰδίοις τὸν λόγον αὐτοῦ ἐν κηρύγματι ὃ ἐπιστεύθην ἐγὼ κατ'
in its own the word of Him in a proclamation which was entrusted I by
4 ἐπιταγὴν τοῦ σωτῆρος ἡμῶν Θεοῦ, Τίτῳ γνησίῳ τέκνῳ
(the) command of the Savior of us, God, to Titus a true child
κατὰ κοινὴν πίστιν· χάρις, ἔλεος, εἰρήνη ἀπὸ Θεοῦ πατρός,
according to a common faith: Grace, mercy, peace from God (the) Father
καὶ Κυρίου Ἰησοῦ Χριστοῦ τοῦ σωτῆρος ἡμῶν.
and (the) Lord Jesus Christ, the Savior of us.
5 Τούτου χάριν κατέλιπόν σε ἐν Κρήτῃ, ἵνα τὰ λείποντα
For this cause I left you in Crete, that the things lacking
ἐπιδιορθώσῃ, καὶ καταστήσῃς κατὰ πόλιν πρεσβυτέρους,
you set in order, and appoint in every city elders,
6 ὡς ἐγώ σοι διεταξάμην· εἴ τίς ἐστιν ἀνέγκλητος, μιᾶς
as I you ordered; if anyone is blameless, of one
γυναικὸς ἀνήρ, τέκνα ἔχων πιστά, μὴ ἐν κατηγορίᾳ ἀσωτίας
wife husband, children having believing, not in accusation of looseness
7 ἢ ἀνυπότακτα. δεῖ γὰρ τὸν ἐπίσκοπον ἀνέγκλητον εἶναι,
or unruly. it behoves For the overseer blameless to be,
ὡς Θεοῦ οἰκονόμον· μὴ αὐθάδη, μὴ ὀργίλον, μὴ πάροινον,
as of God a steward, not self-pleasing, not passionate, not given to wine,
8 μὴ πλήκτην, μὴ αἰσχροκερδῆ, ἀλλὰ φιλόξενον, φιλάγαθον,
not a quarreler, not greedy of ill gain, but hospitable, a lover of good,
9 σώφρονα, δίκαιον, ὅσιον, ἐγκρατῆ, ἀντεχόμενον τοῦ κατὰ
discreet, just, holy, temperate, clinging to the according to
τὴν διδαχὴν πιστοῦ λόγου, ἵνα δυνατὸς ᾖ καὶ παρακαλειν
the teaching faithful word, that able he may be both to exhort
ἐν τῇ διδασκαλίᾳ τῇ ὑγιαινούσῃ, καὶ τοὺς ἀντιλέγοντας
by the teaching sound, and those contradicting
ἐλέγχειν.
to convict.
10 Εἰσὶ γὰρ πολλοὶ καὶ ἀνυπότακτοι, ματαιολόγοι καὶ
there are For many indeed unruly men, empty talkers, and
11 φρεναπάται, μάλιστα οἱ ἐκ περιτομῆς, οὓς δεῖ ἐπιστομίζειν·
mind-deluders, especially those of circumcision, of whom must (you) stop the mouth
οἵτινες ὅλους οἴκους ἀνατρέπουσι, διδάσκοντες ἃ μὴ δεῖ,
who whole houses overturn, teaching things not right,

ought not for the sake of ill gain. 12 One of them, a prophet of their own, said: Cretans *are* always liars, evil beasts, lazy gluttons. 13 This testimony is true; for which cause convict them severely, that they may be sound in the faith, 14 not listening to Jewish myths and commandments of men, having turned away from the truth. 15 Truly, all things *are* pure to the pure; but to the ones having been defiled and unbelieving, nothing is pure, but even their mind and conscience has been defiled. 16 They profess to know God, but by *their* works they deny *Him,* being abominable and disobedient, and reprobate to every good work.

CHAPTER 2

1 But you speak things which become sound doctrine: 2 aged men to be temperate, sensible, discreet, sound in faith, in love, in patience; 3 aged women likewise in reverent behavior, not slanderers, not having been enslaved by much wine, teachers of good, 4 that they might train the young women to be lovers of husbands, lovers of children, 5 discreet, chaste, keepers at home, good, subject to their own husbands, so that the word of God may not be spoken against; 6 the younger men in the same way exhort to be discreet; 7 having shown yourself a pattern of good works about all things, in teaching, in purity, sensibleness, incorruption, *in* sound speech, not to be condemned; that he who is opposed may not be ashamed, having nothing bad to say about you. 9 Let slaves be subject to *their* own masters, well-pleasing in all things, not speaking against *them,* 10 not stealing, but showing all good faith, that they may adorn the teaching of our Savior God in all things. 11 For the grace of God which brings salvation appeared to all men, 12 instructing us

12 αἰσχροῦ κέρδους χάριν. εἶπέ τις ἐξ αὐτῶν, ἴδιος αὐτῶν
ill gain for the sake of. said One of them, an own of them
προφήτης, Κρῆτες ἀεὶ ψεῦσται, κακὰ θηρία, γαστέρες ἀργαί.
prophet, Cretans (are) always liars, evil beasts, gluttons idle.
13 ἡ μαρτυρία αὕτη ἐστὶν ἀληθής. δι' ἣν αἰτίαν ἔλεγχε αὐτοὺς
witness This is true; for which cause convict them
14 ἀποτόμως, ἵνα ὑγιαίνωσιν ἐν τῇ πίστει, μὴ προσέχοντες
severely, that they may be sound in the faith, not listening
Ἰουδαϊκοῖς μύθοις καὶ ἐντολαῖς ἀνθρώπων ἀποστρεφομένων
to Jewish myths and commandments of men having perverted
15 τὴν ἀλήθειαν· πάντα μὲν καθαρὰ τοῖς καθαροῖς· τοῖς δὲ
the truth. All things indeed (are) clean to the clean, to those but
μεμιασμένοις καὶ ἀπίστοις οὐδὲν καθαρόν· ἀλλὰ μεμίανται
having been defiled and unbelieving nothing (is) clean, but has been defiled
16 αὐτῶν καὶ ὁ νοῦς καὶ ἡ συνείδησις. Θεὸν ὁμολογοῦσιν
of them even the mind and the conscience. God They profess
εἰδέναι, τοῖς δὲ ἔργοις ἀρνοῦνται, βδελυκτοὶ ὄντες καὶ
to know, by the but works they deny (Him), abominable being and
ἀπειθεῖς καὶ πρὸς πᾶν ἔργον ἀγαθὸν ἀδόκιμοι.
disobedient and to every work good reprobate.

CHAPTER 2

1 Σὺ δὲ λάλει ἃ πρέπει τῇ ὑγιαινούσῃ διδασκαλίᾳ· πρεσ-
you But speak things which becomes the sound teaching. Aged
2 βύτας νηφαλίους εἶναι, σεμνούς, σώφρονας, ὑγιαίνοντας τῇ
men temperate to be, sensible, discreet, sound in the
3 πίστει, τῇ ἀγάπῃ, τῇ ὑπομονῇ· πρεσβύτιδας ὡσαύτως ἐν
faith; in love, in patience; aged women likewise in
καταστήματι ἱεροπρεπεῖς, μὴ διαβόλους, μὴ οἴνῳ πολλῷ
behavior reverent, not slanderers, not wine by much
4 δεδουλωμένας, καλοδιδασκάλους, ἵνα σωφρονίζωσι τὰς νέας
having been enslaved, teachers of good, that they may train the young women
5 φιλάνδρους εἶναι, φιλοτέκνους, σώφρονας, ἁγνάς, οἰκουρούς,
lovers of husbands to be, child-lovers, discreet, chaste, homeworkers,
ἀγαθάς, ὑποτασσομένας τοῖς ἰδίοις ἀνδράσιν, ἵνα μὴ ὁ λόγος
good, being subject to the own husbands, that not the word
6 τοῦ Θεοῦ βλασφημῆται· τοὺς νεωτέρους ὡσαύτως παρακάλει
of God be blasphemed. The younger men likewise exhort
7 σωφρονεῖν· περὶ πάντα σεαυτὸν παρεχόμενος τύπον καλῶν
to be discreet;about all things yourself showing a pattern of good
ἔργων, ἐν τῇ διδασκαλίᾳ ἀδιαφθορίαν, σεμνότητα, ἀφθ-
works, in the teaching, in purity, sensibleness, incor-
8 αρσίαν, λόγον ὑγιῆ, ἀκατάγνωστον, ἵνα ὁ ἐξ ἐναντίας
ruption, speech sound, irreprehensible, that he of opposition
9 ἐντραπῇ, μηδὲν ἔχων περὶ ὑμῶν λέγειν φαῦλον. δούλους ἰδίοις
be ashamed, nothing having about us to say bad. Slaves to own
δεσπόταις ὑποτάσσεσθαι, ἐν πᾶσιν εὐαρέστους εἶναι, μὴ
masters to be subject in all things well-pleasing to be, not
10 ἀντιλέγοντας, μὴ νοσφιζομένους, ἀλλὰ πίστιν πᾶσαν ἐνδει-
contradicting, not stealing, but faith all
κνυμένους ἀγαθήν, ἵνα τὴν διδασκαλίαν τοῦ σωτῆρος ἡμῶν
showing good, that the teaching of the Savior of us,
11 Θεοῦ κοσμῶσιν ἐν πᾶσιν. ἐπεφάνη γὰρ ἡ χάρις τοῦ Θεοῦ ἡ
God, they may adorn in all things. appeared For the grace of God which
12 σωτήριος πᾶσιν ἀνθρώποις, παιδεύουσα ἡμᾶς ἵνα, ἀρνησά-
saving to all men, instructing us that having

that having denied ungodliness and worldly lusts, we should live discreetly and righteously and godly in the present age, [13]looking for the blessed hope and appearance of the glory of our great God and Savior Jesus Christ, [14]who gave Himself on our behalf, that He might redeem us from all iniquity, and purify a special people for Himself, zealous of good works.

[15]Speak these things, and exhort, and convict with all authority. Let no one despise you.

CHAPTER 3

[1]Remind them to be subject to rulers and authorities, to be obedient, to be ready in every good work; [2]to speak evil of no one, not quarrelsome, *but* forbearing, having displayed all meekness to all men. [3]For we also once *were* disobedient, senseless, led astray, slaving for various lusts and pleasures, living in malice and envy, hateful, hating one another. [4]But when the kindness and love of God our Savior toward man appeared, not by works in righteousness which we had done, but according to His mercy He saved us, through *the* washing of regeneration and renewal of *the* Holy Spirit, [6]which He poured out on us richly through Jesus Christ our Savior, [7]that being justified by His grace, we should become heirs according to *the* hope of eternal life. [8]Faithful is the word, and concerning all things I desire you to strongly affirm that the *ones* believing God should take thought to maintain good works. These things are good and profitable to men. [9]But keep back from questionings, and genealogies, and arguments, and quarrels of law, for they are

μενοι τὴν ἀσέβειαν καὶ τὰς κοσμικὰς ἐπιθυμίας, σωφρόνως καὶ
denied ungodliness and worldly lusts, discreetly and
13 δικαίως καὶ εὐσεβῶς ζήσωμεν ἐν τῷ νῦν αἰῶνι, προσδεχό-
righteously and godly we might live in the present age, expecting
μενοι τὴν μακαρίαν ἐλπίδα καὶ ἐπιφάνειαν τῆς δόξης τοῦ
the blessed hope and appearance of the glory of the
14 μεγάλου Θεοῦ καὶ σωτῆρος ἡμῶν Ἰησοῦ Χριστοῦ, ὃς ἔδωκεν
great God and Savior of us, Jesus Christ, who gave
ἑαυτὸν ὑπὲρ ἡμῶν, ἵνα λυτρώσηται ἡμᾶς ἀπὸ πάσης
Himself on behalf of us, that He might redeem us from all
ἀνομίας, καὶ καθαρίσῃ ἑαυτῷ λαὸν περιούσιον, ζηλωτὴν
iniquity and cleanse for Himself a people special, zealous
καλῶν ἔργων.
of good works.

15 Ταῦτα λάλει, καὶ παρακάλει, καὶ ἔλεγχε μετὰ πάσης
These things speak, and exhort, and convict with all
ἐπιταγῆς. μηδείς σου περιφρονείτω.
authority. no one you Let despise.

CHAPTER 3

1 Ὑπομίμνησκε αὐτοὺς ἀρχαῖς καὶ ἐξουσίαις ὑποτάσσεσθαι,
Remind them to rulers and authorities to be subject,
2 πειθαρχεῖν, πρὸς πᾶν ἔργον ἀγαθὸν ἑτοίμους εἶναι, μηδένα
to be obedient, in every work good ready to be, no one
βλασφημεῖν, ἀμάχους εἶναι, ἐπιεικεῖς, πᾶσαν ἐνδεικνυμένους
to speak evil of, uncontentious to be, forbearing, all showing forth
3 πρᾳότητα πρὸς πάντας ἀνθρώπους. ἦμεν γάρ ποτε καὶ
meekness to all men. were For then also
ἡμεῖς ἀνόητοι, ἀπειθεῖς, πλανώμενοι, δουλεύοντες ἐπιθυμίαις
we senseless, disobedient, led astray, slaving for lusts
καὶ ἡδοναῖς ποικίλαις, ἐν κακίᾳ καὶ φθόνῳ διάγοντες,
and pleasures various, in evil and envy living;
4 στυγητοί, μισοῦντες ἀλλήλους. ὅτε δὲ ἡ χρηστότης καὶ ἡ
hateful, hating one another. when But the kindness and
5 φιλανθρωπία ἐπεφάνη τοῦ σωτῆρος ἡμῶν Θεοῦ, οὐκ ἐξ
love toward man appeared of the Savior of us God, not by
ἔργων τῶν ἐν δικαιοσύνῃ ὧν ἐποιήσαμεν ἡμεῖς, ἀλλὰ κατὰ
works in righteousness which had done we, but according to
τὸν αὐτοῦ ἔλεον ἔσωσεν ἡμᾶς, διὰ λουτροῦ παλιγγενεσίας
the of Him mercy He saved us, through (the) washing of regeneration
6 καὶ ἀνακαινώσεως Πνεύματος Ἁγίου, οὗ ἐξέχεεν ἐφ' ἡμᾶς
and renewal of (the) Spirit Holy, which He poured out on us
7 πλουσίως, διὰ Ἰησοῦ Χριστοῦ τοῦ σωτῆρος ἡμῶν, ἵνα
richly through Jesus Christ the Savior of us, that
δικαιωθέντες τῇ ἐκείνου χάριτι, κληρονόμοι γενώμεθα κατ'
being justified by the of that One grace, heirs we might become according to
8 ἐλπίδα ζωῆς αἰωνίου. πιστὸς ὁ λόγος, καὶ περὶ τούτων
(the) hope of life eternal. Faithful (is) the word, and as to these things
βούλομαί σε διαβεβαιοῦσθαι, ἵνα φροντίζωσι καλῶν ἔργων
I desire you to strongly affirm that may take thought of good works
προΐστασθαι οἱ πεπιστευκότες τῷ Θεῷ. ταῦτά ἐστι τὰ
to maintain those having believed God. These things are
9 καλὰ καὶ ὠφέλιμα τοῖς ἀνθρώποις· μωρὰς δὲ ζητήσεις καὶ
good and profitable to men. foolish But questionings and
γενεαλογίας καὶ ἔρεις καὶ μάχας νομικὰς περιΐστασο· εἰσὶ
genealogies, and arguments, and quarrels of law keep back from; they are

unprofitable and vain. 10 After the first and second warning, avoid a man of heresy, 11 knowing that such a one has been perverted, being self-condemned. 12 When I shall send Artemas to you, or Tychicus, hasten to come to me at Neapolis. For I have decided to winter there. 13 Diligently set forward Zenas the lawyer, and Apollos, that nothing be lacking to them. 14 And let ours also learn to maintain good works for necessary uses, that they may not be without fruit.

15 All those with me greet you. Greet those who love us in *the* faith.

Grace *be* with you all. Amen.

10 γὰρ ἀνωφελεῖς καὶ μάταιοι. αἱρετικὸν ἄνθρωπον μετὰ μίαν
for unprofitable and vain. A heretic man after one
11 καὶ δευτέραν νουθεσίαν παραιτοῦ, εἰδὼς ὅτι ἐξέστραπται ὁ
and a second warning avoid, knowing that has been perverted
τοιοῦτος, καὶ ἁμαρτάνει, ὢν αὐτοκατάκριτος.
such a one and sins, being self-condemned.

12 Ὅταν πέμψω Ἀοτεμᾶν πρός σε ἢ Τυχικόν, σπούδασον
When I shall send Artemas to you, or Tychicus, hasten
ἐλθεῖν πρός με εἰς Νικόπολιν· ἐκεῖ γὰρ κέκρικα παραχειμάσαι.
to come to me at Nicopolis; there for I have decided to winter.
13 Ζηνᾶν τὸν νομικὸν καὶ Ἀπολλὼ σπουδαίως πρόπεμψον,
Zenas the lawyer and Apollos urgently set forward,
14 ἵνα μηδὲν αὐτοῖς λείπῃ. μανθανέτωσαν δὲ καὶ οἱ ἡμέτεροι
that nothing to them be lacking. let learn And also our (own)
καλῶν ἔργων προΐστασθαι εἰς τὰς ἀναγκαίας χρείας, ἵνα μὴ
of good works to maintain for necessary uses, that not
ὦσιν ἄκαρποι.
they be without fruit.

15 Ἀσπάζονταί σε οἱ μετ' ἐμοῦ πάντες. ἄσπασαι τοὺς
Greet you those with me all. Greet those
φιλοῦντας ἡμᾶς ἐν πίστει.
loving us in faith.

Ἡ χάρις μετὰ πάντων ὑμῶν. ἀμήν.
Grace (be) with all you. Amen.

ΠΑΥΛΟΥ
PAUL
Η ΠΡΟΣ
THE TO
ΦΙΛΗΜΟΝΑ ΕΠΙΣΤΟΛΗ
PHILEMON EPISTLE

KING JAMES II VERSION

THE EPISTLE TO PHILEMON

1 Paul, *a* prisoner of Christ Jesus, and Timothy the brother, to Philemon the beloved and our fellow-worker, 2 and to Apphia the beloved, and to Archippus our fellow-soldier, and to the church in your house: 3 Grace to you and peace from God our Father and *the* Lord Jesus Christ.

4 I thank my God always making mention of you in my prayers, 5 hearing of your love and faith which you have toward the Lord Jesus and toward all the saints, 6 so that the fellowship of your faith may operate in a full knowledge of every good thing in you for Jesus Christ. 7 For we have much joy and encouragement over your love, because the hearts of the saints have been refreshed through you, brother.

8 Therefore, having much boldness in Christ to enjoin you *to do* what *is* becoming — 9 rather because of love I entreat, being such a one as Paul *the* aged, and now also a prisoner of Jesus Christ. 10 I entreat you concerning my child Onesimus, whom I fathered in my bonds, 11 the *one* once worthless to you, but now useful to you and to me; whom I sent back. 12 Even receive him, that is, my heart; 13 whom I resolved to hold with myself, that for you he might minister to me in the bonds of the gospel. 14 But I was willing to do nothing without your consent

1 Παῦλος δέσμιος Χριστοῦ Ἰησοῦ, καὶ Τιμόθεος ὁ ἀδελφός,
Paul, a prisoner of Christ Jesus, and Timothy the brother,
2 Φιλήμονι τῷ ἀγαπητῷ καὶ συνεργῷ ἡμῶν, καὶ Ἀπφίᾳ τῇ
to Philemon the beloved and fellow-worker to us, and to Apphia the
ἀγαπητῇ, καὶ Ἀρχίππῳ τῷ συστρατιώτῃ ἡμῶν, καὶ τῇ
beloved, and to Archippus the fellow-soldier of us, and to the
3 κατ' οἶκόν σου ἐκκλησίᾳ· χάρις ὑμῖν καὶ εἰρήνη ἀπὸ Θεοῦ
at house of you church: Grace to you and peace from God
πατρὸς ἡμῶν καὶ Κυρίου Ἰησοῦ Χριστοῦ.
(the) Father of us and (the) Lord Jesus Christ.
4 Εὐχαριστῶ τῷ Θεῷ μου, πάντοτε μνείαν σου ποιούμενος
I thank the God of me, always mention of you making
5 ἐπὶ τῶν προσευχῶν μου, ἀκούων σου τὴν ἀγάπην, καὶ τὴν
at the prayers of me, hearing of you the love and the
πίστιν ἣν ἔχεις πρὸς τὸν Κύριον Ἰησοῦν καὶ εἰς πάντας τοὺς
faith which you have to the Lord Jesus, and to all the
6 ἁγίους, ὅπως ἡ κοινωνία τῆς πίστεώς σου ἐνεργὴς γένηται
saints, so as the fellowship of the faith of you operative may be
ἐν ἐπιγνώσει παντὸς ἀγαθοῦ τοῦ ἐν ὑμῖν εἰς Χριστὸν Ἰησοῦν.
in a full knowledge of every good thing in you for Christ Jesus.
7 χαρὰν γαρ ἔχομεν πολλὴν καὶ παράκλησιν ἐπὶ τῇ ἀγάπῃ
joy For we have much, and encouragement over the love
σου, ὅτι τὰ σπλάγχνα τῶν ἁγίων ἀναπέπαυται διὰ σοῦ,
of you, that the bowels of the saints have been refreshed through you,
ἀδελφέ.
brother.
8 Διὸ πολλὴν ἐν Χριστῷ παρρησίαν ἔχων ἐπιτάσσειν σοι
Therefore, much in Christ boldness having to enjoin you
9 τὸ ἀνῆκον, διὰ τὴν ἀγάπην μᾶλλον παρακαλῶ, τοιοῦτος
the thing fitting, because of love rather I beseech; such a one
ὢν ὡς Παῦλος πρεσβύτης, νυνὶ δὲ καὶ δέσμιος Ἰησοῦ
being as Paul (the) aged one, now and also a prisoner of Jesus
10 Χριστοῦ. παρακαλῶ σε περὶ τοῦ ἐμοῦ τέκνου, ὃν ἐγέννησα ἐν
Christ. I beseech you concerning the of me child, whom I fathered in
11 τοῖς δεσμοῖς μου, Ὀνήσιμον, τόν ποτέ σοι ἄχρηστον, νυνὶ δὲ
the bonds of me, Onesimus, the (one) then to you useless, now but
12 σοὶ καὶ ἐμοὶ εὔχρηστον, ὃν ἀνέπεμψα· σὺ δὲ αὐτόν, τοῦτ' ἔστι
to you and to me useful, whom I sent back to you, even him, this is,
13 τὰ ἐμὰ σπλάγχνα, προσλαβοῦ· ὃν ἐγὼ ἐβουλόμην πρὸς
the of me bowels, receive (him), whom I resolved with
ἐμαυτὸν κατέχειν, ἵνα ὑπὲρ σοῦ διακονῇ μοι ἐν τοῖς δεσμοῖς
myself to hold, that for you he minister to me in the bonds
14 τοῦ εὐαγγελίου· χωρὶς δὲ τῆς σῆς γνώμης οὐδὲν ἠθέλησα
of the gospel. without But your consent nothing I was willing

in order that your good might not be by way of necessity, but by way of willingness. [15]For perhaps for this he was separated for an hour, that you might receive him eternally; [16]no longer as a slave, but beyond a slave, a beloved brother, especially to me, and how much more to you, both in *the* flesh and in the Lord.

[17]Then if you have me as a partner, receive him as me. [18]And if he wronged you *in* anything, or owes, put this to my account. [19]I, Paul, wrote with my hand; I will repay; that I not say to you that you even owe yourself to me also. [20]Yes, brother, *that* I may have your help in *the* Lord, refresh my bowels in *the* Lord. [21]Trusting to your obedience, I wrote to you, knowing that you will do even beyond what I say. [22]But at once prepare lodging for me; for I hope that through your prayers I shall be given to you.

[23]My fellow-prisoner in Christ Jesus, Epaphras, [24]Mark, Aristarchus, Demas, Luke, my fellow-workers, greet you.

[25]The grace of our Lord Jesus Christ *be* with your spirit. Amen.

ποιῆσαι, ἵνα μὴ ὡς κατὰ ἀνάγκην τὸ ἀγαθόν σου ᾖ, ἀλλὰ
to do, that not as by way of necessity the good of you be, but
15 κατὰ ἑκούσιον. τάχα γὰρ διὰ τοῦτο ἐχωρίσθη πρὸς ὥραν,
by way of willingness. perhaps For for this he was separated for an hour,
16 ἵνα αἰώνιον αὐτὸν ἀπέχῃς· οὐκέτι ὡς δοῦλον, ἀλλ' ὑπὲρ
that eternally him you might receive; no longer as a slave, but beyond
δοῦλον, ἀδελφὸν ἀγαπητόν, μάλιστα ἐμοί, πόσῳ δὲ μᾶλλον
a slave, a brother beloved, especially to me, how much and more
17 σοὶ καὶ ἐν σαρκὶ καὶ ἐν Κυρίῳ. εἰ οὖν ἐμὲ ἔχεις κοινωνόν,
to you both in flesh and in (the) Lord. if Then me you have a partner,
18 προσλαβοῦ αὐτὸν ὡς ἐμέ. εἰ δέ τι ἠδίκησέ σε ἢ ὀφείλει, τοῦτο
receive him as me. if And anything he wronged you, or owes, this
19 ἐμοὶ ἐλλόγει· ἐγὼ Παῦλος ἔγραψα τῇ ἐμῇ χειρί, ἐγὼ ἀπο-
to me reckon: I Paul wrote with my hand, I will
20 τίσω· ἵνα μὴ λέγω σοι ὅτι καὶ σεαυτόν μοι προσοφείλεις. ναί,
repay, that not I say to you that indeed yourself to me you owe also. Yes,
ἀδελφέ, ἐγώ σου ὀναίμην ἐν Κυρίῳ· ἀνάπαυσόν μου τὰ
brother, I of you may have help in (the) Lord, refresh of me the
21 σπλάγχνα ἐν Κυρίῳ. πεποιθὼς τῇ ὑπακοῇ σου ἔγραψά
bowels in (the) Lord. Having trusted to the obedience of you, I wrote
22 σοι, εἰδὼς ὅτι και ὑπὲρ ὃ λέγω ποιήσεις. ἅμα δὲ καὶ ἑτοίμαζέ
to you at
you, knowing that even beyond what I say will do. once And prepare
μοι ξενίαν· ἐλπίζω γὰρ οτι διὰ τῶν προσευχῶν ὑμῶν
for me lodging, I hope for that through the prayers of you
χαρισθήσομαι ὑμῖν.
I shall be given to you.
23 Ἀσπάζονταί σε Ἐπαφρᾶς ὁ συναιχμάλωτός μου ἐν
Greet you Epaphras the fellow-captive of me in
24 Χριστῷ Ἰησοῦ, Μάρκος, Ἀρίσταρχος, Δημᾶς, Λουκᾶς, οἱ
Christ Jesus, Mark, Aristarchus, Demas, Luke, the
συνεργοί μου.
fellowworkers of me.
25 Ἡ χάρις τοῦ Κυρίου ἡμῶν Ἰησοῦ Χριστοῦ μετὰ τοῦ
The grace of the Lord of us, Jesus Christ, with the
πνεύματος ὑμῶν. ἀμήν.
spirit of you (be). Amen.

ΠΑΥΛΟΥ ΤΟΥ ΑΠΟΣΤΟΛΟΥ
PAUL THE APOSTLE

Η ΠΡΟΣ
THE TO

ΕΒΡΑΙΟΥΣ ΕΠΙΣΤΟΛΗ
(THE) HEBREWS EPISTLE

KING JAMES II VERSION

THE EPISTLE TO *THE* HEBREWS

CHAPTER 1

1 In many times and in many ways of old, God spoke to the fathers in the prophets; 2 in these last days *He* spoke to us in *the* Son, whom He appointed heir of all; through whom He indeed made the ages; 3 who being *the* shining splendor of *His* glory, and the express image of His essence, and upholding all things by the word of His power, having made purification of our sins through Himself, *He* sat down on *the* right of the Majesty on high, 4 having become so much better than the angels, He has inherited a name more excellent than they. 5 For to which of the angels did He ever say, "You are My Son; today I have begotten You"? And again, "I will be a Father to Him, and He shall be a Son to Me." 6 And again, when He brought the Firstborn into the world, He said, "And let all *the* angels of God worship Him." 7 And as to the angels, He said, "Who makes His angels spirits, and His ministers a flame of fire;" 8 but as to the Son, "Your throne, *O* God, *is* forever and ever, A sceptre of righteousness *is* the sceptre of Your kingdom; 9 You have loved righteousness and hated lawlessness, because of this God, Your God, has anointed You *with* the oil of gladness above Your companions." 10 And, "You, Lord, at *the* beginning founded the earth, and the heavens are works of

CHAPTER 1

1 Πολυμερῶς καὶ πολυτρόπως πάλαι ὁ Θεὸς λαλήσας τοῖς
In many times and in many ways of old God spoke to the
2 πατράσιν ἐν τοῖς προφήταις, ἐπ' ἐσχάτων τῶν ἡμερῶν τού-
fathers by the prophets, in (the) last days of
των ἐλάλησεν ἡμῖν ἐν υἱῷ, ὃν ἔθηκε κληρονόμον πάντων, δι'
these spoke to us in (the) Son, whom He appointed heir of all, through
3 οὗ καὶ τοὺς αἰῶνας ἐποίησεν, ὃς ὢν ἀπαύγασμα τῆς δόξης
whom indeed the ages He made; who being (the) radiance of the glory
καὶ χαρακτὴρ τῆς ὑποστάσεως αὐτοῦ, φέρων τε τὰ πάντα
and the express image of the essence of Him, upholding and all things
τῷ ῥήματι τῆς δυνάμεως αὐτοῦ, δι' ἑαυτοῦ καθαρισμὸν
by the word of the power of Him, through Himself cleansing
ποιησάμενος τῶν ἁμαρτιῶν ἡμῶν, ἐκάθισεν ἐν δεξιᾷ τῆς
having made of the sins of us, sat down on (the) right the
4 μεγαλωσύνης ἐν ὑψηλοῖς, τοσούτῳ κρείττων γενόμενος τῶν
Majesty on high; by so much better becoming (than) the
ἀγγέλων, ὅσῳ διαφορώτερον παρ' αὐτοὺς κεκληρονόμηκεν
angels, as a more excellent than them He has inherited
5 ὄνομα. τίνι γὰρ εἶπέ ποτε τῶν ἀγγέλων, Υἱός μου εἶ σύ, ἐγὼ
name. to which For said He ever of the angels, Son of Me are you, I
σήμερον γεγέννηκά σε; καὶ πάλιν, Ἐγὼ ἔσομαι αὐτῷ εἰς
today have begotten You? And again, I will be to Him for
6 πατέρα, καὶ αὐτὸς ἔσται μοι εἰς υἱόν; ὅταν δὲ πάλιν εἰσα-
a Father, and He shall be to me for a Son? when And again He
γάγῃ τὸν πρωτότοκον εἰς τὴν οἰκουμένην λέγει, Καὶ προσ-
brings the Firstborn into the habitable world He says, And let
7 κυνησάτωσαν αὐτῷ πάντες ἄγγελοι Θεοῦ. καὶ πρὸς μὲν τοὺς
worship Him all angels of God. And as to the
ἀγγέλους λέγει, Ὁ ποιῶν τοὺς ἀγγέλους αὐτοῦ πνεύματα,
angels, He says, The (One) making the angels of Him spirits,
8 καὶ τοὺς λειτουργοὺς αὐτοῦ πυρὸς φλόγα· πρὸς δὲ τὸν υἱόν,
and the ministers of Him of fire a flame as to but the Son,
Ὁ θρόνος σου, ὁ Θεός, εἰς τὸν αἰῶνα τοῦ αἰῶνος· ῥάβδος
The throne of You, God, (is) to the ages of the ages, (the) rod
9 εὐθύτητος ἡ ῥάβδος τῆς βασιλείας σου. ἠγάπησας δικαιο-
of uprightness (is the) rod of the kingdom of You. You loved righteous-
σύνην, καὶ ἐμίσησας ἀνομίαν· διὰ τοῦτο ἔχρισέ σε ὁ Θεός, ὁ
ness, and hated lawlessness; therefore anointed You God, the
10 Θεός σου, ἔλαιον ἀγαλλιάσεως παρὰ τοὺς μετόχους σου. καί,
God of You, (with) oil of gladness above the partners of You. And:
Σὺ κατ' ἀρχάς, Κύριε, τὴν γῆν ἐθεμελίωσας, καὶ ἔργα τῶν
You at (the) beginning Lord the earth founded, and works of the

Your hands. [11]They will vanish away, but You will continue; and *they* will all become old, like a garment, [12]and You shall fold them up like a covering, and *they* shall be changed. But You are the same, and Your years shall not fail." [13]But to which of the angels did He ever say, "Sit at My right *hand* until I place Your enemies *as* a footstool of Your feet"? [14]Are they not all ministering spirits for service, being sent out because of the *ones* being about to inherit salvation?

CHAPTER 2

[1]For this reason we ought to give the more earnest heed to the things heard, that we should not slip away at any time. [2]For the word spoken by angels was confirmed, and every transgression and disobedience received a just repayment, [3]how shall we escape *if we* neglect so great a salvation? Which having received a beginning to be spoken through the Lord, was confirmed to us by the ones hearing, [4]God bearing witness with *them* by both miracles and wonders, and by various works of power, even by distribution *of the* Holy Spirit, according to His will.

[5]For He did not put the coming world under angels, about which we speak, [6]but one fully testified somewhere, saying, "What is man, that You are mindful of him; or the son of man, that You look upon Him? [7]You made him a little less than *the* angels; You crowned him with glory and honor, and. You set him over the works of Your hands; [8]You put all things under his feet." For in putting all things under him, He left nothing not subjected to him. but now we do not see all things being subjected to him; [9]but we do see Jesus crowned with glory and honor, who on account of the suffering of death *was* made a little less than the angels, so that by

11 χειρῶν σού εἰσιν οἱ οὐρανοί· αὐτοὶ ἀπολοῦνται, σὺ δὲ δια-
hands of You are the heavens; they will perish, You but will
12 μένεις· καὶ πάντες ὡς ἱμάτιον παλαιωθήσονται, καὶ ὡσεὶ
remain and all as a garment shall become old, and as
περιβόλαιον ἑλίξεις αὐτοὺς καὶ ἀλλαγήσονται· σὺ δὲ ὁ αὐτὸς
a covering You shall roll them, and shall be changed. You but the same
13 εἶ, καὶ τὰ ἔτη σου οὐκ ἐκλείψουσι. πρὸς τίνα δὲ τῶν
are, and the years of You not shall fail. to which But of the
ἀγγέλων εἴρηκέ ποτε, Κάθου ἐκ δεξιῶν μου, ἕως ἂν θῶ τοὺς
angels has He said at any time, Sit on (the) right of Me, until I put the
14 ἐχθρούς σου ὑποπόδιον τῶν ποδῶν σου ; οὐχὶ πάντες εἰσὶ
enemies of You a footstool of the feet of You. not all Are they
λειτουργικὰ πνεύματα, εἰς διακονίαν ἀποστελλόμενα διὰ
ministering spirits for service being sent out because of
τοὺς μέλλοντας κληρονομεῖν σωτηρίαν ;
those being about to inherit salvation?

CHAPTER 2

1 Διὰ τοῦτο δεῖ περισσοτέρως ἡμᾶς προσέχειν τοῖς ἀκου-
For this reason ought more abundantly us to give heed to the things
2 σθεῖσι, μή ποτε παραρρυῶμεν. εἰ γὰρ ὁ δι' ἀγγέλων
heard, lest at any time we should slip away. if For the through angels
λαληθεὶς λόγος ἐγένετο βέβαιος, καὶ πᾶσα παράβασις καὶ
spoken word was confirmed, and every transgression and
3 παρακοὴ ἔλαβεν ἔνδικον μισθαποδοσίαν, πῶς ἡμεῖς ἐκφευ-
disobedience received a just recompense, how we shall escape
ξόμεθα τηλικαύτης ἀμελήσαντες σωτηρίας ; ἥτις, ἀρχὴν
so great neglecting a salvation? Which a beginning
λαβοῦσα λαλεῖσθαι διὰ τοῦ Κυρίου, ὑπὸ τῶν ἀκουσάντων
having received to be spoken via the Lord, by the (ones) hearing
4 εἰς ἡμᾶς ἐβεβαιώθη, συνεπιμαρτυροῦντος τοῦ Θεοῦ σημείοις
to us was confirmed, bearing witness with God by signs
τε καὶ τέρασι, καὶ ποικίλαις δυνάμεσι, καὶ Πνεύματος Ἁγίου
both and wonders, and by various works of power and (the) Spirit Holy
μερισμοῖς, κατὰ τὴν αὐτοῦ θέλησιν.
by distribution, according to the of Him will.

5 Οὐ γὰρ ἀγγέλοις ὑπέταξε τὴν οἰκουμένην τὴν μέλλουσαν,
not For to angels subjected He the habitable world coming,
6 περὶ ἧς λαλοῦμεν. διεμαρτύρατο δέ πού τις λέγων, Τί
about which we speak. solemnly witnessed But somewhere one, saying, What
ἐστιν ἄνθρωπος, ὅτι μιμνήσκῃ αὐτοῦ ; ἢ υἱὸς ἀνθρώπου,
is man that You remember him? Or the son of man
7 ὅτι ἐπισκέπτῃ αὐτόν ; ἠλάττωσας αὐτὸν βραχύ τι παρ'
that You observed him? You made less him a little than
ἀγγέλους· δόξῃ καὶ τιμῇ ἐστεφάνωσας αὐτόν, καὶ κατέ-
the angels with glory and with honor You crowned him; and,
8 στησας αὐτὸν ἐπὶ τὰ ἔργα τῶν χειρῶν σου· πάντα ὑπέταξας
You set him over the works of the hands of You; all things You subjected
ὑποκάτω τῶν ποδῶν αὐτοῦ. ἐν γὰρ τῷ ὑποτάξαι αὐτῷ
under the feet of him. in order For to subject to him
τὰ πάντα, οὐδὲν ἀφῆκεν αὐτῷ ἀνυπότακτον. νῦν δὲ οὔπω
all things, nothing He left to him not subjected. now But not yet
9 ὁρῶμεν αὐτῷ τὰ πάντα ὑποτεταγμένα. τὸν δὲ βραχύ τι
do we see to him all things having been subjected. the (One) But a little
παρ' ἀγγέλους ἠλαττωμένον βλέπομεν Ἰησοῦν, διὰ τὸ
than the angels having been made less we see, Jesus, because of the

the grace of God He might taste of death for every *son.* 10 For it was fitting for Him, because of whom, and through whom *are* all things, bringing many sons to glory, to perfect *Him as* the Author of their salvation through sufferings. 11 For both He sanctifying and the *one* being sanctified *are* all of one; for which cause He is not ashamed to call them brothers, 12 saying, "I will announce Your name to My brothers; I will sing to You in *the* midst of the church." 13 And again, "I will be trusting on Him." And again, "Behold, I and the children whom God gave to Me."

14 Since, then, the children have partaken of flesh and blood, in like manner He Himself also shared the same things, that through death He might cause to cease the *one* having the power of death, that is, the Devil; 15 and might set these free, as many as by fear of death were subject to slavery through all the *time* to live. 16 For indeed He does not take hold of angels, but He takes hold of *the* seed of Abraham. 17 Therefore, He ought by all means to become like *His* brothers, that He might become a merciful and faithful High Priest *in* the things respecting God, in order to make propitiation for the sins of *His* people. 18 For in what He has suffered, being tried, He is able to help those having been tried.

CHAPTER 3

1 Therefore, holy brothers, called *to be* partakers of a heavenly *calling,* consider the Apostle and High Priest of our confession, Christ Jesus, 2 being faithful to Him who appointed Him, as also Moses in all his house. 3 For He was counted worthy of more glory than Moses, by so much as the *one* having built the house has more honor the house. 4 For every house is built by someone; but He who built all things *is* God. 5 And Moses

πάθημα τοῦ θανάτου δόξῃ καὶ τιμῇ ἐστεφανωμένον, ὅπως
suffering of death with glory and with honor having been crowned so as,

10 χάριτι Θεοῦ ὑπὲρ παντὸς γεύσηται θανάτου. ἔπρεπε γὰρ
by grace God's for every (son) He might taste of death. it was fitting For

αὐτῷ, δι' ὃν τὰ πάντα, καὶ δι' οὗ τὰ πάντα, πολλοὺς υἱοὺς
for Him, because of whom, and through whom all things many sons

εἰς δόξαν ἀγαγόντα, τὸν ἀρχηγὸν τῆς σωτηρίας αὐτῶν
to glory bringing, the Author of the salvation of them

11 διὰ παθημάτων τελειῶσαι. ὅ τε γὰρ ἁγιάζων καὶ οἱ ἁγιαζό-
through sufferings to perfect. He both For sanctifying and the (one) being

μενοι, ἐξ ἑνὸς πάντες· δι' ἣν αἰτίαν οὐκ ἐπαισχύνεται
sanctified of one all (are); for which cause not He is ashamed

12 ἀδελφοὺς αὐτοὺς καλεῖν, λέγων, Ἀπαγγελῶ τὸ ὄνομά σου
brothers them to call, saying, I will announce the name of You

13 τοῖς ἀδελφοῖς μου, ἐν μέσῳ ἐκκλησίας ὑμνήσω σε. καὶ πάλιν,
to the brothers of Me; in (the) midst of (the) church I will hymn You. And again,

Ἐγὼ ἔσομαι πεποιθὼς ἐπ' αὐτῷ. καὶ πάλιν, Ἰδοὺ ἐγὼ καὶ
I will be trusting on Him. And again, Behold, I and

14 τὰ παιδία ἅ μοι ἔδωκεν ὁ Θεός. ἐπεὶ οὖν τὰ παιδία κεκοινώ-
the children whom to Me gave God. Since, then, the children have partaken

νηκε σαρκὸς καὶ αἵματος, καὶ αὐτὸς παραπλησίως μετέσχε
of flesh and blood, also Himself, in like manner He shared

τῶν αὐτῶν, ἵνα διὰ τοῦ θανάτου καταργήσῃ τὸν τὸ κράτος
the same things, that through the death He might annul the (one) the power

15 ἔχοντα τοῦ θανάτου, τοῦτ' ἔστι τὸν διάβολον, καὶ ἀπαλ-
having of death, this is the Devil, and might set

λάξῃ τούτους, ὅσοι φόβῳ θανάτου διὰ παντὸς τοῦ ζῆν
free these, as many as by fear of death through all the (time) to live

16 ἔνοχοι ἦσαν δουλείας. οὐ γὰρ δήπου ἀγγέλων ἐπιλαμβά-
subject were to slavery. not For indeed of angels He takes hold,

17 νεται, ἀλλὰ σπέρματος Ἀβραὰμ ἐπιλαμβάνεται. ὅθεν ὤφειλε
but of (the) seed of Abraham He takes hold. Therefore He ought

κατὰ πάντα τοῖς ἀδελφοῖς ὁμοιωθῆναι, ἵνα ἐλεήμων γένηται
by all means to the brothers to become like, that a merciful He might be

καὶ πιστὸς ἀρχιερεὺς τὰ πρὸς τὸν Θεόν, εἰς τὸ ἱλάσκεσθαι
and faithful High Priest (in) the things as to God, in order to make propitiation for

18 τὰς ἁμαρτίας τοῦ λαοῦ. ἐν ᾧ γὰρ πέπονθεν αὐτὸς πειρα-
the sins of the people. in what For has suffered He, having been

σθείς, δύναται τοῖς πειραζομένοις βοηθῆσαι.
tempted, He is able those being tempted to help.

CHAPTER 3

1 Ὅθεν, ἀδελφοὶ ἅγιοι, κλήσεως ἐπουρανίου μέτοχοι,
Therefore, brothers holy, called (to be) of a heavenly sharers,

κατανοήσατε τὸν ἀπόστολον καὶ ἀρχιερέα τῆς ὁμολογίας
consider the Apostle and High Priest of the confession

2 ἡμῶν Χριστὸν Ἰησοῦν, πιστὸν ὄντα τῷ ποιήσαντι αὐτόν,
of us, Christ Jesus, faithful being to the (One) making Him (these)

3 ὡς καὶ Μωσῆς ἐν ὅλῳ τῷ οἴκῳ αὐτοῦ. πλείονος γὰρ δόξης
as also Moses in all the house of him. of more For glory

οὗτος παρὰ Μωσῆν ἠξίωται, καθ' ὅσον πλείονα τιμὴν ἔχει
this (One) than Moses has been counted worthy, by so much as more honor has (than)

4 τοῦ οἴκου ὁ κατασκευάσας αὐτόν. πᾶς γὰρ οἶκος κατασκευά-
the house the (one) having built it. every For house is prepared

5 ζεται ὑπό τινος· ὁ δὲ τὰ πάντα κατασκευάσας, Θεός. καὶ
by someone, He but all things having prepared (is) God. And

truly *was* faithful in all his house as a ministering servant, for a testimony of the things going to be spoken;

[6]but Christ as Son over His house, whose house we are, if we should hold fast the boldness and rejoicing of the hope firm to the end.
[7]For this reason even as the Holy Spirit says, "Today, if you will hear His voice, [8]do not harden your hearts, as in the provocation, in the day of temptation in the wilderness, [9]where your fathers tempted Me, testing Me, and saw My works forty years. [10]Because of this, I was angry with that generation, and said, They always go astray in heart; and they did not know My ways; [11]so I swore in My wrath, They shall not enter into My rest." [12]Watch, brothers, lest perhaps shall be in any one of you a heart of evil unbelief in falling away from *the* living God. [13]But exhort yourselves each day, as long as it is being called today, that not any of you be hardened by *the* deceit of sin. [14]For we have become sharers of Christ, if truly we hold the beginning of the assurance firm to *the* end; [15]*as* in the saying, "Today, if you hear His voice, do not harden your hearts, as in the provocation." [16]For hearing, some provoked *Him*, but not all those coming out of Egypt through Moses. [17]But with whom was He angry forty years? *Was it* not with the ones sinning, whose corpses fell in the wilderness? [18]And to whom did He swear *they would* not enter into His rest, except to those not obeying? [19]And we see that they were not able to enter in because of unbelief.

CHAPTER 4

[1]Therefore, let us fear lest perhaps a promise being left

Μωσῆς μὲν πιστὸς ἐν ὅλῳ τῷ οἴκῳ αὐτοῦ ὡς θεράπων, εἰς
Moses indeed (was) faithful in all the house of him as a servant, for
6 μαρτύριον τῶν λαληθησομένων· Χριστὸς δὲ ὡς υἱὸς ἐπὶ τὸν
a testimony of the things having been spoken; Christ but as a Son over the
οἶκον αὐτοῦ· οὗ οἶκός ἐσμεν ἡμεῖς, ἐάνπερ τὴν παρρησίαν καὶ
house of Him, of whom a house are we, if truly the confidence and
τὸ καύχημα τῆς ἐλπίδος μέχρι τέλους βεβαίαν κατάσχωμεν.
the boast of the hope until (the) end firm we hold fast.
7 διό, καθὼς λέγει τὸ Πνεῦμα τὸ Ἅγιον, Σήμερον ἐὰν τῆς
Therefore, as says the Spirit – Holy, Today, if the
8 φωνῆς αὐτοῦ ἀκούσητε, μὴ σκληρύνητε τὰς καρδίας ὑμῶν,
voice of Him you hear, do not harden the hearts of you,
ὡς ἐν τῷ παραπικρασμῷ, κατὰ τὴν ἡμέραν τοῦ πειρασμοῦ
as in the provocation in the day of the temptation
9 ἐν τῇ ἐρήμῳ, οὗ ἐπείρασάν με οἱ πατέρες ὑμῶν, ἐδοκίμασάν
in the wilderness, when tempted Me the fathers of you, testing
10 με, καὶ εἶδον τὰ ἔργα μου τεσσαράκοντα ἔτη. διὸ προσ-
Me, and saw the works of Me forty years. Therefore I was
ώχθισα τῇ γενεᾷ ἐκείνῃ, καὶ εἶπον, Ἀεὶ πλανῶνται τῇ καρδίᾳ·
angry with generation that, and I said, Always they err in the heart;
11 αὐτοὶ δὲ οὐκ ἔγνωσαν τὰς ὁδούς μου· ὡς ὤμοσα ἐν τῇ ὀργῇ
they and not did know the ways of Me; as I swore in the wrath
12 μου, Εἰ εἰσελεύσονται εἰς τὴν κατάπαυσίν μου. βλέπετε,
of Me, If they shall enter into the rest of Me. Watch,
ἀδελφοί, μή ποτε ἔσται ἔν τινι ὑμῶν καρδία πονηρὰ ἀπιστίας
brothers, lest perhaps shall be in anyone of you a heart evil of unbelief
13 ἐν τῷ ἀποστῆναι ἀπὸ Θεοῦ ζῶντος· ἀλλὰ παρακαλεῖτε
in departing from God a living; but exhort
ἑαυτοὺς καθ' ἑκάστην ἡμέραν, ἄχρις οὗ τὸ σήμερον καλεῖται,
yourselves each day, while today it is being called,
14 ἵνα μὴ σκληρυνθῇ τις ἐξ ὑμῶν ἀπάτῃ τῆς ἁμαρτίας· μέτοχοι
that not be hardened anyone of you by (the) deceit of sin. sharers
γὰρ γεγόναμεν τοῦ Χριστοῦ, ἐάνπερ τὴν ἀρχὴν τῆς ὑπο-
For we have become of Christ, if truly the beginning of the
15 στάσεως μέχρι τέλους βεβαίαν κατάσχωμεν· ἐν τῷ λέγεσθαι,
assurance until (the) end firm we hold fast. In the saying
Σήμερον ἐὰν τῆς φωνῆς αὐτοῦ ἀκούσητε, μὴ σκληρύνητε τὰς
Today, if the voice of Him you hear, do not harden the
16 καρδίας ὑμῶν, ὡς ἐν τῷ παραπικρασμῷ. τινὲς γὰρ ἀκού-
hearts of you, as in the provocation. some For
σαντες παρεπίκραναν, ἀλλ' οὐ πάντες οἱ ἐξελθόντες ἐξ
hearing provoked, but not all those coming out of
17 Αἰγύπτου διὰ Μωσέως. τίσι δὲ προσώχθισε τεσσαράκοντα
Egypt through Moses. with whom But was He angry forty
ἔτη; οὐχὶ τοῖς ἁμαρτήσασιν, ὧν τὰ κῶλα ἔπεσεν ἐν τῇ
years? Not with those sinning, of whom the corpses fell in the
18 ἐρήμῳ; τίσι δὲ ὤμοσε μὴ εἰσελεύσεσθαι εἰς τὴν κατάπαυσιν
wilderness? to whom And swore He not to enter into the rest
19 αὐτοῦ, εἰ μὴ τοῖς ἀπειθήσασι: καὶ βλέπομεν ὅτι οὐκ ἠδυνή-
of Him, except to those not obeying? And we see that not they were
θησαν εἰσελθεῖν δι' ἀπιστίαν.
able to enter in because of unbelief.

CHAPTER 4

1 Φοβηθῶμεν οὖν μή ποτε καταλειπομένης ἐπαγγελίας
let us fear Therefore, lest perhaps being left a promise

to enter into His rest, any of you might seem to come short. [2]For, indeed, we have had the gospel preached *to us*, even as they also; but the word did not profit those hearing *it*, not having been mixed with faith in the ones who heard. [3]For we, the ones believing, enter into the rest, even as He said, "As I swore in My wrath, they shall not enter into My rest," though the works had come into being from *the* foundation of the world. [4]For He has spoken somewhere about the seventh *day* this way, "And God rested from all His works in the seventh day." [5]And in this *place* again, "They shall not enter into My rest." [6]Therefore, since it remains *for* some to enter into it, and those who formerly heard the gospel did not enter in on account of disobedience, [7]He again marks out a certain day, saying in David, "Today"— after so long a time, according as it has been said— "Today, if you hear His voice, do not harden your hearts." [8]For if Joshua gave them rest, then He would not have afterwards spoken about another day. [9]So, then, there remains a rest to the people of God. [10]For He entering into His rest, *He* Himself also rested from His works, as God *had done* from His own.

[11]Therefore, let us labor to enter into that rest, that not anyone fall in the same example of disobedience. [12]For the word of God *is* living, and powerfully working, and sharper than every two-edged sword, even piercing as far as *the* dividing apart of both soul and spirit, of both joints and marrow, and able to judge of the thoughts and intentions of the heart; [13]and there is no creature unrevealed before Him; but all things *are* naked and laid open to His eyes, with whom *is* our account.

[14]Therefore, having a great High Priest *who* has passed through the heavens, Jesus

εἰσελθεῖν εἰς τὴν κατάπαυσιν αὐτοῦ, δοκῇ τις ἐξ ὑμῶν
to enter into the rest of Him, seems anyone of you
2 ὑστερηκέναι. καὶ γάρ ἐσμεν εὐηγγελισμένοι, καθάπερ
to come short. indeed For we are having had the gospel preached, even as
κἀκεῖνοι· ἀλλ' οὐκ ὠφέλησεν ὁ λόγος τῆς ἀκοῆς ἐκείνους, μὴ
those also; but did not profit the word of hearing those, not
3 συγκεκραμένος τῇ πίστει τοῖς ἀκούσασιν. εἰσερχόμεθα γὰρ
having been mixed with faith in those hearing. we enter For
εἰς τὴν κατάπαυσιν οἱ πιστεύσαντες, καθὼς εἴρηκεν, Ὡς
into the rest, those believing, even as He said, As
ὤμοσα ἐν τῇ ὀργῇ μου, Εἰ εἰσελεύσονται εἰς τὴν κατά-
I swore in the wrath of Me, If they shall enter into the rest
παυσίν μου· καίτοι τῶν ἔργων ἀπὸ καταβολῆς κόσμου
of Me; though the works from (the) foundation of world
4 γενηθέντων. εἴρηκε γάρ που περὶ τῆς ἑβδόμης οὕτω, Καὶ
having come into being, He has said, For somewhere about the seventh (day) thus: And
κατέπαυσεν ὁ Θεὸς ἐν τῇ ἡμέρᾳ τῇ ἑβδόμῃ ἀπὸ πάντων
rested God in the day seventh from all
5 τῶν ἔργων αὐτοῦ· καὶ ἐν τούτῳ πάλιν, Εἰ εἰσελεύσονται εἰς
the works of Him; and in this (place) again, If they shall enter into
6 τὴν κατάπαυσίν μου. ἐπεὶ οὖν ἀπολείπεται τινὰς εἰσελθεῖν
the rest of Me. Since therefore it remains (for) some to enter
εἰς αὐτήν, καὶ οἱ πρότερον εὐαγγελισθέντες οὐκ εἰσῆλθον δι'
into it, and those before having had the gospel preached not entered for
7 ἀπείθειαν, πάλιν τινὰ ὁρίζει ἡμέραν, Σήμερον, ἐν Δαβὶδ
disobedience, again a certain marks out day: Today; in David
λέγων, μετὰ τοσοῦτον χρόνον, καθὼς εἴρηται, Σήμερον ἐὰν
saying after such a time, as he has said, Today, if
τῆς φωνῆς αὐτοῦ ἀκούσητε, μὴ σκληρύνητε τὰς καρδίας
the voice of Him you hear, do not harden the hearts
8 ὑμῶν. εἰ γὰρ αὐτοὺς Ἰησοῦς κατέπαυσεν, οὐκ ἂν περὶ ἄλλης
of you. if For them (Joshua) rested, not concerning another
9 ἐλάλει μετὰ ταῦτα ἡμέρας. ἄρα ἀπολείπεται σαββατισμὸς
he would have spoken after these things day Then remains a sabbath rest
10 τῷ λαῷ τοῦ Θεοῦ. ὁ γὰρ εἰσελθὼν εἰς τὴν κατάπαυσιν αὐτοῦ
to the people of God. He For having entered into the rest of Him,
καὶ αὐτὸς κατέπαυσεν ἀπὸ τῶν ἔργων αὐτοῦ, ὥσπερ ἀπὸ
also Himself rested from the works of Him, as from
11 τῶν ἰδίων ὁ Θεός. σπουδάσωμεν οὖν εἰσελθεῖν εἰς ἐκείνην τὴν
the own (did) God. Let us be eager, therefore, to enter into that
κατάπαυσιν, ἵνα μὴ ἐν τῷ αὐτῷ τις ὑποδείγματι πέσῃ τῆς
rest, that not in the same anyone example falls
12 ἀπειθείας. ζῶν γὰρ ὁ λόγος τοῦ Θεοῦ, καὶ ἐνεργής, καὶ
of disobedience. (is) living For the word of God, and working, and
τομώτερος ὑπὲρ πᾶσαν μάχαιραν δίστομον, καὶ διϊκνού-
sharper than every sword two-mouthed, and piercing
μενος ἄχρι μερισμοῦ ψυχῆς τε καὶ πνεύματος, ἁρμῶν τε καὶ
as far as (the) division of soul both and spirit, of joints both and
13 μυελῶν, καὶ κριτικὸς ἐνθυμήσεων καὶ ἐννοιῶν καρδίας. καὶ
of marrows, and able to judge of thoughts and intentions of a heart; and
οὐκ ἔστι κτίσις ἀφανὴς ἐνώπιον αὐτοῦ· πάντα δὲ γυμνὰ καὶ
not is (a) creature not revealed before Him, all things but (are) naked and
τετραχηλισμένα τοῖς ὀφθαλμοῖς αὐτοῦ πρὸς ὃν ἡμῖν ὁ λόγος.
laid open to the eyes of Him with whom (is) our account.
14 Ἔχοντες οὖν ἀρχιερέα μέγαν, διεληλυθότα τοὺς οὐρανούς,
Having therefore a high priest great, having gone through the heavens,

the Son of God, let us hold fast the confession. [15]For we do not have a High Priest not being able to sympathize with our infirmities, but *One* having been tried in all respects according to *our* likeness, apart from sin. [16]Therefore, let us draw near with confidence to the throne of grace, that we may receive mercy, and we may find grace for help in time of need.

CHAPTER 5

[1]For every high priest from men being taken on behalf of men is appointed *in* the things respecting God, that he may offer both gifts and sacrifices for sins; [2]being able to feel in due measure for those not knowing and having been led astray, since he also is circled about *with* weakness. [3]And because of this he ought to offer for sins as concerning the people and concerning himself. [4]And no one takes the honor to himself, but he being called by God, even as Aaron also. [5]So also Christ did not glorify Himself to become a high priest, but He speaking to Him, "You are My Son; today I have begotten You." [6]As He also says in another, "You *are* a priest forever according to the order of Melchizedek." [7]who in the days of His flesh offering both petitions and entreaties to Him being able to save Him from death, with strong crying and tears, and being heard from *His* godly fear,

[8]though being a Son, He learned obedience from what He suffered; [9]and being perfected, He became *the* Author of eternal salvation to all those obeying Him, [10]having been called out by God *as* a High Priest according to the order of Melchizedek.

[11]Concerning whom we *have* much to say, and hard to interpret, since you have become dull in hearing [12]For indeed because of the time *you are* due to be teachers, you need one to

15 Ἰησοῦν τὸν υἱὸν τοῦ Θεοῦ, κρατῶμεν τῆς ὁμολογίας. οὐ γὰρ
Jesus, the Son of God, let us hold fast the confession. not For
ἔχομεν ἀρχιερέα μὴ δυνάμενον συμπαθῆσαι ταῖς ἀσθενείαις
we have a high priest not being able to sympathize with the infirmities
ἡμῶν, πεπειρασμένον δὲ κατὰ πάντα καθ' ὁμοιότητα, χωρὶς
of us, having been tempted but (One) in all respects according to (our) likeness apart from
16 ἁμαρτίας. προσερχώμεθα οὖν μετὰ παρρησίας τῷ θρόνῳ τῆς
sin, let us draw near Therefore with confidence to the throne —
χάριτος, ἵνα λάβωμεν ἔλεον, καὶ χάριν εὕρωμεν εἰς εὔκαιρον
of grace, that we may receive mercy, and grace we may find for timely
βοήθειαν.
help.

CHAPTER 5

1 Πᾶς γὰρ ἀρχιερεύς, ἐξ ἀνθρώπων λαμβανόμενος, ὑπὲρ
every For high priest out of men having been taken on behalf of
ἀνθρώπων καθίσταται τὰ πρὸς τὸν Θεόν, ἵνα προσφέρῃ
men is appointed (in) the things as to God. that he may offer
2 δῶρά τε καὶ θυσίας ὑπὲρ ἁμαρτιῶν· μετριοπαθεῖν δυνάμενος
gifts both and sacrifices on behalf of sins, to feel due in measure being able
τοῖς ἀγνοοῦσι καὶ πλανωμένοις, ἐπεὶ καὶ αὐτος περίκειται
for those not knowing and being led astray, since also he is encompassed
3 ἀσθένειαν· καὶ διὰ ταύτην ὀφείλει, καθὼς περὶ τοῦ λαοῦ, οὕτω
(with) weakness and for this he ought, as concerning the people, so
4 καὶ περὶ ἑαυτοῦ, προσφέρειν ὑπὲρ ἁμαρτιῶν. καὶ οὐχ ἑαυτῷ
also concerning himself to offer on behalf of sins. And not to himself
τις λαμβάνει τὴν τιμήν, ἀλλὰ ὁ καλούμενος ὑπὸ τοῦ Θεοῦ,
anyone takes the honor, but the (one) being called by God,
5 καθάπερ καὶ ὁ Ἀαρών. οὕτω καὶ ὁ Χριστὸς οὐχ ἑαυτὸν
even as indeed Aaron. So also Christ not Himself
ἐδόξασε γενηθῆναι ἀρχιερέα, ἀλλ' ὁ λαλήσας πρὸς αὐτόν,
glorified to become a high priest, but the (One) speaking to Him:
6 Υἱός μου εἶ σύ, ἐγὼ σήμερον γεγέννηκά σε. καθὼς καὶ ἐν ἑτέρῳ
Son of Me are You, I today have begotten You; as also in another
λέγει, Σὺ ἱερεὺς εἰς τὸν αἰῶνα κατὰ τὴν τάξιν Μελχισεδέκ.
He says, You (are) a priest to the age according to the order of Melchizedek;
7 ὃς ἐν ταῖς ἡμέραις τῆς σαρκὸς αὐτοῦ, δεήσεις τε καὶ ἱκετηρίας
who in the days of the flesh of Him petitions both and entreaties
πρὸς τὸν δυνάμενον σώζειν αὐτὸν ἐκ θανάτου μετὰ κραυγῆς
to the (One) being able to save Him out of death, with crying
ἰσχυρᾶς καὶ δακρύων προσενέγκας, καὶ εἰσακουσθεὶς ἀπὸ τῆς
strong and tears, offering and being heard from the
8 εὐλαβείας, καίπερ ὢν υἱός, ἔμαθεν ἀφ' ὧν ἔπαθε τὴν ὑπακοήν,
godly fear, though being a Son, He learned from (that) which He suffered obedience,
9 καὶ τελειωθεὶς ἐγένετο τοῖς ὑπακούουσιν αὐτῷ πᾶσιν αἴτιος
and having perfected He became those obeying Him to all (the) cause
10 σωτηρίας αἰωνίου· προσαγορευθεὶς ὑπὸ τοῦ Θεοῦ ἀρχιερεὺς
of salvation eternal having been called out by God a High Priest
κατὰ τὴν τάξιν Μελχισεδέκ.
according to the order of Melchizedek.

11 Περὶ οὗ πολὺς ἡμῖν ὁ λόγος καὶ δυσερμήνευτος λέγειν,
Concerning whom much to us the word, and hard to interpret to say,
12 ἐπεὶ νωθροὶ γεγόνατε ταῖς ἀκοαῖς. καὶ γὰρ ὀφείλοντες εἶναι
since dull you have become in the hearing For being due to be
διδάσκαλοι διὰ τὸν χρόνον, πάλιν χρείαν ἔχετε τοῦ διδά-
teachers because of the time, again need you have to

teach you again the rudiments of the beginning of the oracles of God, and you having become *in* need of milk, and not of solid food; [13]for everyone partaking of milk *is* not skilled *in the* word of righteousness, for he is an infant. [14]But solid food is for *the* full-grown ones, who through habit have exercised the faculties for distinguishing both good and bad.

CHAPTER 6

[1]Therefore, leaving the discourse of the beginning of Christ, let us be borne on to full growth, not laying down again a foundation of repentance from dead works, and of faith toward God, [2]of *the* baptisms, of teaching, of laying on of hands, and of resurrection of dead ones, and of eternal judgment. [3]And this we will do, if God permits. [4]For *it is* impossible *for* those being once enlightened, and having tasted of the heavenly gift, and becoming sharers of *the* Holy Spirit, [5]and having tasted *the* good word of God, and *the* works of power of a coming age, [6]and falling away, again to renew to repentance, crucifying to themselves again the Son of God, and putting *Him* to open shame. [7]For the earth drinking in the rain often coming upon it, and producing plants fit for those for whom it is also worked, receives blessing from God; [8]but bearing thorns and thistles, *it is* rejected and near a curse, of which the end *is* for burning.

[9]But, loved ones, even if we indeed speak so, we have been persuaded better things concerning you, even holding fast salvation. [10]For God is not unrighteous, to forget your work and the labor of love which you showed to His name, ministering to the saints, and *now are* ministering. [11]But we desire each of you to

σκειν ὑμᾶς, τίνα τὰ στοιχεῖα τῆς ἀρχῆς τῶν λογίων τοῦ Θεοῦ·
teach you someone the rudiments of the beginning of the oracles of God,
καὶ γεγόνατε χρείαν ἔχοντες γάλακτος, καὶ οὐ στερεᾶς
and you become (in) need having of milk, and not of solid
13 τροφῆς. πᾶς γὰρ ὁ μετέχων γάλακτος ἄπειρος λόγου δι-
food. everyone For partaking of milk (is) not skilled of (the) word
14 καιοσύνης· νήπιος γάρ ἐστι. τελείων δέ ἐστιν ἡ στερεὰ
of righteouesness, an infant for he is; of full-grown but is solid
τροφή, τῶν διὰ τὴν ἕξιν τὰ αἰσθητήρια γεγυμνασμένα
food, of those through habit the faculties exercised
ἐχόντων πρὸς διάκρισιν καλοῦ τε καὶ κακοῦ.
having, for distinguishing good both and bad.

CHAPTER 6

1 Διό, ἀφέντες τὸν τῆς ἀρχῆς τοῦ Χριστοῦ λόγον, ἐπὶ τὴν
Therefore, leaving the of the beginning of Christ discourse, on to
τελειότητα φερώμεθα, μὴ πάλιν θεμέλιον καταβαλλόμενοι
full growth let us be borne, not again a foundation laying down
2 μετανοίας ἀπὸ νεκρῶν ἔργων, καὶ πίστεως ἐπὶ Θεόν, βαπτι-
of repentance from dead works, and of faith toward God, of baptisms,
σμῶν διδαχῆς, ἐπιθέσεώς τε χειρῶν, ἀναστάσεώς τε νεκρῶν,
of teaching, of laying on and of hands, of resurrection and of dead ones
3 καὶ κρίματος αἰωνίου. καὶ τοῦτο ποιήσομεν, ἐάνπερ ἐπι-
and judgment of eternal. And this we will do if indeed
4 τρέπῃ ὁ Θεός. ἀδύνατον γὰρ τοὺς ἅπαξ φωτισθέντας,
permits God. (it is) impossible For (for) those once being enlightened,
γευσαμένους τε τῆς δωρεᾶς τῆς ἐπουρανίου, καὶ μετόχους
tasting and of the gift heavenly, and sharers
5 γενηθέντας Πνεύματος Ἁγίου, καὶ καλὸν γευσαμένους Θεοῦ
becoming Spirit of (the) Holy, and (the) good tasting of God
6 ῥῆμα, δυνάμεις τε μέλλοντος αἰῶνος, καὶ παραπεσόντας,
word, works of power and of a coming age, and falling away
πάλιν ἀνακαινίζειν εἰς μετάνοιαν, ἀνασταυροῦντας ἑαυτοῖς
again to renew to repentance, crucifying again for themselves
7 τὸν υἱὸν τοῦ Θεοῦ καὶ παραδειγματίζοντας. γῆ γὰρ ἡ
the Son of God, and putting (Him) to open shame. earth For
πιοῦσα τὸν ἐπ᾽ αὐτῆς πολλάκις ἐρχόμενον ὑετόν, καὶ
drinking the upon it often coming rain, and
τίκτουσα βοτάνην εὔθετον ἐκείνοις δι᾽ οὓς καὶ γεωργεῖται,
producing plants fit for those for whom indeed it is worked
8 μεταλαμβάνει εὐλογίας ἀπὸ τοῦ Θεοῦ· ἐκφέρουσα δὲ ἀκάνθας
receives blessing from God; bringing forth but thorns
καὶ τριβόλους, ἀδόκιμος καὶ κατάρας ἐγγύς, ἧς τὸ τέλος εἰς
and thistles (it is) disapproved and a curse near, of which the end (is) for
καῦσιν.
burning.

9 Πεπείσμεθα δὲ περὶ ὑμῶν, ἀγαπητοί, τὰ κρείττονα καὶ
we have been persuaded But about you, loved ones, the things better even
10 ἐχόμενα σωτηρίας, εἰ και οὕτω λαλοῦμεν· οὐ γὰρ ἄδικος ὁ
holding fast salvation, if indeed so we speak. not For unjust
Θεὸς ἐπιλαθέσθαι τοῦ ἔργου ὑμῶν, καὶ τοῦ κόπου τῆς
God (is) to be forgetful of the work of you, and of the labor
ἀγάπης ἧς ἐνδείξασθε εἰς τὸ ὄνομα αὐτοῦ, διακονήσαντες
of love which you showed to the name of Him, having ministered
11 τοῖς ἁγίοις καὶ διακονοῦντες. ἐπιθυμοῦμεν δὲ ἕκαστον ὑμῶν
to the saints, and (now) ministering. we desire But each one of you

show the same eagerness, to the full assurance of the hope to *the* end; [12]that you be not dull, but imitators of those who through faith and long-suffering *are* inheriting the promises.

[13]For God having made promise to Abraham, since He had no greater to swear by, *He* swore by Himself, [14]saying, "Surely blessing I will bless you, and multiplying I will multiply you." [15]And so, being long-suffering, he obtained the promise. [16]For men indeed swear by the greater, and an oath to make things sure *is* to them the end of all gainsaying. [17]In which way, desiring to more fully declare to the heirs of the promise the unchangeableness of His counsel, God interposed by an oath, [18]that through two unchangeable things, in which *it was* not possible *for* God to lie, we might have a strong consolation, those having fled to lay hold on the hope set before *us*, [19]which we have as an anchor of the soul, both certain and sure, and entering into the inner *side* of the veil; [20]where Jesus entered *as* forerunner for us, having become a High Priest forever, according to the order of M[illegible]lchizedek.

τὴν αὐτὴν ἐνδείκνυσθαι σπουδὴν πρὸς τὴν πληροφορίαν τῆς
the same to show eagerness to the full assurance of the
12 ἐλπίδος ἄχρι τέλους· ἵνα μὴ νωθροὶ γένησθε, μιμηταὶ δὲ
hope unto (the) end, lest dull you become; imitators but
τῶν διὰ πίστεως καὶ μακροθυμίας κληρονομούντων τὰς
of those through faith and long-suffering inheriting the
ἐπαγγελίας.
promises.

13 Τῷ γὰρ Ἀβραὰμ ἐπαγγειλάμενος ὁ Θεός, ἐπεὶ κατ'
For to Abraham having made promise God, since by
14 οὐδενὸς εἶχε μείζονος ὀμόσαι, ὤμοσε καθ' ἑαυτοῦ, λέγων,
no one he had greater to swear, swore by Himself, saying,
Ἦ μὴν εὐλογῶν εὐλογήσω σε, καὶ πληθύνων πληθυνῶ σε.
If surely blessing I will bless you, and multiplying I will multiply you.
15 καὶ οὕτω μακροθυμήσας ἐπέτυχε τῆς ἐπαγγελίας. ἄνθρωποι
16 And so being long-suffering, he obtained the promise. men
μὲν γὰρ κατὰ τοῦ μείζονος ὀμνύουσι, καὶ πάσης αὐτοῖς
indeed For by the greater swear, and of all (is) to them
17 ἀντιλογίας πέρας εἰς βεβαίωσιν ὁ ὅρκος. ἐν ᾧ περισσότερον
contradiction an end for confirmation the oath. In which more abundantly
βουλόμενος ὁ Θεὸς ἐπιδεῖξαι τοῖς κληρονόμοις τῆς ἐπαγ-
resolving God to show to the heirs of the promise
γελίας τὸ ἀμετάθετον τῆς βουλῆς αὐτοῦ, ἐμεσίτευσεν ὅρκῳ
the unchangeableness of the counsel of Him, He interposed by an oath,
18 ἵνα διὰ δύο πραγμάτων ἀμεταθέτων, ἐν οἷς ἀδύνατον
that through two things unchangeable, in which (it was) impossible
ψεύσασθαι Θεόν, ἰσχυρὰν παράκλησιν ἔχωμεν οἱ κατα-
to lie God, a strong consolation we might have, those
19 φυγόντες κρατῆσαι τῆς προκειμένης ἐλπίδος· ἣν ὡς ἄγκυραν
having fled to lay hold of the set before (us) hope; which as an anchor
ἔχομεν τῆς ψυχῆς ἀσφαλῆ τε καὶ βεβαίαν, καὶ εἰσερχομένην
we have of the soul, secure both and firm, and entering
20 εἰς τὸ ἐσώτερον τοῦ καταπετάσματος· ὅπου πρόδρομος ὑπὲρ
into the inner (side) of the veil, where a forerunner for
ἡμῶν εἰσῆλθεν Ἰησοῦς, κατὰ τὴν τάξιν Μελχισεδὲκ ἀρχιερεὺς
us entered, Jesus, according to the order of Melchizedek a high priest
γενόμενος εἰς τὸν αἰῶνα.
becoming to the age.

CHAPTER 7

[1]For this Melchizedek, king of Salem, priest of the most high God, the *one* meeting Abraham returning from the slaughter of the kings, and blessing him; [2]to whom also Abraham divided a tenth from all—first being interpreted, king of righteousness; and then also king of Salem, which is, king of peace, [3]without father, without mother, without pedigree, nor beginning of days, nor having end of life, but having been made like the Son of God, *he* remains a priest in perpetuity.

CHAPTER 7

1 Οὗτος γὰρ ὁ Μελχισεδέκ, βασιλεὺς Σαλήμ, ἱερεὺς τοῦ Θεοῦ
this For Melchizedek, king of Salem, priest of God
τοῦ ὑψίστου, ὁ συναντήσας Ἀβραὰμ ὑποστρέφοντι ἀπὸ τῆς
the most high, the (one) meeting Abraham returning from the
2 κοπῆς τῶν βασιλέων καὶ εὐλογήσας αὐτόν, ᾧ καὶ δεκάτην
slaughter of the kings and blessing him, to whom indeed a tenth
ἀπὸ πάντων ἐμέρισεν Ἀβραάμ (πρῶτον μὲν ἑρμηνευόμενος
from all divided Abraham firstly being interpreted,
βασιλεὺς δικαιοσύνης, ἔπειτα δὲ καὶ βασιλεὺς Σαλήμ, ὅ ἐστι
king of righteousness, then and also king of Salem, which is,
3 βασιλεὺς εἰρήνης· ἀπάτωρ, ἀμήτωρ, ἀγενεαλόγητος, μήτε
king of peace, without father, without mother, without pedigree, nor
ἀρχὴν ἡμερῶν μήτε ζωῆς τέλος ἔχων, ἀφωμοιωμένος δὲ τῷ
beginning of days, nor of life end having, having been made like but the
υἱῷ τοῦ Θεοῦ), μένει ἱερεὺς εἰς τὸ διηνεκές.
Son of God — remains a priest in perpetuity.

[4]Now behold how great this *one was,* to whom even the patriarch Abraham gave a tenth of the spoils; [5]and indeed those of the sons of Levi receiving the priesthood have a command to tithe the people according to the Law —that is, from their brothers, though coming forth out of Abraham's loins— [6]but he not counting *his* pedigree from them has tithed Abraham, and has blessed the *one* having the promises. [7]But without contradiction, the lesser is blessed by the better. [8]And here dying men indeed receive tithes, but there having been witnessed that he lives; [9]and as a word to say, through Abraham Levi also, the *one* receiving tithes, has been tithed. [10]For he was yet in his father's loins when Melchizedek met him.

[11]Truly, then, if perfection was through the Levitical priestly office—for the people has been given Law under it —why yet need *for* another priest to arise according to the order of Melchizedek, and not to be called according to the order of Aaron? [12]For the priestly office having been changed, of necessity a change of law also occurs. [13]For the *One* of whom these things are said has partaken of another tribe from which no one has given devotion at the altar. [14]For it is clear that our Lord has risen out of Judah, as to which tribe Moses spoke nothing concerning priesthood. [15]And it is still more abundantly clear *that* if another priest arises according to the likeness of Melchizedek, [16]who has not become *so* according to a law of a fleshly command, but according to *the* power of an indissoluble life—[17]for it is testified, "You *are* a priest forever according to the order of Melchizedek." [18]For a voiding of *the* preceding command comes about because of its weakness and unprofitableness; [19]for the Law perfected nothing, but a bringing in of a better hope, through which we draw near to God. [20]And by how much *it was* not apart from *the* swearing of an oath

4 Θεωρεῖτε δὲ πηλίκος οὗτος, ᾧ καὶ δεκάτην Ἀβραὰμ ἔδωκεν
this to even
behold Now how great (one was) whom a tenth Abraham gave
5 ἐκ τῶν ἀκροθινίων ὁ πατριάρχης. καὶ οἱ μὲν ἐκ τῶν υἱῶν
of the spoils the patriarch. And those of the sons
Λευὶ τὴν ἱερατείαν λαμβάνοντες ἐντολὴν ἔχουσιν ἀποδεκα-
of Levi the priesthood receiving a commandment have to tithe
τοῦν τὸν λαὸν κατὰ τὸν νόμον, τοῦτ' ἔστι τοὺς ἀδελφοὺς
the people according to the law, this is the brothers
6 αὐτῶν, καίπερ ἐξεληλυθότας ἐκ τῆς ὀσφύος Ἀβραάμ· ὁ δὲ
of them, though having come forth out of the loins of Abraham; he but
μὴ γενεαλογούμενος ἐξ αὐτῶν δεδεκάτωκε τὸν Ἀβραάμ, καὶ
not counting (his) pedigree from them has tithed Abraham, and
7 τὸν ἔχοντα τὰς ἐπαγγελίας εὐλόγηκε. χωρὶς δὲ πάσης ἀντι-
the (one) having the promises (he) has blessed. without And all con-
8 λογίας, τὸ ελαττον ὑπὸ τοῦ κρείττονος εὐλογεῖται. καὶ ὧδε
tradiction, the lesser by the better is blessed. And here
μὲν δεκάτας ἀποθνήσκοντες ἄνθρωποι λαμβάνουσιν· ἐκεῖ δέ,
indeed tithes dying men receive, there but
9 μαρτυρούμενος ὅτι ζῇ. καί, ὡς ἔπος εἰπεῖν, διὰ Ἀβραὰμ καὶ
being witnessed that he lives. And as a word to say, through Abraham also
10 Λευὶ ὁ δεκάτας λαμβάνων δεδεκάτωται· ἔτι γὰρ ἐν τῇ ὀσφύϊ
Levi, the (one) tithes receiving, has been tithed. yet For in the loins
τοῦ πατρὸς ἦν, ὅτε συνήντησεν αὐτῷ ὁ Μελχισεδέκ.
of the father he was when met him Melchizedek.
11 Εἰ μὲν οὖν τελείωσις διὰ τῆς Λευϊτικῆς ἱερωσύνης ἦν (ὁ
If therefore perfection through the Levitical priestly office was, the
λαὸς γὰρ ἐπ' αὐτῇ νενομοθέτητο), τίς ἔτι χρεία, κατὰ τὴν
people for under it has been given law, why yet need according to the
τάξιν Μελχισεδὲκ ἕτερον ἀνίστασθαι ἱερέα, καὶ οὐ κατὰ τὴν
order of Melchizedek another to arise priest, and not according to the
12 τάξιν Ἀαρὼν λέγεσθαι; μετατιθεμένης γὰρ τῆς ἱερωσύνης,
order of Aaron to be said? being changed For the priestly office,
13 ἐξ ἀνάγκης καὶ νόμου μετάθεσις γίνεται. ἐφ' ὃν γὰρ λέγεται
of necessity also of law a change occurs. of whom For are said
ταῦτα, φυλῆς ἑτέρας μετέσχηκεν, ἀφ' ἧς οὐδεὶς προσέσχηκε
these things, tribe of another has partaken, from which no one has given devotion
14 τῷ θυσιαστηρίῳ. πρόδηλον γὰρ ὅτι ἐξ Ἰούδα ἀνατέταλκεν
at the altar. it is clear For that out of Judah has risen
ὁ Κύριος ἡμῶν, εἰς ἣν φυλὴν οὐδὲν περὶ ἱερωσύνης Μωσῆς
the Lord of us, as to which tribe nothing concerning priesthood Moses
15 ἐλάλησε. καὶ περισσότερον ἔτι κατάδηλόν ἐστιν, εἰ κατὰ τὴν
spoke. And more abundantly still quite clear is it, if according to the
16 ὁμοιότητα Μελχισεδὲκ ἀνίσταται ἱερεὺς ἕτερος, ὃς οὐ κατὰ
likeness of Melchizedek arises priest another, who not according to
νόμον ἐντολῆς σαρκικῆς γέγονεν, ἀλλὰ κατὰ δύναμιν ζωῆς
(the) law of a command fleshly has become, but according to (the) power life
17 ἀκαταλύτου· μαρτυρεῖ γὰρ ὅτι Σὺ ἱερεὺς εἰς τὸν αἰῶνα κατὰ
of an indissoluble. it is testified for: — You (are) a priest to the age according to
18 τὴν τάξιν Μελχισεδέκ. ἀθέτησις μὲν γὰρ γίνεται προαγούσης
the order of Melchizedek. an annulment For comes about of (the) preceding
19 ἐντολῆς, διὰ τὸ αὐτῆς ἀσθενὲς καὶ ἀνωφελές· οὐδὲν γὰρ
command, because of the of it weak(ness) and unprofitable(ness), nothing for
ἐτελείωσεν ὁ νόμος, ἐπεισαγωγὴ δὲ κρείττονος ἐλπίδος, δι'
perfected the law, a bringing in but of a better hope, through
20 ἧς ἐγγίζομεν τῷ Θεῷ. καὶ καθ' ὅσον οὐ χωρὶς ὁρκωμοσίας
which we draw-near to God. And by how much (it was) not without oath-taking

—for those are priests without *the* swearing of an oath; [21] but He having become *so* with *the* swearing of an oath by the *One* saying to Him, "*The* Lord swore, and will not change *His* mind, You are a Priest forever according to the order of Melchizedek"—[22] by so much Jesus has become Surety of a better covenant. [23] And they truly are many priests, being hindered from continuing because of death; [24] but He has the priesthood not to be passed on, because of His living forever. [25] From this also He is able to save to the uttermost those who come to God through Him, ever living to intercede for them.

[26] For such a High Priest was fitting for us: holy, harmless, undefiled, and separated from sinners, and having become higher than the heavens; [27] who has no need, as do the high priests, to offer sacrifices day by day, first for His own sins, then for those of the people. For He did this once for all, offering up Himself. [28] For the Law makes men high priest who have infirmity, but the word of the swearing of an oath, after the Law, *appoints the* Son forever, having been perfected.

CHAPTER 8

[1] Now a summary of the things being said *is*: We have such a High Priest, who sat down on *the* right of the throne of the Majesty in Heaven, [2] Minister of the holies, and of the true tabernacle which the Lord pitched, and not man.

[3] For every high priest is set in place to offer both gifts and sacrifices; from which *it is* necessary *for* this One also to have something which He may offer. [4] for if indeed He were on earth, He would not even be a priest, there being those priests offering gifts according to the Law. [5] who

21 (οἱ μὲν γὰρ χωρὶς ὁρκωμοσίας εἰσὶν ἱερεῖς γεγονότες, ὁ δὲ
—those for without oath-taking are priests having become He but
μετὰ ὁρκωμοσίας, διὰ τοῦ λέγοντος πρὸς αὐτόν, Ὤμοσε
with oath-taking through the (One) saying to Him, swore
Κύριος καὶ οὐ μεταμεληθήσεται, Σὺ ἱερεὺς εἰς τὸν αἰῶνα κατὰ
(the) Lord, and not will change (His) mind, You a priest to the age; by
22 τὴν τάξιν Μελχισεδέκ)· κατὰ τοσοῦτον κρείττονος διαθήκης
the order of Melchizedek— by so much of a better covenant
γέγονεν ἔγγυος Ἰησοῦς. καὶ οἱ μὲν πλείονές εἰσι γεγονότες
23 **has become surety Jesus. And those indeed many are, having become**
ἱερεῖς, διὰ τὸ θανάτῳ κωλύεσθαι παραμένειν· ὁ δέ, διὰ τὸ
24 **priests because of by death being prevented to continue; He but, because of**
μένειν αὐτὸν εἰς τὸν αἰῶνα, ἀπαράβατον ἔχει τὴν ἱερωσύνην.
remaining Him to the age, not to be passed on has the priestly office
ὅθεν καὶ σῴζειν εἰς τὸ παντελὲς δύναται τοὺς προσερχο-
25 **from which truly to save to perfection He is able those drawing near**
μένους δι' αὐτοῦ τῷ Θεῷ, πάντοτε ζῶν εἰς τὸ ἐντυγχάνειν
through Him to God, ever living to intercede
ὑπὲρ αὐτῶν.
on behalf of them.
26 Τοιοῦτος γὰρ ἡμῖν ἔπρεπεν ἀρχιερεύς, ὅσιος, ἄκακος,
such For to us was fitting a High Priest, holy, harmless,
ἀμίαντος, κεχωρισμένος ἀπὸ τῶν ἁμαρτωλῶν, καὶ ὑψηλό-
undefiled, having been separated from sinners, and higher
27 τερος τῶν οὐρανῶν γενόμενος· ὃς οὐκ ἔχει καθ' ἡμέραν
than the heavens becoming; who not has day by day
ἀνάγκην, ὥσπερ οἱ ἀρχιερεῖς, πρότερον ὑπὲρ τῶν ἰδίων
need, as do the high priests, firstly for the own
ἁμαρτιῶν θυσίας ἀναφέρειν, ἔπειτα τῶν τοῦ λαοῦ· τοῦτο
sins sacrifices to offer up, then (for) those of the people; this
28 γὰρ ἐποίησεν ἐφάπαξ, ἑαυτὸν ἀνενέγκας. ὁ νόμος γὰρ
for He did once for all, Himself offering up. the law For
ἀνθρώπους καθίστησιν ἀρχιερεῖς, ἔχοντας ἀσθένειαν· ὁ
men appoints high priests having infirmity; the
λόγος δὲ τῆς ὁρκωμοσίας τῆς μετὰ τὸν νόμον, υἱὸν εἰς τὸν
word but of the oath-taking after the law (appoints) a Son to the
αἰῶνα τετελειωμένον.
age, having been perfected.

CHAPTER 8

1 Κεφάλαιον δὲ ἐπὶ τοῖς λεγομένοις· τοιοῦτον ἔχομεν
a summary Now over the things being said, such we have
ἀρχιερέα, ὃς ἐκάθισεν ἐν δεξιᾷ τοῦ θρόνου τῆς μεγαλωσύνης
a High Priest, who sat at (the) right of the throne of the Majesty
2 ἐν τοῖς οὐρανοῖς, τῶν ἁγίων λειτουργός, καὶ τῆς σκηνῆς τῆς
in Heaven, of the holy things a minister, and of the tabernacle
3 ἀληθινῆς, ἣν ἔπηξεν ὁ Κύριος, καὶ οὐκ ἄνθρωπος. πᾶς γὰρ
true, which raised up the Lord, and not man. every For
ἀρχιερεὺς εἰς τὸ προσφέρειν δῶρά τε καὶ θυσίας καθίσταται·
high priest to offer gifts both and sacrifices is appointed;
4 ὅθεν ἀναγκαῖον ἔχειν τι καὶ τοῦτον ὃ προσενέγκῃ. εἰ μὲν γὰρ
from which (it is) needful to have something also this One which He may offer. if truly For
ἦν ἐπὶ γῆς, οὐδ' ἂν ἦν ἱερεύς, ὄντων τῶν ἱερέων τῶν
He were on earth, He would not be a priest, being those priests
5 προσφερόντων κατὰ τὸν νόμον τὰ δῶρα, οἵτινες ὑποδείγματι
offering according to the law the gifts; who an example

serve *the* pattern and shadow of heavenly things, even as Moses divinely warned, being about to make the tabernacle: "For He says, See that you make all things according to the pattern shown to you in the mount." 6 But now He has gotten a more excellent ministry, by so much He is a Mediator of a better covenant, which has been enacted on better promises. 7 For if that first was faultless, place would not have been sought for a second. 8 For finding fault, He said to them, "Behold, days are coming, says *the* Lord, and I will make an end on the house of Israel, and on the house of Judah; a new covenant *shall be*, 9 not according to the covenant which I made with their fathers in *the* day of My taking hold of their hand to lead them out of *the* land of Egypt; because they did not continue in My covenant, and I did not regard them, says *the* Lord." 10 "Because this *is* the covenant which I will covenant with the house of Israel after those days, says *the* Lord, giving My laws into their mind, and I will write them on their hearts, and I will be their God, and they shall be My people. 11 And they shall no more teach each one his neighbor, and each one his brother, saying, Know the Lord; because all shall know Me, from the least of them to their great ones. 12 For I will be merciful to their unrighteousnesses, and I will not at all remember their sins and their lawless deeds." 13 In the saying, "New," He has made the first old. And the thing having been made old and growing aged *is* near disappearing.

καὶ σκιᾷ λατρεύουσι τῶν ἐπουρανίων, καθὼς κεχρημάτισται
and a shadow serve of the heavenly things, as has been warned
Μωσῆς μέλλων ἐπιτελεῖν τὴν σκηνήν, Ὅρα, γάρ φησι,
Moses being about to make the tabernacle,: see For, He says,
ποιήσῃς πάντα κατὰ τὸν τύπον τὸν δειχθέντα σοι ἐν τῷ ὄρει.
you make all things according to the pattern shown to you in the mount.
6 νυνὶ δὲ διαφορωτέρας τέτευχε λειτουργίας, ὅσῳ καὶ κρείτ-
now And a more excellent He has gotten ministry, by so much of a
τονός ἐστι διαθήκης μεσίτης, ἥτις ἐπὶ κρείττοσιν ἐπαγγελίαις
better He is covenant Mediator, which on better promises
7 νενομοθέτηται. εἰ γὰρ ἡ πρώτη ἐκείνη ἦν ἄμεμπτος, οὐκ ἂν
has been enacted. if For first that was faultless, not would
8 δευτέρας ἐζητεῖτο τόπος. μεμφόμενος γὰρ αὐτοῖς λέγει, Ἰδού,
of a second have been sought place. finding fault For them He says, Behold,
ἡμέραι ἔρχονται, λέγει Κύριος, καὶ συντελέσω ἐπὶ τὸν οἶκον
days are coming, says (the) Lord, and I will make an end upon the house
9 Ἰσραὴλ καὶ ἐπὶ τὸν οἶκον Ἰούδα διαθήκην καινήν· οὐ κατὰ
of Israel, and upon the house of Judah, covenant a new, not according to
τὴν διαθήκην ἣν ἐποίησα τοῖς πατράσιν αὐτῶν ἐν ἡμέρᾳ
the covenant which I made with the fathers of them, in (the) day
ἐπιλαβομένου μου τῆς χειρὸς αὐτῶν ἐξαγαγεῖν αὐτοὺς ἐκ
taking hold Me the hand of them to lead forth them out of
γῆς Αἰγύπτου· ὅτι αὐτοὶ οὐκ ἐνέμειναν ἐν τῇ διαθήκῃ μου,
(the) land of Egypt, because they not continued in the covenant of Me,
10 κἀγὼ ἠμέλησα αὐτῶν, λέγει Κύριος. ὅτι αὕτη ἡ διαθήκη ἣν
and I not regarded them, says (the) Lord. Because this the covenant which
διαθήσομαι τῷ οἴκῳ Ἰσραὴλ μετὰ τὰς ἡμέρας ἐκείνας, λέγει
I will covenant with the house of Israel after days those, says
Κύριος, διδοὺς νόμους μου εἰς τὴν διανοιαν αὐτῶν, καὶ ἐπὶ
(the) Lord, giving laws of Me into the mind of them, and on
καρδίας αὐτῶν ἐπιγράψω αὐτούς· καὶ ἔσομαι αὐτοῖς εἰς Θεόν,
hearts of them I will write them, and I will be to them for God,
11 καὶ αὐτοὶ ἔσονταί μοι εἰς λαόν. καὶ οὐ μὴ διδάξωσιν ἕκαστος
and they will be to Me for a people; and not at all may they teach each one
τὸν πλησίον αὐτοῦ, καὶ ἕκαστος τὸν ἀδελφὸν αὐτοῦ, λέγων,
the neighbor of him, and each one the brother of him, saying,
Γνῶθι τὸν Κύριον· ὅτι πάντες εἰδήσουσί με, ἀπὸ μικροῦ
Know the Lord; because all will know Me, from little
12 αὐτῶν ἕως μεγάλου αὐτῶν. ὅτι ἵλεως ἔσομαι ταῖς ἀδικίαις
of them unto (the) great of them. Because merciful I will be to the righteous-nesses
αὐτῶν, καὶ τῶν ἁμαρτιῶν αὐτῶν καὶ τῶν ἀνομιῶν αὐτῶν
of them; and the sins of them , and the lawlessnesses of them,
13 οὐ μὴ μνησθῶ ἔτι. ἐν τῷ λέγειν, Καινήν, πεπαλαίωκε τὴν
not at all I may remember still. In the saying, New, He has made old the
πρώτην. τὸ δὲ παλαιούμενον καὶ γηράσκον, ἐγγὺς ἀφανι-
first; the thing and being made old and growing aged (is) near dis-
σμοῦ.
appearing.

CHAPTER 9

1 Truly, then, the first *tabernacle* also had ordinances of service, and the worldly holy place. 2 For the first tabernacle was prepared, in which *was* both the lampstand and the table, and the setting out of the loaves,

CHAPTER 9

1 Εἶχε μὲν οὖν καὶ ἡ πρώτη δικαιώματα λατρείας, τό τε
had So then also the first (tabernacle) ordinances of service, the and
2 ἅγιον κοσμικόν. σκηνὴ γὰρ κατεσκευάσθη ἡ πρώτη, ἐν ᾗ ἥ
holy place worldly. a tabernacle For was prepared, the first, in which the
τε λυχνία καὶ ἡ τράπεζα καὶ ἡ πρόθεσις τῶν ἄρτων, ἥτις
both lampstand and the table, and the setting out of the loaves, which

which is called holy; [3]but behind the second veil *is* a tabernacle, that called Holy of Holies, having a golden altar, and the ark of the covenant covered around on all sides with gold, in which *was* the golden pot having the manna, and Aaron's rod that budded, and the tablets of the covenant; [5]and above it *the* cherubim of glory overshadowing the mercy-seat—about which now is not *time* to speak piece by piece. [6]And these having been prepared thus, the priests go into the first tablenacle through all, completing the services. [7]But into the second the high priest *goes* alone once *in* the year, not without blood, which he offers for himself and the ignorances of the people; [8]the Holy Spirit signifying *by* this *that* the way of the Holies has not yet been made manifest, the first tabernacle still having standing; [9]which *is* a parable for the present time, in which both gifts and sacrifices are offered, *that* as regards conscience, not being able to perfect the *one* serving, [10]but only on foods and drinks, and various washings, and fleshly ordinances, until *the* time of setting things right has been imposed.

[11]But Christ having appeared *as* a High Priest of the coming good things, through the greater and more perfect tabernacle not made with hands, that is, not of this creation, [12]nor through *the* blood of goats and of calves, but through *His* own blood, *He* entered once for all into the Holies, having procured everlasting redemption. [13]For if the blood of bulls and goats, and ashes of a heifer sprinkling those having been defiled, sanctifies to the purity of the flesh, [14]by how much more the blood of Christ, who through *the* eternal Spirit offered Himself without spot to God, shall purify your conscience from dead

3 λέγεται ἅγια. μετὰ δὲ τὸ δεύτερον καταπέτασμα σκηνὴ ἡ
is called Holy; after and the second veil a tabernacle, that
4 λεγομένη ἅγια ἁγίων, χρυσοῦν ἔχουσα θυμιατήριον, καὶ
called Holy of Holies, golden having an altar, and
τὴν κιβωτὸν τῆς διαθήκης περικεκαλυμμένην πάντοθεν
the ark of the covenant having been covered around on all sides
χρυσίῳ, ἐν ᾗ στάμνος χρυσῆ ἔχουσα τὸ μάννα, καὶ ἡ ῥάβδος
with gold, in which a pot golden having the manna, and the rod
5 Ἀαρὼν ἡ βλαστήσασα, καὶ αἱ πλάκες τῆς διαθήκης· ὑπερ-
of Aaron budded, and the tablets of the covenant, above
άνω δὲ αὐτῆς Χερουβὶμ δόξης κατασκιάζοντα τὸ ἱλαστή-
and it cherubim of glory overshadowing the mercy-
6 ριον· περὶ ὧν οὐκ ἔστι νῦν λέγειν κατὰ μέρος. τούτων δὲ οὕτω
seat, about which not is now to speak piece by piece. these And thus
κατεσκευασμένων, εἰς μὲν τὴν πρώτην σκηνὴν διὰ παντὸς
having been prepared, into the first tabernacle through all
7 εἰσίασιν οἱ ἱερεῖς, τὰς λατρείας ἐπιτελοῦντες· εἰς δὲ τὴν
go the priests the services completing, into but the
δευτέραν ἅπαξ τοῦ ἐνιαυτοῦ μόνος ὁ ἀρχιερεύς, οὐ χωρὶς
second once (in) the year (goes) alone the high priest, not without
αἵματος, ὃ προσφέρει ὑπὲρ ἑαυτοῦ καὶ τῶν τοῦ λαοῦ ἀγνοη-
blood,, which he offers for himself and the of the people ignorances;
8 μάτων· τοῦτο δηλοῦντος τοῦ Πνεύματος τοῦ Ἁγίου, μήπω
this showing the Spirit Holy, not yet
πεφανερῶσθαι τὴν τῶν ἁγίων ὁδόν, ἔτι τῆς πρώτης σκηνῆς
having been revealed the of the Holies way, yet the first tabernacle
9 ἐχούσης στάσιν· ἥτις παραβολὴ εἰς τὸν καιρὸν τὸν ἐνεστη-
having standing, which (was) a parable for the time present,
κότα, καθ' ὃν δῶρά τε καὶ θυσίαι προσφέρονται, μὴ δυνά-
according to which gifts both and sacrifices are being offered, not being
10 μεναι κατὰ συνείδησιν τελειῶσαι τὸν λατρεύοντα, μόνον
able as to conscience to perfect the (one) serving, only
ἐπὶ βρώμασι καὶ πόμασι καὶ διαφόροις βαπτισμοῖς καὶ
on foods and drinks and various washings, even
δικαιώμασι σαρκός, μέχρι καιροῦ διορθώσεως ἐπικείμενα.
ordinances of flesh, until a time of setting things right being imposed.
11 Χριστὸς δὲ παραγενόμενος ἀρχιερεὺς τῶν μελλόντων
Christ But having appeared (as) a High Priest of the coming
ἀγαθῶν, διὰ τῆς μείζονος καὶ τελειοτέρας σκηνῆς, οὐ
good things, through the greater and more perfect tabernacle not
12 χειροποιήτου, τοῦτ' ἔστιν, οὐ ταύτης τῆς κτίσεως, οὐδὲ δι'
made with hands, this is not of this creation; nor through
αἵματος τράγων καὶ μόσχων, διὰ δὲ τοῦ ἰδίου αἵματος
blood of goats and of calves, through but the own blood
εἰσῆλθεν ἐφάπαξ εἰς τὰ ἅγια, αἰωνίαν λύτρωσιν εὑράμενος.
entered once for all into the Holies, eternal redemption having found.
13 εἰ γὰρ τὸ αἷμα ταύρων καὶ τράγων, καὶ σποδὸς δαμάλεως
if For the blood of bulls and goats, and ashes of a heifer
ῥαντίζουσα τοὺς κεκοινωμένους, ἁγιάζει πρὸς τὴν τῆς
sprinkling those having been polluted sanctifies to the of the
14 σαρκὸς καθαρότητα, πόσῳ μᾶλλον τὸ αἷμα τοῦ Χριστοῦ,
flesh cleanness, by how much more the blood of Christ,
ὃς διὰ Πνεύματος αἰωνίου ἑαυτὸν προσήνεγκεν ἄμωμον τῷ
who through (the) Spirit Eternal Himself offered without spot
Θεῷ, καθαριεῖ τὴν συνείδησιν ὑμῶν ἀπὸ νεκρῶν ἔργων, εἰς
to God, will cleanse the conscience of you from dead works, for

works for *the* serving of *the* living God! [15]And because of this He is Mediator of a new covenant, so that, death having occurred for redemption of transgressions under the first covenant, those having been called out might receive the promise of the everlasting inheritance.

[16]For where a covenant *is*, *the* death of him covenanting must be offered. [17]For a covenant is affirmed over *those* dead, since it never has force when he covenanting *is* living. [18]From which: Neither the first was dedicated without blood. [19]For every command according to Law being spoken by Moses to all the people, taking the blood of the calves and goats, with water and scarlet wool and hyssop, he sprinkled both the scroll and all the people, [20]saying, This *is* the blood of the covenant which God enjoined to you. [21]And he likewise sprinkled both the tabernacle and the service vessels with the blood. [22]And almost all things are cleansed by blood according to the Law; and apart from shedding of blood no remission occurs. [23]Then *it was* needful the figures of the things in the heavens to be cleansed *with* these; but the heavenly things by better sacrifices than these. [24]For Christ did not enter into *the* Holies made by hand, types of the true things, but into Heaven itself, now to appear in the presence of God on our behalf— [25]not that He often should offer Himself, even as the high priest enters into the Holies year by year with blood of others; [26]since He must often have suffered from *the* foundation of the world. But now once, at the completion of the ages, He has been manifested for putting away of sin through the sacrifice of Himself. [27]And as it is reserved to men once to die, and after this Judgment; [28]so being once offered to bear *the* sins of many, Christ shall appear

15 τὸ λατρεύειν Θεῷ ζῶντι ; καὶ διὰ τοῦτο διαθήκης καινῆς
serving God of (the) living. And therefore covenant of a new
μεσίτης ἐστίν, ὅπως, θανάτου γενομένου εἰς ἀπολύτρωσιν
Mediator He is, so as death having occurred for redemption
τῶν ἐπὶ τῇ πρώτῃ διαθήκῃ παραβάσεων, τὴν ἐπαγγελίαν
of the under the first covenant transgressions, , the promise
16 λάβωσιν οἱ κεκλημένοι τῆς αἰωνίου κληρονομίας. ὅπου γὰρ
may receive those being called of the eternal inheritance. where (is) For
17 διαθήκη, θάνατον ἀνάγκη φέρεσθαι τοῦ διαθεμένου. διαθήκη
a covenant (the) death (is) needful to be offered of him covenanting a covenant
γὰρ ἐπὶ νεκροῖς βεβαία, ἐπεὶ μή ποτε ἰσχύει ὅτε ζῇ ὁ διαθέ-
for over (those) dead (is) firm, since not ever has it strength when living he cove-
18 μενος. ὅθεν οὐδ᾽ ἡ πρώτη χωρὶς αἵματος ἐγκεκαίνισται.
nanting. From which neither the first without blood was dedicated.
λαληθείσης γὰρ πάσης ἐντολῆς κατὰ νόμον ὑπὸ Μωϋσέως
having been spoken For every command according to law by Moses
19 παντὶ τῷ λαῷ, λαβὼν τὸ αἷμα τῶν μόσχων καὶ τράγων,
to all the people, taking the blood of the calves and of goats,
μετὰ ὕδατος καὶ ἐρίου κοκκίνου καὶ ὑσσώπου, αὐτό τε τὸ
with water and wool scarlet and hyssop, it(self) both the
20 βιβλίον καὶ πάντα τὸν λαὸν ἐρράντισε, λέγων, Τοῦτο τὸ
scroll and all the people he sprinkled, saying, This (is) the
21 αἷμα τῆς διαθήκης ἧς ἐνετείλατο πρὸς ὑμᾶς ὁ Θεός. καὶ τὴν
blood of the covenant which enjoined to you God. both the
σκηνὴν δὲ καὶ πάντα τὰ σκεύη τῆς λειτουργίας τῷ αἵματι
tabernacle And and all the vessels of the service with the blood
22 ὁμοίως ἐρράντισε. καὶ σχεδὸν ἐν αἵματι πάντα καθαρίζεται
likewise he sprinkled. And almost by blood all things are cleansed
κατὰ τὸν νόμον, καὶ χωρὶς αἱματεκχυσίας οὐ γίνεται ἄφεσις.
according to the law, and without bloodshedding no there comes remission.
23 Ἀνάγκη οὖν τὰ μὲν ὑποδείγματα τῶν ἐν τοῖς οὐρανοῖς,
(It was) needful, then, the examples of the things in the heavens
τούτοις καθαρίζεσθαι, αὐτὰ δὲ τὰ ἐπουράνια κρείττοσι
these to be cleansed; them(selves) But the heavenly things by better
24 θυσίαις παρὰ ταύτας. οὐ γὰρ εἰς χειροποίητα ἅγια εἰσῆλθεν
sacrifices than these. not For into made by hand Holies entered
ὁ Χριστός, ἀντίτυπα τῶν ἀληθινῶν, ἀλλ᾽ εἰς αὐτὸν τὸν
Christ, figures of the true things, but into it(self)
οὐρανόν, νῦν ἐμφανισθῆναι τῷ προσώπῳ τοῦ Θεοῦ ὑπὲρ
Heaven, now to appear in the presence of God for
25 ἡμῶν· οὐδ᾽ ἵνα πολλάκις προσφέρῃ ἑαυτόν, ὥσπερ ὁ
us; not that often He should offer Himself, even as the
ἀρχιερεὺς εἰσέρχεται εἰς τὰ ἅγια κατ᾽ ἐνιαυτὸν ἐν αἵματι
high priest enters into the Holies year by year with blood
26 ἀλλοτρίῳ· ἐπεὶ ἔδει αὐτὸν πολλάκις παθεῖν ἀπὸ καταβολῆς
of others—since must He often have suffered from foundation
κόσμου· νῦν δὲ ἅπαξ ἐπὶ συντελείᾳ τῶν αἰώνων εἰς ἀθέτησιν
of (the) world—now but once at the completion of the ages for putting away
27 ἁμαρτίας διὰ τῆς θυσίας αὐτοῦ πεφανέρωται. καὶ καθ᾽ ὅσον
of sin through the sacrifice of Him He has been revealed. And as
ἀπόκειται τοῖς ἀνθρώποις ἅπαξ ἀποθανεῖν, μετὰ δὲ τοῦτο
it is reserved to men once to die, after and this
28 κρίσις· οὕτως ὁ Χριστός, ἅπαξ προσενεχθεὶς εἰς τὸ πολλῶν
judgment, so Christ, once having been offered of many
ἀνενεγκεῖν ἁμαρτίας, ἐκ δευτέρου χωρὶς ἁμαρτίας ὀφθήσεται
to bear sins, a second (time) without sin will appear

a second *time* without sin to those expecting Him for salvation.

CHAPTER 10

[1]For the Law having a shadow of the coming good things, not the image itself of *those* things, year by year with the same sacrifices which they offer continually never are able to perfect the ones drawing near, [2]since they would not have ceased to be offered because of those serving not still having conscience of sins, having once been cleansed. [3]But in these *there is* a remembrance of sins year by year— [4]for *it is* not possible *for the* blood of bulls and goats to take away sins. [5]For this reason, coming into the world, He says, "Sacrifice and offering You did not desire, but You prepared a body for Me. [6]You did not delight in burnt offerings and *sacrifices* as to sins. [7]Then I said, Lo, I come—in *the* roll of the Book, it was written concerning Me—to do Your will, *O* God."

[8]Above, saying, "You did not desire sacrifice and offering and burnt offerings and *sacrifices* as to sins," which are offered according to the Law, [9]then He said, "Lo, I come to do Your will, *O* God." He takes away the first in order that He may set up the second; [10]by which will we are sanctified through the offering of the body of Jesus Christ once for all. [11]And indeed every priest stands day by day ministering, and often offering the same sacrifices, which can never take away sins. [12]But He, offering but one sacrifice for sins, sat down in perpetuity at *the* right *hand* of God, [13]from then on expecting until His enemies are placed *as* a footstool of His feet. [14]For by one offering He has perfected forever the ones being sanctified.

[15]And the Holy Spirit bears witness to us also. For after

τοῖς αὐτὸν ἀπεκδεχομένοις, εἰς σωτηρίαν.
to those Him expecting for salvation.

CHAPTER 10

1 Σκιὰν γὰρ ἔχων ὁ νόμος τῶν μελλόντων ἀγαθῶν, οὐκ
a shadow For having the law of the coming good things, not
αὐτὴν τὴν εἰκόνα τῶν πραγμάτων, κατ' ἐνιαυτὸν ταῖς
it(self) the image of those things, year by year with the
αὐταῖς θυσίαις ἃς προσφέρουσιν εἰς τὸ διηνεκές, οὐδέποτε
same sacrifices which they offer continually never
2 δύναται τοὺς προσερχομένους τελειῶσαι. ἐπεὶ οὐκ ἂν
are able those drawing near to perfect. ; since not would
ἐπαύσαντο προσφερόμεναι, διὰ τὸ μηδεμίαν ἔχειν ἔτι συνείδη-
they have ceased being offered because of not having still conscience
3 σιν ἁμαρτιῶν τοὺς λατρεύοντας, ἅπαξ κεκαθαρμένους ; ἀλλ'
of sins those serving, once having been cleansed; but
4 ἐν αὐταῖς ἀνάμνησις ἁμαρτιῶν κατ' ἐνιαυτόν· ἀδύνατον γὰρ
in them a remembrance of sins year by year; it is impossible for
5 αἷμα ταύρων καὶ τράγων ἀφαιρεῖν ἁμαρτίας. διὸ εἰσερχό-
blood of bulls and of goats to take away sins. Therefore entering
μενος εἰς τὸν κόσμον λέγει, Θυσίαν καὶ προσφορὰν οὐκ
into the world, He says, Sacrifice and offering not
6 ἠθέλησας, σῶμα δὲ κατηρτίσω μοι· ὁλοκαυτώματα καὶ περὶ
You desired, a body but You prepared for Me; burnt offerings and (sacrifices) as to
7 ἁμαρτίας οὐκ εὐδόκησας· τότε εἶπον, Ἰδού, ἥκω (ἐν κεφαλίδι
sins not You were pleased. Then I said, Behold, I come—in a heading
βιβλίου γέγραπται περὶ ἐμοῦ) τοῦ ποιῆσαι, ὁ Θεός, τὸ
of (the) Book it was written about Me — to do God the
8 θέλημά σου. ἀνώτερον λέγων ὅτι Θυσίαν καὶ προσφορὰν
will of You. Above saying that sacrifice and offering
καὶ ὁλοκαυτώματα καὶ περὶ ἁμαρτίας οὐκ ἠθέλησας, οὐδὲ
and burnt offerings and (sacrifices) as to sins not You desired, nor
9 εὐδόκησας (αἵτινες κατὰ τὸν νόμον προσφέρονται), τότε
were pleased — which according to the law are offered — then
εἴρηκεν. Ἰδού, ἥκω τοῦ ποιῆσαι, ὁ Θεός, τὸ θέλημά σου.
He said, Behold, I come to do God the will of You.
10 ἀναιρεῖ τὸ πρῶτον, ἵνα τὸ δεύτερον στήσῃ. ἐν ᾧ θελήματι
He takes away the first, that the second He may set up, by which will
ἡγιασμένοι ἐσμὲν διὰ τῆς προσφορᾶς τοῦ σώματος τοῦ
sanctified we are through the offering of the body
11 Ἰησοῦ Χριστοῦ ἐφάπαξ. καὶ πᾶς μὲν ἱερεὺς ἕστηκε καθ'
of Jesus Christ once for all. And every indeed priest stands day
ἡμέραν λειτουργῶν, καὶ τὰς αὐτὰς πολλάκις προσφέρων
by day ministering, and the same often offering
12 θυσίας, αἵτινες οὐδέποτε δύνανται περιελεῖν ἁμαρτίας· αὐτὸς
sacrifices, which never can take away sins; He
δὲ μίαν ὑπὲρ ἁμαρτιῶν προσενέγκας θυσίαν εἰς τὸ διηνεκές,
but one on behalf of sins having offered sacrifice, in perpetuity,
13 ἐκάθισεν ἐν δεξιᾷ τοῦ Θεοῦ, τὸ λοιπὸν ἐκδεχόμενος ἕως
sat down at (the) right of God, from then on expecting until
14 τεθῶσιν οἱ ἐχθροὶ αὐτοῦ ὑποπόδιον τῶν ποδῶν αὐτοῦ. μιᾷ
are put the enemies of Him (as) a footstool of the feet of Him. by one
γὰρ προσφορᾷ τετελείωκεν εἰς τὸ διηνεκὲς τοὺς ἁγιαζο-
For offering He has perfected in perpetuity those being sanct-
15 μένους. μαρτυρεῖ δὲ ἡμῖν καὶ τὸ Πνεῦμα τὸ Ἅγιον· μετὰ γὰρ
ified. witnesses And to us also the Spirit Holy; after for

having said before, 16 "This *is* the covenant which I will covenant to them after those days, says *the* Lord: Giving My laws on their hearts, and I will write them on their minds; 17 and I will not at all still remember their sins and their lawless deeds." 18 But where forgiveness of these *is,* there *is* no longer offering concerning sins.

19 Therefore, brothers, having confidence for the entering of the Holies by the blood of Jesus, 20 which He consecrated for us, a new and living way through the veil, that is, His flesh; 21 and *having* a great priest over the house of God, 22 let us draw near with a true heart in full assurance of faith, *our* hearts having been sprinkled from an evil conscience, and *our* body having been washed in pure water; 23 let us hold fast the confession of the hope without yielding, for He who has promised *is* faithful. 24 And let us consider one another, to incitement of love and of good works, 25 not forsaking the assembling of ourselves, as *is the* custom of some, but exhorting, and so much more as you see the Day drawing near.

26 For *if* we *are* willfully sinning after receiving the full knowledge of the truth, there remains no more sacrifice concerning sins, 27 but a certain fearful expectation of judgment and zealous fire being about to consume the adversaries. 28 Anyone not regarding *the* Law of Moses dies without pities on *the word of* two or three witnesses. 29 How much worse punishment do you think he will be thought worthy *to receive* having trampled on the Son of God, and having counted the blood of the covenant in which he was sanctified common, and having insulted the Spirit of grace? 30 For we know Him who has said, "Vengeance *belongs* to Me; I will repay, says *the* Lord." And again, "*The* Lord will

16 τὸ προειρηκέναι, Αὕτη ἡ διαθήκη ἣν διαθήσομαι πρὸς
having said before. This (is) the covenant which I will covenant to
αὐτοὺς μετὰ τὰς ἡμέρας ἐκείνας, λέγει Κύριος, διδοὺς νόμους
them after days those, says (the) Lord: Giving laws
μου ἐπὶ καρδίας αὐτῶν, καὶ ἐπὶ τῶν διανοιῶν αὐτῶν
of Me on hearts of them, also on the minds of them
17 ἐπιγράψω αὐτούς· καὶ τῶν ἁμαρτιῶν αὐτῶν καὶ τῶν
I will write them, and the sins of them and the
18 ἀνομιῶν αὐτῶν οὐ μὴ μνησθῶ ἔτι. ὅπου δὲ ἄφεσις τούτων,
lawlessnesses of them not at all I will remember still. where Now forgiveness of these (is),
οὐκέτι προσφορὰ περὶ ἁμαρτίας.
no longer (is) offering concerning sins.
19 Ἔχοντες οὖν, ἀδελφοί, παρρησίαν εἰς τὴν εἴσοδον τῶν
Having, therefore, brothers, confidence for the entering of the
20 ἁγίων ἐν τῷ αἵματι Ἰησοῦ, ἣν ἐνεκαίνισεν ἡμῖν ὁδὸν
Holies by the blood of Jesus, which He consecrated for us, a way
πρόσφατον καὶ ζῶσαν, διὰ τοῦ καταπετάσματος, τοῦτ᾽
new and living through the veil, this
21 ἔστι, τῆς σαρκὸς αὐτοῦ, καὶ ἱερέα μέγαν ἐπὶ τὸν οἶκον τοῦ
is, the flesh of Him; and (having) a priest great over the house
22 Θεοῦ, προσερχώμεθα μετὰ ἀληθινῆς καρδίας ἐν πληρο-
of God, let us draw near with a true heart in full
φορίᾳ πίστεως, ἐρραντισμένοι τὰς καρδίας ἀπὸ συνειδήσεως
assurance of faith, having been sprinkled the hearts from a conscience
23 πονηρᾶς, καὶ λελουμένοι τὸ σῶμα ὕδατι καθαρῷ· κατέχω-
evil, and having been washed the body water in clean; let us hold
μεν τὴν ὁμολογίαν τῆς ἐλπίδος ἀκλινῆ, πιστὸς γὰρ ὁ
fast the confession of the hope unyieldingly, faithful for (is) He
24 ἐπαγγειλάμενος· καὶ κατανοῶμεν ἀλλήλους εἰς παροξυσμὸν
having promised; and let us consider one another to incitement
25 ἀγάπης καὶ καλῶν ἔργων, μὴ ἐγκαταλείποντες τὴν ἐπισυν-
of love and of good works, not forsaking the assembling
αγωγὴν ἑαυτῶν, καθὼς ἔθος τισίν, ἀλλὰ παρακαλοῦντες,
of ourselves as (the) custom of some (is), but exhorting,
καὶ τοσούτῳ μᾶλλον, ὅσῳ βλέπετε ἐγγίζουσαν τὴν ἡμέραν.
and by so much more as you see drawing near the Day.
26 Ἑκουσίως γὰρ ἁμαρτανόντων ἡμῶν μετὰ τὸ λαβεῖν τὴν
willfully For sinning us after receiving the
ἐπίγνωσιν τῆς ἀληθείας, οὐκέτι περὶ ἁμαρτιῶν ἀπολείπεται
full knowledge of the truth, no more concerning sins remains
27 θυσία, φοβερὰ δέ τις ἐκδοχὴ κρίσεως, καὶ πυρὸς ζῆλος
a sacrifice, fearful but some expectation of judgment, and of fire zeal
28 ἐσθίειν μέλλοντος τοὺς ὑπεναντίους. ἀθετήσας τις νόμον
to consume being about the adversaries. disregarding Anyone law
Μωσέως χωρὶς οἰκτιρμῶν ἐπὶ δυσὶν ἢ τρισὶ μάρτυσιν
of Moses without pities on (the word of) two or three witnesses
29 ἀποθνήσκει· πόσῳ, δοκεῖτε, χείρονος ἀξιωθήσεται τιμωρίας
dies; by how much think you of worse will be thought worthy (to receive) punishment
ὁ τὸν υἱὸν τοῦ Θεοῦ καταπατήσας, καὶ τὸ αἷμα τῆς διαθή-
he the Son of God having trampled, and the blood of the cove-
κης κοινὸν ἡγησάμενος ἐν ᾧ ἡγιάσθη, καὶ τὸ Πνεῦμα τῆς
nant common having deemed by which he was sanctified, and the Spirit
30 χάριτος ἐνυβρίσας; οἴδαμεν γὰρ τὸν εἰπόντα, Ἐμοὶ ἐκδίκη-
of grace having insulted; we know for the (One) having said, To Me (is) ven-
σις, ἐγὼ ἀνταποδώσω, λέγει Κύριος· καὶ πάλιν, Κύριος
geance, I will repay, says (the) Lord; and again, (The) Lord

judge His people." 31 *It is* a fearful thing to fall into *the* hands of *the* living God.

32 But call to mind the former days in which being enlightened you endured much conflict of sufferings; 33 partly being exposed both to reproaches and to afflictions; and partly having become partners of those so conducting themselves. 34 For also you suffered together in my bonds; and you accepted the seizure of your possessions with joy, knowing yourselves to have a better possession in Heaven. 35 Then do not throw away your confidence, which has great reward. 36 For you have need of patience, that having done the will of God you may obtain the promise. 37 For yet a very little *and* the *One* coming will come, and will not delay. 38 But the just shall live by faith; and if he draws back, My soul is not pleased in him. 39 But we are not of *those* drawing back to destruction, but of faith, to *the* preservation of *the* soul.

CHAPTER 11

1 Now faith is of *things* hoped for, *the* substantiation, the evidence of things not being seen. 2 For by this the elders obtained witness. 3 By faith we understand the worlds to have been framed by *the* word of God, so that the things seen not to have come into being out of things that appear.

4 By faith Abel offered a greater sacrifice than Cain, by which he obtained witness to be righteous, God testifying over his gifts; and through it, having died, he yet speaks. 5 By faith Enoch was translated *so as* not to see death, and was not found, because God translated him. For before his translation, he had obtained witness to have been pleasing to God. 6 But without faith it is impossible to please *God*. For it is right *that* the *one* drawing near to God should believe that He

31 κρινεῖ τὸν λαὸν αὐτοῦ. φοβερὸν τὸ ἐμπεσεῖν εἰς χεῖρας Θεοῦ
will judge the people of Him. A fearful thing (it is) to fall into (the) hands God
ζῶντος.
of (the) living.

32 Ἀναμιμνήσκεσθε δὲ τὰς πρότερον ἡμέρας, ἐν αἷς φωτι-
call to mind But the former days in which having

33 σθέντες πολλὴν ἄθλησιν ὑπεμείνατε παθημάτων· τοῦτο μέν,
been enlightened much struggle you endured of sufferings; this
ὀνειδισμοῖς τε καὶ θλίψεσι θεατριζόμενοι· τοῦτο δέ, κοινωνοὶ
to reproaches both and to afflictions being exposed; this and, sharers

34 τῶν οὕτως ἀναστρεφομένων γενηθέντες. καὶ γὰρ τοῖς
of those so living having become. indeed For in the
δεσμοῖς μου συνεπαθήσατε, καὶ τὴν ἁρπαγὴν τῶν ὑπαρχόν-
bonds of me you suffered together, and the seizure of the possessions
των ὑμῶν μετὰ χαρᾶς προσεδέξασθε, γινώσκοντες ἔχειν ἐν
of you with joy you accepted, knowing to have in

35 ἑαυτοῖς κρείττονα ὕπαρξιν ἐν οὐρανοῖς καὶ μένουσαν. μὴ
yourselves a better possession in Heaven and abiding. do not
ἀποβάλητε οὖν τὴν παρρησίαν ὑμῶν, ἥτις ἔχει μισθαποδο-
cast away Therefore the confidence of you, which has reward

36 σίαν μεγάλην. ὑπομονῆς γὰρ ἔχετε χρείαν, ἵνα τὸ θέλημα
great. of patience For you have need, that the will

37 τοῦ Θεοῦ ποιήσαντες κομίσησθε τὴν ἐπαγγελίαν. ἔτι γὰρ
of God having done, you may obtain the promise. yet For

38 μικρὸν ὅσον ὅσον, Ὁ ἐρχόμενος ἥξει, καὶ οὐ χρονιεῖ. ὁ δὲ
little a very, the coming (One) will come, and not delay; the but
δίκαιος ἐκ πίστεως ζήσεται· καὶ ἐὰν ὑποστείληται, οὐκ
just by faith will live, and if he draws back, not

39 εὐδοκεῖ ἡ ψυχή μου ἐν αὐτῷ. ἡμεῖς δὲ οὐκ ἐσμὲν ὑποστολῆς
is pleased the soul of Me in him. we But not are of (those) drawing
εἰς ἀπώλειαν, ἀλλὰ πίστεως εἰς περιποίησιν ψυχῆς.
to destruction, but of faith to possession of (the) soul.

CHAPTER 11

1 Ἔστι δὲ πίστις ἐλπιζομένων ὑπόστασις, πραγμάτων
is Now faith of things being hoped (the) substance, of things

2 ἔλεγχος οὐ βλεπομένων. ἐν ταύτῃ γὰρ ἐμαρτυρήθησαν οἱ
(the) evidence not being seen. by this For obtained witness the

3 πρεσβύτεροι. πίστει νοοῦμεν κατηρτίσθαι τοὺς αἰῶνας
elders. By faith we understand to have been framed the worlds
ῥήματι Θεοῦ, εἰς τὸ μὴ ἐκ φαινομένων τὰ βλεπόμενα γεγονέ-
by a word of God, so as not out of things appearing the things seen to have come

4 ναι. πίστει πλείονα θυσίαν Ἄβελ παρὰ Κάϊν προσήνεγκε τῷ
into being. By faith a greater sacrifice Abel than Cain offered
Θεῷ, δι' ἧς ἐμαρτυρήθη εἶναι δίκαιος, μαρτυροῦντος ἐπὶ τοῖς
to God, by which he obtained witness to be righteous, testifying over the
δώροις αὐτοῦ τοῦ Θεοῦ· καὶ δι' αὐτῆς ἀποθανὼν ἔτι λαλεῖ.
gifts of him God, and through it having died yet he speaks.

5 πίστει Ἐνὼχ μετετέθη τοῦ μὴ ἰδεῖν θάνατον, καὶ οὐχ
By faith Enoch was translated not to see death, and not
εὑρίσκετο, διότι μετέθηκεν αὐτὸν ὁ Θεός· πρὸ γὰρ τῆς μεταθέ-
was found, because translated him God. before For the trans-

6 σεως αὐτοῦ μεμαρτύρηται εὐηρεστηκέναι τῷ Θεῷ· χωρὶς δὲ
lating of him he obtained witness to have been pleasing to God; without but
πίστεως ἀδύνατον εὐαρεστῆσαι· πιστεῦσαι γὰρ δεῖ τὸν
faith it is impossible to please (God); to believe for it is right the (one)

is, and *that* He becomes a rewarder to the ones seeking Him out. 7 Being warned by God about the things not yet having been seen, Noah moved with fear prepared an ark for *the* salvation of his house; through which he condemned the world, and became heir of the righteousness according to faith.

8 Having been called out by faith, Abraham obeyed to go forth to a place which he was going to receive for an inheritance, and went out not understanding where he went. 9 By faith he resided as a foreigner in a land of promise, living in tents with Isaac and Jacob, the co-heirs of the same promise; 10 for he looked for a city having the foundation of which the builder and maker *is* God. 11 Also by faith Sarah herself received power for conceiving seed even beyond *the* time of age, *and* gave birth, since she deemed the *One* having promised *to be* faithful. 12 Because of this came into being from one—and that *from* one having died—*seed* even as the stars of the heaven in multitude, and countless as sand by the seaside.

13 These all died by way of faith, not having received the promises, but they seeing from afar, and being persuaded, and having embraced and confessed that they are aliens and sojourners on the earth. 14 For those saying such things make clear that they seek a fatherland. 15 And truly if they remembered that from which they came out, they had time to return. 16 But now they stretch forth to a better, that is, a heavenly *land*. Therefore, God is not ashamed *of* them, to be called their God; for He prepared a city for them.

17 Being tested, Abraham by faith offered up Isaac; and he receiving the promises was offering up the only-

προσερχόμενον τῷ Θεῷ, ὅτι ἔστι, καὶ τοῖς ἐκζητοῦσιν αὐτὸν
approaching God that He is, and to those seeking out Him
7 μισθαποδότης γίνεται. πίστει χρηματισθεὶς Νῶε περὶ τῶν
a rewarder He becomes. By faith having been warned by God Noah about the things
μηδέπω βλεπομένων, εὐλαβηθεὶς κατεσκεύασε κιβωτὸν εἰς
not yet being seen, , moved with fear prepared an ark for
σωτηρίαν τοῦ οἴκου αὐτοῦ· δι' ἧς κατέκρινε τὸν κόσμον, καὶ
(the) salvation of the house of him, by which he condemned the world, and
8 τῆς κατὰ πίστιν δικαιοσύνης ἐγένετο κληρονόμος. πίστει
of the according to faith righteousness became heir. By faith
καλούμενος Ἀβραὰμ ὑπήκουσεν ἐξελθεῖν εἰς τὸν τόπον ὃν
having been called, Abraham obeyed to go forth to a place which
ἤμελλε λαμβάνειν εἰς κληρονομίαν, καὶ ἐξῆλθε μὴ ἐπιστά-
he was about to receive for an inheritance, and went forth not under-
9 μενος ποῦ ἔρχεται. πίστει παρῴκησεν εἰς τὴν γῆν τῆς ἐπαγ-
standing where he went. By faith he sojourned in a land of
γελίας, ὡς ἀλλοτρίαν, ἐν σκηναῖς κατοικήσας μετὰ Ἰσαὰκ
promise, as a foreigner, in tents dwelling with Isaac
καὶ Ἰακώβ, τῶν συγκληρονόμων τῆς ἐπαγγελίας τῆς αὐτῆς·
and Jacob, the co-heirs of the promise same;
10 ἐξεδέχετο γὰρ τὴν τοὺς θεμελίους ἔχουσαν πόλιν, ἧς τεχνίτης
looked forward for to the the foundation having city, of which builder
11 καὶ δημιουργὸς ὁ Θεός. πίστει καὶ αὐτὴ Σάρρα δύναμιν εἰς
and maker (was) God. By faith also her(self) Sarah power for
καταβολὴν σπέρματος ἔλαβε, καὶ παρὰ καιρὸν ἡλικίας
conception of seed received even beyond time of age,
12 ἔτεκεν, ἐπεὶ πιστὸν ἡγήσατο τὸν ἐπαγγειλάμενον. διὸ καὶ
gave birth, since faithful she deemed the (One) having promised. Therefore
ἀφ' ἑνὸς ἐγεννήθησαν, καὶ ταῦτα νενεκρωμένου, καθὼς τὰ
from one came into being —and that (of) one having died — even as the
ἄστρα τοῦ οὐρανοῦ τῷ πλήθει, καὶ ὡσεὶ ἄμμος ἡ παρὰ τὸ
stars of the heaven in multitude, and as sand by the
χεῖλος τῆς θαλάσσης ἡ ἀναρίθμητος.
lip of the sea countless.
13 Κατὰ πίστιν ἀπέθανον οὗτοι πάντες, μὴ λαβόντες τὰς
By way of faith died these all, not having received the
ἐπαγγελίας, ἀλλὰ πόρρωθεν αὐτὰς ἰδόντες, καὶ πεισθέντες,
promises, but from afar them seeing, and being persuaded
καὶ ἀσπασάμενοι, καὶ ὁμολογήσαντες ὅτι ξένοι καὶ παρ-
and having embraced, and having confessed that aliens and so-
14 επίδημοί εἰσιν ἐπὶ τῆς γῆς. οἱ γὰρ τοιαῦτα λέγοντες ἐμφανί-
journers they are on the earth. those For such things saying make
15 ζουσιν ὅτι πατρίδα ἐπιζητοῦσι. καὶ εἰ μὲν ἐκείνης ἐμνη-
clear that a fatherland they seek. And if indeed that they
16 μόνευον ἀφ' ἧς ἐξῆλθον, εἶχον ἂν καιρὸν ἀνακάμψαι. νυνὶ δὲ
remembered from which they came out, they had time to return. now But
κρείττονος ὀρέγονται, τοῦτ' ἔστιν, ἐπουρανίου· διὸ οὐκ
a better stretch forth to, this is, a heavenly. Therefore not
ἐπαισχύνεται αὐτοὺς ὁ Θεός, Θεὸς ἐπικαλεῖσθαι αὐτῶν
is ashamed (of) them God, God to be called of them;
ἡτοίμασε γὰρ αὐτοῖς πόλιν.
He prepared for them a city.
17 Πίστει προσενήνοχεν Ἀβραὰμ τὸν Ἰσαὰκ πειραζόμενος,
By faith offered up Abraham Isaac, being tested,
καὶ τὸν μονογενῆ προσέφερεν ὁ τὰς ἐπαγγελίας ἀναδεξά-
and the only-begotten was offering up the (one) the promises having

begotten, [18]as to whom it was said, "In Isaac your Seed shall be called;" [19]reckoning that God *was* able to raise even from *the* dead; from where indeed he obtained him in a parable. [20]Concerning coming things, Isaac by faith blessed Jacob and Esau. [21]Dying Jacob by faith blessed each of the sons of Joseph, and worshiped on the top of his staff. [22]Dying Joseph by faith remembered concerning the Exodus of the sons of Israel, and gave orders concerning his bones. [23]Moses being born was by faith hidden by his parents three months, because they saw the child *was* beautiful; and they did not fear the king's decree. [24]Having become great, Moses by faith refused to be called son of Pharaoh's daughter, [25]having chosen rather to suffer affliction with the people of God than for a time to have enjoyment of sin; [26]having counted the reproach of Christ greater than the riches of Egypt, for he was looking to the reward. [27]By faith he left Egypt, not fearing the anger of the king; for he kept on as seeing the Invisible *One*. [28]By faith he made the Passover, and the sprinkling of blood, that the destroyer of the firstborn might not touch them. [29]By faith they passed through the Red Sea, as through dry *land*; *by* which trial the Egyptians were swallowed. [30]By faith the walls of Jericho fell down, having been circled for seven days. [31]By faith Rahab the harlot did not perish with those disobeying, having received the spies with peace.

[32]And what more may I say? For the times will fail me telling about Gideon, Barak, and also Samson and Jephthah, and also David and Samuel, and the prophets, [33]who through faith overcame kingdoms, worked out righteousness, obtained

18 μενος, πρὸς ὃν ἐλαλήθη ὅτι Ἐν Ἰσαὰκ κληθήσεταί σοι
accepted, as to whom it was spoken —: In Isaac shall be called of you
19 σπέρμα· λογισάμενος ὅτι καὶ ἐκ νεκρῶν ἐγείρειν δυνατὸς ὁ
the seed, reckoning that even from (the) dead to raise (was) able
20 Θεός· ὅθεν αὐτὸν καὶ ἐν παραβολῇ ἐκομίσατο. πίστει περὶ
God, from where him truly in a parable he obtained. By faith concerning
μελλόντων εὐλόγησεν Ἰσαὰκ τὸν Ἰακὼβ καὶ τὸν Ἠσαῦ.
coming things blessed Isaac Jacob and Esau.
21 πίστει Ἰακὼβ ἀποθνήσκων ἕκαστον τῶν υἱῶν Ἰωσὴφ
By faith Jacob dying each of the sons of Joseph
εὐλόγησε, καὶ προσεκύνησεν ἐπὶ τὸ ἄκρον τῆς ῥάβδου αὐτοῦ.
blessed, and worshipped on the top of the staff of him.
22 πίστει Ἰωσὴφ τελευτῶν περὶ τῆς ἐξόδου τῶν υἱῶν Ἰσραὴλ
By faith Joseph dying concerning the exodus of the sons of Israel
ἐμνημόνευσε, καὶ περὶ τῶν ὀστέων αὐτοῦ ἐνετείλατο.
remembered, and concerning the bones of him gave orders.
23 πίστει Μωσῆς γεννηθεὶς ἐκρύβη τρίμηνον ὑπὸ τῶν πατέρων
By faith Moses having been born was hidden three months by the parents
αὐτοῦ, διότι εἶδον ἀστεῖον τὸ παιδίον· καὶ οὐκ ἐφοβήθησαν
of him, because they saw (was) fair the child, and not they feared
24 τὸ διάταγμα τοῦ βασιλέως. πίστει Μωσῆς μέγας γενόμενος
the decree of the king. By faith Moses great having become
25 ἠρνήσατο λέγεσθαι υἱὸς θυγατρὸς Φαραω, μᾶλλον ἑλόμενος
refused to be called son of (the) daughter of Pharaoh, rather choosing
συγκακουχεῖσθαι τῷ λαῷ τοῦ Θεοῦ ἢ πρόσκαιρον ἔχειν
to suffer affliction with the people of God, than for a time to have
26 ἁμαρτίας ἀπόλαυσιν· μείζονα πλοῦτον ἡγησάμενος τῶν
of sin enjoyment, greater riches deeming (than) the
ἐν Αἰγύπτῳ θησαυρῶν τὸν ὀνειδισμὸν τοῦ Χρίστοῦ· ἀπέ-
of Egypt treasures the reproach of Christ; he was
27 βλεπε γὰρ εἰς τὴν μισθαποδοσίαν. πίστει κατέλιπεν
looking for to the reward. By faith he left
Αἴγυπτον, μὴ φοβηθεὶς τὸν θυμὸν τοῦ βασιλέως· τὸν γὰρ
Egypt, not fearing the anger of the king; the for
28 ἀόρατον ὡς ὁρῶν ἐκαρτέρησε. πίστει πεποίηκε τὸ πάσχα
invisible (One) as seeing he kept on. By faith he made the Passover
καὶ τὴν πρόσχυσιν τοῦ αἵματος, ἵνα μὴ ὁ ὀλοθρεύων τὰ
and the sprinkling of blood, that not He destroying the
29 πρωτότοκα θίγῃ αὐτῶν. πίστει διέβησαν τὴν ἐρυθρὰν
firstborns should touch them. By faith they went through the Red
θάλασσαν ὡς διὰ ξηρᾶς· ἧς πεῖραν λαβόντες οἱ Αἰγύπτιοι
Sea as through dry, which trial taking the Egyptians
30 κατεπόθησαν. πίστει τὰ τείχη Ἰεριχὼ ἔπεσε, κυκλωθέντα
were swallowed. By faith the walls of Jericho fell, having been circled
31 ἐπὶ ἑπτὰ ἡμέρας. πίστει Ῥαὰβ ἡ πόρνη οὐ συναπώλετο
during seven days. By faith Rahab the harlot did not perish
τοῖς ἀπειθήσασι, δεξαμένη τοὺς κατασκόπους μετ᾽ εἰρήνης.
with those disobeying, receiving the spies with peace.
32 καὶ τί ἔτι λέγω; ἐπιλείψει γάρ με διηγούμενον ὁ χρόνος περὶ
And what still may I say? will fail For me telling the times concerning
Γεδεών, Βαράκ τε καὶ Σαμψὼν καὶ Ἰεφθάε, Δαβίδ τε καὶ
Gideon, Barak, both and Samson and Jephthah, David both and
33 Σαμουὴλ καὶ τῶν προφητῶν· οἳ διὰ πίστεως κατηγωνίσαντο
Samuel, and the prophets, who through faith overcame
βασιλείας, εἰργάσαντο δικαιοσύνην, ἐπέτυχον ἐπαγγελιῶν,
kingdoms, worked out righteousness, obtained promises,

promises, stopped the
mouths of lions, 34 quenched
the power of fire, escaped *the*
mouths of *the* sword, acquired power from weakness,
became strong in war, made
armies of foreigners to yield.
35 Women received their
dead by resurrection; but
others were beaten to death,
not accepting deliverance,
that they might obtain a
better resurrection. 36 And
others received trial of mockings and of floggings; yea,
more, of bonds and of prison;
37 they were stoned; they
were tried; they were sawn in
two; they died by murder of
sword; they went about in
sheepskins *and* in goatskins,
being in need, being afflicted, being ill-treated; 38 of
whom the world was not
worthy, wandering in
deserts, and mountains, and
caves, and the holes of the
earth. 39 And having obtained
witness through the faith,
these all did not obtain the
promise, 40 God having foreseen something better concerning us, that they should
not be perfected apart from
us.

CHAPTER 12

1 So therefore we, having
such a cloud of witnesses
encircling us, having laid
aside every weight and the
easily-surrounding sin, let us
through patience run the race
set before us, 2 looking to
the Author and Finisher of *our*
faith, Jesus, who because of
the joy set before Him
endured *the* cross, despising
the shame, and sat down at
the right of the throne of
God. 3 For consider Him
who had endured such gainsaying of sinners against
Himself, that you do not grow
weary, fainting in your souls.
4 You did not yet resist unto
blood, wrestling against sin.
5 And you have forgotten the
exhortation which *He* speaks
with you, as with sons, "My
sons, do not despise the
chastening of *the* Lord, nor

34 ἔφραξαν στόματα λεόντων, ἔσβεσαν δύναμιν πυρός, ἔφυγον
stopped mouths of lions, quenched (the) power of fire, escaped
στόματα μαχαίρας, ἐνεδυναμώθησαν ἀπὸ ἀσθενείας, ἐγενή-
mouths of (the) sword, acquired power from weakness, became
θησαν ἰσχυροὶ ἐν πολέμῳ, παρεμβολὰς ἔκλιναν ἀλλοτρίων.
strong in war, armies made to yield of foreigners.
35 ἔλαβον γυναῖκες ἐξ ἀναστάσεως τοὺς νεκροὺς αὐτῶν· ἄλλοι
received women by resurrection the dead of them; others
δὲ ἐτυμπανίσθησαν, οὐ προσδεξάμενοι τὴν ἀπολύτρωσιν,
but were beaten to death, not accepting deliverance,
36 ἵνα κρείττονος ἀναστάσεως τύχωσιν· ἕτεροι δὲ ἐμπαιγμῶν
that a better resurrection they might obtain; others and of mockings
καὶ μαστίγων πεῖραν ἔλαβον, ἔτι δὲ δεσμῶν καὶ φυλακῆς·
and of floggings trial received, more and, bonds and of prison;
37 ἐλιθάσθησαν, ἐπρίσθησαν, ἐπειράσθησαν, ἐν φόνῳ μαχαίρας
they were stoned, they were tried, they were sawn apart, by murder of sword
ἀπέθανον· περιῆλθον ἐν μηλωταῖς, ἐν αἰγείοις δέρμασιν,
they died, they went about in sheepskins, in goatskins,
38 ὑστερούμενοι, θλιβόμενοι, κακουχούμενοι (ὧν οὐκ ἦν ἄξιος
being in need, being afflicted, being ill-treated, of whom not was worthy
ὁ κόσμος), ἐν ἐρημίαις πλανώμενοι καὶ ὄρεσι καὶ σπηλαίοις
the world, over deserts wandering and mountains and caves
39 καὶ ταῖς ὀπαῖς τῆς γῆς. καὶ οὗτοι πάντες, μαρτυρηθέντες
and the holes of the earth. And these all having obtained witness
40 διὰ τῆς πίστεως, οὐκ ἐκομίσαντο τὴν ἐπαγγελίαν, τοῦ
through the faith did not obtain the promise,
Θεοῦ περὶ ἡμῶν κρεῖττόν τι προβλεψαμένου, ἵνα μὴ χωρὶς
God concerning us better something having foreseen, that not without
ἡμῶν τελειωθῶσι.
us they should be perfected.

CHAPTER 12

1 Τοιγαροῦν καὶ ἡμεῖς, τοσοῦτον ἔχοντες περικείμενον ἡμῖν
So therefore also we, such having encircling us
νέφος μαρτύρων, ὄγκον ἀποθέμενοι πάντα καὶ τὴν εὐπερί-
a cloud of witnesses, weight laying aside every and the easily sur-
στατον ἁμαρτίαν, δι' ὑπομονῆς τρέχωμεν τὸν προκείμενον
rounding sin, through patience let us run the set before
2 ἡμῖν ἀγῶνα, ἀφορῶντες εἰς τὸν τῆς πίστεως ἀρχηγὸν καὶ
us race, looking to the of the faith Author and
τελειωτὴν Ἰησοῦν, ὅς, ἀντὶ τῆς προκειμένης αὐτῷ χαρᾶς,
Finisher, Jesus, who against the set before Him joy
ὑπέμεινε σταυρόν, αἰσχύνης καταφρονήσας, ἐν δεξιᾷ τε τοῦ
endured (the) cross, (the) shame despising, at (the) right of the
3 θρόνου τοῦ Θεοῦ ἐκάθισεν. ἀναλογίσασθε γὰρ τὸν τοιαύτην
throne of God sat down. consider For the (One) such
ὑπομεμενηκότα ὑπὸ τῶν ἁμαρτωλῶν εἰς αὐτὸν ἀντιλογίαν,
having endured by of sinners against Himself contradiction,
4 ἵνα μὴ κάμητε ταῖς ψυχαῖς ὑμῶν ἐκλυόμενοι. οὔπω μέχρις
lest you grow weary in the souls of you fainting Not yet unto
αἵματος ἀντικατέστητε πρὸς τὴν ἁμαρτίαν ἀνταγωνιζόμε-
blood you resisted against sin wrestling,
5 νοι· καὶ ἐκλέλησθε τῆς παρακλήσεως, ἥτις ὑμῖν ὡς υἱοῖς
and you have forgotten the exhortation, which with you as with sons
διαλέγεται, Υἱέ μου, μὴ ὀλιγώρει παιδείας Κυρίου, μηδὲ
(He) speaks: Son of Me, do not despise (the) chastening of (the) Lord, nor

faint *while* being corrected by Him. [6]For whom *the* Lord loves, He disciplines, and whips every son whom He receives." [7]If you endure discipline, God is dealing with you as with sons; for who is *the* son whom a father does not discipline? [8]But if you are without discipline, of which all have become sharers, then you are bastards, and not sons. [9]Furthermore, we have had fathers of our flesh *as* correctors, and we respected *them.* Shall we not much more be subject to the Father of spirits, and we shall live? [10]For they truly disciplined *us* for a few days according to the things seeming good to them; but He for *our* profit, in order *for us* to partake of His holiness. [11]And all discipline for the present indeed does not seem to be joyous, but grievous; but afterward it gives back peaceable fruit of righteousness to the ones having been exercised by it.

[12]For this reason, straighten up the hands hanging alongside, and the enfeebled knees; [13]and make straight tracks for your feet, that the lame not be turned aside, but rather healed.

[14]Eagerly pursue peace and holiness with all, without which no one will see the Lord, [15]watching diligently that no root of bitterness growing up may disturb you, and through this many be defiled; [16]lest any fornicator, or profane one—as Esau, who for one feeding gave up his birthright; [17]for you know also that afterwards desiring to inherit the blessing, he was rejected, for he found no place of repentance, although seeking it with tears.

[18]For you have drawn near to *the* mountain being touched, and having been lit with fire, and to gloom, and darkness, and tempest, [19]and to a sound of trumpet, and to a voice of words, which those hearing begged not a word be added to them; [20]for they could not bear that

6 ἐκλύου ὑπ' αὐτοῦ ἐλεγχόμενος· ὃν γὰρ ἀγαπᾷ Κύριος
faint by Him being corrected, whom for loves (the) Lord

7 παιδεύει· μαστιγοῖ δὲ πάντα υἱὸν ὃν παραδέχεται. εἰ
He disciplines, whips and every son whom He receives. If

παιδείαν ὑπομένετε, ὡς υἱοῖς ὑμῖν προσφέρεται ὁ Θεός· τίς
discipline you endure, as with sons with you is dealing God, who

8 γάρ ἐστιν υἱὸς ὃν οὐ παιδεύει πατήρ; εἰ δὲ χωρίς ἐστε
for is son, whom not disciplines a father? if But without you are

παιδείας, ἧς μέτοχοι γεγόνασι πάντες, ἄρα νόθοι ἐστὲ καὶ
discipline, of which sharers have become all, then bastards you are and

9 οὐχ υἱοί. εἶτα τοὺς μὲν τῆς σαρκὸς ἡμῶν πατέρας εἴχομεν
not sons. Moreover the of the flesh of us fathers we had

παιδευτάς, καὶ ἐνετρεπόμεθα· οὐ πολλῷ μᾶλλον ὑποταγησό-
(as) correctors, and we respected (them); not much more shall we be subject

10 μεθα τῷ πατρὶ τῶν πνευμάτων, καὶ ζήσομεν; οἱ μὲν γὰρ
to the Father of spirits, and we shall live? they truly For

πρὸς ὀλίγας ἡμέρας κατὰ τὸ δοκοῦν αὐτοῖς ἐπαίδευον· ὁ δὲ
for a few days according to the seeming thing good to them disciplined. He But

ἐπὶ τὸ συμφέρον, εἰς τὸ μεταλαβεῖν τῆς ἁγιότητος αὐτοῦ.
for the profit, to partake of the holiness of Him.

11 πᾶσα δὲ παιδεία πρὸς μὲν τὸ παρὸν οὐ δοκεῖ χαρᾶς εἶναι,
all And discipline for indeed the present does not seem of joy to be,

ἀλλὰ λύπης· ὕστερον δὲ καρπὸν εἰρηνικὸν τοῖς δι' αὐτῆς
but of grief; later but fruit peaceable to those through it

12 γεγυμνασμένοις ἀποδίδωσι δικαιοσύνης. διὸ τὰς παρειμένας
having been exercised it gives back of righteousness. Therefore the alongside

13 χεῖρας καὶ τὰ παραλελυμένα γόνατα ἀνορθώσατε· καὶ
hands and the enfeebled knees straighten up, and

τροχιὰς ὀρθὰς ποιήσατε τοῖς ποσὶν ὑμῶν, ἵνα μὴ τὸ χωλὸν
tracks straight make for the feet of you, that not the lame

ἐκτραπῇ, ἰαθῇ δὲ μᾶλλον.
be turned aside, be healed but rather.

14 Εἰρήνην διώκετε μετὰ πάντων, καὶ τὸν ἁγιασμόν, οὗ
peace Follow with all, and holiness, which

15 χωρὶς οὐδεὶς ὄψεται τὸν Κύριον· ἐπισκοποῦντες μή τις
without no one will see the Lord, watching diligently lest any

ὑστερῶν ἀπὸ τῆς χάριτος τοῦ Θεοῦ· μή τις ῥίζα πικρίας
lack from the grace of God, lest any root of bitterness

16 ἄνω φύουσα ἐνοχλῇ, καὶ διὰ ταύτης μιανθῶσι πολλοί· μή
up growing disturb, and through this be defiled many; lest

τις πόρνος, ἢ βέβηλος, ὡς Ἠσαῦ, ὃς ἀντὶ βρώσεως μιᾶς
any fornicator, or profane one, as Esau, who for feeding one

17 ἀπέδοτο τὰ πρωτοτόκια αὐτοῦ. ἴστε γὰρ ὅτι καὶ μετέπειτα,
gave up the birthright of him. you know for that indeed afterwards

θέλων κληρονομῆσαι τὴν εὐλογίαν, ἀπεδοκιμάσθη· μετανοίας
desiring to inherit the blessing, he was rejected, of repentance

γὰρ τόπον οὐχ εὗρε, καίπερ μετὰ δακρύων ἐκζητήσας αὐτήν.
for place not he found, though with tears seeking it.

18 Οὐ γὰρ προσεληλύθατε ψηλαφωμένῳ ὄρει, καὶ κεκαυ-
not For you have drawn near being touched (the) mountain, and having

19 μένῳ πυρί, καὶ γνόφῳ, καὶ σκότῳ, καὶ θυέλλῃ, καὶ σάλπιγ-
been lit with fire, and to gloom and darkness and tempest, and of trumpet

γος ἤχῳ, καὶ φωνῇ ῥημάτων, ἧς οἱ ἀκούσαντες παρῃτή-
to a sound, and to a voice of words, which those hearing begged

20 σαντο μὴ προστεθῆναι αὐτοῖς λόγον· οὐκ ἔφερον γὰρ τὸ
not to be added to them a word; not they bore for that

which was enjoined: "Even if a beast touches the mountain, it will be stoned, or shot through with a dart." 21 And so fearful was the thing appearing, Moses said, "I am terrified and trembling." 22 But you have drawn near to Mount Zion, even the city of *the* living God, to a heavenly Jerusalem, and to myriads of angels, 23 and to an assembly, a church of the firstborn ones having been enrolled in Heaven; and to God *the* judge of all; and to spirits of just ones who have been perfected; 24 and to Jesus *the* Mediator of a new covenant, and to blood of sprinkling speaking better things than *that* of Abel. 25 Watch *that* you do not refuse the *One* speaking; for if these did not escape who refused Him who divinely warned *them* on earth, much rather we, those turning away from Heaven; 26 whose voice shook the earth then, but now He has promised, saying, "Yet once I will shake not only the earth, but the heaven." 27 Now the *words*, "Yet once" makes clear the removal of the *things* being shaken, as having been made, so that the things not shaken may remain. 28 Therefore, receiving an unshakeable kingdom, let us have grace, through which we may serve God pleasingly, with reverence and awe; 29 for also, "Our God *is* a consuming fire."

CHAPTER 13

1 Let brotherly love continue. 2 Do not forget hospitality, for by this some unknowingly took in angels as guests. 3 Be mindful of the prisoners, as having been bound with *them*; of those ill-treated, as also being in the body yourselves. 4 Marriage *is* honorable in all, and the bed undefiled; but God will judge fornicators and adulterers. 5 *Set your* way of life without money-loving, being satisfied with present things; for He has said, "I will never leave you, nor will I ever forsake you." 6 So that we

διαστελλόμενον, Κἂν θηρίον θίγῃ τοῦ ὄρους, λιθοβοληθη-
being enjoined: If even a beast touches the mountain, it will be stoned;
21 σεται ἢ βολίδι κατατοξευθήσεται· καί, οὕτω φοβερὸν ἦν τὸ
or with a dart shot through; and, so fearful was the thing
φανταζόμενον, Μωσῆς εἶπεν, Ἔκφοβός εἰμι καὶ ἔντρομος.
appearing, Moses said: terrified I am, and trembling.
22 ἀλλὰ προσεληλύθατε Σιὼν ὄρει, καὶ πόλει Θεοῦ ζῶντος,
But you have drawn near Zion Mount, and a city God of (the) living.
23 Ἱερουσαλὴμ ἐπουρανίῳ, καὶ μυριάσιν ἀγγέλων, πανηγύρει
Jerusalem to a heavenly, and to myriads of angels, to an assembly
καὶ ἐκκλησίᾳ πρωτοτόκων ἐν οὐρανοῖς ἀπογεγραμμένων,
and, a church of firstborn ones in Heaven having been enrolled,
καὶ κριτῇ Θεῷ πάντων, καὶ πνεύμασι δικαίων τετελειω-
and (the) judge God of all, and to spirits of just ones having been
24 μένων, καὶ διαθήκης νέας μεσίτῃ Ἰησοῦ, καὶ αἵματι ῥαντι-
perfected, and covenant of a new Mediator to Jesus, and to blood of
25 σμοῦ κρείττονα λαλοῦντι παρὰ τὸ Ἄβελ. βλέπετε μὴ
sprinkling better things speaking than (that) of Abel. Watch (that) not
παραιτήσησθε τὸν λαλοῦντα. εἰ γὰρ ἐκεῖνοι οὐκ ἔφυγον, τὸν
you refuse the (One) speaking; if for these did not escape
ἐπὶ τῆς γῆς παραιτησάμενοι χρηματίζοντα, πολλῷ μᾶλλον
on the earth refusing (the One) divinely warning, much rather
26 ἡμεῖς οἱ τὸν ἀπ' οὐρανῶν ἀποστρεφόμενοι· οὗ ἡ φωνὴ τὴν
we, those from Heaven turning away; of whom the voice the
γῆν ἐσάλευσε τότε, νῦν δὲ ἐπήγγελται, λέγων, Ἔτι ἅπαξ
earth shook then, now but He has promised, saying, Yet once
27 ἐγὼ σείω οὐ μόνον τὴν γῆν, ἀλλὰ καὶ τὸν οὐρανόν. τὸ δέ,
I shake not only the earth, but also the Heaven. (the words) Now,
Ἔτι ἅπαξ, δηλοῖ τῶν σαλευομένων τὴν μετάθεσιν, ὡς
Yet once, makes clear of the (things) being shaken the removal, as
28 πεποιημένων, ἵνα μείνῃ τὰ μὴ σαλευόμενα. διὸ βασιλείαν
having been made, that may remain the things not shaken. Therefore kingdom
ἀσάλευτον παραλαμβάνοντες, ἔχωμεν χάριν, δι' ἧς λα-
an unshakeable receiving, let us have grace, through which we
29 τρεύωμεν εὐαρέστως τῷ Θεῷ μετὰ αἰδοῦς καὶ εὐλαβείας· καὶ
may serve well-pleasingly God with reverence and fear; truly
γὰρ ὁ Θεὸς ἡμῶν πῦρ καταναλίσκον.
for the God of us fire a consuming (is).

CHAPTER 13

1 Ἡ φιλαδελφία μενέτω. τῆς φιλοξενίας μὴ ἐπιλανθάνεσθε·
brotherly love Let remain. of hospitality Be not forgetful,
2 διὰ ταύτης γὰρ ἔλαθόν τινες ξενίσαντες ἀγγέλους. μιμνή-
3 through this for unknowingly some entertained angels. Be
σκεσθε τῶν δεσμίων, ὡς συνδεδεμένοι· τῶν κακουχουμένων,
mindful of the prisoners, as being bound with (them), of those ill-treated,
4 ὡς καὶ αὐτοὶ ὄντες ἐν σώματι. τίμιος ὁ γάμος ἐν πᾶσι, καὶ ἡ
as also yourselves, being in the body. honorable marriage (is) in all, and the
5 κοίτη ἀμίαντος· πόρνους δὲ καὶ μοιχοὺς κρινεῖ ὁ Θεός. ἀφιλ-
bed undefiled; fornicators but and adulterers will judge God. (Let be)
άργυρος ὁ τρόπος, ἀρκούμενοι τοῖς παροῦσιν· αὐτὸς γὰρ
without money-loving the way of life, being satisfied with the present things; He for
6 εἴρηκεν, Οὐ μή σε ἀνῶ, οὐδ' οὐ μή σε ἐγκαταλίπω. ὥστε
has said, Not at all you will I leave, nor in any way you will I forsake. So that
θαρροῦντας ἡμᾶς λέγειν, Κύριος ἐμοὶ βοηθός, καὶ οὐ φοβηθή-
may confidently we say, (The) Lord to me (is) a helper, and not I will be

may boldly say, *The* Lord *is* my helper, and I will not be afraid —what shall man do to me? [7]Remember your leaders who spoke the word of God to you, considering the issue of *their* conduct, imitate *their* faith: [8]Jesus Christ, the same yesterday and today and forever. [9]Do not be carried away by various and strange teaching; for *it is* good *that* the heart be confirmed by grace, not by foods, in which those walking *in them* were not profited. [10]We have an altar of which those serving the tabernacle have no authority to eat. [11]For of what blood of animals is brought by the high priest into the Holies concerning sins, of these the bodies are burned outside the camp. [12]Therefore, that He might sanctify the people by His own blood, Jesus also suffered outside the gate. [13]So now let us go forth to Him outside the camp, bearing His reproach. [14]For we do not have here a continuing city, but we seek the *city* coming. [15]Then through Him let us offer up a sacrifice of praise to God always, that is, *the* fruit of the lips, confessing to His name. [16]But do not be forgetful of doing good and sharing, for God is well-pleased with such sacrifices. [17]Obey those taking the lead of you, and submit, for they watch for your souls, giving account, that they may do this with joy, and not *with* groaning, for this *would be* no profit to you.

[18]Pray for us, for we are persuaded that we have a good conscience, in all things wishing to behave well. [19]But I much more urge *you* to do this, that I may sooner be restored to you.

[20]Now the God of peace, He leading up out of *the*

σομαι τί ποιήσει μοι ἄνθρωπος.
afraid; what shall do to me man?
7 Μνημονεύετε τῶν ἡγουμένων ὑμῶν, οἵτινες ἐλάλησαν ὑμῖν
Remember the leaders of you, who spoke to you
τὸν λόγον τοῦ Θεοῦ· ὧν ἀναθεωροῦντες τὴν ἔκβασιν τῆς
the word of God, of whom considering the issue of the
8 ἀναστροφῆς, μιμεῖσθε τὴν πίστιν. Ἰησοῦς Χριστὸς χθὲς καὶ
conduct, imitate (their) faith. Jesus Christ yesterday and
9 σήμερον ὁ αὐτός, καὶ εἰς τοὺς αἰῶνας. διδαχαῖς ποικίλαις καὶ
today (is) the same, even to the ages. teaching By various and
ξέναις μὴ περιφέρεσθε· καλὸν γὰρ χάριτι βεβαιοῦσθαι τὴν
strange not do be carried away; good (it is) for by grace to be confirmed the
καρδίαν, οὐ βρώμασιν, ἐν οἷς οὐκ ὠφελήθησαν οἱ περιπατή-
heart, not by foods, by which not were profited those walking.
10 σαντες. ἔχομεν θυσιαστήριον, ἐξ οὗ φαγεῖν οὐκ ἔχουσιν
We have an altar of which to eat not have
11 ἐξουσίαν οἱ τῇ σκηνῇ λατρεύοντες. ὧν γὰρ εἰσφέρεται ζώων
authority those the tabernacle serving. of what For is brought animals
τὸ αἷμα περὶ ἁμαρτίας εἰς τὰ ἅγια διὰ τοῦ ἀρχιερέως, τούτων
the blood concerning sins into the Holies via the high priest, of these
12 τὰ σώματα κατακαίεται ἔξω τῆς παρεμβολῆς. διὸ καὶ
the bodies are burned outside the camp. Therefore indeed
Ἰησοῦς, ἵνα ἁγιάσῃ διὰ τοῦ ἰδίου αἵματος τὸν λαόν, ἔξω τῆς
Jesus, that He might sanctify through the own blood the people, outside the
13 πύλης ἔπαθε. τοίνυν ἐξερχώμεθα πρὸς αὐτὸν ἔξω τῆς παρ-
gate suffered. So let us go forth to Him outside the
14 εμβολῆς, τὸν ὀνειδισμὸν αὐτοῦ φέροντες. οὐ γὰρ ἔχομεν ὧδε
camp, the reproach of Him bearing. not For we have here
15 μένουσαν πόλιν, ἀλλὰ τὴν μέλλουσαν ἐπιζητοῦμεν. δι'
a continuing city, but the (one) coming we seek. 'Through
αὐτοῦ οὖν ἀναφέρωμεν θυσίαν αἰνέσεως διὰ παντὸς τῷ Θεῷ,
Him, therefore, let us offer up a sacrifice of praise always to God,
τοῦτ' ἔστι, καρπὸν χειλέων ὁμολογούντων τῷ ὀνόματι
this is, (the) fruit of the lips, confessing to the name
16 αὐτοῦ. τῆς δὲ εὐποιΐας καὶ κοινωνίας μὴ ἐπιλανθάνεσθε·
of Him. of the But doing good and sharing, do not be forgetful;
17 τοιαύταις γὰρ θυσίαις εὐαρεστεῖται ὁ Θεός. πείθεσθε τοῖς
with such for sacrifices is well-pleased God. Obey those
ἡγουμένοις ὑμῶν, καὶ ὑπείκετε· αὐτοὶ γὰρ ἀγρυπνοῦσιν
leading of you, and submit to (them), they for watch
ὑπὲρ τῶν ψυχῶν ὑμῶν, ὡς λόγον ἀποδώσοντες· ἵνα μετὰ
for the souls of you, an account giving, that with
χαρᾶς τοῦτο ποιῶσι, καὶ μὴ στενάζοντες· ἀλυσιτελὲς γὰρ
joy this they may do, and not (with) groaning.; profitless for
ὑμῖν τοῦτο.
to you this (would be).
18 Προσεύχεσθε περὶ ἡμῶν· πεποίθαμεν γὰρ ὅτι καλὴν
Pray concerning us, we are persuaded for that a good
συνείδησιν ἔχομεν, ἐν πᾶσι καλῶς θέλοντες ἀναστρέφεσθαι.
conscience we have, in all well desiring to conduct (ourselves).
19 περισσοτέρως δὲ παρακαλῶ τοῦτο ποιῆσαι, ἵνα τάχιον
more abundantly But I exhort (you) this to do, that sooner
ἀποκατασταθῶ ὑμῖν.
I may be restored to you.
20 Ὁ δὲ Θεὸς τῆς εἰρήνης, ὁ ἀναγαγὼν ἐκ νεκρῶν τὸν
the Now God of peace, He having led up out of (the) dead, the

dead, the great Shepherd of
the sheep, in *the* blood of *the*
everlasting covenant, our
Lord Jesus [21] perfect you in
every good work, to do His
will, doing in you that *which*
is pleasing in His sight,
through Jesus Christ, to
whom *be* the glory forever
and ever. Amen.
[22] And I exhort you,
brothers, endure the word of
exhortation, for I indeed
wrote to you by *a* few *words*.
[23] You know the brother,
Timothy, with whom if I
come sooner, having been
freed, I will see you.
[24] Greet all those leading
you, also all the saints. Those
from Italy greet you.
[25] Grace *be* with you all.
Amen.

ποιμένα τῶν προβάτων τὸν μέγαν ἐν αἵματι διαθήκης
Shepherd of the sheep great, in (the) blood of a covenant
21 αἰωνίου, τὸν Κύριον ἡμῶν Ἰησοῦν, καταρτίσαι ὑμᾶς ἐν
eternal, the Lord of us, Jesus, perfect you in
παντὶ ἔργῳ ἀγαθῷ εἰς τὸ ποιῆσαι τὸ θέλημα αὐτοῦ, ποιῶν
every work good, in order to do the will of Him, doing
ἐν ὑμῖν τὸ εὐάρεστον ἐνώπιον αὐτοῦ, διὰ Ἰησοῦ Χριστοῦ·
in you the thing pleasing before Him, through Jesus Christ,
ᾧ ἡ δόξα εἰς τοὺς αἰῶνας τῶν αἰώνων. ἀμήν.
to whom (be) the glory to the ages of the ages. Amen.
22 Παρακαλῶ δὲ ὑμᾶς, ἀδελφοί, ἀνέχεσθε τοῦ λόγου τῆς
I exhort And you, brothers, endure the word
23 παρακλήσεως· καὶ γὰρ διὰ βραχέων ἐπέστειλα ὑμῖν. γινώ-
of exhortation; indeed for through few (words) I wrote to you. Know
σκετε τὸν ἀδελφὸν Τιμόθεον ἀπολελυμένον, μεθ' οὗ, ἐὰν τάχιον
the brother, Timothy, having been freed, with whom, if sooner
ἔρχηται, ὄψομαι ὑμᾶς.
I come, I will see you.
24 Ἀσπάσασθε πάντας τοὺς ἡγουμένους ὑμῶν, καὶ πάντας
Greet all those leading of you, and all
τοὺς ἁγίους. ἀσπάζονται ὑμᾶς οἱ ἀπὸ τῆς Ἰταλίας.
the saints. greet you Those from Italy.
25 Ἡ χάρις μετὰ πάντων ὑμῶν. ἀμήν.
Grace (be) with all of you. Amen.

ΙΑΚΩΒΟΥ
OF JAMES
ΕΠΙΣΤΟΛΗ ΚΑΘΟΛΙΚΗ
EPISTLE GENERAL

KING JAMES II VERSION

THE GENERAL EPISTLE OF JAMES

CHAPTER 1

[1] James, a slave of God and of *the* Lord Jesus Christ, to the twelve tribes in the Dispersion, greeting. [2] My brothers, count *it* all joy when you fall into various temptations,[3] knowing that the proving of your faith works patience. [4] But let patience have *its* perfect work, that you may be perfect and entire, lacking nothing.

[5] But if any of you lacks wisdom, let him ask from God, *who* gives to all freely and with no reproach, and it will be given to him. [6] But let him ask in faith, doubting nothing. For the *one* who doubts is like a wave of *the* sea, being driven by wind and being tossed; [7] for do not let that man suppose that he will receive anything from the Lord— [8] *he is* a double-souled man, not dependable in all his ways.

[9] But let *the* lowly brother rejoice in his lifting up; [10] and the rich one *rejoice* in his humiliation, because he will pass away like *the* flower of *the* grass. [11] For the sun rose with the hot wind and dried up the grass, and its flower fell out, and the beauty of its appearance perished—so also the rich one will fade away in his ways.

[12] Blessed *is the* man who endures temptation, because having been approved he will receive the crown of life which the Lord promised to the ones loving Him.

CHAPTER 1

1 Ἰάκωβος, Θεοῦ καὶ Κυρίου Ἰησοῦ Χριστοῦ δοῦλος, ταῖς
James, of God and of (the) Lord Jesus Christ a slave, to the
δώδεκα φυλαῖς ταῖς ἐν τῇ διασπορᾷ, χαίρειν.
twelve tribes in the dispersion, greeting.
2 Πᾶσαν χαρὰν ἡγήσασθε, ἀδελφοί μου, ὅταν πειρασμοῖς
all joy Count (it), brothers of me, when you fall
3 περιπέσητε ποικίλοις, γινώσκοντες ὅτι τὸ δοκίμιον ὑμῶν τῆς
into various temptations, knowing that the proving of you the
4 πίστεως κατεργάζεται ὑπομονήν· ἡ δὲ ὑπομονὴ ἔργον
faith works patience. And patience work
τέλειον ἐχέτω, ἵνα ἦτε τέλειοι καὶ ὁλόκληροι, ἐν μηδενὶ λειπό-
perfect let it have, that you may be perfect and entire, in nothing lacking.
μενοι.

5 Εἰ δέ τις ὑμῶν λείπεται σοφίας, αἰτείτω παρὰ τοῦ διδόντος
if But any of you lacks wisdom, let him ask from giving
Θεοῦ πᾶσιν ἁπλῶς, καὶ μὴ ὀνειδίζοντος, καὶ δοθήσεται αὐτῷ.
God to all freely, and not reproaching, and it will be given to him.
6 αἰτείτω δὲ ἐν πίστει, μηδὲν διακρινόμενος· ὁ γὰρ διακρινό-
let him ask But in faith, nothing doubting, the (one) for doubting
μενος ἔοικε κλύδωνι θαλάσσης ἀνεμιζομένῳ καὶ ῥιπιζομένῳ.
(is) like a wave of (the) sea, being driven by wind and tossed.
7 μὴ γὰρ οἰέσθω ὁ ἄνθρωπος ἐκεῖνος ὅτι λήψεταί τι παρὰ τοῦ
not For let suppose man that that he will receive any-thing from the
8 Κυρίου. ἀνὴρ δίψυχος ἀκατάστατος ἐν πάσαις ταῖς ὁδοῖς
Lord, a man two-souled undependable in all the ways
αὐτοῦ.
of him.

9 Καυχάσθω δὲ ὁ ἀδελφὸς ὁ ταπεινὸς ἐν τῷ ὕψει αὐτοῦ· ὁ
10 let boast But the brother humble in the height of him; the
δὲ πλούσιος ἐν τῇ ταπεινώσει αὐτοῦ· ὅτι ὡς ἄνθος χόρτου
and the rich one in the humiliation of him, because as a flower of grass
11 παρελεύσεται. ἀνέτειλε γὰρ ὁ ἥλιος σὺν τῷ καύσωνι, καὶ
he will pass away. rose For the sun with the hot wind and
ἐξήρανε τὸν χόρτον, καὶ τὸ ἄνθος αὐτοῦ ἐξέπεσε, καὶ ἡ εὐπρέ-
dried the grass, and the flower of it fell out, and the beauty
πεια τοῦ προσώπου αὐτοῦ ἀπώλετο· οὕτω καὶ ὁ πλούσιος
of the appearance of it perished; so also the rich one
ἐν ταῖς πορείαις αὐτοῦ μαρανθήσεται.
in the goings of him will fade away.
12 Μακάριος ἀνὴρ ὃς ὑπομένει πειρασμόν· ὅτι δόκιμος γενό-
Blessed (the) man who endures temptation, because approved having
μενος λήψεται τὸν στέφανον τῆς ζωῆς, ὃν ἐπηγγείλατο ὁ
become he will receive the crown of life, which promised the
13 Κύριος τοῖς ἀγαπῶσιν αὐτόν. μηδεὶς πειραζόμενος λεγέτω
Lord to those loving Him. no one being tempted Let say,

[13] Let no one being tempted say, I am tempted from God. For God is not tempted by evils, and He tempts no one. [14] But each one is tempted by *his* lusts, having been drawn out and having been seduced *by them.* [15] Then having conceived lust brings forth sin. And sin being fully formed brings forth death. [16] Do not go astray, my beloved brothers, [17] every *act of* giving good and every perfect gift is from above, coming down from the Father of lights, with whom is no change or shadow of turning. [18] Having purposed, He brought us forth by *the* word of truth, for us to be a certain firstfruit of His creatures.

[19] So that, my beloved brothers, let every man be swift to hear, slow to speak, slow to wrath. [20] For *the* wrath of man does not work out *the* righteousness of God. [21] On account of this, having put aside all filthiness and overflowing of evil, in meekness receive the implanted word being able to save your soul. [22] But become doers of *the* word, and not hearers only, deceiving yourselves. [23] Because if anyone *is* a hearer of *the* word, and not a doer, this one is like a man studying his natural face in a mirror, [24] for he studied himself, and has gone away, and immediately *he* forgot what he was like. [25] But the *one* looking into the perfect law of liberty, and continuing in *it,* this one not having become a forgetful hearer, but a doer of *the* work, this one will be blessed in his doing. [26] If anyone thinks to be religious among you, *yet* not bridling his tongue, but deceiving his heart, this one's religion *is* vain. [27] Pure and undefiled religion before God and *the* Father is this: to visit orphans and widows in their afflictionsand to keep oneself unspotted from the world.

ὅτι Ἀπὸ τοῦ Θεοῦ πειράζομαι· ὁ γὰρ Θεὸς ἀπείραστός ἐστι
From God I am tempted. For God not tempted is
14 κακῶν, πειράζει δὲ αὐτὸς οὐδένα· ἕκαστος δὲ πειράζεται,
by evils, tempts and He no one. each one But is tempted
15 ὑπὸ τῆς ἰδίας ἐπιθυμίας ἐξελκόμενος καὶ δελεαζόμενος. εἶτα
by the own lusts being drawn out and being seduced; then
ἡ ἐπιθυμία συλλαβοῦσα τίκτει ἁμαρτίαν· ἡ δὲ ἁμαρτία
lust having conceived produces sin; and sin
16 ἀποτελεσθεῖσα ἀποκύει θάνατον. μὴ πλανᾶσθε, ἀδελφοί
being fully formed brings forth death. Do not go astray, brothers
17 μου ἀγαπητοί. πᾶσα δόσις ἀγαθὴ καὶ πᾶν δώρημα τέλειον
of me beloved. Every giving good and every gift perfect
ἄνωθέν ἐστι, καταβαῖνον ἀπὸ τοῦ πατρὸς τῶν φώτων, παρ'
from above is, coming down from the Father of lights, with
18 ᾧ οὐκ ἔνι παραλλαγή, ἢ τροπῆς ἀποσκίασμα. βουληθεὶς
whom not there is variation or of turning shadow. Having purposed
ἀπεκύησεν ἡμᾶς λόγῳ ἀληθείας, εἰς τὸ εἶναι ἡμᾶς ἀπαρχήν
He brought forth us by a word of truth, for to be us firstfruit
τινα τῶν αὐτοῦ κτισμάτων.
a certain of the of Him creatures.
19 Ὥστε, ἀδελφοί μου ἀγαπητοί, ἔστω πᾶς ἄνθρωπος ταχὺς
So that, , brothers of me beloved, let be every man swift
εἰς τὸ ἀκοῦσαι, βραδὺς εἰς τὸ λαλῆσαι, βραδὺς εἰς ὀργήν·
to hear, slow to speak, slow to wrath;
20 ὀργὴ γὰρ ἀνδρὸς δικαιοσύνην Θεοῦ οὐ κατεργάζεται. διὸ
(the) wrath for of man (the) righteousness of God not works. Therefore,
21 ἀποθέμενοι πᾶσαν ῥυπαρίαν καὶ περισσείαν κακίας, ἐν πραΰ-
putting away all filthiness and overflowing of evil, in meek-
τητι, δέξασθε τὸν ἔμφυτον λόγον, τὸν δυνάμενον σῶσαι τὰς
ness receive the implanted word being able to save the
22 ψυχὰς ὑμῶν. γίνεσθε δὲ ποιηταὶ λόγου, καὶ μὴ μόνον
soul of you. become And doers of the word, and not only
23 ἀκροαταί, παραλογιζόμενοι ἑαυτούς. ὅτι εἴ τις ἀκροατὴς
hearers, deceiving yourselves. Because if anyone a hearer
λόγου ἐστὶ καὶ οὐ ποιητής, οὗτος ἔοικεν ἀνδρὶ κατανοοῦντι
of (the) word is, and not a doer, this one is like a man perceiving
24 τὸ πρόσωπον τῆς γενέσεως αὐτοῦ ἐν ἐσόπτρῳ· κατενόησε
the face of the birth of him in a mirror; he perceived
γὰρ ἑαυτὸν καὶ ἀπελήλυθε, καὶ εὐθέως ἐπελάθετο ὁποῖος ἦν.
for himself and has gone away, and immediately forgot what sort he was.
25 ὁ δὲ παρακύψας εἰς νόμον τέλειον τὸν τῆς ἐλευθερίας καὶ
he But having looked into law perfect the of freedom, and
παραμείνας, οὗτος οὐκ ἀκροατὴς ἐπιλησμονῆς γενόμενος
continuing, this one not a hearer of forgetfulness becoming,
ἀλλὰ ποιητὴς ἔργου, οὗτος μακάριος ἐν τῇ ποιήσει αὐτοῦ
but a doer of (the) work, this one blessed in the doing of him
26 ἔσται. εἴ τις δοκεῖ θρῆσκος εἶναι ἐν ὑμῖν, μὴ χαλιναγωγῶν
will be. If anyone thinks religious to be among you, not bridling
γλῶσσαν αὐτοῦ, ἀλλ' ἀπατῶν καρδίαν αὐτοῦ, τούτου
the tongue of him, but deceiving (the) heart of himself, this one's
27 μάταιος ἡ θρησκεία. θρησκεία καθαρὰ καὶ ἀμίαντος παρὰ
vain the religion (is). religion Clean and undefiled before
τῷ Θεῷ καὶ πατρὶ αὕτη ἐστίν, ἐπισκέπτεσθαι ὀρφανοὺς καὶ
God and Father this is, to visit orphans and
χήρας ἐν τῇ θλίψει αὐτῶν, ἄσπιλον ἑαυτὸν τηρεῖν ἀπὸ τοῦ
widows in the affliction of them, unspotted himself to keep from the

CHAPTER 2

[1] My brothers, do not with partiality to persons have the faith of our Lord Jesus Christ, the *Lord* of glory. [2] for if a gold-fingered man in splendid clothing comes into your synagogue, and a poor one in shabby clothing also comes in; [3] and you look on the *one* wearing the splendid clothing, and say to him, You sit here comfortably; and to the poor one you say, You stand there, or, Sit here under my footstool; [4] did you not also make a difference among yourselves and became judges *with* evil thoughts? [5] Hear, my beloved brothers, did not God choose the poor of this world *to be* rich in faith, and heirs of the kingdom which He promised to the *ones* loving Him? [6] But you dishonored the poor one. Do not the rich ones oppress you, and they drag you to judgment seats? [7] Do they not blaspheme the good Name called on you? [8] If you truly fulfill *the* royal law according to the Scripture, "You shall love your neighbor as yourself," you do well. [9] But if you have partiality to persons, you work sin, having been found guilty as transgressers by the law. [10] For whoever shall keep all the law, but stumbles in one, he has become guilty of all. [11] For He who said, "You shall not commit adultery," also said, "You shall not murder." But if you do not commit adultery, but commit murder, you have become a transgressor of *the* law. [12] So speak and so do as being about to be judged by *the* law of liberty. [13] For Judgment *will be* without mercy to those not doing mercy. And mercy rejoices over judgment.

[14] My brothers, what *is* the gain if anyone says *he* has faith, but he does not have works? Is faith able to save him? [15] But if a brother or a

κόσμου.
world.

CHAPTER 2

1 Ἀδελφοί μου, μὴ ἐν προσωποληψίαις ἔχετε τὴν πίστιν
Brothers of me, not in respects of persons have the faith
2 τοῦ Κυρίου ἡμῶν Ἰησοῦ Χριστοῦ τῆς δόξης. ἐὰν γὰρ εἰσ-
the Lord of us, Jesus Christ, of the (Lord) of glory if For
έλθῃ εἰς τὴν συναγωγὴν ὑμῶν ἀνὴρ χρυσοδακτύλιος ἐν
comes into the synagogue of you a man gold-fingered, in
ἐσθῆτι λαμπρᾷ, εἰσέλθῃ δὲ καὶ πτωχὸς ἐν ῥυπαρᾷ ἐσθῆτι,
clothing fancy, comes in and also a poor one in shabby clothing,
3 καὶ ἐπιβλέψητε ἐπὶ τὸν φοροῦντα τὴν ἐσθῆτα τὴν λαμπράν,
and you look on the (one) wearing the clothing fancy,
καὶ εἴπητε αὐτῷ, Σὺ κάθου ὧδε καλῶς, καὶ τῷ πτωχῷ
and say to him, You sit here well, and to the poor one
εἴπητε, Σὺ στῆθι ἐκεῖ, ἢ κάθου ὧδε ὑπὸ τὸ ὑποπόδιόν μου·
you say, You stand there, or sit here under the footstool of me,
4 καὶ οὐ διεκρίθητε ἐν ἑαυτοῖς, καὶ ἐγένεσθε κριταὶ διαλογισμῶν
even did make a not difference among yourselves, and became judges thoughts
5 πονηρῶν; ἀκούσατε, ἀδελφοί μου ἀγαπητοί. οὐχ ὁ Θεὸς
of evil? Hear, brothers of me beloved, Did not God
ἐξελέξατο τοὺς πτωχοὺς τοῦ κόσμου τούτου, πλουσίους
choose the poor world of this rich
ἐν πίστει, καὶ κληρονόμους τῆς βασιλείας ἧς ἐπηγγείλατο
in faith, and heirs of the kingdom which He promised
6 τοῖς ἀγαπῶσιν αὐτόν; ὑμεῖς δὲ ἠτιμάσατε τὸν πτωχόν. οὐχ
to those loving Him, you But dishonored the poor one. Do not
οἱ πλούσιοι καταδυναστεύουσιν ὑμῶν, καὶ αὐτοὶ ἕλκουσιν
the rich ones oppress you, and they drag
7 ὑμᾶς εἰς κριτήρια; οὐκ αὐτοὶ βλασφημοῦσι τὸ καλὸν ὄνομα
you to judgment seats? Do not they blaspheme the good name
8 τὸ ἐπικληθὲν ἐφ' ὑμᾶς; εἰ μέντοι νόμον τελεῖτε βασιλικόν,
called upon you? If indeed law you fulfill a royal,
κατὰ τὴν γραφήν, Ἀγαπήσεις τὸν πλησίον σου ὡς σεαυ-
according to the Scripture: You shall love the neighbor of you as your-
9 τόν, καλῶς ποιεῖτε· εἰ δὲ προσωποληπτεῖτε, ἁμαρτίαν ἐργά-
self, well you do; if but you respect persons, sin you work,
10 ζεσθε, ἐλεγχόμενοι ὑπὸ τοῦ νόμου ὡς παραβάται. ὅστις γὰρ
being reproved by the law as transgressors, (he) who For
ὅλον τὸν νόμον τηρήσει, πταίσει δὲ ἐν ἑνί, γέγονε πάντων
all the law keeps, stumbles but in one, he has become of all
11 ἔνοχος. ὁ γὰρ εἰπών, Μὴ μοιχεύσῃς, εἶπε καί, Μὴ φονεύσῃς·
guilty. he For saying, Do not do adultery, said also, Do not murder;
εἰ δὲ οὐ μοιχεύσεις, φονεύσεις δέ, γέγονας παραβάτης νόμου.
if but not you do adultery, murder but, you have become a transgressor of law
12 οὕτω λαλεῖτε καὶ οὕτω ποιεῖτε, ὡς διὰ νόμου ἐλευθερίας
So speak and so do, as through a law of freedom
13 μέλλοντες κρίνεσθαι. ἡ γὰρ κρίσις ἀνίλεως τῷ μὴ ποιήσαντι
being about to be judged. the For Judgment will be unmerciful to those not doing
ἔλεος· καὶ κατακαυχᾶται ἔλεος κρίσεως.
mercy; and exults over mercy judgment.
14 Τί τὸ ὄφελος, ἀδελφοί μου, ἐὰν πίστιν λέγῃ τις ἔχειν, ἔργα
What (is) the profit, brothers of me, if faith says anyone to have, works
15 δὲ μὴ ἔχῃ; μὴ δύναται ἡ πίστις σῶσαι αὐτόν; ἐὰν δὲ
but not he has? Is able the faith to save him? if But

sister is naked and may be lacking in daily food, [16] and anyone may say to them, Go in peace, be warmed and filled—but does not give them the things the body needs—what gain *is it*? [17] So also faith, if it does not have works, is dead by itself. [18] But someone will say, You have faith, and I have works. Show me your faith apart from your works, and I will show you my faith by my works. [19] You believe that God is one. You do well; even the demons believe and shudder. [20] But will you know, O vain man, that faith apart from works is dead? [21] Was not our father Abraham justified by works, offering up his son Isaac on the altar? [22] You see that faith worked with his works, and by the works the faith was made complete. [23] And the Scripture was fulfilled, saying, "And Abraham believed God, and it was counted to him for righteousness; and he was called, Friend of God." [24] You see, then, that a man is justified by works, and not by faith only. [25] But in the same way Rahab the harlot was also justified by works, having received the messengers, and sending *them* out by another way. [26] For as the body is dead apart from *the* spirit, so also faith is dead apart from works.

ἀδελφὸς ἢ ἀδελφὴ γυμνοὶ ὑπάρχωσι καὶ λειπόμενοι ὦσι
a brother or a sister naked be, and lacking may be
16 τῆς ἐφημέρου τροφῆς, εἴπῃ δέ τις αὐτοῖς ἐξ ὑμῶν, Ὑπάγετε
of daily food, says and anyone to them of you, Go
ἐν εἰρήνῃ, θερμαίνεσθε καὶ χορτάζεσθε, μὴ δῶτε δὲ αὐτοῖς
in peace, be warmed and filled, not you give but them
17 τὰ ἐπιτήδεια τοῦ σώματος, τί τὸ ὄφελος; οὕτω καὶ ἡ πίστις,
the necessities of the body, what (is) the profit? So indeed faith,
18 ἐὰν μὴ ἔργα ἔχῃ, νεκρά ἐστι καθ' ἑαυτήν. ἀλλ' ἐρεῖ τις, Σὺ
if not works it has, dead is by itself. But will say one, You
πίστιν ἔχεις, κἀγὼ ἔργα ἔχω· δεῖξόν μοι τὴν πίστιν σου
faith have, and I works have: show me the faith of you
χωρὶς τῶν ἔργων σου, κἀγὼ δείξω σοι ἐκ τῶν ἔργων μου
without the works of you, and I will show you by the works of me
19 τὴν πίστιν μου. σὺ πιστεύεις ὅτι ὁ Θεὸς εἷς ἐστί· καλῶς
the faith of me. You believe that God one is? well
20 ποιεῖς· καὶ τὰ δαιμόνια πιστεύουσι, καὶ φρίσσουσι. θέλεις
You do; also the demons believe and tremble. are you willing
δὲ γνῶναι, ὦ ἄνθρωπε κενέ, ὅτι ἡ πίστις χωρὶς τῶν ἔργων
But to know, O man vain, that faith without works
21 νεκρά ἐστιν; Ἀβραὰμ ὁ πατὴρ ἡμῶν οὐκ ἐξ ἔργων ἐδικαιώθη,
dead is? Abraham the father of us not by works Was justified
ἀνενέγκας Ἰσαὰκ τὸν υἱὸν αὐτοῦ ἐπὶ τὸ θυσιαστήριον;
offering up Isaac the son of him on the altar?
22 βλέπεις ὅτι ἡ πίστις συνήργει τοῖς ἔργοις αὐτοῦ, καὶ ἐκ τῶν
You see that faith worked with the works of him, and by the
23 ἔργων ἡ πίστις ἐτελειώθη; καὶ ἐπληρώθη ἡ γραφὴ ἡ
works the faith was perfected, and was fulfilled the Scripture,
λέγουσα, Ἐπίστευσε δὲ Ἀβραὰμ τῷ Θεῷ, καὶ ἐλογίσθη
saying, believed And Abraham God, and it was counted
24 αὐτῷ εἰς δικαιοσύνην, καὶ φίλος Θεοῦ ἐκλήθη. ὁρᾶτε τοίνυν
to him for righteousness, and friend of God he was called. You see then
ὅτι ἐξ ἔργων δικαιοῦται ἄνθρωπος, καὶ οὐκ ἐκ πίστεως μόνον.
that by works is justified a man, and not by faith only.
25 ὁμοίως δὲ καὶ Ῥαὰβ ἡ πόρνη οὐκ ἐξ ἔργων ἐδικαιώθη, ὑποδε-
likewise And also Rahab the harlot not by works was justified, enter-
ξαμένη τοὺς ἀγγέλους, καὶ ἑτέρᾳ ὁδῷ ἐκβαλοῦσα; ὥσπερ
taining the messengers, and by another way sending out? as
26 γὰρ τὸ σῶμα χωρὶς πνεύματος νεκρόν ἐστιν, οὕτω καὶ ἡ
For the body without spirit dead is, so also
πίστις χωρὶς τῶν ἔργων νεκρά ἐστι.
faith without works dead is.

CHAPTER 3

[1] My brothers, do not be many teachers, knowing that we will receive greater judgment. [2] For we all stumble *in* many *ways*. If anyone does not stumble in word, this *one is* a mature man, able also to bridle the whole body. [3] Behold, we put bits in the mouths of the horses, for them to obey us; and we turn about their whole body.

CHAPTER 3

1 Μὴ πολλοὶ διδάσκαλοι γίνεσθε, ἀδελφοί μου, εἰδότες ὅτι
not many teachers Become, brothers of me, knowing that
2 μεῖζον κρίμα ληψόμεθα. πολλὰ γὰρ πταίομεν ἅπαντες. εἴ
greater judgment we will receive. (in) many For (ways) we stumble all. If
τις ἐν λόγῳ οὐ πταίει, οὗτος τέλειος ἀνήρ, δυνατὸς χαλιν-
anyone in word not stumbles, this (is) a mature man, able to
3 αγωγῆσαι καὶ ὅλον τὸ σῶμα. ἰδού, τῶν ἵππων τοὺς χαλι-
bridle also the whole body. Behold, of the horses the bits
νοὺς εἰς τὰ στόματα βάλλομεν πρὸς τὸ πείθεσθαι αὐτοὺς
in the mouths we put, for to obey them
4 ἡμῖν, καὶ ὅλον τὸ σῶμα αὐτῶν μετάγομεν. ἰδού, καὶ τὰ
us, and whole the body of them we turn about. Behold, also the

4 Behold, the ships also, being so great, and being driven by violent winds, *they are* directed by a very small rudder, where the impulse of the *one* steering purposes. 5 So also the tongue is a little member, and boasts great things. Behold, how little a fire kindles how large a forest! 6 And the tongue *is* a fire, the world of iniquity. So the tongue is set among our members, spotting all the body, and inflaming the course of nature, and having been inflamed by Hell. 7 For every species of beasts, both of birds, of creeping things, and of sea-animals, is tamed, and has been tamed by the human species; 8 but no one of men is able to tame the tongue—it is an evil that cannot be restrained, full of death-dealing poison. 9 By this we bless God and the Father, and by this we curse men having come into being according to *the* image of God. 10 Out of the same mouth comes forth blessing and cursing. My brothers, it is not fitting *for* these things to be so. 11 *Does* the fountain out of the same hole send forth the sweet and the bitter? 12 My brothers, is a fig-tree able to produce olives, or a vine figs? So neither *can* a fountain produce *both* salt and sweet water.

13 Who is wise and knowing among you? Let him show his works by *his* good behavior, in meekness of wisdom. 14 But if you have bitter jealousy and contention in your heart, do not boast and lie against the truth. 15 This is not the wisdom coming down from above, but *is* earthly, beastly, devilish. 16 For where jealousy and contention *are*, there *is* confusion and every foul deed. 17 But the wisdom from above is firstly truly pure, then peaceable, forbearing, yielding, full of mercy and of good fruits, not partial and not pretended. 18 And *the* fruit of

πλοῖα, τηλικαῦτα ὄντα, καὶ ὑπὸ σκληρῶν ἀνέμων ἐλαυνό-
ships so great being, and by hard winds being
μενα, μετάγεται ὑπὸ ἐλαχίστου πηδαλίου, ὅπου ἂν ἡ ὁρμὴ
driven, is directed by a very little rudder, where the impulse
5 τοῦ εὐθύνοντος βούληται. οὕτω καὶ ἡ γλῶσσα μικρὸν μέλος
of the (one) steering purposes. So also the tongue a little member
ἐστί, καὶ μεγαλαυχεῖ. ἰδού, ὀλίγον πῦρ ἡλίκην ὕλην
is, and great things boasts. Behold, how little a fire how great wood
6 ἀνάπτει. καὶ ἡ γλῶσσα πῦρ, ὁ κόσμος τῆς ἀδικίας· οὕτως
kindles; and the tongue (is) a fire, the world of iniquity; so
ἡ γλῶσσα καθίσταται ἐν τοῖς μέλεσιν ἡμῶν, ἡ σπιλοῦσα
the tongue is set among the members of us, spotting
ὅλον τὸ σῶμα, καὶ φλογίζουσα τὸν τροχὸν τῆς γενέσεως,
all the body, and inflaming the course of nature,
7 καὶ φλογιζομένη ὑπὸ τῆς γεέννης. πᾶσα γὰρ φύσις θηρίων
and being inflamed by Gehenna. every For nature of beasts
τε καὶ πετεινῶν, ἑρπετῶν τε καὶ ἐναλίων, δαμάζεται καὶ
both and of birds of reptiles both and of sea animals, is tamed and
8 δεδάμασται τῇ φύσει τῇ ἀνθρωπίνῃ· τὴν δὲ γλῶσσαν
has been tamed by the nature human; the but tongue
οὐδεὶς δύναται ἀνθρώπων δαμάσαι· ἀκατάσχετον κακόν,
no one is able of men to tame; (it is) an an unrestrainable evil,
9 μεστὴ ἰοῦ θανατηφόρου. ἐν αὐτῇ εὐλογοῦμεν τὸν Θεὸν καὶ
full of poison death-dealing. By this we bless God and
πατέρα, καὶ ἐν αὐτῇ καταρώμεθα τοὺς ἀνθρώπους τοὺς καθ'
(the) Father, and by this we curse men according to
10 ὁμοίωσιν Θεοῦ γεγονότας· ἐκ τοῦ αὐτοῦ στόματος ἐξέρχεται
(the) image of God having come into being, out of the same mouth comes forth
εὐλογία καὶ κατάρα. οὐ χρή, ἀδελφοί μου, ταῦτα οὕτω
blessing and cursing. not It is fitting, brothers of me, these things so
11 γίνεσθαι. μήτι ἡ πηγὴ ἐκ τῆς αὐτῆς ὀπῆς βρύει τὸ γλυκὺ
to be. (Does) the fountain out of the same hole send forth the sweet
12 καὶ τὸ πικρόν; μὴ δύναται, ἀδελφοί μου, συκῆ ἐλαίας
and the bitter? Is able, brothers of me, a fig-tree olives
ποιῆσαι, ἢ ἄμπελος σῦκα; οὕτως οὐδεμία πηγὴ ἁλυκὸν καὶ
to produce, or a vine figs? So neither a fountain salt and
γλυκὺ ποιῆσαι ὕδωρ.
sweet to produce water.

13 Τίς σοφὸς καὶ ἐπιστήμων ἐν ὑμῖν; δειξάτω ἐκ τῆς καλῆς
Who (is) wise and knowing among you? Let him show by the good
14 ἀναστροφῆς τὰ ἔργα αὐτοῦ ἐν πραΰτητι σοφίας. εἰ δὲ ζῆλον
behavior the works of him in meekness of wisdom. if But jealousy
πικρὸν ἔχετε καὶ ἐρίθειαν ἐν τῇ καρδίᾳ ὑμῶν, μὴ κατα-
bitter you have, and contention in the heart of you, do not exult
15 καυχᾶσθε καὶ ψεύδεσθε κατὰ τῆς ἀληθείας. οὐκ ἔστιν αὕτη ἡ
over and lie against the truth. not is This the
σοφία ἄνωθεν κατερχομένη, ἀλλ' ἐπίγειος, ψυχική, δαι-
wisdom from above coming down, but (is) earthly, beastly
16 μονιώδης. ὅπου γὰρ ζῆλος καὶ ἐρίθεια, ἐκεῖ ἀκαταστασία καὶ
devilish. where For jealousy and contention, there (is) confusion and
17 πᾶν φαῦλον πρᾶγμα. ἡ δὲ ἄνωθεν σοφία πρῶτον μὲν ἁγνή
every foul deed. the But from above wisdom firstly truly pure
ἐστιν, ἔπειτα εἰρηνική, ἐπιεικής, εὐπειθής, μεστὴ ἐλέους καὶ
is, then peaceable, forbearing, yielding, full of mercy and
18 καρπῶν ἀγαθῶν, ἀδιάκριτος καὶ ἀνυπόκριτος. καρπὸς δὲ τῆς
fruits of good, not partial and not pretended. (the) fruit And

righteousness is sown in peace for those making peace.

CHAPTER 4

[1] From where do wars and fightings among you *come*? *Is it* not from this, from your lusts warring in your members? [2] You desire and do not have. You murder, and are jealous, and are not able to obtain. You fight and you war, and you do not have, because you do not ask *God*. [3] You ask, and do not receive, because you ask wrongly, in order that you may spend on your lusts. [4] Adulterers and adulteresses! Do you not know that the friendship of the world is enmity *with* God? Whoever, then, purposes to be a friend of the world is shown to be an enemy of God. [5] Or do you think that vainly the Scripture says, "The spirit which has dwelt in us yearns with envy"? [6] But He gives greater grace. Because of this it says, "God sets *Himself* against proud ones; but He gives grace to humble ones." [7] Then be subject to God. Resist the Devil, and he will flee from you. [8] Draw near to God, and He will draw near to you. Cleanse your hands, sinners. And purify *your* hearts, double-minded ones: [9] be distressed, and mourn, and weep. Let your laughter be turned to mourning, and *your* joy into shame. [10] Be humbled before the Lord, and He will exalt you.

[11] Do not speak against one another, brothers. He that speaks against a brother, and *is* judging a brother, *he* speaks against law, and judges law. But if you judge law, you are not a doer of law, but a judge. [12] One is the Lawgiver, who is able to save and to destroy. Who are you who judges another?

[13] Come now, those saying, Today or tomorrow we will go into this city, and we will spend one year there, and we will trade and will make a profit; [14] who do not

δικαιοσύνης ἐν εἰρήνῃ σπείρεται τοῖς ποιοῦσιν εἰρήνην.
of righteousness in peace is sown for those making peace.

CHAPTER 4

1 Πόθεν πόλεμοι καὶ μάχαι ἐν ὑμῖν; οὐκ ἐντεῦθεν, ἐκ τῶν
From where (come) wars and fights among you? Not from this, from the
ἡδονῶν ὑμῶν τῶν στρατευομένων ἐν τοῖς μέλεσιν ὑμῶν;
lusts of you warring in the members of you?
2 ἐπιθυμεῖτε, καὶ οὐκ ἔχετε· φονεύετε καὶ ζηλοῦτε, καὶ οὐ δύνα-
You desire, and not have; you murder and are jealous, and not are
σθε ἐπιτυχεῖν· μάχεσθε καὶ πολεμεῖτε, οὐκ ἔχετε δέ, διὰ τὸ μὴ
able to obtain; you fight and you war. do not you have and, because not
3 αἰτεῖσθαι ὑμᾶς· αἰτεῖτε, καὶ οὐ λαμβάνετε, διότι κακῶς
ask you; you ask, and not you receive, because wrongly
4 αἰτεῖσθε, ἵνα ἐν ταῖς ἡδοναῖς ὑμῶν δαπανήσητε. μοιχοὶ καὶ
you ask, that on the lusts of you you may waste. Adulterers and
μοιχαλίδες, οὐκ οἴδατε ὅτι ἡ φιλία τοῦ κόσμου ἔχθρα τοῦ
adulteresses, do not you know that the friendship of the world enmity
Θεοῦ ἐστίν; ὃς ἂν οὖν βουληθῇ φίλος εἶναι τοῦ κόσμου,
of God is? Whoever, therefore, purposes a friend to be of the world,
5 ἐχθρὸς τοῦ Θεοῦ καθίσταται. ἢ δοκεῖτε ὅτι κενῶς ἡ γραφὴ
an enemy of God is shown to be. Or do you think that vainly the Scripture
λέγει, Πρὸς φθόνον ἐπιποθεῖ τὸ πνεῦμα ὃ κατῴκησεν ἐν ἡμῖν
says: to envy yearns 'The spirit which has dwelt in us?
6 μείζονα δὲ δίδωσι χάριν· διὸ λέγει, Ὁ Θεὸς ὑπερηφάνοις
greater But He gives grace, therefore it says: God proud ones
7 ἀντιτάσσεται, ταπεινοῖς δὲ δίδωσι χάριν. ὑποτάγητε οὖν
sets (Himself) against, to humble ones but He gives grace. Be subject, therefore
τῷ Θεῷ· ἀντίστητε τῷ διαβόλῳ, καὶ φεύξεται ἀφ᾽ ὑμῶν.
to God; oppose the devil, and he will flee from you.
8 ἐγγίσατε τῷ Θεῷ, καὶ ἐγγιεῖ ὑμῖν· καθαρίσατε χεῖρας,
Draw near to God, and He will draw near to you. Cleanse (the) hands,
9 ἁμαρτωλοί, καὶ ἁγνίσατε καρδίας, δίψυχοι. ταλαιπωρή-
sinners, and purify (your) hearts, two-souled ones. Be distressed
σατε καὶ πενθήσατε καὶ κλαύσατε· ὁ γέλως ὑμῶν εἰς πένθος
and mourn and weep, the laughter of you to mourning
10 μεταστραφήτω, καὶ ἡ χαρὰ εἰς κατήφειαν. ταπεινώθητε
let it be turned, and the joy to shame. Be humbled
ἐνώπιον τοῦ Κυρίου, καὶ ὑψώσει ὑμᾶς.
before the Lord, and He will exalt you.

11 Μὴ καταλαλεῖτε ἀλλήλων, ἀδελφοί. ὁ καταλαλῶν
Do not speak against one another, brothers. He speaking against
ἀδελφοῦ, καὶ κρίνων τὸν ἀδελφὸν αὐτοῦ, καταλαλεῖ νόμου,
a brother, and judging the brother of him, speaks against law,
καὶ κρίνει νόμον· εἰ δὲ νόμον κρίνεις, οὐκ εἶ ποιητὴς νόμου,
and judges law; if and law you judge, not you are a doer of law,
12 ἀλλὰ κριτής. εἷς ἐστὶν ὁ νομοθέτης, ὁ δυνάμενος σῶσαι καὶ
but a judge. One is the Lawgiver, who is able to save and
ἀπολέσαι· σὺ τίς εἶ ὃς κρίνεις τὸν ἕτερον;
to destroy; you who are who judges the other?

13 Ἄγε νῦν οἱ λέγοντες, Σήμερον ἢ αὔριον πορευσόμεθα εἰς
Come now those saying, Today or tomorrow we will go into
τήνδε τὴν πόλιν, καὶ ποιήσομεν ἐκεῖ ἐνιαυτὸν ἕνα, καὶ
this city, and we will spend there year one, and
14 ἐμπορευσόμεθα, καὶ κερδήσομεν· οἵτινες οὐκ ἐπίστασθε τὸ
we will trade and will make a profit; who not know of the

know of the morrow; for what *is* your life? For it is a mist, which for a little *while* appears, and then disappears. [15]Instead of you saying, If the Lord wills, even we will live, and we will do this or that; [16]but now you boast in your presumptions. All such boasting is evil. [17]Therefore, to *anyone* knowing to do good, and not doing *it*, it is sin to him.

CHAPTER 5

[1]Come now, rich ones, weep, howling over your hardships coming on. [2]Your riches have rotted, and your garments have become moth-eaten. [3]Your gold and silver have rusted over, and their poison will be a testimony to you, and will eat your flesh as fire. You heaped treasure in *the* last days. [4]Behold, the wages of the workmen reaping your fields cries out, being kept back by you. And the cries of the ones reaping have entered into the ears of *the* Lord of Hosts. [5]You lived luxuriously on the earth, and lived in self-gratification; you nourished your hearts as in a day of slaughter; [6]you condemned; you murdered the righteous—he does not resist you.

[7]Therefore, brothers, be long-suffering until the coming of the Lord. Behold, the farmer awaits the precious fruit of the earth, being long-suffering over it until it may receive *the* early and the latter rain. [8]You also be long-suffering. Set your hearts firmly, because the coming of the Lord has drawn near. [9]Do not murmur against one another, brothers, that you not be condemned. Behold, *the* Judge stands before the door. [10]My brothers, *as* an example of suffering ill, and of long-suffering, take the prophets who spoke in the name of *the* Lord. [11]Behold, we call those blessed who

τῆς αὔριον. ποία γὰρ ἡ ζωὴ ὑμῶν ; ἀτμὶς γάρ ἐστιν ἡ πρὸς
morrow; what for the life of you; a mist for it is, which for
15 ὀλίγον φαινομένη, ἔπειτα δὲ ἀφανιζομένη. ἀντὶ τοῦ λέγειν
a little (while) appears, then and disappears. Instead of saying
ὑμᾶς, Ἐὰν ὁ Κύριος θελήσῃ, καὶ ζήσομεν, καὶ ποιήσομεν
you, If the Lord wills, even we will live, and we will do
16 τοῦτο ἢ ἐκεῖνο. νῦν δὲ καυχᾶσθε ἐν ταῖς ἀλαζονείαις ὑμῶν·
this or that. now But you boast in the vauntings of you;
17 πᾶσα καύχησις τοιαύτη πονηρά ἐστιν. εἰδότι οὖν καλὸν
all boastings such evil is. to (one) knowing Then good
ποιεῖν καὶ μὴ ποιοῦντι, ἁμαρτία αὐτῷ ἐστίν.
to do, and not doing (it), sin to him it is.

CHAPTER 5

1 Ἄγε νῦν οἱ πλούσιοι, κλαύσατε ὀλολύζοντες ἐπὶ ταῖς
Come now rich ones, weep, crying aloud over the
2 ταλαιπωρίαις ὑμῶν ταῖς ἐπερχομέναις. ὁ πλοῦτος ὑμῶν
hardships of you coming upon. The riches of you
3 σέσηπε, καὶ τὰ ἱμάτια ὑμῶν σητόβρωτα γέγονεν· ὁ χρυσὸς
have rotted, and the garments of you moth-eaten have become; the gold
ὑμῶν καὶ ὁ ἄργυρος κατίωται, καὶ ὁ ἰὸς αὐτῶν εἰς μαρτύ-
of you and the silver have rusted over, and the poison of them for a test-
ριον ὑμῖν ἔσται, καὶ φάγεται τὰς σάρκας ὑμῶν ὡς πῦρ.
imony to you will be, and will eat the flesh of you as fire.
4 ἐθησαυρίσατε ἐν ἐσχάταις ἡμέραις. ἰδού, ὁ μισθὸς τῶν
You heaped treasure in (the) last days. Behold, the wages of the
ἐργατῶν τῶν ἀμησάντων τὰς χώρας ὑμῶν, ὁ ἀπεστερη-
workmen having reaped the fields of you being kept
μένος ἀφ' ὑμῶν, κράζει· καὶ αἱ βοαὶ τῶν θερισάντων εἰς τὰ
back from you cries out, and the cries of those having reaped into the
5 ὦτα Κυρίου Σαβαὼθ εἰσεληλύθασιν. ἐτρυφήσατε ἐπὶ τῆς
ears of (the) Lord of Hosts have entered. You lived luxuriously on the
γῆς καὶ ἐσπαταλήσατε· ἐθρέψατε τὰς καρδίας ὑμῶν ὡς ἐν
earth, and lived riotously, you nourished the hearts of you as in
6 ἡμέρᾳ σφαγῆς. κατεδικάσατε, ἐφονεύσατε τὸν δίκαιον· οὐκ
a day of slaughter. You condemned, you murdered the righteous; not
ἀντιτάσσεται ὑμῖν.
he resists you.

7 Μακροθυμήσατε οὖν, ἀδελφοί, ἕως τῆς παρουσίας τοῦ
Be longsuffering, therefore, brothers, until the presence of the
Κυρίου. ἰδού, ὁ γεωργὸς ἐκδέχεται τὸν τίμιον καρπὸν τῆς
Lord. Behold, the farmer awaits the precious fruit of the
γῆς, μακροθυμῶν ἐπ' αὐτῷ, ἕως ἂν λάβῃ ὑετὸν πρώϊμον
earth, being longsuffering over it until it may receive rain (the) early
8 καὶ ὄψιμον. μακροθυμήσατε καὶ ὑμεῖς, στηρίξατε τὰς καρδίας
and latter. Be longsuffering also you, establish the hearts
9 ὑμῶν, ὅτι ἡ παρουσία τοῦ Κυρίου ἤγγικε. μὴ στενάζετε κατ'
of you, because the coming of the Lord has drawn near. not Murmur against
ἀλλήλων, ἀδελφοί, ἵνα μὴ κατακριθῆτε· ἰδού, ὁ κριτὴς πρὸ
one another, brothers, that not you be judged; behold, the Judge before
10 τῶν θυρῶν ἕστηκεν. ὑπόδειγμα λάβετε τῆς κακοπαθείας,
the door stands. an example Take of suffering ill,
ἀδελφοί μου, καὶ τῆς μακροθυμίας, τοὺς προφήτας οἳ
brothers of me, and of longsuffering: the prophets who
11 ἐλάλησαν τῷ ὀνόματι Κυρίου. ἰδού, μακαρίζομεν τοὺς
spoke in the name of (the) Lord. Behold, we count blessed those

endure. You have heard *of*
the patience of Job, and you
saw the end of *the* Lord, that
the Lord is full of tender
mercy and pity.
12 But before all things, my
brothers, do not swear,
neither by the heaven, nor by
the earth, nor any other
oath. But let your yes be yes,
and the no, no, that you may
not fall under judgment.
13 Does anyone suffer ill
among you? Let him pray. Is
anyone cheerful? Let him
praise. 14 Is any among you
sick? Let him call the elders of
the church, and let them pray
over him, anointing him with
oil in the name of the Lord.
15 And the prayer of faith will
cure those being sick, and
the Lord will raise him up.
And if he may have committed sin, it will be forgiven
him.
16 Confess faults to one
another, and pray for one
another, that you may be
healed. *The* prayer of a
righteous one is very powerful, having been made effective. 17 Elijah was a man of
like feeling to us, and he
prayed in prayer *for it* not to
rain; and it did not rain on the
earth three years and six
months. 18 And he prayed
again, and the heaven gave
rain, and the earth caused its
fruit to sprout.
19 Brothers, if anyone
among you goes astray from
the truth, and anyone turns
back, 20 know that the *one*
turning a sinner from *the*
error of his way will save *the*
soul from death, and will hide
a multitude of sins.

ὑπομένοντας· τὴν ὑπομονὴν Ἰὼβ ἠκούσατε, καὶ τὸ τέλος
enduring. the patience of Job You heard (of), and the end
Κυρίου εἴδετε, ὅτι πολύσπλαγχνός ἐστιν ὁ Κύριος καὶ
of (the) Lord you saw, that very compassionate is the Lord and
οἰκτίρμων.
pitying.
12 Πρὸ πάντων δέ, ἀδελφοί μου, μὴ ὀμνύετε, μήτε τὸν
before all things But, brothers of me, do not swear, neither by the
οὐρανόν, μήτε τὴν γῆν, μήτε ἄλλον τινὰ ὅρκον· ἤτω δὲ
heaven, nor by the earth, nor other any oath; let be but
ὑμῶν τὸ ναί, ναί, καὶ τὸ οὔ, οὔ· ἵνα μὴ ὑπὸ κρίσιν πέσητε.
of you the yes, yes, and the no, no, that not under judgment you fall.
13 Κακοπαθεῖ τις ἐν ὑμῖν; προσευχέσθω. εὐθυμεῖ τις;
Suffers ill any among you? Let him pray. Is cheerful any?
14 ψαλλέτω. ἀσθενεῖ τις ἐν ὑμῖν; προσκαλεσάσθω τοὺς πρεσ-
Let him sing. Is infirm any among you? Let him summon the
βυτέρους τῆς ἐκκλησίας, καὶ προσευξάσθωσαν ἐπ' αὐτόν,
elders of the church, and let them pray over him,
15 ἀλείψαντες αὐτὸν ἐλαίῳ ἐν τῷ ὀνόματι τοῦ Κυρίου· καὶ ἡ
having anointed him with oil in the name of the Lord. And the
εὐχὴ τῆς πίστεως σώσει τὸν κάμνοντα, καὶ ἐγερεῖ αὐτὸν ὁ
prayer of faith will cure those being sick, and will raise him the
Κύριος· κἂν ἁμαρτίας ᾖ πεποιηκώς, ἀφεθήσεται αὐτῷ.
Lord; and if sin he may be having done it will be forgiven him.
16 ἐξομολογεῖσθε ἀλλήλοις τὰ παραπτώματα, καὶ εὔχεσθε
Confess to one another the offenses, and pray
ὑπὲρ ἀλλήλων, ὅπως ἰαθῆτε. πολὺ ἰσχύει δέησις δικαίου
for one another, so as you may be healed. Much is a strong petition of one righteous
17 ἐνεργουμένη. Ἠλίας ἄνθρωπος ἦν ὁμοιοπαθὴς ἡμῖν, καὶ
being made effective. Elijah a man was of like feeling to us, and
προσευχῇ προσηύξατο τοῦ μὴ βρέξαι· καὶ οὐκ ἔβρεξεν ἐπὶ
in prayer he prayed not to rain, and not it rained on
18 τῆς γῆς ἐνιαυτοὺς τρεῖς καὶ μῆνας ἕξ. καὶ πάλιν προσηύξατο,
the earth years three and months six. And again he prayed,
καὶ ὁ οὐρανὸς ὑετὸν ἔδωκε, καὶ ἡ γῆ ἐβλάστησε τὸν καρπὸν
and the heaven rain gave, and the earth produced the fruit
αὐτῆς.
of it.
19 Ἀδελφοί, ἐάν τις ἐν ὑμῖν πλανηθῇ ἀπὸ τῆς ἀληθείας, καὶ
Brothers, if anyone among you errs from the truth, and
20 ἐπιστρέψῃ τις αὐτόν, γινωσκέτω ὅτι ὁ ἐπιστρέψας ἁμαρ-
turns anyone him, know that the (one) turning a
τωλὸν ἐκ πλάνης ὁδοῦ αὐτοῦ σώσει ψυχὴν ἐκ θανάτου, καὶ
sinner from (the) error of way of him will save (the) soul from death, and
καλύψει πλῆθος ἁμαρτιῶν.
will hide a multitude of sins.

KING JAMES II VERSION

THE FIRST GENERAL EPISTLE OF PETER

CHAPTER 1

[1] Peter, an apostle of Jesus Christ, to *the* elect sojourners of *the* dispersion of Pontus, of Galatia, of Cappadocia, of Asia, and of Bithynia, [2] according to the foreknowledge of God the Father, in sanctification of *the* Spirit to obedience and sprinkling of *the* blood of Jesus Christ: Grace and peace be multiplied to you.

[3] Blessed *be* the God and Father of our Lord Jesus Christ, He according to His great mercy having regenerated us to a living hope through *the* resurrection of Jesus Christ from *the* dead, [4] to an inheritance incorruptible and undefiled, and unfading, having been kept in Heaven for you [5] by *the* power of God, having been guarded through faith to a salvation ready to be revealed in *the* last time; [6] in which you exult, yet a little *while*, if need be, grieving in manifold trials, [7] that the proving of your faith, much more precious than perishing gold, but having been proved through fire, may be found to praise and honor and glory at *the* revelation of Jesus Christ; [8] whom you love, not having seen *Him*; in whom you exult with unspeakable joy, and have glorified; believing in *Him*, yet not seeing, [9] obtaining the end of your faith, the salvation of *your* souls.

[10] About which salvation the prophets sought out and searched out, prophesying concerning the grace for you, [11] searching for what, or what sort of time the Spirit of Christ made clear within them; testifying beforehand of the sufferings *belonging* to Christ, and the glories after

ΠΕΤΡΟΥ

OF PETER

ΕΠΙΣΤΟΛΗ ΚΑΘΟΛΙΚΗ ΠΡΩΤΗ

EPISTLE GENERAL FIRST

CHAPTER 1

1 Πέτρος, ἀπόστολος Ἰησοῦ Χριστοῦ, ἐκλεκτοῖς παρεπιδή-
Peter, an apostle of Jesus Christ, to (the) elect sojourners
μοις διασπορᾶς Πόντου, Γαλατίας, Καππαδοκίας, Ἀσίας,
of (the) dispersion of Pontus, of Galatia, of Cappadocia, of Asia,
2 καὶ Βιθυνίας, κατὰ πρόγνωσιν Θεοῦ πατρός, ἐν ἁγιασμῷ
and of Bithynia, according to foreknowledge God's, the Father, in sanctification
Πνεύματος, εἰς ὑπακοὴν καὶ ῥαντισμὸν αἵματος Ἰησοῦ
of (the) Spirit, to obedience and sprinkling of (the) blood of Jesus
Χριστοῦ· χάρις ὑμῖν καὶ εἰρήνη πληθυνθείη.
Christ: Grace to you, and peace, be multiplied.
3 Εὐλογητὸς ὁ Θεὸς καὶ πατὴρ τοῦ Κυρίου ἡμῶν Ἰησοῦ
Blessed (be) the God and Father of the Lord of us, Jesus
Χριστοῦ, ὁ κατὰ τὸ πολὺ αὐτοῦ ἔλεος ἀναγεννήσας ἡμᾶς
Christ, the (One) according to much of Him mercy, having regenerated us
εἰς ἐλπίδα ζῶσαν δι' ἀναστάσεως Ἰησοῦ Χριστοῦ ἐκ νεκρῶν,
to a hope living through (the) resurrection of Jesus Christ from (the) dead
4 εἰς κληρονομίαν ἄφθαρτον καὶ ἀμίαντον καὶ ἀμάραντον,
to an inheritance incorruptible and undefiled and unfading,
5 τετηρημένην ἐν οὐρανοῖς εἰς ὑμᾶς, τοὺς ἐν δυνάμει Θεοῦ
having been kept in Heaven for you by (the) power of God,
φρουρουμένους διὰ πίστεως εἰς σωτηρίαν ἑτοίμην ἀποκαλυ-
being guarded through faith to a salvation ready to be reveal-
6 φθῆναι ἐν καιρῷ ἐσχάτῳ. ἐν ᾧ ἀγαλλιᾶσθε, ὀλίγον ἄρτι,
ed in time (the) last. In which you exult, a little yet
7 εἰ δέον ἐστί, λυπηθέντες ἐν ποικίλοις πειρασμοῖς, ἵνα τὸ
if needful it is grieving by manifold trials, that the
δοκίμιον ὑμῶν τῆς πίστεως πολὺ τιμιώτερον χρυσίου τοῦ
proving of you of the faith, much more precious than gold
ἀπολλυμένου, διὰ πυρὸς δὲ δοκιμαζομένου, εὑρεθῇ εἰς
of perishing, through fire yet being proved, may be found to
ἔπαινον καὶ τιμὴν καὶ δόξαν ἐν ἀποκαλύψει Ἰησοῦ Χριστοῦ·
praise and honor and glory at (the) revelation of Jesus Christ;
8 ὃν οὐκ ἰδόντες ἀγαπᾶτε, εἰς ὃν ἄρτι μὴ ὁρῶντες, πιστεύοντες
whom not having seen, you love, in whom yet not seeing, believing,
9 δέ, ἀγαλλιᾶσθε χαρᾷ ἀνεκλαλήτῳ καὶ δεδοξασμένῃ, κομιζό-
but; you exult with joy unspeakable and glorified, obtaining
μενοι τὸ τέλος τῆς πίστεως ὑμῶν, σωτηρίαν ψυχῶν.
the end of the faith of you, (the) salvation of (your) souls.
10 περὶ ἧς σωτηρίας ἐξεζήτησαν καὶ ἐξηρεύνησαν προφῆται οἱ
About which salvation sought out and searched out prophets the
11 περὶ τῆς εἰς ὑμᾶς χάριτος προφητεύσαντες· ἐρευνῶντες εἰς
concerning the for you grace prophesying, searching for
τίνα ἢ ποῖον καιρὸν ἐδήλου τὸ ἐν αὐτοῖς Πνεῦμα Χριστοῦ,
what or what sort of time made clear the in them Spirit of Christ,
προμαρτυρόμενον τὰ εἰς Χριστὸν παθήματα, καὶ τὰς μετὰ
testifying beforehand of the (belonging) to Christ sufferings, and the after

these. 12 to whom it was revealed that not to themselves, but to you they ministered the same things, which now were announced to you by those having preached the gospel to you in *the* Holy Spirit sent from Heaven—into which things angels long to look into.

13 Therefore, girding up the loins of your mind, being sober, perfectly hope on the grace being brought to you at *the* revelation of Jesus Christ, 14 as obedient children, not in ignornace fashioning yourselves to your former lusts, 15 but according to the Holy One who has called you, you also become holy in all conduct; 16 because it has been written, "Be holy, because I am holy." 17 And if you call on *Him as* Father, He judging without respect to persons, according to the work of each one, pass the time of your sojourning in fear, 18 knowing that not with corruptible things, silver or gold, you were redeemed from your worthless way of life handed down from *your* fathers, 19 but with precious blood of Christ, as of an unblemished and unspotted lamb, 20 indeed having been foreknown before *the* foundation of *the* world, but revealed in *the* last times because of you, 21 the ones believing in God through Him, He raising Him from *the* dead, and giving glory to Him so that your faith and hope may be in God. 22 Purifying your souls in the obedience of the truth through *the* Spirit to unpretended brotherly love, love one another fervently out of a pure heart, 23 having been born again, not by corruptible seed, but incorruptible; through the living word of God, and remaining forever. 24 Because all flesh *is* as grass, and all *the* glory of men as *the* flower of grass—the grass was dried, and its flower fell out—

25 but *the* word of *the* Lord remains forever. And this is the word preached as gospel

12 ταῦτα δόξας. οἷς ἀπεκαλύφθη ὅτι οὐχ ἑαυτοῖς, ἡμῖν δὲ
these glories. To whom it was revealed that not to themselves to you but
διηκόνουν αὐτά, ἃ νῦν ἀνηγγέλη ὑμῖν διὰ τῶν εὐαγγελισα-
they ministered the same, which now were announced to you through those having preached
μένων ὑμᾶς ἐν Πνεύματι Ἁγίῳ ἀποσταλέντι ἀπ' οὐρανοῦ,
the gospel to you in (the) Spirit Holy sent from Heaven,
εἰς ἃ ἐπιθυμοῦσιν ἄγγελοι παρακύψαι.
into which things long angels to look into.
13 Διὸ ἀναζωσάμενοι τὰς ὀσφύας τῆς διανοίας ὑμῶν,
Therefore, girding up the loins of the mind of you,
νήφοντες, τελείως ἐλπίσατε ἐπὶ τὴν φερομένην ὑμῖν χάριν
being sober, perfectly hope on the being brought to you grace
14 ἐν ἀποκαλύψει Ἰησοῦ Χριστοῦ· ὡς τέκνα ὑπακοῆς, μὴ
at (the) revelation of Jesus Christ. As children of obedience, not
συσχηματιζόμενοι ταῖς πρότερον ἐν τῇ ἀγνοίᾳ ὑμῶν ἐπιθυ-
fashioning yourselves to the formerly in the ignorance of you lusts,
15 μίαις, ἀλλὰ κατὰ τὸν καλέσαντα ὑμᾶς ἅγιον καὶ αὐτοὶ ἅγιοι
but according to the having called you Holy one, also yourselves holy
16 ἐν πάσῃ ἀναστροφῇ γενήθητε· διότι γέγραπται, Ἅγιοι
in all conduct become. Because it has been written: holy
17 γένεσθε, ὅτι ἐγὼ ἅγιός εἰμι. καὶ εἰ πατέρα ἐπικαλεῖσθε τὸν
Be, because I holy am. And if (as) Father you call on (Him), the (One)
ἀπροσωπολήπτως κρίνοντα κατὰ τὸ ἑκάστου ἔργον, ἐν
without respect to persons judging according to the of each one work, in
18 φόβῳ τὸν τῆς παροικίας ὑμῶν χρόνον ἀναστράφητε· εἰδότες
fear the of the sojourning of you time pass, knowing
ὅτι οὐ φθαρτοῖς, ἀργυρίῳ ἢ χρυσίῳ, ἐλυτρώθητε ἐκ τῆς
that not with corruptible things, silver or gold, you were redeemed from the
19 ματαίας ὑμῶν ἀναστροφῆς πατροπαραδότου, ἀλλὰ τιμίῳ
worthless of you living handed down from fathers, but with precious
20 αἵματι ὡς ἀμνοῦ ἀμώμου καὶ ἀσπίλου Χριστοῦ, προεγνω-
blood, as of a lamb unblemished and unspotted, of Christ, having been
σμένου μὲν πρὸ καταβολῆς κόσμου, φανερωθέντος δὲ ἐπ'
foreknown before (the) foundation of (the) world, revealed but in
21 ἐσχάτων τῶν χρόνων δι' ὑμᾶς, τοὺς δι' αὐτοῦ πιστεύοντας
(the) last of the times because of you, those through Him believing
εἰς Θεόν, τὸν ἐγείραντα αὐτὸν ἐκ νεκρῶν, καὶ δόξαν αὐτῷ
in God, the (One) raising Him from (the) dead, and glory to Him
22 δόντα, ὥστε τὴν πίστιν ὑμῶν καὶ ἐλπίδα εἶναι εἰς Θεόν. τὰς
having given, so as the faith of you and hope to be in God. The
ψυχὰς ὑμῶν ἡγνικότες ἐν τῇ ὑπακοῇ τῆς ἀληθείας διὰ Πνεύ-
souls of you having purified in the obedience of the truth, through (the)
ματος εἰς φιλαδελφίαν ἀνυπόκριτον, ἐκ καθαρᾶς καρδίας
Spirit to brotherly love unpretended, from (the) pure heart
23 ἀλλήλους ἀγαπήσατε ἐκτενῶς· ἀναγεγεννημένοι οὐκ ἐκ
one another love fervently, having been regenerated not by
σπορᾶς φθαρτῆς. ἀλλὰ ἀφθάρτου διὰ λόγου ζῶντος Θεοῦ
seed corruptible, but incorruptible through word (the) living of God
24 καὶ μένοντος εἰς τὸν αἰωνα. διότι πᾶσα σὰρξ ὡς χόρτος,
and remaining to the age. Because all flesh (is) as grass,
καὶ πᾶσα δόξα ἀνθρώπου ὡς ἄνθος χόρτου. ἐξηράνθη ὁ
and all (the) glory of man as (the) flower of grass; was dried the
25 χόρτος, καὶ τὸ ἄνθος αὐτοῦ ἐξέπεσε· τὸ δὲ ῥῆμα Κυρίου
grass, and the flower of it fell out, the but word of (the) Lord
μένει εἰς τὸν αἰῶνα. τοῦτο δέ ἐστι τὸ ῥῆμα τὸ εὐαγγελισθὲν
remains to the age. this And is the word preached as gospel

to you.

CHAPTER 2

[1]Then laying aside all malice, and all guile, and hypocrisies, and envies, and all evil words, [2]as newborn babes desire the pure spiritual milk, that you may grow by it; [3]if indeed you tasted that the Lord *is* good. [4]Having drawn near to *Him*, a living Stone, indeed having been rejected by men, but elect, precious with God; [5]you also as living stones are being built a spiritual house, a holy priesthood, to offer spiritual sacrifices acceptable to God through Jesus Christ. [6]Because of this, it is also contained in the Scripture, "Behold, I lay in Zion an elect, precious Stone, a Corner-foundation; and the *one* believing in Him shall never in any way be ashamed."

[7]Then to you who believe *belongs* the honor. But to disobeying ones, *He is the* Stone which those building rejected—this One became *the* Head-of-the-corner, [8]and a Stone-of-stumbling, and a Rock-of-offense to those disobeying, stumbling at the word, to which they were also appointed. [9]But you are an elect race, a royal priesthood, a holy nation, a people for possession, so that you may openly speak of the *One* who has called you out of darkness into His marvelous light; [10]*you* who then were not a people, but now God's people; the one not pitied *then* but now pitied.

[11]Beloved, I exhort *you* as sojourners and aliens to abstain from fleshly lusts which war against the soul; [12]having your behavior good among the nations, in that which they speak against you as evildoers, by observing *your* good works, they may glorify God in a day of visitation.

εἰς ὑμᾶς.
to you.

CHAPTER 2

1 Ἀποθέμενοι οὖν πᾶσαν κακίαν καὶ πάντα δόλον καὶ
laying aside Then all malice and all guile, and
2 ὑποκρίσεις καὶ φθόνους καὶ πάσας καταλαλιάς, ὡς ἀρτιγέν-
hypocrisies, and envies, and all evil words, as newborn
νητα βρέφη, τὸ λογικὸν ἄδολον γάλα ἐπιποθήσατε, ἵνα ἐν
babes, the spiritual pure milk desire, that by
3 αὐτῷ αὐξηθῆτε, εἴπερ ἐγεύσασθε ὅτι χρηστὸς ὁ Κύριος· πρὸς
4 it you may grow, if indeed you tasted that good the Lord (is), to
ὃν προσερχόμενοι, λίθον ζῶντα, ὑπὸ ἀνθρώπων μὲν ἀποδε-
whom drawing near, a stone living, by men indeed having
5 δοκιμασμένον, παρὰ δὲ Θεῷ ἐκλεκτόν, ἔντιμον, καὶ αὐτοὶ
been rejected by but God elect, precious, also yourselves
ὡς λίθοι ζῶντες οἰκοδομεῖσθε οἶκος πνευματικός, ἱεράτευμα
as stones living are being built a house spiritual, a priesthood
ἅγιον, ἀνενέγκαι πνευματικὰς θυσίας εὐπροσδέκτους τῷ
holy, to offer spiritual sacrifices acceptable
6 Θεῷ διὰ Ἰησοῦ Χριστοῦ. διὸ καὶ περιέχει ἐν τῇ γραφῇ,
to God through Jesus Christ. Because indeed it is contained in the Scripture:
Ἰδού, τίθημι ἐν Σιὼν λίθον ἀκρογωνιαῖον, ἐκλεκτόν, ἔντιμον·
Behold, I lay in Zion a stone corner foundation elect, precious,
7 καὶ ὁ πιστεύων ἐπ' αὐτῷ οὐ μὴ καταισχυνθῇ. ὑμῖν οὖν ἡ
and the (one) believing on Him not at all shall be shamed. To you, then, the
τιμὴ τοῖς πιστεύουσιν· ἀπειθοῦσι δέ, Λίθον ὃν ἀπεδοκί-
honor, those believing. to disobeying ones, But a stone which rejected
μασαν οἱ οἰκοδομοῦντες, οὗτος ἐγενήθη εἰς κεφαλὴν γωνίας,
those building. This (One) came to be for Head of (the) corner,
8 καί, Λίθος προσκόμματος καὶ πέτρα σκανδάλου· οἳ προσ-
and, a Stone-of-stumbling, and a Rock- of-offense to those
9 κόπτουσι τῷ λόγῳ ἀπειθοῦντες· εἰς ὃ καὶ ἐτέθησαν. ὑμεῖς
stumbling at the word disobeying, to which indeed they were appointed. you
δὲ γένος ἐκλεκτόν, βασίλειον ἱεράτευμα, ἔθνος ἅγιον, λαὸς
But a race elect, a royal priesthood, a nation holy, a people
εἰς περιποίησιν, ὅπως τὰς ἀρετὰς ἐξαγγείλητε τοῦ ἐκ
for possession, so as the virtues you may tell out of the (One) from
σκότους ὑμᾶς καλέσαντος εἰς τὸ θαυμαστὸν αὐτοῦ φῶς·
darkness you having called into the marvelous of Him light;
10 οἱ ποτὲ οὐ λαός, νῦν δὲ λαὸς Θεοῦ· οἱ οὐκ ἠλεημένοι, νῦν δὲ
who then not a people, now but people God's, those not pitied, now but
ἐλεηθέντες.
pitied.

11 Ἀγαπητοί, παρακαλῶ ὡς παροίκους καὶ παρεπιδή-
Beloved, I exhort (you) as sojourners and aliens
μους, ἀπέχεσθαι τῶν σαρκικῶν ἐπιθυμιῶν, αἵτινες στρατεύον-
to abstain from fleshly lusts, which war
12 ται κατὰ τῆς ψυχῆς· τὴν ἀναστροφὴν ὑμῶν ἐν τοῖς ἔθνεσιν
against the soul, the behavior of you among the nations
ἔχοντες καλήν, ἵνα, ἐν ᾧ καταλαλοῦσιν ὑμῶν ὡς κακοποιῶν
having good, that in which they speak against you as evildoers,
ἐκ τῶν καλῶν ἔργων, ἐποπτεύσαντες, δοξάσωσι τὸν Θεὸν
by the good works having witnessed, they may glorify God
ἐν ἡμέρᾳ ἐπισκοπῆς.
in a day of visitation.

[13]Then be in obedience to every ordinance of men because of the Lord; whether to a king, as being supreme; [14] or to governors, as through Him having indeed been sent for vengeance *on* evildoers— but praise *on* welldoers— [15] because so is the will of God, doing good to silence the ignorance of foolish men; [16] as free, and not having freedom as a cover of evil, but as slaves of God; [17] honor all, love the brotherhood, fear God, honor the king.

[18] Servants, be obedient to *your* masters in all fear, not only to those good and forbearing, but also to the perverse *ones*. [19] For this *is* a grace, if because of conscience *toward* God anyone bears grief, suffering unjustly. [20] For what glory *is it* if you patiently endure *while* sinning and being buffeted? [21] For you were called to this, for even Christ suffered on our behalf, leaving behind an example for us, that you should follow His steps; [22] who did not sin, nor was guile found in His mouth; [23] who, being reviled, did not revile in return; suffering, He did not threaten, but gave *Himself* up to Him judging righteously; [24] who Himself bore in His body our sins onto the tree; that dying to sins, we might live to righteousness; of whom, by His wound, you were healed. [25] For you were straying sheep, but now you *are* turned to the Shepherd and Overseer of your souls.

CHAPTER 3

[1] Likewise, wives, submitting yourselves to *your* own husbands, that even if any disobey the word, through

13 Ὑποτάγητε οὖν πάσῃ ἀνθρωπίνῃ κτίσει διὰ τὸν Κύριον·
Be obedient, then, to every of men ordinance because of the Lord;
14 εἴτε βασιλεῖ, ὡς ὑπερέχοντι· εἴτε ἡγεμόσιν, ὡς δι' αὐτοῦ
whether to a king as being supreme, or to governors, as through Him
πεμπομένοις εἰς ἐκδίκησιν μὲν κακοποιῶν, ἔπαινον δὲ
having been sent for vengeance indeed (on) evildoers, praise but
15 ἀγαθοποιῶν. ὅτι οὕτως ἐστὶ τὸ θέλημα τοῦ Θεοῦ, ἀγαθο-
of welldoers; because so is the will of God, doing
ποιοῦντας φιμοῦν τὴν τῶν ἀφρόνων ἀνθρώπων ἀγνωσίαν·
good to silence the of foolish men ignorance;
16 ὡς ἐλεύθεροι, καὶ μὴ ὡς ἐπικάλυμμα ἔχοντες τῆς κακίας τὴν
as free, and not as a cover having of evil
17 ἐλευθερίαν, ἀλλ' ὡς δοῦλοι Θεοῦ. πάντας τιμήσατε. τὴν
freedom, but as slaves of God. all Honor,
ἀδελφότητα ἀγαπᾶτε. τὸν Θεὸν φοβεῖσθε. τὸν βασιλέα
the brotherhood love, God fear, the king
τιμᾶτε.
honor.

18 Οἱ οἰκέται, ὑποτασσόμενοι ἐν παντὶ φόβῳ τοῖς δεσπόταις,
Servants, be obedient in all fear to the masters (of you),
οὐ μόνον τοῖς ἀγαθοῖς καὶ ἐπιεικέσιν, ἀλλὰ καὶ τοῖς σκολιοῖς.
not only to the good and forbearing, but also to the perverse.
19 τοῦτο γὰρ χάρις, εἰ διὰ συνείδησιν Θεοῦ ὑποφέρει τις
this For (is) a grace, if because of conscience of God bears anyone
20 λύπας, πάσχων ἀδίκως. ποῖον γὰρ κλέος, εἰ ἁμαρτάνοντες
grief, suffering unjustly. what For glory (is it) if sinning
καὶ κολαφιζόμενοι ὑπομενεῖτε; ἀλλ' εἰ ἀγαθοποιοῦντες καὶ
and being buffeted you patiently endure? But if doing good and
21 πάσχοντες ὑπομενεῖτε, τοῦτο χάρις παρὰ Θεῷ. εἰς τοῦτο
suffering you patiently endure, this (is) a grace from God. to this
γὰρ ἐκλήθητε, ὅτι καὶ Χριστὸς ἔπαθεν ὑπὲρ ἡμων, ἡμῖν
For you were called because even Christ suffered on behalf of us, for us
ὑπολιμπάνων ὑπογραμμόν, ἵνα ἐπακολουθήσητε τοῖς
leaving behind an example that you should follow the
22 ἴχνεσιν αὐτοῦ· ὃς ἁμαρτίαν οὐκ ἐποίησεν, οὐδὲ εὑρέθη δόλος
steps of Him; who sin did not do, nor was found guile
23 ἐν τῷ στόματι αὐτοῦ· ὃς λοιδορούμενος οὐκ ἀντελοιδόρει,
in the mouth of Him; who being reviled did not revile in return;
24 πάσχων οὐκ ἠπείλει, παρεδίδου δὲ τῷ κρίνοντι δικαίως· ὃς
suffering, not He threatened, gave (Himself) but to the (one) judging righteously, who
τὰς ἁμαρτίας ἡμῶν αὐτὸς ἀνήνεγκεν ἐν τῷ σώματι αὐτοῦ
the sins of us Himself carried up in the body of Him
ἐπὶ τὸ ξύλον, ἵνα, ταῖς ἁμαρτίαις ἀπογενόμενοι, τῇ δικαιο-
onto the tree, that to sins dying, to righteous-
25 σύνῃ ζήσωμεν· οὗ τῷ μώλωπι αὐτοῦ ἰάθητε. ἦτε γὰρ ὡς
ness we might live; of whom by the wound of Him you were healed. you were For as
πρόβατα πλανώμενα· ἀλλ' ἐπεστράφητε νῦν ἐπὶ τὸν ποι-
sheep wandering, but you turned now to the
μένα καὶ ἐπίσκοπον τῶν ψυχῶν ὑμῶν.
Shepherd and Overseer of the souls of you.

CHAPTER 3

1 Ὁμοίως, αἱ γυναῖκες, ὑποτασσόμεναι τοῖς ἰδίοις ἀν-
Likewise, wives, submitting yourselves to the own
δράσιν, ἵνα, καὶ εἴ τινες ἀπειθοῦσι τῷ λόγῳ, διὰ τῆς τῶν
husbands, that even if any disobey the word, through the of the

the behavior of the wives, they will without a word be won, [2]observing your pure behavior in fear. [3]Of whom let it not be the outward *act* of braiding of hairs, and of putting gold around, or of clothing, *the* adorning of garments, [4]but the hidden man of the heart, in the incorruptible *adornment* of the meek and quiet spirit, which is of great value before God. [5]For so once indeed the holy women hoping on God adorned themselves, submitting themselves to their own husbands, [6]as Sarah obeyed Abraham, calling him lord; whose children you became, doing good, and fearing no terror. [7]Likewise, husbands, dwelling together according to knowledge, as with a weaker vessel, the female, bestowing honor, as truly *being* co-heirs of *the* grace of life, not cutting off your prayers.

[8]And, finally, *be* all of one mind, sympathetic, loving *the* brothers, tenderhearted, friendly, [9]not giving back evil for evil, or reviling against reviling; but, on the contrary, *give* blessing; knowing that you were called to this in order that you might inherit blessing. [10]For the *one* desiring to love life, and to see good days, let him restrain his tongue from evil, even his lips not to speak guile. [11]Let him turn aside from evil, and let him do good. Let him seek peace, and pursue it; [12]because the eyes of *the* Lord *are* on the righteous, and His ears *open* to their prayer. But *the* face of *the* Lord *is* against *any* doing bad things.

[13]And who *is* the *one* harming you, if you become imitators of the good? [14]But if you truly suffer because of righteousness, *you are* blessed. [15]But sanctify the Lord God in your hearts, and always *be* ready to give an

2 γυναικῶν ἀναστροφῆς ἄνευ λόγου κερδηθήσωνται, ἐπο-
wives behavior, without a word they will be won, having

3 πτεύσαντες τὴν ἐν φόβῳ ἁγνὴν ἀναστροφὴν ὑμῶν. ὧν ἔστω
witnessed the in fear pure behavior of you. Of whom let it be

οὐχ ὁ ἔξωθεν ἐμπλοκῆς τριχῶν, καὶ περιθέσεως χρυσίων,
not the outward of braiding of hairs, and of putting around gold (jewelry)

4 ἢ ἐνδύσεως ἱματίων κόσμος· ἀλλ' ὁ κρυπτὸς τῆς καρδίας
or of clothing of garments adorning; but the hidden of the heart

ἄνθρωπος, ἐν τῷ ἀφθάρτῳ τοῦ πρᾳέος καὶ ἡσυχίου πνεύ-
man, in the incorruptible of the meek and quiet spirit

5 ματος, ὅ ἐστιν ἐνώπιον τοῦ Θεοῦ πολυτελές. οὕτω γάρ ποτε
which is before God of great value. so For then

καὶ αἱ ἅγιαι γυναῖκες αἱ ἐλπίζουσαι ἐπὶ τὸν Θεὸν ἐκόσμουν
also the holy women hoping on God adorned

6 ἑαυτάς, ὑποτασσόμεναι τοῖς ἰδίοις ἀνδράσιν· ὡς Σάρρα
themselves, submitting themselves to the own husbands, as Sarah

ὑπήκουσε τῷ Ἀβραάμ, κύριον αὐτὸν καλοῦσα, ἧς ἐγενήθητε
obeyed Abraham, lord him calling, of whom you became

τέκνα, ἀγαθοποιοῦσαι καὶ μὴ φοβούμεναι μηδεμίαν πτόησιν.
children, doing good and fearing no terror.

7 Οἱ ἄνδρες ὁμοίως, συνοικοῦντες κατὰ γνῶσιν, ὡς ἀσθενε-
Husbands likewise, dwelling together according to knowledge, as with a

στέρῳ σκεύει τῷ γυναικείῳ ἀπονέμοντες τιμήν, ὡς καὶ
weaker vessel the female, bestowing honor, as truly

συγκληρονόμοι χάριτος ζωῆς, εἰς τὸ μὴ ἐκκόπτεσθαι τὰς
co-heirs of (the) grace of life, unto not cutting off the

προσευχὰς ὑμῶν.
prayers of you.

8 Τὸ δὲ τέλος, πάντες ὁμόφρονες, συμπαθεῖς, φιλάδελφοι,
And finally, all of one mind, sympathetic, loving (the) brothers,

9 εὔσπλαγχνοι, φιλόφρονες· μὴ ἀποδιδόντες κακὸν ἀντὶ κακοῦ,
tenderhearted, friendly, not giving back evil against evil,

ἢ λοιδορίαν ἀντὶ λοιδορίας· τοὐναντίον δὲ εὐλογοῦντες,
or reviling against reviling, on the contrary but, blessing,

εἰδότες ὅτι εἰς τοῦτο ἐκλήθητε, ἵνα εὐλογίαν κληρονομήσητε.
knowing that to this you were called that blessing you might inherit.

10 Ὁ γὰρ θέλων ζωὴν ἀγαπᾶν, καὶ ἰδεῖν ἡμέρας ἀγαθάς,
the (one) For desiring life to love, and to see days good,

παυσάτω τὴν γλῶσσαν αὐτοῦ ἀπὸ κακοῦ, καὶ χείλη αὐτοῦ
let him hold back the tongue of him from evil, even (the) lips of him

11 τοῦ μὴ λαλῆσαι δόλον· ἐκκλινάτω ἀπὸ κακοῦ, καὶ ποιησάτω
not to speak guile; let him turn away from evil, and let him do

12 ἀγαθόν· ζητησάτω εἰρήνην, καὶ διωξάτω αὐτήν. ὅτι οἱ
good; let him seek peace and pursue it; because the

ὀφθαλμοὶ Κυρίου ἐπὶ δικαίους, καὶ ὦτα αὐτοῦ εἰς δέησιν
eyes of (the) Lord (are) on the righteous, and His ears (open) to petition

αὐτῶν· πρόσωπον δὲ Κυρίου ἐπὶ ποιοῦντας κακά.
of them; (the) face but of (the) Lord against (any) doing evil things.

13 Καὶ τίς ὁ κακώσων ὑμᾶς, ἐὰν τοῦ ἀγαθοῦ μιμηταὶ γένησθε;
And who (is) he harming you, if of the good imitators you become?

14 ἀλλ' εἰ καὶ πάσχοιτε διὰ δικαιοσύνην, μακάριοι· τὸν δὲ
But if truly you suffer because of righteousness, blessed (are you). the But

15 φόβον αὐτῶν μὴ φοβηθῆτε, μηδὲ ταραχθῆτε· Κύριον δὲ τὸν
fear of them do not fear, nor be troubled, Lord but the

Θεὸν ἁγιάσατε ἐν ταῖς καρδίαις ὑμῶν· ἕτοιμοι δὲ ἀεὶ πρὸς
God sanctify in the hearts of you ready and always to

answer to everyone asking you a reason concerning the hope in you, with meekness and fear, [16] having a good conscience, that while they speak against you as evildoers, they may be shamed, those falsely accusing your good behavior in Christ. [17] For *it is* better, if the will of God wills *it,* to suffer *for* doing good than *for* doing evil. [18] Because even Christ once suffered concerning sins, the just for the unjust, that He might bring you to God; indeed being put to death in *the* flesh, but made alive in the Spirit; [19] in which also, going in to the spirits in prison, He then proclaimed [20] to disobeying ones, when the longsuffering of God waited in *the* days of Noah, an ark having been prepared in which a few, that is, eight souls, were saved through water. [21] Which figure now also saves us, baptism—not a putting away of *the* filth of *the* flesh, but *the* answer of a good conscience toward God through *the* resurrection of Jesus Christ, [22] who going into Heaven is at *the* right of God, *the* angels, and authorities, and powers being subjected to Him.

CHAPTER 4

[1] Therefore, Christ having suffered for us in *the* flesh, you also arm yourselves with the same mind, because the *one* suffering in flesh has ceased from sin, [2] for *him* to live in *the* lusts of men, but in *the* will of God the remaining time in *the* flesh. [3] For *the* time of life having passed *is* sufficient for us to have worked out the will of the nations, having gone *on* in wantonness, lusts, drunkennesses, parties, carousings, and unlawful idolatries; [4] in which they are surprised, you not running with *them* into the same overflow of unsaved *acts,* blaspheming; [5] who will give account to Him having readiness to judge *the* living and dead.

ἀπολογίαν παντὶ τῷ αἰτοῦντι ὑμᾶς λόγον περὶ τῆς ἐν ὑμῖν
give an answer to everyone asking you a word concerning the in you
16 ἐλπίδος, μετὰ πραΰτητος καὶ φόβου· συνείδησιν ἔχοντες
hope; with meekness and fear, conscience having
ἀγαθήν, ἵνα, ἐν ᾧ καταλαλῶσιν ὑμῶν ὡς κακοποιῶν,
a good, that while they speak against you as evildoers,
καταισχυνθῶσιν οἱ ἐπηρεάζοντες ὑμῶν τὴν ἀγαθὴν ἐν
they may be shamed , those abusing of you the good in
17 Χριστῷ ἀναστροφήν. κρεῖττον γὰρ ἀγαθοποιοῦντας, εἰ
Christ behavior. (it is) better For doing good if
18 θέλει τὸ θέλημα τοῦ Θεοῦ, πάσχειν, ἢ κακοποιοῦντας. ὅτι
wills the will of God, to suffer, than (for) doing evil. Because
καὶ Χριστὸς ἅπαξ περὶ ἁμαρτιῶν ἔπαθε, δίκαιος ὑπὲρ
even Christ once concerning sins suffered, the just for
ἀδίκων, ἵνα ἡμᾶς προσαγάγῃ τῷ Θεῷ, θανατωθεὶς μὲν
the unjust, that you He might bring to God, being put to death truly
19 σαρκί, ζωοποιηθεὶς δὲ τῷ πνεύματι, ἐν ᾧ καὶ τοῖς ἐν φυλακῇ
in (the) flesh, made alive but in the Spirit; in which also to the in prison
20 πνεύμασι πορευθεὶς ἐκήρυξεν, ἀπειθήσασί ποτε, ὅτε ἅπαξ
spirits going He proclaimed to disobeying ones then, when once
ἐξεδέχετο ἡ τοῦ Θεοῦ μακροθυμία ἐν ἡμέραις Νῶε, κατα-
waited the of God longsuffering in (the) days of Noah, having
σκευαζομένης κιβωτοῦ, εἰς ἣν ὀλίγαι, τοῦτ' ἔστιν ὀκτὼ
been prepared an ark, in which a few, this is, eight
21 ψυχαί, διεσώθησαν δι' ὕδατος· ᾧ καὶ ἡμᾶς ἀντίτυπον νῦν
souls, were saved through water. Which also us figure now
σώζει βάπτισμα, οὐ σαρκὸς ἀπόθεσις ῥύπου, ἀλλὰ συνειδή-
saves, baptism, not of (the) flesh a putting away of (the) filth, but of a conscience
σεως ἀγαθῆς ἐπερώτημα εἰς Θεόν, δι' ἀναστάσεως Ἰησοῦ
good an answer toward God, through (the) resurrection of Jesus
22 Χριστοῦ, ὅς ἐστιν ἐν δεξιᾷ τοῦ Θεοῦ, πορευθεὶς εἰς οὐρανόν,
Christ, who is at (the) right of God, having gone into Heaven,
ὑποταγέντων αὐτῷ ἀγγέλων καὶ ἐξουσιῶν καὶ δυνάμεων.
being subjected to Him angels and authorities and powers.

CHAPTER 4

1 Χριστοῦ οὖν παθόντος ὑπὲρ ἡμῶν σαρκί, καὶ ὑμεῖς τὴν
Christ Therefore having suffered for us in (the) flesh, also you the
αὐτὴν ἔννοιαν ὁπλίσασθε· ὅτι ὁ παθὼν ἐν σαρκί, πέπαυται
same mind arm yourselves, because he suffering in (the) flesh has ceased
2 ἁμαρτίας· εἰς τὸ μηκέτι ἀνθρώπων ἐπιθυμίαις, ἀλλὰ θελή-
from sin; for the no longer of men in (the) lusts, but in (the) will
3 ματι Θεοῦ τὸν ἐπίλοιπον ἐν σαρκὶ βιῶσαι χρόνον. ἀρκετὸς
of God the remaining in (the) flesh to live time. sufficient
γὰρ ἡμῖν ὁ παρεληλυθὼς χρόνος τοῦ βίου τὸ θέλημα τῶν
For to us the having passed away time of life of the will of the
ἐθνῶν κατεργάσασθαι, πεπορευμένους ἐν ἀσελγείαις, ἐπιθυ-
nations having worked out, having gone (on) in wantonness, lusts,
μίαις, οἰνοφλυγίαις, κώμοις, πότοις, καὶ ἀθεμίτοις εἰδωλο-
drunkennesses, parties, carousings, and unlawful idol-
4 λατρείαις· ἐν ᾧ ξενίζονται, μὴ συντρεχόντων ὑμῶν εἰς τὴν
atries. While they are surprised not running with you into the
5 αὐτὴν τῆς ἀσωτίας ἀνάχυσιν, βλασφημοῦντες· οἳ ἀποδώ-
same of dissoluteness overflow, blaspheming; who will give
σουσι λόγον τῷ ἑτοίμως ἔχοντι κρῖναι ζῶντας καὶ νεκρούς.
account to the (One) ready having to judge living and dead.

6 For to this *end* also the gospel was preached to *the* dead, that they might be judged according to men in *the* flesh, but might live according to God in *the* Spirit.

7 But the end of all things has drawn near. Be of sound mind, then, and be sensible to prayers; 8 and above all things having fervent love to yourselves, because love will cover a multitude of sins. 9 Be hospitable to one another without murmurings, 10 each one as he received a gift, ministering it to yourselves as good stewards of *the* manifold grace of God. 11 If anyone speaks, *let it be* as the words of God; if anyone ministers, as by strength which God supplies, that in all things God may be glorified through Jesus Christ; to whom is the glory and the might forever and ever. Amen.

12 Beloved, do not be astonished *at* the fiery trial happening among you for your testing, as *if* a surprise *were* occurring; 13 but according as you share the sufferings of Christ, rejoice; so that you may rejoice exultingly at the revelation of His glory.

14 If you are reviled in *the* name of Christ, *you are* blessed, because the Spirit of God and of glory rests on you. Truly, according to them, He is blasphemed; but according to you, He is glorified. 15 For do not let any of you suffer as a murderer, or a thief, or an evildoer, or as a meddler. 16 But if *he suffers* as a Christian, do not let him be ashamed, but to glorify God in this respect. 17 Because the time *has come* to begin the judgment from the house of God; and if firstly from us, what *will be* the end of the ones disobeying the gospel of God? 18 And if the righteous is scarcely saved, where will the ungodly and sinner appear? 19 So as indeed the ones suffering according to God's will, as to a faithful Creator, let them commit their souls in welldoing.

6 εἰς τοῦτο γὰρ καὶ νεκροῖς εὐηγγελίσθη, ἵνα κριθῶσι μὲν κατὰ
for this For indeed to dead ones was preached the gospel that they might be judged in- deed accord- ing to
ἀνθρώπους σαρκί, ζῶσι δὲ κατὰ Θεὸν πνεύματι.
men in (the) flesh; might live but according to God in (the) Spirit.

7 Πάντων δὲ τὸ τέλος ἤγγικε· σωφρονήσατε οὖν καὶ
of all things But the end has drawn near. Be disciplined, then, and
8 νήψατε εἰς τὰς προσευχάς· πρὸ πάντων δὲ τὴν εἰς ἑαυτοὺς
be sensible to prayers; before all things and to yourselves
ἀγάπην ἐκτενῆ ἔχοντες, ὅτι ἡ ἀγάπη καλύψει πλῆθος
love fervent having, because love will cover a multitude
9 ἁμαρτιῶν· φιλόξενοι εἰς ἀλλήλους ἄνευ γογγυσμῶν·
of sins. Be hospitable to one another without murmurings;
10 ἕκαστος καθὼς ἔλαβε χάρισμα, εἰς ἑαυτοὺς αὐτὸ διακονοῦν-
each one as he received a gift, to yourselves it ministering
11 τες, ὡς καλοὶ οἰκονόμοι ποικίλης χάριτος Θεοῦ· εἴ τις λαλεῖ,
as good stewards of (the) manifold grace of God; If any speaks,
ὡς λόγια Θεοῦ· εἴ τις διακονεῖ, ὡς ἐξ ἰσχύος ἧς χορηγεῖ ὁ
as (the) words of God; if any ministers, as by strength which supplies
Θεός· ἵνα ἐν πᾶσι δοξάζηται ὁ Θεὸς διὰ Ἰησοῦ Χριστοῦ,
God, that in all things may be glorified God through Jesus Christ,
ᾧ ἐστιν ἡ δόξα καὶ τὸ κράτος εἰς τοὺς αἰῶνας τῶν αἰώνων.
to whom is the glory and the might to the ages of the ages.
μήν.
Amen.

12 Ἀγαπητοί, μὴ ξενίζεσθε τῇ ἐν ὑμῖν πυρώσει πρὸς πειρα-
Beloved, do not be astonished (at the) among you fiery trial for trial
13 σμὸν ὑμῖν γινομένῃ, ὡς ξένου ὑμῖν συμβαίνοντος· ἀλλὰ καθὸ
of you happening, as a surprise to you occurring, but as
κοινωνεῖτε τοῖς τοῦ Χριστοῦ παθήμασι, χαίρετε, ἵνα καὶ ἐν
you share the of Christ sufferings, rejoice, that also at
14 τῇ ἀποκαλύψει τῆς δόξης αὐτοῦ χαρῆτε ἀγαλλιώμενοι. εἰ
the revelation of the glory of Him you may rejoice exultingly If
ὀνειδίζεσθε ἐν ὀνόματι Χριστοῦ, μακάριοι· ὅτι τὸ τῆς δόξης
you are reviled in (the) name of Christ, blessed (are you), for the of glory
καὶ τὸ τοῦ Θεοῦ Πνεῦμα ἐφ' ὑμᾶς ἀναπαύεται· κατὰ μὲν
and the of God Spirit on you rests; according to truly
15 αὐτοὺς βλασφημεῖται, κατὰ δὲ ὑμᾶς δοξάζεται. μὴ γάρ τις
them, He is blasphemed; according to but you, He is glorified. not For any
ὑμῶν πασχέτω ὡς φονεύς, ἢ κλέπτης, ἢ κακοποιός, ἢ ὡς
of you let suffer as a murderer, or a thief, or an evildoer, or as
16 ἀλλοτριοεπίσκοπος· εἰ δὲ ὡς Χριστιανός, μὴ αἰσχυνέσθω,
a meddler; if but as a Christian, not let him be ashamed,
17 δοξαζέτω δὲ τὸν Θεὸν ἐν τῷ μέρει τούτῳ. ὅτι ὁ καιρὸς τοῦ
to glorify but God in respect this. Because the time
ἄρξασθαι τὸ κρίμα ἀπὸ τοῦ οἴκου τοῦ Θεοῦ· εἰ δὲ πρῶτον
to begin the judgment from the house of God; if and firstly
ἀφ' ἡμῶν, τί τὸ τέλος τῶν ἀπειθούντων τῷ τοῦ Θεοῦ
from us, what (will be) the end of those disobeying the of God
18 εὐαγγελίῳ; καὶ εἰ ὁ δίκαιος μόλις σώζεται, ὁ ἀσεβὴς καὶ
gospel? And if the righteous one scarcely is saved, the ungodly and
19 ἁμαρτωλὸς ποῦ φανεῖται; ὥστε καὶ οἱ πάσχοντες κατὰ τὸ
sinner where will appear? So as indeed those suffering according to
θέλημα τοῦ Θεοῦ, ὡς πιστῷ κτίστῃ παρατιθέσθωσαν τὰς
will God's, as to a faithful Creator, let them commit the
ψυχὰς ἑαυτῶν ἐν ἀγαθοποιΐᾳ.
souls of themselves in welldoing.

CHAPTER 5

[1] I, a fellow-elder, exhort the elders among you, *I being* also witness of the sufferings of Christ, and being sharer of the about to be revealed glory: [2] Shepherd the flock of God among you, exercising oversight, not by compulsion, but willingly; nor eagerly for base gain, but readily; [3] nor as exercising lordship over the ones allotted *to you*, but becoming examples of the flock. [4] And *at* the appearing of the Chief Shepherd, you will receive the never-fading crown of glory. [5] Likewise, younger ones be subject to older ones; and all being subject to one another. Put on humility, because God sets *Himself* against proud ones, but He gives grace to humble ones. [6] Then be humbled under the mighty hand of God, that He may exalt you in time; [7] casting all your anxiety onto Him, because it matters to Him concerning you. [8] Be sensible, watch, because your adversary *the* Devil walks about seeking someone he may devour; [9] whom firmly resist in the faith, knowing the same sufferings *that are* in the world are being completed in your brotherhood. [10] Now the God of all grace, the *One* calling you to His eternal glory in Christ Jesus, *you* having suffered a little, *He* Himself will perfect, confirm, make *you* strong *and* establish you. [11] To Him *be* the glory and the might forever and ever. Amen.

[12] I wrote to you by a few *words* by way of Silvanus the faithful brother, as I reckon, exhorting and witnessing this to be *the* true grace of God, in which you stand. [13] The fellow-elected in Babylon greet you; also Mark my son. [14] Greet one another with a kiss of love.

CHAPTER 5

1 Πρεσβυτέρους τοὺς ἐν ὑμῖν παρακαλῶ ὁ συμπρεσβύτερος
elders The among you I exhort, the (one) a fellow-elder (being),
καὶ μάρτυς τῶν τοῦ Χριστοῦ παθημάτων, ὁ καὶ τῆς μελλού-
and witness of the of Christ sufferings, the also of the being
2 σης ἀποκαλύπτεσθαι δόξης κοινωνός· ποιμάνατε τὸ ἐν ὑμῖν
about to be revealed glory sharer; shepherd the among you
ποίμνιον τοῦ Θεοῦ, ἐπισκοποῦντες μὴ ἀναγκαστῶς, ἀλλ᾽
flock of God, exercising oversight not by compulsion, but
3 ἑκουσίως· μηδὲ αἰσχροκερδῶς, ἀλλὰ προθύμως· μηδ᾽ ὡς
willingly, nor eagerly for base gain, but readily; nor as
κατακυριεύοντες τῶν κλήρων, ἀλλὰ τύποι γινόμενοι τοῦ
exercising lordship over the allotments, but examples becoming of the
4 ποιμνίου. καὶ φανερωθέντος τοῦ ἀρχιποίμενος, κομιεῖσθε τὸν
flock; and (at) the appearing of the chief Shepherd, you will receive the
5 ἀμαράντινον τῆς δόξης στέφανον. ὁμοίως, νεώτεροι, ὑποτά-
unfading of glory crown. Likewise, younger ones be sub-
γητε πρεσβυτέροις· πάντες δὲ ἀλλήλοις ὑποτασσόμενοι, τὴν
ject to older ones; all and to one another being subject,
ταπεινοφροσύνην ἐγκομβώσασθε· ὅτι ὁ Θεὸς ὑπερηφάνοις
humility put on, because God proud ones
6 ἀντιτάσσεται, ταπεινοῖς δὲ δίδωσι χάριν. ταπεινώθητε
sets (Himself) against, to humble ones but He gives grace. Be humbled,
οὖν ὑπὸ τὴν κραταιὰν χεῖρα τοῦ Θεοῦ, ἵνα ὑμᾶς ὑψώσῃ ἐν
then, under the mighty hand of God, that you He may exalt in
7 καιρῷ, πᾶσαν τὴν μέριμναν ὑμῶν ἐπιρρίψαντες ἐπ᾽ αὐτόν,
time; all the anxiety of you casting onto Him,
8 ὅτι αὐτῷ μέλει περὶ ὑμῶν. νήψατε, γρηγορήσατε, ὅτι ὁ
because to Him it matters concerning you. Be sensible, watch, because the
ἀντίδικος ὑμῶν διάβολος, ὡς λέων ὠρυόμενος, περιπατεῖ
adversary of you, (the) devil, as a lion roaring walks about
9 ζητῶν τίνα καταπίῃ· ᾧ ἀντίστητε στερεοὶ τῇ πίστει,
seeking someone he may devour; whom resist firm in the faith,
εἰδότες τὰ αὐτὰ τῶν παθημάτων τῇ ἐν κόσμῳ ὑμῶν ἀδελ-
knowing the same sufferings in the in (the) world of you brother-
10 φότητι ἐπιτελεῖσθαι. ὁ δὲ Θεὸς πάσης χάριτος, ὁ καλέσας
hood are being completed. the Now God of all grace, the (One) calling
ἡμᾶς εἰς τὴν αἰώνιον αὐτοῦ δόξαν ἐν Χριστῷ Ἰησοῦ, ὀλίγον
us to the eternal of Him glory in Christ Jesus, a little
παθόντας αὐτὸς καταρτίσαι ὑμᾶς, στηρίξαι, σθενώσαι,
having suffered Himself perfect you, confirm, strengthen,
11 θεμελιώσαι. αὐτῷ ἡ δόξα καὶ τὸ κράτος εἰς τοὺς αἰῶνας τῶν
establish (you). To Him the glory and the might to the ages of the
αἰώνων. ἀμήν.
ages. Amen.
12 Διὰ Σιλουανοῦ ὑμῖν τοῦ πιστοῦ ἀδελφοῦ, ὡς λογίζομαι,
Through Silvanus to you the faithful brother, as I reckon,
δι᾽ ὀλίγων ἔγραψα, παρακαλῶν καὶ ἐπιμαρτυρῶν ταύτην
via a few (words) I wrote, exhorting and witnessing this
13 εἶναι ἀληθῆ χάριν τοῦ Θεοῦ εἰς ἣν ἑστήκατε. ἀσπάζεται
to be (the) true grace of God, in which you stand. Greets
ὑμᾶς ἡ ἐν Βαβυλῶνι συνεκλεκτή, καὶ Μάρκος ὁ υἱός μου.
you the in Babylon fellow-elected, and Mark the son of me.
14 ἀσπάσασθε ἀλλήλους ἐν φιλήματι ἀγάπης.
Greet one another with a kiss of love.

Peace *be* to you, all those in Christ Jesus. Amen.

Εἰρήνη ὑμῖν πᾶσι τοῖς ἐν Χριστῷ Ἰησοῦ. ἀμήν.
Peace to you, all those in Christ Jesus. Amen.

ΠΕΤΡΟΥ
OF PETER

ΕΠΙΣΤΟΛΗ ΚΑΘΟΛΙΚΗ ΔΕΥΤΕΡΑ
EPISTLE GENERAL SECOND

KING JAMES II VERSION

THE SECOND GENERAL EPISTLE OF PETER

CHAPTER 1

[1]Simon Peter, a slave of Jesus Christ, to those equally precious with us, having obtained faith in *the* righteousness of our God and our Savior, Jesus Christ: [2]Grace to you, and peace be multiplied by a full knowledge of God, and of Jesus our Lord.

[3]As His divine power has given to us all things pertaining to life and godliness through the full knowledge of the *One* calling us through glory and virtue, [4]by which means He has given to us the very great and precious promises, so that through these you might be partakers of *the* divine nature, escaping from the corruption in *the* world by lust. [5]But also in this very thing, bringing in all diligence, filling out your faith *with* virtue; and virtue *with* knowledge; [6]and knowledge *with* self-control; and self-control *with* patience; and patience *with* godliness; [7]and godliness *with* brotherly love; and brotherly love *with* love. [8]For these things being in you, and abounding, makes *you* not barren, not unfruitful in our Lord Jesus Christ. [9]For the *one* in whom these things *are* not present is blind, being short-sighted, taking on forgetfulness of the cleansing of his sins in time past.

[10]Therefore, brothers, rather be diligent to make sure of your calling and election; for doing these things, you will not ever fall. [11]For so will be richly furnished to you the entrance into the everlasting kingdom of our Lord and Savior, Jesus

CHAPTER 1

1 Σίμων Πέτρος, δοῦλος καὶ ἀπόστολος Ἰησοῦ Χριστοῦ,
Simon Peter, a slave and apostle of Jesus Christ,
τοῖς ἰσότιμον ἡμῖν λαχοῦσι πίστιν ἐν δικαιοσύνῃ τοῦ Θεοῦ
to those equally precious with us having obtained faith in (the) righteousness of the God
2 ἡμῶν καὶ σωτῆρος ἡμῶν Ἰησοῦ Χριστοῦ· χάρις ὑμῖν καὶ
of us and Savior of us, Jesus Christ: Grace to you and
εἰρήνη πληθυνθείη ἐν ἐπιγνώσει τοῦ Θεοῦ, καὶ Ἰησοῦ τοῦ
peace be multiplied by a full knowledge of God, and of Jesus the
3 Κυρίου ἡμῶν· ὡς πάντα ἡμῖν τῆς θείας δυνάμεως αὐτοῦ τὰ
Lord of us. As all things to us the divine power of Him
πρὸς ζωὴν καὶ εὐσέβειαν δεδωρημένης, διὰ τῆς ἐπιγνώσεως
as to life and godliness having been given, through the full knowledge
4 τοῦ καλέσαντος ἡμᾶς διὰ δόξης καὶ ἀρετῆς· δι' ὧν τὰ μέγιστα
of the (One) calling us via glory and virtue, through which the very great
ἡμῖν καὶ τίμια ἐπαγγέλματα δεδώρηται, ἵνα διὰ τούτων
to us and precious promises He has given, that through these
γένησθε θείας κοινωνοὶ φύσεως, ἀποφυγόντες τῆς ἐν κόσμῳ
you might be of a divine partakers nature, escaping from the in (the) world
5 ἐν ἐπιθυμίᾳ φθορᾶς. καὶ αὐτὸ τοῦτο δέ, σπουδὴν πᾶσαν
by lust corruption. also in this very thing But, diligence all
παρεισενέγκαντες, ἐπιχορηγήσατε ἐν τῇ πίστει ὑμῶν τὴν
bringing in, fill out in the faith of you
6 ἀρετήν, ἐν δὲ τῇ ἀρετῇ τὴν γνῶσιν, ἐν δὲ τῇ γνώσει τὴν
virtue; with and virtue, knowledge; with and knowledge,
ἐγκράτειαν, ἐν δὲ τῇ ἐγκρατείᾳ τὴν ὑπομονήν, ἐν δὲ τῇ
self-control; with and self-control, patience; with and
7 ὑπομονῇ τὴν εὐσέβειαν, ἐν δὲ τῇ εὐσεβείᾳ τὴν φιλαδελφίαν,
patience, godliness, with and godliness, brotherly love;
8 ἐν δὲ τῇ φιλαδελφίᾳ τὴν ἀγάπην. ταῦτα γὰρ υμῖν ὑπάρ-
with and brotherly love, love. these things For in you being
χοντα καὶ πλεονάζοντα, οὐκ ἀργοὺς οὐδὲ ἀκάρπους καθί-
and abounding, not barren not unfruitful
στησιν εἰς τὴν τοῦ Κυρίου ἡμῶν Ἰησοῦ Χριστοῦ ἐπίγνωσιν.
makes (you) in the of the Lord of us Jesus Christ full knowledge.
9 ᾧ γὰρ μὴ πάρεστι ταῦτα, τυφλός ἐστι, μυωπάζων, λήθην
(he) in whom For not is present these things, blind is, being short-sighted, forgetful
10 λαβὼν τοῦ καθαρισμοῦ τῶν πάλαι αὐτοῦ ἁμαρτιῶν. διὸ
taking of the cleansing of the in time past of him sins. Therefore
μᾶλλον, ἀδελφοί, σπουδάσατε βεβαίαν ὑμῶν τὴν κλῆσιν
rather, brothers, be diligent sure of you the calling
καὶ ἐκλογὴν ποιεῖσθαι· ταῦτα γὰρ ποιοῦντες οὐ μὴ πταίσητέ
and election to make; these things for doing not at all you will fall
11 ποτε· ουτω γὰρ πλουσίως ἐπιχορηγηθήσεται ὑμῖν ἡ εἴσοδος
ever. so For richly will be furnished to you the entrance
εἰς τὴν αἰώνιον βασιλείαν τοῦ Κυρίου ἡμῶν καὶ σωτῆρος
into the eternal kingdom of the Lord of us and Savior,

Christ.
12 For this reason I will not neglect to cause you to remember always concerning these things, though *you* know and have been confirmed in the present truth.
13 But I deem *it* right, so long as I am in this tabernacle, to stir you up by a reminder,
14 knowing that the putting off of my tabernacle is soon, as indeed our Lord made clear to me.
15 And I will also be diligent to cause you to always have memory of these things after my departure.
16 For not following fables which had been cleverly devised, but becoming eyewitnesses of the majesty of Jesus Christ, we made known to you the power and coming of our Lord.
17 For receiving honor and glory from God *the* Father—such a voice being borne to Him from the magnificent glory, "This is My Son, the Beloved, in whom I was well-pleased,"
18 even we heard this voice being borne out of Heaven, being with Him in the holy mountain—
19 and we have the more established prophetic word, in which you do well to take heed, as to a lamp shining in a murky place, until day dawns and the Daystar rises in your hearts;
20 knowing this first, that every prophecy of Scripture did not come into being of *its* own interpretation;
21 for prophecy was not at any time borne by *the* will of man, but having been borne along by *the* Holy Spirit, holy men of God spoke.

CHAPTER 2

1 But false prophets were also among the people, as also false teachers will be among you, who will secretly bring in destructive heresies, and denying the Master who has bought them, bringing swift destruction on themselves.
2 And many will

Ἰησοῦ Χριστοῦ.
Jesus Christ.
12 Διὸ οὐκ ἀμελήσω ὑμᾶς ἀεὶ ὑπομιμνήσκειν περὶ τούτων,
Therefore not I will neglect you always to cause to remember about these,
καίπερ εἰδότας, καὶ ἐστηριγμένους ἐν τῇ παρούσῃ ἀληθείᾳ.
though knowing and having been confirmed in the present truth.
13 δίκαιον δὲ ἡγοῦμαι, ἐφ' ὅσον εἰμὶ ἐν τούτῳ τῷ σκηνώματι,
right And I deem (it), so long as I am in this tabernacle,
14 διεγείρειν ὑμᾶς ἐν ὑπομνήσει· εἰδὼς ὅτι ταχινή ἐστιν ἡ
to arouse you by a reminder, knowing that soon is the
ἀπόθεσις τοῦ σκηνώματός μου, καθὼς καὶ ὁ Κύριος ἡμῶν
putting off of the tabernacle of me, as indeed the Lord of us,
15 Ἰησοῦς Χριστὸς ἐδήλωσέ μοι. σπουδάσω δὲ καὶ ἑκάστοτε
Jesus Christ, made clear to me. I will be diligent And also always
ἔχειν ὑμᾶς μετὰ τὴν ἐμὴν ἔξοδον τὴν τούτων μνήμην
to have you after my departure the of these things memory
16 ποιεῖσθαι. οὐ γὰρ σεσοφισμένοις μύθοις ἐξακολουθήσαντες
to cause. not For having been cleverly devised fables following,
ἐγνωρίσαμεν ὑμῖν την τοῦ Κυρίου ἡμῶν Ἰησοῦ Χριστοῦ
we made known to you the of the Lord of us, Jesus Christ,
δύναμιν καὶ παρουσίαν, ἀλλ' ἐπόπται γενηθέντες τῆς
power and coming, but eyewitnesses having become of the
17 ἐκείνου μεγαλειότητος. λαβὼν γὰρ παρὰ Θεοῦ πατρὸς
of that (One) majesty. receiving For from God (the) Father
τιμὴν καὶ δόξαν, φωνῆς ἐνεχθείσης αὐτῷ τοιᾶσδε ὑπὸ τῆς
honor and glory, a voice being borne to Him such from the
μεγαλοπρεποῦς δόξης, Οὗτός ἐστιν ὁ υἱός μου ὁ ἀγαπητός,
magnificent glory: This is the Son of Me, the Beloved,
18 εἰς ὃν ἐγὼ εὐδόκησα· καὶ ταύτην τὴν φωνὴν ἡμεῖς ἠκού-
in whom I was well-pleased. And this voice we heard
σαμεν ἐξ οὐρανοῦ ἐνεχθεῖσαν, σὺν αὐτῷ ὄντες ἐν τῷ ὄρει τῷ
out of Heaven being borne, with Him being in the mountain
19 ἁγίῳ. καὶ ἔχομεν βεβαιότερον τὸν προφητικὸν λόγον, ᾧ
holy. And we have more firm the prophetic word, in whic
καλῶς ποιεῖτε προσέχοντες, ὡς λύχνῳ φαίνοντι ἐν αὐχμηρῷ
well you do taking heed, as to a lamp shining in murky
τόπῳ, ἕως οὗ ἡμέρα διαυγάσῃ, καὶ φωσφόρος ἀνατείλῃ ἐν
place, until day dawns, and the Daystar rises in
20 ταῖς καρδίαις ὑμῶν· τοῦτο πρῶτον γινώσκοντες, ὅτι πᾶσα
the hearts of you; this firstly knowing, that every
21 προφητεία γραφῆς ἰδίας ἐπιλύσεως οὐ γίνεται. οὐ γὰρ
prophecy of Scripture of (its) own unloosing did not come into being. not For
θελήματι ἀνθρώπου ἠνέχθη ποτὲ προφητεία, ἀλλ' ὑπὸ
by (the) will of man was borne at any time prophecy, but by
Πνεύματος Ἁγίου φερόμενοι ἐλάλησαν ἅγιοι Θεοῦ ἄνθρωποι.
(the) Spirit Holy being borne along spoke (the) holy of God men.

CHAPTER 2

1 Ἐγένοντο δὲ καὶ ψευδοπροφῆται ἐν τῷ λαῷ, ὡς καὶ ἐν
there were But also false prophets among the people, as also amon
ὑμῖν ἔσονται ψευδοδιδάσκαλοι, οἵτινες παρεισάξουσιν
you will be false teachers, who will secretly bring in
αἱρέσεις ἀπωλείας, καὶ τὸν ἀγοράσαντα αὐτοὺς δεσπότην
heresies of destruction, and the having bought them Master
2 ἀρνούμενοι, ἐπάγοντες ἑαυτοῖς ταχινὴν ἀπώλειαν. καὶ
denying, bringing on themselves swift destruction. And

follow their destructive ways, by whom the way of truth will be evil spoken of. 3 And by covetousness, with well-turned words, they will use you for gain—for whom judgment of old does not linger, and their destruction does not slumber. 4 For if God did not spare sinning angels, but delivered *them* to chains of darkness, thrust down into Tartarus, having been kept to judgment; 5 and did not spare *the* ancient world, but preserved Noah *the* eighth, a herald of righteousness, bringing a flood on a world of ungodly ones; 6 and covering the cities *of* Sodom and Gomorrah with ashes, *He* condemned *them* with an overthrow, setting an example to men intending to live ungodly. 7 And He delivered righteous Lot, who had been oppressed by the behavior of the lawless in lustfulness. 8 For that righteous one living among them day after day, in seeing and in hearing, *his* righteous soul *was* tormented with *their* lawless deeds.

9 *But the* Lord knows to deliver the godly out of temptation, and to keep the unjust for a day of judgment, being punished, 10 and most of all those going after flesh in *the* lust of defilement, and despising rulership, darers, self-satisfied; they do not tremble *at* glories, speaking evil; 11 where angels being greater in strength and power do not bring a reproaching charge before *the* Lord. 12 But these as unreasoning natural beasts, having been born for capture and corruption, speaking evil in that *of* which they are ignorant, they shall utterly perish in their corruption, 13 being about to receive *the* wages of unrighteousness, deeming indulgence in the day *to be* pleasure; reveling *in* spots and blemishes, feasting along with you in their deceits; 14 having eyes full of an adulteress, and never ceasing from sin; alluring unsettled souls; having a heart busied *with* covetousness; cursed children; 15 forsaking a straight path,

πολλοὶ ἐξακολουθήσουσιν αὐτῶν ταῖς ἀπωλείαις, δι' οὓς
many will follow of them the destructive ways, by whom
3 ἡ ὁδὸς τῆς ἀληθείας βλασφημηθήσεται. καὶ ἐν πλεονεξίᾳ
the way of the truth will be evil spoken of. And by covetousness
πλαστοῖς λόγοις ὑμᾶς ἐμπορεύσονται· οἷς τὸ κρίμα ἔκπαλαι
with well-turned words you they will use for gain; for whom the judgment of old
4 οὐκ ἀργεῖ, καὶ ἡ ἀπώλεια αὐτῶν οὐ νυστάζει. εἰ γὰρ ὁ
not lingers, and the destruction of them not slumbers. if For
Θεὸς ἀγγέλων ἁμαρτησάντων οὐκ ἐφείσατο, ἀλλὰ σειραῖς
God angels sinning did not spare, but to chains
5 ζόφου ταρταρώσας παρέδωκεν εἰς κρίσιν τετηρημένους· καὶ
of darkness thrust down into Tartarus delivered (them) to judgment having been kept; and
ἀρχαίου κόσμου οὐκ ἐφείσατο, ἀλλ' ὄγδοον Νῶε δικαιοσύνης
(the) ancient world not spared, but (the) eighth, Noah, of righteousness
6 κήρυκα ἐφύλαξε, κατακλυσμὸν κόσμῳ ἀσεβῶν ἐπάξας· καὶ
a herald preserved, a flood a world of ungodly ones bringing on; and
πόλεις Σοδόμων καὶ Γομόρρας τεφρώσας καταστροφῇ
the cities, Sodom and Gomorrah, covering with ashes by an overthrow
7 κατέκρινεν, ὑπόδειγμα μελλόντων ἀσεβεῖν τεθεικώς· καὶ
condemned, an example of men intending to live ungodly setting; and
δίκαιον Λώτ, καταπονούμενον ὑπὸ τῆς τῶν ἀθέσμων ἐν
righteous Lot, having been oppressed by the of the lawless in
8 ἀσελγείᾳ ἀναστροφῆς, ἐρρύσατο (βλέμματι γὰρ καὶ ἀκοῇ ὁ
lustfulness conduct delivered — in seeing for and hearing, the
δίκαιος, ἐγκατοικῶν ἐν αὐτοῖς, ἡμέραν ἐξ ἡμέρας ψυχὴν
righteous one dwelling among them day after day (his) soul
9 δικαίαν ἀνόμοις ἔργοις ἐβασάνιζεν)· οἶδε Κύριος εὐσεβεῖς
righteous with (the) lawless works tormented — knows (the) Lord the godly
ἐκ πειρασμῶν ῥύεσθαι, ἀδίκους δὲ εἰς ἡμέραν κρίσεως κολαζο-
out of temptation to deliver, the unjust but for a day of judgment being
10 μένους τηρεῖν· μάλιστα δὲ τοὺς ὀπίσω σαρκὸς ἐν ἐπιθυμίᾳ
punished to keep; most of all and the after flesh in lust
μιασμοῦ πορευομένους, καὶ κυριότητος καταφρονοῦντας.
of defilement (ones) going, and dominion despising,
τολμηταί, αὐθάδεις, δόξας οὐ τρέμουσι βλασφημοῦντες·
darers, self-satisfied, glories not they tremble (at), speaking evil,
11 ὅπου ἄγγελοι, ἰσχύϊ καὶ δυνάμει μείζονες ὄντες, οὐ φέρουσι
where angels in strength and in power greater being do not bring
12 κατ' αὐτῶν παρὰ Κυρίῳ βλάσφημον κρίσιν. οὗτοι δέ, ὡς
against them before (the) Lord a reproaching charge. these But, as
ἄλογα ζῶα φυσικὰ γεγενημένα εἰς ἅλωσιν καὶ φθοράν, ἐν
unreasoning beasts natural having been born for capture and corruption, in
οἷς ἀγνοοῦσι βλασφημοῦντες, ἐν τῇ φθορᾷ αὐτῶν καταφθαρή-
which they are ignorant (of) speaking evil; in the corruption of them, they shall utterly
13 σονται, κομιούμενοι μισθὸν ἀδικίας, ἡδονὴν ἡγούμενοι τὴν
perish; being about to receive wages of wrong, (as) pleasure deeming
ἐν ἡμέρᾳ τρυφήν, σπῖλοι καὶ μῶμοι, ἐντρυφῶντες ἐν ταῖς
in (the) day indulgence, spots and blemishes revelling (in); in the
14 ἀπάταις αὐτῶν συνευωχούμενοι ὑμῖν, ὀφθαλμοὺς ἔχοντες
deceits of them feasting along with you; eyes having
μεστοὺς μοιχαλίδος καὶ ἀκαταπαύστους ἁμαρτίας, δελεά-
full of an adulteress, and not ceasing from sin, alluring
ζοντες ψυχὰς ἀστηρίκτους, καρδίαν γεγυμνασμένην πλεονε-
souls unsettled; a heart having been busied covet-
15 ξίαις ἔχοντες, κατάρας τέκνα· καταλιπόντες τὴν εὐθεῖαν ὁδὸν
ousness having; of curse children; forsaking a straight way,

they went astray, following the way of Balaam the *son* of Beor, who loved *the* wages of unrighteousness, [16] but had reproof of *his* own transgression—the dumb ass speaking in a man's voice held back the prophet's madness.

[17] These are springs without water, clouds being driven by tempest, for whom blackness of darkness is kept forever. [18] For speaking great swelling *words* of vanity, by *the* lusts of the flesh, by unbridled lusts, they allure those who *were* escaping the ones living in error, [19] promising them freedom, though themselves being slaves of corruption; for by whom anyone has been overcome, even to this one he has been enslaved. [20] For if by a full knowledge of the Lord and Savior, Jesus Christ, *they* have escaped the defilements of the world, and again being entangled, *they* have been overcome by these, *and their* last *state is* worse than the first. [21] For it was better for them not to have fully known the way of righteousness, than fully knowing to turn from the holy commandment delivered to them. [22] But the *word* of the true proverb has happened to them: *The* dog turning to *his* own vomit; and, *the* sow to wallowing *in* mud.

CHAPTER 3

[1] Beloved, I now write this second epistle to you, in which by reminder I stir up your sincere mind to remember [2] the words having been spoken before by the holy prophets, and those of the apostles, by us, *by* the Lord and Savior; [3] first, knowing this, that during *the* last days scoffers will come, walking according to their own lusts, [4] and saying, Where is the promise of His coming? For since the fathers

ἐπλανήθησαν, ἐξακολουθήσαντες τῇ ὁδῷ τοῦ Βαλαὰμ τοῦ
they erred, following the way of Balaam the (son

16 Βοσόρ, ὃς μισθὸν ἀδικίας ἠγάπησεν, ἔλεγξιν δὲ ἔσχεν ἰδίας
of Beor, who (the) wages of wrong loved, reproof and had of own

παρανομίας· ὑποζύγιον ἄφωνον, ἐν ἀνθρώπου φωνῇ φθεγξά-
transgression; ass a dumb with of a man voice speaking

17 μενον, ἐκώλυσε τὴν τοῦ προφήτου παραφρονίαν. οὗτοί εἰσι
restrained the of the prophet madness. These are

πηγαὶ ἄνυδροι, νεφέλαι ὑπὸ λαίλαπος ἐλαυνόμεναι, οἷς ὁ
springs without water, clouds by tempest being driven, for whom the

18 ζόφος τοῦ σκότους εἰς αἰῶνα τετήρηται. ὑπέρογκα γὰρ
blackness of darkness to ages is kept. overswollen (words) For

ματαιότητος φθεγγόμενοι, δελεάζουσιν ἐν ἐπιθυμίαις σαρκός,
of vanity speaking, they allure by (the) lusts of (the) flesh

ἐν ἀσελγείαις, τοὺς ὄντως ἀποφυγόντας τοὺς ἐν πλάνῃ
in unbridled lusts, those indeed escaping the (ones) in error

19 ἀναστρεφομένους, ἐλευθερίαν αὐτοῖς ἐπαγγελλόμενοι, αὐτοὶ
living, freedom to them promising, themselves

δοῦλοι ὑπάρχοντες τῆς φθορᾶς· ᾧ γάρ τις ἥττηται, τούτῳ
slaves being of corruption; by whom for any- one has been defeated, to this one

20 καὶ δεδούλωται. εἰ γὰρ ἀποφυγόντες τὰ μιάσματα τοῦ
also he has been enslaved. if For having escaped the defilements of the

κόσμου ἐν ἐπιγνώσει τοῦ Κυρίου καὶ σωτῆρος Ἰησοῦ Χρι-
world by a full knowledge of the Lord and Savior Jesus Christ,

21 στοῦ, τούτοις δὲ πάλιν ἐμπλακέντες ἡττῶνται, γέγονεν αὐτοῖς
by these and again being entangled have been defeated, have become to them

τὰ ἔσχατα χείρονα τῶν πρώτων. κρεῖττον γὰρ ἦν αὐτοῖς
the last things worse (than) the first. better For it was for them

μὴ ἐπεγνωκέναι τὴν ὁδὸν τῆς δικαιοσύνης, ἢ ἐπιγνοῦσιν
not to have fully known the way of righteousness, than fully knowing

ἐπιστρέψαι ἐκ τῆς παραδοθείσης αὐτοῖς ἁγίας ἐντολῆς.
to turn from the delivered to them holy commandment

22 συμβέβηκε δὲ αὐτοῖς τὸ τῆς ἀληθοῦς παροιμίας, Κύων
has happened But to them the (word) of the true proverb: (the) dog

ἐπιστρέψας ἐπὶ τὸ ἴδιον ἐξέραμα, καί, Ὗς λουσαμένη εἰς
turning to the own vomit; and, (The) sow washed, to

κύλισμα βορβόρου.
wallowing of mud.

CHAPTER 3

1 Ταύτην ἤδη, ἀγαπητοί, δευτέραν ὑμῖν γράφω ἐπιστολήν,
This now, beloved, second to you I write epistle,

ἐν αἷς διεγείρω ὑμῶν ἐν ὑπομνήσει τὴν εἰλικρινῆ διάνοιαν,
in which I arouse you by reminder the sincere mind,

2 μνησθῆναι τῶν προειρημένων ῥημάτων ὑπὸ τῶν ἁγίων
to remember the having been before spoken words by the holy

προφητῶν, καὶ τῆς τῶν ἀποστόλων ἡμῶν ἐντολῆς τοῦ
prophets, and the of the apostles by us command of the

3 Κυρίου καὶ σωτῆρος· τοῦτο πρῶτον γινώσκοντες, ὅτι
Lord and Savior; this firstly knowing, that

ἐλεύσονται ἐπ' ἐσχάτου τῶν ἡμερῶν ἐμπαῖκται, κατὰ τὰς
will come during (the) last of the days scoffers, according to the

4 ἰδίας αὐτῶν ἐπιθυμίας πορευόμενοι, καὶ λέγοντες, Ποῦ
own of them lusts walking, and saying, Where

ἐστὶν ἡ ἐπαγγελία τῆς παρουσίας αὐτοῦ; ἀφ' ἧς γὰρ οἱ
is the promise of the coming of Him? from which for the

fell asleep, all things continue this way from *the* beginning of creation. [5]For this is hidden from them *by their* willing *it so,* that heavens were of old, and earth by water, and through water, being held together by the word of God, [6]through which the world that then *was,* being flooded by water, perished. [7]But the heavens and the earth now, having been stored up by the same word, are being kept for fire to a day of judgment and destruction of ungodly men.

[8]But let not this one thing be hidden *from* you, beloved, that one day with *the* Lord *is* as a thousand years, and a thousand years as one day. [9]The Lord is not slow *as to* the promise, as some deem slowness, but is longsuffering toward us, not having purposed any *of us* to perish, but all *of us* to come to repentance. [10]But the day of *the* Lord will come as a thief in *the* night, in which the heavens will pass away with rushing sound, and *the* elements burning will be dissolved, and earth and the works in it will be burned up. [11]Then all these being *about* to be dissolved, what sort ought you to be in holy behavior and godliness, [12]looking for and hastening the coming of the Day of God, through which *the* heavens being set afire will be dissolved, and *the* elements will melt? [13]But according to His promise, we look for new heavens and a new earth, in which righteousness dwells.

[14]Therefore, beloved, looking for these things, be diligent, spotless, and without blemish, to be found in peace by Him. [15]And think of the long-suffering of our Lord *as* salvation, as also our beloved brother Paul wrote to you, according to the wisdom given to him; [16]as also in all *His* epistles, speaking in them concerning these things, in which are some things hard to understand, which the unlearned and unsettled pervert, as also

πατέρες ἐκοιμήθησαν, πάντα οὕτω διαμένει ἀπ' ἀρχῆς
fathers fell asleep, all things so remain (the) from beginning
5 κτίσεως. λανθάνει γὰρ αὐτοὺς τοῦτο θέλοντας, ὅτι οὐρανοὶ
of creation. is hidden (from) For them this (by their) willing, that heavens
ἦσαν ἔκπαλαι, καὶ γῆ ἐξ ὕδατος καὶ δι' ὕδατος συνεστῶσα,
were of old, and earth by water, and through water having been held together
6 τῷ τοῦ Θεοῦ λόγῳ, δι' ὧν ὁ τότε κόσμος ὕδατι κατακλυ-
by the of God word, by which the then world by water being
7 σθεὶς ἀπώλετο· οἱ δὲ νῦν οὐρανοὶ καὶ ἡ γῆ τῷ αὐτῷ λόγῳ
flooded perished; the But now heavens and the earth by the same word
τεθησαυρισμένοι εἰσί, πυρὶ τηρούμενοι εἰς ἡμέραν κρίσεως
having been stored up are for fire being kept unto a day of judgment
καὶ ἀπωλείας τῶν ἀσεβῶν ἀνθρώπων.
and destruction of ungodly men.
8 Ἓν δὲ τοῦτο μὴ λανθανέτω ὑμᾶς, ἀγαπητοί, ὅτι μία
one But this thing not let be hidden (from) you, beloved, that one
ἡμέρα παρὰ Κυρίῳ ὡς χίλια ἔτη, καὶ χίλια ἔτη ὡς ἡμέρα
day with (the) Lord (is) as a thousand years and a thousand years as day
9 μία. οὐ βραδύνει ὁ Κύριος τῆς ἐπαγγελίας, ὥς τινες βραδυ-
one. not is slow The Lord of the promise, as some slowness
τῆτα ἡγοῦνται· ἀλλὰ μακροθυμεῖ εἰς ἡμᾶς, μὴ βουλόμενός
deem, but is longsuffering toward us, not purposing
τινας ἀπολέσθαι, ἀλλὰ πάντας εἰς μετάνοιαν χωρῆσαι.
any to perish, but all to repentance to come.
10 ἥξει δὲ ἡ ἡμέρα Κυρίου ὡς κλέπτης ἐν νυκτί, ἐν ᾗ οἱ οὐρανοὶ
will come But the day of (the) Lord as a thief in (the) night, in which the heavens
ῥοιζηδὸν παρελεύσονται, στοιχεῖα δὲ καυσούμενα λυθή-
with rushing sound will pass away, (the) elements and burning will be
11 σονται, καὶ γῆ καὶ τὰ ἐν αὐτῇ ἔργα κατακαήσεται. τούτων
dissolved, and earth and the in it works will be burned up. these things
οὖν πάντων λυομένων, ποταποὺς δεῖ ὑπάρχειν ὑμᾶς ἐν
Then all being dissolved, what sort ought to be you in
12 ἁγίαις ἀναστροφαῖς καὶ εὐσεβείαις, προσδοκῶντας καὶ
holy behavior and godliness, looking for and
σπεύδοντας τὴν παρουσίαν τῆς τοῦ Θεοῦ ἡμέρας, δι' ἣν
rushing the coming of the of God day, for which
οὐρανοὶ πυρούμενοι λυθήσονται, καὶ στοιχεῖα καυσούμενα
(the) heavens being set afire will be dissolved, and (the) elements burning
13 τήκεται; καινοὺς δὲ οὐρανοὺς καὶ γῆν καινὴν κατὰ τὸ
will melt. new But heavens and an earth new according to the
ἐπάγγελμα αὐτοῦ προσδοκῶμεν, ἐν οἷς δικαιοσύνη κατοικεῖ.
promise of Him we look for, in which righteousness dwells.
14 Διό, ἀγαπητοί, ταῦτα προσδοκῶντες, σπουδάσατε
Therefore, beloved, these things looking for, be diligent,
15 ἄσπιλοι καὶ ἀμώμητοι αὐτῷ εὑρεθῆναι ἐν εἰρήνῃ. καὶ τὴν
spotless and without blemish, by Him to be found in peace, and the
τοῦ Κυρίου ἡμῶν μακροθυμίαν σωτηρίαν ἡγεῖσθε, καθὼς
of the Lord of us longsuffering salvation deem, as
καὶ ὁ ἀγαπητὸς ἡμῶν ἀδελφὸς Παῦλος κατὰ τὴν αὐτῷ
also the beloved of us brother, Paul, according to the to him
16 δοθεῖσαν σοφίαν ἔγραψεν ὑμῖν· ὡς καὶ ἐν πάσαις ταῖς
given wisdom, wrote to you, as also in all (his)
ἐπιστολαῖς, λαλῶν ἐν αὐταῖς περὶ τούτων· ἐν οἷς ἐστι δυσνόη-
epistles, speaking in them concerning these, in which are hard to understand
τά τινα, ἃ οἱ ἀμαθεῖς καὶ ἀστήρικτοι στρεβλοῦσιν, ὡς καὶ τὰς
some things, which the unlearned and unsettled pervert, as also the

they do the rest of the Scriptures, to *their* own destruction. [17]Then beloved, you knowing beforehand, watch lest being led away by the error of the lawless you fall from *your* own steadfastness.

[18]But grow in grace and knowledge of our Lord and Savior, Jesus Christ. To Him *be* the glory, both now and to *the* day of eternity. Amen.

17 λοιπὰς γραφάς, πρὸς τὴν ἰδίαν αὐτῶν ἀπώλειαν. ὑμεῖς οὖν,
remaining Scriptures, to the own of them destruction. You, then,
ἀγαπητοί, προγινώσκοντες φυλάσσεσθε, ἵνα μή, τῇ τῶν
beloved, knowing beforehand, watch lest by the of the
ἀθέσμων πλάνῃ συναπαχθέντες, ἐκπέσητε τοῦ ἰδίου στηριγ-
lawless error being led away you fall from the own steadfast-
18 μοῦ. αὐξάνετε δὲ ἐν χάριτι καὶ γνώσει τοῦ Κυρίου ἡμῶν καὶ
ness; grow but in grace and knowledge of the Lord of us and
σωτῆρος Ἰησοῦ Χριστοῦ. αὐτῷ ἡ δόξα καὶ νῦν καὶ εἰς
Savior, Jesus Christ. To Him (be) the glory both now and to
ἡμέραν αἰῶνος. ἀμήν.
a day of age. Amen.

KING JAMES II VERSION

THE FIRST GENERAL EPISTLE OF JOHN

CHAPTER 1

[1] *We announce to you* what was from *the* beginning, what we have heard, what we have seen with our eyes, what we beheld, and *what* our hands touched, as regards the Word of life. And the Life was revealed, and we have seen, and we bear witness, and we announce to you the everlasting Life which was with the Father, and was revealed to us. [3] We announce to you what we have seen, and *what* we have heard, that you also may have fellowship with us. And truly our fellowship *is* with the Father and with His Son, Jesus Christ. [4] And we write these things to you, that your joy may be full.

[5] And this is the message which we have heard from Him, and we announce to you: God is light, and no darkness is in Him—none. If we say that we have fellowship with Him, and we walk in darkness, we lie and are not practicing the truth. But if we walk in the light, as He is in the light, we have fellowship with one another, and the blood of His Son Jesus Christ cleanses us from all sin. [8] If we say that we have no sin, we deceive ourselves, and the truth is not in us. [9] If we confess our sins, He is faithful and righteous that He may forgive us the sins, and may cleanse us from all unrighteousness. [10] If we say that we have not sinned, we make Him a liar, and His word is not in us.

ΙΩΑΝΝΟΥ

OF JOHN

ΕΠΙΣΤΟΛΗ ΚΑΘΟΛΙΚΗ ΠΡΩΤΗ

EPISTLE GENERAL FIRST

CHAPTER 1

1 Ὃ ἦν ἀπ' ἀρχῆς, ὃ ἀκηκόαμεν, ὃ ἑωράκαμεν τοῖς ὀφθαλ-
What was from (the) beginning what we have heard, what we have seen with the eyes
μοῖς ἡμῶν, ὃ ἐθεασάμεθα, καὶ αἱ χεῖρες ἡμῶν ἐψηλάφησαν
of us, what we beheld, and the hands of us touched,
2 περὶ τοῦ λόγου τῆς ζωῆς (καὶ ἡ ζωὴ ἐφανερώθη, καὶ
concerning the Word of life —and the Life was revealed, and
ἑωράκαμεν, καὶ μαρτυροῦμεν, καὶ ἀπαγγέλλομεν ὑμῖν τὴν
we have seen, and we bear witness, and we announce to you the
ζωὴν τὴν αἰώνιον, ἥτις ἦν πρὸς τὸν πατέρα, καὶ ἐφανερώθη
Life everlasting, which was with the Father, and was revealed
3 ἡμῖν)· ὃ ἑωράκαμεν καὶ ἀκηκόαμεν, ἀπαγγέλλομεν ὑμῖν,
to us— what we have seen, and we have heard, we announce to you,
ἵνα καὶ ὑμεῖς κοινωνίαν ἔχητε μεθ' ἡμῶν· καὶ ἡ κοινωνία δὲ
that also you fellowship may have with us, truly fellowship And
ἡ ἡμετέρα μετὰ τοῦ πατρὸς καὶ μετὰ τοῦ υἱοῦ αὐτοῦ Ἰησοῦ
our (is) with the Father and with the Son of Him, Jesus
4 Χριστοῦ· καὶ ταῦτα γράφομεν ὑμῖν, ἵνα ἡ χαρὰ ὑμῶν ᾖ
Christ. And these things write to you, that the joy of you be
πεπληρωμένη.
fulfilled.

5 Καὶ αὕτη ἐστὶν ἡ ἀγγελία ἣν ἀκηκόαμεν ἀπ' αὐτοῦ καὶ
And this is the message which we have heard from Him, and
ἀναγγέλλομεν ὑμῖν, ὅτι ὁ Θεὸς φῶς ἐστί, καὶ σκοτία ἐν αὐτῷ
we announce to you, that God light is, and darkness in Him
6 οὐκ ἔστιν οὐδεμία. ἐὰν εἴπωμεν ὅτι κοινωνίαν ἔχομεν μετ'
not is, none. If we say that fellowship we have with
αὐτοῦ, καὶ ἐν τῷ σκότει περιπατῶμεν, ψευδόμεθα, καὶ οὐ
Him, and in the darkness we walk, we lie, and not
7 ποιοῦμεν τὴν ἀλήθειαν· ἐὰν δὲ ἐν τῷ φωτὶ περιπατῶμεν,
are doing the truth. if But in the light we walk,
ὡς αὐτός ἐστιν ἐν τῷ φωτί, κοινωνίαν ἔχομεν μετ' ἀλλήλων,
as He is in the light, fellowship we have with one another,
καὶ τὸ αἷμα Ἰησοῦ Χριστοῦ τοῦ υἱοῦ αὐτοῦ καθαρίζει ἡμᾶς
and the blood of Jesus Christ the Son of Him cleanses us
8 ἀπὸ πάσης ἁμαρτίας. ἐὰν εἴπωμεν ὅτι ἁμαρτίαν οὐκ ἔχομεν,
from all sin. If we say that sin not we have,
9 ἑαυτοὺς πλανῶμεν, καὶ ἡ ἀλήθεια οὐκ ἔστιν ἐν ἡμῖν. ἐὰν
ourselves we deceive, and the truth not is in us. If
ὁμολογῶμεν τὰς ἁμαρτίας ἡμῶν, πιστός ἐστι καὶ δίκαιος
we confess the sins of us, faithful He is and righteous,
ἵνα ἀφῇ ἡμῖν τὰς ἁμαρτίας, καὶ καθαρίσῃ ἡμᾶς ἀπὸ πάσης
that He may forgive us the sins, and may cleanse us from all
10 ἀδικίας. ἐὰν εἴπωμεν ὅτι οὐχ ἡμαρτήκαμεν, ψεύστην ποιοῦ-
unrighteousness. If we say that not we have sinned, a liar we
μεν αὐτόν, καὶ ὁ λόγος αὐτοῦ οὐκ ἔστιν ἐν ἡμῖν.
make Him, and the word of Him not is in us.

CHAPTER 2

[1] My little children, I write these things to you so that you do not sin. And if anyone sins, we have an advocate with the Father, Jesus Christ *the* righteous. [2] And He is *the* propitiation relating to our sins, and not relating to ours only, but also relating to all the world. [3] And by this we know that we have known Him, if we keep His commands. [4] The *one* saying, I have known Him, and not keeping His commands is a liar, and the truth is not in that one. [5] But whoever keeps His word, truly in this one the love of God has been perfected. By this we know that we are in Him. [6] The *one* saying to rest in Him ought so to walk himself as that *One* walked. [7] Brothers, I do not write a new commandment to you, but an old commandment which you had from *the* beginning. The old commandment is the word which you heard from *the* beginning. [8] Again I write a new commandment to you which is true in Him and in us, because the darkness is passing away, and the true Light already shines. [9] The *one* saying to be in the light, and hating his brother, is in the darkness until now. [10] The *one* loving his brother rests in the light, and no offense is in him. [11] But the *one* hating his brother is in the darkness, and walks in the darkness, and does not know where he is going, because the darkness blinded his eyes.

[12] Little children, I write to you because you have been forgiven *your* sins through His name. [13] Fathers, I write to you because you have known Him from *the* beginning. I write to you, young men, because you have overcome the evil one. I write to you, young ones, because you have known the Father. [14] Young men, I wrote to

CHAPTER 2

1 Τεκνία μου, ταῦτα γράφω ὑμῖν, ἵνα μὴ ἁμάρτητε. καὶ ἐάν
Little children of me, these I write to you, that not you sin. And if
τις ἁμάρτῃ, παράκλητον ἔχομεν πρὸς τὸν πατέρα, Ἰησοῦν
anyone sins, an advocate we have with the Father, Jesus
2 Χριστὸν δίκαιον· καὶ αὐτὸς ἱλασμός ἐστι περὶ τῶν ἁμαρτιῶν
Christ (the) righteous; and He a propitiation is concerning the sins
ἡμῶν· οὐ περὶ τῶν ἡμετέρων δὲ μόνον, ἀλλὰ καὶ περὶ ὅλου
of us; not concerning ours and only, but also concerning all
3 τοῦ κόσμου. καὶ ἐν τούτῳ γινώσκομεν ὅτι ἐγνώκαμεν αὐτόν,
the world. And by this we know that we have known Him,
4 ἐὰν τὰς ἐντολὰς αὐτοῦ τηρῶμεν. ὁ λέγων, Ἔγνωκα αὐτόν,
if the commands of Him we keep. The (one) saying, I have known Him,
καὶ τὰς ἐντολὰς αὐτοῦ μὴ τηρῶν, ψεύστης ἐστί, καὶ ἐν τούτῳ
and the commands of Him not keeping a liar is, and in this one
5 ἡ ἀλήθεια οὐκ ἔστιν· ὃς δ' ἂν τηρῇ αὐτοῦ τὸν λόγον, ἀληθῶς
the truth not is. whoever But keeps of Him the word, truly
ἐν τούτῳ ἡ ἀγάπη τοῦ Θεοῦ τετελείωται. ἐν τούτῳ γινώ-
in this one the love of God has been perfected. By this we know
6 σκομεν ὅτι ἐν αὐτῷ ἐσμέν· ὁ λέγων ἐν αὐτῷ μένειν ὀφείλει,
that in Him we are. The (one) saying in Him to remain ought
καθὼς ἐκεῖνος περιεπάτησε, καὶ αὐτὸς οὕτω περιπατεῖν.
as that (One) walked, also himself so to walk.
7 Ἀδελφοί, οὐκ ἐντολὴν καινὴν γράφω ὑμῖν, ἀλλ' ἐντολὴν
Brothers, not a commandment new I write to you, but a commandment
παλαιάν, ἣν εἴχετε ἀπ' ἀρχῆς· ἡ ἐντολὴ ἡ παλαιά ἐστιν ὁ
old, which you had from (the) beginning the commandment old is the
8 λόγος ὃν ἠκούσατε ἀπ' ἀρχῆς. πάλιν ἐντολὴν καινὴν γράφω
word which you have heard from (the) beginning. Again commandment new I write
ὑμῖν, ὅ ἐστιν ἀληθὲς ἐν αὐτῷ καὶ ἐν ὑμῖν· ὅτι ἡ σκοτία παρ-
to you, what is true in Him and in us, because the darkness is
9 άγεται, καὶ τὸ φῶς τὸ ἀληθινὸν ἤδη φαίνει. ὁ λέγων ἐν τῷ φωτὶ
passing away, and the light true already shines. He saying in the light
εἶναι καὶ τὸν ἀδελφὸν αὐτοῦ μισῶν, ἐν τῇ σκοτίᾳ ἐστὶν ἕως
to be and the brother of him hating in the darkness is until
10 ἄρτι. ὁ ἀγαπῶν τὸν ἀδελφὸν αὐτοῦ ἐν τῷ φωτὶ μένει, καὶ
now. He loving the brother of him, in the light rests, and
11 σκάνδαλον ἐν αὐτῷ οὐκ ἔστιν. ὁ δὲ μισῶν τὸν ἀδελφὸν
offense in him not is. the (one) But hating the brother
αὐτοῦ ἐν τῇ σκοτίᾳ ἐστί, καὶ ἐν τῇ σκοτίᾳ περιπατεῖ, καὶ οὐκ
of him, in the darkness is, and in the darkness walks, and not
οἶδε ποῦ ὑπάγει, ὅτι ἡ σκοτία ἐτύφλωσε τοὺς ὀφθαλμοὺς
knows where he is going; for the darkness blinded the eyes
αὐτοῦ.
of him.
12 Γραφω ὑμῖν, τεκνία, ὅτι ἀφέωνται ὑμῖν αἱ ἁμαρτίαι διὰ
I write to you, little children, for have been forgiven you the sins because of
13 τὸ ὄνομα αὐτοῦ. γράφω ὑμῖν, πατέρες, ὅτι ἐγνώκατε τὸν
the name of Him. I write to you, fathers, because you have known the (One)
ἀπ' ἀρχῆς. γράφω ὑμῖν, νεανίσκοι, ὅτι νενικήκατε τὸν πονη-
from beginning. I write to you, young men, because you have overcome the evil
14 ρόν. γράφω ὑμῖν, παιδία, ὅτι ἐγνώκατε τὸν πατέρα. ἔγραψα
one. I wrote to you, young ones, for you have known the Father. I wrote
ὑμῖν, πατέρες, ὅτι ἐγνώκατε τὸν ἀπ' ἀρχῆς. ἔγραψα ὑμῖν,
to you, fathers, because you have known the (One) from beginning. I wrote to you,

you because you are strong, and the word of God abides in you, and you have overcome the evil one. 15 Do not love the world. If anyone loves the world, the love of the Father is not in him, 16 because all that which *is* in the world: the lust of the flesh, and the lust of the eye, and the pride of life, is not of the Father, but is of the world. 17 And the world is passing away, and its lust. But the *one* doing the will of God abides forever.

18 Young ones, it is a last hour, and as you heard that the antichrist is coming, even now many antichrists have risen up; from which you know that it is a last hour. 19 They went out from us, but they were not of us. For if they were of us, they would have remained with us; but *they left* so that it might be revealed that they are not of us. 20 And you have an anointing from the Holy One, and you know all things. 21 I did not write to you because you do not know the truth, but because you know it, and because every lie is not of the truth. 22 Who is the liar, except the *one* denying, *saying* that Jesus is not the Christ? This is the antichrist, the *one* denying the Father and the Son. 23 Everyone denying the Son neither has the Father. The *one* confessing the Son also has the Father. 24 Then what you heard from *the* beginning, let it abide in you. If what you heard from *the* beginning abides in you, you will abide in both the Father and in the Son. 25 And this is the promise which He promised us: everlasting life.

26 I wrote these things to you concerning the ones leading you astray. 27 And the anointing which you received from Him abides in you, and you have no need that anyone teach you. But as His anointing teaches you concerning all things, and is true, and is not a lie, and as

νεανίσκοι, ὅτι ἰσχυροί ἐστε, καὶ ὁ λόγος τοῦ Θεοῦ ἐν ὑμῖν
young men, that strong you are, and the word of God in you

15 μένει, καὶ νενικήκατε τὸν πονηρόν. μὴ ἀγαπᾶτε τὸν κόσμον,
remains, and you have overcome the evil one. Do not love the world,

μηδὲ τὰ ἐν τῷ κόσμῳ. ἐάν τις ἀγαπᾷ τὸν κόσμον, οὐκ ἔστιν
nor the things in the world. If anyone loves the world, not is

16 ἡ ἀγάπη τοῦ πατρὸς ἐν αὐτῷ. ὅτι πᾶν τὸ ἐν τῷ κόσμῳ, ἡ
the love of the Father in him; because all that which (is) in the world, the

ἐπιθυμία τῆς σαρκός, καὶ ἡ ἐπιθυμία των ὀφθαλμῶν, καὶ ἡ
lust of the flesh, and the lust of the eye, and the

ἀλαζονεία τοῦ βίου, οὐκ ἔστιν ἐκ τοῦ πατρός, ἀλλ' ἐκ τοῦ
pride of life, not is of the Father, but of the

17 κόσμου ἐστί. καὶ ὁ κόσμος παράγεται, καὶ ἡ ἐπιθυμία αὐτοῦ·
world is. And the world is passing away, and the lust of it;

ὁ δὲ ποιῶν τὸ θέλημα τοῦ Θεοῦ μένει εἰς τὸν αἰῶνα.
he but doing the will of God remains to the age.

18 Παιδία, ἐσχάτη ὥρα ἐστί· καὶ καθὼς ἠκούσατε ὅτι ὁ
Young ones, a last hour it is, and as you heard that the

ἀντίχριστος ἔρχεται, καὶ νῦν ἀντίχριστοι πολλοὶ γεγόνασιν·
antichrist is coming, even now antichrists many have arisen;

19 ὅθεν γινώσκομεν ὅτι ἐσχάτη ὥρα ἐστίν. ἐξ ἡμῶν ἐξῆλθον,
from which you know that a last hour it is. From us they went out,

ἀλλ' οὐκ ἦσαν ἐξ ἡμῶν· εἰ γὰρ ἦσαν ἐξ ἡμῶν, μεμενήκεισαν
but not they were of us; if for they were of us, they would have remained

ἂν μεθ' ἡμῶν· ἀλλ' ἵνα φανερωθῶσιν ὅτι οὐκ εἰσὶ πάντες
with us; but that it might be revealed that not they are all

20 ἐξ ἡμῶν. καὶ ὑμεῖς χρίσμα ἔχετε ἀπὸ τοῦ ἁγίου, καὶ οἴδατε
of us And you an anointing have from the Holy One, and you know

21 πάντα. οὐκ ἔγραψα ὑμῖν, ὅτι οὐκ οἴδατε τὴν ἀλήθειαν, ἀλλ'
all. Not I wrote to you because not you know the truth, but

ὅτι οἴδατε αὐτήν, καὶ ὅτι πᾶν ψεῦδος ἐκ τῆς ἀληθείας οὐκ
because you know it, and because every lie of the truth not

22 ἔστι. τίς ἐστιν ὁ ψεύστης, εἰ μὴ ὁ ἀρνούμενος ὅτι Ἰησοῦς οὐκ
is. Who is the liar, except the (one) denying that Jesus not

ἔστιν ὁ Χριστός; οὗτός ἐστιν ὁ ἀντίχριστος, ὁ ἀρνούμενος
is the Christ? This is the antichrist, the (one) denying

23 τὸν πατέρα καὶ τὸν υἱόν. πᾶς ὁ ἀρνούμενος τὸν υἱὸν οὐδὲ
the Father and the Son. Everyone denying the Son neither

τὸν πατέρα ἔχει· ὁ ὁμολογῶν τὸν υἱὸν καὶ τὸν πατέρα ἔχει.
the Father has; the (one) confessing the Son also the Father has.

24 ὑμεῖς οὖν ὃ ἠκούσατε ἀπ' ἀρχῆς, ἐν ὑμῖν μενέτω. ἐὰν ἐν
you then What you heard from (the) beginning, in you let it remain. If in

ὑμῖν μείνῃ ὃ ἀπ' ἀρχῆς ἠκούσατε, καὶ ὑμεῖς ἐν τῷ υἱῷ καὶ
you remains what from (the) beginning you heard, both you in the Son and

25 ἐν τῷ πατρὶ μενεῖτε. καὶ αὕτη ἐστὶν ἡ ἐπαγγελία ἣν αὐτὸς
in the Father will remain. And this is the promise which He

26 ἐπηγγείλατο ἡμῖν, τὴν ζωὴν τὴν αἰώνιον. ταῦτα ἔγραψα
promised us, the life everlasting. These things I wrote

27 ὑμῖν περὶ τῶν πλανώντων ὑμᾶς. καὶ ὑμεῖς, τὸ χρίσμα ὃ
to you concerning those leading astray you. And you the anointing which

ἐλάβετε ἀπ' αὐτοῦ ἐν ὑμῖν μένει, καὶ οὐ χρείαν ἔχετε ἵνα τις
received from Him in you remains, and no need you have that anyone

διδάσκῃ ὑμᾶς· ἀλλ' ὡς τὸ αὐτὸ χρίσμα διδάσκει ὑμᾶς περὶ
teach you; but as the of Him anointing teaches you concerning

πάντων, καὶ ἀληθές ἐστι, καὶ οὐκ ἔστι ψεῦδος, καὶ καθὼς
all things, and true is, and not is a lie, and as

He taught you, abide in Him. [28]And now, little children, abide in Him, that when He is revealed we may have confidence, and not be shamed from Him in His coming. [29]If you know that He is righteous, know that everyone doing righteousness has been born of Him.

CHAPTER 3

[1]See what manner of love the Father has given us, that we may be called children of God. For this reason the world does not know us, because it did not know Him. [2]Beloved, now we are the children of God, and it was not yet revealed what we shall be. But we know that if He appears, we shall be like Him, because we shall see Him as He is. [3]And everyone having this hope on Him purifies himself, even as that *One* is pure. [4]Everyone practicing sin also practices lawlessness, and sin is lawlessness. [5]And you know that He was revealed that He might bear our sins; and sin is not in Him.

[7]Little children, let no one lead you astray; the *one* practicing righteousness is righteous, even as He is righteous. [8]The *one* practicing sin is of the Devil, because the Devil sins from *the* beginning. For this the Son of God was revealed, that He undo the works of the Devil. [9]Everyone having been begotten of God does not sin, because His seed abides in him, and he is not able to sin, because he has been born of God. [10]By this the children of God and the children of the Devil are revealed: Everyone not practicing righteousness is not of God; also the *one* not loving his brother. [11]Because this is the message which you heard from *the* beginning, that we should love one another, [12]not as Cain was

28 ἐδίδαξεν ὑμᾶς, μενεῖτε ἐν αὐτῷ. καὶ νῦν, τεκνία, μένετε ἐν
He taught you, remain in Him. And now, little children, remain in
αὐτῷ· ἵνα ὅταν φανερωθῇ, ἔχωμεν παρρησίαν, καὶ μὴ
in Him, that when He is revealed we may have confidence, and not
29 αἰσχυνθῶμεν ἀπ' αὐτοῦ ἐν τῇ παρουσίᾳ αὐτοῦ. ἐὰν εἰδῆτε
be shamed from Him in the coming of Him. If you know
ὅτι δίκαιός ἐστι, γινώσκετε ὅτι πᾶς ὁ ποιῶν τὴν δικαιοσύνην
that righteous He is, know that everyone doing the righteousness,
ἐξ αὐτοῦ γεγέννηται.
of Him has been born.

CHAPTER 3

1 Ἴδετε ποταπὴν ἀγάπην δέδωκεν ἡμῖν ὁ πατήρ, ἵνα τέκνα
See what manner of love has given us the Father, that children
Θεοῦ κληθῶμεν. διὰ τοῦτο ὁ κόσμος οὐ γινώσκει ἡμᾶς, ὅτι
of God we may be called. Therefore the world not knows us, because
2 οὐκ ἔγνω αὐτόν. ἀγαπητοί, νῦν τέκνα Θεοῦ ἐσμέν, καὶ οὔπω
not it knew Him. Beloved, now children of God we are, and not yet
ἐφανερώθη τί ἐσόμεθα· οἴδαμεν δὲ ὅτι ἐὰν φανερωθῇ, ὅμοιοι
was it revealed what we shall be, we know but that if He is revealed, like
3 αὐτῷ ἐσόμεθα, ὅτι ὀψόμεθα αὐτὸν καθώς ἐστι. καὶ πᾶς ὁ
Him we shall be, because we shall see Him as He is. And everyone
ἔχων τὴν ἐλπίδα ταύτην ἐπ' αὐτῷ ἁγνίζει ἑαυτόν, καθὼς
having hope this on him purifies himself, as
4 ἐκεῖνος ἁγνός ἐστι. πᾶς ὁ ποιῶν τὴν ἁμαρτίαν, καὶ τὴν
that (One) pure is. Everyone doing sin, also
5 ἀνομίαν ποιεῖ· καὶ ἡ ἁμαρτία ἐστὶν ἡ ἀνομία. καὶ οἴδατε ὅτι
lawlessness does; and sin is lawlessness. And you know that
ἐκεῖνος ἐφανερώθη, ἵνα τὰς ἁμαρτίας ἡμῶν ἄρῃ· καὶ ἁμαρτία
that (One) was revealed that the sins of us He might bear, and sin
6 ἐν αὐτῷ οὐκ ἔστι. πᾶς ὁ ἐν αὐτῷ μένων οὐχ ἁμαρτάνει· πᾶς
in Him not is. Everyone in Him remaining not sins; everyone
ὁ ἁμαρτάνων οὐχ ἑώρακεν αὐτόν, οὐδὲ ἔγνωκεν αὐτόν.
sinning not has seen Him, nor known Him.
7 τεκνία, μηδεὶς πλανάτω ὑμᾶς· ὁ ποιῶν τὴν δικαιοσύνην
Little children, no one let lead astray you; he doing righteousness
8 δίκαιός ἐστι, καθὼς ἐκεῖνος δίκαιός ἐστιν· ὁ ποιῶν τὴν
righteous is, even as that One righteous is. The (one) doing
ἁμαρτίαν ἐκ τοῦ διαβόλου ἐστίν, ὅτι ἀπ' ἀρχῆς ὁ διάβολος
sin of the Devil is, because from (the) beginning the Devil
ἁμαρτάνει. εἰς τοῦτο ἐφανερώθη ὁ υἱὸς τοῦ Θεοῦ, ἵνα λύσῃ
sins. For this was revealed the Son of God, that He undo
9 τὰ ἔργα τοῦ διαβόλου. πᾶς ὁ γεγεννημένος ἐκ τοῦ Θεοῦ
the works of the Devil. Everyone having been begotten of God
ἁμαρτίαν οὐ ποιεῖ, ὅτι σπέρμα αὐτοῦ ἐν αὐτῷ μένει· καὶ οὐ
sin not does, because seed of Him in him remains; and not
10 δύναται ἁμαρτάνειν, ὅτι ἐκ τοῦ Θεοῦ γεγέννηται. ἐν τούτῳ
he is able to sin, because of God he has been born. By this
φανερά ἐστι τὰ τέκνα τοῦ Θεοῦ καὶ τὰ τέκνα τοῦ διαβόλου·
revealed are the children of God and the children of the Devil:
πᾶς ὁ μὴ ποιῶν δικαιοσύνην οὐκ ἔστιν ἐκ τοῦ Θεοῦ, καὶ ὁ μὴ
everyone not doing righteousness not is of God; also he not
11 ἀγαπῶν τὸν ἀδελφὸν αὐτοῦ. ὅτι αὕτη ἐστὶν ἡ ἀγγελία ἣν
loving the brother of him. Because this is the message which
12 ἠκούσατε ἀπ' ἀρχῆς, ἵνα ἀγαπῶμεν ἀλλήλους· οὐ καθὼς
you heard from (the) beginning, that we should love one another; not as

of the evil one, and killed his brother. And for what did he kill him? Because his works were evil, but the things of his brother *were* righteous.

[13] Do not marvel, my brothers, if the world hates you. [14] We know that we have passed from death to life because we love the brothers. The *one* not loving the brother remains in death. [15] Everyone hating the brother is a murderer, and you know that every murderer does not have everlasting life abiding in him.

[16] By this we have known the love of God, because that *One* laid down His soul for us; and on behalf of the brothers we ought to lay down *our* souls. [17] Whoever has the means of life of the world, and sees his brother having need, and shuts up his bowels from him, how does the love of God abide in him?

[18] My little children, let us not love in word, or in tongue, but in deed and in truth. [19] And in this we shall know that we are of the truth, and shall persuade our hearts, [20] that if our heart accuses us, *we know* that God is greater than our heart and knows all things. [21] Beloved, if our heart does not accuse us, we have confidence with God. [22] And whatever we ask, we receive from Him, because we keep His commandments, and we do the things pleasing before Him. [23] And this is His commandment, that we should believe the name of His Son, Jesus Christ, and love one another, even as He gave command to us. [24] And the *one* keeping His commandments abides in Him, and He in him. And by this we know that He abides in us, by the Spirit which He gave to us.

Κάϊν ἐκ τοῦ πονηροῦ ἦν, καὶ ἔσφαξε τὸν ἀδελφὸν αὐτοῦ. καὶ
Cain of the evil one was, and killed the brother of him; and
χάριν τίνος ἔσφαξεν αὐτόν; ὅτι τὰ ἔργα αὐτοῦ πονηρὰ ἦν,
for what did he kill him? Because the works of him evil were;
τὰ δὲ τοῦ ἀδελφοῦ αὐτοῦ δίκαια.
the things but of the brother of him righteous.
13 Μὴ θαυμάζετε, ἀδελφοί μου, εἰ μισεῖ ὑμᾶς ὁ κόσμος· ἡμεῖς
14 Do not marvel, brothers of me, if hates you the world. We
οἴδαμεν ὅτι μεταβεβήκαμεν ἐκ τοῦ θανάτου εἰς τὴν ζωήν, ὅτι
know that we have passed from death to life, because
ἀγαπῶμεν τοὺς ἀδελφούς. ὁ μὴ ἀγαπῶν τὸν ἀδελφόν,
we love the brothers. The (one) not loving the brother
15 μένει ἐν τῷ θανάτῳ. πᾶς ὁ μισῶν τὸν ἀδελφὸν αὐτοῦ ἀνθρω-
remains in death. Everyone hating the brother of him a murderer
ποκτόνος ἐστί· καὶ οἴδατε ὅτι πᾶς ἀνθρωποκτόνος οὐκ ἔχει
is, and you know that every murderer not has
16 ζωὴν αἰώνιον ἐν αὐτῷ μένουσαν. ἐν τούτῳ ἐγνώκαμεν τὴν
life everlasting in him remaining. By this we have known the
ἀγάπην τοῦ Θεοῦ, ὅτι ἐκεῖνος ὑπὲρ ἡμῶν τὴν ψυχὴν αὐτοῦ
love of God, because that (One) for us the soul of Him
ἔθηκε· καὶ ἡμεῖς ὀφείλομεν ὑπὲρ τῶν ἀδελφῶν τὰς ψυχὰς
laid down; and we ought on behalf of the brothers the souls
17 τιθέναι. ὃς δ' ἂν ἔχῃ τὸν βίον τοῦ κόσμου, καὶ θεωρῇ τὸν
to lay down. Whoever has the means of life of the world, and beholds the
ἀδελφὸν αὐτοῦ χρείαν ἔχοντα, καὶ κλείσῃ τὰ σπλάγχνα
brother of him need having, and shuts up the bowels
αὐτοῦ ἀπ' αὐτοῦ, πῶς ἡ ἀγάπη τοῦ Θεοῦ μένει ἐν αὐτῷ;
of him from him, how the love of God remains in him?
18 τεκνία μου, μὴ ἀγαπῶμεν λόγῳ μηδὲ γλώσσῃ ἀλλ' ἔργῳ
Little children of me, not let us love in word, nor in tongue, but in work
19 καὶ ἀληθείᾳ. καὶ ἐν τούτῳ γινώσκομεν ὅτι ἐκ τῆς ἀληθείας
and truth. And in this we shall know that of the truth
ἐσμέν, καὶ ἔμπροσθεν αὐτοῦ πείσομεν τὰς καρδίας ἡμῶν,
we are, and before Him shall persuade the heart of us,
20 ὅτι ἐὰν καταγινώσκῃ ἡμῶν ἡ καρδία, ὅτι μείζων ἐστὶν ὁ
that if accuses of us the heart, that greater is
21 Θεὸς τῆς καρδίας ἡμῶν, καὶ γινώσκει πάντα. ἀγαπητοί,
God (than) the heart of us and knows all things. Beloved,
ἐὰν ἡ καρδία ἡμῶν μὴ καταγινώσκῃ ἡμῶν, παρρησίαν
if the heart of us not accuses us, confidence
22 ἔχομεν πρὸς τὸν Θεόν, καὶ ὃ ἐὰν αἰτῶμεν, λαμβάνομεν παρ'
we have with God, and whatever we ask we receive from
αὐτοῦ, ὅτι τὰς ἐντολὰς αὐτοῦ τηροῦμεν, καὶ τὰ ἀρεστὰ
Him, because the commandments of Him we keep, and the things pleasing
23 ἐνώπιον αὐτοῦ ποιοῦμεν. καὶ αὕτη ἐστὶν ἡ ἐντολὴ αὐτοῦ,
before Him we do. And this is the commandment of Him,
ἵνα πιστεύσωμεν τῷ ὀνόματι τοῦ υἱοῦ αὐτοῦ Ἰησοῦ Χρι-
that we should believe the name of the Son of Him, Jesus Christ,
στοῦ, καὶ ἀγαπῶμεν ἀλλήλους, καθὼς ἔδωκεν ἐντολὴν ἡμῖν.
and love one another, even as He gave command to us.
24 καὶ ὁ τηρῶν τὰς ἐντολὰς αὐτοῦ ἐν αὐτῷ μένει, καὶ αὐτὸς ἐν
And he keeping the commandments of Him in Him remains, and He in
αὐτῷ. καὶ ἐν τούτῳ γινώσκομεν ὅτι μένει ἐν ἡμῖν, ἐκ τοῦ
him. And by this we know that He remains in us, by the
Πνεύματος οὗ ἡμῖν ἔδωκεν.
Spirit which to us He gave.

CHAPTER 4

1 Beloved, do not believe every spirit, whether they are from God; for many false prophets have gone forth into the world. 2 By this know the Spirit of God: every spirit which confesses that Jesus Christ has come in *the* flesh is from God. 3 And every spirit which does not confess that Jesus Christ has come in *the* flesh is not from God; and this is the antichrist which you heard is coming, and now is already in the world. 4 Little children, you are of God and have overcome them, because He in you is greater than he in the world. 5 They are of the world; therefore they speak of the world, and the world hears them. 6 We are of God; the *one* knowing God hears us. Whoever is not of God does not hear us. From this we know the spirit of truth and the spirit of error.

7 Beloved, let us love one another, because love is of God, and everyone who loves has been born of God, and knows God. 8 The *one* who does not love has not known God, because God is love. 9 By this the love of God was revealed in us, because His Son, the Only-begotten, God has sent into the world that we might live through Him. 10 In this is love, not that we loved God, but that He loved us, and sent His Son *to be* a propitiation relating to our sins. 11 Beloved, if God so loved us, we also ought to love one another. 12 No one has seen God at any time. If we love one another, God abides in us, and His love having been perfected is in

CHAPTER 4

1 Ἀγαπητοί, μὴ παντὶ πνεύματι πιστεύετε, ἀλλὰ δοκι-
Beloved not every spirit believe, but test
μάζετε τὰ πνεύματα, εἰ ἐκ τοῦ Θεοῦ ἐστίν· ὅτι πολλοὶ
the spirits, if of God they are, because many
2 ψευδοπροφῆται ἐξεληλύθασιν εἰς τὸν κόσμον. ἐν τούτῳ
false prophets have gone forth into the world. By this
γινώσκετε τὸ Πνεῦμα τοῦ Θεοῦ· πᾶν πνεῦμα ὃ ὁμολογεῖ
know the Spirit of God: every spirit which confesses
Ἰησοῦν Χριστὸν ἐν σαρκὶ ἐληλυθότα ἐκ τοῦ Θεοῦ ἐστί·
Jesus Christ in (the) flesh having come, of God is.
3 καὶ πᾶν πνεῦμα ὃ μὴ ὁμολογεῖ τὸν Ἰησοῦν Χριστὸν ἐν
and every spirit which not confesses Jesus Christ in
σαρκὶ ἐληλυθότα, ἐκ τοῦ Θεοῦ οὐκ ἔστι· καὶ τοῦτό ἐστι τὸ
(the) flesh having come, of God not is; and this is the
τοῦ ἀντιχρίστου, ὃ ἀκηκόατε ὅτι ἔρχεται, καὶ νῦν ἐν τῷ
antichrist which you heard that it is coming, and now in the
4 κόσμῳ ἐστὶν ἤδη. ὑμεῖς ἐκ τοῦ Θεοῦ ἐστέ, τεκνία, καὶ
world is already. You of God are, little children, and
νενικήκατε αὐτούς· ὅτι μείζων ἐστὶν ὁ ἐν ὑμῖν ἢ ὁ ἐν τῷ
have overcome them, because greater is the (One) in you than the (one) in the
5 κόσμῳ. αὐτοὶ ἐκ τοῦ κόσμου εἰσί· διὰ τοῦτο ἐκ τοῦ κόσμου
world. They of the world are; therefore of the world
6 λαλοῦσι, καὶ ὁ κόσμος αὐτῶν ἀκούει. ἡμεῖς ἐκ τοῦ Θεοῦ
they speak, and the world them hears. We of God
ἐσμέν· ὁ γινώσκων τὸν Θεόν, ἀκούει ἡμῶν· ὃς οὐκ ἔστιν ἐκ
are; the (one) knowing God hears us; (he) who not is of
τοῦ Θεοῦ, οὐκ ἀκούει ἡμῶν. ἐκ τούτου γινώσκομεν τὸ
God not hears us. From this we know the
πνεῦμα τῆς ἀληθείας καὶ τὸ πνεῦμα τῆς πλάνης.
spirit of truth, and the spirit of error.

7 Ἀγαπητοί, ἀγαπῶμεν ἀλλήλους· ὅτι ἡ ἀγάπη ἐκ τοῦ
Beloved, let us love one another, because love of
Θεοῦ ἐστί, καὶ πᾶς ὁ ἀγαπῶν ἐκ τοῦ Θεοῦ γεγέννηται, καὶ
God is, and everyone loving, of God has been born, and
8 γινώσκει τὸν Θεόν. ὁ μὴ ἀγαπῶν οὐκ ἔγνω τὸν Θεόν· ὅτι
knows God. The (one) not loving not knew God, because
9 ὁ Θεὸς ἀγάπη ἐστίν. ἐν τούτῳ ἐφανερώθη ἡ ἀγάπη τοῦ
God love is. By this was revealed the love
Θεοῦ ἐν ἡμῖν, ὅτι τὸν υἱὸν αὐτοῦ τὸν μονογενῆ ἀπέσταλκεν
of God in us, because the Son of Him the only-begotten has sent
10 ὁ Θεὸς εἰς τὸν κόσμον, ἵνα ζήσωμεν δι' αὐτοῦ. ἐν τούτῳ
God into the world, that we might live through Him. In this
ἐστὶν ἡ ἀγάπη, οὐχ ὅτι ἡμεῖς ἠγαπήσαμεν τὸν Θεόν, ἀλλ'
is love, not that we loved God, but
ὅτι αὐτὸς ἠγάπησεν ἡμᾶς, καὶ ἀπέστειλε τὸν υἱὸν αὐτοῦ
that He loved us, and sent the Son of Him
11 ἱλασμὸν περὶ τῶν ἁμαρτιῶν ἡμῶν. ἀγαπητοί, εἰ οὕτως ὁ
a propitiation concerning the sins of us. Beloved, if so
Θεὸς ἠγάπησεν ἡμᾶς, καὶ ἡμεῖς ὀφείλομεν ἀλλήλους ἀγαπᾷν.
God loved us, also we ought one another to love.
12 Θεὸν οὐδεὶς πώποτε τεθέαται· ἐὰν ἀγαπῶμεν ἀλλήλους,
God No one ever has beheld; if we love one another,
ὁ Θεὸς ἐν ἡμῖν μένει, καὶ ἡ ἀγάπη αὐτοῦ τετελειωμένη
God in us remains, and the love of Him having been perfected

us. 13 By this we know that we abide in Him, and He in us, because of His Spirit He has given to us. 14 And we have beheld and bear witness that the Father has sent the Son *as* Savior of the world. 15 Whoever confesses that Jesus is the Son of God, God abides in him, and he in God. 16 And we have known and have believed the love which God has in us. God is love, and the *one* abiding in love abides in God, and God in him. 17 Love has been perfected with us by this, that we have confidence in the day of judgment, that as He is, we also are in this world.

18 There is no fear in love, but perfect love casts out fear, because fear has punishment; and the *one* fearing has not been perfected in love. 19 We love Him because He first loved us. 20 If anyone says, I love God, and hates his brother, he is a liar. For the *one* not loving his brother whom he has seen, how is he able to love God whom he has not seen? 21 And we have this commandment from Him, that the *one* who loves God also loves his brother.

CHAPTER 5

1 Everyone who believes that Jesus is the Christ has been born of God. And everyone who loves Him who begets also loves the *one* who has been born of Him. 2 By this we know that we love the children of God when we love God and keep His commandments. 3 For this is the love of God, that we keep His commandments; and His commandments are not heavy. 4 Because everything having been born of God overcomes the world, and this is the victory overcoming the

13 ἐστὶν ἐν ἡμῖν. ἐν τούτῳ γινώσκομεν ὅτι ἐν αὐτῷ μένομεν καὶ
is in us. By this we know that in Him we remain, and
αὐτὸς ἐν ἡμῖν, ὅτι ἐκ τοῦ Πνεύματος αὐτοῦ δέδωκεν ἡμῖν.
He in us, because of the Spirit of Him He has given us.
14 καὶ ἡμεῖς τεθεάμεθα καὶ μαρτυροῦμεν ὅτι ὁ πατὴρ ἀπέσταλκε
And we we have beheld and bear witness that the Father has sent
15 τὸν υἱὸν σωτῆρα τοῦ κόσμου. ὃς ἂν ὁμολογήσῃ ὅτι Ἰησοῦς
the Son (as) Savior of the world. Whoever confesses that Jesus
ἐστὶν ὁ υἱὸς τοῦ Θεοῦ, ὁ Θεὸς ἐν αὐτῷ μένει, καὶ αὐτὸς ἐν
is the Son of God, God in him remains, and he in
16 τῷ Θεῷ. καὶ ἡμεῖς ἐγνώκαμεν καὶ πεπιστεύκαμεν τὴν ἀγάπην
God. And we have known and have believed the love
ἣν ἔχει ὁ Θεὸς ἐν ἡμῖν. ὁ Θεὸς ἀγάπη ἐστί, καὶ ὁ μένων ἐν τῇ
which has God in us. God love is, and he remaining in
17 ἀγάπῃ, ἐν τῷ Θεῷ μένει, καὶ ὁ Θεὸς ἐν αὐτῷ. ἐν τούτῳ τετε-
love, in God remains, and God in him. By this has
λείωται ἡ ἀγάπη μεθ' ἡμῶν, ἵνα παρρησίαν ἔχωμεν ἐν τῇ
been perfected love with us, that confidence we have in the
ἡμέρᾳ τῆς κρίσεως, ὅτι καθὼς ἐκεῖνός ἐστι, καὶ ἡμεῖς ἐσμὲν ἐν
day of judgment, that as that (One) is, also we are in
18 τῷ κόσμῳ τούτῳ. φόβος οὐκ ἔστιν ἐν τῇ ἀγάπῃ, ἀλλ' ἡ
world this. Fear not is in love, but
τελεία ἀγάπη ἔξω βάλλει τὸν φόβον, ὅτι ὁ φόβος κόλασιν
perfect love out casts fear, because fear punishment
19 ἔχει ὁ δὲ φοβούμενος οὐ τετελείωται ἐν τῇ ἀγάπῃ. ἡμεῖς
has, the (one) and fearing not has been perfected in love. We
20 ἀγαπῶμεν αὐτόν, ὅτι αὐτὸς πρῶτος ἠγάπησεν ἡμᾶς. ἐάν
love Him, because He first loved us. If
τις εἴπῃ ὅτι Ἀγαπῶ τὸν Θεόν, καὶ τὸν ἀδελφὸν αὐτοῦ μισῇ,
anyone says, I love God, and the brother of him hates,
ψεύστης ἐστίν· ὁ γὰρ μὴ ἀγαπῶν τὸν ἀδελφὸν αὐτοῦ ὃν
a liar he is; the (one) for not loving the brother of him whom
21 ἑώρακε, τὸν Θεὸν ὃν οὐχ ἑώρακε πῶς δύναται ἀγαπᾷν; καὶ
he has seen, God whom not he has seen, how is he able to love? And
ταύτην τὴν ἐντολὴν ἔχομεν ἀπ' αὐτοῦ, ἵνα ὁ ἀγαπῶν τὸν
this commandment we have from Him, that the (one) loving
Θεόν, ἀγαπᾷ καὶ τὸν ἀδελφὸν αὐτοῦ.
God, loves also the brother of him.

CHAPTER 5

1 Πᾶς ὁ πιστεύων ὅτι Ἰησοῦς ἐστὶν ὁ Χριστός, ἐκ τοῦ Θεοῦ
Everyone believing that Jesus is the Christ, of God
γεγέννηται· καὶ πᾶς ὁ ἀγαπῶν τὸν γεννήσαντα ἀγαπᾷ καὶ
has been born; and everyone loving the (One) begetting, loves also
2 τὸν γεγεννημένον ἐξ αὐτοῦ. ἐν τούτῳ γινώσκομεν ὅτι
the (one) having been born of Him. By this we know that
ἀγαπῶμεν τὰ τέκνα τοῦ Θεοῦ, ὅταν τὸν Θεὸν ἀγαπῶμεν,
we love the children of God, whenever God we love,
3 καὶ τὰς ἐντολὰς αὐτοῦ τηρῶμεν. αὕτη γάρ ἐστιν ἡ ἀγάπη
and the commandments of Him we keep. this For is the love
τοῦ Θεοῦ, ἵνα τὰς ἐντολὰς αὐτοῦ τηρῶμεν· καὶ αἱ ἐντολαὶ
of God, that the commandments of Him we keep; and the commands
4 αὐτοῦ βαρεῖαι οὐκ εἰσίν. ὅτι πᾶν τὸ γεγεννημένον ἐκ τοῦ
of Him heavy not are, because everything having been born of
Θεοῦ νικᾷ τὸν κόσμον· καὶ αὕτη ἐστὶν ἡ νίκη ἡ νικήσασα τὸν
God overcomes the world, and this is the victory overcoming the

world, our faith. [5]Who is the *one* overcoming the world except the *one* who believes that Jesus is the Son of God? [6]This is the *One* coming through water and blood, Jesus Christ, not by the water only, but by the water and the blood. And the Spirit is the *One* witnessing, because the Spirit is the truth. *[7]For there are three bearing witness in Heaven: the Father, the Word, and the Holy Spirit; and these three are one.* [8]And there are three who bear witness on the earth: The Spirit, and the water, and the blood; and the three are to the one. [9]If we receive the witness of men, the witness of God is greater, because this is the witness of God which he has witnessed about His Son. [10]The *one* believing in the Son of God has the witness in himself. The *one* not believing God has made Him a liar, because he has not believed in the witness which God has witnessed concerning His Son. [11]And this is the witness, that God gave us everlasting life, and this life is in His Son. [12]The *one* having the Son has life. The *one* not having the Son of God does not have life.

[13]I wrote these things to you, the ones believing in the name of the Son of God, that you may know that you have everlasting life, and that you may believe in the name of the Son of God. [14]And this is the confidence we have toward Him, that if we ask anything according to His will, He hears us. [15]And if we know that He hears us, whatever we ask, we know that we have the requests which we have asked from Him.

[16]If anyone sees his brother sinning a sin unto death, he shall ask, and He shall give life to him, to the ones not sinning unto death. There is a sin unto death. I do not say that he should ask

5 κόσμον. ἡ πίστις ἡμῶν. τίς ἐστιν ὁ νικῶν τὸν κόσμον, εἰ μὴ ὁ
world, the faith of us. Who is the (one) over-coming the world, except the (one)
6 πιστεύων ὅτι Ἰησοῦς ἐστὶν ὁ υἱὸς τοῦ Θεοῦ ; οὗτός ἐστιν ὁ
believing that Jesus is the Son of God? This is the (One)
ἐλθὼν δι᾽ ὕδατος καὶ αἵματος, Ἰησοῦς ὁ Χριστός· οὐκ ἐν τῷ
coming through water and blood, Jesus Christ; not by the
ὕδατι μόνον, ἀλλ᾽ ἐν τῷ ὕδατι καὶ τῷ αἵματι. καὶ τὸ Πνεῦμά
water only, but by the water and the blood. And the Spirit
7 ἐστι τὸ μαρτυροῦν, ὅτι τὸ Πνεῦμά ἐστιν ἡ ἀλήθεια. ὅτι τρεῖς
is the (One) witnessing, because the Spirit is the truth. (Because three
εἰσὶν οἱ μαρτυροῦντες ἐν τῷ οὐρανῷ, ὁ πατήρ, ὁ λόγος, καὶ
there are bearing witness in Heaven, the Father, the Word, and
8 τὸ Ἅγιον Πνεῦμα· καὶ οὗτοι οἱ τρεῖς ἕν εἰσι. καὶ τρεῖς εἰσὶν
the Holy Spirit, and these three One is.) And three there are
οἱ μαρτυροῦντες ἐν τῇ γῇ, τὸ Πνεῦμα, καὶ τὸ ὕδωρ, καὶ τὸ
who bear witness on the earth, the Spirit, and the water, and the
9 αἷμα· καὶ οἱ τρεῖς εἰς τὸ ἕν εἰσιν. εἰ τὴν μαρτυρίαν τῶν
blood; and the three to the one are. If the witness
ἀνθρώπων λαμβάνομεν, ἡ μαρτυρία τοῦ Θεοῦ μείζων ἐστίν·
of men we receive, the witness of God greater is,
ὅτι αὕτη ἐστὶν ἡ μαρτυρία τοῦ Θεοῦ, ἣν μεμαρτύρηκε περὶ
because this is the witness of God, which He has witnessed about
10 τοῦ υἱοῦ αὐτοῦ. ὁ πιστεύων εἰς τὸν υἱὸν τοῦ Θεοῦ ἔχει τὴν
the Son of Him. The (one) believing in the Son of God has the
μαρτυρίαν ἐν ἑαυτῷ· ὁ μὴ πιστεύων τῷ Θεῷ ψεύστην πεποί-
witness in himself. The (one) not believing God a liar has
ηκεν αὐτόν, ὅτι οὐ πεπίστευκεν εἰς τὴν μαρτυρίαν, ἣν
made Him, because not he has believed in the witness which
11 μεμαρτύρηκεν ὁ Θεὸς περὶ τοῦ υἱοῦ αὐτοῦ. καὶ αὕτη ἐστὶν
has witnessed God concerning the Son of Him. And this is
ἡ μαρτυρία, ὅτι ζωὴν αἰώνιον ἔδωκεν ἡμῖν ὁ Θεός, καὶ αὕτη
the witness, that life everlasting gave us God, and this
12 ἡ ζωὴ ἐν τῷ υἱῷ αὐτοῦ ἐστίν. ὁ ἔχων τὸν υἱὸν ἔχει τὴν ζωήν·
life in the Son of Him is. The (one) having the Son has life,
ὁ μὴ ἔχων τὸν υἱὸν τοῦ Θεοῦ τὴν ζωὴν οὐκ ἔχει.
he not having the Son of God. life not has.
13 Ταῦτα ἔγραψα ὑμῖν τοῖς πιστεύουσιν εἰς τὸ ὄνομα τοῦ
These things I wrote to you, those believing in the name of the
υἱοῦ τοῦ Θεοῦ, ἵνα εἰδῆτε ὅτι ζωὴν ἔχετε αἰώνιον, καὶ ἵνα
Son of God, that you may know that life you have eternal, and that
14 πιστευητε εἰς τὸ ὄνομα τοῦ υἱοῦ τοῦ Θεοῦ. καὶ αὕτη ἐστὶν
you may believe in the name of the Son of God. And this is
ἡ παρρησία ἣν ἔχομεν πρὸς αὐτόν, ὅτι ἐάν τι αἰτώμεθα
the confidence which we have toward Him, that if anything we ask
15 κατὰ τὸ θέλημα αὐτοῦ, ἀκούει ἡμῶν· καὶ ἐὰν οἴδαμεν ὅτι
according to the will of Him, He hears us. And if we know that
ἀκούει ἡμῶν, ὃ ἂν αἰτώμεθα, οἴδαμεν ὅτι ἔχομεν τὰ
He hears us, whatever we ask, we know that we have the
16 αἰτήματα ἃ ᾐτήκαμεν παρ᾽ αὐτοῦ. ἐάν τις ἴδῃ τὸν ἀδελφὸν
requests which we have asked from Him. If anyone sees the brother
αὐτοῦ ἁμαρτάνοντα ἁμαρτίαν μὴ πρὸς θάνατον, αἰτήσει,
of him sinning a sin not unto death, he shall ask,
καὶ δώσει αὐτῷ ζωὴν τοῖς ἁμαρτάνουσι μὴ πρὸς θάνατον.
and He will give to him life to those sinning not unto death.
ἔστιν ἁμαρτία πρὸς θάνατον· οὐ περὶ ἐκείνης λέγω ἵνα
There is a sin unto death; not concerning that I say that

about that. [17] All unrighteousness is sin, and there is a sin not unto death.

[18] We know that everyone having been born of God does not sin, but the *one* born of God guards himself, and the evil one does not touch him. [19] We know that we are of God, and the whole world lies in evil. [20] And we know that the Son of God has come, and has given to us an understanding that we might know the true *One*, and we are in the true *One*, in His Son Jesus Christ. This is the true God, and the life everlasting.

[21] Little children, guard yourself from idols. Amen.

17 ἐρωτήσῃ. πᾶσα ἀδικία ἁμαρτία ἐστί· καὶ ἔστιν ἁμαρτία οὐ
he should ask. All unrighteousness sin is, and there is a sin not
πρὸς θάνατον.
unto death.
18 Οἴδαμεν ὅτι πᾶς ὁ γεγεννημένος ἐκ τοῦ Θεοῦ οὐχ ἁμαρ-
We know that everyone having been born of God not sins,
τάνει· ἀλλ᾽ ὁ γεννηθεὶς ἐκ τοῦ Θεοῦ τηρεῖ ἑαυτόν, καὶ ὁ
but the (one) born of God keeps himself, and the
19 πονηρὸς οὐχ ἅπτεται αὐτοῦ. οἴδαμεν ὅτι ἐκ τοῦ Θεοῦ
evil one does not touch him. We know that of God
20 ἐσμέν, καὶ ὁ κόσμος ὅλος ἐν τῷ πονηρῷ κεῖται. οἴδαμεν δὲ
we are, and the world whole in evil lies. we know And
ὅτι ὁ υἱὸς τοῦ Θεοῦ ἥκει, καὶ δέδωκεν ἡμῖν διάνοιαν ἵνα
that the Son of God is come, and has given to us an understanding that
γινώσκωμεν τὸν ἀληθινόν· καί ἐσμεν ἐν τῷ ἀληθινῷ, ἐν τῷ
we might know the true (One), and we are in the true (One), in the
υἱῷ αὐτοῦ Ἰησοῦ Χριστῷ. οὗτός ἐστιν ὁ ἀληθινὸς Θεός,
Son of Him, Jesus Christ. This is the true God,
21 καὶ ἡ ζωὴ αἰώνιος. Τεκνία, φυλάξατε ἑαυτοὺς ἀπὸ τῶν
and the life everlasting. Little children, guard yourselves from
εἰδώλων. ἀμήν.
idols. Amen.

ΙΩΑΝΝΟΥ
JOHN
ΕΠΙΣΤΟΛΗ ΔΕΥΤΕΡΑ
EPISTLE SECOND

KING JAMES II VERSION

THE SECOND EPISTLE OF JOHN

1 The elder to *the* elect lady
and her children, whom I
love in truth; and not I only,
but also all those who have
known the truth, 2 because
of the truth remaining
among us, and will be with
us forever. 3 Grace, mercy,
peace from God *the* Father
and from *the* Lord Jesus
Christ, the Son of the Father,
in truth and love.
4 I rejoiced greatly be-
cause I found your children
walking in truth, as we
received command from the
Father. 5 And I now request
you, lady, not writing as a
new commandment, but
one which we had from *the*
beginning, that we should
love one another. 6 And this
is love, that we should walk
according to His command-
ments. This is the commandment, even as you heard from
the beginning, that you
should walk in it. 7 Because
many deceivers went out into
the world, those not confessing Jesus Christ to have
come in *the* flesh—this is the
deceiver and the antichrist.
8 Watch yourselves, that
we may not lose the things
we worked out, but that we
may receive a full reward.
9 Everyone transgressing
and not abiding in the teaching of Christ does not have
God. The *one* abiding in the
teaching of Christ, this one
has the Father and the Son.
10 If anyone comes to you
and does not bear this teaching, do not receive him into
the house, and do not speak
a greeting to him. 11 For the
one speaking a greeting

1 Ὁ πρεσβύτερος ἐκλεκτῇ κυρίᾳ καὶ τοῖς τέκνοις αὐτῆς,
The elder to (the) elect lady and the children of her,
οὓς ἐγὼ ἀγαπῶ ἐν ἀληθείᾳ, καὶ οὐκ ἐγὼ μόνος, ἀλλὰ καὶ
whom I love in truth, and not I only, but also
2 πάντες οἱ ἐγνωκότες τὴν ἀλήθειαν, διὰ τὴν ἀλήθειαν τὴν
all those who have known the truth, because of the truth
3 μένουσαν ἐν ἡμῖν, καὶ μεθ' ἡμῶν ἔσται εἰς τὸν αἰῶνα· ἔσται
remaining among us, and with us will be unto the age. will be
μεθ' ὑμῶν χάρις, ἔλεος, εἰρήνη παρὰ Θεοῦ πατρός, καὶ παρὰ
with you Grace, mercy, peace, from God (the) Father, and from
Κυρίου Ἰησοῦ Χριστοῦ τοῦ υἱοῦ τοῦ πατρός, ἐν ἀληθείᾳ καὶ
(the) Lord Jesus Christ the Son of the Father, in truth and
ἀγάπῃ.
love.
4 Ἐχάρην λίαν ὅτι εὕρηκα ἐκ τῶν τέκνων σου περιπατοῦν-
I rejoiced greatly because I found of the children of you walking
τας ἐν ἀληθείᾳ, καθὼς ἐντολὴν ἐλάβομεν παρὰ τοῦ πατρός.
in truth, as commandment we received from the Father.
5 καὶ νῦν ἐρωτῶ σε, κυρία, οὐχ ὡς ἐντολὴν γράφων σοι καινήν,
And now I request you, lady, not as a command writing to you new,
6 ἀλλὰ ἣν εἴχομεν ἀπ' ἀρχῆς, ἵνα ἀγαπῶμεν ἀλλήλους. καὶ
but which we had from (the) beginning, that we should love one another. And
αὕτη ἐστὶν ἡ ἀγάπη, ἵνα περιπατῶμεν κατὰ τὰς ἐντολας
this is love, that we should walk according to the commands
αὐτοῦ. αὕτη ἐστὶν ἡ ἐντολή, καθὼς ἠκούσατε ἀπ' ἀρχῆς,
of Him. This is the command, as you heard from (the) beginning
7 ἵνα ἐν αὐτῇ περιπατῆτε. ὅτι πολλοὶ πλάνοι εἰσῆλθον εἰς τὸν
that in it you should walk. Because many deceivers went out into the
κόσμον, οἱ μὴ ὁμολογοῦντες Ἰησοῦν Χριστὸν ἐρχόμενον ἐν
world, those not confessing Jesus Christ coming in
8 σαρκί. οὗτός ἐστιν ὁ πλάνος καὶ ὁ ἀντίχριστος. βλέπετε
(the) flesh. This is the deceiver and the antichrist. Watch
ἑαυτούς, ἵνα μὴ ἀπολέσωμεν ἃ εἰργασάμεθα, ἀλλὰ μισθὸν
yourselves, lest we may lose the things we worked out, but a reward
9 πλήρη ἀπολάβωμεν. πᾶς ὁ παραβαίνων καὶ μὴ μένων ἐν
full we may receive. Everyone transgressing and not abiding in
τῇ διδαχῇ τοῦ Χριστοῦ, Θεὸν οὐκ ἔχει· ὁ μένων ἐν τῇ
the teaching of Christ, God not has. The (one) abiding in the
διδαχῇ τοῦ Χριστοῦ, οὗτος καὶ τὸν πατέρα καὶ τὸν υἱὸν
teaching of Christ, this one even the Father and the Son
10 ἔχει. εἴ τις ἔρχεται πρὸς ὑμᾶς, καὶ ταύτην τὴν διδαχὴν οὐ
has. If anyone comes to you, and this teaching not
φέρει, μὴ λαμβάνετε αὐτὸν εἰς οἰκίαν, καὶ χαίρειν αὐτῷ μὴ
bears, not do receive him into (the) house, and a greeting to him not
11 λέγετε· ὁ γὰρ λέγων αὐτῷ χαίρειν κοινωνεῖ τοῖς ἔργοις
do speak. he For speaking to him a greeting shares in the works

shares in his evil works.

[12] Having many things to write to you, I do not intend *to speak* by means of paper and ink, but I am hoping to come to you, and to speak mouth to mouth, that your joy may be full.

[13] The children of your elect sister greet you.

Amen.

αὐτοῦ τοῖς πονηροῖς.
of him evil.
12 Πολλὰ ἔχων ὑμῖν γράφειν οὐκ ἠβουλήθην διὰ χάρτου
Many things having to you to write, not I intend by means of paper
καὶ μέλανος· ἀλλὰ ἐλπίζω ἐλθεῖν πρὸς ὑμᾶς, καὶ στόμα πρὸς
and ink, but I am hoping to come to you, and mouth to
13 στόμα λαλῆσαι, ἵνα ἡ χαρὰ ἡμῶν ᾖ πεπληρωμένη. ἀσπά-
mouth to speak, that the joy of us may be fulfilled. greet
ζεταί σε τὰ τέκνα τῆς ἀδελφῆς σου τῆς ἐκλεκτῆς. ἀμήν.
you The children of the sister of you elect. Amen.

KING JAMES II VERSION

THE THIRD EPISTLE OF JOHN

1 The elder to Gaius the beloved, whom I love in truth.

2 Beloved, in regard to all things, I pray *for* you to do well, and to be in health, as your soul does well. 3 For I rejoiced greatly *at* *the* coming of *the* brothers, also bearing witness of you in the truth, as you walk in truth. 4 I have no greater joy than these things, that I hear my children are walking in truth.

5 Beloved, you do faithfully whatever you work for the brothers and for the strangers, 6 who bore witness of you before *the* church, whom you will do well to send forward worthily of God. 7 For on behalf of His name they went out, taking nothing from the Gentiles. 8 Therefore, we ought to entertain such *men*, that we may become co-workers in the truth.

9 I wrote to the church, but he loving to be first of them, Diotrephes, does not receive us. 10 Because of this, if I come, I will recall his works which he does, ranting against us with evil words. And not being satisfied *with* these, neither does he receive the brothers; and those intending *it* he prevents, and thrusts them out from the church.

11 Beloved, do not imitate the bad, but the good. The *one* doing good is of God; but the *one* doing bad has not seen God.

12 Witness has been borne to Demetrius by all, and by the truth itself. And we also bear witness, and you know

ΙΩΑΝΝΟΥ
OF JOHN

ΕΠΙΣΤΟΛΗ ΤΡΙΤΗ
EPISTLE THIRD

1 Ὁ πρεσβύτερος Γαΐῳ τῷ ἀγαπητῷ, ὃν ἐγὼ ἀγαπῶ ἐν
The elder to Gaius the beloved, whom I love in
ἀληθείᾳ.
truth.
'Αγαπητέ, περὶ πάντων εὔχομαί σε εὐοδοῦσθαι καὶ
2 Beloved, concerning all things I pray you to do well, and
3 ὑγιαίνειν, καθὼς εὐοδοῦταί σου ἡ ψυχή. ἐχάρην γὰρ λίαν,
to be in health, as does well of you the soul. I rejoiced For greatly,
ἐρχομένων ἀδελφῶν καὶ μαρτυρούντων σου τῇ ἀληθείᾳ,
coming (the) brothers and bearing witness of you in the truth
4 καθὼς σὺ ἐν ἀληθείᾳ περιπατεῖς. μειζοτέραν τούτων οὐκ
as you in truth walk. greater (than) these things not
ἔχω χαράν, ἵνα ἀκούω τὰ ἐμὰ τέκνα ἐν ἀληθείᾳ περι-
I have joy, that I hear my children in (the) truth are
πατοῦντα.
walking.
5 'Αγαπητέ, πιστὸν ποιεῖς ὃ ἐὰν ἐργάσῃ εἰς τοὺς ἀδελφοὺς
Beloved, faithfully you do whatever you work for the brothers
6 καὶ εἰς τοὺς ξένους, οἳ ἐμαρτύρησάν σου τῇ ἀγάπῃ ἐνώπιον
and for the strangers, who bore witness of you in the love in sight of
ἐκκλησίας· οὓς καλῶς ποιήσεις προπέμψας ἀξίως τοῦ Θεοῦ.
(the) church, whom well you will do sending forward worthily of God.
7 ὑπὲρ γὰρ τοῦ ὀνόματος αὐτοῦ ἐξῆλθον μηδὲν λαμβάνοντες
on behalf of For the name of Him they went out, nothing taking
8 ἀπὸ τῶν ἐθνῶν. ἡμεῖς οὖν ὀφείλομεν ἀπολαμβάνειν τοὺς
from the Gentiles. We therefore ought to entertain
τοιούτους, ἵνα συνεργοὶ γινώμεθα τῇ ἀληθείᾳ.
such (men) that co-workers we may become in the truth.
9 Ἔγραψα τῇ ἐκκλησίᾳ· ἀλλ' ὁ φιλοπρωτεύων αὐτῶν
I wrote to the church, but the (one) loving to be first of them,
10 Διοτρεφὴς οὐκ ἐπιδέχεται ἡμᾶς. διὰ τοῦτο, ἐὰν ἔλθω,
Diotrephes, not does receive us. Therefore, If I come,
ὑπομνήσω αὐτοῦ τὰ ἔργα ἃ ποιεῖ, λόγοις πονηροῖς φλυαρῶν
I will recall of him the works which he does, with words evil prating against
ἡμᾶς· καὶ μὴ ἀρκούμενος ἐπὶ τούτοις, οὔτε αὐτὸς ἐπιδέχεται
us, and not being satisfied on these, neither he receives
τοὺς ἀδελφούς, καὶ τοὺς βουλομένους κωλύει, καὶ ἐκ τῆς
the brothers, and those intending (to do so), he prevents, and from th
11 ἐκκλησίας ἐκβάλλει. ἀγαπητέ, μὴ μιμοῦ τὸ κακόν, ἀλλὰ τὸ
church thrusts out. Beloved, not do imitate the bad, but the
ἀγαθόν. ὁ ἀγαθοποιῶν ἐκ τοῦ Θεοῦ ἐστίν· ὁ δὲ κακοποιῶν
good. The (one) doing good of God is; the (one) but doing ill
12 οὐχ ἑώρακε τὸν Θεόν. Δημητρίῳ μεμαρτύρηται ὑπὸ
not has seen God. To Demetrius witness has been borne by
πάντων, καὶ ὑπ' αὐτῆς τῆς ἀληθείας· καὶ ἡμεῖς δὲ μαρτυροῦ-
all, and by its (own) self the truth; also we and bear witness

that our witness is true.

[13]I had many things to write, but I do not desire to write by means of pen and ink. [14]But I am hoping to see you at once, and we will speak mouth to mouth.

[15]Peace to you. The friends greet you. Greet the friends by name.

μεν, καὶ οἴδατε ὅτι ἡ μαρτυρία ἡμῶν ἀληθής ἐστι.
and you know that the witness of us true is.

13 Πολλὰ εἶχον γράφειν, ἀλλ' οὐ θέλω διὰ μέλανος καὶ
Many things I had to write, but not I desire via ink and

14 καλάμου σοι γράψαι· ἐλπίζω δὲ εὐθέως ἰδεῖν σε, καὶ στόμα
pen to you to write; I am hoping but at once to see you, and mouth

15 πρὸς στόμα λαλήσομεν. εἰρήνη σοι. ἀσπάζονταί σε οἱ
to mouth we will speak. Peace to you. Greet you The

φίλοι. ἀσπάζου τοὺς φίλους κατ' ὄνομα.
friends. Greet the friends by name.

ΙΟΥΔΑ
JUDE
ΕΠΙΣΤΟΛΗ ΚΑΘΟΛΙΚΗ
EPISTLE GENERAL

KING JAMES II VERSION

THE GENERAL EPISTLE OF JUDE

[1] Jude, a slave of Jesus Christ, and brother of James, to the *ones* called in God *the* Father, having been loved, and having been kept to Jesus Christ. [2] Mercy, and peace, and love be multiplied to you.

[3] Having made all haste to write to you about the common salvation, beloved, I had need to write to you *to* exhort you to earnestly contend for the faith once delivereded to the saints. [4] For certain men crept in secretly, those having been of old marked out to this condemnation, ungodly ones perverting the grace of God for unbridled lust, and denying the only Master, God, and our Lord Jesus Christ.

[5] But I intend to remind you, you once knowing these things, that the Lord having saved a people out of *the* land of Egypt, in the second place destroyed the ones not believing. [6] And those angels not having kept their first place, but having deserted *their* dwelling-place, He has kept in everlasting chains under darkness for *the* judgment of a great Day; [7] as Sodom and Gomorrah, and the cities around them, in like manner to these, committing fornication, and going away after other flesh, laid down an example beforetimes, undergoing vengeance of everlasting fire. [8] Likewise, indeed, also those dreaming ones even defile flesh, and despise rulership, and speak evil of glories. [9] But Michael the archangel, when contending with the Devil, he argued about the body of Moses, *but* he dared not bring a judg-

1 Ἰούδας Ἰησοῦ Χριστοῦ δοῦλος, ἀδελφὸς δὲ Ἰακώβου,
Jude, of Jesus Christ a slave, brother and of James,
τοῖς ἐν Θεῷ πατρὶ ἡγιασμένοις, καὶ Ἰησοῦ Χριστῷ τετηρη-
to those in God (the) Father having been loved, and by Jesus Christ having been
2 μένοις, κλητοῖς· ἔλεος ὑμῖν καὶ εἰρήνη καὶ ἀγάπη πληθυνθείη.
kept, called: Mercy to you and peace and love be multiplied.
3 Ἀγαπητοί, πᾶσαν σπουδὴν ποιούμενος γράφειν ὑμῖν περὶ
Beloved, all haste making to write to you about
τῆς κοινῆς σωτηρίας, ἀνάγκην ἔσχον γράψαι ὑμῖν, παρα-
the common salvation, necessity I had to write to you, ex-
καλῶν ἐπαγωνίζεσθαι τῇ ἅπαξ παραδοθείσῃ τοῖς ἁγίοις
horting to earnestly contend for the once delivered to the saints
4 πίστει. παρεισέδυσαν γάρ τινες ἄνθρωποι, οἱ πάλαι προγε-
faith, crept in For certain men, those of old having been
γραμμένοι εἰς τοῦτο τὸ κρίμα, ἀσεβεῖς, τὴν τοῦ Θεοῦ ἡμῶν
previously written into this judgment, ungodly ones, the of the God of us
χάριν μετατιθέντες εἰς ἀσέλγειαν, και τὸν μόνον δεσπότην
grace, perverting for unbridled lust, and the only Master
Θεόν, καὶ Κύριον ἡμῶν Ἰησοῦν Χριστὸν ἀρνούμενοι.
God, and Lord of us, Jesus Christ denying.
5 Ὑπομνῆσαι δὲ ὑμᾶς βούλομαι, εἰδότας ὑμᾶς ἅπαξ τοῦτο,
to remind But you I intend, knowing you once these things,
ὅτι ὁ Κύριος, λαὸν ἐκ γῆς Αἰγύπτου σώσας, τὸ δεύτερον
that the Lord people out of land of Egypt having saved, in the second place
6 τοὺς μὴ πιστεύσαντας ἀπώλεσεν. ἀγγέλους τε τοὺς μὴ
those not believing He destroyed; angels and those not
τηρήσαντας τὴν ἑαυτῶν ἀρχήν, ἀλλὰ ἀπολιπόντας τὸ
having kept the of themselves first place, but having deserted the
ἴδιον οἰκητήριον, εἰς κρίσιν μεγάλης ἡμέρας δεσμοῖς ἀϊδίοις
own dwelling-place, for (the) Judgment of a great Day in chains eternal
7 ὑπὸ ζόφον τετήρηκεν. ὡς Σόδομα καὶ Γόμορρα, καὶ αἱ περὶ
under blackness He has kept.; as Sodom and Gomorrah and the around
αὐτὰς πόλεις, τὸν ὅμοιον τουτοις τρόπον ἐκπορνευσασαι,
them cities, in the similar to these manner committing fornication
καὶ ἀπελθοῦσαι ὀπισω σαρκὸς ἑτέρας, πρόκεινται δεῖγμα,
and going away after flesh other. laid beforetimes an example
8 πυρὸς αἰωνίου δίκην ὑπέχουσαι. ὁμοίως μέντοι καὶ ουτοι
of fire everlasting vengeance undergoing. Likewise indeed also these
ἐνυπνιαζόμενοι σάρκα μὲν μιαίνουσι, κυριότητα δὲ ἀθετοῦσι,
dreaming (ones) flesh even defile, lordship and despise,
9 δόξας δὲ βλασφημοῦσιν. ὁ δὲ Μιχαὴλ ὁ ἀρχάγγελος, ὅτε τῷ
glories and speak evil of. But Michael the archangel, when with the
διαβόλῳ διακρινόμενος διελέγετο περὶ τοῦ Μωσέως σώ-
Devil contending, he argued about the of Moses
ματος, οὐκ ἐτόλμησε κρίσιν ἐπενεγκεῖν βλασφημίας, ἀλλ'
body, not he dared a judgment to bring of blasphemy, but

ment of blasphemy, but said, Let *the* Lord rebuke you! [10] But what things they do not know, they speak evil of these. And what things they understand naturally, like the animals without reason, they are corrupted by these.

[11] Woe to them, because they went in the way of Cain, and gave themselves to the error of Balaam *for* reward, and perished in the gainsaying of Korah! [12] These are sunken rocks in your love feasts, feasting together with you, feeding themselves without fear, waterless clouds being carried about by winds; fruitless autumn trees, having died twice, having been plucked up by the roots; [13] wild waves of *the* sea foaming up their shames; wandering stars for whom blackness of darkness has been kept forever.

[14] And Enoch, *the* seventh from Adam, also prophesied to these, saying, Behold, *the* Lord came with myriads of His saints, [15] to do judgment against all, and to rebuke all the ungodly of them concerning all their ungodly works which they ungodly did, and concerning all the hard things ungodly sinners spoke against Him. [16] These are murmurers, complainers, leading lives according to their lusts, and their mouth speaks proud things, admiring faces for the sake of gain. [17] But you, beloved, remember the words spoken before by the apostles of our Lord Jesus Christ, [18] because they told you that at *the* last time there will be mockers according to their lusts, leading ungodly lives. [19] These are the *ones* setting themselves apart, animal-like ones, not having *the* Spirit.

[20] But you, beloved, building yourselves up by your most holy faith, praying in *the* Holy Spirit, [21] keep yourselves in *the* love of God, eagerly awaiting the mercy of our Lord Jesus Christ to

10 εἶπεν, Ἐπιτιμήσαι σοι Κύριος. οὗτοι δὲ ὅσα μὲν οὐκ οἴδασι
said, Let rebuke you (the) Lord. these But what things not they know,
βλασφημοῦσιν· ὅσα δὲ φυσικῶς, ὡς τὰ ἄλογα ζῶα, ἐπί-
they speak evil of; what things and naturally—as the without reason animals—they
11 στανται, ἐν τούτοις φθείρονται. οὐαὶ αὐτοῖς· ὅτι τῇ ὁδῷ τοῦ
understand, by these they are corrupted. Woe to them, because in the way
Κάϊν ἐπορεύθησαν, καὶ τῇ πλάνῃ τοῦ Βαλαὰμ μισθοῦ
of Cain they went, and to the error of Balaam (for) reward
12 ἐξεχύθησαν, καὶ τῇ ἀντιλογίᾳ τοῦ Κορὲ ἀπώλοντο. οὗτοί
gave themselves, and in the gainsaying of Korah perished! These
εἰσιν ἐν ταῖς ἀγάπαις ὑμῶν σπιλάδες, συνευωχούμενοι ὑμῖν,
are in the love feasts of you rocky reefs feasting together with you,
ἀφόβως ἑαυτοὺς ποιμαίνοντες· νεφέλαι ἄνυδροι, ὑπὸ
without fear themselves feeding, clouds waterless by
ἀνέμων περιφερόμεναι· δένδρα φθινοπωρινά, ἄκαρπα, δὶς
winds having been carried about trees autumn without fruit, twice
13 ἀποθανόντα, ἐκριζωθέντα· κύματα ἄγρια θαλάσσης, ἐπ-
having died, having been uprooted, waves wild of (the) sea
αφρίζοντα τὰς ἑαυτῶν αἰσχύνας· ἀστέρες πλανῆται, οἷς ὁ
foaming up the of themselves shames, stars wandering, for whom
14 ζόφος τοῦ σκότους εἰς τὸν αἰῶνα τετήρηται. προεφήτευσε
blackness of darkness to the age has been kept. prophesied
δὲ καὶ τούτοις ἕβδομος ἀπὸ Ἀδὰμ Ἐνώχ, λέγων, Ἰδού,
And also to these (the) seventh from Adam, Enoch, saying, Behold,
15 ἦλθε Κύριος ἐν μυριάσιν ἁγίαις αὐτοῦ, ποιῆσαι κρίσιν κατὰ
came (the) Lord with myriads saints of Him, to do judgment against
πάντων, καὶ ἐξελέγξαι πάντας τοὺς ἀσεβεῖς αὐτῶν περὶ
all, and to rebuke all the ungodly of them concerning
πάντων τῶν ἔργων ἀσεβείας αὐτῶν ὧν ἠσέβησαν, καὶ περὶ
all the works ungodly of them which they ungodly did, and about
πάντων τῶν σκληρῶν ὧν ἐλάλησαν κατ' αὐτοῦ ἁμαρτωλοὶ
all the hard things which spoke against Him sinners
16 ἀσεβεῖς. οὗτοί εἰσι γογγυσταί, μεμψίμοιροι, κατὰ τὰς
ungodly. These are murmurers, complainers, according to the
ἐπιθυμίας αὐτῶν πορευόμενοι, καὶ τὸ στόμα αὐτῶν λαλεῖ
lusts of them following and the mouth of them speaks
ὑπέρογκα, θαυμάζοντες πρόσωπα ὠφελείας χάριν.
proud things, admiring faces gain for tne sake of
17 Ὑμεῖς δέ, ἀγαπητοί, μνήσθητε τῶν ῥημάτων τῶν
you But, beloved, remember the words
προειρημένων ὑπὸ τῶν ἀποστόλων τοῦ Κυρίου ἡμῶν
spoken before by the apostles of the Lord of us,
18 Ἰησοῦ Χριστοῦ· ὅτι ἔλεγον ὑμῖν, ὅτι ἐν ἐσχάτῳ χρόνῳ
Jesus Christ, because they told you that at (the) last time
ἔσονται ἐμπαῖκται, κατὰ τὰς ἑαυτῶν ἐπιθυμίας πορευό-
will be mockers according to the of themselves lusts following
19 μενοι τῶν ἀσεβειῶν. οὗτοί εἰσιν οἱ ἀποδιορίζοντες ἑαυτούς,
the ungodly. These are they dividing apart themselves,
20 ψυχικοί, Πνεῦμα μὴ ἔχοντες. ὑμεῖς δέ, ἀγαπητοί, τῇ ἁγιω-
animal-like, (the) Spirit not having. you But, beloved by the most
τάτῃ ὑμῶν πίστει ἐποικοδομοῦντες ἑαυτούς, ἐν Πνεύματι
holy of you faith building up yourselves, in (the) Spirit
21 Ἁγίῳ προσευχόμενοι, ἑαυτοὺς ἐν ἀγάπῃ Θεοῦ τηρήσατε,
Holy praying, yourselves in (the) love of God keep,
προσδεχόμενοι τὸ ἔλεος τοῦ Κυρίου ἡμῶν Ἰησοῦ Χριστοῦ
eagerly awaiting the mercy of the Lord of us, Jesus Christ

everlasting life. [22]And pity some, making distinction. [23]But save others with fear, snatching *them* out of the fire, hating even the garment having been stained from the flesh.

[24]Now to Him being able to keep you without stumbling, and to set *you* before His glory without blemish, with unspeakable joy, [25]to *the* only wise God, our Savior, *be* glory and majesty and might and authority, even now and forever. Amen.

22 εἰς ζωὴν αἰώνιον. καὶ οὓς μὲν ἐλεεῖτε διακρινόμενοι· οὓς δὲ
23 to life everlasting. And some pity, making distinction, others But
ἐν φόβῳ σώζετε, ἐκ τοῦ πυρὸς ἁρπάζοντες, μισοῦντες καὶ
with fear save, out of the fire snatching (them), hating even
τὸν ἀπὸ τῆς σαρκὸς ἐσπιλωμένον χιτῶνα.
the from the flesh stained garment.
24 Τῷ δὲ δυναμένῳ φυλάξαι ὑμᾶς ἀπταίστους, καὶ στῆσαι
to Him Now being able to keep you without stumbling, and to set
κατενώπιον τῆς δόξης αὐτοῦ ἀμώμους ἐν ἀγαλλιάσει,
(you) before the glory of Him without blemish with exultation,
25 μόνῳ σοφῷ Θεῷ σωτῆρι ἡμῶν, δόξα καὶ μεγαλωσύνη,
to (the) only wise God Savior of us, (be) glory and
κράτος καὶ ἐξουσία, καὶ νῦν καὶ εἰς πάντας τοὺς αἰῶνας.
might and majesty, even now and to all the ages.
ἀμήν.
Amen.

shares in his evil works.

[12]Having many things to write to you, I do not intend *to speak* by means of paper and ink, but I am hoping to come to you, and to speak mouth to mouth, that your joy may be full.

[13]The children of your elect sister greet you. Amen.

αὐτοῦ τοῖς πονηροῖς.
of him evil.
12 Πολλὰ ἔχων ὑμῖν γράφειν οὐκ ἠβουλήθην διὰ χάρτου
Many things having to you to write, not I intend by means of paper
καὶ μέλανος· ἀλλὰ ἐλπίζω ἐλθεῖν πρὸς ὑμᾶς, καὶ στόμα πρὸς
and ink, but I am hoping to come to you, and mouth to
13 στόμα λαλῆσαι, ἵνα ἡ χαρὰ ἡμῶν ᾖ πεπληρωμένη. ἀσπά-
mouth to speak, that the joy of us may be fulfilled. greet
ζεταί σε τὰ τέκνα τῆς ἀδελφῆς σου τῆς ἐκλεκτῆς. ἀμήν.
you The children of the sister of you elect. Amen.

that our witness is true.

[13]I had many things to write, but I do not desire to write by means of pen and ink. [14]But I am hoping to see you at once, and we will speak mouth to mouth.

[15]Peace to you. The friends greet you. Greet the friends by name.

μεν, καὶ οἴδατε ὅτι ἡ μαρτυρία ἡμῶν ἀληθής ἐστι.
and you know that the witness of us true is.
13 Πολλὰ εἶχον γράφειν, ἀλλ᾽ οὐ θέλω διὰ μέλανος καὶ
Many things I had to write, but not I desire via ink and
14 καλάμου σοι γράψαι· ἐλπίζω δὲ εὐθέως ἰδεῖν σε, καὶ στόμα
pen to you to write; I am hoping but at once to see you, and mouth
15 πρὸς στόμα λαλήσομεν. εἰρήνη σοι. ἀσπάζονταί σε οἱ
to mouth we will speak. Peace to you. Greet you The
φίλοι. ἀσπάζου τοὺς φίλους κατ᾽ ὄνομα.
friends. Greet the friends by name.

KING JAMES II VERSION

THE HOLY REVELATION OF JOHN THE DIVINE

CHAPTER 1

[1]A revelation of Jesus Christ, which God gave to Him to show to His slaves things which must occur quickly. And He signified *by* sending through His angel to His slave, John, [2]who testified of the word of God and the witness of Jesus Christ, even as many as he saw. [3]Blessed *is* the *one* reading, and those hearing, the words of this prophecy, and keeping the things having been written; for the time *is* near.

[4]John to the seven churches in Asia: Grace to you, and peace, from the *One* who is, and who was, and who *is* coming, the Almighty; and from the seven spirits which are before His throne; even from Jesus Christ the faithful witness, the Firstborn from the dead, and the Ruler of kings of the earth. To Him loving us, and freeing us from our sins by His blood, [6]and made us kings and priests to God and His Father. To Him *is* the glory and the might forever and ever. Amen.

[7]Behold, He comes with the clouds, and every eye will see Him, and those who pierced Him, and all the tribes of the earth will wail due to Him. Yes, Amen.

[8]I am the Alpha and the Omega, *the* beginning and *the* End, says the Lord, the *One* who is, and who was, and who *is* coming—the Almighty.

[9]I, John, even your brother and co-sharer in the afflic-

ΑΠΟΚΑΛΥΨΙΣ
REVELATION
ΤΟΥ ΑΓΙΟΥ
THE HOLY
ΙΩΑΝΝΟΥ ΤΟΥ ΘΕΟΛΟΓΟΥ
OF JOHN THE DIVINE

CHAPTER 1

1 Ἀποκάλυψις Ἰησοῦ Χριστοῦ, ἣν ἔδωκεν αὐτῷ ὁ Θεὸς
A revelation of Jesus Christ, which gave to Him God,
δεῖξαι τοῖς δούλοις αὐτοῦ, ἃ δεῖ γενέσθαι ἐν τάχει, καὶ ἐσή-
to show to the slaves of Him things which must occur with speed; and He
μανεν ἀποστείλας διὰ τοῦ ἀγγέλου αὐτοῦ τῷ δούλῳ αὐτοῦ
signified sending through the angel of Him to the slave of Him,
2 Ἰωάννῃ, ὃς ἐμαρτύρησε τὸν λόγον τοῦ Θεοῦ καὶ τὴν μαρτυ-
John, who testified of the word of God and the witness
3 ρίαν Ἰησοῦ Χριστοῦ, ὅσα τε εἶδε. μακάριος ὁ ἀναγινώσκων,
of Jesus Christ, as many as even he saw. Blessed the (one) reading
καὶ οἱ ἀκούοντες τοὺς λόγους τῆς προφητείας καὶ τηροῦντες
and those hearing the words of the prophecy, and keeping
τὰ ἐν αὐτῇ γεγραμμένα· ὁ γὰρ καιρὸς ἐγγύς.
the things in it having been written, the for time (is) near.
4 Ἰωάννης ταῖς ἑπτὰ ἐκκλησίαις ταῖς ἐν τῇ Ἀσίᾳ· χάρις ὑμῖν
John to the seven churches in Asia: Grace to you
5 καὶ εἰρήνη ἀπὸ τοῦ ὁ ὢν καὶ ὁ ἦν καὶ ὁ ἐρχόμενος· καὶ ἀπὸ
and peace from He being and who was and who (is) coming, the Almighty.
τῶν ἑπτὰ πνευμάτων ἅ ἐστιν ἐνώπιον τοῦ θρόνου αὐτοῦ·
the seven spirits which are before the throne of Him.
καὶ ἀπὸ Ἰησοῦ Χριστοῦ, ὁ μάρτυς ὁ πιστός, ὁ πρωτότοκος
and from Jesus Christ the witness faithful, the firstborn
ἐκ τῶν νεκρῶν, καὶ ὁ ἄρχων τῶν βασιλέων τῆς γῆς. τῷ
out of the dead, and the ruler of the kings of the earth. To the (One)
ἀγαπήσαντι ἡμᾶς, καὶ λούσαντι ἡμᾶς ἀπὸ τῶν ἁμαρτιῶν
loving us, and having loosed us from the sins
6 ἡμῶν ἐν τῷ αἵματι αὐτοῦ· καὶ ἐποίησεν ἡμᾶς βασιλεῖς καὶ
of us by the blood of Him, and made us kings and
ἱερεῖς τῷ Θεῷ καὶ πατρὶ αὐτοῦ· αὐτῷ ἡ δόξα καὶ τὸ κράτος
priests to the God and Father of Him, to Him (is) the glory and the might
7 εἰς τοὺς αἰῶνας τῶν αἰώνων. ἀμήν. ἰδού, ἔρχεται μετὰ τῶν
to the ages of the ages. Amen. Behold, He comes with the
νεφελῶν, καὶ ὄψεται αὐτὸν πᾶς ὀφθαλμός, καὶ οἵτινες αὐτὸν
clouds, and will see Him every eye and those who Him
ἐξεκέντησαν· καὶ κόψονται ἐπ' αὐτὸν πᾶσαι αἱ φυλαὶ τῆς
pierced, and will wail due to Him all the tribes of the
γῆς. ναί, ἀμήν.
earth. Yes, Amen.
8 Ἐγώ εἰμι τὸ Α καὶ τὸ Ω, ἀρχὴ καὶ τέλος, λέγει ὁ Κύριος,
I am the Alpha and the Omega, beginning and ending, says the Lord,
ὁ ὢν καὶ ὁ ἦν καὶ ὁ ἐρχόμενος, ὁ παντοκράτωρ.
the being (One) and was and (is) coming, the Almighty.
9 Ἐγὼ Ἰωάννης, ὁ καὶ ἀδελφὸς ὑμῶν καὶ συγκοινωνὸς ἐν
I, John, the even brother of you, and co-sharer in

tion, and in the kingdom and patience of Jesus Christ, came to be in the island called Patmos because of the word of God, and because of the witness of Jesus Christ. 10 I came to be in *the* Spirit on the Lord's day, and I heard behind me a great voice, as of a trumpet, 11 saying, I am the Alpha and the Omega, the First and the Last; and, What you see, write in a roll, and send to the seven churches of Asia: to Ephesus, and to Smyrna, and to Pergamos, and to Thyatira, and to Sardis, and to Philadelphia, and to Laodicea. 12 And I turned to see the voice which spoke with me. 13 And turning, I saw seven golden lampstands, and in *the* midst of the seven lampstands *One* like *the* Son of man, having been clothed to *the* feet, and having been girded with a golden girdle at the breasts. 14 And His head and hair *were* white as white wool, as snow, and His eyes as a flame of fire; 15 and His feet like burnished metal having been fired in a furnace; and His voice as a sound of many waters; 16 and having in His right hand seven stars; and a sharp, two-edged sword proceeding out of His mouth; and His face shining as the sun in its power. 17 And when I saw Him, I fell at His feet, as dead. And He put His right hand on me, saying to me, Do not fear. I am the First and the Last, 18 and the Living One; and I became dead; and, behold, I am living forever and ever. Amen. And I have the keys to Hades, and of death. 19 Write what things you saw, and what things are, and what things are about to occur after these things. 20 The mystery of the seven stars which you saw on My right, and the seven golden lampstands: the seven stars are angels of the

τῇ θλίψει καὶ ἐν τῇ βασιλείᾳ καὶ ὑπομονῇ Ἰησοῦ Χριστοῦ,
the affliction and in the kingdom and patience of Jesus Christ,
ἐγενόμην ἐν τῇ νήσῳ τῇ καλουμένῃ Πάτμῳ, διὰ τὸν λόγον
came to be in the island being called Patmos, for the word
10 τοῦ Θεοῦ καὶ διὰ τὴν μαρτυρίαν Ἰησοῦ Χριστοῦ. ἐγενόμην
of God and because of the witness of Jesus Christ. I came to be
ἐν Πνεύματι ἐν τῇ Κυριακῇ ἡμέρᾳ· καὶ ἤκουσα ὀπίσω μου
(the) Spirit on the (of) the Lord day, and I heard behind me
11 φωνὴν μεγάλην ὡς σάλπιγγος, λεγούσης. Ἐγώ εἰμι τὸ Α καὶ
voice great, as of a trumpet, saying, I am the Alpha and
τὸ Ω, ὁ πρῶτος καὶ ὁ ἔσχατος· καί, Ὃ βλέπεις γράψον εἰς
the Omega, the First and the Last; and, What you see write in
βιβλίον, καὶ πέμψον ταῖς ἑπτὰ ἐκκλησίαις ταῖς ἐν Ἀσίᾳ, εἰς
a roll, and send to the seven churches in Asia, to
Ἔφεσον, καὶ εἰς Σμύρναν, καὶ εἰς Πέργαμον, καὶ εἰς Θυάτειρα,
Ephesus, and to Smyrna, and to Pergamos, and to Thyatira,
καὶ εἰς Σάρδεις, καὶ εἰς Φιλαδέλφειαν, καὶ εἰς Λαοδίκειαν.
and to Sardis, and to Philadelphia, and to Laodicea.
12 καὶ ἐπέστρεψα βλέπειν τὴν φωνὴν ἥτις ἐλάλησε μετ᾽ ἐμοῦ.
And I turned to see the voice which spoke with me.
13 καὶ ἐπιστρέψας εἶδον ἑπτὰ λυχνίας χρυσᾶς, καὶ ἐν μέσῳ
And having turned I saw seven lampstands of gold, and in (the) midst
τῶν ἑπτὰ λυχνιῶν ὅμοιον υἱῷ ἀνθρώπου, ἐνδεδυμένον
of the seven lampstands (One) like (the) Son of man, having been clothed
ποδήρη, καὶ περιεζωσμένον πρὸς τοῖς μαστοῖς ζώνην
to (the) feet, and having been girded with at the breasts a girdle
14 χρυσῆν. ἡ δὲ κεφαλὴ αὐτοῦ καὶ αἱ τρίχες λευκαὶ ὡσεὶ ἔριον
of gold. the And head of Him, and the hair white as wool
λευκόν, ὡς χιών· καὶ οἱ ὀφθαλμοὶ αὐτοῦ ὡς φλὸξ πυρός·
white, as snow, and the eyes of Him as a flame of fire,
15 καὶ οἱ πόδες αὐτοῦ ὅμοιοι χαλκολιβάνῳ, ὡς ἐν καμίνῳ
and the feet of Him like burnished metal as in a furnace
πεπυρωμένοι· καὶ ἡ φωνὴ αὐτοῦ ὡς φωνὴ ὑδάτων πολλῶν.
having been fired, and the voice of Him as a sound of waters many,
16 καὶ ἔχων ἐν τῇ δεξιᾷ αὐτοῦ χειρὶ ἀστέρας ἑπτά· καὶ ἐκ τοῦ
and having in the right of Him hand stars seven, and out of the
στόματος αὐτοῦ ῥομφαία δίστομος ὀξεῖα ἐκπορευομένη· καὶ
mouth of Him a sword two-mouthed sharp proceeding, and
17 ἡ ὄψις αὐτοῦ, ὡς ὁ ἥλιος φαίνει ἐν τῇ δυνάμει αὐτοῦ. καὶ ὅτε
the face of Him as the sun shines in the power of it. And when
εἶδον αὐτόν, ἔπεσα πρὸς τοὺς πόδας αὐτοῦ ὡς νεκρός· καὶ
I saw Him, I fell at the feet of Him as dead; and
ἐπέθηκε τὴν δεξιὰν αὐτοῦ χεῖρα ἐπ᾽ ἐμέ, λέγων μοι, Μὴ
He placed the right of Him hand on me, saying to me, Not
18 φοβοῦ· ἐγώ εἰμι ὁ πρῶτος καὶ ὁ ἔσχατος, καὶ ὁ ζῶν, καὶ
fear; I am the First and the Last, and the living One, and
ἐγενόμην νεκρός, καὶ ἰδού, ζῶν εἰμὶ εἰς τοὺς αἰῶνας τῶν
I became dead, and, behold, living I am to the ages of the
αἰώνων, ἀμήν· καὶ ἔχω τὰς κλεῖς τοῦ ᾅδου καὶ τοῦ θανάτου.
ages, Amen. And I have the keys of Hades and of death.
19 γράψον ἃ εἶδες, καὶ ἅ εἰσι. καὶ ἃ μέλλει γίνεσθαι μετὰ ταῦτα·
Write what things you saw, and what things are, and what things are about to occur after these things.
20 τὸ μυστήριον τῶν ἑπτὰ ἀστέρων ὧν εἶδες ἐπὶ τῆς δεξιᾶς
The mystery of the seven stars which you saw on the right
μου, καὶ τὰς ἑπτὰ λυχνίας τὰς χρυσᾶς. οἱ ἑπτὰ ἀστέρες
of Me, and the seven lampstands of gold the seven stars

seven churches; and the seven lampstands you saw are seven churches.

CHAPTER 2

1 To the angel of the Ephesian church, write: 2 These things says the *One* holding the seven stars in His right *hand,* He walking in *the* midst of the seven lampstands: I know your works, and your labor, and your patience, and that you cannot bear evil ones; and *you* tried those pretending to be apostles, and are not, and found them *to be* liars. 3 And *I know* you bore up and have had patience, and for My name's sake you have labored and have not wearied. 4 But I have against you that you left your first love. 5 Then remember from where you have fallen, and repent, and do the first works. And if not, I am coming to you quickly, and will remove your lampstand from its place, unless you repent. 6 But you have this, that you hate the works of the Nicolaitans, which I also hate. 7 The *one* who has an ear, hear what the Spirit says to the churches. To the *one* overcoming, I will give to him to eat of the Tree of Life which is in *the* midst of the Paradise of God.

8 And to the angel of Smyrna, write: 9 These things says the First and the Last, who became dead and lived: I know your works and the affliction, and the poverty, but you are rich. And *I know* the evil speaking of those saying themselves to be Jews, and they are not, but *are* a synagogue of Satan. 10 Do not at all fear what you are about to suffer. Behold, the Devil is about to throw you into prison, so that you may be tried, and you will have affliction ten days. Be faithful until death, and I will give you the crown of life. 11 The *one* who has an ear, hear what the Spirit says to

ἄγγελοι τῶν ἑπτὰ ἐκκλησιῶν εἰσί· καὶ αἱ ἑπτὰ λυχνίαι ἃς
angels of the seven churches are, and the seven lampstands
εἶδες ἑπτὰ ἐκκλησίαι εἰσί.
you saw seven churches are.

CHAPTER 2

1 Τῷ ἀγγέλῳ τῆς Ἐφεσίνης ἐκκλησίας γράψον,
To the angel of the Ephesian church write:
Τάδε λέγει ὁ κρατῶν τοὺς ἑπτὰ ἀστέρας ἐν τῇ δεξιᾷ
These things says the (One) holding the seven stars in the right
αὐτοῦ, ὁ περιπατῶν ἐν μέσῳ τῶν ἑπτὰ λυχνιῶν τῶν
of Him, the (One) walking in (the) midst of the seven lampstands
2 χρυσῶν· Οἶδα τὰ ἔργα σου, καὶ τὸν κόπον σου, καὶ τὴν
of gold: I know the works of you, and the labor of you, and the
ὑπομονήν σου, καὶ ὅτι οὐ δύνῃ βαστάσαι κακούς, καὶ
patience of you, and that you cannot bear evil ones; and
ἐπειράσω τοὺς φάσκοντας εἶναι ἀποστόλους καὶ οὐκ εἰσί,
(you) tried those pretending to be apostles, and not are,
3 καὶ εὗρες αὐτοὺς ψευδεῖς, καὶ ἐβάστασας καὶ ὑπομονὴν ἔχεις,
and found them liars; and you bore up and patience have,
4 καὶ διὰ τὸ ὄνομά μου κεκοπίακας καὶ οὐ κέκμηκας. ἀλλ' ἔχω
even due to the name of Me you have labored, and not have wearied. But I have
5 κατὰ σοῦ, ὅτι τὴν ἀγάπην σου τὴν πρώτην ἀφῆκας. μνημό-
against you that the love of you the first you left. Remember
νευε οὖν πόθεν ἐκπέπτωκας, καὶ μετανόησον, καὶ τὰ πρῶτα
therefore whence you have fallen, and repent, and the first
ἔργα ποίησον· εἰ δὲ μή, ἔρχομαί σοι ταχύ, καὶ κινήσω τὴν
works do; if and not, I am coming to you quickly, and will move the
6 λυχνίαν σου ἐκ τοῦ τόπου αὐτῆς, ἐὰν μὴ μετανοήσῃς. ἀλλὰ
lampstand of you from the place of it, unless you repent. But
τοῦτο ἔχεις, ὅτι μισεῖς τὰ ἔργα τῶν Νικολαϊτῶν, ἃ κἀγὼ
this you have, that you hate the works of the Nicolaitans, which I also
7 μισῶ. ὁ ἔχων οὖς ἀκουσάτω τί τὸ Πνεῦμα λέγει ταῖς ἐκκλη-
hate. The (one) having an ear, hear what the Spirit says to the churches.
σίαις. τῷ νικῶντι δώσω αὐτῷ φαγεῖν ἐκ τοῦ ξύλου τῆς ζωῆς,
To the (one) overcoming I will give to him to eat of the tree of life,
ὅ ἐστιν ἐν μέσῳ τοῦ παραδείσου τοῦ Θεοῦ.
which is in (the) midst of the Paradise of God.
8 Καὶ τῷ ἀγγέλῳ τῆς ἐκκλησίας Σμυρναίων γράψον,
And to the angel of the church of Smyrna write:
Τάδε λέγει ὁ πρῶτος καὶ ὁ ἔσχατος, ὃς ἐγένετο νεκρὸς καὶ
These things says the First and the Last, who became dead and
9 ἔζησεν· Οἶδά σου τὰ ἔργα καὶ τὴν θλῖψιν καὶ τὴν πτωχείαν
lived: I know of you the works and the affliction and the poverty,
(πλούσιος δὲ εἶ), καὶ τὴν βλασφημίαν τῶν λεγόντων Ἰου-
rich but you are, and the evil speaking of those saying Jews
δαίους εἶναι ἑαυτούς, καὶ οὐκ εἰσίν, ἀλλὰ συναγωγὴ τοῦ
to be themselves, and not they are, but a synagogue of
10 Σατανᾶ. μηδὲν φοβοῦ ἃ μέλλεις πάσχειν· ἰδού, μέλλει βαλεῖν
Satan. Not at all do fear what you are about to suffer. Behold, is about to cast
ἐξ ὑμῶν ὁ διάβολος εἰς φυλακήν, ἵνα πειρασθῆτε· καὶ ἕξετε
of you the Devil into prison, that you may be tried, and you will have
θλῖψιν ἡμερῶν δέκα. γίνου πιστὸς ἄχρι θανάτου, καὶ δώσω
affliction days ten. Be faithful until death, and I will give
11 σοι τὸν στέφανον τῆς ζωῆς. ὁ ἔχων οὖς ἀκουσάτω τί τὸ
you the crown of life. The (one) having an ear, hear what the

the churches. The *one* overcoming will not at all be hurt by the second death.

[12]And to the angel of the church in Pergamos, write:

[13]These things says the *One* having the sharp, two-edged sword: I know your works, and where you dwell, where the throne of Satan *is*. And you hold My name, and did not deny My faith even in the days in which Antipas *was* My faithful witness; who was killed alongside you, where Satan dwells. [14]But I have a few things against you, that you have there those holding the teachings of Balaam, who taught Balak to throw a stumbling-block before the sons of Israel, to eat idol-sacrifices, and to commit fornication. [15]So you also have those holding the teaching of the Nicolaitans, which thing I hate. [16]Repent! But if not, I will come to you quickly, and I will make war with them by the sword of My mouth. [17]The *one* who has an ear, hear what the Spirit says to the churches. To the *one* overcoming, I will give him to eat from the hidden manna. And I will give to him a white stone, and on the stone a new name having been written, which no one knows except the *one* receiving *it*.

[18]And to the angel of the church in Thyatira, write:

These things says the Son of God, the *One* having His eyes as a flame of fire, and His feet like burnished metal: [19]I know your works, and the love, and the ministry, and the faith, and your patience, and your works; and the last more than the first. [20]But I have a few things against you, that you allow the woman Jezebel, she saying herself *to be* a prophetess, to teach, and to cause My slaves to go astray, and to commit fornication, and to eat idol-sacrifices. [21]And I gave time to her that she might repent of her forni-

Πνεῦμα λέγει ταῖς ἐκκλησίαις. ὁ νικῶν οὐ μὴ ἀδικηθῇ ἐκ τοῦ
Spirit says to the churches. The (one) over-coming not at all will be hurt by the
θανάτου τοῦ δευτέρου.
death second.

12 Καὶ τῷ ἀγγέλῳ τῆς ἐν Περγάμῳ ἐκκλησίας γράψον,
And to the angel of the in Pergamos church write:
Τάδε· λέγει ὁ ἔχων τὴν ῥομφαίαν τὴν δίστομον τὴν
These things says the (One) having the sword two-mouthed
13 ὀξεῖαν· Οἶδα τὰ ἔργα σου καὶ ποῦ κατοικεῖς, ὅπου ὁ θρόνος
sharp: I know the works of you and where you dwell, where the throne
τοῦ Σατανᾶ· καὶ κρατεῖς τὸ ὄνομά μου, καὶ οὐκ ἠρνήσω τὴν
(is) of Satan; and you hold the name of Me, and not did deny the
πίστιν μου καὶ ἐν ταῖς ἡμέραις ἐν αἷς Ἀντίπας ὁ μάρτυς μου,
faith of Me even in the days in which (was) Antipas the witness of Me
ὁ πιστός, ὃς ἀπεκτάνθη παρ' ὑμῖν, ὅπου κατοικεῖ ὁ Σατανᾶς.
faithful, who was killed alongside you, where dwells Satan.
14 ἀλλ' ἔχω κατὰ σοῦ ὀλίγα, ὅτι ἔχεις ἐκεῖ κρατοῦντας τὴν
But I have against you a few things, for you have there those holding the
διδαχὴν Βαλαάμ, ὃς ἐδίδασκε τὸν Βαλὰκ βαλεῖν σκάνδαλον
teachings of Balaam, who taught Balak to throw a stumbling-block
ἐνώπιον τῶν υἱῶν Ἰσραήλ, φαγεῖν εἰδωλόθυτα καὶ πορνεῦ-
before the sons of Israel, to eat idol sacrifices and to commit
15 σαι. οὕτως ἔχεις καὶ σὺ κρατοῦντας τὴν διδαχὴν τῶν
forni-cation. So have also you those holding the teaching of the
16 Νικολαϊτῶν· ὃ μισῶ. μετανόησον· εἰ δὲ μή, ἔρχομαί σοι
Nicolaitans which thing I hate. Repent! if But not, I will come to you
ταχύ, καὶ πολεμήσω μετ' αὐτῶν ἐν τῇ ῥομφαίᾳ τοῦ στό-
quickly, and I will make war with them by the sword of the mouth
17 ματός μου. ὁ ἔχων οὖς ἀκουσάτω τί τὸ Πνεῦμα λέγει ταῖς
of Me. The (one) having an ear, hear what the Spirit says to the
ἐκκλησίαις. τῷ νικῶντι δώσω αὐτῷ φαγεῖν ἀπὸ τοῦ μάννα
churches To the (one) over-coming, I will give him to eat from the manna
τοῦ κεκρυμμένου, καὶ δώσω αὐτῷ ψῆφον λευκήν, καὶ ἐπὶ
hidden. And I will give to him a stone white, and on
τὴν ψῆφον ὄνομα καινὸν γεγραμμένον, ὃ οὐδεὶς ἔγνω εἰ μὴ
the stone a name new being written, which no one knows except
ὁ λαμβάνων.
the (one) receiving (it).

18 Καὶ τῷ ἀγγέλῳ τῆς ἐν Θυατείροις ἐκκλησίας γράψον,
And to the angel of the in Thyatira church write:
Τάδε λέγει ὁ υἱὸς τοῦ Θεοῦ, ὁ ἔχων τοὺς ὀφθαλμοὺς αὐτοῦ
These things says the Son of God, the (One) having the eyes of Him
ὡς φλόγα πυρός, καὶ οἱ πόδες αὐτοῦ ὅμοιοι χαλκολιβάνῳ·
as a flame of fire, and the feet of Him like burnished metal:
19 Οἶδά σου τὰ ἔργα, καὶ τὴν ἀγάπην καὶ τὴν διακονίαν, καὶ
I know of you the works, and the love and the ministry, and
τὴν πίστιν καὶ τὴν ὑπομονήν σου, καὶ τὰ ἔργα σου, καὶ τὰ
the faith and the patience of you, and the works of you, and the
20 ἔσχατα πλείονα τῶν πρώτων. ἀλλ' ἔχω κατὰ σοῦ ὀλίγα
last more than the first. But I have against you a few things,
ὅτι ἐᾷς τὴν γυναῖκα Ἰεζαβήλ, τὴν λέγουσαν ἑαυτὴν προφῆ-
that you allow the woman Jezebel, the (one) saying herself a prophet-
τιν, διδάσκειν καὶ πλανᾶσθαι ἐμοὺς δούλους πορνεῦσαι καὶ
tess, to teach and to cause to err My slaves to commit forni-cation and
21 εἰδωλόθυτα φαγεῖν. καὶ ἔδωκα αὐτῇ χρόνον ἵνα μετανοήσῃ
idol sacrifices to eat. And I gave to her time that she might repent

cation. And she did not repent. 22 Behold, I am throwing her into a bed, and those committing adultery with her into great affliction, unless they repent of their works. 23 And I will kill her children with death; and all the churches will know that I am the *One* searching the inner parts and hearts. And I will give to each of you according to your works. 24 But I say to you and to the rest in Thyatira, as many as do not have this teaching, and who did not know the deep things of Satan, as they say: I am not casting another burden on you; 25 but what you have, hold until I shall come. 26 And the *one* overcoming, and the *one* keeping My works until *the* end, I will give to him authority over the nations, 27 and he will shepherd them with an iron staff—they are broken as clay vessels—as I also have received from My Father. 28 And I will give to him the morning star. 29 The *one* who has an ear, hear what the Spirit says to the churches.

CHAPTER 3

1 And to the angel of the church in Sardis, write:

These things says the *One* having the seven spirits of God, and the seven stars: I know your works, that you have the name that you live, and are dead. 2 Be watching, and establish the things left, which are about to die. For I have not found your works being fulfilled before God. 3 Then remember how you received and heard, and keep, and repent. If, then, you do not watch, I will come upon you like a thief, and you will not at all know what hour I come upon you. 4 You also have a few names in Sardis which did not defile their robes, and they shall walk with Me in white because they are worthy. 5 The *one* overcoming, this *one* shall be clothed in white garments, and I will not at all blot his name out of the

22 ἐκ τῆς πορνείας αὐτῆς, καὶ οὐ μετενόησεν. Ἰδού, ἐγὼ βάλλω
of the fornication of her, and not she repented. Behold, I am casting

αὐτὴν εἰς κλίνην, καὶ τοὺς μοιχεύοντας μετ' αὐτῆς εἰς θλίψιν
her into a bed, and those committing adultery with her into affliction

23 μεγάλην, ἐὰν μὴ μετανοήσωσιν ἐκ τῶν ἔργων αὐτῶν. καὶ τὰ
great, unless they may repent of the works of them. And the

τέκνα αὐτῆς ἀποκτενῶ ἐν θανάτῳ· καὶ γνώσονται πᾶσαι
children of her I will kill with death; and will know all

αἱ ἐκκλησίαι ὅτι ἐγώ εἰμι ὁ ἐρευνῶν νεφροὺς καὶ καρδίας·
the churches that I am the (One) searching kidneys and hearts,

24 καὶ δώσω ὑμῖν ἑκάστῳ κατὰ τὰ ἔργα ὑμῶν. ὑμῖν δὲ
and I will give to you each according to the works of you. to you But

λέγω καὶ λοιποῖς τοῖς ἐν Θυατείροις, ὅσοι οὐκ ἔχουσι τὴν
I say and to the rest in Thyatira, as many as not have

διδαχὴν ταύτην, καὶ οἵτινες οὐκ ἔγνωσαν τα βάθη τοῦ
teaching this, and who not did know the deep things

25 Σατανᾶ, ὡς λέγουσιν, Οὐ βαλῶ ἐφ' ὑμᾶς ἄλλο βάρος. πλὴν
of Satan, as they say, not I am casting on you another load, but

26 ὃ ἔχετε κρατήσατε, ἄχρις οὗ ἂν ἥξω. καὶ ὁ νικῶν καὶ ὁ
what you have hold until I shall come. And the over-(one) coming and he

τηρῶν ἄχρι τέλους τὰ ἔργα μου, δώσω αὐτῷ ἐξουσίαν ἐπὶ
keeping until (the) end the works of Me, I will give him authority over

27 τῶν ἐθνῶν· καὶ ποιμανεῖ αὐτοὺς ἐν ῥάβδῳ σιδηρᾷ· ὡς τὰ
the nations, and he will shepherd them with a staff iron, as

σκεύη τὰ κεραμικά, συντρίβεται· ὡς κἀγὼ εἴληφα παρὰ τοῦ
vessels clay, they are broken, as I also have received from the

28 πατρός μου· καὶ δώσω αὐτῷ τὸν ἀστέρα τὸν πρωϊνόν.
Father of Me, and I will give him the star morning.

29 ὁ ἔχων οὖς ἀκουσάτω τί τὸ Πνεῦμα λέγει ταῖς ἐκκλησίαις.
he having an ear, hear what the Spirit says to the churches.

CHAPTER 3

1 Καὶ τῷ ἀγγέλῳ τῆς ἐν Σάρδεσιν ἐκκλησίας γράψον,
And to the angel of the in Sardis church write:

Τάδε λέγει ὁ ἔχων τὰ ἑπτὰ πνεύματα τοῦ Θεοῦ καὶ τοὺς
These things says He having the seven spirits of God, and the

ἑπτὰ ἀστέρας· Οἶδά σου τὰ ἔργα, ὅτι τὸ ὄνομα ἔχεις ὅτι
seven stars: I know of you the works, that the name you have that

2 ζῇς, καὶ νεκρὸς εἶ. γίνου γρηγορῶν, καὶ στήριξον τὰ λοιπὰ
you live, and dead are. Be watching, and establish the things left

ἃ μέλλει ἀποθανεῖν· οὐ γὰρ εὕρηκά σου τὰ ἔργα πεπληρω-
which are about to die; not for I have found of you the works being ful-

3 μένα ἐνώπιον τοῦ Θεοῦ. μνημόνευε οὖν πῶς εἴληφας καὶ
filled before God Remember, then, how you received and

ἤκουσας, καὶ τήρει, καὶ μετανόησον. ἐὰν οὖν μὴ γρηγορή-
heard, and keep, and repent. If, then, not you watch,

4 σῃς, ἥξω ἐπί σε ὡς κλέπτης, καὶ οὐ μὴ γνῷς ποίαν ὥραν
I will come on you as a thief, and not at all you know what hour

ἥξω ἐπί σε. ἔχεις ὀλίγα ὀνόματα καὶ ἐν Σάρδεσιν, ἃ οὐκ
I come on you. You have a few names also in Sardis which not

ἐμόλυναν τὰ ἱμάτια αὐτῶν· καὶ περιπατήσουσι μετ' ἐμοῦ ἐν
defile the robes of them, and they shall walk with Me in

5 λευκοῖς, ὅτι ἄξιοί εἰσιν. ὁ νικῶν, οὗτος περιβαλεῖται ἐν
white, because worthy they are. he overcoming, he shall be clothed in

ἱματίοις λευκοῖς· καὶ οὐ μὴ ἐξαλείψω τὸ ὄνομα αὐτοῦ ἐκ τῆς
garments white, and not at all will I blot the name of him out of the

Book of Life; and I will acknowledge his name before My Father, and before His angels. [6]The *one* who has an ear, hear what the Spirit says to the churches.

[7]And to the angel of the church in Philadelphia, write

These things says the Holy One, the True One, the *One* having the key of David, the *One* opening, and no one shuts; and shuts, and no one opens: [8]I know your works. Behold, I have given a door being opened before you, and no one is able to shut it, for you have a little power and have kept My word, and have not denied My name. [9]Behold, I give out of the synagogue of Satan those saying themselves to be Jews, and they are not, but they lie. Behold, I will make them come, and bow down before your feet, and they shall know that I loved you. [10]Because you kept the word of My patience, I also will keep you out of the hour of trial which is going to come on all the habitable world in order to try those dwelling on the earth. [11]Behold, I am coming quickly. Hold what you have that no one take your crown. [12]The *one* overcoming, I will make him a pillar in the temple of My God, and he shall not go out any more. And I will write the name of My God on him, and the name of the city of My God, the new Jerusalem which comes down out of Heaven from My God, and My new name. [13]The *one* who has an ear, hear what the Spirit says to the churches. [14]And to the angel of the church of Laodicea, write:

These things says the Amen, the faithful and true Witness, the Head of the creation of God: [15]I know your works, that you are neither hot nor cold. I would that you were cold, or hot. [16]So, because you are luke-

βίβλου τῆς ζωῆς, καὶ ἐξομολογήσομαι τὸ ὄνομα αὐτοῦ
Scroll of Life, and I will acknowledge the name of him
ἐνώπιον τοῦ πατρός μου, καὶ ἐνώπιον τῶν ἀγγέλων αὐτοῦ.
before the Father of Me, and before the angels of Him.
6 ὁ ἔχων οὖς ἀκουσάτω τί τὸ Πνεῦμα λέγει ταῖς ἐκκλησίαις.
The (one) having an ear, hear what the Spirit says to the churches.
7 Καὶ τῷ ἀγγέλῳ τῆς ἐν Φιλαδελφείᾳ ἐκκλησίας γράψον,
And to the angel of the in Philadelphia church write:
Τάδε λέγει ὁ ἅγιος, ὁ ἀληθινός, ὁ ἔχων τὴν κλεῖδα τοῦ
These things says the Holy One, the True One, He having the key
Δαβίδ, ὁ ἀνοίγων καὶ οὐδεὶς κλείει, καὶ κλείει καὶ οὐδεὶς
of David, the (One) opening and no one shuts, and shuts, and no one
8 ἀνοίγει· Οἶδά σου τὰ ἔργα (ἰδού, δέδωκα ἐνώπιόν σου θύραν
opens: I know of you the works. Behold, I have given before you a door
ἀνεῳγμένην, καὶ οὐδεὶς δύναται κλεῖσαι αὐτήν), ὅτι μικρὰν
being opened, and no one is able to shut it, because a little
ἔχεις δύναμιν, καὶ ἐτήρησάς μου τὸν λόγον, καὶ οὐκ ἠρνήσω
you have power, and have kept of Me the word, and not denied
9 τὸ ὄνομά μου. ἰδού, δίδωμι ἐκ τῆς συναγωγῆς τοῦ Σατανᾶ,
the name of Me. Behold, I give out of the synagogue of Satan,
τῶν λεγόντων ἑαυτοὺς Ἰουδαίους εἶναι, καὶ οὐκ εἰσίν, ἀλλὰ
those saying themselves Jews to be, and not they are, but
ψεύδονται· ἰδού, ποιήσω αὐτοὺς ἵνα ἥξωσι καὶ προσκυνή-
they lie; behold, I will make them that they shall come and shall
σωσιν ἐνώπιον τῶν ποδῶν σου, καὶ γνῶσιν ὅτι ἐγὼ
bow before the feet of you, and they shall know that I
10 ἠγάπησά σε. ὅτι ἐτήρησας τὸν λόγον τῆς ὑπομονῆς μου,
loved you. Because you kept the word of the patience of Me,
κἀγώ σε τηρήσω ἐκ τῆς ὥρας τοῦ πειρασμοῦ, τῆς μελλούσης
I also you will keep out of the hour of trial being about
ἔρχεσθαι ἐπὶ τῆς οἰκουμένης ὅλης, πειράσαι τοὺς κατοι-
to come upon the habitable world all, to try those dwelling
11 κοῦντας ἐπὶ τῆς γῆς. ἰδού, ἔρχομαι ταχύ· κράτει ὃ ἔχεις, ἵνα
on the earth. Behold, I am coming quickly; hold what you have that
12 μηδεὶς λάβῃ τὸν στέφανόν σου. ὁ νικῶν, ποιήσω αὐτὸν
no one take the crown of you. The (one) over-coming I will make him
στύλον ἐν τῷ ναῷ τοῦ Θεοῦ μου, καὶ ἔξω οὐ μὴ ἐξέλθῃ ἔτι,
a pillar in the temple of the God of Me, and out not at all he will go yet,
καὶ γράψω ἐπ' αὐτὸν τὸ ὄνομα τοῦ Θεοῦ μου, καὶ τὸ ὄνομα
and I will write on him the name of the God of Me, and the name
τῆς πόλεως τοῦ Θεοῦ μου, τῆς καινῆς Ἱερουσαλήμ, ἣ κατα-
of the city of the God of Me, the new Jerusalem which comes
βαίνει ἐκ τοῦ οὐρανοῦ ἀπὸ τοῦ Θεοῦ μου, καὶ τὸ ὄνομά μου
down out of Heaven from the God of Me, and the name of Me
13 τὸ καινόν. ὁ ἔχων οὖς ἀκουσάτω τί τὸ Πνεῦμα λέγει ταῖς
new. The (one) having an ear, hear what the Spirit says to the
ἐκκλησίαις.
churches.
14 Καὶ τῷ ἀγγέλῳ τῆς ἐκκλησίας Λαοδικέων γράψον,
And to the angel of the church in Laodicea write:
Τάδε λέγει ὁ Ἀμήν, ὁ μάρτυς ὁ πιστὸς καὶ ἀληθινός, ἡ
These things says the Amen, the Witness faithful and true, the
15 ἀρχὴ τῆς κτίσεως τοῦ Θεοῦ· Οἶδά σου τὰ ἔργα, ὅτι οὔτε
Head of the creation of God: I know of you the works, that neither
16 ψυχρὸς εἶ οὔτε ζεστός· ὄφελον ψυχρὸς εἴης ἢ ζεστός. οὕτως
cold are you, nor hot; I would that cold you were, or hot. So

warm, and neither cold nor hot, I am about to vomit you out of My mouth. [17]Because you say, I am rich, and I am made rich, and I have need of nothing, and do not know that you are wretched and miserable and poor and blind and naked. [18]I advise you to buy from Me gold having been fired by fire, that you may be rich; and white garments, that you may be clothed, and your shame and nakedness may not be revealed. And anoint your eyes with eye-salve, that you may see. [19]I, as many as I love, I rebuke and I chasten. Be zealous, then, and repent. [20]Behold, I stand at the door and knock. If anyone hears My voice and opens the door, I will go in to him, and I will dine with him, and he with Me. [21]The *one* overcoming, I will give to him to sit with Me in My throne, as I also overcame and sat with My Father in His throne. [22]The *one* who has an ear, hear what the Spirit says to the churches.

ὅτι χλιαρὸς εἶ, καὶ οὔτε ψυχρὸς οὔτε ζεστός, μέλλω σε ἐμέσαι
because luke-warm you are, and neither cold nor hot, I am about you to vomit
17 ἐκ τοῦ στόματός μου. ὅτι λέγεις ὅτι Πλούσιός εἰμι, καὶ
out of the mouth of Me. Because you say, — rich I am, and
πεπλούτηκα, καὶ οὐδενὸς χρείαν ἔχω, καὶ οὐκ οἶδας ὅτι σὺ
I am made rich, and of nothing need I have, and not know that you
εἶ ὁ ταλαίπωρος καὶ ἐλεεινὸς καὶ πτωχὸς καὶ τυφλὸς καὶ
are the wretched (one) and miserable and poor and blind and
18 γυμνός· συμβουλεύω σοι ἀγοράσαι παρ' ἐμοῦ χρυσίον
naked, I advise you to buy from Me gold
πεπυρωμένον ἐκ πυρός, ἵνα πλουτήσῃς, καὶ ἱμάτια λευκά,
having been fired by fire, that you may be rich; and garments white,
ἵνα περιβάλῃ, καὶ μὴ φανερωθῇ ἡ αἰσχύνη τῆς γυμνότητός
that you be clothed, and not may be revealed the shame and the nakedness
σου· καὶ κολλούριον ἔγχρισον τοὺς ὀφθαλμούς σου, ἵνα
of you, and with eyesalve anoint the eyes of you, that
19 βλέπῃς. ἐγὼ ὅσους ἐὰν φιλῶ, ἐλέγχω καὶ παιδεύω· ζήλωσον
you may see. I as many if I love, I rebuke, and I chasten; be zealous
20 οὖν καὶ μετανόησον. ἰδού, ἕστηκα ἐπὶ τὴν θύραν καὶ κρούω·
then, and repent. Behold, I stand at the door and knock;
ἐάν τις ἀκούσῃ τῆς φωνῆς μου, καὶ ἀνοίξῃ τὴν θύραν,
If anyone hear the voice of Me, and opens the door,
εἰσελεύσομαι πρὸς αὐτόν, καὶ δειπνήσω μετ' αὐτοῦ, καὶ
I will enter to him, and I will dine with him, and
21 αὐτὸς μετ' ἐμοῦ. ὁ νικῶν, δώσω αὐτῷ καθίσαι μετ' ἐμοῦ
he with Me. The (one) overcoming I will give to him to sit with Me
ἐν τῷ θρόνῳ μου, ὡς κἀγὼ ἐνίκησα, καὶ ἐκάθισα μετὰ τοῦ
in the throne of Me, as I also overcame and sat with the
22 πατρός μου ἐν τῷ θρόνῳ αὐτοῦ. ὁ ἔχων οὖς ἀκουσάτω τί
Father of Me in the throne of Him. The (one) having an ear, hear what
τὸ Πνεῦμα λέγει ταῖς ἐκκλησίαις.
the Spirit says to the churches.

CHAPTER 4

[1]After these things I saw. And behold, a door being opened in Heaven. And I heard the first voice as a trumpet speaking with me, saying, Come up here, and I will show you what needs to happen after these things. [2]And at once I became in spirit. And, behold, a throne was set in Heaven, and *One* sitting on the throne. [3]And the *One* sitting was in appearance like a jasper stone, and a sardius; and a rainbow *was* around the throne, in appearance like an emerald. [4]And around the throne *I saw* twenty-four elders sitting, having been clothed in white garments. And they had golden crowns

CHAPTER 4

1 Μετὰ ταῦτα εἶδον, καὶ ἰδού, θύρα ἠνεῳγμένη ἐν τῷ
After these things I saw, and behold, a door having been opened in
οὐρανῷ, καὶ ἡ φωνὴ ἡ πρώτη ἣν ἤκουσα ὡς σάλπιγγος
Heaven, and the voice first which I heard as a trumpet
λαλούσης μετ' ἐμοῦ, λέγουσα, Ἀνάβα ὧδε, καὶ δείξω σοι
speaking with me, saying, Come up here, and I will show you
2 ἃ δεῖ γενέσθαι μετὰ ταῦτα. καὶ εὐθέως ἐγενόμην ἐν πνεύματι·
what needs to occur after these things. And at once I became in spirit,
και ιδου, θρονος ἔκειτο ἐν τῷ οὐρανῷ, καὶ ἐπὶ τοῦ θρόνου
and behold, a throne was set in Heaven, and on the throne
3 καθήμενος· καὶ ὁ καθήμενος ἦν ὅμοιος ὁράσει λίθῳ ἰάσπιδι
(One) sitting, and the (One) sitting was like in appearance a stone jasper;
καὶ σαρδίνῳ· καὶ ἶρις κυκλόθεν τοῦ θρόνου ὁμοία ὁράσει
and a sardius, and a rainbow (was) around the throne like in appearance
4 σμαραγδίνῳ. καὶ κυκλόθεν τοῦ θρόνου θρόνοι εἴκοσι καὶ
to an emerald And around the throne (I saw) thrones twenty and
τέσσαρες· καὶ ἐπὶ τοὺς θρόνους εἶδον τοὺς εἴκοσι καὶ τέσσαρας
four, and on the thrones I saw twenty and four
πρεσβυτέρους καθημένους, περιβεβλημένους ἐν ἱματίοις
elders sitting, having been clothed in garments
λευκοῖς, καὶ ἔσχον ἐπὶ τὰς κεφαλὰς αὐτῶν στεφάνους
white, and they had on the heads of them crowns

on their heads. [5]And out of the throne come forth lightnings and thunders and voices. And seven lamps of fire *are* burning before the throne, which are the seven Spirits of God; [6]and a glassy sea before the throne, like crystal. And in *the* midst of the throne and around the throne *were* four living creatures full of eyes before and behind.

[7]And the first living creature *was* like a lion; and the second living creature like a calf; and the third living creature having a face like a man; and the fourth living creature like an eagle flying. [8]And the four living creatures each one had six wings around, and within being full of eyes. And they had no rest day and night, saying, Holy, holy, holy, Lord God Almighty, the *One who* was, and is, and *is* coming! [9]And when the living creatures shall give glory and honor and thanks to the *One* sitting on the throne, to the *One* living forever and ever, [10]the twenty-four elders fall down before Him sitting on the throne; and they will worship the *One* living forever and ever, and will throw their crowns before the throne, saying, [11]Lord, You are worthy to receive the glory and the honor and the power, because You created all things, and through Your will they exist and were created.

CHAPTER 5

[1]And I saw on the right of the *One* sitting on the throne a book having been written within and on the back, having been sealed with seven seals. [2]And I saw a mighty angel proclaiming with a great voice: Who is worthy to open the book, and to loosen its seals? [3]And no one in Heaven was able, nor on the earth, nor underneath the earth, to open the book,

5 χρυσοῦς. καὶ ἐκ τοῦ θρόνου ἐκπορεύονται ἀστραπαὶ καὶ
of gold. And out of the throne come forth lightnings and
βρονταὶ καὶ φωναί. καὶ ἑπτὰ λαμπάδες πυρὸς καιόμεναι
thunders and voices. And seven lamps of fire (are) burning
ἐνώπιον τοῦ θρόνου, αἵ εἰσι τὰ ἑπτὰ πνεύματα τοῦ Θεοῦ·
before the throne, which are the seven Spirits of God;
6 καὶ ἐνώπιον τοῦ θρόνου θάλασσα ὑαλίνη, ὁμοία κρυστάλλῳ.
and before the throne sea a glassy like to crystal;
καὶ ἐν μέσῳ τοῦ θρόνου καὶ κύκλῳ τοῦ θρόνου τέσσαρα ζῶα
and in (the) midst of the throne and around the throne four living creatures
7 γέμοντα ὀφθαλμῶν ἔμπροσθεν καὶ ὄπισθεν. καὶ τὸ ζῶον
full of eyes before and behind, and the living creature
τὸ πρῶτον ὅμοιον λέοντι, καὶ τὸ δεύτερον ζῶον ὅμοιον
first (was) like a lion, and the second living creature like
μόσχῳ, καὶ τὸ τρίτον ζῶον ἔχον τὸ πρόσωπον ὡς ἄνθρωπος,
a calf, and the third living creature having the face as of a man,
8 καὶ τὸ τέταρτον ζῶον ὅμοιον ἀετῷ πετωμένῳ. καὶ τέσσαρα
and the fourth living creature like an eagle flying. And (the) four
ζῶα, ἓν καθ' ἑαυτὸ εἶχον ἀνὰ πτέρυγας ἓξ κυκλόθεν, καὶ
living creatures one by one having each wings six around, and
ἔσωθεν γέμοντα ὀφθαλμῶν, καὶ ἀνάπαυσιν οὐκ ἔχουσιν
within being full of eyes; and respite not they have
ἡμέρας καὶ νυκτός, λέγοντα, Ἅγιος, ἅγιος, ἅγιος Κύριος ὁ
day and night, saying, Holy, holy, holy, Lord
9 Θεὸς ὁ παντοκράτωρ, ὁ ἦν καὶ ὁ ὢν καὶ ὁ ἐρχόμενος. καὶ
God, the Almighty, the (One who) was and is and (is) coming. And
ὅταν δώσουσι τὰ ζῶα δόξαν καὶ τιμὴν καὶ εὐχαριστίαν τῷ
when shall give the living creatures glory and honor and thanks to the (One)
καθημένῳ ἐπὶ τοῦ θρόνου, τῷ ζῶντι εἰς τοὺς αἰῶνας τῶν
sitting on the throne, to the (One) living to the ages of the
10 αἰώνων, πεσοῦνται οἱ εἴκοσι καὶ τέσσαρες πρεσβύτεροι
ages, will fall down the twenty and four elders
ἐνώπιον τοῦ καθημένου ἐπὶ τοῦ θρόνου, καὶ προσκυνοῦσι τῷ
before the (One) sitting on the throne, and they will worship the (One)
ζῶντι εἰς τοὺς αἰῶνας τῶν αἰώνων, καὶ βάλλουσι τοὺς
living to the ages of the ages, and will cast the
11 στεφάνους αὐτῶν ἐνώπιον τοῦ θρόνου, λέγοντες, Ἄξιος εἶ,
crowns of them before the throne, saying, worthy are You
Κύριε, λαβεῖν τὴν δόξαν καὶ τὴν τιμὴν καὶ τὴν δύναμιν· ὅτι σὺ
Lord, to receive the glory and the honor and the power because You
ἔκτισας τὰ πάντα, καὶ διὰ τὸ θέλημά σου εἰσὶ καὶ ἐκτίσθησαν.
created all things, and because of the will of You they exist and were created.

CHAPTER 5

1 Καὶ εἶδον ἐπὶ τὴν δεξιὰν τοῦ καθημένου ἐπὶ τοῦ θρόνου
And I saw on the right of the (One) sitting on the throne
βιβλίον γεγραμμένον ἔσωθεν καὶ ὄπισθεν, κατεσφραγισμένον
a scroll having been written within and on the back, having been sealed
2 σφραγῖσιν ἑπτά. καὶ εἶδον ἄγγελον ἰσχυρὸν κηρύσσοντα
with seals seven,. And I saw an angel strong proclaiming
φωνῇ μεγάλῃ, Τίς ἐστιν ἄξιος ἀνοῖξαι τὸ βιβλίον, καὶ λῦσαι
with a voice great, Who is worthy to open the scroll, and to loosen
3 τὰς σφραγῖδας αὐτοῦ; καὶ οὐδεὶς ἠδύνατο ἐν τῷ οὐρανῷ,
the seals of it? And no one was able in Heaven,
οὐδὲ ἐπὶ τῆς γῆς, οὐδὲ ὑποκάτω τῆς γῆς, ἀνοῖξαι τὸ βιβλίον,
nor on the earth, nor underneath the earth, to open the scroll

4 οὐδὲ βλέπειν αὐτό. καὶ ἐγὼ ἔκλαιον πολλά, ὅτι οὐδεὶς ἄξιος
nor to see it. And I wept much, because no one worthy
εὑρέθη ἀνοῖξαι καὶ ἀναγνῶναι τὸ βιβλίον, οὔτε βλέπειν αὐτό.
was found to open and to read the scroll, nor to see it.
5 καὶ εἷς ἐκ τῶν πρεσβυτέρων λέγει μοι, Μὴ κλαῖε· ἰδού,
And one of the elders says to me, Not do weep; behold,
ἐνίκησεν ὁ λέων ὁ ὢν ἐκ τῆς φυλῆς Ἰούδα, ἡ ῥίζα Δαβίδ,
overcame the Lion being of the tribe of Judah, the Root of David,
ἀνοῖξαι τὸ βιβλίον καὶ λῦσαι τὰς ἑπτὰ σφραγῖδας αὐτοῦ.
to open the scroll and to loose the seven seals of it.
6 καὶ εἶδον, καὶ ἰδού, ἐν μέσῳ τοῦ θρόνου καὶ τῶν τεσσάρων
And I saw and behold, in (the) midst of the throne and of the four
ζώων, καὶ ἐν μέσῳ τῶν πρεσβυτέρων, ἀρνίον ἑστηκὸς ὡς
living creatures, and amidst the elders, a Lamb standing as
ἐσφαγμένον, ἔχον κέρατα ἑπτὰ καὶ ὀφθαλμοὺς ἑπτά, οἵ εἰσι
having been slain, having horns seven and eyes seven, which are
τὰ ἑπτὰ τοῦ Θεοῦ πνεύματα τὰ ἀπεσταλμένα εἰς πᾶσαν τὴν
the seven of God Spirits, having been sent out into all the
7 γῆν. καὶ ἦλθε, καὶ εἴληφε τὸ βιβλίον ἐκ τῆς δεξιᾶς τοῦ
earth. And He came, and took the scroll out of the right of the
8 καθημένου ἐπὶ τοῦ θρόνου. καὶ ὅτε ἔλαβε τὸ βιβλίον, τὰ
(One) sitting on the throne. And when He took the scroll, the
τέσσαρα ζῶα καὶ οἱ εἰκοσιτέσσαρες πρεσβύτεροι ἔπεσον
four living creatures and the twenty-four elders fell down
ἐνώπιον τοῦ ἀρνίου, ἔχοντες ἕκαστος κιθάρας, καὶ φιάλας
before the Lamb, having each one harps, and bowls
χρυσᾶς γεμούσας θυμιαμάτων, αἵ εἰσιν αἱ προσευχαὶ τῶν
of gold full of incenses, which are the prayers of the
9 ἁγίων. καὶ ᾄδουσιν ᾠδὴν καινήν, λέγοντες, Ἄξιος εἶ λαβεῖν
saints. And they sing a song new, saying, Worthy are You to receive
τὸ βιβλίον, καὶ ἀνοῖξαι τὰς σφραγῖδας αὐτοῦ· ὅτι ἐσφάγης,
the scroll, and to open the seals of it, because You were slain
καὶ ἠγόρασας τῷ Θεῷ ἡμᾶς ἐν τῷ αἵματί σου ἐκ πάσης φυλῆς
and purchased the God of us by the blood of You out of every tribe
10 καὶ γλώσσης καὶ λαοῦ καὶ ἔθνους, καὶ ἐποίησας ἡμᾶς τῷ Θεῷ
and tongue and people and nation, and made us to the God
11 ἡμῶν βασιλεῖς καὶ ἱερεῖς, καὶ βασιλεύσομεν ἐπὶ τῆς γῆς. καὶ
of us kings and priests, and we shall reign over the earth. And
εἶδον, καὶ ἤκουσα φωνὴν ἀγγέλων πολλῶν κυκλόθεν τοῦ
I saw, and I heard a sound of angels many around the
θρόνου καὶ τῶν ζώων καὶ τῶν πρεσβυτέρων· καὶ ἦν ὁ
throne, and the living creatures and of the elders, and was the
ἀριθμὸς αὐτῶν μυριάδες μυριάδων, καὶ χιλιάδες χιλιάδων,
number of them myriads of myriads, and thousands of thousands,
12 λέγοντες φωνῇ μεγάλῃ, Ἄξιόν ἐστι τὸ ἀρνίον τὸ ἐσφαγ-
saying with a voice great, Worthy is the Lamb having been
μένον λαβεῖν τὴν δύναμιν καὶ πλοῦτον καὶ σοφίαν καὶ
slain to receive the power and riches and wisdom and
13 ἰσχὺν καὶ τιμὴν καὶ δόξαν καὶ εὐλογίαν. καὶ πᾶν κτίσμα ὅ
strength and honor and glory and blessing. And every creature which
ἐστιν ἐν τῷ οὐρανῷ, καὶ ἐν τῇ γῇ, καὶ ὑποκάτω τῆς γῆς, καὶ
is in Heaven, and in the earth, and underneath the earth, and
ἐπὶ τῆς θαλάσσης ἅ ἐστι, καὶ τὰ ἐν αὐτοῖς πάντα, ἤκουσα
on the sea the things that are, and the things in them all, I heard
λέγοντας, Τῷ καθημένῳ ἐπὶ τοῦ θρόνου καὶ τῷ ἀρνίῳ ἡ
saying, To the (one) sitting on the throne and to the Lamb the

nor to see it. 4 And I wept very much, because no one worthy was found to open and to read the book, nor to see it. 5 And one of the elders said to me, Do not weep. Behold, the Lion being of the tribe of Judah, the Root of David, overcame *so as* to open the book, and to loose its seven seals. 6 And I saw, and behold, in *the* midst of the throne, and of the four living creatures, and in *the* midst of the elders, *was* a Lamb standing, as having been slain, having seven horns and seven eyes, which are the seven Spirits of God, having been sent out into all the earth. 7 And He came and took the book out of the right of Him sitting on the throne. 8 And when He took the book, the four living creatures, and the twenty-four elders, fell down before the Lamb, each one having harps, and golden bowls full of incenses, which are the prayers of the saints. 9 And they sing a new song, saying, Worthy are You to receive the book, and to open its seals, because You were slain, and by Your blood purchased us out of every tribe and tongue and people and nation, 10 and made us kings and priests to our God; and we shall reign over the earth. 11 And I saw, and I heard a sound of many angels around the throne, and the living creatures, and the elders, and their number was myriads of myriads, and thousands of thousands,

12 saying with a great voice, Worthy is the Lamb having been slain to receive the power and riches and wisdom and strength and honor and glory and blessing. 13 And every creature which is in Heaven, and in the earth, and the things that are on the sea, and the things in all of them, I heard saying, To Him sitting on the throne, and to

the Lamb *be* the blessing and the honor and the glory and the might forever and ever. [14]And the four living creatures said, Amen. And the twenty-four elders fell down and worshiped *the* Living One forever and ever.

CHAPTER 6

[1]And I saw when the Lamb opened one of the seals. And I heard one of the four living creatures, like a sound of thunder, saying, Come and see. [2]And I saw, and behold, a white horse! And the *one* sitting on it had a bow. And a crown was given to him, and he went out overcoming, and that he might overcome.

[3]And when He opened the second seal, I heard the second living creature saying, Come and see. [4]And another horse went out, red. And it was given to the *one* sitting on *it* to take peace from the earth, and that they should slay one another. And a great sword was given to him.

[5]And when he opened the third seal, I heard the third living creature saying, Come and see. And I saw. And, behold, a black horse. And the *one* sitting on it having a balance in his hand. [6]And I heard a voice in *the* midst of the four living creatures saying, A choenix of wheat *for* a denarius, and three choenixes of barley *for* a denarius; and do not harm the oil and the wine.

[7]And when He opened the fourth seal, I heard a voice of the fourth living creature saying, Come and see. [8]And I saw, and behold, a pale green horse, and the name of the *one* sitting on it *was* Death; and Hades followed after him. And *it* was given to them to kill over the fourth of the earth with sword, and with famine, and with death, and by the wild beasts of the earth.

εὐλογία καὶ ἡ τιμὴ καὶ ἡ δόξα καὶ τὸ κράτος εἰς τοὺς αἰῶνας
blessing and the honor and the glory and the might to the ages
14 τῶν αἰώνων. καὶ τὰ τέσσαρα ζῶα ἔλεγον, Ἀμήν. καὶ οἱ
of the ages. And the four living creatures said, Amen; and the
εἰκοσιτέσσαρες πρεσβύτεροι ἔπεσαν καὶ προσεκύνησαν
twenty-four elders fell down and worshiped
ζῶντι εἰς τοὺς αἰῶνας τῶν αἰώνων.
(the) Living One to the ages of the ages.

CHAPTER 6

1 Καὶ εἶδον ὅτε ἤνοιξε τὸ ἀρνίον μίαν ἐκ τῶν σφραγίδων,
And I saw when opened the Lamb one of the seals
καὶ ἤκουσα ἑνὸς ἐκ τῶν τεσσάρων ζώων λέγοντος, ὡς φωνῆς
and I heard one of the four living creatures saying, as of a sound
2 βροντῆς, Ἔρχου καὶ βλέπε. καὶ εἶδον, καὶ ἰδού, ἵππος
of thunder, Come and see; and I saw. And behold, a horse
λευκός, καὶ ὁ καθήμενος ἐπ᾽ αὐτῷ ἔχων τόξον· καὶ ἐδόθη
white, and the (one) sitting on it having a bow, and was given
αὐτῷ στέφανος, καὶ ἐξῆλθε νικῶν, καὶ ἵνα νικήσῃ.
to him a crown, and he went out over-coming, and that he might overcome.
3 Καὶ ὅτε ἤνοιξε τὴν δευτέραν σφραγῖδα, ἤκουσα τοῦ
And when He opened the second seal, I heard the
4 δευτέρου ζώου λέγοντος, Ἔρχου καὶ βλέπε. καὶ ἐξῆλθεν
second living creature saying, Come and see. And went out
ἄλλος ἵππος πυρρός· καὶ τῷ καθημένῳ ἐπ᾽ αὐτῷ ἐδόθη
another horse, red; and to the (one) sitting on it was given
αὐτῷ λαβεῖν τὴν εἰρήνην ἀπὸ τῆς γῆς, καὶ ἵνα ἀλλήλους
to him to take peace from the earth, and that one another
σφάξωσι· καὶ ἐδόθη αὐτῷ μάχαιρα μεγάλη.
they shall slay; and was given to him a sword great.
5 Καὶ ὅτε ἤνοιξε τὴν τρίτην σφραγῖδα, ἤκουσα τοῦ τρίτου
And when He opened the third seal, I heard the third
ζώου λέγοντος, Ἔρχου καὶ βλέπε. καὶ εἶδον, καὶ ἰδού, ἵππος
living creature saying, Come and see And I saw, and behold, a horse
μέλας, καὶ ὁ καθήμενος ἐπ᾽ αὐτῷ ἔχων ζυγὸν ἐν τῇ χειρὶ
black, and the (one) sitting on it having a balance in the hand
6 αὐτοῦ. καὶ ἤκουσα φωνὴν ἐν μέσῳ τῶν τεσσάρων ζώων
of him. And I heard a voice in (the) midst of the four living creatures
λέγουσαν, Χοῖνιξ σίτου δηναρίου, καὶ τρεῖς χοίνικες κριθῆς
saying, A choenix of wheat (for) a denarius, and three choenixes of barley
δηναρίου· καὶ τὸ ἔλαιον καὶ τὸν οἶνον μὴ ἀδικήσῃς.
(for) a denarius; and the oil and the wine not harm.
7 Καὶ ὅτε ἤνοιξε τὴν σφραγῖδα τὴν τετάρτην, ἤκουσα
And when He opened the seal fourth, I heard
8 φωνὴν τοῦ τετάρτου ζώου λέγουσαν, Ἔρχου καὶ βλέπε. καὶ
(the) voice of the fourth living creature saying, Come and see. And
εἶδον, καὶ ἰδού, ἵππος χλωρός, καὶ ὁ καθήμενος ἐπάνω
I saw. And behold, a horse pale green, and the (one) sitting upon
αὐτοῦ, ὄνομα αὐτῷ ὁ θάνατος, καὶ ὁ ᾅδης ἀκολουθεῖ μετ᾽
it, name to him death, and Hades followed with
αὐτοῦ. καὶ ἐδόθη αὐτοῖς ἐξουσία ἀποκτεῖναι ἐπὶ τὸ τέταρτον
him, and was given to them authority to kill over the fourth
τῆς γῆς ἐν ῥομφαίᾳ καὶ ἐν λιμῷ καὶ ἐν θανάτῳ, καὶ ὑπὸ τῶν
of the earth with sword and with famine and with death, and by the
θηρίων τῆς γῆς.
wild beasts of the earth.

9 And when He opened the fifth seal, I saw under the altar the souls of those having been slain for the word of God, and for the witness which they had. 10 And they cried with a great voice, saying, Until when, holy and true Master, do You not judge and take vengeance *for* our blood, from those dwelling on the earth? 11 And there was given to each one a white robe. And it was said to them that they should rest a little time, until might be fulfilled also *the number* of their fellow-slaves and their brothers, those being about to be killed, even as they.

12 And I saw when He opened the sixth seal. And behold, a great earthquake occurred. And the sun became black as sackcloth made of hair; and the moon became as blood; 13 and the stars of the heaven fell to the earth, as a fig-tree being shaken by the wind casts its unripe figs. 14 And *the* heaven departed like a scroll being rolled up. And every mountain and island were moved out of their places. 15 And the kings of the earth, and the great ones, and the rich ones, and the commanders, and the powerful ones, and every slave, and every freeman, hid themselves in the caves and in the rocks of the mountains. 16 And they said to the mountains and to the rocks, Fall on us, and hide us from *the* face of the *One* sitting on the throne, and from the wrath of the Lamb, 17 because the great day of His wrath has come and who is able to stand?

9 Καὶ ὅτε ἤνοιξε τὴν πέμπτην σφραγῖδα, εἶδον ὑποκάτω
And when He opened the fifth seal I saw underneath
τοῦ θυσιαστηρίου τὰς ψυχὰς τῶν ἐσφαγμένων διὰ τὸν λόγον
the altar the souls of those having been slain for the word
10 τοῦ Θεοῦ, καὶ διὰ τὴν μαρτυρίαν ἣν εἶχον, καὶ ἔκραζον φωνῇ
of God, and for the witness which they had. And they cried with a voice
μεγάλῃ, λέγοντες, Ἕως πότε, ὁ δεσπότης, ὁ ἅγιος καὶ ὁ ἀλη-
great saying, Until when, Master holy and true,
θινός, οὐ κρίνεις καὶ ἐκδικεῖς τὸ αἷμα ἡμῶν ἀπὸ τῶν κατοι-
not do You judge and avenge the blood of us from those dwelling
11 κούντων ἐπὶ τῆς γῆς; καὶ ἐδόθησαν ἑκάστοις στολαὶ λευκαί,
on the earth? And was given to each one a robe white,
καὶ ἐρρέθη αὐτοῖς ἵνα ἀναπαύσωνται ἔτι χρόνον μικρόν, ἕως
and it was said to them that they should rest yet a time little, until
οὗ πληρώσονται καὶ οἱ σύνδουλοι αὐτῶν καὶ οἱ ἀδελφοὶ
should be fulfilled also the fellow-slaves of them and the brothers
αὐτῶν, οἱ μέλλοντες ἀποκτείνεσθαι ὡς καὶ αὐτοί.
of them, those being about to be killed as also they.
12 Καὶ εἶδον ὅτε ἤνοιξε τὴν σφραγῖδα τὴν ἕκτην, καὶ ἰδού,
And I saw when He opened the seal sixth, and behold,
σεισμὸς μέγας ἐγένετο, καὶ ὁ ἥλιος ἐγένετο μέλας ὡς σάκκος
an earthquake great occurred, and the sun became black as sackcloth
13 τρίχινος, καὶ ἡ σελήνη ἐγένετο ὡς αἷμα, καὶ οἱ ἀστέρες τοῦ
made of hair, and the moon became as blood, and the stars of the
οὐρανοῦ ἔπεσαν εἰς τὴν γῆν, ὡς συκῆ βάλλει τοὺς ὀλύνθους
heaven fell to the earth, as a fig-tree casts the unripe figs
14 αὐτῆς, ὑπὸ μεγάλου ἀνέμου σειομένη. καὶ οὐρανὸς ἀπεχω-
of it, by a great wind being shaken. And (the) heaven departed
ρίσθη ὡς βιβλίον εἱλισσόμενον, καὶ πᾶν ὄρος καὶ νῆσος ἐκ
as a scroll being rolled up, and every mountain and island out
15 τῶν τόπων αὐτῶν ἐκινήθησαν. καὶ οἱ βασιλεῖς τῆς γῆς, καὶ
of the places of them were moved. And the kings of the earth, and
οἱ μεγιστᾶνες, καὶ οἱ πλούσιοι, καὶ οἱ χιλίαρχοι, καὶ οἱ
the great ones, and the rich, and the chiliarchs, and the
δυνατοί, καὶ πᾶς δοῦλος καὶ πᾶς ἐλεύθερος, ἔκρυψαν ἑαυτοὺς
powerful, and every slave, and every freeman, hid themselves
16 εἰς τὰ σπήλαια καὶ εἰς τὰς πέτρας τῶν ὀρέων, καὶ λέγουσι
in the caves and in the rocks of the mountains; and they say
τοῖς ὄρεσι καὶ ταῖς πέτραις, Πέσετε ἐφ' ἡμᾶς, καὶ κρύψατε
to the mountains and to the rocks, Fall on us and hide
ἡμᾶς ἀπὸ προσώπου τοῦ καθημένου ἐπὶ τοῦ θρόνου, καὶ
us from (the) face of Him sitting on the throne, and
17 ἀπὸ τῆς ὀργῆς τοῦ ἀρνίου· ὅτι ἦλθεν ἡ ἡμέρα ἡ μεγάλη
from the wrath of the Lamb, because came the day great
τῆς ὀργῆς αὐτοῦ, καὶ τίς δύναται σταθῆναι;
of the wrath of Him, and who is able to stand?

CHAPTER 7

1 And after these things I saw four angels standing on the four corners of the earth, holding the four winds of the earth, that wind should not blow on the earth, nor on the sea, nor on every tree. 2 And I saw another angel

1 Καὶ μετὰ ταῦτα εἶδον τέσσαρας ἀγγέλους ἑστῶτας ἐπὶ τὰς
And after these things I saw four angels standing on the
τέσσαρας γωνίας τῆς γῆς, κρατοῦντας τοὺς τέσσαρας
four corners of the earth,, holding the four
ἀνέμους τῆς γῆς, ἵνα μὴ πνέῃ ἄνεμος ἐπὶ τῆς γῆς, μήτε ἐπὶ
winds of the earth, that not should blow wind on the earth, nor on
2 τῆς θαλάσσης, μήτε ἐπὶ πᾶν δένδρον. καὶ εἶδον ἄλλον
the sea, nor on every tree. And I saw another

coming up from *the* rising of the sun, having a seal of *the* living God. And he cried with a great voice to the four angels to whom it was given to them to harm the earth and the sea, saying, 3 Do not harm the earth, nor the sea, nor the trees, until we seal the slaves of our God on their foreheads. 4 And I heard the number of those having been sealed: one hundred forty-four thousands, having

5 Out of *the* tribe of Judah, twelve thousand having been sealed. Out of *the* tribe of Reuben, twelve thousand having been sealed. Out of *the* tribe of Gad, twelve thousand having been sealed.

6 Out of *the* tribe of Asher, twelve thousand having been sealed. Out of *the* tribe of Naphtali, twelve thousand having been sealed. Out of *the* tribe of Manasseh, twelve thousand having been sealed.

7 Out of *the* tribe of Simeon, twelve thousand having been sealed. Out of *the* tribe of Levi, twelve thousand having been sealed. Out of *the* tribe of Issachar, twelve thousand having been sealed.

8 Out of *the* tribe of Zebulun, twelve thousand having been sealed. Out of *the* tribe of Joseph, twelve thousand having been sealed. Out of *the* tribe of Benjamin, twelve thousand having been sealed.

9 After these things I saw, and behold, a great crowd which no one was able to number them, out of every nation, even tribes and peoples and tongues standing in front of the throne, and before the Lamb, having been clothed *with* white robes, and palms *were* in their hands. 10 And they cry with a loud voice, saying, Salvation to our God sitting on the throne, and to the Lamb.

11 And all the angels stood around the throne, and the elders, and the four living

ἄγγελον ἀναβαίνοντα ἀπὸ ἀνατολῆς ἡλίου, ἔχοντα σφρα-
angel coming up from (the) rising of (the) sun, having a seal
γῖδα Θεοῦ ζῶντος· καὶ ἔκραξε φωνῇ μεγάλῃ τοῖς τέσσαρσι
of God (the) living, and he cried with a voice great to the four
ἀγγέλοις, οἷς ἐδόθη αὐτοῖς ἀδικῆσαι τὴν γῆν καὶ τὴν
angels to whom it was given to them to harm the earth and the
3 θάλασσαν, λέγων, Μὴ ἀδικήσητε τὴν γῆν, μήτε τὴν θάλασ-
sea, saying, Not do harm the earth, nor the sea
σαν, μήτε τὰ δένδρα, ἄχρις οὗ σφραγίσωμεν τοὺς δούλους
nor the trees, until we may seal the slaves
4 τοῦ Θεοῦ ἡμῶν ἐπὶ τῶν μετώπων αὐτῶν. καὶ ἤκουσα τὸν
of the God of us on the foreheads of them. And I heard the
ἀριθμὸν τῶν ἐσφραγισμένων, ρμδ΄ χιλιάδες, ἐσφραγισμένοι
number of those having been sealed, 144 thousands, having been sealed
ἐκ πάσης φυλῆς υἱῶν Ἰσραήλ.
out of every tribe of (the) sons of Israel:
5 Ἐκ φυλῆς Ἰούδα, ιβ΄ χιλιάδες ἐσφραγισμένοι·
Of (the) tribe of Judah, twelve thousands having been sealed.
Ἐκ φυλῆς Ῥουβήν, ιβ΄ χιλιάδες ἐσφραγισμένοι·
Of (the) tribe of Reuben, twelve thousands having been sealed.
Ἐκ φυλῆς Γάδ, ιβ΄ χιλιάδες ἐσφραγισμένοι·
Of (the) tribe of Gad, twelve thousands having been sealed.
6 Ἐκ φυλῆς Ἀσήρ, ιβ΄ χιλιάδες ἐσφραγισμένοι·
Of (the) tribe of Asher, twelve thousands having been sealed.
Ἐκ φυλῆς Νεφθαλείμ, ιβ΄ χιλιάδες ἐσφραγισμένοι·
Of (the) tribe of Napthali, twelve thousands having been sealed.
Ἐκ φυλῆς Μανασσῆ, ιβ΄ χιλιάδες ἐσφραγισμένοι·
Of (the) tribe of Manasseh, twelve thousands having been sealed.
7 Ἐκ φυλῆς Συμεών, ιβ΄ χιλιάδες ἐσφραγισμένοι·
Of (the) tribe of Simeon, twelve thousands having been sealed.
Ἐκ φυλῆς Λευΐ, ιβ΄ χιλιάδες ἐσφραγισμένοι·
Of (the) tribe of Levi, twelve thousands having been sealed.
Ἐκ φυλῆς Ἰσαχάρ, ιβ΄ χιλιάδες ἐσφραγισμένοι·
Of (the) tribe of Issachar, twelve thousands having been sealed.
8 Ἐκ φυλῆς Ζαβουλών, ιβ΄ χιλιάδες ἐσφραγισμένοι·
Of (the) tribe of Zebulun, twelve thousands having been sealed.
Ἐκ φυλῆς Ἰωσήφ, ιβ΄ χιλιάδες ἐσφραγισμένοι·
Of (the) tribe of Joseph, twelve thousands having been sealed.
Ἐκ φυλῆς Βενιαμίν, ιβ΄ χιλιάδες ἐσφραγισμένοι.
Of (the) tribe of Benjamin, twelve thousands having been sealed.
9 Μετὰ ταῦτα εἶδον, καὶ ἰδού, ὄχλος πολύς, ὃν ἀριθμῆσαι
After these things I saw, and behold, a crowd much, which to number
αὐτὸν οὐδεὶς ἠδύνατο, ἐκ παντὸς ἔθνους καὶ φυλῶν καὶ
them no one was able, out of every nation, even tribes and
λαῶν καὶ γλωσσῶν, ἑστῶτες ἐνώπιον τοῦ θρόνου καὶ
peoples and tongues, standing before the throne and
ἐνώπιον τοῦ ἀρνίου, περιβεβλημένοι στολὰς λευκάς, καὶ
before the Lamb, having been clothed (with) robes white, and
10 φοίνικες ἐν ταῖς χερσὶν αὐτῶν· καὶ κράζοντες φωνῇ μεγάλῃ,
palms in the hands of them. And they cry with a voice great,
λέγοντες, Ἡ σωτηρία τῷ Θεῷ ἡμῶν τῷ καθημένῳ ἐπὶ τοῦ
saying, Salvation to the God of us sitting on the
11 θρόνου, καὶ τῷ ἀρνίῳ. καὶ πάντες οἱ ἄγγελοι ἑστήκεσαν
throne, and to the Lamb. And all the angels stood
κύκλῳ τοῦ θρόνου καὶ τῶν πρεσβυτέρων καὶ τῶν τεσ-
around the throne, and of the elders, and of the four

creatures. And *they* fell before the throne on their faces, and worshiped God, [12] saying, Amen. Blessing and glory and wisdom and thanksgiving and honor and power and strength to our God forever and ever. Amen.

[13] And one of the elders answered, saying to me, These, the ones having been clothed *in* the white robes, who are they, and from where did they come? [14] And I said to him, Sir, you know. And he said to me, These are those coming out of the great tribulation; and *they* washed their robes and whitened them in the blood of the Lamb. [15] Because of this they are before the throne of God, and serve Him day and night in His temple. And He sitting on the throne will spread *His skirt* over them. [16] And they will not hunger still, nor will they thirst still, nor at all shall fall on them the sun, nor any *kind of* heat. [17] Because the Lamb in the midst of the throne will shepherd them, and will lead them on *the* fountains of living waters; and God will wipe off every tear from their eyes.

σάρων ζώων, καὶ ἔπεσον ἐνώπιον τοῦ θρόνου ἐπὶ πρόσ-
living creatures, and they fell before the throne on (the)
12 ωπον αὐτῶν, καὶ προσεκύνησαν τῷ Θεῷ, λέγοντες, Ἀμήν·
face of them, and worshiped God, saying, Amen,
ἡ εὐλογία καὶ ἡ δόξα καὶ ἡ σοφία καὶ ἡ εὐχαριστία καὶ ἡ
blessing and glory and wisdom and thanksgiving and
τιμὴ καὶ ἡ δύναμις καὶ ἡ ἰσχὺς τῷ Θεῷ ἡμῶν εἰς τοὺς αἰῶνας
honor and power and strength to the God of us to the ages
τῶν αἰώνων. ἀμήν.
of the ages. Amen.

13 Καὶ ἀπεκρίθη εἷς ἐκ τῶν πρεσβυτέρων, λέγων μοι, Οὗτοι
And answered one of the elders, saying to me, These,
οἱ περιβεβλημένοι τὰς στολὰς τὰς λευκάς, τίνες εἰσί, καὶ πόθεν
those having been clothed (in) robes the white, **who are they, and from where**
14 ἦλθον; καὶ εἴρηκα αὐτῷ, Κύριε, σὺ οἶδας. καὶ εἶπέ μοι, Οὗτοί
came they? And I said to him, Sir, you know. And he told me, These
εἰσιν οἱ ἐρχόμενοι ἐκ τῆς θλίψεως τῆς μεγάλης, καὶ ἔπλυναν
are those coming out of the affliction great, and they washed
τὰς στολὰς αὐτῶν, καὶ ἐλεύκαναν αὐτὰς ἐν τῷ αἵματι τοῦ
the robes of them, and whitened them in the blood of the
15 ἀρνίου. διὰ τοῦτό εἰσιν ἐνώπιον τοῦ θρόνου τοῦ Θεοῦ,
Lamb. Therefore are they before the throne of God,
καὶ λατρεύουσιν αὐτῷ ἡμέρας καὶ νυκτὸς ἐν τῷ ναῷ αὐτοῦ·
and serve Him day and night in the temple of Him,
16 καὶ ὁ καθήμενος ἐπὶ τοῦ θρόνου σκηνώσει ἐπ' αὐτούς. οὐ
and the (One) sitting on the throne tabernacled over them. not
πεινάσουσιν ἔτι, οὐδὲ διψήσουσιν ἔτι, οὐδὲ μὴ πέσῃ ἐπ'
they will hunger longer, nor will they thirst longer, nor not shall fall on
17 αὐτοὺς ὁ ἥλιος, οὐδὲ πᾶν καῦμα· ὅτι τὸ ἀρνίον τὸ ἀνὰ
them the sun, nor every (kind of) heat, because the Lamb in the
μέσον τοῦ θρόνου ποιμανεῖ αὐτούς, καὶ ὁδηγήσει αὐτοὺς ἐπὶ
midst of the throne will shepherd them, and will lead them upon
ζώσας πηγὰς ὑδάτων, καὶ ἐξαλείψει ὁ Θεὸς πᾶν δάκρυον
living fountains of waters and will wipe off God every tear
ἀπὸ τῶν ὀφθαλμῶν αὐτῶν.
from the eyes of them.

CHAPTER 8

[1] And when He opened the seventh seal, a silence occurred in Heaven, about a half-hour. [2] And I saw the seven angels who stood before God, and seven trumpets were given to them. [3] And another angel came and stood on the altar, having a golden censer. And many incenses were given to him, that he give *them* with the prayers of all the saints on the golden altar before the throne.

[4] And the smoke of the incenses went up with the prayers of the saints out of

1 Καὶ ὅτε ἤνοιξε τὴν σφραγῖδα τὴν ἑβδόμην, ἐγένετο σιγὴ
And when He opened the seal seventh, occurred a silence
2 ἐν τῷ οὐρανῷ ὡς ἡμιώριον. καὶ εἶδον τοὺς ἑπτὰ ἀγγέλους οἳ
in Heaven about a half-hour. And I saw the seven angels who
ἐνώπιον τοῦ Θεοῦ ἑστήκασι, καὶ ἐδόθησαν αὐτοῖς ἑπτὰ
before God stood, and were given to them seven
σάλπιγγες.
trumpets.

3 Καὶ ἄλλος ἄγγελος ἦλθε, καὶ ἐστάθη ἐπὶ τὸ θυσιαστήριον,
And another angel came and stood on the altar
ἔχων λιβανωτὸν χρυσοῦν· καὶ ἐδόθη αὐτῷ θυμιάματα πολλά,
having a censer of gold, and was given to him incenses many,
ἵνα δώσῃ ταῖς προσευχαῖς τῶν ἁγίων πάντων ἐπὶ τὸ θυσια-
that he give with the prayers of the saints all on the altar
4 στήριον τὸ χρυσοῦν τὸ ἐνώπιον τοῦ θρόνου. καὶ ἀνέβη ὁ
of gold before the throne. And went up the
καπνὸς τῶν θυμιαμάτων ταῖς προσευχαῖς τῶν ἁγίων ἐκ
smoke of the incenses with the prayers of the saints out of

the hand of the angel before God. [5]And the angel has taken the censer, and has filled it from the fire of the altar, and cast *it* into the earth; and sounds and thunders and lightnings and earthquakes occurred.

[6]And the seven angels having the seven trumpets prepared themselves, that they might trumpet. [7]And the first angel trumpeted. And hail and fire mixed with blood occurred. And it was cast onto the earth; and the third *part* of the trees was burned; and all green grass was burned down.

[8]And the second angel trumpeted. And a great mountain burning with fire was thrown into the sea. And the third *part* of the sea became blood; [9]and the third *part* of the creatures having souls died in the sea; and the third *part* of the ships was destroyed.

[10]And the third angel trumpeted. And a great burning star, like a lamp, fell out of the heaven. And it fell onto the third *part* of the rivers, and onto the fountain of waters. [11]And the name of the star is said *to be* Wormwood. And the third *part* of the waters became *changed* into wormwood. And many men died from the waters, because they were bitter.

[12]And the fourth angel trumpeted. And the third *part* of the sun, and the third *part* of the moon, and the third of the stars, was struck, that the third *part* of them might be darkened, and the third of the day might not appear, and the night likewise.

[13]And I saw, and I heard one angel flying in mid-heaven, saying with a great voice, Woe! Woe to those dwelling on the earth, from the rest of *the* voices of the trumpet of the three angels being about to trumpet.

5 χειρὸς τοῦ ἀγγέλου ἐνώπιον τοῦ Θεοῦ. καὶ εἴληφεν ὁ
(the) hand of the angel before God. And has taken the
ἄγγελος τὸ λιβανωτόν, καὶ ἐγέμισεν αὐτὸ ἐκ τοῦ πυρὸς τοῦ
angel the censer, and filled it from the fire of the
θυσιαστηρίου, καὶ ἔβαλεν εἰς τὴν γῆν· καὶ ἐγένοντο φωναὶ καὶ
altar, and cast it into the earth, and occurred sounds and
βρονταὶ καὶ ἀστραπαὶ καὶ σεισμός.
thunders and lightnings and an earthquake.

6 Καὶ οἱ ἑπτὰ ἄγγελοι οἱ ἔχοντες τὰς ἑπτὰ σάλπιγγας
And the seven angels having the seven trumpets
ἡτοίμασαν ἑαυτοὺς ἵνα σαλπίσωσι.
prepared themselves that they might trumpet.

7 Καὶ ὁ πρῶτος ἄγγελος ἐσάλπισε, καὶ ἐγένετο χάλαζα καὶ
And the first angel trumpeted, and occurred hail and
πῦρ μεμιγμένα αἵματι, καὶ ἐβλήθη εἰς τὴν γῆν· καὶ τὸ τρίτον
fire being mixed with blood, and it was cast to the earth, and the third (part)
τῶν δένδρων κατεκάη, καὶ πᾶς χόρτος χλωρὸς κατεκάη.
of the trees was burned down and all grass green was burned down

8 Καὶ ὁ δεύτερος ἄγγελος ἐσάλπισε, καὶ ὡς ὄρος μέγα πυρὶ
And the second angel trumpeted, and as a mountain great with fire
καιόμενον ἐβλήθη εἰς τὴν θάλασσαν· καὶ ἐγένετο τὸ τρίτον
burning it was cast into the sea; and became the third (part)
9 τῆς θαλάσσης αιμα· καὶ ἀπέθανε τὸ τρίτον τῶν κτισμάτων
of the sea blood, and died the third (part) of the creatures
τῶν ἐν τῇ θαλάσσῃ, τὰ ἔχοντα ψυχάς, καὶ τὸ τρίτον τῶν
in the sea those having souls; and the third (part) of the
πλοίων διεφθάρη
ships was destroyed.

10 Καὶ ὁ τρίτος ἄγγελος ἐσάλπισε, καὶ ἔπεσεν ἐκ τοῦ οὐρανοῦ
And the third angel trumpeted, and fell out of the heaven
ἀστὴρ μέγας καιόμενος ὡς λαμπάς, καὶ ἔπεσεν ἐπὶ τὸ τρίτον
a star great burning as a lamp, and it fell onto the third (part
11 τῶν ποταμῶν, καὶ ἐπὶ τὰς πηγὰς ὑδάτων. καὶ τὸ ὄνομα τοῦ
of the rivers, and onto the fountains of waters. And the name of the
ἀστέρος λέγεται Ἄψινθος· καὶ γίνεται τὸ τρίτον τῶν ὑδάτων
star is said (to be) Wormwood. And became the third (part) of the waters
εἰς ἄψινθον, καὶ πολλοι ἀνθρώπων ἀπέθανον ἐκ τῶν ὑδάτων,
into wormwood, and many of men died from the waters,
ὅτι ἐπικράνθησαν.
because they were bitter.

12 Καὶ ὁ τέταρτος ἄγγελος ἐσάλπισε, καὶ ἐπλήγη τὸ τρίτον
And the fourth angel trumpeted, and was struck the third (part)
τοῦ ἡλίου καὶ τὸ τρίτον τῆς σελήνης καὶ τὸ τρίτον τῶν
of the sun and the third (part) of the moon and the third (part) of the
ἀστέρων, ἵνα σκοτισθῇ το τρίτον αὐτῶν, καὶ ἡ ἡμέρα μὴ
stars, that might be darkened the third of them, and the day not
φαίνῃ τὸ τρίτον αὐτῆς, καὶ ἡ νὺξ ὁμοίως.
might appear the third of it, and the night likewise.

13 Καὶ εἶδον, καὶ ἤκουσα ἑνὸς ἀγγέλου πετωμένου ἐν μεσου-
And I saw, and I heard one angel flying in mid-
ρανήματι, λέγοντος φωνῇ μεγάλῃ, Οὐαί, οὐαί, οὐαί τοῖς
heaven, saying, with a voice great, Woe! Woe! Woe to those
κατοικοῦσιν ἐπὶ τῆς γῆς, ἐκ τῶν λοιπῶν φωνῶν τῆς σάλ-
dwelling on the earth, from the rest of (the) voices of the
πιγγος τῶν τριῶν ἀγγέλων τῶν μελλόντων σαλπίζειν.
trumpet of the three angels being about to trumpet.

CHAPTER 9

[1]And the fifth angel trumpeted. And I saw a star out of the heaven falling onto the earth. And the key of the abyss was given to it. [2]And he opened the pit of the abyss. And smoke went up out of the pit, like smoke of a great furnace. And the sun was darkened, and the air, by the smoke of the pit. [3]And out of the smoke locusts came forth to the earth. And authority was given to them, as the scorpions of the earth have authority. [4]And it was said to them that they should not harm the grass of the earth, nor every green thing, nor every tree, except only the men who do not have the seal of God on their foreheads. [5]And it was given to them that they should not kill them, but that they be tormented five months. And their torment *is* as *the* torment of a scorpion when it stings a man. [6]And in those days men will seek death, and they will not find it. And they will long to die, yet death will flee from them.

[7]And the likenesses of the locusts *were* like horses having been prepared for war; and crowns like gold on their heads; and their faces like the faces of men. [8]And they had hairs like *the* hairs of women; and their teeth were like *those* of lions. [9]And they had breastplates like iron breastplates; and the sound of their wings *was* like chariots of many horses sound, running to war. [10]And they have tails like scorpions, and their stings were in their tails; and they *have* authority to harm men five months. [11]And they have a king over them, the angel of the abyss. In Hebrew his name *was*

CHAPTER 9

1 Καὶ ὁ πέμπτος ἄγγελος ἐσάλπισε, καὶ εἶδον ἀστέρα ἐκ τοῦ
And the fifth angel trumpeted, and I saw a star out of
οὐρανοῦ πεπτωκότα εἰς τὴν γῆν, καὶ ἐδόθη αὐτῷ ἡ κλεὶς
heaven having fallen onto the earth. And was given to it the key
2 τοῦ φρέατος τῆς ἀβύσσου. καὶ ἤνοιξε τὸ φρέαρ τῆς ἀβύσσου,
to the pit of the abyss. and he opened the pit of the abyss;
και ἀνέβη καπνὸς ἐκ τοῦ φρέατος ὡς καπνὸς καμίνου
and went up a smoke out of the pit as smoke of a furnace
μεγάλης, καὶ ἐσκοτίσθη ὁ ἥλιος καὶ ὁ ἀὴρ ἐκ τοῦ καπνοῦ
great And was darkened the sun and the air from the smoke
3 τοῦ φρέατος. καὶ ἐκ τοῦ καπνοῦ ἐξῆλθον ἀκρίδες εἰς τὴν γῆν,
of the pit. And out of the smoke came forth locusts to the earth,
καὶ ἐδόθη αὐταῖς ἐξουσία, ὡς ἔχουσιν ἐξουσίαν οἱ σκορπίοι
and was given to them authority as have authority the scorpions
4 τῆς γῆς. καὶ ἐρρέθη αὐταῖς ἵνα μὴ ἀδικήσωσι τὸν χόρτον
of the earth. And it was said to them that not they should harm the grass
τῆς γῆς, οὐδὲ πᾶν χλωρόν, οὐδὲ πᾶν δένδρον, εἰ μὴ τοὺς
of the earth, nor every green thing, nor every tree, except the
ἀνθρώπους μόνους οἵτινες οὐκ ἔχουσι τὴν σφραγῖδα τοῦ
men only who not have the seal
5 Θεοῦ ἐπὶ τῶν μετώπων αὐτῶν. καὶ ἐδόθη αὐταῖς ἵνα μὴ
of God on the foreheads of them. And it was given to them that not
ἀποκτείνωσιν αὐτούς, ἀλλ' ἵνα βασανισθῶσι μῆνας πέντε·
they should kill them, but that they be tormented months five;
καὶ ὁ βασανισμὸς αὐτῶν ὡς βασανισμὸς σκορπίου, ὅταν
and the torment of them (is) as (the) torment of a scorpion when
6 παίσῃ ἄνθρωπον. καὶ ἐν ταῖς ἡμέραις ἐκείναις ζητήσουσιν
it stings a man. And in days those will seek
οἱ ἄνθρωποι τὸν θάνατον, καὶ οὐχ εὑρήσουσιν αὐτόν·
men death, and not they will find it,
καὶ ἐπιθυμήσουσιν ἀποθανεῖν, καὶ φεύξεται ὁ θάνατος ἀπ'
and they will long to die, and will flee death from
7 αὐτῶν. καὶ τὰ ὁμοιώματα τῶν ἀκρίδων ὅμοια ἵπποις ἡτοι-
them. And the likenesses of the locusts like horses having
μασμένοις εἰς πόλεμον, καὶ ἐπὶ τὰς κεφαλὰς αὐτῶν ὡς
been prepared for war, and on the heads of them as
στέφανοι ὅμοιοι χρυσῷ, καὶ τὰ πρόσωπα αὐτῶν ὡς
crowns like gold; and the faces of them as
8 πρόσωπα ἀνθρώπων. καὶ εἶχον τρίχας ὡς τρίχας γυναικῶν,
the faces of men; and they had hairs as hairs of women;
9 καὶ οἱ ὀδόντες αὐτῶν ὡς λεόντων ἦσαν. καὶ εἶχον θώρακας
and the teeth of them as of lions were; and they had breastplates
ὡς θώρακας σιδηροῦς, καὶ ἡ φωνὴ τῶν πτερύγων αὐτῶν
as breastplates iron; and the sound of the wings of them
ὡς φωνὴ ἁρμάτων ἵππων πολλῶν τρεχόντων εἰς πόλεμον.
as sound chariots of horses many running to war.
10 καὶ ἔχουσιν οὐρὰς ὁμοίας σκορπίοις, καὶ κέντρα ἦν ἐν ταῖς
And they have tails like scorpions, and stings were in the
οὐραῖς αὐτῶν· καὶ ἡ ἐξουσία αὐτῶν ἀδικῆσαι τοὺς ἀνθρώ-
tails of them and the authority of them (is) to harm men
11 πους μῆνας πέντε. καὶ ἔχουσιν ἐπ' αὐτῶν βασιλέα τὸν
months five. And they have over them a king, the
ἄγγελον τῆς ἀβύσσου· ὄνομα αὐτῷ Ἑβραϊστὶ Ἀβαδδών,
angel of the abyss, name to him in Hebrew, Abaddon,

Abaddon, and in Greek he
has *the* name Apollyon.
12 The first woe has
departed; behold, after these
things yet comes two woes.
13 And the sixth angel
trumpeted. And I heard one
voice out of the four horns of
the golden altar before God,
14 saying to the sixth angel
who had the trumpet,
Release the four angels,
those having been bound at
the great river Euphrates.
15 And the four
angels were released, those
having been prepared for the
hour and day and month and
year, that they should kill the
third *part* of men.
16 And the number of the
armies of the cavalry *was* two
myriads of myriads; and I
heard their number. 17 And
so I saw in the vision the
horses, and those sitting on
them, having fire-colored
breastplates, even dusky red
and brimstone-like; and the
heads of the horses as heads
of lions; and out of their
mouths comes fire and
smoke and brimstone. 18 By
these three were killed the
third *part* of men, by the fire,
and by the smoke, and by the
brimstone coming out of
their mouths. 19 For their
authority is in their mouth,
and in their tails; for their tails
are like snakes, having
heads, and they do harm with
them.

20 And the rest of men,
those not killed by these
plagues, did not repent of the
works of their hands, that
they will not worship
demons, and golden idols,
and silver, and bronze, and
wooden *idols*, which neither
are able to see, nor hear, nor
walk. 21 And they did not
repent of their murders, nor
of their sorceries, nor of their
fornications, nor of their
thefts.

12 καὶ ἐν τῇ Ἑλληνικῇ ὄνομα ἔχει Ἀπολλύων. ἡ οὐαὶ ἡ μία
and in the Greek (the) name he has (is) Apollyon. The woe one
ἀπῆλθεν· ἰδού, ἔρχονται ἔτι δύο οὐαὶ μετὰ ταῦτα.
has departed; behold, comes yet two woes after these things.
13 Καὶ ὁ ἕκτος ἄγγελος ἐσάλπισε, καὶ ἤκουσα φωνὴν μίαν ἐκ
And the sixth angel trumpeted. And I heard a voice one out o
τῶν τεσσάρων κεράτων τοῦ θυσιαστηρίου τοῦ χρυσοῦ
the four horns of the altar of gold
14 τοῦ ἐνώπιον τοῦ Θεοῦ, λέγουσαν τῷ ἕκτῳ ἀγγέλῳ ὃς εἶχε
before God, saying to the sixth angel who had
τὴν σάλπιγγα, Λῦσον τοὺς τέσσαρας ἀγγέλους τοὺς δεδε-
the trumpet, Loose the four angels, those having
15 μένους ἐπὶ τῷ ποταμῷ τῷ μεγάλῳ Εὐφράτῃ. καὶ ἐλύθησαν
been bound at the river great Euphrates. And were loosed
οἱ τέσσαρες ἄγγελοι οἱ ἡτοιμασμένοι εἰς τὴν ὥραν καὶ
the four angels, those having been prepared for the hour and
ἡμέραν καὶ μῆνα καὶ ἐνιαυτόν, ἵνα ἀποκτείνωσι τὸ τρίτον
day and month and year, that they should kill the third (part)
16 τῶν ἀνθρώπων. καὶ ὁ ἀριθμὸς στρατευμάτων τοῦ ἱππικοῦ
of men. And the number of the armies of the cavalry
17 δύο μυριάδες μυριάδων· καὶ ἤκουσα τὸν ἀριθμὸν αὐτῶν. καὶ
two myriads of myriads; and I heard the number of them. And
οὕτως εἶδον τοὺς ἵππους ἐν τῇ ὁράσει, καὶ τοὺς καθημένους
thus I saw the horses in the vision, and those sitting
ἐπ' αὐτῶν, ἔχοντας θώρακας πυρίνους καὶ ὑακινθίνους
on them, having breastplates fire-colored and dusky red
καὶ θειώδεις· καὶ αἱ κεφαλαὶ τῶν ἵππων ὡς κεφαλαὶ λεόντων,
and brimstone-like; and the heads of the horses as heads of lions;
καὶ ἐκ τῶν στομάτων αὐτῶν ἐκπορεύεται πῦρ καὶ καπνὸς
and out of the mouths of them proceeds fire and smoke
18 καὶ θεῖον. ὑπὸ τῶν τριῶν τούτων ἀπεκτάνθησαν τὸ τρίτον
and brimstone. By three these were killed the third (part)
τῶν ἀνθρώπων, ἐκ τοῦ πυρὸς καὶ ἐκ τοῦ καπνοῦ καὶ ἐκ τοῦ
of men, from the fire and from smoke and from the
19 θείου τοῦ ἐκπορευομένου ἐκ τῶν στομάτων αὐτῶν. ἡ γὰρ
brimstone coming out from the mouths of them. the For
ἐξουσία αὐτῶν ἐν τῷ στόματι αὐτῶν ἐστί, καὶ ἐν ταῖς οὐραῖς
authority of them in the mouth of them is, and in the tails
αὐτῶν· αἱ γὰρ οὐραὶ αὐτῶν ὅμοιαι ὄφεσιν, ἔχουσαι κεφαλάς,
of them; the for tails of them (are) like snakes, having heads
20 καὶ ἐν αὐταῖς ἀδικοῦσι. καὶ οἱ λοιποὶ τῶν ἀνθρώπων, οἳ οὐκ
and with them they do harm. And the rest of men, who not
ἀπεκτάνθησαν ἐν ταῖς πληγαῖς ταύταις, οὐ μετενόησαν ἐκ
were killed by plagues these, not repented of
τῶν ἔργων τῶν χειρῶν αὐτῶν, ἵνα μὴ προσκυνήσωσι τὰ
the works of the hands of them, that not they will worship
δαιμόνια, καὶ εἴδωλα τὰ χρυσᾶ καὶ τὰ ἀργυρᾶ καὶ τὰ
demons and idols gold and silver and
χαλκᾶ καὶ τὰ λίθινα καὶ τὰ ξύλινα, ἃ οὔτε βλέπειν δύναται,
bronze and stone and wood which neither to see are able,
21 οὔτε ἀκούειν, οὔτε περιπατεῖν· καὶ οὐ μετενόησαν ἐκ τῶν
nor to hear, nor to walk; and not they repented of the
φόνων αὐτῶν, οὔτε ἐκ τῶν φαρμακειῶν αὐτῶν, οὔτε ἐκ τῆς
murders of them, nor of the sorceries of them, nor of the
πορνείας αὐτῶν, οὔτε ἐκ τῶν κλεμμάτων αὐτῶν.
fornications of them nor of the thefts of them.

CHAPTER 10

1 And I saw another strong angel coming down out of Heaven, having been clothed *with* a cloud, and a rainbow on the head; and his face as the sun, and his feet as pillars of fire. 2 And he had in his hand a little book having been opened. And he placed his right foot on the sea, the left on the land, 3 and cried with a great voice, as a lion roars. And when he cried, the seven thunders spoke their sounds. 4 And when the seven thunders spoke their sounds, I was about to write. And I heard a voice out of Heaven saying to me, Seal what things the seven thunders spoke, and do not write these things. 5 And the angel whom I saw standing on the sea and on the land lifted his hand to Heaven, 6 and swore by Him living forever and ever, who created the heaven and the things in it, and the earth and the things in it, and the sea and the things in it, that time shall no longer be; 7 but in the days of the voice of the seventh angel, whenever he is about to trumpet, was even ended the mystery of God, as He announced to His slaves, the prophets.

8 And the voice which I heard out of Heaven *was* again speaking to me, and saying, Go, take the little book having been opened in the hand of the angel standing on the sea and on the land. 9 And I went away toward the angel, saying to him, Give the little book to me. And he said to me, Take and eat it up, and it will be sweet as honey. 10 And I took the little book out of the angel's hand, and ate it up. And it was sweet like honey

CHAPTER 10

1 Καὶ εἶδον ἄλλον ἄγγελον ἰσχυρὸν καταβαίνοντα ἐκ τοῦ
And I saw another angel strong coming down out of

οὐρανοῦ, περιβεβλημένον νεφέλην, καὶ ἶρις ἐπὶ τῆς κεφαλῆς,
Heaven, having been clothed (with) a cloud, and a rainbow on the head.

καὶ τὸ πρόσωπον αὐτοῦ ὡς ὁ ἥλιος, καὶ οἱ πόδες αὐτοῦ ὡς
and the face of him as the sun, and the feet of him as

2 στῦλοι πυρός· καὶ εἶχεν ἐν τῇ χειρὶ αὐτοῦ βιβλαρίδιον
pillars of fire, and he had in the hand of him a little scroll

ἀνεῳγμένον· καὶ ἔθηκε τὸν πόδα αὐτοῦ τὸν δεξιὸν ἐπὶ τὴν
having been opened. And he placed the foot of him the right on the

3 θάλασσαν, τὸν δὲ εὐώνυμον ἐπὶ τὴν γῆν, καὶ ἔκραξε φωνῇ
sea, the and left on the land, and cried with a voice

μεγάλῃ ὥσπερ λέων μυκᾶται· καὶ ὅτε ἔκραξεν, ἐλάλησαν αἱ
great as a lion roars. And when he cried, spoke the

4 ἑπτὰ βρονταὶ τὰς ἑαυτῶν φωνάς. καὶ ὅτε ἐλάλησαν αἱ ἑπτὰ
seven thunders the of themselves voices. And when spoke the seven

βρονταὶ τὰς φωνὰς ἑαυτῶν, ἔμελλον γράφειν· καὶ ἤκουσα
thunders the voices of themselves, I was about to write; and I heard

φωνὴν ἐκ τοῦ οὐρανοῦ, λέγουσάν μοι, Σφράγισον ἃ ἐλά-
a voice out of Heaven, saying to me, Seal what things

5 λησαν αἱ ἑπτὰ βρονταί, καὶ μὴ ταῦτα γράψῃς. καὶ ὁ
spoke the seven thunders, and not these things write. And the

ἄγγελος ὃν εἶδον ἑστῶτα ἐπὶ τῆς θαλάσσης καὶ ἐπὶ τῆς γῆς
angel whom I saw standing on the sea and on the land

6 ἦρε τὴν χεῖρα αὐτοῦ εἰς τὸν οὐρανόν, καὶ ὤμοσεν ἐν τῷ
lifted the hand of him to Heaven, and swore by Him

ζῶντι εἰς τοὺς αἰῶνας τῶν αἰώνων, ὃς ἔκτισε τὸν οὐρανὸν
living to the ages of the ages, who created the heaven

καὶ τὰ ἐν αὐτῷ, καὶ τὴν γῆν καὶ τὰ ἐν αὐτῇ, καὶ τὴν θάλασ-
and the things in it, and the earth and the things in it, and the sea

7 σαν καὶ τὰ ἐν αὐτῇ, ὅτι χρόνος οὐκ ἔσται ἔτι· ἀλλ' ἐν ταῖς
and the things in it, that time not shall be longer, but in the

ἡμέραις τῆς φωνῆς τοῦ ἑβδόμου ἀγγέλου, ὅταν μέλλῃ
days of the voice of the seventh angel, whenever he is about

σαλπίζειν, καὶ τελεσθῇ τὸ μυστήριον τοῦ Θεοῦ, ὡς εὐηγ-
to trumpet, even may be ended the mystery of God, as He

8 γέλισε τοῖς ἑαυτοῦ δούλοις τοῖς προφήταις. καὶ ἡ φωνὴ ἣν
preached to the of Himself slaves the prophets. And the voice which

ἤκουσα ἐκ τοῦ οὐρανοῦ, πάλιν λαλοῦσα μετ' ἐμοῦ, καὶ
I heard out of Heaven, again speaking with me, and

λέγουσα, Ὕπαγε, λάβε τὸ βιβλαρίδιον τὸ ἠνεῳγμένον ἐν
saying, Go, take the little scroll having been opened in

τῇ χειρὶ ἀγγέλου τοῦ ἑστῶτος ἐπὶ τῆς θαλάσσης καὶ ἐπὶ
the hand of the angel standing on the sea and on

9 τῆς γῆς. καὶ ἀπῆλθον πρὸς τὸν ἄγγελον, λέγων αὐτῷ, Δός
the land. And I went away toward the angel, saying to him, Give

μοι τὸ βιβλαρίδιον. καὶ λέγει μοι, Λάβε καὶ κατάφαγε αὐτό·
to me the little scroll. And he said to me, Take and eat up it,

καὶ πικρανεῖ σου τὴν κοιλίαν, ἀλλ' ἐν τῷ στόματί σου ἔσται
and it will embitter of you the belly, but in the mouth of you it will be

10 γλυκὺ ὡς μέλι. καὶ ἔλαβον τὸ βιβλαρίδιον ἐκ τῆς χειρὸς τοῦ
sweet as honey. And I took the little scroll out of the hand of the

ἀγγέλου, καὶ κατέφαγον αὐτό, καὶ ἦν ἐν τῷ στόματί μου
angel and devoured it, and it was in the mouth of me

in my mouth; and when I ate it, my belly was made bitter. [11] And he said to me, You must again prophesy before peoples and nations and tongues and many kings.

CHAPTER 11

[1] And a reed like a staff was given to me, and the angel stood, saying, Rise and measure the temple of God and the altar, and those worshiping in it. [2] And cast aside the outside court of the temple, and do not measure it. For it was given to the nations, and they will trample the holy city forty-two months. [3] And I will give to My two witnesses, and they will prophesy a thousand, two hundred and sixty days, dressed *in* sackcloth. [4] These are the two olive trees, and the two lampstands, standing before the God of the earth. [5] And if anyone desires to harm them, fire comes out of their mouth and devours their enemies. And if anyone desires to harm them, so it is right for him to be killed.

[6] These have the authority to shut up the heaven, that no rain may rain in the days of their prophecy. And they have authority over the waters, to turn them into blood, and to strike the earth *with* every plague, as often as they desire. [7] And when they complete their witness, the beast coming up out of the abyss will make war with them, and will overcome them, and will kill them. [8] And their bodies *will be* on the street of the great city, which spiritually is called Sodom, and Egypt—where our Lord was crucified. [9] And *some* from the peoples and tribes and tongues and nations will see their bodies three days and a half; and they do not allow their bodies

ὡς μέλι, γλυκύ· καὶ ὅτε ἔφαγον αὐτό, ἐπικράνθη ἡ κοιλία
as honey, sweet; and when I ate it, was made bitter the belly
11 μου. καὶ λέγει μοι, Δεῖ σε πάλιν προφητεῦσαι ἐπὶ λαοῖς καὶ
of me. And he says to me, must You again prophesy before peoples and
ἔθνεσι καὶ γλώσσαις καὶ βασιλεῦσι πολλοῖς.
nations and tongues and kings many.

CHAPTER 11

1 Καὶ ἐδόθη μοι κάλαμος ὅμοιος ῥάβδῳ, καὶ ὁ ἄγγελος
And was given to me a reed like a staff, and the angel
εἱστήκει, λέγων, Ἔγειραι, καὶ μέτρησον τὸν ναὸν τοῦ Θεοῦ,
stood, saying, Rise and measure the temple of God,
2 καὶ τὸ θυσιαστήριον, καὶ τοὺς προσκυνοῦντας ἐν αὐτῷ. καὶ
and the altar, and those worshiping in it. And
τὴν αὐλὴν τὴν ἔξωθεν τοῦ ναοῦ ἔκβαλε ἔξω, καὶ μὴ αὐτὴν
the court outside of the temple cast outside, and not it
μετρήσῃς, ὅτι ἐδόθη τοῖς ἔθνεσι· καὶ τὴν πόλιν τὴν ἁγίαν
do measure, for it was given to the nations, and the city holy
3 πατήσουσι μῆνας τεσσαράκοντα δύο. καὶ δώσω τοῖς δυσὶ
they will trample months forty-two. And I will give to the two
μάρτυσί μου, καὶ προφητεύσουσιν ἡμέρας χιλίας διακοσίας
witnesses of Me, and they will prophesy days a thousand, two hundred
4 ἑξήκοντα περιβεβλημένοι σάκκους. οὗτοί εἰσιν αἱ δύο ἐλαῖαι,
sixty, having been clothed (in) sackcloth. These are the two olive-trees,
καὶ αἱ δύο λυχνίαι αἱ ἐνώπιον τοῦ Θεοῦ τῆς γῆς ἑστῶσαι.
and the two lampstands before the God of the earth standing.
5 καὶ εἴ τις αὐτοὺς θέλῃ ἀδικῆσαι, πῦρ ἐκπορεύεται ἐκ τοῦ
And if anyone them desires to harm, fire proceeds out of the
στόματος αὐτῶν, καὶ κατεσθίει τοὺς ἐχθροὺς αὐτῶν· καὶ εἴ
mouth of them and devours the enemies of them; and if
τις αὐτοὺς θέλῃ ἀδικῆσαι, οὕτω δεῖ αὐτὸν ἀποκτανθῆναι.
anyone them desires to harm, thus it behoves him to be killed.
6 οὗτοι ἔχουσιν ἐξουσίαν κλεῖσαι τὸν οὐρανόν, ἵνα μὴ βρέχῃ
These have authority to shut the heaven, that not may rain
ὑετὸς ἐν ἡμέραις αὐτῶν τῆς προφητείας· καὶ ἐξουσίαν ἔχου-
rain in days of them of the prophecy, and authority they
σιν ἐπὶ τῶν ὑδάτων, στρέφειν αὐτὰ εἰς αἷμα, καὶ πατάξαι
have over the waters, to turn them into blood, and to strike
7 τὴν γῆν πάσῃ πληγῇ, ὁσάκις ἐὰν θελήσωσι. καὶ ὅταν
the earth (with) every plague, as often as if they desire. And whenever
τελέσωσι τὴν μαρτυρίαν αὐτῶν, τὸ θηρίον τὸ ἀναβαῖνον ἐκ
they finish the witness of them, the beast coming up out of
τῆς ἀβύσσου ποιήσει πόλεμον μετ᾽ αὐτῶν, καὶ νικήσει
the abyss will make war with them, and will overcome
8 αὐτούς, καὶ ἀποκτενεῖ αὐτούς. καὶ τὰ πτώματα αὐτῶν ἐπὶ
them, and will kill them. And the bodies of them on
τῆς πλατείας πόλεως τῆς μεγάλης, ἥτις καλεῖται πνευ-
the street of city the great, which is called spirit-
ματικῶς Σόδομα καὶ Αἴγυπτος, ὅπου καὶ ὁ Κύριος ἡμῶν
ually Sodom, and, Egypt, where indeed the Lord of us
9 ἐσταυρώθη. καὶ βλέψουσιν ἐκ τῶν λαῶν καὶ φυλῶν καὶ
was crucified. And will see (some) from the peoples and tribes and
γλωσσῶν καὶ ἐθνῶν τὰ πτώματα αὐτῶν ἡμέρας τρεῖς καὶ
tongues and nations the bodies of them days three and
ἥμισυ, καὶ τὰ πτώματα αὐτῶν οὐκ ἀφήσουσι τεθῆναι εἰς
a half; and the bodies of them not they allow to be placed in

to be put in a tomb. [10]And those living on the earth will rejoice over them, and will make merry. And they will send one another gifts, because these two prophets tormented those living on the earth.

[11]And after three days and a half, a spirit of life from God entered into them, and they stood on their feet. And great fear fell on the ones beholding them.

And they heard a great voice out of Heaven saying to them, Come up here. And they went up into Heaven in the cloud. And their enemies saw them. [13]And in that hour a great earthquake occurred, and the tenth *part* of the city fell. And there were killed in the earthquake seven thousand names of men. And the rest became terrified, and gave glory to the God of Heaven.

[14]The second woe passed away. And, behold, the third woe is coming quickly.

[15]And the seventh angel trumpeted. And there were great voices in Heaven, saying, The kingdoms of the world became our Lord's, even of His Christ; and He shall reign forever *and* ever. [16]And the twenty-four elders sitting before God on their thrones fell on their faces and worshiped God, [17]saying, We thank You, Lord God Almighty, the *One* who is, and who was, and who *is* coming, because You took Your great power and reigned. [18]And the nations were full of wrath; and Your wrath came, and the time of the judging of the dead, and to give the reward to Your slaves the prophets, and to the saints, and to the ones fearing Your name—to the small and to the great—and

10 μνήματα. καὶ οἱ κατοικοῦντες ἐπὶ τῆς γῆς χαροῦσιν ἐπ'
a tomb. And those dwelling on the earth will rejoice over
αὐτοῖς, καὶ εὐφρανθήσονται, καὶ δῶρα πέμψουσιν ἀλλήλοις,
them and will make merry. And gifts they will send one another
ὅτι οὗτοι οἱ δύο προφῆται ἐβασάνισαν τοὺς κατοικοῦντας
because these two prophets tormented those dwelling
11 ἐπὶ τῆς γῆς. καὶ μετὰ τὰς τρεῖς ἡμέρας καὶ ἥμισυ, πνεῦμα
on the earth. And after the three days and a half, a spirit
ζωῆς ἐκ τοῦ Θεοῦ εἰσῆλθεν ἐπ' αὐτούς καὶ ἔστησαν ἐπὶ
of life out of God entered into them, and they stood on
τοὺς πόδας αὐτῶν, καὶ φόβος μέγας ἔπεσεν ἐπὶ τοὺς θεωροῦν-
the feet of them, and fear great fell on those beholding
12 τας αὐτούς. καὶ ἤκουσαν φωνὴν μεγάλην ἐκ τοῦ οὐρανοῦ,
them. And they heard a voice great out of Heaven
λέγουσαν αὐτοῖς, Ἀνάβητε ὧδε. καὶ ἀνέβησαν εἰς τὸν
saying to them, Come up here. And they went up into
οὐρανὸν ἐν τῇ νεφέλῃ, καὶ ἐθεώρησαν αὐτοὺς οἱ ἐχθροὶ
Heaven in the cloud; and beheld them the enemies
13 αὐτῶν. καὶ ἐν ἐκείνῃ τῇ ὥρᾳ ἐγένετο σεισμὸς μέγας, καὶ τὸ
of them. And in that hour occurred an earthquake great, and the
δέκατον τῆς πόλεως ἔπεσε, καὶ ἀπεκτάνθησαν ἐν τῷ σεισμῷ
tenth (part) of the city fell, and were killed in the earthquake
ὀνόματα ἀνθρώπων, χιλιάδες ἑπτά· καὶ οἱ λοιποὶ ἔμφοβοι
names of men, thousands seven, and the rest terrified
ἐγένοντο, καὶ ἔδωκαν δόξαν τῷ Θεῷ τοῦ οὐρανοῦ.
became, and gave glory to the God of Heaven.
14 Ἡ οὐαὶ ἡ δευτέρα ἀπῆλθεν· καὶ ἰδού, ἡ οὐαὶ ἡ τρίτη
The woe second passed away; and behold, the woe third
ἔρχεται ταχύ.
is coming quickly.

15 Καὶ ὁ ἕβδομος ἄγγελος ἐσάλπισε, καὶ ἐγένοντο φωναὶ
And the seventh angel trumpeted. And there were voices
μεγάλαι ἐν τῷ οὐρανῷ, λέγουσαι, Ἐγένοντο αἱ βασιλεῖαι
great in Heaven, saying, became The kingdoms
τοῦ κόσμου, τοῦ Κυρίου ἡμῶν, καὶ τοῦ Χριστοῦ αὐτοῦ,
of the world of the Lord of us, and of the Christ of Him,
16 καὶ βασιλεύσει εἰς τοὺς αἰῶνας τῶν αἰώνων. καὶ οἱ εἴκοσι καὶ
and He shall reign to the ages of the ages. And the twenty and
τέσσαρες πρεσβύτεροι οἱ ἐνώπιον τοῦ Θεοῦ καθήμενοι ἐπὶ
four elders before God sitting on
τοὺς θρόνους αὐτῶν, ἔπεσαν ἐπὶ τὰ πρόσωπα αὐτῶν, καὶ
the thrones of them, fell on the faces of them, and
17 προσεκύνησαν τῷ Θεῷ, λέγοντες, Εὐχαριστοῦμέν σοι, Κύριε
worshiped God, saying, We thank You, Lord
ὁ Θεὸς ὁ παντοκράτωρ, ὁ ὢν καὶ ὁ ἦν καὶ ὁ ἐρχόμενος,
God Almighty, the (One) being, and who was, and who (is) coming,
ὅτι εἴληφας τὴν δύναμίν σου τὴν μεγάλην, καὶ ἐβασίλευσας.
because You took the power of You **great, and reigned.**
18 καὶ τὰ ἔθνη ὠργίσθησαν, καὶ ἦλθεν ἡ ὀργή σου, καὶ ὁ
And the nations were wrathful, and came the wrath of You, and the
καιρὸς τῶν νεκρῶν κριθῆναι, καὶ δοῦναι τὸν μισθὸν τοῖς
time of the dead to be judged and to give the reward to the
δούλοις σου τοῖς προφήταις καὶ τοῖς ἁγίοις καὶ τοῖς φοβου-
slaves of You, to the prophets and to the saints, and to those fearing
μένοις τὸ ὄνομά σου, τοῖς μικροῖς καὶ τοῖς μεγάλοις, καὶ
the name of You, to the small and to the great, and

to destroy those destroying the earth. 19 And the temple of God in Heaven was opened, and the ark of His covenant was seen in His temple, and lightnings, and voices, and thunders, and earthquake, and a great hail occurred.

CHAPTER 12

1 And a great sign was seen in Heaven, a woman having been clothed *with* the sun, and the moon *was* underneath her feet, and on her head a crown of twelve stars; 2 and having *a babe* in womb. She cries, being in labor, and having been distressed to bear. 3 And another sign was seen in Heaven. And, behold, a great red dragon having seven heads and ten horns! And on his heads *were* seven diadems. 4 and his tail drew the third *part* of the stars of the heaven. And *he* throws them to the earth. And the dragon stood before the woman being about to bear, so that when she bears he might devour her child. 5 And she bore a son, a male, who is going to shepherd all the nations with an iron staff. And her child was caught away to God, and to His throne. 6 And the woman fled into the wilderness, where she had a place, *it* having been prepared from God, that there they might nourish her a thousand two hundred *and* sixty days.

7 And war occurred in Heaven, Michael and his angels making war against the dragon. And the dragon and his angels made war, 8 but they did not have strength, nor was place even found *for* them in Heaven. 9 And the great dragon—the old serpent being called Devil, and, Satan, he deceiving the whole habitable world—was cast onto the

διαφθεῖραι τοὺς διαφθείροντας τὴν γῆν.
to destroy those destroying the earth.
19 Καὶ ἠνοίγη ὁ ναὸς τοῦ Θεοῦ ἐν τῷ οὐρανῷ, καὶ ὤφθη ἡ
And was opened the temple of God in Heaven, and was seen the
κιβωτὸς τῆς διαθήκης αὐτοῦ ἐν τῷ ναῷ αὐτοῦ· καὶ ἐγένοντο
ark of the covenant of Him in the temple of Him, and occurred
ἀστραπαὶ καὶ φωναὶ καὶ βρονταὶ καὶ σεισμὸς καὶ χάλαζα
lightnings and voices and thunders and an earthquake and a hail
μεγάλη.
great.

CHAPTER 12

1 Καὶ σημεῖον μέγα ὤφθη ἐν τῷ οὐρανῷ, γυνὴ περιβεβλη-
And a sign great was seen in Heaven a woman having been
μένη τὸν ἥλιον. καὶ ἡ σελήνη ὑποκάτω τῶν ποδῶν αὐτῆς,
clothed (with) the sun, and the moon underneath the feet of her,
2 καὶ ἐπὶ τῆς κεφαλῆς αὐτῆς στέφανος ἀστέρων δώδεκα· καὶ
and on the head of her a crown of stars twelve, and
ἐν γαστρὶ ἔχουσα, κράζει ὠδίνουσα, καὶ βασανιζομένη
in womb having; she cries, being in travail, and having been distressed
3 τεκεῖν. καὶ ὤφθη ἄλλο σημεῖον ἐν τῷ οὐρανῷ, καὶ ἰδού,
to bear. And was seen another sign in Heaven, and behold,
δράκων μέγας πυρρός, ἔχων κεφαλὰς ἑπτὰ καὶ κέρατα δέκα,
a dragon great red, having heads seven and horns ten,
4 καὶ ἐπὶ τὰς κεφαλὰς αὐτοῦ διαδήματα ἑπτά. καὶ ἡ οὐρὰ
and on the heads of him diadems seven, and the tail
αὐτοῦ σύρει τὸ τρίτον τῶν ἀστέρων τοῦ οὐρανοῦ, καὶ
of him draws the third (part) of the stars of heaven, and
ἔβαλεν αὐτοὺς εἰς τὴν γῆν· καὶ ὁ δράκων ἕστηκεν ἐνώπιον
throws them to the earth. And the dragon stood before
τῆς γυναικὸς τῆς μελλούσης τεκεῖν, ἵνα, ὅταν τέκῃ, τὸ τέκνον
the woman being about to bear, that, when she bears, the child
5 αὐτῆς καταφάγῃ. καὶ ἔτεκεν υἱὸν ἄρρενα, ὃς μέλλει ποι-
of her he may devour. And she bore a son, a male, who is about to
μαίνειν πάντα τὰ ἔθνη ἐν ῥάβδῳ σιδηρᾷ· καὶ ἡρπάσθη τὸ
shepherd all the nations with a staff iron. And was seized the
6 τέκνον αὐτῆς πρὸς τὸν Θεὸν καὶ τὸν θρόνον αὐτοῦ. καὶ ἡ
child of her to God and the throne of Him. And the
γυνὴ ἔφυγεν εἰς τὴν ἔρημον, ὅπου ἔχει τόπον ἡτοιμασμένον
woman fled into the wilderness, where she has a place having been prepared
ἀπὸ τοῦ Θεοῦ, ἵνα ἐκεῖ τρέφωσιν αὐτὴν ἡμέρας χιλίας
from God, that there they might nourish her days a thousand
διακοσίας ἑξήκοντα.
two hundred (and) sixty.
7 Καὶ ἐγένετο πόλεμος ἐν τῷ οὐρανῷ· ὁ Μιχαὴλ καὶ οἱ
And occurred war in Heaven, Michael and the
ἄγγελοι αὐτοῦ ἐπολέμησαν κατὰ τοῦ δράκοντος· καὶ ὁ
angels of him made war against the dragon. And the
8 δράκων ἐπολέμησε, καὶ οἱ ἄγγελοι αὐτου, καὶ οὐκ ἴσχυσαν,
dragon warred, and the angels of him, and not they had strength,
9 οὔτε τόπος εὑρέθη αὐτῶν ἔτι ἐν τῷ οὐρανῷ. καὶ ἐβλήθη
not even place was found of them still in Heaven. And was cast
ὁ δράκων ὁ μέγας, ὁ ὄφις ὁ ἀρχαῖος, ὁ καλούμενος διάβολος
the dragon great, the serpent old, being called Devil
καὶ ὁ Σατανᾶς, ὁ πλανῶν τὴν οἰκουμένην ὅλην· ἐβλήθη
and Satan the (one) deceiving the habitable world whole; was cast

earth, and his angels were cast with him. [10]And I heard a great voice saying in Heaven, Now has come the salvation and power and the kingdom of our God, and the authority of His Christ, because the accuser of our brothers is thrown down, the *one* accusing them before our God day and night. [11]And they overcame him because of the blood of the Lamb, and because of the word of their testimony. And they did not love their soul *even* until death. [12]Because of this, be glad, the heavens and those tabernacling in them. Woe *to* the ones dwelling on the earth, and in the sea, because the Devil came down to you having great anger, knowing that he has a little time!

[13]And when the dragon saw that he was cast onto the earth, he pursued the woman who bore the male. [14]And two wings of the great eagle were given to the woman, that she might fly into the wilderness, to her place, where she is fed there a time, and times, and half a time, away from *the* serpent's face. [15]And the serpent threw water out of his mouth after the woman, that he might cause her *to be* carried off *by the* river. [16]And the earth helped the woman, and the earth opened its mouth and swallowed the river which the dragon threw out of his mouth. [17]And the dragon was enraged over the woman, and went away to make war with the rest of her seed, those keeping the commandments of God, and having the testimony of Jesus Christ.

CHAPTER 13

[1]And I stood on the sand of the sea.

And I saw a beast coming up out of the sea, having

εἰς τὴν γῆν, καὶ οἱ ἄγγελοι αὐτοῦ μετ' αὐτοῦ ἐβλήθησαν.
onto the earth, and the angels of him with him were cast.
10 καὶ ἤκουσα φωνὴν μεγάλην λέγουσαν ἐν τῷ οὐρανῷ, Ἄρτι
And I heard a voice great saying in Heaven, Now
ἐγένετο ἡ σωτηρία καὶ ἡ δύναμις καὶ ἡ βασιλεία τοῦ Θεοῦ
has come into being the salvation and the power and the kingdom of the God
ἡμῶν, καὶ ἡ ἐξουσία τοῦ Χριστοῦ αὐτοῦ· ὅτι κατεβλήθη
of us, and the authority of the Christ of Him, because is thrown down
ὁ κατήγορος τῶν ἀδελφῶν ἡμῶν, ὁ κατηγορῶν αὐτῶν
the accuser of the brothers of us, the (one) accusing them
11 ἐνώπιον τοῦ Θεοῦ ἡμῶν ἡμέρας καὶ νυκτός. καὶ αὐτοὶ
before the God of us day and night. And they
ἐνίκησαν αὐτὸν διὰ τὸ αἷμα τοῦ ἀρνίου, καὶ διὰ τὸν λόγον
overcame him because of the blood of the Lamb, and because of the word
τῆς μαρτυρίας αὐτῶν, καὶ οὐκ ἠγάπησαν τὴν ψυχὴν αὐτῶν
of the witness of them; and not they loved the soul of them
12 ἄχρι θανάτου. διὰ τοῦτο εὐφραίνεσθε, οἱ οὐρανοὶ καὶ οἱ ἐν
until death. Therefore, be glad, the heavens and those in
αὐτοῖς σκηνοῦντες· οὐαὶ τοῖς κατοικοῦσι τὴν γῆν καὶ τὴν
them tabernacling. Woe (to) those inhabiting the earth and the
θάλασσαν, ὅτι κατέβη ὁ διάβολος πρὸς ὑμᾶς ἔχων θυμὸν
sea, because came down the Devil to you having anger
μέγαν, εἰδὼς ὅτι ὀλίγον καιρὸν ἔχει.
great, knowing that a little time he has.
13 Καὶ ὅτε εἶδεν ὁ δράκων ὅτι ἐβλήθη εἰς τὴν γῆν, ἐδίωξε τὴν
And when saw the dragon that he was cast onto the earth, he pursued the
14 γυναῖκα ἥτις ἔτεκε τὸν ἄρρενα. καὶ ἐδόθησαν τῇ γυναικὶ
woman who bore the male. And were given to the woman
δύο πτέρυγες τοῦ ἀετοῦ τοῦ μεγάλου, ἵνα πέτηται εἰς τὴν
two wings of the eagle great, that she may fly into the
15 ἔρημον εἰς τὸν τόπον αὐτῆς, ὅπου τρέφεται ἐκεῖ καιρόν, καὶ
wilderness, to the place of her, where she is nourished there a time, and
καιρούς, καὶ ἥμισυ καιροῦ, ἀπὸ προσώπου τοῦ ὄφεως. καὶ
times, and half a time, from (the) face of the serpent. And
ἔβαλεν ὁ ὄφις ὀπίσω τῆς γυναικὸς ἐκ τοῦ στόματος αὐτοῦ
cast the serpent after the woman out of the mouth of him
ὕδωρ ὡς ποταμόν, ἵνα ταύτην ποταμοφόρητον ποιήσῃ.
water as a river, that she carried off (a) river he might make.
16 καὶ ἐβοήθησεν ἡ γῆ τῇ γυναικί, καὶ ἤνοιξεν ἡ γῆ τὸ στόμα
And helped the earth the woman, and opened the earth the mouth
αὐτῆς, καὶ κατέπιε τὸν ποταμὸν ὃν ἔβαλεν ὁ δράκων ἐκ τοῦ
of it and swallowed the river which cast the dragon out of the
17 στόματος αὐτοῦ. καὶ ὠργίσθη ὁ δράκων ἐπὶ τῇ γυναικί, καὶ
mouth of him. And was enraged the dragon over the woman, and
ἀπῆλθε ποιῆσαι πόλεμον μετὰ τῶν λοιπῶν τοῦ σπέρματος
went away to make war with the rest of the seed
αὐτῆς, τῶν τηρούντων τὰς ἐντολὰς τοῦ Θεοῦ καὶ ἐχόντων
of her, those keeping the commandments of God, and having
τὴν μαρτυρίαν τοῦ Ἰησοῦ Χριστοῦ
the witness of Jesus Christ.

CHAPTER 13

1 καὶ ἐστάθην ἐπὶ τὴν ἄμμον τῆς θαλάσσης.
And I stood on the sand of the sea.
Καὶ εἶδον ἐκ τῆς θαλάσσης θηρίον ἀναβαῖνον, ἔχον κεφαλὰς
And I saw out of the sea a beast coming up, having heads

seven heads and ten horns, and on his horns ten diadems, and on its head names of blasphemy. 2 And the beast which I saw was like a leopard, and its feet as of a bear, and its mouth as a lion's mouth. And the dragon gave its power to it, and its throne, and great authority. 3 And I saw one of its heads, as having been slain to death, and its deadly wound was healed. And all the earth marveled after the beast.

4 And they worshiped the dragon who gave authority to the beast; and they worshiped the beast, saying, Who *is* like the beast; who is able to make war with it?

5 And a mouth speaking great things was given to it, and blasphemies. And authority to act forty-two months was given to it. 6 And it opened its mouth in blasphemy toward God, to blaspheme His name and His tabernacle, and those tabernacling in Heaven. 7 And it was given to it to war with the saints, and to overcome them. And authority was given to it over every tribe and tongue and nation.

8 And all those dwelling in the earth will worship it, *those* of whom the names have not been written in the Book of Life of the Lamb having been slain, from *the* foundation of *the* world. 9 If anyone has an ear, let him hear. 10 If anyone will kill by a sword, by a sword he must be killed. Here is the patience and the faith of the saints.

11 And I saw another beast coming up out of the earth. And it had two horns like a lamb, but spoke like a dragon. 12 And it executes all the authority of the first beast before it. And it causes

ἑπτὰ καὶ κέρατα δέκα, καὶ ἐπὶ τῶν κεράτων αὐτοῦ δέκα
seven and horns ten, and on the horns of it ten
διαδήματα, καὶ ἐπὶ τὰς κεφαλὰς αὐτοῦ ὄνομα βλασφημίας.
diadems, and on the heads of it names of blasphemy.
2 καὶ τὸ θηρίον, ὃ εἶδον, ἦν ὅμοιον παρδάλει, καὶ οἱ πόδες
And the beast which I saw was like a leopard, and the feet
αὐτοῦ ὡς ἄρκτου, καὶ τὸ στόμα αὐτοῦ ὡς στόμα λέοντος·
of it as of a bear, and the mouth of it as (the) mouth of a lion.
καὶ ἔδωκεν αὐτῷ ὁ δράκων τὴν δύναμιν αὐτοῦ, καὶ τὸν
And gave to it the dragon the power of it and the
3 θρόνον αὐτοῦ, καὶ ἐξουσίαν μεγάλην. καὶ εἶδον μίαν τῶν
throne of it and authority great. And I saw one of the
κεφαλῶν αὐτοῦ ὡς ἐσφαγμένην εἰς θάνατον· καὶ ἡ πληγὴ τοῦ
heads of it as having been slain to death, and the wound of the
θανάτου αὐτοῦ ἐθεραπεύθη· καὶ ἐθαύμασεν ὅλη ἡ γῆ ὀπίσω
death of it was healed. And marveled all the earth after
4 τοῦ θηρίου· καὶ προσεκύνησαν τὸν δράκοντα ὃς ἔδωκεν
the beast; and they worshiped the dragon who gave
ἐξουσίαν τῷ θηρίῳ, καὶ προσεκύνησαν τὸ θηρίον, λέγοντες,
authority to the beast, and they worshiped the beast, saying,
Τίς ὅμοιος τῷ θηρίῳ; τίς δύναται πολεμῆσαι μετ' αὐτοῦ;
Who (is) like the beast, who is able to make war with it?
5 καὶ ἐδόθη αὐτῷ στόμα λαλοῦν μεγάλα καὶ βλασφημίας· καὶ
And was given to it a mouth speaking great things and blasphemies; and
6 ἐδόθη αὐτῷ ἐξουσία ποιῆσαι μῆνας τεσσαράκοντα δύο. καὶ
was given to it authority to act months forty- two. And
ἤνοιξε τὸ στόμα αὐτοῦ εἰς βλασφημίαν πρὸς τὸν Θεόν,
it opened the mouth of it in blasphemy toward God,
βλασφημῆσαι τὸ ὄνομα αὐτοῦ, καὶ τὴν σκηνὴν αὐτοῦ, καὶ
to blaspheme the name of Him, and the tabernacle of Him, and
7 τοὺς ἐν τῷ οὐρανῷ σκηνοῦντας. καὶ ἐδόθη αὐτῷ πόλεμον
those in Heaven tabernacling. And was given to it war
ποιῆσαι μετὰ τῶν ἁγίων, καὶ νικῆσαι αὐτούς· καὶ ἐδόθη
to make with the saints, and to overcome them. And was given
αὐτῷ ἐξουσία ἐπὶ πᾶσαν φυλὴν καὶ γλῶσσαν καὶ ἔθνος.
to it authority over every tribe and tongue and nation
8 καὶ προσκυνήσουσιν αὐτῷ πάντες οἱ κατοικοῦντες ἐπὶ τῆς
And will worship it all those dwelling on the
γῆς, ὧν οὐ γέγραπται τὰ ὀνόματα ἐν τῇ βίβλῳ τῆς ζωῆς
earth, of whom not was written the names in the Scroll of Life
9 τοῦ ἀρνίου ἐσφαγμένου ἀπὸ καταβολῆς κόσμου. εἴ τις ἔχει
of the Lamb having been slain from (the) foundation of world. If any-one have
10 οὖς, ἀκουσάτω. εἴ τις αἰχμαλωσίαν συνάγει, εἰς αἰχμαλω-
an ear, let him hear. If anyone captivity gathers into captivity
σίαν ὑπάγει· εἴ τις ἐν μαχαίρᾳ ἀποκτενεῖ, δεῖ αὐτὸν ἐν
he goes. If anyone by a sword will kill, must he by
μαχαίρᾳ ἀποκτανθῆναι. ὧδέ ἐστιν ἡ ὑπομονὴ καὶ ἡ πίστις
a sword be killed. Here is the patience and the faith
τῶν ἁγίων.
of the saints.

11 Καὶ εἶδον ἄλλο θηρίον ἀναβαῖνον ἐκ τῆς γῆς, καὶ εἶχε
And I saw another beast coming up out of the earth, and it had
12 κέρατα δύο ὅμοια ἀρνίῳ, καὶ ἐλάλει ὡς δράκων. καὶ τὴν
horns two like a lamb, and spoke as a dragon. And the
ἐξουσίαν τοῦ πρώτου θηρίου πᾶσαν ποιεῖ ἐνώπιον αὐτοῦ.
authority of the first beast all it does before it.

that the earth and those dwelling in it should worship the first beast, of which was healed its deadly wound. [13]And it does great signs, that even fire it causes to come down out of the heaven onto the earth before men. [14]And it deceives those dwelling on the earth, because of the signs which were given to it to do before the beast, saying to those dwelling on the earth to make an image to the beast who has the wound of the sword, and lived. [15]And was given to it to give a spirit to the image of the beast, so that the image of the beast might even speak, and might cause as many as would not worship the image of the beast to be killed. [16]And the small and the great, and the rich and the poor, and the freemen and the slaves, it causes that they give to them a mark on their right hand, or on their foreheads, [17]even that not any could buy or sell, except those having the mark of the name of the beast, or the number of its name. [18]Here is wisdom: Let him having reason count the number of the beast, for it is *the* number of a man—and its number *is* six hundred *and* sixty-six.

CHAPTER 14

[1]And I saw, and behold, *the* Lamb standing on Mount Zion! And with Him *were* a hundred *and* forty-four thousands, having the name of His Father written on their foreheads. [2]And I heard a sound out of Heaven, as a sound of many waters, and as a sound of great thunder. Also I heard a sound of harpers harping on their harps. [3]And they sing as a new song before the throne, and before the four living creatures and the elders. And no one was able

καὶ ποιεῖ τὴν γῆν καὶ τοὺς κατοικοῦντας ἐν αὐτῇ ἵνα
And it makes the earth and those dwelling in it that
προσκυνήσωσι τὸ θηρίον τὸ πρῶτον, οὗ ἐθεραπεύθη ἡ
they should worship the beast the first, of which was healed the
13 πληγὴ τοῦ θανάτου αὐτοῦ. καὶ ποιεῖ σημεῖα μεγάλα, ἵνα
wound of death of it. And it does signs great, that
καὶ πῦρ ποιῇ καταβαίνειν ἐκ τοῦ οὐρανοῦ εἰς τὴν γῆν
even fire it makes to come down out of the heaven onto the earth
14 ἐνώπιον τῶν ἀνθρώπων. καὶ πλανᾷ τοὺς κατοικοῦντας
before men. And it deceives those dwelling
ἐπὶ τῆς γῆς διὰ τὰ σημεῖα ἃ ἐδόθη αὐτῷ ποιῆσαι ἐνώπιον
on the earth, because of the signs which were given it to do before
τοῦ θηριου, λέγων τοῖς κατοικουσιν ἐπὶ τῆς γῆς ποιῆσαι
the beast, saying to those dwelling on the earth to make
εἰκόνα τῷ θηρίῳ ὃ ἔχει τὴν πληγὴν τῆς μαχαίρας καὶ ἔζησε.
an image to the beast who has the wound of the sword, and lived.
15 καὶ ἐδόθη αὐτῷ δοῦναι πνεῦμα τῇ εἰκόνι τοῦ θηρίου, ἵνα καὶ
And was given to it to give a spirit to the image of the beast, that even
λαλήσῃ ἡ εἰκὼν τοῦ θηρίου, καὶ ποιήσῃ, ὅσοι ἂν μὴ
might speak the image of the beast, and might make as many as not
προσκυνήσωσι τὴν εἰκόνα τοῦ θηρίου, ἵνα ἀποκτανθῶσι.
would worship the image of the beast, that (they) be killed.
16 καὶ ποιεῖ πάντας, τοὺς μικροὺς καὶ τοὺς μεγάλους, καὶ τοὺς
And it makes all, the small and the great, and the
πλουσίους καὶ τοὺς πτωχούς, καὶ τοὺς ἐλευθέρους καὶ τοὺς
rich and the poor, and the freemen and the
δούλους, ἵνα δώσῃ αὐτοῖς χάραγμα ἐπὶ τῆς χειρὸς αὐτῶν
slaves, that it may give to them a mark on the hand of them
17 τῆς δεξιᾶς, ἢ ἐπὶ τῶν μετώπων αὐτῶν, καὶ ἵνα μή τις
right, or on the foreheads of them, even that not any
δύνηται ἀγοράσαι ἢ πωλῆσαι, εἰ μὴ ὁ ἔχων τὸ χάραγμα ἢ
could buy or sell, except he having the mark, or
18 τὸ ὄνομα τοῦ θηρίου ἢ τὸν ἀριθμὸν τοῦ ὀνόματος αὐτοῦ. ὧδε
the name of the beast, or the number of the name of it. Here
ἡ σοφία ἐστίν. ὁ ἔχων τὸν νοῦν ψηφισάτω τὸν ἀριθμὸν τοῦ
wisdom is. The (one) having reason let him count the number of the
θηρίου· ἀριθμὸς γὰρ ἀνθρώπου ἐστί, καὶ ὁ ἀριθμὸς αὐτοῦ χξς'
beast; (the) number for of a man it is. And the number of it (is) 666.

CHAPTER 14

1 Καὶ εἶδον, καὶ ἰδού, ἀρνίον ἑστηκὸς ἐπὶ τὸ ὄρος Σιών, καὶ
And I saw, and behold, (the) Lamb standing on the mount Zion, and
μετ' αὐτοῦ ἑκατὸν τεσσαρακοντατέσσαρες χιλιάδες, ἔχουσαι
with Him a hundred (and) forty-four thousands, having
τὸ ὄνομα τοῦ πατρὸς αὐτοῦ γεγραμμένον ἐπὶ τῶν μετώπων
the name of the Father of Him having been written on the foreheads
2 αὐτῶν. καὶ ἤκουσα φωνὴν ἐκ τοῦ οὐρανοῦ, ὡς φωνὴν ὑδάτων
of them. And I heard a sound out of Heaven, as a sound of waters
πολλῶν, καὶ ὡς φωνὴν βροντῆς μεγάλης· καὶ φωνὴν ἤκουσα
many, and as a sound of thunder great; and a sound I heard
3 κιθαρῳδῶν κιθαριζόντων ἐν ταῖς κιθάραις αὐτῶν. καὶ
of harpers harping on the harps of them. And
ᾄδουσιν ὡς ᾠδὴν καινὴν ἐνώπιον τοῦ θρόνου, καὶ ἐνώπιον
they sing as a song new before the throne, and before
τῶν τεσσάρων ζώων καὶ τῶν πρεσβυτέρων· καὶ οὐδεὶς ἠδύ-
the four living creatures and the elders; and no one could

to learn the song except the hundred *and* forty-four thousands, those having been redeemed from the earth. [4] These are the ones who were not defiled with women, for they are virgins. These are the ones following the Lamb wherever He may go. These were redeemed from among men *as* first-fruit to God and to the Lamb. [5] And no guile was found in their mouth, for they are without blemish before the throne of God. [6] And I saw another angel flying in mid-heaven, having an everlasting gospel to proclaim to those dwelling on the earth, even *to* every nation and tribe and tongue and people, [7] saying in a great voice, Fear God, and give glory to Him, because the hour of His judgment has come; and, Worship Him who has made the heaven, and the earth, and the sea, and the fountain of waters. [8] And another angel followed, saying, The great city, Babylon, has fallen, has fallen; because of the wine of the anger of her fornication, *she* has made all nations to drink. [9] And a third angel followed them, saying in a great voice, If anyone worships the beast and its image, and receives a mark on his forehead, or in his hand, [10] he also shall drink of the wine of the anger of God having been mixed undiluted in the cup of His wrath. And *he* will be tormented by fire and brimstone before the holy angels and before the Lamb. [11] And the smoke of their torment goes up forever *and* ever. And they have no rest night and day, the ones worshiping the beast and its image, even if anyone receives the mark of its name. [12] Here *is the* patience of the saints

νατο μαθεῖν τὴν ᾠδήν, εἰ μὴ αἱ ἑκατὸν τεσσαρακοντατέσ-
to learn the song, except the hundred (and) forty-four
4 σαρες χιλιάδες, οἱ ἠγορασμένοι ἀπὸ τῆς γῆς. οὗτοί εἰσιν οἳ
thousands, those being redeemed from the earth. These are who
μετὰ γυναικῶν οὐκ ἐμολύνθησαν· παρθένοι γάρ εἰσιν. οὗτοί
with women not were defiled, virgins for they are. These
εἰσιν οἱ ἀκολουθοῦντες τῷ ἀρνίῳ ὅπου ἂν ὑπάγῃ. οὗτοι
are those following the Lamb wherever He may go. These
ἠγοράσθησαν ἀπὸ τῶν ἀνθρώπων, ἀπαρχὴ τῷ Θεῷ καὶ τῷ
were from men firstfruit to God and to the
5 ἀρνίῳ. καὶ ἐν τῷ στόματι αὐτῶν οὐχ εὑρέθη δόλος· ἄμωμοι
Lamb. And in the mouth of them not was found guile; unmarked
γάρ εἰσιν ἐνώπιον τοῦ θρόνου τοῦ Θεοῦ.
for they are before the throne of God.
6 Καὶ εἶδον ἄλλον ἄγγελον πετώμενον ἐν μεσουρανήματι,
And I saw another angel flying in mid-heaven,
ἔχοντα εὐαγγέλιον αἰώνιον, εὐαγγελίσαι τοὺς κατοικοῦντας
having a gospel everlasting to preach to those dwelling
ἐπὶ τῆς γῆς, καὶ πᾶν ἔθνος καὶ φυλὴν καὶ γλῶσσαν καὶ λαόν,
on the earth, even every nation and tribe and tongue and people,
7 λέγοντα ἐν φωνῇ μεγάλῃ, Φοβήθητε τὸν Θεόν, καὶ δότε αὐτῷ
saying in a voice great, Fear God, and give to Him
δόξαν, ὅτι ἦλθεν ἡ ὥρα τῆς κρίσεως αὐτοῦ, καὶ προσκυνή-
glory, because came the hour of the judgment of Him; and, Worship
σατε τῷ ποιήσαντι τὸν οὐρανὸν καὶ τὴν γῆν καὶ τὴν θάλασ-
Him having made the heaven and the earth and the sea
σαν καὶ πηγὰς ὑδάτων.
and fountains of waters.
8 Καὶ ἄλλος ἄγγελος ἠκολούθησε, λέγων, Ἔπεσεν ἔπεσε
And another angel followed, saying, Fell, fell
Βαβυλὼν ἡ πόλις ἡ μεγάλη, ὅτι ἐκ τοῦ οἴνου τοῦ θυμοῦ τῆς
Babylon the city great, because of the wine of the anger of the
πορνείας αὐτῆς πεπότικε πάντα ἔθνη.
fornication of her she made to drink all nations.
9 Καὶ τρίτος ἄγγελος ἠκολούθησεν αὐτοῖς, λέγων ἐν φωνῇ
And a third angel followed them, saying in a voice
μεγάλῃ, Εἴ τις τὸ θηρίον προσκυνεῖ καὶ τὴν εἰκόνα αὐτοῦ,
great, If anyone the beast worships and the image of it,
καὶ λαμβάνει χάραγμα ἐπὶ τοῦ μετώπου αὐτοῦ, ἢ ἐπὶ τὴν
and receives a mark on the forehead of him, or on the
10 χεῖρα αὐτοῦ, καὶ αὐτὸς πίεται ἐκ τοῦ οἴνου τοῦ θυμοῦ τοῦ
hand of him, even he shall drink of the wine of the anger of the
Θεοῦ, τοῦ κεκερασμένου ἀκράτου ἐν τῷ ποτηρίῳ τῆς ὀργῆς
God, having been mixed undiluted in the cup of the wrath
αὐτοῦ, καὶ βασανισθήσεται ἐν πυρὶ καὶ θείῳ ἐνώπιον τῶν
of Him, and will be tormented by fire and brimstone before the
11 ἁγίων ἀγγέλων, καὶ ἐνώπιον τοῦ ἀρνίου· καὶ ὁ καπνὸς τοῦ
holy angels, and before the Lamb. And the smoke of the
βασανισμοῦ αὐτῶν ἀναβαίνει εἰς αἰῶνας αἰώνων· καὶ οὐκ
torment of them goes up to ages of ages; and not
ἔχουσιν ἀνάπαυσιν ἡμέρας καὶ νυκτὸς οἱ προσκυνοῦντες τὸ
have rest day and night those worshiping the
θηρίον καὶ τὴν εἰκόνα αὐτοῦ, καὶ εἴ τις λαμβάνει τὸ χάραγμα
beast and the image of it; even if anyone receives the mark
12 τοῦ ὀνόματος αὐτοῦ. ὧδε ὑπομονὴ τῶν ἁγίων ἐστίν· ὧδε
of the name of it. Here (the) patience of the saints is. Here

here *are* the ones keeping the command of God, and the faith of Jesus. [13]And I heard a voice out of Heaven saying to me, Write: Blessed *are* the dead, the ones dying in *the* Lord from now. Yes, says the Spirit, they shall rest from their labors, and their works follow with them. [14]And I saw, and behold, a white cloud; and on the cloud *One* sitting, like *the* Son of man, having on His head a golden crown, and in His hand a sharp sickle. [15]And another angel went forth out of the Temple, crying in a great voice to the *One* sitting on the cloud, Send Your sickle and reap, because Your hour to reap has come, because the harvest of the earth was dried. [16]And the *One* sitting on the cloud thrust His sickle on the earth, and the earth was reaped.

[17]And another angel went forth out of the temple in heaven, he also having a sharp sickle. [18]And another angel went forth out of the altar having authority over the fire. And he spoke with a great cry to the *one* having the sharp sickle, saying, Send your sharp sickle and gather the clusters of the vine of the earth, because its grapes are ripened. [19]And the angel thrust his sickle into the earth and gathered the vine of the earth, and threw into the winepress of the great anger of God. [20]And the winepress was trodden outside the city, and blood went out of the winepress until the bridles of the horses, from a thousand, six hundred stadia.

οἱ τηροῦντες τὰς ἐντολὰς τοῦ Θεοῦ καὶ τὴν πίστιν Ἰησοῦ.
those keeping the commandments of God and the faith of Jesus.
13 Καὶ ἤκουσα φωνῆς ἐκ τοῦ οὐρανοῦ λεγούσης μοι, Γράψον,
And I heard a voice out of Heaven saying to me, Write:
Μακάριοι οἱ νεκροὶ οἱ ἐν Κυρίῳ ἀποθνήσκοντες ἀπ᾽ ἄρτι·
Blessed (are) the dead, those in (the) Lord dying from now.
ναί, λέγει τὸ Πνεῦμα, ἵνα ἀναπαύσωνται ἐκ τῶν κόπων
Yes, says the Spirit, that they shall rest from the labors
αὐτῶν· τὰ δὲ ἔργα αὐτῶν ἀκολουθεῖ μετ᾽ αὐτῶν.
of them; the and works of them follow with them.
14 Καὶ εἶδον, καὶ ἰδού, νεφέλη λευκή, καὶ ἐπὶ τὴν νεφέλην
And I saw, and behold, a cloud white, and on the cloud
καθήμενος ὅμοιος υἱῷ ἀνθρώπου, ἔχων ἐπὶ τῆς κεφαλῆς
(One) sitting like (the) Son of man, having on the head
αὐτοῦ στέφανον χρυσοῦν, καὶ ἐν τῇ χειρὶ αὐτοῦ δρέπανον
of Him a crown of gold and in the hand of Him a sickle
15 ὀξύ. καὶ ἄλλος ἄγγελος ἐξῆλθεν ἐκ τοῦ ναοῦ, κράζων ἐν
sharp. And another angel went forth out of the temple, crying in
μεγάλῃ φωνῇ τῷ καθημένῳ ἐπὶ τῆς νεφέλης, Πέμψον τὸ
a great voice to the (One) sitting on the cloud, Send the
δρέπανόν σου καὶ θέρισον· ὅτι ἦλθέ σοι ἡ ὥρα τοῦ θερίσαι,
sickle of You and reap because came You the hour to reap,
16 ὅτι ἐξηράνθη ὁ θερισμὸς τῆς γῆς. καὶ ἔβαλεν ὁ καθήμενος
because was dried the harvest of the earth. And thrust the (One) sitting
ἐπὶ τὴν νεφέλην τὸ δρέπανον αὐτοῦ ἐπὶ τὴν γῆν. καὶ
on the cloud the sickle of Him on the earth, and
ἐθερίσθη ἡ γῆ.
was reaped the earth.
17 Καὶ ἄλλος ἄγγελος ἐξῆλθεν ἐκ τοῦ ναοῦ τοῦ ἐν τῷ
And another angel went forth out of the temple in
18 οὐρανῷ, ἔχων καὶ αὐτὸς δρέπανον ὀξύ. καὶ ἄλλος ἄγγελος
Heaven, having also he a sickle sharp. And another angel
ἐξῆλθεν ἐκ τοῦ θυσιαστηρίου, ἔχων ἐξουσίαν ἐπὶ τοῦ πυρός,
went forth out of the altar, having authority over the fire,
καὶ ἐφώνησε κραυγῇ μεγάλῃ τῷ ἔχοντι τὸ δρέπανον τὸ ὀξύ,
and he spoke with a cry great to the (one) having the sickle sharp,
λέγων, Πέμψον σου τὸ δρέπανον τὸ ὀξὺ καὶ τρύγησον τοὺς
saying, Send of you the sickle sharp and gather the
βότρυας τῆς ἀμπέλου τῆς γῆς, ὅτι ἤκμασαν αἱ σταφυλαὶ
clusters of the vine of the earth, because are ripened the grapes
19 αὐτῆς. καὶ ἔβαλεν ὁ ἄγγελος τὸ δρέπανον αὐτοῦ εἰς τὴν γῆν,
of it. And thrust the angel the sickle of him into the earth,
καὶ ἐτρύγησε τὴν ἄμπελον τῆς γῆς, καὶ ἔβαλεν εἰς τὴν ληνὸν
and gathered the vine of the earth, and threw into the winepress
20 τοῦ θυμοῦ τοῦ Θεοῦ τὴν μεγάλην. καὶ ἐπατήθη ἡ ληνὸς
of the anger of God great. And was trodden the winepress
ἔξω τῆς πόλεως, καὶ ἐξῆλθεν αἷμα ἐκ τῆς ληνοῦ ἄχρι τῶν
outside the city, and went out blood out of the winepress until the
χαλινῶν τῶν ἵππων, ἀπὸ σταδίων χιλίων ἑξακοσίων.
bridles of the horses, from stadia a thousand six hundred.

CHAPTER 15

[1]And I saw another sign in Heaven, great and marvelous: seven angels having the last

CHAPTER 15

1 Καὶ εἶδον ἄλλο σημεῖον ἐν τῷ οὐρανῷ μέγα καὶ θαυμα-
And I saw another sign in Heaven, great and marvelous
στόν, ἀγγέλους ἑπτὰ ἔχοντας πληγὰς ἑπτὰ τὰς ἐσχάτας,
angels seven having plagues seven the last,

plagues, because the anger of God was completed in them. [2]And I saw, as a glassy sea having been mixed with fire. And the ones overcoming the beast, and its image, and its mark, of the number of its name, *were* standing on the glassy sea, having harps of God. [3]And they sing the song of Moses the slave of God, and the song of the Lamb, saying, Great and marvelous *are* Your works, Lord God Almighty, true and righteous *are* Your ways, King of the nations. [4]Who will not fear You, Lord, and glorify Your name? For *You* only are holy. For all the nations will come and will worship before You, because Your righteousnesses were made known. [5]And after these things I saw; and behold, the temple of the tabernacle of the testimony in Heaven was opened! [6]And the seven angels having the seven plagues came forth out of the temple, having been clothed *in* clean and bright linen, and golden bands having been girded around the breasts. [7]And one of the four living creatures gave to the seven angels seven golden bowls filled with the anger of the living God, forever *and* ever. [8]And the temple was filled with *the* smoke of the glory of God, and with His power. And no one was able to enter into the temple until the seven plagues of the seven angels should be finished.

ὅτι ἐν αὐταῖς ἐτελέσθη ὁ θυμὸς τοῦ Θεοῦ.
because in them was completed the anger of God.
2 Καὶ εἶδον ὡς θάλασσαν ὑαλίνην μεμιγμένην πυρί, καὶ
And I saw as a sea glassy having been mixed with fire, and
τοὺς νικῶντας ἐκ τοῦ θηρίου καὶ ἐκ τῆς εἰκόνος αὐτοῦ καὶ
those overcoming of the beast and of the image of it, and
ἐκ τοῦ χαράγματος αὐτοῦ, ἐκ τοῦ ἀριθμοῦ τοῦ ὀνόματος
of the mark of it, of the number of the name
αὐτοῦ, ἑστῶτας ἐπὶ τὴν θάλασσαν τὴν ὑαλίνην, ἔχοντας
of it, standing on the sea glassy, having
3 κιθάρας τοῦ Θεοῦ. καὶ ᾄδουσι τὴν ᾠδὴν Μωσέως τοῦ δούλου
harps of God. And they sing the song of Moses the slave
τοῦ Θεοῦ, καὶ τὴν ᾠδὴν τοῦ ἀρνίου, λέγοντες, Μεγάλα
of God, and the song of the Lamb, saying, Great
καὶ θαυμαστὰ τὰ ἔργα σου, Κύριε ὁ Θεὸς ὁ παντοκράτωρ·
and marvelous the works of You, Lord God Almighty,
4 δίκαιαι καὶ ἀληθιναὶ αἱ ὁδοί σου, ὁ βασιλεὺς τῶν ἁγίων. τίς
righteous and true the ways of You, the King of the saints Who
οὐ μὴ φοβηθῇ σε, Κύριε, καὶ δοξάσῃ τὸ ὄνομά σου; ὅτι
in no way fear You, Lord, and glorify the name of You? For
μόνος ὅσιος· ὅτι πάντα τὰ ἔθνη ἥξουσι καὶ προσκυνή-
(You) only (are) holy, for all the nations will come and will worship
σουσιν ἐνώπιόν σου, ὅτι τὰ δικαιώματά σου ἐφανερώθησαν.
before You, because the righteousnesses of You were revealed.
5 Καὶ μετὰ ταῦτα εἶδον, καὶ ἰδού, ἠνοίγη ὁ ναὸς τῆς σκηνῆς
And after these things I saw, and behold, was opened the temple of the tent
6 τοῦ μαρτυρίου ἐν τῷ οὐρανῷ· καὶ ἐξῆλθον οἱ ἑπτὰ ἄγγελοι
of the testimony in Heaven; and came forth the seven angels
ἔχοντες τὰς ἑπτὰ πληγὰς ἐκ τοῦ ναοῦ, ἐνδεδυμένοι λίνον
having the seven plagues out of the temple, being clothed (with) linen
καθαρὸν καὶ λαμπρόν, καὶ περιεζωσμένοι περὶ τὰ στήθη
clean and bright, and having been girded around the breasts
7 ζώνας χρυσᾶς. καὶ ἓν ἐκ τῶν τεσσάρων ζώων ἔδωκε τοῖς
(with) girdles of gold And one of the four living creatures gave to the
ἑπτὰ ἀγγέλοις ἑπτὰ φιάλας χρυσᾶς γεμούσας τοῦ θυμοῦ
seven angels seven bowls of gold filled of the anger
8 τοῦ Θεοῦ τοῦ ζῶντος εἰς τοὺς αἰῶνας τῶν αἰώνων. καὶ
of God the living, to the ages of the ages. And
ἐγεμίσθη ὁ ναὸς καπνοῦ ἐκ τῆς δόξης τοῦ Θεοῦ, καὶ ἐκ τῆς
was filled the temple of smoke of the glory of God, and of the
δυνάμεως αὐτοῦ· καὶ οὐδεὶς ἠδύνατο εἰσελθεῖν εἰς τὸν ναόν,
power of Him. And no one could enter into the temple,
ἄχρι τελεσθῶσιν αἱ ἑπτὰ πληγαὶ τῶν ἑπτὰ ἀγγέλων.
until should be finished the seven plagues of the seven angels.

CHAPTER 16

[1]And I heard a great voice out of the temple saying to the seven angels, Go and pour out the bowls of the anger of God onto the earth. [2]And the first went away and poured out his bowl onto the earth. And a bad and evil sore

1 Καὶ ἤκουσα φωνῆς μεγάλης ἐκ τοῦ ναοῦ, λεγούσης τοῖς
And I heard a voice great out of the temple, saying to the
ἑπτὰ ἀγγέλοις, Ὑπάγετε, καὶ ἐκχέατε τὰς φιαλας τοῦ θυμοῦ
seven angels, Go, and pour out the bowls of the anger
τοῦ Θεοῦ εἰς τὴν γῆν.
of God onto the earth.
2 Καὶ ἀπῆλθεν ὁ πρῶτος, καὶ ἐξέχεε τὴν φιάλην αὐτοῦ ἐπὶ
And went away the first, and poured out the bowl of him onto
τὴν γῆν· καὶ ἐγένετο ἕλκος κακὸν καὶ πονηρὸν εἰς τοὺς
the earth; and it became a sore bad and evil into the

came upon the men, the ones having the mark of the beast, and the ones worshiping its image.
[3]And the second angel poured out his bowl onto the sea. And it became blood, as of a dead one, and every soul of life died in the sea.
[4]And the third angel poured out his bowl onto the rivers, and onto the fountains of the waters; and it became blood. [5]And I heard the angel of the waters saying, Righteous is *the* Lord, the *One* who is, and who was, and who will be, because You judged these things, [6]since they poured out *the* blood of the saints and of *the* prophets; and You gave blood to them to drink, for they were deserving.
[7]And I heard another out of the altar saying, Yes, Lord God Almighty, Your judgments *are* true and righteous. [8]And the fourth angel poured out his bowl onto the sun. And it was given to him to burn men with fire. [9]And men were burned *with* great heat. And they blasphemed the name of God, the *One* having authority over these plagues—and they did not repent to give Him glory:

give Him glory. [10]
the fifth angel poured

[10]And the fifth angel poured out his bowl onto the throne of the beast. And its kingdom became darkened; and they gnawed their tongues from the pain. [11]And they blasphemed the God of Heaven, from their pains and from their sores. And they did not repent of their works.
[12]And the sixth angel poured out his bowl onto the great river Euphrates, and its water was dried up so that might be prepared the way of the kings from *the* rising of *the* sun. [13]And I saw three unclean spirits like frogs out of the mouth of the

ἀνθρώπους τοὺς ἔχοντας τὸ χάραγμα τοῦ θηρίου, καὶ τοὺς
men having the mark of the beast, and those
τῇ εἰκόνι αὐτοῦ προσκυνοῦντας.
the image of it worshiping.
3 Καὶ ὁ δεύτερος ἄγγελος ἐξέχεε τὴν φιάλην αὐτοῦ εἰς τὴν
And the second angel poured out the bowl of him onto the
θάλασσαν· καὶ ἐγένετο αἷμα ὡς νεκροῦ, καὶ πᾶσα ψυχὴ
sea; and it became blood, as of a dead one, and every soul
ζῶσα ἀπέθανεν ἐν τῇ θαλάσσῃ.
living died in the sea.
4 Καὶ ὁ τρίτος ἄγγελος ἐξέχεε τὴν φιάλην αὐτοῦ εἰς τοὺς
And the third angel poured out the bowl of him onto the
ποταμοὺς καὶ εἰς τὰς πηγὰς τῶν ὑδάτων· καὶ ἐγένετο αἷμα.
rivers and onto the fountains of the waters; and it became blood.
5 καὶ ἤκουσα τοῦ ἀγγέλου τῶν ὑδάτων λέγοντος, Δίκαιος,
And I heard the angel of the waters saying, Righteous
Κύριε, εἶ, ὁ ὢν καὶ ὁ ἦν καὶ ὁ ἐσόμενος, ὅτι ταῦτα ἔκρινας·
Lord You are: He being, who was and who will be, because these You judged;
6 ὅτι αἷμα ἁγίων καὶ προφητῶν ἐξέχεαν, καὶ αἷμα αὐτοῖς
since (the) blood of saints and of prophets they poured out; and blood to them
7 ἔδωκας πιεῖν· ἄξιοι γάρ εἰσι. καὶ ἤκουσα ἄλλου ἐκ τοῦ
You gave to drink; deserving for they are. And I heard another out of the
θυσιαστηρίου λέγοντος, Ναί, Κύριε ὁ Θεὸς ὁ παντοκράτωρ,
altar saying, Yes, Lord God Almighty,
ἀληθιναὶ καὶ δίκαιαι αἱ κρίσεις σου.
true and righteous the judgments of You.
8 Καὶ ὁ τέταρτος ἄγγελος ἐξέχεε τὴν φιάλην αὐτοῦ ἐπὶ τὸν
And the fourth angel poured out the bowl of him onto the
ἥλιον· καὶ ἐδόθη αὐτῷ καυματίσαι τοὺς ἀνθρώπους ἐν πυρί.
sun, and it was given to it to burn the men with fire.
9 καὶ ἐκαυματίσθησαν οἱ ἄνθρωποι καῦμα μέγα, καὶ ἐβλασφή-
And were burned men (with) heat great, and they blas-
μησαν τὸ ὄνομα τοῦ Θεοῦ τοῦ ἔχοντος ἐξουσίαν ἐπὶ τὰς
phemed the name of God, the (One) having authority over
πληγὰς ταύτας, καὶ οὐ μετενόησαν δοῦναι αὐτῷ δόξαν.
plagues these; and not they repented to give Him glory.
10 Καὶ ὁ πέμπτος ἄγγελος ἐξέχεε τὴν φιάλην αὐτοῦ ἐπὶ τὸν
And the fifth angel poured out the bowl of him onto the
θρόνον τοῦ θηρίου· καὶ ἐγένετο ἡ βασιλεία αὐτοῦ ἐσκοτω-
throne of the beast; and became the kingdom of it darkened,
μένη· καὶ ἐμασσῶντο τὰς γλώσσας αὐτῶν ἐκ τοῦ πόνου,
and they gnawed the tongues of them from the pain;
11 καὶ ἐβλασφήμησαν τὸν Θεὸν τοῦ οὐρανοῦ ἐκ τῶν πόνων
and they blasphemed the God of Heaven from the pains
αὐτῶν καὶ ἐκ τῶν ἑλκῶν αὐτῶν, καὶ οὐ μετενόησαν ἐκ τῶν
of them and from the sores of them; and not they repented of the
ἔργων αὐτῶν.
works of them.
12 Καὶ ὁ ἕκτος ἄγγελος ἐξέχεε τὴν φιάλην αὐτοῦ ἐπὶ τὸν
And the sixth angel poured out the bowl of him onto the
ποταμὸν τὸν μέγαν τὸν Εὐφράτην· καὶ ἐξηράνθη τὸ ὕδωρ
river great Euphrates, and was dried up the water
αὐτοῦ, ἵνα ἑτοιμασθῇ ἡ ὁδὸς τῶν βασιλέων τῶν ἀπὸ
of it, that might be prepared the way of the kings from
13 ἀνατολῶν ἡλίου. καὶ εἶδον ἐκ τοῦ στόματος τοῦ δράκοντος,
(the) rising of (the) sun. And I saw out of the mouth of the dragon,

dragon, and out of the mouth of the beast, and out of the mouth of the false prophet. [14]For they are spirits of demons doing signs, which go forth to the kings of the earth, even of the whole habitable world to gather them together to the war of the great day of God Almighty. [15]Behold, I am coming as a thief. Blessed *is* the *one* watching and keeping his garments, that he does not walk naked, and they see his shame. [16]And He gathered them in the place having been called in Hebrew, Armageddon.

[17]And the seventh angel poured out his bowl into the air, and a great voice came from the throne from the temple of Heaven, saying, It has happened! [18]And voices and thunders and lightnings occurred. And a great earthquake occurred, such as did not occur since man came into being on the earth, such a huge earthquake, so great! [19]And the great city came to be into three parts, and the cities of the nations fell. And Babylon the great was remembered before God, to give to her the cup of the wine of the anger of His wrath. [20]And every island fled away, and mountains were not found. [21]And a great hail, as the size of a talent, comes down out of the heaven upon men. And men blasphemed God from the plague of the hail, because the its plague is exceedingly great.

CHAPTER 17

[1]And one of the seven angels having the seven bowls came and spoke with me, saying to me, Come, I will show you the judgment of the great harlot sitting on the many waters, [2]with whom the kings of the earth committed fornication, and

καὶ ἐκ τοῦ στόματος τοῦ θηρίου, καὶ ἐκ τοῦ στόματος τοῦ
and out of the mouth of the beast, and out of the mouth of the
ψευδοπροφήτου, πνεύματα τρία ἀκάθαρτα ὅμοια βατρά-
false prophet, spirits three unclean like frogs;
14 χοις· εἰσὶ γὰρ πνεύματα δαιμόνων ποιοῦντα σημεῖα, ἃ
they are for spirits of demons doing signs, which
ἐκπορεύεται ἐπὶ τοὺς βασιλεῖς τῆς γῆς καὶ τῆς οἰκουμένης
go forth to the kings of the earth, even of the habitable world
ὅλης, συναγαγεῖν αὐτοὺς εἰς τὸν πόλεμον τῆς ἡμέρας ἐκείνης
whole, to assemble them to the war of day that
15 τῆς μεγάλης τοῦ Θεοῦ τοῦ παντοκράτορος. (Ἰδού,
the great (day) of God Almighty. Behold,
ἔρχομαι ὡς κλέπτης. μακάριος ὁ γρηγορῶν καὶ τηρῶν τὰ
I am coming as a thief, blessed the (one) watching and keeping the
ἱμάτια αὐτοῦ, ἵνα μὴ γυμνὸς περιπατῇ, καὶ βλέπωσι τὴν
garments of him, that not naked he may walk, and they may see the
16 ἀσχημοσύνην αὐτοῦ.) καὶ συνήγαγεν αὐτοὺς εἰς τὸν τόπον
shame of him. And he assembled them in the place
τὸν καλούμενον Ἑβραϊστὶ Ἀρμαγεδδών.
having been called in Hebrew, Armageddon.
17 Καὶ ὁ ἕβδομος ἄγγελος ἐξέχεε τὴν φιάλην αὐτοῦ εἰς τὸν
And the seventh angel poured out the bowl of him into the
ἀέρα· καὶ ἐξῆλθε φωνὴ μεγάλη ἀπὸ τοῦ ναοῦ τοῦ οὐρανοῦ,
air, and came a voice great from the temple of Heaven,
18 ἀπὸ τοῦ θρόνου, λέγουσα, Γέγονε. καὶ ἐγένοντο φωναὶ καὶ
from the throne, saying, It has happened. And occurred voices and
βρονταὶ καὶ ἀστραπαί, καὶ σεισμὸς ἐγένετο μέγας, οἷος οὐκ
thunders and lightnings, and an earthquake occurred great such as not
ἐγένετο ἀφ᾽ οὗ οἱ ἄνθρωποι ἐγένοντο ἐπὶ τῆς γῆς, τηλι-
occurred from when men came into being on the earth, such a
19 κοῦτος σεισμός, οὕτω μέγας. καὶ ἐγένετο ἡ πόλις ἡ μεγάλη
huge earthquake, so great. And came to be the city great
εἰς τρία μέρη, καὶ αἱ πόλεις τῶν ἐθνῶν ἔπεσον· καὶ Βαβυλὼν
into three parts, and the cities of the nations fell. And Babylon
ἡ μεγάλη ἐμνήσθη ἐνώπιον τοῦ Θεοῦ, δοῦναι αὐτῇ τὸ ποτή-
the great was remembered before God, to give to her the cup
20 ριον τοῦ οἴνου τοῦ θυμοῦ τῆς ὀργῆς αὐτοῦ. καὶ πᾶσα νῆσος
of the wine of the anger of the wrath of Him. And every island
21 ἔφυγε, καὶ ὄρη οὐχ εὑρέθησαν. καὶ χάλαζα μεγάλη, ὡς ταλαν-
fled, and mountains not were found. And a hail great, as talent-
τιαία, καταβαίνει ἐκ τοῦ οὐρανοῦ ἐπὶ τοὺς ἀνθρώπους· καὶ
sized, comes down out of the heaven on men, and
ἐβλασφήμησαν οἱ ἄνθρωποι τὸν Θεὸν ἐκ τῆς πληγῆς
blasphemed men God from the plague
τῆς χαλάζης· ὅτι μεγάλη ἐστὶν ἡ πληγὴ αὐτῆς σφόδρα.
of the hail, because great is the plague of it exceedingly

CHAPTER 17

1 Καὶ ἦλθεν εἷς ἐκ τῶν ἑπτὰ ἀγγέλων τῶν ἐχόντων τὰς
And came one of the seven angels having the
ἑπτὰ φιάλας, καὶ ἐλάλησε μετ᾽ ἐμοῦ, λέγων μοι, Δεῦρο, δείξω
seven bowls, and spoke with me, saying to me, Come, I will show
σοι τὸ κρίμα τῆς πόρνης τῆς μεγάλης, τῆς καθημένης ἐπὶ τῶν
you the judgment of the harlot great sitting on the
2 ὑδάτων τῶν πολλῶν· μεθ᾽ ἧς ἐπόρνευσαν οἱ βασιλεῖς τῆς
waters many, with whom committed fornication the kings of the

became drunk from the wine of her fornication, those inhabiting the earth. [3] And he carried away me into a desert, by *the* Spirit. And I saw a woman sitting on a scarlet beast, filled *with* names of blasphemy, having seven heads and ten horns. [4] And the woman was clothed *in* purple and scarlet, and being gilded with gold and precious stone and pearls, having a golden cup in her hand, filled *with* abominations and unclean things of her fornication. [5] And on her forehead *was* a name having been written: MYSTERY, BABYLON THE GREAT, THE MOTHER OF THE HARLOTS AND OF THE ABOMINATIONS OF THE EARTH.

[6] And I saw the woman being drunk from the blood of the saints, and from the blood of the witnesses of Jesus. And I marveled, seeing her *with* a great marveling. [7] And the angel said to me, Why did you marvel? I will tell you the mystery of the woman, and of the beast supporting her, the *one* having the seven heads and the ten horns. [8] The beast which you saw was, and is not, and is about to come up out of the abyss, and goes to perdition. And those dwelling on the earth will marvel, *the ones* whose names have not been written on the Book of Life from *the* foundation of *the* world, seeing the beast, that it was a thing, and is not, yet now is. [9] Here is the mind having wisdom: the seven heads are seven mountains, where the woman sits on them. [10] And *the* kings are seven. The five fell, and the one is, and the other has not yet come. And when he does come, he must remain a little. [11] And the beast which was, and is not, even he is *the* eighth, and is of the seven, and goes to perdition. [12] And the ten horns you saw are ten kings, who not yet have received a kingdom, but will receive authority as kings one hour

γῆς, καὶ ἐμεθύσθησαν ἐκ τοῦ οἴνου τῆς πορνείας αὐτῆς οἱ
earth, and became drunk from the wine of the fornication of her, those
3 κατοικοῦντες τὴν γῆν. καὶ ἀπήνεγκέ με εἰς ἔρημον ἐν
inhabiting the earth. And he carried away me into a desert by
Πνεύματι· καὶ εἶδον γυναῖκα καθημένην ἐπὶ θηρίον κόκκινον,
(the) Spirit. And I saw a woman sitting on beast scarlet,
γέμον ὀνομάτων βλασφημίας, ἔχον κεφαλὰς ἑπτὰ καὶ κέρατα
full of names of blasphemy, having heads seven and horns
4 δέκα. καὶ ἡ γυνὴ ἦν περιβεβλημένη πορφύρᾳ καὶ κοκκίνῳ,
ten. And the woman was clothed (in) purple and scarlet,
καὶ κεχρυσωμένη χρυσῷ καὶ λίθῳ τιμίῳ καὶ μαργαρίταις,
and being gilded with gold and stone precious and pearls,
ἔχουσα χρυσοῦν ποτήριον ἐν τῇ χειρὶ αὐτῆς, γέμον βδε-
having a golden cup in the hand of her, full of
5 λυγμάτων καὶ ἀκαθάρτητος πορνείας αὐτῆς, καὶ ἐπὶ τὸ
abominations and uncleanness of (the) fornication of her. And on the
μέτωπον αὐτῆς ὄνομα γεγραμμένον, Μυστήριον, Βαβυλὼν
forehead of her a name having been written: MYSTERY, BABYLON
ἡ μεγάλη, ἡ μήτηρ τῶν πορνῶν καὶ τῶν βδελυγμάτων τῆς
THE GREAT, The Mother of the Harlots and of the Abominations of the
6 γῆς. καὶ εἶδον τὴν γυναῖκα μεθύουσαν ἐκ τοῦ αἵματος τῶν
Earth. And I saw the woman being drunk from the blood of the
ἁγίων, καὶ ἐκ τοῦ αἵματος τῶν μαρτύρων Ἰησοῦ. καὶ
saints, and from the blood of the witnesses of Jesus. And
7 ἐθαύμασα, ἰδὼν αὐτήν, θαῦμα μέγα. καὶ εἶπέ μοι ὁ
I marveled seeing her (with) a marvel great. And said to me the
ἄγγελος, Διατί ἐθαύμασας; ἐγώ σοι ἐρῶ τὸ μυστήριον τῆς
angel, Why did you wonder? I you will tell the mystery of the
γυναικός, καὶ τοῦ θηρίου τοῦ βαστάζοντος αὐτήν, τοῦ
woman, and of the beast supporting her, the (one)
8 ἔχοντος τὰς ἑπτὰ κεφαλὰς καὶ τὰ δέκα κέρατα. τὸ θηρίον, ὃ
having the seven heads and the ten horns. The beast which
εἶδες, ἦν, καὶ οὐκ ἔστι, καὶ μέλλει ἀναβαίνειν ἐκ τῆς ἀβύσσου,
you saw was, and not is, and is about to come up out of the abyss,
καὶ εἰς ἀπώλειαν ὑπάγειν. καὶ θαυμάσονται οἱ κατοικοῦντες
and to perdition goes; and will marvel those dwelling
ἐπὶ τῆς γῆς, ὧν οὐ γέγραπται τὰ ὀνόματα ἐπὶ τὸ βιβλίον
on the earth, of whom not has been written the names on the Scroll
τῆς ζωῆς ἀπὸ καταβολῆς κόσμου, βλέποντες τὸ θηρίον ὅ, τι
of Life from (the) foundation of (the) world, seeing the beast, that a thing
9 ἦν, καὶ οὐκ ἔστι, καίπερ ἔστιν. ὧδε ὁ νοῦς ὁ ἔχων σοφίαν. αἱ
it was, and not is, although it is. Here (is) the mind having wisdom. The
ἑπτὰ κεφαλαὶ ὄρη εἰσὶν ἑπτά, ὅπου ἡ γυνὴ κάθηται ἐπ'
seven heads mountains are seven, where the woman sits on
10 αὐτῶν. καὶ βασιλεῖς ἑπτά εἰσιν· οἱ πέντε ἔπεσαν, καὶ ὁ εἷς
them; and kings seven are: the five fell, and the one
ἔστιν, ὁ ἄλλος οὔπω ἦλθε· καί, ὅταν ἔλθῃ, ὀλίγον αὐτὸν δεῖ
is, the other not yet came, and when he comes, a little he must
11 μεῖναι. καὶ τὸ θηρίον ὃ ἦν, καὶ οὐκ ἔστι, καὶ αὐτὸς ὄγδοός
remain. And the beast which was, and not is, even he eighth
12 ἐστι, καὶ ἐκ τῶν ἑπτά ἐστι, καὶ εἰς ἀπώλειαν ὑπάγει. καὶ τὰ
is, and of the seven it is, and to perdition goes. And the
δέκα κέρατα, ἃ εἶδες, δέκα βασιλεῖς εἰσίν, οἵτινες βασιλείαν
ten horns which you saw, ten kings are, who a kingdom
οὔπω ἔλαβον, ἀλλ' ἐξουσίαν ὡς βασιλεῖς μίαν ὥραν λαμβά-
not yet received, but authority as kings one hour receive

with the beast. 13 These have one mind, and their power and authority they shall give up to the beast.
14 These will make war with the Lamb, and the Lamb will overcome them, because He is Lord of lords and King of kings, and the ones with Him *are the* called and elect and faithful ones.

15 And he says to me, The waters which you saw, where the harlot sits, are peoples and crowds and nations and tongues. 16 And the ten horns which you saw on the beast, these will hate the harlot, and will make her desolated and naked. And *they* will eat her flesh, and will burn her down with fire.
17 For God gave into their hearts to do His mind, and to act in one mind, and to give their kingdom to the beast, until the words of God shall be fulfilled. 18 And the woman whom you saw is the great city, having a kingdom over the kings of the earth.

CHAPTER 18

1 And after these things I saw another angel coming down out of Heaven having great authority, and the earth was lighted up from his glory. 2 And he cried in a strong, great voice, saying, Babylon the great has fallen! *It* has fallen, and it has become a dwelling-place of demons, and a prison of every unclean spirit, and a prison of every unclean bird, even having been hated; 3 because of the wine of the anger of her fornication *which* all the nations have drunk, even the kings of the earth have committed fornication with her, and the merchants of the earth became rich from the power of her luxury.

4 And I heard another voice out of Heaven saying, My people, come out of her, that you may not share in her sins,

13 νουσι μετὰ τοῦ θηρίου. οὗτοι μίαν γνώμην ἔχουσι, και τὴν
with the beast. These one mind have, and the
δύναμιν καὶ τὴν ἐξουσίαν ἑαυτῶν τῷ θηρίῳ διαδιδώσουσιν.
power and the authority of themselves to the beast they shall give up.
14 οὗτοι μετὰ τοῦ ἀρνίου πολεμήσουσι, καὶ τὸ ἀρνίον νικήσει
These with the Lamb will make war, and the Lamb will overcome
αὐτούς, ὅτι Κύριος κυρίων ἐστὶ καὶ Βασιλεὺς βασιλέων, καὶ
them, because Lord of lords He is and King of kings, and
15 οἱ μετ᾽ αὐτοῦ, κλητοὶ καὶ ἐκλεκτοὶ καὶ πιστοί. καὶ λέγει μοι,
those with Him (the) called and elect and faithful ones. And he says to me,
Τὰ ὕδατα, ἃ εἶδες, οὗ ἡ πόρνη κάθηται, λαοὶ καὶ ὄχλοι εἰσί,
The waters which you saw, where the harlot sits, peoples and crowds are,
16 καὶ ἔθνη καὶ γλῶσσαι. καὶ τὰ δέκα κέρατα, ἃ εἶδες, ἐπὶ τὸ
even nations and tongues. And the ten horns which you saw on the
θηρίον, οὗτοι μισήσουσι τὴν πόρνην, καὶ ἠρημωμένην
beast, these will hate the harlot, and desolated
ποιήσουσιν αὐτὴν καὶ γυμνήν, καὶ τὰς σάρκας αὐτῆς
will make her and naked, and the flesh of her
17 φάγονται, καὶ αὐτὴν κατακαύσουσιν ἐν πυρί. ὁ γὰρ Θεὸς
they will eat, and her will burn down with fire. For God
ἔδωκεν εἰς τὰς καρδίας αὐτῶν ποιῆσαι τὴν γνώμην αὐτοῦ,
gave into the hearts of them to do the mind of Him,
καὶ ποιῆσαι μίαν γνώμην, καὶ δοῦναι τὴν βασιλείαν αὐτῶν
and to do one mind, and to give the kingdom of them
18 τῷ θηρίῳ, ἄχρι τελεσθῇ τὰ ῥήματα τοῦ Θεοῦ. καὶ ἡ γυνή,
to the beast, until shall be completed the words of God. And the woman
ἣν εἶδες, ἐστὶν ἡ πόλις ἡ μεγάλη, ἡ ἔχουσα βασιλείαν ἐπὶ
whom you saw is the city great, having a kingdom over
τῶν βασιλέων τῆς γῆς.
the kings of the earth.

CHAPTER 18

1 Καὶ μετὰ ταῦτα εἶδον ἄλλον ἄγγελον καταβαίνοντα ἐκ
And after these things I saw another angel coming down out of
τοῦ οὐρανοῦ, ἔχοντα ἐξουσίαν μεγάλην· καὶ ἡ γῆ ἐφωτίσθη
Heaven, having authority great, and the earth was lighted up
2 ἐκ τῆς δόξης αὐτοῦ. καὶ ἔκραξεν ἐν ἰσχύϊ, φωνῇ μεγάλῃ,
from the glory of him. And he cried in a strong, with a a voice great,
λέγων, Ἔπεσεν ἔπεσε Βαβυλὼν ἡ μεγάλη, καὶ εγένετο
saying, Fell, fell Babylon the great, and has become
κατοικητήριον δαιμόνων, καὶ φυλακὴ παντὸς πνεύματος
a dwelling-place of demons, and a prison of every spirit
ἀκαθάρτου, καὶ φυλακὴ παντὸς ὀρνέου ἀκαθάρτου καὶ
unclean, and a prison of every bird unclean and
3 μεμισημένου. ὅτι ἐκ τοῦ οἴνου τοῦ θυμοῦ τῆς πορνείας αὐτῆς
being hated, because of the wine of the anger of the fornication of her
πέπωκε πάντα τὰ ἔθνη, καὶ οἱ βασιλεῖς τῆς γῆς μετ᾽ αὐτῆς
have drunk all the nations, and the kings of the earth with her
ἐπόρνευσαν, καὶ οἱ ἔμποροι τῆς γῆς ἐκ τῆς δυνάμεως τοῦ
committed fornication, and the merchants of the earth from the power of the
στρήνους αὐτῆς ἐπλούτησαν.
luxury of her became rich.
4 Καὶ ἤκουσα ἄλλην φωνὴν ἐκ τοῦ οὐρανοῦ, λεγουσαν,
And I heard another voice out of Heaven, saying,
Ἐξέλθετε ἐξ αὐτῆς ὁ λαός μου, ἵνα μὴ συγκοινωνήσητε ταῖς
Come out of her, people of Me, that not you share in the

and that you may not receive of her plagues; 5 because her sins joined together, *even* up to Heaven, and God remembered her unjust deeds. 6 Give back to her as also she gave back to you, and double to her double, according to her works. In the cup which she mixed, mix to her double. 7 By what things she glorified herself, and luxuriated, by so much give back to her torment and mourning. Because she says in her heart, I sit *as* a queen, and I am not a widow; and I do not see mourning at all. 8 Because of this, in one day her plagues shall come: death, and mourning, and famine; and she will be consumed with fire, because *the* Lord God judging her *is* strong. 9 And the kings of the earth will weep for her, and will wail over her, those having fornicated and having luxuriated with her, when they see the smoke of her burning, 10 standing from afar because of the fear of her torment, saying, Woe! Woe to the great city, Babylon the strong city! For in one hour your judgment came.

11 And the merchants of the earth weep and mourn over her, because no one buys their cargo any more, 12 cargo of gold, and silver, and of precious stone, and of pearls, and of fine linen, and of purple, and of silk, and of scarlet, and all thyine wood, and every ivory vessel, and every vessel of very precious wood, and of bronze, and of iron, and of marble, 13 and cinnamon, and incenses, and ointment, and frankincense, and wine, and oil, and fine meal, and wheat, and beasts, and sheep, and horses, and chariots, and of bodies and souls of men. 14 And the ripe fruits of the lust of your soul went away from you, and all the fat things, and the bright things

ἁμαρτίαις αὐτῆς, καὶ ἵνα μὴ λάβητε ἐκ τῶν πληγῶν αὐτῆς·
sins of her, and that not you receive of the plagues of her;
5 ὅτι ἐκολλήθησαν αὐτῆς αἱ ἁμαρτίαι ἄχρι τοῦ οὐρανοῦ, καὶ
because joined together of her the sins up to Heaven, and
6 ἐμνημόνευσεν ὁ Θεὸς τὰ ἀδικήματα αὐτῆς. ἀπόδοτε αὐτῇ
remembered God the unjust deeds of her. Return to her
ὡς καὶ αὐτὴ ἀπέδωκεν ὑμῖν, καὶ διπλώσατε αὐτῇ διπλᾶ
as also she returned to you, and double to her double
κατὰ τὰ ἔργα αὐτῆς· ἐν τῷ ποτηρίῳ ᾧ ἐκέρασε κεράσατε
according to the works of her; in the cup in which she mixed, mix
7 αὐτῇ διπλοῦν. ὅσα ἐδόξασεν ἑαυτὴν καὶ ἐστρηνίασε,
to her double By what things she glorified herself and luxuriated,
τοσοῦτον δότε αὐτῇ βασανισμὸν καὶ πένθος· ὅτι ἐν τῇ
by so much give to her torment and mourning. Because in the
καρδίᾳ αὐτῆς λέγει, Κάθημαι βασίλισσα, καὶ χήρα οὐκ εἰμί,
heart of her she says, I sit a queen, and a widow not I am,
8 καὶ πένθος οὐ μὴ ἴδω. διὰ τοῦτο ἐν μιᾷ ἡμέρᾳ ἥξουσιν αἱ
and mourning not at all I see. Therefore in one day shall come the
πληγαὶ αὐτῆς, θάνατος καὶ πένθος καὶ λιμός, καὶ ἐν πυρὶ
plagues of her, death and mourning and famine, and with fire
κατακαυθήσεται, ὅτι ἰσχυρὸς Κύριος ὁ Θεὸς ὁ κρίνων αὐτήν.
she will be consumed, because strong (is the) Lord God judging her.
9 καὶ κλαύσονται αὐτήν, καὶ κόψονται ἐπ' αὐτῇ οἱ βασιλεῖς τῆς
And will weep for her, and will wail over her the kings of the
γῆς οἱ μετ' αὐτῆς πορνεύσαντες καὶ στρηνιάσαντες, ὅταν
earth, those with her having fornicated and having luxuriated, when
10 βλέπωσι τὸν καπνὸν τῆς πυρώσεως αὐτῆς, ἀπὸ μακρόθεν
they see the smoke of the burning of her, from afar
ἑστηκότες διὰ τὸν φόβον τοῦ βασανισμοῦ αὐτῆς, λέγοντες,
standing because of the fear of the torment of her, saying,
Οὐαί, οὐαί, ἡ πόλις ἡ μεγάλη Βαβυλὼν ἡ πόλις ἡ ἰσχυρά,
Woe! Woe, to the city great, Babylon, the city strong,
11 ὅτι ἐν μιᾷ ὥρᾳ ἦλθεν ἡ κρίσις σου. καὶ οἱ ἔμποροι τῆς γῆς
for in one hour came the judgment of you. And the merchants of the earth
κλαίουσι καὶ πενθοῦσιν ἐπ' αὐτῇ, ὅτι τὸν γόμον αὐτῶν
weep and mourn over her, because the cargo of them
12 οὐδεὶς ἀγοράζει οὐκέτι· γόμον χρυσοῦ, καὶ ἀργύρου, καὶ
no one buys no more, cargo of gold, and of silver, and
λίθου τιμίου, καὶ μαργαρίτου, καὶ βύσσου, καὶ πορφύρας,
of stone precious, and of pearls, and of fine linen, and of purple,
καὶ σηρικοῦ, καὶ κοκκίνου· καὶ πᾶν ξύλον θύϊνον, καὶ πᾶν
and of silk, and of scarlet, and all wood sandarac, and every
σκεῦος ἐλεφάντινον, καὶ πᾶν σκεῦος ἐκ ξύλου τιμιωτάτου,
vessel ivory, and every vessel of wood very precious,
13 καὶ χαλκοῦ, καὶ σιδήρου, καὶ μαρμάρου· καὶ κινάμωμον, καὶ
and of bronze, and of iron, and of marble, and cinnamon, and
θυμιάματα, καὶ μύρον, καὶ λίβανον, καὶ οἶνον, καὶ ἔλαιον,
incenses, and ointment, and frankincense, and wine, and oil,
καὶ σεμίδαλιν, καὶ σῖτον, καὶ κτήνη, καὶ πρόβατα· καὶ ἵππων,
and fine meal, and wheat, and beasts, and sheep, and horses,
14 καὶ ῥεδῶν, καὶ σωμάτων· καὶ ψυχὰς ἀνθρώπων. καὶ ἡ
and chariots, and of bodies, and souls of men. And the
ὀπώρα τῆς ἐπιθυμίας τῆς ψυχῆς σου ἀπῆλθεν ἀπὸ σοῦ, καὶ
ripe fruits of the lust of the soul of you went away from you, and
πάντα τὰ λιπαρὰ καὶ τὰ λαμπρὰ ἀπῆλθεν ἀπὸ σοῦ, καὶ
all the fat things, and the bright things went away from you, and

went away from you, and they will find them no more, not at all. [15]The merchants of these, the ones being enriched from her, will stand from afar because of the fear of her torment, weeping and mourning; [16]and saying, Woe! Woe *to* the great city having been clothed in linen and purple and scarlet, and having been gilded with gold and precious stone, and pearls! [17]For in one hour such great wealth was desolated. And every ship-pilot and all company on the ships, and the sailors, and as many as work the sea, stood from afar, [18]and cried out, seeing the smoke of her burning, saying, What *is* the great city? [19]And they threw dust on their heads, and cried out, weeping and mourning, saying, Woe! Woe *to* the great city, by which all those having ships in the sea were rich, from her costliness, because in one hour she was ruined. [20]Rejoice over her, Heaven, and the holy apostles, and the prophets, because God judged your judgment on her.

[21]And one strong angel lifted a stone like a great millstone, and threw *it* into the sea, saying, This way, on an impulse, Babylon the great city will be thrown down, and *it* will never more be found. [22]And the sound of harpers, and of musicians, and flutists, and of trumpeters will never more be heard in you. And the sound of a mill will never more be heard in you. [23]And the light of a lamp *will* never more shine in you. And *the* voice of the bridegroom and bride will never more be heard in you. For your merchants were the great ones of the earth, for by your sorcery all the nations were misled. [24]And in her was found *the* blood of prophets, and of saints, and of all the ones having been slain on the earth.

15 οὐκέτι οὐ μὴ εὑρήσῃς αὐτά. οἱ ἔμποροι τούτων, οἱ πλουτή-
no more, not at all, they will find them. The merchants of these, those being
σαντες ἀπ' αὐτῆς, ἀπὸ μακρόθεν στήσονται διὰ τὸν φόβον
enriched from her, from afar will stand because of the fear
16 τοῦ βασανισμοῦ αὐτῆς, κλαίοντες καὶ πενθοῦντες, καὶ
of the torment of her, weeping and mourning and
λέγοντες, Οὐαί, οὐαί, ἡ πόλις ἡ μεγάλη, ἡ περιβεβλημένη
saying, Woe, woe, the city great, having been clothed in
βύσσινον καὶ πορφυροῦν καὶ κόκκινον, καὶ κεχρυσωμένη ἐν
linen and purple and scarlet, and having been gilded with
17 χρυσῷ καὶ λίθῳ τιμίῳ καὶ μαργαρίταις· ὅτι μιᾷ ὥρᾳ ἠρη-
gold and stone precious, and pearls; because in one hour was
μώθη ὁ τοσοῦτος πλοῦτος. καὶ πᾶς κυβερνήτης, καὶ πᾶς ἐπὶ
desolated such great wealth. And every helmsman and all on
τῶν πλοίων ὁ ὅμιλος, καὶ ναῦται, καὶ ὅσοι τὴν θάλασσαν
the ships the company, and sailors, and as many as the sea
18 ἐργάζονται, ἀπὸ μακρόθεν ἔστησαν, καὶ ἔκραζον, ὁρῶντες
work, from afar stood, and cried out seeing
τὸν καπνὸν τῆς πυρώσεως αὐτῆς, λέγοντες, Τίς ὁμοία τῇ
the smoke of the burning of her, saying, What (is) like the
19 πόλει τῇ μεγάλῃ; καὶ ἔβαλον χοῦν ἐπὶ τὰς κεφαλὰς αὐτῶν,
city great? And they threw dust on the heads of them,
καὶ ἔκραζον κλαίοντες καὶ πενθοῦντες, λέγοντες, Οὐαί, οὐαί,
and cried out weeping and mourning, saying, Woe! Woe,
ἡ πόλις ἡ μεγάλη, ἐν ᾗ ἐπλούτησαν πάντες οἱ ἔχοντες πλοῖα
(to) the city great, by which were rich all those having ships
ἐν τῇ θαλάσσῃ ἐκ τῆς τιμιότητος αὐτῆς, ὅτι μιᾷ ὥρᾳ ἠρη-
in the sea, from the costliness of her, because in one hour was
20 μώθη. εὐφραίνου ἐπ' αὐτήν, οὐρανέ, καὶ οἱ ἅγιοι ἀπόστολοι,
she ruined. Be glad over her, Heaven, and the holy apostles
καὶ οἱ προφῆται, ὅτι ἔκρινεν ὁ Θεὸς τὸ κρίμα ὑμῶν ἐξ αὐτῆς.
and the prophets, because judged God the judgment of you upon her.
21 Καὶ ἦρεν εἷς ἄγγελος ἰσχυρὸς λίθον ὡς μύλον μέγαν, καὶ
And lifted one angel strong a stone as a millstone great, and
ἔβαλεν εἰς τὴν θάλασσαν, λέγων, Οὕτως ὁρμήματι βληθή-
threw (it) into the sea, saying, Thus on an impulse will be
22 σεται Βαβυλὼν ἡ μεγάλη πόλις, καὶ οὐ μὴ εὑρεθῇ ἔτι. καὶ
thrown Babylon the great city, and not at all will be found yet. An
φωνὴ κιθαρῳδῶν καὶ μουσικῶν καὶ αὐλητῶν καὶ σαλπιστῶν
sound of harpers, and of musicians, and flutists, and of trumpeters,
οὐ μὴ ἀκουσθῇ ἐν σοὶ ἔτι. καὶ πᾶς τεχνίτης πάσης τέχνης
not at all will be heard in you longer, and every craftsman of every craft
οὐ μὴ εὑρεθῇ ἐν σοὶ ἔτι, καὶ φωνὴ μύλου οὐ μὴ ἀκουσθῇ ἐν
not at all will be found in you longer; and sound of a mill not at all be heard in
23 σοὶ ἔτι, καὶ φῶς λύχνου οὐ μὴ φανῇ ἐν σοὶ ἔτι, καὶ φωνὴ
you longer; and light of a lamp not at all (will) shine in you still; and voice
νυμφίου καὶ νύμφης οὐ μὴ ἀκουσθῇ ἐν σοὶ ἔτι· ὅτι οἱ ἔμποροί
of groom and bride not at all will be heard in you still. For the merchants
σου ἦσαν οἱ μεγιστᾶνες τῆς γῆς· ὅτι ἐν τῇ φαρμακείᾳ σου
of you were the great ones of the earth, for by the sorcery of you
24 ἐπλανήθησαν πάντα τὰ ἔθνη. καὶ ἐν αὐτῇ αιμα προφητῶν
were misled all the nations, and in her (the) blood of prophets
καὶ ἁγίων εὑρέθη, καὶ πάντων τῶν ἐσφαγμένων ἐπὶ τῆς γῆς.
and saints was found, and of all those having been slain on the earth.

CHAPTER 19

1 Καὶ μετὰ ταῦτα ἤκουσα φωνὴν ὄχλου πολλοῦ μεγάλην
And after these things I heard a voice of a crowd much great
ἐν τῷ οὐρανῷ, λέγοντος, Ἀλληλούϊα· ἡ σωτηρία καὶ ἡ
in Heaven, saying, Hallelujah! The salvation and the
2 δόξα καὶ ἡ τιμὴ καὶ ἡ δύναμις Κυρίῳ τῷ Θεῷ ἡμῶν· ὅτι
glory and the honor and the power of(the) Lord God of us, because
ἀληθιναὶ καὶ δίκαιαι αἱ κρίσεις αὐτοῦ· ὅτι ἔκρινε τὴν πόρνην
true and righteous the judgments of Him, for He judged the harlot
τὴν μεγάλην, ἥτις ἔφθειρε τὴν γῆν ἐν τῇ πορνείᾳ αὐτῆς,
great, who defiled the earth with the fornication of her,
καὶ ἐξεδίκησε τὸ αἷμα τῶν δούλων αὐτοῦ ἐκ τῆς χειρὸς αὐτῆς.
and He avenged the blood of the slaves of Him out of the hand of her.
3 καὶ δεύτερον εἴρηκαν, Ἀλληλούϊα· καὶ ὁ καπνὸς αὐτῆς
And secondly, they said, Hallelujah! And the smoke of her
4 ἀναβαίνει εἰς τοὺς αἰῶνας τῶν αἰώνων. καὶ ἔπεσαν οἱ
goes up to the ages of the ages. And fell down the
πρεσβύτεροι οἱ εἴκοσι καὶ τέσσαρες, καὶ τὰ τέσσαρα ζῶα,
elders twenty and four, and the four living creatures,
καὶ προσεκύνησαν τῷ Θεῷ τῷ καθημένῳ ἐπὶ τοῦ θρόνου,
and worshiped God sitting on the throne
5 λέγοντες, Ἀμήν· Ἀλληλούϊα. καὶ φωνὴ ἐκ τοῦ θρόνου
saying, Amen! Hallelujah! And a voice from the throne
ἐξῆλθε, λέγουσα, Αἰνεῖτε τὸν Θεὸν ἡμῶν πάντες οἱ δοῦλοι
came out, saying, Praise the God of us, all the slaves
αὐτοῦ, καὶ οἱ φοβούμενοι αὐτόν, καὶ οἱ μικροὶ καὶ οἱ μεγάλοι.
of Him, and those fearing Him, even the small and the great.
6 καὶ ἤκουσα ὡς φωνὴν ὄχλου πολλοῦ, καὶ ὡς φωνὴν ὑδάτων
And I heard as a sound of a crowd much, and as a sound of waters
πολλῶν, καὶ ὡς φωνὴν βροντῶν ἰσχυρῶν, λέγοντας,
many, and as a sound thunders of strong, saying,
Ἀλληλούϊα· ὅτι ἐβασίλευσε Κύριος ὁ Θεὸς ὁ παντοκράτωρ.
Hallelujah, because reigned (the) Lord God Almighty.
7 χαίρωμεν καὶ ἀγαλλιώμεθα, καὶ δῶμεν τὴν δόξαν αὐτῷ·
Let us rejoice and let us exult, and we will give the glory to Him,
ὅτι ἦλθεν ὁ γάμος τοῦ ἀρνίου, καὶ ἡ γυνὴ αὐτοῦ ἡτοίμασεν
because came the marriage of the Lamb, and the wife of Him prepared
8 ἑαυτήν. καὶ ἐδόθη αὐτῇ ἵνα περιβάληται βύσσινον καθαρὸν
herself, and it was given to her that she be clothed (with) fine linen clean
καὶ λαμπρόν· τὸ γὰρ βύσσινον τὰ δικαιώματά ἐστι τῶν
and bright; the for fine linen the righteousnesses is of the
9 ἁγίων. καὶ λέγει μοι, Γράψον, Μακάριοι οἱ εἰς τὸ δεῖπνον
saints. And he says to me, Write: Blessed those to the supper
τοῦ γάμου τοῦ ἀρνίου κεκλημένοι. καὶ λέγει μοι, Οὗτοι οἱ
of the marriage of the Lamb having been called. And he says to me, These
10 λόγοι ἀληθινοί εἰσι τοῦ Θεοῦ. καὶ ἔπεσον ἔμπροσθεν τῶν
words true are of God, And I fell before the
ποδῶν αὐτοῦ προσκυνῆσαι αὐτῷ· καὶ λέγει μοι, Ὅρα μή·
feet of him to worship him; and he says to me, See, do not.
σύνδουλός σου εἰμὶ καὶ τῶν ἀδελφῶν σου τῶν ἐχόντων τὴν
A fellow-slave of you I am, and of the brothers of you, having the
μαρτυρίαν τοῦ Ἰησοῦ· τῷ Θεῷ προσκύνησον· ἡ γὰρ
witness of Jesus; To God, give worship. the For
μαρτυρία τοῦ Ἰησοῦ ἐστὶ τὸ πνεῦμα τῆς προφητείας.
witness of Jesus is the spirit of prophecy.

CHAPTER 19

1 And after these things, I heard a great voice of a numerous crowd in Heaven, saying, Hallelujah! The salvation and the glory and the honor and the power of *the* Lord our God! 2 For true and righteous *are* His judgments, because He judged the great harlot who defiled the earth with her forni-cation. And He avenged the blood of His slaves out of her hand. 3 And secondly they said, Hallelujah! Also her smoke goes up forever *and* ever. 4 And the twenty-four elders, and the four living creatures fell down and worshiped God sitting on the throne, saying, Amen! Hallelujah! 5 And a voice came out from the throne, saying, Praise our God, all His slaves, and the ones fearing Him, the small and the great.

6 And I heard as a sound of a numerous crowd, and as a sound of many waters, and as a sound of strong thunders, saying, Hallelujah! Because *the* Lord God Almighty reigned. 7 Let us rejoice and let us exult, and we will give glory to Him, because the marriage of the Lamb came, and His wife prepared herself. 8 And it was given to her that she be clothed *in* fine linen, pure and bright; for the fine linen is the righteousnesses of the saints.

9 And he says to me, Write: Blessed *are* the ones having been called to the supper of the marriage of the Lamb. And he says to me, These words of God are true. 10 And I fell before his feet to worship him, but he said to me, See, do not *do it*! I am your fellow-slave, and of your brothers, having the testimony of Jesus. Worship God. For the testimony of Jesus is the spirit of prophecy.

11 And I saw Heaven being opened. And, behold! A white horse, and He sitting on it having been called Faithful and True. And He judges and makes war in righteousness. 12 And His eyes *were* as a flame of fire, and on His head many diadems having a name that had been written, which no one knows except Himself; 13 and having been clothed *in* a garment which had been dipped in blood. And His name is called The Word of God.

14 And the armies in Heaven followed Him on white horses, being dressed *in* fine linen, white and pure. 15 And out of His mouth goes forth a sharp sword, that with it He might smite the nations. And He will shepherd them with an iron rod. And He treads the winepress of the wine of the anger and of the wrath of God Almighty. 16 And He has on His garment and on His thigh a name having been written: KING OF KINGS AND LORD OF LORDS.

11 Καὶ εἶδον τὸν οὐρανὸν ἀνεῳγμένον, καὶ ἰδού, ἵππος
And I saw Heaven having been opened, and behold, a horse
λευκός, καὶ ὁ καθήμενος ἐπ' αὐτόν, καλούμενος πιστὸς καὶ
white, and the (One) sitting on it being called faithful and
12 ἀληθινός, καὶ ἐν δικαιοσύνῃ κρίνει καὶ πολεμεῖ. οἱ δὲ ὀφθαλμοὶ
true. And in righteousness He judges and wars. the And eyes
αὐτοῦ ὡς φλὸξ πυρός, καὶ ἐπὶ τὴν κεφαλὴν αὐτοῦ διαδήματα
of Him as a flame of fire, and on the head of Him diadems
πολλά· ἔχων ὄνομα γεγραμμένον ὃ οὐδε οἶδεν εἰ μὴ αὐτός,
many, having a name having been written which no one knows except Him;
13 καὶ περιβεβλημένος ἱμάτιον βεβαμμένον αἵματι· καὶ καλεῖται
and being clothed (in) a garment having been dipped in blood, and is called
14 τὸ ὄνομα αὐτοῦ, Ὁ λόγος τοῦ Θεοῦ. καὶ τὰ στρατεύματα
the name of Him, The Word of God. And the armies
ἐν τῷ οὐρανῷ ἠκολούθει αὐτῷ ἐφ' ἵπποις λευκοῖς, ἐνδεδυ-
in Heaven followed Him on horses white, having been
15 μένοι βύσσινον λευκὸν καὶ καθαρόν. καὶ ἐκ τοῦ στόματος
dressed (in) fine linen, white and clean. And out of the mouth
αὐτοῦ ἐκπορεύεται ῥομφαία ὀξεῖα, ἵνα ἐν αὐτῇ πατάσσῃ τὰ
of Him goes forth a sword sharp, that with it He may smite the
ἔθνη· καὶ αὐτὸς ποιμανεῖ αὐτοὺς ἐν ῥάβδῳ σιδηρᾷ· καὶ αὐτὸς
nations; and He will shepherd them with a rod iron. And He
πατεῖ τὴν ληνὸν τοῦ οἴνου τοῦ θυμοῦ καὶ τῆς ὀργῆς τοῦ
treads the press of the wine of the anger and of the wrath
16 Θεοῦ τοῦ παντοκράτορος. καὶ ἔχει ἐπὶ τὸ ἱμάτιον καὶ ἐπὶ τὸν
of God Almighty. And He has on the garment and on the
μηρὸν αὐτοῦ ὄνομα γεγραμμένον, Βασιλεὺς βασιλέων καὶ
thigh of Him a name having been written: KING OF KINGS, AN
Κύριος κυρίων.
LORD OF LORDS.

17 And I saw one angel standing in the sun. And he cried with a great voice, saying to all the birds flying in mid-heaven, Come and gather together to the supper of the great God, 18 that you may eat *the* flesh of kings, and *the* flesh of commanders, and *the* flesh of strong ones, and of the *ones* sitting on them, and *the* flesh of all, both freemean and slaves, even of *the* small and great.

19 And I saw the beast and the kings of the earth, and their armies being assembled to make war with the *One* sitting on the horse, and with His army. 20 And the beast was seized, and with this *one* the false prophet doing signs before it, by which he deceived those having received the mark of the beast, and those

17 Καὶ εἶδον ἕνα ἄγγελον ἑστῶτα ἐν τῷ ἡλίῳ· καὶ ἔκραξε
And I saw one angel standing in the sun and he cried
φωνῇ μεγάλῃ, λέγων πᾶσι τοῖς ὀρνέοις τοῖς πετωμένοις ἐν
with a voice great, saying to all the birds flying in
μεσουρανήματι, Δεῦτε καὶ συνάγεσθε εἰς τὸ δεῖπνον τοῦ
mid-heaven, Come and gather together to the supper of the
18 μεγάλου Θεοῦ, ἵνα φάγητε σάρκας βασιλέων, καὶ σάρκας
great God, that you may eat (the) flesh of kings, and (the) flesh
χιλιάρχων, καὶ σάρκας ἰσχυρῶν, καὶ σάρκας ἵππων καὶ τῶν
of chiliarchs, and (the) flesh of strong ones, and (the) flesh of horses, and of the
καθημένων ἐπ' αὐτῶν, καὶ σάρκας πάντων, ἐλευθέρων τε καὶ
sitting on them, and (the) flesh of all, freemen both and
δούλων, καὶ μικρῶν καὶ μεγάλων.
slaves, even of (the) small and great.
19 Καὶ εἶδον τὸ θηρίον, καὶ τοὺς βασιλεῖς τῆς γῆς, καὶ τὰ
And I saw the beast, and the kings of the earth, and the
στρατεύματα αὐτῶν συνηγμένα ποιῆσαι πόλεμον μετὰ τοῦ
armies of them being assembled to make war with the (One)
καθημένου ἐπὶ τοῦ ἵππου, καὶ μετὰ τοῦ στρατεύματος αὐτοῦ
sitting on the horse, and with the army of Him.
20 καὶ ἐπιάσθη τὸ θηρίον, καὶ μετὰ τούτου ὁ ψευδοπροφήτης
And was seized the beast and with this (one) the false prophet
ὁ ποιήσας τὰ σημεῖα ἐνώπιον αὐτοῦ, ἐν οἷς ἐπλάνησε τοὺς
doing the signs before it, by which he misled those
λαβόντας τὸ χάραγμα τοῦ θηρίου, καὶ τοὺς προσκυνοῦντας
having received the mark of the beast, and those worshiping

worshiping its image. The two were thrown alive into the Lake of Fire burning with brimstone. 21 And the rest were killed with the sword of the *One* sitting on the horse, *it* having gone out of His mouth. And all the birds were filled from their flesh.

CHAPTER 20

1 And I saw an angel coming down out of Heaven, having the key of the abyss, and a great chain on his hand. 2 And he laid hold of the dragon, the old serpent who is *the* Devil, and Satan, and bound him a thousand years, 3 and threw him into the abyss, and shut him up, and sealed over him, that he should not still mislead the nations, until the thousand years are fulfilled. And after these things, he must be set loose a little time.

4 And I saw thrones, and they sat on them. And judgment was given to them, and the souls of the *ones* having been beheaded because of the witness of Jesus, and because of the word of God, and who had not worshiped the beast nor its image, and had not received the mark on their forehead and on their hand. And they lived and reigned with Christ a thousand years. 5 But the rest of the dead did not live again until the thousand years were ended. This *is* the first resurrection. 6 Blessed and holy *is* the *one* having part in the first resurrection. The second death has no authority over these, but they will be priests of God and of Christ, and will reign with Him a thousand years.

7 And whenever the thousand years are ended, Satan will be set loose out of his prison, 8 and he will go to mislead the nations in the

τῇ εἰκόνι αὐτοῦ ζῶντες ἐβλήθησαν οἱ δύο εἰς τὴν λίμνην τοῦ
the image of it; living were thrown the two into the Lake
21 πυρὸς τὴν καιομένην ἐν τῷ θείῳ· καὶ οἱ λοιποὶ ἀπεκτάνθησαν
of Fire burning with brimstone. And the rest were killed
ἐν τῇ ῥομφαίᾳ τοῦ καθημένου ἐπὶ τοῦ ἵππου, τῇ ἐκπορευο-
with the sword of the (One) sitting on the horse, having gone
μένῃ ἐκ τοῦ στόματος αὐτοῦ· καὶ πάντα τὰ ὄρνεα ἐχορτάσθη-
forth out of the mouth of Him, and all the birds were filled
σαν ἐκ τῶν σαρκῶν αὐτῶν.
from the flesh of them.

CHAPTER 20

1 Καὶ εἶδον ἄγγελον καταβαίνοντα ἐκ τοῦ οὐρανοῦ,
And I saw an angel coming down out of Heaven,
ἔχοντα τὴν κλεῖδα τῆς ἀβύσσου, καὶ ἅλυσιν μεγάλην ἐπὶ
having the key of the abyss, and a chain great on
2 τὴν χεῖρα αὐτοῦ. καὶ ἐκράτησε τὸν δράκοντα, τὸν ὄφιν τὸν
the hand of him. And he laid hold of the dragon, the serpent
ἀρχαῖον, ὅς ἐστι διάβολος καὶ Σατανᾶς, καὶ ἔδησεν αὐτὸν
old, who is Devil and Satan, and bound him
3 χίλια ἔτη, καὶ ἔβαλεν αὐτὸν εἰς τὴν ἄβυσσον, καὶ ἔκλεισεν
a thousand years, and threw him into the abyss, and shut up
αὐτόν, καὶ ἐσφράγισεν ἐπάνω αὐτοῦ, ἵνα μὴ πλανήσῃ τὰ
him, and sealed over him, that not he should mislead the
ἔθνη ἔτι, ἄχρι τελεσθῇ τὰ χίλια ἔτη· καὶ μετὰ ταῦτα δεῖ
nations still, until are ended the thousand years; and after these things must
αὐτὸν λυθῆναι μικρὸν χρόνον.
he be loosed a little time.

4 Καὶ εἶδον θρόνους, καὶ ἐκάθισαν ἐπ' αὐτούς, καὶ κρίμα
And I saw thrones, and they sat on them, and judgment
ἐδόθη αὐτοῖς· και τὰς ψυχὰς τῶν πεπελεκισμένων διὰ τὴν
was given to them, and the souls of those having been beheaded due to the
μαρτυρίαν Ἰησοῦ, καὶ διὰ τὸν λόγον τοῦ Θεοῦ, καὶ οἵτινες
witness of Jesus, and because of the word of God, and who
ού προσεκύνησαν τῷ θηρίῳ, οὔτε τὴν εἰκόνα αὐτοῦ, καὶ
not had worshiped the beast nor the image of it, and
οὐκ ἔλαβον τὸ χάραγμα ἐπὶ τὸ μέτωπον αὐτῶν, καὶ ἐπὶ
not received the mark on the forehead of them, and on
τὴν χεῖρα αὐτῶν· καὶ ἔζησαν, καὶ ἐβασίλευσαν μετὰ
the hand of them; and they lived and reigned with
5 Χριστοῦ χίλια ἔτη. οἱ δὲ λοιποὶ τῶν νεκρῶν οὐκ ἀνέζησαν
Christ a thousand years. the But rest of the dead not did live again
ἕως τελεσθῇ τὰ χίλια ἔτη. αὕτη ἡ ἀνάστασις ἡ πρώτη.
until, were ended the thousand years. This (is) the resurrection first.
6 μακάριος καὶ ἅγιος ὁ ἔχων μέρος ἐν τῇ ἀναστάσει τῇ πρώτῃ·
Blessed and holy the (one) having part in the resurrection first;
ἐπὶ τούτων ὁ θάνατος ὁ δεύτερος οὐκ ἔχει ἐξουσίαν, ἀλλ'
over these the death second not has authority, but
ἔσονται ἱερεῖς τοῦ Θεοῦ καὶ τοῦ Χριστοῦ, καὶ βασιλεύσουσι
they will be priests of God and of Christ, and will reign
μετ' αὐτοῦ χίλια ἔτη.
with Him a thousand years.
7 Καὶ ὅταν τελεσθῇ τὰ χίλια ἔτη, λυθήσεται ὁ Σατανᾶς ἐκ
And whenever are ended the thousand years will be loosed Satan out of
8 τῆς φυλακῆς αὐτοῦ, καὶ ἐξελεύσεται πλανῆσαι τὰ ἔθνη τὰ
the prison of him, and he will go out to mislead the nations

four corners of the earth—Gog and Magog—to assemble them in war, whose number *is* as the sand of the sea. [9]And they went up over the breadth of the land and encircled the camp of the saints, and the beloved city. And fire from God came down out of Heaven and burned them down. [10]And the Devil misleading them was thrown into the Lake of Fire and Brimstone, where the beast and the false prophet *were*. And they were tormented day and night forever *and* ever.

[11]And I saw a great white throne, and the *One* sitting on it, from whose face the earth and the heaven fled; and a place was not found for them. [12]And I saw the dead, the small and the great, standing before God. And books were opened. And another book was opened, which is the *Book* of Life. And the dead were judged out of the things written in the books, according to their works. [13]And the sea gave up the dead in it. And death and Hades gave up the dead in them. And they were each judged according to their works. [14]And death and Hades were thrown into the Lake of Fire. This is the second death. [15]And if anyone was not found having been written in the Book of Life, he was thrown into the Lake of Fire.

CHAPTER 21

[1]And I saw a new heaven and a new earth, for the first heaven and the first earth passed away, and the sea no longer is. [2]And I, John, saw the holy city, New Jerusalem, coming down out of Heaven from God, having been prepared as a bride, having been adorned for her Husband. [3]And I heard a great voice out of Heaven, saying, Behold, the

ἐν ταῖς τέσσαρσι γωνίαις τῆς γῆς, τὸν Γὼγ καὶ τὸν Μαγώγ,
in the four corners of the earth, Gog and Magog,
συναγαγεῖν αὐτοὺς εἰς πόλεμον· ὧν ὁ ἀριθμὸς ὡς ἡ ἄμμος
to assemble them in war, of whom the number (is) as the sand
9 τῆς θαλάσσης. καὶ ἀνέβησαν ἐπὶ τὸ πλάτος τῆς γῆς, καὶ
of the sea. And they went up over the breadth of the land and
ἐκύκλωσαν τὴν παρεμβολὴν τῶν ἁγίων καὶ τὴν πόλιν τὴν
encircled the camp of the saints, and the city
ἠγαπημένην· καὶ κατέβη πῦρ ἀπὸ τοῦ Θεοῦ ἐκ τοῦ οὐρανοῦ,
beloved, and came down fire from God out of Heaven
10 καὶ κατέφαγεν αὐτούς. καὶ ὁ διάβολος ὁ πλανῶν αὐτοὺς
and burned down them. And the Devil misleading them
ἐβλήθη εἰς τὴν λίμνην τοῦ πυρὸς καὶ θείου, ὅπου τὸ θηρίον
was thrown into the Lake of Fire and brimstone, where the beast
καὶ ὁ ψευδοπροφήτης· καὶ βασανισθήσονται ἡμέρας καὶ
and the false prophet (were); and they will be tormented day and
νυκτὸς εἰς τοὺς αἰῶνας τῶν αἰώνων.
night to the ages of the ages.

11 Καὶ εἶδον θρόνον λευκὸν μέγαν, καὶ τὸν καθήμενον ἐπ' αὐτοῦ
And I saw a throne white great, and the (One) sitting on it,
οὗ ἀπὸ προσώπου ἔφυγεν ἡ γῆ καὶ ὁ οὐρανός, καὶ τόπος
of whom from (the) face fled the earth and the heaven; and a place
12 οὐχ εὑρέθη αὐτοῖς. καὶ εἶδον τοὺς νεκρούς, μικροὺς καὶ
not was found for them. And I saw the dead, (the) small and
μεγάλους, ἑστῶτας ἐνώπιον τοῦ Θεοῦ, καὶ βιβλία ἠνεῴχθη-
great, standing before God, and scrolls were opened.
σαν· καὶ βιβλίον ἄλλο ἠνεῴχθη, ὅ ἐστι τῆς ζωῆς· καὶ ἐκρί-
And Scroll another was opened, which is the (Scroll) of Life. And were
θησαν οἱ νεκροὶ ἐκ τῶν γεγραμμένων ἐν τοῖς βιβλίοις, κατὰ
judged the dead out of those having been written in the scrolls, according to
13 τὰ ἔργα αὐτῶν. καὶ ἔδωκεν ἡ θάλασσα τοὺς ἐν αὐτῇ νεκρούς,
the works of them. And gave the sea the in it dead,
καὶ ὁ θάνατος καὶ ὁ ᾅδης ἔδωκαν τοὺς ἐν αὐτοῖς νεκρούς· καὶ
and death and Hades gave the in them dead; and
14 ἐκρίθησαν ἕκαστος κατὰ τὰ ἔργα αὐτῶν. καὶ ὁ θάνατος καὶ
they were judged each one according to their works. And death and
ὁ ᾅδης ἐβλήθησαν εἰς τὴν λίμνην τοῦ πυρός· οὗτός ἐστιν ὁ
Hades were thrown into the Lake of Fire. This is the
15 δεύτερος θάνατος. καὶ εἴ τις οὐχ εὑρέθη ἐν τῇ βίβλῳ τῆς ζωῆς
second death. And if anyone not was found in the Scroll of Life
γεγραμμένος, ἐβλήθη εἰς τὴν λίμνην τοῦ πυρός.
having been written, he was thrown into the Lake of Fire.

CHAPTER 21

1 Καὶ εἶδον οὐρανὸν καινὸν καὶ γῆν καινήν· ὁ γὰρ πρῶτος
And I saw a heaven new and an earth new; the for first
οὐρανὸς καὶ ἡ πρώτη γῆ παρῆλθε, καὶ ἡ θάλασσα οὐκ ἔστιν
heaven and the first earth went away, and the sea not is
2 ἔτι. καὶ ἐγὼ Ἰωάννης εἶδον τὴν πόλιν τὴν ἁγίαν, Ἱερουσαλὴμ
still. And I John, saw the city holy, Jerusalem
καινήν, καταβαίνουσαν ἀπὸ τοῦ Θεοῦ ἐκ τοῦ οὐρανοῦ, ἡτοι-
New, coming down from God out of Heaven, having
3 μασμένην ὡς νύμφην κεκοσμημένην τῷ ἀνδρὶ αὐτῆς. καὶ
been prepared as a bride having been adorned for the Husband of her. And
ἤκουσα φωνῆς μεγάλης ἐκ τοῦ οὐρανοῦ, λεγούσης, Ἰδού, ἡ
I heard a voice great out of Heaven, saying, Behold, the

tabernacle of God with men! And He will tabernacle with them, and they will be His people, and God Himself will be with them as their God. [4]And God will wipe away every tear from their eyes. And death shall be no longer, nor mourning, nor outcry, nor pain will be any longer, for the first things passed away. [5]And the *One* sitting on the throne said, Behold, I make all things new. And He says to me, Write, because these words are faithful and true.

[6]And He said to me, It is done! I am the Alpha and the Omega, the Beginning and the End. To the *one* thirsting, I will freely give of the fountain of the water of life. [7]The *one* overcoming will inherit all things, and I will be God to him, and he will be the son to Me. [8]But for the cowardly and unbelieving, and those having become foul, and murderers, and fornicators, and sorcerers, and idolaters, and all the lying ones, their part *will be* in the Lake burning with fire and brimstone, which is *the* second death.

[9]And one of the seven angels came to me, he having the seven bowls being filled *with* the seven last plagues, and spoke with me, saying, Come, I will show you the bride, the wife of the Lamb. [10]And he carried me in spirit onto a great and high mountain, and showed me the great city, holy Jerusalem, coming down out of Heaven from God, [11]having the glory of God. And its light *was* like a very precious stone, as a jasper stone, being clear as crystal, [12]and having a great and high wall, having twelve gates, and twelve angels at the gates, and names having been inscribed, which is of the twelve tribes of the sons of Israel. [13]From *the* east, three gates; from *the* north, three gates; from *the* south, three gates; and from *the* west, three gates.

σκηνὴ τοῦ Θεοῦ μετὰ τῶν ἀνθρώπων, καὶ σκηνώσει μετ
tabernacle of God with men! And He will tabernacle with
αὐτῶν, καὶ αὐτοὶ λαοὶ αὐτοῦ ἔσονται, καὶ αὐτὸς ὁ Θεὸς ἔσται
them, and they peoples of Him will be, and Himself God will be
4 μετ' αὐτῶν, Θεὸς αὐτῶν· καὶ ἐξαλείψει ὁ Θεὸς πᾶν δάκρυον
with them (the) God of them. And will wipe away God every tear
ἀπὸ τῶν ὀφθαλμῶν αὐτῶν, καὶ ὁ θάνατος οὐκ ἔσται ἔτι· οὔτε
from the eyes of them; and death not will be longer, nor
πένθος, οὔτε κραυγή, οὔτε πόνος οὐκ ἔσται ἔτι· ὅτι τὰ πρῶτα
mourning, nor outcry, nor pain not will be longer, for the things first
5 ἀπῆλθον. καὶ εἶπεν ὁ καθήμενος ἐπὶ τοῦ θρόνου, Ἰδού,
went away. And said the (One) sitting on the throne, Behold,
καινὰ πάντα ποιῶ. καὶ λέγει μοι, Γράψον· ὅτι οὗτοι οἱ λόγοι
new all things I make. And He says to me, Write, because these words
6 ἀληθινοὶ καὶ πιστοί εἰσι. καὶ εἶπέ μοι, Γέγονε. ἐγώ εἰμι τὸ
true and faithful are; and He said to me, It is done, I am the
Α καὶ τὸ Ω, ἡ ἀρχὴ καὶ τὸ τέλος. ἐγὼ τῷ διψῶντι δώσω ἐκ
Alpha and the Omega, the Head and the End. I to (the one) thirsting will give of
7 τῆς πηγῆς τοῦ ὕδατος τῆς ζωῆς δωρεάν. ὁ νικῶν κληρονομή-
the fountain of the water of life freely. The (one) overcoming will in-
σει πάντα, καὶ ἔσομαι αὐτῷ Θεός, καὶ αὐτὸς ἔσται μοι ὁ υἱός.
herit all things, and I will be to him God, and he will be to Me the son.
8 δειλοῖς δὲ καὶ ἀπίστοις καὶ ἐβδελυγμένοις καὶ φονεῦσι καὶ
to fearful But and unbelieving and abominable and murderers and
πόρνοις καὶ φαρμακεῦσι καὶ εἰδωλολάτραις, καὶ πᾶσι τοῖς
fornicators and sorcerers and idolaters and all the
ψευδέσι, τὸ μέρος αὐτῶν ἐν τῇ λίμνῃ τῇ καιομένῃ πυρὶ καὶ
lying ones, the part of them in the Lake burning with fire and
θείῳ, ὅ ἐστι δεύτερος θάνατος.
brimstone, which is (the) second death.
9 Καὶ ἦλθε πρός με εἷς τῶν ἑπτὰ ἀγγέλων τῶν ἐχόντων τὰς
And came to me one of the seven angels, he having the
ἑπτὰ φιάλας τὰς γεμούσας τῶν ἑπτὰ πληγῶν τῶν ἐσχάτων,
seven bowls being filled of the seven plagues last,
καὶ ἐλάλησε μετ' ἐμοῦ, λέγων, Δεῦρο, δείξω σοι τὴν νύμφην
and spoke with me, saying, Come, I will show you the bride,
10 τοῦ ἀρνίου τὴν γυναῖκα. καὶ ἀπήνεγκέ με ἐν Πνεύματι ἐπ'
of the Lamb the wife. And he carried me in Spirit onto
ὄρος μέγα καὶ ὑψηλόν, καὶ ἔδειξέ μοι τὴν πόλιν τὴν μεγάλην,
a mount great and high, and showed me the city great,
τὴν ἁγίαν Ἱερουσαλήμ, καταβαίνουσαν ἐκ τοῦ οὐρανοῦ
Holy Jerusalem coming down out of Heaven
11 ἀπὸ τοῦ Θεοῦ, ἔχουσαν τὴν δόξαν τοῦ Θεοῦ· καὶ ὁ φωστὴρ
from God having the glory of God. And the lighting
αὐτῆς ὅμοιος λίθῳ τιμιωτάτῳ, ὡς λίθῳ ἰάσπιδι κρυσταλλί-
of it (was) like a stone very precious, as stone a jasper being clear as
12 ζοντι· ἔχουσάν τε τεῖχος μέγα καὶ ὑψηλόν, ἔχουσαν πυλῶνας
crystal, having and wall a great and high, having gates
δώδεκα, καὶ ἐπὶ τοῖς πυλῶσιν ἀγγέλους δώδεκα, καὶ ὀνόματα
twelve, and at the gates angels twelve, and names
ἐπιγεγραμμένα, ἅ ἐστι τῶν δώδεκα φυλῶν τῶν υἱῶν Ἰσραήλ.
having been inscribed, which are of the twelve tribes of the sons of Israel.
13 ἀπ' ἀνατολῆς, πυλῶνες τρεῖς· ἀπὸ βορρᾶ, πυλῶνες τρεῖς·
From (the) east, gates three; from (the) north, gates three;
ἀπὸ νότου, πυλῶνες τρεῖς· καὶ ἀπὸ δυσμῶν, πυλῶνες τρεῖς.
from (the) south, gates three; and from (the) west gates three.

[14]And the wall of the city had twelve foundations, and in them *the* names of the twelve apostles of the Lamb. [15]And he speaking with me had a golden reed, that he may measure the city, and its gates, and its wall. [16]And the city lies four-cornered, even its length as much as the width also. And he measured the city with the reed at twelve thousand stadia; the length and the width and the height of it are equal. [17]And he measured its wall, a hundred *and* forty-four cubits, a measure of a man, which is of an angel. [18]And the structure of its wall *was* jasper; and the city *was* pure gold, like pure glass. [19]And the foundation of the wall of the city having been adorned with every precious stone: The first foundation, jasper; the second, sapphire; the third, chalcedony; the fourth, emerald; [20]the fifth, sardonyx; the sixth, sardius; the seventh, chrysolite; the eighth, beryl; the ninth, topaz; the tenth, chrysoprasus; the eleventh, hyacinth; the twelfth, amethyst. [21]And the twelve gates *were* twelve pearls; respectively each one of the gates was of one pearl. And the street of the city *was* pure gold, as transparent glass. [22]And I saw no temple in it, for *the* Lord God Almighty is its temple, even the Lamb.

[23]And the city had no need of the sun, nor of the moon, that they might shine in it, for the glory of God illuminated it, even its lamp *is* the Lamb. [24]And the nations of the ones saved will walk in its light; and the kings of the earth bring their glory and honor into it. [25]And its gates may not at all be shut by day, for no night will be there. [26]And they

14 καὶ τὸ τεῖχος τῆς πόλεως ἔχον θεμελίους δώδεκα, καὶ ἐν
And the wall of the city having foundations twelve, and in
15 αὐτοῖς ὀνόματα τῶν δώδεκα ἀποστόλων τοῦ ἀρνίου. καὶ
them names of the twelve apostles of the Lamb. And
ὁ λαλῶν μετ' ἐμοῦ εἶχε κάλαμον χρυσοῦν, ἵνα μετρήσῃ τὴν
he speaking with me had a reed of gold, that he may measure the
16 πόλιν, καὶ τοὺς πυλῶνας αὐτῆς, καὶ τὸ τεῖχος αὐτῆς. καὶ
city, and the gates of it, and the wall of it. And
ἡ πόλις τετράγωνος κεῖται, καὶ τὸ μῆκος αὐτῆς τοσοῦτόν
the city four-cornered lies, and the length of it so much
ἐστιν ὅσον καὶ τὸ πλάτος. καὶ ἐμέτρησε τὴν πόλιν τῷ
is as much as also the width. And he measured the city with the
καλάμῳ ἐπὶ σταδίων δώδεκα χιλιάδων· τὸ μῆκος καὶ τὸ
reed at stadia twelve thousands; the length and the
17 πλάτος καὶ τὸ ὕψος αὐτῆς ἴσα ἐστί. καὶ ἐμέτρησε τὸ τεῖχος
width and the height of it equal are. And he measured the wall
αὐτῆς ἑκατὸν τεσσαρακοντατεσσάρων πηχῶν, μέτρον
of it, a hundred (and) forty-four cubits, a measure
18 ἀνθρώπου, ὅ ἐστιν ἀγγέλου. καὶ ἦν ἡ ἐνδόμησις τοῦ τείχους
of a man, which is of an angel. And was the structure of the wall
αὐτῆς, ἴασπις· καὶ ἡ πόλις χρυσίον καθαρόν, ὁμοία ὑάλῳ
of it jasper; and the city (was) gold clean, like glass
19 καθαρῷ. καὶ οἱ θεμέλιοι τοῦ τείχους τῆς πόλεως παντὶ λίθῳ
clean. And the foundations of the wall of the city with every stone
τιμίῳ κεκοσμημένοι. ὁ θεμέλιος ὁ πρῶτος, ἴασπις· ὁ δεύτερος,
precious was adorned; the foundation first, jasper; the second,
20 σάπφειρος· ὁ τρίτος, χαλκηδών· ὁ τέταρτος, σμάραγδος· ὁ
sapphire; the third, chalcedony; the fourth, emerald; the
πέμπτος, σαρδόνυξ· ὁ ἕκτος, σάρδιος· ὁ ἕβδομος, χρυσόλιθος·
fifth, sardonyx; the sixth, sardius; the seventh, chrysolite;
ὁ ὄγδοος, βήρυλλος· ὁ ἔννατος, τοπάζιον· ὁ δέκατος,
the eighth, beryl; the ninth, topaz; the tenth,
χρυσόπρασος· ὁ ἑνδέκατος, ὑάκινθος· ὁ δωδέκατος, ἀμέ-
chrysoprasus; the eleventh hyacinth; the twelfth, ame-
21 θυστος. καὶ οἱ δώδεκα πυλῶνες, δώδεκα μαργαρῖται· ἀνὰ
thyst. And the twelve gates (were) twelve pearls; respectively
εἷς ἕκαστος τῶν πυλώνων ἦν ἐξ ἑνὸς μαργαρίτου· καὶ ἡ
one each of the gates was of one pearl. And the
πλατεῖα τῆς πόλεως χρυσίον καθαρόν, ὡς ὕαλος διαφανής.
street of the city (was) of gold clean, as glass transparent.
22 καὶ ναὸν οὐκ εἶδον ἐν αὐτῇ· ὁ γὰρ Κύριος ὁ Θεὸς ὁ παντο-
And a temple not I saw in it, the for Lord God
23 κράτωρ ναὸς αὐτῆς ἐστί, καὶ τὸ ἀρνίον. καὶ ἡ πόλις οὐ
Almighty temple of it is, and the Lamb. And the city not
χρείαν ἔχει τοῦ ἡλίου, οὐδὲ τῆς σελήνης, ἵνα φαίνωσιν ἐν
need has of the sun, nor of the moon, that they might shine in
αὐτῇ· ἡ γὰρ δόξα τοῦ Θεοῦ ἐφώτισεν αὐτήν, καὶ ὁ λύχνος
it, the for glory of God enlightened it, and the lamp
24 αὐτῆς τὸ ἀρνίον. καὶ τὰ ἔθνη τῶν σωζομένων ἐν τῷ φωτὶ
of it (is) the Lamb. And the nations of those saved in the light
αὐτῆς περιπατήσουσι· καὶ οἱ βασιλεῖς τῆς γῆς φέρουσι τὴν
of it will walk; and the kings of the earth bring the
25 δόξαν καὶ τὴν τιμὴν αὐτῶν εἰς αὐτήν. καὶ οἱ πυλῶνες
glory and the honor of them into it. And the gates
26 αὐτῆς οὐ μὴ κλεισθῶσιν ἡμέρας (νὺξ γὰρ οὐκ ἔσται ἐκεῖ) καὶ
of it not at all may be shut by day —night for not will be there— and

will b[illegible] the glory and the honor of the nations into it. [27]And all profaning may not at all enter into it, or *any* making an abomination or a lie; but only the ones having been written in the Book of Life of the Lamb.

27 οἴσουσι τὴν δόξαν καὶ τὴν τιμὴν τῶν ἐθνῶν εἰς αὐτήν· καὶ
they will bring the glory and the honor of the nations into it. And
οὐ μὴ εἰσέλθῃ εἰς αὐτὴν πᾶν κοινοῦν, καὶ ποιοῦν βδέλυγμα
not at all may enter into it all profaning, and (any) making an abomination
καὶ ψεῦδος· εἰ μὴ οἱ γεγραμμένοι ἐν τῷ βιβλίῳ τῆς ζωῆς τοῦ
and a lie, except those having been written in the Scroll of Life of the
ἀρνιου.
Lamb.

CHAPTER 22

[1]And he showed me a pure river of water of life, bright as crystal, coming forth out of the throne of God and of the Lamb. [2]In *the* midst of its street and of the river, from here and from there, *was* a tree of life producing twelve fruits: according to one month each yielding its fruit. And the leaves of the tree *were* for healing of the nations. [3]And every curse will no longer be. And the throne of God and the Lamb will be in it; and His slaves will serve Him. [4]And they will see His face; and His name *will be* on their foreheads. [5]And night will not be there; and they have no need of a lamp or a light of *the* sun, because *the* Lord God will shed light on them. And they shall reign forever *and* ever. [6]And he said to me, These words *are* faithful and true. And *the* Lord God of the holy prophets sent His angel to show His slaves what must happen quickly. [7]Behold, I am coming quickly. Blessed *is* the *one* keeping the words of the prophecy of this Book.

[8]And I, John, *was* the *one* seeing and hearing these things. And when I heard and saw, I fell down to worship before the feet of the angel showing me these things. [9]And he said to me, See, stop! For I am your fellow-slave, and of your brothers the prophets, and of the *ones* keeping the

1 καὶ ἔδειξέ μοι καθαρὸν ποταμὸν ὕδατος ζωῆς, λαμ-
And he showed me a clean river of water of life,
πρὸν ὡς κρύσταλλον, ἐκπορευόμενον ἐκ τοῦ θρόνου τοῦ Θεοῦ
bright as crystal, coming forth out of the throne of God
2 καὶ τοῦ ἀρνίου. ἐν μέσῳ τῆς πλατείας αὐτῆς, καὶ τοῦ
and of the Lamb. In (the) midst of the street of it, and of the
ποταμοῦ ἐντεῦθεν καὶ ἐντεῦθεν, ξύλον ζωῆς, ποιοῦν καρποὺς
river, from here and from there, a tree of life, producing fruits
δώδεκα, κατὰ μῆνα ἕνα ἕκαστον ἀποδιδοῦν τὸν καρπὸν
twelve, according to month one each yielding the fruit
αὐτοῦ· καὶ τὰ φύλλα τοῦ ξύλου εἰς θεραπείαν τῶν ἐθνῶν.
of it. And the leaves of the tree (will be) for healing of the nations.
3 καὶ πᾶν κατανάθεμα οὐκ ἔσται ἔτι· καὶ ὁ θρόνος τοῦ Θεοῦ καὶ
And every curse not will be longer. And the throne of God and
τοῦ ἀρνίου ἐν αὐτῇ ἔσται· καὶ οἱ δοῦλοι αὐτοῦ λατρεύσουσιν
of the Lamb in it will be, and the slaves of Him will do service
4 αὐτῷ, καὶ ὄψονται τὸ πρόσωπον αὐτοῦ· καὶ τὸ ὄνομα
to Him, and they will see the face of Him, and the name
5 αὐτοῦ ἐπὶ τῶν μετώπων αὐτῶν. καὶ νὺξ οὐκ ἔσται ἐκεῖ, καὶ
of Him (will be) on the foreheads of them. And night not will be there, and
χρείαν οὐκ ἔχουσι λύχνου καὶ φωτὸς ἡλίου, ὅτι Κύριος ὁ
need not they have of a lamp and a light of sun, because (the) Lord
Θεὸς φωτίζει αὐτούς· καὶ βασιλεύσουσιν εἰς τοὺς αἰῶνας τῶν
God will enlighten them, and they will reign to the ages of the
αἰώνων.
ages.

6 Καὶ εἶπέ μοι, Οὗτοι οἱ λόγοι πιστοὶ καὶ ἀληθινοί· καὶ
And he said to me, These words (are) faithful and true, and
Κύριος ὁ Θεὸς τῶν ἁγίων προφητῶν ἀπέστειλε τὸν ἄγγελον
(the) Lord God of the holy prophets sent the angel
αὐτοῦ δεῖξαι τοῖς δούλοις αὐτοῦ ἃ δεῖ γενέσθαι ἐν τάχει.
of Him to show the slaves of Him what must happen with speed.
7 Ἰδού, ἔρχομαι ταχύ. μακάριος ὁ τηρῶν τοὺς λόγους τῆς
Behold, I am coming quickly. Blessed the (one) keeping the words of the
προφητείας τοῦ βιβλίου τούτου.
prophecy of Scroll this.

8 Καὶ ἐγὼ Ἰωάννης ὁ βλέπων ταῦτα καὶ ἀκούων. καὶ ὅτε
And I, John, the (one) seeing these things and hearing; and when
ἤκουσα καὶ ἔβλεψα, ἔπεσα προσκυνῆσαι ἔμπροσθεν τῶν
I heard and saw, I fell down to worship before the
9 ποδῶν τοῦ ἀγγέλου τοῦ δεικνύοντός μοι ταῦτα. καὶ λέγει
feet of the angel showing me these things. And he says
μοι, Ὅρα μή· σύνδουλός σου γάρ εἰμι, καὶ τῶν ἀδελφῶν σου
to me, See, no! a fellow-slave of you For I am, and of the brothers of you,
τῶν προφητῶν, καὶ τῶν τηρούντων τοὺς λόγους τοῦ
the prophets, and of those keeping the words

words of this Book. Do worship to God.

[10]And he said to me, Seal the words of the prophecy of this Book, because the time is near. [11]The *one* acting unjustly, let him still act unjustly; and the filthy, let *him* still be filthy; and the righteous, let *him* still *do* righteousness; and the holy, let *him* still be holy.

[12]And, behold, I am coming quickly, and My reward *is* with Me, to give to each as his work is. [13]I am the Alpha and the Omega, the Beginning and the End, the First and the Last. [14]Blessed *are* the *ones* doing His commands, that their authority will be over the tree of life, and by the gates they may enter into the city. [15]But outside *are* the dogs, and the sorcerers, and the fornicators, and the murderers, and the idolaters, and everyone loving and making a lie.

[16]I, Jesus, sent My angel to testify these things to you over the churches. I am the Root and Offspring of David, the bright and morning Star.

[17]And the Spirit and the bride say, Come! And the *one* hearing, let him say, Come! And the *one* thirsting, let *him* come; and the *one* desiring, let him take of the water of life freely.

[18]For I testify together with everyone hearing the words of the prophecy of this Book: If anyone adds to these things, God will add upon him the plagues having been written in this Book. [19]And if anyone takes away from the words of *the* Book of this prophecy, God will take away his part from *the* Book of Life, and out of the holy city, and of the things having been written in this Book.

[20]The *One* testifying these things says, Yes, I am coming quickly. Amen. Yes, come, Lord Jesus!

[21]The grace of our Lord Jesus Christ *be* with all of you. Amen.

βιβλίου τούτου· τῷ Θεῷ προσκύνησον.
Scroll of this. To God, do worship.
10 Καὶ λέγει μοι, Μὴ σφραγίσῃς τοὺς λόγους τῆς προφητείας
And he says to me, seal not the words of the prophecy
11 τοῦ βιβλίου τούτου· ὅτι ὁ καιρὸς ἐγγύς ἐστιν. ὁ ἀδικῶν
Scroll of this, because the time near is. He acting unjustly
ἀδικησάτω ἔτι· καὶ ὁ ῥυπῶν ῥυπωσάτω ἔτι· καὶ ὁ δίκαιος
let him act unjustly still; and the filthy, let be filthy still; and the righteous,
12 δικαιωθήτω ἔτι· καὶ ὁ ἅγιος ἁγιασθητω ἔτι. καὶ ἰδού,
righteousness (do) still; and the holy, let him be holy still. And behold,
ἔρχομαι ταχύ, καὶ ὁ μισθός μου μετ' ἐμοῦ, ἀποδοῦναι ἑκάστῳ
I am coming quickly, and My reward (is) with Me, to render to each
13 ὡς τὸ ἔργον αὐτοῦ ἔσται. ἐγώ εἰμι τὸ Α καὶ τὸ Ω, ἀρχὴ
as the work of him is. I am the Alpha and the Omega the Head
14 καὶ τέλος, ὁ πρῶτος καὶ ὁ ἔσχατος. μακάριοι οἱ ποιουντες
and End, the First and the Last. Blessed (are) those doing
τὰς ἐντολὰς αὐτοῦ, ἵνα ἔσται ἡ ἐξουσία αὐτῶν ἐπὶ τὸ ξύλον
the commands of Him, that will be the authority of them over the tree
τῆς ζωῆς, καὶ τοῖς πυλῶσιν εἰσέλθωσιν εἰς τὴν πόλιν.
of life, and by the gates they may enter into the city
15 ἔξω δὲ οἱ κύνες καὶ οἱ φαρμακοὶ καὶ οἱ πόρνοι καὶ οἱ φονεῖς
outside But the dogs and the sorcerers, and the fornicators and the murderers
καὶ οἱ εἰδωλολάτραι, καὶ πᾶς ὁ φιλῶν καὶ ποιῶν ψεῦδος.
and the idolaters, and everyone loving and making a lie.
16 Ἐγὼ Ἰησοῦς ἔπεμψα τὸν ἄγγελόν μου μαρτυρῆσαι
I, Jesus, sent the angel of Me to witness
ὑμῖν ταῦτα ἐπὶ ταις ἐκκλησίαις. ἐγώ εἰμι ἡ ῥίζα καὶ τὸ γένος
to you these things over the churches. I am the root and the offspring
τοῦ Δαβίδ, ὁ ἀστὴρ ὁ λαμπρὸς καὶ ὀρθρινός.
of David, the Star bright and morning.
17 Καὶ τὸ Πνεῦμα καὶ ἡ νύμφη λέγουσιν, Ἐλθέ. καὶ ὁ ἀκούων
And the Spirit and the bride say, Come! And he hearing,
εἰπάτω, Ἐλθέ. καὶ ὁ διψῶν ἐλθέτω· καὶ ὁ θέλων λαμβανέτω
let him say, Come! And he thirsting let come; and he willing, let him take
τὸ ὕδωρ ζωῆς δωρεάν.
of the water of life freely.
18 Συμμαρτυροῦμαι γὰρ παντὶ ἀκούοντι τοὺς λόγους τῆς
I testify together For everyone hearing the words of the
προφητείας τοῦ βιβλίου τούτου, Ἐάν τις ἐπιτιθῇ πρὸς
prophecy of Scroll this, If anyone add to
ταῦτα, ἐπιθήσει ὁ Θεὸς ἐπ' αὐτὸν τὰς πληγὰς τὰς γεγραμ-
these things, will add God upon him the plagues having been
19 μένας ἐν βιβλίῳ τούτῳ· καὶ ἐάν τις ἀφαιρῇ ἀπὸ τῶν λόγων
written in Scroll this; and if anyone take away from the words
βίβλου τῆς προφητείας ταύτης, ἀφαιρήσει ὁ Θεὸς τὸ μέρος
of (the) Scroll of prophecy this, will take away God the part
αὐτοῦ ἀπὸ βίβλου τῆς ζωῆς, καὶ ἐκ τῆς πόλεως τῆς ἁγίας,
of him from (the) Scroll of Life, and out of the city holy,
καὶ τῶν γεγραμμένων ἐν βιβλίῳ τούτῳ.
and of the things having been written in Scroll this.
20 Λέγει ὁ μαρτυρῶν ταῦτα, Ναί, ἔρχομαι ταχύ. ἀμήν. Ναί,
says The (One) testifying these things, Yes, I am coming quickly. Amen. Yes,
21 ἔρχου, Κύριε Ἰησοῦ. Ἡ χάρις τοῦ Κυρίου ἡμῶν Ἰησοῦ
come, Lord Jesus. The grace of the Lord of us, Jesus
Χριστοῦ μετὰ πάντων ὑμῶν. αμήν.
Christ, (be) with all of you. Amen.

586759
THE SOUND
ALTERNATIVE